Between Alpine and Mediterranean influences

Alto Adige is a land of great contrasts. The vineyards are located at elevations between 200 and 1,000 metres, kissed by the Mediterranean sun, flourishing in the Alps.

altoadigewines.com

Gambero Rosso

2021

ITALIAN WINES

VINI D'ITALIA 2021
GAMBERO ROSSO®

Senior Editors
Marco Sabellico
Gianni Fabrizio
Giuseppe Carrus

Co-editor
Lorenzo Ruggeri

Technical Directors
William Pregentelli

Special Contributors
Stefania Annese
Antonio Boco
Paolo De Cristofaro
Paolo Zaccaria

Regionali Coordinators
Nino Aiello
Francesco Beghi
Nicola Frasson
Massimo Lanza
Gianni Ottogalli
Nereo Pederzolli
Pierpaolo Rastelli

Contributors
Sergio Bonanno
Giorgio Buloncelli
Michele Bressan
Pasquale Buffa
Dionisio Castello
Stefano Ghisletta
Giacomo Mojoli
Franco Pallini
Leonardo Romanelli
Giulia Sampognaro
Herbert Taschler
Cinzia Tosetti

Other Contributors
Giovanni Angelucci
Stefano Barone
Enrico Battistella
Carlotta Ozino Caligaris
Pietro Chirco
Palmiro Ciccarelli
Giambeppe Colombano
Francesco D'Angelo
Emilio Del Fante
Franco Fusco
Davide Giachino
Giovanni Lanzillo
Alessandro Mancuso
Roberto Mattozzi
Sandro Milei
Michele Muraro
Alberto Parrinello
Davide Pelucchi
Dario Piccinelli
Nicola Piccinini
Massimo Ponzanelli
Mirko Rainer
Federico Ranieri
Filippo Rapini
Riccardo Rossetti
Jacopo Rossi
Maurizio Rossi
Yukari Sato
Simona Silvestri
Sabrina Somigli
Marzio Taccetti
Anna Valli
Andrea Vannelli
Henry W. Visentin
Danilo Zannella

Editorial Secretary
Giulia Sciortino

Layout
Marina Proietti

Publisher
Gambero Rosso S.p.A.
via Ottavio Gasparri, 13/17
00152 Roma
tel. 06/551121 -fax 06/55112260
www.gamberorosso.it
email: gambero@gamberorosso.it

Managing Editor Books
Laura Mantovano

Graphics
Chiara Buosi

Commercial Director
Francesco Dammicco

Editorial product distribution and sales manager
Eugenia Durando

Production
Angelica Sorbara

Translation
Jordan De Maio

Assistant translator
Jane Upchurch

Advertising Sales Agency:
Class Pubblicità SpA
Milano, Via Marco Burigozzo, 5
tel. 02 58219522
Per informazioni commerciali: mprestileo@class.it

Distribution
USA and Canada
by ACC ART BOOKS, 6 West 18th Street, Suite 4B
New York, NY 10011
UK and Australia
by ACC ART BOOKS Sandy Lane, Old Martlesham,
Woodbridge, Suffolk IP12 4SD - United Kingdom
Italy
by Messaggerie Libri S.p.A.
via Verdi, 8 - 20090 Assago (MI)

The final edit of Italian Wines was completed on 10 September 2020

ISBN 978-88-6641-216-8

Printed in Italy for
Gambero Rosso Holding S.p.A
in October 2020 by
FP Design srl
Via Atto Tigri, 11
00197 Roma

SUMMARY

REGIONS

INDEX

THE GUIDE

This year's edition of Italian Wines is all about records. In a year plagued by severe difficulties, dramatic even, which shook, and continue to shake, the world, the Italian wine industry and our team of passionate tasters have responded commendably. It's an achievement that aptly demonstrates the extraordinary vitality of Italian wine, which has once again proven to be a leader in terms of exports, even during a year as difficult as 2020. First of all, we tasted many more wines than in previous editions (about 2,000). This points to how indispensable our publication is for producers. Tasting over 46,000 wines was an incredible feat if we consider the complexity of Italian wine and its geography, from Pantelleria to Ticino (even if it's in Switzerland, we include it in the guide), and the conditions in which we had to operate.

And so on to the first record, that of the number of printed pages: 1056 in all. This brought the total number of producers reviewed to an eye-popping 2645, over 100 more than last year. 34 years ago, when the first edition was being drafted (465 wineries and about 1400 wines tasted), such a thing would have been unthinkable. In this edition you'll find some 24,638 wines reviewed. During the months of lockdown, when we wondered whether it would even be possible to publish the guide, we wouldn't have bet on it either. But alas, there's a reason why it's called 'The Bible of Italian Wine'.

Indeed, Every year our guide is translated into English, German, Chinese and Japanese, serving as a must-have tool for wine lovers and professionals around the world. Undoubtedly, credit for this success goes to the team of enophiles and experts who dedicate weeks every year to their work of tasting (strictly blind) thousands of wines throughout Italy. Over the years we've selected more than sixty people, all seasoned tasters, for their expertise and reliability.

Our initial tastings, which were condensed into two months, provided an accurate and objective snapshot of Italian enology. 2300 wines were then selected to participate in our final round, with a spectacular 467 emerging with the legendary Tre Bicchieri. Considering that we only award one Tre Biccheri per producer, it should be said many of the 1800 wines awarded Due Bicchieri were just as deserving. This is indeed a record, but in a year as plagued by troubles as 2020 it takes on an even greater importance. It's true that along the way we discovered great, and in some cases outstanding, vintages, like 2015 in Montalcino, and 2016 in Barolo. But it's equally true that Italian wine is thriving both in terms of quantity and quality, and the 1% of superb wines awarded Tre Bicchieri represent a country that towers globally.

Our philosophy, our vision of wine-making, is encapsulated in our special awards: here you'll find small artisan selections vinified in amphorae alongside prestigious, international best-sellers. The Red of the Year award goes to Pio Cesare's sumptuous 2016 Barolo Ornato. A wine of spectacular finesse, elegance and longevity that will be a joy to follow over the years, it tops off a superlative performance not only by this historic producer but by all of Langa. The White of the Year comes from Valle d'Aosta: it's Rosset Terroir's Sopraquota 900 '19. It's a wine of unspeakable finesse, a child of truly heroic viticulture. The Sparkler of the Year hails from Lombardy. It's the Oltrepò

Pavese Pinot Nero Dosaggio Zero Farfalla Cave Privée '11, crafted by Ballabio, the historic Casteggio producer brilliantly brought back into vogue by the Nevelli family. The Rosé of the Year is Luigi Cataldi Madonna's Cerasuolo d'Abruzzo Piè delle Vigne '18. It's a rosé of charm, generosity, characterized by structure and color, a child of Abruzzo tradition reinterpreted in light of modern enological science. The Meditation Wine of the Year (this year it's not 'Sweet Wine of the Year') is a spectacular Vernaccia di Oristano Antico Gregori by Contini—vintage 1976 (no, that's not a typo) It's a wine you'll never forget. Finally, the Best Value for Money award goes to Vigneti Le Monde's Friuli Pinot Bianco '19, a superb Friulian white that's accessible to everyone.

This year our Solidarity Award (one we hold very dear) also goes to Friuli. It's for Villa Russiz, a producer that's also a foundation. For decades, they've kept alive the Adele Cerruti Foster Home for youth in difficulty. The Award for Sustainable Viticulture goes to a great Sicilian winery, Firriato, which in addition to offering great wines, has always been committed to this important, though challenging, cause. Our 2021 Viticulturist of the Year is a woman, Antonella Lombardo. In her winery, in the 'Riviera dei Gelsomini' (Calabria), she forges true gems, overseeing every stage of production, from pruning her vineyards to the cellar. This year's Up-and-Coming Winery is Ridolfi, in Montalcino. An ambitious and growing winery, this year they took home Tre Bicchieri, for the first time, with an extraordinary Brunello di Montalcino '15. A new special award, Cooperative of the Year, goes to San Michele Appiano in Alto Adige. We felt that it was important to recognize the world of co-ops, and no winery could represent them with such authority. Finally, our Winery of the Year is the Marzotto family's Santa Margherita Group, which brings together important Italian brands, from Ca' del Bosco to Cà Maiol in Lombardy, to Kettmeir in Alto Adige, Lamole in Chianti Classico and Mesa in Sardinia. Each submitted wines of outstanding quality, an achievement that starts with the parent company. You'll also find our Tre Bicchieri Verdi, awarded wines that are also certified organic or biodynamic (now 126, 27% of the total, a figure that makes us proud). Finally, we make note of award-winning wines available for under €15 (79 this year).

This year we welcome Giuseppe Carrus to our editorial team, a step that recognizes his 15 years of passionate work for the guide and his extraordinary expertise. Lorenzo Ruggeri, who has always been a key part of Gambero Rosso publications in Italy and throughout the world, will step in to fill his shoes as assistant editor. More and more, Gambero Rosso, with its magazines and guides, video and digital content, its events organized annually on every continent, is the brand that represents high-profile Italian enology and gastronomy at a global level.

Marco Sabellico, Gianni Fabrizio, Giuseppe Carrus

We would like to thank:

The Bolzano EOS Chamber of Commerce, Consorzio Vini Alto Adige, the Wine Roads of Arezzo, the Marche Institute for Jesi Wine (IMT) and VINEA of Offida, Brescia Wine Association, the Valbormida Carcare Training Consortium (SV), Committee for the Tuscan Coast's Great Cru, Assovini Sicilia, the E. del Giudice Viticultural Innovation Centre in Marsala. We'd also like to thank the following protection consortiums: Gavi, Barolo, Barbaresco, Alba, Langhe and Dogliani, Colli Tortonesi, Nebbiolo dell'Alto Piemonte, Caluso, Carema and Canavese, Valtellina, Oltrepò Pavese, Franciacorta, Valcalepio, Mantua Wines, Valcamonica, San Colombano, Lugana, Valtenesi, Conegliano Valdobbiadene, Soave, Valpolicella, Consorzio Colli Euganei, Consorzio Colli Berici, the Trento Wine Consortium, and then the Lambrusci Modenesi Historic Wines Consortium, as well as Lambrusco di Modena, the Romagna Wine Consortium, those of Bolgheri, Brunello di Montalcino, Chianti Classico, San Gimignano, Montepulciano, Chianti Colli Fiorentini, Chianti Rufina, Morellino di Scansano, Maremma Toscana, Montecucco, Carmignano, Orvieto, Montefalco, the Piceno Wines Consortium and, finally, the DOC Sicilia Wines Consortium. We'd also like to thank the Roero Enoteca Regionale, that of Nizza Monferrato, Canelli and Astesana, the Cantina Comunale I Sörì in Diano d'Alba, the Bottega del Vino in Dogliani, Carpe Diem restaurant in Montaione, the Calidario in Venturina, the Città del Gusto in Rome, the Basilicata Enoteca Regionale in Venosa, that of Caneva in Mogliano Veneto, the Casa e Putia restaurant in Messina, Andrea Conconi and the whole team of Ticinowine and the Azienda Agraria Cantonale di Mezzana. Finally, a sincere thanks to all our team, who passionately supported us in realizing Italian Wines, from local tastings to drafting the profiles all the way to writing, editing and publishing the volume itself, and to all those we've worked with down through the years.

And a special thanks to Danilo Zannella, coordinator of all our tastings.

I TRE BICCHIERI 2021

VALLE D'AOSTA

Wine	Producer	Page
Sopraquota 900 '19	Rosset Terroir	41
Valle d'Aosta Chambave Muscat Flétri '18	La Vrille	41
Valle d'Aosta Chardonnay Cuvée Bois '18	Les Crêtes	37
Valle d'Aosta Chardonnay Mains et Cœur '18	Maison Anselmet	36
Valle d'Aosta Petite Arvine '19	Elio Ottin	40
Valle d'Aosta Pinot Gris '19	Lo Triolet	39

PIEDMONT

Wine	Producer	Page
Alta Langa Brut Rosé 60 Mesi Ris. '13	Colombo - Cascina Pastori	99
Alta Langa Extra Brut Ris. '15	Coppo	102
Alta Langa Pas Dosé Zero Ris. '14	Enrico Serafino	179
Barbaresco Crichët Pajé '12	Roagna	168
Barbaresco Currà '15	Sottimano	181
Barbaresco Martinenga Camp Gros Ris. '15	Tenute Cisa Asinari dei Marchesi di Grésy	96
Barbaresco Rabajà '16	Bruno Rocca	169
Barbaresco Rabajà Ris. '13	Giuseppe Cortese	104
Barbaresco Rombone '16	Fiorenzo Nada	143
Barbaresco Roncaglie Ris. '15	Socré	180
Barbaresco Vallegrande '17	Ca' del Baio	74
Barbera d'Asti Sup. La Luna e i Falò '18	Vite Colte	193
Barbera d'Asti Sup. V. La Mandorla '18	Luigi Spertino	182
Barbera del M.to Albarola '16	Tacchino	184
Barbera del M.to Sup. Cantico della Crosia '17	Vicara	190
Barolo '16	Bartolo Mascarello	133
Barolo Arborina '16	Elio Altare	51
Barolo Bric dël Fiasc '16	Paolo Scavino	177
Barolo Brunate '16	Giuseppe Rinaldi	166
Barolo Cannubi '16	G. B. Burlotto	72
Barolo Cannubi '16	Poderi Luigi Einaudi	108
Barolo Castelletto '16	Fortemasso	113
Barolo Cerequio '16	Michele Chiarlo	93
Barolo Cerretta '16	Brandini	67
Barolo Cerretta Luigi Baudana '16	G. D. Vajra	188
Barolo del Comune di Castiglione Falletto V. V. '15	Cascina Fontana	84
Barolo Falletto V. Le Rocche Ris. '14	Bruno Giacosa	120
Barolo Ginestra Ris. '12	Paolo Conterno	100
Barolo Lazzarito '16	Casa E. di Mirafiore	79
Barolo Liste '15	Giacomo Borgogno & Figli	63
Barolo Meriame '16	Paolo Manzone	129
Barolo Monfortino Ris. '14	Giacomo Conterno	100
Barolo Monprivato '15	Giuseppe Mascarello e Figlio	134
Barolo Monvigliero '16	F.lli Alessandria	48
Barolo Monvigliero '16	Bel Colle	57
Barolo Ornato '16	Pio Cesare	157
Barolo Parafada '16	Massolino - Vigna Rionda	135
Barolo Pressenda '16	Abbona	44
Barolo Rive '16	Negretti	144
Barolo Rocche dell'Annunziata '16	Renato Corino	103

LIGURIA

LOMBARDY

Franciacorta Dosage Zéro '11	Castello Bonomi	249
Franciacorta Dosage Zéro Naturae '16	Barone Pizzini	239
Franciacorta Dosage Zéro Vintage Collection Noir '11	Ca' del Bosco	246
Franciacorta Dosaggio Zero Ris. '13	Lo Sparviere	275
Franciacorta Extra Brut '15	Ricci Curbastro	271
Franciacorta Extra Brut EBB '15	Mosnel	265
Franciacorta Extra Brut Extreme Palazzo Lana Ris. '09	Guido Berlucchi & C.	241
Franciacorta Non Dosato Grande Cuvée Alma	Bellavista	240
Lugana Fabio Contato Ris. '18	Cà Maiol	245
Lugana Madreperla Ris. '18	Perla del Garda	267
Lugana Menasasso Ris. '16	Selva Capuzza	274
Nature M. Cl.	Monsupello	263
OP Buttafuoco Storico V. Solenga '16	Fiamberti	256
OP M. Cl. Extra Brut Rosé NorEma '17	Calatroni	248
OP Pinot Nero Brut M. Cl. 1870 '16	Giorgi	258
OP Pinot Nero Dosaggio Zero Farfalla Cave Privée '11	Ballabio	238
OP Pinot Nero Pernice '17	Conte Vistarino	252
OP Rosso Cavariola Ris. '16	Bruno Verdi	278
Valtellina Sforzato Corte di Cama '18	Mamete Prevostini	260
Valtellina Sfursat 5 Stelle '17	Nino Negri	265
Valtellina Sup. Grumello Ris. '17	Dirupi	254
Valtellina Sup. Sassella Nuova Regina Ris. '13	Ar.Pe.Pe	238
Valtellina Sup. Valgella Carteria Ris. '16	Sandro Fay	255
Valtènesi Chiaretto Molmenti '17	Costaripa	253

CANTON TICINO

Ticino Merlot Carato Ris. '17	Vini Angelo Delea	299
Ticino Rosso di Chiara '17	Paolo Basso Wine	298

TRENTINO

L'Ora Nosiola '15	Toblino	321
Teroldego Rotaliano Luigi Ris. '16	Dorigati	312
Trentino Müller Thurgau Viàch '19	Corvée	311
Trentino Pinot Nero V. Cantanghel '17	Maso Cantanghel	316
Trentino Riesling '19	Pojer & Sandri	319
Trentino Vino Santo Arèle '07	Pravis	319
Trento Brut Altemasi Blanc de Noirs '16	Cavit	310
Trento Brut Aquila Reale '10	Cesarini Sforza	311
Trento Brut Cuvée dell'Abate Ris. '09	Abate Nero	308
Trento Brut Giulio Ferrari Riserva del Fondatore '09	Ferrari	313
Trento Brut Madame Martis Ris. '10	Maso Martis	316
Trento Brut Nature '14	Moser	318
Trento Brut Rotari Flavio Ris. '12	Mezzacorona	317
Trento Dosaggio Zero Letrari Ris. '14	Letrari	315

ALTO ADIGE

A. A. Bianco Grande Cuvée Beyond the Clouds '18	Elena Walch	356
A. A. Cabernet Sauvignon Freienfeld Ris. '16	Cantina Kurtatsch	341

Vino	Produttore	Pag.
A. A. Chardonnay Sanct Valentin '18	Cantina Produttori San Michele Appiano	348
A. A. Gewürztraminer Nussbaumer '18	Cantina Tramin	353
A. A. Lagrein Abtei Muri Ris. '17	Cantina Convento Muri-Gries	344
A. A. Lagrein Taber Ris. '18	Cantina Bolzano	329
A. A. Merlot V. Kressfeld Ris. '16	Tenuta Kornell	340
A. A. Müller Thurgau Feldmarschall von Fenner '18	Tiefenbrunner	352
A. A. Pinot Bianco Sirmian '19	Nals Margreid	345
A. A. Pinot Bianco Tyrol '18	Cantina Meran	344
A. A. Pinot Nero Trattmann Ris. '17	Cantina Girlan	334
A. A. Santa Maddalena Cl. '19	Tenuta Waldgries	356
A. A. Sauvignon Lafóa '18	Cantina Colterenzio	332
A. A. Sauvignon Renaissance Ris. '17	Gumphof Markus Prackwieser	336
A. A. Spumante Extra Brut M. Cl. 1919 Ris. '14	Kettmeir	338
A. A. Terlano Pinot Bianco Vorberg Ris. '17	Cantina Terlano	352
A. A. Val Venosta Riesling '18	Falkenstein Franz Pratzner	334
A. A. Valle Isarco Sylvaner '19	Strasserhof Hannes Baumgartner	350
A. A. Valle Isarco Sylvaner R '18	Köfererhof Günther Kerschbaumer	339
A. A. Valle Isarco Veltliner Praepositus '18	Abbazia di Novacella	328
VENETO		
Amarone della Valpolicella '16	Famiglia Cottini Monte Zovo	395
Amarone della Valpolicella Campo dei Gigli '16	Tenuta Sant'Antonio	427
Amarone della Valpolicella Case Vecie '15	Brigaldara	378
Amarone della Valpolicella Cl. '16	Allegrini	368
Amarone della Valpolicella Cl. '13	Secondo Marco	429
Amarone della Valpolicella Cl. Albasini '13	Villa Spinosa	443
Amarone della Valpolicella Cl. Ca' Florian Ris. '12	Tommasi Viticoltori	435
Amarone della Valpolicella Cl. Capitel Monte Olmi Ris. '15	F.lli Tedeschi	433
Amarone della Valpolicella Cl. Leone Zardini Ris. '13	Pietro Zardini	445
Amarone della Valpolicella Cl. Mazzano '12	Masi	409
Amarone della Valpolicella Cl. Monte Ca' Bianca Ris. '15	Lorenzo Begali	372
Amarone della Valpolicella Cl. Ris. '09	Giuseppe Quintarelli	422
Amarone della Valpolicella Cl. Sant'Urbano '16	Speri	430
Amarone della Valpolicella Mai Dire Mai '13	Pasqua - Cecilia Beretta	420
Bardolino Sup. Pràdicà '18	Corte Gardoni	392
Capitel Croce '19	Roberto Anselmi	369
Cartizze Brut La Rivetta	Villa Sandi	443
Colli Berici Carmenere Carminium '16	Inama	405
Colli Euganei Cabernet Borgo delle Casette Ris. '16	Il Filò delle Vigne	399
Colli Euganei Merlot Ris. '15	Vignalta	441
Conegliano Valdobbiadene Rive di Soligo Extra Brut '19	BiancaVigna	373

Wine	Producer	Page
Custoza Sup. Amedeo '18	Cavalchina	387
Custoza Sup. Ca' del Magro '18	Monte del Frà	413
Frank! '18	Barollo	371
Lessini Durello Dosaggio Zero M. Cl. Ris. '14	Casa Cecchin	385
Lessini Durello Pas Dosé M. Cl. Amedeo Ris. '15	Ca' Rugate	381
Lugana Molceo Ris. '18	Ottella	420
Lugana Sergio Zenato Ris. '17	Zenato	446
Madre '18	Italo Cescon	389
Riesling Renano Collezione di Famiglia '16	Roeno	424
Soave Cl. Calvarino '18	Leonildo Pieropan	421
Soave Cl. Campo Vulcano '19	I Campi	382
Soave Cl. La Froscà '18	Gini	402
Soave Sup. Il Casale '18	Agostino Vicentini	440
Soave Sup. Runcata '18	Dal Cero Tenuta Corte Giacobbe	395
Valdobbiadene Brut Ius Naturae '19	Bortolomiol	376
Valdobbiadene Brut Particella 68 '19	Sorelle Bronca	378
Valdobbiadene Extra Dry Casté '19	Merotto	411
Valdobbiadene Extra Dry Giustino B '19	Ruggeri & C.	425
Valdobbiadene Rive di Collalto Extra Brut '19	Borgoluce	375
Valdobbiadene Rive di Refrontolo Brut Col Del Forno '19	Andreola	368
Valpolicella Cl. Sup. Campo Morar '17	Viviani	444
Valpolicella Cl. Sup. Ognisanti '18	Bertani	372
Valpolicella Sup. Brolo dei Giusti '15	Cantina Valpantena Verona	438

FRIULI VENEZIA GIULIA

Wine	Producer	Page
Braide Alte '18	Livon	490
Capo Martino '18	Jermann	487
Collio '18	Edi Keber	487
Collio Bianco Blanc di Blanchis Ris. '17	Ronco Blanchis	508
Collio Bianco Broy '18	Eugenio Collavini	474
Collio Bianco Fosarin '18	Ronco dei Tassi	508
Collio Friulano '19	Schiopetto	512
Collio Friulano '18	Tenuta Stella	518
Collio Friulano Rassauer '19	Castello di Spessa	472
Collio Pinot Bianco '19	Doro Princic	503
Collio Pinot Bianco '19	Villa Russiz	527
Collio Pinot Grigio '19	Polje	501
Collio Sauvignon '19	Tenuta Borgo Conventi	464
Collio Sauvignon '19	Tiare - Roberto Snidarcig	520
Collio Sauvignon Ris. '16	Russiz Superiore	511
Eclisse '18	La Roncaia	506
FCO Bianco Myò I Fiori di Leonie '18	Zorzettig	531
FCO Biancosesto '18	Tunella	521
FCO Friulano '19	Torre Rosazza	521
FCO Sauvignon Liende '18	La Viarte	523
FCO Sauvignon Zuc di Volpe '19	Volpe Pasini	529
Friuli Isonzo Friulano I Ferretti '18	Tenuta Luisa	490
Friuli Isonzo Sauvignon Piere '18	Vie di Romans	524
Friuli Pinot Bianco '19	Vigneti Le Monde	489
Miklus Natural Art Ribolla Gialla '15	Draga - Miklus	480
Ribolla Gialla Selezione '10	Damijan Podversic	500

EMILIA ROMAGNA		
Arvange Pas Dosé M. Cl.	Cantina Valtidone	570
C. B. Pignoletto Frizzante '19	Floriano Cinti	549
Lambrusco di Sorbara Brut Rosé M. Cl. '15	Cantina della Volta	545
Lambrusco di Sorbara del Fondatore '19	Cleto Chiarli Tenute Agricole	549
Lambrusco di Sorbara Leclisse '19	Alberto Paltrinieri	560
Lambrusco di Sorbara V. del Cristo '19	Cavicchioli	547
MaraMia Sangiovese '18	Tenuta Mara	557
Reggiano Lambrusco Concerto '19	Ermete Medici & Figli	557
Romagna Albana Passito Scaccomatto '16	Fattoria Zerbina	573
Romagna Albana Secco A '19	Fattoria Monticino Rosso	558
Romagna Sangiovese Modigliana I Probi Ris. '17	Villa Papiano	572
Romagna Sangiovese Predappio Calisto Ris. '16	Stefano Berti	543
Romagna Sangiovese Predappio Godenza '18	Noelia Ricci	562
Romagna Sangiovese Predappio Le Lucciole Ris. '17	Chiara Condello	550
Romagna Sangiovese Sup. Primo Segno '18	Villa Venti	572
TUSCANY		
Alessandro Dal Borro Syrah '16	Il Borro	597
Aria di Caiarossa '16	Caiarossa	601
Baron'Ugo '16	Monteraponi	668
Bolgheri Rosso Rute '18	Guado al Melo	649
Bolgheri Rosso Sup. Grattamacco '17	Grattamacco	648
Bolgheri Rosso Sup. Le Gonnare '17	Fabio Motta	674
Bolgheri Rosso Sup. Ornellaia '17	Ornellaia	676
Bolgheri Rosso Villa Donoratico '18	Tenuta Argentiera	587
Bolgheri Rosso Volpolo '18	Podere Sapaio	709
Bolgheri Sup. Sassicaia '17	Tenuta San Guido	707
Bolgheri Varvàra '18	Castello di Bolgheri	612
Brunello di Montalcino '15	Baricci	592
Brunello di Montalcino '15	Camigliano	602
Brunello di Montalcino '15	Casisano	608
Brunello di Montalcino '15	Le Chiuse	620
Brunello di Montalcino '15	Donatella Cinelli Colombini	622
Brunello di Montalcino '15	Tenuta Fanti	636
Brunello di Montalcino '15	Le Macioche	660
Brunello di Montalcino '15	Poggio di Sotto	690
Brunello di Montalcino '15	Ridolfi	698
Brunello di Montalcino '15	Tenuta di Sesta	717
Brunello di Montalcino Giodo '15	Giodo	646
Brunello di Montalcino Madonna delle Grazie '15	Il Marroneto	663
Brunello di Montalcino Ripe al Convento di Castelgiocondo Ris. '14	Castelgiocondo	609
Brunello di Montalcino Tenuta Nuova '15	Casanova di Neri	608
Brunello di Montalcino V. del Suolo '15	Argiano	587
Brunello di Montalcino V. Schiena d'Asino '15	Mastrojanni	665
Brunello di Montalcino V. Spuntali '15	Val di Suga	725
Brunello di Montalcino Vignavecchia '15	San Polo	708
Campo di Camagi Cabernet Franc '18	Tenuta di Trinoro	717
Carmignano Ris. '17	Tenuta Le Farnete - Cantagallo	637
Carmignano Ris. '17	Piaggia	683

Orma '18	Orma	675
Paleo Rosso '17	Le Macchiole	659
Pinot Nero '17	Podere della Civettaja	623
Solaia '17	Marchesi Antinori	586
Valdarno di Sopra Merlot Galatrona '17	Fattoria Petrolo	682
Vernaccia di S. Gimignano Carato '17	Montenidoli	667
Vernaccia di S. Gimignano Ris. '16	Panizzi	679
Vernaccia di San Gimignano L'Albereta Ris. '17	Il Colombaio di Santa Chiara	628
Volta di Bertinga '16	Bertinga	594

MARCHE

Arshura '17	Valter Mattoni	780
Castelli di Jesi Verdicchio Cl. Ambrosia Ris. '17	Vignamato	798
Castelli di Jesi Verdicchio Cl. Ergo Sum Ris. Mirizzi '16	Montecappone - Mirizzi	781
Castelli di Jesi Verdicchio Cl. Rincrocca Ris. '17	La Staffa	792
Castelli di Jesi Verdicchio Cl. Salmariano Ris. '17	Marotti Campi	779
Castelli di Jesi Verdicchio Cl. V. Il Cantico della Figura Ris. '17	Andrea Felici	773
Conero Campo San Giorgio Ris. '16	Umani Ronchi	795
Falerio Pecorino Onirocep '19	Pantaleone	783
Kupra '17	Oasi degli Angeli	782
Offida Pecorino '19	Tenuta Santori	789
Offida Pecorino Artemisia '19	Tenuta Spinelli	792
Offida Pecorino Vignagiulia '19	Emanuele Dianetti	772
Piceno Sup. Morellone '16	Le Caniette	762
Rosso Piceno Sup. Roggio del Filare '17	Velenosi	797
Verdicchio dei Castelli di Jesi Cl. Sup. Ghiffa '18	Cològnola Tenuta Musone	768
Verdicchio dei Castelli di Jesi Cl. Sup. Massaccio '18	Tenute San Sisto Fazi Battaglia	788
Verdicchio dei Castelli di Jesi Cl. Sup. Qudì '18	Roberto Venturi	797
Verdicchio dei Castelli di Jesi Cl. Sup. Ylice '18	Poderi Mattioli	779
Verdicchio di Matelica Cambrugiano Ris. '17	Belisario	759
Verdicchio di Matelica Collestefano '19	Collestefano	767
Verdicchio di Matelica Senex Ris. '15	Bisci	759

UMBRIA

Adarmando Trebbiano Spoletino '18	Giampaolo Tabarrini	824
Brecciaro Ciliegiolo '18	Leonardo Bussoletti	809
Cervaro della Sala '18	Castello della Sala	811
Fiorfiore Grechetto '18	Roccafiore	822
Mattone Bianco Trebbiano '19	Briziarelli	809
Montefalco Rosso Lampante Ris. '17	Tenute Lunelli Castelbuono	816
Montefalco Rosso Pomontino '18	Tenuta Bellafonte	808
Montefalco Sagrantino Collepiano '16	Arnaldo Caprai	810
Montefalco Sagrantino Medeo '16	Romanelli	822
Montefalco Sagrantino Molino dell'Attone '15	Antonelli - San Marco	806
Orvieto Cl. Sup. Luigi e Giovanna '17	Barberani	807
Orvieto Cl. Villa Barbi '19	Decugnano dei Barbi	813

Todi Grechetto Sup. Colle Nobile '18	Tudernum	826
Torgiano Rosso Rubesco V. Monticchio Ris. '16	Lungarotti	816

LAZIO

Anthium '19	Casale del Giglio	834
Fiorano Rosso '15	Tenuta di Fiorano	843
Frascati Sup. '19	Castel de Paolis	836
Habemus '18	San Giovenale	843
Poggio della Costa '19	Sergio Mottura	840
Roma Rosso Ed. Limitata '17	Poggio Le Volpi	842
Sodale '18	Falesco Famiglia Cotarella	838

ABRUZZO

8½ Pecorino '19	Villa Medoro	868
Abruzzo Pecorino Castello di Semivicoli '19	Masciarelli	861
Abruzzo Pecorino Sup. Tegèo '18	Codice Vino	856
Cerasuolo d'Abruzzo '19	Emidio Pepe	863
Cerasuolo d'Abruzzo Giusi '19	Tenuta Terraviva	864
Cerasuolo d'Abruzzo Piè delle Vigne '18	Cataldi Madonna	854
Montepulciano d'Abruzzo '15	Valentini	866
Montepulciano d'Abruzzo Amorino '16	Castorani	853
Montepulciano d'Abruzzo Colline Teramane Zanna Ris. '15	Dino Illuminati	859
Montepulciano d'Abruzzo Mo Ris. '16	Cantina Tollo	865
Montepulciano d'Abruzzo Vign. Sant'Eusanio '18	Valle Reale	867
Trebbiano d'Abruzzo Bianchi Grilli per la Testa '18	Torre dei Beati	865
Trebbiano d'Abruzzo Solàrea '18	Agriverde	852
Tullum Pecorino Biologico '19	Feudo Antico	858

MOLISE

Molise Rosso Don Luigi Ris. '16	Di Majo Norante	874

CAMPANIA

Campi Flegrei Falanghina Cruna deLago '18	La Sibilla	900
Campi Flegrei Piedirosso Colle Rotondella '19	Cantine Astroni	879
Core Bianco '19	Montevetrano	892
Costa d'Amalfi Furore Bianco Fiorduva '19	Marisa Cuomo	884
Falanghina del Sannio Janare Senete '19	La Guardiense	891
Falanghina del Sannio Sant'Agata dei Goti V. Segreta '18	Mustilli	892
Falanghina del Sannio Svelato '19	Terre Stregate	901
Falanghina del Sannio Taburno '19	Fontanavecchia	888
Fiano di Avellino '19	Colli di Lapio	883
Fiano di Avellino '19	Tenuta Scuotto	899
Fiano di Avellino Alimata '18	Villa Raiano	903
Fiano di Avellino Pietramara '19	I Favati	886
Fiano di Avellino Tognano '17	Rocca del Principe	896
Greco di Tufo '19	Fonzone	889
Greco di Tufo Claudio Quarta Special Edition '19	Sanpaolo di Claudio Quarta	898
Greco di Tufo G '19	Di Meo	885
Morrone Pallagrello Bianco '18	Alois	878
Pian di Stio '19	San Salvatore 1988	898

Taurasi '16	Donnachiara	886
Taurasi '15	Fiorentino	888
Taurasi V. Cinque Querce '13	Salvatore Molettieri	891
Taurasi V. Macchia dei Goti '16	Antonio Caggiano	881
Zagreo '18	I Cacciagalli	880

BASILICATA

Aglianico del Vulture Donato D'Angelo '17	Donato D'Angelo di Filomena Ruppi	916
Aglianico del Vulture Gricos '18	Grifalco	917
Aglianico del Vulture Il Repertorio '18	Cantine del Notaio	915
Aglianico del Vulture Nocte '16	Terra dei Re	920
Aglianico del Vulture Sup. Serpara '16	Re Manfredi Cantina Terre degli Svevi	919
Aglianico del Vulture Titolo '18	Elena Fucci	916

PUGLIA

1943 del Presidente '18	Cantine Due Palme	928
Askos Verdeca '19	Masseria Li Veli	932
Brindisi Rosso Susumaniello Oltremé '18	Tenute Rubino	938
Castel del Monte Rosso Bolonero '19	Torrevento	942
Collezione Privata Cosimo Varvaglione Old Vines Negroamaro '17	Varvaglione 1921	944
Gioia del Colle Primitivo 17 Vign. Montevella '17	Polvanera	936
Gioia del Colle Primitivo Muro Sant'Angelo Contrada Barbatto '17	Tenute Chiaromonte	927
Gioia del Colle Primitivo Ris. '17	Plantamura	935
Gioia del Colle Primitivo Sellato '18	Tenuta Viglione	945
Gioia del Colle Primitivo Senatore '17	Coppi	927
Onirico '18	Terre dei Vaaz	940
Orfeo Negroamaro '18	Cantine Paolo Leo	931
Otto '18	Carvinea	925
Primitivo di Manduria Lirica '18	Produttori di Manduria	937
Primitivo di Manduria Piano Chiuso 26 27 63 Ris. '17	Masca del Tacco	933
Primitivo di Manduria Raccontami '18	Vespa Vignaioli per Passione	944
Primitivo di Manduria Sessantanni '17	Cantine San Marzano	939
Primitivo di Manduria Sinfarosa Zinfandel '18	Felline	929

CALABRIA

Cirò Rosso Cl. Sup. Duca San Felice Ris. '18	Librandi	956
Esmen Tetra '18	Tenuta del Travale	959
Grisara Pecorello '19	Roberto Ceraudo	954
Moscato Passito '19	Luigi Viola	959
Pi Greco '19	Antonella Lombardo	956

SICILY

Cerasuolo di Vittoria Giambattista Valli '18	Feudi del Pisciotto	975
Cerasuolo di Vittoria Il Para Para '17	Poggio di Bortolone	985
Etna Bianco Alta Mora '19	Alta Mora	967
Etna Bianco Arcuria '18	Graci	979
Etna Bianco Pietrarizzo '19	Tornatore	991
Etna Bianco Trainara '18	Generazione Alessandro	978

Etna Rosso Barbagalli '17	Pietradolce	984
Etna Rosso Contrada Santo Spirito Part. 468 '16	Palmento Costanzo	983
Etna Rosso Erse Contrada Moscamento 1911 '17	Tenuta di Fessina	989
Etna Rosso Lenza di Munti 720 slm '17	Cantine Nicosia	981
Etna Rosso Passorosso '18	Passopisciaro	983
Etna Rosso Qubba '18	Monteleone	980
Etna Rosso San Lorenzo '18	Girolamo Russo	988
Etna Rosso V. Vico Prephylloxera '17	Tenute Bosco	970
Etna Rosso Zottorinoto Ris. '16	Cottanera	973
Faro '18	Le Casematte	972
Malvasia delle Lipari Passito '19	Caravaglio	971
Passito di Pantelleria Ben Ryé '17	Donnafugata	974
Salealto Tenuta Ficuzza '18	Cusumano	974
Sicilia Catarrato V. di Mandranova '18	Alessandro di Camporeale	966
Sicilia Chardonnay V. San Francesco Tenuta Regaleali '18	Tasca d'Almerita	989
Sicilia Mandrarossa Cartagho '18	Cantine Settesoli	988
Sicilia Nero d'Avola Saia '18	Feudo Maccari	976
Sicilia Perricone Furioso '17	Assuli	967
Sicilia Perricone Ribeca '15	Firriato	977
Sicilia Zibibbo Al Qasar '19	Rallo	986

SARDINIA

Alghero Torbato Catore '18	Tenute Sella & Mosca	1021
Cannonau di Sardegna Cl. Dule '17	Giuseppe Gabbas	1010
Cannonau di Sardegna Mamuthone '17	Giuseppe Sedilesu	1020
Cannonau di Sardegna Naniha '18	Tenute Perdarubia	1017
Cannonau di Sardegna Nepente di Oliena Pro Vois Ris. '15	F.lli Puddu	1018
Capichera V. T. '17	Capichera	1005
Carignano del Sulcis 6 Mura Ris. '17	Cantina Giba	1011
Carignano del Sulcis Sup. Terre Brune '16	Cantina Santadi	1019
Nuracada Bovale '18	Audarya	1004
Su' Nico '18	Su Entu	1022
Turriga '16	Argiolas	1004
Vermentino di Gallura Sup. Sciala '19	Surrau	1022
Vermentino di Sardegna Stellato '19	Pala	1016
Vernaccia di Oristano Antico Gregori '76	Attilio Contini	1007
Vernaccia di Oristano Ris. '68	Silvio Carta	1006

THE BEST

RED OF THE YEAR

BAROLO ORNATO '16 - PIO CESARE

WHITE OF THE YEAR

SOPRAQUOTA 900 '19 - ROSSET TERROIR

SPARKLER OF THE YEAR

OP PINOT NERO DOSAGGIO ZERO FARFALLA CAVE PRIVÉE '11
BALLABIO

ROSÈ OF THE YEAR

CERASUOLO D'ABRUZZO PIÈ DELLE VIGNE '18
CATALDI MADONNA

MEDITATION WINE OF THE YEAR

VERNACCIA DI ORISTANO ANTICO GREGORI '76 - CONTINI

BEST VALUE FOR MONEY

FRIULI PINOT BIANCO '19 – VIGNETI LE MONDE

WINERY OF THE YEAR

SANTA MARGHERITA GRUPPO VINICOLO

CA' DEL BOSCO, CÀ MAIOL, KETTMEIR, LAMOLE DI LAMOLE, MESA

COOPERATIVE OF THE YEAR

SAN MICHELE APPIANO

UP-AND-COMING WINERY

RIDOLFI

GROWER OF THE YEAR

ANTONELLA LOMBARDO

AWARD FOR SUSTAINABLE VITICULTURE

FIRRIATO

SOLIDARITY AWARD

VILLA RUSSIZ

TRE BICCHIERI VERDI

With our Tre Bicchieri Verdi we make note of those wines made with certified organic or biodynami-cally cultivated grapes (here indicated in red). This year there were a record 126 in all, 27% of the total wines awarded. It's an important figure that attests to a growing focus on ecology, from micro wineries to large producers, all of whom are taking on the many challenges associated with sustai-nable winemaking.

Aglianico del Vulture Gricos '18	Grifalco	**Basilicata**
Aglianico del Vulture Titolo '18	Elena Fucci	**Basilicata**
Alessandro Dal Borro Syrah '16	Il Borro	**Tuscany**
Amarone della Valpolicella Cl. Sant'Urbano '16	Speri	**Veneto**
Aria di Caiarossa '16	Caiarossa	Tuscany
Arvange Pas Dosé M. Cl.	Cantina Valtidone	**Emilia Romagna**
Barbaresco Currà '15	Sottimano	**Piedmont**
Barbaresco Rabajà '16	Bruno Rocca	**Piedmont**
Barbera d'Asti Sup. La Luna e i Falò '18	Vite Colte	**Piedmont**
Barbera del M.to Sup. Cantico della Crosia '17	Vicara	Piedmont
Barolo Cerretta '16	Brandini	**Piedmont**
Barolo Lazzarito '16	Casa E. di Mirafiore	**Piedmont**
Barolo Liste '15	Giacomo Borgogno & Figli	**Piedmont**
Barolo Meriame '16	Paolo Manzone	**Piedmont**
Barolo Villero '16	Brovia	**Piedmont**
Baron'Ugo '16	Monteraponi	**Tuscany**
Bolgheri Rosso Sup. Grattamacco '17	Grattamacco	**Tuscany**
Bolgheri Rosso Volpolo '18	Podere Sapaio	**Tuscany**
Brecciaro Ciliegiolo '18	Leonardo Bussoletti	**Umbria**
Brunello di Montalcino '15	Le Chiuse	**Tuscany**
Brunello di Montalcino '15	Poggio di Sotto	**Tuscany**
Brunello di Montalcino Giodo '15	Giodo	**Tuscany**
Campi Flegrei Piedirosso Colle Rotondella '19	Cantine Astroni	**Campania**
Cannonau di Sardegna Naniha '18	Tenute Perdarubia	**Sardinia**
Cannonau di Sardegna Nepente di Oliena Pro Vois Ris. '15	F.lli Puddu	**Sardinia**
Cartizze Brut La Rivetta	Villa Sandi	**Veneto**
Castelli di Jesi Verdicchio Cl. Rincrocca Ris. '17	La Staffa	**Marche**
Castelli di Jesi Verdicchio Cl. V. Il Cantico della Figura Ris. '17	Andrea Felici	**Marche**
Cerasuolo d'Abruzzo '19	Emidio Pepe	Abruzzo
Cerasuolo d'Abruzzo Giusi '19	Tenuta Terraviva	**Abruzzo**

Cerasuolo d'Abruzzo Piè delle Vigne '18	Cataldi Madonna	**Abruzzo**
Chianti Cl. '18	Badia a Coltibuono	**Tuscany**
Chianti Cl. '17	Val delle Corti	**Tuscany**
Chianti Cl. Lamole '18	I Fabbri	**Tuscany**
Chianti Cl. Montaperto '17	Fattoria Carpineta Fontalpino	**Tuscany**
Chianti Cl. Ris. '17	Bibbiano	**Tuscany**
Chianti Cl. Ris. '17	Castello di Albola	**Tuscany**
Chianti Cl. Ris. '17	Castello di Volpaia	**Tuscany**
Chianti Cl. Ris. '17	Tenuta di Lilliano	**Tuscany**
Chianti Cl. V. Istine '18	Istine	**Tuscany**
Colli Berici Carmenere Carminium '16	Inama	**Veneto**
Colline Lucchesi Tenuta di Valgiano '16	Tenuta di Valgiano	**Tuscany**
Collio Friulano '18	Tenuta Stella	**Friuli Venezia Giulia**
Conegliano Valdobbiadene Rive di Soligo Extra Brut '19	BiancaVigna	**Veneto**
Conero Campo San Giorgio Ris. '16	Umani Ronchi	**Marche**
Cortona Syrah '17	Stefano Amerighi	**Tuscany**
Duemani '17	Duemani	**Tuscany**
Etna Bianco Arcuria '18	Graci	**Sicily**
Etna Rosso Contrada Santo Spirito Part. 468 '16	Palmento Costanzo	**Sicily**
Etna Rosso Lenza di Munti 720 slm '17	Cantine Nicosia	**Sicily**
Etna Rosso San Lorenzo '18	Girolamo Russo	**Sicily**
Etna Rosso V. Vico Prephylloxera '17	Tenute Bosco	**Sicily**
Falerio Pecorino Onirocep '19	Pantaleone	**Marche**
Faro '18	Le Casematte	**Sicily**
Fiano di Avellino Alimata '18	Villa Raiano	**Campania**
Fiorano Rosso '15	Tenuta di Fiorano	**Lazio**
Franciacorta Brut Eronero '12	Ferghettina	**Lombardy**
Franciacorta Dosage Zéro Naturae '16	Barone Pizzini	**Lombardy**
Franciacorta Dosage Zéro Vintage Collection Noir '11	Ca' del Bosco	**Lombardy**
Franciacorta Extra Brut EBB '15	Mosnel	**Lombardy**
Franciacorta Extra Brut Extreme Palazzo Lana Ris. '09	Guido Berlucchi & C.	**Lombardy**
Gioia del Colle Primitivo 17 Vign. Montevella '17	Polvanera	**Puglia**
Gioia del Colle Primitivo Ris. '17	Plantamura	**Puglia**
Gioia del Colle Primitivo Sellato '18	Tenuta Viglione	**Puglia**
Gioia del Colle Primitivo Senatore '17	Coppi	**Puglia**
Grisara Pecorello '19	Roberto Ceraudo	**Calabria**
Guardiavigna '16	Podere Forte	**Tuscany**
Habemus '18	San Giovenale	**Lazio**
L'Ora Nosiola '15	Toblino	**Trentino**
La Gioia '16	Riecine	**Tuscany**
La Regola '17	Podere La Regola	**Tuscany**
Lugana Madreperla Ris. '18	Perla del Garda	**Lombardy**
Madre '18	Italo Cescon	**Veneto**

Malvasia delle Lipari Passito '19	Caravaglio	**Sicily**
MaraMia Sangiovese '18	Tenuta Mara	**Emilia Romagna**
Molise Rosso Don Luigi Ris. '16	Di Majo Norante	**Molise**
Montecucco Sangiovese Poggio Lombrone Ris. '16	Colle Massari	**Tuscany**
Montefalco Rosso Lampante Ris. '17	Tenute Lunelli - Castelbuono	**Umbria**
Montefalco Sagrantino Medeo '16	Romanelli	**Umbria**
Montefalco Sagrantino Molino dell'Attone '15	Antonelli - San Marco	**Umbria**
Montepulciano d'Abruzzo Amorino '16	Castorani	**Abruzzo**
Montepulciano d'Abruzzo Vign. Sant'Eusanio '18	Valle Reale	**Abruzzo**
Moscato Passito '19	Luigi Viola	**Calabria**
Nambrot '17	Tenuta di Ghizzano	**Tuscany**
Nobile di Montepulciano '17	Salcheto	**Tuscany**
Offida Pecorino '19	Tenuta Santori	**Marche**
Oreno '18	Tenuta Sette Ponti	**Tuscany**
Orfeo Negroamaro '18	Cantine Paolo Leo	**Puglia**
Orvieto Cl. Sup. Luigi e Giovanna '17	Barberani	**Umbria**
Otto '18	Carvinea	**Puglia**
Pian di Stio '19	San Salvatore 1988	**Campania**
Piceno Sup. Morellone '16	Le Caniette	**Marche**
Pinot Nero '17	Podere della Civettaja	**Tuscany**
Poggio della Costa '19	Sergio Mottura	**Lazio**
Primitivo di Manduria Sessantanni '17	Cantine San Marzano	**Puglia**
Primitivo di Manduria Sinfarosa Zinfandel '18	Felline	**Puglia**
Reggiano Lambrusco Concerto '19	Ermete Medici & Figli	**Emilia Romagna**
Ribolla Gialla Selezione '10	Damijan Podversic	**Friuli Venezia Giulia**
Roero Mompissano Ris. '17	Cascina Ca' Rossa	**Piedmont**
Romagna Sangiovese Modigliana I Probi Ris. '17	Villa Papiano	**Emilia Romagna**
Romagna Sangiovese Sup. Primo Segno '18	Villa Venti	**Emilia Romagna**
Sicilia Catarrato V. di Mandranova '18	Alessandro di Camporeale	**Sicily**
Sicilia Nero d'Avola Saia '18	Feudo Maccari	**Sicily**
Sicilia Perricone Furioso '17	Assuli	**Sicily**
Sicilia Perricone Ribeca '15	Firriato	**Sicily**
Sicilia Zibibbo Al Qasar '19	Rallo	**Sicily**
Soave Cl. Calvarino '18	Leonildo Pieropan	**Veneto**
Soave Cl. La Froscà '18	Gini	**Veneto**
Taurasi '16	Donnachiara	**Campania**
Trebbiano d'Abruzzo Bianchi Grilli per la Testa '18	Torre dei Beati	**Abruzzo**
Trebbiano d'Abruzzo Solàrea '18	Agriverde	**Abruzzo**
Trentino Pinot Nero V. Cantanghel '17	Maso Cantanghel	**Trentino**
Trentino Riesling '19	Pojer & Sandri	**Trentino**
Trento Brut Madame Martis Ris. '10	Maso Martis	**Trentino**

Tullum Pecorino Biologico '19	Feudo Antico	**Abruzzo**
Valdarno di Sopra Merlot Galatrona '17	Fattoria Petrolo	**Tuscany**
Valle d'Aosta Chambave Muscat Flétri '18	La Vrille	**Valle d'Aosta**
Verdicchio dei Castelli di Jesi Cl. Sup. Ghiffa '18	Cològnola - Tenuta Musone	**Marche**
Verdicchio dei Castelli di Jesi Cl. Sup. Ylice '18	Poderi Mattioli	**Marche**
Verdicchio di Matelica Collestefano '19	Collestefano	**Marche**
Verdicchio di Matelica Senex Ris. '15	Bisci	**Marche**
Vernaccia di Oristano Antico Gregori '76	Attilio Contini	**Sardinia**
Vernaccia di Oristano Ris. '68	Silvio Carta	**Sardinia**
Vernaccia di S. Gimignano Carato '17	Montenidoli	**Tuscany**
Vernaccia di San Gimignano L'Albereta Ris. '17	Il Colombaio di Santa Chiara	**Tuscany**
Zagreo '18	I Cacciagalli	**Campania**

TABLE OF VINTAGES FROM 1995 TO 2018

	ALTO ADIGE BIANCO	LUGANA / SOAVE	FRIULI BIANCO
2006	3	3	5
2007	3	4	5
2008	3	4	3
2009	4	5	4
2010	5	4	2
2011	3	3	3
2012	4	3	4
2013	4	4	4
2014	2	3	3
2015	4	4	5
2016	5	5	5
2017	3	4	4
2018	4	5	5
2019	5	4	4

TABLE OF VINTAGES

VERDICCHIO DEI CASTELLI DI JESI	FIANO DI AVELLINO	GRECO DI TUFO	FRANCIACORTA
5	4	4	4
2	3	2	3
4	3	5	5
4	3	4	3
5	5	5	3
1	3	2	5
4	4	4	4
5	5	3	5
3	3	3	3
3	4	3	3
5	5	4	4
2	3	3	4
4	5	4	
4	4	4	

TABLE OF VINTAGES

	BARBARESCO	BAROLO	AMARONE	CHIANTI CLASSICO
1995	3	3	5	5
1996	5	5	3	4
1997	3	3	4	4
1998	3	4	3	3
1999	5	4	3	5
2000	3	3	4	4
2001	5	5	5	5
2002	2	2	3	2
2003	2	2	3	2
2004	4	4	4	4
2005	3	3	4	3
2006	3	4	3	3
2007	3	3	5	4
2008	4	4	4	4
2009	2	2	3	3
2010	5	5	4	5
2011	4	4	4	3
2012	3	3	3	3
2013	5	5	4	4
2014	3	2	2	3
2015	4	4	4	4
2016	5	5	5	5
2017	3			3
2018				4

TABLE OF VINTAGES

BRUNELLO DI MONTALCINO	BOLGHERI	TAURASI	MONTEPULCIANO D'ABRUZZO	ETNA ROSSO
5	4	3	5	3
2	3	3	4	2
4	4	4	4	3
4	5	2	4	3
5	5	5	2	4
3	3	2	4	3
5	5	4	5	4
2	2	3	2	2
3	2	4	3	3
4	3	4	4	3
3	3	3	4	4
4	4	3	3	4
4	4	4	5	5
3	4	5	3	5
2	5	3	2	3
5	3	4	2	4
4	4	2	4	5
3	4	3	3	4
5	5	4	4	3
2	2	3	2	5
4	4	4	4	3
	4	3	3	5
	3		3	3
	4			4

STARS

58

Gaja (Piedmont)

45

Ca' del Bosco (Lombardy)

39

Elio Altare (Piedmont)

38

La Spinetta (Piedmont)

36

Allegrini (Veneto)
Valentini (Abruzzo)

34

Castello di Fonterutoli (Tuscany)

32

Bellavista (Lombardy)
Giacomo Conterno (Piedmont)
Jermann (Friuli Venezia Giulia)
Tenuta San Guido (Tuscany)
Cantina Produttori San Michele Appiano (Alto Adige)

31

Castello della Sala (Umbria)
Ferrari (Trentino)
Masciarelli (Abruzzo)

30

Planeta (Sicily)

29

Poliziano (Tuscany)
Tasca d'Almerita (Sicily)
Cantina Tramin (Alto Adige)
Vie di Romans (Friuli Venezia Giulia)

28

Marchesi Antinori (Tuscany)
Fèlsina (Tuscany)
Bruno Giacosa (Piedmont)
Leonildo Pieropan (Veneto)

27

Feudi di San Gregorio (Campania)
Ornellaia (Tuscany)

26

Argiolas (Sardinia)
Cantina Bolzano (Alto Adige)
Arnaldo Caprai (Umbria)
Castello di Ama (Tuscany)
Livio Felluga (Friuli Venezia Giulia)
Nino Negri (Lombardy)
Paolo Scavino (Piedmont)
Schiopetto (Friuli Venezia Giulia)
Villa Russiz (Friuli Venezia Giulia)

25

Falesco - Famiglia Cotarella (Lazio)
Tenute Sella & Mosca (Sardinia)
Cantina Terlano (Alto Adige)

24

Ca' Viola (Piedmont)
Cantina Colterenzio (Alto Adige)
Fontodi (Tuscany)
Gravner (Friuli Venezia Giulia)
Isole e Olena (Tuscany)
Vietti (Piedmont)

23

Michele Chiarlo (Piedmont)
Les Crêtes (Valle d'Aosta)
Montevetrano (Campania)
Barone Ricasoli (Tuscany)
San Leonardo (Trentino)
Volpe Pasini (Friuli Venezia Giulia)
Elena Walch (Alto Adige)

22
Ca' Rugate (Veneto)
Cascina La Barbatella (Piedmont)
Castellare di Castellina (Tuscany)
Domenico Clerico (Piedmont)
Cantina Kaltern (Alto Adige)
Le Macchiole (Tuscany)
Montevertine (Tuscany)

21
Castello del Terriccio (Tuscany)
Cataldi Madonna (Abruzzo)
Cusumano (Sicily)
Donnafugata (Sicily)
Ruffino (Tuscany)
Cantina Santadi (Sardinia)
Serafini & Vidotto (Veneto)
Sottimano (Piedmont)

20
Abbazia di Novacella (Alto Adige)
Antoniolo (Piedmont)
Dorigo (Friuli Venezia Giulia)
Firriato (Sicily)
Gioacchino Garofoli (Marche)
Elio Grasso (Piedmont)
Lis Neris (Friuli Venezia Giulia)
Livon (Friuli Venezia Giulia)
Monsupello (Lombardy)
Cantina Convento Muri-Gries (Alto Adige)
Fiorenzo Nada (Piedmont)
Giuseppe Quintarelli (Veneto)
Bruno Rocca (Piedmont)
Ronco dei Tassi (Friuli Venezia Giulia)
Franco Toros (Friuli Venezia Giulia)
Umani Ronchi (Marche)
Venica & Venica (Friuli Venezia Giulia)

★

19
Roberto Anselmi (Veneto)
Casanova di Neri (Tuscany)
Coppo (Piedmont)
Matteo Correggia (Piedmont)
Massolino - Vigna Rionda (Piedmont)
Palari (Sicily)
Doro Princic (Friuli Venezia Giulia)
San Patrignano (Emilia Romagna)
Luciano Sandrone (Piedmont)
Velenosi (Marche)
Le Vigne di Zamò
(Friuli Venezia Giulia)
Fattoria Zerbina (Emilia Romagna)

18
Lorenzo Begali (Veneto)
Bertani (Veneto)
Brancaia (Tuscany)
Castello Banfi (Tuscany)
Conterno Fantino (Piedmont)
Kuenhof - Peter Pliger (Alto Adige)
Mastroberardino (Campania)
Fattoria Petrolo (Tuscany)

17
Abbona (Piedmont)
Bucci (Marche)
Cavit (Trentino)
Di Majo Norante (Molise)
Grattamacco (Tuscany)
Librandi (Calabria)
Lungarotti (Umbria)
Bartolo Mascarello (Piedmont)
Masi (Veneto)
Pietracupa (Campania)
Querciabella (Tuscany)
Albino Rocca (Piedmont)
Rocca di Frassinello (Tuscany)
San Felice (Tuscany)
Tenuta Sant'Antonio (Veneto)
Speri (Veneto)
Suavia (Veneto)
Tenuta Unterortl - Castel Juval
(Alto Adige)
Vignalta (Veneto)
Viviani (Veneto)

16
F.lli Alessandria (Piedmont)
Aldo Conterno (Piedmont)
Romano Dal Forno (Veneto)
Ferghettina (Lombardy)
Tenuta di Ghizzano (Tuscany)
Dino Illuminati (Abruzzo)
Malvirà (Piedmont)
Miani (Friuli Venezia Giulia)
La Monacesca (Marche)
Sergio Mottura (Lazio)
Piaggia (Tuscany)

Russiz Superiore (Friuli Venezia Giulia)
Valle Reale (Abruzzo)

15

Giulio Accornero e Figli (Piedmont)
Biondi - Santi Tenuta Greppo (Tuscany)
Boscarelli (Tuscany)
Ca' del Baio (Piedmont)
Cavalchina (Veneto)
Tenute Cisa Asinari dei Marchesi di Grésy (Piedmont)
Elvio Cogno (Piedmont)
Eugenio Collavini (Friuli Venezia Giulia)
Poderi Luigi Einaudi (Piedmont)
Falkenstein Franz Pratzner (Alto Adige)
Tenute Ambrogio e Giovanni Folonari (Tuscany)
Frescobaldi (Tuscany)
Elena Fucci (Basilicata)
Köfererhof - Günther Kerschbaumer (Alto Adige)
Leone de Castris (Puglia)
Mamete Prevostini (Lombardy)
Monchiero Carbone (Piedmont)
Nals Margreid (Alto Adige)
Oasi degli Angeli (Marche)
Graziano Prà (Veneto)
Produttori del Barbaresco (Piedmont)
Aldo Rainoldi (Lombardy)
Tenuta di Valgiano (Tuscany)
Villa Medoro (Abruzzo)
Roberto Voerzio (Piedmont)
Zenato (Veneto)

14

Avignonesi (Tuscany)
Bricco Rocche - Bricco Asili (Piedmont)
Brovia (Piedmont)
Piero Busso (Piedmont)
Cascina Ca' Rossa (Piedmont)
Castello di Albola (Tuscany)
Castello di Volpaia (Tuscany)
Cantine Due Palme (Puglia)
Ettore Germano (Piedmont)
Gini (Veneto)
Cantina Girlan (Alto Adige)
Edi Keber (Friuli Venezia Giulia)
Cantina Kurtatsch (Alto Adige)
Franco M. Martinetti (Piedmont)
Fattoria Le Pupille (Tuscany)
Ronco del Gelso (Friuli Venezia Giulia)
Torrevento (Puglia)
Uberti (Lombardy)
Villa Sparina (Piedmont)

13

Maison Anselmet (Valle d'Aosta)
Braida (Piedmont)
Brigaldara (Veneto)
Cavalleri (Lombardy)
Tenuta Col d'Orcia (Tuscany)
Colle Massari (Tuscany)
Marisa Cuomo (Campania)
Dorigati (Trentino)
Le Due Terre (Friuli Venezia Giulia)
Foradori (Trentino)
Galardi (Campania)
Maculan (Veneto)
Marchesi di Barolo (Piedmont)
Vigneti Massa (Piedmont)
Pecchenino (Piedmont)
Poggio di Sotto (Tuscany)
Tenute Rubino (Puglia)
Salvioni (Tuscany)
Giampaolo Tabarrini (Umbria)
Tenute del Cerro (Tuscany)
Tormaresca (Puglia)
Torraccia del Piantavigna (Piedmont)
Tua Rita (Tuscany)
G. D. Vajra (Piedmont)

12

Abate Nero (Trentino)
Gianfranco Alessandria (Piedmont)
Azelia (Piedmont)
Benanti (Sicily)
Guido Berlucchi & C. (Lombardy)
Cà Maiol (Lombardy)
I Campi (Veneto)
Fattoria Carpineta Fontalpino (Tuscany)
Castello dei Rampolla (Tuscany)
Tenute Chiaromonte (Puglia)
Cleto Chiarli Tenute Agricole (Emilia Romagna)
Colli di Lapio (Campania)
Còlpetrone (Umbria)
Cottanera (Sicily)
Feudi del Pisciotto (Sicily)
Feudo Maccari (Sicily)

Giuseppe Gabbas (Sardinia)
Giorgi (Lombardy)
Franz Haas (Alto Adige)
Lo Triolet (Valle d'Aosta)
Cantine Lunae Bosoni (Liguria)
Mastrojanni (Tuscany)
Ermete Medici & Figli (Emilia Romagna)
Orma (Tuscany)
Ottella (Veneto)
Pio Cesare (Piedmont)
Dario Raccaro (Friuli Venezia Giulia)
Rocche dei Manzoni (Piedmont)
Ruggeri & C. (Veneto)
Tenute San Sisto - Fazi Battaglia (Marche)
Luigi Spertino (Piedmont)
Tiefenbrunner (Alto Adige)

11

Badia a Coltibuono (Tuscany)
Borgo San Daniele (Friuli Venezia Giulia)
Bruna (Liguria)
Tenuta di Capezzana (Tuscany)
Capichera (Sardinia)
Castello di Monsanto (Tuscany)
Castello di Spessa (Friuli Venezia Giulia)
F.lli Cigliuti (Piedmont)
Paolo Conterno (Piedmont)
Corte Sant'Alda (Veneto)
Guerrieri Rizzardi (Veneto)
Gumphof - Markus Prackwieser (Alto Adige)
Letrari (Trentino)
Giuseppe Mascarello e Figlio (Piedmont)
La Massa (Tuscany)
Cantina Meran (Alto Adige)
Monte del Frà (Veneto)
Poderi e Cantine Oddero (Piedmont)
Pietradolce (Sicily)
Poggio Le Volpi (Lazio)
Polvanera (Puglia)
Prunotto (Piedmont)
Re Manfredi - Cantina Terre degli Svevi (Basilicata)
Podere Sapaio (Tuscany)
Tenuta Sette Ponti (Tuscany)
F.lli Tedeschi (Veneto)
Villa Sandi (Veneto)
Luigi Viola (Calabria)
Tenuta Waldgries (Alto Adige)

10

Nicola Balter (Trentino)
Belisario (Marche)
Enzo Boglietti (Piedmont)
Giacomo Borgogno & Figli (Piedmont)
Carvinea (Puglia)
Castello di Cigognola (Lombardy)
Castorani (Abruzzo)
Cavallotto - Tenuta Bricco Boschis (Piedmont)
Famiglia Cecchi (Tuscany)
Ceretto (Piedmont)
Giovanni Corino (Piedmont)
Hilberg - Pasquero (Piedmont)
Tenuta J. Hofstätter (Alto Adige)
Inama (Veneto)
Alois Lageder (Alto Adige)
Tenuta di Lilliano (Tuscany)
Merotto (Veneto)
Monte Rossa (Lombardy)
Montenidoli (Tuscany)
Elio Ottin (Valle d'Aosta)
Paternoster (Basilicata)
Le Piane (Piedmont)
Poggio Antico (Tuscany)
Riecine (Tuscany)
Giuseppe Rinaldi (Piedmont)
Rocca delle Macìe (Tuscany)
Giovanni Rosso (Piedmont)
Girolamo Russo (Sicily)
Enrico Serafino (Piedmont)
Tacchino (Piedmont)
Tenimenti Luigi d'Alessandro (Tuscany)
Tenuta delle Terre Nere (Sicily)
Torre dei Beati (Abruzzo)
Agostino Vicentini (Veneto)
Villa Matilde Avallone (Campania)
Conti Zecca (Puglia)

HOW TO USE THE GUIDE

WINERY INFORMATION

CELLAR SALES
PRE-BOOK VISITS
ACCOMODATION
RESTAURANT SERVICE

ANNUAL PRODUCTION
HECTARES UNDER VINE
SUSTAINABLE WINERY

VITICULTURE METHOD
- certified biodynamic
- certified organic

N.B. The figures related here are provided annually by the producers.
The publisher is not responsible for eventual errors or inconsistencies.

SYMBOLS

○ WHITE WINE
⊙ ROSÈ
● RED WINE

RATINGS

🍷 MODERATELY GOOD TO GOOD WINES IN THEIR RESPECTIVE CATEGORIES
🍷🍷 VERY GOOD TO EXCELLENT WINES IN THEIR RESPECTIVE CATEGORIES
🍷🍷 VERY GOOD TO EXCELLENT WINES THAT WENT FORWARD TO THE FINAL TASTINGS
🍷🍷🍷 EXCELLENT WINES IN THEIR RESPECTIVE CATEGORIES

WINES RATED IN PREVIOUS EDITIONS OF THE GUIDE ARE INDICATED BY WHITE GLASSES (🍷, 🍷🍷, 🍷🍷🍷), PROVIDED THEY ARE STILL DRINKING AT THE LEVEL FOR WHICH THE ORIGINAL AWARD WAS MADE.

STAR ★

INDICATES WINERIES THAT HAVE WON TEN TRE BICCHIERI AWARDS FOR EACH STAR

PRICE RANGES

1 up to 5 euro	2 from € 5.01 to € 10.00
3 from € 10.01 to € 15.00	4 from € 15.01 to € 20.00
5 from € 20.01 to € 30.00	6 from € 30.01 to € 40.00
7 from € 40.01 to € 50.00	8 more than € 50.01

PRICES INDICATED REFER TO AVERAGE PRICES IN WINE STORES

ASTERISK *

INDICATES ESPECIALLY GOOD VALUE WINES

ABBREVIATIONS

A. A.	Alto Adige	P.R.	Peduncolo Rosso (red bunchstem)
C.	Colli	P.	Prosecco
Cl.	Classico	Rif. Agr.	Riforma Agraria (agrarian reform)
C.S.	Cantina Sociale (co-operative winery)	Ris.	Riserva
CEV	Colli Etruschi Viterbesi	Sel.	Selezione
Cons.	Consorzio	Sup.	Superiore
Coop.Agr.	Cooperativa Agricola (farming co-operative)	TdF	Terre di Franciacorta
C. B.	Colli Bolognesi	V.	Vigna (vineyard)
C. P.	Colli Piacentini	Vign.	Vigneto (vineyard)
Et.	Etichetta (label)	V. T.	Vendemmia Tardiva (late harvest)
FCO	Friuli Colli Orientali	V. V.	Vecchia Vigna/Vecchie Vigne (old vine /old vines)
M.	Metodo (method)		
M.to	Monferrato		
OP	Oltrepò Pavese		

VALLE D'AOSTA

It's true that Valle d'Aosta, in proportion to the hectares under vine (about 400), is the region that obtains the most Tre Bicchieri. Of course we have great respect and also a pinch of admiration for the growers who, every year, cultivate their vineyards with the attention and care one might bring to a garden, even if these are often difficult to reach on foot and even more exhausting to work. Nevertheless, our awards have nothing to do with this more sentimental form of appreciation. Our awards are for the great wines, and only the great wines, that a region is capable of producing. If we think that for a long time the vineyards were planted close to farmhouses for mere convenience, without any kind of study of soil or microclimate, or of how the different grape varieties might interact, then we can understand how Valle d'Aosta's qualitative potential is still largely unknown. Unfortunately, it's difficult to ask vigneron and co-ops to take on this burden, even just a little. In recent years we've detected a passion and enthusiasm (more with private growers than public wineries or cooperatives) that's led to a desire to seek out new directions. Nevertheless, Valle d'Aosta's quality is largely uniform and evenly distributed—indeed, like last year, the region earned 6 Tre Bicchieri. The big difference compared to the past is that, despite last year's praise for the region's rich ampelography, in this edition only whites were awarded, including a passito. This is certainly not a rejection of its grape varieties and reds, which still performed well and will return to shine in the future. Rather, it's a confirmation of our suspicions. We have long argued that the morphological and climatic peculiarities of 'The Valley', with its considerable day-night temperature swings, facilitate the production of fresh and fragrant whites, currently more sought after by consumers. Rosset Terroir's Petite Arvine Sopraquota 900 '19 took home the award for White of the Year, thanks to its aromatic finesse and gustatory tension, serving as a clear example of just how well suited Valle d'Aosta's vineyards are for the production of world-class whites. Elio Ottin also demonstrated his familiarity with the grape of Swiss origin. Tre Bicchieri for Anselmet and Les Crêtes (Chardonnay) and Lo Triolet (Pinot Gris), true Italian icons. Finally, we close by mentioning La Vrille, who belong to a small group of elite Italian growers, as demonstrated this year by their Muscat Flétri.

★Maison Anselmet

FRAZ. VEREYTAZ, 30
11018 VILLENEUVE [AO]
TEL. +39 0165904851
www.maisonanselmet.it

CELLAR SALES
PRE-BOOKED VISITS
ANNUAL PRODUCTION 80,000 bottles
HECTARES UNDER VINE 11.50

The Anselmet family have always had an eye on technological developments that can increase the quality of their wines, but they also use it to reduce chemical treatments in the vineyard. For some years now the winery, situated in the heart of the Torrette sub-zone, has been managed by Giorgio, who oversees the vineyards and winemaking with the help of the whole family. The level of their entire range is constantly growing, making use primarily of Aosta's indigenous grapes, without neglecting, of course, international varieties, especially Chardonnay, a true mainstay. The Chardonnay Mains et Cœur is excellent, a wine of great finesse, intense and complex with spicy notes that adorn its fruit while the palate is governed by a nice balance. The Pinot Nero Semel Pater is always a treat: strawberries and blueberries mix with peppery nuances; the palate enchants for its tannic finesse and richness. The Chardonnay Elevé en fût de chêne was highly appreciated by virtue of its fresh, long flavor.

○ Valle d'Aosta Chardonnay Mains et Cœur '18	🍷🍷🍷 6
○ Valle d'Aosta Chardonnay Élevé en Fût de Chêne '18	🍷🍷 5
● Valle d'Aosta Pinot Noir Semel Pater '18	🍷🍷 7
● Valle d'Aosta Syrah Henri '18	🍷🍷 6
○ Valle d'Aosta Chardonnay Élevé en Fût de Chêne '15	🍷🍷🍷 5
○ Valle d'Aosta Chardonnay Mains et Cœur '16	🍷🍷🍷 6
● Valle d'Aosta Pinot Noir Semel Pater '17	🍷🍷🍷 7
● Valle d'Aosta Pinot Noir Semel Pater '13	🍷🍷🍷 8

Château Feuillet

LOC. CHÂTEAU FEUILLET, 12
11010 SAINT PIERRE
TEL. +39 3287673880
www.chateaufeuillet.it

CELLAR SALES
ACCOMMODATION AND RESTAURANT SERVICE
ANNUAL PRODUCTION 45,000 bottles
HECTARES UNDER VINE 6.00
VITICULTURE METHOD Certified Biodynamic

With his Château Feuillet, Maurizio Fiorano operates in one of Aosta's best areas for viticulture, the central part of the region, Petit Rouge wine country. Maurizio processes his grapes with the utmost respect for local tradition, and even though Château Feuillet is a relatively young producer, his wines are an expression of the territory. The vineyard is mostly dedicated to native grape varieties, even though, as often happens in these parts, international grapes play an important role in their delicious range. Their entire range put in a strong performance. We appreciated the still-young and vinous Syrah, a wine characterized by delicate, fresh tannins. The Torrette Supérieur exhibits nice typicity with its pleasant palate. We tasted a nice version of the Petite Arvine, floral and citrusy, simple in the mouth and very pleasant. The Fumin pours an impenetrable red, opening on aromas of black fruit mixed with hints of cinchona, coming through full and juicy on the palate.

● Valle d'Aosta Fumin '19	🍷🍷 4
○ Valle d'Aosta Petite Arvine '19	🍷🍷 4
● Valle d'Aosta Syrah '19	🍷🍷 4
● Valle d'Aosta Torrette Sup. '18	🍷🍷 4
○ Valle d'Aosta Petite Arvine '12	🍷🍷🍷 3*
○ Valle d'Aosta Petite Arvine '11	🍷🍷🍷 3*
○ Valle d'Aosta Petite Arvine '10	🍷🍷🍷 3*
● Valle d'Aosta Fumin '18	🍷🍷 4
● Valle d'Aosta Fumin '17	🍷🍷 4
● Valle d'Aosta Fumin '16	🍷🍷 4
○ Valle d'Aosta Petite Arvine '18	🍷🍷 3*
○ Valle d'Aosta Petite Arvine '16	🍷🍷 3
● Valle d'Aosta Syrah '18	🍷🍷 3
● Valle d'Aosta Syrah '17	🍷🍷 3
● Valle d'Aosta Torrette Sup. '17	🍷🍷 3
● Valle d'Aosta Torrette Sup. '16	🍷🍷 3*
● Valle d'Aosta Torrette Sup. '15	🍷🍷 3

★★Les Crêtes

loc. Villetos, 50
11010 Aymavilles [AO]
Tel. +39 0165902274
www.lescretes.it

CELLAR SALES
PRE-BOOKED VISITS
ANNUAL PRODUCTION 200,000 bottles
HECTARES UNDER VINE 25.00
SUSTAINABLE WINERY

Les Crêtes has always been a driving force and model for all of Aosta's producers. A grafting of new forces has brought vitality to the winery, but if new technologies and new experiments are pushing their standards of quality higher and higher, this doesn't mean that traditional wines are neglected. Their selection, which has always been an expression of the territory and representative of the region, draws both on native grapes and international varieties. We don't have enough space to describe the quality of all the producer's wines, but we can say that they all stand out for their structure and elegance. The Petite Arvine exhibits floral and fruity scents made tantalizing by a mineral finish, coming through long and vital on t he palate. The Chardonnay was also up to snuff—aromatically broad, balanced and clean. Fine grain tannins characterize the ink-colored Fumin; the Pinot Nero also delivered.

Wine	Rating
○ Valle d'Aosta Chardonnay Cuvée Bois '18	𝕐𝕐𝕐 7
● Valle d'Aosta Nebbiolo Sommet '17	𝕐𝕐 6
○ Valle d'Aosta Petite Arvine Fleur V. Devin Ros '18	𝕐𝕐 5
● Valle d'Aosta Fumin '18	𝕐𝕐 5
● Valle d'Aosta Pinot Nero Revei '17	𝕐𝕐 7
○ Valle d'Aosta Chardonnay Cuvée Bois '17	𝕐𝕐𝕐 6
○ Valle d'Aosta Chardonnay Cuvée Bois '16	𝕐𝕐𝕐 6
○ Valle d'Aosta Chardonnay Cuvée Bois '13	𝕐𝕐𝕐 6
○ Valle d'Aosta Chardonnay Cuvée Bois '10	𝕐𝕐𝕐 6
○ Valle d'Aosta Chardonnay Cuvée Bois '09	𝕐𝕐𝕐 6
● Valle d'Aosta Nebbiolo Sommet '15	𝕐𝕐𝕐 6

La Crotta di Vegneron

p.zza Roncas, 2
11023 Chambave [AO]
Tel. +39 016646670
www.lacrotta.it

CELLAR SALES
PRE-BOOKED VISITS
RESTAURANT SERVICE
ANNUAL PRODUCTION 200,000 bottles
HECTARES UNDER VINE 40.00

Founded in 1980, today this cooperative producer avails itself of about 120 growers, all constantly monitored by regional and in-house technicians to ensure that their grapes are healthy and of excellent quality. Their 40 hectares, made up of very small plots, are cultivated with passion and attention, and give rise to a not insignificant number of wines (confirming the territory's prowess when it comes viticulture). Obviously great attention is paid to native grape varieties, and each wine seeks to best express its innate typicity. The quality of their Moscato Passito di Chambave is by now a guarantee. It's a classy wine, elegant, always harmonious and balanced. Aromatically, it goes all in on honey sensations, dried fruit and nuts. In the mouth it's alluring, spectacular as usual. We also very much appreciated their new Fumin, with its fragrances of black berries. It has vigorous tannins and plushness to sell. Their Moscato, which matures at length, is excellent. The Malvoisie di Nus also put in a good performance.

Wine	Rating
○ Valle d'Aosta Chambave Moscato Passito Prieuré '18	𝕐𝕐 5
● Valle d'Aosta Fumin La Griffe des Lions '18	𝕐𝕐 5
○ Valle d'Aosta Chambave Muscat Attente '17	𝕐𝕐 4
○ Valle d'Aosta Nus Malvoisie '19	𝕐𝕐 4
○ Valle d'Aosta Chambave Moscato Passito Prieuré '15	𝕐𝕐𝕐 5
○ Valle d'Aosta Chambave Moscato Passito Prieuré '13	𝕐𝕐𝕐 5
○ Valle d'Aosta Chambave Moscato Passito Prieuré '12	𝕐𝕐𝕐 5
○ Valle d'Aosta Chambave Moscato Passito Prieuré '11	𝕐𝕐𝕐 5
● Valle d'Aosta Fumin Esprit Follet '09	𝕐𝕐𝕐 3

Cave Gargantua

FRAZ. CLOS CHATEL, 1
11020 GRESSAN [AO]
TEL. +39 3299271999
www.cavegargantua.it

ANNUAL PRODUCTION 25,000 bottles
HECTARES UNDER VINE 4.50

The Dora Baltea cuts through the Aosta Valley from the northwest to the southeast. It's well known that most of the vineyards are cultivated on the left side of the valley, 'l'ardet', an area that enjoys more favorable exposure. That's not the case with Nadir and Laurent Cuneaz's winery, which is situated in Gressan, in the 'envers', a territory that's certainly more difficult, but when cultivated with dedication and passion can give rise to great wines. Their production figures are smaller, but the quality of their wines is notable, and every year they always provide some pleasant surprises. Tantalizing, elegant and complex, the Torrette Supérieur offers up delicious, fruity notes that close with nuances of tobacco. Decidedly balanced in the mouth, with velvety and powerful tannins, it's a wine of great character. Medicinal herbs and plenty of freshness mark the Mon Dadà. The harmonious Impasse is redolent of red berries and spices, anticipating a richly-structured palate. The well-made Daphne opens with pleasing spicy notes, while the pleasant and vibrant Pinot Gris is never banal.

Wine	Rating
● Valle d'Aosta Torrette Sup. Labiè '18	🍷🍷 4
○ Mon Dadà	🍷🍷 5
○ Valle d'Aosta Bianco Daphne	🍷🍷 5
○ Valle d'Aosta Pinot Grigio '19	🍷🍷 5
● Valle d'Aosta Rosso Impasse Elevée Fût de Chêne '18	🍷🍷 5
○ Valle d'Aosta Chardonnay Daphne '16	🍷🍷 5
● Valle d'Aosta Pinot Noir '16	🍷🍷 3*
● Valle d'Aosta Rosso Impasse '15	🍷🍷 5
● Valle d'Aosta Rosso Impasse Elevée Fût de Chêne '16	🍷🍷 5
● Valle d'Aosta Torrette Sup. Labiè '17	🍷🍷 4
● Valle d'Aosta Torrette Sup. Labiè '16	🍷🍷 4
● Valle d'Aosta Vin de la Fée '18	🍷🍷 5
● Vin de la Fée '16	🍷🍷 5

Grosjean

FRAZ. OLLIGNAN, 2
11020 QUART [AO]
TEL. +39 0165775791
www.grosjeanvins.it

CELLAR SALES
PRE-BOOKED VISITS
ANNUAL PRODUCTION 120,000 bottles
HECTARES UNDER VINE 12.00
VITICULTURE METHOD Certified Organic

The Grosjean family are part of the region's winemaking past. They've been documented as part of the Aosta Valley's agricultural fabric since 1781, but it was only in 1968 that they began to bottle and market their wines. Today they're on the third generation, but what's most striking is the passion that its current leaders have inherited from their fathers and uncles. Commitment, study, knowledge and practice have elevated the quality of their wines, which are now known throughout the world. Typicity and tradition characterize their entire range, though without neglecting a general shift towards organic production. The Chardonnay is lively and vivid, pleasant to the nose with floral and vegetal primaries reminiscent of herbs and acacia flowers, then fruit, apple and damson. Nice structure, very fresh. The vibrant, elegant Petite Arvine features citrusy notes only to explode in the mouth. Vibrant aromas for the Fumin, with marked tannins—it's still young. We also recommend their nice Pinot Nero.

Wine	Rating
○ Valle d'Aosta Chardonnay '19	🍷🍷 4
○ Valle d'Aosta Petite Arvine V. Rovettaz '19	🍷🍷 4
● Valle d'Aosta Fumin '18	🍷🍷 5
● Valle d'Aosta Pinot Noir V. Tzeriat '18	🍷🍷 4
● Valle d'Aosta Fumin '06	🍷🍷🍷 4
● Valle d'Aosta Fumin V. Rovettaz '07	🍷🍷🍷 5
○ Valle d'Aosta Petite Arvine V. Rovettaz '09	🍷🍷🍷 4
● Valle d'Aosta Cornalin V. Rovettaz '16	🍷🍷 5
● Valle d'Aosta Fumin V. Rovettaz '16	🍷🍷 5
● Valle d'Aosta Fumin V. Rovettaz '14	🍷🍷 5
○ Valle d'Aosta Petite Arvine V. Rovettaz '18	🍷🍷 4
● Valle d'Aosta Pinot Noir '11	🍷🍷 3*

★Lo Triolet

loc. Junod, 7
11010 Introd [AO]
Tel. +39 016595437
www.lotriolet.vievini.it

CELLAR SALES
PRE-BOOKED VISITS
ANNUAL PRODUCTION 42,000 bottles
HECTARES UNDER VINE 5.00

Triolet is one of the Aosta Valley's historic producers. Over the years it has always sought, and found, the right harmony between traditional winemaking and a modern vision. Although most of their attention is dedicated to white grapes and wines, especially Pinot Grigio, Marco Martin has never neglected red wines, obtaining, harvest after harvest, increasingly interesting results. Attentive to principles of integrated pest management, he works his vineyards with total respect for the surrounding mountain environment. The great quality, and above all the continuity, of one of the most successful Pinot Grigios in Italy comes as no surprise. Vibrant and elegant on the nose with notes of white fruit, pear and apricot, and great structure on the palate—it's in a league of its own. Nice performance for the Fumin, with its fruity and somewhat woodland aromas, soft in the mouth. We also appreciated the Pinot Grigio: maturation in barriques makes for a spicy, rich and powerful wine. Pleasant and nicely-balanced, the Coteau Barrage's notes of violet and red berries surprised us.

○ Valle d'Aosta Pinot Gris '19	🍷🍷🍷 4*
● Valle d'Aosta Fumin '18	🍷🍷 5
● Valle d'Aosta Coteau Barrage '18	🍷🍷 6
○ Valle d'Aosta Pinot Gris Élevé en Barriques '18	🍷🍷 6
● Valle d'Aosta Fumin '16	🍷🍷🍷 5
○ Valle d'Aosta Pinot Gris '18	🍷🍷🍷 4*
○ Valle d'Aosta Pinot Gris '16	🍷🍷🍷 5
○ Valle d'Aosta Pinot Gris '15	🍷🍷🍷 5
○ Valle d'Aosta Pinot Gris '14	🍷🍷🍷 3*
○ Valle d'Aosta Pinot Gris '13	🍷🍷🍷 3*
○ Valle d'Aosta Pinot Gris '12	🍷🍷🍷 3*
○ Valle d'Aosta Pinot Gris '09	🍷🍷🍷 3
○ Valle d'Aosta Pinot Gris '08	🍷🍷🍷 3*
○ Valle d'Aosta Pinot Gris '05	🍷🍷🍷 3*
○ Valle d'Aosta Pinot Gris Élevé en Barriques '10	🍷🍷🍷 5

Cave Mont Blanc de Morgex et La Salle

fraz. La Ruine
Chemin des Îles, 31
11017 Morgex [AO]
Tel. +39 0165800331
www.caveduvinblanc.com

CELLAR SALES
PRE-BOOKED VISITS
ANNUAL PRODUCTION 140,000 bottles
HECTARES UNDER VINE 19.00

Prié Blanc is a special grape variety grown exclusively in the villages of Morgex and La Salle. Here ungrafted vines are cultivated with very low pergolas and enjoy a rather short vegetative cycle, a characteristic that allows the plant to survive and produce excellent grapes, even in the extreme climate of the north. Step by step, this cooperative follows the growers of the area, all of whom oversee the small plots that host the grapes for their famous Blanc de Morgex and La Salle. There's always plenty happening when it comes to their sparkling wines. This year we tasted the Cuvée du Prince. Very fine and persistent perlage, on the nose it's fragrant with notes of mountain herbs and hay—on the palate it's fresh and balanced, long and persistent. The pleasantly pervasive Blanc de Blanc offers up aromas of white fruit and an intriguing palate. We also tasted a nice version of their La Piagne.

○ Valle d'Aosta Blanc de Morgex et de La Salle Brut Blanc du Blanc M. Cl.	🍷🍷 5
○ Valle d'Aosta Blanc de Morgex et de La Salle Brut Nature Cuvée du Prince M. Cl. '12	🍷🍷 6
○ Valle d'Aosta Blanc de Morgex et de La Salle La Piagne '18	🍷 5
○ Valle d'Aosta Blanc de Morgex et de La Salle Brut Blanc du Blanc M. Cl. '15	🍷🍷 4
○ Valle d'Aosta Blanc de Morgex et de La Salle Brut Blanc du Blanc M. Cl. '16	🍷🍷 5
○ Valle d'Aosta Blanc de Morgex et de La Salle Pas Dosé Glacier M. Cl. '16	🍷🍷 5

★Elio Ottin

Fraz. Porossan Neyves, 209
11100 Aosta
Tel. +39 3474071331
www.ottinvini.it

CELLAR SALES
PRE-BOOKED VISITS
ANNUAL PRODUCTION 60,000 bottles
HECTARES UNDER VINE 8.00
SUSTAINABLE WINERY

Elio Ottin's wine adventure began in 2007, and in little more than a decade, with dedication and intelligence, he has reached the heights of regional excellence. But his greatest success, as he himself defines it, is his son Nicolas, who today, after several experiences abroad, is collaborating more and more actively in the winery. Their range is focused mainly on indigenous grapes, Petit Rouge, Fumin and Petite Arvine, but there are also excellent wines drawing on international grape varieties, foremost Pinot Nero, which is interpreted with sensitivity and without excess. Choosing their best wine is getting more and more difficult, but once again the Petite Arvine stands out. Vibrant and elegant on the nose with fresh, floral and fruity sensations, it shines for the velvety elegance of its palate, which proves powerful and long. The spectacular Fumin pours an impenetrable red, the prelude to pervasive aromas of blackberry coulis and sweet spices, and an extremely balanced, long palate.

Wine	Rating
○ Valle d'Aosta Petite Arvine '19	🍷🍷🍷 4*
● Valle d'Aosta Fumin '18	🍷🍷 5
● Valle d'Aosta Pinot Noir L'Emerico '17	🍷🍷 6
○ Valle d'Aosta Petite Arvine Nuances '18	🍷🍷 5
● Valle d'Aosta Fumin '12	🍷🍷🍷 3*
○ Valle d'Aosta Petite Arvine '17	🍷🍷🍷 4*
○ Valle d'Aosta Petite Arvine '16	🍷🍷🍷 5
○ Valle d'Aosta Petite Arvine '15	🍷🍷🍷 5
○ Valle d'Aosta Petite Arvine '14	🍷🍷🍷 4*
○ Valle d'Aosta Petite Arvine '12	🍷🍷🍷 3*
○ Valle d'Aosta Petite Arvine '11	🍷🍷🍷 3*
○ Valle d'Aosta Petite Arvine '10	🍷🍷🍷 3*
● Valle d'Aosta Pinot Noir L'Emerico '16	🍷🍷🍷 6
○ Valle d'Aosta Petite Arvine '18	🍷🍷 4
○ Valle d'Aosta Petite Arvine Nuances '17	🍷🍷 5

Ermes Pavese

s.da Pineta, 26
11017 Morgex [AO]
Tel. +39 0165800053
www.ermespavese.it

CELLAR SALES
PRE-BOOKED VISITS
ANNUAL PRODUCTION 32,000 bottles
HECTARES UNDER VINE 6.00
VITICULTURE METHOD Certified Organic

This family-run winery was founded by Ermes in 1999 and has since grown into one of the territory's most thriving producers. And now his children, Nathan and Ninive, are providing additional support. Here at the foot of Mont Blanc there's little land for agriculture, thus viticulture is an extreme sport. Grapes are cultivated over more than a hundred plots, but their efforts are rewarded by the quality of their wines, their character and bond to tradition, making for a true expression of the territory. The Blanc de Morgex et de La Salle is a very well-typed wine, pleasant in its aromas of mountain flowers, all harmonized by a marked minerality, In the mouth it comes through long and clean. Once again their selection of bubbly met with approval, with the Metodo Classico presented in three versions: 18, 24 and 36 months. All were fresh and exhibited a nice balance of flavor. This year the news is their Ventanni, an original interpretation of Priè Blanc characterized by appley aromas on the nose, and a long, fresh palate.

Wine	Rating
○ Valle d'Aosta Vin Blanc de Morgex et La Salle '19	🍷🍷 4
○ Priè Ventanni	🍷🍷 5
○ Valle d'Aosta Vin Blanc de Morgex et La Salle Pavese Pas Dosé M.Cl. XVIII '16	🍷🍷 5
○ Valle d'Aosta Vin Blanc de Morgex et La Salle Pavese Pas Dosé M.Cl. XXIV '16	🍷🍷 5
○ Valle d'Aoste Blanc de Morgex et de La Salle Pavese XXXVI Pas Dosé M. Cl. '15	🍷🍷 5
○ Valle d'Aosta Vin Blanc de Morgex et La Salle '18	🍷🍷 4
○ Valle d'Aoste Blanc de Morgex et de La Salle Pavese XXXVI Pas Dosé M. Cl. '13	🍷🍷 5

Rosset Terroir

loc. Torrent de Maillod, 4
11020 Quart [AO]
Tel. +39 0165774111
www.rosseterroir.it

CELLAR SALES
ANNUAL PRODUCTION 30,000 bottles
HECTARES UNDER VINE 7.00

The recent investments made are a tangible sign of how much Nicola Rosset believes in Valdostan. The result is a new cellar and a structure equipped with modern technology, but that still bear the hallmarks of tradition. After an initial period dedicated to international grape varieties, the focus has shifted increasingly to native grapes. So it is that while the land in Saint Cristophe is home to Chardonnay, Cornalin and Petit Rouge, in Chambave we find local Moscato and in Villeneuve they cultivate Petite Arvine and Pinot Grigio. The Sopraquota, which by now demonstrates real consistence in terms of quality, remains a spearhead of their range. Intense floral scents are accompanied by hints of herbs and fruits, with mandarin standing out. On the palate it proves immense, yet balanced and fresh, with a long, pleasantly savory finish. It's our White of the Year. Spices and dark fruit characterize the Syrah, a fine and elegant wine. The alluring Petite Arvine is vibrant and vivid, balanced in structure and pleasantly long at the finish.

Wine	Rating	Price
○ Sopraquota 900 '19	▼▼▼	4*
● Valle d'Aosta Syrah '18	▼▼	4
○ Valle d'Aosta Petite Arvine '19	▼▼	5
○ Sopraquota 900 '18	▽▽▽	4*
● Valle d'Aosta Cornalin '16	▽▽▽	4*
● Valle d'Aosta Cornalin '15	▽▽▽	4*
● Valle d'Aosta Syrah '13	▽▽▽	4*
○ Valle d'Aosta Chardonnay '18	▽▽	5
○ Valle d'Aosta Chardonnay '17	▽▽	4
○ Valle d'Aosta Chardonnay '16	▽▽	4
● Valle d'Aosta Cornalin '17	▽▽	4
○ Valle d'Aosta Pinot Gris '18	▽▽	5
○ Valle d'Aosta Pinot Gris '17	▽▽	5
● Valle d'Aosta Syrah '17	▽▽	5
● Valle d'Aosta Syrah '15	▽▽	4
● Valle d'Aosta Syrah '14	▽▽	4

La Vrille

loc. Grangeon, 1
11020 Verrayes [AO]
Tel. +39 0166543018
www.lavrille.it

CELLAR SALES
PRE-BOOKED VISITS
ACCOMMODATION AND RESTAURANT SERVICE
ANNUAL PRODUCTION 18,000 bottles
HECTARES UNDER VINE 3.90
VITICULTURE METHOD Certified Organic
SUSTAINABLE WINERY

In the shadow of the Avic and Emilius mountains, in a natural amphitheater along the Via Francigena and just a stone's throw from Aosta, we find La Vrille's vineyards. Hervé Deguillame is its owner. French by birth, he's a shy person and very attentive to environmental concerns. He's also well known in the region for his love of his ancestors' land. His range is dedicated almost entirely to native grapes, while his passito, made with Muscat di Chambave, is perennially among the best in the country. Their Muscat passito has become a must. Consistent in quality, it's always marked by alluring honey sensations and great harmony on the palate—a wine you can't do without. This year the Pinot Nero also delivers; clean on the nose, it's fresh, complex and long in the mouth. Characteristic aromas feature in the Muscat Secco, a wine that surprises with its intriguing, juicy palate. We also appreciated the full, potent Fumin.

Wine	Rating	Price
○ Valle d'Aosta Chambave Muscat Flétri '18	▼▼▼	7
● Valle d'Aosta Pinot Noir '17	▼▼	5
○ Valle d'Aosta Chambave Muscat '18	▼▼	5
● Valle d'Aosta Fumin '16	▼▼	6
○ Valle d'Aosta Chambave Muscat '12	▽▽▽	4*
○ Valle d'Aosta Chambave Muscat Flétri '17	▽▽▽	7
○ Valle d'Aosta Chambave Muscat Flétri '16	▽▽▽	7
○ Valle d'Aosta Chambave Muscat Flétri '15	▽▽▽	7
○ Valle d'Aosta Chambave Muscat Flétri '14	▽▽▽	7
○ Valle d'Aosta Chambave Muscat Flétri '11	▽▽▽	6

Caves Cooperatives de Donnas

via Roma, 97
11020 Donnas [AO]
Tel. +39 0125807096
www.donnasvini.it

CELLAR SALES
PRE-BOOKED VISITS
ANNUAL PRODUCTION 150,000 bottles
HECTARES UNDER VINE 26.00

- ● Valle d'Aosta Donnas '17 — 🍷🍷 5
- ● Valle d'Aosta Donnas Napoléon '17 — 🍷🍷 4
- ● Valle d'Aosta Donnas Sup. Vieilles Vignes '16 — 🍷🍷 5

André Pellissier

fraz. Bussan Dessous, 17
11010 Saint Pierre [AO]
Tel. +39 3405704029
info@pellissierwine.it

CELLAR SALES
ANNUAL PRODUCTION 7,000 bottles
HECTARES UNDER VINE 2.00

- ● Valle d'Aosta Syrah '18 — 🍷🍷 4
- ● Bouquet XXVIII — 🍷🍷 4
- ● Valle d'Aosta Fumin '17 — 🍷🍷 4
- ● Valle d'Aosta Torrette Sup. '18 — 🍷🍷 4

La Plantze

fraz. Vereytaz,30
11018 Villeneuve [AO]
Tel. +39 3460571193
www.laplantze.eu

CELLAR SALES
PRE-BOOKED VISITS
ANNUAL PRODUCTION 10,000 bottles
HECTARES UNDER VINE 4.00

- ○ Trii Rundin Pinot Gris '19 — 🍷🍷 4
- ● Valle d'Aosta El Teemp '18 — 🍷🍷 4
- ● Valle d'Aosta Torrette Sup. '18 — 🍷🍷 5

Cave des Onze Communes

loc. Urbains, 14
11010 Aymavilles [AO]
Tel. +39 0165902912
www.caveonzecommunes.it

CELLAR SALES
PRE-BOOKED VISITS
ANNUAL PRODUCTION 460,000 bottles
HECTARES UNDER VINE
VITICULTURE METHOD Certified Organic

- ● Valle d'Aosta Fumin '18 — 🍷🍷 5
- ○ Valle d'Aosta Gewürztraminer '19 — 🍷🍷 4
- ○ Valle d'Aosta Petite Arvine '19 — 🍷🍷 4

Pianta Grossa

via Roma, 213
11020 Donnas [AO]
Tel. +39 3480077404
www.piantagrossadonnas.it

CELLAR SALES
PRE-BOOKED VISITS
ANNUAL PRODUCTION 10,000 bottles
HECTARES UNDER VINE 2.50

- ● Valle d'Aosta Donnas Georgos '17 — 🍷🍷 7
- ● Valle d'Aosta Nebbiolo Dessus '18 — 🍷🍷 5
- ● Valle d'Aosta Nebbiolo 396 '18 — 🍷 4

La Source

loc. Bussan Dessous, 1
11010 Saint Pierre
Tel. +39 0165904038
www.lasource.it

CELLAR SALES
PRE-BOOKED VISITS
ACCOMMODATION AND RESTAURANT SERVICE
ANNUAL PRODUCTION 40,000 bottles
HECTARES UNDER VINE 7.00

- ○ Valle d'Aosta Chardonnay '16 — 🍷🍷 3
- ● Valle d'Aosta Syrah '15 — 🍷🍷 3
- ● Valle d'Aosta Torrette Sup. '15 — 🍷 3

PIEDMONT

Despite the extraordinarily difficult circumstances that affected food services and viticulture, Piedmont's producers showed that they know how to fight. Some, like Flavio Roddolo, postponed bottling, and so you won't find him in this edition. The results, however, on the whole, are remarkable, and every year it becomes more and more difficult to limit the number of Tre Bicchieri awarded. 2016, hailed as a vintage for the ages for Nebbiolo, lived up to its promise, with no less than 29 wines out of 32 earning recognition. Of these 29 Tre Bicchieri, 25 are Barolos, 2 are Barbarescos and 2 come from Upper Piedmont. The greatness of 2016's Barolo, widely known, was attested to by some 32 Tre Bicchieri and our award for Red of the Year, which goes to Pio Cesare and their extraordinary Barolo Ornato. As quality grows, especially in the most prestigious appellations, our work becomes more and more difficult. With 45 Tre Bicchieri out of a regional total of 75, Nebbiolo continues to reign supreme. Fortunately, the spread of lesser known cultivars is also increasing. Tortona's Timorasso received 2 awards, while in the area of Castagnole Monferrato, Ruché saw its second Tre Bicchieri. Luca Ferraris's intoxicating Clàsic, which has done so much to relaunch the grape, deserves special praise. Monferrato Casalese's Grignolino, in the new aged version, maintains its 2 Tre Bicchieri, rewarding the Monferace association that's leading the project. It's also worth noting the remarkable performance put in by Piedmont's bubbly, which saw 4 wines take home golds, including 3 from Alta Langa, a rapidly expanding appellation. 6 wineries earned Tre Bicchieri for the first time—5 if we consider the Barolo Lazzarito '16 produced by Casa E. di Mirafiore, (which is, in reality, its own business now, having recently broken off from Fontanafredda). That's almost 10% of the total awarded. Here they are: Socré with their Barbaresco Roncaglie Riserva '15; La Masera and their Erbaluce di Caluso Anima dAnnata '17; La Toledana and the Gavi del Comune di Gavi Vigne Rade '19; Castellari Bergaglio with their notable Gavi Pilin '14; and finally Luca Ferraris, mentioned above.

460 Casina Bric

Loc. Cascina Bricco
via Sorello, 1a
12060 Barolo [CN]
Tel. +39 335283468
www.casinabric-barolo.it

CELLAR SALES
PRE-BOOKED VISITS
ANNUAL PRODUCTION 45,000 bottles
HECTARES UNDER VINE 10.00

Enologist Gianluca Viberti's new cellar in Serralunga d'Alba is now operating at full capacity, and we'll be able to appreciate the results with their line of 2019s. In any case, their Barolo and Guarene vineyards continue to prove quite valid. The former gives rise to Barolo appellation wines primarily, with the Bricco delle Viole always in great form. The latter hosts the grapes used for their sparkling wines, drawing on the Nebbiolo d'Alba appellation. Among these, the Metodo Classico Brut Nature Rosé 48 Months and the more approachable Brut Rosé Cuvée 970, elaborated with the Charmat technique, are consistent standouts. The youthful Barolo Bricco delle Viole '16 stands out for its notable olfactory impact, characterized by herbs, cinchona-quinine and licorice together with a harmonious, well-structured palate. The fresh Barolo del comune di Barolo '16 is just a bit more marked by oak, simple, forthright, and impeccably crafted. The enjoyable, fruity white prevails among the new line of daily drinkers called Mesdì ('midday').

● Barolo Bricco delle Viole '16	🍷🍷 7
⊙ Nebbiolo d'Alba Brut Nature Rosé Origo-Ginis 60 mesi '14	🍷🍷 5
● Barolo del Comune di Barolo '16	🍷🍷 6
○ Langhe Arneis Ansì '19	🍷🍷 6
○ Mesdì Bianco	🍷🍷 3
⊙ Nebbiolo d'Alba Brut Rosé Cuvée 970	🍷🍷 5
● Langhe Rosso Ansì '17	🍷 4
● Mesdì Rosso	🍷 3
● Barolo '13	♡♡ 6
● Barolo Bricco delle Viole '15	♡♡ 7
● Barolo Bricco delle Viole '14	♡♡ 7
● Barolo Bricco delle Viole '13	♡♡ 7
● Barolo del Comune di Barolo '15	♡♡ 6
● Barolo del Comune di Serralunga d'Alba '14	♡♡ 6

★Abbona

B.go San Luigi, 40
12063 Dogliani [CN]
Tel. +39 0173721317
www.abbona.com

CELLAR SALES
PRE-BOOKED VISITS
ACCOMMODATION
ANNUAL PRODUCTION 350,000 bottles
HECTARES UNDER VINE 50.00

It's not easy to reach the goal of having a high-level range of wines. Marziano Abbona has succeeded with flying colors, as shown by the national and foreign awards that are no longer limited to the Papà Celso or Barolo Cerviano but that now concern the Nebbiolo d'Alba Bricco Barone as well as Langhe Bianco, Barolo Pressenda and single-vintage Alta Langa Extra Brut. Fifty years of harvests crowned by well-deserved successes. An important notice for wine tourists: in addition to quality wines and the owner's amiability, they've recently added the possibility of staying in elegant rooms overlooking their picturesque underground cellar. The Barolo Cerviano-Merli is back with the rich 2016 vintage: grace and finesse characterize its fruity aromas, all enriched by a delicate oak background. But it's the Pressenda that dominates thanks to a robust and decisive 2016 version, with beautiful aromas of cinchona-quinine and vivid tannins. We also appreciated the surprising and very pleasant Barbera d'Alba Rinaldi '18.

● Barolo Pressenda '16	🍷🍷🍷 7
● Barbera d'Alba Rinaldi '18	🍷🍷 4
● Barolo Cerviano-Merli '16	🍷🍷 8
● Dogliani Papà Celso '19	🍷🍷 4
○ Alta Langa Extra Brut '15	🍷🍷 5
● Dogliani San Luigi '19	🍷🍷 3
○ Langhe Bianco Cinerino '19	🍷🍷 5
● Nebbiolo d'Alba Bricco Barone '18	🍷🍷 4
● Barolo Cerviano '10	♡♡♡ 7
● Barolo Terlo Ravera '08	♡♡♡ 6
● Dogliani Papà Celso '18	♡♡♡ 4*
● Dogliani Papà Celso '17	♡♡♡ 4*
● Dogliani Papà Celso '16	♡♡♡ 4*
● Dogliani Papà Celso '15	♡♡♡ 4*
● Dogliani Papà Celso '13	♡♡♡ 4*
● Dogliani Papà Celso '11	♡♡♡ 3*

Anna Maria Abbona

FRAZ. MONCUCCO, 21
12060 FARIGLIANO [CN]
TEL. +39 0173797228
www.annamariabbona.it

CELLAR SALES
PRE-BOOKED VISITS
ANNUAL PRODUCTION 85,000 bottles
HECTARES UNDER VINE 20.00

More and more the husband and wife team of Anna Maria Abbona and Franco Schellino can count on the contribution of their children Federico and Lorenzo, bearing in mind that the winery has gradually expanded and that today the estate hosts not only Dolcetto but also Nebbiolo grapes for Barolo, Riesling, Nascetta and Barbera. The 15 wines that make up their selection are all marked by rich personality, testifying to the family's passion for the vineyard and cellar. Their always reliable portfolio of Dogliani DOCG is headed by their San Bernardo, which is made with grapes from very old vines, while every year the Monforte d'Alba Barolo Bricco San Pietro proves increasingly impressive and well-defined. Rare harmony features in the very youthful Dogliani Sorí dij But '19, a wine endowed with remarkable structure and an alluring, fresh vein that delights the palate. It's an elegant hymn to Dogliani's fruity richness. We found the very enjoyable Dogliani Superiore Maioli '18 sumptuous amidst aromas of blackberry and bitter almond, with a succulent palate underlined by close-knit, soft tannins.

● Dogliani Sorì Dij But '19	▼▼▼ 3*
● Barolo Bricco San Pietro '16	▼▼ 7
● Dogliani Sup. Maioli '18	▼▼ 3*
● Barolo d el Comune di Monforte d'Alba '16	▼▼ 6
● Langhe Dolcetto '19	▼▼ 2*
● Langhe Nebbiolo '17	▼▼ 3
○ Langhe Riesling L'Alman '18	▼▼ 3
● Barbera d'Alba '19	▼ 3
○ Langhe Nascetta Netta '19	▼ 3
○ Netta Brut	▼ 4
● Dogliani Sup. San Bernardo '12	▽▽▽ 4*
● Dogliani Sup. San Bernardo '11	▽▽▽ 4*
● Dogliani Sup. San Bernardo '16	▽▽ 4

F.lli Abrigo

LOC. BERFI
VIA MOGLIA GERLOTTO, 2
12055 DIANO D'ALBA [CN]
TEL. +39 017369104
www.abrigofratelli.it

CELLAR SALES
PRE-BOOKED VISITS
ANNUAL PRODUCTION 100,000 bottles
HECTARES UNDER VINE 27.00

The winery got its start in 1935 with the acquisition of Cascina dei Berfi, but the most important step in terms of production came in 1976, when Ernesto Abrigo graduated from the Alba School of Enology. Since then, the family have dedicated themselves primarily to the area's flagship wine, Dolcetto di Diano d'Alba. A major step forward was taken recently when the 2013 Barolo Ravera was marketed for the first time together with an Alta Langa sparkler, which his brilliant son Walter believes in greatly. It's a winery of rare beauty and quality, which emerges through wisdom and care in all their wines. Definitely worth a visit. The Barbera d'Alba Superiore is rightly among the best of Langhe's 2018s: elegant and spicy without any particular contribution of oak, in the mouth it has plenty of pulp, freshness and balance. We also appreciated the soft and elegant Langhe Nebbiolo '18, just touched by a hint of oak, though not coarse—it's a highly pleasant wine. Plum and almond feature in the appealing and supple Diano '19.

● Barbera d'Alba Sup. '18	▼▼ 3*
● Diano d'Alba '19	▼▼ 2*
○ Langhe Bianco Lumiè '19	▼▼ 2*
● Langhe Nebbiolo '18	▼▼ 3
○ Alta Langa Brut Sivà '15	▼ 5
● Barolo Ravera '16	▼ 7
● Barbera d'Alba Sup. '17	▽▽ 3
● Barbera d'Alba Sup. '16	▽▽ 3
● Barolo Ravera '15	▽▽ 7
● Barolo Ravera '14	▽▽ 7
● Diano d'Alba '18	▽▽ 2*
● Diano d'Alba Sorì dei Berfi '15	▽▽ 3*
● Diano d'Alba Sup. '16	▽▽ 3*
● Diano d'Alba Sup. Pietrin '17	▽▽ 3
● Dolcetto di Diano d'Alba '17	▽▽ 2*

Giovanni Abrigo

VIA SANTA CROCE, 9
12055 DIANO D'ALBA [CN]
TEL. +39 017369345
www.abrigo.it

CELLAR SALES
PRE-BOOKED VISITS
ANNUAL PRODUCTION 40,000 bottles
HECTARES UNDER VINE 10.00

As well expressed by the great gastronome Giovanni Goria, 'Dolcetto is round, dense and pulpy, as well as fragrant and cheerful'. Add to this the fact that it has little acidity and is rich in sugars and it's easy to understand why it was once used, fresh off the vine, as a restorative cure for children. The Abrigo family have been cultivating and vinifying these grapes since 1968, with results that are sure to delight the palate and prices that are more than accessible. In recent years Giorgio, who's increasingly helped by his sons Giorgio and Sergio, has also managed to dedicate himself to Barolo thanks to a plot in the prized Ravera cru. And it's the Barolo Ravera '16 that leads this year's selection: elegant red fruit and tobacco make for a clear, focused complexity, while the palate comes through austere and rich, with tannins serving as a solid backbone. Black fruits and beautiful freshness characterize the persuasive Barbera d'Alba Marminela '18, a well-orchestrated and tantalizing wine. The fruity and vegetable Nebbiolo d'Alba '18 is another gem.

Wine	Rating
● Barolo Ravera '16	🍷🍷 6
● Barbera d'Alba Marminela '18	🍷🍷 2*
● Nebbiolo d'Alba '18	🍷🍷 3
● Dolcetto di Diano d'Alba Sorì dei Crava '19	🍷 2
● Barbera d'Alba Marminela '17	YY 2*
● Barbera d'Alba Marminela '16	YY 2*
● Barbera d'Alba Marminela '15	YY 2*
● Barolo Ravera '15	YY 6
● Barolo Ravera '14	YY 6
● Diano d'Alba Sup. Garabei '15	YY 2*
● Dolcetto di Diano d'Alba '17	YY 2*
● Dolcetto di Diano d'Alba Sup. Garabei '16	YY 2*
● Dolcetto Diano d'Alba Sup. Garabei '17	YY 2*
● Nebbiolo d'Alba '17	YY 3

Orlando Abrigo

VIA CAPPELLETTO, 5
12050 TREISO [CN]
TEL. +39 0173630533
www.orlandoabrigo.com

CELLAR SALES
PRE-BOOKED VISITS
ACCOMMODATION
ANNUAL PRODUCTION 100,000 bottles
HECTARES UNDER VINE 23.00
SUSTAINABLE WINERY

We find Giovanni Abrigo at the helm of a winery whose splendid, modern cellar is perfectly integrated with the territory, embellished with a guest house for a true 'agritourism' experience. The vineyards have now reached full maturity, with Barbaresco Meruzzano and Montersino serving as the flagships, giving rise to particularly rich, compact and powerful wines. Their style is rooted in succulent, dense and well-structured wines, capable of expressing complexity and depth of flavor. The Barbaresco Rongalio Riserva proved worthy of our finals, offering up notes of watermelon well combined with a delicate vegetal stroke and a dark, spicy twist. On the palate it's full, juicy, with a close-knit and progressive tannic texture. The Barbaresco Meruzzano '17 stands out for its character, lovely aromatic freshness and notable length—its tannins are creamy and fine. The 2016 Barbaresco Montersino is classic in its notes of tobacco and licorice.

Wine	Rating
● Barbaresco Rongalio Ris. '15	🍷🍷 8
● Barbaresco Meruzzano '17	🍷🍷 6
● Barbaresco Montersino '16	🍷🍷 7
● Barbera d'Alba Sup. Mervisano '16	🍷🍷 4
● Nebbiolo d'Alba Valmaggiore '17	🍷🍷 5
○ Langhe Très Plus '18	🍷 3
● Barbaresco Meruzzano '16	YY 5
● Barbaresco Meruzzano '15	YY 5
● Barbaresco Meruzzano '14	YY 5
● Barbaresco Montersino '15	YY 7
● Barbaresco Rongalio Ris. '14	YY 8
● Barbaresco Rongalio Ris. '13	YY 8
● Barbaresco Rongalio Ris. '12	YY 8
○ Langhe Sauvignon D'Amblè '17	YY 2*
○ Langhe Très Plus '17	YY 3
○ Langhe Très Plus '16	YY 3
● Nebbiolo d'Alba Valmaggiore '15	YY 5

★Giulio Accornero e Figli

Cascina Ca' Cima, 1
15049 Vignale Monferrato [AL]
Tel. +39 0142933317
www.accornerovini.it

CELLAR SALES
PRE-BOOKED VISITS
ACCOMMODATION
ANNUAL PRODUCTION 100,000 bottles
HECTARES UNDER VINE 22.00
SUSTAINABLE WINERY

The winery created by the Accornero family deserves a place among those producers writing the enological history of the territory. Here tradition, new technology and an unmistakable style come together to create extraordinary interpretations of Piedmont's native grapes, wines that highlight the characteristics of the varieties used through an exemplary expression of 'terroir'. Additionally, Ermanno has recently begun working with Ruché. In fact, their Monferrato Rosso Viarì, first released with the 2019 harvest, is born from the grape. An outstanding performance points up the great care dedicated to their entire range. Giulin, by virtue of a longer period of maturation in wood barrels, exhibits the qualities of a great Piedmontese red. The Il Vigne Vecchie, a Grignolino matured in wood, and the Grignolino Bricco del Bosco are characterized by their superb olfactory suite. We recommend the new addition, the Viarì. The rest of their selection is all exceptionally well made.

Wine	Rating	Price
● Grignolino del M.to Casalese Monferace Bricco del Bosco V. V. '16	🍷🍷🍷	6
● Barbera del M.to Giulin '17	🍷🍷	4
● Grignolino del M.to Casalese Bricco del Bosco '19	🍷🍷	4
● M.to Girotondo '17	🍷🍷	4
● Barbera del M.to Sup. Cima '15	🍷🍷	7
● Casorzo Brigantino '19	🍷🍷	2*
● M.to Freisa La Bernardina '19	🍷🍷	3
● M.to Rosso Viarì '19	🍷🍷	3
● Piemonte Barbera Campomoro '18	🍷🍷	3
● Barbera del M.to Giulin '15	🍷🍷🍷 (past)	3*
● Barbera del M.to Sup. Bricco Battista '15	🍷🍷🍷 (past)	5
● Grignolino del M.to Casalese Bricco del Bosco V. Vecchie '15	🍷🍷🍷 (past)	6

Marco e Vittorio Adriano

Fraz. San Rocco Seno d'Elvio, 13a
12051 Alba [CN]
Tel. +39 0173362294
www.adrianovini.it

CELLAR SALES
PRE-BOOKED VISITS
ANNUAL PRODUCTION 160,000 bottles
HECTARES UNDER VINE 27.00
SUSTAINABLE WINERY

Rigorous, airy and austere wines: that's the style adopted by a winery that uses only large Slavonian oak barrels for its elegant and expressive Nebbiolos. Drawing on roots that go back to the early 20th century, in San Rocco Seno d'Elvio (a few kilometers from Alba), two brothers, two wives and the lively, enthusiastic, young Michela (who carries on the export business) created a lovely family business. For several years the producer has employed a green philosophy, both in the vineyard and in the cellar, certifying a level of quality that's complemented by great prices. The floral timbres of the Barbaresco Sanadaive '17 are delicious, expressed amidst nuances of violet and hay. In the mouth it's rich, full, structured and very long. The Barbaresco Basarin '17 exhibits a more evolved profile, with a soft and creamy tannic texture, while the Barbaresco Basarin Riserva '15 proves pleasantly spicy, warm and ripe in its notes of cinchona and dried flowers. A note of merit for the Barbera d'Alba, a vibrant wine that unfolds progressively on hints of juniper and small red berries.

Wine	Rating	Price
● Barbaresco Sanadaive '17	🍷🍷	5
● Barbaresco Basarin '17	🍷🍷	5
● Barbaresco Basarin Ris. '15	🍷🍷	5
● Barbera d'Alba Sup. '18	🍷🍷	2*
● Langhe Freisa Lica '18	🍷🍷	2*
● Langhe Nebbiolo Cainassa '17	🍷	3
○ Moscato d'Asti Maddalena '19	🍷	3
● Barbaresco Basarin '16	🍷🍷 (past)	5
● Barbaresco Basarin '15	🍷🍷 (past)	5
● Barbaresco Basarin '14	🍷🍷 (past)	5
● Barbaresco Basarin Ris. '13	🍷🍷 (past)	6
● Barbaresco Sanadaive '16	🍷🍷 (past)	5
● Barbaresco Sanadaive '15	🍷🍷 (past)	5
● Barbaresco Sanadaive '14	🍷🍷 (past)	5
● Barbera d'Alba Sup. '17	🍷🍷 (past)	2*
○ Langhe Sauvignon Basarico '15	🍷🍷 (past)	3

Claudio Alario

via Santa Croce, 23
12055 Diano d'Alba [CN]
Tel. +39 0173231808
www.alarioclaudio.it

CELLAR SALES
PRE-BOOKED VISITS
ANNUAL PRODUCTION 46,000 bottles
HECTARES UNDER VINE 10.00

We met Claudio Alario in 1990, and for 30 years we've been tasting his wines with pleasure, recommending them unhesitatingly to lovers of pure, simple bottles. Approachable and without pretense, sometimes they're even a little rustic, but always rich in personality. That's not to say that there haven't been any changes. In fact, two Barolos have been created—Sorano da Serralunga and Riva Rocca da Verduno—and the winery has been equipped with numerous steel tanks, including rotomacerators, which allow the separate vinification of each plot. Soon young Matteo and Francesco will be making their presence felt as well. The Riva Rocca is splendid: initial blackcurrant whiffs combine with a sophisticated liquorice sensation that borders on truffle, while the palate comes through taut, bold and harmonious, with a finish that already offers up elegant hints of tar. The Sorano is another standout, with its nice foreground of fruit, a delicate background of spices, and docile tannins. The rest of their selection is excellent, as usual.

Wine	Glasses	
● Barolo Riva Rocca '16	▼▼	5
● Dolcetto di Diano d'Alba Sorì Costa Fiore '19	▼▼	2*
● Barbera d'Alba Valletta '18	▼▼	4
● Barolo Sorano '16	▼▼	6
● Dolcetto di Diano d'Alba Sorì Montagrillo '19	▼▼	2*
● Nebbiolo d'Alba Cascinotto '18	▼▼	4
● Barolo Sorano '05	▽▽▽	7
● Barbera d'Alba Valletta '17	▽▽	4
● Barolo Riva Rocca '15	▽▽	5
● Barolo Sorano '15	▽▽	6
● Barolo Sorano '14	▽▽	6
● Dolcetto di Diano d'Alba Sorì Montagrillo '18	▽▽	2*
● Nebbiolo d'Alba Cascinotto '17	▽▽	4

★F.lli Alessandria

via B. Valfré, 59
12060 Verduno [CN]
Tel. +39 0172470113
www.fratellialessandria.it

CELLAR SALES
PRE-BOOKED VISITS
ANNUAL PRODUCTION 90,000 bottles
HECTARES UNDER VINE 15.00

This charming winery, owned by the Alessandria family since 1870, is one of the few, true creators of Barolo when understood as a substantial, dry and still wine capable of improving for decades, and made according to the teachings of Paolo Francesco Staglieno (who's still of great interest today and well documented in the book 'Il vino del generale: lettere dell'enologo di Re Carlo Alberto' (by Mainardi and Berta). Today, Vittore is overseeing production, with outstanding results not only when it comes to their three Barolos but across the entire range. Our advice is also to taste their delicious Verduno Pelaverga Speziale. Complexity and elegance feature in the splendid Barolo Monvigliero '16, a wine that offers up an elegant and vibrant aromatic suite of red flowers and sweet spices, then leaves room for a measured, classic palate: well-orchestrated, lively, long and charming. Just more assertive and slightly marked by the wood, the Gramolere '16 is still a clear, focused and convincing wine. Kudos to the delicious Rossoluna '17, made with Barbera, Nebbiolo and Freisa.

Wine	Glasses	
● Barolo Monvigliero '16	▼▼▼	6
● Barolo Gramolere '16	▼▼	6
● Barolo San Lorenzo di Verduno '16	▼▼	6
● Barolo '16	▼▼	5
● Langhe Rossoluna '17	▼▼	4
● Verduno Pelaverga Speziale '19	▼▼	3
● Langhe Nebbiolo Prinsiot '18	▼	3
● Barolo Gramolere '11	▽▽▽	6
● Barolo Gramolere '10	▽▽▽	6
● Barolo Monvigliero '15	▽▽▽	6
● Barolo Monvigliero '14	▽▽▽	6
● Barolo Monvigliero '13	▽▽▽	6
● Barolo Monvigliero '12	▽▽▽	6
● Barolo Monvigliero '09	▽▽▽	6
● Barolo S. Lorenzo '08	▽▽▽	6

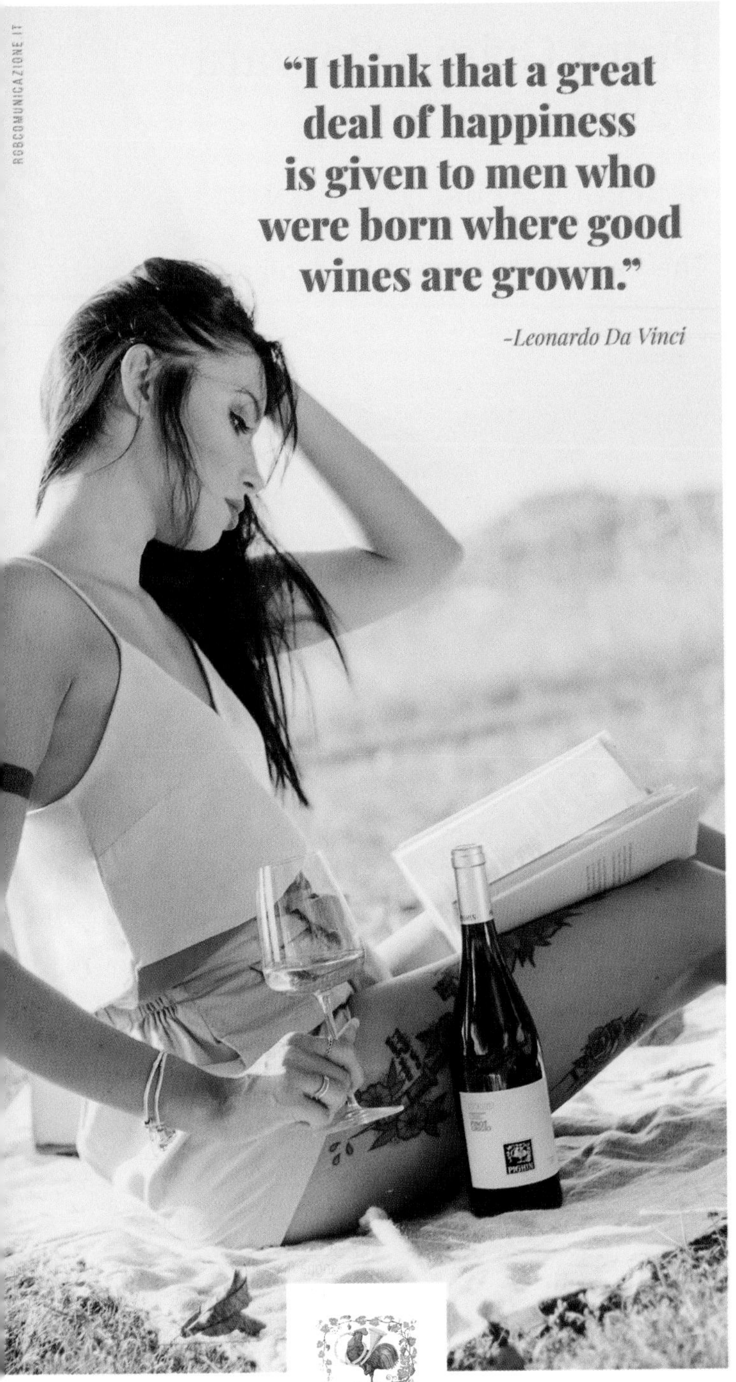
"I think that a great deal of happiness is given to men who were born where good wines are grown."
-Leonardo Da Vinci
PINOT GRIGIO
PIGHIN

Pinot Grigio Corvara
Valdadige doc
GENEROUS / PURE / AUTHENTIC
The Perfect Balance in Valdadige
VITICOLTORI DAL 1607 - MADE IN ITALY
ALBINO®
ARMANI
1607
Corvara
PINOT GRIGIO
Valdadige
denominazione di origine controllata
albinoarmani.com

★Gianfranco Alessandria

LOC. MANZONI, 13
12065 MONFORTE D'ALBA [CN]
TEL. +39 017378576
www.gianfrancoalessandria.com

CELLAR SALES
PRE-BOOKED VISITS
ANNUAL PRODUCTION 50,000 bottles
HECTARES UNDER VINE 7.00

The vineyard from which the Alessandria family obtains most of their grapes is in the San Giovanni cru, facing east/southeast, a position that guarantees, in addition to notable structure, a marked freshness to the grapes. Combine this with the fact that Gianfranco has always been a convinced supporter of thinning out and you get richness and concentration. The rest happens in the cellar, where new French oak is used frequently, lending a refined elegance to their award-winning Barolo San Giovanni and Barbera d'Alba Vittoria. All the the wines submitted this year have something to offer, though they're led by an exquisite version of their 'basic' Barolo. 2016, a great year, gave rise to fresh, liquorice aromas combined with a juicy, well-orchestrated palate—very enjoyable. The rich San Giovanni '16 is more youthful and still marked by oak. The tasty, drinkable Barbera d'Alba is a must, as is the seductive Langhe Nebbiolo, both 2018s. Their famous Barbera d'Alba Vittoria '17 is a potent wine characterized by sensations of vanilla.

Wine	Rating
● Barolo '16	🍷🍷 6
● Barolo San Giovanni '16	🍷🍷 8
● Barbera d'Alba '18	🍷🍷 3
● Barbera d'Alba Vittoria '17	🍷🍷 5
● Langhe Nebbiolo '18	🍷🍷 4
● Barbera d'Alba Vittoria '15	🍷🍷🍷 5
● Barbera d'Alba Vittoria '11	🍷🍷🍷 5
● Barbera d'Alba Vittoria '96	🍷🍷🍷 6
● Barolo '93	🍷🍷🍷 6
● Barolo S. Giovanni '04	🍷🍷🍷 7
● Barolo S. Giovanni '01	🍷🍷🍷 7
● Barolo S. Giovanni '00	🍷🍷🍷 7
● Barolo S. Giovanni '99	🍷🍷🍷 8

Marchesi Alfieri

P.ZZA ALFIERI, 28
14010 SAN MARTINO ALFIERI [AT]
TEL. +39 0141976015
www.marchesialfieri.it

CELLAR SALES
PRE-BOOKED VISITS
ACCOMMODATION
ANNUAL PRODUCTION 130,000 bottles
HECTARES UNDER VINE 21.00
SUSTAINABLE WINERY

Supported by Mario Olivero, sisters Emanuela, Antonella and Giovanna oversee a producer founded in the mid-1980s in the historic castle of the Marquis Alfieri in San Martino. Reds dominate, and when it comes to the grapes cultivated, Barbera Astigiana takes center stage, but their vineyards also see a significant share of Nebbiolo, Grignolino and Pinot Nero, which is used to produce a Blanc de Noir Metodo Classico. It's a multifaceted array of cultivars that gives rise to a solid and territorial range of wines. The Barbera d'Asti Superiore Alfiera '17 is always at the fore, with its aromas of cinchona-quinine, ripe black fruits, and spices that lend character and complexity. On the palate it has superb structure and volume, well supported by acidity. Other excellent bottles include the Barbera d'Asti La Tota '18, an elegant wine in its notes of berries, rich in pulp, long and balanced, and the Piedmont Grignolino Sansoero '19, a captivating and pleasant drink in which floral and pepper sensations stand out.

Wine	Rating
● Barbera d'Asti La Tota '18	🍷🍷 3*
● Barbera d'Asti Sup. Alfiera '17	🍷🍷 5
● Piemonte Grignolino Sansoero '19	🍷🍷 3*
○ Blanc de Noir Extra Brut M. Cl. '16	🍷🍷 5
● M.to Rosso Sostegno '18	🍷🍷 2*
● Piemonte Pinot Nero San Germano '17	🍷🍷 5
● Terre Alfieri Nebbiolo Costa Quaglia '17	🍷🍷 4
● Barbera d'Asti Sup. Alfiera '07	🍷🍷🍷 5
● Barbera d'Asti Sup. Alfiera '05	🍷🍷🍷 5
● Barbera d'Asti Sup. Alfiera '01	🍷🍷🍷 5
● Barbera d'Asti Sup. Alfiera '00	🍷🍷🍷 5
● Barbera d'Asti Sup. Alfiera '99	🍷🍷🍷 5
● Barbera d'Asti La Tota '17	🍷🍷 3*
● Barbera d'Asti Sup. Afiera '16	🍷🍷 5
● Terre Alfieri Nebbiolo Costa Quaglia '16	🍷🍷 4

Cantina Alice Bel Colle

REG. STAZIONE, 9
15010 ALICE BEL COLLE [AL]
TEL. +39 014474103
www.cantinaalicebc.it

CELLAR SALES
PRE-BOOKED VISITS
ANNUAL PRODUCTION 100,000 bottles
HECTARES UNDER VINE 370.00

Alice Bel Colle's 100 grower members cover about 350 hectares. Founded in 1955, the winery has mostly focused on the production of Barbera. Over the years, thanks also to the acquisition of modern equipment, the range of products has expanded, especially in favor of the area's classic, aromatic sweet wines: Moscato and Brachetto. Today it's a modern and dynamic producer with high ranking consultants, such as Beppe Caviola, and that energy also recently affected their commendably designed labels. This year their selection shines, with the Barbera d'Asti from the 360° line at the top. Intense, with nice crunchy fruit, it unfolds on notes of aromatic herbs, coming through fresh and sapid on the palate, with a long finish rich in pulp. The Alix is very rich, almost opulent, but youthful and fruity. The Dolcetto d'Acqui features red berries and jam on a lovely structure, with harmonious tannins. We found the Barbera d'Asti, Le Casette di Alice, to be pleasant.

- ● Barbera d'Asti Collezione 360° Al Casò '19 — TT 2*
- ● Barbera d'Asti Sup. Alix '17 — TT 3*
- ● Barbera d'Asti Le Casette di Alice '19 — TT 2*
- ● Dolcetto d'Acqui Collezione 360 ° Coste di Muiran '17 — TT 3
- ○ Asti Dolce M. Cl. — T 5
- ● Brachetto d'Acqui Le Casette di Alice '19 — T 2
- ○ Moscato d'Asti Le Casette di Alice '19 — T 2
- ● Barbera d'Asti '17 — YY 3
- ● Barbera d'Asti Al Casò '16 — YY 2*
- ● Barbera d'Asti Al Casò '15 — YY 2*
- ● Barbera d'Asti Filari Sociali '16 — YY 2*
- ● Barbera d'Asti Le Casette di Alice '18 — YY 2*
- ● Barbera d'Asti Sup. Alix '16 — YY 3*
- ● Barbera d'Asti Sup. Alix '14 — YY 3
- ● Barbera d'Asti Sup. Alix '13 — YY 3

Giovanni Almondo

VIA SAN ROCCO, 26
12046 MONTÀ [CN]
TEL. +39 0173975256
www.giovannialmondo.com

PRE-BOOKED VISITS
ANNUAL PRODUCTION 130,000 bottles
HECTARES UNDER VINE 18.00
SUSTAINABLE WINERY

Domenico Almondo, flanked by his sons Federico and Stefano, has for years been a leader in Roero. The vineyards, cultivated with an approach inspired by the principles of biodynamics, are located in Montà d'Alba. Arneis, some of which go back 60 years, can be found in the northern part of the municipality, on sandy and acidic soils at about 400 meters above sea level, while the red grapes grow in more calcareous soils at lower elevations between 200 and 300 meters. The wines proposed are among the most interesting of the territory in terms of complexity and elegance. The Roero Arneis Bricco delle Ciliegie is always one of the best in the appellation. The 2019 offers up aromas of citrus fruits and Mediterranean scrub, with floral and herb nuances, while the palate proves linear, sapid and plucky. It's on par with the Roero Bric valdiana '17, a wine characterized by hints of berries and wisteria, a palate of nice depth and fine tannins—crunchy and impressively long.

- ○ Roero Arneis Bricco delle Ciliegie '19 — TT 3*
- ● Roero Bric Valdiana '17 — TT 5
- ● Roero '18 — TT 3
- ○ Roero Arneis Le Rive del Bricco delle Ciliegie '16 — YYY 4*
- ● Roero Bric Valdiana '11 — YYY 5
- ● Roero Bric Valdiana '07 — YYY 5
- ● Roero Bric Valdiana '03 — YYY 5
- ● Roero Bric Valdiana '01 — YYY 4
- ● Roero Bric Valdiana '00 — YYY 4*
- ● Roero Giovanni Almondo Ris. '13 — YYY 5
- ● Roero Giovanni Almondo Ris. '11 — YYY 5
- ● Roero Giovanni Almondo Ris. '09 — YYY 5
- ○ Roero Arneis Bricco delle Ciliegie '18 — YY 3*
- ○ Roero Arneis Le Rive del Bricco delle Ciliegie '18 — YY 4
- ● Roero Bric Valdiana '15 — YY 5

★★★Elio Altare

Fraz. Annunziata, 51
12064 La Morra [CN]
Tel. +39 017350835
www.elioaltare.com

CELLAR SALES
PRE-BOOKED VISITS
ANNUAL PRODUCTION 70,000 bottles
HECTARES UNDER VINE 11.00

Elio Altare represents the concept of 'modern Barolo'at the highest quality levels, having created a style in which Nebbiolo is at the fore. And so small French barrels are used, though in a way that oak is never invasive or smothering. Rotomacerators and short fermentation are also employed, but substance and tannins are extracted as to allow a healthy longevity. Low yields in the vineyard and close attention to the concentration/ripeness of the grapes are also key. Elio's capable daughter Silvia is now at the helm and has already shown that she is able to maintain the excellence that has made the winery famous throughout the world. We appreciated the delicious Barolo Arborina '16, a particularly complex and multifaceted wine in which fresh red fruit sensations combine with persuasive hints of licorice only to give way to a powerful, perfectly balanced palate. Even with the cool 2014 harvest, the Barolo Vigna Bricco del cru Cerretta di Serralunga d'Alba manages to express commendable mouthfeel, coming through rich and pervasive.

Wine	Rating	Price
● Barolo Arborina '16	▼▼▼	8
● Barolo '16	▼▼	8
● Barolo Cerretta V. Bricco Ris. '14	▼▼	8
● Langhe Giàrborina '18	▼▼	8
● Dolcetto d'Alba '19	▼▼	3
● Langhe La Villa '18	▼▼	8
● Langhe Larigi '18	▼▼	8
● Langhe Nebbiolo '19	▼▼	4
● Barbera d'Alba '19	▼	3
● Barolo Arborina '09	▽▽▽	8
● Barolo Cerretta V. Bricco '11	▽▽▽	8
● Barolo Cerretta V. Bricco '10	▽▽▽	8
● Barolo Cerretta V. Bricco Ris. '13	▽▽▽	8
● Langhe Larigi '13	▽▽▽	8
● Langhe Larigi '12	▽▽▽	8
● Langhe Rosso Giàrborina '16	▽▽▽	8

Amalia Cascina in Langa

Loc. Sant'Anna, 85
12065 Cuneo
Tel. +39 0173789013
www.cascinaamalia.it

CELLAR SALES
PRE-BOOKED VISITS
ACCOMMODATION
ANNUAL PRODUCTION 40,000 bottles
HECTARES UNDER VINE 8.00
SUSTAINABLE WINERY

Now on its 18th year, Gigi Boffa's winery has officially reached adulthood. The producer is supported by his son Paolo, and expert consultants like Piero Ballario and Gian Piero Romana. And the results have been excellent, with Barolos that are increasingly recognized by wine critics. The core of production centers on Nebbiolo grown in the Le Coste and Bussia crus, but the area of Sant'Anna, where the winery and the family B&B are located, is important as well. Indeed it's always been famous for its Dolcetto and Barbera grapes. Nice complexity features in the Barolo Le Coste di Monforte '16, a wine redolent of red berries, tobacco and licorice. It unfolds gradually, steadily with balance and decisive character. Beautiful harmony in the Barolo Bussia '16, with hints of licorice and black berries giving way to a fresh and already well-balanced palate. The fruity Barbera d'Alba Superiore '17 exhibits notable structure, while the satisfying Dolcetto d'Alba '18 proves more delicate and drinkable. The elegant Langhe Nebbiolo '17 also deserves a taste.

Wine	Rating	Price
● Barolo Bussia '16	▼▼	6
● Barolo Le Coste di Monforte '16	▼▼	6
● Barbera d'Alba Sup. '17	▼▼	4
● Dolcetto d'Alba '18	▼▼	3
○ Langhe Rossese Bianco '18	▼	4
● Barbera d'Alba '17	▽▽	4
● Barbera d'Alba Sup. '16	▽▽	4
● Barbera d'Alba Sup. '15	▽▽	4
● Barolo '14	▽▽	6
● Barolo '13	▽▽	6
● Barolo Bussia '15	▽▽	6
● Barolo Bussia '13	▽▽	6
● Barolo Le Coste di Monforte '15	▽▽	6
● Barolo Le Coste di Monforte '13	▽▽	6
○ Langhe Rossese Bianco '17	▽	4

Antichi Vigneti di Cantalupo

via Michelangelo Buonarroti, 5
28074 Ghemme [NO]
Tel. +39 0163840041
www.cantalupo.net

CELLAR SALES
PRE-BOOKED VISITS
ANNUAL PRODUCTION 180,000 bottles
HECTARES UNDER VINE 35.00

A focus on the value of the Nebbiolo grape, a production philosophy rooted in classically-styled wine and a rigorous respect for the environment are the points that define this important and acclaimed winery, a true model for Northern Piedmont. It's also worth highlighting the praiseworthy choice to release certain wines (premium selections such as Collis Breclemae and Abate di Cluny) only after lengthy aging in the cellar. Another sign of Alberto Arlunno's professionalism and his respect for the consumer is that these wines aren't produced during sub-par years. Liquorice and blond tobacco feature in the complex Collis Breclemae '13, a fleshy, full wine that also exhibits an appealingly delicateness. Once again the fruity and lively Nebbiolo Il Mimo 2019 demonstrates that it's among the region's most interesting rosés, while the Vespolina Villa Horta '18 sees elegant aromas of fresh red fruit adorned by tantalizing white pepper. Strawberries and sweet spices characterize the alluring Primigenia '18, a wine made mainly with Nebbiolo.

● Ghemme Collis Breclemae '13	▼▼ 7
⊙ Colline Novaresi Nebbiolo Il Mimo '19	▼▼ 2*
● Colline Novaresi Primigenia '18	▼▼ 2*
● Colline Novaresi Vespolina Villa Horta '18	▼▼ 2*
○ Carolus Bianco N. M.	▼ 2
● Ghemme '05	▽▽▽ 4
● Ghemme Collis Breclemae '00	▽▽▽ 6
○ Carolus '17	▽▽ 2*
● Colline Novaresi Abate di Cluny '11	▽▽ 5
⊙ Colline Novaresi Nebbiolo Il Mimo '17	▽▽ 2*
● Colline Novaresi Rosso Primigenia '17	▽▽ 2*
● Colline Novaresi Vespolina Villa Horta '16	▽▽ 2*
● Ghemme Cantalupo Anno Primo '11	▽▽ 5
● Ghemme Collis Breclemae '11	▽▽ 7
● Ghemme Collis Carellae '11	▽▽ 6

★★Antoniolo

c.so Valsesia, 277
13045 Gattinara [VC]
Tel. +39 0163833612
antoniolovini@bmm.it

CELLAR SALES
PRE-BOOKED VISITS
ANNUAL PRODUCTION 60,000 bottles
HECTARES UNDER VINE 12.00

The winery founded by Mario Antoniolo and now run by his grandchildren Lorella (a tireless ambassador of Nebbiolo in Northern Piedmont) and Alberto (who follows the production side) just recently passed its 70-year milestone. The three selections of Gattinara, led by a consistently superb Osso San Grato, do a superb job representing the appellation. Soft, lingering drinkability is accompanied by elegantly tamed tannins, the result of stringent selection criteria in the vineyard and long maturation in oak barrels, mostly sizable. Splendid success for all three Gattinara Reserves thanks to a favorable 2016. The Osso San Grato, however, put in the best performance, taking home Tre Bicchieri thanks to alluring aromas of gentian, dark tobacco and red berries, the prelude to an assertive, powerful and juicy palate that's destined to mellow for many years. A touch of iodine and rough tannins, though not aggressive, characterize the Riserva—no cru is mentioned, but it's a real marvel. We also appreciated the San Francesco, rich in liquorice and dense in pulp.

● Gattinara Osso San Grato Ris. '16	▼▼▼ 8
● Gattinara Ris. '16	▼▼ 6
● Gattinara San Francesco Ris. '16	▼▼ 8
● Coste della Sesia Nebbiolo Juvenia '18	▼▼ 4
⊙ Bricco Lorella Rosato '19	▼ 3
● Gattinara Vign. Castelle '00	▽▽▽ 6
● Gattinara Vign. Castelle '99	▽▽▽ 5
● Gattinara Vign. Osso S. Grato '06	▽▽▽ 6
● Gattinara Vign. Osso S. Grato '05	▽▽▽ 6
● Gattinara Vign. Osso S. Grato '04	▽▽▽ 6
● Gattinara Vign. Osso S. Grato '01	▽▽▽ 6
● Gattinara Vign. S. Francesco '06	▽▽▽ 5
● Gattinara Vign. S. Francesco '05	▽▽▽ 6
● Gattinara Vign. S. Francesco '03	▽▽▽ 6
● Gattinara Vign. S. Francesco '01	▽▽▽ 6

Odilio Antoniotti

fraz. Casa del Bosco
v.lo Antoniotti, 5
13868 Sostegno [BI]
Tel. +39 0163860309
antoniottiodilio@libero.it

CELLAR SALES
PRE-BOOKED VISITS
ANNUAL PRODUCTION 15,000 bottles
HECTARES UNDER VINE 4.50

Despite the brilliant success they've been having with consumers, Odilio and Mattia Antoniotti continue to take small steps, carefully selecting their grapes in the vineyards and marketing only the best of their wines, as is evident just by observing the relationship between the area under vine and bottles sold. Nebbiolo takes center stage, giving rise primarily to an always rich and long-lived Bramaterra, the result of an absolutely natural and environmentally friendly production approach. Indeed, their philosophy is such that the winery has joined the ViniVeri consortium. The fresh 2016 harvest gave rise to a particularly fruity Bramaterra, with bold vegetal hints that make for a decidedly youthful and lively drink—it will be able to mellow in the bottle for many years. The Coste della Sesia Nebbiolo '17 overcame the hot summer for clear, focused and rich aromas of raspberries, strawberries and spices.

Wine	Rating
● Bramaterra '16	🍷🍷 6
● Coste della Sesia Nebbiolo '17	🍷🍷 4
● Bramaterra '10	🍷🍷🍷 3*
● Coste della Sesia Nebbiolo '15	🍷🍷🍷 3*
● Bramaterra '15	🍷🍷 6
● Bramaterra '14	🍷🍷 5
● Bramaterra '13	🍷🍷 4
● Bramaterra '12	🍷🍷 4
● Bramaterra '11	🍷🍷 3*
● Bramaterra '09	🍷🍷 3*
● Bramaterra '08	🍷🍷 3*
● Bramaterra '07	🍷🍷 3*
● Coste della Sesia Nebbiolo '16	🍷🍷 4

F.lli Aresca

via Pontetto, 8a
14047 Mombercelli [AT]
Tel. +39 0141955128
www.arescavini.it

CELLAR SALES
PRE-BOOKED VISITS
ANNUAL PRODUCTION 180,000 bottles
HECTARES UNDER VINE 12.00
SUSTAINABLE WINERY

Situated in in the hills of Mombercelli, the Aresca family's farm got its start in 1952, under brothers Luigi and Piero. Since the 1970s they've been focusing on viticulture and bottling their own wine. Their range centers on Barbera, obviously, but wines from other appellations are also represented, such as Dolcetto di Ovada, Barolo, Roero Arneis and Gavi. Their style is modern, but respectful of the territory of provenance, with a production approach that tries to be as minimally invasive as possible. The Aresca family's winery enters the main section of our guide thanks to a series of wines of excellent craftsmanship, with the Nizza San Luigi '17 standing out. Spicy and violet fragrances are accompanied by notes of tobacco and liquorice. On the palate it's generous and complex, with a lingering, characterful finish. Among the other wines tasted we especially enjoyed the Barbera d'Asti La Moretta '18, a supple and fresh wine, juicy and well-balanced.

Wine	Rating
● Nizza Barbera San Luigi '17	🍷🍷 5
● Barbera d'Asti La Moretta '18	🍷🍷 2*
● Barbera d'Asti Sup. La Rossa '17	🍷🍷 3
● Grignolino d'Asti Testabalorda '19	🍷🍷 2*
● Barbera d'Asti La Moretta '17	🍷🍷 2*
● Barbera d'Asti La Moretta '16	🍷🍷 2*
● Barbera d'Asti Superiore La Rossa '15	🍷🍷 3
● Grignolino d'Asti '17	🍷🍷 2*
● Grignolino d'Asti Testabalorda '18	🍷🍷 2*
● Nizza San Luigi '16	🍷🍷 5
● Nizza San Luigi '15	🍷🍷 5

L'Armangia

FRAZ. SAN GIOVANNI, 122
14053 CANELLI [AT]
TEL. +39 0141824947
www.armangia.it

CELLAR SALES
PRE-BOOKED VISITS
ACCOMMODATION
ANNUAL PRODUCTION 95,000 bottles
HECTARES UNDER VINE 11.00
SUSTAINABLE WINERY

Brought to life over thirty years ago by Ignazio Giovine in Canelli, where the family have been producing grapes and wines since the mid-19th century, the property hosts a multifaceted array of cultivars. The vineyards around the winery are mostly dedicated to white grapes, mainly Moscato, while Moasca, San Marzano Oliveto and Castel Boglione give rise to primarily red grapes: Nebbiolo, Freisa, Merlot, Cabernet and, of course, Barbera. With the help of his wife, Giuliana, Ignazio now signs off on an extremely reliable and stylistically recognizable battery of wines. Their two Nizzas stand out: the Titon '17 is broad on the nose, with floral, fruity, rain-soaked earth sensations accompanied by iodine aromas; the palate is rich in fruit, of considerable structure, well supported by a vibrant acidity that lends length and freshness. The Vignali Riserva '16 features ripe cherry and rose fragrances and a close-knit tannic texture, a sapid and charmingly complex wine.

Wine	Glasses	Price
● Nizza Titon '17	TT	4
● Nizza Vignali Ris. '16	TT	5
● Barbera d'Asti Sopra Berruti '18	TT	2*
○ Lorenzo MariaSole Dosaggio Zero M. Cl. '14	TT	4
○ M.to Bianco EnnEEnnE '18	TT	2*
○ Moscato d'Asti Canelli '19	TT	2*
○ Piemonte Chardonnay Pratorotondo '19	TT	2*
○ Piemonte Chardonnay Robi & Robi '18	TT	4
○ Lorenzo MariaSole Dosaggio Zero M. Cl. '13	YY	4
○ Lorenzo MariaSole Pas Dosé M. Cl.	YY	4
● Nizza Titon '16	YY	4
● Nizza Titon '15	YY	4
○ Piemonte Chardonnay Pratorotondo '18	YY	2*

Ascheri

VIA PIUMATI, 23
12042 BRA [CN]
TEL. +39 0172412394
www.ascherivini.it

CELLAR SALES
PRE-BOOKED VISITS
ACCOMMODATION AND RESTAURANT SERVICE
ANNUAL PRODUCTION 240,000 bottles
HECTARES UNDER VINE 40.00

Bolstered by a wine-making history that goes back to 1880, and a surname that's also one of Verduno's geographical mentions, Matteo Ascheri, active president of the consortium for the protection of Barolo, has built an important production center in the heart Bra. The winery is certainly worth a visit, in part because the winery is accompanied by food and accommodation facilities. Most of their vineyards, primarily Nebbiolo, are situated in Serralunga d'Aba and Verduno, while on the hill of Bra Syrah and Viognier are also cultivated. This year they submitted an overall selection of excellent quality, starting with their 2016 Barolos. Elegant in its aromas of bottled cherries, the Sorano exhibits nice roundness on the palate. The youthful and racy Ascheri offers up licorice sensations and a hint of vanilla together with good tannins. An excellent performance for the Viognier Montalupa Bianco, which recalls the great white wines of the Rhone for its complexity and character.

Wine	Glasses	Price
● Barolo Sorano '16	TT	6
○ Langhe Bianco Montalupa '16	TT	4
○ Ascheri Brut M. Cl.	TT	5
● Barolo '16	TT	5
● Barolo Ascheri '16	TT	5
● Barolo Coste & Bricco '16	TT	6
● Barolo Pisapola '16	TT	5
○ Langhe Arneis Cristina Ascheri '19	TT	2*
● Langhe Dolcetto Nirane '19	TT	4
● Langhe Nebbiolo S. Giacomo '18	TT	4
● Langhe Rosso Montalupa '15	T	4
● Verduno Pelaverga '19	T	2
● Barolo Sorano '00	YYY	5
● Barolo Sorano Coste & Bricco '06	YYY	5
● Barolo Coste & Bricco '10	YY	6
● Barolo Sorano '10	YY	5

★Azelia

via Alba Barolo, 143
12060 Castiglione Falletto [CN]
Tel. +39 017362859
www.azelia.it

CELLAR SALES
PRE-BOOKED VISITS
ANNUAL PRODUCTION 80,000 bottles
HECTARES UNDER VINE 16.00
SUSTAINABLE WINERY

Two main characteristics define Luigi Scavino and his son Lorenzo's approach to winemaking: elegance and power. Concentration of flavor and aromatic substances within the grapes is achieved both by very strict thinning and by the presence of particularly old vines, which alone contribute to avoiding excesses while conferring decidedly soft tannins. Elegance derives first and foremost, of course, from the Nebbiolo grape, which has some of the most complex and fascinating aromas among the thousands of varieties vinified. Luigi's passion for studying the different barrels used for the maturation of Barolo takes care of the rest. Extremely elegant aromas feature in the Bricco Fiasco '16, with its notes of herbs, red fruits and liquorice heralding a palate rich in substance, long, of rare harmony and pleasantness. The San Rocco '16 is even weightier in the mouth, well endowed with texture and pervasive tannins. The Barolo Cerretta '16 is certainly among the best of its kind, majestic even. Once again the elegant Dolcetto d'Alba Bricco dell'Oriolo performed well.

Wine	Rating
● Barolo Bricco Fiasco '16	TT 8
● Barolo Cerretta '16	TT 8
● Barolo San Rocco '16	TT 8
● Barbera d'Alba Punta '16	TT 5
● Barolo '16	TT 6
● Barolo Margheria '16	TT 8
● Dolcetto d'Alba Bricco dell'Oriolo '18	TT 3
● Langhe Nebbiolo '18	TT 4
● Barolo Bricco Fiasco '12	YYY 8
● Barolo Bricco Fiasco '09	YYY 8
● Barolo Bricco Fiasco '01	YYY 7
● Barolo Margheria '06	YYY 7
● Barolo S. Rocco '11	YYY 8
● Barolo S. Rocco '08	YYY 8
● Barolo Voghera Brea Ris. '01	YYY 8

Barbaglia

via Dante, 54
28010 Cavallirio [NO]
Tel. +39 016380115
www.vinibarbaglia.it

CELLAR SALES
PRE-BOOKED VISITS
ANNUAL PRODUCTION 25,000 bottles
HECTARES UNDER VINE 4.50

As required by production regulations, Sergio Barbaglia combines a small percentage of Vespolina with Nebbiolo to make his Boca, obtaining aroms particularly rich in notes of roses and delicate spices. The property is very small, but his brilliant daughter Silvia is making her contribution to expanding and making use of their main production facility. The landscape in which the vineyards are located is particularly evocative, with Monte Rosa as a backdrop to the many woods and sparse plots of vines here, serving as a symbol of the desire to revitalize local winemaking traditions. Right from the color, the Boca '16 looks lovely, youthful, pouring a nice, dense and lively ruby red. The nose is vibrant and focused, with red and black berries giving way to rhubarb and iodine—great complexity and finesse. On the palate it's tantalizing and fleshy, with dense but not aggressive tannins and a long characterful finish that foretells of great things to come. Sensations of damson and beeswax feature in the more than pleasant Bianco Lucino '19.

Wine	Rating
● Boca '16	TT 5
○ Colline Novaresi Bianco Lucino '19	TT 3
● Colline Novaresi Vespolina Ledi '19	T 3
● Boca '15	YY 5
● Boca '13	YY 5
● Boca '12	YY 5
○ Colline Novaresi Bianco Lucino '17	YY 3*
● Colline Novaresi Croatina '13	YY 2*
● Colline Novaresi Nebbiolo Il Silente '17	YY 3
● Colline Novaresi Nebbiolo Il Silente '15	YY 3*
● Colline Novaresi Vespolina Ledi '17	YY 3
● Colline Novaresi Vespolina Ledi '15	YY 3

Osvaldo Barberis

B.TA VALDIBÀ, 42
12063 DOGLIANI [CN]
TEL. +39 017370054
www.osvaldobarberis.com

CELLAR SALES
PRE-BOOKED VISITS
ANNUAL PRODUCTION 20,000 bottles
HECTARES UNDER VINE 8.00
VITICULTURE METHOD Certified Organic

It seems that many of older consumers are a bit perplexed by the recent tendency to produce powerful, alcoholic Dolcettos, accustomed as they were to a simple, approachable mealtime wine. Our advice, which holds for everyone, is to taste Osvaldo Barberis's Dogliani, which is never too muscular but always rich in personality and captivating plum aromas. Never over-structured, it's endowed with a rare ability to pair with food. Their range is enriched by two selections that revolve around Nebbiolo and two others based on Barbera, as well as a valid Langhe Nascetta Anì white. The lively Dogliani Puncin '19 is a commendably classic wine, combining characteristic hints of blackberry and bitter almond with fresh notes of blackcurrant; the palate is just as charming, harmonious, juicy and with just a hint of tannins. The Dogliani Valdibà '19, with its lovely aromas of red berries, is a little more stiff, forthright. The tasty Langhe Barbera Brichat '19 is particularly complex, just a bit coarse. The Nascetta Anì '19 proves citrusy and well structured.

Wine	Rating
● Dogliani Puncin '19	🍷🍷 3*
● Dogliani Valdibà '19	🍷🍷 3
● Langhe Barbera Brichat '19	🍷🍷 2*
○ Langhe Nascetta Anì '19	🍷🍷 3
● Barbera d'Alba Cesca '18	🍷 3
● Dogliani Avrì '19	🍷 3
● Barbera d'Alba Cesca '17	🍷🍷 3
● Barbera d'Alba Cesca '16	🍷🍷 3
● Barbera d'Alba Cesca '15	🍷🍷 3
● Dogliani Puncin '17	🍷🍷 3
● Dogliani Sup. Puncin '16	🍷🍷 3
● Dogliani Valdibà '18	🍷🍷 3*
● Dogliani Valdibà '17	🍷🍷 2*
● Dogliani Valdibà '16	🍷🍷 2*
○ Langhe Nascetta Anì '18	🍷🍷 3
● Langhe Nebbiolo Muntajà '16	🍷🍷 3

Batasiolo

FRAZ. ANNUNZIATA, 87
12064 LA MORRA [CN]
TEL. +39 017350130
www.batasiolo.com

CELLAR SALES
PRE-BOOKED VISITS
ANNUAL PRODUCTION 2,500,000 bottles
HECTARES UNDER VINE 130.00

An area of about 120 hectares unfolds across 9 farmsteads. About half of these are planted Nebbiolo grapes, 5 excellent Barolo crus: Briccolina, Cerequio, Brunate, Bussia and Boscareto. At this last there's also an elegant resort with a spa, a fine restaurant and a lovely view of the vineyards. But not only Barolo is produced, the range includes the red wines Barbaresco, Barbera d'Alba, Dolcetto d'Alba, and whites made with Cortese, Arneis, Sauvignon, Pinot Bianco and Moscato grapes. A multifaceted range is enriched by a few highly worthy crus, with the Barolo Cerequio '16 standing out. It's the child of an excellent vintage, representing the cultivar and an extraordinary terroir, with its elegance and harmony, exceptionally well. Their historic flagship, the Barolo Briccolina '16 is equally valid for its polish, balancing balsamic and spicy nuances with gustatory depth. As per tradition, the firmly structured and ageworthy Boscareto '15 is still austere.

Wine	Rating
● Barolo Briccolina '16	🍷🍷 8
● Barolo Cerequio '16	🍷🍷 7
● Barbera d'Alba Sovrana '18	🍷🍷 4
● Barolo '16	🍷🍷 6
● Barolo Boscareto '15	🍷🍷 7
● Barolo Brunate '16	🍷🍷 7
○ Batasiolo Brut M. Cl. '14	🍷🍷 3
○ Langhe Chardonnay Vign. Morino '18	🍷🍷 5
● Langhe Nebbiolo '18	🍷🍷 3
○ Roero Arneis '19	🍷 3
● Barolo Boscareto '05	🍷🍷🍷 7
● Barolo Briccolina '15	🍷🍷🍷 8
● Barolo Corda della Briccolina '90	🍷🍷🍷 7
● Barolo Corda della Briccolina '89	🍷🍷🍷 7
● Barolo Corda della Briccolina '88	🍷🍷🍷 7

Bava

s.da Monferrato, 2
14023 Cocconato [AT]
Tel. +39 0141907083
www.bava.com

CELLAR SALES
PRE-BOOKED VISITS
ACCOMMODATION
ANNUAL PRODUCTION 490,000 bottles
HECTARES UNDER VINE 55.00

The Bava family's enological roots date back to the early-20th century, while their agricultural roots go all the way back to the 17th century. In the 1970s they took over the Cocchi brand, creating a production base in Cocconato, on the slopes of Monferrato Astigiano, and later expanding into Langa di Agliano and Castiglione Falletto. Nebbiolo, Barbera and Moscato are the foundation of a range in which even lesser known typologies, such as Ruchè, Malvasia di Castelnuovo Don Bosco and Albarossa, are represented. The producer's various faces were all represented in our finals. The Nizza Piano Alto '17 features aromas of black berries enriched by notes of rose, cocoa and cinchona-quinine, while the palate proves rich in fruit, with well-managed tannins supporting a long finish. The Alta Langa Brut TotoCorde '15 offers up citrus notes and white fruit, proving beautifully structured and full on the palate, while the juicy and complex Barolo Scarrone '15 stands out for its austere tannic texture.

○ Alta Langa Brut TotoCorde '15	5
● Nizza Barbera Piano Alto '17	4
⊙ Alta Langa Brut Rösa '15	6
● Barbera d'Asti Li Bera '18	3
● Barolo Scarrone '16	7
● Barolo Scarrone '15	7
○ Alta Langa Brut Bianc 'd Bianc '15	6
○ Piemonte Chardonnay Thou Bianc '19	3
○ Alta Langa Brut Bianc 'd Bianc Giulio Cocchi '12	6
○ Alta Langa Brut Bianc 'd Bianc Giulio Cocchi '10	6
○ Alta Langa Pas Dosé '12	6
○ Alta Langa Pas Dosé Giulio Cocchi '08	6
● Nizza Piano Alto '16	4
● Nizza PianoAlto '15	4

Bel Colle

fraz. Castagni, 56
12060 Verduno [CN]
Tel. +39 0172470196
www.belcolle.eu

CELLAR SALES
PRE-BOOKED VISITS
ANNUAL PRODUCTION 180,000 bottles
HECTARES UNDER VINE 14.00

In the summer of 2015 Bel Colle, the historic winery founded 45 years ago in Borgo Castani (a hamlet of Verduno) by brothers Franco and Carlo Pontiglione, and Giuseppe Priola, became part of the Bosio Family Estates group. The wines exhibit a truly admirable stylistic precision, both in the area of Barbaresco and Barolo, thanks in part to wonderful crus such as Pajorè, or the legendary Monvigliero. In the cellar their work is highly respectful of the grapes, with measured extractions, making for wines with excellent tannic balance. The Barolo Monvigliero '16 is sumptuous with its fragrant, complex aromas, from raspberry to rose, pepper and liquorice. In the mouth it's majestic in volume, character and finesse, with a long finish. The Pajorè '17 is delicate and airy, classic in its fruity, balsamic strokes; in the mouth it's velvety, ethereal and nuanced. The Barolo Symposium '16 is very convincing and balanced. A note of merit for the Alta Langa of the same vintage, which exhibits character and complexity in a weave of vibrant freshness.

● Barolo Monvigliero '16	6
● Barbaresco Pajoré '17	5
○ Alta Langa Extra Brut Cuvée Valentina '16	6
● Barbaresco Boschi dei Signori Bosio '17	5
● Barolo 10 Anni Ris. '09	7
● Barolo Bosco dei Signori Bosio '16	5
● Barolo Simposio '16	6
● Nebbiolo d'Alba La Reala '18	3
● Barbera d'Alba Sup. Le Masche '18	3
● Barbera d'Asti Sup. Nuwanda '18	3
○ Langhe Nas-cëtta '19	3
● Barbaresco Pajoré '16	5
● Barbaresco Pajoré '15	5
● Barolo Monvigliero '09	5

Bera

loc. Cascina Palazzo
via Castellero, 12
12050 Neviglie [CN]
Tel. +39 0173630500
www.bera.it

CELLAR SALES
PRE-BOOKED VISITS
RESTAURANT SERVICE
ANNUAL PRODUCTION 180,000 bottles
HECTARES UNDER VINE 30.00

The vineyards owned by the Bera family are among the best in Neviglie. Situated near the winery, they span elevations ranging from 300 to 400 meters on calcareous soils mixed with clay and tuff. The result is a range of wines, especially Moscato, of great expressive clarity and drinkability. And we shouldn't forget their Nebbiolo da Barbaresco, which is cultivated in the famous Rabajà, Basarin and Serraboella crus, as well as other interesting selections of Dolcetto, Barbera, Pinot Nero and Chardonnay. The entire range presented is of excellent quality. Among the wines produced in Asti, the Moscato d'Asti Su Reimond '19 stands out with its notes of tropical fruit and medicinal herbs; it's a complex wine, of good finesse, rich in pulp, with a long finish. From those from Langhe, the Barbaresco Serraboella '16 most impressed with its spicy aromas accompanied by notes of tobacco, red fruit and liquorice. On the palate it's superbly rich, but also fresh, with elegant, well-integrated tannins.

● Barbaresco Serraboella '16	TT 8
○ Moscato d'Asti Su Reimond '19	TT 4
○ Asti '19	TT 4
● Barbaresco '16	TT 6
● Barbaresco Rabajà Ris. '13	TT 8
● Barbaresco Serraboella '17	TT 8
● Barbera d'Alba Sup. La Lena '17	TT 5
○ Dell'Um.be '16	TT 5
● Langhe Nebbiolo Alladio '16	TT 5
○ Moscato d'Asti '19	TT 4
○ Alta Langa Bera Brut '16	T 6
○ Alta Langa Bera Brut '12	YY 3
● Barbaresco Basarin Ris. '11	YY 7
○ Moscato d'Asti '18	YY 3
○ Moscato d'Asti '17	YY 2*
○ Moscato d'Asti Su Reimond '18	YY 3*
○ Moscato d'Asti Su Reimond '17	YY 3*

Cinzia Bergaglio

via Gavi, 29
15060 Tassarolo [AL]
Tel. +39 0143342203
www.vinicinziabergaglio.it

CELLAR SALES
PRE-BOOKED VISITS
ANNUAL PRODUCTION 30,000 bottles
HECTARES UNDER VINE 9.00

Despite its small size, Cinzia Bergaglio's winery is one Gavi's leading producers, thanks to minimalist and precise style throughout every stage of production. In the vineyard, great attention is paid to the quality of the grapes and the utmost respect is shown for the environment, while in the cellar their approach is minimally invasive, aimed entirely at making wines with a strong territorial identity. And so it is that Rovereto and Tassarolo are expressed in a range centered on the Cortese grape. The Grifone delle Roveri '19 is an amazing interpretation of the typology, intense in its floral and fruity aromas, which then veer to notes of ferns and minerals. On the palate it's powerful and rich, with a nice, persistent and sapid finish. The Gavi La Fornace held its own—it's elegant and complex, with a broad gustatory phase and a long finish.

○ Gavi del Comune di Gavi Grifone delle Roveri '19	TT 2*
○ Gavi La Fornace '19	TT 2*
○ Gavi del Comune di Gavi Grifone delle Roveri '18	YY 2*
○ Gavi del Comune di Gavi Grifone delle Roveri '16	YY 2*
○ Gavi del Comune di Gavi Grifone delle Roveri '15	YY 2*
○ Gavi del Comune di Gavi Grifone delle Roveri '14	YY 2*
○ Gavi La Fornace '18	YY 2*
○ Gavi La Fornace '17	YY 2*
○ Gavi La Fornace '16	YY 2*
○ Gavi La Fornace '15	YY 2*
○ Gavi La Fornace '14	YY 2*
○ Gavi La Fornace '13	YY 2*

Nicola Bergaglio

FRAZ. ROVERETO
LOC. PEDAGGERI, 59
15066 GAVI [AL]
TEL. +39 0143682195
nicolabergaglio@alice.it

CELLAR SALES
PRE-BOOKED VISITS
ANNUAL PRODUCTION 140,000 bottles
HECTARES UNDER VINE 17.00
SUSTAINABLE WINERY

Nicola Bergaglio is part of Gavi's history, making this wine known around the world and garnering ever-greater attention. Their secret? A perfect terroir for cultivating Cortese, a grape that seems to offer up its best only around here. Their production style is certainly well defined, honed through new technology, making for wines of great complexity, but that haven't lost their naturalness and balance. To all this we must add the time and experience gained over the years (the first harvest came in 1970, thus 2020 represents their 50-year anniversary). An inviting, vital color heralds fine, elegant aromas: fresh herbs and white fruit, which continue on a palate rich in pulp, with a long, sapid finish. This is the excellent Minaia '19. As often happens, what we consider the 'basic' version is just a bit more ready than its big brother. The mineral phase is unveiled, preceded by hints of ferns and notes of camphor, on a tense, vibrant palate, with a long finish.

○ Gavi del Comune di Gavi Minaia '19	🍷🍷🍷 4*
○ Gavi del Comune di Gavi '19	🍷🍷 3*
○ Gavi del Comune di Gavi Minaia '18	🍷🍷🍷 4*
○ Gavi del Comune di Gavi Minaia '17	🍷🍷🍷 4*
○ Gavi del Comune di Gavi Minaia '15	🍷🍷🍷 4*
○ Gavi del Comune di Gavi Minaia '14	🍷🍷🍷 4*
○ Gavi del Comune di Gavi Minaia '11	🍷🍷🍷 4*
○ Gavi del Comune di Gavi Minaia '10	🍷🍷🍷 4
○ Gavi del Comune di Gavi Minaia '09	🍷🍷🍷 4
○ Gavi del Comune di Gavi '18	🍷🍷 2*
○ Gavi del Comune di Gavi '17	🍷🍷 2*
○ Gavi del Comune di Gavi '16	🍷🍷 2*
○ Gavi del Comune di Gavi '15	🍷🍷 2*
○ Gavi del Comune di Gavi Et. Bianca '14	🍷🍷 3*
○ Gavi del Comune di Gavi Minaia '13	🍷🍷 4
○ Gavi del comune di Gavi' Minaia' '16	🍷🍷 4

Bersano

P.ZZA DANTE, 21
14049 NIZZA MONFERRATO [AT]
TEL. +39 0141720211
www.bersano.it

CELLAR SALES
PRE-BOOKED VISITS
ANNUAL PRODUCTION 1,300,000 bottles
HECTARES UNDER VINE 230.00

If the Bersano brand has become one of the most important in the region, it's thanks primarily to the agricultural research work that has allowed the producer to expand into practically each of Piedmont's main districts. The original center of production winds around the farmsteads located between Monferrato and Langhe. This was progressively expanded with acquisitions that have made it possible to include other important typologies in their range, such as Cortese di Gavi. This year the Nizza Cremosina '18 takes center stage. A nose of lovely intensity and finesse features hints of cherry, tobacco and spices, while the palate proves powerful and rich in pulp, with a long, harmonious finish. We also appreciated the excellent Nizza Generala Riserva '17, a rich wine, very compact, with notes of ripe black fruit still just a bit covered by wood. It's also worth mentioning the Arturo Bersano Brut '17, with its flowery aromas and a taut, subtle, austere palate.

● Nizza Cremosina '18	🍷🍷 3*
● Nizza Generala Ris. '17	🍷🍷 5
○ Arturo Bersano Brut M. Cl. '17	🍷🍷 4
● Barbera d'Asti Sup. Costalunga '18	🍷🍷 3
⊙ Arturosé Brut M. Cl. '17	🍷 4
○ Gavi del Comune di Gavi '19	🍷 3
● Barbera d'Asti Sup. Generala '97	🍷🍷🍷 5
● Nizza Generala Ris. '16	🍷🍷🍷 5
○ Artur.O Brut Pas Dosè M. Cl.	🍷🍷 4
● Barbera d'Asti Costalunga '17	🍷🍷 2*
● Barbera d'Asti Sup. Cremosina '16	🍷🍷 3*
● Barolo Badarina '13	🍷🍷 7
● Barolo Badarina Ris. '12	🍷🍷 7
● Piemonte Pinot Nero La Prata '16	🍷🍷 4
● Ruché di Castagnole M.to San Pietro Realto '17	🍷🍷 3

Franco Boasso - Gabutti

B.TA GABUTTI, 3A
12050 SERRALUNGA D'ALBA [CN]
TEL. +39 0173613165
www.gabuttiboasso.com

CELLAR SALES
PRE-BOOKED VISITS
ACCOMMODATION
ANNUAL PRODUCTION 25,000 bottles
HECTARES UNDER VINE 7.00

The Gabutti cru has always been considered one of the most important in all of Barolo, as evidenced by extensive documentation that goes all the way back to 1880 with Lorenzo Fantini's viticultural 'Monograph' of Cuneo, and later Renato Ratti's 1976 Barolo Map, 1990 Atlas of Langhe Vineyards, and finally Alessandro Masnaghetti's recent Barolo MGA. And it's here that the core of Ezio Boasso's winery can be found. Boasso owns other plots planted with Nebbiolo, among which the cru Margheria stands out. In addition to their traditionally-styled range, they offer accommodations at the recommended I Grappoli B&B. Fresh and rich in fruity scents, the delicious Barolo Gabutti '16 is made with grapes cultivated in slightly sandier soil than the other important crus of Serralunga that flank it. The result is a unique softness of taste. The powerful Margheria '16 is just a bit oakier, while the Barolo (which uses the name of the local appellation) is already more open and mature. Kudos to the lively and pleasant Dolcetto d'Alba '19.

- ● Barolo Gabutti '16 — 6
- ● Barolo del Comune di Serralunga d'Alba '16 — 5
- ● Barolo Margheria '16 — 6
- ● Dolcetto d'Alba '19 — 2*
- ● Langhe Nebbiolo '18 — 3
- ● Barolo Gabutti '13 — 6
- ● Barolo Margheria '05 — 5*
- ● Barbera d'Alba Sup. '17 — 2*
- ● Barolo del Comune di Serralunga d'Alba '15 — 5
- ● Barolo Gabutti '15 — 6
- ● Barolo Gabutti '14 — 6
- ● Barolo Margheria Ris. '13 — 7
- ● Langhe Nebbiolo '17 — 3

★Enzo Boglietti

VIA FONTANE, 18A
12064 LA MORRA [CN]
TEL. +39 017350330
www.enzoboglietti.com

CELLAR SALES
PRE-BOOKED VISITS
ANNUAL PRODUCTION 100,000 bottles
HECTARES UNDER VINE 22.50
VITICULTURE METHOD Certified Organic
SUSTAINABLE WINERY

As Enzo Boglietti points out, since the winery was founded in 1991 priority has been given to keeping the personality of each single vineyard intact, and today this approach is even more perceptible thanks to a reduction in the use of those new and somewhat invasive oak barrels that a certain market required until about ten years ago. Even the vineyards, managed by his brother Gianni, are evolving in pursuit of greater sustainability, as evidenced by recent organic certification. When it comes to the quality of their wines, elegance is always at the fore. As demonstrated by the Barolo Arione '16, with its foreground of red berries on a background of blond tobacco and cinchona. On the palate it exhibits a particularly soft and pervasive tannic grip. Delicate smoky hints introduce the Case Nere '16, a wine with a lively, rich and evenly developing palate. The young and racy Brunate and Fossati (from the same, powerful vintage) need more time in the bottle. The elegance of the pleasant Langhe Nebbiolo '18 also impressed.

- ● Barolo Arione '16 — 8
- ● Barolo Case Nere '16 — 8
- ● Barolo Brunate '16 — 8
- ● Barolo Fossati '16 — 8
- ● Langhe Nebbiolo '18 — 4
- ● Barbera d'Alba '18 — 3
- ● Barolo Boiolo '16 — 7
- ● Dolcetto d'Alba Tiglineri '18 — 3
- ● Barolo Arione '06 — 8
- ● Barolo Arione '05 — 8
- ● Barolo Brunate '13 — 8
- ● Barolo Brunate '01 — 8
- ● Barolo Case Nere '04 — 8
- ● Barolo Case Nere '99 — 8
- ● Barolo V. Arione '07 — 8

La Bollina

via Monterotondo, 58
15069 Serravalle Scrivia [AL]
Tel. +39 014361984
www.labollina.it

CELLAR SALES
PRE-BOOKED VISITS
ACCOMMODATION AND RESTAURANT SERVICE
ANNUAL PRODUCTION 200,000 bottles
HECTARES UNDER VINE 28.00

Bollina is overlooked by a splendid Liberty-style villa, which today houses 4 accommodation facilities. Surrounding the main building is a centuries-old estate (for enthusiasts there's even a 9-hole golf course). It's a charming property nestled in historic Gavi. 7 wines are produced in their modern, well-equipped cellar, mainly using native grapes: 2 Gavis, 1 Monferrato Chiaretto (made with Nebbiolo), 2 Monferrato Rossos (Barbera), and 2 Monferrato Biancos (Chardonnay). Theirs are modern wines, an expression of a territory with deep roots in viticulture. Doing the honors this year is a splendid version of the Gavi Ventola: intense and complex, aromas of fresh herbs and white fruit rise up on a mineral background. Balance and harmony characterize the palate, rich in pulp with a lingering finish. The 'basic' Gavi is less complex, with a more classic profile and an easy, fresh palate. We also appreciated the pleasant, 2018 version of the Bricchetta.

Wine	Rating
○ Gavi Ventola '19	▼▼ 3*
○ Gavi '19	▼▼ 3
● M.to Rosso Bricchetta '18	▼▼ 3
⊙ M.to Chiaretto Tinetta '19	▼ 3
○ Gavi '18	▽▽ 3*
○ Gavi Ventola '18	▽▽ 3
○ M.to Bianco Armason '18	▽▽ 3

Bondi

s.da Cappellette, 73
15076 Ovada [AL]
Tel. +39 0131299186
www.bondivini.it

CELLAR SALES
PRE-BOOKED VISITS
ANNUAL PRODUCTION 20,000 bottles
HECTARES UNDER VINE 5.00

This family-run producer concentrates exclusively on red wines. Their range faithfully expresses an area known for its viticulture, combining it with the Bondi family's gift for artisan winemaking. The resulting wines are elegant and aromatically persistent, powerful and rich in personality. A unique quality of their range, which sees around 20 thousand bottles produced, is longevity, a characteristic that we also find in their Dolcettos, a grape that usually expresses its best in the first two or three years of life, but which here proves capable of thrills even over the long term. The Barbera del Monferrato Superiore Ruvrin plays on the power of its olfactory profile. Mature blackberry on notes of spices and tobacco anticipate a rich, fresh palate, with a lingering finish. The Ansensò has a very youthful appearance and nose, with the influence of maturation in wood barrels emerging perceptibly. But a strong foundation, excellent grapes, guarantees growth and good aging prospects.

Wine	Rating
● Barbera del M.to Sup. Ruvrin '17	▼▼ 4
● M.to Rosso Ansensò '17	▼▼ 5
● Ovada D'Uien '17	▼ 3
● Barbera del M.to Banaiotta '17	▽▽ 4
● Barbera del M.to Ruvrin '10	▽▽ 4
● Barbera del M.to Sup. Ruvrin '15	▽▽ 4
● Dolcetto di Ovada Nani '17	▽▽ 2*
● Dolcetto di Ovada Nani '16	▽▽ 2*
● Dolcetto di Ovada Nani '15	▽▽ 2*
● M.to Rosso Ansensò '15	▽▽ 4
● M.to Rosso Ansensò '11	▽▽ 4
● Nani	▽▽ 3*
● Ovada D'Uien '16	▽▽ 3*
● Ovada D'Uien '15	▽▽ 3*
● Ovada D'Uien '13	▽▽ 3
● Ovada D'Uien '11	▽▽ 4

Marco Bonfante

s.da Vaglio Serra, 72
14049 Nizza Monferrato [AT]
Tel. +39 0141725012
www.marcobonfante.com

CELLAR SALES
PRE-BOOKED VISITS
ANNUAL PRODUCTION 250,000 bottles
HECTARES UNDER VINE 13.00
SUSTAINABLE WINERY

Rooted in a history of production that spans some eight generations, siblings Marco and Micaela Bonfante created their own winery in the early 2000s and in just a few seasons have managed to emerge as one of the most notable operating in Asti and beyond. In fact, their Nizza Monferrato vineyards are joined by others throughout the region. The result is a rich and versatile range that's representative of Piedmont's most prestigious appellations and that's constantly appreciated for its cleanness and vigour. A solid overall performance for Bonfante, with the Barbaresco '17 standing out. It's a multifaceted wine, marked by aromas of dried aromatic herbs and tobacco, camphor and black berries. On the palate it exhibits good structure and length. The Barolo Bussia '15 proves balanced and dynamic, with notes of cinchona-quinine and licorice, and a long, gutsy finish, while the Barbera d'Asti Superiore Menego '16 features notes of cherry, undergrowth and rain-soaked earth followed by a powerful, dense, fruity palate.

Wine	Rating
● Barbaresco '17	TT 4
● Barbera d'Asti Sup. Menego '16	TT 4
● Barolo Bussia '15	TT 6
● M.to Rosso Duedidue '16	TT 4
○ Gavi di Gavi I Ronchetti '19	T 2
○ Roero Arneis Persté '19	T 2
● Barbera d'Asti Sup. Menego '15	YY 4
● Barbera d'Asti Sup. Stella Rossa '16	YY 2*
● Barolo Bussia '14	YY 6
● Barolo Bussia '13	YY 6
● Langhe Nebbiolo Imma '16	YY 4
● M.to Rosso Duedidue '15	YY 4
○ Moscato d'Asti '17	YY 2*
● Nizza Bricco Bonfante Ris. '15	YY 5
● Nizza Bricco Bonfante Ris. '14	YY 5

Gilberto Boniperti

via Vittorio Emanuele, 43/45
28010 Barengo [NO]
Tel. +39 0321997123
www.bonipertivignaioli.com

CELLAR SALES
ANNUAL PRODUCTION 12,000 bottles
HECTARES UNDER VINE 3.50

In the always interesting and varied array of northern Piedmont's great reds, Fara is characterized by a limited presence of Nebbiolo, only between 50-70%, so as to leave more room for Vespolina and Uva Rara. Gilberto Boniperti, an expert enologist, has developed his own dosage for his Fara Barton, which provides for only 30% Vespolina, which brings a certain liveliness, especially in terms of aromas. We also recommend his Colline Novaresi Vespolina Favolalunga, a wine that's aged only in steel and is marked by an alluring drinkability. The Fara Bartön does a nice job expressing the hot 2017 summer, endowed as it is with vibrant aromas of ripe fruit and a palate characterized by a consistent tannic grip—it will improve even more in the bottle. Fresh and lively, the Nebbiolo Carlin '18 proves elegant in its hints of raspberries, the prelude to a well-orchestrated and enticing palate. The Vespolina Favolalunga '18 opens on notes of ripe cherries, while a harmonious palate sees the addition of white pepper nuances.

Wine	Rating
● Fara Bartön '17	TT 5
● Colline Novaresi Nebbiolo Carlin '18	TT 4
● Colline Novaresi Vespolina Favolalunga '18	TT 3
⊙ Rosadisera	T 3
● Fara Bartön '15	YYY 5
● Colline Novaresi Barbera Barblin '17	YY 4
● Colline Novaresi Barbera Barblin '16	YY 4
● Colline Novaresi Nebbiolo Carlin '17	YY 4
● Colline Novaresi Nebbiolo Carlin '16	YY 4
● Colline Novaresi Nebbiolo Carlin '15	YY 4
● Colline Novaresi Vespolina Favolalunga '17	YY 3
● Fara Bartön '16	YY 5

Borgo Maragliano

via San Sebastiano, 2
14051 Loazzolo [AT]
Tel. +39 014487132
www.borgomaragliano.com

CELLAR SALES
PRE-BOOKED VISITS
ANNUAL PRODUCTION 365,000 bottles
HECTARES UNDER VINE 39.00
SUSTAINABLE WINERY

A marvellous estate situated at around 450 metres above sea level on the slopes of Loazzolo: it's here that Carlo Galliano and Silvio Quirico created Borgo Maragliano, one of the most reputed brands in Piedmont. Influenced by the particular sandy, tufaceous and calcareous soils, their Moscato-based wines point up the variety's versatility, both when it comes to their Metodo Classico sparklers and their naturally sweet wines. These gems form part of an elegantly contemporary range together with selections made with Chardonnay, Riesling, Brachetto and Pinot Nero. Their range of Metodo Classicos is splendid. The harmonious and very fresh Giuseppe Galliano Brut Nature '15, with its fine and persistent beading, unveils flowery notes, pastry-shop sensations and toasted hazelnut. The Giovanni Galliano Brut Rosé '16 sees red fruit aromas followed by a balanced, plucky palate. The Dogma Blanc de Noirs '16 is complex, with aromas of bread crust, dried fruit and notes, and a palate that plays above all on power.

Wine	Rating
○ Dogma Blanc de Noirs M. Cl. '16	▼▼ 5
⊙ Giovanni Galliano Brut Rosé M. Cl. '16	▼▼ 5
○ Giuseppe Galliano Brut Nature M. Cl. '15	▼▼ 5
○ El Calié '19	▼▼ 2*
○ Federico Galliano Brut Nature M. Cl. '17	▼▼ 5
○ Francesco Galliano Blanc de Blancs M. Cl. '17	▼▼ 4
○ Moscato d'Asti La Caliera '19	▼▼ 3
○ Piemonte Chardonnay Crevoglio '19	▼▼ 2*
○ Giuseppe Galliano Ris. Brut M. Cl. '01	▽▽▽ 4*
⊙ Giovanni Galliano Brut Rosé M. Cl. '15	▽▽▽ 5
○ Giuseppe Galliano Brut Nature M. Cl. '13	▽▽▽ 5
○ Dogma Blanc de Noirs M. Cl. '15	▽▽ 5
○ Federico Galliano Brut Nature M. Cl. '16	▽▽ 5
○ Giuseppe Galliano Brut Nature M. Cl. '14	▽▽ 5

★Giacomo Borgogno & Figli

via Gioberti, 1
12060 Barolo [CN]
Tel. +39 017356108
www.borgogno.com

CELLAR SALES
PRE-BOOKED VISITS
ANNUAL PRODUCTION 250,000 bottles
HECTARES UNDER VINE 34.00
VITICULTURE METHOD Certified Organic
SUSTAINABLE WINERY

The Liste, Fossati and Cannubi crus are at the heart of the winery's portfolio of wines, giving rise primarily to Barolos and an always-sumptuous reserve. But young Andrea Farinetti has followed with acquisitions in Madonna di Como, an area famous for its exquisite Dolcetto d'Alba, where the elevations allow for the cultivation of Riesling as well. This was followed by plots of Timorasso in Tortona and Barbera in Monferrato. Soon we'll be talking about Etna as well. The Barolo Liste '15 sees sensations of herbs and fresh hay combine with powerful, red fruit. In the mouth it's vivid, structured, rich and pervasive: Tre Bicchieri. The complex, powerful and well-orchestrated Barolo Riserva '13 features raspberry hints, licorice and camphor. In the palate it's got both pulp and close-knit tannins. The floral, silky and long 'entry-level' Barolo '15 is no less impressive. The valid Timorasso Derthona '18 proves rich in elegant olfactory nuances.

Wine	Rating
● Barolo Liste '15	▼▼▼ 8
● Barolo '15	▼▼ 7
● Barolo Ris. '13	▼▼ 8
● Barolo Cannubi '15	▼▼ 8
● Barolo Fossati '15	▼▼ 8
○ Colli Tortonesi Timorasso Derthona '18	▼▼ 7
● Langhe Nebbiolo No Name '16	▼▼ 6
● Barbera d'Alba Sup. '18	▼ 5
● Barbera d'Asti Cascina Valle Asinari '18	▼ 6
● Barbera d'Asti Sup. Cascina Valle Asinari '18	▼ 6
○ Langhe Riesling Era Ora '18	▼ 5
● Nizza Cascina Valle Asinari '17	▼ 5
● Barolo Liste '11	▽▽▽ 8
● Barolo Liste '10	▽▽▽ 8
● Barolo Ris. '11	▽▽▽ 8

Boroli

via Pugnane, 4
12060 Castiglione Falletto [CN]
Tel. +39 017362927
www.boroli.it

CELLAR SALES
PRE-BOOKED VISITS
ACCOMMODATION AND RESTAURANT SERVICE
ANNUAL PRODUCTION 200,000 bottles
HECTARES UNDER VINE 32.00
SUSTAINABLE WINERY

The Boroli family have privately-owned plots in prestigious sites such as Castiglione Falletto, Barolo and La Morra, including cult vineyards known worldwide such as Cerequio or Villero, names that speak to the hearts of great wine lovers. The vines go back anywhere from 20 to 40 years, and are painstakingly manicured. Yields are particularly low, while in the cellar they prefer top-quality oak, small barrels especially, making for a solid and very reliable range of wines. This year they submitted a smaller selection than usual, only two wines, both Barolos from the favorable 2016 vintage. The Villero offers up aromas of ripe raspberry, quinine and licorice. The palate comes through succulent, the finish long and well sustained. With the Barolo Brunella floral strokes are more pronounced, while its tannic texture is still quite compact and austere. Time in the bottle will smooth things out.

- Barolo Brunella '16 8
- Barolo Villero '16 8
- Barolo Villero '01 6
- Barolo Villero '00 4*
- Barolo '14 6
- Barolo '12 6
- Barolo '11 6
- Barolo Brunella '15 8
- Barolo Brunella '14 8
- Barolo Brunella '13 8
- Barolo Cerequio '15 8
- Barolo Cerequio '14 8
- Barolo Cerequio '13 8
- Barolo Cerequio '12 7
- Barolo Villero '15 8
- Barolo Villero '13 8
- Barolo Villero '12 7

Agostino Bosco

via Fontane, 24
12064 La Morra [CN]
Tel. +39 0173509466
www.barolobosco.com

CELLAR SALES
PRE-BOOKED VISITS
ANNUAL PRODUCTION 28,000 bottles
HECTARES UNDER VINE 5.50
SUSTAINABLE WINERY

Rightly proud of his acclaimed Barolo, Andrea Bosco is celebrating his winery's fortieth anniversary by reaffirming his conviction that 'Barbera d'Alba deserves to be appreciated all over the world, as long as careful attention is paid both in the vineyard and during aging in oak'. The two Baroloare selections are always valid: with the Neirane, which is cultivated on rather sandy soil, proving more approachable and open, and the austere La Serra more in need of aging. With the 2016 harvest, both shined during our tastings, with the La Serra cru offering up elegant notes of sweet spices and raspberry, combined with a palate that's both pulpy and still slightly tannic. The Neirane tends more towards scents of licorice, tobacco and herbs, while the palate already proves well balanced and highly enjoyable. Fresh and almost balsamic on the nose, the Barbera d'Alba Superiore Volupta '18 comes through austere on the palate, closing with notes of rhubarb.

- Barolo La Serra '16 6
- Barolo Neirane '16 6
- Barbera d'Alba Sup. Volupta '18 4
- Langhe Nebbiolo Rurem '18 4
- Barbera d'Alba Sup. Volupta '17 3*
- Barbera d'Alba Sup. Volupta '16 3*
- Barbera d'Alba Sup. Volupta '15 3
- Barolo La Serra '15 6
- Barolo La Serra '14 6
- Barolo La Serra '13 6
- Barolo Neirane '15 5
- Barolo Neirane '14 5
- Barolo Neirane '13 5
- Dolcetto d'Alba Vantrin '15 2*
- Langhe Nebbiolo Rurem '17 3
- Langhe Nebbiolo Rurem '15 3

Giacomo Boveri

FRAZ. MONTALE CELLI
VIA COSTA VESCOVATO, 15
15050 COSTA VESCOVATO [AL]
TEL. +39 0131838223
www.vignetiboveri.it

CELLAR SALES
PRE-BOOKED VISITS
ANNUAL PRODUCTION 25,000 bottles
HECTARES UNDER VINE 9.00

Although he has solid family roots in agriculture, Giacomo Boveri has only emerged in our guide over the last few years ago thanks to a series of characterful Timorassos. Today we can count him as among the most interesting producers working with the grape. Only native varieties are used (in addition to the already-mentioned Timorasso, there's Cortese, Barbera, Croatina and Freisa), with an elegant stylistic approach, one that brings out the grapes' characteristic aromas, despite the exuberance of alcohol that has marked the latest vintages. The Bricco della Ginestra features nice, ripe fruit on notes of sweet spices and cocoa; on the palate it's rich and intense, with acidity lengthening a lingering finish. The Muntà l'è Ruma is commendable, rich and vibrant with a nice, fresh, sapid finish—very long. The Piccolo Derthona drinks easy and fresh, very enticing. We also appreciated the intriguing, complex Freisa La Cappelletta.

● Colli Tortonesi Barbera Sup. Bricco della Ginestra '15	🍷🍷 3*
● Colli Tortonesi Freisa La Cappelletta '16	🍷🍷 3
○ Colli Tortonesi Timorasso Muntà L'è Ruma '17	🍷🍷 5
○ Piccolo Derthona '19	🍷🍷 3
○ Colli Tortonesi Timorasso Lacrime del Bricco '17	🍷 5
○ Colli Tortonesi Timorasso Lacrime del Bricco '16	🍷🍷 4
○ Colli Tortonesi Timorasso Lacrime del Bricco '15	🍷🍷 4
○ Colli Tortonesi Timorasso Muntà L'è Ruma '16	🍷🍷 4
○ Colli Tortonesi Timorasso Muntà L'è Ruma '15	🍷🍷 4

Luigi Boveri

LOC. MONTALE CELLI
VIA XX SETTEMBRE, 6
15050 COSTA VESCOVATO [AL]
TEL. +39 0131838165
www.boveriluigi.com

CELLAR SALES
PRE-BOOKED VISITS
ANNUAL PRODUCTION 80,000 bottles
HECTARES UNDER VINE 22.00

Luigi and his wife, Germana, have made an important contribution to local winemaking history, playing a leading role in the revolution of the 1990s together with a small, exemplary group of producers who helped change the fortunes of this Alessandria district. A strong bond with local tradition is well evidenced by the robust use of native grapes. The heart of production lies with Timorasso and Barbera-based wines, and Luigi's stylistic approach highlights great elegance and persistence, as well as notable longevity. The Poggio Delle Amarene '17 express its unique attributes with a very sophisticated, elegant version. It's intense, with sweet spices of oak combining with notes of tobacco and cinchona-quinine. The powerful Timorasso Derthona features a fresh, sapid finish. The Filari di Timorasso has notable gustatory-olfactory substance, but still hasn't peaked.

● Colli Tortonesi Barbera Poggio delle Amarene '17	🍷🍷 5
○ Colli Tortonesi Timorasso Derthona '18	🍷🍷 5
○ Colli Tortonesi Timorasso Derthona Filari di Timorasso '18	🍷🍷 6
● Colli Tortonesi Barbera Boccanera '19	🍷 3
○ Colli Tortonesi Cortese Terre del Prete '19	🍷 3
○ Colli Tortonesi Timorasso Derthona '11	🍷🍷🍷 4*
○ Colli Tortonesi Timorasso Filari di Timorasso '12	🍷🍷🍷 5
○ Colli Tortonesi Timorasso Filari di Timorasso '07	🍷🍷🍷 3
○ Colli Tortonesi Timorasso Derthona Filari di Timorasso '17	🍷🍷 5
○ Colli Tortonesi Timorasso Derthona Filari di Timorasso '16	🍷🍷 5

Gianfranco Bovio

FRAZ. ANNUNZIATA
B.TA CIOTTO, 63
12064 LA MORRA [CN]
TEL. +39 017350667
www.boviogianfranco.com

CELLAR SALES
PRE-BOOKED VISITS
ANNUAL PRODUCTION 65,000 bottles
HECTARES UNDER VINE 8.50

The winery bears the name of Gianfranco, who left us five years ago but is still very much alive in the memory of food lovers all over the world, having personally managed the Belvedere restaurant from 1963 to 2007, the first to receive a Michelin star in Piedmont. It wasn't long, however, before Belvedere's wine list included Gianfranco's own Barolos, made with grapes mostly from excellent La Morra crus. His daughter Alessandra is carrying forward and expanding the producer, offering Barolos inspired by the most rigorous and traditional classicism with remarkable constancy. All the 2016 Barolos submitted put in spectacular performances. The Gattera is complex, calling up dried herbs together with more youthful hints of raspberry, while the palate comes through dense, with a discreet acidity lending dynamism. The highly elegant and licorice-scented Arborina successfully plays more on finesse than power. The multifaceted Parussi opens with tobacco aromas before giving way to an elegant hint of white truffle.

Wine	Rating
● Barolo Gattera '16	TT 7
● Barolo Parussi '16	TT 8
● Barolo Rocchettevino '16	TT 7
● Barolo '16	TT 6
● Barolo Arborina '16	TT 7
● Barbera d'Alba Sup. Regiaveja '18	T 4
● Dolcetto d'Alba Dabbene '19	T 2
● Langhe Nebbiolo Firagnetti '18	T 4
● Barolo Bricco Parussi Ris. '01	YYY 6
● Barolo Gattera '11	YYY 6
● Barolo Rocchettevino '06	YYY 5*
● Barolo V. Arborina '90	YYY 6
● Barolo Arborina '15	YY 6
● Barolo Gattera '15	YY 6

★Braida

LOC. CIAPPELLETTE
S.DA PROV.LE 27, 9
14030 ROCCHETTA TANARO [AT]
TEL. +39 0141644113
www.braida.it

CELLAR SALES
PRE-BOOKED VISITS
ACCOMMODATION
ANNUAL PRODUCTION 700,000 bottles
HECTARES UNDER VINE 70.00
SUSTAINABLE WINERY

For over half a century Braida has been one of Piedmont's most beloved wineries. Founded by Giuseppe Bologna (known as Braida) with his son Giacomo, it's now managed by his grandchildren Giuseppe and Raffaella. The property winds its way across five estates and gives rise to precise stylistic interpretations. Mango d'Alba and Trezzo Tinella host their white grapes and Moscato, while Costigliole d'Asti and Castelnuovo Calcea are dedicated to the tastiest reds and in Rocchetta Tanaro we find the vineyards whose grapes are used for their barbera-based classics, such as Bricco dell'Uccellone and Bricco della Bigotta. These two wines weren't presented, leaving the limelight to the Barbera d'Asti Ai Suma, which comes in two versions. On the nose, the 2016 offers up rich notes of red berries accompanied by nuances of sweet spices, making for a long, powerful, juicy palate. The 2017 is denser, more extractive, with oak still in the foreground, but it's got great energy and complexity. It's also worth mentioning the sapid, long and citrusy Langhe Chardonnay Asso di Fiori '18.

Wine	Rating
● Barbera d'Asti Ai Suma '17	TT 7
● Barbera d'Asti Ai Suma '16	TT 7
● Grignolino d'Asti Limonte '19	TT 3
○ Langhe Chardonnay Asso di Fiori '18	TT 5
○ Langhe Nascetta La Regina '19	TT 3
○ Langhe Bianco Il Fiore '19	T 3
○ Langhe Riesling Re di Fiori '18	T 3
○ Moscato d'Asti Vigna senza Nome '19	T 3
● Barbera d'Asti Ai Suma '04	YYY 7
● Barbera d'Asti Bricco dell'Uccellone '15	YYY 7
● Barbera d'Asti Bricco dell'Uccellone '12	YYY 7
● Barbera d'Asti Bricco dell'Uccellone '09	YYY 6
● Barbera d'Asti Bricco dell'Uccellone '05	YYY 6
● Barbera d'Asti Bricco dell'Uccellone '03	YYY 6
● Barbera d'Asti Bricco della Bigotta '07	YYY 6
● Barbera d'Asti Bricco della Bigotta '06	YYY 6
● Barbera d'Asti Montebruna '11	YYY 3*

Brandini

Fraz. Brandini, 16
12064 La Morra [CN]
Tel. +39 017350266
www.agricolabrandini.com

CELLAR SALES
PRE-BOOKED VISITS
ACCOMMODATION AND RESTAURANT SERVICE
ANNUAL PRODUCTION 80,000 bottles
HECTARES UNDER VINE 15.00
VITICULTURE METHOD Certified Organic
SUSTAINABLE WINERY

Piero Bagnasco has vast experience as an administrator of wineries, so it's not surprising that he thought to provide his daughters with a winery that would set its sights immediately on high quality. This is the direction that Giovanna and Serena, the latter a graduate of the University of Gastronomic Sciences in Pollenzo, are taking, with the active participation of expert enological consultant Beppe Caviola. The original vineyards situated in the highest part of La Morra, organic from the outset, have been accompanied by important acquisitions, in particular in Serralunga d'Alba, where the Cerretta and Meriame crus are already giving rise to wines of absolute excellence. The well-made Barolo Annunziata '16 is lively, tantalizing, flowery and juicy, while the more liquorice-leaning Cerretta proves weighty and classically styled. The Barolo R 56 '16 is just a bit more immediate and youthful. The fruity Langhe Nebbiolo Filari Corti '17 is among the best of its kind. We also appreciated the pulpy and fruity Barbera d'Alba Superiore Rocche del Santo '18.

- ● Barolo Cerretta '16 ▼▼▼ 8
- ● Barolo Annunziata '16 ▼▼ 8
- ● Langhe Nebbiolo Filari Corti '17 ▼▼ 4
- ● Barbera d'Alba Sup. Rocche del Santo '18 ▼▼ 5
- ● Barolo R56 '16 ▼▼ 8
- ● Barolo del Comune di La Morra '16 ▼ 7
- ● Barolo del Comune di La Morra '14 ▽▽▽ 8
- ● Barolo R56 '15 ▽▽▽ 8
- ● Barolo Resa 56 '13 ▽▽▽ 8
- ● Barolo Resa 56 '12 ▽▽▽ 8
- ● Barolo Resa 56 '11 ▽▽▽ 7
- ● Barolo Resa 56 '10 ▽▽▽ 7

Brangero

via Provinciale, 26
12055 Diano d'Alba [CN]
Tel. +39 017369423
www.brangero.com

PRE-BOOKED VISITS
ANNUAL PRODUCTION 50,000 bottles
HECTARES UNDER VINE 9.00

Marco Brangero is firmly at the helm, overseeing the winery situated in the upper part of the hill overlooking Diano d'Alba. In the vineyard we find Piedmont's classic grapes: Dolcetto is accompanied by Barbera, Nebbiolo and Arneis, with a few rows dedicated to international varieties as well. In addition, from a small plot in Verduno (the glorious Monvigliero cru) Marco also produces two Barolos. Marco's winemaking commitment goes beyond regional boundaries—in fact, for several years now, he has also led La Ginestraia, a Ligurian winery in the province of Imperia. Elegant in its sensations of rose and liquorice, the Barolo Monvigliero '16 delivers rich, juicy texture, delicate and progressive tannins, and a classy finish. The Alta Langa Extra Brut '15 impresses with its notes of toasted bread and plum—it has fine beading and a fresh, dry finish. Rich aromas of butter and hazelnut characterize the Centofile Chardonnay, a wine that finishes on a spicy whiff.

- ● Barolo Monvigliero '16 ▼▼ 6
- ○ Alta Langa Extra Brut '15 ▼▼ 5
- ○ Langhe Chardonnay Centofile '18 ▼▼ 3
- ● Barbera d'Alba Sup. La Soprana '18 ▼ 3
- ● Barbera d'Alba La Soprana '13 ▽▽ 3
- ● Barolo Monvigliero '15 ▽▽ 6
- ● Barolo Monvigliero '14 ▽▽ 6
- ● Barolo Monvigliero '12 ▽▽ 6
- ● Dolcetto di Diano d'Alba Sörì Cascina Rabino '16 ▽▽ 2*
- ● Dolcetto di Diano d'Alba Sörì Rabino Soprano '17 ▽▽ 2*
- ● Dolcetto di Diano d'Alba Sörì Rabino Soprano '15 ▽▽ 2*
- ● Langhe Nebbiolo Quattro Cloni '16 ▽▽ 4
- ● Langhe Nebbiolo Quattro Cloni '15 ▽▽ 4
- ● Langhe Rosso Tremarzo '15 ▽▽ 4

Brema

via Pozzomagna, 9
14045 Incisa Scapaccino [AT]
Tel. +39 014174019
www.vinibrema.com

CELLAR SALES
PRE-BOOKED VISITS
ANNUAL PRODUCTION 150,000 bottles
HECTARES UNDER VINE 25.00
SUSTAINABLE WINERY

Umberto Brema represents the fifth generation to work for a producer whose history goes back centuries. These deep roots emerge when it comes to Barbera, especially, a benchmark cultivar for Monferrato Astigiano that's interpreted here in various versions (differentiated according to territory, production technique and style). Indeed, the estate's vineyards span Nizza Monferrato, Fontanile d'Asti, Incisa Scapaccino, Mombaruzzo, San Marzano Oliveto and Sessame d'Asti: six districts that express different temperaments with precision and verve. Once again two classics prove to be among the best of their kind. The Nizza A Luigi Veronelli '17 unveils aromas of tobacco, licorice and cherry, while the palate proves taut and long. The Barbera d'Asti Superiore Volpettona '17 plays more on fruity hints of black damson and plum accompanied by spicy hints—the palate is dense, almost chewy, but without heaviness. In fact it finishes long and juicy.

- Barbera d'Asti Sup. Volpettona '17 — TT 5
- Nizza A Luigi Veronelli '17 — TT 6
- Barbera d'Asti Ai Cruss '18 — TT 3
- Barbera d'Asti Sup. Nizza A Luigi Veronelli '12 — YYY 6
- Barbera d'Asti Sup. Nizza A Luigi Veronelli '06 — YYY 6
- Barbera d'Asti Ai Cruss '17 — YY 3
- Barbera d'Asti Ai Cruss '16 — YY 2*
- Barbera d'Asti Sup. Nizza A Luigi Veronelli '13 — YY 6
- Barbera d'Asti Sup. Volpettona '16 — YY 5
- Barbera d'Asti Sup. Volpettona '15 — YY 5
- Barbera d'Asti Sup. Volpettona '14 — YY 5
- Barbera del M.to Vivace Castagni '17 — YY 2*
- Nizza A Luigi Veronelli '16 — YY 6
- Nizza A Luigi Veronelli '15 — YY 6

Giacomo Brezza & Figli

via Lomondo, 4
12060 Barolo [CN]
Tel. +39 0173560921
www.brezza.it

CELLAR SALES
PRE-BOOKED VISITS
ACCOMMODATION AND RESTAURANT SERVICE
ANNUAL PRODUCTION 100,000 bottles
HECTARES UNDER VINE 20.00
VITICULTURE METHOD Certified Organic
SUSTAINABLE WINERY

Just a stone's throw from Barolo, a historic brand ignites the enthusiasm of true wine lovers. Brezza is wine, hospitality and catering in the great Piedmontese tradition (indeed, the first bottles date back to 1910). Today their wines, which mature slowly in medium and large Slavonian oak casks, are made with grapes from vineyards in Barolo (Castellero, Cannubi, Sarmassa and Sarmassa Vigna Bricco, offered in a Riserva version), as well as Monforte d'Alba, Novello, Diano d'Alba and Alba. Their pale but bright color evidences a very classic style, rich in contours and acidic contrast, designed for long aging in bottle. We begin with the excellent Barbera d'Alba Superiore '17, a juicy wine in its aromas of currant and licorice; it's supple, vibrant and very tasty on the palate. Traditional in its hints of dried herbs and quinine, the Barolo Cannubi '16 proves austere on the palate, tending more to the charm of spices than fruit. Compact in its tannic texture, the powerful Barolo Sarmassa '16 is also vivid in its tones of raspberry and tobacco. As usual, the rest of their selection also performed quite well.

- Barbera d'Alba Sup. '17 — TT 4
- Barolo Cannubi '16 — TT 7
- Barolo Sarmassa '16 — TT 7
- Barbera d'Alba V. Santa Rosalia '18 — TT 3
- Barolo '16 — TT 6
- Barolo Castellero '16 — TT 6
- Langhe Nebbiolo '19 — TT 3
- Barolo Bricco Sarmassa '08 — YYY 7
- Barolo Bricco Sarmassa '07 — YYY 7
- Barolo Cannubi '01 — YYY 6
- Barolo Cannubi '96 — YYY 6
- Barolo Sarmassa '11 — YYY 6
- Barolo Sarmassa '05 — YYY 6
- Barolo Sarmassa '04 — YYY 6
- Barolo Sarmassa '03 — YYY 6
- Barolo Sarmassa V. Bricco Ris. '11 — YYY 7

Gallino Domenico Bric Castelvej

Madonna Loreto, 70
12043 Canale [CN]
Tel. +39 017398108
www.briccastelvej.com

CELLAR SALES
PRE-BOOKED VISITS
ANNUAL PRODUCTION 100,000 bottles
HECTARES UNDER VINE 12.40

Founded by Domenico Gallino in 1956, today Bric Castelvej is run by his son-in-law Mario Repellino and son Cristiano. The wines produced are traditional, but also rich in character, made with grapes from vineyards located in the municipality of Canale, on Roero's classic, sandy soils, with layers of silt and calcareous clay. The area's traditional grapes are grown, starting with Arneis, Nebbiolo and Barbera, and moving on to Dolcetto, Favita, Grignolino, Bonarda. There are also a few international varieties, such as Viognier and Chardonnay. The Roero Panera Alta Riserva '17 is excellent, with flowery aromas accompanied by nuances of berries and incense; in the mouth it's harmonious, long with dense tannins, nice body, and sensations of blood orange. The rest of the range is also well crafted, in particular the multifaceted and complex Roero Arneis Vigna Bricco Novara '19, with its notes of white fruit and Mediterranean scrub. The Roero '17, with its hints of violet and tobacco, is beautifully structured and long.

Wine	Rating
● Roero Panera Alta Ris. '17	TT 6
● Barbera d'Alba '19	TT 2*
● Barbera d'Alba Sup. V. Mompassiano '17	TT 2*
● Roero '17	TT 4
○ Roero Arneis '19	TT 2*
○ Roero Arneis V. Bricco Novara '19	TT 3
○ San Vittore '19	TT 2*
● Barbera d'Alba Sup. V. Mompassiano '18	T 2
○ Langhe Favorita '19	T 2
● Langhe Nebbiolo '19	T 3
● Nebbiolo d'Alba Selezione Il Pilone '19	T 2
● Barbera d'Alba '18	YY 2*
○ Nebbiolo d'Alba Selezione Il Pilone '18	YY 2*
● Roero '16	YY 4
● Roero Panera Alta Ris. '16	YY 6

Bric Cenciurio

via Roma, 24
12060 Barolo [CN]
Tel. +39 017356317
www.bricenciurio.com

CELLAR SALES
PRE-BOOKED VISITS
ANNUAL PRODUCTION 50,000 bottles
HECTARES UNDER VINE 15.00

Fiorella Sacchetto has found strong professional support in her and her husband's (Franco Pittatore) children. Alessandro works in the cellar and Alberto in vineyard management. The family's properties in Roero give rise to two perennially-valid Arneis, while the Barolo Coste di Rose and Monrobiolo di Bussia Barolo originate in the town of Barolo itself. A favorable combination of two vineyards located on the opposite banks of the Tanaro river has made for a convincing Langhe Riesling as well. A blend of various crus has produced a particularly convincing 'basic' Barolo '16, one marked by a polished classicism, both in its fruity and spicy aromas and on a palate made pervasive by commendable pulp. Equally elegant, the Coste di Rose '16 is already open on pleasant, pronounced hints of tar and juniper—it's not very powerful, but displays excellent harmony on the palate. The citrusy and fresh Sito dei Fossili, made with Arneis, is also excellent

Wine	Rating
● Barolo '16	TT 6
● Barolo Coste di Rose '16	TT 7
● Barolo Monrobiolo di Bussia '16	TT 6
● Langhe Nebbiolo '19	TT 4
○ Langhe Riesling '18	TT 3
○ Roero Arneis Sito dei Fossili '19	TT 3
○ Sito dei Fossili V. T.	TT 5
○ Roero Arneis '19	T 3
● Barolo '15	YY 5
● Barolo Coste di Rose '15	YY 6
● Barolo Coste di Rose Ris. '13	YY 7
● Barolo Monrobiolo di Bussia '15	YY 6
● Langhe Nebbiolo '17	YY 4
○ Langhe Riesling '17	YY 2*
○ Roero Arneis '18	YY 3

Bricco dei Guazzi

via Vittorio Veneto, 23
15030 Olivola [AL]
Tel. +39 0422864511
www.briccodeiguazzi.it

PRE-BOOKED VISITS
ANNUAL PRODUCTION 100,000 bottles
HECTARES UNDER VINE 35.00
SUSTAINABLE WINERY

Bricco dei Guazzi is situated on a historically important property, with the original cellar built in the 15th century under the Guazzo family's residential villa. It was then enlarged several times, until the definitive renovation came in the past years, which has given it its current characteristics. The excellent conservation of the ancient building can be admired in the cellar, where their wines mature, as well as the tasting room adjacent to the cellar's lowest floor. Albarossa, Barbera, Merlot and Chardonnay give rise to their five wines. The Piemonte Albarossa is one of the most interesting wines tasted this year. Intense on the nose, it's marked by vegetal aromas and sweet spices on notes of powder and quinine. On the palate it's soft and rich in pulp, with a nice, fresh and persistent finish. The Barbera d'Asti features lovely, enticing fruit and notes of cocoa; it's powerful and rich on the palate, with a very intense finish supported by elegant tannins. The other wines tasted are also of note.

Wine	Rating
● Barbera d'Asti '18	▼▼ 2*
● Piemonte Albarossa '18	▼▼ 5
○ Gavi del Comune di Gavi '19	▼▼ 3
● M.to Rosso La Presidenta '18	▼▼ 3
● Barbera d'Asti '16	▽▽ 2*
● M.to Rosso La Presidenta '17	▽▽ 3
● Piemonte Albarossa '16	▽▽ 5
○ Piemonte Chardonnay '18	▽▽ 3

Bricco Maiolica

fraz. Ricca
via Bolangino, 7
12055 Diano d'Alba [CN]
Tel. +39 0173612049
www.briccomaiolica.it

CELLAR SALES
PRE-BOOKED VISITS
ACCOMMODATION
ANNUAL PRODUCTION 110,000 bottles
HECTARES UNDER VINE 24.00
SUSTAINABLE WINERY

It's not the crisis in the Dolcetto wine market that has led Beppe Accomo to increasingly focus on the value of other varieties from his vast estate. In fact, he has always been convinced that the soils of Diano d'Alba are more than suitable for other grapes, and he's proving it with vineyards that have over the last 30 years hosted Chardonnay, Pinot Nero, Sauvignon and Nebbiolo. It's precisely from the this last that his greatest successes have come, first with Nebbiolo d'Alba Cumot, which is consistently among the best of its kind, and since 2012 with a convincing Barolo Contadin. In any case, as always, his Diano d'Alba makes for clear, focused and enjoyable drinking. The Barolo del comune di Diano d'Alba Contadin '16 has already reached a precious and enjoyable gustatory harmony, with plenty of fruity pulp on the one hand and a notable tannic component on the other, making for an elegant, multifaceted whole. Bold, complex and of great gustatory richness, we also appreciated the Pensiero Infinito '16, which has preserved incredible freshness.

Wine	Rating
● Barolo del Comune di Diano d'Alba Contadin '16	▼▼ 8
○ Langhe Chardonnay Pensiero Infinito '16	▼▼ 6
● Barbera d'Alba Sup. V. Vigia '17	▼▼ 5
● Nebbiolo d'Alba Sup. Cumot '17	▼▼ 5
● Dolcetto di Diano d'Alba '19	▼ 3
● Langhe Pinot Nero Perlei '17	▼ 5
● Barbera d'Alba V. Vigia '98	▽▽▽ 4*
● Diano d'Alba Sup. Sörì Bricco Maiolica '07	▽▽▽ 3*
● Nebbiolo d'Alba Cumot '11	▽▽▽ 5
● Nebbiolo d'Alba Cumot '10	▽▽▽ 4*
● Nebbiolo d'Alba Cumot '09	▽▽▽ 4*
● Nebbiolo d'Alba Sup. Cumot '13	▽▽▽ 5
● Barbera d'Alba Sup. V. Vigia '16	▽▽ 5
● Nebbiolo d'Alba Sup. Cumot '16	▽▽ 5

Francesco Brigatti

via Olmi, 31
28019 Suno [NO]
Tel. +39 032285037
www.vinibrigatti.it

CELLAR SALES
PRE-BOOKED VISITS
ANNUAL PRODUCTION 25,000 bottles
HECTARES UNDER VINE 6.50

In order to emphasize the olfactory characteristics of Nebbiolo in northern Piedmont, terms such as 'quinine', 'pencil lead', 'rust', 'blood', 'rhubarb', 'gentian', 'flint', 'tamarind', 'iron' and 'black pepper' are often used. In short, one might think of greater rusticity with respect to Langhe or Roero. But we shouldn't believe that these nuances are the main characteristics of the area's great reds. These remain small red berry fruits, balsamic sensations, violet and rose petals, as skilled winemaker Francesco Brigatti's elegant Ghemme Oltre Il Bosco demonstrates. Two elegant Colline Novaresi Nebbiolos, the Möt Frei and the Möt Ziflon also stand out. The lovely Mötfrei '17 features a foreground of red berries succeeded by licorice and cinchona, lending character and complexity to its sophisticated olfactory suite. On the palate it's full-bodied, with elegant tannins and notable character, finishing pleasant and very long. The pleasant MötZiflon '17 is just a bit less lively and multifaceted, while the Barbera Campazzi '18 stands out for its clear, focused and commendable drinkability.

Wine	Rating
● Colline Novaresi Nebbiolo V. Mötfrei '17	🍷 3*
● Colline Novaresi Barbera Campazzi '19	🍷🍷 3
● Colline Novaresi Nebbiolo MötZiflon '17	🍷🍷 3
● Ghemme Oltre il Bosco '16	🍷🍷 5
○ Colline Novaresi Bianco Mottobello '19	🍷 3
● Colline Novaresi Uva Rara Selvalunga '19	🍷 3
● Colline Novaresi Vespolina Maria '19	🍷 3
● Colline Novaresi Barbera Campazzi '18	🍷🍷 3
● Colline Novaresi Nebbiolo Mötfrei '16	🍷🍷 3
● Colline Novaresi Nebbiolo MötZiflon '16	🍷🍷 3*
● Colline Novaresi Vespolina Maria '18	🍷🍷 3
● Ghemme Oltre il Bosco '15	🍷🍷 4

Broccardo

loc. Manzoni, 22
12065 Monforte d'Alba [CN]
Tel. +39 017378180
www.broccardo.it

CELLAR SALES
PRE-BOOKED VISITS
ANNUAL PRODUCTION 90,000 bottles
HECTARES UNDER VINE 13.00
SUSTAINABLE WINERY

The Broccardo family, with their long experience of working in the vineyard, patiently waited for the right moment to take the plunge: it was 2009 when bottling and commercialization finally began. Filippo has shown that he knows how to interpret Langa's classic red grapes, foremost Nebbiolo (obviously), and the resulting wines are of sure quality, led by four selections of Barolo which, starting next year, will be accompanied by a fifth. Thanks to the family's efforts, and good enological support, the wines released in 2020 pleasantly surprised our tasting panel, as can be seen from the below table. Among the 2016 Barolos, the Bricco San Pietro stood out, moving amidst rose and licorice only to reveal soft tannins and a long finish of fine classicism. The I Tre Pais, an early drinker from Monforte, Novello and Barolo, is just a bit less powerful but nicely crafted, while the Paiagallo already proves well-orchestrated and enjoyable.

Wine	Rating
● Barolo Bricco San Pietro '16	🍷🍷 6
● Barolo I Tre Pais '16	🍷🍷 5
● Barolo Paiagallo '16	🍷🍷 7
● Barbera d'Alba La Martina '18	🍷🍷 2*
● Barolo Ravera '16	🍷🍷 7
● Langhe Nebbiolo Il Giò Pì '18	🍷 3
● Barbera d'Alba La Martina '16	🍷🍷 4
● Barolo Bricco San Pietro '15	🍷🍷 6
● Barolo Bricco San Pietro '14	🍷🍷 7
● Barolo I Tre Pais '15	🍷🍷 5
● Langhe Nebbiolo '16	🍷🍷 5
● Langhe Nebbiolo Il Giò Pì '17	🍷🍷 3

★Brovia

via Alba-Barolo, 145
12060 Castiglione Falletto [CN]
Tel. +39 017362852
www.brovia.net

CELLAR SALES
PRE-BOOKED VISITS
ANNUAL PRODUCTION 75,000 bottles
HECTARES UNDER VINE 15.00
VITICULTURE METHOD Certified Organic
SUSTAINABLE WINERY

Brovia is proof of a great vineyard's ability to create great wine. Here, fifty years ago, the legendary Giacinto Brovia created spectacular Barolos without applying any special techniques, just serious work and tradition. When the skills and care applied today by his daughter Elena and her husband, Alex Sanchez, are added, the result is true masterpieces, including the few other wines that make up their portfolio, in particular the Barbera and Dolcetto d'Alba, always elegant and full of personality. Perfect classicism and extraordinary complexity characterize the clear, focused Barolo Brea Vigna Ca' Mia '16, a wine rich in red berry aromas, sweet tobacco, and liquorice. On the palate it's powerful and close-knit, evolving towards an elegance that will be many years in the making. Fresher and more delicate, the bewitching Villero '16 proves graceful and sumptuous in its fine fragrances of roses. Sunny herbs and raspberries feature in the harmonious Rocche di Castiglione '16.

● Barolo Villero '16	🍷🍷🍷	8
● Barolo Brea V. Ca' Mia '16	🍷🍷	8
● Barolo Rocche di Castiglione '16	🍷🍷	8
● Barbera d'Alba Sorì del Drago '18	🍷🍷	4
● Barolo '16	🍷🍷	7
● Barolo Garblèt Sué '16	🍷🍷	8
● Barolo Brea V. Ca' Mia '10	🍷🍷🍷	8
● Barolo Brea Vigna Ca' Mia '15	🍷🍷🍷	8
● Barolo Ca' Mia '09	🍷🍷🍷	8
● Barolo Monprivato '90	🍷🍷🍷	8
● Barolo Rocche di Castiglione '12	🍷🍷🍷	8
● Barolo Villero '13	🍷🍷🍷	8
● Barolo Villero '11	🍷🍷🍷	8
● Barolo Villero '10	🍷🍷🍷	8

G. B. Burlotto

via Vittorio Emanuele, 28
12060 Verduno [CN]
Tel. +39 0172470122
www.burlotto.com

CELLAR SALES
PRE-BOOKED VISITS
ACCOMMODATION
ANNUAL PRODUCTION 60,000 bottles
HECTARES UNDER VINE 15.00

Fabio Alessandria is extremely attached to Langhe's winemaking traditions, but he says that honoring the past also means improving it, and that means constantly updating and revisiting tradition as well. And so respect for his Nebbiolo grapes translates into fermentation with the stems, into delicate crushing by foot, and the never excessive presence of oak. His Barolos—foremost the Cannubi and Monvigliero cru—are now highly prized and sought after everywhere, but the rest of his selection is also expertly crafted and worth tasting, from his Sauvignon to the Pelaverga and the always exquisite base-level Barolo. The Barolo Cannubi '16 is complex and elegant, offering up fresh red berries together with more mature hints of licorice. On the palate it exhibits perfect, smooth harmony, proving long and multifaceted, with an enlivening acidic vein: Tre Bicchieri. The Monvigliero '16 is extraordinarily complex, but their whole selection is commendable, with particular praise for the taut, complex and elegant Sauvignon Dives '18.

● Barolo Cannubi '16	🍷🍷🍷	7
● Barolo Monvigliero '16	🍷🍷	7
○ Langhe Sauvignon Dives '18	🍷🍷	3*
● Barbera d'Alba Aves '18	🍷🍷	4
● Barolo '16	🍷🍷	6
● Barolo Acclivi '16	🍷🍷	6
● Langhe Nebbiolo '18	🍷🍷	3
● Verduno Pelaverga '19	🍷🍷	3
● Barolo Acclivi '11	🍷🍷🍷	6
● Barolo Acclivi '07	🍷🍷🍷	6
● Barolo Cannubi '12	🍷🍷🍷	7
● Barolo Monvigliero '10	🍷🍷🍷	7
● Barolo Cannubi '15	🍷🍷	7

★Piero Busso

VIA ALBESANI
12052 NEIVE [CN]
TEL. +39 017367156
www.bussopiero.com

CELLAR SALES
PRE-BOOKED VISITS
ACCOMMODATION
ANNUAL PRODUCTION 45,000 bottles
HECTARES UNDER VINE 11.50
SUSTAINABLE WINERY

Piero Busso loves to express himself freely and is endowed with an intellectual honesty that has earned him great esteem from Langhe's producers, even when they've felt a bit criticized. He also wants his Barbaresco to express freely and fully the characteristics of each individual vineyard—hence the choice to offer four single cru wines, as well as a small and highly prized selection made with old vines. We highly recommend a visit to the winery, where research and experimentation with fermentation and aging continue thanks in part to increased support from his capable son Pierguido. Multifaceted and delicious, the Barbaresco San Stunet '16 opens on licorice and a touch of blood oranges only to come through sapid, lively, structured and well balanced on the palate (despite the presence of tannins that are still discernible). The Gallina '16 features a captivating bouquet and enjoyably fresh taste. The Mondino '17 is simpler but immediately pleasant. A lovely note of tar and sweet oak feature in the complex Barbaresco Albesani Vigna Borgese '16.

Wine	Rating
● Barbaresco Albesani V. Borgese '16	TT 7
● Barbaresco Gallina '16	TT 8
● Barbaresco S. Stunet '16	TT 8
● Barbaresco Mondino '17	TT 6
○ Langhe Sauvignon Arbè '18	TT 4
● Barbera d'Alba '18	T 2
● Barbera d'Alba S. Stefanetto '18	T 5
● Barbaresco Albesani V. Borgese '15	YYY 7
● Barbaresco Borgese '09	YYY 6
● Barbaresco Borgese '08	YYY 6
● Barbaresco Gallina '12	YYY 8
● Barbaresco Gallina '11	YYY 8
● Barbaresco Gallina '09	YYY 8
● Barbaresco S. Stefanetto '07	YYY 7
● Barbaresco S. Stunet '11	YYY 7

Ca' Bianca

REG. SPAGNA, 58
15010 ALICE BEL COLLE [AL]
TEL. +39 0144745420
www.cantinacabianca.it

CELLAR SALES
PRE-BOOKED VISITS
ANNUAL PRODUCTION 555,000 bottles
HECTARES UNDER VINE 24.00

This Gruppo Italiano Vini producer is a dynamic and vital winery, constantly on the cutting edge in terms of technology, and so well positioned to maximize the value of their grapes. In recent years we've noticed further steps forward, which have allowed their range to achieve a notable level of quality. Production revolves around Piedmont's classic grapes, from Nebbiolo, Barbera and Dolcetto for their reds, to Arneis and Cortese di Gavi for their white wines. A selection of dessert wines, made with Moscato and Brachetto, complete their range. Crisp fruit sensations emerge, making the Barbera D'Asti Superiore extremely pleasant to drink. While the Chersì is still in a period of growth, it has the potential to improve further with time in the bottle. The balanced and vibrant Roero Arneis enriches itself on the palate with a fresh and sapid finish. The Moscato D'Asti is a pleasant and enticing drink.

Wine	Rating
● Barbera d'Asti Sup. '18	TT 2*
● Barbera d'Asti Sup. Chersì '17	TT 4
○ Moscato d'Asti '19	TT 2*
○ Roero Arneis '19	TT 2*
● Dolcetto d'Acqui '19	T 2
○ Gavi '19	T 2
● Barbera d'Asti Sup. Antè '17	YY 2*
● Barbera d'Asti Sup. Antè '16	YY 3
● Barbera d'Asti Sup. Chersì '16	YY 4
● Barbera d'Asti Sup. Chersì '15	YY 5
● Barbera d'Asti Sup. Chersì '14	YY 5
● Barbera d'Asti Teis '17	YY 3
● Dolcetto d'Acqui '17	YY 3
○ Gavi '18	YY 3
○ Gavi '17	YY 3
○ Moscato d'Asti '18	YY 2*

Ca' d' Gal

FRAZ. VALDIVILLA
S.DA VECCHIA DI VALDIVILLA, 1
12058 SANTO STEFANO BELBO [CN]
TEL. +39 0141847103
www.cadgal.it

CELLAR SALES
PRE-BOOKED VISITS
ACCOMMODATION AND RESTAURANT SERVICE
ANNUAL PRODUCTION 95,000 bottles
HECTARES UNDER VINE 12.00

An idea as simple as it was audacious: to demonstrate with his own bottles how Moscato d'Asti is much more than a beverage to be uncorked at parties. This is how Alessandro Boido managed to establish himself as an absolute benchmark for the typology, forging on the hills of Santo Stefano Belbo sweet and sparkling wines suitable for all occasions and also capable of aging well to boot. This is particularly true of their Vigna Vecchia, which is flanked by three other Moscato-based wines and still wines made with Chardonnay, Sauvignon, Pinot Nero, Barbera and Freisa. Alessandro Boido submitted a splendid line-up for tasting. The Moscato d'Asti Canelli Sant'Ilario '19 is broad and complex on the nose, with aromas ranging from medicinal herbs to rosemary, candied lemon, pineapple and saffron, all followed by a palate of considerable volume and richness. In the mouth it manages to balance sapidity and acidity, making for a long finish. We also appreciated the elegant and fresh Moscato d'Asti Lumine '19.

Wine	Rating	Price
○ Moscato d'Asti Canelli Sant'Ilario '19	▼▼▼	4*
○ Moscato d'Asti Lumine '19	▼▼	3*
○ Asti '19	▼▼	3
○ Moscato d'Asti Canelli Sant'Ilario '16	▽▽▽	4*
○ Moscato d'Asti Canelli Sant'Ilario '15	▽▽▽	3*
○ Moscato d'Asti V. V. '11	▽▽▽	3*
○ Asti	▽▽	3
○ Asti	▽▽	3
○ Moscato d"Asti Vite Vecchia '14	▽▽	7
○ Moscato d'Asti Canelli Sant'Ilario '18	▽▽	4
○ Moscato d'Asti Canelli Sant'Ilario '17	▽▽	4
○ Moscato d'Asti Lumine '18	▽▽	3
○ Moscato d'Asti Lumine '17	▽▽	3
○ Moscato d'Asti Lumine '16	▽▽	3
○ Moscato d'Asti Lumine '15	▽▽	3*
○ Moscato d'Asti V. Vecchia '10	▽▽	7
○ Moscato d'Asti Vite Vecchia '15	▽▽	7

★Ca' del Baio

VIA FERRERE SOTTANO, 33
12050 TREISO [CN]
TEL. +39 0173638219
www.cadelbaio.com

CELLAR SALES
PRE-BOOKED VISITS
ANNUAL PRODUCTION 130,000 bottles
HECTARES UNDER VINE 25.00

Federica, Paola and Valentina Grasso, without recourse to hierarchies of age or skill, are now serving as the driving force behind a cohesive family business. 'Mamma' Luciana and 'Papà' Giulio share in the work, helping out on a daily basis. Together they've built one of the most prestigious producers in the Barbaresco and Langa area. Their range, which is consistently reliable and draws on a variety of grapes, from white cultivars to Barbaresco crus, is a touchstone both in Italy and the world. Aromas of roses, raspberries and herbs figure centrally in the commendable Barbaresco Asili Riserva '15. On the palate, pronounced (but not mouth-drying) tannins come together with a fruity component that persists up to a long finish. Floral and liquorice sensations feature in the highly pleasant Barbaresco Pora '16, with its structured and assertive flavor. Fresh (in spite of the vintage) and powerful, the Vallegrande '17 comes through broad and mouthfilling on the palate. The Langhe Riesling is always a sure bet.

Wine	Rating	Price
● Barbaresco Vallegrande '17	▼▼▼	5
● Barbaresco Asili Ris. '15	▼▼	8
● Barbaresco Pora '16	▼▼	6
● Barbaresco Autinbej '17	▼▼	5
○ Langhe Riesling Fré '18	▼▼	3
● Barbaresco Asili '15	▽▽▽	6
● Barbaresco Asili '12	▽▽▽	6
● Barbaresco Asili '10	▽▽▽	6
● Barbaresco Asili '09	▽▽▽	5
● Barbaresco Asili Ris. '11	▽▽▽	8
● Barbaresco Pora '10	▽▽▽	6
● Barbaresco Pora '06	▽▽▽	6
● Barbaresco Valgrande '08	▽▽▽	5
● Barbaresco Vallegrande '16	▽▽▽	5
● Barbaresco Vallegrande '14	▽▽▽	5

Ca' Romé

S.DA RABAJÀ, 86
12050 BARBARESCO [CN]
TEL. +39 0173635126
www.carome.com

CELLAR SALES
PRE-BOOKED VISITS
ANNUAL PRODUCTION 30,000 bottles
HECTARES UNDER VINE 5.00

It was in 1980 when Romano Marengo decided to create his own small, well-studied winery whose waxed and polished terracotta floor demonstrates just how much care and attention is paid to each detail. The small size of the property, which comprises excellent crus in both Barbaresco and Serralunga d'Alba, has always allowed him to personally oversee, with the help of his wife, Olimpia, all stages of production. The children have integrated harmoniously, with skilled Giuseppe looking after enology and daughter Paola managing the sales side of things. The Barbaresco Maria di Brün delivers. The nose is enticing, complex and delicate, marked by notes of rose and cocoa; on the palate it's rich in fruity pulp, which bodes well for magnificent aging. The vibrant Chiaramanti '17 is a bit more vegetal and licorice scented, powerfu and very long. Splendid personality emerges in the dynamic and stylish Barolo Rapet '16.

Wine	Rating
● Barbaresco Chiaramanti '17	TT 8
● Barbaresco Maria di Brün '16	TT 8
● Barolo Rapet '16	TT 8
● Barbaresco Rio Sordo '17	TT 6
● Barolo Cerretta '16	TT 8
● Barbaresco Maria di Brün '13	YYY 8
● Barbaresco Sorì Rio Sordo '06	YYY 6
● Barolo Rapet '14	YYY 7
● Barolo Rapet '11	YYY 7
● Barolo Rapet '08	YYY 7
● Barolo V. Cerretta '09	YYY 7
● Barbaresco Chiaramanti '16	YY 7
● Barbaresco Maria di Brün '15	YY 8
● Barolo Cerretta '15	YY 7
● Barolo Rapet '15	YY 7

★★Ca' Viola

B.TA SAN LUIGI, 11
12063 DOGLIANI [CN]
TEL. +39 017370547
www.caviola.com

CELLAR SALES
PRE-BOOKED VISITS
ACCOMMODATION AND RESTAURANT SERVICE
ANNUAL PRODUCTION 70,000 bottles
HECTARES UNDER VINE 10.00

Beppe Caviola is a great enologist, as demonstrated by the success of the wineries he advises all over Italy, but above all he remains a convinced wine artisan. Rather than relying on the data obtained in his well-equipped analysis laboratory, he avails himself of his exceptional skill as a taster. The fame of his winery gradually grew out of the Dolcetto and Barbera d'Alba he made from old vines in Montelupo Albese. And then he crossed the ocean, with the arrival of his Barolo Sottocastello di Novello, a quintessential Nebbiolo aged according to a commendably classical approach. And this is the birthplace of the Riserva '13, a wine marked by a pleasant citrus touch on the nose, coming through weighty and austere on the long palate. The harmonious Barolo Sottocastello di Novello '16 is even more fruity and captivating. Caviola confirms its skill with Barbera in both selections, both the long, progressive and mouthfilling Bric du Luv '17, and the elegant, pleasant Brichet '18. A brilliant debut for the noteworthy Rosato Rita, a very pleasant wine made with Nebbiolo grapes.

Wine	Rating
● Barolo Sottocastello di Novello '16	TTT 8
● Barolo Caviot '16	TT 8
● Barolo Sottocastello di Novello Ris. '13	TT 8
● Barbera d'Alba Bric du Luv '17	TT 5
● Barbera d'Alba Brichet '18	TT 4
● Dolcetto d'Alba Vilot '19	TT 3
● Langhe Nebbiolo Giblin '18	TT 5
○ Langhe Riesling Clem '18	TT 5
⊙ Langhe Rosato Rita '19	TT 4
● Barbera d'Alba Bric du Luv '12	YYY 5
● Barbera d'Alba Bric du Luv '10	YYY 5
● Barolo Sottocastello '06	YYY 7
● Barolo Sottocastello di Novello '11	YYY 8
● Barolo Sottocastello di Novello '10	YYY 7
● Barolo Sottocastello di Novello '08	YYY 7

Fabrizia Caldera

fraz. Portacomaro Stazione, 53
14100 Asti
Tel. +39 0141296154
www.vinicaldera.it

CELLAR SALES
PRE-BOOKED VISITS
ACCOMMODATION
ANNUAL PRODUCTION 95,000 bottles
HECTARES UNDER VINE 22.00

Founded by the legendary Signor Prospero in the early 1900s in Asti, the winery led today by Fabrizia Caldera (with the help of her husband, Roberto Rossi, and her son Fabio) is one of Monferrato's historic family producers. With respect to its origins, their vineyards and ampelography have progressively expanded, making it possible to offer a vast range rooted mainly in traditional wine typologies. Balmèt, Harmonius and the Il Giullare make up their trio of Barberas, but we regularly see excellent results with Moscato, Cortese, Viognier, Chardonnay, Ruchè, Grignolino and Dolcetto as well. This year the most notable results came from the wines made with these grapes. The Ruché di Castagnole Monferrato Prevost '19 is at the top of its game, with notes of rose and red fruit heralding a dense palate of great structure, but it's also balanced, with a long finish. The Grignolino d'Asti Leserre '19 proves classic in its aromas of white pepper, and a rich palate in which close-knit tannins are already well integrated.

- ● Grignolino d'Asti Leserre '19 — YY 3*
- ● Ruché di Castagnole Monferrato Prevost '19 — YY 4
- ● Barbera d'Asti Harmonius '17 — YY 3
- ○ Piemonte Viognier Viò '19 — YY 3
- ● Ruché di Castagnole Monferrato Xenio '18 — YY 3
- ● Barbera d'Asti Sup. Balmèt '17 — Y 4
- ○ Monferrato Bianco Forestè '18 — Y 6
- ● Barbera d'Asti '15 — yy 3
- ● Barbera d'Asti Sup. Balmèt '16 — yy 4
- ● Grignolino d'Asti Leserre '18 — yy 3
- ● Grignolino d'Asti Leserre '17 — yy 2*
- ● Ruché di Castagnole Monferrato Prevost '18 — yy 4
- ● Ruché di Castagnole Monferrato Prevost '17 — yy 3

Cantina del Nebbiolo

via Torino, 17
12050 Vezza d'Alba [CN]
Tel. +39 017365040
www.cantinadelnebbiolo.com

CELLAR SALES
PRE-BOOKED VISITS
ANNUAL PRODUCTION 300,000 bottles
HECTARES UNDER VINE 300.00
VITICULTURE METHOD Certified Organic

This historic winery, founded in 1959 from the ashes of the Parish Cooperative Winery of Vezza d'Alba, which dates back to 1901, is one of the most important in the region. 170 members give rise to more than 20 different wines, all made exclusively with native grape varieties, foremost Nebbiolo, obviously from the most prestigious appellations of Langa and Roero. The wines offered are traditionally styled, exhibiting territorial identity and technical precision. This year's Barbarescos are in the limelight. The Riserva '15 features notes of tobacco and dried aromatic herbs, with a charming, delicately salty appeal, a palate rich in pulp, dense tannins and a long finish. The Meruzzano '17 sees smoky notes of juniper followed by a supple yet characterful, clearly focused and dynamic palate. Other well-made selections include the sapid and citrusy Roero Arneis '19, the Barolo Perno '16, whose tannins are harmonious and elegant (though it's a bit marked by oak), and the Barbera d'Alba Superiore '17, a fruity, assertive wine.

- ● Barbaresco Meruzzano '17 — YY 5
- ● Barbaresco Ris. '15 — YY 6
- ● Barbaresco '17 — YY 4
- ● Barbera d'Alba Sup. '17 — YY 2*
- ● Barolo Perno '16 — YY 5
- ○ Langhe Nascetta Riveverse '18 — YY 2*
- ● Nebbiolo d'Alba V. Valmaggiore '18 — YY 3
- ○ Roero Arneis '19 — YY 2*
- ○ Roero Arneis Arenarium '19 — YY 2*
- ● Barbera d'Alba '18 — Y 2
- ○ Langhe Favorita '19 — Y 2
- ● Nebbiolo d'Alba '18 — Y 2
- ● Barbaresco '16 — yy 4
- ● Barbaresco Meruzzano '16 — yy 5
- ● Barbaresco Meruzzano Ris. '15 — yy 5
- ● Barolo Perno '15 — yy 5
- ○ Roero Arneis '18 — yy 2*

Cantina del Pino

s.da Ovello, 31
12050 Barbaresco [CN]
Tel. +39 0173635147
www.cantinadelpino.com

ANNUAL PRODUCTION 35,000 bottles
HECTARES UNDER VINE 7.00

It's with great affection that we remember Renato Vacca, one of the most esteemed vintners of his generation, who left us last March. In 1997, together with his father he created this famous brand to carry on the legacy of Domizio Cavazza, creator of Barbaresco and the farm's previous owner. It was Renato who planted the pine, still visible, that serves as the winery's symbol. Among the crus he developed with extraordinary tenacity we remember Ovello, foremost, followed by Gallina, vineyards expressed in the bottle with a careful, delicate hand capable of gently drawing out the attributes of each. The Albesani Barbaresco features lovely, fresh fruit and harmony in its hints of dried rose and gentian, with delicately salty strokes lending character and complexity; the palate has harmony and measured, balanced tannins, the finish is long and well-orchestrated. The spicier Barbaresco Ovello of the same vintage is fine and pleasant in its measured, balsamic finish. Soft, red fruit sensations and a creamy palate characterize the Barbaresco '16.

● Barbaresco Albesani '16	▼▼ 7
● Barbaresco Ovello '16	▼▼ 7
● Barbaresco '16	▼▼ 5
● Barbaresco '04	YYY 5*
● Barbaresco '03	YYY 4*
● Barbaresco Albesani '14	YYY 7
● Barbaresco Albesani '05	YYY 6
● Barbaresco Ovello '13	YYY 7
● Barbaresco Ovello '07	YYY 6
● Barbaresco Ovello '99	YYY 5
● Barbaresco '15	YY 5
● Barbaresco '14	YY 5
● Barbaresco '13	YY 5
● Barbaresco Albesani '13	YY 7
● Barbaresco Gallina '14	YY 7
● Barbaresco Ovello '15	YY 7
● Barbaresco Ovello '14	YY 7

La Caplana

via Circonvallazione, 4
15060 Bosio [AL]
Tel. +39 0143684182
www.lacaplana.com

CELLAR SALES
PRE-BOOKED VISITS
ANNUAL PRODUCTION 120,000 bottles
HECTARES UNDER VINE 5.00

Bosio is a small county in Piedmont situated in the northern Ligurian Apennines and bordering Genoa. So it's easy to imagine that here agriculture has more to do with mountains than hills, with steep slopes playing an important role in how the grapes ripen together with the winds coming in off the sea. The Guido family cultivate Cortese, Dolcetto, Barbera and Chardonnay in this area. Natalino's wines are characterized by a modern, non-invasive style, with an attentive use of wood and a preference for clean, varietal aromas. Their Gavis are excellent, exhibiting a vibrant, complex olfactory spectrum: flowery, mature white fruit aromas and hints of almond anticipate a powerful, fresh palate with a long, sapid finish. The Narcys is an excellent example of Dolcetto di Ovada, with lovely fruit that stretches on notes of bitter almond and cocoa. On the palate it's intense, with silky tannins and a long finish. We also appreciate the intriguing Barbera d'Asti; the rest of their selection is also well made.

○ Gavi '19	▼▼ 2*
● Barbera d'Asti '18	▼▼ 3
● Dolcetto di Ovada Narcys '16	▼▼ 3
○ Gavi del Comune di Gavi '19	▼ 2
○ Gavi Villa Vecchia '19	▼ 2
○ Piemonte Chardonnay '19	▼ 2
● Barbera d'Asti '17	YY 3
● Barbera d'Asti Rubis '16	YY 3
● Barbera d'Asti Rubis '15	YY 3
● Dolcetto di Ovada '17	YY 2*
● Dolcetto di Ovada Narcys '17	YY 3*
● Dolcetto di Ovada Narcys '15	YY 3*
○ Gavi '18	YY 2*
○ Gavi del Comune di Gavi '18	YY 2*
○ Gavi del Comune di Gavi '17	YY 2*
○ Gavi del Comune di Gavi '16	YY 2*
○ Gavi Villa Vecchia '18	YY 2*

Pierangelo Careglio

loc. Aprato, 15
12040 Baldissero d'Alba [CN]
Tel. +39 3339905448
www.cantinacareglio.it

CELLAR SALES
PRE-BOOKED VISITS
ANNUAL PRODUCTION 35,000 bottles
HECTARES UNDER VINE 9.00
SUSTAINABLE WINERY

Founded in 1986 by Pierangelo Careglio, this small family business has followed the path of many producers in Roero, moving from fruit cultivation to wine production, thanks in part to the arrival of the new generation in the form of Pierangelo's son Andrea. Their vineyards are situated both on the sandy, marine soils typical of Roero, and on soils with a greater presence of limestone and clay. The wines offered are modern, but still leave room for the expression of a strong territorial identity. The Careglio family earned themselves a place in our main section this year. The Roero Arneis '19 offers up notes of pear and aromatic herbs on the nose, while the palate exhibits notable structure and richness of fruit, but also sapidity, length and lovely acidity. The Roero '17, on the other hand, is characterized by aromas of berries, hints of quinine, tobacco and spices followed by a palate that's austere, but also long, persistent and juicy on the finish.

Wine	Glasses	Price
● Roero '17	**YY**	5
○ Roero Arneis '19	**YY**	3*
● Barbera d'Alba '18	**YY**	4
○ Langhe Favorita '19	**YY**	2*
○ Roero Arneis Savij '16	**YY**	5
● Langhe Nebbiolo '18	**Y**	2
● Barbera d'Alba '17	YY	4
● Barbera d'Alba '15	YY	2*
● Roero '16	YY	5
● Roero '13	YY	2*
○ Roero Arneis '17	YY	2*
○ Roero Arneis '16	YY	2*
○ Roero Arneis Savij '15	YY	5

Tenuta Carretta

loc. Carretta, 2
12040 Piobesi d'Alba [CN]
Tel. +39 0173619119
www.tenutacarretta.it

CELLAR SALES
PRE-BOOKED VISITS
ACCOMMODATION AND RESTAURANT SERVICE
ANNUAL PRODUCTION 500,000 bottles
HECTARES UNDER VINE 85.00

Since 1985 the Miroglio family have been running this historic estate, situated in an area known since the 15th century for its wine grapes. In addition to the single, 35-hectare vineyard that extends like an amphitheater around the cellar, the Miroglio family have, over the years, added a series of plots in some of Piedmont's most prestigious appellations, from Cannubi in Barolo to Treiso in Barbaresco, to parcels in the Alta Langa area, all leading up to the recent acquisition of Malgrà, in the heart of Asti, making for a wide range of wines. The Roero Bric Paradiso Riserva '15 is fine and complex on the nose, with notes of fresh red fruit, tobacco and liquorice, and a dense palate, with fine tannins, rich fruit and a long finish. The Barolo Cannubi Collezione Rag. Franco Miroglio Riserva '14 is also excellent, classic in its notes of orange peel, making for a juicy, pleasant palate. A solid performance by the other wines submitted as well.

Wine	Glasses	Price
● Barolo Cannubi Collezione Ragionier Franco Miroglio Ris. '14	**YY**	8
● Roero Bric Paradiso Ris. '15	**YY**	6
● Barbaresco Cascina Bordino Ris. '14	**YY**	8
● Barbaresco Garassino '16	**YY**	7
● Barolo Cannubi '15	**YY**	8
○ Gavi del Comune di Gavi Poggio Basco Malgrà '19	**YY**	2*
○ Roero Arneis Cayega '19	**YY**	4
● Langhe Nebbiolo Podio '18	**Y**	5
⊙ Langhe Rosato Cereja '19	**Y**	4
● Barbaresco Garassino '15	YY	5
● Barolo Cannubi Collezione Rag. Franco Miroglio Ris. '12	YY	8
● Barolo Cannubi Selezione Franco Miroglio Ris. '13	YY	8

Casa E. di Mirafiore

via Alba, 15
12050 Serralunga d'Alba [CN]
Tel. +39 0173626111
www.mirafiore.it

CELLAR SALES
PRE-BOOKED VISITS
ACCOMMODATION AND RESTAURANT SERVICE
ANNUAL PRODUCTION 200,000 bottles
HECTARES UNDER VINE 25.00
VITICULTURE METHOD Certified Organic
SUSTAINABLE WINERY

The brand, founded in 1878 by Alberto Emanuele di Mirafiore and owned by the Farinetti family since 2008, has become its own independent producer. Most of the vineyards are situated in Serralunga d'Alba, where the excellent Lazzarito cru (hence the name of the Barolo) is accompanied by plots of Barbera and Dolcetto along with Pinot Nero and Chardonnay (used for their bubbly). And that's not to mention Nebbiolo, which is cultivated in the more than valid Paiagallo vineyard in Barolo. An independent winemaking cellar is already being planned—detailed information will be forthcoming in our guide. Sophisticated and complex, the Barolo Lazzarito '16 offers up elegant aromas of raspberries, citrus fruits and licorice, coming through weighty and voluminous in the mouth, long and of a polished classicism. The Paiagallo tends more to mint and fresh herbs on the nose, while on the palate it's firm and powerful, clear and focused. Plenty of fruity pulp and gentle touches of tar feature in the mature Riserva '13. Kudos to the 'basic' Barolo '16, a harmonious, charming wine.

Wine	Rating
● Barolo Lazzarito '16	🍷🍷🍷 8
● Barolo Paiagallo '16	🍷🍷 8
● Barolo Ris. '13	🍷🍷 8
○ Alta Langa Brut Blanc de Noir '15	🍷🍷 5
● Barbera d'Alba Sup. '18	🍷🍷 5
● Barolo '16	🍷🍷 7
● Langhe Rosso Pietra Magica '17	🍷🍷 5
● Langhe Nebbiolo '18	🍷 5
● Barolo Paiagallo '13	🍷🍷🍷 7
● Barolo Paiagallo '12	🍷🍷🍷 7
● Barolo Ris. '04	🍷🍷🍷 8

La Casaccia

via D. Barbano, 10
15034 Cella Monte [AL]
Tel. +39 0142489986
www.lacasaccia.biz

CELLAR SALES
PRE-BOOKED VISITS
ANNUAL PRODUCTION 25,000 bottles
HECTARES UNDER VINE 6.70
VITICULTURE METHOD Certified Organic

Cella Monte is one of Italy's most charming villages, a home to the Pietra da Cantoni (Cantoni Stone) and a stop along the 'Infernot route' (the old cellars dug into tuff, typical of Casale Monferrato), a historical, cultural and natural setting that can't help but touch on the world of wine as well. La Casaccia, whose roots go back to 1700, still fulfils its original function today: it's here that the the Rava family's organic wines, made using Monferrato's grapes, are matured and aged. The 2019 version of their Poggeto is interesting. It opens with notes of tobacco and pepper, only to continue fresh and vibrant on the palate with a long finish. The Monfiorenza has a rather austere, ethereal bouquet, with aromas of jam on notes of resin. In the mouth it stands out with character and intensity, and a nice, fresh, lingering finish.

Wine	Rating
● Grignolino del M.to Casalese Poggeto '18	🍷🍷 3
● M.to Freisa Monfiorenza '18	🍷🍷 3
● Barbera del M.to Giuanìn '18	🍷 3
● Grignolino del M.to Casalese Ernesto '14	🍷 3
● Barbera del M.to Bricco dei Boschi '15	🍷🍷 3
● Barbera del M.to Calichè '15	🍷🍷 3
● Grignolino del M.to Casalese Ernesto '13	🍷🍷 3
● Grignolino del M.to Casalese Ernesto '12	🍷🍷 3*
● Grignolino del M.to Casalese Poggeto '17	🍷🍷 3*
● Grignolino del M.to Casalese Poggeto '16	🍷🍷 2*
● Grignolino del M.to Casalese Poggeto '15	🍷🍷 2*
○ La Casaccia Brut M.Cl. '15	🍷🍷 4

Casalone

via Marconi, 100
15040 Lu e Cuccaro Monferrato
Tel. +39 0131741280
www.casalone.it

CELLAR SALES
PRE-BOOKED VISITS
ANNUAL PRODUCTION 50,000 bottles
HECTARES UNDER VINE 10.00

The territory of the new municipality of Lu and Cuccaro is an area historically well suited to viticulture. Here the Casalone family have built this solid, artisan winery. About ten hectares of vineyards grow in mainly clayey-calcareous soils divided between Bricchi Santa Maria, Morlantino and San Benedetto. A dozen or so wines are produced, serving as an expression of a territorial bond and the initiative of the new generation, who now lead the producer. A lovely version of the Brut Metodo Classico, from Malvasia Greca grapes got things started. It's intense and complex on the nose, with aromas of dried flowers and saffron rising on notes of honey. On the palate it shows great structure and a long close. Antique gold in color, the Monvasia passito opens on aromas of dried fruit and apricot, coming through dense on the palate, but well balanced by acidity. We recommend the Rus. The other wines tasted are also interesting.

Wine	Rating
● M.to Rosso Rus '16	🍷🍷 3
○ Monvasia Brut M. Cl.	🍷🍷 4
○ Monvasia Mosto Parzialmente Fermentato	🍷🍷 2*
○ Monvasia Passito '18	🍷🍷 3
● Barbera del M.to Sup. Rubermillo '16	🍷 3
● Barbera d'Asti Rubermillo '13	🍷🍷 3
● Barbera del M.to Sup. Bricco Morlantino '15	🍷🍷 3*
● Barbera del M.to Sup. Bricco Morlantino '11	🍷🍷 2*
● Barbera del M.to Sup. Rubermillo '15	🍷🍷 3
● M.to Rosso Rus '12	🍷🍷 3
● Monferrato Rosso Fandamat '14	🍷🍷 2*
○ Monvasia Brut M. Cl. 60 mesi '13	🍷🍷 4
● Piemonte Grignolino I Canonici di Lu '15	🍷🍷 4
● Piemonte Grignolino La Caplëtta '15	🍷🍷 3*

Cascina Barisél

reg. San Giovanni, 30
14053 Canelli [AT]
Tel. +39 3394165913
www.barisel.it

CELLAR SALES
PRE-BOOKED VISITS
ANNUAL PRODUCTION 35,000 bottles
HECTARES UNDER VINE 4.50
SUSTAINABLE WINERY

Active since the mid-1980s, the Penna family have managed, harvest after harvest, to establish Cascina Barisèl as among the most interesting producers operating in Asti. Everything revolves around the calcareous terrain of Canelli, which hosts their private vineyards and the area's most representative varieties: foremost Barbera, Dolcetto and Moscato. To complete the ampelography, and their versatile range, there are plots cultivated with Favorita, Chardonnay and Pinot Nero (used to produce a Metodo Classico sparkler). This year we were especially impressed with the Nizza Vigna dei Pilati Riserva '15, with its notes of cocoa, spices and black berries followed by a palate of great power and acidity, finishing balanced, long and juicy. The Barbera d'Asti Superiore La Cappelletta '17 also delivered, featuring aromas of cinchona-quinine, juniper and pencil lead, and a rich, pulpy, beautifully sapid palate. A special mention for the Enrico Penna Extra Brut Metodo Classico '15, a sparkler that's at once vibrant and creamy.

Wine	Rating
● Barbera d'Asti Sup. La Cappelletta '17	🍷🍷 4
● Nizza V. dei Pilati Ris. '15	🍷🍷 6
● Barbera d'Asti Sup. Listoria '18	🍷🍷 3
○ Enrico Penna Extra Brut M. Cl. '15	🍷🍷 5
○ Moscato d'Asti Canelli '19	🍷🍷 2*
● Barbera d'Asti '19	🍷 2
● Barbera d'Asti '18	🍷🍷 2*
● Barbera d'Asti '17	🍷🍷 2*
● Barbera d'Asti Sup. La Cappelletta '16	🍷🍷 4
● Barbera d'Asti Sup. La Cappelletta '15	🍷🍷 4
● Barbera d'Asti Sup. Listoria '17	🍷🍷 3
● Barbera d'Asti Sup. Listoria '16	🍷🍷 3*
● Barbera d'Asti Sup. Nizza V. dei Pilati '13	🍷🍷 6
○ Enrico Penna Brut M. Cl. '15	🍷🍷 5
● Moscato d'Asti Canelli '17	🍷🍷 2*
○ Moscato d'Asti Canelli '16	🍷🍷 2*

Cascina Bongiovanni

loc. Uccellaccio
via Alba Barolo, 3
12060 Castiglione Falletto [CN]
Tel. +39 0173262184
www.cascinabongiovanni.com

CELLAR SALES
PRE-BOOKED VISITS
ACCOMMODATION
ANNUAL PRODUCTION 50,000 bottles
HECTARES UNDER VINE 7.20
SUSTAINABLE WINERY

It's full steam ahead for Davide Mozzone, now at the helm of the winery founded in 1950 by Giovanni Bongiovanni. Eight hectares of vineyards are cultivated in Castiglione Falletto, Serralunga d'Alba, Monforte d'Alba, Diano d'Alba and San Pietro in Govone. Their catalog of wines is rich and broad, ranging from early-drinkers to ageworthy selections, all proposed with a style that nicely balances tradition and modernity, with spicy contributions that are never excessive or out of place. The Barolo Pernanno '16 exhibits a particularly complex character, dark in its fruit and rich in hints of wood tar and dried herbs on a juicy palate. Intense in its toasty profile, the Barbera d'Alba '18 is characterized by an elegant, supple and dynamic palate. The Barolo '16 is also excellent, standing out for its harmonious and firm structure. The rest of the range also performed notably.

● Barolo Pernanno '16	TT	7
● Barbera d'Alba '18	TT	4
● Barolo '16	TT	6
● Dolcetto d'Alba '19	TT	3
○ Langhe Arneis '19	TT	3
● Langhe Nebbiolo '18	TT	4
● Dolcetto di Diano d'Alba '19	T	3
● Barolo Pernanno '01	YYY	6
● Barolo '15	YY	6
● Barolo Pernanno '15	YY	7
● Barolo Pernanno '14	YY	7
● Barolo Pernanno '13	YY	7
● Barolo Ris. '13	YY	8
● Langhe Nebbiolo '17	YY	4
● Langhe Rosso Faletto '17	YY	4

★Cascina Ca' Rossa

loc. Cascina Ca' Rossa, 56
12043 Canale [CN]
Tel. +39 017398348
www.cascinacarossa.com

CELLAR SALES
PRE-BOOKED VISITS
ANNUAL PRODUCTION 90,000 bottles
HECTARES UNDER VINE 16.00
VITICULTURE METHOD Certified Organic

For years now Angelo Ferrio, one of the most inspired interpreters of Roero and its Nebbiolo, has been producing some of the best Roero in terms of typicality, finesse and elegance. The vineyards, situated in Canale, Santo Stefano Roero and Vezza d'Alba, comprise outstanding cru, including the old plots of Audinaggio in historic Valmaggiore, Mompissano and Le Coste. In addition to Roero, they make successful Roero Arneis and Barbera d'Alba, as well as a classic Birbet. Once again, their various crus performed at truly high levels. The Roero Mompissano Riserva '17 won us over. Elegant in its notes of undergrowth and black fruits, it's got tannins of great finesse, fresh, with a long, tasty finish. The charming Roero Valmaggiore Audinaggio '18 is always of great finesse and tension, with nice mouthfeel and sapidity, it's juicy and long, while the Roero Le Coste '17 proves complex and gutsy, offering up spicy, black fruit sensations.

● Roero Mompissano Ris. '17	TTT	5
● Roero Le Coste '17	TT	5
● Roero Valmaggiore V. Audinaggio '18	TT	5
○ Roero Arneis Merica '19	TT	3
● Barbera d'Alba Mulassa '04	YYY	4*
● Roero Audinaggio '07	YYY	5
● Roero Audinaggio '06	YYY	5
● Roero Audinaggio '01	YYY	5
● Roero Mompissano Ris. '13	YYY	5
● Roero Mompissano Ris. '12	YYY	5
● Roero Mompissano Ris. '10	YYY	5
● Roero Mompissano Ris. '07	YYY	6
● Roero Valmaggiore V. Audinaggio '17	YYY	5
● Roero Valmaggiore V. Audinaggio '16	YYY	5
● Roero Valmaggiore V. Audinaggio '15	YYY	5

Cascina Chicco

via Valentino, 14
12043 Canale [CN]
Tel. +39 0173979411
www.cascinachicco.com

CELLAR SALES
PRE-BOOKED VISITS
ANNUAL PRODUCTION 435,000 bottles
HECTARES UNDER VINE 50.00
SUSTAINABLE WINERY

In recent years, the Faccenda family have been able to find the right balance between their Roero roots and a new commitment to Barolo. The winery, founded in Canale in 1950 with a hectare of vineyards, now comprises properties in the municipalities of Canale, Vezza d'Alba, Castellinaldo and Castagnito, as well as eight hectares in Monforte d'Alba. Their wines are grounded in native grape varieties and are styled so as to strike the right balance between technical precision and territorial character. With the splendid Barolo Rocche di Castelletto '16 hints of tobacco and liquorice are at the fore, followed by notes of raspberry, anise and rose, while the palate proves rich in fruit, with silky tannins—it's a drink of great balance and complexity. Almost on the same level, the Barolo Ginestra Riserva '13 is characterized by notes of undergrowth and dried flowers, long and velvety in its tannic texture. Their Roeros are also of excellent quality, in particular the pleasant, fruity Barbera d'Alba Bric Loira '18.

Wine	Rating
● Barolo Rocche di Castelletto '16	▼▼▼ 5
● Barbera d'Alba Bric Loira '18	▼▼ 4
● Barolo Ginestra Ris. '13	▼▼ 8
○ Arcass	▼▼ 4
⊙ Cuvée Zero Extra Brut Rosé M. Cl. '16	▼▼ 4
● Langhe Nebbiolo '19	▼▼ 3
● Nebbiolo d'Alba Mompissano '18	▼▼ 4
○ Roero Arneis Anterisio '19	▼▼ 3
● Roero Valmaggiore Ris. '17	▼▼ 4
● Barbera d'Alba Granera Alta '19	▼ 3
○ Cuvée Zero Extra Brut M. Cl. '16	▼ 4
● Roero Montespinato '18	▼ 3
○ Arcàss Passito '04	▽▽▽ 4
● Barbera d'Alba Bric Loira '98	▽▽▽ 4*
● Barolo Ginestra Ris. '11	▽▽▽ 8
● Nebbiolo d'Alba Mompissano '99	▽▽▽ 3*
● Roero Valmaggiore Ris. '12	▽▽▽ 4*

Cascina Corte

fraz. San Luigi
b.ta Valdiberti, 33
12063 Dogliani [CN]
Tel. +39 0173743539
www.cascinacorte.it

CELLAR SALES
PRE-BOOKED VISITS
ACCOMMODATION
ANNUAL PRODUCTION 30,000 bottles
HECTARES UNDER VINE 5.00
VITICULTURE METHOD Certified Organic
SUSTAINABLE WINERY

The bet that began 20 years ago paid off. Since then Sandro Barosi has been recognized as a great interpreter of Dolcetto and, even more so, as a master of a style that focuses on nature and not technology, on respect for the environment and not on chemical additives. Another important aspect is research and experimentation: amphorae are combined with steel and oak, flowers and plants are grown in the grassy vineyard rows, and their famous Dogliani Vigna Pirochetta has been accompanied by a line of Langhe DOC that spans Nascetta, Riesling and Nebbiolo. Everyone agrees on the freshness and vegetal profile of the Dogliani Superiore Pirochetta Vecchie Vigne '18, which plays on the elegance of fruit and multifaceted details of Dolcetto. The Dogliani San Luigi '19 is more powerful, richer, endowed with intense red berries and hints of almond. The golden Langhe Riesling '19 is intense and decisive, destined to open further in the next few years but already appreciable for to its citrus notes and hearty acidity.

Wine	Rating
● Dogliani San Luigi '19	▼▼ 3
● Dogliani Sup. Pirochetta V. V. '18	▼▼ 3
● Langhe Barbera '18	▼▼ 3
○ Langhe Riesling '19	▼▼ 3
● L'Imprevisto	▼ 5
● Langhe Barbera Amphorae '18	▼ 3
○ Langhe Nascetta '19	▼ 3
● Langhe Nebbiolo Amphorae '18	▼ 4
● Dogliani Vecchie V. Pirochetta '08	▽▽▽ 3*
● Barbetto	▽▽ 2*
● Dogliani '15	▽▽ 3*
● Dogliani Sup. Pirochetta V. V. '17	▽▽ 3*
● Dogliani Sup. Pirochetta V. V. '15	▽▽ 3
● Dogliani Sup. Pirochetta V. V. Anfora '17	▽▽ 3
● Langhe Nebbiolo '17	▽▽ 4
● Langhe Nebbiolo Anfora '17	▽▽ 4

Cascina delle Rose

FRAZ. TRE STELLE
S.DA RIO SORDO, 58
12050 BARBARESCO [CN]
TEL. +39 0173638292
www.cascinadellerose.it

CELLAR SALES
PRE-BOOKED VISITS
ACCOMMODATION
ANNUAL PRODUCTION 30,000 bottles
HECTARES UNDER VINE 5.00
VITICULTURE METHOD Certified Organic

Bu now young Davide, son of the winery's still-active founder, Giovanna Rizzolio, has taken over agronomic management, which he looks after with exemplary passion and respect, so much so that he has rejected the idea of enlarging the vineyards for fear that it might prevent him from personally overseeing each row. Her other son, Riccardo, has established himself as well, seeing to the needs of their passionate clients. Their production philosophy is rooted in tradition, which is interpreted with elegance and adherence to the territory, as consistently demonstrated by their prized Barbaresco Rio Sordo. The rich Barbaresco Rio Sordo '17 exhibits excellent structure—it's a wine that's as elegant in its fruity aromas as it is assertive on the palate, thanks to nice tannins. Intriguing today, it will grow even more charming over time. Fresh, with slight balsamic hints, the Barbaresco Tre Stelle '17 is already more open and enjoyable. The Dolcetto d'Alba A Elizabeth '19 offers up particularly alluring aromas.

Wine	Rating
● Barbaresco Rio Sordo '17	TT 7
● Barbaresco Tre Stelle '17	TT 7
● Dolcetto d'Alba A Elizabeth '19	TT 3
● Langhe Nebbiolo '19	T 4
● Barbaresco Rio Sordo '16	YYY 7
● Barbaresco Rio Sordo '15	YY 5
● Barbaresco Tre Stelle '16	YY 7
● Barbaresco Tre Stelle '15	YY 5
● Barbera d'Alba '17	YY 3
● Barbera d'Alba '16	YY 4
● Barbera d'Alba Sup. Donna Elena '15	YY 4
● Dolcetto d'Alba A Elizabeth '18	YY 3
● Langhe Nebbiolo '18	YY 4
● Langhe Nebbiolo '16	YY 4

Cascina Fonda

VIA SPESSA, 29
12052 MANGO [CN]
TEL. +39 0173677877
www.cascinafonda.com

CELLAR SALES
PRE-BOOKED VISITS
ACCOMMODATION
ANNUAL PRODUCTION 110,000 bottles
HECTARES UNDER VINE 12.00

Cascina Fonda was founded in the late-1980s, when brothers Massimo and Marco decided to start bottling the wines produced on the family estate (planted in the early 1960s by their father, Secondino). Their range centers on Moscato, which is offered in different versions according to the unique qualities highlighted by plots in Mango and Neive. There's also a commendable battery of traditional reds, in particular Nebbiolo da Barbaresco and Dolcetto, not to mention their Brachetto. The Asti Spumante Bel Piasì opens on lovely, fresh notes of sage and peach, followed by a palate that plays more on finesse than on sweetness, well supported by acidity, finishing long. Among the best of its kind, the Moscato d'Asti Canelli '19 proves rich in aromas of peach and candied fruit, rosemary and mint, coming through harmonious and balanced in the mouth, long and elegant. The Moscato Spumante Tardivo, a balsamic wine rich in fruit, is also well made.

Wine	Rating
○ Asti Spumante Bel Piasì '19	TT 2*
○ Moscato d'Asti Canelli '19	TT 2*
○ Driveri Extra Brut M. Cl.	TT 5
○ Moscato d'Asti Bel Piano '19	TT 2*
○ Tardivo Moscato Spumante	TT 3
○ Asti Bel Piasì '18	YY 2*
○ Asti Bel Piasì '16	YY 2*
○ Asti Spumante Bel Piasì '15	YY 2*
○ Brut Nature	YY 4
● Dolcetto d'Alba Brusalino '14	YY 2*
○ La Tardja '16	YY 3*
○ Moscato d'Asti Bel Piano '18	YY 2*
○ Moscato d'Asti Bel Piano '16	YY 2*
○ Moscato d'Asti Bel Piano '14	YY 2*
○ Moscato Spumante Chiara Blanc	YY 3
○ Moscato Spumante Tardivo '14	YY 3*
○ Moscato Spumante Tardivo '12	YY 3*

Cascina Fontana

Loc. Perno
v.lo della Chiesa, 2
12065 Monforte d'Alba [CN]
Tel. +39 0173789005
www.cascinafontana.com

CELLAR SALES
PRE-BOOKED VISITS
ANNUAL PRODUCTION 26,000 bottles
HECTARES UNDER VINE 5.00
SUSTAINABLE WINERY

While maintaining absolutely artisanal dimensions, Mario Fontana is proud to have surrounded himself with a fine team of collaborators, who over the years have integrated well with his project, resulting in pure, forthright wines, direct in their expression of the grape. The spaces for winemaking and ageing have also been expanded, with the sole aim of allowing the yeasts on the musts to carry out their work harmoniously and for their Barolo to mature comfortably in oak. The results have been notable in quality terms, with both wine lovers and critics making their approval known. Just one wine was ready for this year's tasting. The Barolo del comune di Castiglione Falletto Vecchie Vigne '15 is intense and rich in aromas of tobacco and dried flowers, but with fruit still discernible; the palate is harmonious and warm, with austere but not dry tannins. Its fruity pulp is pleasantly vital right up to a long finish.

● Barolo del Comune di Castiglione Falletto V. V. '15	7
● Barolo '12	6
● Barolo '10	7
● Barbera d'Alba '17	3
● Barbera d'Alba '16	3
● Barbera d'Alba '14	3
● Barbera d'Alba '13	3
● Barbera d'Alba '11	5
● Barolo '15	6
● Barolo '14	6
● Barolo '13	6
● Barolo '11	6
● Barolo del Comune di Castiglione Falletto V. V. '13	7

Cascina Gilli

fraz. Nevissano, 36
14022 Castelnuovo Don Bosco [AT]
Tel. +39 0119876984
www.cascinagilli.it

CELLAR SALES
PRE-BOOKED VISITS
ANNUAL PRODUCTION 100,000 bottles
HECTARES UNDER VINE 12.00
SUSTAINABLE WINERY

Cascina Gilli is one of lower Monferrato's most surprising producers. Led by Gianni Vergnano, together with Giovanni Matteis, Gianpiero Gerbi and Giann's son Paolo, it deserves credit for having gradually brought attention to otherwise neglected areas and varieties. In the vineyards around the winery, on the hill of Cornareto (in Castelnuovo Don Bosco), they cultivate the grapes for their Malvasia and Freisa, while Albugnano and the Schierano hill in Passerano Marmorito host their Bonarda and Barbera. With the 2018 vintage, the Freisa d'Asti Il Forno once again proves to be a touchstone for the type. Vibrant and elegant on the nose, flowery notes, black fruit and pepper aromas emerge. It has a pulpy mouthfeel and considerable structure, with pronounced but well-managed tannins and a long finish of great character. As usual the rest of the range is well made, including the Barbera d'Asti Le More '18, a wine rich in pulp, long and persistent with hints of undergrowth, cocoa and spices.

● Freisa d'Asti Il Forno '18	2*
● Barbera d'Asti Le More '18	3
● Barbera d'Asti Sup. Dedica '17	4
● Freisa d'Asti Sup. Arvelé '16	3
● Malvasia di Castelnuovo Don Bosco '19	2*
● Barbera d'Asti Le More '16	2*
● Barbera d'Asti Le More '15	2*
● Barbera d'Asti Sup. Dedica '16	3
● Dlicà	3
● Freisa d'Asti Arvelé '15	3*
● Freisa d'Asti Il Forno '17	2*
● Freisa d'Asti Il Forno '16	2*
● Freisa d'Asti Il Forno '15	2*
● Malvasia di Castelnuovo Don Bosco '18	2*
● Malvasia di Castelnuovo Don Bosco '17	2*
● Malvasia di Castelnuovo Don Bosco '16	2*
● Piemonte Bonarda Sernù '16	2*

Cascina Guido Berta

Loc. Saline, 63
14050 San Marzano Oliveto [AT]
Tel. +39 0141856731
www.cascinaguidoberta.com

CELLAR SALES
PRE-BOOKED VISITS
ANNUAL PRODUCTION 68,000 bottles
HECTARES UNDER VINE 20.00

San Marzano Oliveto, Calamandrana and Agliano Terme: these are the three towns in Monferrato Astigiano that host the vineyards owned by Guido Berta and his family. For over twenty years the producer has stood out for the valuable work being done with Barbera, especially, and one of its most appealing expressions: Nizza. But we certainly shouldn't overlook the care and stylistic consistency that tie together their entire range, which is rounded out by Chardonnay, Moscato and Nebbiolo, all distinct for their exemplary mix of vivacity and tension. The Nizza Canto di Luna once again proves well made. The 2017 sees notes of black berries and spices followed by a sapid palate of good acidic freshness, lacking just a hint of fruit. The Barbera d'Asti Superiore '17 offers up notes of cinchona-quinine and wet earth, and has a rich, harmonious palate, while the Piedmont Chardonnay '18 features notes of white fruit and sweet spices on a mineral background, making for a fresh, long, characterful finish.

Wine	Rating	Price
● Barbera d'Asti Sup. '17	🍷🍷	4
● Nizza Canto di Luna '17	🍷🍷	5
○ Piemonte Chardonnay '18	🍷🍷	4
● Barbera d'Asti '18	🍷	3
● M.to Rosso '17	🍷	5
○ Moscato d'Asti '19	🍷	3
● Barbera d'Asti '17	YY	3*
● Barbera d'Asti Le Rondini '16	YY	3
● Barbera d'Asti Sup. '16	YY	3
● M.to Rosso '16	YY	4
○ Moscato d'Asti '17	YY	3
○ Moscato d'Asti '16	YY	3
● Nizza Canto di Luna '16	YY	5
● Nizza Canto di Luna '15	YY	5
● Nizza Canto di Luna '14	YY	5

★★Cascina La Barbatella

s.da Annunziata, 55
14049 Nizza Monferrato [AT]
Tel. +39 0141701434
www.labarbatella.com

CELLAR SALES
PRE-BOOKED VISITS
ANNUAL PRODUCTION 25,000 bottles
HECTARES UNDER VINE 4.00

A decade has already passed since Lorenzo and Cinzia Perego took over the business founded in the early 1980s by Angelo Sonvico, starting with a farmhouse (called 'La Barbatella') situated on the slopes of Nizza Monferrato. It's a contiguous tract of land characterized by sandy-calcareous soils, dedicated foremost to Barbera (naturally), which here exhibits a slender, elegant quality. The grape is flanked by other native and international varieties, making for a contemporary and always reliable range of wines. The Nizza La Vigna dell'Angelo is back with Tre Bicchieri. The 2017 is splendid, alternating aromas of ripe fruit and spices by way of cocoa, licorice and pencil lead, while the palate amazes for its depth, elegance and length. The Nizza La Vigna dell'Angelo Riserva '16 is also excellent, rich in fruit with remarkable structure, with ripe cherry, cinchona-quinine and a spicy background on which acidity is grafted, making for a balanced, fresh finish.

Wine	Rating	Price
● Nizza La V. dell'Angelo '17	🍷🍷🍷	5
● Nizza La V. dell'Angelo Ris. '16	🍷🍷	5
● Barbera d'Asti La Barbatella '18	🍷🍷	3
○ M.to Bianco Non È '18	🍷🍷	3
● M.to Rosso Ruanera '17	🍷🍷	2*
● M.to Rosso Sonvico '15	🍷🍷	6
○ M.to Bianco Noè '18	🍷	3
● Barbera d'Asti Sup. Nizza V. dell'Angelo '11	YYY	5
● Barbera d'Asti Sup. Nizza V. dell'Angelo '07	YYY	5
● M.to Rosso Mystère '01	YYY	6
● M.to Rosso Sonvico '09	YYY	6
● M.to Rosso Sonvico '06	YYY	5
● M.to Rosso Sonvico '04	YYY	5
● M.to Rosso Sonvico '03	YYY	5
● Nizza La V. dell'Angelo '14	YYY	5

Cascina Luisin

s.da Rabajà, 34
12050 Barbaresco [CN]
Tel. +39 0173635154
cascinaluisin@gmail.com

PRE-BOOKED VISITS
ANNUAL PRODUCTION 30,000 bottles
HECTARES UNDER VINE 8.00

Rightly famous thanks to more than a century of history in quality winemaking, today Cascina Luisin is run by Roberto Minuto, great-grandson of its founder, Luigi. It's a strictly family-run business, whose style sees long maceration on the skins and the use of Slavonian oak barrels, though they're always very attentive to gustatory finesse. The Minutos have demonstrated that they're skilled interpreters of the Nebbiolo grape, which is offered in a variety of Langhe appellations. Starting with the very well-made Barbaresco Riserva '15, a wine of polished and fine classicism, already richly harmonious on its pervasive palate, of rare pleasantness. Equally well balanced is the Barolo del comune di Serralunga d'Alba Léon '15, a wine rich in red berries in alcohol, warm, with soft tannins that lend power to the palate. The persuasive Barbaresco Rabajà '16 is just a bit more modern, with a slight spicy note, while the velvety Asili '16 proves delicate and elegant.

● Barbaresco Rabajà '16	🍷🍷 6
● Barbaresco Ris. '15	🍷🍷 6
● Barolo del Comune di Serralunga d'Alba Léon '15	🍷🍷 7
● Barbaresco Asili '16	🍷🍷 6
● Barbaresco Paolin '16	🍷🍷 6
● Langhe Nebbiolo Maggiur '18	🍷🍷 3
○ Roero Arneis Ave '19	🍷 2

Cascina Morassino

s.da Bernino, 10
12050 Barbaresco [CN]
Tel. +39 3471210223
morassino@gmail.com

CELLAR SALES
PRE-BOOKED VISITS
ANNUAL PRODUCTION 20,000 bottles
HECTARES UNDER VINE 4.50
SUSTAINABLE WINERY

We are used to talking about Roberto Bianco as serious and scrupulous, a lover of the countryside and the cellar rather than public relations. But when you visit him you begin to see on his face and on his hands the signs of the harvests he has overseen since he founded the winery in 1984. The main Nebbiolo vineyards are situated in two of the appellation's top crus: Ovello and Cottà. They are the source of consistently harmonious and balanced wines that always exhibit the finest olfactory elegance and a lively, intense palate. Their Barbera and Dolcetto d'Alba are equally well crafted. Only two Barbaresco were submitted for tasting. A scalding 2017 brought many difficulties, both in the vineyard and in the cellar. That's why the famous Barbaresco Ovello lacks its usual freshness this year, proving rich in dried hay on the nose and marked by coarse tannins on the palate. The Morassino is not dissimilar, though it exhibits more balance on the palate.

● Barbaresco Morassino '17	🍷🍷 5
● Barbaresco Ovello '17	🍷🍷 6
● Barbaresco Morassino '09	YYY 5
● Barbaresco Ovello '14	YYY 6
● Barbaresco Morassino '16	YY 5
● Barbaresco Morassino '15	YY 5
● Barbaresco Morassino '14	YY 5
● Barbaresco Morassino '13	YY 5
● Barbaresco Morassino '12	YY 5
● Barbaresco Ovello '16	YY 6
● Barbaresco Ovello '15	YY 6
● Barbaresco Ovello '13	YY 6

Cascina Salicetti

via Cascina Salicetti, 2
15050 Montegioco [AL]
Tel. +39 0131875192
www.cascinasalicetti.it

CELLAR SALES
PRE-BOOKED VISITS
ANNUAL PRODUCTION 25,000 bottles
HECTARES UNDER VINE 16.00

Enologist Anselmo Franzosi leads a producer that has distinguished itself over the years for the quality of its wines. The turning point came about thanks to a greater commitment to vineyard management and the increasingly precise use of advanced technologies during winemaking. The result is a range of modern wines that highlight the attributes of the area's native cultivars, as well as the territory's prowess for winemaking. Local grapes give rise to genuine, forthright wines that exhibit a strong propensity for aging. The 2018 version of the Timorasso Ombra di Luna is elegant, with citrus aromas on a mineral background and a vibrant, sapid palate. The Colli Tortonesi Rosso Il Seguito is characteristic, varietal, with a rather soft profile that makes it an easy drinker. The Mont'Effe is a Dolcetto with aromas tending to herbaceous sensations on a fresh, intense palate of nice length. The affable Montarlino proves pleasant.

Wine	Rating
○ Colli Tortonesi Timorasso Ombra di Luna '18	TT 4
○ Colli Tortonesi Cortese Montarlino '18	TT 4
● Colli Tortonesi Dolcetto Mont'Effe '19	TT 2*
● Colli Tortonesi Rosso Il Seguito '18	TT 2*
○ Colli Tortonesi Timorasso Ombra di Luna '15	YYY 4*
○ Colli Tortonesi Timorasso Ombra di Luna '17	YY 4
○ Colli Tortonesi Timorasso Ombra di Luna '16	YY 4
○ Colli Tortonesi Timorasso Ombra di Luna '13	YY 4
○ Colli Tortonesi Timorasso Ombra di Luna '11	YY 3*

Francesca Castaldi

via Novembre, 6
28072 Briona [NO]
Tel. +39 0321826045
www.cantinacastaldi.it

CELLAR SALES
PRE-BOOKED VISITS
ANNUAL PRODUCTION 20,000 bottles
HECTARES UNDER VINE 6.30
SUSTAINABLE WINERY

If you say 'Francesca Castaldi' you can't help but think of Fara. The bond that links this winery to the small and historic appellation (the DOC was founded in 1969) of Upper Piedmont is very strong. Francesca's Fara has a unique character for its expression and complexity, bolstered by strong, red soils rich in minerals, careful vineyard management and a minimally-invasive approach in the cellar. The Vespolina grape lends lightness and spiciness, making for a wine of great charm. The 2016 Fara made it to our finals thanks to aromas ranging from cinchona-quinine to licorice, then iodine and rhubarb on a lovely bed of raspberry. The palate is characterful thanks to dense tannins, making for a mature, complex finish. The delicious Colline Novaresi Nebbiolo Bigin '18 features subtle notes of watermelon and licorice; it's powerful in the mouth, with elegant tannins and pulp lending a generous, velvety sensation, finishing long and subtle. Character and freshness characterize the Colline Novaresi Bianco Lucia '19 an Erbaluce.

Wine	Rating
● Fara '16	TT 5
○ Colline Novaresi Bianco Lucia '19	TT 3
● Colline Novaresi Nebbiolo Bigin '18	TT 3
● Colline Novaresi Uva Rara Valceresole '19	TT 3
● Colline Novaresi Vespolina Nina '19	T 3
○ Colline Novaresi Bianco Lucia '17	YY 3
○ Colline Novaresi Bianco Lucia '16	YY 3
● Colline Novaresi Nebbiolo Bigin '15	YY 3
⊙ Colline Novaresi Rosato Rosa Alba '17	YY 3
● Colline Novaresi Vespolina Nina '16	YY 3
● Fara '15	YY 5
● Fara '14	YY 5
● Fara '13	YY 5

Castellari Bergaglio

FRAZ. ROVERETO, 136R
15066 GAVI [AL]
TEL. +39 0143644000
www.castellaribergaglio.it

CELLAR SALES
PRE-BOOKED VISITS
ANNUAL PRODUCTION 90,000 bottles
HECTARES UNDER VINE 11.00

Castellari Bergaglio has played an important role for the history of the area's winemaking traditions. 11 hectares of vineyards give rise to a series of wines that faithfully express its soils. These are wines of great personality, firmly guided by Marco Bergaglio, who's never been one to follow the markets or fashion, keeping faith in a classic, traditional notion of Gavi and producing an interesting range centered on Cortese. Four still wines are offered along with a Metodo Classico and a passito. A difficult vintage like 2014 spawned a masterpiece. The Pilin is an extremely elegant, complex wine, with aromas of dried herbs and grains on notes of incense. On the palate it's sensational for the power it releases and an endless finish. The Rolona features a structured, intense and persistent nose-palate profile. The other wines tasted are also of excellent craftsmanship.

○ Gavi Pilin '14	🍷🍷🍷 5
○ Gavi del Comune di Gavi Rolona '19	🍷🍷 3*
○ Gavi del Comune di Gavi Rovereto Vignavecchia '17	🍷🍷 3
○ Gavi del Comune di Tassarolo Fornaci '19	🍷🍷 2*
○ Gavi Brut Ardé M. Cl. '11	🍷🍷 4
○ Gavi del Comune di Gavi Rolona '18	🍷🍷 3
○ Gavi del Comune di Gavi Rolona '17	🍷🍷 3*
○ Gavi del Comune di Gavi Rovereto Vignavecchia '16	🍷🍷 3*
○ Gavi del Comune di Tassarolo Fornaci '18	🍷🍷 2*
○ Gavi del Comune di Tassarolo Fornaci '17	🍷🍷 2*
○ Gavi del Comune di Tassarolo Fornaci '16	🍷🍷 2*

Castello di Gabiano

VIA SAN DEFENDENTE, 2
15020 GABIANO [AL]
TEL. +39 0142945004
www.castellodigabiano.com

CELLAR SALES
PRE-BOOKED VISITS
ACCOMMODATION AND RESTAURANT SERVICE
ANNUAL PRODUCTION 130,000 bottles
HECTARES UNDER VINE 24.00

The charming estate of Castello di Gabiano overlooks the Po valley, in what has, since the 8th century, been considered a strategic position. The property covers 260 hectares, 24 of which are under vine: among the rows mostly native grape varieties can be found, Barbera, Freisa and Grignolino, though international grapes also make an appearance in the form of Chardonnay, Sauvignon and Pinot Nero. The cellar, upgraded for a modern winemaking approach, is entrusted to the care of enologist Mario Ronco, who has been on board since 2007. The Gabiano Riserva: A Matilde Giustiniani exhibits an intense and multifaceted olfactory spectrum. Sweet spices and tobacco emerge on a still-fruity background, anticipating a very elegant palate that's rich in flesh, long and sapid. The Gavius is intense and multifaceted on the nose, while the palate proves full-bodied and rich, stretching sapid through a long finish. The other wines tasted are also notable.

● Gabiano Ris. A Matilde Giustiniani '15	🍷🍷 8
● Barbera d'Asti La Braja '18	🍷🍷 4
● Grignolino del M.to Casalese Il Ruvo '19	🍷🍷 4
○ M.to Bianco Corte '19	🍷🍷 4
● M.to Rosso Gavius '18	🍷🍷 5
○ Piemonte Chardonnay Castello '17	🍷🍷 8
● Piemonte Pinot Nero '18	🍷🍷 3
● Rubino di Cantavenna '17	🍷🍷 5

Castello di Neive

c.so Romano Scagliola, 205
12052 Neive [CN]
Tel. +39 017367171
www.castellodineive.it

CELLAR SALES
PRE-BOOKED VISITS
ACCOMMODATION
ANNUAL PRODUCTION 170,000 bottles
HECTARES UNDER VINE 26.00
SUSTAINABLE WINERY

The 18th-century castle was purchased by the Stupino family back in 1964 and since then their enological approach has always been faithful to tradition, following the approach set out by Italo, the winery's still very active director. Since then, research has never stopped, with different grape varieties, clones, typologies and methods of aging all explored, from Arneis to Metodo Classico, from Pinot Nero to Riesling. The main vineyards from which their Barbaresco is made are situated in two top-level crus, Santo Stefano and Gallina. Visitors can taste the different selections in their welcoming 'Casetta del Castello' reception area. The Barbaresco Albesani Santo Stefano Riserva '15 exhibits an elegant, complex aromatic suite, with raspberry and medicinal herbs at the fore; the palate is powerful and long, pulpy and pervasive, still a bit hard by virtue of its weighty, though welcome, tannic presence. The Barbaresco Gallina '17 is among the best of the vintage, proving rich in sweet spices and red berries, harmonious and already nicely supple on a long palate.

Wine	Rating
● Barbaresco Albesani Santo Stefano Ris. '15	🍷🍷 8
● Barbaresco Gallina '17	🍷🍷 7
● Barbaresco Albesani Santo Stefano '17	🍷🍷 7
● Barbera d'Alba Sulfites Free '18	🍷🍷 5
○ Langhe Riesling '18	🍷🍷 5
○ Piemonte Pinot Nero M. Cl. '14	🍷🍷 5
● Barbaresco '17	🍷 6
● Barbera d'Alba Sup. '18	🍷 6
● Barbaresco Albesani S. Stefano '12	🍷🍷🍷 6
● Barbaresco Albesani S. Stefano Ris. '12	🍷🍷🍷 8
● Barbaresco Albesani S. Stefano Ris. '11	🍷🍷🍷 8
● Barbaresco Albesani Santo Stefano Ris. '13	🍷🍷🍷 8
● Barbaresco S. Stefano Ris. '01	🍷🍷🍷 7
● Barbaresco S. Stefano Ris. '99	🍷🍷🍷 7
● Barbaresco Albesani Santo Stefano '16	🍷🍷 8

Castello di Tassarolo

loc. Alborina, 1
15060 Tassarolo [AL]
Tel. +39 0143342248
www.castelloditassarolo.it

CELLAR SALES
PRE-BOOKED VISITS
ANNUAL PRODUCTION 130,000 bottles
HECTARES UNDER VINE 20.00
VITICULTURE METHOD Certified Organic
SUSTAINABLE WINERY

We can consider Castello di Tassarolo to be one of the most important producers in Gavi, for the Spinola family's millennia of history, but also because, since 2006, the winery has been at the forefront of the low environmental impact movement. They were among the first in the area to implement biodynamic management, which has redefined the style of their wines. Their range is quite wide, drawing mostly on Cortese. The other varieties used are Barbera and Cabernet Sauvignon, which give rise to the Piemonte Barbera, a Monferrato Chiaretto and a Monferrato Rosso. In this edition of the guide, we tasted only a part of the wines in production. The Gavi del Comune di Tassarolo Il Castello features apricot aromas on almond notes, anticipating a fresh, long palate. The Marchesi Spinola has a style more focused on maceration, which brings out a slight tannic note on the finish. The Sparkling Spinola is a pleasant drink.

Wine	Rating
○ Gavi del Comune di Tassarolo Il Castello '19	🍷🍷 3
○ Gavi del Comune di Tassarolo Sparkling Spinola '19	🍷 2
○ Gavi del Comune di Tassarolo Spinola '19	🍷 2
○ Gavi del Comune di Tassarolo Alborina '16	🍷🍷 3*
○ Gavi del Comune di Tassarolo Alborina '15	🍷🍷 3
○ Gavi del Comune di Tassarolo Il Castello '18	🍷🍷 3*
○ Gavi del Comune di Tassarolo Il Castello '16	🍷🍷 3*
○ Gavi del Comune di Tassarolo Spinola '17	🍷🍷 2*

Castello di Uviglie

via Castello di Uviglie, 73
15030 Rosignano Monferrato [AL]
Tel. +39 0142488132
www.castellodiuviglie.com

CELLAR SALES
PRE-BOOKED VISITS
ANNUAL PRODUCTION 90,000 bottles
HECTARES UNDER VINE 25.00

This Rosignano Monferrato winery is undoubtedly among those that have contributed to the territory's enological revival. The property brings together the centuries-old history of the Uviglie estate with the technology of a modern winery. Mainly indigenous grapes are used for a range in which the area's classic wines are represented (international varieties contribute to the creation of fragrant whites). A modern style, the careful use of oak (but also fibreglass-lined concrete), and a focus on the attributes of the grapes are the main characteristics pursued by Simone Lupano. Barbera and Grignolino are among the company's strong suits. The Pico Gonzaga is intense on the nose with fine aromas of mulberry, blackberry and blackcurrant on notes of cocoa. In the mouth a lovely freshness regulates the richness of its flesh, only to finish long. The Grignolino '19 is vibrant, with beautiful notes of pepper on a vegetal background. On the palate it's fresh and intense, with characterful tannins. The other wines tasted are also of note.

- ● Barbera del M.to Sup. Pico Gonzaga '17 TT 5
- ● Grignolino del M.to Casalese San Bastiano '19 TT 3*
- ● Barbera del M.to Bricco del Conte '19 TT 2*
- ● Barbera del M.to Sup. Le Cave '18 TT 3
- ● Grignolino del M.to Casalese Monferace San Bastiano Terre Bianche '15 TT 5
- ○ Le Cave Extra Brut M. Cl. '16 TT 5
- ○ Piemonte Chardonnay Ninfea '19 TT 2*
- ● Barbera del M.to Sup. Le Cave '16 YYY 3*
- ● Barbera del M.to Sup. Le Cave '13 YYY 3*
- ● Barbera del M.to Sup. Le Cave '09 YYY 3*
- ● Barbera del M.to Sup. Le Cave '07 YYY 3*
- ● Barbera del M.to Sup. Pico Gonzaga '13 YYY 5
- ● Barbera del M.to Sup. Pico Gonzaga '07 YYY 4*

Castello di Verduno

via Umberto I, 9
12060 Verduno [CN]
Tel. +39 0172470284
www.cantinecastellodiverduno.it

CELLAR SALES
PRE-BOOKED VISITS
ACCOMMODATION AND RESTAURANT SERVICE
ANNUAL PRODUCTION 68,000 bottles
HECTARES UNDER VINE 10.00
SUSTAINABLE WINERY

The marvelous castle owned by Gabriella Burlotto and Franco Bianco brings with it stories of the Savoy family and King Carlo Alberto. Today, thanks to the valuable support of their three daughters and respective families, it's become an elegant hotel and first-rate restaurant, which serve as perfect complements to the winery and farm stay. Ten hectares of well-kept vineyards unfold in Barbaresco (Faset and Rabajà) and Barolo (Massara and Monvigliero). The wines are classic, aged in large barrels—the extraordinarily pleasant Pelaverga is a must. We start with an enjoyable Verduno Basadone, highly pleasant in its flashes of pepper and its freshness, its light, airy palate, delicately tannic, and a well-sustained finish. The excellent Barbaresco Rabajà Riserva '15 focuses on fresh, fragrant red fruit, then tobacco and liquorice. It combines finesse and flesh in a progressively unfolding texture for a characterful finish. The 2017 version of the Barbaresco Rabajà-Bas is particularly rich and structured, with generous mouthfeel and flesh.

- ● Barbaresco Rabajà Ris. '15 TT 8
- ● Verduno Basadone '19 TT 3*
- ● Barbaresco Rabajà '17 TT 6
- ● Barbaresco Rabajà-Bas '17 TT 6
- ● Barolo Massara '16 TT 6
- ● Barbaresco Rabajà '04 YYY 6
- ● Barolo Massara '08 YYY 6
- ● Barolo Massara '01 YYY 6
- ● Barolo Monvigliero Ris. '08 YYY 7
- ● Barolo Monvigliero Ris. '04 YYY 7
- ● Barbaresco '16 YY 5
- ● Barbaresco Rabajà '16 YY 6
- ● Barbaresco Rabajà-Bas '16 YY 6
- ● Barolo '15 YY 5
- ● Barolo Massara '15 YY 6
- ● Barolo Monvigliero Ris. '13 YY 7
- ● Verduno Basadone '18 YY 3*

La Caudrina

via Valle Bera, 10
12053 Castiglione Tinella [CN]
Tel. +39 0141855126
www.caudrina.it

CELLAR SALES
PRE-BOOKED VISITS
ANNUAL PRODUCTION 200,000 bottles
HECTARES UNDER VINE 25.00

Romano Dogliotti's vineyards of Moscato are situated in the municipality of Castiglione Tinella, on mainly calcareous marly soils, and go back, on average, more than 40 years. Barbera, Nebbiolo and Dolcetto are grown on an estate in Nizza Monferrato, while Chardonnay is grown in a vineyard in Ottiglio Monferrato. The wines are traditionally styled, with particular attention paid to ensuring both typicity and aromatic precision. La Caudrina returns with style. One of the best of its kind, the Moscato d'Asti La Galeisa '19 is vibrant on the nose with notes of tropical fruit, peach and candied fruit, and rich, sweet on the palate, but balanced by nice acidity, making for a long, pleasant finish. The Nizza Montevenere '16 is just as good, of great classicism in its aromas of cherry and wet earth, with tannins discernible but well managed, it's bright and plucky. The other wines presented are also well made.

Wine	Glasses	Price
○ Moscato d'Asti La Galeisa '19	▼▼	3*
● Nizza Montevenere '16	▼▼	3*
○ Asti La Selvatica	▼▼	3
● Barbera d'Asti La Solista '18	▼▼	2*
● Barbera d'Asti La Solista '17	▼▼	2*
○ Moscato d'Asti La Caudrina '19	▼▼	3
○ Piemonte Chardonnay Mej '17	▼▼	3
● Barbera d'Asti La Solista '13	YY	2*
● Barbera d'Asti La Solista '12	YY	2*
○ Moscato d'Asti '13	YY	3*
○ Moscato d'Asti La Caudrina '15	YY	3
○ Moscato d'Asti La Caudrina '12	YY	3*
○ Moscato d'Asti La Galeisa '15	YY	3
○ Moscato d'Asti La Galeisa '14	YY	3
○ Moscato d'Asti La Galeisa '13	YY	3
○ Piemonte Moscato Passito Redento '11	YY	4

★Cavallotto
Tenuta Bricco Boschis

loc. Bricco Boschis
via Alba-Monforte
12060 Castiglione Falletto [CN]
Tel. +39 017362814
www.cavallotto.com

CELLAR SALES
PRE-BOOKED VISITS
ANNUAL PRODUCTION 110,000 bottles
HECTARES UNDER VINE 25.00
VITICULTURE METHOD Certified Organic

As Alfio Cavallotto emerges from the huge oak barrel that he'd been cleaning of sediment he welcomes us with a smile. He's proud of the combination of traditional tools, such as his giant wooden containers, with the most modern winemaking techniques adopted here. The winery's name is synonymous not only with the highest quality, but also with rigorous respect for the environment, made possible through herbs, minerals and infusions that have long since replaced chemical treatments. The result is best appreciated in their Barolo Bricco Boschis, a wine that represents the essence of classical style and the purity of Nebbiolo. Only two Barolos were submitted for tasting this year. The Bricco Boschis '16 opens with clear, focused aromas of raspberry and herbs, the prelude to a sumptuous palate of rare harmony, with acidity, tannins and fruity pulp all exquisitely combined—a masterpiece. More mature and austere, the Riserva Vigna San Giuseppe '13 stands out for a full finish that veers towards sensations of rhubarb.

Wine	Glasses	Price
● Barolo Bricco Boschis '16	▼▼	8
● Barolo Bricco Boschis V. San Giuseppe Ris. '13	▼▼	8
● Barolo Bricco Boschis '12	YYY	8
● Barolo Bricco Boschis '05	YYY	6
● Barolo Bricco Boschis '04	YYY	7
● Barolo Bricco Boschis V. S. Giuseppe Ris. '05	YYY	8
● Barolo Bricco Boschis V. S. Giuseppe Ris. '01	YYY	7
● Barolo Bricco Boschis V. S. Giuseppe Ris. '00	YYY	7
● Barolo Bricco Boschis V. S. Giuseppe Ris. '99	YYY	7
● Barolo Vignolo Ris. '06	YYY	8
● Barolo Vignolo Ris. '04	YYY	8

Le Cecche

via Moglia Gerlotto, 10
12055 Diano d'Alba [CN]
Tel. +39 3316357664
www.lececche.it

CELLAR SALES
PRE-BOOKED VISITS
ANNUAL PRODUCTION 35,000 bottles
HECTARES UNDER VINE 8.00
SUSTAINABLE WINERY

What might have seemed a pastime twenty years ago is further establishing itself year after year, and Jean Jules de Bruyne is now at the helm of a producer that offers a range of fine wines, without exception. It soon became a benchmark for elegant Dolcetto in the Diano d'Alba DOCG zone, but for a few seasons now they've also been offering well-crafted Barolo, thanks in part to the expertise of the experienced enologist Piero Ballario. The fruits of the new vineyards acquired in Bossolasco, in Alta Langa, are expected soon. Impressive quality for their entire selection this year. The Fiammingo, an original blend of Merlot, Nebbiolo and Barbera, is as elegant as it is balanced, reaching the heights of pleasantness. Among their valid Barolos, it's worth emphasizing the power and clear complexity of the Bricco San Pietro '16. The fragrant Langhe Bianco '19, a peculiar and successful blend of Manzoni Bianco and Timorasso, also deserves praise.

Wine	Glasses	Price
● Barolo Bricco San Pietro '16	2 (black)	6
● Langhe Rosso Fiammingo '18	2 (black)	4
● Barolo Borzone '16	2 (black)	5
● Barolo Sorano '16	2 (black)	6
● Diano d'Alba '19	2 (black)	2*
○ Langhe Bianco '19	2 (black)	2*
● Langhe Rosso '19	2 (black)	2*
● Nebbiolo d'Alba '17	2 (black)	3
● Barbera d'Alba '17	2 (white)	3
● Barolo Borzone '15	2 (white)	6
● Barolo Bricco San Pietro '15	2 (white)	6
● Barolo Sorano '15	2 (white)	5
● Diano d'Alba '18	2 (white)	2*
● Langhe Rosso Fiammingo '17	2 (white)	3
● Nebbiolo d'Alba '16	2 (white)	3

★Ceretto

loc. San Cassiano, 34
12051 Alba [CN]
Tel. +39 0173282582
www.ceretto.com

CELLAR SALES
PRE-BOOKED VISITS
RESTAURANT SERVICE
ANNUAL PRODUCTION 900,000 bottles
HECTARES UNDER VINE 130.00
VITICULTURE METHOD Certified Organic
SUSTAINABLE WINERY

The Ceretto family entered the world of wine in 1937, and evolved in a way that's emblematic of Langhe's development. In the first decades, production was based heavily on grapes purchased in the markets of Alba, where hundreds of growers and their wagons converged. The 1970s saw the production of wines from the great Barbaresco and Barolo crus, then in 1985 the brilliant Blangé was created, an Arneis that was an immediate global success. While the hectares of vineyards continued to increase, since 2010 there has also been a growing adherence to organic farming, resulting in wines deservedly praised by critics and consumers. The mastery of the cellarman emerges clearly from the finesse with which their 2017 Barbarescos were made, taking into account the hot vintage. We start with the 'basic' version, which is a gem of elegance and roundness in the mouth. The Asili is the perfect expression of classicism, not very rich in structure but alluring, clear and harmonious. Lovely notes of liquorice and elegant tannins characterize the splendid Prapò '16.

Wine	Glasses	Price
● Barbaresco '17	2 (black)	6
● Barbaresco Asili '17	2 (black)	8
● Barolo Bricco Rocche '16	2 (black)	8
● Barolo Prapò '16	2 (black)	8
● Barbaresco Bernardot '17	2 (black)	8
● Barolo '16	2 (black)	7
● Barolo Brunate '16	2 (black)	8
● Barolo Bussia '16	2 (black)	8
● Nebbiolo d'Alba '18	2 (black)	5
○ Langhe Arneis Blangé '19	1 (black)	4
● Barbaresco Asili '16	3 (white)	8
● Barbaresco Asili '15	3 (white)	8
● Barbaresco Asili '13	3 (white)	8
● Barolo Bricco Rocche '13	3 (white)	8

Cerutti

via Canelli, 205
14050 Cassinasco [AT]
Tel. +39 0141851286
www.cascinacerutti.it

CELLAR SALES
PRE-BOOKED VISITS
ANNUAL PRODUCTION 25,000 bottles
HECTARES UNDER VINE 8.00
SUSTAINABLE WINERY

Gianmario represents the fourth generation of Cerutti family to run the winery founded by his great-grandfather Enrico in the 1930s. The vineyards are situated around the farmhouse in two areas. Cassinasco has a cool climate and sandy soils, conditions that prove ideal for the cultivation of Moscato and Chardonnay. Canelli is warmer, and the soils see a greater presence of silt and clay, more suitable for Barbera. Pinot Nero and Cortese are also grown. The Moscato d'Asti Canelli Surì Sandrinet '19 is among the best of its kind, with notes of saffron, sage, peach and medicinal herbs followed by a palate of great complexity and finesse, with vibrant acidity. The Barbera d'Asti '19 is a classic standard-label Barbera, with cherry notes, flesh and a finish that plays on freshness, peasantness. The tasty and balanced Alta Langa Brut Cuvée Enrico Cerutti '16 is also excellent, characterized by aromas of white fruit and toasted bread, beautiful finesse.

Wine	Rating
● Barbera d'Asti '19	🍷🍷 3*
○ Moscato d'Asti Canelli Surì Sandrinet '19	🍷🍷 3*
○ Alta Langa Brut Cuvée Enrico Cerutti '16	🍷🍷 5
● Barbera d'Asti Sup. Föje Rùsse '17	🍷 4
○ Cortese dell'Alto M.to '19	🍷 3
○ Alta Langa Brut Cuvée Enrico Cerutti '15	🍷🍷 3
● Barbera d'Asti '17	🍷🍷 2*
● Barbera d'Asti '15	🍷🍷 2*
● Barbera d'Asti Sup. Föje Rùsse '16	🍷🍷 4
● Barbera d'Asti Sup. Föje Rùsse '15	🍷🍷 4
● Barbera d'Asti Sup. Foje Russe '12	🍷🍷 4
○ Enrico Cerutti Brut M. Cl.	🍷🍷 3
○ Moscato d'Asti Canelli Surì Sandrinet '18	🍷🍷 2*
○ Moscato d'Asti Canelli Surì Sandrinet '16	🍷🍷 2*
○ Moscato d'Asti Canelli Surì Sandrinet '15	🍷🍷 2*
○ Piemonte Chardonnay Riva Granda '17	🍷🍷 3
○ Piemonte Chardonnay Riva Granda '15	🍷🍷 3

★★Michele Chiarlo

s.da Nizza-Canelli, 99
14042 Calamandrana [AT]
Tel. +39 0141769030
www.michelechiarlo.it

CELLAR SALES
PRE-BOOKED VISITS
ACCOMMODATION
ANNUAL PRODUCTION 1,100,000 bottles
HECTARES UNDER VINE 150.00
SUSTAINABLE WINERY

3 production centers, a dozen or so vineyards, more than 20 wines and virtually complete representation of the region's most reputed appellations. These are just a few of the numbers that summarize the importance of the brand founded by Michele Chiarlo in the 1950s. Just take a look at their crus in Langhe, Monferrato and Alessandrino: Cerequio, Cannubi, Asili, Faset for Barolo and Barbaresco, La Court for Nizza, Rovereto for Gavi... Their range highlights the best qualities of Nebbiolo, Barbera, Cortese, Moscato and many other varieties, both native and international. The Barolo Cerequio '16 is splendid, characterized by notes of mint and aniseed, licorice and fresh red fruit of superb clarity, while the palate proves harmonious, full, with a dense, progressively unfolding tannic texture that lends character and length. Among their Langhe selections, the Barolo Cannubi '16 stands out, coming through elegant, long and fresh. Among their Astis, the Nizza La Court Riserva '17 once again delivered, with its spicy notes, compactness and a nice sapidity.

Wine	Rating
● Barolo Cerequio '16	🍷🍷🍷 8
● Barolo Cannubi '16	🍷🍷 8
● Barolo Cerequio Ris. '13	🍷🍷 8
● Nizza La Court Ris. '17	🍷🍷 6
● Barbaresco Faset '17	🍷🍷 8
○ Gavi del Comune di Gavi Rovereto '19	🍷🍷 3
● Nizza Cipressi '18	🍷🍷 4
● Piemonte Albarossa '17	🍷 3
● Barbera d'Asti Sup. Nizza La Court '13	🍷🍷🍷 5
● Barbera d'Asti Sup. Nizza La Court '12	🍷🍷🍷 5
● Barbera d'Asti Sup. Nizza La Court '09	🍷🍷🍷 5
● Barolo Cerequio '10	🍷🍷🍷 7
● Barolo Cerequio '09	🍷🍷🍷 7
● Barolo Cerequio '07	🍷🍷🍷 7
● Nizza La Court Ris. '15	🍷🍷🍷 6

Chionetti

FRAZ. FRAZ. SAN LUIGI
B.TA VALDIBERTI, 44
12063 DOGLIANI [CN]
TEL. +39 017371179
www.chionettiquinto.com

CELLAR SALES
PRE-BOOKED VISITS
ANNUAL PRODUCTION 83,000 bottles
HECTARES UNDER VINE 15.00
VITICULTURE METHOD Certified Organic
SUSTAINABLE WINERY

Nicola Chionetti is absolutely convinced of the potential of Dogliani made exclusively with Dolcetto grapes, so much so that he wanted to join the classic wines of his famous grandfather Quinto—Briccolero and San Luigi—with the rich La Costa. It's a wine that undergoes a very delicate stay in large barrels and so is released a year after vintage. He's equally convinced that his production range would be made complete through a version of Langhe's most famous wine, and so it is that they're offering their first Barolos, for the moment just a few thousand bottles, accompanied by the Nebbiolo La Chiusa. Plenty of fruity pulp and oak are still evident in the well-made Barolo Parussi '16, a wine with a concentrated, youthful tannicity on the palate. Full-bodied, intriguing and rich in black berries, we also appreciated the assertive Dogliani Briccolero '19, while the San Luigi '19 is already more expressive and open, moving easily from fresh herbs to cocoa. Ripe cherries and a nice alcoholic warmth characterize the complex Barbera d'Alba Vigna San Sebastiano '18.

Wine	Rating
● Barolo Parussi '16	▼▼ 7
● Dogliani Briccolero '19	▼▼ 3*
● Barbera d'Alba V. San Sebastiano '18	▼▼ 4
● Dogliani San Luigi '19	▼▼ 3
○ Langhe Riesling '19	▼▼ 3
● Barolo Bussia V. Pianpolvere '16	▼ 6
● Langhe Nebbiolo La Chiusa '18	▼ 4
● Dolcetto di Dogliani Briccolero '07	▽▽▽ 3*
● Dolcetto di Dogliani Briccolero '04	▽▽▽ 3*
● Barolo Bussia V. Pianpolvere '15	▽▽ 6
● Barolo Primo '15	▽▽ 6
● Dogliani Briccolero '18	▽▽ 3
● Dogliani Briccolero '17	▽▽ 3*
● Dogliani La Costa '17	▽▽ 4
● Dogliani San Luigi '18	▽▽ 3
● Dogliani San Luigi '17	▽▽ 3*

Ciabot Berton

FRAZ. SANTA MARIA, 1
12064 LA MORRA [CN]
TEL. +39 017350217
www.ciabotberton.it

CELLAR SALES
PRE-BOOKED VISITS
ANNUAL PRODUCTION 70,000 bottles
HECTARES UNDER VINE 14.00

A cellar with a view. The Oberto family obtains first-class expressions from their vineyards, which host mainly Nebbiolo. Winemaking was already underway as early as the 19th century, but it was only around the 1960s that the winery began bottling under its own brand. Today, Marco is managing the producer, bolstered by plots in historic crus such as Roggeri, Bricco San Biagio, Rive, Cappallotti, Pira and Rocchettevino. In addition to Nebbiolo, other regional classics are cultivated, Dolcetto, Barbera and Favorita. Aromatic freshness is common throughout their range. The tannic texture of the Barolo Rocchettevino '15 is highly commendable, clear in its toasty and spicy hints, it's a harmonious wine, to say the least, creamy in texture, with a balanced and well-sustained finish. The Barolo '15 also proves highly pleasant—its fruit is fleshy and the finish expansive. A note of merit for the Barbera d'Alba Fisetta '18, dark in its fruit, tantalizing in its aromas of freshly-mown grass and licorice, which adorn a soft structure, rich in flavor.

Wine	Rating
● Barolo Rocchettevino '15	▼▼ 6
● Barbera d'Alba Fisetta '18	▼▼ 2*
● Barolo '15	▼▼ 5
● Barolo del Comune di La Morra '16	▼▼ 5
● Barolo Roggeri '15	▼▼ 6
● Dolcetto d'Alba Rutuin '18	▼▼ 2*
● Langhe Nebbiolo 3 Utin '18	▼ 3
● Barbera d'Alba Fisetta '17	▽▽ 3
● Barbera d'Alba V. Bricco S. Biagio '17	▽▽ 4
● Barbera d'Alba V. Bricco S. Biagio '16	▽▽ 4
● Barolo del Comune di La Morra '13	▽▽ 5
● Barolo Rocchettevino '14	▽▽ 6
● Barolo Rocchettevino '13	▽▽ 6
● Barolo Rocchettevino '12	▽▽ 6
● Barolo Roggeri '13	▽▽ 6
● Langhe Nebbiolo 3 Utin '16	▽▽ 3

Cieck

Cascina Castagnola, 2
10090 San Giorgio Canavese [TO]
Tel. +39 0124330522
www.cieck.it

CELLAR SALES
PRE-BOOKED VISITS
ANNUAL PRODUCTION 85,000 bottles
HECTARES UNDER VINE 12.00

Remo Falconieri started in 1985 and the results were positive, in particular thanks to the Alladium, a passito that immediately earned a place as one the best of its kind nationally. It's truly a sight to observe, during winter visits to the winery, hundreds of bunches hanging for months so as to concentrate the grapes' sugar and mineral richness. We shouldn't forget the excellent results obtained with their Metodo Classico and still whites, among which we recommend both the classic Misobolo and the new Erbaluce di Caluso T. This year we saw a nice performance from the Erbaluce di Caluso T '18, made with grapes from the famous Misobolo vineyard, harvested late (in November). It preserves a nice acidity, proving beautifully dry even in the presence of a rather broad, pervasive palate. On the nose it has a fine floral component that makes it quite pleasing. The easy Erbaluce di Caluso '19 is simple and immediately expressive, while a splendid oxidative style features in the Erbaluce di Caluso Passito Alladium Riserva '06.

Wine	Rating
○ Erbaluce di Caluso Passito Alladium Ris. '06	🍷🍷 6
○ Erbaluce di Caluso T '18	🍷🍷 3
○ Erbaluce di Clauso Passito Alladium '13	🍷🍷 5
● Canavese Nebbiolo '17	🍷 3
○ Erbaluce di Caluso '19	🍷 2
○ Erbaluce di Caluso Extra Brut M. Cl. San Giorgio '17	🍷 4
○ Erbaluce di Caluso Passito Alladium '06	🍷🍷🍷 5
○ Caluso Passito Alladium Ris. '05	🍷🍷 5
○ Erbaluce di Caluso Brut San Giorgio '16	🍷🍷 4
○ Erbaluce di Caluso Passito Alladium '10	🍷🍷 5
○ Erbaluce di Caluso T '16	🍷🍷 3*

★F.lli Cigliuti

via Serraboella, 17
12052 Neive [CN]
Tel. +39 0173677185
www.cigliuti.it

CELLAR SALES
PRE-BOOKED VISITS
ANNUAL PRODUCTION 30,000 bottles
HECTARES UNDER VINE 7.50

The property in the Serraboella cru—which covers about 25 hectares—enjoys a particularly favorable exposure and elevation. It's here that since 1964 Renato Cigliuti has personally harvested his most prized grapes, with results that have made this small winery a member of the Barbaresco elite. Their agricultural approach is particularly attentive to the health of the land, so much so that artificial products are banned and for fertilization green manure cropping is used. The owner's capable daughters Claudia and Silvia are proving apt at carrying forward a legacy of quality. The rich 2016 harvest gave rise to a selection marked by abundant structure. The Barbaresco Serraboella is strong and powerful, a bit tannic, with a nose that combines hints of tanned leather with small red berries. The Vie Erte features a graceful palate and a slightly fresher nose that veers towards mint. Modern and enveloped by oak, both of their 2017 Barbera d'Albas prove pleasant.

Wine	Rating
● Barbaresco Serraboella '16	🍷🍷 8
● Barbaresco Vie Erte '16	🍷🍷 6
● Barbera d'Alba V. Serraboella '17	🍷🍷 4
● Langhe Nebbiolo '18	🍷🍷 5
● Barbera d'Alba Campass '17	🍷 5
● Barbaresco '83	🍷🍷🍷 6
● Barbaresco Serraboella '13	🍷🍷🍷 8
● Barbaresco Serraboella '11	🍷🍷🍷 7
● Barbaresco Serraboella '10	🍷🍷🍷 7
● Barbaresco Serraboella '09	🍷🍷🍷 7
● Barbaresco Serraboella '01	🍷🍷🍷 6
● Barbaresco Serraboella '00	🍷🍷🍷 6
● Barbaresco V. Erte '04	🍷🍷🍷 6
● Barbaresco Serraboella '15	🍷🍷 8
● Barbaresco Serraboella '14	🍷🍷 8
● Barbaresco Vie Erte '15	🍷🍷 6
● Barbaresco Vie Erte '14	🍷🍷 6

★Tenute Cisa Asinari dei Marchesi di Grésy

loc. Martinenga
s.da della Stazione, 21
12050 Barbaresco [CN]
Tel. +39 0173635222
www.marchesidigresy.com

CELLAR SALES
PRE-BOOKED VISITS
ACCOMMODATION
ANNUAL PRODUCTION 200,000 bottles
HECTARES UNDER VINE 35.00
SUSTAINABLE WINERY

The producer has ancient origins, but it was Alberto di Grésy (accompanied by his children for a few years now) who brought the winery into the firmament of Langhe's quality producers. Their success is thanks not only to the splendid Martinenga estate, which gives rise to wines of great elegance and a highly valued longevity, but also a deliberate style rooted in the finesse and delicacy that the powerful Nebbiolo grape is capable of offering. Complexity, aromatic clarity and territoriality have thus become the winery's true and distinctive hallmarks. Aromatically, the Barbaresco Martinenga Camp Gros Riserva '15 is of wonderful classicism and finesse, with a soft background of ripe red berries on which the first elegant hints of liquorice are emerging; the palate is firm, almost austere, with delicate tannins already well integrated with its rich pulp. The assertive Gaiun '16, very pleasant and full of personality, is still slightly marked by sweet hints of oak. The warm Martinenga '17 is a polished wine of charming harmony.

Wine	Rating
● Barbaresco Martinenga Camp Gros Ris. '15	🍷🍷🍷 8
● Barbaresco Martinenga '17	🍷🍷 8
● Barbaresco Martinenga Gaiun '16	🍷🍷 8
● Dolcetto d'Alba Monte Aribaldo '18	🍷🍷 3
● Langhe Nebbiolo '19	🍷🍷 4
○ Langhe Sauvignon '19	🍷🍷 4
● M.to Rosso Merlot DaSolo '12	🍷🍷 5
● Langhe Rosso Virtus '12	🍷 6
○ Moscato d'Asti La Serra '19	🍷 2
● Barbaresco Camp Gros Martinenga '09	🍷🍷🍷 8
● Barbaresco Camp Gros Martinenga '08	🍷🍷🍷 8
● Barbaresco Camp Gros Martinenga Ris. '13	🍷🍷🍷 8
● Barbaresco Martinenga Camp Gros Ris. '12	🍷🍷🍷 8

★★Domenico Clerico

loc. Manzoni, 67
12065 Monforte d'Alba [CN]
Tel. +39 017378171
www.domenicoclerico.com

PRE-BOOKED VISITS
ANNUAL PRODUCTION 110,000 bottles
HECTARES UNDER VINE 21.00

Giuliana Viberti has been demonstrating her determination since taking over the winery where she collaborates with Oscar Arrivabene. Their production style follows the direction established by Domenico Clerico, with their Barolo, from excellent vineyards in Monforte and Serralunga d'Alba, continuing to prove well structured, elegant and rich in aromas, though without the prevalence of oak that characterized it in the 1990s. The range comprises nine superb wines, all made with the area's classic grapes, with Nebbiolo followed by Barbera and Dolcetto. Their 2016 Barolos put in a splendid performance. The Aeroplanservaj,famous for its artistic labels, is outstanding for its elegance and power, rich in fruit but already endowed with hints of licorice. The palate is well-orchestrated, rich and long, fresh in its youth but already appreciable. The 'basic' version is also commendable, even fruitier and just a bit less assertive. The famous Pajana, from the magical Ginestra cru, demonstrates its noble origins through minty notes and elegant gustatory development.

Wine	Rating
● Barolo '16	🍷🍷 6
● Barolo del Comune di Serralunga d'Alba Aeroplanservaj '16	🍷🍷 7
● Barolo Pajana '16	🍷🍷 8
● Barolo Ciabot Mentin '16	🍷🍷 8
● Barolo Percristina '10	🍷🍷 8
● Dolcetto d'Alba Visadì '18	🍷🍷 3
● Langhe Rosso Arte '17	🍷🍷 5
● Barbera d'Alba Trevigne '17	🍷 6
● Langhe Nebbiolo Capisme-e '18	🍷 5
● Barolo Ciabot Mentin '08	🍷🍷🍷 8
● Barolo Ciabot Mentin Ginestra '05	🍷🍷🍷 8
● Barolo Ciabot Mentin Ginestra '04	🍷🍷🍷 8
● Barolo Ciabot Mentin Ginestra '01	🍷🍷🍷 7
● Barolo Ciabot Mentin Ginestra '99	🍷🍷🍷 8
● Barolo Percristina '01	🍷🍷🍷 8
● Barolo Percristina '99	🍷🍷🍷 8

★Elvio Cogno

a Ravera, 2
2060 Novello [CN]
el. +39 0173744006
www.elviocogno.com

ELLAR SALES
RE-BOOKED VISITS
CCOMMODATION
NNUAL PRODUCTION 90,000 bottles
IECTARES UNDER VINE 15.00
ITICULTURE METHOD Certified Organic
USTAINABLE WINERY

bout thirty wineries and fifteen versions of Barolo center on the Ravera cru, which with ts 50 hectares of Nebbiolo is one of the nost important in the whole territory, not ust for its size but also for the resulting quality. Here, Valter Fissore and Nadia Cogno have splendid positions, with Bricco Pernice and Vigna Elena standing out. And despite its name, Cascina Nuova is able to have the success that it does thanks in part o the particularly old vines here. The cellar has been repeatedly enlarged with underground spaces, making it charming and worth a visit. The well-orchestrated Barolo Ravera '16 is rich in red berry sensations and flowers, from raspberry to violet, and endowed with a palate rich in character, already particularly balanced, with a charming, sweet liquorice finish. We also appreciated the rich and pulpy Barolo Ravera Bricco Pernice '15, the child of a vintage dense in fresh fruit, which makes for a juicy pleasantness. The Barolo Ravera Vigna Elena Riserva '14, a memorable, ively wine, also delivered.

Wine	Glasses	Score
● Barolo Ravera '16	TT	8
● Barolo Ravera Bricco Pernice '15	TT	8
● Barolo Ravera V. Elena Ris. '14	TT	8
● Barbaresco Bordini '17	TT	5
● Barolo Cascina Nuova '16	TT	6
● Dolcetto d'Alba Mandorlo '19	TT	3
○ Langhe Nascetta del Comune di Novello Anas-Cëtta '19	TT	4
● Barbera d'Alba Bricco dei Merli '18	T	4
● Barolo Bricco Pernice '11	YYY	8
● Barolo Bricco Pernice '09	YYY	8
● Barolo Bricco Pernice '08	YYY	8
● Barolo Ravera '11	YYY	7
● Barolo Ravera Bricco Pernice '13	YYY	8
● Barolo Ravera Bricco Pernice '12	YYY	8
● Barolo Ravera V. Elena Ris. '13	YYY	8

Col dei Venti

s.da Comunale Balbi, 25
12053 Castiglione Tinella [CN]
Tel. +39 0141793071
www.coldeiventi.com

PRE-BOOKED VISITS
ANNUAL PRODUCTION 35,000 bottles
HECTARES UNDER VINE 10.00

Ornella Cordara's winery is turning 18. This strictly family-run producer draws on the main appellations of Langhe and Monferrato, and has all the necessary internal skills to make quality wines, thanks in part to the active collaboration of her two children, Sara (who has a degree in Enology) and Ivan (Economics). Production has its beating heart in Moscato d'Asti, which reaches about 20,000 bottles a year, but there are also smaller selections as well, such as Barolo Debútto, which are handled with great skill. As is nicely demonstrated by the 2016 version, a particularly elegant wine, graceful and harmonious, rich in red fruit and hints of cinchona-quinine that make an encore on a long finish. The elegant Barbaresco Túfoblu '17 is pleasant, just veiled by a youthful touch of oak. Lovely aromas of plum and a touch of toast feature in the clear, fresh Barbera d'Asti Petràia '17. It's a good winery that's growing in both quantity and quality.

Wine	Glasses	Score
● Barolo Debútto '16	TT	8
● Barbaresco Túfoblu '17	TT	8
● Barbera d'Asti Petràia '17	TT	3
○ Infiore Brut	T	3
● Barbaresco Túfoblu '16	YY	6
● Barbaresco Túfoblu '15	YY	6
● Barbaresco Túfoblu '14	YY	6
● Barbaresco Túfoblu '13	YY	6
● Barbera d'Alba Sopralta '15	YY	3
● Barbera d'Asti '15	YY	2*
● Barbera d'Asti Sup. '11	YY	3
● Barolo Debútto '15	YY	7
● Barolo Debútto '14	YY	7
● Barolo Debutto '13	YY	7
● Barolo Debútto '12	YY	6
● Barolo Debútto '11	YY	6
● Langhe Nebbiolo Lampio '17	YY	4

Poderi Colla

FRAZ. SAN ROCCO SENO D'ELVIO, 82
12051 ALBA [CN]
TEL. +39 0173290148
www.podericolla.it

CELLAR SALES
PRE-BOOKED VISITS
ANNUAL PRODUCTION 150,000 bottles
HECTARES UNDER VINE 26.00

The winery was founded in 1994, though documents attest to its presence in the sector as far back as the 1700s. Beppe Colla, born in 1930, would take part in drawing up the production regulations for the Alba appellations, and in the 1960s he began an innovative path of separately vinifying the best areas while introducing the use of the word 'cru'. Manual work and limited, fertilization were other contributions. A strong focus on protecting the environment has been a key objective from the start. In the 1950s Beppe's son Tino was born, and he would go on to become the key figure together with his daughter Federica and grandson Pietro. The profile of the Barbaresco Roncaglie '17 is highly charming, clear in its fragrant red fruit, notes of tobacco and bark; the palate is powerful, dynamic, the finish long and nicely expressed. Intense in its smoky texture and dark fruit, the Langhe Bricco del Drago '16 demonstrates a perfect balance between flesh and tannic texture. The austere, classic Barolo Dardi Le Rose '16 will surely follow in the footsteps of the family's superb Barolos.

● Barbaresco Roncaglie '17	🍷🍷	6
● Barolo Bussia Dardi Le Rose '16	🍷🍷	6
● Langhe Bricco del Drago '16	🍷🍷	4
● Nebbiolo d'Alba Drago '18	🍷🍷	3
○ Pietro Colla Blanc de Noirs Extra Brut M. Cl. '16	🍷🍷	5
● Barbera d'Alba Costa Bruna '18	🍷	3
● Langhe Pinot Nero Campo Romano '17	🍷	4
⊙ Nebbiolo d'Alba Rosé Extra Brut M. Cl. '13	🍷	5
● Barbaresco Roncaglie '16	🍷🍷 (white)	6
● Barbaresco Roncaglie '15	🍷🍷 (white)	6
● Barolo Bussia Dardi Le Rose '15	🍷🍷 (white)	6
● Barolo Bussia Dardi Le Rose '14	🍷🍷 (white)	6
● Dolcetto d'Alba Pian Balbo '18	🍷🍷 (white)	2*

La Colombera

LOC. VHO
S.DA COMUNALE PER VHO, 7
15057 TORTONA [AL]
TEL. +39 0131867795
www.lacolomberavini.it

CELLAR SALES
PRE-BOOKED VISITS
ANNUAL PRODUCTION 80,000 bottles
HECTARES UNDER VINE 24.00
SUSTAINABLE WINERY

The Semino family bring competence and commitment to this estate on the hills of Vho, just over Tortona. The first La Colombera dates back to 1998, and so about 20 years have passed since the first Timorasso was harvested, 2 decades that have changed the territory's economy and transformed La Colombera into the dynamic and modern producer that we know today. Their products have reached an extraordinary level of quality across the board, starting with their excellent basic wines, thus demonstrating the care and passion that the family put into their work. The Montino, like a beacon in the night, is always surprising for the fragrance of its aromas and for its elegance, which contain its gustatory power. Mineral hints on notes of flint characterize the Derthona, a rich, intense and very long Timorasso. Very youthful and brilliant in color, we also appreciated the Barbera Elisa. The Vegia Rampana '19 is a fresh and juicy Barbera. Try their Croatinas as well.

○ Colli Tortonesi Timorasso Il Montino '18	🍷🍷🍷	5
○ Colli Tortonesi Timorasso Derthona '18	🍷🍷	4
● Colli Tortonesi Barbera Elisa '17	🍷🍷	4
○ Colli Tortonesi Cortese Bricco Bartolomeo '19	🍷🍷	2*
● Colli Tortonesi Croatina Arché '18	🍷🍷	4
● Colli Tortonesi Croatina La Romba '19	🍷🍷	3
● Colli Tortonesi Rosso Suciaja '17	🍷🍷	4
○ Colli Tortonesi Timorasso Il Montino '17	🍷🍷🍷 (white)	5
○ Colli Tortonesi Timorasso Il Montino '16	🍷🍷🍷 (white)	5
○ Colli Tortonesi Timorasso Il Montino '13	🍷🍷🍷 (white)	5
○ Colli Tortonesi Timorasso Il Montino '09	🍷🍷🍷 (white)	5

Colombo - Cascina Pastori

reg. Cafra, 172b
14051 Bubbio [AT]
Tel. +39 0144852807
www.colombovino.it

CELLAR SALES
PRE-BOOKED VISITS
ANNUAL PRODUCTION 40,000 bottles
HECTARES UNDER VINE 10.00
SUSTAINABLE WINERY

Cascina Pastori's project formed in the early 2000s out of Antonio Colombo's passion for wine. The internationally renowned cardiologist later sought out the expertise of the prodigious enologist Riccardo Cotarella. The estate's vineyards are situated in the hills, inside a charming amphitheatre that faces southeast and where the marly-calcareous soils prove ideal for the cultivation of Pinot Nero, Chardonnay and Moscato, all interpreted favorably according to a modern style in which wines are vinified according to their plot. The Piemonte Pinot Nero Maxima always performs at high levels. The 2016 is particularly broad on the nose, with aromas of red fruit, cinchona-quinine, licorice, tobacco and spices. The palate proves gutsy and powerful, with elegant tannins and a long finish. Rich and balanced, fresh and characterful, the Alta Langa Brut Rosé Reserve 60 Months '13 testifies to the significant progress made with sparkling wines, exhibiting fine, persistent beading, notes of berries and pastry. A well-deserved Tre Bicchieri.

- ⊙ Alta Langa Brut Rosé 60 Mesi Ris. '13 — TTT 5
- ○ Piemonte Chardonnay Blanc de Blancs 60 Mesi M. Cl. '14 — TT 4
- ● Piemonte Pinot Nero Maxima '16 — TT 5
- ● Piemonte Pinot Nero Apertura '16 — YYY 4*
- ● Piemonte Pinot Nero Apertura '15 — YYY 3*
- ⊙ Alta Langa Brut Rosé Silvì Ris. '12 — YY 5
- ○ Piemonte Chardonnay Onisia '18 — YY 2*
- ○ Piemonte Chardonnay Spumante Blanc de Blancs 48 Mesi M. Cl. '14 — YY 5
- ○ Piemonte Chardonnay Spumante Blanc de Blancs Andrè M. Cl. '13 — YY 5
- ● Piemonte Pinot Nero Apertura '14 — YY 3*
- ● Piemonte Pinot Nero Apertura '13 — YY 3
- ● Piemonte Pinot Nero Apertura Maxima '12 — YY 8

Diego Conterno

via Montà, 27
12065 Monforte d'Alba [CN]
Tel. +39 0173789265
www.diegoconterno.it

CELLAR SALES
PRE-BOOKED VISITS
ANNUAL PRODUCTION 40,000 bottles
HECTARES UNDER VINE 7.50

The turning point came in 2003: Diego, taking advantage of his experience at Conterno Fantino, decided to go his own way. Today he oversees 7 hectares with the valuable support of his son Stefano, who's increasingly central to this successful, family-run winery. The cellar enjoys a panoramic position, with a view overlooking the hills of Monforte as far as the eye can see to the Alps of Cuneo. Among their Barolo cru wines, we find Le Coste and Ginestra, which mature in small, 600-liter French barrels, in addition to versions of Barbera and Nascetta. They have, however, decided to postpone release of the Barolo Ginestra '16. Classic, with measured strokes of dried herbs, tobacco and quinine, the Barolo of Monforte d'Alba '16 has clear margins for evolution in the bottle. Elegant and very focused, the Barolo '16 offers up fresh and fragrant red fruit sensations, coming through elegant and nicely calibrated on the palate; the finish has length and a very pleasant balsamic stroke. We also appreciated the clear, focused and enticing Nascetta '19.

- ● Barolo del comune di Monforte d'Alba '16 — TT 7
- ● Barbera d'Alba Ferrione '18 — TT 3
- ● Barolo '16 — TT 6
- ○ Langhe nascetta '19 — TT 3
- ● Nebbiolo d'Alba Baluma '18 — TT 4
- ● Barolo Le Coste '09 — YYY 6
- ● Barbera d'Alba Ferrione '16 — YY 3
- ● Barolo '15 — YY 6
- ● Barolo '14 — YY 6
- ● Barolo '13 — YY 6
- ● Barolo Ginestra '15 — YY 7
- ● Barolo Ginestra '14 — YY 7
- ● Barolo Ginestra '13 — YY 7
- ○ Langhe Nascetta '18 — YY 3
- ○ Langhe Nascetta '17 — YY 3
- ● Nebbiolo d'Alba Baluma '15 — YY 3

★★★Giacomo Conterno

LOC. ORNATI, 2
12065 MONFORTE D'ALBA [CN]
TEL. +39 017378221
www.conterno.it

PRE-BOOKED VISITS
ANNUAL PRODUCTION 60,000 bottles
HECTARES UNDER VINE 23.00

The search for perfection continues, and it must be said that Roberto Conterno always comes close with his Monfortino, which has become one of the most sought-after wines in the world. Many awards have encouraged the producer to enlarge his range through major acquisitions in crus suitable for the production of Barolo in the beloved territory of Serralunga d'Aba, like Cerretta and Arione. We also suggest trying his two fine—and accessible—Barbera d'Albas. A little higher up in Piedmont, but always with the Nebbiolo grape at the fore, he has also acquired the historic Nervi winery, which is treated separately in the guide. With the 2014 version, their famous Barolo Monfortino once again proves magnificent. Notes of dried herbs and licorice emerge on a background wrought of bright red fruit; the palate is alluring, with a freshness that accompanies its velvety tannins: Tre Bicchieri. The long and licorice-scented Barolo Arione '16 is a must, exemplary in its finesse, gustatory development and complexity.

● Barolo Monfortino Ris. '14	TTT 8
● Barbera d'Alba V. Francia '18	TT 5
● Barolo Arione '16	TT 8
● Barolo Francia '16	TT 8
● Barolo Cerretta '16	TT 8
● Barbera d'Alba V. Cerretta '18	T 5
● Barolo Cascina Francia '06	YYY 8
● Barolo Cerretta '14	YYY 8
● Barolo Francia '12	YYY 8
● Barolo Francia '10	YYY 8
● Barolo Monfortino Ris. '13	YYY 8
● Barolo Monfortino Ris. '10	YYY 8
● Barolo Monfortino Ris. '08	YYY 8
● Barolo Monfortino Ris. '06	YYY 8
● Barolo Monfortino Ris. '05	YYY 8
● Barolo Monfortino Ris. '04	YYY 8
● Barolo Monfortino Ris. '02	YYY 8

★Paolo Conterno

LOC. GINESTRA, 34
12065 MONFORTE D'ALBA [CN]
TEL. +39 017378415
www.paoloconterno.com

CELLAR SALES
PRE-BOOKED VISITS
ACCOMMODATION
ANNUAL PRODUCTION 180,000 bottles
HECTARES UNDER VINE 37.00
SUSTAINABLE WINERY

Let's travel back in time, to 1886, when Paolo Conterno founded Ginestra, selecting the best soils and positions to cultivate Nebbiolo, Barbera and Dolcetto with extraordinary care. The work continued over time with great dedication and expertise, and today it's Giorgio leading a producer that's increasingly appreciated across major world markets. His work goes beyond Langa, in fact he also manages the Antico Podere Sant'Uffizio in Asti and Monferrato, as well as Ortaglia in Pratolino, north of Florence. The Barolo Ginestra '16 exhibits an intense and complex toasty profile, demonstrating that it's still in a stage of full youthfulness, with a still-austere palate, vibrant acidic vein and character. Tre Bicchieri for the modern, complex and fine Barolo Ginestra Riserva '12, an elegant wine with beautiful notes of dried herbs and tobacco on a clear, red berry background; in the mouth it proves harmonious, with dense tannins supported by nice, soft, rich, full flesh. The finish is very long.

● Barolo Ginestra Ris. '12	TTT 8
● Barolo Ginestra '16	TT 8
● Barbera d'Asti Bricco '18	TT 3
● Barolo Riva del Bric '16	TT 6
○ Langhe Arneis A Val '19	TT 4
● Barolo Ginestra '10	YYY 8
● Barolo Ginestra '06	YYY 8
● Barolo Ginestra '05	YYY 8
● Barolo Ginestra Ris. '11	YYY 8
● Barolo Ginestra Ris. '10	YYY 8
● Barolo Ginestra Ris. '09	YYY 8
● Barolo Ginestra Ris. '08	YYY 8
● Barolo Ginestra Ris. '06	YYY 8
● Barolo Ginestra Ris. '05	YYY 8
● Barolo Ginestra Ris. '01	YYY 8
● Barbera d'Alba La Ginestra '17	YY 4
● Barbera d'Asti Bricco '17	YY 3

Contratto

via G. B. Giuliani, 56
14053 Canelli [AT]
Tel. +39 0141823349
www.contratto.it

CELLAR SALES
PRE-BOOKED VISITS
ANNUAL PRODUCTION 140,000 bottles
HECTARES UNDER VINE 21.00

A property that stands shoulder-to-shoulder with the most prestigious maisons of Champagne, and the experience and energy of a figure like Giorgio Rivetti, are helping to rewrite the history of a sparkling wine producer that's important for both the region and the country. Quality wine can't be rushed—it's with this in mind that Contratto has been evolving of late. Their extraordinary patrimony of vineyards in Alta Langa will serve as another piece in the gradual construction of a great viticultural mosaic. The line-up submitted this year proved valid across the board, with the Special Cuvée Extra Brut '12 standing out for its gustatory definition, olfactory complexity and sapidity. The Piemonte Pas Dosé '15 is also excellent—powerful, tasty and harmonious with its linear, mineral profile. And we can't forget the De Miranda Metodo Classico, made with Moscato, an alluring wine, fascinating in its uniqueness.

Wine	Rating
○ Piemonte Pas Dosé M. Cl. '15	🍷🍷 5
○ Special Cuvée Extra Brut M. Cl. '12	🍷🍷 5
○ Alta Langa Pas Dosé Blanc de Blancs For England '16	🍷🍷 6
○ Alta Langa Pas Dosé For England Blanc de Noir '16	🍷🍷 6
⊙ Alta Langa Pas Dosé For England Rosé '16	🍷🍷 6
○ De Miranda M. Cl. '13	🍷🍷 5
○ Asti De Miranda M. Cl. '00	🍷🍷🍷 5
○ Asti De Miranda M. Cl. '97	🍷🍷🍷 5
○ Asti De Miranda M. Cl. '96	🍷🍷🍷 5
● Barolo Cerequio '99	🍷🍷🍷 8
● Barolo Cerequio Tenuta Secolo '97	🍷🍷🍷 8
○ Millesimato Pas Dosé M. Cl. '13	🍷🍷🍷 5

Vigne Marina Coppi

via Sant'Andrea, 5
15051 Castellania [AL]
Tel. +39 0131837089
www.vignemarinacoppi.com

CELLAR SALES
PRE-BOOKED VISITS
ANNUAL PRODUCTION 25,000 bottles
HECTARES UNDER VINE 4.50

Francesco Bellocchio, a pragmatic and forward-thinking man, embarked on an extraordinary venture in the early 2000s. Starting from scratch, in Castellania, the birthplace of his grandfather Fausto, he managed to reached levels of excellence in just a few years, thanks especially to his Fausto, a wine of extraordinary elegance that has received numerous awards. In addition to his Timorasso, we'd like to point out interesting offerings made with Barbera, Nebbiolo and Favorita. For the whites, maturation includes 6-10 months on the fine lees, in steel, and further aging in the bottle. Their reds see 12-18 months in medium-large oak barrels. The Fausto opens on classic hints of minerals and flinty notes. On the palate it's vibrant, with acidity that lingers across a sapid, long finish. The Francesca focuses more on floral, fruity sensations. We also recommend the Barbera Sant'Andrea, with its nice, crunchy fruit and juicy, mouth-watering palate. The other wines tasted are also well made.

Wine	Rating
○ Colli Tortonesi Timorasso Fausto '18	🍷🍷 6
● Colli Tortonesi Barbera Sant'Andrea '19	🍷🍷 3
● Colli Tortonesi Barbera Sup. I Grop '16	🍷🍷 5
○ Colli Tortonesi Favorita Marine '18	🍷🍷 5
● Colli Tortonesi Rosso Lindin '17	🍷🍷 5
○ Colli Tortonesi Timorasso Francesca '19	🍷🍷 3
○ Colli Tortonesi Timorasso Fausto '15	🍷🍷🍷 6
○ Colli Tortonesi Timorasso Fausto '12	🍷🍷🍷 6
○ Colli Tortonesi Timorasso Fausto '11	🍷🍷🍷 6
○ Colli Tortonesi Timorasso Fausto '10	🍷🍷🍷 6
○ Colli Tortonesi Timorasso Fausto '09	🍷🍷🍷 6
○ Colli Tortonesi Timorasso Fausto '17	🍷🍷 6
○ Colli Tortonesi Timorasso Fausto '16	🍷🍷 6
○ Colli Tortonesi Timorasso Fausto '14	🍷🍷 6

★Coppo

via Alba, 68
14053 Canelli [AT]
Tel. +39 0141823146
www.coppo.it

CELLAR SALES
PRE-BOOKED VISITS
ANNUAL PRODUCTION 420,000 bottles
HECTARES UNDER VINE 52.00

Long known for the quality of their Barbera d'Asti, from the simplest Avvocata to the most complex Pomorosso or Riserva della Famiglia, Coppo has often reminded us that he's also a great interpreter of Chardonnay aged in oak (Monteriolo and Chardonnay Riserva della Famiglia). With the arrival of a young team, not only have their wines adapted to today's tastes, reducing the use of new wood, but they're working with the territory in an organic way, drawing on the new appellations even with their premium selections: Nizza for their Barberas and Alta Langa for their Metodo Classico bubbly. In a line-up without weak points, it was difficult to choose the best, especially because this year they presented the splendid 2017 Nizzas: the powerful and pulpy Pontiselli and the more austere Bric del Marquis. But for the first time, our Tre Bicchieri goes to the Alta Langa Riserva Coppo, which with the 2015 harvest offers up a magnificent citrusy nose rich in yeast sensations, and a classy, harmonious gustatory profile.

○ Alta Langa Extra Brut Ris. '15	🍷🍷🍷 6
● Nizza Barbera Pontiselli '17	🍷🍷 8
● Nizza Barbera Riserva della Famiglia '15	🍷🍷 8
○ Piero Coppo Riserva del Fondatore Extra Brut '09	🍷🍷 8
● Barbera d'Asti Camp du Rouss '18	🍷🍷 4
● Barbera d'Asti L'Avvocata '19	🍷🍷 3
● Bric del Marchese '17	🍷🍷 8
⊙ Clelia Coppo Brut Rosé M. Cl.	🍷🍷 5
○ Gavi La Rocca '19	🍷🍷 3
○ Luigi Coppo Brut M. Cl.	🍷🍷 4
○ Moscato d'Asti Canelli Moncalvina '19	🍷🍷 3
○ Piemonte Chardonnay Riserva della Famiglia '15	🍷🍷 8
● Barbera d'Asti Sup. Nizza Riserva della Famiglia '09	🍷🍷🍷 8

★Giovanni Corino

fraz. Annunziata, 25b
12064 La Morra [CN]
Tel. +39 0173509452
www.corino.it

CELLAR SALES
PRE-BOOKED VISITS
ANNUAL PRODUCTION 50,000 bottles
HECTARES UNDER VINE 9.50

The new Barolo comes from a cru called Bricco Manescotto, a name that, for the moment, is used only by Giuliano Corino's winery. It's a southwest facing hill situated at an average elevation of 250 meters, and the first results are promising. The style is, as with the other selections of Barolo from Arborina and Giachini, decidedly modern and elegant, with charming fruity and spicy scents deriving in part from aging in French oak. The winery is deservedly famous for their elegant Barbera d'Alba, the Ciabot dù Re, as well. An endless trail of sweet tannins characterizes the Barolo Bricco Manescotto '16, a wine whose elegant nose combines notes of red fruits with more mature hints of herbs in the sun. A fresher, more youthful style features in the fine Arborina '16, endowed with a splendid backbone of enticing acidity. The Giachini '16 goes all in on finesse, favoring gentle drinkability and a soft, smooth palate over sheer might, much like the pleasantly minty, harmonious, cosseting Barolo del comune di La Morra '16

● Barolo Arborina '16	🍷🍷 8
● Barolo Bricco Manescotto '16	🍷🍷 7
● Barolo del Comune di La Morra '16	🍷🍷 6
● Barolo Giachini '16	🍷🍷 8
● Langhe Nebbiolo '18	🍷🍷 3
● Barbera d'Alba '18	🍷 3
● Barbera d'Alba Ciabot dù Re '17	🍷🍷🍷 5
● Barbera d'Alba V. Pozzo '97	🍷🍷🍷 5
● Barbera d'Alba V. Pozzo '96	🍷🍷🍷 5
● Barolo Giachini '12	🍷🍷🍷 7
● Barolo Giachini '11	🍷🍷🍷 7
● Barolo Rocche '01	🍷🍷🍷 7
● Barolo Rocche '90	🍷🍷🍷 7
● Barolo V. Giachini '89	🍷🍷🍷 7
● Barolo V. V. '99	🍷🍷🍷 8
● Barolo V. V. '98	🍷🍷🍷 8

Renato Corino

fraz. Annunziata
b.go Pozzo, 49a
12064 La Morra [CN]
Tel. +39 0173500349
www.renatocorino.it

CELLAR SALES
PRE-BOOKED VISITS
ANNUAL PRODUCTION 50,000 bottles
HECTARES UNDER VINE 7.00

Despite its small size, in 15 years of activity Renato Corino's winery has created a name for itself as one of the most well-established producers in Barolo. The approach is innovative, with low yields and somewhat new French oak used. A few stylistic touches are applied to each vintage, guaranteeing ever greater quality. And with the arrival of his son Stefano, new experiments and further challenges are being undertaken. Agronomic management is aimed at maximum respect for the environment, with remarkable results for Barolos and the Barbera d'Alba Pozzo. Their 2016 Barolos are superb, starting with the Roncaglie cru, a wine that stands out for its harmony and finesse, rather than power. The complex, intense Rocche dell'Annunziata is even more multifaceted, with raspberry and delicate oak; in the mouth it's long, fascinating, endowed with pulp and just as much acidity. The municipally-denominated Barolo isn't so powerful but surprising for its vitality and elegance. A spicy background and fine red fruit mark the vital, fresh Arborina.

● Barolo Rocche dell'Annunziata '16	🍷🍷🍷 8
● Barolo del Comune di La Morra '16	🍷🍷 6
● Barolo Roncaglie '16	🍷🍷 8
● Barolo Arborina '16	🍷🍷 7
● Dolcetto d'Alba '19	🍷🍷 3
● Langhe Nebbiolo '19	🍷🍷 3
● Barbera d'Alba '19	🍷 3
● Barolo Rocche dell'Annunziata '14	🍷🍷🍷 8
● Barolo Rocche dell'Annunziata '11	🍷🍷🍷 8
● Barolo Rocche dell'Annunziata '10	🍷🍷🍷 7
● Barolo Rocche dell'Annunziata '09	🍷🍷🍷 7
● Barolo Vign. Rocche '06	🍷🍷🍷 7
● Barolo Vign. Rocche '04	🍷🍷🍷 8
● Barolo Vign. Rocche '03	🍷🍷🍷 8

Cornarea

via Valentino, 150
12043 Canale [CN]
Tel. +39 017365636
www.cornarea.com

CELLAR SALES
PRE-BOOKED VISITS
ACCOMMODATION
ANNUAL PRODUCTION 90,000 bottles
HECTARES UNDER VINE 14.00

The Bovone family was among the first in Roero to believe in the quality of Arneis and it boasts some of the oldest vineyards, planted between 1975 and 1978. A single, contiguous property surrounds the winery on the Cornarea hill, where the calcareous clay soil is rich in magnesium. Only two grapes are cultivated: Arneis and Nebbiolo. Their various wines, all technically well made, exhibit great character and typicity. The Roero Arneis is a true classic. The 2019 opens on notes of kaiser pear and jasmine, it has nice structure and sapidity, with a long, pleasant finish. The very well-crafted Roero '17 offers up aromas of black berries, spices and liquorice, while in the mouth it's consistent and smooth, with a delicate tannic texture. Other well-made selections include the Roero Arneis En Ritard '16, with its resin and rosemary whiffs, the Mapoi Brut Metodo Classico, a pervasive wine in its notes of tropical fruit, and the alluring, balanced Tarasco Passito '16.

● Roero '17	🍷🍷 4
○ Roero Arneis '19	🍷🍷 3*
○ Mapoi Brut M. Cl.	🍷🍷 4
○ Roero Arneis En Ritard '16	🍷🍷 3
○ Tarasco Passito '16	🍷🍷 5
● Nebbiolo d'Alba '17	🍷 3
○ Enritard '14	🍷🍷 3
● Nebbiolo d'Alba '16	🍷🍷 3
● Roero '16	🍷🍷 4
● Roero '15	🍷🍷 4
● Roero '14	🍷🍷 4
○ Roero Arneis '18	🍷🍷 3*
○ Roero Arneis '17	🍷🍷 3*
○ Roero Arneis '16	🍷🍷 3*
○ Roero Arneis En Ritard '15	🍷🍷 3*
○ Tarasco Passito '15	🍷🍷 5
○ Tarasco Passito '14	🍷🍷 5

★Matteo Correggia

loc. Garbinetto
via Santo Stefano Roero, 124
12043 Canale [CN]
Tel. +39 0173978009
www.matteocorreggia.com

CELLAR SALES
PRE-BOOKED VISITS
ANNUAL PRODUCTION 150,000 bottles
HECTARES UNDER VINE 20.00
VITICULTURE METHOD Certified Organic

Some 35 years have passed since Matteo Correggia decided to create a winery capable of bringing the name and quality of Roero to the world. Today it's one of the best known and most significant producers in Roero wine country. The estate's vineyards are all located in Canale, apart from a small estate in Santo Stefano Roero that gives rise to their Le Marne Grigie. In recent years, the work in the vineyards has been accompanied by constant research in the cellar, ranging from the use of amphora for vinification to adoption of the screw cap. The Roero Ròche d'Ampsèj Riserva '16 sees hints of undergrowth and porcini mushrooms followed by a palate rich in fruit, tannic and sapid. The other Roero, the La Val dei Preti '17, exhibits aromas of Mediterranean scrub and black berries, coming through fresh on the palate, with nice mouthfeel and tannins that are still perceptible but fine and well managed. The Barbera d'Alba Superiore Marun '17 is a highly pleasant drink, juicy and rich in texture all at once.

● Barbera d'Alba Sup. Marun '17	🍷🍷 5
● Roero La Val dei Preti '17	🍷🍷 5
● Roero Ròche d'Ampsèj Ris. '16	🍷🍷 6
○ Roero Arneis La Val dei Preti '14	🍷🍷 3
● Barbera d'Alba Marun '04	YYY 5
● Barbera d'Alba Marun '99	YYY 5
● Roero Ròche d'Ampsèj '04	YYY 6
● Roero Ròche d'Ampsèj '01	YYY 6
● Roero Ròche d'Ampsèj '00	YYY 6
● Roero Ròche d'Ampsèj '99	YYY 6
● Roero Ròche d'Ampsèj Ris. '14	YYY 6
● Roero Ròche d'Ampsèj Ris. '09	YYY 6
● Roero Ròche d'Ampsèj Ris. '07	YYY 6
● Roero Ròche d'Ampsèj Ris. '06	YYY 6

Giuseppe Cortese

s.da Rabajà, 80
12050 Barbaresco [CN]
Tel. +39 0173635131
www.cortesegiuseppe.it

CELLAR SALES
PRE-BOOKED VISITS
ACCOMMODATION
ANNUAL PRODUCTION 58,000 bottles
HECTARES UNDER VINE 9.00
SUSTAINABLE WINERY

We find the Cortese siblings, Pier Carlo and Tiziana (together with the latter's husband), at the helm of this boutique producer founded by Giuseppe in the early 1970s. The core of production is concentrated on the hill of Rabajà, a cru that gives rise to two Barbarescos, one a standard-label version, the other a reserve. This year sees the release of a third Barbaresco, a basic version that accentuates the winery's trademark lightness. Their wines mature in large oak barrels, making for a solid range, starting with a Langhe Nebbiolo and Barbera d'Alba that are daily-drinking delights. The fine, subtly whispered yet complex aromas of the Barbaresco Rabajà '17 make for a captivating red. A flowery background and spices anticipate plenty of flavor and expressive lightness on the finish. Intense and ripe in its notes of red berries, quinine and licorice, the Barbaresco Rabajà Riserva '13 is still quite youthful, with plenty of acidic freshness. Dense tannins and a vibrant energy mean it has a very long and bright future. Tre Bicchieri.

● Barbaresco Rabajà Ris. '13	🍷🍷🍷 8
● Barbaresco Rabajà '17	🍷🍷 7
● Barbaresco '17	🍷🍷 5
● Barbera d'Alba '19	🍷🍷 3
● Langhe Nebbiolo '18	🍷🍷 4
● Langhe Dolcetto '19	🍷 2
● Barbaresco Rabajà '16	YYY 6
● Barbaresco Rabajà '15	YYY 6
● Barbaresco Rabajà '11	YYY 5
● Barbaresco Rabajà '10	YYY 5
● Barbaresco Rabajà '08	YYY 5
● Barbaresco Rabajà Ris. '96	YYY 8
● Barbaresco Rabajà Ris. '11	YY 8
● Barbera d'Alba '18	YY 3
● Barbera d'Alba Morassina '15	YY 3
● Langhe Nebbiolo '17	YY 3*
● Langhe Nebbiolo '16	YY 3*

Clemente Cossetti

via Guardie, 1
14043 Castelnuovo Belbo [AT]
Tel. +39 0141799803
www.cossetti.it

CELLAR SALES
PRE-BOOKED VISITS
ACCOMMODATION AND RESTAURANT SERVICE
ANNUAL PRODUCTION 500,000 bottles
HECTARES UNDER VINE 28.00

For four generations now, the Cossetti family have been a consistent presence in the Monferrato wine-growing and wine-producing scene. Alongside selections from their privately-owned vineyards, all situated in Castelnuovo Belbo on medium-textured, clayey soils rich in minerals, and planted mainly with Barbera, the producer offers wines from other territories as well, thus covering some of Piedmont's most important appellations. The wines produced are well made and modern in style. Cossetti's range is solid, reliable. The well-made Nizza Cribelletto '17 sees aromas of red fruit and tobacco followed by a palate of nice complexity and depth. The Barbera d'Asti Gelsomora '18 is classic in its aromas of sweet spices, tobacco and fresh cherries, with a rich palate well supported by acidity. Characteristic and alluring, the Ruchè '19 proves rich in varietal aromas of rose and blackberry, and bold on the palate. The Grignolino '19 is softer and gentler than usual.

- ● Barbera d'Asti Gelsomora '18 TT 2*
- ● Barbera d'Asti Venti di Marzo '18 TT 3
- ● Grignolino d'Asti Gelsomora '19 TT 2*
- ● Nizza Crivelletto '17 TT 4
- ● Ruché di Castagnole M.to '19 TT 3
- ● Barbera d'Asti La Vigna Vecchia '15 YY 2*
- ● Barbera d'Asti Sup. La Vigna Vecchia '17 YY 2*
- ● Grignolino d'Asti '17 YY 2*
- ● Grignolino d'Asti Gelsomora '18 YY 2*
- ○ Moscato d'Asti La Vita '15 YY 2*
- ● Nizza '16 YY 4
- ● Nizza '15 YY 4
- ● Piemonte Albarossa Amartè '14 YY 3
- ● Ruché di Castagnole M.to '17 YY 3
- ● Ruché di Castagnole M.to '16 YY 3
- ● Ruché di Castagnole Monferrato '15 YY 3

Stefanino Costa

b.ta Benna, 5
12046 Montà [CN]
Tel. +39 0173976336
ninocostawine@gmail.com

CELLAR SALES
PRE-BOOKED VISITS
ANNUAL PRODUCTION 50,000 bottles
HECTARES UNDER VINE 9.50

Stefanino Costa and his son Alessandro lead the family business with passion and competence. In recent years production has grown significantly in terms of quality, making for wines of great technical clarity and aromatic precision, both their reds and Arneis, which are today among the best of their kind. The vineyards are situated in the municipalities of Canale, Montà and Santo Stefano Roero and grow in the sandy soils characteristic of the Tanaro river's left bank. Another nice performance for the Roero Arneis Sarun saw the 2019 version take home Tre Bicchieri. On the nose it offers up hints of aromatic herbs, spices and yellow fruit, while the palate proves rich, full, almost salty, with a long, dynamic finish. The Roero Gepin Riserva '15 also delivered, with its balsamic and red fruit whiffs accompanied by spicy nuances, and a gutsy palate, with tannins detectable but marked by a lovely finesse, all topped off by a pleasant, juicy finish.

- ○ Roero Arneis Sarun '19 TTT 3*
- ● Roero Gepin Ris. '15 TT 5
- ○ Langhe Bianco Ricordi '18 TT 3
- ○ Roero Arneis Seminari '19 TT 3
- ○ Roero Arneis Sarun '18 YYY 3*
- ○ Roero Arneis Sarun '17 YYY 3*
- ● Roero Gepin '13 YYY 4*
- ● Roero Gepin '12 YYY 4*
- ● Roero Gepin '11 YYY 4*
- ● Roero Gepin '10 YYY 4*
- ○ Roero Arneis Sarun '15 YY 3*
- ○ Roero Arneis Seminari '17 YY 3*
- ● Roero Gepin '15 YY 4
- ● Roero Gepin '14 YY 4

Tenuta Cucco

via Mazzini, 10
12050 Serralunga d'Alba [CN]
Tel. +39 0173613003
www.tenutacucco.it

CELLAR SALES
PRE-BOOKED VISITS
ACCOMMODATION
ANNUAL PRODUCTION 70,000 bottles
HECTARES UNDER VINE 13.00
VITICULTURE METHOD Certified Organic

The Rossi Cairo family's adherence to organic viticulture is a convinced and central choice, as demonstrated by the adoption of biodynamic principles for La Raia di Gavi since 2003. The purchase of this prized estate and its charming headquarters took place in 2015, and the decision was made immediately to aim for high quality, as demonstrated by collaborations with expert technicians such as Piero Ballario for the cellar and Gian Piero Romana for viticulture. The winery's productive heart is situated in the Cerrati cru, which gives rise to a Barolo that's particularly rich on the palate. The Barolo Cerrati '16 landed a place in our finals, proving vibrant and elegant in its fragrant notes of red fruit, dried flowers and orange peel. In the mouth it's rich and pulpy, warm and pervasive, with notable length. The more evolved Barolo del Comune di Serralunga d'Alba '16 offers up charming hints of undergrowth and tobacco followed by a particularly dense tannic texture and long, austere finish.

● Barolo Cerrati '16	🍷🍷	8
● Barolo del Comune di Serralunga d'Alba '16	🍷🍷	6
● Langhe Nebbiolo '19	🍷🍷	4
● Barolo Cerrati '15	🍷🍷	7
● Barolo Cerrati '14	🍷🍷	7
● Barolo Cerrati '13	🍷🍷	7
● Barolo Cerrati V. Cucco Ris. '13	🍷🍷	8
● Barolo Cerrati V. Cucco Ris. '12	🍷🍷	8
● Barolo Cerrati V. Cucco Ris. '11	🍷🍷	8
● Barolo del Comune di Serralunga d'Alba '15	🍷🍷	6
● Barolo del Comune di Serralunga d'Alba '14	🍷🍷	6
○ Langhe Chardonnay '16	🍷🍷	3
● Langhe Rosso '16	🍷🍷	4

Giovanni Daglio

via Montale Celli, 10
15050 Costa Vescovato [AL]
Tel. +39 0131838262
www.vignetidaglio.com

CELLAR SALES
ANNUAL PRODUCTION 15,000 bottles
HECTARES UNDER VINE 10.00

Winemakers are judged, above all, by how they manage so-called 'inferior' vintages. Just taste the 2014 version of Giovanni Daglio's Cantico to understand the good, quality work being done by this winery. Giovanni has proven capable of producing whites, with Timorasso, and reds. His Barbera Basinass, Dolcetto Nibiö and Croatina Zerbo are often masterful interpretations of Tortona's native grapes. The Negher, made with the rare Moscato Nero grape, which Giovanni has dried slightly in the vineyard, is a separate project. The Cantico and the Derthona are characterful Timorassos, splendid examples of this typology united by elegant traits. The former opens on intense mineral notes of flint, exploding in the mouth for its freshness and body only to endure endlessly. The latter is redolent of citrus fruits on a mineral background; it has a sumptuous, rich and very long palate.

○ Colli Tortonesi Timorasso Cantico '18	🍷🍷	4
○ Colli Tortonesi Timorasso Derthona '18	🍷🍷	4
● Colli Tortonesi Barbera Basinas '16	🍷🍷	4
○ Colli Tortonesi Timorasso Cantico '17	🍷🍷	4
○ Colli Tortonesi Timorasso Cantico '16	🍷🍷	4
○ Colli Tortonesi Timorasso Cantico '15	🍷🍷	4
○ Colli Tortonesi Timorasso Cantico '13	🍷🍷	4
○ Colli Tortonesi Timorasso Derthona '17	🍷🍷	4
○ Colli Tortonesi Timorasso Derthona '15	🍷🍷	4
○ Colli Tortonesi Timorasso Derthona Cantico '14	🍷🍷	4

Deltetto

c.so Alba, 43
12043 Canale [CN]
Tel. +39 0173979383
www.deltetto.com

CELLAR SALES
PRE-BOOKED VISITS
ANNUAL PRODUCTION 170,000 bottles
HECTARES UNDER VINE 21.00
VITICULTURE METHOD Certified Organic
SUSTAINABLE WINERY

Antonio Deltetto has been a leader in the Roero wine firmament for several years now. Certified organic since 2017, production focuses on the classics of the Roero area drawing on grape varieties such as Arneis and Nebbiolo, Barbera and Favorita, which are accompanied by bottles from other prestigious appellations, like Barolo and Gavi. A modern style, attention to territorial identity, technical clarity and aromatic precision are defining characteristics of their range. A fine overall performance for the Deltetto family's wines. The Roero Arneis Daivej '19 opens on intense, flowery and fresh herb sensations, followed by notes of white fruit; the palate is rich in flesh, sapid, plucky and nicely balanced by acidic freshness. The Roero Braja Riserva '17, with its hints of tea leaves and red berries, proves complex in the mouth, with nice substance and depth. Finally the Deltetto Extra Brut '14 is full and creamy, characterized by notes of butter and bread crust.

Wine	Rating
○ Deltetto Extra Brut M. Cl. '14	TT 5
○ Roero Arneis Daivej '19	TT 3*
● Roero Braja Ris. '17	TT 4
○ Alta Langa Brut '16	TT 5
● Barolo Parussi '15	TT 6
⊙ Deltetto Brut Rosé M. Cl.	TT 4
○ Roero Arneis San Defendente '18	TT 3
● Roero Gorrini '18	TT 3
● Langhe Pinot Nero 777 '18	T 3
○ Roero Arneis San Michele '19	T 3
● Barolo Parussi '14	YY 6
○ Deltetto Brut M. Cl. '15	YY 4
● Langhe Pinot Nero 777 '17	YY 3
● Roero Braja Ris. '16	YY 4
● Roero Gorrini '17	YY 3*

Gianni Doglia

via Annunziata, 56
14054 Castagnole delle Lanze [AT]
Tel. +39 0141878359
www.giannidoglia.it

CELLAR SALES
PRE-BOOKED VISITS
ANNUAL PRODUCTION 110,000 bottles
HECTARES UNDER VINE 16.00
SUSTAINABLE WINERY

With kindness and humility, but now with a certain confidence as well, Gianni tells visitors about his methods in the vineyard and in the cellar, which he says are simple and natural, the most important thing being the care and attention necessary to make flawless wines (indeed, not just flawless, but full of qualities, we might add). He's now recognized as a great interpreter of Moscato d'Asti, so much so that many of his colleagues turn to him for advice. But his Barbera is outstanding as well, and not just the premium versions (Nizza and Genio) but also the affordable, clear, focused and fresh Bosco Donne, a wine aged entirely in steel. The Moscato d'Asti Casa di Bianca '19 is splendid. Notes of peach and sage are accompanied by medicinal herbs, mint and lime, all followed by a subtle yet close-knit palate, long and harmonious. The Nizza Viti Vecchie '18 is also excellent, with complex aromas of cinchona-quinine merging with tobacco and spices. In the mouth it's juicy, sapid, marked by great character and length.

Wine	Rating
○ Moscato d'Asti Casa di Bianca '19	TTT 3*
○ Moscato d'Asti '19	TT 3*
● Nizza V. V. '18	TT 5
● Barbera d'Asti Bosco Donne '19	TT 3
● Barbera d'Asti Sup. Genio '18	TT 4
● Grignolino d'Asti '19	TT 3
● Barbera d'Asti Sup. Genio '12	YYY 4*
○ Moscato d'Asti Casa di Bianca '17	YYY 5
○ Moscato d'Asti Casa di Bianca '16	YYY 3*
○ Moscato d'Asti Casa di Bianca '15	YYY 3*
○ Moscato d'Asti Casa di Bianca '18	YYY 3*
● Barbera d'Asti Sup. Genio '17	YY 4
● Grignolino d'Asti '18	YY 2*
○ Moscato d'Asti '18	YY 3*
○ Moscato d'Asti '17	YY 4
● Nizza '16	YY 6
● Nizza V. V. '17	YY 5

Dosio

REG. SERRADENARI, 6
12064 LA MORRA [CN]
TEL. +39 017350677
www.dosiovigneti.com

CELLAR SALES
PRE-BOOKED VISITS
ACCOMMODATION
ANNUAL PRODUCTION 65,000 bottles
HECTARES UNDER VINE 11.00

The winery, founded in 1974 by the skilled and tireless Beppe Dosio, underwent considerable changes over the years due to the arrival of its new owners, the Lenci family, and consequent organizational changes. Their range is characterized both by a precise observance of classical expression, which is the case with most of their wines, foremost Barolo, and innovative selections marked by the prominence of oak, as with the Langhe Nebbiolo Barilà and Dolcetto d'Alba Nassone. The innovative Eventi is made with Merlot. Theirs is a range that goes all in on technical polish and pleasantness of flavor. It's led by the Barolo Fossati '15 a wine rich in fruit, clean and delicate, with gentle tannins and discreet freshness. Just a little more youthful, and with foregrounded aromas of oak, the Serradenari '16 comes through weighty, austere on the palate. Aromas of cinchona and a mouthfilling alcohol characterize the structured, 'basic' Barolo, while the Barbera d'Alba Superiore '17 proves highly pleasant in its notes of red berries and sweet oak.

Wine	Rating	Price
● Barbera d'Alba Sup. '17	🍷🍷	4
● Barolo '16	🍷🍷	6
● Barolo Fossati '15	🍷🍷	7
● Barolo Serradenari '16	🍷🍷	7
● Dolcetto d'Alba Sup. Nassone '18	🍷🍷	3
⊙ Per Ti Rosato '19	🍷🍷	3
● Dolcetto d'Alba '19	🍷	3
● Barolo Fossati '13	🍷🍷 (white)	7
● Barolo Fossati Ris. '12	🍷🍷 (white)	8
● Barolo Fossati Ris. '11	🍷🍷 (white)	8
● Barolo Serradenari '15	🍷🍷 (white)	7
● Barolo Serradenari '13	🍷🍷 (white)	6
● Barolo Serradenari '12	🍷🍷 (white)	6
● Langhe Momenti '16	🍷🍷 (white)	5
● Langhe Nebbiolo Barilà '15	🍷🍷 (white)	5

★Poderi Luigi Einaudi

LOC. CASCINA TECC
B.TA GOMBE, 31/32
12063 DOGLIANI [CN]
TEL. +39 017370191
www.poderieinaudi.com

CELLAR SALES
PRE-BOOKED VISITS
ACCOMMODATION
ANNUAL PRODUCTION 350,000 bottles
HECTARES UNDER VINE 60.00
SUSTAINABLE WINERY

Founded in 1897, the winery's gift for Barolo has grown consistently since it first began producing the wine in 1958. Credit goes to major investments both in new prestigious vineyards, from Cannubi to Monvigliero, and in the cellar, where the spaces and the barrel stock have undergone renovations. But we shouldn't forget their Dogliani Vigna Tecc either, a wine that's a true flagship for the appellation and deserves to be known by all enophiles. Today Poderi Luigi Einaudi is firmly in the hands of Matteo Sardagna Einaudi, who's supported by a qualified team and expert consultants like Beppe Caviola and Gian Piero Romana. The Cannubi cru doesn't betray its well-deserved fame: the 2016 vintage's fresh, lively grapes made for a harmonious structure and soft tannins, unfolding rich and elegant in the mouth. The pleasant Ludo '16, made with grapes from the Bussia, Cannubi and Terlo vineyards, is just a bit more austere. Lovely aromas of red berries and toasty notes feature in the Bussia '16, blackberries and cocoa in the enchanting Dogliani Superiore Tecc '18, a soft, succulent wine.

Wine	Rating	Price
● Barolo Cannubi '16	🍷🍷🍷	8
● Barolo Bussia '16	🍷🍷	8
● Dogliani Sup. Tecc '18	🍷🍷	4
● Barolo Ludo '16	🍷🍷	6
● Barolo Terlo V. Costa Grimaldi '16	🍷🍷	7
● Dogliani '19	🍷	3
● Langhe Barbera '17	🍷	3
● Langhe Nebbiolo '19	🍷	4
● Barolo Cannubi '15	🍷🍷🍷 (white)	8
● Barolo Cannubi '11	🍷🍷🍷 (white)	8
● Barolo Cannubi '10	🍷🍷🍷 (white)	8
● Barolo Costa Grimaldi '05	🍷🍷🍷 (white)	8
● Barolo Costa Grimaldi '01	🍷🍷🍷 (white)	7
● Barolo nei Cannubi '00	🍷🍷🍷 (white)	8
● Dogliani Sup. V. Tecc '10	🍷🍷🍷 (white)	3*
● Dogliani V. Tecc '06	🍷🍷🍷 (white)	4
● Langhe Rosso Luigi Einaudi '04	🍷🍷🍷 (white)	5

F.lli Facchino

loc. Val del Prato, 210
15078 Rocca Grimalda [AL]
Tel. +39 014385401
www.vinifacchino.it

CELLAR SALES
PRE-BOOKED VISITS
RESTAURANT SERVICE
ANNUAL PRODUCTION 80,000 bottles
HECTARES UNDER VINE 31.00

The Facchino brothers' winery is located in Val del Prato, a hilly area with picturesque views near the medieval village of Rocca Grimalda, situated not far from Ovada. Today Giorgio and Diego represent the second generation of family to oversee management. Having come of age in an exemplary wine-growing tradition, they've proven to have the right skills to lead the producer towards a bright future. At the heart of their range we find a series of native regional grapes, presented with elegance and attention to detail, thanks to the moderate use of oak. The two Ovadas are expertly crafted. The Poggiobello, youthful and brilliant, is characterized by pronounced fruit and a harmonious, lingering palate. Carasöi behaves like an older brother, steady and serious, with more complex aromas, a powerful palate and nicely calibrated tannins. The Terre del Re has great potential, but we'll only know who it really is with more time in the bottle. We also recommend the Albarossa and the basic Dolcetto.

Wine	Rating
● Barbera del M.to Terre del Re '17	▼▼ 3
● Dolcetto di Ovada '18	▼▼ 2*
● Ovada Carasöi '17	▼▼ 3
● Ovada Poggiobello '17	▼▼ 3
● Piemonte Albarossa Note d'Autunno '16	▼▼ 3
● Barbera del M.to '19	▼ 2
○ Cortese dell'Alto M.to Pacialan '19	▼ 2
● Barbera del M.to '16	▽▽▽ 2*
● Barbera del M.to '18	▽▽ 2*
● Barbera del M.to Terre del Re '15	▽▽ 2*
○ Cortese dell'Alto M.to Pacialan '16	▽▽ 2*
● Dolcetto di Ovada '17	▽▽ 2*
● Dolcetto di Ovada '16	▽▽ 2*
● Dolcetto di Ovada Poggiobello '16	▽▽ 2*
● Dolcetto di Ovada Poggiobello '15	▽▽ 2*
● Ovada Carasöi '15	▽▽ 3

Tenuta Il Falchetto

fraz. Ciombi
via Valle Tinella, 16
12058 Santo Stefano Belbo [CN]
Tel. +39 0141840344
www.ilfalchetto.com

CELLAR SALES
PRE-BOOKED VISITS
ANNUAL PRODUCTION 280,000 bottles
HECTARES UNDER VINE 50.00

Bricco Paradiso, Lovetta, Lurei, Pian Scorrone, Vigna del Ciabot in Agliano Terme, Vigneto del Fant in Calosso, Marini and Il Falchetto in Santo Stefano Belbo. A veritable dream team of estates and vineyards, situated in Cuneo and Asti, serves as the viticultural foundation for the Forno family's production venture. They're all areas renowned for both Barbera and Moscato, though we shouldn't forget the results achieved of late with Chardonnay, Dolcetto, Cabernet Sauvignon, Merlot, Pinot Nero. Once again, the Moscato d'Asti Canelli Ciombo '19 is among the best in the appellation. Fresh, fine and long, it's characterized by great harmony, classic in its notes of white fruit and sage, with nuances of candied fruit and chlorophyll. The Barbera d'Asti Superiore Lürei '17 is also outstanding, unveiling complex aromas of cocoa, tobacco and black berries, and a powerful, flavorful palate, with tight-knit tannins and lovely acidity. We also appreciated the elegant, assertive, berry-scented Piedmont Pinot Noir Solo '17.

Wine	Rating
● Barbera d'Asti Sup. Lurei '17	▼▼ 3*
○ Moscato d'Asti Canelli Ciombo '19	▼▼ 2*
● Piemonte Pinot Nero Solo '17	▼▼ 4
● Barbera d'Asti Pian Scorrone '19	▼▼ 2*
● Barbera d'Asti Sup. Bricco Paradiso '17	▼▼ 4
○ Moscato d'Asti Canelli Tenuta del Fant '19	▼▼ 2*
● Nizza Bricco Roche Ris. '16	▼▼ 6
○ Moscato d'Asti Canelli Ciombo '17	▽▽▽ 2*
● Barbera d'Asti Pian Scorrone '17	▽▽ 2*
● Barbera d'Asti Sup. Bricco Paradiso '16	▽▽ 4
○ Moscato d'Asti Canelli Ciombo '18	▽▽ 2*
○ Moscato d'Asti Canelli Tenuta del Fant '17	▽▽ 2*
○ Moscato d'Asti Tenuta del Fant '18	▽▽ 2*
○ Piemonte Sauvignon Pian Craie '18	▽▽ 3*

Benito Favaro

S.DA CHIUSURE, 1BIS
10010 PIVERONE [TO]
TEL. +39 012572606
www.cantinafavaro.it

CELLAR SALES
PRE-BOOKED VISITS
ANNUAL PRODUCTION 20,000 bottles
HECTARES UNDER VINE 3.50
VITICULTURE METHOD Certified Organic

Benito and Camillo Favaro's winery, which is about to turn twenty, is situated in the area from which their most important wine, Erbaluce di Caluso Le Chiusure, takes its name (more than 8,000 bottles are produced annually). Their other selection, called 13 Mesi because aging is longer than usual for the area, is also highly notable. Camillo is doing an outstanding job demonstrating that Erbaluce, a wine that's naturally endowed with strong acidity, acquires roundness on the palate and aromatic complexity thanks to long maturation, which mainly involve steel together with concrete and a light touch of wood. As elegant as it is rich, the Erbaluce di Caluso Le Chiusure '18 benefited nicely from the long period of maturation in the cellar, proving variegated on the nose with fine notes of herbs and wax. On the palate shows substance, with excellent freshness and an exquisite note of almond on the finish. The 13 Mesi is equally complex but at the moment a little less well orchestrated. Red berries feature in the powerful, pleasant Rossomeraviglia '18.

Wine	Rating
○ Erbaluce di Caluso Le Chiusure '18	YY 3*
○ Erbaluce di Caluso 13 Mesi '18	YY 4
● Rossomeraviglia '18	YY 5
○ Erbaluce di Caluso 13 Mesi '17	YYY 4*
○ Erbaluce di Caluso 13 Mesi '16	YYY 3*
○ Erbaluce di Caluso Le Chiusure '16	YYY 2*
○ Erbaluce di Caluso Le Chiusure '13	YYY 2*
○ Erbaluce di Caluso Le Chiusure '12	YYY 2*
○ Erbaluce di Caluso Le Chiusure '11	YYY 2*
○ Erbaluce di Caluso Le Chiusure '10	YYY 2*
○ Erbaluce di Caluso 13 Mesi '15	YY 3*
○ Erbaluce di Caluso Le Chiusure '17	YY 3*
○ Erbaluce di Caluso Le Chiusure '15	YY 2*
● Rossomeraviglia '17	YY 5
● Rossomeraviglia '16	YY 5
● Rossomeraviglia '15	YY 5

Giacomo Fenocchio

LOC. BUSSIA, 72
12065 MONFORTE D'ALBA [CN]
TEL. +39 017378675
www.giacomofenocchio.com

CELLAR SALES
PRE-BOOKED VISITS
ACCOMMODATION
ANNUAL PRODUCTION 95,000 bottles
HECTARES UNDER VINE 16.00
SUSTAINABLE WINERY

Claudio Fenocchio's attitude towards Barolo is apparently simple. In fact, he humbly declares that he adheres to classical tradition, starting with long maceration of the skins and aging in large Slavonian oak barrels. But tasting his Barolos one can grasp a stylistic precision that's a clear indication of a refined sensitivity. Indeed over the years, it's earned the winery a well-deserved reputation. Its heart beats in the Bussia vineyards in Monforte d'Alba, but the crus of Castiglione Falletto (Villero) and Barolo (Cannubi) are also of great importance. Only 2016 Barolos were submitted for tasting. The classic Bussia exhibits proportion and harmony: characteristic notes of red berries and a hint of rose stand out in its lovely, clean aromatic suite, while the palate features exquisite balance, with a long acidic backbone that makes for gratifying drinkability. Notes closer to sweet tobacco and oak mark the Cannubi, a wine that shows an unexpected power and a certain tannicity in the mouth. The weighty Villero is just a bit more vegetal.

Wine	Rating
● Barolo Bussia '16	YY 6
● Barolo Cannubi '16	YY 7
● Barolo Castellero '16	YY 6
● Barolo Villero '16	YY 7
● Barolo Bussia '11	YYY 6
● Barolo Bussia '09	YYY 6
● Barolo Bussia 90 Dì Ris. '12	YYY 8
● Barolo Bussia 90 Dì Ris. '10	YYY 8
● Barolo Bussia 90 Dì Ris. '13	YY 8
● Barolo Cannubi '15	YY 7
● Barolo Castellero '15	YY 6
● Barolo Villero '15	YY 7

Ferrando

via Torino, 599
10015 Ivrea [TO]
Tel. +39 0125633550
www.ferrandovini.it

CELLAR SALES
PRE-BOOKED VISITS
ANNUAL PRODUCTION 50,000 bottles
HECTARES UNDER VINE 5.00

Today Andrea and Roberto Ferrando are leading this praiseworthy winery. Bolstered by a history of five generations of family, it's one of Canavese's most important producers. Two Carema are made with grapes cultivated on just two hectares planted exclusively with Nebbiolo. They differ only in that the elegant Etichetta Nera is consistently a bit rounder and more powerful, while the Etichetta Bianca is more approachable and smooth. It's a similar story with their Erbaluce di Caluso: the Cariola is more long-lived and structured, the La Torrazza just a bit less rich. Their range also includes a Metodo Classico Pas Dosé and a sumptuous Passito. Elegant notes of bottled cherries feature in the valid Carema Etichetta Nera '16, all accompanied by a lovely touch of toasted oak; on the palate it exhibits notable vitality, with soft tannins that build an already commendable gustatory grace. The Etichetta Bianca '16 is decidedly youthful and fruity, also rich in aromatic herbs. Notable olfactory finesse characterizes the Erbaluce di Caluso Cariola '19.

- ● Carema Et. Nera '16 🍷🍷 7
- ● Carema Et. Bianca '16 🍷🍷 5
- ○ Erbaluce di Caluso Cariola '19 🍷🍷 3
- ○ Erbaluce di Caluso Pas Dosé M. Cl. '13 🍷🍷 5
- ○ Erbaluce di Caluso La Torrazza '19 🍷 3
- ● Carema Et. Bianca '12 YYY 5
- ● Carema Et. Nera '11 YYY 7
- ● Carema Et. Nera '09 YYY 6
- ● Carema Et. Nera '08 YYY 6
- ● Carema Et. Nera '07 YYY 6
- ● Carema Et. Nera '06 YYY 6
- ● Carema Et. Nera '05 YYY 6
- ● Carema Et. Nera '01 YYY 5
- ● Carema Et. Nera '15 YY 7
- ● Carema Et. Nera '13 YY 7
- ○ Erbaluce di Caluso Cariola '18 YY 3*
- ○ Erbaluce di Caluso La Torrazza '17 YY 3*

Luca Ferraris

loc. Rivi, 7
s.da prov.le 14
14030 Castagnole Monferrato [AT]
Tel. +39 0141292202
www.ferrarisagricola.it

CELLAR SALES
PRE-BOOKED VISITS
ANNUAL PRODUCTION 220,000 bottles
HECTARES UNDER VINE 21.00
SUSTAINABLE WINERY

It was 1999 when Luca Ferraris decided to put the business founded in the 1920s by his great-grandmother Teresa back on track. One of the first to focus heavily on the potential of Ruchè di Castagnole Monferrato, the project has grown gradually over time, thanks in part to a collaboration with Californian Randall Grahm. The range offers four stylistically differentiated versions of Ruchè (Clàsic, Sant'Eufemia, Vigna del Parroco and Opera Prima per il Fondatore), alongside Barbera, Grignolino, Viognier and Chardonnay. Luca Ferraris presented two versions of Ruché di Castagnole Monferrato this year. Between the two, the Clàsic '19 won us over with its rich, fruity aromas, elegant notes of rose on the nose and a palate of considerable volume, soft, but also long, balanced and properly aromatic. The Barbera d'Asti Superiore Ca' Mongross Viti Centenarie '17 is also excellent, standing out for its black fruit sensations, hints of rain-soaked earth, tobacco and cinchona-quinine, the prelude to a close-woven, rich and velvety palate.

- ● Ruchè di Castagnole M.to Clàsic '19 🍷🍷🍷 3*
- ● Barbera d'Asti Sup. Ca' Mongross Viti Centenarie '17 🍷🍷 4
- ● Ruchè di Castagnole M.to Sant'Eufemia '19 🍷🍷 3
- ○ Pimonte Viognier Sensazioni '19 🍷 3
- ● Ruchè di Castagnole M.to Clàsic '18 YY 2*
- ● Ruchè di Castagnole M.to Clàsic '17 YY 2*
- ● Ruchè di Castagnole M.to Sant'Eufemia '18 YY 3
- ● Ruchè di Castagnole M.to Sant'Eufemia '17 YY 3
- ● Ruchè di Castagnole M.to V. del Parroco '18 YY 3*

Roberto Ferraris

REG. DOGLIANO, 33
14041 AGLIANO TERME [AT]
TEL. +39 0141954234
www.robertoferraris.com

CELLAR SALES
PRE-BOOKED VISITS
ANNUAL PRODUCTION 70,000 bottles
HECTARES UNDER VINE 12.00
SUSTAINABLE WINERY

The producer led by Roberto Ferraris, and situated in Agliano Terme, is dedicated entirely to Monferrato Astigiano's traditional reds. The property's vineyards are characterized by limey-calcareous soils with little clay, making it extremely well suited to the cultivation of Grignolino, Nebbiolo and Barbera, naturally, which comes in five different versions. Their wines are differentiated according to the type of vinification and maturation. Only stainless steel is used for the I Suôrí and Nobbio, small oak barrels for the Bisavolo and La Cricca, and 18 months of French oak for the Nizza Liberta (from the vineyard of the same name in Castelnuovo Calcea). Their selection of Barberas is outstanding, in particular the Barbera d'Asti Superiore Bisavolo '18, which sees notes of ripe red berries, pencil lead and tobacco followed by a pervasive, rich palate, perfectly balanced by acidity. We also appreciated the Barbera d'Asti I Suôrí '18, a fresh and harmonious wine, energetic in its fresh notes of cherry and plum, with a long, juicy finish.

- Barbera d'Asti I Suôrì '18 — 2 red glasses 2*
- Barbera d'Asti Sup. Bisavolo '18 — 2 red glasses 3*
- Barbera d'Asti Nobbio '18 — 2 red glasses 3
- Barbera d'Asti Sup. La Cricca '18 — 2 red glasses 4
- Nizza Liberta '17 — 2 red glasses 5
- Nizza Liberta '15 — 3 glasses 5
- Barbera d'Asti Nobbio '17 — 2 glasses 3
- Barbera d'Asti Nobbio '16 — 2 glasses 3*
- Barbera d'Asti Sup. Bisavolo '17 — 2 glasses 3*
- Barbera d'Asti Sup. Bisavolo '16 — 2 glasses 3
- Barbera d'Asti Sup. Bisavolo '15 — 2 glasses 4
- Barbera d'Asti Sup. La Cricca '17 — 2 glasses 4
- Barbera d'Asti Sup. La Cricca '16 — 2 glasses 4
- Barbera d'Asti Sup. La Cricca '15 — 2 glasses 5
- Barbera d'Asti Sup. La Cricca '13 — 2 glasses 3*
- Nizza Liberta '16 — 2 glasses 5

Carlo Ferro

FRAZ. SALERE, 41
14041 AGLIANO TERME [AT]
TEL. +39 3282818967
www.ferrovini.com

CELLAR SALES
PRE-BOOKED VISITS
ANNUAL PRODUCTION 15,000 bottles
HECTARES UNDER VINE 12.00

Barbera, Dolcetto, Grignolino, Nebbiolo and a few rows of Cabernet Sauvignon: only red grapes are grown in the Ferro family's vineyards, situated around 300 meters elevation on the slopes of Agliano Terme (a bridge between Langhe and Monferrato) and managed according to principles of sustainable agriculture. Launched over a century ago, it's now one of the most solid producers in the area, thanks to a range that's traditionally styled, though certainly not dated, and that's managed to shine particularly bright in recent years. Once again the range of wines presented proves to be reliable and well made. The Barbera d'Asti Giulia '18 offers up notes of black olives, rosemary and cherry, while the palate proves compact, dense, balanced by a marked acidity that lends considerable length. The Barbera d'Asti Superiore Notturno '17 is more austere, but also of lovely pulp and character, while the Nizza La Corazziera '17 is still marked by aromas of wood, but rich in fruit, with considerable volume.

- Barbera d'Asti Giulia '18 — 2 red glasses 2*
- Barbera d'Asti Sup. Notturno '17 — 2 red glasses 3
- Nizza La Carrozziera '17 — 2 red glasses 4
- M.to Rosso Paolo '16 — 1 red glass 4
- Barbera d'Asti Giulia '16 — 2 glasses 2*
- Barbera d'Asti Giulia '15 — 2 glasses 2*
- Barbera d'Asti Sup. Notturno '16 — 2 glasses 3
- Barbera d'Asti Sup. Notturno '15 — 2 glasses 2*
- Barbera d'Asti Sup. Notturno '15 — 2 glasses 3*
- Barbera d'Asti Sup. Notturno '14 — 2 glasses 3
- Barbera d'Asti Sup. Roche '16 — 2 glasses 4
- Barbera d'Asti Sup. Roche '13 — 2 glasses 3
- M.to Rosso Paolo '13 — 2 glasses 4
- Nizza La Carrozziera '16 — 2 glasses 4
- Nizza La Corazziera '15 — 2 glasses 4

Fontanafredda

LOC. FONTANAFREDDA
VIA ALBA, 15
12050 SERRALUNGA D'ALBA [CN]
TEL. +39 0173626111
www.fontanafredda.it

CELLAR SALES
PRE-BOOKED VISITS
ACCOMMODATION AND RESTAURANT SERVICE
ANNUAL PRODUCTION 8,500,000 bottles
HECTARES UNDER VINE 100.00
VITICULTURE METHOD Certified Organic
SUSTAINABLE WINERY

This striking estate became famous in 1858, when it was purchased by King Vittorio Emanuele II. Since then it has always been an important benchmark for all of Barolo. It's enough to think that at the end of WW I 200 people lived and worked in this splendid village. Since 2009, when the entire complex was purchased by the Farinetti family, production has gained great momentum, especially in terms of quality, and today Fontanafredda, together with its sister Casa di E.Mirafiore, offers a range of quality wines. Finesse and complexity characterize the Barolo Fontanafredda Vigna La Rosa '16, a wine born in what is probably their estate's loveliest plot: red berries and tobacco emerge along with a hint of citrus fruit, while the palate proves beautifully structured, gentle without being too soft, long, clear and focused. The well-made Alta Langa Brut Nature Vigna Gatinera '11 is crisp but not sharp, with delicate notes of yeast—a wine that's sure to charm.

● Barolo Fontanafredda V. La Rosa '16	🍷🍷 8
○ Alta Langa Brut Nature V. Gatinera '11	🍷🍷 6
● Barolo Fontanafredda Proprietà in Fontanafredda '16	🍷🍷 8
● Barolo Silver '16	🍷🍷 8
○ Langhe Riesling Marin '18	🍷🍷 4
○ Roero Arneis Val di Tana '19	🍷🍷 3
● Barolo del Comune di Serralunga d'Alba '16	🍷 7
○ Roero Arneis Pradalupo '19	🍷 3
● Barolo Fontanafredda V. La Rosa '07	🍷🍷🍷 7
● Barolo Lazzarito V. La Delizia '04	🍷🍷🍷 8
● Barolo Lazzarito V. La Delizia '01	🍷🍷🍷 7
● Barolo V. La Rosa '04	🍷🍷🍷 7
● Barolo V. La Rosa '00	🍷🍷🍷 7

Fortemasso

LOC. CASTELLETTO, 21
12065 MONFORTE D'ALBA [CN]
TEL. +39 0173328148
www.fortemasso.it

CELLAR SALES
ANNUAL PRODUCTION 27,000 bottles
HECTARES UNDER VINE 5.20

The Agricole Gussalli Beretta group immediately focused on quality and, in less than 10 years, it's managed to earn its Langhe winery a place among Barolo's most renowned producers. Credit goes to targeted investments that began with the decision to make an important vineyard of Nebbiolo in the Castelletto cru available to its local consultants. A characteristic feature of this plot is that it combines the classic power of Monforte d'Alba Barolo with a remarkable freshness of taste, tje result of the grapes' natural acidity, which guarantees an enticing drinkability. We appreciated the lovely Barolo Castelletto '16. Its initial impact on the nose moves on notes of raspberry and tobacco, making for nice finesse and complexity; then comes a background of mint supported by nice alcohol; powerful, rich and very long, a discreet sensation of freshness emerges along with a slight diluting of alcohol. Fresh rose petals and a wisp of wet earth characterize the balanced and enjoyable Langhe Nebbiolo '19.

● Barolo Castelletto '16	🍷🍷🍷 6
● Langhe Nebbiolo '19	🍷🍷 3
● Barbera d'Alba '18	🍷 3
● Barolo Castelletto Ris. '13	🍷🍷🍷 8
● Barbera d'Alba '17	🍷🍷 3
● Barbera d'Alba '16	🍷🍷 3
● Barbera d'Alba '15	🍷🍷 3
● Barolo Castelletto '15	🍷🍷 6
● Barolo Castelletto '14	🍷🍷 6
● Barolo Castelletto '13	🍷🍷 6
● Langhe Nebbiolo '17	🍷🍷 3
● Langhe Nebbiolo '16	🍷🍷 3

Davide Fregonese

VIA RODDINO, 10/1
12050 SERRALUNGA D'ALBA [CN]
TEL. +39 3409643637
www.davidefregonese.com

ANNUAL PRODUCTION 5,000 bottles
HECTARES UNDER VINE 1.00

First finance, then wine. Not only to drink it (as he has always done), but above all to make it. This is biography of Davide Fregonese, one of Langa's most recent arrivals. A hectare is divided between two crus, Cerretta and Prapò, making for two Barolos plus a Langhe Rosso made in Serralunga d'Alba. There's no tradition here, only a great passion for excellent wine, foremost Piedmontese and French. A friendship with Davide Rosso (of Giovanni Rosso) turned his dream into a business, and the two are now collaborators. They're also working together on a project on Mt. Etna. Their range is limited, but the quality is outstanding, with two contiguous, yet very different, crus. The Prapò '16 offers up complex aromas of licorice and tobacco, enriched by a clear vein of raspberries, while the palate reveals a finesse in its tannic texture that's unexpected for such a powerful wine. The Cerretta is just a bit less harmonious.

Wine	Rating
● Barolo Prapò '16	TT 7
● Barolo Cerretta '16	TT 7
● Barolo Cerretta '15	YY 7
● Barolo Prapò '15	YY 7

La Fusina

FRAZ. SANTA LUCIA, 33
12063 DOGLIANI [CN]
TEL. +39 017370488
www.lafusina.com

CELLAR SALES
PRE-BOOKED VISITS
ANNUAL PRODUCTION 80,000 bottles
HECTARES UNDER VINE 20.00
SUSTAINABLE WINERY

For more than a century the Abbona family have been cultivating their splendid property in Santa Lucia, a place we recommend that all wine tourists visit. Over time, the vineyards have gradually expanded, as testified to by their Barolo and Alta Langa, but the productive heart continues to beat for Dolcetto, and for the Dogliani DOCG they produce. The winery is now run by Massimo, who's decided to avail himself of a collaboration with talented enological consultants (in part in light of further expansion). The Dogliani Superiore San Luigi Cavagné '18 moves from red berries to almond sensations by way of elegant vegetal notes. In the mouth it has good pulp and tannins that are just a bit punchy. The Santa Lucia '19 is even more complex and decisive—it will continue to grow for years in the bottle. The well-made Barolo Perno '16 is particularly delicate, pleasantly spicy and smooth on the palate. The pleasant Chardonnay '19 is also worth tasting, rich in acacia flowers and mineral hints.

Wine	Rating
● Barolo Perno '16	TT 6
● Dogliani Santa Lucia '19	TT 4
● Dogliani Sup. Luigi Cavagnè '18	TT 3
○ Langhe Chardonnay '19	TT 2*
● Langhe Nebbiolo '19	TT 3
○ Alta Langa Pas Dosé '16	T 5
● Barbera d'Alba Sup. La Castella '18	T 4
○ Alta Langa Extra Brut '16	YY 5
● Barbera d'Alba '18	YY 3
● Barbera d'Alba '17	YY 3
● Barbera d'Alba '16	YY 3
● Barolo '14	YY 5
● Barolo Perno '15	YY 6
● Dogliani Gombe '17	YY 2*
● Dogliani Gombe '16	YY 2*
● Dogliani Sup. Cavagnè '16	YY 3

Gaggino

S.DA SANT'EVASIO, 29
15076 OVADA [AL]
TEL. +39 0143822345
www.gaggino.it

PRE-BOOKED VISITS
ACCOMMODATION
ANNUAL PRODUCTION 150,000 bottles
HECTARES UNDER VINE 70.00
SUSTAINABLE WINERY

Over the years the name Gaggino has become increasingly associated with Dolcetto di Ovada, thanks to the invaluable work done by a winery that has always believed strongly in the variety and territory. Today Dolcetto, which is sometimes mistreated by the market (abroad and nationally), once again represents a wonderful territory, a fact that has brought to light its deep historical roots. Their range also includes masterful interpretations of Barbera del Monferrato, complete with a selection of expertly-crafted entry-level wines, serving as further proof of the good, quality work being done here. This year saw a superb performance for Gaggino's prized selections. The Convivio once again made an appearance in the finals with its classy olfactory suite and fruit that lengthens an already-persistent palate. The Ticco is vibrant on the nose, with exquisite tertiary aromas of jam preceding a powerful, fresh palate. Both the Barbera Lazzarina and the Dolcetto di Ovada 19 are commendably crafted.

● Ovada Convivio '18	🍷🍷🍷 3*
● Barbera del M.to Sup. Ticco '17	🍷🍷 4
● Barbera del M.to La Lazzarina '19	🍷🍷 2*
● Dolcetto di Ovada Sedìci '19	🍷🍷 2*
○ Gavi '19	🍷🍷 3
⊙ Piemonte Rosato Sedìci Rosé '19	🍷 2
● Ovada Convivio '17	🍸🍸🍸 3*
● Ovada Convivio '16	🍸🍸🍸 3*
● Ovada Convivio '13	🍸🍸🍸 2*
● Barbera del M.to La Lazzarina '18	🍸🍸 2*
● Barbera del M.to La Lazzarina '16	🍸🍸 2*
● Barbera del M.to Ticco '16	🍸🍸 4
● Dolcetto di Ovada '17	🍸🍸 2*
● Dolcetto di Ovada '16	🍸🍸 2*
● Dolcetto di Ovada Sedìci '18	🍸🍸 2*
● Ovada Convivio '15	🍸🍸 3*
● Piemonte Rosso Passito '17	🍸🍸 3

Poderi Gianni Gagliardo

FRAZ. SANTA MARIA
B.GO SERRA DEI TURCHI, 88
12064 LA MORRA [CN]
TEL. +39 017350829
www.gagliardo.it

CELLAR SALES
PRE-BOOKED VISITS
ANNUAL PRODUCTION 180,000 bottles
HECTARES UNDER VINE 25.00

The name Gianni Gagliardo has only appeared on their bottles since 1986, but the producer's winemaking history began as early as the mid-19th century, with properties in Monferrato, Roero and Langhe. A tireless promoter of Barolo on both sides of the ocean, their philosophy is now firmly focused on a style of absolute classicism, carefully selecting their grapes and drawing on long aging in large wood barrels. The result is some 8 different types of increasingly-successful Barolo. Red and black berries feature in the complex aromas of the Barolo Lazzarito Vigna Preve '16, giving way to a full-bodied palate, where dense and close-knit tannins are well harmonized with rich, fruity pulp. The less powerful Barolo Mosconi '16 is fresh and elegant, easy and deliciously drinkable. The Fossati '16 is just a bit austere, with scents of cinchona and sunny herbs accompanying a dynamic palate. The pleasant Barolo del comune di La Morra '16 is down-to-earth and approachable.

● Barolo Lazzarito V. Preve '16	🍷🍷 8
● Barbera d'Asti Tenuta Garetto '18	🍷🍷 3
● Barolo del Comune di La Morra '16	🍷🍷 7
● Barolo Fossati '16	🍷🍷 7
● Barolo Mosconi '16	🍷🍷 7
● Nebbiolo d'Alba Sup. San Ponzio '17	🍷🍷 5
● Barolo Castelletto '16	🍷 7
● Barolo Monvigliero '16	🍷 7
● Roero Arneis '19	🍷 2
● Barolo '10	🍸🍸 5
● Barolo '08	🍸🍸 5
● Barolo Cannubi '08	🍸🍸 8
● Barolo Preve '07	🍸🍸 8
● Barolo Serre '10	🍸🍸 8
● Barolo Serre '09	🍸🍸 8
● Barolo Preve Ris. '06	🍸 8

★★★★★Gaja

via Torino, 18
12050 Barbaresco [CN]
Tel. +39 0173635158
info@gaja.com

ANNUAL PRODUCTION 350,000 bottles
HECTARES UNDER VINE 92.00

His father Giovanni's teachings were well received and now, with the same charisma and determination, he's transmitting that knowledge to his children (Gaia, Rosanna and Giovanni): ideas, strategies, wine culture, but above all love and respect for the territory. Angelo Gaja needs no introduction—his winery is a model in Piedmont, in Italy, and abroad. The range produced is, today more than ever, a true distillation of Langa, despite the fact that its qualities are universally recognized and respected. Two prized selections, the Sperss and Sorì Tildin, captain a top-notch line-up. Between the two, the Barolo, bolstered by the (great) 2016 vintage, won out. The complexity of its nose is stunning, but in the mouth it's even more fascinating: superb balance, with vigor making the wine come alive while tannins lend rhythm to a palate that seems to never end. The Sorì Tildin is more immediately expressive, pervasive and creamy, incredible for its flavor and freshness. The 2017 San Lorenzo and Barbaresco are also first rate.

Wine	Glasses	Price
● Barolo Sperss '16	▼▼▼	8
● Barbaresco '17	▼▼	8
● Barbaresco San Lorenzo '17	▼▼	8
● Barbaresco Sorì Tildin '17	▼▼	8
● Barbaresco Costa Russi '17	▼▼	8
● Barbaresco '09	▽▽▽	8
● Barbaresco '08	▽▽▽	8
● Barbaresco Costa Russi '13	▽▽▽	8
● Barbaresco Sorì Tildin '16	▽▽▽	8
● Barbaresco Sorì Tildin '15	▽▽▽	8
● Barbaresco Sorì Tildin '14	▽▽▽	8
● Langhe Nebbiolo Costa Russi '10	▽▽▽	8
● Langhe Nebbiolo Costa Russi '08	▽▽▽	8
● Langhe Nebbiolo Costa Russi '07	▽▽▽	8
● Langhe Nebbiolo Sorì Tildin '11	▽▽▽	8
● Langhe Nebbiolo Sperss '11	▽▽▽	8

Filippo Gallino

fraz. Valle del Pozzo, 63
12043 Canale [CN]
Tel. +39 017398112
www.filippogallino.com

CELLAR SALES
PRE-BOOKED VISITS
ACCOMMODATION
ANNUAL PRODUCTION 100,000 bottles
HECTARES UNDER VINE 14.00
SUSTAINABLE WINERY

An important historical figure for Roero's wine, Filippo Gallino is now joined at the helm by his children Laura and Gianni. The vineyards are all situated in the municipality of Canale, mainly around the winery headquarters, on sandy and clayey soils, while production centers on the territory's grapes (Arneis, Barbera, Brachetto and Nebbiolo). In the vineyard a traditional management style has been adopted, while and in the cellar the approach is modern, making for wines that are pleasant, rich in fruit and notably territorial. Filippo Gallino's wines are always reliable. This year we particularly appreciated the Barbera d'Alba '18, vibrant on the nose with its aromas of red berries and sweet spices, and a consistent, rich palate, still a bit marked by oak, but with nice sapidity and a long, pleasant finish. Other very well made selections include the taut and juicy Langhe Nebbiolo Licin '18, with its balsamic whiffs and notes of Mediterranean scrub, all accompanied by nuances of red berries, and the Roero Arneis '19, a fresh, supple and citrusy wine.

Wine	Glasses	Price
● Barbera d'Alba '18	▼▼	2*
● Langhe Nebbiolo Licin '18	▼▼	3
○ Moda Veja	▼▼	4
○ Roero Arneis '19	▼▼	2*
● Langhe Nebbiolo '18	▼	2
○ Roero Arneis 4 Luglio '18	▼	4
● Barbera d'Alba Sup. '05	▽▽▽	4*
● Barbera d'Alba Sup. '04	▽▽▽	4*
● Roero '06	▽▽▽	4*
● Roero Sup. '03	▽▽▽	3
● Roero Sup. '01	▽▽▽	5
● Roero Sup. '99	▽▽▽	5
● Barbera d'Alba '17	▽▽	2*
○ Roero Arneis 4 Luglio '16	▽▽	3
● Roero Sorano Ris. '15	▽▽	5

Garesio

LOC. SORDO, 1
12050 SERRALUNGA D'ALBA [CN]
TEL. +39 3667076775
www.garesiovini.it

CELLAR SALES
PRE-BOOKED VISITS
ANNUAL PRODUCTION 85,000 bottles
HECTARES UNDER VINE 25.00
VITICULTURE METHOD Certified Organic

In just ten years of activity the Garesio family have brought home important results. They work on a dual track. On the one hand there's Asti, and Barbera grapes, which give rise to two Nizzas. Then there's Langa and Serralunga d'Alba: different versions of Barolo are produced here, including the prestigious Cerretta cru. The style of winemaking involves rather long maceration and the use of medium-large, French and Austrian oak barrels. The Nizza Riserva '16 earned a place in our finals. Notes of quinine and rain-soaked earth embellish dark, ripe fruit; in the mouth it's weighty, with great structure that's well balanced by acidity. The Nizza '17 is more light-bodied, a well-balanced wine overall. Waiting for next year's release of the Cerretta '16, we saw a solid performance from the Barolo Giannetto, with its clear strokes of flowers and spices, its fleshy and sapid palate. A final note of merit for the elegant and airy Langhe Nebbiolo '18.

● Nizza Ris. '16	🍷🍷 5
● Barolo del Comune di Serralunga d'Alba '16	🍷🍷 6
● Barolo Gianetto '16	🍷🍷 6
● Langhe Nebbiolo '18	🍷🍷 4
○ M.to Bianco Resilio '19	🍷🍷 3
● Nizza '17	🍷🍷 4
● Barbera d'Asti Sup. Sage '18	🍷 3
● Barolo Cerretta '15	🍷🍷🍷 7
● Barolo del Comune di Serralunga d'Alba '15	🍷🍷 5
● Barolo del Comune di Serralunga d'Alba '14	🍷🍷 5
● Langhe Nebbiolo '16	🍷🍷 3
● Nizza '16	🍷🍷 4
● Nizza '15	🍷🍷 4

Cantine Garrone

VIA SCAPACCINO, 36
28845 DOMODOSSOLA [VB]
TEL. +39 0324242990
www.cantinegarrone.it

CELLAR SALES
PRE-BOOKED VISITS
ACCOMMODATION
ANNUAL PRODUCTION 50,000 bottles
HECTARES UNDER VINE 10.00

The Garrone family's winery has reached the century mark. Over this time it's operated in various capacities: as bottlers of wines purchased outside the area, as wine merchants and, finally, as producers of their own grapes, mainly Nebbiolo, which is grown on their small property. In addition to these vineyards, there are those that fall under the Association of Ossola Agricultural Producers. Their ageing cellar is located in a structure that dates back to the 14th century in Oira di Crevoladossola, where you'll also find their charming B&B (which we recommend to wine tourists for a number of reasons, including the beautiful landscape). This year the Nebbiolo Superiore Prünent Diecibrente '16 stood out. Airy and complex, it's endowed with a rare harmony, thanks to supple tannins and beautiful, fruity pulp. The Prünent '17 alternates wild strawberries with iodine and licorice in a combination of fine elegance. The Cà d'Maté '17, made with Nebbiolo and Croatina, is still a bit muted but has lovely structure.

● Valli Ossolane Nebbiolo Sup. Prünent '17	🍷🍷 5
● Valli Ossolane Nebbiolo Sup. Prünent Diecibrente '16	🍷🍷 6
● Valli Ossolane Rosso Cà d'Maté '17	🍷🍷 4
● Valli Ossolane Rosso Tarlap '18	🍷🍷 3
○ Valli Ossolane Bianco La Gera '19	🍷 4
● Valli Ossane Rosso Cà d'Maté '13	🍷🍷 3
● Valli Ossane Rosso Cà d'Maté '11	🍷🍷 3
● Valli Ossolane Nebbiolo Sup. Prünent '16	🍷🍷 5
● Valli Ossolane Nebbiolo Sup. Prünent '12	🍷🍷 4
● Valli Ossolane Nebbiolo Sup. Prünent '11	🍷🍷 4
● Valli Ossolane Nebbiolo Sup. Prünent Diecibrente '15	🍷🍷 6
● Valli Ossolane Rosso Cà d'Maté '16	🍷🍷 4
● Valli Ossolane Rosso Tarlàp '13	🍷🍷 2*
● Valli Ossolane Rosso Tarlàp '12	🍷🍷 2*

Gaudio - Bricco Mondalino

C.NE REG. MONDALINO, 5
15049 VIGNALE MONFERRATO [AL]
TEL. +39 0142933204
www.gaudiovini.it

CELLAR SALES
PRE-BOOKED VISITS
ANNUAL PRODUCTION 100,000 bottles
HECTARES UNDER VINE 19.50
SUSTAINABLE WINERY

The Gaudio Family's vineyards are divided up among the municipalities of Vignale, Camagna and Casorzo. Barbera, Grignolino, Freisa, Cortese, and Malvasia are all cultivated, but international grapes are represented in the form of two plots of Merlot and Syrah. The heart of production centers on native grapes, which are offered in different versions: matured in steel and oak (mostly small, barriques and tonneaux). Among the producer's best selections, we must certainly include their Malvasia di Casorzo, usually one of the most notable in the area, and the Grignolino Metodo Classico Margot (which spends 36 months on the lees). The Zerolegno uplifted us with its nice, crisp fruit on aromas of black berries, all made more complex by light, smoky notes. It's rich and intense on the palate, with an energetic, long finish. The Grignolino, Gaudio is characterized by great typicity, with floral aromas on notes of pepper and tobacco. In the mouth it's balanced and vibrant, with austere though characterful tannins. The other wines tasted are also well made.

● Barbera d'Asti Zerolegno '18	🍷🍷 4
● Grignolino del M.to Casalese Gaudio '19	🍷🍷 3*
● Barbera d'Asti Il Bergantino '17	🍷🍷 4
● Barbera del M.to Sup. '17	🍷🍷 2*
● Grignolino del M.to Casalese Monte della Sala '17	🍷 4
● Barbera d'Asti Zerolegno '17	ΥΥ 4
● Barbera del M.to Sup. '16	ΥΥ 2*
● Barbera del M.to Sup. '15	ΥΥ 2*
● Grignolino del M.to Casalese '17	ΥΥ 3
● Grignolino del M.to Casalese Bricco Mondalino '17	ΥΥ 3
● Grignolino del M.to Casalese Bricco Mondalino '13	ΥΥ 2*
● Grignolino del M.to Casalese Monte della Sala '13	ΥΥ 4

Generaj

B.TA TUCCI, 4
12046 MONTÀ [CN]
TEL. +39 0173976142
www.generaj.it

CELLAR SALES
PRE-BOOKED VISITS
ANNUAL PRODUCTION 50,000 bottles
HECTARES UNDER VINE 12.00
SUSTAINABLE WINERY

Giuseppe Viglione runs the family winery founded in 1947. The vineyards of Generaj are situated in the northernmost part of Roero on various soils, ranging from sandy to more calcareous terrain and mixed gravel, at elevations spanning 350-450 meters. In keeping with Arneis tradition, Barbera and Nebbiolo are the main grapes grown. The result is a modern style that exhibits nice freshness and richness of fruit, expressing the best of what the territory has to offer. Giuseppe Viglione's wines put in an excellent performance, starting with the Roero Bric Aût Riserva '16 with its aromas of black berries, Asian spices and quinine; in the mouth it's juicy, complex and pleasant, with a fine tannic texture. The Roero Bric Aût '17 is fresh and approachable with flowery hints accompanied by red berries, the Roero Arneis Bric Varomaldo '19 sapid and fruity, while the Barbera d'Alba Superiore Ca' d' Pistola '17 is classic in its whiffs of undergrowth. We also appreciated the Pas Dosé 60 Mesi Metodo Classico '13, full and rich in fruit.

● Roero Bric Aût Ris. '16	🍷🍷 5
● Barbera d'Alba Sup. Cà d' Pistola '17	🍷🍷 3
○ Generaj Pas Dosè 60 Mesi M. Cl. '13	🍷🍷 5
○ Roero Arneis Bric Varomaldo '19	🍷🍷 2*
● Roero Bric Aût '17	🍷🍷 4
○ Roero Arneis Quindicilune Ris. '18	🍷 3
○ Generaj Brut M. Cl. '15	ΥΥ 5
○ Roero Arneis Bric Varomaldo '18	ΥΥ 2*
○ Roero Arneis Bric Varomaldo '17	ΥΥ 2*
○ Roero Arneis Quindicilune Ris. '17	ΥΥ 3
● Roero Bric Aût '16	ΥΥ 4
● Roero Bric Aût Ris. '15	ΥΥ 5
● Roero Bric Aût Ris. '14	ΥΥ 5

★Ettore Germano

LOC. CERRETTA, 1
12050 SERRALUNGA D'ALBA [CN]
TEL. +39 0173613528
www.ettoregermano.com

CELLAR SALES
PRE-BOOKED VISITS
ACCOMMODATION
ANNUAL PRODUCTION 140,000 bottles
HECTARES UNDER VINE 20.00
SUSTAINABLE WINERY

We can finally let tourists know that Sergio Germano's new cellar is at their disposal, complete with a welcoming tasting room. The space has been structured to serve the winery's three identities: reds foremost, then still whites, finally their Metodo Classico bubbly. In all cases Sergio, who took over the helm in 1993, has proven to be a true master. The power and classicism of his Barolo is splendid, his Riesling Hérzu a perennial champion, and his Alta Langa are always exemplary. Unembellished but rich, bolstered by one of Barolo's most famous terroirs, the Vignarionda '15 proves a gem of fruit accented by broad sweet spices, while the palate comes through austere, licorice-scented, without overdoing it in terms of structure. The delicately balsamic Cerretta '16 is also sophisticated, coming through long across a well-orchestrated palate. The Barbera d'Alba Superiore della Madre is one of 2017's best. And their whites continue to stand out, with the Alta Langa Brut proving taut, fresh and sapid, while the Hérzu is finely mineral.

Wine	Rating
● Barolo Cerretta '16	🍷🍷 7
● Barolo Lazzarito Ris. '14	🍷🍷 8
● Barolo Vignarionda '15	🍷🍷 8
○ Langhe Riesling Hérzu '18	🍷🍷 5
○ Alta Langa Extra Brut '16	🍷🍷 5
● Barbera d'Alba Sup. V. della Madre '17	🍷🍷 5
● Barolo del Comune di Serralunga d'Alba '16	🍷🍷 6
● Barolo Prapò '16	🍷🍷 8
● Langhe Nebbiolo '19	🍷🍷 3
● Rosanna Nebbiolo Extra Brut M. Cl. Rosé	🍷🍷 5
● Barolo Lazzarito Ris. '13	🍷🍷🍷 (empty) 8
● Barolo Lazzarito Ris. '12	🍷🍷🍷 (empty) 8
● Barolo Lazzarito Ris. '11	🍷🍷🍷 (empty) 8

La Ghibellina

FRAZ. MONTEROTONDO, 61
15066 GAVI [AL]
TEL. +39 0143686257
www.laghibellina.it

CELLAR SALES
PRE-BOOKED VISITS
RESTAURANT SERVICE
ANNUAL PRODUCTION 60,000 bottles
HECTARES UNDER VINE 17.00

Twenty years after its founding, La Ghibellina is proving to be a modern producer, well integrated in the Monterotondo wine scene. Production is focused mainly on Cortese, which gives rise to two characterful still wines and two Metodo Classicos, with different maturation times on the lees. They also offer a rosé made with Barbera and two reds, the Pituj and Nero del Montone, monovarietal Barberas. Their range is characterized by an elegant, modern style. The Gavi Altius has character and personality, intense in its aromas of citrus peel and tropical fruit, it enters powerful and dense in the mouth; on the finish it reveals an intriguing tannic note, only to continue long and sapid. The Mainìn is vibrant on the nose with aromas of lime and apple on a mineral background. On the palate, nice pulp comes to the fore on a fresh, sapid finish. The other wines tasted are also well made.

Wine	Rating
○ Gavi del Comune di Gavi Altius '18	🍷🍷 5
○ Gavi del Comune di Gavi Mainìn '19	🍷🍷 3
○ Gavi del Comune di Gavi Brut M. Cl.	🍷 4
● M.to Rosso Pituj '18	🍷 4
⊙ Piemonte Rosato Sandrino '19	🍷 2
○ Gavi del Comune di Gavi Altius '16	🍷🍷 (empty) 5
○ Gavi del Comune di Gavi Altius '14	🍷🍷 (empty) 5
○ Gavi del Comune di Gavi Brut M. Cl. Cuvée Marina '12	🍷🍷 (empty) 5
○ Gavi del Comune di Gavi Brut M. Cl. Cuvée Marina '11	🍷🍷 (empty) 7
○ Gavi del Comune di Gavi Mainìn '18	🍷🍷 (empty) 3*
○ Gavi del Comune di Gavi Mainìn '17	🍷🍷 (empty) 3*
○ Gavi del Comune di Gavi Mainìn '16	🍷🍷 (empty) 3*
○ Gavi del Comune di Gavi Mainìn '15	🍷🍷 (empty) 3*
○ Gavi del Comune di Gavi Mainìn '14	🍷🍷 (empty) 3*
● M.to Rosso Pituj '17	🍷🍷 (empty) 4

★★Bruno Giacosa

via XX Settembre, 52
12052 Neive [CN]
Tel. +39 017367027
www.brunogiacosa.it

ANNUAL PRODUCTION 300,000 bottles
HECTARES UNDER VINE 20.00
SUSTAINABLE WINERY

Bruno Giacosa told us that, in the course of his 50 vintages, he's never wanted to make great changes to the style of his wines. Yet due to phytosanitary treatments, he was forced to make slow and continuous modifications dictated by grapes that slowly weakened over the years. And so it is that he gradually reduced the maceration time, which in his early days could be up to 100 days, and adopted large French oak barrels, which he found a little softer and kinder than Slavonian oak. This is how his Barolo and Barbaresco reserves, two wines of international renown, came to be. Bright and sophisticated in its rich aromas, the Barolo Falletto Vigna Le Rocche Riserva '14 proves fresh in the mouth, of a rare harmony, with mature tannins only enriching its delicious, fruity pulp. The Barbaresco Rabajà '16 is spectacular on the nose, with violets, roots and licorice blending into a true symphony, while the palate is as powerful as it is silky, making for a bewitching drinkability.

● Barolo Falletto V. Le Rocche Ris. '14	🍷🍷🍷 8
● Barbaresco Asili '17	🍷🍷 8
● Barbaresco Rabajà '16	🍷🍷 8
● Barolo Falletto '16	🍷🍷 8
○ Roero Arneis '19	🍷 4
● Barbaresco Asili '05	YYY 8
● Barbaresco Asili Ris. '07	YYY 8
● Barbaresco Asili Ris. '04	YYY 8
● Barbaresco Rabajà Ris. '01	YYY 8
● Barbaresco Santo Stefano '83	YYY
● Barolo Falletto '07	YYY 8
● Barolo Falletto '04	YYY 8
● Barolo Falletto '01	YYY 8
● Barolo Le Rocche del Falletto '05	YYY 8
● Barolo Le Rocche del Falletto '04	YYY 8
● Barolo Le Rocche del Falletto Ris. '01	YYY 8

Carlo Giacosa

s.da Ovello, 9
12050 Barbaresco [CN]
Tel. +39 0173635116
www.carlogiacosa.it

CELLAR SALES
PRE-BOOKED VISITS
ANNUAL PRODUCTION 42,000 bottles
HECTARES UNDER VINE 5.50
SUSTAINABLE WINERY

There are only eight hectares of vineyards in the Montefico cru and only six wineries bear it on their label. Nevertheless, it's a famous name among Barbaresco enthusiasts, as for generations its Nebbiolo has been considered among the most elegant in the area. It's here that Maria Grazia Giacosa, a convinced supporter of traditional aging methods, gets the grapes for the wine that's made her small winery famous. A blend of grapes from three different vineyards gives rise to the Riserva di Barbaresco Luca, another notable selection. There are 9 wines in all, each characterized by pleasant fruity scents and accessible prices. Raspberry, licorice and golden-leaf tobacco mark the traditional and elegant Barbaresco Luca Riserva '15, a complex, long wine, velvety on the palate and just enriched by tannins. Notes of herbs in the sun and sweet oak characterize the Montefico '17, the result of a particularly hot vintage, which limited its acidity.

● Barbaresco Luca Ris. '15	🍷🍷 7
● Barbaresco Montefico '17	🍷🍷 6
● Langhe Nebbiolo Maria Grazia '18	🍷 4
● Langhe Pinot Nero '18	🍷 5
● Barbaresco Montefico '15	YYY 6
● Barbaresco Montefico '08	YYY 5*
● Barbaresco Luca Ris. '14	YY 7
● Barbaresco Montefico '16	YY 6
● Barbaresco Narin '16	YY 6
● Barbaresco Narin '15	YY 5
● Barbera d'Alba Mucin '16	YY 3
● Barbera d'Alba Sup. Lina '17	YY 3
● Barbera d'Alba Sup. Lina '16	YY 4
● Langhe Nebbiolo Maria Grazia '17	YY 4

Giovanni Battista Gillardi

Cascina Corsaletto, 69
12060 Farigliano [CN]
Tel. +39 017376306
www.gillardi.it

CELLAR SALES
PRE-BOOKED VISITS
ANNUAL PRODUCTION 50,000 bottles
HECTARES UNDER VINE 9.00

Walking with Giacolino in the steep amphitheatre of Dolcetto grapevines in summer takes us back several years, when we used to do this walk with his father, Giovanni Battista, a great interpreter of the cultivar. And it really is strange how little has changed. It's only a little warmer than it was then and many vines are much more developed and knotty due to their age. The plots here give rise to two classically-styled Dogliani marked by enjoyable drinkability, the slimmer and suppler Maestra and the slightly denser and weightier Cursalet, both of which should be tried three or four years from bottling. And meanwhile in Barolo their new operation is growing. Several wines, including the famous Dogliani Maestra and the Langhe Harys, were still in the vat or barrel at the time of our tasting, so the scorecard below is smaller than usual. The small Vignane cru, situated in front of the famous Cannubi looking towards Monforte, gave rise to a Barolo '16 with nice personality, in which hints of rain-soaked earth, sweet oak and red fruit blend. The palate is already round and enticing.

Wine	Rating
● Barolo Vignane '16	🍷🍷 6
● Dogliani Cursalet '19	🍷🍷 3*
● Dogliani Maestra '19	🍷🍷 3*
● Barolo '16	🍷🍷 6
● Langhe Nebbiolo '18	🍷🍷 4
● Barolo '15	YY 6
● Barolo '14	YY 6
● Barolo del Comune di Barolo '13	YY 4
● Barolo Vignane '15	YY 6
● Barolo Vignane '13	YY 6
● Dogliani Cursalet '18	YY 3
● Dogliani Cursalet '17	YY 3*
● Dogliani Cursalet '16	YY 3*
● Dogliani Maestra '18	YY 3
● Dogliani Maestra '17	YY 3
● Langhe Harys '17	YY 7
● Langhe Nebbiolo '17	YY 4

La Gironda

s.da Bricco, 12
14049 Nizza Monferrato [AT]
Tel. +39 0141701013
www.lagironda.com

CELLAR SALES
PRE-BOOKED VISITS
ANNUAL PRODUCTION 60,000 bottles
HECTARES UNDER VINE 9.00
SUSTAINABLE WINERY

The producer managed by Susanna Galandrino together with her husband, Alberto Adamo, is one of the most notable in Asti. Founded by her father, Agostino, in the early 2000s, they've always drawn inspiration from principles of sustainability. Two outstanding sites for cultivating Barbera, Bricco di Nizza and Chiesavecchia di Calamandrana, are interpreted with a contemporary style, but their range is enriched with selections from Sauvignon, Moscato, Brachetto, Cabernet Sauvignon and Nebbiolo, not to mention Metodo Classico made with Chardonnay and Pinot Nero. The Nizza Le Nicchie '17 features aromas of plum and cherry, accompanied by cocoa and licorice, while the palate proves rich in fruit, well supported by a fine acidity, making for a long, harmonious finish. It's on par with the Nizza Riserva Ago '15, characterized by notes of quinine, greater structure and austerity—it's a compact, plucky wine. The other wines tasted are also well made, in particular the fresh and pleasant Moscato d'Asti.

Wine	Rating
● Nizza Ago Ris. '15	🍷🍷 7
● Nizza Le Nicchie '17	🍷🍷 5
● Barbera d'Asti La Lippa '19	🍷🍷 3
○ Galandrino Brut M. Cl. '15	🍷🍷 5
○ Moscato d'Asti '19	🍷🍷 3
● Barbera d'Asti Sup. Nizza Le Nicchie '11	YYY 5
● Barbera d'Asti La Gena '16	YY 3
● Barbera d'Asti La Gena '15	YY 3*
● Barbera d'Asti La Lippa '16	YY 2*
● Barbera d'Asti Sup. La Gena '17	YY 3*
○ Galandrino Brut M. Cl. '14	YY 3
● M.to Rosso Chiesavecchia '16	YY 4
● M.to Rosso Soul '15	YY 5
○ Moscato d'Asti '17	YY 2*
● Nizza Le Nicchie '16	YY 5
● Nizza Le Nicchie '15	YY 5

Tenuta La Giustiniana

FRAZ. ROVERETO, 5
15066 GAVI [AL]
TEL. +39 0143682132
www.lagiustiniana.it

CELLAR SALES
PRE-BOOKED VISITS
ANNUAL PRODUCTION 200,000 bottles
HECTARES UNDER VINE 39.00

La Giustiniana has played an important role in the history of Gavi. The Giustiniani family bought what was a 13th-century Benedictine agricultural property, where wine was already being produced, and transformed it into a splendid neoclassical estate. All this took place in the early 17th century. Over time changes of ownership have never interrupted the viticultural work done here, lending prestige to Rovereto, one of the most area's most notable districts for the quality of its grapes. Their selection includes three Gavis, one basic version and two crus, Lugarara and Montessora. The Montessora opens with elegant notes of chamomile on citrus peel and a mineral background. On the palate it's full-bodied and vibrant, with acidity accentuating a sapid, very long finish. The Lugarara is elegant and intense, with herbaceous hints on a mineral background. The gustatory phase reveals excellent structure for body and freshness, with a sapid, persistent finish that's still evolving.

- ○ Gavi del Comune di Gavi Montessora '19 🍷🍷 4
- ○ Gavi del Comune di Gavi Lugarara '19 🍷🍷 3
- ○ Gavi del Comune di Gavi Il Nostro Gavi '12 YY 4
- ○ Gavi del Comune di Gavi Lugarara '18 YY 3*
- ○ Gavi del Comune di Gavi Lugarara '17 YY 3
- ○ Gavi del Comune di Gavi Lugarara '16 YY 3*
- ○ Gavi del Comune di Gavi Lugarara '15 YY 3
- ○ Gavi del Comune di Gavi Montessora '18 YY 4
- ○ Gavi del Comune di Gavi Montessora '17 YY 4
- ○ Gavi del Comune di Gavi Montessora '16 YY 4
- ○ Gavi del Comune di Gavi Montessora '15 YY 4

★★Elio Grasso

LOC. GINESTRA, 40
12065 MONFORTE D'ALBA [CN]
TEL. +39 017378491
www.eliograsso.it

PRE-BOOKED VISITS
ANNUAL PRODUCTION 90,000 bottles
HECTARES UNDER VINE 18.00
SUSTAINABLE WINERY

The Grasso family's winery enjoys one of the most beautiful views of the vineyards of Langhe. In fact there are views both of the unique Ginestra di Monforte district and of Serralunga d'Alba's series of famous crus. Entering the cellar we discover the large, underground space where both the barrels for maturation and the bottles for aging rest. Elio Grasso started in 1978 and proved a skilled forerunner of the Barolo revolution that would unfold a few years later. His son Gianluca has proven capable of expressing elegance and finesse in his selections, starting with the careful cultivation of the grapes. The Barolo Ginestra Casa Maté '16 is certainly destined for a long and favorable evolution, considering that it's already powerful and harmonious, complex and long. The nose is characterized by liquorice and sweet oak sensations, the palate by pervasive structure and an elegant finish on golden-leaf tobacco. The Gavarini Chiniera '16 moves on a similar track, offering up lovely red berry aromas and quinine.

- ● Barbera d'Alba V. Martina '17 🍷🍷 5
- ● Barolo Gavarini Chiniera '16 🍷🍷 8
- ● Barolo Ginestra Casa Maté '16 🍷🍷 8
- ● Barolo Rüncot Ris. '13 🍷🍷 8
- ● Barolo Gavarini Chiniera '09 YYY 8
- ● Barolo Gavarini V. Chiniera '06 YYY 8
- ● Barolo Gavarini V. Chiniera '01 YYY 7
- ● Barolo Gavarini V. Chiniera '00 YYY 7
- ● Barolo Ginestra Casa Maté '15 YYY 8
- ● Barolo Ginestra Casa Maté '12 YYY 8
- ● Barolo Ginestra Casa Maté '07 YYY 8
- ● Barolo Ginestra V. Casa Maté '05 YYY 8
- ● Barolo Ginestra V. Casa Maté '04 YYY 8
- ● Barolo Ginestra V. Casa Maté '03 YYY 7
- ● Barolo Rüncot '01 YYY 8
- ● Barolo Rüncot '00 YYY 8
- ● Barolo Rüncot '99 YYY 8

Silvio Grasso

fraz. Annunziata, 112
12064 La Morra [CN]
Tel. +39 3355273168
www.silviograsso.com

CELLAR SALES
PRE-BOOKED VISITS
ANNUAL PRODUCTION 80,000 bottles
HECTARES UNDER VINE 14.00

In addition to their basic version, the Grasso family produces some five Barolos named after the respective crus in which the grapes are grown, demonstrating their attention to the specific characteristics and personality of each individual vineyard. Their production style is decidedly modern, with persuasive hints of the French barriques used serving as the olfactory backdrop early on (with the sole exception of the Barolo Turné, for which traditional winemaking and ageing principles are applied). Theirs is an entirely interesting range based on elegance rather than power, with the Barolo Bricco Luciani earning the most accolades. Two very different 2016 Barolos take center stage. The Bricco Manzoni is modern and elegant, with a fine blend of liquorice, sweet oak and fresh fruit followed by a pulpy palate that's already pleasantly harmonious. On the other hand we find the steady, traditional style of the Turné, a wine wrought of spicy aromas and sensations of undergrowth, the prelude to a well-structured palate. The Bricco Luciani '16 is still marked by oak.

● Barolo Bricco Manzoni '16	🍷🍷 8
● Barolo Turnè '16	🍷🍷 7
● Barolo Annunziata V. Plicotti '16	🍷🍷 7
● Barolo Il Contadino Ris. '13	🍷🍷 6
● Barolo '16	🍷 5
● Barolo Bricco Luciani '16	🍷 7
● Barolo Giachini '16	🍷 6
● Barolo Bricco Luciani '04	🍷🍷🍷 7
● Barolo Bricco Luciani '01	🍷🍷🍷 6
● Barolo Bricco Luciani '96	🍷🍷🍷 6
● Barolo Bricco Luciani '95	🍷🍷🍷 6
● Barolo Bricco Luciani '90	🍷🍷🍷 6
● Barolo Bricco Manzoni '10	🍷🍷🍷 7
● Barolo Bricco Luciani '97	🍷🍷

Bruna Grimaldi

via Parea, 7
12060 Grinzane Cavour [CN]
Tel. +39 0173262094
www.grimaldibruna.it

CELLAR SALES
PRE-BOOKED VISITS
ANNUAL PRODUCTION 70,000 bottles
HECTARES UNDER VINE 15.00
VITICULTURE METHOD Certified Organic

The Badarina cru comprises almost 20 hectares of Nebbiolo cultivated at over 400 meters elevation in close contact with Serralunga d'Alba's other famous vineyards. This is the production heart of the winery owned by Bruna Grimaldi and her husband, Franco Fiorino, which her son Simone works at with passion today. And it's here that the grapes for their Barolo are cultivated. It's a wine that combines the area's characteristic power with a stimulating burst of freshness that lends drinkability. From the less famous but increasingly appreciated Bricco Ambrogio in Roddi, at an average elevation of 250 meters, comes a less structured but elegant Barolo. In the aromas of the Barolo Badarina '16, tobacco and licorice combine with a pleasant touch of mint; the palate has an imposing structure in which acidity and tannins integrate nicely with its fruity pulp, and an elegant finish. The Bricco Ambrogio '16 is more subtly expressed and vegetal, while the Barolo Camilla '16 is still slightly aggressive.

● Barolo Badarina '16	🍷🍷 6
● Barbera d'Alba Sup. Scassa '17	🍷🍷 3
● Barolo Bricco Ambrogio '16	🍷🍷 6
● Barolo Camilla '16	🍷🍷 5
● Dolcetto d'Alba San Martino '19	🍷🍷 2*
● Nebbiolo d'Alba Bonurei '18	🍷🍷 4
○ Langhe Arneis '19	🍷 2
● Barbera d'Alba Sup. Scassa '16	🍷🍷 3*
● Barbera d'Alba Sup. Scassa '15	🍷🍷 3
● Barolo Badarina '15	🍷🍷 6
● Barolo Badarina '14	🍷🍷 6
● Barolo Bricco Ambrogio '15	🍷🍷 6
● Barolo Bricco Ambrogio '14	🍷🍷 5
● Barolo Camilla '15	🍷🍷 5
● Dolcetto d'Alba '17	🍷🍷 2*
○ Langhe Arneis '18	🍷🍷 2*
● Nebbiolo d'Alba '16	🍷🍷 3

Fratelli Grimaldi

loc. San Grato, 15
12058 Santo Stefano Belbo [CN]
Tel. +39 0141840341
www.fratelligrimaldi.it

CELLAR SALES
PRE-BOOKED VISITS
ANNUAL PRODUCTION 100,000 bottles
HECTARES UNDER VINE 18.00
SUSTAINABLE WINERY

Literally 'The Mayor's House', Ca' du Sindic is the historic name of the Grimaldi family's farmstead. Sergio decided to revive it in the late 1980s with the help of his parents, Ilario and Vittorina. Supported today by his wife, Angela, together with their children Paolo and Ilaria, he oversees a first-rate set of vineyards, which embody the potential of the hills of Santo Stefano Belbo. The plots of San Grato, San Maurizio and Moncucco serve as the core of an original range grounded in Brachetto, Barbera, Dolcetto, Pinot Nero and Moscato. The Moscato d'Asti Canelli Vigna Moncucco is always of excellent quality. The 2019 vintage is all about freshness, with a nice balance between sweetness and acidity on the palate and a long, pleasant finish. The Moscato d'Asti Vigna San Maurizio '19 is also excellent. We appreciated the way it perfectly balances sweetness and acidity, even if it lacks just a bit of structure and length.

Wine	Rating
○ Moscato d'Asti V. Moncucco '19	▼▼ 3*
○ Moscato d'Asti V. San Maurizio '19	▼▼ 3
○ Moscato d'Asti Capsula Argento '19	▼ 3
⊙ Ventuno Brut Rosé '18	▼ 3
○ Alta Langa Brut '15	YY 4
● Barbera d'Asti San Grato '15	YY 2*
● Barbera d'Asti SanGrato '17	YY 2*
○ Moscato d'Asti Ca' du Sindic '18	YY 3*
○ Moscato d'Asti Ca' du Sindic '17	YY 3
○ Moscato d'Asti Ca' du Sindic Capsula Oro '16	YY 3
○ Moscato d'Asti Capsula Argento '16	YY 3
○ Moscato d'Asti V. Moncucco '18	YY 3
○ Moscato d'Asti V. Moncucco '17	YY 3*
○ Moscato d'Asti V. Moncucco '16	YY 3*
○ Moscato d'Asti V. Moncucco '15	YY 3*
○ Ventuno Brut '14	YY 3

Giacomo Grimaldi

via Luigi Einaudi, 8
12060 Barolo [CN]
Tel. +39 0173560536
www.giacomogrimaldi.com

CELLAR SALES
PRE-BOOKED VISITS
ANNUAL PRODUCTION 50,000 bottles
HECTARES UNDER VINE 13.00

Young Alberto Grimaldi can't wait to try his hand at vinifying and aging Barolo, so he's studying enology and gaining experience with his capable father, Ferruccio. The winery is geared to Nebbiolo, which is cultivated in vineyards located on both sides of the Tanaro river. On the left is the famous and impervious Valmaggiore vineyard, which gives rise to their always elegant Nebbiolo d'Alba. The Le Coste cru is located in the immediate vicinity of the winery, with very old vines resulting in a perennially harmonious and enticing Barolo. The Barolo Sotto Castello di Novello is a little more vivacious and tannic. In fact, with the 2016 vintage, it's fruity and tarry, with tannins that are still punchy, prolonging a palate of nice structure and finesse. In the absence of the Le Coste '16, the Ravera proves well-balanced, full-bodied and graceful: it's a Barolo of great elegance. Beautiful personality even features in the 'basic' 2016, a wine that's measured in its body but endowed with elegant licorice.

Wine	Rating
● Barolo Ravera '16	▼▼ 7
● Barolo '16	▼▼ 7
● Barolo Sotto Castello di Novello '16	▼▼ 6
● Nebbiolo d'Alba V. Valmaggiore '18	▼ 4
● Barolo Sotto Castello di Novello '05	YYY 6
● Barolo '13	YY 6
● Barolo '12	YY 6
● Barolo Le Coste '15	YY 7
● Barolo Le Coste '14	YY 7
● Barolo Le Coste '13	YY 7
● Barolo Le Coste '12	YY 7
● Barolo Sotto Castello di Novello '15	YY 6
● Barolo Sotto Castello di Novello '14	YY 6
● Barolo Sotto Castello di Novello '13	YY 6
● Barolo Sotto Castello di Novello '12	YY 6
● Nebbiolo d'Alba V. Valmaggiore '17	YY 4
○ Roero Arneis '18	YY 2*

★Hilberg - Pasquero

via Bricco Gatti, 16
12040 Priocca [CN]
Tel. +39 0173616197
www.hilberg-pasquero.com

CELLAR SALES
PRE-BOOKED VISITS
ANNUAL PRODUCTION 23,000 bottles
HECTARES UNDER VINE 8.00
VITICULTURE METHOD Certified Organic

One of Roero's historical producers, Miclo Pasquero and Annette Hilberg's winery offers exclusively red wines made with the area's traditional grapes: Barbera, Brachetto and Nebbiolo. Their vineyards are located all around the winery, on Bricco Gatti, just above Priocca, on loamy and marly soils, and in Monteforche and Bricco Stella. Their range of balanced and well-structured wines are the result of a combination of traditional viticulture and the careful use of oak in the cellar. This year's Nebbiolo d'Alba '17 stands out among an expertly-crafted selection. Vibrant on the nose, it offers up mint, aromatic herbs and cocoa sensations, coming through austere but long, full and fleshy on the palate. The Barbera d'Alba sulla Stella '19 features aromas of black cherry, quinine and sweet oak, while the palate is dense and powerful, but fresh and juicy as well, with a finish that's nicely supported by acidity. The Nebbiolo d'Alba sul Monte '18 features raspberry and licorice whiffs, while in the mouth it's harmonious, characterized by tannins of beautiful finesse.

Wine	Rating
● Nebbiolo d'Alba '17	▼▼ 6
● Barbera d'Alba Sulla Stella '19	▼▼ 5
● Nebbiolo d'Alba Sul Monte '18	▼▼ 6
● Vareij '19	▼▼ 4
● Barbera d'Alba Sup. '17	▼ 6
● Barbera d'Alba '18	▽▽ 3*
● Barbera d'Alba Stella '17	▽▽ 3*
● Barbera d'Alba Sup. '16	▽▽ 5
● Nebbiolo d'Alba '16	▽▽ 5
● Nebbiolo d'Alba Sul Monte '17	▽▽ 5
● Nebbiolo d'Alba Sul Monte '16	▽▽ 5
● Nebbiolo d'Alba Sup. '15	▽▽ 5
● Vareij '18	▽▽ 3
● Vareij '17	▽▽ 3

Ioppa

fraz. Mauletta
via delle Pallotte, 10
28078 Romagnano Sesia [NO]
Tel. +39 0163833079
www.viniioppa.it

CELLAR SALES
PRE-BOOKED VISITS
ANNUAL PRODUCTION 140,000 bottles
HECTARES UNDER VINE 20.50

Generation after generation, here it's been a continuous process of modernization and expansion, which means that today the Ioppa family are managing a rather sizable winery for the area. Their passion is for the Nebbiolo grape, obviously, which they are skilled at growing and transforming into wine. Indeed, both their Ghemme and the Colline Novaresi Nebbiolo are exquisitely crafted, not to mention the enticing highly drinkable rosé. Their approach to vinification is classic, with rather long fermentation and the prevalence of Slavonian oak for aging. They did an extraordinary job interpreting the 2015 vintage, as evidenced by some 4 wines. The sophisticated Ghemme Santa Fé opens with aromas of tobacco, liquorice and gentian, only to unfold with delicate tannins on the palate. The more youthful and fruitier Balsina exhibits notable structure and a lively freshness, while the commendable 'basic' Ghemme is just a little more vivacious and forthright. The spunky Vespolina Mauletta offers up plenty of spiciness on the nose.

Wine	Rating
● Colline Novaresi Vespolina Mauletta '15	▼▼ 3*
● Ghemme Balsina '15	▼▼ 6
● Ghemme Santa Fé '15	▼▼ 6
● Ghemme '15	▼▼ 4
● Colline Novaresi Nebbiolo '19	▼ 3
⊙ Colline Novaresi Nebbiolo Rusin '19	▼ 2
○ San Grato Bianco	▼ 2
● Ghemme Balsina '13	▽▽▽ 6
● Ghemme '11	▽▽ 4
● Ghemme '07	▽▽ 4
● Ghemme Bricco Balsina '08	▽▽ 6
● Ghemme Bricco Balsina '07	▽▽ 4
● Ghemme Santa Fè '07	▽▽ 6
● Ghemme Santa Fè '06	▽▽ 6

Isolabella della Croce

Loc. Saracchi
Regione Caffi, 3
14051 Loazzolo [AT]
Tel. +39 014487166
www.isolabelladellacroce.it

CELLAR SALES
PRE-BOOKED VISITS
ANNUAL PRODUCTION 90,000 bottles
HECTARES UNDER VINE 14.00

The Isolabella della Croce family founded the producer in 2001, in the Loazzolo appellation, in 'Langa Astigiana'. The vineyards grow in calcareous-marly soils at about 500 meters above sea level, in an area with a particularly cool climate, thanks in part to large wooded areas. The main vines cultivated are Moscato, Chardonnay and Pinot Nero. Barbera, on the other hand, is cultivated on an estate in Calamandrana, in Nizza. Their wines are of a modern style. The Piemonte Pinot Nero Bricco del Falco put in yet another splendid performance. The 2016 version offers up notes of fresh red fruit, dried herbs and licorice, while the palate comes through rich but elegant, with a dense tannic texture and a long finish. The Nizza Augusta '16 is excellent, with its aromas of blackberry and coffee, it's got great concentration and just as much acidity. The Piedmont Chardonnay Solum '18 also delivered, with its fragrances of acacia flowers and white fruit, it's both elegant and complex.

Wine	Rating
● Piemonte Pinot Nero Bricco del Falco '16	▼▼▼ 5
● Nizza Augusta '16	▼▼ 4
○ Piemonte Chardonnay Solum '18	▼▼ 4
● Barbera d'Asti Sup. Serena '17	▼▼ 4
○ Moscato d'Asti Canelli Valdiserre '19	▼▼ 3
○ Piemonte Sauvignon '19	▼▼ 3
● Nizza Augusta '14	▽▽▽ 4*
● Piemonte Pinot Nero Bricco del Falco '15	▽▽▽ 5
● Nizza Augusta '15	▽▽ 4
○ Piemonte Chardonnay Solum '17	▽▽ 4
● Piemonte Pinot Nero Bricco del Falco '14	▽▽ 5
● Piemonte Pinot Nero Bricco del Falco '13	▽▽ 5

Tenuta Langasco

Fraz. Madonna di Como, 10
12051 Alba [CN]
Tel. +39 0173286972
www.tenutalangasco.it

CELLAR SALES
PRE-BOOKED VISITS
ANNUAL PRODUCTION 60,000 bottles
HECTARES UNDER VINE 22.00

The Sacco family have been running this estate since 1979. Situated in a favorable position on a hill overlooking the towers of Alba, it offers evocative views of the surrounding landscape. Claudio's range of wines is wide and reliable, ranging from Langhe Arneis to Nebbiolo d'Alba, Moscato d'Asti and Dolcetto Madonna di Como (of which a cru is also produced, the Vigna Miclet), as well as an interesting Langhe Favorita and Brachetto. In short, plenty of tradition offered at reasonable prices, considering the quality you get in the bottle. The Barbera d'Alba Sorì '18 put in a nice performance, opening with elegant smoky notes, from tobacco to liquorice, anticipating a highly enjoyable palate. It's rhythmic and dynamic with a fresh, long finish. Fragrant aromas of blackberry and almond characterize the Dolcetto d'Alba Vigna Madonna di Como '19, a wine that finishes precise and very pleasant.

Wine	Rating
● Barbera d'Alba Sorì '18	▼▼ 3
● Dolcetto d'Alba V. Madonna di Como '19	▼▼ 2*
● Nebbiolo d'Alba Sorì Coppa '18	▼▼ 4
● Barbera d'Alba V. Madonna di Como '18	▼ 2
● Barbera d'Alba Sorì '17	▽▽ 3
● Barbera d'Alba Sortì '17	▽▽ 3
● Barbera d'Alba V. Madonna di Como '17	▽▽ 2*
● Barbera d'Alba V. Madonna di Como '16	▽▽ 2*
● Dolcetto d'Alba Madonna di Como V. Miclet '16	▽▽ 3*
● Dolcetto d'Alba Madonna di Como V. Miclet '15	▽▽ 3*
● Dolcetto d'Alba V. Madonna di Como '16	▽▽ 2*
● Dolcetto d'Alba V. Miclet '17	▽▽ 3
● Langhe Saccorosso '15	▽▽ 4
● Nebbiolo d'Alba Sorì Coppa '17	▽▽ 4
● Nebbiolo d'Alba Sorì Coppa '15	▽▽ 4

Ugo Lequio

via del Molino, 10
12057 Neive [CN]
Tel. +39 0173677224
www.ugolequio.it

CELLAR SALES
PRE-BOOKED VISITS
ANNUAL PRODUCTION 30,000 bottles

The grapes purchased from long-trusted growers are carefully processed at this Molino di Neive winery's cellar. Their pride and joy is Gallina, one of the most inspired crus of the Barbaresco appellation, which Ugo Lequio has been expressing in the glass with constancy and sensitivity for some time now, honoring one of the noblest and most prestigious vineyards in Neive. Their approach includes medium-long maceration and maturation in mid-sized French oak barrels; vibrant and spicy in youth, their wines need time in the bottle to find the right rhythm. The Barbera d'Alba Superiore Vigna Gallina '17 is a must. It's certainly among the best of its kind, with a classic, elegant fruity profile, a creamy, thick, pervasive palate, rich in freshness and acid contrast, and a finish that's lively, acute and characterful. Whiffs of medicinal herbs and small red berries characterize the Barbaresco Gallina '17, a powerful, warm and mature drink.

Wine	Rating
● Barbera d'Alba Sup. V. Gallina '17	🍷🍷 4
● Barbaresco Gallina '17	🍷🍷 6
● Langhe Nebbiolo '18	🍷🍷 4
○ Langhe Arneis '19	🍷 3
● Barbaresco Gallina '16	♡♡ 6
● Barbaresco Gallina '15	♡♡ 6
● Barbaresco Gallina '14	♡♡ 6
● Barbaresco Gallina '13	♡♡ 5
● Barbaresco Gallina '12	♡♡ 5
● Barbaresco Gallina '11	♡♡ 5
● Barbaresco Gallina Ris. '10	♡♡ 6
● Barbera d'Alba Sup. Gallina '12	♡♡ 4
● Barbera d'Alba Sup. V. Gallina '16	♡♡ 4
● Barbera d'Alba Sup. V. Gallina '15	♡♡ 4
● Barbera d'Alba Sup. V. Gallina '14	♡♡ 4
● Langhe Nebbiolo '17	♡♡ 4
● Langhe Nebbiolo '15	♡♡ 4

Malabaila di Canale

via Madonna dei Cavalli, 93
12043 Canale [CN]
Tel. +39 017398381
www.malabaila.com

CELLAR SALES
PRE-BOOKED VISITS
ANNUAL PRODUCTION 100,000 bottles
HECTARES UNDER VINE 22.00
SUSTAINABLE WINERY

The winery owned by the Carrega Malabaila family and Valerio Falletti has been a recognized leader in Roero for several years now. The estate's vineyards—cultivated according to tradition mainly with Arneis, Barbera and Nebbiolo—can all be found on a large, 90-hectare estate. The sandy marl soil that characterizes the left bank of the Tanaro river gives rise to a range of modern wines marked by territorial identity and pleasantness. This year the Roero Bric Volta '17 made it into our finals, with its aromas of red berries and violets, spicy nuances, a medium-bodied, smooth palate rich in flesh, and long, elegant tannins. Other well-made selections include the Roero Castelletto Riserva '16, which is marked by nice complexity and texture, the Roero Arneis Le Tre '19, sapid and citrus, the Nebbiolo d'Alba Bric Merli '17, rich in hints of blackberry and aniseed, and the Langhe Nebbiolo Aja '19, a supple and pleasantly approachable wine.

Wine	Rating
● Roero Bric Volta '17	🍷🍷 3*
● Langhe Nebbiolo Aja '19	🍷🍷 4
● Nebbiolo d'Alba Bric Merli '17	🍷🍷 3
○ Roero Arneis Le Tre '19	🍷🍷 2*
● Roero Castelletto Ris. '16	🍷🍷 5
● Barbera d'Alba Sup. Mezzavilla '17	🍷 3
○ Roero Arneis Pradvaj '19	🍷 3
● Barbera d'Alba Giardino '16	♡♡ 2*
● Barbera d'Alba Sup. Mezzavilla '16	♡♡ 3
● Nebbiolo d'Alba Bric Merli '16	♡♡ 3*
○ Roero Arneis Le Tre '18	♡♡ 2*
● Roero Castelletto Ris. '15	♡♡ 5
● Roero Castelletto Ris. '14	♡♡ 4

★Malvirà

LOC. CANOVA
VIA CASE SPARSE, 144
12043 CANALE [CN]
TEL. +39 0173978145
www.malvira.com

CELLAR SALES
PRE-BOOKED VISITS
ACCOMMODATION AND RESTAURANT SERVICE
ANNUAL PRODUCTION 300,000 bottles
HECTARES UNDER VINE 42.00

For several years Massimo and Roberto Damonte have been leaders in Roero, both for their wines and for their splendid relais, Villa Tiboldi, situated on the Trinità hill just above the winery. The estate vineyards, which include prestigious additional geographical indications (MGA), mainly host the area's three traditional grapes: Arneis, Barbera and Nebbiolo. Their wines are characterized by their ageability and territorial identity, and that holds for their Barolo as well, a wine cultivated in the MGA Boiolo in La Morra. This year the Damonte brothers submitted a truly top-level range, starting with the two 2019 Roero Arneis crus. The Renesio is splendid, spicy and citrusy, of great length and complexity, with a finish well supported by sapidity, while the S.S. Trinità proves sapid and assertive, playing more on white fruit. Among the reds the Roero Vigna Renesio Riserva '16 stands out with its flowery sensations and orange peel notes, fine tannins and a juicy finish.

Wine	Rating
○ Roero Arneis Renesio '19	TTT 3*
○ Roero Arneis S. S. Trinità '19	TT 3*
● Roero V. Renesio Ris. '16	TT 5
● Barbera d'Alba '18	TT 3
● Barolo Boiolo '16	TT 7
○ Roero Arneis '19	TT 2*
○ Roero Arneis V. Saglietto '18	TT 3
● Roero Trinità Ris. '16	TT 5
● Roero V. Mombeltramo Ris. '16	TT 5
● Roero Bio '17	T 3
○ Roero Arneis Renesio '18	YYY 3*
● Barbera d'Alba S. Michele '17	YY 3
● Barolo Boiolo '15	YY 7
○ Roero Arneis S. S. Trinità '18	YY 3*
● Roero Trinità Ris. '15	YY 5
● Roero V. Mombeltramo Ris. '15	YY 5

Giovanni Manzone

VIA CASTELLETTO, 9
12065 MONFORTE D'ALBA [CN]
TEL. +39 017378114
www.manzonegiovanni.com

CELLAR SALES
PRE-BOOKED VISITS
ANNUAL PRODUCTION 45,000 bottles
HECTARES UNDER VINE 7.50
SUSTAINABLE WINERY

At the time we met Giovanni Manzone, his was the only winery in Langhe to produce Rossese Bianco. A rather rare wine made with the Ligurian grape of the same name, it's endowed with floral and citrus scents, with good structure and a certain freshness on the palate. But the winery, in which his wife, Rita Roggero, and his children Mauro and Mirella actively collaborate, is even more famous for its Barolo: the floral and classic Castelletto, the fruitier and more robust Gramolere, the complex and powerful Bricat. Notable vineyard elevations guarantee a constant and vital freshness of taste. With the Barolo Gramolere Riserva, the fresh 2013 harvest made for alluring balsamic nuances combined with a delicate touch of oak and red berries, all of which give way to a vital palate, with tannins well blended in its rich pulp. Obviously the Gramolere '16 is more impetuous and vivacious, destined to evolve well in the bottle. We also recommend the elegant Rossese Bianco Rosserto '17, an aromatically sophisticated and subtle wine.

Wine	Rating
● Barolo Gramolere '16	TT 6
● Barolo Gramolere Ris. '13	TT 8
● Barolo Bricat '16	TT 6
● Barolo Castelletto '16	TT 6
○ Langhe Rossese Bianco Rosserto '17	TT 3
● Langhe Nebbiolo Il Crutin '18	T 3
● Barolo Bricat '05	YYY 6
● Barolo Castelletto '09	YYY 5
● Barolo Gramolere Ris. '05	YYY 7
● Barolo Le Gramolere '04	YYY 6
● Barolo Le Gramolere Ris. '01	YYY 7
● Barolo Le Gramolere Ris. '00	YYY 7
● Barolo Le Gramolere Ris. '99	YYY 7
● Barolo Bricat '15	YY 6
● Barolo Castelletto '15	YY 6
● Barolo Gramolere '15	YY 6

Paolo Manzone

Loc. Meriame, 1
12050 Serralunga d'Alba [CN]
Tel. +39 0173613113
www.barolomeriame.com

CELLAR SALES
PRE-BOOKED VISITS
ACCOMMODATION
ANNUAL PRODUCTION 85,000 bottles
HECTARES UNDER VINE 10.00
VITICULTURE METHOD Certified Organic
SUSTAINABLE WINERY

The winery has been active since 1970, but it was only in 1999 that Paolo Manzone, bolstered in part by his wife Luisella Corino's vineyards, brought its current enological operations to life. At the center of it all is the powerful Meriame cru, which, obviously, gives rise to the Barolo of the same name. It's flanked by valid vineyards in the adjacent municipality of Sinio, where mainly Dolcetto, Barbera and Nebbiolo grapes are grown. Their award-winning Riserva consistently proves a particularly velvety and elegant Barolo, while the Meriame is a bit more vivacious and tannic. The farmstay lodging is enchanting. The olfactory spectrum of the Barolo Meriame '16 is characterized by clear hints of golden-leaf tobacco and aromatic herbs on a delicate background of well-toasted oak; in the mouth, the soft presence of alcohol is detectable, but a perfect acid-tannic balance guarantees notable and gratifying drinkability. The elegant Nebbiolo d'Alba Mirinè is among the most successful 2018s of its kind, with delicious balsamic hints and a palate of polished harmony.

Wine	Rating
● Barolo Meriame '16	3 Glasses 7
● Nebbiolo d'Alba Mirinè '18	2 Glasses 4
● Barbera d'Alba Sup. Fiorenza '18	2 Glasses 3
● Barolo del Comune di Serralunga d'Alba '16	2 Glasses 6
● Dolcetto d'Alba Magna '19	2 Glasses 2*
● Langhe Rosso Luvì '17	2 Glasses 4
○ Roero Arneis Reysu' '19	2 Glasses 3
● Barolo Ris. '13	3 White Glasses 7
● Barolo Ris. '11	3 White Glasses 7
● Barbera d'Alba Sup. Fiorenza '17	2 White Glasses 3
● Barolo del Comune di Serralunga d'Alba '15	2 White Glasses 6
● Barolo Meriame '15	2 White Glasses 7
● Barolo Ris. '12	2 White Glasses 7
● Nebbiolo d'Alba Mirinè '17	2 White Glasses 3
○ Roero Arneis Reysù '18	2 White Glasses 3

Marcalberto

via Porta Sottana, 9
12058 Santo Stefano Belbo [CN]
Tel. +39 0141844022
www.marcalberto.it

CELLAR SALES
PRE-BOOKED VISITS
ANNUAL PRODUCTION 40,000 bottles
HECTARES UNDER VINE 6.50

The Cane family's winery is now considered one of the best sparkling wine 'maison' in Italy. In recent years Piero Cane and his sons Alberto and Marco have managed to grow and improve, both in the vineyard and in the cellar, creating a producer that represents the excellence of Piedmont's Metodo Classico, an increasingly known and appreciated wine. Their vineyards are situated in Loazzolo, Calosso, Cossano Belbo and Santo Stefano Belbo, on marly-calcareous soils situated at 300-550 meters elevation. Like clockwork, their outstanding range once again demonstrates its superb quality, thanks to the Marcalberto Pas Dosé Blanc de Blancs. Complex notes of plum and white flowers are accompanied by dried fruit, nuts and bread crust; it's got great depth, with a freshness and structure of the highest quality. The Alta Langa Extra Brut Millesimo2mila16 '16 sees elegant aromas of white fruit and rusks followed by a creamy palate rich in pulp, but it's also long and gutsy. We also appreciated the fine, complex and alluring Rosé.

Wine	Rating
○ Marcalberto Pas Dosé Blanc de Blancs M. Cl.	3 Glasses 4
○ Alta Langa Extra Brut Millesimo2Mila16 '16	2 Glasses 5
⊙ Marcalberto Brut Rosé M. Cl.	2 Glasses 4
○ Marcalberto Brut Sansannée M. Cl.	2 Glasses 4
○ Marcalberto Nature M. Cl. Senza Aggiunta di Solfiti	2 Glasses 6
● Piemonte Pinot Nero Lavorare Stanca '17	2 Glasses 5
○ Alta Langa Extra Brut Millesimo2Mila15 '15	3 White Glasses 5
○ Marcalberto Extra Brut Millesimo2Mila12 M. Cl. '12	3 White Glasses 5
○ Marcalberto Extra Brut Millesimo2Mila13 M. Cl. '13	3 White Glasses 5
⊙ Marcalberto Brut Rosé M. Cl.	2 White Glasses 4

Poderi Marcarini

P.ZZA MARTIRI, 2
12064 LA MORRA [CN]
TEL. +39 017350222
www.marcarini.it

CELLAR SALES
PRE-BOOKED VISITS
ACCOMMODATION
ANNUAL PRODUCTION 125,000 bottles
HECTARES UNDER VINE 20.00

Siblings Andrea, Chiara and Elisa Marchetti represent the sixth generation of Marcarini family to work here in La Morra. The producer, whose roots go back to the mid-19th century, avails itself of two of Langa's best crus, Brunate and La Serra, vineyards near to one another, but different in terms of the character and moods they express in the bottle. About 20 hectares in total are covered, with the Sargentin estate in Neviglie and Muschiadivino in Montaldo Roero giving rise to Dolcetto, Barbera, Moscato and Arneis grapes. This year they presented a smaller selection than usual, but there's still plenty to say. The Barolo La Serra '16 opens with beautiful flowery and balsamic notes embellishing delicate, red fruit; the palate is more subtle than it is powerful, with a vivid acidic vein lending rhythm to a classy, characterful weave. The Barolo del comune di La Morra '16 is clear, focused and precise in its fruit, graceful in its extraction, already highly pleasant, juicy and multifaceted.

Wine	Rating
● Barolo La Serra '16	TT 7
● Barolo del Comune di La Morra '16	TT 7
● Barolo Brunate '05	YYY 6
● Barolo Brunate '03	YYY 6
● Barolo Brunate '01	YYY 6
● Barolo Brunate '99	YYY 6
● Barolo Brunate '96	YYY 6
● Barolo Brunate Ris. '85	YYY 6
● Dolcetto d'Alba Boschi di Berri '96	YYY 4*
● Barolo Brunate '15	YY 7
● Barolo Brunate '14	YY 7
● Barolo Brunate '13	YY 7
● Barolo del Comune di La Morra '15	YY 7
● Barolo La Serra '15	YY 7
● Barolo La Serra '14	YY 7
● Barolo La Serra '13	YY 7

★Marchesi di Barolo

VIA ROMA, 1
12060 BAROLO [CN]
TEL. +39 0173564400
www.marchesibarolo.com

CELLAR SALES
PRE-BOOKED VISITS
RESTAURANT SERVICE
ANNUAL PRODUCTION 1,500,000 bottles
HECTARES UNDER VINE 200.00

200 years ago Marquis Carlo Tancredi Falletti married Juliette Colbert Maulévrier, great-granddaughter of the 'Sun King' and the woman who understood Nebbiolo's potential (indeed, it's thanks to her that cellars were built to make wine with the grape). It's a story that still lives on today thanks to Anna and Ernesto Abbona, along with their children Davide and Valentina, a family who are carrying on an important legacy, balancing tradition and innovation while preserving a part of the history of Barolo, Castello Falletti and 200 hectares of vineyards in Langhe, Roero and Monferrato. The Barolo Cannubi '16 delivers charming sensations of dried flowers and liquorice; the palate is characterized by fine, fragrant red fruit, coming through powerful and rhythmic, with an intense tannic structure; the finish is long and full of character. The Barolo Sarmassa '16 is even more polished and compact, multifaceted in its whiffs of earth and spices. The Barolo Coste di Rose '16 is more delicate and floral, the Barbaresco Rio Sordo Cascina Bruciata Riserva '15 powerful, mature and intense.

Wine	Rating
● Barolo Cannubi '16	TT 8
● Barolo Sarmassa '16	TT 8
● Barbaresco Rio Sordo Cascina Bruciata '16	TT 5
● Barbaresco Rio Sordo Cascina Bruciata Ris. '15	TT 6
● Barolo Coste di Rose '16	TT 8
● Barolo del Comune di Barolo '16	TT 8
● Barolo Cannubi '14	YYY 8
● Barolo Cannubi '12	YYY 8
● Barolo Cannubi '11	YYY 8
● Barolo Cannubi '10	YYY 8
● Barolo Sarmassa '09	YYY 8
● Barolo Sarmassa '08	YYY 7
● Barolo Sarmassa '07	YYY 7
● Barolo Sarmassa '06	YYY 7
● Barolo Sarmassa '05	YYY 7

Marchesi Incisa della Rocchetta

via Roma, 66
14030 Rocchetta Tanaro [AT]
Tel. +39 0141644647
www.marchesiincisawines.it

CELLAR SALES
PRE-BOOKED VISITS
ACCOMMODATION AND RESTAURANT SERVICE
ANNUAL PRODUCTION 120,000 bottles
HECTARES UNDER VINE 17.00
SUSTAINABLE WINERY

Set harmoniously within the Rocchetta Tanaro Natural Park, the Incisa della Rocchetta family's vineyard plots unfold along the area's clayey-sandy hills. Primarily Barbera, Grignolino and Pinot Nero are cultivated here (this last since the end of the 19th century), with a few rows reserved for Merlot as well. Arneis, Moscato and Nebbiolo da Barolo come from other vineyards, acquired later in Langhe and Roero. In the absence of the Barbera, we tasted a Grignolino d'Asti '19 that's at the top of its game, one of the year's best. It's intense on the nose with notes of herbs and pepper. On the palate it's balanced, without excessive tannins, unfolding progressively, superbly, finishing long and pleasant. The Piedmont Pinot Noir Marchese Leopoldo '18 is also well made, characterized by nice richness and volume. Soft and pervasive, it's also got beautiful length.

Wine	Rating
● Grignolino d'Asti '19	▼▼ 3*
● Piemonte Pinot Nero Marchese Leopoldo '18	▼▼ 5
⊙ Piemonte Rosato Futurosa '19	▼ 3
● Barbera d'Asti Sup. Sant' Emiliano '15	▽▽▽ 5
● Barbera d'Asti Sup. Sant' Emiliano '17	▽▽ 5
● Barbera d'Asti Sup. Sant' Emiliano '16	▽▽ 5
● Barbera d'Asti Valmorena '18	▽▽ 3
● Barbera d'Asti Valmorena '17	▽▽ 3
● Barbera d'Asti Valmorena '16	▽▽ 3
● Grignolino d'Asti '18	▽▽ 3
● Grignolino d'Asti '17	▽▽ 3
● Grignolino d'Asti '16	▽▽ 3
● Piemonte Pinot Nero Barbera Rollone '17	▽▽ 3
● Piemonte Pinot Nero Barbera Rollone '16	▽▽ 3

Mario Marengo

loc. Serra Denari, 2a
12064 La Morra [CN]
Tel. +39 017350115
marengo@cantinamarengo.it

CELLAR SALES
PRE-BOOKED VISITS
ANNUAL PRODUCTION 38,000 bottles
HECTARES UNDER VINE 7.50
SUSTAINABLE WINERY

The Marengo family have been making wine in La Morra for four generations—that is, since the producer was founded in 1899. Marco Marengo is carrying on that tradition, managing 7 hectares of privately-owned vineyards. He's left his father's style behind, and that of his grandfather before him, giving voice to an innovative approach: in the vineyard only copper and sulphur are used, while winemaking calls for short fermentations. A commendable team performance saw two wines reach our finals. The Barolo Bricco delle Viole '16 is elegant in its notes of small red berries and flowers, delicate in its aromatic profile, vibrant acidity and long finish. The Barolo Brunate '16 is slightly behind in terms of maturity but has the energy and substance to evolve well in the coming years, supported by nice pulp, dense tannic extraction, and well-calibrated structure.

Wine	Rating
● Barolo Bricco delle Viole '16	▼▼ 6
● Barolo Brunate '16	▼▼ 7
● Barolo '16	▼▼ 5
● Nebbiolo d'Alba V. Valmaggiore '17	▼▼ 4
● Barbera d'Alba V. Pugnane '18	▼ 3
● Dolcetto d'Alba '19	▼ 2
● Barolo Brunate '12	▽▽▽ 7
● Barolo Brunate '11	▽▽▽ 7
● Barolo Brunate '09	▽▽▽ 6
● Barolo Brunate '07	▽▽▽ 6
● Barolo Brunate '06	▽▽▽ 6
● Barolo Brunate '05	▽▽▽ 6
● Barolo Brunate '04	▽▽▽ 6
● Barbera d'Alba V. Pugnane '16	▽▽ 3*
● Barolo Bricco delle Viole '14	▽▽ 6
● Barolo Brunate '15	▽▽ 7
● Barolo Brunate '14	▽▽ 7

Claudio Mariotto

s.da per Sarezzano, 29
15057 Tortona [AL]
Tel. +39 0131868500
www.claudiomariotto.it

CELLAR SALES
PRE-BOOKED VISITS
ANNUAL PRODUCTION 100,000 bottles
HECTARES UNDER VINE 24.00

We often talk about Timorasso's longevity, but sometimes tangible proof is in order. We know that wines aged for 6, 7 or 10 years hold up well over time, but retasting the Pitasso 2004 left us floored by its extraordinary aromatic freshness and elegance. Claudio Mariotto never ceases to amaze, as eclectic as he is, as clear, elegant and generous his wines are. And we aren't just talking about Timorasso, but also Barbera, Dolcetto, Croatina, Freisa, Cortese and Moscato. And there are some forays in the pipeline that have also aroused our curiosity. This year they submitted a line-up for the ages. The Pitasso exudes enchanting mineral hints playing on notes of petrol, all followed by a palate that impresses for its elegance and length. The Cavallina is its twin but seems slightly more evolved, with a highly characterful finish that's almost tannic. The Derthona features an impeccable nose-palate symmetry, while the Bricco San Michele is perhaps the simplest of the four, but what elegance!

Wine	Rating
○ Colli Tortonesi Timorasso Pitasso '18	▼▼▼ 6
○ Colli Tortonesi Timorasso Bricco San Michele '18	▼▼ 4
○ Colli Tortonesi Timorasso Cavallina '18	▼▼ 5
○ Colli Tortonesi Timorasso Derthona '18	▼▼ 5
● Colli Tortonesi Barbera Vhò '16	▼▼ 4
● Colli Tortonesi Croatina Montemirano '16	▼▼ 4
● Colli Tortonesi Freisa Braghè '18	▼▼ 3
○ Colli Tortonesi Bianco Pitasso '06	▽▽▽ 5
○ Colli Tortonesi Bianco Pitasso '05	▽▽▽ 4
○ Colli Tortonesi Timorasso Derthona Pitasso '17	▽▽▽ 6
○ Colli Tortonesi Timorasso Pitasso '13	▽▽▽ 6
○ Colli Tortonesi Timorasso Pitasso '12	▽▽▽ 6
○ Colli Tortonesi Timorasso Pitasso '08	▽▽▽ 5

Marsaglia

via Madama Mussone, 2
12050 Castellinaldo [CN]
Tel. +39 0173213048
www.cantinamarsaglia.it

CELLAR SALES
PRE-BOOKED VISITS
ANNUAL PRODUCTION 80,000 bottles
HECTARES UNDER VINE 15.00

At Marsaglia the whole family is involved, from Marina and Emilio to their children Enrico and Monica. The estate's vineyards are located in Castellinaldo, but grow in different soils. Closer to Canale, where their main cru, Brich d'America, is situated, the area's characteristic sandy soil dominates, while closer to Castagnito the terrain is more compact. The wines offered, which are grounded in Roero's classic grape varieties (especially Arneis, Barbera and Nebbiolo), prove technically well crafted and pleasantly drinkable. The Roero Brich d'America '16 features aromas of black berries, oak and spices followed by a dense, full palate, with hints of sweet fruit well balanced by sapidity. The Barbera d'Alba Superiore Castellinaldo '17 is juicy and rich in fruit, with nice texture and structure, while the Barbera d'Alba San Cristoforo '18 proves fresh and pleasant. We also found the sapid and assertive Roero Arneis Serramiana '19 notable, with its fragrances of citrus fruits and Mediterranean shrub.

Wine	Rating
● Barbera d'Alba S. Cristoforo '18	▼▼ 3
● Barbera d'Alba Sup. Castellinaldo '17	▼▼ 4
○ Roero Arneis Serramiana '19	▼▼ 3
● Roero Brich d'America '16	▼▼ 4
⊙ Langhe Rosato Rustichel '19	▼ 4
● Nebbiolo d'Alba San Pietro '18	▼ 3
● Barbera d'Alba Sup. Castellinaldo '16	▽▽ 4
● Barbera d'Alba Sup. Castellinaldo '15	▽▽ 4
● Nebbiolo d'Alba San Pietro '15	▽▽ 3
○ Roero Arneis Armonia '16	▽▽ 3
○ Roero Arneis Serramiana '18	▽▽ 3*
○ Roero Arneis Serramiana '17	▽▽ 3
● Roero Brich d'America '15	▽▽ 4
● Roero Brich d'America '14	▽▽ 4

★Franco M. Martinetti

via San Francesco da Paola, 18
10123 Torino
Tel. +39 0118395937
www.francomartinetti.it

PRE-BOOKED VISITS
ANNUAL PRODUCTION 1,200,000 bottles
HECTARES UNDER VINE 5.00

A sophisticated wine and food expert, Franco Martinetti began proposing his own wines in 1974, when consumption in Italy still centered on demijohns and bulk wines. Over the years he has expanded his range, continuing to avail himself of collaborations with prestigious wineries, covering Langhe and Monferrato's main typologies, both whites and reds. And he has managed to enter the not-so-easy world of Barolo with notable results, even though he has established himself internationally mainly with his perennially elegant Barbera d'Asti, Gavi and Timorasso. The Barolo Marasco '16 put in an excellent performance. Rich and elegant, it's still slightly marked by oak on the nose, long and austere on the palate. The 2018 version of the Barbera d'Asti Bric dei Banditi is very well crafted, as bold, firm and progressive in its development as ever. Beautiful notes of herbs and peach characterize the charming Timorasso Biancofranco '19, a soft, round wine that proves satisfyingly drinkable.

● Barbera d'Asti Sup. Bric dei Banditi '18	TT 4
● Barolo Marasco '16	TT 8
○ Colli Tortonesi Timorasso Biancofranco '19	TT 5
○ Colli Tortonesi Timorasso Martin '19	TT 6
○ Gavi Minaia '19	TT 5
● M.to Rosso sul Bric '18	TT 6
● Barbera d'Asti Sup. Montruc '06	YYY 5
● Barbera d'Asti Sup. Montruc '01	YYY 5
● Barbera d'Asti Sup. Montruc '96	YYY 5
● Barolo Marasco '01	YYY 7
● Barolo Marasco '00	YYY 7
○ Colli Tortonesi Timorasso Martin '12	YYY 6
○ Gavi Minaia '14	YYY 5
● M.to Rosso Sul Bric '10	YYY 6
● M.to Rosso Sul Bric '09	YYY 6
● M.to Rosso Sul Bric '00	YYY 5

★Bartolo Mascarello

via Roma, 15
12060 Barolo [CN]
Tel. +39 017356125

CELLAR SALES
PRE-BOOKED VISITS
ANNUAL PRODUCTION 30,000 bottles
HECTARES UNDER VINE 5.00

Mascarello's Barolo has always been made by blending grapes from four small vineyards, harvested at the same time and aged together in large oak vats. Without a doubt, the cru that sets the style is the one located in a splendid and sunny part of Cannubi, the most famous and time-honored name in all of Barolo. Maria Teresa Mascarello is carrying forward, adding just a touch of finesse and stylistic precision to what has always been a wine appreciated by lovers of the most classic and purest Barolo. A century of history for a winery made famous by an outstanding, unforgettable Bartolo. Thanks to a perfect vintage, one as complete and complex as 2016, Bartolo Mascarello's Barolo reaches truly remarkable heights in terms of expressiveness and depth. Balsamic hints integrate with a suite of violets and licorice, contributing, together with a silky and multifaceted tannic texture, to a gustatory profile of unique charm.

● Barolo '16	TTT 8
● Barolo '15	YYY 8
● Barolo '13	YYY 8
● Barolo '12	YYY 8
● Barolo '11	YYY 8
● Barolo '10	YYY 8
● Barolo '09	YYY 8
● Barolo '07	YYY 8
● Barolo '06	YYY 8
● Barolo '05	YYY 8
● Barolo '01	YYY 8
● Barolo '99	YYY 8
● Barolo '98	YYY 8
● Barolo '89	YYY 8
● Barolo '85	YYY 8
● Barolo '84	YYY 8
● Barolo '83	YYY 8

★Giuseppe Mascarello e Figlio

via Borgonuovo, 108
12060 Monchiero [CN]
Tel. +39 0173792126
www.mascarello1881.com

CELLAR SALES
PRE-BOOKED VISITS
ANNUAL PRODUCTION 60,000 bottles
HECTARES UNDER VINE 13.50

The winery was built in 1919 just outside the Barolo production zone, nevertheless the wine has been central from the outset, thanks in particular to the splendid Monprivato cru. Owned almost entirely by the Mascarello family and universally recognized as one of the most prestigious in the whole area, it gives rise to the famous Monprivato and the rare Ca' d' Morissio. The style of winemaking is classic and calls for long aging in bottle, which holds for the Barolo made in the Villero and Santo Stefano di Perno vineyards as well. Only 3 wines were submitted for tasting. The Barolo Monprivato '15 exhibits great finesse and harmony, coming through intense, with fruity notes of raspberry before turning to more complex hints of iodine and tobacco—a mineral, rooty sensation makes for commendable complexity. The palate unfolds progressively, deep, with balanced tannins and acidity, and a long, harmonious finish. The pulpy Barbera d'Alba Scudetto '18 is characterized by lovely plum hints and sensations that call up wooden barrels.

● Barolo Monprivato '15	🍷🍷🍷 8
● Babera D'Alba Scudetto '18	🍷🍷 6
● Langhe Nebbiolo '18	🍷🍷 7
● Barolo Monprivato '13	YYY 8
● Barolo Monprivato '12	YYY 8
● Barolo Monprivato '11	YYY 8
● Barolo Monprivato '10	YYY 8
● Barolo Monprivato '09	YYY 8
● Barolo Monprivato '08	YYY 8
● Barolo Monprivato '01	YYY 8
● Barolo Monprivato '85	YYY 8
● Barolo S. Stefano di Perno '98	YYY 8
● Barolo Villero '96	YYY 8
● Barolo Monprivato '14	YY 8
● Barolo Perno V. Santo Stefano '14	YY 8
● Barolo Villero '14	YY 8
● Barolo Villero '13	YY 8

La Masera

s.da San Pietro, 32
10010 Piverone [TO]
Tel. +39 0113164161
www.lamasera.it

CELLAR SALES
PRE-BOOKED VISITS
ANNUAL PRODUCTION 25,000 bottles
HECTARES UNDER VINE 5.00
SUSTAINABLE WINERY

The project continues to grow and what began as something of a lark is becoming a producer increasingly attentive to the precision and clarity of its range, now composed of 12 wines. As the winery's 5 founders are keen to point out, the desire is to interpret Canavese in the best way, carrying forward the winemaking legacy of their grandparents without giving up the opportunities represented by new cellar techniques. The Erbaluce di Caluso Anima dAnnata '17 is characterized by splendid aromatic freshness, moving amidst medicinal herbs and hints of aniseed on a suite of great finesse. The palate is notable, delicately fresh, long and clear. Equally complex, the Macaria version sees a touch of wood joining Asian fruits on a back palate of considerable structure. In this beautiful land of whites, we also mention the valid Barbera Monte Gerbido '17 and the highly pleasant Spumante Brut Masilé '13.

○ Erbaluce di Caluso Anima dAnnata '17	🍷🍷🍷 3*
○ Erbaluce di Caluso Macaria '17	🍷🍷 3*
● Canavese Barbera Monte Gerbido '17	🍷🍷 2*
○ Erbaluce di Caluso Anima '19	🍷🍷 3
○ Erbaluce di Caluso Brut M. Cl. Masilé '13	🍷🍷 5
○ Erbaluce di Caluso Passito Ris. Venanzia '06	🍷🍷 4
● Canavese Rosso '18	🍷 2
○ Caluso Passito Venanzia '12	YY 5
● Canavese Rosso '17	YY 2*
● Canavese Rosso '16	YY 2*
○ Erbaluce di Caluso Anima '18	YY 3
○ Erbaluce di Caluso Anima '17	YY 3*
○ Erbaluce di Caluso Anima '16	YY 2*
○ Erbaluce di Caluso Anima d'Annata '16	YY 3
○ Erbaluce di Caluso Brut Masilé '14	YY 5

★Vigneti Massa

P.ZZA G. CAPSONI, 10
15059 MONLEALE [AL]
TEL. +39 013180302
massa@vignetimassa.com

CELLAR SALES
PRE-BOOKED VISITS
ANNUAL PRODUCTION 120,000 bottles
HECTARES UNDER VINE 25.00
SUSTAINABLE WINERY

For some time now Walter Massa, undoubtedly the best known producer in Tortona, has achieved fame beyond local borders. Over the years Walter has executed his style of winemaking with a courage and determination matched by few, without a thought for market trends. His range, from Timorasso to Barbera, Croatina and Freisa (Moscato as well), is an expression of the great artisan's talent. Power, intensity and longevity serve as its defining qualities. Just a few lines to describe a great story that has changed the direction of the region's whites. The Sterpi opens vibrant on citrus aromas that quickly give way to mineral sensations with notes of petrol. It's sumptuous on the palate, with an acidity that lengthens a sapid finish. The Derthona is broad, with floral aromas on a mineral base and a full-bodied, rich flavor. Their other wines are quite valid, starting with the Costa del Vento, which can surprise after a few years of aging.

Wine	Rating
○ Derthona '18	⚲⚲ 5
○ Sterpi '18	⚲⚲ 6
○ Anarchia Costituzionale '19	⚲⚲ 3
○ Costa del Vento '18	⚲⚲ 6
○ Montecitorio '18	⚲⚲ 6
● Sentieri '19	⚲⚲ 4
⊙ Libertà '19	⚲ 2
○ Colli Tortonesi Timorasso Derthona '06	⚲⚲⚲ 5
○ Colli Tortonesi Timorasso Sterpi '08	⚲⚲⚲ 7
○ Colli Tortonesi Timorasso Sterpi '07	⚲⚲⚲ 7
○ Costa del Vento '15	⚲⚲⚲ 6
○ Costa del Vento '12	⚲⚲⚲ 6
○ Derthona '09	⚲⚲⚲ 5
○ Derthona Sterpi '16	⚲⚲⚲ 6
○ Montecitorio '11	⚲⚲⚲ 6
○ Montecitorio '10	⚲⚲⚲ 6
○ Sterpi '13	⚲⚲⚲ 6

★Massolino - Vigna Rionda

P.ZZA CAPPELLANO, 8
12050 SERRALUNGA D'ALBA [CN]
TEL. +39 0173613138
www.massolino.it

CELLAR SALES
PRE-BOOKED VISITS
ANNUAL PRODUCTION 290,000 bottles
HECTARES UNDER VINE 42.00

Parafada, Margheria and Vigna Rionda on the western side of Serralunga d'Alba; Parussi, in Castiglione Falletto: it's from these areas that the Massolino family, active producers since 1896, get their most celebrated wines. Their style does a nice job bringing together richness and power, tannic intensity and length, while their range, which is wide but reliable across the board, comprises wines made with Nebbiolo, Barbera, Dolcetto, Chardonnay and Moscato grapes. Tre Bicchieri for the Barolo Parafada, a wine of nice aromatic freshness in its notes of red berries, tobacco and liquorice. On the palate it's complex and fine, rich in flavor and gustatory tension. The Barolo Vigna Rionda '14 exhibits the usual level of detail and depth, it's just a bit clenched at the end. The excellent Barolo '16 is dynamic and lean in its sapid, balsamic profile. A note of merit for the Riesling '18, an elegant wine in its delicate smoky hints.

Wine	Rating
● Barolo Parafada '16	⚲⚲⚲ 8
● Barolo '16	⚲⚲ 5
● Barolo Vigna Rionda Ris. '14	⚲⚲ 8
● Barolo Margheria '16	⚲⚲ 8
● Barolo Parussi '16	⚲⚲ 8
● Dolcetto d'Alba '19	⚲⚲ 2*
○ Langhe Chardonnay '18	⚲⚲ 3
○ Langhe Riesling '18	⚲⚲ 4
● Barbera d'Alba '19	⚲ 3
● Langhe Nebbiolo '18	⚲ 4
○ Moscato d'Asti '19	⚲ 2
● Barolo Parafada '11	⚲⚲⚲ 8
● Barolo Vigna Rionda Ris. '11	⚲⚲⚲ 8
● Barolo Vigna Rionda Ris. '10	⚲⚲⚲ 8
● Barolo Vigna Rionda Ris. '08	⚲⚲⚲ 8
● Barolo Vigna Rionda Ris. '06	⚲⚲⚲ 8
● Barolo Vigna Rionda Ris. '05	⚲⚲⚲ 8

Tiziano Mazzoni

via Roma, 73
28010 Cavaglio d'Agogna [NO]
Tel. +39 3488200635
www.vinimazzoni.it

CELLAR SALES
PRE-BOOKED VISITS
ANNUAL PRODUCTION 20,000 bottles
HECTARES UNDER VINE 4.50
SUSTAINABLE WINERY

Gilles Mazzoni has worked well with his father, Tiziano, in managing this small producer. Their wines, all made with great enological sensitivity, do an outstanding job expressing the characteristics of the grape varieties and vineyards of origin. Production regulations provide that Ghemme can be made with a minimum of 85% Nebbiolo, but here they've always preferred 100%, saving their Vespolina for a separate and special, delectably drinkable selection. But when it comes to Nebbiolo, Monteregio is consistently among the appellation's best. Quinine, licorice and sunny herbs characterize the commendable Ghemme Ai Livelli '15, a wine that's powerful and still a bit austere in the mouth thanks to the presence of a nice acidity. The more immediately expressive and youthful Ghemme dei Mazzoni performed nicely on the palate, benefiting from the excellent 2016 vintage. Strawberries and a hint of rhubarb mark the elegant and harmonious Nebbiolo del Monteregio '18.

Wine	Rating
● Ghemme Ai Livelli '15	ΨΨ 6
● Colline Novaresi Nebbiolo del Monteregio '18	ΨΨ 3
● Ghemme dei Mazzoni '16	ΨΨ 5
● Colline Novaresi Vespolina Il Ricetto '19	Ψ 3
○ Iris	Ψ 4
● Ghemme dei Mazzoni '12	ΨΨΨ 5
● Colline Novaresi Nebbiolo del Monteregio '17	ΨΨ 4
● Colline Novaresi Nebbiolo del Monteregio '16	ΨΨ 3
● Colline Novaresi Vespolina Il Ricetto '18	ΨΨ 4
● Ghemme Ai Livelli '13	ΨΨ 6
● Ghemme dei Mazzoni '15	ΨΨ 5
○ Iris	ΨΨ 4

Tenuta La Meridiana

via Tana Bassa, 5
14048 Montegrosso d'Asti [AT]
Tel. +39 0141956172
www.tenutalameridiana.com

CELLAR SALES
PRE-BOOKED VISITS
ANNUAL PRODUCTION 100,000 bottles
HECTARES UNDER VINE 10.00
SUSTAINABLE WINERY

Gianpiero Bianco and Federico Primo represent the fifth generation of family to work at Tenuta La Meridiana, an estate that's been acclaimed as one of Monferrato's best since the 19th century. Historically, the focus has been on Barbera, a grape whose attributes are highlighted through varying styles and territorial interpretations, resulting in a diverse battery of wines. All it takes is a look at their monovarietals and blends of Chardonnay, Cortese, Favorita, Arneis, Moscato, Nebbiolo and Malaga to get an appreciation for a range that surprises for character and vigor. The two 2018 Barbera d'Asti Superiores presented are truly lovely. The Bricco Sereno features notes of ripe cherries, cocoa and roasted coffee, which lend complexity and character to a palate rich in fruit. In the mouth it's nicely supported by acidity, which ensures freshness and balance. The Tra La Terra e Il Cielo sees aromas of blackberries and ripe plums combine with spicy hints of oak, all followed by a palate of great structure, with acidity and alcohol in harmony, and a long, sapid finish.

Wine	Rating
● Barbera d'Asti Sup. Bricco Sereno '18	ΨΨ 4
● Barbera d'Asti Sup. Tra la Terra e il Cielo '18	ΨΨ 5
○ M.to Bianco Puntet '19	ΨΨ 3
○ Ouverture Brut M. Cl.	ΨΨ 5
● Barbera d'Asti Le Gagie '18	Ψ 3
● Barbera d'Asti Le Quattro Terre '19	Ψ 2
● Barbera d'Asti Le Gagie '17	ΨΨ 3
● Barbera d'Asti Le Quattro Terre '18	ΨΨ 2*
● Barbera d'Asti Le Quattro Terre '17	ΨΨ 2*
● Barbera d'Asti Sup. Bricco Sereno '17	ΨΨ 4
● Barbera d'Asti Sup. Tra la Terra e il Cielo '17	ΨΨ 5
● Barbera d'Asti Sup. Tra la Terra e il Cielo '16	ΨΨ 5
● Barbera d'Asti Vitis '17	ΨΨ 2*
● M.to Rosso Rivaia '15	ΨΨ 5

La Mesma

FRAZ. MONTEROTONDO, 7
15066 GAVI [AL]
TEL. +39 0143342012
www.lamesma.it

CELLAR SALES
PRE-BOOKED VISITS
ACCOMMODATION
ANNUAL PRODUCTION 52,000 bottles
HECTARES UNDER VINE 25.00
VITICULTURE METHOD Certified Organic

Years ago we described La Mesma as one of the most interesting, new producers in the Gaviese wine scene. Today we find a solid and dynamic winery, fresh off organic certification. Their range, made mainly with Cortese, shows great attention to detail. From their entry-level selections on up, their wines are more than captivating by virtue of their intensity and character. Behind it all is an original enological style that's capable of emphasizing and giving depth to aroma. In the absence of the Gavi Riserva, we were consoled by their other splendid wines. The Indi is vibrant, vital, with aromas of plum and apple on a vegetal background. On the palate it expresses great harmony, with a freshness that lengthens a lovely, sapid finish. The Etichetta Gialla sees vegetal aromas give way to floral and mineral notes; in the mouth it features great balance and a very long finish. The Brut Metodo Classico is also excellent.

Wine	Rating
○ Gavi del Comune di Gavi Et. Gialla '19	🍷🍷 3*
○ Gavi del Comune di Gavi Indi '19	🍷🍷 4
○ Gavi Brut M. Cl. '14	🍷🍷 5
○ Gavi V. della Rovere Verde Ris. '17	ΨΨΨ 5
○ Gavi V. della Rovere Verde Ris. '15	ΨΨΨ 5
○ Gavi Brut M. Cl. '13	ΨΨ 5
○ Gavi Brut M. Cl. '11	ΨΨ 5
○ Gavi del Comune di Gavi 10 Anni '08	ΨΨ 2*
○ Gavi del Comune di Gavi Et. Gialla '18	ΨΨ 3*
○ Gavi del Comune di Gavi Et. Gialla '17	ΨΨ 3
○ Gavi del Comune di Gavi Et. Gialla '16	ΨΨ 2*
○ Gavi del Comune di Gavi Et. Nera '18	ΨΨ 3
○ Gavi del Comune di Gavi Et. Nera '17	ΨΨ 3*
○ Gavi del Comune di Gavi Et. Nera '16	ΨΨ 3*
○ Gavi del Comune di Gavi Indi '18	ΨΨ 4
○ Gavi del Comune di Gavi Indi '17	ΨΨ 4
○ Gavi V. della Rovere Verde Ris. '16	ΨΨ 5

Mauro Molino

FRAZ. ANNUNZIATA GANCIA, 111A
12064 LA MORRA [CN]
TEL. +39 017350814
www.mauromolino.com

CELLAR SALES
PRE-BOOKED VISITS
ANNUAL PRODUCTION 95,000 bottles
HECTARES UNDER VINE 12.00
SUSTAINABLE WINERY

Mauro Molino's winery is about to celebrate 40 years of activity. In 1982 Mauro decided to set up his own winery and take part in the small winemaking revolution that was about to unfold in Langhe. The size is still the same, with the addition of a Barbera d'Asti, which comes from the Molino family's homeland, while their Barolos, led by an always-interesting Conca, make up the lion's share. His son Matteo has been fully active for 15 years and is proving to be a capable interpreter of Nebbiolo, which ages in small oak barrels in a cellar that's well worth a visit. Only Barolos were submitted for tasting. The Conca '16 opens on ripe red berries and hints of liquorice, coming through rich in personality; hints of sweet wood are very perceptible, but its structure is remarkable, thus creating a complex dialog between oak and Nebbiolo's flesh. The Barolo '16 draws more on classicism. It's contained in its power but with a clear olfactory cleanness. Vanilla and tar dominate in the pleasant La Serra '16, a wine that features a beautiful finish on rhubarb.

Wine	Rating
● Barolo Conca '16	🍷🍷 7
● Barolo La Serra '16	🍷🍷 7
● Barolo '16	🍷🍷 5
● Barolo Bricco Luciani '16	🍷 6
● Barbera d'Alba V. Gattere '00	ΨΨΨ 5
● Barbera d'Alba V. Gattere '97	ΨΨΨ 7
● Barbera d'Alba V. Gattere '96	ΨΨΨ 7
● Barolo Gallinotto '11	ΨΨΨ 6
● Barolo Gallinotto '03	ΨΨΨ 6
● Barolo Gallinotto '01	ΨΨΨ 6
● Barolo V. Conca '00	ΨΨΨ 7
● Barolo V. Conca '97	ΨΨΨ 7
● Barolo V. Conca '96	ΨΨΨ 7
● Barolo '15	ΨΨ 5
● Barolo Bricco Luciani '15	ΨΨ 6
● Barolo Conca '15	ΨΨ 7
● Barolo Gallinotto '15	ΨΨ 6

F.lli Monchiero

via Alba Monforte, 49
12060 Castiglione Falletto [CN]
Tel. +39 017362820
www.monchierovini.it

CELLAR SALES
PRE-BOOKED VISITS
ANNUAL PRODUCTION 40,000 bottles
HECTARES UNDER VINE 12.00
SUSTAINABLE WINERY

Among the many documents and texts that testify to the excellent quality level of Rocche di Castiglione, there are two of particular interest. One is the collection of testimonies of merchants, who have always been willing to pay a higher price for its grapes. The other was written by Professor Ferdinando Vignolo Lutati in 1930, 'The Nebbiolo grown here is suitable for producing Barolo with a distinct aroma, making it highly prized'. And it's here that Vittorio Monchiero and his family cultivate the grapes for the winery's flagship product, sometimes also offered as a Riserva. Their Barolo del comune di Castiglione Falletto '16 has the tannic development of a superb wine, austere and decisive on the nose with dried flowers accompanied by the first hints of licorice. Excellent. Just a little less powerful, but of exquisite craftsmanship, the elegant Barolo Montanello '16 is characterized by sensations owing to its time aging in oak. The Barolo '16 more than convinced, revealing aromatic herbs and tobacco whiffs, with the fruity component serving only as a background.

Wine	Rating
● Barolo del comune di Castiglione Falletto '16	▼▼ 8
● Barolo Montanello '16	▼▼ 5
● Barolo '16	▼▼ 5
● Nebbiolo d'Alba '18	▼▼ 3
● Barbera d'Alba Sup. '17	▼ 3
● Barbera d'Alba Sup. '16	▽▽ 3
● Barbera d'Alba Sup. '15	▽▽ 3
● Barolo Montanello '14	▽▽ 5
● Barolo Montanello Ris. '13	▽▽ 5
● Barolo Rocche di Castiglione '15	▽▽ 5
● Barolo Rocche di Castiglione '13	▽▽ 5
● Barolo Rocche di Castiglione Ris. '13	▽▽ 7
● Barolo Rocche di Castiglione Ris. '12	▽▽ 7
○ Langhe Arneis '18	▽▽ 2*
● Langhe Nebbiolo '17	▽▽ 3

★Monchiero Carbone

via Santo Stefano Roero, 2
12043 Canale [CN]
Tel. +39 017395568
www.monchierocarbone.com

CELLAR SALES
PRE-BOOKED VISITS
ANNUAL PRODUCTION 190,000 bottles
HECTARES UNDER VINE 30.00
SUSTAINABLE WINERY

Year after year, Monchiero Carbone affirms its status as one of Roero's most significant and renowned producers, with a series of wines that are now true stylistic and qualitative benchmarks for the whole territory. Francesco and Lucrezia Monchiero manage some of the most beautiful vineyards in the territory, including Monbirone, Renesio and Sru, which are cultivated with the area's classic grapes. The wines produced bring together territorial character with complexity, elegance and great aromatic clarity. By now the Roero Arneis Cecu d'la Biunda is a model for the appellation. The 2019 offers up hints of Mediterranean scrub and pomegranate on the nose, accompanied by floral notes, while the palate proves sapid, rich in fruit, long and assertive. Two Roeros are also outstanding: the Srü '17, fresh and fruity, with red berry notes and aromatic herbs, and the Printi Riserva '16, a powerful and complex wine with spicy notes. Tannins are still at the fore, but it's got great finesse, a long and juicy drink.

Wine	Rating
○ Roero Arneis Cecu d'La Biunda '19	▼▼▼ 3*
● Roero Printi Ris. '16	▼▼ 6
● Roero Srü '17	▼▼ 4
● Barbera d'Alba Pelisa '18	▼▼ 2*
○ Roero Arneis Recit '19	▼▼ 3
○ Roero Arneis Cecu d'la Biunda '17	▽▽▽ 3*
● Roero Printi Ris. '15	▽▽▽ 6
● Barbera d'Alba Monbirone '16	▽▽ 5
● Barbera d'Alba Pelisa '17	▽▽ 2*
○ Langhe Bianco Tamardì '18	▽▽ 2*
○ Roero Arneis Cecu d'La Biunda '18	▽▽ 3*
○ Roero Arneis Recit '18	▽▽ 3
● Roero Printi Ris. '14	▽▽ 5
● Roero Srü '16	▽▽ 4
● Roero Srü '15	▽▽ 4

La Montagnetta

FRAZ. BRICCO CAPPELLO, 4
14018 ROATTO [AT]
TEL. +39 335309361
www.lamontagnetta.com

CELLAR SALES
PRE-BOOKED VISITS
ANNUAL PRODUCTION 50,000 bottles
HECTARES UNDER VINE 10.00

Domenico Capello is deservedly recognized as the true standard bearer of Freisa, a traditional grape variety long neglected (and not only because of its controversial agronomic profile). Still-dry, sparkling, spumante or rosé: La Montagnetta's range includes almost every version with results that stand out for quality and character. The same care is reserved for Barbera, Bonarda, Chardonnay, Sauvignon and Viognier, cultivated in the fruitful vineyards of Roatto, San Paolo Solbrito and Piovà Massaia. The Barbera d'Asti Pi-Cit '19 is a splendid standard-label Barbera d'Asti with crisp and fresh notes of cherry and plum, and an assertive, well-balanced, well-structured and freshly acidic palate. The Barbera d'Asti Superiore Piovà '17 is characterized by ripe fruit aromas of great finesse and a rich, long palate, well supported by tannic texture. A note of merit for the Freisa d'Asti Superiore Bugianen '16, one of the best of its kind.

Wine	Rating
● Barbera d'Asti Pi Cit '19	🍷🍷 2*
● Barbera d'Asti Sup. Piovà '17	🍷🍷 4
● Freisa d'Asti I Ronchi '19	🍷🍷 2*
● Freisa d'Asti Sup. Bugianen '16	🍷🍷 4
○ Piemonte Chardonnay La Fiur '19	🍷🍷 2*
● Piemonte Bonarda Frizzante La Mossa '19	🍷 2
⊙ Piemonte Rosato Il Ciaret '19	🍷 2
● Barbera d'Asti Pi Cit '17	YY 2*
● Barbera d'Asti Pi-Cit '18	YY 2*
● Barbera d'Asti Sup. Piovà '16	YY 4
● Barbera d'Asti Sup. Piova '15	YY 4
● Freisa d'Asti Sup. Bugianen '15	YY 4
● Freisa d'Asti Sup. Bugianen '14	YY 4
○ M.to Bianco A Stim '18	YY 3

Montalbera

VIA MONTALBERA, 1
14030 CASTAGNOLE MONFERRATO [AT]
TEL. +39 0119433311
www.montalbera.it

CELLAR SALES
PRE-BOOKED VISITS
ANNUAL PRODUCTION 550,000 bottles
HECTARES UNDER VINE 184.00
SUSTAINABLE WINERY

As they cover over half of the vineyards suitable for growing Ruchè di Castagnole Monferrato, Montalbera is by far the producer of reference for the unusual Asti appellation, which comes in various versions. But the selection of grapes cultivated by the Morando family is much more broad based: the parcels cultivated with Viognier, Grignolino and Barbera are flanked by those reserved for Nebbiolo, Moscato and Chardonnay, from the estates of La Morra, Barbaresco, Neive and Castiglione Tinella. Once again their Ruché di Castagnole Monferrato della Montalbera perform at top levels. The Laccento '19 features hints of roses and pepper, red fruit and tobacco. The palate is powerful, but also marked by great finesse and harmony, with soft, close-knit tannins and beautiful length. La Tradizione '19 is more austere, but still quite persistent, with notes of flowers and dried herbs. The Barbera d'Asti Superiore Nuda '18, with its raspberries notes, citrus fruits, spicy and earthy nuances, proves supple and rich in fruit.

Wine	Rating
● Ruchè di Castagnole M.to Laccento '19	🍷🍷🍷 4*
● Barbera d'Asti Sup. Nuda '18	🍷🍷 5
● Ruchè di Castagnole M.to La Tradizione '19	🍷🍷 3*
● Barbera d'Asti Solo Acciaio '19	🍷🍷 3
● Grignolino d'Asti Grignè '19	🍷🍷 3
● Ruchè di Castagnole M.to Limpronta '17	🍷🍷 5
● Barbera d'Asti Nuda '15	YYY 5
● Ruché di Castagnole M.to La Tradizione '15	YYY 3*
● Ruché di Castagnole M.to Laccento '18	YYY 4*
● Ruché di Castagnole M.to Laccento '16	YYY 3*
● Barbera d'Asti Sup. Nuda '16	YY 5

Tenuta Montemagno

via Cascina Valfossato, 9
14030 Montemagno [AT]
Tel. +39 014163624
www.tenutamontemagno.it

CELLAR SALES
PRE-BOOKED VISITS
ACCOMMODATION AND RESTAURANT SERVICE
ANNUAL PRODUCTION 140,000 bottles
HECTARES UNDER VINE 15.00
SUSTAINABLE WINERY

An old farmhouse dating back to the 16th century serves as the fulcrum of the decidedly charming setting in which Montemagno is immersed. The cellar, and adjacent relais, is surrounded by vineyards with the Alps providing the backdrop. The experience is amplified by the quality of their production, which is manicured down to the last detail. Enologist Gianfranco Cordero brings great skill to his work, managing to bring out the aromatic qualities of his whites and ennoble the structure of his reds without the invasive use of oak. A wide range of wines is forged mainly from indigenous grape varieties. The overall performance of the wines submitted for tasting points up the quality of their entire range. The Barolo Soranus features an intense and persistent nose-palate profile. Their Ruchés prove pleasant: the Nobilis behaves elegantly, with its flowery aromas on spicy notes. The Invictus is more fruit-forward, adorned with floral notes and aromatic herbs. The other wines tasted are also exceptionally well made.

● Barolo Soranus '15	🍷🍷 6
○ Brut M. Cl. 36 Mesi	🍷🍷 5
● Grignolino d'Asti Ruber '19	🍷🍷 2*
○ M.to Bianco Musae '19	🍷🍷 3
○ M.to Bianco Nymphae '19	🍷🍷 2*
● Ruché di Castagnole M.to Invictus '19	🍷🍷 3
● Ruché di Castagnole M.to Nobilis '19	🍷🍷 3
● Barbera d'Asti Austerum '17	🍷🍷 3
● Barbera d'Asti Austerum '16	🍷🍷 3
● Barbera d'Asti Sup. Mysterium '16	🍷🍷 4
● Barbera d'Asti Sup. Mysterium '15	🍷🍷 4
● Grignolino d'Asti Ruber '18	🍷🍷 2*
● Grignolino d'Asti Ruber '17	🍷🍷 2*
○ M.to Bianco Solis Vis '18	🍷🍷 3
● M.to Rosso Violae '18	🍷 2

La Morandina

loc. Morandini, 11
12053 Castiglione Tinella [CN]
Tel. +39 0141855261
www.lamorandina.com

CELLAR SALES
PRE-BOOKED VISITS
ANNUAL PRODUCTION 100,000 bottles
HECTARES UNDER VINE 20.00

For more than 30 years brothers Giulio and Paolo Morando have worked to transform the historic family business, present in the territory of Castiglione Tinella since the 17th century, into an important producer that offers a series of wines, fruit of their privately-owned vineyards, which host grapes from Moscato to Barbera and Barbaresco. There are 4 properties, with their Moscato d'Asti cultivated in Castiglione Tinella and their Barbaresco in Neive. In Montegrosso d'Asti their vines going back as far as 100 years and give rise to their Barbera d'Asti Superiore Varmat. La Morandina is back in the guide with great style, thanks to a series of truly expertly crafted wines. The Barbera d'Asti Superiore Varmat '17 sees notes of blackberries and blackcurrants accompanied by spicy and toasty nuances. A powerful palate follows, but there's lively acidity that accentuates a long, juicy finish. The Moscato d'Asti Canelli '19 features elegant aromas of sage and peach, vibrant acidity and great freshness—it's a fine, elegant wine.

● Barbera d'Asti Sup. Varmat '17	🍷🍷 6
○ Moscato d'Asti Canelli '19	🍷🍷 2*
● Barbaresco '16	🍷🍷 6
● Barbera d'Asti Zucchetto '18	🍷🍷 4
○ Langhe Chardonnay '18	🍷🍷 3

Diego Morra

via Cascina Mosca, 37
12060 Verduno [CN]
Tel. +39 3284623209
www.morrawines.com

CELLAR SALES
PRE-BOOKED VISITS
ANNUAL PRODUCTION 40,000 bottles
HECTARES UNDER VINE 32.00

The three intertwined Ms that make up the winery's logo are derived from Morra (the family name), Monvigliero (the most important cru, where the cellar is also located) and Mosca, the name of the property where they operate. The area under vine is considerable for Langhe, especially if you take into account that of the 30 hectares total, 16 are cultivated with Nebbiolo grapes for Barolo. A combination of grapes from Verduno and La Morra give rise to their new Barolo Zinzasco. Pleasing aromas of strawberries, licorice and aromatic herbs give way to a soft and velvety palate, already well-balanced and free of roughness. Equally valid is the Barolo Monvigliero '16, just a bit more spicy and tantalizing on the nose, with a nice, pervasive grip on the palate. The 2016 'basic' Barolo is a marvel of finesse, endowed with considerable personality. We also appreciated the delicate, cherry-scented and satisfying Langhe Nebbiolo '18.

Wine	Glasses	Price
● Barolo Monvigliero '16	TT	7
● Barolo Zinzasco '16	TT	6
● Barbera d'Alba '18	TT	3
● Barolo '16	TT	6
● Langhe Nebbiolo '18	TT	3
○ Langhe Chardonnay '19	T	3
⊙ Langhe Rosato '19	T	3
● Barbera d'Alba '16	YY	3
● Barolo '14	YY	6
● Barolo '12	YY	6
● Barolo Monvigliero '15	YY	7
● Barolo Monvigliero '14	YY	6
● Barolo Monvigliero '12	YY	6
● Dolcetto d'Alba '17	YY	2*
● Langhe Nebbiolo '14	YY	3
● Verduno Pelaverga '17	YY	3

Stefanino Morra

loc. San Pietro
via Castagnito, 50
12050 Castellinaldo [CN]
Tel. +39 0173213489
www.morravini.it

CELLAR SALES
PRE-BOOKED VISITS
ANNUAL PRODUCTION 75,000 bottles
HECTARES UNDER VINE 12.00
SUSTAINABLE WINERY

Founded almost a century ago, in 1925, the Morra family's business has been run for over 30 years by Stefanino, who for some time now has been joined by his son Luca. The estate vineyards are mainly to be found in Castellinaldo, on sandy soils crossed by marl and layers of limestone, and host the area's classic grapes: Arneis, Barbera, Brachetto, Favorita and Nebbiolo. The wines produced are well made, generous and classic in style. It was their so-called 'basic' wines that most impressed this year.The Roero Arneis '19 unveils white-fleshed fruit aromas on the nose, accompanied by nuances of melon and aromatic herbs, while the palate proves plucky, well supported by sapidity, with a highly pleasant finish. The Barbera d'Alba '17 exhibits nice texture, coming through rich in fruit with notes of red berries and pomegranate, while the Roero '17, with its tannins still quite perceptible, plays more on notes of spices and Mediterranean scrub.

Wine	Glasses	Price
○ Roero Arneis '19	TT	2*
● Barbera d'Alba '17	TT	3
● Roero '17	TT	3
● Barbera d'Alba Castellinaldo '17	T	4
● Barbera d'Alba Castlè '17	T	5
● Barbera d'Alba '16	YY	3*
● Barbera d'Alba Castellinaldo '15	YY	4
● Roero '16	YY	3*
● Roero '14	YY	3
○ Roero Arneis '17	YY	2*
○ Roero Arneis '16	YY	2*
○ Roero Arneis V. San Pietro '17	YY	3
○ Roero Arneis Vign. San Pietro '15	YY	3
● Roero Sräi Ris. '15	YY	5

F.lli Mossio

fraz. Cascina Caramelli
via Montà, 12
12050 Rodello [CN]
Tel. +39 0173617149
www.mossio.com

CELLAR SALES
PRE-BOOKED VISITS
ACCOMMODATION
ANNUAL PRODUCTION 50,000 bottles
HECTARES UNDER VINE 10.00
SUSTAINABLE WINERY

Viticulture and winemaking began in 1967 with the purchase of a classic Langa farmstead, whose basement proved perfect for aging Dolcetto in steel tanks. Since then the Mossio family have worked with confidence, as well as commercial success, to make their wines known. Their classically-styled range features purity of fruit and notable, but never excessive, structure. They are also helped by higher elevations, which can surpass 400 metres, as in the case of the company's flagship, the always-exquisite Dolcetto d'Alba Bricco Caramelli. The forward-thinking decision to postpone the marketing of new vintages has further enhanced the enticing drinkability of their entire range. These true 'artists of Dolcetto' have managed to find the perfect balance in their Gamus, owing to the hot summer of 2017. Thanks to the elevation of the vineyard, a rewarding freshness emerges, while a delicate, year-long maturation in used oak ensures that all the grape's characteristic, fruity complexity is expressed, making for an alluring drink.

Wine	Rating
● Dolcetto d'Alba Sup. Gamvs '17	🍷🍷 4
● Dolcetto d'Alba Piano delli Perdoni '18	🍷🍷 2*
● Dolcetto d'Alba Sup. Bricco Caramelli '18	🍷🍷 3
● Langhe Nebbiolo Luen '16	🍷🍷 4
● Barbera d'Alba '18	🍷 4
● Barbera d'Alba '16	🍷🍷 4
● Dolcetto d'Alba Piano delli Perdoni '17	🍷🍷 2*
● Dolcetto d'Alba Piano delli Perdoni '16	🍷🍷 2*
● Dolcetto d'Alba Sup. Bricco Caramelli '17	🍷🍷 3
● Dolcetto d'Alba Sup. Bricco Caramelli '16	🍷🍷 3
● Langhe Nebbiolo Luen '15	🍷🍷 4
● Langhe Rosso '16	🍷🍷 4
● Langhe Rosso '15	🍷🍷 4

Musso

via D. Cavazza, 5
12050 Barbaresco [CN]
Tel. +39 0173635129
www.mussobarbaresco.it

CELLAR SALES
PRE-BOOKED VISITS
ANNUAL PRODUCTION 80,000 bottles
HECTARES UNDER VINE 10.00

The producer was founded in 1929 by Sebastiano Musso, in a difficult period for viticulture. Indeed, the great turning point came in 1968, when Sebastiano's son Augusto decided to vinify and bottle the grapes from their vineyards and, moreover, acquire plots in Pora and Rio Sordo. Today, the capable Valter Musso is overseeing the winery's activities, availing himself of the support of his son Emanuele and grandson Luca Accornero. The Pora cru delivered splendid results. The modern Riserva di Barbaresco '15 offers pervasive toasty aromas together with clear hints of fresh, lively fruit; the palate is full and pulpy, velvety even, very long and enticing. The Pora '17 unveils sweet spices and red berries on the nose, together with a powerful mouth, with close-knit and assertive (though not aggressive) tannins. Theirs is a notable range, overall, with a highly elegant Barbera d'Alba '18 and a sophisticated, subtle and herbaceous Roero Arneis '19 standing out.

Wine	Rating
● Barbaresco Pora '17	🍷🍷 6
● Barbaresco Pora Ris. '15	🍷🍷 6
● Barbaresco Rio Sordo '17	🍷🍷 6
● Barbera d'Alba '17	🍷🍷 3
● Dolcetto d'Alba '19	🍷🍷 2*
● Langhe Pinot Nero '18	🍷🍷 2*
○ Roero Arneis '19	🍷🍷 3
● Barbaresco '17	🍷 5
● Barbera d'Alba Sup. Brua '18	🍷 4
● Barbaresco Pora '16	🍷🍷 6
● Barbaresco Rio Sordo '16	🍷🍷 6
● Barbaresco Rio Sordo '15	🍷🍷 5
● Barbera d'Alba '16	🍷🍷 3
● Barbera d'Alba Sup. Brua '16	🍷🍷 4
● Langhe Nebbiolo '18	🍷🍷 4

Ada Nada

loc. Rombone
via Ausario, 12
12050 Treiso [CN]
Tel. +39 0173638127
www.adanada.it

CELLAR SALES
PRE-BOOKED VISITS
ACCOMMODATION AND RESTAURANT SERVICE
ANNUAL PRODUCTION 45,000 bottles
HECTARES UNDER VINE 9.00

The winery led by Elvio, together with his wife Anna Lisa and daughters Elisa, Serena and Emma, is well worth a visit. It's housed in a beautiful 18th-century farmhouse, which includes excellent guest accommodations. Founded in 1919 by Carlo Nada, today it's bolstered by prestigious crus such as Valeirano and Rombone, offered both in the Elisa and in the Riserva Cichin, made with grapes from the oldest plots. Their Barbarescos mature in large, 3000-liter oak barrels, making for a consummately classic style. A trio of Barbarescos proved more than convincing, starting with the Barbaresco Rombone Cichin Riserva '15. Aromas of blackberries and roots herald a creamy tannic structure and a long, well-sustained finish, rich in flavor. Fresh in its hints of mint and medicinal herbs, the Barbaresco Valeirano '17 is already quaffable and juicy on the palate, thanks to a well-profiled mouthfeel. The aromatically clear, focused and polished Barbaresco Elisa '17 exhibits balance and nice harmony.

● Barbaresco Cichin Ris. '15	TT	6
● Barbaresco Valeirano '17	TT	5
● Barbaresco Rombone Elisa '17	TT	5
● Barbaresco Rombone Elisa '16	YYY	5
● Barbaresco Cichin Ris. '13	YY	6
● Barbaresco Cichin Ris. '12	YY	6
● Barbaresco Rombone Elisa '15	YY	5
● Barbaresco Valeirano '16	YY	5
● Barbaresco Valeirano '15	YY	5
● Barbaresco Valeirano '14	YY	5
● Barbera d'Alba Sup. Salgà '16	YY	3
● Langhe Nebbiolo Serena '18	YY	3
○ Langhe Sauvignon Neta '18	YY	2*
○ Langhe Sauvignon Neta '17	YY	2*

★★Fiorenzo Nada

via Ausario, 12c
12050 Treiso [CN]
Tel. +39 0173638254
www.nada.it

CELLAR SALES
PRE-BOOKED VISITS
ANNUAL PRODUCTION 45,000 bottles
HECTARES UNDER VINE 10.00
SUSTAINABLE WINERY

This winery has been in our guidebook since its first year of publication. It was 1988, Fiorenzo was 63 years old and had already demonstrated his greatness as a vigneron. Bruno Nada had grown passionate about wine while still teaching, while his son Danilo was learning to walk. It was a success story wrought of beautiful vineyards—Rombone, Manzola and the recent Montaribaldi—combined with a sensibility of rare finesse and a strong desire to excel. The entire range, which is small, lives up to its reputation, with the Langhe Rosso Seifile (80% Barbera and 20% Nebbiolo) a perennial standout. Highly elegant, rich in small black berries and spices, the Barbaresco Rombone '16 is just slightly adorned by a veil of oak and a tantalizing whiff of cocoa on the finish; the palate aptly interprets the richness of the vintage, and is already well balanced. The exquisite Seifile '16 is enriched by a fresh, vegetal touch, which lends complexity, while in the mouth it reveals the quiet presence of tannins and joyful vitality of acidity—just a touch.

● Barbaresco Rombone '16	TTT	8
● Langhe Rosso Seifile '16	TT	8
● Barbaresco Manzola '16	TT	7
● Barbaresco Montaribaldi '16	TT	8
● Barbera d'Alba '18	TT	4
● Langhe Nebbiolo '18	T	4
● Barbaresco Manzola '08	YYY	6
● Barbaresco Manzola '06	YYY	6
● Barbaresco Montaribaldi '15	YYY	7
● Barbaresco Montaribaldi '14	YYY	7
● Barbaresco Montaribaldi '13	YYY	7
● Barbaresco Rombone '12	YYY	7
● Barbaresco Rombone '10	YYY	7
● Barbaresco Rombone '09	YYY	7
● Barbaresco Rombone '07	YYY	7
● Barbaresco Rombone '06	YYY	7

Cantina dei Produttori Nebbiolo di Carema

via Nazionale, 32
10010 Carema [TO]
Tel. +39 0125811160
www.caremadoc.it

CELLAR SALES
PRE-BOOKED VISITS
RESTAURANT SERVICE
ANNUAL PRODUCTION 65,000 bottles
HECTARES UNDER VINE 20.00

The stone pillars that support Carema's pergolas are a historical and cultural patrimony kept alive and productive above all thanks to this praiseworthy cooperative winery, which collects the Nebbiolo grapes from dozens of small growers in this corner of Piedmont near Aosta. Their two main wines are the Carema and Carema Riserva, but the potential of this town and its 795 inhabitants is also represented by other bottles, with the Metodo Classico Nebbiolo, called Villanova, starting to gain attention. The Carema Riserva '16 is characterized by an interesting olfactory fullness, with vibrant notes of aromatic herbs, and good supporting alcohol; as is the want of both the vintage and the vineyard, the palate delivers a hearty acidity accompanied by moderate tannins, making for an overall drink of good, fruity substance. We find the same freshness and structure, though slightly more diluted, in the Canavese Nebbiolo Paré '18.

- ● Carema Et. Bianca Ris. '16 — 🍷🍷 4
- ● Canavese Nebbiolo Parè '18 — 🍷 2
- ● Carema Et. Bianca '07 — 🍷🍷🍷 3*
- ● Carema Et. Bianca Ris. '11 — 🍷🍷🍷 3*
- ● Carema Et. Bianca Ris. '09 — 🍷🍷🍷 3*
- ● Carema Et. Bianca Ris. '08 — 🍷🍷🍷 3*
- ● Canavese Nebbiolo Parè '17 — 🍷🍷 2*
- ● Carema Et. Bianca Ris. '15 — 🍷🍷 4
- ● Carema Et. Bianca Ris. '12 — 🍷🍷 3
- ● Carema Et. Bianca Ris. '10 — 🍷🍷 3*
- ● Carema Et. Nera '16 — 🍷🍷 3
- ● Carema Et. Nera '15 — 🍷🍷 3
- ● Carema Et. Nera '14 — 🍷🍷 3
- ● Carema Et. Nera '13 — 🍷🍷 2*
- ● Carema Et. Nera '12 — 🍷🍷 2*
- ● Carema Et. Nera '11 — 🍷🍷 2*
- ● Carema Ris. '13 — 🍷🍷 4

Negretti

fraz. Santa Maria, 53
12064 La Morra [CN]
Tel. +39 0173509850
www.negrettivini.com

CELLAR SALES
ANNUAL PRODUCTION 50,000 bottles
HECTARES UNDER VINE 13.00

Given that their winery is in excellent health, it's clear that brothers Ezio and Massimo Negretti have managed to make the most of the family business. 13 hectares of vineyards are situated in the hills of La Morra (the Rive and Bettolotti crus) and Bricco Ambrogio di Roddi. By now their style is well established, with great attention shown in the vineyard, intense and well-calibrated extractions, and wines of balanced spiciness. In the cellar they use barrels of different sizes (225 or 2500 liters) and origins (France and Austria). Tre Bicchieri for the Barolo Rive '16 with its elegant aromas amidst wild strawberries, tobacco and sweet spices; on the palate it's elegant and complex, medium-bodied, with creamy tannins and a long, dynamic finish. We also appreciated the Barolo '16, an airy wine in its notes of liquorice, fresh flowers and raspberries. Elegant and classic, it's got a powerful palate and tannic finesse. The Barolo Mirau '16 is more austere in its tannic texture, with a charming, spicy stroke.

- ● Barolo Rive '16 — 🍷🍷🍷 7
- ● Barolo Bricco Ambrogio '16 — 🍷🍷 7
- ● Barolo Mirau '16 — 🍷🍷 6
- ● Barbera d'Alba Sup. '17 — 🍷🍷 3
- ● Barolo '16 — 🍷🍷 6
- ○ Langhe Chardonnay Dadà '18 — 🍷🍷 4
- ● Nebbiolo d'Alba Minot '17 — 🍷 4
- ● Barolo Bricco Ambrogio '14 — 🍷🍷🍷 6
- ● Barolo Rive '15 — 🍷🍷🍷 6
- ● Barolo '15 — 🍷🍷 6
- ● Barolo '13 — 🍷🍷 6
- ● Barolo Bricco Ambrogio '15 — 🍷🍷 6
- ● Barolo Bricco Ambrogio '13 — 🍷🍷 6
- ● Barolo Bricco Ambrogio '09 — 🍷🍷 6
- ● Barolo Rive '14 — 🍷🍷 6
- ● Barolo Rive '13 — 🍷🍷 6

Angelo Negro

FRAZ. SANT' ANNA , 1
12040 MONTEU ROERO [CN]
TEL. +39 017390252
www.angelonegro.it

CELLAR SALES
PRE-BOOKED VISITS
ANNUAL PRODUCTION 350,000 bottles
HECTARES UNDER VINE 60.00
SUSTAINABLE WINERY

In Monteu Roero, the vineyards of Ciabot San Giorgio, Prachiosso and Serra Lupini all give rise to their classic Roero wines (together with San Vittore in Canale), while Basarin in Neive hosts their Barbaresco and Baudana in Serralunga d'Alba their Barolo. The Negro family's great vineyards have grown in recent years, and not just in Roero but Langhe as well. All their many wines, which feature great aromatic clarity, are made with native grape varieties and are marked by a classic style of remarkable typicity and territorial identity. On the nose the Roero Sudisfá Riserva '17 offers up notes of Mediterranean scrub, with balsamic and sweet citrus whiffs, while the palate proves large in volume, rich in fruit, with close-knit, but fine tannins and a long, juicy finish. The Roero Ciabot San Giorgio Riserva '17 is fresh and relaxed, of notable finesse, with hints of black fruit, violet and spices. Their Langa selections are also of high quality, in particular the Barolo del Comune di Serralunga d'Alba '16, a classic wine marked by nice complexity and finesse.

Wine	Rating	
● Roero Sudisfà Ris. '17	▼▼▼	6
● Barolo del Comune di Serralunga d'Alba '16	▼▼	7
● Roero Ciabot San Giorgio Ris. '17	▼▼	5
● Barbaresco Basarin '15	▼▼	5
○ Roero Arneis Serra Lupini '19	▼▼	3
○ Roero Arneis Sette Anni '13	▼▼	7
● Roero Prachiosso '18	▼▼	4
● Roero Sudisfà Ris. '16	▽▽▽	6
● Barbaresco Basarin '16	▽▽	5
○ Roero Arneis Perdaudin '18	▽▽	4
○ Roero Arneis Sette Anni '12	▽▽	7
● Roero Ciabot San Giorgio '16	▽▽	5
● Roero Prachiosso '16	▽▽	4

Lorenzo Negro

FRAZ. SANT'ANNA, 55
12040 MONTEU ROERO [CN]
TEL. +39 017390645
www.negrolorenzo.com

CELLAR SALES
PRE-BOOKED VISITS
ANNUAL PRODUCTION 35,000 bottles
HECTARES UNDER VINE 8.00
SUSTAINABLE WINERY

For 15 years now Lorenzo Negro's winery has been a stable presence in the Roero firmament, offering a range of modern wines that exhibit aromatic clarity while expressing the characteristics of the territory and its native grape varieties. The winery in Monteu Roero is situated at the top of the Serra Lupini hill, surrounded by vineyards at elevations of about 300 meters. Here we find the classic sandy soils that characterize the left bank of the Tanaro, with layers of silt and clay. The Roero S. Francesco Riserva '16 is elegant in its aromas of red berries and flowers on a background of spices, with a harmonious, dynamic palate in which a close-knit, velvety tannic texture makes for a long finish, properly austere. Other well-made selections include the Barbera d'Alba Superiore La Nanda '16, fresh and pleasantly sapid with hints of black berries and Mediterranean scrub, and the Roero Arneis '19, with its aromas of kaiser pear and its consistent, well-sustained palate.

Wine	Rating	
● Roero S.Francesco Ris. '16	▼▼	3*
● Barbera d'Alba Sup. La Nanda '16	▼▼	3
● Langhe Nebbiolo '17	▼▼	2*
○ Roero Arneis '19	▼▼	2*
● Roero Prachiosso '17	▼▼	3
● Barbera d'Alba '17	▼	2
● Barbera d'Alba '16	▽▽	2*
● Barbera d'Alba '15	▽▽	2*
○ Roero Arneis '18	▽▽	2*
○ Roero Arneis Brut M. Cl. '12	▽▽	4
● Roero Prachiosso '16	▽▽	3*
● Roero Prachiosso '15	▽▽	3*
● Roero S.Francesco Ris. '15	▽▽	3*
● Roero San Francesco Ris. '14	▽▽	3

Nervi Conterno

c.so Vercelli, 117
13045 Gattinara [VC]
Tel. +39 0163833228
www.nervicantine.it

CELLAR SALES
PRE-BOOKED VISITS
ANNUAL PRODUCTION 120,000 bottles
HECTARES UNDER VINE 27.00

The transition from the old ownership, which still holds 10% of the business, to the new one was a smooth one. Indeed Roberto Conterno, who declared in 2018, 'It's a fantastic area', has high regard for the wines made here with Nebbiolo, under the supervision of the Norwegian Erling Astrup. Both were and are convinced that of the area's great potential and that further developments in quality are possible. Investments and renovations are already moving in that direction, and positive results are already starting to show. As is nicely demonstrated by the complex Gattinara Valferana '16, rich in red berries, hints of iodine and gentian; the palate plays on finesse, with delicate, silky tannins adding length. Even more multifaceted, the Molsino '16 is characterized by rose and raspberry, all lending aromatic vitality, while the palate excels in persistence and harmony. The tasty Gattinara from the warm 2017 vintage is just a bit more decisive and immediately expressive.

Wine	Rating
● Gattinara V. Molsino '16	🍷🍷 7
● Gattinara V. Valferana '16	🍷🍷 6
● Gattinara '17	🍷🍷 5
● Gattinara Podere dei Ginepri '01	🍷🍷🍷 5
● Gattinara Vign. Molsino '00	🍷🍷🍷 5
● Colline Novaresi Spanna '15	🍷🍷 3
● Gattinara '15	🍷🍷 5
● Gattinara '15	🍷🍷 4
● Gattinara '13	🍷🍷 4
● Gattinara Molsino '11	🍷🍷 5
● Gattinara V. Molsino '14	🍷🍷 7
● Gattinara V. Molsino '13	🍷🍷 7
● Gattinara V. Molsino '12	🍷🍷 5
● Gattinara V. Valferana '14	🍷🍷 6
● Gattinara V. Valferana '13	🍷🍷 6

Silvano Nizza

fraz. Balla Lora 29a
12040 Santo Stefano Roero [CN]
Tel. +39 017390516
www.nizzasilvano.it

CELLAR SALES
PRE-BOOKED VISITS
ANNUAL PRODUCTION 65,000 bottles
HECTARES UNDER VINE 8.00

It was Silvano Nizza who founded the producer in 2001, taking up the family tradition started by his father, Sandro, and uncle Alfredo 50 years earlier. Arneis, Barbera, Brachetto and Nebbiolo are cultivated in their vineyards, situated mainly next to the Ca' Boscarone farmhouse in Santo Stefano Roero, and in the municipalities of Canale and Montà. Although unabashedly modern, their wines seek to best express the characteristics of the grape varieties and territories of origin. The Barbera d'Alba Superiore Crua '17 opens on aromas of great finesse, plum and cherry well accompanied by spicy nuances. A harmonious palate of great character follows, rich in fruit and well supported by acidic freshness. The Roero Arneis Il Santo Stefano '17, with its notes of white fruit and almond, proves interesting, of notable typicity, with a consistent, long palate of nice texture and flavor. Finally the Roero '17 exhibits nice tension amidst sensations of alpine herbs and black fruits.

Wine	Rating
● Barbera d'Alba Sup. Crua '17	🍷🍷 4
● Nebbiolo d'Alba '18	🍷🍷 4
● Roero '17	🍷🍷 5
○ Roero Arneis '19	🍷🍷 3
○ Roero Arneis Il Santo Stefano Limited Edition '17	🍷🍷 3
● Barbera d'Alba '15	🍷🍷 4
● Barbera d'Alba Sup. Crua '16	🍷🍷 4
● Roero '16	🍷🍷 5
● Roero '15	🍷🍷 5
○ Roero Arneis '18	🍷🍷 3
○ Roero Arneis '17	🍷🍷 3
● Roero Ca' Boscarone Ris. '14	🍷🍷 6

Noah

via Forte, 48
13862 Brusnengo [BI]
Tel. +39 3201510906
info@noah.wine

CELLAR SALES
PRE-BOOKED VISITS
ANNUAL PRODUCTION 15,000 bottles
HECTARES UNDER VINE 4.50
SUSTAINABLE WINERY

Andrea Mosca and Giovanna Pepe Diaz's first harvest took place in 2011, but their ultimate goal was already quite clear: cultivate only the territory's classic grapes, i.e. mainly Nebbiolo, using environmentally friendly agricultural practices combined with a traditional winemaking style. Hence the choice to use Slavonian oak for both fermentation and aging, with positive results in terms of flavor. The surface area under vine has slightly increased since then and allows them to produce, in addition to the award-winning Lessona and Bramaterra, a splendid Croatina and an experimental Rosso Noah. With the 2016 vintage, Noah once again demonstrates its ability and precision in interpreting both Lessona and Bramaterra. The former proves to be rich and impressive by virtue of its remarkable tannic qualities, which strengthen the palate in the wake of berry fruit and quinine sensations on the nose. The Bramaterra offers up elegant rose and violet petal aromas, coming through pulpy and elegant in the mouth.

● Bramaterra '16	▼▼ 5
● Lessona '16	▼▼ 6
● Coste della Sesia Rosso Noah '19	▼▼ 4
● Coste della Sesia Rosso Noah '18	▼▼ 4
● Coste della Sesia Rosso Dalla Mesola '18	▼ 3
● Bramaterra '12	▽▽▽ 5
● Bramaterra '15	▽▽ 5
● Bramaterra '14	▽▽ 5
● Bramaterra '13	▽▽ 5
● Coste della Sesia Croatina '15	▽▽ 5
● Lessona '15	▽▽ 5
● Lessona '14	▽▽ 5

★Poderi e Cantine Oddero

fraz. Santa Maria
via Tetti, 28
12064 La Morra [CN]
Tel. +39 017350618
www.oddero.it

CELLAR SALES
PRE-BOOKED VISITS
ANNUAL PRODUCTION 150,000 bottles
HECTARES UNDER VINE 35.00
VITICULTURE METHOD Certified Organic
SUSTAINABLE WINERY

Mariacristina and Mariavittoria Oddero avail themselves of one of the region's most prestigious sets of vineyards, thanks to the inheritance left by their father, Giacomo. Among their plots, we can mention Villero and Rocche di Castiglione (Castiglione Folletto), Brunate in La Morra, Mondoca di Bussia Soprana in Monforte d'Alba, and Vignarionda in Serralunga. Their style proves classic, polished, with a marked sensitivity when it comes to extraction and using oak barrels of various sizes, making for wines that age beautifully over time. Fine, potent and harmonious, the Barolo Vigna Rionda Riserva '13 exhibits aromatic freshness and spicy complexity on a rich, multifaceted and highly persistent palate. The delicately salty character of the Barolo Brunate '16 is peculiar. It's a wine rich in spicy sensations, with a close-knit, gradually unfolding tannic texture, sure to improve with age. Masterful harmony, finesse and balance characterize the Barolo '16, an already pleasant and juicy drink.

● Barolo Rocche di Castiglione '16	▼▼ 8
● Barolo Vignarionda Ris. '13	▼▼ 8
● Barolo Villero '16	▼▼ 8
● Barbaresco Gallina '17	▼▼ 7
● Barbera d'Alba Sup. '17	▼▼ 4
● Barolo Brunate '16	▼▼ 8
● Barolo Bussia V. Mondoca Ris. '14	▼▼ 8
● Langhe Nebbiolo '18	▼▼ 5
● Nizza Barbera '17	▼ 4
● Barbaresco Gallina '16	▽▽ 6
● Barbera d'Asti Sup. Nizza '15	▽▽ 4
● Barolo '15	▽▽ 6
● Barolo Brunate '15	▽▽ 8
● Barolo Bussia V. Mondoca Ris. '13	▽▽ 8
● Barolo Vignarionda Ris. '11	▽▽ 8
● Barolo Villero '15	▽▽ 8

Figli Luigi Oddero Tenuta Parà

fraz. Santa Maria
loc. Tenuta Parà, 95
12604 La Morra [CN]
Tel. +39 0173500386
www.figliluigioddero.it

CELLAR SALES
PRE-BOOKED VISITS
ANNUAL PRODUCTION 110,000 bottles
HECTARES UNDER VINE 20.00
SUSTAINABLE WINERY

The winery got its start thanks to a curious man. As Mario Soldati once described him, Luigi Oddero was a 'country gentleman' who combined past and future, tradition and vision. His wife followed her husband's footsteps, together with their children. Their wines have reached peaks of true excellence thanks to a defined style that expresses a peculiar aromatic freshness, thanks in part to prestigious plots like Rive and Santa Maria di La Morra, Scarrone, Vigna Rionda and Rombone. This it's worth noting that this year saw yet another strong overall performance. 3 wines earned a place in our finals. Great character, structure and length characterize the excellent Barolo Rocche Rivera '16, a wine capable of calibrating power and energy with a particular grace and finesse. The Barbaresco Rombone '17 is vivid in its freshness and aromatic precision, with a distinctly balsamic finish on notes of juniper and mint. The Barolo Vigna Rionda Riserva '14 proves to be a brilliant interpretation of the vintage.

Wine	Glasses	Price
● Barbaresco Rombone '17	▼▼	6
● Barolo Rocche Rivera '16	▼▼	8
● Barolo Vigna Rionda Ris. '14	▼▼	8
● Barolo '16	▼▼	8
● Langhe Nebbiolo '18	▼▼	6
● Barbera d'Alba '18	▼	6
● Barolo Vigna Rionda '13	▽▽▽	8
● Barolo Vigna Rionda '10	▽▽▽	8
● Barbaresco Rombone '16	▽▽	6
● Barbaresco Rombone '15	▽▽	6
● Barbaresco Rombone '14	▽▽	8
● Barbera d'Alba '17	▽▽	6
● Barolo '15	▽▽	8
● Barolo '13	▽▽	8
● Barolo Rocche Rivera '13	▽▽	6
● Barolo Specola '11	▽▽	8
● Barolo Vigna Rionda '12	▽▽	8

Tenuta Olim Bauda

via Prata, 50
14045 Incisa Scapaccino [AT]
Tel. +39 0141702171
www.tenutaolimbauda.it

CELLAR SALES
PRE-BOOKED VISITS
ANNUAL PRODUCTION 200,000 bottles
HECTARES UNDER VINE 30.00
SUSTAINABLE WINERY

A historic producer founded in the 1960s by the Bertolino family, today Tenuta Olim Bauda is managed by siblings Dino, Diana and Giovanni. This agricultural business has grown gradually over time, putting together several estates in the municipalities of Nizza Monferrato, Isola d'Asti, Fontanile, Castelnuovo Calcea and Gavi, which host the grapes best suited to the zone. We find mainly Barbera and Moscato, but Cortese, Chardonnay, Grignolino, Nebbiolo and Freisa are all well represented as well. Once again, the Bertolino family's Barberas are first-rate. On the nose the Nizza Riserva '17 brings out beautiful notes of blackberry and ripe cherry, with nuances of earth and tobacco, while the palate exhibits structure and flesh, but also elegance in its development, finishing long. The Barbera d'Asti Superiore Le Rocchette '17 plays on red berry sensations, citrus fruits and sweet spices, followed by a bold body of beautiful fullness, with a nice, flavorful finish.

Wine	Glasses	Price
● Nizza Ris. '17	▼▼▼	5
● Barbera d'Asti Sup. Le Rocchette '17	▼▼	4
● Barbera d'Asti La Villa '19	▼▼	3
○ Moscato d'Asti Centive '19	▼▼	3
● Barbera d'Asti Sup. Nizza '13	▽▽▽	5
● Barbera d'Asti Sup. Nizza '12	▽▽▽	5
● Barbera d'Asti Sup. Nizza '11	▽▽▽	5
● Barbera d'Asti Sup. Nizza '08	▽▽▽	5
● Barbera d'Asti Sup. Nizza '07	▽▽▽	5
● Barbera d'Asti Sup. Nizza '06	▽▽▽	5
● Nizza '15	▽▽▽	5
● Nizza Ris. '16	▽▽▽	5
● Barbera d'Asti La Villa '18	▽▽	3*
● Freisa d'Asti '16	▽▽	4
○ Gavi del Comune di Gavi '18	▽▽	3
○ Moscato d'Asti Centive '18	▽▽	3*
● Nebbiolo d'Alba San Pietro '17	▽▽	4

Orsolani

via Michele Chiesa, 12
10090 San Giorgio Canavese [TO]
Tel. +39 012432386
www.orsolani.it

CELLAR SALES
PRE-BOOKED VISITS
ANNUAL PRODUCTION 140,000 bottles
HECTARES UNDER VINE 19.00

The highly-active Gigi Orsolani is leading one of the area's historic wineries, serving as a true international ambassador of Erbaluce di Caluso, convinced as he is that the white that can stand shoulder-to-shoulder with the best. He's also convinced of the pergola method for vineyard management, which allows efficient selection of the grapes cultivated, at different times, for his Metodo Classico sparkling wine, still white version and passito. They also produce 60,000 bottles per year of La Rustìa, a wine we strongly recommend trying (even after a few years in bottle). The La Rustìa '19 put in a truly superb performance. First produced in 1985, ever since it's been an icon of the appellation. On the nose it's rich in herbs and white flowers, followed by a lovely gustatory pulp that's not without an enticing freshness. The Cuvée Tradition '13 also proves top-notch. It's a vibrant, fine Metodo Classico that offers up notes of dried herbs and bread crust; the palate is harmonious, with a perfectly integrated dosage and a long finish.

Wine	Rating
○ Erbaluce di Caluso La Rustìa '19	▼▼▼ 3*
○ Caluso Extra Brut Cuvée Tradizione '13	▼▼ 5
● Canavese Rosso Acini Sparsi '18	▼▼ 3
○ Erbaluce di Caluso Vintage '16	▼▼ 5
○ Caluso Passito Sulè '15	▼ 5
○ Caluso Passito Sulé '04	▽▽▽ 5
○ Caluso Passito Sulé '98	▽▽▽ 5
○ Erbaluce di Caluso La Rustia '15	▽▽▽ 3*
○ Erbaluce di Caluso La Rustia '13	▽▽▽ 3*
○ Erbaluce di Caluso La Rustia '12	▽▽▽ 3*
○ Erbaluce di Caluso La Rustia '11	▽▽▽ 3*
○ Erbaluce di Caluso La Rustia '10	▽▽▽ 2*
○ Erbaluce di Caluso La Rustia '09	▽▽▽ 2*
● Canavese Rosso Acini Sparsi '17	▽▽ 3
○ Erbaluce di Caluso La Rustia '18	▽▽ 3*

Pace

fraz. Madonna di Loreto
loc. Cascina Pace, 52
12043 Canale [CN]
Tel. +39 3384323245
www.pacevini.it

CELLAR SALES
PRE-BOOKED VISITS
ANNUAL PRODUCTION 60,000 bottles
HECTARES UNDER VINE 22.00

For four generations the Negro family have worked in agriculture, ever since the purchase of the farm in 1934. Today the producer is managed by brothers Dino and Pietro, who formally established the winery in 1996. The vineyards are located on a hill overlooking Canale, in an area called Pace, one of the most heavily wooded and coolest in the municipality. Here the medium textured soil hosts primarily the area's classic grape varieties: Arneis, Barbera, Favorita and Nebbiolo. The wines proposed are traditionally styled. The family are back in our main section. The Roero Riserva '15 really delivers; its aromas of licorice and tobacco lend complexity to hints of fresh red berry fruit, while the palate proves harmonious, rich in fruit, but also marked by elegant tannins and a juicy, sapid finish. Other well-made selections include the fresh and pleasant Brut Metodo Classico '16, and the Roero Arneis '19, which has nice texture, rich in fruit. The Roero Arneis Giuan from Pas '11 is less brilliant than the splendid 2010 version.

Wine	Rating
● Roero Ris. '15	▼▼ 5
○ Brut M. Cl. '16	▼▼ 5
○ Langhe Favorita '19	▼▼ 2*
○ Roero Arneis '19	▼▼ 2*
● Barbera d'Alba '18	▼ 2
● Barbera d'Alba Sup. '17	▼ 5
● Langhe Nebbiolo '18	▼ 2
○ Roero Arneis Giuan da Pas '11	▼ 7
● Barbera d'Alba '17	▽▽ 2*
○ Langhe Favorita '17	▽▽ 2*
○ Roero Arneis '17	▽▽ 3*
○ Roero Arneis Giuan da Pas '10	▽▽ 7
● Roero Ris. '13	▽▽ 5

Paitin

FRAZ. BRICCO DI NEIVE
VIA SERRABOELLA, 20
12052 NEIVE [CN]
TEL. +39 017367343
www.paitin.it

CELLAR SALES
PRE-BOOKED VISITS
ACCOMMODATION
ANNUAL PRODUCTION 90,000 bottles
HECTARES UNDER VINE 18.00
VITICULTURE METHOD Certified Organic
SUSTAINABLE WINERY

Of the three sub-varieties of Nebbiolo, Lampia, Michet and Rosé, this last is the most controversial, with some scholars even claiming that it's its own cultivar. For those few producers who still vinify it as a monovarietal, Rosé still delivers excellent results. The Pasquero Elia family (Giovanni and Silvano, who are increasingly supported by young Luca) demonstrate the grape's potential with their Barbaresco Sorì Paitin. The winery also stands out for its interesting Barbera d'Alba Campolive, which is made with grapes from a steep, not windy vineyard where olive trees were grown in past centuries. Both Barbarescos proposed represent exquisite interpretations of the warm 2017 vintage. The Serraboella is rich in red berries, with a very slight hint of sweet oak; it's powerful in the mouth, with delicate tannins. Even more elegant, the decidedly harmonious Serraboella Sorì Paitin plays on fine hints of licorice and rose petals. The valid Riserva Vecchie Vigne of 2015 is more closed and austere. Kudos to the well-crafted Nebbiolo Starda '18, absolutely first-rate

- Barbaresco Serraboella '17 🍷🍷 6
- Barbaresco Serraboella Sorì Paitin '17 🍷🍷 7
- Barbaresco Sorì Paitin V. V. '15 🍷🍷 8
- Langhe Nebbiolo Starda '18 🍷🍷 4
- Nebbiolo d'Alba Ca Veja '17 🍷🍷 5
- Barbera d'Alba Serra '18 🍷 3
- Barbera d'Alba Sup. Campolive '17 🍷 5
- Barbaresco Sorì Paitin '07 🥂🥂🥂 5
- Barbaresco Sorì Paitin '04 🥂🥂🥂 5
- Barbaresco Sorì Paitin '97 🥂🥂🥂 5
- Barbaresco Sorì Paitin '95 🥂🥂🥂 7
- Barbaresco Sorì Paitin V. V. '04 🥂🥂🥂 7
- Barbaresco Sorì Paitin V. V. '01 🥂🥂🥂 7
- Barbaresco Sorì Paitin V. V. '99 🥂🥂🥂 8
- Langhe Paitin '97 🥂🥂🥂 5

Palladino

P.ZZA CAPPELLANO, 9
12050 SERRALUNGA D'ALBA [CN]
TEL. +39 0173613108
www.palladinovini.com

CELLAR SALES
ANNUAL PRODUCTION 180,000 bottles
HECTARES UNDER VINE 11.00

Founded in 1974, Palladino initially specialised in the selection of grapes cultivated by Serralunga's local growers. Then came the cellar and finally bottling. Over the years, certain prestigious plots have been acquired directly, including the Ornato and Parafada crus, not to mention their small plot in San Bernardo, which has repeatedly earned Tre Bicchieri thanks to its Barolo Riserva. The range centers on 11 wines, all made with southern Piedmont's classic grape varieties and available at quite accessible prices. Ever so slightly dried violet accompanies raspberry and fine, sweet spices in the intense Barolo Ornato '16, creating a complexity of considerable character; the palate is very rich, with a compelling and delicate tannic texture that lends fullness and structure. The Barolo Parafada '16 is also of great elegance, with ripe peach and fresh red flowers creating a beautiful blend of finesse, while the palate proves classic, powerful, long and progressive.

- Barolo Ornato '16 🍷🍷 6
- Barolo Parafada '16 🍷🍷 6
- Barbera d'Alba Sup. Bricco delle Olive '17 🍷🍷 3
- Langhe Nebbiolo '18 🍷🍷 3
- Barolo del Comune di Serralunga d'Alba '16 🍷 5
- Barolo San Bernardo Ris. '13 🥂🥂🥂 8
- Barbera d'Alba Sup. Bricco delle Olive '16 🥂🥂 3
- Barolo del Comune di Serralunga d'Alba '14 🥂🥂 5
- Barolo del Comune di Serraunga d'Alba '15 🥂🥂 5
- Barolo Ornato '15 🥂🥂 6
- Barolo Parafada '15 🥂🥂 6
- Nebbiolo d'Alba '17 🥂🥂 3

F.lli Parusso

loc. Bussia, 55
12065 Monforte d'Alba [CN]
Tel. +39 017378257
www.parusso.com

CELLAR SALES
PRE-BOOKED VISITS
ANNUAL PRODUCTION 125,000 bottles
HECTARES UNDER VINE 25.00
SUSTAINABLE WINERY

The producer now boasts 120 years of activity, even though it was only in 1971 that Armando Parusso took over the business and began introducing their bottles to the world. His sons Marco and Tiziana have given a further boost, conferring a remarkable personality on their Barolo, one constituted of organic and biodynamic farming, new French oak and great maturity of fruit. Nebbiolo continues to give rise to a Metodo Classico sparkling wine of guaranteed elegance and pleasantness. For exceptional vintages they also produce a prestigious Barolo Riserva and a Barolo Bussia Riserva Oro. With the 2018 vintage, the Rovella once again demonstrates that it's one of Italy's most interesting Sauvignon, thanks to multifaceted aromas of citrus and pineapple, while the palate is certainly voluminous and pervasive, though without ever becoming heavy. Their 2016 Barolos are characterized by mature notes, which are always grounded in cocoa and chocolate as well as quinine, with tannins always quite vivid and tight-knit.

Wine	Glasses	Price
● Barolo Bussia Riserva Oro '12	TT	8
● Barolo Mariondino '16	TT	8
○ Langhe Sauvignon Rovella '18	TT	5
● Barolo '16	TT	7
● Barolo Mosconi '16	TT	8
○ Parusso Brut M. Cl. '15	TT	6
● Barolo Bussia '16	T	8
● Barolo '15	YY	6
● Barolo '14	YY	6
● Barolo Bussia '15	YY	8
● Barolo Bussia Ris. '10	YY	8
● Barolo Mariondino '15	YY	7
● Barolo Mosconi '15	YY	8
○ Parusso Brut M. Cl. '14	YY	6

Agostino Pavia e Figli

loc. Molizzo, 3
14041 Agliano Terme [AT]
Tel. +39 0141954125
www.agostinopavia.it

CELLAR SALES
PRE-BOOKED VISITS
ACCOMMODATION
ANNUAL PRODUCTION 75,000 bottles
HECTARES UNDER VINE 9.00

A viticultural node that connects Langhe and Monferrato perfectly, Agliano Terme hosts the winery run by Giuseppe and Mauro Pavia in the district of Bologna, as well as most of their vineyards (though they also have some plots in Montegrosso). Naturally, most of the vineyards host Barbera, but the wines made with Grignolino, Dolcetto and Syrah show a well-rounded stylistic skill that's recognizable in its measured, though flavorful touch, both when it comes to their base offering and their premium selections. The Barbera d'Asti proposed are always of excellent craftsmanship. On the nose the Superior Moliss '17 offers up aromas of quinine and juniper berries, with a close-woven, powerful palate that plays especially on the richness of alcohol and fruit. The Superior La Mareschialla '17 sees notes of roasted coffee and cocoa followed by a palate rich in pulp, still marked by the presence of oak, but with a long, juicy finish. The Monferrato Rosso Talin '17, a blend of Barbera (85%) and Syrah, also proves quite generous.

Wine	Glasses	Price
● Barbera d'Asti Sup. La Marescialla '17	TT	4
● Barbera d'Asti Sup. Moliss '17	TT	3
● M.to Rosso Talin '17	TT	3
⊙ Piemonte Rosato '19	T	2
● Piemonte Rosso i Tre Volti '15	T	2
● Barbera d'Asti Blina '17	YY	2*
● Barbera d'Asti Blina '15	YY	2*
● Barbera d'Asti Casareggio '16	YY	2*
● Barbera d'Asti Sup. La Marescialla '16	YY	4
● Barbera d'Asti Sup. Moliss '16	YY	3
● Barbera d'Asti Sup. Moliss '14	YY	3
● Grignolino d'Asti '18	YY	2*
● Grignolino d'Asti '16	YY	2*
● M.to Rosso Talin '16	YY	3

★Pecchenino

B.TA VALDIBERTI, 59
12063 DOGLIANI [CN]
TEL. +39 017370686
www.pecchenino.com

CELLAR SALES
PRE-BOOKED VISITS
ACCOMMODATION
ANNUAL PRODUCTION 130,000 bottles
HECTARES UNDER VINE 28.00
SUSTAINABLE WINERY

Attilio and Orlando Pecchenino have been managing the winery since 1987 with outstanding results in the world of Dogliani DOGCG. The wine is offered in different versions, from the always elegant Sirì d'Jermu to the powerful Bricco Botti (which makes use of an extra year of aging in the cellar), to the fresh and fruity San Luigi. The skilled brothers have also proceeded with a gradual expansion of the vineyards, acquiring plots mainly suited to the production of Barolo in the municipality of Monforte d'Alba. The family's latest passion is Metodo Classico. Made with Nebbiolo, it already started gaining attention with the first trial in 2015. On the palate the Barolo Le Coste di Monforte '16 is a model of harmony, with alcohol, acidity and tannins perfectly blended and perfectly balanced; its lovely nose features plenty of fruit and a fine hint of oak. It's similar to the successful style exhibited by the Barolo San Giuseppe '16, with a structure that unfolds progressively, and isn't too rich. The Barolo Bussia '16 is just a bit more vegetal, with hints of herbs in the sun and citrus.

● Barolo Le Coste di Monforte '16	▼▼ 7
○ Alta Langa Pas Dosé Psea '16	▼▼ 5
● Barbera d'Alba Quass '19	▼▼ 4
● Barolo Bussia '16	▼▼ 7
● Barolo San Giuseppe '16	▼▼ 6
● Dogliani San Luigi '19	▼▼ 3
● Langhe Nebbiolo Bricco Ravera '17	▼▼ 3
● Dogliani Sup. Sirì d'Jermu '18	▼ 4
○ Langhe Chardonnay Maestro '19	▼ 3
○ Alta Langa Pas Dosé Psea '15	▽▽ 5
● Barolo Bussia '15	▽▽ 7
● Barolo San Giuseppe '15	▽▽ 6
● Dogliani San Luigi '18	▽▽ 3*
● Dogliani Sup. Bricco Botti '16	▽▽ 4
● Dogliani Sup. Sirì d'Jermu '17	▽▽ 4
● Dogliani Sup. Sirì d'Jermu '16	▽▽ 4

Magda Pedrini

LOC. CA' DA' MEO
VIA PRATOLUNGO, 163
15066 GAVI [AL]
TEL. +39 0143667923
www.magdapedrini.it

CELLAR SALES
PRE-BOOKED VISITS
ANNUAL PRODUCTION 90,000 bottles
HECTARES UNDER VINE 11.50
SUSTAINABLE WINERY

The picturesque winery of Magda Pedrini is situated in Gavi, on the road that leads to the hamlet of Pratolungo, an area bordering Arquata, Gavi and Serravalle Scrivia. It's a territory bound up with noble Genoese families, and can boast deep agricultural and viticultural roots. Today predominantly Cortese and Barbera are used, for a range that comprises 4 wines: 2 characterful Gavi del Comune di Gavi, a Gavi del Comune di Gavi Brut Metodo Classico (that spends 42 months on the lees) and the Pettirosso, a Monferrato Rosso made with Barbera and Cabernet Sauvignon. The Gavi del Comune di Gavi Magda features an impressive olfactory spectrum: chamomile and exotic fruit on a mineral background, aromas that converge in an intense, full-bodied and sapid palate, finishing long. The Ad Lunam unveils an intense, persistent aromatic suite, with hints of plum and dried fruit on mineral notes. In the mouth it's full-bodied, with acidity and sapidity lengthening a lingering finish.

○ Gavi del Comune di Gavi Magda '19	▼▼ 3*
○ Gavi del Comune di Gavi ad Lunam '19	▼▼ 3
○ Gavi del Comune di Gavi ad Lunam '18	▽▽ 3*
○ Gavi del Comune di Gavi Domino '14	▽▽ 4
○ Gavi del Comune di Gavi E' '17	▽▽ 3
○ Gavi del Comune di Gavi E' '16	▽▽ 3*
○ Gavi del Comune di Gavi E' '15	▽▽ 3
○ Gavi del Comune di Gavi La Piacentina '17	▽▽ 3*
○ Gavi del Comune di Gavi La Piacentina '16	▽▽ 3
○ Gavi del Comune di Gavi La Piacentina '15	▽▽ 3
○ Gavi del Comune di Gavi Magda '18	▽▽ 3*

Pelassa

B.GO TUCCI, 43
12046 MONTÀ [CN]
TEL. +39 0173971312
www.pelassa.com

CELLAR SALES
ANNUAL PRODUCTION 80,000 bottles
HECTARES UNDER VINE 14.00

Founded in 1960 by Mario Pelassa, the producer is now run by his sons Daniele and Davide. The estate's vineyards are located in Montà d'Alba, in the northernmost part of the municipality, a fresh and wooded area. These give rise to wines rooted mainly in the area's traditional grapes, Arneis, Barbera and Nebbiolo. There are also other plots in Verduno, where Barolo is produced. Their selection is well made, pleasant and rich in fruit, but at the same time full bodied and structured. With the 2017 vintage the Roero Antaniolo Riserva once again delivered during our final tastings. Hints of tea leaves and citrus fruits rise up out of the glass, while the palate, though still marked by oak, is rich in pulp, long and beautifully harmonious. It's on par with the Barolo San Lorenzo di Verduno '16, with its hints of red berries and balsamic nuances on the nose, and a palate characterized by elegant tannic texture and good substance. The other wines tasted are also well made.

Wine	Rating
● Barolo San Lorenzo di Verduno '16	🍷🍷 6
● Roero Antaniolo Ris. '17	🍷🍷 4
● Nebbiolo d'Alba Sot '17	🍷 3
○ Roero Arneis San Vito '19	🍷 3
● Barbera d'Alba Sup. San Pancrazio '17	🍷🍷 3
● Barbera d'Alba Sup. San Pancrazio '15	🍷🍷 3
● Barolo '12	🍷🍷 6
● Barolo San Lorenzo '15	🍷🍷 6
● Barolo San Lorenzo di Verduno '13	🍷🍷 6
● Nebbiolo d'Alba Sot '14	🍷🍷 3
● Nebbiolo d'Alba Sot '12	🍷🍷 3
● Roero Antaniolo Ris. '16	🍷🍷 4
● Roero Antaniolo Ris. '15	🍷🍷 4
● Roero Antaniolo Ris. '13	🍷🍷 4
○ Roero Arneis San Vito '18	🍷🍷 3
○ Roero Arneis San Vito '17	🍷🍷 3*
○ Roero Arneis San Vito '16	🍷🍷 2*

Pelissero

VIA FERRERE, 10
12050 TREISO [CN]
TEL. +39 0173638430
www.pelissero.com

CELLAR SALES
PRE-BOOKED VISITS
ANNUAL PRODUCTION 250,000 bottles
HECTARES UNDER VINE 43.00
SUSTAINABLE WINERY

The tireless Giorgio Pelissero looks after his winery and his customers with equal passion, so you can find him, depending on the season, overseeing fermentation of his Nebbiolo grapes, at Tokyo airport, giving instructions on pruning a certain vineyard, or presenting his Barbaresco in a wine shop in Rome. The panoramic cellar is equipped with the most modern technology, but Giorgio always wants to emphasize his deep respect for the intrinsic characteristics of each cru, taking care that winemaking is also respectful of the personality of each cultivar. In the absence of their Barbarescos, whose release has been postponed until next year, the Barbera d'Alba Tulin '17 shines, combining notes of ripe cherries and toasted hints with an opulent but still lively acidic vigor. The Barbera d'Alba Piani '18 seems more open and immediately expressive. The Moscato d'Asti '19 is satisfying and convincing, calling up fresh sage on the nose and coming through pleasantly soft on the palate. The two 2019 Dolcetto d'Albas are also excellent.

Wine	Rating
● Barbera d'Alba Tulin '17	🍷🍷 5
● Barbera d'Alba Piani '18	🍷🍷 3
● Dolcetto d'Alba Augenta '19	🍷🍷 3
○ Langhe Favorita '19	🍷🍷 2*
○ Langhe Riesling Rigadin '19	🍷🍷 3
○ Moscato d'Asti '19	🍷🍷 2*
● Dolcetto d'Alba Munfrina '19	🍷 2
● Barbaresco Vanotu '08	🍷🍷🍷 8
● Barbaresco Vanotu '07	🍷🍷🍷 8
● Barbaresco Vanotu '06	🍷🍷🍷 8
● Barbaresco Vanotu '01	🍷🍷🍷 7
● Barbaresco Nubiola '16	🍷🍷 5
● Barbaresco Vanotu '16	🍷🍷 8
● Barbera d'Alba Piani '17	🍷🍷 3*
● Barbera d'Alba Tulin '16	🍷🍷 5

Pasquale Pelissero

Cascina Crosa, 2
12052 Neive [CN]
Tel. +39 017367376
www.pasqualepelissero.com

CELLAR SALES
PRE-BOOKED VISITS
ANNUAL PRODUCTION 35,000 bottles
HECTARES UNDER VINE 8.00

Ornella Pelissero stays away from the spotlight and media attention, preferring instead to continue with her family's reserved style, which emphasizes artisanal craftsmanship both in the vineyard and in the cellar. And, even with her young son Simone becoming more and more active, her range follows this classical Langhe approach: no draconian thinning out, no rotomacerators, rather long fermentations, only large oak barrels never used invasively. The resulting wines have purity of fruit and great drinkability as their strong points, from Dolcetto d'Alba to their always convincing Barbaresco. Only two wines were submitted for tasting. The Barbaresco San Giuliano Bricco is particularly complex and elegant, certainly among the most successful of the warm 2017 vintage: black and red berries merge with hints of liquorice, anticipating a soft, relaxed palate that's not devoid of substance but nevertheless shows excellent balance—a very pleasant drink. Alcohol-steeped cherries and a touch of oak characterize the elegant, supple Cascina Crosa '17.

- Barbaresco San Giuliano Bricco '17 TT 5
- Barbaresco Cascina Crosa '17 TT 4
- Barbaresco Bricco San Giuliano '14 YY 5
- Barbaresco Bricco San Giuliano '12 YY 5
- Barbaresco Cascina Crosa '16 YY 4
- Barbaresco Cascina Crosa '14 YY 4
- Barbaresco Cascina Crosa '13 YY 4
- Barbaresco Ciabot Ris. '13 YY 5
- Barbaresco Ciabot Ris. '12 YY 4
- Barbaresco Ciabot Ris. '10 YY 4
- Barbaresco San Giuliano Bricco '16 YY 5
- Barbaresco San Giuliano Bricco '15 YY 5
- Barbaresco San Giuliano Bricco '13 YY 5
- Barbera d'Alba Anna '17 YY 2*

Pertinace

loc. Pertinace, 2/5
12050 Treiso [CN]
Tel. +39 0173442238
www.pertinace.com

CELLAR SALES
PRE-BOOKED VISITS
ANNUAL PRODUCTION 700,000 bottles
HECTARES UNDER VINE 100.00

The cooperative producer Pertinace brings together 17 members. Together they bring great care and dedication to their work of cultivating about 90 hectares of vineyards in Treiso. Founded by Mario Barbero in 1973, Pertinace has reached high quality levels while maintaining competitive prices, and the winery is now represented on major world markets. The main variety grown is Nebbiolo, which is flanked by Dolcetto, Barbera, Chardonnay and Moscato, for a total annual production that exceeds 600 thousand bottles. The Barbaresco Nervo '16 features vibrant whiffs of red berries, tobacco and violet on the nose, while on the palate it has medium body, proving full, and harmonious with fine tannins and a rich, fruity finish. The Barbaresco Castellizzano '17 is plush in tones of cherry and mint, combining a mature profile with a finish of nice aromatic freshness. Toastier, spicier sensations characterize the 2017 Barbaresco Marcarini.

- Barbaresco Castellizzano '17 TT 5
- Barbaresco '17 TT 5
- Barbaresco Marcarini '17 TT 5
- Barbaresco Nervo '17 TT 5
- Dolcetto d'Alba '19 TT 3
- Barbera d'Alba '18 T 3
- Langhe Nebbiolo '18 T 3
- Barbaresco '16 YY 5
- Barbaresco '15 YY 5
- Barbaresco Castellizzano '16 YY 5
- Barbaresco Marcarini '16 YY 5
- Barbaresco Marcarini '15 YY 5
- Barbaresco Nervo '16 YY 5
- Barbaresco Nervo '15 YY 5
- Barbera d'Alba '17 YY 3
- Dolcetto d'Alba '18 YY 3

Pescaja

via San Matteo, 59
14010 Cisterna d'Asti [AT]
Tel. +39 0141979711
www.pescaja.com

PRE-BOOKED VISITS
ANNUAL PRODUCTION 200,000 bottles
HECTARES UNDER VINE 23.50

Pescaja, the winery founded by Beppe Guido, is unique in bringing together three territories that are all near to each other but quite different in terms of history, appellations of origin and winemaking traditions: Roero, Terre Alfieri and Nizza. The cellar is situated in Cisterna d'Asti, where you'll also find the original vineyard, acquired in 1990, growing in mainly sandy soils. They also have plots in Nizza Monferrato, acquired in 1998, where the soil is more calcareous. The wines offered are well crafted, modern, rich in fruit and pleasant. This year Beppe Guido proposed a solid and well-crafted set of wines. The Nizza Solneri '17 is classic in its aromas of ripe black berries and wet earth, making for a palate rich in fruit and well supported by acidity. The Barbera d'Asti Soliter '19 is fresh and gutsy, going all in on notes of undergrowth and cherry, with a highly pleasant finish, while the Terre Alfieri Arneis Solei '19 sees aromas of white fruit and citrus followed by a consistent palate, sapid and well-sustained.

Wine	Rating
○ Monferrato Bianco Solo Luna '18	🍷🍷 5
● Nizza Solneri '17	🍷🍷 5
● Barbera d'Asti Soliter '19	🍷🍷 2*
● Monferrato Rosso Solis '17	🍷🍷 5
○ Roero Arneis '19	🍷🍷 3
○ Terre Alfieri Arneis Solei '19	🍷🍷 2*
● Terre Alfieri Nebbiolo Tuké '18	🍷🍷 3
● Barbera d'Asti Soliter '18	ΨΨ 2*
● Barbera d'Asti Soliter '17	ΨΨ 2*
○ Monferrato Bianco Solo Luna '17	ΨΨ 5
● Monferrato Rosso Solis '16	ΨΨ 3
● Nizza Solneri '16	ΨΨ 4
● Nizza Solneri '15	ΨΨ 4
⊙ Piemonte Rosato Le Fleury '18	ΨΨ 2*
○ Roero Arneis '18	ΨΨ 3
○ Terre Alfieri Arneis Solei '18	ΨΨ 2*
○ Terre Alfieri Arneis Sololuce '17	ΨΨ 2*

★Le Piane

p.zza Matteotti, 1
28010 Boca [NO]
Tel. +39 3483354185
www.bocapiane.com

CELLAR SALES
PRE-BOOKED VISITS
ANNUAL PRODUCTION 60,000 bottles
HECTARES UNDER VINE 10.00
SUSTAINABLE WINERY

In 1998 Christopf Künzli arrived in Boca from Switzerland, determined to bet on the great potential not only of Northern Piedmont's Nebbiolo but also on the promise of an almost extinct appellation, Boca. These bets paid off thanks to a deep and forward-thinking conviction: traditional agronomic techniques, and in particular the maggiorina training system, could be preserved, while also protecting the environment without relying on artificial chemicals. Quality has grown steadily, and today Le Piane is a winery known and appreciated throughout the world. The soils of the area (the porphyry of the Valsesia supervulcano) contribute heavily to the expression of the magnificent Boca '16. From the terrain it draws its indomitable, sapid, wild character, rich in gentian aromas. The Bianko '18, made with Erbaluce, is also splendid, exhibiting a structure on the palate that's almost that of a red.

Wine	Rating
● Boca '16	🍷🍷🍷 8
○ Bianko '18	🍷🍷 3*
● Mimmo '17	🍷 5
● Piane '17	🍷 6
● Boca '15	ΨΨΨ 8
● Boca '12	ΨΨΨ 8
● Boca '11	ΨΨΨ 8
● Boca '10	ΨΨΨ 7
● Boca '08	ΨΨΨ 7
● Boca '06	ΨΨΨ 6
● Boca '05	ΨΨΨ 6
● Boca '04	ΨΨΨ 6
● Boca '03	ΨΨΨ 6
● La Maggiorina '18	ΨΨ 3
● Mimmo '16	ΨΨ 5
● Piane '12	ΨΨ 6
● Piane '11	ΨΨ 5

Le Pianelle

S.DA FORTE, 24
13862 BRUSNENGO [BI]
TEL. +39 3478772726
www.lepianelle.com

PRE-BOOKED VISITS
ANNUAL PRODUCTION 12,000 bottles
HECTARES UNDER VINE 3.00

Dieter Heuskel and Peter Dipoli's venture in Northern Piedmont has achieved a certain maturity. Already appreciated in Alto Adige, the producers' results here say it all, thanks to important work done on many tiny parcels (50 plots for a total of 4 hectares), a detailed knowledge of the terrain, and work in the cellar that's increasingly calibrated and graceful. At about 500 meters above sea level, the soils are rich in porphyry red sand of volcanic origin and crushed rocks. Their flagship wine is the Bramaterra, made with Nebbiolo grapes and smaller shares of Croatina and Vespolina. Just from its color the magnificent Bramaterra '16 entices. It's intense in its graceful nuances, first spicy and then just a bit herbaceous. In the mouth it has a measured weight, with crunchy red fruit and a very tasty flavor, finishing long and characterful. Accentuated color and structure for the typology are rendering the Rosato Al Posto dei Fiori '19 a model: it has flesh, density and length.

Wine	Rating
● Bramaterra '16	▼▼ 8
⊙ Coste della Sesia Rosato Al Posto dei Fiori '19	▼▼ 3
● Coste della Sesia Rosso Al Forte '17	▼▼ 5
● Bramaterra '15	▽▽ 8
● Bramaterra '14	▽▽ 8
● Bramaterra '13	▽▽ 8
● Bramaterra '12	▽▽ 8
● Bramaterra '11	▽▽ 8
⊙ Coste della Sesia Rosato Al Posto dei Fiori '18	▽▽ 3
⊙ Coste della Sesia Rosato Al Posto dei Fiori '17	▽▽ 3
⊙ Coste della Sesia Rosato Al Posto dei Fiori '16	▽▽ 3
⊙ Coste della Sesia Rosato Al Posto dei Fiori '15	▽▽ 3

Pico Maccario

VIA CORDARA, 87
14046 MOMBARUZZO [AT]
TEL. +39 0141774522
www.picomaccario.com

CELLAR SALES
PRE-BOOKED VISITS
ANNUAL PRODUCTION 650,000 bottles
HECTARES UNDER VINE 100.00

Founded in the second half of the 1990s, the Maccario family's winery is a sort of 'château' surrounded by a single, contiguous vineyard of about 70 hectares on the hills of Mombaruzzo, one of the best areas for the production of Nizza and Barbera in general. Available in four versions, differentiated according to style and territory, the Asti grape is at the core of a modern range that's completed by Chardonnay, Sauvignon, Favorita, Freisa, Merlot and Cabernet. The 2019 version of the Barbera d'Asti Lavignone Barbera d'Asti once again demonstrates that it's a delicious, standard-label Barbera. Notes of fresh red berries accompany vegetal nuances, while on the palate it's supple, but also long and pleasant. The Nizza Tre Roveri '18 exhibits excellent body, with notes of dried mushrooms and cherry. The Barbera d'Asti Superiore Epico '18 plays on complexity and the density of its tannins, while the Barbera d'Asti Villa della Rosa '19 proves medium bodied and well supported by acidity.

Wine	Rating
● Nizza Tre Roveri '18	▼▼▼ 4*
● Barbera d'Asti Lavignone '19	▼▼ 3*
● Barbera d'Asti Sup. Epico '18	▼▼ 6
● Barbera d'Asti Villa della Rosa '19	▼▼ 2*
○ M.to Bianco Vita '19	▼ 5
● Barbera d'Asti Lavignone '18	▽▽▽ 3*
● Barbera d'Asti Lavignone '17	▽▽▽ 3*
● Barbera d'Asti Sup. Epico '15	▽▽▽ 5
● Barbera d'Asti Lavignone '16	▽▽ 3
● Barbera d'Asti Sup. Epico '17	▽▽ 6
● Barbera d'Asti Sup. Epico '16	▽▽ 5
● Barbera d'Asti Sup. Tre Roveri '16	▽▽ 4
● Barbera d'Asti Sup. Tre Roveri '15	▽▽ 4
● Barbera d'Asti Villa della Rosa '18	▽▽ 2*
● Barbera d'Asti Villa della Rosa '17	▽▽ 2*
● Barbera d'Asti Villa della Rosa '16	▽▽ 2*
● Nizza Tre Roveri '17	▽▽ 4

★Pio Cesare

via Cesare Balbo, 6
12051 Alba [CN]
Tel. +39 0173440386
www.piocesare.it

PRE-BOOKED VISITS
ANNUAL PRODUCTION 420,000 bottles
HECTARES UNDER VINE 75.00
SUSTAINABLE WINERY

Pio Cesare made this producer a leader in Langhe, working to both expand the area under vine and construct an extensive team of expert agronomists and enologists. And so it is that a few bottles exported around Europe starting back in 1881 has grown into a brand present in restaurants the world over, with increasing recognition from wine critics. Outstanding quality and expressiveness pervade their range, with the Barolo Ornato, Barbaresco Il Bricco and Chardonnay Piodilei regularly in the spotlight. The lively and expressive Barolo Ornato '16 exhibits magnificent personality. It's rich in red berry sensations, with a delicious hint of licorice, exceptionally long and harmonious on the palate, with a suffused, austere halo that brings out its charm and substance. For us this excellent Ornato is our Red Wine of the Year. The lovely, 'basic' 2016 Barolo is just a little more impetuous, but rich in pulp, offering plenty of gustatory satisfaction. The Barbaresco Il Bricco '16 is characterized by notable complexity and delicate harmony.

● Barolo Ornato '16	TTT 8
● Barbaresco Il Bricco '16	TT 8
● Barolo Mosconi '16	TT 8
○ Langhe Chardonnay Piodilei '17	TT 6
● Barolo '16	TT 8
○ Langhe Sauvignon Blanc '19	TT 4
● Barbera d'Alba Sup. Fides V. Mosconi '18	T 6
● Barolo Ornato '13	YYY 8
● Barolo Ornato '12	YYY 8
● Barolo Ornato '11	YYY 8
● Barolo Ornato '10	YYY 8
● Barolo Ornato '09	YYY 8
● Barolo Ornato '08	YYY 8
● Barolo Ornato '06	YYY 8
● Barolo Ornato '05	YYY 8

Luigi Pira

via XX Settembre, 9
12050 Serralunga d'Alba [CN]
Tel. +39 0173613106
www.piraluigi.it

CELLAR SALES
PRE-BOOKED VISITS
ANNUAL PRODUCTION 50,000 bottles
HECTARES UNDER VINE 12.00

The Luigi Pira winery, whose viticultural roots go way back, became famous for its Barolo in the late 1990s, when American critics noticed that a new star had been born. Gianpaolo Pira had recently taken over the reins and had made two choices: on the one hand to work the grapes from the famous family owned crus as best as possible, and on the other to adopt cutting-edge equipment, with horizontal fermentation vessels and fine, small French oak barrels for ageing. Their range is made up entirely of reds, with the Barolo Marenca often contending for first place with the more acclaimed Vignarionda. The combination of grapes from various estate crus gave rise to a more than interesting Barolo del comune di Serralunga d'Alba '16, with beautiful red and black berries marking the nose and a long, alluring palate characterized by measured tannic grip. Fresh and vibrant notes of liquorice and tobacco adorn the clean, fruity aromatic background of the Barolo Vigna Rionda '16, while the palate proves bold and pleasant.

● Barolo del Comune di Serralunga d'Alba '16	TT 5
● Barolo Marenca '16	TT 7
● Barbera d'Alba Sup. '18	TT 3
● Barolo Margheria '16	TT 6
● Barolo Vigna Rionda '16	TT 8
● Langhe Nebbiolo '18	TT 3
● Barolo Marenca '11	YYY 7
● Barolo Marenca '09	YYY 7
● Barolo Marenca '08	YYY 7
● Barolo V. Marenca '01	YYY 7
● Barolo V. Marenca '97	YYY 8
● Barolo V. Rionda '06	YYY 8
● Barolo V. Rionda '04	YYY 8
● Barolo V. Rionda '00	YYY 8
● Barolo Vignarionda '12	YYY 8
● Barolo Margheria '15	YY 6

E. Pira & Figli Chiara Boschis

via Vittorio Veneto, 1
12060 Barolo [CN]
Tel. +39 017356247
www.pira-chiaraboschis.com

CELLAR SALES
PRE-BOOKED VISITS
ANNUAL PRODUCTION 35,000 bottles
HECTARES UNDER VINE 8.50
VITICULTURE METHOD Certified Organic

Few of our readers had the opportunity to meet the winery's original founder, who left us in the 1970s after becoming famous for his wines and for being the last producer to crush grapes with his feet. Chiara Boschis, who came into action in 1980, not only wanted to maintain the artisanal size of the winery, but she wanted to create her own Barolo, one with a charming, modern style born from grapes grown with the utmost respect for the environment. If the great Gigi Pira boasted making wine without the help of any kind of machinery, Chiara has managed without chemicals. The best Barolo Mosconi proposed so far is a 2016: its aromas range from violet to red berries by ways of herbs on a delicate hint of elegant oak, while the palate proves rich, long and always perfectly balanced. Particularly fresh and lively, we also appreciated the alluring Barolo Via Nuova '16, already an elegantly drinkable wine. And Chiara never ceases to impress with her modern-yet-classic interpretations of the Cannubi cru.

Wine	Glasses	Price
● Barolo Cannubi '16	TT	8
● Barolo Mosconi '16	TT	8
● Barolo Via Nuova '16	TT	8
● Barbera d'Alba Sup. '18	TT	5
● Langhe Nebbiolo '18	TT	6
● Dolcetto d'Alba '19	T	4
● Barolo '94	YYY	7
● Barolo Cannubi '11	YYY	8
● Barolo Cannubi '10	YYY	8
● Barolo Cannubi '06	YYY	8
● Barolo Cannubi '05	YYY	8
● Barolo Cannubi '00	YYY	8
● Barolo Cannubi '97	YYY	8
● Barolo Cannubi '96	YYY	8
● Barolo Ris. '90	YYY	8

Guido Platinetti

via Roma, 60
28074 Ghemme [NO]
Tel. +39 3389945783
www.platinettivini.com

CELLAR SALES
PRE-BOOKED VISITS
ANNUAL PRODUCTION 25,000 bottles
HECTARES UNDER VINE 8.00

Brothers Stefano and Andrea have made the most of this historic Ghemme producer's long tradition of winemaking. Indeed, their five hectares of vineyards are well manicured. Their pride and joy is Ronco al Maso, a southwest facing hill whose soils are rich in mineral components. Theirs are wines of great charm, offered at a very attractive price. In addition to Nebbiolo, a cornerstone, we find Barbera and Vespolina, making for a solidly traditional battery of wines that faithfully reflect the characteristics of the DOCG. The Ghemme Vigna Ronco al Maso '16 proves vibrant with lovely notes of red fruit and slightly vegetal hints lending complexity—subtle and youthful. On the palate it's fresh, juicy, with close-knit tannins and a nice, elegant, harmonious finish. Captivating with its young fruitiness and stylish, peppery profile, the Vespolina '19 is simple and very pleasant to drink, but also endowed with character and expressiveness on the finish.

Wine	Glasses	Price
● Ghemme V. Ronco al Maso '16	TT	5
● Colline Novaresi Nebbiolo '18	TT	3
● Colline Novaresi Vespolina '19	TT	3
● Colline Novaresi Rosso Guido '19	T	3
● Ghemme V. Ronco al Maso '15	YYY	4*
● Colline Novaresi Nebbiolo '17	YY	3
● Colline Novaresi Nebbiolo '16	YY	3
● Colline Novaresi Nebbiolo '14	YY	3
● Colline Novaresi Nebbiolo '11	YY	3
● Colline Novaresi Rosso Guido '18	YY	3
● Colline Novaresi Vespolina '18	YY	3
● Colline Novaresi Vespolina '17	YY	3
● Colline Novaresi Vespolina '16	YY	2*
● Colline Novaresi Vespolina '14	YY	2*
● Ghemme V. Ronco al Maso '13	YY	4
● Ghemme V. Ronco Maso '12	YY	4
● Ghemme V. Ronco Maso '10	YY	4

Marco Porello

c.so Alba, 71
12043 Canale [CN]
Tel. +39 0173979324
www.porellovini.it

CELLAR SALES
PRE-BOOKED VISITS
ANNUAL PRODUCTION 130,000 bottles
HECTARES UNDER VINE 15.00

Marco Porello has been running the family business, founded in the 1930s, for a quarter of a century. The estate vineyards are located in two municipalities. In Vezza d'Alba, the predominantly sandy and mineral-rich marine soil hosts Arneis, Favorita and Nebbiolo. In Canale the medium-dense calcareous-clayey soil gives rise to Barbera, Brachetto and Nebbiolo. Their range is marked by cleanness, finesse and freshness of the fruit. The two Roeros proposed this year are excellent. The Torretta '17 is vibrant on the nose, with beautiful harmony amidst fresh fruit and sweet oak, and of notable structure on the palate. Tannins are pronounced, still a bit rough, but it's juicy, coming through with a long, vigorous finish. The Roero San Michele Riserva '16 is characterized by aromas of liqueur cherries and Mediterranean scrub, all followed by a rather supple palate, medium-bodied and highly pleasant.

Wine	Rating	Price
● Roero San Michele Ris. '16	▼▼	5
● Roero Torretta '17	▼▼	4
● Langhe Nebbiolo '18	▼▼	3
○ Roero Arneis '19	▼▼	2*
○ Roero Arneis Camestri '19	▼▼	3
● Barbera d'Alba Mommiano '19	▼	2
○ Langhe Favorita '19	▼	2
● Roero Torretta '06	▽▽▽	3*
● Roero Torretta '04	▽▽▽	3*
● Nebbiolo d'Alba '16	▽▽	3
○ Roero Arneis '18	▽▽	2*
○ Roero Arneis '17	▽▽	2*
○ Roero Arneis Camestri '18	▽▽	3
○ Roero Arneis Camestri '17	▽▽	3*
○ Roero San Michele Ris. '15	▽▽	3
● Roero Torretta '16	▽▽	4
● Roero Torretta '15	▽▽	4

Guido Porro

via Alba, 1
12050 Serralunga d'Alba [CN]
Tel. +39 0173613306
www.guidoporro.com

CELLAR SALES
PRE-BOOKED VISITS
ACCOMMODATION
ANNUAL PRODUCTION 35,000 bottles
HECTARES UNDER VINE 8.00

It's full steam ahead for Guido Porro's winery in Serralunga d'Alba, a property surrounded by vineyards that practically form a single, contiguous estate. Here in the heart of Lazzarito, the producer's historic cru, they forge wines with a strong sapid and balsamic profile. In all, four Barolos are produced. The last chronologically is the prestigious Vigna Rionda, the result of parcels once owned by Tommaso Canale. Vinification takes place in steel and concrete, with maturation in Slavonian barrels to follow. Deep and airy earthy hints features in the Barolo Vigna Rionda '16, a substantive red capable of expressing a complex gustatory weave without ever losing its verve and flavor. The finish is overwhelming, its aging potential enormous. Tre Bicchieri. The Barolo Vigna Lazzairasco '16 was also in our finals. A vibrant wine in its notes of tobacco and licorice, the finish is austere and lengthy. The rest of their range also exhibits commendable craftsmanship.

Wine	Rating	Price
● Barolo Vigna Rionda '16	▼▼▼	8
● Barolo Gianetto '16	▼▼	5
● Barolo V. Lazzairasco '16	▼▼	5
● Barbera d'Alba V. Santa Caterina '19	▼▼	3
● Lange Nebbiolo Camilu '19	▼	4
● Barolo V. Lazzairasco '13	▽▽▽	5
● Barolo V. Lazzairasco '12	▽▽▽	5
● Barolo V. Lazzairasco '11	▽▽▽	5
● Barolo V. Lazzairasco '09	▽▽▽	5
● Barolo V. Lazzairasco '07	▽▽▽	5
● Barolo Vigna Rionda '15	▽▽▽	8
● Barolo Gianetto '15	▽▽	5
● Barolo V. Lazzairasco '15	▽▽	5
● Barolo V. Lazzairasco '14	▽▽	5
● Barolo V. Santa Caterina '15	▽▽	5
● Barolo V. Santa Caterina '14	▽▽	5
● Barolo Vigna Rionda '14	▽▽	8

Post dal Vin
Terre del Barbera

Fraz. Possavina
via Salie, 19
14030 Rocchetta Tanaro [AT]
Tel. +39 0141644143
www.postdalvin.it

CELLAR SALES
PRE-BOOKED VISITS
ANNUAL PRODUCTION 80,000 bottles
HECTARES UNDER VINE 100.00

Rocchetta Tanaro, Cortiglione and Masio: it's here that we find most of the plots of Barbera overseen by Post dal Vin's 200 growers. The historic Monferrato Astigiano cooperative winery, which has been active for over 60 years, offers a range that's divided into various lines amidst base offerings, select wines and crus. Production is carried out at two sites: one equipped with cutting edge equipment for winemaking and storage, the other with a retail point where both bottled and bulk wines are sold. This cooperative producer submitted a lovely range of Barbera d'Astis this year. The Maricca '19 features hints of plum, a pulpy palate and a distinct acidic note. The Superiore Castagnassa '18 offers up black fruit sensations on the nose, followed by a rich, powerful and characterful palate. The Rebarba '17 once again plays on fullness and volume, with earthy notes and quinine, and a long, gutsy finish. Finally, the 'basic' 2019 is a classic, standard-label Barbera, fresh and pleasant.

- ● Barbera d'Asti '19 TT 1*
- ● Barbera d'Asti Maricca '19 TT 2*
- ● Barbera d'Asti Rebarba '17 TT 3
- ● Barbera d'Asti Sup. Castagnassa '18 TT 3
- ● Barbera d'Asti '17 YY 1*
- ● Barbera d'Asti Maricca '18 YY 2*
- ● Barbera d'Asti Maricca '17 YY 2*
- ● Barbera d'Asti Maricca '16 YY 2*
- ● Barbera d'Asti Maricca '14 YY 2*
- ● Barbera d'Asti Rebarba '16 YY 2*
- ● Barbera d'Asti Sup. Briccofiore '16 YY 2*
- ● Barbera d'Asti Sup. Briccofiore '15 YY 2*
- ● Barbera d'Asti Sup. BriccoFiore '14 YY 2*
- ● Barbera d'Asti Sup. Castagnassa '17 YY 3
- ● Barbera d'Asti Sup. Castagnassa '16 YY 3
- ● Barbera d'Asti Sup. Castagnassa '14 YY 2*
- ● Barbera del M.to La Matutona '15 YY 2*

Diego Pressenda
La Torricella

Loc. Sant'Anna, 98
12065 Monforte d'Alba [CN]
Tel. +39 017378327
www.diegopressenda.it

CELLAR SALES
PRE-BOOKED VISITS
ACCOMMODATION AND RESTAURANT SERVICE
ANNUAL PRODUCTION 50,000 bottles
HECTARES UNDER VINE 13.00
SUSTAINABLE WINERY

The Pressenda family pay close attention to elegance, both in their wines and when receiving guests. The enological part is entrusted to young Silvia, whose work is growing with admirable constancy, drawing on a patrimony cultivated mainly in Monforte (though they also have a presence in cool Roddino, where a part of the grapes destined for their Riesling are cultivated). Elevations are, however, always considerable, between 450 and 500 meters above sea level, which guarantees a lovely acidic strength in their wines. The intense and complex Barolo Barbadelchi '16 moves on rose sensations and licorice, all on a background of tantalizing strawberry; the palate is velvety and vital, progressively unfolding, delicate but long. Darker notes of quinine-cinchona characterize the stiff Le Coste di Monforte '16, while the elegant Bricco San Pietro '16 exhibits commendable harmony. Incense and whiffs of beeswax feature in the powerful and highly pleasant Langhe Riesling '18.

- ● Barolo Barbadelchi '16 TT 6
- ● Barolo Bricco San Pietro '16 TT 7
- ● Barolo Le Coste di Monforte '16 TT 7
- ● Langhe Nebbiolo '18 TT 3
- ○ Langhe Riesling '18 TT 3
- ● Barolo Barbadelchi '13 YY 6
- ● Barolo Bricco San Pietro '15 YY 7
- ○ Langhe Riesling '17 YY 3
- ○ Langhe Riesling '16 YY 3
- ● Nebbiolo d'Alba Il Donato '17 YY 4
- ● Nebbiolo d'Alba Il Donato '15 YY 4

La Prevostura

via Cascina Prevostura, 1
13853 Lessona [BI]
Tel. +39 0158853188
www.laprevostura.it

CELLAR SALES
PRE-BOOKED VISITS
RESTAURANT SERVICE
ANNUAL PRODUCTION 15,000 bottles
HECTARES UNDER VINE 5.50

The winery managed by brothers Marco and Davide Bellini is about to turn twenty. And it's full speed ahead, not so much in terms of quantity, which remains limited by the few prized hectares of property available, as quality. The winery's name comes from its most prestigious vineyard, which gives rise to about 5,000 bottles of Lessona every year. Here Nebbiolo is marked by fruity characteristics and particularly broad, fresh aromas. The Bramaterra, their other flagship wine, is also made with Nebbiolo, but in this case it sees the addition of smaller shares of Vespolina and Croatina. For the moment the latter is absent, thus the elegant and complex Lessona '16 steals the limelight. Elegant notes of tobacco and liquorice combine with lovely, focused and youthful red fruit; the palate plays on elegance and harmony, with silky tannins unfolding amidst weighty, fruity pulp. Made mainly based with Nebbiolo (together with Croatina and Vespolina), the tantalizing Piemonte Rosso Garsun '18 is more approachable, and a bit rustic.

Wine	Rating
● Lessona '16	TT 5
⊙ Piemonte Rosato Corinna '19	TT 3
● Piemonte Rosso Garsum '18	TT 3
● Lessona '12	YYY 5
● Bramaterra '12	YY 5
● Bramaterra '11	YY 5
● Coste della Sesia Rosso Muntacc '13	YY 3*
● Coste della Sesia Rosso Muntacc '12	YY 3*
● Coste della Sesia Rosso Muntacc '11	YY 3
● Coste della Sesia Rosso Muntacc '10	YY 3
● Lessona '13	YY 5
● Lessona '11	YY 5
● Lessona '09	YY 5
⊙ Piemonte Rosato Corinna '16	YY 3

Prinsi

via Gaia, 5
12052 Neive [CN]
Tel. +39 017367192
www.prinsi.it

CELLAR SALES
PRE-BOOKED VISITS
ANNUAL PRODUCTION 60,000 bottles
HECTARES UNDER VINE 14.50

With great affection, we say goodbye to Franco Lequio, who passed away last March, though not before fully transmitting his love and respect for the land to his son Daniele. Minimal interventions in the cellar and deep knowledge of the individual plots give rise to authentic, territorial wines, starting with their Barbarescos: the structured and powerful Fausoni, which needs time and is therefore used for the reserve, the more subtle and aromatically airy Gaia Principe, and the Gallina, a wine of rare harmony and bewitching roundness. Once again the producer submitted a highly worthy line-up of wines. Aromas of wild berries and liquorice characterize the Barbaresco Gaia-Principe '17. Subtle and complex on the nose, it comes through powerful and dynamic in the mouth, finishing rich in energy and vitality. The Barbaresco Riserva Fausoni '15 is more mature in its notes of undergrowth and tobacc. Elegant and complex, the Gallina exhibits a harmonious tannic texture and great length.

Wine	Rating
● Barbaresco Gaia Principe '17	TT 5
● Barbaresco Gallina '17	TT 5
● Barbaresco Fausoni Ris. '15	TT 6
● Barbera d'Alba Sup. Much '17	T 3
○ Langhe Arneis Il Nespolo '19	T 3
● Barbaresco Gaia Principe '16	YY 5
● Barbaresco Gaia Principe '15	YY 5
● Barbaresco Gaia Principe '14	YY 5
● Barbaresco Gaia Principe '13	YY 5
● Barbaresco Gallina '16	YY 5
● Barbaresco Gallina '15	YY 5
● Barbaresco Gallina '14	YY 5
● Barbaresco Gallina '13	YY 5
● Barbaresco Gallina '12	YY 5
● Barbera d'Alba Sup. Il Bosco '17	YY 3
● Barbera d'Alba Sup. Il Bosco '16	YY 3

★Produttori del Barbaresco

via Torino, 54
12050 Barbaresco [CN]
Tel. +39 0173635139
www.produttoridelbarbaresco.com

CELLAR SALES
PRE-BOOKED VISITS
ACCOMMODATION
ANNUAL PRODUCTION 540,000 bottles
HECTARES UNDER VINE 105.00

As Eleonora Guerini wisely recalls in her great illustrated book of Italian wine, cooperation came about to facilitate new economic, social and professional opportunities. It was with these intentions that the praiseworthy cooperative agricultural society Produttori del Barbaresco was founded in 1894, and then reconstituted in 1958. It soon became an international benchmark for its wines, all grounded entirely in Nebbiolo. And so it was that new opportunities soon turned into successes and prestige, especially for the consistent quality exhibited by their nine reserves and by the always gratifying basic Barbaresco. In 2015 only 10,000 bottles of the extraordinary Barbaresco Pajé '15 were produced from the vineyards of two small vine growers. The elegant aromas call up raspberry, cinchona-quinine and liquorice, while the palate is powerful and rich in fruity pulp, with harmonious tannins—a gem. The exceptional value of the series of 2015 reserves shouldn't overshadow the delicate Barbaresco '17.

Wine	Rating	Price
● Barbaresco Montestefano Ris. '15	🍷🍷	6
● Barbaresco Muncagota Ris. '15	🍷🍷	6
● Barbaresco Pajè Ris. '15	🍷🍷	6
● Barbaresco Rio Sordo Ris. '15	🍷🍷	6
● Barbaresco '17	🍷🍷	5
● Barbaresco Asili Ris. '15	🍷🍷	6
● Barbaresco Montefico Ris. '15	🍷🍷	6
● Barbaresco Ovello Ris. '15	🍷🍷	6
● Barbaresco Pora Ris. '15	🍷🍷	6
● Barbaresco Rabajà Ris. '15	🍷🍷	6
● Barbaresco Asili Ris. '13	🍷🍷🍷	6
● Barbaresco Ovello Ris. '09	🍷🍷🍷	6
● Barbaresco Vign. in Montestefano Ris. '05	🍷🍷🍷	6
● Barbaresco Vign. in Ovello Ris. '08	🍷🍷🍷	6
● Barbaresco Vign. in Pora Ris. '07	🍷🍷🍷	6

Cantina Produttori del Gavi

via Cavalieri di Vittorio Veneto, 45
15066 Gavi [AL]
Tel. +39 0143642786
www.cantinaproduttoridelgavi.it

CELLAR SALES
PRE-BOOKED VISITS
ANNUAL PRODUCTION 300,000 bottles
HECTARES UNDER VINE 220.00

The work being done in this Gavi winery is as positive as ever, capable of combining high quality standards and notable production volumes. What's surprising is the attention to detail that distinguishes their entire range, from their basic wines on up, thus confirming the good, quality work being done here. The style is modern, aimed at highlighting the aromas of great native grapes, such as Cortese di Gavi. Behind this success are strict policies stipulated with growers, and the skills of enologist Andrea Pancotti. A splendid set of wines were presented, evidence of the great intrinsic quality of the entire range. The Mille951 opens on aromas of ferns and musk on mineral notes; in the mouth it's taut and rich, with great persistence. The Maddalena is vibrant on aromas of fresh herbs and almond, with mineral notes. On the palate it's powerful, with vibrant acidity and a long finish. It will go far. The other wines tasted are also of note.

Wine	Rating	Price
○ Gavi del Comune di Gavi Mille951 '19	🍷🍷	3*
○ Gavi Maddalena '19	🍷🍷	2*
○ Gavi Brut M. Cl.	🍷🍷	4
○ Gavi del Comune di Gavi GG '18	🍷🍷	3
○ Gavi G '18	🍷🍷	3
○ Gavi Il Forte '19	🍷🍷	2*
○ Gavi del Comune di Gavi GG '15	🍷🍷🍷	3*
○ Gavi del Comune di Gavi Bio '18	🍷🍷	3*
○ Gavi del Comune di Gavi GG '17	🍷🍷	3
○ Gavi del Comune di Gavi Mille951 '18	🍷🍷	3*
○ Gavi del Comune di Gavi Mille951 '17	🍷🍷	3*
○ Gavi del Comune di Gavi Primi Grappoli '18	🍷🍷	3
○ Gavi G '17	🍷🍷	3
○ Gavi Il Forte '18	🍷🍷	2*
○ Gavi Il Forte '17	🍷🍷	2*
○ Gavi Maddalena '18	🍷🍷	2*

★Prunotto

c.so Barolo, 14
12051 Alba [CN]
Tel. +39 0173280017
www.prunotto.it

CELLAR SALES
PRE-BOOKED VISITS
ACCOMMODATION
ANNUAL PRODUCTION 800,000 bottles
HECTARES UNDER VINE 55.00

The large cellar, where grapes from the vast property scattered throughout southern Piedmont come together, is located in Alba, while visitors are welcomed in the farmhouse in Monforte d'Alba. It's here that their valid Barolo, Bussia and Vigna Colonnello are made together with the famous Barbera d'Alba Pian Romualdo, produced by Prunotto since 1961. To stay on the subject of Barbera, their other flagship is the Nizza Costamiòle, a wine that's consistently held up a standard-bearer of Monferrato. The Antinori family's range, overseen by enologist Gianluca Torrengo, is rooted in close observance of the most sophisticated tradition. Elegant fruity and vegetal hints feature in the harmonious Barbaresco Bric Turot '17, a wine endowed with a palate of discreet consistency and overall pleasantness—it has no rough points. Rose petals and lovely spicy notes characterize the elegant Barolo Bussia '16, dynamic and progressively unfolding on a well-balanced palate. The modern Nizza Costamiòle Riserva '17 sees softer sensations, fresh.

Wine	Rating
● Barbaresco Bric Turot '17	🍷🍷 6
● Barolo Bussia '16	🍷🍷 8
● Barbaresco '17	🍷🍷 5
● Barbaresco Secondine '17	🍷🍷 8
● Barolo '16	🍷🍷 6
● Barolo Bussia V. Colonnello Ris. '14	🍷🍷 8
● M.to Mompertone '17	🍷🍷 2*
● Nizza Costamiole Ris. '17	🍷🍷 4
● Barbera d'Asti Costamiòle '99	🍷🍷🍷 4*
● Barbera d'Asti Costamiòle '96	🍷🍷🍷 6
● Barolo Bussia '01	🍷🍷🍷 8
● Barolo Bussia '99	🍷🍷🍷 8
● Barolo Bussia '98	🍷🍷🍷 8
● Barolo Bussia '96	🍷🍷🍷 8
● Barolo Bussia '85	🍷🍷🍷 8

La Raia

s.da Monterotondo, 79
15067 Novi Ligure [AL]
Tel. +39 0143743685
www.la-raia.it

CELLAR SALES
PRE-BOOKED VISITS
ACCOMMODATION
ANNUAL PRODUCTION 150,000 bottles
HECTARES UNDER VINE 50.00
VITICULTURE METHOD Certified Biodynamic
SUSTAINABLE WINERY

Tenimenti Rossi Cairo has invested considerable resources into Gavi and La Raia, one of its crown jewels, since 2003, launching a wide-ranging project that focuses on the relationship between land, architecture and culture. Biodynamic vineyard management forms part of this naturalistic approach, along with pastures and arable land, making for a colorful, 180-hectare puzzle (50 of which are under vine). The winery is managed by brilliant enologist Clara Milani, and their range now includes five selections: three Gavis, differentiated according to characteristics and aging, and two Barbera reds. A masterful performance saw two wines in our finals, both superb examples of their kind. The Gavi Riserva is a whirlwind of aromas: white fruit on herbs and notes of flint. On the palate it's juicy and sapid, with taut acidity and an endless finish. The Pisè is intense and multifaceted, exuding aromas of honey, dried herbs and almond on notes of camphor. In the mouth it's firm and powerful, with a long finish. We also appreciated the pleasant, entry-level Gavi.

Wine	Rating
○ Gavi Pisè '17	🍷🍷 5
○ Gavi V. della Madonnina Ris. '18	🍷🍷 3*
○ Gavi '19	🍷🍷 3
○ Gavi V. della Madonnina Ris. '16	🍷🍷🍷 3*
○ Gavi '18	🍷🍷 3
○ Gavi '17	🍷🍷 3
○ Gavi '16	🍷🍷 3*
○ Gavi '15	🍷🍷 3*
○ Gavi Pisè '15	🍷🍷 5
○ Gavi Ris. '15	🍷🍷 3*
○ Gavi V. della Madonnina Ris. '17	🍷🍷 3*
● Piemonte Barbera '18	🍷🍷 3
● Piemonte Barbera '16	🍷🍷 3
● Piemonte Barbera Largé '15	🍷🍷 4

Renato Ratti

FRAZ. ANNUNZIATA, 7
12064 LA MORRA [CN]
TEL. +39 017350185
www.renatoratti.com

CELLAR SALES
PRE-BOOKED VISITS
ACCOMMODATION
ANNUAL PRODUCTION 350,000 bottles
HECTARES UNDER VINE 35.00

The vast property significant production volumes possible across nine wines, all closely linked to the area's classic grapes: Nebbiolo, Barbera and Dolcetto. The only exceptions are the white I Cedri, made with Sauvignon, and the Merlot that's combined with Barbera for their Villa Pattono, a wine they've been making since 1982. The three Barolos come from vineyards not far from the beautiful wine cellar, which is worth a visit for the panoramic tasting room as well. Although they are all near, it's interesting to note that the Rocche dell'Annunziata is consistently fresher and more fragrant than the fruitier Conca. We suggest trying both. A sophisticated, traditional style characterizes the youthful Barolo Marcenasco '16, a long, alluring wine bursting with raspberry and liquorice, with silky tannins and rich flesh. Just a little more mature, the appealing Barolo Conca '16 is characterized by sweet tobacco and alcohol-steeped fruit, while the palate shows nice, pervasive alcohol and a certain tannic austerity. The powerful Barolo Rocche dell'Annunziata '16 is still rather closed and stiff.

● Barolo Conca '16	▼▼ 8
● Barolo Marcenasco '16	▼▼ 6
● Barbera d'Asti Sup. Villa Pattono '18	▼▼ 4
● Barolo Rocche dell'Annunziata '16	▼▼ 8
○ Langhe Chardonnay Brigata '19	▼▼ 3
● Langhe Nebbiolo Reggimento '17	▼ 5
● Barolo Rocche '06	▽▽▽ 8
● Barolo Rocche Marcenasco '84	▽▽▽ 6
● Barolo Rocche Marcenasco '83	▽▽▽ 6
● Barbera d'Alba Battaglione '18	▽▽ 3
● Barolo Conca '15	▽▽ 8
● Barolo Conca '14	▽▽ 8
● Barolo Marcenasco '15	▽▽ 6
● Barolo Marcenasco '14	▽▽ 6
● Barolo Rocche dell'Annunziata '15	▽▽ 8
● M.to Rosso Villa Pattono '16	▽▽ 5
○ Piemonte Sauvignon I Cedri '18	▽▽ 2*

Réva

LOC. SAN SEBASTIANO, 68
12065 MONFORTE D'ALBA [CN]
TEL. +39 0173789269
www.revamonforte.it

CELLAR SALES
PRE-BOOKED VISITS
ACCOMMODATION AND RESTAURANT SERVICE
ANNUAL PRODUCTION 35,000 bottles
HECTARES UNDER VINE 8.00
SUSTAINABLE WINERY

A property that's as multifaceted as it is welcoming brings together a restaurant with elegant rooms, vineyards and a splendid wine cellar. Here they live by the dictum, 'We are free from the burden of tradition, we are inspired by influences of a different nature'. This might lead one to think of enological upheavals, but in reality their wines are classic. Tasting them one can, at most, notice an attempt to make Barolo of great finesse without tannic harshness. Langhe's power and structure, however, are always at the fore. Violet and tar lead a rich, clear suite of aromas. The Barolo Cannubi '16 is still at a stage where it's finding harmony. In the coming years it will continue to blunt the oak note that was still a bit intrusive at the time of tasting; tannins are discernible while the finish is of considerable length. The well-made 'basic' 2016 Barolo is fruitier and more multifaceted, with a pleasant freshness and elegance.

● Barolo Cannubi '16	▼▼ 8
● Barolo '16	▼▼ 5
● Barbera d'Alba Sup. '18	▼ 4
● Nebbiolo d'Alba '18	▼ 3
● Barbera d'Alba Sup. '15	▽▽ 3
● Barolo '15	▽▽ 5
● Barolo '14	▽▽ 5
● Barolo '13	▽▽ 5
● Barolo '12	▽▽ 5
● Barolo Ravera '15	▽▽ 7
● Barolo Ravera '13	▽▽ 7
● Barolo Ravera '12	▽▽ 7
○ Langhe Bianco Grey '18	▽▽ 3
○ Langhe Bianco Grey '17	▽▽ 3
● Nebbiolo d'Alba '17	▽▽ 3
● Nebbiolo d'Alba '16	▽▽ 3*
● Nebbiolo d'Alba '15	▽▽ 3

Carlo & Figli Revello

FRAZ. SANTA MARIA
12064 LA MORRA [CN]
TEL. +39 3356765021
www.carlorevello.com

PRE-BOOKED VISITS
ANNUAL PRODUCTION 25,000 bottles
HECTARES UNDER VINE 7.00

The final touches are now being put on Carlo Revello's new enological project, with the production infrastructure in place both in the vineyard and in the cellar. The enological style here, which is based on a return to classicism, benefits from Carlo's personal supervision, while young Erik is beginning to put into practice what he learned during his enological studies. Their range is comprised entirely of red wines, made with Dolcetto, Barbera and—above all—Nebbiolo, with their Barolo coming foremost from the precious Rocche dell'Annunziata and Giachini crus. The Barolo '16 is decidedly complex and multifaceted, with a background of red berry and nice alcohol; in the mouth it's dense, of great volume, with velvety sensations filling a long palate. The Barolo R.G. '16 is vibrant, with lovely notes of mint and liquorice opening a nose of polished typicity—hints of raspberry and tobacco emerge; the palate is potent, rich, still not very expansive, but acidity is present across a long finish. Their 2019s go all in on freshness and finesse.

Wine	Rating
● Barolo '16	TT 5
● Barolo R.G. '16	TT 7
● Barbera d'Alba Sup. '19	TT 3
● Dolcetto d'Alba '19	TT 2*
● Langhe Nebbiolo '19	T 3
● Barbera d'Alba '16	YY 3
● Barbera d'Alba Sup. '17	YY 3
● Barolo '15	YY 5
● Barolo '14	YY 5
● Barolo '13	YY 5
● Barolo R.G. '15	YY 7
● Barolo R.G. '14	YY 7
● Barolo R.G. '13	YY 7

F.lli Revello

FRAZ. ANNUNZIATA, 103
12064 LA MORRA [CN]
TEL. +39 017350276
www.revellofratelli.it

CELLAR SALES
PRE-BOOKED VISITS
ACCOMMODATION
ANNUAL PRODUCTION 45,000 bottles
HECTARES UNDER VINE 8.00
SUSTAINABLE WINERY

The winery's first Barolo was bottled in 1967, a now mythical vintage, by blending grapes of different origins. Their current production structure, which dates back to the 1990s, focuses on the individual crus. Their four La Morra vineyards, enriched in 2013 by the first Barolo Cerretta (from Serralunga d'Alba), are appreciated for their elegance, which revolves around plush structure and the sophisticated aromas of Nebbiolo grapes, embellished by the use of French casks, some new. The harmonious Barbera d'Alba Ciabot du Re is also a consistently good performer. The Barolo Cerretta '16 is a magnificent interpretation, perfectly representing the characteristics of the beautiful Serralunga d'Alba vineyard: red and black berries combine with a characteristic, refined balsamic note, while the palate expresses all its power, proving elegant and harmonious, with an alluring, clear, minty finish. Liquorice and dried rose petals feature in the Barolo Giachini '16, a wine of fine classicism, with a dynamic freshness.

Wine	Rating
● Barolo Cerretta '16	TTT 7
● Barolo Giachini '16	TT 7
● Barolo '16	TT 5
● Barolo Conca '16	TT 7
● Barolo Gattera '16	TT 6
● Barbera d'Alba Ciabot du Re '05	YYY 5
● Barbera d'Alba Ciabot du Re '00	YYY 5
● Barolo '93	YYY 5
● Barolo Rocche dell'Annunziata '01	YYY 8
● Barolo Rocche dell'Annunziata '00	YYY 8
● Barolo Rocche dell'Annunziata '97	YYY 8
● Barolo V. Conca '99	YYY 7
● Barbera d'Alba Ciabot du Re '16	YY 5
● Barolo Conca '15	YY 7
● Barolo Gattera '15	YY 6
● Barolo Giachini '15	YY 7
● Barolo Giachini '14	YY 7

Michele Reverdito

FRAZ. RIVALTA
B.TA GARASSINI, 74B
12064 LA MORRA [CN]
TEL. +39 017350336
www.reverdito.it

CELLAR SALES
PRE-BOOKED VISITS
ANNUAL PRODUCTION 100,000 bottles
HECTARES UNDER VINE 24.00

Despite the size of the winery today, siblings Michele and Sabina Reverdito have not renounced personal oversight of all stages of production, from the vineyard to the cellar. And they are celebrating twenty years of activity by consolidating on the one hand an increasingly traditional approach to winemaking and aging, and on the other changes in the vineyard, where artificial chemicals are now a thing of the past. The search for purity of the fruit has led to the first amphorae being used in the cellar for the delicious Pelaverga, while their Barolo ages in large oak barrels. Barolo La Serra '16 shows great character and just as much finesse, with beautiful ripe red fruit making its presence felt on a veil of sweet tobacco; the palate is of prestigious classicism, lovely tannic strength and alluring harmony. Slightly more balsamic notes feature in the pervasive Badarina '16—a round, well-balanced palate closes on an elegant citrus note.

● Barolo Badarina '16	ΥΥ 8
● Barolo La Serra '16	ΥΥ 8
● Barbera d'Alba Delia '17	ΥΥ 4
● Barolo Ascheri '16	ΥΥ 6
● Barolo Bricco Cogni '16	ΥΥ 7
○ Langhe Nascetta '18	Υ 3
● Langhe Nebbiolo Simane '18	Υ 3
● Barolo Bricco Cogni '04	ΥΥΥ 6
● Barolo Ascheri '14	ΥΥ 8
● Barolo Ascheri '13	ΥΥ 5
● Barolo Badarina '15	ΥΥ 7
● Barolo Bricco Cogni '15	ΥΥ 6
● Barolo Bricco Cogni '14	ΥΥ 8
● Barolo Bricco Cogni '13	ΥΥ 6
● Barolo Castagni '14	ΥΥ 7
● Langhe Nebbiolo Simane '16	ΥΥ 4
● Langhe Nebbiolo Simane '15	ΥΥ 3

★Giuseppe Rinaldi

VIA MONFORTE, 5
12060 BAROLO [CN]
TEL. +39 017356156
www.rinaldigiuseppe.com

CELLAR SALES
PRE-BOOKED VISITS
ANNUAL PRODUCTION 35,000 bottles
HECTARES UNDER VINE 6.50

The label bearing the name 'Giuseppe Rinaldi' has become emblematic of Barolo rich in personality, changing with every harvest, pure in its natural vitality, devoid of any artifice in the cellar. And increasingly international wine lovers are rewarding this forthright, spontaneous style, one that can be, at times, even rustic but always represents a perfect expression of Nebbiolo. Beppe Rinaldi, the splendid raconteur of Langhe and nature, has left us, so today it is his daughters Carlotta and Marta who are furthering their commitment to the winery. Their research and experimentation includes increasingly sustainable cultivation practices. Sensations of forest undergrowth and red berries feature in the timid Barolo Brunate '16, a wine that's a bit closed in aromatically and still reluctant to indulge at this point—it still has a ways to go; the palate is marked by youthful tannins and a nice long finish. The Tre Tine '16 moves on a similar track, but it's got more freshness and liveliness on the nose, while the palate is still compact, exhibiting an appealing austerity.

● Barolo Brunate '16	ΥΥΥ 8
● Barolo Tre Tine '16	ΥΥ 7
● Barolo Brunate '15	ΥΥΥ 8
● Barolo Brunate '13	ΥΥΥ 7
● Barolo Brunate '11	ΥΥΥ 7
● Barolo Brunate-Le Coste '07	ΥΥΥ 7
● Barolo Brunate-Le Coste '06	ΥΥΥ 7
● Barolo Brunate-Le Coste '01	ΥΥΥ 6
● Barolo Brunate-Le Coste '00	ΥΥΥ 6
● Barolo Brunate-Le Coste '97	ΥΥΥ 6
● Barolo Cannubi S. Lorenzo-Ravera '04	ΥΥΥ 6
● Barolo Brunate '14	ΥΥ 7
● Barolo Brunate '12	ΥΥ 7
● Barolo Tre Tine '15	ΥΥ 7
● Barolo Tre Tine '14	ΥΥ 7
● Barolo Tre Tine '13	ΥΥ 7
● Barolo Tre Tine '12	ΥΥ 7

Francesco Rinaldi & Figli

via Crosia, 30
12060 Barolo [CN]
Tel. +39 0173440484
www.rinaldifrancesco.it

CELLAR SALES
PRE-BOOKED VISITS
ACCOMMODATION
ANNUAL PRODUCTION 70,000 bottles
HECTARES UNDER VINE 11.00

Founded in 1970, the winery now managed by Piera and Paola Rinaldi has two particularly important vineyards within Barolo: Cannubi and Brunate. In both cases the property is situated in the heart of the cru, in the part best exposed to the sun. Their Barolo is aged in large Slavonian oak barrels, which allows it to mature slowly. Our advice is to taste their wine after a few years of bottle aging because, as Burton Anderson pointed out in his Great Atlas of Italian Wine, 'Barolo acquires finesse only with time'. The Cannubi '16 put in a notable performance. Vibrant, multifaceted aromas alternate red berries with dried rose by way of tobacco, violet and a fresh nuance of aniseed and licorice; the palate is of exquisite proportion and character, with fine, but discernible tannins and adequate pulp leading right up to a long finish. The less developed Brunate '16 is delicately spicy, with the occasional citrusy hint.

Wine	Rating
● Barolo Brunate '16	🍷🍷 7
● Barolo Cannubi '16	🍷🍷 7
● Barbaresco '14	♀♀ 5
● Barbaresco '13	♀♀ 5
● Barbera d'Alba '13	♀♀ 3
● Barolo Brunate '15	♀♀ 7
● Barolo Brunate '13	♀♀ 7
● Barolo Brunate '12	♀♀ 7
● Barolo Brunate '11	♀♀ 6
● Barolo Brunate '10	♀♀ 7
● Barolo Cannubi '15	♀♀ 7
● Barolo Cannubi '14	♀♀ 7
● Barolo Cannubi '13	♀♀ 7
● Barolo Cannubi '12	♀♀ 7
● Barolo Cannubi '11	♀♀ 7
● Barolo Cannubi '10	♀♀ 7
● Barolo Cannubi Ris. '13	♀♀ 7

Massimo Rivetti

via Rivetti, 22
12052 Neive [CN]
Tel. +39 017367505
www.rivettimassimo.it

CELLAR SALES
PRE-BOOKED VISITS
ANNUAL PRODUCTION 70,000 bottles
HECTARES UNDER VINE 25.00

The Serraboella cru, with its 15 hectares of Nebbiolo, gives rise to a particularly structured Barbaresco that's marked by good, fruity pulp and substantive tannins. It's here that Massimo Rivetti creates his two most important wines, Barbaresco Serraboella and a reserve version of the same, taking care to pick healthy, pure bunches free of any chemical contamination. The Barbaresco Froi, which is cultivated organically in the beautiful, sunny vineyard around the cellar, is more relaxed and linear. The Riserva '15 Barbaresco Serraboella Riserva '15 is a demanding wine, compact, thanks to strong aromas that alternate red berries with spices and a perceptible note of juniper, while the palate exhibits nice, vivid tannins—it will improve further with time in the bottle. The pleasant Barbaresco '17 plays more on elegance than on robustness. The Barolo '16, from a hectare of vineyards in La Morra, also did well.

Wine	Rating
● Barbaresco Serraboella Ris. '15	🍷🍷 6
● Barbaresco '17	🍷🍷 5
● Barolo '16	🍷🍷 5
● Barbaresco '14	♀♀ 5
● Barbaresco '13	♀♀ 5
● Barbaresco Froi '16	♀♀ 6
● Barbaresco Froi '15	♀♀ 6
● Barbaresco Froi '14	♀♀ 6
● Barbaresco Froi '13	♀♀ 5
● Barbaresco Serraboella '13	♀♀ 7
● Barbaresco Serraboella Ris. '14	♀♀ 6
● Barbera d'Alba Sup. Froi '16	♀♀ 2*
● Barbera d'Alba Sup. V. Serraboella '16	♀♀ 4
● Barbera d'Alba Sup. V. Serraboella '12	♀♀ 4
● Langhe Nebbiolo Avene '17	♀♀ 3
● Langhe Nebbiolo Avene '15	♀♀ 3
● Langhe Pinot Nero '15	♀♀ 3

Rizzi

VIA RIZZI, 15
12050 TREISO [CN]
TEL. +39 0173638161
www.cantinarizzi.it

CELLAR SALES
PRE-BOOKED VISITS
ACCOMMODATION
ANNUAL PRODUCTION 90,000 bottles
HECTARES UNDER VINE 40.00
SUSTAINABLE WINERY

The Dellapiana family's winery is one of the most appreciated in Barbaresco, an appellation that is becoming more and more famous all over the world. The secret to their success is being able to draw on some of its most popular crus, maximum attention throughout all stages of production and a very correct pricing policy (despite the high demand). Four Barbarescos are produced, all aged in mid-sized Slavonian oak barrels. The Barbaresco Riserva Rizzi Vigna Boito '15 handily earned a place in our finals. It's a red of character, capable of calibrating structure and acidity on a very wide, juicy weave, with fleshy, ripe fruit; the finish is well-sustained and long. An airy balsamic whiff characterizes the Barbaresco Pajoré '17, a pure wine in its hints of rose and raspberry. In the mouth it's delicate, graceful, with a finish enlivened by a sapid vigor.

Wine	Glasses	Price
● Barbaresco Pajorè '17	▼▼	6
● Barbaresco Rizzi V. Boito Ris. '15	▼▼	8
● Barbaresco Nervo '17	▼▼	6
● Barbaresco Rizzi '17	▼▼	5
● Barbera d'Alba '17	▼▼	3
● Dolcetto d'Alba '19	▼▼	3
○ Langhe Chardonnay '19	▼	3
● Langhe Nebbiolo '18	▼	4
● Barbaresco Boito Ris. '10	▽▽▽	6
● Barbaresco Nervo '14	▽▽▽	6
● Barbaresco Nervo '16	▽▽	6
● Barbaresco Nervo '15	▽▽	6
● Barbaresco Pajorè '16	▽▽	6
● Barbaresco Pajorè '15	▽▽	6
● Barbaresco Rizzi '16	▽▽	5
● Barbaresco Rizzi Boito Ris. '14	▽▽	7
● Langhe Nebbiolo '17	▽▽	4

Roagna

LOC. PAJÉ
S.DA PAGLIERI, 7
12050 BARBARESCO [CN]
TEL. +39 0173635109
www.roagna.com

CELLAR SALES
PRE-BOOKED VISITS
ANNUAL PRODUCTION 50,000 bottles
HECTARES UNDER VINE 15.00

Here they've got two reasons to celebrate: father Alfredo is on his 50th vintage, while his son Luca celebrates his first 20 years of activity, continuing with a winemaking style based on naturalness in the vineyard and rigorous tradition in the cellar. This doesn't mean stopping. To the joy of I Paglieri's many fans, new plots of land have been acquired in Barbaresco, as well as a vineyard where their Timorasso Derthona is cultivated. Even their Barolo, already bolstered by the beautiful Rocche di Castiglione vineyard (where the Pira originates) has been increased thanks to new plots in the municipality of Barolo. Medicinal herbs and liquorice feature in the sumptuous, elegant Crichët Pajé '12, with its elegant, rich palate, delicate and harmonious, and an enchanting touch of freshness. Among their Barbarescos the potent Montefico Vecchie Viti '15 stands out, while the Asili is a bit more rustic. Excellent results for their 2015 Barolos as well. The Vecchie Viti is elegant and complex, the Pira harmonious and velvety.

Wine	Glasses	Price
● Barbaresco Crichët Pajé '12	▼▼▼	8
● Barbaresco Montefico V. V. '15	▼▼	8
● Barolo Pira '15	▼▼	8
● Barolo Pira V. V. '15	▼▼	8
● Barbaresco Asili V. V. '15	▼▼	8
● Barbaresco Pajé '15	▼▼	8
● Barbaresco Pajè V. V. '15	▼▼	8
○ Derthona Montemarzino '18	▼▼	8
● Langhe Rosso '15	▼▼	3
● Barbaresco Asili V. Viti '13	▽▽▽	8
● Barbaresco Asili V. Viti '07	▽▽▽	8
● Barbaresco Crichët Pajé '11	▽▽▽	8
● Barbaresco Crichët Pajé '08	▽▽▽	8
● Barbaresco Crichët Pajé '06	▽▽▽	8
● Barbaresco Crichët Pajé '05	▽▽▽	8
● Barbaresco Crichët Pajé '04	▽▽▽	8
● Barbaresco Pajé '11	▽▽▽	8

★Albino Rocca

s.da Ronchi, 18
12050 Barbaresco [CN]
Tel. +39 0173635145
www.albinorocca.com

CELLAR SALES
PRE-BOOKED VISITS
ANNUAL PRODUCTION 100,000 bottles
HECTARES UNDER VINE 18.00
SUSTAINABLE WINERY

The Rocca sisters, who are supported in the cellar by Paola's husband, Carlo Castellengo, operate in a splendid location, both for its panoramic position and, more so, for the underground spaces/ winemaking facilities available, making the winery worthy of one of the most prestigious names in Barbaresco. Their Nebbiolo vineyards, which lend their names to the various selections, are situated in famous local cru: Vigna Loreto nell'Ovello, Ronchi, Montersino and Cottà. The Barbaresco Angelo, first produced in 2013 and dedicated to their father, is a blend of all these. The Barbaresco Ronchi does a nice job interpreting the powerful 2016 vintage, avoiding edges and hardness in favor of an overall roundness: the nose is rich in flowers and red berries, as well as a tantalizing smoky note, while on the palate it's soft, with tannins governed by a nice pervasiveness. The 2017 Barbarescos are a bit stiffer, with the Cottà and Montersino offering a discernible note of bitter almond on the finish and the famous Ovello Vigna Loreto playing on fresh, vegetal hints.

Wine	Glasses	Price
● Barbaresco Ovello V. Loreto '17	🍷🍷	6
● Barbaresco Ronchi '16	🍷🍷	6
● Barbaresco Cottà '17	🍷🍷	5
● Barbaresco Montersino '17	🍷🍷	6
● Barbaresco Angelo '13	YYY	5
● Barbaresco Ovello V. Loreto '16	YYY	6
● Barbaresco Ovello V. Loreto '11	YYY	6
● Barbaresco Ovello V. Loreto '09	YYY	6
● Barbaresco Ovello V. Loreto '07	YYY	6
● Barbaresco Ronchi '10	YYY	6
● Barbaresco Vign. Brich Ronchi '05	YYY	6
● Barbaresco Vign. Brich Ronchi '03	YYY	6
● Barbaresco Vign. Brich Ronchi '00	YYY	6
● Barbaresco Vign. Brich Ronchi Ris. '06	YYY	8
● Barbaresco Vign. Brich Ronchi Ris. '04	YYY	8
● Barbaresco Vign. Loreto '04	YYY	6

★★Bruno Rocca

s.da Rabajà, 60
12050 Barbaresco [CN]
Tel. +39 0173635112
www.brunorocca.it

CELLAR SALES
PRE-BOOKED VISITS
ANNUAL PRODUCTION 70,000 bottles
HECTARES UNDER VINE 15.00
VITICULTURE METHOD Certified Organic

Francesco Rocca has unquestionable skills, both in the vineyard and in the cellar, where he is making his own important contribution to the already acclaimed enological approach carved out by his father Bruno going back to 1978. There are mainly two objectives. One is to be able to protect the vineyards, already certified organic, by treating them as little as possible, especially by reducing copper. In the cellar, in addition to further reducing sulphur, their intention is to maintain the elegance for which these wines are famous by using larger barrels whose influence is felt less. Fine harmony characterizes the Rabajà '16, a complex wine that tames the strength of the vintage in favor of a soft complexity in which tannins and acidity complement a pervasive, fruity flesh. Equally graceful and charming, the Currà '16 is just slightly more assertive in its powerful fruitiness. The velvety Maria Adelaide '13 is sumptuous and structured, with freshness and power making for a gustatory profile of rare richness. The 2014 reserves are also splendid.

Wine	Glasses	Price
● Barbaresco Rabajà '16	🍷🍷🍷	8
● Barbaresco Currà '16	🍷🍷	8
● Barbaresco Maria Adelaide '13	🍷🍷	8
● Barbaresco Rabajà Ris. '14	🍷🍷	8
● Barbaresco '17	🍷🍷	7
● Barbaresco Currà Ris. '14	🍷🍷	8
● Barbaresco Coparossa '04	YYY	8
● Barbaresco Currà Ris. '13	YYY	8
● Barbaresco Currà Ris. '12	YYY	8
● Barbaresco Maria Adelaide '07	YYY	8
● Barbaresco Maria Adelaide '04	YYY	8
● Barbaresco Maria Adelaide '01	YYY	8
● Barbaresco Rabajà '13	YYY	8
● Barbaresco Rabajà '12	YYY	8
● Barbaresco Rabajà '11	YYY	8
● Barbaresco Rabajà '10	YYY	8
● Barbaresco Rabajà '09	YYY	8

Rocche Costamagna

via Vittorio Emanuele, 8
12064 La Morra [CN]
Tel. +39 0173509225
www.rocchecostamagna.it

CELLAR SALES
PRE-BOOKED VISITS
ACCOMMODATION
ANNUAL PRODUCTION 95,000 bottles
HECTARES UNDER VINE 15.80

Rocche dell'Annunziata is one of the most famous cru in all of Barolo, and deservedly so thanks to its 25 hectares of Nebbiolo facing south at elevations spanning 250-360 meters. It's here that Alessandro Locatelli's winery has its productive heart, bolstered by a long tradition of winemaking, as evidenced by 19th-century documents testifying to the fact. In addition to their Barolo Rocche dell'Annunziata, which is sometimes offered as a reserve, the winery produces the area's classic reds, led by a formidable Barbera Superiore, and a white made with Arneis. The fruity spectrum of the Barolo Rocche dell'Annunziata '16 is particularly broad and variegated, rising up over a delicate hint of sunny herbs and sweet tobacco; the palate is equally complex, balancing tannins and pulp for a prestigious harmony. Fine, tanned-leather notes feature in the highly enjoyable Barolo Rocche dell'Annunziata Bricco Francesco Riserva '13, a soft and pervasive wine.

- ● Barbera d'Alba Sup. Rocche delle Rocche '17 — TT 4
- ● Barolo Rocche dell'Annunziata '16 — TT 6
- ● Barolo Rocche dell'Annunziata Bricco Francesco Ris. '13 — TT 8
- ● Barbera d'Alba '18 — TT 3
- ● Barolo '16 — TT 5
- ○ Langhe Arneis '19 — T 3
- ● Barolo Rocche dell'Annunziata '04 — YYY 5
- ● Barbera d'Alba '17 — YY 3
- ● Barbera d'Alba '16 — YY 3
- ● Barbera d'Alba Sup. Rocche delle Rocche '15 — YY 4
- ● Barolo '15 — YY 5
- ● Barolo Rocche dell'Annunziata '15 — YY 6
- ● Barolo Rocche dell'Annunziata '14 — YY 6
- ● Langhe Nebbiolo Roccardo '17 — YY 3

Il Rocchin

loc. Vallemme, 39
15066 Gavi [AL]
Tel. +39 0143642228
www.ilrocchin.it

CELLAR SALES
PRE-BOOKED VISITS
ANNUAL PRODUCTION 50,000 bottles
HECTARES UNDER VINE 20.00

The Zerbo family established the winery in 1982. Today Bruno's children Angelo and Francesca run the business, though despite his age, their tireless father still makes his opinion heard. The estate now spans over 100 hectares, 44 of which are under vine. Most of the vineyards are planted with Cortese, Barbera and Dolcetto. A dozen wines are in production, with different interpretations of Cortese and Barbera offered, including a monovarietal Dolcetto made with grapes from the San Cristoforo vineyard. Il Rocchin submitted a balanced line-up. In the absence of Il Bosco, we were presented another Gavi del Comune di Gavi. Vibrant on the nose, it opens on aromas of wisteria and chamomile with mineral notes. On the palate it's rich and intense, with fine acidic support sustaining a long finish. The basic Gavi is less complex, but with an excellent olfactory spectrum. We also appreciated the easy and fresh Dolcetto di Ovada.

- ● Dolcetto di Ovada '18 — TT 2*
- ○ Gavi '19 — TT 3
- ○ Gavi del Comune di Gavi '19 — TT 2*
- ● Barbera del M.to Il Basacco '17 — YY 3*
- ● Barbera del M.to Il Basacco '16 — YY 3
- ● Dolcetto di Ovada '16 — YY 2*
- ● Dolcetto di Ovada '15 — YY 2*
- ○ Gavi del Comune di Gavi '17 — YY 2*
- ○ Gavi del Comune di Gavi '16 — YY 2*
- ○ Gavi del Comune di Gavi '15 — YY 2*
- ○ Gavi del Comune di Gavi '14 — YY 2*
- ○ Gavi del Comune di Gavi Il Bosco '18 — YY 3
- ○ Gavi del Comune di Gavi Il Bosco '17 — YY 3*
- ○ Gavi del Comune di Gavi Il Bosco '16 — YY 3*
- ○ Gavi del Comune di Gavi Il Bosco '15 — YY 3*

★Giovanni Rosso

via Roddino, 10/1
12050 Serralunga d'Alba [CN]
Tel. +39 0173613340
www.giovannirosso.com

CELLAR SALES
PRE-BOOKED VISITS
ANNUAL PRODUCTION 130,000 bottles
HECTARES UNDER VINE 18.00

In his twenty years of activity in the winery, Davide Rosso has managed to demonstrate how it's possible to combine power and sophistication, structure and elegance, complexity and drinkability. From his stories, wine tourists will be able to appreciate how much attention and detail goes into the creation of Barolos that have conquered consumers and critics worldwide. And if the small selection of Vigna Rionda is difficult to get your hands on, wine lovers can easily enjoy four other Barolos all made with the same level of skill. The Barolo Vigna Rionda Ester Canale Rosso '16 exhibits a spectacular palate. It's as firm as it is harmonious, multifaceted and progressive in its development. Aromatically it exhibits textbook classicism: spices, red berries and a slight hint of tobacco in the background. The elegant Barolo Serra '16 is fruitier and more immediately expressive, with delicate tannins reinforcing a pervasive pulp. The Langhe Nebbiolo Ester Canale Rosso '17 is magnificent.

Wine	Glasses	Price
● Barolo Vigna Rionda Ester Canale Rosso '16	🍷🍷🍷	8
● Barolo Cerretta '16	🍷🍷	8
● Barolo Serra '16	🍷🍷	8
● Langhe Nebbiolo Ester Canale Rosso '17	🍷🍷	8
● Barolo del Comune di Serralunga d'Alba '16	🍷🍷	5
● Langhe Nebbiolo '18	🍷	5
● Barolo Cerretta '12	🍸🍸🍸	8
● Barolo Serra '15	🍸🍸🍸	8
● Barolo Vigna Rionda Ester Canale Rosso '14	🍸🍸🍸	8
● Barolo Vigna Rionda Ester Canale Rosso '13	🍸🍸🍸	8
● Barolo Vigna Rionda Ester Canale Rosso '11	🍸🍸🍸	8

Poderi Rosso Giovanni

p.zza Roma 36/37
14041 Agliano Terme [AT]
Tel. +39 0141954006
www.rossowines.it

CELLAR SALES
PRE-BOOKED VISITS
ANNUAL PRODUCTION 55,000 bottles
HECTARES UNDER VINE 12.00
SUSTAINABLE WINERY

Managed according to principles of sustainable agriculture, the Rosso family's vineyards can be found in Cascina Perno and Cascina San Sebastiano, historic cultivation sites on the slopes of Agliano Terme. Poderi Rosso Giovanni has been active for three generations, with Lionello now at the helm. He deserves credit for consolidating a winery whose versatility is evident both in terms of production and style, one that's managed to express the different faces of Asti's Barbera with four versions differentiated according to vinification and aging (steel, barriques and mid-sized casks). The Nizza Gioco dell'Oca Riserva '17 features aromas of berries and sweet spices and a palate of great concentration, but it's also long and balanced. Of the two Barbera d'Asti Superiores, the Cascina Perno '18 is fresher and sustained by acidity, with tones of cherry and licorice, while the Carlinet '17 is characterized by a return to extractive sensations, all nicely orchestrated, with nice aromatic clarity. We also appreciated the pleasantly approachable Barbera d'Asti San Bastian '19.

Wine	Glasses	Price
● Nizza Gioco dell'Oca Ris. '17	🍷🍷	6
● Barbera d'Asti San Bastian '19	🍷🍷	2*
● Barbera d'Asti Sup. Carlinet '17	🍷🍷	4
● Barbera d'Asti Sup. Cascina Perno '18	🍷🍷	3
● Barbera d'Asti Podere San Bastian '14	🍸🍸	2*
● Barbera d'Asti San Bastian '17	🍸🍸	2*
● Barbera d'Asti San Bastian '15	🍸🍸	2*
● Barbera d'Asti Sup. Carlinet '16	🍸🍸	4
● Barbera d'Asti Sup. Carlinet '15	🍸🍸	4
● Barbera d'Asti Sup. Carlinet '13	🍸🍸	4
● Barbera d'Asti Sup. Cascina Perno '17	🍸🍸	3*
● Barbera d'Asti Sup. Cascina Perno '16	🍸🍸	3*
● Barbera d'Asti Sup. Cascina Perno '15	🍸🍸	3
● Barbera d'Asti Sup. Cascina Perno '14	🍸🍸	3
● Barbera d'Asti Sup. Gioco dell'Oca '16	🍸🍸	6
● Barbera d'Asti Sup. Gioco dell'Oca '15	🍸🍸	6
● Barbera d'Asti Sup. Gioco dell'Oca '13	🍸🍸	6

Josetta Saffirio

loc. Castelletto, 39
12065 Monforte d'Alba [CN]
Tel. +39 0173787278
www.josettasaffirio.com

CELLAR SALES
PRE-BOOKED VISITS
ANNUAL PRODUCTION 30,000 bottles
HECTARES UNDER VINE 5.00
VITICULTURE METHOD Certified Organic
SUSTAINABLE WINERY

Sara Vezza continues to prove a capable interpreter of Barolo, which gives rise to three wines. The grapes grown in her beautiful Castelletto cru are always endowed with lively personality and remarkable complexity. At the top is the Riserva, which comes from vines planted in 1948, but they're all outstanding. And she's just as convinced of Metodo Classico, made with both Nebbiolo and more classic Chardonnay or Pinot Nero, so much so that she's acquired a considerable estate in cool Roddino at over 400 meters above sea level. The fragrant and long-lived Langhe Rossese Bianco also deserves mentioning. The Barolo Persiera '16 is vibrant and very fruit-forward, characterized by sweet spices on the nose together with an alluring liquorice. Tannins are perceptible, but wrapped up nicely in pulpy juice, making for good volume right up to a long, elegant finish. The 2014 reserve of the Barolo Millenovecento48 is more austere and pleasantly vegetal.

Wine	Rating
● Barolo Persiera '16	TT 8
● Barolo del Comune di Monforte d'Alba '16	TT 5
● Barolo Millenovecento48 Ris. '14	TT 8
○ Langhe Rossese Bianco '18	TT 3
⊙ Nebbiolo d'Alba Brut Rosé M. Cl. '17	TT 5
● Barolo '89	YYY 6
● Barolo '88	YYY 6
● Barolo del Comune di Monforte d'Alba '15	YY 5
● Barolo Millenovecento48 Ris. '13	YY 8
● Barolo Millenovecento48 Ris. '12	YY 8
● Barolo Millenovecento48 Ris. '11	YY 8
● Barolo Persiera '15	YY 8
● Barolo Persiera '14	YY 8
● Langhe Nebbiolo '15	YY 3
○ Langhe Rossese Bianco '16	YY 3

San Fereolo

loc. San Fereolo
b.ta Valdibà, 59
12063 Dogliani [CN]
Tel. +39 0173742075
www.sanfereolo.com

PRE-BOOKED VISITS
ANNUAL PRODUCTION 46,000 bottles
HECTARES UNDER VINE 12.00

In her thirty years of activity, Nicoletta Bocca has always sought to realize the great potential of Dolcetto, a grape that in Doglianese can prove long-lived and rich in personality. Herein we find two central features of her approach. On the one hand, each vine and vineyard is cultivated in a precise way that respects nature, while favoring the most direct expression of the vineyard's peculiarities. On the other hand, her bottles age for a few years in the cellar before being put on the market so as to enhance her Dogliani's aromatic and gustatory qualities. Blackberry, spices and tanned-leather feature in the rich Dogliani Superiore Vigne Dolci '18, a wine with remarkable structure. The complex Dogliani Superiore San Fereolo '13, which goes so far as to call up white truffle, is characterized by a firm, austere profile. The Langhe Rosso 1593 '09, made with Dolcetto, is endowed with a very strong personality, though it's just a tiny bit edgy.

Wine	Rating
● Dogliani Sup. San Fereolo '13	TT 2*
● Dogliani Sup. Vigne Dolci '18	TT 3
● Langhe Nebbiolo Il Provinciale '16	TT 5
● Langhe Rosso 1593 '09	TT 5
● Dogliani Sup. Vigneti Dolci '17	YYY 3*
● Dolcetto di Dogliani S. Fereolo '99	YYY 2
● Dogliani Sup. '17	YY 3
● Dogliani Valdibà '13	YY 3*
● Dolcetto di Dogliani Valdibà '10	YY 3*
○ Langhe Bianco Coste di Riavolo '11	YY 3
○ Langhe Bianco Coste di Riavolo '10	YY 3
● Langhe Nebbiolo Il Provinciale '09	YY 3
● Langhe Rosso 1593 '07	YY 5
● Langhe Rosso Il Provinciale '10	YY 4

Tenuta San Sebastiano

Cascina San Sebastiano, 41
15040 Lu [AL]
Tel. +39 0131741353
www.dealessi.it

CELLAR SALES
PRE-BOOKED VISITS
ANNUAL PRODUCTION 70,000 bottles
HECTARES UNDER VINE 9.00

Roberto De Alessi is one of the most brilliant winemakers operating in this corner of Piedmont. Moreover, since his son Fabio has been at his side, he's managed to reconnect with the determination that comes with being in your 30s. His passion has forged great wines over the years, such as the Barbera Mepari or the Grignolino Monfiorato, splendid expressions of the attributes of native grape varieties. He also makes a Nebbiolo, the Capolinea, and a Pinot Nero, the Sol-Do. Production reaches about 70 thousand bottles per year, and includes a charming passito, the LV, made with Moscato Bianco and Gewürztraminer. The Grignolino Monfiorato 2015 is amazing. Extremely multifaceted and elegant on the nose, tobacco aromas merge with notes of pepper, cinchona-quinine and coffee. On the palate it stands out for its power and richness, which manage to absorb you, and a sapid, endless finish. The Mepari features nice olfactory taste and will benefit further from more time in the bottle. The other wines tasted are also well made.

- ● Piemonte Grignolino Monfiorato '15 — TT 4
- ● Barbera del M.to Sup. Mepari '18 — TT 4
- ○ LV Quinquagesimaquinta Mansio Passito '17 — TT 4
- ● M.to Rosso Dalera '16 — TT 3
- ● Piemonte Grignolino '19 — TT 2*
- ○ M.to Bianco Sperilium '19 — T 2
- ● Barbera del M.to '16 — YY 2*
- ● Barbera del M.to Sup. Mepari '17 — YY 4
- ● Barbera del M.to Sup. Mepari '16 — YY 4
- ● Barbera del M.to Sup. Mepari '15 — YY 4
- ● M.to Rosso Capolinea '16 — YY 2*
- ● M.to Rosso Dalera '16 — YY 3
- ● M.to Rosso Dalera '15 — YY 3
- ● Piemonte Grignolino '18 — YY 2*
- ● Piemonte Grignolino Monfiorato '13 — YY 4
- ● Piemonte Grignolino Monfiorato '12 — YY 4

★Luciano Sandrone

via Pugnane, 4
12060 Barolo [CN]
Tel. +39 0173560023
www.sandroneluciano.com

PRE-BOOKED VISITS
ANNUAL PRODUCTION 110,000 bottles
HECTARES UNDER VINE 27.00
SUSTAINABLE WINERY

Luciano Sandrone is a key figure for understanding Barolo's worldwide success and evolution. In fact, he was one of the first (having debuted in 1978) to use small wood barrels, forging a highly original style that departed from tradition. In just a few years that style has set a standard, encouraging other producers to question their own approaches. Luciano, with the help of his brother Luca and daughter Barbara, continues to offer neoclassical wines of great prestige that express famous plots such as Cannubi Boschis (Barolo Aleste) or Le Vigne, where Novello, Serralunga, Castiglione Falletto and Barolo all converge. An elegant profile of spices introduces the Barolo Aleste '16, a classic wine in its notes of cinchona-quinine, tobacco and black pepper. In the mouth it exhibits fruit of unique fragrance and flavor, at once rich, dense and dynamic, while the finish is long and multifaceted. The powerful Barolo Le Vigne '16 is even more intense, with well-calibrated earthy scents, showing considerable energy and tension.

- ● Barolo Aleste '16 — TT 8
- ● Barolo Le Vigne '16 — TT 8
- ● Barbera d'Alba '18 — TT 5
- ● Dolcetto d'Alba '18 — TT 3
- ● Nebbiolo d'Alba Valmaggiore '18 — TT 5
- ● Barolo Aleste '15 — YYY 8
- ● Barolo Cannubi Boschis '11 — YYY 8
- ● Barolo Cannubi Boschis '10 — YYY 8
- ● Barolo Cannubi Boschis '08 — YYY 8
- ● Barolo Cannubi Boschis '07 — YYY 8
- ● Barolo Cannubi Boschis '06 — YYY 8
- ● Barolo Cannubi Boschis '05 — YYY 8
- ● Barolo Cannubi Boschis '04 — YYY 8
- ● Barolo Cannubi Boschis '03 — YYY 8
- ● Barolo Cannubi Boschis '01 — YYY 8
- ● Barolo Cannubi Boschis '00 — YYY 8

Tenuta Santa Caterina

via Guglielmo Marconi, 17
14035 Grazzano Badoglio [AT]
Tel. +39 0141925108
www.tenuta-santa-caterina.it

CELLAR SALES
PRE-BOOKED VISITS
ACCOMMODATION
ANNUAL PRODUCTION 50,000 bottles
HECTARES UNDER VINE 23.00

Last year, Tenuta Santa Caterina received our special Up-and-Coming Winery Award and Tre Bicchieri for their Grignolino Monferace: two awards that confirmed its upward trajectory since debuting in the guide. The venture was well planned by Carlo Alleva, with the collaboration of Mario Ronco, a nationally acclaimed enologist, his goal being to bring out the attributes of local grape varieties. This is especially true of Grignolino and Freisa, two grapes elevated to the heights of excellence. The wines submitted are outstanding. The Monferace unfolds rich and intense, with aromas of cinchona-quinine and pepper on a slightly evolved note, which lends even more complexity. Multifaceted and vibrant, the Arlandino is well anchored to fruity aromas accompanied by hints of pepper and bark. The Silente delle Marne is sensational, with sweet notes of oak emerging on candied citrus and a mineral background. We recommend their other wines as well.

Wine	Glasses	Price
● Grignolino d'Asti Monferace '15	TTT	5
● Grignolino d'Asti Arlandino '18	TT	3*
○ M.to Bianco Silente delle Marne '15	TT	5
● Barbera d'Asti Sup. Setecàpita '16	TT	5
● Barbera d'Asti Sup. V. Lina '17	TT	3
○ M.to Bianco Salidoro '18	TT	3
● M.to Rosso Illegale '17	TT	3
● Grignolino d'Asti M '13	YYY	5
● Barbera d'Asti Sup. Setecàpita '15	YY	5
● Barbera d'Asti Sup. Setecàpita '13	YY	5
● Barbera d'Asti Sup. V. Lina '16	YY	3
● Barbera d'Asti Sup. V. Lina '15	YY	3*
● Barbera d'Asti Sup. V. Lina '14	YY	3
● Freisa d'Asti Sorì di Giul '15	YY	5
● Grignolino d'Asti Arlandino '17	YY	3*
● Grignolino d'Asti Arlandino '16	YY	3
● Grignolino d'Asti M2012 '12	YY	3*

Paolo Saracco

via Circonvallazione, 6
12053 Castiglione Tinella [CN]
Tel. +39 0141855113
www.paolosaracco.it

CELLAR SALES
PRE-BOOKED VISITS
ANNUAL PRODUCTION 600,000 bottles
HECTARES UNDER VINE 46.00

Divided into more than ten properties in the municipalities of Calosso, Castagnole Lanze, Castiglione Tinella and Santo Stefano Belbo, the vineyards overseen by the Saracco family are characterized by elevations ranging from 300 to 500 meters, as well as sandy, silty and calcareous soils. These conditions have proven ideal for amplifying the polyphonic expressions of Moscato d'Asti, a wine that the producer has specialized in over time, though without neglecting equally personal selections made with Chardonnay, Riesling, Pinot Nero and Barbera. This historic producer's Moscatos are always excellent. The Piemonte Moscato d'Autunno '19 sees distinct hints of sage followed by a palate of considerable volume, playing more on sweet tones of honey and candied fruit than in the past, and beautiful length. The complex and balanced Moscato d'Asti '19 features aromas of peach and ripe melon, with a beautifully structured palate. The sapid Langhe Chardonnay Prasué '19 is also well made, with notes of white flesh fruit.

Wine	Glasses	Price
○ Moscato d'Asti '19	TT	3*
○ Piemonte Moscato d'Autunno '19	TT	3*
○ Langhe Chardonnay Prasué '19	TT	3
○ Langhe Riesling '19	TT	3
○ Moscato d'Asti '16	YYY	3*
○ Langhe Chardonnay Prasué '18	YY	3
○ Langhe Chardonnay Prasué '16	YY	3
○ Moscato d'Asti '18	YY	3*
○ Moscato d'Asti '17	YY	3*
○ Piemonte Moscato d'Autunno '18	YY	3*
○ Piemonte Moscato d'Autunno '17	YY	3*
○ Piemonte Moscato d'Autunno '16	YY	3*
● Piemonte Pinot Nero '17	YY	5

Roberto Sarotto

via Ronconuovo, 13
12050 Neviglie [CN]
Tel. +39 0173630228
www.robertosarotto.com

CELLAR SALES
PRE-BOOKED VISITS
ANNUAL PRODUCTION 700,000 bottles
HECTARES UNDER VINE 84.00
SUSTAINABLE WINERY

Roberto Sarotto's winery is one of the largest and most varied in the region, thanks to a set of privately-owned vineyards that spans more than 50 hectares, plus another 30 that are rented. Plots can be found in Barolo, Barbaresco, Gavi and Asti, making for a range that covers the classic appellations with room for innovative projects and new stylistic directions. Their wines are of great intensity and aromatic richness, mature and spicy, pervasive and soft, and come at an affordable price. These year their selection was a bit less lively than in the past. The Barbaresco Gaia-Principe '17 is soft and distinctly toasty, with a sweet, fruity profile, warm and mature on the palate. The two Gavis, in particular the vibrant and powerful Bric Sassi '19, shine as well.

○ Gavi del Comune di Gavi Bric Sassi Tenuta Manenti '19	TT 3*
● Barbaresco Gaia Principe '17	TT 6
○ Gavi Aurora '19	TT 2*
○ Langhe Arneis Runcneuv '19	TT 2*
○ Piemonte Chardonnay Puro '19	TT 3
● Barbera d'Alba Elena la Luna '18	T 4
● Barolo Audace '16	T 4
● Barbaresco Currà Ris. '14	YY 5
● Barbaresco Gaia Principe '16	YY 6
● Barbaresco Gaia Principe '15	YY 6
● Barolo Audace '15	YY 4
● Barolo Audace '14	YY 4
● Barolo Briccobergera '13	YY 4
○ Gavi del Comune di Gavi Bric Sassi '18	YY 2*
○ Langhe Arneis Runcneuv '18	YY 2*
○ Piemonte Chardonnay Puro '18	YY 3

Scagliola

via San Siro, 42
14052 Calosso [AT]
Tel. +39 0141853183
www.scagliolavini.com

CELLAR SALES
PRE-BOOKED VISITS
ANNUAL PRODUCTION 200,000 bottles
HECTARES UNDER VINE 37.00

The Scagliola family's production venture, whose roots go back to the 1930s, is grounded in two principal agricultural centers. The original production base can be found on the hills of Calosso, at about 400 metres elevation in the hamlet of San Siro, an area that stands out for its sandy-tufaceous soils with calcareous strips, a mix that's particularly well suited to Barbera reds. Marly-sandy soils, on the other hand, characterize their vineyards in Canelli, where Moscato is cultivated. Though we shouldn't forget the other varieties that make up their wide and reliable range. The Barbera d'Asti Superiore Sansì Antologia '17 exhibits great complexity on the nose, with aromas of dried herbs and cocoa accompanied by rain-soaked earth and plum, and a velvety, potent, notably fresh palate. The Moscato d'Asti Volo di Farfalle '19 is also excellent. Hints of tropical fruit, candied fruit, citrus and sage make for a wine that's both complex and fresh. Elegant and characterful, the Barbera d'Asti Frem '18 sees spicy and ripe cherry notes give way to a sapid, juicy palate.

● Barbera d'Asti Frem '18	TT 4
● Barbera d'Asti Sup. SanSì Antologia '17	TT 8
○ Moscato d'Asti Volo di Farfalle '19	TT 3*
● Barbera d'Asti Sup. SanSì '18	TT 6
● M.to Rosso Azörd '18	TT 5
● Nizza Foravia '18	TT 5
○ Piemonte Chardonnay Casot Dan Vian '19	TT 3
● Nizza Foravia '17	T 5
● Barbera d'Asti Sup. SanSì Sel. '01	YYY 6
● Barbera d'Asti Sup. SanSì Sel. '00	YYY 6
● Barbera d'Asti Sup. SanSì Sel. '99	YYY 5
● Barbera d'Asti Sup. SanSì '17	YY 6
● Barbera d'Asti Sup. SanSì Antologia '16	YY 8
● M.to Rosso Azörd '17	YY 5
○ Moscato d'Asti Primo Bacio '18	YY 3
○ Moscato d'Asti Volo di Farfalle '18	YY 3*

Simone Scaletta

Loc. Manzoni, 61
12065 Monforte d'Alba [CN]
Tel. +39 3484912733
www.simonescaletta.it

CELLAR SALES
PRE-BOOKED VISITS
ACCOMMODATION
ANNUAL PRODUCTION 35,000 bottles
HECTARES UNDER VINE 7.00

Young Simone Scaletta forges wines of great personality from his five hectares of property in Monforte d'Alba. These combine a rigorous territorial identity with pronounced pleasantness and vibrant character. Behind everything is a minimally-invasive philosophy and absolute respect for the environment in his vineyards (Viglioni, Sarsera, Chirlet and Autin 'd Madama). In the cellar non-invasive extraction is preferred, making for a distinct style and good prices (in light of the intrinsic quality of the wines). The Barbera d'Alba Superiore Sarsera '18 is vivid in its balsamic profile, nicely orchestrating flesh and acidity for an expansive and very satisfying drink. The Dolcetto d'Alba Viglioni '19 also delivers. It's one of the best of its kind, multifaceted and complex, flavorful, and of great impact on the palate. We also appreciated the pervasive and deep Barolo Bricco San Pietro Chirlet '16.

Wine	Rating
● Barbera d'Alba Sup. Sarsera '18	TT 5
● Barolo Bussia '16	TT 8
● Barolo Chirlet Bricco San Pietro '16	TT 8
● Dolcetto d'Alba Viglioni '19	TT 3
● Langhe Nebbiolo Autin 'd Madama '18	TT 5
● Langhe Nebbiolo Autin 'd Professor '19	T 5
● Barbera d'Alba Sup. Sarsera '17	YY 5
● Barbera d'Alba Sup. Sarsera '16	YY 5
● Barbera d'Alba Sup. Sarsera '15	YY 4
● Barolo Bricco San Pietro Chirlet '14	YY 8
● Barolo Bussia '15	YY 8
● Barolo Bussia '14	YY 8
● Barolo Chirlet '15	YY 6
● Barolo Ris. '13	YY 7
● Dolcetto d'Alba Viglioni '17	YY 2*
● Langhe Nebbiolo Autin 'd Madama '16	YY 5
● Langhe Nebbiolo Autin 'd Madama '15	YY 4

Giorgio Scarzello e Figli

via Alba, 29
12060 Barolo [CN]
Tel. +39 017356170
/www.scarzellobarolo.com

CELLAR SALES
PRE-BOOKED VISITS
ANNUAL PRODUCTION 45,000 bottles
HECTARES UNDER VINE 5.50

Young Federico Scarzello has just surpassed his 30th vintage. Initially he accompanied his father, Giorgio, but now he's on his own, bolstered by his enological studies and enthusiasm for his work. The property is still small but it revolves around one of the most famous and appreciated crus of the entire appellation, Sarmassa, which gives rise to their Barolo Vigna Merenda (a wine that's often highly rated by independent critics). Respect for the consumer and for the characteristics of each vintage is such that, to give a recent example, Federico preferred to market the notable 2013 version one year after the release of the simpler 2014. The new Barolo Boschetti '15 is elegant and potent, with nice freshness both on the nose and on the palate. Sensations of alcohol-steeped fruit feature in the warmer Barolo Sarmassa Vigna Merenda '15, a gentle wine, pervasive in the mouth. The Barolo del comune di Barolo '15 is even more harmonious and balanced at the moment, slightly smoky, with soft tannins. Black berries and red flowers feature in the lively Barbera d'Alba Superiore '17.

Wine	Rating
● Barolo del Comune di Barolo '15	TT 7
● Barolo Sarmassa V. Merenda '15	TT 8
● Barbera d'Alba Sup. '17	TT 5
● Barolo Boschetti '15	TT 8
● Langhe Nebbiolo '18	TT 4
● Barolo Sarmassa V. Merenda '10	YYY 6
● Barolo V. Merenda '99	YYY 5
● Barbera d'Alba Sup. '15	YY 4
● Barolo del Comune di Barolo '14	YY 5
● Barolo del Comune di Barolo '13	YY 5
● Barolo del Comune di Barolo '10	YY 5
● Barolo Sarmassa V. Merenda '13	YY 6
● Barolo Sarmassa V. Merenda '12	YY 6
● Langhe Nebbiolo '17	YY 3
● Langhe Nebbiolo '16	YY 3

★★Paolo Scavino

FRAZ. GARBELLETTO
VIA ALBA-BAROLO, 157
12060 CASTIGLIONE FALLETTO [CN]
TEL. +39 017362850
www.paoloscavino.com

CELLAR SALES
PRE-BOOKED VISITS
ANNUAL PRODUCTION 130,000 bottles
HECTARES UNDER VINE 29.00

In addition to their reserve wines and certain unique selections, Enrico Scavino, one of the most celebrated producers in the Langhe, now offers seven Barolo crus. The common characteristic is elegance, but the personality of each individual vineyard is on display, from the rich and pulpy Prapò to the softer and rounder Monvigliero, the fruit-rich Ravera and the floral, majestic Bric dël Fiasc. Such successes have been made possible thanks to wisdom and research, experimenting with innovative winemaking systems, comparing oak of different origins and sizes, protecting the grapes with anti-hail nets and only offering guaranteed excellence. Fresh and vibrant notes of undergrowth characterize the sophisticated Bric dël Fiasc, a rich and potent wine on the palate, supported by nice alcohol. Dried herbs and a hint of licorice feature in the complex Bricco Ambrogio, a wine that's not lacking in acidity or harmony on the palate. The Ravera stands out for its well-integrated citrus hints, finishing elegant and warm.

- Barolo Bric dël Fiasc '16 ▼▼▼ 8
- Barolo Bricco Ambrogio '16 ▼▼ 8
- Barolo Carobric '16 ▼▼ 8
- Barolo Ravera '16 ▼▼ 7
- Barolo Cannubi '16 ▼▼ 8
- Barolo Enrico Scavino '16 ▼▼ 7
- Barolo Monvigliero '16 ▼▼ 8
- Barolo Prapò '16 ▼▼ 7
- Barolo Bric dël Fiasc '15 ▽▽ 8
- Barolo Bricco Ambrogio '15 ▽▽ 8
- Barolo Cannubi '15 ▽▽ 8
- Barolo Carobric '15 ▽▽ 8
- Barolo Enrico Scavino '15 ▽▽ 7
- Barolo Monvigliero '15 ▽▽ 8
- Barolo Prapò '15 ▽▽ 7
- Barolo Rocche dell'Annunziata Ris. '13 ▽▽ 8

Schiavenza

VIA MAZZINI, 4
12050 SERRALUNGA D'ALBA [CN]
TEL. +39 0173613115
www.schiavenza.com

CELLAR SALES
PRE-BOOKED VISITS
RESTAURANT SERVICE
ANNUAL PRODUCTION 46,000 bottles
HECTARES UNDER VINE 11.00
SUSTAINABLE WINERY

After lunch at the exquisite, nearby family trattoria, we suggest that wine tourists visit the cellar, which is as minimalist and traditional as it is a rich enological patrimony. Only three types of red grapes are vinified here, aptly representing Serralunga d'Alba's prowess for viticulture: Barbera, Dolcetto and, above all, Nebbiolo. Excellent and famous crus give rise to their Barolos: Broglio, Prapò and Cerretta. The first is fruity and pulpy, the second enriched by tannins, the third exhibits rare power. The Barolo del comune di Serralunga d'Alba, a blend of several vineyards, is a perennially balsamic, well-crafted wine. The four 2016 Barolos put in a splendid performance, with the municipally-denominated selection just getting the better of it. A profile of splendid classicism is well represented by rich, spicy notes and rose petals; on the palate it has a soft, progressive tannic grip, never too assertive, with a long, austere finish. Beautiful licorice features in the juicy Prapò, while the Broglio proves rich in pulp.

- Barolo Broglio '16 ▼▼ 6
- Barolo del Comune di Serralunga d'Alba '16 ▼▼ 5
- Barolo Prapò '16 ▼▼ 7
- Barolo Cerretta '16 ▼▼ 6
- Barolo Broglio '11 ▽▽▽ 5
- Barolo Broglio '05 ▽▽▽ 5
- Barolo Broglio '04 ▽▽▽ 5
- Barolo Broglio Ris. '08 ▽▽▽ 7
- Barolo Broglio Ris. '04 ▽▽▽ 5
- Barolo Prapò '08 ▽▽▽ 6
- Barolo Broglio '15 ▽▽ 6
- Barolo Cerretta '15 ▽▽ 6
- Barolo del Comune di Serralunga d'Alba '15 ▽▽ 5
- Barolo Prapò '15 ▽▽ 7
- Langhe Nebbiolo '17 ▽▽ 4

Mauro Sebaste

fraz. Gallo d'Alba
via Garibaldi, 222bis
12051 Alba [CN]
Tel. +39 0173262148
www.maurosebaste.it

CELLAR SALES
PRE-BOOKED VISITS
ANNUAL PRODUCTION 120,000 bottles
HECTARES UNDER VINE 30.00
SUSTAINABLE WINERY

The 30-year-old winery overseen by Mauro Sebaste and his family boasts important vineyards in many appellations scattered throughout Langhe, Monferrato and Roero. Mauro has declared that his main efforts, when he decided to open his own winery in 1991, were devoted to finding the best land. Hence the choice of Serralunga Alba for Barolo; Alba and Diano for Nebbiolo; Vezza, Corneliano and Monteu for Roero Arneis; Santa Rosalia d'Alba for Barbera, Dolcetto and Freisa; Vinchio for Barbera d'Asti and Nizza; Gavi for the Gavi DOCG; and Mango for Moscato d'Asti. The tasty 2014 Riserva Ghè opts more for elegance than power, with a nice touch of sweet oak on a nose refreshed by a pleasant touch of resin; it's round and harmonious on the palate, with restrained tannins. Just a bit fruitier, the Barolo Trèsüri '16 is softened by virtue of maturation in oak barrels. The notable Nizza Costemonghisio '17 guarantees pleasantness.

Wine	Rating
● Barolo Ghe Ris. '14	🍷🍷 8
● Barolo Tresuri '16	🍷🍷 6
● Nizza Barbera Costemonghisio '17	🍷🍷 5
● Barolo Cerretta '16	🍷 8
● Nebbiolo d'Alba Parigi '18	🍷 5
● Barbera d'Alba Sup. Centobricchi '16	YY 5
● Barolo Cerretta '15	YY 6
● Barolo Cerretta '14	YY 6
● Barolo Ghè Ris. '12	YY 8
● Barolo Prapò '11	YY 7
● Barolo Trèsürì '15	YY 6
● Barolo Trèsürì '14	YY 6
● Nizza Costemonghisio '16	YY 4
● Nizza Costemonghisio '15	YY 4

F.lli Seghesio

loc. Castelletto, 19
12065 Monforte d'Alba [CN]
Tel. +39 017378108
www.fratelliseghesio.com

CELLAR SALES
PRE-BOOKED VISITS
ANNUAL PRODUCTION 55,000 bottles
HECTARES UNDER VINE 10.00

The whole Seghesio family, overseen by Riccardo, is involved both in cultivating the steep vineyards with the utmost respect for the environment, and in their beautiful cellar, where we find French, wooden barrels of various sizes. It's a pleasant, secluded place with a panoramic view, and we highly recommend a visit. The area's classic red grapes are cultivated, foremost Nebbiolo, though there's also Barbera and Dolcetto, with a small concession made for international grapes in the experimental Langhe Rosso Bouquet. Only three wines were submitted for tasting. Red berries and liquorice characterize the complex Barolo La Villa '16, a wine endowed with a lively freshness, harmonious and progressively unfolding on a lovely, pulpy palate, closing on hints of sweet tobacco. Pleasing vegetal notes and red fruits feature in the very classic Barolo '16, a wine that rewards the palate with its gustatory balance. The elegant Barbera d'Alba La Chiesa '17 is just slightly marked by oak, but also rich in an enlivening acidity.

Wine	Rating
● Barbera d'Alba La Chiesa '17	🍷🍷 6
● Barolo La Villa '16	🍷🍷 7
● Barolo '16	🍷🍷 7
● Barbera d'Alba Vign. della Chiesa '00	YYY 4*
● Barbera d'Alba Vign. della Chiesa '97	YYY 4*
● Barolo La Villa '10	YYY 7
● Barolo Vign. La Villa '04	YYY 6
● Barolo Vign. La Villa '99	YYY 7
● Barolo Vign. La Villa '91	YYY 6
● Barbera d'Alba '16	YY 3
● Barolo '13	YY 7
● Barolo '12	YY 7
● Barolo La Villa '15	YY 7
● Barolo La Villa '14	YY 7
● Barolo La Villa '13	YY 7
● Barolo La Villa '12	YY 7
● Langhe Rosso Bouquet '14	YY 4

Tenute Sella

via IV Novembre, 130
13060 Lessona [BI]
Tel. +39 01599455
www.tenutesella.it

CELLAR SALES
PRE-BOOKED VISITS
ANNUAL PRODUCTION 70,000 bottles
HECTARES UNDER VINE 22.50
SUSTAINABLE WINERY

The founding of the Sella family winery dates back to 1671. That alone should provide a good introduction to a name that aptly represents the potential of Northern Piedmont's Nebbiolo, foremost through their always noteworthy selections of Lessona and Bramaterra. Their most important wine, the Lessona Omaggio a Quintino Sella, is dedicated to the statesman who repeatedly served as Minister of Finance between 1862 and 1873, as well founding the Italian Geological Society. Here it's always and only Nebbiolo, which holds for their Metodo Classico as well, while their other wines also draw on traditional Croatian and Vespolina. The long stay in the bottle made for a poised and harmonious San Sebastiano allo Zoppo '11, a wine that plays more on relaxed, mature sensations than fresh and youthful ones. The Bramaterra '13 is quite vivid, with aromas of tobacco and cinchona-quinine combining with a nice tannicity on the palate. 2018 confirms the great elegance of the Orbello, a successful blend of five grapes, foremost Nebbiolo.

Wine	Rating
● Coste della Sesia Rosso Orbello '18	🍷🍷 3*
● Bramaterra '13	🍷🍷 5
⊙ Coste della Sesia Rosato Majoli '19	🍷🍷 3
● Lessona '14	🍷🍷 5
● Lessona S. Sebastiano allo Zoppo '11	🍷🍷 6
● Bramaterra I Porfidi '11	🍷 5
● Bramaterra I Porfidi '07	🍷🍷🍷 5
● Bramaterra I Porfidi '05	🍷🍷🍷 5
● Bramaterra I Porfidi '03	🍷🍷🍷 5
● Lessona Omaggio a Quintino Sella '06	🍷🍷🍷 7
● Lessona Omaggio a Quintino Sella '05	🍷🍷🍷 6
● Lessona S. Sebastiano allo Zoppo '04	🍷🍷🍷 5
● Lessona S. Sebastiano allo Zoppo '01	🍷🍷🍷 5
● Bramaterra '12	🍷🍷 5
● Lessona '13	🍷🍷 5

★Enrico Serafino

c.so Asti, 5
12043 Canale [CN]
Tel. +39 0173970474
www.enricoserafino.it

CELLAR SALES
PRE-BOOKED VISITS
ANNUAL PRODUCTION 350,000 bottles
HECTARES UNDER VINE 60.00
SUSTAINABLE WINERY

A historic winery in Roero (now owned by the Krause family), Enrico Serafino comprises 60 hectares of vineyards spanning Roero, Langhe and Monferrato. 25 of these are owned, while the other 35 are rented (but worked directly by their agronomists). The territory's classic grapes are grown, in addition to Chardonnay and Pinot Nero for their Alta Langa. All the wines offered are well made, with increasing attention paid to territorial expression. Serafino's selection of Alta Langas is splendid, establishing the producer as one of the best in Italy when it comes to bubbly. The Pas Dosé Zero Riserva '14, with its fine and well-sustained bead, sees hints of bread crust, spices and Mediterranean scrub followed by a rich, complex palate, long, with a sapid, gutsy finish. The Pas Dosé Zero 140 Riserva '07 charms, exhibiting nice length, but also an austere profile, while the Brut Oudeis Rosé '16 proves elegant and flowery.

Wine	Rating
○ Alta Langa Pas Dosé Zero Ris. '14	🍷🍷🍷 7
⊙ Alta Langa Brut Oudeis Rosé de Saignée '16	🍷🍷 5
○ Alta Langa Pas Dosé Zero 140 '07	🍷🍷 8
● Roero Oesio '17	🍷🍷 5
○ Alta Langa Brut Oudeis '16	🍷🍷 5
○ Alta Langa Extra Brut Blanc de Blancs Propago '16	🍷🍷 7
● Barolo Briccolina '15	🍷🍷 8
● Barolo del Comune di Serralunga d'Alba '16	🍷🍷 8
● Barolo Monclivio '16	🍷🍷 6
● Langhe Nebbiolo Picotener '18	🍷🍷 5
○ Moscato d'Asti Black Limited Edition '19	🍷🍷 4
● Barbera d'Alba Sup. S. Defendente '17	🍷 5
○ Alta Langa Pas Dosé Zéro Ris. '13	🍷🍷🍷 7

La Smilla

via Garibaldi, 7
15060 Bosio [AL]
Tel. +39 0143684245
www.lasmilla.it

CELLAR SALES
ANNUAL PRODUCTION 100,000 bottles
HECTARES UNDER VINE 5.00

Danilo Guido, who grew up in the world of wine, has been running the family's historic winery in the center of Bosio for some time now. Production centers on the region's native grape varieties, with a focus on the territories of Gavi and Dolcetto di Ovada, as well as Barbera. The result is a solid, well-defined range characterized by a modern style, and respectful of tradition, territory and varietal characteristics. The Gavi del Comune di Gavi '19 is vibrant, with fruity aromas on sensations of herbs, dried fruit and nuts; in the mouth it's fresh and harmonious. The Dolcetto di Ovada is starting to highlight tertiary aromas of spices and cocoa on a harmonious, persistent palate, with rather pronounced tannins. The intriguing Gavi Brut Metodo Classico was also received well, with its nice, complex, vibrant nose and a potent, fresh palate.

Wine	Rating
● Dolcetto di Ovada '18	▼▼ 2*
○ Gavi Brut M. Cl. '16	▼▼ 3
○ Gavi del Comune di Gavi '19	▼▼ 2*
● Barbera d'Asti '18	▼ 2
○ Gavi '19	▼ 2
● M.to Rosso Calicanto '17	▼ 3
● Barbera d'Asti '17	▽▽ 2*
● Dolcetto di Ovada '17	▽▽ 2*
● Dolcetto di Ovada '15	▽▽ 2*
○ Gavi '18	▽▽ 2*
○ Gavi '17	▽▽ 2*
○ Gavi Brut M. Cl. '14	▽▽ 3
○ Gavi del Comune di Gavi '18	▽▽ 2*
○ Gavi del Comune di Gavi '17	▽▽ 2*
○ Gavi del Comune di Gavi '16	▽▽ 2*
○ Gavi I Bergi '16	▽▽ 3
○ Gavi I Bergi '15	▽▽ 3*

Socré

s.da Terzolo, 7
12050 Barbaresco [CN]
Tel. +39 3487121685
www.socre.it

CELLAR SALES
PRE-BOOKED VISITS
ANNUAL PRODUCTION 30,000 bottles
HECTARES UNDER VINE 5.50

The solidity of the millennia-old granite boulders with which he designed and built his winery are a metaphor for the rocky energy and tenacious passion with which architect Marco Piacentino continues to grow the quality and image of his wines. He's achieved increasing critical and commercial success through wines ranging from the ever surprising Chardonnay Paint It Black to the classic Barbaresco Roncaglie, as well as many simpler selections: a basic Barbaresco, Barbera d'Alba and Langhe Freisa. A passion for the Metodo Classico, now made with Nebbiolo, will give birth to new selections in their Alta Langa line. The Barbaresco Roncaglie Riserva '15 sees seductive hints of tar and mint re-emerge on a long finish. It's an enchantingly harmonious, elegant and fresh wine. On its third release, with the 2018, the Paint It Black wreaks havoc on the sleepy world of Langa Chardonnay. Olfactory whiffs of hazelnut, citrus fruits and sweet spices give way to a palate that's rich and pervasive, but also endowed with an enticing freshness.

Wine	Rating
● Barbaresco Roncaglie Ris. '15	▼▼▼ 8
○ Langhe Chardonnay Paint it Black '18	▼▼ 5
● Barbaresco '17	▼▼ 6
● Barbaresco Roncaglie '16	▼▼ 7
● Barbera d'Asti '17	▼▼ 3
● Cisterna d'Asti De Scapin '17	▼▼ 4
● Langhe Freisa '18	▼▼ 4
● Langhe Nebbiolo '17	▼▼ 4
● Barbera d'Alba Sup. '17	▼ 5
● Barbaresco '16	▽▽ 5
● Barbaresco '15	▽▽ 5
● Barbaresco Roncaglie '15	▽▽ 6
● Barbaresco Roncaglie '14	▽▽ 6
○ Langhe Chardonnay Paint It Black '17	▽▽ 3*
○ Langhe Chardonnay Paint It Black '16	▽▽ 3*
● Langhe Freisa '17	▽▽ 3

Giovanni Sordo

FRAZ. GARBELLETTO
VIA ALBA BAROLO, 175
12060 CASTIGLIONE FALLETTO [CN]
TEL. +39 017362853
www.sordogiovanni.it

CELLAR SALES
PRE-BOOKED VISITS
ACCOMMODATION
ANNUAL PRODUCTION 350,000 bottles
HECTARES UNDER VINE 53.00

The winery has a centuries-old history behind it, but 2014 was a watershed year with the inauguration of their splendid new headquarters, a cellar as charming as it is well-equipped, presentation of new selections of Barolo, and important awards from wine critics. Giorgio Sordo is determined to bring his operation to the heights of excellence in Langhe, bolstered by some 8 top-level crus and 10 Barolos (including 2 reserves). It's an estate that we strongly recommend visiting and which also has one of the most attractive tasting rooms in the area. The Barolo Rocche di Castiglione '16 is a wine of great character, faithful to the best of tradition, combining classic hints of licorice and tobacco with a fine, refreshing note of aniseed; the palate is as majestic as it is velvety, and never too soft, charmingly austere. The exquisite Gabutti '16 is fruitier and more youthful, showing more harmony than muscle on the palate. The Valmaggiore '17 is another must.

Wine	Glasses	Score
● Barolo Gabutti '16	▼▼	7
● Barolo Rocche di Castiglione '16	▼▼	7
● Barbera d'Alba Sup. Massucchi '16	▼▼	4
● Barolo '16	▼▼	6
● Barolo Monprivato '15	▼▼	8
● Nebbiolo d'Alba V. Valmaggiore '17	▼▼	5
● Barolo Monvigliero '16	▼	7
○ Roero Arneis Garblet Suè '19	▼	3
● Barolo '15	▽▽	5
● Barolo Gabutti '15	▽▽	7
● Barolo Monvigliero '14	▽▽	7
● Barolo Monvigliero '13	▽▽	7
● Barolo Parussi '14	▽▽	7
● Barolo Parussi '13	▽▽	7
● Barolo Perno '13	▽▽	7
● Barolo Rocche di Castiglione '15	▽▽	7
● Dolcetto d'Alba '18	▽▽	3

★★Sottimano

LOC. COTTÀ, 21
12052 NEIVE [CN]
TEL. +39 0173635186
www.sottimano.it

CELLAR SALES
PRE-BOOKED VISITS
ANNUAL PRODUCTION 85,000 bottles
HECTARES UNDER VINE 18.00
VITICULTURE METHOD Certified Organic

Rino Sottimano is a true leader in the world of Barbaresco, but every time we visit he also lets us taste his Maté, a nice Brachetto that we recommend for its delicious drinkability. His son Andrea is proving to be up to the task and continues in his pursuit of natural grapes and elegant wine. Thanks to gradual acquisitions of vineyards, their production is increasingly focused on Barbaresco, which this close-knit and hospitable family offers six selections of. It's awfully difficult to rank them as they are all so impeccably crafted. Notable olfactory intensity features in the delicious, elegant Barbaresco Currà '15, with its notes of dried herbs and licorice followed by tobacco and raspberry; the palate is potent, with nice softness brought out by alcohol and consistent pulp, all up to a long, harmonious finish. The Basarin '16 is rather austere—it's got a bright future. The splendid Pajoré proves complex and powerful.

Wine	Glasses	Score
● Barbaresco Currà '15	▼▼▼	8
● Barbaresco Basarin '16	▼▼	7
● Barbaresco Pajoré '17	▼▼	7
● Barbaresco Cottà '17	▼▼	7
● Barbaresco Cottà '15	▽▽▽	7
● Barbaresco Cottà '05	▽▽▽	7
● Barbaresco Currà '12	▽▽▽	8
● Barbaresco Currà '10	▽▽▽	8
● Barbaresco Currà '08	▽▽▽	7
● Barbaresco Currà '04	▽▽▽	6
● Barbaresco Pajoré '16	▽▽▽	7
● Barbaresco Pajoré '14	▽▽▽	7
● Barbaresco Pajoré '10	▽▽▽	7
● Barbaresco Pajoré '08	▽▽▽	7
● Barbaresco Ris. '10	▽▽▽	8
● Barbaresco Ris. '05	▽▽▽	8
● Barbaresco Ris. '04	▽▽▽	8

★Luigi Spertino

via Lea, 505
14047 Mombercelli [AT]
Tel. +39 0141959098
luigi.spertino@libero.it

CELLAR SALES
PRE-BOOKED VISITS
ANNUAL PRODUCTION 40,000 bottles
HECTARES UNDER VINE 9.00

The growth of Asti's wines owes much to the great bottles produced by the Spertino family using grapes cultivated in the evocative, steep vineyards of Mombercelli. Today we find Mauro at the helm, who continues the work of his father, Luigi, with an eye to reviving long-marginalized cultivars, such as Grignolino. Indeed, their forward-thinking vision is paying dividends, as evidenced by the universal praise for their entire range, which has consistently shone for its varietal fidelity and natural drinkability—and that includes their Barbera, Pinot Nero and Cortese selections as well. The Barbera La Mandorla '18, probably the best ever, is back in great form in this edition, having benefited from the contribution of what should have become the second vintage of the Mandorla Edizione Speciale (after the 2014). The result is a Barbera that, like few others, manages to express its extraordinary richness with ease. Acidity and tannins perfectly balance an endless finish.

- ● Barbera d'Asti Sup. V. La Mandorla '18 TTT 8
- ● Barbera d'Asti '18 TT 4
- ● Grignolino d'Asti '19 TT 3*
- ● Grignolino d'Asti Margherita Barbero '19 TT 3*
- ○ Piemonte Cortese Vilet '17 TT 7
- ○ Piemonte Pinot Nero Brut Nature M. Cl. Cuvée della Famiglia '16 TT 7
- ● Barbera d'Asti Sup. La Mandorla '13 YYY 8
- ● Barbera d'Asti Sup. V. La Mandorla '16 YYY 8
- ● Barbera d'Asti Sup. V. La Mandorla '15 YYY 8
- ● Barbera d'Asti Sup. V. La Mandorla Edizione La Grisa '14 YYY 8
- ● Grignolino d'Asti '18 YYY 3*

★★★La Spinetta

via Annunziata, 17
14054 Castagnole delle Lanze [AT]
Tel. +39 0141877396
www.la-spinetta.com

CELLAR SALES
PRE-BOOKED VISITS
ACCOMMODATION
ANNUAL PRODUCTION 500,000 bottles
HECTARES UNDER VINE 100.00
SUSTAINABLE WINERY

The winery's size allows for respectable production volumes, thanks to a large vineyard that spans Monferrato and Langhe. The greatest international success has come from their Barbaresco, with their Gallina, Starderi and Valeirano cru competing for supremacy, but the Barolo Campè alone has managed to revitalize the Grinzane Cavour area for the production of Nebbiolo. We shouldn't forget that the winery, founded in 1977, was initially dedicated mainly to Moscato and Barbera d'Asti, which it still expertly produces. This year it's the elegant Starderi cru that stands out about the 2017 Barbarescos proposed. On the nose, fresh fruit emerges along with cherries and strawberries. The palate is magnificent for its consistency and pervasiveness, with dense, well-rounded tannins lending complexity. The 2016 Barolo Campè is splendid. Here red berries and elegant oak turn harmoniously together with spices, giving way to bitter cocoa; in the mouth it's voluminous, pulpy, with a pleasantly fresh note.

- ● Barbaresco Starderi '17 TT 8
- ● Barbera d'Asti Sup. Bionzo '17 TT 6
- ● Barolo Campè '16 TT 8
- ● Barbaresco Gallina '17 TT 8
- ● Barbaresco Valeirano '17 TT 8
- ● Barbaresco Vign. Bordini '17 TT 7
- ● Barolo Vign. Garretti '16 TT 7
- ○ Colli Tortonesi Timorasso Piccolo Derthona '19 TT 5
- ○ Langhe Bianco '17 TT 6
- ○ Moscato d'Asti Bricco Quaglia '19 TT 3
- ○ Piemonte Moscato Passito Oro '11 TT 6
- ○ Piemonte Chardonnay Lidia '17 T 8
- ● Barbaresco Gallina '11 YYY 8
- ● Barbaresco Vign. Starderi '07 YYY 8
- ● Barbera d'Asti Sup. Bionzo '09 YYY 6
- ● Barolo Campè '08 YYY 8

Marchese Luca Spinola

FRAZ. ROVERETO
LOC. CASCINA MASSIMILIANA, 97
15066 GAVI [AL]
TEL. +39 0143682514
www.marcheselucaspinola.it

CELLAR SALES
PRE-BOOKED VISITS
ANNUAL PRODUCTION 30,000 bottles
HECTARES UNDER VINE 15.00
VITICULTURE METHOD Certified Organic

The Spinola family's small winery is bolstered by solid agricultural roots. Today Andrea Spinola is carrying on thanks to time-honored family vineyards situated in Rovereto and Tassarolo. Their range, certified organic, features three wines that focus on environmental sustainability and proper management of natural resources, all in the name of preserving the qualities of the territory of origin. Cortese serves as a cornerstone and is interpreted with a contemporary style that's capable of lending prestige to the wines of the past. See, for example, the Marquis col Fondo, made with the Metodo Ancestrale. The Gavi del Comune di Gavi Carlo put in a fine performance, with aromas of dried herbs and hints of almond lending complexity; on the palate it's fresh, sapid, with a nice, lingering finish. The Gavi del Comune di Tassarolo opts more for flowery, citrus aromas with mineral notes; on the palate it's fresh and vibrant, with a sapid finish. The Massimiliano, which features a complex nose-palate profile, is still evolving.

Wine	Rating
○ Gavi del Comune di Gavi Carlo '19	▼▼ 3*
○ Gavi del Comune di Tassarolo '19	▼▼ 2*
○ Gavi del Comune di Gavi Massimiliano '18	▼ 3
○ Gavi del Comune di Gavi '16	▽▽ 2*
○ Gavi del Comune di Gavi '15	▽▽ 2*
○ Gavi del Comune di Gavi Carlo '18	▽▽ 3*
○ Gavi del Comune di Gavi Carlo '17	▽▽ 2*
○ Gavi del Comune di Gavi Et. Blu '14	▽▽ 2*
○ Gavi del Comune di Gavi Massimiliano '17	▽▽ 3*
○ Gavi del Comune di Gavi Tenuta Massimiliana '16	▽▽ 3*
○ Gavi del Comune di Gavi Tenuta Massimiliana '15	▽▽ 3
○ Gavi del Comune di Gavi Tenuta Massimiliana '14	▽▽ 3

Giuseppe Stella

S.DA BOSSOLA, 8
14055 COSTIGLIOLE D'ASTI [AT]
TEL. +39 0141966142
www.stellavini.com

CELLAR SALES
PRE-BOOKED VISITS
ANNUAL PRODUCTION 50,000 bottles
HECTARES UNDER VINE 12.00

The producer founded in the 1920's by Domenico Stella is situated in Costigliole d'Asti, an authentic production center in Monferrato. Today it's run by Giuseppe, along with his sons Massimo and Paolo, who've contributed to further consolidating their already reliable battery of wines. These are made with both native and international varieties: Barbera, Dolcetto, Grignolino for the red grapes, Cortese, Chardonnay and Moscato for the whites. Theirs is a traditional range, perfect to accompany a meal. The Barbera d'Asti Superiore Giaiet '17, with its jammy notes of red fruit on a citrus background, has richness, volume and a long, sapid finish. The Barbera d'Asti Superiore Il Maestro '17 sees aromas of ripe black fruit and cinchona-quinine followed by a close-woven, dense palate, well supported by acidity, while the Piedmont Chardonnay Giaiet '19 features mineral notes before unveiling a palate that's powerful and rich, but still highly drinkable.

Wine	Rating
● Barbera d'Asti Sup. Giaiet '17	▼▼ 4
● Barbera d'Asti Sup. Il Maestro '17	▼▼ 5
● Grignolino d'Asti Sufragio '18	▼▼ 3
○ Piemonte Chardonnay Giaiet '19	▼▼ 4
● Barbera d'Asti Stravisan '18	▼ 3
● Freisa d'Asti Convento '17	▼ 3
● Barbera d'Asti Stravisan '17	▽▽ 2*
● Barbera d'Asti Stravisan '13	▽▽ 2*
● Barbera d'Asti Stravisan '11	▽▽ 2*
● Barbera d'Asti Sup. Giaiet '16	▽▽ 3
● Barbera d'Asti Sup. Giaiet '11	▽▽ 3
● Barbera d'Asti Sup. Il Maestro '16	▽▽ 4
● Barbera d'Asti Sup. Il Maestro '12	▽▽ 4
● Freisa d'Asti Convento '16	▽▽ 3*
● Grignolino d'Asti Sufragio '14	▽▽ 3
● Grignolino d'Asti Vign. Sufragio '10	▽▽ 2*

Sulin

v.le Pininfarina, 14
14035 Grazzano Badoglio [AT]
Tel. +39 0141925136
www.sulin.it

CELLAR SALES
PRE-BOOKED VISITS
ANNUAL PRODUCTION 220,000 bottles
HECTARES UNDER VINE 19.50

The Fracchia family have always adopted an ethical and sustainable approach to viticulture, one that goes beyond the requirements of organic farming. Years ago a deep bond with the territory and an instinct for the preservation of biodiversity drove them to invest time and money into selecting a Barbera clone from one of their almost century-old vineyards. From those few vines a successful path emerged, generating the Ornella vineyard from which their Barbera del Monferrato Superiore Barbera is born. The next bet? Two wines made with native, almost extinct vines: Slarina and Baratuciat. The Monferace Brasal is an extremely elegant, complex wine. Notes of pepper, tobacco and liquorice converge on the palate, where it's elegant and full-bodied, with a very long finish. The charming Centum reveals aromas of blackcurrant syrup on light vegetal notes, anticipating a generous, full-bodied palate with well-modulated tannins and a lingering finish. The other wines tasted are also very well made.

- ● Barbera del M.to Centum '18 — TT 3*
- ● Piemonte Grignolino Monferace Brasal '16 — TT 5
- ● Barbera del M.to Sup. Ornella Memoriae '09 — TT 5
- ● Casorzo Voület '19 — TT 2*
- ● Grignolino del M.to Casalese '19 — TT 2*
- ● M.to Rosso Adriano '17 — TT 2*
- ○ Piemonte Chardonnay Memoriae '14 — TT 3
- ● Barbera del M.to '17 — YY 2*
- ● Barbera del M.to Sup. Ornella '16 — YY 5
- ● Barbera del M.to Sup. Ornella '15 — YY 5
- ● Casorzo Voület '18 — YY 2*
- ● M.to Rosso Adriano '16 — YY 3
- ● Piemonte Grignolino Monferace Brasal '15 — YY 5

★Tacchino

via Martiri della Benedicta, 26
15060 Castelletto d'Orba [AL]
Tel. +39 0143830115
www.luigitacchino.it

CELLAR SALES
PRE-BOOKED VISITS
ANNUAL PRODUCTION 120,000 bottles
HECTARES UNDER VINE 12.00

Romina and Alessio lead one of the area's most vibrant wineries, thanks to a rare spirit of initiative combined with a strong passion for their work. Their wines, every type and level, benefit from the extreme care shown, and their top selections frequently make appearances during our tasting finals. Indeed, we've tasted many greats over the years, making Tacchino one of the region's most distinguished producers. At the heart of it all is the valuable work done with Dolcetto di Ovada, which despite its peculiarities once risked falling into oblivion. Their range is characterized by a clear, modern style. The line-up presented this year really needs no comment. The Du Riva and Albarola do an outstanding job interpreting their respective typologies. The Albarola, perhaps, is a bit readier, offering up a nose-palate profile of great character. Tre Bicchieri. We definitely recommend the Monferrato Rosso Di Fatto, and especially the Barbera del Monferrato '18, a juicy, enticing drink.

- ● Barbera del M.to Albarola '16 — TTT 5
- ● Dolcetto di Ovada Sup. Du Riva '16 — TT 4
- ● Barbera del M.to '18 — TT 3
- ● Dolcetto di Ovada '18 — TT 2*
- ○ Gavi del Comune di Gavi '19 — TT 3
- ● M.to Rosso Di Fatto '17 — TT 4
- ● Dolcetto di Ovada '16 — YYY 2*
- ● Dolcetto di Ovada '15 — YYY 2*
- ● Dolcetto di Ovada Sup. Du Riva '15 — YYY 4*
- ● Dolcetto di Ovada Sup. Du Riva '13 — YYY 4*
- ● Dolcetto di Ovada Sup. Du Riva '12 — YYY 5
- ● Dolcetto di Ovada Sup. Du Riva '11 — YYY 5

Michele Taliano

c.so A. Manzoni, 24
12046 Montà [CN]
Tel. +39 0173975658
www.talianomichele.com

CELLAR SALES
PRE-BOOKED VISITS
ANNUAL PRODUCTION 60,000 bottles
HECTARES UNDER VINE 12.00

Founded in 1930, the Taliano family winery is now run by brothers Alberto and Ezio. The estates are situated in Roero, in the municipality of Montà, and Langa, in the Barbaresco appellation (in San Rocco Seno d'Elvio). Mostly native grapes are cultivated, starting with Arneis, Barbera and Nebbiolo, as well as Brachetto, Dolcetto, Favorita and Moscato, together with small quantities of Sauvignon and Cabernet Sauvignon. The wines produced are modern, well-balanced and beautifully aromatic. This year the two Barbarescos stand out. The Montersino Tera Mia Riserva '13 sees a bouquet of ripe red berries and liquorice followed by an expansive palate with well-managed tannins, while the Montersino Ad Altiora '16 is still a bit clenched, but fresh, spunky and rich in fruit. The Barbera d'Alba Superiore Laboriosa '16 is generous, with nice verve and sapidity, while the Barbera d'Alba A Bon Rendre '19 proves supple and quaffable.

Wine	Rating
● Barbaresco Montersino Ad Altiora '16	🍷🍷 5
● Barbaresco Montersino Tera Mia Ris. '13	🍷🍷 5
● Barbera d'Alba Sup. Laboriosa '16	🍷🍷 3
● Roero Ròche Dra Bòssora Ris. '16	🍷🍷 3
● Barbera d'Alba A Bon Rendre '19	🍷 2
● Dolcetto d'Alba Ciabot '19	🍷 2
○ Langhe Favorita Fiori e Frutti '19	🍷 2
● Barbaresco Montersino Ad Altiora '15	🍷🍷 5
● Barbaresco Montersino Ad Altiora '14	🍷🍷 5
● Barbaresco Montersino Tera Mia Ris. '12	🍷🍷 5
● Barbera d'Alba A Bon Rendre '18	🍷🍷 2*
● Barbera d'Alba Sup. '14	🍷🍷 3
○ Roero '14	🍷🍷 2*
○ Roero Arneis '17	🍷🍷 2*
○ Roero Arneis Serni '18	🍷🍷 2*
○ Roero Arneis U R Nice '17	🍷🍷 2*
● Roero Ròche dra Bòssora Ris. '15	🍷🍷 3*

Tenuta Tenaglia

s.da Santuario di Crea, 5
15020 Serralunga di Crea [AL]
Tel. +39 0142940252
www.tenutatenaglia.it

CELLAR SALES
PRE-BOOKED VISITS
ACCOMMODATION
ANNUAL PRODUCTION 100,000 bottles
HECTARES UNDER VINE 30.00
SUSTAINABLE WINERY

Tenuta Tenaglia is situated below the Sanctuary of the Madonna di Crea, in an enviable, panoramic position. The higher elevations also benefit the vineyards—indeed, the favorable mesoclimate and temperature swings facilitate slow and regular ripening of the grapes. Production is entrusted to Roberto Imarisio, an experienced enologist, who tends towards a modern style, with the careful use of oak aimed at preserving the grapes' characteristic aromas. Barbera and Grignolino serve as cornerstones. The Emozioni pours a bright, ruby-red, the prologue to a multifaceted, persistent nose: sweet spices combine with cinchona-quinine and cocoa with a light touch of mocha. In the mouth it opens rich and intense, very well-orchestrated and endlessly long. The Giorgio Tenaglia, with more time in the bottle, could reveal its true potential. The Cappella III is an excellent drink. The other wines tasted are also worth noting.

Wine	Rating
● Barbera d'Asti Sup. Emozioni '15	🍷🍷 6
● Barbera d'Asti Giorgio Tenaglia '17	🍷🍷 4
● Barbera del M.to Cappella III '19	🍷🍷 2*
● Grignolino del M.to Casalese '19	🍷🍷 2*
● Grignolino del M.to Casalese Monferace '16	🍷🍷 6
⊙ M.to Chiaretto Edenrose '19	🍷🍷 2*
○ Piemonte Chardonnay '19	🍷 3
● Barbera d'Asti Emozioni '99	🍷🍷🍷 4*
● Grignolino del M.to Casalese '17	🍷🍷🍷 2*
● Barbera d'Asti Bricco '18	🍷🍷 3
● Barbera del M.to Sup. 1930 Una Buona Annata '15	🍷🍷 5
● Grignolino del M.to Casalese '18	🍷🍷 2*
● Grignolino del M.to Casalese '16	🍷🍷 2*
● Grignolino del M.to Casalese Monferace '15	🍷🍷 6

Terre del Barolo

via Alba - Barolo, 8
12060 Castiglione Falletto [CN]
Tel. +39 0173262053
www.arnaldorivera.com

CELLAR SALES
PRE-BOOKED VISITS
ANNUAL PRODUCTION 3,000,000 bottles
HECTARES UNDER VINE 600.00
VITICULTURE METHOD Certified Organic
SUSTAINABLE WINERY

Only four years ago the line of wines named after the winery's founder, Arnaldo Rivera, was created, and the results are already outstanding, as evidenced by numerous awards from critics on both sides of the ocean. The project was carried out in collaboration with a number of growers whose grapes are then worked according to the strictest quality protocols in collaboration with qualified agronomists and enologists. The result is 11 wines, including eight Barolo crus, each representing the perfect expression of its territory, with vineyards ranging from Vignarionda to Bussia and Monvigliero. Our tasting of the 2016 Barolos begins with a sumptuous, complex Monvigliero endowed with fresh red fruit and an austere palate of classic harmony. A delicate whiff of sweet oak features in the alluring Vigna Rionda, with its powerful tannic texture and enchanting persistence. Liquorice and cinchona characterize the Castello, a wine rich in detail and nicely balanced.

Wine	Rating	
● Barolo Monvigliero '16	🍷🍷	6
● Barolo Vignarionda '16	🍷🍷	7
● Barolo Bussia '16	🍷🍷	6
● Barolo Castello '16	🍷🍷	6
● Barolo Ravera '16	🍷🍷	6
● Barolo Rocche di Castiglione '16	🍷🍷	7
● Barolo Undicicomuni '16	🍷🍷	5
○ Langhe Nascetta del Comune di Novello '18	🍷🍷	3
● Barolo Vignarionda Arnaldo Rivera '13	YYY	7
● Barolo Boiolo '15	YY	5
● Barolo Castello '15	YY	6
● Barolo Monvigliero '15	YY	6
● Barolo Rocche di Castiglione '15	YY	7
● Barolo Undicicomuni '15	YY	5
● Barolo Vignarionda '15	YY	7

La Toledana

loc. Sermoira, 5
15066 Gavi [AL]
Tel. +39 0141837211
www.latoledana.it

CELLAR SALES
PRE-BOOKED VISITS
ANNUAL PRODUCTION 160,000 bottles
HECTARES UNDER VINE 28.00

The winery gets its name from the charming, mid-16th century rural villa, enlarged by the Gambiaso family in the late 19th century. The vineyards around the property host the grapes for their Gavi del Comune di Gavi Toledana and Spumante Metodo Italiano Toledana. The Cascina La Doria is situated in San Cristoforo, a small town about 3 kilometres from Gavi and another historic production areas for Cortese wines. Here the vineyards, which are situated on the left bank of the Lemme, give rise to a single wine, the Gavi La Doria. The Gavi Vigne Rade opens with a complex, multifaceted bouquet: aromas of mimosa and acacia blossom on a mineral background converge in a vibrant, fresh, sapid palate, finishing long. Aromas of wisteria and linden on more complex mineral notes are the hallmark of the La Doria, an intense wine, with a sapid, fresh gustatory phase and a persistent finish.

Wine	Rating	
○ Gavi del Comune di Gavi Vigne Rade '19	🍷🍷🍷	5
○ Gavi La Doria San Cristoforo '19	🍷🍷	3*
● Barolo Lo Zoccolaio '15	YY	5
● Barolo Ravera Lo Zoccolaio Ris. '12	YY	7
○ Gavi del Comune di Gavi La Toledana '18	YY	5
○ Gavi del Comune di Gavi La Toledana '17	YY	5
○ Gavi del Comune di Gavi La Toledana '16	YY	5
○ Gavi del Comune di Gavi La Toledana '15	YY	5
○ Gavi del Comune di Gavi V.Rade Foglio 46 '18	YY	5
○ Gavi La Doria '17	YY	3
○ Gavi La Doria '16	YY	3
● Langhe Baccanera Lo Zoccolaio '16	YY	3

★Torraccia del Piantavigna

via Romagnano, 20
28074 Ghemme [NO]
Tel. +39 0163840040
www.torracciadelpiantavigna.it

CELLAR SALES
PRE-BOOKED VISITS
ANNUAL PRODUCTION 150,000 bottles
HECTARES UNDER VINE 38.00
SUSTAINABLE WINERY

Alessandro Francoli became famous first for his grappas and then, over the last twenty years, for this winery, which has gradually developed thanks to the arrival of the Ponti family. The aim was to relaunch Northern Piedmont's two DOCG wines, Ghemme and Gattinara, offering reds marked by great structure, suitable for aging and always endowed with the elegance that Nebbiolo can express. The success achieved comes down to serious work in the vineyards and a multifaceted production approach, skilfully carried out by enologist Mattia Donna, with the support of Beppe Caviola. The property is well worth the visit. The Gattinara '16 features commendable harmony on the palate, with a fruity, tannic sensation that's nicely balanced right up to a long, elegant finish. The Ghemme '15 is a bit harder, more decisive, with both oak and vegetal notes lending complexity. The rest of their selection proves pleasantly simple and enjoyably drinkable.

Wine	Rating
● Gattinara '16	🍷🍷 6
● Ghemme '15	🍷🍷 6
● Colline Novaresi Nebbiolo Tre Confini '18	🍷🍷 3
○ Colline Novaresi Bianco ErbaVoglio '19	🍷 3
● Colline Novaresi Nebbiolo Neb '18	🍷 4
⊙ Colline Novaresi Nebbiolo Rosato Barlàn '19	🍷 3
● Gattinara '15	🍷🍷🍷 6
● Gattinara '09	🍷🍷🍷 5
● Ghemme '13	🍷🍷🍷 6
● Ghemme '11	🍷🍷🍷 6
● Ghemme '10	🍷🍷🍷 5
● Ghemme Ris. '07	🍷🍷🍷 5
● Ghemme V. Pelizzane '11	🍷🍷🍷 6
● Ghemme V. Pelizzane '10	🍷🍷🍷 6

Giancarlo Travaglini

via delle Vigne, 36
13045 Gattinara [VC]
Tel. +39 0163833588
www.travaglinigattinara.it

CELLAR SALES
PRE-BOOKED VISITS
ANNUAL PRODUCTION 250,000 bottles
HECTARES UNDER VINE 55.00
SUSTAINABLE WINERY

In 1958 Giancarlo Travaglini began to pursue his dream of realizing a Gattinara based on aromatic elegance, as well as on the gustatory power naturally inherent in Nebbiolo. The results have been appreciated throughout the world. His capable daughter Cinzia is carrying forward, maintaining high quality standard and expanding both the vineyard and the cellar, which now includes a nice tasting room. Their Riserva, as well as the base-level Gattinara and Tre Vigne are of exquisite craftsmanship. The Gattinara Riserva and the Tre Vigne del 2015 were released at the same time. The former features a refined aromatic elegance followed by a dense, progressive drinkability made possible by notable structure and a welcome acidity. The latter is just a bit more austere on the palate, preceded by alluring hints of tobacco, gentian and liquorice. Despite the warm 2017 vintage, we also appreciated the Gattinara, fresh and very lively on the nose.

Wine	Rating
● Gattinara Ris. '15	🍷🍷🍷 6
● Gattinara Tre Vigne '15	🍷🍷 6
● Gattinara '17	🍷🍷 5
● Coste della Sesia Nebbiolo '19	🍷 4
● Il Sogno '16	🍷 8
● Gattinara Ris. '13	🍷🍷🍷 7
● Gattinara Ris. '12	🍷🍷🍷 7
● Gattinara Ris. '06	🍷🍷🍷 6
● Gattinara Ris. '04	🍷🍷🍷 5
● Gattinara Ris. '01	🍷🍷🍷 5
● Gattinara Tre Vigne '04	🍷🍷🍷 5
● Coste della Sesia Nebbiolo '18	🍷🍷 3
● Gattinara '15	🍷🍷 6
● Gattinara '14	🍷🍷 6
● Gattinara '13	🍷🍷 6
● Gattinara Tre Vigne '14	🍷🍷 7
● Il Sogno '15	🍷🍷 8

★G. D. Vajra

FRAZ. VERGNE
VIA DELLE VIOLE, 25
12060 BAROLO [CN]
TEL. +39 017356257
www.gdvajra.it

PRE-BOOKED VISITS
ACCOMMODATION
ANNUAL PRODUCTION 350,000 bottles
HECTARES UNDER VINE 60.00
SUSTAINABLE WINERY

Aldo Vaira's personality, together with his academic background in agriculture, has always led to a technical, somewhat unimaginative approach to problems of enology, convinced as he is that respect for nature doesn't mean relying on chance but rather studying the ripening of the grapes and then working methodically during vinification. But he's still able, even after almost 50 seasons, to get excited by his Nebbiolo during the delicate and always complex harvest period. The vineyards are located mainly in Barolo and Serralunga d'Alba, with results that are consistently rewarded by critics and consumers. The extraordinary Barolo Cerretta Luigi Baudana '16 unveils a notable, multifaceted aromatic complexity that moves from rose to licorice, from raspberry to dried herbs—a fantastic olfactory pinwheel. In the mouth it's enchanting, long and graceful, with tannins and acidity lending vitality. Their Barolo vineyards gave rise to a magnificent Bricco delle Viole '16.

Wine	Rating	
● Barolo Cerretta Luigi Baudana '16	▼▼▼	6
● Barolo Baudana Luigi Baudana '16	▼▼	6
● Barolo Bricco delle Viole '16	▼▼	8
● Barolo Coste di Rose '16	▼▼	8
● Barbera d'Alba Sup. '17	▼▼	5
● Barolo Ravera '16	▼▼	8
○ Langhe Bianco Dragon '19	▼▼	4
○ Langhe Riesling '19	▼▼	5
● Barolo Baudana Luigi Baudana '09	▽▽▽	6
● Barolo Bricco delle Viole '15	▽▽▽	8
● Barolo Bricco delle Viole '12	▽▽▽	8
● Barolo Bricco delle Viole '10	▽▽▽	8
● Barolo Bricco delle Viole '05	▽▽▽	8
● Barolo Bricco delle Viole '01	▽▽▽	8
● Barolo Bricco delle Viole '00	▽▽▽	8
● Barolo Cerretta Luigi Baudana '08	▽▽▽	6
○ Langhe Bianco '02	▽▽▽	5

Valfaccenda

FRAZ. MADONNA LORETO
LOC. VAL FACCENDA, 43
12043 CANALE [CN]
TEL. +39 3397303837
www.valfaccenda.it

CELLAR SALES
PRE-BOOKED VISITS
ACCOMMODATION
ANNUAL PRODUCTION 22,000 bottles
HECTARES UNDER VINE 3.50
VITICULTURE METHOD Certified Organic
SUSTAINABLE WINERY

For generations, the Faccenda family have lived in a valley between Canale and Cisterna called Valle Faccenda. The winery, founded by Luca Faccenda in 2010, draws on vineyards cultivated exclusively with Arneis and Nebbiolo. Located a stone's throw from the farmhouse, on the hills bordering le Rocche, they're flanked by other vineyards rented in other parts of Roero. All grow in the sandy soil typical of the area. The wines proposed are traditional, the result of an approach that seeks to be as minimally invasive as possible, both in the vineyard and in the cellar. The charming Roero '19, made with Arneis grapes partially macerated on the skins, proves broad on the nose, with notes of yellow fruit, beeswax and incense. In addition to fruity tones, the palate exhibits a pronounced sapidity, almost salty, with a pleasant, bitterish finish. The Roero Valmaggiore '17 sees hints of red berries, Mediterranean scrub and cinchona-quinine followed by a palate rich in pulp and structure, finishing supple, juicy.

Wine	Rating	
● Roero '19	▼▼	5
● Roero V. Valmaggiore Ris. '17	▼▼	6
● Roero '18	▼▼	5
● Roero '16	▽▽	4
● Roero '15	▽▽	4
● Roero '14	▽▽	4
● Roero '13	▽▽	4
● Roero Ris. '15	▽▽	6
● Roero V. Valmaggiore Ris. '16	▽▽	6
● Roero V. Valmaggiore Ris. '14	▽▽	4
● Roero V. Valmaggiore Ris. '13	▽▽	4
● Vindabeive '15	▽▽	3

Mauro Veglio

FRAZ. ANNUNZIATA
LOC. CASCINA NUOVA, 50
12064 LA MORRA [CN]
TEL. +39 0173509212
www.mauroveglio.com

CELLAR SALES
PRE-BOOKED VISITS
ANNUAL PRODUCTION 115,000 bottles
HECTARES UNDER VINE 22.00
SUSTAINABLE WINERY

Mauro Veglio is convinced that elegance is the main strength of the Barolo from La Morra and the important crus of Arborina, Gattera and Rocche dell'Annunziata. Thus he feels that his primary task is to maintain this elegance, starting first of all with the use of the highest quality French oak. The Barolo from Monforte d'Alba, in the Castelletto cru, however, sees a different approach, with free rein given to the power that characterizes the area's grape. Though when it comes to fermentation and aging, his methods are not dissimilar. His wife, Daniela Saffirio, and grandson Alessandro Veglio are the other pillars of this fine winery. The cosseting Barolo Gattera '16 exhibits a modern style, without excesses, rich in red berries and a touch of sweet oak that's well integrated with its rich mouthfeel. The elegant, liquorice-scented Arborina '16 also proves pleasantly fresh in the mouth. Elegant, clear and focused fruity aromas feature in the Barolo Paiagallo '16, a wine that makes a notable, harmonious impact on the palate.

Wine	Rating
● Barolo Arborina '16	TT 7
● Barolo Gattera '16	TT 7
● Barolo Paiagallo '16	TT 8
● Barbera d'Alba Cascina Nuova '18	TT 5
● Barolo '16	TT 6
● Barolo Castelletto '16	TT 7
● Barbera d'Alba '18	YY 3
● Barbera d'Alba Cascina Nuova '17	YY 5
● Barbera d'Alba Cascina Nuova '16	YY 5
● Barolo '15	YY 5
● Barolo Arborina '15	YY 7
● Barolo Castelletto '15	YY 7
● Barolo Castelletto '14	YY 7
● Barolo Gattera '15	YY 7
● Barolo Rocche dell'Annunziata '15	YY 8
● Barolo Rocche dell'Annunziata '14	YY 8
● Dolcetto d'Alba '18	YY 2*

Giovanni Viberti

FRAZ. VERGNE
VIA DELLE VIOLE, 30
12060 BAROLO [CN]
TEL. +39 017356192
www.viberti-barolo.com

CELLAR SALES
PRE-BOOKED VISITS
RESTAURANT SERVICE
ANNUAL PRODUCTION 205,000 bottles
HECTARES UNDER VINE 23.00
SUSTAINABLE WINERY

Today at the helm we find we find Claudio Viberti, operating in the highest part of the municipality of Barolo, at elevations spanning 400-550 meters above sea level. Their wines need time to find harmony and balance in the bottle, which explains the choice to release three Barolo reserves (the Bricco delle Viole, San Pietro and La Volta). The style is classic, with calibrated extraction in conical vats and untoasted barrels. We highly recommend the traditional food offered at the Buon Padre restaurant, where house wines have been served since 1923. The Barolo Buon Padre '16 offers up aromas of cinchona-quinine, licorice and raspberries, graceful in its measured structure; tannins are refined, progressively unfolding, the finish long, rich in flavor and energy. The complex and elegant Barolo Bricco delle Viole Riserva '14 features notes of tanned leather and dried flowers, coming through light and expressive on the palate. Notes of mint and pepper characterize the fleshy Barolo Ravera Riserva '14, a wine that still has to find the perfect balance.

Wine	Rating
● Barolo Buon Padre '16	TT 6
● Barolo Bricco delle Viole Ris. '14	TT 7
● Barolo Ravera Ris. '14	TT 8
● Langhe Nebbiolo '18	TT 4
● Barbera d'Alba La Gemella '19	T 3
○ Langhe Chardonnay Rinato '18	T 5
● Barbera d'Alba La Gemella '17	YY 3
● Barbera d'Alba Sup. Bricco Airoli '15	YY 4
● Barolo Bricco delle Viole Ris. '13	YY 8
● Barolo Buon Padre '15	YY 6
● Barolo Buon Padre '14	YY 6
● Barolo Ravera Ris. '13	YY 8
● Dolcetto d'Alba Sup. '17	YY 3
● Dolcetto d'Alba Sup. '16	YY 3
● Langhe Dolbà '17	YY 2*
● Langhe Dolbà '16	YY 2*
● Langhe Nebbiolo '17	YY 3

Vicara

via Madonna delle Grazie, 5
15030 Rosignano Monferrato [AL]
Tel. +39 0142488054
www.vicara.it

CELLAR SALES
PRE-BOOKED VISITS
ANNUAL PRODUCTION 200,000 bottles
HECTARES UNDER VINE 37.00
VITICULTURE METHOD Certified Biodynamic

One of Vicara's great skills has been its ability to manage and interpret native grape varieties, something they've proven increasingly adept at with each passing harvest. The wines, whether they be standard-label or reserves aged in wood, manage to amaze us year after year for the elegance of their aromas and their explosive fruit, as is the case with the Barbera Volpuva, or the spicy finesse of the Grignolino. Then there's their premium selections, the Cantico della Crosia and the Uccelletta, making for an exquisite range that expresses an extraordinary territory. We start with the award-winning Grignolino G. Sophisticated and elegant, it unveils spicy aromas on notes of red berries before giving way to a palate of great class, with harmonious tannins and a very long finish. The Cantico della Crosia opens on aromas of red berries accompanied by hints of cinchona-quinine and licorice; in the mouth it's lovely, with great freshness to balance its flesh and a long, juicy finish. The other wines tasted are also of note.

- ● Barbera del M.to Sup. Cantico della Crosia '17 — 3 glasses 4*
- ● Grignolino del M.to Casalese G '19 — 2 glasses 4
- ● Barbera del M.to Cascina La Rocca 33 '17 — 2 glasses 4
- ● Barbera del M.to Volpuva '19 — 2 glasses 3
- ● Grignolino del M.to Casalese Monferace Uccelletta '16 — 2 glasses 4
- ○ M.to Airales '19 — 2 glasses 3
- ● Grignolino del M.to Casalese °G '15 — 3 glasses (previous) 4*
- ● Barbera del M.to Sup. Cantico della Crosia '16 — 2 glasses (previous) 4
- ● Barbera del M.to Volpuva '18 — 2 glasses (previous) 3
- ● Grignolino del M.to Casalese G '18 — 2 glasses (previous) 4
- ● Grignolino del M.to Casalese Uccelletta Monferace '15 — 2 glasses (previous) 4

★★Vietti

p.zza Vittorio Veneto, 5
12060 Castiglione Falletto [CN]
Tel. +39 017362825
www.vietti.com

CELLAR SALES
PRE-BOOKED VISITS
ANNUAL PRODUCTION 300,000 bottles
HECTARES UNDER VINE 40.00

Luca Currado Vietti is not only the winery's managing director, he's also the enologist responsible for every production choice, both agronomically and in the cellar. The level of quality with which Vietti is now associated internationally is absolute, both when it comes to their more famous and expensive selections, headed by the Barolo Villero Riserva, and their simpler wines, with the Langhe Nebbiolo Perbacco, which undergoes two years of aging in oak, standing out. The Krause family, owners since 2016, continue with the acquisition of important vineyards, and not only in Langhe. The Barolo Villero Riserva '13 exhibits textbook complexity, opening on ripe red fruits and alluring notes of licorice and tar. In the mouth it's dense, memorable, almost austere, rich in pulp, with delicate tannins. Elegant, sweet notes of tobacco and a hint of oak feature in the aromatically splendid Lazzarito '16, a wine whose palate is powerful and vivid. Their outstanding range also includes the fantastic Barbaresco Masseria '16.

- ● Barolo Villero Ris. '13 — 3 glasses 8
- ● Barolo Lazzarito '16 — 2 glasses 8
- ● Barolo Ravera '16 — 2 glasses 8
- ● Barolo Rocche di Castiglione '16 — 2 glasses 8
- ● Barbaresco Masseria '16 — 2 glasses 8
- ● Barbera d'Alba Scarrone V. Vecchia '18 — 2 glasses 6
- ● Barbera d'Alba Tre Vigne '18 — 2 glasses 3
- ● Barbera d'Alba V. Scarrone '18 — 2 glasses 5
- ● Barolo Brunate '16 — 2 glasses 8
- ● Barolo Castiglione '16 — 2 glasses 7
- ○ Roero Arneis '19 — 2 glasses 3
- ● Langhe Nebbiolo Perbacco '17 — 1 glass 4
- ● Barolo Ravera '12 — 3 glasses (previous) 8
- ● Barolo Rocche '08 — 3 glasses (previous) 8
- ● Barolo Rocche di Castiglione '11 — 3 glasses (previous) 8
- ● Barolo Villero Ris. '07 — 3 glasses (previous) 8
- ● Barolo Villero Ris. '06 — 3 glasses (previous) 8

Villa Giada

reg. Ceirole, 10
14053 Canelli [AT]
Tel. +39 0141831100
www.villagiada.wine

CELLAR SALES
PRE-BOOKED VISITS
ACCOMMODATION AND RESTAURANT SERVICE
ANNUAL PRODUCTION 180,000 bottles
HECTARES UNDER VINE 25.00
SUSTAINABLE WINERY

Cascina Dani in Agliano Terme (loose, medium-textured soil), Cascina del Parroco in Calosso (a small plateau overlooking the valley of Rio Nizza), Cascina Ceirole in Canelli (the original vineyard and adjacent cellar): these three farms are the foundation of the range produced by the Faccio family (aka Villa Giada), using mainly Barbera and Moscato. It's a veteran winery that still avails itself of a picturesque bottle cellar dating back to the late-18th century for the maturation of its most important bottles, the pride of an enological selection without weak points. The Nizza Dani '17 still isn't very expressive on the nose, but we find pleasant hints of cherry and black cherry nevertheless, with slightly spicy whiffs. The palate is fruit forward, of remarkable volume, with a long finish. Other well-made selections include the Barbera d'Asti Superiore Quercia '18, a bit too marked by oak, but of nice softness and complexity, and the rich, sapid Barbera d'Asti Surì '19, with its aromas of cinchona-quinine and juniper.

● Nizza Dani '17	🍷🍷 4
● Barbera d'Asti Sup. Quercia '18	🍷🍷 3
● Barbera d'Asti Surì '19	🍷🍷 2*
○ Moscato d'Asti Canelli '19	🍷🍷 2*
● Barbera d'Asti Ajan '19	🍷 2
● Barbera d'Asti Ajan '16	🍷🍷 2*
● Barbera d'Asti Sup. La Quercia '17	🍷🍷 3
● Barbera d'Asti Sup. La Quercia '16	🍷🍷 3*
● Barbera d'Asti Surì '18	🍷🍷 2*
● Gamba di Pernice	🍷🍷 3*
○ Moscato d'Asti Canelli '17	🍷🍷 2*
○ Moscato d'Asti Canelli '16	🍷🍷 2*
○ Moscato d'Asti Surì '15	🍷🍷 2*
● Nizza Bricco Dani '15	🍷🍷 4
● Nizza Dedicato '16	🍷🍷 5
● Nizza Dedicato '15	🍷🍷 5
○ Piemonte Chardonnay Cortese Manè '17	🍷🍷 2*

★Villa Sparina

fraz. Monterotondo, 56
15066 Gavi [AL]
Tel. +39 0143633835
www.villasparina.it

PRE-BOOKED VISITS
ACCOMMODATION AND RESTAURANT SERVICE
ANNUAL PRODUCTION 550,000 bottles
HECTARES UNDER VINE 65.00

In hills of Monterotondo, the Moccagatta family have created one of the territory's most important estates, one adorned with a beautiful four-star hotel, a renowned restaurant and a winery par excellence. A spectacular panoramic view heralds the high-level sensorial experiences of which they're capable. As far as their wines are concerned, their most important selections are faithful representations of the territory: two Corteses (a basic version and the Monterotondo cru), two Barberas (with the Rivalta serving as a great example of the typology), and their Brut Metodo Classico Blanc de Blancs. The line-up presented sees their premium wines take center stage. The Monterotondo is complex and multifaceted, with aromas of ripe fruit accompanied by notes of citrus and camphor. The 10 Anni is extraordinarily complex, with fragrances of dried herbs and spices on a background of saffron and incense. The Gavi del Comune di Gavi is a wine of great intensity and persistence. The other wines tasted are also excellent.

○ Gavi del Comune di Gavi '19	🍷🍷 3*
○ Gavi del Comune di Gavi Monterotondo '17	🍷🍷 6
○ Gavi del Comune di Gavi Villa Sparina 10 anni '09	🍷🍷 3*
● Barbera del M.to '18	🍷🍷 3
○ Brut Villa Sparina Blanc de Blancs M. Cl.	🍷🍷 3
○ Gavi del Comune di Gavi Monterotondo '14	🍷🍷🍷 6
○ Gavi del Comune di Gavi Monterotondo '12	🍷🍷🍷 6
○ Gavi del Comune di Gavi Monterotondo '16	🍷🍷🍷 6
○ Gavi del Comune di Gavi Monterotondo '15	🍷🍷🍷 6

Viticoltori Associati di Vinchio Vaglio Serra

frAz. reg. San Pancrazio, 1
s.da prov.le 40 km. 3,75
14040 Vinchio [AT]
Tel. +39 0141950903
www.vinchio.com

CELLAR SALES
PRE-BOOKED VISITS
ANNUAL PRODUCTION 1,200,000 bottles
HECTARES UNDER VINE 450.00

Some 200 growers, more than 450 hectares of vineyards cultivated, and about 50 different wines produced: figures like this give us a snapshot of Cantina Sociale di Vinchio Vaglio Serra's production capacity. Founded in the late 1950s by a group of just 19 growers, the winery has grown over time and earned recognition well beyond the borders of Monferrato Astigiano. The two municipalities named in the winery's trademark host the bulk of their vineyards, but a significant share can also be found in Castelnuovo Belbo, Castelnuovo Calcea, Cortiglione, Incisa Scapaccino, Mombercelli and Nizza. The excellent Nizza Laudana Riserva '16 features aromas of plum and blackberry, all accompanied by notes of rain-soaked earth, with a rich, dense palate, and a long finish well supported by acidity. The Barbera d'Asti 50 Vigne Vecchie '18 also delivered, playing more on notes of spices and cocoa, it's both elegant and complex, nicely supple and immediately expressive. As usual, the other wines tasted are also well made.

Wine	Rating
● Barbera d'Asti V. V. 50° '18	TT 3*
● Nizza Laudana Ris. '16	TT 4
● Barbera d'Alba Sup. I Tre Vescovi '18	TT 3
● Barbera d'Alba Sup. V. V. '17	TT 5
● Barbera d'Asti Sorì dei Mori '19	TT 2*
● Barbera d'Asti Sup. Sei Vigne Insynthesis '15	TT 7
● Grignolino d'Asti Le Nocche '19	TT 2*
● Barbera d'Asti La Leggenda '19	T 2
○ Moscato d'Asti Valamasca '19	T 2
● Barbera d'Asti Sup. Sei Vigne Insynthesis '01	YYY 6
● Barbera d'Asti 50° Vigne Vecchie '17	YY 3*
● Barbera d'Asti Sup. I Tre Vescovi '17	YY 3*
● Barbera d'Asti Sup. Vigne Vecchie '16	YY 5
○ Moscato d'Asti Valamasca '18	YY 2*
● Nizza Laudana Ris. '15	YY 4

Virna

via Alba, 24
12060 Barolo [CN]
Tel. +39 017356120
www.virnabarolo.it

CELLAR SALES
PRE-BOOKED VISITS
ANNUAL PRODUCTION 60,000 bottles
HECTARES UNDER VINE 12.00

Virna Borgogno, a graduate in enology, and her sister Ivana, the administrative and commercial director, operate in a winery situated at the foot of Barolo, right where the historic Cannubi vineyard begins to unfold. 12 hectares are cultivated: in Barolo we find Cannubi, Sarmassa and Preda, while Novello includes Monforte and La Morra, which give rise to the Barolo Noi. In the cellar they use oak barrels of various sizes, with a preference for mid-size casks, and medium-large barrels. Red flowers and a touch of strawberry combine with a background of elegant liquorice in the Barolo Sarmassa '16, a complex wine, of rare balance, endowed with a powerful palate, rich in soft tannins. The Riserva di Barolo '13 is still quite fruity, marked by a precise classicism and excellent harmony. Even the municipally-denominated Barolo deserves praise, thanks to its multifaceted olfactory spiciness and a vivid, close-focused, seductive palate.

Wine	Rating
● Barolo del Comune di Barolo '16	TT 6
● Barolo Ris. '13	TT 5
● Barolo Sarmassa '16	TT 8
● Barolo Cannubi '16	TT 8
● Langhe Nebbiolo '17	TT 3
● Barbera d'Alba San Giovanni '17	T 3
● Barolo Noi '16	T 6
● Langhe Rosso Le Sorelle '17	T 3
● Barbera d'Alba La '17	YY 3
● Barolo Cannubi '15	YY 8
● Barolo Cannubi Boschis '14	YY 6
● Barolo del Comune di Barolo '15	YY 6
● Barolo del Comune di Barolo '14	YY 6
● Barolo Sarmassa '15	YY 8
● Barolo Sarmassa '14	YY 6

Vite Colte

via Bergesia, 6
12060 Barolo [CN]
Tel. +39 0173564611
www.vitecolte.it

CELLAR SALES
PRE-BOOKED VISITS
ANNUAL PRODUCTION 1,200,000 bottles
HECTARES UNDER VINE 300.00
VITICULTURE METHOD Certified Organic
SUSTAINABLE WINERY

Over the years Terre da Vino's premium line wines, Vite Colte (Est. 1980), has found increasing definition. At the base is a shared agronomic protocol that brings together 180 members who cover a total of no less than 300 hectares of vineyards. Vintage after vintage, their range exhibits greater adherence to the traditional characteristics of the area's wines, bolstered by prized plots in the municipalities of Barolo and Serralunga d'Alba. Their rich portfolio touches on Nebbiolo, Barbera, Dolcetto, Arneis, Cortese and Moscato. The Barbera d'Asti La Luna e i Falò '18 is a wine of exemplary aromatic finesse, complex and fragrant in its minty touch, it has harmony, silky tannins and a finish full of enticing hints of earth and spices. We also appreciated the Barbaresco Spezie Riserva '10—a great vintage made for a multifaceted, deep wine, evolved and ample, refreshed by a final minty background and a classy finish. The Barolo del Comune di Serralunga d'Alba Essenze '15 also delivered, proving rich in fruit and pulp.

- ● Barbera d'Asti Sup. La Luna e i Falò '18 — 3*
- ● Barbaresco Spezie Ris. '10 — 6
- ● Barolo del Comune di Serralunga d'Alba Essenze '15 — 7
- ● Barbaresco La Casa in Collina '17 — 5
- ● Barolo del Comune di Barolo Essenze '16 — 7
- ● Barolo del Comune di Monforte d'Alba Essenze '15 — 7
- ● Barolo Paesi Tuoi '16 — 6
- ○ Piemonte Moscato Passito La Bella Estate '18 — 5
- ● Barbera d'Asti Sup. La Luna e i Falò '17 — 3*
- ○ Piemonte Moscato Passito La Bella Estate '16 — 5

Voerzio Martini

s.da Loreto, 3
12064 La Morra [CN]
Tel. +39 0173509194
voerzio.gianni@tiscali.it

CELLAR SALES
PRE-BOOKED VISITS
ANNUAL PRODUCTION 54,000 bottles
HECTARES UNDER VINE 12.00

Mirko and Federica Martini, the former a graduate in Enology, the latter in Gastronomic Sciences, have drawn on their youthful enthusiasm for the world of wine to create a new, uniquely dynamic producer, drawing on the deep, qualified experience of winemaker/cellarman Gianni Voerzio as well. Their range is based on three central principles: prized vineyards (which will continue to grow), very low yields in the vineyard, and non-invasive French oak for barrel aging. Year after year, the results are increasingly notable. Elegant, fresh fruit and sweet spices feature in the aromatically lovely Barolo La Serra '16, a wine that exhibits freshness in the mouth, as well as excellent length right up to a finish where you can perceive an elegant note of oak. Liquorice-scented and smoothly harmonious, we also appreciated (and highly recommend tasting) the 'basic' Barolo '16. The modern Barbera d'Alba Superiore Ciabot della Luna '18 is among the best of the vintage, vivid and progressively unfolding across a pervasive palate.

- ● Barbera d'Alba Ciabot della Luna '18 — 5
- ● Barolo La Serra '16 — 8
- ● Barolo '16 — 6
- ○ Langhe Arneis Bricco Cappellina '19 — 3
- ● Langhe Nebbiolo Ciabot della Luna '18 — 5
- ● Barbera d'Alba Ciabot della Luna '17 — 5
- ● Barbera d'Alba Ciabot della Luna '16 — 4
- ● Barbera d'Alba Ciabot della Luna '15 — 4
- ● Barolo '15 — 6
- ● Barolo La Serra '15 — 8
- ● Barolo La Serra '13 — 8
- ○ Langhe Arneis Bricco Cappellina '17 — 3
- ● Langhe Nebbiolo Ciabot della Luna '16 — 5

499

loc. Camo
via Roma, 3
12058 Santo Stefano Belbo [CN]
Tel. +39 0141840155
www.499vino.it

- Langhe Freisa '18 — 🍷🍷 3
- Langhe Freisa Coste dei Fre '16 — 🍷🍷 3

Tenuta Alemanni

fraz. Cherli Inferiore, 64
15070 Tagliolo Monferrato [AL]
Tel. +39 0143896229
tenutaalemanni@gmail.com

CELLAR SALES
ACCOMMODATION
ANNUAL PRODUCTION 10,000 bottles
HECTARES UNDER VINE 4.00
SUSTAINABLE WINERY

- ○ M.to Bianco Tre Lune '13 — 🍷🍷 3
- ● M.to Rosso Aimemi '11 — 🍷🍷 4

Alemat

via Giardini, 19
15020 Ponzano Monferrato [AL]
Tel. +39 335268464
www.alemat.it

ANNUAL PRODUCTION 20,000 bottles
HECTARES UNDER VINE 5.50
SUSTAINABLE WINERY

- ● Grignolino del M.to Casalese Monferace '16 — 🍷🍷 4
- ● Barbera d'Asti Praie '19 — 🍷🍷 4
- ● Grignolino d'Asti Emilio '19 — 🍷🍷 2*

Paolo Angelini

Cascina Cairo, 10
15039 Ozzano Monferrato [AL]
Tel. +39 3468549015
www.societaagricolaangelinipaolo.com

CELLAR SALES
PRE-BOOKED VISITS
ANNUAL PRODUCTION 80,000 bottles
HECTARES UNDER VINE 40.00
SUSTAINABLE WINERY

- ● Barbera del M.to First '19 — 🍷🍷 2*
- ● Grignolino del M.to Casalese Arbian '19 — 🍷🍷 2*
- ● Grignolino del M.to Casalese Monferace Golden Arbian '15 — 🍷🍷 6

Antica Cascina dei Conti di Roero

loc. Val Rubiagno, 2
12040 Vezza d'Alba [CN]
Tel. +39 017365459
www.oliveropietro.it

CELLAR SALES
PRE-BOOKED VISITS
ANNUAL PRODUCTION 90,000 bottles
HECTARES UNDER VINE 13.50
SUSTAINABLE WINERY

- ⊙ Nebbiolo d'Alba Brut Rosè M. Cl. Maria Teresa '17 — 🍷🍷 4
- ○ Roero Arneis Sru Ris. '18 — 🍷🍷 3
- ● Roero V. Sant'Anna Ris. '16 — 🍷🍷 4

Anzivino

c.so Valsesia, 162
13045 Gattinara [VC]
Tel. +39 0163827172
www.anzivino.it

CELLAR SALES
PRE-BOOKED VISITS
ACCOMMODATION AND RESTAURANT SERVICE
ANNUAL PRODUCTION 40,000 bottles
HECTARES UNDER VINE 6.00
SUSTAINABLE WINERY

- ● Gattinara '15 — 🍷🍷 4
- ● Gattinara Ris. '15 — 🍷🍷 5
- ● Gattinara Cesare Ris. '15 — 🍷 8

L'Astemia Pentita

via Crosia, 40
12060 Barolo [CN]
Tel. +39 0173560501
www.astemiapentita.it

CELLAR SALES
PRE-BOOKED VISITS
ANNUAL PRODUCTION 70,000 bottles
HECTARES UNDER VINE 15.00
SUSTAINABLE WINERY

● Barolo Cannubi '16	🍷🍷 8
● Barolo Cannubi Ris. '14	🍷🍷 8
● Barolo Terlo '16	🍷🍷 8
○ Langhe Nascetta '19	🍷🍷 3

Paolo Avezza

reg. Monforte, 62
14053 Canelli [AT]
Tel. +39 0141822296
www.paoloavezza.com

CELLAR SALES
PRE-BOOKED VISITS
ANNUAL PRODUCTION 35,000 bottles
HECTARES UNDER VINE 8.00

○ Alta Langa Dosaggio Zero '16	🍷🍷 5
● Barbera d'Asti '18	🍷🍷 3
● Nizza '17	🍷🍷 5
● Nizza Ris. '15	🍷🍷 6

Melchiorre Balbiano

via Vittorio Emanuele, 1
10020 Andezeno [TO]
Tel. +39 0119434214

● Freisa di Chieri Federico I Il Barbarossa '18	🍷🍷 3
● Freisa di Chieri Sup. V. Villa della Regina '16	🍷🍷 5
● Freisa di Chieri Surpreisa '19	🍷 2

Baldissero

via Roma, 29
12050 Treiso [CN]
Tel. +39 3334420201
www.baldisserovini.it

CELLAR SALES
PRE-BOOKED VISITS
ANNUAL PRODUCTION 11,000 bottles
HECTARES UNDER VINE 7.00

● Barbaresco '17	🍷🍷 5
● Langhe Nebbiolo '18	🍷🍷 3

Cantina Sociale Barbera dei Sei Castelli

via Opessina, 41
14040 Castelnuovo Calcea [AT]
Tel. +39 0141957137
www.barberaseicastelli.it

CELLAR SALES
PRE-BOOKED VISITS
ANNUAL PRODUCTION 80,000 bottles
HECTARES UNDER VINE 650.00

● Nizza '17	🍷🍷 5
● Barbera d'Asti 50 Anni di Barbera '18	🍷🍷 3
● Grignolino d'Asti '19	🍷🍷 2*
● Nizza Angelo Brofferio Ris. '16	🍷 6

Fabrizio Battaglino

loc. Borgonuovo
via Montaldo Roero, 44
12040 Vezza d'Alba [CN]
Tel. +39 0173658156
www.battaglino.com

CELLAR SALES
PRE-BOOKED VISITS
ANNUAL PRODUCTION 25,000 bottles
HECTARES UNDER VINE 5.00

○ Roero Arneis San Michele '19	🍷🍷 3*
● Barbera d'Alba Munbèl '18	🍷🍷 3
○ Nebula Brut Nature '16	🍷 4
● Roero Colla Ris. '16	🍷 5

Battaglio - Briccogrilli

LOC. BORBORE
VIA SALERIO, 15
12040 VEZZA D'ALBA [CN]
TEL. +39 017365423
www.battaglio.com

CELLAR SALES
PRE-BOOKED VISITS
ANNUAL PRODUCTION 36,000 bottles
HECTARES UNDER VINE 5.00

- ○ Amus V.T. 🍷🍷 5
- ● Barbaresco Battaglio '17 🍷🍷 6
- ● Barbaresco Serragrilli '17 🍷🍷 7
- ● Nebbiolo d'Alba Riverte '18 🍷 4

Antonio Bellicoso

FRAZ. MOLISSO, 5A
14048 MONTEGROSSO D'ASTI [AT]
TEL. +39 0141953233
antonio.bellicoso@alice.it

CELLAR SALES
PRE-BOOKED VISITS
ANNUAL PRODUCTION 15,000 bottles
HECTARES UNDER VINE 4.00
SUSTAINABLE WINERY

- ● Barbera d'Asti Amormio '19 🍷🍷 3
- ● Barbera d'Asti Merum '18 🍷🍷 5
- ● Freisa d'Asti '19 🍷 3

Piero Benevelli

LOC. SAN GIUSEPPE, 13
12065 MONFORTE D'ALBA [CN]
TEL. +39 017378416
www.barolobenevelli.com

ANNUAL PRODUCTION 50,000 bottles
HECTARES UNDER VINE 10.00

- ● Barolo Le Coste di Monforte '16 🍷🍷 6
- ● Barolo Ravera di Monforte '16 🍷🍷 7
- ● Barolo Mosconi '16 🍷 6

Paolo Berta

S.DA SAN MICHELE, 42
14049 NIZZA MONFERRATO [AT]
TEL. +39 3483536205
viniberta@gmail.com

- ● Barbera d'Asti Evolution '17 🍷🍷 3*
- ● Nizza La Berta '16 🍷🍷 3
- ● Barbera d'Asti Belmon '17 🍷 2
- ● Barbera d'Asti Sup. Valbeccara '17 🍷 3

Bianchi

VIA ROMA, 37
28070 SIZZANO [NO]
TEL. +39 0321810004
www.bianchibiowine.it

CELLAR SALES
PRE-BOOKED VISITS
ANNUAL PRODUCTION 150,000 bottles
HECTARES UNDER VINE 21.00
VITICULTURE METHOD Certified Organic

- ● Ghemme '12 🍷🍷 4
- ○ Colline Novaresi Bianco Luminae '12 🍷🍷 2*
- ● Gattinara Vign. Valferana Ris. '10 🍷🍷 4
- ● Sizzano '14 🍷 4

Silvano Bolmida

LOC. BUSSIA 30
12065 MONFORTE D'ALBA [CN]
TEL. +39 0173789877
www.silvanobolmida.com

CELLAR SALES
PRE-BOOKED VISITS
ANNUAL PRODUCTION 30,000 bottles
HECTARES UNDER VINE 6.00

- ● Barolo Bussia '16 🍷🍷 5
- ● Barolo Bussia Ris. '13 🍷🍷 7
- ● Barolo Bussia V. dei Fantini '16 🍷🍷 5

F.lli Serio & Battista Borgogno

loc. Cannubi
via Crosia,12
12060 Barolo [CN]
Tel. +39 017356107
www.borgognoseriobattista.it

CELLAR SALES
PRE-BOOKED VISITS
ANNUAL PRODUCTION 60,000 bottles
HECTARES UNDER VINE 7.50

- ● Barolo '16 🍷🍷 5
- ● Barolo Cannubi '16 🍷🍷 6
- ○ Langhe Nascetta '19 🍷 3

Francesco Boschis

b.ta Pianezzo, 57
12063 Dogliani [CN]
Tel. +39 017370574
www.boschisfrancesco.it

CELLAR SALES
PRE-BOOKED VISITS
ANNUAL PRODUCTION 35,000 bottles
HECTARES UNDER VINE 10.00

- ● Dogliani Sup. V. dei Prey '18 🍷🍷 2*
- ● Dogliani Sup. V. Sorì San Martino '17 🍷🍷 2*
- ● Dogliani V. in Pianezzo '18 🍷🍷 2*
- ○ Langhe Sauvignon V. dei Garisin '19 🍷🍷 3

La Briccolina

via Roddino, 7
12050 Serralunga d'Alba [CN]
Tel. +39 3282217094
labriccolina@gmail.com

ANNUAL PRODUCTION 3,000 bottles
HECTARES UNDER VINE 5.50

- ● Barolo Briccolina '16 🍷🍷 5

Bussia Soprana

loc. Bussia, 88a
12065 Monforte d'Alba [CN]
Tel. +39 039305182
www.bussiasoprana.it

CELLAR SALES
PRE-BOOKED VISITS
ANNUAL PRODUCTION 40,000 bottles
HECTARES UNDER VINE 14.00

- ● Barolo Mosconi '16 🍷🍷 7
- ● Barolo Bussia V. Colonnello '16 🍷🍷 7
- ● Barolo Bussia V. Gabutti '16 🍷🍷 8
- ● Nizza '17 🍷🍷 5

Oreste Buzio

via Piave, 13
15049 Vignale Monferrato [AL]
Tel. +39 0142933197
www.orestebuzio.altervista.org

CELLAR SALES
PRE-BOOKED VISITS
ANNUAL PRODUCTION 25,000 bottles
HECTARES UNDER VINE 6.00
VITICULTURE METHOD Certified Organic

- ● Grignolino del M.to Casalese '19 🍷🍷 3
- ● Piemonte Albarossa Al Barba Carlo '17 🍷🍷 4
- ● Barbera del M.to '19 🍷 2

Cà Bensi

loc. Cascina Bensi, 31a
15070 Tagliolo Monferrato [AL]
Tel. +39 014389194
www.ca-bensi.it

ANNUAL PRODUCTION 30,000 bottles
HECTARES UNDER VINE 8.80

- ● Dolcetti di Ovada Poggio San Pietro '16 🍷🍷 2*
- ○ M.to Bianco '19 🍷🍷 2*
- ● Ovada Moongiardin '16 🍷🍷 3

Ca' Brusà

loc. Manzoni, 25
12065 Monforte d'Alba [CN]
Tel. +39 017378169
www.cabrusa.com

PRE-BOOKED VISITS
ACCOMMODATION AND RESTAURANT SERVICE
ANNUAL PRODUCTION 30,000 bottles
HECTARES UNDER VINE 5.50

- ● Barbera d'Alba Sup. Cunca d'Or '17 — 🍷🍷 4
- ● Barolo del Comune di Monforte d'Alba Menico '16 — 🍷🍷 5
- ● Barolo Vai Ris. '10 — 🍷🍷 7

Ca' Nova

via San Isidoro, 1
28010 Bogogno [NO]
Tel. +39 0322863406
www.cascinacanova.it

CELLAR SALES
PRE-BOOKED VISITS
ACCOMMODATION
ANNUAL PRODUCTION 45,000 bottles
HECTARES UNDER VINE 10.00

- ⊙ Colline Novaresi Nebbiolo Aurora '19 — 🍷🍷 2*
- ○ Colline Novaresi Bianco Rugiada '19 — 🍷 2
- ● Colline Novaresi Nebbiolo Bocciolo '19 — 🍷 2

Cagliero

via Monforte, 34
12060 Barolo [CN]
Tel. +39 017356172
www.cagliero.com

- ● Barolo Ravera '16 — 🍷🍷 5
- ● Barolo Ravera '15 — 🍷🍷 5
- ● Barolo Terlo '16 — 🍷🍷 5

Marco Canato

fraz. Fons Salera
loc. Ca' Baldea, 19/3
15049 Vignale Monferrato [AL]
Tel. +39 00393409193882
www.canatovini.it

CELLAR SALES
PRE-BOOKED VISITS
ANNUAL PRODUCTION 30,000 bottles
HECTARES UNDER VINE 11.00

- ● Barbera del M.to Gambaloita '19 — 🍷🍷 3
- ● Barbera del M.to Sup. La Baldea '16 — 🍷🍷 4
- ● Grignolino del M.to Casalese Celio '19 — 🍷🍷 3

La Carlina

via Valle Talloria, 35
12060 Grinzane Cavour [CN]
Tel. +39 0173262926
www.lacarlina.com

ACCOMMODATION
ANNUAL PRODUCTION 50,000 bottles
HECTARES UNDER VINE 25.00

- ● Barbera d'Asti Sup. Bionzo '17 — 🍷🍷 3*
- ● Barolo '16 — 🍷🍷 6

Davide Carlone

via Monsignor Sagliaschi, 8
28075 Grignasco [NO]
Tel. +39 3290987672
www.
aziendaagricoladavidecarlone.wordpress.com

ANNUAL PRODUCTION 35,000 bottles
HECTARES UNDER VINE 7.00

- ● Boca '16 — 🍷🍷 5
- ● Boca Adele '16 — 🍷🍷 6
- ● Coste della Sesia Nebbiolo '18 — 🍷🍷 3
- ● Colline Novaresi Croatina '17 — 🍷 3

Casavecchia

via Roma, 2
12055 Diano d'Alba [CN]
Tel. +39 017369321
www.cantinacasavecchia.com

CELLAR SALES
PRE-BOOKED VISITS
ANNUAL PRODUCTION 45,000 bottles
HECTARES UNDER VINE 10.00

- ● Barbera d'Alba Sup. '16 — 🍷🍷 3
- ● Nebbiolo d'Alba V. Piadvenza '16 — 🍷🍷 4
- ● Barolo del Comune di Castiglione Falletto '13 — 🍷 5

Cascina Adelaide

via Aie Sottane, 14
12060 Barolo [CN]
Tel. +39 0173560503
www.cascinaadelaide.com

CELLAR SALES
PRE-BOOKED VISITS
ANNUAL PRODUCTION 50,000 bottles
HECTARES UNDER VINE 9.50

- ● Barolo Baudana '16 — 🍷🍷 7
- ● Barolo Cannubi '16 — 🍷🍷 8

Cascina Alberta

via Alba, 5
12050 Treiso [CN]
Tel. +39 0173638047
www.calberta.it

CELLAR SALES
PRE-BOOKED VISITS
ACCOMMODATION
ANNUAL PRODUCTION 35,000 bottles
HECTARES UNDER VINE 9.00
VITICULTURE METHOD Certified Organic
SUSTAINABLE WINERY

- ● Barbaresco Giacone '17 — 🍷🍷 6
- ● Barbera d'Alba '18 — 🍷🍷 3
- ● Langhe Nebbiolo '18 — 🍷 3
- ○ Langhe Riesling '18 — 🍷 4

Cascina Ballarin

fraz. Annunziata, 115
12064 La Morra [CN]
Tel. +39 017350365
www.cascinaballarin.it

CELLAR SALES
PRE-BOOKED VISITS
ACCOMMODATION
ANNUAL PRODUCTION 60,000 bottles
HECTARES UNDER VINE 9.00
VITICULTURE METHOD Certified Organic
SUSTAINABLE WINERY

- ● Barolo Bricco Rocca '16 — 🍷🍷 7
- ● Barolo Bussia '16 — 🍷🍷 7
- ● Barolo Tre Ciabót '16 — 🍷🍷 6

Cascina del Monastero

fraz. Annunziata, 112a
12064 La Morra [CN]
Tel. +39 0173509245
www.cascinadelmonastero.it

CELLAR SALES
PRE-BOOKED VISITS
ACCOMMODATION
ANNUAL PRODUCTION 40,000 bottles
HECTARES UNDER VINE 12.00
VITICULTURE METHOD Certified Organic
SUSTAINABLE WINERY

- ● Barbera d'Alba Sup. Parroco '15 — 🍷🍷 5
- ● Barolo Perno '15 — 🍷🍷 5
- ● Barolo Bricco Luciani '16 — 🍷 6
- ● Langhe Nebbiolo Monastero '16 — 🍷 3

Cascina Galarin

loc. Carossi, 12
14054 Castagnole delle Lanze [AT]
Tel. +39 0141878586
www.galarin.it

CELLAR SALES
PRE-BOOKED VISITS
ACCOMMODATION
ANNUAL PRODUCTION 30,000 bottles
HECTARES UNDER VINE 7.00
VITICULTURE METHOD Certified Organic

- ● Barbera d'Asti Le Querce '18 — 🍷🍷 3
- ● Barbera d'Asti Sup. Tinella '17 — 🍷🍷 5
- ○ Moscato d'Asti Prà Dône '19 — 🍷 3

Cascina Garitina

via Gianola, 20
14040 Castel Boglione [AT]
Tel. +39 0141762162
www.cascinagaritina.it

CELLAR SALES
PRE-BOOKED VISITS
ANNUAL PRODUCTION 150,000 bottles
HECTARES UNDER VINE 23.00

- ● Barbera d'Asti Bricco Garitta '18 🍷🍷 3
- ● Barbera d'Asti Sup. Caranti '17 🍷🍷 4
- ● Nizza 900 58-61 '17 🍷🍷 5
- ● Nizza 900 Neuvsent Margherita '17 🍷🍷 6

Cascina Gentile

s.da prov.le per San Cristoforo, 11
15060 Capriata d'Orba [AL]
Tel. +39 0143468975
www.cascinagentile.tumblr.com

CELLAR SALES
PRE-BOOKED VISITS
ANNUAL PRODUCTION 30,000 bottles
HECTARES UNDER VINE 10.00
SUSTAINABLE WINERY

- ○ Colli Tortonesi Timorasso Derthona '17 🍷🍷 3
- ● Ovada Le Parole Servon Tanto Ris. '17 🍷🍷 3
- ● Piemonte Barbera Mat '17 🍷🍷 3

Cascina Lo Zoccolaio

loc. Boschetti, 4
12060 Barolo [CN]
Tel. +39 0141837211
www.cascinalozoccolaio.it

CELLAR SALES
ANNUAL PRODUCTION 128,000 bottles
HECTARES UNDER VINE 22.00

- ● Barolo '16 🍷🍷 5
- ● Barolo Ravera Ris. '14 🍷🍷 6
- ● Langhe Rosso Baccanera '17 🍷🍷 3
- ● Barbera d'Alba Sup. Suculè '17 🍷 3

Cascina Massara Gian Carlo Burlotto

via Capitano Laneri, 6
12060 Verduno [CN]
Tel. +39 0172470152
www.cantinamassara.it

CELLAR SALES
PRE-BOOKED VISITS
ANNUAL PRODUCTION 80,000 bottles
HECTARES UNDER VINE 10.00

- ● Barbera d'Alba '18 🍷🍷 3
- ● Barolo Massara '15 🍷🍷 8
- ● Barolo Monvigliero '15 🍷🍷 7
- ● Verduno Pelaverga '19 🍷🍷 3

Cascina Melognis

via San Pietro, 10
12036 Revello [CN]
Tel. +39 0175257395
cascina.melognis@gmail.com

ANNUAL PRODUCTION 15,000 bottles
HECTARES UNDER VINE 4.00

- ● Colline Saluzzesi Ardy '18 🍷🍷 3
- ● Colline Saluzzesi Divicaroli '19 🍷🍷 3
- ● Novamen '18 🍷🍷 4
- ⊙ Sinespina '19 🍷 3

Cascina Montagnola

s.da Montagnola, 1
15058 Viguzzolo [AL]
Tel. +39 3480742701
www.cascinamontagnola.com

CELLAR SALES
PRE-BOOKED VISITS
ANNUAL PRODUCTION 30,000 bottles
HECTARES UNDER VINE 10.00

- ○ Colli Tortonesi Timorasso Morasso '18 🍷🍷 4
- ○ Risveglio 🍷🍷 4
- ○ Colli Tortonesi Cortese Dunin '19 🍷 3

Cascina Mucci

LOC. MUCCI, 2
12050 RODDINO [CN]
TEL. +39 3496201920
www.cascinamucci.it

CELLAR SALES
PRE-BOOKED VISITS
ANNUAL PRODUCTION 13,000 bottles
HECTARES UNDER VINE 1.85

- ● Barbera d'Alba Sup. '17 — 🍷🍷 4
- ● Langhe Rosso '16 — 🍷🍷 5

Cascina Rabaglio

S.DA RABAJÀ, 8
12050 BARBARESCO [CN]
TEL. +39 3388885031
www.cascinarabaglio.com

- ● Barbaresco Gaia Principe '17 — 🍷🍷 5
- ● Langhe Nebbiolo '18 — 🍷🍷 3
- ● Barbera d'Alba Sup. '17 — 🍷 5
- ● Dolcetto d'Alba '19 — 🍷 3

Cascina Val del Prete

S.DA SANTUARIO, 2
12040 PRIOCCA [CN]
TEL. +39 0173616534
www.valdelprete.com

CELLAR SALES
PRE-BOOKED VISITS
ANNUAL PRODUCTION 55,000 bottles
HECTARES UNDER VINE 11.00
VITICULTURE METHOD Certified Organic

- ● Barbera d'Alba Serra dè Gatti '19 — 🍷🍷 3
- ● Barbera d'Alba Sup. Carolina '17 — 🍷🍷 5
- ● Nebbiolo d'Alba '16 — 🍷🍷 3
- ● Roero Bricco Medica '17 — 🍷 3

Cascina Vano

VIA RIVETTI, 9
12057 NEIVE [CN]
TEL. +39 017367263
www.cascinavano.com

PRE-BOOKED VISITS
ANNUAL PRODUCTION 30,000 bottles
HECTARES UNDER VINE 8.00

- ● Barbaresco Canova '16 — 🍷🍷 5
- ● Barbaresco Pilone nei Rivetti '15 — 🍷🍷 4

Pietro Cassina

VIA IV NOVEMBRE, 171
13583 LESSONA [BI]
TEL. +39 3332518903
www.pietrocassina.com

CELLAR SALES
PRE-BOOKED VISITS
ACCOMMODATION
ANNUAL PRODUCTION 18,000 bottles
HECTARES UNDER VINE 6.00
SUSTAINABLE WINERY

- ● Coste della Sesia Vespolina Tèra Rùssa '12 — 🍷🍷 7
- ○ Lessona Pidrin '14 — 🍷🍷 5

Renzo Castella

VIA ALBA, 15
12055 DIANO D'ALBA [CN]
TEL. +39 017369203
renzocastella@virgilio.it

CELLAR SALES
PRE-BOOKED VISITS
ANNUAL PRODUCTION 20,000 bottles
HECTARES UNDER VINE 8.00

- ● Dolcetto di Diano d'Alba '19 — 🍷🍷 2*
- ● Dolcetto di Diano d'Alba Sorì della Rivolia '19 — 🍷🍷 2*
- ● Langhe Nebbiolo Madonnina '18 — 🍷🍷 2*

Castello di Castellengo

via Castello, 31
13836 Cossato [BI]
Tel. +39 3383543101
www.centovigne.it

ACCOMMODATION
ANNUAL PRODUCTION 25,000 bottles
HECTARES UNDER VINE 6.50

- ● Coste della Sesia Nebbiolo Il Centovigne '16 🍷🍷 4
- ⊙ Coste della Sesia Rosato Il Rosa '19 🍷 3
- ● Rosso della Motta '18 🍷 3

Cavalier Bartolomeo

via Alba Barolo, 55
12060 Castiglione Falletto [CN]
Tel. +39 017362866
www.cavalierbartolomeo.com

ANNUAL PRODUCTION 15,000 bottles
HECTARES UNDER VINE 3.50

- ● Barolo Altenasso '16 🍷🍷 6
- ● Barolo San Lorenzo '16 🍷🍷 6

Davide Cavelli

via Provinciale, 77
15010 Prasco [AL]
Tel. +39 0144375706
www.cavellivini.com

ANNUAL PRODUCTION 60,000 bottles
HECTARES UNDER VINE 10.50

- ● Ovada Bricco Le Zerbe '17 🍷🍷 3*
- ● Dolcetto di Ovada Le Zerbe '19 🍷🍷 2*
- ○ Cortese dell'Alto M.to Pertiassa '19 🍷 2

La Chiara

loc. Vallegge, 24/2
15066 Gavi [AL]
Tel. +39 0143642293
www.lachiara.it

CELLAR SALES
PRE-BOOKED VISITS
ANNUAL PRODUCTION 190,000 bottles
HECTARES UNDER VINE 26.00

- ○ Gavi del Comune di Gavi Groppella '18 🍷🍷 2*
- ○ Gavi del Comune di Gavi '19 🍷🍷 2*
- ○ Gavi del Comune di Gavi Et. Nera '18 🍷🍷 3

Il Chiosso

v.le Guglielmo Marconi 45-47a
13045 Gattinara [VC]
Tel. +39 0163826739
www.ilchiosso.it

CELLAR SALES
PRE-BOOKED VISITS
ANNUAL PRODUCTION 80,000 bottles
HECTARES UNDER VINE 12.00

- ● Fara '17 🍷🍷 3*
- ● Colline Novaresi Vespolina '19 🍷🍷 4
- ● Gattinara '15 🍷🍷 5
- ● Ghemme '15 🍷🍷 4

Cantina Clavesana

fraz. Madonna della Neve, 19
12060 Clavesana [CN]
Tel. +39 0173790451
www.inclavesana.it

CELLAR SALES
PRE-BOOKED VISITS
ANNUAL PRODUCTION 3,400,000 bottles
HECTARES UNDER VINE 320.00
VITICULTURE METHOD Certified Organic
SUSTAINABLE WINERY

- ● Barbera d'Alba Sup. Terra '17 🍷🍷 3
- ● Barolo Mito '15 🍷🍷 5
- ● Dogliani Sup. Terra '18 🍷🍷 3
- ● Dogliani Terra '19 🍷🍷 2*

Aldo Clerico

loc. Manzoni, 69
12065 Monforte d'Alba [CN]
Tel. +39 0173209981
www.aldoclerico.it

CELLAR SALES
PRE-BOOKED VISITS
ANNUAL PRODUCTION 30,000 bottles
HECTARES UNDER VINE 8.00

Wine	Glasses	
● Barbera d'Alba '18	🍷🍷	3
● Dogliani '19	🍷🍷	2*
● Barolo Ginestra '16	🍷	8
● Dolcetto d'Alba '19	🍷	2

Colle Manora

loc. Colle Manora
s.da Bozzola, 5
15044 Quargnento [AL]
Tel. +39 0131219252
www.collemanora.it

CELLAR SALES
PRE-BOOKED VISITS
ACCOMMODATION
ANNUAL PRODUCTION 100,000 bottles
HECTARES UNDER VINE 21.00
SUSTAINABLE WINERY

Wine	Glasses	
● Barbera d'Asti Sup. Manora '17	🍷🍷	3
○ M.to Bianco Mimosa '19	🍷🍷	2*
● M.to Rosso Barchetta '17	🍷🍷	3
● Piemonte Albarossa Ray '17	🍷🍷	3

Cortino - Produttori Dianesi

via S. Croce, 1/bis
12055 Diano d'Alba [CN]
Tel. +39 017369221
www.produttoridianesi.com

Wine	Glasses	
○ Alta Langa Brut '16	🍷🍷	4
● Barbera d'Alba Luisella '17	🍷🍷	3
● Barolo del Comune di Serralunga d'Alba '16	🍷🍷	5

Cantine Crosio

via Roma, 75
10010 Candia Canavese [TO]
Tel. +39 0119836048
www.cantinecrosio.it

CELLAR SALES
RESTAURANT SERVICE
ANNUAL PRODUCTION 40,000 bottles
HECTARES UNDER VINE 9.00

Wine	Glasses	
● Canavese Nebbiolo Gemini '17	🍷🍷	3
○ Erbaluce di Caluso Erbalus '19	🍷🍷	2*
○ Erbaluce di Caluso Brut Incanto '15	🍷	4
○ Erbaluce di Caluso Primavigna '19	🍷	3

Cuvage

Stradale Alessandria, 90
15011 Acqui Terme [AL]
Tel. +39 0144371600
www.cuvage.com

ANNUAL PRODUCTION 80,000 bottles
HECTARES UNDER VINE 200.00

Wine	Glasses	
○ Alta Langa Brut '16	🍷🍷	4
○ Brut Blanc de Blancs M. Cl.	🍷🍷	3
⊙ Nebbiolo d'Alba Brut Rosé M.Cl. '16	🍷🍷	3
○ Pas Dosé Cuvage de Cuvage M. Cl.	🍷🍷	3

Dacapo

s.da Asti Mare, 4
14041 Agliano Terme [AT]
Tel. +39 0141964921
www.dacapo.it

CELLAR SALES
PRE-BOOKED VISITS
ANNUAL PRODUCTION 45,000 bottles
HECTARES UNDER VINE 8.00
VITICULTURE METHOD Certified Organic
SUSTAINABLE WINERY

Wine	Glasses	
● Nizza V. Dacapo Ris. '16	🍷🍷	5
● Barbera d'Asti Sup. Valrionda '17	🍷🍷	3
● Grignolino d'Asti Renard '19	🍷🍷	3
● Ruchè di Castagnole M.to Majoli '19	🍷🍷	3

Duilio Dacasto

FRAZ. VIANOCE, 26
14041 AGLIANO TERME [AT]
TEL. +39 3339828612
www.dacastoduilio.com

ANNUAL PRODUCTION 24,000 bottles
HECTARES UNDER VINE 8.00

- ● Barbera d'Asti La Maestra '18 🍷🍷 3*
- ● Nizza Moncucco '17 🍷🍷 4
- ○ Piemonte Chardonnay Bourg '19 🍷🍷 3

Cantina Delsignore

C.SO VERCELLI, 88
13045 GATTINARA [VC]
TEL. +39 0163833777
www.cantinadelsignore.com

PRE-BOOKED VISITS
ANNUAL PRODUCTION 19,500 bottles
HECTARES UNDER VINE 3.00

- ● Gattinara Il Putto Vendemmiatore '16 🍷🍷 5
- ● Gattinara Borgofranco Ris. '15 🍷🍷 6

Fogliati

VIA PUGNANE, 8
12060 CASTIGLIONE FALLETTO [CN]
TEL. +39 3333230410
www.poderifogliati.it

ANNUAL PRODUCTION 6,800 bottles
HECTARES UNDER VINE 3.00

- ● Barolo Bussia '16 🍷🍷 8
- ● Langhe Nebbiolo '18 🍷🍷 4

Livia Fontana

VIA FONTANA, 1
12060 CASTIGLIONE FALLETTO [CN]
TEL. +39 017362844
www.liviafontana.it

- ● Barolo Fontanin '16 🍷🍷 5
- ● Barbera d'Alba Sup. '17 🍷🍷 3
- ● Langhe Nebbiolo '18 🍷🍷 4
- ● Barolo Villero '16 🍷 8

Fontanabianca

LOC. BORDINI, 15
12057 NEIVE [CN]
TEL. +39 017367195
www.fontanabianca.it

CELLAR SALES
PRE-BOOKED VISITS
ANNUAL PRODUCTION 90,000 bottles
HECTARES UNDER VINE 16.00

- ● Barbaresco '17 🍷🍷 5
- ● Barbaresco Bordini '17 🍷🍷 6
- ○ Langhe Arneis '19 🍷🍷 2*
- ● Langhe Nebbiolo '18 🍷 3

Forteto della Luja

REG. CANDELETTE, 4
14051 LOAZZOLO [AT]
TEL. +39 014487197
www.fortetodellaluja.it

CELLAR SALES
PRE-BOOKED VISITS
ANNUAL PRODUCTION 50,000 bottles
HECTARES UNDER VINE 11.00
VITICULTURE METHOD Certified Organic

- ○ Loazzolo V. T. Piasa Rischei '16 🍷🍷 6
- ○ Moscato d'Asti Canelli '19 🍷🍷 3
- ● M.to Rosso Le Grive '18 🍷 4

Giovanni e Lorenzo Frea

fraz. San Rocco
12040 Montaldo Roero [CN]
Tel. +39 017240254
aziendagricolafrea@libero.it

ANNUAL PRODUCTION 30,000 bottles
HECTARES UNDER VINE 7.00

- ● Barbera d'Alba La Padruna '18 — 🍷🍷 3
- ○ Roero Arneis Galarà '19 — 🍷🍷 2*
- ● Roero Muschiavin '18 — 🍷🍷 3
- ● Nebbiolo d'Alba Sarzurì '18 — 🍷 3

Gagliasso

borgata Torriglione, 7
12064 La Morra [CN]
Tel. +39 017350180
www.gagliassovini.it

CELLAR SALES
PRE-BOOKED VISITS
RESTAURANT SERVICE
ANNUAL PRODUCTION 50,000 bottles
HECTARES UNDER VINE 12.50

- ● Barolo Rocche dell'Annunziata '16 — 🍷🍷 6
- ● Barolo Torriglione '16 — 🍷🍷 6
- ● Barolo Tre Utin '16 — 🍷🍷 6
- ● Barolo Ris. '13 — 🍷 8

Pierfrancesco Gatto

via Vittorio Emanuele II, 13
14030 Castagnole Monferrato [AT]
Tel. +39 0141292149
vinigatto@libero.it

CELLAR SALES
PRE-BOOKED VISITS
ANNUAL PRODUCTION 60,000 bottles
HECTARES UNDER VINE 8.00

- ● Barbera d'Asti Sup. Iolanda '17 — 🍷🍷 3*
- ● Barbera d'Asti Robiano '19 — 🍷🍷 2*
- ● Barbera d'Asti Vigna Serra '18 — 🍷🍷 3
- ● Ruché di Castagnole M.to Caresana '19 — 🍷🍷 3

F.lli Giacosa

via XX Settembre, 64
12052 Neive [CN]
Tel. +39 017367013
www.giacosa.it

CELLAR SALES
PRE-BOOKED VISITS
ANNUAL PRODUCTION 600,000 bottles
HECTARES UNDER VINE 51.00
VITICULTURE METHOD Certified Organic
SUSTAINABLE WINERY

- ● Barolo Bussia '16 — 🍷🍷 7
- ● Barbaresco Basarin V. Gianmaté '17 — 🍷 7
- ● Barbera d'Alba Maria Gioana '17 — 🍷 6

Le Ginestre

s.da Grinzane, 15
12050 Grinzane Cavour [CN]
Tel. +39 0173262910
www.leginestre.com

SUSTAINABLE WINERY

- ● Barolo Sotto Castello di Novello '16 — 🍷🍷 6
- ● Langhe Nebbiolo '18 — 🍷🍷 3
- ● Dolcetto d'Alba '19 — 🍷 3

La Giribaldina

fraz. San Vito, 39
14042 Calamandrana [AT]
Tel. +39 0141718043
www.giribaldina.com

CELLAR SALES
PRE-BOOKED VISITS
ACCOMMODATION
ANNUAL PRODUCTION 65,000 bottles
HECTARES UNDER VINE 11.00

- ● Barbera d'Asti Cavalbianc '19 — 🍷🍷 2*
- ○ M.to Bianco Ferro di Cavallo '19 — 🍷🍷 3
- ● Nizza Cala delle Mandrie '17 — 🍷🍷 4

Gozzelino

S.DA BRICCO LÙ, 7
14055 COSTIGLIOLE D'ASTI [AT]
TEL. +39 0141966134
www.gozzelinovini.com

CELLAR SALES
PRE-BOOKED VISITS
ANNUAL PRODUCTION 100,000 bottles
HECTARES UNDER VINE 30.00

- ● Barbera d'Asti Ciabot d'la Mandorla '18 — 2*
- ● Barbera d'Asti Sup. Ciabot d'la Mandorla '17 — 3
- ● Grignolino d'Asti Bric d'la Riva '19 — 2*

Tenute Guardasole

FRAZ. ISELLA, 35
28075 GRIGNASCO [NO]
TEL. +39 0163411693
www.tenuteguardasole.it

- ● Boca '16 — 6
- ● Pio Decimo '18 — 5
- ● Virgilio '18 — 4

Clemente Guasti

C.SO IV NOVEMBRE, 80
14049 NIZZA MONFERRATO [AT]
TEL. +39 0141721350
www,clemente.guasti.it

CELLAR SALES
PRE-BOOKED VISITS
ANNUAL PRODUCTION 120,000 bottles
HECTARES UNDER VINE 10.00

- ● Barbera d'Asti Sup. Severa '16 — 3
- ○ Moscato d'Asti Santa Teresa '19 — 3
- ● Barbera d'Asti Sup. Boschetto Vecchio '16 — 4
- ● Nizza Barcarato '16 — 5

Paride Iaretti

VIA PIETRO MICCA, 23B
13045 GATTINARA [VC]
TEL. +39 0163826899
www.parideiaretti.it

CELLAR SALES
PRE-BOOKED VISITS
ANNUAL PRODUCTION 15,000 bottles
HECTARES UNDER VINE 5.00

- ● Gattinara V. Valferana '16 — 8
- ● Coste della Sesia Nebbiolo Velut Luna '18 — 3
- ● Gattinara Pietro '16 — 5
- ● Gattinara Ris. '15 — 7

Franco Ivaldi

S.DA CARANZANO, 211
15016 CASSINE [AL]
TEL. +39 348 7492231
www.francoivaldivini.com

ANNUAL PRODUCTION 40,000 bottles
HECTARES UNDER VINE 7.00

- ● Dolcetto d'Acqui Sup. La Uèca '18 — 3*
- ● Barbera d'Asti La Guerinotta '19 — 2*
- ● Barbera d'Asti Sup. La Balzana '17 — 4
- ● Dolcetto d'Acqui La Moschina '19 — 2*

Lagobava

FRAZ. CA' BERGANTINO, 5
15049 VIGNALE MONFERRATO [AL]
TEL. +39 3476900656
www.lagobava.it

CELLAR SALES
PRE-BOOKED VISITS
ANNUAL PRODUCTION 14,000 bottles
HECTARES UNDER VINE 6.00
VITICULTURE METHOD Certified Organic
SUSTAINABLE WINERY

- ● M.to Rosso L'Amo '16 — 6
- ● M.to Rosso Lagobava '12 — 4

Gianluigi Lano

FRAZ. SAN ROCCO SENO D'ELVIO
S.DA BASSO, 38
12051 ALBA [CN]
TEL. +39 0173286958
www.lanovini.it

CELLAR SALES
PRE-BOOKED VISITS
ANNUAL PRODUCTION 40,000 bottles
HECTARES UNDER VINE 6.00

- ● Barbaresco Rocche Massalupo '16 🍷🍷 5
- ● Barbera d'Alba Sup. V. Altavilla '16 🍷🍷 3
- ● Langhe Lanot '16 🍷 3
- ● Langhe Nebbiolo '18 🍷 4

Le Marie

VIA SAN DEFENDENTE, 6
12032 BARGE [CN]
TEL. +39 0175345159
www.lemarievini.eu

CELLAR SALES
PRE-BOOKED VISITS
RESTAURANT SERVICE
ANNUAL PRODUCTION 45,000 bottles
HECTARES UNDER VINE 9.50

- ○ Festina Lente '18 🍷🍷 5
- ○ Pas Dosé M. Cl. 🍷🍷 5
- ● Piemonte Pinot Nero Noir de Mariette '18 🍷🍷 3
- ○ Blanc de Lissart 🍷 3

Le Strette

VIA LE STRETTE, 1F
12060 NOVELLO [CN]
TEL. +39 0173744002
www.lestrette.com

CELLAR SALES
PRE-BOOKED VISITS
ANNUAL PRODUCTION 23,000 bottles
HECTARES UNDER VINE 6.50
VITICULTURE METHOD Certified Organic
SUSTAINABLE WINERY

- ● Barolo Bergeisa '16 🍷🍷 6
- ● Barolo Corini-Pallaretta '16 🍷🍷 6
- ○ Langhe Nas-cëtta del Comune di Novello Pasinot '18 🍷🍷 5

Liedholm

LOC. VILLA BOEMIA, 41A
VIA PER CUCCARO
15043 LU E CUCCARO MONFERRATO
TEL. +39 0332798836
www.liedholm.com

CELLAR SALES
PRE-BOOKED VISITS
ACCOMMODATION
ANNUAL PRODUCTION 60,000 bottles
HECTARES UNDER VINE 10.00

- ● Barbera d'Asti '15 🍷🍷 3
- ○ Grenoli 🍷🍷 3
- ● Grignolino del M.to Casalese '19 🍷🍷 2*

Lodali

V.LE RIMEMBRANZA, 5
12050 TREISO [CN]
TEL. +39 0173638109
www.lodali.it

CELLAR SALES
PRE-BOOKED VISITS
ACCOMMODATION AND RESTAURANT SERVICE
ANNUAL PRODUCTION 90,000 bottles
HECTARES UNDER VINE 15.00

- ● Barolo Lorens '16 🍷🍷 7
- ● Barbaresco Lorens '17 🍷🍷 7
- ● Barbaresco Rocche dei 7 Fratelli '17 🍷🍷 5
- ● Barolo Bricco Ambrogio '16 🍷🍷 5

Maccagno

VIA BONORA, 29
12043 CANALE [CN]
TEL. +39 0173979438
www.cantinamaccagno.it

CELLAR SALES
PRE-BOOKED VISITS
ANNUAL PRODUCTION 50,000 bottles
HECTARES UNDER VINE 12.00

- ● Barbera d'Alba Sup. Arcalè '17 🍷🍷 4
- ● Nebbiolo d'Alba '16 🍷🍷 3
- ○ Roero Arneis '19 🍷 2
- ● Roero La Perla Nera Ris. '14 🍷 5

Podere Macellio

VIA ROMA, 18
10014 CALUSO [TO]
TEL. +39 0119833511
www.erbaluce-bianco.it

CELLAR SALES
PRE-BOOKED VISITS
ANNUAL PRODUCTION 25,000 bottles
HECTARES UNDER VINE 3.50

- ○ Erbaluce di Caluso Extra Brut 🍷🍷 3
- ○ Erbaluce di Caluso '19 🍷 2

Cantine Macrì

VIA GIUSEPPE AVALLE, 13
14042 CALAMANDRANA [AT]
TEL. +39 014175643
www.cantinemacri.it

PRE-BOOKED VISITS
ANNUAL PRODUCTION 150,000 bottles
HECTARES UNDER VINE 23.00

- ● Nizza Federica '17 🍷🍷 4
- ○ Moscato d'Asti Dulcis in Fundo '19 🍷🍷 2*

Marenco

P.ZZA VITTORIO EMANUELE II, 10
15019 STREVI [AL]
TEL. +39 0144363133
www.marencovini.com

CELLAR SALES
PRE-BOOKED VISITS
ACCOMMODATION
ANNUAL PRODUCTION 250,000 bottles
HECTARES UNDER VINE 80.00
SUSTAINABLE WINERY

- ● Barbera d'Asti Bassina '18 🍷🍷 3
- ○ M.to Bianco Carialoso '18 🍷🍷 3
- ○ Moscato d'Asti Scrapona '19 🍷 3
- ○ Moscato d'Asti Strev '19 🍷 2

Mirù

P.ZZA ANTONELLI, 24
28074 GHEMME [NO]
TEL. +39 0163840032
www.aziendaagricolamiru.it

- ● Ghemme V. Cavenago Ris. '15 🍷🍷 5
- ● Colline Novaresi Nebbiolo N50 '18 🍷🍷 3
- ● Colline Novaresi Vespolina N54 '19 🍷🍷 3
- ○ Colline Novaresi Bianco Piriet '19 🍷 2

Moccagatta

S.DA RABAJÀ, 46
12050 BARBARESCO [CN]
TEL. +39 0173635228
www.moccagatta.eu

CELLAR SALES
PRE-BOOKED VISITS
ANNUAL PRODUCTION 65,000 bottles
HECTARES UNDER VINE 12.00
SUSTAINABLE WINERY

- ● Barbaresco Cole '17 🍷🍷 8
- ● Barbaresco Bric Balin '17 🍷 7

Molino

VIA AUSARIO, 5
12050 TREISO [CN]
TEL. +39 0173638384
www.molinovini.com

CELLAR SALES
PRE-BOOKED VISITS
ANNUAL PRODUCTION 80,000 bottles
HECTARES UNDER VINE 16.00
SUSTAINABLE WINERY

- ● Barbaresco Ausario Ris. '15 🍷🍷 8
- ● Barbaresco Teorema '17 🍷🍷 6
- ● Barbera d'Alba Sup. '18 🍷 4
- ● Piemonte Rosso Selvaggia '19 🍷 3

Montaribaldi

FRAZ. TRE STELLE
S.DA NICOLINI ALTO, 12
12050 BARBARESCO [CN]
TEL. +39 0173638220
www.montaribaldi.com

CELLAR SALES
PRE-BOOKED VISITS
ANNUAL PRODUCTION 100,000 bottles
HECTARES UNDER VINE 23.00

- ● Barbaresco Ricü '15 🍷🍷 6
- ● Barbaresco Sorì Montaribaldi '16 🍷🍷 5
- ● Dolcetto d'Alba Vagnona '19 🍷🍷 2*
- ● Barbera d'Alba Dü Gir '17 🍷 4

Paolo Monti

FRAZ. CAMIE
LOC. SAN SEBASTIANO, 39
12065 MONFORTE D'ALBA [CN]
TEL. +39 017378391
www.paolomonti.com

CELLAR SALES
PRE-BOOKED VISITS
ANNUAL PRODUCTION 50,000 bottles
HECTARES UNDER VINE 16.00

- ● Barbera d'Alba Sup. '16 🍷🍷 7
- ● Nebbiolo d'Alba Sup. '17 🍷🍷 5
- ● Barolo del Comune di Monforte d'Alba '16 🍷 7

Le More Bianche

VIA ADELE ALFIERI, 35
12050 MAGLIANO ALFIERI [CN]
TEL. +39 3456141980
www.lemorebianche.com

ANNUAL PRODUCTION 15,000 bottles
HECTARES UNDER VINE 3.50

- ● Barbera d'Alba '18 🍷🍷 3
- ● Langhe Nebbiolo Nebiulin '19 🍷🍷 4
- ● Roero San Bernardo '17 🍷🍷 5
- ● Barbera d'Alba Sup. '18 🍷 5

Morgassi Superiore

CASE SPARSE SERMORIA, 7
15066 GAVI [AL]
TEL. +39 0143642007
www.morgassisuperiore.it

CELLAR SALES
PRE-BOOKED VISITS
ANNUAL PRODUCTION 130,000 bottles
HECTARES UNDER VINE 20.00

- ○ Gavi del Comune di Gavi Volo '18 🍷🍷 4
- ○ Gavi del Comune di Gavi Tuffo '19 🍷🍷 3
- ○ M.to Bianco Timorgasso '18 🍷 4

Cantina Sociale di Nizza

S.DA ALESSANDRIA, 57
14049 NIZZA MONFERRATO [AT]
TEL. +39 0141721348
www.nizza.it

CELLAR SALES
PRE-BOOKED VISITS
ANNUAL PRODUCTION 200,000 bottles
HECTARES UNDER VINE 560.00
VITICULTURE METHOD Certified Organic
SUSTAINABLE WINERY

- ● Barbera d'Asti Le Pole '18 🍷🍷 2*
- ● Barbera d'Asti Sup. Magister '18 🍷🍷 3
- ○ Piemonte Chardonnay Labrì '19 🍷 2

Massimo Pastura Cascina La Ghersa

VIA CHIARINA, 2
14050 MOASCA [AT]
TEL. +39 0141856012
www.laghersa.it

CELLAR SALES
PRE-BOOKED VISITS
ACCOMMODATION
ANNUAL PRODUCTION 150,000 bottles
HECTARES UNDER VINE 20.00

- ● Barbera d'Asti Sup. Camparò '18 🍷🍷 4
- ● Barbera d'Asti Sup. Nizza Collezione 10 Anni '10 🍷🍷 7
- ● Nizza Muaschae Ris. '17 🍷 6

Elio Perrone

via San Martino, 2
12053 Castiglione Tinella [CN]
Tel. +39 0141855803
www.elioperrone.it

CELLAR SALES
PRE-BOOKED VISITS
ANNUAL PRODUCTION 250,000 bottles
HECTARES UNDER VINE 19.00
SUSTAINABLE WINERY

● Barbera d'Asti Sup. Mongovone '18	🍷🍷 5
○ Moscato d'Asti Sourgal '19	🍷🍷 2*
● Barbera d'Asti Tasmorcan '19	🍷 3

Fabio Perrone

fraz. Valdivilla, 69
12058 Santo Stefano Belbo [CN]
Tel. +39 0141847123
www.fabioperrone.com

CELLAR SALES
PRE-BOOKED VISITS
ANNUAL PRODUCTION 90,000 bottles
HECTARES UNDER VINE 15.00

● Barbera d'Asti Sup. '18	🍷🍷 5
● Langhe Nebbiolo Ciabot '18	🍷🍷 3
○ Moscato d'Asti Cascina Galletto '19	🍷🍷 2*
○ Langhe Favorita Parroco '19	🍷 2

Armando Piazzo

fraz. San Rocco di Seno d'Elvio, 31
12051 Alba [CN]
Tel. +39 017335689
www.piazzo.it

CELLAR SALES
PRE-BOOKED VISITS
ACCOMMODATION
ANNUAL PRODUCTION 500,000 bottles
HECTARES UNDER VINE 70.00
SUSTAINABLE WINERY

● Barolo Sottocastello di Novello Ris. '10	🍷🍷 7
● Barbaresco '17	🍷🍷 5
● Barbaresco Nervo V. Giaia Ris. '15	🍷🍷 6
● Barolo '16	🍷🍷 5

Poderi dei Bricchi Astigiani

fraz. Repergo
via Ritane, 7
14057 Isola d'Asti [AT]
Tel. +39 0141958974
www.bricchiastigiani.it

CELLAR SALES
PRE-BOOKED VISITS
ANNUAL PRODUCTION 40,000 bottles
HECTARES UNDER VINE 15.00
VITICULTURE METHOD Certified Organic

● Barbera d'Asti '18	🍷🍷 2*
○ Piemonte Pinot Nero Blanc de Noirs M. Cl.	🍷🍷 4
● Barbera d'Asti Sup. Bricco del Perg '17	🍷 3
⊙ Piemonte Rosato Bricco Preje '19	🍷 2

Paolo Giuseppe Poggio

via Roma, 67
15050 Brignano Frascata [AL]
Tel. +39 0131784929
www.cantinapoggio.com

CELLAR SALES
PRE-BOOKED VISITS
ANNUAL PRODUCTION 18,000 bottles
HECTARES UNDER VINE 3.50

● Colli Tortonesi Barbera Campo La Bà '18	🍷🍷 2*
● Colli Tortonesi Rosso Prosone '18	🍷🍷 2*
○ Colli Tortonesi Timorasso Ronchetto '18	🍷🍷 3

Pomodolce

via IV Novembre, 7
15050 Montemarzino [AL]
Tel. +39 0131878135
www.pomodolce.it

CELLAR SALES
PRE-BOOKED VISITS
RESTAURANT SERVICE
ANNUAL PRODUCTION 14,000 bottles
HECTARES UNDER VINE 4.00
VITICULTURE METHOD Certified Organic

○ Colli Tortonesi Timorasso Derthona Diletto '18	🍷🍷 4
○ Colli Tortonesi Timorasso Grue '18	🍷🍷 5
● Colli Tortonesi Monleale Marsen '14	🍷 4

Maurizio Ponchione

VIA R. SACCO, 9A
12040 GOVONE [CN]
TEL. +39 017358149
www.ponchionemaurizio.com

CELLAR SALES
PRE-BOOKED VISITS
ANNUAL PRODUCTION 35,000 bottles
HECTARES UNDER VINE 11.00

- ● Roero Arneis Monfrini '19 — 🍷🍷 3
- ● Roero Monfrini '16 — 🍷🍷 3
- ● Barbera d'Alba Donia '16 — 🍷 3
- ● Barbera d'Alba Monfrini '16 — 🍷 3

Giovanni Prandi

FRAZ. CASCINA COLOMBÈ
VIA FARINETTI, 5
12055 DIANO D'ALBA [CN]
TEL. +39 017369248
www.prandigiovanni.it

CELLAR SALES
PRE-BOOKED VISITS
ANNUAL PRODUCTION 20,000 bottles
HECTARES UNDER VINE 5.00
SUSTAINABLE WINERY

- ● Dolcetto di Diano d'Alba Sorì Colombè '19 — 🍷🍷 2*
- ● Nebbiolo d'Alba '18 — 🍷🍷 3
- ● Barbera d'Alba '19 — 🍷 2
- ○ Langhe Arneis '19 — 🍷 2

Punset

VIA ZOCCO, 2
12052 NEIVE [CN]
TEL. +39 01736707267072
www.punset.com

CELLAR SALES
PRE-BOOKED VISITS
ACCOMMODATION
ANNUAL PRODUCTION 100,000 bottles
HECTARES UNDER VINE 17.00
VITICULTURE METHOD Certified Organic
SUSTAINABLE WINERY

- ● Barbaresco San Cristoforo Campo Quadro '14 — 🍷🍷 6
- ● Barbera d'Alba '19 — 🍷🍷 3
- ● Langhe Nebbiolo '18 — 🍷🍷 4

Raineri

LOC. PANEROLE, 24
12060 NOVELLO [CN]
TEL. +39 3396009289
www.rainerivini.com

CELLAR SALES
PRE-BOOKED VISITS
ANNUAL PRODUCTION 40,000 bottles
HECTARES UNDER VINE 6.00
SUSTAINABLE WINERY

- ● Dogliani Zovetto '19 — 🍷🍷 2*
- ● Barolo Castelletto '16 — 🍷🍷 8
- ● Langhe Nebbiolo Snart '19 — 🍷🍷 3
- ● Barolo Perno '16 — 🍷 8

Vigneti Repetto

LOC. CASTELLAZZO
15050 MONTEMARZINO [AL]
TEL. +39 3494669501
www.vignetirepetto.it

ANNUAL PRODUCTION 60,000 bottles
HECTARES UNDER VINE 24.00

- ○ Colli Tortonesi Timorasso Derthona Quadro '18 — 🍷🍷 4
- ○ Colli Tortonesi Timorasso Derthona Origo '18 — 🍷🍷 4

Ressia

VIA CANOVA, 28
12052 NEIVE [CN]
TEL. +39 0173677305
www.ressia.com

CELLAR SALES
PRE-BOOKED VISITS
ANNUAL PRODUCTION 3,000 bottles
HECTARES UNDER VINE 5.50
SUSTAINABLE WINERY

- ● Barbaresco Canova Serie Oro Ris. '15 — 🍷🍷 7
- ● Barbaresco Canova '17 — 🍷🍷 5
- ○ Evien '19 — 🍷🍷 2*

Pietro Rinaldi

FRAZ. MADONNA DI COMO
12051 ALBA [CN]
TEL. +39 0173360090
www.pietrorinaldi.com

CELLAR SALES
PRE-BOOKED VISITS
ACCOMMODATION
ANNUAL PRODUCTION 70,000 bottles
HECTARES UNDER VINE 10.00

- ● Barolo '16 🍷🍷 6
- ● Barolo Monvigliero '16 🍷🍷 6
- ○ Langhe Arneis Hortensia '16 🍷🍷 2*
- ● Barbera d'Alba Sup. Bricco Cichetta '17 🍷 4

Silvia Rivella

LOC. MONTESTEFANO, 17
12050 BARBARESCO [CN]
TEL. +39 0173635040
www.agriturismorivella.it

CELLAR SALES
PRE-BOOKED VISITS
ACCOMMODATION AND RESTAURANT SERVICE
ANNUAL PRODUCTION 10,000 bottles
HECTARES UNDER VINE 1.50

- ● Barbaresco '17 🍷🍷 7
- ● Barbaresco Montestefano '17 🍷🍷 7

Rizieri

CASCINA RICCHINO
12055 DIANO D'ALBA [CN]
TEL. +39 0173468540
www.rizieri.com

CELLAR SALES
PRE-BOOKED VISITS
ANNUAL PRODUCTION 22,000 bottles
HECTARES UNDER VINE 6.50

- ● Barbera d'Alba Sbilauta '19 🍷🍷 4
- ● Barbera d'Alba Sup. '17 🍷🍷 4
- ● Barolo '16 🍷🍷 5
- ● Nebbiolo d'Alba '17 🍷🍷 3

Tenuta Rocca

LOC. ORNATI, 19
12065 MONFORTE D'ALBA [CN]
TEL. +39 017378412
www.tenutarocca.com

CELLAR SALES
PRE-BOOKED VISITS
ACCOMMODATION
ANNUAL PRODUCTION 90,000 bottles
HECTARES UNDER VINE 15.00

- ● Barolo '16 🍷🍷 6
- ● Barolo Bussia '16 🍷🍷 7
- ● Barolo del Comune di Serralunga d'Alba '16 🍷🍷 8

Rolfo - Ca' di Cairè

B.GO VALLE CASETTE, 52
12046 MONTÀ [CN]
TEL. +39 0173971263
www.emanuelerolfo.it

PRE-BOOKED VISITS
ANNUAL PRODUCTION 38,000 bottles
HECTARES UNDER VINE 5.00

- ● Nebbiolo d'Alba Ca 'd Pilat '17 🍷🍷 3
- ○ Roero Arneis '19 🍷🍷 2*
- ● Barbera d'Alba '16 🍷 3

Gigi Rosso

STRADA ALBA-BAROLO, 34
12060 CASTIGLIONE FALLETTO [CN]
TEL. +39 0173262369
www.gigirosso.com

CELLAR SALES
PRE-BOOKED VISITS
ANNUAL PRODUCTION 196,000 bottles
HECTARES UNDER VINE 25.00

- ● Barolo Rocche Mariondino '15 🍷🍷 8
- ● Barolo Bricco San Pietro '16 🍷🍷 6

F.lli Rovero

loc. Valdonata
fraz. San Marzanotto, 218
14100 Asti
Tel. +39 0141592460
www.rovero.it

CELLAR SALES
PRE-BOOKED VISITS
ANNUAL PRODUCTION 90,000 bottles
HECTARES UNDER VINE 20.00

- ● Barbera d'Asti Sanpansè '19 — 🍷🍷 2*
- ● Barbera d'Asti Sup. Rouvè '17 — 🍷🍷 4
- ● Barbera d'Asti Sup. Vign. Gustin '18 — 🍷🍷 3
- ● Grignolino d'Asti Vign. La Casalina '18 — 🍷🍷 2*

Podere Ruggeri Corsini

loc. Bussia Bovi 18
12065 Monforte d'Alba [CN]
Tel. +39 017378625
www.ruggericorsini.it

CELLAR SALES
PRE-BOOKED VISITS
ANNUAL PRODUCTION 80,000 bottles
HECTARES UNDER VINE 12.00
SUSTAINABLE WINERY

- ● Barolo Bricco San Pietro '16 — 🍷🍷 5
- ● Barbera d'Alba '18 — 🍷🍷 2*
- ● Barolo Bussia Corsini '16 — 🍷🍷 6
- ● Langhe Nebbiolo '18 — 🍷🍷 3

San Biagio

fraz. Santa Maria
San Biagio, 98
12064 La Morra [CN]
Tel. +39 017350214
www.barolosanbiagio.com

CELLAR SALES
PRE-BOOKED VISITS
ANNUAL PRODUCTION 45,000 bottles
HECTARES UNDER VINE 20.00

- ● Barolo Bricco San Biagio '16 — 🍷🍷 5
- ● Barolo Pria-Capalot '16 — 🍷🍷 5
- ● Barbaresco Montersino '17 — 🍷 5
- ● Barolo Sorano '15 — 🍷 5

Cantine Sant'Agata

reg. Mezzena, 19
14030 Scurzolengo [AT]
Tel. +39 0141203186
www.santagata.com

CELLAR SALES
PRE-BOOKED VISITS
RESTAURANT SERVICE
ANNUAL PRODUCTION 150,000 bottles
HECTARES UNDER VINE 12.00

- ● Ruché di Castagnole M.to 'Na Vota '19 — 🍷🍷 3
- ● Ruchè di Castagnole M.to Il Cavaliere '19 — 🍷🍷 2*
- ● Ruchè di Castagnole M.to Pro Nobis '17 — 🍷 4

Santa Clelia

reg. Rossana, 7
10035 Mazzè [TO]
Tel. +39 0119835187
www.santaclelia.it

CELLAR SALES
PRE-BOOKED VISITS
ANNUAL PRODUCTION 70,000 bottles
HECTARES UNDER VINE 12.00
VITICULTURE METHOD Certified Organic
SUSTAINABLE WINERY

- ○ Erbaluce di Caluso Essenthia '19 — 🍷🍷 3
- ○ Erbaluce di Caluso Ypa '19 — 🍷 3

Sassi - San Cristoforo

via Pastura, 10
12052 Neive [CN]
Tel. +39 0173677122
www.sassisancristoforo.com

CELLAR SALES
PRE-BOOKED VISITS
ANNUAL PRODUCTION 10,000 bottles
HECTARES UNDER VINE 1.30

- ● Barbaresco '17 — 🍷🍷 4
- ● Barbaresco San Cristoforo '16 — 🍷🍷 5
- ● Barbaresco San Cristoforo Ris. '15 — 🍷🍷 6
- ● Langhe Nebbiolo '18 — 🍷🍷 3

Antica Casa Vinicola Scarpa

via Montegrappa, 6
14049 Nizza Monferrato [AT]
Tel. +39 0141721331
www.scarpavini.it

CELLAR SALES
PRE-BOOKED VISITS
ANNUAL PRODUCTION 120,000 bottles
HECTARES UNDER VINE 30.00

- Barbera d'Asti CasaScarpa '17 — 2*
- Barbera d'Asti I Bricchi '15 — 4
- M.to Freisa '17 — 4
- M.to Rosso Rouchet '17 — 5

Segni di Langa

loc. Ravinali, 25
12060 Roddi [CN]
Tel. +39 3803945151
www.segnidilanga.it

CELLAR SALES
PRE-BOOKED VISITS
ACCOMMODATION
ANNUAL PRODUCTION 15,000 bottles
HECTARES UNDER VINE 3.50
SUSTAINABLE WINERY

- Barolo '16 — 6
- Barbera d'Alba Sup. '18 — 4
- Nebbiolo d'Alba '18 — 4

Collina Serragrilli

fraz. Serragrilli
via Serragrilli, 30
12052 Neive [CN]
Tel. +39 0173677010
www.serragrilli.it

CELLAR SALES
PRE-BOOKED VISITS
ANNUAL PRODUCTION 100,000 bottles
HECTARES UNDER VINE 15.00

- Barbaresco Starderi '17 — 7
- Barbera d'Alba Serraia '17 — 2*
- Langhe Nebbiolo Bailè '17 — 3
- Barbaresco Serragrilli '17 — 6

Sette

loc. Ponteverde, 74
14049 Nizza Monferrato [AT]
Tel. +39 3803945151
www.sette.wine

HECTARES UNDER VINE 5.00

- Nizza V. V. '18 — 4
- Barbera d'Asti '19 — 3

Vini Silva

Cascine Rogge, 1b
10011 Agliè [TO]
Tel. +39 3473075648
www.silvavini.com

CELLAR SALES
PRE-BOOKED VISITS
ANNUAL PRODUCTION 50,000 bottles
HECTARES UNDER VINE 12.00

- ○ Erbaluce di Caluso Dry Ice '19 — 2*
- ○ Erbaluce di Caluso Tre Ciochè '19 — 2

Poderi Sinaglio

fraz. Ricca
via Sinaglio, 5
12055 Diano d'Alba [CN]
Tel. +39 0173612209
www.poderisinaglio.it

CELLAR SALES
PRE-BOOKED VISITS
ACCOMMODATION
ANNUAL PRODUCTION 35,000 bottles
HECTARES UNDER VINE 13.00

- Barbera d'Alba Erta '18 — 3
- Dolcetto di Diano d'Alba Sorì Bric Maiolica '19 — 2*
- Nebbiolo d'Alba Giachet '18 — 3

Francesco Sobrero

via Pugnane, 5
12060 Castiglione Falletto [CN]
Tel. +39 017362864
www.sobrerofrancesco.it

CELLAR SALES
PRE-BOOKED VISITS
ACCOMMODATION
ANNUAL PRODUCTION 90,000 bottles
HECTARES UNDER VINE 16.00

- ● Barolo Ciabot Tanasio '16 🍷🍷 6
- ● Barolo Parussi '16 🍷🍷 7

Terre Astesane

via Marconi, 42
14047 Mombercelli [AT]
Tel. +39 0141959155
www.terreastesane.it

CELLAR SALES
PRE-BOOKED VISITS
ANNUAL PRODUCTION 100,000 bottles
HECTARES UNDER VINE 240.00

- ● Grignolino d'Asti Ganassa '19 🍷🍷 2*
- ● Nizza Mumbersé '17 🍷🍷 3
- ● Barbera d'Asti La '19 🍷 2
- ● Barbera d'Asti Sup. Savej '17 🍷 2

Terre dei Santi

via San Giovanni, 6
14022 Castelnuovo Don Bosco [AT]
Tel. +39 0119876117
www.terredeisanti.it

CELLAR SALES
PRE-BOOKED VISITS
ANNUAL PRODUCTION 350,000 bottles
HECTARES UNDER VINE 300.00

- ● Barbera d'Asti '18 🍷🍷 2*
- ● Barbera d'Asti L'Alfiere '17 🍷🍷 3
- ● Freisa d'Asti Zaffo '17 🍷🍷 3
- ● Freisa di Chieri '19 🍷 2

Terre di Sarizzola

fraz. Sarizzola
via Appennini, 41
15050 Costa Vescovato [AL]
Tel. +39 3381222128
www.terredisarizzola.com

ANNUAL PRODUCTION 18,000 bottles
HECTARES UNDER VINE 8.00

- ○ Colli Tortonesi Timorasso Derthona '18 🍷🍷 4
- ● Colli Tortonesi Barbera Sup. M.....e '16 🍷🍷 6
- ○ Colli Tortonesi TImorasso Biancornetto '17 🍷🍷 4

Terre Sabaude Produttori di Govone

via Umberto I, 46
12040 Govone [CN]
Tel. +39 017358120
www.produttorigovone.com

- ● Barbera d'Alba Sup. Borbonica Terre Sabaude '17 🍷🍷 3
- ○ Roero Arneis Terre Sabaude '19 🍷🍷 2*

Tibaldi

s.da San Giacomo, 49
12060 Pocapaglia [CN]
Tel. +39 0172421221
www.cantinatibaldi.com

CELLAR SALES
ANNUAL PRODUCTION 35,000 bottles
HECTARES UNDER VINE 7.00

- ○ Roero Arneis Pas Dosé Ritasté M. Cl. '15 🍷🍷 3
- ● Roero Le Passere '17 🍷🍷 3
- ○ Roero Arneis Bricco delle Passere '18 🍷 3

Trediberri

B.TA TORRIGLIONE, 4
12064 LA MORRA [CN]
TEL. +39 3391605470
www.trediberri.com

CELLAR SALES
PRE-BOOKED VISITS
ANNUAL PRODUCTION 50,000 bottles
HECTARES UNDER VINE 8.00
VITICULTURE METHOD Certified Organic

- ● Barolo '16 🍷🍷 5
- ● Barolo Rocche dell'Annunziata '16 🍷🍷 7
- ● Langhe Nebbiolo '19 🍷🍷 2*
- ● Barbera d'Alba '19 🍷 2

Poderi Vaiot

BORGATA LAIONE, 43
12046 MONTÀ [CN]
TEL. +39 0173976283
www.poderivaiot.it

ANNUAL PRODUCTION 25,000 bottles
HECTARES UNDER VINE 4.00

- ○ Roero Arneis Franco '19 🍷🍷 2*
- ● Roero Pierin '17 🍷🍷 3
- ● Nebbiolo d'Alba Sessantadì '18 🍷 3
- ○ Val del Moro M. Cl. 🍷 5

Valdinera

VIA CAVOUR, 1
12040 CORNELIANO D'ALBA [CN]
TEL. +39 0173619881
www.valdinera.com

CELLAR SALES
PRE-BOOKED VISITS
ANNUAL PRODUCTION 160,000 bottles
HECTARES UNDER VINE 20.00

- ● Nebbiolo d'Alba Sontuoso '16 🍷🍷 4
- ● Roero San Carlo Ris. '16 🍷🍷 5
- ● Barbera d'Alba Sup. '18 🍷 3
- ● Nebbiolo d'Alba '18 🍷 3

La Vecchia Posta

VIA MONTEBELLO, 2
15050 AVOLASCA [AL]
TEL. +39 0131876254
www.lavecchiaposta-avolasca.com

CELLAR SALES
PRE-BOOKED VISITS
ACCOMMODATION AND RESTAURANT SERVICE
ANNUAL PRODUCTION 13,000 bottles
HECTARES UNDER VINE 4.00
VITICULTURE METHOD Certified Organic

- ● Colli Tortonesi Barbera Languia '16 🍷🍷 4
- ○ Colli Tortonesi Timorasso Derthona Il Selvaggio '18 🍷🍷 4
- ● Rosso Ciliegio '19 🍷🍷 3

Alberto Voerzio

B.GO BRANDINI, 1A
12064 LA MORRA [CN]
TEL. +39 3333927654
www.albertovoerzio.com

CELLAR SALES
ANNUAL PRODUCTION 13,000 bottles
HECTARES UNDER VINE 6.00
SUSTAINABLE WINERY

- ● Barolo Castagni '16 🍷🍷 6
- ● Barolo La Serra '16 🍷🍷 7
- ● Langhe Nebbiolo '17 🍷🍷 6
- ● Barbera d'Alba '17 🍷 3

La Zerba

LOC. ZERBA, 1
15060 TASSAROLO [AL]
TEL. +39 0143342259
www.la-zerba.it

CELLAR SALES
PRE-BOOKED VISITS
ANNUAL PRODUCTION 90,000 bottles
HECTARES UNDER VINE 12.00
VITICULTURE METHOD Certified Organic

- ● Piemonte Barbera Bio '18 🍷🍷 2*
- ○ Gavi del Comune di Tassarolo Anfora '18 🍷 3
- ○ Gavi del Comune di Tassarolo Terrarossa '19 🍷 2

LIGURIA

Liguria, a coastal territory about 350 km long, may appear uniform. In reality it's anything but. To the west it's enclosed by the Maritime Alps and by the Ligurian Apennines that open up near Levante. The mountains are crossed longitudinally by several valleys, and it's here, historically, that viticulture has taken on various forms, leading to different enological traditions and wines. This year the region managed to express this diversity as never before, with 8 award-winning wines serving as a beautiful representation of Liguria's individual grape varieties. As a district, Levante is compact, offering the highest quality: here Vermentino is the undisputed prince grape, and this year we particularly appreciated it thanks to 4 major producers. Lunae Bosoni presented an excellent version of their Nera, a white characterized by fascinating exotic scents; the Federici brothers' Baia del Sole manages to express all the grape's minerality through the Sarticola; Giacomelli, with their Pianacce, stood out for its exemplary Mediterranean touch; finally Zangani's Vermentino Superiore Boceda proves to be a wine of notable structure, but still elegant and harmonious. The diversity that characterizes the region's west saw several different typologies awarded. The Luvaira, a Dolceacqua by Giovanna Maccario, is a true champion of complexity, but also deliciously drinkable, while Massimo Alessandri's Rossese proves to be a harmonious, elegant drink, taking home its first Tre Bicchieri. Among the whites, the personality of Pigato emerges with 2 great bottles: Bruna's multi-award winning U Baccan and another first timer, the Pigato di Albenga Saleasco by historic producer Marcello Calleri. Riviera Ligure and Dolceacqua to the west, Colli di Luni to the east. Pigato, Vermentino and Rossese. This is the region's patrimony, though we mustn't forget its smaller, but still important, appellations. One of these is Cinque Terre, an area of undisputed beauty that still manages (fortunately) to spawn unique wines such as the Sciacchetrà: a Passito cultivated on its famous terraced vineyards, immersed in a landscape of absolute beauty.

Massimo Alessandri

via Costa Parrocchia, 42
18020 Ranzo [IM]
Tel. +39 018253458
www.massimoalessandri.it

CELLAR SALES
PRE-BOOKED VISITS
RESTAURANT SERVICE
ANNUAL PRODUCTION 35,000 bottles
HECTARES UNDER VINE 7.00

Massimo, Alessandri's owner and factotum, produces a range of wines that's long proved extremely reliable in terms of quality. An attentive winemaker who has invested a lot in technical and human terms, his flagship wines include the Viorus, made with 80% Viognier and 20% Roussanne. It's a wine that's celebrating more than 15 years of production. Fermentation is exclusively on the fine lees, without maceration on the skins. This combines with maturation in 600-liter barrels, making for complex and unique flavor. The excellent Rossese Costa de Vigne '18 pours a vibrant ruby garnet, the prelude to notes of cinchona and bark, cocoa and red berries. In the mouth it's warm and harmonious with pleasant pulp, vital tannins and good length. The Pigato Vigne Vegie '18 proves complex in its notes of citrus fruits, mint and tobacco, all expressed in an elegant body, pervasive and long. The Pigato Costa de Vigne '19 and Granaccia '18 are also well made.

● Riviera Ligure di Ponente Rossese Costa de Vigne '18	🍷🍷🍷 4*
○ Riviera Ligure di Ponente Pigato Vigne Vëggie '18	🍷🍷 4
● Riviera Ligure di Ponente Granaccia '18	🍷🍷 4
○ Riviera Ligure di Ponente Pigato Costa de Vigne '19	🍷🍷 3
○ Riviera Ligure di Ponente Vermentino Costa de Vigne '19	🍷 3
○ Viorus '18	🍷 5
● Riviera Ligure di Ponente Granaccia '17	🍷🍷 4
● Riviera Ligure di Ponente Granaccia '15	🍷🍷 4
○ Riviera Ligure di Ponente Pigato Costa de Vigne '18	🍷🍷 3
● Riviera Ligure di Ponente Rossese Costa de Vigne '17	🍷🍷 4
○ Riviera Ligure di Ponente Vermentino Costa de Vigne '18	🍷🍷 3*

Tenuta Anfosso

c.so Verbone, 175
18036 Soldano [IM]
Tel. +39 0184289906
www.tenutaanfosso.it

CELLAR SALES
ACCOMMODATION
ANNUAL PRODUCTION 23,000 bottles
HECTARES UNDER VINE 4.50

Alessandro Anfosso, together with his wife, Marisa (who oversees sales), continues to invest in new terrain in Pini di Soldano. It's an abandoned vineyard situated at about 400 meters elevation in the upper part of the 'Pini' geographical indication (soon to be replanted with red grapes). The venture, which began in 2002, is bearing fruit to the point that Alessandro's son (owner of E Prie) is following in his father's footsteps, experimenting with new production approaches and turning in good results. The 2018 vintage was favorable, to say the least, for Tenuta Anfosso's Dolceacqua. A bright garnet color, the Superiore Fulavin unfolds amidst suggestions of licorice and tobacco, bark and dried flowers, lending a nice, gently vibrant sapidity to the palate. Shades of red fruit and spices, licorice and cocoa introduce the Poggio Pini, a wine that brings together character and length on the palate.

● Dolceacqua Sup. Fulavin '18	🍷🍷 5
● Dolceacqua Sup. Poggio Pini '18	🍷🍷 5
● Dolceacqua Sup. '18	🍷🍷 4
● Dolceacqua Sup. Luvaira '18	🍷🍷 5
● Dolceacqua E Prie '19	🍷 4
● Dolceacqua '15	🍷🍷 4
● Dolceacqua Sup. '17	🍷🍷 4
● Dolceacqua Sup. '16	🍷🍷 4
● Dolceacqua Sup. '13	🍷🍷 4
● Dolceacqua Sup. Fulavin '16	🍷🍷 5
● Dolceacqua Sup. Fulavin '13	🍷🍷 4
● Dolceacqua Sup. Luvaira '17	🍷🍷 5
● Dolceacqua Sup. Luvaira '16	🍷🍷 5
● Dolceacqua Sup. Luvaira '13	🍷🍷 4
● Dolceacqua Sup. Poggio Pini '16	🍷🍷 5
● Dolceacqua Sup. Poggio Pini '15	🍷🍷 4
● Dolceacqua Sup. Poggio Pini '12	🍷🍷 4

Arrigoni

via Sarzana, 224
19126 La Spezia
Tel. +39 0187504060
www.arrigoni1913.it

CELLAR SALES
PRE-BOOKED VISITS
ACCOMMODATION AND RESTAURANT SERVICE
ANNUAL PRODUCTION 150,000 bottles
HECTARES UNDER VINE 18.00
SUSTAINABLE WINERY

The Arrigoni farm is composed of two distinct realities. The first is situated in San Gimignano and the second in La Spezia, Liguria. Here cultivation is spread over a wide territory that starts in Castelnuovo Magra-La Colombera, in the Colli di Luni DOC zone, and reaching into Ricò del Golfo, in the hinterland of Cinque Terre. In the coastal part, work is concentrated on two small estates, one in Volastra and the other in the beautiful village of Vernazza. These microstructures are essential for working the grapes from local vineyards. Cascina dei Peri '19 is a vibrant Vermentino marked by notes of Mediterranean scrubland and rosemary, white fruit and citrus. Elegant and complex, it expresses firm structure and a sapid pleasantness across a long finish. The fresh, elegant Prefect '19 features a background of mineral and fruity hints, all of which develop harmoniously on the palate.

Wine	Rating
○ Colli di Luni Vermentino Il Prefetto '19	🍷🍷 3*
○ Colli di Luni Vermentino La Cascina dei Peri '19	🍷🍷 3*
○ Cinque Terre Pipato '19	🍷🍷 3
○ Cinque Terre Sciacchetrà Passito Rosa di Maggio '09	🍷🍷 8
○ Cinque Terre Sciacchetrà Rosa di Maggio '16	🍷🍷 8
○ Cinque Terre Tra I Monti '18	🍷🍷 3*
○ Cinque Terre Tra I Monti '17	🍷🍷 3*
○ Colli di Luni Vermentino La Cascina dei Peri '18	🍷🍷 3
○ Colli di Luni Vermentino V. del Prefetto '18	🍷🍷 3
○ Colli di Luni Vermentino V. del Prefetto '17	🍷🍷 3

Laura Aschero

p.zza Vittorio Emanuele, 7
18027 Pontedassio [IM]
Tel. +39 0183710307
www.lauraaschero.it

CELLAR SALES
PRE-BOOKED VISITS
ANNUAL PRODUCTION 65,000 bottles
HECTARES UNDER VINE 50.00

The winery remains a family-run business, even if growing demand for their product and a desire to enlarge their range in the future is pushing the owners to search for new spaces. They're known above all for their whites, which derive from vineyards located mainly in Monti and Posai, at about 150 meters above sea level, along the Impero river valley. Although small in quantity, the last harvest generated healthy fruit harvested at the proper ripeness. Marco and Carla support their daughter Bianca, who for years now has taken over full control of the producer. Glossy greenish highlights introduce the Pigato '19, a wine marked by vibrant notes of medicinal herbs and white fruit, sensations that unfold harmoniously on an elegantly fresh, long palate. The less vivid Vermentino '19 features aromas of white fruit and Mediterranean herbs on a measured body, while the pleasant Rossese '19 is characterized by vibrant aromas of red fruit and nice persistence.

Wine	Rating
○ Riviera Ligure di Ponente Pigato '19	🍷🍷 3*
● Riviera Ligure di Ponente Rossese '19	🍷 3
○ Riviera Ligure di Ponente Vermentino '19	🍷 3
○ Riviera Ligure di Ponente Vermentino '10	🍷🍷🍷 3*
○ Riviera Ligure di Ponente Pigato '18	🍷🍷 3*
○ Riviera Ligure di Ponente Pigato '17	🍷🍷 3
○ Riviera Ligure di Ponente Pigato '16	🍷🍷 3
○ Riviera Ligure di Ponente Pigato '15	🍷🍷 3*
○ Riviera Ligure di Ponente Pigato '13	🍷🍷 3*
○ Riviera Ligure di Ponente Pigato '11	🍷🍷 3*
○ Riviera Ligure di Ponente Vermentino '18	🍷🍷 3
○ Riviera Ligure di Ponente Vermentino '17	🍷🍷 3
○ Riviera Ligure di Ponente Vermentino '16	🍷🍷 3

La Baia del Sole - Federici

Fraz. Luni Antica
via Forlino, 3
19034 Luni [SP]
Tel. +39 0187661821
www.cantinefederici.com

CELLAR SALES
PRE-BOOKED VISITS
ANNUAL PRODUCTION 180,000 bottles
HECTARES UNDER VINE 35.00

The Federici family's winery is constantly growing. Three new hectares of Vermentino Bianco and a smaller share of Vermentino Nero have been planted. One part is in Palvotrisia, in Castelnuovo Magra, at an elevation of about 200 meters, while the remaining plots are situated on three large hillocks in Luni, San Martino. And although the last harvest saw a slight decrease in quantity, production has been strengthened thanks to a nearby walkway built for the museum of Luni, which has helped to fuel visits to the winery. The Vermentino Sarticola '19 is a superb wine. A lively, bright straw-yellow color is the prelude to vibrant notes of dried herbs, all enriched by hints of apricot and iodine. On the palate it's complex, with nice mineral structure and a surprising elegance, coming through fresh on a long finish. The Vermentino Oro d'Isée '19 features great vigor and complexity.

- ○ Colli di Luni Vermentino Sarticola '19 ▼▼▼ 5
- ○ Colli di Luni Vermentino Oro D'Ise'e '19 ▼▼ 4
- ○ Colli di Luni Bianco Glaudius '19 ▼▼ 3
- ○ Colli di Luni Vermentino Solaris '19 ▼▼ 3
- ○ Colli di Luni Bianco Muri Grandi '19 ▼ 2
- ⊙ Prima Brezza Rosato '19 ▼ 3
- ○ Colli di Luni Vermentino Sarticola '15 ▽▽▽ 4*
- ○ Colli di Luni Bianco Gladius '17 ▽▽ 2*
- ○ Colli di Luni Vermentino Oro d'Ise'e '18 ▽▽ 4
- ○ Colli di Luni Vermentino Oro d'Ise'e '17 ▽▽ 4
- ○ Colli di Luni Vermentino Sarticola '18 ▽▽ 5
- ○ Colli di Luni Vermentino Sarticola '17 ▽▽ 5
- ○ Colli di Luni Vermentino Sarticola '16 ▽▽ 4
- ○ Colli di Luni Vermentino Solaris '18 ▽▽ 3*
- ○ Colli di Luni Vermentino Solaris '17 ▽▽ 3*

Maria Donata Bianchi

via Merea, 101
18013 Diano Arentino [IM]
Tel. +39 0183498233
www.aziendaagricolabianchi.it

CELLAR SALES
PRE-BOOKED VISITS
ACCOMMODATION
ANNUAL PRODUCTION 30,000 bottles
HECTARES UNDER VINE 4.00

Marta Trevia, fresh off a degree in enology and viticulture, is the bridge between the past and the present for a winery that combines a modern approach that's rapid in adapting and in communication with ancient knowledge, varietal identity and territorial expression. It is she who today has the task of growing Maria Donata Bianchi and her ideas are very clear. With the conversion to organic farming and plans to enlarge their vineyards, the future is looking bright. A multifaceted wine that's true to type in its aromas of white fruit, Mediterranean scrub and grapefruit, the Pigato '19 is fine and complex on the palate, dense and harmonious, thanks to its firm structure and lively acidity. The Vermentino '19 fully convinces with its buoyant fruity profile, all brought out by nuances of dried herbs. On the palate it exhibits a sunnier touch, before giving way to a delicately almond finish.

- ○ Riviera Ligure di Ponente Pigato '19 ▼▼ 3*
- ○ Riviera Ligure di Ponente Vermentino '19 ▼▼ 3
- ○ Riviera Ligure di Ponente Pigato '12 ▽▽▽ 3*
- ○ Riviera Ligure di Ponente Vermentino '09 ▽▽▽ 3
- ○ Riviera Ligure di Ponente Vermentino '07 ▽▽▽ 3*
- ○ Antico Sfizio '18 ▽▽ 4
- ○ Riviera Ligure di Ponente Pigato '18 ▽▽ 3
- ○ Riviera Ligure di Ponente Pigato '17 ▽▽ 3
- ○ Riviera Ligure di Ponente Pigato '16 ▽▽ 3
- ○ Riviera Ligure di Ponente Pigato '14 ▽▽ 3*
- ○ Riviera Ligure di Ponente Vermentino '18 ▽▽ 3*
- ○ Riviera Ligure di Ponente Vermentino '17 ▽▽ 3

BioVio

fraz. Bastia
via Crociata, 24
17031 Albenga [SV]
Tel. +39 018220776
www.biovio.it

CELLAR SALES
PRE-BOOKED VISITS
ACCOMMODATION
ANNUAL PRODUCTION 60,000 bottles
HECTARES UNDER VINE 9.00
VITICULTURE METHOD Certified Organic

Caterina Vio is showing increased productive capacity and skill. Their range is welcoming a new wine, a sort of experiment with Pigato grapes processed without added sulphites. Harvests see the selection of the healthiest bunches, which are then cryo-macerated for 24 hours before fermentation with only indigenous yeasts. The winery is also planning a future plot in Vallette, in the foothills of Bastia di Albenga, which will be planted with Granaccia. The addition of the grape, which is already cultivated in the territory, will increase the variety of their range. A vibrant body adorned with light notes of caramel, the Pigato Grand Père '18 exhibits remarkably full texture accompanied by soft hints of ripe yellow fruit, all of which goes back to maceration (while enriching its long palate). A nice mix of medicinal herbs and Mediterranean scrub, fruit and spices, characterize the Ma René '19, a wine that closes with great structure and beautiful harmony. An excellent performance for the Granaccia Gigò '19 as well.

Wine	Rating
○ Riviera Ligure di Ponente Pigato Grand Père '18	🍷🍷🍷 5
○ Riviera Ligure di Ponente Pigato Ma René '19	🍷🍷 3*
● Gigò Granaccia '19	🍷🍷 3
○ Riviera Ligure di Ponente Pigato Essenza '19	🍷 4
● Riviera Ligure di Ponente Rossese U Bastiò '19	🍷 3
○ Riviera Ligure di Ponente Pigato Bon in da Bon '17	🍷🍷🍷 5
○ Riviera Ligure di Ponente Pigato Bon in da Bon '16	🍷🍷🍷 5
○ Riviera Ligure di Ponente Pigato Bon in da Bon '15	🍷🍷🍷 2*
○ Riviera Ligure di Ponente Vermentino Aimone '11	🍷🍷🍷 2*

Bregante

via Unità d'Italia, 47
16039 Sestri Levante [GE]
Tel. +39 018541388
www.cantinebregante.it

CELLAR SALES
PRE-BOOKED VISITS
ANNUAL PRODUCTION 120,000 bottles
HECTARES UNDER VINE 1.00

Sergio Sanguineti oversees the winery he inherited from Ferdinando Bregante, father of his wife, Simona. Over time he has specialized in vinification, exploring various production techniques. In addition to traditional typlogies, including Metodo Charmat Moscato, we find a sparkling wine made with Genoese Bianchetta, the territory's principal grape variety. It's a single-vintage Metodo Classico, worked only in steel and the bottle, with 18 months on the lees. The grapes are harvested early so as to preserve the proper acidity. Suggestions of peach and apricot, with a distant musky hint give way to a palate made tasty and dynamic by virtue of its close-knit bristle. This is, in short, the Moscato '19, a rich and pleasant wine. Subtle yet intense in its aromas of wild flowers and ferns, the Bianchetta Genovese '19 proves delicate, elegant and fresh, topped off by a pleasant finish.

Wine	Rating
○ Golfo del Tigullio Portofino Moscato '19	🍷🍷 3*
○ Golfo del Tigullio Baia delle Favole Brut M. Cl.	🍷🍷 5
○ Golfo del Tigullio Portofino Bianchetta Genovese '19	🍷🍷 2*
○ Golfo del Tigullio Portofino Bianco '19	🍷🍷 2*
● Golfo del Tigullio Portofino Ciliegiolo '19	🍷🍷 2*
○ Golfo del Tigullio Portofino Vermentino '19	🍷 2
○ Golfo del Tigullio Portofino Bianchetta Genovese '17	🍷🍷 2*
○ Golfo del Tigullio Portofino Bianco '18	🍷🍷 2*
○ Golfo del Tigullio Portofino Bianco '17	🍷🍷 2*
● Golfo del Tigullio Portofino Ciliegiolo '18	🍷🍷 2*
○ Golfo del Tigullio Portofino Moscato '18	🍷🍷 3
○ Golfo del Tigullio Portofino Moscato '17	🍷🍷 3
○ Golfo del Tigullio Portofino Vermentino '16	🍷🍷 2*

★Bruna

FRAZ. BORGO
VIA UMBERTO I, 81
18020 RANZO [IM]
TEL. +39 0183318082
www.brunapigato.it

CELLAR SALES
PRE-BOOKED VISITS
ANNUAL PRODUCTION 40,000 bottles
HECTARES UNDER VINE 8.50

The winery, now in the second year of the organic certification process, experienced a significant decrease in production but has maintained the high quality standards set with the 2019 vintage. Abundant spring rains accompanied by low temperatures inhibited full development of their grapes, leading to the formation of loose bunches suitable for distinguished wines. Their organizational structure hasn't undergone any changes: Roberto is mainly responsible for overseeing the vineyards, while his wife, Francesca, handles the office. Both also work in the cellar, with all the various jobs that requires. The Pigato U Baccan '19 pours a vibrant, vivid color, anticipating complex notes of mint and rosemary, which open to white fruit. On the palate it's fresh, exhibiting great harmony and undisputed elegance. A faint straw-yellow with greenish highlights, the Pigato Majè '19 also plays on officinal and balsamic sensations, unfolding tense and elegant before finishing on a slightly bitterish note.

○ Riviera Ligure di Ponente Pigato U Baccan '18	🍷🍷🍷	6
○ Riviera Ligure di Ponente Pigato Le Russeghine '19	🍷🍷	4
● Bansigu '18	🍷🍷	3
○ Riviera Ligure di Ponente Pigato Majè '19	🍷🍷	3
○ Riviera Ligure di Ponente Vermentino '19	🍷	4
○ Riviera Ligure di Ponente Pigato U Baccan '16	🍷🍷🍷 (open)	5
○ Riviera Ligure di Ponente Pigato U Baccan '15	🍷🍷🍷 (open)	5
○ Riviera Ligure di Ponente Pigato U Baccan '13	🍷🍷🍷 (open)	5
○ Riviera Ligure di Ponente Pigato U Baccan '12	🍷🍷🍷 (open)	5

Cantine Calleri

LOC. SALEA
REG. FRATTI, 2
17031 ALBENGA [SV]
TEL. +39 018220085
www.cantinecalleri.com

ANNUAL PRODUCTION 55,000 bottles
HECTARES UNDER VINE 6.00

The commitment and professionalism that Marcello Calleri has always brought to vinifying his grapes, chosen with meticulousness year after year by trusted growers, is now undisputed. His love for his work, combined with the enological expertise he's gained, are behind wines of such great quality. A new selection has expanded their production range: it's a Pigato, from Salea, that's bottled after a 4-month stay in new barriques and long maturation in steel tanks. The Pigato Saleasco '19 is a great wine, extremely elegant in its aromas of apricot, rosemary and Mediterranean herbs. It combines complexity and class, broad sapidity and nice freshness, with a long and rich yet supple finish. The Vermentino Muzzazzi '19 also exhibits a fine elegance, a pleasant structure and nice harmony, but their entire range stands out for its personality and naturalness.

○ Riviera Ligure di Ponente Pigato di Albenga Saleasco '19	🍷🍷🍷	3*
○ Riviera Ligure di Ponente Vermentino I Müzazzi '19	🍷🍷	3*
● Dolceacqua '18	🍷🍷	3
○ Riviera Ligure di Ponente Pigato di Albenga '19	🍷🍷	3
○ Riviera Ligure di Ponente Pigato di Albenga Il Calleri '17	🍷🍷	4
○ Riviera Ligure di Ponente Pigato di Albenga Saleasco '18	🍷🍷 (open)	3*
○ Riviera Ligure di Ponente Pigato di Albenga Saleasco '17	🍷🍷 (open)	3*
○ Riviera Ligure di Ponente Vermentino '18	🍷🍷 (open)	3
● Rossese di Dolceacqua '17	🍷🍷 (open)	3

Cheo

via Brigate Partigiane, 1
19018 Vernazza [SP]
Tel. +39 0187821189
www.cheo.it

CELLAR SALES
PRE-BOOKED VISITS
ANNUAL PRODUCTION 13,000 bottles
HECTARES UNDER VINE 2.00
SUSTAINABLE WINERY

Vernazza is a small village in the Cinqueterre. It's here that Bartolo Lercari has his roots, and it's here that with his wife, Lise, after years at the University of Pisa, he's built his current life and work. The main property under vine is gorgeous. Accessible almost exclusively by monorail, here order and beauty come together, enriching the charming coastal landscape. A man of undisputed intelligence and broad vision, Bartolo painstakingly cares for every little detail of his vineyards, which are manicured with diligence and constancy vine for vine. Vibrant notes of caramel, toffee and candied orange on a sophisticated background of incense and liquorice introduce the Sciacchetrà '17. It's a wine of great complexity, with a harmonious, deep body that's able to deliver a long, truly classic finish. The Perciò '19 plays more on fresh sensations of herbs and medicinal plants, though it's just as endowed with pulp and balance.

Wine	Glasses	Price
○ Cinque Terre Sciacchetrà '17	▼▼	8
○ Cinque Terre Perciò '19	▼▼	4
● Liguria di Levante '18	▼▼	3
○ Cinque Terre Bianco Mavà '19	▼	4
○ Cheo Bianco '18	▽▽	3
● Cheo Rosso '17	▽▽	4
○ Cinque Terre Cheo '17	▽▽	3
○ Cinque Terre Cheo '16	▽▽	3
○ Cinque Terre Mavà '17	▽▽	4
○ Cinque Terre Perciò '18	▽▽	4
○ Cinque Terre Perciò '17	▽▽	4
○ Cinque Terre Perciò '16	▽▽	4
○ Cinque Terre Perciò '15	▽▽	4
○ Cinque Terre Sciacchetrà '16	▽▽	8
○ Cinque Terre Sciacchetrà '15	▽▽	8
○ Cinque Terre Sciacchetrà '14	▽▽	8
○ Cinque Terre Sciacchetrà '13	▽▽	8

Cantina Cinque Terre

fraz. Manarola
loc. Groppo
19010 Riomaggiore [SP]
Tel. +39 0187920435
www.cantinacinqueterre.com

PRE-BOOKED VISITS
ANNUAL PRODUCTION 200,000 bottles
HECTARES UNDER VINE 45.00

Situated on high, in the beautiful village of Riomaggiore, Cantina 5 Terre has made significant investments to improve its accommodation facilities and better welcome wine tourists, who increasingly come up to visit the paths and vineyards overlooking the sea. The upper part of the operational center, which is used for drying the grapes for their Sciacchetrà, has been improved. It's a fixed structure with large windows and a room that will serve as a space for meeting and tasting wines. The Costa de Campu '19 is quite delicate, proving simple and approachable in its nuances of fresh herbs and ferns. On the palate it exhibits nice harmony across a long, final stroke. The Sciacchetrà '18, which is an antique gold color, has plenty of extraction, with fragrances of apricot, honey and candied orange giving way to a palate of lively acidity, making for a broad, pleasant drink. Excellent results for the Cinque Terre Pergole Sparse and Vigne Alte '19 as well.

Wine	Glasses	Price
○ Cinque Terre Costa de Campu '19	▼▼	3*
○ Sciacchetrà '18	▼▼	6
○ Cinque Terre Pergole Sparse '19	▼▼	3
○ Cinque Terre Vigne Alte '19	▼▼	3
○ Cinque Terre Costa da' Posa '19	▼	3
○ Cinque Terre '18	▽▽	2*
○ Cinque Terre '17	▽▽	2*
○ Cinque Terre Costa da' Posa '18	▽▽	3
○ Cinque Terre Costa da' Posa '17	▽▽	3
○ Cinque Terre Costa de Campu '18	▽▽	3
○ Cinque Terre Costa de Campu '17	▽▽	3
○ Cinque Terre Pergole Sparse '17	▽▽	3
○ Cinque Terre Sciacchetrà '17	▽▽	6
○ Cinque Terre Sciacchetrà '15	▽▽	6
○ Cinque Terre Sciacchetrà Ris. '12	▽▽	6
○ Cinque Terre Vigne Alte '18	▽▽	3*
○ Cinque Terre Vigne Alte '17	▽▽	3*

Fontanacota

FRAZ. PONTI
VIA PROVINCIALE, 137
18100 PORNASSIO [IM]
TEL. +39 3339807442
www.fontanacota.it

CELLAR SALES
PRE-BOOKED VISITS
ANNUAL PRODUCTION 40,000 bottles
HECTARES UNDER VINE 6.00

The winery's headquarters are located in Pornassio, but Marina and her brother Fabio are expanding into other neighboring municipalities, thus enriching Fontanacota's range of wines. In addition to the vineyard already planted in Dolcedo, the new plots include, in the hinterland of San Giorgio, another small parcel of Granaccia that will go into production in the coming years. In the meantime, young Andreas and Ludovico are working on the new website, which includes two projects: the first is an e-commerce platform and the second is for communications concerning their new tasting room, planned for the area above the cellar. The Pigato '19 stands out for its beautiful notes of citrus and apricot, all enriched by hints of chlorophyll and Mediterranean scrub. Complexity and class distinguish the palate, which is supported by nice acidity and a classy finish. The Vermentino '19 is soft, lively and very youthful. It enters on fruit, minty nuances and slightly dried herbs.

○ Riviera Ligure di Ponente Pigato '19	🍷🍷 3*
● Ormeasco di Pornassio Sup. '18	🍷🍷 4
● Riviera Ligure di Ponente Rossese '19	🍷🍷 3
○ Riviera Ligure di Ponente Vermentino '19	🍷🍷 3
● Ormeasco di Pornassio '18	🍷 3
○ Riviera Ligure di Ponente Pigato '11	🍷🍷🍷 3*
○ Riviera Ligure di Ponente Vermentino '18	🍷🍷🍷 3*
● Ormeasco di Pornassio '17	🍷🍷 3
● Ormeasco di Pornassio Sup. '17	🍷🍷 3
○ Riviera Ligure di Ponente Pigato '18	🍷🍷 3*
○ Riviera Ligure di Ponente Pigato '17	🍷🍷 3
○ Riviera Ligure di Ponente Pigato '16	🍷🍷 3
● Riviera Ligure di Ponente Rossese '17	🍷🍷 3
○ Riviera Ligure di Ponente Vermentino '17	🍷🍷 3

Giacomelli

VIA PALVOTRISIA, 134
19030 CASTELNUOVO MAGRA [SP]
TEL. +39 3496301516
www.azagricolagiacomelli.com

CELLAR SALES
PRE-BOOKED VISITS
ANNUAL PRODUCTION 100,000 bottles
HECTARES UNDER VINE 12.00
SUSTAINABLE WINERY

At Giacomelli, work is nearing completion on the new cellar, which has seen the expansion of the spaces already in use and the restoration of the old concrete tanks, which will be fixed up and covered with fiberglass. The aim is to produce wines that follow in the footsteps of tradition. As for the vineyards, a small plot has been planted in the town of Luni. Vermentino Nero, a grape that's enjoying great success in the area, will be cultivated. Youthful and explosive, the Pianacce '19 offers up gorgeous notes of white fruit and mint on a background of citrus. Elegant and complex on the palate, it comes through rich and sapid, with a long finish and plenty of character. With its intense floral and citrus aromas, the Boboli '19 expresses Vermentino's compelling character, combining elegance, fresh flavor and persistence. The Vermentino Paduletti '19 and Giardino dei Vescovi '18 also performed exceptionally well.

○ Colli di Luni Vermentino Pianacce '19	🍷🍷🍷 3*
○ Colli di Luni Vermentino Boboli '19	🍷🍷 4
○ Colli di Luni Vermentino Giardino dei Vescovi '18	🍷🍷 5
○ Colli di Luni Vermentino Paduletti '19	🍷🍷 2*
● Liguria di Levante Pergole Basse '19	🍷 3
○ Colli di Luni Vermentino Boboli '17	🍷🍷🍷 4*
○ Colli di Luni Vermentino Pianacce '18	🍷🍷🍷 3*
○ Colli di Luni Bianco Paduletti '16	🍷🍷 2*
○ Colli di Luni Vermentino Boboli '18	🍷🍷 4
○ Colli di Luni Vermentino Boboli '13	🍷🍷 4
○ Colli di Luni Vermentino Giardino dei Vescovi '17	🍷🍷 5
○ Colli di Luni Vermentino Paduletti '18	🍷🍷 2*
○ Colli di Luni Vermentino Pianacce '17	🍷🍷 3
○ Colli di Luni Vermentino Pianacce '16	🍷🍷 2*
○ Colli di Luni Vermentino Pianacce '15	🍷🍷 2*

La Ginestraia

via Steria
18100 Cervo [IM]
Tel. +39 3482613723
www.laginestraia.com

ANNUAL PRODUCTION 50,000 bottles
HECTARES UNDER VINE 7.00

Finally Mauro Leporieri and Marco Brangero are working on the new plot of Vermentino in the municipality of Cervo, just above the village of San Bartolomeo al Mare. It's situated about 400 meters above sea level, and positioned in such a way that it covers the entire hill from southeast to southwest. Four different clones of Vermentino can be found, the result will be a single selection wine that will enrich their collection of whites. A second piece of important news is authorization to build the new cellar. The Pigato '19 exhibits a profile rich in fruit, supported by assertive freshness and an enticing herbaceous stroke. The Pigato Le Marige '19 is also lively, with hints of ripe white fruit adorning a body of nice harmony and a fairly long finish. Clean, sincere and pleasant, the Vermentino '19 plays more on the primaries.

Wine	Rating
○ Riviera Ligure di Ponente Pigato '19	🍷🍷 3
○ Riviera Ligure di Ponente Pigato Le Marige '19	🍷🍷 5
○ Riviera Ligure di Ponente Vermentino '19	🍷🍷 3
○ Riviera Ligure di Ponente Pigato Le Marige '18	YYY 5
○ Riviera Ligure di Ponente Pigato Le Marige '15	YYY 3*
○ Riviera Ligure di Ponente Pigato Via Maestra '16	YYY 5
○ Riviera Ligure di Ponente Pigato '18	YY 3*
○ Riviera Ligure di Ponente Pigato Le Marige '17	YY 3
○ Riviera Ligure di Ponente Pigato Via Maestra '15	YY 3*
○ Riviera Ligure di Ponente Vermentino '17	YY 3

Ka' Manciné

fraz. San Martino
via Maciurina, 7
18036 Soldano [IM]
Tel. +39 339 3965477
www.kamancine.it

CELLAR SALES
PRE-BOOKED VISITS
ANNUAL PRODUCTION 20,000 bottles
HECTARES UNDER VINE 3.00

Alessandro Anfosso, assisted by his wife, Marisa (who oversees the sales side of things), continues to invest with new terrain in Pini di Soldano. It's an abandoned vineyard, situated at about 400 meters elevation in the upper part of the 'Pini' geographical indication, and will be replanted with red grapes. The venture, which began in 2002, is turning in excellent results, to the point that Alessandro's son, owner of E Prie, is following in his father's footsteps and having success with new production approaches. The Galeae Angè Ris. '18 exhibits a youthful contour, with intense fruity notes accompanied by deeper nuances of bark and spices. A pulpy, austere temperament is particularly evident across its long palate. Lively and ebullient, but just as complex, the Galeae '19 with its jubilant red fruits and pepper is enriched by a light and appetizing 'green' sensation. The Beragna '19 is also very promising.

Wine	Rating
● Dolceacqua Galeae Angè Ris. '18	🍷🍷 3*
● Dolceacqua Beragna '19	🍷🍷 3
● Dolceacqua Galeae '19	🍷🍷 3
⊙ Sciakk '19	🍷 3
○ Tabaka '19	🍷 3
● Dolceacqua Beragna '17	YYY 3*
● Dolceacqua Beragna '16	YYY 3*
● Dolceacqua Galeae '13	YYY 3*
● Dolceacqua Beragna '18	YY 3
● Dolceacqua Beragna '15	YY 3*
● Dolceacqua Galeae '18	YY 3
● Dolceacqua Galeae '17	YY 3*
● Dolceacqua Galeae '16	YY 3*
● Dolceacqua Galeae Angè Ris. '17	YY 3*
● Dolceacqua Galeae Angè Ris. '16	YY 3*
● Dolceacqua Galeae Angè Ris. '15	YY 3
● Dolceacqua Galeae Angè Ris. '14	YY 3*

Ottaviano Lambruschi

via Olmarello, 28
19030 Castelnuovo Magra [SP]
Tel. +39 0187674261
www.ottavianolambruschi.com

CELLAR SALES
PRE-BOOKED VISITS
ANNUAL PRODUCTION 36,000 bottles
HECTARES UNDER VINE 10.00

An addition to the production facility has been completed, and even if the area will be used in the near future mainly as a tasting room, this will allow Fabio Lambruschi to work more easily. In the meantime a new wine is going into production, one whose grapes are harvested higher up in the Costa Marina cru. After vinification in steel at a controlled temperature, these undergo a brief stay on the skins. Only a few bottles bear the Superiore name. Youthful and vibrant, the Il Maggiore '19 is a mineral-rich Vermentino with a lovely salty streak, potent flavor, and long, austere finish. The Superiore '19 opens on pleasant hints of medicinal and Mediterranean herbs, ferns and citrus fruits. The Costa Marina '19 also proved excellent, with its full body supported by a lively iodine skeleton.

○ Colli di Luni Vermentino Il Maggiore '19	🍷🍷 5
○ Colli di Luni Vermentino Sup. '19	🍷🍷 3*
○ Colli di Luni Vermentino '19	🍷🍷 3
○ Colli di Luni Vermentino Costa Marina '19	🍷🍷 4
● Liguria di Levante Maniero '19	🍷 2
○ Colli di Luni Vermentino Costa Marina '16	🍷🍷🍷 4*
○ Colli di Luni Vermentino Costa Marina '11	🍷🍷🍷 4*
○ Colli di Luni Vermentino Costa Marina '09	🍷🍷🍷 3
○ Colli di Luni Vermentino Il Maggiore '15	🍷🍷🍷 5
○ Colli di Luni Vermentino Il Maggiore '14	🍷🍷🍷 5
○ Colli di Luni Vermentino Il Maggiore '13	🍷🍷🍷 5
○ Colli di Luni Vermentino Il Maggiore '12	🍷🍷🍷 4*
○ Colli di Luni Vermentino Sarticola '08	🍷🍷🍷 3*

★Cantine Lunae Bosoni

via Bozzi, 63
19034 Luni [SP]
Tel. +39 0187669222
www.cantinelunae.com

CELLAR SALES
PRE-BOOKED VISITS
ANNUAL PRODUCTION 550,000 bottles
HECTARES UNDER VINE 80.00

Paolo Bosoni's winemaking ventures, supported for years by his sons Diego and Debora, have been moving towards study and research, with respect for biodiversity, starting with soil analysis based on a precise territorial identity and increasingly sustainable viticulture. Among the area's local grape varieties, we'd like to mention Albarola, which in recent years has been supporting the quality of Vermentino Bianco and increasingly meeting with approval. Attention is also being paid to Vermentino Nero, a variety cultivated by only a few producers in the small area of Lunigiana. The Vermentino Cavagino '19 is very promising. Notes of sage and ripe yellow-fleshed fruit (melon and apricot) feature on the nose, while the palate comes through sophisticated and complex, unleashing a mix of freshness and flavor in commendable harmony through a tantalizing finish. The Etichetta Nera '19 is on par with its predecessors, with a lively, long palate amplified by sweet aromas of dried herbs and spices. The full and elegant Numero Chiuso '16 also did well.

○ Colli di Luni Vermentino Lunae Et. Nera '19	🍷🍷🍷 4*
○ Colli di Luni Vermentino Cavagino '19	🍷🍷 5
○ Colli di Luni Vermentino Numero Chiuso '16	🍷🍷 7
○ Colli di Luni Vermentino Albarola '19	🍷🍷 4
○ Colli di Luni Vermentino Et. Grigia '19	🍷🍷 3
● Colli di Luni Rosso Niccolò V Ris. '13	🍷 5
○ Labianca '19	🍷 3
○ Colli di Luni Vermentino Et. Nera '15	🍷🍷🍷 4*
○ Colli di Luni Vermentino Lunae Et. Nera '18	🍷🍷🍷 4*
○ Colli di Luni Vermentino Lunae Et. Nera '17	🍷🍷🍷 4*
○ Colli di Luni Vermentino Lunae Et. Nera '16	🍷🍷🍷 4*

Maccario Dringenberg

via Torre, 3
18036 San Biagio della Cima [IM]
Tel. +39 0184289947
maccariodringenberg@yahoo.it

CELLAR SALES
PRE-BOOKED VISITS
ANNUAL PRODUCTION 23,000 bottles
HECTARES UNDER VINE 4.00

Giovanna Maccario and her husband, Goetz Dringenberg, continue to grow their winery. Starting this year in the municipality of Ventimiglia they'll have a new vineyard that will be recognized in the future with the 'Sette Camini' geographical mention. At about 480 meters above sea level and facing the sea, at the foot of Mount Grammondo in the Maritime Alps, the 50-year-old plot is already planted with red grapes. The soil is calcareous and of marine origin, rich in minerals and fossils, with a beautiful south-southeast exposure. Among their elegant battery of Dolceacquas, the Posaù Biamonti '18 stands out most. Vibrant and racy, tannic and sapid, it closes with a long, flavorful stroke. The Luvaira '18 is even more surprising. A vibrant, lively color anticipates rich red fruit on hints of cigar and bark. The Dolceacqua '19 is also excellent, offering up notes of tobacco and dried flowers before a warm, tannic palate and a dynamic finish.

Wine	Rating
● Rossese di Dolceacqua Sup. Luvaira '18	▼▼▼ 4*
● Rossese di Dolceacqua '19	▼▼ 3*
● Rossese di Dolceacqua Posaù Biamonti '18	▼▼ 5
● Rossese di Dolceacqua Sup. Brae '19	▼▼ 3
● Rossese di Dolceacqua Sup. Curli '18	▼▼ 3
● Dolceacqua Sup. Vign. Posaù '13	▽▽▽ 3*
● Rossese di Dolceacqua Posaù Biamonti '17	▽▽▽ 5
● Rossese di Dolceacqua Sup. Vign. Luvaira '07	▽▽▽ 4*
● Rossese di Dolceacqua Sup. Vign. Posaù '10	▽▽▽ 3*
● Rossese di Dolceacqua Sup. Vign. Posaù '08	▽▽▽ 3
● Rossese di Dolceacqua '18	▽▽ 3*
● Rossese di Dolceacqua '17	▽▽ 3*

Maixei

loc. Regione Porto
18035 Dolceacqua [IM]
Tel. +39 0184205015
www.maixei.it

CELLAR SALES
PRE-BOOKED VISITS
ANNUAL PRODUCTION 45,000 bottles
HECTARES UNDER VINE 10.00

An important merger with two other producers operating in the territory has brought a breath of fresh air to Maixei. The brand remains the same, but the current enological production will be flanked by oil and flowers, reaching wider and more diversified markets. On the other hand, agronomist Pasquale Restuccia and enologist Fabio Corradi will be able to directly oversee agricultural processing. The 2019 vintage saw a reduction in the quantity of white grapes harvested, while there was an increase in the share of red grapes provided by their growers. Quinine, licorice and tobacco, the Dolceacqua Sup. '18 proves classic, to say the least, with its sophisticated body and a background of ripe red fruit. In the mouth it's elegant and somewhat austere due to its solid tannic texture before finishing long and pleasant. The Barbadirame '18 is close on its heels, playing more on sweet and spicy tones of cocoa and pepper while the palate comes through soft, warm and pervasive.

Wine	Rating
● Dolceacqua Sup. '18	▼▼ 4
● Dolceacqua Sup. Barbadirame '18	▼▼ 4
● Dolceacqua '19	▼ 3
● Dolceacqua '18	▽▽ 3*
● Dolceacqua '15	▽▽ 3
● Dolceacqua '14	▽▽ 3*
● Dolceacqua Sup. '16	▽▽ 4
● Dolceacqua Sup. '15	▽▽ 4
● Dolceacqua Sup. '14	▽▽ 4
● Dolceacqua Sup. '13	▽▽ 4
● Dolceacqua Sup. Barbadirame '17	▽▽ 4
● Dolceacqua Sup. Barbadirame '16	▽▽ 4
● Dolceacqua Sup. Barbadirame '15	▽▽ 4
● Mistral '15	▽▽ 4
○ Riviera Ligure di Ponente Riviera dei Fiori Vermentino '17	▽▽ 3
○ Riviera Ligure di Ponente Vermentino '18	▽▽ 3

La Pietra del Focolare

via Isola, 76
19034 Luni [SP]
Tel. +39 0187662129
www.lapietradelfocolare.it

CELLAR SALES
PRE-BOOKED VISITS
ANNUAL PRODUCTION 30,000 bottles
HECTARES UNDER VINE 6.00
SUSTAINABLE WINERY

The winery is still managed by Laura and her husband Stefano, while at their side they have a new agronomist who's working according to the dictates of organic farming. The 2019 harvest saw a slight decrease in quantity, which combined with careful viticultural management to make it possible to bring healthy, high-quality grapes to the cellar. The choice of working without added sulfites is accompanied by other new experiments, such as the use of non-vitrified terracotta amphorae, which are suitable for the production of wines with long maceration on the skins. The Vermentino Superiore Solarancio '19 features intense fragrances of fruit, rosemary and medicinal herbs, then unfolds on the palate with commendable harmony and complexity. The Augusto '19 stands out for its aromas of fresh herbs, citrus fruits and mint, emphasizing the sophisticated, racy style before a long finish. The Villa Linda '19 also plays on a classic weave of ripe white fruit.

Wine	Rating
○ Colli di Luni Vermentino Augusto '19	🍷🍷 3*
○ Colli di Luni Vermentino Sup. Solarancio '19	🍷🍷 4
○ Colli di Luni Vermentino Sup. Villa Linda '19	🍷🍷 4
○ Colli di Luni Vermentino Augusto '18	🍷🍷 3
○ Colli di Luni Vermentino Augusto '16	🍷🍷 3
○ Colli di Luni Vermentino Augusto '15	🍷🍷 3
○ Colli di Luni Vermentino L'Aura di Sarticola '16	🍷🍷 6
○ Colli di Luni Vermentino Solarancio '15	🍷🍷 4
○ Colli di Luni Vermentino Sup. Solarancio '18	🍷🍷 4
○ Colli di Luni Vermentino Sup. Villa Linda '18	🍷🍷 4
○ Colli di Luni Vermentino Sup. Villa Linda '17	🍷🍷 4
○ Vigna delle Rose '17	🍷🍷 3*

Poggio dei Gorleri

fraz. Diano Gorleri
via San Leonardo
18013 Diano Marina [IM]
Tel. +39 0183495207
www.poggiodeigorleri.com

CELLAR SALES
PRE-BOOKED VISITS
ACCOMMODATION
ANNUAL PRODUCTION 80,000 bottles
HECTARES UNDER VINE 10.50

Davide Merano continues Poggio dei Gorleri's production and hospitality activities together with his wife, Cristina, his father, Giampiero, and mother, Rosella. This year they're proposing two new selections: the first is from a plot of about two hectares located in the wide basin below the village of Arnasco, one of the best areas for growing Pigato. The second is a wine made with Granaccia grapes from a one-hectare plot in Garzelli, in the Impero valley. Yet another great performance for Poggio dei Gorleri, starting with their Pigato Albium '17, a wine characterized by complex aromas of fruit peels and dried herbs, coming through rich and original on the palate. The Pigato Arveglio '19 is also very pleasant with its intense notes of ripe white fruit, medicinal herbs and citrus peel. Their Cian di Previ '18 and Shalok '17, powerful yet racy Granaccia reds, are improving.

Wine	Rating
○ Riviera Ligure di Ponente Pigato Albium '17	🍷🍷 5
○ Riviera Ligure di Ponente Pigato Arveglio '19	🍷🍷 5
● Riviera Ligure di Ponente Granaccia Cian di Previ '18	🍷🍷 5
● Riviera Ligure di Ponente Granaccia Shalok '17	🍷🍷 5
○ Riviera Ligure di Ponente Pigato Cycnus '19	🍷🍷 3
○ Riviera Ligure di Ponente Pigato Albium '15	🍷🍷🍷 5
○ Riviera Ligure di Ponente Pigato Albium '13	🍷🍷🍷 5
○ Riviera Ligure di Ponente Pigato Albium '10	🍷🍷🍷 5
○ Riviera Ligure di Ponente Pigato Cycnus '13	🍷🍷🍷 3*

Terenzuola

via Vercalda, 14
54035 Fosdinovo [MS]
Tel. +39 0187670387
www.terenzuola.it

PRE-BOOKED VISITS
ANNUAL PRODUCTION 180,000 bottles
HECTARES UNDER VINE 18.00

Ivan Giuliani is a young wine-grower from Lunigiana who for years has been living with the difficulties of a territory that is, to say the least, peculiar from an environmental, viticultural and productive standpoint. Located on the border between Liguria and Tuscany, where the Colli di Luni appellation crosses regional borders, thus standardizing cultivation, Ivan continues to develop the 'Lunigiana Storico' project. And despite all the pitfalls deriving from cultivating different grape varieties, the winery continues to grow in hectares and quality. Pleasantly vivid, the Vermentino Superiore Fosso di Corsano '19 exhibits a firm alcohol structure in the mid palate, proving round and mineral. Rich in extract and very clean, the Vermentino Nero Permano '17 comes through vibrant in fruit, which broadens after a delicately vegetal opening. The Cinque Terre '19 features aromas of fresh herbs, lively acidity and a supple palate.

Wine	Rating
○ Cinque Terre '19	TT 4
○ Colli di Luni Vermentino Sup. Fosso di Corsano '19	TT 4
● Merla della Miniera '17	TT 4
● Permano Vermentino Nero '17	TT 8
● Vermentino Nero V. Basse '18	TT 3
○ Colli di Luni Vermentino Sup. Fosso di Corsano '18	YYY 4*
○ Colli di Luni Vermentino Sup. Fosso di Corsano '17	YYY 3*
○ Colli di Luni Vermentino Sup. Fosso di Corsano '16	YYY 3*
○ Colli di Luni Vermentino Sup. Fosso di Corsano '11	YYY 3*
○ Cinque Terre Sciacchetrà Ris. '16	YY 8
● Merla della Miniera '16	YY 4
● Vigne Basse '17	YY 3*

Terre Bianche

loc. Arcagna
18035 Dolceacqua [IM]
Tel. +39 018431426
www.terrebianche.com

CELLAR SALES
PRE-BOOKED VISITS
ACCOMMODATION
ANNUAL PRODUCTION 55,000 bottles
HECTARES UNDER VINE 8.50
SUSTAINABLE WINERY

The 2019 vintage saw high levels of quality and a drop in quantity. For this reason Filippo Rondelli and his partner, Franco Locani, decided not to make the selection of Pigato Arcana Bianco and to concentrate instead only on their freshest and most approachable wines, those characterized by a strong sapidity that's very appreciated at this stage by international markets. As far as the producer's vineyards are concerned, management of a plot already under vine in Tramontina, Dolceacqua, will allow them to increase their range in the near future. A thick, bright ruby garnet, the Bricco Arcagna '18 opens with tantalizing hints of red fruit and sweet spices as if to announce the pleasantly casual character that we discover in its long, harmonious palate. And once again pulpy, peppery sensations draw the contours of the Dolceacqua '19, an elegant and complex drink.

Wine	Rating
● Dolceacqua '19	TT 4
● Dolceacqua Bricco Arcagna '18	TT 6
● Dolceacqua Terrabianca '18	TT 5
○ Riviera Ligure di Ponente Pigato '19	TT 3
○ Riviera Ligure di Ponente Pigato Arcana '18	TT 5
○ Riviera Ligure di Ponente Vermentino '19	TT 3
● Dolceacqua Bricco Arcagna '14	YYY 5
● Dolceacqua Bricco Arcagna '12	YYY 5
● Rossese di Dolceacqua '12	YYY 3*
● Rossese di Dolceacqua Bricco Arcagna '17	YYY 6
● Rossese di Dolceacqua Bricco Arcagna '09	YYY 4
● Rossese di Dolceacqua Bricco Arcagna '08	YYY 5

Vis Amoris

Loc. Caramagna
s.da per Vasia, 1
18100 Imperia
Tel. +39 3483959569
www.visamoris.it

CELLAR SALES
PRE-BOOKED VISITS
ANNUAL PRODUCTION 24,000 bottles
HECTARES UNDER VINE 3.50
VITICULTURE METHOD Certified Organic
SUSTAINABLE WINERY

Young Simone's presence at the winery is becoming more and more significant. After his degree in viticulture and enology in Alba, Roberto Tozzi's young son is now fully involved in production, pursuing organic agricultural practices with increasing determination. All stages of production are now entirely in his hands, from care of the vineyards to the work in the cellar, where fermentation is carried out with indigenous yeasts and the use of sulfites has been greatly reduced, as has the number of clarifiying agents. Still focused on youthful sensations, the Sogno '18 is a pleasant yet complex Pigato that exhibits a rich, Mediterranean profile and an elegant mineral vein. In the mouth it's buttery and fine, developing fluently. We found the Brut Metodo Classico, with its delicate perlage and aromas of citrus and bread crust, interesting. We also shouldn't forget the good performances put in by the Pigato '19, Domè and Verum.

○ Riviera Ligure di Ponente Pigato Sogno '18	🍷🍷 4
○ Vis Amoris Brut M.Cl.	🍷🍷 5
○ Riviera Ligure di Ponente Pigato Domè '19	🍷 4
○ Riviera Ligure di Ponente Pigato Verum '19	🍷 3
○ Riviera Ligure di Ponente Pigato Sogno '17	🍷🍷 4
○ Riviera Ligure di Ponente Pigato Sogno '16	🍷🍷 4
○ Riviera Ligure di Ponente Pigato Sogno '15	🍷🍷 4
○ Riviera Ligure di Ponente Pigato Verum '18	🍷🍷 3*
○ Riviera Ligure di Ponente Pigato Verum '17	🍷🍷 3*

Zangani

loc. Ponzano Superiore
via Gramsci, 46
19037 Santo Stefano di Magra [SP]
Tel. +39 0187632406
www.zangani.it

CELLAR SALES
PRE-BOOKED VISITS
ACCOMMODATION AND RESTAURANT SERVICE
ANNUAL PRODUCTION 40,000 bottles
HECTARES UNDER VINE 10.00

The Zangani family's winery is managed by young recruits: Filippo is in charge of production, sales and administration, his brother Michele is involved in finance, and his cousin Rossana oversees marketing and communication. In memory of their grandparents, Gemma and Alberto (who founded the winery in the 1960s), there's a new Vermentino Nero called 'Gemma'. Almost all of the estate's vineyards are now fully operative, significantly increasing the range of wines offered. Brilliant and bright, the Vermentino Boceda '19 offers up lovely notes of pear and citrus on a pleasant iodine background that's even more pronounced on the palate. Pervasive and structured, it unravels harmoniously, without sacrificing more complex nuances. The Mortedo '19 exhibits a similar profile. Here Mediterranean shrub and coastal scents emerge on a minty background while the palate combines richness and character.

○ Colli di Luni Vermentino Sup. Boceda '19	🍷🍷🍷 4*
○ Colli di Luni Vermentino Mortedo '19	🍷🍷 4
○ Colli di Luni Albarola Feletti '19	🍷🍷 3
● Gemma Vermentino Nero '19	🍷🍷 3
● Marfi Rosso '19	🍷🍷 2*
○ Colli di Luni Vermentino Sup. Boceda '18	🍷🍷🍷 4*
○ Boceda '16	🍷🍷 3
○ Colli di Luni Vermentino Mortedo '18	🍷🍷 3*
○ Colli di Luni Vermentino Mortedo '17	🍷🍷 3
○ Colli di Luni Vermentino Sup. Boceda '17	🍷🍷 4
○ Marfi Bianco '18	🍷🍷 2*
○ Marfi Bianco '16	🍷🍷 2*
● Marfi Rosso '18	🍷🍷 2*
○ Mortedo '16	🍷🍷 2*

Michele Alessandri

via Umberto I, 15
18020 Ranzo [IM]
Tel. +39 0183318114
az.alessandricarlo@libero.it

CELLAR SALES
PRE-BOOKED VISITS
ANNUAL PRODUCTION 23,000 bottles
HECTARES UNDER VINE 2.13

● Pornassio '19	🍷🍷 3
○ Riviera Ligure di Ponente Pigato '19	🍷🍷 3
● Pornassio Sciac-Trà '19	🍷 3
○ Riviera Ligure di Ponente Vermentino '19	🍷 2

aMaccia

fraz. Borgo
via Umberto I, 54
18020 Ranzo [IM]
Tel. +39 0183318003
www.amaccia.it

CELLAR SALES
PRE-BOOKED VISITS
ACCOMMODATION
ANNUAL PRODUCTION 25,000 bottles
HECTARES UNDER VINE 3.80
SUSTAINABLE WINERY

○ Riviera Ligure di Ponente Pigato '19	🍷🍷 3
● Ormeasco di Pornassio Sciac-trà '19	🍷 3
○ Riviera Ligure di Ponente Vermentino '19	🍷 3

Berry and Berry

via Matteotti, 2
17020 Balestrino [SV]
Tel. +39 3332805368
www.berryandberry.it

CELLAR SALES
PRE-BOOKED VISITS
ANNUAL PRODUCTION 8,500 bottles
HECTARES UNDER VINE 2.00

○ Campulou '18	🍷🍷 5
○ Baitinin '19	🍷 4
⊙ Lappazucche '19	🍷 4

Cantine Bondonor

via Isola Alta, 53
19034 Luni [SP]
Tel. +39 3488713641
www.cantinebondonor.it

ANNUAL PRODUCTION 15,000 bottles
HECTARES UNDER VINE 3.00

○ Colli di Luni Vermentino Lunaris '19	🍷🍷 3
● Atrum '16	🍷 3
⊙ RosaLuna '19	🍷 3

Andrea Bruzzone

via Bolzaneto, 96r
16162 Genova
Tel. +39 0107455157
www.andreabruzzonevini.it

CELLAR SALES
PRE-BOOKED VISITS
ANNUAL PRODUCTION 10,000 bottles
HECTARES UNDER VINE 2.00
SUSTAINABLE WINERY

○ Val Polcèvera Bianchetta Genovese Bunassa '19	🍷🍷 3*
○ Equinozio '19	🍷🍷 2*
○ Val Polcèvera Coronata La Superba '19	🍷🍷 3

Luca Calvini

via Solaro, 76/78a
18038 Sanremo [IM]
Tel. +39 0184660242
www.luigicalvini.com

CELLAR SALES
PRE-BOOKED VISITS
ANNUAL PRODUCTION 50,000 bottles
HECTARES UNDER VINE 3.50
SUSTAINABLE WINERY

○ Riviera Ligure di Ponente Pigato '19	🍷🍷 3
○ Riviera Ligure di Ponente Vermentino Gold Label '19	🍷🍷 5
○ Riviera Ligure di Ponente Vermentino '19	🍷 3

Cascina Praiè

loc. Colla Micheri
s.da Castello, 20
17051 Andora [SV]
Tel. +39 019602377
www.cascinapraievino.it

CELLAR SALES
PRE-BOOKED VISITS
ANNUAL PRODUCTION 50,000 bottles
HECTARES UNDER VINE 8.50

○ Riviera Ligure di Ponente Vermentino Colla Micheri '19 — 3*
○ Riviera Ligure di Ponente Pigato Il Canneto '19 — 3

I Cerri

via Garibotti
19012 Carro [SP]
Tel. +39 3485102780
www.icerrivaldivara.it

ANNUAL PRODUCTION 8,000 bottles
HECTARES UNDER VINE 1.00

○ Cian dei Seri '19 — 3
● Fonte Dietro il Sole '19 — 3
○ Campo Grande '19 — 3
○ Poggio alle Api '19 — 3

La Colombiera

loc. Montecchio, 92
19030 Castelnuovo Magra [SP]
Tel. +39 0187674265
info@cantinalacolombiera.it

HECTARES UNDER VINE

○ Colli di Luni Vermentino 3 Vigne '19 — 3*
● Colli di Luni Rosso '18 — 4
○ Colli di Luni Vermentino Celsus '18 — 4

Deperi

fraz. Caneto, 2
18020 Ranzo [IM]
Tel. +39 0183318143
www.deperi.eu

PRE-BOOKED VISITS
ANNUAL PRODUCTION 50,000 bottles
HECTARES UNDER VINE 5.00

○ Riviera Ligure di Ponente Pigato '19 — 3
○ Riviera Ligure di Ponente Vermentino Colombera '19 — 3
○ Riviera Ligure di Ponente Vermentino '19 — 3

Durin

via Roma, 202
17037 Ortovero [SV]
Tel. +39 0182547007
www.durin.it

CELLAR SALES
PRE-BOOKED VISITS
ACCOMMODATION
ANNUAL PRODUCTION 150,000 bottles
HECTARES UNDER VINE 17.50
SUSTAINABLE WINERY

○ Riviera Ligure di Ponente Pigato '19 — 3*
● Alicante '18 — 3
○ Riviera Ligure di Ponente Pigato Geva '19 — 3
○ Riviera Ligure di Ponente Vermentino '19 — 3

Gajaudo

loc. Bunda
s.da prov.le 7
18035 Isolabona [IM]
Tel. +39 0184208095
www.gajaudo.it

CELLAR SALES
PRE-BOOKED VISITS
RESTAURANT SERVICE
ANNUAL PRODUCTION 110,000 bottles
HECTARES UNDER VINE 10.00

○ Riviera Ligure di Ponente Vermentino Pejuna '19 — 4
○ Riviera Ligure di Ponente Pigato '19 — 3
○ Riviera Ligure di Ponente Vermentino '19 — 3

Podere Grecale

LOC. BUSSANA
VIA CIOUSSE
18038 SANREMO [IM]
TEL. +39 01841955158
www.poderegrecale.it

ANNUAL PRODUCTION 22,000 bottles
HECTARES UNDER VINE 4.00

- ● Riviera Ligure di Ponente Granaccia Sup. Beusi '18 ΨΨ 4
- ○ Riviera Ligure di Ponente Pigato '19 ΨΨ 3
- ○ Riviera Ligure di Ponente Vermentino '19 Ψ 3

Guglierame

VIA CASTELLO, 4
18024 PORNASSIO [IM]
TEL. +39 3475696718
www.ormeasco-guglierame.it

CELLAR SALES
ANNUAL PRODUCTION 15,000 bottles
HECTARES UNDER VINE 2.50

- ● Ormeasco di Pornassio '18 ΨΨ 4
- ⊙ Ormeasco di Pornassio Sciac-trà '19 Ψ 4
- ● Ormeasco di Pornassio Sup. '17 Ψ 5

Tenuta La Ghiaia

VIA FALCINELLO, 127
19038 SARZANA [SP]
TEL. +39 0187627307
www.tenutalaghiaia.it

CELLAR SALES
ACCOMMODATION
ANNUAL PRODUCTION 45,000 bottles
HECTARES UNDER VINE 5.50

- ○ Colli di Luni Vermentino '19 ΨΨ 3
- ○ Colli di Luni Vermentino Atys '19 ΨΨ 3
- ○ Ithaa '19 Ψ 4

Lupi

VIA MAZZINI, 9
18026 PIEVE DI TECO [IM]
TEL. +39 018336161
www.casalupi.it

CELLAR SALES
PRE-BOOKED VISITS
ANNUAL PRODUCTION 160,000 bottles
HECTARES UNDER VINE 12.00

- ○ Riviera Ligure di Ponente Pigato Petraie '18 ΨΨ 3*
- ○ Riviera Ligure di Ponente Vermentino Serre '18 ΨΨ 3*

Il Monticello

VIA GROPPOLO, 7
19038 SARZANA [SP]
TEL. +39 0187621432
www.ilmonticello.it

CELLAR SALES
PRE-BOOKED VISITS
ACCOMMODATION
ANNUAL PRODUCTION 68,000 bottles
HECTARES UNDER VINE 10.00
VITICULTURE METHOD Certified Biodynamic

- ○ Colli di Luni Vermentino Groppolo '19 ΨΨ 3*
- ○ Colli di Luni Vermentino Poggio Paterno '18 ΨΨ 3
- ○ Passito dei Neri '18 ΨΨ 4

Gino Pino

FRAZ. MISSANO
VIA PODESTÀ, 31
16030 CASTIGLIONE CHIAVARESE [GE]
TEL. +39 0185408036
pinogino.az.agricola@tin.it

ANNUAL PRODUCTION 25,000 bottles
HECTARES UNDER VINE 3.50

- ● Golfo del Tigullio Portofino Ciliegiolo '19 ΨΨ 3
- ○ Golfo del Tigullio Portofino Moscato '19 ΨΨ 3
- ○ Golfo del Tigullio Portofino Bianchetta Genovese '19 Ψ 3

Possa

via San Antonio, 72
19017 Riomaggiore [SP]
Tel. +39 0187920959
www.possa.it

CELLAR SALES
PRE-BOOKED VISITS
ANNUAL PRODUCTION 7,000 bottles
HECTARES UNDER VINE 1.50

- ○ Cinque Terre Sciacchetrà '17 ⚲⚲ 8
- ○ Cinque Terre '19 ⚲ 5
- ● Renfursà '18 ⚲ 8

Edoardo Primo

via Aurelia, 190
19030 Castelnuovo Magra [SP]
Tel. +39 340 6739118
www.edoardoprimo.it

CELLAR SALES
ANNUAL PRODUCTION 30,000 bottles
HECTARES UNDER VINE 7.00

- ○ Colli di Luni Vermentino Cà' Duà '19 ⚲⚲ 3*
- ○ Colli di Luni Vermentino Ma Teo '19 ⚲⚲ 3

Podere Lavandaro

via Castiglione
54035 Fosdinovo [MS]
Tel. +39 018768202
www.poderelavandaro.it

CELLAR SALES
PRE-BOOKED VISITS
ANNUAL PRODUCTION 25,000 bottles
HECTARES UNDER VINE 5.00

- ○ Colli Di Luni Vermentino '19 ⚲⚲ 3*
- ● Vignanera '18 ⚲⚲ 3
- ● Vermentino Nero '19 ⚲ 3

Natale Sassarini

loc. Pian del Corso 1
19016 Monterosso al Mare [SP]
Tel. +39 0187818063
cantinasassarini.com

HECTARES UNDER VINE

- ○ Cinque Terre Bucce '18 ⚲⚲ 3*
- ○ Cinque Terre '19 ⚲ 4
- ○ Cinque Terre Campo al Sole '19 ⚲ 3

Terre di Levanto

loc. San Gottardo, 1

19015 Levanto [SP]
Tel. +39 3395432482
www.terredilevanto.com

CELLAR SALES
PRE-BOOKED VISITS
ANNUAL PRODUCTION 2,500 bottles
HECTARES UNDER VINE 2.50
SUSTAINABLE WINERY

- ● Colline di Levanto Rosso di Mare '18 ⚲⚲ 3
- ● Colline di Levanto Ciliegiolo '18 ⚲ 3
- ● Colline di Levanto Costa de Brassú '18 ⚲ 3

Innocenzo Turco

via Bertone, 7a
17040 Quiliano [SV]
Tel. +39 0192000026
www.innocenzoturco.it

CELLAR SALES
PRE-BOOKED VISITS
ACCOMMODATION AND RESTAURANT SERVICE
ANNUAL PRODUCTION 6,000 bottles
HECTARES UNDER VINE 2.50

- ● Riviera Ligure di Ponente Granaccia Cappuccini '17 ⚲⚲ 5
- ⊙ In Rosa '19 ⚲⚲ 3
- ○ Riviera Ligure di Ponente Pigato '19 ⚲⚲ 3

LOMBARDY

Looking at the numbers, Lombardy is the top region in terms of area dedicated to agriculture, 69% of the territory, with 50 thousand producers working the land. As far as wine is concerned, 22,900 hectares are under vine, with the province of Pavia dominating. Oltrepò Pavese alone produces 65% of the region's wine. The portrait that emerges from our tastings? An extremely positive one, vital even, starting with the number of Tre Bicchieri awarded: 27 (an absolute record). Lombardy once again demonstrates its prowess for bubbly. It is, by far, the Italian region with the most award-winning sparkling wines, all made using the 'Metodo Classico'. Franciacorta took home 10 Tre Bicchieri, demonstrating an increasingly evident solidity; the appellation is doing very well, both in terms of sustainability (it's almost entirely managed organically), and in terms of quality. The use of sugar is increasingly limited, while its cuvées are acquiring greater definition and character, with Pinot Nero making its way into a role occupied historically by Chardonnay. And speaking of the most difficult grape variety in the world, Oltrepò's Pinot Nero Metodo Classicos landed 5 Tre Bicchieri. Among these was a big one: our special Sparkler of the Year award. It went to Ballabio, with their Oltrepò Pavese Pinot Nero Metodo Classico, the Farfalla Cave Privée Dosaggio Zero '11, a cuvée that does an outstanding job expressing the potential of an area with deep historical roots in sparkling wine, and that has finally regained its identity. In the glass there's character, gustatory tension, all the freshness of the Upper Versa Valley, an area where acidity and flavor go hand in hand. The area's other Tre Bicchieri come from the red wine sector, with a fine Pinot Nero, a powerful Buttafuoco Storico and an Oltrepò Pavese Rosso that bears the name of its vineyard, Bruno Verdi's Cavariola. Lugana also put in another characterful performance. It's a terroir that has now reached full maturity, with 3 wines awarded in our guide this year, and many more appreciated all over the world. If we move a few kilometers, to Valtènesi, we find a rosè that's gaining new momentum. Chiaretto, the so-called 'one night wine', can age with extraordinary grace and complexity, as demonstrated by Mattia Vezzola's Molmenti, made with Groppello grapes. Completing the line-up of Tre Bicchieri are 5 gems from Valtellina: Ar.Pe.Pe, Fay, Dirupi, Mamete Prevostini and Nino Negri. Theses producers capture the breath of the Alps in the bottle.

Marchese Adorno

via Garlassolo, 30
27050 Retorbido [PV]
Tel. +39 0383374404
www.marcheseadorno-wines.it

CELLAR SALES
PRE-BOOKED VISITS
ANNUAL PRODUCTION 250,000 bottles
HECTARES UNDER VINE 85.00

Further changes have come at the winery owned by the Adorno family since 1834. Vineyard management is now in the hands of Paolo Fiocchi, while Samuele Paraboschi, the young enologist from Piacenza, oversees winemaking. The estate is large and well-structured, with arable land in the plains and 60 hectares of hillside vineyards that reach up to almost 400 meters above sea level. Rigorous soil mapping of the property's very different terroirs is aimed at obtaining the best results from each grape variety. The Rile Nero '17 easily earned a place in our finals by virtue of an elegant, fragrant nose in which blackberry and blueberry are accompanied by spices and star anise. The palate, which enters on sensations of undergrowth, proves consistent, balanced and integral. Elegant tones also feature in the delicious Riesling Renano Arcolaio '18, a wine characterized by ripe yellow fruits, nice vigour and a hint of minerality. Rich and persistent, the Barbera Vigna del Re '17 features aromas of wild cherry and cocoa.

● OP Pinot Nero Rile Nero '17	🍷🍷 5
● OP Barbera V. del Re '17	🍷🍷 4
○ OP Riesling Arcolaio '18	🍷🍷 3
● Cliviano '18	🍷 3
● OP Barbera Poggio Marino '18	🍷 3
● OP Bonarda Costa del Sole '19	🍷 3
● OP Pinot Nero Brugherio '18	🍷 2
● OP Pinot Nero Rile Nero '15	🍷🍷🍷 5
● OP Barbera V. del Re '16	🍷🍷 4
● OP Barbera V. del Re '15	🍷🍷 4
● OP Pinot Nero Brugherio '17	🍷🍷 2*
● OP Pinot Nero Brugherio '16	🍷🍷 2*
● OP Pinot Nero Brugherio '15	🍷🍷 2*
● OP Pinot Nero Rile Nero '16	🍷🍷 5
○ OP Riesling Arcolaio '17	🍷🍷 3*
○ OP Riesling Arcolaio '16	🍷🍷 3*

F.lli Agnes

via Campo del Monte, 1
27040 Rovescala [PV]
Tel. +39 038575206
www.fratelliagnes.it

CELLAR SALES
PRE-BOOKED VISITS
ANNUAL PRODUCTION 120,000 bottles
HECTARES UNDER VINE 21.00

From Luigi and Alberto to Sergio and Cristiano, theirs is a true legacy of winemaking in the cradle of Bonarda. Good terrain, rigorous grape selection, the choice to use 'Pignola' clones (i.e. Croatina, with smaller and more compact bunches), no compromises in the vineyard and in the cellar: year after year, harvest after harvest, this winery reaffirms its status as a leader for the whole territory when it comes to Bonarda in all its various forms. Our preferences were for the Campo del Monte '19, a Bonarda with slightly overripe fruity tones, owing to the year, with residual sugars that integrate nicely in its notable structure. The Cresta del Ghiffi '19 is just a step behind. As usual it tends to be semi-sweetish, marked by aromas of roses and small fruits. The Loghetto '18 is a well-made still characterized by almonds, soft fruit and sugars.

● OP Bonarda Frizzante Campo del Monte '19	🍷🍷 2*
● Loghetto '18	🍷🍷 5
● OP Bonarda Frizzante Cresta del Ghiffi '19	🍷🍷 2*
● Poculum '15	🍷 4
● Possessione del Console '18	🍷 3
● OP Bonarda Vivace Campo del Monte '15	🍷🍷🍷 2*
● OP Bonarda Frizzante Campo del Monte '18	🍷🍷 2*
● OP Bonarda Frizzante Campo del Monte '17	🍷🍷 2*
● OP Bonarda Vivace Campo del Monte '16	🍷🍷 2*

Antica Fratta

via Fontana, 11
25040 Monticelli Brusati [BS]
Tel. +39 030652068
www.anticafratta.it

CELLAR SALES
PRE-BOOKED VISITS
ANNUAL PRODUCTION 350,000 bottles
HECTARES UNDER VINE 35.00

Even if this winery is part of the Guido Berlucchi Group, it has total autonomy when it comes to vineyard management and wine production. It's headquartered in a restored 19th-century building now used as a venue for events and receptions of all kinds. Once the property of a rich wine merchant, one of its peculiar features are the beautiful vaulted cellars, which are laid out in the shape of a Greek cross. The level of their Franciacorta, which ages in the "Cantinon" (the name by which the building is known locally) is always very high. The Essence Nature '15 perfectly represents Fratta's style: it's a crisp, sapid, spirited and harmonious Franciacorta, soft in its fruit and delicate in its sparkle, a quality it shares with the Essence Noir Extra Brut '15 with its beautiful copper highlights and hints of peach and red berries. But the entire range shines for its cleanness and elegance.

○ Franciacorta Nature Essence '15	🍷🍷 5
○ Franciacorta Brut Cuvée Real	🍷🍷 4
○ Franciacorta Brut Essence '15	🍷🍷 5
○ Franciacorta Brut Essence Rosé '15	🍷🍷 6
○ Franciacorta Extra Brut Essence Noir '15	🍷🍷 6
○ Franciacorta Satèn Essence	🍷 5
○ Franciacorta Brut Essence '14	🍷🍷 5
○ Franciacorta Brut Essence '13	🍷🍷 5
○ Franciacorta Essence Noir '14	🍷🍷 6
○ Franciacorta Nature Essence '14	🍷🍷 5
○ Franciacorta Nature Essence '13	🍷🍷 5
○ Franciacorta Nature Essence '11	🍷🍷 5
⊙ Franciacorta Rosé Essence '14	🍷🍷 5
○ Franciacorta Rosé Essence '11	🍷🍷 5
○ Franciacorta Satèn Essence '11	🍷🍷 5
○ Franciacorta Satèn Essence '11	🍷🍷 5

Antinori - Tenuta Montenisa

fraz. Calino
via Paolo VI, 62
25046 Cazzago San Martino [BS]
Tel. +39 0307750838
www.tenutamontenisa.it

CELLAR SALES
ANNUAL PRODUCTION 300,000 bottles
HECTARES UNDER VINE 60.00

More than 20 years have passed since the Antinori family decided to establish a presence in Franciacorta as well, acquiring the estate owned by the Conti Maggi family. The rebirth of Montenisa began in 1999, with the renovation of the historic manor house and vineyards. Production has grown over time, and currently their range includes two lines: the basic Franciacorta and their reserves, which are produced only in the most favorable vintages. The Satèn Donna Cora '15 is among the best of this classic Franciacorta typology: it has a bead of remarkable finesse, lovely notes of ripe white fruit on the nose as well as on the palate, where it proves sapid, fresh and long. The Rosé is lean, fresh and vital, while we appreciated the Cuvée Royale for its cleanness and elegant mineral, citrus vein.

○ Franciacorta Satèn Donna Cora '15	🍷🍷 6
○ Franciacorta Brut Cuvée Royale	🍷🍷 5
⊙ Franciacorta Brut Rosé	🍷🍷 5
○ Franciacorta Brut Blanc de Blancs	🍷 5
○ Franciacorta Brut Conte Aimo '07	🍷🍷 8
○ Franciacorta Brut Conte Aimo Ris. '09	🍷🍷 8
○ Franciacorta Brut Contessa Maggi '11	🍷🍷 7
○ Franciacorta Brut Contessa Maggi '06	🍷🍷 7
○ Franciacorta Brut Contessa Maggi Ris. '07	🍷🍷 7
○ Franciacorta Brut Satèn Donna Cora '11	🍷🍷 6

Ar.Pe.Pe

via del Buon Consiglio, 4
23100 Sondrio
Tel. +39 0342214120
www.arpepe.com

CELLAR SALES
PRE-BOOKED VISITS
ANNUAL PRODUCTION 100,000 bottles
HECTARES UNDER VINE 13.00

The Pelizzati Perego family, four generations of vintners, express all the character and charm of Valtellina in their wines. The decision to put their products to market only after a long stay in the bottle certainly paid off, and today their range is increasingly multifaceted and solid, while keeping faith with a style that plays on intense yet fresh and airy sensations, rich in acidity, and complex, spicy nuances. The Riserva Nuova Regina '13 is a wine of great class. It has a crystalline clarity, with aromas of dried herbs and sweet spices mixed with fresh red fruit. The palate is notable, fine, with nice pulp that harmonizes its long finish. The excellent and complex Riserva Buon Consiglio '13 features notes of cinchona, licorice, pepper and tar. The palate is harmonious, with balanced fruit, dense tannins and a long finish. The Riserva Ultimi Raggi '13 proves vital, with notes of strawberry jam, spices and herbs. In the mouth it's characterful and impressive, elegant, with a very long finish.

● Valtellina Sup. Sassella Nuova Regina Ris. '13	🍷🍷🍷 8
● Valtellina Sup. Grumello Buon Consiglio Ris. '13	🍷🍷 8
● Valtellina Sup. Sassella Ultimi Raggi Ris. '13	🍷🍷 8
● Rosso di Valtellina '18	🍷🍷 4
● Valtellina Sup. Il Pettirosso '17	🍷🍷 5
● Valtellina Sup. Inferno Sesto Canto Ris. '13	🍷🍷 8
● Valtellina Sup. Sassella V. Regina Ris. '09	🍷🍷🍷 8
● Valtellina Sup. Grumello Rocca De Piro '15	🍷🍷 5
● Valtellina Sup. Sassella Rocce Rosse Ris. '09	🍷🍷 7
● Valtellina Sup. Sassella Stella Retica '15	🍷🍷 5

Ballabio

via San Biagio, 32
27045 Casteggio [PV]
Tel. +39 0383805878
www.ballabiowinery.it

PRE-BOOKED VISITS
ANNUAL PRODUCTION 100,000 bottles
HECTARES UNDER VINE 60.00
SUSTAINABLE WINERY

More than a hundred years have passed since Angelo Ballabio founded what has been for some time a benchmark winery for the whole of Oltrepò Pavese, in part because of a conviction that the area's quality Pinot Nero could be used to make Metodo Classico rather than being sold in Piedmont. And so, after much work, the producer has relaunched, taking advantage of a cutting-edge cellar and rigorous protocols to make sparkling wines that are increasingly linear in style and convincing in their interpretation of Pinot Nero. This year Ballabio's range is enriched with a new gem: the Dosaggio Zero '11, a sparkling wine of extraordinary purity, balance and clarity, the pure strength of Pinot Noir tamed in a bottle. It's powerful and elegant at the same time, with very fine bubbles and an endless finish. It's our Sparkler of the Year. As usual the rest of their wines performed at high levels, with a special mention for the excellent Rosé.

○ OP Pinot Nero Dosaggio Zero Farfalla Cave Privée '11	🍷🍷🍷 7
○ Farfalla Extra Brut M. Cl.	🍷🍷 5
⊙ Farfalla Extra Brut M. Cl. Rosé	🍷🍷 4
○ Farfalla Zero Dosage M. Cl.	🍷🍷 5
● OP Bonarda V. delle Cento Pertiche '15	🍷🍷 3
● OP Bonarda V. delle Cento Pertiche '13	🍷🍷 3
● OP Bonarda V. delle Cento Pertiche '11	🍷🍷 2*
○ OP Pinot Grigio Clastidium '15	🍷🍷 3
○ Pinot Grigio Clastidium '16	🍷🍷 2*

I Barisei

via Bellavista, 1a
25030 Erbusco [BS]
Tel. +39 0307356069
www.ibarisei.it

CELLAR SALES
PRE-BOOKED VISITS
ACCOMMODATION
ANNUAL PRODUCTION 90,000 bottles
HECTARES UNDER VINE 40.00

The Bariselli family have been cultivating land and producing wine in Franciacorta since 1898. In the 1970s red grapes were accompanied by Chardonnay, planted so as to meet the needs of producers operating in the nascent Franciacorta production zone. In 1993 Gian Mario Bariselli decided to start producing on his own with the small brand Solive. It was an immediate success. In 2002 the new cellar was built in Erbusco, and since 2006 the bottles have been sold under the brand I Barisèi. They only use grapes from their privately-owned 40 hectares, situated in some of the appellation's best positions. The Brut Sempiterre is exemplary of I Barisèi's style: it pours a brilliant straw yellow, exhibiting very fine beading and creamy mousse; it opens elegant and caressing on the palate, coming through sapid and clean in its notes of peach and Amalfi lemon. The Extra Brut Mariadri '12 is just as well-crafted: captivating in its pastry notes and vanilla, it proves deep, multifaceted, vital and full on the palate.

○ Franciacorta Brut Sempiterre	🍷🍷	6
○ Franciacorta Extra Brut Mariadri '12	🍷🍷	5
○ Franciacorta Natura '14	🍷	6
○ Franciacorta Natura '13	☐☐	6
⊙ Franciacorta Rosé '13	☐☐	6
○ Franciacorta Satèn '14	☐☐	6

Barone Pizzini

via San Carlo, 14
25050 Provaglio d'Iseo [BS]
Tel. +39 0309848311
www.baronepizzini.it

CELLAR SALES
PRE-BOOKED VISITS
ACCOMMODATION
ANNUAL PRODUCTION 290,000 bottles
HECTARES UNDER VINE 55.00
VITICULTURE METHOD Certified Organic
SUSTAINABLE WINERY

Silvano Brescianini is bursting with energy. It was he who created this lovely producer situated just a stone's throw from Lake Iseo, in western Franciacorta, but he's also the president of the Franciacorta Consortium, where he's supported by the commitment of the consortium's other members (and not only in economic terms). Over the years Silvano has led Barone Pizzini to become a touchstone in terms of environmental sustainability, organic and biodynamic cultivation, all the while producing first-rate wines. With the Dosaggio Zero Naturae '16 the maison takes home yet another Tre Bicchieri, affirming their perfectly-calibrated approach, splendid vineyards and a cellar that's at the cutting edge, as well as sustainable. You'll be impressed by its lean but authoritative profile, the cleanness of its fruit and a subtle, minty stroke that makes it irresistible. But the whole range performs at high levels.

○ Franciacorta Dosage Zéro Naturae '16	🍷🍷🍷	5
○ Franciacorta Dosaggio Zero Animante LA	🍷🍷	5
○ Franciacorta Extra Brut Animante	🍷🍷	5
⊙ Franciacorta Extra Brut Rosé Edizione '16	🍷🍷	5
● San Carlo '17	🍷🍷	5
○ Tesi 2 Extra Brut M. Cl.	🍷🍷	5
○ Curtefranca Bianco Polzina '19	🍷	3
○ Franciacorta Brut Golf 1927	🍷	5
○ Franciacorta Brut Satèn Edizione '16	🍷	5
○ Franciacorta Brut Naturae '13	☐☐☐	5
○ Franciacorta Brut Naturae '11	☐☐☐	5
○ Franciacorta Brut Nature '10	☐☐☐	5
○ Franciacorta Dosaggio Zero Bagnadore Ris. '11	☐☐☐	7

★★★Bellavista

via Bellavista, 5
25030 Erbusco [BS]
Tel. +39 0307762000
www.bellavistawine.it

CELLAR SALES
PRE-BOOKED VISITS
ANNUAL PRODUCTION 1,400,000 bottles
HECTARES UNDER VINE 190.00
SUSTAINABLE WINERY

The group led by Vittorio Moretti is a true powerhouse of wine, both in Italy and beyond. Bellavista is the flagship of a group that comprises six wineries in Franciacorta, Tuscany and Sardinia. The constant work of the family team calls for continuous improvements and momentum towards the future, with the creation of new wines and prestigious acquisitions such as the Santissima Annunciata, the beautiful convent situated atop Mount Orfano, with its vineyards and adjacent wine cellar (currently under renovation). It was hard to choose between the soft and elegant complexity of the Pas Operé '14 and the fresh, citrusy pluck of the Alma Non Dosato, but in the end the latter prevailed with its beautiful fruity vein and touch of mandarin peel. Tre Bicchieri. We shouldn't forget the Riserva Vittorio Moretti '13, a Franciacorta of rare depth and harmony. But the whole range is excellent.

Wine	Rating
○ Franciacorta Non Dosato Grande Cuvée Alma	▼▼▼ 6
○ Franciacorta Extra Brut Vittorio Moretti Ris. '13	▼▼ 8
○ Franciacorta Pas Operé '14	▼▼ 8
○ Franciacorta Brut Teatro alla Scala '15	▼▼ 7
○ Franciacorta Brut Teatro alla Scala '13	▽▽▽ 7
○ Franciacorta Extra Brut Vittorio Moretti Ris. '08	▽▽▽ 8
○ Franciacorta Extra Brut Vittorio Moretti Ris. '06	▽▽▽ 8
○ Franciacorta Gran Cuvée Pas Operé '06	▽▽▽ 8
○ Franciacorta Pas Operé '10	▽▽▽ 7
○ Franciacorta Pas Operé '09	▽▽▽ 7

F.lli Berlucchi

fraz. Borgonato
via Broletto, 2
25040 Corte Franca [BS]
Tel. +39 030984451
www.fratelliberlucchi.it

CELLAR SALES
PRE-BOOKED VISITS
ANNUAL PRODUCTION 380,000 bottles
HECTARES UNDER VINE 70.00

The 16th-century Casa delle Colonne is the demesne where Pia Donata Berlucchi and her daughter Tilli Rizzo produce Franciacorta of style and personality, drawing on 70 hectares of property. The splendid vaulted frescoed cellars are notable, as is their Franciacorta. It's divided into two lines: Freccianera (single-vintages) and Casa delle Colonne (reserves). For over 2 decades the producer has adopted a low-impact cultivation approach. Their Riserva Casa delle colonne are always top-notch, as is demonstrated by the Brut '13, a wine characterized by a lovely, bright straw-yellow color tinted green, very fine bead and a complex nose. It's at once fresh and complex in its hints of yeast but also citrus and white fruit. The Freccianera Rosa '16 is delicious in its aromas of small red berries, while the clear, focused and racy Freccianera Nature '16 also delivered.

Wine	Rating
○ Franciacorta Brut Casa delle Colonne Ris. '13	▼▼ 8
○ Franciacorta Brut Freccianera '15	▼▼ 6
○ Franciacorta Nature Freccianera '16	▼▼ 7
⊙ Franciacorta Rosé Freccianera Rosa '16	▼▼ 6
○ Franciacorta Satèn '16	▼▼ 7
○ Curtefranca Bianco Ca' Brusade '19	▼ 3
○ Franciacorta Brut 25	▼ 6
○ Franciacorta Brut Casa delle Colonne Ris. '12	▽▽ 8
○ Franciacorta Brut Freccianera '14	▽▽ 6
○ Franciacorta Casa delle Colonne Zero Ris. '12	▽▽ 8
○ Franciacorta Nature Freccianera '15	▽▽ 7
⊙ Franciacorta Rosé Freccianera '15	▽▽ 6
⊙ Franciacorta Rosé Freccianera Rosa '14	▽▽ 6
○ Franciacorta Satèn '15	▽▽ 7

★Guido Berlucchi & C.

Loc. Borgonato
P.zza Duranti, 4
25040 Corte Franca [BS]
Tel. +39 030984381
www.berlucchi.it

CELLAR SALES
PRE-BOOKED VISITS
ACCOMMODATION
ANNUAL PRODUCTION 4,400,000 bottles
HECTARES UNDER VINE 115.00
VITICULTURE METHOD Certified Organic
SUSTAINABLE WINERY

Franco Ziliani and Guido Berlucchi, a partnership that began more than 60 years ago, changed the destiny of Italian enology. In fact it was they who invented Franciacorta in that magical year 1961, which is now commemorated on the bottles of an entire range of wines. Berlucchi went on to became an internationally renowned brand, and for the past 10 years Arturo, Franco's son, an enologist and president of the group, has practically refounded the business, thanks in part to the fundamental contribution of his sister Cristina and brother Paolo. If Guido Berlucchi's entire range is outstanding, and without weak points, it's also true that in those vintages when they release selections from their Palazzo Lana line, plenty of thrills are assured. So here we are with the Riserva Extrême '09, a monovarietal Pinot Noir that, after more than 9 years of maturation on the lees, proves to be in dazzling form, complex, elegant, fresh and deep as never before. It's beautifully accompanied by the Brut 61 and the 61 Blanc de Blancs Nature '13.

Wine	Glasses	Score
○ Franciacorta Extra Brut Extreme Palazzo Lana Ris. '09	▼▼▼	8
○ Franciacorta Brut 61	▼▼	5
○ Franciacorta Nature Blanc de Blancs 61 '13	▼▼	8
○ Franciacorta Nature 61 '13	▼▼	8
⊙ Franciacorta Nature Rosé 61 '13	▼▼	8
⊙ Franciacorta Rosé 61	▼	5
○ Franciacorta Satèn 61	▼	5
○ Franciacorta Nature 61 '10	▽▽▽	7
○ Franciacorta Extra Brut Extreme Palazzo Lana Ris. '07	▽▽▽	7
○ Franciacorta Nature 61 '12	▽▽▽	7
○ Franciacorta Nature 61 '11	▽▽▽	7
○ Franciacorta Nature 61 '09	▽▽▽	5
○ Franciacorta Satèn Palazzo Lana '06	▽▽▽	6

Cantina Bersi Serlini

via Cereto, 7
25050 Provaglio d'Iseo [BS]
Tel. +39 0309823338
www.bersiserlini.it

CELLAR SALES
PRE-BOOKED VISITS
ACCOMMODATION AND RESTAURANT SERVICE
ANNUAL PRODUCTION 200,000 bottles
HECTARES UNDER VINE 30.00
VITICULTURE METHOD Certified Organic

The estate's origins date back to the Middle Ages, when the Cluniac monks of the Abbey of San Pietro in Lamosa built a grange to make wine and preserve the monks' various agricultural products. The estate has been owned by the Bersi Serlini family since 1886, and its subsequent expansion and renovation have led to it becoming an important producer in Franciacorta. Maddalena and Chiara Bersi Serlini continue the family tradition with enthusiasm. The Satèn di Maddalena e Chiara is one of the most interesting wines tasted this year in Franciacorta. It pours a beautiful, bright straw-yellow tinted green, with minute, well-sustained beading. On the nose it opens with vibrant notes of white fruit, vanilla and acacia honey, coming through creamy-sapid, soft and lingering on the palate. The Blanc de Blancs Anniversario is also outstanding. Proposed only in magnum, it's a soft and leisurely wine characterized by elegant hints of peach.

Wine	Glasses	Score
○ Franciacorta Brut Anniversario	▼▼	5
○ Franciacorta Brut Satèn	▼▼	5
○ Franciacorta Brut Cuvée n. 4 '16	▼▼	6
○ Franciacorta Demi Sec Nuvola	▼▼	4
○ Franciacorta Brut Anteprima	▼	5
⊙ Franciacorta Brut Rosé Rosa Rosae '14	▼	5
○ Franciacorta Brut '11	▽▽	5
○ Franciacorta Brut Cuvée n. 4 '15	▽▽	6
○ Franciacorta Brut Cuvée n. 4 '13	▽▽	6
○ Franciacorta Brut Cuvée n. 4 '12	▽▽	5
○ Franciacorta Brut Cuvée n. 4 '10	▽▽	5
○ Franciacorta Extra Brut '15	▽▽	6
○ Franciacorta Extra Brut '14	▽▽	6
○ Franciacorta Extra Brut '13	▽▽	6
○ Franciacorta Extra Brut '12	▽▽	6
○ Franciacorta Extra Brut '11	▽▽	6
○ Franciacorta Extra Brut '10	▽▽	6

Bertè & Cordini Francesco Montagna

via Cairoli, 67
27043 Broni [PV]
Tel. +39 038551028
www.bertecordini.it

CELLAR SALES
PRE-BOOKED VISITS
ACCOMMODATION
ANNUAL PRODUCTION 700,000 bottles
HECTARES UNDER VINE 18.00

This time-honored winery (its foundation dates back to 1895) has been owned for over forty years by the Bertè and Cordini families, who have kept its original name. It's changed and evolved with the passing of time, first under the guidance of Natale Bertè, who was able to bring it to its current levels. Now it's his son Matteo and grandson Luca (both enologists), with the support of the latter's sister, Marzia, who are overseeing production. Their range is large and diverse, with certain peaks of excellence, especially when it comes to Metodo Classico. The very well-made Cuvée Tradizione '16 is redolent of mint, grapefruit and mandarin. It's a spirited wine with fine sparkle. The Cuvée della Casa features more mature, evolved sensations well supported by acidity. Very well-typed and clean in its aromas of berries with streaks of aromatic herbs, the Pinot Noir '18 closes on a pleasant almondy note. Plenty of citrus for the pleasant, simple, supple Cruasé.

○ OP Brut M. Cl. Cuvée Tradizione '16	🍷🍷 5
● OP Pinot Nero '18	🍷🍷 3
○ OP Pinot Nero Brut M. Cl. Cuvée della Casa	🍷🍷 5
⊙ OP Cruasé	🍷 5
○ OP Pinot Nero Brut M. Cl. Cuvée Nero d'Oro	🍷 5
○ OP Sauvignon Masaria '18	🍷 2
○ OP Brut M. Cl. Cuvée Tradizione '15	🍷🍷 5
○ OP Brut M. Cl. Cuvée Tradizione '14	🍷🍷 5
○ OP Pinot Nero Dosage Zéro M. Cl. Oblio '10	🍷🍷 7
○ OP Sauvignon Masaria '17	🍷🍷 2*
○ OP Pinot Nero Brut M. Cl. Cuvée Tradizione '13	🍷 5

F.lli Bettini

loc. San Giacomo
via Nazionale, 4a
23036 Teglio [SO]
Tel. +39 0342786068
www.vinibettini.it

CELLAR SALES
PRE-BOOKED VISITS
ANNUAL PRODUCTION 200,000 bottles
HECTARES UNDER VINE 15.00

Once again this solid wine producer in Teglio earned a place in our main section, bolstered by over 130 years of deep-rooted tradition in wine. Their range highlights the peculiarities of a unique territory, one capable of a fragrant, alpine character that is, at the same time, marked by an enviable power and aromatic richness. Their style calls for rich, mature wines, with their premium selections aged carefully in small oak barrels. Dense and spicy, these are capable of long aging in bottle, where they find rhythm and balance. Pietro Bettini's skill in making delicious Sforzato is a sure bet. The Sfursat '15 is a perfect example, offering up exotic notes of tamarind and coffee cream. The palate is austere and complex, with a soft and prolonged finish. Intense and elegant, the Valgella Vigna La Cornella '16 features nuances of ripe fruit and spices. The palate is firm and juicy, the finish long.

● Sforzato di Valtellina '15	🍷🍷 6
● Valtellina Sup. Ris. Sant'Andrea '15	🍷🍷 5
● Valtellina Sup. Valgella V. La Cornella '16	🍷🍷 5
● Valtellina Sup. Sassella Reale '16	🍷 5
● Sforzato di Valtellina '13	🍷🍷 6
● Sforzato di Valtellina Fruttaio di Spina '13	🍷🍷 7
● Valtellina Sup. Inferno Prodigio '15	🍷🍷 5
● Valtellina Sup. La Botte Ventitrè Ris. '09	🍷🍷 3
● Valtellina Sup. Sassella Reale '15	🍷🍷 5

Bisi

LOC. CASCINA SAN MICHELE
FRAZ. VILLA MARONE, 70
27040 SAN DAMIANO AL COLLE [PV]
TEL. +39 038575037
www.aziendagricolabisi.it

CELLAR SALES
PRE-BOOKED VISITS
ANNUAL PRODUCTION 90,000 bottles
HECTARES UNDER VINE 30.00

We have never hidden our admiration for Claudio Bisi, a 'true' vigneron in every sense. A man of few words and clear ideas, he maniacally looks after every detail both in the vineyard and in the cellar. A pioneer of the so-called green harvest and low yields, for years he's been called crazy by the area's older population in a part of Italy where most grapes were (and still are) sold by the quintal. Claudio's wines are polished and complex, to drink and enjoy over the long-term. Dense, powerful, redolent of black fruits, tobacco and spices, the Barbera Roncolongo '17 is Claudio Bisi's calling card, a wine to be uncorked even in twenty years. The notable Calonga '17 is a vibrant, deep Pinot Noir marked by hints of small berries. Some big pieces are missing, like the Barbera Senz'Aiuto and the Ultrapadum, which aren't yet ready, but the whole range is, as usual, outstanding.

Wine	Rating	Price
● Calonga Pinot Nero '17	🍷🍷	5
● Roncolongo Barbera '17	🍷🍷	5
● OP Bonarda Vivace La Peccatrice '19	🍷🍷	2*
● Pezzabianca Barbera '18	🍷🍷	3
● Pramattone Croatina '18	🍷🍷	2*
● Calonga Pinot Nero '16	🍷🍷 (white)	5
● Calonga Pinot Nero '15	🍷🍷 (white)	5
● OP Bonarda Vivace La Peccatrice '18	🍷🍷 (white)	2*
● OP Bonarda Vivace La Peccatrice '17	🍷🍷 (white)	2*
● OP Pinot Nero Calonga '13	🍷🍷 (white)	3
● Pezzabianca Barbera '17	🍷🍷 (white)	3
● Pezzabianca Barbera '15	🍷🍷 (white)	3
● Roncolongo Barbera '16	🍷🍷 (white)	5
● Roncolongo Barbera '15	🍷🍷 (white)	5
● Roncolongo Barbera '14	🍷🍷 (white)	5
● Roncolongo Barbera '12	🍷🍷 (white)	3

La Boscaiola Vigneti Cenci

VIA RICCAFANA
25033 COLOGNE [BS]
TEL. +39 0307156386
www.vigneticenci.com

CELLAR SALES
PRE-BOOKED VISITS
ANNUAL PRODUCTION 50,000 bottles
HECTARES UNDER VINE 6.00

Giuliana Cenci and her son Maurizio are carrying forward their work at La Boscaiola, the beautiful winery in Cologne born out of Nelson Cenci's passion for the territory, its people and its wine. In the 1970s Nelson, a doctor (but foremost a mountaineer and writer), began planting vines on his estate, which gradually grew thanks in part to the valuable support of Giuliana and excellent professionals. The Franciacorta Brut Sessanta '09 landed the maison a place in our finals. It pours a lovely, bright straw-yellow, with creamy mousse and fine beading. On the nose it opens with fruit, flowers and citrus, all of which dissolve on toasty notes and vanilla. On the palate it's sapid, rich and deep, elegantly combing complexity and approachability. The Extra Brut boasts a beautiful, fresh mineral vein, while the Brut La Capinera goes all in on the freshness of fruit and citrus.

Wine	Rating	Price
○ Franciacorta Brut Sessanta '09	🍷🍷	6
○ Franciacorta Brut La Capinera	🍷🍷	5
○ Franciacorta Extra Brut Nelson Cenci	🍷🍷	6
⊙ Franciacorta Rosé La Capinera	🍷🍷	5
● Ritorno	🍷🍷	4
○ Franciacorta Pas Dosé Zero	🍷	5
○ Franciacorta Satèn La Via della Seta	🍷	5
○ Franciacorta Brut Nelson Cenci L'Insolita '11	🍷🍷 (white)	6
○ Franciacorta Brut Sessanta '10	🍷🍷 (white)	6

Bosio

FRAZ. TIMOLINE
VIA M. GATTI, 4
25040 CORTE FRANCA [BS]
TEL. +39 0309826224
www.bosiofranciacorta.it

CELLAR SALES
PRE-BOOKED VISITS
ANNUAL PRODUCTION 120,000 bottles
HECTARES UNDER VINE 20.00
VITICULTURE METHOD Certified Organic
SUSTAINABLE WINERY

The brother and sister team of Cesare and Laura Bosio are the beating heart of this modern Franciacorta producer. Born out of a small family-owned farm, today it's an important touchstone in the territory, thanks to Cesare's agronomic qualities and Laura's innate entrepreneurial skills. The property has expanded to 30 hectares, and gives rise to a wide range of Franciacorta and local still wines. The Extra Brut Boschedòr '15 easily earned a place in our final tastings thanks to an elegant complexity that manages to emerge on the nose as well as on the palate. Sensations of polyflora honey and spices don't come at the expense of a lively freshness, all accentuated by notes of white fruit and citrus. It's beautiful and long in its fruity finish. We also appreciated the sapid, creamy, clear and citrusy Nature '15.

○ Franciacorta Extra Brut Boschedòr '15	🍷🍷 6
○ Franciacorta Brut	🍷🍷 5
○ Franciacorta Nature '15	🍷🍷 6
⊙ Franciacorta Pas Dosé Rosé Girolamo Bosio Ris. '13	🍷🍷 8
⊙ Franciacorta Rosé Extra Brut '16	🍷🍷 6
○ Franciacorta Satèn	🍷 5
○ Franciacorta Pas Dosé Girolamo Bosio Ris. '09	🍷🍷🍷 5
○ Franciacorta Extra Brut Boschedòr '13	🍷🍷 6
⊙ Franciacorta Extra Brut Rosé '14	🍷🍷 5
○ Franciacorta Pas Dosè Girolamo Bosio Ris. '12	🍷🍷 8
⊙ Franciacorta Pas Dosè Rosè Girolamo Bosio Ris. '11	🍷🍷 8
⊙ Franciacorta Rosé Extra Brut '15	🍷🍷 5

Alessio Brandolini

FRAZ. BOFFALORA, 68
27040 SAN DAMIANO AL COLLE [PV]
TEL. +39 038575232
www.alessiobrandolini.com

CELLAR SALES
PRE-BOOKED VISITS
ANNUAL PRODUCTION 70,000 bottles
HECTARES UNDER VINE 11.00
SUSTAINABLE WINERY

For some years now Alessio Brandolini has been managing the family producer, aiming to make the most of each individual vineyard by planting the most suitable grapes. In the meantime, he's expanded the winery by creating a beautiful tasting room with a view of the vineyards. The area's traditional grapes are cultivated, from Croatina to Barbera, Pinot Nero and Malvasia—this last has always been present in the eastern part of Oltrepò Pavese due to its proximity to Piacenza. There's also a small selection of sparkling wines from which we expect outstanding results. Their new Pinot Noir sparkler, the I Ger '14, captivates for its almost coppery colour, slightly oxidative style, backbone and fleshiness, and long finish. The delicious Barbera Il Pozzo '18 is fruity and compact with notes of currant, liquorice and mint—an energetic, supple wine. Another piece of news is the Il Costante '17, a bottle-fermented Croatina with personality. There's nothing banal about the battery of wines presented by Alessio Brandolini.

○ I Ger Pas Dosé M. Cl. '14	🍷🍷 5
● Il Pozzo Barbera '18	🍷🍷 3*
● Il Beneficio '16	🍷🍷 4
● Il Costante Croatina FB '17	🍷🍷 3
⊙ Note d'Agosto Extra Brut M. Cl. Rosé '16	🍷🍷 5
● Al Negres Pinot Nero '18	🍷 4
○ Il Bardughino Malvasia '19	🍷 2
● Il Soffio Croatina '19	🍷 2
○ Luogo d'Agosto Pas Dosé M. Cl. '16	🍷 5
● OP Bonarda Frizzante Il Cassino '19	🍷 2
⊙ Brut M. Cl. Rosé Note d'Agosto '13	🍷🍷 5
○ Il Bardughino '16	🍷🍷 2*
○ Il Bardughino Malvasia '18	🍷🍷 2*
● Il Beneficio '15	🍷🍷 4
● Il Beneficio '14	🍷🍷 4
● Il Beneficio '13	🍷🍷 4
● Il Soffio Croatina '18	🍷🍷 2*

★Cà Maiol

via Colli Storici, 119
25015 Desenzano del Garda [BS]
Tel. +39 0309910006
www.camaiol.it

CELLAR SALES
PRE-BOOKED VISITS
ACCOMMODATION
ANNUAL PRODUCTION 940,000 bottles
HECTARES UNDER VINE 112.00
SUSTAINABLE WINERY

Ca' Majol was founded in 1967 by Milano's Walter Contato, a lover of this territory south of Lake Garda. In 1996 the winery passed to his sons, while a few years ago it became part of the Santa Margherita group, which allowed for a further boost in terms of quality and sales. 110 hectares of vineyards divided into various estates, an 18th-century central property and modern underground cellars make this producer a benchmark for the area. An excellent performance for Ca' Majol, with the Lugana Riserva '18 standing out in our tastings for its elegance, depth and pleasantness. It pours a bright, straw-yellow, the prelude to a complex nose in which fruit combines with oak and incense. In the mouth it's rich, dense and sapid by virtue of a lovely acidity. Crisp and taut, the Prestige '19 is marked by creamy, white fruit sensations, while the Valtènesi Fabio Contato '16 exhibits nice structure, elegant tannins and length.

○ Lugana Fabio Contato Ris. '18	🍷🍷🍷 6
○ Lugana Prestige '19	🍷🍷 4
○ Lugana Molin '19	🍷🍷 5
● Valtènesi Riviera del Garda Cl. Rosso Fabio Contato '16	🍷🍷 5
⊙ Valtènesi Riviera del Garda Cl. Chiaretto Roseri '19	🍷 4
○ Lugana Molin '16	🍷🍷🍷 3*
○ Lugana Sel. Fabio Contato '16	🍷🍷🍷 5
○ Lugana Molin '18	🍷🍷 3*
○ Lugana Molin '17	🍷🍷 3*
○ Lugana Sel. Fabio Contato Ris. '17	🍷🍷 5
○ Lugana Sup. Sel. Fabio Contato '15	🍷🍷 5

Cà Tessitori

via Matteotti, 15
27043 Broni [PV]
Tel. +39 038551495
www.catessitori.it

CELLAR SALES
PRE-BOOKED VISITS
ANNUAL PRODUCTION 120,000 bottles
HECTARES UNDER VINE 40.00

With founder Luigi steadily at the helm and his sons Giovanni and Francesco acting as indispensable supports, this winery has been able to carve out a respectable place for itself in the region's wine firmament. The gradual abandonment of oak and a return to concrete tanks has led to the creation of wines with remarkable personality, very much linked to the soil (divided into two large plots distinct from each other) and the vintages. In recent years, Metodo Classico has become increasingly important, and seems to have found the right direction after some stylistic adjustments. Both versions of the Metodo Classico Pas Dosé deliver. The M.V. '16 is more complex, deep, variegated and long at the finish, while the LB9 is more powerful, immediate, juicy and mineral. Two different but very interesting Pinot Noir sparklers. One of the best of the vintage, the Bonarda Frizzante Sempà '19 is full, vivid, creamy in its deep red fruit.

○ OP Pinot Nero Dosaggio Zero M. Cl. M.V. '16	🍷🍷 5
● Borghesa Rosso '19	🍷🍷 3
● Oltremodo '18	🍷🍷 3
● OP Bonarda Frizzante Sempà '19	🍷🍷 2*
○ OP Pinot Nero Dosaggio Zero M. Cl. LB9	🍷🍷 5
○ Agòlo '19	🍷 2
○ Agòlo '18	🍷🍷 2*
○ Agòlo '17	🍷🍷 2*
● Borghesa Rosso '17	🍷🍷 3
● Marona Barbera '15	🍷🍷 4
● Oltremodo '17	🍷🍷 3*
● OP Bonarda Frizzante '18	🍷🍷 2*
● OP Bonarda Vivace '16	🍷🍷 2*
○ OP Pinot Nero Brut M. V. '12	🍷🍷 4
○ OP Pinot Nero M. Cl. Dosaggio Zero LB9 '14	🍷🍷 5

★★★★Ca' del Bosco

via Albano Zanella, 13
25030 Erbusco [BS]
Tel. +39 0307766111
www.cadelbosco.com

CELLAR SALES
PRE-BOOKED VISITS
ACCOMMODATION
ANNUAL PRODUCTION 1,800,000 bottles
HECTARES UNDER VINE 245.40
VITICULTURE METHOD Certified Organic
SUSTAINABLE WINERY

Maurizio Zanella transformed what was once the summer holiday home of his mother, Annamaria Clementi, into one of the most important, modern and innovative wineries in Italy. The turning point came with acquisition by the colossus Santa Margherita, leading to an infusion of fresh capital that allowed the explosive Maurizio and his indispensable enologist Stefano Capelli to achieve extraordinary results nationally and beyond. Certainly the white and rosé versions of their Annamaria Clementi cuvée are highlights of Italian bubbly, and should be considered great, elite Italian wines. Yet tasting the Vintage Collection Dosage Zéro Noir '11 we experienced a thrill of unstoppable pleasure worthy of Tre Bicchieri. Broad and deep, elegant and complex, irresistibly rich in fruit and freshness. Unforgettable.

Wine	Glasses	
○ Franciacorta Dosage Zéro Vintage Collection Noir '11	▼▼▼	8
○ Curtefranca Chardonnay '16	▼▼	8
○ Franciacorta Dosaggio Zero Cuvée Annamaria Clementi Ris. '10	▼▼	8
⊙ Franciacorta Extra Brut Rosé Cuvée Annamaria Clementi Ris. '10	▼▼	8
○ Curtefranca Bianco Corte del Lupo '18	▼▼	7
● Curtefranca Rosso Corte del Lupo '17	▼▼	6
○ Franciacorta Brut ì Vintage Collection '15	▼▼	8
○ Franciacorta Dosage Zéro Vintage Collection '15	▼▼	8
○ Franciacorta Extra Brut Cuvée Prestige	▼▼	6
○ Franciacorta Extra Brut Cuvée Prestige Rosé	▼▼	7
● Maurizio Zanella '16	▼▼	8

Ca' del Gè

fraz. Ca' del Gè, 3
27040 Montalto Pavese [PV]
Tel. +39 0383870179
www.cadelge.com

CELLAR SALES
PRE-BOOKED VISITS
ANNUAL PRODUCTION 160,000 bottles
HECTARES UNDER VINE 45.00

It was Enzo Padroggi who, several years ago, gave a boost to quality viticulture at this beautiful winery. The estate's white soils are very suitable for Pinot Nero and, above all, for Riesling, which is something of a symbol. His legacy today is being carried forward by his children, Carlo, Stefania and Sara, who oversee viticulture with low environmental impact on the property's two plots. Montalto Pavese is characterized by the above-mentioned chalk soil while Cigognola is better suited to traditional red grapes such as Croatina and Barbera. We appreciated the creamy, sapid and vibrant Metodo Classico '15, a well-structured, clear, focused wine marked by fine sparkle. The Il Marinoni (Rhine Riesling) and Filagn Long (Italic), both 2019s, prove very good in their variety. The former is taut, redolent of medicinal herbs (which foretells of nice aging power), while the second is simpler, flowery, sapid and fresh.

Wine	Glasses	
○ OP Pinot Nero Brut M. Cl. '15	▼▼	5
● Costa del Vento Pinot Nero '19	▼▼	2*
○ Filagn Long Riesling '19	▼▼	3
○ Il Marinoni Riesling '19	▼▼	3
● OP Bonarda Frizzante La Fidela '18	▼▼	4
○ Brinà Riesling '19	▼	2
○ Brinà Riesling '18	▽▽	2*
○ Brinà Riesling '17	▽▽	2*
○ Brut M. Cl. '13	▽▽	5
○ Filagn Long Riesling '18	▽▽	3
● OP Bonarda Frizzante La Fidela '16	▽▽	4
○ OP Brut Cà del Gé '13	▽▽	5
○ OP Pinot Nero Brut M. Cl. '11	▽▽	3
○ OP Pinot Nero Brut M. Cl. '10	▽▽	3*
○ OP Riesling Brinà '16	▽▽	2*
○ OP Riesling Brinà '15	▽▽	2*

Ca' di Frara

via Casa Ferrari, 1
27040 Mornico Losana [PV]
Tel. +39 0383892299
www.cadifrara.com

CELLAR SALES
PRE-BOOKED VISITS
ANNUAL PRODUCTION 400,000 bottles
HECTARES UNDER VINE 46.00

Though it's seen its ups and downs, for over twenty years now the Bellani family's winery, under Luca, has grown into one of Oltrepò Pavese's most important producers. Drawing on excellent vineyards, particularly on chalky and calcareous soil, and the construction of a new, larger and more efficient cellar, every year they produce wines of absolute value and great personality, starting with Riesling and Metodo Classico, without forgetting their reds. Amidst a wide variety of wines and products, Luca Bellani always manages to deliver some surprises. One example is the rosé Oltre Il Classico. Fine in its sparkle, it's an elegant, vibrant wine redolent of roses and small berries. The Pinot Grigio '18 returns to its previous splendour. A mainstay for 20 years now, it's characterized by great typicity, fleshiness, fragrance and length.

⊙ Oltre il Classico Extra Brut M. Cl. Rosé	🍷🍷 5
○ Pinot Grigio '18	🍷🍷 3*
⊙ OP Pinot Nero Pas Dosé M. Cl. Luca Bellani Centoventi Rosé	🍷🍷 5
○ OP Riesling Oliva Ris. '18	🍷🍷 4
● Il Frater '16	🍷 5
⊙ Oltre il Classico Nature Noir M. Cl.	🍷 5
○ OP Riesling Oliva Ris. '16	🍷🍷🍷 4*
● Il Frater '15	🍷🍷 5
● Io Rosso '15	🍷🍷 5
● Mornico Pinot Nero '15	🍷🍷 5
○ Oliva Riesling Ris. '17	🍷🍷 4
● OP Pinot Nero Mornico Parcella 4 Ris. '16	🍷🍷 5
○ OP Riesling '15	🍷🍷 4
○ OP Riesling Sup. '16	🍷🍷 2*

Ca' Lojera

loc. Rovizza
via 1866, 19
25019 Sirmione [BS]
Tel. +39 0457551901
www.calojera.com

CELLAR SALES
PRE-BOOKED VISITS
ANNUAL PRODUCTION 140,000 bottles
HECTARES UNDER VINE 20.00

Ca' Lojera (the 'House of the Wolves') is a touchstone in the southern part of Lake Garda, where the white morainic clay serves as the ideal soil for Turbiana, the local Trebbiano grape that gives rise to Lugana. For many years Franco and Ambra Tiraboschi have been painstakingly overseeing the property, with a particular attention to tradition and respect for the land. Their work on the cultivar has allowed them to bring out not only its freshness but also its remarkable aging capacity. Three excellent performances for their three Lugana dei Tiraboschi. The Riserva del Lupo '17 was in the finals, as usual. It's a great white that combines tension and minerality with more complex hints of vanilla, talcum powder and ripe white fruit. The Lugana Superiore '17 is exemplary, sapidly fresh and taut. The fruity and focused Lugana '19 is slightly less complex, though still enticing and fresh.

○ Lugana del Lupo Ris. '17	🍷🍷 4
○ Lugana '19	🍷🍷 3
○ Lugana Sup. '17	🍷🍷 4
○ Lugana '18	🍷🍷 3
○ Lugana '16	🍷🍷 3
○ Lugana '15	🍷🍷 3
○ Lugana '14	🍷🍷 3
○ Lugana Riserva del Lupo '16	🍷🍷 5
○ Lugana Riserva del Lupo '15	🍷🍷 5
○ Lugana Riserva del Lupo '14	🍷🍷 5
○ Lugana Sup. '16	🍷🍷 3
○ Lugana Sup. '15	🍷🍷 3
○ Lugana Sup. '14	🍷🍷 3
○ Lugana Sup. '13	🍷🍷 3

Calatroni

loc. Casa Grande, 7
27040 Montecalvo Versiggia [PV]
Tel. +39 038599013
www.calatronivini.it

CELLAR SALES
PRE-BOOKED VISITS
RESTAURANT SERVICE
ANNUAL PRODUCTION 70,000 bottles
HECTARES UNDER VINE 15.00
SUSTAINABLE WINERY

With great attention we've been following this winery's evolution over the last few years. Much progress has been made since it was founded in 1964 by Luigi Calatroni. Now that the fourth generation has arrived with Stefano and enologist Cristian, they're working to highlight the attributes of the vineyards, located on mainly white soils. Rhine Riesling and Pinot Nero are the principal grapes cultivated. The development of the former and the Metodo Classico obtained from the latter have often allowed their range to stand out for its maturity and personality, despite the inevitable ups and downs. The Norema '17, a wine the color of rose-water, proves elegant on the nose, with red berries accompanied by aromatic herbs and aniseed. In the mouth it exhibits fine sparkle, coming through clear, long and supple. Elegance also features in the Pinot 64 '16, a flowery, mineral wine, sapid and highly drinkable. The Riserva della Famiglia '12 is a more demanding rosé, evolved, mature and multi-faceted amidst fruit and spices.

Wine	Rating
⊙ OP M. Cl. Extra Brut Rosé NorEma '17	▼▼▼ 4*
● OP Bonarda Frizzante Vigiò '19	▼▼ 2*
⊙ OP Pas Dosé M. Cl. Riserva della Famiglia Rosé '12	▼▼ 6
○ OP Riesling Campo Dottore '19	▼▼ 3
○ Pinot Nero Brut 64 M. Cl. '16	▼▼ 4
● OP Pinot Nero Fioravanti '19	▼ 3
⊙ OP Pinot Nero M. Cl. NorEma Rosé '13	▽▽▽ 4*
○ Pinot Nero Brut 64 M. Cl. '11	▽▽▽ 5
● OP Bonarda Frizzante Vigiò '17	▽▽ 2*
● OP Pinot Nero Fioravanti '18	▽▽ 3
○ OP Riesling Viticoltori in Montecalvo '14	▽▽ 5
○ Pinot Nero Brut 64 M. Cl. '15	▽▽ 4
○ Pinot Nero Brut 64 M. Cl. '14	▽▽ 4
○ Riesling '15	▽▽ 2*

Il Calepino

via Surripe, 1
24060 Castelli Calepio [BG]
Tel. +39 035847178
www.ilcalepino.it

CELLAR SALES
PRE-BOOKED VISITS
ANNUAL PRODUCTION 230,000 bottles
HECTARES UNDER VINE 15.00

For many years now, the winery managed by brothers Franco and Marco Plebani has focused on the production of Metodo Classico sparkling wines. On the other hand, only the course of the river Oglio, just outside Lake Iseo, separates Il Calepino from the westernmost part of Franciacorta. This is to say that the soils and microclimates are similar and very suitable for the planting of Pinot Nero and Chardonnay. This is also demonstrated by the complexity these grapes gain by long aging on the lees. Like last year, this year's Non Dosato was slightly preferred to the historic Riserva Fra' Ambrogio '11. It's dry, clear and mineral, redolent of herbs and exotic fruit. Balanced and linear, it doesn't give an inch all the way through a long finish. And about that Fra' Ambrogio: it's always rich and opulent, exuding sensations of dried and candied fruit. It has the breadth and creamy bubbles that one would expect. The Blanc de Blancs and Rosé are also very good.

Wine	Rating
○ Non Dosato M. Cl.	▼▼ 4
○ Fra Ambrogio Brut M. Cl. '11	▼▼ 5
⊙ Rosé Brut M. Cl.	▼▼ 5
○ Terre del Colleoni B.D.B. Brut M. Cl.	▼▼ 4
○ Il Calepino Brut M. Cl. '13	▼ 4
● Merlot M.A.S '15	▼ 5
● Valcalepio Rosso Surìe Ris. '15	▼ 3
○ Brut M. Cl. Fra' Ambrogio Ris. '10	▽▽ 4
○ Brut M. Cl. Non Dosato '11	▽▽ 4
● Kalòs Cabernet '15	▽▽ 5
○ Terre del Colleoni B.D.B. Brut M. Cl.	▽▽ 4
● Valcalepio Rosso '15	▽ 2

CastelFaglia - Monogram

fraz. Calino
loc. Boschi, 3
25046 Cazzago San Martino [BS]
Tel. +39 0307751042
www.cavicchioli.it

CELLAR SALES
PRE-BOOKED VISITS
ANNUAL PRODUCTION 350,000 bottles
HECTARES UNDER VINE 22.00

Enologist Sandro Cavicchioli is heir to a family of Modena winemakers who need no introduction. He creates notable Franciacorta (especially when it comes to the Monogram line) in a cellar carved in the morainic hills that stretch towards the Faglia di Calino castle, and that also host his terraced vineyards. Owned by Cavicchioli, the winery operates with the belief that high-end Franciacorta should be differentiated from that destined for wider consumption. Sandro Cavicchioli's selection has no weak points, only strengths. The most dazzling this year is certainly the Monogram Zero '16, a cuvée made with Chardonnay and a small percentage of Pinot Noir. It exhibits clear fruit and beautiful fleshiness, with nuances of tobacco and elegant notes of chamomile. The Satèn, with its floral aromas, is excellent, as is the rest of their range.

○ Franciacorta Monogram Zero '16 TT 5
○ Franciacorta Brut TT 4
○ Franciacorta Brut Blanc de Blancs Monogram TT 5
○ Franciacorta Brut Monogram '13 TT 5
⊙ Franciacorta Brut Rosé TT 4
⊙ Franciacorta Monogram Brut Rosé '12 TT 5
○ Franciacorta Monogram Satèn '14 TT 5
○ Franciacorta Satèn TT 5
○ Franciacorta Satèn Monogram TT 5
○ Franciacorta Brut Monogram '12 YY 5
○ Franciacorta Brut Monogram '11 YY 5
○ Franciacorta Dosage Zéro '15 YY 5
○ Franciacorta Dosage Zero Monogram '15 YY 5
○ Franciacorta Monogram Satèn '13 YY 5
○ Franciacorta Monogram Zero '15 YY 5
○ Franciacorta Satèn Monogram Zero '14 YY 5

Castello Bonomi

loc. Franciacorta
via San Pietro, 46
25030 Coccaglio [BS]
Tel. +39 0307721015
www.castellobonomi.it

CELLAR SALES
PRE-BOOKED VISITS
ANNUAL PRODUCTION 100,000 bottles
HECTARES UNDER VINE 24.00
SUSTAINABLE WINERY

The Paladins are a Venetian family with estates in Friuli, Tuscany, and for some years now also Franciacorta. Castello Bonomi is situated at the foot of Monte Orfano. The estate takes its name from the beautiful Art Nouveau villa at the entrance to the property. Drawing on the area's calcareous soil, brothers Carlo and Roberto make wines of great expressiveness and longevity, thanks in part to the contribution of Pinot Nero, which has found an ideal habitat on these soils. The Dosage Zéro '11 made its presence felt in our final tastings, bringing Tre Bicchieri back to the maison of Bonomi, or rather, Paladin. This cuvée of equal parts Chardonnay and Pinot Noir matures at length on the lees, unleashing great determination and elegance in the glass. Complex, smoky notes and minerals don't sacrifice the clarity of its citrus foot sensations, which ensure depth and pleasantness. The Satèn '14 is among the best ever.

○ Franciacorta Dosage Zéro '11 TTT 7
○ Franciacorta Satèn '14 TT 6
○ Franciacorta Brut Cuvée 22 TT 6
○ Franciacorta Brut CruPerdu '14 T 6
⊙ Franciacorta Brut Rosé T 7
○ Franciacorta Extra Brut Lucrezia Et. Nera Ris. '08 T 8
○ Franciacorta Extra Brut Lucrezia Et. Nera '04 YYY 8
○ Franciacorta Brut Cru Perdu '11 YY 7
○ Franciacorta Brut CruPerdu Ris. '09 YY 7
○ Franciacorta Dosage Zéro '12 YY 7
○ Franciacorta Dosage Zéro Gran Cuvée del Laureato '10 YY 8
○ Franciacorta Extra Brut Cuvée Lucrezia '06 YY 8
○ Franciacorta Extra Brut Cuvée Lucrezia Et. Bianca Ris. '08 YY 8

★Castello di Cigognola

P.ZZA CASTELLO, 1
27040 CIGOGNOLA [PV]
TEL. +39 0385284828
www.castellodicigognola.com

CELLAR SALES
PRE-BOOKED VISITS
ANNUAL PRODUCTION 75,000 bottles
HECTARES UNDER VINE 30.00

The Castle of Cigognola was founded in 1212 to guard access to the Scuropasso Valley. After the end of feudalism it hosted a Renaissance court, while as early as the turn of the 19th century it was being used for wine production. This beautiful and splendidly manicured estate, which is also a center of research on ancient local varieties and new grapes (in collaboration with the University of Milan), has for some years now been focusing on quality, changing certain objectives and concentrating mainly on Metodo Classico. The delicious Cuvée 'more Pas Dosé is a potent, linear, fragrant Metodo Classico characterized by rich, ripe fruit, and a long finish. Great with food. We appreciated the new Barbera Barberasso '18 for its fragrant nose of mint and wild cherry, and, above all, its juicy, fresh, expansive palate, with slight residual sugars integrating very well with a lively acidity.

○ 'More Pas Dosé M. Cl.	🍷🍷🍷 4*
○ 'More Brut M. Cl.	🍷🍷 4
● Barberasso Barbera '18	🍷🍷 4
● OP Barbera Dodicidodici '16	🍷🍷 3
○ OP Pinot Nero Pas Dosé M. Cl. Cuvée dell'Angelo '13	🍷🍷 5
○ 'More Brut M. Cl. '11	🍷🍷🍷 4*
○ 'More Brut M. Cl. '10	🍷🍷🍷 4*
● OP Barbera Castello di Cigognola '07	🍷🍷🍷 6
● OP Barbera Castello di Cigognola '06	🍷🍷🍷 6
● OP Barbera Dodicidodici '11	🍷🍷🍷 3*
● OP Barbera Poggio Della Maga '05	🍷🍷🍷 7
○ OP Brut M. Cl. 'More '12	🍷🍷🍷 4*
○ OP Pinot Nero Brut M. Cl. 'More '13	🍷🍷🍷 4*
○ OP Pinot Nero Brut M. Cl. 'More '08	🍷🍷🍷 4*

Castello di Gussago La Santissima

VIA MANICA, 8
25064 GUSSAGO [BS]
TEL. +39 0302525267
www.castellodigussago.it

CELLAR SALES
PRE-BOOKED VISITS
ANNUAL PRODUCTION 130,000 bottles
HECTARES UNDER VINE 21.00
VITICULTURE METHOD Certified Organic
SUSTAINABLE WINERY

On the Colle della Santissima, in Gussago, in the early 2000s, the Gozio family renovated an old Dominican convent, renovating a cellar built in 1941 and transforming it into a modern structure. Active since 2005, the winery draws exclusively on the grapes from its 20 hectares of privately-owned vineyards, separately fermenting the individual plots, some of which reach elevations of 450 meters above sea level, at the foot of the abbey. The entire production chain is managed with an eye towards sustainability. The Extra Brut Rosé Inganni '15 is a forthright and sincere Franciacorta, among the best tasted this year. Kidding aside, we appreciated the wine dedicated to the famous Gussago painter Angelo Inganni for its lovely, bright pale pink color, its complex and fine nose of berries, strawberries and cherries, and for its assertive, structured palate, like a true Pinot Noir. But their entire range is growing.

⊙ Franciacorta Extra Brut Rosé Inganni '15	🍷🍷 5
○ Curtefranca Bianco Malandrino '18	🍷🍷 4
● Curtefranca Rosso Pomaro '17	🍷🍷 4
○ Franciacorta Brut Nobleblanc	🍷🍷 5
○ Franciacorta Club Cuvée Satèn '15	🍷🍷 5
○ Franciacorta Brut Noblenoir	🍷 5
○ Franciacorta Extra Brut Operacento Ris. '10	🍷 7
○ Franciacorta Pas Dosé '14	🍷 5
○ Curtefranca Bianco Malandrino '15	🍷🍷 5
● Curtefranca Rosso Pomaro '15	🍷🍷 4
● Curtefranca Rosso Pomaro '13	🍷🍷 4
○ Franciacorta Brut Sel. Gozio '13	🍷🍷 6
⊙ Franciacorta Extra Brut Rosé '14	🍷🍷 5
○ Franciacorta Pas Dosé '12	🍷🍷 5
○ Franciacorta Pas Dosé 800 '14	🍷🍷 5

★Cavalleri

via Provinciale, 96
25030 Erbusco [BS]
Tel. +39 0307760217
www.cavalleri.it

PRE-BOOKED VISITS
ANNUAL PRODUCTION 200,000 bottles
HECTARES UNDER VINE 42.00
VITICULTURE METHOD Certified Organic

The name Cavalleri appeared on a 1450 notarial deed, testifying to the family's deep roots in Franciacorta. Gian Paolo and his son Giovanni, the winery's founders, launched the business in 1968 and contributed to the birth of the appellation. Giovanni's daughters, Maria and Giulia, and the fourth generation represented by Francesco and Diletta, are responsible for carrying on the family tradition, managing the 42 hectares of property in accordance with principles of sustainability. The Cavalleri range, which this year once again saw two cuvées in our finals, is always top-notch. The Pas Dosé '15 offers up beautiful whiffs of white peach and citrus fruit on the nose, all made complex by notes of medicinal herbs. In the mouth it comes through crisp, relaxed and sapid. It's flanked by a rosé that was among the best tasted, fragrant and delicate in its bouquet of flowers and berries; the palate is more austere and structured. Their historic Curtefranca are also excellent.

Wine	Rating
⊙ Franciacorta Brut Rosé '15	▼▼ 6
○ Franciacorta Pas Dosé '15	▼▼ 6
○ Curtefranca Bianco V. Rampaneto '19	▼▼ 4
● Curtefranca Rosso V. Tajardino '16	▼▼ 5
○ Franciacorta Brut Blanc de Blancs	▼▼ 5
○ Franciacorta Satèn '16	▼▼ 6
○ Franciacorta Brut Collezione '05	▽▽▽ 6
○ Franciacorta Brut Collezione Esclusiva Giovanni Cavalleri '05	▽▽▽ 8
○ Franciacorta Brut Collezione Esclusiva Giovanni Cavalleri '04	▽▽▽ 7
○ Franciacorta Brut Collezione Esclusiva Giovanni Cavalleri '01	▽▽▽ 7
○ Franciacorta Collezione Grandi Cru '08	▽▽▽ 6
○ Franciacorta Pas Dosé '07	▽▽▽ 5
○ Franciacorta Pas Dosé Au Contraire '01	▽▽▽ 7
○ Franciacorta Pas Dosé R. D. '06	▽▽▽ 6

Contadi Castaldi

loc. Fornace Biasca
via Colzano, 32
25030 Adro [BS]
Tel. +39 0307450126
www.contadicastaldi.it

CELLAR SALES
PRE-BOOKED VISITS
ANNUAL PRODUCTION 1,000,000 bottles
HECTARES UNDER VINE 150.00
SUSTAINABLE WINERY

Vittorio Moretti's idea to build a new cellar by renovating Adro's old furnaces dates back to the 1990s. This idea paid off, since over the years Contadi Castaldi's Franciacorta has reached remarkable levels of quality, building on a modern, assertive style. The wines are made through careful selection of grapes, both from privately-owned vineyards and from many third-party growers, with a total of over 130 hectares covered. Franciacorta Zèro is probably the wine that best represents the producer. The Cuvée '16, mostly Pinot Nero (as always), offers up a beautiful bouquet characterized by notes of lavender, blueberry and berries. On the palate it's dry and sapid, though not austere, closing long on soft notes of ripe fruit. The Satèn '16 is subtle but pulpy in its fruit, persuasive, taut and focused.

Wine	Rating
○ Franciacorta Zèro '16	▼▼ 6
○ Franciacorta Brut	▼▼ 5
○ Franciacorta Satèn '16	▼▼ 5
⊙ Franciacorta Brut Rosé	▼ 5
○ Franciacorta Brut Satèn Soul '11	▽▽▽ 6
○ Franciacorta Satèn '15	▽▽▽ 6
○ Franciacorta Satèn Soul '06	▽▽▽ 6
○ Franciacorta Satèn Soul '05	▽▽▽ 6
○ Franciacorta Zero '14	▽▽▽ 5
○ Franciacorta Zero '12	▽▽▽ 5
○ Franciacorta Zero '09	▽▽▽ 5
○ Franciacorta Brut Satèn '12	▽▽ 6
○ Franciacorta Pinònero Natura '11	▽▽ 7
○ Franciacorta Satèn '14	▽▽ 6
○ Franciacorta Satèn '11	▽▽ 5
○ Franciacorta Zero '15	▽▽ 5
○ Franciacorta Zero '13	▽▽ 5

Conte Vistarino

fraz. Villa Fornace, 11
27040 Rocca de' Giorgi [PV]
Tel. +39 0385241171
www.contevistarino.it

CELLAR SALES
PRE-BOOKED VISITS
ANNUAL PRODUCTION 350,000 bottles
HECTARES UNDER VINE 200.00

When someone says, 'Conte Vistarino', you immediately think of Pinot Nero. In fact, clones of this noble grape variety from Champagne were introduction here, in the heart of the Scuropasso Valley, in the mid-19th century for the production of Metodo Classico sparkling wines. The winery, which covers 800 hectares (120 of which are vineyards), has recently opened a new cellar and, at the same time, identified the best areas for the creation of three different crus of Pinot Nero (to be vinified on the skins), while their sparkling wine grapes are cultivated at higher elevations. Vistarino's work on his Pinot Noir crus is commendable, both for the quality of the wines and for the stylistic differences made possible by the different terroirs. This year the Pernice '17, the oldest cru, earned accolades by virtue of its splendid, untarnished aromas as well as its sapid, substantive and supple palate. The Bertone is very elegant, as usual, while the Tavernetto exhibits deep sensations of black berries and undergrowth.

Wine	Rating
● OP Pinot Nero Pernice '17	▼▼▼ 6
● OP Pinot Nero Bertone '17	▼▼ 6
● OP Pinot Nero Tavernetto '17	▼▼ 5
○ Cépage Brut M. Cl.	▼ 5
○ OP Pinot Nero Pas Dosé M. Cl. 1865 '15	▼ 5
● Bertone Pinot Nero '15	▽▽▽ 5
● Bertone Pinot Nero '13	▽▽▽ 5
○ OP Pinot Nero Brut M. Cl. Conte Vistarino 1865 '08	▽▽▽ 4*
● OP Pinot Nero Pernice '06	▽▽▽ 4*
● Tavernetto Pinot Nero '16	▽▽▽ 3*
● OP Pinot Nero Pernice '12	▽▽ 5
● Pernice Pinot Nero '15	▽▽ 5
● Pernice Pinot Nero '13	▽▽ 5
● Tavernetto Pinot Nero '15	▽▽ 3*

Corte Aura

via Colzano, 13
25030 Adro [BS]
Tel. +39 030 7357281
www.corteaura.it

CELLAR SALES
PRE-BOOKED VISITS
ANNUAL PRODUCTION 100,000 bottles
HECTARES UNDER VINE 6.00

A few years ago Federico Fossati, a Franciacorta enthusiast, decided to renovate an old farmhouse, transforming it into a winery with ambitious plans. To aim high, he decided to avail himself of the support of Pierangelo Bonomi, one of the area's long-time enologists. Pending forthcoming acquisitions, they integrate the grapes cultivated on six hectares of privately-owned vineyards with targeted purchases from local growers, and the resulting quality testifies to the good work being done. The accolades that two Fossati cuvées earned during our tastings demonstrate why the producer is in our main section. One is the Brut, exemplary for its balance and freshness, it's sapid and taut, rich in fruity notes and creamy sparkle. The other is the Satèn, an interpretation we appreciated. It plays on floral scents, with sensations of ripe white fruit on the palate and a softness that lends opulence rather than sweetness.

Wine	Rating
○ Franciacorta Brut	▼▼ 5
○ Franciacorta Brut Satèn	▼▼ 5
○ Franciacorta Pas Dosé Insé	▼▼ 5
⊙ Franciacorta Brut Rosè	▼ 5
○ Franciacorta Brut Satèn '13	▽▽ 5
○ Franciacorta Pas Dosé Insè '12	▽▽ 7
○ Franciacorta Satèn '10	▽▽ 6

La Costa

FRAZ. COSTA
VIA GALBUSERA NERA, 2
23888 PEREGO [LC]
TEL. +39 0395312218
www.la-costa.it

CELLAR SALES
PRE-BOOKED VISITS
RESTAURANT SERVICE
ANNUAL PRODUCTION 30,000 bottles
HECTARES UNDER VINE 12.00
VITICULTURE METHOD Certified Organic

This lovely winery, situated in the heart of the regional park of Montevecchia and the Curone valley, in the Brianza region of Lecco, has demonstrated the quality of its range by consistently getting into our final round of tastings. The Crippa family oversee 12 hectares of vineyards, organically managed and surrounded by woods, providing highly original interpretations of international varieties that have found a home on the mineral and limestone-rich soils here. The stylistically perfect Solesta '17 continues to improve. It's subtle and complex, with notes of rosemary accompanied by petrol and white fruit. The palate has fresh acidity, with a long finish and character. Vibrant, with nuances of currant and plum, we also appreciated the Serìz '17. In the mouth it's pulpy, with a multifaceted, long finish. The San Giobbe '17 performed well, with its black pepper sensations and jam, and a lingering finish, as did the delicious Brigante Bianco '19, a fruity and fresh wine.

Wine	Glasses	
○ Solesta '17	▼▼	5
○ Brigante Bianco '19	▼▼	3
● Brigante Rosso '17	▼▼	3
● San Giobbe '17	▼▼	5
● Serìz '17	▼▼	4
○ Brigante Bianco '17	▽▽	3
● Brigante Rosso '16	▽▽	3
○ Incrediboll Extra Brut M. Cl. '16	▽▽	5
● San Giobbe '16	▽▽	5
● Serìz '16	▽▽	4
○ Solesta '16	▽▽	5
○ Solesta '15	▽▽	4
○ Solesta '14	▽▽	4
● Vino del Quindici '15	▽▽	6

Costaripa

VIA COSTA, 1A
25080 MONIGA DEL GARDA [BS]
TEL. +39 0365502010
www.costaripa.it

CELLAR SALES
PRE-BOOKED VISITS
ANNUAL PRODUCTION 400,000 bottles
HECTARES UNDER VINE 40.00

At his winery, Mattia Vezzola is doing research work that's a touchstone not only for Valtènesi and the entire Garda area, but also for those who want to discover the aging potential of a typology such as still rosé wines. The other face of the winery is its sparkling wine, so they would have to be represented in the line that bears the Vezzola name: Metodo Classicos made with traditional Chardonnay and Pinot Nero grapes. His sons Nicole and Gherardo have been working side by side with their father for some years now. With its third success in our finals, the Chiaretto Molmenti, 2017 is by now a classic, with its beautiful, pale antique-pink color, a complex bouquet in which fruit meets mineral and spicy notes, and a crisp, fresh palate, rich in echoes of red berries and herbs, yet incredibly deep and long. From the more immediately expressive Chiaretto Rosamara '19, an irresistible wine, to the more mature Metodo Classico cuvées like the Grande Annata '15, each wine deserves a taste.

Wine	Glasses	
⊙ Valtènesi Chiaretto Molmenti '17	▼▼▼	5
○ Brut Grande Annata '15	▼▼	5
⊙ Costaripa Brut Rosé '15	▼▼	4
○ Mattia Vezzola Brut	▼▼	5
⊙ Mattia Vezzola Rosé	▼▼	5
⊙ Valtènesi Chiaretto RosaMara '19	▼▼	2*
○ Mattia Vezzola Cremant	▼	5
⊙ Valtènesi Chiaretto Molmenti '16	▽▽▽	5
⊙ Valtènesi Chiaretto Molmenti '15	▽▽▽	3*
○ Brut Grande Annata '14	▽▽	5
○ Mattia Vezzola Brut	▽▽	5
⊙ Mattia Vezzola Brut Rosé	▽▽	5
⊙ Valtènesi Chiaretto Molmenti '13	▽▽	2*
⊙ Valtènesi Chiaretto RosaMara '18	▽▽	2*
⊙ Valtènesi Chiaretto RosaMara '17	▽▽	3

Derbusco Cives

via Provinciale, 83
25030 Erbusco [BS]
Tel. +39 0307731164
www.derbuscocives.com

CELLAR SALES
PRE-BOOKED VISITS
RESTAURANT SERVICE
ANNUAL PRODUCTION 96,000 bottles
HECTARES UNDER VINE 12.00

Citizens of Erbusco', as the Latin name reads, was founded recently by a group of friends. Dario and Giuseppe Vezzoli, Luigi Dotti, Paolo Brescianini and Vanni Bordiga wanted to underline the centrality of this town, which can be considered the capital of Franciacorta, working 12 hectares of property in a sustainable way and making their wines using Franciacorta must for refermentation. The Doppio Erre Di (delayed dégorgement, recently degorged...) represents the producer's philosophy at its best, focusing on long maturation of the yeasts, soft crushing and bottle fermentation according to the 'ancestral method'. The version tasted this year also charms for its elegance and harmony, for its fruity and citrus whiffs, its calm assertiveness. The whole range is excellent, with a special mention for the 2013 Brut and Extra Brut Grand Taille.

Wine	Rating
○ Franciacorta Brut Doppio Erre Di	🍷🍷 5
○ Franciacorta Brut '13	🍷🍷 6
○ Franciacorta Brut Doppio Erre DV	🍷🍷 5
○ Franciacorta Extra Brut Grand Taille '13	🍷🍷 7
○ Franciacorta Brut Crisalis '16	🍷 7
○ Franciacorta Brut '12	🍷🍷 6
○ Franciacorta Brut '11	🍷🍷 6
○ Franciacorta Brut '10	🍷🍷 6
○ Franciacorta Brut Crisalis '12	🍷🍷 6
○ Franciacorta Brut Crisalis '11	🍷🍷 6
○ Franciacorta Extra Brut '12	🍷🍷 8
○ Franciacorta Extra Brut '11	🍷🍷 8
○ Franciacorta Extra Brut '10	🍷🍷 8
⊙ Franciacorta Rosé '14	🍷🍷 6

Dirupi

loc. Madonna di Campagna
via Grumello, 1
23020 Montagna in Valtellina [SO]
Tel. +39 3472909779
www.dirupi.com

CELLAR SALES
PRE-BOOKED VISITS
ANNUAL PRODUCTION 35,000 bottles
HECTARES UNDER VINE 7.00
SUSTAINABLE WINERY

The duo of Davide Fasolini and Pierpaolo di Franco have managed to create one of the most surprising Italian wineries of late, one that's gained in complexity and dynamism. They took over a handful of steep plots, and, at the same time, planted new vineyards in a strategic position, enriching their production with crus that we are only just now appreciating. In their bottles there's all the lightness of the mountain air, a dose of easiness, a desire to have fun doing something rewarding for yourself. An excellent line-up of wines were presented, one star after another, starting with the Inferno Guast '17 which features very fine, fruity aromas of great harmony and freshness, enriched with spices and dried flowers. The palate is majestic, with tannins combining with pulp for a personal, long finish. The Grumello Riserva '17 is intense and elegant, with beautiful notes of licorice and red fruits. In the mouth it's balanced, with juicy fruit, very fine tannins and a long finish. The Sforzato '18 is rich and elegant, but not weighed down by the use of raisined grapes.

Wine	Rating
● Valtellina Sup. Grumello Ris. '17	🍷🍷🍷 7
● Sforzato di Valtellina Vino Sbagliato '18	🍷🍷 6
● Valtellina Sup. Inferno Guast '17	🍷🍷 6
● Rosso di Valtellina Olè '19	🍷🍷 3
● Valtellina Sup. Dirupi '18	🍷🍷 4
● Valtellina Sup. Grumello Gess '17	🍷🍷 5
● Valtellina Sup. Dirupi '16	🍷🍷🍷 4*
● Valtellina Sup. Dirupi Ris. '14	🍷🍷🍷 6
● Valtellina Sup. Grumello Dirupi Ris. '16	🍷🍷🍷 7
● Sforzato di Valtellina Vino Sbagliato '17	🍷🍷 6
● Valtellina Sup. Dirupi '17	🍷🍷 4

Luca Faccinelli

via Medici, 3a
23030 Chiuro [SO]
Tel. +39 3470807011
www.lucafaccinelli.it

CELLAR SALES
PRE-BOOKED VISITS
ANNUAL PRODUCTION 20,000 bottles
HECTARES UNDER VINE 3.00
SUSTAINABLE WINERY

It's full-steam-ahead for the winery founded by Luca Faccinelli in 2007. Here in Chiuro, at the foot of the Alps, we find the fascinating and complex territory that is Valtellina. The vineyards unfold in the Grumello subzone between 400 and 650 meters above sea level, with incredible slopes that reach grades of 70%. Here they work only by hand, with passion and enthusiasm, making for a battery of wines that just keeps getting better. All the wines presented by Luca Faccinelli, a passionate and dynamic Grumello producer, validate last year's good debut. The Tell '16 impressed with its notable fruit and overall finesse. Its tannins are gentle, the finish fresh and long. We also appreciated the Grumello Riserva '17, with its nuances of black pepper and dried flowers—in the mouth it's structured, with an enticing finish. The Ortensio Lando '17 is aromatically intense, with fruit still emerging, while the palate is weighty and evolving favorably. Great notes of raspberry characterize the Rosso di Valtellina '18, an elegant and fresh wine.

Wine	Glasses	Price
● Valtellina Sup. Grumello Tell '16	🍷🍷	5
● Rosso di Valtellina Matteo Bandello '18	🍷🍷	4
● Valtellina Sup. Grumello Ortensio Lando '17	🍷🍷	5
● Valtellina Sup. Grumello Ris. '17	🍷🍷	6
● Rosso di Valtellina Matteo Bandello '17	🍷🍷	4
● Valtellina Sup. Grumello Ortensio Lando '16	🍷🍷	5
● Valtellina Sup. Grumello Ris. '16	🍷🍷	6
● Valtellina Sup. Grumello Tell '15	🍷🍷	5
● Valtellina Sup. Ortensio Lando '13	🍷🍷	5
● Valtellina Sup. Ortensio Lando '10	🍷🍷	5

Sandro Fay

loc. San Giacomo
via Pila Caselli, 1
23030 Teglio [SO]
Tel. +39 0342786071
www.vinifay.it

CELLAR SALES
PRE-BOOKED VISITS
ANNUAL PRODUCTION 38,000 bottles
HECTARES UNDER VINE 13.00

In many ways the winery founded in 1973 by Sandro Fay, in the heart of the Valgella subzone, represents a model. The studies carried out over the years on environmental sustainability and the effect of altimetry have guaranteed increasingly interesting results, keeping the producer ahead of the competition. At the helm is Marco Fay, one of the most authoritative figures in the region. This Riserva Carteria '16 is a marvelous alchemy, a harmonious synthesis of 'the three Fs': fruit, freshness and finesse, with floral and peppery notes, a rich palate, long and pulpy finish. The Valtellina Superiore Costa Bassa '17 is elegant, always striking the perfect balance between 'top and pop'. It's fruity, with complex nuances of tobacco and licorice, the palate is harmonious, delicious. The Cà Morei '17 is intense in its bouquet, with red berries. The palate is bold, the finish long and voluminous. We found the Chardonnay Sottocastello '19 original and nicely interpreted, vibrant in the mouth, with floral and white peach on the nose.

Wine	Glasses	Price
● Valtellina Sup. Valgella Carterìa Ris. '16	🍷🍷🍷	6
● Valtellina Sup. Costa Bassa '17	🍷🍷	4
● Valtellina Sup. Valgella Ca' Morèi '17	🍷🍷	5
○ Sottocastello Chardonnay '18	🍷🍷	4
● Valtellina Sup. Sassella Il Glicine '17	🍷🍷	5
● Sforzato di Valtellina Ronco del Picchio '16	🍷🍷🍷	6
● Valtellina Sforzato Ronco del Picchio '10	🍷🍷🍷	6
● Valtellina Sforzato Ronco del Picchio '09	🍷🍷🍷	6
● Valtellina Sforzato Ronco del Picchio '02	🍷🍷🍷	6
● Valtellina Sup. Valgella Cà Moréi '13	🍷🍷🍷	5
● Sforzato di Valtellina Ronco del Picchio '14	🍷🍷	6
● Valtellina Sup. Valgella Ca' Morèi '16	🍷🍷	5
● Valtellina Sup. Valgella Carterìa Ris. '15	🍷🍷	6

★Ferghettina

via Saline, 11
25030 Adro [BS]
Tel. +39 0307451212
www.ferghettina.it

CELLAR SALES
PRE-BOOKED VISITS
ANNUAL PRODUCTION 500,000 bottles
HECTARES UNDER VINE 190.00
VITICULTURE METHOD Certified Organic

Ferghettina got its start in 1990, when Roberto Gatti and his wife, Andreina, took over management of the original 4 hectares of vineyards in Erbusco. From then on, it was a continued growth, up to the approximately 200 hectares managed today. In the meantime, construction of their new headquarters began in Adro in 2002 and was completed in 2005, while 2016 saw further expansion (completed 2 years later). In short, it can't be said that the Gattis—now joined by their children Laura and Matteo, both enologists—rest on their laurels. This year the wine that most impressed among their rich and multifaceted range is the Eronero Brut '12, which should considered one of the most accomplished expressions of Pinot Nero in Franciacorta. It has structure, finesse, fruity flesh, and is pervaded by a subtle elegance that makes for a long, harmonious finish. Impeccable mousse. Tre Bicchieri. But from the Rosé '16 to the non-vintage Brut, every bottle is excellent, including their stills.

Wine	Rating	
○ Franciacorta Brut Eronero '12	TTT	6
○ Franciacorta Brut	TT	4
○ Franciacorta Satèn '16	TT	5
● Baladello Merlot '15	TT	5
● Curtefranca Rosso '18	TT	2*
○ Franciacorta Brut Milledì '16	TT	5
⊙ Franciacorta Brut Rosé '16	TT	5
○ Franciacorta Extra Brut '14	TT	6
○ Franciacorta Extra Brut '09	YYY	5
○ Franciacorta Extra Brut '06	YYY	5
○ Franciacorta Extra Brut '05	YYY	5
○ Franciacorta Pas Dosé 33 Ris. '10	YYY	6
○ Franciacorta Pas Dosé 33 Ris. '09	YYY	6
○ Franciacorta Pas Dosé 33 Ris. '07	YYY	6
○ Franciacorta Pas Dosé 33 Ris. '06	YYY	6
○ Franciacorta Pas Dosé Riserva 33 '11	YYY	6

Fiamberti

via Chiesa, 17
27044 Canneto Pavese [PV]
Tel. +39 038588019
www.fiambertivini.it

CELLAR SALES
PRE-BOOKED VISITS
ANNUAL PRODUCTION 140,000 bottles
HECTARES UNDER VINE 18.00

The Fiamberti family's winery sees father Ambrogio dedicated primarily to traditional sparkling wines, while his son Giulio works mainly with Metodo Classico and Buttafuoco Storico. Their vineyards are situated in very different locations, with different soils and aspects. As per tradition, they produce all types of wines, white, red, still, sparkling, semi-sparkling, all of them of high quality. Their two crus of Buttafuoco Storico are their crown jewels, while their selection of sparkling wines keep getting better. Spices, ripe blackberry, chocolate and, above all, clear balsamic scents: the Solinga Valley of Canneto is fully expressed in the Buttafuoco Storico Vigna Solenga '16, a dense and dark, potent and elegant wine. The Sacca del Prete '16, their other cru, is more alcoholic, marked by notes of licorice, tobacco and undergrowth. Balance, fruit and a nice aromatic suite feature in the young Buttafuoco Il Cacciatore '18. The citrusy Cruasé also proves well made.

Wine	Rating	
● OP Buttafuoco Storico V. Solenga '16	TTT	5
● OP Buttafuoco Storico V. Sacca del Prete '16	TT	5
● OP Buttafuoco Il Cacciatore '18	TT	3
⊙ OP Cruasé	TT	4
● OP Bonarda La Briccona '19	T	2
○ OP Pinot Nero Brut M. Cl.	T	4
○ OP Riesling Ida '19	T	2
● OP Sangue di Giuda Lella '19	T	2
● OP Buttafuoco Storico V. Sacca del Prete '15	YYY	5
● OP Bonarda La Briccona '18	YY	2*
● OP Buttafuoco Il Cacciatore '16	YY	3
● OP Buttafuoco Storico V. Sacca del Prete '13	YY	4
● OP Buttafuoco Storico V. Solenga '15	YY	4

Finigeto

loc. Cella, 27
27040 Montalto Pavese [PV]
Tel. +39 328 7095347
www.finigeto.com

CELLAR SALES
PRE-BOOKED VISITS
ACCOMMODATION
ANNUAL PRODUCTION 80,000 bottles
HECTARES UNDER VINE 42.00

This year we welcome the winery founded by Aldo Dellavalle in 2005 into our main section. We've been following its evolution for some years now, and it's clear that the work carried out by Aldo with enologist Marco Terzoni is bearing fruit. The project came out of a deeply-rooted passion, but the cellar was only built in 2012, all following principles of eco-compatible architecture while respecting the style of the territory. The resulting wines show a strong personality and distinctly varietal character. The Riesling Lo Spavaldo '19 features the characteristic profile we'd expect from a young Rhine Riesling: delicious scents of chamomile and aromatic herbs, yellow fruit, a spirited, graceful palate. It will age well, as demonstrated by our reassessment of the 2018, in which an intriguing mineral vein is starting to emerge. A nice performance for the Bonarda Frizzante La Grintosa '19, a long, expansive drink with sensations of berries and a pleasantly almondy finish. Polished and supple, juicy in its ripe fruit, the Barbera Il Ribaldo '19 runs on a similar track.

- ○ Lo Spavaldo Riesling Renano '19 ▼▼ 3*
- ○ Il Fermo Chardonnay '19 ▼▼ 3
- ● OP Barbera Il Ribaldo '19 ▼▼ 3
- ● OP Bonarda Frizzante La Grintosa '19 ▼▼ 3
- ● OP Bonarda Il Baldo '19 ▼▼ 3
- ○ OP Pinot Nero Brut M. Cl. '05 ▼ 6
- ● OP Pinot Nero Il Nirò Ris. '17 ▼ 5
- ○ Il Fermo Chardonnay '18 ▽▽ 3
- ○ Lo Spavaldo Riesling Renano '16 ▽▽ 3
- ○ Lo Spavaldo Riesling Renano '14 ▽▽ 2*
- ● OP Barbera Il Ribaldo '13 ▽▽ 3
- ● OP Pinot Nero Il Nirò '16 ▽▽ 5
- ● OP Pinot Nero Il Nirò '15 ▽▽ 5
- ● OP Pinot Nero Il Nirò '14 ▽▽ 3
- ○ OP Riesling Lo Spavaldo '18 ▽▽ 2*

Enrico Gatti

via Metelli, 9
25030 Erbusco [BS]
Tel. +39 0307267999
www.enricogatti.it

CELLAR SALES
PRE-BOOKED VISITS
ANNUAL PRODUCTION 120,000 bottles
HECTARES UNDER VINE 17.00

Family management of the producer founded in 1975 by Enrico Gatti continues to bear fruit. Their modern, underground and thermo-conditioned cellar was built in 2005, expanded and modernized 3 times in successive phases. It's here that Lorenzo and Paola Gatti, with Paola's husband, Enzo Balzarini, process the grapes from their 17 hectares of property, all situated in the municipality of Erbusco, forging Franciacorta wines that faithfully express to the terroir. Stylistically, the Nature is right in Gatti's wheelhouse. Bolstered by beautiful vineyards in the heart of the appellation, every year they provide a compelling interpretation, both with the vintage version and non-vintage. The 2014 exhibits a creamy fruit, lovely structure and overall harmony enlivened by citrus notes. Beautiful notes of pineapple and fresh almond characterize the Brut 'sans année'. We also appreciated the Satèn '16, with its nice, delicately salty vein.

- ○ Franciacorta Nature '14 ▼▼ 6
- ○ Franciacorta Brut ▼▼ 5
- ○ Franciacorta Brut Satèn '16 ▼▼ 5
- ○ Franciacorta Nature ▼▼ 5
- ○ Franciacorta Brut '05 ▽▽▽ 6
- ○ Franciacorta Nature '07 ▽▽▽ 5
- ○ Franciacorta Satèn '05 ▽▽▽ 5
- ○ Franciacorta Satèn '03 ▽▽▽ 5
- ○ Franciacorta Satèn '02 ▽▽▽ 4
- ○ Franciacorta Satèn '01 ▽▽▽ 4
- ○ Franciacorta Satèn '00 ▽▽▽ 5
- ○ Franciacorta Brut Satèn '15 ▽▽ 5
- ○ Franciacorta Brut Satèn '14 ▽▽ 5
- ○ Franciacorta Brut Satèn '13 ▽▽ 5
- ○ Franciacorta Nature '13 ▽▽ 6
- ○ Franciacorta Nature '11 ▽▽ 6
- ○ Franciacorta Satèn '12 ▽▽ 5

★Giorgi

FRAZ. CAMPONOCE, 39A
27044 CANNETO PAVESE [PV]
TEL. +39 0385262151
www.giorgi-wines.it

CELLAR SALES
PRE-BOOKED VISITS
ANNUAL PRODUCTION 1,600,000 bottles
HECTARES UNDER VINE 60.00

For years the new generation, represented by Fabiano Giorgi, his sister Eleonora and his wife, Ileana (they also have the precious support of father Antonio) have changed the face of this winery, reaching peaks of absolute excellence especially with their Pinot Nero Metodo Classico, achieving a style that has gradually grown in elegance and definition. But there are many wines to keep an eye on, starting with their Buttafuoco Storico. The enology team is composed of Andrea Bonfanti and Matteo Olcelli, under the supervision of Stefano Testa. This year we tasted one of the best ever versions of the award-winning 1870. The 2016, with its decidedly coppery color, features variegated aromas ranging from flowers to pastry, citrus fruits and aniseed. Fine and persistent bubble lend creaminess to a full, elegant, deep palate. The Top Zero is a vigorous Pas Dosé. In terms of their Metodo Classicos, a citrusy Rosé and a soft, ingratiating Gerry Scotti also stand out.

Wine	Rating
○ OP Pinot Nero Brut M. Cl. 1870 '16	TTT 5
○ Top Zero Pas Dosé M. Cl.	TT 6
⊙ 1870 M. Cl. Rosé	TT 4
● OP Buttafuoco Gerry Scotti 56 '16	TT 3
○ OP Extra Brut M. Cl. Gerry Scotti	TT 4
● OP Pinot Nero Monteroso '18	TT 3
○ OP Riesling Il Bandito '19	TT 4
○ Fusion M. Cl. '16	T 4
● OP Bonarda La Gallina '19	T 2
○ OP Pinot Nero Brut M. Cl. Gianfranco Giorgi '17	T 5
● OP Sangue di Giuda '19	T 3
○ OP Pinot Nero Brut 1870 '12	YYY 5
○ OP Pinot Nero Brut 1870 '11	YYY 5
○ OP Pinot Nero Brut M. Cl. 1870 '14	YYY 5

Isimbarda

FRAZ. CASTELLO
CASCINA ISIMBARDA
27046 SANTA GIULETTA [PV]
TEL. +39 0383899256
www.isimbarda.com

CELLAR SALES
PRE-BOOKED VISITS
ANNUAL PRODUCTION 130,000 bottles
HECTARES UNDER VINE 40.00

This winery is situated in one of Oltrepò Pavese's most charming areas. Here, where the feud of the Marquises Isimbardi stood in the 17th century and where quality wine was already being produced in the 19th century, it's as if you're in Tuscany (the rows of cypress trees help). 40 hectares of vineyards, with soils of varying composition, from limestone and marl to clay, give rise to local wines, starting with Rhine Riesling, their crown jewel, with an eye to sparkling wine production as well. The new La Fleur '18 shows how bottle aging can only benefit Oltrepò Pavese's Rhine Riesling, especially when cultivated in the right areas. More mature fruit than flowers serve as a counterbalance to the grape's characteristic minerality, which has emerged with time. Flavorful on the palate, it has a long finish and excellent aging potential. The historic Vigna Martina is a standard-label Riesling that's very enjoyable in its floral bouquet. The delicious Cruasé is a fruity, balsamic wine.

Wine	Rating
○ OP Riesling La Fleur '18	TT 4
⊙ OP Cruasé	TT 4
○ OP Pinot Nero Brut M. Cl. Blanc de Noir	TT 4
○ OP Riesling Renano V. Martina '19	TT 3
● Costa di Annibale Croatina '19	T 3
● OP Barbera Monplò '19	T 3
○ OP Pinot Nero Brut M. Cl. Première Cuvée	T 4
○ OP Pinot Nero Pas Dosé M. Cl. Sniper	T 5
● OP Pinot Nero V. dei Giganti '16	YY 3
● OP Pinot Nero V. del Cardinale '16	YY 4
○ OP Riesling Renano V. Martina '18	YY 3
○ OP Riesling Renano V. Martina '17	YY 3*
○ OP Riesling Renano V. Martina '16	YY 2*

Cantina Sociale La Versa

via F. Crispi, 15
27047 Santa Maria della Versa [PV]
Tel. +39 0385798411
www.laversa.it

CELLAR SALES
PRE-BOOKED VISITS
ANNUAL PRODUCTION 5,000,000 bottles
HECTARES UNDER VINE 1300.00

After a period of ups and downs, in 2017 Terre d'Oltrepò, together with the Trentino giant Cavit, saved this historic brand (Est. 1905) from bankruptcy. In late 2019 control passed entirely into the hands of Terre d'Oltrepò. The estate's history, traditions and even the bottles stored in its cellars all make it an emblem of the glories of yesteryear, when the late Duke Denari was able to bring the La Versa brand to national and international fame. Meanwhile, the involvement of a star like Riccardo Cotarella is a clear sign of new life. So will this time be different? The Testarossa '15 is a sophisticated Metodo Classico characterized by the energy of Pinot Nero, both aromatically and in its perlage—an exemplary wine. Pinot Nero, fermented with skin contact, gave rise to another notable selection. It's youthful, pleasantly rustic, with a juicy palate and fine tannins. Highly drinkable. Their standard-label Riesling and Pinot Grigio exhibit a small but pleasant varietal correspondence.

Wine	Glasses
○ Testarossa Brut M. Cl. '15	🍷🍷 5
● OP Pinot Nero '19	🍷🍷 3
○ OP Pinot Grigio '19	🍷 2
○ OP Riesling '19	🍷 2
○ Testarossa Principio Brut M. Cl. '08	🍷 6
● OP Barbera '12	YY 2*
● OP Barbera Fermo La Versa '11	YY 2*
○ OP Moscato di Volpara '13	YY 2*

Lantieri de Paratico

loc. Colzano
via Videtti (ingresso da via 2 Agosto)
25031 Capriolo [BS]
Tel. +39 030736151
www.lantierideparatico.it

CELLAR SALES
PRE-BOOKED VISITS
ACCOMMODATION AND RESTAURANT SERVICE
ANNUAL PRODUCTION 140,000 bottles
HECTARES UNDER VINE 20.00
VITICULTURE METHOD Certified Organic

More than a thousand years of history link Brescia's Lantieri de Paratico family to Franciacorta. Already in 1500, when the noble family moved to Capriolo, the wine produced here, known as 'Rubino di Corte Franca', was widespread and appreciated in Italian and European courts. In the historic property, whose 17th century vaults watch over their wines while they age, Fabio Lantieri built the modern cellar where he makes excellent Franciacorta from organically-grown grapes. The Arcadia Brut '16 once again demonstrates that it's one of the appellation's most interesting cuvées, gaining access to our final tastings. Made with Chardonnay (80%) and Pinot Nero, it matures over 42 months on the lees before disgorgement. It has a very fine beading, a delicate, floral and fruity bouquet, while on the palate it's pulpy, sapid and rich in ripe fruit notes, supported by a rich acidity. The very pleasant Brut is citrusy, fresh and racy, but with a soft, vanilla finish.

Wine	Glasses
○ Franciacorta Brut Arcadia '16	🍷🍷 5
○ Franciacorta Brut	🍷🍷 5
⊙ Franciacorta Brut Rosé	🍷🍷 5
○ Franciacorta Extra Brut	🍷🍷 5
○ Franciacorta Satèn	🍷🍷 5
○ Franciacorta Brut Arcadia '13	YYY 5
○ Franciacorta Nature Origines Ris. '12	YYY 7
○ Franciacorta Brut Arcadia '15	YY 5
○ Franciacorta Brut Arcadia '14	YY 5
○ Franciacorta Brut Arcadia '12	YY 5
○ Franciacorta Brut Arcadia '11	YY 5
○ Franciacorta Brut Arcadia '10	YY 5
○ Franciacorta Extra Brut Origines Ris. '10	YY 7
○ Franciacorta Nature Origines Ris. '13	YY 7
○ Franciacorta Nature Origines Ris. '11	YY 7

Lazzari

via Mella, 49
25020 Capriano del Colle [BS]
Tel. +39 0309747387
www.lazzarivini.it

CELLAR SALES
PRE-BOOKED VISITS
ANNUAL PRODUCTION 40,000 bottles
HECTARES UNDER VINE 9.50
VITICULTURE METHOD Certified Organic
SUSTAINABLE WINERY

Davide Lazzari knows his family's land meter-by-meter. For four generations they've been cultivating vines with incredible passion on a small hill that rises up on the plains south of Brescia. The producer is organic, powered by photovoltaic panels, to protect the environment as much as possible. Their wines are authentic, forthright, sometimes extravagant, but always the result of attention and love for the land. Lime and pineapple sensations characterize the white dedicated to Davide's grandfather Fausto. In the mouth it exhibits flesh, coming through linear and spirited. The Berzamì '19, 100% Marzemino, is characterized by the immediate, fruity fragrances of the grape, with a fresh palate. The Rosso Adagio '17 is the traditional wine: a blend of 4 grapes, it features wild and black cherry notes that bind together compact, ripe fruit. As we said last year, the Bastian Contrario, made with botrytised Turbiana grapes fermented and aged in barriques, is true to its name. The 2018 sees vanilla dominate over exotic fruit.

Wine	Rating
○ Capriano del Colle Bianco Fausto '19	🍷🍷 2*
● Capriano del Colle Marzemino Berzamì '19	🍷🍷 2*
● Capriano del Colle Rosso Adagio '17	🍷🍷 2*
○ Capriano del Colle Bianco Sup. Bastian Contrario '18	🍷 6
○ Capriano del Colle Bianco Fausto '18	🍷🍷 2*
○ Capriano del Colle Bianco Fausto '16	🍷🍷 2*
○ Capriano del Colle Bianco Sup. Bastian Contrario '16	🍷🍷 6
● Capriano del Colle Rosso Riserva degli Angeli '15	🍷🍷 4
● Capriano del Colle Rosso Riserva degli Angeli Ris. '16	🍷🍷 5

★Mamete Prevostini

loc. San Vittore
via Don Primo Lucchinetti, 63
23020 Sondrio
Tel. +39 034341522
www.mameteprevostini.com

CELLAR SALES
PRE-BOOKED VISITS
RESTAURANT SERVICE
ANNUAL PRODUCTION 180,000 bottles
HECTARES UNDER VINE 20.00
SUSTAINABLE WINERY

The winery managed by Mamete Prevostini is a model of environmental sustainability. They also offer a range that's solid and complete in all respects, with lean, airy wines redolent of mountains, and reserves that exhibit great concentration and deep gustatory sensations. Being able to grow in elegance, consistently producing a wine that year after year reaches the heights of excellence, is not a simple or obvious feat. But, the exception confirms the rule and the 2018 version of the Sforzato Corte di Cama amazes with its multifaceted personality. Aromas of herbs and licorice accompany red berries and mint. The palate surfs on austere tannins and sensations of ripe red berries. The San Lorenzo '18, a wine of great class and finesse, is marked by notes of red berries and spices. In the mouth it's rich, powerful, with a long finish. The Sforzato Albareda '18 is deliberately complex, with nuances of dried rose and a full, long, elegant palate.

Wine	Rating
● Valtellina Sforzato Corte di Cama '18	🍷🍷🍷 6
● Valtellina Sforzato Albareda '18	🍷🍷 6
● Valtellina Sup. Sassella San Lorenzo '18	🍷🍷 6
● Valtellina Sup. Inferno La Cruus '18	🍷🍷 5
● Valtellina Sup. Ris. '15	🍷🍷 5
● Valtellina Sforzato Albareda '15	🍷🍷🍷 6
● Valtellina Sforzato Albareda '13	🍷🍷🍷 6
● Valtellina Sforzato Corte di Cama '17	🍷🍷🍷 6
● Valtellina Sup. Sassella San Lorenzo '16	🍷🍷🍷 6
● Valtellina Sforzato Albareda '17	🍷🍷 6
● Valtellina Sup. Sassella Sommarovina '17	🍷🍷 5

Manuelina

FRAZ. RUINELLO DI SOTTO, 3A
27047 SANTA MARIA DELLA VERSA [PV]
TEL. +39 0385278247
Fraz. Ruinello di Sotto 3/a

CELLAR SALES
PRE-BOOKED VISITS
ANNUAL PRODUCTION 230,000 bottles
HECTARES UNDER VINE 22.00

The Achilli family's winery has made it into our main section. Its roots go back to the middle of the last century, with Luigi Achilli and his brother Guido. The baton then passed to Paolo and Antonio, Luigi's sons, and now to the third generation, with a concomitant change of name (Manuela is one of Paolo's daughters) so as to avoid being confused with other wineries in the area. Manuelina proposes modern wines, technically impeccable yet firmly linked to the territory. Right from its aromatic suite, the Solo Nero '18 proves an elegant Pinot Noir, varietal in its fragrances, with aromatic herbs softening focused fruit. A complex, polished, broad and deep palate gives way to a characterful finish. The terroir's aromatic herbs also feature in the Riesling Filare 52 '18, a wine redolent of peach and mint, exhibiting a vigor and personality in which mineral sensations are just emerging. Their bubbly also performed well, with a special mention for the excellent Rosé 145 '15, fragrant and juicy in its red berries.

Wine	Rating	Price
● OP Pinot Nero Solo Nero '18	🍷🍷	4
⊙ OP Pinot Nero Brut M. Cl. 145 Rosè '15	🍷🍷	4
○ OP Riesling Filare 52 '18	🍷🍷	3
○ OP Pinot Nero Brut M. Cl. 137 '16	🍷	4
○ Brut Pas Dosè '15	🍷🍷	3
○ OP Pinot Nero Brut M. Cl. 137 '13	🍷🍷	4
⊙ OP Pinot Nero Brut M. Cl. 145 Rosé '13	🍷🍷	3
● OP Pinot Nero Solo Nero '16	🍷🍷	3
● OP Sangue di Giuda Il Traditore '17	🍷🍷	2*
○ OP Pinot Nero Brut M. Cl. 137 '15	🍷	4

Le Marchesine

VIA VALLOSA, 31
25050 PASSIRANO [BS]
TEL. +39 030657005
www.lemarchesine.it

CELLAR SALES
PRE-BOOKED VISITS
ANNUAL PRODUCTION 450,000 bottles
HECTARES UNDER VINE 43.00
SUSTAINABLE WINERY

For at least 5 generations Brescia's time-honored Biatta family have been working in the world of wine. But it was in 1985 that Giovanni, starting with 3 hectares of vineyards, founded Le Marchesine. Since then, the producer has steadily expanded to its current 47 hectares. Today Loris Biatta is at the helm, together with his children Alice and Andrea. They're supported by the invaluable guidance of sparkling wine expert Jean-Pierre Valade. Once again, the Secolo Novo Brut '12 put in an outstanding performance. After almost five years of maturation on the lees, this Blanc de Blancs pours a beautiful, bright straw-yellow tinted green, the prologue to elegant scents of honey, butter and flowers, as well as white fruit. On the palate it exhibits structure, freshness, elegant sapidity and a long, complex finish of fruit and chestnut honey. But from the Satèn '16 to the non-vintage Brut, the whole range is excellent.

Wine	Rating	Price
○ Franciacorta Brut Secolo Novo '12	🍷🍷🍷	7
○ Franciacorta Brut	🍷🍷	4
○ Franciacorta Blanc de Blancs '12	🍷🍷	6
⊙ Franciacorta Brut Rosé '16	🍷🍷	6
○ Franciacorta Brut Satèn '16	🍷🍷	6
○ Franciacorta Extra Brut	🍷🍷	5
○ Franciacorta Brut '04	🍷🍷🍷	5
○ Franciacorta Brut Blanc de Noir '09	🍷🍷🍷	5
○ Franciacorta Brut Secolo Novo '05	🍷🍷🍷	7
○ Franciacorta Dosage Zero Secolo Novo Ris. '11	🍷🍷🍷	8
⊙ Franciacorta Brut Rosé '15	🍷🍷	6
○ Franciacorta Brut Satèn '15	🍷🍷	6
○ Franciacorta Brut Secolo Novo '11	🍷🍷	8
○ Franciacorta Extra Brut Blanc de Noirs '15	🍷🍷	6

Tenuta Mazzolino

via Mazzolino, 34
27050 Corvino San Quirico [PV]
Tel. +39 0383876122
www.tenuta-mazzolino.com

CELLAR SALES
PRE-BOOKED VISITS
ANNUAL PRODUCTION 100,000 bottles
HECTARES UNDER VINE 20.00

Mazzolino, a villa with an Italian-style garden and spectacular views, has been owned by the Braggiotti family since 1980. It was Giacomo Bologna himself who advised Enrico Braggiotti to vinify Pinot Nero on the skins, at the time with Giancarlo Scaglione, two icons of Piedmont's wine history. Then came outside help from France in the form of Kyriakos Kinigopoulos, thus they were able to recreate a patch of Burgundy in Oltrepò by drawing on Pinot Nero and Chardonnay in all their forms. For three years technical direction has been entrusted to the Piacenza enologist Stefano Malchiodi. Spices, healthy berries, fullness and depth: the Noir '17 is a Pinot Noir of class and substance. It's clear to see that it's got great aging prospects. The two sparklers also deliver: a racy Blanc de Blanc '16 proves redolent of wisteria and tropical fruits, while an elegant Cruasé features berries and lively acidity. The Blanc '18 is a Chardonnay with some personality. We just need some patience while its oak integrates more fully.

Wine	Rating
● OP Pinot Nero Noir '17	▼▼ 5
○ Chardonnay Blanc '18	▼▼ 3
○ Mazzolino Blanc de Blancs Brut M. Cl. '16	▼▼ 4
⊙ OP Cruasé Mazzolino	▼▼ 4
○ Camarà Chardonnay '19	▼ 2
● Terrazze Pinot Nero '19	▼ 3
● OP Pinot Nero Noir '12	▽▽▽ 5
● OP Pinot Nero Noir '10	▽▽▽ 5
● OP Pinot Nero Noir '09	▽▽▽ 5
● OP Pinot Nero Noir '08	▽▽▽ 5
● OP Pinot Nero Noir '07	▽▽▽ 5
● OP Pinot Nero Noir '06	▽▽▽ 5
○ Mazzolino Blanc de Blancs Brut M. Cl. '15	▽▽ 4
● OP Pinot Nero Noir '16	▽▽ 5
● OP Pinot Nero Noir '15	▽▽ 5

Mirabella

via Cantarane, 2
25050 Rodengo Saiano [BS]
Tel. +39 030611197
www.mirabellafranciacorta.it

CELLAR SALES
PRE-BOOKED VISITS
ACCOMMODATION
ANNUAL PRODUCTION 350,000 bottles
HECTARES UNDER VINE 45.00
SUSTAINABLE WINERY

In 1979 Teresio Schiavi, enologist, founded Mirabella with a group of vine-growing friends. Nowadays the producer, with its 50 hectares of vineyards, modern cellar and low-environmental impact, is run by administrator Francesco Bracchi together with Teresio's children Alessandro (enologist) and Alberto (commercial director). Almost half a million bottles are produced, and their constantly-growing range includes wines with low or no added sulphites. 2012 made for one of the most interesting reserves in the appellation.The Zero Døm Dosage is a cuvée of Chardonnay (60%) Pinot Nero (25%) and Bianco vinified partly in steel and partly (30%) in oak, before maturing on the lees over 7 years. It has soft, vanilla scents, opulence of fruit and a creamy mousse, fading long on notes of tropical fruit. The excellent Demetra Extra Brut '13 is a crisp, spirited and well profiled wine.

Wine	Rating
○ Franciacorta Pas Dosé Døm Ris. '12	▼▼ 7
○ Franciacorta Brut Edea	▼▼ 5
⊙ Franciacorta Brut Rosé	▼▼ 5
○ Franciacorta Exra Brut Demetra '13	▼▼ 5
○ Franciacorta Brut Satèn	▼ 5
○ Franciacorta Dosaggio Zero Dom Ris. '09	▽▽ 6
○ Franciacorta Dosaggio Zero Døm Ris. '11	▽▽ 7
○ Franciacorta Exra Brut Demetra '12	▽▽ 5
○ Franciacorta Extra Brut '09	▽▽ 5
○ Franciacorta Pinot Nero Brut Nature '15	▽▽ 6

★★Monsupello

via San Lazzaro, 5
27050 Torricella Verzate [PV]
Tel. +39 0383896043
www.monsupello.it

CELLAR SALES
PRE-BOOKED VISITS
ANNUAL PRODUCTION 260,000 bottles
HECTARES UNDER VINE 50.00

The winery led by Pierangelo and Laura, children of the never-forgotten Carlo Boatti (one of the first to believe in the quality of Oltrepò Pavese's wines) continues to be a benchmark for the territory. Skilfully managed by enologist Marco Bertelegni, it has for years been one of the best sparkling wine producers in Italy. All their wines, however, are noteworthy, whites and reds, young or aged, not to mention those sparklers, which continue to represent an important local market. Once again the Nature di Monsupello hits the mark. Bright in its slightly coppery color, it's an exemplary Metodo Classico redolent of anise, aromatic herbs and small berries, coming through taut and mineral, sapid right up to a long finish. We also appreciated the Rosé, fleshy in its fruit and highly expressive in its aromas of berries. The Brut—which we refuse to define as 'entry-level'—once again proves well made, full and ripe. The entirely new Extra Brut Blanc de Blancs proves elegant in its hints of spices and pastries, pleasant in its creamy sparkle.

Wine	Rating
○ Nature M. Cl.	▼▼▼ 4
⊙ Brut M. Cl. Rosé	▼▼ 4
○ Extra Brut Blanc de Blancs M. Cl.	▼▼ 5
○ Brut M. Cl.	▼▼ 5
● OP Bonarda Vivace Vaiolet '19	▼ 2
● Podere La Borla '16	▼ 3
○ Riesling '19	▼ 2
○ Brut M. Cl. '13	▽▽▽ 5
○ OP Brut Classese '06	▽▽▽ 5
○ OP Brut Classese '04	▽▽▽ 5
○ Brut M. Cl. '14	▽▽ 5
● Pinot Nero 3309 '09	▽▽ 3
● Pinot Nero Junior '16	▽▽ 3
○ Riesling '16	▽▽ 2*

★Monte Rossa

fraz. Bornato
via Monte Rossa, 1
25040 Cazzago San Martino [BS]
Tel. +39 030725066
www.monterossa.com

CELLAR SALES
PRE-BOOKED VISITS
ANNUAL PRODUCTION 500,000 bottles
HECTARES UNDER VINE 70.00

The Rabotti family's winery is part of the history of Franciacorta. Paolo Rabotti, in fact, with the support of his wife, Paola, has been selling wine since its foundation in 1972, and was among the first to abandon the production of still wines in favor of bubbly. Today the business is entrusted to his son Emanuele, who's flanked by Oscar Farinetti. They oversee 70 hectares of vineyards, situated in different terroirs, which, every year, give rise to about 500 thousand bottles of top-quality wine. Once again we very much appreciated the Brut P. R., the wine that best represents this historical maison today. It's a cuvée of Chardonnay and 35% reserve wines from previous vintages, about 22 different vineyards. It's linear, focused, sapid and fruity, supported by a fresh acidic vein and closing long on notes of fruit. The two Cabochons, the Doppiozero and Brut, also held their own but frankly we expected more emotions.

Wine	Rating
○ Franciacorta Brut P. R.	▼▼ 5
○ Franciacorta Brut Nature Cabochon Doppiozero '14	▼▼ 8
○ Franciacorta Brut Prima Cuvée	▼▼ 5
○ Franciacorta Brut Satèn Sansevé	▼▼ 5
○ Franciacorta Brut Cabochon Fuoriserie N. 022	▼ 8
○ Franciacorta Non Dosato Coupé	▼ 5
⊙ Franciacorta Rosé Flamingo	▼ 5
○ Franciacorta Brut Cabochon '05	▽▽▽ 6
○ Franciacorta Brut Cabochon '04	▽▽▽ 6
○ Franciacorta Brut Cabochon '03	▽▽▽ 6
○ Franciacorta Brut Cabochon '01	▽▽▽ 6
○ Franciacorta Brut Cabochon '99	▽▽▽ 7
○ Franciacorta Brut Cabochon '98	▽▽▽ 6
○ Franciacorta Brut Cabochon '97	▽▽▽ 6

La Montina

FRAZ. BAIANA, 17
25040 MONTICELLI BRUSATI [BS]
TEL. +39 030653278
www.lamontina.com

CELLAR SALES
PRE-BOOKED VISITS
RESTAURANT SERVICE
ANNUAL PRODUCTION 400,000 bottles
HECTARES UNDER VINE 70.00
VITICULTURE METHOD Certified Organic

Founded in 1987, La Montina is owned by the Bozza brothers, Vittorio, Giancarlo and Alberto. The winery takes its name from the historic Montini family property, the birthplace of Pope Paul VI. Today the producer has more than 70 hectares of vineyards located in seven municipalities in Franciacorta. Their headquarters is a beautiful villa where, in addition to their large and modern underground cellar, we find elegant accommodations. The new generation, represented by Michele and Daniele Bozza, is bringing new energy to the business, whose quality continues to grow. La Montina's range has no weak points. Topping our preferences this year is the Brut '12, with its beautiful spicy tones, rich in fruit, structure and freshness. The Rosé Extra Brut shows off its acidic backbone and tension, ensuring a pleasant, fresh drink on berry sensations, while the Satèn expresses an elegant complexity in which mineral and vanilla notes emerge, closing long on hints of fruit and lime blossom.

Wine	Rating
○ Franciacorta Brut '12	▼▼ 5
⊙ Franciacorta Extra Brut Rosé	▼▼ 5
⊙ Franciacorta Rosé Demi Sec	▼▼ 4
○ Franciacorta Satèn	▼▼ 5
○ Franciacorta Brut	▼ 5
○ Franciacorta Extra Brut	▼ 4
○ Franciacorta Brut '05	∇∇∇ 5
○ Franciacorta Extra Brut Vintage Ris. '05	∇∇∇ 6
○ Franciacorta Extra Brut Vintage Ris. '04	∇∇∇ 6
○ Franciacorta Brut '11	∇∇ 5
○ Franciacorta Pas Dosé Baiana Ris. '11	∇∇ 5

Monzio Compagnoni

VIA NIGOLINE, 98
25030 ADRO [BS]
TEL. +39 0307457803
www.monziocompagnoni.com

CELLAR SALES
PRE-BOOKED VISITS
ANNUAL PRODUCTION 170,000 bottles
HECTARES UNDER VINE 17.00

Marcello Monzio Compagnoni, a long-time vine dresser, created a new winery in Franciacorta 30 years ago where he could live out his passion for Metodo Classico sparkling wine, which went hand in hand with the excellent products made on the family estate in nearby Valcalepio. In the modern Adro cellar he produces a well-crafted range of Franciacorta from 14 hectares of estate vineyards, doing the same in Scanzorosciate with the wines of Valcalepio. The Blanc de Noir Riserva '09 is the wine that most impressed this year. It pours a lovely, bright straw-yellow with copper highlights, heralding a complex and rich nose that sees nuances of toast and yeast followed by spicy, red berry notes. In the mouth it's rich and deep, with a pleasant fruity finish and a delicate smoky stroke. The Satèn, in the producer's classic style, opens amidst creamy notes of fruit and citron, while the pleasant, delectable Brut Cuvée adheres to fashion, coming through sapid and fruity.

Wine	Rating
○ Franciacorta Nature Blanc de Noir Monti della Corte Ris. '09	▼▼ 7
○ Curtefranca Bianco Ronco della Seta '19	▼▼ 3
○ Franciacorta Brut '15	▼▼ 5
○ Franciacorta Brut Cuvée alla Moda	▼▼ 5
○ Franciacorta Extra Brut '12	▼▼ 5
○ Franciacorta Satèn '15	▼▼ 6
○ Franciacorta Extra Brut '04	∇∇∇ 5
○ Franciacorta Extra Brut '03	∇∇∇ 5
○ Curtefranca Bianco della Seta '15	∇∇ 4
○ Curtefranca Bianco Ronco della Seta '18	∇∇ 3
○ Franciacorta Brut '14	∇∇ 5
○ Franciacorta Brut '13	∇∇ 6
○ Franciacorta Brut '12	∇∇ 5
○ Franciacorta Satèn '13	∇∇ 6

Mosnel

Fraz. Camignone
c.da Barboglio, 14
25050 Passirano [BS]
Tel. +39 030653117
www.mosnel.com

CELLAR SALES
PRE-BOOKED VISITS
RESTAURANT SERVICE
ANNUAL PRODUCTION 250,000 bottles
HECTARES UNDER VINE 41.00
VITICULTURE METHOD Certified Organic

It's definitely worth visiting Mosnel's 16th-century property. There's a beautifully restored villa, where Giulio and Lucia Barzanò welcome guests, while, in contrast to the estate's ancient charm, there's also a very modern cellar, where the some of the area's best Franciacorta is produced. Children of Emanuela Barzanò Barboglio, a true pioneer of Franciacorta, Giulio and Lucia represent the fifth generation of family to make wine. The 40 hectares of vineyards that surround the estate are organically farmed. The 2015 version of the Extra Brut EBB that Giulio and Lucia dedicated to their mother did exceptionally well for itself. Sapid, elegant, deep, creamy in its mousse, it's one of the most representative wines of the terroir. The Pas Dosé is sapid, clear and crisp in its fruit, while the Satèn '16 sees delicate vanilla and floral hints followed by a soft, elegant palate that's not without a nice acidic tension. But every wine in their range has something to offer.

Wine	Rating	
○ Franciacorta Extra Brut EBB '15	🍷🍷🍷	7
○ Franciacorta Satèn '16	🍷🍷	6
○ Franciacorta Brut	🍷🍷	5
⊙ Franciacorta Brut Rosé	🍷🍷	5
○ Franciacorta Nature Bio	🍷🍷	4
○ Franciacorta Pas Dosé	🍷🍷	5
⊙ Franciacorta Pas Dosè Parosé '15	🍷🍷	7
○ Franciacorta Extra Brut EBB '09	ϒϒϒ	5
○ Franciacorta Pas Dosé QdE Ris. '04	ϒϒϒ	6
○ Franciacorta Pas Dosé Ris. '08	ϒϒϒ	8
○ Franciacorta Satèn '15	ϒϒϒ	6
○ Franciacorta Satèn '05	ϒϒϒ	5
○ Franciacorta Extra Brut EBB '14	ϒϒ	7
○ Franciacorta Extra Brut EBB '13	ϒϒ	7
⊙ Franciacorta Pas Dosè Parosé '14	ϒϒ	7
⊙ Franciacorta Pas Dosè Parosé '12	ϒϒ	7
○ Franciacorta Satèn '14	ϒϒ	5

★★Nino Negri

via Ghibellini
23030 Chiuro [SO]
Tel. +39 0342485211
www.ninonegri.it

CELLAR SALES
PRE-BOOKED VISITS
RESTAURANT SERVICE
ANNUAL PRODUCTION 800,000 bottles
HECTARES UNDER VINE 160.00
SUSTAINABLE WINERY

Nino Negri represents a beautiful slice of Valtellina's wine. in terms of its history, the producer's size, the quality of their wines, and for the intense work done to promote their products internationally. At the helm we find director Danilo Trocco. Guests are welcome to visit the cellar, which is dug into the rock of Castello Quadrio. Here incredible vintages give you a sense of the long journey made by a brand now owned by Gruppo Italiano Vini. The 5 Stelle '17 balances power, drinkability and finesse, and not only, thanks to lovely notes of tobacco, licorice, spices, red berries and tanned leather. In the mouth its tannins are close-knit, but there's also plenty of pulp, while the finish comes through long and harmonious. The Sasso Rosso '17 surprises with its sensations of dried roses, raspberry and tobacco. The palate is polished, progressively unfolding and long. The excellent Vigneto Fracia '17 stands out for its notes of dried herbs crossed by ripe raspberry. Elegantly expressive of the territory, in the mouth it shows balanced pulp.

Wine	Rating	
● Valtellina Sfursat 5 Stelle '17	🍷🍷🍷	8
● Valtellina Sup. Grumello Sassorosso '17	🍷🍷	5
● Valtellina Sup. Inferno Carlo Negri '17	🍷🍷	5
● Valtellina Sup. Vign. Fracia '17	🍷🍷	6
● Valtellina Sfursat Carlo Negri '17	🍷🍷	6
● Valtellina Sup. Sassella Le Tense '17	🍷🍷	5
● Valtellina Sfursat 5 Stelle '16	ϒϒϒ	8
● Valtellina Sfursat 5 Stelle '15	ϒϒϒ	8
● Valtellina Sfursat 5 Stelle '10	ϒϒϒ	7
● Valtellina Sfursat 5 Stelle '09	ϒϒϒ	7
● Valtellina Sfursat Carlo Negri '11	ϒϒϒ	8
● Valtellina Sup. Vign. Fracia '08	ϒϒϒ	6
● Valtellina Sfursat Carlo Negri '16	ϒϒ	6

Noventa

LOC. BOTTICINO MATTINA
VIA MERANO, 28
25080 BOTTICINO [BS]
TEL. +39 0302691500
www.noventabotticino.it

CELLAR SALES
PRE-BOOKED VISITS
ANNUAL PRODUCTION 45,000 bottles
HECTARES UNDER VINE 11.00
VITICULTURE METHOD Certified Organic

The Noventa family, especially Pierangelo and his daughter Alessandra, must be given credit for having believed in the potential of this very small appellation, which includes a handful of producers in Brescia and Lake Garda. For over 4 decades they've been stubbornly working these vineyards, situated at elevations of 450 meters and organically managed for some time now. The result is a range of powerful reds, increasingly elegant over the years. While their star performer, the Gobbio, rests in the cellar for a while longer, the producer submitted an excellent Pià della Tesa '18, a Botticine that pours a lovely, ruby-red, the prelude to spicy notes and blueberry sensations. In the mouth it shows nicely balanced acidity and remarkable finesse. The Colle degli Ulivi '18 is deliciously drinkable, while we found the rosé L'Aura '19, made with Schiava, simply irresistible in its aromas of rose and white peach.

Wine	Rating
● Botticino Pià de la Tesa '18	🍷🍷 5
● Botticino Colle degli Ulivi '18	🍷🍷 4
⊙ L'Aura '19	🍷🍷 3
● Botticino Gobbio '17	YYY 5
● Botticino Gobbio '16	YYY 5
● Botticino Colle degli Ulivi '17	YY 2*
● Botticino Colle degli Ulivi '16	YY 2*
● Botticino Gobbio '15	YY 5
● Botticino Pià de la Tesa '15	YY 3
● Botticino Pià de la Tesa '12	YY 3
● Botticino Pià de la Tesa '11	YY 3
● Botticino Pià della Tesa '17	YY 3
● Botticino Pià della Tesa '16	YY 3
● Botticino V. del Gobbio '11	YY 5
● Botticino V. del Gobbio '10	YY 5
● Botticino V. del Gobbio 50 '12	YY 5
⊙ L'Aura Schiava '18	YY 3

Oltrenero

LOC. BOSCO
27049 ZENEVREDO [PV]
TEL. +39 0385245326
www.ilbosco.com

CELLAR SALES
PRE-BOOKED VISITS
ANNUAL PRODUCTION 1,000,000 bottles
HECTARES UNDER VINE 152.00

A lot has changed since 1987 when the Zonin family decided to invest in Oltrepò Pavese by purchasing the estate which, in medieval times, formed part of the Monastery of Santa Maria Teodote. The hectares of vineyards, all privately owned, have increased from the initial 30 to 152. Naturally, the focus was immediately on the area's traditional grapes, starting with Croatina and Barbera. But the greatest work has been done with Pinot Nero, present in Oltrepò since the 19th century, through identifying terroirs and clones suitable for both sparkling wine and reds. The Poggio Pelato once again demonstrates its ability to evolve over the years. The 2017 is a mature Pinot Noir, very fruity, rich and dense, aromatically varietal, interpreted in the classic Oltrepò Pavese style. As for their Oltrenero Metodo Classicos, the Nature '15 exhibits texture, intensity and nice finesse in its sparkle. The Rosé features small berries and citrus on the nose, and a nice acidity on the palate that compensates for residual sugar. The same holds for the Brut, a wine redolent of pear, peach and apricot.

Wine	Rating
⊙ OP Pinot Nero Brut Rosé	🍷🍷 3
○ OP Pinot Nero Nature M. Cl. Oltrenero '15	🍷🍷 6
● OP Pinot Nero Poggio Pelato '17	🍷🍷 4
○ OP Pinot Nero Brut M. Cl. Oltrenero	🍷 5
○ OP Pinot Nero Nature M. Cl Oltrenero '13	YYY 6
○ OP Pinot Nero Nature M. Cl Oltrenero '14	YY 6
○ OP Pinot Nero Nature M. Cl. Oltrenero '10	YY 6

Pasini San Giovanni

FRAZ. RAFFA
VIA VIDELLE, 2
25080 PUEGNAGO SUL GARDA [BS]
TEL. +39 0365651419
www.pasinisangiovanni.it

CELLAR SALES
PRE-BOOKED VISITS
ANNUAL PRODUCTION 300,000 bottles
HECTARES UNDER VINE 36.00
VITICULTURE METHOD Certified Organic
SUSTAINABLE WINERY

Founded by Andrea Pasini in 1958, the family business is now managed by cousins Luca, Sara, Laura and Paolo Pasini, the third generation of viticulturists to work 36 hectares of property straddling the Valtènesi and Lugana appellations. Over the years the cellar has been modernized and, since 2009, powered by photovoltaic panels. Attention to the environment and eco-sustainability have also led to organic certification. This year we most appreciated the Valtènesi Il Valtènesi '18. Fresh, sapid, crisp in its fruit and highly enjoyable to drink, it's a red of great cleanness and freshness—delicious, as perhaps every Groppello should be. The Dosaggio Zero Ceppo 326, a Metodo Classico rosé made with Groppello and Chardonnay, has remarkable finesse, while the Chiaretto Rosagreen '19 proves sapid, fresh and enticing in its fruit.

Wine	Rating
⊙ Brut M. Cl. Rosé Ceppo 326	TT 4
○ Lugana Busocaldo Ris. '18	TT 5
⊙ Valtènesi Chiaretto Rosagreen '19	TT 3
● Valtènesi Il Valtènesi '18	TT 3
○ Extra Brut M. Cl. 100%	T 4
○ Lugana Il Lugana '19	T 3
⊙ Valtènesi Il Chiaretto '19	T 3
○ 100% Extra Brut M. Cl.	YY 4
○ Lugana Bio '18	YY 2*
● Valtènesi '16	YY 2*
● Valtènesi Arzane '15	YY 3
⊙ Valtènesi Chiaretto Rosagreen '18	YY 3
● Valtènesi Il Groppello '17	YY 3
⊙ Valtènesi Riviera del Garda Cl. Chiaretto Rosagreen '17	YY 3

Perla del Garda

VIA FENIL VECCHIO, 9
25017 LONATO [BS]
TEL. +39 0309103109
www.perladelgarda.it

CELLAR SALES
PRE-BOOKED VISITS
ANNUAL PRODUCTION 120,000 bottles
HECTARES UNDER VINE 30.00
VITICULTURE METHOD Certified Organic
SUSTAINABLE WINERY

Through patient work, in the year 2000 brother and sister Giovanna and Ettore Prandini revived viticulture on the family estate, a property that goes back generations. Production started in 2006, in a modern, three-level cellar that allows for gravity-flow winemaking. 30 hectares are mainly cultivated with Turbiana, and give rise to multifaceted Lugana. Organic certification is already in place, testifying to their commitment to environmental sustainability. The Lugana Riserva Madreperla '18 stood out in our tastings and earned the second award for this lovely Lake Garda producer. It pours a brilliant straw-yellow, anticipating a nose rich in fruit with elegant strokes of aromatic herbs and citrus. On the palate it's rich, deep and full, with a beautiful sapid and mineral vein, closing alluringly on white fruit. It's a tension and freshness that we find in the pulpy Lugana Bio '19. The valid Garda Brut, made with Chardonnay, proves harmonious and sapid, the Brio Brut fresh and drinkable, while the Brut Nature '12 is more complex and deep, though a bit over-mature.

Wine	Rating
○ Lugana Madreperla Ris. '18	TTT 4*
○ Garda Brut M. Cl.	TT 6
○ Lugana Perla Bio '19	TT 2*
○ Lugana Brio Brut	T 3
○ Lugana Perla '19	T 3
○ Perla Brut Nature M. Cl. '12	T 3
⊙ Valtènesi Chiaretto '19	T 3
○ Lugana Sup. Madonna della Scoperta '17	YYY 4*
● Garda Merlot Leonatus '15	YY 4
○ Lugana Bio '16	YY 2*
○ Lugana Brut Nature M. Cl. '11	YY 7
○ Lugana Madreperla '16	YY 4
○ Lugana Perla '17	YY 3
○ Lugana Perla '16	YY 3
○ Lugana Perla Bio '18	YY 2*

Andrea Picchioni

fraz. Camponoce, 4
27044 Canneto Pavese [PV]
Tel. +39 0385262139
www.picchioniandrea.it

CELLAR SALES
PRE-BOOKED VISITS
ACCOMMODATION
ANNUAL PRODUCTION 70,000 bottles
HECTARES UNDER VINE 10.00
VITICULTURE METHOD Certified Organic
SUSTAINABLE WINERY

The story of Andrea Picchioni and his small winery serves as a model. He built it at the age of twenty, acquiring and reviving old, steep, abandoned vineyards in the Solinga Valley, learning how to make wine and improve it, year after year, in small steps. All the while he listened to the opinions of those he trusted and took advantage of the precious support of his parents. Harvest after harvest, these small steps began to emerge in his wines, especially those intended for aging, so much so that that now they represent true benchmarks for the territory. A powerful and elegant red, the Bricco Riva Bianca '17 is a still-youthful Buttafuoco, owing to the hot year. It needs more time than the 2016 to relax and develop a close-knit weave of fine tannins and ripe fruit. Racy, balsamic and harmonious, we also appreciated the Pinot Nero Arfena '18. Characteristic notes of mint herald a tight, fruity, broad and multifaceted Rosso d'Asia '17. The Bonarda Ipazia '19 is among the best of the vintage.

● Arfena Pinot Nero '18	🍷🍷 4
● OP Buttafuoco Bricco Riva Bianca '17	🍷🍷 4
● Da Cima a Fondo '18	🍷🍷 3
● OP Bonarda Vivace Ipazia '19	🍷🍷 2*
● Rosso d'Asia '17	🍷🍷 4
● OP Buttafuoco Solinghino '19	🍷 3
⊙ Profilo Pas Dosé M. Cl. Rosé '10	🍷 6

Pratello

via Pratello, 26
25080 Padenghe sul Garda [BS]
Tel. +39 0309907005
www.pratello.com

CELLAR SALES
ACCOMMODATION AND RESTAURANT SERVICE
ANNUAL PRODUCTION 600,000 bottles
HECTARES UNDER VINE 31.00
VITICULTURE METHOD Certified Organic

Vincenzo Bertola brings passion to his winery, which boasts over 150 years of history and a beautiful farmstead behind the Castle of Padenghe, in a breathtaking, hillside position overlooking Lake Garda and Valtènesi. The estate spans more than 70 hectares, and includes organically-farmed vineyards and olive trees. 31 are under vine, mostly high-density plots (from 6250-8500 feet per hectare) designed for quality wine production. Pratello is a compete producer, where arable land and livestock farming coexist in a sustainable ecosystem, of which Vincenzo is a scrupulous guardian. Vincenzo's range is vast and covers Garda's appellations. The Lugana Catulliano '19 is excellent, sapid-fruity and pulpy, supported by a beautiful acidity, as is the Riesling '19 with its lovely hints of grapefruit and petrol. We also appreciated the smooth and spicy Lugana 90+10 '19, and the Garda Spumante, with its beautiful peachy tones and spectrum of aromatic herbs. The creamy and soft Garda Pinot Grigio '19 also performed well.

○ Garda Chardonnay Brut M. Cl.	🍷🍷 4
○ Garda Riesling '19	🍷🍷 3
○ Lugana 90+10 Il Rivale '19	🍷🍷 4
○ Lugana Catulliano '19	🍷🍷 3
○ Pinot Grigio '19	🍷🍷 3
○ Lieti Conversari '18	🍷 4
⊙ Valtènesi Chiaretto Sant'Emiliano '19	🍷 3
○ Lieti Conversari '16	🍷🍷 4
○ Lugana 90+10 '17	🍷🍷 3
○ Lugana Catulliano '16	🍷🍷 4
○ Riesling '16	🍷🍷 3*
⊙ Valtènesi Chiaretto Sant'Emiliano '16	🍷🍷 3
⊙ Valtènesi Riviera del Garda Cl. Chiaretto Sant'Emiliano '17	🍷🍷 3
● Valtènesi Torrazzo '17	🍷🍷 3

Prime Alture

via Madonna, 109
27045 Casteggio [PV]
Tel. +39 038383214
www.primealture.it

CELLAR SALES
PRE-BOOKED VISITS
ACCOMMODATION AND RESTAURANT SERVICE
ANNUAL PRODUCTION 40,000 bottles
HECTARES UNDER VINE 8.00

In 2006, Roberto Lechiancole decided to focus on Oltrepò Pavese, creating this beautiful winery on a Casteggio foothill (there's also a restaurant and a splendid resort, run by his wife, Anna, and daughter Simona, with themed rooms and a saltwater swimming pool). The views of the plains and the vineyards surrounding the winery are remarkable. After changing hands a few times, winemaking is now under the supervision of expert Jean-François Coquard, a French enologist who's at home in Oltrepò. Io per Te is a Metodo Classico made entirely with Pinot Noir and that rests for at least 36 months on the lees. Characteristic red fruits emerge from this white sparkler, with beautiful light scents that follow through on a rather broad palate, made creamy thanks to the finesse of its bubbles. The Ssopra Riva '19 is an original blend of Chardonnay (40%) and Moscato Bianco (60%) that combines the tropical firmness of the former with the aromaticity of the latter, making for a pleasant and racy drink.

○ OP Pinot Nero Brut M. Cl. Io per Te	🍷🍷 6
○ Sopra Riva '19	🍷🍷 3
● Bordo Bosco Pinot Noir '19	🍷 4
● L'Altra Metà del Cuore '17	🍷 5
● Centopercento Pinot Noir '15	🍷🍷 5
● Centopercento Pinot Noir '14	🍷🍷 5
● Centopercento Pinot Noir '13	🍷🍷 5
● Centopercento Pinot Noir '12	🍷🍷 4
○ Il Bianco 60&40 '17	🍷🍷 4
○ Io per Te Brut M. Cl.	🍷🍷 5
● L'Altra Metà del Cuore Merlot '12	🍷🍷 3
● Monsieur Pinot Noir '16	🍷🍷 5
○ Sopra Riva '18	🍷🍷 3

Quadra

via Sant'Eusebio, 1
25033 Cologne [BS]
Tel. +39 0307157314
www.quadrafranciacorta.it

CELLAR SALES
PRE-BOOKED VISITS
RESTAURANT SERVICE
ANNUAL PRODUCTION 170,000 bottles
HECTARES UNDER VINE 32.00

The producer was founded in 2003 by entrepreneur Ugo Ghezzi, who's assisted by his children Cristina and Marco. In 2008 the team saw the arrival of enologist Mario Falcetti, who took over management. Currently, Quadra owns 32 hectares of vineyards, organically cultivated. Particular attention is paid to Pinot Bianco and Pinot Nero, and through research Falcetti has identified specific vineyards able to express the best qualities of the vines. The spirit of research and experimentation that drives Falcetti and his team is well expressed in Quadra's cuvées. The Qvée 72 '12 is an Extra Brut made with Chardonnay and Pinot Nero (20%) vinified and aged in wood barrels (small and not new). It rests 75 months on the lees before disgorgement. Delicate and deep, it's complex, dry and soft, closing long on notes of fruit. The Qblack, made with Pinot Nero, and the rest of the range, are all worth taking note of.

○ Franciacorta Quvée 72 Ris. '12	🍷🍷 5
○ Franciacorta Brut QBlack	🍷🍷 5
○ Franciacorta Dosaggio Zéro Eretiq '13	🍷🍷 6
○ Franciacorta Dosaggio Zero QZero Ris. '13	🍷🍷 5
○ Franciacorta Satèn QSaten '15	🍷🍷 6
⊙ Franciacorta Brut QRosé	🍷 5
○ Franciacorta Brut Vegan	🍷 4
○ Franciacorta Dosaggio Zero EretiQ '11	🍷🍷 6
○ Franciacorta Dosaggio Zero QZero '11	🍷🍷 5
○ Franciacorta Dosaggio Zero QZero '10	🍷🍷 5
○ Franciacorta Extra Brut Cuvée 55 '10	🍷🍷 5
○ Franciacorta Extra Brut Quvée 58 Ris. '11	🍷🍷 5
○ Franciacorta QSatèn '14	🍷🍷 5
○ Franciacorta QSatèn '12	🍷🍷 5
○ Franciacorta QSatèn '11	🍷🍷 5
○ Franciacorta Satèn QSatèn '13	🍷🍷 5

Francesco Quaquarini

LOC. MONTEVENEROSO
VIA CASA ZAMBIANCHI, 26
27044 CANNETO PAVESE [PV]
TEL. +39 038560152
www.quaquarinifrancesco.it

CELLAR SALES
PRE-BOOKED VISITS
ANNUAL PRODUCTION 650,000 bottles
HECTARES UNDER VINE 60.00
VITICULTURE METHOD Certified Organic

The Quaquarini family's winery, managed by father Francesco and his children Umberto (enologist) and Maria Teresa, is typical for Oltrepò Pavese. A medium/large producer for the territory, for many years it's been organically cultivated, always managing to offer good quality at affordable prices. Many different wines are produced, as is normal for the area, with sparkling wines representing their core business. We are still waiting for the star performer, which is certainly within the family's reach. Once again the Buttafuoco Guasca '16 proves compact in its ripe fruit, coming through spicy, tasty and vibrant on the palate. Rich, redolent of mint, cocoa and dark berry fruits, the Barbera Poggio Anna '16 is balanced and weighty. Pleasant and harmonious, with its floral fragrances and hints of white fruit, the Classese '13 proves fine in its sparkle. As always the Sangue di Giuda '19 is among the best in its class, sapid and fragrant of red fruits and rosemary, nicely balancing sweetness, tannins and acidity.

Wine	Rating
● OP Buttafuoco La Guasca '16	TT 4
● OP Buttafuoco Storico V. Pregana '16	TT 6
○ OP Pinot Nero Brut M. Cl. Classese '13	TT 4
● OP Sangue di Giuda '19	TT 2*
● Poggio Anna Barbera '16	TT 3
● OP Bonarda Riva di Sass '19	T 3
● OP Pinot Nero Blau '17	T 3
● OP Barbera Poggio Anna '12	YY 2*
● OP Bonarda Riva di Sass '17	YY 3
● OP Buttafuoco Storico V. Pregana '15	YY 6
● OP Buttafuoco Storico V. Pregana '13	YY 6
● OP Pinot Nero Blau '14	YY 3
● OP Pinot Nero Blau '13	YY 3
● OP Sangue di Giuda '18	YY 2*
● OP Sangue di Giuda '17	YY 2*
● OP Sangue di Giuda '16	YY 2*
● OP Sangue di Giuda '15	YY 2*

★Aldo Rainoldi

FRAZ. CASACCE
VIA STELVIO, 128
23030 CHIURO [SO]
TEL. +39 0342482225
www.rainoldi.com

CELLAR SALES
PRE-BOOKED VISITS
ANNUAL PRODUCTION 180,000 bottles
HECTARES UNDER VINE 9.60

Aldo Rainoldi is a true ambassador of Valtellina. His wines shine a light on the unique attributes of a singular territory, whether it be his clear and airy Sassellas or rich and powerful Sfursats (indeed, a recent re-evaluation of the Ca' Rizzieri '97 literally entranced us, demonstrating the wine's extraordinary aging potential). In addition to leading the winery, founded in 1925, Aldo is also busy serving as President of the Consorzio Vini Valtellina. The Sassella Riserva '16 is a splendid interpretation of the territory and Alpine Nebbiolo. A lovely olfactory harmony sees red fruit in the foreground, blending with tanned leather, dried herbs and noble wood. The palate is rich, unfolding progressively, of rare elegance. The Sforzato Ca' Rizzieri '17 is excellent, as always, sophisticated, with notes of tobacco and licorice, fresh cherries and plenty of fruit. In the mouth it's voluptuous, but not heavy. The Grumello Riserva '15 is multifaceted, with cinchona and berries. On the palate it's full-bodied, exhibiting nice class and character, long on the finish.

Wine	Rating
● Valtellina Sfursat Ca' Rizzieri '17	TT 6
● Valtellina Sup. Grumello Ris. '15	TT 6
● Valtellina Sup. Sassella Ris. '16	TT 5
● Valtellina Sfursat '08	YYY 5
● Valtellina Sfursat Fruttaio Ca' Rizzieri '15	YYY 6
● Valtellina Sfursat Fruttaio Ca' Rizzieri '11	YYY 6
● Valtellina Sfursat Fruttaio Ca' Rizzieri '10	YYY 6
● Valtellina Sfursat Fruttaio Ca' Rizzieri '09	YYY 6
● Valtellina Sfursat Fruttaio Ca' Rizzieri '06	YYY 6
● Valtellina Sup. Grumello Ris. '13	YYY 6
● Valtellina Sup. Sassella Ris. '13	YYY 5
● Valtellina Sup. Sassella Ris. '12	YYY 5
● Valtellina Sup. Sassella Ris. '06	YYY 5

Rebollini

LOC. SBERCIA
27040 BORGORATTO MORMOROLO [PV]
TEL. +39 0383872295
www.rebollini.it

CELLAR SALES
PRE-BOOKED VISITS
ANNUAL PRODUCTION 100,000 bottles
HECTARES UNDER VINE 35.00
SUSTAINABLE WINERY

Founded in the early 20th century, this western-Oltrepò winery has been owned and run by the Rebollini family from the beginning. Today Gabriele Rebollini is firmly at the helm of a producer that has expanded into neighboring municipalities with the purchase of plots suitable for Pinot Nero and Rhine Riesling. Their vineyards are managed according to principles of integrated pest management, while their wines, never banal, always show great personality. The Brut Nature '16 features an elegant floral bouquet accompanied by notes of yellow fruit. In the mouth it exhibits very fine sparkle widening with substance and fullness, moving towards a nice, clear finish. The Re Noir '16 is a spicy Pinot Noir fermented with skin contact. On the nose it's marked by small ripe fruit and hints of coffee, while on the palate it proves expansive and well orchestrated. Citrus, mandarin in particular, feature in the stylized and mature Cruasé '15, while the Riesling '18 is in that phase typical of Rhine Riesling in which it veers towards tertiaries.

Wine	Rating
⊙ OP Cruasé '15	🍷🍷 4
○ OP Pinot Nero Brut Nature M. Cl. '16	🍷🍷 5
● OP Pinot Nero Re Noir '16	🍷🍷 4
○ OP Riesling '18	🍷🍷 2*
○ Brut Nature M. Cl. '12	YY 5
● OP Bonarda '15	YY 4
● OP Bonarda Frizzante Sel. '16	YY 3
○ OP Pinot Nero Brut M. Cl. '11	YY 4
○ OP Pinot Nero Brut Nature M. Cl. '12	YY 5
○ OP Riesling '17	YY 2*
○ OP Riesling '16	YY 2*
○ OP Riesling '14	YY 4

Ricci Curbastro

VIA ADRO, 37
25031 CAPRIOLO [BS]
TEL. +39 030736094
www.riccicurbastro.it

CELLAR SALES
PRE-BOOKED VISITS
ACCOMMODATION
ANNUAL PRODUCTION 200,000 bottles
HECTARES UNDER VINE 27.00
SUSTAINABLE WINERY

Originally from Romagna, where they still own a farm, the Ricci Curbastro family came to Franciacorta in the 13th century. The producer founded by Gualberto has been run for years by his agronomist son Riccardo, who has expanded and modernized the estate by 32 hectares, 27.5 of which are under vine. Modern Franciacorta is now forged in their underground cellar, together with the support of enologists Annalisa Massetti and Andrea Rudelli and now Riccardo's son, Gualberto Jr, as well. The winery is a leader of sustainability in Italy. Once again the maison took home Tre Bicchieri. Three candidates, all of them outstanding, but at the photo finish it's the excellent Extra Brut '15 who takes the cake. It's a cuvée of equal parts Chardonnay and Pinot Nero matured at least 42 months on the lees before disgorgement. Elegant, thick, creamy, complex and rich in fruit, it's supported by a lovely, spirited acidity wrapped in creamy sparkle. The Satèn '16 is excellent, as always. The Extra Brut MR '09 is also worth a taste.

Wine	Rating
○ Franciacorta Extra Brut '15	🍷🍷🍷 5
○ Franciacorta Extra Brut Museum Release '09	🍷🍷 6
○ Franciacorta Satèn '16	🍷🍷 5
○ Brolo dei Passoni Passito '12	🍷🍷 4
○ Franciacorta Brut	🍷🍷 4
○ Franciacorta Dosaggio Zero Gualberto '10	🍷🍷 6
⊙ Franciacorta Rosé	🍷🍷 5
● Curtefranca Rosso V. Santella del Gröm '14	🍷 3
○ Franciacorta Demi Sec	🍷 4
○ Franciacorta Brut Museum Release '07	YYY 6
○ Franciacorta Extra Brut '12	YYY 5
○ Franciacorta Satèn '15	YYY 5
○ Franciacorta Satèn '14	YYY 5

Ronco Calino

loc. Quattro Camini
fraz. Torbiato
via Fenice, 45
25030 Adro [BS]
Tel. +39 0307451073
www.roncocalino.it

CELLAR SALES
PRE-BOOKED VISITS
ANNUAL PRODUCTION 70,000 bottles
HECTARES UNDER VINE 13.00
VITICULTURE METHOD Certified Organic
SUSTAINABLE WINERY

In what used to be the refuge of the great Brescian pianist Arturo Benedetti Michelangeli, the Bergamasque industrialist Paolo Radici found the perfect place to live out his passion for wine. After purchasing the estate in 1996, construction of its lovely underground cellar began in 1999. Since 2002, his wife, Lara Imberti Radici, has also been a fundamental part of the business, with agronomic and enological support provided by Pierluigi Donna and Leonardo Valenti. While this lovely producer's vintage and special edition wines are still aging, we'd like to point out 3 excellent non-vintage bottles that give us a sense of the Radici winery's upward trajectory: a fresh, sapid and fragrant Brut with a lovely, delicately salty vein, a Satèn with intense fruity notes and a coloring of aromatic herbs and a Rosé Radijan characterized by beautiful notes of peach and berries. It's also worth mentioning the elegant and full-bodied Curtefranca Rosso Ponènt '17.

● Curtefranca Rosso Ponènt '17	4
○ Franciacorta Brut	5
⊙ Franciacorta Brut Rosé Radijan	5
○ Franciacorta Satèn	5
○ Curtefranca Bianco Leànt '19	3
○ Curtefranca Bianco Leànt '18	3
○ Curtefranca Bianco Lèant '17	3
● Curtefranca Rosso Ponènt '16	4
● Curtefranca Rosso Ponènt '15	4
● Curtefranca Rosso Ponènt '12	4
○ Franciacorta Brut '12	5
○ Franciacorta Brut '11	5
○ Franciacorta Brut '10	5
○ Franciacorta Brut Nature '15	5
○ Franciacorta Brut Nature '12	5
○ Franciacorta Brut Nature '11	5
● L'Arturo Pinot Nero '15	5

Rossetti & Scrivani

via Costaiola, 23
27054 Montebello della Battaglia [PV]
Tel. +39 038383169
www.rossettiescrivani.it

ANNUAL PRODUCTION 100,000 bottles
HECTARES UNDER VINE 10.00

Situated in a beautiful position on the hills over Casteggio, the Rossetti and Scrivani families' winery has changed its approach several times over time. In recent years, the La Costaiola brand represents their traditional local wines, while the Rossetti & Scrivani brand was created specifically for Metodo Classico sparkling wines made with Pinot Nero. And thanks to the work of Fabio Rossetti in the vineyard, his enologist brother Michele in the winery and support from their cousin Simona, their selection of sparkling wines are increasingly proving to be well crafted. The Nature, redolent of small fruits and aromatic herbs, is crisp, linear, mature, with a softness made possible by the creaminess of its very fine sparkle. Wild berries also feature in the Brut Rosé, with hints of citrus fruits emerging as well, while in the mouth it proves supple and racy. The new Extra Brut Rosé is more full-bodied and substantive, while the Brut, characterized by melon and grapefruit sensations, is rounded out by residual sugars.

○ Brut Nature M. Cl.	4
⊙ Brut M. Cl. Rosé	4
○ Extra Brut M. Cl. Rosé	4
○ Brut M. Cl.	4

San Cristoforo

FRAZ. VILLA
VIA VILLANUOVA, 2
25030 ERBUSCO [BS]
TEL. +39 0307760482
www.sancristoforo.eu

CELLAR SALES
PRE-BOOKED VISITS
ANNUAL PRODUCTION 80,000 bottles
HECTARES UNDER VINE 10.00
SUSTAINABLE WINERY

San Cristoforo is a small producer founded in 1992 by Bruno Dotti and his wife, Claudia. It's a strictly family-run producer, with his daughter Celeste now a permanent member of the team. The ten hectares acquired over the years are personally overseen by Bruno, while the winery has been expanded and renovated, and the quality of their Franciacorta is constantly growing. Year after year, this family-run maison stands out for the consistent quality and stylistic cleanness of its wines. This year we'd like to point out, in particular, the Pas Dosé '15, with its harmonious and crystalline profile, elegant on the nose in its notes of white fruit, aromatic herbs and honey, coming through linear, fresh and dry on the palate, with creamy mousse. The excellent Brut ND is sapid and deep, while the intriguing Celeste Pas Dosé '11 offers up complex sensations of spices and medicinal herbs.

Wine	Glasses	Score
○ Franciacorta Pas Dosé '15	▼▼	6
○ Franciacorta ND	▼▼	6
○ Franciacorta Pas Dosé Celeste '11	▼▼	8
○ Franciacorta Brut '15	▼	6
○ Franciacorta Brut	▼	4
○ Franciacorta Brut '14	▽▽	6
○ Franciacorta Brut '13	▽▽	6
○ Franciacorta Brut '11	▽▽	6
○ Franciacorta Dosaggio Zero '11	▽▽	6
○ Franciacorta Pas Dosé '14	▽▽	6
○ Franciacorta Pas Dosé '13	▽▽	6
○ Franciacorta Pas Dosé '12	▽▽	6
○ Franciacorta Pas Dosé '10	▽▽	6
○ Franciacorta Pas Dosé Celeste '10	▽▽	8

Scuropasso - Roccapietra

FRAZ. SCORZOLETTA, 40/42
27043 PIETRA DE' GIORGI [PV]
TEL. +39 038585143
www.scuropasso.it

CELLAR SALES
PRE-BOOKED VISITS
ANNUAL PRODUCTION 200,000 bottles
HECTARES UNDER VINE 15.00

Slowly but surely, Fabio Marazzi has overcome the inevitable hindrances to build on the family business and create a winery focused on his great passions: Metodo Classico and Buttafuoco. He's also paid particular attention to its environmental impact. Indeed, the winery is completely powered by renewable energy, while the vineyards are being converted to organic. For some years now he's been joined by his daughter Flavia, another driving force on the road to quality. What a personality shines through for the Cruasé Roccapietra '14! Rich and compact, bursting with sensations of red berries, notes of wheat and liquorice. On the palate it proves full and ebullient while maintaining rhythm, finishing with energy and flavor. The very well-crafted Vigna Pian Long '17 is a fruity Buttafuoco Storico characterized by a broad suite of spices and herbs, from mint to rosemary. The Brut Roccapietra '15 is citrusy, mature and rich, while the Buttafuoco Lunapiena '14 proves warm and robust with sensations of cherry tart.

Wine	Glasses	Score
● OP Buttafuoco Storico V. Pian Long '17	▼▼	4
⊙ OP Cruasé Roccapietra '14	▼▼	4
○ OP Brut M. Cl Roccapietra '15	▼▼	4
● OP Buttafuoco Lunapiena '14	▼▼	3
● OP Buttafuoco Costa Barosine '17	▼	4
○ Roccapietra Pas Dosé M. Cl. '14	▼	4
○ Roccapietra Pas Dosé M. Cl. '13	▽▽▽	4*
● OP Buttafuoco '15	▽▽	4
● OP Buttafuoco Lunapiena '13	▽▽	3
● OP Buttafuoco Scuropasso '16	▽▽	3
● OP Buttafuoco Storico Lunapiena '13	▽▽	3*
⊙ OP Cruasé Roccapietra '13	▽▽	4
⊙ OP Cruasé Roccapietra '12	▽▽	4
○ Roccapietra Pas Dosé M. Cl. '12	▽▽	4

Selva Capuzza

FRAZ. SAN MARTINO DELLA BATTAGLIA
LOC. SELVA CAPUZZA
25010 DESENZANO DEL GARDA [BS]
TEL. +39 0309910381
www.selvacapuzza.it

CELLAR SALES
PRE-BOOKED VISITS
ACCOMMODATION AND RESTAURANT SERVICE
ANNUAL PRODUCTION 300,000 bottles
HECTARES UNDER VINE 25.00
SUSTAINABLE WINERY

Selva Capuzza is a lovely, 50-hectare estate located in the amphitheater of the morainic hills in southern Lake Garda. It's divided into vineyards, olive groves and woods (born as a site for cultivating truffle). The producer, whose history goes back centuries, grows six native grape varieties, divided into three contiguous appellations, exclusively in privately-owned vineyards. Luca Formentini brings passion to his work of overseeing the property, which also includes a restaurant and guest rooms, with a particular focus on sustainability. The 2016 reserve version of the Lugana Menasasso also stood out in our finals. It's a complex white, structured but above all elegant. It pours a vibrant straw-yellow, opening up on a fresh and complex bouquet, with creamy notes of ripe, white fruit followed by fresh nuances of aromatic herbs. On the palate it's firm, pulpy and full, pervaded by a fresh acidity that gives way to a long and fresh, citrus finish. From the Chiaretto San Donino '19 to the San Martino '19 the whole range is excellent.

Wine	Rating
○ Lugana Menasasso Ris. '16	▼▼▼ 3*
○ Lugana San Vigilio '19	▼▼ 3
○ Lugana Selva '19	▼▼ 4
○ San Martino della Battaglia Campo del Soglio '19	▼▼ 4
⊙ Valtènesi Chiaretto San Donino '19	▼▼ 2*
○ Hirundo Brut	▼ 3
● Riviera Del Garda Bresciano Groppello San Biagio '18	▼ 3
○ Lugana Menasasso Ris. '15	▽▽▽ 3*
○ Lugana San Vigilio '18	▽▽ 3
○ Lugana Selva '18	▽▽ 4
○ San Martino della Battaglia Campo del Soglio '18	▽▽ 4
⊙ Valtènesi Chiaretto San Donino '18	▽▽ 2*

Le Sincette

LOC. PICEDO
VIA ROSARIO, 44
25080 POLPENAZZE DEL GARDA [BS]
TEL. +39 0365651471
www.lesincette.it

CELLAR SALES
PRE-BOOKED VISITS
ANNUAL PRODUCTION 30,000 bottles
HECTARES UNDER VINE 10.00
VITICULTURE METHOD Certified Biodynamic

Sincette Picedo was founded in 1979 by entrepreneur Ruggero Brunori as a winery that would respect the environment as much as possible through low-impact practices. After renovating the Cascina La Pertica, thanks in part to the support of director Andrea Salvetti various renowned enologists and technicians have followed one another over the years, first for the purposes of obtaining organic certification and then, after meeting with Jacques Mell, for biodynamic conversion. The Groppello '18, which we also tasted last year, is a great red. It's still redolent of berries, with smooth tannins, clear and fresh, with a beautiful structure and enticing palate. It's one of those wines that, in addition to interpreting a difficult grape, traces a path forward. The Colombaio '17 is more relaxed, rich and pulpy in its ripe red fruit, floral and spicy. Finally, kudos to the Chiaretto, a wine vinified in amphora. It pours a beautiful pale and bright pink color, and it's delicious to drink.

Wine	Rating
⊙ Valtènesi Chiaretto '19	▼▼ 3*
● Il Colombaio '17	▼▼ 4
● Garda Cl. Groppello '18	▽▽ 2*
● Garda Cl. Groppello '14	▽▽ 2*
● Garda Cl. Groppello '13	▽▽ 2*
● Ronco del Garda '13	▽▽ 2*
⊙ Valtenesi Chiaretto '18	▽▽ 2*
⊙ Valtenesi Chiaretto '12	▽▽ 2*

Lo Sparviere

via Costa
25040 Monticelli Brusati [BS]
Tel. +39 030652382
www.losparviere.com

CELLAR SALES
PRE-BOOKED VISITS
ANNUAL PRODUCTION 120,000 bottles
HECTARES UNDER VINE 30.00

The Gussalli Beretta family, led by Ugo, owns a large group of estates. In addition to Lo Sparviere in Franciacorta, they own ForteMasso in Langhe, Steinhaus in Alto Adige, Castello di Radda in Chianti Classico and Orlandi Contucci Ponno in Abruzzo. The winery dates back to the 16th century and owes its name to the sparrowhawk depicted on the coat of arms of the living room fireplace of the manor house. The fact that the Beretta family is also serious about agriculture is made evident by the prize-winning Lo Sparviere, one of the most important brands in Franciacorta. This year the honor goes to the Dosaggio Zero Riserva '13, a wine that makes complexity and depth its distinctive traits. Aromatic herbs, candied citrus fruit, smoky notes and a fresh, lemony element... In the glass you'll find all this, wrapped in a creamy mousse and mineral sapidity.

Wine	Glasses	Price
○ Franciacorta Dosaggio Zero Ris. '13	🍷🍷🍷	6
○ Franciacorta Extra Brut	🍷🍷	5
○ Franciacorta Satèn	🍷🍷	6
⊙ Franciacorta Brut Rosé Monique	🍷	5
○ Franciacorta Brut '13	🍸🍸🍸	5
○ Franciacorta Brut '12	🍸🍸🍸	5
○ Franciacorta Dosaggio Zero Ris. '08	🍸🍸🍸	6
○ Franciacorta Extra Brut '13	🍸🍸🍸	6
○ Franciacorta Extra Brut '09	🍸🍸🍸	5
○ Franciacorta Extra Brut '08	🍸🍸🍸	5
○ Franciacorta Extra Brut '07	🍸🍸🍸	5
○ Franciacorta Brut '14	🍸🍸	5
○ Franciacorta Dosaggio Zero Riserva '12	🍸🍸	6
○ Franciacorta Extra Brut '12	🍸🍸	6

Conti Thun

via Masserino 2
25080 Puegnago sul Garda [BS]
Tel. +39 0365651757
www.contithun.com

ANNUAL PRODUCTION 25,000 bottles
HECTARES UNDER VINE 12.00

Vittorio Sommo and Ilona Thun chose Puegnago as their residence, spawning this promising producer. It's made up of twelve hectares of vineyards (and two of olive groves) in the heart of the Valtènesi, around the lovely, perfectly restored 19th-century agricultural court where their picturesque cellars are housed (rural accommodations are available as well is practiced). A few years ago they began restoring the vineyards and cellar, and thanks in part to a high-level technical staff, their work is now bearing fruit. Despite the fact that the winery is just on its second harvest, the Chiaretto Vino Rosa '17 explores the aging potential of this fascinating typology. The result is a complex and rich but sapid, lean wine. It's pleasant and enjoyable, qualities innate to Groppello, the grape that dominates the blend. The Rosé Bolle di Michaela is creamy, with beautiful hints of rose, raspberry, currant and blueberry. We also appreciated the sapid and fruity Riesling Vasca 59 '19.

Wine	Glasses	Price
⊙ Brut Rosé Bolle di Michaela	🍷🍷	4
○ Riesling Vasca 59 '19	🍷🍷	3
⊙ Vinorosa '17	🍷🍷	5
○ Bolle di Gioia Brut '19	🍷	3
⊙ Valtenesi Chiaretto Michaela '19	🍷	4
● Valtènesi Leonardo '18	🍷	4
⊙ Valtenesi Chiaretto Michaela '18	🍸🍸	4

Torrevilla

via Emilia, 4
27050 Torrazza Coste [PV]
Tel. +39 038377003
www.torrevilla.it

CELLAR SALES
PRE-BOOKED VISITS
ANNUAL PRODUCTION 3,000,000 bottles
HECTARES UNDER VINE 650.00

Since 2008, 100 years after the founding of Torrazza Coste and under Massimo Barbieri, Torrevilla has decided to embark on an important development path. Collaboration with the University of Milan and the Riccagioia Research Center has made it possible to carry out an in-depth zoning study on its vineyards, with the help of four weather stations. The progress made by their wines in recent years is palpable, and the recent acquisition of historic brand Il Montù brings an additional 70 hectares in Valle Versa. We very much appreciated the Nature Riserva 110 '16, a complex and multifaceted sparkler redolent of flowers and aromatic herbs—sapid and spunky, creamy in the finesse and persistence of its sparkle. The Pinot Noir Riserva '17 also put in a good performance, proving fruity and energetic, varietal in the lovely, classic Oltrepò Pavese style. The Bonarda La Genisia Bio '18 is a still wine made with grapes grown organically. It exhibits close-knit, mature tannins, hints of plum and undergrowth, as well as nice backbone.

Wine	Rating
○ OP Pinot Nero Brut Nature M. Cl. 110 '16	🍷🍷 5
● OP Bonarda La Genisia Bio '18	🍷🍷 3
● OP Pinot Nero 110 Noir Ris. '17	🍷🍷 4
○ OP Pinot Nero Brut Nature M. Cl. La Genisia	🍷🍷 5
● OP Barbera La Genisia Bio '18	🍷 2
○ OP Cortese Garlà '19	🍷 2
○ OP Riesling Sup. La Genisia '19	🍷 3
● OP Barbera La Genisia '18	ΥΥ 2*
● OP Barbera La Genisia Bio '17	ΥΥ 2*
● OP Bonarda La Genisia Bio '17	ΥΥ 2*
○ OP Pinot Grigio La Genisia Ramato '18	ΥΥ 3
○ OP Pinot Nero Brut Nature M. Cl. 110 Ris. '14	ΥΥ 5
○ OP Riesling Sup. La Genisia '18	ΥΥ 3

Pietro Torti

fraz. Castelrotto, 9
27047 Montecalvo Versiggia [PV]
Tel. +39 038599763
www.pietrotorti.it

CELLAR SALES
PRE-BOOKED VISITS
ACCOMMODATION
ANNUAL PRODUCTION 40,000 bottles
HECTARES UNDER VINE 18.00
VITICULTURE METHOD Certified Organic

Sandro Torti, son of Pietro, has been running the family business since 1990, flanked in recent years by his daughter Chiara. Five generations of Torti have succeeded one another in overseeing their vineyards in Montecalvo, which are now organically managed. Sandro is basically a wine artisan, adopting a minimally-invasive approach in the countryside, limited use of sulphites and selected yeasts, etc. In short, his are wines that must often be interpreted and, above all, prove sensitive to the climate of individual vintages. This year Sandro submitted a truly notable Metodo Classico, undoubtedly his best. Complex on the nose, with scents ranging from citrus fruits to berries accompanied by marine and mineral suggestions, a very slight, fascinating oxidative tendency emerges, while the palate proves rich and creamy. The delicious Bonarda La Riva '19 is dark, close-knit and rustic, marked by typicity, with a broad palate and almondy finish. The Campo Rivera '17 is a mature, close-knit and fleshy Barbera redolent of wild cherry and raspberry.

Wine	Rating
○ OP Pinot Nero Brut M. Cl. '15	🍷🍷 4
○ Fagù '19	🍷🍷 2*
● OP Barbera Campo Rivera '17	🍷🍷 4
● OP Bonarda Frizzante La Riva '19	🍷🍷 2*
● OP Pinot Nero Mobi '16	🍷 4
● Uva Rara '18	🍷 3
○ Fagù '16	ΥΥ 2*
● OP Barbera Campo Rivera '16	ΥΥ 4
● OP Barbera Campo Rivera '15	ΥΥ 4
● OP Barbera Campo Rivera '12	ΥΥ 4
● OP Bonarda Verzello '17	ΥΥ 2*
● OP Bonarda Vivace '16	ΥΥ 2*
⊙ OP Cruasé '13	ΥΥ 4
⊙ OP Cruasé '12	ΥΥ 4
○ OP Pinot Nero Brut M. Cl. Torti '13	ΥΥ 4

Travaglino

LOC. TRAVAGLINO
27040 CALVIGNANO [PV]
TEL. +39 0383872222
www.travaglino.it

CELLAR SALES
PRE-BOOKED VISITS
ACCOMMODATION AND RESTAURANT SERVICE
ANNUAL PRODUCTION 200,000 bottles
HECTARES UNDER VINE 80.00

This historic winery, whose core property consists of an ancient monastery converted into a manor house, has been owned by the Comi family for over 150 years, thanks to Cavalier Vincenzo. It was his grandson who, in the 1960s, revolutionized the estate by zoning the land. And now more grandchildren, Cristina and Alessandro Cerri Comi, are relaunching the name, thanks primarily to two grapes: Rhine Riesling and Pinot Nero. In the cellar Achille Bergomi operates in support of Donato Lanati with the Enosis laboratory. Campo della Fojada is a historic Rhine Riesling cru in Oltrepò, and the 2019 version once again proves it's got plenty of substance, even if it's still at the beginning. Clear aromas of peach, plum and tropical fruits are accompanied by floral hints and a touch of honey—nice backbone on the palate and a satisfying finish. The Riserva del Fondatore '11 is a Metodo Classico that rests at length on the lees. Mature on the nose, it proves well-structured and supported by a still-detectable acidity on the palate.

○ OP Riesling Campo della Fojada '19	🍷🍷 3*
○ OP Pinot Nero Brut M. Cl. Gran Cuvée '16	🍷🍷 4
○ OP Pinot Nero Brut M. Cl. Vincenzo Comi Riserva del Fondatore '11	🍷🍷 5
○ OP Pinot Nero Brut M. Cl. Cuvée 59	🍷 4
● OP Pinot Nero Poggio della Buttinera '17	🍷 5
● OP Pinot Nero Pernero '18	🍷🍷 3
● OP Pinot Nero Poggio della Buttinera '16	🍷🍷 5
● OP Pinot Nero Poggio della Buttinera '15	🍷🍷 5
○ OP Riesling Campo della Fojada '18	🍷🍷 3
○ OP Riesling Campo della Fojada '17	🍷🍷 3*
○ OP Riesling Campo della Fojada Ris. '16	🍷🍷 3*
○ OP Riesling Campo della Fojada Ris. '14	🍷🍷 3*

★Uberti

LOC. SALEM
VIA E. FERMI, 2
25030 ERBUSCO [BS]
TEL. +39 0307267476
www.ubertivini.it

PRE-BOOKED VISITS
ANNUAL PRODUCTION 180,000 bottles
HECTARES UNDER VINE 26.00
VITICULTURE METHOD Certified Organic
SUSTAINABLE WINERY

A notarial deed certifies that on Saturday October 12th, 1793, Agostino Uberti bought a small farmhouse with vineyards in Salem, in Erbusco. Until the 1970s, viticulture was flanked by other traditional agricultural activities. Then another Agostino Uberti arrived, and it was he who decided to focus only on wine by carrying out, together with his wife, Eleonora, the first Franciacorta grape harvest in 1978. After several acquisitions, his daughters Silvia (enologist) and Francesca (administration) are also on board. We very much appreciated the Comarì del Salem '13 that we tasted this year. It nicely expresses the attributes of this historic Franciacorta cru, with delicate mousse, and a clear, focused, complex nose dominated by hints of white fruit, yeasts and aromatic herbs. The palate, soft and deep, is notable. The Rosé Francesco I is among the best tasted this year, like many of this historic producer's cuvées. It's clear they're headed in the right direction.

○ Franciacorta Extra Brut Comarì del Salem '13	🍷🍷🍷 6
○ Curtefranca Bianco Maria Medici '17	🍷🍷 4
○ Franciacorta Brut Francesco I	🍷🍷 5
⊙ Franciacorta Brut Rosé Francesco I	🍷🍷 5
○ Franciacorta Dosaggio Zero Sublimis Ris. '12	🍷🍷 7
○ Franciacorta Satèn Magnificentia '16	🍷🍷 6
● Rosso dei Frati Priori '16	🍷🍷 5
○ Franciacorta Extra Brut Francesco I	🍷 5
○ Franciacorta Brut Comarì del Salem '00	🍷🍷🍷 6
○ Franciacorta Extra Brut Comarì del Salem '03	🍷🍷🍷 6
○ Franciacorta Extra Brut Comarì del Salem '02	🍷🍷🍷 6
○ Franciacorta Extra Brut Comarì del Salem '01	🍷🍷🍷 6

Vanzini

fraz. Barbaleone, 7
27040 San Damiano al Colle [PV]
Tel. +39 038575019
www.vanzini-wine.com

CELLAR SALES
PRE-BOOKED VISITS
ANNUAL PRODUCTION 600,000 bottles
HECTARES UNDER VINE 27.00

If we are talking about sparkling wines produced with the area's classic grapes, the winery owned by siblings Antonio, Michela and Pierpaolo Vanzini is as reliable as they come. Their Bonarda, Sangue di Giuda and Moscato are always at the top during our tastings, thanks in part to the skill of enologist Pierpaolo. The same goes for the extra dry Metodo Martinotti white and rosé, made entirely with their own Pinot Nero grapes, an absolute guarantee of pleasantness. But even among their still wines it's not uncommon to find highly interesting bottles. The Sangue di Giuda '19 is a lovely red sparkler with a purplish mousse, bursting with crisp red berry aromas. On the palate it's not excessively sweet, nicely balancing sugar, acidity and tannins. As usual the two Extra Dry Metodo Martinotti Lungo sparklers (100% Pinot Nero) prove very pleasant, with a note of merit for the rosé, with its alluring fruity nuances.

Wine	Rating
● OP Sangue di Giuda '19	▼▼ 3
⊙ Pinot Nero Extra Dry Rosé	▼▼ 3
○ Assedio Moscato '19	▼ 2
● OP Barbera La Desiderata '19	▼ 2
● OP Bornarda Frizzante Con Tatto '19	▼ 2
○ Pinot Nero Extra Dry	▼ 3
● OP Barbera La Desiderata '17	▽▽ 2*
● OP Bonarda '16	▽▽ 2*
● OP Bonarda Frizzante '18	▽▽ 2*
● OP Rosso Barbaleone '15	▽▽ 5
● OP Sangue di Giuda '18	▽▽ 3
● OP Sangue di Giuda '17	▽▽ 3
● OP Sangue di Giuda '16	▽▽ 3
● OP Sangue di Giuda '15	▽▽ 3

Bruno Verdi

via Vergomberra, 5
27044 Canneto Pavese [PV]
Tel. +39 038588023
www.brunoverdi.it

CELLAR SALES
PRE-BOOKED VISITS
ANNUAL PRODUCTION 90,000 bottles
HECTARES UNDER VINE 12.00

We never get tired of singing the praises of Paolo Verdi, a vigneron who's personally overseen his property since he was twenty years old as a result of his father's death (Paolo wanted to keep his name as the company brand). Since then, year after year, he's been learning about his land and vineyards, taking care of them painstakingly, all supported by his mother, Carla, his sister Monica, then his wife, Enrica, and finally by his son Jacopo. And thanks to his efforts, he's built one of the area's most commendable producers, one that's capable of excellent wines. The 2016 Cavariola is one of the best versions ever of this historic red wine: ripe berry fruit, chocolate and mint sensations herald a powerful and juicy palate that admirably balances alcohol, fine tannins, acidity and structure, with a long almond finish. A top-notch range also features two Metodo Classicos: the full and creamy Vergomberra '15, just a bit less taut than usual, and the Cruasé, which impresses for its compact fruit and finesse.

Wine	Rating
● OP Rosso Cavariola Ris. '16	▼▼▼ 5
⊙ OP Cruasé Extra Brut	▼▼ 5
○ OP Extra Brut M. Cl. Vergomberra '15	▼▼ 5
● OP Bonarda Frizzante Possessione di Vergombera '19	▼▼ 2*
● OP Buttafuoco '19	▼▼ 2*
● OP Barbera Campo del Marrone '18	▼ 4
○ OP Riesling V. Costa '18	▼ 3
○ OP Dosage Zero Vergomberra '12	▽▽▽ 5
○ OP Pinot Nero Dosage Zéro M. Cl. Vergomberra '13	▽▽▽ 5
● OP Rosso Cavariola Ris. '10	▽▽▽ 5
● OP Rosso Cavariola Ris. '07	▽▽▽ 4
● OP Buttafuoco '18	▽▽ 2*
○ OP Pinot Nero M. Cl. Dosage Zero Vergomberra '14	▽▽ 5

Vigne Olcru

via Buca, 26
27047 Santa Maria della Versa [PV]
Tel. +39 0385799958
www.vigneolcru.com

PRE-BOOKED VISITS
ANNUAL PRODUCTION 190,000 bottles
HECTARES UNDER VINE 29.00
SUSTAINABLE WINERY

In 2013 brothers Massimiliano and Matteo Brambilla decided to move to Oltrepò Pavese from Brianza to create a new winery in the Upper Versa Valley. And so it was that they founded Vigne Olcru, a futuristic winery not only in terms of its architecture but also in terms of research, which is carried out in collaboration with the Department of Agricultural and Environmental Sciences at the University of Milan, under the supervision of Professor Leonardo Valenti. Numerous Pinot Nero clones have been planted, and in recent years their wines have experienced a remarkable surge in quality. Like last year, the wine we appreciated the most is the Victoria '16, an undosed rosé with complex and intriguing aromas of clear berry fruit accompanied by hints of citrus and ginger. In the mouth it's structured yet supple and dynamic. Lovely varietal fruit features in the Enigma Nero '19, a fresh and fluent wine, while the Antico Tralcio '17, a characteristic blend of Oltrepò Pavese's native grapes, offers up red berry sensations and cocoa, as well as a firm tannic weave.

Wine	Rating
⊙ Victoria Pas Dosé M. Cl. Rosé '16	🍷🍷 7
● Antico Tralcio '17	🍷🍷 4
● Enigma Nero Pinot Nero '19	🍷🍷 3
○ Verve Pas Dosé M. Cl. '14	🍷🍷 5
● OP Bonarda Frizzante Buccia Rossa '18	🍷 4
○ Virtus Pas Dosé M. Cl. '16	🍷 4
● Coppiere Nero Pinot Nero '16	🍸🍸 4
● Enigma Nero Pinot Nero '17	🍸🍸 3
○ Verve Extra Brut M. Cl. '13	🍸🍸 4
⊙ Victoria Pas Dosé M. Cl. Rosé '14	🍸🍸 7
○ Virtus Brut M. Cl. '13	🍸🍸 4

Villa Crespia

via Valli, 31
25030 Adro [BS]
Tel. +39 0307451051
www.villacrespia.it

PRE-BOOKED VISITS
ANNUAL PRODUCTION 360,000 bottles
HECTARES UNDER VINE 60.00
VITICULTURE METHOD Certified Organic
SUSTAINABLE WINERY

60 hectares planted with vines on Franciacorta's 6 specific terroirs, identified by the zoning work carried out in the early 1990s (called 'production units'); a large, modern, 3-floor underground cellar where grapes are processed using gravity flow, without mechanical tools: this is the profile of the property owned by the Muratori family, who named the winery after a sort of Medieval wine that underwent secondary fermentation before it was a commonplace practice. The Millè Brut '08 earned a place in our finals with its beautiful bouquet of hawthorn flowers, apple, and white peach fruit. It's an elegant cuvée, fresh and taut, despite long maturation on the lees—it fades out lingering and full on notes of apricot, hazelnut and vanilla. The Numerozero proves gratifying and generous, while the Extra Brut Rosé Brolese is rich in fruit and sapidity. But the entire range is excellent and deserves to be tried.

Wine	Rating
○ Franciacorta Brut Millè Ris. '08	🍷🍷 5
○ Franciacorta Brut Millè '12	🍷🍷 5
○ Franciacorta Dosaggio Zero Cisiolo	🍷🍷 5
○ Franciacorta Dosaggio Zero Numerozero	🍷🍷 5
⊙ Franciacorta Extra Brut Rosé Brolese	🍷🍷 5
○ Franciacorta Brut Novalia	🍷 5
○ Franciacorta Brut Satèn Cesonato	🍷 5
○ Franciacorta Dosaggio Zero Francesco Iacono Ris. '04	🍸🍸🍸 7
○ Franciacorta Brut Millè '11	🍸🍸 5
○ Franciacorta Brut Millé '10	🍸🍸 5
○ Franciacorta Brut Millè '09	🍸🍸 5
○ Franciacorta Brut Millè Ris. '07	🍸🍸 5
○ Franciacorta Dosaggio Zero Francesco Iacono Ris. '11	🍸🍸 7

Villa Franciacorta

FRAZ. VILLA
VIA VILLA, 12
25040 MONTICELLI BRUSATI [BS]
TEL. +39 030652329
www.villafranciacorta.it

PRE-BOOKED VISITS
ACCOMMODATION AND RESTAURANT SERVICE
ANNUAL PRODUCTION 300,000 bottles
HECTARES UNDER VINE 37.00

The producer's history began in 1960, when Alessandro Bianchi, who unfortunately left us recently, decided to buy the medieval property called Villa. Since the 1960s, they've been excavating to build tunnels and cellars in the heart of the Madonna della Rosa hill, with the twofold aim of obtaining an optimal environment for bottle aging and minimizing its visual impact. On the hillside we find terraced vineyards, reaching up to Villa Gradoni, a splendid resort in a unique setting. The business is now run by Alessandra Bianchi and her husband, Paolo Piziol. The Villa's cuvées and wines are excellent again this year. Two cuvées, the Pas Dosé Diamant '15 and the Brut Emozione '16, earned a place in our finals. The former is elegant and deep in its fruit, owing to a 15% share of Pinot Nero, which lends it authority, while the latter is crisp, sapid, taut and fruity, truly enjoyable. But from the Riserva '11 to the Mon Satèn '16 and the Brut Cuvétte '15 every bottle deserves great attention.

○ Franciacorta Brut Emozione '16	🍷🍷	5
○ Franciacorta Pas Dosé Diamant '15	🍷🍷	6
● Bianchi Roncalli '15	🍷🍷	6
● Curtefranca Rosso Gradoni '15	🍷🍷	5
○ Franciacorta Brut Cuvette '15	🍷🍷	5
○ Franciacorta Brut Sel. Ris. '11	🍷🍷	6
○ Franciacorta Extra Brut Extra Blu '15	🍷🍷	6
○ Franciacorta Mon Satèn '16	🍷🍷	5
○ Franciacorta Brut Emozione '09	🍷🍷🍷	5
⊙ Franciacorta Brut Rosé Boké '12	🍷🍷🍷	5
○ Franciacorta Extra Brut '98	🍷🍷🍷	4*
○ Franciacorta Brut Cuvette '12	🍷🍷	5
○ Franciacorta Brut Emozione '15	🍷🍷	5
○ Franciacorta Brut Emozione '14	🍷🍷	5
○ Franciacorta Brut Emozione 40 Ris. '08	🍷🍷	5
○ Franciacorta Mon Satèn '15	🍷🍷	5
○ Franciacorta Pas Dosé Diamant '13	🍷🍷	6

Chiara Ziliani

VIA FRANCIACORTA, 7
25050 PROVAGLIO D'ISEO [BS]
TEL. +39 030981661
www.cantinachiaraziliani.it

PRE-BOOKED VISITS
ANNUAL PRODUCTION 400,000 bottles
HECTARES UNDER VINE 31.00
SUSTAINABLE WINERY

Chiara Ziliani's winery is situated on a morainic hill south of Lake Iseo, where many of its 17 hectares of vineyards unfold on terraced plots. At the top is the winery, where more than 20 wines, divided into 5 lines (not only Franciacorta, but also traditional stills), are made. A peculiarity of the estate is the planting patterns used in the vineyards, which make for high densities, up to 7100 vines per hectare. Amid their vast range, we mention the wines that most impressed. The Extra Brut Ziliani C '16 is intense on the nose and the palate, harmonious and alluring in its notes of peach and white apple, it shows fine beading and beautiful depth, closing long and enticing on fruit. From the same line, the Satèn '16 is characterized by vigor, creaminess and beautiful iodine notes, while the Pas Dosé '16 proves structured, harmonious and mineral. The Brut Conte di Provaglio is rich in character and freshness, while the Brut Duca d'Iseo stood out for its citrus and red fruit sensations.

○ Franciacorta Extra Brut Ziliani C '16	🍷🍷	4
○ Franciacorta Brut Conte di Provaglio	🍷🍷	3
○ Franciacorta Brut Duca d'Iseo	🍷🍷	5
○ Franciacorta Brut Noir Ziliani C '16	🍷🍷	5
○ Franciacorta Pas Dosé Ziliani C '16	🍷🍷	5
○ Franciacorta Satèn Duca d'Iseo	🍷🍷	3
○ Franciacorta Satèn Ziliani C '16	🍷🍷	5
○ Franciacorta Brut Satèn Conte di Provaglio	🍷	3
○ Franciacorta Brut Ziliani C	🍷	3
○ Franciacorta Satèn Ziliani C	🍷	3
○ Franciacorta Brut Gran Cuvée Italo Ziliani Ris. '12	🍷🍷	5
○ Franciacorta Brut Noir Ziliani C '15	🍷🍷	4
⊙ Franciacorta Brut Rosé Ziliani C '14	🍷🍷	5
○ Franciacorta Brut Satèn Ziliani C '15	🍷🍷	4
○ Franciacorta Extra Brut Ziliani C '15	🍷🍷	4

1701

P.ZZA MARCONI, 6
25046 CAZZAGO SAN MARTINO [BS]
TEL. +39 0307750875
www.1701franciacorta.it

CELLAR SALES
PRE-BOOKED VISITS
ANNUAL PRODUCTION 60,000 bottles
HECTARES UNDER VINE 10.50
VITICULTURE METHOD Certified Biodynamic

○ Franciacorta Dosaggio Zero	🍷🍷 7
○ Franciacorta Dosaggio Zero Vintage Ris. '13	🍷🍷 7
○ Franciacorta Satèn '15	🍷🍷 6

Elisabetta Abrami

VIA VICINALE DELLE FOSCHE
25050 PROVAGLIO D'ISEO [BS]
TEL. +39 0306857185
www.vinielisabettaabrami.it

CELLAR SALES
ACCOMMODATION
ANNUAL PRODUCTION 60,000 bottles
HECTARES UNDER VINE 15.00
VITICULTURE METHOD Certified Organic

○ Franciacorta Extra Brut 3V Ris. '10	🍷🍷 6
○ Franciacorta Brut '13	🍷🍷 5
○ Franciacorta Satèn	🍷🍷 5
⊙ Franciacorta Brut Rosé	🍷 6

Alberelle

VIA ISONZO, 37
25038 ROVATO [BS]
TEL. +39 0307709050
info@agriturismoalberelle.it

HECTARES UNDER VINE

○ Franciacorta Brut '16	🍷🍷 5
○ Franciacorta Satèn '16	🍷🍷 5
⊙ Franciacorta Brut Rosé '15	🍷 5

Annibale Alziati

LOC. SCAZZOLINO, 55
27040 ROVESCALA [PV]
TEL. +39 038575261
www.gaggiarone.it

CELLAR SALES
PRE-BOOKED VISITS
ANNUAL PRODUCTION 100,000 bottles
HECTARES UNDER VINE 21.00
VITICULTURE METHOD Certified Organic
SUSTAINABLE WINERY

● La Barbera '18	🍷🍷 3
● O.P. Bonarda Gaggiarone V. V. '16	🍷🍷 5

Tenuta Ambrosini

VIA DELLA PACE, 58
25046 CAZZAGO SAN MARTINO [BS]
TEL. +39 0307254850
www.tenutambrosini.it

ANNUAL PRODUCTION 55,000 bottles
HECTARES UNDER VINE 8.00

⊙ Franciacorta Brut Rosé Ambrosé '15	🍷🍷 6
○ Franciacorta Extra Brut '15	🍷🍷 5
○ Franciacorta Satèn '15	🍷🍷 5

Ascesa

VIA RIBOLATTI 42
23020 TRESIVIO [SO]
TEL. +39 340 4132048
www.ascesavini.com

HECTARES UNDER VINE

● Rosso di Valtellina Ascesa '18	🍷🍷 4
● Valtellina Sup. Ascesa '18	🍷🍷 5

Giovanni Avanzi

via Trevisago, 19
25080 Manerba del Garda [BS]
Tel. +39 0365551013
www.avanzi.net

CELLAR SALES
PRE-BOOKED VISITS
RESTAURANT SERVICE
ANNUAL PRODUCTION 600,000 bottles
HECTARES UNDER VINE 63.00

- ○ Garda Dorobianco '19 — 🍷🍷 3
- ⊙ Riviera del Garda Cl. Brut Rosé — 🍷🍷 2*
- ○ Lugana di Sirmione '19 — 🍷 2

Balgera

c.so M. Quadrio, 26
23030 Chiuro [SO]
Tel. +39 0342482203
www.vinibalgera.it

CELLAR SALES
PRE-BOOKED VISITS
ANNUAL PRODUCTION 75,000 bottles
HECTARES UNDER VINE

- ● Sforzato di Valtellina Solstizio '13 — 🍷🍷 8
- ● Valtellina Sup. Valgella Ris. Pizaméi '13 — 🍷🍷 7
- ● Valtellina Sup. Valgella Ris. Quigna '13 — 🍷🍷 7

Barboglio De Gaioncelli

fraz. Colombaro
via Nazario Sauro
25040 Corte Franca [BS]
Tel. +39 0309826831
www.barbogliodegaioncelli.it

CELLAR SALES
PRE-BOOKED VISITS
RESTAURANT SERVICE
ANNUAL PRODUCTION 90,000 bottles
HECTARES UNDER VINE 60.00

- ○ Franciacorta Satèn '15 — 🍷🍷 5
- ● Pinot Nero Guido Costa '15 — 🍷🍷 5
- ○ Franciacorta Extra Dry 1875 — 🍷 4

Bèlon du Bèlon

via Rampaneto,10/12
25030 Erbusco [BS]
Tel. +39 3351433774
www.franciacortabelon.it

PRE-BOOKED VISITS
ANNUAL PRODUCTION 47,500 bottles
HECTARES UNDER VINE 6.50
SUSTAINABLE WINERY

- ⊙ Franciacorta Brut Rosé — 🍷🍷 6
- ○ Franciacorta Pas Dosè Vintage 120 Mesi Riserva del Fondatore '09 — 🍷🍷 8

Cantina Sociale Bergamasca

via Bergamo, 10
24060 San Paolo d'Argon [BG]
Tel. +39 035951098
www.cantinabergamasca.it

CELLAR SALES
PRE-BOOKED VISITS
ANNUAL PRODUCTION 650,000 bottles
HECTARES UNDER VINE 90.00

- ○ Sottosopra Brut Cl. — 🍷🍷 3
- ○ Terre del Colleoni Incrocio Manzoni 6013 '19 — 🍷🍷 5
- ⊙ Schiava '19 — 🍷 3

Bertagna

loc. Bande
s.da Madonna della Porta, 14
46040 Cavriana [MN]
Tel. +39 037682211
www.cantinabertagna.it

CELLAR SALES
PRE-BOOKED VISITS
ANNUAL PRODUCTION 160,000 bottles
HECTARES UNDER VINE 17.00

- ● Rosso del Barone '18 — 🍷🍷 3
- ○ Montevolpe Bianco '19 — 🍷 3
- ● Rosso del Chino '17 — 🍷 3

Bonfadini

fraz. Clusane
via L. di Bernardo, 87
25049 Iseo [BS]
Tel. +39 0309826721
www.bonfadini.it

CELLAR SALES
PRE-BOOKED VISITS
ANNUAL PRODUCTION 120,000 bottles
HECTARES UNDER VINE 12.00

- ⊙ Franciacorta Brut Opera Rosé '16 🍷🍷 5
- ○ Franciacorta Nature Veritas 🍷🍷 6
- ○ Franciacorta Nature Victus '16 🍷🍷 8
- ○ Franciacorta Satèn Carpe Diem '16 🍷🍷 5

Bosco Longhino

fraz. Molino Marconi
27047 Santa Maria della Versa [PV]
Tel. +39 0385798049
www.boscolonghino.it

PRE-BOOKED VISITS
ACCOMMODATION AND RESTAURANT SERVICE
ANNUAL PRODUCTION 200,000 bottles
HECTARES UNDER VINE 29.00

- ○ Campo dei Fitti Pinot Grigio '19 🍷🍷 3
- ● Sangue di Giuda '19 🍷🍷 2*
- ● OP Bonarda Frizzante '19 🍷 2
- ○ OP Pinot Nero Pas Dosé Casto M. Cl. '16 🍷 3

Bricco dei Roncotti

fraz. Vigalone, 132
27044 Canneto Pavese [PV]
Tel. +39 3663025432
www.briccodeironcotti.it

ANNUAL PRODUCTION 4,000 bottles
HECTARES UNDER VINE 2.70

- ● Mistero '17 🍷🍷 3
- ● Nido della Tempesta Frizzante '19 🍷🍷 2*
- ● Roncotto '16 🍷🍷 4

Bulgarini

loc. Vaibò, 1
25010 Pozzolengo [BS]
Tel. +39 030918224
www.vini-bulgarini.com

CELLAR SALES
ANNUAL PRODUCTION 750,000 bottles
HECTARES UNDER VINE 40.00

- ○ Lugana '19 🍷🍷 2*
- ○ Lugana 010 '19 🍷🍷 3
- ○ Lugana Sup. Cà Vaibò '17 🍷🍷 2*
- ⊙ Riviera del Garda Cl. Chiaretto '19 🍷 2

Patrizia Cadore

loc. Campagna Bianca
25010 Pozzolengo [BS]
Tel. +39 0309918138
www.vinicadore.eu

ANNUAL PRODUCTION 25,000 bottles
HECTARES UNDER VINE 8.50

- ○ Lugana '19 🍷🍷 3
- ○ Lugana Campagna Bianca '19 🍷🍷 4
- ○ San Martino della Battaglia 50° Anniversario '17 🍷🍷 4

Andrea Calvi

fraz. Vigalone, 13
27044 Canneto Pavese [PV]
Tel. +39 038560034
www.andreacalvi.it

CELLAR SALES
PRE-BOOKED VISITS
ANNUAL PRODUCTION 100,000 bottles
HECTARES UNDER VINE 26.00

- ● OP Bonarda Frizzante '19 🍷🍷 2*
- ○ OP Pinot Nero M. Cl. Brut 🍷🍷 4

Davide Calvi

FRAZ. PALAZZINA, 24
27040 CASTANA [PV]
TEL. +39 038582136
www.vinicalvi.it

CELLAR SALES
PRE-BOOKED VISITS
ANNUAL PRODUCTION 45,000 bottles
HECTARES UNDER VINE 8.00

- ● OP Buttafuoco V. Montarzolo '16 🍷🍷 4
- ● OP Bonarda '19 🍷 2
- ● OP Pinot Nero Marion '16 🍷 3

Camillucci

VIA DELLE SELVE, 1
25038 PADERNO FRANCIACORTA [BS]
TEL. +39 0307702739
www.camilucci.it

PRE-BOOKED VISITS
ANNUAL PRODUCTION 50,000 bottles
HECTARES UNDER VINE 6.00

- ○ Franciacorta Brut Ammonites 🍷🍷 5
- ○ Franciacorta Brut Nature St.06 Ris. '06 🍷🍷 8
- ○ Franciacorta Extra Brut Anthologie Blanc '14 🍷🍷 6

Camossi

VIA METELLI, 5
25030 ERBUSCO [BS]
TEL. +39 0307268022
www.camossi.it

CELLAR SALES
PRE-BOOKED VISITS
ANNUAL PRODUCTION 60,000 bottles
HECTARES UNDER VINE 30.00

- ○ Franciacorta Dosaggio Zero CR 142 Ris. '07 🍷🍷 8
- ○ Franciacorta Extra Brut Pietro Camossi Ris. '10 🍷🍷 8

Le Cantorie

VIA CASTELLO DI CASAGLIO, 24/25
25064 GUSSAGO [BS]
TEL. +39 0302523723
www.lecantorie.it

ANNUAL PRODUCTION 75,000 bottles
HECTARES UNDER VINE 12.00

- ⊙ Franciacorta Rosé Rosi delle Margherite 🍷🍷 4
- ○ Franciacorta Satèn Armonia 🍷🍷 5
- ● Cellatica Rosso Giulia '17 🍷 3

Cantrina

VIA COLOMBERA, 7
25081 BEDIZZOLE [BS]
TEL. +39 3356362137
www.cantrina.it

CELLAR SALES
ANNUAL PRODUCTION 35,000 bottles
HECTARES UNDER VINE 7.90
VITICULTURE METHOD Certified Organic

- ○ Riné '18 🍷🍷 3
- ⊙ Rosanoire '19 🍷🍷 2*
- ⊙ Valtènesi Chiaretto '19 🍷 3
- ● Zerdì '17 🍷 3

Cascina Gnocco

FRAZ. LOSANA, 45
27040 MORNICO LOSANA [PV]
TEL. +39 038383499
www.cascinagnocco.it

CELLAR SALES
PRE-BOOKED VISITS
ANNUAL PRODUCTION 60,000 bottles
HECTARES UNDER VINE 13.00

- ● Orione '16 🍷🍷 4

Cascina Piano

LOC. ANGERA
VIA VALCASTELLANA, 33
21021 ANGERA [VA]
TEL. +39 0331930928
www.cascinapiano.it

CELLAR SALES
PRE-BOOKED VISITS
ANNUAL PRODUCTION 23,000 bottles
HECTARES UNDER VINE 3.00

○ Mott Carè	🍷🍷 4
● Sebuino '18	🍷 3

Castello di Luzzano

LOC. LUZZANO, 5
27040 ROVESCALA [PV]
TEL. +39 0523863277
www.castelloluzzano.com

CELLAR SALES
PRE-BOOKED VISITS
ACCOMMODATION AND RESTAURANT SERVICE
ANNUAL PRODUCTION 120,000 bottles
HECTARES UNDER VINE 76.00

● Mesy '16	🍷 6
● OP Bonarda Frizzante Sommossa '19	🍷 2

Castelveder

VIA BELVEDERE, 4
25040 MONTICELLI BRUSATI [BS]
TEL. +39 030652308
www.castelveder.it

CELLAR SALES
PRE-BOOKED VISITS
ANNUAL PRODUCTION 70,000 bottles
HECTARES UNDER VINE 11.00

○ Franciacorta Brut	🍷🍷 4
⊙ Franciacorta Brut Rosé	🍷🍷 5
○ Franciacorta Extra Brut	🍷🍷 5
○ Franciacorta Satèn	🍷 5

Le Chiusure

FRAZ. PORTESE
VIA BOSCHETTE, 2
25010 SAN FELICE DEL BENACO [BS]
TEL. +39 0365626243
www.lechiusure.net

CELLAR SALES
PRE-BOOKED VISITS
ACCOMMODATION
ANNUAL PRODUCTION 24,000 bottles
HECTARES UNDER VINE 4.00

⊙ Valtènesi Riviera del Garda Chiaretto Roseti '18	🍷🍷 4
⊙ Valtènesi Riviera del Garda Cl. Chiaretto '19	🍷🍷 3

Il Cipresso

FRAZ. TRIBULINA
VIA CERRI, 2
24020 SCANZOROSCIATE [BG]
TEL. +39 0354597005
www.ilcipresso.info

CELLAR SALES
PRE-BOOKED VISITS
ANNUAL PRODUCTION 20,000 bottles
HECTARES UNDER VINE 4.00

○ Valcalepio Bianco Melardo '19	🍷🍷 2*
● Valcalepio Rosso Bartolomeo Ris. '13	🍷🍷 4
● Moscato di Scanzo Serafino '16	🍷 6
● Valcalepio Rosso Dionisio '17	🍷 3

Citari

FRAZ. SAN MARTINO DELLA BATTAGLIA
LOC. CITARI, 2
25015 DESENZANO DEL GARDA [BS]
TEL. +39 0309910310
www.citari.it

CELLAR SALES
PRE-BOOKED VISITS
ANNUAL PRODUCTION 150,000 bottles
HECTARES UNDER VINE 21.00
SUSTAINABLE WINERY

○ Lugana Conchiglia '19	🍷🍷 4
○ Lugana Sorgente '19	🍷🍷 3
○ San Martino della Battaglia Il Vecchio Vigneto '18	🍷 3

Battista Cola

VIA INDIPENDENZA, 3
25030 ADRO [BS]
TEL. +39 0307356195
www.colabattista.it

CELLAR SALES
PRE-BOOKED VISITS
ANNUAL PRODUCTION 60,000 bottles
HECTARES UNDER VINE 9.00
SUSTAINABLE WINERY

○ Franciacorta Brut '15	🍷🍷 5
○ Franciacorta Extra Brut	🍷🍷 4
○ Curtefranca Bianco '19	🍷 2
● Curtefranca Rosso '18	🍷 2

Colline della Stella - Arici

VIA FORCELLA,70
25064 GUSSAGO [BS]
TEL. +39 3478039339
www.collinedellastella.com

CELLAR SALES
PRE-BOOKED VISITS
ANNUAL PRODUCTION 50,000 bottles
HECTARES UNDER VINE 10.00

○ Franciacorta Dosaggio Zero Francesco Arici Ris. '11	🍷🍷 6
○ Franciacorta Dosaggio Zero '15	🍷🍷 5
○ Franciacorta Dosaggio Zero Uno '15	🍷🍷 5

Cordero San Giorgio

LOC. CASTELLO, 1
27046 SANTA GIULETTA [PV]
TEL. +39 0383899168
www.poderesangiorgio.it

CELLAR SALES
PRE-BOOKED VISITS
ACCOMMODATION AND RESTAURANT SERVICE
ANNUAL PRODUCTION 250,000 bottles
HECTARES UNDER VINE 24.00

● OP Pinot Nero TiaMat '19	🍷🍷 3*
○ OP Pinot Grigio Katari '19	🍷🍷 3
○ Ramé '19	🍷🍷 3
⊙ Piasa Rosato '19	🍷 2

Tenuta La Costa

FRAZ. COSTA, 68
27040 CASTANA [PV]
TEL. +39 0385241527
www.tenutalacosta.com

CELLAR SALES
PRE-BOOKED VISITS
ANNUAL PRODUCTION 50,000 bottles
HECTARES UNDER VINE 10.50

○ OP Pinot Nero Extra Brut M. Cl. '10	🍷🍷 4
⊙ OP Pinot Nero Rosé Brut M. Cl. '12	🍷 5

La Costaiola

FRAZ. COSTAIOLA
VIA COSTAIOLA, 25
27054 MONTEBELLO DELLA BATTAGLIA [PV]
TEL. +39 038383169
www.lacostaiola.it

CELLAR SALES
ACCOMMODATION
ANNUAL PRODUCTION 90,000 bottles
HECTARES UNDER VINE 15.00

● Briccaia '18	🍷🍷 3
⊙ Nové Brut Rosé M. Cl.	🍷🍷 3
○ Nové Brut M. Cl.	🍷 3
● Pinot Nero '19	🍷 3

De Toma

VIA BATTISTI, 7
24020 SCANZOROSCIATE [BG]
TEL. +39 035657329

CELLAR SALES
PRE-BOOKED VISITS
ANNUAL PRODUCTION 5,000 bottles
HECTARES UNDER VINE 2.50

● Moscato di Scanzo '17	🍷🍷 7
● Cardinale '17	🍷🍷 5

Due Pini

loc. Picedo
via Novaglio, 16
25080 Polpenazze del Garda [BS]
Tel. +39 0365675123
www.viniduepini.it

PRE-BOOKED VISITS
ANNUAL PRODUCTION 40,000 bottles
HECTARES UNDER VINE 6.00
VITICULTURE METHOD Certified Organic

- ○ Garda Riesling Emanuela '19 ₸₸ 3
- ● Riviera del Garda Cl. Sup. Rosso Samantha '16 ₸₸ 3
- ⊙ Valtènesi Chiaretto Grazie '19 ₸ 3

Lorenzo Faccoli

via Cava, 7
25030 Coccaglio [BS]
Tel. +39 0307722761
www.faccolifranciacorta.it

CELLAR SALES
PRE-BOOKED VISITS
ANNUAL PRODUCTION 55,000 bottles
HECTARES UNDER VINE 5.50

- ⊙ Franciacorta Brut Rosé ₸₸ 5
- ○ Franciacorta Extra Brut ₸₸ 5

Fejoia

via Medolago, 40
24020 Scanzorosciate [BG]
Tel. +39 035668363
www.fejoia.it

CELLAR SALES
PRE-BOOKED VISITS
ANNUAL PRODUCTION 9,000 bottles
HECTARES UNDER VINE 2.10

- ● Moscato di Scanzo '11 ₸₸ 7

Il Feudo Nico

via San Rocco, 63
27040 Mornico Losana [PV]
Tel. +39 0383892452

ANNUAL PRODUCTION 40,000 bottles
HECTARES UNDER VINE 16.00

- ○ Maria Antonietta Pas Dosé M. Cl. '15 ₸ 5
- ○ OP Pinot Grigio Schiavighetto '19 ₸ 2

La Fiòca

fraz. Nigoline
via Villa, 13b
25040 Corte Franca [BS]
Tel. +39 0309826313
www.lafioca.com

CELLAR SALES
PRE-BOOKED VISITS
ACCOMMODATION AND RESTAURANT SERVICE
ANNUAL PRODUCTION 40,000 bottles
HECTARES UNDER VINE 5.00
VITICULTURE METHOD Certified Organic

- ○ Franciacorta Dosaggio Zero Nudo ₸₸ 7
- ○ Franciacorta Extra Brut Ris. '10 ₸₸ 6
- ○ Franciacorta Satèn ₸₸ 5
- ● Rosso del Diavolo Allegro ₸ 5

La Fiorita

via Maglio, 10
25020 Ome [BS]
Tel. +39 030652279
www.lafioritafranciacorta.com

CELLAR SALES
PRE-BOOKED VISITS
ACCOMMODATION AND RESTAURANT SERVICE
ANNUAL PRODUCTION 94,000 bottles
HECTARES UNDER VINE 10.00

- ○ Franciacorta Brut ₸₸ 4
- ○ Franciacorta Dosage Zéro Calicanto '15 ₸₸ 5
- ○ Franciacorta Dosaggio Zero ₸₸ 4
- ○ Franciacorta Satèn ₸₸ 5

Le Fracce

fraz. Mairano
via Castel del Lupo, 5
27045 Casteggio [PV]
Tel. +39 038382526
www.lefracce.com

CELLAR SALES
PRE-BOOKED VISITS
ANNUAL PRODUCTION 180,000 bottles
HECTARES UNDER VINE 40.00

- ● OP Barbera Garboso '18 — 🍷🍷 3
- ○ OP Pinot Grigio Levriere '19 — 🍷🍷 3
- ● OP Rosso Cirgà '15 — 🍷🍷 3
- ⊙ Bussolera Grand Rosé Brut — 🍷 5

I Gessi

fraz. Cascina Fossa, 8
27050 Oliva Gessi [PV]
Tel. +39 0383896606
www.cantineigessi.it

CELLAR SALES
PRE-BOOKED VISITS
ACCOMMODATION
ANNUAL PRODUCTION 160,000 bottles
HECTARES UNDER VINE 41.00

- ● Barbera '16 — 🍷🍷 3
- ○ Maria Cristina Brut M. Cl. — 🍷🍷 3
- ⊙ Maria Cristina Rosé Brut M. Cl. — 🍷 3

Giorgio Gianatti

via dei Portici, 82
23020 Montagna in Valtellina [SO]
Tel. +39 0342380033
gianatti.giorgio@alice.it

CELLAR SALES
PRE-BOOKED VISITS
ANNUAL PRODUCTION 8,000 bottles
HECTARES UNDER VINE 2.00

- ● Valtellina Rosso '16 — 🍷🍷 4
- ● Valtellina Sup. Grumello '15 — 🍷🍷 3

Giubertoni

fraz. San Nicolò Po
via Papa Giovanni XXIII
46031 Bagnolo San Vito [MN]
Tel. +39 0376252762
www.cantinegiubertoni.it

ANNUAL PRODUCTION 100,000 bottles
HECTARES UNDER VINE 20.00

- ● Il Vecchio Ponte '19 — 🍷🍷 2*
- ● Lambrusco Mantovano G Rosso '19 — 🍷🍷 2*
- ● Il Bel Angelin '19 — 🍷 2

Giuseppe Guglielmini

via del Nerone, 9
27010 Miradolo Terme [PV]
Tel. +39 038277183
az.guglielmini@libero.it

HECTARES UNDER VINE

- ● La Bertona '16 — 🍷🍷 3
- ● San Colombano '18 — 🍷🍷 2*
- ○ San Colombano Bianco '19 — 🍷 2

Tenuta La Vigna

Cascina La Vigna
25020 Capriano del Colle [BS]
Tel. +39 0309748061
www.tenutalavigna.it

CELLAR SALES
PRE-BOOKED VISITS
ANNUAL PRODUCTION 35,000 bottles
HECTARES UNDER VINE 6.00

- ○ Brut M. Cl. Anna Botti — 🍷🍷 4
- ○ Brut M. Cl. Nature Ugo Botti — 🍷🍷 5
- ● Capriano del Colle Montebruciato Ris. '16 — 🍷 5
- ● Capriano del Colle Rosso Rubinera '18 — 🍷 3

Lebovitz

fraz. Governolo
v.le Rimembranze, 4
46037 Roncoferraro [MN]
Tel. +39 0376668115
www.lebovitz.it

CELLAR SALES
PRE-BOOKED VISITS
ANNUAL PRODUCTION 1,000,000 bottles
HECTARES UNDER VINE

● Al Scagarün '19	🍷🍷 1*
● Lambrusco Mantovano Rosso dei Concari '19	🍷🍷 2*
● Sedamat '19	🍷🍷 1*

Locatelli Caffi

via A. Moro, 6
24060 Chiuduno [BG]
Tel. +39 035838308
www.locatellicaffi.it

HECTARES UNDER VINE

● I Cardinài '15	🍷🍷 4
○ TdC Claudun Brut M. Cl. '16	🍷🍷 3
○ Valcalepio Bianco '19	🍷 2

Francesco Maggi

fraz. Costiolo, 87
27044 Canneto Pavese [PV]
Tel. +39 038560233
www.maggifrancesco.it

HECTARES UNDER VINE

● OP Buttafuoco Abbondanza '19	🍷🍷 3
● OP Buttafuoco Storico V. Costera '16	🍷 3
● OP Riesling Essenza '19	🍷 2

Majolini

loc. Valle
via A. Manzoni, 3
25050 Ome [BS]
Tel. +39 0306527378
www.majolini.it

CELLAR SALES
PRE-BOOKED VISITS
ANNUAL PRODUCTION 180,000 bottles
HECTARES UNDER VINE 20.00
VITICULTURE METHOD Certified Organic
SUSTAINABLE WINERY

○ Franciacorta Brut Blanc de Noir	🍷🍷 5
○ Franciacorta Pas Dosé Aligi Sassu '15	🍷🍷 5
○ Franciacorta Extra Brut Disobbedisco	🍷 5

Malavasi

loc. Casina Sacco, 1
fraz. San Giacomo
25010 Pozzolengo [BS]
Tel. +39 0309918759
www.malavasivini.it

ANNUAL PRODUCTION 100,000 bottles
HECTARES UNDER VINE 10.00

⊙ Garda Bresciano Chiaretto Rosa del Lago '19	🍷🍷 3
● Mulinero '16	🍷🍷 6
○ Lugana Camilla '19	🍷 3

Mantì

Via Iseo 76
25030 Erbusco [BS]
Tel. +39 0306813398
info@manti.wine

HECTARES UNDER VINE

○ Franciacorta Brut	🍷🍷 5
○ Franciacorta Extra Brut	🍷🍷 5
○ Franciacorta Satèn	🍷🍷 5

Marangona

loc. Marangona 1
25010 Pozzolengo [BS]
Tel. +39 030919379
www.marangona.com

CELLAR SALES
PRE-BOOKED VISITS
ANNUAL PRODUCTION 30,000 bottles
HECTARES UNDER VINE 30.00

- ○ Lugana '19 — 🍷🍷 2*
- ○ Lugana Tre Campane '18 — 🍷🍷 3

Marsadri

loc. Raffa di Puegnago
via Nazionale, 26
25080 Puegnago sul Garda [BS]
Tel. +39 0365651005
www.cantinamarsadri.it

PRE-BOOKED VISITS
ANNUAL PRODUCTION 200,000 bottles
HECTARES UNDER VINE 15.00
SUSTAINABLE WINERY

- ○ Lugana Brolo '19 — 🍷🍷 3
- ● Riviera del Garda Cl. Rosso Del Pioppo Sup. '18 — 🍷🍷 4
- ● Riviera del Garda Groppello Brolo '18 — 🍷 3

Martilde

fraz. Croce, 4a
27040 Rovescala [PV]
Tel. +39 0385756280
www.martilde.it

CELLAR SALES
PRE-BOOKED VISITS
ANNUAL PRODUCTION 30,000 bottles
HECTARES UNDER VINE 15.00
VITICULTURE METHOD Certified Organic

- ● La Strega, la Gazza e il Pioppo Barbera '13 — 🍷🍷 4
- ○ Dedica Malvasia '19 — 🍷 2
- ● Nina Pinot Nero '18 — 🍷 2

Medolago Albani

via Redona, 12
24069 Trescore Balneario [BG]
Tel. +39 035942022
www.medolagoalbani.it

CELLAR SALES
PRE-BOOKED VISITS
ANNUAL PRODUCTION 200,000 bottles
HECTARES UNDER VINE 23.00

- ○ Brut M. Cl. '18 — 🍷🍷 3
- ⊙ Brut Rosè M. Cl. '17 — 🍷🍷 3
- ● Valcalepio Rosso I Due Lauri Ris. '16 — 🍷 4
- ● Villa Redona Cabernet '17 — 🍷 3

Il Molino di Rovescala

loc. Molino, 2
27040 Rovescala [PV]
Tel. +39 339 4739924
www.ilmolinodirovescala.it/

CELLAR SALES
PRE-BOOKED VISITS
ANNUAL PRODUCTION 40,000 bottles
HECTARES UNDER VINE 23.00
SUSTAINABLE WINERY

- ○ Felice Riesling '19 — 🍷🍷 3
- ○ Madone Malvasia '19 — 🍷 3
- ● OP Bonarda Povromme '18 — 🍷 3

Monte Alto

Via Luigi di Bernardo, 98
25049 Iseo [BS]
Tel. +39 3478693294

HECTARES UNDER VINE

- ○ Franciacorta Brut PR — 🍷🍷 5
- ○ Franciacorta Extra Brut — 🍷🍷 5

Monte Cicogna

via delle Vigne, 6
25080 Moniga del Garda [BS]
Tel. +39 0365503200
www.montecicogna.it

CELLAR SALES
PRE-BOOKED VISITS
ACCOMMODATION
ANNUAL PRODUCTION 150,000 bottles
HECTARES UNDER VINE 30.00

○ Lugana Imperiale '19	🍷🍷 2*
⊙ Riviera del Garda Cl. Chiaretto Siclì '19	🍷🍷 3
○ Lugana S.Caterina '19	🍷 2

Tenuta Monte Delma

via Valenzano, 23
25050 Passirano [BS]
Tel. +39 0306546161
www.montedelma.it

CELLAR SALES
PRE-BOOKED VISITS
ANNUAL PRODUCTION 100,000 bottles
HECTARES UNDER VINE 20.00

○ Franciacorta Brut	🍷🍷 4
○ Franciacorta Brut Satèn	🍷🍷 5
○ Franciacorta Pas Dosé '14	🍷🍷 5
⊙ Franciacorta Brut Rosé	🍷 5

Montelio

via D. Mazza, 1
27050 Codevilla [PV]
Tel. +39 0383373090
montelio.gio@alice.it

CELLAR SALES
PRE-BOOKED VISITS
ACCOMMODATION AND RESTAURANT SERVICE
ANNUAL PRODUCTION 130,000 bottles
HECTARES UNDER VINE 27.00

● Comprino Merlot '17	🍷🍷 4
⊙ Il Fiorile Brut Rosé	🍷🍷 4
○ OP Riesling Il Nadòt '19	🍷 2

Montonale

loc. Conta, 4a
25015 Desenzano del Garda [BS]
Tel. +39 0309103358
www.montonale.it

ANNUAL PRODUCTION 140,000 bottles
HECTARES UNDER VINE 30.00

○ Lugana Montunal '19	🍷🍷 4
○ Lugana Orestilla '18	🍷🍷 5
○ Primessenza Brut M. Cl. '17	🍷 5

Riccardi - Nettare dei Santi

via Capra, 17
20078 San Colombano al Lambro [MI]
Tel. +39 0371200523
www.nettaredeisanti.it

CELLAR SALES
PRE-BOOKED VISITS
ANNUAL PRODUCTION 600,000 bottles
HECTARES UNDER VINE 40.00

○ Domm Pas Dosè M. Cl. '14	🍷🍷 6
● San Colombano V. Roverone Ris. '17	🍷🍷 3
○ Brut M. Cl. Domm '16	🍷 4
○ Passito di Verdea '18	🍷 3

Oselara

s.da Vicinale della Bazzola, 1
25010 Pozzolengo [BS]
Tel. +39 347 229 5623
www.oselara.it

CELLAR SALES
PRE-BOOKED VISITS
ANNUAL PRODUCTION 50,000 bottles
HECTARES UNDER VINE 14.00

○ Lugana Terra Dorata '19	🍷🍷 3
○ Oselara Brut M. Cl.	🍷🍷 3

Panigada - Banino

via della Vittoria, 13
20078 San Colombano al Lambro [MI]
Tel. +39 0371898795
www.banino.it

CELLAR SALES
PRE-BOOKED VISITS
ANNUAL PRODUCTION 30,000 bottles
HECTARES UNDER VINE 5.00
SUSTAINABLE WINERY

○ Aureum '17	🍷🍷 4
● Banino Rosso Frizzante '19	🍷 2
● San Colombano Banino Tranquillo '17	🍷 2

La Perla

loc. Tresenda
via Valgella, 29b
23036 Teglio [SO]
Tel. +39 3462878894
www.vini-laperla.com

CELLAR SALES
PRE-BOOKED VISITS
ANNUAL PRODUCTION 20,000 bottles
HECTARES UNDER VINE 3.30
SUSTAINABLE WINERY

● Sforzato di Valtellina Quattro Soli '15	🍷🍷 7
○ La Perla Extra Brut M. Cl. '17	🍷🍷 4
● Valtellina Sup. Elisa Ris. '14	🍷🍷 5
● Valtellina Sup. La Mossa '15	🍷🍷 5

Pian del Maggio

via Iseo,108
25030 Erbusco [BS]
Tel. +39 3355638610
www.piandelmaggio.it

CELLAR SALES
PRE-BOOKED VISITS
ANNUAL PRODUCTION 25,000 bottles
HECTARES UNDER VINE 1.80

○ Franciacorta Brut Proscenio	🍷🍷 4

Piccolo Bacco dei Quaroni

fraz. Costamontefedele
27040 Montù Beccaria [PV]
Tel. +39 038560521
www.piccolobaccodeiquaroni.it

CELLAR SALES
PRE-BOOKED VISITS
RESTAURANT SERVICE
ANNUAL PRODUCTION 35,000 bottles
HECTARES UNDER VINE 10.00
VITICULTURE METHOD Certified Organic

● OP Bonarda Vivace Mons Acutus '19	🍷 2
○ OP Riesling Il Pozzo '18	🍷 2

Pilandro

fraz. San Martino della Battaglia
loc. Pilandro, 1
25015 Desenzano del Garda [BS]
Tel. +39 0309910363
www.pilandro.it

CELLAR SALES
PRE-BOOKED VISITS
ANNUAL PRODUCTION 300,000 bottles
HECTARES UNDER VINE 33.00

○ Lugana '19	🍷🍷 2*
○ Lugana Terecrea '19	🍷🍷 3

La Piotta

loc. Piotta, 2
27040 Montalto Pavese [PV]
Tel. +39 0383870178
www.padroggilapiotta.it

CELLAR SALES
PRE-BOOKED VISITS
ANNUAL PRODUCTION 90,000 bottles
HECTARES UNDER VINE 20.00
VITICULTURE METHOD Certified Organic

○ OP Pinot Nero Nature M. Cl. '16	🍷🍷 4
○ OP Pinot Nero Brut M. Cl. Talento '16	🍷 4

Priore

FRAZ. CALINO
VIA SALA, 41
25046 CAZZAGO SAN MARTINO [BS]
TEL. +39 0307254710
www.aziendaagricolapriore.it

HECTARES UNDER VINE

- ○ Franciacorta Brut 🍷🍷 5
- ○ Franciacorta Brut Lihander '15 🍷🍷 5
- ○ Franciacorta Satèn 🍷 5

Quattro Terre

FRAZ. BORGONATO
VIA RISORGIMENTO, 11
25040 CORTE FRANCA [BS]
TEL. +39 030984312
www.quattroterre.it

CELLAR SALES
PRE-BOOKED VISITS
ACCOMMODATION AND RESTAURANT SERVICE
ANNUAL PRODUCTION 50,000 bottles
HECTARES UNDER VINE 10.00

- ○ Franciacorta Brut 940 Ris. '11 🍷🍷 8
- ○ Franciacorta Extra Brut Sinequal 🍷🍷 6
- ○ Franciacorta Satèn Luna Mea 🍷🍷 5
- ⊙ Franciacorta Brut Rosé l'Acrobata '16 🍷 6

Cantina Sociale Cooperativa di Quistello

VIA ROMA, 46
46026 QUISTELLO [MN]
TEL. +39 0376618118
www.cantinasocialequistello.it

CELLAR SALES
PRE-BOOKED VISITS
ANNUAL PRODUCTION 1,000,000 bottles
HECTARES UNDER VINE 330.00
SUSTAINABLE WINERY

- ● Gran Rosso del Vicariato di Quistello '19 🍷🍷 2*
- ● Rossissimo '19 🍷🍷 2*
- ⊙ 80 Vendemmie Rosato '19 🍷 2

Tenuta Quvestra

LOC. CASE NUOVE 9
27047 SANTA MARIA DELLA VERSA [PV]
TEL. +39 3476014109
www.quvestra.it

CELLAR SALES
PRE-BOOKED VISITS
ACCOMMODATION
ANNUAL PRODUCTION 35,000 bottles
HECTARES UNDER VINE 12.00

- ● OP Croatina '15 🍷🍷 3
- ○ OP Pinot Nero Brut Symposium 🍷🍷 4
- ● OP Rosso Sinfonia in Rosso '17 🍷 3

Ricchi

FRAZ. RICCHI
VIA FESTONI, 13D
46040 MONZAMBANO [MN]
TEL. +39 0376800238
www.cantinaricchi.it

CELLAR SALES
PRE-BOOKED VISITS
ANNUAL PRODUCTION 300,000 bottles
HECTARES UNDER VINE 40.00

- ○ Aroma 85 M. Cl. 🍷🍷 3
- ○ Essenza Zero Pas Dosé M. Cl. '14 🍷🍷 4
- ○ Espressione 8 Brut M. Cl. '14 🍷 4

La Rifra

LOC. PILANDRO, 2
25010 DESENZANO DEL GARDA [BS]
TEL. +39 0309108023
claudiofraccaroli@virgilio.it

ANNUAL PRODUCTION 130,000 bottles
HECTARES UNDER VINE 17.00

- ○ Lugana Il Bepi Ris. '17 🍷🍷 3
- ○ Lugana Libiam '19 🍷🍷 2*
- ○ Follie Follie Brut 🍷 3
- ○ Lugana Brut 🍷 2

San Michele

via Parrocchia, 57
25020 Capriano del Colle [BS]
Tel. +39 0309444091
www.sanmichelevini.it

CELLAR SALES
PRE-BOOKED VISITS
ANNUAL PRODUCTION 70,000 bottles
HECTARES UNDER VINE 16.00
VITICULTURE METHOD Certified Organic

- ● Capriano del Colle Rosso Carme '18 🍷🍷 2*
- ○ Belvedere Brut M. Cl. 🍷 4
- ○ Capriano del Colle Bianco Netto '19 🍷 2
- ● Capriano del Colle Marzemino '19 🍷 2

Santa Lucia

via Verdi, 6
25030 Erbusco [BS]
Tel. +39 0307769814
www.santaluciafranciacorta.it

CELLAR SALES
PRE-BOOKED VISITS
ANNUAL PRODUCTION 100,000 bottles
HECTARES UNDER VINE 28.00
VITICULTURE METHOD Certified Organic

- ○ Franciacorta Brut 🍷🍷 5
- ○ Franciacorta Satèn 🍷🍷 5
- ⊙ Franciacorta Brut Rosé 🍷 5

Santus

via Badia, 68
25060 Cellatica [BS]
Tel. +39 0308367074
www.santus.it

CELLAR SALES
PRE-BOOKED VISITS
ANNUAL PRODUCTION 50,000 bottles
HECTARES UNDER VINE 9.50
VITICULTURE METHOD Certified Organic

- ○ Franciacorta Brut '15 🍷🍷 5
- ⊙ Franciacorta Rosé Zero '15 🍷🍷 5
- ○ Franciacorta Dosaggio Zero '15 🍷 5

Tenuta Scerscé

via Stelvio, 18
23037 Tirano [SO]
Tel. +39 3461542970
www.tenutascersce.it

CELLAR SALES
PRE-BOOKED VISITS
ANNUAL PRODUCTION 22,000 bottles
HECTARES UNDER VINE 2.50
SUSTAINABLE WINERY

- ● Valtellina Sforzato Infinito '17 🍷🍷 6
- ● Rosso di Valtellina Nettare '18 🍷🍷 3
- ● Valtellina Sup. Essenza '17 🍷🍷 5

Scolari

loc. Puegnano sul Garda
fraz. Raffa
via Nazionale, 38
25080 Brescia
Tel. +39 0365651002
www.cantinescolari.it

HECTARES UNDER VINE

- ○ Lugana '19 🍷🍷 2*
- ○ Lugana et Azzurra '19 🍷🍷 3
- ⊙ Valtènesi Chiaretto Bellerica '19 🍷🍷 3

Sullali

via Costa di Sopra, 22
25030 Erbusco [BS]
Tel. +39 3930206080
info@sullali.com

ANNUAL PRODUCTION 10,000 bottles
HECTARES UNDER VINE 3.50

- ○ Franciacorta Extra Brut Blanc de Noirs 🍷🍷 5
- ○ Franciacorta Brut 🍷 4
- ○ Franciacorta Extra Brut Blanc de Blancs 🍷 5

Tenute del Garda

via Burago, 1
25080 Calvagese della Riviera [BS]
Tel. +39 0309919000
www.tenutedelgarda.it

CELLAR SALES
PRE-BOOKED VISITS
ANNUAL PRODUCTION 50,000 bottles
HECTARES UNDER VINE 23.00

- ○ Garda Riesling '17 🍷🍷 2*
- ⊙ Valtènesi Chiaretto '19 🍷🍷 3

Benedetto Tognazzi

fraz. Caionvico
via Sant'Orsola, 161
25135 Brescia
Tel. +39 0302692695
www.tognazzivini.it

CELLAR SALES
PRE-BOOKED VISITS
ANNUAL PRODUCTION 80,000 bottles
HECTARES UNDER VINE 12.00
SUSTAINABLE WINERY

- ● Botticino Cobio '17 🍷🍷 5
- ○ Lugana Cascina Ardea '19 🍷🍷 2*
- ● Botticino Uve di Mattina '17 🍷 3

La Travaglina

fraz. Castello
via Travaglina, 1
27046 Santa Giuletta [PV]
Tel. +39 0383899195
www.latravaglina.it

CELLAR SALES
PRE-BOOKED VISITS
ANNUAL PRODUCTION 230,000 bottles
HECTARES UNDER VINE 30.50

- ○ Martinburgo Brut M. Cl. 🍷🍷 4
- ● OP Pinot Nero Casaia '17 🍷🍷 3
- ● OP Rosso 3 Lune '15 🍷 3

Triacca

via Nazionale, 121
23030 Villa di Tirano [SO]
Tel. +39 0342701352
www.triacca.eu

CELLAR SALES
PRE-BOOKED VISITS
RESTAURANT SERVICE
ANNUAL PRODUCTION 450,000 bottles
HECTARES UNDER VINE 40.00

- ● Valtellina Sforzato San Domenico '16 🍷🍷 6
- ● Valtellina Sup. Casa La Gatta '17 🍷🍷 5
- ● Valtellina Sup. Casa La Gatta Ris. '16 🍷🍷 5

Valdamonte

fraz. Valdamonte, 58
27047 Santa Maria della Versa [PV]
Tel. +39 038579665
www.valdamonte.it

CELLAR SALES
PRE-BOOKED VISITS
RESTAURANT SERVICE
ANNUAL PRODUCTION 17,000 bottles
HECTARES UNDER VINE 16.00
VITICULTURE METHOD Certified Organic
SUSTAINABLE WINERY

- ○ 347 M.S.L.M. Bianco '19 🍷 3
- ● 347 M.S.L.M. Rosso '19 🍷 2
- ● OP Bonarda Frizzante Novecento '19 🍷 2

Agricola Vallecamonica

via XXV Aprile, 11
25040 Artogne [BS]
Tel. +39 3355828410
www.vinivallecamonica.com

CELLAR SALES
PRE-BOOKED VISITS
ANNUAL PRODUCTION 20,000 bottles
HECTARES UNDER VINE 4.50

- ○ Bianco dell'Annunciata '17 🍷🍷 3
- ○ Estremo Adamamus Extra Brut M. Cl. '16 🍷🍷 6
- ○ Bianco delle Colture '17 🍷 3

Le Vedute

Via Monte Orfano, snc
25038 Rovato [BS]
Tel. +39

HECTARES UNDER VINE
SUSTAINABLE WINERY

- ○ Franciacorta Dosaggio Zero 🍷🍷 5
- ○ Franciacorta Satèn 🍷🍷 5

Vercesi del Castellazzo

via Aureliano, 36
27040 Montù Beccaria [PV]
Tel. +39 0385262098
www.vercesidelcastellazzo.it

CELLAR SALES
PRE-BOOKED VISITS
ANNUAL PRODUCTION 80,000 bottles
HECTARES UNDER VINE 13.00

- ○ Gugiarolo Pinot Nero in Bianco '19 🍷🍷 2*
- ● Clà Barbera '18 🍷 2
- ● Fatila Croatina '15 🍷 4

Giuseppe Vezzoli

via Costa Sopra, 22
25030 Erbusco [BS]
Tel. +39 0307267579
www.vezzolivini.it

CELLAR SALES
PRE-BOOKED VISITS
ANNUAL PRODUCTION 200,000 bottles
HECTARES UNDER VINE 63.00

- ○ Franciacorta Brut '15 🍷🍷 6
- ○ Franciacorta Nefertiti Dizeta '13 🍷🍷 6
- ○ Franciacorta Brut 🍷 5
- ○ Franciacorta Dosage Zero 🍷 5

Vigna Dorata

fraz. Calino
via Sala, 80
25046 Cazzago San Martino [BS]
Tel. +39 0307254275
www.vignadorata.it

CELLAR SALES
PRE-BOOKED VISITS
ANNUAL PRODUCTION 70,000 bottles
HECTARES UNDER VINE 8.00

- ○ Franciacorta Brut 🍷🍷 5
- ○ Franciacorta Nature 🍷🍷 5
- ○ Franciacorta Satèn 🍷🍷 5

Villa Domizia

via Marconi, 1
24060 Torre de' Roveri [BG]
Tel. +39 035580701
www.villadomizia.it

HECTARES UNDER VINE

- ● Valcalepio Rosso Gaudes '16 🍷🍷 2*
- ○ TdC Incrocio Manzoni Punto Uno '19 🍷 3
- ● TdC Incrocio Terzi Punto Zero '18 🍷 2

Zatti

via Lanfranchi, 10
25080 Calvagese della Riviera [BS]
Tel. +39 3464273907
www.cantinazatti.it

ANNUAL PRODUCTION 10,000 bottles
HECTARES UNDER VINE 2.00

- ⊙ Brut Rosé Sandriolè M. Cl. 🍷🍷 5
- ○ Garda Riesling Gep '18 🍷🍷 3

CANTON TICINO

Here we are with Ticino back in our guide for the fourth year. It's a regional presence that, in the past, had enriched our publication but had then gone missing for several years. Cultural and linguistic affinities, and territorial contiguity, convinced us to resume the custom. And we're happy for having done so, because once again we tasted a number of excellent wines, thanks in part to the passionate and skilled team of Ticino tasters who made it all easy (as well as possible). Cantone comprises a range of excellent terroirs when it comes to viticulture, which has been practiced here since time immemorial. It's enough to visit the region, admire its steep pre-Alpine slopes, terraced and covered with vineyards, to understand how important wine-growing is for the land, Ticino's history and culture (and not only in the material sense of culture). Of course, most of the wines we reviewed are based on Merlot, the variety with which the area is most identified today. After phylloxera, in 1907, the Bordeaux grape replaced the local grapes and hybrids that were popular at the time, and became the hegemonic cultivar. In recent years, although its supremacy remains clear, we've seen a flourishing rediscovery of local varieties, primarily Bondola, and experimentation with many Italian and international varieties, both in Sopraceneri and Sottoceneri. As for Merlot, it's interpreted in different styles: as a light and fruity summer wine, but also in full-bodied selections matured in barriques, where it's concentrated and suitable for laying down. Even when vinified off-the-skins, as a white, it can be convincing. This year, in the end, we awarded 2 producers: Lugano's Paolo Basso Wine, with their Rosso di Chiara '17, an excellent Bordeaux blend, and Losone's Angelo Delea, whose elegant Ticino Merlot Carato Riserva '17 once again demonstrates why Delea is a top producer. 2 awards but many wines, some 22, made it to our final tastings. Ticino is growing, and we can attest to the fact.

Agriloro

via Prella, 14
6852 Genestrerio
Tel. +39 +41916405454
www.agriloro.ch

CELLAR SALES
PRE-BOOKED VISITS
ANNUAL PRODUCTION 180,000 bottles
HECTARES UNDER VINE 20.00

The owner, Meinrad C. Perler, grew up in the canton of Fribourg in a family of farmers. In 1981 he decided to purchase Tenimento dell'Ör in the municipality of Arzo, thus returning to his origins. Then he set about renewing the estate. Being enthusiastic about experimentation, he created an ampelographical vineyard containing 600 varieties in order to study their different characteristics. In 2002, he bought Tenuta La Prella in Genestrerio. Today he produces 23 different wines, giving space to unusual grapes for the canton. He uses natural vinegrowing and winemaking methods that respect the environment as much as possible. Sottobosco '17 stood out during tasting for its weight, balance and well-integrated tannins; the complex finish reveals nice sapidity. Their Casimiro '16, a blend of 11 varieties, and Granito '18, a worthy white wine, were also impressive.

Wine	Rating
● Ticino Rosso Sottobosco '17	🍷🍷 7
● Casimiro '16	🍷🍷 5
○ Ticino Bianco Granito '18	🍷🍷 5
● Ticino Merlot Riserva da l'Ör '17	🍷 7
● Ticino Pinot Nero '17	🍷 5
● Casimiro '15	YY 5
○ Ticino Bianco Granito '16	YY 5
● Ticino Merlot La Prella Ris. '16	YY 6
● Ticino Merlot La Prella Ris. '15	YY 6
● Ticino Rosso Sottobosco '15	YY 6
● Ticino Sottobosco '16	YY 6

Paolo Basso Wine

c.so Pestalozzi, 3
6901 Lugano
Tel. +39 +41919220810
www.paolobassowine.ch

CELLAR SALES
PRE-BOOKED VISITS
ANNUAL PRODUCTION 20,000 bottles
HECTARES UNDER VINE 6.00

Paolo Basso comes from an intense career as a sommelier, where he won the title of best sommelier in the world in 2013 (and in Europe in 2010). His passion for wine is also due to the fact he resides in one of the best-known vinegrowing villages in Ticino. This spurred him on to become a producer, helped by the best agronomists and winemakers in the region, who make up a team with very specific expertise. The line dedicated to his daughter Chiara reflects Paolo's precision and meticulous nature. The Il Bianco di Chiara '18 is a classic Merlot fermented off the skins that plays on freshness and finesse. The Il Rosso di Chiara '17 is a classic Bordeaux blend and one of the best reds from Ticino that made it into this guide. Exhibiting great class, it comes through elegant and velvety, with all the components showing great balance. Tre Bicchieri.

Wine	Rating
● Ticino Rosso di Chiara '17	🍷🍷🍷 6
○ Ticino Bianco di Chiara '18	🍷 5

Tenuta Castello di Morcote

S.DA AL CASTEL, 27
6921 VICO MORCOTE
TEL. +39 +41919961230
www.castellodimorcote.ch

CELLAR SALES
PRE-BOOKED VISITS
ANNUAL PRODUCTION 60,000 bottles
HECTARES UNDER VINE 13.00

Castello di Morcote extends over a vast promontory surrounded by Lake Ceresio, where Ticino's unique soil gives rise to a thriving, unspoilt natural landscape. In the heart of the estate, in a panoramic position overlooking the lake, we find the 15th-century castle. The property, family-run since 1930, has adopted a careful viticultural approach, manually applying organic practices so as to obtain quality grapes, making for authentic wines that are an expression of the territory. Our tastings highlighted top-level wines. The Castello di Morcote Riserva '17 expresses sweet balsamic notes and a vigorous, fresh palate, with nice tannins; the finish is sapid and lingering. Their Castello di Morcote '18 plays on fresh fruit and fragrance; it proves fine and elegant, showing lots of zip, making for pleasant drinking.

- ● Ticino Merlot Castello di Morcote Ris. '17 — 🍷🍷 8
- ● Ticino Merlot Castello di Morcote '18 — 🍷🍷 7
- ○ Ticino Merlot Bianc Castello di Morcote '19 — 🍷 7

Vini Angelo Delea

VIA ZANDONE, 11
6616 LOSONE
TEL. +39 +41917910817
www.delea.ch

CELLAR SALES
PRE-BOOKED VISITS
ANNUAL PRODUCTION 550,000 bottles
HECTARES UNDER VINE 24.00
SUSTAINABLE WINERY

The winery was set up in 1983 by Angelo Delea, whose aim was to produce quality wines. Today Angelo shares the work with his sons, Cesare and Davide, who maintain the excellent levels achieved, as well as bringing new stimulus and ideas. The care they take in production makes for an interesting wine selection using grapes grown in the Locarno area. Carato Riserva '17 confirms the excellent results of previous years. Featuring ripe fruit and spices on the nose, the palate proves fresh and caressing, with elegant tannins and a long, lingering finish. Tre Bicchieri. The Carato '17 is a classic, pleasant wine, with nice, fresh fruit. It shows good structure, coming through intense and spicy. Finesse and elegance are its main features. The Carato Bianco '18 conveys pleasant sensations and this generous, balanced wine reveals a moderate taste development.

- ● Ticino Merlot Carato Ris. '17 — 🍷🍷🍷 8
- ● Ticino Merlot Carato '17 — 🍷🍷 8
- ○ Ticino Bianco Carato '18 — 🍷🍷 7
- ○ Ticino Il Sauvignon '19 — 🍷 4
- ● Ticino Merlot Saleggi Losone '18 — 🍷 4
- ● Ticino Merlot Carato '16 — 🍷🍷🍷 5
- ○ Ticino Carato Bianco '17 — 🍷🍷 4
- ○ Ticino Carato Bianco '15 — 🍷🍷 4
- ● Ticino Diamante '15 — 🍷🍷 8
- ● Ticino Diamante '13 — 🍷🍷 8
- ○ Ticino Il Sauvignon '17 — 🍷🍷 3
- ○ Ticino Il Sauvignon '16 — 🍷🍷 3
- ● Ticino Merlot Carato Ris. '16 — 🍷🍷 6
- ● Ticino Merlot Carato Ris. '15 — 🍷🍷 6
- ● Ticino Merlot Saleggi '16 — 🍷🍷 4

Gialdi Vini - Brivio

via Vignoo, 3
6850 Mendrisio
Tel. +39 +41916403030
www.gialdi.ch

CELLAR SALES
PRE-BOOKED VISITS
ANNUAL PRODUCTION 1,000,000 bottles
HECTARES UNDER VINE 140.00

The winery founded in 1953 is now run by Feliciano Gialdi. The first ten years were dedicated to selling wines and it was only in 1985 that they focussed on producing their own. Since 2001, the work of Alfred Demartin and a group of vinegrowers has helped the winery to reach the heights of Ticino winemaking. In 2018, when the Brivio brand was added to their range of wines sold, it became the largest winery in the canton, but this doesn't stop them producing wines of absolute quality. They produce about thirty wines. During these tastings, the Brivio Riflessi d'Epoca '17, made with grapes grown in Mendrisiotto vineyards, stood out for its constant steadiness. Brivio Vigna d'Antan also impressed for its precise, balanced and elegant aromas, with a palate expressing great energy and length. The Sassi Grossi, made in the north of the canton, still manages to develop its potential over the years.

Wine	Score
● Ticino Rosso Brivio Vigna D'Antan '17	6
● Ticino Merlot Brivio Riflessi d'Epoca '17	7
● Ticino Merlot Sassi Grossi '17	7
● Ticino Rosso Estro '16	6
● Ticino Brivio Merlot Riflessi d'Epoca '15	5
● Ticino Merlot Arzo '13	5
● Ticino Merlot Platinum '15	8
● Ticino Merlot Riflessi d'Epoca '16	5
● Ticino Merlot Sassi Grossi '16	7
● Ticino Merlot Sassi Grossi '15	6
● Ticino Merlot Sassi Grossi '13	6
● Ticino Merlot Trentasei '13	7
● Ticino Merlot Trentasei '10	7

Hauser

via Cantonale, 42
6594 Contone - Gambarogno
Tel. +39 +41792375452
www.vinohauser.ch

CELLAR SALES
PRE-BOOKED VISITS
ANNUAL PRODUCTION 35,000 bottles
HECTARES UNDER VINE 7.50

Urs Hauser moved to Ticino at the age of 25 to learn Italian after finishing his studies in engineering. It should have been a brief stay, but his relationship with this land had an unexpected outcome. He gradually developed a passion for viticulture and taught himself the rudiments of winemaking. Today he works just over seven hectares of vineyards divided into about twenty plots of land, dominated by Merlot. Urs' winery has made it into our Guide thanks to a thoroughly impressive selection. All of their wines were very well-made; Le Cime '17 stood out for its pleasant, well-integrated oaky notes, velvety tannins, perfect balance and energy at the finish. Kudos. Stella '16 reveals great pleasantness, nice freshness of fruit and palate, well-integrated tannins and notable complexity.

Wine	Score
● Ticino Rosso Le Cime '17	7
● Ticino Merlot Bella Stasera '16	5
● Ticino Merlot Dopo Mezzanotte '16	6
● Ticino Merlot Stella '16	7
○ Ticino Bianco Tutto Bene '18	4

Cantina Kopp von der Crone Visini

via Noga, 2
6917 Barbengo
Tel. +39 +41916829616
www.cantinabarbengo.ch

CELLAR SALES
PRE-BOOKED VISITS
ANNUAL PRODUCTION 40,000 bottles
HECTARES UNDER VINE 7.00

The Kopp von der Crone Visini winery in Barbengo was formed by the merger between the Kopp von der Crone and Vini Visini wineries in 2006, though they already collaborated in the old Melide cellars. Today the vineyard surface area of about seven hectares is divided between municipalities in Mendrisio, Lugano and Bellinzona; Merlot is planted on 70% of this land. Anna Barbara Von der Crone and Paolo Visini use integrated production methods in the vineyard. Their wines exhibit character and strength. Irto '16 offers up balanced aromas, good volume, elegant tannins and a marked fresh finish. Scalin '17 is on top form: its nose conveys fresh sensations alternating between red fruit and nuances of herbs. It exhibits vigour, well-integrated tannins and a tempting finish. Their Balin '17 is also excellent and full of character, but needs further maturation in bottle.

Wine	Rating
● Ticino Rosso Irto '16	🍷🍷 7
● Ticino Rosso Scalin '17	🍷🍷 5
● Ticino Rosso Balin '17	🍷🍷 7
● Balin '15	🍷🍷 6
● Irto '13	🍷🍷 6
● Scala '15	🍷🍷 6

Istituto Agrario Cantonale di Mezzana

via S. Gottardo, 1
6877 Coldrerio
Tel. +39 +41918166201
www.mezzana.ch

CELLAR SALES
PRE-BOOKED VISITS
ANNUAL PRODUCTION 65,000 bottles
HECTARES UNDER VINE 10.00

Since 1915, the Agricultural Institute in Mezzana has been a compulsory stepping stone for anyone undertaking professional training in the agricultural sector. On a surface area of about 50 hectares, young trainees apply themselves to vinegrowing, arable farming, fodder production and fruit and vegetable farming. Vinegrowing specialization is divided between work in the vineyard or cellar. The winery, run by Daniele Maffei and winemaker Nicola Caimi, covers 10 hectares of vineyards in lower Mendrisio, planted with Merlot, Chardonnay, Pinot Bianco, Viognier and Doral. This is a continually expanding farm where young people can learn the tricks of the trade. The wines they produce guarantee typicity and the ones we tasted confirm the good work carried out. Bongio '17 is classic, fruity and pleasantly spicy, with well-balanced components. Ronco '18 proves fragrant and tempting to drink.

Wine	Rating
● Ticino Merlot Bongio '17	🍷🍷 5
● Ticino Merlot Ronco '18	🍷🍷 5

Moncucchetto

via Marietta Crivelli Torricelli, 27
6900 Lugano
Tel. +39 +41919677060
www.moncucchetto.ch

CELLAR SALES
PRE-BOOKED VISITS
RESTAURANT SERVICE
ANNUAL PRODUCTION 30,000 bottles
HECTARES UNDER VINE 6.50

The history of the Lucchini family dates back to 1919 when they bought a hillside estate in the heart of Lugano. Eighty years later the new cellar designed by architect Mario Botta was built precisely on this site. The area called Moncucchetto is surrounded by vineyards whose grapes produce wines full of personality. Today, Lisetta and Niccolò Lucchini, aided by their very capable winemaker Cristina Monico, are getting much-deserved recognition thanks to their great efforts. Their wines, which are gradually becoming better known, manage to convey important sensations. Collina d'Oro Agra '17 is our favorite for the moment. This wine draws on freshness and balance, while its density and abundant, but fine-grained, tannins look hopeful for aging. Moncucchetto Riserva '16 comes through vigorous, with the right amount of tannin and a finish that reveals a very pleasant aromatic expression.

Wine	Rating
● Ticino Rosso Collina d'Oro Agra '17	🍷🍷 6
● Ticino Merlot Moncucchetto Ris. '16	🍷🍷 6
○ Ticino Bianco dell'Arco '19	🍷 4
○ Ticino Bianco dell'Arco '18	🍷🍷 5
○ Ticino Bianco Moncucchetto '17	🍷🍷 4
● Ticino Merlot L'Arco '17	🍷🍷 5
● Ticino Merlot Moncucchetto '17	🍷🍷 6
● Ticino Merlot Moncucchetto '16	🍷🍷 6
○ Ticino Sauvignon '17	🍷🍷 5

Mondò

via Al Mondò, 3
6514 Sementina
Tel. +39 +41918574558
www.aziendamondo.ch

CELLAR SALES
PRE-BOOKED VISITS
ANNUAL PRODUCTION 50,000 bottles
HECTARES UNDER VINE 7.00

Giorgio Rossi's completely family-run Mondò winery is situated in the Sementin hills. Their love for the land and careful management of the hillside terrain and vineyards, are a natural condition for obtaining good, healthy grapes with the necessary characteristics for making excellent wines. In addition to Merlot, they also grow Bondola, the only native grape in Ticino - especially in Sopra Ceneri. This decision enables them to safeguard the tradition of Ticino winegrowing. During tasting, the Ronco dei Ciliegi '17 delivers once again for balance and ripe, velvety tannins, livened up by a distinctive fresh finish. Scintilla '17 enjoys the benefits of a good vintage and proves fruity and pleasantly balsamic; we liked its finesse and lovely finish. Bondola del Nonu Mario '18 expresses all its original character, with assertive acidity and a certain rustic charm. It could be laid down for ten years or so.

Wine	Rating
● Ticino Rosso Ronco dei Ciliegi '17	🍷🍷 7
● Ticino Merlot Scintilla '17	🍷🍷 6
○ Ticino Bianco Crudéll '18	🍷 6
● Ticino Bondola del Nonu Mario '18	🍷 4
● Ticino Mondò '15	🍷🍷 7
● Ticino Mondò '13	🍷🍷 7
● Ticino Ronco dei Ciliegi '15	🍷🍷 6
● Ticino Ronco dei Ciliegi '13	🍷🍷 6

Cantina Monti

via dei Ronchi
6936 Cademario
Tel. +39 +41916053475
www.cantinamonti.ch

CELLAR SALES
PRE-BOOKED VISITS
ANNUAL PRODUCTION 30,000 bottles
HECTARES UNDER VINE 5.00
SUSTAINABLE WINERY

Ivo Monti is the son of the great Sergio, remembered by Ticino vinegrowers as the president of Federviti of Lugano for years. From the winery's terrace, you can enjoy the view over the steep vineyards of Ronchi di Cademario, in Malcantone. The winery's philosophy is based on low yields in the vineyard, making for optimum grape ripening. The careful attention paid to every detail, both in the choice of barrique, toasting and corks, has helped the winery achieve levels of excellence. This was also confirmed by our tastings this year. Merlot grapes grown in five different vineyards produce this splendid Rosso dei Ronchi '17, a fresh, close-knit, elegant and deep wine. Their Canto della Terra '18 proves juicy, with velvety tannins, power and zip. The Rovere '17 may be less complex, but it offers up great pleasure and perfectly expresses the winery's style. All these wines generally age very well.

Wine	Rating
● Ticino Merlot Canto della Terra '18	🍷🍷 8
● Ticino Rosso Malcantone Rosso dei Ronchi '17	🍷🍷 7
● Ticino Merlot Rovere '17	🍷🍷 6
● Ticino Rosso SM '18	🍷🍷 7
○ Ticino Bianco di Cademario '18	🍷 5

Tamborini Vini

via Serta, 18
6814 Lamone
Tel. +39 +41919357545
www.tamborinivini.ch

CELLAR SALES
PRE-BOOKED VISITS
ANNUAL PRODUCTION 700,000 bottles
HECTARES UNDER VINE 30.00

Tamborini is a continually developing winery; initially working in wine sales, they began vinifying their own grapes at the end of the 1970s, spurred on by Claudio Tamborini. Today's generation has brought new drive that has made the winery even more modern. The 30 hectares of vineyards are scattered over the Lugano hills. They sport a wide range of wines covering different commercial areas. The best expressions come from Merlot, which manages to produce concentrated wines that are sometimes elegant, depending on the area where the grapes are grown. Comano '17 features a particularly elegant and refined structure. San Zeno Costamagna '17, on the other hand, exhibits intense notes of black fruit and spices; the palate reveals a dense, powerful structure. Credi '17, the red wine of their young daughter Valentina, expresses tenacity, nice freshness and tannins still to be matured in the bottle.

Wine	Rating
● Ticino Merlot San Zeno Costamagna '17	🍷🍷 7
● Ticino Merlot San Zeno Trentalune '17	🍷🍷 8
● Ticino Merlot Comano '17	🍷🍷 8
○ Ticino Bianco Espe n.5 '19	🍷 5
○ Ticino Bianco Mosaico '18	🍷 5
● Ticino Credi Valentina WineCollection '17	🍷 8
● Ticino Credi '15	🍷🍷 7
● Ticino Merlot Castelrotto '16	🍷🍷 6
● Ticino Merlot Comano '15	🍷🍷 7
● Ticino Merlot San Domenico '16	🍷🍷 4
● Ticino Merlot San Domenico '15	🍷🍷 7
● Ticino Merlot San Zeno Costamagna '15	🍷🍷 7
● Ticino Merlot San Zeno Trentalune '16	🍷🍷 7
● Ticino Merlot Tenuta San Rocco '16	🍷🍷 4
● Ticino Merlot V. V. '15	🍷🍷 4
○ Ticino Vivi '17	🍷🍷 5

Tenuta Vitivinicola Trapletti

via P. F. Mola, 34
6877 Coldrerio
Tel. +39 +41916301150
www.viticoltori.ch/trapletti

CELLAR SALES
PRE-BOOKED VISITS
ANNUAL PRODUCTION 40,000 bottles
HECTARES UNDER VINE 4.00

Enrico Trapletti is a volatile character who carries out his projects with great diligence. The culture of the land was instilled into him at a very young age. He began making wine in the early 1990s and, over time, the winery became his main activity. Among the several ideas he has come up with over the years, he deserves credit for relaunching the Nebbiolo grape variety in Ticino, which was already present in the nineteenth century before Merlot came along. Today he produces 15 wines made with just as many grape varieties. The wines we tasted are part of the historic selection that made them famous on a national level. Their Culdrée '17 (the dialect name for Coldrerio) comes from old vines: the prowess of this dense but energetic high-profile wine can be seen in the tannin extraction. Trapletti '17 reveals nice personality and expresses all its fragrance, with ripe fruit and pleasant balance.

● Ticino Merlot Culdrée '17	▼▼ 8
● Ticino Merlot Trapletti '17	▼▼ 6
● Ticino Merlot Terra Creda '18	▼ 6
● Ticino Merlot Culdrée '17	▽▽ 7
● Ticino Merlot Culdrée '15	▽▽ 7
● Ticino Merlot Culdrée '13	▽▽ 7
● Ticino Vino del Monte S. Giorgio '17	▽▽ 5
● Trapletti Rosso '13	▽▽ 5

Valsangiacomo Vini

v.le alle Cantine, 6
6850 Mendrisio
Tel. +39 +41916836053
www.valswine.ch

CELLAR SALES
PRE-BOOKED VISITS
ANNUAL PRODUCTION 250,000 bottles
HECTARES UNDER VINE 20.00

The winery was founded in 1831, but it was only at the start of the 1900s that it took on an important role as a benchmark in Canton Ticino winegrowing. Continuity is ensured by both the territorial and generational link. Today, Uberto Valsangiacomo enthusiastically follows in his father Cesare's footsteps. The 20 hectares of vineyards are scattered over the Mendrisiotto hills and mainly grow Merlot. The winery produces quality wines that have become classics on the Swiss winemaking scene. Aging takes place in the characteristic Mendrisio cellars at the foot of Monte Generoso, where the wines enjoy perfect natural conditions of temperature and humidity. The Gran Segreto Bianco '18 features complex aromas of ripe fruit, spices, vanilla and toasting; the fresh, sapid palate exhibits a lingering taste. The 1831 '18 reveals sweet fruit, while pepper tickles the nose and the palate comes through direct and fresh, with nice structure.

○ Ticino Merlot Bianco GranSegreto '18	▼▼ 6
● Ticino Syrah 1831 '18	▼▼ 6
● Ticino Merlot Rubro '16	▼ 7
○ Ticino Gransegreto Fondo del Bosco '16	▽▽ 5
● Ticino Merlot Loverciano '16	▽▽ 5
● Ticino Merlot Piccolo Ronco '15	▽▽ 5
● Ticino Merlot Piccolo Ronco '13	▽▽ 5

Bianchi

S.DA DA RÖV, 24
6822 AROGNO
TEL. +39 +41762732050
www.bianchi.bio

CELLAR SALES
PRE-BOOKED VISITS
ANNUAL PRODUCTION 12,000 bottles
HECTARES UNDER VINE 6.00

- ● Ticino Syrah Piaz '18 — 🍷🍷 6
- ○ Ticino Bianco Alma '19 — 🍷 5
- ○ Ticino Bianco None '19 — 🍷 5

Cagi - Cantina Giubiasco

VIA LINOLEUM, 11
6512 GIUBIASCO
TEL. +39 +41918572531
www.cagivini.ch

PRE-BOOKED VISITS
ANNUAL PRODUCTION 600,000 bottles
SUSTAINABLE WINERY

- ● Ticino Merlot Camorino '17 — 🍷🍷 5
- ● Ticino Merlot Monte Carasso '17 — 🍷🍷 5
- ● Ticino Rosso Enigma '16 — 🍷🍷 5
- ○ Ticino Bianco di Merlot Ris. '18 — 🍷 4

Castello di Cantone

LOC. RANCATE
VIA MUNICIPIO, 6
6825 MENDRISIO
TEL. +39 +41916404434
www.castellodicantone.ch

- ● Ticino Rosso Negromante '17 — 🍷🍷 7
- ● Ticino Merlot Castello di Cantone Ris. '17 — 🍷🍷 8
- ○ Ticino Merlot Bianco Galanthus '19 — 🍷 7
- ● Ticino Rosso Ungulus '16 — 🍷 8

Cantina Cavallini

LOC. VALLE DI MUGGIO
6838 CABBIO
TEL. +39 +41916841579
cantinacavallini@gmail.com

HECTARES UNDER VINE 3.00

- ● Ticino Merlot Pedrinate '16 — 🍷🍷 6
- ● Cabernet '18 — 🍷 6

Cantina Cristini e Figli

AI SCARSITT, 6
6528 CAMORINO
TEL. +39 +41787761161
cristini@ticino.com

- ● Ticino Merlot Antares '18 — 🍷🍷 6
- ● Ticino Rosso Synthesis '17 — 🍷🍷 6

Robin Garzoli

6673 MAGGIA
TEL. +39 +41917531863
www.rombolau.ch

- ● Ticino Acqua Reale '18 — 🍷🍷 5
- ● Ticino Rombolau '17 — 🍷🍷 6

Matteo Huber Tenuta Arca Rubra

via P. Moretto, 9
6924 Sorengo
Tel. +39 +41919508373
www.arcarubra.ch

- ● Ticino Rosso Note di Notte '17 🍷🍷 7
- ● Ticino Merlot Arca Rubra '17 🍷🍷 6
- ● Ticino Merlot Primo Segno '19 🍷 5
- ○ Ticino Sauvignon Arca Clara '19 🍷 6

Hubervini

6998 Monteggio
Tel. +39 +41916081754
www.hubervini.ch

- ○ Ticino Bianco Volpe Alata '18 🍷🍷 5
- ● Ticino Merlot Fustoquattro '18 🍷🍷 4
- ● Ticino Rosso Costera Ris. '17 🍷🍷 6
- ● Ticino Rosso Montagna Magica '17 🍷 7

Monzeglio

via privata dei Gelsi, 5
6807 Taverne
Tel. +39 +41794714102
www.vinimonzeglio.ch

- ● Ticino Rosso Tre Sorelle '18 🍷🍷 5
- ● Ticino Merlot Filari della Luna '18 🍷🍷 6
- ● Ticino Rosso Terra Viva '18 🍷🍷 5
- ○ Ticino Bianco di Luna '19 🍷 4

Parravicini

via alle Corti, 55
6873 Corteglia
Tel. +39 +41916302175
www.parravicini.ch

- ● Ticino Rosso I Cavri '17 🍷🍷 6

Tenuta Pian Marnino

Al Gaggioletto, 2
6515 Gudo
Tel. +39 +41918590960
www.pianmarnino.com

PRE-BOOKED VISITS
ANNUAL PRODUCTION 20,000 bottles
HECTARES UNDER VINE 5.00

- ● Ticino Merlot Oro di Gudo '16 🍷🍷 7
- ● Ticino Rosso Tre Ori di Gudo '15 🍷 7

Theilervini

via Cademario, 135
6935 Bosco Luganese
Tel. +39 +41916046078
www.theilervini.ch

SUSTAINABLE WINERY

- ● Ticino Merlot Corifeo '17 🍷🍷 7
- ● Ticino Merlot Dives '17 🍷🍷 6

TRENTINO

When it comes to Trentino, the wines awarded in our 2021 edition of the guide are as varied as ever, with some 14 bottles recognized. A record, in every sense, as a total number and for the rise of Trentodoc sparklers, which continue to stimulate production in the Dolomite valleys, amidst Alpine lakes and porphyry rocks. It should be pointed out that among these, you won't find some of the best known and established bottles because several wineries (foremost San Leonardo), together with renowned Teroldego growers (De Vescovi) and prestigious Brioso Cuvées (see Balter) decided to extend the bottle aging of their most important products. Tasting, however, was merely postponed until next year. But awards weren't lacking, nor were some exciting new additions: from Pojer & Sandri's vibrant Riesling to the Passito par excellence, Pravis's Vino Santo. Then there's a white that can face the test of time, Toblino's Ora, made with Nosiola. Half a decade (it's a vintage 2015) has lent further complexity to a white made with one of the area's great native grapes. Among the wines back in the limelight, we find Corvée's Müller Thurgau, as well as the Pinot Nero that the Simoni family produces at Maso Cantanghel. We also shouldn't forget the amazing (that's not an exaggeration) Teroldego Rotaliano proposed by the Dorigati family, named 'Luigi' in honour of one of their ancestors. Trento's sparklers are captained by the Lunelli family's usual Giulio Ferrari, an unmistakable model, an international must that's leading an increasingly formidable line-up of Dolomitic bubbly. Then there's the fabulous Abate Nero '09 made by the late Luciano Lunelli, a Trentino wine patriarch, a sparkling wine master who inspired many other producers to bet on Trentodoc. One of these is Francesco Moser, the cycling champ who, with his children, makes a first-rate Nature. Trento's large cooperatives also delivered: Cavit, with their new Blanc de Noirs '16, Mezzacorona with the Flavio '12, and the Aquila Reale '10 by Cesarini Sforza. We also shouldn't forget Lucia Letrari with their Dosaggio Zero '14, nor the authoritative Madame Martis '10 by Maso Martis. All rigorously authentic wines that faithfully express the mountains in which they're forged.

★Abate Nero

via Sponda Trentina, 45
38121 Trento
Tel. +39 0461246566
www.abatenero.it

CELLAR SALES
ANNUAL PRODUCTION 65,000 bottles
HECTARES UNDER VINE 65.00

Unfortunately, Luciano Lunelli has left us after an illness. He was the founder of Abate Nero, a figure of the highest authority in Trentino. Abate Nero is a beautiful winery, and over the years they've been able to offer great Metodo Classico, serving as authentic interpreters of mountain sparkling wines. It's now managed by his close family, his daughter Roberta and Roberto Sebastiani, who treasure Luciano's precious teachings. All their cuvées exhibit finesse and elegance, charm and great character. The Cuvée dell'Abate '09 handily took home our Tre Bicchieri. It has the unmistakable strength of a classic Trento wine and just as much vigor of taste; it comes through appealing, redolent of ripe wheat and autumnal apples grown in the Dolomites, with an intriguing complex vibrancy. The other three standard bearers of this exquisite version performed quite well, especially the Domini '13.

Wine	Rating
○ Trento Brut Cuvée dell'Abate Ris. '09	▼▼▼ 6
○ Trento Brut Abate Nero	▼▼ 5
○ Trento Brut Domini '13	▼▼ 5
⊙ Trento Brut Rosé Abate Nero	▼▼ 5
○ Trento Brut Cuvée dell'Abate Ris. '04	▽▽▽ 6
○ Trento Brut Cuvée dell'Abate Ris. '03	▽▽▽ 5
○ Trento Brut Cuvée dell'Abate Ris. '02	▽▽▽ 5
○ Trento Brut Cuvée dell'Abate Ris. '01	▽▽▽ 5
○ Trento Brut Domini '10	▽▽▽ 5
○ Trento Brut Domini '07	▽▽▽ 5
○ Trento Brut Domini '05	▽▽▽ 5
○ Trento Brut Domini Nero '10	▽▽▽ 5
○ Trento Brut Domini Nero '08	▽▽▽ 5
○ Trento Domìni Nero '09	▽▽▽ 5
⊙ Trento Brut Domini Rosé '13	▽▽ 5

★Nicola Balter

via Vallunga II, 24
38068 Rovereto [TN]
Tel. +39 0464430101
www.balter.it

CELLAR SALES
PRE-BOOKED VISITS
ANNUAL PRODUCTION 80,000 bottles
HECTARES UNDER VINE 10.00

As far back as 1975 this charming plateau overlooking Rovereto was singled out as an excellent site for growing notable, quality wine grapes. The farm is beautiful, surrounded by woodlands amidst stone walls and a unique fortified tower, evidence of past territorial conflicts. Nicola Balter and his two children, Clementina and Giacomo, have maintained the original charm of the rural property, digging a cellar perfect for Metodo Classico production beneath the vineyards. While awaiting further development of their most important Trento wines, Nicola Balter submitted the still and non-vintage sparkling wines. The exquisite Cabernet Sauvignon opens the discussion: full and energizing, it reveals great character on the palate and notes of plum and redcurrant jam on the nose. Other traditional wines include the Traminer (which proves unusual both for the production area and winemaking style) - and we mustn't forget the simple and charming Trento Brut and Rosé wines.

Wine	Rating
● Cabernet Sauvignon '17	▼▼ 4
○ Trento Brut Balter	▼▼ 4
⊙ Trento Rosé Balter	▼▼ 5
● Lagrein Merlot '18	▼ 3
○ Traminer '19	▼ 4
○ Barbanico '97	▽▽▽ 4*
○ Trento Balter Ris. '06	▽▽▽ 5
○ Trento Balter Ris. '05	▽▽▽ 5
○ Trento Balter Ris. '04	▽▽▽ 5
○ Trento Balter Ris. '01	▽▽▽ 5
○ Trento Dosaggio Zero Ris. '10	▽▽▽ 7
○ Trento Pas Dosé Balter Ris. '13	▽▽▽ 6
○ Trento Pas Dosé Balter Ris. '12	▽▽▽ 6
○ Trento Pas Dosé Balter Ris. '11	▽▽▽ 5
○ Trento Pas Dosé Balter Ris. '09	▽▽▽ 5

Bellaveder

FRAZ. FAEDO
LOC. MASO BELVEDERE, 1
38010 SAN MICHELE ALL'ADIGE [TN]
TEL. +39 0461650171
www.bellaveder.it

CELLAR SALES
PRE-BOOKED VISITS
ANNUAL PRODUCTION 70,000 bottles
HECTARES UNDER VINE 12.00
SUSTAINABLE WINERY

Tranquillo Lucchetta carries on his work with humility, without flaunting success or making a fuss. The splendid vineyards for which he's responsible are set in two diametrically opposed areas but share in their high quality, while the winery is headquartered on the hillsides leading to Faedo. Other plots are located in in the Valle dei Laghi, on the promontory overlooking Lake Garda and the Brenta Dolomites. Depending on the vineyard, various types of grapes are cultivated. This year a Burgundy-style Pinot Nero stood out from the rest: very expressive, finely-tuned spicy notes, a generous palate, but velvety with a lovely evolving pressure. The juicy Riesling features a relaxed progression and clear varietal expression, with hints of petrol, ready to stand the test of time. The Trento Nature also impressed for its liveliness and focused aromas. The Sauvignon performed well, while the Mansum, made with Lagrein grapes, proved less captivating, being still too young.

Wine	Rating
● Trentino Pinot Nero Faedi '17	ŸŸ 5
○ Trentino Riesling Faedi '18	ŸŸ 3
○ Trento Brut Nature '15	ŸŸ 6
○ Faedi Sauvignon '19	Ÿ 3
● Trentino Lagrein Mansum '17	Ÿ 5
● Trentino Lagrein Mansum '16	ΥΥ 5
● Trentino Lagrein Mansum '15	ΥΥ 5
● Trentino Lagrein Mansum '12	ΥΥ 4
○ Trentino Müller Thurgau San Lorenz '18	ΥΥ 5
○ Trentino Müller Thurgau San Lorenz '13	ΥΥ 2*
● Trentino Pinot Nero Faedi '15	ΥΥ 6
● Trentino Pinot Nero Faedi Ris. '16	ΥΥ 5
○ Trentino Riesling '16	ΥΥ 3*
○ Trento Brut Nature Ris. '12	ΥΥ 5
○ Trento Brut Nature Ris. '12	ΥΥ 6
○ Trento Brut Nature Ris. '11	ΥΥ 5

Borgo dei Posseri

LOC. POZZO BASSO, 1
38061 ALA [TN]
TEL. +39 0464671899
www.borgodeiposseri.com

CELLAR SALES
PRE-BOOKED VISITS
ANNUAL PRODUCTION 60,000 bottles
HECTARES UNDER VINE 21.00
VITICULTURE METHOD Certified Organic
SUSTAINABLE WINERY

The effects of climate change are visible in the Little Dolomites, the mountains over Ala and the Vallagarina. Here viticulture is reaching higher elevations, trying to exploit better microclimates. Recently the area has become popular among those determined to work the steep slopes over the Adige. Borgo dei Possèri has been a forerunner of this new frontier and continues to serve as an example of research and innovation. Management is in the hands of Martin Mainenti and Maria Marangoni, the two families responsible for a range closely linked to the territory. The goal was certainly ambitious: to vinify Pinot Nero grown in the high hills to produce a wine with character, free from trends and full of mountainous expressions. They hit the bullseye. The Paradis Plus '17 is an invigorating wine with a vivid color and sensory range, several spicy overtones and nice suppleness. Their other wines prove just as sound, such as the Paradis, the Rocol, the Müller Thurgau and the two Trentos (Tananai Zero and the classic Tananai brut).

Wine	Rating
● Trentino Pinot Nero Paradis Plus '17	ŸŸ 3*
○ Müller Thurgau '19	ŸŸ 4
● Paradis Pinot Nero '16	ŸŸ 3
● Trentino Merlot Rocol '17	ŸŸ 3
○ Trento Brut Tananai '16	ŸŸ 5
○ Trento Dosaggio Zero Tananai '14	ŸŸ 5
○ Arliz Gewürztraminer '19	Ÿ 3
○ Furiel Sauvignon '19	Ÿ 4
○ Malusèl '18	Ÿ 3
○ Cuvée Malusel '15	ΥΥ 4
○ Malusèl '16	ΥΥ 3
● Paradis Plus Pinot Nero '16	ΥΥ 3
○ Quaron Müller Thurgau '18	ΥΥ 4
● Rocol Merlot '16	ΥΥ 3
○ Trento Brut Tananai '15	ΥΥ 5
○ Trento Brut Tananai '14	ΥΥ 5

Bossi Fedrigotti

via Unione, 43
38068 Rovereto [TN]
Tel. +39 0456832511
www.masi.it

CELLAR SALES
PRE-BOOKED VISITS
ANNUAL PRODUCTION 120,000 bottles
HECTARES UNDER VINE 40.00
SUSTAINABLE WINERY

The history of Trentino's wine is largely linked to the Bossi Fedrigotti family, a dynasty whose roots go back to the early 1500's. They were among the main innovators in various sectors and the first to sell wine in Europe, thanks to high-ranking relatives in the Austro-Hungarian Empire. They were also the creators of the first Bordeaux-style red, the Fojaneghe, produced as early as 1961. For some years now, management has been in the hands of Masi Agricola, which aims to protect all of this historic winery's peculiarities. Once again their classic sparklers nicely represent a producer, well-known for producing Bordeaux-style wines (their Fojaneghe is currently aging further). The Trento Conte Federico offers up a range of aromas redolent of bergamot orange and cotton candy, while the palate exhibits an enjoyable liveliness. As for still wines, their Marzemino (with a part of the grapes dried) impressed the most, while the Vign'Asmara, made with Pinot Grigio grapes, proves simple and drinkable.

○ Trento Conte Federico Ris. '16	🍷🍷	5
● Trentino Marzemino Mas'Est '19	🍷🍷	3
○ Vign'Asmara Pinot Grigio '19	🍷	4
● Fojaneghe Rosso '12	🍷🍷🍷	5
○ Trento Brut Conte Federico Ris. '12	🍷🍷🍷	5
● Fojaneghe Rosso '15	🍷🍷	5
● Fojaneghe Rosso '13	🍷🍷	5
○ Trentino Bianco Vign'Asmara '16	🍷🍷	4
● Trentino Teroldego Mas'Est '16	🍷🍷	3
○ Trentino Vign'Asmara '17	🍷🍷	4
○ Trento Brut Conte Federico Ris. '15	🍷🍷	5
○ Trento Brut Conte Federico Ris. '13	🍷🍷	5
○ Vign'Asmara '15	🍷🍷	4
○ Vign'Asmara '14	🍷🍷	4

★Cavit

via del Ponte, 31
38040 Trento
Tel. +39 0461381711
www.cavit.it

CELLAR SALES
PRE-BOOKED VISITS
ANNUAL PRODUCTION 70,000,000 bottles
HECTARES UNDER VINE 5500.00

Cavit perfectly represents the concept of cooperation when it comes to producing wine. We're talking about an enological giant that's in constant expansion, and has recently proven able to involve the Cantina La Vis and the Cesarini Sforza sparkling wine producer in its various business activities. Here enormous volumes of wine can be sold, and at the same time, they respect the small properties overseen by their growers (more than 5 thousand!) through the selection of authentic crus. Their range is quite diverse. Some lines are for international exports, others for large-scale distribution nationally. This year the Tre Bicchieri go to the Blanc di Noirs, which succeeds over the formidable Graal, both powerful Trento wines. The award-winning wine exhibits an extremely compact and bright color, and plays on tones of plum, sweet spices and jasmine. The palate comes through creamy, without citrine harshness or excess sugar. Their popular Nosiola was also outstanding. The elegant Pinot Nero (Brusafer) delivered once again, alongside a delightful Altemasi Rosé.

○ Trento Brut Altemasi Blanc de Noirs '16	🍷🍷🍷	5
○ Trentino Nosiola Bottega Vinai '19	🍷🍷	2*
○ Trento Brut Altemasi Graal Ris. '13	🍷🍷	7
● Trentino Pinot Nero Sup. Brusafer '17	🍷🍷	4
⊙ Trento Altemasi Rosé	🍷🍷	4
○ Maso Torresella Cuvée '18	🍷	4
○ Trentino Bianco Sup. Rupe Re '17	🍷	4
● Trentino Rosso Sup. Quattro Vicariati '17	🍷	4
○ Trento Brut Altemasi Graal Ris. '12	🍷🍷🍷	6
○ Trento Brut Altemasi Graal Ris. '10	🍷🍷🍷	6
○ Trento Brut Altemasi Graal Ris. '09	🍷🍷🍷	6
○ Trento Brut Altemasi Graal Ris. '08	🍷🍷🍷	6
○ Trento Brut Altemasi Graal Ris. '06	🍷🍷🍷	6

Cesarini Sforza

FRAZ. RAVINA
VIA STELLA, 9
38123 TRENTO
TEL. +39 0461382200
www.cesarinisforza.com

CELLAR SALES
PRE-BOOKED VISITS
ANNUAL PRODUCTION 1,000,000 bottles
HECTARES UNDER VINE 800.00
SUSTAINABLE WINERY

A recent partnership with the giant Cavit in no way affects the autonomy of this historic Trentino producer. Its ability to operate is greater in all respects, and that includes careful selection of wines destined to become vivacious, authentic sparklers of the Dolomites. Their Trentodocs, which are flanked by some excellent versions of Charmat Method Nereo Cavazzani, once again prove they're archetypes of solid sparkling wine evolution, all in the name of elegance and extreme drinkability. It doesn't disappoint this time, either: the Trento Aquila Reale easily wins our Tre Bicchieri. Thanks to the supple texture and precise aromas, with clear hints of petit fours and mountain grass, the wine exhibits elegance and harmony with a very lingering finish. Their Brut delivered again, while the Rosè came through very sapid, sound and reliable.

Wine	Rating
○ Trento Brut Aquila Reale '10	🍷🍷🍷 7
○ Trento Brut	🍷🍷 5
⊙ Trento Brut Rosé	🍷🍷 5
○ Trento Aquila Reale Ris. '05	🍷🍷🍷 7
○ Trento Aquila Reale Ris. '02	🍷🍷🍷 7
○ Trento Brut Aquila Reale Ris. '09	🍷🍷🍷 6
○ Trento Extra Brut 1673 Ris. '11	🍷🍷🍷 5
○ Trento Extra Brut Tridentum '09	🍷🍷🍷 4*
○ Trento Aquila Reale Ris. '08	🍷🍷 6
○ Trento Aquila Reale Ris. '06	🍷🍷 7
○ Trento Brut Nature Noir 1673 '12	🍷🍷 5
⊙ Trento Brut Rosé Ris. '11	🍷🍷 4
○ Trento Brut Tridentum '12	🍷🍷 4
○ Trento Extra Brut 1673 Ris. '12	🍷🍷 5
○ Trento Extra Brut 1673 Ris. '10	🍷🍷 5
⊙ Trento Rosè 1673 '13	🍷🍷 5

Corvée

LOC. BEDIN, 1
38034 LISIGNAGO [TN]
TEL. +39 3440260170
www.corvee.wine

CELLAR SALES
PRE-BOOKED VISITS
ANNUAL PRODUCTION 50,000 bottles
HECTARES UNDER VINE 13.60

The direction of this innovative winery, founded just a few harvests ago by a group of far-sighted entrepreneurs, continues unabated. The first move was to involve some good winemakers from the Cembra Valley, where they're based. Then the emerging sparkling wine producer Opera was purchased after suffering from problems of an exclusively managerial nature. Now the enological staff is led by the Piedmontese Beppe Caviola and the young Moreno Nardin, a Cembrano native, while production is focusing on some authentic Trentino delights, including sparklers. The link between variety and territory proves to be a winner once again. Because Müller Thurgau and the Cembra Valley reach perfect harmony in the Viàch, the wine that wins the producer yet another Tre Bicchieri. With a fuller body and fine aromas, it exhibits glossiness and captivating drinkability. The sure hand of the cellarmen draws on other features of Cembra Valley vintages, from Pinot Nero to Traminer, Lagrein and Sauvignon, not to mention their two classic Trentos.

Wine	Rating
○ Trentino Müller Thurgau Viàch '19	🍷🍷🍷 4*
● Trentino Pinot Nero Agole '18	🍷🍷 6
● Trentino Lagrein Passo della Croce '18	🍷🍷 5
○ Trentino Sauvignon Bisù '19	🍷🍷 5
○ Trento Brut	🍷🍷 5
⊙ Trento Rosè	🍷🍷 5
○ Trentino Chardonnay Quaràs '19	🍷 5
○ Trentino Müller Thurgau Viàch '18	🍷🍷🍷 4*
○ Trentino Müller Thurgau Viàch '17	🍷🍷🍷 4*
● Trentino Lagrein Passo della Croce '17	🍷🍷 5
● Trentino Pinot Nero Agole '17	🍷🍷 6
● Trentino Pinot Nero Agole '16	🍷🍷 6
○ Trentino Sauvignon Bisù '18	🍷🍷 5
○ Trentino Traminer Clongiàn '18	🍷🍷 5

De Vescovi Ulzbach

P.ZZA GARIBALDI, 12
38016 MEZZOCORONA [TN]
TEL. +39 04611740050
www.devescoviulzbach.it

CELLAR SALES
PRE-BOOKED VISITS
ANNUAL PRODUCTION 20,000 bottles
HECTARES UNDER VINE 3.50

This small, confident agricultural estate is owned by a dynasty of vine-growers who have always guarded Campo Rotaliano. Here Teroldego takes center stage, and the young Giulio De Vescovi Ulzbach vinifies the grape in pursuit of its maximum expression, and not just varietal, but also territorial. His other wines (he also experiments with some classic sparklers from grapes grown at around 1000 meters) have become cult classics, winning awards and inspiring other winemakers in the area to try their hand at the so-called TeroldeGO(R)evolution. Trusting that some of their wines (especially Vigilius) will improve with time resting in the cellar, the winery only submitted two versions of Teroldego and a wine made with local grapes (including Groppello di Revò). This latter is the Kino Nero, a wine honoring Father Eusebio Chini, seventeenth-century missionary and explorer of California, a figure linked to the historical affairs of the De Vescovi family. Their Teroldego wines feature a lovely appearance and sure drinkability, as guaranteed by this skilled Rotaliano producer.

Wine	Glasses	Price
● Kino Nero '16	▼▼	4
● Teroldego Rotaliano '18	▼▼	3
⊙ Teroldego Rotaliano Kretzer '19	▼	3
● Teroldego Rotaliano '15	▽▽▽	3*
● Teroldego Rotaliano V. Le Fron '16	▽▽▽	6
● Teroldego Rotaliano Vigilius '12	▽▽▽	5
● Kino Nero '15	▽▽	4
● Teroldego Rotaliano '17	▽▽	3
● Teroldego Rotaliano '16	▽▽	3*
● Teroldego Rotaliano '14	▽▽	3*
● Teroldego Rotaliano '13	▽▽	3
● Teroldego Rotaliano '12	▽▽	3*
● Teroldego Rotaliano Vigilius '16	▽▽	5
● Teroldego Rotaliano Vigilius '15	▽▽	5
● Teroldego Rotaliano Vigilius '13	▽▽	5

★Dorigati

VIA DANTE, 5
38016 MEZZOCORONA [TN]
TEL. +39 0461605313
www.dorigati.it

CELLAR SALES
PRE-BOOKED VISITS
ANNUAL PRODUCTION 100,000 bottles
HECTARES UNDER VINE 10.00
SUSTAINABLE WINERY

For 5 generations, home and cellar have characterizedthe Dorigati family's property in Mezzocorona. Theirs is a dynasty of true vigneron, scholars of agrarian evolution and pioneers of sparkling wine, a love they've never abandoned, despite their excellent Teroldego. Cousins Paolo and Michele are among those promoting the TeroldeGO(R) evolution. For years now they've also been innovating by drawing on Rebo, a native variety that, this year, they've blended with Teroldego and Sauvignon for the latest addition to their range. However, they won the Tre Bicchieri with their "house wine", a Teroldego dedicated to Luigi Dorigati. This wine is thrilling to say the least, one of the best tasted in Trentino in the last decade: fragrant with a meaty succulence, it features an exquisite texture, caressing and very classy. Another very enjoyable Riserva di Teroldego, Diedri, also proved outstanding. The new Planus, on the other hand, needs further rest in the bottle, but the character of a great wine can already be felt.

Wine	Glasses	Price
● Teroldego Rotaliano Luigi Ris. '16	▼▼▼	6
● Planus '18	▼▼	4
● Teroldego Rotaliano Diedri Ris. '17	▼▼	5
● Teroldego Rotaliano '18	▼	4
● Teroldego Rotaliano Luigi Ris. '13	▽▽▽	6
○ Trento Brut Methius Ris. '09	▽▽▽	6
○ Trento Brut Methius Ris. '08	▽▽▽	6
○ Trento Brut Methius Ris. '06	▽▽▽	6
○ Trento Brut Methius Ris. '05	▽▽▽	6
○ Trento Brut Methius Ris. '04	▽▽▽	6
○ Trento Brut Methius Ris. '03	▽▽▽	6
○ Trento Brut Methius Ris. '02	▽▽▽	6
○ Trento Brut Methius Ris. '00	▽▽▽	6
○ Trento Brut Methius Ris. '98	▽▽▽	6
○ Trento Methius Ris. '95	▽▽▽	4
○ Trento Methius Ris. '92	▽▽▽	4*

Endrizzi

loc. Masetto, 2
38010 San Michele all'Adige [TN]
Tel. +39 0461650129
www.endrizzi.it

CELLAR SALES
PRE-BOOKED VISITS
ANNUAL PRODUCTION 600,000 bottles
HECTARES UNDER VINE 55.00
SUSTAINABLE WINERY

Cultivate beauty and do it naturally. This is the production philosophy driving the esteemed Endrici family's work, a philosophy that emerges through a range of wines that perfectly balance typicity, global tendencies and sustainability, both in the vineyard and in the cellar. On the hill of Faedo, near the scenic Castel Monreale, birds chirp among the bunches of grapes, serving as true ecological guides and authentic symbols of the Endrizzi family's wines. Some of the wines submitted certainly stand out this year. Starting with the Gran Maestro, a powerful red made with slightly dried Teroldego grapes, making for a sumptuous, deep, almost all-embracing wine. A second wine worthy of our finals is the Trento Masetto Privé, a decade-old Riserva, with a perfectly sound lively, racy texture and a fresh, delicately salty finish. Masetto Dulcis, an uplifting, late harvest meditation wine also deserves a mention.

● Gran Masetto '15	▼▼	8
○ Trento Dosaggio Zero Masetto '10	▼▼	8
○ Masetto Dulcis '17	▼▼	5
● Teroldego Rotaliano Sup. Leoncorno '17	▼	4
● Gran Masetto '14	▽▽	8
● Gran Masetto '13	▽▽	8
● Gran Masetto '12	▽▽	8
○ Masetto Bianco '15	▽▽	3
● Teroldego Rotaliano Leoncorno Ris. '15	▽▽	5
● Teroldego Rotaliano Sup. Leocorno Ris. '16	▽▽	4
○ Trento Brut Pian Castello Ris. '12	▽▽	4
⊙ Trento Brut Piancastello Rosè Ris. '13	▽▽	5
○ Trento Masetto Privè '09	▽▽	8
○ Trento Piancastello '13	▽▽	5

★★★Ferrari

via del Ponte, 15
38123 Trento
Tel. +39 0461972311
www.ferraritrento.com

CELLAR SALES
PRE-BOOKED VISITS
RESTAURANT SERVICE
ANNUAL PRODUCTION 5,800,000 bottles
HECTARES UNDER VINE 100.00
SUSTAINABLE WINERY

The Lunelli family's dynamism is commensurate with the effervescence of their exclusive Trentodocs. They continuously strengthen their activities, designing a spectacular 'Cathedral of Wine', but above all they manage to produce wines more and more representative of the Ferrari brand. Everything revolves around a balance between body and acidity, vivaciousness and a sapid raciness. The style that emerges across their range, from the classic brut to the most prized cuvèe, is inimitable, the result of increasingly ecological viticulture carried out by Ruben Larentis, their talented chef de cave. We could call their Trentos the magnificient 7. All feature a marked, unmistakable identity. The Giulio Ferrari, (the traditional version even better than the new rosé), exhibits great charm and wins another Tre Bicchieri. It's an incredible mix of style, creaminess and tempting acidity that verges on absolute perfection. The others also obtained very high scores, especially the outstanding Perlé. Hats off!

○ Trento Brut Giulio Ferrari Riserva del Fondatore '09	▼▼▼	8
⊙ Trento Brut Giulio Ferrari Riserva del Fondatore Rosé '08	▼▼	8
○ Trento Brut Perlé Bianco Ris. '12	▼▼	7
○ Trento Extra Brut Perlé Nero Ris. '12	▼▼	8
○ Trento Perlé Zero Cuvée Zero 13	▼▼	8
○ Trento Brut Maximum	▼▼	6
○ Trento Extra Brut Riserva Lunelli '12	▼▼	8
○ Trento Brut Giulio Ferrari Riserva del Fondatore '08	▽▽▽	8
○ Trento Brut Giulio Ferrari Riserva del Fondatore '06	▽▽▽	8
○ Trento Brut Giulio Ferrari Riserva del Fondatore '05	▽▽▽	8

Cantina d' Isera

via al Ponte, 1
38060 Isera [TN]
Tel. +39 0464433795
www.cantinaisera.it

CELLAR SALES
PRE-BOOKED VISITS
ANNUAL PRODUCTION 500,000 bottles
HECTARES UNDER VINE 200.00
VITICULTURE METHOD Certified Organic

In this part of Vallagarina, Marzemino is synonymous with Isera, the village on the right bank of the river Adige that has for centuries served as an agricultural hub for the grape and wine of the same name. The producer is a bulwark of the 'marzemina' tradition, although their range of wines is wide and draws on basalt vineyards located at various elevations on Mount Baldo and the mountains leading to Lake Garda. Picturesque terraces, fields where grapes find the ideal climate and exposure, a terroir that allows Marzemino—as well as varieties suitable for sparkling wine—to evolve splendidly. Corè, a careful selection of Marzemino d'Isera, made it to our finals for the first time ever. It proves gracefully easy to drink, but just as elegant, with a purplish color and hints of Parma violets on both the nose and palate. The other version of Marzemino also performed well, as did several other still red wines, without forgetting the Riserva di Trento.

Wine	Rating	Price
● Trentino Marzemino Sup. Corè '17	🍷🍷	4
⊙ Schiava '19	🍷🍷	3
● Trentino Cabernet Sauvignon '18	🍷🍷	3
● Trentino Lagrein '18	🍷🍷	3
● Trentino Marzemino '18	🍷🍷	3
● Trentino Marzemino Bio '18	🍷🍷	3
● Trentino Merlot '18	🍷🍷	3
● Trentino Rebo '18	🍷🍷	3
○ Trento Extra Brut Ris. '15	🍷🍷	5
○ Trentino Chardonnay '19	🍷	3
○ Trentino Gewürztraminer '19	🍷	3
○ Trentino Müller Thurgau '19	🍷	2
○ Trento Brut Ris. '15	🍷	5
● Trentino Marzemino Et. Verde '17	🍸🍸	3
○ Trento Brut Ris. '13	🍸🍸	5
○ Trento Extra Brut '13	🍸🍸	5

La Vis - Valle di Cembra

via Carmine, 7
38015 Lavis [TN]
Tel. +39 0461440111
www.la-vis.com

CELLAR SALES
PRE-BOOKED VISITS
ACCOMMODATION
ANNUAL PRODUCTION 1,000,000 bottles
HECTARES UNDER VINE 750.00
SUSTAINABLE WINERY

Vis, a viticultural tour de force, has left its mark on the evolution of outstanding cooperative wine production in Trentino. After overcoming certain management problems, it's once again partnered with Cavit, though while maintaining maximum autonomy when it comes to the commitment of its members and their properties. The diversity of the areas cultivated, from the valley floor to the high hills, in Lavis, Pressano and in the villages leading up there, near Fiemme, allow for a wide range of commendable wines, all produced at the Cembra Cantina di Montagna and the classic Lavis. The most convincing surprise was a Pinot Bianco from Cantina Cembra. It comes through eminent, with linear aromas and the assertive structure of a true Alpine wine. Then the red grape blend Ritratto - from the classic La Vis line - stepped onto the podium. However, Lavis has decided to focus on more "popular" wines, assigning its "crus" to a future date. Here is an easily approachable, varietal and flavorsome Sauvignon, followed by an aromatic Trentino-style Riesling.

Wine	Rating	Price
● Ritratto Rosso '15	🍷🍷	5
○ Trentino Pinot Bianco V. Cembra '19	🍷🍷	3*
● Teroldego '19	🍷🍷	3
○ Trentino Kerner V. Cembra '19	🍷🍷	3
○ Trentino Nosiola '19	🍷🍷	3
○ Trentino Riesling '19	🍷🍷	3
○ Trentino Sauvignon '19	🍷🍷	3
○ Trentino Müller Thurgau '19	🍷	3
○ Trentino Chardonnay '19	🍷	3
● Trentino Lagrein '19	🍷	3
○ Trentino Müller Thurgau V. Cembra '18	🍷	3
● Trentino Pinot Nero V. Cembra '19	🍷	3
○ Trentino Müller Thurgau V. delle Forche '14	🍸🍸🍸	3*
○ Trentino Müller Thurgau V. delle Forche '13	🍸🍸🍸	3*

★Letrari

via Monte Baldo, 13/15
38068 Rovereto [TN]
Tel. +39 0464480200
www.letrari.it

CELLAR SALES
PRE-BOOKED VISITS
ANNUAL PRODUCTION 160,000 bottles
HECTARES UNDER VINE 23.00

Lucia Letrari sunny but determined, able to combine a strong dose of genuineness with precision, cleanness and aromatic transparency. Lucia, in her work, manages to be a vinedresser, sparkling wine maker and 'enopromoter' without any discontinuity—and she does so with stubbornness and plenty of enthusiasm. No doubt, she inherited all these qualities from her father, the late Nello, a regional patriarch, a person who aptly transmitted the teachings that continue to consolidate Letrari's prestige through great Trentodoc sparkling wines. The Dosaggio Zero Riserva '14 leaves behind the other five Metodo Classico wines from this estate to proudly win the Tre Bicchieri, though the Quore also performed well: both possess an elegant, very slow perlage and highlight hints of crusty bread, with a pinch of floral aromas and flint, making for a warm, captivating finish. The Riserva dedicated to the founder, Leonello Letrari, proves just as pleasant: a signature Trento wine that gratifies the senses and relishes the drinkability.

○ Trento Dosaggio Zero Letrari Ris. '14	🍷🍷🍷 6
○ Trento Brut Quore Ris. '13	🍷🍷 6
○ Trento Brut 976 Riserva del Fondatore '09	🍷🍷 8
○ Trento Brut Letrari Ris. '14	🍷🍷 5
● Ballistarius '15	🍷 5
○ Trento Brut '17	🍷 5
○ Trento Cuvèe Blanche	🍷 4
○ Trento Brut 976 Riserva del Fondatore '05	🍷🍷🍷 8
○ Trento Brut Letrari Ris. '09	🍷🍷🍷 5
○ Trento Brut Letrari Ris. '08	🍷🍷🍷 5
○ Trento Brut Letrari Ris. '07	🍷🍷🍷 5
○ Trento Brut Ris. '10	🍷🍷🍷 5
⊙ Trento Brut Rosé +4 '09	🍷🍷🍷 6
○ Trento Dosaggio Zero Letrari Ris. '12	🍷🍷🍷 6
○ Trento Dosaggio Zero Ris. '11	🍷🍷🍷 6

Mas dei Chini

fraz. Martignano
via Bassano, 3
38121 Trento
Tel. +39 0461821513
www.cantinamasdeichini.it

CELLAR SALES
ANNUAL PRODUCTION 55,000 bottles
HECTARES UNDER VINE 30.00

For centuries the word 'maso' referred to a rural farmhouse in the Dolomites. Mas dei Chini, on the other hand, is a modern re-proposal of an archetype, transformed into an evocative cellar dug out of the rock and equipped with a series of spaces for hospitality and food. Graziano Chini, a well-known Trentino businessman who deals with automobile brands, has dedicated great resources to his winery on the hill of Trento, near Calisio, amidst sunny vineyards that have proven ideal for cultivating sparkling wine grapes. The Nature just misses out on the top award, while still searching for further complexity. This thoroughbred Trento features a precise, elegant palate. The stylish and polished Carlo V comes through rich, spot-on, with nice acid backbone and pure opulence. The simpler versions (the Trento Brut and Rosè) always prove pleasant. Mas dei Chini is not just about sparkling wines: they also make nice still wines and have launched a project to produce Vida Rubina, an unusual red made with native varieties from the Dolomites.

○ Trento Nature Inkino '12	🍷🍷 6
○ Trento Inkino Brut	🍷🍷 6
○ Trento Inkino Carlo V Ris. '11	🍷🍷 6
⊙ Trento Inkino Rosé	🍷🍷 4
● Vida Rubina '17	🍷🍷 4
○ Theodor Manzoni Bianco '19	🍷 4
○ Trentino Gewürztraminer '19	🍷 3
● Trentino Lagrein '19	🍷 4
○ Inkino Brut Riserva '10	🍷🍷 5
● Trentino Lagrein '18	🍷🍷 4
○ Trento Inkino Carlo V Ris. '10	🍷🍷 6
○ Trento Inkino Nature '11	🍷🍷 6
○ Trento Inkino Rosè Nature	🍷🍷 6

Maso Cantanghel

via Carlo Sette, 21
38015 Lavis [TN]
Tel. +39 0461246353
www.masocantanghel.eu

CELLAR SALES
PRE-BOOKED VISITS
ANNUAL PRODUCTION 20,000 bottles
HECTARES UNDER VINE 8.50
VITICULTURE METHOD Certified Organic
SUSTAINABLE WINERY

Federico Simoni, who's been carrying on the family business for over ten years in the Monfort winery in Lavis, has a kind temperament, a quality that's reflected in his wines. It's a kindness that dampens the austere image of the Austro-Hungarian fort depicted on their labels, a symbol of the Maso Cantanghel vineyards that unfold around the Fort of Civezzano. Simone is a convinced connoisseur of Trentino's historic grape varieties. He selects artisan wines without wavering in his pursuit of charming reds and whites, Pinot Nero especially. The Pinot Nero put in an excellent performance again this year, winning the Tre Bicchieri for the third time in a row. Though still young, this red shows great character, expressive notes of wild berries and spices and a polished, elegant palate. Also outstanding were the SotSàs, a cuvée made with white grapes, and a juicy Pinot Grigio. As for Casata Monfort, Lavis' mother cellar, we liked the Nosiola Corylus and the Gewürztraminer '19.

Wine	Glasses	Price
● Trentino Pinot Nero V. Cantanghel '17	🍷🍷🍷	5
○ Corylus Nosiola Casata Monfort '16	🍷🍷	4
○ SotSàs Cuvée '18	🍷🍷	3
○ Trentino Gewürztraminer Casata Monfort '19	🍷🍷	3
● Trentino Lagrein Casata Monfort '18	🍷🍷	3
○ Trentino Pinot Grigio '18	🍷🍷	3
○ Trentino Sauvignon V. Cantanghel '19	🍷🍷	3
○ Trento Brut Casata Monfort	🍷🍷	4
⊙ Trento Brut Rosé Casata Monfort	🍷🍷	5
○ Trentino Gewürztraminer V. Caselle '19	🍷	4
○ Trentino Müller Thurgau Casata Monfort '19	🍷	2
● Trentino Pinot Nero Casata Monfort '18	🍷	3

Maso Martis

loc. Martignano
via dell'Albera, 52
38121 Trento
Tel. +39 0461821057
www.masomartis.it

CELLAR SALES
PRE-BOOKED VISITS
ANNUAL PRODUCTION 65,000 bottles
HECTARES UNDER VINE 12.00
VITICULTURE METHOD Certified Organic

The vineyards surround their recently-expanded cellar. Bristling rows of Chardonnay, Pinot Nero and Meunier climb up Mount Calisio, recreating the original appearance of the hill overlooking the city of Trento below. The Stelzer family, in this unique enclave of biodiversity snatched from urbanization, practice agronomic techniques in complete harmony with nature, carefully selecting the grapes destined to become their Trentodocs. The news this year is a sparkling wine produced solely from Meunier grapes, the result of long experimentation common to all their cuvées. The Cuvée Madame Martis hits the bullseye, thanks to the infinitesimal liveliness of its bubbles, complex aromas redolent of mountain flowers and fruit (hawthorn, wild peach) and a never-ending finish - a commendable quality in outstanding sparkling wines. The other Trento wines performed well, particularly the Dosaggio Zero Riserva Bio, the Brut Bio and the exquisite Rosé.

Wine	Glasses	Price
○ Trento Brut Madame Martis Ris. '10	🍷🍷🍷	8
○ Trento Dosaggio Zero Maso Martis Ris. Bio '16	🍷🍷	5
○ Trento Brut Maso Martis Bio	🍷🍷	5
⊙ Trento Brut Maso Martis Rosé Bio '16	🍷🍷	5
○ Trento Brut Madame Martis Ris. '09	🍷🍷🍷 (white)	8
○ Trento Brut Madame Martis Ris. '08	🍷🍷🍷 (white)	8
○ Trento Dosaggio Zero Ris. '12	🍷🍷🍷 (white)	6
○ Trento Dosaggio Zero Ris. '11	🍷🍷🍷 (white)	5
○ Trento Brut Maso Martis Ris. '13	🍷🍷 (white)	6
⊙ Trento Brut Maso Martis Rosè Bio '15	🍷🍷 (white)	5
○ Trento Dosaggio Zero '13	🍷🍷 (white)	5
○ Trento Dosaggio Zero Maso Martis Ris. Bio '15	🍷🍷 (white)	5
⊙ Trento Extra Brut Rosé Bio Ris. '13	🍷🍷 (white)	5

Maso Poli

loc. Masi di Pressano, 33
38015 Lavis [TN]
Tel. +39 0461871519
www.masopoli.com

CELLAR SALES
PRE-BOOKED VISITS
ANNUAL PRODUCTION 75,000 bottles
HECTARES UNDER VINE 13.00

Let time unfold naturally in an ancient land shaped by the toil of atavistic winegrowers, and then challenge modernity with wines that draw on the past so as to embrace the future. This is the Togn sisters's aim, and in the space of a few vintages, they've managed to establish their operation at their Gajerhof in Roverè della Luna and at the same time develop the vineyards around Maso Poli, over Lavis. One of the most recent choices was to extend the aging of all their wines, and for this reason the vault was enlarged. You will find both these wines, under two distinct labels, here on this page. Maso Poli stands out as a very fragrant, drinkable Traminer, but we mustn't forget the red Marmoran, made with Teroldego and Lagrein grapes. The Gajerhof rises to the occasion with two versions of Teroldego, a special Riserva and a vintage version. The Müller Thurgau and Lagrein prove exquisitely made and able to meet the rising demand from abroad.

● Teroldego Rotaliano Gaierhof '18	🍷🍷 4
● Teroldego Rotaliano Sup. Ris. Gaierhof '16	🍷🍷 5
○ Trentino Gewürztraminer '19	🍷🍷 4
○ Trentino Müller Thurgau Gaierhof '19	🍷🍷 3
○ Trentino Riesling '19	🍷🍷 4
● Trentino Sorni Rosso Marmoram '17	🍷🍷 5
● Trentino Lagrein '19	🍷 3
○ Trentino Nosiola '19	🍷 3
○ Trentino Nosiola Gaierhof '19	🍷 2
● Trentino Pinot Nero Sup. '17	🍷 3
○ Trentino Gewürztraminer '17	🍷🍷 4
● Trentino Marmoram '16	🍷🍷 5
○ Trentino Riesling '18	🍷🍷 4
○ Trentino Traminer '18	🍷🍷 3
○ Trento Brut Ris. '13	🍷🍷 6

Mezzacorona

via del Teroldego, 1e
38016 Mezzocorona [TN]
Tel. +39 0461616399
www.mezzacorona.it

CELLAR SALES
PRE-BOOKED VISITS
ACCOMMODATION
ANNUAL PRODUCTION 48,000,000 bottles
HECTARES UNDER VINE 2800.00

Large production volumes at competitive prices: the Mezzacorona Group divides its time between Trentino and Sicily, respecting the territory while taking advantage of the brand's enormous commercial potential. Here we find a range of wines that are easy to approach and enologically perfect while also driving absolutely commendable, unique micro-productions. And if Pinot Grigio and Teroldego are the cornerstones of their still wines, we mustn't forget their elegant and fine Trentodoc sparklers. With its mixed style of strength and finesse, the great Trento wine, Flavio, firmly keeps hold of the Tre Bicchieri. It wins you over with its varied tones of citrus, lime and mandarin, and exhibits excellent balance between sapidity and acid backbone. All these features emerge in their other Trento wines: from Alpe Regis to Cuvée 28. However, Mezzacorona mainly produces still wines. The two whites from the Musivum line performed well, while the Chardonnay Riserva captains a lovely selection made by Castel Firmian.

○ Trento Brut Rotari Flavio Ris. '12	🍷🍷🍷 8
○ Trentino Chardonnay Castel Firmian Ris. '18	🍷🍷 5
● Nerofino '17	🍷🍷 4
● Teroldego Rotaliano Sup. Ris. Castel Firmian '16	🍷🍷 5
○ Trentino Gewürztraminer Sup. Castel Firmian '18	🍷🍷 3
○ Trentino Müller Thurgau Musivum '17	🍷🍷 6
○ Trentino Pinot Grigio Musivum '16	🍷🍷 6
○ Trentino Sauvignon Castel Firmian '19	🍷🍷 5
○ Trento Cuvée 28°	🍷🍷 4
○ Trento Pas Dosé Rotari AlpeRegis '14	🍷🍷 6
● Teroldego Rotaliano Castel Firmian '19	🍷 3
● Trentino Nosiola Castel Fimian '18	🍷 3
● Trentino Pinot Nero Castel Firmian '18	🍷 3

Moser

FRAZ. GARDOLO DI MEZZO
VIA CASTEL DI GARDOLO, 5
38121 TRENTO
TEL. +39 0461990786
www.mosertrento.com

CELLAR SALES
PRE-BOOKED VISITS
ACCOMMODATION
ANNUAL PRODUCTION 120,000 bottles
HECTARES UNDER VINE 17.00

Francesco Moser hasn't lost the sparkle of the expert cyclist, putting all his sporting experience at the service of a singular enotour. With the support of his children (especially Carlo, a great sparkling wine maker, but also Francesca, who deals in sales, and Ignazio, a certified enologist, TV and social network star) he runs his beautiful winery in the hills over Gardolo di Trento. Impeccable management has also involved a cousin of theirs, Matteo Moser, who in a few years has become one of the best 'chef de cave' for Trendodoc wines. Their captivating Nature features Mediterranean aromas, crusty bread and the wheat that generates it. The elegant, vibrant, deep palate finishes with a blast of irresistible acidity. It keeps pace with the 51,151, a sparkling wine dedicated to the hour record set by Moser. Some of the still wines worth highlighting include a Gewürztraminer with great balance of taste.

Wine	Rating	Price
○ Trento Brut Nature '14	🍷🍷🍷	5
○ Trentino Gewürztraminer Maso Warth '19	🍷🍷	3*
○ Trentino Riesling Renano Maso Warth '18	🍷🍷	3
○ Trento Brut 51,151	🍷🍷	5
○ Trentino Chardonnay Maso Warth '19	🍷	3
○ Trentino Moscato Giallo Maso Warth '19	🍷	3
○ Trento Brut Nature '12	🍷🍷🍷 (white)	5
○ Trentino Chardonnay '18	🍷🍷 (white)	2*
○ Trentino Traminer Aromatico '18	🍷🍷 (white)	3
○ Trento Brut Nature '13	🍷🍷 (white)	5
○ Trento Brut Nature '11	🍷🍷 (white)	5
⊙ Trento Extra Brut Rosé '15	🍷🍷 (white)	5

Pisoni Spumanti

LOC. SARCHE
FRAZ. PERGOLESE DI LASINO
VIA SAN SIRO, 7A
38076 MADRUZZO [TN]
TEL. +39 0461564106
www.pisoni.it

CELLAR SALES
PRE-BOOKED VISITS
ANNUAL PRODUCTION 23,500 bottles
HECTARES UNDER VINE 16.00

Pisoni represents a dynasty of vinedressers who have been working since 1852 in the basin that stretches out over Lake Garda. They have always cultivated vineyards at high elevations, committed to the protection of the area's native varieties—Nosiola above all. They also make wine from dried grapes for the rare Vino Santo. Additionally, they distill all the pomace from the harvest on their own and offer traditional Trentino brandies. For some seasons they have differentiated their family skills, separating their purely agricultural activities (Pisoni Vini, dedicated only to still wines) from those related to grappa and the classic bubbly that we review here. An exuberant Nature, with a captivating, creamy body, lovely sparkle and a vigorous, fruity finish stood out during our finals. The charming Riserva dedicated to Erminia Segalla, the Pisoni family's historic grandmother, rests on the lees for 96 months. Their other 2016s also proved well made.

Wine	Rating	Price
○ Trento Brut Nature '16	🍷🍷	5
○ Trento Extra Brut Blanc de Noirs '16	🍷🍷	5
○ Trento Extra Brut Erminia Segalla '11	🍷🍷	6
○ Trento Brut '16	🍷	5
⊙ Trento Brut Rosé '16	🍷	5

Pojer & Sandri

FRAZ. FAEDO
LOC. MOLINI, 4
38010 SAN MICHELE ALL'ADIGE [TN]
TEL. +39 0461650342
www.pojeresandri.it

CELLAR SALES
PRE-BOOKED VISITS
ACCOMMODATION
ANNUAL PRODUCTION 200,000 bottles
HECTARES UNDER VINE 26.00
VITICULTURE METHOD Certified Organic

From an enological point of view, the duo have left their mark on the evolution of the Dolomites over the last half century. Mario Pojer and Fiorentino Sandri have revolutionized winemaking techniques and grape selection while experimenting with unusual varieties, distilled pomace, fruit and more, without neglecting an exquisite line of vinegars. All this to transform Faedo, the wine-growing village where they operate, into a true hotbed of ideas. It's all come together through early-drinking wines, sparkling wines, full-bodied reds and other rarities deriving from lengthy aging, but also absolutely natural cultivation techniques. The deep, austere Riesling turned out to be a real surprise this year. It's the first time that this variety has won the Tre Bicchieri in Trentino. It exhibits a bright green-gold color and a pure nose, thanks to notes of pepper and lime. It will be interesting to see how it evolves to appreciate its tertiary aromas. The palate comes through stylish and elegant, not intrusive in the least, with marked personality.

Wine	Rating	Price
○ Trentino Riesling '19	🍷🍷🍷	4*
⊙ Ballo del Contadino Brut Rosé	🍷🍷	5
○ Essenzia '18	🍷🍷	5
● Faye Rosso '16	🍷🍷	6
○ Ballo del Contadino Extra Brut	🍷	6
● Rodel Pianezzi Pinot Nero '17	🍷	5
○ Faye Bianco '08	⚲⚲⚲	5
○ Faye Bianco '01	⚲⚲⚲	5
● Faye Rosso '05	⚲⚲⚲	5
● Faye Rosso '00	⚲⚲⚲	5
● Faye Rosso '94	⚲⚲⚲	5
● Faye Rosso '93	⚲⚲⚲	5
● Rodel Pianezzi Pinot Nero '09	⚲⚲⚲	5
○ Faye Bianco '15	⚲⚲	5
○ Faye Bianco '13	⚲⚲	5
● Faye Rosso '12	⚲⚲	6
● Rodel Pianezzi Pinot Nero '16	⚲⚲	5

Pravis

LOC. LE BIOLCHE, 1
38076 LASINO [TN]
TEL. +39 0461564305
www.pravis.it

CELLAR SALES
PRE-BOOKED VISITS
ANNUAL PRODUCTION 200,000 bottles
HECTARES UNDER VINE 32.00

Pravis enjoys vineyards that mark the rhythm of the alpine landscape, suspended between the blue of the lakes (Garda is in the background)and the clear sky of the Brenta Dolomites. The winery, adjacent to Castel Madruzzo, draws on the area's classic grapes and cultivates them with the utmost respect for biodiversity. For some years now its three founding members, who are friends, have involved their respective children, with young Erika Pedrini serving as enologist and her sister Giulia as marketing manager, while Alessio and Silvio Chistè oversee the vineyards. The Valle dei Laghi has turned out to be a kind of 'Holy Land' for wines made with dried Nosiola grapes to produce the rare Vino Santo. The 2007 version is the proud winner of our Tre Bicchieri. Every aspect of this meditation wine comes through very long, never cloying, with youthful grip that leads you to think that further development is in store. The unusual Stravino di Stravino (made with super-ripe grapes and fermented in acacia wood) and the Kerner Le Biolche '19 also put in a nice performance.

Wine	Rating	Price
○ Trentino Vino Santo Arèle '07	🍷🍷🍷	6
○ Le Biolche Kerner '19	🍷🍷	3
○ Stravino di Stravino '18	🍷🍷	4
○ Teramara Sauvignon '19	🍷	4
● Fratagranda '10	⚲⚲⚲	4*
● Fratagranda '09	⚲⚲⚲	4*
● Fratagranda '07	⚲⚲⚲	4
○ Stravino di Stravino '99	⚲⚲⚲	4*
○ Vino Santo Arèle '06	⚲⚲⚲	6
○ l'Ora '14	⚲⚲	5
● Madruzzo Pinot Nero '16	⚲⚲	3
○ Müller Thurgau San Thomà '18	⚲⚲	2*
○ Nosiola Le Frate '18	⚲⚲	2*
○ Soliva '12	⚲⚲	6
● Syrae '16	⚲⚲	5
● Syrae '15	⚲⚲	5

Agraria Riva del Garda

loc. San Nazzaro, 4
38066 Riva del Garda [TN]
Tel. +39 0464552133
www.agririva.it

CELLAR SALES
PRE-BOOKED VISITS
ANNUAL PRODUCTION 250,000 bottles
HECTARES UNDER VINE 280.00

Diversify to innovate without ever upsetting the agricultural customs of Lake Garda's Trentino Riviera: this is the work carried out by the cooperative producer Agririva, a business that's long been active in promoting good taste. They make some of the area's most renowned extra-virgin olive oil, protect local gastronomic specialties and involve their members in precise viticulture that respects the local habitat. A wide range is offered, mainly wines from international grapes, but these exhibit a typicity that's decidedly representative of Garda. Once again, the painstaking selection of Pinot Nero delivers a great wine. The credit goes to the continual commitment that is widely applied in the vineyard here (under organic management). The Maso Elèsi is a very versatile, elegant wine that you rarely come across on the land lapped by Lake Garda. The Trento Brezza, a sparkling wine named after the wind that blows in the lake-like hollow, also did well.

- ● Trentino Pinot Nero Sup. Maso Elèsi '16 — 🍷🍷 4
- ○ Trento Brut Brezza — 🍷🍷 4
- ● Maso Lizzone '17 — 🍷 3
- ● Trentino Merlot Sup. Crèa '17 — 🍷 4
- ● Maso Lizzone '16 — YY 4
- ● Maso Lizzone '15 — YY 3
- ○ Trentino Chardonnay Loré '18 — YY 3
- ○ Trentino Chardonnay Loré '16 — YY 3
- ● Trentino Gère '16 — YY 3
- ● Trentino Lagrein Sasèra '17 — YY 4
- ● Trentino Lagrein Sasera '15 — YY 4
- ● Trentino Riva'Ldego '17 — YY 2*
- ● Trentino Sup. Pinot Nero Elesi '15 — YY 4
- ○ Trentino Traminer Aromatico La Prea '16 — YY 3

★★San Leonardo

loc. San Leonardo, 1
38063 Avio [TN]
Tel. +39 0464689004
www.sanleonardo.it

CELLAR SALES
PRE-BOOKED VISITS
ANNUAL PRODUCTION 270,000 bottles
HECTARES UNDER VINE 40.00
VITICULTURE METHOD Certified Organic
SUSTAINABLE WINERY

Respect for the land, authoritative vineyard care, a classic dedication to wine and a clear, forward-thinking global vision. The marquise Guerrieri Gonzaga family, Carlo and his young son Anselmo, have made Tenuta San Leonardo, a magical place with a long history behind it, even more fascinating. It's situated in an area that even before the year 1000 had been under vine, a bastion of rural traditions with an Italian-Habsburg imprint that, over time, has grown into an undisputed leader for ageworthy reds. But now it's ready to bet on other typologies, from sparkling wines to superb whites. They always respect time. This is why you won't find the new vintage of San Leonardo or their other important wines on the sheet. They wait patiently for further significant evolution in bottle, for new quality challenges. Space is given to their two 'pop' wines: the Terre, a perfectly amalgamated Cabernet and Merlot, and the Vette, made with 100% Sauvignon. These two simple wines exhibit great class and excellent drinkability.

- ● Terre di San Leonardo '17 — 🍷🍷 3*
- ○ Vette di San Leonardo '19 — 🍷🍷 3
- ● Carmenère '07 — YYY 8
- ● San Leonardo '15 — YYY 8
- ● San Leonardo '14 — YYY 8
- ● San Leonardo '13 — YYY 8
- ● San Leonardo '11 — YYY 8
- ● San Leonardo '10 — YYY 7
- ● San Leonardo '08 — YYY 7
- ● San Leonardo '07 — YYY 7
- ● San Leonardo '06 — YYY 7
- ● San Leonardo '05 — YYY 7
- ● San Leonardo '04 — YYY 7
- ● San Leonardo '03 — YYY 7
- ● San Leonardo '01 — YYY 7
- ● San Leonardo '00 — YYY 7
- ● Villa Gresti '03 — YYY 6

Toblino

FRAZ. SARCHE
VIA LONGA, 1
38076 MADRUZZO [TN]
TEL. +39 0461564168
www.toblino.it

PRE-BOOKED VISITS
RESTAURANT SERVICE
ANNUAL PRODUCTION 400,000 bottles
HECTARES UNDER VINE 700.00
VITICULTURE METHOD Certified Organic
SUSTAINABLE WINERY

The name Toblino evokes Trentino's lake and the castle where even Attila the Hun found some peace. But it's also the name of an innovative co-op. Over the years Toblino has been able to involve its members in careful conversions to organic while also taking pains to respect the vineyards' natural dispositions. These are scattered in a valley kissed by the breezes of Lake Garda and Brenta Dolomites. Director Carlo De Biasi is assisted by a staff that includes Luca D'Attoma. Their wines range from Trentodoc to the rare Vino Santo. All have achieved widespread praise, including a much-deserved Tre Bicchieri. An outstanding performance from a unique Nosiola, with a few vintages behind it, but still very youthful: the Ora is a sunny white, with notes of tropical fruit and captivating sapidity. Their Vin Santo Passito is another success story, while the new selection from organic viticulture draws on a Manzoni Bianco, a succulent Lagrein and a classic Chardonnay. The Nature sparkling wine proved impeccable.

○ L'Ora Nosiola '15	🍷🍷🍷 3*
○ Trentino Vino Santo '04	🍷🍷 6
○ Trentino Chardonnay Foll '18	🍷🍷 5
● Trentino Lagrein Las '16	🍷🍷 6
○ Trentino Manzoni Bianco Da Fora '18	🍷🍷 5
○ Trento Brut Antares '16	🍷🍷 4
○ Trento Nature Antares '16	🍷🍷 5
● eLimarò '15	🍷 3
○ Trentino Vino Santo '03	🍷🍷🍷 6
○ Kerner '18	🍷🍷 2*
● Teroldego Bio '16	🍷🍷 2*
⊙ Trentino Lagrein Kretzer '18	🍷🍷 2*
○ Trentino Nosiola Largiller '12	🍷🍷 3
● Trentino Pinot Nero '16	🍷🍷 2*
● Trentino Rebo Elimarò '17	🍷🍷 2*
○ Trentino Vino Santo '02	🍷🍷 6

Vallarom

LOC. VO' SINISTRO
FRAZ. MASI, 21
38063 AVIO [TN]
TEL. +39 0464684297
www.vallarom.it

CELLAR SALES
PRE-BOOKED VISITS
ACCOMMODATION AND RESTAURANT SERVICE
ANNUAL PRODUCTION 35,000 bottles
HECTARES UNDER VINE 7.00
VITICULTURE METHOD Certified Organic
SUSTAINABLE WINERY

At Vallarom, nature takes back its ancestral dimension while respecting the healthy vigour of the vines overseen by Filippo and Barbara Scienza. Together with their young son Riccardo, the couple have transformed their farm into a bastion of highly eco-sustainable vineyards. Cultivation is strictly organic, carried out both through the revival of old varieties and the proper cultivation of certain international grapes, like Shiraz. The result is sincere wines with a marked typicity, authentically Trentino and also certified vegan. Their most outstanding wine was a red made with Syrah grapes. It features a lovely dark color and spicy aromas ranging from meadow flowers to minty herbs; the taste proves elegant, with well-paced tannins marked by a slight edginess from the quick aging. The Pinot Nero, with more taste backbone than sensory overtones, also made a nice impression.

● Pinot Nero '18	🍷🍷 4
● Syrah '17	🍷🍷 5
○ Chardonnay '18	🍷 4
○ Moscato Giallo '19	🍷 3
○ Vadum Caesaris '19	🍷 3
● Cabernet Sauvignon Bio '13	🍷🍷 3
○ Enantio '15	🍷🍷 3
● Flufluns '15	🍷🍷 4
● Fufluns '11	🍷🍷 4
○ Trentatrè '18	🍷🍷 3
○ Trentatrè '16	🍷🍷 3
● Trentino Marzemino Bio '15	🍷🍷 3
○ Vadum Caesaris '17	🍷🍷 3*
○ Vadum Caesaris '16	🍷🍷 3
● Vallagarina Pinot Nero '15	🍷🍷 4
○ Vo' '14	🍷🍷 4
○ Vo' '13	🍷🍷 4

Villa Corniole

FRAZ. VERLA
VIA AL GREC', 23
38030 GIOVO [TN]
TEL. +39 0461695067
www.villacorniole.com

CELLAR SALES
PRE-BOOKED VISITS
ACCOMMODATION
ANNUAL PRODUCTION 75,000 bottles
HECTARES UNDER VINE 10.00
SUSTAINABLE WINERY

Villa Corniole is managed with great skill by a group of four women: Maddalena Pellegrini and her three daughters, Sara, Linda and Sabina. The cellar is dug entirely into red porphyry, while the vineyards unfold on the hills surrounding the Avisio riverbed, as well as comprising plots on the valley floor in Campo Rotaliano (especially their red grapes). Winemaking is entrusted to Mattia Clementi, an enologist and great promoter of the wines of his native Valle Cembra, starting with Müller Thurgau. With this last harvest they've expanded their range, updated their image and made their Trentodoc more elegant and fine. The Teroldego 7 Pergole comes through positively charming, full-bodied and velvety. Its aromas redolent of cranberries and chocolatey overtones lead into a taut, inviting palate, with a gratifyingly spicy finish. The Kròz (whose name recalls porphyry, a common mineral in Cembra) also proved an excellent wine with a certain aromatic evolution. The Müller Thurgau Pietramontis impressed and their other wines, including the Trentodoc ones, were sound, as always.

- ● Teroldego Rotaliano 7 Pergole '16 — TT 6
- ○ Kròz '18 — TT 5
- ○ Pinot Grigio Ramato '18 — TT 3
- ● Trentino Lagrein '18 — TT 4
- ○ Trentino Müller Thurgau Sup. Pietramontis '19 — TT 3
- ○ Trento Dosaggio Zero Salísa '15 — TT 5
- ● Trentino Pinot Nero Sagum '18 — T 5
- ○ Trento Brut Salísa '16 — T 5
- ○ Kròz '17 — YY 5
- ○ Kròz '16 — YY 5
- ● Teroldego Rotaliano 7 Pergole '15 — YY 6
- ● Teroldego Rotaliano 7 Pergole '13 — YY 6
- ● Trentino Lagrein Petramontis '17 — YY 4
- ○ Trentino Müller Thurgau Petramontis '17 — YY 4
- ○ Trento Brut Salísa '15 — YY 5

Roberto Zeni

FRAZ. GRUMO
VIA STRETTA, 2
38010 SAN MICHELE ALL'ADIGE [TN]
TEL. +39 0461650456
www.zeni.tn.it

CELLAR SALES
PRE-BOOKED VISITS
ANNUAL PRODUCTION 150,000 bottles
HECTARES UNDER VINE 14.00
VITICULTURE METHOD Certified Organic

The decision to cultivate with organic methods has led the Zeni family to revive not only impervious, high hill vineyards, but also return to more sustainable winemaking practices, in part through minimalist bottles and packaging. There's no doubting their dedication to their crown jewels, starting with Teroldego. It's a wine that's always at the fore, made with select grapes from Campo Rotaliano and their Maso Nero vineyards on high, over Lavis. The Zeni have demonstrated their prowess as highly experienced vigneron and sparkling wine makers, but they're also distillers and skilled brewers. A classic sparkling wine stood out during our tastings. This Trento Maso Nero Rosé initially exhibits an austere character, but then immediately softens with light overtones of rose petals, redcurrants and ginger; the palate shows nice balance between roundness, acid backbone and long sapidity. The still wines didn't perform quite so well, but were generally well made.

- ⊙ Trento Maso Nero Rosé '15 — TT 5
- ○ Trentino Nosiola Palustella '19 — TT 2*
- ○ Trento Brut Maso Nero '16 — TT 5
- ● Ternet Schwarzhof Teroldego '17 — T 5
- ● Trentino Moscato Rosa — T 4
- ● Ternet Schwarzhof Teroldego '10 — YYY 5
- ● Teroldego Rotaliano Pini '13 — YYY 6
- ● Teroldego Rotaliano Pini '12 — YYY 6
- ● Teroldego Rotaliano Pini '09 — YYY 6
- ● Ternet Schwarzhof Teroldego '15 — YY 5
- ● Teroldego Rotaliano Lealbere '18 — YY 3*
- ● Teroldego Rotaliano Lealbere '16 — YY 3
- ● Teroldego Rotaliano Pini '15 — YY 6
- ● Teroldego Rotaliano Ternet Schwarzhof '16 — YY 5
- ○ Trentino Nosiola Schwarzhof '18 — YY 2*

Cantina Aldeno

via Roma, 76
38060 Aldeno [TN]
Tel. +39 0461842511
www.cantinaaldeno.com

CELLAR SALES
PRE-BOOKED VISITS
ANNUAL PRODUCTION 240,000 bottles
HECTARES UNDER VINE 340.00

○ San Zeno Bianco '17	🍷🍷 4
● Trentino Merlot Ris. '16	🍷🍷 4
○ Trento Extra Brut Altinum Ris. '13	🍷🍷 5
○ Trento Pas Dosé Altinum '16	🍷🍷 5

Bolognani

via Stazione, 19
38015 Lavis [TN]
Tel. +39 0461246354
www.bolognani.com

CELLAR SALES
PRE-BOOKED VISITS
ANNUAL PRODUCTION 60,000 bottles
HECTARES UNDER VINE 4.40

○ Sanròc '18	🍷🍷 4
○ Sauvignon '19	🍷🍷 3
○ Trento Extra Brut PerNilo '13	🍷🍷 5
○ Nosiola '19	🍷 3

Cantina Sociale di Trento

via dei Viticoltori, 2/4
38123 Trento
Tel. +39 0461920186
www.cantinasocialetrento.it

CELLAR SALES
PRE-BOOKED VISITS
ANNUAL PRODUCTION 250,000 bottles
HECTARES UNDER VINE 50.00
SUSTAINABLE WINERY

● Trentino Marzemino Sup. dei Ziresi '18	🍷🍷 2*
○ Trentino Riesling Renano '18	🍷🍷 4
○ Trento Brut Zèll	🍷🍷 5
⊙ Trento Brut Zèll Rosé	🍷 5

Comai

via San Cassiano, 9
38066 Riva del Garda [TN]
Tel. +39 0464553485
www.agriturcomai.com

○ Trentino Chardonnay '18	🍷🍷 4
● Busat Rosso '18	🍷🍷 5
○ Busat Bianco '19	🍷 4
● Rebo Morer '17	🍷 4

Cantina De Vigili

via Molini, 28
38017 Mezzolombardo [TN]
Tel. +39 349 554 3239
www.cantinadevigili.it

ANNUAL PRODUCTION 20,000 bottles
HECTARES UNDER VINE 3.00

● Teroldego Rotaliano Sup. Ottaviano Ris. '17	🍷🍷 5
○ Trentino Chardonnay Terre Bianche '19	🍷🍷 4
⊙ Teroldego Rosato '19	🍷 4
● Teroldego Rotaliano '18	🍷 4

Delaiti

via Lucianer, 3
38060 Aldeno [TN]
Tel. +39 33986188299
www.cantinadelaiti.it

● Borgognoni Rosso '18	🍷🍷 4
● Merlot '18	🍷🍷 4
● Merà Largo	🍷 4
○ Zerla Bianco '19	🍷 4

Marco Donati

via Cesare Battisti, 41
38016 Mezzocorona [TN]
Tel. +39 0461604141
www.cantinadonatimarco.it

CELLAR SALES
PRE-BOOKED VISITS
ANNUAL PRODUCTION 100,000 bottles
HECTARES UNDER VINE 20.00
SUSTAINABLE WINERY

- ● Teroldego Rotaliano Bagolari '18 ҮҮ 4
- ● Trentino Lagrein '18 ҮҮ 4
- ○ Trentino Müller Thurgau Albeggio '19 Ү 4
- ○ Trentino Nosiola Sole Alto '19 Ү 3

Eredi di Cobelli Aldo

loc. Sorni
fraz. Panizza di Sopra
s.da del Vino, 22
38015 Lavis [TN]
Tel. +39 3319672482
www.cobelli.it

CELLAR SALES
PRE-BOOKED VISITS
ANNUAL PRODUCTION 6,000 bottles
HECTARES UNDER VINE 7.50

- ● Ert Pinot Nero '17 ҮҮ 5
- ● Teroldego Grill '16 ҮҮ 4
- ○ Trentino Sorni Bianco Arlevo '18 Ү 4
- ○ Trentino Traminer Gess '16 Ү 5

Etyssa

loc. Moià, 4
38121 Trento
Tel. +39 3938922784
www.etyssaspumanti.it

ANNUAL PRODUCTION 3,500 bottles
HECTARES UNDER VINE 14.00

- ○ Trento Extra Brut Cuvée N. 4 '15 ҮҮ 5

Furletti

via Sega, 36
38066 Riva del Garda [TN]
Tel. +39 3475228641
www.furlettiwines.com

- ○ Furlet Bianco '19 ҮҮ 4
- ● Furlet Rosso '18 Ү 5
- ○ Trentino Pinot Grigio Ris. '18 Ү 4

Grigoletti

via Garibaldi, 12
38060 Nomi [TN]
Tel. +39 0464834215
www.grigoletti.com

CELLAR SALES
PRE-BOOKED VISITS
ANNUAL PRODUCTION 60,000 bottles
HECTARES UNDER VINE 7.00

- ● Gonzalier '15 ҮҮ 5
- ○ San Martim V. T. ҮҮ 4
- ○ Trentino Chardonnay L'Opera '19 ҮҮ 3
- ● Trentino Merlot Antica Vigna '17 ҮҮ 4

Lagertal

via A. Pesenti, 1
38060 Villa Lagarina [TN]
Tel. +39 0422836790
info@lagertal.com

ANNUAL PRODUCTION 25,000 bottles
HECTARES UNDER VINE 2.00

- ○ Trento Lagertal Extra Brut ҮҮ 5
- ○ Trentino Chardonnay Merum '18 Ү 4
- ○ Trentino Goldtraminer '19 Ү 4

Martinelli

via Castello, 10
38016 Mezzocorona [TN]
Tel. +39 3388288686
www.cantinamartinelli.com

ANNUAL PRODUCTION 12,000 bottles
HECTARES UNDER VINE 3.00

- ● Teroldego Rotaliano Maso Chini '16 🍷🍷 5
- ● Teroldego Rotaliano Single Barrel '18 🍷🍷 5
- ○ Trentino Chardonnay Barrel Aged '18 🍷🍷 4
- ● Teroldego Rotaliano Martinelli '17 🍷 4

Tenuta Maso Corno

loc. Valbona
38061 Ala [TN]
Tel. +39 0464421130
www.tenutamasocorno.it

PRE-BOOKED VISITS
ANNUAL PRODUCTION 10,000 bottles
HECTARES UNDER VINE 5.00

- ● Trentino Pinot Nero Santa Maria Ris. '11 🍷🍷 6
- ○ Trento Giulio Larcher Pas Dosé Clou '14 🍷🍷 5
- ○ Trentino Chardonnay '16 🍷 5
- ○ Trento Giulio Larcher Pas Dosé '15 🍷 5

Maso Grener

loc. Masi di Pressano
38015 Lavis [TN]
Tel. +39 0461871514
www.masogrener.it

CELLAR SALES
PRE-BOOKED VISITS
ANNUAL PRODUCTION 18,000 bottles
HECTARES UNDER VINE 3.00

- ○ Maso Grener '19 🍷🍷 4
- ● Trentino Pinot Nero V. Bindesi '18 🍷🍷 5
- ○ Nosiola '19 🍷 4
- ○ Trentino Chardonnay V. Tratta '19 🍷 4

Pisoni Agricola

loc. Sarche
fraz. Pergolese di Madruzzo
via San Siro, 7a
38076 Madruzzo [TN]
Tel. +39 0461563214
www.pisonivini.it

CELLAR SALES
PRE-BOOKED VISITS
ANNUAL PRODUCTION 23,500 bottles
HECTARES UNDER VINE 16.00

- ○ Trentino Vino Santo '06 🍷🍷 6
- ● Reboro '15 🍷🍷 6
- ● Pinot Nero '17 🍷 5

Ress

via Roma, 103
38010 San Michele all'Adige [TN]
Tel. +39 3478511776
spumanti.ress@gmail.com

- ⊙ Trento Brut Maria Rosa Rosé 🍷🍷 6
- ○ Trento Brut 🍷🍷 5

Revì

via Florida, 10
38060 Aldeno [TN]
Tel. +39 0461843155
www.revispumanti.com

CELLAR SALES
PRE-BOOKED VISITS
ANNUAL PRODUCTION 20,000 bottles
HECTARES UNDER VINE 1.70
VITICULTURE METHOD Certified Organic

- ⊙ Trento Extra Brut Cavaliere Nero Rosé 🍷🍷 5
- ○ Trento Revì Paladino Extra Brut '14 🍷🍷 7

Cantina Rotaliana

via Trento, 65b
38017 Mezzolombardo [TN]
Tel. +39 0461601010
www.cantinarotaliana.it

CELLAR SALES
PRE-BOOKED VISITS
ACCOMMODATION
ANNUAL PRODUCTION 800,000 bottles
HECTARES UNDER VINE 330.00
SUSTAINABLE WINERY

- ● Teroldego Rotaliano Clesurae '17 — 6
- ● Teroldego Rotaliano Sup. Ris. '17 — 4
- ○ Trentino Chardonnay '19 — 4
- ○ Trento Extra Brut — 4

Cantina Sociale Roverè della Luna

via IV Novembre, 9
38030 Roverè della Luna [TN]
Tel. +39 0461658530
www.csrovere1919.it

CELLAR SALES
ANNUAL PRODUCTION 100,000 bottles
HECTARES UNDER VINE 420.00

- ● Trentino Pinot Nero V. Feldi '17 — 5
- ○ Trento Extra Brut Vervè Ris. '13 — 5
- ● Trentino Lagrein V. Rigli '17 — 3

Sajini Fasanotti

via Marconi, 40
38065 Mori [TN]
Tel. +39 3457504713
www.tenutesajnifasanotti.it

SUSTAINABLE WINERY

- ○ Trentino Extra brut Cuvée Senza Pensieri — 5
- ● Trentino Merlot Ris. Conversus '15 — 5
- ⊙ Trentino Pinot Grigio Ramato Crescendo '19 — 5

Marco Tonini

fraz. Folaso
via A. Rosmini, 8
38060 Isera [TN]
Tel. +39 3404991043
www.marcotonini.it

CELLAR SALES
PRE-BOOKED VISITS
ANNUAL PRODUCTION 13,500 bottles
HECTARES UNDER VINE 5.00
VITICULTURE METHOD Certified Organic

- ○ Trento Brut Nature Marco Tonini '17 — 5
- ○ Trento Nature Le Grile Ris. '14 — 6
- ● Trentino Marzemino Sup. di Isera '18 — 3

Vin de la Neu

fraz. Coredo
via San Romedio, 8
38012 Predaia [TN]
Tel. +39 3474116854
www.vindelaneu.it

ANNUAL PRODUCTION 508 bottles
HECTARES UNDER VINE 0.35

- ○ Vin de la Neu '18 — 8

Zanotelli

v.le 4 Novembre, 52
38034 Cembra [TN]
Tel. +39 0461683131
www.zanotelliwines.com

CELLAR SALES
PRE-BOOKED VISITS
ANNUAL PRODUCTION 40,000 bottles
HECTARES UNDER VINE 11.00

- ○ Trentino Riesling '19 — 4
- ○ Trentino Gewürztraminer '19 — 4
- ● Trentino Pinot Nero Sup. '18 — 5
- ○ Trento Brut Forneri '15 — 5

ALTO ADIGE

Few appellations can boast the variety of soils, elevations, exposures and climates that Alto Adige has. It's a region that stretches across valleys, plateaus outstanding for viticulture, slopes that are sunny during the day and refreshed by breezes at night, from the Mediterranean basin of Bolzano to the cool, high vineyards on the Mendola or Renon. This diverse appellation hosts many grape varieties, from the historic Lagrein, Schiava and Traminer, to more recently introduced varieties, like Chardonnay, Sauvignon and Bordeaux grapes. It's an agricultural fabric that's managed by a varied set of producers: cooperatives, historic estates, and small, family-run businesses. Together they cover a few thousand hectares of exceptional vineyards while maintaining a very high standard of quality. It's up to growers to highlight the attributes of the area, expressing the warmth of the shores of Lake Kaltern with thick Cabernets, such as Cantina di Cortaccia's Freienfeld, the freshness of plots cultivated at 1000+ meters elevation, like Tiefenbrunner does with their Müller Thurgau Feldmarshall, or the inseparable link between the Eisack Valley and Sylvaner, as is clearly seen in the wines of Köfererhof and Strasserhof. Then there are areas such as Oltradige or Burgraviato, where elegance characterizes the best bottles, from Merano's Pinot Bianco Tyrol to Colterenzio's Sauvignon Lafóa, from Girlan's Pinot Nero Trattmann to Gumphof's Sauvignon Renaissance. Riesling has found its ideal habitat in the Eisack and Vinschgau valleys, while the hills surrounding the capital see Lagrein and Schiava competing for the best positions, with the former giving rise to compact and deep wines, and the latter spawning San Maddalena, a wine capable of expressing the warmth of the territory, bringing together richness and simplicity. The sparkling wine sector is attracting more and more attention, with many producers looking with interest at the world of bubbly, following the path traced for decades by Kettmeier and Lorenz Martini. Underlining the positive work being done by the region's 'social wineries' is San Michele Appiano, which has clearly demonstrated how this sector can be fundamental for the development of a territory. For its efforts we've named it our Cooperative of the Year.

★★Abbazia di Novacella

FRAZ. NOVACELLA
VIA ABBAZIA, 1
39040 VARNA/VAHRN [BZ]
TEL. +39 0472836189
www.abbazianovacella.it

CELLAR SALES
PRE-BOOKED VISITS
RESTAURANT SERVICE
ANNUAL PRODUCTION 650,000 bottles
HECTARES UNDER VINE 26.00

The Abbey of Novacella stands out among the vineyards like a precious gem in a piece of jewelery. The rows of vines seem to protect the ancient buildings and the modern wine cellar from the outside, resulting in a perfect blend of history, tradition and modernity. The plots that unfold in the Bressanone basin and give rise to their white wines form the backbone of the winery, while Bolzano and Cornaiano host the parcels where their red grapes are cultivated. Grüner Veltliner, one of the last grapes to be planted in the Eisack Valley, has pretty much found an ideal habitat here, as the Praepositus '18 testifies to. On the nose it offers up vibrant nuances of ripe yellow fruit and dried flowers, with a soft, smoky nuance in the background. The palate is sapid, dynamic and very long. The Pinot Grigio '19 (from the same line) also delivers, proving rich and harmonious, and making the most of the bond between variety and territory.

- ○ A. A. Valle Isarco Veltliner Praepositus '18 — TTT 3*
- ○ A. A. Valle Isarco Riesling Praepositus '18 — TT 5
- ● A. A. Moscato Rosa Praepositus '18 — TT 5
- ○ A. A. Pinot Bianco Quota Insolitus '18 — TT 5
- ○ A. A. Sauvignon '19 — TT 3
- ○ A. A. Valle Isarco Gewürztraminer Praepositus '18 — TT 5
- ○ A. A. Valle Isarco Kerner Praepositus '18 — TT 4
- ○ A. A. Valle Isarco Kerner Praepositus Passito '18 — TT 5
- ○ A. A. Valle Isarco Pinot Grigio Praepositus '18 — TT 4
- ○ A. A. Valle Isarco Sylvaner '19 — TT 3
- ○ A. A. Valle Isarco Riesling Praepositus '13 — YYY 4*

Tenuta Baron Di Pauli

VIA CANTINE, 12
39052 CALDARO/KALTERN [BZ]
TEL. +39 0471963696
www.barondipauli.com

CELLAR SALES
PRE-BOOKED VISITS
ANNUAL PRODUCTION 46,000 bottles
HECTARES UNDER VINE 15.00

Tenuta Baron di Pauli boasts a long history of winemaking. The winery has always been adept at interpreting the wonderful Oltradige district, the area surrounding Lake Caldaro where a third of the province's vineyards are situated. Soils dominated by limestone and porphyry, a mild climate in Arzenhof and warmer, sunnier Söll, allow the winery flexibility in choosing the best area for each cultivar. The style of production alternates between a focus on the varietal profile of the grape and on the complexity that allows for lengthy aging. Just how good a territory it is for Bordeaux grapes is evidenced by the Arzio '17, which offers up dark fruit aromas and spices on the nose, with a fresh vegetal note lending dynamism to a harmonious and supple palate. When it comes to their whites, we appreciated the exotic and flowery richness of the Gewürztraminer Exil '19. A pervasive impact gives way to rigor and lightness, more by virtue of sapidity than acidity.

- ○ A. A. Gewürztraminer Exil '19 — TT 6
- ● A. A. Lagrein Carano Ris. '17 — TT 5
- ● A. A. Merlot Cabernet Arzio Ris. '17 — TT 6
- ○ A. A. Sauvignon Kinesis '19 — TT 4
- ○ Enosi '19 — TT 3
- ● A. A. Arzio Merlot Cabernet '05 — YY 6
- ○ A. A. Enosi '04 — YY 3
- ○ A. A. Gewürztraminer Exilissi '07 — YY 6
- ○ A. A. Gewürztraminer Exilissi '03 — YY 6
- ● A. A. Lago di Caldaro Cl. Sup. Kalkofen '07 — YY 3*
- ● A. A. Lago di Caldaro Cl. Sup. Kalkofen '06 — YY 3*
- ○ Enosi '08 — YY 3*
- ○ Enosi '06 — YY 3*

Bessererhof - Otmar Mair

LOC. NOVALE DI PRESULE, 10
39050 FIÈ ALLO SCILIAR/VÖLS AM SCHLERN [BZ]
TEL. +39 0471601011
www.bessererhof.it

CELLAR SALES
PRE-BOOKED VISITS
ANNUAL PRODUCTION 40,000 bottles
HECTARES UNDER VINE 4.50

The winery operated by Otmar Mair and his wife, Rosmarie, is situated in Novale di Fiè allo Sciliar, just a stone's throw from Bolzano yet far from the warm city basin. Here, the influence of the cool currents that pass through the Eisack Valley confer lightness and fragrance to the grapes, making for wines with a supple, racy profile. The vineyards span a handful of hectares at elevations ranging from 350 to 800 metres, and host primarily white grape varieties. The Pinot Bianco Ris. '16 testifies to these conditions, with its elegant notes of white-fleshed fruit and flowers, and a subtle background of oak. Juicy and supple, it unfolds on the palate by virtue of exquisite acidity. The younger version, a 2019 matured only in steel, also delivers: fresh varietal scents are echoed by a dynamic, tapered palate that wins you over with its finesse and balance.

○ A. A. Pinot Bianco Ris. '16	🍷🍷	3*
○ A. A. Pinot Bianco '19	🍷🍷	3
○ A. A. Sauvignon '19	🍷🍷	4
○ A. A. Valle Isarco Kerner '19	🍷🍷	4
○ A. A. Chardonnay Ris. '17	🍷	3
○ A. A. Gewürztraminer '19	🍷	4
○ A. A. Moscato Giallo '19	🍷	4
● Roan Zweigelt '16	🍷	4
○ A. A. Chardonnay '05	🍷🍷 (white)	3*
○ A. A. Chardonnay Ris. '07	🍷🍷 (white)	3
○ A. A. Pinot Bianco '16	🍷🍷 (white)	3*
○ A. A. Pinot Bianco '11	🍷🍷 (white)	3*
○ A. A. Sauvignon '18	🍷🍷 (white)	4

★★Cantina Bolzano

VIA SAN MAURIZIO, 36
39100 BOLZANO/BOZEN
TEL. +39 0471270909
www.cantinabolzano.com

CELLAR SALES
PRE-BOOKED VISITS
ANNUAL PRODUCTION 3,000,000 bottles
HECTARES UNDER VINE 350.00
SUSTAINABLE WINERY

Cantina di Bolzano is the result of a series of mergers involving a number of cooperatives in the region's capital. Today it's one of Alto Adige's most important wineries, thanks in part to a large area of land cultivated by over 200 grower members. Gries is certainly one of their cornerstones, but over time they've added plots at elevations of up to 1,000 metres on the Renon plateau, behind the city. The range proposed by Stefan Filippi is notable and varied, characterized by a focus on the bond between grape and vineyard. The producer on via San Maurizio has hit the mark, offering a selection once more led by the Lagrein Taber Ris. '18. Its close-knit, brilliant color heralds a fresh and elegant aromatic suite amidst berries, licorice and medicinal herbs: it doesn't impress for its power, but rather for its ability to unfold elegant and taut with fine, smooth tannins. The Santa Maddalena Moar '18 is just marvelous.

● A. A. Lagrein Taber Ris. '18	🍷🍷🍷	6
○ A. A. Gewürztraminer Kleinstein '19	🍷🍷	5
● A. A. Santa Maddalena Cl. Moar Ris. '18	🍷🍷	4
● A. A. Cabernet Mumelter Ris. '18	🍷🍷	6
● A. A. Lagrein - Merlot Mauritius '17	🍷🍷	5
● A. A. Lagrein Prestige Line Ris. '18	🍷🍷	4
○ A. A. Moscato Giallo Passito Vinalia '18	🍷🍷	3
○ A. A. Pinot Bianco Dellago '19	🍷🍷	4
● A. A. Pinot Nero Thalman Ris. '17	🍷🍷	5
● A. A. Santa Maddalena Cl. Huck am Bach '19	🍷🍷	3
○ A. A. Sauvignon Greel Ris. '18	🍷🍷	4
○ A. A. Sauvignon Mock '19	🍷🍷	4
● A. A. Lagrein Taber Ris. '17	🍷🍷🍷 (white)	6
● A. A. Lagrein Taber Ris. '16	🍷🍷🍷 (white)	6
● A. A. Lagrein Taber Ris. '15	🍷🍷🍷 (white)	6

Josef Brigl

loc. San Michele
via Madonna del Riposo, 3
39057 Appiano/Eppan [BZ]
Tel. +39 0471662419
www.brigl.com

CELLAR SALES
PRE-BOOKED VISITS
ACCOMMODATION
ANNUAL PRODUCTION 1,000,000 bottles
HECTARES UNDER VINE 50.00
SUSTAINABLE WINERY

Among the region's winemakers, the Brigl family have one of the longest traditions behind them. Seven centuries of experience and knowledge make them an absolute leader of Alto Adige. In recent years we have witnessed a decisive change of direction, with wines no longer limited to technical perfection but which explore the deep bond between vineyard and grape, between the harvest and the vision of the 'kellermeister', with a new selection of wines distinguished by the year in which the winery was founded: 1309. Their most important wines are made with grapes from single plots, true jewels managed entirely by the producers themselves. Among these we find the Lake Caldaro, a 2019 from the Windegg vineyard. It pours a bright ruby color, intensely fragrant of berries and spices, with a supple, juicy and extraordinarily sapid palate. The same cru also gives rise to a rich and bewitching Gewürztraminer '19.

● A. A. Lago di Caldaro Cl. V. Windegg '19	TT 3*
○ A. A. Gewürztraminer V. Windegg '19	TT 3
○ A. A. Pinot Bianco V. Haselhof '19	TT 3
● A. A. Pinot Nero Haslhof Ris. '18	TT 3
○ A. A. Sauvignon V. Rielerhof '19	T 3
○ A. A. Pinot Grigio Windegg '11	YYY 3*
○ A. A. Gewürztraminer V. Windegg '17	YY 3*
○ A. A. Gewürztraminer Windegg '15	YY 3*
● A. A. Lago di Caldaro Scelto Cl. Sup. Windegg '09	YY 2*
● A. A. Lagrein Briglhof '11	YY 5
● A. A. Lagrein Briglhof Ris. '10	YY 5
● A. A. Santa Maddalena Rielerhof '06	YY 2*
○ A. A. Sauvignon '07	YY 2*
○ A. A. Terlano Drei König Hof '10	YY 2*

Brunnenhof Kurt Rottensteiner

loc. Mazzon
via degli Alpini, 5
39044 Egna/Neumarkt [BZ]
Tel. +39 0471820687
www.brunnenhof-mazzon.it

CELLAR SALES
PRE-BOOKED VISITS
ANNUAL PRODUCTION 35,000 bottles
HECTARES UNDER VINE 5.50
VITICULTURE METHOD Certified Organic

Kurt Rottensteiner's estate spans a handful of hectares in one of Bolzano's most interesting areas, Mazzon, where Pinot Nero is cultivated. These west-facing vineyards, situated at elevations between 350-500 meters above sea level, have proven capable of capturing all the summer heat but cool down at night with the currents coming in off the mountains. The resulting wines are so energetic that they must be tamed in order to gain in tension and elegance. A brilliant performance for the Pinot Nero Ris. '16 with its dark fruit sensations enriched by floral and spicy nuances, a deep and earthy aromatic spectrum that follows through to a decisive palate, with acidity and tannins supporting its rigorous, long development. The Lagrein '18 is diametrically opposed, playing on more immediate timbres of fruit, with a juicy and gradual palate. Among the whites, we point out the soft and pervasive Chardonnay '18.

● A. A. Pinot Nero Mazzon Ris. '17	TT 5
○ A. A. Chardonnay '18	TT 4
● A. A. Lagrein '18	TT 5
○ Eva Manzoni Bianco '19	TT 4
○ A. A. Gewürztraminer '19	T 4
● A. A. Lagrein V. V. '17	YY 4
● A. A. Lagrein V. V. '16	YY 3
● A. A. Lagrein V. V. '15	YY 3
● A. A. Pinot Nero Mazzon Ris. '15	YY 5
● A. A. Pinot Nero Mazzon V. Zis Ris. '15	YY 5
● A. A. Pinot Nero Ris. '16	YY 5
● A. A. Pinot Nero V. Zis Ris. '16	YY 5
○ Eva '18	YY 4
○ Eva '17	YY 4

Castel Sallegg

v.lo di Sotto, 15
39052 Caldaro/Kaltern [BZ]
Tel. +39 0471963132
www.castelsallegg.it

CELLAR SALES
PRE-BOOKED VISITS
ANNUAL PRODUCTION 170,000 bottles
HECTARES UNDER VINE 30.00

The area surrounding Lake Caldaro is occupied primarily by warm and sunny vineyards, still largely cultivated with Schiava. At the base the vines grow sparsely but get increasingly thick as they climb up the slopes of Mendola. Eventually they seem to disappear entirely into the woods at an elevation of over 600 meters, a point where the evening breeze allows the grapes to capture the finest aromas. This is the territory of choice for Castel Sallegg, a winery that boasts almost two centuries of history. Their range sees wines marked by their varietal profile alternate with more complex and ambitious selections. The only thing missing this year is that crowning stroke, for the rest we can say that theirs is an outstanding selection. The Moscato Rosa '17 is a late-harvest wine that expresses ripe, enticing fruit on the nose, sensations exalted in the mouth, where it reveals firmness and excellent balance between sweetness and acidity. We also appreciated the Merlot Nussleiten '16, a red that plays more on elegance than on power.

- ● A. A. Moscato Rosa V. T. '17 🍷🍷 7
- ○ A. A. Bianco Ars Lyrica '17 🍷🍷 4
- ● A. A. Cabernet Sauvignon Ris. '17 🍷🍷 5
- ○ A. A. Gewürztraminer '19 🍷🍷 3
- ● A. A. Lago di Caldaro Cl. Sup. Bischofsleiten '19 🍷🍷 3
- ● A. A. Merlot Cabernet Chorus Madrigal Ris. '17 🍷🍷 5
- ● A. A. Merlot Nussleiten '16 🍷🍷 6
- ● A. A. Merlot Ris. '17 🍷🍷 4
- ● A. A. Pinot Nero '18 🍷🍷 3
- ○ A. A. Terlano Pinot Bianco Pratum '17 🍷🍷 5
- ○ A. A. Moscato Giallo '19 🍷 3
- ● A. A. Lago di Caldaro Scelto Sup. Bischofsleiten '15 🍷🍷🍷 2*
- ● A. A. Lago di Caldaro Cl. Sup. Bischofsleiten '18 🍷🍷 3*

Castelfeder

via Portici, 11
39040 Egna/Neumarkt [BZ]
Tel. +39 0471820420
www.castelfeder.it

CELLAR SALES
PRE-BOOKED VISITS
ANNUAL PRODUCTION 400,000 bottles
HECTARES UNDER VINE 20.00

The Giovannett family is an authoritative interpreter of Bassa Atesina, the southernmost wine-growing area of the province, which stretches from the bottom of the Adige valley at 200 metres above sea level to over 1,000 metres at the top. A variety of soils, vineyard positions and elevations allow flexibility in identifying the best area for each grape. Great attention is paid to Pinot Nero, which takes advantage of three different soil and climate types: Mazon, Glen and Buchholz, making for an interesting enological puzzle. At Giovannett, great attention is paid to Pinot Nero, with some four versions of the wine produced. Our preference goes to the Burgum Novum '17 because of the sense of completeness that it expresses, both in its sophisticated, deep aromas and in the firmness and elegance of its palate. Mazon, Glen and Buchholz '18 also perform on excellent levels, each exploring the link between vineyard and grape in its own way. Both the Chardonnay Burgum Novum '17 and Pinot Bianco Tecum '18 are also very good.

- ○ A. A. Chardonnay Burgum Novum Ris. '17 🍷🍷 4
- ○ A. A. Pinot Bianco Tecum Ris. '18 🍷🍷 3*
- ● A. A. Pinot Nero Burgum Novum Ris. '17 🍷🍷 5
- ● A. A. Lagrein Burgum Novum Ris. '17 🍷🍷 4
- ○ A. A. Pinot Bianco Vom Stein '19 🍷🍷 3
- ● A. A. Pinot Nero Glen '18 🍷🍷 3
- ○ A. A. Sauvignon Burgum Novum '17 🍷🍷 4
- ● A.A. Pinot Nero Buchholz '18 🍷🍷 5
- ● A.A. Pinot Nero Mazon '18 🍷🍷 6
- ○ Raif Sauvignon '19 🍷🍷 3
- ○ A. A. Gewürztraminer Vom Lehm '19 🍷 3
- ○ A. A. Gewürztraminer Vom Lehm '15 🍷🍷🍷 3*
- ○ A. A. Pinot Bianco Tecum '10 🍷🍷🍷 3*

★★Cantina Colterenzio

loc. Cornaiano/Girlan
s.da del Vino, 8
39057 Appiano/Eppan [BZ]
Tel. +39 0471664246
www.colterenzio.it

CELLAR SALES
PRE-BOOKED VISITS
ANNUAL PRODUCTION 1,600,000 bottles
HECTARES UNDER VINE 300.00
SUSTAINABLE WINERY

Cantina di Colterenzio was founded in 1960 in the village of the same name in Oltradige by a handful of winegrowers eager to leave the work of being merchants behind and develop the value of their production. The few original farmers have grown to around 300, but the main plots continue to be concentrated around the villages of Cornaiano and San Michele. These are complemented by small estates scattered throughout Atesina wine country. In the cellar, Martin Lemayr and his staff interpret each member's harvest with sensitivity and precision. The Lafóa line remains their range's guiding light, with four wines that do an outstanding job interpreting the bond between the grape variety and the territory. The Sauvignon '18 isn't an aromatically explosive wine, but wins you over little by little: first the floral notes, then white fruit, finally a slight vegetal nuance that lends lightness and freshness; its generous palate is governed by sapidity and acidity.

○ A. A. Sauvignon Lafóa '18	▼▼▼ 5
● A. A. Cabernet Sauvignon Lafóa '17	▼▼ 7
○ A. A. Chardonnay Lafóa '18	▼▼ 5
○ A. A. Gewürztraminer Lafóa '18	▼▼ 5
○ A. A. Gewürztraminer Perelise '19	▼▼ 3
○ A. A. Pinot Bianco Berg '18	▼▼ 4
● A. A. Pinot Nero Villa Nigra Ris. '17	▼▼ 5
● A. A. Schiava Menzen '19	▼▼ 2*
● A. A. Cabernet Sauvignon Lafóa '16	▽▽▽ 7
● A. A. Cabernet Sauvignon Lafóa '12	▽▽▽ 7
○ A. A. Chardonnay Lafóa '16	▽▽▽ 5
○ A. A. Chardonnay Lafóa '15	▽▽▽ 5
○ A. A. Sauvignon Lafóa '14	▽▽▽ 5

Hartmann Donà

via Raffein, 8
39010 Cermes/Tscherms [BZ]
Tel. +39 3292610628
hartmann.dona@rolmail.net

ANNUAL PRODUCTION 35,000 bottles
HECTARES UNDER VINE 4.65

Hartmann Donà represents an Alto Adige that's different from what's expected. Sometimes technical expertise tends to dilute the expression of a territory, superb wines that are just lacking a pinch of soul. In this case, however, the direction taken and the strong sensitivity of the producer manages to mediate these two aspects. The resulting wines are never banal, able to explore the hidden potential of the area and grapes, even those less noble, or by virtue of lengthy aging in the cellar. The Schiava Liquid Stone Granit '18 debuts with a bang. Made with grapes grown on soils rich in granite, the terrain lends volume and tannic vigor to the wine, qualities reminiscent of the rock itself. The Chardonnay Donà d'Or '13, which is released after slow maturation, offers up mature and complex aromas in which yellow-fleshed fruit is crossed by notes of minerals and dried flowers; the palate comes through full, taut and vital.

○ A. A. Chardonnay Donà D'Or '13	▼▼ 5
○ A. A. Pinot Bianco '19	▼▼ 3
○ A. A. Sauvignon '19	▼▼ 4
○ Donà Blanc '16	▼▼ 5
● Schiava Liquid Stone Granit '18	▼▼ 5
○ Blanc de Rouge Extra Brut M. Cl.	▼ 3
○ A. A. Chardonnay Donà D'Or '10	▽▽ 5
● A.A. Pinot Nero Donà Noir '11	▽▽ 3*
● A.A. Pinot Nero Donà Noir '09	▽▽ 3*
○ Donà Blanc '13	▽▽ 5
○ Donà Blanc '12	▽▽ 3*
● Donà Noir '08	▽▽ 3*
● Donà Rouge '08	▽▽ 3*
● Donà Rouge '07	▽▽ 3*

Tenuta Ebner Florian Unterthiner

fraz. Campodazzo, 18
39054 Renon/Ritten [BZ]
Tel. +39 0471353386
www.weingutebner.it

CELLAR SALES
PRE-BOOKED VISITS
RESTAURANT SERVICE
ANNUAL PRODUCTION 20,000 bottles
HECTARES UNDER VINE 4.50

The Renon plateau rises behind Bolzano, an area that's bordered by the Eisack Valley and the Val Sarentina and is characterised by an agricultural landscape that quickly gives way to the Alps. This is where Florian and Brigitte Unterthiner's operate, just a few kilometres from the capital. Here in Campodazzo the acidic pressure and aromatic clarity typical of the wines of the Eisack Valley merge with the maturity and fullness of the Bolzano basin. Production centers on white grape varieties. Their selection just keeps getting better, with our preferences going to the area's classic whites. The Grüner Veltliner '19 is immediately gratifying on the nose, offering up elegant notes of white fruit, dried flowers and a characteristic smoky hint in the background. In the mouth it stretches gracefully, supported by acidity, proving long and juicy. Even fresher, more dynamic and approachable, the Pinot Bianco '19 features a supple, racy palate.

○ A. A. Pinot Bianco '19	🍷🍷 3*
○ A. A. Valle Isarco Grüner Veltliner '19	🍷🍷 3*
● A. A. Pinot Nero Ris. '17	🍷🍷 4
○ A. A. Sauvignon '19	🍷🍷 3
○ A. A. Valle Isarco Gewürztraminer '19	🍷🍷 4
○ A. A. Valle Isarco Grüner Veltliner Ris. '18	🍷🍷 4
● Zweigelt '18	🍷🍷 4
● A. A. Pinot Nero '18	🍷 3
● A. A. Schiava '19	🍷 2
○ A. A. Pinot Bianco '17	🍷🍷 3*
○ A. A. Sauvignon '15	🍷🍷 3*
○ A. A. Valle Isarco Grüner Veltliner '18	🍷🍷 3*
○ A. A. Valle Isarco Grüner Veltliner '15	🍷🍷 3*

Egger-Ramer

via Guncina, 5
39100 Bolzano/Bozen
Tel. +39 0471280541
www.egger-ramer.com

CELLAR SALES
PRE-BOOKED VISITS
ANNUAL PRODUCTION 120,000 bottles
HECTARES UNDER VINE 14.00

The Egger Ramer family business has been active in Bolzano for almost a century and a half. It's a historic producer, one that operates along two tracks: on the one hand there are the patches of land dedicated to the whites of Appiano, San Paolo and Frangarto, on the other hand we find the basin's classic varieties, i.e. Schiava and Lagrein. The latter serves as the real productive cornerstone of their range, with various territorial interpretations offered, including that deriving from the sandy Kristan vineyard, located in Gries. And in this last round of tastings, the cru gave rise to one of their best performers: the 2018 delivers with its aromas of black fruit and spices, sensations that steady the palate while maintaining a fine balance between power and suppleness. The Riserva '17, from the same plot, follows a similar aromatic path, while its tannic texture proves softer and silkier. On the white front, we appreciated the gratifyingly fresh Pinot Bianco '19.

○ A. A. Gewürztraminer '19	🍷🍷 3
● A. A. Lagrein Gries '19	🍷🍷 2*
● A. A. Lagrein Gries Kristan '18	🍷🍷 3
● A. A. Lagrein Gries Kristan Ris. '17	🍷🍷 3
○ A. A. Pinot Bianco '19	🍷🍷 2*
● A. A. Santa Maddalena Cl. Reisegger '19	🍷🍷 2*
○ A.A. Moscato Giallo '19	🍷🍷 3
● Ottanta '18	🍷🍷 6
● A. A. Lagrein Gries Tenuta Kristan Ris. '11	🍷🍷 5
● A. A. Lagrein Gries Tenuta Kristan Ris. '10	🍷🍷 5
● A. A. Lagrein Gries Tenuta Kristan Ris. '09	🍷🍷 5
● A. A. Lagrein Kristan '17	🍷🍷 3*
● A. A. Lagrein Kristan '09	🍷🍷 3*

★Falkenstein Franz Pratzner

via Castello, 19
39025 Naturno/Naturns [BZ]
Tel. +39 0473666054
www.falkenstein.bz

CELLAR SALES
PRE-BOOKED VISITS
ANNUAL PRODUCTION 90,000 bottles
HECTARES UNDER VINE 12.00

The Vinschgau Valley is the smallest wine-growing area in the province of Atesina. About fifty hectares represent less than 1% of the province's production. Yet the low rainfall conditions, combined with a lean, sandy soil rich in schist and gneiss, make for grapes with an unmistakable character, combining aromatic freshness with a ripeness that's hard to find elsewhere. Franz Pratzner, together with his wife, Bernadette, is a true leader in the area, availing himself of a dozen hectares dedicated almost exclusively to white varieties. Leading the group, as usual, is the Riesling, with an impressive 2018 version: matured in large barrels, it offers up scents ranging from ripe white fruit to dried flowers, with nascent notes of petrol that will gain in prominence in the coming years. The palate comes through firm, dynamic and exhilarating. The Alte Rebe '17 is amazing—only a handful of bottles of this energetic, powerful reserve are produced.

- ○ A. A. Val Venosta Riesling '18 — 🍷🍷🍷 5
- ○ A. A. Val Venosta Riesling Alte Rebe '17 — 🍷🍷 5
- ○ A. A. Val Venosta Pinot Bianco '18 — 🍷🍷 4
- ○ A. A. Val Venosta Pinot Bianco Phileo '16 — 🍷🍷 5
- ● A. A. Val Venosta Pinot Nero '18 — 🍷🍷 5
- ○ A. A. Val Venosta Sauvignon '18 — 🍷🍷 4
- ○ A. A. Val Venosta Riesling '15 — 🍷🍷🍷 5
- ○ A. A. Val Venosta Riesling '14 — 🍷🍷🍷 5
- ○ A. A. Val Venosta Riesling '13 — 🍷🍷🍷 5
- ○ A. A. Val Venosta Riesling '12 — 🍷🍷🍷 5
- ○ A. A. Val Venosta Riesling '11 — 🍷🍷🍷 5
- ○ A. A. Val Venosta Riesling '10 — 🍷🍷🍷 5

★Cantina Girlan

loc. Cornaiano
via San Martino, 24
39057 Appiano/Eppan [BZ]
Tel. +39 0471662403
www.girlan.it

CELLAR SALES
PRE-BOOKED VISITS
ANNUAL PRODUCTION 1,500,000 bottles
HECTARES UNDER VINE 220.00

Alto Adige has largest presence of cooperatives, and these are often at the top of national wine production. Girlan has experienced difficult times in past decades, but today it's one of the most interesting wineries in the region thanks to a close-knit staff led by Gerhard Kofler in the cellar, and Oscar Lorandi in administration. Great attention is paid to traditional grape varieties, foremost Schiava, but also to the successful combination of international varieties and their growers' best vineyards. It's no coincidence that the most interesting results come from their Pinot Nero, a true feather in their cap. The Trattmann '17 offers up vibrant aromas of wild fruit and undergrowth, while the palate unfolds vigorously thanks to its nice acidity, making for a long, elegant finish. An even more rigorous selection comes from the same vineyard, the Vigna Ganger, which we won't review due to the few bottles produced.

- ● A. A. Pinot Nero Trattmann Ris. '17 — 🍷🍷🍷 8
- ○ A. A. Chardonnay Flora '18 — 🍷🍷 5
- ● A. A. Schiava Gschleier Alte Reben '18 — 🍷🍷 3*
- ○ A. A. Bianco Cuvée Flora '18 — 🍷🍷 4
- ○ A. A. Gewürztraminer Flora '18 — 🍷🍷 6
- ○ A. A. Gewürztraminer V.T. Pasithea Oro '18 — 🍷🍷 6
- ○ A. A. Pinot Bianco Flora Ris. '18 — 🍷🍷 3
- ○ A. A. Pinot Bianco Platt&Riegl '19 — 🍷🍷 3
- ● A. A. Pinot Nero Patricia '18 — 🍷🍷 3
- ○ A. A. Sauvignon Flora '18 — 🍷🍷 4
- ○ A. A. Sauvignon Indra '19 — 🍷🍷 3
- ● A. A. Schiava Fass N° 9 '19 — 🍷🍷 3
- ● A. A. Pinot Nero Trattmann Mazon Ris. '15 — 🍷🍷🍷 8
- ● A. A. Pinot Nero Trattmann Ris. '16 — 🍷🍷🍷 8

Glögglhof - Franz Gojer

FRAZ. SANTA MADDALENA
VIA RIVELLONE, 1
39100 BOLZANO/BOZEN
TEL. +39 0471978775
www.gojer.it

CELLAR SALES
PRE-BOOKED VISITS
ACCOMMODATION
ANNUAL PRODUCTION 55,000 bottles
HECTARES UNDER VINE 7.40

The agricultural fabric that distinguishes the wine-growing area around Bolzano is made up of a dense network of small farms where, often times, just a few thousand meters of vineyards are cultivated near the cellar. Franz Gojer, together with his son Florian and his wife, Maria Luise, oversee one such property at the foot of Santa Maddalena. Over time they've expanded to include sites in Cornedo all'Isarco, thus making for a solid range of whites. Their beating heart remains faithfully linked to their plots outside Bolzano, which give rise to a fantastic 2017 version of their Lagrein Riserva. Aromatically it's dominated by ripe red fruit, with nuances of oak, spices and dried flowers in the background; its long, elegant palate is rich, sapid, and marked by nice tension. The Vigna Rondell '18 is a classic Santa Maddalena that combines richness and souplesse on a highly enjoyable palate that never slows down.

Wine	Rating
● A. A. Lagrein Ris. '17	🍷🍷 4
● A. A. Santa Maddalena Rondell '19	🍷🍷 3*
○ A. A. Kerner Karneid '19	🍷🍷 3
● A. A. Santa Maddalena Cl. '19	🍷🍷 2*
● A. A. Schiava Alte Reben '19	🍷 2
● A. A. Santa Maddalena Cl. Rondell '18	YYY 3*
● A. A. Santa Maddalena Cl. Rondell '16	YYY 3*
● A. A. Santa Maddalena Cl. Rondell '15	YYY 3*
● A. A. Lagrein '14	YY 3*
● A. A. Lagrein Ris. '16	YY 4
● A. A. Lagrein Ris. '15	YY 4
● A. A. Santa Maddalena Cl. Rondell '17	YY 3*

Griesbauerhof
Georg Mumelter

VIA RENCIO, 66
39100 BOLZANO/BOZEN
TEL. +39 0471973090
www.griesbauerhof.it

CELLAR SALES
PRE-BOOKED VISITS
ANNUAL PRODUCTION 30,000 bottles
HECTARES UNDER VINE 3.80

Georg Mumelter's winery is located in Rencio, a small village situated between the course of the Eisack river and the hills of Santa Maddalena. It's an area surrounded by vineyards and yet, at the same time, it's just a stone's throw from the Bolzano city center. Although they offer a wide range of wines, the heart of the production is dedicated to Schiava and Lagrein, the main grape varieties of this 'Mediterranean' corner nestled among Alpine peaks. The soils are rich in sand and porphyry, perfect for the territory's historic varieties to ripen and give rise to wines capable of combining souplesse and power. Rather than pursue a richness that it doesn't possess, the Schiava Isarcus '18 focuses on a simple purity, with its fresh, spicy scents, and discernible but not overwhelming fleshy fruit. In the mouth it's sapid and taut, unfolding unhesitatingly. The Lagrein Riserva '17 moves on a different track: fruit dominates the aromatic spectrum, while the palate is more consistent and powerful, well supported by its tannic weave.

Wine	Rating
● Isarcus Schiava '18	🍷🍷 3*
● A. A. Lagrein Ris. '17	🍷🍷 5
○ A. A. Pinot Bianco '18	🍷🍷 3
○ A. A. Pinot Grigio '19	🍷🍷 3
● A. A. Santa Maddalena Cl. '19	🍷🍷 2*
● A. A. Lagrein Ris. '09	YYY 5
● A. A. Cabernet Sauvignon Ris. '16	YY 3
● A. A. Lagrein '13	YY 3*
● A. A. Lagrein Ris. '16	YY 5
● A. A. Lagrein Ris. '10	YY 5
● A. A. Merlot Spitz '17	YY 3
○ A. A. Pinot Grigio '18	YY 3
● A. A. Santa Maddalena Cl. '18	YY 2*

Gummerhof - Malojer

via Weggestein, 36
39100 Bolzano/Bozen
Tel. +39 0471972885
www.malojer.it

CELLAR SALES
PRE-BOOKED VISITS
ANNUAL PRODUCTION 100,000 bottles
HECTARES UNDER VINE 18.00

There was a time when the city of Bolzano was much smaller than the one we know today. A few kilometers from the old town center the houses would disappear and you could easily find yourself in the middle of vineyards. The Malojer winery testifies to this past, with a beautiful courtyard, now surrounded by houses, located a few hundred meters from the vineyards. Today it houses all the facilities and a pretty wine shop with garden, while the plots (partly owned and partly overseen by independent growers) are located between the Bolzano basin and Ritten mountains. The Lagrein Ris. '17 put in an excellent performance, drawing on a warm year to entice with its scents of red fruits, spices and dried flowers: the fullness of its palate is well governed by acidity and tannins, making for nice harmony. The Bautzanum '17, a blend of Cabernet and Lagrein, follows a similar gustatory style, with crisp, juicy hints of red fruit combining with fresh nuances of herbs.

- ● A. A. Lagrein Ris. '17 — 🍷🍷 4
- ● A. A. Cabernet Lagrein Cuvée Bautzanum Ris. '17 — 🍷🍷 4
- ○ A. A. Gewürztraminer Kui '19 — 🍷🍷 3
- ○ A. A. Pinot Bianco Kreiter '19 — 🍷🍷 3
- ● A. A. Pinot Nero Ris. '17 — 🍷🍷 4
- ○ A. A. Sauvignon Gur zu Sand '19 — 🍷🍷 3
- ○ A. A. Valle Isarco Sylvaner Kreiter '19 — 🍷🍷 2*
- ○ A. A. Bianco Cuvée Bautzanum '19 — 🍷 4
- ○ A. A. Chardonnay Justinus '19 — 🍷 3
- ○ A. A. Müller Thurgau Kreiter '19 — 🍷 2
- ● A. A. Santa Maddalena Cl. Loamer '19 — 🍷 2
- ● A. A. Lagrein Gries '09 — 🍸🍸🍸 2*
- ● A. A. Lagrein Gummerhof zu Gries '14 — 🍸🍸 3*
- ● A. A. Lagrein Ris. '15 — 🍸🍸 4
- ● A. A. Lagrein Ris. '12 — 🍸🍸 4

★Gumphof Markus Prackwieser

fraz. Novale di Presule
s.da di Fié, 11
39050 Fiè allo Sciliar/Völs am Schlern [BZ]
Tel. +39 0471601190
www.gumphof.it

CELLAR SALES
PRE-BOOKED VISITS
ANNUAL PRODUCTION 60,000 bottles
HECTARES UNDER VINE 7.00
SUSTAINABLE WINERY

Markus Prackwieser operates in the Eisack Valley, in Novale di Presule to be precise, a hamlet of Fié allo Sciliar. Don't let the location deceive you—here climate and traditions have little in common with the enclave of Chiusa or Bressanone. Indeed, it's an area that's more affected by the warmth of the Bolzano basin, and that lends itself wonderfully to the ripening of less algid, edgy grapes, thus achieving a harmony and poise that are in many ways unique. A few hectares of vineyards serve as the basis of an outstanding range of wines. Once again the Renaissance Ris. '17 proves at the top of its game. This Sauvignon goes well beyond its varietal character, offering up complex, iridescent aromas in which exotic fruit is suddenly replaced by floral notes and then mineral hints. Sapid and long, with a sharpish acidity, it enters on the palate with lightness and decisiveness, right up to a long,enthralling finish. The increasingly impressive Pinot Nero Praesulis '18 is also gaining in elegance.

- ○ A. A. Sauvignon Renaissance Ris. '17 — 🍷🍷🍷 4*
- ○ A. A. Pinot Bianco Mediaevum '19 — 🍷🍷 3
- ○ A. A. Pinot Bianco Praesulis '19 — 🍷🍷 4
- ● A. A. Pinot Nero Praesulis '18 — 🍷🍷 5
- ● A. A. Schiava Mediaevum '19 — 🍷🍷 4
- ○ A. A. Pinot Bianco Praesulis '17 — 🍸🍸🍸 4*
- ○ A. A. Pinot Bianco Praesulis '15 — 🍸🍸🍸 3*
- ○ A. A. Pinot Bianco Praesulis '14 — 🍸🍸🍸 3*
- ○ A. A. Pinot Bianco Praesulis '06 — 🍸🍸🍸 3*
- ○ A. A. Sauvignon Praesulis '13 — 🍸🍸🍸 4*
- ○ A. A. Sauvignon Praesulis '09 — 🍸🍸🍸 3
- ○ A. A. Sauvignon Praesulis '07 — 🍸🍸🍸 3*
- ○ A. A. Sauvignon Praesulis '04 — 🍸🍸🍸 3*
- ○ A. A. Sauvignon Renaissance '16 — 🍸🍸🍸 4*
- ○ A. A. Sauvignon Renaissance '14 — 🍸🍸🍸 4*

★Franz Haas

via Villa, 6
39040 Montagna/Montan [BZ]
Tel. +39 0471812280
www.franz-haas.it

CELLAR SALES
PRE-BOOKED VISITS
ANNUAL PRODUCTION 400,000 bottles
HECTARES UNDER VINE 55.00
SUSTAINABLE WINERY

Franz Haas is certainly one of the winemakers who has most contributed to making the world aware of the potential of Mount Corno, an area situated between Mazzon, Glen and Montagna. It's a choice location for Pinot Nero in Italy, as the delicate Burgundian variety has found a way to bind itself inextricably to the territory. Franz's vineyards span many hectares in this area, though we shouldn't forget that Franz's desire to experiment has led him to explore unusual areas such as plots at 1,000 meters elevation in Aldino. The most interesting reactions this year concern their whites, with the Manna '18 leading our preferences. A blend of five varieties grown between 350 and 800 meters above sea level, it offers up complex aromas ranging from white fruit to oregano, with a delicate botrytic sensation. The palate is highly sapid, supple and taut, revealing a strong character. The Sauvignon '18 is simpler and more intelligible, playing on elegance and harmony.

○ A. A. Sauvignon '18	🍷🍷	5
○ Manna '18	🍷🍷	5
○ A. A. Pinot Bianco Lepus '19	🍷🍷	3
● A. A. Pinot Nero '18	🍷🍷	5
● A. A. Pinot Nero Schweizer '16	🍷🍷	6
○ Moscato Giallo '19	🍷🍷	5
○ Petit Manseng '18	🍷🍷	3
● A. A. Moscato Rosa '12	🍸🍸🍸	5
● A. A. Moscato Rosa '11	🍸🍸🍸	5
● A. A. Pinot Nero Schweizer '13	🍸🍸🍸	6
● A. A. Pinot Nero Schweizer '02	🍸🍸🍸	5
● A. A. Pinot Nero Schweizer '01	🍸🍸🍸	5
○ A. A. Sauvignon '13	🍸🍸🍸	5
○ Manna '17	🍸🍸🍸	5
○ Manna '07	🍸🍸🍸	4
○ Manna '05	🍸🍸🍸	4
○ Manna '04	🍸🍸🍸	4

Haderburg

fraz. Pochi
via Albrecht Dürer, 3
39040 Salorno/Salurn [BZ]
Tel. +39 0471889097
www.haderburg.it

CELLAR SALES
PRE-BOOKED VISITS
ANNUAL PRODUCTION 100,000 bottles
HECTARES UNDER VINE 12.00
VITICULTURE METHOD Certified Biodynamic

Pochi di Salorno is a sort of small plateau situated at elevations ranging from 400 to 600 meters above sea level and serves as a border between the provinces of Bolzano and Trento. For some time now, at 3 Via Dürer, Alois Ochsenreiter has been applying biodynamic concepts at his property here, and today Haderburg is one of the few certified wineries in the region. The vineyards extend around the Hausmannhof farm, while above Chiusa, at Obermairlhof, we find the Eisack Valley's traditional grapes. Made with Chardonnay and a share of Pinot Nero, the Pas Dosé '16 features fine, well-sustained sparkle. On the nose it exudes aromas of ripe yellow fruit, with a classy nuance of chalk in the background; the palate reveals an indomitable, spirited and flavorful character, making for an energetic, linear and plucky drink. The Riesling Obermairlhof '18 exhibits a similar profile, debuting with a slightly closed nose before turning pleasantly gratifying and juicy.

○ A. A. Pinot Grigio Salurn Pfatten '18	🍷🍷	5
● A. A. Pinot Nero Hausmannhof Ris. '16	🍷🍷	6
○ A. A. Spumante Brut M. Cl.	🍷🍷	5
○ A. A. Spumante Pas Dosé M. Cl. '16	🍷🍷	5
○ A. A. Valle Isarco Riesling Obermairlhof '18	🍷🍷	3
○ A. A. Gewürztraminer '18	🍷	3
○ A. A. Valle Isarco Sylvaner Obermairlhof '05	🍸🍸🍸	3*
● A. A. Pinot Nero Hausmannhof Ris. '10	🍸🍸	6
○ A. A. Spumante Brut	🍸🍸	5
○ A. A. Spumante Hausmannhof Brut M. Cl. Ris. '09	🍸🍸	5
○ A. A. Spumante Hausmannhof Brut M. Cl. Ris. '08	🍸🍸	5

★★Cantina Kaltern

via Cantine, 12
39052 Caldaro/Kaltern [BZ]
Tel. +39 0471963149
www.kellereikaltern.com/it

CELLAR SALES
PRE-BOOKED VISITS
ANNUAL PRODUCTION 3,400,000 bottles
HECTARES UNDER VINE 480.00

Kaltern is the largest cooperative winery in the province of Bolzano, cultivating almost 500 hectares of land. The grower members bring passion and expertise to their work of exploring the historic wine-growing areas around Lake Caldaro. Technical management is overseen by Andrea Moser and his staff, who in recent years have managed to confer a clearly discernible style to the entire range. Two different lines are offered: on the one hand there are their simple wines, which exhibit a strong varietal profile, and on the other there are selections that express more markedly their territorial identity. The Lake of Caldaro Quintessenz '19 never fails to deliver class—it's a glass that entices you to drink from its bright, brilliant color. On the nose notes of berries and flowers emerge, while on the palate it impresses with its ability to handle richness and lightness. The Pinot Bianco '18, on the other hand, expresses greater depth and aromatic complexity, all enriched by a sapid, long and juicy palate.

Wine	Glasses	Price
● A. A. Lago di Caldaro Cl. Sup. Quintessenz '19	🍷🍷	3*
○ A. A. Pinot Bianco Quintessenz '18	🍷🍷	5
○ A. A. Bianco Solos '19	🍷🍷	3
● A. A. Cabernet Sauvignon Quintessenz Ris. '17	🍷🍷	5
○ A. A. Gewürztraminer Campaner '19	🍷🍷	3
● A. A. Lago di Caldaro Cl. Sup. Leuchtenberg '19	🍷🍷	2*
● A. A. Lagrein Lareith Ris. '17	🍷🍷	5
○ A. A. Moscato Giallo Passito Quintessenz '16	🍷🍷	6
○ A. A. Pinot Bianco Vial '19	🍷🍷	3
● A. A. Pinot Nero Saltner Ris. '17	🍷🍷	4
○ A. A. Sauvignon Quintessenz '18	🍷🍷	5
○ A. A. Sauvignon Stern '19	🍷🍷	3
○ A. A. Pinot Bianco Quintessenz '17	🍷🍷🍷	5

Kettmeir

via delle Cantine, 4
39052 Caldaro/Kaltern [BZ]
Tel. +39 0471963135
www.kettmeir.com

CELLAR SALES
PRE-BOOKED VISITS
ACCOMMODATION
ANNUAL PRODUCTION 290,000 bottles
HECTARES UNDER VINE 55.00

Unlike many other producers in Atesina, Kettmeir hasn't focused on an all-inclusive range that comprises all the region's varieties. Rather, they've made specific choices, with the intention of developing only those varieties that are best suited to their well-manicured vineyards. And so it is that great attention is paid to sparkling wine and bolder selections made with only a few cultivars. Indeed, precision and sensitivity are key elements of Josef Romen's management approach, resulting in a range that alternates straightforward, approachable wines with ageworthy selections that need time to reveal their hidden, deepest qualities. The cool 2014 harvest made for a fantastic Extra Brut 1919. This Chardonnay and Pinot Nero sparkler features delicate and persistent bead. Its aromas call up ripe white fruit and notes of toasted bread, while in the mouth mineral nuances contribute to an energetic palate of great tension. The Pinot Bianco Athesis '18 is the essence of elegance.

Wine	Glasses	Price
○ A. A. Spumante Extra Brut M. Cl. 1919 Ris. '14	🍷🍷🍷	6
○ A. A. Pinot Bianco Athesis '18	🍷🍷	4
○ A. A. Chardonnay '19	🍷🍷	3
○ A. A. Chardonnay V. Maso Reiner '18	🍷🍷	4
● A. A. Moscato Rosa Athesis '16	🍷🍷	5
○ A. A. Müller Thurgau Athesis '18	🍷🍷	4
○ A. A. Pinot Bianco '19	🍷🍷	3
○ A. A. Pinot Grigio '19	🍷🍷	3
● A. A. Pinot Nero V. Maso Reiner '17	🍷🍷	4
○ A. A. Spumante Brut Athesis '17	🍷🍷	4
⊙ A. A. Spumante Brut Athesis Rosé '17	🍷🍷	5
○ A. A. Spumante Pas Dosé '15	🍷🍷	4
○ A. A. Spumante Extra Brut M. Cl. 1919 Ris. '13	🍷🍷🍷	6
○ A. A. Spumante Extra Brut M. Cl. 1919 Ris. '12	🍷🍷🍷	6

Tenuta Klosterhof Oskar Andergassen

loc. Clavenz, 40
39052 Caldaro/Kaltern [BZ]
tel. +39 0471961046
www.garni-klosterhof.com

CELLAR SALES
PRE-BOOKED VISITS
ACCOMMODATION AND RESTAURANT SERVICE
ANNUAL PRODUCTION 38,000 bottles
HECTARES UNDER VINE 5.00

Like other small producers in the territory, the Andergassen family divides its commitments between management of their hotel and their wine-growing activities near the town of Caldaro. Today wine production is increasingly central to the project, with a small but well-equipped cellar that satisfies all the needs of their five hectares of property. Among the red grape varieties, Schiava takes center stage, but great attention is paid to Pinot Nero. Among the whites, Pinot Bianco is the cultivar of reference. Exemplary in its aromas of wild fruit and undergrowth, the Pinot Nero Schwarze Madonna '17 reveals a pleasantly gutsy palate well defined by acidity and tannins. The Merlot Nussbaum Ris. '17 also delivers: clear hints of red fruit combine with notes of oak, while its fruit emerges even more clearly on the palate, finding support and length in its lush flavor.

- ● A. A. Pinot Nero Schwarze Madonna '17 ▼▼ 5
- ● A. A. Lago di Caldaro Cl. Sup. Plantaditsch '18 ▼▼ 2*
- ○ A. A. Pinot Bianco Acapella '18 ▼▼ 3
- ● A.A. Merlot Nussbaum Ris. '17 ▼▼ 4
- ○ A. A. Moscato Giallo Birnbaum '19 ▼ 3
- ⊙ A. A. Pinot Nero Rosé Summer '19 ▼ 4
- ● A. A. Merlot Ris. '16 ▽▽ 4
- ○ A. A. Moscato Giallo Birnbaum '18 ▽▽ 3
- ○ A. A. Pinot Bianco Ris. '15 ▽▽ 3*
- ● A. A. Pinot Nero Panigl '14 ▽▽ 5
- ● A. A. Pinot Nero Schwarze Madonna '16 ▽▽ 5
- ● A. A. Pinot Nero Schwarze Madonna '15 ▽▽ 5

★Köfererhof Günther Kerschbaumer

fraz. Novacella
via Pusteria, 3
39040 Varna/Vahrn [BZ]
Tel. +39 3474778009
www.koefererhof.it

CELLAR SALES
PRE-BOOKED VISITS
RESTAURANT SERVICE
ANNUAL PRODUCTION 80,000 bottles
HECTARES UNDER VINE 10.00

Leaving the Bolzano basin and following the course of the Eisack river, the panorama suddenly narrows and climbs. In about forty kilometers we reach the enclave of Varna, where Italy's northernmost wineries can be found. Among these is Günther Kerschbaumer's estate. The winemaker takes advantage of the elevations and the cool climate here, where significant day-night temperature swings are common, for a range dedicated entirely to whites and characterized by richness and acidic tension. The Sylvaner R '18 is exemplary by virtue of its elegant aromas of white fruit combined with smoky notes and straw; in the mouth it opens full and powerful, then lengthens under the pressure of its hammering acidity, finishing clear and crisp. The Veltliner '18 features more immediate and fragrant scents, while the palate proves broad and highly pleasant. We also appreciated the sapid and spunky Riesling '18.

- ○ A. A. Valle Isarco Sylvaner R '18 ▼▼▼ 5
- ○ A. A. Valle Isarco Riesling '18 ▼▼ 5
- ○ A. A. Valle Isarco Veltliner '18 ▼▼ 4
- ○ A. A. Valle Isarco Gewürztraminer '19 ▼▼ 4
- ○ A. A. Valle Isarco Kerner '19 ▼▼ 3
- ○ A. A. Valle Isarco Müller Thurgau '19 ▼▼ 3
- ○ A. A. Valle Isarco Pinot Grigio '19 ▼▼ 3
- ○ A. A. Valle Isarco Sylvaner '19 ▼▼ 3
- ○ A. A. Valle Isarco Pinot Grigio '15 ▽▽▽ 3*
- ○ A. A. Valle Isarco Pinot Grigio '13 ▽▽▽ 3*
- ○ A. A. Valle Isarco Pinot Grigio '12 ▽▽▽ 3*
- ○ A. A. Valle Isarco Pinot Grigio '11 ▽▽▽ 3*
- ○ A. A. Valle Isarco Riesling '16 ▽▽▽ 5
- ○ A. A. Valle Isarco Sylvaner '16 ▽▽▽ 3*
- ○ A. A. Valle Isarco Sylvaner R '17 ▽▽▽ 5
- ○ A. A. Valle Isarco Sylvaner R '13 ▽▽▽ 5

Tenuta Kornell

fraz. Settequerce
via Cosma e Damiano, 6
39018 Terlano/Terlan [BZ]
Tel. +39 0471917507
www.kornell.it

CELLAR SALES
PRE-BOOKED VISITS
ANNUAL PRODUCTION 120,000 bottles
HECTARES UNDER VINE 15.00

Leaving Bolzano and moving in the direction of Merano, you eventually reach Settequerce, where the valley floor abruptly stops and gives way to the slopes that separate the Adige Valley from the Val Sarentina. It's here that we find Florian Brigl's winery. Florian is an attentive and sensitive interpreter of an area that's almost like a Mediterranean oasis in the heart of the Alps. So don't look for wines that are overly fragrant or linear. Indeed, Florian takes advantage of the very special climatic conditions here for wines that combine maturity and elegance. This year their selection put in a performance for the ages, thanks to a series of extraordinarily territorial and expertly crafted wines. The Merlot Kressfeld '16 saw sensations of plum, fine herbs and spices follow through on a full palate governed by acidity and smooth tannic texture. The Aichberg and Oberberg '18 are two whites of character and finesse.

- ● A. A. Merlot V. Kressfeld Ris. '16 — TTT 5
- ○ A. A. Sauvignon Oberberg '18 — TT 6
- ○ A.A. Bianco Aichberg '18 — TT 4
- ● A. A. Cabernet Sauvignon Staffes Ris. '17 — TT 5
- ● A. A. Lagrein Greif '19 — TT 3
- ● A. A. Lagrein Staffes Ris. '17 — TT 5
- ● A. A. Merlot Staffes Ris. '17 — TT 5
- ○ A. A. Pinot Bianco Eich '19 — TT 4
- ○ A. A. Pinot Grigio Gris '19 — TT 4
- ● A. A. Pinot Nero Marith '19 — TT 6
- ○ A. A. Sauvignon Cosmas '19 — TT 3
- ○ A. A. Gewürztraminer Damian '19 — T 4
- ● A. A. Lagrein Staffes Ris. '16 — YYY 5
- ● A. A. Lagrein Staves Ris. '14 — YYY 5
- ● A. A. Lagrein Staves Ris. '12 — YYY 5
- ● A. A. Merlot V. Kressfeld Ris. '15 — YY 5

★Kuenhof - Peter Pliger

loc. La Mara, 110
39042 Bressanone/Brixen [BZ]
Tel. +39 0472850546
www.kuenhof.com

CELLAR SALES
PRE-BOOKED VISITS
ANNUAL PRODUCTION 38,000 bottles
HECTARES UNDER VINE 6.00
SUSTAINABLE WINERY

The Eisack Valley does not offer large expanses of vineyards. There are no plateaus or tablelands where viticulture can prevail. Each single parcel has literally been snatched from the mountain, which climbs up to over 800 meters above sea level. Peter Pliger, together with his wife, Brigitte, is one of the producers who best represents this small and winding district, an area dominated by the presence of grape varieties that aren't developed elsewhere, such as Sylvaner and Veltliner, or that can benefit from ideal conditions, as in the case of Riesling. This year the only thing missing was that crowning stroke, but the battery of wines tasted was, as always, outstanding. The Sylvaner '19, which pours a pale straw-yellow, is bursting with aromas: white fruit, flowers and a hint of smoke in the background. In the mouth it's taut, long and penetrating, with a nice final stretch. The Kaiton '19 is redolent of flowers and citrus fruits, while on the palate it wins you over with its tension and harmony.

- ○ A. A. Valle Isarco Riesling Kaiton '19 — TT 4
- ○ A. A. Valle Isarco Sylvaner '19 — TT 3*
- ○ A. A. Valle Isarco Veltliner '19 — TT 4
- ○ A. A. Valle Isarco Gewürztraminer '19 — TT 3
- ○ A. A. Valle Isarco Grüner Veltliner '15 — YYY 3*
- ○ A. A. Valle Isarco Riesling Kaiton '16 — YYY 3*
- ○ A. A. Valle Isarco Riesling Kaiton '12 — YYY 4*
- ○ A. A. Valle Isarco Riesling Kaiton '11 — YYY 4*
- ○ A. A. Valle Isarco Riesling Kaiton '10 — YYY 4
- ○ A. A. Valle Isarco Riesling Kaiton '07 — YYY 3*
- ○ A. A. Valle Isarco Sylvaner '18 — YYY 3*
- ○ A. A. Valle Isarco Sylvaner '14 — YYY 3*
- ○ A. A. Valle Isarco Sylvaner '13 — YYY 3*
- ○ A. A. Valle Isarco Sylvaner '08 — YYY 3
- ○ A. A. Valle Isarco Sylvaner '06 — YYY 3*
- ○ A. A. Valle Isarco Veltliner '09 — YYY 3*

★Cantina Kurtatsch

Loc. Breitbach
S.da del Vino, 23
39040 Cortaccia/Kurtatsch [BZ]
Tel. +39 0471880115
www.cantina-kurtatsch.it

CELLAR SALES
PRE-BOOKED VISITS
ANNUAL PRODUCTION 1,500,000 bottles
HECTARES UNDER VINE 190.00
SUSTAINABLE WINERY

An absolute leader in the Bassa Atesina (South Tyrolean Unterland), Cantina di Cortaccia is the southernmost cooperative in the region. From the wide valley floor of the Adige, the vines climb rapidly towards the Mendola, at 700 meters elevation, on the coolest sites in Penon, and then again up to around 900 meters in Graun. Othmar Donà knows how to manage grapes from such a complex territorial puzzle, dedicating the most significant plots to each selection. The result is a range of wines characterized by a strong territorial identity. Their simpler wines, on the other hand, exalt the qualities of the cultivar. It's certainly not news that Cortaccia is one of the few regional sites where Bordeaux varieties thrive, but their Cabernet Sauvignon Freienfeld '16 put in a jaw-dropping performance. Intense and complex aromas serve as the prelude to an energetic palate outlined by dense and smooth tannins. We also note, with pleasure, the excellent Spumante Pas Dosé Ris. '14, a new addition.

Wine	Glasses	
● A. A. Cabernet Sauvignon Freienfeld Ris. '16	▼▼▼	6
○ A. A. Chardonnay Freienfeld Ris. '17	▼▼	7
○ A. A. Gewürztraminer Brenntal Ris. '18	▼▼	5
○ A. A. Blanc de Blancs Pas Dosé M. Cl. 600 Ris. '14	▼▼	5
● A. A. Merlot Brenntal Ris. '17	▼▼	6
○ A. A. Müller Thurgau Graun '19	▼▼	3
○ A. A. Pinot Grigio Penóner '18	▼▼	4
● A. A. Pinot Nero Mazon Ris. '17	▼▼	6
○ A. A. Sauvignon Kofl '18	▼▼	4
○ Aruna V. T. '18	▼▼	6
● Ushas Moscato Rosa Passito '18	▼▼	6
● A. A. Schiava Sonntaler Alte Reben '19	▼	3
○ A. A. Gewürztraminer Brenntal Ris. '16	▽▽▽	5
○ A. A. Gewürztraminer Brenntal Ris. '15	▽▽▽	5
○ A. A. Gewürztraminer Brenntal Ris. '14	▽▽▽	5

Laimburg

Loc. Laimburg, 6
39040 Vadena/Pfatten [BZ]
Tel. +39 0471969590
www.laimburg.bz.it

CELLAR SALES
PRE-BOOKED VISITS
ANNUAL PRODUCTION 100,000 bottles
HECTARES UNDER VINE 20.00
SUSTAINABLE WINERY

Not all of Italy's wine-growing territories can count on the precious work carried out by the Laimburg Experimental Center, one of the most reliable sources for information on the synergy between variety and territory. Behind it all are vineyards that explore a little bit of each of the region's wine districts, and supply grapes for the Vadena winery. Here commendably crafted wines take shape, divided between their 'Podere' wines, which are simpler and more approachable, and the 'Selezione Maniero', which comprises their most ambitious selections. This last line includes the Sauvignon Passito Saphir '18, a wine made with grapes harvested in early December. It pours a lovely, bright, golden-straw color, while the nose is characterized by ripe aromas amidst sensations of caramel and biscuit, all of which bind to its rich palate, decidedly sweet but balanced thanks to a nice sapidity. A good performance from their Merlot '17, a full and harmonious wine, as well.

Wine	Glasses	
● A. A. Cabernet Sauvignon Sass Roà Ris. '17	▼▼	5
○ A. A. Gewürztraminer Elyònd Ris. '17	▼▼	4
● A. A. Lago di Caldaro Cl. Sup. Vernacius Solemnis '18	▼▼	3
● A. A. Lagrein Barbagòl Ris. '17	▼▼	5
● A. A. Merlot Ris. '17	▼▼	4
○ A. A. Pinot Bianco Musis '19	▼▼	3
○ A. A. Riesling '18	▼▼	4
○ A. A. Sauvignon Oyèll Ris. '17	▼▼	4
○ A. A. Sauvignon Passito Saphir '18	▼▼	6
● A.A. Moscato Rosa Passito '18	▼▼	6
● Col de Réy '16	▼▼	6
○ Dòa '17	▼	4
● A. A. Lagrein Barbagòl Ris. '16	▽▽	5
○ A. A. Pinot Bianco '17	▽▽	2*
○ A. A. Pinot Bianco Musis '18	▽▽	3*

Klaus Lentsch

s.da Reinsperg, 18a
39057 Appiano/Eppan [BZ]
Tel. +39 0471967263
www.klauslentsch.eu

CELLAR SALES
PRE-BOOKED VISITS
ANNUAL PRODUCTION 50,000 bottles
HECTARES UNDER VINE 6.00

Even if the history of Klaus Lentsch's winery is relatively recent, we are talking about a family that has a deep-rooted connection with regional viticulture. The adventure began a few years ago, but the few hectares of vineyards at the entrance to the Eisack valley have quickly grown into a dozen, thanks to acquisitions in the areas of San Paolo and Bronzoll. Their selection, which exhibits reliable and commendable craftsmanship, centers on Pinot Nero, which is interpreted in two versions: one that's fragrant and approachable, the other deeper and more complex. Their most notable wines come from the Eisack Valley estate, including an impressive Veltliner '18 this year. Its time in the barrel lends depth and richness: complex aromas of white fruit reveal notes of dried flowers and smoky hints, all brought out by an energetic, tense and assertive palate. The Pinot Nero Bachgart '17 is exemplary, immediately expressive in its sensations of undergrowth, with a supple, juicy palate.

○ A. A. Valle Isarco Veltliner Eichberg '18	🍷🍷	4
○ A. A. Gewürztraminer Amperg '19	🍷🍷	2*
● A. A. Lagrein Amperg Ris. '17	🍷🍷	4
○ A. A. Pinot Bianco Amperg '19	🍷🍷	3
● A. A. Pinot Nero Bachgart '17	🍷🍷	4
● A. A. Pinot Nero Bachgart '13	♀♀♀	4*
○ A. A. Gewürztraminer Fuchslahn '16	♀♀	2*
○ A. A. Grüner Veltliner Eichberg '16	♀♀	3
○ A. A. Pinot Grigio '17	♀♀	2*
● A. A. Pinot Nero Bachgart '16	♀♀	4
● A. A. Pinot Nero Bachgart Ris. '16	♀♀	5
○ A. A. Valle Isarco Veltliner Eichberg '17	♀♀	4

Loacker Schwarhof

loc. Sankt Justina, 3
39100 Bolzano/Bozen
Tel. +39 0471365125
www.loacker.bio

CELLAR SALES
PRE-BOOKED VISITS
ANNUAL PRODUCTION 60,000 bottles
HECTARES UNDER VINE 7.00
VITICULTURE METHOD Certified Organic
SUSTAINABLE WINERY

The Loacker family's winery is located on the slopes of the Santa Maddalena hills, small slopes near Bolzano that seem to lie in the sun to catch its rays, refreshed by the breezes of the Eisack and Ritten valleys. In this scenic landscape we find vineyards that have been cultivated according to biodynamic principles for years, hosting both area's traditional varieties and international ones as well. It's an ideal habitat for generous, characterful wines capable of perfectly expressing the area's warmth. Expert skill is on display when it comes to Lagrein, as evidenced by the Gran Lareyn '18. Its intense though not impenetrable color anticipates aromas dominated by ripe, dark fruit refreshed by mineral whiffs and undergrowth, all of which we find perfectly expressed in the mouth where it's potent yet supple, sapid, dry and assertive. The rest of their selection is also in great form, starting with the Iwain Merlot '18.

● A. A. Lagrein Gran Lareyn Ris. '18	🍷🍷	5
● A. A. Santa Maddalena Morit '19	🍷🍷	3
● Kastlet '16	🍷🍷	5
○ Tasnim Sauvignon '19	🍷🍷	4
○ Timeless '11	🍷🍷	8
● Ywain Merlot '18	🍷🍷	4
○ A. A. Gewürztraminer Atagis '19	🍷	4
● A. A. Merlot Ywain '04	♀♀♀	4*
○ A. A. Gewürztraminer Atagis '17	♀♀	4
● A. A. Lagrein Gran Lareyn Ris. '16	♀♀	5
● A. A. Lagrein Gran Lareyn Ris. '15	♀♀	4
● Kastlet '15	♀♀	5
● Lagrein Gran Lareyn '17	♀♀	4
● Ywain '16	♀♀	4

Manincor

Loc. San Giuseppe al Lago, 4
39052 Caldaro/Kaltern [BZ]
Tel. +39 0471960230
www.manincor.com

CELLAR SALES
PRE-BOOKED VISITS
ANNUAL PRODUCTION 330,000 bottles
HECTARES UNDER VINE 50.00
VITICULTURE METHOD Certified Biodynamic
SUSTAINABLE WINERY

Owned by the count Göess-Enzemberg family, Manincor is one of Alto Adige's most representative wineries. Situated near Lake Kaltern, its many hectares of property are overseen according to the dictates of biodynamic agriculture. The grapes are then processed by Helmut Zozin in their beautiful, low-environmental impact cellar in San Giuseppe al Lago. The vineyards unfold around the heart of their production facilities, stretching from the shores of the lake to the highest area of Mason, not to mention plots near Terlano. Three 2018 whites topped our preferences: the Eichhorn, Sophie and Tannenberg. The first is a youthfully fruity Pinot Blanc, energetic and long on the palate. The second is a Chardonnay that delivers a sapid palate, rich and taut at the same time. Finally there's the Sauvignon, a wine dominated by exotic and floral sensations, all of which follow through coherently on the palate, where oak is perfectly integrated.

○ A. A. Terlano Chardonnay Sophie '18	🍷🍷 6
○ A. A. Terlano Pinot Bianco Eichhorn '18	🍷🍷 5
○ A. A. Terlano Sauvignon Tannenberg '18	🍷🍷 5
● A. A. Pinot Nero Mason '18	🍷🍷 6
○ A. A. Terlano Réserve della Contessa '19	🍷🍷 4
● Cassiano '18	🍷🍷 6
○ A. A. Terlano Pinot Bianco Eichhorn '16	🍸🍸🍸 5
○ A. A. Terlano Pinot Bianco Eichhorn '15	🍸🍸🍸 5
○ A. A. Terlano Pinot Bianco Eichhorn '13	🍸🍸🍸 5
○ A. A. Terlano Pinot Bianco Eichhorn '12	🍸🍸🍸 5
○ A. A. Terlano Pinot Bianco Eichhorn '10	🍸🍸🍸 4
○ A. A. Terlano Pinot Bianco Eichhorn '09	🍸🍸🍸 4
○ A. A. Terlano Sauvignon Tannenberg '13	🍸🍸🍸 5
○ Le Petit '17	🍸🍸 8

Lorenz Martini

Loc. Cornaiano/Girlan
via Pranzoll, 2d
39057 Appiano/Eppan [BZ]
Tel. +39 0471664136
lorenz-martini.jimdo.com

CELLAR SALES
PRE-BOOKED VISITS
ANNUAL PRODUCTION 20,000 bottles
HECTARES UNDER VINE 3.00

Lorenz Martini is among the few producers in Alto Adige that have chosen to concentrate all their efforts on a single wine, in his case a sparkling wine produced with grapes grown in Cornaiano, Appiano Monte and Cologna. Elevations ranging from 500 to 800 meters prove indispensable towards preserving the acidity that's key to Lorenz's stylistic approach. Only Chardonnay, Pinot Bianco and Pinot Nero arrive at his small cellar in Via Pranzoll, where all vinification is carried out. As happened with 2011, when there's a great vintage they make an important reserve, the Comitissa Gold. It's a Brut sparkler of rare precision and depth, with hints of white fruit chasing notes of toasted bread, dried flowers and mineral hints. In the mouth it unfolds with grace and tension, proving long, sapid and fascinating. The Comitissa Pas Dosé '16 moves on a fresher register, intact and fragrant in its expression of fruit and flowers.

○ A. A. Spumante Brut Comitissa Gold Gran Riserva '11	🍷🍷 8
○ A. A. Spumante Pas Dosé Comitissa Ris. '16	🍷🍷 5
○ A. A. Brut Comitissa Ris. '10	🍸🍸 5
○ A. A. Brut Comitissa Ris. '09	🍸🍸 5
○ A. A. Spumante Brut Comitissa Gold Gran Riserva '06	🍸🍸 5
○ A. A. Spumante Brut Comitissa Ris. '12	🍸🍸 5
○ A. A. Spumante Pas Dosé Comitissa Ris. '15	🍸🍸 5
○ A. A. Spumante Pas Dosé Comitissa Ris. '13	🍸🍸 5

★Cantina Meran

via Cantina, 9
39020 Marlengo/Marling [BZ]
Tel. +39 0473447137
www.kellereimeran.it

CELLAR SALES
ANNUAL PRODUCTION 1,300,000 bottles
HECTARES UNDER VINE 265.00

The cooperative overseen by Kaspar Platzer has Stefan Kapfinger as its technical director, while his staff perfectly interpret the territory of Burgraviato. The producer comprises almost 400 grower members who cultivate small plots of land in various areas, from Lana to the Vinschgau Valley, from the bottom of the valley up to 1,000 meters elevation. Unlike most other cooperatives, the vineyards can be found almost exclusively in the same area as the cellar, with Schiava and Pinot Bianco serving as cornerstones. It's hard to choose the best of the lot, with a selection this good. The classy Pinot Bianco Tyrol '18 stands out with its broad and still young aromatic spectrum, winning you over for the generosity and harmony of a palate that seems to never end. The Pinot Nero Zeno '17 is another classy drink, deep in its aromas and marked by firm elegance on the palate.

Wine	Rating	Price
○ A. A. Pinot Bianco Tyrol '18	🍷🍷🍷	4*
○ A. A. Moscato Giallo Passito Sissi '17	🍷🍷	6
● A. A. Pinot Nero Zeno Ris. '17	🍷🍷	4
○ A. A. Chardonnay Goldegg Ris. '17	🍷🍷	4
○ A. A. Gewürztraminer Graf '19	🍷🍷	3
● A. A. Lagrein Segen Ris. '17	🍷🍷	4
● A. A. Meranese Schickenburg Graf '18	🍷🍷	3
● A. A. Merlot Freiherr Ris. '17	🍷🍷	5
○ A. A. Sauvignon Mervin '18	🍷🍷	4
○ A. A. Val Venosta Pinot Bianco '19	🍷🍷	3
○ A.A. Spumante Brut Meran 36 Ris. '16	🍷🍷	5
○ A. A. Val Venosta Kerner '19	🍷	4
○ A. A. Pinot Bianco Tyrol '16	🍷🍷🍷 (outline)	4*
○ A. A. Pinot Bianco Tyrol '15	🍷🍷🍷 (outline)	4*
○ A. A. Sauvignon Mervin '14	🍷🍷🍷 (outline)	4*

★★Cantina Convento Muri-Gries

p.zza Gries, 21
39100 Bolzano/Bozen
Tel. +39 0471282287
www.muri-gries.com

CELLAR SALES
ANNUAL PRODUCTION 650,000 bottles
HECTARES UNDER VINE 55.00
SUSTAINABLE WINERY

Passing through the gates of the Abbey of Muri Gries is a bit like going back in time. The winery and its most important vineyards are situated in the town center, and all the activities come back to the Abbot, as was also the case in ancient times. Following tradition, it's kellermeister Christian Werth's responsibility to interpret the grapes of this sizable estate (Klosteranger is their crown jewel). The property is rounded out by vineyards in Appiano, where mostly white grape varieties are cultivated. As the Lagrein Klosteranger is still aging, the Lagrein Abtei Muri Riserva '17 caught our attention. Bright and thick in color, on the nose it offers up vibrant aromas in which dark fruit has plenty of company: sensations of violet, undergrowth and ink emerge, while the palate comes through powerful and decisive, finding its length thanks to bursting acidity. The Pinot Bianco '17 of the same line is aromatically deep and harmonious on the palate.

Wine	Rating	Price
● A. A. Lagrein Abtei Muri Ris. '17	🍷🍷🍷	5
○ A. A. Terlano Pinot Bianco Abtei Muri Ris. '17	🍷🍷	5
⊙ A. A. Lagrein Kretzer '19	🍷🍷	3
● A. A. Pinot Nero Abtei Muri Ris. '17	🍷🍷	5
● A. A. Santa Maddalena Cl. '19	🍷🍷	2*
○ A. A. Terlano Pinot Bianco '19	🍷🍷	3
● A. A. Lagrein Abtei Muri Ris. '14	🍷🍷🍷 (outline)	5
● A. A. Lagrein Abtei Muri Ris. '12	🍷🍷🍷 (outline)	5
● A. A. Lagrein Abtei Muri Ris. '11	🍷🍷🍷 (outline)	5
● A. A. Lagrein Abtei Muri Ris. '10	🍷🍷🍷 (outline)	5
● A. A. Lagrein Abtei Muri Ris. '09	🍷🍷🍷 (outline)	5
● A. A. Lagrein Abtei Ris. '07	🍷🍷🍷 (outline)	5
● A. A. Lagrein V. Klosteranger Ris. '15	🍷🍷🍷 (outline)	8
● A. A. Pinot Nero Abtei Muri Ris. '15	🍷🍷🍷 (outline)	5

★Nals Margreid

via Heiligenberg, 2
39010 Nalles/Nals [BZ]
Tel. +39 0471678626
www.kellerei.it

CELLAR SALES
PRE-BOOKED VISITS
ANNUAL PRODUCTION 1,000,000 bottles
HECTARES UNDER VINE 173.00
SUSTAINABLE WINERY

The cooperative in Via Heiligenberg is the result of the unusual fusion of two very distant producers: Nalles is located at the northern end of the Atesina wine-growing district, while Magrè, almost on the border with Trentino, represents its southern limit. It's a veritable viticultural puzzle that the numerous members cultivate following the guidelines set by kellermeister Harald Schraffl. Together they highlight the attributes of extremely diverse territories, to say the least, and are supported by Gottfried Pollinger, whose deep knowledge of the world of wine is an invaluable asset. The Pinot Bianco Sirmian '19 put in a performance for the ages with its aromas of white fruit, flowers and mineral hints; in the mouth it doesn't astound for power, but wins you over with delicacy and decision, proving tense, energetic and very long—a true champion. The Pinot Nero Jura '17 also put in a notable performance: nuances of undergrowth and rain-soaked earth follow through on a full and juicy palate.

Wine	Rating	Price
○ A. A. Pinot Bianco Sirmian '19	🍷🍷🍷	5
○ A. A. Pinot Grigio Punggl '19	🍷🍷	5
● A. A. Pinot Nero Jura Ris. '17	🍷🍷	6
○ A. A. Chardonnay Baron Salvadori Ris. '17	🍷🍷	6
○ A. A. Chardonnay Magred '19	🍷🍷	4
● A. A. Lagrein Gries Ris. '17	🍷🍷	5
● A. A. Merlot Cabernet Anticus Ris. '17	🍷🍷	7
○ A. A. Moscato Giallo Passito Baronesse '17	🍷🍷	7
○ A. A. Pinot Bianco Penon '19	🍷🍷	3
○ A. A. Sauvignon Mantele '19	🍷🍷	5
● A. A. Schiava Galea '19	🍷🍷	3
○ A. A. Pinot Bianco Sirmian '18	🍷🍷🍷 (previous)	5
○ A. A. Pinot Bianco Sirmian '17	🍷🍷🍷 (previous)	5
○ A. A. Pinot Bianco Sirmian '16	🍷🍷🍷 (previous)	5

Ignaz Niedrist

loc. Cornaiano/Girlan
via Ronco, 5
39057 Appiano/Eppan [BZ]
Tel. +39 0471664494
www.ignazniedrist.com

CELLAR SALES
PRE-BOOKED VISITS
ANNUAL PRODUCTION 50,000 bottles
HECTARES UNDER VINE 10.00
SUSTAINABLE WINERY

Founded discreetly in the late 1980s using the family vineyards in Ronco, the adventure of Ignaz Niedrist and his wife, Elisabeth, has grown into a solid producer that's also exploring the territories of Mühlweg in Cornaiano, Untersteiner in Appiano Monte and Gries in Bolzano. Each variety is cultivated in its most well-suited plot, so much so that their range is constituted almost exclusively of single-vineyard wines. These express the deep bond that a conscientious and environmentally-friendly approach manages to transmit from the soil to the grapes. The Pinot Nero Riserva '17 just fell short of a gold. Aromatically it unravels slowly: first earthy notes and undergrowth, then wild red berries, finally medicinal herbs, which lend lightness and freshness. In the mouth it reveals consistency and pluck, letting through a long and elegant development. The Lagrein Berger Gei '17 is diametrically opposed: vibrant in dark, fruity notes, winning over the palate with power and rigor.

Wine	Rating	Price
● A. A. Pinot Nero Ris. '17	🍷🍷	6
● A. A. Lagrein Berger Gei Ris. '17	🍷🍷	5
○ A. A. Sauvignon Porphyr & Kalk '18	🍷🍷	4
○ Trias '18	🍷🍷	4
○ A. A. Pinot Bianco Limes '18	🍷	5
○ A. A. Riesling Berg '11	🍷🍷🍷 (previous)	4*
○ A. A. Terlano Pinot Bianco '12	🍷🍷🍷 (previous)	3*
○ A. A. Terlano Sauvignon '10	🍷🍷🍷 (previous)	3
○ Trias '14	🍷🍷🍷 (previous)	4*
● A. A. Lagrein Berger Gei Ris. '16	🍷🍷 (previous)	5
● A. A. Lagrein Berger Gei Ris. '15	🍷🍷 (previous)	4
● A. A. Pinot Nero Vom Kalk '16	🍷🍷 (previous)	8
○ A. A. Sauvignon Limes '16	🍷🍷 (previous)	4

Pfannenstielhof Johannes Pfeifer

via Pfannestiel, 9
39100 Bolzano/Bozen
Tel. +39 0471970884
www.pfannenstielhof.it

CELLAR SALES
PRE-BOOKED VISITS
ANNUAL PRODUCTION 43,000 bottles
HECTARES UNDER VINE 4.00

Unlike many producers in Santa Maddalena who have extended their reach into other districts, the Pfeifer family have remained faithful to the territory and its grapes, Schiava and Lagrein. Surrounded by vineyards, the winery is located in Rencio, enclosed between the mixed gravelly sands of the Eisack and the dolomitic porphyry of the hillside, a choice area for growing Bolzano's native grapes. Their range fully explores the expressiveness of these places, at times exalting their more approachable, enjoyable qualities, and at others delving into deeper, more complex sensations. The thick and intensely-colored Lagrein '17 expresses all the character of Bolzanino through rich aromas dominated by ripe fruit, which slowly give way to spices, smoky notes and medicinal herbs. On the palate it's powerful and decisive, gaining tension thanks to fresh acidity. Intense and enticing, the Santa Maddalena '19 wins you over by virtue of its sapidity and pleasantness.

● A. A. Lagrein Ris. '17	TT 5
● A. A. Lagrein vom Boden '19	TT 3
● A. A. Santa Maddalena Cl. '19	TT 3
⊙ Lagrein Rosé '19	TT 3
● A. A. Santa Maddalena Cl. '14	YYY 3*
● A. A. Lagrein Ris. '14	YY 5
● A. A. Lagrein Ris. '12	YY 5
● A. A. Santa Maddalena Cl. '18	YY 3*
● A. A. Santa Maddalena Cl. '17	YY 3*
● A. A. Santa Maddalena Cl. '16	YY 3*
● A. A. Santa Maddalena Cl. '15	YY 3*

Tenuta Pfitscher

via Dolomiti, 17
39040 Montagna/Montan [BZ]
Tel. +39 04711681317
www.pfitscher.it

CELLAR SALES
PRE-BOOKED VISITS
ANNUAL PRODUCTION 60,000 bottles
HECTARES UNDER VINE 7.00

The Pfitscher family's winery, a splendid structure designed to have a low environmental and energy impact, can be found nestled among the vineyards of Montagna, the cradle of Bolzano/Bozen Pinot Nero. The vineyards cultivated explore all of Bassa Atesina (South Tyrolean Unterland), with the grapes most in need of heat grown mainly in Cortaccia, Egna and Ora, and those that do best in cooler climates concentrated on the Montagna side and in the Eisack Valley, in Fié allo Sciliar (the only vineyard that's not near the cellar). This year their selection performed quite well, with the Sauvignon Mathias standing out. Made with grapes from the Kathreinerfelder vineyard, located at 900 meters elevation in Fiè, it offers up vibrant, smoky notes of ripe yellow fruit, which reemerge on a substantive palate. Here it unfolds with ease, gaining tension and finesse thanks to its hammering acidity. The Pinot Nero Matan '17, nuanced aromatically with a long, supple palate, also delivers.

○ A. A. Sauvignon Mathias Ris. '18	TT 4
○ A. A. Gewürztraminer Rutter Ris. '18	TT 4
● A. A. Lagrein Griesfeld '17	TT 5
● A. A. Pinot Nero Fuchsleiten '18	TT 4
● A. A. Pinot Nero Matan Ris. '17	TT 5
○ A. A. Sauvignon Saxum '19	TT 4
○ A. A. Chardonnay Arvum '18	YY 3
○ A. A. Gewürztraminer Rutter Ris. '17	YY 4
● A. A. Lagrein Griesfeld '16	YY 5
● A. A. Lagrein Kotznloater '09	YY 5
● A. A. Pinot Nero Matan '08	YY 5
● A. A. Pinot Nero Matan Ris. '16	YY 5
○ A. A. Sauvignon Mathias Ris. '17	YY 4
○ A. A. Sauvignon Saxum '18	YY 4

Tenuta Ritterhof

S.DA DEL VINO, 1
39052 CALDARO/KALTERN [BZ]
TEL. +39 0471963298
www.ritterhof.it

CELLAR SALES
PRE-BOOKED VISITS
RESTAURANT SERVICE
ANNUAL PRODUCTION 300,000 bottles
HECTARES UNDER VINE 40.00

The Roner family's winery is managed confidently by Ludwig Kaneppele, an expert in the world of wine who spares no effort when it comes to improving production. He's flanked by a competent and passionate staff who oversee the estate's own vineyards and the numerous growers who contribute to their outstanding selection. The heart of the vineyards is concentrated in Oltradige, Bassa Atesina (the South Tyrolean Unterland) and the Bolzano basin, and the grapes chosen are those best suited to each territory. The Gewürztraminer Auratus '19 is the usual, classic white, offering up intoxicating aromas of orange blossom flowers, exotic fruit and spices; in the mouth its ebullient richness finds enough supporting sapidity to stretch and unfold harmoniously. Aromatically vibrant in its notes of red fruit and fine herbs, the Cabernet Sauvignon Gratus '16 plays on generous flavor, coming through soft, powerful and warm on the palate.

Wine	Rating
○ A. A. Gewürztraminer Auratus '19	🍷🍷 5
● A.A. Cabernet Sauvignon Gratus '16	🍷🍷 5
○ A. A. Gewürztraminer '19	🍷🍷 3
● A. A. Lago di Caldaro Cl. Sup. Novis '19	🍷🍷 3
● A. A. Lagrein '19	🍷🍷 3
○ A. A. Pinot Bianco '19	🍷🍷 2*
● A. A. Pinot Nero Dignus Crescendo '16	🍷🍷 5
○ A.A. Pinot Grigio Opes '18	🍷🍷 4
● Perlhofer Crescendus '17	🍷🍷 5
○ A. A. Pinot Bianco Verus '19	🍷 3
● A. A. Santa Maddalena Perlhof '19	🍷 2
○ A. A. Sauvignon '19	🍷 2
○ A. A. Gewürztraminer Auratus '18	🍷🍷🍷 5
○ A. A. Gewürztraminer Auratus '17	🍷🍷🍷 5
○ A. A. Gewürztraminer Auratus '16	🍷🍷🍷 4*

Tenuta Hans Rottensteiner

FRAZ. GRIES
VIA SARENTINO, 1A
39100 BOLZANO/BOZEN
TEL. +39 0471282015
www.rottensteiner.wine

CELLAR SALES
PRE-BOOKED VISITS
ANNUAL PRODUCTION 450,000 bottles
HECTARES UNDER VINE 90.00

The Rottensteiner family's production adventure began after the Second World War, when Hans founded a company that exported wine in demijohns to Switzerland. After more than half a century, the business has changed radically: only bottled wine is produced and the winery avails itself of some of the region's most beautiful plots. What hasn't changed is the passion with which the family dedicates itself to viticulture, overseeing a range that does a superb job expressing the territory, with their crown jewels represented by the estate's loveliest vineyards. The Pinot Bianco Carnol '19 pours a delicate color, anticipating a delicate aromatic suite: fragrances of white fruit echo floral nuances, while the palate comes through juicy, supple and pleasant. The Chardonnay '19 features more vibrant and fruity aromas, while the mouth exhibits nice texture, with perky acidity lending tension and vertical rhythm. Finally a special mention for the harmonious Santa Maddalena Premstallerhof '19.

Wine	Rating
○ A. A. Chardonnay '19	🍷🍷 2*
○ A. A. Gewürztraminer Passito Cresta '18	🍷🍷 6
○ A. A. Pinot Bianco Carnol '19	🍷🍷 3
● A. A. Santa Maddalena Cl. V. Premstallerhof '19	🍷🍷 3
○ A. A. Sauvignon '19	🍷🍷 3
● A. A.Lagrein Gries Select Ris. '17	🍷🍷 5
○ A.A. Pinot Grigio '19	🍷🍷 3
○ A .A. Gewürztraminer Cancenai '19	🍷 4
● A. A. Schiava V. Kristplonerhof '19	🍷 2
● A. A. Cabernet Select Ris. '12	🍷🍷 5
● A. A. Lagrein Grieser Select Ris. '15	🍷🍷 5
● A. A. Santa Maddalena Cl. V. Premstallerhof '18	🍷🍷 3*

★★★Cantina Produttori San Michele Appiano

VIA CIRCONVALLAZIONE, 17/19
39057 APPIANO/EPPAN [BZ]
TEL. +39 0471664466
www.stmichael.it

CELLAR SALES
PRE-BOOKED VISITS
ANNUAL PRODUCTION 2,200,000 bottles
HECTARES UNDER VINE 380.00

The cooperative of San Michele Appiano has been a cornerstone of the wine renaissance that's unfolded in Alto Adige in recent decades. A group of more than 300 families have contributed to a renewal of viticulture and wine production under the leadership of Hans Terzer, who's still firmly in charge of the winery today. Looking back on its history, one realizes how it's been a continuous flow of improvements and new paths, at times highlighted by the birth of a new product, but always visible in the consistent quality of their wines. The wines tasted for this year's edition put in an impressive performance. The Chardonnay Sanct Valentin '18 topped our preferences: on the nose fruit fuses perfectly with nuances of oak, nicely rounded out by a mineral background; on the palate it's sapid, rich and harmonious. We also want to point out some limited edition wines, real treats worth seeking out, like the Appius '15, or the Wine Collection Pinot Nero and Sauvignon. For all these reasons, San Michele Appiano is our Cooperative of the Year.

- ○ A. A. Chardonnay Sanct Valentin '18 🍷🍷🍷 5
- ○ A. A. Pinot Bianco Sanct Valentin '18 🍷🍷 5
- ● A. A. Pinot Nero Sanct Valentin Ris. '17 🍷🍷 5
- ● A. A. Cabernet Merlot Sanct Valentin Ris. '17 🍷🍷 5
- ○ A. A. Gewürztraminer Passito Comtess '18 🍷🍷 7
- ○ A. A. Gewürztraminer Sanct Valentin '19 🍷🍷 5
- ○ A. A. Pinot Bianco Schulthauser '19 🍷🍷 3
- ○ A. A. Pinot Grigio Sanct Valentin '18 🍷🍷 5
- ○ A. A. Sauvignon Sanct Valentin '19 🍷🍷 5
- ○ A. A. Pinot Bianco Sanct Valentin '17 🍷🍷🍷 5
- ○ A. A. Pinot Bianco Sanct Valentin '15 🍷🍷🍷 6
- ○ A. A. Pinot Grigio Sanct Valentin '14 🍷🍷🍷 5
- ● A. A. Pinot Nero Sanct Valentin Ris. '15 🍷🍷🍷 5

Cantina Produttori San Paolo

LOC. SAN PAOLO
VIA CASTEL GUARDIA, 21
39057 APPIANO/EPPAN [BZ]
TEL. +39 0471662183
www.stpauls.wine

CELLAR SALES
PRE-BOOKED VISITS
ANNUAL PRODUCTION 1,200,000 bottles
HECTARES UNDER VINE 175.00
SUSTAINABLE WINERY

San Paolo is a small hamlet of Appiano. In 1907 a few thousand of its inhabitants founded Cantina Produttori. Today the cooperative and its members cover almost 200 hectares, scattered mainly throughout the territory of Oltradige, at elevations ranging from 300 to 700 meters and on soils that vary greatly in terms of composition. Their range is divided into three lines designed to highlight the varietal aspects of the wines as well as the territory's richness and complexity. Because of Dieter Haas's new presidency and the unfortunate problems encountered during the spring, their most ambitious wines have been left to mature in their cellar at Via Castel Guardia. Many convincing wines, however, were tasted, polished expressions of their respective grape varieties, such as the Pinot Grigio Löss or the Pinot Bianco Plötzner, both 2019s and both marked by their gustatory dynamism.

- ○ A. A. Brut Praeclarus 🍷🍷 5
- ○ A. A. Chardonnay Fuxberg '19 🍷🍷 3
- ○ A. A. Gewürztraminer Kössler '17 🍷🍷 3
- ○ A. A. Pinot Bianco Kössler '19 🍷🍷 3
- ○ A. A. Pinot Bianco Plötzner '19 🍷🍷 3
- ○ A. A. Pinot Grigio Kössler '19 🍷🍷 3
- ○ A. A. Pinot Grigio Löss '19 🍷🍷 3
- ● A. A. Pinot Nero Kössler '19 🍷🍷 3
- ● A. A. Pinot Nero Luzia '19 🍷🍷 3
- ○ A. A. Sauvignon Gfill '19 🍷🍷 3
- ● A. A. Schiava Missianer '19 🍷🍷 2*
- ○ A. A. Spumante Brut Praeclarus 🍷🍷 5
- ○ Aurie Petit Manseng '18 🍷🍷 5
- ○ A. A. Gewürztraminer Justina '19 🍷 3
- ○ A. A. Pinot Bianco Passion '09 🍷🍷🍷 4
- ○ A. A. Pinot Bianco Passion Ris. '11 🍷🍷🍷 4*

Tenuta Seeperle

LOC. SAN GIUSEPPE AL LAGO, 28
39052 CALDARO/KALTERN [BZ]
TEL. +39 0471960158
www.seeperle.it

ANNUAL PRODUCTION 15,000 bottles
HECTARES UNDER VINE 2.00

Ingrid and Arhur Rainer's adventure in the world of wine began less than twenty years ago, when for the first time grapes from the family vineyards were fermented on their own. Since then, a lot has changed and what used to be a small hotel storage room, which housed the steel tanks and wood barrels, has become a chaotic little wine cellar where passion reigns supreme. With the exception of a small property in Magrè, the vineyards are concentrated in the area of Caldaro, from the shores of the lake to the highest plots of Pianizza. They offer a wide selection, often with a rather limited number of bottles produced, as is the case with the Seitensprung '18, a Pinot Bianco matured in oak and redolent of ripe fruit and flowers, all embellished by toastiness. In the mouth it's almost perfect: sapid, dynamic and drinkable. Steel and oak for the Lake Caldaro Scheinheilig '19, a fresh, enticing and enjoyable drink.

● A. A. Lago di Caldaro Cl. Sup. Scheinheilig '19	🍷🍷	4
● A. A. Lago di Caldaro Cl. Sup. Waschecht '19	🍷🍷	4
○ A. A. Pinot Bianco Chardonnay '19	🍷🍷	5
○ A. A. Pinot Bianco Leidenschaft '19	🍷🍷	2*
○ A. A. Pinot Bianco Seitensprung Ris. '18	🍷🍷	5
○ A. A. Sauvignon Echt Geil '18	🍷🍷	4
● A.A. Cabernet Höhepunkt Ris. '15	🍷🍷	5
○ A. A. Gewürztraminer Scharf '19	🍷	4
● Rotlicht '17	🍷	4
● A. A. Lago di Caldaro Cl. Sup. Scheinheilig '17	♀♀	4
● A. A. Lago di Caldaro Cl. Sup. Waschecht '17	♀♀	4
○ A. A. Pinot Bianco Leidenschaft '17	♀♀	2*

Peter Sölva & Söhne

VIA DELL'ORO, 33
39052 CALDARO/KALTERN [BZ]
TEL. +39 0471964650
www.soelva.com

CELLAR SALES
PRE-BOOKED VISITS
ANNUAL PRODUCTION 75,000 bottles
HECTARES UNDER VINE 12.00

The Sölva family's winery is one of the oldest in the region, a business that opened its doors in the mid-18th century and that's passed from one generation to the next up to present day. The vineyards lie mainly in the area of Lake Kaltern, but there are also plots close to the historic cellar, which is about to be expanded and improved. The desire to produce high quality wines, combined with the maturation of recently planted vineyards, led to the end of their simplest line of wines, I Vigneti, as of 2019. The Amistar Edizione Rossa '16 is a Bordeaux blend made with a substantial share of Lagrein, partially harvested when overripe. On the nose it expresses all the area's warmth in its aromas of sweet, fleshy red fruit, while in the mouth it surprises for its combination of power, grace and tension. The Cuvée Bianco '18 (from the same line) is a blend of Chardonnay, mostly, and Sauvignon characterized by a full and harmonious profile.

● Amistar Edizione Rossa '16	🍷🍷	6
○ A. A. Gewürztramimer DeSilva '18	🍷🍷	4
● A. A. Lagrein I Vigneti '18	🍷🍷	3
○ Amistar Cuvée Bianco '18	🍷🍷	6
● Amistar Cuvée Rosso Ris. '17	🍷🍷	5
○ A. A. Sauvignon DeSilva '18	🍷	4
○ A. A. Terlano Pinot Bianco DeSilva '10	♀♀♀	3
○ A. A. Terlano Pinot Bianco DeSilva '09	♀♀♀	3
● A. A. Cabernet Franc Amistar '15	♀♀	5
● A. A. Lago di Caldaro Cl. Sup. Peterleiten DeSilva '18	♀♀	2*
● A. A. Lagrein I Vigneti '17	♀♀	3
○ A. A. Sauvignon DeSilva '17	♀♀	4
○ Amistar Cuvée Bianco '17	♀♀	6

Stachlburg Baron von Kripp

via Mitterhofer, 2
39020 Parcines/Partschins [BZ]
Tel. +39 0473968014
www.stachlburg.com

CELLAR SALES
PRE-BOOKED VISITS
ANNUAL PRODUCTION 30,000 bottles
HECTARES UNDER VINE 7.00
VITICULTURE METHOD Certified Organic

The Kripp family's historic estate is situated at the entrance to the Vinschgau Valley, an area that has been divided between viticulture and the much more widespread practice of apple cultivation since time immemorial. The farm that unfolds on Via Mitterhofer, which extends for a handful of hectares, is no exception. Their vineyards unfold in Paracines, Andriano and Naturno, at elevations between 300 and 650 meters. Organic management for over twenty years testifies to an approach in which respect for the environment is a major priority along with minimally-invasive practices in the cellar. The Pinot Nero '17 consistently expresses the valley's qualities: a faint color anticipates subtle aromas, with wild fruit intertwining with notes of fine herbs and undergrowth; the palate is light, taut and perfectly supported by acidity. The Merlot '17 exhibits a similar profile, though still seems to be in search of the right aromatic harmony amidst fruit, spices and oak; in the mouth it unfold light and supple.

Wine	Rating
● A. A. Merlot Ris. '17	TT 5
○ A. A. Terlano Sauvignon '19	TT 3
○ A. A. Val Venosta Pinot Bianco '19	TT 3
● A. A. Val Venosta Pinot Nero '17	TT 5
○ A. A. Pinot Grigio '18	T 2
○ A. A. Val Venosta Chardonnay '19	T 4
○ A. A. Valle Venosta Pinot Bianco '13	YYY 3*
○ A. A. Valle Venosta Pinot Bianco '10	YYY 3*
● A. A. Merlot Ris. '16	YY 5
○ A. A. Val Venosta Chardonnay '18	YY 4
○ A. A. Val Venosta Pinot Bianco '18	YY 3
● A. A. Val Venosta Pinot Nero '16	YY 5
● A. A. Val Venosta Pinot Nero Eustachius Ris. '15	YY 6
○ Praesepium V. T. '16	YY 5

Strasserhof Hannes Baumgartner

fraz. Novacella
loc. Unterrain, 8
39040 Varna/Vahrn [BZ]
Tel. +39 0472830804
www.strasserhof.info

CELLAR SALES
PRE-BOOKED VISITS
ACCOMMODATION
ANNUAL PRODUCTION 45,000 bottles
HECTARES UNDER VINE 5.50

It almost seems as if the Eisack Valley abandons wine-growing shortly after the village of Chiusa. But then comes Novacella, where the vineyards reemerge for one final hurrah as the landscape widens and softens before winding in the direction of the Brenner Pass or the Puster Valley. It's here that Hannes Baumgartner operates, overseeing the family farm at 700 meters above sea level. A handful of hectares perched between stone walls capture the sun's rays during the day and at night are invigorated by the cool mountain winds. Such conditions are ideal for white wines characterized by tension and finesse. A convincing selection this year, to say the least, captained by the remarkable Sylvaner '19: aromas of flowers and white fruits give way to smoky notes, while in the mouth it proves taut, spirited and linear. The new Cuvée AnJo '18, a blend of their best grapes, expresses olfactory depth and great harmony on the palate, while the Riesling '19, an aromatically citrusy wine, perfectly balances sweetness and acidity.

Wine	Rating
○ A. A. Valle Isarco Sylvaner '19	TTT 3*
○ A. A. Valle Isarco Riesling '19	TT 4
○ A. A. Sauvignon '19	TT 3
○ A. A. Valle Isarco Grüner Veltliner '19	TT 3
○ A. A. Valle Isarco Kerner '19	TT 3
○ Cuvée AnJo '18	TT 5
○ A. A. Valle Isarco Riesling '12	YYY 3*
○ A. A. Valle Isarco Riesling '11	YYY 3*
○ A. A. Valle Isarco Veltliner '10	YYY 3*
○ A. A. Valle Isarco Veltliner '09	YYY 3*
○ A. A. Valle Isarco Riesling '18	YY 4
○ A. A. Valle Isarco Veltliner '18	YY 3*

Stroblhof

loc. San Michele
via Piganò, 25
39057 Appiano/Eppan [BZ]
Tel. +39 0471662250
www.stroblhof.it

CELLAR SALES
PRE-BOOKED VISITS
ANNUAL PRODUCTION 40,000 bottles
HECTARES UNDER VINE 5.20

Travelling through the wine-growing area of Appiano one might get the impression of a rather uniform territory with a few differences due to vineyard elevations. But in reality there are marked variations, so much so that near Stroblhof evening and night temperatures are considerably lower than in the center of the village. Rosi Hanny and Andreas Nicolussi-Leck take advantage of these environmental conditions for wines that draw on the cool climate and the sunniness of the vineyards near the Mendola woods. The Pinot Nero Riserva '17 points up these very conditions, with a nose that debuts shyly on notes of berries before letting through deeper aromas of rain-soaked earth and spices. In the mouth it doesn't astound for power, but rather wins you over with its tension and length, proving harmonious and elegant. The Pinot Bianco Strahler '19, one of their great classics, plays on the freshness of white fruit and flowers, with a tapered, very long palate.

● A. A. Pinot Nero Ris. '17	🍷🍷 6
○ A. A. Chardonnay Schwarzhaus '19	🍷🍷 4
○ A. A. Pinot Bianco Strahler '19	🍷🍷 4
● A. A. Pinot Nero Pigeno '17	🍷🍷 5
○ A. A. Sauvignon Nico '19	🍷 4
○ A. A. Pinot Bianco Strahler '09	YYY 3*
● A. A. Pinot Nero Ris. '15	YYY 6
● A. A. Pinot Nero Ris. '05	YYY 5
○ A. A. Chardonnay Schwarzhaus '11	YY 3*
○ A. A. Pinot Bianco Strahler '17	YY 4
● A. A. Pinot Nero Pigeno '14	YY 5
● A. A. Pinot Nero Ris. '16	YY 6
● A. A. Pinot Nero Ris. '13	YY 6
● A. A. Pinot Nero Ris. '11	YY 6

Taschlerhof - Peter Wachtler

loc. Mara, 107
39042 Bressanone/Brixen [BZ]
Tel. +39 0472851091
www.taschlerhof.com

CELLAR SALES
PRE-BOOKED VISITS
ANNUAL PRODUCTION 30,000 bottles
HECTARES UNDER VINE 4.20

Peter Wachtler's winery is located at +600 meters above sea level in the southern part of Brixen/Bressanone, in La Mara. The area is home to extraordinarily steep, southeast facing vineyards. These grow in soil rich in schist and host the Eisack Valley's most representative grapes, in particular Sylvaner, Riesling and the ever-present Kerner. The warmth of the day, followed by cool night winds, confers richness of fruit and great acidity to the grapes, making for a profile of remarkable finesse. And elegance is the true hallmark of their Riesling '19: the nose is a whirlwind of citrus fruits, fresh flowers and a delicately smoky hint. In the mouth it reveals all its youth, with a sharp, plucky palate—all the credentials to improve further in the bottle. The Sylvaner Lahner '18 offers up more mature, deeper notes of yellow fruit, straw and dried flowers; the palate comes through full and well refreshed by acidity.

○ A. A. Valle Isarco Riesling '19	🍷🍷 4
○ A. A. Valle Isarco Sylvaner Lahner '18	🍷🍷 5
○ A. A. Valle Isarco Gewürztraminer '19	🍷🍷 4
○ A. A. Valle Isarco Kerner '19	🍷🍷 4
○ A. A. Valle Isarco Sylvaner '19	🍷🍷 3
○ A. A. Valle Isarco Riesling '14	YYY 4*
○ A. A. Valle Isarco Sylvaner '15	YYY 3*
○ A. A. Valle Isarco Sylvaner Lahner '16	YYY 5
○ A. A. Valle Isarco Riesling '18	YY 4
○ A. A. Valle Isarco Sylvaner '17	YY 3*
○ A. A. Valle Isarco Sylvaner '16	YY 3*
○ A. A. Valle Isarco Sylvaner Lahner '17	YY 5

★★Cantina Terlano

via Silberleiten, 7
39018 Terlano/Terlan [BZ]
Tel. +39 0471257135
www.cantina-terlano.com

CELLAR SALES
PRE-BOOKED VISITS
ANNUAL PRODUCTION 1,500,000 bottles
HECTARES UNDER VINE 190.00

Terlano is divided rather sharply between the left and right banks of the Adige river. Closer to Terlano the terrain is red, rich in porphyry and with very little fine soil, while near Andriano, whose co-op winery merged with Terlano, the presence of the Mendola Pass makes for yellow calcareous-clay, medium-textured soil. Rudi Kofler brings great sensitivity in tending to grapes shaped by such different conditions. Cooler or warmer positions, elevations ranging from 250 to 900 meters all come together in a selection in which elegance and longevity are distinctive features. The Vorberg '19 is at the top of its game. It's a Pinot Bianco that explores the typology's richer, deeper side. On the nose it's dominated by notes of ripe white fruit and dried flowers, with moderate oak in the background, while the palate reveals its fullness and poise, unfolding nicely through the finish. Both both wineries perform at the highest levels, and the rare Cuvée Terlaner I° is a real privilege to taste.

○ A. A. Terlano Pinot Bianco Vorberg Ris. '17	🍷🍷🍷	5
○ A. A. Terlano Pinot Bianco Rarity '07	🍷🍷	8
○ A. A. Terlano Sauvignon Quarz '18	🍷🍷	6
○ A. A. Chardonnay Doran Andriano Ris. '17	🍷🍷	4
○ A. A. Gewürztraminer Lunare '18	🍷🍷	6
● A. A. Lagrein Porphyr Ris. '17	🍷🍷	6
● A. A. Lagrein Tor di Lupo Andriano Ris. '17	🍷🍷	4
● A. A. Merlot Gant Andriano Ris. '17	🍷🍷	4
● A. A. Pinot Nero Monticol Ris. '17	🍷🍷	5
○ A. A. Terlano Chardonnay Kreuth '18	🍷🍷	4
○ A. A. Terlano Cuvée '19	🍷🍷	4
○ A. A. Terlano Nova Domus Ris. '17	🍷🍷	6
○ A. A. Terlano Sauvignon Winkl '19	🍷🍷	3
○ A. A. Terlano Sauvignon Quarz '17	🍸🍸🍸	6

★Tiefenbrunner

fraz. Niclara
via Castello, 4
39040 Cortaccia/Kurtatsch [BZ]
Tel. +39 0471880122
www.tiefenbrunner.com

CELLAR SALES
PRE-BOOKED VISITS
RESTAURANT SERVICE
ANNUAL PRODUCTION 650,000 bottles
HECTARES UNDER VINE 78.00

Looking at the area where Tiefenbrunner is located, one might think of a winery that produces rich, mature wines, the result of viticulture characterized by a warm, sunny climate as well as a natural setting that is in some ways more southern than alpine. The reality is the opposite. Due to the position of vineyards that reach high mountain elevations towards the Mendola Pass, the winery's style is linear and spirited. Christof Tiefenbrunner, together with kellermeister Stephan Rohregger, interprets the South Tyrolean Unterland with rigor and finesse. Once more the Feldmarschall put in a performance for the ages. The 2018 is redolent of citrus and mineral scents, dried flowers and spices, all of which animate a full palate marked by great acidic tension. The Sauvignon Rachtl Riserva '17 indulges slowly, first with its sulphurous tones, then with nuances of white fruit and aromatic herbs, sensations that follow through on an energetic, progressively unfolding palate.

○ A. A. Müller Thurgau Feldmarschall von Fenner '18	🍷🍷🍷	6
○ A. A. Chardonnay V. Au Ris. '17	🍷🍷	3*
○ A. A. Sauvignon V. Rachtl Ris. '17	🍷🍷	4
● A. A. Cabernet Merlot Linticlarus Cuvée Ris. '17	🍷🍷	6
● A. A. Cabernet Sauvignon V. Toren Ris. '16	🍷🍷	8
○ A. A. Gewürztraminer Tardus V.T. '16	🍷🍷	6
○ A. A. Gewürztraminer Turmhof '18	🍷🍷	5
● A. A. Lagrein Turmhof '18	🍷🍷	3
○ A. A. Pinot Bianco Anna '18	🍷🍷	3
● A. A. Pinot Nero Turmhof '18	🍷🍷	3
○ A. A. Sauvignon Turmhof '18	🍷🍷	4
● A. A. Schiava Turmhof '19	🍷🍷	2*
○ A. A. Müller Thurgau Feldmarschall von Fenner '17	🍸🍸🍸	6

★★Cantina Tramin

s.da del Vino, 144
39040 Termeno/Tramin [BZ]
Tel. +39 0471096633
www.cantinatramin.it

CELLAR SALES
PRE-BOOKED VISITS
ANNUAL PRODUCTION 1,500,000 bottles
HECTARES UNDER VINE 250.00

The cooperative led by Willy Sturz extends throughout Bassa Atesina (South Tyrolean Unterland), with 300 members active in the areas of Tramin, Egna, Ora and Montagna. Gewürztraminer is certainly the grape variety with which this sunny area is most associated, but the possibility of cultivating at high elevations makes for a highly worthy range in which even grapes in need of cooler climates are represented. Careful viticultural management by its growers and winemaking aimed at highlighting the attributes of each individual plot form the basis of Cantina Tramin's success. The Nussbaumer '18 features intense aromas of candied citrus fruits, spices and orange blossom, all of which we find on a palate that's powerful yet elegant, taut and long by virtue of sapidity. The Pinot Grigio Unterebner '18 is one of the best in the region: a wine that combines richness and elegance. Finally, we mention the great work being done with Chardonnay, which has led to the Troy, a limited edition wine.

○ A. A. Gewürztraminer Nussbaumer '18	𝕐𝕐𝕐	5
○ A. A. Gewürztraminer Terminum V. T. '17	𝕐𝕐	7
○ A. A. Pinot Grigio Unterebner '18	𝕐𝕐	5
○ A. A. Bianco Stoan '18	𝕐𝕐	4
● A. A. Cabernet Merlot Loam Ris. '18	𝕐𝕐	5
○ A. A. Gewürztraminer Selida '19	𝕐𝕐	3
● A. A. Lagrein Urban Ris. '18	𝕐𝕐	5
○ A. A. Pinot Bianco Moriz '19	𝕐𝕐	2*
● A. A. Pinot Nero Maglen Ris. '17	𝕐𝕐	5
● A. A. Pinot Nero Marjun '18	𝕐𝕐	4
○ A. A. Sauvignon Pepi '19	𝕐𝕐	3
● A. A. Schiava Freisinger '19	𝕐𝕐	3
○ A. A. Gewürztraminer Nussbaumer '17	YYY	5

Erbhof Unterganzner Josephus Mayr

fraz. Cardano
via Campiglio, 15
39053 Bolzano/Bozen
Tel. +39 0471365582
www.mayr-unterganzner.it

CELLAR SALES
PRE-BOOKED VISITS
ANNUAL PRODUCTION 65,000 bottles
HECTARES UNDER VINE 9.00

Josephus Mayr has been able to give Santa Maddalena a new profile, one that's not content with immediate pleasantness and roundness of fruit, but that explores complexity and multifaceted structure through depth, stratification and harmony. At the base of it all is the great precision with which the family vineyards are managed. These lie close to the course of the Eisack river and have, over time, found development at the Kampenn farmstead. Two very different soil types, even if they're both grounded in porphyry, give rise to a range in which reds tend to dominate. Mayr has managed to highlight Lagrein's attributes through a distinct style, as expressed by the Riserva '17. Its compact and inky color anticipates scents of ripe dark fruit embellished by smoky hints, spices and violet. Full and powerful, its tannins are compensated for by its generous palate, which proves balanced and highly drinkable. The Composition Reif '17 is a rich, powerful a Bordeaux blend topped off with a spray of Lagrein.

● A. A. Lagrein Ris. '17	𝕐𝕐	5
⊙ A. A. Lagrein Kretzer Rosato V. T. '19	𝕐𝕐	3
● A. A. Santa Maddalena Cl. Heilman '18	𝕐𝕐	3
○ A. A. Sauvignon Platt & Pignat '19	𝕐𝕐	3
● Composition Reif '17	𝕐𝕐	6
● Lamarein '17	𝕐𝕐	6
● A. A. Lagrein Ris. '13	YYY	5
● A. A. Lagrein Ris. '11	YYY	5
● A. A. Cabernet Ris. '14	YY	5
● A. A. Lagrein Ris. '16	YY	5
● A. A. Lagrein Ris. '15	YY	5
● A. A. Lagrein Ris. '14	YY	5
● A. A. Santa Maddalena Cl. '17	YY	3*
● Composition Reif '15	YY	6
● Lamarein '15	YY	6

Untermoserho Georg Ramoser

via Santa Maddalena, 36
39100 Bolzano/Bozen
Tel. +39 0471975481
untermoserhof@rolmail.net

CELLAR SALES
PRE-BOOKED VISITS
ACCOMMODATION
ANNUAL PRODUCTION 30,000 bottles
HECTARES UNDER VINE 3.70

Georg Ramoser's small estate unfolds across a handful of hectares below the small church of St. Magdalena, on the enchanting hill at the gates of the capital of Bolzano. The loose, sunlit soils, which have long hosted the Schiavo grape, are refreshed at night by the currents coming in from the Eisack valley or descending off the Renon plateau, allowing the grapes to ripen well and rich in aromas. Production follows two main stylistic lines: finesse and tension for the lighter wines, power and structure for Lagrein and Merlot. The Santa Maddalena Hub '18, made with grapes from their oldest vineyards, offers up a multifaceted bouquet on the nose, with red fruit meeting medicinal herbs and delicious spices. In the mouth tension governs delicately, making for a highly drinkable wine. The Lagrein Riserva '17 pours a dark color, heralding intensely fruity and peppery aromas; in the mouth it impresses for its warm, pervasive touch, all nicely invigorated by tannins.

● A. A. Lagrein Ris. '17	🍷🍷 4
● A. A. Santa Maddalena Cl. Hub '18	🍷🍷 3*
○ A. A. Chardonnay Morain '18	🍷🍷 3
● A. A. Merlot Ris. '17	🍷🍷 4
● A. A. Santa Maddalena Cl. '19	🍷🍷 3
● A. A. Lagrein Scuro Ris. '03	🍷🍷🍷 4*
● A. A. Santa Maddalena Cl. Hueb '16	🍷🍷🍷 3*
● A. A. Lagrein Ris. '16	🍷🍷 4
● A. A. Lagrein Ris. '08	🍷🍷 4
● A. A. Lagrein Untermoserhof Ris. '11	🍷🍷 5
● A. A. Lagrein Untermoserhof Ris. '10	🍷🍷 4
● A. A. Santa Maddalena Cl. Hueb '17	🍷🍷 3*

★Tenuta Unterortl Castel Juval

loc. Juval, 1b
39020 Castelbello Ciardes/Kastelbell Tschars [BZ]
Tel. +39 0473667580
www.unterortl.it

CELLAR SALES
PRE-BOOKED VISITS
ANNUAL PRODUCTION 33,000 bottles
HECTARES UNDER VINE 4.00

Martin Aurich and his wife Gisela run one of the region's smallest and most renowned wineries, perched on the spurs that lead from the wide and sunny Vinschgau valley to the more hidden Schnalstal valley. A handful of hectares have literally been snatched from the mountain, small patches that have hosted Riesling, in particular, for over 20 years, though there's also a bit of Pinot Bianco, Pinot Nero, Müller Thurgau and old local varieties. Painstaking care in the vineyard is complemented by a production approach that seeks to bring out the best of each single batch of grapes. Made with grapes from the oldest and best-exposed vineyards, the Riesling Unterortl '19 offers up vibrant notes of flowers and citrus fruits, sensations that follow through on a dynamic, sapid palate. The Windbichel vineyard gives rise to a few thousand bottles of a deeper and more complex Riesling, as evidenced by the 2018: floral and exotic fruit scents are echoed by a succulent and very long palate.

○ A. A. Val Venosta Riesling Unterortl '19	🍷🍷 4
○ A. A. Val Venosta Riesling Windbichel '18	🍷🍷 5
○ A. A. Val Venosta Pinot Bianco '19	🍷🍷 2*
● A. A. Val Venosta Pinot Nero Ris. '17	🍷🍷 5
○ A. A. Val Venosta Riesling Gletscherschliff '19	🍷🍷 3
○ A. A. Val Venosta Pinot Bianco Castel Juval '13	🍷🍷🍷 3*
○ A. A. Val Venosta Riesling '14	🍷🍷🍷 4*
○ A. A. Val Venosta Riesling Unterortl '15	🍷🍷🍷 4*
○ A. A. Val Venosta Riesling Weingarten Windbichel '16	🍷🍷🍷 5
○ A. A. Val Venosta Riesling Windbichel '17	🍷🍷🍷 5
○ A. A. Val Venosta Riesling Windbichel '15	🍷🍷🍷 5

Cantina Produttori Valle Isarco

via Coste, 50
39043 Chiusa/Klausen [BZ]
Tel. +39 0472847553
www.cantinavalleisarco.it

CELLAR SALES
PRE-BOOKED VISITS
ANNUAL PRODUCTION 900,000 bottles
HECTARES UNDER VINE 150.00
SUSTAINABLE WINERY

About 20 members founded Cantina della Valle Isarco in the early 1960s. Today the number of members has grown to 130, and about 150 hectares are covered along the valley, often small patches of land that had to be teased out of the mountain at elevations of anywhere from 300-1000 meters above sea level. These are dedicated, almost exclusively, to the white grape varieties used in their range, which is characterized by elegance and tension. The Aristos line represents their premium offerings, wines obtained only from the best vineyards worked by the most adept members. The Grüner Veltliner '19 pours a delicate straw-yellow color, introducing aromas of white fruit and hay; in the mouth it reveals a supple body perfectly supported by acidity and a sapid verve. The Sylvaner '19 is still marked by very youthful aromas, but in the mouth it changes pace, proving full, dynamic and endowed with great length, which allows it to close clean and harmonious.

Wine	Rating
○ A. A. Valle Isarco Sylvaner Aristos '19	🍷🍷 4
○ A. A. Valle Isarco Veltliner Aristos '19	🍷🍷 3*
○ A. A. Pinot Bianco Aristos '19	🍷🍷 4
○ A. A. Sauvignon Aristos '19	🍷🍷 4
○ A. A. Valle Isarco Gewürztraminer Aristos '19	🍷🍷 4
○ A. A. Valle Isarco Kerner Aristos '19	🍷🍷 4
○ A. A. Valle Isarco Kerner Passito Nectaris '18	🍷🍷 6
○ A. A. Valle Isarco Kerner Sabiona '18	🍷🍷 5
○ A. A. Valle Isarco Müller Thurgau Aristos '19	🍷🍷 4
○ A. A. Valle Isarco Pinot Grigio Aristos '19	🍷🍷 4
○ A. A. Valle Isarco Riesling Aristos '19	🍷🍷 4
○ A. A. Valle Isarco Sylvaner Sabiona '18	🍷🍷 5

Von Blumen

fraz. Pochi, 18/Bulcholz, 18
39040 Salorno/Salurn [BZ]
Tel. +39 0457230110
www.vonblumenwine.com

CELLAR SALES
PRE-BOOKED VISITS
ANNUAL PRODUCTION 44,000 bottles
HECTARES UNDER VINE 11.00
SUSTAINABLE WINERY

Only a short time ago Roberta, Cristina and Giuseppe Fugatti acquired an important property in Pochi di Salorno: a little more than 10 hectares in an enchanting position, at about 500 meters above sea level. Primarily the grapes that do best on these calcareous and porphyry soils are cultivated. Year after year the quality of their wines has grown more constant and noticeable. The decision to delay the release of their most ambitious wines confirms the farsightedness with which they operate. The Pinot Bianco Flowers '18 pours a lovely, bright color, heralding an aromatic suite in which ripe fruit has plenty of company: floral and mineral notes emerge along with a pinch of oak that still needs to integrate. The palate is sapid and harmonious, elegantly stretching towards a crisp finish. The Pinot Nero '18 is also notable, a varietal and almost exemplary expression of the grape that wins you over with its harmony and pleasantness.

Wine	Rating
○ A. A. Pinot Bianco Flowers Selection '18	🍷🍷 5
○ A. A. Gewürztraminer '19	🍷🍷 4
● A. A. Lagrein '18	🍷🍷 4
○ A. A. Pinot Bianco '19	🍷🍷 3
● A. A. Pinot Nero '19	🍷🍷 4
○ A. A. Sauvignon '19	🍷🍷 3
○ A. A. Gewürztraminer '18	🍷🍷 4
● A. A. Lagrein '17	🍷🍷 4
○ A. A. Pinot Bianco Flowers '16	🍷🍷 5
○ A. A. Pinot Bianco Flowers Selection '17	🍷🍷 5
○ A. A. Pinot Bianco Flowers Selection '15	🍷🍷 5
○ A. A. Pinot Bianco Flowers Selection '14	🍷🍷 3*
○ A. A. Sauvignon Flowers Selection '17	🍷🍷 5

★★Elena Walch

via A. Hofer, 1
39040 Termeno/Tramin [BZ]
Tel. +39 0471860172
www.elenawalch.com

CELLAR SALES
RESTAURANT SERVICE
ANNUAL PRODUCTION 550,000 bottles
HECTARES UNDER VINE 65.00

The historic producer owned by Elena Walch cultivates over 30 hectares of land in some of Bassa Atesina and Oltradige's most fruitful areas. Highlights include the Kastelaz and Castel Ringberg vineyards (the former overlooks the small village of Tramin from above, the latter is a gentle east-facing slope near Kaltern). Other small tracts form a prized viticultural patrimony, making for a high-profile range of wines. If their more ambitious wines refer back to the vineyard of origin, the Grande Cuvée Beyond The Clouds is, instead, a selection of the best grapes. The 2018 put in a performance for the ages: the nose captures a whirlwind of fruits, flowers and spices, all of which is brought out on a palate where the watchword is 'elegance'. The Lagrein Riserva '17, made with grapes from the Castel Ringberg estate, is characterized by dark, fruity aromas, with smoky notes more evident on its full, rigorous palate.

Wine	Rating
○ A. A. Bianco Grande Cuvée Beyond the Clouds '18	🍷🍷🍷 7
○ A. A. Gewürztraminer V. Kastelaz '19	🍷🍷 5
● A. A. Lagrein V. Castel Ringberg Ris. '17	🍷🍷 5
● A. A. Cabernet Sauvignon V. Castel Ringberg Ris. '17	🍷🍷 8
○ A. A. Chardonnay V. Castel Ringberg Ris. '17	🍷🍷 7
● A. A. Merlot V. Kastelaz Ris. '17	🍷🍷 6
○ A. A. Pinot Bianco Kristallberg '18	🍷🍷 4
● A. A. Pinot Nero Ludwig '17	🍷🍷 5
○ A. A. Sauvignon V. Castel Ringberg '19	🍷🍷 4
○ A. A. Bianco Beyond the Clouds '16	🍷🍷🍷 7
○ A. A. Gewürztraminer Kastelaz '13	🍷🍷🍷 5
○ A. A. Gewürztraminer V. Kastelaz '18	🍷🍷🍷 5
● A. A. Lagrein Castel Ringberg Ris. '11	🍷🍷🍷 5

★Tenuta Waldgries

loc. Santa Giustina, 2
39100 Bolzano/Bozen
Tel. +39 0471323603
www.waldgries.it

CELLAR SALES
PRE-BOOKED VISITS
ANNUAL PRODUCTION 65,000 bottles
HECTARES UNDER VINE 8.20

Santa Maddalena is situated just a stone's throw from Bolzano: south-east facing slopes traditionally dedicated to Schiavo and Lagrein. This is the home of the Plattner family's historic winery, a producer that over the last few decades has expanded its wine-growing patrimoney to the area of Appiano (where Christian planted Sauvignon) and Cornaiano (where Pinot Bianco is grown). For the rest, all their attention goes to Bolzano's two classic grapes, which are accompanied by Moscato Rosa as well. The Santa Maddalena '19 put in a fantastic performance, offering up vibrant aromas of wild fruit, violet and spices, all of which carry over on a sapid, harmonious and highly pleasant palate. Energetic and sophisticated, the Pinot Bianco Isos '17 alternates sulphurous notes with toasty hints. A wide range of Lagrein are offered, with the Roblinus de' Waldgries '17 topping our preferences, an aromatically deep wine that's close-knit and gutsy on the palate.

Wine	Rating
● A. A. Santa Maddalena Cl. '19	🍷🍷🍷 3*
● A. A. Lagrein Roblinus de Waldgries '17	🍷🍷 8
○ A. A. Pinot Bianco Isos Ris. '17	🍷🍷 4
● A. A. Lagrein Mirell Ris. '17	🍷🍷 6
● A. A. Lagrein Ris. '17	🍷🍷 5
● A. A. Moscato Rosa '18	🍷🍷 5
● A. A. Lagrein Mirell '09	🍷🍷🍷 6
● A. A. Lagrein Mirell Ris. '15	🍷🍷🍷 6
● A. A. Lagrein Scuro Mirell '08	🍷🍷🍷 6
● A. A. Santa Maddalena Cl. Antheos '16	🍷🍷🍷 5
● A. A. Santa Maddalena Cl. Antheos '13	🍷🍷🍷 4*
● A. A. Santa Maddalena Cl. Antheos '12	🍷🍷🍷 4*
● A. A. Santa Maddalena Cl. Antheos '11	🍷🍷🍷 4*

Wassererhof

loc. Novale di Fiè, 21
39050 Fiè allo Sciliar/Völs am Schlern [BZ]
Tel. +39 0471724114
www.wassererhof.com

CELLAR SALES
PRE-BOOKED VISITS
RESTAURANT SERVICE
ANNUAL PRODUCTION 35,000 bottles
HECTARES UNDER VINE 4.00

In the late 1990s, the Mock family acquired ownership of an old farm near a spring in Novale di Fiè, the Wassererhof. In just a couple of years, the building was perfectly restored, giving rise to the farmstead and trattoria. The property is run by two brothers. Andreas is head of the kitchen, while Christoph takes care of viticultural and enological management. The vineyards are concentrated mainly around the cellar, in the southern part of the Eisack Valley and in the Costa area of Bolzano, where red grape varieties are grown. The Pinot Grigio '18 stood out among their reliable selection of wines, playing on a lovely combination of ripe fruit and toasty notes, which harken back to the use of oak, while in the mouth it proves rich, sapid and juicy. The Sauvignon '18 is characterized by more mature exotic fruit, aromas that anticipate a racy palate of good length. The only red presented this year was the Cabernet Riserva '17, which exhibits nice consistency and precision.

Wine	Glasses	Price
● A. A. Cabernet Ris. '17	**YY**	3
○ A. A. Pinot Bianco '18	**YY**	3
○ A. A. Pinot Grigio '18	**YY**	3
○ A. A. Sauvignon '18	**YY**	3
○ A. A. Sauvignon Ris. '17	**YY**	4
● A. A. Cabernet Ris. '16	YY	3
● A. A. Cabernet Ris. '15	YY	3
○ A. A. Pinot Bianco '17	YY	3
○ A. A. Pinot Bianco '16	YY	3
○ A. A. Pinot Bianco '15	YY	3
○ A. A. Pinot Grigio '17	YY	3
● A. A. Santa Maddalena Cl. '17	YY	3
● A. A. Santa Maddalena Cl. Mumelterhof '15	YY	3
○ A. A. Sauvignon '17	YY	3
○ A. A. Sauvignon '15	YY	3
○ A.A. Sauvignon '16	YY	3

Josef Weger

loc. Cornaiano/Girlan
via Casa del Gesù, 17
39057 Appiano/Eppan [BZ]
Tel. +39 0471662416
www.wegerhof.it

CELLAR SALES
PRE-BOOKED VISITS
ACCOMMODATION AND RESTAURANT SERVICE
ANNUAL PRODUCTION 80,000 bottles
HECTARES UNDER VINE 8.00

This historic Cornaiano winery has been run by the Weger family for 6 generations. Their bond with territory's viticulture and wines has never waned, even in the darkest years, and over time the Wegers began exploring sales as well as production, with the establishment of a wholesale distribution company in Austria that's still owned by the family today. The vineyards span fewer than 10 hectares in Bassa Atesina (South Tyrolean Unterland) and Oltradige, in Cornaiano in particular. The Maso delle Rose line represents the top of their range, as demonstrated once more by the Pinot Bianco '18, the result of blending equal parts of wines matured in steel and oak. The nose reveals notes of ripe fruit, flowers and a slightly spicy nuance; in the mouth it comes through supple, juicy and satisfying. The Sauvignon '18 is clear and focused in its vegetal aromas, approachable and pleasant on the palate.

Wine	Glasses	Price
○ A. A. Gewürztraminer Maso delle Rose '18	**YY**	3
● A. A. Merlot Maso delle Rose '16	**YY**	5
○ A. A. Pinot Bianco Maso delle Rose '18	**YY**	4
○ A. A. Sauvignon Maso delle Rose '18	**YY**	4
● Joanni Maso delle Rose '17	**Y**	4
○ A. A. Gewürztraminer Artyo '18	YY	3
● A. A. Merlot Maso delle Rose '13	YY	5
○ A. A. Müller Thurgau Pursgla '18	YY	3
○ A. A. Pinot Bianco Maso delle Rose '13	YY	4
○ A. A. Pinot Bianco Maso delle Rose '10	YY	4
○ A. A. Pinot Grigio Ried '18	YY	3
● A. A. Pinot Nero Maso delle Rose '16	YY	5
○ A. A. Sauvignon Myron '18	YY	3

Weingut Niklas Dieter Sölva

loc. San Nicolò
via delle Fontane, 31a
39052 Caldaro/Kaltern [BZ]
Tel. +39 0471963434
www.niklaserhof.it

CELLAR SALES
PRE-BOOKED VISITS
ANNUAL PRODUCTION 50,000 bottles
HECTARES UNDER VINE 7.00

The area around Lake Caldaro provides the necessary temperatures and sunshine for those grapes most in need of heat to ripen. However, you only have to climb a little towards Mendola to find a completely different climate, one marked by greater temperature fluctuations and much cooler nights, ideal for more delicate, white varieties. The Sölva family cultivate vineyards in these two areas, making for a range of great stylistic precision. Matured in steel, the Lake Caldaro Hecht is made with grapes from their Barleit plots. The 2019 is a memorable version by virtue of small wild red berry hints that follow through on a dynamic, juicy, immediately pleasant palate. Their Prutznai vineyards give rise to the DJJ Riserva '17, a Merlot with a mature, enticing profile dominated by red fruit and enriched by a background of spices and oak. In the mouth it's full, powerful, well governed by dense tannic texture.

- ● A. A. Lago di Caldaro Cl. Sup. Hect Klaser '19 — 🍷🍷 2*
- ○ A. A. Kerner Luxs '19 — 🍷🍷 3
- ● A. A. Lagrein Bos Taurus Mondevinum Ris. '17 — 🍷🍷 4
- ● A. A. Lagrein Cabernet Klaser Stoanadler Ris. '17 — 🍷🍷 4
- ● A. A. Merlot DJJ Ris. '17 — 🍷🍷 4
- ○ A. A. Pinot Bianco Salamander Klaser Ris. '17 — 🍷🍷 4
- ○ A. A. Sauvignon Doxs '19 — 🍷🍷 3
- ○ A. A. Kerner Libellula Mondevinum Ris. '17 — 🍷 4
- ○ A. A. Pinot Bianco Hos '19 — 🍷 3
- ○ A. A. Pinot Bianco Klaser Ris. '15 — 🍸🍸🍸 4*
- ● A. A. Lago di Caldaro Cl. Sup. Klaser '17 — 🍸🍸 2*
- ○ A. A. Pinot Bianco Hos '18 — 🍸🍸 3*

Peter Zemmer

s.da del Vino, 24
39040 Cortina Sulla Strada del Vino/Kurtinig [BZ]
Tel. +39 0471817143
www.peterzemmer.com

CELLAR SALES
PRE-BOOKED VISITS
ANNUAL PRODUCTION 500,000 bottles
HECTARES UNDER VINE 65.00

Peter Zemmer's cellar is located on the wine road in Cortina, the only municipality in the province of Adige on the plains, at the bottom of the Adige valley. The vineyards extend over many hectares and stretch in several directions, climbing up the hills to elevations of almost 1,000 meters. Each variety is cultivated in the best suited areas. In the lower hills we find mainly Pinot Grigio and Chardonnay, at 800 meters Caprile hosts Müller Thurgau, and at 1,000 meters Kofl provides the best conditions for their Pinot Nero. Their most ambitious wines are aging for another year, but in the meantime the excellent Pinot Blanc '19 kept us company. Fresh aromas call up white-fleshed fruit and flowers, while in the mouth it expresses all its territorial qualities, proving taut and dynamic. The Pinot Nero Rolhüt '19 plays on varietal nuances and a supple, juicy, highly pleasant palate. The intriguing Müller Thurgau Caprile '19 is an aromatically delicate wine, highly sapid on the palate.

- ○ A. A. Gewürztraminer Frauenrigl '18 — 🍷🍷 3
- ○ A. A. Müller Thurgau Caprile '19 — 🍷🍷 3
- ○ A. A. Pinot Bianco '19 — 🍷🍷 3
- ○ A. A. Pinot Grigio '19 — 🍷🍷 3
- ● A. A. Pinot Nero Rolhütt '19 — 🍷🍷 4
- ○ A. A. Riesling '19 — 🍷🍷 2*
- ○ A. A. Sauvignon '19 — 🍷🍷 3
- ○ A. A. Chardonnay '19 — 🍷 2
- ○ A. A. Pinot Grigio Giatl Ris. '15 — 🍸🍸🍸 3*
- ○ A. A. Chardonnay Crivelli Ris. '16 — 🍸🍸 4
- ○ A. A. Chardonnay Crivelli Ris. '15 — 🍸🍸 4
- ○ A. A. Chardonnay V. Crivelli Ris. '17 — 🍸🍸 4
- ○ A. A. Pinot Grigio Giatl Ris. '17 — 🍸🍸 3*
- ○ A. A. Pinot Grigio Giatl Ris. '16 — 🍸🍸 3*

Baron Longo

via Val di Fiemme 30
39044 Egna/Neumarkt [BZ]
Tel. +39 0471 820007
www.baronlongo.com

ANNUAL PRODUCTION 30,000 bottles
HECTARES UNDER VINE 17.00

○ Liebenstein '18	🍷🍷 6
● Wellenburg '17	🍷🍷 6
○ Hohenstein Gewürztraminer '18	🍷 6

Baron Widmann

Endergasse, 3
39040 Cortaccia/Kurtatsch [BZ]
Tel. +39 0471880092
www.baron-widmann.it

CELLAR SALES
PRE-BOOKED VISITS
ANNUAL PRODUCTION 35,000 bottles
HECTARES UNDER VINE 15.00

● A. A. Cabernet Merlot V. Auhof '16	🍷🍷 7
○ A. A. Sauvignon '18	🍷🍷 3
○ Weiss '18	🍷 4

Befehlhof

via Vezzano, 14
39028 Silandro/Schlanders [BZ]
Tel. +39 0473742197
www.befehlhof.it

CELLAR SALES
PRE-BOOKED VISITS
ANNUAL PRODUCTION 7,000 bottles
HECTARES UNDER VINE 1.20

○ A. A. Val Venosta Pinot Bianco '19	🍷🍷 4
○ Jera '19	🍷🍷 3
○ A. A. Val Venosta Riesling '19	🍷 5
● Zweigelt '18	🍷 5

Bergmannhof

loc. San Paolo
Riva di Sotto, 46
39050 Appiano/Eppan [BZ]
Tel. +39 0471637082
www.bergmannhof.it

CELLAR SALES
PRE-BOOKED VISITS
ANNUAL PRODUCTION 13,000 bottles
HECTARES UNDER VINE 2.20

○ A. A. Chardonnay Ris. '17	🍷🍷 5
● A.A. Lagrein Ris. '17	🍷🍷 5
● Hoamet '17	🍷🍷 4
● Kalch '16	🍷 6

Castello Rametz

loc. Maia Alta
via Labers, 4
39012 Merano/Meran [BZ]
Tel. +39 0473211011
www.rametz.com

CELLAR SALES
PRE-BOOKED VISITS
RESTAURANT SERVICE
ANNUAL PRODUCTION 400,000 bottles
HECTARES UNDER VINE 8.00

● A. A. Pinot Nero Castello '15	🍷🍷 5
○ A. A. Sauvignon '19	🍷🍷 3
○ Castel Monreale Extra Brut '15	🍷🍷 5
○ A. A. Riesling '19	🍷 3

Tenuta Donà

fraz. Riva di Sotto
39057 Appiano/Eppan [BZ]
Tel. +39 0473221866
www.weingut-dona.com

CELLAR SALES
PRE-BOOKED VISITS
ACCOMMODATION
ANNUAL PRODUCTION 30,000 bottles
HECTARES UNDER VINE 6.00

○ A. A. Sauvignon '19	🍷🍷 5
● A. A. Schiava '19	🍷🍷 3
○ A. A. Pinot Bianco '19	🍷 3

Eichenstein

VIA CASTEL GATTO, 34
39012 MERANO/MERAN [BZ]
TEL. +39 3442820179
www.eichenstein.it

ANNUAL PRODUCTION 25,000 bottles
HECTARES UNDER VINE 4.50
SUSTAINABLE WINERY

- ● A. A. Merlot Cabernet Franc Baccara Ris. '17 🍷🍷 5
- ● A. A. Pinot Nero Amantus '18 🍷🍷 4
- ○ A. A. Sauvignon Stein '18 🍷🍷 5

Schloss Englar

LOC. PIGENO, 42
39057 APPIANO/EPPAN [BZ]
TEL. +39 0471662628
www.weingut-englar.com

ANNUAL PRODUCTION 15,000 bottles
HECTARES UNDER VINE 7.00

- ○ A. A. Chardonnay Ris. '17 🍷🍷 5
- ○ A. A. Pinot Bianco '18 🍷🍷 3
- ○ A. A. Pinot Bianco Ris. '17 🍷🍷 5
- ● A. A. Pinot Nero '17 🍷 4

Fliederhof - Stefan Ramoser

LOC. SANTA MADDALENA DI SOTTO, 33
39100 BOLZANO/BOZEN
TEL. +39 0471979048
www.fliederhof.it

CELLAR SALES
PRE-BOOKED VISITS
ANNUAL PRODUCTION 25,000 bottles
HECTARES UNDER VINE 2.40

- ● A. A. Santa Maddalena Cl. Gran Marie '18 🍷🍷 4
- ● A. A. Lagrein Ris. '17 🍷🍷 5

Haidenhof

VIA MONTELEONE, 17
39010 CERMES/TSCHERMS [BZ]
TEL. +39 0473562392
www.haidenhof.it

CELLAR SALES
PRE-BOOKED VISITS
RESTAURANT SERVICE
ANNUAL PRODUCTION 30,000 bottles
HECTARES UNDER VINE 3.50

- ○ A. A. Kerner '19 🍷🍷 3
- ● A. A. Pinot Nero '18 🍷🍷 5
- ○ A. A. Sauvignon V. Ofenweingarten '18 🍷🍷 5
- ○ A.A. Sauvignon '19 🍷🍷 2*

Himmelreichhof

VIA CONVENTO, 15A
39020 CASTELBELLO CIARDES/KASTELBELL TSCHARS [BZ]
TEL. +39 0473624417
www.himmelreich-hof.info

ANNUAL PRODUCTION 20,000 bottles
HECTARES UNDER VINE 3.50

- ○ A.A. Val Venosta Riesling Geieregg '18 🍷🍷 4

Kandlerhof

VIA SANTA MADDALENA DI SOTTO, 30
39100 BOLZANO/BOZEN
TEL. +39 0471973033
www.kandlerhof.it

ANNUAL PRODUCTION 20,000 bottles
HECTARES UNDER VINE 2.00

- ○ A. A. Sauvignon '19 🍷🍷 4
- ● A. A. Lagrein '19 🍷 3

Tenuta Kränzelhof Graf Franz Pfeil

via Palade, 1
39010 Cermes/Tscherms [BZ]
Tel. +39 0473564549
www.kraenzelhof.it

CELLAR SALES
PRE-BOOKED VISITS
ANNUAL PRODUCTION 35,000 bottles
HECTARES UNDER VINE 6.00

- ○ Dorado Passito '17 — 🍷🍷 6
- ● Libra Kunstwerk der Natur Pinot Nero '17 — 🍷🍷 6
- ● Sagittarius '15 — 🍷🍷 7

Larcherhof - Spögler

via Rencio, 82
39100 Bolzano/Bozen
Tel. +39 0471365034
larcherhof@yahoo.de

CELLAR SALES
PRE-BOOKED VISITS
ANNUAL PRODUCTION 30,000 bottles
HECTARES UNDER VINE 5.00

- ● A. A. Lagrein '17 — 🍷🍷 3
- ● A. A. Lagrein Rivelaun Ris. '16 — 🍷🍷 4
- ○ A. A. Pinot Grigio '19 — 🍷 3
- ● A.A. Santa Maddalena Cl. '19 — 🍷 2

Lehengut

via delle Fonti, 2
39020 Colsano
Tel. +39 3487562676
www.lehengut.it

ANNUAL PRODUCTION 10,000 bottles
HECTARES UNDER VINE 3.00
VITICULTURE METHOD Certified Organic

- ○ A. A. Val Venosta Riesling '19 — 🍷🍷 3
- ○ A. A. Val Venosta Pinot Bianco '19 — 🍷 3

Lieselehof Werner Morandell

via Kardatsch, 6
39052 Caldaro/Kaltern [BZ]
Tel. +39 3299011593
www.lieselehof.com

CELLAR SALES
PRE-BOOKED VISITS
ACCOMMODATION
ANNUAL PRODUCTION 20,000 bottles
HECTARES UNDER VINE 3.00
VITICULTURE METHOD Certified Organic

- ○ Julian '19 — 🍷🍷 3
- ○ Sweet Claire '18 — 🍷🍷 6
- ○ Vino del Passo '19 — 🍷🍷 6
- ○ Lieselehof Brut '16 — 🍷 7

Marinushof - Heinrich Pohl

loc. Maragno
s.da Vecchia, 9b
39020 Castelbello Ciardes/Kastelbell Tschars [BZ]
Tel. +39 0473624717
www.marinushof.it

CELLAR SALES
PRE-BOOKED VISITS
ACCOMMODATION
ANNUAL PRODUCTION 20,000 bottles
HECTARES UNDER VINE 2.20
SUSTAINABLE WINERY

- ○ A. A. Val Venosta Pinot Grigio '19 — 🍷🍷 4
- ● A. A. Val Venosta Pinot Nero '18 — 🍷🍷 5
- ○ A. A. Val Venosta Riesling '19 — 🍷 4
- ● Zweigelt Primus '18 — 🍷 5

K. Martini & Sohn

loc. Cornaiano
via Lamm, 28
39057 Appiano/Eppan [BZ]
Tel. +39 0471663156
www.martini-sohn.it

CELLAR SALES
PRE-BOOKED VISITS
ANNUAL PRODUCTION 230,000 bottles
HECTARES UNDER VINE 30.00

- ○ A. A. Pinot Bianco V. V. '17 — 🍷🍷 7
- ● A. A. Pinot Nero Palladium '18 — 🍷🍷 4
- ○ A. A. Sauvignon Palladium '19 — 🍷🍷 3
- ○ A. A. Chardonnay Maturum '18 — 🍷 4

Maso Thaler

VIA GLENO, 59
39040 MONTAGNA/MONTAN [BZ]
TEL. +39 3388483363
www.masothaler.it

CELLAR SALES
PRE-BOOKED VISITS
ANNUAL PRODUCTION 20,000 bottles
HECTARES UNDER VINE 3.50

- ● A. A. Pinot Nero '17 — 🍷🍷 5
- ● A. A. Pinot Nero 680 Ris. '16 — 🍷🍷 5
- ○ Manzoni Bianco '19 — 🍷🍷 2*
- ○ A. A. Gewürztraminer '19 — 🍷 3

Tenuta Nicolussi-Leck

VIA KREITH, 2
39051 CALDARO/KALTERN [BZ]
TEL. +39 3382963793
www.wein.kaltern.com

- ○ A. A. Gewürztraminer Stephanie '19 — 🍷🍷 4
- ● A. A. Lagrein Sepp '18 — 🍷🍷 3
- ○ A. A. Lago di Caldaro Cl. Sup. 1917 Alexander '19 — 🍷🍷 4

Obermoser H. & T. Rottensteiner

FRAZ. RENCIO
VIA SANTA MADDALENA, 35
39100 BOLZANO/BOZEN
TEL. +39 0471973549
www.obermoser.it

CELLAR SALES
PRE-BOOKED VISITS
ANNUAL PRODUCTION 30,000 bottles
HECTARES UNDER VINE 3.80

- ● A. A. Lagrein Grafenleiten Ris. '17 — 🍷🍷 5

Oberrautner - Anton Schmid

FRAZ. GRIES
VIA M. PACHER, 3
39100 BOLZANO/BOZEN
TEL. +39 0471281440
www.schmid.bz

CELLAR SALES
PRE-BOOKED VISITS
ANNUAL PRODUCTION 110,000 bottles
HECTARES UNDER VINE 10.00

- ● A. A. Lagrein Ris. '16 — 🍷🍷 5
- ● A. A. Lagrein Villa Schmid '18 — 🍷🍷 3
- ● A. A. Lagrein Andrä '18 — 🍷 3

Pacherhof - Andreas Huber

FRAZ. NOVACELLA
V.LO PACHER, 1
39040 VARNA/VAHRN [BZ]
TEL. +39 0472835717
www.pacherhof.com

CELLAR SALES
PRE-BOOKED VISITS
ACCOMMODATION AND RESTAURANT SERVICE
ANNUAL PRODUCTION 90,000 bottles
HECTARES UNDER VINE 8.50

- ○ A. A. Valle Isarco Grüner Veltliner '16 — 🍷🍷🍷 4*
- ○ A. A. Valle Isarco Sylvaner Alte Reben '16 — 🍷🍷🍷 5

Bergkellerei Passeier

VIA DEI LEGNAI, 5A
39015 SAN LEONARDO IN PASSIRIA/SANKT LEONHARD [BZ]
TEL. +39 3479982554
www.bergkellerei.it

ANNUAL PRODUCTION 8,000 bottles
HECTARES UNDER VINE 1.50

- ● A. A. Lagrein Ris. '17 — 🍷🍷 5
- ○ A. A. Pinot Bianco Burgunder '18 — 🍷🍷 5
- ○ A. A. Sauvignon '18 — 🍷🍷 5
- ● Rombo '17 — 🍷 6

Thomas Pichler

FRAZ. VILLA DI MEZZO
VIA DELLE VIGNE, 4A
39052 CALDARO/KALTERN [BZ]
TEL. +39 0471963094
www.thomas-pichler.it

CELLAR SALES
PRE-BOOKED VISITS
ANNUAL PRODUCTION 15,000 bottles
HECTARES UNDER VINE 2.00

- ○ A. A. Pinot Bianco Mitanond '19 — 🍷🍷 4
- ○ A. A. Sauvignon Puiten '18 — 🍷🍷 4
- ○ Anima Vit Est Sauvignon Passito '17 — 🍷 5
- ● Furioso '17 — 🍷 8

Pitzner

VIA CORNEDO, 15
39053 CORNEDO ALL'ISARCO/KARNEID [BZ]
TEL. +39 3384521694
www.pitzner.it

ANNUAL PRODUCTION 16,000 bottles
HECTARES UNDER VINE 3.00

- ● A. A. Lagrein Scharfegg '19 — 🍷🍷 5
- ● Hexagon HX17 '17 — 🍷🍷 7
- ● A. A. Merlot MR18 '18 — 🍷 5
- ○ A. A. Pinot Grigio Finell '19 — 🍷 4

Plonerhof - Erhard Tutzer

VIA TRAMONTANA, 29
39020 MARLENGO/MARLING [BZ]
TEL. +39 0473490525
www.weingut-plonerhof.it

PRE-BOOKED VISITS
ANNUAL PRODUCTION 30,000 bottles
HECTARES UNDER VINE 5.00
SUSTAINABLE WINERY

- ○ A. A. Nörder Cuvée Blanc Mitterberg '19 — 🍷🍷 4
- ● A. A. Pinot Nero '18 — 🍷🍷 4
- ● A. A. Pinot Nero Exclusiv Ris. '16 — 🍷🍷 3
- ○ A. A. Sauvignon '19 — 🍷🍷 3

Prackfolerhof

VIA SPIEGELWEG, 9
39050 FIÈ ALLO SCILIAR/VÖLS AM SCHLERN [BZ]
TEL. +39 0471601532
www.prackfolerhof.it

ANNUAL PRODUCTION 18,000 bottles
HECTARES UNDER VINE 4.50

- ○ A. A. Pinot Bianco '19 — 🍷🍷 4
- ● A. A. Pinot Nero '17 — 🍷🍷 4
- ○ A. A. Sauvignon '19 — 🍷🍷 4

Rielingerhof

SIFFIANER LEITACH, 7
39054 RENON/RITTEN [BZ]
TEL. +39 0471356274
www.rielinger.it

ANNUAL PRODUCTION 20,000 bottles
HECTARES UNDER VINE 3.00

- ○ Kerner '19 — 🍷🍷 4

Tenuta Spitalerhof Günther Oberpertinger

VIA LEITACH, 46
39043 CHIUSA/KLAUSEN [BZ]
TEL. +39 0472847612
www.spitalerhof.it

ANNUAL PRODUCTION 10,000 bottles
HECTARES UNDER VINE 1.60

- ○ Grüner Veltliner '19 — 🍷🍷 4
- ○ Sylvaner Sepp Alte Rebe '19 — 🍷🍷 3
- ○ Grüner Veltliner Muga Selection '18 — 🍷 5

St. Quirinus - Robert Sinn

via Pianizza di Sopra, 4b
39052 Caldaro/Kaltern [BZ]
Tel. +39 3298085003
www.st-quirinus.it

CELLAR SALES
PRE-BOOKED VISITS
ACCOMMODATION
ANNUAL PRODUCTION 12,000 bottles
HECTARES UNDER VINE 2.50
VITICULTURE METHOD Certified Organic

● A. A. Lagrein Badl '18	🍷🍷 4
● A. A. Merlot Ris. '17	🍷🍷 5
○ Planties Weiss '19	🍷🍷 4
○ A. A. Pinot Bianco Solt '19	🍷 4

Thurnhof - Andreas Berger

loc. Aslago
via Castel Flavon, 7
39100 Bolzano/Bozen
Tel. +39 0471288460
www.thurnhof.com

CELLAR SALES
PRE-BOOKED VISITS
ANNUAL PRODUCTION 25,000 bottles
HECTARES UNDER VINE 3.50

● A. A. Cabernet Sauvignon Weinegg Ris. '17	🍷🍷 5
● A. A. Lagrein Ris. '17	🍷🍷 4
○ A. A. Sauvignon 800 '19	🍷 3
⊙ Tirolensis Brut Rosé Ars Vini '16	🍷 5

Tröpfltalhof

via Garnellen, 17
39052 Caldaro/Kaltern [BZ]
Tel. +39 0471964126
www.bioweinhof.it

ANNUAL PRODUCTION 10,000 bottles
HECTARES UNDER VINE 2.30

○ Garnellen Sauvignon Anphora '16	🍷🍷 8
○ LeViogn '18	🍷🍷 5
● Barleith Cabernet Sauvignon '16	🍷 6

Vivaldi - Arunda

via Josef-Schwarz, 18
39010 Meltina/Mölten [BZ]
Tel. +39 0471668033
www.arundavivaldi.it

CELLAR SALES
PRE-BOOKED VISITS
ANNUAL PRODUCTION 90,000 bottles
HECTARES UNDER VINE 12.00

○ A. A. Spumante Brut Nature Zero '16	🍷🍷 6
○ A. A. Spumante Extra Brut Cuvée Muggi '15	🍷🍷 5
⊙ A. A. Spumante Brut Rosé Excellor '16	🍷 6

Wilhelm Walch

via A. Hofer, 1
39040 Termeno/Tramin [BZ]
Tel. +39 0471860172
www.walch.it

CELLAR SALES
PRE-BOOKED VISITS
ANNUAL PRODUCTION 600,000 bottles
HECTARES UNDER VINE 73.00

○ A. A. Gewürztraminer '19	🍷🍷 3
○ A. A. Pinot Bianco '19	🍷🍷 3
○ A. A. Sauvignon Krain '19	🍷🍷 2*
● A. A. Lagrein '19	🍷 2

Weinberghof Christian Bellutti

In der Au, 4a
39040 Termeno/Tramin [BZ]
Tel. +39 0471863224
www.weinberg-hof.com

ANNUAL PRODUCTION 20,000 bottles
HECTARES UNDER VINE 2.80

○ A. A. Gewürztraminer '19	🍷🍷 3
○ A. A. Gewürztraminer Plon '18	🍷🍷 3
● A. A. Lagrein Ris. '17	🍷🍷 4

VENETO

A vast region punctuated by small and large appellations, Veneto once again makes its presence felt in our guide. Starting from the eastern plains, it stretches towards Friuli Venezia Giulia and finishes on the morainic hills that surround the Garda basin, alternating climate conditions and different soil types, from the clayey and gravelly plains that run along the Piave or Livenza rivers, to the volcanic soils of the Euganean Hills, from the basalt of Gambellara and Soave to the limestone of Valpolicella. Its appellations are, at times, contiguous, at times they're separated by a few kilometers of countryside, where vineyards abound nevertheless. While eastern Veneto has embraced the Glera grape with great conviction, the western part of the region has remained faithful to the varieties that have thrived here for centuries, with production alternating the fragrance of Bardolino and Custoza with the power of Valpolicella's Amarone. At the center of it all are the region's winegrowers who, with their work, make a decisive contribution to the management of the territory and the continuation of its traditions, all while developing and promoting that Made in Italy brand that works so well throughout the world. If Valpolicella continues to count on Amarone as its most representative wine, we're seeing a new type of Valpolicella Superiore, one that tends increasingly towards finesse and tension, as embodied perfectly by Bertani's Ognissanti, a wine that's opening up a new, convincing direction. The westernmost part of the region features 3 stars: Cavalchina, Corte Gardoni and Monte del Frà. They interpret a territory that's gone all in on the fragrance and elegance of its wines, almost as if to counterbalance Soave, where Garganega reigns supreme, making for wines characterized by personality and energy. The district of Conegliano Valdobbiadene unveils a series of outstanding wines enriched by the debut of Borgoluce, who've embraced a new form of agriculture, eschewing monoculture and developing in harmony with the environment. Once again the Euganean Hills and Berici demonstrate their aptness when it comes to Bordeaux grape varieties, while we note (with great satisfaction) the success of Lessinia, a little-known territory where the combination of grape varieties allows for the production of highly charming Metodo Classico sparkling wines, as evidenced by Casa Cecchin and Ca' Rugate.

A Mi Manera

FRAZ. LISON
VIA CADUTI PER LA PATRIA, 29
30026 PORTOGRUARO [VE]
TEL. +39 336592660
www.vinicolamimanera.com

CELLAR SALES
PRE-BOOKED VISITS
ANNUAL PRODUCTION 42,000 bottles
HECTARES UNDER VINE 7.00

A mi manera' means 'in my own way'. Antonio Bigai couldn't have chosen a more appropriate name for his winery. The eclectic and unpredictable producer operates in the wide plain enclosed between the provinces of Venice, Treviso and Pordenone. The many rivers that cross the area contribute to alternating soils, the clay and gravel terrain that characterize Lison Pramaggiore. Their range centers on monovarietals, which are flanked by a white and a red that deliberately omit the year of harvest. The role of leader falls to their Cuvée Bianco, a blend of all the grapes grown on the winery, with a prevalence of Tai. Generous aromas on the nose feature a seductive succession of Mediterranean scrub and yellow fruit sensations, which evolve into a dry, sapid palate with great progression. We liked their Cuvée Rosso, on the other hand, for its aromatic fragrance and free and easy drinkability.

Wine	Rating
● Cabernet '18	TT 3
○ Cuvée Bianco Decimoquarto	TT 3
● Cuvée Rosso Duodecimo	TT 3
● Pinot Nero '18	TT 5
● Merlot '18	T 3
● Rosso Vino in Anfora '18	T 4
○ Tai Vino in Anfora '18	T 4
● Cabernet '17	YY 3
○ Malvasia '17	YY 3
○ Malvasia Anfora '17	YY 4
● Merlot '17	YY 2*
● Pinot Nero '17	YY 5
○ Tai '18	YY 3
○ Tai '17	YY 3
○ Chardonnay '18	Y 3
○ Malvasia '18	Y 3

Stefano Accordini

FRAZ. CAVALO
LOC. CAMPAROL, 10
37022 FUMANE [VR]
TEL. +39 0457760138
www.accordinistefano.it

CELLAR SALES
PRE-BOOKED VISITS
ACCOMMODATION AND RESTAURANT SERVICE
ANNUAL PRODUCTION 210,000 bottles
HECTARES UNDER VINE 27.00
VITICULTURE METHOD Certified Organic
SUSTAINABLE WINERY

Cavalo is a sort of amphitheatre that opens to the south, rising to between 550 and 600 metres above sea level. Here the great day-night temperature swings and cool winds that descend from Mount Pastello allow the grapes to ripen while maintaining extraordinary aromatic intensity, as well as an assertive acid and tannic presence. The rest is up to the winemakers, with Tiziano who, helped by his children and grandchildren, skilfully transforms the grapes into bottles of great character, where fullness and acid dynamism coexist in harmony. The tasting of one of their new wines was exemplary: Valpolicella Superiore Stefano '17, named after the founder, brings out the energy of grapes that grow in this area. Aromas dominated by hints of fruit and pepper mingle with nuances of oak, while the wine expands dry and firm on the palate. Their Amarone Acinatico '16 goes along the same lines, although it obviously reveals more power and warmth in the mouth.

Wine	Rating
● Amarone della Valpolicella Cl. Acinatico '16	TT 7
● Valpolicella Sup. Stefano '18	TT 4
● Paxxo '18	TT 4
● Recioto della Valpolicella Cl. Acinatico '18	TT 5
● Valpolicella Cl. '19	TT 2*
● Valpolicella Cl. Bio '19	TT 2*
● Valpolicella Cl. Sup. Ripasso Il Fornetto '15	TT 5
● Valpolicella Cl. Sup. Ripasso Acinatico '18	T 3
● Recioto della Valpolicella Cl. Acinatico '04	YYY 6
● Recioto della Valpolicella Cl. Acinatico '00	YYY 8

Adami

FRAZ. COLBERTALDO
VIA ROVEDE, 27
31020 VIDOR [TV]
TEL. +39 0423982110
www.adamispumanti.it

CELLAR SALES
PRE-BOOKED VISITS
ANNUAL PRODUCTION 700,000 bottles
HECTARES UNDER VINE 12.00

The Prosecco DOCG production zone presents varying geomorphologies: Coneglianese is characterized by gentle hills and rolling vineyards, while on Valdobbiadene's steep and rugged slopes the vineyards seem to cling to the earth's surface. The Adami family has been working here for four generations now, with Armando and Franco interpreting the territories many attributes. The result is a range entirely dedicated to Prosecco and which highlights the harmony and finesse conferred by the terroir. Their top-notch Col Credas '19 manages to bring out the delicate nature of this landscape with pluck and grip. This Prosecco combines floral and white fruit aromas with a dynamic, sometimes acidulous palate, which delivers for firmness and sapidity. Giardino '19 is the result of an even stricter selection than usual; it draws on the aromatic depth and a delicate palate that only the best exposures can offer.

- ○ Valdobbiadene Rive di Colbertaldo Asciutto Vign. Giardino '19 🍷🍷 3*
- ○ Valdobbiadene Rive di Farra di Soligo Brut Col Credas '19 🍷🍷 3*
- ○ Cartizze 🍷🍷 5
- ○ Valdobbiadene Brut Bosco di Gica 🍷🍷 3
- ○ Valdobbiadene Extra Dry Dei Casel 🍷🍷 3
- ○ Prosecco di Treviso Brut Garbel 🍷 2
- ○ Valdobbiadene Rive di Colbertaldo Asciutto Vign. Giardino '16 🍸🍸🍸 3*
- ○ Valdobbiadene Rive di Farra di Soligo Brut Col Credas '13 🍸🍸🍸 3*
- ○ Valdobbiadene Rive di Farra di Soligo Brut Col Credas '12 🍸🍸🍸 3*

Ida Agnoletti

LOC. SELVA DEL MONTELLO
VIA SACCARDO, 55
31040 VOLPAGO DEL MONTELLO [TV]
TEL. +39 0423621555
www.agnoletti.it

CELLAR SALES
PRE-BOOKED VISITS
ANNUAL PRODUCTION 50,000 bottles
HECTARES UNDER VINE 7.00

Montello stands out clearly in the northern part of Treviso province as a sort of outpost of what a few kilometers on becomes the Prealps. A producer with solid farming roots, Ida Agnoletti has been working here for about thirty years, earning herself a leading role as a faithful interpreter of a winemaking tradition in which the focus is more on the countryside than the cellar, and gestures repeated for generations take precedence over innovation. Glera and Bordeaux form the cornerstone of their range. Seneca, a Merlot-heavy Bordeaux blend made with grapes grown in a sixty-year-old vineyard, impressed for its close-focused aromas dotted with wild berries and spices. It moves lithely in the mouth, light and sapid, supported by good acidity that sets apart the best reds in this area. Their intriguing Follia, a Manzoni Bianco with an oxidative style, exhibits balance and character on the palate.

- ● Montello e Colli Asolani Rosso Seneca '17 🍷🍷 3*
- ○ Manzoni Bianco Follia 🍷🍷 3
- ● Montello e Colli Asolani Cabernet Sauvignon Love Is... '18 🍷🍷 3
- ○ PSL Always Frizzante 🍷🍷 2
- ○ Asolo Frizzante Selva n. 55 🍷 2
- ● Montello e Colli Asolani Merlot La Ida '18 🍷 2
- ● Montello e Colli Asolani Merlot La Ida '16 🍸🍸 2*
- ● Montello e Colli Asolani Merlot La Ida '15 🍸🍸 2*
- ● Montello e Colli Asolani Recantina '17 🍸🍸 2*
- ● Montello e Colli Asolani Recantina '16 🍸🍸 2*
- ● Montello e Colli Asolani Recantina '15 🍸🍸 2*
- ● Montello e Colli Asolani Rosso Seneca '16 🍸🍸 3
- ● Montello e Colli Asolani Rosso Seneca '15 🍸🍸 3
- ● Seneca '13 🍸🍸 3
- ● Vita Life is Red '16 🍸🍸 3
- ● Vita Life is Red '15 🍸🍸 3

★★★Allegrini

via Giare, 5
37022 Fumane [VR]
Tel. +39 0456832011
www.allegrini.it

CELLAR SALES
PRE-BOOKED VISITS
ACCOMMODATION AND RESTAURANT SERVICE
ANNUAL PRODUCTION 1,000,000 bottles
HECTARES UNDER VINE 150.00
SUSTAINABLE WINERY

In an area that has enjoyed uninterrupted success for almost thirty years, few wineries have been able to stay the course and expand the area under vine, acquiring only vineyards of great value. The Allegrini family are an exception and today they own one of the most sizable estates in the area, with crown jewels like La Poja, La Grola, Palazzo della Torre, Monte dei Galli and Villa Cavarena and elevations ranging from 150 to over 500 meters above sea level. Their sensational Amarone '16 exploits an excellent vintage to pull off one of the best performances in recent years. Its nose retraces the winery's style, with close-focused aromas and healthy fruit, however it really makes its mark in the mouth: sapidity plays a key role, alongside the distinctive acidic grip that adds lightness and elegance to the palate. Poja '16 and Recioto Giovanni Allegrini '16 remain their usual thoroughbred wines.

Wine	Rating	Price
● Amarone della Valpolicella Cl. '16	🍷🍷🍷	8
● La Poja '16	🍷🍷	8
● Recioto della Valpolicella Cl. Giovanni Allegrini '16	🍷🍷	7
● La Grola '17	🍷🍷	5
○ Lugana Oasi Mantellina '19	🍷🍷	4
● Palazzo della Torre '17	🍷🍷	5
○ Soave Oasi San Giacomo '19	🍷🍷	3
● Valpolicella Cl. '19	🍷🍷	3
● Amarone della Valpolicella Cl. '15	🍷🍷🍷 (past)	8
● Amarone della Valpolicella Cl. '14	🍷🍷🍷 (past)	8
● Amarone della Valpolicella Cl. '13	🍷🍷🍷 (past)	8
● Amarone della Valpolicella Cl. '12	🍷🍷🍷 (past)	8
● Amarone della Valpolicella Cl. '11	🍷🍷🍷 (past)	8
● Amarone della Valpolicella Cl. '10	🍷🍷🍷 (past)	8
● Amarone della Valpolicella Cl. '09	🍷🍷🍷 (past)	8
● Amarone della Valpolicella Cl. '08	🍷🍷🍷 (past)	8

Andreola

fraz. Col San Martino
via Cavre, 19
31010 Farra di Soligo [TV]
Tel. +39 0438989379
www.andreola.eu

CELLAR SALES
PRE-BOOKED VISITS
ANNUAL PRODUCTION 900,000 bottles
HECTARES UNDER VINE 93.00
SUSTAINABLE WINERY

Founded in the late 1980s by Nazzareno Pola, today Andreola is confidently managed by his son Stefano, a young entrepreneur from Conegliano Valdobbiadene. It's a well-developed winery that has quickly moved from being a rural farm to a modern producer dedicated to Prosecco, with estate vineyards that extend into some of the best positions of the appellation, like Rolle, Col San Martino, Refrontolo and Soligo. The Asolo area has been added to these historic vineyards, bearing witness to a never-ending hive of activity. The strength of this territory and their cellar expertise stand out in the Rive di Refrontolo Col del Forno '19. This Brut exhibits green apple and citrus aromas and highlights a dry, dynamic palate, supported by acidity and accompanied with style by the creamy bubbles. Their 26° Primo from the same vintage is made with grapes grown in the Col San Martino vineyards and proves pluckier and more acidulous.

Wine	Rating	Price
○ Valdobbiadene Rive di Refrontolo Brut Col Del Forno '19	🍷🍷🍷	3*
○ Valdobbiadene Rive di Col San Martino Extra Brut 26° Primo '19	🍷🍷	3*
○ Asolo Brut Akelum '19	🍷🍷	3
○ Cartizze Dry '19	🍷🍷	5
○ Valdobbiadene Brut Dirupo '19	🍷🍷	3
○ Valdobbiadene Dry Rive di Rolle V. dei Piai '19	🍷🍷	3
○ Valdobbiadene Dry Sesto Senso '19	🍷🍷	3
○ Pensieri Passito '15	🍷	6
○ Valdobbiadene Extra Dry Dirupo '19	🍷	3
○ Valdobbiadene Extra Dry Rive di Soligo Mas de Fer '19	🍷	3
○ Valdobbiadene Brut Dirupo '17	🍷🍷🍷 (past)	3*
○ Valdobbiadene Rive Di Refrontolo Brut Col Del Forno '18	🍷🍷🍷 (past)	3*

★Roberto Anselmi

via San Carlo, 46
37032 Monteforte d'Alpone [VR]
Tel. +39 0457611488
www.anselmi.eu

CELLAR SALES
PRE-BOOKED VISITS
RESTAURANT SERVICE
ANNUAL PRODUCTION 700,000 bottles
HECTARES UNDER VINE 70.00

Roberto Anselmi's winery is one of the most well-known in the region, bolstered by a range that has helped make Veneto, and the hills of Soave especially, a global center of wine production. The journey began many years ago, when his father's business was transformed into a dynamic producer capable of interpreting the territory and market with sensitivity and precision. Their vineyards unfold entirely on the hills that surround Monteforte, and give rise to a limited number of wines, distinct for their style and elegance. Capitel Foscarino and Capitel Croce, both from the 2019 vintage, seem to be complementary wines: the first one exhibits an almost explosive aromatic expression, revealing a dynamic, racy palate, while the second one offers up more style in both aromas and palate, coming through sapid and well-balanced, very drinkable. Their San Vincenzo, Anselmi's simple white wine, also performed well and delivered for pleasant drinkability.

Wine	Rating
○ Capitel Croce '19	TTT 3*
○ Capitel Foscarino '19	TT 3*
○ I Capitelli Passito '18	TT 6
○ San Vincenzo '19	TT 2*
○ Capitel Croce '18	YYY 3*
○ Capitel Croce '17	YYY 3*
○ Capitel Croce '15	YYY 3*
○ Capitel Croce '09	YYY 3*
○ Capitel Croce '06	YYY 3
○ Capitel Croce '05	YYY 3
○ Capitel Croce '04	YYY 3
○ Capitel Croce '03	YYY 3
○ Capitel Croce '02	YYY 3*
○ Capitel Croce '01	YYY 3
○ Capitel Croce '00	YYY 3

Antolini

via Prognol, 22
37020 Marano di Valpolicella [VR]
Tel. +39 0457755351
www.antolinivini.it

CELLAR SALES
PRE-BOOKED VISITS
ACCOMMODATION
ANNUAL PRODUCTION 60,000 bottles
HECTARES UNDER VINE 9.00
SUSTAINABLE WINERY

Valpolicella's classic heart is made up of a series of valleys that stretch north up the territory, each with different characteristics, making for wines of great character. Pierpaolo and Stefano Antolini mainly operate along the Marano Valley, the area that has kept the landscape most intact and has managed to harmonize with viticulture. Their range is dedicated to the appellation's historic typologies, all interpreted with frankness and authenticity. Their Valpolicella Persegà, only created a few years ago, delivers for quality once again and pulls off a great performance with the 2018 vintage. On the nose, close-focused notes of undergrowth and wild fruit culminate in peppery spices that prove even more marked on the sapid, dynamic palate with a spirited mouthfeel. Their Amarone Moròpio features a more mature, restrained expression, winning over the palate with a fullness and plushness that gradually give way to a more assertive finish.

Wine	Rating
● Valpolicella Cl. Sup. Persegà '18	TT 3*
● Amarone della Valpolicella Cl. Moròpio '16	TT 6
● Corvina '16	TT 2*
● Valpolicella Cl. '19	TT 2*
● Valpolicella Cl. Sup. Ripasso '17	TT 3
● Amarone della Valpolicella Cl. Ca' Coato '16	T 7
○ Elisium Passito	T 5
● Theobroma '13	T 5
● Amarone della Valpolicella Cl. Ca' Coato '15	YY 8
● Amarone della Valpolicella Cl. Moròpio '15	YY 8
● Amarone della Valpolicella Cl. Moròpio '14	YY 8
● Corvina '15	YY 4
● Recioto della Valpolicella Cl. '17	YY 6
● Valpolicella Cl. Sup. Persegà '17	YY 3
● Valpolicella Cl. Sup. Persegà '16	YY 3*

Albino Armani

via Ceradello, 401
37020 Dolcè [VR]
Tel. +39 0457290033
www.albinoarmani.com

CELLAR SALES
PRE-BOOKED VISITS
ANNUAL PRODUCTION 900,000 bottles
HECTARES UNDER VINE 220.00
SUSTAINABLE WINERY

Over the decades, Albino Armani has managed to give the family business a wide-ranging dimension, widening its boundaries from his native Valdadige to Valpolicella, and then further east to Friuli. The beating heart and the control room, however, remain faithfully linked to the land of passage that is the Adige Valley. Here international varieties are cultivated alongside native ones, creating a mix that leads to some very notable wines. Their many impressive wines include Foja Tonda '16, made with Casetta which adds aromas of ripe red fruit and spice, following onto a dry palate with good tannic structure. Our favorite white, on the other hand, was a Friuli Grave Sauvignon, which makes the most of the cool 2019 vintage to confer exotic aromas with good intensity spruced up by distinctive green overtones. The palate comes through supple and dynamic, ending with a dry, long finish.

Wine	Rating
● Amarone della Valpolicella Cl. '16	🍷🍷 5
○ Friuli Grave Sauvignon '19	🍷🍷 2*
○ Valdadige Pinot Grigio Corvara '19	🍷🍷 2*
● Valdadige Terra dei Forti Casetta Foja Tonda '16	🍷🍷 3
○ Trento Dosaggio Zero '15	🍷 4
○ Valdadige Terra dei Forti Pinot Grigio Colle Ara '19	🍷 2
● Amarone della Valpolicella Cl. '15	🍷🍷 5
● Amarone della Valpolicella Cl. Cuslanus '13	🍷🍷 6
● Amarone della Valpolicella Cl. Cuslanus '12	🍷🍷 6
○ Campo Napoleone Sauvignon '17	🍷🍷 2*
● Valdadige Terra dei Forti Foja Tonda '14	🍷🍷 3
● Valpolicella Cl. Sup. Egle '17	🍷🍷 2*
● Valpolicella Cl. Sup. Ripasso '16	🍷🍷 3

Balestri Valda

via Monti, 44
37038 Soave [VR]
Tel. +39 0457675393
www.vinibalestrivalda.com

CELLAR SALES
PRE-BOOKED VISITS
ACCOMMODATION
ANNUAL PRODUCTION 65,000 bottles
HECTARES UNDER VINE 16.00
VITICULTURE METHOD Certified Organic
SUSTAINABLE WINERY

To reach the winery managed by Laura Rizzotto and her father, Guido, you have to go into the heart of the classic area north of Soave and climb up the buttresses. Then, suddenly, a landscape of rare harmony will open before your eyes. The cellar, which was built a few decades ago, seems always to have been there. It integrates perfectly with the environment, surrounded by woods and vineyards. Both in the countryside and in the winery their work is aimed at sustainability and reducing their impact on the environment. An excellent performance from Soave Sengialta '17, made with grapes grown in the vineyard of the same name located on the highly basaltic and calcareous soils that mark this slope of the appellation. Aromas of white fruit gradually give way to floral and benzine notes. The palate displays a lot of character and leads to a balanced, dynamic mouthfeel, closing with a dry, sapid finish.

Wine	Rating
○ Soave Cl. Sengialta '17	🍷🍷 4
○ Soave Cl. '19	🍷🍷 2*
○ Soave Cl. Lunalonga '17	🍷🍷 3
○ Libertate '17	🍷 3
○ Libertate '16	🍷🍷 3
○ Soave Cl. '18	🍷🍷 2*
○ Soave Cl. '17	🍷🍷 2*
○ Soave Cl. '16	🍷🍷 2*
○ Soave Cl. Lunalonga '12	🍷🍷 3*
○ Soave Cl. Vign. Sengialta '16	🍷🍷 3
○ Soave Cl. Vign. Sengialta '15	🍷🍷 3
○ Soave Cl. Vign. Sengialta '14	🍷🍷 2*
○ Soave Cl. Vign. Sengialta '13	🍷🍷 2*
○ Soave Cl. Vign. Sengialta '12	🍷🍷 2*

Barollo

via Rio Serva, 4b
31022 Preganziol [TV]
Tel. +39 0422633014
www.barollo.com

CELLAR SALES
PRE-BOOKED VISITS
ANNUAL PRODUCTION 88,000 bottles
HECTARES UNDER VINE 45.00
SUSTAINABLE WINERY

The vast strip of plains that stretches from Venice to Treviso comprises large swathes of vineyards dedicated to quality viticulture. It's an area that has, in recent years, begun spawning first-rate producers and wines. Marco and Nicola Barollo operate here in an area that unfolds from the hills to the sea, resisting the invasion of Prosecco and carving out a leading role in the regional wine scene. Their solid range is characterized by a clear, elegant style. Frank ! '18 is an example of this style of monovarietal Cabernet Franc. The nose offers up aromas of very ripe red fruit refreshed by spicy and pleasantly vegetal notes, which follow onto a well-made, supple, dynamic palate that is not overly structured. Alfredo Barollo '13 proved an intriguing traditional method sparkling wine made with Chardonnay grapes, which delivered for aromatic complexity and tidy palate.

Wine	Rating
● Frank! '18	🍷🍷🍷 5
○ Alfredo Barollo Brut M. Cl. Ris. '13	🍷🍷 5
● Venezia Merlot Frater '19	🍷🍷 3
○ Prosecco di Treviso Brut '19	🍷 2
○ Venezia Chardonnay Frater '19	🍷 3
● Frank! '17	🥂🥂🥂 4*
○ Chardonnay '16	🥂🥂 4
● Frank! '16	🥂🥂 4
● Frank! '15	🥂🥂 4
● Frank! '14	🥂🥂 4
● Frank! '13	🥂🥂 4
○ Piave Chardonnay '17	🥂🥂 5
○ Piave Chardonnay '15	🥂🥂 4
○ Venezia Chardonnay Frater '18	🥂🥂 3
● Venezia Merlot Frater '18	🥂🥂 3
● Venezia Merlot Frater '17	🥂🥂 3
● Piave Merlot Frater '15	🥂 2

Le Battistelle

fraz. Brognoligo
via Sambuco, 110
37032 Monteforte d'Alpone [VR]
Tel. +39 0456175621
www.lebattistelle.it

CELLAR SALES
PRE-BOOKED VISITS
ANNUAL PRODUCTION 22,000 bottles
HECTARES UNDER VINE 9.00
SUSTAINABLE WINERY

Gelmino and Cristina Dal Bosco's winery is one of the most interesting in Soave, an exquisitely family-run business that avails itself of a property that's limited in size but unfolds across some of the best and most beautiful positions in the appellation. Fewer than ten hectares, characterized by dark, volcanic soil, are dedicated exclusively to the area's classic grapes, making for a rich, plucky style that's redolent of authenticity. Their Roccolo del Durlo '18 proved simply splendid. This Soave is made exclusively with Garganega grapes grown in vineyards lying on basalt soils at 250 meters of elevation, on a very steep slope held up by dry stone walls. The nose offers up immediate notes of ripe fruit, which give way to charming overtones of minerals and dried flowers. The wine changes pace on the palate, extending with grip and traction. Their Battistelle '18 also impressed with its more approachable fruity notes.

Wine	Rating
○ Soave Cl. Roccolo del Durlo '18	🍷🍷 3*
○ Passito della Gloria '18	🍷🍷 6
○ Soave Cl. Le Battistelle '18	🍷🍷 3
○ Soave Cl. Montesei '19	🍷🍷 2*
○ Soave Brut Settembrino '19	🍷 3
○ Soave Cl. Battistelle '14	🥂🥂 3
○ Soave Cl. Le Battistelle '17	🥂🥂 3*
○ Soave Cl. Le Battistelle '16	🥂🥂 3
○ Soave Cl. Le Battistelle '15	🥂🥂 3
○ Soave Cl. Montesei '18	🥂🥂 2*
○ Soave Cl. Montesei '17	🥂🥂 2*
○ Soave Cl. Montesei '16	🥂🥂 2*
○ Soave Cl. Roccolo del Durlo '17	🥂🥂 3*
○ Soave Cl. Roccolo del Durlo '16	🥂🥂 3*
○ Soave Cl. Roccolo del Durlo '15	🥂🥂 3*
○ Soave Cl. Roccolo del Durlo '14	🥂🥂 3

★Lorenzo Begali

via Cengia, 10
37020 San Pietro in Cariano [VR]
Tel. +39 0457725148
www.begaliwine.it

CELLAR SALES
PRE-BOOKED VISITS
ANNUAL PRODUCTION 90,000 bottles
HECTARES UNDER VINE 12.00

If the success that has overwhelmed Valpolicella has, on the one hand, brought wellbeing and development to the territory, on the other hand it has seen the birth of wineries that have often only aimed for profit. Lorenzo Begali has managed to maintain his territorial roots, becoming one of the most appreciated producers of the appellation. His children Tiliana and Giordano round out the team, working to produce a solid range that's respectful of tradition and characterized by energetic wines of great character. After spending five years in the dark cellar in Via Cengia, their Riserva '15 del Monte Ca' Bianca can finally see the light of day. This unique Amarone features close-focused, fragrant aromas of fruit and spices, while the palate pulls off a performance that highlights its character to the full. The impact is vigorous, but the mouthfeel manages to unfold with tension and suppleness, thanks to the distinctive crisp acidity of these wines and supported by a pleasant, close-knit, rugged tannic texture.

Wine	Rating
● Amarone della Valpolicella Cl. Monte Ca' Bianca Ris. '15	🍷🍷🍷 8
● Valpolicella Cl. Sup. Siora '17	🍷🍷 3*
● Amarone della Valpolicella Cl. '16	🍷🍷 6
● Tigiolo '16	🍷🍷 5
● Valpolicella Cl. Sup. Ripasso La Cengia '18	🍷🍷 3
● Valpolicella Cl. '19	🍷 2
● Amarone della Valpolicella Cl. Monte Ca' Bianca '13	🍷🍷🍷 8
● Amarone della Valpolicella Cl. Monte Ca' Bianca '12	🍷🍷🍷 8
● Amarone della Valpolicella Cl. Monte Ca' Bianca '11	🍷🍷🍷 8
● Amarone della Valpolicella Cl. Monte Ca' Bianca '10	🍷🍷🍷 8
● Amarone della Valpolicella Cl. Vign. Monte Ca' Bianca '09	🍷🍷🍷 8

★Bertani

via Asiago, 1
37023 Grezzana [VR]
Tel. +39 0458658444
www.bertani.net

CELLAR SALES
PRE-BOOKED VISITS
ANNUAL PRODUCTION 1,800,000 bottles
HECTARES UNDER VINE 200.00
SUSTAINABLE WINERY

The Angelini family's great group has in Bertani its prized-pony, a winery that has managed to face the challenges of the modern market with precision and respect for tradition. If Amarone Classico represents a cornerstone for the entire appellation, the Bertani Cru project is proving even more interesting, focusing on Valpolicella wines that, rather than give in to international taste, express the potential of each single vineyard. Le Miniere '19 offers a whirlwind of aromas, where cherry and pepper suddenly encounter rose overtones. The palate comes through sapid and graceful with an exhilarating progression. Their Ognisanti '18, on the other hand, reinterprets the aromas with more depth and elegance, indicating a more interesting direction to follow for the Verona wine type. The palate plays more on tension and finesse than power, proving dynamic and very lingering.

Wine	Rating
● Valpolicella Cl. Sup. Ognisanti '18	🍷🍷🍷 5
● Valpolicella Cl. Le Miniere '19	🍷🍷 4
● Amarone della Valpolicella Valpantena '17	🍷🍷 7
● Secco Bertani Vintage '17	🍷🍷 4
○ Soave Sereole '19	🍷🍷 3
○ Soave Vintage '18	🍷🍷 4
● Valpolicella '19	🍷🍷 3
● Valpolicella Ripasso '18	🍷🍷 4
● Amarone della Valpolicella Cl. '11	🍷🍷🍷 8
● Amarone della Valpolicella Cl. '10	🍷🍷🍷 8
● Amarone della Valpolicella Cl. '09	🍷🍷🍷 8
● Amarone della Valpolicella Cl. '08	🍷🍷🍷 8
● Amarone della Valpolicella Cl. '07	🍷🍷🍷 8
● Amarone della Valpolicella Cl. '06	🍷🍷🍷 8
● Amarone della Valpolicella Cl. '05	🍷🍷🍷 8
● Amarone della Valpolicella Cl. '04	🍷🍷🍷 8

BiancaVigna

LOC. OGLIANO
VIA MONTE NERO, 8
31015 CONEGLIANO [TV]
TEL. +39 0438788403
www.biancavigna.it

CELLAR SALES
PRE-BOOKED VISITS
ACCOMMODATION
ANNUAL PRODUCTION 600,000 bottles
HECTARES UNDER VINE 32.00
VITICULTURE METHOD Certified Organic
SUSTAINABLE WINERY

Founded a few years ago, Elena and Enrico Moschetta's winery has undertaken a path matched by few in the territory: finding a way for the appellation's different identities to coexist under the same roof, from cultivation to winemaking, from fermentation to marketing. Often the historic producers are only involved in a part of the supply chain, but Biancavigna brings them all together, making for a range that draws on the vineyards situated mainly in the eastern part of the DOCG. To understand how much the territory influences a wine type such as Prosecco, just taste these two flagship wines produced near each other: Rive di Ogliano and Rive di Soligo '19. The first one expresses all the style and balance the appellation has to offer, with mature, inviting aromas that enrich the sapid, juicy palate. The second one, on the other hand, explores its more hidden, confident soul, consisting of less explosive aromas and a palate that reveals an unexpected assertive, almost sharp, tension.

Wine	Rating
○ Conegliano Valdobbiadene Rive di Soligo Extra Brut '19	▼▼▼ 3*
○ Conegliano Valdobbiadene Rive di Ogliano Extra Brut '19	▼▼ 3*
○ Conegliano Valdobbiadene Brut '19	▼▼ 3
○ Conegliano Valdobbiadene Brut Biologico '19	▼▼ 3
○ Conegliano Valdobbiadene Brut Nature Sui Lieviti '19	▼▼ 3
○ Conegliano Valdobbiadene Extra Dry '19	▼▼ 3
○ Prosecco Brut	▼▼ 3
○ Prosecco Extra Dry	▼▼ 3
⊙ Cuvée 1931 Brut Rosé	▼ 2
○ Prosecco Frizzante	▼ 2
○ Conegliano Valdobbiadene Rive di Ogliano Brut Nature '18	▽▽▽ 3*
○ Conegliano Valdobbiadene Rive di Ogliano Brut Nature '17	▽▽▽ 3*

Bisol 1542

FRAZ. SANTO STEFANO
VIA FOLLO, 33
31049 VALDOBBIADENE [TV]
TEL. +39 0423900138
www.bisol.it

CELLAR SALES
PRE-BOOKED VISITS
ANNUAL PRODUCTION 4,500,000 bottles
HECTARES UNDER VINE 55.00

As far back as anyone can remember, the historic maison at Via Follo has been one of the mainstays of the Treviso appellation, thanks to its eminent past and a strong presence in the territory's best areas for wine-growing. In addition to the estate vineyards, the producer avails itself of local growers, followed throughout the year, who provide the grapes for a highly reliable, consistent and wide range of wines. Indeed, all the appellation's typologies are represented and interpreted in pursuit of fragrance and harmony. Their outstanding Brut is made with grapes grown in the most beautiful vineyards in the Guia area, perched on extremely steep slopes. The 2019 vintage brought a refined aromatic expression, dominated by notes of pear and apple, complemented by a fresh floral expression. The sapid palate is supported by creamy bubbles and expands with elegance and style. Their Extra Dry Rive di Campea '19 conveys a more approachable fruity expression.

Wine	Rating
○ Valdobbiadene Rive di Guia Brut Relio '19	▼▼ 4
○ Cartizze Dry '19	▼▼ 5
○ Valdobbiadene Brut Crede '19	▼▼ 3
○ Valdobbiadene Extra Dry Molera '19	▼▼ 3
○ Valdobbiadene Rive di Campea Dry '19	▼▼ 3
○ Valdobbiadene Brut Jeio	▼ 3
○ Valdobbiadene Extra Dry Jeio	▼ 3
○ P. di Valdobbiadene Dry Garnei '95	▽▽▽ 2*
○ Cartizze '18	▽▽ 5
○ Valdobbiadene Brut Crede '18	▽▽ 3
○ Valdobbiadene Brut Crede '17	▽▽ 4
○ Valdobbiadene Brut Rive di Guia Relio '18	▽▽ 4
○ Valdobbiadene Extra Dry Molera '18	▽▽ 3

Bolla

FRAZ. PEDEMONTE
VIA A. BOLLA, 3
37029 SAN PIETRO IN CARIANO [VR]
TEL. +39 0456836555
www.bolla.it

CELLAR SALES
PRE-BOOKED VISITS
ANNUAL PRODUCTION 9,560,000 bottles
HECTARES UNDER VINE 264.00

Large producers often make reliable but not particularly personal wines. Christian Zulian has been able to take the historic winery of Pedemonte in other directions, exploring in depth the potential of the territory and its grapes, all in pursuit of modern wines with ancient roots. The utmost care is brought to selecting the best grapes and subdividing them according to the areas of origin, making for a range that brings together integrity and tradition. In recent years, their Amarone Le Origini has shown significant growth and proved itself once again with the tasting of the Riserva '15. It seems slow and almost reluctant to offer up its suite of aromas, consisting of overripe fruit and spices, while the palate comes through assertive and confident, revealing a full body well-supported by acidity and tannins, with a long, charming finish. Their Rhetico from the same vintage, on the other hand, expresses sweeter, juicier fruit on the nose, following through onto a full, powerful palate.

- ● Amarone della Valpolicella Cl. Le Origini Ris. '15 — 🍷🍷6
- ● Amarone della Valpolicella Cl. '15 — 🍷🍷5
- ● Amarone della Valpolicella Cl. Rhetico '15 — 🍷🍷5
- ⊙ Bardolino Chiaretto Cl. La Canestraia '19 — 🍷🍷2*
- ● Valpolicella Cl. Sup. Ripasso '17 — 🍷🍷2*
- ● Valpolicella Cl. Sup. Ripasso Le Poiane '17 — 🍷🍷3
- ○ Lugana '19 — 🍷2
- ○ Soave Cl. Retrò '19 — 🍷2
- ○ Soave Cl. Sup. Tufaie '18 — 🍷2
- ● Amarone della Valpolicella Cl. '14 — 🍷🍷5 (white)
- ● Amarone della Valpolicella Cl. Le Origini Ris. '13 — 🍷🍷7 (white)
- ● Amarone della Valpolicella Cl. Le Origini Ris. '12 — 🍷🍷7 (white)
- ● Amarone della Valpolicella Cl. Rhetico '13 — 🍷🍷7 (white)

Bonotto delle Tezze

FRAZ. TEZZE DI PIAVE
VIA DUCA D'AOSTA, 36
31028 VAZZOLA [TV]
TEL. +39 0438488323
www.bonottodelletezze.it

CELLAR SALES
PRE-BOOKED VISITS
ANNUAL PRODUCTION 150,000 bottles
HECTARES UNDER VINE 48.00

Antonio Bonotto's farm unfolds for a few dozen hectares along the banks of the Piave river, land that over the centuries has seen a succession of agricultural activities, gone through periods of absence and abundance while remaining faithful to its past and traditions. Today the it's largely dedicated to viticulture, with soils dominated by gravel alternating with clay, creating a sort of puzzle in which each grape variety finds its ideal home. Barabane '17 is made with 100% Carmenere grown in a small vineyard on stony soil near a river. It ages in oak for over a year and exhibits intense aromas of wild fruit and pepper, while the dry palate comes through supple and juicy. The Raboso Potestà '17, on the other hand, explores the lighter, more fragrant features of the local rebel variety, offering up fresh, spicy aromas, while the distinctive acid proves fundamental for expanding and unfolding the palate.

- ● Piave Carmenere Barabane '17 — 🍷🍷3
- ● Piave Malanotte '15 — 🍷🍷6
- ● Piave Raboso Potestà '17 — 🍷🍷3
- ○ Manzoni Bianco '19 — 🍷2
- ● Piave Merlot Spezza '17 — 🍷3
- ● Ribelle Raboso Frizzante — 🍷2
- ● Piave Malanotte '14 — 🍷🍷6 (white)
- ● Piave Malanotte '13 — 🍷🍷6 (white)
- ● Piave Malanotte '12 — 🍷🍷6 (white)
- ● Piave Raboso Potestà '15 — 🍷🍷3 (white)
- ● Raboso Passito '14 — 🍷🍷5 (white)

Borgo Stajnbech

via Belfiore, 109
30020 Pramaggiore [VE]
Tel. +39 0421799929
www.borgostajnbech.com

CELLAR SALES
PRE-BOOKED VISITS
ANNUAL PRODUCTION 90,000 bottles
HECTARES UNDER VINE 15.00

Giuliano Valent's winery can be found in the heart of the plain that lies between the provinces of Venice and Pordenone. It's a position that's almost equidistant from the sea and the hills, and so it enjoys the influences of the Adriatic basin and the fresh breezes blowing in from the Pre-Alps. About fifteen hectares, mostly dedicated to the international varieties cultivated in the territory for some decades now, give rise to a range that centers more on elegance than power. The wine that charmed us most was their Lison 150, from the 2018 vintage. Its suite of aromas, consisting of fresh flowers and vegetal overtones, leads to a close-focused note of white fruit, while the palate relaxes with grace and sapidity, expanding gently. As for the reds, we were impressed by their Rosso Stajnbech '16, a blend of Refosco and Cabernet Sauvignon which expresses freshness and suppleness.

Wine	Rating
○ Bosco della Donna Sauvignon '19	▼▼ 4
○ Lison Cl. 150 '18	▼▼ 3
○ Stajnbech Bianco '17	▼▼ 4
● Stajnbech Rosso '16	▼▼ 4
● Cabernet Sauvignon '18	▼ 3
○ Chardonnay '19	▼ 3
● Lison Pramaggiore Refosco P. R. '18	▼ 3
● Malbec '18	▼ 3
○ Pinot Grigio delle Venezie '19	▼ 3
○ Bosco della Donna Sauvignon '18	▽▽ 3
○ Lison Cl. 150 '17	▽▽ 3
● Lison-Pramaggiore Refosco P. R. '17	▽▽ 3
● Malbech '17	▽▽ 2*
● Merlot '17	▽▽ 3
● Merlot '16	▽▽ 3
● Refosco P. R. '16	▽▽ 2*
○ Stajnbech Bianco '16	▽▽ 3

Borgoluce

loc. Musile, 2
31058 Susegana [TV]
Tel. +39 0438435287
www.borgoluce.it

CELLAR SALES
PRE-BOOKED VISITS
ACCOMMODATION AND RESTAURANT SERVICE
ANNUAL PRODUCTION 250,000 bottles
HECTARES UNDER VINE 70.00

In the span of a few decades, Borgoluce has grown into one of the most interesting wineries in Conegliano Valdobbiadene, developing and benefiting from the enormous patrimony at its disposal. Many hectares of vineyards stretch throughout the heart of the hills of Susegana, but ample space is also left to woodland, pasture and activities related to animal husbandry. All stages of production are carried out at their new winery, which was designed to have a low environmental impact, making for a range of great rigor and quality. Their Rive di Collalto Brut '19 perfectly expresses precision and quality. This Prosecco succeeds in the difficult task of combining the distinctive style and simplicity of this wine type with the depth and delicacy conferred by the Collalto vineyard. The Extra Dry version, with lower residual sugar, expresses more approachable fruity notes on the palate. Lastly, their 'on-the-lees' version came out really well.

Wine	Rating
○ Valdobbiadene Rive di Collalto Extra Brut '19	▼▼▼ 3*
⊙ Rosariflesso Extra Brut	▼▼ 3
○ Valdobbiadene Brut	▼▼ 3
○ Valdobbiadene Brut Nature sui Lieviti '19	▼▼ 3
○ Valdobbiadene Extra Dry	▼▼ 3
○ Valdobbiadene Rive di Collalto Extra Dry '19	▼▼ 3
○ Valdobbiadene Rive di Collalto Brut '18	▽▽ 3*
○ Valdobbiadene Rive di Collalto Brut '17	▽▽ 3*
○ Valdobbiadene Rive di Collalto Extra Dry '18	▽▽ 3
○ Valdobbiadene Rive di Collalto Extra Dry '17	▽▽ 3

Borin Vini & Vigne

FRAZ. MONTICELLI
VIA DEI COLLI, 5
35043 MONSELICE [PD]
TEL. +39 042974384
www.viniborin.it

CELLAR SALES
PRE-BOOKED VISITS
ANNUAL PRODUCTION 105,000 bottles
HECTARES UNDER VINE 28.00

Monticelli is a small village located in a strip of plain wedged in the Euganean Hills and facing west. It's here that we find Gianni and Teresa Borin's winery, in an area surrounded by vineyards (these are accompanied by properties in the upper Arquà Petrarca). The full-time support of sons Francesco and Gianpaolo, which has brought new enthusiasm and energy to the producer, is now proving essential to management of the winery and its thirty hectares of vineyards. Their wines are impeccably crafted, crowned by some truly outstanding selections. Their Cabernet Sauvignon Coldivalle '18 is a new little gem that breaks with the winery's style. Compared to other important selections, it appears more refreshing and dynamic, starting with the aromas dominated by juicy red fruit and contrasted by notes of spice and pencil lead. The full, crisp palate is supported by good acidity and a vigorous tannic texture that comes through pleasantly rugged. Among their whites, worthy of mention is their excellent sapid Corte Borin '18.

● Colli Euganei Cabernet Sauvignon Coldivalle '18	🍷🍷 3*
● Coldivalle Syrah '17	🍷🍷 3
● Colli Euganei Cabernet Sauvignon Mons Silicis Ris. '17	🍷🍷 4
● Colli Euganei Cabernet Sauvignon V. Costa '17	🍷🍷 3
○ Colli Euganei Manzoni Bianco Corte Borin '18	🍷🍷 3
● Colli Euganei Merlot Rocca Chiara Ris. '17	🍷🍷 4
○ Colli Euganei Chardonnay V. Bianca '18	🍷 3
○ Colli Euganei Fior d'Arancio Fiore di Gaia '19	🍷 2
○ Colli Euganei Pinot Bianco Archino '19	🍷 2
○ Pinot Grigio delle Venezie '19	🍷 2
○ Colli Euganei Chardonnay V. Bianca '17	🍷🍷 3

Bortolomiol

VIA GARIBALDI, 142
31049 VALDOBBIADENE [TV]
TEL. +39 04239749
www.bortolomiol.com

CELLAR SALES
PRE-BOOKED VISITS
RESTAURANT SERVICE
ANNUAL PRODUCTION 2,100,000 bottles
HECTARES UNDER VINE 5.00
SUSTAINABLE WINERY

Maria Elena, Elvira, Luisa and Giuliana Bortolomiol have successfully assumed the reigns of the winery founded by their father, Giuliano, immediately after the Second World War and turned it into one of the most appreciated brands in the world of sparkling wines. A dense network of local growers have proven an invaluable asset, as has the estate vineyards, which are overseen with the utmost respect for the environment. A new venture just outside Montalcino is the fulfillment of Giuliano's Tuscan dream. The task of leading the wide range of sparkling wines made with grapes grown in vineyards in the historic area goes to Ius Naturae. This Brut made the most of the excellent 2019 vintage to express close-focused aromas of white fruit and flowers, which follow through onto a dry, taut palate supported by acidity and refreshingly sapid bubbles. We found their Segreto di Giuliano '17 a very interesting, precise, sound Sangiovese.

○ Valdobbiadene Brut Ius Naturae '19	🍷🍷🍷 5
● Il Segreto di Giuliano '17	🍷🍷 6
○ Valdobbiadene Brut Prior '19	🍷🍷 4
○ Valdobbiadene Rive di Santo Stefano Brut Nature 70th Anniversario '17	🍷🍷 6
○ Valdobbiadene Rive San Pietro di Barbozza Brut Grande Cuvée del Fondatore Motus Vitae '18	🍷🍷 5
○ Cartizze '19	🍷 5
○ Valdobbiadene Extra Brut Audax 3.0 '19	🍷 4
○ Valdobbiadene Extra Dry Banda Rossa Special Reserve '19	🍷 4
○ Valdobbiadene Rive San Pietro di Barbozza Brut Grande Cuvée del Fondatore Motus Vitae '16	🍷🍷🍷 5

Carlo Boscaini

via Sengia, 15
37015 Sant'Ambrogio di Valpolicella [VR]
Tel. +39 0457731412
www.boscainicarlo.it

CELLAR SALES
PRE-BOOKED VISITS
ACCOMMODATION
ANNUAL PRODUCTION 60,000 bottles
HECTARES UNDER VINE 14.00

Within Valpolicella's classic heart, Sant'Ambrogio is closest to Lake Garda. It's here that we find the Boscaini family's winery, in an area separated from Valdadige only by a group of hills. About fifteen hectares are dedicated primarily to the territory's historic varieties, with just a sprinkling of white grapes to boot. The winery follows a style closely linked to tradition, making for a range with energetic character and gratifying drinkability. The Valpolicella Ca' Bussin '18 put in a convincing performance. It's a bottle that shows how even the simplest wines can have character and endure over the years. Aromas of cherry and pepper are perfectly recognizable, even in the mouth where it's lean, juicy and tasty. Greater aromatic depth characterizes the Amarone Riserva '12, with fruit growing sweeter and more mature, enriched by notes of medicinal herbs. It has greater volume on the palate but is able to unfold with the same grace, making for gratifying drinkability.

- ● Amarone della Valpolicella Cl. Ris. '12 ▼▼ 7
- ● Valpolicella Cl. Ca' Bussin '18 ▼▼ 2*
- ● Valpolicella Cl. Sup. La Preosa '17 ▼▼ 3
- ● Amarone della Valpolicella Cl. San Giorgio '15 ▽▽ 6
- ● Amarone della Valpolicella Cl. San Giorgio '13 ▽▽ 6
- ● Amarone della Valpolicella Cl. San Giorgio '12 ▽▽ 6
- ● Recioto della Valpolicella Cl. La Sengia '14 ▽▽ 4
- ● Valpolicella Cl. Ca' Bussin '16 ▽▽ 2*
- ● Valpolicella Cl. Sup. La Preosa '14 ▽▽ 3
- ● Valpolicella Cl. Sup. Ripasso Zane '16 ▽▽ 4
- ● Valpolicella Cl. Sup. Ripasso Zane '15 ▽▽ 4
- ● Valpolicella Cl. Sup. Ripasso Zane '13 ▽▽ 4

Bosco del Merlo

via Postumia, 12
30020 Annone Veneto [VE]
Tel. +39 0422768167
www.boscodelmerlo.it

CELLAR SALES
PRE-BOOKED VISITS
ANNUAL PRODUCTION 950,000 bottles
HECTARES UNDER VINE 90.00

The winery headed by Carlo and Roberto Paladin is one of the region's cornerstones, a large producer that operates mainly in the flat area stretching along the Adriatic coast between Veneto and Friuli, though they've also expanded into Franciacorta and Chianti Classico. Their Veneto wines are structured into two distinct brands: Paladin, which is dedicated to early-drinking wines, and Bosco del Merlo, which explores the potential of each grape variety in its most suitable vineyard. Their Roggio dei Roveri perfectly displays its potential. This Riserva from the 2017 vintage features aromas of red fruit and spices, enriched with floral nuances that refresh the aromas. In the mouth the wine unfolds with tension and sapidity, supported by an assertive tannic weight. As for their whites, we were impressed by the Sauvignon Turranio '19, dominated by floral and vegatal notes which follow onto a dynamic, pleasant palate.

- ● Lison Pramaggiore Refosco P. R. Roggio dei Roveri Ris. '17 ▼▼ 5
- ○ Friuli Sauvignon Turranio '19 ▼▼ 6
- ● Lison Pramaggiore Merlot Campo Camino Ris. '17 ▼▼ 4
- ● Lison Pramaggiore Rosso Vineargenti Ris. '17 ▼▼ 5
- ○ Pinot Grigio delle Venezie '19 ▼ 2
- ○ Pinot Grigio delle Venezie Tudajo '19 ▼ 3
- ○ Prosecco Brut Paladin '19 ▼ 3
- ○ Ribolla Gialla Iside '19 ▼ 3
- ○ Valdobbiadene Brut ▼ 3
- ● Lison Pramaggiore Merlot Campo Camino Ris. '16 ▽▽ 6
- ● Lison Pramaggiore Refosco P. R. Roggio dei Roveri Ris. '16 ▽▽ 6
- ○ Lison-Pramaggiore Sauvignon Turranio '18 ▽▽ 6

★Brigaldara

fraz. San Floriano
via Brigaldara, 20
37029 San Pietro in Cariano [VR]
Tel. +39 0457701055
www.brigaldara.it

CELLAR SALES
PRE-BOOKED VISITS
ANNUAL PRODUCTION 300,000 bottles
HECTARES UNDER VINE 50.00
SUSTAINABLE WINERY

The winery headed by Stefano Cesari spans about fifty hectares in some of Valpolicella's most beautiful areas, from the appellation's classic heart to its eastern part. The western wines are more subtle and play on elegance, drawing on the cool climate of the Marano valley for tension and suppleness. Their Marcellise and Grezzana wines are more powerful and assertive, playing instead on ripeness of fruit, making for greater fullness and warmth. Amarone Case Vecie made the most of the excellent 2015 vintage to offer up a suite of aromas dominated by ripe red fruit, enriched with nuances ranging between notes of spice and cut flowers. It enters the mouth confidently and powerfully, then gradually tightens up thanks to assertive tannins. We were also impressed by their Valpolicella Superiore '18 of the same name, which expresses aromas of wild fruit and undergrowth, displaying striking dynamism and pressure on the palate.

Wine	Rating
● Amarone della Valpolicella Case Vecie '15	▼▼▼ 8
● Valpolicella Sup. Case Vecie '18	▼▼ 4
● Amarone della Valpolicella Cavolo '15	▼▼ 6
○ Soave '19	▼▼ 3
● Valpolicella Sup. Ripasso Il Vegro '18	▼▼ 4
● Valpolicella '19	▼ 3
● Amarone della Valpolicella Case Vecie '13	▽▽▽ 6
● Amarone della Valpolicella Case Vecie '07	▽▽▽ 7
● Amarone della Valpolicella Cl. '13	▽▽▽ 6
● Amarone della Valpolicella Cl. '10	▽▽▽ 7
● Amarone della Valpolicella Cl. '06	▽▽▽ 6
● Amarone della Valpolicella Ris. '07	▽▽▽ 8

Sorelle Bronca

fraz. Colbertaldo
via Martiri, 20
31020 Vidor [TV]
Tel. +39 0423987201
www.sorellebronca.com

CELLAR SALES
PRE-BOOKED VISITS
ACCOMMODATION
ANNUAL PRODUCTION 350,000 bottles
HECTARES UNDER VINE 24.00

In the district of Conegliano Valdobbiadene there are few wineries that have been able to resist the temptations of the market and maintained a production approach linked only to their own vineyards, putting the bond between wine and vineyard first. Antonella and Ersiliana Bronca are an exception. For many years they've been overseeing two dozen hectares in the hilly strip of land that stretches from Valdobbiadene towards Conegliano, cultivating mostly Glera, but smaller plots dedicated to red grapes as well. Once again their two "single vineyard" Valdobbiadene wines head Antonella and Ersiliana's selection. Particella '68 is a Brut that explores the seductive, delicate qualities of the wine type, featuring aromas of yellow fruit and flowers which follow through onto the sapid, well-balanced, enthralling palate. Their 232, on the other hand, features edgier aromas, dominated by fresher fruit and vegetal overtones. In the mouth it reveals a dry, assertive and lingering profile.

Wine	Rating
○ Valdobbiadene Brut Particella 68 '19	▼▼▼ 4*
○ Valdobbiadene Extra Brut Particella 232 '19	▼▼ 5
● Ardesco '17	▼▼ 4
○ Colli di Conegliano Bianco Delico '19	▼▼ 3
○ Valdobbiadene Brut	▼▼ 3
○ Valdobbiadene Extra Dry	▼▼ 3
● Colli di Conegliano Rosso Ser Bele '09	▽▽▽ 5
● Colli di Conegliano Rosso Ser Bele '05	▽▽▽ 5
○ Valdobbiadene Brut Nature Particella 232 '18	▽▽▽ 5
○ Valdobbiadene Brut Particella 68 '15	▽▽▽ 4*
○ Valdobbiadene Brut Particella 68 '13	▽▽▽ 4*
○ Colli di Conegliano Bianco Delico '17	▽▽ 3

Luigi Brunelli

via Cariano, 10
37029 San Pietro in Cariano [VR]
Tel. +39 0457701118
www.brunelliwine.com

CELLAR SALES
PRE-BOOKED VISITS
ACCOMMODATION
ANNUAL PRODUCTION 120,000 bottles
HECTARES UNDER VINE 14.00

The Brunelli family's winery is situated in the western part of San Pietro in Cariano, a sort of flat strip of land that unfolds in the direction of Fumane. The winery is surrounded by vineyards, most of which are dedicated to the simplest selections. When it comes to their more ambitious wines, they draw on plots situated at over 400 meters above sea level, where vines have been growing for half a century. The style alternates between dynamic, racy wines and versions where concentration emerges as a key feature. Amarone Campo del Titari '15 displays distinctive richness and concentration. On the nose, it offers up aromas of overripe red fruit and spices, while the mature, caressing palate is dotted with sweet, smooth tannins. The Ripasso Pa' Riondo '17 also exhibits a mature and generous style, with sweet, appealing fruit following onto a palate with good concentration and suppleness. Their Valpolicella Superiore from the 2018 vintage comes through fresher, dynamic and racy.

● Amarone della Valpolicella Cl. Campo del Titari Ris. '15	🍷🍷 8
● Amarone della Valpolicella Cl. '16	🍷🍷 8
● Recioto della Valpolicella Cl. '18	🍷🍷 5
● Valpolicella Cl. Sup. '18	🍷🍷 3
● Valpolicella Cl. Sup. Ripasso Pa' Riondo '17	🍷🍷 4
● Corte Cariano '18	🍷 2
● Amarone della Valpolicella Cl. Campo del Titari '97	🍷🍷🍷 8
● Amarone della Valpolicella Cl. Campo del Titari '96	🍷🍷🍷 8
● Amarone della Valpolicella Cl. '15	🍷🍷 8
● Amarone della Valpolicella Cl. Campo del Titari Ris. '13	🍷🍷 8
● Amarone della Valpolicella Cl. Campo Inferi Ris. '13	🍷🍷 8

Buglioni

fraz. Corrubbio
via Campagnole, 55
37029 San Pietro in Cariano [VR]
Tel. +39 0456760681
www.buglioni.it

CELLAR SALES
PRE-BOOKED VISITS
ACCOMMODATION
ANNUAL PRODUCTION 170,000 bottles
HECTARES UNDER VINE 48.00

It's been almost thirty years since the Buglioni family launched its winemaking venture in Valpolicella, and today Mariano's is one of the fastest growing. The estate unfolds around the Corrubbio winery and in Sant'Ambrogio, for a total of about 50 hectares, mostly devoted to the appellation's traditional vines. Since the beginning, Diego Bertoni has been working in full harmony with Mariano, and together they've brought about a marked increase in quality in recent years. Their Valpolicella L'(Im)perfetto '17 plays on mature, close-focused, well-defined fruit, enriched with overtones of medicinal herbs and pepper. These follow through even clearer on the palate, where the wine comes through mouthfilling, becoming thinner around the acidity and tannic weight. Their Amarone Il Lussurioso '16 exhibits a more mature and generous aromatic expression, offering up a supple, plush palate, closing with a lovely dry sensation.

● Amarone della Valpolicella Cl. Il Lussurioso '16	🍷🍷 7
● Valpolicella Cl. Sup. L'(Im)perfetto '17	🍷🍷 4
● Valpolicella Cl. Sup. Ripasso Il Bugiardo '17	🍷🍷 5
○ Lugana Musa '19	🍷 2
● Amarone della Valpolicella Cl. Il Lussurioso '15	🍷🍷 7
● Amarone della Valpolicella Cl. Il Lussurioso '13	🍷🍷 7
● Valpolicella Cl. Sup. L'(Im)perfetto '16	🍷🍷 4
● Valpolicella Cl. Sup. L'Imperfetto '15	🍷🍷 4
● Valpolicella Cl. Sup. L'Imperfetto '14	🍷🍷 5
● Valpolicella Cl. Sup. Ripasso Il Bugiardo '16	🍷🍷 5

Ca' La Bionda

Fraz. Valgatara
via Bionda, 4
37020 Marano di Valpolicella [VR]
Tel. +39 0456801198
www.calabionda.it

CELLAR SALES
PRE-BOOKED VISITS
ACCOMMODATION
ANNUAL PRODUCTION 150,000 bottles
HECTARES UNDER VINE 29.00
VITICULTURE METHOD Certified Organic

Alessandro and Nicola Castellani are not only talented winegrowers and wine producers, they also possess sensitivity, poise and measure, qualities that have allowed them to establish a vision of what Valpolicella's wine is, and the potential the territory represents. About thirty hectares of organically managed hectares unfold in the Marano valley, almost contiguously, providing the grapes for a range entirely dedicated to tradition, and interpreted with tension and elegance. Their Riserva '12 Ravazzol offers up a suite of aromas with great depth, dominated by hints of very ripe fruit, refreshed by spices and moderate oak. The solid, caressing, warm palate manages to tighten up with precision and grip. We also liked their Superiore Casal Vegri '18, a Valpolicella that plays on aromatic freshness and impresses for its elegant, supple palate.

- ● Amarone della Valpolicella Cl. Vign. di Ravazzol Ris. '12 — TT 8
- ● Valpolicella Cl. Sup. Campo Casal Vegri '18 — TT 6
- ● Amarone della Valpolicella Cl. '15 — TT 8
- ○ Bianco del Casal '19 — TT 3
- ● Valpolicella Cl. '19 — TT 4
- ● Amarone della Valpolicella Cl. Vign. di Ravazzol '13 — YYY 8
- ● Amarone della Valpolicella Cl. Vign. di Ravazzol '11 — YYY 8
- ● Valpolicella Cl. Sup. Campo Casal Vegri '17 — YYY 6
- ● Valpolicella Cl. Sup. Campo Casal Vegri '15 — YYY 6
- ● Valpolicella Cl. Sup. Campo Casal Vegri '11 — YYY 5

Ca' Lustra - Zanovello

loc. Faedo
via San Pietro, 50
35030 Cinto Euganeo [PD]
Tel. +39 042994128
www.calustra.it

CELLAR SALES
PRE-BOOKED VISITS
ANNUAL PRODUCTION 160,000 bottles
HECTARES UNDER VINE 25.50
VITICULTURE METHOD Certified Organic
SUSTAINABLE WINERY

Marco and Linda Zanovello's estate is a landmark of Euganean viticulture. Founded by father Franco in 1977, it's since pursued not only organoleptic excellence in its wines, but also expression of this wonderful territory's attributes. Many hectares of property, only partly dedicated to viticulture, are scattered throughout the Euganean Hills Park, at times on volcanic soil, at times on terrain characterized by ancient marine material, making for a selection of great solidity and character. Sasso Nero and Girapoggio, both from the excellent 2016 vintage, are thoroughbreds from the Zanovello winery. One is a Merlot, the other a Cabernet, both perfectly express the sunniness of the hills, without forgoing grip and tension. The first revolves around central fruit, gradually giving way to notes of medicinal herbs and undergrowth, with a sound, juicy palate and a great finish. The second starts off more closed (almost hidden), but then it comes through with a sapid, enthralling palate.

- ● Colli Euganei Cabernet Girapoggio '16 — TT 3*
- ● Colli Euganei Merlot Sassonero '16 — TT 3*
- ○ Colli Euganei Bianco '19 — TT 3
- ○ Colli Euganei Fior d'Arancio Spumante Dolce '19 — TT 3
- ● Colli Euganei Merlot Cinto Alto '17 — TT 3
- ● Colli Euganei Rosso Moro Polo '16 — TT 2*
- ● Colli Euganei Rosso Natio '15 — TT 5
- ○ Il Boschetto '17 — TT 3
- ○ Moscato di Retia Passito — TT 3
- ○ Roverello Chardonnay '16 — T 3
- ● Colli Euganei Cabernet Girapoggio '05 — YYY 3
- ○ Colli Euganei Fior d'Arancio Passito '07 — YYY 4
- ● Colli Euganei Merlot Sassonero Villa Alessi '05 — YYY 3
- ● Colli Euganei Cabernet Girapoggio '15 — YY 3*
- ● Colli Euganei Merlot Sassonero '15 — YY 3*

Ca' Orologio

VIA CA' OROLOGIO, 7A
35030 BAONE [PD]
TEL. +39 042950099
www.caorologio.com

CELLAR SALES
PRE-BOOKED VISITS
ACCOMMODATION
ANNUAL PRODUCTION 30,000 bottles
HECTARES UNDER VINE 10.00
VITICULTURE METHOD Certified Organic
SUSTAINABLE WINERY

The southern part of the Euganean Hills has in Baone its epicentre. It's a small village surrounded by some of the most beautiful vineyards in the appellation, and it's here, inside the splendid Villa Ca' Orologio, that Mariagioia Rosellini launched her winery. She's managed to capture the sunny, almost Mediterranean character of this corner of Veneto, transforming it into voluptuous, energetic wines. Organic management of the 10-hectare estate gives rise to a reliable selection of great personality. Their Relógio '18 is a blend of Carmenère and Cabernet Franc which impresses right from its bright appearance. The nose offers up close-focused notes of wild berries and spices, which contrast with a curious note of pencil lead. The solid palate is supported by lively, crisp tannins that confer lightness and traction to a palate that unfolds with elegance and tension. Their aromatic Calaòne '18 features a more mature and sunny expression and reveals more acidity on the juicy palate.

Wine	Rating
● Colli Euganei Rosso Calaóne '18	🍷🍷 4
● Relógio '18	🍷🍷 5
○ Salaróla '19	🍷🍷 3
⊙ Salarosa '19	🍷 3
● Colli Euganei Rosso Calaóne '05	🍷🍷🍷 3*
● Relógio '09	🍷🍷🍷 4*
● Relógio '07	🍷🍷🍷 4
● Relógio '06	🍷🍷🍷 4
● Relógio '04	🍷🍷🍷 4*
● Colli Euganei Rosso Calaóne '17	🍷🍷 4
● Colli Euganei Rosso Calaóne '16	🍷🍷 4
● Lunisóle '16	🍷🍷 4
● Relógio '17	🍷🍷 5
● Relógio '16	🍷🍷 5
● Relógio '15	🍷🍷 5
○ Salaróla '18	🍷🍷 3
○ Salaróla '17	🍷🍷 3

★★Ca' Rugate

VIA PERGOLA, 36
37030 MONTECCHIA DI CROSARA [VR]
TEL. +39 0456176328
www.carugate.it

CELLAR SALES
PRE-BOOKED VISITS
ACCOMMODATION
ANNUAL PRODUCTION 700,000 bottles
HECTARES UNDER VINE 90.00
SUSTAINABLE WINERY

Founded after the Second World War by Fulvio 'Beo' Tessari, the turning point came in 1986 when the first bottles were produced under the Ca' Rugate brand. It was Fulvio's grandson Michele, in the early part of the new millennium, who took the winery to a new level, expanding the area under vine to almost ninety hectares in some of the most important appellations of Verona: Soave, Valpolicella and Lessinia. Today the vines are in the process of being converted to organic and the winery has become a real driving force for Soave. However, the most convincing results come from Lessinia, the Amedeo Pas Dosé '15, a sparkler of refined aromatic expression and gutsy acidic tension. A very different profile characterizes the Amarone Punta 470 '16, a wine with a mature yet extraordinarily fresh aromatic profile. It wins you over for the way the palate gradually unfolds. The Monte Alto '18 and Fiorentine '18 explore the more mature and alluring side of Garganega, pointing up great sensitivity in the cellar.

Wine	Rating
○ Lessini Durello Pas Dosé M. Cl. Amedeo Ris. '15	🍷🍷🍷 5
● Amarone della Valpolicella Punta 470 '16	🍷🍷 7
○ Recioto di Soave La Perlara '16	🍷🍷 5
○ Soave Cl. Monte Alto '18	🍷🍷 3*
○ Soave Cl. Monte Fiorentine '18	🍷🍷 3*
● Recioto della Valpolicella L'Eremita '17	🍷🍷 5
○ Soave Cl. San Michele '19	🍷🍷 2*
○ Soave Cl. Sup. Bucciato '18	🍷🍷 4
○ Studio '18	🍷🍷 4
● Valpolicella Rio Albo '19	🍷🍷 2*
● Valpolicella Sup. Campo Lavei '18	🍷🍷 4
● Valpolicella Sup. Ripasso Campo Bastiglia '18	🍷🍷 4
○ Soave Cl. Monte Alto '16	🍷🍷🍷 3*
○ Soave Cl. Monte Fiorentine '17	🍷🍷🍷 3*

Giuseppe Campagnola

FRAZ. VALGATARA
VIA AGNELLA, 9
37020 MARANO DI VALPOLICELLA [VR]
TEL. +39 0457703900
www.campagnola.com

CELLAR SALES
PRE-BOOKED VISITS
ANNUAL PRODUCTION 5,000,000 bottles
HECTARES UNDER VINE 157.00

The historic producer of Marano is now on its fifth generation of family, and what began as an activity aimed at making wines for the family tavern has become a large producer whose vineyards can be found in Valpolicella, near Lake Garda and in the Friulian plain. For their Valpolicellas, in addition to its own vineyards, the winery draws on a collaboration with about fifty local growers, who provide additional grapes. The grapes used to make the winery's two flagship wines are grown in the Marano district: Amarone Ris. '15 and Valpolicella Superiore '18, both dedicated to grandma Caterina Zardini. The first one wins you over with its intense and close-focused aromas of overripe fruit and spices, which come through even cleaner on the invigorating, solid palate. The second one plays more on fresh, sound fruit that follows onto a tapered palate, marked by a distinctive vibrant closure.

Wine	Rating
● Amarone della Valpolicella Cl. Caterina Zardini Ris. '15	🍷🍷 6
● Recioto della Valpolicella Cl. Casotto del Merlo '17	🍷🍷 5
● Valpolicella Cl. Sup. Caterina Zardini '18	🍷🍷 4
● Valpolicella Cl. Sup. Ripasso '18	🍷🍷 3
● Roccolo del Lago Corvina Veronese V. T. '18	🍷 3
○ Soave Cl. Vign. Monte Foscarino Le Bine '19	🍷 3
● Valpolicella Cl. Le Bine '19	🍷 3
● Amarone della Valpolicella Cl. Caterina Zardini '04	🍷🍷🍷 6
● Amarone della Valpolicella Cl. Caterina Zardini '01	🍷🍷🍷 6
● Amarone della Valpolicella Cl. Caterina Zardini '99	🍷🍷🍷 6
● Valpolicella Cl. Sup. Caterina Zardini '05	🍷🍷🍷 3*

★I Campi

LOC. ALLODOLA
FRAZ. CELLORE D'ILLASI
VIA DELLE PEZZOLE, 3
37032 ILLASI [VR]
TEL. +39 0456175915
www.icampi.it

CELLAR SALES
PRE-BOOKED VISITS
ANNUAL PRODUCTION 80,000 bottles
HECTARES UNDER VINE 12.00

Founded almost as a lark about fifteen years ago, I Campi has become Flavio Prà's primary job, with the winemaker considerably reducing his work as a consultant. His ten hectares of hillside plots can be found in Soave and Valpolicella, where volcanic soils alternate with marine marl, making for a range dedicated exclusively to traditional wines. The style is well defined according to the types: elegance and suppleness feature in their whites, while fullness and energy characterize their reds. The excellent 2019 vintage enabled them to produce a very precise Soave Campo Vulcano, with intense aromas of white-fleshed fruit and flowers, which wins over the palate with its length and elegance. Lunghi '16, on the other hand, reveals a varied suite of aromas consisting of spices and wild berries. In the mouth, the body is well-supported by acidity, which lengthens and refines the palate. Their Valpolicella Superiore proves approachable and fragrant with an exhilarating mouthfeel.

Wine	Rating
○ Soave Cl. Campo Vulcano '19	🍷🍷🍷 3*
● Amarone della Valpolicella Campi Lunghi '16	🍷🍷 6
● Valpolicella Sup. '18	🍷🍷 3*
○ Pinot Grigio delle Venezie '19	🍷🍷 2*
○ Soave Campo Base '19	🍷🍷 2*
● Valpolicella Sup. Bio '18	🍷🍷 3
● Valpolicella Sup. Ripasso Bio '18	🍷🍷 3
○ Lugana Campo Argilla '19	🍷 2
○ Soave Cl. Campo Vulcano '18	🍷🍷🍷 3*
○ Soave Cl. Campo Vulcano '15	🍷🍷🍷 3*
○ Soave Cl. Campo Vulcano '13	🍷🍷🍷 3*
○ Soave Cl. Campo Vulcano '12	🍷🍷🍷 3*
○ Soave Cl. Campo Vulcano '11	🍷🍷🍷 5
○ Soave Cl. Campo Vulcano '10	🍷🍷🍷 3*
● Valpolicella Sup. Ripasso Campo Ciotoli '13	🍷🍷🍷 3*

Canevel Spumanti

FRAZ. SACCOL
VIA ROCCAT E FERRARI, 17
31049 VALDOBBIADENE [TV]
TEL. +39 0423975940
www.canevel.it

CELLAR SALES
PRE-BOOKED VISITS
ANNUAL PRODUCTION 900,000 bottles
HECTARES UNDER VINE 26.00
VITICULTURE METHOD Certified Organic
SUSTAINABLE WINERY

This historic Saccol producer became part of the Boscaini family's group a few years ago, a move that's brought innovation and expertise to winery operating in a continuously evolving sector, Treviso sparkling winemaking. Today Canevel Spumanti avails itself of a rich, organically-managed estate, which is accompanied by vineyards cultivated by a dense group of local growers. The latter, who are followed step-by-step by Masi's technical staff, provide the grapes for a range that has in Valdobbiadene DOCG its flagship. Their top-notch Campofalco '19 is a Valdobbiadene Brut that offers up a unique suite of aromas dominated by exotic and yellow-fleshed fruit. On tasting, it is striking for its rich taste sensations, revealing a rich profile with good concentration. Their Extra Brut runs along similar lines and, thanks to its lower residual sugar, exhibits a palate with a drier, racier progression. Their Cartizze, on the other hand, plays on more pervasive, mature aromas and features a creamy, soft palate.

Wine	Rating
○ Valdobbiadene Brut Campofalco '19	🍷🍷 3*
○ Cartizze Dry '19	🍷🍷 5
○ Valdobbiadene Extra Brut Terre Del Faè '19	🍷🍷 3
○ Valdobbiadene Brut Campofalco Vign. Monfalcon '17	🍷🍷🍷 5
○ Valdobbiadene Dosaggio Zero Vign. Del Faè '18	🍷🍷🍷 3*
○ Cartizze '18	🍷🍷 4
○ Cartizze '17	🍷🍷 4
○ Valdobbiadene Brut Campofalco '18	🍷🍷 3
○ Valdobbiadene Brut Setàge '18	🍷🍷 4
○ Valdobbiadene Dosaggio Zero Vign. del Faè '17	🍷🍷 4
○ Valdobbiadene Dosaggio Zero Vign. del Faè '16	🍷🍷 4
○ Valdobbiadene Extra Dry Il Millesimato '18	🍷🍷 5

La Cappuccina

FRAZ. COSTALUNGA
VIA SAN BRIZIO, 125
37032 MONTEFORTE D'ALPONE [VR]
TEL. +39 0456175036
www.lacappuccina.it

CELLAR SALES
PRE-BOOKED VISITS
RESTAURANT SERVICE
ANNUAL PRODUCTION 310,000 bottles
HECTARES UNDER VINE 42.00
VITICULTURE METHOD Certified Organic
SUSTAINABLE WINERY

Now that the shift to 'organic' is almost obligatory for many producers in the wine-growing sector, the choice made more than thirty years ago by the Tessari brothers appears all the more visionary and pioneering. Today more than 40 hectares overseen by Elena, Pietro and Sisto, are divided into three areas: San Brizio and Monte Stelle in Costalunga, and Pergola in Val d'Alpone, near Montecchia di Crosara. Their style privileges elegance and tension for the whites, richness and power for the reds. The Tessari family have submitted a high-quality wine selection, led by their shining Soave Monte Stelle '19, made with grapes grown in vinyeards located in the Soave Classico area. It offers up delicate floral and white fruit aromas, while the palate displays great tension and suppleness, highlighting elegance and length. Their San Brizio '18 plays on more mature and complex aromas, dominated by hints of yellow-fleshed fruit which come through close-focused on a precise, soft palate.

Wine	Rating
○ Soave Cl. Monte Stelle '19	🍷🍷 4
● Campo Buri '16	🍷🍷 5
○ Soave '19	🍷🍷 3
○ Soave Fontégo '19	🍷🍷 3
○ Soave San Brizio '18	🍷🍷 5
○ Filòs Brut	🍷 2
● Camp Buri Cabernet Sauvignon '95	🍷🍷🍷 5
○ Basaltik Sauvignon '18	🍷🍷 2*
● Campo Buri '15	🍷🍷 4
○ Recioto di Soave Arzimo '16	🍷🍷 5
○ Recioto di Soave Arzimo '15	🍷🍷 5
○ Soave '18	🍷🍷 2*
○ Soave Fontégo '18	🍷🍷 3
○ Soave Cl. Monte Stelle '18	🍷🍷 3*
○ Soave San Brizio '17	🍷🍷 3*
○ Soave San Brizio '16	🍷🍷 3*
○ Villa Buri Brut M. Cl. '09	🍷🍷 5

Le Carline

via Carline, 24
30020 Pramaggiore [VE]
Tel. +39 0421799741
www.lecarline.com

CELLAR SALES
PRE-BOOKED VISITS
ANNUAL PRODUCTION 400,000 bottles
HECTARES UNDER VINE 18.00
VITICULTURE METHOD Certified Organic

Daniele Piccinin was ahead of his time in embracing the dictates of organic farming out of a deep personal conviction. This was back when production was often more aimed at increasing quantity than developing the deep bond between vineyard and territory. Today the winery on Via Carline is a benchmark for Lison Pramaggiore, the great Venetian denomination enclosed between the Prealps and the sea. Alongside the grapes that have characterized the Veneto plain for decades, more and more space is being dedicated to PIWI (fungus-resistant) varieties—perhaps the new frontier of organic farming. Their excellent Carlino Rosso is a Bordeaux blend that makes the most of the 2015 vintage to confer complex aromas and a sapid, well-balanced palate. Their Dogale is the usual Verduzzo sweet Passito wine with a delicate aromatic expression and charming palate. Also worthy of mention is their Resiliens Bianco, a blend of all the new varieties planted, interpreted with richness, sapidity and tension.

Wine	Rating
● Carline Rosso '15	🍷🍷 3
○ Dogale Passito	🍷🍷 4
○ Resiliens '19	🍷🍷 3
○ Diana Brut M. Cl.	🍷 4
○ Lison-Pramaggiore Chardonnay '18	🍷 3
● Venezia Cabernet Franc '18	🍷 3
○ Diana Brut M. Cl. '16	🍷🍷 4
○ Diana Brut M. Cl. '15	🍷🍷 4
● Lison-Pramaggiore Merlot '16	🍷🍷 2*
● Lison-Pramaggiore Refosco P. R. '18	🍷🍷 2*
○ Resiliens '18	🍷🍷 3

Carpenè Malvolti

via Antonio Carpenè, 1
31015 Conegliano [TV]
Tel. +39 0438364611
www.carpene-malvolti.com

CELLAR SALES
PRE-BOOKED VISITS
ANNUAL PRODUCTION 5,300,000 bottles
HECTARES UNDER VINE 26.00
SUSTAINABLE WINERY

Carpené Malvolti is one of the best known wineries in Prosecco Superiore, a producer active for over a century and a half and which the world of sparkling wines owes a great deal to. The Carpené family's commitment is a constant one: personally oversee the work of highlighting the attributes of the territory and the wine that best represents it. While only a few vineyards are cultivated directly, a large number of growers contribute to a range focused on sparkling wines. Their Brut 1924 is a Prosecco Superiore with distinctive apple and pear aromas, refreshed by floral notes and a palate that impresses for its delicate and creamy bubbles. The wine harks back to the original version from 1924, the first to inextricably link the name Prosecco to the Conegliano hills. Their Cartizze offers up a more appealing, soft and caressing palate.

Wine	Rating
○ Cartizze 1868	🍷🍷 5
○ Conegliano Valdobbiadene Brut 1924	🍷🍷 3
⊙ Brut Rosé	🍷 3
○ Conegliano Valdobbiadene Brut 1868	🍷 3
○ Conegliano Valdobbiadene Extra Dry 1868	🍷 3
○ Tarvisium Brut M. Cl.	🍷 5
○ Conegliano Valdobbiadene Dry Cuvée Oro	🍷🍷 3*
○ Conegliano Valdobbiadene Extra Dry PVXINVM '17	🍷🍷 8
○ Conegliano Valdobbiadene Extra Dry PVXINVM '14	🍷🍷 5

Casa Cecchin

via Agugliana, 11
36054 Montebello Vicentino [VI]
Tel. +39 0444649610
www.casacecchin.it

CELLAR SALES
PRE-BOOKED VISITS
ANNUAL PRODUCTION 30,000 bottles
HECTARES UNDER VINE 3.00
SUSTAINABLE WINERY

The territory of Lessinia can be divided into two zones. The larger, higher area is often still used for grazing and alpine cheese production. The foothills, whose elevations can range from 5-600 meters above sea level, are occupied by vineyards in the positions that are best suited to grape cultivation. The undisputed queen of this territory is Durella, which the Cecchin family transforms into sparkling wines of great personality and tension by drawing on the grape's plucky, acidic verve. The 2014 vintage enabled them to produce an excellent Riserva, a "zero dosage" which offers up delicate aromas of flowers, white fruit and mineral hints. Then it changes pace in the mouth, all the aromatic shyness is overwhelmed by a dynamic palate with great sapidity, supported by an acid backbone that expands the palate, proving one of the best versions we have tasted. Their Nostrum '15, on the other hand, comes through fuller and compact, winning over the palate with assertiveness and grip.

Wine	Rating
○ Lessini Durello Dosaggio Zero M. Cl. Ris. '14	TTT 5
○ Lessini Durello Extra Brut M. Cl. Nostrum '15	TT 5
○ Montebello Passito '16	TT 5
○ Durello Passito Montebello '15	YY 5
○ Il Durello '16	YY 2*
○ Lessini Durello Brut M. Cl. Nostrum '14	YY 4
○ Lessini Durello Brut M. Cl. Nostrum '13	YY 4
○ Lessini Durello Dosaggio Zero M. Cl. '11	YY 5
○ Lessini Durello Extra Brut M. Cl. Nostrum '12	YY 4
○ Lessini Durello Il Durello '14	YY 2*
○ Lessini Durello Pietralava '14	YY 2*
○ Pietralava '18	YY 3
○ Pietralava '17	YY 3

Casa Roma

via Ormelle, 19
31020 San Polo di Piave [TV]
Tel. +39 0422855339
www.casaroma.com

CELLAR SALES
PRE-BOOKED VISITS
ANNUAL PRODUCTION 200,000 bottles
HECTARES UNDER VINE 15.00

Luigi Peruzzeto's winery is situated in the flat area between the Treviso pre-Alps and the sea, just a stone's throw from the Piave river. Here, where clay alternates with the gravelly and pebbly soil that characterizes the terrain closest to the river, they've been cultivating vines for as long as anyone can remember. For over a century many international varieties have found a home in this corner of Veneto, thus we find them alongside native grapes like Raboso and Marzemina Bianca. Their range of wines draw on these varieties, resulting in standard-label sparkling wines that express the varietal character of the grapes and reserves dedicated to traditional cultivars. The undisputed king of the cellar is the Raboso variety, which brought all its weight to bear in the 2013 vintage. It proves faint, almost hidden, on the nose, allowing its aromas of red fruit and spices to gradually emerge. The palate wins you over for the way it manages to handle body with weight and lightness.

Wine	Rating
● Peruzzet Cabernet Sauvignon '19	TT 2*
○ Peruzzet Manzoni Bianco '19	TT 2*
● Piave Malanotte '14	TT 6
○ Piave Manzoni Bianco San Dordi '18	TT 3
● Piave Raboso '13	TT 4
● Peruzzet Carmènere '19	T 2
○ Peruzzet Chardonnay '19	T 2
⊙ Peruzzet Manzoni Moscato Rosato Dolce	T 2
● Peruzzet Merlot	T 2
○ Pinot Grigio delle Venezie Peruzzet '19	T 2
● Piave Carmènere Peruzzet '18	YY 2*
● Piave Malanotte '12	YY 6
○ Piave Manzoni Bianco Peruzzet '18	YY 2*
○ Piave Manzoni Bianco San Dordi '17	YY 3
● Piave Raboso '12	YY 4
● Piave Raboso Peruzzet '13	YY 4

Case Paolin

via Madonna Mercede, 55
31040 Volpago del Montello [TV]
Tel. +39 0423871433
www.casepaolin.it

CELLAR SALES
PRE-BOOKED VISITS
ANNUAL PRODUCTION 145,000 bottles
HECTARES UNDER VINE 16.00
VITICULTURE METHOD Certified Organic
SUSTAINABLE WINERY

The Pozzobon family winery was founded in the 1970s, when Emilio bought the estate that the family had been sharecropping for generations. Today his sons, Diego, Adelino and Mirco, are at the helm, and have developed the winemaking business by shuttering the property's other activities and moving the core plots from the plains, where the winery is located, to the slopes of Montello. Glera, Manzoni Bianco and Bordeaux varieties are all organically cultivated. Once again this year, the San Carlo leads the selection of wines submitted. It's a Bordeaux that plays on fruit, finding its completion in delicate nuances of oak. In the mouth it's full and soft, closing with a long, crisp finish. The Asolo Brut, a Prosecco Superiore dominated by fruity aromas, is also interesting. Full and mature on the palate, it's well accompanied by bubbles.

● Montello e Colli Asolani Rosso San Carlo '16	TT 5
○ Asolo Brut	TT 3
○ Costa degli Angeli Manzoni Bianco '19	TT 3
● Rosso del Milio '18	TT 3
○ Asolo Frizzante Col Fondo	T 3
● Cabernet '19	T 2
○ Prosecco di Treviso Extra Dry	T 2
● Cabernet '17	YY 2*
○ Costa degli Angeli Manzoni '16	YY 3*
○ Costa degli Angeli Manzoni Bianco '18	YY 3
● Montello e Colli Asolani Rosso San Carlo '15	YY 5
● Rosso del Milio '17	YY 3
● Rosso del Milio '16	YY 3
● Rosso del Milio '15	YY 3

Michele Castellani

fraz. Valgatara
via Granda, 1
37020 Marano di Valpolicella [VR]
Tel. +39 0457701253
www.castellanimichele.it

CELLAR SALES
PRE-BOOKED VISITS
ANNUAL PRODUCTION 300,000 bottles
HECTARES UNDER VINE 50.00

Sergio Castellani's winery is situated in Valgatara, at the entrance of the Marano valley, where wineries often mix with small artisan activities. Their 50 hectares of vineyards, some of which are owned and some of which are rented, unfold along the slopes of the nearby hills, where the territory's traditional grapes are accompanied by smaller plots dedicated to international varieties. Theirs is a range of great rigor and concentration, whatever the typology. Their Amarones pursue the pleasantness of super-ripe fruit, in part through relatively short work in the cellar, the idea being to maintain the primacy of varietal expression. The Cinquestelle Collezione Ca' del Pipa '17 delivered for its generosity and tension, all supported by good acidity and assertive tannins. The Campo Casalin '17, on the other hand, expresses more of a raisiny note, coming through softer and more pervasive on the palate.

● Amarone della Valpolicella Cl. Campo Casalin I Castei '17	TT 6
● Amarone della Valpolicella Cl. Cinquestelle Collezione Ca' del Pipa '17	TT 7
● Recioto della Valpolicella Cl. Monte Fasenara I Castei '18	TT 5
● Sergio '16	TT 4
● Valpolicella Cl. Campo del Biotto I Castei '19	T 2
● Valpolicella Cl. Sup. Ripasso Costamaran I Castei '18	T 3
● Recioto della Valpolicella Cl. Le Vigne Ca' del Pipa '99	YYY 6
● Amarone della Valpolicella Cl. Cinquestelle Collezione Ca' del Pipa '15	YY 7

Castello di Roncade

VIA ROMA, 141
31056 RONCADE [TV]
TEL. +39 0422708736
www.castellodironcade.com

CELLAR SALES
PRE-BOOKED VISITS
ANNUAL PRODUCTION 200,000 bottles
HECTARES UNDER VINE 45.00

The Ciani Bassetti family acquired the property of Castello di Roncade during the first post-war period, and today it's an agricultural leader in the plains enclosed between Venice and Treviso. The splendid 16th-century residence, circumscribed by walls in the center of Roncade, is surrounded by more than a hundred hectares of vineyards, mostly red Bordeaux varieties, but there are also native grape varieties such as Raboso and the ubiquitous Glera. For some years now the cellar has moved to a modern and well-equipped facility in Mogliano Veneto. The Bianco dell'Arnasa '18 is a monovarietal Chardonnay that matures in small oak barrels. The nose reveals mature, still-crisp yellow fruit, with delicate spicy notes rising up from the background. Rather than surprising for concentration and power, the palate expands with elegance and tension. Made with raisined Raboso grapes, the Baroness Ilaria '15 features aromas of super-ripe fruit and a tantalizing sweetness.

Wine	Rating
● Baronessa Ilaria Raboso Passito '15	▼▼ 5
○ Venezia Chardonnay Bianco dell'Arnasa '18	▼▼ 3
○ Baronessa Isabella Brut	▼ 3
○ Manzni Bianco '19	▼ 3
○ Patriarca Extra Dry	▼ 3
● Piave Cabernet '18	▼ 3
● Piave Merlot '18	▼ 3
● Piave Raboso dell'Arnasa '16	▼ 3
● Baronessa Ilaria Raboso Passito '13	▽▽ 5
● Piave Raboso dell'Arnasa '15	▽▽ 3
● Piave Raboso dell'Arnasa '14	▽▽ 3
● Piave Raboso dell'Arnasa '12	▽▽ 2*
○ Venezia Chardonnay dell'Arnasa '17	▽▽ 2*
● Villa Giustinian '12	▽▽ 3

★Cavalchina

LOC. CAVALCHINA
FRAZ. CUSTOZA
VIA SOMMACAMPAGNA, 7
37066 SOMMACAMPAGNA [VR]
TEL. +39 045516002
www.cavalchina.com

CELLAR SALES
PRE-BOOKED VISITS
ANNUAL PRODUCTION 445,000 bottles
HECTARES UNDER VINE 50.00

Luciano and Franco Piona's winery was one of the first to relaunch the area that from the southeastern shore of Lake Garda opens up to include the surrounding hills, where vines destined for Bardolino alternate with those for Custoza. Over the years the property has expanded through acquisitions along the Mincio, into Valpolicella and finally into Lugana as well. Luciano and Franco interpret these very different areas with a broad-based production style. This year they submitted a selection of superb precision, captained by the house champion, the Custoza Amedeo '18. It pours a faint straw-yellow, while on the nose it offers up a broad array of aromas. Notes of exotic fruit intersect with fresher hints of flowers and citrus fruits. On the palate it succeeds in the difficult task of combining solidity and finesse, once again proving one of the region's most interesting whites. The Amarone '16 also delivered, playing on the centrality of fruit and generous flavor.

Wine	Rating
○ Custoza Sup. Amedeo '18	▼▼▼ 3*
● Amarone della Valpolicella Torre D'Orti '16	▼▼ 6
● Bardolino Casella '17	▼▼ 5
○ Custoza '19	▼▼ 2*
● Garda Cabernet Sauvignon Falcone Prendina '17	▼▼ 4
○ Garda Riesling Prendina '19	▼▼ 3
● Valpolicella Sup. Ripasso Torre d'Orti '18	▼▼ 3
● Valpolicella Torre d'Orti '18	▼▼ 3
⊙ Bardolino Chiaretto '19	▼ 2
○ Lugana L'Lac '19	▼ 3
○ Custoza Sup. Amedeo '17	▽▽▽ 3*
○ Custoza Sup. Amedeo '16	▽▽▽ 3*
○ Custoza Sup. Amedeo '15	▽▽▽ 2*
○ Custoza Sup. Amedeo '14	▽▽▽ 3*

Cavazza

c.da Selva, 22
36054 Montebello Vicentino [VI]
Tel. +39 0444649166
www.cavazzawine.com

CELLAR SALES
PRE-BOOKED VISITS
ACCOMMODATION
ANNUAL PRODUCTION 860,000 bottles
HECTARES UNDER VINE 150.00
SUSTAINABLE WINERY

The Cavazza family boasts a strong and well-rooted link with Gambellara, one that began almost a century ago and runs right up to present day. The few original hectares have swiftly increased. The late 1980s, in particular, were a period of rapid growth, with the acquisition of the Cicogna estate on the nearby Berici Hills, a property that's a real jewel today. Production remains firmly linked to these two territories, with entry-level wines characterized by great varietal expressiveness and premium selections where the strength of the vineyards emerges. The Cabernet '16 from the Cicogna estate draws on ripe fruit, which stands out clearly against a background of spices and Mediterranean scrub. Great ripeness in the mouth leads into a broad palate well-supported by sapidity, with a long and balanced finish. In Gambellara, on the other hand, all the class of their Creari '17 comes out in an original interpretation of this Vicenza white wine that plays on aromatic complexity and powerful palate.

● Colli Berici Cabernet Cicogna '16	🍷🍷 5
● Fornetto '17	🍷🍷 4
○ Gambellara Cl. Bocara '19	🍷🍷 2*
○ Gambellara Cl. Creari '17	🍷🍷 3
● Cicogna Syrah '15	🍷🍷 5
● Colli Berici Cabernet Cicogna '15	🍷🍷 4
● Colli Berici Cabernet Cicogna '13	🍷🍷 4
● Colli Berici Merlot Cicogna '16	🍷🍷 5
● Colli Berici Tai Rosso Corallo '16	🍷🍷 3
● Fornetto '16	🍷🍷 3
○ Gambellara Cl. Bocara '17	🍷🍷 2*
○ Gambellara Cl. Creari '16	🍷🍷 3*
○ Gambellara Cl. La Bocara '16	🍷🍷 2*
○ Gambellara Cl. La Bocara '15	🍷🍷 2*
● Syrhae Cicogna '16	🍷🍷 4

Giorgio Cecchetto

fraz. Tezze di Piave
via Piave, 67
31028 Vazzola [TV]
Tel. +39 043828598
www.rabosopiave.com

CELLAR SALES
PRE-BOOKED VISITS
ANNUAL PRODUCTION 200,000 bottles
HECTARES UNDER VINE 73.00
SUSTAINABLE WINERY

After a tumultuous stretch through the dolomites, the course of the Piave river grows gradually calmer as it reaches Tezze di Piave. Here its bed, scattered with white pebbles, gets wider and gradually disappears into the Treviso countryside. It's here that we find Giorgio Cecchetto's winery. In thirty years the estate has grown, expanded into the areas of Motta di Livenza and Cornuda, making for a range that expresses a strong link with the identity of the varieties cultivated, starting with the characteristic Turbose. 2017 brought with it an aromatic suite dominated by fruity sensations, which the Piave Raboso offers with great intensity and clarity, all underlined by a discreet, almost hidden presence of oak. On the palate, the wine opens with generosity and fullness, tapering and finishing with characteristic acidity. The Sante Rosso '18 also convinced. It's a monovarietal Merlot marked by fruity suggestions and a full, pervasive and warm palate.

● Piave Raboso '17	🍷🍷 3
● RP Passito di Raboso	🍷🍷 4
● Sante Rosso '18	🍷🍷 4
● Cabernet Sauvignon '19	🍷 2
○ Manzoni Bianco '19	🍷 2
● Carmenère '18	🍷🍷 2*
● Malanotte Gelsaia '13	🍷🍷 5
○ Manzoni Bianco '15	🍷🍷 2*
● Piave Malanotte Gelsaia '16	🍷🍷 5
● Piave Raboso '16	🍷🍷 3
● Piave Raboso '15	🍷🍷 3
● Piave Raboso '13	🍷🍷 3
● Piave Raboso '12	🍷🍷 3
⊙ Rosa Bruna Cuvée 21 Brut M. Cl. '12	🍷🍷 3
● Sante Rosso '16	🍷🍷 4

Gerardo Cesari

Loc. Sorsei, 3
37010 Cavaion Veronese [VR]
Tel. +39 0456260928
www.cesariverona.it

CELLAR SALES
PRE-BOOKED VISITS
ANNUAL PRODUCTION 1,500,000 bottles
HECTARES UNDER VINE 120.00
SUSTAINABLE WINERY

The Cesari family's historic winery comprises plots in Verona's most important appellations, from Valpolicella to Custoza, from Lugana to Bardolino. More than a hundred hectares of vineyards give rise to the grapes that are then transported to their Cavaion Veronese and Fumane cellars, only to be aged for anywhere from a few months, in the case of the more youthful versions, to many years for their premium Amarone reserves. Their range is never aimed at strength, pursuing tension and elegance instead. The Il Bosco vineyard in Castelrotto gives rise to the grapes for their Amarone of the same name. A 2015 made mostly with Corvina (with a share of Rondinella), it offers up intense notes of sweet, overripe fruit, which we find perfectly expressed on the palate where oak is responsible for tying the sensations together. The Bosan '11, a pervasive and warm reserve, is more evolved aromatically.

Wine	Rating
● Amarone della Valpolicella Cl. Il Bosco '15	TT 7
● Amarone della Valpolicella Cl. Bosan Ris. '11	TT 8
● Valpolicella Ripasso Sup. Bosan '17	TT 5
● Amarone della Valpolicella Cl. '16	T 6
○ Lugana Cento Filari '19	T 3
● Valpolicella Sup. Ripasso Mara '18	T 3
● Amarone della Valpolicella Cl. '14	YY 5
● Amarone della Valpolicella Cl. Bosan Ris. '10	YY 8
● Amarone della Valpolicella Cl. Bosan Ris. '09	YY 8
● Amarone della Valpolicella Cl. Il Bosco '13	YY 6
● Amarone della Valpolicella Cl. Il Bosco '12	YY 6
● Valpolicella Sup. Ripasso Bosan '16	YY 4

Italo Cescon

fraz. Roncadelle
p.zza dei Caduti, 3
31024 Ormelle [TV]
Tel. +39 0422851033
www.cesconitalo.it

CELLAR SALES
PRE-BOOKED VISITS
ANNUAL PRODUCTION 930,000 bottles
HECTARES UNDER VINE 115.00
VITICULTURE METHOD Certified Organic
SUSTAINABLE WINERY

Piave is riddled with producers that once made simple, approachable wines, but today have thrown themselves headlong into Prosecco. Domenico, Gloria and Graziella Cescon, on the other hand, have chosen a different path, expanding their property, adopting organic management, and developing their vineyards by focusing on the grape variety that best suits the soil conditions. The result is a range of outstanding wines, including a couple of real gems. This year the Cescon brothers submitted a top selection, with the Madre leading among our favorites. A 2018 monovarietal Manzoni Bianco, on the nose it offers up intense notes of exotic fruit and dried flowers, all of which reemerge on an energetic palate of great sapidity. Pinot Grigio also got a lot of attention. Several versions explore the potential of a great grape that's too often reserved for ordinary production. The Integro '18 is complex on the nose, tense and plucky on the palate.

Wine	Rating
○ Madre '18	TTT 5
● Amaranto 72 Ris. '15	TT 6
● Piave Raboso Rabià Ris. '13	TT 7
○ Pinot Grigio delle Venezie Integro Tesirare '18	TT 3
○ Pinot Grigio delle Venezie Macerato Tesirare '18	TT 5
○ Pinot Grigio delle Venezie Tralcetto '19	TT 3
● Tralcetto Merlot '18	TT 3
○ Madre '17	YYY 5
○ Madre '16	YYY 5
○ Madre '14	YYY 4*
● Amaranto 72 Ris. '13	YY 6
● Chieto '16	YY 4
● Tralcetto Merlot '17	YY 3
○ Tralcetto Pinot Grigio '18	YY 3

Clementi

FRAZ. VALGATARA
VIA GNIREGA, 2
37020 MARANO DI VALPOLICELLA [VR]
TEL. +39 3472534456
www.vini-clementi.com

CELLAR SALES
PRE-BOOKED VISITS
ANNUAL PRODUCTION 25,000 bottles
HECTARES UNDER VINE 12.50
SUSTAINABLE WINERY

In the late 1960s, the Clementi family acquired a historic property in the heart of Valpolicella Classica, in Gnirega, along the limestone divide that separates the Marano and Negrar valleys. The vineyards lie in this area, at elevations spanning 300–400 meters, and are mainly exposed to the south and west. In the cellar the utmost attention is paid to traditional wines, which are interpreted by combining the concentration conferred by partial drying of the grapes with aromatic integrity and tension. The Amarone '11 has been submitted after a long period in the cellar. This wine features aromas of overripe fruit and spices, enriched with nuances of still slightly forward oak. The generous palate is well-controlled by tannins. Their Ripasso '16 is even more interesting, with its pleasantly light appearance, floral aromas and a palate that unfolds with grace and grip, proving very pleasant.

Wine	Rating
● Amarone della Valpolicella Cl. '11	🍷🍷 8
● Valpolicella Cl. Sup. '17	🍷🍷 4
● Valpolicella Cl. Sup. Ripasso '16	🍷🍷 5

Coffele

VIA ROMA, 5
37038 SOAVE [VR]
TEL. +39 0457680007
www.coffele.it

CELLAR SALES
PRE-BOOKED VISITS
ANNUAL PRODUCTION 120,000 bottles
HECTARES UNDER VINE 25.00
VITICULTURE METHOD Certified Organic

Soave Classico is characterized by a very dense weave of hills. The eastern slopes are dominated by lava basalt, while the western ones are rich in limestone. Chiara and Alberto Coffele lead the family winery in Castelcerino, one of the highest points of the appellation, situated almost between the two soil typologies and bolstered by a single, contiguous vineyard that stretches for many hectares. Their range is almost entirely dedicated to Soave's classic wines. This year's selection has no weak points, with four wines that do an outstanding job representing Soave's territory and traditions. The Alzari '18 is a honed blend of fresh and slightly dried Garganega matured in large casks. On the nose it proves multifaceted and subtle, dominated by notes of fruit. On the palate it moves sapid and light, finishing crisp and very long. The Recioto Le Sponde '18, a passito of rare integrity and juice, is explosive as usual.

Wine	Rating
○ Recioto di Soave Cl. Le Sponde '18	🍷🍷 5
○ Soave Cl. Alzari '18	🍷🍷 3*
○ Soave Cl. Ca' Visco '19	🍷🍷 3
○ Soave Cl. Castel Cerino '19	🍷🍷 3
○ Recioto di Soave Cl. Le Sponde '09	🍷🍷🍷 5
○ Soave Cl. Ca' Visco '14	🍷🍷🍷 3*
○ Soave Cl. Ca' Visco '05	🍷🍷🍷 3*
○ Soave Cl. Ca' Visco '04	🍷🍷🍷 2
○ Soave Cl. Ca' Visco '03	🍷🍷🍷 2
○ Recioto di Soave Cl. Le Sponde '16	🍷🍷 5
○ Recioto di Soave Cl. Le Sponde '15	🍷🍷 5
○ Recioto di Soave Cl. Le Sponde '14	🍷🍷 5
○ Soave Cl. Alzari '17	🍷🍷 3*
○ Soave Cl. Alzari '16	🍷🍷 3*
○ Soave Cl. Ca' Visco '18	🍷🍷 3*
○ Soave Cl. Ca' Visco '16	🍷🍷 3*
○ Soave Cl. Ca' Visco '15	🍷🍷 3*

Conte Collalto

via XXIV Maggio, 1
31058 Susegana [TV]
Tel. +39 0438435811
www.cantine-collalto.it

CELLAR SALES
PRE-BOOKED VISITS
ACCOMMODATION
ANNUAL PRODUCTION 850,000 bottles
HECTARES UNDER VINE 164.00
SUSTAINABLE WINERY

This Susegana winery's history goes well back, having got its start as a donation from Berengario II sometime before the year 1000. Today Isabella Collalto de Croÿ is at the helm, managing the large estate on the slopes of the Treviso foothills. Maximum attention is paid to Glera, the undisputed queen in this part of Veneto, even if there's no lack of international varieties or unexpected varieties, such as the numerous crossbreeds invented by Professor Manzoni in the years after the First World War. The outstanding Ponte Rosso is a Prosecco Superiore from a vineyard near Castello di San Salvatore, an area characterized by clayey soil and a perfect southern exposure. Clear, fruity sensations of green apple rise up on the nose, while in the mouth it proves energetic, taut and well supported by acidity. The San Salvatore explores the more appealing, approachable qualities of the typology. A mature, fruity nose is exalted by a harmonious, sapid palate caressed by bubbles.

○ Conegliano Valdobbiadene Extra Brut Ponte Rosso '19	🍷🍷 3*
○ Conegliano Valdobbiadene Brut San Salvatore '19	🍷🍷 3
● Incrocio Manzoni 2.15 '18	🍷🍷 2*
● Piave Cabernet Torrai Ris. '15	🍷🍷 5
○ Rosabianco '19	🍷🍷 2*
○ Conegliano Valdobbiadene Dry Dame '19	🍷 3
○ Conegliano Valdobbiadene Extra Dry Gaio '19	🍷 3
○ Conegliano Valdobbiadene Rive di Collalto Brut Isabella '18	🍷 4
○ Manzoni Bianco '19	🍷 2
⊙ Violette Extra Dry Rosé	🍷 2
○ Conegliano Valdobbiadene Extra Dry Gaio '18	🍷🍷 3

Le Colture

loc. Santo Stefano
via Follo, 5
31049 Valdobbiadene [TV]
Tel. +39 0423900192
www.lecolture.com

CELLAR SALES
PRE-BOOKED VISITS
ACCOMMODATION
ANNUAL PRODUCTION 750,000 bottles
HECTARES UNDER VINE 40.00

The Ruggeri family have always placed great value on the land, both arable and not. In an area where the land is often cultivated by local farmers while large producers process their harvests, the Ruggeri family has tried to keep the supply chain together, working more than half of the vineyards they need for their production themselves. Glera takes center stage, giving rise to a complete and reliable range of sparkling wines. The grapes for the Gerardo come from the best, steepest vineyards in Santo Stefano. It's a brut that alternates characteristic notes of apple and wisteria flowers with fresh vegetal nuances. In the mouth it's marked by sapidity and acid tension, unfolding decisively towards a crisp, plucky finish. The Dry Pianer exhibits an entirely different profile, playing on more expressive, ripe fruit and a smooth palate caressed by bubbles.

○ Valdobbiadene Rive di Santo Stefano Brut Gerardo '19	🍷🍷 3*
○ Cartizze	🍷🍷 5
○ Valdobbiadene Brut Fagher	🍷🍷 3
○ Valdobbiadene Dry Cruner	🍷🍷 3
○ Valdobbiadene Extra Dry Pianer	🍷🍷 3
○ Valdobbiadene Prosecco Frizzante Mas	🍷 3
○ Valdobbiadene Brut Rive di Santo Stefano Gerardo '16	🍷🍷 3
○ Valdobbiadene Rive di Santo Stefano Brut Gerardo '18	🍷🍷 3*
○ Valdobbiadene Rive di Santo Stefano Brut Gerardo '15	🍷🍷 3

Corte Adami

Circonvallazione Aldo Moro, 32
37038 Soave [VR]
Tel. +39 0456190218
www.corteadami.it

CELLAR SALES
PRE-BOOKED VISITS
ANNUAL PRODUCTION 170,000 bottles
HECTARES UNDER VINE 37.00
SUSTAINABLE WINERY

After a long history of cultivating vineyards for local cooperatives, a few years ago the Adami family decided to change course and restructure in such a way that they can now personally oversee all stages of production. Today Giulia, Martina and Andrea are at the helm, guiding a producer that operates in both Soave and Valpolicella, and giving rise to a reliable, constantly growing selection of wines. Although the winery's heart beats in Soave, the most interesting results this year come from Valpolicella, with a Superiore that offers up intense notes of underbrush and cherry refreshed by a vital peppery nuance. The palate impresses less for its power than for its tension and length. When it comes to their whites, it's worth pointing out the concentrated flavor of their Vigna della Corte, a late-harvest monovarietal Garganega matured in steel.

● Amarone della Valpolicella '16	TT 6
○ Soave '19	TT 2*
○ Soave Sup. V. della Corte '18	TT 3
● Valpolicella Sup. '17	TT 3
● Valpolicella Sup. Ripasso '17	TT 4
○ Recioto di Soave '15	T 4
○ Soave Cl. Cimalta '19	T 2
● Valpolicella '19	T 2
● Amarone della Valpolicella '15	YY 6
● Amarone della Valpolicella '14	YY 6
○ Soave '17	YY 2*
○ Soave Cl. Cimalta '17	YY 2*
○ Soave Decennale '16	YY 3
○ Soave Sup. V. della Corte '17	YY 3
○ Soave Sup. V. della Corte '16	YY 3
● Valpolicella Sup. Ripasso '16	YY 4
● Valpolicella Sup. Ripasso '14	YY 3

Corte Gardoni

loc. Gardoni, 5
37067 Valeggio sul Mincio [VR]
Tel. +39 0456370270
www.cortegardoni.it

CELLAR SALES
PRE-BOOKED VISITS
ANNUAL PRODUCTION 180,000 bottles
HECTARES UNDER VINE 25.00

Mattia, Stefano and Andrea Piccoli oversee the winery founded by their father, Gianni, in the wine-growing district south of Lake Garda and along the Mincio river. These gentle hills, often barely mentioned, were originally orchards, but for years now they've hosted vineyards, all managed with the utmost respect for the environment and with an experienced eye for quality. Their wines, which focus primarily on the two local appellations, Bardolino and Custoza, highlight the finesse conferred by both the territory and grapes cultivated. The Bardolino Pràdicà '18 put in an excellent performance. It's a red that, in spite of its reserved, almost edgy aromatic profile, comes through with a rare energy on the palate, proving sapid, supple and long. The Custoza Mael '18 exhibits the opposite profile. Great aromatic, elegant and floral thrust gives way to a palate that plays on grip and tension. Finally we mention their excellent Bardolino Le Fontane '19, a juicy and highly pleasant wine.

● Bardolino Sup. Pràdicà '18	TTT 3*
⊙ Bardolino Chiaretto Nichesole '19	TT 2*
○ Custoza Mael '18	TT 3*
● Bardolino Le Fontane '19	TT 2*
● Becco Rosso '18	TT 3
○ Custoza Greoto '19	T 2
● Bardolino Sup. Pràdicà '16	YYY 3*
○ Bianco di Custoza Mael '09	YYY 2*
○ Bianco di Custoza Mael '08	YYY 2*
○ Custoza Mael '13	YYY 3*
○ Custoza Mael '11	YYY 3*
● Bardolino Le Fontane '18	YY 2*
● Bardolino Le Fontane '16	YY 2*
● Bardolino Sup. Pradicà '15	YY 3*
● Becco Rosso '16	YY 3
○ Custoza '17	YY 2*
○ Custoza Mael '16	YY 3*

Corte Moschina

via Moschina, 1
37030 Roncà [VR]
Tel. +39 0457460788
www.cortemoschina.it

CELLAR SALES
PRE-BOOKED VISITS
ANNUAL PRODUCTION 95,000 bottles
HECTARES UNDER VINE 35.00
SUSTAINABLE WINERY

To the east Soave borders Gambellara. The two territories are joined by the volcanic soil that characterizes both and the prevalence of Garganega, the undisputed queen of these hills. Patrizia Niero's winery unfolds primarily in Soave, with the occasional plot on the Lessinia hills, where Durella takes center stage. Their range, which is grounded in these two cultivars, highlights the winery's roots in these two different territories and their traditions. The Soave Evaos '18 gave an excellent performance: intense aromas of ripe white fruit on a nose that wins you over with its continual pace, without weak points, right through to the long finish. As for their sparkling wines made with Durella grapes, we really liked the Riserva Valgrande '13, with its nose of fruity notes mingling well with crusty bread and yeast. The palate reveals a richer, more substantial profile than expected, proving sapid, dry and generous.

○ Soave Evaos '18	🍷🍷 3*
○ Lessini Durello Dosaggio Zero Valgrande M. Cl. Ris. '13	🍷🍷 5
○ Lessini Durello Extra Brut Valgrande M. Cl.	🍷🍷 4
○ Recioto di Soave Incanto '17	🍷🍷 4
○ Soave Roncathe '19	🍷🍷 3
○ Soave Sup. I Tarai '18	🍷🍷 4
○ Lessini Durello Brut M. Cl. '13	🍷🍷 4
○ Lessini Durello Brut M. Cl. 60 Mesi Ris. '12	🍷🍷 5
○ Lessini Durello Brut Nature M. Cl. Ris. '11	🍷🍷 5
○ Recioto di Soave Incanto '15	🍷🍷 4
○ Soave Evaos '17	🍷🍷 3*
○ Soave Roncathe '18	🍷🍷 2*
○ Soave Sup. I Tarai '17	🍷🍷 3
○ Soave Sup. I Tarai '16	🍷🍷 3*

Corte Rugolin

fraz. Valgatara
via Rugolin, 1
37020 Marano di Valpolicella [VR]
Tel. +39 0457702153
www.corterugolin.it

CELLAR SALES
PRE-BOOKED VISITS
ANNUAL PRODUCTION 80,000 bottles
HECTARES UNDER VINE 13.00
SUSTAINABLE WINERY

In a territory like Valpolicella, which is constantly evolving, the Coati family's winery represents a haven for exclusively traditional cultivars and wines closely linked to the historic Veronese appellation. The vineyards are mostly distributed around the Valgatara cellar, at the entrance to the Marano valley, but also reach into the hills of Castelrotto and San Giorgio. Their wines offer aromatic clarity and a richness that's well contrasted by the acidity of the area's grapes. Their outstanding Amarone Crosara de le Strie from the 2015 vintage pulled out a great performance. Its approachable nose is dominated by sensations of very ripe fruit, while the palate reveals notes of bitter cocoa and spices alongside fruit, making for a wine with a powerful body and continual development, closing with a warm, soft finish. Their Ripasso '17 was also interesting, playing on fresher, intact fruit and exhibiting a supple, elegant palate.

● Amarone della Valpolicella Cl. Crosara de le Strie '15	🍷🍷 7
● Valpolicella Cl. Rugolin '19	🍷🍷 3
● Valpolicella Cl. Sup. Ripasso '17	🍷🍷 5
● Amarone della Valpolicella Cl. Crosara de le Strie '13	🍷🍷 7
● Amarone della Valpolicella Cl. Crosara de le Strie '12	🍷🍷 7
● Amarone della Valpolicella Cl. Monte Danieli Ris. '12	🍷🍷 8
● Recioto della Valpolicella Cl. '17	🍷🍷 5
● Recioto della Valpolicella Cl. '15	🍷🍷 5
● Valpolicella Cl. Sup. Ripasso '16	🍷🍷 5
● Valpolicella Cl. Sup. Ripasso '15	🍷🍷 5
● Valpolicella Cl. Sup. San Giorgio '16	🍷🍷 5

★Corte Sant'Alda

loc. Fioi
via Capovilla, 28
37030 Mezzane di Sotto [VR]
Tel. +39 0458880006
www.cortesantalda.it

CELLAR SALES
PRE-BOOKED VISITS
ACCOMMODATION
ANNUAL PRODUCTION 90,000 bottles
HECTARES UNDER VINE 19.00
VITICULTURE METHOD Certified Biodynamic

Marinella Camerani's winery was founded almost by chance more than thirty years ago. What might have seemed like a quest for freedom has, year after year, become one of Valpolicella's most notable wineries, first in terms of the quality of the wines and then, gradually, thanks to an increasingly firm awareness of the central role that nature plays in our lives. Today the facts count more than certifications. Indeed, here vines aren't guided, but rather accompanied through the seasons, and their wine is on a virtuous path that represents a new frontier for the producer. After last year's exploit, the Valpolicella Ca' Fiui '19 proves once again to be one of the most interesting reds in the appellation. The intense aromas of wild berries and spices feature a fresh, inviting floral note beneath. Its solid, supple palate wins over even the most experienced enthusiast. The Campi Magri '17, on the other hand, is a Ripasso exhibiting aromas of undergrowth and moist earth, with a dynamic, enthralling palate.

● Valpolicella Ca' Fiui '19	🍷🍷 3*
● Valpolicella Sup. Ripasso Campi Magri '17	🍷🍷 5
⊙ Agathe '19	🍷🍷 4
● Amarone della Valpolicella Ruvain/Torrente Adalia '16	🍷🍷 8
● Recioto della Valpolicella '17	🍷🍷 6
● Recioto della Valpolicella Roasan/Fiorire Adalia '16	🍷🍷 6
○ Soave '19	🍷🍷 3
● Valpolicella Laute/Gente Adalia '19	🍷🍷 3
● Valpolicella Sup. Ripasso Balt/Bosco Adalia '18	🍷🍷 4
○ Inti '19	🍷 3
○ Soave Singan/Cantare Adalia '19	🍷 3
● Valpolicella Ca' Fiui '18	🍷🍷🍷 3*
● Valpolicella Sup. Mithas '12	🍷🍷🍷 8

Costa Arente

loc. Costa, 86
37023 Grezzana [VR]
Tel. +39 0422864511
www.arente.it

ANNUAL PRODUCTION 46,000 bottles
HECTARES UNDER VINE 17.00
SUSTAINABLE WINERY

A few years ago the large group headed by Generali acquired the splendid estate of Costa Arente, a property that spans many hectares in Valpantena, the only subzone in the Valpolicella appellation other than 'Classica'. A wide and sunny valley characterized by gravelly soil, as it approaches the hills the presence of clay and limestone increases, making it ideal for bringing traditional grapes to maturity. Only three wines are produced, all closely tied to the appellation while expressing the warmth of these hills. The outstanding Ripasso '17 offers up intense aromas of super-ripe red fruit, refreshed by spicy overtones. The generous palate expresses the Mediterranean character of this corner of Valpolicella and the wine reveals sapidity and good tannic weight. Their Amarone '16 plays on fruit that steals the limelight, while the palate features the distinctive trait of this valley, sapidity, which governs its pace.

● Amarone della Valpolicella Valpantena '16	🍷🍷 8
● Valpolicella Valpantena Sup. Ripasso '17	🍷🍷 4
● Valpolicella Valpantena '18	🍷 3
● Amarone della Valpolicella '15	🍷🍷 7
● Amarone della Valpolicella '13	🍷🍷 7
● Valpolicella Valpantena '17	🍷🍷 3

Famiglia Cottini Monte Zovo

LOC. ZOVO, 23A
37013 CAPRINO VERONESE [VR]
TEL. +39 0457281301
www.montezovo.com

CELLAR SALES
PRE-BOOKED VISITS
ACCOMMODATION AND RESTAURANT SERVICE
ANNUAL PRODUCTION 1,000,000 bottles
HECTARES UNDER VINE 140.00
SUSTAINABLE WINERY

Diego Cottini's winery is located at the northern end of the province of Verona, where the hills become increasingly steep and the Adige valley emerges ominously. Their many hectares of vineyards in eastern Valpolicella, Tregnago and Sirmione are destined both for the production of Bardolino and for their more creative selections, while the Civaie estate hosts the grapes for their Lugana wines. The style, which is precise and well interpreted by Diego's son Michele, features clear varietal expression and excellent solidity. The quality of their Amarone stands out from the large selection of wines, which range from historic Verona appellations to more creative wines. It offers up aromas of sweet, very ripe fruit, enriched with balsamic, oaky overtones. The wine opens warm and soft in the mouth, progressing into a generous, powerful palate well-supported by tannins. The Ripasso '18, on the other hand, features fresher, intact fruit, with a warm, soft palate.

- ● Amarone della Valpolicella '16 🍷🍷🍷 8
- ● Crocevento Pinot Nero '17 🍷🍷 6
- ○ Lugana Ca' del Perlago '19 🍷🍷 3
- ● Valpolicella Sup. Ripasso '18 🍷🍷 5
- ● Calinverno '16 🍷 5
- ○ Oltremonte Sauvingon '19 🍷 4
- ● Amarone della Valpolicella '15 🍸🍸🍸 8
- ● Amarone della Valpolicella '14 🍸🍸🍸 8
- ● Amarone della Valpolicella '13 🍸🍸 7
- ● Amarone della Valpolicella '12 🍸🍸 6
- ● Ca' Linverno '14 🍸🍸 4
- ● Calinverno '15 🍸🍸 5
- ● Valpolicella Sup. '15 🍸🍸 4
- ● Valpolicella Sup. Ripasso '17 🍸🍸 5
- ● Valpolicella Sup. Ripasso '16 🍸🍸 5
- ● Valpolicella Sup. Ripasso '15 🍸🍸 4
- ● Valpolicella Sup. Ripasso '14 🍸🍸 4

Dal Cero Tenuta Corte Giacobbe

VIA MOSCHINA, 11
37030 RONCÀ [VR]
TEL. +39 0457460110
www.dalcerofamily.it

CELLAR SALES
PRE-BOOKED VISITS
ANNUAL PRODUCTION 300,000 bottles
HECTARES UNDER VINE 40.00

The areas of Roncà and Terrossa, on the slopes of the Calvarina, Crocetta and Duello volcanoes, represent a new frontier for Soave. It's a wilder territory than the appellation's classic heart, still rich in woods and uncultivated land, where vineyards have to be teased out of the mountainside but enjoy great day-night temperature swings and constant breezes. The Dal Cero family operates here, bolstered by an indissoluble bond with the land and its fruits, serving as a modern and yet time-honored interpreter of Scaligera's white wine. The Soave Runcata '18 perfectly represents the territory. Vibrant aromas rise up out of the glass, fresh yet mature. On the palate it alternates the poise of oak with the unpredictability of acidity. When it comes to their Valpolicella reds, we appreciated the frankness of the Ripasso '17, a wine that offers up aromas of fruit and spices. It's still quite fresh, winning over the palate for its flavor and tension.

- ○ Soave Sup. Runcata '18 🍷🍷🍷 5
- ○ Brut M. Cl. 🍷🍷 4
- ○ Soave Roncà Monte Clavarina '19 🍷🍷 2*
- ● Valpolicella '18 🍷🍷 3
- ● Valpolicellla Sup. Ripasso '17 🍷🍷 4
- ○ Soave Sup. Runcata '17 🍸🍸🍸 3*
- ○ Soave Sup. Vign. Runcata '14 🍸🍸🍸 2*
- ○ Lessini Durello Dosaggio Zero Cuvée Augusto M. Cl. '13 🍸🍸 5
- ○ Lessini Durello Dosaggio Zero M. Cl. Augusto '12 🍸🍸 5
- ○ Soave Sup. Vign. Runcata '16 🍸🍸 5
- ○ Soave Sup. Vign. Runcata '15 🍸🍸 4

Dal Maso

c.da Selva, 62
36054 Montebello Vicentino [VI]
Tel. +39 0444649104
www.dalmasovini.com

CELLAR SALES
PRE-BOOKED VISITS
RESTAURANT SERVICE
ANNUAL PRODUCTION 300,000 bottles
HECTARES UNDER VINE 30.00
SUSTAINABLE WINERY

Nicola Dal Maso is confidently leading the winery founded by his father, Luigino, in 1975 (though the family's agricultural roots in the area go back to the late 19th century). Alongside him, his sisters Silvia and Anna oversee the entire commercial and administrative side of the business, making for one of the area's most notable producers. Today their vineyards, which are distributed equally between Gambellara/Lessinia and the Berici Hills, give rise to reds of great generosity and dynamism, and whites of great finesse and tension. The Dal Maso brothers submitted an excellent selection this year, with our personal favorites being the Colli Berici reds. In the running for the top position are Terra dei Rovi and Merlot Casara Roveri, both from the 2017 vintage. The first is a Bordeaux blend with an intense aromatic expression and elegant palate, while the second conveys almost explosive fruit on the nose, with rigour and grip on a very precise palate.

● Colli Berici Merlot Casara Roveri '17	🍷🍷 5
● Colli Berici Rosso Terra dei Rovi '17	🍷🍷 6
● Colli Berici Cabernet Casara Roveri '17	🍷🍷 3
● Colli Berici Tai Rosso Colpizzarda '17	🍷🍷 5
● Colli Berici Tai Rosso Montemitorio '18	🍷🍷 3
○ Gambellara Ca' Fischele '19	🍷🍷 3
○ Gambellara Riva del Molino '18	🍷🍷 3
○ Lessini Durello Pas Dosé M. Cl. Ris. '16	🍷🍷 5
● Montebelvedere Cabernet '18	🍷🍷 3
○ Lessini Durello Brut	🍷 3
● Colli Berici Merlot Casara Roveri '15	♡♡♡ 5
○ Gambellara Cl. Riva del Molino '07	♡♡♡ 2*
● Colli Berici Merlot Casara Roveri '16	♡♡ 5
● Colli Berici Tai Rosso Colpizzarda '16	♡♡ 5
○ Lessini Durello Pas Dosé M. Cl. Ris. '15	♡♡ 5
○ Recioto di Gambellara Cl. Riva dei Perari '17	♡♡ 5

Sandro De Bruno

via Santa Margherita, 26
37030 Montecchia di Crosara [VR]
Tel. +39 0456540465
www.sandrodebruno.it

ANNUAL PRODUCTION 80,000 bottles
HECTARES UNDER VINE 22.00

Sandro De Bruno's winery is located at the bottom of the valley that separates the village of Monteforte from that of Roncà, a large alluvial stretch that collects the basaltic detritus from the surrounding hills. His vineyards climb up one of the most interesting and lesser known areas of the appellation, the slopes of Mount Calvarina, which made a decisive contribution to the genesis of Soave. In the large and well-equipped cellar, their wines age at length before being released on the market. The Soave Colli Scaligeri '18 is an interesting wine with aromas reminiscent of ripe white fruit and dried flowers, which gradually give way to clearer mineral notes. The palate expresses good body, allowing the more vibrant and pleasantly rustic character of Garganega emerge. The grapes used to produce the Extra Brut 60 from the 2010 vintage are grown in nearby Lessinia. This sparkling wine exhibits complex aromas and a dry, dynamic, gutsy palate.

○ Lessini Durello Extra Brut M. Cl. 60 '10	🍷🍷 5
○ Soave '19	🍷🍷 3
○ Soave Colli Scaligeri '18	🍷🍷 2*
○ Lessini Durello Extra Brut M. Cl. 100 Ris. '10	🍷 5
○ Lessini Durello Extra Brut M. Cl. 36 '15	🍷 5
○ Soave Sup. Monte San Piero '18	🍷 3
○ Lessini Durello Extra Brut M. Cl. Ris. '10	♡♡ 5
○ Soave '17	♡♡ 3
○ Soave Colli Scaligeri '16	♡♡ 2*
○ Soave Sup. Monte San Piero '16	♡♡ 3

De Faveri

FRAZ. BOSCO
VIA SARTORI, 21
31020 VIDOR [TV]
TEL. +39 0423987673
www.defaverispumanti.it

CELLAR SALES
PRE-BOOKED VISITS
ANNUAL PRODUCTION 900,000 bottles
HECTARES UNDER VINE 31.50

Lucio and Mirella De Faveri founded their winery in the late 1970s, and since then their direction has always been illuminated by a desire to produce Prosecco in the best way possible. Today, they are joined by their children Giorgia and Giordano, who are involved in the commercial and production side, respectively. The estate's vineyards cover about 15 hectares in the historic heart, with another 6 hectares in the extended zone. Local growers provide the rest of the grapes needed to complete their range. The excellent Brut '19 from their Etichetta Nera line, conveys all its finesse right from the perlage, launched by floral aromas accompanied by juicy ripe white fruit. The palate comes through stylish, supported by acidity and the presence of bubbles, leaving it to the sweetness to add balance. The Brut G&G, on the other hand, seems less expressive on the nose, however its stylish and sapid palate wins you over.

○ Valdobbiadene Brut	🍷🍷 2*
○ Valdobbiadene Brut G&G '19	🍷🍷 3
○ Valdobbiadene Brut Nera '19	🍷🍷 2*
○ Valdobbiadene Extra Dry Nera	🍷🍷 2*
○ Cartizze	🍷 4
⊙ Extra Dry Rosé	🍷 2
○ Valdobbiadene Extra Dry	🍷 2

De Stefani

VIA CADORNA, 92
30020 FOSSALTA DI PIAVE [VE]
TEL. +39 042167502
www.de-stefani.it

CELLAR SALES
PRE-BOOKED VISITS
ANNUAL PRODUCTION 500,000 bottles
HECTARES UNDER VINE 60.00
SUSTAINABLE WINERY

The De Stefani family's bond with viticulture dates back to the second half of the 1800s, but it was with Tiziano's arrival in the late 1950s that the producer acquired the profile that we know today. His son Alessandro is now at the helm, overseeing an estate whose core has shifted from the original vineyards of Refrontolo to the Piave plain, Fossalta and Monastier, where an increasingly environmentally-friendly approach to wine-growing prevails. Their wines have a clear style, one that's focused on the varietal expression of the grapes. Olmera '18 is a blend of slightly dried Tai aged in oak and Sauvignon fermented entirely in steel. The result is a white wine where fresh notes alternate with overripe ones, while the palate opens full and well-supported by acidity and sapidity. Of their reds, we were impressed by the Venezia '17, a full, fresh Bordeaux blend with aromatic notes and a supple, juicy palate.

○ Olmera '18	🍷🍷 5
● Piave Malanotte '15	🍷🍷 3
● Solèr '17	🍷🍷 4
○ Valdobbiadene Brut Nature Rive di Refrontolo '19	🍷🍷 3
● Venezia Rosso '17	🍷🍷 4
○ Vènis '19	🍷🍷 3
● Kreda '16	🍷 6
○ Pinot Grigio delle Venezie '19	🍷 3
○ Prosecco Frizzante Col Fondo '18	🍷 4
○ Valdobbiadene Brut '19	🍷 3
● Kreda '15	🍷🍷 6
○ Olmera '17	🍷🍷 5
○ Olmera '16	🍷🍷 5
● Solèr '16	🍷🍷 4
○ Valdobbiadene Brut Nature Rive di Refrontolo '18	🍷🍷 2*

Conte Emo Capodilista La Montecchia

via Montecchia, 16
35030 Selvazzano Dentro [PD]
Tel. +39 049637294
www.lamontecchia.it

CELLAR SALES
PRE-BOOKED VISITS
ACCOMMODATION
ANNUAL PRODUCTION 144,000 bottles
HECTARES UNDER VINE 30.00
SUSTAINABLE WINERY

The Euganean Hills are made up of a dense weave of volcanic slopes that cover a 10 X 15 km area to the southwest of Padua. It's a relatively small territory, but it's extremely varied, with a decidedly more Mediterranean climate and vegetation to the south. Giordano Emo Capodilista oversees about thirty hectares of vineyards here, both in the warmer and cooler parts of the territory, making for a solid and reliable selection of wines. The grapes used for Villa Capodilista, a Bordeaux blend with a dash of Raboso, are grown in Selvazzano. It offers up very fresh aromas that follow through onto a dynamic, supple palate. Their outstanding Cuore di Donna Daria is a kind of Solera method Fior d'Arancio Passito containing different percentages of vintages from 2002 to 2015. Exotic, with hints of Mediterranean scrub and Nocino walnut liqueur, it exhibits an exhilarating palate where sapidity contrasts sweetness.

● Colli Euganei Rosso Villa Capodilista '15	▼▼ 5
○ Cuore di Donna Daria	▼▼ 8
● Carmenère Progetto Recupero '16	▼▼ 3
○ Colli Euganei Fior d'Arancio Spumante Dolce	▼▼ 2*
● Godimondo Cabernet Franc '19	▼▼ 2*
○ Piuchebello Bianco '19	▼▼ 2*
○ Acinidoro '17	▼ 4
○ Colli Euganei Pinot Bianco Rolandino '19	▼ 2
● Forzaté Raboso '15	▼ 2
● Baon '15	▽▽▽ 7
● Colli Euganei Cabernet Sauvignon Ireneo '12	▽▽▽ 4*
○ Colli Euganei Fior d'Arancio Passito Donna Daria '06	▽▽▽ 5

Farina

loc. Pedemonte
via Bolla, 11
37029 San Pietro in Cariano [VR]
Tel. +39 0457701349
www.farinawines.com

CELLAR SALES
PRE-BOOKED VISITS
ANNUAL PRODUCTION 800,000 bottles
HECTARES UNDER VINE 45.00

Even if it's a relatively young outfit, the Farina family's winery boasts a strong and well-rooted viticultural tradition in Valpolicella. Today Claudio, Elena and Alessandro run a producer that makes full use of its own vineyards, while also relying on collaborations with local winegrowers who are followed step-by-step throughout the year before delivering their harvests to Via Bolla in Pedemonte. The range focuses mainly on Valpolicella, but Verona's other production areas have a presence as well. Grapes grown in old vineyards in Masua, San Pietro in Cariano, produce the Ripasso Montecorna '18. The wine ages in large barrels and barriques, making for intense notes of very ripe red fruit, refreshed by subtle spices. In the mouth the wine comes through soft and caressing, winning you over with its stylish palate. Their Ripasso '17 proves more approachable on the nose and juicy on the palate.

● Amarone della Valpolicella Cl. '17	▼▼ 5
● Valpolicella Cl. Sup. Ripasso '18	▼▼ 2*
● Valpolicella Cl. Sup. Ripasso Montecorna '18	▼▼ 3
● Corte Conti Cavalli '17	▼ 4
● Nodo d'Amore '18	▼ 3
○ Nodo d'Amore '18	▼ 3
● Amarone della Valpolicella Cl. '16	▽▽ 5
● Amarone della Valpolicella Cl. Montefante Ris. '13	▽▽ 8
● Amarone della Valpolicella Cl. Montefante Ris. '12	▽▽ 8
● Amarone della Valpolicella Cl. Montefante Ris. '11	▽▽ 8
● Valpolicella Cl. Sup. Ripasso '17	▽▽ 2*
● Valpolicella Cl. Sup. Ripasso Montecorna '17	▽▽ 3

Fattori

FRAZ. TERROSSA
VIA OLMO, 4
37030 RONCÀ [VR]
TEL. +39 0457460041
www.fattoriwines.com

CELLAR SALES
PRE-BOOKED VISITS
ANNUAL PRODUCTION 280,000 bottles
HECTARES UNDER VINE 72.00
SUSTAINABLE WINERY

Antonio Fattori's winery is bolstered by a network of vineyards that span some three different territories. If the Soave area, and Roncà in particular, serves as their base, their holdings in Lessinia and Valpolicella are more recent. Their whites play on aromatic fragrance, while their reds combine fragrance with structure and ageworthiness. The owners are also taking their first steps in sparkling wine production. The Valpolicella Col de la Bastia '18 offers up intensely fruity aromas on the nose, embellished with balsamic notes of incense and cyclamen that add freshness and cohesion. In the mouth, the wine comes through light and refined, featuring sensations of great elegance and pressure. The Roncha '17, on the other hand, is a Trebbiano di Soave with faint, delicately floral aromas and a pleasantly rustic, dynamic palate that conveys solidity.

Wine	Glasses	Price
○ Lessini Durello Non Dosato M. Cl. 60 '13	🍷🍷	6
○ Roncha Trebbiano '17	🍷🍷	3
○ Soave Danieli '19	🍷🍷	2*
○ Soave Motto Piane '18	🍷🍷	4
● Valpolicella Sup. Col de la Bastia '18	🍷🍷	3
● Amarone della Valpolicella Col de La Bastia '16	🍷	6
● Amarone della Valpolicella Ris. '15	🍷	8
○ Lessini Durello Brut M. Cl. 60 '13	🍷	6
○ Soave Cl. Runcaris '19	🍷	2
● Amarone della Valpolicella Col de La Bastia '15	🍸🍸	6
○ Soave Cl. Runcaris '17	🍸🍸	2*
○ Soave Motto Piane '17	🍸🍸	4
● Valpolicella Sup. Ripasso Col de la Bastia '17	🍸🍸	5

Il Filò delle Vigne

VIA TERRALBA, 14
35030 BAONE [PD]
TEL. +39 042956243
www.ilfilodellevigne.it

CELLAR SALES
PRE-BOOKED VISITS
ANNUAL PRODUCTION 50,000 bottles
HECTARES UNDER VINE 22.00

Carlo Giordani's Filò delle Vigne spans over twenty hectares in the southern part of the Euganean Hills, the warmest and most Mediterranean area that Veneto can offer. Here, on gentle slopes characterized by volcanic soils, Bordeaux varieties have found the ideal habitat to ripen, steadily taking on a fruity profile where vegetal notes fade into the background. Matteo Zanaica oversees both the vineyards and the winery, making for a range that's decidedly limited in numbers, but full of charm and personality. It's difficult to choose which was their best wine this year, with Borgo delle Casette and Casa del Merlo competing for the role. The first is a 2016 Cabernet with a rich profile, compact but supple at the same time. The second, on the other hand, is a 2017 Merlot featuring intensely fruity overtones and a powerful palate, perfectly supported by acidity and tannins. Lastly, the Cecilia di Baone, a Cabernet aged in concrete, exhibits an approachable, sunny character.

Wine	Glasses	Price
● Colli Euganei Cabernet Borgo delle Casette Ris. '16	🍷🍷🍷	5
● Colli Euganei Merlot Casa del Merlo '17	🍷🍷	5
● Colli Euganei Cabernet Cecilia di Baone Ris. '17	🍷🍷	3
● Io di Baone '16	🍷🍷	3
○ Terralba di Baone '19	🍷🍷	3
● Volo '19	🍷	3
● Colli Euganei Cabernet Borgo delle Casette Ris. '12	🍸🍸🍸	5
● Colli Euganei Cabernet Borgo delle Casette Ris. '10	🍸🍸🍸	5
● Colli Euganei Cabernet Borgo delle Casette Ris. '06	🍸🍸🍸	5
● Colli Euganei Merlot Casa del Merlo '16	🍸🍸🍸	5

Silvano Follador

loc. Follo
fraz. Santo Stefano
via Callonga, 11
31040 Valdobbiadene [TV]
Tel. +39 0423900295
www.silvanofollador.it

CELLAR SALES
PRE-BOOKED VISITS
ANNUAL PRODUCTION 20,000 bottles
HECTARES UNDER VINE 3.50

In recent years, Conegliano Valdobbiadene has undergone major transformations, with large producers intensifying their relationship with local growers so as to ensure they have enough quality grapes to meet their production needs. Then there are the small wineries, like Silvano and Alberta Follador's, which have preferred to draw exclusively on their own vineyards, even when it means limited production capacities. A handful of biodynamically managed hectares hectares give rise to a range marked by character and finesse. Only traditional grapes, mainly Glera with the occasional use of Bianchetta, Perera and Verdiso, make up the base for the Valdobbiadene Extra Brut '19. This sparkling wine with elegant aromas of white fruit and flowers, features a dynamic palate with great finesse, supported by sapidity and acidity. Their Metodo Classico, made with grapes from the 2018 vintage, explores the more concealed qualities of the appellation: complexity and longevity.

○ Valdobbiadene Extra Brut '19	▼▼ 5
○ Valdobbiadene Extra Brut M. Cl. '18	▼▼ 3
○ Cartizze Brut '08	▽▽▽ 4
○ Valdobbiadene Brut Nature '18	▽▽▽ 5
○ Valdobbiadene Brut Nature '16	▽▽▽ 5
○ Bianco Fermo '18	▽▽ 3
○ Bianco Fermo '17	▽▽ 3
○ Bianco Fermo '16	▽▽ 3
○ Cartizze Brut Nature '13	▽▽ 4
○ Cartizze Brut Nature M. Cl. '16	▽▽ 4
○ Valdobbiadene Brut Nature '17	▽▽ 5
○ Valdobbiadene Brut Nature '15	▽▽ 4
○ Valdobbiadene Brut Nature '14	▽▽ 4
○ Valdobbiadene Brut Nature '13	▽▽ 4
○ Valdobbiadene Brut Nature M. Cl. '17	▽▽ 3
○ Valdobbiadene Sup. Brut Dosaggio Zero M. Cl. '12	▽▽ 3

Le Fraghe

loc. Colombara, 3
37010 Cavaion Veronese [VR]
Tel. +39 0457236832
www.fraghe.it

CELLAR SALES
PRE-BOOKED VISITS
ACCOMMODATION
ANNUAL PRODUCTION 120,000 bottles
HECTARES UNDER VINE 28.00
VITICULTURE METHOD Certified Organic

The love story between Matilde Poggi and Le Fraghe began with the 1984 harvest, but their courtship goes back further, to childhood summers and harvests, memories of the warm scents of Lake Garda, the Alpine currents of Valdadige, and the reassuring presence of Mount Baldo in the background. Today the vineyards are managed organically and their entire range revolves around traditional grapes, with the only exception being a bit of Cabernet Sauvignon and Franc destined for their only Quaiare. The grapes used to produce Brol Grande '18 are grown in vineyards in the Classico area. This Bardolino isn't just a fresh, easy-drinking wine, but explores all of its development potential. Corvina and Rondinella are fermented separately, then aged in large barrels, making for a wine with complex aromas ranging from ripe fruit to spices and a palate that manages to come through rich, but supple and taut. The Bardolino '19 also proved very good, with its intact, crisp, juicy fruit.

⊙ Bardolino Chiaretto Rodon '19	▼▼ 3*
● Bardolino Cl. Brol Grande '18	▼▼ 4
● Bardolino '19	▼▼ 3
○ Camporego Garganega '19	▼▼ 3
● Bardolino Cl. Brol Grande '15	▽▽▽ 3*
● Bardolino Cl. Brol Grande '12	▽▽▽ 3*
● Bardolino Cl. Brol Grande '11	▽▽▽ 3*
● Bardolino '18	▽▽ 2*
● Bardolino '17	▽▽ 2*
● Bardolino '16	▽▽ 2*
● Bardolino '15	▽▽ 2*
⊙ Bardolino Chiaretto Ròdon '18	▽▽ 2*
⊙ Bardolino Chiaretto Rodon '16	▽▽ 2*
● Bardolino Cl. Brol Grande '16	▽▽ 3*
○ Camporengo Garganega '18	▽▽ 2*
○ Camporengo Garganega '17	▽▽ 2*
⊙ Bardolino Chiaretto Ròdon '17	▽ 2

Franchetto

fraz. Terrossa
via Binelli, 2
37030 Roncà [VR]
Tel. +39 0457460287
www.cantinafranchetto.com

ANNUAL PRODUCTION 35,000 bottles
HECTARES UNDER VINE 15.00

The Franchetto family's farm spans two very distinct areas: one near the winery, in Terrossa, where about ten hectares of Garganega are dedicated to the production of Soave. Here the red soil is rich in minerals, thanks to the disintegration of ancient volcanoes. The second can be found going up the Alpone Valley, where viticultural activity begins to merge with the alpine landscape. Here we find 5 hectares dedicated to Durella, making for a range that's rather limited in terms of bottles produced, but of great expressive strength. As well as being their most famous wine, the Soave La Capelina '19 best represents their production philosophy. The nose features clean sensations of crisp ripe white fruit, with faint floral notes in the background. In the mouth the wine reveals a dry, lean body that expands perfectly around the sapid acidity. The intriguing Pinot Grigio Val Serina proved approachable and very pleasant.

○ Pinot Grigio delle Venezie Val Serina '19	🍷🍷 3
○ Soave La Capelina '19	🍷🍷 3
○ Soave Recorbian '17	🍷🍷 3
○ Lessini Durello Brut M.Cl. Ris. '14	🍷🍷 5
○ Soave La Capelina '18	🍷🍷 3
○ Soave Recorbian '16	🍷🍷 3

Gamba

loc. Valgatara
via Gnirega, 19
37020 Marano di Valpolicella [VR]
Tel. +39 0456801714
www.vinigamba.it

CELLAR SALES
PRE-BOOKED VISITS
ANNUAL PRODUCTION 90,000 bottles
HECTARES UNDER VINE 15.00
SUSTAINABLE WINERY

The Aldrighetti brothers' cellar is literally immersed in the vineyards that unfold along the ridge that separates the Marano and Negrar valleys. A handful of hectares are cultivated with Verona's traditional pergola vines, exclusively the area's historic varieties, making for a range that's classic and supported, above all, by acidity, the valley's true trademark. To satisfy production needs, they also rely on vineyards cultivated by local growers operating in the same area. They submitted an excellent selection of wines this year, with our favorite being the Amarone Campedel '16. Its aromas seem concealed, almost reluctant to reveal themselves, while herbs add a touch of freshness to the sweet, super-ripe fruit, inviting you to taste it. In the mouth the wine confidently wins over the palate, it is rich with good concentration, supported and governed by solid tannins. The Amarone Le Quare from the same vintage proved fresher on the nose and supple in the mouth.

● Amarone della Valpolicella Cl. Campedel '16	🍷🍷 8
● Amarone della Valpolicella Cl. Le Quare '16	🍷🍷 6
● Valpolicella Cl. Sup. Campedel '17	🍷🍷 5
● Valpolicella Cl. Sup. Ripasso Campedel '17	🍷🍷 5
● Valpolicella Cl. Sup. Ripasso Le Quare '17	🍷🍷 3
● Valpolicella Cl. Le Quare '19	🍷 3
● Amarone della Valpolicella Cl. Campedel '15	🍷🍷 7
● Amarone della Valpolicella Cl. Campedel Ris. '12	🍷🍷 8
● Amarone della Valpolicella Cl. Le Quare '15	🍷🍷 6

Giannitessari

via Prandi, 10
37030 Roncà [VR]
Tel. +39 0457460070
www.giannitessari.wine

CELLAR SALES
PRE-BOOKED VISITS
ANNUAL PRODUCTION 350,000 bottles
HECTARES UNDER VINE 50.00
SUSTAINABLE WINERY

Gianni Tessari's winery is situated in Roncà, a small village in Verona that's nestled among the vineyards near the border between Soave and Gambellara. The estate itself spans three different appellations: Soave, Lessinia and Colli Berici, and each is interpreted with an eye to the specific characteristics that make it unique. Complexity and elegance for Soave, decisiveness and almost an penetrating quality in Lessinia, and finally Berici, which gives rise to reds characterized by fleshiness of fruit. Their most interesting wine comes from the Monte Lessini territory. This Metodo Classico '13 rests on the lees for over 5 years and offers up elegant aromas, where notes of crusty bread are quickly concealed by assertive minerality, leaving floral nuances in the background. In the mouth it proves confident and juicy with good grip. The Tai Rosso '18, on the other hand, comes from the Colli Berici area and features fruity aromas and a dynamic palate.

○ Lessini Durello Extra Brut M. Cl. 60 '13	🍷🍷 6
● Colli Berici Tai Rosso '18	🍷🍷 3
● Due Rosso '17	🍷🍷 2*
○ Lessini Durello Brut M. Cl. 36	🍷🍷 5
○ Soave Cl. Perinato Pigno '18	🍷🍷 4
○ Soave Cl. Scalette Tenda '19	🍷🍷 3
● Colli Berici Rosso Pian Alto '16	🍷 5
○ Soave Cl. Pigno Gianni Tessari '13	YYY 3*
● Colli Berici Tai Rosso '17	YY 2*
○ Lessini Durello Extra Brut M. Cl. 120 Mesi '08	YY 5
○ Lessini Durello Extra Brut M. Cl. 120 Mesi '06	YY 5
○ Lessini Durello Extra Brut M. Cl. 60 Mesi '10	YY 5
○ Soave Cl. Pigno '17	YY 3
○ Soave Cl. Pigno '16	YY 3*

★Gini

via Matteotti, 42
37032 Monteforte d'Alpone [VR]
Tel. +39 0457611908
www.ginivini.com

CELLAR SALES
PRE-BOOKED VISITS
ANNUAL PRODUCTION 200,000 bottles
HECTARES UNDER VINE 58.00
VITICULTURE METHOD Certified Organic

The Gini brothers' winery is among those that have contributed decisively to the success of Soave in recent decades. A sizable tract of land is cultivated in the heart of the classic area, vineyards that in many cases go back more than a century, hosting exclusively Garganega and Trebbiano di Soave. The new challenge, however, concerns Valpolicella, a territory that's being explored by Claudio and Sandro on the easternmost slope and now sees only two wines, Amarone and Valpolicella Superiore. Their whole selection is dedicated to Soave this year, with two outstanding performances from the 2018 vintage, Salvarenza and Froscà. The first expresses completely, deeply ripe fruit, embellished by spicy, marine notes. The palate proves rich, powerful and supple at the same time. The second exhibits crisp, lively fruit, accompanied by floral notes that give way to shy mineral overtones. The dry, sapid palate shows good progression and closes with an elegant finish.

○ Soave Cl. La Froscà '18	🍷🍷🍷 4*
○ Recioto di Soave Renobilis '13	🍷🍷 4
○ Soave Cl. Contrada Salvarenza V. V. '18	🍷🍷 5
○ Recioto di Soave Cl. Col Foscarin '13	🍷🍷 4
○ Soave Cl. '19	🍷🍷 3
○ Soave Cl. Contrada Salvarenza V. V. '14	YYY 5
○ Soave Cl. Contrada Salvarenza V. V. '09	YYY 5
○ Soave Cl. Contrada Salvarenza V. V. '08	YYY 5
○ Soave Cl. Contrada Salvarenza V. V. '07	YYY 5
○ Soave Cl. La Froscà '11	YYY 4*
○ Soave Cl. La Froscà '06	YYY 4*
○ Soave Cl. La Froscà '05	YYY 4*
○ Soave Cl. Sup. Contrada Salvarenza V. V. '00	YYY 5
○ Soave Cl. Sup. La Froscà '99	YYY 4*
○ Soave Cl. Sup. La Froscà '97	YYY 4*

Giusti Wine

via del Volante, 4
31040 Nervesa della Battaglia [TV]
Tel. +39 0422720198
www.giustiwine.com

CELLAR SALES
PRE-BOOKED VISITS
ACCOMMODATION
ANNUAL PRODUCTION 200,000 bottles
HECTARES UNDER VINE 75.00
SUSTAINABLE WINERY

Ermenegildo Giusti's winery is situated near Montello, a modest mountainous relief of red soil that stands out sharply north of Treviso. Many hectares are cultivated, mostly on the plain at the foot of the hill, for the grapes dedicated to their simplest selections, while their more ambitious wines avail themselves of the vineyards that stretch along the dolines that characterize the hillside. The range focuses on Prosecco, but there's no lack of Bordeauxs, and we shouldn't forget their traditional 'Recantina' either. Giusti's excellent version of the Asolo Extra Brut has garnered attention from the world of Prosecco. Its nose reveals sensations of white fruit that merge with floral and yeasty nuances. In the mouth the wine expands gracefully, revealing grip and a juicy, gratifying palate. As for the still wines, without their champion Umberto I°, our attention was drawn to the Chardonnay Dei Carni '19, which came through dynamic and very pleasant.

● Amarone della Valpolicella Cl. '15	▼▼ 8
○ Asolo Extra Brut	▼▼ 2*
○ Chardonnay dei Carni '19	▼▼ 3
○ Asolo Extra Dry	▼ 2
● Montello e Colli Asolani Rosso Antonio '17	▼ 4
○ Pinot Grigio delle Venezie Longheri '19	▼ 3
● Amarone della Valpolicella Cl. '14	▽▽ 8
● Antonio '15	▽▽ 5
○ Longheri Pinot Grigio '17	▽▽ 3
● Montello e Colli Asolani Recantina Augusto '17	▽▽ 5
● Montello e Colli Asolani Recantina Augusto '16	▽▽ 5
● Montello e Colli Asolani Rosso Umberto I° '15	▽▽ 8
● Valpolicella Cl. Sup. '16	▽▽ 5

La Giuva

via Trezzolano, 20c
37141 Verona
Tel. +39 3421117089
www.lagiuva.com

CELLAR SALES
PRE-BOOKED VISITS
ANNUAL PRODUCTION 20,000 bottles
HECTARES UNDER VINE 9.50
VITICULTURE METHOD Certified Organic

Trezzolano is a lesser-known area, even among regional winemakers, yet the conditions for quality viticulture are all there: elevation, position, light, a soil lean in organic matter but rich in minerals, and constant air circulation that allows the grapes to ripen regularly. A few years ago Albero Malesani, together with his daughters Giulia and Valentina, brought to life a winery that explores this potential, with a range marked by a crisp, healthy, vibrant style. Their vintage Valpolicella was exemplary at tasting, with intense aromas of cherry, pepper and fresh flowers. In the mouth the body proves lean and the wine expands racy, with a very pleasant finish. The new Amarone Aristide is dedicated to the father. It makes the most of the 2015 vintage to offer up a suite of aromas dominated by super-ripe red fruit, which progresses and expands on a dynamic palate, where concentration is well-supported by the tannic texture and acid backbone.

● Amarone della Valpolicella L'Aristide '15	▼▼ 8
● Recioto della Valpolicella '17	▼▼ 6
● Valpolicella Sup. Il Rientro '17	▼▼ 5
● Valpolicello Il Valpo '19	▼▼ 4
● Amarone della Valpolicella '15	▽▽ 7
● Amarone della Valpolicella '13	▽▽ 7
● Amarone della Valpolicella '12	▽▽ 7
● Recioto della Valpolicella '16	▽▽ 6
● Recioto della Valpolicella '15	▽▽ 6
● Valpolicella Il Valpo '18	▽▽ 3
● Valpolicella Il Valpo '17	▽▽ 3
● Valpolicella Il Valpo '16	▽▽ 3
● Valpolicella Il Valpo '15	▽▽ 3
● Valpolicella Sup. Il Rientro '16	▽▽ 5
● Valpolicella Sup. Il Rientro '15	▽▽ 5
● Valpolicella Sup. Il Rientro '14	▽▽ 5
● Valpolicella Sup. Il Rientro '13	▽▽ 5

Gorgo

FRAZ. CUSTOZA
LOC. GORGO
37066 SOMMACAMPAGNA [VR]
TEL. +39 045516063
www.cantinagorgo.com

ANNUAL PRODUCTION 350,000 bottles
HECTARES UNDER VINE 50.00

The appellations of Bardolino and Custoza, which stretch along the morainic hills southeast of the Garda basin, exhibit very similar characteristics. Gorgo, a winery founded by Roberto Bricolo and now confidently managed by his daughter Roberta and her young, skilled staff, has been operating here for almost half a century. The vineyards are managed organically and their range is closely linked to the two territories, highlighting the qualities of finesse and suppleness that have always distinguished the wines of lower Garda. This year the absolute star is Custoza, with two versions reaching our finals. Their Summa '18, made with overripe grapes, expresses mature fruity aromas, while the solid palate gives way to the first mineral notes. The San Michelin '19, on the other hand, plays on aromatic finesse. This single vineyard wine is dotted with floral and crisp white fruit aromas that win over the palate with the lightness and sapidity typical of this wine from Verona.

○ Custoza San Michelin '19	🍷🍷 2*
○ Custoza Sup. Summa '18	🍷🍷 2*
⊙ Bardolino Chiaretto '19	🍷🍷 2*
● Ca' Nova '16	🍷🍷 3
○ Custoza '19	🍷🍷 2*
● Bardolino '19	🍷 2
● Bardolino '18	🍷🍷 2*
⊙ Bardolino Chiaretto '18	🍷🍷 2*
○ Custoza '18	🍷🍷 2*
○ Custoza San Michelin '18	🍷🍷 2*
○ Custoza San Michelin '17	🍷🍷 2*
○ Custoza San Michelin '16	🍷🍷 2*
○ Custoza Sup. Summa '17	🍷🍷 2*
○ Custoza Sup. Summa '16	🍷🍷 2*
○ Custoza Sup. Summa '15	🍷🍷 2*

Gregoletto

FRAZ. PREMAOR
VIA SAN MARTINO, 83
31050 MIANE [TV]
TEL. +39 0438970463
www.gregoletto.com

CELLAR SALES
PRE-BOOKED VISITS
ANNUAL PRODUCTION 200,000 bottles
HECTARES UNDER VINE 18.00

Luigi Gregoletto does more than just make wine—he expresses a territory, its customs and crops. Fewer than 20 hectares immersed in the hills separating the Pre-Alps from the Po Valley host Glera, but other grapes as well, which is, unfortunately, not such a common occurrence of late. Here we find traditional varieties like Verdiso and Manzoni Bianco, as well as international Bordeaux varieties, which have been cultivated in the area for over a century. Many wines were bottled too late this year, also due to the pandemic last spring, but there were still some pleasant surprises from Gregoletto. Their excellent Conegliano Valdobbiadene Monte Corbino is a Prosecco Superiore with aromas of ripe apple and pear that wins you over with its approachable taste and pleasantly rustic palate. One of the most interesting wines from the area is the Prosecco Frizzante Sui Lieviti, a stylish, sapid wine with an enthralling palate.

● Cabernet '17	🍷🍷 3
○ Conegliano Valdobbiadene Extra Dry Monte Corbino	🍷🍷 3
○ Prosecco di Treviso Frizzante '19	🍷🍷 3
○ Prosecco di Treviso Frizzante sui Lieviti '19	🍷🍷 3
● Colli di Conegliano Rosso '15	🍷🍷 5
○ Conegliano Valdobbiadene Prosecco Tranquillo '18	🍷🍷 2*
○ Conegliano Valdobbiadene Prosecco Tranquillo '16	🍷🍷 2*
○ Conegliano Valdobbiadene Prosecco Tranquillo '15	🍷🍷 2*
● Merlot '17	🍷🍷 3
● Merlot '16	🍷🍷 3
○ Pinot Bianco '18	🍷🍷 3
○ Verdiso '18	🍷🍷 3

★Guerrieri Rizzardi

S.DA CAMPAZZI, 2
37011 BARDOLINO [VR]
TEL. +39 0457210028
www.guerrieri-rizzardi.it

CELLAR SALES
PRE-BOOKED VISITS
ANNUAL PRODUCTION 700,000 bottles
HECTARES UNDER VINE 100.00
SUSTAINABLE WINERY

The address indicates Bardolino as the winery's headquarters, but we're talking about one of the most beautiful estates in Verona, about a hundred hectares spread throughout the most important appellations of the province. Indeed, Agostino and Giuseppe Rizzardi carry out their work in Bardolino, Soave, Valpolicella and Valdadige, interpreting wines closely linked to tradition, highlighting the qualities of elegance and tension that distinguish the territory's classic grape varieties. Their excellent Amarone Calcarole '15 features very deep aromas of super-ripe fruit surrounded by balsamic, spicy notes. The palate seems to be caressed by softness, except for the sudden revival of acidity and a pleasantly rustic tannic texture, resulting in great balance. The Clos Roareti '17, on the other hand, is a Merlot with complex, layered aromas that win you over for their solidity and length.

● Amarone della Valpolicella Cl. Calcarole '15	🍷🍷 8
● Bardolino Cl. Cuvée XV '19	🍷🍷 2*
● Bardolino Cl. Tacchetto '18	🍷🍷 2*
● Clos Roareti '17	🍷🍷 5
● Munus '18	🍷🍷 3
⊙ Rosa Rosae '19	🍷🍷 2*
○ Soave Cl. Cuvée XX '19	🍷🍷 2*
○ Soave Cl. Ferra '17	🍷🍷 3
⊙ Bardolino Chiaretto Cl. Keya '19	🍷 2
○ Recioto di Soave '18	🍷 4
● Amarone della Valpolicella Cl. Calcarole '13	🍸🍸🍸 8
● Amarone della Valpolicella Cl. Calcarole '11	🍸🍸🍸 8
● Amarone della Valpolicella Cl. Villa Rizzardi '13	🍸🍸🍸 7

★Inama

LOC. BIACCHE, 50
37047 SAN BONIFACIO [VR]
TEL. +39 0456104343
www.inamaaziendaagricola.it

CELLAR SALES
PRE-BOOKED VISITS
ANNUAL PRODUCTION 450,000 bottles
HECTARES UNDER VINE 62.00
VITICULTURE METHOD Certified Organic

In the early 1990s, Stefano Inama took over the reins of the family business, a producer focused on Soave and its territory. Today, 30 years later, alongside him are his sons Matteo, Alessio and Luca, while its center of gravity has moved in the direction of the Berici Hills. The property's many hectares are managed with the utmost respect for the environment, through a minimally invasive approach, so that their wines are capable of expressing the territory even before highlighting their varietal attributes. A great performance from the Carminium '16, a wine that offers up intense hints of black fruit that quickly give way to spices and medicinal herbs. The generous, rich palate is not weighed down but remains anchored to the tannic and acid backbone, proving long and charming. The Bradisismo from the same vintage remains more moderate for the time being. This Bordeaux blend plays on finesse rather than power.

● Colli Berici Carmenere Carminium '16	🍷🍷🍷 5
● Bradisismo '16	🍷🍷 5
○ Soave Cl. Vign. di Carbonare '17	🍷🍷 4
○ Soave Cl. Vign. di Foscarino '17	🍷🍷 4
○ Soave Cl. Vign. Du Lot '17	🍷 4
● Bradisismo '08	🍸🍸🍸 5
● Colli Berici Carmenère Oratorio di San Lorenzo Ris. '09	🍸🍸🍸 6
○ Sauvignon Vulcaia Fumé '96	🍸🍸🍸 4
○ Soave Cl. Vign. di Foscarino '08	🍸🍸🍸 4
○ Soave Cl. Vign. Du Lot '05	🍸🍸🍸 2*
○ Soave Cl. Vign. Du Lot '01	🍸🍸🍸 4
○ Soave Cl. Vign. Du Lot '00	🍸🍸🍸 4*
○ Soave Cl. Vign. Du Lot '99	🍸🍸🍸 4*
○ Soave Cl. Vign. Du Lot '96	🍸🍸🍸 4*
● Bradisismo '12	🍸🍸 5
○ Soave Cl. Vign. di Foscarino '14	🍸🍸 4

Le Morette

FRAZ. SAN BENEDETTO DI LUGANA
V.LE INDIPENDENZA, 19D
37019 PESCHIERA DEL GARDA [VR]
TEL. +39 0457552724
www.lemorette.it

CELLAR SALES
PRE-BOOKED VISITS
ANNUAL PRODUCTION 450,000 bottles
HECTARES UNDER VINE 40.00
SUSTAINABLE WINERY

The clay shores that surround the southern Garda basin are home to Turbiana, the ancient cultivar that gives rise to Lugana. It's a grape whose vegetative life is long, meaning the vine has more time to absorb the soil's minerals, thus gaining in personality and sapidity. Bolstered by their experiences as vigneron and nurserymen, Fabio and Paolo Zenato, who also know the territory and its principal grape well, give rise to a selection marked by notable quality and typicality. The Lugana Riserva '17, after a long stay in the cellar, opens with an impressive suite of aromas. Faint and almost shy at first, ripe peachy fruit emerge, gradually giving way to toasty notes of Mediterranean scrub and flowers. In the mouth it's firm and crisp, perfectly supported by acidity and sapidity, finishing long and alluring. The Benedictus also delivered. Made with grapes from a single vineyard, it exhibits more expressed fruit and a dynamic, gradually unfolding palate.

⊙ Bardolino Chiaretto Cl. '19	🍷🍷 2*
○ Lugana Ris. '17	🍷🍷 4
● Bardolino Cl. '19	🍷🍷 2*
○ Lugana Benedictus '18	🍷🍷 3
○ Lugana Mandolara '19	🍷🍷 3
○ Brut M. Cl. Trentaseimesi	🍷 4
● Perseo '17	🍷 5
⊙ Bardolino Chiaretto Cl. '18	ΥΥ 2*
● Bardolino Cl. '18	ΥΥ 2*
○ Lugana Benedictus '17	ΥΥ 3
○ Lugana Benedictus '16	ΥΥ 3
○ Lugana Mandolara '18	ΥΥ 3
○ Lugana Mandolara '17	ΥΥ 3
○ Lugana Ris. '16	ΥΥ 4
○ Lugana Ris. '15	ΥΥ 4
○ Lugana Ris. '13	ΥΥ 4

Loredan Gasparini

FRAZ. VENEGAZZÙ
VIA MARTIGNAGO ALTO, 23
31040 VOLPAGO DEL MONTELLO [TV]
TEL. +39 0423870024
www.loredangasparini.it

CELLAR SALES
PRE-BOOKED VISITS
ANNUAL PRODUCTION 450,000 bottles
HECTARES UNDER VINE 60.00
SUSTAINABLE WINERY

The Palla family's farm stretches along the southern slopes of Montello, where the red terrain is rich in detritus left by the Piave River as it washes out of the Alps. It's an area also characterized by sinkholes, which pock the woods and vineyards. The area under vine is extensive, with Bordeaux varieties alternating with Glera. However this large estate gives rise to a limited range of wines, the result of an approach that focuses on individual vineyards and their ability to highlight different characteristics. Their most important offering, the Capo di Stato '16, is a blend of the best lots of Cabernet Sauvignon, Franc, Merlot and Malbec, mainly from the historic vineyard called '100 piante' planted in the immediate post-war period. On the nose it proves more immediate and fragrant than usual, while on the palate it comes through relaxed with the usual class, one wrought of spirited tension and a substantive tannic weave. The Rosso della Casa '16 exhibits a similar aromatic profile, proving juicy and approachable on the palate.

● Montello e Colli Asolani Venegazzù Sup. Capo di Stato '16	🍷🍷 8
● Montello e Colli Asolani Cabernet Sauvignon '18	🍷🍷 3
● Montello e Colli Asolani Venegazzù Rosso della Casa '16	🍷🍷 6
● Malbec '19	🍷 4
● Montello e Colli Asolani Cabernet Sauvignon '16	ΥΥ 3
● Montello e Colli Asolani Merlot Falconera '16	ΥΥ 3
● Montello e Colli Asolani Rosso Capo di Stato '13	ΥΥ 7
● Montello e Colli Asolani Venegazzù Rosso della Casa '15	ΥΥ 4
● Montello e Colli Asolani Venegazzù Sup. Capo di Stato '15	ΥΥ 6

★Maculan

via Castelletto, 3
36042 Breganze [VI]
Tel. +39 0445873733
www.maculan.net

CELLAR SALES
PRE-BOOKED VISITS
ANNUAL PRODUCTION 650,000 bottles
HECTARES UNDER VINE 50.00

The hilly strip of land that stretches from Thiene towards Bassano del Grappa and Valsugana represents the Breganze production area, an uninterrupted succession of hills whose southern slopes experience the warmth of the plains and are, at the same time, crossed by the cool breezes descending down from the north. The Maculan family is certainly a symbol of this territory, thanks to a 50-hectare vineyard and a range of wines that has brought both prestige and recognition to the territory and the entire region. Maculan has shown true skill when it comes wines made with partially dried grapes, with the Acininobili '16 putting in one for the ages. The grapes (100% Vespaiola) are harvested only when completely affected by botrytis. After a long stay in barriques, the wine offers up a complex bouquet dominated by notes of candied fruit and spices, while in the mouth sweetness is perfectly contrasted by sapidity. The Fratta '16, a Bordeaux blend of great richness and harmony, is also excellent.

○ Acininobili '15	🍷🍷 8
● Fratta '16	🍷🍷 8
○ Breganze Torcolato '16	🍷🍷 6
● Cornorotto Marzemino '17	🍷🍷 3
○ Ferrata Chardonnay '18	🍷🍷 4
○ Ferrata Sauvignon '19	🍷🍷 4
○ Pino & Toi '19	🍷🍷 2*
● Breganze Pinot Nero '18	🍷 3
● Cabernet '18	🍷 3
⊙ Costadolio '19	🍷 2
○ Dindarello '19	🍷 4
○ Tre Volti Brut M. Cl.	🍷 3
● Breganze Cabernet Fratta '87	🍷🍷🍷 3*
● Breganze Cabernet Sauvignon Palazzotto '05	🍷🍷🍷 4
● Breganze Cabernet Sauvignon Palazzotto '04	🍷🍷🍷 4*

Manara

loc. San Floriano
via Don Cesare Biasi, 53
37029 San Pietro in Cariano [VR]
Tel. +39 0457701086
www.manaravini.it

CELLAR SALES
PRE-BOOKED VISITS
ANNUAL PRODUCTION 150,000 bottles
HECTARES UNDER VINE 11.00
SUSTAINABLE WINERY

Few wineries can boast a set of vineyards like the one overseen by the Manara brothers. It may be small in size but it's a prized patrimony, just over 10 hectares in some of the best parts of the 'Classica' appellation. Viticulture is traditional, with the pergola still dominating, their choice of grapes is bound up with local tradition, and their work in the cellar aims to be minimally invasive, respectful of the time needed to allow their wines to fully express their character. The Valpolicella Vecio Belo '17 comes from a vineyard in San Pietro in Cariano where no selection is made for Amarone and the entire harvest is dedicated to this wine. Matured only in steel, it offers up an aromatic bouquet of berries and spices, with a curious vegetal background. In the mouth it moves supplely and with tension, proving pleasant and highly drinkable. The Amarone Corte Manara '16 is more mature in its aromatic expression, while in the mouth it comes through firm and harmonious.

● Amarone della Valpolicella Cl. Corte Manara '16	🍷🍷 5
● Amarone della Valpolicella Cl. Postera '14	🍷🍷 6
● Recioto della Valpolicella Cl. Moronalto '17	🍷🍷 5
● Valpolicella Cl. Sup. Vecio Belo '17	🍷🍷 2*
● Guido Manara '15	🍷 6
● Valpolicella Cl. Val Polesela '19	🍷 2
● Amarone della Valpolicella Cl. '00	🍷🍷🍷 5
● Amarone della Valpolicella Cl. Corte Manara '13	🍷🍷 5
● Amarone della Valpolicella Cl. Postera '13	🍷🍷 6
● Valpolicella Cl. Sup. Ripasso Le Morete '17	🍷🍷 3

Le Marognole

LOC. VALGATARA
VIA MAROGNOLE, 7
37020 MARANO DI VALPOLICELLA [VR]
TEL. +39 0457755114
www.lemarognole.it

CELLAR SALES
PRE-BOOKED VISITS
ANNUAL PRODUCTION 15,000 bottles
HECTARES UNDER VINE 5.50

About fifteen years ago, in 2004, Fabio Corsi took the plunge and assumed the reins of the family business, transforming it from a grape producer to a wine producer. The vineyards span a handful of hectares in the Valgatara area, at the entrance to the Marano valley, with the best plots reaching elevations of over 300 meters. The countryside features the traditional pergola system while in the cellar a more modern style is pursued, one that offers integrity of fruit as well as power. The grapes used for the Recioto '17 are cultivated in the Campo Gerico vineyard. It's a wine that offers up curiously spicy and vegetal aromas, leaving super-ripe fruit just in the background. In the mouth an evident sweetness is perfectly contrasted by acidity as the wine lengthens and closes dry. The Ripasso '16 is fresher, fruitier and spicier, while in the mouth it broadens on more pervasive sensations, only to close around acidity.

● Recioto della Valpolicella Cl. CampoGerico '17	🍷🍷 4
● Valpolicella Cl. '18	🍷🍷 3
● Valpolicella Cl. Sup. Ripasso '16	🍷🍷 3
⊙ El Marascar '19	🍷 2
● El Nane '16	🍷 5
● Amarone della Valpolicella Cl. CampoRocco '15	🍷🍷 5
● Amarone della Valpolicella Cl. CampoRocco '13	🍷🍷 5
● Recioto della Valpolicella Cl. CampoGerico '16	🍷🍷 4
● Valpolicella Cl. Sup. Ripasso '14	🍷🍷 3

Masari

LOC. MAGLIO DI SOPRA
C.DA BEVILACQUA, 2A
36078 VALDAGNO [VI]
TEL. +39 0445410780
www.masari.it

CELLAR SALES
PRE-BOOKED VISITS
ANNUAL PRODUCTION 55,000 bottles
HECTARES UNDER VINE 10.00
VITICULTURE METHOD Certified Organic
SUSTAINABLE WINERY

Massimo Dal Lago and Arianna Tessari have created one of the most beautiful wineries in the region, one that's not only focused on how to get the best out of its vineyards, but also looks at how to manage agriculture without depleting natural resources. It's a winery where viticulture is central but not hegemonic, where the vineyards are surrounded by forest and pasture, making for a range that aims to express the intrinsic bond between the individual vineyards and the grape variety best suited to them. The selection submitted by Massimo and Arianna this year is one with no weak points. It's led by a great version of their Monte Pulgo '13. A monovarietal Merlot produced only during vintages in which the grapes, selected from a limestone-rich vineyard at 400 meters elevation, reach the proper ripeness. On the nose it's broad and elegant, with notes of ripe fruit intersecting with spices and mineral hints. In the mouth it changes direction, combining concentration and elegance.

● Monte Pulgo '13	🍷🍷 8
○ Agnobianco '19	🍷🍷 3
● Costa Nera Pinot Nero '18	🍷🍷 4
● San Lorenzo Pinot Nero '17	🍷🍷 7
● Vicenza Rosso San Martino '16	🍷🍷 3
○ Agnobianco '18	🍷🍷 3
○ Agnobianco '17	🍷🍷 3
○ AgnoBianco '15	🍷🍷 2*
● Costa Nera Pinot Nero '17	🍷🍷 4
○ Doro Passito '15	🍷🍷 5
● Masari '16	🍷🍷 6
● Masari '15	🍷🍷 6
● Masari '13	🍷🍷 5
● Monte Pulgo '11	🍷🍷 8
● San Lorenzo Pinot Nero '16	🍷🍷 7
● Vicenza Rosso San Martino '13	🍷🍷 3*

★Masi

fraz. Gargagnago
via Monteleone, 26
37015 Sant'Ambrogio di Valpolicella [VR]
Tel. +39 0456832511
www.masi.it

CELLAR SALES
PRE-BOOKED VISITS
ACCOMMODATION
ANNUAL PRODUCTION 3,950,000 bottles
HECTARES UNDER VINE 550.00
SUSTAINABLE WINERY

Sandro Boscaini is still guiding this large Gargagnago-based winery, interpreting a territory that has contributed to making the area known throughout the world. Their vineyards span several different territories: Verona forms the core, obviously, but they have collaborations in Tuscany, Friuli, Valdadige, historic Prosecco and, finally, a large estate in Argentina. A skilled technical group led by his son Raffaele oversees production. Only an Amarone could lead this year's selection, the Mazzano '12. Made with grapes cultivated on the highest hills over Negrar, it offers up intense notes of overripe fruit and bitter cocoa, all enriched by balsamic nuances of medicinal herbs. The palate exhibits great concentration and solidity supported by a substantive tannic weave. The Costasera is a 2015 reserve that's generous in its aromas and marked by great extractive force.

- ● Amarone della Valpolicella Cl. Mazzano '12 — 🍷🍷🍷 8
- ● Amarone della Valpolicella Cl. Costasera Ris. '15 — 🍷🍷 8
- ● Valpolicella Cl. Sup. Toar '17 — 🍷🍷 4
- ● Osar '13 — 🍷 8
- ○ Soave Cl. Sup. Colbaraca '18 — 🍷 3
- ● Amarone della Valpolicella Cl. Campolongo di Torbe '12 — 🍸🍸🍸 8
- ● Amarone della Valpolicella Cl. Campolongo di Torbe '11 — 🍸🍸🍸 8
- ● Amarone della Valpolicella Cl. Campolongo di Torbe '09 — 🍸🍸🍸 8
- ● Amarone della Valpolicella Cl. Costasera Ris. '13 — 🍸🍸🍸 8
- ● Amarone della Valpolicella Cl. Costasera Ris. '09 — 🍸🍸🍸 8

Masottina

loc. Castello Roganzuolo
via Bradolini, 54
31020 San Fior [TV]
Tel. +39 0438400775
www.masottina.it

CELLAR SALES
ANNUAL PRODUCTION 1,200,000 bottles
HECTARES UNDER VINE 300.00

The Dal Bianco family's story goes well back, when right after WW II they founded Masottina. Theirs has been a gradual but steady path of growth that's avoided the spotlight, perhaps because the family are more concerned with shoring up the foundations than riding the success of sparkling wine. Today the area under vine is extensive, with their crown jewels concentrated in Ogliano for the world of Prosecco and in Gorgo al Monticano for their still wines. More and more attention is being dedicated to the world of bubbly, with the wines obtained from the best positions in Ogliano leading the way. The Brut '19 opens with aromas dominated by white-fleshed fruit, embellished by delicately floral nuances. These reemerge on a firm, crisp palate marked by commendable tension. The Extra Dry version plays more on fruit and a tasty, harmonious palate, all perfectly accompanied by sparkle.

- ○ Conegliano Valdobbiadene Rive di Ogliano Brut R.D.O. '19 — 🍷🍷 4
- ○ Conegliano Valdobbiadene Brut — 🍷🍷 4
- ○ Conegliano Valdobbiadene Extra Dry — 🍷🍷 4
- ○ Conegliano Valdobbiadene Rive di Ogliano Extra Dry R.D.O. '19 — 🍷🍷 4
- ● Aether Ai Palazzi '18 — 🍷 4
- ○ Colli di Conegliano Bianco Rizzardo '16 — 🍷 8
- ○ Pinot Grigio delle Venezie Dorsoduro '19 — 🍷 4
- ○ Prosecco Extra Brut — 🍷 2
- ● Colli di Conegliano Rosso Montesco '15 — 🍸🍸 6
- ○ Conegliano Valdobbiadene Rive di Ogliano Brut Contrada Granda '18 — 🍸🍸 5
- ○ Conegliano Valdobbiadene Rive di Ogliano Brut Contrada Granda '17 — 🍸🍸 5
- ○ Conegliano Valdobbiadene Rive di Ogliano Extra Dry '18 — 🍸🍸 5

Roberto Mazzi e Figli

loc. San Peretto
via Crosetta, 8
37024 Negrar [VR]
Tel. +39 0457502072
www.robertomazzi.it

CELLAR SALES
PRE-BOOKED VISITS
ACCOMMODATION AND RESTAURANT SERVICE
ANNUAL PRODUCTION 50,000 bottles
HECTARES UNDER VINE 8.00

Within Valpolicella's classic heart, the Negrar valley is perhaps the one area that has most suffered from urbanization, with an influx of small villas that today can be seen scattered along the hills. In San Peretto, however, time seems to have stopped, with Antonio and Stefano Mazzi's winery situated by an old watermill, perfectly integrated with the rural landscape and surrounded by vineyards. A limited number of bottles are produced, while their style strikes a balance between modernity and tradition. Their two Valpolicella Superiores delivered plenty of gratification. The Sanperetto and Poiega are both 2017s. The former plays on aromatic freshness and a flavor profile that stretches supplely around its acidic thrust. The second features more mature, pervasive fruit, while in the mouth it reveals good concentration and harmony. The Recioto Calcarole '17 offers up intensely fruity aromas and a firm palate of great precision.

- ● Valpolicella Cl. Sup. Poiega '17 — 🍷🍷 4
- ● Valpolicella Cl. Sup. Sanperetto '17 — 🍷🍷 3*
- ● Amarone della Valpolicella Castel '15 — 🍷🍷 7
- ● Libero '16 — 🍷🍷 5
- ● Recioto della Valpolicella Cl. Le Calcarole '17 — 🍷🍷 5
- ● Valpolicella Cl. '19 — 🍷🍷 3
- ● Amarone della Valpolicella Cl. Punta di Villa '11 — YYY 7
- ● Valpolicella Cl. Sup. Sanperetto '11 — YYY 3*
- ● Amarone della Valpolicella Cl. Punta di Villa '13 — YY 7
- ● Amarone della Valpolicella Cl. Punta di Villa '12 — YY 7
- ● Recioto della Valpolicella Cl. Le Calcarole '13 — YY 5
- ● Valpolicella Cl. Sup. Poiega '16 — YY 4

Menegotti

loc. Acquaroli, 7
37069 Villafranca di Verona [VR]
Tel. +39 0457902611
www.menegotticantina.com

CELLAR SALES
PRE-BOOKED VISITS
ACCOMMODATION
ANNUAL PRODUCTION 250,000 bottles
HECTARES UNDER VINE 30.00
SUSTAINABLE WINERY

The hills surrounding the southern shore of Lake Garda ripple like a stone thrown in water, an echo of the advance and dissolution of an ancient glacier. They're also a choice area for Bardolino and Custoza, the two wines that represent the history of this territory. Antonio and Andrea Menegotti have been able to take a new direction, emphasizing the production of Metodo Classico sparkling wines that, alongside traditional typlogies, also make use of the territory's historic cultivars. The interesting Pas Dosé is a monovarietal Corvina, vinified off-the-skins, that makes use of a long stay on the lees before disgorgement. On the nose we detect notes of apples, pears and brioche all of which reemerge on the palate, where the wine unfolds decisively, perfectly supported by acidity and accompanied by a delicate, subtle weft of bubbles. When it comes to their stills, we appreciated the Bardolino, a wine marked by good aromatic freshness—relaxed and satisfying.

- ● Bardolino '19 — 🍷🍷 2*
- ○ Brut M. Cl. '15 — 🍷🍷 4
- ○ Lugana '19 — 🍷🍷 3
- ○ Pas Dosé M. Cl. '14 — 🍷🍷 7
- ⊙ Bardolino Chiaretto '19 — 🍷 2
- ○ Custoza '19 — 🍷 2
- ○ Extra Brut M. Cl. — 🍷 4
- ○ Extra Dry M. Cl. — 🍷 3
- ⊙ Bardolino Chiaretto '18 — YY 2*
- ○ Brut M. Cl. '15 — YY 4
- ○ Brut M. Cl. '14 — YY 4
- ○ Custoza '18 — YY 2*
- ○ Custoza '16 — YY 2*
- ○ Custoza Sup. Elianto '17 — YY 3*
- ○ Custoza Sup. Elianto '16 — YY 3*
- ○ Custoza Sup. Elianto '15 — YY 3
- ● Mezzacosta '15 — YY 3

★Merotto

FRAZ. COL SAN MARTINO
VIA SCANDOLERA, 21
31010 FARRA DI SOLIGO [TV]
TEL. +39 0438989000
www.merotto.it

CELLAR SALES
PRE-BOOKED VISITS
ANNUAL PRODUCTION 610,000 bottles
HECTARES UNDER VINE 28.00

Graziano Merotto is a shy producer, a man of few words who's strongly tied to his land. He's also capable of almost unexpected verve and sensitivity. Over the years he's managed to grow the winery in his image, remaining deeply bound to the Prosecco of these hills, the fruit of the only Glera cultivated along the gentle slopes that suddenly become steep, rendering it an area that's as gorgeous as it is arduous to climb. His range explores all the potential of the Treviso grape variety, interpreted with a keen eye to sapidity and harmony. The winery in Via Scandolera has taken a fairly clear direction, with the Castè and Graziano Merotto leading the way. The first is an Extra Dry redolent of white fruit and flowers, and wins over the palate with its rare precision and pleasantness, proving harmonious in its fusion of sugars, sapidity and bubbles. The second is the classic prized-pony, delicate in its aromatic suite, exploding in a sapid, crisp and highly elegant palate.

Wine	Rating
○ Valdobbiadene Extra Dry Castè '19	TTT 4*
○ Valdobbiadene Rive di Col San Martino Brut Cuvée del Fondatore Graziano Merotto '19	TT 4
○ Cartizze	TT 5
● Rosso Dogato '16	TT 4
○ Royam Passito di Collina '13	TT 5
○ Valdobbiadene Brut Bareta	TT 3
○ Valdobbiadene Brut Integral '19	TT 3
○ Valdobbiadene Dry La Primavera di Barbara '19	TT 3
○ Valdobbiadene Extra Dry Colbelo	TT 3
⊙ Grani di Nero Brut Rosé	T 3
○ Valdobbiadene Brut Rive di Col San Martino Cuvée del Fondatore Graziano Merotto '18	YYY 4*

Ornella Molon

FRAZ. CAMPODIPIETRA
VIA RISORGIMENTO, 40
31040 SALGAREDA [TV]
TEL. +39 0422804807
www.ornellamolon.it

CELLAR SALES
PRE-BOOKED VISITS
RESTAURANT SERVICE
ANNUAL PRODUCTION 500,000 bottles
HECTARES UNDER VINE 42.00
SUSTAINABLE WINERY

Ornella Molon and Giancarlo Traverso's winery has always lent prestige to the territory of Piave, a generous land where vineyards extend almost as far as the eye can see. Today Glera takes center stage, but Ornella hasn't wanted to bend to fashion, so she's also remained faithful to the territory's historical varieties. Their range is divided into two lines: one that focuses on varietal aromas and another, more ambitious selection, that pursues complexity and character. Raboso, a historical grape that's well represent in the area, is a difficult one to tame, characterized as it is by decidedly late ripening and an extremely rigid organoleptic profile linked to acidity and tannins. At Molon they managed to rein it in, with the Malanotte '14 offering up aromas of overripe red fruit and a solid palate well supported by acidity. The Piave Raboso '15 is aromatically fresher and supple in the mouth, while the Vite Rossa '16 proves an elegant Bordeaux blend with good depth.

Wine	Rating
○ Bianco di Ornella Passito Selezione '16	TT 5
● Piave Malanotte Selezione '14	TT 7
● Piave Raboso Selezione '15	TT 5
● Venezia Merlot Selezione '16	TT 4
● Vite Rossa Selezione '16	TT 4
● Èros Selezione '17	T 3
○ Prosecco di Treviso Brut	T 2
○ Prosecco Extra Dry	T 2
○ Traminer Selezione '19	T 3
○ Bianco di Ornella Passito '15	YY 5
○ Bianco di Ornella Passito '14	YY 5
● Piave Malanotte '12	YY 8
● Piave Merlot Rosso di Villa '15	YY 5
● Piave Raboso '13	YY 5
○ Traminer '17	YY 3
● Venezia Merlot Rosso di Villa '13	YY 6

Monte Cillario

FRAZ. PARONA DI VALPOLICELLA
VIA SANTA CRISTINA, 1B
37124 VERONA
TEL. +39 045941387
www.montecillariovini.com

CELLAR SALES
PRE-BOOKED VISITS
ANNUAL PRODUCTION 65,000 bottles
HECTARES UNDER VINE 30.00
SUSTAINABLE WINERY

The Marchesini family owns a rather large set of vineyards, mostly in Valpolicella, close to the city of Verona and reaching up to the northernmost districts. On the flat terrain in Quar the grapes for their base offering are cultivated, while for their most ambitious wines the family has vineyards on Monte Cillario and on the slopes of San Dionigi. Although production volumes are still limited, their range has been divided into two lines with different ambitions. On the nose the Ripasso Excellentia '17 offers up vibrant notes of red fruit and forest undergrowth accompanied by a discreet background of oak. In the mouth the wine comes through soft and pervasive, relaxing with elegance around acidity and proving long and highly pleasant. Among their Amarones, we preferred the Casa Erbisti '16 by virtue of its ripe, fruity expression and palate that's soft but enlivened by tannins.

● Amarone della Valpolicella Casa Erbisti '16	🍷🍷 6
● Amarone della Valpolicella EgoSum '16	🍷🍷 5
● Valpolicella Essentia '19	🍷🍷 2*
● Valpolicella Sup. Borgo Antico '17	🍷🍷 3
● Valpolicella Sup. Ripasso Excellentia '17	🍷🍷 3
● Valpolicella Marchesini '19	🍷 3
● Valpolicella Sup. Ripasso I Berari '17	🍷 4
● Amarone della Valpolicella Casa Erbisti '15	🍷🍷 6
● Amarone della Valpolicella Casa Erbisti '14	🍷🍷 6
● Amarone della Valpolicella Ego Sum '15	🍷🍷 6
● Valpolicella Essentia '17	🍷🍷 3
● Valpolicella Marchesini '17	🍷🍷 3
● Valpolicella Sup. Euphoria '16	🍷🍷 3
● Valpolicella Sup. Ripasso Excellentia '16	🍷🍷 4

Monte dall'Ora

LOC. CASTELROTTO
VIA MONTE DALL'ORA, 5
37029 SAN PIETRO IN CARIANO [VR]
TEL. +39 0457704462
www.montedallora.com

CELLAR SALES
PRE-BOOKED VISITS
ANNUAL PRODUCTION 35,000 bottles
HECTARES UNDER VINE 6.00
VITICULTURE METHOD Certified Organic

Castelrotto stands out as somewhat isolated from the other hills, overlooking the course of the Adige river and, further on, the town of Scaligera. At the top is a small, 19th-century church and, a little further down, Carlo Venturini's estate, a property surrounded by rows of vines, villas and historic plots. Here a handful of hectares are cultivated according to the dictates of organic farming, with a wink at biodynamic principles, making for a style that perfectly balances tradition and modernity, drawing on the supple, fragrant characteristics of the area's native cultivars. The Stropa put in a great performance. Aged at length in the cellar, it's an Amarone that calls up the fruits of the 2012 harvest. Cherry intersects with notes of spices and crushed flowers, while the palate opens rich and consistent, gaining finesse and tension thanks to a smooth tannic weave and a racy vein of acidity. The Ripasso Sausto '17 is also excellent, with red fruits finding freshness in Corvinone's green, spicy note.

● Amarone della Valpolicella Cl. Stropa '12	🍷🍷 8
● Valpolicella Cl. Sup. Ripasso Sausto '17	🍷🍷 5
● Valpolicella Cl. Saseti '19	🍷🍷 2*
● Valpolicella Cl. Sup. Camporenzo '17	🍷🍷 4
● Valpolicella Cl. Sup. San Giorgio '16	🍷🍷 5
● Valpolicella Cl. Sup. Camporenzo '15	🍷🍷🍷 4*
● Valpolicella Cl. Sup. Camporenzo '13	🍷🍷🍷 4*
● Valpolicella Cl. Sup. Camporenzo '11	🍷🍷🍷 4*
● Valpolicella Cl. Sup. Camporenzo '10	🍷🍷🍷 4*
● Valpolicella Cl. Sup. Ripasso Saustò '07	🍷🍷🍷 5
● Amarone della Valpolicella Cl. Stropa '11	🍷🍷 8
● Amarone della Valpolicella Cl. Stropa '10	🍷🍷 8
● Recioto della Valpolicella Cl. Sant' Ulderico '12	🍷🍷 6

★Monte del Frà

s.da per Custoza, 35
37066 Sommacampagna [VR]
Tel. +39 045510490
www.montedelfra.it

CELLAR SALES
PRE-BOOKED VISITS
ANNUAL PRODUCTION 1,000,000 bottles
HECTARES UNDER VINE 197.00
SUSTAINABLE WINERY

Literally immersed in the vineyards that unfold along the gentle hills of Custoza, the Bonomo brothers' winery is an absolute landmark of Verona's wine. Their bond with the land is as close as ever, so much so that even their venture in Valpolicella, which began a few years ago, has seen the family committed to acquiring the best plots available in the area's classic heart. Today 200-hectares of vineyards give rise to a range that has elegance and finesse as its guiding principles. The 2018 harvest brought with it an aromatic suite dominated by ripe, pulpy yellow fruit, which in the Ca' del Magro finds support in notes of dried flowers and citrus. In the mouth the wine unfolds gracefully and evenly, proving sapid and very long. The Scarnocchio '15, an Amarone reserve, took home a silver medal. Intensely fruity and spicy on the nose, in the mouth its volume is perfectly governed by acidity and tannins.

○ Custoza Sup. Ca' del Magro '18	🍷🍷🍷 3*
● Amarone della Valpolicella Cl. Scarnocchio Tenuta Lena di Mezzo Ris. '15	🍷🍷 8
● Amarone della Valpolicella Cl. Tenuta Lena di Mezzo '16	🍷🍷 8
○ Custoza '19	🍷🍷 2*
● Valpolicella Cl. Sup. Ripasso Tenuta Lena di Mezzo '18	🍷🍷 3
● Valpolicella Cl. Sup. Tenuta Lena di Mezzo '18	🍷🍷 3
● Bardolino '19	🍷 2
⊙ Bardolino Chiaretto '19	🍷 2
● Valpolicella Cl. Tenuta Lena di Mezzo '19	🍷 2
○ Custoza Sup. Ca' del Magro '17	🍷🍷🍷 3*
○ Custoza Sup. Ca' del Magro '16	🍷🍷🍷 3*
○ Custoza Sup. Ca' del Magro '15	🍷🍷🍷 3*

Monte Santoccio

loc. Santoccio, 6
37022 Fumane [VR]
Tel. +39 3496461223
www.montesantoccio.it

CELLAR SALES
ANNUAL PRODUCTION 55,000 bottles
HECTARES UNDER VINE 7.00

Nicola Ferrari and his wife Laura operate on a handful of hectares mainly along the divide that separates the Marano and Fumane valleys (they also have a beautiful plot in the innermost part of the latter). When it comes to vineyard management, a traditional approach in the older plots alternates with rows of vines in the more recent ones. In the cellar, on the other hand, a beautiful stylistic synthesis between modernity and tradition comes together, resulting in wines that do not pursue aromatic complexity and gustatory tension rather than power for its own sake. The exemplary Ripasso '18 offers up healthy, ripe fruit on the nose, all underlined by aromatic herbs and a discreet spiciness in the background. In the mouth it proves racy, lengthening with precision and lightness. Their Amarone, on the other hand, a 2015, revolves around ripe, fleshy fruit, while in the mouth its fullness is never exaggerated, making for an invigorating, vital palate.

● Amarone della Valpolicella Cl. '15	🍷🍷 7
● Valpolicella Cl. Sup. '18	🍷🍷 2*
● Valpolicella Cl. Sup. Ripasso '18	🍷🍷 4
● Santoccio '18	🍷 4
● Valpolicella Cl. '19	🍷 2
● Amarone della Valpolicella Cl. '15	🍷🍷 7
● Amarone della Valpolicella Cl. '13	🍷🍷 7
● Amarone della Valpolicella Cl. '12	🍷🍷 7
● Recioto della Valpolicella Cl. '15	🍷🍷 5
● Recioto della Valpolicella Cl. Amandorlato '14	🍷🍷 5
● Valpolicella Cl. Sup. '15	🍷🍷 2*
● Valpolicella Cl. Sup. '14	🍷🍷 2*
● Valpolicella Cl. Sup. Ripasso '15	🍷🍷 4
● Valpolicella Cl. Sup. Ripasso '13	🍷🍷 4

Monte Tondo

loc. Monte Tondo
via San Lorenzo, 89
37038 Soave [VR]
Tel. +39 0457680347
www.montetondo.it

CELLAR SALES
PRE-BOOKED VISITS
ACCOMMODATION
ANNUAL PRODUCTION 200,000 bottles
HECTARES UNDER VINE 32.00

Gino Magnabosco's winery avails itself of vineyards situated primarily in Soave Classico, then branch out into the flatlands on Mount Gazzo in Caldiero, and finally in Campiano, where the grapes for their Valpolicella reds are grown. The heart of production, however, remains firmly rooted in Soave and benefits from some of the best positions on Mount Foscarino. Their production style focuses on lightness and fragrance for their simpler selections, richness and complexity for the most ambitious ones. The Foscarin Slavinus '18 pours a straw-yellow, anticipating the maturity of its aromas. The fruit comes through sweet, ready to be enjoyed, already embellished by hints of petrol and gravel, all of which we find perfectly expressed in a palate of great firmness and breadth, supported by good acidic vivacity. When it comes to their reds we enjoyed the Valpolicella San Pietro, a 2018 superior appreciated for its light and dynamic style.

Wine	Rating
○ Soave Cl. Sup. Foscarin Slavinus '18	TT 4
○ Soave Cl. Casette Foscarin '18	TT 3
○ Soave Cl. Monte Tondo '19	TT 2*
● Valpolicella Sup. San Pietro '18	TT 2*
○ Soave Brut	T 3
● Valpolicella Ripasso Campo Grande '17	T 4
○ Soave Cl. Monte Tondo '06	YYY 2*
● Amarone della Valpolicella '15	YY 6
● Amarone della Valpolicella '14	YY 6
● Amarone della Valpolicella Ris. '11	YY 6
○ Soave Cl. Casette Foscarin '17	YY 3*
○ Soave Cl. Casette Foscarin '16	YY 3*
○ Soave Cl. Sup. Foscarin Slavinus '17	YY 4
○ Soave Cl. Sup. Foscarin Slavinus '16	YY 4

Cantina Sociale di Monteforte d'Alpone

via XX Settembre, 24
37032 Monteforte d'Alpone [VR]
Tel. +39 0457610110
www.cantinadimonteforte.it

CELLAR SALES
PRE-BOOKED VISITS
ANNUAL PRODUCTION 3,000,000 bottles
HECTARES UNDER VINE 1300.00

The evolution of Verona's wine has led to a profound rethinking of the role that cooperative wineries can play. The one led by the steady hand of Gaetano Tobin, on the other hand, has remained faithful to its historical role, cultivating a large area of vineyards with the support of its members and limiting bottling only to the best batches, around 30% of total production. Soave takes center stage, naturally, with a range of fine wines offered at very attractive prices. This year the winery in Via XX Settembre submitted a limited number of wines, but the Soave Foscarino '19 was in great form. A monovarietal Garganega that matures almost exclusively in steel, on the nose it features vibrant suggestions of white-fleshed fruit and flowers while the palate unfolds with grace and tension, finishing crisp and long. The simpler Vicar '19 also did well, playing on fruity fragrance and a supple, highly pleasant palate.

Wine	Rating
○ Soave Cl. Foscarino '19	TT 3*
○ Soave Cl. Clivus '19	TT 2*
○ Soave Cl. Il Vicario '19	TT 2*
● Prima Pietra '18	T 3
○ Soave Cl. Sup. Vign. di Castellaro '15	YYY 2*
● Amarone della Valpolicella Tolotti '16	YY 5
○ Recioto di Soave Cl. Sigillo '15	YY 3
○ Soave Cl. Clivus '17	YY 2*
○ Soave Cl. Foscarino '17	YY 3
○ Soave Cl. Foscarino '16	YY 3*
○ Soave Cl. Il Vicario '18	YY 2*
○ Soave Cl. Sup. Castellaro '17	YY 2*
○ Soave Cl. Sup. Castellaro '16	YY 2*
○ Soave Cl. Vicario '17	YY 2*
● Valpolicella Ripasso Clivus '17	YY 2*

Montegrande

via Torre, 2
35030 Rovolon [PD]
Tel. +39 0495226276
www.vinimontegrande.it

CELLAR SALES
PRE-BOOKED VISITS
ANNUAL PRODUCTION 250,000 bottles
HECTARES UNDER VINE 30.00

Even if they've been growing grapes here since time immemorial, the Euganean Hills have never bowed entirely to their presence. Indeed, here vineyards are surrounded by woods, Mediterranean scrub and occasionally meadows, in a landscape dotted with small villages and historic villas. It's here that Raffaele and Paola Cristofanon run the family business, a producer deeply rooted in the territory and one that has, in the last decade, taken significant steps forward, offering whites marked by their varietal character and reds that do an outstanding job expressing a sunny, Mediterranean territory. Produced for the first time in 2016, the Merlot Luigi Cristofanon has made believers out of us thanks to a broad-based and still-evolving aromatic profile in which fruit is crossed by fresher notes of medicinal herbs and spices. On the palate it is of a superior category: opening rich and powerful, it finds dynamism and continuity under the pressure of its acidity, closing with a pleasantly rough finish.

Wine	Rating	Price
● Colli Euganei Merlot Luigi Cristofanon Ris. '16	▼▼	4
○ Colli Euganei Bianco Erto '19	▼▼	2*
○ Colli Euganei Chardonnay San Giorgio '17	▼▼	4
● Colli Euganei Merlot Corterocco '18	▼▼	2*
● Colli Euganei Rosso Momi '18	▼▼	2*
● Colli Euganei Cabernet Borgomoro '18	▼	2
○ Colli Euganei Pinot Bianco Marani '19	▼	2
○ Colli Euganei Serprino Brut	▼	2
● Colli Euganei Cabernet Borgomoro '17	▽▽	3
● Colli Euganei Cabernet Sereo Ris. '16	▽▽	3
● Colli Euganei Merlot Corterocco '17	▽▽	3
● Colli Euganei Rosso Ottomano Ris. '16	▽▽	4
● Colli Euganei Rosso Ottomano Ris. '15	▽▽	4
● Colli Euganei Rosso V. delle Roche Ris. '16	▽▽	3

Monteversa

via Monte Versa, 1024
35030 Vo' [PD]
Tel. +39 0499941092
www.monteversa.it

CELLAR SALES
PRE-BOOKED VISITS
ANNUAL PRODUCTION 23,000 bottles
HECTARES UNDER VINE 17.00
VITICULTURE METHOD Certified Organic

The Voltazza family winery has been active for a few years in the southwestern part of the Euganean Hills Regional Park. The vineyards, however, were planted decades earlier (only a small part have been recently replaced). The overall picture, therefore, is one of a dense set of vineyards in some of the appellation's best positions, and a family eager to produce great wines. To this end, the presentation of their flagship has been postponed to allow the wine to age a bit longer in the cellar. The Animaversa Chardonnay '18 is at the top of its game. It's a fruity wine, enticing on the nose, while in the mouth its generosity seems almost hidden, leaving room for an energetic, sapid palate marked by great tension. When it comes to their reds, we enjoyed the Versacinto '18, a Bordeaux blend appreciated for the clarity of its red fruit and crispness of flavor.

Wine	Rating	Price
○ Animaversa Chardonnay '18	▼▼	4
● Colli Euganei Rosso Versacinto '18	▼▼	3
○ Primaversa Frizzante '19	▼	3
● Colli Euganei Cabernet Animaversa '12	▽▽	4
○ Colli Euganei Fior d'Arancio Spumante '18	▽▽	4
○ Colli Euganei Fior d'Arancio Spumante '16	▽▽	4
○ Colli Euganei Manzoni Bianco Animaversa '17	▽▽	3
● Colli Euganei Rosso Animaversa '16	▽▽	4
● Colli Euganei Rosso Animaversa '15	▽▽	4
● Colli Euganei Rosso Animaversa '13	▽▽	4
● Colli Euganei Rosso Versacinto '16	▽▽	3
○ Versavò '17	▽▽	2*
○ Versavò '15	▽▽	2*

Marco Mosconi

VIA PARADISO, 5
37031 ILLASI [VR]
TEL. +39 0456529109
www.marcomosconi.it

CELLAR SALES
PRE-BOOKED VISITS
ANNUAL PRODUCTION 25,000 bottles
HECTARES UNDER VINE 10.00

Over the last few years Marco Mosconi has found his direction, freeing himself from a style centered at concentration—which, especially in the Illasi valley, has long dominated—and embracing an approach where tension, elegance and suppleness are essential for counteracting richness. About ten hectares of vineyards are mostly dedicated to red grapes, though a small share of Garganega is cultivated as well. This year they submitted an unusual selection for tasting, with all their most important wines left to rest in the cellar. To compensate we tasted a top-notch passito made with Marco's small amount of Garganega. Harking all the way back to 2006, the wine offers up complex aromas of dried figs, caramel and exotic, balsamic notes. In the mouth sweetness is well represented, but not cumbersome, while the wine finds balance via a notable sapidity.

Wine	Rating
○ Passito '06	TT 7
● Corvina '19	TT 3
○ Soave Corte Paradiso '19	TT 2*
● Valpolicella Sup. '13	YYY 5
● Valpolicella Sup. '12	YYY 5
● Amandorlato '15	YY 3
● Amarone della Valpolicella '13	YY 8
● Amarone della Valpolicella '12	YY 8
○ Soave Corte Paradiso '18	YY 2*
○ Soave Corte Paradiso '17	YY 2*
○ Soave Rosetta '18	YY 3
○ Soave Rosetta '15	YY 3
● Turan '15	YY 3
● Turan '13	YY 3
● Valpolicella Montecurto '16	YY 3
● Valpolicella Sup. '15	YY 5
● Valpolicella Sup. '14	YY 5

Mosole

LOC. CORBOLONE
VIA ANNONE VENETO, 60
30029 SANTO STINO DI LIVENZA [VE]
TEL. +39 0421310404
www.mosole.com

CELLAR SALES
PRE-BOOKED VISITS
ANNUAL PRODUCTION 230,000 bottles
HECTARES UNDER VINE 30.00

At first glance, the wide plain that stretches from Venice towards Friuli looks all the same, but if we dig down below the first 20 centimetres, we discover an extremely varied world, where the gravelly soils that meet near the main watercourses alternate with clays and silt. Lucio Mosole, who works on such clay terrain, is an authentic interpreter of the territory and brings great sensitivity to his work. This is how he manages to bring out the freshness of his more approachable selections, and the character and finesse of his premium versions. The Cabernet Hora Sexta '17 is a splendid wine, one that manages to express the territory through a fruity presence that, true to its origins, is circumscribed by a clear vegetality and hints of medicinal herbs. On the palate it proves generous, supple and juicy. The Ad Nonam is a passito that plays on exotic, citrus notes while in the mouth it reveals a pronounced sweetness balanced by acidity.

Wine	Rating
○ Ad Nonam Passito '18	TT 5
● Lison Pramaggiore Cabernet Hora Sexta '17	TT 5
● Lison Pramaggiore Merlot Ad Nonam '17	TT 6
○ Tai '19	TT 3
○ Venezia Pinot Grigio '19	TT 3
● Lison Pramaggiore Refosco P. R. '19	T 3
○ Sauvignon '19	T 3
○ Venezia Chardonnay '19	T 3
○ Ad Nonam Passito '17	YY 4
○ Hora Prima '17	YY 4
○ Hora Prima '16	YY 4
● Lison-Pramaggiore Cabernet Hora Sexta '16	YY 4
● Lison-Pramaggiore Merlot Ad Nonam '16	YY 5
○ Venezia Chardonnay '18	YY 2*
● Venezia Merlot '18	YY 2*

Il Mottolo

LOC. LE CONTARINE
VIA COMEZZARA, 13
35030 BAONE [PD]
TEL. +39 3479456155
www.ilmottolo.it

CELLAR SALES
PRE-BOOKED VISITS
ANNUAL PRODUCTION 30,000 bottles
HECTARES UNDER VINE 8.00

Sergio Fortin came to viticulture in adulthood, driven by a passion for wine that's matched by few. Together with his friend Roberto Dalla Libera, he created Il Mottolo, a beautiful winery situated in the southern part of the Euganean Hills. Here the heat makes itself felt, so the problem is not achieving ripeness but maintaining freshness and finesse. A few hectares are cultivated, mainly red Bordeaux varieties, making for a range that does an outstanding job expressing this Mediterranean corner of Veneto. The Serro once again put in a performance for the ages. 2017 brought out the usual aromatic spectrum, with fruit complemented by notes of spices, flowers and undergrowth. In the mouth its fullness is perfectly balanced by acidity, while a long finish is marked by a tannic presence. The Vignanima '17 is richer in its fruity expression, endowed with energy and verve.

Wine	Rating
● Colli Euganei Carménère Vignànima '17	🍷🍷 5
● Colli Euganei Rosso Serro '17	🍷🍷 4
● Comezzara Merlot '18	🍷🍷 3
○ Le Contarine '19	🍷🍷 3
● V. Marè Cabernet '18	🍷 3
● Colli Euganei Rosso Serro '16	🍸🍸🍸 4*
● Colli Euganei Rosso Serro '11	🍸🍸🍸 3*
● Colli Euganei Rosso Serro '10	🍸🍸🍸 3*
● Colli Euganei Rosso Serro '09	🍸🍸🍸 3*
○ Colli Euganei Fiori d'Arancio Passito Luna del Pozzo '16	🍸🍸 3
○ Le Contarine '17	🍸🍸 2*
● Merlot Comezzara '17	🍸🍸 2*
● Serro '15	🍸🍸 4
● V. Marè Cabernet '17	🍸🍸 2*
● V. Marè Cabernet '16	🍸🍸 2*

Mulin di Mezzo

VIA MOLIN DI MEZZO,16
30020 ANNONE VENETO [VE]
TEL. +39 0422 769398
www.mulindimezzo.com

PRE-BOOKED VISITS
ANNUAL PRODUCTION 40,000 bottles
HECTARES UNDER VINE 6.00

The Lison Pramaggiore appellation extends over the Venetian plains in the direction of Pordenone, just a stone's throw from the sea and just south of the Pre-Alps. The area is mainly dedicated to the production of light, supple wines, which Paolo Lazzarin is determined to reinterpret. His vineyards, which only span a handful of hectares, grow in a soil dominated by clay, which confers an unusual pluck to the grapes. These are cultivated according to an extremely selective approach, making for a solid and rich selection of wines. That Annone is one of the cradles of Tai isn't news, but the Lison '19 once again proves it. Vibrant aromas are dominated by yellow fruit and flowers, while the palate comes through full, energetic and highly sapid. The Sauvignon '19 is tantalising and fresh, while when it comes to their reds, we point out the excellent results put in by their Cabernet Franc '18, an aromatically fresh wine that's juicy, supple and very pleasant on the palate.

Wine	Rating
○ Lison Cl. '19	🍷🍷 2*
● Rosso Molino '18	🍷🍷 3
○ Sauvignon '19	🍷🍷 2*
● Venezia Cabernet Franc '18	🍷🍷 3
● Lison Pramaggiore Merlot '17	🍷 3
● Venezia Cabernet Sauvignon '18	🍷 3
● Il Priore '10	🍸🍸 4
○ Lison Cl. '18	🍸🍸 2*
○ Lison Cl. '17	🍸🍸 2*
○ Lison Cl. '16	🍸🍸 2*
○ Lison Cl. Blanc '18	🍸🍸 2*
○ Lison Pramaggiore Chardonnay '17	🍸🍸 2*
● Lison Pramaggiore Merlot '16	🍸🍸 2*
● Rosso Molino '17	🍸🍸 2*
● Rosso Molino '15	🍸🍸 2*

Musella

LOC. FERRAZZE
VIA FERRAZZETTE, 2
37036 SAN MARTINO BUON ALBERGO [VR]
TEL. +39 045973385
www.musella.it

CELLAR SALES
PRE-BOOKED VISITS
ACCOMMODATION
ANNUAL PRODUCTION 150,000 bottles
HECTARES UNDER VINE 25.00
VITICULTURE METHOD Certified Biodynamic
SUSTAINABLE WINERY

Maddalena Pasqua's property is located inside the ancient Musella estate, gentle hills enclosed by walls, a true green oasis just a stone's throw from the Scaligera town center. What was once an environmentally friendly approach to agriculture has, over the years, evolved into biodynamic management of the entire property. The result is a range in which the appellation's classic wines, all interpreted with personality, are complemented by couple of more creative offerings. The Ripasso '16 put in one for the ages, a performance wrought of tension and aromatic elegance. Ripe wild fruits are echoed by notes of medicinal herbs and pepper, while in the mouth it comes through crisp, juicy and thrilling. Three Amarones were submitted, with our preference going to the Senza Titolo '11, a wine that pours a light color, anticipating complex, almost tertiary aromas, with alcohol-steeped fruit letting through mineral hints and licorice. In the mouth it widens delicate and sapid, finishing crisp and relaxed.

Wine	Rating
● Valpolicella Sup. Ripasso '16	▼▼ 4
● Amarone della Valpolicella '14	▼▼ 6
● Amarone della Valpolicella Ris. '15	▼▼ 6
● Amarone della Valpolicella Senza Titolo '11	▼▼ 8
● Monte del Drago '15	▼▼ 5
● Valpolicella Sup. '18	▼▼ 3
○ Drago Bianco '18	▼ 3
○ Fibio Pinot Bianco '18	▼ 3
● Amarone della Valpolicella Ris. '07	▽▽▽ 6
● Valpolicella Sup. '13	▽▽▽ 3*
● Valpolicella Sup. '12	▽▽▽ 2*
● Amarone della Valpolicella '12	▽▽ 6
○ Drago Bianco '16	▽▽ 3
● Valpolicella Sup. '16	▽▽ 3*
● Valpolicella Sup. '15	▽▽ 3*
● Valpolicella Sup. '14	▽▽ 3*

Nardello

VIA IV NOVEMBRE, 56
37032 MONTEFORTE D'ALPONE [VR]
TEL. +39 0457612116
www.nardellovini.it

CELLAR SALES
PRE-BOOKED VISITS
ANNUAL PRODUCTION 75,000 bottles
HECTARES UNDER VINE 16.00
SUSTAINABLE WINERY

Slowly Federica and Daniele Nardello are developing the family business, bolstered by a vineyard that extends for more than 15 hectares and has in Monte Tondo and Zoppega its crown jewels. Here, in the southern end of the 'zona classica', Daniele has gradually modified the old pergola vineyards to reduce the vigor of the grapes while preserving their healthiness (their newest vineyards are cultivated with the guyot system). Only the best batches of grapes are used for a range that focuses primarily on appellation designated wines. And Monte Zoppega hosts the grapes for their Soave '18, a wine redolent of ripe, juicy, yellow-fleshed fruit, with a discreet, almost hidden presence of oak lurking in the background. In the mouth it broadens delicately, proving pervasive and soft. The Turbian '19 exhibits greater aromatic freshness and gustatory tension, making use of a notable share of Trebbiano di Soave.

Wine	Rating
○ Soave Cl. Meridies '19	▼▼ 2*
○ Soave Cl. Monte Zoppega '18	▼▼ 4
○ Soave Cl. Turbian '19	▼▼ 3
○ Blanc de Fe' '19	▼ 3
○ Recioto di Soave Suavissimus '16	▽▽ 4
○ Recioto di Soave Suavissimus '14	▽▽ 4
○ Soave Cl. Meridies '18	▽▽ 2*
○ Soave Cl. Meridies '17	▽▽ 2*
○ Soave Cl. Monte Zoppega '17	▽▽ 4
○ Soave Cl. Monte Zoppega '16	▽▽ 4
○ Soave Cl. Monte Zoppega '15	▽▽ 3*
○ Soave Cl. Turbian '18	▽▽ 3
○ Soave Cl. V. Turbian '17	▽▽ 3*
○ Soave Cl. V. Turbian '16	▽▽ 2*

Nicolis

via Villa Girardi, 29
37029 San Pietro in Cariano [VR]
Tel. +39 0457701261
www.vininicolis.com

CELLAR SALES
PRE-BOOKED VISITS
ANNUAL PRODUCTION 220,000 bottles
HECTARES UNDER VINE 42.00
SUSTAINABLE WINERY

Present in the territory of Valpolicella for generations, the Nicolis family's winery is defined by tradition. Today the property extends for many hectares within the classic area, for a traditionally-styled range dedicated to the appellation's classic typologies. At the helm we find brothers Giancarlo and Giuseppe, with the former carefully overseeing the vineyards and the second serving as a sensitive interpreter in the cellar. Almost a decade after harvest, the Ambrosan '11, their most ambitious Amarone, sees the light of day. On the nose, its fruit comes through super ripe, almost jammy, enriched by the presence of medicinal herbs and deep mineral notes, which confer a certain aromatic lightness. A generous palate opens strikingly, only to unfold gracefully by virtue of its acidity. The Seccal '17 also delivered. It's a Ripasso with a youthful profile and a supple, dynamic, highly pleasant palate.

- Amarone della Valpolicella Cl. Ambrosan '11 — 🍷🍷 8
- Amarone della Valpolicella Cl. '15 — 🍷🍷 6
- Valpolicella Cl. Sup. Ripasso Seccal '17 — 🍷🍷 4
- Amarone della Valpolicella Cl. Ambrosan '06 — YYY 7
- Amarone della Valpolicella Cl. Ambrosan '98 — YYY 7
- Amarone della Valpolicella Cl. Ambrosan '93 — YYY 6
- Amarone della Valpolicella Cl. '13 — YY 6
- Amarone della Valpolicella Cl. '12 — YY 6
- Amarone della Valpolicella Cl. '11 — YY 6
- Amarone della Valpolicella Cl. Ambrosan '10 — YY 7
- Amarone della Valpolicella Cl. Ambrosan '09 — YY 7

Novaia

via Novaia, 1
37020 Marano di Valpolicella [VR]
Tel. +39 0457755129
www.novaia.it

CELLAR SALES
PRE-BOOKED VISITS
ANNUAL PRODUCTION 50,000 bottles
HECTARES UNDER VINE 7.00
VITICULTURE METHOD Certified Organic
SUSTAINABLE WINERY

If the valley floors of Valpolicella Classica are experiencing urbanization, all it takes is to move a few hundred meters to find oneself, as if by magic, in a landscape characterized by vineyards (until a few decades ago, cherry and olive trees also contended for the best positions, but they've since been thinned out to a few patches here and there). The Vaona family organically cultivates one of the most untarnished and beautiful corners of Valpolicella, producing a range of wines linked strongly to tradition and marked by great personality. Marano hit the mark this year, with the Amarone Corte Vaona '15 topping our preferences. On the nose it opens shy, decidedly closed, only to broaden, little by little, releasing super-ripe fruit crossed by notes of herbs and spices, with a reserved but deep mineral note lurking in the background. On the palate it reveals great texture and a highly pleasant tannic rusticity. We also appreciated the vibrant, juicy, highly drinkable Ripasso '17.

- Amarone della Valpolicella Cl. Corte Vaona '15 — 🍷🍷 6
- Recioto della Valpolicella Cl. Le Novaje '18 — 🍷🍷 5
- Valpolicella Cl. '19 — 🍷🍷 3
- Valpolicella Cl. Sup. I Cantoni '17 — 🍷🍷 4
- Valpolicella Cl. Sup. Ripasso '17 — 🍷🍷 4
- Amarone della Valpolicella Cl. Corte Vaona '13 — YY 6
- Amarone della Valpolicella Cl. Corte Vaona '12 — YY 6
- Amarone della Valpolicella Cl. Le Balze Ris. '13 — YY 7
- Recioto della Valpolicella Cl. Le Novaje '17 — YY 4
- Valpolicella Cl. '18 — YY 3
- Valpolicella Cl. '17 — YY 3
- Valpolicella Cl. Sup. I Cantoni '16 — YY 4
- Valpolicella Cl. Sup. Ripasso '16 — YY 4

★Ottella

FRAZ. SAN BENEDETTO DI LUGANA
LOC. OTTELLA
37019 PESCHIERA DEL GARDA [VR]
TEL. +39 0457551950
www.ottella.it

CELLAR SALES
PRE-BOOKED VISITS
ANNUAL PRODUCTION 350,000 bottles
HECTARES UNDER VINE 40.00

The winemaking venture launched many years ago by Lodovico Montresor together with his sons Francesco and Michele has grown into one of Lugana's most beautiful estates. Over the years, the producer has expanded the area under vine, first in the direction of Ponti sul Mincio, where the red grapes are cultivated, and in recent years in Valpolicella, in Romagnano, where they cultivate about twenty hectares of traditional grape varieties. The winery's heart, however, remains in Lugana, where it seeks to bring out the wines' varietal qualities and ageworthiness. Once again the Lugana Molceo topped our list of preferences. The 2018 version of this reserve features vibrant suggestions of ripe fruit refreshed by subtle vegetal and floral notes. On the palate its generosity is perfectly contrasted by acidity and a vital, juicy sapidity. Their Valpolicella reds are also beginning to find their way, with an excellent Ripasso Ripa della Volta '18 that won us over for its mature aromas and the harmony of its rich palate.

Wine	Rating
○ Lugana Molceo Ris. '18	TTT 4*
● Campo Sireso '17	TT 4
○ Lugana '19	TT 2*
○ Lugana Le Creete '19	TT 3
○ Nasomatto '19	TT 2*
○ Prima Luce Passito '14	TT 5
⊙ RosesRoses '19	TT 2*
● Valpolicella Ripasso Ripa della Volta '17	TT 4
● Gemei '19	T 2
○ Lugana Back to Silence '19	T 2
○ Lugana Molceo Ris. '17	YYY 4*
○ Lugana Molceo Ris. '16	YYY 4*
○ Lugana Molceo Ris. '15	YYY 4*
○ Lugana Molceo Ris. '14	YYY 4*
○ Lugana Molceo Ris. '13	YYY 4*
○ Lugana Molceo Ris. '12	YYY 4*

Pasqua - Cecilia Beretta

LOC. SAN FELICE EXTRA
VIA BELVEDERE, 135
37131 VERONA
TEL. +39 0458432111
www.pasqua.it

CELLAR SALES
PRE-BOOKED VISITS
ANNUAL PRODUCTION 15,500,000 bottles
HECTARES UNDER VINE 322.00

Today this Verona winery stands as one of the most interesting producers operating in the area, with a vast area cultivated and a management approach that's not limited to producing good quality wines. Indeed, here their goal is also to carefully interpret the deep bond that binds each vineyard to its grapes. If Pasqua has undergone major changes in recent years, today it's time for Cecilia Beretta, the family producer, to offer a renewed range of wines marked by great personality. This year the winery at Via Belvedere submitted a limited selection for tasting. The Amarone Mai Dire Mai pours a thick ruby red, only to release little by little its fruity aromas—these are followed by mineral hints and forest undergrowth, with spices waiting in the wings. In the mouth it's rich, close-knit and assertive, making for a drink that's hard to forget. The Famiglia Pasqua '16 is diametrically opposed, playing on aromatic freshness and harmony of flavor.

Wine	Rating
● Amarone della Valpolicella Mai Dire Mai '13	TTT 8
● Amarone della Valpolicella Famiglia Pasqua '16	TT 6
○ Soave Cl. Brognoligo Cecilia Beretta '19	TT 3*
● Amarone della Valpolicella Cl. Terre di Cariano Cecilia Beretta Ris. '15	TT 8
● Valpolicella Sup. Mai dire Mai '15	TT 6
● Amarone della Valpolicella Cl. Terre di Cariano '04	YYY 8
● Amarone della Valpolicella Famiglia Pasqua '13	YYY 6
● Amarone della Valpolicella Mai Dire Mai '12	YYY 8
● Amarone della Valpolicella Pasqua Mai dire Mai '11	YYY 8

★★Leonildo Pieropan

via Matteotti
37038 Soave [VR]
Tel. +39 0456190171
www.pieropan.it

CELLAR SALES
PRE-BOOKED VISITS
ANNUAL PRODUCTION 550,000 bottles
HECTARES UNDER VINE 70.00
VITICULTURE METHOD Certified Organic

If Soave is recognized as a quality wine today, a part of the credit must certainly go to the Pieropan family's winery, now managed by brothers Dario and Andrea under the watchful eye of mother Teresita. A large estate, which today reaches into both classic Soave and eastern Valpolicella, is comprised of about seventy organically managed hectares. These give rise to a range of wines that plays more on elegance and longevity than on richness and immediacy. This year the Pieropan brothers submitted a battery of wines dedicated entirely to Soave, with the Valpolicella reds left to age in the cellar. The Calvarino '18 offers up intense fruity suggestions echoed by Trebbiano di Soave's fresher and more floral notes. In the mouth it tends towards suppleness and a spirited energy only to reveal sapidity and harmony. The La Rocca '18 is richer, deeper and more mineral, endowed with a full, satisfying palate.

Wine	Rating
○ Soave Cl. Calvarino '18	🍷🍷🍷 4*
○ Soave Cl. La Rocca '18	🍷🍷 5
○ Recioto di Soave Cl. Le Colombare '16	🍷🍷 5
○ Soave Cl. '19	🍷🍷 3
○ Soave Cl. Calvarino '17	☐☐☐ 4*
○ Soave Cl. Calvarino '16	☐☐☐ 4*
○ Soave Cl. Calvarino '15	☐☐☐ 4*
○ Soave Cl. Calvarino '13	☐☐☐ 4*
○ Soave Cl. Calvarino '09	☐☐☐ 4*
○ Soave Cl. Calvarino '08	☐☐☐ 4
○ Soave Cl. Calvarino '07	☐☐☐ 4
○ Soave Cl. La Rocca '14	☐☐☐ 5
○ Soave Cl. La Rocca '12	☐☐☐ 5
○ Soave Cl. La Rocca '11	☐☐☐ 5
○ Soave Cl. La Rocca '10	☐☐☐ 5

Piovene Porto Godi

fraz. Toara di Villaga
via Villa, 14
36021 Villaga [VI]
Tel. +39 0444885142
www.piovene.com

CELLAR SALES
PRE-BOOKED VISITS
ACCOMMODATION
ANNUAL PRODUCTION 120,000 bottles
HECTARES UNDER VINE 40.00
SUSTAINABLE WINERY

The Piovene family's estate unfolds in the enclave of Toara, a sort of large amphitheatre that opens to the southeast in the southern part of the Berici Hills. Around the historic villa, which also houses the cellar, woods and vineyard rows alternate with meadows and farmland, making for a landscape where vineyards are only one of many natural features. Their range, which focuses on red wines, takes advantage of the particularly hot and dry summer months to highlight a rich style dominated by ripe fruit. The Merlot Fra I Broli '16 exhibits an extraordinarily youthful aromatic profile dominated by ripe fruit and embellished by floral hints and forest undergrowth. In the mouth it opens even more youthful, revolving around fruity notes and riding acidity to a long, vibrant finish. The Thovara '16 appears more closed on the nose, developing a crisp, dynamic and pleasantly rough palate. Finally, we make note of the excellent Polveriera Rosso '18, a fragrant and juicy Bordeaux.

Wine	Rating
● Colli Berici Merlot Fra i Broli '16	🍷🍷 4
● Colli Berici Tai Rosso Thovara '16	🍷🍷 5
○ Colli Berici Garganega '19	🍷🍷 2*
● Colli Berici Tai Rosso Riveselle '19	🍷🍷 2*
● Polveriera Rosso '18	🍷🍷 2*
○ Colli Berici Pinot Bianco Polveriera '19	🍷 2
○ Colli Berici Sauvignon Fostine '19	🍷 2
● Colli Berici Cabernet Vign. Pozzare '12	☐☐☐ 4*
● Colli Berici Cabernet Vign. Pozzare '07	☐☐☐ 3
● Colli Berici Cabernet Vign. Pozzare '16	☐☐ 4
● Colli Berici Cabernet Vign. Pozzare '15	☐☐ 4
○ Colli Berici Pinot Bianco Polveriera '18	☐☐ 2*
○ Colli Berici Sauvignon Vign. Fostine '18	☐☐ 2*
● Colli Berici Tai Rosso Thovara '15	☐☐ 5
● Polveriera Rosso '17	☐☐ 2*
○ Sauvignon Campigie '17	☐☐ 3

★Graziano Prà

via della Fontana, 31
37032 Monteforte d'Alpone [VR]
Tel. +39 0457612125
www.vinipra.it

CELLAR SALES
PRE-BOOKED VISITS
ACCOMMODATION
ANNUAL PRODUCTION 350,000 bottles
HECTARES UNDER VINE 35.00
VITICULTURE METHOD Certified Organic
SUSTAINABLE WINERY

The dark, almost black soil of Monte Grande immediately lays bare its volcanic origin. It's here that we find the winery owned by Graziano Prà, whose property has grown to almost 40 hectares. His vineyards also reach into the limestone hills between the valleys of Tregnago and Mezzane, an area that gives rise to their Valpolicellas. Graziano interprets these very different soils with sensitivity, highlighting the mineral complexity that characterizes the whites and the fragrant finesse that higher elevations confer to the reds. It's difficult to choose which of the wines presented this year is the best, as the entire lot delivers in all respects. The Monte Grande '18 is the classic prized white, marked by an aromatic profile that, in addition to white fruit, is already exhibiting its first mineral hints. In the mouth it comes through elegant, taut and highly drinkable. The Staforte '18 moves on a more subdued register but one of character, with a juicy and long palate.

Wine	Rating
○ Soave Cl. Monte Grande '18	🍷🍷 4
○ Soave Cl. Staforte '18	🍷🍷 3*
● Amarone della Valpolicella Morandina '15	🍷🍷 7
○ Soave Cl. Colle Sant'Antonio '16	🍷🍷 5
○ Soave Cl. Otto '19	🍷🍷 3
● Valpolicella Sup. Ripasso Morandina '18	🍷🍷 4
● Valpolicella Morandina '19	🍷 3
○ Soave Cl. Monte Grande '16	🥂🥂🥂 4*
○ Soave Cl. Monte Grande '11	🥂🥂🥂 4*
○ Soave Cl. Monte Grande '08	🥂🥂🥂 4
○ Soave Cl. Staforte '15	🥂🥂🥂 3*
○ Soave Cl. Staforte '14	🥂🥂🥂 4*
○ Soave Cl. Staforte '13	🥂🥂🥂 4*
○ Soave Cl. Staforte '11	🥂🥂🥂 4*
○ Soave Cl. Staforte '08	🥂🥂🥂 4

★★Giuseppe Quintarelli

via Cerè, 1
37024 Negrar [VR]
Tel. +39 0457500016
vini@giuseppequintarelli.it

CELLAR SALES
PRE-BOOKED VISITS
ANNUAL PRODUCTION 60,000 bottles
HECTARES UNDER VINE 10.00

The success of Valpolicella over the last twenty years has led many producers to expand the area under vine and increase production. At the Quintarelli family's winery this isn't the case. The vineyards cover ten hectares, the same as always, and production is below 100,000 bottles even during the best vintages. Today Francesco and Lorenzo Quintarelli have taken things over from their parents, and lead the winery according to tradition. Here they produce wines that need time to offer up their best, revealing an extraordinary fusion of richness, complexity and lightness. More than a decade after the harvest, the Quintarelli family are presenting the Amarone Riserva '09, a wine of rare stylistic precision that offers a fruity bouquet with a shifting outline streaked by notes of underbrush and spices that follow one another in succession. The palate opens rich and decisive, unfolding and lightening instant after instant, finishing long and warm.

Wine	Rating
● Amarone della Valpolicella Cl. Ris. '09	🍷🍷🍷 8
● Valpolicella Cl. Sup. '13	🍷🍷 7
● Amarone della Valpolicella Cl. '11	🥂🥂🥂 8
● Amarone della Valpolicella Cl. '09	🥂🥂🥂 8
● Amarone della Valpolicella Cl. '06	🥂🥂🥂 8
● Amarone della Valpolicella Cl. '03	🥂🥂🥂 8
● Amarone della Valpolicella Cl. '98	🥂🥂🥂 8
● Amarone della Valpolicella Cl. '97	🥂🥂🥂 8
● Amarone della Valpolicella Cl. Ris. '07	🥂🥂🥂 8
● Amarone della Valpolicella Cl. Sup. Monte Cà Paletta '00	🥂🥂🥂 8
● Recioto della Valpolicella Cl. '01	🥂🥂🥂 8
● Recioto della Valpolicella Cl. '95	🥂🥂🥂 5
● Recioto della Valpolicella Cl. Monte Ca' Paletta '97	🥂🥂🥂 8
● Valpolicella Cl. Sup. '99	🥂🥂🥂 7

Quota 101

VIA MALTERRENO, 12
35038 TORREGLIA [PD]
TEL. +39 0495211322
www.quota101.com

CELLAR SALES
PRE-BOOKED VISITS
ACCOMMODATION
ANNUAL PRODUCTION 45,000 bottles
HECTARES UNDER VINE 18.00
VITICULTURE METHOD Certified Organic
SUSTAINABLE WINERY

The winery's name refers to the elevation at which the cellar is situated. It's a small but functional structure immersed in the Euganean Hills, surrounded by vineyards and woods that seem to shield it from the outside. Roberto Gardina, together with his wife Natalia and daughters Silvia and Roberta, acquired the property a few years ago, but already they've brought about a marked change of pace with respect to the past. Organic vineyard management, respect for biodiversity, pursuit of a style that, in addition to being good knows how to express its territory of provenance, are the pillars on which their production philosophy is based. The Cabernet Sauvignon '16 put in an excellent performance. It's redolent of ripe fruit and spices, with a subtle nuance of pencil lead lurking in the background. In the mouth it doesn't pursue concentration and power, but wins you over with its purity, coming through fine, long and juicy. The Merlot Silvano '18 offers a fresher, tastier share of ripe fruit, while in the mouth it exhibits body and an energetic, highly pleasant palate.

- ● Colli Euganei Cabernet Poggio Ameno '18 — 🍷🍷 2*
- ● Colli Euganei Cabernet Sauvignon '16 — 🍷🍷 5
- ○ Colli Euganei Chardonnay '18 — 🍷🍷 3
- ● Colli Euganei Merlot Silvano '18 — 🍷🍷 2*
- ○ Colli Euganei Fior d'Arancio Spumante Dolce '19 — 🍷 3
- ○ Garganega '18 — 🍷 2
- ○ Colli Euganei Fior d'Arancio '16 — 🍷🍷 3
- ○ Colli Euganei Fior d'Arancio Passito Il Gelso di Lapo '16 — 🍷🍷 5
- ○ Colli Euganei Fior d'Arancio Passito Il Gelso di Lapo '15 — 🍷🍷 5
- ○ Colli Euganei Manzoni Bianco '18 — 🍷🍷 3
- ○ Colli Euganei Manzoni Bianco '16 — 🍷🍷 3
- ● Colli Euganei Rosso Ortone '16 — 🍷🍷 4
- ● Colli Euganei Rosso Ortone '15 — 🍷🍷 4

Le Ragose

FRAZ. ARBIZZANO
VIA RAGOSE, 1
37024 NEGRAR [VR]
TEL. +39 0457513241
www.leragose.com

CELLAR SALES
PRE-BOOKED VISITS
ANNUAL PRODUCTION 130,000 bottles
HECTARES UNDER VINE 18.00
SUSTAINABLE WINERY

The Galli brothers' estate unfolds along the divide that separates the Negrar Valley from the lesser-known Quinzano Valley, with vineyards that still enjoy the protection of the forest and are constantly caressed by the breeze. Paolo and Marco know that you can't rush, that their wines need time to achieve harmony and full expressiveness to narrate the season, the vineyard and tradition. A limited number of bottles, all closely linked to the appellation, are produced. The Amarone '10, presented a decade after the harvest, is exemplary. On the nose fruit blends perfectly with notes of undergrowth and medicinal herbs, with a subtle mineral hint rising up from below. In the mouth it unfolds supple, pleasantly spirited, proving energetic and vibrant. The Le Sassine '16 offers up scents dominated by overripe red fruit, while in the mouth it reveals a more dynamic and supple palate, serving as a perfect example of contemporary tradition.

- ● Amarone della Valpolicella Cl. '10 — 🍷🍷 7
- ● Amarone della Valpolicella Cl. Marta Galli '10 — 🍷🍷 7
- ● Recioto della Valpolicella Cl. '16 — 🍷🍷 5
- ● Valpolicella Cl. Sup. Marta Galli '16 — 🍷🍷 5
- ● Valpolicella Cl. Sup. Ripasso Le Sassine '16 — 🍷🍷 4
- ● Amarone della Valpolicella Cl. '88 — 🍷🍷🍷 7
- ● Amarone della Valpolicella Cl. '86 — 🍷🍷🍷 7
- ● Amarone della Valpolicella Cl. Caloetto '06 — 🍷🍷🍷 7
- ● Amarone della Valpolicella Cl. Marta Galli '05 — 🍷🍷🍷 8
- ● Amarone della Valpolicella Cl. '08 — 🍷🍷 7
- ● Amarone della Valpolicella Cl. Caloetto '07 — 🍷🍷 7
- ● Recioto della Valpolicella Cl. '15 — 🍷🍷 5
- ● Valpolicella Cl. Sup. Marta Galli '15 — 🍷🍷 5

Roeno

via Mama, 5
37020 Brentino Belluno [VR]
Tel. +39 0457230110
www.cantinaroeno.com

CELLAR SALES
PRE-BOOKED VISITS
ACCOMMODATION AND RESTAURANT SERVICE
ANNUAL PRODUCTION 400,000 bottles
HECTARES UNDER VINE 80.00
SUSTAINABLE WINERY

The panorama that dominates the eastern shore of Lake Garda is constituted of a series of small, gentle hills that slope down towards the Po Valley. When you reach Rivoli, however, things change radically: you enter the Valdadige and suddenly it's an almost alpine landscape, with vineyards stretching out across the valley floor and the first spurs rising up. The Fugatti family operate here, serving as a careful and sensitive interpreter of a borderland that unites Veneto and Trentino, and dedicating themselves to a range that highlights the attributes of the area's classic grape varieties. The Riesling Collezione di Famiglia '16 is still one of the best in Italy, a wine that, after long ageing in the cellar, delivers complex aromas, with exotic fruit intersecting with mineral notes, unleashing an energetic, sapid, enthralling palate. The Cristina '17 is a refined and harmonious late-harvest wine marked by measured sweetness, all well contrasted by acidity, while the Rivoli '17 is a robust Pinot Grigio characterized by great development.

- ○ Riesling Renano Collezione di Famiglia '16 — 🍷🍷🍷 6
- ○ Cristina V. T. '17 — 🍷🍷 5
- ○ Valdadige Terra dei Forti Pinot Grigio Rivoli '17 — 🍷🍷 5
- ● La Rua Marzemino '19 — 🍷🍷 2*
- ○ Praecipuus Riesling Renano '18 — 🍷🍷 4
- ○ Valdadige Pinot Grigio Tera Alta '19 — 🍷🍷 2*
- ● Valdadige Terra dei Forti Enantio '17 — 🍷🍷 4
- ● Valdadige Terra dei Forti Enantio 1865 Pre-Fillossera Ris. '15 — 🍷🍷 6
- ○ Cristina V. T. '13 — YYY 5
- ○ Riesling Renano Collezione di Famiglia '15 — YYY 6
- ○ Riesling Renano Collezione di Famiglia '13 — YYY 6
- ○ Riesling Renano Collezione di Famiglia '12 — YYY 6

Rubinelli Vajol

loc. Vajol
fraz. San Floriano
via Paladon, 31
37029 San Pietro in Cariano [VR]
Tel. +39 0456839277
www.rubinellivajol.it

CELLAR SALES
PRE-BOOKED VISITS
ACCOMMODATION
ANNUAL PRODUCTION 70,000 bottles
HECTARES UNDER VINE 10.00

The Rubinelli family's winery is situated in the Vajol basin, a small depression between San Pietro in Cariano and San Floriano that hosts the estate vineyards. In this natural amphitheatre, the tuff terraces are dense with vines, with all the available spaces divided equally between the youngest, guyot-trained plots, and the oldest, which still rely on the traditional pergola. Their range is dedicated entirely to traditional wines, interpreted with an eye to the suppleness of the area's historic cultivars. This year represents a small pause for reflection for Rubinelli, with their most important wines left to age in pursuit of more expressive harmony. Thus our attention turns to the Ripasso '16, a wine that, rather than ape Amarone, exhibits a character wrought of elegant aromas, with fruit embellished by floral hints and undergrowth—in the mouth it reveals a supple profile and great dynamism. The Valpolicella '19 is fresh, racy and juicy.

- ● Valpolicella Cl. '19 — 🍷🍷 2*
- ● Valpolicella Cl. Sup. Ripasso '16 — 🍷🍷 4
- ● Amarone della Valpolicella Cl. '13 — YY 7
- ● Amarone della Valpolicella Cl. '12 — YY 7
- ● Amarone della Valpolicella Cl. '11 — YY 7
- ● Amarone della Valpolicella Cl. '10 — YY 6
- ● Recioto della Valpolicella Cl. '13 — YY 6
- ● Recioto della Valpolicella Cl. '12 — YY 6
- ● Valpolicella Cl. Sup. '15 — YY 4
- ● Valpolicella Cl. Sup. '14 — YY 4
- ● Valpolicella Cl. Sup. '12 — YY 4
- ● Valpolicella Cl. Sup. '11 — YY 4
- ● Valpolicella Cl. Sup. Ripasso '15 — YY 4
- ● Valpolicella Cl. Sup. Ripasso '14 — YY 5
- ● Valpolicella Cl. Sup. Ripasso '12 — YY 5

★Ruggeri & C.

fraz. Zecchei
via Prà Fontana, 4
31049 Valdobbiadene [TV]
Tel. +39 04239092
www.ruggeri.it

CELLAR SALES
PRE-BOOKED VISITS
ANNUAL PRODUCTION 1,600,000 bottles
HECTARES UNDER VINE 28.00
SUSTAINABLE WINERY

Despite the great success that Prosecco is experiencing, the producer in Via Prà Fontana hasn't changed its rhythms or its way of working, focusing on constancy and its bond with the many local growers on whom it relies for its grapes. The cellar is equipped with 5 presses and two completely separate delivery lines, which guarantees optimal management of the incoming grapes even in hectic moments. Their range is dedicated almost exclusively to DOCG Prosecco. 2019 made for a Giustino B. whose aromatic profile is marked by superb elegance, with ripe fruit constantly refreshed by notes of flowers and citrus fruits. In the mouth it's a classic Prosecco, with sweetness contrasted more by sapidity than by acidity and supported by creamy bubbles. The Vecchie Viti '19, on the other hand, explores the typology's hidden, edgy soul, revealing faint fragrances and an energetic, almost sharp palate.

Wine	Rating
○ Valdobbiadene Extra Dry Giustino B '19	🍷🍷🍷 5
○ Valdobbiadene Brut Vecchie Viti '19	🍷🍷 5
○ Cartizze Brut	🍷🍷 5
○ Cartizze Dry	🍷🍷 5
○ Valdobbiadene Dry Santo Stefano	🍷🍷 4
○ Valdobbiadene Extra Dry Giall'Oro	🍷🍷 4
○ Valdobbiadene L'Extra Brut '19	🍷🍷 4
○ Valdobbiadene Brut Quartese	🍷 4
○ Valdobbiadene Extra Brut Saltèr	🍷 4
○ Valdobbiadene Brut Vecchie Viti '14	🍸🍸🍸 4*
○ Valdobbiadene Extra Dry Giustino B. '18	🍸🍸🍸 5
○ Valdobbiadene Extra Dry Giustino B. '17	🍸🍸🍸 5
○ Valdobbiadene Extra Dry Giustino B. '16	🍸🍸🍸 4*
○ Valdobbiadene Extra Dry Giustino B. '15	🍸🍸🍸 4*

Le Salette

via Pio Brugnoli, 11c
37022 Fumane [VR]
Tel. +39 0457701027
www.lesalette.it

CELLAR SALES
PRE-BOOKED VISITS
ANNUAL PRODUCTION 130,000 bottles
HECTARES UNDER VINE 20.00

Franco Scamperle's winery is situated in the small village of Fumane, a district overlooked by the Sanctuary of Ragose and its cypress trees. His 20 hectares of vineyards are situated here together with plots in Sant'Ambrogio and San Floriano, and in Valpolicella Classica. In the cellar Franco pursues a style that manages to combine tradition and modern sensibilities. The richness brought about by partial drying of the grapes isn't an end in-and-of-itself, but rather serves the expression of rich, generous and yet supple wines. The Amarone Pergole Vece '16 is made with a selection of grapes harvested on old pergolas from the winery's best vineyards. Aged in barriques for more than two years, today it offers up intense notes of fruit and spices, which we reemerge on a rich, sapid, lively palate. The Marega, on the other hand, which is from a single vineyard, is fresher and more dynamic.

Wine	Rating
● Amarone della Valpolicella Cl. Pergole Vece '16	🍷🍷 8
● Amarone della Valpolicella Cl. La Marega '16	🍷🍷 6
● Recioto della Valpolicella Cl. Pergole Vece '16	🍷🍷 6
● Valpolicella Cl. '19	🍷 2
● Amarone della Valpolicella Cl. Pergole Vece '05	🍸🍸🍸 8
● Amarone della Valpolicella Cl. Pergole Vece '95	🍸🍸🍸 8
● Amarone della Valpolicella Cl. La Marega '15	🍸🍸 6
● Amarone della Valpolicella Cl. Pergole Vece '15	🍸🍸 8
● Valpolicella Cl. Sup. Ripasso I Progni '17	🍸🍸 3

San Cassiano

via San Cassiano, 17
37030 Mezzane di Sotto [VR]
Tel. +39 0458880665
www.cantinasancassiano.it

CELLAR SALES
PRE-BOOKED VISITS
ANNUAL PRODUCTION 50,000 bottles
HECTARES UNDER VINE 14.00
SUSTAINABLE WINERY

Mirko Sella's winery is situated in the highest part of Mezzane, an area where vineyards and olive groves compete for the best positions, separated by sparse woodlands that testify to a past in which agriculture was more limited. When it comes to their vineyards, the utmost care is taken in an attempt to obtain the healthiest possible grapes and achieve the greatest possible concentration. Indeed, Mirko's style pursues fruity aromatic richness and concentrated flavor. The Valpolicella Le Alene, which is released only after long ageing in the cellar, is exemplary, delivering vibrant notes of fruit preserves, white chocolate and spices. The palate follows the same stylistic path, enticing via great extractive force, coming through pervasive and soft. Despite the difficult year, the Amarone Riserva '14 explores this style even more deeply, proving warm and ripe on the nose, and powerful on the palate.

● Amarone della Valpolicella Ris. '14	🍷🍷 6
● Valpolicella Sup. Le Aléne '15	🍷🍷 4
● Valpolicella '18	🍷 2
● Amarone della Valpolicella '15	🍸🍸 6
● Amarone della Valpolicella '14	🍸🍸 6
● Amarone della Valpolicella '13	🍸🍸 6
● Amarone della Valpolicella '11	🍸🍸 6
● Amarone della Valpolicella Ris. '13	🍸🍸 6
● Recioto della Valpolicella '15	🍸🍸 5
○ Soave '17	🍸🍸 3
● Valpolicella '16	🍸🍸 2*
● Valpolicella '15	🍸🍸 2*
● Valpolicella Sup. Ripasso '14	🍸🍸 3
● Valpolicella Sup. Ripasso '12	🍸🍸 2*

La Sansonina

loc. Sansonina
37019 Peschiera del Garda [VR]
Tel. +39 0457551905
www.sansonina.it

CELLAR SALES
ANNUAL PRODUCTION 35,000 bottles
HECTARES UNDER VINE 13.00

Year after year, Carla Prospero's project becomes more complete. First there was the work of fixing up the vineyards, then the old building that has since become the cellar. Today theirs is a range that has no weak points, dedicated mainly to the two grapes, one native, the other imported, that best represent the territory here along the southern shore of Lake Garda: Turbiana and Merlot. A clear, focused style points up varietal expression and their bond with the territory. The Fermentazione Spontanea '18 is a Lugana that renounces aromatic sweetness and excessive softness only to win you over with an aromatic suite of great depth, with fruit only one element amidst floral and mineral hints, as well as Mediterranean scrub. The palate is crisp, supported by great sapid and acidic pressure. When it comes to their reds, their star player is still aging in the cellar, but we appreciated the fruity fragrance of the Evaluna, a sophisticated, crisp Cabernet.

○ Lugana Fermentazione Spontanea '18	🍷🍷 3*
● Garda Cabernet Evaluna '18	🍷🍷 4
● Garda Cabernet Evaluna '16	🍸🍸 4
● Garda Cabernet Evaluna '15	🍸🍸 4
● Garda Evaluna '14	🍸🍸 4
○ Lugana Fermentazione Spontanea '17	🍸🍸 3
○ Lugana Fermentazione Spontanea '16	🍸🍸 3*
○ Lugana Sansonina '13	🍸🍸 3
○ Lugana Sansonina '12	🍸🍸 3
○ Lugana V. del Morano Verde '15	🍸🍸 4
○ Lugana V. del Morano Verde '14	🍸🍸 3
● Sansonina '17	🍸🍸 6
● Sansonina '16	🍸🍸 6
● Sansonina '14	🍸🍸 6
● Sansonina '13	🍸🍸 6
● Sansonina '12	🍸🍸 6
● Sansonina '10	🍸🍸 6

★Tenuta Sant'Antonio

LOC. SAN ZENO
VIA CERIANI, 23
37030 COLOGNOLA AI COLLI [VR]
TEL. +39 0457650383
www.tenutasantantonio.it

CELLAR SALES
PRE-BOOKED VISITS
ANNUAL PRODUCTION 700,000 bottles
HECTARES UNDER VINE 100.00

The Castagnedi brothers established Tenuta Sant'Antonio in the mid-1990s with the clear intention of aiming for the highest standards of quality. Today the area covered has expanded considerably and their range touches a bit on everything, but the mantra of quality has never waned. The heart of the winery continues to beat on the hill of San Briccio, which lets the character of its white marl soil emerge. Vineyard and cellar management are increasingly focused on limiting their environmental impact. The Amarone Campo dei Gigli '16 is their most representative wine. It pours a sumptuous ruby red, anticipating aromas in which fruit dominates. The presence of more timid, spicy and floral notes will increase with aging. In the mouth it opens rich and pulpy, lengthening by virtue of exquisite acidity. The Bandina '17 is rich and thick, marked by a commendable harmony.

● Amarone della Valpolicella Campo dei Gigli '16	🍷🍷🍷 8
● Valpolicella Sup. La Bandina '17	🍷🍷 5
● Amarone della Valpolicella Antonio Castagnedi '16	🍷🍷 6
● Amarone della Valpolicella Telos '15	🍷🍷 6
○ Soave Monte Ceriani '19	🍷🍷 3
○ Soave V. V. '18	🍷🍷 3
● Valpolicella Sup. Ripasso Monti Garbi '18	🍷🍷 4
○ Pinot Grigio delle Venezie Telos '19	🍷 3
○ Telos Il Bianco '18	🍷 3
● Valpolicella Sup. Telos '17	🍷 4
● Amarone della Valpolicella Campo dei Gigli '15	🍷🍷🍷 8
● Amarone della Valpolicella Campo dei Gigli '13	🍷🍷🍷 8

Santa Margherita

VIA ITA MARZOTTO, 8
30025 FOSSALTA DI PORTOGRUARO [VE]
TEL. +39 0421246111
www.santamargherita.com

CELLAR SALES
PRE-BOOKED VISITS
ANNUAL PRODUCTION 13,000,000 bottles
HECTARES UNDER VINE 135.00

Over the years, the Marzotto family's historic brand has acquired a series of prestigious producers in Tuscany, Alto Adige, Lombardy and Sardinia. At each of these, as with Sant Margherita, the goal has been to achieve the highest quality for each terroir. For this reason, we've decided to recognize the Santa Margherita Group as our Winery of the Year. Their two cornerstones remain Pinot Grigio and Valdobbiadene Prosecco, the former cultivated in Alto Adige, the latter on their Refrontolo estate. The Pinot Grigio Atesino '19 hit the mark. It's a white of rare precision and character, intensely redolent of pears, fresh flowers and a subtle smoky note in the background. The palate is rich, held together more by sapidity than acidity, closing long and elegant. The Rive di Refrontolo '19 is an excellent Prosecco Superiore that doesn't rely on sugar but on the quality of the grapes, making for a wine of great harmony and pleasantness.

○ A. A. Pinot Grigio Impronta del Fondatore '19	🍷🍷 4
○ Valdobbiadene Rive di Refrontolo Extra Brut '19	🍷🍷 4
○ Cartizze Extra Dry	🍷🍷 5
⊙ Riviera del Garda Cl. Chiaretto Stilrose '19	🍷🍷 3
○ Valdobbiadene Brut	🍷🍷 3
○ Valdobbiadene Brut 52 '19	🍷🍷 3
⊙ Brut Rosé	🍷 3
○ Stilwhite '19	🍷 3
○ Valdadige Pinot Grigio '19	🍷 3
○ Valdobbiadene Extra Dry	🍷 3
○ A. A. Pinot Grigio Impronta del Fondatore '18	🍷🍷 3*
○ Valdobbiadene Brut Rive di Refrontolo '18	🍷🍷 3

Santa Sofia

fraz. Pedemonte di Valpolicella
via Ca' Dedé, 61
37029 San Pietro in Cariano [VR]
Tel. +39 0457701074
www.santasofia.com

CELLAR SALES
PRE-BOOKED VISITS
ANNUAL PRODUCTION 550,000 bottles
HECTARES UNDER VINE 53.00

The Begnoni family's cellar is situated on the property of Villa Serego in Santa Sofia. The splendid villa, which was designed by Palladio in 1565, overlooks the plain of Quar that leads to the left bank of the Adige River. The vineyards, on the other hand, are concentrated in the valleys of Fumane, Marano and San Pietro in Cariano, and are cultivated by trustworthy farmers who provide the producer with their grapes. Their own private vineyards, which were acquired in recent years in Valpolicella Orientale, are finally bearing fruit as well. The Amarone '15 put in an excellent performance. Redolent of ripe cherries, it finds freshness in streaks of medicinal herbs. In the mouth the wine reveals full body and succulence, held together perfectly by acidity and tannins but still leaving softness at the center. The Ripasso also delivered. It's somewhat inconspicuous in the glass, but wins over the palate instant after instant by virtue of its suppleness and elegance.

- ● Amarone della Valpolicella Cl. '15 ▼▼ 7
- ● Valpolicella Cl. Sup. Montegradella '17 ▼▼ 4
- ● Valpolicella Sup. Ripasso '17 ▼▼ 4
- ● Amarone della Valpolicella Cl. '13 ▽▽ 7
- ● Amarone della Valpolicella Cl. '12 ▽▽ 7
- ● Amarone della Valpolicella Cl. '12 ▽▽ 7
- ● Amarone della Valpolicella Cl. '11 ▽▽ 7
- ● Recioto della Valpolicella Cl. '11 ▽▽ 5
- ● Valpolicella Cl. '16 ▽▽ 3
- ● Valpolicella Cl. Sup. Montegradella '16 ▽▽ 4
- ● Valpolicella Cl. Sup. Montegradella '15 ▽▽ 4
- ● Valpolicella Sup. Ripasso '16 ▽▽ 4
- ● Valpolicella Sup. Ripasso '15 ▽▽ 4
- ● Valpolicella Sup. Ripasso '14 ▽▽ 4

Santi

via Ungheria, 33
37031 Illasi [VR]
Tel. +39 0456529068
www.cantinasanti.it

CELLAR SALES
PRE-BOOKED VISITS
ANNUAL PRODUCTION 1,430,000 bottles
HECTARES UNDER VINE 53.00

Founded in the mid-19th century, Santi had been owned and managed by the Santi family for over a century before being acquired by the Italian Wine Group, which made it one of its representative producers. Christian Ridolfi relaunched Santi's prospects by focusing on shrewder management of its large estate and restructuring of the cellar, which today sees only large barrels, not only of oak but also, in a small part, of other local woods. Great attention is paid to the production of Ventale, a Valpolicella Superiore made only with fresh grapes. 2018 brought to light aromas that are slow to reveal themselves, almost timid. Wild cherry appears immediately while medicinal herbs, crushed flowers and undergrowth emerge slowly, continuing to enrich its aromatic expression. In the mouth it's medium-bodied, with a pleasantness rooted in a well-orchestrated relationship between acidity, sapidity and tannins, making for a long, juicy palate.

- ● Valpolicella Sup. Ventale '18 ▼▼ 3*
- ● Amarone della Valpolicella Cl. Santico '15 ▼▼ 5
- ○ Lugana Folar '19 ▼▼ 2*
- ● Valpolicella Cl. Sup. Ripasso Solane '17 ▼▼ 3
- ○ Soave Cl. '19 ▼ 2
- ● Amarone della Valpolicella Proemio '05 ▽▽▽ 6
- ● Amarone della Valpolicella Proemio '03 ▽▽▽ 6
- ● Amarone della Valpolicella Proemio '00 ▽▽▽ 5
- ● Valpolicella Cl. Sup. Ripasso Solane '09 ▽▽▽ 3*
- ● Amarone della Valpolicella Cl. Proemio '13 ▽▽ 7
- ● Amarone della Valpolicella Cl. Proemio '12 ▽▽ 7
- ● Valpolicella Cl. Sup. Ripasso Solane '16 ▽▽ 3
- ● Valpolicella Sup. Ventale '17 ▽▽ 3*
- ● Valpolicella Sup. Ventale '16 ▽▽ 3*

Sartori

fraz. Santa Maria
via Casette, 4
37024 Negrar [VR]
Tel. +39 0456028011
www.sartorinet.com

CELLAR SALES
PRE-BOOKED VISITS
ANNUAL PRODUCTION 16,000,000 bottles
HECTARES UNDER VINE 120.00
SUSTAINABLE WINERY

The Sartori family's winery is deeply rooted in Valpolicella, bolstered by more than a century of experience and today counted as one of the territory's largest producers. Only a small part of the vineyards are owned, thus the winery relies both on the support of local growers and collaborations with cooperatives. Their range centers on Valpolicella even if the other Veronese denominations are represented as well. This year, at Sartori, they're only missing that crowning stroke, with a complete battery of wines that faithfully reflects Valpolicella. The Regolo '17 is a Ripasso with a fresh, still youthful aromatic suite in which clear, focused fruit is held up by balsamic sensations. In the mouth it's richer than expected but still sapid, supple and perfectly supported by acidity. The Amarone Reius '15, on the other hand, expresses greater maturity of fruit, offering a generous, harmonious palate.

Wine	Rating
● Amarone della Valpolicella Cl. Reius '15	7
● Recioto della Valpolicella Cl. Rerum '17	5
● Valpolicella Cl. Sup. Montegradella '16	3
● Valpolicella Sup. I Saltari '15	4
● Valpolicella Sup. Ripasso Regolo '17	4
○ Marani '18	2
○ Recioto di Soave Vernus '17	4
● Amarone della Valpolicella Cl. Corte Brà '12	7
● Amarone della Valpolicella Cl. Corte Brà '11	7
● Amarone della Valpolicella Cl. Reius '13	7
● Amarone della Valpolicella I Saltari '12	8
● Amarone della Valpolicella I Saltari '11	8
● Valpolicella Cl. Sup. Montegradella '15	3
● Valpolicella Sup. I Saltari '14	5
● Valpolicella Sup. I Saltari '13	5

Secondo Marco

via Campolongo, 9
37022 Fumane [VR]
Tel. +39 0456800954
www.secondomarco.it

CELLAR SALES
PRE-BOOKED VISITS
ACCOMMODATION
ANNUAL PRODUCTION 75,000 bottles
HECTARES UNDER VINE 15.00

Marco Speri, bolstered by experience working in the family business, brought his winery to life just over a decade ago, building a new cellar on the valley floor of Fumane and inheriting more than ten hectares of vineyards. If in the countryside he opted for the oft-neglected pergola, in the cellar he chose a direction that has in slowness and patience a sort of mantra. His wines are aged at length, using large barrels so as to acquire the qualities of lightness, finesse and harmony that we find throughout his selection. The Amarone '13 is quintessentially elegant, a wine that eschews the muscular style that's raged for decades. Ripe fruit is enriched with notes of Mediterranean scrub, herbs and undergrowth. The palate is supple, steadily balancing sapidity and acidity, proving long and alluring. The Recioto '15 is aromatically fresh and restrained in its sweetness.

Wine	Rating
● Amarone della Valpolicella Cl. '13	8
● Recioto della Valpolicella Cl. '15	6
● Valpolicella Cl. '18	3
● Amarone della Valpolicella Cl. '11	8
● Amarone della Valpolicella Cl. '12	8
● Amarone della Valpolicella Cl. '10	7
● Recioto della Valpolicella Cl. '13	6
● Recioto della Valpolicella Cl. '12	6
● Recioto della Valpolicella Cl. '11	6
● Recioto della Valpolicella Cl. '10	6
● Valpolicella Cl. Sup. Ripasso '15	5
● Valpolicella Cl. Sup. Ripasso '14	5
● Valpolicella Cl. Sup. Ripasso '13	5
● Valpolicella Cl. Sup. Ripasso '12	5
● Valpolicella Cl. Sup. Ripasso '11	4

★★Serafini & Vidotto

via Luigi Carrer, 8
31040 Nervesa della Battaglia [TV]
Tel. +39 0422773281
www.serafinividotto.it

CELLAR SALES
PRE-BOOKED VISITS
ANNUAL PRODUCTION 250,000 bottles
HECTARES UNDER VINE 23.00
SUSTAINABLE WINERY

Francesco Serafini and Antonello Vidotto set up their winery in the late 1980s. The venture, which began with little money but a great desire to get started, has led them to become one of the most important producers in the area and one of Italy's great Bordeaux blenders. The vineyards, which stretch for over 20 hectares along the southeastern slope of Montello, are cultivated with care and with great attention paid to the vitality of the soil. Their range focuses on red grapes, with Cabernet Sauvignon, in particular, playing a predominant role. As the Rosso dell'Abazia is still aging in the cellar, center stage has been occupied by the Phigaia—and it's one of the best versions yet. 2017 made for generous, fruity aromas, which find support in a substantial presence of medicinal herbs and spices. In the mouth it's marked by tannic texture of rare precision, achieving compactness and lightness at the same time. We also appreciated the fragrant, subtle Pinot Nero '17.

- ● Montello e Colli Asolani Phigaia '17 — 🍷🍷 4
- ○ Asolo Brut Bollicine di Prosecco — 🍷🍷 3
- ○ Montello e Colli Asolani Manzoni Bianco '19 — 🍷🍷 3
- ● Montello e Colli Asolani Recantina '19 — 🍷🍷 3
- ○ Phigaia Il Bianco '18 — 🍷🍷 4
- ● Pinot Nero '17 — 🍷🍷 7
- ● Montello e Colli Asolani Il Rosso dell'Abazia '16 — 🍷🍷🍷 6
- ● Montello e Colli Asolani Il Rosso dell'Abazia '15 — 🍷🍷🍷 6
- ● Montello e Colli Asolani Il Rosso dell'Abazia '13 — 🍷🍷🍷 6
- ● Montello e Colli Asolani Il Rosso dell'Abazia '12 — 🍷🍷🍷 5

★Speri

fraz. Pedemonte
via Fontana
37029 San Pietro in Cariano [VR]
Tel. +39 0457701154
www.speri.com

CELLAR SALES
PRE-BOOKED VISITS
ANNUAL PRODUCTION 400,000 bottles
HECTARES UNDER VINE 60.00
VITICULTURE METHOD Certified Organic
SUSTAINABLE WINERY

Going back through the history of the Speri family in Valpolicella means learning about the history of a territory with a great viticultural tradition. Over a century of production and sales, and owners of one of the most beautiful vineyards on Monte Sant'Urbano for over eighty years, the family were among the first to link their wines to their vineyard of origin. The Speri have lived through lean times and international success, remaining faithful to an idea of wine in which territory plays a central role, while limiting production to the typologies provided for by the appellation. This year their selection hit the mark with two wines earning accolades. The Amarone Sant'Urbano '16 drew on an excellent harvest to deliver vibrant notes of ripe fruit and spices. Long and harmonious in the mouth, it wins over the palate with decision and grace. The Valpolicella Sant'Urbano '17 is marked by greater aromatic freshness and a supple, sapid, continuous palate.

- ● Amarone della Valpolicella Cl. Sant'Urbano '16 — 🍷🍷🍷 7
- ● Valpolicella Cl. Sup. Sant'Urbano '17 — 🍷🍷 4
- ● Recioto della Valpolicella Cl. La Roggia '17 — 🍷🍷 6
- ● Valpolicella Cl. '19 — 🍷🍷 3
- ● Valpolicella Cl. Sup. Ripasso '18 — 🍷🍷 4
- ● Amarone della Valpolicella Cl. Sant'Urbano '15 — 🍷🍷🍷 7
- ● Amarone della Valpolicella Cl. Vign. Monte Sant'Urbano '12 — 🍷🍷🍷 7
- ● Amarone della Valpolicella Cl. Vign. Monte Sant'Urbano '09 — 🍷🍷🍷 7
- ● Amarone della Valpolicella Cl. Vign. Sant'Urbano '11 — 🍷🍷🍷 7
- ● Amarone della Valpolicella Vign. Monte Sant'Urbano '13 — 🍷🍷🍷 7

David Sterza

via Casterna, 37
37022 Fumane [VR]
Tel. +39 3471343121
www.davidsterza.it

CELLAR SALES
PRE-BOOKED VISITS
ANNUAL PRODUCTION 40,000 bottles
HECTARES UNDER VINE 4.50

David Sterza and Paolo Mascanzoni run the small family business in Casterna, a tiny village of Fumane nestled among vineyards and off the beaten path. But here they safeguard a form of viticulture that's strongly linked to tradition. The estate, a handful of hectares on the hillside, gives rise to the area's traditional grape varieties, while a small but well-equipped cellar and an immense passion for wine do the rest. If in the countryside the presence of the pergola shows their bond with the past, in the cellar their production style pursues integrity of fruit and fragrance. Year after year the qualitative constancy of Sterza's wines improves, with the Amarone '16 leading our preferences. Ripe and juicy wild fruit rise up out of the glass, crossed by fresher balsamic and floral notes that reemerge brilliantly on the palate. It's a drink of superb solidity and tension. The intriguing Valpolicella Superiore '17 is an elegant wine that doesn't renounce richness and power.

● Amarone della Valpolicella Cl. '16	🍷🍷 6
● Recioto della Valpolicella Cl. '17	🍷🍷 5
● Valpolicella Cl. '19	🍷🍷 2*
● Valpolicella Cl. Sup. '17	🍷🍷 3
● Valpolicella Cl. Sup. Ripasso '18	🍷🍷 3
● Amarone della Valpolicella Cl. '13	🍷🍷🍷 6
● Amarone della Valpolicella Cl. '12	🍷🍷🍷 6
● Amarone della Valpolicella Cl. '15	🍷🍷 6
● Amarone della Valpolicella Cl. '14	🍷🍷 6
● Amarone della Valpolicella Cl. '11	🍷🍷 6
● Recioto della Valpolicella Cl. '15	🍷🍷 5
● Recioto della Valpolicella Cl. '14	🍷🍷 5
● Valpolicella Cl. '17	🍷🍷 2*
● Valpolicella Cl. Sup. Ripasso '17	🍷🍷 3
● Valpolicella Cl. Sup. Ripasso '16	🍷🍷 3
● Valpolicella Cl. Sup. Ripasso '15	🍷🍷 3
● Valpolicella Cl. Sup. Ripasso '14	🍷🍷 3

★Suavia

fraz. Fittà di Soave
via Centro, 14
37038 Soave [VR]
Tel. +39 0457675089
www.suavia.it

CELLAR SALES
PRE-BOOKED VISITS
ANNUAL PRODUCTION 100,000 bottles
HECTARES UNDER VINE 12.00

The Tessari sisters' winery unfolds across Soave Classico's highest areas, in Fittà, where the dark color of the earth and stones lay bare the terrain's volcanic origins. The vineyards extend over the hills and around the cellar, over and below, in search of light, air and warmth. Only Garganega and Trebbiano di Soave are to be found here, making for a range in which even the simplest wines exhibit an indissoluble bond with the territory. Once again the Soave Monte Carbonare leads the way. 2018 delivered another superb version. Subtle and deep, fruit is accompanied by notes of flowers and fine herbs along with mineral hints. The palate brings together richness and suppleness, lengthening with sapidity towards a crisp, clear finish. The Massifitti '17, a monovarietal Trebbiano di Soave, is shyer in its aromatic expression, but on the palate it moves with suppleness and energy.

○ Massifitti '17	🍷🍷 3*
○ Soave Cl. Monte Carbonare '18	🍷🍷 3*
○ Le Rive '17	🍷🍷 4
○ Soave Cl. '19	🍷🍷 2*
○ Soave Cl. Monte Carbonare '17	🍷🍷🍷 3*
○ Soave Cl. Monte Carbonare '16	🍷🍷🍷 3*
○ Soave Cl. Monte Carbonare '15	🍷🍷🍷 3*
○ Soave Cl. Monte Carbonare '14	🍷🍷🍷 3*
○ Soave Cl. Monte Carbonare '12	🍷🍷🍷 3*
○ Soave Cl. Monte Carbonare '11	🍷🍷🍷 3*
○ Soave Cl. Monte Carbonare '10	🍷🍷🍷 3*
○ Soave Cl. Monte Carbonare '09	🍷🍷🍷 3*
○ Soave Cl. Monte Carbonare '08	🍷🍷🍷 3*
○ Soave Cl. Monte Carbonare '07	🍷🍷🍷 3*
○ Soave Cl. Monte Carbonare '06	🍷🍷🍷 3*
○ Soave Cl. Monte Carbonare '05	🍷🍷🍷 3*
○ Soave Cl. Monte Carbonare '04	🍷🍷🍷 3

Sutto

Loc. Campodipietra
via Arzeri, 34/1
31040 Salgareda [TV]
Tel. +39 0422744063
www.sutto.it

CELLAR SALES
PRE-BOOKED VISITS
ACCOMMODATION AND RESTAURANT SERVICE
ANNUAL PRODUCTION 469,000 bottles
HECTARES UNDER VINE 75.00

The Sutto brothers, Stefano and Luigi, travel the world of wine at two speeds. While working in the countryside and the cellar respect for nature's rhythms is an essential factor, but logistics and everything that revolves around production have been approached with a dynamism that's capable of responding to modern needs. Production centers on the large estate in Salgareda but is rounded out by vineyards in the Conegliano Valdobbiadene appellation, making for a style that brings together richness and elegance. The Dogma '17 is a sophisticated Bordeaux blend endowed with an energetic, sapid and pleasantly rough palate. The Rosso di Sutto '18 offers vibrant fruit and floral scents, coming through full, juicy and drinkable on the palate—it's both approachable and gratifying at the same time. When it comes to their whites and Proseccos, we appreciated the evolution of their entire selection.

Wine	Rating
● Dogma Rosso '17	TT 4
○ Bianco di Sutto '19	TT 2*
○ Chardonnay '19	TT 2*
○ Conegliano Valdobbiadene Brut	TT 3
○ Conegliano Valdobbiadene Extra Dry	TT 3
○ Pinot Grigio '19	TT 2*
● Rosso di Sutto '18	TT 4
○ Prosecco Brut	T 2
○ Prosecco Extra Dry	T 3
● Campo Sella '15	YYY 5
○ Bianco di Sutto '18	YY 2*
● Cabernet '18	YY 2*
● Campo Sella '16	YY 5
● Dogma Rosso '16	YY 4
● Merlot '18	YY 2*
○ Pinot Grigio '18	YY 2*

Tamellini

fraz. Costeggiola
via Tamellini, 4
37038 Soave [VR]
Tel. +39 0457675328
piofrancesco.tamellini@tin.it

CELLAR SALES
PRE-BOOKED VISITS
ANNUAL PRODUCTION 250,000 bottles
HECTARES UNDER VINE 27.00

The Tamellini brothers' winery is now twenty years old, but the bond between the family and the land of Soave goes much further back. Gaetano and Pio Francesco are descendants of generations of wine-growers, but their desire to manage the entire production chain themselves led them to abandon the town's cooperative in the late 1990s and begin a new adventure, one dedicated to bringing out the best both of Soave and the limestone hills of Costeggiola. Theirs is a range dedicated almost exclusively to Garganega, with two wines perfectly representing the typology. The fresh, fragrant and juicy Soave '19 is the simpler version, while with the Le Bine de Costiola '18 the aromatic picture becomes more complex and sophisticated. Ripe yellow fruit is echoed by floral and citrus notes, while faint mineral hints emerge from below, needing time to acquire more of a presence. The palate is full, but always supported by a sapid, assertive acidity.

Wine	Rating
○ Soave Cl. Le Bine de Costiola '18	TT 3*
○ Soave '19	TT 2*
○ Soave Cl. Le Bine '04	YYY 3*
○ Soave Cl. Le Bine de Costiola '14	YYY 3*
○ Soave Cl. Le Bine de Costiola '13	YYY 3*
○ Soave Cl. Le Bine de Costiola '11	YYY 3*
○ Soave Cl. Le Bine de Costiola '06	YYY 3*
○ Soave Cl. Le Bine de Costiola '05	YYY 3*
○ Soave '18	YY 2*
○ Soave '17	YY 2*
○ Soave '15	YY 2*
○ Soave '14	YY 2*
○ Soave Cl. '16	YY 2*
○ Soave Cl. '13	YY 2*
○ Soave Cl. Le Bine de Costiola '17	YY 3*
○ Soave Cl. Le Bine de Costiola '16	YY 3*
○ Soave Cl. Le Bine de Costiola '15	YY 3*

Giovanna Tantini

FRAZ. OLIOSI
LOC. I MISCHI
37014 CASTELNUOVO DEL GARDA [VR]
TEL. +39 3488717577
www.giovannatantini.it

CELLAR SALES
PRE-BOOKED VISITS
ACCOMMODATION
ANNUAL PRODUCTION 30,000 bottles
HECTARES UNDER VINE 11.50

Giovanna Tantini's winery is situated in the area south of Lake Garda, a land of glacial origin that's experienced the ice's advance and retreat, a process that left in dowry a soil rich in gravel and limestone, perfect for bringing the area's grapes to maturity. Owned by the family for over a century, the winery began production with the arrival of Giovanna in the early 2000s. Today it's dedicated to classic Garda wines, with a style that privileges finesse over power. The careful work carried out in the countryside and cellar, all with calm and patience, made for a Bardolino '18 redolent of berries, sensations that slowly give way to mineral and spicy notes. In the mouth it's delicate, held together by sapidity and acidity, resulting in a wine that's a joy to drink. The Chiaretto '19 expresses more approachable fruit, while the palate comes through juicy and highly pleasant.

● Bardolino '18	2*
⊙ Bardolino Chiaretto '19	2*
○ Custoza '19	2
● Bardolino '17	2*
● Bardolino '15	2*
● Bardolino '14	2*
⊙ Bardolino Chiaretto '18	2*
⊙ Bardolino Chiaretto '16	2*
⊙ Bardolino Chiaretto '15	2*
○ Custoza '17	2*
● Ettore '14	4
● Ettore '12	4
● Ettore '11	4
● Garda Corvina Ma.Gi.Co. '17	2*

★F.lli Tedeschi

FRAZ. PEDEMONTE
VIA G. VERDI, 4
37029 SAN PIETRO IN CARIANO [VR]
TEL. +39 0457701487
www.tedeschiwines.com

CELLAR SALES
PRE-BOOKED VISITS
ANNUAL PRODUCTION 500,000 bottles
HECTARES UNDER VINE 48.00
SUSTAINABLE WINERY

While Monte Olmi, Lucchine and Fabriseria are the historic origins of the Tedeschi family's property, Maternigo is its present. A splendid estate enclosed by woods is comprised of 30 hectares of vineyards and 50 hectares of woodland at elevations ranging between 200 and 500 meters along the divide that separates the Mezzane and Tregnago valleys. Their range of wines is strongly rooted in the area's historic typologies and features a style whose strong points are its fruity richness and solidity. The Amarone Capitel Monte Olmi '15 points up this style perfectly, with its fragrances of ripe red fruit embellished by the presence of medicinal herbs and spices. The palate opens rich and powerful, unfolding across a backbone of acidity while lengthening its development and pleasantness. The Amarone La Fabriseria '15 is deep in its aromatic expression, endowed with a firm palate and plenty of guts. It's got a bright future.

● Amarone della Valpolicella Cl. Capitel Monte Olmi Ris. '15	8
● Amarone della Valpolicella Cl. La Fabriseria Ris. '15	8
● Amarone della Valpolicella Ansari '16	7
● Valpolicella Cl. Lucchine '19	2*
● Valpolicella Sup. Capitel Nicalò '18	3
● Amarone della Valpolicella Cl. Capitel Monte Olmi '11	8
● Amarone della Valpolicella Cl. Capitel Monte Olmi '07	8
● Amarone della Valpolicella Cl. Capitel Monte Olmi '95	8
● Amarone della Valpolicella Cl. La Fabriseria Ris. '11	8
● Valpolicella Sup. Maternigo '16	5
● Valpolicella Sup. Maternigo '11	4*

Le Tende

via Tende, 35
37017 Lazise [VR]
Tel. +39 0457590748
www.letende.it

CELLAR SALES
PRE-BOOKED VISITS
ANNUAL PRODUCTION 100,000 bottles
HECTARES UNDER VINE 12.50
VITICULTURE METHOD Certified Organic

The Fortuna and Lucillini families' beautiful property unfolds along the hills that surround the eastern shore of Lake Garda. The vineyards are spread over two plots, one for Bardolino Classico, in Cavaion, and one near the 19th-century villa a few hundred meters from the lake. Organic management combined with Mauro Fortuna's keen eye for production allows for a range of refined and elegant wines. The Bardolino Chiaretto '19 shuns the stereotype of a wine centered on fresh, immediate aromas, revealing itself little by little, first berries, then floral notes and finally a faint hint of pepper. In the mouth, however, it changes gear and, supported by a vigorous sapidity, it unfolds, offering up a full, gratifying palate. The Cicisbeo '18, a monovarietal Cabernet Sauvignon, is also worth noting. Fresh and slender, it's endowed with a supple, harmonious palate.

⊙ Bardolino Chiaretto Cl. '19	🍷🍷 2*
● Bardolino Cl. Sup. '18	🍷🍷 3
● Cicisbeo '18	🍷🍷 5
○ Pinot Grigio delle Venezie '19	🍷🍷 3
⊙ Bardolino Chiaretto Brut Voluttà '19	🍷 3
● Bardolino Cl. '19	🍷 2
○ Custoza '19	🍷 2
⊙ Bardolino Chiaretto Cl. '18	🍷🍷 2*
⊙ Bardolino Chiaretto Cl. '17	🍷🍷 2*
● Bardolino Cl. '18	🍷🍷 2*
● Bardolino Cl. '17	🍷🍷 2*
● Bardolino Cl. Sup. '16	🍷🍷 3
● Bardolino Cl. Sup. '15	🍷🍷 3
● Corvina '18	🍷🍷 3
○ Custoza '18	🍷🍷 2*
○ Sabia '16	🍷🍷 2*

Terre di Leone

loc. Porta
via Valpolicella, 6b
37020 Marano di Valpolicella [VR]
Tel. +39 0456895040
www.terredileone.it

CELLAR SALES
PRE-BOOKED VISITS
ANNUAL PRODUCTION 36,000 bottles
HECTARES UNDER VINE 10.00

About fifteen years ago Federico Pellizzari and Chiara Turati founded Terre di Leone, a beautiful winery situated in the highest part of the Marano valley. Fewer than ten hectares lie on tufaceous soils that testify to the terrain's volcanic origins. In the cellar every stage of production is aimed at protecting the integrity of the grapes and their aromas, making for a range rooted in traditional wines that are aged at length before being released to the public. After almost a decade, the Amarone Riserva '11 sees the light of day. It's a wine that reveals itself little by little, renouncing more immediate fruity expressions in favor of dried flowers, medicinal herbs and undergrowth. The palate delivers in spades: powerful and warm, it unfolds with grace and lightness, proving long and subtle. The Valpolicella Superiore '16 exhibits fresher, clearer and more focused aromas, while the palate proves supple, juicy and highly pleasant.

● Amarone della Valpolicella Cl. Ris. '11	🍷🍷 6
● Amarone della Valpolicella Cl. Il Re Pazzo '15	🍷🍷 8
● Dedicatum '15	🍷🍷 6
● Valpolicella Cl. Sup. '16	🍷🍷 5
● Valpolicella Cl. Il Re Pazzo '18	🍷 3
● Valpolicella Sup. Ripasso Il Re Pazzo '18	🍷 5
● Amarone della Valpolicella Cl. '09	🍷🍷 8
● Amarone della Valpolicella Cl. '10	🍷🍷 4
● Amarone della Valpolicella Re Pazzo '12	🍷🍷 8
● Amarone della Valpolicella Re Pazzo '11	🍷🍷 3
● Valpolicella Cl. Sup. '15	🍷🍷 5
● Valpolicella Cl. Sup. '14	🍷🍷 3
● Valpolicella Cl. Sup. Ripasso '15	🍷🍷 4
● Valpolicella Cl. Sup. Ripasso '14	🍷🍷 4
● Valpolicella Re Pazzo '13	🍷🍷 3
● Valpolicella Sup. Ripasso Re Pazzo '11	🍷🍷 4

Tezza

FRAZ. POIANO DI VALPANTENA
VIA STRADELLA MAIOLI, 4
37142 VERONA
TEL. +39 045550267
www.tezzawines.it

CELLAR SALES
PRE-BOOKED VISITS
ANNUAL PRODUCTION 200,000 bottles
HECTARES UNDER VINE 28.00
VITICULTURE METHOD Certified Organic

The Valpantena valley widens warm and gravelly at the gates of Verona, climbing gently in the direction of Grezzana only to narrow as it enters the heart of Lessinia. In the wider, pebbly area, by the residential zone of Poiano, we find the winery operated by the Tezza cousins. The property is perfectly integrated, about thirty hectares of vineyards that extend over the hamlets around the cellar. For years now they've been organically cultivated, hosting mainly traditional grape varieties. The result is a range that alternates fresh, approachable wines with more ambitious, complex selections. The Ripasso Ma Roat '18 offers up sensations of forest floor and aromatic herbs, while in the mouth it reveals a slender body, proving highly drinkable. The Recioto '17, from their more ambitious line, is complex and layered in its aromatic expression. Multifaceted fragrances of overripe fruit, olives in brine and spices emerge. In the mouth sweetness is plenty discernible, but the wine is able to unfold thanks to its sapid and acidic thrust.

- ● Amarone della Valpolicella Corte Majoli '16 🍷🍷 5
- ● Amarone della Valpolicella Valpantena '13 🍷🍷 6
- ● Recioto della Valpolicella Valpantena Brolo delle Giare '17 🍷🍷 6
- ● Valpolicella Sup. Brolo delle Giare '16 🍷🍷 5
- ● Valpolicella Sup. Ripasso Ma Roat '18 🍷🍷 2*
- ● Valpolicella Valpantena Sup. Ripasso '17 🍷🍷 3
- ● Amarone della Valpolicella Valpantena Brolo delle Giare Ris. '13 🍷 7
- ● Amarone della Valpolicella Corte Majoli '18 YY 5
- ● Amarone della Valpolicella Valpantena Brolo delle Giare Ris. '12 YY 7
- ● Valpolicella Sup. Ripasso Corte Majoli '17 YY 3
- ● Valpolicella Sup. Ripasso Ma Roat '17 YY 2*

Tommasi Viticoltori

LOC. PEDEMONTE
VIA RONCHETTO, 4
37029 SAN PIETRO IN CARIANO [VR]
TEL. +39 0457701266
www.tommasi.com

CELLAR SALES
PRE-BOOKED VISITS
ACCOMMODATION AND RESTAURANT SERVICE
ANNUAL PRODUCTION 1,500,000 bottles
HECTARES UNDER VINE 205.00
SUSTAINABLE WINERY

In the early 20th century no one could have imagined that the small Tommasi family business would become the juggernaut we know today. But step by step, generation by generation, the winery grew, maintaining a strong bond with the land and never overreaching. Today the Tommasis manage one of the region's largest producers, drawing on a vast vineyard and a range that has never looked to fashion, but rather to tradition, for inspiration. The Amarone Ca' Florian '12 put in an excellent performance. It's a reserve marked by aromas of great clarity and integrity, with red fruit accompanied by notes of spices and crushed flowers. The palate is full and juicy, supported by a fine tannic texture at the back. The Amarone '16 also delivered. Extraordinarily fresh and vital in its aromas, the palate moves with suppleness and tension, highlighting a vitality that distinguishes it from previous versions.

- ● Amarone della Valpolicella Cl. Ca' Florian Ris. '12 🍷🍷🍷 8
- ● Amarone della Valpolicella Cl. '16 🍷🍷 7
- ● Valpolicella Cl. Sup. Rafael '18 🍷🍷 3
- ● Crearo Conca d'Oro '17 🍷 5
- ○ Lugana Le Fornaci '19 🍷 5
- ● Amarone della Valpolicella Cl. De Buris Ris. '09 YYY 8
- ● Amarone della Valpolicella Cl. De Buris Ris. '08 YYY 7
- ● Amarone della Valpolicella Cl. '15 YY 7
- ● Amarone della Valpolicella Cl. '13 YY 7
- ● Amarone della Valpolicella Cl. Ca' Florian Ris. '11 YY 7
- ● Valpolicella Cl. Sup. Ripasso '17 YY 4
- ● Valpolicella Cl. Sup. Ripasso '15 YY 4

La Tordera

via Alnè Bosco, 23
31020 Vidor [TV]
Tel. +39 0423985362
www.latordera.it

CELLAR SALES
PRE-BOOKED VISITS
ANNUAL PRODUCTION 1,300,000 bottles
HECTARES UNDER VINE 70.00
VITICULTURE METHOD Certified Organic
SUSTAINABLE WINERY

The territory of Valdobbiadene is characterized by a series of hills densely planted with vines and dotted with tiny sheds, testifying to the toil and sweat that have gone into working this gentle yet rugged slopes. The Vettoretti family own some of the splendid area's most beautiful positions but also rely on local growers to provide them with the grapes needed to guarantee production. Their exclusively sparkling selection of wines exhibits a clear, focused style. The best vineyards in Guia provide the grapes for their Extra Brut '19, a wine that calls up unripe apples on the nose, with subtle vegetal sensations contributing to its fresh profile. In the mouth the absence of sweetness makes for a thin, spirited and almost sharp palate. The Tittoni '19 is diametrically opposed. Made with grapes from the banks of the Vidor, it's marked by a summery aromatic profile and a creamy, bewitchingly sweet palate.

Wine	Glasses	Price
○ Cartizze	TT	5
○ Valdobbiadene Rive di Guia Extra Brut Otreval '19	TT	3
○ Valdobbiadene Rive di Vidor Dry Tittoni '19	TT	3
○ Valdobbiadene Brut Brunei	T	3
○ Valdobbiadene Extra Dry Serrai	T	3
○ Valdobbiadene Brut Brunei '17	YY	3
○ Valdobbiadene Rive di Guia Brut Otreval '18	YY	3
○ Valdobbiadene Rive di Guia Brut Otreval '17	YY	3
○ Valdobbiadene Rive di Guida Brut Otreval '16	YY	3
○ Valdobbiadene Brut Brunei '18	Y	3

Trabucchi d'Illasi

loc. Monte Tenda
37031 Illasi [VR]
Tel. +39 0457833233
www.trabucchidillasi.it

CELLAR SALES
PRE-BOOKED VISITS
ANNUAL PRODUCTION 120,000 bottles
HECTARES UNDER VINE 25.00
VITICULTURE METHOD Certified Organic

The Trabucchi family's farm unfolds along the ridge that acts as a divide between the Cazzano valley to the east and the Illasi valley to the west, a generous, blessed land where grapevines thrive. The rest is seen to by careful management both in the countryside, where maximum health and integrity of fruit are the priorities, and in the drying loft and cellar. The result is a selection with a rich style, powerful and fresh all at once, released only after long, slow maturation in the cellar. The Amarone '11 pours a thick ruby-red color, introducing aromas of extraordinary freshness in which fruit comes through fleshy and ripe, refreshed by subtle balsamic and spicy notes that we can trace back to the traditional grape varieties used. On the palate it's striking for its richness and fullness, but it finds balance and tension in acidity and finishes soft and crisp. Despite the difficult year, their intriguing Valpolicella Galante '14 delivers a satisfying and highly pleasant palate.

Wine	Glasses	Price
● Amarone della Valpolicella '11	TT	8
● Valpolicella Sup. Galante '14	TT	4
● Valpolicella Sup. Terre del Cereolo '10	TT	5
● Amarone della Valpolicella '06	YYY	8
● Amarone della Valpolicella '04	YYY	8
● Recioto della Valpolicella Cereolo '05	YYY	8
● Valpolicella Sup. Terre di S. Colombano '03	YYY	4*
● Amarone della Valpolicella '10	YY	8
● Amarone della Valpolicella '09	YY	8
● Amarone della Valpolicella '08	YY	8
● Amarone della Valpolicella Cent'Anni Ris. '10	YY	8
● Valpolicella Sup. '13	YY	3
● Valpolicella Sup. Terre di San Colombano '12	YY	3

Valdo Spumanti

via Foro Boario, 20
31049 Valdobbiadene [TV]
Tel. +39 04239090
www.valdo.com

CELLAR SALES
PRE-BOOKED VISITS
ANNUAL PRODUCTION 9,000,000 bottles
HECTARES UNDER VINE 155.00

The bond between the Bolla family and the world of Treviso sparkling wine began between the two world wars. After WW II the winery took the name that it still uses today. The large quantity of grapes needed to meet the company's needs is guaranteed by the large number of local growers operating in the area, while Gianfranco Zanon and his technical staff manage each batch delivered, allocating it to the most suitable wine typology. In recent years, their range has expanded from Prosecco to sparkling wines made with other grape varieties. The Cuvée di Boj is the classic Prosecco Superiore, with fruit standing out clearly on a background of flowers and sugared almond. In the mouth it's juicy and long with a pleasantness based on harmony between sweetness, acidity and bubbles. The Numero 10 '18, which is produced according to the Metodo Classico, offers more delicate, complex aromas, while in the mouth it proves more close-knit and assertive.

○ Valdobbiadene Brut Cuvée di Boj	🍷🍷 2*
○ Cartizze Cuvée Viviana	🍷🍷 5
○ Valdobbiadene Brut Numero 10 M. Cl. '18	🍷🍷 4
○ Valdobbiadene Extra Dry Cuvée 1926	🍷🍷 2
○ Garda Brut	🍷 2
○ Garda Brut Bio	🍷 2
○ Prosecco di Treviso Extra Dry	🍷 2
○ Valdobbiadene Brut Cuvée del Fondatore '18	🍷🍷 3
○ Valdobbiadene Brut Cuvée del Fondatore '17	🍷🍷 3*
○ Valdobbiadene Brut Cuvée di Boj '18	🍷🍷 2*
○ Valdobbiadene Rive di San Pietro di Barbozza Brut Nature '18	🍷🍷 3*
○ Valdobbiadene Rive di San Pietro di Barbozza Brut Nature '17	🍷🍷 3

Cantina Produttori di Valdobbiadene - Val d'Oca

via San Giovanni, 45
31030 Valdobbiadene [TV]
Tel. +39 0423982070
www.valdoca.com

CELLAR SALES
PRE-BOOKED VISITS
ANNUAL PRODUCTION 13,000,000 bottles
HECTARES UNDER VINE 950.00

Cantina Produttori di Valdobbiadene is made up of about 600 members who cultivate just under a thousand hectares of vineyards scattered throughout the appellation, from the gentle slopes of Conegliano to the steepest and most difficult rims of the Valdobbiadene. Almost the entire range relies on Glera, which the producer receives and transforms into a number of different wines, foremost Prosecco Superiore. The best batches of grapes are used for their Val d'Oca line, the most ambitious selections of all. The Rive di Santo Stefano '19 pours a pale straw-yellow, with a fine perlage that rises to the surface. Subtle notes of green apple, lime blossom and wisteria give way to a palate in which sweetness is quite absent, and the wine unfolds with sapidity and traction. The Rive di San Pietro di Barbozza '19 is more mature in its varietal expression. It's a Prosecco Superiore with a juicy profile, well supported by acidity and lively bubbles.

○ Valdobbiadene Rive di Santo Stefano Extra Brut '19	🍷🍷 4
○ Valdobbiadene Rive di Col San Martino Brut '19	🍷🍷 4
○ Valdobbiadene Rive di San Pietro di Barbozza Brut '19	🍷🍷 4
○ Asolo Extra Dry Bioldo	🍷 2
○ Valdobbiadene Brut Ca' Val '19	🍷 2
○ Valdobbiadene Extra Dry	🍷 2
○ Valdobbiadene Rive di Colbertaldo Extra Dry '19	🍷 4
○ Valdobbiadene Extra Dry Jos '18	🍷🍷 3
○ Valdobbiadene Rive di San Pietro di Barbozza Brut '18	🍷🍷 4
○ Valdobbiadene Rive di Santo Stefano Brut Nature '18	🍷🍷 4

Cantina Valpantena Verona

loc. Quinto
via Colonia Orfani di Guerra, 5b
37142 Verona
Tel. +39 045550032
www.cantinavalpantena.it

CELLAR SALES
PRE-BOOKED VISITS
ANNUAL PRODUCTION 9,000,000 bottles
HECTARES UNDER VINE 750.00
SUSTAINABLE WINERY

Valpolicella has in Cantina della Valpantena a benchmark cooperative, bolstered by an extensive area of land, mainly to the east and to a lesser degree in the 'zona classica', cultivated by about 250 members. When it comes to vineyard management the utmost care is shown, an approach that's complemented by great technical expertise in the cellar, making for an excellent range of wines. Today their efforts are focused on developing the bond between their premium wines and the vineyard of origin. The emblematic Valpolicella Superiore Brolo dei Giusti '15 expresses all the warmth of the Valpantena, proving rich in fruity suggestions and spices, all of which find development on a concentrated, potent palate—though thanks to its exquisite acidity, it still maintains its drinkability. The simpler Amarone, a 2017, intrigues, playing on fruit that still echoes fresh, while the palate is juicy, supple and pleasant. The Torre del Falasco '16 comes through richer, deeper and firmer.

● Valpolicella Sup. Brolo dei Giusti '15	🍷🍷🍷	6
● Amarone della Valpolicella '17	🍷🍷	6
● Amarone della Valpolicella Torre del Falasco '16	🍷🍷	7
○ Lugana Torre del Falasco '19	🍷🍷	3
● Recioto della Valpolicella Tesauro '17	🍷🍷	5
● Valpolicella Sup. Ripasso Torre del Falasco '18	🍷🍷	4
● Valpolicella Sup. Torre del Falasco '18	🍷🍷	3
● Valpolicella Valpantena Ripasso Ritocco '18	🍷🍷	4
○ Baroncino Chardonnay '19	🍷	2
● Torre del Falasco Corvina '19	🍷	2
○ Torre del Falasco Garganega '19	🍷	2
● Amarone della Valpolicella Torre del Falasco '13	🍷🍷 (white)	6

Cantina Valpolicella Negrar

via Ca' Salgari, 2
37024 Negrar [VR]
Tel. +39 0456014300
www.cantinanegrar.it

CELLAR SALES
PRE-BOOKED VISITS
RESTAURANT SERVICE
ANNUAL PRODUCTION 7,000,000 bottles
HECTARES UNDER VINE 700.00

Cantina di Negrar is one of the pillars of cooperation in Valpolicella, a producer whose 230 members cultivate about 700 hectares, mainly in the 'zona classica'. It's been more than 20 years since the quality project was launched, an initiative in which the best plots were identified and memberes were provided with the technical support necessary to ensure the highest quality grapes. Their Domini Veneti line represents their premium, flagship wines, all of which aim to highlight tradition in light of the vineyard of provenance. The best grapes selected from the hills of Marano give rise to their Valpolicella Superiore Pruviniano '17, a wine that doesn't settle for notes of overripe fruit, but ranges from undergrowth to spices, mineral notes and crushed flowers. In the mouth it stretches supplely and racy, unfolding with grace and decisiveness. On the Amarone side, we appreciated the aromatic complexity and soft, pervasive richness of the Mater '12.

● Valpolicella Cl. Sup. Pruviniano Domini Veneti '17	🍷🍷	3*
● Amarone della Valpolicella Cl. Mater Domini Veneti Ris. '12	🍷🍷	8
● Amarone della Valpolicella Cl. PruvinianoDomini Veneti '15	🍷🍷	5
● Valpolicella Cl. Sup. Domini Veneti '17	🍷🍷	3
● Valpolicella Cl. Sup. Ripasso La Casetta Domini Veneti '17	🍷🍷	4
● Valpolicella Cl. Sup. Verjago Domini Veneti '17	🍷🍷	4
● Valpolicella Cl. Sup. Ripasso Pruviniano Domini Veneti '17	🍷	3
● Valpolicella Cl. Sup. Ripasso Vign. di Torbe Domini Veneti '18	🍷	3
● Amarone della Valpolicella Cl. S. Rocco Domini Veneti '08	🍷🍷🍷 (white)	8

Odino Vaona

loc. Valgatara
via Paverno, 41
37020 Marano di Valpolicella [VR]
Tel. +39 0457703710
www.vaona.it

CELLAR SALES
PRE-BOOKED VISITS
ANNUAL PRODUCTION 70,000 bottles
HECTARES UNDER VINE 10.00
SUSTAINABLE WINERY

Alberto Vaona's winery is situated in the heart of the Marano valley, surrounded by vineyards and enclosed among the hills. The property covers about ten hectares on hilly terrain, at elevations ranging from between 200 to 250 meters, which guarantees wines closely bound to the appellation. The producer's style represents a balance between tradition and modernity, richness and suppleness, and is often a favorite among our tasters. The Amarone Pegrandi '13 is released only after a long spell in the cellar. It's a reserve that pours a beautiful, intense ruby red. The nose is marked clearly by suggestions of sweet, ripe fruit, which maintain their integrity, however, and are refreshed by a curious, light note of aromatic herbs. The palate makes a decisive impact, highlighting fullness, maturity and softness, closing sapid and harmonious. The Paverno '16 follows a similar track, offering a slightly more supple and juicy palate.

- ● Amarone della Valpolicella Cl. Pegrandi Ris. '13 — 🍷🍷 8
- ● Amarone della Valpolicella Cl. Paverno '16 — 🍷🍷 5
- ● Valpolicella Cl. Sup. '18 — 🍷🍷 2*
- ● Amarone della Valpolicella Cl. Pegrandi '09 — 🍷🍷🍷 5
- ● Amarone della Valpolicella Cl. Pegrandi '08 — 🍷🍷🍷 5
- ● Amarone della Valpolicella Cl. Pegrandi '15 — 🍷🍷 6
- ● Amarone della Valpolicella Cl. Pegrandi Ris. '12 — 🍷🍷 8
- ● Recioto della Valpolicella Cl. Le Peagnè '16 — 🍷🍷 4
- ● Valpolicella Cl. Sup. Ripasso Pegrandi '17 — 🍷🍷 3
- ● Valpolicella Sup. '17 — 🍷🍷 3

Venturini

fraz. San Floriano
via Semonte, 20
37029 San Pietro in Cariano [VR]
Tel. +39 0457701331
www.viniventurini.com

CELLAR SALES
PRE-BOOKED VISITS
ANNUAL PRODUCTION 130,000 bottles
HECTARES UNDER VINE 15.00
SUSTAINABLE WINERY

Wine belongs to our traditions and has developed along with them. It,s an expression of everyday life, both the past and the present'. It's enough to read these sentences on the Venturini family's website to grasp their bond with the land, its traditions and its wines, and the extent to which that animates Giuseppina, Daniele and Mirco's work. A dozen hectares are dedicated entirely to local grapes cultivated with pergolas, on the terraces that support each patch of land. In the cellar everything happens slowly, each wine is given the time necessary to achieve complete harmony. The Amarone Campomasua '15 is at the top of its game. It's characterized by vibrant aromas of cherries and spices, with a very pleasant note of crushed flowers in the background. In the mouth it's juicy, perfectly combining richness of alcohol and glycerine with acidity and sapidity, making for a harmonious palate—it's got a bright future. The Recioto Le Brugnine '15 delivers complex aromas and a palate marked by a measured, reassuring sweetness.

- ● Amarone della Valpolicella Cl. Campomasua '15 — 🍷🍷 6
- ● Recioto della Valpolicella Cl. Le Brugnine '15 — 🍷🍷 6
- ○ Il Castelliere Passito '12 — 🍷🍷 5
- ● Massimino '16 — 🍷🍷 5
- ● Valpolicella Cl. Sup. Ripasso Semonte Alto '16 — 🍷🍷 4
- ⊙ E...lisa Brut Rosé — 🍷 3
- ● Valpolicella Cl. '19 — 🍷 2
- ● Valpolicella Cl. Sup. Campomasua '17 — 🍷 2
- ● Amarone della Valpolicella Cl. Campomasua '07 — 🍷🍷🍷 6
- ● Amarone della Valpolicella Cl. Campomasua '05 — 🍷🍷🍷 6
- ● Recioto della Valpolicella Cl. Le Brugnine '97 — 🍷🍷🍷 5

★Agostino Vicentini

FRAZ. SAN ZENO
VIA C. BATTISTI, 62C
37030 COLOGNOLA AI COLLI [VR]
TEL. +39 0457650539
www.vinivicentini.com

CELLAR SALES
PRE-BOOKED VISITS
ANNUAL PRODUCTION 100,000 bottles
HECTARES UNDER VINE 20.00

Agostino Vicentini's business started as a fruit producer in that splendid land enclosed within the Colognola ai Colli hills. In 1990 came the turning point, with the gradual transformation of the orchards into vineyards and a firm desire to oversee the entire chain of production. Today the property comprises about twenty hectares of vineyards dedicated exclusively to Soave whites and Valpolicella reds. Intense, forthright, deep wines reveal a strong and indissoluble bond with the territory of provenance. The Casale '18 is a summery Soave that plays on ripe fruit accompanied by notes of dried flowers and Mediterranean scrub. These reemerge on a full, powerful palate, perfectly supported by acidity. The Soave Terrelunghe '19 has taken strides. It's never been this good, with a suite of fresh aromas that give way to a supple, tasty, juicy palate. Their reds also deliver, led by the Palazzo di Campiano '16, a wine that expresses all the elegance of Valpolicella.

Wine	Rating
○ Soave Sup. Il Casale '18	▼▼▼ 3*
○ Exemplum '19	▼▼ 3
○ Recioto di Soave '16	▼▼ 5
○ Soave Vign. Terre Lunghe '19	▼▼ 3
● Valpolicella Sup. '17	▼▼ 3
● Valpolicella Sup. Idea Bacco '15	▼▼ 5
● Valpolicella Sup. Palazzo di Campiano '16	▼▼ 5
● Valpolicella '18	▼ 3
○ Soave Sup. Il Casale '17	▽▽▽ 3*
○ Soave Sup. Il Casale '16	▽▽▽ 3*
○ Soave Sup. Il Casale '15	▽▽▽ 3*
○ Soave Sup. Il Casale '14	▽▽▽ 3*
○ Soave Sup. Il Casale '13	▽▽▽ 3*
○ Soave Sup. Il Casale '12	▽▽▽ 3*
○ Soave Sup. Il Casale '09	▽▽▽ 3*
○ Soave Sup. Il Casale '08	▽▽▽ 3*

Vigna Ròda

LOC. VO'
FRAZ. CORTELÀ
VIA MONTE VERSA, 1569
35030 VO' [PD]
TEL. +39 0499940228
www.vignaroda.com

CELLAR SALES
PRE-BOOKED VISITS
ANNUAL PRODUCTION 52,000 bottles
HECTARES UNDER VINE 17.00

Perhaps today Vò Euganeo is best known for the Covid emergency, but what really defines this small village at the base of the western slopes of the Euganean Hills is its extraordinary viticulture. It's here that Gianni Strazzacappa, together with his wife Elena, runs the family business, fewer than twenty hectares on the gentle hills surrounding the winery, where traditional grapes alternate with Bordeaux varieties present for almost two centuries on this land. Their most important wine, the Scarlatto, was left to rest in the cellar, so our attention was focused on their simpler selections, with the Cabernet Espero '18 topping our preferences. Vibrant notes of red fruit and spices give way to a palate that wins you over with its spontaneity, wrought of immediately gratifying sensations, vibrant tannins and an ebullient pleasantness. The Bianco '19 plays on aromatic delicacy and a subtle, juicy profile, while the Merlot Damerino '18 proves savory and harmonious.

Wine	Rating
○ Colli Euganei Bianco '19	▼▼ 2*
● Colli Euganei Cabernet Espèro '18	▼▼ 3
● Colli Euganei Merlot Il Damerino '18	▼▼ 2*
○ Aroma 2.0 '19	▼ 2
● Colli Euganei Rosso '19	▼ 2
● Colli Euganei Cabernet Espero '16	▽▽ 2*
○ Colli Euganei Fior d'Arancio Passito Petali d'Ambra '12	▽▽ 4
● Colli Euganei Rosso '17	▽▽ 2*
● Colli Euganei Rosso '16	▽▽ 2*
● Colli Euganei Rosso Scarlatto '16	▽▽ 3
● Colli Euganei Rosso Scarlatto '15	▽▽ 3*
● Colli Euganei Rosso Scarlatto '14	▽▽ 3
● Merlot Il Damerino '17	▽▽ 2*
● Merlot Il Damerino '16	▽▽ 2*

Vignale di Cecilia

loc. Fornaci
via Croci, 14
35030 Baone [PD]
Tel. +39 042951420
www.vignaledicecilia.it

PRE-BOOKED VISITS
ANNUAL PRODUCTION 20,000 bottles
HECTARES UNDER VINE 8.00
VITICULTURE METHOD Certified Organic

Paolo Brunello's winery is located behind Baone, almost hidden by vegetation and rolling hills. If there were still the sea here, as there was 30 million years ago, the property would be in a sort of tiny fjord, with the cellar in the lower area and the vineyards along the slopes above (there are another six hectares of hillside vineyards in Arquà Petrarca and Baone as well). All their plots are cultivated organically, with an eye towards biodynamic principles. The Passacaglia '16 is a Bordeaux blend (primarily Merlot). On the nose its aromatic bouquet is dominated by notes of ripe red fruit, with timid hints of medicinal herbs and spices rising up from the background, sensations that are even more expressed on the palate, where the wine proves full, generous and highly pleasant. We also noted the strong, distinct personality of their whites, as is the case with the gutsy fullness of their Cocai '18 or the sapid tension of the Poldo.

● Passacaglia '16	🍷🍷 4
○ Cocài '18	🍷🍷 3
○ Poldo	🍷🍷 3
○ Val di Spin Frizzante	🍷🍷 2
○ Benavides '18	🍷 2
○ Prosecco Campo Nicoletta	🍷 2
○ Benavides '16	🍷🍷 2*
○ Benavides '15	🍷🍷 2*
○ Cocài '16	🍷🍷 3
● Colli Euganei Rosso Covolo '16	🍷🍷 3
● Colli Euganei Rosso Covolo '15	🍷🍷 3
● Colli Euganei Rosso Passacaglia '15	🍷🍷 4
● Colli Euganei Rosso Passacaglia '13	🍷🍷 4
● Colli Euganei Rosso Passacaglia '12	🍷🍷 4
● El Moro Cabernet '16	🍷🍷 3*
● El Moro Cabernet '15	🍷🍷 3

★Vignalta

via Scalette
35032 Arquà Petrarca [PD]
Tel. +39 0429777305
www.vignalta.it

CELLAR SALES
PRE-BOOKED VISITS
ANNUAL PRODUCTION 230,000 bottles
HECTARES UNDER VINE 35.00
SUSTAINABLE WINERY

Vignalta has been exploring the potential of the Euganean territory since its beginnings in the mid-1980s. Today their vineyards not only cover a wide area of land, but are located on some of the territory's best positions. These have proven ideal for consistently and harmoniously bringing to maturity the red Bordeaux grapes that represent the appellation's strength. Vignalta's technical staff combines the area's sunniness with the elegance and suppleness characteristic of the maison. Their new Merlot Riserva '15 debuts with a bang. Deep fragrances of fruit and spices are accompanied by a soft presence of oak in the background. In the mouth it impresses for its sapidity, which, together with acidity, helps to lengthen and lighten a classy drink. Still in a youthful, fragrant phase, the Gemola '15 delivers a firm, crisp and highly elegant palate.

● Colli Euganei Merlot Ris. '15	🍷🍷🍷 5
● Colli Euganei Rosso Gemola '15	🍷🍷 6
○ Agno Casto '18	🍷🍷 4
● Agno Tinto '16	🍷🍷 5
○ Chardonnay '18	🍷🍷 4
● Colli Euganei Carménère Ris. '17	🍷🍷 4
○ Colli Euganei Fiori d'Arancio Passito Alpianae '17	🍷🍷 8
● Colli Euganei Rosso Ris. '15	🍷🍷 3
○ L. H. Moscato '18	🍷🍷 3
○ Pinot Bianco '18	🍷🍷 3
● Pinot Nero '16	🍷🍷 5
○ Colli Euganei Fior d'Arancio Passito Alpianae '12	🍷🍷🍷 5
○ Colli Euganei Fiori d'Arancio Passito Alpianae '16	🍷🍷🍷 5
● Colli Euganei Rosso Gemola '13	🍷🍷🍷 6

Le Vigne di San Pietro

VIA SAN PIETRO, 23
37066 SOMMACAMPAGNA [VR]
TEL. +39 045510016
www.levignedisanpietro.it

CELLAR SALES
PRE-BOOKED VISITS
ANNUAL PRODUCTION 70,000 bottles
HECTARES UNDER VINE 10.00

Carlo Nerozzi's winery is atypical. Straddling the Garda appellations of Bardolino and Custoza, it has never followed the model of large production volumes, simplicity and competitive prices. 40 years after its founding, it covers about ten hectares and never reaches 100,000 bottles, even in the best vintages. Responsible viticulture, obsessive attention to detail and respect for cellar aging times makes for an outstanding range characterized by a combination of complexity and elegance. The Bardolino '18 shuns the stereotype of a drinkable red, offering deep, multi-layered sensations without renouncing pleasantness. In the mouth it proves full and sapid, finishing pleasantly rough. The Refolà '15 is rich, harmonious and juicy, while their Come Un Pino Nero '18 features a multifaceted profile that's sophisticated in its aromas of undergrowth and flowers. On the palate it unfolds with grace and lightness, exhibiting length and good tension.

● Bardolino '18	2 glasses 2*
● Come un Pino Nero '18	2 glasses 4
○ Custoza '19	2 glasses 2*
● Refolà '15	2 glasses 6
⊙ Bardolino Chiaretto CorDeRosa '19	1 glass 2
● Bardolino '14	3 glasses 2*
● Bardolino '11	3 glasses 2*
○ Custoza Sanpietro '16	3 glasses 4*
● Refolà Cabernet Sauvignon '04	3 glasses 6
○ Sud '95	3 glasses 6
⊙ Bardolino Chiaretto CorDeRosa '18	2 glasses 2*
● Bardolino Sup. '17	2 glasses 3*
● Bardolino Sup. '16	2 glasses 3*
● Come un Pino Nero '16	2 glasses 4
○ Custoza Sup. Sanpietro '18	2 glasses 4
○ Custoza Sup. Sanpietro '15	2 glasses 3*

Vigneto Due Santi

V.LE ASIAGO, 174
36061 BASSANO DEL GRAPPA [VI]
TEL. +39 0424502074
www.vignetoduesanti.it

CELLAR SALES
PRE-BOOKED VISITS
ANNUAL PRODUCTION 100,000 bottles
HECTARES UNDER VINE 18.00
SUSTAINABLE WINERY

Bassano del Grappa is a beautiful town located at the foot of the Sette Comuni plateau and at the entrance to the Valsugana valley, a veritable tunnel of cool currents that blow in off the Alps. Adriano and Stefano Zonta operate here, about twenty hectares of hillside vineyards that give rise to a selection of wines grounded in Bordeaux varieties. Rich, intensely fruity and of great stylistic precision, their bottles are the result of a union between the warmth of the plains and the freshness of the hills behind. Their Cabernet Due Santi '17 features vibrant suggestions of ripe wild fruit, with notes of herbs and spices pushing up from the bottom. In the mouth its fullness is perfectly governed by acidity and a tannic weave of great precision. The Cavallare '15 follows a similar aromatic trajectory followed by a palate marked by harmony and pleasantness.

● Breganze Cabernet Due Santi '17	2 glasses 4
● Breganze Rosso Cavallare '15	2 glasses 4
○ Breganze Bianco Rivana '19	2 glasses 2*
● Breganze Cabernet '18	2 glasses 3
● Breganze Merlot '18	2 glasses 2*
○ Breganze Pinot Bianco '19	2 glasses 2*
○ Breganze Sauvignon '19	2 glasses 3
○ Breganze Torcolato '17	2 glasses 5
○ Campo di Fiori Malvasia '19	2 glasses 2*
● Breganze Cabernet Due Santi '14	3 glasses 4*
● Breganze Cabernet Vign. Due Santi '12	3 glasses 4*
● Breganze Cabernet Vign. Due Santi '08	3 glasses 4*
● Breganze Cabernet Vign. Due Santi '07	3 glasses 4
● Breganze Cabernet Vign. Due Santi '05	3 glasses 4
● Breganze Cabernet Vign. Due Santi '04	3 glasses 4

★Villa Sandi

via Erizzo, 113a
31035 Crocetta del Montello [TV]
Tel. +39 04238607
www.villasandi.it

CELLAR SALES
PRE-BOOKED VISITS
ACCOMMODATION AND RESTAURANT SERVICE
ANNUAL PRODUCTION 5,600,000 bottles
HECTARES UNDER VINE 560.00
VITICULTURE METHOD Certified Organic
SUSTAINABLE WINERY

Giancarlo Moretti Polegato leads a producer immersed in Treviso sparkling wines. The activity, which started in the borderland between Montello and Valdobbiadene, has expanded gradually but quickly, with vineyards that now cover many hectares in the various Prosecco appellations, allowing for a complete range that fully explores the potential of the Glera grape. Completing their selection is a small but intriguing line of still wines that has in Corpore its highest expression of quality. The Cartizze La Rivetta is a classic, sophisticated Prosecco Superiore, intensely redolent of white fruit and flowers, with a delicate shade of sugared almond in the background. In the mouth the fusion between bubbles, acidity and sugar is almost perfect, making for a wine that's harmonious and very pleasant. The Amalia Moretti Brut, a blend of Pinot Nero and Chardonnay (with a majority share of the former), offers up clear fragrances of bread crust and yellow-fleshed fruit, while in the mouth it's marked by creaminess and good tension.

Wine	Rating
○ Cartizze Brut La Rivetta	🍷🍷🍷 6
○ Amalia Moretti Brut M. Cl. Ris.	🍷🍷 8
○ Asolo Extra Brut Nero '18	🍷🍷 4
● Montello e Colli Asolani Merlot Còrpore '17	🍷🍷 5
○ Serenissima Brut Opere M. Cl.	🍷🍷 5
○ Valdobbiadene Rive di San Pietro di Barbozza Dry '19	🍷🍷 3
○ Asolo Brut	🍷 3
○ Montello e Colli Asolani Manzoni Bianco '19	🍷 3
● Raboso '16	🍷 3
○ Cartizze Brut V. La Rivetta '11	🍷🍷🍷 4*
○ Cartizze Brut V. La Rivetta '10	🍷🍷🍷 4
○ Cartizze Brut V. La Rivetta '09	🍷🍷🍷 4
○ Valdobbiadene Rive di San Pietro di Barbozza Dry '18	🍷🍷 3

Villa Spinosa

via Jago dall'Ora, 14
37024 Negrar [VR]
Tel. +39 0457500093
www.villaspinosa.it

CELLAR SALES
PRE-BOOKED VISITS
ACCOMMODATION
ANNUAL PRODUCTION 45,000 bottles
HECTARES UNDER VINE 20.00
SUSTAINABLE WINERY

Enrico Cascella approaches his work with the tranquility and serenity of one who has understood that struggling against time and nature is a losing battle, that these must be accommodated if a wine is going to tell its story. His great viticultural patrimony extends over the hills between the Negrar and Marano valleys and is only partially utilized for his winery's production. Don't expect power or exuberance, Villa Spinosa's wines are complex, marked by spiciness and sustained by acidity. The Amarone Albasini '13 is a perfect synthesis of tradition and modernity, a wine whose complex, multi-layered aromatic suite calls up raisins while remaining vital and healthy. The palate is rich but doesn't dwell on concentration—it lengthens and tapers on acidity and sapidity, proving long and charming. The Amarone '16 plays on more fragrant, approachable fruit sensations, while the palate comes through crisp and juicy.

Wine	Rating
● Amarone della Valpolicella Cl. Albasini '13	🍷🍷🍷 8
● Amarone della Valpolicella Cl. '16	🍷🍷 7
● Recioto della Valpolicella Cl. Francesca Finato Spinosa '15	🍷🍷 6
● Valpolicella Cl. '19	🍷 3
● Amarone della Valpolicella Cl. '08	🍷🍷🍷 7
● Amarone della Valpolicella Cl. Albasini '11	🍷🍷🍷 7
● Amarone della Valpolicella Cl. Albasini '10	🍷🍷🍷 7
● Valpolicella Cl. Sup. Ripasso Jago '11	🍷🍷🍷 3*
● Amarone della Valpolicella Cl. '15	🍷🍷 6
● Amarone della Valpolicella Cl. '14	🍷🍷 6
● Amarone della Valpolicella Cl. Guglielmi di Jago 10 Anni '07	🍷🍷 8

Vigneti Villabella

FRAZ. CALMASINO
LOC. CANOVA, 2
37011 BARDOLINO [VR]
TEL. +39 0457236448
www.vignetivillabella.com

CELLAR SALES
PRE-BOOKED VISITS
ACCOMMODATION
ANNUAL PRODUCTION 500,000 bottles
HECTARES UNDER VINE 220.00

Half a century after its foundation, the Cristoforetti and Delibori families' business continues its Verona winemaking journey, with a vast viticultural patrimony that reaches primarily into the territories of Bardolino and Valpolicella, and a management approach that's increasingly focused on reducing their environmental impact, starting with the splendid estate of Villa Cordevigo. In the cellar, the best batches of grapes give rise to a range marked by elegance and varietal expression. The Bardolino Morlongo '18 expresses all that the Garda typology has to offer. It's a wine that, without renouncing pleasantness, offers up articulated aromas and a sapid palate, proving dynamic and of great finesse. The Villa Cordevigo '13, a red made with overripe, slightly dried grapes, exhibits a mature, complex nose, while the palate comes through full, generous and commendably harmonious, unfolding on softer notes.

⊙ Bardolino Chiaretto Cl. Villa Cordevigo '19	🍷🍷 3*
● Bardolino Cl. Morlongo '18	🍷🍷 2*
● Amarone della Valpolicella Cl. '15	🍷🍷 6
● Amarone della Valpolicella Cl. Fracastoro Ris. '11	🍷🍷 7
● Montemazzano Corvina Veronese '18	🍷🍷 3
● Villa Cordevigo Rosso '13	🍷🍷 5
⊙ Bardolino Chiaretto Cl. '19	🍷 2
⊙ Bardolino Chiaretto Cl. Heaven Scent '19	🍷 3
○ Lugana '19	🍷 3
● Valpolicella Cl. Sup. Ripasso '18	🍷 3
● Bardolino Cl. V. Morlongo '14	🥂🥂🥂 2*
● Amarone della Valpolicella Cl. '13	🥂🥂 5
● Amarone della Valpolicella Cl. Fracastoro Ris. '10	🥂🥂 7

★Viviani

VIA MAZZANO, 8
37020 NEGRAR [VR]
TEL. +39 0457500286
www.cantinaviviani.com

CELLAR SALES
PRE-BOOKED VISITS
ANNUAL PRODUCTION 80,000 bottles
HECTARES UNDER VINE 10.00
SUSTAINABLE WINERY

Claudio Viviani is a capable and buoyant winemaker, one who's always ready to question the choices made, convinced as he is that the grapes and the territory of Valpolicella can stand shoulder-to-shoulder with the most important appellations. It all hinges on viticulture, which mustn't be bent to the will of the market, but rather develop in harmony with the environment, following the seasonal trends of the vintage. In the cellar, an artisanal approach is adopted and great patience is shown so that wines are allowed to reach their full expressiveness. The results of a journey that began many years ago, with the planting of the first vineyard, are beginning to show continuity, with a shining Valpolicella Campo Morar '17. On the nose it reveals ripe, spicy fruit, embellished with balsamic nuances and medicinal herbs. In the mouth it exhibits a rich body, well contrasted by acidity and a commendably-crafted tannic weave. The Recioto '16, a wine that's floral on the nose and elegantly sweet on the palate, also delivered.

● Valpolicella Cl. Sup. Campo Morar '17	🍷🍷🍷 5
● Amarone della Valpolicella Cl. '16	🍷🍷 6
● Recioto della Valpolicella Cl. '16	🍷🍷 6
● Amarone della Valpolicella Cl. Casa dei Bepi '13	🥂🥂🥂 8
● Amarone della Valpolicella Cl. Casa dei Bepi '12	🥂🥂🥂 8
● Amarone della Valpolicella Cl. Casa dei Bepi '11	🥂🥂🥂 8
● Amarone della Valpolicella Cl. Casa dei Bepi '10	🥂🥂🥂 8
● Amarone della Valpolicella Cl. Casa dei Bepi '09	🥂🥂🥂 8
● Amarone della Valpolicella Cl. Casa dei Bepi '05	🥂🥂🥂 8
● Valpolicella Cl. Sup. Campo Morar '09	🥂🥂🥂 5

Pietro Zanoni

FRAZ. QUINZANO
VIA ARE ZOVO,16D
37125 VERONA
TEL. +39 0458343977
www.pietrozanoni.it

CELLAR SALES
PRE-BOOKED VISITS
ANNUAL PRODUCTION 25,000 bottles
HECTARES UNDER VINE 7.50

The Quinzano Valley is a small, short valley that wines between the Negrar and Valpantena valleys, reaching up to the outskirts of Scaligera. Still somewhat undeveloped, here vineyards alternate with olive groves and occasional patches of woods. It's an area of rare beauty, and it's here that we find Pietro Zanoni's winery, at 16 Via Are Zovo. The vineyards, which span fewer than 10 hectares, unfold primarily around the cellar and are cultivated with the more efficient guyot system (rather than the traditional pergola). Pietro shows great attention to maturation, making for a selection distinguished by intensely fruity expression and firm structure, as can easily be appreciated in the Valpolicella Superiore '17. The Amarone '15, on the other hand, expresses even sweeter and more mature fruit, enriched with mineral notes and forest undergrowth. In the mouth its impact is warm and potent, but the wine unfolds decisively by virtue of a precise, pleasantly rough tannic weave.

Wine	Rating
● Amarone della Valpolicella '15	🍷🍷 7
● Valpolicella Sup. '17	🍷🍷 3
● Valpolicella Sup. Campo Denari '17	🍷🍷 4
● Valpolicella Sup. Ripasso '17	🍷🍷 4
● Amarone della Valpolicella '14	🍷🍷 7
● Amarone della Valpolicella Zovo '13	🍷🍷 7
● Amarone della Valpolicella Zovo '12	🍷🍷 7
● Amarone della Valpolicella Zovo '11	🍷🍷 7
● Recioto della Valpolicella '11	🍷🍷 5
● Valpolicella Sup. '16	🍷🍷 3
● Valpolicella Sup. '15	🍷🍷 2*
● Valpolicella Sup. '14	🍷🍷 2*
● Valpolicella Sup. '13	🍷🍷 2*
● Valpolicella Sup. Campo Denari '16	🍷🍷 4
● Valpolicella Sup. Campo Denari '15	🍷🍷 4
● Valpolicella Sup. Ripasso '15	🍷🍷 4
● Valpolicella Sup. Ripasso '13	🍷🍷 4

Pietro Zardini

VIA DON P. FANTONI, 3
37029 SAN PIETRO IN CARIANO [VR]
TEL. +39 0456800989
www.pietrozardini.it

CELLAR SALES
PRE-BOOKED VISITS
ANNUAL PRODUCTION 60,000 bottles
HECTARES UNDER VINE 10.00

Behind Pietro Zardini's youthful, almost jaunty air is a long and deep experience in the world of Valpolicella wines, first as a consultant and now increasingly with regard to the family business. The vineyards provide the grapes, Corvina, Corvinone and Rondinella, for a range grounded in tradition. At times these are vinified fresh off the vine, at times they're partially-dried, all in pursuit of a character marked by elegant aromas and racy acid tension. The Amarone dedicated to grandfather Leone Zardini is released only after a long stay in the cellar. The 2013 put in a performance for the ages. On the nose overripe fruit immediately takes center stage, gradually leaving room for balsamic and mineral notes, with pepper just peeping out. The palate perfectly orchestrates richness, alcohol and acidity, proving long and enticing. The Recioto Pietro Junior '18 is approachably pleasant, fragrant and juicy.

Wine	Rating
● Amarone della Valpolicella Cl. Leone Zardini Ris. '13	🍷🍷🍷 8
● Amarone della Valpolicella Pietro Junior '16	🍷🍷 6
● Recioto della Valpolicella Pietro Junior '18	🍷🍷 4
● Valpolicella Sup. Ripasso Pietro Junior '17	🍷🍷 4
○ Lugana Pietro Junior '19	🍷 2
⊙ Rosignol Rosato Brut	🍷 3
● Amarone della Valpolicella Cl. Leone Zardini Ris. '12	🍷🍷🍷 8
● Amarone della Valpolicella Cl. Leone Zardini Ris. '11	🍷🍷🍷 8
● Amarone della Valpolicella Pietro Junior '13	🍷🍷 6
● Valpolicella Sup. Ripasso Pietro Junior '16	🍷🍷 4

★Zenato

via San Benedetto, 8
37019 Peschiera del Garda [VR]
Tel. +39 0457550300
www.zenato.it

CELLAR SALES
PRE-BOOKED VISITS
ANNUAL PRODUCTION 2,000,000 bottles
HECTARES UNDER VINE 95.00

Zenato is one of Verona's great brands, a faithful and contemporary interpreter of the Lugana and Valpolicella appellations. What began many years ago as a collaboration between father Sergio and many local growers, has become a producer that directly oversees a hundred hectares. Nadia and her brother Alberto lead the family business in the same style set by its founder, creating a range that has fruity richness as its leitmotiv. The Lugana Sergio Zenato '17 is a reserve that matures in oak. The nose features a rich aromatic bouquet dominated by ripe yellow fruit, gradually revealing timid citrus, floral and delicately spicy notes. In the mouth it's full, sapid and juicy, unfolding supplely by virtue of acidity. The Amarone Sergio Zenato '15 is summery, pervasive and warm,combining power and tension for a harmonious and very long palate.

○ Lugana Sergio Zenato Ris. '17	🍷🍷🍷 5
● Amarone della Valpolicella Cl. Sergio Zenato Ris. '15	🍷🍷 8
○ Lugana Brut M. Cl. '17	🍷🍷 4
○ Lugana Massoni S. Cristina '19	🍷🍷 3
○ Lugana S. Benedetto '19	🍷🍷 2*
● Valpolicella Cl. Sup. '17	🍷🍷 3
● Valpolicella Sup. Ripasso Ripassa '16	🍷🍷 4
● Cresasso '15	🍷 5
● Amarone della Valpolicella Cl. Sergio Zenato Ris. '11	🍷🍷🍷 8
● Amarone della Valpolicella Cl. Sergio Zenato Ris. '10	🍷🍷🍷 8
● Amarone della Valpolicella Cl. Sergio Zenato Ris. '09	🍷🍷🍷 8
○ Lugana Sergio Zenato Ris. '16	🍷🍷🍷 5
○ Lugana Sergio Zenato Ris. '15	🍷🍷🍷 5

Zeni 1870

via Costabella, 9
37011 Bardolino [VR]
Tel. +39 0457210022
www.zeni.it

CELLAR SALES
PRE-BOOKED VISITS
ANNUAL PRODUCTION 1,000,000 bottles
HECTARES UNDER VINE 25.00

The Zeni family's winery was one of the pioneers of Garda, not only for the quality of a selection that's been in production since WW II, but also for Nino's intuition of the potential the area and its grapes represented. Today, 150 years after its founding, Elena, Federica and Fausto are running the family business, increasingly focused on developing the attributes of Bardolino and Valpolicella, while proposing a reliable range that plays more on elegance and tension than power and volume. I Filari del Nino '19 (a Bardolino dedicated to the producer's father) put in an excellent performance. Made without added sulphur dioxide, it offers up aromas of crisp, healthy wild fruit anticipating a juicy, taut and highly pleasant palate. When it comes to their more structured wines, we appreciated the Amarone Nino Zeni, which reveals its aromas little by little, debuting with jammy fruit only to slowly let through notes of aromatic herbs and spices. In the mouth it's generous and pervasive, refreshed by acidity.

● Amarone della Valpolicella Cl. Nino Zeni '15	🍷🍷 8
● Bardolino Cl. I Filari del Nino '19	🍷🍷 5
● Amarone della Valpolicella Cl. '17	🍷🍷 6
● Amarone della Valpolicella Cl. Vigne Alte '16	🍷🍷 6
⊙ Bardolino Chiaretto Cl. Vigne Alte '19	🍷🍷 2*
● Bardolino Cl. Vigne Alte '19	🍷🍷 2*
● Cruino '15	🍷🍷 6
⊙ Bardolino Chiaretto Cl. Inanfora '18	🍷 2
○ Lugana Marogne '19	🍷 3
○ Lugana Vigne Alte '19	🍷 2
● Valpolicella Sup. Ripasso Marogne '18	🍷 3
● Amarone della Valpolicella Cl. '88	🍷🍷🍷 6
● Amarone della Valpolicella Cl. '16	🍷🍷 6
● Amarone della Valpolicella Cl. Vigne Alte '15	🍷🍷 6

Zonin

via Borgolecco, 9
36053 Gambellara [VI]
Tel. +39 0444640111
www.zonin1821.it

CELLAR SALES
PRE-BOOKED VISITS
ANNUAL PRODUCTION 38,000,000 bottles
HECTARES UNDER VINE 2000.00

This Gambellara winery is one of Italy's largest producers, having operations and interests throughout the peninsula, even abroad, with a presence that branches out into local territories as well. In recent years we've witnessed a decisive step forward for Zonin, and today, in the case of their simplest typologies, their wines exhibit a clear varietal profile while their premium selections are marked by greater complexity and depth. Great attention is paid to Prosecco, of which Zonin is a leading producer. The most interesting piece of news, however, comes from the Euganean Hills, where the Gambellara winery has started a new venture. It's their Ètymo '16, a Bordeaux blend (mostly Merlot) that delights the nose with intense scents of red fruit and Mediterranean scrubland, all exalted on a palate marked by concentration and finesse. The Valdobbiadene Extra Dry Prestige 1821 also delivered. A sparkler with fruity aromas, it plays on the contrast between sweetness and acidity, all well accompanied by bubbles.

- ● Amarone della Valpolicella '17 — 🍷🍷 7
- ● Colli Euganei Rosso Ètymo '16 — 🍷🍷 7
- ○ Valdobbiadene Extra Dry Prestige 1821 — 🍷🍷 3
- ○ Lugana '19 — 🍷 4
- ○ Prosecco Brut Cuvée 1821 — 🍷 4
- ○ Prosecco Extra Dry Black Cuvée — 🍷 4
- ○ Soave Cl. '19 — 🍷 3
- ● Valpolicella Cl. '19 — 🍷 3
- ● Amarone della Valpolicella '16 — ⚲⚲ 6
- ● Amarone della Valpolicella '14 — ⚲⚲ 6
- ○ Friuli Aquileia Pinot Grigio '16 — ⚲⚲ 2*
- ○ Gambellara Cl. Il Giangio '17 — ⚲⚲ 3
- ● Valpolicella Cl. '18 — ⚲⚲ 2*
- ● Valpolicella Sup. Ripasso '17 — ⚲⚲ 4
- ● Valpolicella Sup. Ripasso '16 — ⚲⚲ 3
- ● Valpolicella Sup. Ripasso '15 — ⚲⚲ 3

Zymè

loc. San Floriano
via Ca' del Pipa, 1
37029 San Pietro in Cariano [VR]
Tel. +39 0457701108
www.zyme.it

CELLAR SALES
PRE-BOOKED VISITS
ANNUAL PRODUCTION 120,000 bottles
HECTARES UNDER VINE 30.00
SUSTAINABLE WINERY

Celestino Gaspari boasts a deep knowledge of Valpolicella's territory and traditions. It's a knowledge that he developed over many years working among the appellation's vineyards and wineries and that culminated in the founding of his own business just over 20 years ago. If San Floriano's range is wide and spans a number of different typologies, the best results have come right from Valpolicella, with two outstanding versions of Amarone. The 2015 offers up notes of ripe, spicy red fruit, while the palate reveals fullness and harmony, serving as a perfect example of the typology's classic profile. The Riserva La Mattonara '08 is a trove of all that Amarone can offer: aromatic depth, ripeness of fruit, spices and herbs. In the mouth the wine unfolds supple and long, finishing crisp and clear, thus giving us a glimpse of Celestino's ability to manage even the boldest structures with lightness and tension.

- ● Amarone della Valpolicella Cl. '15 — 🍷🍷 8
- ● Amarone della Valpolicella Cl. La Mattonara Ris. '08 — 🍷🍷 8
- ● Valpolicella Cl. Sup. '17 — 🍷🍷 5
- ○ Il Bianco From Black to White '19 — 🍷 3
- ● Valpolicella Reverie '19 — 🍷 3
- ● Amarone della Valpolicella Cl. '13 — ⚲⚲⚲ 8
- ● Amarone della Valpolicella Cl. '06 — ⚲⚲⚲ 8
- ● Amarone della Valpolicella Cl. La Mattonara Ris. '03 — ⚲⚲⚲ 8
- ● Amarone della Valpolicella Cl. La Mattonara Ris. '01 — ⚲⚲⚲ 8
- ● Amarone della Valpolicella Cl. '11 — ⚲⚲ 8
- ● Harlequin '09 — ⚲⚲ 8
- ● Valpolicella Cl. Sup. '16 — ⚲⚲ 5
- ● Valpolicella Cl. Sup. '15 — ⚲⚲ 5
- ● Valpolicella Cl. Sup. '13 — ⚲⚲ 5

Aldo Adami

frаz. Custoza
via Valbusa, 29
37066 Sommacampagna [VR]
Tel. +39 045516105
www.cantinaaldoadami.com

CELLAR SALES
PRE-BOOKED VISITS
ANNUAL PRODUCTION 130,000 bottles
HECTARES UNDER VINE 10.00

● Bardolino '19	🍷🍷 2*
⊙ Bardolino Chiaretto '19	🍷 2
○ Custoza '19	🍷 2
○ Custoza Sup. Ciampani '18	🍷 3

Ai Galli

via Loredan, 28
30020 Pramaggiore [VE]
Tel. +39 0421799314
www.aigalli.it

CELLAR SALES
PRE-BOOKED VISITS
ACCOMMODATION AND RESTAURANT SERVICE
ANNUAL PRODUCTION 600,000 bottles
HECTARES UNDER VINE 60.00

○ Lison Pramaggiore Verduzzo Passito '15	🍷🍷 4
○ Venezia Chardonnay Et. Sel. '18	🍷🍷 3
○ Tai '19	🍷 2
● Venezia Cabernet Franc Et. Sel. '17	🍷 3

Bacio della Luna

via Rovede, 36
31020 Vidor [TV]
Tel. +39 0423983111
www.baciodellaluna.it

ANNUAL PRODUCTION 2,000,000 bottles
HECTARES UNDER VINE 25.00
VITICULTURE METHOD Certified Organic

Cartizze '19	🍷🍷 5
Valdobbiadene Extra Brut '19	🍷🍷 3
Valdobbiadene Brut '17	🍷 2
Valdobbiadene Extra Dry '19	🍷 2

Beato Bartolomeo da Breganze

via Roma, 100
36042 Breganze [VI]
Tel. +39 0445873112
www.cantinabreganze.it

CELLAR SALES
ANNUAL PRODUCTION 2,500,000 bottles
HECTARES UNDER VINE 700.00

○ Breganze Torcolato '15	🍷🍷 5
● Breganze Cabernet Bosco Grande Ris. '16	🍷 3
● Breganze Cabernet Kilò Ris. '16	🍷 4
● Breganze Merlot Bosco Grande Ris. '16	🍷 3

Bellaguardia

via Ziggiotti
36075 Montecchio Maggiore [VI]
Tel. +39 3480000460
www.bellaguardia.it

○ Extra Brut M. Cl.	🍷🍷 5
○ Lessini Durello Extra Brut Romeo Ris.	🍷🍷 5
○ Lessini Durello Pas Dosè Montecchi	🍷 5
○ Pas Dosè 1920 '16	🍷 5

Bellussi Spumanti

via Erizzo, 215
31049 Valdobbiadene [TV]
Tel. +39 0423983411
www.bellussi.com

CELLAR SALES
PRE-BOOKED VISITS
ANNUAL PRODUCTION 1,300,000 bottles

○ Valdobbiadene Brut	🍷🍷 3
○ Valdobbiadene Extra Dry Belcanto	🍷🍷 3
○ Valdobbiadene Brut Belcanto	🍷 3
○ Valdobbiadene Extra Dry	🍷 3

Alessandro Benini

via Scolara, 2
37030 Lavagno [VR]
Tel. +39 3479208584
www.alebenini.it

○ Soave Balinda '18	🍷🍷 2*
○ Valpolicella Mazzacanà '18	🍷🍷 3
○ Soave Le Macette '17	🍷 2
○ Vespro Albino '18	🍷 3

F.lli Bortolin

fraz. Santo Stefano
via Menegazzi, 5
31049 Valdobbiadene [TV]
Tel. +39 0423900135
www.bortolin.com

CELLAR SALES
PRE-BOOKED VISITS
ANNUAL PRODUCTION 300,000 bottles
HECTARES UNDER VINE 20.00

○ Cartizze	🍷🍷 4
○ Valdobbiadene Brut	🍷🍷 2*
○ Valdobbiadene Brut Rù	🍷🍷 3
○ Valdobbiadene Extra Dry	🍷🍷 2*

Umberto Bortolotti

via Ruio Arcane, 6
31049 Valdobbiadene [TV]
Tel. +39 0423975668
www.bortolotti.com

CELLAR SALES
PRE-BOOKED VISITS
ANNUAL PRODUCTION 975,000 bottles

○ Cartizze	🍷🍷 3
○ Valdobbiadene Rive di Santo Stefano Brut Montagnole '18	🍷🍷 3
○ Valdobbiadene Brut Altena	🍷 2

Ca' Bianca

loc. Fontanafredda
via Cinto, 5
35030 Cinto Euganeo [PD]
Tel. +39 042994288

CELLAR SALES
RESTAURANT SERVICE
ANNUAL PRODUCTION 80,000 bottles
HECTARES UNDER VINE 20.00

● Colli Euganei Cabernet Rittocchino 42 '15	🍷🍷 3
● Colli Euganei Rosso Rossura dei Briganti Ris. '15	🍷🍷 4
● Colli Euganei Merlot Bumagro '15	🍷 3

Ca' dei Maghi

via Ca' dei Maghi, 5
37022 Fumane [VR]
Tel. +39 0457702355
www.cadeimaghi.it

HECTARES UNDER VINE 7.00

● Amarone della Valpolicella Cl. Canova Ris. '13	🍷🍷 8
● Valpolicella Cl. Sup. Maghi '15	🍷🍷 3
● Valpolicella Cl. '19	🍷 2

Canoso

loc. Monteforte d'Alpone
via Roma, 97
37032 Verona
Tel. +39 0456101981
www.canoso.it

CELLAR SALES
PRE-BOOKED VISITS
ANNUAL PRODUCTION 40,000 bottles
HECTARES UNDER VINE 15.00

○ Soave Cl. Fonte '19	🍷🍷 2*
○ Soave Cl. Sup. Verso '17	🍷🍷 3
○ Oltre '17	🍷 4

Cantina del Castello

v.lo Corte Pittora, 5
37038 Soave [VR]
Tel. +39 0457680093
www.cantinacastello.it

CELLAR SALES
PRE-BOOKED VISITS
ANNUAL PRODUCTION 120,000 bottles
HECTARES UNDER VINE 13.00

○ Soave Cl. Castello '19 🍷🍷 2*

Cirotto

via Bassanese, 51
31011 Asolo [TV]
Tel. +39 0423952396
www.cirottovini.com

ANNUAL PRODUCTION 80,000 bottles
HECTARES UNDER VINE 9.00

○ Asolo Brut '19 🍷🍷 2*
○ Sogno Dosage Zéro M. Cl. '15 🍷🍷 7
○ Asolo Extra Dry '19 🍷 4
○ Manzoni Bianco '18 🍷 3

Col Sandago

via Barriera, 41
31058 Susegana [TV]
Tel. +39 043864468
www.colsandago.it

CELLAR SALES
PRE-BOOKED VISITS
ANNUAL PRODUCTION 500,000 bottles
HECTARES UNDER VINE 30.00

○ Conegliano Valdobbiadene Rive di Susegana Dry Undici '19 🍷🍷 3
○ Conegliano Valdobbiadene Rive di Susegana Extra Brut Nature '19 🍷🍷 3

Colli del Soligo

loc. Solighetto
via L. Toffolin, 6
31050 Pieve di Soligo [TV]
Tel. +39 0438840092
www.collisoligo.com

CELLAR SALES
PRE-BOOKED VISITS
ANNUAL PRODUCTION 6,000,000 bottles

○ Valdobbiadene Extra Dry Col del Mez '19 🍷🍷 2*
○ Valdobbiadene Extra Dry Solicum '17 🍷🍷 2*
○ Valdobbiadene Brut Solicum '17 🍷 2
○ Valdobbiadene Rive di Soligo Dry '19 🍷 3

Cantina Colli Euganei

via G. Marconi, 314
35030 Vo' [PD]
Tel. +39 0499940011
www.cantinacollieuganei.it

CELLAR SALES
PRE-BOOKED VISITS
ANNUAL PRODUCTION 3,500,000 bottles
HECTARES UNDER VINE 650.00
VITICULTURE METHOD Certified Organic
SUSTAINABLE WINERY

○ Colli Euganei Moscato Dolce Palazzo del Principe '17 🍷🍷 2*
● Colli Euganei Rosso Notte di Galileo Ris. '17 🍷🍷 3

La Collina dei Ciliegi

fraz. Romagnano
loc. Erbin, 36
37023 Grezzana [VR]
Tel. +39 0459814900
www.lacollinadeiciliegi.it

CELLAR SALES
PRE-BOOKED VISITS
ANNUAL PRODUCTION 60,000 bottles

● Amarone della Valpolicella Ciliegio '15 🍷🍷 8
● Valpolicella Sup. Ripasso Macion '17 🍷🍷 5
● Amarone della Valpolicella '16 🍷 7
● Camponi '18 🍷 2

Collis

via Cappuccini, 6
37032 Monteforte d'Alpone [VR]
Tel. +39 0456108222
www.collisgroup.it

- ● Amarone della Valpolicella Castelforte '15 🍷🍷 5
- ○ Prosecco Extra Dry Castelforte 🍷 2
- ○ Soave Castelforte '19 🍷 2
- ● Valpolicella Ripasso Castelforte '17 🍷 4

Vignaioli Contrà Soarda

s.da Soarda, 26
36061 Bassano del Grappa [VI]
Tel. +39 0424505562
www.contrasoarda.it

CELLAR SALES
PRE-BOOKED VISITS
RESTAURANT SERVICE
ANNUAL PRODUCTION 80,000 bottles
HECTARES UNDER VINE 20.00
VITICULTURE METHOD Certified Organic
SUSTAINABLE WINERY

- ● Breganze Rosso Terre di Lava Ris. '14 🍷🍷 5
- ○ Il Pendio '16 🍷🍷 3
- ○ Breganze Vespaiolo Soarda '19 🍷 3
- ● Vitae Musso '16 🍷 4

Corte Mainente

v.le della Vittoria, 45
37038 Soave [VR]
Tel. +39 0457680303
www.cortemainente.com

CELLAR SALES
PRE-BOOKED VISITS
ANNUAL PRODUCTION 37,000 bottles
HECTARES UNDER VINE 12.00
SUSTAINABLE WINERY

- ○ Soave Cl. Pigno '19 🍷🍷 3
- ○ Soave Cl. Tenda '18 🍷🍷 3
- ○ Recioto di Soave Luna Nova '18 🍷 4
- ○ Soave Netroir '18 🍷 4

Corte Scaletta

fraz. Marcellise
via Cao di Sopra, 19
37036 San Martino Buon Albergo [VR]
Tel. +39 0458740269
www.cortescaletta.it

- ● Valpolicella '18 🍷🍷 3
- ● Valpolicella Sup. '14 🍷🍷 5
- ● Amarone della Valpolicella '13 🍷 7

Paolo Cottini

fraz. Castelrotto
via Belvedere, 29
37029 Verona
Tel. +39 0456837293
www.paolocottini.it

CELLAR SALES
PRE-BOOKED VISITS
ANNUAL PRODUCTION 55,000 bottles
HECTARES UNDER VINE 5.50

- ● Scriba Passito '17 🍷🍷 3
- ● Valpolicella Cl. '19 🍷 2

Valentina Cubi

via Casterna, 60
37022 Fumane [VR]
Tel. +39 0457701806
www.valentinacubi.it

CELLAR SALES
PRE-BOOKED VISITS
ANNUAL PRODUCTION 40,000 bottles
HECTARES UNDER VINE 10.00
VITICULTURE METHOD Certified Organic

- ● Amarone della Valpolicella Cl. Morar '10 🍷🍷 7
- ● Valpolicella Cl. Sup. Ripasso Arusnatico '16 🍷🍷 4
- ● Valpolicella Iperico '19 🍷 2

Cantina di Custoza

VIA STAFFALO,1
37066 SOMMACAMPAGNA [VR]
TEL. +39 045516200
www.cantinadicustoza.it

CELLAR SALES
PRE-BOOKED VISITS
ANNUAL PRODUCTION 4,000,000 bottles
HECTARES UNDER VINE 1000.00
VITICULTURE METHOD Certified Organic

- ○ Custoza Sup. Custodia '18 — 🍷🍷 3*
- ⊙ Bardolino Chiaretto Cl. Val dei Molini '19 — 🍷 3
- ● Bardolino Cl. Val dei Molini '19 — 🍷 3
- ○ Custoza Val dei Molini '19 — 🍷 2

Dal Din

VIA MONTEGRAPPA, 29
31020 VIDOR [TV]
TEL. +39 0423987295
www.daldin.it

CELLAR SALES
PRE-BOOKED VISITS
ANNUAL PRODUCTION 350,000 bottles
HECTARES UNDER VINE 12.00
SUSTAINABLE WINERY

- ○ Valdobbiadene Brut — 🍷🍷 3
- ○ Valdobbiadene Extra Dry — 🍷🍷 3
- ○ Valdobbiadene Brut Dosaggio Zero Ry — 🍷 3
- ○ Valdobbiadene Extra Dry Vidoro '19 — 🍷 2

La Dama

FRAZ. SAN VITO
VIA GIOVANNI QUINTARELLI, 39
37024 NEGRAR [VR]
TEL. +39 0456000728
www.ladamavini.com

ANNUAL PRODUCTION 50,000 bottles
HECTARES UNDER VINE 10.00
VITICULTURE METHOD Certified Organic

- ● Amarone della Valpolicella Cl. '16 — 🍷🍷 7
- ● Valpolicella Cl. Sup. Ca' Besi '17 — 🍷🍷 5
- ● Recioto della Valpolicella Cl. '17 — 🍷 6
- ● Valpolicella Cl. Sup. Ripasso '18 — 🍷 5

DolceVera

LOC. VILLA
VIA SAN ROCCO, 1
37024 NEGRAR [VR]
TEL. +39 0457501045
www.dolceveravini.com

- ● Amarone della Valpolicella Cl. '16 — 🍷🍷 6
- ● Valpolicella Cl. Sup. Ripasso '17 — 🍷🍷 4

Francesco Drusian

FRAZ. BIGOLINO
VIA ANCHE, 1
31049 VALDOBBIADENE [TV]
TEL. +39 0423982151
www.drusian.it

CELLAR SALES
PRE-BOOKED VISITS
ANNUAL PRODUCTION 1,500,000 bottles
HECTARES UNDER VINE 80.00
SUSTAINABLE WINERY

- ○ Valdobbiadene Brut — 🍷🍷 3
- ○ Valdobbiadene Extra Dry — 🍷🍷 3
- ○ Cartizze — 🍷 4
- ○ Valdobbiadene Extra Dry '19 — 🍷 3

Tenute Falezza

VIA BELVEDERE, 35Z
37131 VERONA
TEL. +39 0452221249
www.tenutefalezza.com

- ● Amarone della Valpolicella '16 — 🍷🍷 6
- ● Recioto della Valpolicella '16 — 🍷🍷 6
- ● Valpolicella Cl. Sup. Ripasso '17 — 🍷 4

Fraccaroli

FRAZ. SAN BENEDETTO
LOC. BERRA VECCHIA, 1
37019 PESCHIERA DEL GARDA [VR]
TEL. +39 0457550949
www.fraccarolivini.it

CELLAR SALES
PRE-BOOKED VISITS
ANNUAL PRODUCTION 280,000 bottles
HECTARES UNDER VINE 50.00

○ Lugana 1912 Ris. '16 🍷🍷 4
○ Lugana Pansere '19 🍷🍷 2*
○ Lugana Sup. Campo Serà '18 🍷 2

Cantina Produttori di Fregona

VIA CASTAGNOLA, 50
31010 FREGONA [TV]
TEL. +39 3402706497
www.torchiato.com

○ Colli di Conegliano Torchiato Di Fregona Piera Dolza '15 🍷🍷 5
○ Boschera '19 🍷 3

Garbara

LOC. S.STEFANO
VIA MENEGAZZI, 19
31049 VALDOBBIADENE [TV]
TEL. +39 0423900155
www.garbara.it

CELLAR SALES
PRE-BOOKED VISITS
ANNUAL PRODUCTION 21,000 bottles
HECTARES UNDER VINE 0.90

○ Cartizze Brut Zero 🍷🍷 4
○ Cartizze Extra Dry 🍷🍷 4
○ Valdobbiadene Extra Brut 🍷 4

Fattoria Garbole

LOC. GARBOLE
VIA FRACANZANA, 6
37039 TREGNAGO [VR]
TEL. +39 0457809020
www.fattoriagarbole.it

CELLAR SALES
PRE-BOOKED VISITS
ANNUAL PRODUCTION 15,000 bottles
HECTARES UNDER VINE 6.00

● Amarone della Valpolicella Hatteso '11 🍷🍷 8
● Heletto '12 🍷🍷 6

Gentili

LOC. PESINA
VIA S. ANTONIO, 271
37013 CAPRINO VERONESE [VR]
TEL. +39 3391651823
www.cantinagentili.com

CELLAR SALES
PRE-BOOKED VISITS
ANNUAL PRODUCTION 9,000 bottles
HECTARES UNDER VINE 37.00
SUSTAINABLE WINERY

⊙ Bardolino Chiaretto Dosaggio Zero M. Cl. '17 🍷🍷 5
● Bardolino San Verolo '18 🍷🍷 3
○ Souvignier Gris '18 🍷🍷 4

Natalina Grandi

VIA BTG. VICENZA, 8
36053 GAMBELLARA [VI]
TEL. +39 0444444102
framarin5@interfree.it

○ Gambellara Cl. Colle di Mezzo '18 🍷🍷 4
● Azzardo Merlot '18 🍷 4
○ Gambellara Solo Lei '19 🍷 3
○ Lessini Durello Brut '19 🍷 3

La Farra

VIA SAN FRANCESCO, 44
31010 FARRA DI SOLIGO [TV]
TEL. +39 0438801242
www.lafarra.it

CELLAR SALES
ANNUAL PRODUCTION 200,000 bottles
HECTARES UNDER VINE 20.00

- ○ Valdobbiadene Rive di Farra di Soligo Extra Dry '19 — 🍷🍷 3
- ○ Valdobbiadene Rive di Farra di Soligo Extra Brut '19 — 🍷 3

Latium Morini

VIA FIENILE, 2
37030 MEZZANE DI SOTTO [VR]
TEL. +39 0457834648
www.latiummorini.it

CELLAR SALES
PRE-BOOKED VISITS
ANNUAL PRODUCTION 150,000 bottles
HECTARES UNDER VINE 40.00
SUSTAINABLE WINERY

- ● Valpolicella Sup. Campo Prognai '16 — 🍷🍷 4
- ● Amarone della Valpolicella Campo Leon '15 — 🍷 6
- ○ Amitor '19 — 🍷 2
- ○ Soave '19 — 🍷 2

Lavagnoli

LOC. PIGOZZO
VIA SQUARANTO, 49C
37141 VERONA
TEL. +39 3492801553
famiglialavagnoli99@gmail.com

- ● Amarone della Valpolicella '16 — 🍷🍷 6
- ● Valpolicella Sup. Ripasso '17 — 🍷🍷 3
- ● Pigosso '17 — 🍷 4
- ● Valpolicella '19 — 🍷 2

Lenotti

VIA SANTA CRISTINA, 1
37011 BARDOLINO [VR]
TEL. +39 0457210484
www.lenotti.com

CELLAR SALES
PRE-BOOKED VISITS
ANNUAL PRODUCTION 1,400,000 bottles
HECTARES UNDER VINE 105.00

- ● Amarone della Valpolicella Cl. '15 — 🍷🍷 7
- ⊙ Bardolino Chiaretto Cl. Decus '19 — 🍷 3
- ● Bardolino Cl. Sup. Le Olle '18 — 🍷 3
- ○ Lugana Decus '19 — 🍷 3

Le Mandolare

LOC. BROGNOLIGO
VIA SAMBUCO, 180
37032 MONTEFORTE D'ALPONE [VR]
TEL. +39 0456175083
www.cantinalemandolare.com

CELLAR SALES
PRE-BOOKED VISITS
ANNUAL PRODUCTION 65,000 bottles
HECTARES UNDER VINE 20.00

- ○ Recioto di Soave Cl. Le Schiavette '17 — 🍷🍷 5
- ○ Soave Cl. Menini '19 — 🍷🍷 2*
- ○ Soave Cl. Sup. Monte Sella '16 — 🍷🍷 3
- ○ 3B Trebbiano — 🍷 2

Le Manzane

LOC. BAGNOLO
VIA MASET, 47B
31020 SAN PIETRO DI FELETTO [TV]
TEL. +39 0438486606
www.lemanzane.com

CELLAR SALES
PRE-BOOKED VISITS
ANNUAL PRODUCTION 1,000,000 bottles
HECTARES UNDER VINE 72.00

- ○ Conegliano Valdobbiadene Brut '19 — 🍷🍷 2*
- ○ Conegliano Valdobbiadene Extra Dry '19 — 🍷 3
- ○ Conegliano Valdobbiadene Rive di Manzana Dry Springo Bronze '19 — 🍷 4

Marsuret

loc. Guia di Valdobbiadene
via Barch, 17
31049 Valdobbiadene [TV]
Tel. +39 0423900139
www.marsuret.it

CELLAR SALES
PRE-BOOKED VISITS
ANNUAL PRODUCTION 600,000 bottles
HECTARES UNDER VINE 50.00

- ○ Valdobbiadene Extra Brut Amoler 🍷🍷 3*
- ○ Cartizze 🍷🍷 4
- ○ Valdobbiadene Brut San Boldo 🍷 3
- ○ Valdobbiadene Extra Dry Il Soller 🍷 3

Cantine Maschio

loc. Visnà
via Cadore Mare, 2
31020 Vazzola [TV]
Tel. +39 0438794115
www.cantinemaschio.it

PRE-BOOKED VISITS
ANNUAL PRODUCTION 20,000,000 bottles
HECTARES UNDER VINE 304.00
VITICULTURE METHOD Certified Organic
SUSTAINABLE WINERY

- ○ Valdobbiadene Extra Dry Maschio dei Cavalieri '19 🍷🍷 3
- ○ Valdobbiadene Rive di Col Bertaldo Brut Machio dei Cavalieri '19 🍷🍷 4

Meroni

via Roma, 16a
37015 Sant'Ambrogio di Valpolicella [VR]
Tel. +39 3479186167
www.vinimeroni.com

- ● Amarone della Valpolicella Cl. Il Velluto Ris. '12 🍷🍷 8
- ● Valpolicella Cl. Sup. Il Velluto '14 🍷🍷 5
- ● Valpolicella Cl. Sengia '18 🍷 3

Mionetto

via Colderove, 2
31049 Valdobbiadene [TV]
Tel. +39 04239707
www.mionetto.it

CELLAR SALES
PRE-BOOKED VISITS
ANNUAL PRODUCTION 17,600,000 bottles

- ○ Valdobbiadene Extra Dry 🍷🍷 3
- ○ Valdobbiadene Rive di Guia Brut Nature '18 🍷🍷 3
- ○ Cartizze 🍷 4

Firmino Miotti

via Brogliati Contro, 53
36042 Breganze [VI]
Tel. +39 0445873006
www.firminomiotti.it

CELLAR SALES
PRE-BOOKED VISITS
ANNUAL PRODUCTION 25,000 bottles
HECTARES UNDER VINE 5.00

- ○ Breganze Torcolato '16 🍷🍷 5
- ● Valletta '13 🍷🍷 4
- ○ Breganze Vespaiolo 16.9 '17 🍷 5
- ○ Sampagna Frizzante 🍷 2

Montelvini

fraz. Venegazzù
via Cal Trevigiana, 51
31040 Volpago del Montello [TV]
Tel. +39 04238777
www.montelvini.it

CELLAR SALES
ANNUAL PRODUCTION 5,200,000 bottles
HECTARES UNDER VINE 35.00
SUSTAINABLE WINERY

- ○ Asolo Brut 🍷🍷 2
- ○ Asolo Extra Brut '19 🍷🍷 2*
- ○ Asolo Extra Dry 🍷 2
- ● Montello e Colli Asolani Rosso Zuitér '16 🍷 3

Walter Nardin

loc. Roncadelle
via Fontane, 5
31024 Ormelle [TV]
Tel. +39 0422851622
www.vinwalternardin.it

PRE-BOOKED VISITS
ANNUAL PRODUCTION 350,000 bottles
HECTARES UNDER VINE 20.00

- ● Refosco P. R. La Zerbaia '17 — 🍷🍷 3
- ● Rosso della Ghiaia La Zerbaia '16 — 🍷🍷 4
- ○ Tai La Zerbaia '18 — 🍷🍷 3
- ● Rosso del Nane La Zerbaia '17 — 🍷 2

Pegoraro

via Calbin, 24
36048 Mossano [VI]
Tel. +39 0444886461
www.cantinapegoraro.it

CELLAR SALES
PRE-BOOKED VISITS
ANNUAL PRODUCTION 45,000 bottles
HECTARES UNDER VINE 7.00

- ● Syrah '17 — 🍷🍷 3
- ○ Colli Berici Tai '19 — 🍷 3
- ● Colli Berici Tai Rosso '19 — 🍷 3
- ○ Iose Garganega '18 — 🍷 3

Pian delle Vette

fraz. Vignui
via Teda, 11
32032 Feltre [BL]
Tel. +39 0439302803
www.piandellevette.it

CELLAR SALES
PRE-BOOKED VISITS
ANNUAL PRODUCTION 10,000 bottles
HECTARES UNDER VINE 2.50
SUSTAINABLE WINERY

- ● Granpasso '13 — 🍷🍷 5
- ○ Mat '55 Pas Dosé M.Cl. '12 — 🍷🍷 7
- ● Gnomè '13 — 🍷 4

Il Pianzio

via Pianzio, 66
35030 Galzignano Terme [PD]
Tel. +39 0499130422
www.ilpianzio.it

CELLAR SALES
RESTAURANT SERVICE
HECTARES UNDER VINE 15.00

- ● Colli Euganei Cabernet Jenio '17 — 🍷🍷 2*
- ● Colli Euganei Rosso Eremo Ris. '16 — 🍷🍷 4
- ○ Ca' Nova '17 — 🍷 3
- ● Colli Euganei Rosso '18 — 🍷 3

Albino Piona

fraz. Custoza
via Bellavista, 48
37060 Sommacampagna [VR]
Tel. +39 045516055
www.albinopiona.it

CELLAR SALES
PRE-BOOKED VISITS
ANNUAL PRODUCTION 350,000 bottles
HECTARES UNDER VINE 77.00

- ⊙ Bardolino Chiaretto '19 — 🍷🍷 2*
- ○ Custoza '19 — 🍷🍷 2*
- ○ Verde Piona Frizzante — 🍷 2

Viticoltori Ponte

via Verdi, 50
31047 Ponte di Piave [TV]
Tel. +39 0422858211
www.ponte1948.it

CELLAR SALES
ANNUAL PRODUCTION 15,000,000 bottles
HECTARES UNDER VINE 2500.00
VITICULTURE METHOD Certified Organic

- ○ Sauvignon Campe Dhei '19 — 🍷🍷 2*
- ○ Manzoni Bianco Campe Dhei '19 — 🍷 2
- ○ Prosecco Extra Dry '19 — 🍷 3
- ○ Prosecco Extra Dry — 🍷 2

Umberto Portinari

LOC. BROGNOLIGO
VIA SANTO STEFANO, 2
37032 MONTEFORTE D'ALPONE [VR]
TEL. +39 0456175087
portinarivini@libero.it

CELLAR SALES
PRE-BOOKED VISITS
ANNUAL PRODUCTION 30,000 bottles
HECTARES UNDER VINE 4.00

- ○ Soave Cl. Sup. Ronchetto '18 — ⚲⚲ 4
- ○ Soave Albare '18 — ⚲ 2
- ○ Soave U.P. '19 — ⚲ 3

Possessioni di Serego Alighieri

VIA STAZIONE VECCHIA, 472
37015 SANT'AMBROGIO DI VALPOLICELLA [VR]
TEL. +39 0457703622
serego@seregoalighieri.it

CELLAR SALES
PRE-BOOKED VISITS
ACCOMMODATION
ANNUAL PRODUCTION 350,000 bottles
HECTARES UNDER VINE 120.00

- ● Recioto della Valpolicella Cl. Casal dei Ronchi Serego Alighieri '15 — ⚲⚲ 7
- ● Valpolicella Cl. Sup. Monte Piazzo Serego Alighieri '17 — ⚲⚲ 5

PuntoZero

VIA MONTE PALÙ, 1
36045 LONIGO [VI]
TEL. +39 049659881
www.puntozerowine.it

CELLAR SALES
PRE-BOOKED VISITS
ANNUAL PRODUCTION 16,000 bottles
HECTARES UNDER VINE 11.00

- ● Carmenère '17 — ⚲⚲ 5
- ● Virgola '15 — ⚲⚲ 8
- ● Dimezzo '16 — ⚲ 5
- ● Punto '15 — ⚲ 7

Reassi

VIA A. MANZONI, 9
35030 ROVOLON [PD]
TEL. +39 3475340932
www.reassi.it

CELLAR SALES
PRE-BOOKED VISITS
ACCOMMODATION
ANNUAL PRODUCTION 20,000 bottles
HECTARES UNDER VINE 6.50
VITICULTURE METHOD Certified Organic

- ● Colli Euganei Cabernet Sparviere '17 — ⚲⚲ 3
- ● Colli Euganei Rosso Tre Frazioni '16 — ⚲⚲ 3
- ● Colli Euganei Merlot Archè '16 — ⚲ 3
- ● Vin Bastardo '17 — ⚲ 3

Rechsteiner

FRAZ. PIAVON
VIA FRASSENÈ, 2
31046 ODERZO [TV]
TEL. +39 0422752074
www.rechsteiner.it

CELLAR SALES
PRE-BOOKED VISITS
ACCOMMODATION AND RESTAURANT SERVICE
ANNUAL PRODUCTION 150,000 bottles
HECTARES UNDER VINE 50.00
SUSTAINABLE WINERY

- ● Pinot Nero '17 — ⚲⚲ 2*
- ○ Venezia Manzoni Bianco '19 — ⚲ 2
- ● Venezia Merlot '17 — ⚲ 2
- ○ Venezia Pinot Grigio '19 — ⚲ 2

La Roccola

VIA DIETROMONTE, 10
35030 CINTO EUGANEO [PD]
TEL. +39 042994298
www.laroccola.it

CELLAR SALES
PRE-BOOKED VISITS
RESTAURANT SERVICE
ANNUAL PRODUCTION 100,000 bottles
HECTARES UNDER VINE 18.00
SUSTAINABLE WINERY

- ● Colli Euganei Cabernet Valcinta '18 — ⚲⚲ 4
- ● Colli Euganei Rosso Maroneria '17 — ⚲⚲ 4
- ● Colli Euganei Merlot Giaretta '18 — ⚲ 4

Salatin

via Doge Alvise IV Moncenigo, 57
31016 Cordignano [TV]
Tel. +39 0438995928
www.salatinvini.com

- ● Colli di Conegliano Rosso Le Conche '16 🍷🍷 3
- ○ Valdobbiadene Extra Dry 🍷🍷 3
- ○ Valdobbiadene Brut 🍷 3

Urbano Salvan Vigne del Pigozzo

loc. Pigozzo
via Mincana, 143
35020 Due Carrare [PD]
Tel. +39 049525841
www.salvan.it

CELLAR SALES
PRE-BOOKED VISITS
ANNUAL PRODUCTION 30,000 bottles
HECTARES UNDER VINE 20.00
SUSTAINABLE WINERY

- ● Bagnoli Friularo '15 🍷🍷 5
- ● Colli Euganei Cabernet Sauvignon San Marco '16 🍷🍷 5
- ⊙ Bagnoli Extra Dry Summertime Rosé 🍷 3

San Rustico

fraz. Valgatara
via Pozzo, 2
37020 Marano di Valpolicella [VR]
Tel. +39 0457703348
www.sanrustico.it

CELLAR SALES
PRE-BOOKED VISITS
ANNUAL PRODUCTION 250,000 bottles
HECTARES UNDER VINE 22.00

- ● Amarone della Valpolicella Cl. '15 🍷🍷 6
- ● Amarone della Valpolicella Cl. 150 '15 🍷🍷 7
- ● Valpolicella Cl. '19 🍷 2
- ● Valpolicella Cl. Sup. '18 🍷 2

Sandre

fraz. Campodipietra
via Risorgimento, 16
31040 Salgareda [TV]
Tel. +39 0422804135
www.sandre.it

CELLAR SALES
PRE-BOOKED VISITS
ANNUAL PRODUCTION 100,000 bottles
HECTARES UNDER VINE 35.00

- ● Cuor di Vigna '16 🍷🍷 4
- ○ Acini Bianchi Traminer '19 🍷 2
- ● Piave Merlot '18 🍷 2
- ● Raboso '17 🍷 2

Tenuta Sant'Anna

fraz. Loncon
via Monsignor P. L. Zovatto, 71
30020 Annone Veneto [VE]
Tel. +39 0422864511
www.tenutasantanna.it

CELLAR SALES
PRE-BOOKED VISITS
ANNUAL PRODUCTION 2,800,000 bottles
HECTARES UNDER VINE 140.00

- ○ Cartizze Dry Sior Toni V8+ 🍷🍷 6
- ○ Valdobbiadene Extra Dry 🍷🍷 3
- ○ Prosecco Brut 🍷 3
- ○ Prosecco Extra Dry 🍷 3

Santa Eurosia

fraz. San Pietro di Barbozza
via della Cima, 8
31049 Valdobbiadene [TV]
Tel. +39 0423973236
santaeurosia.it

CELLAR SALES
PRE-BOOKED VISITS
ANNUAL PRODUCTION 270,000 bottles

- ○ Cartizze Dry '19 🍷🍷 5
- ○ Valdobbiadene Extra Brut Zerodue '19 🍷🍷 3
- ○ Valdobbiadene Brut Zerotto '19 🍷 3
- ○ Valdobbiadene Extra Dry Costante '19 🍷 4

Cantina di Soave

v.le della Vittoria, 128
37038 Soave [VR]
Tel. +39 0456139811
www.cantinasoave.it

CELLAR SALES
PRE-BOOKED VISITS
ANNUAL PRODUCTION 3,000,000 bottles
HECTARES UNDER VINE 6000.00
VITICULTURE METHOD Certified Organic
SUSTAINABLE WINERY

- ● Amarone della Valpolicella Rocca Sveva Ris. '15 🍷🍷 8
- ○ Soave Cl. Castelcerino Rocca Sveva '19 🍷 3
- ● Valpolicella Sup. Ripasso Rocca Sveva '15 🍷 4

Spada

via Villa Girardi, 26
37029 San Pietro in Cariano [VR]
Tel. +39 0456801468
www.cantinaspada.it

- ● Amarone della Valpolicella Cl. Ris. '12 🍷🍷 8
- ● Valpolicella Cl. Sup. El Casotto '17 🍷🍷 3
- ● Valpolicella Cl. Sup. Ripasso '17 🍷🍷 3
- ● Valpolicella Cl. '19 🍷 2

Tanoré

fraz. San Pietro di Barbozza
via Mont di Cartizze, 3
31040 Valdobbiadene [TV]
Tel. +39 0423975770
www.tanore.it

CELLAR SALES
PRE-BOOKED VISITS
ANNUAL PRODUCTION 90,000 bottles
HECTARES UNDER VINE 10.00

- ○ Cartizze 🍷🍷 4
- ○ Valdobbiadene Extra Dry 🍷🍷 2*
- ○ Valdobbiadene Brut 🍷 3

Cantina Terra Felice

via Marlunghe, 19
35032 Arquà Petrarca [PD]
Tel. +39 3477025928
www.cantinaterrafelice.it

CELLAR SALES
PRE-BOOKED VISITS
ANNUAL PRODUCTION 45,000 bottles
HECTARES UNDER VINE 10.00

- ● AltaVia Rosso '16 🍷🍷 5
- ● Cabernet '16 🍷🍷 6
- ○ Chardonnay '18 🍷 3
- ● Pinot Nero '16 🍷 7

Terre di San Venanzio Fortunato

via Capitello Ferrari, 1
31049 Valdobbiadene [TV]
Tel. +39 0423974083
Via Capitello Ferrari, 1

ANNUAL PRODUCTION 300,000 bottles

- ○ Valdobbiadene Brut '19 🍷🍷 2*
- ○ Valdobbiadene Dry Fortunato '19 🍷🍷 2*
- ○ Cartizze Brut '19 🍷 5
- ○ Valdobbiadene Extra Dry '19 🍷 3

Davide Vignato

via Capo di Sopra, 39
36053 Gambellara [VI]
Tel. +39 0444 444144
www.davidevignato.it

ANNUAL PRODUCTION 28,000 bottles
HECTARES UNDER VINE 14.00
SUSTAINABLE WINERY

- ○ Gambellara Col Moenia '17 🍷🍷 3
- ○ Gambellara El Gian '18 🍷 3

Vigneti di Ettore

via Casetta di Montecchio, 2
37024 Negrar [VR]
Tel. +39 0457540158
www.vignetidiettore.it

ACCOMMODATION
ANNUAL PRODUCTION 60,000 bottles
HECTARES UNDER VINE 15.00
VITICULTURE METHOD Certified Organic
SUSTAINABLE WINERY

- ● Valpolicella Cl. '19 — 🍷🍷 3
- ● Amarone della Valpolicella Cl. '16 — 🍷 7
- ● Recioto della Valpolicella Cl. '17 — 🍷 5
- ● Valpolicella Cl. Sup. Pavaio '18 — 🍷 3

Villa Angarano

via Contrà San Michele 4b
36061 Bassano del Grappa [VI]
Tel. +39 0424503086
www.levieangarano.com

CELLAR SALES
PRE-BOOKED VISITS
ANNUAL PRODUCTION 30,000 bottles
HECTARES UNDER VINE 8.00
VITICULTURE METHOD Certified Organic

- ○ Breganze Torcolato San Bartolo Ris. '17 — 🍷🍷 5
- ○ Michiel Chardonnay '17 — 🍷🍷 4
- ● Breganze Merlot Masiero '17 — 🍷 3
- ○ Breganze Vespaiolo Brenta '19 — 🍷 3

Villa Canestrari

via Dante Broglio, 2
37030 Colognola ai Colli [VR]
Tel. +39 0457650074
www.villacanestrari.com

CELLAR SALES
PRE-BOOKED VISITS
ANNUAL PRODUCTION 150,000 bottles
HECTARES UNDER VINE 15.00

- ● Amarone della Valpolicella '16 — 🍷🍷 5
- ● Valpolicella Sup. '16 — 🍷🍷 5
- ● Valpolicella Sup. Ripasso I Lasi '16 — 🍷🍷 4
- ● Valpolicella Terre di Lanoli '19 — 🍷 3

Villa Medici

via Campagnol, 9
37066 Sommacampagna [VR]
Tel. +39 045515147
www.cantinavillamedici.it

ANNUAL PRODUCTION 220,000 bottles
HECTARES UNDER VINE 33.00

- ○ Custoza '19 — 🍷🍷 2*
- ○ Custoza Sup. '19 — 🍷🍷 2*
- ● Bardolino '19 — 🍷 2
- ● Bardolino Sup. '17 — 🍷 3

Villa Minelli

via Postioma, 66
31020 Villorba [TV]
Tel. +39 0422912355
www.villaminelli.it

CELLAR SALES
PRE-BOOKED VISITS
ANNUAL PRODUCTION 65,000 bottles
HECTARES UNDER VINE 9.50
SUSTAINABLE WINERY

- ● Cabernet '17 — 🍷🍷 3
- ● Merlot V. V. '16 — 🍷🍷 4
- ○ Chardonnay '19 — 🍷 3
- ● Merlot '17 — 🍷 3

Zardetto

via Martiri delle Foibe, 18
31015 Conegliano [TV]
Tel. +39 0438394969
www.zardettoprosecco.com

CELLAR SALES
ANNUAL PRODUCTION 2,000,000 bottles
HECTARES UNDER VINE 40.00
VITICULTURE METHOD Certified Organic

- ○ Conegliano Valdobbiadene Brut Rive di Ogliano Tre Venti '19 — 🍷🍷 3
- ○ Conegliano Valdobbiadene Extra Brut Viti di San Mor — 🍷🍷 5

FRIULI VENEZIA GIULIA

It seemed as if last year's exploit was an unrepeatable success, yet this year Friuli Venezia Giulia maintained its high quality level and confirmed its excellence. Naturally, the vast majority of awards went to Collio and Colli Orientali, but there were some splendid exceptions, showing that even in the plains, in the right areas, prestigious results can be obtained. This year some 26 wines earned Tre Bicchieri. Sauvignon stands out, having provided 6 of these. 3 were 2019s: Borgo Conventi, Tiare and Volpe Pasini's Zuc di Volpe. 2 more were from 2018: Viarte's Liende and Romans' Pière di Vie. 1 is a 2016 reserve, the Russiz Superiore. Even as a monovarietal, Friuliano (which is behind almost all the region's blends) made a name for itself: there's Schiopetto's, an icon by now, Castello di Spessa's Rassauer and the one produced by Torre Rosazza (all 2019s). They're accompanied by 2018s produced by I Ferretti della Luisa and, for the first time, Tenuta Stella. Speaking of firsts, we mention Polje's Pinot Grigio 19, which beat out the competition. In terms of Pinot Bianco, there were the usual accolades: Doro Princic and Vigneti le Monde, accompanied by an excellent version by Villa Russiz. Closing out the list of monovarietals are 2 whites produced using the ancestral method', with long maceration on the skins. They're the Ribolla Gialla Miklus Natural Art '15 by Draga and the Ribolla Gialla '10 by Damijan Podversic. 9 blends complete the picture: Livon's Braide Alte '18, Jermann's Capo Martino '18, Collavini's Broy '18, Ronco dei Tassi's Fosarin '18, Edi Keber's Collio K '18, Ronco Blanchis's Blanc de Blanchis '17, Tunella's BiancoSesto '18, La Roncaia's Eclisse '18 and Myò by Zorzettig's Fiori di Leonie '18. The fact that only white wines earned Tre Bicchieri attests to just how well suited the territory is to the typology. But there reds, sweet wines and sparklers also stood out during our selections and finals. In closing, we'd like to mention 2 Special Prizes. One is for the Best Value for Money—it's Le Monde's Friuli Pinot Bianco '19. The other is our Solidarity Award, which goes to the Villa Russiz Foundation. For decades Villa Russiz has been using their proceeds to run the Adele Cerruti foster home for youth in difficulty.

Angoris

LOC. ANGORIS, 7
34071 CORMÒNS [GO]
TEL. +39 048160923
www.angoris.com

CELLAR SALES
PRE-BOOKED VISITS
RESTAURANT SERVICE
ANNUAL PRODUCTION 500,000 bottles
HECTARES UNDER VINE 85.00
SUSTAINABLE WINERY

Marta Locatelli has been running this historic winery in Cormons for many years now. Its foundation dates back to 1648 and Locatello Locatelli, who obtained ownership of the estate from the Austrian Emperor Ferdinand III as a reward for his service during the Thirty Years' War. It then passed through several owners, but fate would have it that in 1968, by coincidence, it was acquired by another Locatelli, this time Luciano. The vineyards extend over the most important wine-growing areas of the territory and constitute one of its largest estates. Once again Angoris's wines put in an impeccable overall performance, both the regular, standard-label versions and their reserves. As in previous editions, the wine that most impressed was the Collio Bianco Giulio Locatelli Riserva '18 (Sauvignon, Tocai Friulano and Malvasia Istriana). The Pignolo Giulio Locatelli Riserva '15 also made it into our finals—it's still fruity with an intriguing mineral vein and powerful tannins.

Wine	Rating	Price
○ Collio Bianco Giulio Locatelli Ris. '18	🍷🍷	4
● FCO Pignolo Giulio Locatelli Ris. '15	🍷🍷	5
○ Collio Pinot Grigio '19	🍷🍷	3
○ FCO Chardonnay Spiule Giulio Locatelli Ris. '18	🍷🍷	4
○ FCO Friulano '19	🍷🍷	3
○ FCO Ribolla Gialla '19	🍷🍷	3
● FCO Schioppettino '17	🍷🍷	3
● Friuli Isonzo Pinot Nero Albertina '18	🍷🍷	4
○ Collio Bianco Giulio Locatelli Ris. '17	🍷🍷🍷	4*
○ Collio Bianco Giulio Locatelli Ris. '16	🍷🍷🍷	4*
○ Collio Bianco Giulio Locatelli Ris. '15	🍷🍷🍷	4*
○ FCO Chardonnay Spiule '13	🍷🍷🍷	4*
○ FCO Friulano '15	🍷🍷🍷	3*

Antonutti

FRAZ. COLLOREDO DI PRATO
VIA D'ANTONI, 21
33037 PASIAN DI PRATO [UD]
TEL. +39 0432662001
www.antonuttivini.it

CELLAR SALES
PRE-BOOKED VISITS
ANNUAL PRODUCTION 780,000 bottles
HECTARES UNDER VINE 51.00
SUSTAINABLE WINERY

Casa Vinicola Antonutti is on the brink of turning a hundred. It's a historical, family-run business, with owners Adriana Antonutti and Lino Durandi supported by their children Nicola, Riccardo and Caterina, all of whom have contributed to the winery's growth over time in their own way. As a stylistic choice, their whites don't undergo aging in oak, while their reds, full-bodied and velvety, mature in mid-sized casks. The producer is committed to cultivating Pinot Nero and has a big news in store for next year. The Lindul '16 caresses the palate with velvety sweetness, and leaves it soaked in delicious hints of almond brittle, dried figs, date and melted butter. The Pinot Grigio Ramato '19 is intriguing in color and also on the nose, with fruity whiffs of cherry, raspberry and peach. The Ròs di Murì '16, a blend of Merlot, Cabernet Sauvignon and Refosco, offers up hints of printer's ink, tobacco and coffee.

Wine	Rating	Price
○ Friuli Pinot Grigio Ramato '19	🍷🍷	2*
○ Lindul '16	🍷🍷	6
● Ros di Murì '16	🍷🍷	3
○ Friuli Pinot Grigio '19	🍷	2
● Friuli Refosco dal P. R. '18	🍷	2
○ Friuli Ribolla Gialla On The Move Brut	🍷	3
○ Friuli Sauvignon '19	🍷	2
○ Friuli Traminer Aromatico '19	🍷	2
○ Friuli Grave Pinot Grigio Ramato '16	🍷🍷	3
○ Friuli Grave Traminer Aromatico '17	🍷🍷	3
○ Friuli Pinot Grigio Ramato '18	🍷🍷	3
○ Friuli Traminer Aromatico '18	🍷🍷	3
○ Lindul '15	🍷🍷	6
● Poppone '16	🍷🍷	5
● Ros di Murì '15	🍷🍷	5

Attems

FRAZ. CAPRIVA DEL FRIULI
VIA AQUILEIA, 30
34070 GORIZIA
TEL. +39 0481806098
www.attems.it

CELLAR SALES
PRE-BOOKED VISITS
ANNUAL PRODUCTION 420,000 bottles
HECTARES UNDER VINE 44.00

Owned by the Frescobaldi family since 2000, Attems boasts a fascinating past, one bound up with the history of wine in Friuli Venezia Giulia. In fact, the first document attesting to the Attems dynasty's viticultural landholdings in Collio dates back to the year 1106. A thousand-year-old tradition has made this producer a touchstone, with Count Douglas Attems serving as a key figure. Indeed it was he who founded the Consorzio dei Vini del Collio in 1964, the third in Italy and first in Friuli. For the second year in a row, the Sauvignon Cicinis '18 reached our finals. Special, oval-shaped concrete containers are used for its production. These allow for the formation of convective movements, due to temperature differences, which create currents that stir up the yeasts on the bottom. The Pinot Grigio Ramato '19 is also excellent.

Wine	Glasses	Price
○ Collio Sauvignon Cicins '18	🍷🍷	5
○ Chardonnay '19	🍷🍷	3
○ Collio Ribolla Gialla Trebes '18	🍷🍷	4
○ Pinot Grigio delle Venezie Ramato '19	🍷🍷	3
○ Pinot Grigio delle Venezie '19	🍷	3
○ Ribolla Gialla '19	🍷	3
○ Sauvignon '19	🍷	3
○ Chardonnay '18	🍸🍸	3
○ Chardonnay '17	🍸🍸	3
○ Collio Pinot Grigio '18	🍸🍸	2*
○ Collio Pinot Grigio Ramato '18	🍸🍸	3
○ Collio Ribolla Gialla Trebes '16	🍸🍸	4
○ Collio Sauvignon Blanc Cicinis '16	🍸🍸	5
○ Collio Sauvignon Cicinis '17	🍸🍸	5
○ Pinot Grigio Ramato '16	🍸🍸	3*
○ Sauvignon Blanc '17	🍸🍸	3

Bastianich

LOC. GAGLIANO
VIA DARNAZZACCO, 44/2
33043 CIVIDALE DEL FRIULI [UD]
TEL. +39 0432700943
www.bastianich.com

CELLAR SALES
PRE-BOOKED VISITS
ACCOMMODATION AND RESTAURANT SERVICE
ANNUAL PRODUCTION 270,000 bottles
HECTARES UNDER VINE 35.00

Joe Bastianich and his mother Lidia deserve credit for being true ambassadors of the 'Made in Italy' brand, exporting and promoting the excellence of Italian gastronomy and wine overseas. In 1997 Joe decided to return to his family's homeland, buying a farm on the hills of Buttrio and Premariacco and founding a winery. In 2006 he completed the investment with the acquisition of another property, 20 hectares of vineyards complete with cellar, in Gagliano, near Cividale del Friuli. It now serves as their production headquarters. The excellent performance put in by their 2019s wasn't enough to oust the undisputed dominance of the Vespa Bianco '17 which, once again, landed a place in our finals. A well-proven mix of Chardonnay, Sauvignon and Picolit, it delivers fragrant hints of peach, apricot and acacia honey, satisfying the palate with the weight and crunchiness of its palate.

Wine	Glasses	Price
○ Vespa Bianco '17	🍷🍷	5
○ FCO Friulano '19	🍷🍷	3
○ FCO Pinot Bianco '19	🍷🍷	3
○ FCO Pinot Grigio '19	🍷🍷	3
● FCO Refosco P. R. '18	🍷🍷	3
○ FCO Ribolla Gialla '19	🍷🍷	3
○ FCO Sauvignon '19	🍷	3
○ COF Tocai Friulano Plus '02	🍸🍸🍸	3*
○ Vespa Bianco '04	🍸🍸🍸	4
○ Vespa Bianco '03	🍸🍸🍸	4
○ Vespa Bianco '01	🍸🍸🍸	4
○ Vespa Bianco '00	🍸🍸🍸	3
○ Vespa Bianco '99	🍸🍸🍸	3*
○ Vespa Bianco '16	🍸🍸	5
○ Vespa Bianco '15	🍸🍸	5
● Vespa Rosso '15	🍸🍸	5

Tenuta Borgo Conventi

via Contessa Beretta
34072 Farra d'Isonzo [GO]
Tel. +39 0481888004
www.borgoconventi.it

CELLAR SALES
PRE-BOOKED VISITS
ACCOMMODATION
ANNUAL PRODUCTION 300,000 bottles
HECTARES UNDER VINE 35.00
SUSTAINABLE WINERY

Founded in 1975 by Gianni Vescovo, in April 2019 Borgo Conventi passed from the Folonari family, who'd been looking after it since 2001, to the Moretti Polegato family, owners of the prestigious Tenuta Villa Sandi, one of nearby Veneto's regional jewels. Agronomy and responsibility for production have been entrusted to their in-house enologist Paolo Corso, whose task it is to pursue a philosophy inspired by sustainability and low environmental impact. Among the wines presented this year, the award for best red goes to the Merlot '16 for the pleasan-tness of its aromas, still quite fruity and slightly spicy. However, it's the Sauvignon '19 that really surprises: both on the nose and the palate, it faithfully expresses the grape's aromatic characteri-stics, delivering harmony and balance, and a deep, clean finish. The Schioppettino '16 and Pinot Grigio '19 are also excellent in their categories.

Wine	Glasses	Price
○ Collio Sauvignon '19	▼▼▼	3*
● Collio Merlot '16	▼▼	3*
○ Collio Pinot Grigio '19	▼▼	3
○ Collio Ribolla Gialla '19	▼▼	3
● Schioppettino '16	▼▼	4
○ Collio Friulano '19	▼	3
● Braida Nuova '91	▽▽▽	
● Braida Nuova '13	▽▽	5
● Braida Nuova '12	▽▽	5
○ Collio Chardonnay '18	▽▽	3
○ Collio Friulano '17	▽▽	3
○ Collio Pinot Grigio '18	▽▽	3
○ Collio Ribolla Gialla '18	▽▽	3*
○ Collio Sauvignon '18	▽▽	3
○ Friuli Isonzo Friulano '18	▽▽	2*
○ Friuli Isonzo Pinot Grigio '18	▽▽	3
● Schioppettino '14	▽▽	4

Borgo delle Oche

via Borgo Alpi, 5
33098 Valvasone Arzene [PN]
Tel. +39 0434840640
www.borgodelleoche.it

CELLAR SALES
PRE-BOOKED VISITS
ACCOMMODATION
ANNUAL PRODUCTION 35,000 bottles
HECTARES UNDER VINE 7.00
SUSTAINABLE WINERY

Borgo delle Oche is owned by Luisa Menini, a descendant of a family whose viticultural roots go back many generations. It owes its name to the small village in which it's located, situated in the splendid medieval centre of Valvasone, in the province of Pordenone. Luisa works in perfect synergy with her husband, Nicola Pittini, she in the countryside and he in the cellar. Choosing the path of low yields, they practice quality wine growing, which has earned them a place among the region's best producers, on par with wineries operating at higher elevations. The quality level of their entire range, even if it fluctuates according to seasonal conditions, is particularly notable considering their great prices. This year the Malvasia '18 was the most appreciated, standing out for its intense aromas of hay, wheat and lime blossom honey, and gratifying the palate with its marked minerality. The Traminer Passito Alba '18 and the Pinot Grigio '19 are also excellent.

Wine	Glasses	Price
○ Friuli Malvasia '18	▼▼	3
○ Friuli Pinot Grigio '19	▼▼	2*
○ Terra e Cielo Extra Brut M. Cl. '15	▼▼	4
○ Traminer Passito Alba '18	▼▼	5
○ Friuli Friulano '19	▼	3
○ Friuli Sauvignon '19	▼	3
● Merlot '17	▼	2
● Refosco P. R. '16	▼	3
○ Traminer '19	▼	3
○ Friuli Friulano '17	▽▽	2*
○ Friuli Pinot Grigio '17	▽▽	2*
○ Malvasia '16	▽▽	2*
● Merlot '16	▽▽	2*
● Merlot '15	▽▽	2*
● Refosco P. R. '15	▽▽	3
○ Traminer Aromatico '18	▽▽	2*
○ Traminer Passito Alba '17	▽▽	5

★Borgo San Daniele

via San Daniele, 28
34071 Cormòns [GO]
Tel. +39 048160552
www.borgosandaniele.it

CELLAR SALES
PRE-BOOKED VISITS
ACCOMMODATION
ANNUAL PRODUCTION 60,000 bottles
HECTARES UNDER VINE 18.75
VITICULTURE METHOD Certified Organic
SUSTAINABLE WINERY

A few hectares of vineyards inherited from grandfather Antonio in 1990 inspired the then young brother-sister team of Mauro and Alessandra to change their lives, dedicating themselves exclusively to looking after those precious rows of vines. It was a courageous choice, which immediately paid off. The few wines produced are cared for down to the last detail, fully expressing the potential of the territory. The grapes bear the name Arbis, which means herbs, to remind us that spontaneous herbs are left to grow in the vineyards so as to mitigate the vigor of the vines and the negative effects of monoculture. The Arbis Blanc '17 (Sauvignon, Chardonnay, Pinot Bianco and Tocai Friulano) put in an excellent performance, with its beautiful floral bouquet, which lingers on the palate and even beyond. Equal praise for the Pignolo Arbis Ròs '15 and for two vermouths, one white and one red, called Santòn, which weren't reviewed in the guide but testify, nevertheless, to their embrace of wine-derived products.

Wine	Rating
○ Arbis Blanc '17	TT 5
● Friuli Isonzo Pignolo Arbis Ròs '15	TT 6
○ Friuli Isonzo Friulano '18	TT 4
○ Friuli Isonzo Malvasia '18	TT 4
○ Friuli Isonzo Pinot Grigio '18	TT 4
○ Arbis Blanc '10	YYY 4*
○ Arbis Blanc '09	YYY 4
○ Arbis Blanc '05	YYY 4
○ Friuli Isonzo Arbis Blanc '02	YYY 4
○ Friuli Isonzo Friulano '08	YYY 4*
○ Friuli Isonzo Friulano '07	YYY 4*
○ Friuli Isonzo Pinot Grigio '04	YYY 4
○ Friuli Isonzo Pinot Grigio '99	YYY
○ Friuli Isonzo Tocai Friulano '03	YYY 3
● Gortmarin '03	YYY 5

Borgo Savaian

via Savaian, 36
34071 Cormòns [GO]
Tel. +39 048160725
Via Savaian

CELLAR SALES
PRE-BOOKED VISITS
ANNUAL PRODUCTION 100,000 bottles
HECTARES UNDER VINE 18.00

In Cormons, at the foot of Mount Quarin, in the small village from which it takes its name, Bastiani serves as a classic example of a family-run business. In 2001 Stefano Bastiani, together with his sister Rosanna, took over from their father, Mario, began a new chapter. Fresh off their studies but already experienced, the two handily faced the problems deriving from seasonal variables and after care. Their Borgo Savaian wines have for some time now boasted high quality standards, both the Collio and Friuli Isonzo. The excellent performance put in by their entire range was topped off by the Pinot Grigio '19, which we appreciated for its perfect gustatory balance, this after delighting the nose with strong whiffs of Williams pear, ripe melon and macaroons. The Aransat is a perfectly worthy orange wine. In the last edition we reported it as a curious bottle, but this year it once again demonstrated its great approach, both on the nose and on the palate.

Wine	Rating
○ Collio Pinot Grigio '19	TT 3*
○ Aransat	TT 3
○ Collio Ribolla Gialla '19	TT 3
● Friuli Isonzo Cabernet Franc '18	TT 3
○ Friuli Isonzo Malvasia '19	TT 3
● Tolrem Merlot '15	TT 5
○ Collio Friulano '19	T 3
○ Friuli Isonzo Traminer Aromatico '19	T 3
○ Collio Friulano '18	YY 3
○ Collio Friulano '15	YY 3*
○ Collio Pinot Grigio '18	YY 3
○ Collio Ribolla Gialla '18	YY 3
○ Collio Sauvignon '16	YY 3*
○ Friuli Isonzo Malvasia '18	YY 3*
● Friuli Isonzo Merlot '17	YY 3
○ Friuli Isonzo Sauvignon '18	YY 3

Cav. Emiro Bortolusso

via Oltregorgo, 10
33050 Carlino [UD]
Tel. +39 043167596
www.bortolusso.it

CELLAR SALES
PRE-BOOKED VISITS
ACCOMMODATION
ANNUAL PRODUCTION 120,000 bottles
HECTARES UNDER VINE 40.00

The natural environment in which the winery is situated is one of great beauty. In fact, it overlooks the splendid scenery of the Adriatic Riviera, close to the wildlife oasis of Marano Lagunare. Thus it benefits from the sea breezes that caress the vineyards, allowing the grapes to ripen perfectly and helping to fix varietal aromas. Sergio and Clara Bortolusso, taking advantage of the teachings and experience of their father, Emiro, offer a wide range of high-quality wines at very competitive prices. As usual, they submitted a selection of wines from the last vintage, which we appreciated for the marked expression of the varietal characteristics of each grape variety. The common thread that unites them is minerality, combined with lightness and drinkability. The Sauvignon '19 calls up fragrances of citrus fruits, especially grapefruit, while the Chardonnay '19 proves reminiscent of Malaga ice cream.

Wine	Rating
○ Chardonnay '19	TT 2*
○ Sauvignon '19	TT 2*
○ Friuli Friulano '19	T 2
○ Friuli Pinot Grigio '19	T 2
○ Malvasia '19	T 2
○ Traminer Aromatico '19	T 2
○ Friuli Annia Friulano '17	YY 2*
○ Friuli Annia Malvasia '17	YY 2*
○ Friuli Annia Pinot Grigio '17	YY 2*
○ Friuli Friulano '18	YY 2*
○ Friuli Pinot Grigio '18	YY 2*
○ Malvasia '18	YY 2*
○ Malvasia '17	YY 2*
○ Malvasia '16	YY 2*
○ Sauvignon '18	YY 2*
○ Sauvignon '17	YY 2*

Branko

loc. Zegla, 20
34071 Cormòns [GO]
Tel. +39 0481639826
www.brankowines.com

CELLAR SALES
PRE-BOOKED VISITS
ANNUAL PRODUCTION 45,000 bottles
HECTARES UNDER VINE 9.00

The winery now managed by Igor Erzetic bears the name of his father, Branko. It was he who, in 1950, had the foresight to believe in the territory's potential. Now that small operation has become a benchmark for admirers of Collio's whites. Much of the property under vine can be found around the winery in Zegla, near Cormons, descending gently from the surrounding hills. Igor's wines are exemplary in terms of cleanness and precision, respecting their varietal peculiarities and serving as splendid ambassadors of the territory. Blending Malvasia Istriana, Tocai Friulano and Sauvignon grapes, Igor Branko invented the producer's flagship wine, which, with a play on words, he decided to call 'Capo Branko'. It's a first-rate wine that masterfully brings together softness, fragrance and balance, offering up exquisite aromas of medicinal herbs and tropical fruit. The Friulano '19 is also excellent.

Wine	Rating
○ Capo Branko '19	TT 5
○ Collio Friulano '19	TT 4
○ Collio Chardonnay '19	TT 4
○ Collio Pinot Grigio '19	TT 4
● Red Branko '17	TT 5
○ Collio Pinot Grigio '14	YYY 4*
○ Collio Pinot Grigio '08	YYY 3*
○ Collio Pinot Grigio '07	YYY 3
○ Collio Pinot Grigio '06	YYY 3
○ Collio Pinot Grigio '05	YYY 3
○ Collio Chardonnay '18	YY 4
○ Collio Chardonnay '17	YY 4
○ Collio Chardonnay '16	YY 4
○ Collio Friulano '18	YY 4
○ Collio Sauvignon '16	YY 4
○ Collio Sauvignon '15	YY 4

La Buse dal Lôf

via Ronchi, 90
33040 Prepotto [UD]
Tel. +39 0432701523
www.labusedallof.com

CELLAR SALES
PRE-BOOKED VISITS
ANNUAL PRODUCTION 100,000 bottles
HECTARES UNDER VINE 25.00

Founded in 1972 by Giuseppe Pavan, La Buse dal Lôf is a thriving producer in the regional firmament. Today it's managed by his son Michele, whose philosophy is grounded in Friuli's wine-growing traditions, both in terms of viticulture and the approach to wine-making, which are always respectful of the grapes' varietal characteristics. The vineyards unfold in Prepotto, home of Schioppettino, an area that enjoys an ideal microclimate and Eocene soil that slopes down towards the plain. The Schioppettino di Prepotto '16 and the Cabernet Sauvignon '16, which were not presented in the last edition, are proof of how an extra year of aging can benefit their organoleptic characteristics, both aromas and taste. Among their regular, standard-label versions, we appreciated the Friulano '19 for its marked varietal expression, and the Pinot Grigio '19, for its delicious nuances of dried flowers and rose-water.

Wine	Rating
● FCO Cabernet Sauvignon '16	🍷🍷 4
○ FCO Friulano '19	🍷🍷 3
○ FCO Pinot Grigio '19	🍷🍷 3
● FCO Refosco P. R. '16	🍷🍷 3
● FCO Schioppettino di Prepotto '16	🍷🍷 4
○ FCO Ribolla Gialla '19	🍷 3
○ FCO Sauvignon '19	🍷 3
○ FCO Verduzzo Friulano '17	🍷 3
○ FCO Chardonnay '18	🍷🍷 3
○ FCO Chardonnay '16	🍷🍷 3
○ FCO Friulano '18	🍷🍷 3
● FCO Merlot '17	🍷🍷 3
● FCO Merlot '16	🍷🍷 3
● FCO Refosco P. R. '15	🍷🍷 3
○ FCO Sauvignon '18	🍷🍷 3
● FCO Schioppettino di Prepotto '15	🍷🍷 4
● FCO Schioppettino di Prepotto '13	🍷🍷 4

Valentino Butussi

via Prà di Corte, 1
33040 Corno di Rosazzo [UD]
Tel. +39 0432759194
www.butussi.it

CELLAR SALES
PRE-BOOKED VISITS
ACCOMMODATION
ANNUAL PRODUCTION 110,000 bottles
HECTARES UNDER VINE 20.00
VITICULTURE METHOD Certified Organic
SUSTAINABLE WINERY

One of Corno di Rosazzo's gems, it was Valentino Butussi who founded the winery in 1910. Then came his son Angelo and now the new generation constituted of Tobia, Filippo, Mattia and Erika. Theirs is a high-level family business based on the values of rural culture, team spirit, the proper distribution of work and a sense of responsibility. The conversion of the vineyards to certified organic farming was the logical consequence of respect for the environment and the healthiness of their wines. The Bianco White Angel '18 (Chardonnay, Sauvignon and Pinot Bianco) leads a battery of wines that, especially when it comes to the reserve versions, performs at a very high level in terms of aromatic complexity and gustatory substance. But just getting the better of it are the Rosso Godje Ris. '16, a blend of Refosco and Peduncolo Rosso, and the Sauvignon Genesis '18, a wine characterized by a pleasant hint of aniseed.

Wine	Rating
○ FCO Bianco White Angel '18	🍷🍷 4
● FCO Pignolo '15	🍷🍷 5
○ FCO Pinot Grigio Ramato Madonna d'Aiuto '18	🍷🍷 7
○ FCO Ribolla Gialla '19	🍷🍷 2*
● FCO Rosso Godje Ris. '16	🍷🍷 7
● FCO Rosso Santuari Ris. '16	🍷🍷 5
○ FCO Sauvignon Genesis '18	🍷🍷 4
○ FCO Verduzzo Friulano '17	🍷🍷 3
○ FCO Friulano '19	🍷 2
○ FCO Pinot Grigio '19	🍷 2
○ FCO Sauvignon '19	🍷 3
○ FCO Bianco White Angel '14	🍷🍷 4
○ FCO Chardonnay '17	🍷🍷 2*
● FCO Rosso Santuari Ris. '13	🍷🍷 5
○ FCO Sauvignon Genesis '15	🍷🍷 4

Maurizio Buzzinelli

LOC. PRADIS, 20
34071 CORMÒNS [GO]
TEL. +39 048160902
www.buzzinelli.it

CELLAR SALES
PRE-BOOKED VISITS
ACCOMMODATION
ANNUAL PRODUCTION 120,000 bottles
HECTARES UNDER VINE 35.00

The winery managed by Maurizio Buzzinelli contributes, together with other splendid local producers, to promoting a territory of true excellence along the gentle Pradis hills. It's a kind of amphitheatre, kissed by the sun and the breezes of the nearby Adriatic Sea. Maurizio personally oversees the entire production chain, obtaining outstanding results both from the white grapes grown on the Collio and from red grape varieties. The latter draw on the favorable qualities of the ferrous soils that characterize the Friuli Isonzo denomination. All the wines presented are 2019s, and virtually all of them earned the same score. This testifies to the equal attention paid to each individual grape variety, the producer's ability to preserve their varietal characteristics and bring out the territory's potential. They all exhibit excellent drinkability, proving lean, fruity and fragrant, especially the Ribolla Gialla '19, which excels for its aromatic elegance.

Wine	Rating
○ Collio Chardonnay '19	🍷🍷 3
○ Collio Friulano '19	🍷🍷 3
○ Collio Malvasia '19	🍷🍷 2*
○ Collio Ribolla Gialla '19	🍷🍷 3
○ Collio Sauvignon '19	🍷🍷 3
○ Collio Traminer Aromatico '19	🍷🍷 3
○ Collio Friulano '18	ΥΥ 3*
○ Collio Friulano '17	ΥΥ 3
○ Collio Friulano '16	ΥΥ 3*
○ Collio Malvasia '18	ΥΥ 2*
○ Collio Malvasia '16	ΥΥ 2*
○ Collio Malvasia '15	ΥΥ 2*
○ Collio Pinot Grigio '17	ΥΥ 3
○ Collio Ribolla Gialla '18	ΥΥ 3
○ Collio Sauvignon '17	ΥΥ 3
○ Collio Sauvignon '16	ΥΥ 3
○ Collio Traminer Aromatico '17	ΥΥ 3

Ca' Bolani

VIA CA' BOLANI, 2
33052 CERVIGNANO DEL FRIULI [UD]
TEL. +39 043132670
www.cabolani.it

CELLAR SALES
PRE-BOOKED VISITS
ANNUAL PRODUCTION 1,820,500 bottles
HECTARES UNDER VINE 570.00

Tenuta Ca' Bolani, the region's largest producer, is situated in the heart of the Friuli Aquileia appellation. It was owned by the count Bolani family and acquired by the Zonins in 1970. They restored it to its former glory by renovating the farm center and building a wine cellar equipped with advanced technology. In addition to their well-established selection of whites, their outstanding range includes finely crafted reds, with particular attention to Refosco dal Peduncolo Rosso, a traditional and time-honored grape. The Pinot Bianco Opimio '18 put in an excellent performance. It's a highly balanced and linear wine, with a perfect nose/palate symmetry that plays on fruity and creamy scents. The Sauvignon Aquilis '18 stands out for its fragrance, offering up citrus and vegetable notes. The Refosco P.R. '18 calls up cherry jam and golden-leaf tobacco. Their regular, standard-label versions stand out for their faithful varietal expressions.

Wine	Rating
○ Friuli Aquileia Pinot Bianco Opimio '18	🍷🍷 5
● Friuli Aquileia Refosco P. R. '18	🍷🍷 3
○ Friuli Aquileia Sauvignon Aquilis '18	🍷🍷 5
○ Friuli Aquileia Friulano '19	🍷 4
○ Friuli Aquileia Pinot Bianco '19	🍷 3
○ Friuli Aquileia Pinot Grigio '19	🍷 3
○ Friuli Aquileia Sauvignon '19	🍷 3
○ Friuli Aquileia Traminer Aromatico '19	🍷 3
○ Prosecco Brut	🍷 3
○ Friuli Aquileia Pinot Bianco '09	ΥΥΥ 2*
○ Friuli Aquileia Pinot Grigio '18	ΥΥ 3*
○ Friuli Aquileia Sauvignon Aquilis '16	ΥΥ 5
○ Friuli Aquileia Sauvignon Aquilis '14	ΥΥ 2*

Ca' dei Faggi

FRAZ. RASCHIACCO
VIA CITTÀ DI NAVE, 10
33040 FAEDIS [UD]
TEL. +39 3207460693
www.cadeifaggi.it

PRE-BOOKED VISITS
ACCOMMODATION
ANNUAL PRODUCTION 100,000 bottles
HECTARES UNDER VINE 20.00

Ca' dei Faggi is situated in Raschiacco di Faedis, in the heart of the Friuli Colli Orientali appellation, a time-honored area for producing regional wines thanks to a particularly favorable terroir. The winery, founded in 1912 by the Perabò family, keeps alive a passion for viticulture and enology thanks to Maria and her son Gianni Berton, its current owner. Tradition is expressed in a range of white and red wines of excellent structure and, above all, their Refosco di Faedis, the most representative native local variety. Last year they almost tiptoed into our guide. This year they're back with a selection that comprises all the typologies produced. It's allowed us a wider overview, with pretty flattering results, making this new, lovely winery among the most notable operating in this stretch of hills.

Wine	Rating
○ COF Picolit '17	🍷🍷 7
● FCO Cabernet Franc '19	🍷🍷 2*
○ FCO Friulano '18	🍷🍷 2*
● FCO Merlot '19	🍷🍷 2*
○ FCO Pinot Grigio '19	🍷🍷 2*
● FCO Refosco di Faedis '16	🍷🍷 5
● FCO Refosco P. R. '19	🍷🍷 2*
● FCO Rosso Tre Fadis Neri '17	🍷🍷 5
○ FCO Sauvignon '19	🍷🍷 3
○ FCO Bianco Tre Fradis Blanc '18	🍷 3
○ FCO Ribolla Gialla '19	🍷 2
○ Ribolla Gialla Brut	🍷 2
⊙ Rosè '19	🍷 2
○ FCO Friulano Perabò '17	🍸🍸 3
● FCO Refosco di Faedis '15	🍸🍸 5
● FCO Rosso Tre Fadis Neri '16	🍸🍸 5
○ FCO Sauvignon Perabò '17	🍸🍸 3

Ca' Tullio

VIA BELIGNA, 41
33051 AQUILEIA [UD]
TEL. +39 0431919700
www.catullio.it

CELLAR SALES
PRE-BOOKED VISITS
ANNUAL PRODUCTION 200,000 bottles
HECTARES UNDER VINE 100.00

Ca' Tullio is situated in a large building dating back to the early 20th century and originally used for drying tobacco. In 1994 it was bought by Paolo Calligaris and transformed into a modern, well-equipped production facility. Most of the grapes are cultivated on the hills of Manzano, in Sdricca, in Friuli Colli Orientali, while other vineyards extend around the winery. Here, on the sandy soils of Viola, it's still possible to cultivate ungrafted Traminer. The Friulano '19 leads a series of wines characterized by commendable craftsmanship and varietal expression. It was the one that most impressed for its intensity, complexity and aromatic pleasantness but, above all, for its substance and sapidity. Right behind it is the Chardonnay '19, which offers up delicious flowery hints of lily of the valley and hawthorn, as well as gratifying fruity notes.

Wine	Rating
○ FCO Chardonnay '19	🍷🍷 2*
○ FCO Friulano '19	🍷🍷 2*
● Patriarca Refosco P. R. '18	🍷🍷 3
● FCO Pignolo '16	🍷 3
○ FCO Pinot Grigio '19	🍷 2
○ FCO Ribolla Gialla '19	🍷 3
○ Friuli Aquileia Traminer Viola '19	🍷 2
○ FCO Chardonnay '18	🍸🍸 2*
○ FCO Chardonnay '17	🍸🍸 2*
○ FCO Friulano '18	🍸🍸 2*
○ FCO Friulano '17	🍸🍸 2*
● FCO Pignolo '14	🍸🍸 3
○ FCO Pinot Grigio '18	🍸🍸 2*
○ FCO Pinot Grigio '17	🍸🍸 2*
○ FCO Ribolla Gialla '18	🍸🍸 3
● FCO Schioppettino '15	🍸🍸 3
○ Friuli Aquileia Traminer Viola '18	🍸🍸 2*

Cadibon

LOC. CASALI GALLO, 1
33040 CORNO DI ROSAZZO [UD]
TEL. +39 0432759316
www.cadibon.com

CELLAR SALES
PRE-BOOKED VISITS
ACCOMMODATION
ANNUAL PRODUCTION 50,000 bottles
HECTARES UNDER VINE 14.00
VITICULTURE METHOD Certified Organic

The word 'Cadibon' is a clear invitation to visit the winery. In fact, in local dialect it means, "Here in the winery of the Bon family". The name was chosen in 1977 by Gianni Bon for this flourishing operation, now run by young Luca and Francesca, who are availing themselves of abundant space and state-of-the-art equipment. The courageous choice to opt for natural fermentation has benefited the immediacy of their wines which, although made through a multifaceted process, are distinguished by their freshness and drinkability, as well as enjoying organic certification. The Pinot Grigio '19 topped our preferences for the pleasantness of its bouquet and, above all, for its sapidity and length on the palate. The white Ronco del Nonno '19 (Sauvignon, Chardonnay and Verduzzo Friuliano) brings together elegance and complexity on the nose, while the palate comes through pervasive and velvety. The red Epoca '17 (Merlot and Refosco dal Peduncolo Rosso) proves spicy, structured and juicy.

Wine	Rating
○ Collio Chardonnay '19	▼▼ 4
○ Collio Pinot Grigio '19	▼▼ 3
● Epoca '17	▼▼ 5
○ FCO Friulano Bontaj '19	▼▼ 4
● FCO Merlot '18	▼▼ 3
● FCO Schioppettino '18	▼▼ 3
○ Ronco del Nonno Bianco '19	▼▼ 4
○ Collio Sauvignon '19	▼ 4
● FCO Refosco P. R. '18	▼ 3
○ FCO Ribolla Gialla '19	▼ 4
○ Moscato Giallo '19	▼ 3
○ Collio Sauvignon '18	▽▽ 3
○ Collio Sauvignon Lavoron '18	▽▽ 3
○ FCO Friulano '18	▽▽ 3
○ FCO Malvasia '18	▽▽ 3*
● FCO Merlot '17	▽▽ 3
○ FCO Ribolla Gialla '18	▽▽ 3

Canus

LOC. CASALI GALLO
VIA GRAMOGLIANO, 21
33040 CORNO DI ROSAZZO [UD]
TEL. +39 0432759427
www.canus.it

CELLAR SALES
PRE-BOOKED VISITS
ANNUAL PRODUCTION 60,000 bottles
HECTARES UNDER VINE 18.00

Canus stands perched on the hill of Gramogliano, in Corno di Rosazzo. It has deep roots—in fact, over the years the property has changed owners several times and only in 2004 was it given its current name. Canus is a Latin term that refers the value of wisdom and the benefits of aging. Since 2015 it's been owned by Ottorino Casonato ('Otto' to his friends). His is a story of returning to one's origins, to the countryside abandoned as a boy in pursuit of his dreams. In just a few years he's converted the winery, positioning it among the region's best. This year the honor of participating in our final selections went to the Friulano '18, one of the best in its category, a wine accentuated by scents of bitter almond and pleasantness in the mouth. Kudos to the exotic and elegant Bianco Gramogliano '18 (Sauvignon, Chardonnay and Ribolla Gialla), and the Rosso Mezzo Secolo '13 (Merlot and Refosco dal Peduncolo Rosso), a robust, round wine.

Wine	Rating
○ FCO Friulano '18	▼▼ 4
○ FCO Bianco Gramogliano '18	▼▼ 4
○ FCO Chardonnay '18	▼▼ 4
● FCO Merlot '13	▼▼ 5
● FCO Pignolo '12	▼▼ 6
○ FCO Pinot Grigio '18	▼▼ 4
○ FCO Ribolla Gialla '18	▼▼ 4
● FCO Rosso Mezzo Secolo '13	▼▼ 6
○ FCO Bianco Gramogliano '16	▽▽ 4
○ FCO Chardonnay '17	▽▽ 4
○ FCO Chardonnay '16	▽▽ 4
○ FCO Friulano '17	▽▽ 4
● FCO Merlot '12	▽▽ 5
● FCO Pignolo '11	▽▽ 6
○ FCO Pinot Grigio '17	▽▽ 4
○ FCO Pinot Grigio '16	▽▽ 4
○ FCO Ribolla Gialla '17	▽▽ 4

Fernanda Cappello

s.da di Sequals, 15
33090 Sequals [PN]
Tel. +39 042793291
www.fernandacappello.it

CELLAR SALES
PRE-BOOKED VISITS
RESTAURANT SERVICE
ANNUAL PRODUCTION 90,000 bottles
HECTARES UNDER VINE 126.00
SUSTAINABLE WINERY

In 1988 architect Fernanda Cappello decided to leave her profession in order to devote herself completely to wine, which her father had been involved in since the late 1960s. The estate unfolds on alluvial land between the Cellina and Meduna rivers, just below the Sequals hills, in Pordenone. Increasing ambitions led her to strike up a collaboration with enologist Fabio Coser, and the results have projected the winery to the heights of excellence in western Friuli. The Friulano '19 arouses curiosity with its delicate whiffs of hawthorn, which delight the nose and, above all, for sensations that linger gratifyingly on the palate. The Traminer Aromatico Primo '18 calls up yellow rose, broom, acacia honey and exotic fruit, while in the mouth it proves vivid and long-lasting. The rest of the range also performed well with reviews that, especially in light of the price, deserve consideration.

● Friuli Grave Cabernet Franc '18	▼▼ 2*
○ Friuli Grave Friulano '19	▼▼ 2*
○ Friuli Grave Pinot Grigio '19	▼▼ 2*
○ Friuli Grave Sauvignon '19	▼▼ 2*
○ Friuli Grave Traminer Aromatico Primo '18	▼▼ 3
● Friuli Grave Merlot '16	▼ 2
● Friuli Grave Pinot Nero '18	▼ 2
○ Friuli Grave Traminer Aromatico '19	▼ 2
○ Prosecco Brut	▼ 2
○ Prosecco Extra Dry	▼ 2
○ Friuli Grave Chardonnay Perla dei Sassi '15	▽▽ 3
● Friuli Grave Merlot '14	▽▽ 2*
○ Friuli Grave Pinot Bianco '18	▽▽ 2*
○ Friuli Grave Pinot Grigio '18	▽▽ 2*
○ Friuli Grave Traminer Aromatico '18	▽▽ 2*

Il Carpino

loc. Sovenza, 14a
34070 San Floriano del Collio [GO]
Tel. +39 0481884097
www.ilcarpino.com

CELLAR SALES
PRE-BOOKED VISITS
ANNUAL PRODUCTION 70,000 bottles
HECTARES UNDER VINE 16.00

Despite their agricultural roots, Anna and Franco Sosol went into different lines of work. In 1987, however, they decided to join forces by going back to their rural origins and founding the Il Carpino brand. The family approach allows for, and requires that, all stages of production, from vineyard management to vinification and aging, be overseen carefully. Their niche wines are the result of slow maceration with ancestral techniques, while their Vigna Runc line is vinified in steel. After a long period of bottle aging, their 2016s are in excellent form, taking home very high marks and standing out during our final selections. On the nose the Malvasia '16 is complex and alluring with frequent toasty whiffs reminiscent, surprisingly, of Cognac. The Exordium '16 and Vis Uvae '16 are unique interpretations of Friulian Tocai and Pinot Grigio.

○ Exordium '16	▼▼ 5
○ Malvasia '16	▼▼ 5
○ Vis Uvae '16	▼▼ 5
● Cabernet Sauvignon Special Edition 30 '11	▼▼ 7
○ Collio Bianco V. Runc '10	▽▽▽ 2*
○ Collio Malvasia V. Runc '11	▽▽▽ 3*
○ Malvasia '15	▽▽▽ 5
○ Malvasia '11	▽▽▽ 5
● Rubrum '99	▽▽▽ 3*
○ Chardonnay '12	▽▽ 5
○ Collio Friulano V. Runc '17	▽▽ 3*
○ Collio Ribolla Gialla V. Runc '12	▽▽ 5
○ Exordium '15	▽▽ 5
○ Exordium '13	▽▽ 5
○ Exordium '12	▽▽ 5

Castello di Buttrio

via del Pozzo, 5
33042 Buttrio [UD]
Tel. +39 0432673015
www.castellodibuttrio.it

CELLAR SALES
PRE-BOOKED VISITS
ACCOMMODATION AND RESTAURANT SERVICE
ANNUAL PRODUCTION 60,000 bottles
HECTARES UNDER VINE 25.00

Buttrio's origins date back to the 11th century, and its history is bound up with the Castle, which was destroyed and rebuilt several times. In 1994 the estate was purchased by Marco Felluga, who began transforming it into a wine estate. He then passed it on to his daughter Alessandra, who restored the splendor of the past to those extraordinary walls. The stylistic change introduced by Trentino enologist Hartmann Donà has led to further growth, rewarding Alessandra's always wise choices. Their wines put in an outstanding overall performance, spearheaded by the Sauvignon Ettaro Riserva '18, which earned a place in our finals. A marked hint of citrus is followed by aromas of magnolia, boxwood and wild fennel. We also very much appreciated the Rosso Uve Carate Riserva '15, a monovarietal Merlot redolent of licorice, capers and tobacco.

Wine	Rating	
○ FCO Sauvignon Ettaro Ris. '18	🍷🍷	6
○ FCO Friulano '19	🍷🍷	4
○ FCO Ribolla Gialla '19	🍷🍷	4
● FCO Rosso Uve Carate Ris. '15	🍷🍷	7
○ FCO Sauvignon '19	🍷	3
○ FCO Bianco Mon Blanc '16	🍷🍷	3
○ FCO Bianco Mon Blanc '15	🍷🍷	3
○ FCO Bianco Torre Butria Ris. '13	🍷🍷	5
○ FCO Friulano '18	🍷🍷	4
● FCO Merlot '16	🍷🍷	4
● FCO Merlot Uve Carate Ris. '13	🍷🍷	3*
● FCO Refosco P. R. '16	🍷🍷	4
● FCO Rosso Mon Rouge '14	🍷🍷	3
○ FCO Sauvignon '18	🍷🍷	3
○ FCO Sauvignon '15	🍷🍷	3

★Castello di Spessa

via Spessa, 1
34070 Capriva del Friuli [GO]
Tel. +39 048160445
www.castellodispessa.it

CELLAR SALES
PRE-BOOKED VISITS
ACCOMMODATION AND RESTAURANT SERVICE
ANNUAL PRODUCTION 450,000 bottles
HECTARES UNDER VINE 90.00

Immersed in the greenery of a magnificent Italian garden, the Castle of Spessa stands elegantly in the heart of the Collio. Its origins date back to the 1200s and, for centuries, the manor house was home to Friulian nobility. In 1987 Loretto Pali created the winery there, converting the neighboring vineyards and starting an upward trajectory that soon allowed him to achieve excellence. For some years now he has been benefiting from the skills of expert enologist Enrico Paternoster, to whom he's entrusted the task of conferring leanness and elegance to the intrinsic power of the wines. Once again this year 3 wines were in our finals; the Friulano Rassauer '19 was first in its category, taking home Tre Bicchieri. The Pinot Bianco Santarosa '19 and the Sauvignon Segrè '19 also put in extraordinary performances. Both wines have earned top marks several times in past editions, and have maintained a level of excellence over time that's to be envied.

Wine	Rating	
○ Collio Friulano Rassauer '19	🍷🍷🍷	3*
○ Collio Pinot Bianco Santarosa '19	🍷🍷	3*
○ Collio Sauvignon Segrè '19	🍷🍷	5
○ Collio Pinot Grigio Joy '19	🍷🍷	4
○ Collio Ribolla Gialla Yellow Hills '19	🍷🍷	3
● Friuli Isonzo Merlot '17	🍷🍷	3
○ Friuli Isonzo Pinot Grigio '19	🍷🍷	3
● Friuli Isonzo Cabernet Sauvignon '17	🍷	3
○ Friuli Isonzo Chardonnay '19	🍷	3
○ Friuli Isonzo Friulano '19	🍷	3
○ Collio Pinot Bianco '14	🍷🍷🍷	3*
○ Collio Pinot Bianco '13	🍷🍷🍷	3*
○ Collio Pinot Bianco '11	🍷🍷🍷	3*
○ Collio Pinot Bianco '06	🍷🍷🍷	3*
○ Collio Pinot Bianco Santarosa '18	🍷🍷🍷	3*
○ Collio Sauvignon Segrè '03	🍷🍷🍷	5
○ Collio Tocai Friulano '05	🍷🍷🍷	3*

Castello Sant'Anna

loc. Spessa
via Sant'Anna, 9
33043 Cividale del Friuli [UD]
Tel. +39 0432716289
www.castellosantanna.it

CELLAR SALES
PRE-BOOKED VISITS
ANNUAL PRODUCTION 25,000 bottles
HECTARES UNDER VINE 7.00
VITICULTURE METHOD Certified Organic

Andrea Giaiotti is in charge of managing Castello Sant'Anna, in Spessa di Cividale, a winery founded in 1966 by his grandfather Giuseppe. Once the summer residence of noble families from Cividale, the castle is now surrounded by revived vineyards. Through the patient work of restoration, Andrea reorganized the old plots and then built a new underground cellar that guarantees natural humidity and constant temperatures. He also equipped it with all the necessary infrastructure to work the grapes with the most advanced techniques. The Pinot Grigio '18 repeats last year's splendid performance and regains access to our final selections. Its copper highlights are a hallmark, its aromas make it one of the most interesting and original wines in its category, and the palate comes through sapid and pervasive. A long stay in the bottle made for a Schioppettino '13 that's powerful but under control, mature both in its rich olfactory suite and its gustatory sensations.

Wine	Rating
○ FCO Pinot Grigio '18	🍷🍷 3*
● FCO Cabernet Franc '17	🍷🍷 4
○ FCO Friulano '18	🍷🍷 3
● FCO Merlot '16	🍷🍷 4
● FCO Refosco P. R. '15	🍷🍷 4
○ FCO Ribolla Gialla '18	🍷🍷 3
○ FCO Sauvignon '18	🍷🍷 3
● FCO Schioppettino '13	🍷🍷 5
○ FCO Friulano '17	🍷🍷 3
○ FCO Friulano '16	🍷🍷 3
● FCO Merlot '15	🍷🍷 4
○ FCO Pinot Grigio '17	🍷🍷 3*
○ FCO Pinot Grigio '16	🍷🍷 3
○ FCO Ribolla Gialla '17	🍷🍷 3
○ FCO Ribolla Gialla '16	🍷🍷 3
○ FCO Sauvignon '17	🍷🍷 3
○ FCO Sauvignon '16	🍷🍷 3

Castelvecchio

via Castelnuovo, 2
34078 Sagrado [GO]
Tel. +39 048199742
www.castelvecchio.com

CELLAR SALES
PRE-BOOKED VISITS
ACCOMMODATION AND RESTAURANT SERVICE
ANNUAL PRODUCTION 120,000 bottles
HECTARES UNDER VINE 35.00
SUSTAINABLE WINERY

Splendor and ruin have marked Gorizia Karst over the years. Still today, amidst patches of intact, scenic nature landscapes, the challenge is how to cultivate this difficult terrain, arid and rocky but capable of allying with human interests in unexpected ways. It's here, just above Sagrado, that we find Castelvecchio, owned by the Terraneo family. The untouched nature here offers charming scenery that blends with the property's noble and ancient origins, still visible today in the Renaissance villa and a park dotted with cypresses and ancient oaks. The company's flagship wine is undoubtedly the Malvasia Dileo '19. It's a summery wine, redolent of summer haymaking and Mediterranean shrub. On the palate it combines softness, fragrance and sapidity. The rest of their selection, all ambassadors of Karst's potential, are more or less on a par.

Wine	Rating
○ Carso Malvasia Dileo '19	🍷🍷 4
● Carso Cabernet Sauvignon '17	🍷🍷 3
○ Carso Malvasia '19	🍷🍷 3
○ Carso Pinot Grigio '19	🍷🍷 3
● Carso Refosco P. R. '17	🍷🍷 3
● Carso Terrano '18	🍷🍷 3
○ Carso Vitovska '19	🍷🍷 3
● Sagrado Rosso '16	🍷🍷 5
○ Carso Sauvignon '19	🍷 3
○ Carso Malvasia Dileo '15	🍷🍷🍷 4*
○ Carso Malvasia '18	🍷🍷 3
○ Carso Malvasia '17	🍷🍷 3
○ Carso Malvasia Dileo '18	🍷🍷 4
○ Carso Malvasia Dileo '17	🍷🍷 4
○ Carso Malvasia Dileo '16	🍷🍷 4
○ Carso Malvasia Dileo '14	🍷🍷 4

Tenimenti Civa

FRAZ. BELLAZOIA
VIA SUBIDA, 16
33040 POVOLETTO [UD]
TEL. +39 04321770382
www.tenimenticiva.com

CELLAR SALES
ANNUAL PRODUCTION 1,000,000 bottles
HECTARES UNDER VINE 60.00

In 2016 Valerio Civa decided to put his long experience in the world of wine to use. He took over a cellar and a considerable number of vineyards in Bellazoia di Povoletto and the surrounding area, in the Friuli Colli Orientali appellation, and so founded Tenimenti Civa. In August of 2018 its headquarters, completely renovated, were accompanied by a new production facility, one equipped with technologically advanced equipment, including cellaring tanks and a considerable number of autoclaves for sparkling wine making. The Ribolla Gialla Collezione Privata '19 does a nice job expressing the grape's varietal qualities and, after opening on delicate aromas of wild flowers, lemon wafer and white peach, stands out for its drinkability. The Refosco P. R. Vigneto Bellazoia '18 is redolent of crushed morello cherries, light spices and quinine, while the wine called Ronc Zoiis '18 calls up liquorice root, undergrowth and cigar tobacco.

Wine	Glasses
● FCO Merlot Vign. Bellazoia '18	🍷🍷 5
○ FCO Pinot Grigio Ronc Zoiis '19	🍷🍷 3
● FCO Refosco P. R. Ronc Zoiis '18	🍷🍷 3
● FCO Refosco P. R. Vign. Bellazoia '18	🍷🍷 5
○ FCO Ribolla Gialla Collezione Privata '19	🍷🍷 4
○ FCO Ribolla Gialla Extra Brut Collezione Privata '19	🍷 3
○ FCO Sauvignon Vign. Bellazoia '18	🍷 5
○ FCO Friulano '18	ΥΥ 3
○ FCO Friulano '17	ΥΥ 3
● FCO Merlot V. Bellazoia '17	ΥΥ 3
● FCO Refosco P. R. V. Bellazoia '17	ΥΥ 3
○ FCO Ribolla Gialla '17	ΥΥ 3*
○ FCO Ribolla Gialla Biele Zôe Cuvée '18	ΥΥ 3
○ FCO Sauvignon '18	ΥΥ 3*
○ FCO Sauvignon V. Bellazoia '17	ΥΥ 3
● FCO Schioppettino '17	ΥΥ 3

★Eugenio Collavini

LOC. GRAMOGLIANO
VIA DELLA RIBOLLA GIALLA, 2
33040 CORNO DI ROSAZZO [UD]
TEL. +39 0432753222
www.collavini.it

CELLAR SALES
PRE-BOOKED VISITS
RESTAURANT SERVICE
ANNUAL PRODUCTION 1,200,000 bottles
HECTARES UNDER VINE 140.00
SUSTAINABLE WINERY

Collavini, one of the region's historic producers, bears the surname of its founder, Eugenio, who established it back in 1896. In the 1970s the estate got a further boost from Manlio, with the purchase of an ancient 16th-century manor house in Corno di Rosazzo, which became the family's home and cellar. Manlio was among the first to believe in the potential of sparkling Ribolla Gialla, a wine that is now experiencing moments of great success and popularity. After a further year of bottle aging, the Collio Bianco Broy '18 reappears in great form, once again leading their selection and taking home Tre Bicchieri. The well-proven mix of Friulian Tocai, Chardonnay and Sauvignon wins over the nose with myriad aromatic nuances, and gratifies the palate with its enthralling minerality. The Ribolla Gialla Brut '15, which unveils fragrances of grapefruit and green apple, also delivered.

Wine	Glasses
○ Collio Bianco Broy '18	🍷🍷🍷 6
○ Ribolla Gialla Brut '16	🍷🍷 5
○ Bianco '19	🍷🍷 3
○ Collio Friulano T '19	🍷🍷 3
○ FCO Ribolla Gialla Turian '19	🍷🍷 5
● FCO Schioppettino Turian '13	🍷🍷 5
● Friuli Refosco P. R. Pucino '19	🍷🍷 3
● MoRe '17	🍷🍷 3
○ Il Grigio Brut	🍷 3
○ Collio Bianco Broy '17	ΥΥΥ 6
○ Collio Bianco Broy '15	ΥΥΥ 5
○ Collio Bianco Broy '14	ΥΥΥ 5
○ Collio Bianco Broy '13	ΥΥΥ 5
○ Collio Bianco Broy '11	ΥΥΥ 4*
○ Ribolla Gialla Brut '13	ΥΥΥ 5
○ Ribolla Gialla Dosaggio Zero '15	ΥΥΥ 5

Colle Duga

loc. Zegla, 10
34071 Cormòns [GO]
Tel. +39 048161177
www.colleduga.com

CELLAR SALES
PRE-BOOKED VISITS
ANNUAL PRODUCTION 50,000 bottles
HECTARES UNDER VINE 9.00

Damian Princic, a child of the 1970s, took over management in 1991, creating the Colle Duga brand and immediately pursuing his convictions. There were not many hectares of vines and by drastically lowering yields production dropped of course. The result was a clash with the mentality of his predecessors, who, however, given the quality levels achieved, reconsidered and eventually endorsed the direction. His children Karin and Patrik, who have been contributing for some time, represent the present and a guarantee for the future. With some 3 wines in our finals, Colle Duga once again demonstrates that it's one of the region's best producers. In turns, their few wines perform at the peaks of excellence, thus confirming the overall quality of the entire range. The Collio Bianco '19 (Chardonnay, Malvasia Istriana, Sauvignon and Tocai Friulano) calls up fragrances of citrus fruits and gratifies the palate. The Sauvignon '19 stands out for its pluck, while the Friulano '19 impresses with the softness and fullness of its palate.

Wine	Rating
○ Collio Bianco '19	ΨΨ 4
○ Collio Friulano '19	ΨΨ 3*
○ Collio Sauvignon '19	ΨΨ 3*
○ Collio Chardonnay '19	ΨΨ 3
● Collio Merlot '18	ΨΨ 4
○ Collio Pinot Grigio '19	ΨΨ 3
○ Collio Bianco '16	ΨΨΨ 4*
○ Collio Bianco '11	ΨΨΨ 4*
○ Collio Bianco '08	ΨΨΨ 3*
○ Collio Bianco '07	ΨΨΨ 3
○ Collio Friulano '09	ΨΨΨ 3*
○ Collio Tocai Friulano '06	ΨΨΨ 3*
○ Collio Tocai Friulano '05	ΨΨΨ 3*
○ Collio Bianco '18	ΨΨ 4
○ Collio Friulano '18	ΨΨ 3*
○ Collio Friulano '15	ΨΨ 3*

Colli di Poianis

via Poianis, 23
33040 Prepotto [UD]
Tel. +39 3802925468
www.collidipoianis.it

CELLAR SALES
PRE-BOOKED VISITS
ACCOMMODATION
ANNUAL PRODUCTION 80,000 bottles
HECTARES UNDER VINE 11.00
SUSTAINABLE WINERY

Colli di Poianis is one of the most beautiful parts of Prepotto, the pearl of the Friuli Colli Orientali appellation. Since 1991, Gabriele Marinig has been working to revive native grape varieties, especially Schioppettino, but has also paid great attention to safeguarding the territory, maintaining its original and historical configuration without ever upsetting the peculiarities of the natural landscape. He has worked hard to protect the coexistence of slopes, paths and vineyards that, over time, have created vital micro-balances, generating and preserving biodiversity. During our tastings the Malvasia '19 ranked among the best in its category, earning entry into our final selections. On the nose it calls up yellow peach, tropical fruit, bay leaves and acacia honey, while a combination of fragrance and softness adorns the palate. The Schioppettino di Prepotto '17 stands out for its fragrance and delicious aromas of violet, black cherry and Chinese magnolia.

Wine	Rating
○ FCO Malvasia '19	ΨΨ 4
○ FCO Chardonnay '19	ΨΨ 4
○ FCO Friulano '19	ΨΨ 4
○ FCO Sauvignon '19	ΨΨ 4
● FCO Schioppettino di Prepotto '17	ΨΨ 5
○ FCO Chardonnay '18	ΨΨ 4
○ FCO Chardonnay '17	ΨΨ 4
○ FCO Friulano '18	ΨΨ 4
○ FCO Friulano '17	ΨΨ 4
○ FCO Malvasia '18	ΨΨ 4
○ FCO Malvasia '17	ΨΨ 4
○ FCO Ribolla Gialla '17	ΨΨ 4
● FCO Rosso Ronco della Poiana '16	ΨΨ 5
● FCO Rosso Ronco della Poiana '15	ΨΨ 4
○ FCO Sauvignon '18	ΨΨ 4

Gianpaolo Colutta

via Orsaria, 32a
33044 Manzano [UD]
Tel. +39 0432510654
www.coluttagianpaolo.com

CELLAR SALES
PRE-BOOKED VISITS
ANNUAL PRODUCTION 100,000 bottles
HECTARES UNDER VINE 30.00

The hills of Manzano represent the point from which Friuli Colli Orientali's natural amphitheatre starts. Here, in the area most exposed to the breezes of the nearby Adriatic Sea, Gianpaolo Colutta created his own winery in 1999. Leading the producer today is his daughter Elisabetta, who inherited agricultural roots going back more than a millennium from her mother, Countess Anna di Prampero. The pride of the winery is the replanting of certain vineyards using clones of almost-abandoned and ancient native grape varieties. This year their wines earned similar scores, all quite commendable, confirming the attention paid to the preservation of the unique characteristics of each grape variety, even if the Friulano '19 and the Pinot Grigio '19 only differ slightly. The former stands out for its floral suite of acacia and jasmine, as well as its drinkability, the latter for its lovely, coppery color accompanied by aromas of strawberry, rose, anise and lemon wafer.

Wine	Rating
● FCO Cabernet '18	🍷🍷 3
○ FCO Chardonnay '19	🍷🍷 3
○ FCO Friulano '19	🍷🍷 3
○ FCO Pinot Grigio '19	🍷🍷 3
○ FCO Riesling '19	🍷🍷 4
● FCO Schioppettino '18	🍷🍷 5
○ FCO Sauvignon '19	🍷 3
● FCO Cabernet '17	🍷🍷 (white) 3
● FCO Cabernet '16	🍷🍷 (white) 3
○ FCO Friulano '18	🍷🍷 (white) 3*
○ FCO Pinot Grigio '18	🍷🍷 (white) 3
○ FCO Pinot Grigio '17	🍷🍷 (white) 3
○ FCO Ribolla Gialla '17	🍷🍷 (white) 4
○ FCO Sauvignon '18	🍷🍷 (white) 3
○ FCO Sauvignon '17	🍷🍷 (white) 3
● FCO Schioppettino '17	🍷🍷 (white) 5

Giorgio Colutta

via Orsaria, 32
33044 Manzano [UD]
Tel. +39 0432740315
www.colutta.it

CELLAR SALES
PRE-BOOKED VISITS
ACCOMMODATION
ANNUAL PRODUCTION 140,000 bottles
HECTARES UNDER VINE 21.00

Once better known as Bandut (from the ancient name for an estate holding), Giorgio Colutta's winery has always distinguished itself for its compliance with principles of ecology and sustainability. It's a sensibility that led Giorgio to include Kosher certification, intended for consumption by Jewish faithful, for his range. The plots, which are still managed by vineyard master Antonio Maggio, unfold in Friuli Colli Orientali's prestigious 'Vine and Wine Park'. Last year's whites are joined by a common aromatic pleasantness and drinkability. The Friulano Vecchie Vigne '19 features floral and fruity suggestions that also accompany the palate. The Pinot Grigio '19 offers up vibrant aromas of russet pear, dried flowers and lime blossom honey. The Ribolla Gialla '19 calls up fragrances of citrus fruits, pine resin and mint.

Wine	Rating
○ FCO Friulano V. V. '19	🍷🍷 4
● FCO Pignolo '13	🍷🍷 7
○ FCO Pinot Grigio '19	🍷🍷 3
● FCO Refosco P. R. '15	🍷🍷 3
○ FCO Ribolla Gialla '19	🍷🍷 3
○ FCO Sauvignon V. V. '19	🍷 4
● FCO Cabernet '16	🍷🍷 (white) 3
● FCO Cabernet '15	🍷🍷 (white) 3
○ FCO Chardonnay '18	🍷🍷 (white) 3
○ FCO Friulano '18	🍷🍷 (white) 3
○ FCO Friulano '17	🍷🍷 (white) 3*
● FCO Merlot '15	🍷🍷 (white) 3
○ FCO Pinot Grigio '18	🍷🍷 (white) 3*
○ FCO Pinot Grigio '17	🍷🍷 (white) 3
○ FCO Pinot Grigio '16	🍷🍷 (white) 3
○ FCO Ribolla Gialla '17	🍷🍷 (white) 3

Paolino Comelli

B.GO CASE COLLOREDO, 8
33040 FAEDIS [UD]
TEL. +39 0432711226
www.comelli.it

CELLAR SALES
PRE-BOOKED VISITS
ACCOMMODATION
ANNUAL PRODUCTION 60,000 bottles
HECTARES UNDER VINE 12.50
SUSTAINABLE WINERY

This solid family team made up of Pierluigi Comelli, his wife, Daniela, and their children Nicola and Filippo, is responsible for managing this beautiful farm in Colloredo di Soffumbergo, an area of rare beauty where peace, vines and olive trees reign. The estate came about thanks to the foresight of grandfather Paolino who, in 1946, acquired an old abandoned hamlet and turned it into a farm. Now those decadent rural cottages are farmhouses of rare charm, equipped with every comfort, tastefully furnished in characteristic Friulian style. At the moment of our tastings, they still hadn't bottled the wines from last year's harvest, with the exception of the Pinot Grigio Amplius '19, which received an excellent rating and proved to be among the best in its category. The focus shifted, therefore to a red, the balanced and balsamic Soffumbergo '17 (Merlot and Refosco), and the excellent Picolit '17, a dense and creamy wine.

○ COF Picolit '17	▼▼ 5
○ FCO Pinot Grigio Amplius '19	▼▼ 3
● Soffumbergo '17	▼▼ 4
○ COF Picolit '16	▽▽ 5
○ FCO Bianco Soffumbergo '17	▽▽ 3
○ FCO Bianco Soffumbergo '16	▽▽ 3
○ FCO Friulano '18	▽▽ 3
○ FCO Malvasia '17	▽▽ 3*
○ FCO Malvasia '16	▽▽ 3
● FCO Pignolo '12	▽▽ 5
○ FCO Pinot Grigio Amplius '18	▽▽ 3
○ FCO Pinot Grigio Amplius '17	▽▽ 3
○ FCO Pinot Grigio Amplius '15	▽▽ 3
○ FCO Sauvignon '18	▽▽ 3*
● Soffumbergo '16	▽▽ 4
● Soffumbergo '15	▽▽ 4

Dario Coos

LOC. RAMANDOLO, 5
33045 NIMIS [UD]
TEL. +39 0432790320
www.dariocoos.it

CELLAR SALES
PRE-BOOKED VISITS
ANNUAL PRODUCTION 80,000 bottles
HECTARES UNDER VINE 12.00

Dario Coos is made up of a small group of enthusiasts who oversee management of this beautiful regional producer. Dario represents the fifth generation of expert vigneron to make wine on the steep slopes of Ramandolo. They've always cultivated Verduzzo Giallo here in the northernmost part of Colli Orientali del Friuli, where the hills almost become mountains, the nights are cold, the days are hot and rainfall is high. The variety produces small bunches with thick and resistant skin, making it ideal for drying. The large number of wines submitted for tasting gave us an all-round view of their range. The Picolit '17 broke away from the pack and earned itself a place in our final selections. It calls up cooked pear juice and dried apricot on the nose, winning over the palate with its delicious sweetness. Their reds and the Ramandolo Vendemmia Tardiva '17 also put in an excellent performance, while the Malvasia '19 stood out among their regular, standard-label wines.

○ COF Picolit '17	▼▼ 6
○ Blanc de Blanc Extra Brut M. Cl.	▼▼ 6
○ Friuli Chardonnay '19	▼▼ 4
○ Friuli Friulano '19	▼▼ 3
○ Friuli Malvasia '19	▼▼ 3
○ Friuli Sauvignon '19	▼▼ 3
● Pignolo '16	▼▼ 4
○ Ramandolo V.T. '17	▼▼ 4
● Refosco P. R. '16	▼▼ 4
● Schioppettino '18	▼▼ 4
○ Friuli Pinot Grigio '19	▼ 3
○ Friuli Riesling '19	▼ 3
○ Ramandolo Il Longhino '17	▼ 4
○ Ribolla Gialla '19	▼ 3
○ Ribolla Gialla Brut	▼ 3
⊙ Rosato '19	▼ 3

Cantina Produttori Cormòns

VIA VINO DELLA PACE, 31
34071 CORMÒNS [GO]
TEL. +39 048162471
www.cormons.com

CELLAR SALES
PRE-BOOKED VISITS
ACCOMMODATION AND RESTAURANT SERVICE
ANNUAL PRODUCTION 2,250,000 bottles
HECTARES UNDER VINE 400.00
SUSTAINABLE WINERY

This appreciated winery was born out of a lovely story of cooperation and collaboration. It began in the 1960s when a group of winemakers from Cormonia, unable to work individually, decided to join forces. Alessandro dal Zovo's arrival as general manager coincided with a major shift towards quality. Their range was given a further boost with new selections and the famous 'Vino della Pace', which the best grapes are saved for. Once a message of brotherhood, it's now become emblematic of the winery. This year's great piece of news is the Collio Bianco Territorio '18 which, in its first year of production, earned a place in our finals. It's called 'Territorio' precisely because it's made of only native grapes (Tocai Friulano, Malvasia Istriana and Ribolla Gialla). Aromatically it's very fruit-forward, but also reminiscent of toasted hazelnuts, wild fennel and cotton candy.

Wine	Rating
○ Collio Bianco Territorio '18	▼▼ 3*
○ Collio Friulano '19	▼▼ 3
○ Collio Pinot Bianco '19	▼▼ 3
○ Collio Pinot Grigio '19	▼▼ 3
○ Collio Sauvignon '19	▼▼ 3
○ Friuli Malvasia '19	▼▼ 2*
○ Vino della Pace '18	▼▼ 5
○ Friuli Pinot Grigio '19	▼ 2
○ Friuli Sauvignon '19	▼ 2
○ Collio Bianco '18	▽▽ 3
○ Collio Bianco Collio & Collio '17	▽▽ 3
○ Collio Friuliano '18	▽▽ 3
○ Collio Pinot Grigio '18	▽▽ 3
○ Collio Sauvignon '18	▽▽ 3
○ Friuli Isonzo Malvasia '18	▽▽ 2*
○ Friuli Isonzo Malvasia n.68 '16	▽▽ 2*
○ Vino della Pace '17	▽▽ 5

Crastin

LOC. RUTTARS, 33
34070 DOLEGNA DEL COLLIO [GO]
TEL. +39 0481630310
www.vinicrastin.it

CELLAR SALES
PRE-BOOKED VISITS
ANNUAL PRODUCTION 35,000 bottles
HECTARES UNDER VINE 6.00

Sergio Collarig, sensing the potential of the two and a half hectares of vineyards that he inherited from his father, Olivo, in 1980, decided to plant new plots, abandoning mixed agriculture and specializing in viticulture. He chose to call his winery Crastin in honor of the splendid location immersed in the renowned Ruttars hills. It's a tiny producer, but one that has earned the attention of international markets for its consistent quality, with wines that keep getting better year after year. Not all their wines had been bottled at the time of the tasting, but the samples presented were sufficient to confirm the validity of the winery's range. In particular, the Friulano '19 stood out, moving along the lines of previous vintages with sunny accents reminiscent of dried wild flowers and summer wheat harvests. The Ribolla Gialla '19, which calls up green apple sensations and citron, is also excellent.

Wine	Rating
● Collio Cabernet Franc '18	▼▼ 3
○ Collio Friulano '19	▼▼ 3
● Collio Merlot '17	▼▼ 4
○ Collio Ribolla Gialla '19	▼▼ 3
○ Verduzzo Friulano '16	▼▼ 3
● Collio Cabernet Franc '17	▽▽ 3
○ Collio Friulano '18	▽▽ 3
○ Collio Friulano '17	▽▽ 3
● Collio Merlot '16	▽▽ 4
● Collio Merlot '15	▽▽ 4
○ Collio Pinot Grigio '18	▽▽ 3
○ Collio Pinot Grigio '17	▽▽ 3
○ Collio Ribolla Gialla '18	▽▽ 3
○ Collio Ribolla Gialla '17	▽▽ 3
○ Collio Sauvignon '18	▽▽ 3
○ Collio Sauvignon '17	▽▽ 3
○ Verduzzo Friulano '15	▽▽ 3

di Lenardo

LOC. ONTAGNANO
P.ZZA BATTISTI, 1
33050 GONARS [UD]
TEL. +39 0432928633
www.dilenardo.it

CELLAR SALES
PRE-BOOKED VISITS
ANNUAL PRODUCTION 750,000 bottles
HECTARES UNDER VINE 60.00
SUSTAINABLE WINERY

Massimo di Lenardo inherited from his predecessors a love for the land, as well as innate entrepreneurial skills. With his management, the family business has positioned itself as one of the region's most acclaimed producers. Their wines are rich in nuances thanks to vineyards that extend across the sunny Friulian plains, in different zones with different subsoils and microclimates. The cellar is located in the small town of Ontagnano, a few kilometers from the ramparts of Palmanova, a city known for its original star shape. The Thanks '19 once again demonstrates why it's their flagship wine. For the fourth consecutive year it made it to our finals, ranking among the top wines of its category. It's a blend of several grape varieties: Chardonnay, Sauvignon, Tocai Friulano, Malvasia Istriana and Verduzzo vinified in new, American oak barrels. On the nose it's redolent of amaretto, custard and honey, while the palate proves complex and pervasive.

Wine	Glasses
○ Thanks '19	🍷🍷 4
○ Father's Eyes Chardonnay '19	🍷🍷 3
○ Friuli Friulano Toh! '19	🍷🍷 2*
○ Friulia Pinot Grigio Ramato Gossip '19	🍷🍷 2*
● Just Me Merlot '17	🍷🍷 4
○ Pass The Cookies! '19	🍷🍷 3
● Ronco Nolè '18	🍷🍷 2*
○ Sarà Brut M. Cl. '14	🍷🍷 3
○ Chardonnay '19	🍷 2
○ Friuli Pinot Grigio '19	🍷 2
⊙ Le Nuvole '19	🍷 2
● Merlot '19	🍷 2
○ Ribolla Gialla Brut M. Cl. '18	🍷 3
○ Ribolla Gialla Comemivuoi '19	🍷 2
○ Sauvignon '19	🍷 2

★★Dorigo

S.DA PROV.LE 79
33040 PREMARIACCO [UD]
TEL. +39 0432634161
www.dorigowines.com

CELLAR SALES
PRE-BOOKED VISITS
ANNUAL PRODUCTION 120,000 bottles
HECTARES UNDER VINE 20.00
SUSTAINABLE WINERY

The new, beautiful winery created by Alessio Dorigo has kept approval ratings high for a brand that has been, and remains, a cornerstone of regional viticulture. The generational changing of the guard that saw Alessio taking over from Girolamo has coincided with many developments and given a fresh boost to their entire production line. It's important to remember that, many years ago, Dorigo contributed to a new focus on the value of the region's native cultivars, including Ribolla Gialla, a grape that's now experiencing a period of considerable popularity. In addition to their current, standard-label wines, their Ronc di Juri selections, Metodo Classico sparklers, and reds all performed well, especially the Picolit '18, which delight the nose and palate, distinguishing itself for its finesse and harmony. The Sauvignon Ronc di Juri '18 offers a pleasant bouquet of white peach, sage, honey and vanilla, while the Montsclapade '16 remains complex and powerful both on the nose and on the palate, with vigorous but well-managed tannins.

Wine	Glasses
○ COF Picolit '18	🍷🍷 8
● FCO Rosso Montsclapade '16	🍷🍷 6
○ FCO Sauvignon Ronc di Juri '18	🍷🍷 5
○ Blanc de Blancs Pas Dosé	🍷🍷 5
○ Blanc de Noir Dosage Zéro	🍷🍷 5
○ Dorigo Brut Cuvée	🍷🍷 5
● Dorigo Rosso	🍷🍷 4
○ FCO Friulano '19	🍷🍷 3
○ FCO Friulano Ronc di Juri '18	🍷🍷 5
○ FCO Pinot Grigio '19	🍷🍷 3
○ FCO Ribolla Gialla '19	🍷🍷 3
○ FCO Sauvignon '19	🍷🍷 3
● Pignolo '15	🍷🍷 5
● COF Montsclapade '99	🍷🍷🍷 6
● COF Rosso Montsclapade '06	🍷🍷🍷 6
● COF Rosso Montsclapade '04	🍷🍷🍷 6
● COF Rosso Montsclapade '98	🍷🍷🍷 6

Draga - Miklus

loc. Scedina, 8
34070 San Floriano del Collio [GO]
Tel. +39 0481884182
www.draga-miklus.com

CELLAR SALES
PRE-BOOKED VISITS
ANNUAL PRODUCTION 50,000 bottles
HECTARES UNDER VINE 14.00
SUSTAINABLE WINERY

Draga is one of the many classic, family-run producers that populate the slopes of San Floriano del Collio. Milan Miklus represents the third generation of family to operate here (his sharecropping forefathers took root here in the late 19th century). The vineyards are divided into two plots: Draga, whose excellent position and ideal breezes give rise to wines of great finesse, and Breg, which experiences stronger winds. Here the most resistant varieties of grapes are cultivated before being vinified according to ancient local tradition. Long maceration of the white grapes that make up the Miklus line gives rise to wines that are singular and intriguing both visually and organoleptically (to say the least). Among these is the Ribolla Natural Art '15, a wine that's incredible for its olfactory complexity (from aniseed to candied citron) and its sapid, long palate. We were also surprised by the Friulano '19, which already stands out for its aromatic pleasantness, typicity and complexity, all of which follow through well on the palate.

Wine	Rating
○ Miklus Natural Art Ribolla Gialla '15	ΨΨΨ 6
○ Collio Friulano '19	ΨΨ 3*
○ Collio Pinot Grigio Miklus '17	ΨΨ 6
○ Collio Ribolla Gialla '19	ΨΨ 3
○ Collio Sauvignon '19	ΨΨ 3
○ Collio Malvasia Miklus '10	ΥΥΥ 7
○ Collio Malvasia '18	ΥΥ 3
○ Collio Malvasia Miklus '16	ΥΥ 5
○ Collio Malvasia Miklus '15	ΥΥ 5
○ Collio Malvasia Miklus '14	ΥΥ 4
○ Collio Malvasia Miklus '13	ΥΥ 4
○ Collio Pinot Grigio Miklus '16	ΥΥ 6
○ Collio Ribolla Gialla Miklus Natural Art '14	ΥΥ 5
○ Collio Ribolla Gialla Miklus Natural Art '09	ΥΥ 5
○ Ribolla Gialla Miklus '12	ΥΥ 6

Drius

via Filanda, 100
34071 Cormòns [GO]
Tel. +39 048160998
www.drius.it

CELLAR SALES
PRE-BOOKED VISITS
ANNUAL PRODUCTION 55,000 bottles
HECTARES UNDER VINE 17.00
SUSTAINABLE WINERY

For almost two centuries the Drius family has been setting an example of cohesion and love for the land in the district of Cormons, in an area that straddles the Friuli Isonzo and Collio appellations. Mauro Drius, a true wine craftsman, still plays a key role, but the new generation is already chomping at the bit and ready to take over. His son Denis has been overseeing winemaking for some years now, but it's the compactness of the entire family that has made the producer a top regional performer. This year the news is the release of the Friulano Sensar '18. A wine characterized by a lovely bouquet and a balanced palate, it immediately stood out and earned a place in our finals. In local dialect, 'sensar' means 'broker'. It's a tribute to Sergio, Mauro's father who, until a few years ago, played an active role on the farm, negotiating agricultural products and livestock.

Wine	Rating
○ Friuli Isonzo Friulano Sensar '18	ΨΨ 5
○ Collio Sauvignon '19	ΨΨ 3
○ Friuli Isonzo Bianco Vignis di Siris '18	ΨΨ 4
● Friuli Isonzo Cabernet Sauvignon '18	ΨΨ 4
● Friuli Isonzo Merlot '18	ΨΨ 4
○ Friuli Isonzo Malvasia '19	Ψ 3
○ Collio Tocai Friulano '05	ΥΥΥ 3*
○ Collio Tocai Friulano '02	ΥΥΥ 2*
○ Friuli Isonzo Bianco Vignis di Siris '02	ΥΥΥ 3*
○ Friuli Isonzo Friulano '07	ΥΥΥ 3
○ Friuli Isonzo Malvasia '08	ΥΥΥ 3*
○ Friuli Isonzo Pinot Bianco '09	ΥΥΥ 3*
○ Friuli Isonzo Pinot Bianco '00	ΥΥΥ 3*
○ Friuli Isonzo Bianco Vignis di Siris '16	ΥΥ 3*
○ Friuli Isonzo Chardonnay '18	ΥΥ 3*
○ Friuli Isonzo Pinot Bianco '18	ΥΥ 3*

Ermacora

Fraz. Ipplis
via Solzaredo, 9
33040 Premariacco [UD]
Tel. +39 0432716250
www.ermacora.it

CELLAR SALES
PRE-BOOKED VISITS
ANNUAL PRODUCTION 230,000 bottles
HECTARES UNDER VINE 69.00
SUSTAINABLE WINERY

In 1922 the Ermacora family chose the hill of Ipplis for their vineyards, creating the conditions for the production of fine wines. Brothers Dario and Luciano successfully run a cutting-edge, solid and reliable winery here, one that in recent years has expanded significantly with the purchase of additional vineyards in the crus of Bostonat (Buttrio) and Montsclapade (Orsaria). Working with impeccable synergy, they manage to confer a quality that makes their wines unique while also maintaining typicity and varietal nuances. Despite an excellent performance from all their current-vintage wines, among which we appreciated the Pinot Bianco '19, the top positions are occupied by two wines from previous vintages. The Picolit '16 is dense and juicy on the palate, characterized by aromas of apricot tart, raisins, white chocolate and honey. The Pignolo '14 offers up generous whiffs of dark spices, macerated cherries and cocoa powder, coming through long and pervasive on the palate.

Wine	Rating	
○ COF Picolit '16	▼▼	6
● FCO Pignolo '14	▼▼	5
○ FCO Friulano '19	▼▼	3
○ FCO Pinot Bianco '19	▼▼	3
○ FCO Pinot Grigio '19	▼▼	3
○ FCO Ribolla Gialla '19	▼▼	3
● FCO Rosso Ríul '16	▼▼	4
○ FCO Sauvignon '19	▼▼	3
● FCO Schioppettino '18	▼▼	3
● FCO Merlot '18	▼	3
● COF Pignolo '00	▽▽▽	5
○ COF Picolit '14	▽▽	6
○ FCO Friulano '18	▽▽	3
○ FCO Pinot Bianco '18	▽▽	3*
○ FCO Pinot Bianco '17	▽▽	3*
○ FCO Ribolla Gialla '18	▽▽	3
○ FCO Ribolla Gialla '17	▽▽	3

Fantinel

Fraz. Tauriano
via Tesis, 8
33097 Spilimbergo [PN]
Tel. +39 0427591511
www.fantinel.com

CELLAR SALES
PRE-BOOKED VISITS
RESTAURANT SERVICE
ANNUAL PRODUCTION 5,000,000 bottles
HECTARES UNDER VINE 300.00
SUSTAINABLE WINERY

The Fantinel family avails itself of 300 hectares of vineyards, making it one of the region's largest producers. In 1969 Mario Fantinel bought some vineyards in Dolegna del Collio to satisfy the demands of the guests of the hotel-restaurant he managed in Carnia. Successive generations followed his example, expanding the family patrimony, which now consists of three distinct estates: Tenuta Sant'Helena in Vencò (in Collio), La Roncaia in Nimis (Colli Orientali), and Borgo Tesis in Tauriano di Spilimbergo. Tasting their rich selection of white, red and sparkling wines allows for a complete overview of their range, and the small difference between the scores attests to its validity. Even if only slightly, our preferences went to their blends: the Venkò Sant'Helena '13 (Merlot, Cabernet Franc and Pinot Nero) and the Frontiere Sant'Helena '17 (Tocai Friulano, Pinot Bianco and Chardonnay), both complex on the nose and alluring on the palate.

Wine	Rating	
○ Collio Bianco Frontiere Sant'Helena '17	▼▼	4
● Collio Rosso Venko Sant'Helena '13	▼▼	4
○ Collio Sauvignon Sant'Helena '19	▼▼	3
○ Prosecco Brut One&Only '19	▼▼	3
● Refosco P. R. '14	▼▼	3
○ Sant'Helena Ribolla Gialla '19	▼▼	3
⊙ Brut Rosé One & Only '19	▼	3
○ Collio Pinot Grigio Sant'Helena '19	▼	3
○ Ribolla Gialla Brut	▼	3
● Cabernet Sauvignon '14	▽▽	3
○ Collio Friulano Sant'Helena '18	▽▽	3
○ Collio Friulano Sant'Helena '17	▽▽	3
○ Collio Pinot Grigio Sant'Helena '18	▽▽	3
○ Collio Sauvignon Sant'Helena '18	▽▽	3
○ Ribolla Gialla Sant'Helena '18	▽▽	3

★★Livio Felluga

FRAZ. BRAZZANO
VIA RISORGIMENTO, 1
34071 CORMÒNS [GO]
TEL. +39 048160052
www.liviofelluga.it

PRE-BOOKED VISITS
ANNUAL PRODUCTION 800,000 bottles
HECTARES UNDER VINE 170.00
SUSTAINABLE WINERY

Livio Felluga was always a benchmark in Friulian viticulture and left an important legacy to his four sons, one wrought of tradition, love for the land, and daily challenges. In the 1950s, he successfully intuited something unthinkable at the time in Italy: produce great white wines. Now the winery boasts important hillside vineyards, especially in the Friuli Colli Orientali appellation, and has received a further boost from the acquisition of the historic Abbey of Rosazzo. Among their current-vintage wines, the Sauvignon '19 stood out with its overwhelming power, making it one of the best of its kind. It wins over the nose with its floral notes of lime and magnolia, together with grapefruit, pineapple and papaya, and in the mouth it's vibrant, almost explosive. The Abbey of Rosazzo '17 (Tocai Friulano, Pinot Bianco, Sauvignon, Malvasia and Ribolla Gialla) proves aromatically complex and elegant, while the palate comes through soft and citrusy.

Wine	Rating
○ FCO Sauvignon '19	🍷🍷 4
○ Rosazzo Abbazia di Rosazzo '17	🍷🍷 6
○ FCO Friulano '19	🍷🍷 4
○ FCO Pinot Grigio '19	🍷🍷 4
● FCO Refosco P. R. '16	🍷🍷 4
○ FCO Ribolla Gialla '19	🍷🍷 4
○ COF Bianco Illivio '10	🍸🍸🍸 5
○ COF Rosazzo Bianco Terre Alte '09	🍸🍸🍸 7
○ COF Rosazzo Bianco Terre Alte '08	🍸🍸🍸 7
○ COF Rosazzo Bianco Terre Alte '07	🍸🍸🍸 7
○ COF Rosazzo Bianco Terre Alte '06	🍸🍸🍸 6
○ FCO Bianco Illivio '14	🍸🍸🍸 5
○ Rosazzo Terre Alte '17	🍸🍸🍸 7
○ Rosazzo Terre Alte '16	🍸🍸🍸 7
○ Rosazzo Terre Alte '12	🍸🍸🍸 7
○ Rosazzo Terre Alte '11	🍸🍸🍸 7
○ Terre Alte '87	🍸🍸🍸 7

Marco Felluga

VIA GORIZIA, 121
34072 GRADISCA D'ISONZO [GO]
TEL. +39 048199164
www.marcofelluga.it

CELLAR SALES
PRE-BOOKED VISITS
RESTAURANT SERVICE
ANNUAL PRODUCTION 600,000 bottles
HECTARES UNDER VINE 100.00
SUSTAINABLE WINERY

In 1956 Marco Felluga, now in his late nineties, founded the producer that still bears his name. Today it's run by his son Roberto, who represents the fifth generation of a winemaking dynasty that began in Istria in the second half of the 19th century. Marco was a great innovator, considering all the initiatives he undertook in favour of Gorizia's Collio. It's a reputation now shared with Roberto who, with ever greater commitment, supports the project of developing the longevity of the region's whites by dedicating certain parcels to reserves. The Pinot Grigio Mongris Riserva '17 takes center stage, rising to the peaks of excellence. Elegant hints of petits fours embellish an olfactory spectrum that calls up citrus fruits, alpine butter, dried yellow flowers and polyflora honey. In the mouth it's soft, pervasive and sapid, closing with a vibrant epilogue. The energetic and substantive Molamatta '17 (Pinot Bianco, Tocai Friulano and Ribolla Gialla) is also excellent.

Wine	Rating
○ Collio Pinot Grigio Mongris Ris. '17	🍷🍷 5
○ Collio Bianco Molamatta '17	🍷🍷 5
○ Collio Chardonnay '19	🍷🍷 3
○ Collio Friulano Amani '19	🍷🍷 3
○ Collio Ribolla Gialla Maralba '19	🍷🍷 3
● Collio Rosso Carantan '15	🍷🍷 5
● Ronco dei Moreri Refosco P. R. '15	🍷🍷 4
○ Collio Pinot Grigio Mongris Ris. '16	🍸🍸🍸 5
○ Collio Bianco Molamatta '15	🍸🍸 5
○ Collio Friulano '16	🍸🍸 3*
○ Collio Friulano Amani '18	🍸🍸 3
○ Collio Pinot Grigio Mongris '17	🍸🍸 5
○ Collio Pinot Grigio Mongris Ris. '13	🍸🍸 5
○ Collio Pinot Grigio Mongris Ris. '12	🍸🍸 5
○ Collio Pinot Grigio Mongris Ris. '11	🍸🍸 6
○ Collio Ribolla Gialla Maralba '18	🍸🍸 3

Feudi di Romans

FRAZ. PIERIS
VIA CÀ DEL BOSCO, 16
34075 SAN CANZIAN D'ISONZO [GO]
TEL. +39 048176445
www.ifeudidiromans.it

CELLAR SALES
ANNUAL PRODUCTION 500,000 bottles
HECTARES UNDER VINE 70.00

Taken over by Enzo Lorenzon in the early 1990s, Feudi di Romans is one of Friuli Isonzo's most important producers. Enzo is a charismatic figure, the fulcrum of the business he still runs together with his children Davide and Nicola. It's a classic family winery based on the respect and trust created over the years with the entire staff. Their production philosophy is grounded in sustainability with an environmentally friendly approach to viticulture adopted in the vineyard. For a few harvests now, the role of flagship has fallen on the white grape variety called Sontium, from the ancient name of the Soča river that flows at the edge of the estate. The Sontium '18 (Pinot Bianco, Tocai Friulano and Malvasia Istriana, with a touch of Gewürztraminer) earns top marks again this year. It stands out for its aromatic elegance and, above all, for its creamy yet slender palate.

Wine	Rating	Price
○ Friuli Isonzo Bianco Sontium '18	🍷🍷	5
○ Friuli Isonzo Malvasia '19	🍷🍷	3
○ Friuli Isonzo Pinot Grigio '19	🍷🍷	3
● Friuli Isonzo Pinot Nero '18	🍷🍷	3
● Friuli Isonzo Refosco P. R. '18	🍷🍷	3
○ Friuli Isonzo Sauvignon '19	🍷🍷	3
○ Friuli Isonzo Pinot Bianco '19	🍷	3
○ Ribolla Gialla '19	🍷	3
○ Friuli Isonzo Bianco Sontium '17	🍷🍷 (white)	5
○ Friuli Isonzo Bianco Sontium '16	🍷🍷 (white)	5
○ Friuli Isonzo Malvasia '18	🍷🍷 (white)	3
○ Friuli Isonzo Pinot Bianco '18	🍷🍷 (white)	3
○ Friuli Isonzo Pinot Bianco '17	🍷🍷 (white)	3
○ Friuli Isonzo Pinot Grigio '18	🍷🍷 (white)	3
○ Friuli Isonzo Sauvignon '18	🍷🍷 (white)	3

Fiegl

FRAZ. OSLAVIA
LOC. LENZUOLO BIANCO, 1
34170 GORIZIA
TEL. +39 0481547103
www.fieglvini.com

CELLAR SALES
PRE-BOOKED VISITS
ANNUAL PRODUCTION 180,000 bottles
HECTARES UNDER VINE 30.00
SUSTAINABLE WINERY

Collio Goriziano hill, in the district of Oslavia, in Lenzuolo Bianco, is home to several prestigious wineries. It's a borderland tormented by war, but has forged generations of farmers proud of their land and vineyards. The Fiegl family have lived and worked here for over two centuries. The new generation, represented by Martin, Robert and Matej, has also embraced a production philosophy based on low yields and the use of eco-friendly products, with the utmost respect for nature, thus minimizing environmental impact. The rich sample of wines they always submit allows us to appreciate the entire production line, which is always very convincing. Once again the best results were obtained by the local, traditional wine, the Ribolla Gialla Oslavia '18. Intriguing both in its appearance and bouquet, it unveils intriguing aromas, unfolding progressively on the palate, with an excellent finish.

Wine	Rating	Price
○ Ribolla Gialla di Oslavia '18	🍷🍷	5
○ Collio Friulano '19	🍷🍷	3
○ Collio Malvasia '19	🍷🍷	3
● Collio Merlot Leopold '13	🍷🍷	3
○ Collio Pinot Bianco '19	🍷🍷	3
○ Collio Ribolla Gialla '19	🍷🍷	3
● Collio Rosso Leopold Cuvée Rouge '14	🍷🍷	5
○ Collio Sauvignon '19	🍷🍷	3
⊙ Fiegl Brut Rosé M. Cl.	🍷🍷	5
○ Collio Pinot Grigio '19	🍷	3
○ Collio Friulano '15	🍷🍷🍷 (white)	3*
○ Collio Pinot Grigio '04	🍷🍷🍷 (white)	2*
○ Collio Chardonnay '17	🍷🍷 (white)	3*
○ Collio Friulano '16	🍷🍷 (white)	3*
○ Collio Ribolla Gialla Oslavia '14	🍷🍷 (white)	5
○ Ribolla Gialla di Oslavia '17	🍷🍷 (white)	5

Gigante

via Rocca Bernarda, 3
33040 Corno di Rosazzo [UD]
Tel. +39 0432755835
www.adrianogigante.it

CELLAR SALES
PRE-BOOKED VISITS
ACCOMMODATION
ANNUAL PRODUCTION 100,000 bottles
HECTARES UNDER VINE 25.00

The name Adriano Gigante is bound up with the name of his most famous vineyard of Friulian Tocai: Storico. It's the vineyard around which this splendid winery was founded and still today it represents their pride and joy. The beautiful property stands out on the famous Rocca Bernarda, a cradle of many wine-growing families. Assisted by his wife, Giuliana, in management and by his cousin Ariedo in the vineyards and cellar, Adriano continues the family tradition with a line of superb wines. This year's selection was limited to a group of whites, all from the last harvest. The only exception was the Storico & Friends '18, a blend of indigenous grape varieties (Tocai Friuliano, Malvasia Istriana and Ribolla Gialla) that aims to serve as an ambassador of the area's unique attributes. A full palate is complemented by complex aromas of yellow flowers, aromatic herbs, citrus fruits and pineapple.

Wine	Rating
○ FCO Bianco Storico & Friends '18	🍷🍷 5
○ FCO Chardonnay '19	🍷🍷 3
○ FCO Friulano '19	🍷🍷 3
○ FCO Pinot Grigio '19	🍷🍷 3
○ FCO Ribolla Gialla '19	🍷🍷 3
○ FCO Sauvignon '19	🍷🍷 3
○ Friuli Malvasia '19	🍷🍷 3
○ COF Tocai Friulano Storico '00	🍷🍷🍷
○ COF Tocai Friulano Vign. Storico '06	🍷🍷🍷 4
○ COF Tocai Friulano Vign. Storico '05	🍷🍷🍷 4
○ COF Tocai Friulano Vign. Storico '03	🍷🍷🍷 4
○ FCO Picolit '08	🍷🍷🍷 6
○ FCO Friulano Vign. Storico '17	🍷🍷 4
● FCO Pignolo Ris. '09	🍷🍷 5
● FCO Refosco P. R. Ris. '13	🍷🍷 3*
○ FCO Sauvignon '16	🍷🍷 3*
○ Friuli Malvasia '18	🍷🍷 3*

Gori Wines

via G.B. Gori, 14
33045 Nimis [UD]
Tel. +39 0432878475
www.goriagricola.it

CELLAR SALES
PRE-BOOKED VISITS
ANNUAL PRODUCTION 50,000 bottles
HECTARES UNDER VINE 15.00
VITICULTURE METHOD Certified Organic

Gianpiero Gori (Piero to his friends) created this new winery, one that has ennobled the district of Nimis in the westernmost part of the Friuli Colli Orientali appellation, near the Carnic Pre-Alps. Relying on a skilled staff, Gori has burst out of the gate and now his winery is a leader for the area. The cellar is housed in an architecturally modern, elegant property consisting of three underground floors, which allow the producer to take full advantage of gravity in winemaking. By choice, all their whites are aged for a fairly long period, benefiting the wines' aromatic mix, and especially their generosity and pervasiveness on the palate. The Pinot Nero Nemas I '16 testifies to this part of Friuli's prowess for the grape, while the Ramandolo OrodiNemas '17 stays close to home, drawing on the vineyard to bring out Verduzzo Giallo's potential.

Wine	Rating
○ FCO Chardonnay Giù Giù '18	🍷🍷 3
○ FCO Friulano Bonblanc '18	🍷🍷 3
● FCO Pinot Nero Nemas I '16	🍷🍷 3
○ FCO Ribolla Gialla Blanc di Bianca '18	🍷🍷 3
○ FCO Sauvignon Busseben '18	🍷🍷 3
○ Ramandolo OrodiNemas '17	🍷🍷 5
○ FCO Chardonnay Giùgiù '17	🍷🍷 3
○ FCO Chardonnay Giùgiù '16	🍷🍷 3
○ FCO Friulano Bonblanc '17	🍷🍷 3*
○ FCO Friulano Bonblanc '16	🍷🍷 3
● FCO Pinot Nero Nemas I° '15	🍷🍷 3
○ FCO Sauvignon Busseben '17	🍷🍷 3
○ FCO Sauvignon Busseben '16	🍷🍷 3
● FCO Schioppettino TitaG '16	🍷🍷 3
○ Ramandolo OrodiNemas '16	🍷🍷 4
○ Ramandolo OrodiNemas '15	🍷🍷 4

Gradis'ciutta

loc. Giasbana, 10
34070 San Floriano del Collio [GO]
Tel. +39 0481390237
www.gradisciutta.eu

CELLAR SALES
PRE-BOOKED VISITS
ANNUAL PRODUCTION 100,000 bottles
HECTARES UNDER VINE 20.00

Robert Princic owns the beautiful winery he founded in 1997, when, upon completing his enological studies, he decided to join his father Isidoro in running the family business. The Princic family had produced wine in Kosana, in nearby Slovenia, since 1780. The Habsburg sunset, the Great War and sharecropping led his great-grandfather Filip to settle in San Floriano del Collio. Some vineyards adjacent to the cellar include vines that are over eighty years old, making for a unique patrimony that has been carefully safeguarded. This year the best scores went to the Collio Bianco Riserva '16, a wine produced with the area's most representative grapes (Tocai Friulano, Malvasia Istriana and Ribolla Gialla). After a long period of aging, it unveils golden highlights and evolved aromas of wild flowers, medicinal herbs, candied fruit and honey, only to caresses the palate from sip to sip with pleasant balsamic hints.

Wine	Rating
○ Collio Bianco Ris. '16	TT 5
○ Collio Chardonnay '19	TT 3
○ Collio Friulano '19	TT 3
○ Collio Malvasia '19	TT 3
○ Collio Pinot Grigio '19	TT 3
○ Collio Sauvignon '19	TT 3
● Monsvini '15	TT 5
○ Collio Ribolla Gialla '19	T 3
○ Collio Bianco Bratinis '16	YY 3
○ Collio Bianco Ris. '15	YY 4
○ Collio Chardonnay '18	YY 3*
○ Collio Friulano '18	YY 3
○ Collio Friulano '17	YY 3
○ Collio Malvasia '18	YY 3
○ Collio Malvasia '17	YY 3*
○ Collio Pinot Grigio '18	YY 3

Iole Grillo

via Albana, 60
33040 Prepotto [UD]
Tel. +39 0432713201
www.vinigrillo.it

CELLAR SALES
PRE-BOOKED VISITS
ACCOMMODATION
ANNUAL PRODUCTION 40,000 bottles
HECTARES UNDER VINE 9.00

A beautiful doorway to an 18th-century villa serves as the entrance to Iole Grillo's winery, a property that's been managed for many years now by Iole's daughter Anna Muzzolini, an energetic businesswoman and 'donna del vino'. Originally grounded in Schioppettino, the territory's main grape, the winery has since assumed its own identity, one open to innovation. Anna loves to personally oversee the various stages of production, and relies on support from her husband, Andrea, as well as the proven skills of a highly professional technical staff. Once again, the entire range put in an excellent overall performance. The Sauvignon '18 repeated last year's exploit and regained access to our final selections. The nose unveils varietal whiffs of sage, nettle, boxwood, green pepper and lychee, but it's the wine's gustatory elegance that most surprises and impresses.

Wine	Rating
○ FCO Il Sauvignon '18	TTT 4
○ FCO Friulano '19	TT 3
● FCO Merlot Ris. '17	TT 3
○ FCO Ribolla Gialla '19	TT 3
○ FCO Sauvignon '19	TT 3
● FCO Schioppettino di Prepotto '17	TT 3
○ FCO Verduzzo Friulano '17	TT 3
● FCO Cabernet Sauvignon '15	YY 3
○ FCO Friulano '18	YY 3
○ FCO Friulano '17	YY 3
○ FCO Il Sauvignon '17	YY 4
● FCO Merlot Ris. '15	YY 3
○ FCO Ribolla Gialla '18	YY 3
○ FCO Sauvignon '18	YY 3
○ FCO Sauvignon '17	YY 3
● FCO Schioppettino di Prepotto '16	YY 3
● Rosso Duedonne	YY 3

Albano Guerra

LOC. MONTINA
V.LE KENNEDY, 39A
33040 TORREANO [UD]
TEL. +39 0432715479
www.guerraalbano.it

CELLAR SALES
PRE-BOOKED VISITS
ANNUAL PRODUCTION 65,000 bottles
HECTARES UNDER VINE 11.00

The Guerra family has always cultivated the hills of Montina di Torreano in the northern part of the Friuli Colli Orientali appellation. The turning point, however, came in 1931, when Albano Guerra formalized the winery. Since 1997 this beautiful regional producer has been managed by Dario Guerra, who's personally responsible for both enology and agronomy, practicing a conventional viticulture grounded in ecology and sustainability, following nature's rhythms and minimizing human intervention. The Merlot '18 landed a place in our final selections. It features spicy notes, liquorice and black cherry all well blended, while contained but vivid tannins streamline the palate. The Friulano '19 exudes intense aromas of wild flowers, chamomile, apricot and almond, while the palate proves full and tasty. The Gritul Ris. '13 (Refosco, Merlot and Pignolo) is also excellent.

● FCO Merlot '18	🍷🍷 2*
○ FCO Friulano '19	🍷🍷 2*
○ FCO Malvasia '19	🍷🍷 2*
○ FCO Pinot Grigio '19	🍷🍷 2*
○ FCO Ribolla Gialla '19	🍷🍷 2*
● FCO Rosso Gritul Ris. '13	🍷🍷 4
○ FCO Sauvignon '19	🍷🍷 2*
○ FCO Friulano '18	🍷🍷 2*
● FCO Pignolo Matteo I '10	🍷🍷 5
● FCO Refosco P. R. Ris. '16	🍷🍷 3
● FCO Rosso Gritul Ris. '11	🍷🍷 4
○ FCO Sauvignon '18	🍷🍷 2*
○ Ribolla Gialla Brut Giuliet M. Cl. '16	🍷🍷 3*

Jacùss

FRAZ. MONTINA
V.LE KENNEDY, 35A
33040 TORREANO [UD]
TEL. +39 0432715147
www.jacuss.it

CELLAR SALES
PRE-BOOKED VISITS
ANNUAL PRODUCTION 50,000 bottles
HECTARES UNDER VINE 11.00

Jacùss is the Friulian version of Sandro and Andrea's surname (Iacuzzi). The pair founded the producer in 1990, embracing a trend that in those years led many farming families to convert their land from mixed cultivation to specializing in vineyards. Anchored to the dictates of their ancestors, they chose the varieties best suited to the particular characteristics of each plot and proceeded to significantly modernize the training systems. The results were not long in coming, and allowed the two to stand out in the already-crowded area of Cividale. Among the current-vintage wines, the Sauvignon '19 and Pinot Bianco '19 stand out. Naturally they're very different from each other but both prove highly elegant on the nose. The first unveils fresh whiffs of tart fruit and mint together with floral hints of magnolia, all of which accompany the palate, while the second offers up a delicious note of jasmine, white chocolate and ripe hay, caressing the palate with velvety hints only to close delicately.

○ COF Picolit '13	🍷🍷 6
○ FCO Friulano '19	🍷🍷 3
○ FCO Pinot Bianco '19	🍷🍷 3
● FCO Refosco P. R. '15	🍷🍷 3
○ FCO Sauvignon '19	🍷🍷 3
● FCO Schioppettino Fuc e Flamis '18	🍷🍷 3
○ FCO Verduzzo Friulano '17	🍷🍷 3
○ Friulano Forment '18	🍷🍷 3
○ Bianco Forment '15	🍷🍷 3*
● FCO Cabernet Sauvignon '16	🍷🍷 3
○ FCO Friulano '18	🍷🍷 3
● FCO Merlot '15	🍷🍷 3
○ FCO Pinot Bianco '18	🍷🍷 3
○ FCO Sauvignon '18	🍷🍷 3
● FCO Tazzelenghe '14	🍷🍷 3

★★★Jermann

FRAZ. RUTTARS
LOC. TRUSSIO, 11
34072 DOLEGNA DEL COLLIO [GO]
TEL. +39 0481888080
www.jermann.it

CELLAR SALES
ANNUAL PRODUCTION 900,000 bottles
HECTARES UNDER VINE 170.00
SUSTAINABLE WINERY

It was the 18th century when Stefanus migrated from Austrian Burgenland to the village of Bilijana, now in Slovenia. Later, in 1881, Anton Jermann, Silvio's great-grandfather, moved to Villanova and started the wine business which, in the 1970s, had a major breakthrough thanks to Silvio's genius and imagination. It's a producer that interacts with the world every day, but here there's no shortage of attention to what makes wine great. In the new cellar, technological innovation is skilfully integrated with architectural tradition. In the head-to-head between the Vintage Tunina '18 and the Capo Martino '18 the second took home Tre Bicchieri this year. A blend of only native grape varieties (Malvasia Istriana, Picolit, Ribolla Gialla and Tocai Friulano), it's a true expression of the territory, offering up a flowery bouquet of rare elegance accompanied by fresh, exotic whiffs of fruit salad, all in splendid harmony. Hats off...

Wine	Rating
○ Capo Martino '18	🍷🍷🍷 7
○ Vintage Tunina '18	🍷🍷 7
○ W.... Dreams.... '18	🍷🍷 8
○ Chardonnay '19	🍷🍷 4
○ Pinot Grigio '19	🍷🍷 4
● Red Angel Pinot Nero '17	🍷🍷 4
○ Sauvignon '19	🍷🍷 4
○ Vinnae Ribolla Gialla '19	🍷🍷 4
○ Capo Martino '16	🍷🍷🍷 7
○ Capo Martino '10	🍷🍷🍷 8
○ Pinot Grigio '15	🍷🍷🍷 4*
○ Vintage Tunina '17	🍷🍷🍷 7
○ Vintage Tunina '15	🍷🍷🍷 7
○ Vintage Tunina '13	🍷🍷🍷 6
○ Vintage Tunina '12	🍷🍷🍷 6
○ Vintage Tunina '11	🍷🍷🍷 6
○ W... Dreams... ... ... '12	🍷🍷🍷 8

★Edi Keber

LOC. ZEGLA, 17
34071 CORMÒNS [GO]
TEL. +39 048161184
www.edikeber.it

CELLAR SALES
PRE-BOOKED VISITS
ACCOMMODATION
ANNUAL PRODUCTION 50,000 bottles
HECTARES UNDER VINE 12.00

Keber is synonymous with Collio. More than ten years have passed since we made his decision to produce one wine known, one white that he would call simply 'Collio'. His was nothing more than a return to his origins, as at one time there was no such thing as producing single-variety wines. Tocai Friulano, Malvasia Istriana and Ribolla Gialla were vinified together, and the result was a stylistic complexity that underlined the territory's identity. In last year's edition we praised the courage of their decision to postpone the release of the only white wine produced. The move paid off, benefiting the wine's aromatic balance and gustatory harmony. The Collio '18 unveils delicious, floral aromas of jasmine and acacia blossom, calling up freshly-cut grass from mountain meadows, rich in flowers and wild herbs. In the mouth it's vivid and fragrant, unfolding progressively.

Wine	Rating
○ Collio '18	🍷🍷🍷 3*
○ Collio Bianco '10	🍷🍷🍷 3*
○ Collio Bianco '09	🍷🍷🍷 3
○ Collio Bianco '08	🍷🍷🍷 3*
○ Collio Bianco '04	🍷🍷🍷 3*
○ Collio Bianco '02	🍷🍷🍷 3
○ Collio Tocai Friulano '07	🍷🍷🍷 3
○ Collio Tocai Friulano '06	🍷🍷🍷 3
○ Collio Tocai Friulano '05	🍷🍷🍷 3
○ Collio Tocai Friulano '03	🍷🍷🍷 3*
○ Collio Tocai Friulano '01	🍷🍷🍷 3
○ Collio Tocai Friulano '99	🍷🍷🍷 3*
○ Collio Tocai Friulano '97	🍷🍷🍷 3*
○ Collio Tocai Friulano '95	🍷🍷🍷 3*

Alessio Komjanc

loc. Giasbana, 35
34070 San Floriano del Collio [GO]
Tel. +39 0481391228
www.komjancalessio.com

CELLAR SALES
PRE-BOOKED VISITS
ANNUAL PRODUCTION 80,000 bottles
HECTARES UNDER VINE 24.00
SUSTAINABLE WINERY

When he founded the producer in 1973, Alessio Komjanc's goal was to make wines and olive oil of the highest quality. It's the same goal that his sons, Beniamin, Roberto, Patrik and Ivani, have now set for themselves, and the four are bringing constancy and dedication to climbing the heights of excellence. Peaks can already be glimpsed thanks to the quality demonstrated by their latest vintages. Consultations with Gianni Menotti have been decisive, providing added value to a range that is always up to Collio's high quality standards. The Friulano '19 and the Pinot Nero Dedica '17 repeated last year's splendid performance and earned access to the finals, all in good company with the Pinot Bianco '19, an elegant, flowery, soft and creamy wine. But these are just the tip of the iceberg for a range that faithfully expresses the varietal characteristics of the grapes, as well as clear, focused flavor and exemplary balance.

○ Collio Friulano '19	TT 3*
○ Collio Pinot Bianco '19	TT 3*
● Pinot Nero Dedica '17	TT 4
○ Collio Bianco Bratje '15	TT 3
○ Collio Chardonnay '19	TT 3
● Collio Merlot '16	TT 3
○ Collio Sauvignon '19	TT 3
○ Malvasia '19	TT 2*
○ Collio Ribolla Gialla '19	T 3
○ Collio Friulano '18	YY 3*
○ Collio Friulano '16	YY 3*
○ Collio Pinot Grigio '17	YY 2*
○ Malvasia Istriana '15	YY 3*
● Pinot Nero Dedica '16	YY 4

Kurtin

loc. Novali, 12
34071 Cormòns [GO]
Tel. +39 3488672297
www.kurtin.it

CELLAR SALES
PRE-BOOKED VISITS
ANNUAL PRODUCTION 65,000 bottles
HECTARES UNDER VINE 10.00

Young Alessio Kurtin represents the fourth generation of winemakers to work in Novali, in the heart of Collio, since 1906. He's responsible for agronomic management of the vineyards, while administration is overseen by a corporate group who are working to develop the brand through restyling the labels and relaunching their global image. In the cellar enology is entrusted to the proven experience of Isacco Curtarello, making for a range characterized by deep territorial expression. The Collio Bianco Opera Prima '17 (Pinot Bianco, Chardonnay and Ribolla Gialla) features golden highlights accompanied by aromas of orange blossom, golden apple, anise, acacia honey and amaretto. In the mouth it's juicy yet fragrant, symmetrical and well balanced. The The Sauvignon '19 exudes notes of boxwood, pepper and bay leaf, aromas that follow through on the palate. The Friulano '19, in its simplicity, proves a gratifying drink.

○ Collio Bianco Opera Prima '17	TT 3
○ Collio Friulano '19	TT 3
● Collio Rosso '16	TT 3
○ Collio Sauvignon '19	TT 3
● Diamante Nero '17	TT 3
○ Risposta 110 Ribolla Gialla Brut	TT 3
○ Collio Ribolla Gialla '19	T 3
○ Collio Bianco Opera Prima '16	YY 3
○ Collio Friulano '18	YY 3
○ Collio Friulano '17	YY 3
○ Collio Ribolla Gialla '18	YY 3
● Collio Rosso '15	YY 3
● Collio Rosso '08	YY 4
○ Collio Sauvignon '18	YY 3
● Diamante Nero '16	YY 3
○ Opera Prima Bianco '11	YY 3*

Vigneti Le Monde

loc. Le Monde
via Garibaldi, 2
33080 Prata di Pordenone [PN]
Tel. +39 0434622087
www.lemondewine.com

CELLAR SALES
PRE-BOOKED VISITS
ANNUAL PRODUCTION 700,000 bottles
HECTARES UNDER VINE 85.00
SUSTAINABLE WINERY

Founded in 1970, in 2008 the winery was taken over by Alex Maccan. Le Monde, situated between the banks of the Livenza and Meduna rivers and bordering Veneto, is considered a true cru. Here the mostly calcareous-clayey soils are very different from the gravel of the Friulian plains. Yields per hectare are low and the average age of the vines is over thirty years. Alex's entrepreneurial skills have brought Le Monde to the heights of regional excellence. Looking over the last 10 vintages, an undisputed leader emerges, a wine that has contributed to the success of the entire range: the Pinot Bianco. The 2019 makes elegance its highest virtue and reconquers Tre Bicchieri. It's our Best Value for Money. Power and creaminess characterize the Pratum '17 (Chardonnay, Sauvignon and Pinot Bianco), which offers up sweet notes of honey and pastries.

Wine	Rating
○ Friuli Pinot Bianco '19	🍷🍷🍷 3*
○ Pratum Ris. '17	🍷🍷 4
○ Friuli Chardonnay '19	🍷🍷 3
● Friuli Grave Rosso Inaco Ris. '17	🍷🍷 4
● Friuli Merlot .73 '18	🍷🍷 3
○ Friuli Pinot Grigio '19	🍷🍷 2*
● Friuli Refosco P. R. '18	🍷🍷 3
○ Friuli Friulano '19	🍷 2
○ Friuli Chardonnay '17	🍸🍸🍸 3*
○ Friuli Grave Pinot Bianco '15	🍸🍸🍸 2*
○ Friuli Grave Pinot Bianco '14	🍸🍸🍸 2*
○ Friuli Grave Pinot Bianco '13	🍸🍸🍸 2*
○ Friuli Grave Pinot Bianco '12	🍸🍸🍸 2*
○ Friuli Pinot Bianco '18	🍸🍸🍸 3*
○ Friuli Pinot Bianco '16	🍸🍸🍸 2*

★★Lis Neris

via Gavinana, 5
34070 San Lorenzo Isontino [GO]
Tel. +39 048180105
www.lisneris.it

CELLAR SALES
PRE-BOOKED VISITS
ACCOMMODATION
ANNUAL PRODUCTION 400,000 bottles
HECTARES UNDER VINE 74.00
SUSTAINABLE WINERY

Alvaro Pecorari deserves credit for having transformed a small farm into a wine-growing estate and producer. Slowly but surely Lis Neris has grown to a respectable size such that today it's an important winery for the region and beyond. Their vineyards are situated in four distinct districts: Gris, Picol, Jurosa and Neris. Alvaro has been able to highlight the peculiarities of each single territory and has succeeded in establishing a personal style, taking advantage of strong day-night temperature swings, which help the slow ripening of the grapes, making them more solid and better balanced. The Pinot Grigio Gris '18 offers up alluring hints of lemon cream, marzipan, golden apple, tropical fruit and vanilla pod all on a backdrop of resins and a delicate saltiness. In the mouth it exhibits freshness and flavor. The Chardonnay Jurosa '17 is redolent of candied citrus fruits, hazelnut cream, cooked apple juice and Chinese magnolia. The palate is soft, velvety, with a pleasant iodine finish and a smoky echo.

Wine	Rating
○ Friuli Isonzo Pinot Grigio Gris '18	🍷🍷 5
○ Friuli Isonzo Chardonnay Jurosa '17	🍷🍷 5
○ Friuli Isonzo Friulano La Vila '17	🍷🍷 5
○ Friuli Isonzo Sauvignon Picol '18	🍷🍷 5
○ Friuli Isonzo Pinot Grigio Gris '13	🍸🍸🍸 4*
○ Friuli Isonzo Pinot Grigio Gris '12	🍸🍸🍸 4*
○ Friuli Isonzo Pinot Grigio Gris '11	🍸🍸🍸 4*
○ Lis '15	🍸🍸🍸 5
○ Tal Lùc Cuvée .1.2	🍸🍸🍸 8
○ Tal Lùc Cuvée Speciale	🍸🍸🍸 8
○ Friuli Isonzo Pinot Grigio Gris '17	🍸🍸 5
○ Friuli Isonzo Sauvignon Picol '17	🍸🍸 5

★★Livon

FRAZ. DOLEGNANO
VIA MONTAREZZA, 33
33048 SAN GIOVANNI AL NATISONE [UD]
TEL. +39 0432757173
www.livon.it

CELLAR SALES
PRE-BOOKED VISITS
ACCOMMODATION
ANNUAL PRODUCTION 850,000 bottles
HECTARES UNDER VINE 180.00

Livon, now managed by Valneo and Tonino, is one of the historic brands that have most contributed and continue to contribute to making the region a key player for wine in Italy and the world. The next generational changing of the guard is guaranteed by their children Matteo and Francesca (respectively), who are already integrated and active in the business. In addition to the famous Livon brand, with the icon of the winged woman that represents the parent company, four other producers have been added: RoncAlto in Collio, Villa Chiopris in the Friulian plain, Borgo Salcetino in Tuscany and Colsanto in Umbria. The Braide Alte '18 has taken back its crown and once again earns Tre Bicchieri. It's a wine whose creation goes back to the now-distant 1996 vintage, when Tonino and Valneo planted, in a single vineyard, the 4 varieties that would constitute the blend. A wine that's known and appreciated all over the world, it's been able to evolve over time, adapting to the demands of the market, especially when it comes to the use of oak for aging.

○ Braide Alte '18	▼▼▼	6
○ Collio Friulano Manditocai '18	▼▼	5
○ Collio Bianco Solarco '19	▼▼	4
○ Collio Malvasia Soluna '18	▼▼	3
○ Collio Ribolla Gialla RoncAlto '18	▼▼	3
● TiareBlù '17	▼▼	5
○ Braide Alte '13	▽▽▽	5
○ Braide Alte '11	▽▽▽	5
○ COF Picolit '12	▽▽▽	6
○ Collio Bianco Solarco '17	▽▽▽	3*
○ Collio Bianco Solarco '15	▽▽▽	3*
○ Collio Friulano Manditocai '17	▽▽▽	5
○ Collio Friulano Manditocai '12	▽▽▽	5
○ Collio Friulano Manditocai '10	▽▽▽	5
○ Braide Alte '17	▽▽	6
○ Collio Sauvignon Valbuins '18	▽▽	4

Tenuta Luisa

FRAZ. CORONA
VIA CAMPO SPORTIVO, 13
34070 MARIANO DEL FRIULI [GO]
TEL. +39 048169680
www.tenutaluisa.it

CELLAR SALES
PRE-BOOKED VISITS
ACCOMMODATION
ANNUAL PRODUCTION 350,000 bottles
HECTARES UNDER VINE 100.00
SUSTAINABLE WINERY

Tenuta Luisa has firmly established itself as one of the best wine-growing and producing estates in the region, in particular among those operating in the Friuli Isonzo appellation. Like every family-run business, it bears its simple agricultural origins proudly. In the early 1980s, Eddi Luisa inherited a few hectares of land and began to build its future by moving from mixed agriculture to viticulture. It's since grown to 100 hectares and his sons Michele and Davide are working in perfect harmony, supported by a tight-knit family group. The wines that make up the I Ferretti line, whites and reds, are a cut above the rest. In our finals, for some years now, we've seen the Desiderium '18 and Friulano '18 competing for the top place. This year the second won out, putting in a perfect performance and defeating the fierce competition. It takes home Tre Bicchieri.

○ Friuli Isonzo Friulano I Ferretti '18	▼▼▼	4*
○ Desiderium I Ferretti '18	▼▼	4
○ Friuli Isonzo Friulano '19	▼▼	3
○ Friuli Isonzo Pinot Bianco '19	▼▼	3
○ Friuli Isonzo Sauvignon '19	▼▼	3
● I Ferretti Cabernet Sauvignon '16	▼▼	4
● I Ferretti Refosco P. R. '16	▼▼	4
● Rôl I Ferretti '16	▼▼	5
○ Friuli Isonzo Chardonnay '19	▼	3
○ Ribolla Gialla '19	▼	3
○ Desiderium I Ferretti '17	▽▽▽	4*
○ Desiderium I Ferretti '16	▽▽▽	4*
○ Desiderium I Ferretti '13	▽▽▽	4*
○ Friuli Isonzo Friulano I Ferretti '15	▽▽▽	3*

Magnàs

Loc. Boatina
via Corona, 47
34071 Cormòns [GO]
Tel. +39 048160991
www.magnas.it

CELLAR SALES
PRE-BOOKED VISITS
ACCOMMODATION AND RESTAURANT SERVICE
ANNUAL PRODUCTION 25,000 bottles
HECTARES UNDER VINE 10.00

Magnàs' derives from the time-honored nickname for this branch of the Visintin family, pointing up values like loyalty, pride, dignity and a spirit of sacrifice. Today the small artisan producer is run by Andrea Visintin, who benefits from centuries of family experience in agriculture. The limited number of hectares under vine allows for maximum attention to each single vine. Not many bottles are produced and there are only a few different wines, but the quality is high and prices are very competitive. This year only white wines were submitted for tasting, all from the last harvest and all sharing in the clear aromatic focus that distinguishes each. In short, a respectable team effort with a standout performance from the Friulano '19. It earned a place in our finals by virtue of an elegant varietal profile that binds it to the territory but, above all, for its energy and substance on the palate.

Wine	Rating
○ Collio Friulano '19	🍷🍷 3*
○ Collio Chardonnay '19	🍷🍷 3
○ Collio Pinot Grigio '19	🍷🍷 3
○ Malvasia '19	🍷🍷 3
○ Sauvignon '19	🍷 3
○ Chardonnay '16	🍷🍷 3*
○ Collio Bianco '17	🍷🍷 3
○ Collio Friulano '18	🍷🍷 3
○ Malvasia '18	🍷🍷 3*
● Merlot Neri dal Murzùl '16	🍷🍷 3
○ Pinot Grigio '18	🍷🍷 3
○ Pinot Grigio '15	🍷🍷 3*

Marinig

via Brolo, 41
33040 Prepotto [UD]
Tel. +39 0432713012
www.marinig.it

CELLAR SALES
PRE-BOOKED VISITS
ANNUAL PRODUCTION 25,000 bottles
HECTARES UNDER VINE 9.00
SUSTAINABLE WINERY

As often happens in Friuli's classic family-run farms, where size and workload are on a smaller scale, there's a jack of all trades who oversees management. This role is now entrusted to Valerio Marinig, who's making use of the experience handed down from generation to generation since his great-grandfather Luigi founded the winery a century ago. The vineyards unfold across the hills of Prepotto, where unique morphological and climatic conditions have always allowed for quality cultivation. The Pignolo '15 has aged well, reaching the perfect level with its intriguing mix of black cherry, carob, black pepper and liquorice sensations accompanied by balsamic whiffs of pine resin. The Sauvignon '19 offers up suggestions of magnolia, sage and passionflower, while in the mouth it proves vibrant and vigorous. The Ribolla Gialla '19 also stands out. Apparently it's a simple wine but it exhibits nice acidic tension and a satisfying development.

Wine	Rating
● FCO Pignolo '15	🍷🍷 4
● FCO Cabernet Franc '18	🍷🍷 3
○ FCO Friulano '19	🍷🍷 2*
● FCO Merlot '18	🍷🍷 3
○ FCO Pinot Bianco '19	🍷🍷 2*
○ FCO Ribolla Gialla '19	🍷🍷 3
○ FCO Sauvignon '19	🍷🍷 3
○ FCO Verduzzo Friulano '18	🍷 3
○ Ribolla Gialla Brut	🍷 3
● COF Pignolo '08	🍷🍷 4
○ FCO Friulano '18	🍷🍷 2*
○ FCO Pinot Bianco '18	🍷🍷 2*
● FCO Refosco P. R. '16	🍷🍷 3
● FCO Refosco P. R. '12	🍷🍷 3*
● FCO Rosso Biel Cûr '16	🍷🍷 4
○ FCO Sauvignon '18	🍷🍷 3
● FCO Schioppettino di Prepotto '16	🍷🍷 4

Masùt da Rive

via Manzoni, 82
34070 Mariano del Friuli [GO]
Tel. +39 048169200
www.masutdarive.com

CELLAR SALES
PRE-BOOKED VISITS
ANNUAL PRODUCTION 120,000 bottles
HECTARES UNDER VINE 25.00
SUSTAINABLE WINERY

Masùt da Rive was the name chosen by Silvano Gallo when he formalized the winery. His sons Fabrizio and Marco, who now run it, have grown Masùt da Rive substantially, making it one of the most representative producers in the region. Their wines are increasingly intriguing and convincing, with marked territorial expression that highlights the attributes of the Friuli Isonzo appellation. Particular attention is paid to Pinot Nero, which has earned a role as their flagship wine. The Pinot Bianco '18 once again demonstrates that it's the leader of a cohesive and convincing group of wines. It stands out for the elegance of its aromatic spectrum, which opens on floral scents of lily of the valley and hawthorn only to unveil hints of exotic fruit and acacia honey. The Pinot Nero '18 calls up cherry jam and a beautiful amalgam of spices, which gratify the palate.

Wine	Rating
○ Friuli Isonzo Pinot Bianco '18	🍷🍷 5
○ Friuli Isonzo Chardonnay Maurus '18	🍷🍷 5
○ Friuli Isonzo Pinot Grigio Jesimis '18	🍷🍷 5
● Friuli Isonzo Pinot Nero '18	🍷🍷 5
● Friuli Isonzo Rosso Sassirossi '18	🍷🍷 3
○ Friuli Isonzo Friulano '19	🍷 3
○ Friuli Isonzo Pinot Grigio '19	🍷 3
○ Friuli Isonzo Sauvignon '19	🍷 3
○ Friuli Isonzo Pinot Bianco '17	🍸🍸🍸 5
○ Friuli Isonzo Pinot Bianco '16	🍸🍸🍸 5
○ Friuli Isonzo Chardonnay Maurus '15	🍸🍸 5
○ Friuli Isonzo Pinot Grigio '16	🍸🍸 3*
● Friuli Isonzo Pinot Nero Maurus '12	🍸🍸 6
● Friuli Isonzo Pinot Nero Maurus '11	🍸🍸 6

Davino Meroi

via Stretta, 7b
33042 Buttrio [UD]
Tel. +39 0432673369
www.meroi.wine

CELLAR SALES
PRE-BOOKED VISITS
RESTAURANT SERVICE
ANNUAL PRODUCTION 45,000 bottles
HECTARES UNDER VINE 19.00
SUSTAINABLE WINERY

Current owner Paolo Meroi has brought the winery founded by his father, Davino, to the top of the regional firmament. For many years he's been drawing on the grapes from his historic Vigna Dominin, planted by grandfather Domenico according to the old ways, though in the early 2000s he acquired the Vigna delle Zitelle, also in Buttrio. Paolo has been making use of a precious collaboration with Mirko Degan for some time now. Together they make thrilling, rich, concentrated wines, the result of time-honored techniques in the use of oak. Their whites, which are the result of careful zonal selections, and also the reds, even if they've already been bottled, will undergo a further period of aging. As a result we'll taste them in the next edition of our guide. This year only 3 wines from the 2018 harvest were proposed, but that was enough to confirm the enologist's skill, especially the complexity and juiciness of the Friulano '18.

Wine	Rating
○ FCO Friulano '18	🍷🍷 5
○ FCO Chardonnay '18	🍷🍷 5
○ FCO Ribolla Gialla '18	🍷🍷 5
○ COF Friulano '11	🍸🍸🍸 5
○ COF Friulano '10	🍸🍸🍸 5
● COF Merlot V. Dominin '11	🍸🍸 8
○ FCO Chardonnay '16	🍸🍸 5
○ FCO Chardonnay V. Dominin '16	🍸🍸 5
○ FCO Malvasia Zitelle Durì '16	🍸🍸 5
○ FCO Malvasia Zitelle Durì '13	🍸🍸 6
● FCO Merlot Ros di Buri '13	🍸🍸 5
● FCO Merlot V. Dominin '12	🍸🍸 8
○ FCO Sauvignon '16	🍸🍸 4
○ FCO Sauvignon '15	🍸🍸 4
○ FCO Verduzzo Friulano '13	🍸🍸 5

Modeano

fraz. Modeano
via Casali Modeano, 1
33056 Palazzolo dello Stella [UD]
Tel. +39 043158244
www.modeano.it

CELLAR SALES
PRE-BOOKED VISITS
ANNUAL PRODUCTION 40,000 bottles
HECTARES UNDER VINE 32.00
SUSTAINABLE WINERY

It was 1982 when Emanuela and Gabriele Vialetto, newly married, decided to look after Modeano's vineyards and cellar, continuing a tradition that dates back to the early part of the 20th century. The vines grow in strong but well drained soils and the climate, one of the driest in Friuli, is mitigated by the breezes of the nearby Adriatic Sea. Constant renewal of the vineyards has led to a substantial reduction in yields, something rare in lowland wine-growing, and as a consequence the wines have benefited in olfactory and mineral qualities. The large number of wines tasted, both whites and reds, allowed for a general overview of the winery, with notable results (their prices are certainly not to be underestimated, either). The Pinot Grigio '19 offers up hints of russet pear and macaroons, while in the mouth it proves fragrant and dynamic. We also appreciated the dense and energetic Cabernet Sauvignon '18.

● Friuli Cabernet Sauvignon '18	🍷🍷 2*
○ Friuli Chardonnay '19	🍷🍷 2*
○ Friuli Pinot Grigio '19	🍷🍷 2*
● Friuli Refosco P. R. '18	🍷🍷 2*
● Friulia Merlot '18	🍷🍷 2*
○ Friuli Friulano '19	🍷 2
○ Friuli Sauvignon '19	🍷 2
○ Ribolla Gialla '19	🍷 2
● Friuli Cabernet Sauvignon '16	🍷🍷 2*
○ Friuli Chardonnay '17	🍷🍷 2*
○ Friuli Friulano '18	🍷🍷 2*
○ Friuli Malvasia '17	🍷🍷 2*
○ Friuli Pinot Grigio '18	🍷🍷 2*
○ Friuli Pinot Grigio '17	🍷🍷 2*
● Friuli Refosco P. R. '17	🍷🍷 2*
● Friulia Merlot '17	🍷🍷 2*
○ Ribolla Gialla '17	🍷🍷 2*

Monviert

via Strada di Spessa, 8
33043 Cividale del Friuli [UD]
Tel. +39 0432716172
www.monviert.com

CELLAR SALES
PRE-BOOKED VISITS
ANNUAL PRODUCTION 350,000 bottles
HECTARES UNDER VINE 87.00
SUSTAINABLE WINERY

Three generations of winegrowers and seventy years of history traced the path of the winery known as Ronchi San Giuseppe until 2018. Modernization and a change of image began with the renovation of the production headquarters, which were transformed into a small village reminiscent of the area's characteristic rural properties. But the real turning point came with the change of brand. Today Monviert is represented by a series of wines, the result of careful grape selection, while the rest of their range, called Martagona, reflects a more traditional approach. The Picolit '16 immediately stood out and, with its sweet notes, it won a ticket to our final selections. On the nose, it's redolent of dried apricot and figs, barley candy, honey, dates and cinnamon. A very sweet wine, it's juicy but not at all cloying. The Friulano '18 exhibits a highly territorial profile, with its hints of ripe fruit, almonds and crème brûlée, while the palate comes through pervasive and flavorful.

○ FCO Picolit '16	🍷🍷 6
○ FCO Friulano '18	🍷🍷 5
○ FCO Friulano Martagona '19	🍷🍷 2*
○ FCO Pinot Grigio Martagona '19	🍷🍷 2*
● FCO Refosco P. R. '16	🍷🍷 5
● FCO Refosco P. R. Martagona '17	🍷🍷 2*
○ FCO Sauvignon Martagona '19	🍷🍷 3
● FCO Schioppettino '16	🍷🍷 5
● FCO Schioppettino Martagona '17	🍷🍷 3
○ FCO Ribolla Gialla Martagona '19	🍷 3
○ FCO Ribolla Gialla '18	🍷🍷 2*
○ FCO Sauvignon '18	🍷🍷 2*

Murva - Renata Pizzulin

via Celso Macor, 1
34070 Moraro [GO]
Tel. +39 0432713027
www.murva.it

CELLAR SALES
PRE-BOOKED VISITS
ANNUAL PRODUCTION 15,000 bottles
HECTARES UNDER VINE 4.00
SUSTAINABLE WINERY

Alberto Pelos and Renata Pizzulin are a young couple who, about ten years ago, decided to set up their own winery on the right bank of the So?a river. It was a question of starting from scratch, so the grapes best suited to the soil and climate of each individual plot were chosen. The farm's small size allowed Alberto to choose agronomic practices based on environmental sustainability, and the quality of his wines immediately won the praise of consumers and critics. Their range of wines is increasingly impressive, and the 2018 vintage surpassed expectations. Almost all the wines made it to the threshold of the finals, but one broke through, the Chardonnay Monuments '18, a clear, focused wine on the nose and pleasant in the mouth. It's characterized by aromas of tropical fruit, magnolia, saffron and honey, pervading the palate, then lingering and closing with balsamic notes.

Wine	Rating
○ Friuli Isonzo Chardonnay Monuments '18	▼▼ 4
○ Friuli Isonzo Chardonnay Paladis '18	▼▼ 4
○ Friuli Isonzo Malvasia Melaris '18	▼▼ 4
● Friuli Isonzo Refosco P. R. Murellis '16	▼▼ 4
○ Friuli Isonzo Sauvignon Corvatis '18	▼▼ 4
○ Friuli Isonzo Sauvignon Teolis '18	▼▼ 4
○ Friuli Isonzo Chardonnay Paladis '17	▽▽ 4
○ Friuli Isonzo Chardonnay Paladis '16	▽▽ 4
○ Friuli Isonzo Malvasia Melaris '17	▽▽ 4
○ Friuli Isonzo Sauvignon Corvatis '17	▽▽ 3
○ Friuli Isonzo Sauvignon Teolis '17	▽▽ 4
○ Friuli Isonzo Sauvignon Teolis '16	▽▽ 4

Muzic

loc. Bivio, 4
34070 San Floriano del Collio [GO]
Tel. +39 0481884201
www.cantinamuzic.it

CELLAR SALES
PRE-BOOKED VISITS
ANNUAL PRODUCTION 100,000 bottles
HECTARES UNDER VINE 23.00
SUSTAINABLE WINERY

The Muzic family's adventure in the world of wine began in the early 1960s when they had the opportunity to buy five hectares of vineyards that they were already working as sharecroppers. Now the winery has grown, but it has remained small enough that Giovanni, its current owner, can manage it together with his sons Elija and Fabijan, who have been involved for some time. Mother Orieta provides added value to a very cohesive family group. Once again the Collio Bianco Stare Brajde '18 (Tocai Friulano, Malvasia Istriana and Ribolla Gialla) has what it takes to confirm its status as the producer's flagship, landing a place in the finals. But it's not alone, in fact it's accompanied by a splendid Friulano V. Valeris '19. The first stands out for its aromatic mix and harmony on the palate, while the second excels for its varietal correctness and for its gustatory elegance.

Wine	Rating
○ Collio Bianco Stare Brajde '18	▼▼ 4
○ Collio Friulano V. Valeris '19	▼▼ 3*
○ Collio Chardonnay '19	▼▼ 3
○ Collio Malvasia '19	▼▼ 3
○ Collio Pinot Grigio '19	▼▼ 3
○ Collio Ribolla Gialla '19	▼▼ 3
○ Collio Sauvignon V. Pàjze '19	▼▼ 3
● Friuli Isonzo Merlot '18	▼▼ 3
○ Collio Bianco Stare Brajde '17	▽▽ 3*
○ Collio Bianco Stare Brajde '16	▽▽ 3*
○ Collio Chardonnay '18	▽▽ 3
○ Collio Chardonnay '17	▽▽ 3*
○ Collio Friulano V. Valeris '18	▽▽ 3
○ Collio Pinot Grigio '18	▽▽ 3
○ Collio Ribolla Gialla '18	▽▽ 3
○ Collio Sauvignon V. Pàjze '18	▽▽ 3

Alessandro Pascolo

loc. Ruttars, 1
34070 Dolegna del Collio [GO]
Tel. +39 048161144
www.vinipascolo.com

CELLAR SALES
PRE-BOOKED VISITS
ANNUAL PRODUCTION 25,000 bottles
HECTARES UNDER VINE 7.00
SUSTAINABLE WINERY

Set atop the sunny slopes of the Ruttars hills, Alessandro Pascolo's winery operates at a human scale that allows him to personally oversee all stages of production. The vineyards enjoy ideal exposures and permit Alessandro to masterfully interpret the territory, while also allowing for a strong varietal imprint. Their whites are vinified in steel, while extremely fine-grained mid-sized casks are used the reds. From the last vintage, only the Sauvignon '19 has been bottled, and it was very well received. But Alessandro decided to propose 3 wines from his collection, which are the result of experimentation and subjected to long aging: the Studio di Bianco '16 (Tocai Friulano, Riesling and Sauvignon), which is still fruity and floral, the Dis '15 (Tocai Friulano and Malvasia Istriana) and the Merlot Sveva '16.

Wine	Rating
○ Collio Bianco Studio di Bianco '16	5
● Collio Merlot Sveva '16	5
○ Collio Sauvignon '19	3
○ Dis '15	4
○ Collio Bianco Agnul '17	4
○ Collio Bianco Agnul '16	4
○ Collio Friulano '18	3
○ Collio Malvasia '15	3*
● Collio Merlot Sel. '15	5
○ Collio Pinot Bianco '18	3
○ Collio Sauvignon '18	3
○ Collio Sauvignon '17	3
● Pascal '17	4
● Pascal '16	4

Pierpaolo Pecorari

via Tommaseo, 56
34070 San Lorenzo Isontino [GO]
Tel. +39 0481808775
www.pierpaolopecorari.it

CELLAR SALES
PRE-BOOKED VISITS
ANNUAL PRODUCTION 150,000 bottles
HECTARES UNDER VINE 30.00

In the high plain furrowed by the river Isonzo, the bond between the Pecorari family and the land goes back before anyone can remember. In the early 1970s, Pierpaolo decided to create his own winery, which he still manages together with his son Alessandro. When it comes to winemaking, he's always had a pragmatic philosophy aimed at capturing the best varietal characteristics that each single vine, in accordance with its territorial peculiarities, can express. Their range is comprised of three different lines which take into account the age of each single plot. Both the Sauvignon Kolaus '18 and the Pinot Grigio Olivers '18 are part of their line of crus. They ferment in oak barrels with indigenous yeasts and then mature there for a further 11 months. The former has fresh notes of citrus and kiwi fruit, delivering on the palate with a prolonged and persuasive acidic tension. The second plays on fruity notes of peach and russet pear, while in the mouth it proves soft and balanced.

Wine	Rating
○ Pinot Grigio Olivers '18	5
● Refosco P. R. Tao '16	5
○ Sauvignon Kolaus '18	5
○ Friuli Friulano '19	3
○ Friuli Pinot Grigio '19	3
○ Malvasia '19	3
○ Adsum	4
○ Malvasia '15	3*
● Merlot '16	3
● Merlot Baolar '16	5
○ Pinot Grigio Olivers '12	5
○ Sauvignon '18	3
○ Sauvignon Blanc Altis '11	4
○ Sauvignon Kolaus '17	5

Perusini

LOC. GRAMOGLIANO
VIA DEL TORRIONE, 13
33040 CORNO DI ROSAZZO [UD]
TEL. +39 0432759151
www.perusini.com

CELLAR SALES
PRE-BOOKED VISITS
ACCOMMODATION AND RESTAURANT SERVICE
ANNUAL PRODUCTION 100,000 bottles
HECTARES UNDER VINE 15.00
VITICULTURE METHOD Certified Organic
SUSTAINABLE WINERY

In the late 19th century, when French wines dominated, Giacomo Perusini began selecting native regional grape varieties. He's still credited with having rehabilitated Picolit, the region's pearl, which found its ideal habitat on Rocca Bernarda. His successors were also important for the world of wine, bringing the producer to its current owner, Teresa Perusini. Together with her sons Carlo, Tommaso and Michele, she's taken on the responsibility of further developing the prestigious brand. While waiting for last year's whites, which at the time of tasting hadn't been bottled yet, our attention went to an excellent Rosso del Postiglione '16, a blend of mostly Merlot and Cabernet Sauvignon with a splash of Refosco dal Peduncolo Rosso, for a regional touch. Cloves and black pepper open the nose, then small black fruits, tobacco and balsamic hints close the palate.

○ COF Picolit '16	🍷🍷 8
● FCO Cabernet Franc '17	🍷🍷 3
○ FCO Chardonnay '18	🍷🍷 3
● FCO Merlot '17	🍷🍷 3
● FCO Rosso del Postiglione '16	🍷🍷 3
○ COF Picolit '15	🍷🍷 8
● FCO Cabernet Franc '16	🍷🍷 3
● FCO Cabernet Sauvignon '16	🍷🍷 3
○ FCO Chardonnay '16	🍷🍷 3
○ FCO Friulano '18	🍷🍷 3
● FCO Merlot '16	🍷🍷 3
● FCO Merlot '15	🍷🍷 3
○ FCO Pinot Grigio '18	🍷🍷 3
● FCO Refosco P.R. '16	🍷🍷 3
○ FCO Ribolla Gialla '17	🍷🍷 3
● FCO Rosso del Postiglione '15	🍷🍷 3
○ FCO Sauvignon '18	🍷🍷 3

Petrucco

VIA MORPURGO, 12
33042 BUTTRIO [UD]
TEL. +39 0432674387
www.vinipetrucco.it

CELLAR SALES
PRE-BOOKED VISITS
ANNUAL PRODUCTION 80,000 bottles
HECTARES UNDER VINE 25.00

In 1981 Paolo Petrucco and his wife, Lina, took over a winery whose history is bound up with Italo Balbo. Before the adventurer's plane was shot down over the skies of Libya in 1940, he planted some vineyards on the sunny slopes of the Buttrio hills. Those vines, now of venerable age and deeply rooted in the soil, are a precious asset closely watched over. After careful selection of their grapes, and with the support of skilled enologist Flavio Cabas, they give rise to the Ronco del Balbo reserve, the winery's crown jewel. The Bianco Cabas Ronco del Balbo '18 (Tocai Friulianp, Chardonnay, Malvasia Istriana and Sauvignon) bears the name of its creator, the producer's enologist. In the latest version it's particularly intriguing and elegant. The nose exudes lemongrass, sage, ginger and citron peel, before moving to tantalizing hints of saltiness. The palate comes through soft and well balanced by freshness and flavour.

○ FCO Bianco Cabas Ronco del Balbo '18	🍷🍷 4
○ FCO Friulano '19	🍷🍷 3
○ FCO Malvasia '19	🍷🍷 3
● FCO Merlot Ronco del Balbo '17	🍷🍷 4
● FCO Pignolo '15	🍷🍷 4
○ FCO Sauvignon '19	🍷🍷 3
○ FCO Pinot Bianco '19	🍷 3
● COF Merlot Ronco del Balbo '12	🍷🍷 4
○ FCO Bianco Cabas Ronco del Balbo '17	🍷🍷 4
○ FCO Bianco Cabas Ronco del Balbo '16	🍷🍷 4
● FCO Merlot Ronco del Balbo '16	🍷🍷 4
● FCO Pignolo Ronco del Balbo '13	🍷🍷 5
● FCO Refosco P. R. Ronco del Balbo '17	🍷🍷 4
● FCO Refosco P. R. Ronco del Balbo '15	🍷🍷 4

Petrussa

via Albana, 49
33040 Prepotto [UD]
Tel. +39 0432713192
www.petrussa.it

CELLAR SALES
PRE-BOOKED VISITS
ACCOMMODATION
ANNUAL PRODUCTION 45,000 bottles
HECTARES UNDER VINE 10.00

In 1986 brothers Gianni and Paolo Petrussa took over management of the family business from their parents. They immediately set themselves the objective of highlighting the attributes of their production area, Albana di Prepotto, a narrow strip of land considered the cradle of Schioppettino. The vineyards are divided into small plots located in the northern part of the Friuli Colli Orientali appellation, close to the Julian Pre-alps, in a valley sheltered from strong eastern winds, enjoying an ideal microclimate for the ripening of grapes. Unfortunately the last vintage's whites still hadn't been bottled at the time of our tastings. To compensate, we tasted two versions of Schioppettino di Prepotto from 2017. The one called S. Elena is dark both in color and aromatically, with whiffs of black pepper, cocoa and macerated cherries rising up to the nose, while with the second fruit and spices lend crunchiness and fragrance, streamlining the palate.

Wine	Rating
○ FCO Chardonnay S. Elena '18	🍷🍷 4
● FCO Rosso Petrussa '17	🍷🍷 5
● FCO Schioppettino di Prepotto '17	🍷🍷 5
● FCO Schioppettino di Prepotto S. Elena '17	🍷🍷 5
● COF Schioppettino di Prepotto '12	🍷🍷 5
○ FCO Chardonnay S. Elena '17	🍷🍷 4
○ FCO Friulano '18	🍷🍷 3
○ FCO Pinot Bianco '18	🍷🍷 3
● FCO Rosso Petrussa '16	🍷🍷 5
○ FCO Sauvignon '18	🍷🍷 3
● FCO Schioppettino di Prepotto '16	🍷🍷 5
● FCO Schioppettino di Prepotto '15	🍷🍷 5
● FCO Schioppettino di Prepotto '14	🍷🍷 5
○ Pensiero '16	🍷🍷 5

Norina Pez

via Zorutti, 4
34070 Dolegna del Collio [GO]
Tel. +39 0481639951
www.norinapez.it

CELLAR SALES
PRE-BOOKED VISITS
ANNUAL PRODUCTION 40,000 bottles
HECTARES UNDER VINE 7.00

The producer founded in the early 1980s by Norina Pez has been run for some time now by her son Stefano Bernardis, heir to a family long dedicated to winemaking on the hills of Dolegna del Collio, in the far north of the province of Gorizia. The estate's vineyards extend over the hilly strip between the Isonzo and Judrio rivers, protected by the Julian Alps and open to the breezes of the Adriatic Sea. The microclimate and the peculiarity of the subsoil, composed of Eocene marl and sandstone, create the conditions for a high quality range of wines. Their entire range put in an excellent performance, but the Schioppettino '17 is definitely a cut above the rest. One of the best in its category, it earned access to our finals. The nose offers up suggestions of bottled cherries, licorice root, black pepper, cardamom, cinchona and coffee beans; in the mouth it's dynamic, with lively but mature tannins, all well-balanced by a velvety softness.

Wine	Rating
● Schioppettino '17	🍷🍷 3*
○ Collio Friulano '19	🍷🍷 2*
● Collio Merlot '17	🍷🍷 2*
○ Collio Pinot Grigio '19	🍷🍷 2*
○ Collio Ribolla Gialla '19	🍷🍷 3
○ Collio Sauvignon '19	🍷🍷 2*
● El Neri di Norina '15	🍷🍷 5
○ Collio Chardonnay '19	🍷 2
● Collio Cabernet Franc '16	🍷🍷 2*
● Collio Merlot '16	🍷🍷 2*
○ Collio Pinot Grigio '18	🍷🍷 2*
○ Collio Pinot Grigio '17	🍷🍷 2*
○ Collio Sauvignon '18	🍷🍷 2*
○ Collio Sauvignon '17	🍷🍷 2*
● El Neri di Norina '13	🍷🍷 5
● Schioppettino '16	🍷🍷 3

Roberto Picech

LOC. PRADIS, 11
34071 CORMÒNS [GO]
TEL. +39 048160347
www.picech.com

CELLAR SALES
PRE-BOOKED VISITS
ACCOMMODATION
ANNUAL PRODUCTION 30,000 bottles
HECTARES UNDER VINE 8.00
VITICULTURE METHOD Certified Organic
SUSTAINABLE WINERY

Roberto Picech is an icon for Collio, a true wine artisan, an undisputed leader. Son of Egidio, known as 'the rebel', he inherited his father's vineyards but also the frank, stubborn character that's allowed him to confer a personal identity on his wines. Always open to the new but strongly respectful of tradition, he's always eschewed fashion. For both reds and whites his winemaking style includes prolonged maceration, sometimes for a few days, in order to extract as much aroma as possible. The 3 wines presented are all fundamentally different, however they share a common energy. The Friulano Athena '17 is a summery wine that unveils vibrant aromas of apricot jam, hay and honey while in the mouth it's substantive, varietal, closing on a pleasantly bitter note. It's a mature wine, among the best in its category, and does honor to the cultivar.

Wine	Rating
○ Collio Friulano Athena '17	🍷🍷 5
○ Collio Bianco Jelka '15	🍷🍷 4
● Collio Rosso Ruben Ris. '16	🍷🍷 6
○ Collio Bianco Jelka '11	🍷🍷🍷 4*
○ Collio Pinot Bianco '13	🍷🍷🍷 3*
○ Collio Bianco Athena Magnum '16	🍷🍷 7
○ Collio Bianco Atto Unico '18	🍷🍷 3*
○ Collio Friulano '17	🍷🍷 3
○ Collio Malvasia '17	🍷🍷 3
○ Collio Malvasia '16	🍷🍷 3*
○ Collio Malvasia '14	🍷🍷 3*
○ Collio Pinot Bianco '17	🍷🍷 3*
○ Collio Pinot Bianco '16	🍷🍷 3*
● Collio Rosso '14	🍷🍷 3*
● Collio Rosso Ruben Ris. '15	🍷🍷 6
● Collio Rosso Ruben Ris. '11	🍷🍷 6

Pighin

FRAZ. RISANO
V.LE GRADO, 11/1
33050 PAVIA DI UDINE [UD]
TEL. +39 0432675444
www.pighin.com

CELLAR SALES
PRE-BOOKED VISITS
ANNUAL PRODUCTION 800,000 bottles
HECTARES UNDER VINE 160.00
SUSTAINABLE WINERY

It was 1963 when the three brothers Luigi, Ercole and Fernando Pighin acquired 200 hectares of land belonging to a noble Friulian family, established their business and built the cellar. A few years later they expanded their holdings with the acquisition of another estate in Spessa di Capriva, on the Gorizia Collio. In 2004 management passed to Fernando's family, which includes his wife, Danila, and their children Roberto and Raffaela. A 17th-century Venetian villa, surrounded by a wonderful estate, serves as the producer's headquarters. The Collio Bianco Soreli '18 leads a group of wines interpreted in a modern style, one characterized by linearity, grace and elegant gustatory structure. It's a blend of Ribolla Gialla, Malvasia Istriana and Tocai Friulano, the area's most representative white grapes. In local dialect 'Soreli' means 'sun', and indeed, the nose evokes summer haymaking, wild flowers, sunflowers, ripe fruit and Malaga ice cream.

Wine	Rating
○ Collio Bianco Soreli '18	🍷🍷 5
○ Collio Friulano '19	🍷🍷 3
○ Collio Malvasia '19	🍷🍷 3
○ Collio Pinot Grigio '19	🍷🍷 3
○ Collio Ribolla Gialla '19	🍷🍷 3
○ Collio Sauvignon '19	🍷🍷 3
○ Friuli Grave Friulano '19	🍷🍷 2*
○ Friuli Grave Pinot Grigio '19	🍷 2
○ Friuli Grave Sauvignon '19	🍷 2
○ Ribolla Gialla '19	🍷 2
○ Collio Chardonnay '18	🍷🍷 3
○ Collio Chardonnay '17	🍷🍷 5
○ Collio Malvasia '18	🍷🍷 3
○ Collio Malvasia '17	🍷🍷 5
○ Collio Pinot Grigio '18	🍷🍷 3
○ Collio Ribolla Gialla '17	🍷🍷 5
○ Friuli Grave Chardonnay '17	🍷🍷 4

Pitars

via Tonello, 10
33098 San Martino al Tagliamento [PN]
Tel. +39 043488078
www.pitars.it

CELLAR SALES
PRE-BOOKED VISITS
ANNUAL PRODUCTION 800,000 bottles
HECTARES UNDER VINE 150.00
SUSTAINABLE WINERY

Brothers Loris, Bruno, Mauro and Paolo are the present, while Stefano, Nicola, Jessica and Judy represent the fourth generation, the future of this well-established brand. 'Pitars' is a local word referring to Pittaro, a historic family whose name is bound up with wine production in the vast Friulian plain straddling the Tagliamento river and the provinces of Udine and Pordenone. Their modern cellar, built according to green principles, brings together aesthetics and functionality. The Sauvignon '19 confirmed the splendid performance put in last year; once again it leads a group of wines characterized by excellent craftsmanship. On the nose it maintains its fragrances of citrus fruits and mint, which render the palate supple. In addition to a large number of sparkling wines, this year we tasted a series of blends, both whites and reds, which testify to the producer's willingness to satisfy every market demand.

Wine	Rating
● Brumal '17	🍷🍷 4
○ Cuntrevint '19	🍷🍷 4
● Friuli Refosco P.R. '18	🍷🍷 5
○ Friuli Sauvignon '19	🍷🍷 3
○ Friuli Traminer Aromatico '19	🍷🍷 2*
○ Pas Dosé M. Cl. '17	🍷🍷 5
○ Sèris '19	🍷🍷 4
○ Tèis '19	🍷🍷 3
○ Tureis '17	🍷🍷 4
● Naos '16	🍷 4
○ Prosecco Extra Dry	🍷 2
○ Ribolla Gialla Brut	🍷 2
● Friuli Rosso Brumal '16	🍷🍷 3
○ Friuli Sauvignon '18	🍷🍷 3*
○ Friuli Traminer Aromatico '18	🍷🍷 2*
○ Malvasia '18	🍷🍷 2*
○ Tureis '16	🍷🍷 4

Vigneti Pittaro

via Udine, 67
33033 Codroipo [UD]
Tel. +39 0432904726
www.vignetipittaro.com

CELLAR SALES
PRE-BOOKED VISITS
ACCOMMODATION
ANNUAL PRODUCTION 300,000 bottles
HECTARES UNDER VINE 90.00
SUSTAINABLE WINERY

Piero Pittaro is a prominent figure in the world of wine, and not only in Friuli. During his long journey he has held many institutional positions at an international level, without ever losing contact with the needs of his winery, which he has always managed personally with the precious help of Stefano Trinco, a true jack-of-all-trades. Most of the vineyards surround the historic property in Codroipo, while another five hectares on the beautiful steep hills of Ramandolo give rise to the native grapes for their Ronco Vieri line. The large number of wines in their portfolio is able to satisfy every type of request, but for some time we've focused on their sparkling wines, all rigorously Metodo Classico, and the Ronco Vieri line. The entire range exhibits outstanding quality, led by the Pittaro Et. Oro Pas Dosé M. Cl. '13 whose sublime elegance and crunchy flavor make it the best of the lot.

Wine	Rating
○ Pittaro Et. Oro Pas Dosé M. Cl. '13	🍷🍷 6
○ FCO Friulano Ronco Vieri '18	🍷🍷 3
○ Pittaro Brut Et. Argento M. Cl.	🍷🍷 4
⊙ Pittaro Brut Rosé Pink	🍷🍷 5
○ Pittaro Et. Oro Brut M. Cl. '13	🍷🍷 5
○ Ramandolo Ronco Vieri '16	🍷🍷 3
○ Ribolla Gialla Brut	🍷🍷 5
● FCO Refosco P. R. Ronco Vieri '17	🍷 3
○ FCO Friulano Ronco Vieri '17	🍷🍷 3
○ Pittaro Brut Et. Argento	🍷🍷 4
○ Pittaro Brut Et. Oro '10	🍷🍷 5
○ Pittaro Brut Et. Oro Pas Dosé '09	🍷🍷 6
⊙ Pittaro Brut Rosé Pink	🍷🍷 5
○ Pittaro Et. Oro Brut M. Cl. '12	🍷🍷 5
○ Pittaro Et. Oro Brut M. Cl. '11	🍷🍷 5
○ Pittaro Et. Oro Pas Dosé '11	🍷🍷 6
○ Ribolla Gialla Brut	🍷🍷 5

Denis Pizzulin

via Brolo, 43
33040 Prepotto [UD]
Tel. +39 0432713425
www.pizzulin.com

CELLAR SALES
PRE-BOOKED VISITS
ANNUAL PRODUCTION 35,000 bottles
HECTARES UNDER VINE 11.00
SUSTAINABLE WINERY

Theirs is a small selection, but plenty of passion and innate enological skills have allowed Denis Pizzulin to establish his winery as a benchmark for Prepotto. Situated on the border between Slovenia and Collio, it's a narrow valley protected from the wind and teeming with small family farms that make use of time-honored experience. It's the home of Ribolla Nera, the grape used to produce Schioppettino, a mainstay for the area and for Denis's winery. Nevertheless, here all their wines are afforded equal dignity. Once again this year all the wines obtained very similar, and high, scores. The Schioppettino di Prepotto '17 and Rarisolchi '18 (Pinot Bianco and Sauvignon) were once again well received, while this year's news comes in the form of two 2018s from a new line, called Lastris, which immediately stood out.

Wine	Rating	Price
○ FCO Bianco Rarisolchi '18	▼▼	4
○ FCO Friulano '19	▼▼	3
○ FCO Pinot Grigio '19	▼▼	3
● FCO Pinot Nero Lastris '18	▼▼	5
○ FCO Sauvignon '19	▼▼	3
○ FCO Sauvignon Lastris '18	▼▼	5
● FCO Schioppettino di Prepotto '17	▼▼	5
○ FCO Bianco Rarisolchi '17	▽▽	3*
○ FCO Friulano '18	▽▽	3
○ FCO Friulano '17	▽▽	3
● FCO Merlot Scaglia Rossa Ris. '16	▽▽	5
● FCO Merlot Scaglia Rossa Ris. '15	▽▽	5
○ FCO Pinot Grigio '18	▽▽	3
● FCO Refosco P. R. Ris '16	▽▽	5
○ FCO Sauvignon '18	▽▽	3
● FCO Schioppettino di Prepotto '16	▽▽	5
○ Pinot Bianco '18	▽▽	3

Damijan Podversic

via Brigata Pavia, 61
34170 Gorizia
Tel. +39 048178217
www.damijanpodversic.com

CELLAR SALES
PRE-BOOKED VISITS
ANNUAL PRODUCTION 33,000 bottles
HECTARES UNDER VINE 10.00
VITICULTURE METHOD Certified Organic
SUSTAINABLE WINERY

Damijan Podversic's philosophy of life is linked to farming, aware that working with nature means respecting its rhythms and accepting its challenges. He's been pursuing and perfecting his courageous approach from a young age: low yields in the vineyard, long fermentation on the skins, no cultured yeasts whatsoever, no clarification, no filtration and no temperature control. Such time-honored techniques may seem out of step with the times, but today they're back in the name of respect for nature and the environment. This year, in addition to the usual array of wines released 4 years after harvest, we were offered the chance to taste an amazing Ribolla Gialla '10. What to say... unusual aromas for a wine: toffee, nougat, salted caramel, chestnut honey. But in the mouth there's no question, it goes down with continuity and grace. Tre Bicchieri. The other wines are just as good, especially the powerful and very long Nekaj '16.

Wine	Rating	Price
○ Ribolla Gialla Selezione '10	▼▼▼	8
○ Kaplja '16	▼▼	6
○ Malvasia '16	▼▼	6
○ Nekaj '16	▼▼	6
● Prelit '16	▼▼	6
○ Ribolla Gialla '16	▼▼	6
○ Kaplja '08	▽▽▽	6
○ Malvasia '15	▽▽▽	8
○ Malvasia '13	▽▽▽	8
○ Malvasia '10	▽▽▽	6
○ Malvasia '09	▽▽▽	6
○ Nekaj '14	▽▽▽	6
○ Ribolla Gialla '12	▽▽▽	8
○ Malvasia '14	▽▽	8
○ Nekaj '15	▽▽	6
○ Ribolla Gialla '15	▽▽	8
○ Ribolla Gialla '14	▽▽	8

Isidoro Polencic

Loc. Plessiva, 12
34071 Cormòns [GO]
Tel. +39 048160655
www.polencic.com

CELLAR SALES
PRE-BOOKED VISITS
ACCOMMODATION
ANNUAL PRODUCTION 120,000 bottles
HECTARES UNDER VINE 28.00

Isidoro Polencic, a great master of the vineyard and cellar, founded his winery in 1968 and then led it for many years, growing it to a respectable size for an entirely family-managed operation. Continuity is now entrusted to his three children Elisabetta, Michele and Alex, who have demonstrated truly rare skills considering their young age. The cellar, which is situated in Cormons, is surrounded by a part of the vineyards, while others still are located in various neighboring districts. It's a factor that allows the producer to offer a complete overview of Collio's potential. Michele and Alex once again demonstrated their deep-rooted skill in winemaking. Year after year, they submit wines that are increasingly impressive and elegant. The Pinot Bianco '19 excels for the elegance of its bouquet, with floral notes of jasmine and lily of the valley giving way to whiffs of white chocolate and butter on a balsamic background. The Friulano Fisc '18 is very fruity, even a bit tropical, while in the mouth it proves soft and alluring.

Wine	Rating
○ Collio Chardonnay '19	▼▼ 3
○ Collio Friulano '19	▼▼ 3
○ Collio Friulano Fisc '18	▼▼ 4
○ Collio Pinot Bianco '19	▼▼ 3
○ Collio Pinot Grigio '19	▼▼ 3
○ Oblin Blanc '18	▼▼ 4
○ Collio Friulano Fisc '07	▽▽▽ 3*
○ Collio Pinot Bianco '07	▽▽▽ 3
○ Collio Pinot Grigio '98	▽▽▽ 3*
○ Collio Tocai Friulano '04	▽▽▽ 3*
○ Collio Chardonnay '18	▽▽ 3
○ Collio Friulano '18	▽▽ 3
○ Collio Friulano Fisc '16	▽▽ 4
○ Collio Pinot Grigio '18	▽▽ 3*
○ Collio Pinot Grigio '18	▽▽ 3
○ Collio Sauvignon '18	▽▽ 3
○ Oblin Blanc '17	▽▽ 4

Polje

Loc. Novali, 11
34071 Cormòns [GO]
Tel. +39 047160660
www.polje.com

CELLAR SALES
PRE-BOOKED VISITS
ANNUAL PRODUCTION 64,000 bottles
HECTARES UNDER VINE 12.00

The Polje brand was created by brothers Luigi and Stefano Sutto when they had the opportunity to acquire, in Novali di Cormons, a winery whose foundation dates back to 1926. In choosing the name they were inspired by the sinkholes that characterize the area, called 'polje', formed as a result of the erosion of the Julian Pre-Alps. Successful entrepreneurs in nearby Veneto, the Sutto family ventured into Collio Gorizia in the early 2000s, fell in love with the area and decided to leave their mark here. The ascent of this beautiful winery to the heights of excellence continues. This year, two wines stood out and reached the finals. The Sauvignon '19 teases the nose with intriguing notes of magnolia, sage, green pepper, citron peel and passion fruit, while in the mouth it's clear and vibrant. The Pinot Grigio '19 calls up wild flowers and white peach, progressively unfolding on a soft, fresh and sapid palate. Tre Bicchieri.

Wine	Rating
○ Collio Pinot Grigio '19	▼▼▼ 4*
○ Collio Sauvignon '19	▼▼ 4
○ Collio Bianco Fantazija '19	▼▼ 3
○ Collio Friulano '19	▼▼ 4
○ Collio Ribolla Gialla '19	▼▼ 4
● Collio Rosso '19	▼▼ 4
○ Ribolla Gialla Brut	▼▼ 4
○ Collio Friulano '18	▽▽ 4
○ Collio Friulano '17	▽▽ 3
○ Collio Pinot Grigio '18	▽▽ 4
○ Collio Pinot Grigio '17	▽▽ 3*
○ Collio Ribolla Gialla '18	▽▽ 4
● Collio Rosso '17	▽▽ 4
○ Collio Sauvignon '18	▽▽ 4
○ Collio Sauvignon '17	▽▽ 3*
○ Collio Sauvignon '16	▽▽ 3*

Pradio

FRAZ. FELETTIS
VIA UDINE, 17
33050 BICINICCO [UD]
TEL. +39 0432990123
www.pradio.it

CELLAR SALES
PRE-BOOKED VISITS
ANNUAL PRODUCTION 300,000 bottles
HECTARES UNDER VINE 33.00

Pradio is situated in Felettis, a small town near the city of Palmanova. Owned by the Cielo family, for over a decade it's been run by cousins Luca and Pierpaolo, the fourth generation to lead the winery. The choice, rare in these parts, to drastically reduce yields per hectare has set the producer on a virtuous path towards producing wines of superior quality. Thanks to Gianni Menotti's valuable enological advice, the results haven't been long in coming. Another classy performance for the Starz Bianco '19 (Chardonnay, Sauvignon and Tocai Friulano), which repeated last year's exploit and regained right of access to our finals. The Starz Rosso '16 (Merlot, Cabernet and Refosco) was hot on its heels, proving intriguing on the nose and pervasive to the palate. We also appreciated two new blends, one white and one red, both called Rok.

Wine	Rating
○ Friuli Bianco Starz '19	▼▼ 5
○ Friuli Chardonnay Teraje '19	▼▼ 3
○ Friuli Friulano Gaiare '19	▼▼ 3
● Friuli Grave Rosso Starz '16	▼▼ 5
○ Friuli Pinot Grigio Priara '19	▼▼ 3
○ Friuli Sauvignon Sobaja '19	▼▼ 3
○ Rok Bianco '19	▼▼ 6
● Rok Rosso '17	▼▼ 7
○ Friuli Grave Pinot Grigio Priara '17	YY 3
● Friuli Grave Refosco P.R. Tuaro '16	YY 3
○ Priara Pinot Grigio '18	YY 3
● Roncomoro Merlot '17	YY 2*
○ Starz Bianco '18	YY 5
○ Teraje Chardonnay '18	YY 3
● Tuaro Refosco P. R. '17	YY 3

Primosic

FRAZ. OSLAVIA
LOC. MADONNINA DI OSLAVIA, 3
34170 GORIZIA
TEL. +39 0481535153
www.primosic.com

CELLAR SALES
PRE-BOOKED VISITS
ANNUAL PRODUCTION 210,000 bottles
HECTARES UNDER VINE 32.00

The Primosic family settled on the hill of Oslavia in the late 19th century. Today, Marko and Boris run the winery founded in 1956 by their father Silvestro. Historical documents attest to the fact that the Primosic family supplied wine to the merchants who then transported their precious goods from the hills of the southern Austro-Hungarian Empire to Vienna, its capital. Theirs is a history of family and winemakers that's experiencing a moment of glory thanks to a diversified range, which includes both modern, sophisticated wines, and real jewels made according to time-honored techniques. The Friulano Skin '16 is a truly intriguing wine. As a result of prolonged maceration, it's acquired an antique-gold color with amber highlights, offering up whiffs of blood orange, wild strawberries, ripe melon and toasted hazelnuts. The Ribolla Gialla di Oslavia Riserva '17 exhibits similar qualities, though it's even richer aromatically.

Wine	Rating
○ Collio Ribolla Gialla di Oslavia Ris. '17	▼▼ 7
○ Collio Friulano Skin '16	▼▼ 7
● Collio Merlot '16	▼▼ 4
○ Collio Pinot Grigio '19	▼▼ 4
○ Malvasia '19	▼▼ 3
○ Think Yellow Ribolla Gialla '19	▼▼ 3
○ Collio Chardonnay Gmajne '15	YYY 5
○ Collio Ribolla Gialla di Oslavia Ris. '16	YYY 6
○ Collio Ribolla Gialla di Oslavia Ris. '13	YYY 5
○ Collio Ribolla Gialla di Oslavia Ris. '12	YYY 5
○ Collio Ribolla Gialla di Oslavia Ris. '11	YYY 5

★Doro Princic

Loc. Pradis, 5
34071 Cormòns [GO]
Tel. +39 048160723
doroprincic@virgilio.it

CELLAR SALES
PRE-BOOKED VISITS
ANNUAL PRODUCTION 60,000 bottles
HECTARES UNDER VINE 10.00

The winery was founded by Doro Princic in 1950, but it's thanks to his son Alessandro that the winery has become a guarantee of absolute quality, a pride for Collio and for the whole region. A sly smile shines through under Alessandro's Austro-Hungarian mustache—he's a man of the vineyard, a classic wine artisan, a striking figure both in appearance and character, endowed with an extraordinary balance. Together with his wife Mariagrazia they make an elegantly irresistible couple. Their young son Carlo, an enologist, offers support both in the vineyard and in the cellar. Truly a struggle between giants, an exciting challenge to determine the top position among a series of wines that, each in its category, expresses the highest potential of the individual grapes. By a hair's breadth, for the fourth year in a row, the Pinot Bianco '19 earns Tre Bicchieri for the intrinsic elegance and dynamic synergy of all its components.

Wine	Rating
○ Collio Pinot Bianco '19	🍷🍷🍷 5
○ Collio Friulano '19	🍷🍷 5
○ Collio Malvasia '19	🍷🍷 5
○ Collio Pinot Grigio '19	🍷🍷 5
○ Collio Ribolla Gialla '19	🍷🍷 5
○ Collio Sauvignon '19	🍷🍷 5
○ Collio Friulano '15	🍸🍸🍸 5
○ Collio Malvasia '14	🍸🍸🍸 5
○ Collio Malvasia '13	🍸🍸🍸 5
○ Collio Malvasia '12	🍸🍸🍸 5
○ Collio Malvasia '11	🍸🍸🍸 5
○ Collio Malvasia '10	🍸🍸🍸 4
○ Collio Malvasia '09	🍸🍸🍸 4*
○ Collio Pinot Bianco '18	🍸🍸🍸 5
○ Collio Pinot Bianco '17	🍸🍸🍸 5
○ Collio Pinot Bianco '16	🍸🍸🍸 5

Puiatti

Loc. Zuccole, 4
34076 Romans d'Isonzo [GO]
Tel. +39 0481909608
www.puiatti.com

CELLAR SALES
PRE-BOOKED VISITS
ANNUAL PRODUCTION 450,000 bottles
HECTARES UNDER VINE 46.00
SUSTAINABLE WINERY

Puiatti's wines boast an unmistakable style, one that's aimed at respecting the original, natural characteristics of the grapes. Founded in 1967 by Vittorio Puiatti, the winery has been part of Bertani Domains for some years now. The new ownership has fully embraced the producer's philosophy, building on Vittorio's principles and adapting them to current needs by strengthening the indissoluble bond between humans and the land rather than weakening it. Particular attention is paid to native grape varieties, especially the Ribolla Gialla, which is produced in different versions using innovative technologies. Once again this year we were presented with two Sauvignons: the Archetipi, from the 2018 harvest, is redolent of green apple and citron peel under a veil of sage and rosemary, while the basic version decisively expresses the grape's varietal characteristics. A nice new release is the Ribolla Gialla Extra Brut Metodo Classico, which offers up citrus nuances and fine iodine notes.

Wine	Rating
○ Friuli Sauvignon '19	🍷🍷 3
○ Friuli Sauvignon Archetipi '18	🍷🍷 5
○ Ribolla Gialla Extra Brut M. Cl.	🍷🍷 5
○ Friuli Friulano '19	🍷 3
○ Friuli Pinot Grigio '19	🍷 3
○ Ribolla Gialla '19	🍷 3
○ Collio Sauvignon Archetipi '88	🍸🍸🍸 5
○ Friuli Isonzo Friulano Vuj '16	🍸🍸 3
○ Friuli Pinot Grigio '17	🍸🍸 3
○ Friuli Sauvignon '18	🍸🍸 3
○ Fun Sauvignon '17	🍸🍸 3
○ Ribolla Gialla Archetipi '17	🍸🍸 5
○ Ribolla Gialla Archetipi '16	🍸🍸 5
○ Ribolla Gialla Archetipi '15	🍸🍸 5
○ Sauvignon Archetipi '17	🍸🍸 3
○ Sauvignon Archetipi '16	🍸🍸 3

Teresa Raiz

loc. Marsure di Sotto
via della Roggia, 22
33040 Povoletto [UD]
Tel. +39 0432679556
www.teresaraiz.it

CELLAR SALES
PRE-BOOKED VISITS
ANNUAL PRODUCTION 80,000 bottles
HECTARES UNDER VINE 11.50

Teresa Raiz was the maternal grandmother of Paolo Tosolini, the winery's current owner. She's remembered as an incredible woman, a great wine lover, who lived the land and the countryside as a gift from heaven, one deserving of our gratitude and tireless stewardship. The winery has a strong international bent; for over 30 years it's been exporting Friulian wines around the world. Paolo, fresh off his studies in enology, founded this winery in 1971 at a time of great ferment in the regional wine sector. Since 2003 he has been supported by his son Alessandro. The plots that extend to Marsure di Povoletto constitute their original production base; it contains a set of old vineyards that give rise to exceptional grapes. And it's precisely the Pinot Grigio Le Marsure '19 that crossed the threshold, gaining access to our finals. Floral and fruity aromas precede hints of citrus fruits and notes of vanilla; the palate proves to be of elegant pleasantness.

Wine	Rating
○ Friuli Pinot Grigio Le Marsure '19	🍷🍷 2*
○ FCO Friulano '19	🍷🍷 2*
○ FCO Pinot Grigio '19	🍷🍷 2*
○ FCO Ribolla Gialla '19	🍷🍷 2*
○ Friuli Sauvignon Le Marsure '19	🍷🍷 2*
● Schioppettino '13	🍷🍷 2*
○ Chardonnay Le Marsure '09	🍷🍷 2*
○ COF Ribolla Gialla '08	🍷🍷 3
○ FCO Pinot Grigio '18	🍷🍷 3
○ FCO Ribolla Gialla '18	🍷🍷 3
● FCO Rosso Decano '16	🍷🍷 5
○ Friuli Chardonnay '18	🍷🍷 3
○ Pinot Grigio Le Marsure '08	🍷🍷 2*
○ Sovrej '08	🍷🍷 4*

La Rajade

loc. Petrus, 2
34070 Dolegna del Collio [GO]
Tel. +39 0481639273
www.larajade.it

CELLAR SALES
PRE-BOOKED VISITS
ANNUAL PRODUCTION 50,000 bottles
HECTARES UNDER VINE 6.50

Owned by the Campeotto and Faurlin families, La Rajade is a prized producer, the pride and joy of Dolegna del Collio. The unique positions of the vineyards, which extend over the highest hills and are protected to the north by the Julian Alps, have inspired their name. In fact 'La Rajade' means 'ray of sunshine'. And here, when the sun draws its arc in the sky, it contrasts the low night temperatures, creating strong temperature swings that are ideal for ripening the grapes and engendering primary aromas. Two excellent reds, the Cabernet Sauvignon Ris. '17 and Merlot Ris. '16, took leading positions, with the Bianco Caprizi Ris. '17 (Malvasia Istriana, Chardonnay and Tocai Friulano) just getting the better of them. It has elegant nuances of medicinal herbs, apricot jam, toasted hazelnuts and aniseed, while on the palate it's vivid and structured. Their standard-label 2019s and the Schioppettino '18 are hot on their heels.

Wine	Rating
○ Collio Bianco Caprizi Ris. '17	🍷🍷 5
● Collio Cabernet Sauvignon Ris. '17	🍷🍷 5
● Collio Merlot Ris. '16	🍷🍷 5
○ Collio Sauvignon '19	🍷🍷 3
● Schioppettino '18	🍷🍷 3
○ Collio Ribolla Gialla '19	🍷 3
○ Collio Bianco Caprizi Ris. '16	🍷🍷 5
○ Collio Bianco Caprizi Ris. '15	🍷🍷 5
● Collio Cabernet Sauvignon Ris. '16	🍷🍷 5
● Collio Cabernet Sauvignon Ris. '15	🍷🍷 5
● Collio Rosso '16	🍷🍷 3
○ Collio Sauvignon '18	🍷🍷 3
○ Collio Sauvignon '17	🍷🍷 3
○ Collio Sauvignon '16	🍷🍷 3

Rocca Bernarda

FRAZ. IPPLIS
VIA ROCCA BERNARDA, 27
33040 PREMARIACCO [UD]
TEL. +39 0432716914
www.sagrivit.it

CELLAR SALES
PRE-BOOKED VISITS
ANNUAL PRODUCTION 100,000 bottles
HECTARES UNDER VINE 38.50

Rocca Bernarda is situated in an ancient manor house adorned with four evocative cylindrical towers. These walls, which date back to the mid 1600s, were used over the centuries as a summer residence for noble families from Cividale. It's here that, at the end of the 19th century, Count Asquini's Picolit was reborn, brought here by the Count Perusini family, its owners at the time. In 1977 the Perusini family donated the property to the Order of Malta and, since 2006, the farm has been managed by S.Agri.V.It (Società Agricola Vitivinicola Italiana), one of Italy's largest national agricultural producers. The Picolit '17 performs at levels of the best vintages, and maintains its position at the top of their range. Although it accentuates sweet notes, it exhibits excellent acid backbone in favor of symmetry, balance and harmony on the palate. The Refosco P. R. '18 and the Merlot Centis '17 share in their drinkability, but differ aromatically, with the former playing on notes of tobacco and licorice, while the latter proves fruit-forward.

○ COF Picolit '17	🍷🍷 8
○ FCO Friulano '19	🍷🍷 3
● FCO Merlot Centis '17	🍷🍷 6
● FCO Refosco P. R. '18	🍷🍷 3
○ FCO Ribolla Gialla '19	🍷🍷 3
● FCO Cabernet Franc '18	🍷 3
○ FCO Sauvignon '19	🍷 3
● COF Merlot Centis '99	ΨΨΨ 7
○ COF Picolit '03	ΨΨΨ 7
○ COF Picolit '98	ΨΨΨ 7
○ COF Picolit '97	ΨΨΨ 7
○ COF Picolit '16	ΨΨ 8
● FCO Cabernet Franc '17	ΨΨ 3
○ FCO Friulano '18	ΨΨ 3
● FCO Merlot Centis '16	ΨΨ 6
● FCO Refosco P. R. '17	ΨΨ 3
○ FCO Ribolla Gialla '18	ΨΨ 3

Paolo Rodaro

LOC. SPESSA
VIA CORMONS, 60
33043 CIVIDALE DEL FRIULI [UD]
TEL. +39 0432716066
www.rodaropaolo.it

CELLAR SALES
PRE-BOOKED VISITS
ANNUAL PRODUCTION 250,000 bottles
HECTARES UNDER VINE 64.00
SUSTAINABLE WINERY

After six generations, the winery managed by Paolo Rodaro still bears the name of its original founder. Founded in 1846, it's one of the region's historic producers. Proud of his origins, Paolo prefers to think of himself as a farmer, in the noblest sense of the word, rather than a winemaker. Energetic, affable and talkative, he conveys all his enthusiasm for his work and never misses a chance to sing the praises of the fascinating world of wine. He's always at the forefront, boasting a well-rounded range that's able to satisfy every market need. It's not always possible to test the great aging potential of regional whites as they get sold and consumed before reaching maturity. In the last edition we sang the praises of a 2014 Friulano—this year we do the same for the Sauvignon l'Evoluto '13, a wine of great character, unexpected fragrance and pure emotion.

● FCO Cabernet Sauvignon Romain '13	🍷🍷 5
○ FCO Sauvignon L'Evoluto '13	🍷🍷 6
○ COF Picolit '17	🍷🍷 5
○ FCO Friulano Fiore '19	🍷🍷 4
○ FCO Malvasia Fiore '19	🍷🍷 4
○ FCO Ribolla Gialla Fiore '19	🍷🍷 4
○ FCO Sauvignon Fiore '19	🍷🍷 4
○ Pas Dosé M. Cl. '16	🍷🍷 5
● COF Refosco P. R. Romain '03	ΨΨΨ 6
○ COF Sauvignon Bosc Romain '96	ΨΨΨ 4*
○ FCO Malvasia '16	ΨΨΨ 4*
○ Ronc '00	ΨΨΨ 3
○ FCO Chardonnay '18	ΨΨ 4
○ FCO Malvasia '18	ΨΨ 4
○ FCO Pinot Grigio '18	ΨΨ 4
⊙ Nature M. Cl. Rosé '14	ΨΨ 5

La Roncaia

fraz. Cergneu
via Verdi, 26
33045 Nimis [UD]
Tel. +39 0432790280
www.laroncaia.it

CELLAR SALES
PRE-BOOKED VISITS
ANNUAL PRODUCTION 60,000 bottles
HECTARES UNDER VINE 25.00

La Roncaia, which joined the Fantinel group in 1998, is based in Cergneu, a small hamlet of Nimis and an area made famous by Ramandolo, which is produced here together with Picolit. This irresistible pair of sweet wines, together with the area's renowned whites and reds, adds to the Fantinel family's already rich range, which avails itself of estates both in Collio and Gravel. Thus the producer is able to offer international markets a complete roster of regional specialties. At the top of their range we find a white, the Eclisse '18. Made mostly with Sauvignon and a small though important share of Picolit, it took home Tre Bicchieri. Among its olfactory spectrum we discern candied citrus fruits, broom and golden apple, accompanied by hints of salt and aromatic herbs. On the palate it releases freshness, then expands with repeated fruity hints that endure until its elegant finish.

○ Eclisse '18	TTT	5
○ FCO Pinot Grigio '18	TT	5
○ FCO Friulano '18	TT	4
● FCO Merlot Fusco '15	TT	5
○ FCO Ribolla Gialla '18	TT	4
○ Eclisse '12	YYY	4*
○ Bianco Eclisse '16	YY	5
○ Bianco Eclisse '15	YY	5
○ COF Picolit '15	YY	5
○ COF Picolit '13	YY	5
○ FCO Friulano '17	YY	4
○ FCO Friulano '16	YY	4
○ FCO Friulano '15	YY	4
● FCO Merlot Fusco '14	YY	5
○ FCO Pinot Grigio '17	YY	5
● FCO Refosco P.R. '14	YY	5
○ Ramandolo '15	YY	5

Il Roncal

fraz. Colle Montebello
via Fornalis, 148
33043 Cividale del Friuli [UD]
Tel. +39 0432730138
www.ilroncal.it

CELLAR SALES
PRE-BOOKED VISITS
ANNUAL PRODUCTION 80,000 bottles
HECTARES UNDER VINE 20.00

Martina Moreale is owner and factotum of the entire production chain here at Roncal. With courage and determination she has quickly completed the project started by her husband, Roberto Zorzettig, who died prematurely in 2006. The new cellar, now complete, stands together with the manor house atop Montebello, with rich vegetation and woods surrounding the geometric shapes of the vineyards along the rolling hills. Given the anomalous vintage, we were only able to evaluate a few samples, which were, in any case, sufficient to confirm the producer's high-quality trajectory. The Friulano '19, in particular, offers tantalizing hints of citrus fruits and wild flowers, which intertwine with flowery hints of lime and jasmine and then close with smoky echoes, all of which express the potential of the territory and the grape's varietal characteristics.

○ FCO Friulano '19	TT	4
○ FCO Malvasia '19	TT	4
● FCO Merlot '16	TT	4
○ FCO Ribolla Gialla '19	TT	4
○ FCO Bianco Ploe di Stelis '17	YY	4
○ FCO Bianco Ploe di Stelis '16	YY	4
○ FCO Friulano '18	YY	4
○ FCO Friulano '17	YY	3*
○ FCO Malvasia '18	YY	4
● FCO Merlot '15	YY	3
● FCO Pignolo '11	YY	5
○ FCO Pinot Grigio '17	YY	3
○ FCO Pinot Grigio '16	YY	3*
● FCO Refosco P. R. '16	YY	4
○ FCO Ribolla Gialla '17	YY	3
● FCO Schioppettino '16	YY	5
● FCO Schioppettino '15	YY	4

Il Roncat - Giovanni Dri

FRAZ. RAMANDOLO
VIA PESCIA, 7
33045 NIMIS [UD]
TEL. +39 0432790260
www.drironcat.com

CELLAR SALES
PRE-BOOKED VISITS
ANNUAL PRODUCTION 40,000 bottles
HECTARES UNDER VINE 10.00

Giovanni Dri chose the name 'Roncat' when, in 1968, he founded his winery. In local dialect it refers to a steep hill, sometimes almost impassable, where the cultivation of vines is so difficult as to be considered heroic. On these slopes they've always grown Verduzzo Giallo for Ramandolo, the winery's flagship product. In the large, welcoming and well-equipped cellar, built using only old, natural materials, his daughter Stefania, a graduate in enology, has been working for some time now. Ramandolo and Picolit, with their captivating sweetness, represent the cornerstone of a notable fleet of wines, especially forthright and territorial reds. The Schioppettino Monte dei Carpini '17 bewitches with its interweaving of spices and resins, pervading the palate with an energetic texture. The Pignolo Monte dei Carpini '15 is assertive but well-orchestrated, both on the nose and in the mouth.

Wine	Rating
○ COF Picolit '16	🍷🍷 7
● FCO Merlot '15	🍷🍷 3
● FCO Pignolo Monte dei Carpini '15	🍷🍷 5
● FCO Schioppettino Monte dei Carpini '17	🍷🍷 4
○ Ramandolo Il Roncat '15	🍷🍷 5
○ Sauvignon '18	🍷🍷 4
● FCO Cabernet '16	🍷 3
○ Ramandolo '16	🍷 4
○ COF Picolit '15	🍷🍷 7
○ COF Picolit '14	🍷🍷 7
● FCO Pignolo Monte dei Carpini '14	🍷🍷 5
● FCO Pignolo Monte dei Carpini '13	🍷🍷 5
○ FCO Sauvignon '17	🍷🍷 4
● FCO Schioppettino Monte dei Carpin '13	🍷🍷 4
○ Ramandolo Il Roncat '12	🍷🍷 5
○ Ramandolo Uve Decembrine '13	🍷🍷 5

Ronchi di Manzano

VIA ORSARIA, 42
33044 MANZANO [UD]
TEL. +39 0432740718
www.ronchidimanzano.com

CELLAR SALES
PRE-BOOKED VISITS
ANNUAL PRODUCTION 200,000 bottles
HECTARES UNDER VINE 60.00

Roberta Borghese is a businesswoman with an artisan heart and a touch of innate elegance. Assisted by her daughters Lisa and Nicole, she personally oversees the entire production chain at Ronchi Manzano, from the vineyard to the cellar, bringing a feminine sensitivity that translates into sophisticated, graceful wines. The production style plays on modernity and tradition in a cellar carved from rock, drawing on two underground floors capable of holding large French oak barrels for the maturation of their reds and the fermentation of certain whites. In addition to monovarietals, they make delicious blends, as demonstrated by the Bianco Ellégri (Tocai Friulano, Chardonnay, Sauvignon and Picolit), which has been mentioned several times in previous editions of the guide. This year the Rosazzo Bianco '18 (Tocai Friulano, Sauvignon, Chardonnay and Ribolla Gialla) beat the competition and made it to our finals in the company of a splendid Pignolo '16.

Wine	Rating
● FCO Pignolo '16	🍷🍷 5
○ Rosazzo Bianco '18	🍷🍷 4
○ Bianco Ellègri '19	🍷🍷 3
○ FCO Friulano '19	🍷🍷 3
● FCO Merlot Ronc di Subule '16	🍷🍷 3
● FCO Refosco P. R. '18	🍷🍷 3
● FCO Rosso Brauros '16	🍷🍷 4
○ COF Ellegri '13	🍷🍷🍷 3*
○ COF Friulano '10	🍷🍷🍷 3
○ COF Friulano '09	🍷🍷🍷 3*
● COF Merlot Ronc di Subule '99	🍷🍷🍷 3*
● COF Merlot Ronc di Subule '96	🍷🍷🍷 3*
○ COF Rosazzo Bianco Ellégri '11	🍷🍷🍷 3*
○ Rosazzo Bianco '13	🍷🍷🍷 3*

Ronco Blanchis

via Blanchis, 70
34070 Mossa [GO]
Tel. +39 048180519
www.roncoblanchis.it

CELLAR SALES
PRE-BOOKED VISITS
ANNUAL PRODUCTION 60,000 bottles
HECTARES UNDER VINE 14.00
SUSTAINABLE WINERY

Blanchis hill, one of the highest in Collio, enjoys a wonderful aspect and, as its name suggests, is particularly well suited to the production of great white wines. The producer, founded in 1950, was acquired by the Palla family in the early 2000s, while management has been entrusted to Lorenzo, who's responsible for developing the brand. With keen intuition he chose to concentrate on a few selections and to rely on the enological expertise of Gianni Menotti. Once again this year, with two wines in the finals, their entire range put in a memorable performance. The Blanc di Blanchis Riserva '17 (Chardonnay, Tocai Friulano and Sauvignon) proves extremely elegant, unleashing hints of lime blossom, white peach, mandarin, eucalyptus and citron peel, while the palate comes through energetic and linear. The Sauvignon '19 exudes aromas of dog rose, hawthorn, thyme and sage; in the mouth it enters supple, unfolding slowly with notes of medicinal herbs.

Wine	Rating	Price
○ Collio Bianco Blanc di Blanchis Ris. '17	🍷🍷🍷	5
○ Collio Chardonnay 3 '18	🍷🍷	5
○ Collio Friulano '19	🍷🍷	4
○ Collio Malvasia '19	🍷🍷	4
○ Collio Pinot Grigio '19	🍷🍷	4
○ Collio Sauvignon '19	🍷🍷	4
○ Collio '13	🍷🍷🍷	3*
○ Collio '12	🍷🍷🍷	3*
○ Collio Chardonnay '17	🍷🍷🍷	3*
○ Collio Bianco Ris. '16	🍷🍷	4
○ Collio Blanc de Blanchis '16	🍷🍷	3*
○ Collio Blanc de Blanchis '15	🍷🍷	3*
○ Collio Friulano '18	🍷🍷	4
○ Collio Friulano '17	🍷🍷	4
○ Collio Sauvignon '16	🍷🍷	4

★★Ronco dei Tassi

loc. Montona, 19
34071 Cormòns [GO]
Tel. +39 048160155
www.roncodeitassi.it

CELLAR SALES
PRE-BOOKED VISITS
ANNUAL PRODUCTION 110,000 bottles
HECTARES UNDER VINE 18.00

Founded in 1989 by Fabio Coser, an expert enologist and connoisseur of Collio's potential, Ronco dei Tassi is one of the most flourishing wineries in the regional firmament. Although it has already achieved countless objectives, maintaining its position as a top producer and winning coveted awards, it is still expanding today, setting itself even more ambitious goals. Sons Matteo and Enrico, who have been working alongside their father for some time now, have the task of preserving the producer's identity. The Collio Bianco Fosarin '18 (Pinot Bianco, Tocai Friulano and Malvasia Istriana) has found a proven, winning formula. It's a wine that, as with previous vintages, shines and once again takes home Tre Bicchieri, a concentrate of emotions punctuated by hints of exotic fruit, custard, butter, saffron and candied citron. The Malvasia '19 also remained in a top position.

Wine	Rating	Price
○ Collio Bianco Fosarin '18	🍷🍷🍷	3*
○ Collio Malvasia '19	🍷🍷	3*
○ Collio Friulano '19	🍷🍷	3
○ Collio Picolit '15	🍷🍷	6
○ Collio Pinot Grigio '19	🍷🍷	3
○ Collio Ribolla Gialla '19	🍷🍷	3
○ Collio Sauvignon '19	🍷🍷	3
○ Collio Bianco Fosarin '17	🍷🍷🍷	3*
○ Collio Bianco Fosarin '16	🍷🍷🍷	3*
○ Collio Bianco Fosarin '15	🍷🍷🍷	3*
○ Collio Bianco Fosarin '10	🍷🍷🍷	3
○ Collio Malvasia '15	🍷🍷🍷	3*
○ Collio Malvasia '14	🍷🍷🍷	3*
○ Collio Malvasia '13	🍷🍷🍷	3*
○ Collio Malvasia '12	🍷🍷🍷	3*
○ Collio Malvasia '11	🍷🍷🍷	3*

Ronco delle Betulle

loc. Rosazzo
via Abate Colonna, 24
33044 Manzano [UD]
Tel. +39 3474239162
www.roncodellebetulle.it

CELLAR SALES
PRE-BOOKED VISITS
ANNUAL PRODUCTION 50,000 bottles
HECTARES UNDER VINE 12.00
VITICULTURE METHOD Certified Organic
SUSTAINABLE WINERY

Ronco delle Betulle, a true regional gem, is situated near the famous Abbey of Rosazzo. In 1990 owner Ivana Adami took over management, espousing a simple philosophy focused on the production of high quality wines and building primarily on the peculiarities expressed by the region's native cultivars. Now it's mainly her son Simone at the helm, but Ivana still supervises the work, especially when it comes agronomic management. In a top position we find the Friulano '19, long a house specialty. It opens with a potpourri of medicinal herbs, yellow peach, medlar and citrus fruits, embellished with marine hints. In the mouth it's harmonious, with softness and acid backbone in perfect balance. The Rosazzo '18 (Tocai Friulano, Chardonnay and Sauvignon), another must, is elegant and well-orchestrated on the nose, soft on the palate, where it unfolds with endless rhythm.

Wine	Rating
● FCO Cabernet Franc '17	▼▼ 4
○ FCO Friulano '19	▼▼ 3
● FCO Merlot '17	▼▼ 4
● FCO Pignolo di Rosazzo '14	▼▼ 6
○ FCO Pinot Grigio '19	▼▼ 3
● FCO Refosco P. R. '17	▼▼ 4
○ FCO Sauvignon '19	▼▼ 3
○ Rosazzo '18	▼▼ 5
○ FCO Ribolla Gialla '19	▼ 3
● Narciso Rosso '94	▽▽▽ 4*
● FCO Cabernet Franc '16	▽▽ 3
○ FCO Friulano '18	▽▽ 3
○ FCO Pinot Grigio '18	▽▽ 3
○ FCO Sauvignon '18	▽▽ 3
○ FCO Sauvignon '17	▽▽ 3*
○ Rosazzo '17	▽▽ 5
○ Rosazzo Bianco '15	▽▽ 5

Ronco Scagnèt

loc. Cime di Dolegna, 7
34070 Dolegna del Collio [GO]
Tel. +39 3298536872
www.roncoscagnet.it

PRE-BOOKED VISITS
ANNUAL PRODUCTION 30,000 bottles
HECTARES UNDER VINE 12.00

The Ronco Scagnet brand, unknown to most until some time ago, has come to the fore with a series of wines that, impeccably crafted, captured our attention. Owner Valter Cozzarolo is assisted in management by his son Dimitri. Their vineyards extend over the terraced rolling hills of Collio, where the marl and sandstone subsoil, here known as 'ponca', together with the area's pedoclimate, give rise to wines of great structure, with fruity, intense and varietal aromas. The large number of wines made available certifies the validity of their entire range, which, in light of its competitive prices, works in the consumer's favor. The whites are more or less all on the same level; they differ aromatically, according to the peculiarities of the grapes used, but are all balanced and drinkable. The reds exhibit more body and fair gustatory tension.

Wine	Rating
● Collio Cabernet Franc '18	▼▼ 2*
○ Collio Chardonnay '19	▼▼ 4
○ Collio Friulano '19	▼▼ 4
● Collio Merlot '18	▼▼ 4
○ Collio Pinot Grigio '19	▼▼ 3
○ Collio Sauvignon '19	▼▼ 4
● Schioppettino '17	▼▼ 4
○ Collio Malvasia '18	▼ 2
○ Collio Ribolla Gialla '19	▼ 4
● Collio Cabernet Franc '16	▽▽ 2*
○ Collio Friulano '18	▽▽ 2*
● Collio Merlot '17	▽▽ 2*
○ Collio Pinot Grigio '18	▽▽ 2*
● Collio Refosco P. R. '17	▽▽ 2*
○ Collio Ribolla Gialla '18	▽▽ 2*
○ Collio Sauvignon '18	▽▽ 2*
○ Collio Sauvignon '17	▽▽ 2*

Ronco Severo

via Ronchi, 93
33040 Prepotto [UD]
Tel. +39 04337133440
www.roncosevero.it

CELLAR SALES
PRE-BOOKED VISITS
ANNUAL PRODUCTION 22,000 bottles
HECTARES UNDER VINE 8.00
VITICULTURE METHOD Certified Organic

In 1968 Severo Novello had the opportunity to buy some land in Prepotto, in Colli Orientali del Friuli. He renovated a dilapidated farmhouse and transformed it into a cellar-house. Now the farm that bears his name is run by his son Stefano. A convinced supporter of organic and biodynamic agriculture, Stefano largely makes wine as it was made in the past, without the use of chemicals, cultured yeasts, enzymes, or sulphur dioxide. The musts, even the white ones, remain in contact with the skins for weeks, sometimes even months. The highest score went to the Merlot Artìul Riserva '16, a wine characterized by liquorice hints and notes of clove, powerful and vigorous on the palate. The whites are all 2018s, and share in their characteristic golden-yellow color, tending to amber. On the nose they're intense, marked by whiffs of Mediterranean scrub, dried apricot and almond brittle, while in the mouth they prove sapid and crisp.

● FCO Merlot Artìul Ris. '16	🍷🍷 5
○ FCO Friulano Ris. '18	🍷🍷 4
○ FCO Pinot Grigio '18	🍷🍷 4
● FCO Schioppettino di Prepotto '17	🍷🍷 4
○ Ribolla Gialla '18	🍷🍷 4
○ Severo Bianco '12	🍷🍷🍷 4*
○ FCO Friulano Ris. '17	🍷🍷 4
○ FCO Friulano Ris. '16	🍷🍷 4
○ FCO Friulano Ris. '15	🍷🍷 4
● FCO Merlot Artiûl Ris. '13	🍷🍷 5
○ Ribolla Gialla '17	🍷🍷 4
○ Ribolla Gialla '16	🍷🍷 4
○ Ribolla Gialla '14	🍷🍷 4
○ Severo Bianco '17	🍷🍷 4
○ Severo Bianco '16	🍷🍷 4
○ Severo Bianco '13	🍷🍷 4

Roncùs

via Mazzini, 26
34076 Capriva del Friuli [GO]
Tel. +39 0481809349
www.roncus.it

CELLAR SALES
PRE-BOOKED VISITS
ACCOMMODATION
ANNUAL PRODUCTION 40,000 bottles
HECTARES UNDER VINE 10.00

As an expert winemaker, Marco Perco, owner of Roncús, has managed to imbue his wines with very personal style, combining time-honored cellar practices with modern winemaking techniques. The musts remain in contact with the strictly-indigenous yeasts for many months, accumulating the natural preservatives that guarantee extraordinary aging potential. The vineyard is made up of many small plots, many of which are over fifty years old, scattered throughout the slopes of Capriva del Friuli, in the heart of Collio. The Collio Bianco Vecchie Vigne '16, produced only with native grapes (Malvasia Istriana, Tocai Friulano and Ribolla Gialla), comes to us 4 years after harvest. During this long period of aging, it's been enriched with spicy notes of cinnamon and nutmeg, which combine with an already well-orchestrated aromatic profile of candied fruit, dried flowers and ginger. The substance and pervasiveness of the palate completes the picture.

○ Collio Bianco V. V. '16	🍷🍷 5
○ Collio Friulano '18	🍷🍷 4
○ Reversus Malvasia '18	🍷🍷 5
○ Collio Bianco V. V. '08	🍷🍷🍷 5
○ Roncùs Bianco V. V. '01	🍷🍷🍷 5
○ Collio Bianco '17	🍷🍷 3
○ Collio Bianco '15	🍷🍷 3*
○ Collio Bianco '14	🍷🍷 3
○ Collio Bianco V. V. '15	🍷🍷 5
○ Collio Bianco V. V. '14	🍷🍷 5
○ Collio Bianco V. V. '13	🍷🍷 5
○ Collio Bianco V. V. '12	🍷🍷 5
○ Collio Friulano '16	🍷🍷 4
○ Malvasia '17	🍷🍷 3
○ Pinot Bianco '16	🍷🍷 4
○ Pinot Bianco '15	🍷🍷 4
○ Ribolla Gialla '18	🍷🍷 3

★Russiz Superiore

via Russiz, 7
34070 Capriva del Friuli [GO]
Tel. +39 048180328
www.marcofelluga.it

CELLAR SALES
PRE-BOOKED VISITS
ACCOMMODATION
ANNUAL PRODUCTION 180,000 bottles
HECTARES UNDER VINE 50.00
SUSTAINABLE WINERY

Marco Felluga, a far-sighted innovator par excellence, sensed the potential of the vineyards around the old hamlet of Russiz Superiore, a property whose roots go back to the 13th century. And so he purchased it and settled down within those historic walls. Roberto Felluga, his son, has been managing the 50-hectare estate that extends over the sunny slopes of Collio Goriziano, in Capriva del Friuli, where the grapes thrive thanks to optimal conditions. Roberto has been able to maintain continuity at the producer, reaching increasingly important goals. In past editions, we've repeatedly highlighted the producer's commitment to the production of certain reserves in order to bring out the aging potential of the region's whites. The prize for believing us is a splendid Sauvignon Riserva '16, a concentrate of citrus and fragrant aromas that's elevated on the palate for its crunchiness and tension.

Wine	Rating
○ Collio Sauvignon Ris. '16	▼▼▼ 5
○ Collio Bianco Col Disôre '17	▼▼ 5
● Collio Rosso Riserva degli Orzoni '13	▼▼ 5
● Collio Cabernet Franc '17	▼▼ 4
○ Collio Friulano '19	▼▼ 4
○ Collio Pinot Bianco '19	▼▼ 4
○ Collio Pinot Grigio '19	▼▼ 4
○ Collio Sauvignon '19	▼▼ 4
○ Collio Friulano '16	▽▽▽ 4*
○ Collio Friulano '15	▽▽▽ 4*
○ Collio Friulano '14	▽▽▽ 4*
○ Collio Pinot Bianco '18	▽▽▽ 4*
○ Collio Pinot Bianco '07	▽▽▽ 4
○ Collio Pinot Grigio '11	▽▽▽ 4*
○ Collio Sauvignon '05	▽▽▽ 3
○ Collio Sauvignon '04	▽▽▽ 5
○ Collio Sauvignon Ris. '13	▽▽▽ 5

Marco Sara

fraz. Savorgnano del Torre
via dei Monti, 3a
33040 Povoletto [UD]
Tel. +39 0432666066
www.marcosara.com

CELLAR SALES
PRE-BOOKED VISITS
ANNUAL PRODUCTION 25,000 bottles
HECTARES UNDER VINE 8.00
VITICULTURE METHOD Certified Organic

Marco Sara, together with his wife, Sandra, has been managing this new gem of regional wine production since 2000. Since 2011 all their wines have been certified organic. The vineyards extend over the hilly territory of Povoletto, an area historically constituted of many small wineries divided into a dozen or so plots. This fragmentation means that each single vineyard has a different location, with different exposures and microclimates. Thus cultivars are selected based on their ability to adapt and express their natural qualities in that specific parcel. In the last edition we sang the praises of the Picolit dei Colli Orientali del Friuli '17, while this year we were offered another version of the same vintage but with very distinct characteristics. The Picolit Mufis '17 was produced with grapes completely covered with botrytis cinerea; the result is wine with an amber color, aromas that call up chestnut honey, dates and prunes, and a palate that expands dense and durable.

Wine	Rating
○ COF Picolit Mufis '17	▼▼ 6
○ FCO Bianco Erba Alta '17	▼▼ 5
● FCO Schioppettino '18	▼▼ 4
○ FCO Friulano '19	▼ 3
○ COF Picolit '17	▽▽ 6
○ COF Picolit '16	▽▽ 6
○ COF Picolit '15	▽▽ 6
○ FCO Bianco Erba Alta '16	▽▽ 4
○ FCO Friulano '15	▽▽ 3
○ FCO Friulano Erba Alta '16	▽▽ 4
● FCO Refosco P. R. el Rè '16	▽▽ 4
● FCO Schioppettino '17	▽▽ 4
● FCO Schioppettino '16	▽▽ 4
○ FCO Verduzzo Friulano '17	▽▽ 4
○ FCO Verduzzo Friulano '16	▽▽ 4
○ FCO Verduzzo Friulano '15	▽▽ 4

Sara & Sara

FRAZ. SAVORGNANO DEL TORRE
VIA DEI MONTI, 5
33040 POVOLETTO [UD]
TEL. +39 3393859042
www.saraesara.com

CELLAR SALES
PRE-BOOKED VISITS
ACCOMMODATION
ANNUAL PRODUCTION 25,000 bottles
HECTARES UNDER VINE 7.00
VITICULTURE METHOD Certified Organic
SUSTAINABLE WINERY

Sara & Sara is equivalent to Alessandro & Manuele, two young brothers who have created a prestigious brand for Savorgnano del Torre, a small rural district located in the westernmost part of the Friuli Colli Orientali appellation. Here the territory is rich in rivers and evergreens, while the steep slopes of marl, sandstone and clayey terrain are lashed by the cold northern winds. The vineyards benefit from a unique microclimate that often favors the natural formation of botrytis cinerea on the bunches. Once again this year we were able to taste only a few wines, which don't represent their entire range even if, deriving from three different typologies, they provide a fairly clear sense. The Friulano '18 is highly elegant on the nose, with floral hints of lily of the valley and juniper accompanied by lemon cream and polyflora honey. The Refosco dal Peduncolo Rosso '18 is very spicy with undergrowth whiffs and pencil lead. The Picolit '15 is close-knit on the nose, sweet and pervasive on the palate.

Wine	Rating
○ COF Picolit '15	TT 6
○ FCO Friulano '18	TT 4
● FCO Refosco P. R. '18	TT 4
○ COF Verduzzo Friulano Crei '10	YYY 5
○ COF Friulano '12	YY 3
○ COF Picolit '13	YY 6
○ COF Picolit '12	YY 6
○ COF Picolit '10	YY 5
○ FCO Friulano '17	YY 6
○ FCO Friulano '16	YY 6
○ FCO Picolit '11	YY 6
○ FCO Verduzzo Friulano Crei '13	YY 5
○ FCO Verduzzo Friulano Crei '12	YY 5
○ SaraGialla '17	YY 3
○ Sauvignon '12	YY 2*

★★Schiopetto

VIA PALAZZO ARCIVESCOVILE, 1
34070 CAPRIVA DEL FRIULI [GO]
TEL. +39 048180332
www.schiopetto.it

CELLAR SALES
PRE-BOOKED VISITS
ANNUAL PRODUCTION 190,000 bottles
HECTARES UNDER VINE 30.00
SUSTAINABLE WINERY

The Osteria dei Pompieri (Firemen's Osteria) got its start within the legendary vineyards of Capriva, in memory of the historic site in Udine where Mario Schiopetto began his venture 70 years ago. Wine tourists can sunbathe near the beautiful lake, read a book or walk in the painstakingly manicured woods and old vineyards and, finally, cool off in this beautifully restored building. Emilio and Alessandro Rotolo, with the valuable support of Lorenzo Landi, carry on Mario's mission: making fragrant wines, pleasant but marked by great structure and infinite longevity. In the finals we greeted two pleasantly-surprising new releases: the Ribolla Gialla '19, a fresh, fragrant and graceful wine, and the Podere dei Blumeri Rosso '18 (Merlot and Refosco dal Peduncolo Rosso), a wine redolent of small black berries, coffee beans, humus and tobacco—in the mouth it's lively and alluring. But at the top of the list it's always the same name: the Friulano '19, which for the seventh year in a row takes home Tre Bicchieri.

Wine	Rating
○ Collio Friulano '19	TTT 6
○ Collio Pinot Bianco '19	TT 6
○ Collio Sauvignon '19	TT 6
● Podere dei Blumeri Rosso '18	TT 8
○ Ribolla Gialla '19	TT 5
○ Blanc des Rosis '19	TT 5
○ Collio Malvasia '19	TT 6
○ Collio Pinot Grigio '19	TT 6
● Merlot '19	TT 5
● Rivarossa '18	TT 6
○ Collio Friulano '18	YYY 4*
○ Collio Friulano '17	YYY 4*
○ Collio Friulano '16	YYY 4*
○ Collio Friulano '15	YYY 4*
○ Collio Friulano '14	YYY 4*
○ Collio Friulano '13	YYY 4*
○ Mario Schiopetto Bianco '08	YYY 5

La Sclusa

LOC. SPESSA
VIA STRADA DI SANT'ANNA, 7/2
33043 CIVIDALE DEL FRIULI [UD]
TEL. +39 0432716259
www.lasclusa.it

CELLAR SALES
PRE-BOOKED VISITS
ACCOMMODATION
ANNUAL PRODUCTION 160,000 bottles
HECTARES UNDER VINE 30.00

The trunk of the Zorzettig family tree bears the name of Giobatta, founder of a generation of winegrowers who have been working in Spessa since 1963. There's a winery for every branch, and on one of the largest stands out the name of Gino. A stretch of the Corno river that runs through the vineyards, called La Sclusa, inspired the winery's name, bestowing it with a well-defined identity. Now Gino's sons Germano, Maurizio and Luciano are managing things together as a well-organized family operation. The Friulano 12 Viti '19 proves increasingly impressive, standing out from the pack, and making a solo appearance in our final tastings. Its multifaceted aromatic suite recalls haymaking in mountain meadows, flowers and wild herbs, nectarine peach, mango and salt. The palate comes through balanced, with a considerable glyceric component that's well contrasted by acidity and a pronounced mineral vigor.

Wine	Rating
○ FCO Friulano 12 Viti '19	▼▼ 4
○ FCO Chardonnay '19	▼▼ 3
○ FCO Friulano '19	▼▼ 3
● FCO Malvasia '19	▼▼ 3
● FCO Merlot '18	▼▼ 3
● FCO Refosco P. R. '18	▼▼ 3
○ FCO Ribolla Gialla '19	▼▼ 3
● FCO Rosso del Torrione '17	▼▼ 8
○ Ribolla Gialla Brut	▼ 4
○ COF Picolit '15	▽▽ 6
○ FCO Chardonnay '18	▽▽ 3
○ FCO Chardonnay '17	▽▽ 3
○ FCO Friulano 12 Viti '18	▽▽ 4
○ FCO Pinot Grigio '18	▽▽ 3
○ FCO Ribolla Gialla '18	▽▽ 3
○ FCO Sauvignon '18	▽▽ 3
● FCO Schioppettino '18	▽▽ 3

Marco Scolaris

VIA BOSCHETTO, 4
34070 SAN LORENZO ISONTINO [GO]
TEL. +39 0481809920
www.scolaris.it

CELLAR SALES
PRE-BOOKED VISITS
ANNUAL PRODUCTION 1,100,000 bottles
HECTARES UNDER VINE 25.00
SUSTAINABLE WINERY

The winery founded in 1924 by Giovanni Scolaris is now managed by Gianmarco. He represents the fourth generation and is guaranteeing continuity, though it was his recently-deceased father, Marco, who made the winery a leader in the territory while constantly pursuing a balance between man and nature. Responsibility for production is entrusted to Nevio Fedel. He brings passion and many years of experience to his work of channeling their philosophy into the bottle. The Malvasia '17 exhibits a well-defined profile, calling up pastry sensations and spices, while the palate proves substantive, creamy and very smooth. The Sauvignon '19 is redolent of magnolia, white peach, kiwi and mint; in the mouth it opens and closes with fresh balsamic whiffs. The Friulano '19 offers up citrus fruits and fragrances of wild flowers, while the Merlot '19, though very young, has already reached a respectable balance of flavor.

Wine	Rating
● Collio Cabernet Sauvignon '17	▼▼ 4
○ Collio Friulano '19	▼▼ 4
○ Collio Malvasia '17	▼▼ 4
● Collio Merlot '19	▼▼ 4
○ Collio Sauvignon '19	▼▼ 4
○ Collio Chardonnay '19	▼ 3
○ Collio Ribolla Gialla '19	▼ 4
○ Traminer Aromatico '19	▼ 4
○ Collio Chardonnay '18	▽▽ 3
○ Collio Chardonnay '17	▽▽ 3
○ Collio Friulano '18	▽▽ 3
○ Collio Malvasia '16	▽▽ 3
● Collio Merlot '18	▽▽ 3
● Collio Merlot '16	▽▽ 3
○ Collio Pinot Grigio '18	▽▽ 3
○ Collio Ribolla Gialla '18	▽▽ 3
○ Collio Ribolla Gialla '17	▽▽ 3

Roberto Scubla

FRAZ. IPPLIS
VIA ROCCA BERNARDA, 22
33040 PREMARIACCO [UD]
TEL. +39 0432716258
www.scubla.com

CELLAR SALES
PRE-BOOKED VISITS
ANNUAL PRODUCTION 50,000 bottles
HECTARES UNDER VINE 11.00

In 1991 Roberto Scubla made a life-changing decision to leave the bank he worked at and buy a few hectares of vineyards adjacent to an old farmhouse on the slopes of Rocca Bernarda. For the technical side of things, he availed himself of the valuable advice of Gianni Menotti, a long-time friend who over time has contributed to developing the winery. The vineyards benefit from constant breezes made possible by the unique makeup of the surrounding hills. At the top position we find the Bianco Pomèdes '18 (Pinot Bianco, Tocai Friulano and Rhine Riesling), a wine of great elegance and personality. Fresh hints of lemon balm, mint and sage are the prologue to veiled notes of pastry and sweet spices, while the palate comes through juicy and energetic. The Verduzzo Friulano Passito Cràtis '17 is also among the best of its kind, boasting a sweetness that's well balanced by a vigorous acid thrust.

Wine	Rating
○ FCO Bianco Pomèdes '18	YY 5
○ FCO Sauvignon '19	YY 4
○ FCO Verduzzo Friulano Passito Cràtis '17	YY 6
○ Brut M. Cl.	YY 7
● FCO Cabernet Sauvignon '18	YY 4
○ FCO Friulano '19	YY 4
○ FCO Malvasia Lo Speziale '19	YY 4
● FCO Merlot '18	YY 4
○ FCO Pinot Bianco '19	YY 4
● FCO Refosco P. R. '18	YY 4
○ FCO Ribolla Gialla '19	YY 4
● FCO Rosso Scuro '17	YY 5
○ COF Bianco Pomèdes '04	yyy 4
○ COF Verduzzo Friulano Passito Cràtis '09	yyy 5
○ COF Verduzzo Friulano Passito Cràtis '06	yyy 5
○ COF Verduzzo Friulano Passito Cràtis '04	yyy 5

Ferruccio Sgubin

VIA MERNICO, 8
34070 DOLEGNA DEL COLLIO [GO]
TEL. +39 048160452
www.ferrucciosgubin.it

CELLAR SALES
PRE-BOOKED VISITS
ANNUAL PRODUCTION 100,000 bottles
HECTARES UNDER VINE 20.00

The foundation of Ferruccio Sgubin's winery dates back to 1960, when many family-run producers decided to make a radical change in their approach and specialize in vine cultivation. With constant growth (in terms of territorial expansion), it has arrived at significant dimensions. At the same time, the cellar was modernized. Thanks to the advice of qualified technicians, the quality level of their wines has increased exponentially. The Friulano Petruss '19 stands our with a truly exemplary performance. Decisive on the nose, pronounced varietal expressions lead back to freshly-cut alpine meadows, rich in flowers and wild herbs, candied citrus fruits and almond skin, only to unveil a flavorful, gratifying palate. On the nose the Pinot Bianco '19 proves flowery and elegant, while the palate reveals an unexpected energy.

Wine	Rating
○ Collio Friulano Petruss '19	YY 5
○ Collio Friulano '19	YY 3
● Collio Merlot Redmont '16	YY 4
○ Collio Pinot Bianco '19	YY 3
○ Collio Ribolla Gialla Petruss '19	YY 4
○ Collio Sauvignon Petruss '19	YY 4
○ Collio Friulano '18	yy 3
○ Collio Friulano '17	yy 3
○ Collio Friulano Petrusa '16	yy 3
○ Collio Pinot Bianco '18	yy 3
○ Collio Pinot Bianco '16	yy 3
○ Collio Ribolla Gialla '18	yy 3
○ Collio Ribolla Gialla '17	yy 3
○ Collio Sauvignon '17	yy 3
○ Collio Sauvignon '16	yy 3
● Mirnik '16	yy 4
● Schioppettino '13	yy 2*

Simon di Brazzan

FRAZ. BRAZZANO
VIA SAN ROCCO, 17
34070 CORMÒNS [GO]
TEL. +39 048161182
www.simondibrazzan.com

CELLAR SALES
PRE-BOOKED VISITS
ANNUAL PRODUCTION 70,000 bottles
HECTARES UNDER VINE 13.00
VITICULTURE METHOD Certified Organic

Simon di Brazzan is a splendid winery managed autonomously for over twenty years by Daniele Drius, even if it still bears the name of his grandfather, Enrico Veliscig, a territorial icon who's reached and surpassed the centenarian mark. A convinced supporter of biodynamic viticulture, Daniele abandoned the use of chemical treatments long ago. In the spaces between the vines, the soil is treated with a mix of grasses (green manure cropping) planted in rotation from year to year in alternate rows. At the end of May, after flowering, they are cut and buried. For the fourth year in a row we find the Simon '19, a Friulano Blanc, in the finals, once again demonstrating that it's among the best in its category for the frankness of its aromas and its substance on the palate. The Malvasia '19 offers a sumptuous catwalk of aromatic herbs, dried flowers, candied citrus fruits, acacia honey, dried coconut and sweet spices, and then pervades the palate with style, personality and elegance.

○ Friuli Friulano Blanc di Simon '19	🍷🍷 3*
○ Malvasia '19	🍷🍷 3*
○ Blanc di Simon Tradizion '16	🍷🍷 5
○ Friuli Pinot Grigio '19	🍷🍷 3
○ Ri.nè Blanc '18	🍷🍷 3
○ Sauvignon '19	🍷🍷 3
○ Blanc di Simon '15	🍸🍸 3*
○ Friuli Friulano Blanc di Simon '18	🍸🍸 3*
○ Friuli Friulano Blanc di Simon '17	🍸🍸 3*
○ Friuli Friulano Blanc di Simon '16	🍸🍸 3*
○ Malvasia '18	🍸🍸 3
○ Ri.nè Blanc '17	🍸🍸 3
○ Ri.nè Blanc '16	🍸🍸 3*
○ Ri.nè Blanc '15	🍸🍸 3*
○ Ri.nè Blanc '14	🍸🍸 3*
○ Sauvignon '18	🍸🍸 3*

Sirch

VIA FORNALIS, 277/1
33043 CIVIDALE DEL FRIULI [UD]
TEL. +39 0432709835
www.sirchwine.com

CELLAR SALES
PRE-BOOKED VISITS
ANNUAL PRODUCTION 600,000 bottles
HECTARES UNDER VINE 100.00

In 2002 Luca Sirch was already moving towards producing classic, monovarietal wines, outside any fashion or trend and vinified in a simple, modern way. It's a deceptive philosophy inasmuch as it hides their ambition to obtain subtle complexity and make increasingly elegant wines rich in nuances. Being able to count on the Feudi di San Gregorio distribution network means the producer has recently been able to expand significantly, focusing above all on the appeal of Pinot Grigio on the international market. White wines from the last vintage feature in the set submitted for tasting, and they were on similar lines with last year's commendable performance. The Friulano '19, in particular, stood out for its typicity and pleasantness on the palate. For local residents it's a daily drinker, a summery, straightforward, tasty and balanced wine. We also appreciated the Pinot Grigio '19, which plays on fruity, even exotic sensations.

○ FCO Chardonnay Cladrecis '18	🍷🍷 5
○ FCO Friulano '19	🍷🍷 3
○ FCO Pinot Grigio '19	🍷🍷 3
○ FCO Ribolla Gialla '19	🍷🍷 3
● FCO Rosso Cladrecis '16	🍷 5
○ FCO Sauvignon '19	🍷 3
○ COF Friulano '07	🍸🍸🍸 2*
○ FCO Bianco Cladrecis '14	🍸🍸 3*
○ FCO Chardonnay '18	🍸🍸 3
○ FCO Friulano '18	🍸🍸 3
○ FCO Friulano '17	🍸🍸 3
○ FCO Pinot Grigio '18	🍸🍸 3
● FCO Pinot Nero '18	🍸🍸 3
○ FCO Ribolla Gialla '17	🍸🍸 3
○ FCO Sauvignon '18	🍸🍸 3
○ FCO Sauvignon '17	🍸🍸 3
○ FCO Traminer Aromatico '18	🍸🍸 3

Skerk

FRAZ. SAN PELAGIO
LOC. PREPOTTO, 20
34011 DUINO AURISINA [TS]
TEL. +39 040200156
www.skerk.com

CELLAR SALES
PRE-BOOKED VISITS
RESTAURANT SERVICE
ANNUAL PRODUCTION 22,000 bottles
HECTARES UNDER VINE 7.00
VITICULTURE METHOD Certified Organic

Sandi Skerk is now an icon, one of the best interpreters of viticulture in the Karst region of Trieste. Everything here is done by hand, space is limited and among the thick vegetation scattered vineyards hang in sunny coves overlooking the sea. In the beautiful wine cellar, which is carved out of hard rock and represents a true masterpiece of human ingenuity, mysterious draughts from unreachable inlets guarantee cool temperatures and constant humidity throughout the year. The wines follow a natural process, undergoing prolonged maceration on the skins, and are never clarified or filtered. Only four wines were submitted, but all are outstanding. Year after year, with enviable constancy, Skerk's wines deliver. They don't seem to be affected by the vintage, but are always pearls. The Ograde '18 (Malvasia Istriana, Vitovska, Sauvignon and Pinot Grigio) pours a coppery color, heralding intriguing aromas of pink grapefruit, red orange and saffron, sensations accompanied by balsamic and spicy hints on the palate.

Wine	Rating
○ Malvasia '18	TT 5
○ Ograde '18	TT 5
● Terrano '18	TT 5
○ Vitovska '18	TT 5
○ Carso Malvasia '08	YYY 4
○ Malvasia '13	YYY 5
○ Ograde '17	YYY 5
○ Ograde '16	YYY 5
○ Ograde '15	YYY 5
○ Ograde '12	YYY 5
○ Ograde '11	YYY 5
○ Ograde '10	YYY 4
○ Ograde '09	YYY 4*
○ Malvasia '17	YY 5
○ Malvasia '16	YY 5
○ Vitovska '17	YY 5
○ Vitovska '16	YY 5

Edi Skok

LOC. GIASBANA, 15
34070 SAN FLORIANO DEL COLLIO [GO]
TEL. +39 3408034045
www.skok.it

CELLAR SALES
PRE-BOOKED VISITS
ANNUAL PRODUCTION 38,000 bottles
HECTARES UNDER VINE 11.00

Siblings Edi and Orietta Skok are pure-bred winemakers, proud of their family's farming origins and, while they're deeply attached to local traditions, they've always shown themselves to be open to innovation. For some time now they've renounced the local inclination for long macerations, adopting more modern techniques to preserve the wines' fragrance. They're already working in the new cellar, which is modern and well equipped, and integrates perfectly with the landscape. It's also accented by the charm of the old manor house, which dates back to the 16th century and has always served as the producer's headquarters. The Sauvignon '19 is a true pearl. It had already distinguished itself in the previous vintage, but this version is definitely a cut above. Notes of lemon peel and unripe apple highlight its freshness—they intertwine with floral whiffs of orange blossom and magnolia, as well as aromatic notes of sage and marjoram. In the mouth its sapid tension is well balanced by a notable, velvety glyceric presence.

Wine	Rating
○ Collio Sauvignon '19	TT 3*
○ Collio Bianco Pe Ar '18	TT 3
○ Collio Chardonnay '19	TT 2*
○ Collio Friulano Zabura '19	TT 3
● Collio Merlot Villa Jasbinae '15	TT 3
○ Collio Pinot Grigio '19	TT 3
○ Collio Bianco Pe Ar '17	YY 3
○ Collio Bianco Pe Ar '16	YY 3*
○ Collio Bianco Pe Ar '15	YY 3*
○ Collio Chardonnay '18	YY 2*
○ Collio Chardonnay '17	YY 2*
○ Collio Friulano Zabura '18	YY 3
○ Collio Friulano Zabura '13	YY 3*
○ Collio Friulano Zabura '12	YY 3*
○ Collio Friulano Zabura '11	YY 3*
○ Collio Pinot Grigio '18	YY 3
○ Collio Sauvignon '18	YY 3

Specogna

fraz. Rocca Bernarda, 4
33040 Corno di Rosazzo [UD]
Tel. +39 0432755840
www.specogna.it

CELLAR SALES
PRE-BOOKED VISITS
ACCOMMODATION
ANNUAL PRODUCTION 120,000 bottles
HECTARES UNDER VINE 25.00
VITICULTURE METHOD Certified Organic
SUSTAINABLE WINERY

Michele and Cristian, two explosive brothers, have demonstrated great skill in the fields of enology and communication, leading the winery founded by their grandfather Leonardo to the heights of excellence, so much so that the Specogna brand has earned a preeminent place in some of the most important international markets. A small territory like Friuli Venezia Giulia, and the peculiarities of Rocca Bernarda, have filled the front pages of the most important wine magazines, lending prestige to the entire regional wine sector. Their basic whites wines deserve consideration for their modern style, purity and drinkability, but they risk being overlooked by the power and exuberance of the reserves. We were most impressed with the extraordinary Identità '18 (Tocai Friulano, Malvasia Bianca and Ribolla Gialla), a territorial wine that calls up sensations of harvested wheat, beeswax, coconut and honey on the nose. In the mouth it proves fragrant and vigorous.

○ FCO Bianco Identità '18	TT 6
● FCO Pignolo '14	TT 6
○ FCO Sauvignon Duality '18	TT 6
○ FCO Friulano '19	TT 3
○ FCO Malvasia '19	TT 3
○ FCO Pinot Grigio '19	TT 3
○ FCO Pinot Grigio Ramato Ris. '17	TT 7
● FCO Rosso Oltre '17	TT 6
○ FCO Sauvignon '19	TT 3
○ FCO Bianco Identità '15	YYY 7
○ FCO Bianco Identità '16	YY 7
○ FCO Identità '13	YY 6
○ FCO Malvasia Ris. '16	YY 4
○ FCO Sauvignon Blanc Duality '17	YY 3*
○ FCO Sauvignon Blanc Duality '16	YY 3*
○ FCO Sauvignon Blanc Duality '15	YY 3*

Stanig

via Albana, 44
33040 Prepotto [UD]
Tel. +39 0432713234
www.stanig.it

CELLAR SALES
ACCOMMODATION AND RESTAURANT SERVICE
ANNUAL PRODUCTION 45,000 bottles
HECTARES UNDER VINE 9.00

Among the many family-run wineries that characterize Prepotto, the one managed by brothers Federico and Francesco Stanig stands out. Founded exactly a century ago by their grandfather Giuseppe, its small size and the attention to detail shown throughout all stages of production are its strong points. The vineyards unfold in a valley where soil composition and microclimate prove ideal for the production of reds, starting with Schioppettino. 2019 proved a particularly favorable vintage for the Friulano, a wine enriched by elegant floral aromas of elderflower and dandelion, fruity notes of pear and quince, and finally aromatic herbs, which accompany the palate. The Malvasia '19 draws on the fragrance of iodine notes reminiscent of the sea. The Schioppettino di Prepotto '17 is in line with the best vintages, vigorous and substantive.

○ FCO Friulano '19	TT 3
○ FCO Malvasia '19	TT 3
○ FCO Ribolla Gialla '19	TT 3
● FCO Schioppettino di Prepotto '17	TT 5
● FCO Cabernet '18	T 3
● FCO Merlot '18	T 3
○ Bianco Del Gelso '16	YY 5
○ FCO Friulano '17	YY 3
○ FCO Malvasia '18	YY 3
○ FCO Malvasia '17	YY 3
○ FCO Ribolla Gialla '18	YY 3
○ FCO Ribolla Gialla '17	YY 3
○ FCO Sauvignon '18	YY 3
○ FCO Sauvignon '17	YY 3
● FCO Schioppettino di Prepotto '16	YY 5
● FCO Schioppettino di Prepotto '15	YY 3

Tenuta Stella

LOC. SCRIÒ
VIA SDENCINA, 1
34070 DOLEGNA DEL COLLIO [GO]
TEL. +39 3387875175
www.tenutastellacollio.it

CELLAR SALES
PRE-BOOKED VISITS
ANNUAL PRODUCTION 35,000 bottles
HECTARES UNDER VINE 12.00
VITICULTURE METHOD Certified Organic
SUSTAINABLE WINERY

Tenuta Stella, founded in 2010 by Sergio Stevanato, lies in the highest part of Collio, in the district of Dolegna, Scriò, where the steep slopes guarantee a unique microclimate and ideal exposure to the sun's rays. Management has been entrusted to Erika Barbieri and Alberto Faggiani, an outstanding technical staff who produce certified organic wines. The soils are constituted of marine marl and sandstone. Known locally as 'ponca', it was brought to the surface long ago by the lifting of the Adriatic seabed. The premises were there, and now confirmation has arrived. With a splendid Friulano '18, the doors of the final selections were opened and the first Tre Bicchieri arrived. Golden highlights are the prologue to vibrant aromas of yellow fruit and citrus, all of which satisfy the nose. The palate is rich, pervasive and velvety, well balanced by a vigorous sapid thrust. The other wines tasted confirmed the validity of their range across the board.

Wine	Rating	
○ Collio Friulano '18	▼▼▼	4*
○ Collio Malvasia '18	▼▼	4
● Collio Pinot Nero '18	▼▼	6
○ Collio Ribolla Gialla '18	▼▼	4
○ Frriuli Ribolla Gialla Brut M. Cl.	▼▼	5
● Sdencina '17	▼▼	4
○ Tanni Pas Dosé M. Cl.	▼▼	5
○ Collio Friulano '17	▽▽	4
○ Collio Friulano '16	▽▽	4
○ Collio Friulano '15	▽▽	3*
○ Collio Malvasia '16	▽▽	4
○ Collio Malvasia '15	▽▽	4
○ Collio Ribolla Gialla '17	▽▽	4
○ Collio Ribolla Gialla '16	▽▽	4
○ Collio Ribolla Gialla '15	▽▽	4

Stocco

VIA CASALI STOCCO, 12
33050 BICINICCO [UD]
TEL. +39 0432934906
www.vinistocco.it

CELLAR SALES
PRE-BOOKED VISITS
RESTAURANT SERVICE
ANNUAL PRODUCTION 250,000 bottles
HECTARES UNDER VINE 49.00

In the early part of the last century, the Stocco family settled in the vast plain of Friuli, near Bicinicco, devoting themselves to agriculture in what were later called 'Casali Stocco'. The turning point came in the 1960s, when the producer went from mixed agriculture to wine-growing. It was Francesco who founded the operation, but now it's up to Andrea, Daniela and Paola, the fourth generation, to uphold the family brand, proving that even in a flat land, with its gravel and red soil, you can forge wines of excellent quality. This year we had the chance to taste a variety of wines, which allowed us to evaluate their overall range. Remembering that Due Bicchieri are awarded to wines 'from very good to excellent', the overall performance is decidedly high, especially in light of their prices. We particularly appreciated the curious and pleasant Pinot Grigio Ramato Settantacinque '19, a wine redolent of strawberries and blood orange.

Wine	Rating	
○ Braide Chardonnay '19	▼▼	5
○ Friuli Pinot Grigio Ramato Settantacinque '19	▼▼	3
○ Friuli Pinot Grigio Selvis '19	▼▼	3
○ Malvasia Dai Claps '19	▼▼	2*
● Merlot Motis '18	▼▼	4
● Refosco P. R. Sant'Antoni '18	▼▼	3
○ Traminer Aromatico Dal Borc '19	▼▼	3
○ Ventiduelustri Extra Brut	▼▼	4
● Dal Morar Cabernet Sauvignon '18	▼	2
○ Friuli Grave Friulano Glesis '19	▼	2
○ Ribolla Gialla Brut	▼	3
● Violis Pinot Nero '18	▼	3
○ Chardonnay '18	▽▽	5
○ Malvasia '18	▽▽	2*
○ Traminer Aromatico '18	▽▽	5

Subida di Monte

loc. Subida
via Subida, 6
34071 Cormòns [GO]
Tel. +39 048161011
www.subidadimonte.it

CELLAR SALES
PRE-BOOKED VISITS
ACCOMMODATION
ANNUAL PRODUCTION 45,000 bottles
HECTARES UNDER VINE 9.00

Subida di Monte stands atop a hill overlooking the valley below. It's the work of Luigi Antonutti, a pioneer of quality regional viticulture, who in 1972 succeeded in realizing his dream of managing the winery full-time. The cellar is modern, with ample space for both processing and reception, situated in a strategic position on Collio Goriziano, surrounded by vineyards and unspoilt nature, protected by the Julian Alps and caressed by the salty breezes of the Adriatic Sea. The Sauvignon '19 features aromas of lavender, lily of the valley, abate fetel pear and kiwi, leaving room for a faint balsamic essence. The Pinot Grigio '19 evokes exotic hints of mango and papaya, chamomile flowers and citron peel, while in the mouth it unfolds on fresh and sapid sensations. The elegant Friulano '19 stands out for its balance.

Wine	Rating
○ Collio Friulano '19	TT 3
○ Collio Malvasia '19	TT 3
● Collio Merlot '18	TT 3
○ Collio Pinot Grigio '19	TT 3
○ Collio Sauvignon '19	TT 3
● Collio Cabernet Franc '18	T 3
● Collio Cabernet '17	YY 3
○ Collio Friulano '18	YY 3
○ Collio Friulano '17	YY 3
○ Collio Malvasia '18	YY 3
○ Collio Malvasia '17	YY 3*
● Collio Merlot '17	YY 3
○ Collio Pinot Grigio '18	YY 3
○ Collio Pinot Grigio '17	YY 3
● Collio Rosso Poncaia '16	YY 4
○ Collio Sauvignon '18	YY 3
○ Collio Sauvignon '17	YY 3

Matijaz Tercic

loc. Bucuie, 4a
34070 San Floriano del Collio [GO]
Tel. +39 0481884920
www.tercic.com

CELLAR SALES
PRE-BOOKED VISITS
ANNUAL PRODUCTION 30,000 bottles
HECTARES UNDER VINE 9.50

Matija? Ter?i?'s family has always worked in viticulture and transforming grapes into wine on the hills of San Floriano del Collio, in one of eastern Friuli's foothills most charming areas. On the steep slopes, the rows of vines trace out orderly shapes interspersed with long rows of cherry trees, which accompany the eye all the way down to the splendid valley below. Matija?'s first bottles date back to 1994 and, with continued growth, the producer has established itself as one of the best in the area. Among the few wines presented this year, the Pinot Bianco '18 topped our preferences. On the nose it unveils scents of jasmine, orange blossom, summer hay, abate fetel pear, gooseberry and lemon cream. The palate is pervasive, with a slow, fresh and sapid progression that gives way to a balanced epilogue. The Planta '15, a Chardonnay vinified in French oak barrels, is reminiscent of alpine butter, dill and apricot tart.

Wine	Rating
○ Pinot Bianco '18	TT 3*
○ Planta '15	TT 4
○ Ribolla Gialla '18	TT 4
○ Vino degli Orti '17	TT 3
○ Collio Pinot Grigio '07	YYY 3*
○ Collio Chardonnay '12	YY 3*
● Collio Merlot '15	YY 4
○ Collio Pinot Grigio '17	YY 3
○ Collio Pinot Grigio '16	YY 3
○ Collio Pinot Grigio '12	YY 3*
○ Collio Sauvignon '17	YY 3
○ Collio Sauvignon '16	YY 3*
○ Collio Sauvignon '15	YY 3*
○ Planta '14	YY 4
○ Ribolla Gialla '17	YY 4
○ Vino degli Orti '16	YY 3
○ Vino degli Orti '13	YY 3*

Tiare - Roberto Snidarcig

FRAZ. VENCÒ
LOC. SANT'ELENA, 3A
34070 DOLEGNA DEL COLLIO [GO]
TEL. +39 048162491
www.tiaredoc.com

CELLAR SALES
PRE-BOOKED VISITS
RESTAURANT SERVICE
ANNUAL PRODUCTION 90,000 bottles
HECTARES UNDER VINE 10.00
SUSTAINABLE WINERY

In Friulian dialect, 'tiare' means 'land'. Indeed, it was Roberto Snidarcig's attachment to the land he cultivates that inspired the name for his winery. In small steps, starting with a single hectare on the slopes of Monte Quarin, he managed to grow the producer both in numbers and quality, making it, in a short time, one of the most renowned in the region. Now their headquarters are in Dolegna del Collio, in a new, spacious and well-equipped cellar, where Roberto continues undaunted in pursuit of growth. Last year's wines put it in a sumptuous performance, but so did some backdated selections. Having undergone a clear change of style, the Pinot Grigio Masserè '19 pours a beautiful copper color. Across its long palate, it unveils hints of cooked pear, mango, dried fruit and maple syrup. But the best is, once again, their flagship, the Sauvignon '19, a modern wine of great impact that rises above the competition and takes home Tre Bicchieri.

Wine	Rating
○ Collio Sauvignon '19	TTT 5
○ Collio Friulano '19	TT 4
○ Collio Pinot Grigio Masserè '19	TT 4
○ Collio Sauvignon Empire '17	TT 5
○ Collio Chardonnay '19	TT 3
○ Collio Malvasia '19	TT 3
○ Collio Ribolla Gialla '19	TT 4
○ Il Tiare Sauvignon '19	TT 3
● Pinot Nero Pinuàr '18	TT 5
○ Collio Sauvignon '18	YYY 5
○ Collio Sauvignon '17	YYY 5
○ Collio Sauvignon '16	YYY 5
○ Collio Sauvignon '15	YYY 5
○ Collio Sauvignon '14	YYY 5
○ Collio Sauvignon '13	YYY 3*

★★Franco Toros

LOC. NOVALI, 12
34071 CORMÒNS [GO]
TEL. +39 048161327
www.vinitoros.com

CELLAR SALES
PRE-BOOKED VISITS
ANNUAL PRODUCTION 60,000 bottles
HECTARES UNDER VINE 11.00

Like all greats, Franco Toros attributes the quality of his wines to Mother Nature, but we all know that without the right interpreter the results wouldn't be the same. He's a true artisan, a shy man who moves quietly among his rows of vines, avoiding the commotion. His wines are always distinguished by linearity, frankness, maximum respect for varietal characteristics and, above all, for pleasantness and ease of drinking. They are impeccable wines, territorial, true ambassadors of Collio's unique attributes. It's certainly no coincidence that the two wines that earned the highest accolades find themselves in the finals, challenging the competition in their respective categories. The Friulano '19 plays on fruity notes of yellow peach and golden apple, with aromatic splashes of ginger and rosemary on a smoky background of rare elegance. The Pinot Bianco '19 delights the nose with its floral hints and delicate whiffs of citron and samphire.

Wine	Rating
○ Collio Friulano '19	TT 4
○ Collio Pinot Bianco '19	TT 4
○ Collio Chardonnay '19	TT 4
○ Collio Pinot Grigio '19	TT 4
○ Collio Sauvignon '19	TT 4
○ Collio Friulano '18	YYY 4*
○ Collio Friulano '12	YYY 4*
○ Collio Friulano '11	YYY 4*
○ Collio Friulano '10	YYY 4
○ Collio Friulano '09	YYY 4*
○ Collio Friulano '08	YYY 4*
○ Collio Pinot Bianco '17	YYY 4*
○ Collio Pinot Bianco '14	YYY 4*
○ Collio Pinot Bianco '13	YYY 4*
○ Collio Pinot Bianco '08	YYY 4*
○ Collio Pinot Bianco '07	YYY 4
○ Collio Tocai Friulano '06	YYY 4

Torre Rosazza

FRAZ. OLEIS
LOC. POGGIOBELLO, 12
33044 MANZANO [UD]
TEL. +39 0422864511
www.torrerosazza.com

CELLAR SALES
PRE-BOOKED VISITS
ANNUAL PRODUCTION 200,000 bottles
HECTARES UNDER VINE 90.00
SUSTAINABLE WINERY

Torre Rosazza is Tenute di Genagricola's leading producer (in Friuli, the group includes Poggiobello, Borgo Magredo and Tenuta Sant'Anna). One of the most beautiful regional producers, it's headquartered in the 18th-century Palazzo De Marchi, which stands perched atop a hill, surrounded by two splendid, naturally terraced and perpetually sunny amphitheaters of vineyards. The results achieved are thanks to an outstanding and experienced staff, masterfully orchestrated by Enrico Raddi. This year we tasted fewer wines than usual, but it was enough to confirm the consistent quality of both their whites and reds. The Pignolo '16 earned a top position. The nose offers up hints of small black berries, tar, liquorice, dried tomatoes and cloves, while in the mouth it proves sumptuous, striking. The Friulano '19 stands out among their current, standard-label wines for its aromatic elegance and fragrant flavor. Tre Bicchieri.

Wine	Rating
○ FCO Friulano '19	🍷🍷🍷 3*
● FCO Pignolo '16	🍷🍷 5
○ FCO Pinot Grigio '19	🍷🍷 3
○ FCO Ribolla Gialla '19	🍷🍷 3
● FCO Rosso Altromerlot '16	🍷🍷 5
○ FCO Sauvignon '19	🍷🍷 3
○ COF Pinot Grigio '13	🍷🍷🍷 3*
○ COF Pinot Grigio '12	🍷🍷🍷 3*
○ FCO Pinot Bianco '17	🍷🍷🍷 3*
○ FCO Pinot Bianco '14	🍷🍷🍷 3*
○ FCO Pinot Grigio '18	🍷🍷🍷 3*
○ FCO Pinot Grigio '16	🍷🍷🍷 3*
○ FCO Pinot Grigio '15	🍷🍷🍷 3*
○ FCO Friulano '16	🍷🍷 3*
○ FCO Friulano '15	🍷🍷 3*
○ FCO Ribolla Gialla '18	🍷🍷 3*

Tunella

FRAZ. IPPLIS
VIA DEL COLLIO, 14
33040 PREMARIACCO [UD]
TEL. +39 0432716030
www.tunella.it

CELLAR SALES
PRE-BOOKED VISITS
ANNUAL PRODUCTION 400,000 bottles
HECTARES UNDER VINE 70.00
SUSTAINABLE WINERY

Massimo and Marco Zorzettig, together with their mother, Gabriella, own this splendid winery, the pride of the Friuli Colli Orientali appellation. From a young age they've taken on the burden of running things, making use of the experience passed down from three generations of family. They've always relied on the enological skills of Luigino Zamparo, who grew up with them and contributed to the creation and development of the La Tunella brand. The spacious cellar features advanced technology and commendable architecture. In the finals we find the same two wines as last edition. Both are giants in their respective categories, true ambassadors of the territory as they are produced with a mix of entirely native grapes. The BiancoSesto '18 offers up fresh whiffs of lime and bergamot followed by lemon balm, white peach and tropical fruit. In the mouth it enters soft and the finish is enthralling. Tre Bicchieri, highly deserved.

Wine	Rating
○ FCO Biancosesto '18	🍷🍷🍷 5
● Arcione '16	🍷🍷 5
○ FCO Bianco Noans Dolce '18	🍷🍷 5
○ FCO Friulano '19	🍷🍷 3
○ FCO Malvasia Valmasia '19	🍷🍷 3
○ FCO Pinot Grigio Ramato Col Bajé '18	🍷🍷 5
○ FCO Ribolla Gialla Col del Bliss '18	🍷🍷 5
○ FCO Sauvignon Col Matiss '18	🍷🍷 5
● Pignolo '15	🍷🍷 5
● Schioppettino '17	🍷🍷 5
○ COF BiancoSesto '11	🍷🍷🍷 4*
○ COF BiancoSesto '07	🍷🍷🍷 3
○ FCO Bianco LaLinda '14	🍷🍷🍷 4*
○ FCO Biancosesto '17	🍷🍷🍷 5
○ FCO BiancoSesto '16	🍷🍷🍷 4*
○ Noans '12	🍷🍷🍷 5

Valchiarò

FRAZ. TOGLIANO
VIA DEI LAGHI, 4C
33040 TORREANO [UD]
TEL. +39 0432715502
www.valchiaro.it

CELLAR SALES
PRE-BOOKED VISITS
ANNUAL PRODUCTION 45,000 bottles
HECTARES UNDER VINE 14.00
SUSTAINABLE WINERY

It was 1991 when six small producers from different professional backgrounds decided to create a partnership in which each would provide their grapes to a single winery, thus founding Valchiarò. It's a successful example of collaboration that, almost thirty years later, is still based on mutual esteem, fellowship and team spirit. Important milestones include the construction of a large and modern winery, inaugurated in 2006, where enology is entrusted to the proven expertise of Gianni Menotti. The absence of reds shone a light on the excellent performance of their 2019 whites, even if the best wine tasted was the Verduzzo Friulano '17. It pours a bright, golden-yellow color and delights the nose with aromas of candied citrus fruits, caramelized apple and Catalan cream, plus hints of peach syrup and dried apricot. The palate comes through very sweet but well balanced.

Wine	Rating
○ FCO Verduzzo Friulano '17	▼▼ 4
○ FCO Friulano '19	▼▼ 3
○ FCO Friulano Nexus '19	▼▼ 3
○ FCO Pinot Grigio '19	▼▼ 3
○ FCO Sauvignon '19	▼▼ 3
○ FCO Friulano '18	▽▽ 3
○ FCO Friulano Nexus '18	▽▽ 3*
○ FCO Friulano Nexus '17	▽▽ 3*
○ FCO Friulano Nexus '16	▽▽ 3*
● FCO Merlot Ris. '16	▽▽ 3
● FCO Merlot Ris. '15	▽▽ 3
○ FCO Pinot Grigio '18	▽▽ 3
● FCO Refosco P. R. '15	▽▽ 3
● FCO Rosso Torre Qual Ris. '16	▽▽ 3
● FCO Rosso Torre Qual Ris. '15	▽▽ 3
○ FCO Sauvignon '18	▽▽ 3
○ FCO Verduzzo Friulano '16	▽▽ 4

Valpanera

VIA TRIESTE, 5A
33059 VILLA VICENTINA [UD]
TEL. +39 0431970395
www.valpanera.it

CELLAR SALES
PRE-BOOKED VISITS
ANNUAL PRODUCTION 400,000 bottles
HECTARES UNDER VINE 48.00

Valpanera is one of Friuli Aquileia's most important wineries. Founded by Giampietro Dal Vecchio and now run mainly by his son Giovanni, it has taken on the task of promoting Refosco dal Peduncolo Rosso, the region's most representative red grape variety. Studies and research document that it's thrived in this territory for millennia, here where the soil is clayey and air circulation is constant thanks to the Bora winds. Three different versions of Refosco dal Peduncolo Rosso were submitted, all different types and vintages. The most convincing, classified as a 'Superiore', calls up violets, licorice and pencil lead, while the vivacity of its tannins refreshes the palate. The Riserva is darker, both on the nose and in the mouth, unveiling blackberry sensations and black olives. Finally, the current, standard-label version is characterized by crushed morello cherries and tobacco, coming through lean on the palate.

Wine	Rating
○ Album '19	▼▼ 2*
● Atrum '18	▼▼ 2*
● Friuli Aquileia Refosco P. R. '19	▼▼ 2*
● Friuli Aquileia Refosco P. R. Ris. '15	▼▼ 4
● Friuli Aquileia Refosco P. R. Sup. '17	▼▼ 3
○ Friuli Aquileia Malvasia '19	▼ 2
○ Ribolla Gialla '19	▼ 2
○ Album '18	▽▽ 2*
● Atrum '16	▽▽ 2*
○ Friuli Aquileia Chardonnay '17	▽▽ 3
● Friuli Aquileia Refosco P. R. Ris. '13	▽▽ 5
● Friuli Aquileia Refosco P. R. Sup. '16	▽▽ 3
● Friuli Aquileia Refosco P. R. Sup. '14	▽▽ 3
○ Friuli Aquileia Sauvignon '18	▽▽ 3
○ Friuli Aquileia Sauvignon '17	▽▽ 3

★★Venica & Venica

loc. Cerò, 8
34070 Dolegna del Collio [GO]
Tel. +39 048161264
www.venica.it

CELLAR SALES
PRE-BOOKED VISITS
ACCOMMODATION
ANNUAL PRODUCTION 310,000 bottles
HECTARES UNDER VINE 40.00
SUSTAINABLE WINERY

The Venica family, with a spirit of cohesion common to farming families, has wedded its name to Collio, and the Venica & Venica brand has assumed a role as a true international ambassador for the territory. Dynamism, energy and entrepreneurial spirit enrich this splendid winery, which has managed to capitalize on the vineyards purchased ninety years ago by Daniele, its founder, on Cerò hill. Only whites were presented, all 2019s, and the excellent results highlight the quality of a vintage that was particularly favorable in all respects. Some three wines earned access to our finals, but the others were close behind. The Sauvignon Ronco delle Mele '19 has been in a top position for decades now, and deserves a special mention for its continuity.

Wine	Rating	Price
○ Collio Pinot Bianco Tàlis '19	▼▼	4
○ Collio Pinot Grigio Jesera '19	▼▼	4
○ Collio Sauvignon Ronco delle Mele '19	▼▼	6
○ Collio Friulano Ronco delle Cime '19	▼▼	5
○ Collio Malvasia Pètris '19	▼▼	4
○ Collio Ribolla Gialla L'Adelchi '19	▼▼	4
○ Collio Sauvignon Ronco del Cerò '19	▼▼	5
○ Collio Sauvignon Ronco delle Mele '16	▽▽▽	6
○ Collio Sauvignon Ronco delle Mele '13	▽▽▽	6
○ Collio Sauvignon Ronco delle Mele '12	▽▽▽	6
○ Collio Sauvignon Ronco delle Mele '11	▽▽▽	6

La Viarte

via Novacuzzo, 51
33040 Prepotto [UD]
Tel. +39 0432759458
www.laviarte.it

CELLAR SALES
PRE-BOOKED VISITS
ACCOMMODATION
ANNUAL PRODUCTION 120,000 bottles
HECTARES UNDER VINE 22.00
SUSTAINABLE WINERY

For about ten years now, La Viarte has been managed by its current owner, Alberto Piovan, who deserves credit for having further developed a winery that had already distinguished itself as a leading producer in the Friuli Colli Orientali appellation. La Viarte, which means 'spring' in Friulian dialect, is entrusted to a technical staff of proven experience. With their support it's reached the heights of excellence, especially the Liende line ('legend'), which comprises their most prestigious selections. Another overall performance for the ages for this lovely producer, which is demonstrating a high level of quality constancy. The Sauvignon Liende '18 is a true champion, taking home Tre Bicchieri. The nose is intoxicating with its elegant hints of lemon peel, lime blossom, lemon balm, mint and saffron, while the palate proves to be a whirlwind of emotions. The Malvasia '19 is fresh right out of the gate and already making waves. Hats off.

Wine	Rating	Price
○ FCO Sauvignon Liende '18	▼▼▼	5
○ FCO Friulano '19	▼▼	4
○ FCO Malvasia '19	▼▼	4
○ FCO Chardonnay '19	▼▼	4
○ FCO Friulano Liende '18	▼▼	5
○ FCO Pinot Bianco '19	▼▼	4
○ FCO Pinot Grigio '19	▼▼	4
○ FCO Ribolla Gialla '19	▼▼	4
○ FCO Sauvignon '19	▼▼	4
○ FCO Friulano Liende '17	▽▽▽	5
○ FCO Friulano Liende '16	▽▽▽	5
○ FCO Sauvignon Liende '15	▽▽▽	5
○ FCO Chardonnay Liende '18	▽▽	4
○ FCO Friulano '18	▽▽	4
○ FCO Pinot Bianco '18	▽▽	4
○ FCO Sauvignon '18	▽▽	4
○ FCO Sauvignon Liende '17	▽▽	5

Vidussi

via Spessa, 18
34071 Capriva del Friuli [GO]
Tel. +39 048180072
www.vinimontresor.it

CELLAR SALES
PRE-BOOKED VISITS
ANNUAL PRODUCTION 500,000 bottles
HECTARES UNDER VINE 30.00

Since its foundation, Vidussi has undergone several changes of ownership. As of last year it's part of a notable group of producers. Directed and managed for over twenty years by enologist Luigino De Giuseppe, it has started a new direction, now able to count on the prestige of a well-established brand. The vineyards mostly lie on the pleasant hills of Capriva del Friuli, in the heart of Collio, while other plots are part of the Friuli Colli Orientali and Friuli Isonzo appellations. We reviewed a number of bottles, all of consistently high quality, which testifies to the attention given to each individual wine. If we then compare that to the price, the value of their entire range become evident. The Malvasia '19 is redolent of fresh thyme and ginger; the Ribolla Gialla '19 calls up citrus and unripe fruit, while the Friulano '19 proves reminiscent of summer haymaking and lavender.

Wine	Glasses	Price
● Collio Cabernet Franc '19	TT	3
○ Collio Chardonnay '19	TT	2*
○ Collio Friulano '19	TT	3
○ Collio Malvasia '19	TT	2*
○ Collio Pinot Grigio '19	TT	2*
○ Collio Ribolla Gialla '19	TT	2*
○ Collio Sauvignon '19	TT	3
● FCO Refosco P. R. '19	TT	3
● Schioppettino '19	TT	3
○ Collio Traminer Aromatico '19	T	2
○ Collio Friulano '18	YY	3
○ Collio Malvasia '18	YY	2*
○ Collio Pinot Grigio '18	YY	2*
○ Collio Ribolla Gialla '18	YY	2*
○ Collio Sauvignon '18	YY	3*
○ Collio Traminer Aromatico '18	YY	2*
● Schioppettino '18	YY	3

★★Vie di Romans

loc. Vie di Romans, 1
34070 Mariano del Friuli [GO]
Tel. +39 048169600
www.viedromans.it

CELLAR SALES
PRE-BOOKED VISITS
ANNUAL PRODUCTION 300,000 bottles
HECTARES UNDER VINE 60.00
SUSTAINABLE WINERY

Vie di Romans, founded in 1978 by Gianfranco Gallo, is a true regional gem. The Gallo family have already written a century of history, but the best chapters are being penned today by Gianfranco. With rigorous viticultural choices and personal enological interpretations, Gianfranco confers a style that's distinct for the territorial identity of the vineyards, which fall in the Friuli Isonzo appellation. By now we're accustomed to the dizzyingly high scores that virtually all their range manages to earn and, as with every year, it's difficult to make a final judgement. In the end the wine that shines most brightly, the one that has shown tenacity and class for years, is the Sauvignon Piere '18. The Flors di Uis '18 (Malvasia Istriana, Rhine Riesling and Tocai Friuliano) is hot on its heels, rich in intriguing and intoxicating aromatic nuances.

Wine	Glasses	Price
○ Friuli Isonzo Sauvignon Piere '18	TTT	5
○ Friuli Isonzo Bianco Flors di Uis '18	TT	5
○ Friuli Isonzo Chardonnay Vie di Romans '18	TT	5
○ Friuli Isonzo Sauvignon Vieris '18	TT	5
○ Dut'Un '17	TT	7
○ Friuli Isonzo Chardonnay Ciampagnis '18	TT	5
○ Friuli Isonzo Pinot Grigio Dessimis '18	TT	5
○ Friuli Isonzo Chardonnay Ciampagnis Vieris '13	YYY	4*
○ Friuli Isonzo Friulano Dolée '12	YYY	5
○ Friuli Isonzo Friulano Dolée '11	YYY	4*
○ Friuli Isonzo Sauvignon Piere '17	YYY	5
○ Friuli Isonzo Sauvignon Piere '16	YYY	5
○ Friuli Isonzo Sauvignon Piere '15	YYY	5

Vigna del Lauro

LOC. MONTONA, 19
34071 CORMÒNS [GO]
TEL. +39 0481629549
www.vignadellauro.it

CELLAR SALES
PRE-BOOKED VISITS
ANNUAL PRODUCTION 60,000 bottles
HECTARES UNDER VINE 10.00

Managed by Fabio Coser, former owner of Ronco dei Tassi, Vigna del Lauro got its start in 1994 from a collaboration with a German importer who proposed differentiating production in order to meet the needs of a significant segment of the transalpine market. These consumers preferred coherence, drinkability, varietal identity and, above all, affordable prices. This goal was achieved without ever undermining a philosophy rooted in respect for the grapes, an essential element for the final result. The Sauvignon '19 is a distinctly varietal wine in a highly elegant guise. It's pleasant on the nose but above all on the palate. The Ribolla Gialla '19 is also marked by the grape's characteristic descriptors and is distinguished by its freshness and smoothness on the palate. The Pinot Grigio '19 proves fruity and rich in delicately salty notes that, on the palate, nicely balance its glyceric side.

○ Collio Friulano '19	🍷🍷 3
○ Collio Pinot Grigio '19	🍷🍷 3
○ Collio Sauvignon '19	🍷🍷 3
○ Friuli Isonzo Traminer Aromatico '19	🍷🍷 2*
○ Ribolla Gialla '19	🍷🍷 3
● Friuli Isonzo Cabernet Franc '19	🍷 2
○ Collio Sauvignon '99	🍷🍷🍷 2*
○ Collio Friulano '18	🍷🍷 3
○ Collio Friulano '17	🍷🍷 3
○ Collio Pinot Grigio '18	🍷🍷 3
○ Collio Pinot Grigio '17	🍷🍷 3
○ Collio Sauvignon '18	🍷🍷 3
○ Friuli Isonzo Chardonnay '18	🍷🍷 2*
● Friuli Isonzo Merlot '17	🍷🍷 2*
○ Ribolla Gialla '18	🍷🍷 3
○ Ribolla Gialla '17	🍷🍷 3

Vigna Petrussa

VIA ALBANA, 47
33040 PREPOTTO [UD]
TEL. +39 0432713021
www.vignapetrussa.it

CELLAR SALES
PRE-BOOKED VISITS
ANNUAL PRODUCTION 30,000 bottles
HECTARES UNDER VINE 7.00

Hilde Petrussa, together with her husband, Renato, chose a truly original way to enjoy her retirement when, in 1995, she decided to move back to Albana di Prepotto to take care of the once flourishing family estate that had since fallen into a state of abandonment. She found herself having to convert the vineyards, trying to privilege native grape varieties, especially Ribolla Nera, which gives rise to Schioppettino, and choosing guyot training systems. She also increased the number of vines per hectare and provided for the grassing of the entire area under vine. The Schioppettino di Prepotto '17 pours a beautiful, bright ruby red, the prologue to an intense and variegated olfactory suite in which notes of tobacco merge with coffee beans, milk chocolate, liquorice root and prunes. The palate is soft, with vivid but blunted tannins. The Friulano '19 is also excellent, alternating fruity sensations of yellow peach and medlars with enticing whiffs of thyme and summer savory.

○ COF Picolit '16	🍷🍷 6
○ FCO Friulano '19	🍷🍷 3
● FCO Schioppettino di Prepotto '17	🍷🍷 5
● Refosco P. R. '17	🍷🍷 4
○ Ribolla Gialla '19	🍷 3
○ COF Picolit '15	🍷🍷 6
○ FCO Friulano '18	🍷🍷 3
○ FCO Friulano '17	🍷🍷 3
○ FCO Friulano '15	🍷🍷 3*
● FCO Schioppettino di Prepotto '16	🍷🍷 5
● FCO Schioppettino di Prepotto '15	🍷🍷 5
● FCO Schioppettino di Prepotto Ris. '15	🍷🍷 5
● FCO Schioppettino RiNera '17	🍷🍷 3
● Refosco P. R. '16	🍷🍷 4
○ Richenza '17	🍷🍷 4
○ Richenza '15	🍷🍷 4

Vigna Traverso

via Ronchi, 73
33040 Prepotto [UD]
Tel. +39 0422804807
www.vignatraverso.it

CELLAR SALES
PRE-BOOKED VISITS
RESTAURANT SERVICE
ANNUAL PRODUCTION 100,000 bottles
HECTARES UNDER VINE 22.00
SUSTAINABLE WINERY

For over twenty years Vigna Traverso, once known as Ronco di Castagneto, has been in the hands of the Molon Traverso family, owners of the famous winery based in nearby Veneto. It's managed by Stefano Traverso who, over time, has overseen restructuring of the producer, safeguarding the old vineyards and planting new high-density plots. For some years now he has been working in the new cellar in Prepotto, equipped with modern technology but also with concrete tanks, thus confirming that innovation and tradition can coexist. The Merlot '16 starred in a remarkable performance, obtaining extremely high scores. It opens with mature notes of cherry jam, spices, tanned leather and tobacco, while in the mouth it exhibits muscles, though not in excess. The Bianco Sottocastello '17 (Chardonnay and Sauvignon) is characterized by its usual, intriguing aromas, well blended and gradually unfolding, sensations that accompany its long and fragrant stay on the palate.

Wine	Rating	Price
○ FCO Bianco Sottocastello '17	▼▼	5
● FCO Merlot '16	▼▼	3*
○ FCO Friulano '19	▼▼	3
○ FCO Pinot Grigio '19	▼▼	3
● FCO Rosso Troj '17	▼▼	3
● FCO Schioppettino di Prepotto '16	▼▼	5
● FCO Cabernet Franc '16	▼	3
○ FCO Ribolla Gialla '19	▼	3
○ FCO Sauvignon '18	▼	5
○ FCO Bianco Sottocastello '16	▽▽	5
○ FCO Bianco Sottocastello '15	▽▽	5
○ FCO Bianco Sottocastello '13	▽▽	4
● FCO Refosco P. R. '13	▽▽	3*
● FCO Refosco P. R. '12	▽▽	3*
● FCO Rosso Troj '15	▽▽	4
○ FCO Sauvignon '16	▽▽	3*

★Le Vigne di Zamò

loc. Rosazzo
via Abate Corrado, 4
33044 Manzano [UD]
Tel. +39 0432759693
www.levignedizamo.com

CELLAR SALES
PRE-BOOKED VISITS
ANNUAL PRODUCTION 280,000 bottles
HECTARES UNDER VINE 42.00
SUSTAINABLE WINERY

Long a benchmark for the Friuli Colli Orientali appellation, Le Vigne di Zamò is now the pride and joy of the Fontanafredda group, owned by Oscar Farinetti, creator of Eataly. The winery stands out atop a hill overlooking the famous Abbey of Rosazzo, while the modern, underground cellar merges seamlessly with the landscape and vineyards. The prestigious brand is tied to the name Tullio Zamò, who founded the producer as the last stage of a journey that began in the 1960s. The Friulano No Name '18 is back in one of its best versions, which can be traced back to those that, in previous years, earned top marks. It offers up an elegant bouquet of wild flowers and aromatic herbs, all of which accompany its harmonious palate. The Pinot Bianco Tullio Zamò '17, dedicated to the winery's founder, is redolent of wisteria and pastries, with rich, smoky notes and a soft, creamy palate.

Wine	Rating	Price
○ FCO Pinot Bianco Tullio Zamò '17	▼▼	5
○ Friuli Friulano No Name '18	▼▼	5
○ FCO Chardonnay Ronco delle Acacie '17	▼▼	5
○ FCO Friulano V. 50 Anni '18	▼▼	6
○ FCO Ribolla Gialla '19	▼▼	4
● FCO Rosso Ronco dei Roseti '17	▼▼	6
○ COF Friulano V. Cinquant'Anni '09	▽▽▽	5
○ COF Friulano V. Cinquant'Anni '08	▽▽▽	5
● COF Merlot V. Cinquant'Anni '09	▽▽▽	5
● COF Merlot V. Cinquant'Anni '06	▽▽▽	5
○ COF Tocai Friulano V. Cinquant'Anni '06	▽▽▽	5
○ FCO Friulano No Name '15	▽▽▽	5
○ Friuli Friulano No Name '16	▽▽▽	4*

Villa de Puppi

via Roma, 5
33040 Moimacco [UD]
Tel. +39 0432722461
www.depuppi.it

CELLAR SALES
PRE-BOOKED VISITS
ANNUAL PRODUCTION 70,000 bottles
HECTARES UNDER VINE 25.00
SUSTAINABLE WINERY

Caterina and Valfredo represent the latest generation of the noble de Puppi family who, for as far back as anyone can remember, have dedicated themselves to cultivating their land. Credit for their current success goes to the forward-thinking vision of Count Luigi de Puppi who, at the end of the last century, sensing the potential of the vineyards, proceeded to reorganize them and then handed them down to his young children. The producer's success was later consolidated with the acquisition of about ten hectares of vineyards on the Rosazzo hills. The wines that bear the prestigious Rosa Bosco brand occupy the top four positions in our ranking, and two reached our finals. The Merlot il Boscorosso '15 calls up cherry jam, dark tobacco, cloves and undergrowth, with an oaky background that follows through on the palate. The Sauvignon '16 plays on notes of ripe yellow peach and avocado; in the mouth it's creamy and also highly fragrant.

● Il Boscorosso di Rosa Bosco Merlot '15	🍷🍷 7
○ Sauvignon di Rosa Bosco '16	🍷🍷 5
○ Ribolla Gialla di Rosa Bosco '18	🍷🍷 4
○ Sauvignon '18	🍷🍷 3
○ Cabernet '16	🍷 3
○ Friuli Friulano '18	🍷 3
○ Ribolla Gialla '18	🍷 3
○ Chardonnay '17	ΥΥ 3
○ Friuli Friulano '17	ΥΥ 3
○ Friuli Pinot Grigio '17	ΥΥ 3
● Il Boscorosso di Rosa Bosco Merlot '13	ΥΥ 6
● Refosco P. R. '15	ΥΥ 3
○ Sauvignon '17	ΥΥ 3
○ Sauvignon '16	ΥΥ 3
○ Sauvignon di Rosa Bosco '15	ΥΥ 5
○ Sauvignon di Rosa Bosco '13	ΥΥ 5

★★Villa Russiz

loc. Italia
via Russiz, 4/6
34070 Capriva del Friuli [GO]
Tel. +39 048180047
www.villarussiz.it

CELLAR SALES
PRE-BOOKED VISITS
ANNUAL PRODUCTION 220,000 bottles
HECTARES UNDER VINE 45.00
SUSTAINABLE WINERY

The historic winery of Villa Russiz was founded in 1869 by the French count Teodoro de La Tour, who had moved to Capriva del Friuli with his Austrian wife, Elvine Ritter. He's still recognized as a skilled winemaker, as he imported rooted cuttings from his home town and planted them on the surrounding hills. Soon those vines adapted to perfection and spread like wildfire throughout the area. Since then Villa Russiz has been managed by a public body, which through a foundation runs a shelter for youth in difficulty. For this reason the producer earns our Solidarity Award. The proven substance of the Cabernet Sauvignon Dèfi de la Tour '15 and Merlot Graf de la Tour '15 contributed to a successful team performance that saw some 3 wines reach our finals. Captained by the highly youthful Pinot Bianco '19, the entire line-up proves to be top-notch, pointing to a consistence in quality that once again demonstrates why the producer is one of the region's best.

○ Collio Pinot Bianco '19	🍷🍷🍷 6
● Collio Cabernet Sauvignon Défi de La Tour '15	🍷🍷 8
● Collio Merlot Gräf de La Tour '15	🍷🍷 8
○ Collio Friulano '19	🍷🍷 4
○ Collio Malvasia '19	🍷🍷 6
○ Collio Pinot Grigio '19	🍷🍷 6
○ Collio Sauvignon de La Tour '19	🍷🍷 8
○ Collio Chardonnay Gräfin de La Tour '14	ΥΥΥ 7
○ Collio Friulano '09	ΥΥΥ 4*
○ Collio Malvasia '18	ΥΥΥ 4*
○ Collio Pinot Bianco '16	ΥΥΥ 4*
○ Collio Pinot Bianco '07	ΥΥΥ 3
○ Collio Sauvignon de La Tour '08	ΥΥΥ 5

Tenuta Villanova

FRAZ. VILLANOVA
VIA CONTESSA BERETTA, 29
34072 FARRA D'ISONZO [GO]
TEL. +39 0481889311
www.tenutavillanova.com

CELLAR SALES
PRE-BOOKED VISITS
ANNUAL PRODUCTION 38,000 bottles
HECTARES UNDER VINE 105.00

Villanova, with its more than five centuries of history, is undoubtedly one of the cornerstones of Friulian enology. In 1932 it was acquired by the forward-thinking entrepreneur Arnaldo Bennati. Today it's still managed by his wife, Giuseppina Grossi Bennati, who's supported by their grandson Alberto Grossi. Recently technical direction and production have been entrusted to the experience of enologist Giuseppe Lucido. They've also set in motion a rebranding with a new logo and redesigned labels. Their vineyards are located in the Collio and Friuli Isonzo appellations. Of course, between the hills and the plains there's a significant difference in sun exposure and subsoil, but the scores obtained by their wines show that the difference is minimal. Pinot Grigio, for example, in both versions is highly elegant on the nose, fragrant and citrusy, and with a nice nose-palate symmetry, coming through smooth and substantive in the mouth.

○ Collio Friulano '19	🍷🍷 4
○ Collio Picolit '18	🍷🍷 5
○ Collio Pinot Grigio '19	🍷🍷 3
○ Collio Ribolla Gialla '19	🍷🍷 3
○ Collio Sauvignon '19	🍷🍷 4
○ Friuli Isonzo Chardonnay '19	🍷🍷 2*
○ Friuli Isonzo Malvasia '19	🍷🍷 2*
○ Friuli Isonzo Pinot Grigio '19	🍷🍷 2*
● Friuli Isonzo Refosco P. R. '18	🍷🍷 2*
● Friuli Isonzo Merlot '18	🍷 3
○ Friuli Isonzo Traminer Aromatico '19	🍷 2
○ Collio Chardonnay Monte Cucco '97	🍸🍸🍸 3*
○ Collio Picolit Ronco Cucco '17	🍸🍸 5
○ Collio Pinot Grigio Ronco Cucco '18	🍸🍸 3
○ Collio Ribolla Gialla Ronco Cucco '18	🍸🍸 3
● Fraia '13	🍸🍸 5

Andrea Visintini

VIA GRAMOGLIANO, 27
33040 CORNO DI ROSAZZO [UD]
TEL. +39 0432755813
www.vinivisintini.com

CELLAR SALES
PRE-BOOKED VISITS
ACCOMMODATION
ANNUAL PRODUCTION 140,000 bottles
HECTARES UNDER VINE 35.00
VITICULTURE METHOD Certified Organic
SUSTAINABLE WINERY

On the hills of Corno di Rosazzo there stands a splendid watchtower built in 1560. It was part of the ancient feudal castle of Gramogliano, on the ruins of which today we find the Visintini estate. Of course, over the centuries there have been many owners—this until 1884, when it passed from the Counts Zucco di Cuccagna to the Visintini family. By succession, in 1973, management was entrusted to Andrea Visintini and now his son Oliviero. Together with twins Cinzia and Palmira, they continue with renewed enthusiasm in managing the winery. What most catches the eye when looking at the producer's catalog of wines is the competitiveness of its prices in light of their quality. The Pinot Grigio '19 pours a beautiful coppery color, offering up aromas of yellow muscatel cherry, currant, gooseberry and abate fetel pear; in the mouth it's balanced, pervasive and long. The Friulano Amphora '18 calls up roasted hazelnuts and cooked apple while the palate proves dry, sapid and alluring.

○ FCO Friulano '19	🍷🍷 2*
○ FCO Friulano Amphora '18	🍷🍷 4
● FCO Merlot '18	🍷🍷 2*
○ FCO Pinot Bianco '19	🍷🍷 2*
○ FCO Ribolla Gialla '19	🍷🍷 2*
○ Friuli Pinot Grigio '19	🍷🍷 2*
○ Malvasia '19	🍷🍷 2*
● FCO Merlot Torion Ris. '11	🍷 3
● COF Refosco P. R. '13	🍸🍸 2*
○ FCO Friulano '18	🍸🍸 2*
○ FCO Friulano Amphora '17	🍸🍸 4
● FCO Pignolo Amphora '13	🍸🍸 4
○ FCO Pinot Bianco '18	🍸🍸 2*
○ FCO Pinot Grigio '16	🍸🍸 2*
○ FCO Sauvignon '18	🍸🍸 2*
○ FCO Sauvignon '16	🍸🍸 2*
○ Friuli Pinot Grigio '18	🍸🍸 2*

★★Volpe Pasini

fraz. Togliano
via Cividale, 16
33040 Torreano [UD]
Tel. +39 0432715151
www.volpepasini.it

CELLAR SALES
PRE-BOOKED VISITS
ACCOMMODATION
ANNUAL PRODUCTION 400,000 bottles
HECTARES UNDER VINE 52.00
SUSTAINABLE WINERY

For years we've been writing about the beauty of this winery, talking about its magnificent Venetian villas (Villa Volpe Pasini and Villa Rosa), the centuries-old estate, the vineyards manicured as if they were gardens, as well as the wines, which manage to surprise us every year. Emilio Rotolo has always said that at the center of it all is 'Human effort' and recently he told us, with visible pride, that even in a difficult year like 2020 the producer's activities continued without interruption. By now it's customary to find numerous wines from the Zuc di Volpe line in our finals. This year, however, they are accompanied by a lovely new addition, a white called Cuvée 15.96, a blend of two native grapes, Ribolla Gialla and Malvasia Istriana. It's a territorial wine, of considerable impact, but among a range of very high overall quality, it's the Sauvignon Zuc di Volpe '19 that deservedly regains Tre Bicchieri.

Wine	Glasses	Price
○ FCO Sauvignon Zuc di Volpe '19	▼▼▼	6
○ 15.96 Cuveé Bianco '19	▼▼	4
○ FCO Pinot Bianco Zuc di Volpe '19	▼▼	6
○ FCO Pinot Grigio Zuc di Volpe '19	▼▼	6
○ FCO Ribolla Gialla delle Mura Zuc di Volpe '19	▼▼	6
○ FCO Chardonnay '19	▼▼	5
○ FCO Friulano '19	▼▼	5
● FCO Merlot Togliano '16	▼▼	5
○ FCO Pinot Grigio Grivò '19	▼▼	5
● FCO Refosco P. R. '18	▼▼	5
○ COF Sauvignon Zuc di Volpe '13	▽▽▽	4*
○ FCO Sauvignon Zuc di Volpe '18	▽▽▽	5
○ FCO Sauvignon Zuc di Volpe '17	▽▽▽	5
○ FCO Sauvignon Zuc di Volpe '16	▽▽▽	5
○ FCO Sauvignon Zuc di Volpe '15	▽▽▽	5
○ FCO Sauvignon Zuc di Volpe '14	▽▽▽	5

Francesco Vosca

fraz. Brazzano
via Sottomonte, 19
34071 Cormòns [GO]
Tel. +39 048162135
www.voscavini.it

CELLAR SALES
PRE-BOOKED VISITS
ANNUAL PRODUCTION 60,000 bottles
HECTARES UNDER VINE 10.00
SUSTAINABLE WINERY

Francesco Vosca's is one of those classic family farms with proud agricultural origins that, in the last decades of the last century, decided to progressively abandon mixed cultivation and cattle breeding in order to dedicate themselves exclusively to viticulture. It was an important step for Francesco, not without its unknowns. He was aware of the potential of the territory but also of its challenges, in particular because of the shape of the terrain, which isn't suitable for mechanic cultivation. Unfortunately, this year there were delays in bottling and, therefore, only a few samples were submitted. As a result our attention went to the Malvasia '19, their flagship, which displays a captivating olfactory spectrum that includes exotic fruit, citrus honey, bay leaves, sage and rhubarb. In the mouth, continuous echoes of aromatic herbs gratify its tasty palate.

Wine	Glasses	Price
○ Collio Malvasia '19	▼▼	3
○ Collio Ribolla Gialla '19	▼	3
○ Friuli Isonzo Sauvignon '19	▼	3
○ Collio Friulano '18	▽▽	3
○ Collio Friulano '17	▽▽	3
○ Collio Friulano '16	▽▽	3
○ Collio Malvasia '18	▽▽	3
○ Collio Malvasia '17	▽▽	3
○ Collio Malvasia '16	▽▽	3
● Collio Merlot '15	▽▽	4
○ Collio Ribolla Gialla '18	▽▽	3
○ Collio Ribolla Gialla '17	▽▽	3
○ Collio Ribolla Gialla '16	▽▽	3
○ Friuli Isonzo Chardonnay '17	▽▽	3
○ Friuli Isonzo Pinot Grigio '18	▽▽	3
○ Friuli Isonzo Sauvignon '18	▽▽	3
○ Friuli Isonzo Sauvignon '17	▽▽	3

Zaglia

LOC. FRASSINUTTI
VIA CRESCENZIA, 10
33050 PRECENICCO [UD]
TEL. +39 0431510320
www.zaglia.com

CELLAR SALES
PRE-BOOKED VISITS
ANNUAL PRODUCTION 100,000 bottles
HECTARES UNDER VINE 15.00

Management of the family estate was entrusted to Giorgio Zaglia in the early 1980s. Giorgio immediately introduced a philosophy aimed at the production of wines that would interpret the territory well but, above all, represent high quality standards. The vineyards, which fall in the Friuli Latisana appellation, are characterized by clayey soils rich in mineral salts. They also enjoy the influence of beneficial breezes from the nearby Adriatic Sea, which contribute to a particularly favorable microclimate for cultivating vines. The wines have a clear, focused varietal expression; the quality that unites them is a pronounced minerality, which amplifies their flavor and enlivens the palate. Very competitive prices are added value for the whole range. The Friulano '19 is redolent of wisteria, dry hay and lemon peel while the palate proves full and satisfying. The Pinot Grigio '19 and Chardonnay '19 go hand in hand, delighting the nose and gratifying the palate.

Wine	Rating
○ Friuli Chardonnay '19	🍷🍷 2*
○ Friuli Friulano '19	🍷🍷 2*
○ Friuli Pinot Grigio '19	🍷🍷 2*
● Friuli Refosco P. R. '19	🍷🍷 2*
● Friuli Merlot '19	🍷 2
⊙ Rosato '19	🍷 2
○ Solis Chardonnay Frizzante	🍷 2
● FCO Cabernet Franc Amanti Ris. '15	YY 2*
○ Friuli Chardonnay '16	YY 2*
○ Friuli Friulano '18	YY 2*
○ Friuli Friulano '17	YY 2*
○ Friuli Friulano '16	YY 2*
● Friuli Merlot '18	YY 2*
● Friuli Merlot '17	YY 2*
● Friuli Merlot '16	YY 2*
○ Friuli Pinot Grigio '18	YY 2*
● Friuli Refosco P.R. '18	YY 2*

Zidarich

LOC. PREPOTTO, 23
34011 DUINO AURISINA [TS]
TEL. +39 040201223
www.zidarich.it

CELLAR SALES
PRE-BOOKED VISITS
ANNUAL PRODUCTION 28,000 bottles
HECTARES UNDER VINE 8.00

Benjamin Zidarich is a true winemaker, one of Karst Trieste's best interpreters. The splendid wine cellar, dug into the hard rock, extends over five floors and reaches a depth of 20 meters, with temperature and humidity remaining constant throughout the year. The wines, first aged in casks and then in bottles, rest for years without being affected by the seasonal climate and temperature changes. These wines, in accordance with local tradition (including their whites), are made with maceration of the skins in the must, without temperature control. Zidarich's wines are a precise interpretation of the characteristics of Karst, starting with their intense, bright colors, iodine and delicately salty scents and a pronounced, earthy minerality deriving from the area. All these factors are brought out in the Prulke '18 (Sauvignon, Malvasia Istriana and Vitovska), a wine that offers up myriad aromas on the nose: broom, saffron, cooked apple, toasted almonds, aromatic herbs, delicate spices and salt.

Wine	Rating
○ Kamen Vitovska '18	🍷🍷 7
○ Malvasia '18	🍷🍷 5
○ Prulke '18	🍷🍷 5
○ Vitovska '18	🍷🍷 5
● Terrano '18	🍷🍷 5
○ Carso Malvasia '09	YYY 5
○ Carso Malvasia '06	YYY 5
○ Carso Vitovska V. Collezione '09	YYY 8
○ Prulke '10	YYY 5
○ Prulke '08	YYY 5
○ Kamen Vitovska '17	YY 7
○ Kamen Vitovska '16	YY 7
○ Kamen Vitovska '14	YY 7
○ Malvasia '16	YY 5
○ Malvasia Lehte '15	YY 6
○ Vitovska '17	YY 5
○ Vitovska '16	YY 5

Zorzettig

Fraz. Spessa
S.da Sant'Anna, 37
33043 Cividale del Friuli [UD]
Tel. +39 0432716156
www.zorzettigvini.it

CELLAR SALES
PRE-BOOKED VISITS
ACCOMMODATION
ANNUAL PRODUCTION 800,000 bottles
HECTARES UNDER VINE 120.00
SUSTAINABLE WINERY

Annalisa and Alessandro Zorzettig proudly manage a producer whose family brand, in Spessa di Cividale, has distinguished many generations of winemakers. Annalisa is an innovative and dynamic producer, bursting with ideas, while Alessandro prefers to oversee agronomic management. Despite continuous expansion, the level of quality has never suffered and prices have remained affordable. Excellence comes in the form of their Myò line, made with select grapes and entrusted to the enological expertise of Fabio Coser. Many wines from the Myò line will undergo further aging in the bottle, which allowed us to taste a large number of wines from their basic line, with more than satisfactory results across the entire range. We were also presented a new wine, I Fiori di Leonie '18, whose debut couldn't have been better. It won pole position and handily took home Tre Bicchieri.

- ○ FCO Bianco Myò I Fiori di Leonie '18 — 🍷🍷🍷 5
- ● FCO Rosso Cunfins Segno di Terra '16 — 🍷🍷 5
- ○ FCO Friulano '19 — 🍷🍷 3
- ● FCO Pignolo Myò '15 — 🍷🍷 7
- ○ FCO Ribolla Gialla '19 — 🍷🍷 3
- ● FCO Schioppettino '18 — 🍷🍷 4
- ● FCO Schioppettino Myò '17 — 🍷🍷 6
- ● Friuli Cabernet Sauvignon '19 — 🍷🍷 3
- ● Friuli Merlot '19 — 🍷🍷 3
- ○ Friuli Pinot Bianco '19 — 🍷🍷 3
- ○ Friuli Pinot Grigio '19 — 🍷🍷 3
- ○ Optimum Ribolla Gialla Brut '19 — 🍷🍷 4
- ● FCO Refosco P. R. '19 — 🍷 3
- ○ FCO Sauvignon '19 — 🍷 3
- ○ FCO Pinot Bianco Myò '18 — 🍷🍷🍷 5

Zuani

Loc. Giasbana, 12
34070 San Floriano del Collio [GO]
Tel. +39 0481391432
www.zuanivini.it

CELLAR SALES
PRE-BOOKED VISITS
ACCOMMODATION
ANNUAL PRODUCTION 75,000 bottles
HECTARES UNDER VINE 15.00

Patrizia Felluga's philosophy comes on the heels of years of experience in the vineyards and cellar, all of which combines with her rare entrepreneurial skill. Patrizia, who herself inherited a legacy of winemaking, has managed to pass on her love for the land and viticulture to her children Antonio and Caterina. Collio Bianco Zuani's debut dates back to 2001 and, for many years, it was the producer's only wine, although it comes in two versions: steel and oak. Today it's flanked by other wines from the Sodevo line, which, year after year, keep getting better. The Collio Bianco Zuani Vigne '19 (Chardonnay, Pinot Grigio, Sauvignon and Tocai Friulano in equal parts) exhibits an olfactory suite of rare elegance, introduced by a floral bouquet followed by citrus notes of citron and bergamot, white pepper, lime honey and chalk powder. In the mouth its perfect balance makes it persuasive and harmonious. The reserve is more aristocratic and juicy—a highly classy drink.

- ○ Collio Bianco Zuani Vigne '19 — 🍷🍷 4
- ○ Collio Bianco Zuani Ris. '17 — 🍷🍷 5
- ○ Collio Ribolla Gialla Sodevo '19 — 🍷🍷 3
- ○ Friuli Pinot Grigio Sodevo '19 — 🍷🍷 3
- ○ Collio Bianco Zuani Vigne '10 — 🍷🍷🍷 3
- ○ Collio Bianco Zuani Vigne '07 — 🍷🍷🍷 3
- ○ Collio Bianco Zuani Vigne '18 — 🍷🍷 4
- ○ Collio Bianco Zuani Vigne '17 — 🍷🍷 4
- ○ Collio Bianco Zuani Vigne '16 — 🍷🍷 4
- ○ Collio Bianco Zuani Vigne '15 — 🍷🍷 4
- ○ Collio Bianco Zuani Vigne '13 — 🍷🍷 4

AD Coos

FRAZ. RAMANDOLO
VIA PESCIA, 3
33045 NIMIS [UD]
TEL. +39 3356101320
azienda.ad.coos@gmail.com

CELLAR SALES
PRE-BOOKED VISITS
ANNUAL PRODUCTION 12,000 bottles
HECTARES UNDER VINE 2.50

- ○ FCO Friulano '18 — 🍷🍷 3
- ○ Ramandolo '18 — 🍷🍷 3
- ● Refosco P. R. '18 — 🍷🍷 3
- ○ Sauvignon '18 — 🍷 3

Aquila del Torre

FRAZ. SAVORGNANO DEL TORRE
VIA ATTIMIS, 25
33040 POVOLETTO [UD]
TEL. +39 0432666428
www.aquiladeltorre.it

CELLAR SALES
PRE-BOOKED VISITS
ACCOMMODATION
ANNUAL PRODUCTION 50,000 bottles
HECTARES UNDER VINE 18.00
VITICULTURE METHOD Certified Organic

- ○ FCO At Friulano '18 — 🍷🍷 3
- ○ FCO Bianco Oasi '17 — 🍷🍷 6
- ● FCO At Refosco P. R. '16 — 🍷 3
- ○ FCO At Riesling '16 — 🍷 3

Ascevi - Luwa

LOC. UCLANZI, 24
34070 SAN FLORIANO DEL COLLIO [GO]
TEL. +39 0481884140
www.asceviluwa.it

CELLAR SALES
PRE-BOOKED VISITS
ANNUAL PRODUCTION 200,000 bottles
HECTARES UNDER VINE 30.00

- ○ Collio Pinot Grigio Grappoli '19 — 🍷🍷 2*
- ○ Collio Sauvignon Ronco dei Sassi '19 — 🍷🍷 2*
- ○ Collio Chardonnay Rupis '19 — 🍷 2
- ○ Friuli Isonzo Friulano '19 — 🍷 2

Amandum

VIA F. PETRARCA, 40
34070 MORARO [GO]
TEL. +39 335242566
www.amandum.it

ANNUAL PRODUCTION 35,000 bottles
HECTARES UNDER VINE 2.00

- ○ Friuli Isonzo Friulano '18 — 🍷🍷 4
- ○ Friuli Isonzo Pinot Bianco '18 — 🍷🍷 4
- ○ Friuli Isonzo Pinot Grigio Grey Dop '18 — 🍷 4
- ● Pinot Nero '16 — 🍷🍷 5

Maurizio Arzenton

FRAZ. SPESSA
VIA CORMONS, 221
33043 CIVIDALE DEL FRIULI [UD]
TEL. +39 0432716139
www.arzentonvini.it

CELLAR SALES
PRE-BOOKED VISITS
ANNUAL PRODUCTION 30,000 bottles
HECTARES UNDER VINE 10.00

- ○ FCO Pinot Bianco '19 — 🍷🍷 3
- ○ FCO Sauvignon '19 — 🍷🍷 3
- ○ FCO Friulano '19 — 🍷 3
- ○ FCO Pinot Grigio '19 — 🍷 3

La Bellanotte

S.DA DELLA BELLANOTTE, 3
34072 FARRA D'ISONZO [GO]
TEL. +39 0481888020
www.labellanotte.it

CELLAR SALES
PRE-BOOKED VISITS
ANNUAL PRODUCTION 100,000 bottles
HECTARES UNDER VINE 16.00
VITICULTURE METHOD Certified Organic

- ○ Collio Friulano '19 — 🍷🍷 3
- ○ Friuli Isonzo Sauvignon L'Umberto '19 — 🍷🍷 3
- ○ Friuli Pinot Grigio Conte Lucio '17 — 🍷🍷 5
- ● Friuli Isonzo Merlot Rojadelsonzo '14 — 🍷 5

Tenuta Beltrame

FRAZ. PRIVANO
LOC. ANTONINI, 4
33050 BAGNARIA ARSA [UD]
TEL. +39 0432923670
www.tenutabeltrame.it

CELLAR SALES
PRE-BOOKED VISITS
ANNUAL PRODUCTION 80,000 bottles
HECTARES UNDER VINE 25.00

● Friuli Cabernet '16 — 🍷🍷 3
● Friuli Refosco P. R. '17 — 🍷🍷 3
● Pinot Nero '18 — 🍷🍷 3
● Tazzelenghe '16 — 🍷🍷 6

Blason

LOC. BRUMA
VIA ROMA, 32
34072 GRADISCA D'ISONZO [GO]
TEL. +39 048192414
www.blasonwines.com

CELLAR SALES
PRE-BOOKED VISITS
ANNUAL PRODUCTION 60,000 bottles
HECTARES UNDER VINE 18.00

○ Friuli Isonzo Bruma Bianco '17 — 🍷🍷 3
○ Friuli Isonzo Friulano '19 — 🍷🍷 2*
○ Ribolla Gialla '19 — 🍷🍷 2*
● Cabernet Sauvignon '19 — 🍷 3

Fausta Bolzicco

VIA SAN GIOVANNI, 60
34071 CORMÒNS [GO]
TEL. +39 335258608
aziendabolzicco@libero.it

CELLAR SALES
ANNUAL PRODUCTION 10,000 bottles
HECTARES UNDER VINE 7.50

○ Collio Friulano '19 — 🍷🍷 3
○ Malvasia '19 — 🍷🍷 3
○ Collio Bianco Vignedamont '18 — 🍷 3
○ Collio Ribolla Gialla '19 — 🍷 3

Borgo dei Sapori

S.DA DI PLANEZ, 60
33043 CIVIDALE DEL FRIULI [UD]
TEL. +39 0432732477
www.borgodeisapori.net

CELLAR SALES
PRE-BOOKED VISITS
ANNUAL PRODUCTION 27,000 bottles
HECTARES UNDER VINE 4.00
VITICULTURE METHOD Certified Organic

● FCO Cabernet Franc '18 — 🍷🍷 3
○ FCO Friulano '18 — 🍷🍷 2*
● FCO Merlot '18 — 🍷🍷 3
○ FCO Sauvignon '18 — 🍷🍷 3

Borgo Sant'Andrea

FRAZ. BRAZZACCO
VIA SANT'ANDREA
33030 MORUZZO [UD]
TEL. +39 0432642015
www.borgosantandrea.com

CELLAR SALES
PRE-BOOKED VISITS
RESTAURANT SERVICE
ANNUAL PRODUCTION 30,000 bottles
HECTARES UNDER VINE 21.00

● Friuli Merlot '18 — 🍷🍷 3
○ Friuli Pinot Grigio '18 — 🍷🍷 3
● Friuli Refosco P. R. '18 — 🍷🍷 3
○ Prosecco Brut '18 — 🍷🍷 2*

Tenuta Bosco Albano

FRAZ. CECCHINI
VIA BOSCO DI CECCHINI, 27B
33087 PASIANO DI PORDENONE [PN]
TEL. +39 0434628678
www.boscoalbano.com

CELLAR SALES
PRE-BOOKED VISITS
ACCOMMODATION
ANNUAL PRODUCTION 70,000 bottles
HECTARES UNDER VINE 40.00

○ Friuli Friulano '19 — 🍷🍷 3
○ Pinot Grigio delle Venezie Brut '18 — 🍷🍷 3
○ Ribolla Gialla Brut Nature '17 — 🍷🍷 5
○ Friuli Sauvignon '19 — 🍷 3

Braidot

loc. Versa
via Palmanova, 20 B
34076 Romans d'Isonzo [GO]
Tel. +39 0481908970
www.braidotwines.it

CELLAR SALES
PRE-BOOKED VISITS
ANNUAL PRODUCTION 450,000 bottles
HECTARES UNDER VINE 40.00

- ○ Friuli Friulano '19 🍷🍷 2*
- ○ Ribolla Gialla '19 🍷🍷 2*
- ○ Friuli Pinot Grigio '19 🍷 2
- ○ Friuli Sauvignon Blanc '19 🍷 2

Bressani Giuseppe

via dei Conti, 23
33045 Nimis [UD]
Tel. +39 0432790430
www.bressani.net

ANNUAL PRODUCTION 15,000 bottles
HECTARES UNDER VINE 7.00

- ○ FCO Friulano '18 🍷🍷 3
- ● FCO Merlot '16 🍷🍷 5
- ○ Ramandolo '14 🍷🍷 5
- ● FCO Refosco P. R. '15 🍷 5

Paolo Caccese

loc. Pradis, 6
34071 Cormòns [GO]
Tel. +39 048161062
www.paolocaccese.com

CELLAR SALES
PRE-BOOKED VISITS
ANNUAL PRODUCTION 30,000 bottles
HECTARES UNDER VINE 5.50

- ○ Collio Friulano '18 🍷🍷 4
- ○ Collio Malvasia '18 🍷🍷 4
- ○ Collio Sauvignon '18 🍷🍷 4
- ○ La Veronica 🍷🍷 5

Casasola

fraz. Rosazzo
via Abate Geroldo, 7
33044 Manzano [UD]
Tel. +39 0432759071
www.vinicasasola.it

CELLAR SALES
PRE-BOOKED VISITS
ANNUAL PRODUCTION 8,000 bottles
HECTARES UNDER VINE 11.00

- ● FCO Merlot '18 🍷🍷 3
- ● Pignolo '14 🍷🍷 5
- ○ Riesling Italico '18 🍷🍷 3
- ● FCO Pinot Nero '18 🍷 3

Nicola e Mauro Cencig

via Sottomonte, 171
33044 Manzano [UD]
Tel. +39 3475442235
www.cencig.com

- ○ FCO Friulano '19 🍷🍷 2*
- ● FCO Refosco P. R. '18 🍷🍷 2*
- ○ FCO Sauvignon '19 🍷🍷 2*
- ● FCO Cabernet Franc '18 🍷 2

I Clivi

loc. Gramogliano, 20
33040 Corno di Rosazzo [UD]
Tel. +39 3287269979
www.iclivi.wine

CELLAR SALES
PRE-BOOKED VISITS
ANNUAL PRODUCTION 50,000 bottles
HECTARES UNDER VINE 12.00
VITICULTURE METHOD Certified Organic

- ○ Collio Malvasia '18 🍷🍷 5
- ○ FCO Bianco Galea '18 🍷🍷 4
- ● FCO Merlot Galea '18 🍷🍷 5

Conti Formentini

via Oslavia, 5
34070 San Floriano del Collio [GO]
Tel. +39 0481884131
www.contiformentini.it

CELLAR SALES
PRE-BOOKED VISITS
ANNUAL PRODUCTION 184,200 bottles
HECTARES UNDER VINE 58.00

○ Collio Chardonnay '19	🍷🍷 2*
○ Collio Friulano Furlanà '19	🍷🍷 2*
○ Collio Pinot Grigio '19	🍷🍷 2*
○ Collio Sauvignon Caligo '19	🍷🍷 2*

Cornium

via Aquileia, 79
33040 Corno di Rosazzo [UD]
Tel. +39 3476010132
ariedogigante@alice.it

CELLAR SALES
PRE-BOOKED VISITS
ANNUAL PRODUCTION 20,000 bottles
HECTARES UNDER VINE 12.00

○ FCO Pinot Grigio '19	🍷🍷 3*
○ FCO Friulano '19	🍷🍷 3
● FCO Merlot '16	🍷🍷 3
○ FCO Sauvignon '19	🍷🍷 3

La Cricca

loc. Craoretto, 2
33040 Prepotto [UD]
Tel. +39 3275618717
www.vinilacricca.it

CELLAR SALES
PRE-BOOKED VISITS
ANNUAL PRODUCTION 4,000 bottles
HECTARES UNDER VINE 2.50
SUSTAINABLE WINERY

○ Busart '19	🍷🍷 4
○ FCO Friulano '19	🍷🍷 3
○ FCO Pinot Bianco '19	🍷🍷 4

Marina Danieli

fraz. Caminetto
via Beltrame, 77
33042 Buttrio [UD]
Tel. +39 0432674421
www.marinadanieli.com

CELLAR SALES
PRE-BOOKED VISITS
ANNUAL PRODUCTION 120,000 bottles
HECTARES UNDER VINE 34.00
SUSTAINABLE WINERY

● FCO Cabernet '15	🍷🍷 3
○ FCO Friulano '18	🍷🍷 3
● FCO Merlot Clama '18	🍷🍷 5
● FCO Refosco P. R. '16	🍷🍷 3

Viticoltori Friulani La Delizia

via Udine, 24
33072 Casarsa della Delizia [PN]
Tel. +39 0434869564
www.ladelizia.com

CELLAR SALES
PRE-BOOKED VISITS
ANNUAL PRODUCTION 22,000,000 bottles
HECTARES UNDER VINE 2000.00

● Friuli Merlot Sass Ter' '18	🍷🍷 4
● Friuli Refosco P. R. Sass Ter' '18	🍷🍷 4
○ Jadèr Cuvée Brut	🍷🍷 2*
○ Ribolla Gialla Brut Naonis	🍷 2

Le Due Torri

loc. Vicinale del Judrio
via San Martino, 19
33040 Corno di Rosazzo [UD]
Tel. +39 0432759150
www.le2torri.com

CELLAR SALES
PRE-BOOKED VISITS
RESTAURANT SERVICE
ANNUAL PRODUCTION 50,000 bottles
HECTARES UNDER VINE 10.00
SUSTAINABLE WINERY

○ Friuli Bianco Time Machine '18	🍷🍷 4
○ Friuli Grave Friulano Sup. '18	🍷🍷 2*
● Friuli Grave Rosso Ris. '16	🍷🍷 4

Le Favole

loc. Terra Rossa
via Dietro Castello, 7
33070 Caneva [PN]
Tel. +39 0434735604
www.lefavole-wines.com

CELLAR SALES
PRE-BOOKED VISITS
ACCOMMODATION
ANNUAL PRODUCTION 70,000 bottles
HECTARES UNDER VINE 20.00

● Friuli Annia Refosco P. R. '16	🍷🍷 2*
○ Friuli Friulano '19	🍷🍷 2*
○ Giallo di Roccia Brut M. Cl.	🍷🍷 4
● Friuli Cabernet Franc '18	🍷 2

Forchir

loc. Casali Bianchini
33030 Camino al Tagliamento [UD]
Tel. +39 0432821525
www.forchir.it

CELLAR SALES
PRE-BOOKED VISITS
ANNUAL PRODUCTION 1,200,000 bottles
HECTARES UNDER VINE 240.00
VITICULTURE METHOD Certified Organic
SUSTAINABLE WINERY

○ Friuli Grave Chardonnay Claps '19	🍷🍷 2*
○ Friuli Grave Pinot Bianco Maraveis '19	🍷🍷 3
● Refoscone Refosco P. R. '16	🍷🍷 3
○ Ribolla Gialla Brut	🍷 3

Fossa Mala

via Bassi, 81
33080 Fiume Veneto [PN]
Tel. +39 0434957997
www.fossamala.it

CELLAR SALES
PRE-BOOKED VISITS
ACCOMMODATION AND RESTAURANT SERVICE
ANNUAL PRODUCTION 130,000 bottles
HECTARES UNDER VINE 37.00

○ Friuli Grave Chardonnay '19	🍷🍷 2*
○ Friuli Grave Friulano '19	🍷🍷 2*
○ Vigneti di Familglia Brut	🍷🍷 3
○ Friuli Grave Pinot Grigio '19	🍷 2

Graunar

via Scedina
34070 San Floriano del Collio [GO]
Tel. +39 0481884115
graunarwines@libero.it

○ Collio Picolit '17	🍷🍷 3
○ Collio Pinot Bianco '18	🍷🍷 2*
● Collio Rosso '16	🍷🍷 4
○ Collio Sauvignon '18	🍷🍷 2*

Humar

loc. Valerisce, 20
34070 San Floriano del Collio [GO]
Tel. +39 0481884197
www.humar.it

CELLAR SALES
PRE-BOOKED VISITS
ANNUAL PRODUCTION 60,000 bottles
HECTARES UNDER VINE 12.00

● Collio Cabernet Franc '18	🍷🍷 3
○ Collio Chardonnay '19	🍷🍷 3
○ Collio Friulano '19	🍷🍷 3
○ Collio Pinot Grigio '19	🍷🍷 3

Isola Augusta

via Casali Isola Augusta, 4
33056 Palazzolo dello Stella [UD]
Tel. +39 043158046
www.isolaugusta.com

CELLAR SALES
PRE-BOOKED VISITS
ACCOMMODATION AND RESTAURANT SERVICE
ANNUAL PRODUCTION 270,000 bottles
HECTARES UNDER VINE 65.00
SUSTAINABLE WINERY

○ Friuli Chardonnay Les Iles '18	🍷🍷 3*
● Friuli Cabernet Augusteo '17	🍷🍷 3
○ Ribolla Gialla '19	🍷 2

Lupinc

FRAZ. PREPOTTO, 11B
34011 DUINO AURISINA [TS]
TEL. +39 040200848
www.lupinc.it

CELLAR SALES
PRE-BOOKED VISITS
ANNUAL PRODUCTION 15,000 bottles
HECTARES UNDER VINE 3.00

○ Malvasia '18	🍷🍷 3
○ Stara Brajda '18	🍷🍷 3
● Terrano '18	🍷🍷 3
○ Vitovska '18	🍷🍷 3

La Magnolia

LOC. SPESSA
VIA CORMONS
33043 CIVIDALE DEL FRIULI [UD]
TEL. +39 0432716262
www.vinilamagnolia.it

CELLAR SALES
PRE-BOOKED VISITS
ACCOMMODATION
ANNUAL PRODUCTION 200,000 bottles
HECTARES UNDER VINE 40.00

● FCO Cabernet Sauvignon '19	🍷🍷 3
○ FCO Friulano '19	🍷🍷 2*
○ FCO Ribolla Gialla '19	🍷🍷 3
● Ubi Es '16	🍷 4

Piera Martellozzo 1899

VIA PORDENONE, 33
33080 SAN QUIRINO [PN]
TEL. +39 0434963100
www.piera1899.com

CELLAR SALES
PRE-BOOKED VISITS
ANNUAL PRODUCTION 5,000,000 bottles
HECTARES UNDER VINE 10.00
VITICULTURE METHOD Certified Organic

○ Friuli Chardonnay Terre Magre '19	🍷🍷 2*
● Friuli Merlot Terre Magre '19	🍷🍷 2*
○ Friuli Pinot Grigio Terre Magre '19	🍷🍷 2*
○ Ribolla Gialla Onedis Sel. '19	🍷 3

Vigneti Micossi

LOC. SEDILIS
VIA NIMIS, 20
33017 TARCENTO [UD]
TEL. +39 0432783276
www.vignetimicossi.it

○ Ramandolo '16	🍷🍷 4
● Refosco P. R. '17	🍷🍷 2*
● Schioppettino '18	🍷🍷 4

Mulino delle Tolle

FRAZ. SEVEGLIANO
VIA MULINO DELLE TOLLE, 15
33050 BAGNARIA ARSA [UD]
TEL. +39 0432924723
www.mulinodelletolle.it

CELLAR SALES
PRE-BOOKED VISITS
ACCOMMODATION AND RESTAURANT SERVICE
ANNUAL PRODUCTION 100,000 bottles
HECTARES UNDER VINE 22.00

● Friuli Aquilea Merlot '18	🍷🍷 3
○ Friuli Aquileia Malvasia '19	🍷🍷 2*
○ Friuli Aquileia Sauvignon '19	🍷🍷 2*
○ Friuli Pinot Bianco '19	🍷 3

Obiz

B.GO GORTANI, 2
33052 CERVIGNANO DEL FRIULI [UD]
TEL. +39 043131900
www.obiz.it

CELLAR SALES
PRE-BOOKED VISITS
ANNUAL PRODUCTION 100,000 bottles
HECTARES UNDER VINE 40.00
SUSTAINABLE WINERY

● Friuli Aquileia Merlot '17	🍷🍷 2*
● Friuli Aquileia Refosco P. R. '17	🍷🍷 2*
○ Friuli Friulano '19	🍷🍷 2
● Natissa Rosso '17	🍷 3

Cantina Odoni

FRAZ. LONGERA
34100 TRIESTE
TEL. +39 3409317794
www.cantinaodoni.com

CELLAR SALES
PRE-BOOKED VISITS
RESTAURANT SERVICE
ANNUAL PRODUCTION 50,000 bottles
HECTARES UNDER VINE 6.00

○ Chardonnay '19	🍷🍷 3
○ Sauvignon '19	🍷🍷 2*
○ Malvasia '19	🍷 3
○ Vitovska '19	🍷 3

Orzan

VIA G. MAZZINI, 48
34070 CAPRIVA DEL FRIULI [GO]
TEL. +39 0481809419
www.orzanwines.com

● Cabernet Sauvignon '18	🍷🍷 3
○ Collio Pinot Grigio '18	🍷🍷 3
○ Collio Ribolla Gialla Zal Scur '16	🍷🍷 4
● Merlot Morar '16	🍷🍷 4

Ostrouska

LOC. SAGRADO,1
LOC. SAGRADO,1
34010 SGONICO [TS]
TEL. +39 0402296672
www.ostrouska.it

ANNUAL PRODUCTION 5,000 bottles
HECTARES UNDER VINE 1.50

○ Malvasia '18	🍷🍷 5
○ Vitovska '18	🍷🍷 5
● Terrano '18	🍷 5

Parovel

LOC. CARESANA, 81
LOC. BAGNOLI DELLA ROSANDRA
34018 SAN DORLIGO DELLA VALLE [TS]
TEL. +39 040227050
www.parovel.com

ANNUAL PRODUCTION 35,000 bottles
HECTARES UNDER VINE 11.00

○ Carso Vitovska Onavè '16	🍷🍷 5
○ Matos Nonet '15	🍷🍷 7
○ Visavì '17	🍷🍷 3

Piè di Mont

LOC. PIEDIMONTE DEL CALVARIO
VIA MONTE CALVARIO, 30
34170 GORIZIA
TEL. +39 0481391338
www.piedimont.it

CELLAR SALES
PRE-BOOKED VISITS
ANNUAL PRODUCTION 10,000 bottles
HECTARES UNDER VINE 1.20

○ Blanc de Blanc Pas Dosé M. Cl. '16	🍷🍷 6
○ Brut Cuvée Mill. '13	🍷🍷 6
○ Brut Cuvée Mill. '16	🍷🍷 6

Tenuta Pinni

VIA SANT' OSVALDO, 3
33098 SAN MARTINO AL TAGLIAMENTO [PN]
TEL. +39 0434899464
www.tenutapinni.com

CELLAR SALES
PRE-BOOKED VISITS
ANNUAL PRODUCTION 27,000 bottles
HECTARES UNDER VINE 27.00
SUSTAINABLE WINERY

○ Friuli Pinot Grigio '19	🍷🍷 2*
○ Ribolla Gialla '19	🍷🍷 2*
○ Ribolla Gialla Brut M. Cl.	🍷🍷 5
○ Traminer Aromatico '19	🍷🍷 2*

Flavio Pontoni

via Peruzzi, 8
33042 Buttrio [UD]
Tel. +39 0432674352
www.pontoni.it

CELLAR SALES
PRE-BOOKED VISITS
ACCOMMODATION
ANNUAL PRODUCTION 30,000 bottles
HECTARES UNDER VINE 4.50

- ○ FCO Friulano '19 🍷🍷 2*
- ● FCO Merlot '18 🍷🍷 2*
- ○ FCO Sauvignon '19 🍷🍷 2*
- ● Refosco P. R. '18 🍷🍷 2*

Reguta

via Bassi, 16
33050 Pocenia [UD]
Tel. +39 0432779157
www. reguta.it

CELLAR SALES
PRE-BOOKED VISITS
ACCOMMODATION AND RESTAURANT SERVICE
ANNUAL PRODUCTION 2,500,000 bottles
HECTARES UNDER VINE 270.00

- ● Altropasso Rosso '18 🍷🍷 2*
- ○ Collio Pinot Grigio '19 🍷🍷 3
- ○ Collio Ribolla Gialla '19 🍷🍷 2*
- ○ Friuli Pinot Grigio '19 🍷🍷 2*

Ronco dei Pini

via Ronchi, 93
33040 Prepotto [UD]
Tel. +39 0432713239
www.roncodeipini.it

CELLAR SALES
PRE-BOOKED VISITS
ANNUAL PRODUCTION 90,000 bottles
HECTARES UNDER VINE 15.00

- ○ FCO Friulano '19 🍷🍷 3
- ● FCO Limes Rosso '16 🍷🍷 5
- ● FCO Schiopettino di Prepotto '17 🍷🍷 5
- ○ Ribolla Gialla Brut Tre Lune '19 🍷🍷 3

Ronco Margherita

via XX Settembre, 106a
33094 Pinzano al Tagliamento [PN]
Tel. +39 0432950845
www.roncomargherita.it

CELLAR SALES
PRE-BOOKED VISITS
ANNUAL PRODUCTION 150,000 bottles
HECTARES UNDER VINE 36.00
VITICULTURE METHOD Certified Organic
SUSTAINABLE WINERY

- ○ FCO Friulano '19 🍷🍷 3
- ● Friuli Pinot Nero Anniversario '17 🍷🍷 8
- ● Friuli Refosco P. R. '17 🍷🍷 3
- ○ Ribolla Gialla Gerchia Pas Dosè M. Cl. '15 🍷🍷 5

Russolo

via San Rocco, 58a
33080 San Quirino [PN]
Tel. +39 0434919577
www.russolo.it

CELLAR SALES
PRE-BOOKED VISITS
ANNUAL PRODUCTION 165,000 bottles
HECTARES UNDER VINE 16.00
SUSTAINABLE WINERY

- ● Borgo di Peuma '16 🍷🍷 5
- ○ Doi Raps '18 🍷🍷 4
- ○ Friuli Pinot Grigio Ronco Calaj '19 🍷🍷 3
- ● Pinot Nero Grifo Nero '17 🍷 5

San Simone

loc. Rondover
via Prata, 30
33080 Porcia [PN]
Tel. +39 0434578633
www.sansimone.it

CELLAR SALES
PRE-BOOKED VISITS
ANNUAL PRODUCTION 900,000 bottles
HECTARES UNDER VINE 85.00
SUSTAINABLE WINERY

- ○ Friuli Grave Friulano Case Sugan '18 🍷🍷 3
- ○ Friuli Grave Pinot Grigio Case Sugan '18 🍷🍷 3
- ○ Friuli Grave Pinot Grigio Ramato Case Sugan '18 🍷🍷 3

Scarbolo

FRAZ. LAUZACCO
V.LE GRADO, 4
33050 PAVIA DI UDINE [UD]
TEL. +39 0432675612
www.scarbolo.com

CELLAR SALES
PRE-BOOKED VISITS
RESTAURANT SERVICE
ANNUAL PRODUCTION 160,000 bottles
HECTARES UNDER VINE 28.00
SUSTAINABLE WINERY

- ○ Friuli Grave Chardonnay Lara Sunset Scent '17 — 🍷🍷 4
- ○ Friuli Grave Pinot Grigio Mattia Beyond Pinot '16 — 🍷🍷 4

Skerlj

VIA SALES, 44
34010 SGONICO [TS]
TEL. +39 040229253
www.skerlj.it

CELLAR SALES
PRE-BOOKED VISITS
ACCOMMODATION AND RESTAURANT SERVICE
ANNUAL PRODUCTION 5,000 bottles
HECTARES UNDER VINE 2.00
VITICULTURE METHOD Certified Organic

- ○ Vitovska '17 — 🍷🍷 5
- ○ Malvasia '17 — 🍷🍷 5
- ● Terrano '17 — 🍷🍷 5

Tarlao

VIA SAN ZILI, 41
33051 AQUILEIA [UD]
TEL. +39 043191417
www.tarlao.eu

CELLAR SALES
PRE-BOOKED VISITS
ANNUAL PRODUCTION 30,000 bottles
HECTARES UNDER VINE 6.50

- ○ Friuli Aquileia Friulano Albero del Noce '18 — 🍷🍷 3
- ○ Friuli Aquileia Malvasia Ninive '19 — 🍷🍷 3
- ○ Friuli Aquileia Sauvignon Giona '19 — 🍷🍷 3

Terre del Faet

FRAZ. FAET
V.LE ROMA, 82
34071 CORMÒNS [GO]
TEL. +39 3470103325
www.terredelfaet.it

CELLAR SALES
PRE-BOOKED VISITS
ANNUAL PRODUCTION 24,000 bottles
HECTARES UNDER VINE 4.50

- ○ Collio Bianco del Faet '18 — 🍷🍷 3*
- ○ Collio Friulano '19 — 🍷🍷 3
- ○ Collio Malvasia '19 — 🍷🍷 3
- ○ Collio Pinot Bianco '19 — 🍷 3

Valle

VIA NAZIONALE, 3
33042 BUTTRIO [UD]
TEL. +39 0432674289
www.valle.it

CELLAR SALES
PRE-BOOKED VISITS
ANNUAL PRODUCTION 300,000 bottles
HECTARES UNDER VINE 42.00

- ○ FCO Friulano '19 — 🍷🍷 3
- ○ FCO Pinot Grigio '19 — 🍷🍷 3
- ○ FCO Ribolla Gialla '19 — 🍷🍷 3
- ○ FCO Sauvignon '19 — 🍷🍷 3

Venchiarezza

VIA UDINE, 100
33043 CIVIDALE DEL FRIULI [UD]
TEL. +39 3496829576
info@venchiarezza.it

CELLAR SALES
PRE-BOOKED VISITS
ANNUAL PRODUCTION 40,000 bottles
HECTARES UNDER VINE 8.00
VITICULTURE METHOD Certified Organic

- ○ Blanc de Blancs Pas Dosè M. Cl. — 🍷🍷 4
- ○ Chardonnay '18 — 🍷🍷 2*
- ● Refosco P. R. '18 — 🍷🍷 3
- ○ Vigna del Tempo '19 — 🍷🍷 3

EMILIA ROMAGNA

The area of Lambrusco, where a great transition is underway (the unification of the consortia, planned for 2021), once again sees Sorbara at the fore. Furthermore, the development of 'alternative' variations on the usual second-fermentation approach in autoclaves (i.e. the Metodo Classico and Metodo Ancestrale), should be closely watched., It must be said, however, that when it comes to Lambrusco, the hillside districts are also showing interesting signs, especially Castelvetro and its surroundings. Another dynamic area is Pignoletto, where amidst a host of appellations and typologies, certain wines of note are starting to find their way, especially in terms of their aromatic profiles. Moving up to Parma and Piacenza, in our opinion the consortia aren't giving clear indications about the wines that producers should be focusing on. On the Colli Piacentini the best signs are coming from Metodo Classico, with an award that could inspire the whole area. All this while waiting to understand what Gutturnio wants to do when it grows up, and especially while waiting for Malvasia di Candia Aromatica to develop. The native grape variety that has proven capable of delivering very notable results, even when it comes to aging. Now on to Romagna. Increasingly aware of its own potential, but even more so of its own identity, the part of the region that extends towards the Adriatic comes across as a hotbed of interesting projects amidst recognitions, renewals and new undertakings. We start with Sangiovese. Obviously, we're seeing increased stylistic focus and the pursuit of more acute territorial expressions. There's still a ways to go, but the desire to find an original and singular identity, not always easy (as history has shown), seems to us a very encouraging sign. And what about Albana? We knew it was a versatile variety, but now we're seeing a host of experiments, and there's no lack of excellence either. In general, it must be said that the region's whites also hold their own, with many varieties (such as Rebola Riminese) and as many styles. Speaking of grapes, many of those ancient, indigenous cultivars, bound up with deep tradition, have been dusted off, not only in a nostalgic sense, but with a precise, contemporary vision. An obligatory final note for Emilia Romagna's sweet wines, a typology the region excels at.

Agrintesa

via G. Galilei, 15
48018 Faenza [RA]
Tel. +39 0546941195
www.cantineintesa.it

CELLAR SALES
PRE-BOOKED VISITS
ANNUAL PRODUCTION 350,000 bottles
HECTARES UNDER VINE 44.00

Cantine Intesa is one of the most important cooperatives in Romagna thanks to its unique territorial roots and a modern approach grounded in quality. Their vineyards are concentrated on the hills of Faenza, which have always been well-suited to the cultivation of fine grapes (starting with Sangiovese), while the cellar is located in Modigliana. Here the best batches are vinified using modern technology with maturation and aging carried out underground in oak barrels and barriques. The Albana '19, from the Poderi delle Rose line, is at the top of its game. It's an intense wine, bright yellow in color, with broad aromas, from grape skins to honeyed hints of propolis, closing on refreshing citrus whiffs—it's a close-knit but not immobile, round and excellent drink. The Sangiovese Superiore '19 also delivers, purplish in color and aromatically flowery, it comes through fine and juicy on the palate.

Wine	Rating
○ Romagna Albana Secco Poderi delle Rose '19	▼▼ 2*
● Romagna Sangiovese Sup. '19	▼▼ 3
● Romagna Sangiovese '19	▼ 3
○ Albana di Romagna Secco Poderi delle Rose '15	▽▽ 2*
○ Romagna Albana Secco Poderi delle Rose '18	▽▽ 2*
● Romagna Sangiovese Poderi delle Rose '18	▽▽ 2*
● Romagna Sangiovese Poderi delle Rose '17	▽▽ 2*
● Romagna Sangiovese Poderi delle Rose '15	▽▽ 2*
● Romagna Sangiovese Sup. Poderi delle Rose '15	▽▽ 2*

Balìa di Zola

via Casale, 11
47015 Modigliana [FC]
Tel. +39 0546940577
www.baliadizola.com

CELLAR SALES
PRE-BOOKED VISITS
ANNUAL PRODUCTION 30,000 bottles
HECTARES UNDER VINE 5.00

Balia di Zola was founded in 1999 in Modigliana, on the hills of Faenza, one of Romagna's best territories for cultivating wine grapes. It seems, however, that Balia already existed in the 18th century as an important local agricultural producer. The vineyards share the property with olive trees, broom and woods, in an evocative and uncontaminated natural landscape. The marly-arenaceous soil, endowed with limestone, guarantees fine and ageworthy wines that are also fragrant and flavorful. Over the years they've built a solid operation, starting with the revival of old vineyards. The Sangiovese Modigliana Redinoce '17 behaves like a great wine, a contemporary classic, we could say: a brilliant ruby red, on the nose it offers up forthright aromas of berries and delicately spicy nuances. In the mouth it's austere but not at all edgy—magnificently drinkable. The Sangiovese Superiore Balitore '19 is more compact and penetrating, even if equally rich in flavor and tension. The Albana Isola '19 is worth coming back to in the future, given its extreme youth.

Wine	Rating
● Romagna Sangiovese Modigliana Redinoce Ris. '17	▼▼ 4
● Romagna Sangiovese Sup. Balitore '19	▼▼ 3
○ Romagna Albana Secco Isola '19	▼ 3
● Romagna Sangiovese Sup. Balitore '18	▽▽ 3
● Romagna Sangiovese Sup. Balitore '15	▽▽ 2*
● Romagna Sangiovese Sup. Balitore '14	▽▽ 2*
● Romagna Sangiovese Sup. Redinoce Ris. '14	▽▽ 4
● Sangiovese di Romagna Sup. Redinoce Ris. '13	▽▽ 4

Francesco Bellei & C.

FRAZ. CRISTO DI SORBARA
VIA NAZIONALE, 130/132
41030 BOMPORTO [MO]
TEL. +39 059902009
www.francescobellei.it

CELLAR SALES
PRE-BOOKED VISITS
ANNUAL PRODUCTION 40,000 bottles
HECTARES UNDER VINE 80.00
VITICULTURE METHOD Certified Organic

Theirs is a peculiar approach aimed at the production of bottle-fermented wines. Almost fifty years ago Giuseppe Bellei chose Chardonnay and Pinot Nero to make Metodo Classico sparklers in Lambrusco wine country. In the new millennium, the area's classic grapes, such as Sorbara and Pignoletto, give rise to their Metodo Ancestrale selections. The winery is now situated in the heart of Cristo di Sorbara. For some years now it's been in the hands of the Cavicchioli family, with Sandro Cavicchioli at the helm. The Blanc de Noirs '13 is a monovarietal Pinot Nero Metodo Classico that benefits from long aging on the lees, making for a creamy wine with fine bead, redolent of small red berries and mandarin. It has backbone, structure and a nice, broad finish. The Rosé '16 is linear, clear and citrusy, with aromas of tropical fruits owing to a notable quantity of Chardonnay. We particularly liked the Ancestrale '19, a classic Sorbara, fragrant and well supported by acidity.

○ Cuvée Blanc de Noirs Brut M. Cl. '13	🍷🍷 6
⊙ Cuvée Rosé Brut M. Cl. '16	🍷🍷 5
○ Cuvée Speciale Brut M. Cl. '12	🍷🍷 6
● Lambrusco Ancestrale '19	🍷🍷 3
● Cuvée Rosso Brut M. Cl. '17	🍷 4
○ Pignoletto Ancestrale '18	🍷 3
○ Brut Nature M. Cl. '15	YY 6
⊙ Brut Rosé M. Cl. '15	YY 6
● Brut Rosso M. Cl. '16	YY 4
⊙ Cuvée Brut M. Cl. Rosé '14	YY 5
● Cuvée Brut Rosso M. Cl. '14	YY 3*
○ Cuvée Speciale M. Cl. '12	YY 6
● Lambrusco di Modena Rifermentazione Ancestrale '15	YY 3*
● Modena Lambrusco Rifermentazione Ancestrale '16	YY 3*

Stefano Berti

LOC. RAVALDINO IN MONTE
VIA LA SCAGNA, 18
47121 FORLÌ
TEL. +39 0543488074
www.stefanoberti.it

CELLAR SALES
PRE-BOOKED VISITS
ANNUAL PRODUCTION 40,000 bottles
HECTARES UNDER VINE 6.00

Stefano Berti is one of the most original and charismatic figures operating in Romagna today, even if the roots of his winery date back to the early sixties. The terroir is that of Ravaldino in Monte, in Predappio, where Stefano entered the scene in the early eighties, starting a path that in recent times has started bearing the hoped-for fruits. White grapes have been gradually replaced by black grapes, foremost Sangiovese. There are also less traditional, but equally discriminating selections. The Sangiovese Calisto Riserva '16 is a dazzling wine that brings out the best of a great vintage. The grapes ferment in steel tanks, spontaneously, without added cultured yeasts. Maturation takes place in barriques for 12 months before finishing in the bottle. On the nose it's marked by complex, elegant aromas, while on the palate it's beautifully structured and dynamic, finishing long on hints of undergrowth and liquorice. The Rossetto, a Metodo Ancestrale, is also delicious.

● Romagna Sangiovese Predappio Calisto Ris. '16	🍷🍷🍷 4*
● Romagna Sangiovese Bartimeo '19	🍷🍷 2*
⊙ Rossetto Frizzante	🍷🍷 3
● Romagna Sangiovese Sup. Bartimeo '16	YYY 2*
● Sangiovese di Romagna Sup. Calisto '01	YYY 4
● Romagna Sangiovese Bartimeo '15	YY 2*
● Romagna Sangiovese Predappio Calisto Ris. '15	YY 4

Ca' di Sopra

loc. Marzeno
via Feligara, 15
48013 Brisighella [RA]
Tel. +39 3284927073
www.cadisopra.com

CELLAR SALES
PRE-BOOKED VISITS
ANNUAL PRODUCTION 30,000 bottles
HECTARES UNDER VINE 28.00
SUSTAINABLE WINERY

The Montanari family are responsible for overseeing this notable producer, founded in the late 1960s and modernized in the early years of the new millennium. The vineyards are located in the Marzeno subzone, the smallest of those designated for Romagna Sangiovese. The area is characterized by calcareous-clay soils, elevations ranging from 120-240 meters and an excellent microclimate. An approach that's attentive to nature and minimally-invasive winemaking give rise to an artisanal style that's tasty and perfect with a meal. The excellent Superiore Crepe '19 is a monovarietal Sangiovese that ferments and macerates in steel tanks before maturing in concrete (with a small amount ending up in barriques). A close-woven, flavorful wine, it exhibits nice breadth and tannic maturity, with aromas that call up plums and black cherries, and spicy notes as well. The Sangiovese Marzeno Riserva '17 also delivers. It's more summery in its fruity texture and nicely structured on the palate.

● Romagna Sangiovese Marzeno Cadisopra Ris. '17	🍷🍷 4
● Romagna Sangiovese Sup. Crepe '19	🍷🍷 2*
● Remel '17	🍷 3
● Romagna Sangiovese Marzeno Cadisopra '18	🍷 3
○ Uait '19	🍷 2
○ Romagna Albana Secco Sandrona '18	🍷🍷 3*
○ Romagna Albana Secco Sandrona '17	🍷🍷 3
● Romagna Sangiovese Marzeno '15	🍷🍷 3
● Romagna Sangiovese Marzeno Cà del Rosso '15	🍷🍷 3
● Romagna Sangiovese Sup. Crepe '18	🍷🍷 2*
● Romagna Sangiovese Sup. Crepe '17	🍷🍷 2*
● Romagna Sangiovese Sup. Crepe '15	🍷🍷 2*

Calonga

loc. Castiglione
via Castel Leone, 8
47121 Forlì
Tel. +39 0543753044
www.calonga.it

CELLAR SALES
PRE-BOOKED VISITS
ANNUAL PRODUCTION 30,000 bottles
HECTARES UNDER VINE 8.00

Founded by Maurizio Baravelli in the late 1970s, Calonga is still a family business today, as the founder has since been joined by his sons Lorenzo, Matteo and Francesco. It's located in Castiglione, on the foothills of Forlì and Faenza, where the soils are characterized by the area's characteristic 'molasse' sands. Their vineyards are in line with tradition, with grapes such as Sangiovese, Albana and Pagadebit making up the lion's share. Their work in the fields respects nature while in the cellar they've adopted a balanced approach aimed at highlighting the territory's attributes in a contemporary way. Il Bruno, a new project, calls for Sangiovese to be vinified and matured without the use of oak. In fact, the first release (with the 2018 vintage) is a fragrant red, very elegant and delicate, both aromatically and in the mouth—floral nuances dominate, with a bewitching touch of rose, but tension and acidity are also guaranteed. Truly delicious. We also appreciated the penetrating Pagadebit '19.

● Romagna Sangiovese Sup. Il Bruno '18	🍷🍷 2*
○ Romagna Pagadebit '19	🍷🍷 2*
● Romagna Sangiovese Sup. Michelangiolo Ris. '16	🍷 5
● Ordelaffo '15	🍷🍷 2*
● Ordelaffo '14	🍷🍷 2*
● Romagna Sangiovese Sup. Leggiolo '16	🍷🍷 3
● Romagna Sangiovese Sup. Leggiolo '15	🍷🍷 3
● Romagna Sangiovese Sup. Michelangiolo Ris. '13	🍷🍷 5
● Romagna Sangiovese Sup. Michelangiolo Ris. '12	🍷🍷 4

Tenute Campana

via XXII Aprile 2
41011 Campogalliano [MO]
Tel. +39 059526712
www.tenutecampana.it

CELLAR SALES
PRE-BOOKED VISITS
ANNUAL PRODUCTION 25,000 bottles
HECTARES UNDER VINE 28.00

The farm has been in the hands of the family since the early 1800s, when these alluvial lands, often flooded by the Secchia river, were only cultivated in part with vines, as corn, wheat, sugar beets, pears and cattle breeding were also common. In the 1970s it was Lauro Campana's turn, and she still oversees the property together with her sons Sergio and Mattia. 22 of the estate's 180 hectares are vineyards, all managed in collaboration with the University of Padua. Tenori's wines put in an excellent performance during our tastings. The Sorbara is fragrant, characterized by citrus fruits and raspberries. In the mouth it comes through with sapidity and substance, balance and integrity on a lean, very fragrant palate. The Pignoletto, which pours a vibrant yellow color, proves dense and well developed, redolent of peach, apricot and pineapple. The fresh and compact Lambrusco di Modena is marked by blueberry sensations.

- ● Lambrusco di Modena Dei Tenori — 🍷🍷 2*
- ● Lambrusco di Sorbara Dei Tenori — 🍷🍷 2*
- ○ Pignoletto Dei Tenori — 🍷🍷 2*

Cantina della Volta

via per Modena, 82
41030 Bomporto [MO]
Tel. +39 0597473312
www.cantinadellavolta.com

CELLAR SALES
PRE-BOOKED VISITS
ANNUAL PRODUCTION 130,000 bottles
HECTARES UNDER VINE 16.00

In 2010 Christian Bellei, the descendant of a family that's been producing and marketing Lambrusco di Sorbara for exactly one hundred years, decided to found this winery with the support of some friends. Drawing on the experience gained working in the famous family business, naturally, his primary goal was to produce Metodo Classico Lambrusco, and it can be said that his mission was accomplished, given the quality of a selection that has continued to rise over the years. This year they submitted a lovely selection. We start with the Sorbara Rosé Metodo Classico '15, a sapid, well-structured, pulpy wine with strong personality. Long and elegant, it takes home Tre Bicchieri. The Dosaggio Zero Mattaglio, Chardonnay and 10% Pinot Nero, features hints of bread crust and dried herbs, while the palate exhibits vigor and creaminess. The Prima Volta '16 is an undosed rosé, 100% Sorbara: a very pale color, it's elegant, playing on the finesse of its aromas and bead. The full Il Mattaglio Brut is also marked by creamy bubbles.

- ⊙ Lambrusco di Sorbara Brut Rosé M. Cl. '15 — 🍷🍷🍷 5
- ○ Il Mattaglio Brut M. Cl. — 🍷🍷 5
- ○ Il Mattaglio Dosaggio Zero M. Cl. — 🍷🍷 5
- ⊙ La Prima Volta Dosaggio Zero Rosé M. Cl. '16 — 🍷🍷 5
- ● Lambrusco di Sorbara Rimosso '19 — 🍷 3
- ⊙ Lambrusco di Modena Brut Rosé M. Cl. '13 — 🍷🍷🍷 5
- ⊙ Lambrusco di Modena Brut Rosé M. Cl. '12 — 🍷🍷🍷 5
- ● Lambrusco di Sorbara Rimosso '13 — 🍷🍷🍷 3*
- ● Lambrusco di Sorbara Rimosso '12 — 🍷🍷🍷 3*
- ⊙ La Prima Volta Brut Rosé M. Cl. '15 — 🍷🍷 5
- ⊙ Lambrusco di Sorbara Brut Rosé M. Cl. '14 — 🍷🍷 5

Cantina di Santa Croce

FRAZ. SANTA CROCE
S.DA ST.LE 468 DI CORREGGIO, 35
41012 CARPI [MO]
TEL. +39 059664007
www.cantinasantacroce.it

CELLAR SALES
PRE-BOOKED VISITS
ACCOMMODATION
ANNUAL PRODUCTION 400,000 bottles
HECTARES UNDER VINE 600.00

This cooperative producer's history dates back to the early 20th century, 1907 to be precise. At present it has about 250 members who cultivate mainly Lambrusco Salamino in its native territory. Though we shouldn't forget the other varieties, foremost Sorbara. The terrain, mostly clayey, makes for a Salamino of vigorous rusticity. Winemaker Maurizio Boni knows the characteristics of the grape well, and interprets it in various ways, including a sparkling version. Obviously Salamino di Santa Croce is their cornerstone, starting with a very pleasant and fragrant Spumante Rosé 100 Vendemmie (10% Sorbara) that's nicely supported by acidity. The Secco (here 100% Salamino) has a nice nose of black berries accompanied by a spicy hint—it's lovely in the mouth. The pulpy Vigne Vecchie features blueberry sensations.

⊙ 100 Vendemmie Brut Rosé '19	🍷🍷 2*
● Lambrusco Salamino di Santa Croce Secco '19	🍷🍷 2*
● Lambrusco di Sorbara '19	🍷 2
● Lambrusco Salamino di Santa Croce V. V. '19	🍷 2
○ Pignoletto Brut 100 Vendemmie '19	🍷 2
● Il Castello Lambrusco Secco '16	🍷🍷 1*
● Il Castello Lambrusco Semisecco '17	🍷🍷 1*
● Il Castello Rosso Lambrusco '17	🍷🍷 1*
● Lambrusco di Sorbara '17	🍷🍷 1*
● Lambrusco Salamino di Santa Croce Secco '16	🍷🍷 1*
● Lambrusco Salamino di Santa Croce Secco Tradizione '17	🍷🍷 1*
● Lambrusco Salamino di Santa Croce Secco Tradizione '16	🍷🍷 1*

Cantina di Carpi e Sorbara

VIA CAVATA
41012 CARPI [MO]
TEL. +39 059 643071
www.cantinadicarpiesorbara.it

CELLAR SALES
ANNUAL PRODUCTION 3,200,000 bottles
HECTARES UNDER VINE 2300.00

In 2012, the two historic wineries Cantine di Carpi (founded in 1903) and Sorbara (founded in 1923) decided to merge, creating an organization that now avails itself of 1,200 members and six facilities for winemaking, bottling and storage. Lambrusco di Sorbara takes center stage, but there's plenty more. The area's best known wines are explored in numerous versions, including sparklers, with absolutely convincing results. There's also a wine dedicated to lawyer Gino Friedmann, a key figure for Modena's co-ops. The Sorbara Gino Friedmann (re-fermented in the bottle) is a Metodo Ancestrale marked by intriguing hints of red berries and citrus fruits, from grapefruit to lime; in the mouth it's well supported by acidity, showing nice body and character. The same, but re-fermented in autoclaves, is also lively and spirited, while the other Sorbara Terre della Verdeta plays more on fruity pulp. Once again the Terre dei Pio proves to be a structured Salamino, redolent of blackberry and blueberry, with a classic almond finish.

● Lambrusco di Sorbara Omaggio a Gino Friedmann Rifermentazione Naturale in Bottiglia '19	🍷🍷 3*
● Lambrusco di Sorbara 923 Terre della Verdeta '19	🍷🍷 2*
● Lambrusco di Sorbara Omaggio a Gino Friedmann '19	🍷🍷 2*
● Lambrusco Salamino di Santa Croce 903 Terre dei Pio '19	🍷🍷 2*
● Lambrusco Mantovano 946 Corte del Poggio '19	🍷 2
● Lambrusco Salamino di Santa Croce Dedicato ad Alfredo Molinari '19	🍷 2
● Lambrusco di Sorbara Secco Omaggio a Gino Friedmann '16	🍷🍷🍷 3*
● Lambrusco di Sorbara Secco Omaggio a Gino Friedmann FB '14	🍷🍷🍷 3*

Cavicchioli

via Canaletto, 52
41030 San Prospero [MO]
Tel. +39 059812412
www.cavicchioli.it

CELLAR SALES
PRE-BOOKED VISITS
ANNUAL PRODUCTION 7,424,000 bottles
HECTARES UNDER VINE 90.00

In San Prospero, on April 6, 1928, Umberto Cavicchioli founded what was destined to become one of the most important wineries in the world of Lambrusco. Since 2011 the producer has been part of the giant Gruppo Italiano Vini, but management remains in the hands of the family, represented by Umberto's grandsons, Sandro and Claudio. Many wines are offered, as is to be expected from a producer who puts out ten million bottles a year. Sorbara, in its various versions (including Metodo Classico), always stands out during tastings. Vigna del Cristo always emerges from its territory of choice as a clear, elegant, varietal, fruity and floral Sorbara, balanced and rich. We also appreciated the Millenovecentoventotto, a fruitier, more intense, full-bodied Sorabara with a clear, long finish. The Tre Medaglie moves on a different track, with citrus notes emerging, though precision and a focused clarity are still hallmarks. A very fleshy Grasparossa Col Sassoso also stands out in a range of high quality.

Wine	Rating
● Lambrusco di Sorbara V. del Cristo '19	🍷🍷🍷 2*
● Lambrusco di Sorbara Millenovecentoventotto	🍷🍷 2
● Lambrusco di Sorbara Tre Medaglie	🍷🍷 2
⊙ Lambrusco di Sorbara Brut Rosé del Cristo M. Cl. '16	🍷🍷 4
● Lambrusco Grasparossa di Castelvetro Col Sassoso '19	🍷🍷 2*
● Fieronero Lambrusco Frizzante	🍷 2
● Lambrusco di Modena Millenovecentoventotto	🍷 2
● Lambrusco Grasparossa di Castelvetro Millenovecentoventotto	🍷 2
● Robanera Abboccato	🍷 2
● Lambrusco di Sorbara V. del Cristo '18	🍷🍷🍷 3*
● Lambrusco di Sorbara V. del Cristo '17	🍷🍷🍷 3*
● Lambrusco di Sorbara V. del Cristo '16	🍷🍷🍷 2*

Caviro

via Convertite, 12
48018 Faenza [RA]
Tel. +39 0546629111
www.caviro.it

CELLAR SALES
ANNUAL PRODUCTION 25,000,000 bottles
HECTARES UNDER VINE 31.00

Caviro's production figures already say a lot about its business structure. It's the largest winery in Italy. In fact, its size puts this wine giant into context: a union of about thirty cooperatives and more than 12 thousand winemakers, distributed throughout different regions of the peninsula. Many lines and brands are proposed, including the famous Tavernello, perhaps the most famous Italian wine known to the general public. However, there's no lack of more specialized selections, which center on the vineyards of Romagna. This year we tasted a series of wines from their "Vigneti Romio" project, which is carried out by some of Romagna's most experienced growers cultivating Caviro's best vineyards. Among these was the Sangiovese Superiore Riserva '19, a modern wine characterized by foregrounded notes of coffee, and a vigorous, fruity component. The Trebbiano '19 features vibrant aromas and a complete palate. The Famoso '19 is a step below, but proves supple on the palate.

Wine	Rating
● Romagna Sangiovese Sup. Ris. Vigneti Romio '19	🍷🍷 3
○ Trebbiano Vigneti Romio '19	🍷🍷 2*
○ Famoso Vigneti Romio '19	🍷 2
○ Romagna Albana Secco Romio '17	🍷🍷 2*
○ Romagna Albana Secco Romio '16	🍷🍷 2*
○ Romagna Albana Secco Romio '15	🍷🍷 2*
⊙ Romagna Sangiovese Rosato Portocanale di Cesenatico '18	🍷🍷 2*
● Romagna Sangiovese Sup. Rocca di Cesena Ris. '16	🍷🍷 4
○ Romagna Trebbiano Terre Forti '15	🍷🍷 1*
○ Sono Famoso '17	🍷🍷 2*

Celli

v.le Carducci, 5
47032 Bertinoro [FC]
Tel. +39 0543445183
www.celli-vini.com

CELLAR SALES
PRE-BOOKED VISITS
ANNUAL PRODUCTION 300,000 bottles
HECTARES UNDER VINE 35.00
SUSTAINABLE WINERY

The Sirri and Casadei families designed and planted their estate in the territory of Bertinoro in 1963 and have, since 1985, substantially renovated it. The vineyards grow in calcareous soils characterized by the classic 'spungone' (seabed tufa) and unfold across various plots: Tenuta Maestrina, Tenuta La Massa and Campi di Bracciano. Obviously, the grapes cultivated vary, with both native and international varieties represented, while particular attention has been paid in recent years to Albana. The 2019 version of their Albana Secco I Croppi once again proves stylistically coherent, putting in an excellent performance: redolent of grape skin and ripe citrus fruits, it comes through fleshy and highly flavorful on the palate. The Albana Passito Solara '17 also delivered. Obviously it's softer and more vibrant in its aromas of jam, dried fruit and spices. The Pagadebit Campi di Fratta '19, for lovers of extremely dry whites, is delicious. The Sangiovese Bertinoro Bron & Rusèval Riserva '17 isn't too shabby either.

Wine	Rating
○ Romagna Albana Passito Solara '17	🍷🍷 4
○ Romagna Albana Secco I Croppi '19	🍷🍷 2*
○ Romagna Pagadebit Campi di Fratta '19	🍷🍷 2*
● Romagna Sangiovese Bertinoro Bron & Ruseval Ris '17	🍷🍷 3
○ Romagna Albana Secco I Croppi '17	🍷🍷🍷 2*
○ Romagna Albana Secco I Croppi '16	🍷🍷🍷 2*
○ Romagna Albana Secco I Croppi '15	🍷🍷🍷 2*
○ Romagna Albana Secco I Croppi '18	🍷🍷 2*
● Romagna Sangiovese Sup. Le Grillaie Ris. '16	🍷🍷 2*

Umberto Cesari

via Stanzano, 2160
40024 Castel San Pietro Terme [BO]
Tel. +39 0516947811
www.umbertocesari.it

CELLAR SALES
PRE-BOOKED VISITS
ANNUAL PRODUCTION 3,500,000 bottles
HECTARES UNDER VINE 355.00
SUSTAINABLE WINERY

Umberto Cesari is the name of a great entrepreneur and, consequently, of a great Romagna wine company. The first bottles were produced in 1965 and since then wine production and sales have continued in Italy, but above all abroad. Gradually various goals have been achieved, and Umberto's dream and vision have seen to it that his wines are sold in many parts of the world. The range can't help but reflect the market. Modern and technically impeccable wines are the result of notable extraction and long aging in wood barrels. The Tauleto '14, a monovarietal Sangiovese, is close-knit, full-bodied and austere. The nose offers up hints of tanned leather, resins and black fruit, while the palate proves dense, though slightly restrained by tannins. We appreciated the Colle del Re, an Albana di Romagna passito with vibrant notes of citron and candied fruit. The Liano Bianco '18 (Chardonnay and Sauvignon) and Liano '17 (Sangiovese and Cabernet Sauvignon) are simple but pleasant.

Wine	Rating
○ Romagna Albana Passito Colle del Re '12	🍷🍷 4
● Tauleto '14	🍷🍷 7
● Liano '17	🍷 5
○ Liano Bianco '18	🍷 4
● Resultum '13	🍷 8
● Romagna Sangiovese Sup. Ris. '13	🍷🍷 3
● Romagna Sangiovese Sup. Ris. '12	🍷🍷 3
● Sangiovese di Romagna Laurento Ris. '10	🍷🍷 3

Floriano Cinti

fraz. San Lorenzo
via Gamberi, 48
40037 Sasso Marconi [BO]
Tel. +39 0516751646
www.collibolognesi.com

CELLAR SALES
PRE-BOOKED VISITS
ANNUAL PRODUCTION 95,000 bottles
HECTARES UNDER VINE 24.00

Floriano Cinti is a good winemaker, carrying on with dedication the fine work of bringing out the best of the territory of Bologna. It's a task he's been doing since the early 1990s, with great humility and passion. The wines produced are a mirror of the vineyards from which they come— there's no lack of character, cleanness or pleasantness. Over the years the producer has expanded both in terms of hectares under vine and technology used in the cellar. Inside there are also guest rooms and a restaurant. This year the Pignoletto Frizzante '19 truly surprised. The Colli Bolognesi gave rise to a wine redolent of citrus and tropical fruits, pulpy, fresh, fragrant; on the palate it's very pleasant with a deep, clean finish. Tre Bicchieri. We also appreciated the Bologna Rosso '16, made with Cabernet Sauvignon, Merlot and Barbera: it features notes of jam and nice fruity pulp; the palate's tight but very tasty. The Barbera '18 is pleasant, though simple.

○ C. B. Pignoletto Frizzante '19	3 glasses 2*
● C.B. Bologna Rosso '16	2 glasses 3
● C. B. Barbera '18	1 glass 2
● C.B. Cabernet Sauvignon '15	2 glasses 2*

★Cleto Chiarli Tenute Agricole

via Belvedere, 8
41014 Castelvetro di Modena [MO]
Tel. +39 0593163311
www.chiarli.it

CELLAR SALES
PRE-BOOKED VISITS
ANNUAL PRODUCTION 900,000 bottles
HECTARES UNDER VINE 100.00

If you want to tell the story of Lambrusco Modenese, you can't ignore Cleto Chiarli, a winery whose roots go back to 1860, when the founder decided to produce and bottle wine instead of serving it unbottled to patrons of his Osteria dell'Artigliere. That wine underwent second fermentation in the bottle, which was usual before the advent of technology in the cellar and, specifically, autoclaves. Today production has evolved with the identification of cru for cultivating the best grapes, Sorbara and Grasparossa foremost, and rediscovery of the Metodo Ancestrale. The Lambrusco del Fondatore '19 is a fruit-forward Sorbara whose color is richer than usual, but always a top-notch wine. Two Grasparossas were just as good: the Vigneto Cialdini is linear, balanced, scented with cherry, strawberry and raspberry; the Nivola is more rustic, fruity and fleshy in its shades of small, black berry fruits. The Vecchia Modena Premium, a supple Sorbara with good backbone, is always a sure bet.

● Lambrusco di Sorbara del Fondatore '19	3 glasses 3*
● Lambrusco Grasparossa di Castelvetro Vign. Cialdini '19	2 glasses 3*
● Lambrusco di Sorbara Vecchia Modena Premium '19	2 glasses 3
● Lambrusco Grasparossa di Castelvetro Nivola '19	2 glasses 2*
● Lambrusco Grasparossa di Castelvetro Villa Cialdini '19	2 glasses 2*
○ Pignoletto Modena Brut Modén Blanc '19	1 glass 3
● Pruno Nero Dry	1 glass 3
⊙ Rosé de Noir Brut '19	1 glass 3
● Lambrusco di Sorbara del Fondatore '18	3 glasses 3*
● Lambrusco di Sorbara del Fondatore '17	3 glasses 3*
● Lambrusco di Sorbara del Fondatore '16	3 glasses 3*

Condé

loc. Fiumana di Predappio
via Lucchina, 27
47016 Predappio [FC]
Tel. +39 0543940860
www.conde.it

CELLAR SALES
PRE-BOOKED VISITS
ACCOMMODATION AND RESTAURANT SERVICE
ANNUAL PRODUCTION 150,000 bottles
HECTARES UNDER VINE 77.00
SUSTAINABLE WINERY

In the early 2000s Francesco Condello founded this winery in the subzone of Predappio, certainly one of Romagna's best areas for cultivating wine grapes. The well-manicured vineyards are distributed at elevations spanning 150-350 meters above sea level. Sangiovese plays a central role, obviously, though there are also forays with other varieties. In recent years, agriculture has become increasingly sustainable and the style of their wines has grown in all respects. A super Sangiovese Riserva, the Predappio Raggio Brusa '17, proved just this. Made from a selection of the best grapes grown in the vineyard of the same name, it offers up elegant aromas of fresh flowers, small red and black berries and undergrowth. A slight toasty hint, present but not intrusive, underpins its aromas and accompanies the palate, which is magnificent for texture and tannic cleanness. The Sangiovese Superiore '17 is more immediately expressive but by no means trivial. The Sangiovese Superiore Al Caleri '18 is just a step below.

- ● Romagna Sangiovese Predappio Raggio Brusa Ris. '17 — 🍷🍷 8
- ● Romagna Sangiovese Sup. '17 — 🍷🍷 3
- ● Romagna Sangiovese Sup. Al Caleri '18 — 🍷 2
- ● Romagna Sangiovese Predappio Raggio Brusa Ris. '16 — 🍷🍷 8
- ● Romagna Sangiovese Predappio Ris. '13 — 🍷🍷 6
- ● Romagna Sangiovese Predappio Ris. '12 — 🍷🍷 6
- ● Romagna Sangiovese Predappio Ris. '11 — 🍷🍷 2*
- ● Romagna Sangiovese Sup. '12 — 🍷🍷 3
- ● Sangiovese di Romagna Sup. Ris. '10 — 🍷🍷 2*

Chiara Condello

loc. Fiumana di Predappio
via Lucchina, 27
47016 Predappio [FC]
Tel. +39 0543940860
www.chiaracondello.com

CELLAR SALES
PRE-BOOKED VISITS
ANNUAL PRODUCTION 17,000 bottles
HECTARES UNDER VINE 4.80
SUSTAINABLE WINERY

Chiara Condello is a spin off of Condé, the family estate of the young winemaker after which the former was named. A revelation from last year's edition, their wines represent one of the region's great new developments in terms of identity, style and a contemporary approach. After all, the terroir is highly worthy, and given the producer's sensitivity, it could only be further exalted. Here in Predappio the vineyards by the forest grow at elevations ranging from 150 to 300 meters above sea level on rather lean, calcareous-clayey soils rich in the classic 'spungone' (seabed tufa). In many ways the winery did an impressive job approaching the 2017 harvest, churning out two Sangiovese that dazzle for their purity, style and expressiveness. Le Lucciole Riserva has a graceful texture and flowery aromatic bouquet, with delicious red berries serving as a background. A waltz of raspberries, currants and cherries dance across the palate, making for a wine that's as supple as it is close-woven and deep. The Sangiovese Predappio '17 is similar, though lighter.

- ● Romagna Sangiovese Predappio Le Lucciole Ris. '17 — 🍷🍷🍷 7
- ● Romagna Sangiovese Predappio Chiara Condello '17 — 🍷🍷 4
- ● Romagna Sangiovese Predappio Le Lucciole Ris. '16 — 🍷🍷🍷 7
- ● Romagna Sangiovese Predappio Chiara Condello '16 — 🍷🍷 4

Costa Archi

loc. Serra
via Rinfosco, 1690
48014 Castel Bolognese [RA]
Tel. +39 3384818346
costaarchi.wordpress.com

CELLAR SALES
PRE-BOOKED VISITS
ANNUAL PRODUCTION 16,000 bottles
HECTARES UNDER VINE 11.00

Costa Archi's vineyards and cellar are situated in Castel Bolognese, therefore in the geographic mention of Serra. The small and beautiful estate is overseen by Gabriele Succi, a winemaker of note in Romagna. The vineyards grow in two plots on clayey soil, rich in limestone, at about 150 meters above sea level. The wines continue to exhibit increased stylistic awareness, expressing territorial flavor and moods through careful cultivation practices and an approach to maturation that respects the qualities of the grapes. The GS '15 is a Sangiovese of great character and complexity. It ferments in 7500-liter vats and matures in mid-sized casks for at least a year before moving to concrete. We appreciated its fine fruitiness, with evident spicy hints and echoes of oak anticipating a complex palate—excellent structure and a penetrating, tannic finish. The Monte Brullo Riserva '16 also delivered. We also appreciated the tasty, mineral-rich white Le Barrosche '19.

● GS Sangiovese '15	🍷🍷	5
○ Le Barrosche '19	🍷🍷	3
● Romagna Sangiovese Serra Monte Brullo Ris. '16	🍷🍷	2*
● Romagna Sangiovese Sup. Assiolo '13	🍷🍷🍷	4*
● GS Sangiovese '14	🍷🍷	5
● Romagna Sangiovese Serra Assiolo '17	🍷🍷	3
● Romagna Sangiovese Serra Assiolo '16	🍷🍷	3*
● Romagna Sangiovese Serra Assiolo '15	🍷🍷	2*
● Romagna Sangiovese Serra Monte Brullo Ris. '15	🍷🍷	2*

Cantina Divinja

fraz. Sorbara
via Verdeta 1
41030 Modena
Tel. +39 3391801199
www.cantinadivinja.com

CELLAR SALES
PRE-BOOKED VISITS
ANNUAL PRODUCTION 75,000 bottles
HECTARES UNDER VINE 9.00

The Barbanti family farm, active since the early 20th century, was founded—like many at the time—for the cultivation of fruit, vegetables and arable crops. Over the years the first vineyards of Lambrusco di Sorbara were planted, giving rise to wine, sold mainly in bulk. The popularity of their products and market demand meant that the vineyards were expanded until the complete conversion of the business in 2008, with the construction of the new cellar. The damage caused by the earthquake in 2012 didn't discourage the Barbanti, who saw it as an opportunity to expand and modernize. The Morro is exemplary of Salamino. On the nose it's fruity, redolent of morello cherries and mandarin; in the mouth it's rich and full-flavoured, with a fleshy, pulpy palate that's capable of delivering authentic pleasure. The Sigillo '15 is a well-crafted Metodo Classico made with Sorbara. A brilliant ruby color heralds aromas of berries and medicinal herbs—on the palate it comes through long and fresh. The Unico, a monovarietal Sorbara, is elegant and citrusy.

● Lambrusco di Modena Il Morro	🍷🍷	2*
● Lambrusco di Sorbara Brut Unico	🍷🍷	2*
● Sigillo Brut M. Cl. '15	🍷🍷	4
⊙ Lambrusco di Sorbara Rosé Rosae	🍷	2
● Lambrusco di Sorbara Semisecco Primi Profumi	🍷	2
○ Modena Pignoletto Brut S. Amalia	🍷	2

Drei Donà Tenuta La Palazza

LOC. MASSA DI VECCHIAZZANO
VIA DEL TESORO, 23
47121 FORLÌ
TEL. +39 0543769371
www.dreidona.it

CELLAR SALES
PRE-BOOKED VISITS
ANNUAL PRODUCTION 130,000 bottles
HECTARES UNDER VINE 27.00
SUSTAINABLE WINERY

A historic Romagna producer, Drei Donà owns plots of land on some of the region's most interesting hillsides: Forlì, Castrocaro and Predappio, at the mouth of the valleys of the rivers Rabbi and Montone. Today it's managed by Claudio Drei Donà and his son Enrico, who's eager to usher it into a modern phase, while still aware of the past and what it represents. Great attention is paid to environmental sustainability. The wines themselves are modern but also exhibit character, constancy and great reliability. The Sangiovese Predappio Notturno '18 performed extremely well. Its toastiness is undoubtedly more convincing than in the previous version, as is its sensations of ripe fruit, which span blueberries, blackberries and raspberries. In the mouth intensity and flavor merge in a clear, focused finish. The Sangiovese Superiore Pruno Riserva '16 is also in good form, even if at this stage oak is more present: it's probably worth coming back to later.

- ● Romagna Sangiovese Predappio Notturno '18 — ▼▼ 3*
- ● Romagna Sangiovese Sup. Pruno Ris. '16 — ▼▼ 7
- ● Magnificat '16 — ▼ 5
- ○ Il Tornese '18 — ▽▽ 3
- ● Magnificat '13 — ▽▽ 5
- ● Notturno Sangiovese '14 — ▽▽ 3
- ● Romagna Sangiovese Predappio Notturno '17 — ▽▽ 3*
- ● Romagna Sangiovese Sup. Palazza Ris. '13 — ▽▽ 5
- ● Romagna Sangiovese Sup. Pruno Ris. '15 — ▽▽ 7
- ● Romagna Sangiovese Sup. Pruno Ris. '13 — ▽▽ 5

Emilia Wine

VIA 11 SETTEMBRE 2001, 3
42019 SCANDIANO [RE]
TEL. +39 0522989107
www.emiliawine.eu

ANNUAL PRODUCTION 300,000 bottles
HECTARES UNDER VINE 1900.00

Cooperatives have always represented a strong point for Emilia's economy, especially the agri-food sector. The drive for aggregation continues to this day, as demonstrated by the birth, in 2014, of Emilia Wine, a producer that only strengthens the role of cooperative wineries. The result of the merger of three cooperatives (Arceto, Correggio and Prato di Correggio), it brings together over 700 members with land both in the plains, where Lambrusco is cultivated, and in the foothills of Reggio Emilia, between the rivers Enza and Secchia. Here the grapes for their sparkling wines are grown, along with others. The Perdono '19 is a Salamino-based Lambrusco with a 40% share of Maestri and Malbo Gentile. It has a nice, fragrant nose of blueberry and currant, and an invigorating, fresh palate. The Cardinal Pighin is a robust Grasparossa redolent of berries and undergrowth—tannins are discernible but not intrusive. The Migliolungo, made with Reggio Emilia's classic varieties, sees faint, overripe notes.

- ● Reggiano Lambrusco Il Perdono Cantina di Arceto '19 — ▼▼ 2*
- ● Colli di Scandiano e Canossa Lambrusco Grasparossa Cardinale Pighini Cantina di Arceto '19 — ▼▼ 1*
- ⊙ 1077 Lambrusco Rosato Brut '19 — ▼ 2
- ● Migliolungo Lambrusco Cantina di Arceto '19 — ▼ 2
- ⊙ Colli di Scandiano e di Canossa Lambrusco Rosaspino Cantina di Arceto '17 — ▽▽ 2*
- ● Colli di Scandiano e di Canossa Lambrusco Rossospino Cantina di Arceto '16 — ▽▽ 2*
- ● Reggiano Lambrusco Il Correggio '17 — ▽▽ 2*

Gallegati

VIA LUGO, 182
48018 FAENZA [RA]
TEL. +39 0546621149
www.aziendaagricolagallegati.it

CELLAR SALES
PRE-BOOKED VISITS
ACCOMMODATION
ANNUAL PRODUCTION 15,000 bottles
HECTARES UNDER VINE 6.00

Brothers Antonio and Cesare Gallegati have always had a great passion for wine. After graduating in agriculture, the two decided to launch this beautiful Faenza winery, shaping it according to their ideas with infectious energy. The vineyards grow in clayey-lime soils with a good presence of limestone. In the cellar, their work aims to preserve the integrity of the fruit and overall balance without intervening unnecessarily in the natural process of winemaking, all in pursuit of finesse and drinkability. And their objectives are almost always achieved, while also respecting the vintages. The Corallo Rosso is a delicious Sangiovese, finely adorned with fruity and floral notes, without frills or excess. Above all, it gratifies by virtue of its tapered, dynamic palate, which isn't without a certain complexity. Expert skill when it comes to their whites as well, as demonstrated by the splendid versions of Albana and Trebbiano. The Corallo Giallo '19 features the variety's opulent aromas on a slender and long silhouette. The Corallo Argento '19 is no less good.

Wine	Rating
● Romagna Sangiovese Brisighella Corallo Rosso '18	🍷🍷 2*
○ Romagna Albana Secco Corallo Giallo '19	🍷🍷 3
○ Romagna Trebbiano Corallo Argento '19	🍷🍷 3
○ Colli di Faenza Corallo Bianco '19	🍷 3
○ Albana di Romagna Passito Regina di Cuori Ris. '10	🍷🍷🍷 4*
○ Albana di Romagna Passito Regina di Cuori Ris. '09	🍷🍷🍷 4*
○ Romagna Albana Passito Regina di Cuori Ris. '12	🍷🍷🍷 4*
● Romagna Sangiovese Brisighella Corallo Rosso '17	🍷🍷 2*

Giovannini

VIA PUNTA, 82
40026 IMOLA [BO]
TEL. +39 3389763854
www.vinigiovannini.it

CELLAR SALES
PRE-BOOKED VISITS
ANNUAL PRODUCTION 75,000 bottles
HECTARES UNDER VINE 15.00
VITICULTURE METHOD Certified Organic

Vine growers for three generations, the Giovannini family oversee their property in Imola, an area that's certainly original in the context of the region's agriculture. Over time, founder Garibaldo ceded command to his son Giorgio and then to grandson Jacopo: the entire production and commercial chain is managed directly by the family. Sustainable cultivation guarantees perfect grapes whose qualities are brought out in the cellar by a balanced approach to vinification and maturation; bottle aging takes place in a tunnel dug into the hillside. The Albana Gioja '19 is delicious: despite a hint of sweetness and a certain pronounced alcohol, it maintains a surprising balance and a pleasant citrusy trait that makes sure it will never wear you out. Sensations of fruit peel feature in the vibrant G.G.G. '18, another Albana made with 5-day maceration on the skins and 15 months of maturation in concrete barrels. We also appreciated the nicely complex Cabernet Sauvignon Giocondo '19.

Wine	Rating
○ Romagna Albana Gioja '19	🍷🍷 3*
○ G.G.G. '18	🍷🍷 4
● Giocondo '19	🍷🍷 3
● Giogiò '19	🍷 3
○ Oppalà	🍷 3

Isola

FRAZ. MONGIORGIO
VIA G. BERNARDI, 3
40050 MONTE SAN PIETRO [BO]
TEL. +39 0516768428
info@aziendaagricolaisola.it

CELLAR SALES
PRE-BOOKED VISITS
ANNUAL PRODUCTION 60,000 bottles
HECTARES UNDER VINE 12.50

The Franceschini family have been working their land in Monte San Pietro since 1898, when the cultivation of wine grapes was flanked by other crops, as well as livestock farming, as was normal at the time. In 1957 Giovanni Franceschini founded the winery we know today, dedicating himself to the area's traditional grapes, starting with Grechetto Gentile, used to make Pignoletto Docg in every possible way. Now the producer is run by Marco Franceschini with his wife, Paola, together with their children Gian Luca and Claudia. The Pignoletto Frizzante '19 is one of the best of the appellation. Notes of white fruit and wild flowers form part of its notable fragrance, while the palate comes through supple, flowing and quite broad. The Picrì '19 is the sparkling version, with small quantities of Chardonnay fermented in barriques and Riesling lending complexity. Among their many Pignolettos, we also appreciated a nice Cabernet, the Monte Gorgii '17, a varietal wine characterized by nice substance.

Wine	Rating
○ C. B. Pignoletto Frizzante '19	🍷🍷 2*
● C. B. Cabernet Sauvignon Monte Gorgii '17	🍷🍷 3
○ C. B. Pignoletto Picrì Brut '19	🍷🍷 2*
○ C. B. Pignoletto Sup. '19	🍷 2
○ C. B. Pignoletto Sup. Cl. V. V. '18	🍷 3
○ C. B. Pignoletto Cl. V. V. '13	🍷🍷 3
○ C. B. Pignoletto Picrì Brut '15	🍷🍷 2*

Tenuta La Viola

VIA COLOMBARONE, 888
47032 BERTINORO [FC]
TEL. +39 0543445496
www.tenutalaviola.it

CELLAR SALES
PRE-BOOKED VISITS
ANNUAL PRODUCTION 44,000 bottles
HECTARES UNDER VINE 11.00
VITICULTURE METHOD Certified Organic
SUSTAINABLE WINERY

Tenuta La Viola took its first steps in the early 1960s, when the Gabellini family moved to Bertinoro and bought the first vineyards. It was a very lucky and favorable start, since the vineyards were planted with Sangiovese and Albana, cornerstones among the area's classic varieties today, and bush-trained to boot. Ahead of their time, the family opted for organic farming before it was commonplace, while in 2018 they began experimenting with biodynamic agriculture. Their wines exhibit great personality, though without ever losing sight of balance and cleanness. In this round we were particularly impressed by the Sangiovese Superiore P. Honorii '16, a wine that celebrates Bertinoro's name during the Gothic wars (Petra Honorii). It succeeds brilliantly: bright in color, aromatically nuanced, flavorful and tense on the palate, closing with great verve. The other wines tasted also delivered, starting with their tasty Albana Seccos: the sapid Frangipane '19 and the minerally In Terra '18.

Wine	Rating
● Romagna Sangiovese Bertinoro P. Honorii Ris. '16	🍷🍷 4
○ Romagna Albana Secco Frangipane '19	🍷🍷 2*
○ Romagna Albana Secco In Terra '18	🍷🍷 4
● Romagna Sangiovese Sup. In Terra '18	🍷🍷 4
● Sangiovese di Romagna Sup. Oddone '19	🍷🍷 2*
● Romagna Sangiovese Bertinoro P. Honorii Ris. '15	🍷🍷 4
● Romagna Sangiovese Sup. Il Colombarone '17	🍷🍷 3
● Romagna Sangiovese Sup. In Terra '17	🍷🍷 4

Lini 910

Fraz. Canolo
via Vecchia Canolo, 7
42015 Correggio [RE]
Tel. +39 0522690162
www.lini910.it

CELLAR SALES
PRE-BOOKED VISITS
ANNUAL PRODUCTION 400,000 bottles
HECTARES UNDER VINE 25.00

Lini is back in our main section. Cousins Alicia and Alberto are at the helm of a brand with more than 100 years of history behind it, one that has always focused on quality, even when the world of Lambrusco was thinking about other things. In fact, the Lini have always had an interest in the 'Metodo Classico' and were among the first in Emilia to gain experience in the field. Their great work as consultants has allowed this small family business the opportunity to produce quality Metodo Classico bubbly. Lini's 2015 version is truly a lovely Metodo Classico Rosé. 100% Pinot Nero, it features aromas of citrus fruits, berries and aromatic herbs; the bead is fine, the palate has backbone and elegance. A blend of Salamino and a smaller share of Sorbara, the Labrusca Rosato '19 is notable for its floral aromas—it has character and grit, but maintains its drinkability and pleasantness. 15% Ancellotta, the Rosso offers up fruity aromas, especially blueberry.

- ⊙ Lini 910 M. Cl. Rosé '15 — 🍷🍷 5
- ⊙ Reggiano Lambrusco Labrusca Rosato '19 — 🍷🍷 2*
- ● Reggiano Lambrusco Labrusca Rosso '19 — 🍷 2

Lombardini

via Cavour, 15
42017 Novellara [RE]
Tel. +39 0522654224
www.lombardinivini.it

CELLAR SALES
PRE-BOOKED VISITS
ANNUAL PRODUCTION 800,000 bottles

The Lombardini family have almost a hundred years of experience in the field. The producer is inextricably bound up with Novellara, where Angelo Lombardini, already owner of Bar Roma, founded his winery (it's still at its original location). After the war, the business was taken over by Angelo's five children and, later, by his grandchildren Marco, Angelo and Riccardo, who modernized the facilities. Today the fourth generation of family are at work, overseeing a brand new bottling system that uses nitrogen so as to prevent the wines from coming into contact with oxygen. 80% Salamino and 20% Sorbara, the Il Signor Campanone '19 is a substantive Lambrusco, redolent of blackberry and blueberry, long and balanced. The Rosato del Campanone, made with 10% more Sorbara, is sapid and well-crafted, offering notes of berries and aromatic herbs. Among the "C'era una volta" line, which included an elegant, fragrant Sorbara and a pleasant, fruity Reggiano Secco, we very much appreciated the Amabile, which plays nicely on pulp, sweetness and acidity.

- ● Reggiano Lambrusco Il Signor Campanone '19 — 🍷🍷 2*
- ⊙ Reggian Lambrusco Rosato del Campanone '19 — 🍷🍷 2*
- ● Reggiano Lambrusco Amabile del C'era una Volta '19 — 🍷🍷 2*
- ● Lambrusco di Sorbara del C'era Una Volta '19 — 🍷 2
- ○ Malvasia Spumante Dolce '19 — 🍷 2
- ● Reggiano Lambrusco del C'era Una Volta '19 — 🍷 2
- ● Reggiano Lambrusco Il Campanone '19 — 🍷 2
- ● Reggiano Lambrusco Del C'era Una Volta '18 — 🍷🍷(white) 2*
- ● Reggiano Lambrusco Il Signor Campanone '18 — 🍷🍷(white) 2*

Luretta

LOC. CASTELLO DI MOMELIANO
29010 GAZZOLA [PC]
TEL. +39 0523971070
www.luretta.com

CELLAR SALES
PRE-BOOKED VISITS
ANNUAL PRODUCTION 300,000 bottles
HECTARES UNDER VINE 50.00
VITICULTURE METHOD Certified Organic

The wine names, the labels, the typologies made: everything points to the fact that here in Val Luretta, in the Castle of Momeliano, dating back to the 14th century, there's been very little of what could be called 'normal'. Since 2002, Felice Salamini, a former cattle-breeding globetrotter, has been making original wines in the splendid vaults of his underground cellars. His range is marked by a strong personality, one that Felice (with his wife, Carla, and his son Lucio) obtains from his organically-grown grapes, drawing on low yields and plenty of inspiration. The Selín dl'Armari '18 is a monovarietal Chardonnay that ferments in barriques. It proves interesting in its spicy notes, which enrich a nose bursting with ripe yellow fruits. The Carabas '16 is a fresh Barbera with a lovely balsamic vein, aromas of cherries and undergrowth. The Malvasia Passita Le Rane '15 pours a nice amber color, heralding citrus fruit aromas together with more complex hints of walnut husk and candied fruit.

● C. P. Barbera Carabas '16	🍷🍷 3
○ C. P. Chardonnay Selín dl'Armari '18	🍷🍷 4
○ C. P. Malvasia Passito Le Rane '15	🍷🍷 6
● C. P. Cabernet Sauvignon Corbeau '15	🍷 6
○ C. P. Malvasia Boccadirosa '19	🍷 3
● C. P. Pinot Nero Achab '17	🍷 5
● Gutturnio Sup. L'Ala del Drago '16	🍷 3
○ Principessa Brut M. Cl. '17	🍷 4
● C. P. Barbera Carabas '15	🍷🍷 3
○ C. P. Chardonnay Selín dl'Armari '17	🍷🍷 4
○ C. P. Chardonnay Selín dl'Armari '15	🍷🍷 4
○ C. P. Sauvignon I Nani e le Ballerine '18	🍷🍷 3
○ C. P. Sauvignon I Nani e le Ballerine '16	🍷🍷 3
● Gutturnio Sup. '12	🍷🍷 3
● Pantera '15	🍷🍷 4
○ Principessa Pas Dosé Brut M. Cl. '09	🍷🍷 4
○ Principessa Pas Dosé M. Cl. '10	🍷🍷 4

Manicardi

VIA MASSARONI, 1
41014 CASTELVETRO DI MODENA [MO]
TEL. +39 059799000
www.manicardi.it

CELLAR SALES
PRE-BOOKED VISITS
ANNUAL PRODUCTION 100,000 bottles
HECTARES UNDER VINE 16.90

The producer was founded in the early 1980s thanks to Enzo Manicardi, a man in love with this land and its hills, rich in biodiversity. The vineyards, all south facing, unfold on medium-textured clayey soils continuously fanned by the wind and marked by good day-night temperature swings. In the cellar a modern approach aims to bring out the attributes of the territory's grapes, starting with Lambrusco Grasparossa, Grechetto and Malbo Gentile. We should also mention the presence of a vinegar factory on the beautiful estate. Ca' del Fiore '19 is a Grasparossa from the vineyard of the same name. It's fruity, redolent of small berries and red citrus fruits, In the mouth it has a lovely impact, coming through full-bodied, well supported by acidity, balanced and fine. The Secco '19, another Grasparossa, plays more on aromas of blackberry and blueberry—it's also fruity and enjoyable in the mouth. The Fabula is a curious Spumante Rosé blend of Grasparossa and Grechetto that features flowery aromas and nice backbone.

● Lambrusco Grasparossa di Castelvetro V. Ca' del Fiore '19	🍷🍷 2*
● Lambrusco Grasparossa di Castelvetro '19	🍷🍷 2*
⊙ Fabula Rosé Brut '19	🍷 3
○ Pignoletto Frizzante '19	🍷 2
● Ruby Laury '16	🍷🍷 3

Tenuta Mara

via Ca' Bacchino, 1665
47832 San Clemente [RN]
Tel. +39 0541988870
www.tenutamara.com

CELLAR SALES
PRE-BOOKED VISITS
ACCOMMODATION AND RESTAURANT SERVICE
ANNUAL PRODUCTION 35,000 bottles
HECTARES UNDER VINE 11.00
VITICULTURE METHOD Certified Biodynamic

Tenuta Mara is certainly one of the most original projects to have sprung up recently in Romagna, as well as one of its most ambitious. It was conceived and realized by Giordano Emendatori, who christened the estate with the name of his wife, Mara. It all began in 2000 with the purchase of the land and the planting of the vineyards in the San Clemente area of Rimini. The grape chosen to represent the venture is Sangiovese, worked both in the vineyard and in the cellar using decidedly minimally-invasive, artisan methods. The Maramia '18 matures in conical oak vats, without temperature control and without the addition of cultured yeasts, and macerates on the skins for about a month. On the nose it features vinous aromas of red fruit in gelée, roots and Asian spices; in the mouth it's lively, dynamic and vibrant, finishing with a pronounced acidity. The other Sangiovese Guiry '18 is fainter: floral and spicy in the mouth, more flavorful than full-bodied, it's the perfect companion for good food.

- ● MaraMia Sangiovese '18 🍷🍷🍷 6
- ● Guiry Sangiovese '18 🍷🍷 5
- ● Guiry '16 ΨΨ 5
- ● Guiry Sangiovese '17 ΨΨ 5
- ● MaraMia Sangiovese '16 ΨΨ 6
- ● Maramia Sangiovese '15 ΨΨ 7
- ● Maramia Sangiovese '13 ΨΨ 7
- ● Maramia Sangiovese '12 ΨΨ 4

★Ermete Medici & Figli

loc. Gaida
via I. Newton, 13a
42124 Reggio Emilia
Tel. +39 0522942135
www.medici.it

CELLAR SALES
PRE-BOOKED VISITS
ACCOMMODATION
ANNUAL PRODUCTION 800,000 bottles
HECTARES UNDER VINE 75.00
VITICULTURE METHOD Certified Organic
SUSTAINABLE WINERY

It's not possible to tell the story of Lambrusco Reggiano without talking about the Medici family. Founded by Remigio at the end of the nineteenth century, it was his son Ermete who expanded and modernized the estate, laying the foundations for the production of the quality Lambrusco that we drink today. His work continued with his heirs, until today, with the fourth generation now represented by Alberto Medici. Much of their current work is dedicated to identifying clones and the most well-suited land for the production of their top wines. This year they submitted a spectacular selection (which doesn't comes as a surprise). The Assolo delivers with its wild berry fruit, coming through lively on the nose and palate, with a full, long finish. But it's the Concerto, with its vibrant fruit and perfect balance, that takes home the gold. The I Quercioli delights with its raspberry and blackberry notes. The pleasant GranConcerto '18 stands out for its creaminess. The Phermento '19 is always a sure bet.

- ● Reggiano Lambrusco Concerto '19 🍷🍷🍷 2*
- ● Reggiano Lambrusco Assolo 🍷🍷 2*
- ● Reggiano Lambrusco I Quercioli 🍷🍷 2
- ● Granconcerto Brut M. Cl. '18 🍷🍷 3
- ● Modena Lambrusco Phermento Metodo Ancestrale '19 🍷🍷 3
- ● Reggiano Lambrusco Dolce I Quercioli 🍷🍷 2
- ● Lambrusco di Sorbara I Quercioli 🍷 2
- ● Reggiano Lambrusco Concerto '18 ΨΨΨ 2*
- ● Reggiano Lambrusco Concerto '17 ΨΨΨ 2*
- ● Reggiano Lambrusco Concerto '16 ΨΨΨ 2*
- ● Reggiano Lambrusco Concerto '15 ΨΨΨ 2*
- ● Reggiano Lambrusco Concerto '14 ΨΨΨ 2*
- ● Reggiano Lambrusco Concerto '13 ΨΨΨ 2*
- ● Reggiano Lambrusco Concerto '12 ΨΨΨ 2*
- ● Reggiano Lambrusco Concerto '11 ΨΨΨ 2*
- ● Reggiano Lambrusco Concerto '10 ΨΨΨ 2*

Monte delle Vigne

LOC. OZZANO TARO
VIA MONTICELLO, 22
43046 COLLECCHIO [PR]
TEL. +39 0521309704
www.montedellevigne.it

CELLAR SALES
PRE-BOOKED VISITS
ACCOMMODATION
ANNUAL PRODUCTION 350,000 bottles
HECTARES UNDER VINE 60.00

It was 1983 when Andrea Ferrari began his production adventure, starting with a seven-hectare vineyard estate situated at 300 meters above sea level. In the year 2000 the number of hectares grew to 20, but the turning point came between 2003 and 2004, when developer Paolo Pizzarotti, owner of more than 100 neighboring hectares, became the majority shareholder. At the end of 2006 the new, beautiful winery (underground and powered by solar energy) was inaugurated. The vineyards were converted to organic farming and, in addition to their original selection of still wines, they began producing traditional sparkling wines as well. The Nabucco '18, a blend of Cabernet Sauvignon and Barbera, combines the varietal substance of the former with the acidity of the latter, making for a full, spirited wine, rich and redolent of hay and cherries, long on the finish. The I Calanchi '19, 100% Maestri, is a certified organic Lambrusco, dense and fragrant in its red berry scents. Varietal and supple, we also appreciated the gustatory energy of the Barbera Argille '18.

Wine	Rating
● Nabucco '18	▼▼ 5
● Argille '15	▼▼ 6
● Colli di Parma Lambrusco I Calanchi '19	▼▼ 5
○ Colli di Parma Malvasia Poem '19	▼▼ 3
○ Colli di Parma Sauvignon Bosco Grande '19	▼ 3
○ Callas Malvasia '17	▽▽▽ 4*
○ Callas Malvasia '15	▽▽▽ 4*
● Colli di Parma Rosso MDV '16	▽▽▽ 3*
● Colli di Parma Rosso MDV '14	▽▽▽ 2*
○ Callas Malvasia '14	▽▽ 4
○ Colli di Parma Malvasia Frizzante '15	▽▽ 2*
○ Colli di Parma Malvasia Frizzante '14	▽▽ 2*
○ Colli di Parma Malvasia Poem '14	▽▽ 2*
● Colli di Parma Rosso MDV '18	▽▽ 3
● Colli di Parma Rosso MDV '17	▽▽ 3

Fattoria Monticino Rosso

VIA MONTECATONE, 7
40026 IMOLA [BO]
TEL. +39 054240577
www.fattoriadelmonticinorosso.it

CELLAR SALES
PRE-BOOKED VISITS
ANNUAL PRODUCTION 70,000 bottles
HECTARES UNDER VINE 18.00

A beautiful story ties together memorable business ventures, travels, great returns, entrepreneurial vision and a bond with the territory. It all began in the sixties, when Antonio Zeoli acquired some land on the hills of Imola. Other properties followed, including the one called Monticino Rosso, which gave the producer its name in 1985 and definitively launched an agricultural venture linked to the production of wine grapes and fruit. Today Antonio's sons, Luciano and Gianni, run a modern and well-organized business, one that's capable of offering quality wines on several fronts. Excellent reviews for almost all their wines, but there's no doubt that the winery has a gift for Albana. The Codronchio Secco '18, a late-harvest wine that sees the presence of botrytis, is the family jewel. Nevertheless, we preferred the more immediately expressive Albana Secco A '19. Delicious, racy and juicy, it's a white with plenty of character.

Wine	Rating
○ Romagna Albana Secco A '19	▼▼▼ 2*
○ Romagna Albana Secco Codronchio '18	▼▼ 3*
○ Pas Dosè	▼▼ 4
○ Romagna Albana Passito '16	▼▼ 4
● Romagna Sangiovese Sup. Le Morine Ris. '16	▼▼ 3
○ Romagna Albana Passito '15	▽▽ 4
○ Romagna Albana Secco A '17	▽▽ 2*
○ Romagna Albana Secco A '16	▽▽ 2*
○ Romagna Albana Secco Codronchio Special Edition '16	▽▽ 3
● Romagna Sangiovese Sup. S '18	▽▽ 2*
● Romagna Sangiovese Sup. S '16	▽▽ 2*
● Romagna Sangiovese Sup. S '15	▽▽ 2*

Fattoria Moretto

via Tiberia, 13b
41014 Castelvetro di Modena [MO]
Tel. +39 059790183
www.fattoriamoretto.it

CELLAR SALES
PRE-BOOKED VISITS
ACCOMMODATION
ANNUAL PRODUCTION 65,000 bottles
HECTARES UNDER VINE 10.00
VITICULTURE METHOD Certified Organic
SUSTAINABLE WINERY

A small, family-run business, the winery was founded in 1971 after Antonio Altariva, the founder, came to the area from Pavullo nel Frignano in the 1960s to sign a sharecropping agreement. It was his son Domenico who bought the first land with his home and cellar. But the most important step came in 1991, when the third generation, represented by Fausto and Fabio, decided to start bottling their wine. Today Grasparossa with a strong personality is forged from vineyards managed organically. The Canova '19 is a lovely Grasparossa that features strong acidity on the palate, together with cherry and berry aromas, and notes of herbs. The Semprebon keeps faith with the name: it's a rich, opulent, balanced Grasparossa Amabile. The Tasso is fleshy, more oriented towards black berries, while the Monovitigno comes through nicely on morello cherry sensations—very tasty and linear. We also appreciated the citrusy Pignoletto '19.

Wine	Rating
● Lambrusco Grasparossa di Castelvetro Canova '19	🍷🍷 3*
● Lambrusco Grasparossa di Castelvetro Monovitigno '19	🍷🍷 3
● Lambrusco Grasparossa di Castelvetro Amabile Semprebon '19	🍷🍷 2*
● Lambrusco Grasparossa di Castelvetro Tasso '19	🍷🍷 2*
○ Pignoletto '19	🍷 3
● Lambrusco Grasparossa di Castelvetro Secco Canova '16	🍷🍷 3
● Lambrusco Grasparossa di Castelvetro Secco Canova '15	🍷🍷 3
● Lambrusco Grasparossa di Castelvetro Secco Monovitigno '16	🍷🍷 3
● Lambrusco Grasparossa di Castelvetro Secco Monovitigno '15	🍷🍷 3*

Fattoria Nicolucci

fraz. Predappio Alta
via Umberto I, 21
47016 Predappio [FC]
Tel. +39 0543922361
www.vininicolucci.com

CELLAR SALES
PRE-BOOKED VISITS
ANNUAL PRODUCTION 80,000 bottles
HECTARES UNDER VINE 12.00
SUSTAINABLE WINERY

A historic winery with roots going as far back as 1885, Fattoria Nicolucci has always been bound up with the terroir of Predappio Alta, an area characterized by lean, calcareous and pebbly soils that are ideal for cultivating Sangiovese. Universally appreciated since time immemorial, the house reds are now an absolute benchmark in Romagna. Matured in concrete and large oak barrels, they are proving as tense and deep as ever, managing an admirable synthesis of intensity and harmony. The winery's flagship, consistently among the best reds in the region, is the Vigna del Generale. This year it's presented in a 2015 'Limited Edition', a sort of reserve of a reserve that meets expectations. It's a Sangiovese Superiore of class and complexity, extremely multifaceted aromatically, rich in texture but always able to find bounce and mobility. The 2017 'classic' version is still a bit restrained at this point.

Wine	Rating
● Romagna Sangiovese Sup. Ris. V. del Generale Edizione Limitata '15	🍷🍷 8
● Romagna Sangiovese Sup. V . del Generale Ris. '17	🍷🍷 6
○ Trebbiano '19	🍷🍷 3
● Nero di Predappio '19	🍷 5
● Romagna Sangiovese Sup. Predappio di Predappio V. del Generale Ris. '16	🍷🍷🍷 5
● Romagna Sangiovese Sup. Predappio di Predappio V. del Generale Ris. '15	🍷🍷🍷 5
● Romagna Sangiovese Sup. V. del Generale Ris. '13	🍷🍷🍷 5
● Romagna Sangiovese Sup. Tre Rocche '18	🍷🍷 3

Enio Ottaviani

LOC. SANT'ANDREA IN CASALE
VIA PIAN DI VAGLIA, 17
47832 SAN CLEMENTE [RN]
TEL. +39 0541952608
www.eniottaviani.it

CELLAR SALES
PRE-BOOKED VISITS
ANNUAL PRODUCTION 130,000 bottles
HECTARES UNDER VINE 12.00

Undoubtedly, Enio Ottaviani's winery should be considered a revelation, at least when it comes to Rimini's Sangiovese-based wines. It's not a new venture, but it's demonstrated an ability to adapt in recent times, seeking out and identifying a convincing production style. At the helm are Davide and Massimo Lorenzi, along with their cousins Marco and Milena Tonelli. Together they oversee the vineyards in San Clemente di Rimini, which grow in loamy clay soils and enjoy the sea breeze. Theirs is a new style, never forced, capable of unexpected finesse and aromatic complexity. With our tastings, the overall picture was less clear than in the past, but there were still some standouts, starting with the Romagna Sangiovese Superiore Caciara '19. It pours a faint color, offering up engaging aromas of red fruit and flowers, with pronounced citrus hints. The mouth is on the same wavelength, rather racy, somewhat lean-structured, fresh. We also appreciated the surprising and supple Pagadebit '19.

Wine	Rating
○ Romagna Pagadebit Strati '19	🍷🍷 3
● Romagna Sangiovese Sup. Caciara '19	🍷🍷 3
○ Colli di Rimini Rebola '19	🍷 4
● Romagna Sangiovese Dado '19	🍷 6
○ Romagna Pagadebit Strati '17	YY 2*
● Romagna Sangiovese Caciara '15	YY 3
● Romagna Sangiovese Dado '18	YY 6
● Romagna Sangiovese Primalba Bio '17	YY 2*
● Romagna Sangiovese Sup. Caciara '18	YY 3
● Romagna Sangiovese Sup. Caciara '17	YY 3
● Romagna Sangiovese Sup. Caciara '16	YY 3
● Romagna Sangiovese Sup. Sole Rosso Ris. '15	YY 4
● Romagna Sangiovese Sup. Sole Rosso Ris. '13	YY 4

Alberto Paltrinieri

FRAZ. SORBARA
VIA CRISTO, 49
41030 BOMPORTO [MO]
TEL. +39 059902047
www.cantinapaltrinieri.it

CELLAR SALES
PRE-BOOKED VISITS
ANNUAL PRODUCTION 150,000 bottles
HECTARES UNDER VINE 17.00

First it was grandfather Achille, a chemist and pharmacist with a passion for wine. He's the one who laid the winery's original foundation. Then came father Gianfranco and finally Alberto Paltrinieri, who's managed to create a real gem of regional winemaking, thanks in part to the indispensable support of his wife, Barbara. Here, smack in the middle of Cristo di Sorbara, on the alluvial soils that stretch between the Secchia and Panaro rivers, authentic and elegant Lambrusco wines come to life, expressing a style that's faithful to the territory and to the single cru. A sparkling version is also produced. The elegant and deep Leclisse is a Sorbara that we always like very much, as broad as it is in its floral and fruity scents accompanied by citrus hints. The Piria uses a share of Salamino for its nice, progressively unfolding palate and an encore of citrus and aromatic herbs. The Lariserva is a monovarietal Sorbara sparkler with beautiful, slightly evolved nuances, and a harmonious, linear palate.

Wine	Rating
⊙ Lambrusco di Sorbara Leclisse '19	🍷🍷🍷 3*
● Lambrusco di Sorbara Piria '19	🍷🍷 2*
⊙ Lambrusco di Sorbara Radice '19	🍷🍷 3*
⊙ Lambrusco di Sorbara Brut Lariserva '18	🍷🍷 3
● Solco '19	🍷🍷 2*
⊙ Lambrusco di Modena Grosso Brut M. Cl. '17	🍷 4
● Lambrusco di Sorbara Sant'Agata '19	🍷 2
⊙ Lambrusco di Sorbara Leclisse '18	YYY 3*
● Lambrusco di Sorbara Leclisse '17	YYY 3*
● Lambrusco di Sorbara Leclisse '16	YYY 2*
● Lambrusco di Sorbara Leclisse '10	YYY 3*
● Lambrusco di Sorbara Radice '13	YYY 2*
⊙ Lambrusco di Sorbara Brut Lariserva '17	YY 3
● Lambrusco di Sorbara Sant'Agata '18	YY 2*

Pandolfa

FRAZ. FIUMANA
VIA PANDOLFA, 35
47016 PREDAPPIO [FC]
TEL. +39 0543940073
www.pandolfa.it

CELLAR SALES
PRE-BOOKED VISITS
ACCOMMODATION
ANNUAL PRODUCTION 120,000 bottles
HECTARES UNDER VINE 30.00
VITICULTURE METHOD Certified Organic
SUSTAINABLE WINERY

Pandolfa is a fundamentally important winery, both historically and agriculturally, and has managed to shine thanks to the current efforts of the Cirese family. Its size is also remarkable, as the estate covers over one hundred hectares on the Tuscan-Romagna Apennines, in Fiumana di Predappio. It's one of the cradles of Sangiovese, an area cultivated between 150 and 400 meters above sea level, on soils composed of sandstone and calcareous marl. These conditions form the basis for elegant wines that are never forced, successful in combining flavor, style and suppleness, making them ideal companions for good food. We appreciated the Romagna Sangiovese Superiore Pandolfo Riserva '17, a stalwart among their selection. It features vibrant aromas, owing to the year, nice substance and tannic grip: it's clearly more mature than the previous version, but able to keep intact the basic stylistic idea. The younger Sangiovese was less convincing, at least at the time of our tasting. The rosé Ginevra '19 proves pleasant and delicate.

⊙ Ginevra '19	🍷🍷 2*
● Romagna Sangiovese Sup. Pandolfo Ris. '17	🍷🍷 2*
● Romagna Sangiovese Federico '19	🍷 2
● Romagna Sangiovese Sup. Pandolfo '19	🍷 2
● Romagna Sangiovese Federico '17	🍷🍷 2*
● Romagna Sangiovese Sup. Federico '16	🍷🍷 2*
● Romagna Sangiovese Sup. Pandolfo '16	🍷🍷 2*
● Romagna Sangiovese Sup. Pandolfo Ris. '18	🍷🍷 2*
● Romagna Sangiovese Sup. Pandolfo Ris. '15	🍷🍷 3*

Fattoria Paradiso

FRAZ. CAPOCOLLE
VIA PALMEGGIANA, 285
47032 BERTINORO [FC]
TEL. +39 0543445044
www.fattoriaparadiso.com

CELLAR SALES
PRE-BOOKED VISITS
ACCOMMODATION AND RESTAURANT SERVICE
ANNUAL PRODUCTION 200,000 bottles
HECTARES UNDER VINE 150.00
VITICULTURE METHOD Certified Organic
SUSTAINABLE WINERY

Fattoria Paradiso is a historic winery situated near Bertinoro, on the Apennine foothills. It's a solid producer, in step with the times, conducted with skill and intuition by the Pezzi family. The emphasis has always been on traditional cultivars, including numerous Sangiovese clones and the rare Barbarossa grape, a choice more current than ever, and one that's provided a concrete, fascinating basis for decidedly well-made wines, both in terms of workmanship and stylistic identity. Only grapes from their privately-owned vineyards are used, representing some ten recognized geographic mentions. The Petì Tufi '19 is a Sangiovese Superiore without the frills, as pleasant in its aromas of violet and red fruit as it is fragrant in the mouth. The Sangiovese Superiore Vigna Molino '19 moves on a similar track. The Spungone '19 features delicate floral aromas that call up roses; the Albana Vigna dell'Olivo '19 is fleshy and citrusy, with hints of honey.

● Barbarossa Cuvée Mario Pezzi V. dello Spungone '19	🍷🍷 3
○ Gradisca Muffato '19	🍷🍷 4
○ Romagna Albana Secco V. dell'Olivo '19	🍷🍷 2*
● Romagna Sangiovese Sup. Petì Tufi '19	🍷🍷 3
● Romagna Sangiovese Sup. V. Molino '19	🍷🍷 3
● Lo Spungone '18	🍷🍷 3
○ Romagna Albana Dolce V. del Viale '18	🍷🍷 3
● Romagna Sangiovese Bertinoro V. delle Lepri Ris. '15	🍷🍷 4
● Romagna Sangiovese Sup. Petì Tufi '18	🍷🍷 3
● Romagna Sangiovese Sup. V. del Molino Maestri di Vigna '16	🍷🍷 2*

Pertinello

via Arpineto Pertinello, 2
47010 Galeata [FC]
Tel. +39 0543983156
www.tenutapertinello.it

CELLAR SALES
PRE-BOOKED VISITS
ANNUAL PRODUCTION 70,000 bottles
HECTARES UNDER VINE 15.00
VITICULTURE METHOD Certified Organic

Pertinello is an idea that has found its substance, a fascinating project in all respects. For starters the place itself isn't such an obvious choice: the hills of Alta Val Bidente is an area with an ancient winemaking tradition but that's in need of new energy. Their work is grounded in the revival of old plots of Sangiovese and other cultivars, leading to new vineyards, work that's fundamental in allowing them to bring the best grapes to the cellar. After a few vintages of treading water, their wines have finally returned to their former luster. It may be 'Pertinello's daily-drinker', as they say on the estate, but the Il Bosco '19 is also a Sangiovese that knows how to find complexity and class, even with its graceful, subtle and never excessive style. It's a delight, and for us it deserves to be considered one of the region's best reds. The Memoria di Pertinello is a Sangiovese with a highly original and alluring oxidative style, the Pinot Nero '19 once again proves delicious.

- ● La Memoria di Pertinello — 🍷🍷 8
- ● Romagna Sangiovese Il Bosco di Pertinello '19 — 🍷🍷 2*
- ● Pinot Nero '19 — 🍷🍷 4
- ⊙ La Rosa di Pertinello '19 — 🍷 5
- ○ Riesling '19 — 🍷
- ● Romagna Sangiovese Sup. Il Pertinello '19 — 🍷 3
- ● Colli Romagna Centrale Sangiovese Pertinello '08 — 🍷🍷🍷 3
- ● Colli Romagna Centrale Sangiovese Pertinello '13 — 🍷🍷 3*
- ● Pinot Nero '16 — 🍷🍷 4
- ● Romagna Sangiovese Il Bosco di Pertinello '17 — 🍷🍷 2*
- ● Romagna Sangiovese Modigliana Gemme '16 — 🍷🍷 3

Noelia Ricci

fraz. Fiumana
via Pandolfa, 35
47016 Predappio [FC]
Tel. +39 0543940073
www.noeliaricci.it

CELLAR SALES
PRE-BOOKED VISITS
ACCOMMODATION
ANNUAL PRODUCTION 58,000 bottles
HECTARES UNDER VINE 9.00
SUSTAINABLE WINERY

At Tenuta Pandolfa, a few years ago the Cirese family launched a specialized project focused on a new brand capable of establishing itself quickly. We're talking about Noelia Ricci, an innovative path for Sangiovese di Romagna. At first it was a decidedly minimalist style, breaking with their existing one, then gradually their wines grew more authentic and complete. In short, recent versions seem to have hit their stride, managing to express the terroir with a clear vision, but without predefined schema. The Godenza '18 met expectations. An extremely classy Sangiovese from the Predappio subzone, it's adorned with intensely floral aromas on a background of small berries. In the mouth it has nothing more and nothing less than what it needs, unfolding tasty, dynamic, tapered and fresh across a long finish. The Sangiovese '19 and the Brò '19, a fragrant and racy white, are also excellent.

- ● Romagna Sangiovese Predappio Godenza '18 — 🍷🍷🍷 4*
- ● Romagna Sangiovese Predappio Il Sangiovese '19 — 🍷🍷 3*
- ○ Brò '19 — 🍷🍷 3
- ● Romagna Sangiovese Predappio Godenza '16 — 🍷🍷🍷 4*
- ● Romagna Sangiovese Predappio Il Sangiovese '18 — 🍷🍷🍷 3*
- ● Romagna Sangiovese Sup. Godenza '14 — 🍷🍷🍷 3*
- ● Romagna Sangiovese Sup. Il Sangiovese '16 — 🍷🍷🍷 3*
- ● Romagna Sangiovese Sup. Il Sangiovese '14 — 🍷🍷🍷 2*

Cantine Riunite & Civ

via G. Brodolini, 24
42040 Campegine [RE]
Tel. +39 0522905711
www.riuniteciv.com

CELLAR SALES
ANNUAL PRODUCTION 130,000,000 bottles
HECTARES UNDER VINE 3500.00
SUSTAINABLE WINERY

This important Emilia producer avails itself of 2,600 members, 3,500 hectares of vineyards and 16 associated wineries. These are the figures that make this group the first in Italy in terms of turnover and number of bottles produced. It's a colossus that, beyond its size, has in recent years begun the virtuous work of selecting the best grapes to make top-level wines. To this end, some of their Lambruscos, a benchmark variety for the area that's partially organically cultivated, shine. The Senzatempo is a monovarietal, bottle-fermented Salamino of rare finesse, redolent of blackberry and violet. It has great overall integrity and a clean, precise, satisfying palate. The 1950 Cuvée is a full, fruity and linear blend of Salamino, Marani and Lancellotta. We also appreciated the well-made Pignoletto Spumante P, with its pineapple and lime scents, fine bead and overall pleasantness, as well as the two 1950s, which prove fruity, simple and quaffable.

● Senzatempo Lambrusco	🍷🍷 2
● Lambrusco Grasparossa di Castelvetro Righi	🍷🍷 1
○ Pignoletto Spumante Brut P Righi	🍷🍷 2*
● Reggiano Lambrusco 1950 Secco	🍷🍷 1
● Reggiano Lambrusco Amabile 1950	🍷🍷 1
● Reggiano Lambrusco Cuvèe 1950	🍷🍷 1
● L'Oscuro Lambrusco Semisecco Gaetano Righi	🍷 2
○ Pignoletto Frizzante Arès Righi	🍷 2
● Colli di Scandiano e di Canossa Cabernet Sauvignon Monteleone Albinea Canali '15	🍷🍷 2*
● Lambrusco Grasparossa di Castelvetro Amabile Il Fojonco '17	🍷🍷 2*
● Modena Lambrusco Semisecco Righi '17	🍷🍷 1*
○ Pignoletto Extra Dry Stellato Albinea Canali '17	🍷🍷 2*

Le Rocche Malatestiane

via Emilia, 104
47900 Rimini
Tel. +39 0541743079
www.lerocchemalatestiane.it

CELLAR SALES
PRE-BOOKED VISITS
ANNUAL PRODUCTION 700,000 bottles
HECTARES UNDER VINE 800.00

Le Rocche Malatestiane has vineyards in the Upper Marecchia Valley and in Cattolica, in the Rimini area overlooking Marche. It takes its name from a historic family of rulers and patrons who carried out numerous works, including building forts and fortresses. The current agricultural, viticultural and enological operation centers on Sangiovese and in particular its territorial identity. There are three areas of cultivation: the hinterland of Rimini, Riccione and Coriano; San Clemente, Gemmano and Montescudo; and Verucchio, Torriana and San Paolo. The wine that impressed us the most is the Sangiovese Superiore Sigismondo '19. Made with grapes from Coriano, it's still quite young, a red that plays on delicacy and nuances, as well as on a rather supple palate. On the nose it features aromas of fresh flowers and ripe red berry fruit, though it's not without delicate herbaceous and spicy hints. The I Diavoli '19, from San Clemente and Gemmano, also delivered. The Tre Miracoli '19, from vineyards in Torriana, proved less convincing this year.

● Romagna Sangiovese Sup. S igismondo '19	🍷🍷 2*
● Romagna Sangiovese Sup. I Diavoli '19	🍷🍷 2*
● Romagna Sangiovese Sup. Tre Miracoli '19	🍷 2
● Romagna Sangiovese Sup. Sigismondo '17	🍷🍷🍷 2*
● Romagna Sangiovese Sup. Sigismondo '16	🍷🍷🍷 2*
● Romagna Sangiovese Sup. Tre Miracoli '18	🍷🍷🍷 2*
● Romagna Sangiovese Sup. I Diavoli '14	🍷🍷 2*
● Romagna Sangiovese Sup. Sigismondo '18	🍷🍷 2*

Cantine Romagnoli

LOC. VILLÒ
VIA GENOVA, 20
29020 VIGOLZONE [PC]
TEL. +39 0523870904
www.cantineromagnoli.it

CELLAR SALES
PRE-BOOKED VISITS
ANNUAL PRODUCTION 300,000 bottles
HECTARES UNDER VINE 45.00
SUSTAINABLE WINERY

The property, which dates back to the 19th century, passed to the Romagnoli in 1926, and has since retained the name. Now, next to the original, completely-restored structures, we find the new winery and barrique cellar. Under Alessandro Perini, the producer is investing heavily in Metodo Classico, with a temperature-controlled warehouse for the storage of up to 300,000 bottles. The environment is also a priority, as evidenced by the installation of solar panels and the drafting of the winery's first ever 'sustainability report'. The Pigro Rosé '17 features an elegant weave, delicate scents of berries with floral hints, fine bead and a vital, harmonious, relaxed palate. Staying with their Metodo Classicos, the Dosaggiozero '17 is pleasantly sharp, aromatically mineral and dynamic on the palate, while the Brut '18 proves simpler and harmonious, with fine bubbles as well. The well-made Ortrugo Filanda '18 is mature, sapid, adorned by a nice set of aromatic herbs, while with the Cicotto '18, a Gutturnio, Barbera's lovely, open fruit prevails.

Wine	Rating
○ Il Pigro Dosaggio Zero M. Cl. '17	TT 5
○ Il Pigro Rosé Brut M. Cl. '17	TT 5
○ Colto Vitato della Filanda n. 3 '18	TT 3
● Gutturnio Sup. Colto Vitato del Cicotto n. 21 '18	TT 2*
○ Caravaggio Bianco '19	T 3
● Caravaggio Rosso '18	T 5
○ Il Pigro Brut Cuvée M. Cl. '18	T 4
● Caravaggio '17	YY 5
○ Colto Vitato della Filanda n. 3 '17	YY 3
○ Cuvée Il Pigro Brut M. Cl. '16	YY 4
⊙ Cuvée Il Pigro Brut M. Cl. Rosé '16	YY 4
○ Cuvée Il Pigro Dosaggio Zero M. Cl. '16	YY 4
● Gutturnio Sup. Colto Vitato del Cicotto '17	YY 2*
● Gutturnio Sup. Colto Vitato della Bellaria n. 15 '18	YY 2*

★San Patrignano

VIA SAN PATRIGNANO, 53
47853 CORIANO [RN]
TEL. +39 0541362111
www.spaziosanpa.com

PRE-BOOKED VISITS
RESTAURANT SERVICE
ANNUAL PRODUCTION 500,000 bottles
HECTARES UNDER VINE 110.00
VITICULTURE METHOD Certified Organic

The now historic producer San Patrignano is a complex, multifaceted project on various fronts. It brings together and embraces various elements under the idea of ethical, social enterprise. It's here in Rimini that the winery has its form and substance, starting with the black grape varieties cultivated, such as Sangiovese, and moving on to great international cultivars, especially Cabernet Sauvignon. The wines they produce reveal a modern, contemporary approach that combines fullness and Mediterranean timbres. A blend of Sangiovese, Cabernet and Merlot, the Colli di Rimini Rosso Noi ages in barriques for 12 months. The 2018 is redolent of blackberry, then liquorice and coffee; in the mouth it's rich and dense, with broad tannins. Alluring in its sensations of white peach and balsamic whiffs, the Sauvignon '19 also proves pleasant in the mouth. We were less convinced by the Montepirolo '17, a blend of Cabernet Sauvignon, Merlot and Cabernet Franc aged for a year in barriques.

Wine	Rating
● Colli di Rimini Rosso Noi '18	TT 4
○ Sauvignon '19	TT 3
○ Aulente Bianco '19	T 2
● Montepirolo '17	T 5
● Colli di Rimini Cabernet Sauvignon Montepirolo '15	YYY 4*
● Colli di Rimini Cabernet Sauvignon Montepirolo '13	YYY 4*
● Romagna Sangiovese Sup. Avi Ris. '16	YYY 4*
○ Aulente Bianco '18	YY 2*
● Colli di Rimini Cabernet Sauvignon Montepirolo '16	YY 4

San Valentino

fraz. San Martino in Venti
via Tomasetta, 13
47900 Rimini
Tel. +39 0541752231
www.vinisanvalentino.com

CELLAR SALES
PRE-BOOKED VISITS
ANNUAL PRODUCTION 135,000 bottles
HECTARES UNDER VINE 17.00
VITICULTURE METHOD Certified Organic

San Valentino was founded by the Mascarin family in 1990. It's situated on a side of the Rimini hills that benefits from the sea breeze and faces the Apennines to the west, an interesting territory that has, over time, led the family to embrace organic farming methods. When it comes to the grapes cultivated, they've bet on traditional cornerstones like Sangiovese and Rebola, not to mention Syrah and Cabernet Franc. The good work being done convinced the Aureli family to come on board, allowing the winery to take further steps forward. The Sangiovese Superiore Scabi '18 has more flavor than fragrance: its aromas are still compressed, in need of time in the bottle to blossom completely, but the palate is already perfectly intelligible, tasty, broad and characterful. The Sangiovese Superiore Terra di Covignano Riserva '16 is clearly at a different stage in its evolution, proving broad and spicy with hints of ripe fruit and autumn leaves. The Rebola Scabi '19 is pleasantly approachable.

Wine	Rating
● Luna Nuova '16	🍷🍷 5
● Romagna Sangiovese Sup. Terra di Covignano Ris. '16	🍷🍷 5
● Sangiovese di Romagna Sup. Scabi '18	🍷🍷 2*
○ Colli di Rimini Rebola Scabi Bianco '19	🍷 2
● Romagna Sangiovese Sup. Il Conte di Covignano Ris. '16	🍷 6
○ Colli di Rimini Rebola Scabi Bianco '15	♡♡ 2*
○ Due Bianco '15	♡♡ 3
● Luna Nuova '14	♡♡ 5
● Vivian '14	♡♡ 3*

Tenuta Santa Lucia

via Giardino, 1400
47025 Mercato Saraceno [FC]
Tel. +39 054790441
www.santaluciavinery.it

CELLAR SALES
PRE-BOOKED VISITS
ACCOMMODATION
ANNUAL PRODUCTION 90,000 bottles
HECTARES UNDER VINE 17.00
VITICULTURE METHOD Certified Biodynamic
SUSTAINABLE WINERY

Tenuta Santa Lucia is located in Mercato Saraceno, in the Upper Savio Valley, in a lesser-known part of inland Romagna. The scenic natural landscape is preserved by an extremely respectful viticultural approach rooted in the dictates of organic and biodynamic (certified) agriculture. The grapes cultivated express the history's deep roots (Albana, Famoso, Centesimino and Sangiovese) and a personal tone reverberates throughout their selection. Eschewing conventional modes and styles, they deliver from the first sip. The Albarara '19 once again demonstrates that it's an intense and juicy Albana, enjoyable and capable of delivering weighty (but never cumbersome) pulp: the vineyard, at 400 metres above sea level, certainly works in its favor. The Sangiovese Superiore Taibo '18 also met expectations with its fragrant bouquet of red fruit lengthened by hints of violet and berries—in the mouth it's solid and dynamic. It matures first in 5000-liter conical vats and then in the bottle.

Wine	Rating
○ Romagna Albana Secco Albarara '19	🍷🍷 3
● Romagna Sangiovese Sup. Taibo '18	🍷🍷 3
● Romagna Sangiovese Sup. Sassignolo Ris. '16	🍷 4
○ Occhio di Starna Passito	♡♡ 4
○ Romagna Albana Passito Albarara '11	♡♡ 4
○ Romagna Albana Secco Alba Rara '17	♡♡ 3
○ Romagna Albana Secco Albarara '18	♡♡ 3*
○ Romagna Albana Secco Albarara '16	♡♡ 3*

Tenuta Santini

FRAZ. PASSANO
VIA CAMPO, 33
47853 CORIANO [RN]
TEL. +39 0541656527
www.tenutasantini.com

CELLAR SALES
PRE-BOOKED VISITS
ANNUAL PRODUCTION 40,000 bottles
HECTARES UNDER VINE 22.00

Tenuta Santini is situated in Coriano, on the hills of Rimini. Founded in the 1960s by brothers Giuseppe and Primo Santini, it recently launched a renovation project that has rendered the winery one of the most modern in the area. The vineyards grow in clayey-calcareous soils, in an area where the climate could be called Mediterranean. Sangiovese plays a leading role among the varieties grown, but Bordeaux vines, which are common in this part of the region, are also represented. The wines are beautifully crafted and express a certain territorial identity. At the top of their range is the Beato Enrico '18, a Sangiovese Superiore that combines the intensity of Rimini with a certain expressive grace. It's redolent of black berry fruits, though it's not without some pleasantly spicy hints of liquorice; in the mouth it proves firm, with excellent substance and depth. The Orione '17 is more mature, but able to maintain a certain balance. We also appreciated the Rebola Isotta '19, which plays on sensations of broom.

- ● Romagna Sangiovese Sup. Beato Enrico '18 — 🍷🍷 2*
- ● Romagna Sangiovese Sup. Orione '17 — 🍷🍷 4
- ● Colli di Rimini Battarreo '17 — 🍷 3
- ○ Colli di Rimini Rebola Isotta '19 — 🍷 2
- ● Battarreo '14 — 🍷🍷 3*
- ● Romagna Sangiovese Sup. Beato Enrico '17 — 🍷🍷 2*
- ● Romagna Sangiovese Sup. Beato Enrico '16 — 🍷🍷 2*
- ● Romagna Sangiovese Sup. Beato Enrico '15 — 🍷🍷 2*
- ● Romagna Sangiovese Sup. Cornelianum Ris. '15 — 🍷🍷 4

Cantina Sociale Settecani

VIA MODENA, 184
41014 CASTELVETRO DI MODENA [MO]
TEL. +39 059702505
www.cantinasettecani.it

CELLAR SALES
ANNUAL PRODUCTION 1,000,000 bottles
HECTARES UNDER VINE 530.00

Founded by 48 members in 1923, Settecani now boasts almost 200 growers. The winery is still to be found in the hamlet of Settecani di Castelvetro, in the heart of Grasparossa wine country, and it's the main grape grown here on the Modena Apennine foothills (Grechetto Gentile is the other principal grape cultivated). Always in step with the times, in 2017 the producer undertook an extensive project aimed at environmental sustainability, which includes renovating the winery, training its members, and reducing water consumption in the countryside. We start with two impeccable 2019 Grasparossas. The dry version features compact fruit and iodine, delicately salty, fresh scents, while the Amabile goes all in on crisp wild berry aromas, and nice overall integrity as well. 7note is a sparkling Pignoletto Spumante redolent of peach and apricot, with nice backbone and substance. The frank and fragrant Pignoletto Frizzante of the Vini del Re line offers up citrus and pineapple notes.

- ● Lambrusco Grasparossa di Castelvetro Amabile '19 — 🍷🍷 1*
- ● Lambrusco Grasparossa di Castelvetro Secco '19 — 🍷🍷 1
- ○ Pignoletto Frizzante Secco Vini del Re — 🍷🍷 2*
- ○ Pignoletto Spumante 7note — 🍷🍷 2*
- ⊙ Lambrusco di Modena Rosato Vini del Re '19 — 🍷 2
- ● Lambrusco Grasparossa di Castelvetro DiVino '19 — 🍷 2
- ○ Pignoletto di Modena '19 — 🍷 1*
- ● Lambrusco Grasparossa di Castelvetro Secco '15 — 🍷🍷 1*
- ● Lambrusco Grasparossa di Castelvetro Secco Divino '15 — 🍷🍷 1*
- ● Lambrusco Grasparossa di Castelvetro Secco Vini del Re '15 — 🍷🍷 1*

Terre Cevico

via Fiumazzo, 72
48022 Lugo [RA]
Tel. +39 0545284711
www.gruppocevico.com

CELLAR SALES
PRE-BOOKED VISITS
ANNUAL PRODUCTION 50,000,000 bottles
HECTARES UNDER VINE 7000.00

Founded in 1963, Cevico is one of the most important cooperatives in the region. Today about five thousand members bring their grapes to the processing and bottling facilities in Lugo di Romagna, Forlì and Reggio Emilia. Such large production figures have led, naturally, to the birth of various projects and brands, some of which are rather limited in quantity and sought after in terms of quality, like Galassi, Sancrispino, Ronco, Romandiola, Bernardi. Among their various lines, we very much appreciated the Novilunio '18, a Romandiola DOC. It's a modern red, but capable of good rhythm, offering up notes of violets and berries accompanied by sensations of plum, which just peep out and enlarge its aromatic suite. Oak is evident but doesn't smother its fruit and will blend further in the bottle; a fleshy palate sees solid tannic support. Excellent performance for the Sangiovese Galassi '19 as well.

- ● Romagna Sangiovese Sup. Romandiola Novilunio '18 — 🍷🍷 2*
- ● Romagna Sangiovese Vign. Galassi '19 — 🍷🍷 2*
- ○ Romagna Albana Secco Massellina '19 — 🍷 2
- ● Romagna Sangiovese Sup. Massellina 138 '19 — 🍷 3
- ○ Albana di Romagna Secco Nova Luna '18 — 🍷🍷 3
- ● Romagna Sangiovese La Romandiola Il Malatesta '18 — 🍷🍷 3
- ● Romagna Sangiovese La Romandiola Nova Luna '18 — 🍷🍷 3
- ● Romagna Sangiovese Sup. Vign. Galassi '17 — 🍷🍷 2*
- ● Romagna Sangiovese Sup. Vign. Galassi '16 — 🍷🍷 2*
- ● Romagna Sangiovese Sup. Vign. Galassi '15 — 🍷🍷 2*

Torre San Martino

via Morana, 14
47015 Modigliana [FC]
Tel. +39 0546940102
www.torre1922.it

CELLAR SALES
PRE-BOOKED VISITS
ANNUAL PRODUCTION 45,000 bottles
HECTARES UNDER VINE 15.00

Torre San Martino is situated in one of the three valleys of Modigliana that rise up towards the Apennines—Acerreta to be precise. Here the producer avails itself of an extraordinary viticultural patrimony, with some of their vines dating back to the 1920s. They are spectacular not only for their age, as at certain points they form veritable natural amphitheaters. Elevations reach 300 metres, while the soils are the area's classic clay, resulting in a distinct style: reds that are intense and firmly structured, but always well balanced and deep. As usual the Sangiovese Vigna 1922 delivered. The 2017 vintage inevitably expresses greater maturity, both aromatically and in the mouth: it's a quite vibrant red, marked by aromas of fruit (plum, black cherry and blueberry) adorned by a certain roastiness. The palate comes through full, powerful, with excellent structure and tannic substance. We'll be sure to follow its evolution in the bottle.

- ● Romagna Sangiovese Modigliana V. 1922 '17 — 🍷🍷 7
- ● Flos Arenaria '17 — 🍷 5
- ● Romagna Sangiovese Modigliana Gemme '18 — 🍷 5
- ● Romagna Sangiovese Modigliana Sup. V. 1922 Ris. '13 — 🍷🍷🍷 6
- ● Romagna Sangiovese Sup. Gemme '14 — 🍷🍷🍷 3*
- ● Sangiovese di Romagna V. 1922 Ris. '11 — 🍷🍷🍷 6
- ● Romagna Sangiovese Modigliana Sup. Gemme '15 — 🍷🍷 3*
- ● Romagna Sangiovese Modigliana V. 1922 '16 — 🍷🍷 7
- ● Romagna Sangiovese Modigliana V. 1922 '15 — 🍷🍷 5

La Tosa

LOC. LA TOSA
29020 VIGOLZONE [PC]
TEL. +39 0523870727
www.latosa.it

CELLAR SALES
PRE-BOOKED VISITS
RESTAURANT SERVICE
ANNUAL PRODUCTION 110,000 bottles
HECTARES UNDER VINE 19.00
VITICULTURE METHOD Certified Organic

Stefano and Ferruccio Pizzamiglio have a special history. Both left Milan and their previous careers to return to their native hills and to build a benchmark producer for the viticulture of the area. The farmhouse was purchased in 1980, together with some land, initially to relax on weekends. Four years later the winery was born. From there the producer has been on an upward trajectory, with a style that culminates in the interpretation of traditional grape varieties. The Malvasia secca Sorriso di Cielo is always a sure bet. Varietal and fragrant, with scents ranging from passion fruit to aromatic herbs, from citron to pineapple, it made it into our finals by virtue of its expressive, full-bodied and supple palate, and a sapid, balanced finish. The Ora Felice '18 is a Malvasia passito in which candied citrus fruits and orange peel emerge clean and fragrant. The TerreDellaTosa '19 is a youthful Gutturnio, in which Barbera's acidity and cherry aromas lend freshness.

○ C. P. Malvasia Sorriso di Cielo '19	🍷🍷 4
● Gutturnio Sup. TerredellaTosa '19	🍷🍷 3
○ L'Ora Felice Malvasia Passito '18	🍷🍷 5
● C. P. Cabernet Sauvignon Luna Selvatica '18	🍷 5
○ C. P. Sauvignon '19	🍷 3
● Gutturnio Sup. Vignamorello '18	🍷 4
● C. P. Cabernet Sauvignon Luna Selvatica '06	🍷🍷🍷 5
● C. P. Cabernet Sauvignon Luna Selvatica '04	🍷🍷🍷 5
● C. P. Cabernet Sauvignon Luna Selvatica '97	🍷🍷🍷 5
● C. P. Cabernet Sauvignon Luna Selvatica '17	🍷🍷 5
○ C. P. Malvasia Sorriso di Cielo '18	🍷🍷 3
● Gutturnio Sup. Vignamorello '17	🍷🍷 4

Tre Monti

FRAZ. BERGULLO
VIA LOLA, 3
40026 IMOLA [BO]
TEL. +39 0542657116
www.tremonti.it

CELLAR SALES
PRE-BOOKED VISITS
ANNUAL PRODUCTION 200,000 bottles
HECTARES UNDER VINE 40.00
VITICULTURE METHOD Certified Organic
SUSTAINABLE WINERY

At Tre Monti generations of family are working together to carry the winery into the future. Indeed, founded in the 1970s, it has since shown great family continuity. Their vineyards are concentrated on the farms of Bergullo (in the hills of Imola) and Petrignone (in Forlivese). Albana and Sangiovese are cultivated together with other local and international varieties. Special attention, however, is reserved for the Romagna white grape variety par excellence, which is offered in various versions, all of which are truly intriguing and successful. The white Thea '19 performs spectacularly well. It's an unusual Petit Manseng in the land of Romagna. A bright, vibrant yellow color is the prelude to expressive aromas of grape skin and white peach accompanied by a very original touch of saffron. The palate is fleshy and creamy, austere and gratifying, closing on mineral and citrus sensations. The Albana Vitalba '19 also delivered, offering up something more in terms of pulp and tannins; we were less convinced by the Vigna Rocca '19.

○ Romagna Albana Secco Vitalba '19	🍷🍷 4
○ Thea '19	🍷🍷 4
○ Anablà	🍷 3
○ Romagna Albana V. Rocca '19	🍷 2
● Colli di Imola Boldo '97	🍷🍷🍷 3*
○ Romagna Albana Secco Vitalba '18	🍷🍷🍷 4*
● Sangiovese di Romagna Sup. Petrignone Ris. '08	🍷🍷🍷 3*
● Sangiovese di Romagna Sup. Petrignone Ris. '07	🍷🍷🍷 4
● Sangiovese di Romagna Sup. Petrignone Ris. '06	🍷🍷🍷 3
○ Romagna Albana V. Rocca '18	🍷🍷 2*
○ Romagna Albana V. Rocca '17	🍷🍷 2*
● Romagna Sangiovese Sup. Campo di Mezzo '17	🍷🍷 2*
● Romagna Sangiovese Sup. Petrignone Ris. '16	🍷🍷 3

Trerè

loc. Monticoralli
via Casale, 19
48018 Faenza [RA]
Tel. +39 054647034
www.trere.com

CELLAR SALES
PRE-BOOKED VISITS
ACCOMMODATION AND RESTAURANT SERVICE
ANNUAL PRODUCTION 150,000 bottles
HECTARES UNDER VINE 35.00
SUSTAINABLE WINERY

Founded in the early 1960s by Valeriano Trerè, over time this producer has grown both in terms of wine produced and awareness. It's situated on the hills of Faenza, where the original plots were purchased, and has since expanded. It's also worth mentioning the investments made in the hospitality sector, as guests are offered the possibility of having an all-round experience in the wine-growing heart of the region. When it comes to the grapes cultivated, from the outset they've focused on native varieties, making for aptly modern wines that aren't lacking in character either. Many wines were tasted, including the excellent Sangiovese Superiore Violeo Riserva '16. Vinified in steel tanks and aged in barriques for 18 months, it features aromas of black berries adorned with spicy touches; the palate is juicy, balanced nicely by tannic substance, finishing on sensations of roots. A step below, but still delicious, the Sangiovese Vigna dello Sperone '19 is obviously more immediate and fresh. We also point out the excellent Re Famoso '19.

Wine	Rating
● Romagna Sangiovese Sup. Violeo Ris. '16	🍷🍷 5
○ Re Famoso '19	🍷🍷 2*
● Romagna Sangiovese Lôna Bôna '19	🍷🍷 2*
● Romagna Sangiovese Sup. Amarcord d'un Ross Ris. '17	🍷🍷 3
● Romagna Sangiovese Sup. V. dello Sperone '19	🍷🍷 2*
○ Re Famoso '18	🍷🍷 2*
○ Romagna Albana Secco Arlùs '17	🍷🍷 2*
● Romagna Sangiovese Lona Bona '18	🍷🍷 2*
● Romagna Sangiovese Lôna Bôna '17	🍷🍷 2*
● Romagna Sangiovese Sup. Sperone '18	🍷🍷 2*

Marta Valpiani

via Bagnolo, 158
47011 Castrocaro Terme e Terra del Sole [FC]
Tel. +39 0543769598
www.vinimartavalpiani.it

CELLAR SALES
PRE-BOOKED VISITS
ANNUAL PRODUCTION 19,000 bottles
HECTARES UNDER VINE 11.50

Marta Valpiani, which is named after the winery's owner and founder, got its start in 1999 in Castrocaro Terme. Today her daughter Elisa Mazzavillani is leading things. It was she, especially, who gave the producer its extraordinary driving force, reshaping the existing organization and perfecting an increasingly convincing stylistic formula. A new cellar signals that things are moving in the right direction, and is proving perfect for processing the grapes from the vineyards of geographical mention. The result is a nuanced selection of wines, delicate, floral and highly drinkable. A benchmark for Romagna's wine, the Sangiovese Crete Azzurre '18 features an elegant nose, intensely floral and delicately fruity; on the palate it's intriguing, appetizing, with nice texture—it's just a little held back by lively tannins and dilution by alcohol at the end. Simpler but still well made, the Sangiovese Superiore '18 is a juicy, stylistically coherent wine.

Wine	Rating
● Romagna Sangiovese Castrocaro e Terra del Sole Crete Azzurre '18	🍷🍷 3*
● Romagna Sangiovese Sup. '18	🍷🍷 2*
○ Delyus '19	🍷 2
● La Farfalla '19	🍷 2
● Romagna Sangiovese Castrocaro e Terra del Sole Crete Azzurre '15	🍷🍷🍷 3*
○ Marta Valpiani Bianco '17	🍷🍷 3
○ Romagna Albana Secco Madonna dei Fiori '18	🍷🍷 3
● Romagna Sangiovese Castrocaro e Terra del Sole Crete Azzurre '16	🍷🍷 3*
● Romagna Sangiovese Sup. '17	🍷🍷 2*

Cantina Valtidone

via Moretta, 58
29011 Borgonovo Val Tidone [PC]
Tel. +39 0523846411
www.cantinavaltidone.it

CELLAR SALES
PRE-BOOKED VISITS
ANNUAL PRODUCTION 6,500,000 bottles
HECTARES UNDER VINE 1100.00
VITICULTURE METHOD Certified Organic
SUSTAINABLE WINERY

Founded in 1966, Cantina Valtidone has grown in numbers (from 16 to 220 members), in size and, especially in recent years, in the desire to produce more and better wines. Great attention is paid to selecting the best grapes for traditional, well-structured Piacenza wines represented by their '50 Vendemmie' line, which is made with vines planted in the sixties. The new challenge, launched thanks to enologist Francesco Fissore, is Metodo Classico. This year's new release is the Arvange, a Pinot Nero-based Pas Dosé that spends 44 months on the lees. Pleasantly evolved, sapid, linear and powerful, it exhibits very fine bead—Tre Bicchieri for this truly lovely Metodo Classico. We also appreciated the Perlage. A small percentage of extra Chardonnay makes for aromas of herbs, peach and lime, while the Magnum version, which spends 60 months on the lees, features hints of pastry and bread crust. The full-bodied Bollo Rosso '16 is a balsamic, spicy Gutturnio Riserva. The whole range, starting from the 50 Vendemmie line, performs at high levels.

Wine	Rating
○ Arvange Pas Dosé M. Cl.	▼▼▼ 4*
○ Perlage Brut M. Cl.	▼▼ 4
● Gutturnio Bollo Rosso Ris. '16	▼▼ 4
● Gutturnio Cl. Sup. 50 Vendemmie '19	▼▼ 3
○ Perlage Brut M. Cl. Magnum	▼▼ 6
○ C. P. Malvasia 50 Vendemmie '19	▼ 3
○ Colli Piacentini Malvasia Spumante Dolce Venus '19	▼ 3
● Gutturnio Frizzante 50 Vendemmie '19	▼ 3
○ Zefiro Ortrugo '19	▼ 2
● C. P. Barbera Castelli del Duca Ranuccio '11	▽▽ 2*
● C. P. Bonarda Castelli del Duca Ottavio '11	▽▽ 2*
○ C. P. Malvasia 50 Vendemmie '17	▽▽ 2*
● Gutturnio Bollo Rosso Ris. '15	▽▽ 4
● Gutturnio Cl. Sup 50 Vendemmie '18	▽▽ 3

VentiVenti - Il Borghetto

loc. s.da prov.le 5
via della Saliceta, 15
41036 Medolla [MO]
Tel. +39 3440330771
www.ventiventi.it

CELLAR SALES
PRE-BOOKED VISITS
ANNUAL PRODUCTION 40,000 bottles
HECTARES UNDER VINE 30.00
VITICULTURE METHOD Certified Organic

VentiVenti is the Razzaboni family's dream come true. Vittorio, already owner of Il Borghetto, together with his sons Riccardo, Andrea and Tommaso, has created a beautiful winery. The name is dedicated to the year in which the cellar was completed, a year that marked the beginning of a project involving 18 hectares of vineyards (they own almost 50 hectares total), with another 11 soon to be planted. Lambrusco di Sorbara, Salamino di Santa Croce, Pignoletto and Ancellotta, as well as some international grapes, are grown in the area north of Modena. The Ricanto Rosato '18 is delicious in its fruity and floral notes. Blackberries, currants and cherries anticipate a fresh, graceful palate, with a linear development and a crystalline, clean finish. Among the sparkling wines, the VentiVenti Rosé Metodo Classico, a characteristic and fragrant Lambrusco di Modena, stands out. We found the Lambrusco Salamino di Santa Croce Brut, another Metodo Classico, interesting, even if a bit rustic.

Wine	Rating
⊙ Lambrusco di Modena Brut Rosé M. Cl.	▼▼ 5
⊙ Ricanto Rosato '18	▼▼ 4
⊙ Lambrusco Salamino Santa Croce Brut M. Cl.	▼ 4

Venturini Baldini

FRAZ. RONCOLO
VIA TURATI, 42
42020 QUATTRO CASTELLA [RE]
TEL. +39 0522249011
www.venturinibaldini.it

CELLAR SALES
PRE-BOOKED VISITS
RESTAURANT SERVICE
ANNUAL PRODUCTION 90,000 bottles
HECTARES UNDER VINE 35.00
VITICULTURE METHOD Certified Organic
SUSTAINABLE WINERY

The current business came to light in 1976 under the Venturini Baldini family. The 16th-century Villa Manodori, built on the foundations of a structure dating back to the times of Matilde di Canossa, serves as the heart of the property. 32 hectares of vineyards have been organically farmed for years on hills that reach almost 400 meters elevation. In addition to Lambrusco, the producer focuses on native grape varieties such as Malbo Gentile, Spergola and Montericco. The estate is now owned by the Prestia family, who avail themselves of the guidance of Carlo Ferrini. The Cadelvento is a Brut Rosato made with 70% Sorbara and 30% Grasparossa. It always stands out thanks to its forthright aromas of berries, blackberry and blueberry in particular, accompanied by aromatic herbs, wild flowers and citrus fruits. In the mouth it's consistent, broad, fresh and fragrant. The Marquis Manodori '19, a blend of four grapes (Maestri, Marani, Grasparossa and Salamino, in equal parts) proves well made, very fruit-forward and balanced in its residual sugars.

Wine	Rating
⊙ Reggiano Lambrusco Brut Rosato Cadelvento	🍷🍷 3*
● Reggiano Lambrusco Marchese Manodori '19	🍷🍷 2*
○ Brut M. Cl. '15	🍷 4
⊙ Reggiano Lambrusco Brut Cadelvento Rosé '18	🍷🍷🍷 3*
⊙ Reggiano Lambrusco Brut Cadelvento Rosé '17	🍷🍷🍷 3*
● Reggiano Lambrusco Marchese Manodori '16	🍷🍷🍷 3*
● Reggiano Lambrusco Brut Rubino del Cerro '17	🍷🍷 3
● Reggiano Lambrusco Marchese Manodori '17	🍷🍷 3*
⊙ Reggiano Lambrusco Rosato Spumante Secco Cadelvento '15	🍷🍷 3

Villa di Corlo

LOC. BAGGIOVARA
S.DA CAVEZZO, 200
41126 MODENA
TEL. +39 059510736
www.villadicorlo.com

CELLAR SALES
PRE-BOOKED VISITS
ANNUAL PRODUCTION 100,000 bottles
HECTARES UNDER VINE 16.50
VITICULTURE METHOD Certified Organic

Maria Antonietta Munari oversees this beautiful estate in southwest Modena, in one of the best areas for Grasparossa di Castelvetro. Higher up, at over 300 meters above sea level, on slopes mostly facing south / southeast, we find Pignoletto and some international grapes, including Chardonnay, which is used for their Metodo Classico sparklers. In the attic of the beautiful villa two traditional balsamic vinegars are also produced. As of 2012, the producer is powered entirely by photovoltaic panels. They submitted an excellent selection of Grasparossa di Castelvetro. The Corleto has a fragrant, fresh nose, while in the mouth it unfolds, balancing tannins and residual sugars nicely. The Secco offers up lovely notes of ripe berries, with blackberry and blueberry at the fore, fruity sensations that return in the mouth across a long finish. The Olimpia, the sweet version, is also characterized by nice, broad and ripe fruit.

Wine	Rating
● Lambrusco Grasparossa di Castelvetro Corleto	🍷🍷 2*
● Lambrusco Grasparossa di Castelvetro Secco	🍷🍷 2*
● Lambrusco Grasparossa di Castelvetro Semisecco Olimpia	🍷🍷 2*
● Lambrusco di Sorbara Primevo	🍷 2
● Lambrusco di Sorbara Primevo '18	🍷🍷 2*
● Lambrusco Grasparossa di Castelvetro Corleto '18	🍷🍷 2*
● Lambrusco Grasparossa di Castelvetro Corleto '17	🍷🍷 2*
● Lambrusco Grasparossa di Castelvetro Semisecco Olimpia Bio '18	🍷🍷 2*
● Lambrusco Grasparossa di Castelvetro Villa di Corlo '18	🍷🍷 2*

Villa Papiano

via Ibola, 24
47015 Modigliana [FC]
Tel. +39 3381041271
www.villapapiano.it

CELLAR SALES
PRE-BOOKED VISITS
ANNUAL PRODUCTION 50,000 bottles
HECTARES UNDER VINE 10.00
VITICULTURE METHOD Certified Organic
SUSTAINABLE WINERY

Villa Papiano belongs to the Bordini family, a 'loaded' name when it comes to Romagna's wine. Francesco is mainly involved in the stylistic and production front together with Maria Rosa, Giampaolo and Enrica. The territory is bound up with the Apennines by the National Park of the Casentino Forests, where the woods are fringed by lean soils and the hills reach higher. These characteristics confer flavor, mineral sensations and expressive depth, proving a perfect combination and revealing skilled production techniques. The Sangiovese Modigliana Probi Riserva '17 thumbs its nose at the vintage and soars, earning itself a place among Romagna's best wines. It's marked by excellent aromatic coherence, both on the nose and in the mouth, amidst sensations of blood orange, wild flowers and small berries; on the palate it exhibits commendable texture, with tannin as strong as they are tasty. It's a great wine that will only continue to improve in the bottle. The Sangiovese Superiore Papesse '19 is young but ageworthy.

- ● Romagna Sangiovese Modigliana I Probi Ris. '17 — 🍷🍷🍷 4*
- ● Romagna Sangiovese Sup. Le Papesse '19 — 🍷🍷 3
- ● Centesimino '16 — 🍷 4
- ● Romagna Sangiovese Modigliana I Probi di Papiano Ris. '15 — ☐☐☐ 4*
- ● Romagna Sangiovese Modigliana I Probi di Papiano Ris. '14 — ☐☐☐ 4*
- ● Romagna Sangiovese Modigliana I Probi di Papiano Ris. '13 — ☐☐☐ 3*
- ● Romagna Sangiovese Modigliana I Probi Ris. '16 — ☐☐ 6
- ● Romagna Sangiovese Sup. Le Papesse '18 — ☐☐ 3

Villa Venti

loc. Villaventi di Roncofreddo
via Doccia, 1442
47020 Forlì
Tel. +39 0541949532
www.villaventi.it

CELLAR SALES
PRE-BOOKED VISITS
ACCOMMODATION
ANNUAL PRODUCTION 30,000 bottles
HECTARES UNDER VINE 7.00
VITICULTURE METHOD Certified Organic

We find Villa Venti beyond the Rubicon, on the slopes of the hills of Roncofreddo and Longiano, in the province of Cesena overlooking the sea. Here Mauro Giardini and Davide Castellucci work in harmony with nature and the rhythms of the seasons. The vineyard is part of an agricultural ecosystem that finds in wine the symbol of their production philosophy: the secret is clean agriculture, combined with a style capable of innovating on the recent past, especially when it comes to Sangiovese. And so it is that we get to enjoy selections that are as pure as they are tasty, offered in various versions and drawing on different cultivars. The delicious Primo Segno '18 topped our preferences. It's a Sangiovese Superiore that gives up a bit of compactness so as to bring its usual finesse to the highest levels. In short, airy aromas of fresh flowers and raspberries, a racy and juicy palate, and a long, sapid finish. We also appreciated the amusing Centesimino '19, with its aromas of rose and its supremely fresh palate.

- ● Romagna Sangiovese Sup. Primo Segno '18 — 🍷🍷🍷 3*
- ● Centesimino A '19 — 🍷🍷 4
- ● Romagna Sangiovese Sup. Primo Segno '17 — ☐☐☐ 3*
- ● Sangiovese di Romagna Longiano Primo Segno '11 — ☐☐☐ 3*
- ● Romagna Sangiovese Longiano Ris. '16 — ☐☐ 5
- ● Romagna Sangiovese Sup. Primo Segno '16 — ☐☐ 3*
- ● Sangiovese di Romagna Sup. Primo Segno '13 — ☐☐ 3*

★Fattoria Zerbina

FRAZ. MARZENO
VIA VICCHIO, 11
48018 FAENZA [RA]
TEL. +39 054640022
www.zerbina.com

CELLAR SALES
PRE-BOOKED VISITS
ANNUAL PRODUCTION 220,000 bottles
HECTARES UNDER VINE 33.00

Cristina Geminiani is the face, heart and hands of Fattoria Zerbina, one of Romagna wine's classic producers. After all, its beginnings are well in the past. In 1966 the farm was purchased, the vineyards were planted and the first wines were made. The subzone is that of Marzeno, with its red clay and futuristic head-trained viticulture, while Albana and Sangiovese have grown in importance, generating impressive successes especially on the sweet wines front. The present is evolving, as usual with an eye to the future. The Albana Passito Scaccomatto is one of Italy's benchmark sweet wines, and the 2016 is no exception. Indeed it elevates the typology, proving simply marvelous in its delicately floral notes, which sew together an elegant weave supported by sensations of white peach, tropical fruit and almonds. Hints of spice emerge as well, all on an iodine background that balances the palate—a masterpiece destined to endure over time.

Wine	Rating
○ Romagna Albana Passito Scaccomatto '16	🍷🍷🍷 7
○ Romagna Albana Secco Bianco di Ceparano '19	🍷🍷 2*
○ Romagna Trebbiano Ceregio Bianco '19	🍷🍷 2*
○ Tergeno '19	🍷🍷 3
● Romagna Sangiovese Marzeno Pietramora Ris. '16	🍷 5
● Romagna Sangiovese Sup. Ceregio '19	🍷 2
○ Albana di Romagna Passito AR Ris. '06	🍷🍷🍷 8
● Marzieno '08	🍷🍷🍷 4*
○ Romagna Albana Passito Scaccomatto '13	🍷🍷🍷 6
● Sangiovese di Romagna Sup. Pietramora Ris. '11	🍷🍷🍷 5
● Sangiovese di Romagna Sup. Pietramora Ris. '08	🍷🍷🍷 6

Zucchi

LOC. SAN LORENZO
VIA VIAZZA, 64
41030 SAN PROSPERO [MO]
TEL. +39 059908934
www.vinizucchi.it

CELLAR SALES
PRE-BOOKED VISITS
ACCOMMODATION
ANNUAL PRODUCTION 130,000 bottles
HECTARES UNDER VINE 10.00
SUSTAINABLE WINERY

Zucchi is situated in Lambrusco di Sorbara wine country where its founder, Bruno Zucchi, began making his own starting in the 1950s. He's been flanked by his son Davide and his wife, Maura, while Silvia Zucchi, an enologist, represents the third generation of family to support the winery. Thanks to the knowledge she acquired in Italy and abroad, she's managed to raise the quality of their wines even further, offering Sorbara in various versions, all true to the territory. The selections that undergo bottle fermentation are also interesting. The Marascone is a Lambrusco from Modena made with 100% Santa Croce Salamino. It has a nice, fresh nose of berries, blueberry and raspberry, fruity sensations that return intact on the palate, where it's pulpy, making for a rich, tasty drink. We also appreciated the Rito, a sparkling Sorbara rosé redolent of wild rose, mandarin and lime. In the mouth it proves elegant and plucky.

Wine	Rating
⊙ Lambrusco di Sorbara Brut Rosé Rito	🍷🍷 3
● Modena Lambrusco Marascone	🍷🍷 2*
● Lambrusco di Sorbara Dosaggio Zero M. Cl. '17	🍷 2
● Lambrusco di Sorbara Rito '14	🍷🍷🍷 2*
● Lambrusco di Sorbara Secco Rito '15	🍷🍷🍷 2*
● Lambrusco di Modena Marascone '16	🍷🍷 2*
● Lambrusco di Sorbara Dosaggio Zero M. Cl.'16	🍷🍷 5
● Lambrusco di Sorbara Dosaggio Zero M. Cl. '13	🍷🍷 2*
● Lambrusco di Sorbara Et. Bianca '17	🍷🍷 2*
● Lambrusco di Sorbara Fermentato in Questa Bottiglia '17	🍷🍷 3
● Lambrusco di Sorbara Rito '16	🍷🍷 3
● Lambrusco di Sorbara Secco '15	🍷🍷 2*
● Modena Lambrusco Marascone '17	🍷🍷 2*

Albinea Canali

FRAZ. CANALI
VIA TASSONI, 213
42123 REGGIO EMILIA
TEL. +39 0522569505
www.albineacanali.it

CELLAR SALES
PRE-BOOKED VISITS
ANNUAL PRODUCTION 492,000 bottles
HECTARES UNDER VINE 150.00
VITICULTURE METHOD Certified Organic
SUSTAINABLE WINERY

- ● Colli di Scandiano e Canossa Lambrusco Grasparossa Amabile Codarossa 🍷🍷 2*
- ⊙ Rosé Pas Dosé M. Cl. 🍷🍷 5

Vittorio Assirelli

VIA MONTE DEL RE, 31P
40060 DOZZA [BO]
TEL. +39 0542678303
www.cantinadavittorio.com

- ○ Romagna Albana Passito Piccolo Fiore '15 🍷🍷 4
- ○ Romagna Albana Secco L'Albena d'Doza '19 🍷🍷 2*
- ● Romagna Sangiovese Sup. Ris. '16 🍷🍷 2*

Riccardo Ballardini

VIA PIDEURA, 50
48013 BRISIGHELLA [RA]
TEL. +39 0543 700925
www.ballardinivini.it

CELLAR SALES
PRE-BOOKED VISITS
ANNUAL PRODUCTION 100,000 bottles
HECTARES UNDER VINE 30.00

- ○ Romagna Albana Secco Leggiadro '19 🍷🍷 3
- ● Romagna Sangiovese Sup. V. Le Case '19 🍷🍷 3
- ● Romagna Sangiovese Sup. Torricello Ris. '17 🍷 3

Conte Otto Barattieri di San Pietro

VIA DEI TIGLI, 100
29020 VIGOLZONE [PC]
TEL. +39 0523875111
ottobarattieri@libero.it

CELLAR SALES
PRE-BOOKED VISITS
ANNUAL PRODUCTION 120,000 bottles
HECTARES UNDER VINE 34.00

- ○ C. P. Vin Santo Albarola '09 🍷🍷 6
- ● Cabernet Sauvignon '16 🍷🍷 4
- ○ La Berganzina Sauvignon '19 🍷🍷 3

Tenuta Bonzara

LOC. SANCHIERLO
VIA SANCHIERLO, 37A
40050 MONTE SAN PIETRO [BO]
TEL. +39 0516768324
www.bonzara.it

CELLAR SALES
PRE-BOOKED VISITS
ACCOMMODATION AND RESTAURANT SERVICE
ANNUAL PRODUCTION 70,000 bottles
HECTARES UNDER VINE 13.60

- ● C. B. Bologna Rosso '18 🍷🍷 3
- ● Negretto #1.0 '18 🍷🍷 2*
- ○ Pignoletto Passito U' Pasa '17 🍷 5

Branchini

FRAZ. TOSCANELLA DI DOZZA
VIA MARSIGLIA, 3
40060 DOZZA [BO]
TEL. +39 054253778
branchini1858@libero.it

- ○ Romagna Albana Secco Dutia '19 🍷🍷 2*
- ● Romagna Sangiovese Sup. Contrà Grande '18 🍷🍷 2*
- ○ Romagna Albana Passito D'or Luce '16 🍷 3

Ca' de' Medici

loc. Cadè
via della Stazione, 34
42040 Reggio Emilia
Tel. +39 0522942141
www.cademedici.it

CELLAR SALES
PRE-BOOKED VISITS

- ● Colli di Scandiano e di Canossa Lambrusco Grasparossa Remigio 100 ŦŦ 2*
- ● Reggiano Lambrusco Scuro Piazza San Prospero ŦŦ 2*

Cantina di Soliera

via Carpi Ravarino, 529
41011 Soliera [MO]
Tel. +39 0522942135
www.cantinadisoliera.it

ANNUAL PRODUCTION 20,000 bottles
HECTARES UNDER VINE 5.00
SUSTAINABLE WINERY

- ● Lambrusco Grasparossa di Castelvetro Amabile ŦŦ 2*
- ● Lambrusco Salamino di Santa Croce Semisecco ŦŦ 2*

Tenuta Casali

via della Liberazione, 32
47025 Mercato Saraceno [FC]
Tel. +39 0547690334
www.tenutacasali.it

PRE-BOOKED VISITS
ANNUAL PRODUCTION 95,000 bottles
HECTARES UNDER VINE 18.00

- ● Romagna Sangiovese San Vinicio Quarto Sole Ris '17 ŦŦ 3
- ● Romagna Sangiovese Sup. V. Palazzina '18 ŦŦ 2*

Casali Viticultori

fraz. Pratissolo
via delle Scuole, 7
42019 Scandiano [RE]
Tel. +39 0522855441
www.casalivini.it

CELLAR SALES
PRE-BOOKED VISITS
ANNUAL PRODUCTION 1,500,000 bottles
HECTARES UNDER VINE 48.00

- ● Colli di Scandiano e di Canossa Lambrusco Secco Feudi del Boiardo '19 ŦŦ 2*
- ● Reggiano Lambrusco Secco Pra di Bosso '19 ŦŦ 2*

Castelluccio

loc. Poggiolo di Sotto
via Tramonto, 15
47015 Modigliana [FC]
Tel. +39 0546942486
www.ronchidicastelluccio.it

CELLAR SALES
PRE-BOOKED VISITS
ACCOMMODATION
ANNUAL PRODUCTION 85,000 bottles
HECTARES UNDER VINE 16.00

- ● Romagna Sangiovese Sup. Le More '19 ŦŦ 3
- ● Ronco delle Ginestre '15 Ŧ 5
- ○ Sauvignon Blanc '19 Ŧ 5

Collina del Tesoro

loc. Massa di Vecchiazzano
via del Tesoro, 18
47121 Forlì
Tel. +39 3490513709
www.lacollinadeltesoro.it

CELLAR SALES
ANNUAL PRODUCTION 60,000 bottles
HECTARES UNDER VINE 24.00
VITICULTURE METHOD Certified Organic

- ● Romagna Sangiovese Predappio Nature SSA '19 ŦŦ 3
- ● Romagna Sangiovese Sup. Roserosse '16 Ŧ 4

Corte d'Aibo

via Marzatore, 15
40050 Monteveglio [BO]
Tel. +39 051832583
www.cortedaibo.it

CELLAR SALES
PRE-BOOKED VISITS
ANNUAL PRODUCTION 90,000 bottles
HECTARES UNDER VINE 18.00
VITICULTURE METHOD Certified Organic

- ● C. B. Barbera Frizzante '18 🍷🍷 2*
- ● Meriggio '18 🍷🍷 3
- ● C. B. Cabernet Sauvignon '15 🍷 4

Ferraia - Roberto Manara

loc. Vicomarino, 140
29010 Ziano Piacentino [PC]
Tel. +39 0523860209
www.ferraiawinery.it

CELLAR SALES
PRE-BOOKED VISITS
ANNUAL PRODUCTION 150,000 bottles
HECTARES UNDER VINE 40.00

- ○ C. P. Ortrugo Frizzante '19 🍷🍷 2*
- ● Gutturnio Cl. Sup. Le Staffe '19 🍷 3
- ● Gutturnio Frizzante '19 🍷 2

Stefano Ferrucci

via Casolana, 3045
48014 Castel Bolognese [RA]
Tel. +39 0546651068
www.stefanoferrucci.it

CELLAR SALES
PRE-BOOKED VISITS
ANNUAL PRODUCTION 130,000 bottles
HECTARES UNDER VINE 16.00

- ○ Romagna Albana Passito Domus Aurea '18 🍷🍷 5
- ● Romagna Sangiovese Sup. Domus Caia Ris. '17 🍷🍷 5

Fondo Cà Vecja

loc. Ponticelli
via Montanara, 333
40020 Imola [BO]
Tel. +39 0542665194
www.fondocavecja.com

CELLAR SALES
PRE-BOOKED VISITS
ACCOMMODATION
ANNUAL PRODUCTION 40,000 bottles
HECTARES UNDER VINE 19.00
SUSTAINABLE WINERY

- ○ Romagna Albana Querciola '19 🍷🍷 2*
- ○ Due Pievi Manzoni Bianco '19 🍷🍷 2*
- ○ Colvento Sauvignon '19 🍷 3

Paolo Francesconi

loc. Sarna
via Tuliero, 154
48018 Faenza [RA]
Tel. +39 054643213
www.francesconipaolo.it

CELLAR SALES
PRE-BOOKED VISITS
ANNUAL PRODUCTION 20,000 bottles
HECTARES UNDER VINE 8.40
VITICULTURE METHOD Certified Biodynamic
SUSTAINABLE WINERY

- ● Romagna Sangiovese Sup. Limbecca '17 🍷🍷 3
- ● Rosso '19 🍷🍷 2*
- ● Vite in Fiore '19 🍷 3

Maria Galassi

fraz. Paderno
via Via Casetta, 688
47522 Cesena [FC]
Tel. +39 3387230288
www.galassimaria.it

CELLAR SALES
PRE-BOOKED VISITS
ACCOMMODATION
ANNUAL PRODUCTION 40,000 bottles
HECTARES UNDER VINE 30.00
VITICULTURE METHOD Certified Organic
SUSTAINABLE WINERY

- ○ Romagna Albana Secco La Sgnòra '19 🍷🍷 3
- ○ Fiaba '19 🍷 3

Garuti

FRAZ. SORBARA
VIA PER SOLARA, 6
41030 BOMPORTO [MO]
TEL. +39 059902021
www.garutivini.it

ANNUAL PRODUCTION 120,000 bottles
HECTARES UNDER VINE 30.00

- ⊙ Lambrusco di Sorbara Brut Rosato Valentina '19 — 3
- ● Lambrusco di Sorbara Dante Secco '19 — 2*
- ● Lambrusco di Sorbara Garuti Secco '19 — 2

La Grotta

LOC. SAIANO
VIA CIMADORI, 621
47023 CESENA [FC]
TEL. +39 0547326368
www.lagrottavini.it

CELLAR SALES
PRE-BOOKED VISITS
ANNUAL PRODUCTION 30,000 bottles
HECTARES UNDER VINE 12.00
VITICULTURE METHOD Certified Organic
SUSTAINABLE WINERY

- ● Romagna Sangiovese Sup. Cleto Ris. '16 — 4
- ● Romagna Sangiovese Sup. Mazapegul '19 — 2*
- ○ Romagna Albana Secco Damadora '19 — 3

Giovanna Madonia

LOC. VILLA MADONIA
VIA DE' CAPPUCCINI, 130
47032 BERTINORO [FC]
TEL. +39 0543444361
www.giovannamadonia.it

CELLAR SALES
PRE-BOOKED VISITS
RESTAURANT SERVICE
ANNUAL PRODUCTION 60,000 bottles
HECTARES UNDER VINE 16.00

- ● Romagna Sangiovese Bertinoro Ombroso Ris. '17 — 5
- ● Romagna Sangiovese Sup. Fermavento '18 — 3
- ● Tenentino '19 — 2*

Manaresi

LOC. POD. BELLA VISTA
VIA BERTOLONI , 14/16
40069 ZOLA PREDOSA [BO]
TEL. +39 3358032189
www.manaresi.net

CELLAR SALES
PRE-BOOKED VISITS
ANNUAL PRODUCTION 45,000 bottles
HECTARES UNDER VINE 11.00
SUSTAINABLE WINERY

- ● C. B. Rosso Controluce '17 — 4
- ● C. B. Merlot '18 — 3
- ○ Colli Bolognesi Pignoletto Cl. Sup. '18 — 3

Marchesi di Ravarino

VIA RUGGINENTA, 2107
41017 RAVARINO [MO]
TEL. +39 3358190101
www.marchesidiravarino.it

ANNUAL PRODUCTION 30,000 bottles
HECTARES UNDER VINE 15.00

- ● Lambrusco di Sorbara Baby Magnum '19 — 3

Merlotta

VIA MERLOTTA, 1
40026 IMOLA [BO]
TEL. +39 054241740
info@merlotta.com

ANNUAL PRODUCTION 400,000 bottles
HECTARES UNDER VINE 45.00
SUSTAINABLE WINERY

- ● Romagna Albana V.T. Fondatori GP '19 — 2*
- ○ Colli di Imola Chardonnay Grifaia '19 — 2
- ● Romagna Sangiovese Sup. Petali di Viola '19 — 3

Cantina Mingazzini

via Lamberti, 50
40059 Medicina [BO]
Tel. +39 0518513669
www.cantinamingazzini.it

○ Pignoletto Frizzante Euporja '19 🍷🍷 2*
● Romagna Sangiovese Sup. Alcjone '19 🍷🍷 2*
○ Pignoletto Dionjso '19 🍷 2

Montevecchio Isolani

via San Martino, 5
Monte San Pietro [BO]
Tel. +39 051231434
www.montevecchioisolani.it

● C. B. Rosso Bologna Ris. '12 🍷🍷 3
● C. B. Rosso Bologna Bio '16 🍷 2
○ Pignoletto Sup. '18 🍷 2

Moro - Rinaldini

fraz. Calerno
via Andrea Rivasi, 27
42049 Sant'Ilario d'Enza [RE]
Tel. +39 0522679190
www.rinaldinivini.it

CELLAR SALES
PRE-BOOKED VISITS
ANNUAL PRODUCTION 120,000 bottles
HECTARES UNDER VINE 15.50

⊙ Rosé Lambrusco Secco 🍷🍷 2*
● Vigna del Picchio '15 🍷 3

Opera 02 - Ca' Montanari

fraz. Levizzano Rangone
via Medusia, 32
41014 Castelvetro di Modena [MO]
Tel. +39 059741019
www.opera02.it

CELLAR SALES
PRE-BOOKED VISITS
ACCOMMODATION AND RESTAURANT SERVICE
ANNUAL PRODUCTION 75,000 bottles
HECTARES UNDER VINE 20.00
VITICULTURE METHOD Certified Organic
SUSTAINABLE WINERY

● Lambrusco di Modena Brut '19 🍷🍷 3
● Lambrusco di Modena Demi-Sec '19 🍷🍷 2*
● Lambrusco Grasparossa di Castelvetro Brut Operapura '19 🍷 3

Tenuta Palazzona di Maggio

via Panzacchi, 16
40064 Ozzano dell'Emilia [BO]
Tel. +39 051798982
www.palazzonadimaggio.it

CELLAR SALES
PRE-BOOKED VISITS
ANNUAL PRODUCTION 32,000 bottles
HECTARES UNDER VINE 15.50

● Romagna Sangiovese Sup. Ulziano '18 🍷🍷 2*
● Romagna Sangiovese Sup. Le Armi Ris. '16 🍷🍷 5

Pezzuoli

via Vignola, 136
41053 Maranello [MO]
Tel. +39 0536948800
www.pezzuoli.it

CELLAR SALES
PRE-BOOKED VISITS
ANNUAL PRODUCTION 220,000 bottles
HECTARES UNDER VINE 120.00

● Lambrusco Grasparossa di Castelvetro Pietra Scura '19 🍷🍷 1*
● Lambrusco di Sorbara Pietra Rossa '19 🍷🍷 1*

Piccolo - Brunelli

s.da San Zeno, 1
47010 Galeata [FC]
Tel. +39 3468020206
www.piccolobrunelli.it

CELLAR SALES
PRE-BOOKED VISITS
ACCOMMODATION
ANNUAL PRODUCTION 23,000 bottles
HECTARES UNDER VINE 20.00
SUSTAINABLE WINERY

- ● Romagna Sangiovese Predappio Cesco 1938 '18 🍷🍷 3*
- ● Romagna Sangiovese Sup. Il Conte Pietro '18 🍷 2

Podere dell'Angelo

via Rodella, 38r
47923 Vergiano
Tel. +39 3397542711
www.vinidellangelo.it

- ● Colli di Rimini Sangiovese Fulgor '19 🍷🍷 2*
- ● Romagna Sangiovese Sup. Angelico '18 🍷🍷 3
- ● Rosso dell'Angelo '19 🍷🍷 2*

Poderi dal Nespoli 1929

loc. Nespoli
Villa Rossi, 50
47012 Civitella di Romagna [FC]
Tel. +39 0543989911
www.poderidalnespoli.com

CELLAR SALES
PRE-BOOKED VISITS
ACCOMMODATION
ANNUAL PRODUCTION 1,000,000 bottles
HECTARES UNDER VINE 180.00
SUSTAINABLE WINERY

- ● Romagna Sangiovese Sup. Il Nespoli Ris '17 🍷🍷 4
- ● Romagna Borgo dei Guidi '17 🍷 5

Il Poggiarello

loc. Scrivellano di Statto
29020 Travo [PC]
Tel. +39 0523957241
www.ilpoggiarellovini.it

CELLAR SALES
PRE-BOOKED VISITS
ANNUAL PRODUCTION 100,000 bottles
HECTARES UNDER VINE 20.00

- ● Gutturnio Frizzante Lo Spago '19 🍷🍷 3
- ○ Perticato Beatrice Quadri Malvasia '18 🍷🍷 4
- ○ Ortrugo Frizzante Lo Spago '19 🍷 3

QuintoPasso

loc. Sozzigalli
via Canale, 267
41019 Soliera [MO]
Tel. +39 0593163311
www.quintopasso.it

CELLAR SALES
ANNUAL PRODUCTION 40,000 bottles
HECTARES UNDER VINE 12.00

- ⊙ Modena Brut Rosé M. Cl. '16 🍷🍷 5
- ○ Pas Dosè M. Cl. '16 🍷 5

Podere Riosto

via di Riosto, 12
40065 Pianoro [BO]
Tel. +39 051777109
www.podereriosto.it

CELLAR SALES
PRE-BOOKED VISITS
ACCOMMODATION
ANNUAL PRODUCTION 80,000 bottles
HECTARES UNDER VINE 15.80
SUSTAINABLE WINERY

- ● C. B. Barbera '16 🍷🍷 2*
- ● C. B. Cabernet Sauvignon Grifone '15 🍷🍷 2*
- ○ C. B. Pignoletto Sup. '19 🍷 2

SaDiVino

loc. Trivella Sant'Agostino
via Trivella, 16a
47016 Predappio [FC]
Tel. +39 3665949948
www.sadivino.com

CELLAR SALES
ANNUAL PRODUCTION 12,000 bottles
HECTARES UNDER VINE 6.00
SUSTAINABLE WINERY

- ● Romagna Sangiovese Predappio Maestroso Ris. '16 — 🍷🍷 5
- ● Romagna Sangiovese Sup. Solfatara Ris. '16 — 🍷🍷 4

Spalletti Colonna di Paliano

via Sogliano, 104
47039 Savignano sul Rubicone [FC]
Tel. +39 0541945111
www.spalletticolonnadipaliano.com

CELLAR SALES
PRE-BOOKED VISITS
RESTAURANT SERVICE
ANNUAL PRODUCTION 250,000 bottles
HECTARES UNDER VINE 52.00

- ● Romagna Sangiovese Sup. Principe di Ribano '19 — 🍷🍷 2*
- ● Romagna Sangiovese Sup. Rocca di Ribano V. della Croce '17 — 🍷🍷 3

Terraquilia

via Marano, 583
41052 Guiglia [MO]
Tel. +39 059931023
www.terraquilia.it

CELLAR SALES
PRE-BOOKED VISITS
ANNUAL PRODUCTION 70,000 bottles
HECTARES UNDER VINE 9.00
VITICULTURE METHOD Certified Organic

- ● Falconero Zero Metodo Ancestrale '18 — 🍷🍷 3
- ⊙ Sanrosé Zero Metodo Ancestrale '18 — 🍷🍷 3

Tozzi

via Renzuno, 16
48032 Casola Valsenio [RA]
Tel. +39 0544525311
www.cantinatozzi.it

- ○ Romagna Albana Passito Ally '17 — 🍷🍷 3
- ○ Romagna Albana Secco Tantalilli '18 — 🍷🍷 2*

Consorzio Vini di San Marino

loc. Borgo Maggiore
fraz. Valdragone
s.da Serrabolino, 89
47893 San Marino
Tel. +39 0549903124
www.consorziovini.sm

CELLAR SALES
PRE-BOOKED VISITS
ANNUAL PRODUCTION 650,000 bottles
HECTARES UNDER VINE 120.00
SUSTAINABLE WINERY

- ○ Ribolla di San Marino '19 — 🍷🍷 2*
- ● Sangiovese Sup. di San Marino '18 — 🍷🍷 2*
- ○ Biancale di San Marino '19 — 🍷 2
- ○ Caldese di San Marino '18 — 🍷 4

Zanasi

loc. Cavidole
via Settecani Cavidole, 53/A
41051 Castelnuovo Rangone [MO]
Tel. +39 059537052
www.zanasi.net

ANNUAL PRODUCTION 210,000 bottles
HECTARES UNDER VINE 22.00

- ● Lambrusco Grasparossa di Castelvetro Sassostorno '18 — 🍷🍷 3
- ● Lambrusco Grasparossa di Castelvetro Bruno Zanasi '19 — 🍷🍷 2*

TUSCANY

Tuscany has been helped, of course, by some very good vintages for its premium wines and reserves, such as 2015 and 2016, and by years that play off one another, like sunny 2017 and cooler 2018. In no other region (with the sole exception of Piedmont, perhaps) have producers' profits been so consistently reinvested in their vineyards, wineries and professional growth. On Tuscan soil we find the country's best enological talents, great international groups, great wine families such as Antinori and Frescobaldi who have been making wine since the late 1300s, all challenging each other. The magical hills of Chianti Classico, Montalcino, Bolgheri and the Maremma are an irresistible magnet for those who feel capable of making great wines. During our final tastings, 366 wines were reviewed, and we can assure you that between those that earned Tre Bicchieri and the 276 wines that finished with Due Bicchieri, the difference is very little. Breaking down the geography, Chianti Classico is in the lead, with 22 wines from the region's beating heart earning Tre Bicchieri, together with Montalcino, which this year saw 18 Brunello di Montalcinos taking home golds (the best result ever, thanks to an excellent 2015). But Tuscany's other prestigious areas delivered as well: Bolgheri with 8, Vino Nobile di Montepulciano with 5, Carmignano with 2, Rufina with 1, San Gimignano with 3, while smoking-hot Maremma scored 7 awards (2 Morellino di Scasanos and 5 IGTs), Montecucco 2, passing through Cortona to Parrina and the small appellation of Orbetello, which offers a view of the Argentario promontory. Ant that's not to mention the region's Supertuscans and the great classics that bear its name, mainstays in wine collections worldwide. Paying tribute to Tuscany's vitality and verve, we greet all the producers that have, for the first time, earned Tre Bicchieri: they are Bertinga, Bibbiano, Caiarossa, Casisano, La Madonnina, San Polo and Ridolfi. This last, acquired in 2011 by Giuseppe Valter Peretti and expertly managed by Gianni Maccari, surprised us with its classic style, which is increasingly focused and sophisticated. As a result it's our Up-and-Coming Winery of the Year.

Abbadia Ardenga

FRAZ. TORRENIERI
VIA ROMANA, 139
53028 MONTALCINO [SI]
TEL. +39 0577834150
www.abbadiardengapoggio.it

CELLAR SALES
PRE-BOOKED VISITS
ANNUAL PRODUCTION 40,000 bottles
HECTARES UNDER VINE 10.00

Situated in Torrenieri, a famous district in the northeastern part of Montalcino, Abbadia Ardenga is owned by the Società di Esecutori di Pie Disposizioni di Siena. In the past it was a Benedictine convent and staging post along the Via Francigena. Today it is the headquarters of a producer that's consistently at the top of the district, thanks in part to their vigorous Brunello, made through modular maceration and patient maturation in medium and large barrels. The Brunello Vigna Piaggia '15 put in an excellent performance. It's an intense and refined red that opens on notes of red fruit, tobacco and cinchona-quinine. On the palate it's harmonious, progressively unfolding, showing a nice overall depth, mature tannins and only a slight vegetal dissonance. The Brunello '15 is elegant and long, rather warm in its alcohol, closing on notes of camphor and liquorice. We also appreciated the pleasant Sant'Antimo Vin santo '07.

Wine	Rating
● Brunello di Montalcino V. Piaggia '15	🍷🍷 5
● Brunello di Montalcino '15	🍷🍷 5
○ Sant'Antimo Vin Santo '07	🍷 6
● Brunello di Montalcino '14	🍷🍷 5
● Brunello di Montalcino Ris. '13	🍷🍷 6
● Brunello di Montalcino Ris. '12	🍷🍷 6
● Brunello di Montalcino V. Piaggia '14	🍷🍷 5
● Brunello di Montalcino V. Piaggia '13	🍷🍷 5
● Brunello di Montalcino V. Piaggia '12	🍷🍷 5

Acquabona

LOC. ACQUABONA, 1
57037 PORTOFERRAIO [LI]
TEL. +39 0565933013
www.acquabonaelba.it

CELLAR SALES
PRE-BOOKED VISITS
ANNUAL PRODUCTION 90,000 bottles
HECTARES UNDER VINE 18.00

As far back as 1700 there are documents testifying to the presence of the farm, whose name comes from a source of fresh water in the area. The wine-growing business came about in the 1950s, and after 30 years they specialized in the crop. Credit goes to the management expertise of 3 Lombard agronomists, who are still at the helm and have made Acquabuona one of the most important producers in the territory of Elba. The Elba Vermentino '19 is highly intriguing, with fresh, aromatic notes of tarragon, marjoram, apple, damson and gooseberries; in the mouth it's warm, tasty, juicy and enticing, with a long finish. The very pleasant Voltraio '15, made with Syrah and Merlot, is aromatically rich and firm on the palate. The 2016 version of the Elba Aleatico Passito also delivered, offering up sweet tones of jam and cinnamon spices. On the palate it's creamy, pervasive, making for a rich, tasty and quite broad finish.

Wine	Rating
● Elba Aleatico Passito '16	🍷🍷 3
● Elba Rosso Ris. '17	🍷🍷 4
○ Elba Vermentino '19	🍷🍷 3
● Voltraio '15	🍷🍷 4
○ Elba Ansonica '19	🍷 3
○ Elba Bianco '19	🍷 2
⊙ Elba Rosato	🍷 2
● Elba Aleatico Passito '12	🍷🍷 3
○ Elba Ansonica '18	🍷🍷 3
○ Elba Bianco '18	🍷🍷 2*
● Elba Rosso '16	🍷🍷 2*
○ Elba Vermentino '17	🍷🍷 3
● Voltraio '14	🍷🍷 4
● Voltraio '13	🍷🍷 4

Agricoltori del Chianti Geografico

LOC. MULINACCIO, 10
53013 GAIOLE IN CHIANTI [SI]
TEL. +39 0577749489
www.chiantigeografico.it

CELLAR SALES
PRE-BOOKED VISITS
ACCOMMODATION
ANNUAL PRODUCTION 1,100,000 bottles
HECTARES UNDER VINE 100.00

The producer was founded in 1961 by 17 vine growers from Radda, Gaiole and Castellina in Chianti who decided to join forces and form a cooperative. Although work began immediately, with the creation of the first wine, the first collective harvest came in 1965. 1972 saw the construction of the cellar, which was accompanied more recently (1989) by one in San Gimignano. After periods of great success and less prosperous years, in 2018 the cooperative was purchased by Tenute Piccini. For us the best wine this year is the Chianti Classico Montegiachi Ris. '16, pleasant in its aromatic suite of Mediterranean herbs, plums and cherries. The palate opens warm, well structured, with strong tannins and progressive development. The other Riserva '16, the Contessa di Radda, is also tasty: it has a fruity nose of cherry, a racy, relaxed body, a fresh acidic vein and a well-sustained finish on floral sensations.

Wine	Rating
● Chianti Cl. Montegiachi Ris. '16	🍷🍷 4
● Chianti Cl. Contessa di Radda Ris. '16	🍷🍷 3
● La Pevera '16	🍷🍷 5
○ Vernaccia di San Gimignano Borgo alla Terra '19	🍷🍷 2*
● Chianti Cl. Montegiachi Ris. '09	🍷🍷🍷 4*
● Chianti Cl. Montegiachi Ris. '07	🍷🍷🍷 4
● Chianti Cl. Montegiachi Ris. '05	🍷🍷🍷 4
● Chianti Cl. '13	🍷🍷 3
● Chianti Cl. Contessa di Radda '13	🍷🍷 3
● Chianti Cl. Lucignano '12	🍷🍷 3
● Chianti Cl. Montegiachi Ris. '12	🍷🍷 4
● Chianti Cl. Montegiachi Ris. '11	🍷🍷 4
● Chianti Cl. Montegiachi Ris. '10	🍷🍷 4
● Ferraiolo '13	🍷🍷 5

Agrisole Podere Pellicciano

LOC. LA SERRA, 64
56028 SAN MINIATO [PI]
TEL. +39 0571409825
www.agri-sole.it

CELLAR SALES
PRE-BOOKED VISITS
ANNUAL PRODUCTION 30,000 bottles
HECTARES UNDER VINE 7.00

The Caputo family is leading a venture that started in 2003, initially at the behest of Gerardo and Concetta, who wanted to find a place in the countryside where they could spend some time, but then transformed the property into a serious project. A passion for agriculture and winemaking gradually blossomed and soon it was unstoppable, so much so that it also involved their sons, who've made it their main occupation. Federico is involved both in the vineyard and in the cellar, while Fabio oversees hospitality and direct sales. The Malvasia Nera '16 is interesting, almost explosive on the nose with intense aromas of raspberries and blackberries, all presented on a well-expressed body, fresh in its acidity, with a juicy, sapid finish. The Colorino '16 is also well made, exhibiting intense aromas of ink, blueberries and currants, with vegetal hints of bay leaf to close; the palate highlights rich structure and appetizing flavor. The rest of the range also performed well.

Wine	Rating
● Colorino '16	🍷🍷 6
● Mafefa '16	🍷🍷 2*
○ Mafefa Bianco '19	🍷🍷 3
● Malvasia Nera '16	🍷🍷 2*
● Chianti Sanminiatello '18	🍷 3
● Chianti San Miniatello '16	🍷🍷 3*
● Mafefa '12	🍷🍷 2*
○ Mafefa Bianco '18	🍷🍷 3
○ Mafefa Bianco '17	🍷🍷 3
● Mafefa Rosso '15	🍷🍷 4
● Malvasia Nera '12	🍷🍷 2*
○ Trebbiano '16	🍷🍷 3
○ Trebbiano '15	🍷🍷 4
○ Vin Santo del Chianti Griso '10	🍷🍷 5
○ Vin Santo Pisano Bianco di San Torpè '09	🍷🍷 2*

Maurizio Alongi

Loc. Monti di Sotto, 25
53013 Gaiole in Chianti [SI]
Tel. +39 3389878937
www.maurizioalongi.it

ANNUAL PRODUCTION 4,500 bottles
HECTARES UNDER VINE 1.30
VITICULTURE METHOD Certified Organic

Here in a small, remote corner of Gaiole in Chianti, Barbischio Maurizio Alongi is making wine rooted in the territory itself. His is a small but excellent vineyard, cultivated with Sangiovese, Canaiolo, Colorino and Malvasia Nera, whose origins go back some forty years. With patience, he has brought it back to full production efficiency, growing the grapes for his unique wine, which, thanks to the cleanness and precision of his production approach, faithfully express the territory. The Chianti Classico Vigna Barbischio Riserva '17 brilliantly overcomes a complicated vintage, in perfect harmony with a subzone like Gaiole, which can weather even the hottest vintages. Indeed, the wine exhibits an elegant, delicate olfactory profile that plays on the intersection of flowers, fruits and spicy, earthy hints, the prologue to a nice, subtle taste progression, with a tannic texture that makes its presence felt.

● Chianti Cl. V. Barbischio Ris. '17	🍷🍷 5
● Chianti Cl. V. Barbischio Ris. '16	🍷🍷🍷 5
● Chianti Cl. V. Barbischio Ris. '15	🍷🍷 5

Altesino

Loc. Altesino, 54
53024 Montalcino [SI]
Tel. +39 0577806208
www.altesino.it

CELLAR SALES
PRE-BOOKED VISITS
ACCOMMODATION
ANNUAL PRODUCTION 250,000 bottles
HECTARES UNDER VINE 49.00

Founded in the 1970s by the Consonni family, Altesino is one of the producers that has made Montalcino great, having brought about a real sea change in terms of territorial awareness. One of the first wineries to offer a cru of Brunello (Montosoli, a benchmark toponym in the northern district), in the early 2000s the property was acquired by Elisabetta Gnudi Angelini, who has further strengthened its viticultural and productive capacities, making it a stylistic bedrock that brings together innovation and classicism, and not only when it comes to Sangiovese. The Brunello Montosoli '15 marks Elisabetta's return into our guide (her daughter Alessandra is now permanently at her side). It's a red of structure, backbone and finesse, with lovely notes of ripe cherries and cinchona-quinine on the nose, opening harmoniously on the palate and closing long, exhibiting ripe fruit and smooth tannins. The Brunello '15 is also notable, structured and harmonious. The Rosso '18 is pleasant and quite mature.

● Brunello di Montalcino Montosoli '15	🍷🍷 8
● Brunello di Montalcino '15	🍷🍷 6
● Rosso di Montalcino '18	🍷 3
● Brunello di Montalcino '13	🍷🍷 6
● Brunello di Montalcino '11	🍷🍷 6
● Brunello di Montalcino Montosoli '13	🍷🍷 8
● Brunello di Montalcino Montosoli '12	🍷🍷 8
● Brunello di Montalcino Montosoli '11	🍷🍷 8
● Brunello di Montalcino Our 40th Harvest '12	🍷🍷 7
● Brunello di Montalcino Ris. '10	🍷🍷 8
● Rosso di Montalcino '16	🍷🍷 3
● Toscana Rosso '14	🍷🍷 3

Fattoria Ambra

via Lombarda, 85
59015 Carmignano [PO]
Tel. +39 3358282552
www.fattoriaambra.it

CELLAR SALES
PRE-BOOKED VISITS
ANNUAL PRODUCTION 80,000 bottles
HECTARES UNDER VINE 20.00
VITICULTURE METHOD Certified Organic

Owned by the Romei Rigoli family since the mid-19th century, Fattoria Ambra (whose name comes from a poem written by Lorenzo de' Medici)spans 20 hectares of hilltop vineyards planted with Sangiovese and smaller shares of Cabernet Sauvignon, Canaiolo, Trebbiano and Vermentino. Beppe Rigoli, owner and winemaker, has identified four cru that he bottles separately, thus recreating in Carmignano the French agronomic idea of developing individual plots. The Carmignano Santa Cristina in Pilli '17 is excellent. It has ripe red berry sensations, hints of jam, and slightly vegetal notes of tobacco. In the mouth it's warm, full-bodied, with well-defined tannins and a fresh finish, without excessive roughness. The two 2016 reserves are pleasant: the Elzana, with its intriguing balsamic notes, nice pulp and power, and the juicy, warm Montalbiolo, with its intense, fruity hints of cherry. We also mention the velvety and pervasive Vin Santo '11.

Wine	Rating	
● Carmignano Santa Cristina in Pilli '17	▼▼	3*
● Barco Reale '19	▼▼	2*
● Carmignano Elzana Ris. '16	▼▼	5
● Carmignano Montalbiolo Ris. '16	▼▼	5
○ Trebbiano '19	▼▼	2*
○ Vin Santo di Carmignano '11	▼▼	5
⊙ Barco Reale Rosato '19	▼	2
● Carmignano Santa Cristina in Pilli '16	▽▽▽	3*
● Carmignano Santa Cristina in Pilli '15	▽▽▽	3*
● Carmignano Elzana Ris. '15	▽▽	5
● Carmignano Elzana Ris. '13	▽▽	5
● Carmignano Montalbiolo Ris. '15	▽▽	5
● Carmignano Montalbiolo Ris. '13	▽▽	5
● Carmignano Montefortini Podere Lombarda '15	▽▽	3

Stefano Amerighi

loc. Poggiobello di Farneta
52044 Cortona [AR]
Tel. +39 0575648340
www.stefanoamerighi.it

CELLAR SALES
PRE-BOOKED VISITS
ANNUAL PRODUCTION 35,000 bottles
HECTARES UNDER VINE 8.50
VITICULTURE METHOD Certified Biodynamic
SUSTAINABLE WINERY

Sustainable viticulture and a biodynamic agricultural approach mean that pruning and working the land are carried out in accordance with the moon and the planets. For phytosanitary protection, only copper and sulphur are used together with macerates and natural herbal teas. And no additives are used in winemaking. Stefano Amerighi is a leader of the sector. In addition to following through on his intention to produce wine from a single grape, Syrah, which exhibits its best qualities here, he's carrying out new experiments, both with Sangiovese and with Pecorino, this time in the Marche. This year there's a new addition that completes their range of Syrah, now offered in three versions and vintages. The 2017 impressed the most, with its complex, multifaceted bouquet of aromatic and medicinal herbs and ink combined with hints of coffee, chocolate and ripe black fruit. The palate is soft and juicy, concentrated but with a fresh, sapid, vital finish.

Wine	Rating	
● Cortona Syrah '17	▼▼▼	5
● Cortona Syrah Apice '16	▼▼	6
● Cortona Syrah Julie and Julia '18	▼▼	4
● Cortona Syrah '16	▽▽▽	5
● Cortona Syrah '15	▽▽▽	5
● Cortona Syrah '14	▽▽▽	5
● Cortona Syrah '11	▽▽▽	5
● Cortona Syrah '10	▽▽▽	5
● Cortona Syrah '09	▽▽▽	5
● Cortona Syrah '13	▽▽	5
● Cortona Syrah '12	▽▽	5
● Cortona Syrah Apice '15	▽▽	6
● Cortona Syrah Apice '14	▽▽	6
● Cortona Syrah Apice '13	▽▽	6
● Cortona Syrah Apice '11	▽▽	6
● Cortona Syrah Apice '10	▽▽	6

★★Marchesi Antinori

via Cassia per Siena, 133
50026 San Casciano in Val di Pesa [FI]
Tel. +39 05523595
www.antinori.it

CELLAR SALES
PRE-BOOKED VISITS
ACCOMMODATION AND RESTAURANT SERVICE
ANNUAL PRODUCTION 1,700,000 bottles
HECTARES UNDER VINE 324.00

Without a doubt, Antinori is the most famous Tuscan wine brand in the world. Needless to say, despite the family's massive presence in the region, their "propensity" for Chianti Classico is evident. The Florentine brand has concentrated its most important strategies here, starting with their Bargino winery. This is not to forget their wine, naturally, which, especially in the recent past, has exhibited a mix of old and new stylistic approaches. The 2017 version once again demonstrated that their Solaia is a great Tuscan red. It's an elegant blend of Cabernet Sauvignon, Franc and Sangiovese from a part of the Tignanello estate that gives rise to their other great red. It pours a dark ruby-red color, anticipating a vibrant, rich, dynamic nose, full of red and black berries, spices, balsamic and minty hints elegantly blended with oak. On the palate it's juicy, taut, vibrant, with velvety tannins, very long. We also recommend the excellent Tignanello '17.

Wine	Rating
● Solaia '17	TTT 8
● Chianti Cl. Gran Selezione Badia a Passignano '17	TT 6
● Chianti Cl. Pèppoli '18	TT 3*
● Tignanello '17	TT 8
● Chianti Cl. Marchese Antinori Ris. '17	TT 6
● Chianti Cl. Villa Antinori Ris. '17	TT 4
● Villa Antinori Rosso '17	TT 4
○ Villa Antinori Tenuta Monteloro Pinot Bianco '19	TT 3
○ Villa Antinori Bianco '19	T 2
● Chianti Cl. Marchese Antinori Ris. '15	YYY 5
● Solaia '16	YYY 8
● Tignanello '13	YYY 8
● Tignanello '09	YYY 8

Tenuta di Arceno

loc. Arceno
fraz. San Gusmé
53010 Castelnuovo Berardenga [SI]
Tel. +39 0577359346
www.tenutadiarceno.com

CELLAR SALES
PRE-BOOKED VISITS
ANNUAL PRODUCTION 250,000 bottles
HECTARES UNDER VINE 92.00

Near Castelnuovo Berardenga, the "capital" of the southernmost area of Chianti Classico, we find the increasingly convincing, American-owned Tenuta di Arceno (Kendall-Jackson Group), which produces wines of impeccable quality and craftsmanship. From Chianti's Sangiovese, with its clean, modern style and a focus on not detracting from personality and character, to Bordeaux-based blends that exhibit the same care and elegance. The Chianti Classico Riserva '17 features polished aromas ranging from ripe red berries to spices, anticipating an equally convincing, juicy and well-sustained palate. The Chianti Classico Gran Selezione Strada al Sasso '17 is just as well made, with more concentrated aromas and a tight, consistent palate. The two 'Super Tuscans' are impeccable: Valadorna (Merlot) and Arcanum (Cabernet Sauvignon, Cabernet Franc and Petit Verdot), both 2016s.

Wine	Rating
● Chianti Cl. Ris. '17	TTT 5
● Chianti Cl. Gran Selezione Strada al Sasso '17	TT 6
● Arcanum '16	TT 8
● Valadorna '16	TT 8
● Chianti Cl. '18	T 4
● Chianti Cl. '17	YYY 4*
● Valadorna '13	YYY 8
● Arcanum '15	YY 8
● Arcanum '13	YY 8
● Chianti Cl. '16	YY 4
● Chianti Cl. '15	YY 3
● Chianti Cl. Gran Selezione Strada al Sasso '15	YY 6
● Chianti Cl. Ris. '16	YY 5
● Chianti Cl. Ris. '15	YY 5
● Il Fauno di Arcanum '14	YY 6

Tenuta Argentiera

loc. I Pianali
fraz. Donoratico
via Aurelia, 412a
57022 Castagneto Carducci [LI]
Tel. +39 0565773176
www.argentiera.eu

CELLAR SALES
PRE-BOOKED VISITS
ANNUAL PRODUCTION 450,000 bottles
HECTARES UNDER VINE 76.00

Argentiera is one of the most important and prestigious wineries in Bolgheri. The name calls to mind the silver mines once located in the area, while the estate's vineyards are matched by few. Today the majority shareholder of the property is the Austrian industrialist Stanislaus Turnauer, a great wine lover. He's flanked by Federico Zileri, who guarantees the continuity of the project. It's evident that all this, from their splendid vineyards to the technical expertise brought to winemaking, is a guarantee of elegance, of incomparable style and quality. And this was the case for the Bolgheri Rosso Villa Donoratico '18, one of the appellation's best wines this year. It plays on detail and precision in blending its various components. Its aromatic suite is bright with commendable fruit that's able to bind wonderfully with toasted and balsamic sensations. In the mouth it's pervasive and tasty, making for a dynamic and deep drink.

- ● Bolgheri Rosso Villa Donoratico '18 — 5
- ● Bolgheri Rosso Sup. '17 — 8
- ● Bolgheri Rosso Poggio ai Ginepri '18 — 4
- ● Bolgheri Sup. '11 — 8
- ● Bolgheri Sup. Argentiera '10 — 7
- ● Bolgheri Sup. Argentiera '06 — 7
- ● Bolgheri Sup. Argentiera '05 — 7
- ● Bolgheri Sup. Argentiera '04 — 7
- ● Bolgheri Rosso Poggio ai Ginepri '17 — 4
- ● Bolgheri Rosso Sup. '16 — 8
- ● Bolgheri Rosso Sup. '14 — 8
- ● Bolgheri Rosso Sup. '13 — 8
- ● Bolgheri Rosso Villa Donoratico '17 — 5
- ● Bolgheri Rosso Villa Donoratico '15 — 5
- ● Bolgheri Sup. Argentiera '15 — 8
- ● Bolgheri Villa Donoratico '13 — 5
- ○ Poggio ai Ginepri Bianco '17 — 3

Argiano

loc. Sant'Angelo in Colle
53024 Montalcino [SI]
Tel. +39 0577844037
www.argiano.net

CELLAR SALES
PRE-BOOKED VISITS
ACCOMMODATION
ANNUAL PRODUCTION 330,000 bottles
HECTARES UNDER VINE 55.00

Argiano's is a centuries-old story. A splendid estate located at the southwestern edge of Montalcino, from the 16th century onward it belonged to various noble Tuscan families. In 2013 it was bought by Bernardino Sani, who as of 2015 has also branded its wines. Their range is bound up with the peculiarities of an area that is, in many ways, Mediterranean, characterized by limestone and clayey marl. Their Sangioveses and international grapes, matured both in small barrels and Slavonian oak, prove naturally generous and broad. Our tastings painted a picture of a winery that's one of the appellation's top performers. Just take the Vigna del Suolo '15, a wine that enchants with its elegance and expressive depth. It's a great Brunello, fruity and spicy, with fresh citrus notes that introduce a powerful but incredibly harmonious palate. Ripe plum, floral and spicy notes feature in the Brunello '15, notes of black berries, cocoa and spices for the Solengo '17.

- ● Brunello di Montalcino V. del Suolo '15 — 8
- ● Brunello di Montalcino '15 — 8
- ● Rosso di Montalcino '18 — 5
- ● Solengo '17 — 8
- ● Brunello di Montalcino Ris. '88 — 7
- ● Brunello di Montalcino Ris. '85 — 7
- ● Solengo '97 — 6
- ● Solengo '95 — 6
- ● Brunello di Montalcino '13 — 7
- ● Brunello di Montalcino '12 — 7
- ● Non Confunditur '13 — 3
- ● Rosso di Montalcino '16 — 4
- ● Rosso di Montalcino '12 — 3

Arrighi

loc. Pian del Monte, 1
57036 Porto Azzurro [LI]
Tel. +39 3356641793
www.arrighivigneolivi.it

CELLAR SALES
PRE-BOOKED VISITS
ANNUAL PRODUCTION 30,000 bottles
HECTARES UNDER VINE 6.00

Arrighi can be considered an indigenous operation, since the family have been in Elba for generations and wine-growing has always been an important part of production. In the 1970s, due to a boom in tourism, the surface area of the vineyards was reduced, until its current owner, Antonio, decided to start again with enthusiasm in making wine, as well as overseeing guest accommodations. Thus began the long work of identifying the native grapes that could thrive on the estate, as well as testing great international varieties. Many wines were submitted, starting with the Tresse '17: made with Syrah, Sangiovese and Sagrantino, it has a broad-based bouquet of liquorice and coffee, with hints of toasted pine nuts. In the mouth it enters warm, with nice weight and proper acidity, making for a pleasant finish. The original Hermia '19 is a Viognier matured in amphora, with fresh notes of aromatic herbs and tropical fruit. In the mouth it's tasty and pulpy, fresh on the finish.

Wine	Glasses	
● Elba Aleatico Passito Silosò '19	2 (black)	5
○ Elba Ansonica Valerius '19	2 (black)	4
○ Elba Bianco Illagiù '19	2 (black)	3
● Elba Rosso Centopercento '19	2 (black)	5
○ Hermia '19	2 (black)	4
● Tresse '17	2 (black)	5
○ V.I.P. Anfora Viognier '19	2 (black)	4
○ Elba Ansonica Mattanto '19	1 (black)	3
○ Elba Vermentino Arembapampane '19	1 (black)	4
● Elba Aleatico Passito Silosò '18	2 (white)	5
● Elba Aleatico Passito Silosò '17	2 (white)	5
● Elba Aleatico Passito Silosò '16	2 (white)	5
○ Elba Bianco Illagiù '18	2 (white)	3
● Tresse '16	2 (white)	5
○ Valerium Vinum Anfora '17	2 (white)	4

Artimino

fraz. Artimino
v.le Papa Giovanni XXIII, 1
59015 Carmignano [PO]
Tel. +39 0558751423
www.artimino.com

CELLAR SALES
PRE-BOOKED VISITS
ACCOMMODATION AND RESTAURANT SERVICE
ANNUAL PRODUCTION 420,000 bottles
HECTARES UNDER VINE 88.00

Artimino was first an Etruscan settlement, then a medieval village and, finally, a favourite haunt of the Medicis. The family chose it for the construction of one of their most important residences: the Villa dei Cento Camini, also known as 'La Ferdinanda', which is an integral part of the estate. The property, which has belonged to the Olmo family (famous for their bicycles) since the 1980s, stretches across more than 700 hectares, of which almost ninety are vineyards and spans two appellations (Carmignano and Chianti Montalbano). The property also hosts more than 17 thousand olive trees. The Carmignano Poggilarca '17 is delicious with its broad olfactory suite, fruity notes of cherry and plum that blend well with spicy hints of cloves and sensations of aromatic herbs, rosemary. The palate is polished, with crisp tannins, balanced freshness and a progressively unfolding finish. The Chianti Montalbano '18 surprises with its nice, delicate nose of red berries, and a soft, clear palate.

Wine	Glasses	
● Carmignano Poggilarca '17	2 (black)	3*
● Carmignano V. Grumarello Ris. '14	2 (black)	4
● Chianti Montalbano '18	2 (black)	2*
● Iris '16	2 (black)	5
● Vin Santo di Carmignano Occhio di Pernice '13	2 (black)	5
⊙ Barco Reale Rosato Vin Ruspo '19	1 (black)	2
● Carmignano Poggilarca '15	2 (white)	3
● Carmignano V. Grumarello Ris. '13	2 (white)	4
● Carmignano V. Grumarello Ris. '12	2 (white)	4
● Iris '15	2 (white)	5
● Vin Santo di Carmignano Occhio di Pernice '12	2 (white)	5
● Vin Santo di Carmignano Occhio di Pernice '10	2 (white)	5
● Vin Santo di Carmignano Occhio di Pernice '09	2 (white)	5

Assolati

fraz. Montenero
pod. Assolati, 47
58040 Castel del Piano [GR]
Tel. +39 0564954146
www.assolati.it

CELLAR SALES
PRE-BOOKED VISITS
ACCOMMODATION
ANNUAL PRODUCTION 18,000 bottles
HECTARES UNDER VINE 5.00

Based in Montenero d'Orcia, Floriano Giannetti's winery is one of the Montecucco producers who've managed to offer intriguing, original reds with ever-greater continuity. This happens especially when the earthy character of the local Sangiovese, which can be too decisive at times, is properly contrasted by a fresh, balanced progression of flavor. It's a feat that's difficult to achieve with regularity in an area this hot, where summers can often be torrid. But the winery is up to the task by virtue of its great stylistic awareness. The Montecucco Rosso '18 exhibits lovely personality, proving approachably pleasant to drink with aromatic nuances that call up wild herbs, cherries, spices and mint, an enticing mix. On the palate it's juicy and rich in contrast, with vivid and flavorful tannins and well-sustained acidic verve. The well-made Dionysos '19, a monovarietal Vermentino marked by precise, fragrant aromas, proves sapid and supple in the mouth.

● Montecucco Rosso '18	🍷🍷 2*
○ Dionysos '19	🍷🍷 2*
● Montecucco Rosso '15	YY 2*
● Montecucco Rosso '14	YY 2*
● Montecucco Rosso '12	YY 2*
● Montecucco Rosso '11	YY 2*
● Montecucco Sangiovese '16	YY 3
● Montecucco Sangiovese '15	YY 3
● Montecucco Sangiovese '14	YY 3
● Montecucco Sangiovese '13	YY 3
● Montecucco Sangiovese Ris. '16	YY 4
● Montecucco Sangiovese Ris. '15	YY 4
● Montecucco Sangiovese Ris. '13	YY 4
● Montecucco Sangiovese Ris. '12	YY 3
● Montecucco Sangiovese Ris. '10	YY 3

★Avignonesi

fraz. Valiano
via Colonica, 1
53045 Montepulciano [SI]
Tel. +39 0578724304
www.avignonesi.it

CELLAR SALES
PRE-BOOKED VISITS
ACCOMMODATION AND RESTAURANT SERVICE
ANNUAL PRODUCTION 500,000 bottles
HECTARES UNDER VINE 169.00
VITICULTURE METHOD Certified Organic

Owned by Virginie Saverys, this historic winery, which is now flying the Belgian flag, is based in Valiano in one of the most important 'subzones' of Montepulciano. It firmly occupies a significant place among the leaders of the Nobile appellation. Their current portfolio of wines focuses on balance and good character, the result of rigorous work, especially in the vineyard, where the winery has adopted detailed internal zoning and cultivation practices that are decidedly respectful of the environment. With its clear aromas of fragrant red berry fruit and spices, the Nobile Poggetto di Sopra '16 benefited from a particularly interesting year in Montepulciano. In the mouth it's just as good, proving juicy and well-sustained. The floral and graceful Rosso di Montepulciano '18 impresses most for its fresh and relaxed palate, which makes for delicious and enticing drinkability.

● Nobile di Montepulciano Poggetto di Sopra '16	🍷🍷 7
● Rosso di Montepulciano '18	🍷🍷 3
● 50 & 50 '16	🍷 8
● Da-Di '19	🍷 6
● Desiderio '17	🍷 6
● Grifi '17	🍷 6
● 50 & 50 Avignonesi e Capannelle '99	YYY 8
● 50 & 50 Avignonesi e Capannelle '97	YYY 8
● Nobile di Montepulciano '12	YYY 4*
○ Vin Santo '98	YYY 8
○ Vin Santo '96	YYY 8
○ Vin Santo '95	YYY 8
○ Vin Santo '93	YYY 8
● Vin Santo Occhio di Pernice '97	YYY 8
● Vin Santo Occhio di Pernice '93	YYY 8
○ Vin Santo Occhio di Pernice '90	YYY 8

★Badia a Coltibuono

loc. Badia a Coltibuono
53013 Gaiole in Chianti [SI]
Tel. +39 0577746110
www.coltibuono.com

CELLAR SALES
PRE-BOOKED VISITS
ACCOMMODATION AND RESTAURANT SERVICE
ANNUAL PRODUCTION 240,000 bottles
HECTARES UNDER VINE 62.00
VITICULTURE METHOD Certified Organic
SUSTAINABLE WINERY

Territorial to the core, Badia a Coltibuono's wines are some of the most stylistically discernible examples of the Chianti Classico appellation. In spite of fashion and changes in climate, they have managed to maintain a unique and inimitable character, demonstrating that the power of terroir sometimes exceeds all else. Their vineyards, which have been cultivated organically since 2000, are mostly located in Monti in Chianti, a southern offshoot of the Gaiole subzone bordering Castelnuovo Berardenga. With its light and precise aromatic traits, the Chianti Classico '18 offers up fragrances of flowers and wild grass, topped off by spicy touches. The wine gives its best in the mouth, where it's delicious, elegant, mouth-watering and flavorful. The Colmaia '19, monovarietal Sangiovese, goes all in on drinkability, with a fragrant, full palate, and fresh, fruity aromas. The Chianti Classico Cultus Boni Riserva '16, with its more austere, dense profile, is also well made.

- ● Chianti Cl. '18 ▼▼▼ 4*
- ● Chianti Cl. Cultus Boni Ris. '16 ▼▼ 5
- ● Colmaia '19 ▼▼ 3
- ● Chianti Cl. '15 ▽▽▽ 4*
- ● Chianti Cl. '13 ▽▽▽ 3*
- ● Chianti Cl. '12 ▽▽▽ 3*
- ● Chianti Cl. '06 ▽▽▽ 3*
- ● Chianti Cl. Cultus Boni '15 ▽▽▽ 4*
- ● Chianti Cl. Cultus Boni '09 ▽▽▽ 4*
- ● Chianti Cl. Ris. '09 ▽▽▽ 5
- ● Chianti Cl. Ris. '07 ▽▽▽ 5
- ● Chianti Cl. Ris. '04 ▽▽▽ 5
- ● Chianti Cetamura '17 ▽▽ 2*
- ● Chianti Cl. '17 ▽▽ 4
- ● Chianti Cl. '16 ▽▽ 4
- ● Chianti Cl. Ris. '16 ▽▽ 5
- ● Collebello '16 ▽▽ 2*

Badia di Morrona

via del Chianti, 6
56030 Terricciola [PI]
Tel. +39 0587658505
www.badiadimorrona.it

CELLAR SALES
PRE-BOOKED VISITS
ACCOMMODATION AND RESTAURANT SERVICE
ANNUAL PRODUCTION 500,000 bottles
HECTARES UNDER VINE 110.00

The Gaslini Alberti family's Badia di Morrona is simply gorgeous, starting with the property's abbey, which dates back to the year 1000 and 600 hectares of land that stretch for as far as the eye can see. When it comes to wine, here in Terricciola, an area situated between Pisa and Volterra, the gorgeous landscapes are gradually finding their own stylistic definition. On this front, Morrona's selection has played (and continues to play) a central role, with a surprising increase in quality in recent years. The VignAlta '17 performed very well, especially for the year. Elegant and fresh, complex and linear, it has ripe, clear and focused fruit wrapped in a notable toastiness. Pulpy, smooth tannins feature in the Taneto '17, while, as usual, the I Sodi del Paretaio '19 proves balanced and tasty. The fresh and jolly Vermentino Felciaio '19 offers up balanced aromas on a delicate palate.

- ● Chianti I Sodi del Paretaio '19 ▼▼ 2*
- ● Terre di Pisa Sangiovese VignaAlta '17 ▼▼ 5
- ● N'antia '17 ▼▼ 5
- ● Taneto '17 ▼▼ 3
- ○ Felciaio '19 ▼ 2
- ● Terre di Pisa Sangiovese VignaAlta '16 ▽▽▽ 5
- ● Chianti I Sodi del Paretaio '18 ▽▽ 2*
- ● Chianti I Sodi del Paretaio '17 ▽▽ 2*
- ● N'antia '16 ▽▽ 5
- ● N'antia '15 ▽▽ 5
- ● Taneto '16 ▽▽ 3*
- ● Taneto '15 ▽▽ 3*
- ● VignaAlta '15 ▽▽ 5
- ○ Vin Santo del Chianti '13 ▽▽ 4

Alfonso Baldetti

LOC. PIETRAIA, 71A
52044 CORTONA [AR]
TEL. +39 057567077
www.baldetti.com

CELLAR SALES
PRE-BOOKED VISITS
ANNUAL PRODUCTION 100,000 bottles
HECTARES UNDER VINE 15.00
SUSTAINABLE WINERY

The Baldetti family's deep-rooted history continues, with Alfonso still firmly in charge of the winery, together with his sons Daniele and Gianluca. It was Mario Baldetti, father of the current owner, who gave impetus to the wine business, but it was a time when many wineries weren't bottling. The creation of the first DOC wines in the area, first Bianco Vergine della Valdichiana, and more recently Cortona Syrah, has allowed for a definitive transformation into a modern producer. The Crano '16, a Syrah, sees aromas of raspberry and currant softened by spicy notes of pepper and hints of tanned leather. On the palate it's firm, rich in texture and a calibrated freshness for a finish of convincing length. The Marius '17, a monovarietal Sangiovese, is more traditional aromatically, initially dominated by notes of plum and cherry, then hints of aromatic herbs. It's supple on the palate, fresh and relaxed on the finish.

Wine	Rating
● Cortona Sangiovese Marius '17	▼▼ 3
● Cortona Syrah Crano '16	▼▼ 4
Cortona Vin Santo Leopoldo '05	▼▼ 5
○ Brut M. Cl. '16	▼ 4
○ Chagrè '19	▼ 2
⊙ Piet Rosè '19	▼ 3
○ Chagré '18	▽▽ 3
● Cortona Crano '11	▽▽ 3
● Cortona Sangiovese Marius '12	▽▽ 4
● Cortona Syrah Crano '15	▽▽ 5
● Cortona Syrah Crano '12	▽▽ 4
○ Cortona Vin Santo Leopoldo '03	▽▽ 5

Baracchi

LOC. CEGLIOLO, 21
52044 CORTONA [AR]
TEL. +39 0575612679
www.baracchiwinery.com

CELLAR SALES
PRE-BOOKED VISITS
ACCOMMODATION AND RESTAURANT SERVICE
ANNUAL PRODUCTION 140,000 bottles
HECTARES UNDER VINE 32.00
SUSTAINABLE WINERY

The Baracchi family has been involved in wine production for five generations. Riccardo has created, near the winery, a resort with hotel, restaurant and spa, around which a part of the vineyards grow. Helped by his son Benedetto, he practices modern viticulture, listening to the territory, favoring Syrah, which has found its ideal habitat in the area. Traditional grape varieties are treated in alternative ways, like his sparkling Trebbiano and Sangiovese. Another piece of news is the planting of Pinot Nero. Their entire range was well received, starting with the Cortona Syrah Smeriglio '17. It has a multifaceted bouquet, with notes of cherry and tobacco followed by elegant spices, pepper, juniper and aromatic herbs. On the palate it's pleasant and juicy, with calibrated tannins and a lively finish. The Vin Santo '12 is very charming, with an array of aromas ranging from hazelnut to honey by way of dates and dried figs.

Wine	Rating
● Cortona Syrah Smeriglio '17	▼▼ 4
● Cortona Sangiovese Smeriglio '18	▼▼ 4
● Cortona Syrah Ris. '16	▼▼ 6
○ Cortona Vin Santo Il Mio Vin Santo '12	▼▼ 6
● O'Lillo '18	▼▼ 2*
● Ardito '16	▼ 6
○ Astore '19	▼ 3
○ O'Lilla '19	▼ 3
● Ardito '15	▽▽ 6
○ Astore '18	▽▽ 3
● Cortona Cabernet Ris. '15	▽▽ 6
● Cortona Cabernet Ris. '13	▽▽ 6
● Cortona Syrah Ris. '15	▽▽ 6
● Cortona Syrah Smeriglio '16	▽▽ 4
● Cortona Syrah Smeriglio '15	▽▽ 4
● Cortona Syrah Smeriglio '14	▽▽ 4

Fattoria dei Barbi

loc. Podernovi, 170
53024 Montalcino [SI]
Tel. +39 0577841111
www.fattoriadeibarbi.it

CELLAR SALES
PRE-BOOKED VISITS
ACCOMMODATION AND RESTAURANT SERVICE
ANNUAL PRODUCTION 600,000 bottles
HECTARES UNDER VINE 66.00

Now managed by Stefano Cinelli Colombini, Fattoria dei Barbi is one of the few wineries in Montalcino that can boast being 'historic'. Its large estate is concentrated in the eastern part of the area, near the renowned town of Podernovi, well known by enthusiasts and travellers who come to visit the wine cellar-museum or treat themselves to a pleasant break in the Taverna of the same name. Their range remains anchored to a selection of classic Brunellos and Rossos built to age well over long periods of time. The 2015 vintage gave rise to two truly remarkable wines. The Vigna del Fiore has all the qualities of a classic, from its expressive depth to its gustatory tension, wholesome fruit and those complex notes that indicate glorious things to come. It's flanked by a harmonious Brunello '15, a classy, characterful wine with lovely hints of tobacco and licorice. The Rosso '18 is also delicious.

Wine	Rating	
● Brunello di Montalcino '15	TT	5
● Brunello di Montalcino V. del Fiore '15	TT	7
● Rosso di Montalcino '18	TT	3
● Brunello di Montalcino '14	YY	5
● Brunello di Montalcino '13	YY	5
● Brunello di Montalcino Ris. '13	YY	7
● Brunello di Montalcino Ris. '12	YY	7
● Brunello di Montalcino Ris. '11	YY	7
● Brunello di Montalcino V. del Fiore '13	YY	7
● Brunello di Montalcino V. del Fiore '12	YY	7
● Brunello di Montalcino V. del Fiore '11	YY	7
● Rosso di Montalcino '17	YY	3
● Rosso di Montalcino '16	YY	3
● Rosso di Montalcino '15	YY	3

Baricci

loc. Colombaio di Montosoli, 13
53024 Montalcino [SI]
Tel. +39 0577848109
www.baricci.it

CELLAR SALES
PRE-BOOKED VISITS
ANNUAL PRODUCTION 30,000 bottles
HECTARES UNDER VINE 5.00

A cru par excellence in northern Montalcino, Montosoli makes its unmistakable voice heard thanks to Rossos and Brunellos moulded at Podere Colombaio. Robust and at the same time racy, taut and tasty, they are in every way 'intergenerational' wines: long maturation in 2000 and 4000-liter Slavonian oak barrels are only a small part of a broader vision, which focuses primarily on the attributes of the six parcels adjacent to the winery. Thus the pioneering work performed by Nello Baricci is carried on by his son-in-law Pietro Buffi and grandsons Federico and Francesco. Baricci is one of those producers that makes it difficult, every year, to choose between excellent Brunellos and charming Rossos. This year, thanks to a favorable 2015, the former edges out the still-delicious latter. A deep, clear ruby red, the Brunello '15 opens on notes of ripe cherry, blackcurrant and blackberry, all of which fade to hints of humus, spice and cinchona-quinine. On the palate it's powerful, assertive, with elegant tannins and an extraordinary overall harmony.

Wine	Rating	
● Brunello di Montalcino '15	TTT	6
● Rosso di Montalcino '18	TT	4
● Brunello di Montalcino '14	YYY	6
● Brunello di Montalcino '10	YYY	6
● Brunello di Montalcino '09	YYY	5
● Brunello di Montalcino '07	YYY	5
● Brunello di Montalcino '83	YYY	5
● Brunello di Montalcino Nello Ris. '10	YYY	6
● Rosso di Montalcino '16	YYY	4*
● Rosso di Montalcino '15	YYY	4*
● Brunello di Montalcino '13	YY	6
● Brunello di Montalcino '12	YY	6
● Brunello di Montalcino Nello Ris. '12	YY	6

Basile

pod. Monte Mario
58044 Cinigiano [GR]
Tel. +39 0564993227
www.basilessa.it

CELLAR SALES
PRE-BOOKED VISITS
ANNUAL PRODUCTION 50,000 bottles
HECTARES UNDER VINE 8.00
VITICULTURE METHOD Certified Organic
SUSTAINABLE WINERY

Founded in 1999 on the Monte Mario estate, the Basile family's winery has quickly gained a well-deserved reputation thanks to its Sangiovese, which is offered in a variety of styles that fully demonstrate the propensity of the areas where it's cultivated. And so it is that Cinigiano has become, in a sense, the "capital" of the Montecucco appellation. There are no trade secrets here, only rigorous work in the vineyard, starting with organic cultivation and an approach to winemaking that eschews shortcuts or unnecessary interference with the natural process of winemaking. The Sangiovese Ad Agio Riserva once again demonstrated that it's one of the best in its class. The 2016 version exhibits a fragrant aromatic profile of red fruit, spices and balsamic hints. In the mouth it tends to persistence and balance. The juicy and supple Sangiovese Cartacanta '17 plays on warm, vibrant, Mediterranean aromas. The rest of their selection also performed well.

Wine	Rating
● Montecucco Sangiovese Ad Agio Ris. '16	🍷🍷 5
● Montecucco Sangiovese Cartacanta '17	🍷🍷 3
● Maremma Toscana Rosso Comandante '17	🍷 4
○ Montecucco Vermentino Arteteca '19	🍷 3
● Montecucco Sangiovese Ad Agio Ris. '15	YYY 5
● Montecucco Sangiovese Ad Agio Ris. '14	YYY 5
● Montecucco Sangiovese Ad Agio Ris. '12	YYY 5
● Maremma Toscana Rosso Comandante '16	YY 4
● Montecucco Sangiovese Ad Agio Ris. '13	YY 5
● Montecucco Sangiovese Ad Agio Ris. '11	YY 5
● Montecucco Sangiovese Cartacanta '16	YY 3
● Montecucco Sangiovese Cartacanta '15	YY 3
● Montecucco Sangiovese Cartacanta '13	YY 3
● Montecucco Sangiovese Cartacanta '12	YY 3

Pietro Beconcini

fraz. La Scala
via Montorzo, 13a
56028 San Miniato [PI]
Tel. +39 0571464785
www.pietrobeconcini.com

CELLAR SALES
PRE-BOOKED VISITS
ANNUAL PRODUCTION 110,000 bottles
HECTARES UNDER VINE 15.00

In the mid-1950s, Leonardo Beconcini's grandfather bought the farm on which he was a sharecropper from the Marquis Ridolfi. The property was passed down to Leonardo through his father, Pietro. Here there was a vineyard of Tempranillo, an Iberian vine that may have been brought to San Miniato by pilgrims on the Via Francigena and from Santiago de Compostela. Leonardo and his partner, Eva, cultivate it, combining it with Sangiovese, Canaiolo, Colorino, Malvasia Bianca and Nera. They and other winemakers contribute to making the area known, thanks to the Consorzio dei Vignaioli di San Miniato. The Maurleo, a blend of Sangiovese and Malvasia Nera, is always tantalizing, with ink, tanned leather and liquorice sensations on a fruity plum base characterizing the 2018. The palate is potent, strong on the tannic side, with a finish on bay leaves and balsamic hints. The Ixe '18, 100% Tempranillo, is powerful on the nose, with a juicy, lively body. The Vin Santo Aria '09 is a sweetly classic wine.

Wine	Rating
● IXE Tempranillo '18	🍷🍷 3
● Terre di Pisa Maurleo '18	🍷🍷 3
● Vin Santo del Chianti Occhio di Pernice Aria '09	🍷🍷 7
○ Bianco Vea '19	🍷 4
● Chianti '19	🍷 2
● Reciso '17	🍷 5
⊙ Rosato Fresco di Nero '19	🍷 2
● IXE Tempranillo '17	YY 3
● Ixe Tempranillo '16	YY 3
● Maurleo '16	YY 3
● Maurleo '15	YY 2*
● Reciso '16	YY 5
○ Vin Santo del Chianti Caratello '09	YY 6
● Vin Santo del Chianti Occhio di Pernice Aria '08	YY 7

Bertinga

loc. Le Terrazze di Adine
53013 Gaiole in Chianti [SI]
Tel. +39 0577746218
www.bertinga.it

ANNUAL PRODUCTION 40,000 bottles
HECTARES UNDER VINE 23.00

Maksim Kashirin and Anatoly Korneev created Bertinga (named after the property's most famous vineyard) from a section of land that once belonged to Castello di Ama, together with La Porta di Vertine (also in Gaiole). So far, the range is divided into 4 wines, all obtained from their privately-owned 23 hectares, with Sangiovese and Merlot making up the lion's share. Elisa Ascani, agronomist, coordinates a first-rate technical team. She also has the support of prestigious international consultants. The finishing touches are being put on their new cellar. That the producer's goal is uncompromising quality and highlighting the attributes of the terroir is evident from tasting the Sassi Chiusi '16, a blend of Sangiovese and Merlot from three vineyards: Adine, Bertinga and Vertine. The big surprise, however, was the Volta di Bertinga '16, which seemed to us, in its fresh and enticing depth, simply the best Italian Merlot tasted this year. We also appreciated the charming Bertinga '16, a blend, and Punta di Adine '16, a monovarietal Sangiovese.

● Volta di Bertinga '16	🍷🍷🍷 8
● Bertinga '16	🍷🍷 6
● Punta di Adine '16	🍷🍷 8
● Sassi Chiusi '16	🍷🍷 5

Bibbiano

via Bibbiano, 76
53011 Castellina in Chianti [SI]
Tel. +39 0577743065
www.bibbiano.com

CELLAR SALES
PRE-BOOKED VISITS
ACCOMMODATION
ANNUAL PRODUCTION 140,000 bottles
HECTARES UNDER VINE 30.00
VITICULTURE METHOD Certified Organic
SUSTAINABLE WINERY

This Castellina in Chianti winery, now run by Tommaso Marrocchesi, has always exhibited respect, both in the cellar and in the vineyard, for the traditions and territory to which it belongs. It's an approach that has allowed it to succeed in building a coherent, personal and in a certain sense classic style of wine, which is still discernible today. No doubt, part of it is the unmistakable mark left by Giulio Gambelli, but it's also the result of a desire to safeguard a precise expressive quality and a particular character of the wines, which consistently reveal a comforting continuity. The Chianti Classico Riserva '17 features elegant aromas dominated by a lush, fruity bouquet, accompanied by spices and smoky touches. In the mouth it's consistent, yet racy, complex and tonic. The primaries are a bit closed with the Gran Selezione Vigna del Capannino '16, though it's compensated by a juicy, sapid palate. The two 2013 Vin Santo San Lorenzo a Bibbianos are a triumph of enological classicism.

● Chianti Cl. Ris. '17	🍷🍷🍷 4*
● Chianti Cl. Gran Selezione V. del Capannino '16	🍷🍷 5
○ Vin Santo del Chianti Cl. San Lorenzo a Bibbiano '13	🍷🍷 5
○ Vin Santo del Chianti Cl. San Lorenzo a Bibbiano Occhio di Pernice '13	🍷🍷 5
● Chianti Cl. '18	🍷 3
● Chianti Cl. '17	🍸🍸 3
● Chianti Cl. '16	🍸🍸 3*
● Chianti Cl. '15	🍸🍸 3
● Chianti Cl. '14	🍸🍸 3
● Chianti Cl. Gran Selezione V. del Capannino '15	🍸🍸 5
● Chianti Cl. Montornello Ris. '13	🍸🍸 4
● Chianti Cl. Ris. '16	🍸🍸 4
● Chianti Cl. Ris. '15	🍸🍸 4

Bindella

FRAZ. ACQUAVIVA
VIA DELLE TRE BERTE, 10A
53045 MONTEPULCIANO [SI]
TEL. +39 0578767777
www.bindella.it

CELLAR SALES
PRE-BOOKED VISITS
ANNUAL PRODUCTION 190,000 bottles
HECTARES UNDER VINE 52.00

When it comes to Montepulciano producers, the winery owned by Swiss Rudolf Bindella really does seem to be one that has taken the most significant steps lately towards becoming a great Sangiovese di Montepulciano powerhouse. At the same time they've also been highlighting the attributes of certain subzones, such as Vallocaia, Santa Maira and Fossolupaio. Increasingly, the Acquaviva winery has shown the ability to offer a range defined by its solid consistency and personality, widespread quality and an elegant, focused style, as well as exhibiting an excellent propensity for aging. The Nobile di Montepulciano I Quadri '17 is a convincingly rich, aromatic, fruity, floral and spicy wine, proving that it's one of the best of its kind by virtue of an extraordinary palate, vivid and rich in chiaroscuro—truly great. The Nobile '17 is equally on the mark, with its clean fragrances and sapid, flavorful palate. The fragrant and juicy Rosso di Montepulciano Fossolupaio '18 proves highly enjoyable as well.

Wine	Glasses	Price
● Nobile di Montepulciano I Quadri '17	🍷🍷🍷	5
● Nobile di Montepulciano '17	🍷🍷	4
⊙ Gemella Rosato '19	🍷🍷	3
● Rosso di Montepulciano Fossolupaio '18	🍷🍷	3
● Nobile di Montepulciano Vallocaia Ris. '16	🍷	6
● Nobile di Montepulciano I Quadri '16	🍸🍸🍸	5
● Nobile di Montepulciano I Quadri '13	🍸🍸🍸	5
● Nobile di Montepulciano I Quadri '12	🍸🍸🍸	5
● Nobile di Montepulciano '16	🍸🍸	4
● Nobile di Montepulciano I Quadri '15	🍸🍸	5
● Nobile di Montepulciano Vallocaia Ris. '15	🍸🍸	6
● Rosso di Montepulciano Fossolupaio '17	🍸🍸	3

★Biondi - Santi Tenuta Greppo

LOC. VILLA GREPPO, 183
53024 MONTALCINO [SI]
TEL. +39 0577848023
www.biondisanti.it

HECTARES UNDER VINE 26.00

Seasoned leaders in the world of wine with the Champagne producer Piper-Heidsieck and the Château la Verrerie in Rodano, the French holding company Epi Group has for some years now had the precious Biondi Santi brand in its portfolio as well. The winery is a symbol of Montalcino and has, like no other, embodied the indomitable spirit of Brunello. At the helm today is Giampiero Bertolini, who's increasingly determined to harmoniously link past and future, protecting the rigorous style of Greppo and further benefiting from the work of internal zoning. Our visit to the winery and tasting the wines still to be released (still in the barrel) confirm the extraordinary skill of the team of professionals who lead this historic maison today. The Riserva '12, unfortunately, reflects a period of transition, with all its uncertainties. It's a great wine that still struggles to find the magical harmony of previous vintages and—we bet—those to come. The Rosso di Montalcino is excellent with its 'small' Brunello character.

Wine	Glasses	Price
● Brunello di Montalcino Ris. '12	🍷🍷	8
● Rosso di Montalcino '16	🍷🍷	7
● Brunello di Montalcino '12	🍸🍸🍸	8
● Brunello di Montalcino '10	🍸🍸🍸	8
● Brunello di Montalcino '09	🍸🍸🍸	8
● Brunello di Montalcino '06	🍸🍸🍸	7
● Brunello di Montalcino '04	🍸🍸🍸	8
● Brunello di Montalcino '03	🍸🍸🍸	8
● Brunello di Montalcino '01	🍸🍸🍸	8
● Brunello di Montalcino Ris. '10	🍸🍸🍸	8
● Brunello di Montalcino Ris. '07	🍸🍸🍸	8
● Brunello di Montalcino Ris. '06	🍸🍸🍸	8
● Brunello di Montalcino Ris. '04	🍸🍸🍸	8
● Brunello di Montalcino Ris. '01	🍸🍸🍸	8
● Brunello di Montalcino Ris. '99	🍸🍸🍸	8
● Brunello di Montalcino Ris. '95	🍸🍸🍸	8

Tenuta di Biserno

LOC. PALAZZO GARDINI
P.ZZA GRAMSCI, 9
57020 BIBBONA [LI]
TEL. +39 0586671099
www.biserno.it

ANNUAL PRODUCTION 160,000 bottles
HECTARES UNDER VINE 99.00

For a long time, Lodovico Antinori had been cultivating the dream of discovering something new. And so, supported by his family and Umberto Mannoni, he went in search of a new, great terroir, and found one on the hills of Bibbona. The estate is beautiful, punctuated by vineyards and a villa that stands out on the highest hill. Here Antinori has renewed a fruitful collaboration with Michel Rolland, proving capable of sculpting modern, international wines, in which extraction and aging in oak make for pulp and intensity. Among the wines tasted this year, the Insoglio del Cinghiale '18 stands out. It's a blend of Syrah, Cabernet Franc, Merlot and Petit Verdot that calls up aromas of small berries on a background of coffee nuances; on the palate it's rather free and pleasant, accented by peppery notes. The Pino '17 is also excellent, more powerful and spicy, enveloped by unique smoky sensations. The Bianco Occhione '19 and the Rosso Biserno '17 are no less good.

● Insoglio del Cinghiale '18	TT 4
● Biserno '17	TT 8
● Il Pino di Biserno '17	TT 6
○ Occhione '19	TT 4
● Biserno '10	YYY 8
● Biserno '08	YYY 6
● Il Pino di Biserno '09	YYY 6
● Biserno '15	YY 8
● Biserno '13	YY 8
● Biserno '12	YY 8
● Biserno '11	YY 8
● Il Pino di Biserno '16	YY 6
● Il Pino di Biserno '14	YY 6
● Il Pino di Biserno '11	YY 6
● Insoglio del Cinghiale '16	YY 4
● Insoglio del Cinghiale '15	YY 4
⊙ Sof '18	YY 3

Borgo Salcetino

LOC. LUCARELLI
53017 RADDA IN CHIANTI [SI]
TEL. +39 0577733541
www.livon.it

PRE-BOOKED VISITS
ANNUAL PRODUCTION 95,000 bottles
HECTARES UNDER VINE 15.00
SUSTAINABLE WINERY

This Chianti estate, owned by the well-known Livon family (wine producers from Friuli), is located in the heart of the Radda in Chianti subzone. Their vineyards grow on one of the best hills of this particular area, next to some of the most significant plots of the entire Chianti Classico appellation. Their style is undoubtedly sound, with a clearly modern approach preserving all the charm of Radda in Chianti wines, unaltered, while exhibiting a commendable precision of execution. The Chianti Classico Gran Selezione I Salci '16 features vibrant, fruity and spicy sensations with hints of pencil lead and licorice to finish a complex aromatic picture. In the mouth it's deep, articulate and juicy, with great flavor and a satisfying sweetness. The olfactory spectrum of the Chianti Classico Lucarello Riserva '16 is more uncertain, marked for the most part by smoky accents of oak that we also find on a tight and, at times, clenched palate.

● Chianti Cl. Gran Selezione I Salci '16	TT 6
● Chianti Cl. Lucarello Ris. '16	T 4
● Chianti Cl. '16	YYY 3*
● Chianti Cl. '15	YYY 3*
● Chianti Cl. '14	YYY 3*
● Chianti Cl. '13	YYY 3*
● Chianti Cl. '11	YYY 3*
● Chianti Cl. Lucarello Ris. '15	YYY 4*
● Rossole '12	YYY 3*
● Chianti Cl. '17	YY 3
● Chianti Cl. '10	YY 3
● Chianti Cl. Gran Selezione I Salci '15	YY 6
● Chianti Cl. Lucarello Ris. '13	YY 4
● Chianti Cl. Lucarello Ris. '12	YY 4
● Chianti Cl. Lucarello Ris. '11	YY 4
● Chianti Cl. Lucarello Ris. '10	YY 4

Il Borro

FRAZ. SAN GIUSTINO VALDARNO
LOC. IL BORRO, 1
52020 LORO CIUFFENNA [AR]
TEL. +39 055977053
www.ilborro.it

CELLAR SALES
PRE-BOOKED VISITS
ACCOMMODATION AND RESTAURANT SERVICE
ANNUAL PRODUCTION 160,000 bottles
HECTARES UNDER VINE 45.00
VITICULTURE METHOD Certified Organic

This historic estate was passed down from the dal Borro family to some of the most important families in Europe. This until 1993, when Ferruccio Ferragamo decided to buy the entire estate and to revive, protect and develop its 700 hectares, the village and the villas. The first wine produced was in 1999, which came after taking the time necessary to identify the most well-suited land for the grape varieties chosen. Then there was the new cellar—more hectares of vineyards followed. The greatest commitment undertaken in recent years has concerned the conversion to biodynamic. Alessandro Del Borro '16 is a monovarietal Syrah produced only in magnums. On the nose it has fresh aromas of underbrush on a fruity base of blackberry and currant before meeting spicy hints of pepper and closing on minty, slightly smoky nuances. In the mouth it opens pulpy but not heavy, with a captivating spicy aftertaste. The Bolle di Borro '14 is a fun Metodo Classico made with Sangiovese.

● Alessandro Dal Borro Syrah '16	🍷🍷🍷 8
⊙ Brut Bolle di Borro '14	🍷🍷 8
● Valdarno di Sopra Petruna '18	🍷🍷 6
● Polissena '17	🍷 5
● Il Borro '16	🍸🍸🍸 7
● Alessandro Dal Borro '15	🍸🍸 8
● Il Borro '15	🍸🍸 7
● Il Borro '12	🍸🍸 7
● Petruna Sangiovese in Anfora '17	🍸🍸 6
● Petruna Sangiovese in Anfora '16	🍸🍸 6
● Pian di Nova '16	🍸🍸 3
● Pian di Nova '15	🍸🍸 3
● Polissena '16	🍸🍸 5
● Polissena '15	🍸🍸 5

★Boscarelli

LOC. CERVOGNANO
VIA DI MONTENERO, 28
53045 MONTEPULCIANO [SI]
TEL. +39 0578767277
www.poderiboscarelli.com

CELLAR SALES
PRE-BOOKED VISITS
ANNUAL PRODUCTION 100,000 bottles
HECTARES UNDER VINE 14.00

The De Ferrari family arrived in Montepulciano in the early 1960s. The winery they founded, which takes its name from the area, gets its grapes mainly from Cervognano, one of the best subzones of Nobile. The producer has always made authentic and long-lived wines, the result of continued reflection and the gradual improvement of their Sangiovese—and theirs is one of the best versions in the entire appellation. With the 2016 version, their Nobile di Montepulciano Il Nocio once again proves that it's a benchmark. Forward-fruit joins with slightly earthy and spicy hints; in the mouth it's juicy and sapid, with sweet-acid contrasts that enliven the palate. The delicious Nobile '17 is right on its heels. Once again a special mention for the Prugnolo '19, Rosso di Montepulciano, a highly drinkable, delectable wine, to say the least. The rest of their range proves more than reliable.

● Nobile di Montepulciano Il Nocio '16	🍷🍷🍷 8
● Nobile di Montepulciano '17	🍷🍷 5
● Rosso di Montepulciano Prugnolo '19	🍷🍷 3*
● Nobile di Montepulciano Costa Grande '16	🍷🍷 5
● Nobile di Montepulciano Et. Bianca Ris. '16	🍷🍷 6
● De Ferrari '18	🍷 3
● Nobile di Montepulciano '16	🍸🍸🍸 5
● Nobile di Montepulciano Il Nocio '13	🍸🍸🍸 8
● Nobile di Montepulciano Il Nocio '12	🍸🍸🍸 8
● Nobile di Montepulciano Il Nocio '11	🍸🍸🍸 8
● Nobile di Montepulciano Nocio dei Boscarelli '10	🍸🍸🍸 8
● Nobile di Montepulciano Nocio dei Boscarelli '09	🍸🍸🍸 8

★Brancaia

Loc. Poppi, 42
53017 Radda in Chianti [SI]
Tel. +39 0577742007
www.brancaia.it

CELLAR SALES
PRE-BOOKED VISITS
ACCOMMODATION AND RESTAURANT SERVICE
ANNUAL PRODUCTION 550,000 bottles
HECTARES UNDER VINE 80.00
VITICULTURE METHOD Certified Organic
SUSTAINABLE WINERY

Owned by the Swiss Widmer family since 1981, Brancaia has a solid foundation in terms of its vineyards, which span two different subzones of the Chianti Classico appellation: Castellina and Radda. What makes the personality and character of the producer's wines so clearly discernible, however, is a stylistic approach of rare finesse, which characterizes their entire range. Even if the grapes derive from completely different soil and climate conditions, it's an expressive 'fil rouge' that we also find in the wines from their Maremma vineyards. The Chianti Classico Riserva '17 exhibits impeccable execution in a modern key, with aromas that alternate fruity notes with spicy accents, smoky hints, evocative touches of chocolate and pencil lead. In the mouth it develops soft and sweet, complex on a dense, pervasive structure. The Blu '17 is a juicy and satisfying blend of Cabernet Sauvignon, Sangiovese and Merlot.

● Brancaia Il Blu '18	🍷🍷 7
● Chianti Cl. Ris. '17	🍷🍷 5
● Il Blu '17	🍷🍷 8
● Tre '18	🍷🍷 3
● Chianti Cl. '18	🍷 4
○ Il Bianco '19	🍷 3
● Ilatraia '17	🍷 7
● Brancaia Il Blu '08	🍷🍷🍷 8
● Brancaia Il Blu '07	🍷🍷🍷 7
● Brancaia Il Blu '06	🍷🍷🍷 6
● Chianti Cl. Brancaia '13	🍷🍷🍷 4*
● Chianti Cl. Ris. '14	🍷🍷🍷 5
● Chianti Cl. Ris. '13	🍷🍷🍷 5
● Chianti Cl. Ris. '11	🍷🍷🍷 5
● Chianti Cl. Ris. '10	🍷🍷🍷 4*
● Chianti Cl. Ris. '09	🍷🍷🍷 7

Brunelli - Le Chiuse di Sotto

Loc. Podernovone, 157
53024 Montalcino [SI]
Tel. +39 0577849337
www.giannibrunelli.it

CELLAR SALES
PRE-BOOKED VISITS
ACCOMMODATION AND RESTAURANT SERVICE
ANNUAL PRODUCTION 30,000 bottles
HECTARES UNDER VINE 6.50
SUSTAINABLE WINERY

Two hectares in Le Chiuse di Sotto (northern Montalcino) and four and a half hectares in Podernovone (southeast) are divided into the parcels of Olmo, Oliva, Quercia and Gelso. It's a special viticultural and pedoclimatic patchwork that expresses the airy and energetic qualities of Sangiovese authored by Maria Laura Vacca, Adriano Brunelli and a close-knit family team. Matured in 2000 and 3000 liter oak casks, their Rossos and Brunellos are consistently among the upper echelons of those produced in Montalcino. The Brunello '15 once again demonstrates that it's a wine of great intensity, as is the style of their Le Chiuse di Sotto line. It's rich in texture, fruit, with an earthy, rustic character that will take time to soften, but it has plenty of substance. In the meantime we'll enjoy the Amor Costante '16, a well-made blend of Merlot and Sangiovese with a rich, fruity character and nice harmony.

● Brunello di Montalcino '15	🍷🍷 6
● Amor Costante '16	🍷🍷 5
● Amor Costante '05	🍷🍷🍷 5
● Brunello di Montalcino '14	🍷🍷🍷 6
● Brunello di Montalcino '12	🍷🍷🍷 6
● Brunello di Montalcino '10	🍷🍷🍷 6
● Amor Costante '15	🍷🍷 5
● Brunello di Montalcino '13	🍷🍷 6
● Brunello di Montalcino '11	🍷🍷 6
● Brunello di Montalcino '09	🍷🍷 6
● Brunello di Montalcino Ris. '13	🍷🍷 8
● Brunello di Montalcino Ris. '10	🍷🍷 8
● Rosso di Montalcino '17	🍷🍷 4
● Rosso di Montalcino '16	🍷🍷 4
● Rosso di Montalcino '13	🍷🍷 4
● Rosso di Montalcino '12	🍷🍷 4
● Brunello di Montalcino Ris. '12	🍷 8

Bruni

fraz. Fonteblanda
s.da vic.le Migliorina, 6
58015 Orbetello [GR]
Tel. +39 0564885445
www.aziendabruni.it

CELLAR SALES
ANNUAL PRODUCTION 500,000 bottles
HECTARES UNDER VINE 48.00

Marco and Moreno Bruni's winery is not only significant for the consistency, in terms of quality, of its wines, which are of impeccable craftsmanship, but also for keen decision-making. The most evident example is the decision to focus on a monovarietal Alicante, or Grenache or Cannonau or, to piece together Maremma's enological history, a wine made from uva Spagna ('Spanish grapes'). It's their Oltreconfine, which debuted with the 2013 vintage and whose first versions were aged in barriques. Today the wine, which has graduated to large oak barrels, increasingly exhibits an elegant, balanced style. By now a solid benchmark for Maremma's reds, the 2018 version of their Alicante Oltreconfine hits the absolute peaks of excellence, proving elegant and of impeccable craftsmanship. The Perlaia '19, a Vermentino with an original, balanced style, deserves special praise, especially in light of the hot area. The Morellino Laire Riserva '17 also delivers.

- ● Maremma Toscana Alicante Oltreconfine '18 — TTT 6
- ● Morellino Di Scansano Laire Ris. '17 — TT 5
- ○ Perlaia Vermentino '19 — TT 4
- ○ Maremma Toscana Vermentino Plinio '19 — TT 3
- ● Grenache Oltreconfine '13 — YYY 2*
- ● Maremma Toscana Alicante Oltreconfine '15 — YYY 6
- ● Maremma Toscana Grenache Oltreconfine '16 — YYY 6
- ● Maremma Toscana Oltreconfine '17 — YYY 5
- ● Maremma Toscana Grenache Oltreconfine '14 — YY 5
- ○ Maremma Toscana Vermentino Perlaia V. T. '18 — YY 3*
- ● Morellino di Scansano Laire Ris. '13 — YY 4

Alejandro Bulgheroni Family Vineyards

fraz. Vagliagli
loc. Dievole, 6
53019 Castelnuovo Berardenga [SI]
Tel. +39 0577322613
www.dievole.it

CELLAR SALES
PRE-BOOKED VISITS
ACCOMMODATION AND RESTAURANT SERVICE
ANNUAL PRODUCTION 350,000 bottles
HECTARES UNDER VINE 80.00

Alejandro Bulgheroni Family Vineyards is a veritable enological mosaic. The Argentine oil magnate, who was already operating in the wine world with companies in Uruguay and Argentina, built it in a short time (starting in 2012) by acquiring land and wineries in some of Tuscany's best terroirs. Needless to say, excellence is their goal: Dievole and Certosa di Pontignano in Chianti Classico, Podere Brizio and Poggio Landi in Montalcino, Tenuta Le Colonne and Tenuta Meraviglia in Bolgheri. The Chianti Classico Novecento Riserva '17 is redolent of ripe red berries, wild herb and spices, topped off by smoky accents and undergrowth. In the mouth it has nice texture, stretching vivid and well contrasted, sapid—a well-sustained and juicy palate finishes on an encore of fruit. The Chianti Classico '18, with its lovely Chianti character, is fragrant and flavorful. The wines of their Bolgheri estates are also excellent.

- ● Chianti Cl. Novecento Ris. Dievole '17 — TT 5
- ● Bolgheri Rosso Sup. Maestro di Cava Tenuta Meraviglia '17 — TT 7
- ● Chianti Cl. Dievole '18 — TT 4
- ● Plenum Tenuta Le Colonne '18 — TT 4
- ● Chianti Cl. Novecento Ris. Dievole '14 — YYY 5
- ● Chianti Cl. '13 — YY 4
- ● Chianti Cl. Dievole '17 — YY 4
- ● Chianti Cl. Dievole '15 — YY 4
- ● Chianti Cl. Gran Selezione V. di Sessina Dievole '16 — YY 7
- ● Chianti Cl. Gran Selezione V. di Sessina Dievole '15 — YY 7
- ● Chianti Cl. La Vendemmia '12 — YY 3
- ● Chianti Cl. Novecento Ris. Dievole '16 — YY 5
- ● Chianti Cl. Ris. '13 — YY 5

Bulichella

loc. Bulichella, 131
57028 Suvereto [LI]
Tel. +39 0565829892
www.bulichella.it

CELLAR SALES
PRE-BOOKED VISITS
ACCOMMODATION AND RESTAURANT SERVICE
ANNUAL PRODUCTION 60,000 bottles
HECTARES UNDER VINE 17.00
VITICULTURE METHOD Certified Organic

The history of Bulichella is quite interesting. It was founded in 1993 by 4 families who left their respective homes to create a community where they could raise their children together and work on a project linked to the land. All this until 1999, when Marisa and Hideyuki Miyakawa bought the entire property and began an adventure that continues to this day: to emphasize the pioneering choice, at least in the area, to follow the dictates of organic farming. Wines can be shipped directly, and aren't without a certain originality. The excellent Montecristo '17 is a blend of Cabernet, Merlot and Petit Verdot. It has a multifaceted nose of cherry and blackberry, with spicy hints of cloves, reaching vegetal tones; in the mouth it has nice weight, a pervasive impact, a fresh, acidic vein, and a dynamic, long finish. The Syrah Hide '17 is enticing: pepper combines with lively balsamic nuances, then fruity notes of currant. The palate is creamy and rich, with subtle tannins and a pleasantly sapid finish.

● Suvereto Montecristo '17	🍷🍷 2*
● Suvereto Coldipietre Rosse '17	🍷🍷 5
● Syrah Hide '17	🍷🍷 5
⊙ Rosato Sol Sera '19	🍷 3
○ Vermentino Tuscanio '19	🍷 3
● Hyde '16	YY 5
● Suvereto Cabernet Coldipietrerosse '13	YY 5
● Suvereto Coldipietre Rosse '16	YY 5
● Suvereto Coldipietre Rosse '15	YY 5
● Suvereto Montecristo '16	YY 2*
● Suvereto Montecristo '15	YY 2*

Buondonno Casavecchia alla Piazza

loc. La Piazza, 37
53011 Castellina in Chianti [SI]
Tel. +39 0577749754
www.buondonno.com

CELLAR SALES
PRE-BOOKED VISITS
ACCOMMODATION
ANNUAL PRODUCTION 40,000 bottles
HECTARES UNDER VINE 11.00
VITICULTURE METHOD Certified Organic
SUSTAINABLE WINERY

Casavecchia alla Piazza, which lends its name to the winery Buondonno, is a property with deep agricultural roots. In 1988 agronomists Gabriele Buondonno and Valeria Sodano became the owners, launching their enological project. The choice to cultivate the vineyards organically came almost immediately, in a period when this type of approach was a pioneering one. In the cellar, as well, they've adopted non-invasive methods, with maturation carried out in large wood barrels. The result is a range of wines with a decidedly Chianti-like character, pleasant and at the same time complex. Made with grapes from vines still tree-trained on maples (from the sharecropping era), the Lemme Lemme is what one would call an 'old-fashioned Chianti'. A blend of Sangiovese, Canaiolo, Malvasia Nera, Colorino and Trebbiano, it matures in ceramic for 12 months. The 2018 has a fragrant olfactory profile, while in the mouth it's delectable, sapid and juicy. The Chianti Classico '18 is just as pleasant.

● Chianti Cl. '18	🍷🍷 4
● Lemme Lemme '18	🍷🍷 6
● Cabernet Franc '18	🍷🍷 5
● Chianti Cl. Ris. '17	🍷🍷 5
● Chianti Cl. Casavecchia alla Piazza '15	YYY 3*
● Chianti Cl. '09	YY 3
● Chianti Cl. Casavecchia alla Piazza '17	YY 3
● Chianti Cl. Casavecchia alla Piazza '16	YY 3*
● Chianti Cl. Casavecchia alla Piazza Ris. '16	YY 3*
● Chianti Cl. Casavecchia alla Piazza Ris. '15	YY 3
● Chianti Cl. Ris. '13	YY 5
● Chianti Cl. Ris. '08	YY 5
● Chianti Cl. Ris. '07	YY 5
● Lemme Lemme '16	YY 6

Caccia al Piano 1868

Loc. Bolgheri
via Bolgherese, 279
57022 Castagneto Carducci [LI]
Tel. +39 0565763394
www.berlucchi.it

CELLAR SALES
PRE-BOOKED VISITS
ANNUAL PRODUCTION 127,000 bottles
HECTARES UNDER VINE 18.00
SUSTAINABLE WINERY

Caccia al Piano is owned by the Ziliani family (originally from Franciacorta). Today Arturo, Paolo and Cristina, in addition to Guido Berlucchi, lead this beautiful, 30-hectare estate in the heart of the appellation. A new, modern cellar has been built on the Via Bolgherese, following the inspiration of their father Franco, who bought the property from the Della Gherardesca family in 2003. The estate's vineyards, Le Grottine, San Biagio and Caccia al Piano, which are planted at high density on different soils, give rise to Cabernet Sauvignon and Franc, Syrah, Merlot, Petit Verdot and Vermentino grapes. With the maturity of their vineyards (the oldest go back about 20 years), Caccia al Piano's wines are showing signs of stylistic maturity and territorial adherence. The Levia Gravia '16, which reached our finals, proves it. This elegant blend of Cabernet Sauvignon, Franc and Merlot comes from their San Biagio vineyard, at 210 meters above sea level. It has lush, crisp fruit, velvety tannins and delicate Mediterranean fragrances. The other wines tasted are also quite valid.

● Bolgheri Rosso Sup. Levia Gravia '16	🍷🍷 7
● Bolgheri Rosso Ruit Hora '17	🍷🍷 4
● Grottaia Rosso '19	🍷🍷 3
● Bolgheri Levia Gravia '05	YY 7
● Bolgheri Rosso Ruit Hora '16	YY 4
● Bolgheri Ruit Hora '15	YY 4
● Bolgheri Sup. Levia Gravia '13	YY 7
● Bolgheri Sup. Levia Gravia '08	YY 7
● Bolgheri Sup. Levia Gravia '06	YY 7
● Grottaia Rosso '18	YY 3*
● Grottaia Rosso '16	YY 3

Caiarossa

Loc. Serra all'Olio, 59
56046 Riparbella [PI]
Tel. +39 0586699016
www.caiarossa.com

CELLAR SALES
PRE-BOOKED VISITS
ANNUAL PRODUCTION 130,000 bottles
HECTARES UNDER VINE 32.00
VITICULTURE METHOD Certified Biodynamic

Situated in the southernmost part of the province of Pisa, not far from the sea, Caiarossa is dedicated to principles of biodynamic agriculture. Syrah, Cabernet Sauvignon and Franc, Sangiovese, Merlot, Chardonnay and Viognier all grow well here. In the winery itself, which is structured on four levels and designed according to principles of Feng Shui, winemaking is powered by gravity. Because of its colors, location, and construction techniques used, it's been included in the Toscana Wine Architecture project, which is promoted by the region of Tuscany and comprises 14 wineries all chosen for their peculiarities. The Aria di Caiarossa '16, a blend of Cabernet Franc, Merlot, Syrah and Petit Verdot, took home Tre Bicchieri. A minty bouquet drives a fruity profile wrought of delicious berries, while the palate exhibits great balance, with tannins blended with alcohol, a refreshing acidic backbone and an appetizing finish. The Caiarossa '16 is more austere but very pleasant.

● Aria di Caiarossa '16	🍷🍷🍷 5
● Caiarossa '17	🍷🍷 6
○ Caiarossa Bianco '18	🍷🍷 5
● Pergolaia '16	🍷🍷 3
● Aria di Caiarossa '15	YY 5
● Aria di Caiarossa '13	YY 5
○ Bianco '17	YY 4
● Caiarossa '16	YY 6
● Caiarossa '13	YY 6
● Caiarossa '12	YY 6
○ Oro di Caiarossa '14	YY 6
● Pergolaia '15	YY 3
● Pergolaia '13	YY 3

Camigliano

LOC. CAMIGLIANO
VIA D'INGRESSO, 2
53024 MONTALCINO [SI]
TEL. +39 0577844068
www.camigliano.it

CELLAR SALES
PRE-BOOKED VISITS
ANNUAL PRODUCTION 350,000 bottles
HECTARES UNDER VINE 92.00
SUSTAINABLE WINERY

It was the late 1950's when the Ghezzi family decided to renovate the centuries-old property of Camigliano, transforming it into the beating heart of production. It's a bond testified to by a long series of Brunellos that have with surgical precision recreated the Mediterranean atmosphere of this enclave in the western part of Montalcino, almost in Maremma. Aged in medium and large French oak barrels, there are now three versions: the Paesaggio Inatteso, the 'standard-label' version and the Gualto Riserva. The Brunello '15 stood out in our finals, bringing Camigliano its second award. It's a Brunello with structure and generosity, but one that manages to express an elegance, balance and cleanness of fruit associated with wines from further north. In the mouth it's harmonious, long, irresistible. The Paesaggio Inatteso '15 is softer, subtler, while the Poderuccio '18 proves modern and enjoyable. The other wines tasted are also valid.

● Brunello di Montalcino '15	TTT 6
● Brunello di Montalcino Paesaggio Inatteso '15	TT 7
⊙ Gamal Rosato '19	TT 2*
● Poderuccio '18	TT 2*
○ Gamal '19	T 2
● Brunello di Montalcino Gualto Ris. '12	YYY 8
● Brunello di Montalcino '14	YY 6
● Brunello di Montalcino '13	YY 6
● Brunello di Montalcino '12	YY 6
● Brunello di Montalcino '11	YY 6
● Brunello di Montalcino Gualto Ris. '13	YY 8
● Brunello di Montalcino Paesaggio Inatteso '12	YY 7
● Brunello di Montalcino Ris. '11	YY 6
● Rosso di Montalcino '17	YY 3
● Rosso di Montalcino '15	YY 3

Antonio Camillo

LOC. PIANETTI DI MONTEMERANO
58014 MANCIANO [GR]
TEL. +39 3391525224
www.antoniocamillo.it

CELLAR SALES
PRE-BOOKED VISITS
ANNUAL PRODUCTION 95,000 bottles
HECTARES UNDER VINE 17.00
VITICULTURE METHOD Certified Organic

Antonio Camillo's work embodies the most intimate qualities of the Maremma wine world today, and his marked, frank humanity makes this an even more significant achievement. The wines he has crafted have quietly made a name for themselves, thanks primarily to an approach to Ciliegiolo that's like nothing else in the recent past. These stand out for their clearly discernible style, original features and distinct personality. On the other hand, in many ways Morellino Sangiovese remains a work in progress, but one that's showing good results. With its aromas of small red fruits and herbs, spices and flint, the Vallerana Alta '18 exhibits an irresistible, mouth-watering and tasty palate —it's an elegant, vivid Ciliegiolo. Equally successful, albeit with a simpler and more casual approach, the Ciliegiolo '19 offers up fragrant aromas and a weighty palate, seeming to open the way to a great version of its older brother.

● Ciliegiolo '19	TT 3*
● Vallerana Alta Ciliegiolo '18	TT 5
● Morellino di Scansano '19	T 3
● Maremma Toscana Ciliegiolo V. Vallerana Alta '16	YYY 5
● Maremma Toscana Ciliegiolo V. Vallerana Alta '15	YYY 6
● Maremma Toscana Ciliegiolo V. Vallerana Alta '14	YYY 3*
● Ciliegiolo '18	YY 3
● Maremma Toscana Ciliegiolo '17	YY 3
● Maremma Toscana Ciliegiolo V. Vallerana Alta '13	YY 3*
● Maremma Toscana Ciliegiolo V. Vallerana Alta '12	YY 3*
● Maremma Toscana Ciliegiolo V. Vallerana Alta '11	YY 3*

Campo alla Sughera

LOC. CACCIA AL PIANO
S.DA PROV.LE BOLGHERESE, 280
57020 BOLGHERI [LI]
TEL. +39 0565766936
www.campoallasughera.com

CELLAR SALES
PRE-BOOKED VISITS
ACCOMMODATION
ANNUAL PRODUCTION 110,000 bottles
HECTARES UNDER VINE 16.50

This splendid estate is managed by the German Knauf family, successful entrepreneurs with valuable winemaking experience in their homeland. The property is gorgeous, and attention has been shown to every detail, starting with the cellar. The vineyards are, needless to say, excellent, growing in light soils caressed by the sea breeze. Divided into 15 micro-sites, each of the 38 plots gets tailored care, making for an elegant and flavorful range of wines, 'Bolgheri' in the best sense of the word. For us the most convincing wine tasted this year was the Bolgheri Rosso Adeo '18. Supported by measured fruit, it virtuously combines expressive integrity and aromatic maturity across a clear, focused and dynamic palate, as fresh as it is deep, with great flavor and a long finish. Truly a performance to remember. The Bolgheri Superiore Arnione '17 is warmer and marked by toastiness, while the Bianco Arioso '19 proves pleasantly fresh.

- ● Bolgheri Rosso Adeo '18 **YY** 5
- ○ Arioso '19 **Y** 5
- ● Bolgheri Rosso Sup. Arnione '17 **Y** 6
- ● Bolgheri Sup. Arnione '06 YYY 6
- ○ Bolgheri Achenio '12 YY 5
- ● Bolgheri Adeo '12 YY 4
- ○ Bolgheri Bianco Achenio '16 YY 5
- ● Bolgheri Rosso Adeo '17 YY 5
- ● Bolgheri Rosso Adeo '16 YY 5
- ● Bolgheri Rosso Sup. Arnione '15 YY 6
- ● Bolgheri Sup. Arnione '14 YY 6
- ● Bolgheri Sup. Arnione '11 YY 6
- ● Campo alla Sughera Rosso '15 YY 8

Canalicchio - Franco Pacenti

LOC. CANALICCHIO DI SOPRA, 6
53024 MONTALCINO [SI]
TEL. +39 0577849277
www.canalicchiofrancopacenti.it

CELLAR SALES
PRE-BOOKED VISITS
RESTAURANT SERVICE
ANNUAL PRODUCTION 40,000 bottles
HECTARES UNDER VINE 10.00

Founded in the 1960s by Rosildo and then converted into a bottler in 1988, the winery, now managed by Franco Pacenti, takes its name from one of the most reputable locations in the northern part of Montalcino. At Franco's side are his children Lisa, Serena and Lorenzo, who share in the work of overseeing 10 or so hectares of land cultivated exclusively with Sangiovese. Situated at around 300 meters above sea level on Canalicchi's characteristic clayey-stony soils, these give rise to traditionally-styled Rossos and Brunellos aged in medium-large Slavonian oak barrels. We very much appreciated the Brunello '15. It's intense, close-woven, rich in fruit and balance, supported by a brilliant acidic vein that carries its fruit through a long finish adorned with soft tannins and fresh Mediterranean herbs. The Rosso '17 is even more expressive, pouring a lovely ruby garnet color, complex on the nose in its notes of morello cherry, tobacco and mint, coming through harmonious and long on the palate. Intensity, complexity and mature notes feature in the Brunello Rosildo 15.

- ● Brunello di Montalcino '15 **YY** 7
- ● Brunello di Montalcino Rosildo '15 **YY** 8
- ● Rosso di Montalcino '17 **YY** 3
- ● Brunello di Montalcino '04 YYY 5
- ● Brunello di Montalcino '14 YY 7
- ● Brunello di Montalcino '12 YY 5
- ● Brunello di Montalcino '11 YY 5
- ● Brunello di Montalcino '10 YY 5
- ● Brunello di Montalcino Ris. '10 YY 7
- ● Rosso di Montalcino '16 YY 3
- ● Rosso di Montalcino '15 YY 3
- ● Rosso di Montalcino '13 YY 3
- ● Rosso di Montalcino '10 YY 3

Canalicchio di Sopra

Loc. Casaccia, 73
53024 Montalcino [SI]
Tel. +39 0577848316
www.canalicchiodisopra.com

CELLAR SALES
PRE-BOOKED VISITS
ACCOMMODATION
ANNUAL PRODUCTION 55,000 bottles
HECTARES UNDER VINE 15.00

Siblings Simonetta, Marco and Francesco Ripaccioli are now fully in control of the winery founded in the 1960s by their grandfather Primo Pacenti, and later consolidated by their father, Pier Luigi. It's a producer that's made the most of the two districts (I Canalicchi and Montosoli) that host the estate's vineyards in northern Montalcino. With the 2015 vintage, their standard-label Brunello and Riserva are joined by La Casaccia, the first official cru in the history of Canalicchio di Sopra. It's a natural choice, considering the extensive work of mapping the parcels, all vinified separately. The cru La Casaccia '15 plays on vibrant and clear fruit. A youthful exuberance is accompanied by notes of aromatic and medicinal herbs, spices and delicate smoky nuances. It's soft and rich in the mouth, with smooth tannins. The Brunello '15 has a more classic profile and a more measured expressiveness, but it's clear and focused, taut and beautifully harmonious. The Rosso '18, a 'mini' Brunello, made it into our finals by virtue of its fruity notes, backbone and structure. Truly delicious.

● Rosso di Montalcino '18	🍷🍷 3*
● Brunello di Montalcino '15	🍷🍷 6
● Brunello di Montalcino La Casaccia '15	🍷🍷 8
● Brunello di Montalcino '10	🍷🍷🍷 6
● Brunello di Montalcino '07	🍷🍷🍷 6
● Brunello di Montalcino '06	🍷🍷🍷 6
● Brunello di Montalcino '04	🍷🍷🍷 6
● Brunello di Montalcino Ris. '10	🍷🍷🍷 8
● Brunello di Montalcino Ris. '07	🍷🍷🍷 8
● Brunello di Montalcino Ris. '04	🍷🍷🍷 7
● Brunello di Montalcino Ris. '01	🍷🍷🍷 7
● Brunello di Montalcino '13	🍷🍷 6
● Brunello di Montalcino Ris. '13	🍷🍷 8
● Brunello di Montalcino Ris. '12	🍷🍷 8
● Rosso di Montalcino '17	🍷🍷 3
● Rosso di Montalcino '15	🍷🍷 3*

Capanna

Loc. Capanna, 333
53024 Montalcino [SI]
Tel. +39 0577848298
www.capannamontalcino.com

CELLAR SALES
PRE-BOOKED VISITS
ACCOMMODATION AND RESTAURANT SERVICE
ANNUAL PRODUCTION 80,000 bottles
HECTARES UNDER VINE 23.00

Owned by the Cencioni family since the 1950s, Capanna is situated in the northern part of Montalcino, on a bright hill adjacent to the hillock of Montosoli, an area marked by elevations of around 300 meters and tough marl soil. Led by Patrizio with the support of his son Amedeo, the producer is universally appreciated for its Sangiovese da Brunello, regularly recognizable for its lush, vivacious character. Theirs is a great history enriched by their Capanna Suites (farmstay accommodations, spa and wine club) and restaurant Il Passaggio. The Brunello '15 made it into our finals: it's an intense wine, rich, exuberant in its fruit, gracefully supported by a fresh acidic backbone and smooth, caressing tannins. Harmonious and warm, it's just a bit dried by alcohol on the finish. The Moscadello Vendemmia Tardiva '17, with its lovely antique gold color, hints of dates and dried figs, is worth mentioning as well.

● Brunello di Montalcino '15	🍷🍷 7
○ Moscadello di Montalcino '19	🍷🍷 3
○ Moscadello di Montalcino V. T. '17	🍷🍷 5
● Sant'Antimo Rosso '17	🍷🍷 4
● Rosso di Montalcino '18	🍷 3
● Brunello di Montalcino Ris. '10	🍷🍷🍷 8
● Brunello di Montalcino Ris. '06	🍷🍷🍷 7
● Brunello di Montalcino Ris. '04	🍷🍷🍷 7
● Brunello di Montalcino Ris. '90	🍷🍷🍷 6
● Rosso di Montalcino '15	🍷🍷🍷 3*
● Brunello di Montalcino '14	🍷🍷 6
● Brunello di Montalcino '13	🍷🍷 6
● Brunello di Montalcino 50° Vendemmia Ris. '13	🍷🍷 8
● Brunello di Montalcino Ris. '12	🍷🍷 8
○ Moscadello di Montalcino V. T. '15	🍷🍷 4
● Rosso di Montalcino '17	🍷🍷 3

★Tenuta di Capezzana

loc. Seano
via Capezzana, 100
59015 Carmignano [PO]
Tel. +39 0558706005
www.capezzana.it

CELLAR SALES
PRE-BOOKED VISITS
ACCOMMODATION AND RESTAURANT SERVICE
ANNUAL PRODUCTION 400,000 bottles
HECTARES UNDER VINE 75.00
VITICULTURE METHOD Certified Organic

Capezzana, one of Tuscany's oldest producers, has been making wine since 804. In the 1920s, the Contini Bonacossi family bought the property, which was then expanded with two neighboring farms. Thus Tenuta di Capezzana was born, an estate that found in Ugo Contini Bonacossi a true leader and developer. Today his children carry on his work: Beatrice, flanked by her sister Benedetta, winemaker, and her brother Filippo, who's responsible for the production of oil and the financial side of things.
And when it comes to the most recent generation, Serena oversees hospitality and Gaddo the fields. The UCB '16, a monovarietal Sangiovese, put in an excellent performance. On the nose it exhibits nice, strong fruit, with slight notes of Mediterranean scrub. On the palate it opens pulpy, sapid, elegant and harmonious, closing long and creamy. The Carmignano Trefiano Riserva '16 unveils a mature nose characterized by medicinal herbs, jammy hints and assorted spices; the palate is soft, juicy and quite open.

● UCB Ugo Contini Bonacossi '16	**YY** 7
● Carmignano Trefiano Ris. '16	**YY** 6
● Carmignano Villa di Capezzana 10 Anni '10	**YY** 5
● Carmignano Villa di Capezzana '07	YYY 4
● Carmignano Villa di Capezzana '05	YYY 4
● Carmignano Villa di Capezzana '99	YYY 5
● Ghiaie della Furba '01	YYY 5
● Ghiaie della Furba '98	YYY 5
○ Vin Santo di Carmignano Ris. '12	YYY 6
○ Vin Santo di Carmignano Ris. '10	YYY 6
○ Vin Santo di Carmignano Ris. '09	YYY 6
○ Vin Santo di Carmignano Ris. '08	YYY 6
○ Vin Santo di Carmignano Ris. '07	YYY 6
○ Vin Santo di Carmignano Ris. '05	YYY 5

Caprili

fraz. Tavernelle
loc. Caprili, 268
53024 Montalcino [SI]
Tel. +39 0577848566
www.caprili.it

CELLAR SALES
PRE-BOOKED VISITS
ACCOMMODATION
ANNUAL PRODUCTION 75,000 bottles
HECTARES UNDER VINE 21.00
SUSTAINABLE WINERY

The Bartolommei family's production adventure began in the 1960s with the acquisition of the noble Castelli-Martinozzi family's Caprili estate. Now managed energetically by young Giacomo, the estate has become a benchmark for those looking for a radiant though complex Sangiovese da Brunello. Such interpretations are consistent with the pedoclimatic characteristics of southwest Montalcino. Here their various, distinct vineyards are cultivated before maturing separately in large barrels. The Brunello '15 pours a dark ruby color, then opens on notes of red fruit, which turn to quinine and liquorice. The palate is also dense and close-knit, rich in texture and fruit, with oaky and toasty nuances. It's an excellent wine, but will need some time before discovering the magic of the best vintages. The Moscadello '19, with its lovely floral nose, proves well made: delicately sweet and fresh. The Rosso '18 performs on good levels, though we would have expected more.

● Brunello di Montalcino '15	**YY** 6
○ Moscadello di Montalcino '19	**YY** 3
● Rosso di Montalcino '18	**Y** 3
● Brunello di Montalcino '13	YYY 6
● Brunello di Montalcino '10	YYY 6
● Brunello di Montalcino '06	YYY 7
● Brunello di Montalcino AdAlberto Ris. '10	YYY 8
● Brunello di Montalcino Ris. '08	YYY 7
● Brunello di Montalcino Ris. '06	YYY 7
● Brunello di Montalcino Ris. '04	YYY 5
● Brunello di Montalcino '14	YY 6
● Brunello di Montalcino '12	YY 6
● Brunello di Montalcino AdAlberto Ris. '12	YY 8
● Rosso di Montalcino '16	YY 3*
● Rosso di Montalcino '15	YY 3

Tenuta Carleone

loc. Castiglioni
53017 Radda in Chianti [SI]
Tel. +39 0577735613
www.carleone.it

CELLAR SALES
PRE-BOOKED VISITS
ANNUAL PRODUCTION 35,000 bottles
HECTARES UNDER VINE 15.00
VITICULTURE METHOD Certified Organic

Karl Egger, an industrialist with a passion for wine, began his winemaking project in 2012. Along the way, he's certainly enjoyed the insights of Sean O'Callaghan, a winemaker who's had plenty of success in the Chianti hills. The Austrian-owned winery is located in the subzone of Radda in Chianti, a decisive element that, from the beginning, has conferred personality and character on the producer's wines, which are capable of expressing all the elegance and consistence of which Sangiovese is capable. The 2017 version of their Uno, a monovarietal Sangiovese, proves generous, bringing together aromas of ripe red berries accompanied by spicy and smoky touches. In the mouth it's sweet and well-sustained, with full, tasty tannins. The Guercio '17, another Sangiovese, is good, with fruity aromas and a pervasive development of flavor. Aromatically the Chianti Classico '17 is not completely focused, but the wine finds its strong point on a light, flavorful palate.

● Il Guercio '18	🍷🍷 7
● Uno '17	🍷🍷 8
● Chianti Cl. '17	🍷🍷 5
● Chianti Cl. '15	🍸🍸🍸 5
● Uno '16	🍸🍸🍸 8
● Chianti Cl. '16	🍸🍸 5
● Il Due '15	🍸🍸 6
● Il Guercio '17	🍸🍸 7
● Il Guercio '16	🍸🍸 7
● Il Guercio '15	🍸🍸 7

★Fattoria Carpineta Fontalpino

fraz. Montaperti
loc. Carpineta
53019 Castelnuovo Berardenga [SI]
Tel. +39 0577369219
www.carpinetafontalpino.it

CELLAR SALES
PRE-BOOKED VISITS
ACCOMMODATION
ANNUAL PRODUCTION 100,000 bottles
HECTARES UNDER VINE 23.00
VITICULTURE METHOD Certified Organic

The winery overseen by siblings Gioia and Filippo Cresti is situated just a stone's throw from Montaperti, in the Gallo Nero subzone of Castelnuovo Berardenga. For some time now, they've been producing wines of solid and consistent quality—wines with a close-knit style and a modern approach capable of expressing the most characteristic qualities of their territory of origin, both when it comes to DOC and IGT. Here unhesitating craftsmanship comes together with generous and clearly discernible personality. The growth of this Castelnuovo Berardenga producer's line of Chianti Classicos is increasingly evident. The Chianti Classico Montaperto '17 is one of the best of its kind, both in terms of its technical precision and for its stylistic personality and consistency: on the nose it offers up lush, spicy fruitiness, while a fragrant sapidity characterizes a pleasantly satisfying palate—it's difficult not to go back for seconds.

● Chianti Cl. Montaperto '17	🍷🍷🍷 4*
● Chianti Cl. Dofana '17	🍷🍷 4
● Chianti Cl. Fontalpino '18	🍷🍷 3*
● Chianti Cl. Dofana '16	🍸🍸🍸 4*
● Chianti Cl. Fontalpino '17	🍸🍸🍸 3*
● Chianti Cl. Montaperto '15	🍸🍸🍸 4*
● Do ut des '13	🍸🍸🍸 5
● Do ut des '12	🍸🍸🍸 5
● Do ut des '11	🍸🍸🍸 5
● Do ut des '10	🍸🍸🍸 5
● Do ut des '09	🍸🍸🍸 5
● Do ut des '07	🍸🍸🍸 5
● Dofana '10	🍸🍸🍸 7
● Dofana '07	🍸🍸🍸 8
● Chianti Cl. Montaperto '16	🍸🍸 4
● Do ut des '16	🍸🍸 5
● Do ut des '15	🍸🍸 5

Carpineto

loc. Dudda, 17b
50022 Greve in Chianti [FI]
Tel. +39 0558549086
www.carpineto.com

CELLAR SALES
PRE-BOOKED VISITS
ANNUAL PRODUCTION 1,500,000 bottles
HECTARES UNDER VINE 165.00

Founded in 1967 by Giovanni Carlo Sacchet and Antonio Mario Zaccheo, today Carpineto boasts several properties, from the Dudda Estate (Greve in Chianti) to that of Gaville (Upper Valdarno), Gavorrano in Maremma, Montepulciano (perhaps the most important production area) and Montalcino (Il Forteto del Drago, their most recent acquisition). It's a multi-layered mosaic of properties held together by their shared Tuscan heritage, making for a small wine 'empire' of significant quality. The Nobile di Montepulciano Riserva '16, a red of great character and complexity, topped our preferences. Notes of tobacco, spices and black fruit anticipate a deep and balanced palate, with mature tannins and a clean finish. Their Brunello '15, whose grapes are cultivated in Montalcino, is another characterful bottle, marked by notes of quinine and liquorice, and a powerful palate with a fruit-forward finish. The Rosso di Montalcino '17 is youthful, but well made and, thanks to the vintage, already showing a structure similar to its older brother.

● Nobile di Montepulciano Ris. '16	🍷🍷 5
● Brunello di Montalcino '15	🍷🍷 7
● Rosso di Montalcino '17	🍷🍷 5

Casa alle Vacche

fraz. Pancole
loc. Lucignano, 73a
53037 San Gimignano [SI]
Tel. +39 0577955103
www.casaallevacche.it

CELLAR SALES
PRE-BOOKED VISITS
ACCOMMODATION AND RESTAURANT SERVICE
ANNUAL PRODUCTION 120,000 bottles
HECTARES UNDER VINE 28.00
SUSTAINABLE WINERY

During the 19th century, the oldest building on the farm was used as a stable, hence the name of the property ('vacche' means 'cows'). For generations, the Ciappi family have dedicated themselves to cultivating the land and producing wine and oil. For about twenty years now they've also dealt in hospitality, thanks to farmstay accommodations. Integrated farming techniques have long been adopted, which testifies to the attention shown to the environment and the land. Brothers Fernando and Lorenzo represent the latest generation of family to oversee the estate. Among their Vernaccias, the best performance came from the Crocus Riserva '17 whose nose is enlivened by hints of honey and apricot, accompanied by vanilla. The palate is soft, enticing, with a balanced acidic vein and a long, enjoyable finish. The current, 'standard-label' 2019 is pleasant, more traditional in its aromas of almond and apple, with some floral hints; in the mouth it's well-structured, smooth and clean.

○ Vernaccia di S. Gimignano '19	🍷🍷 2*
○ Vernaccia di S. Gimignano Crocus Ris. '17	🍷🍷 3
○ Vernaccia di S. Gimignano I Macchioni '19	🍷🍷 2*
● Acantho '16	🍷 3
● Chianti Colli Senesi Cinabro '16	🍷 3
⊙ Raffy Rosato '19	🍷 2
○ Sangiovese Bianco '19	🍷 2
● Merlot '16	🍷🍷 2*
○ Vernaccia di S. Gimignano Crocus Ris. '16	🍷🍷 3*
○ Vernaccia di S. Gimignano Crocus Ris. '14	🍷🍷 3
○ Vernaccia di S. Gimignano I Macchioni '18	🍷🍷 2*

★Casanova di Neri

POD. FIESOLE
53024 MONTALCINO [SI]
TEL. +39 0577834455
www.casanovadineri.com

PRE-BOOKED VISITS
ACCOMMODATION
ANNUAL PRODUCTION 225,000 bottles
HECTARES UNDER VINE 63.00

Torrenieri, Sesta, Cava dell'Onyx, Podernuovo, Poderuccio and Cerretalto: these are just some of the districts that form the viticultural framework for the winery led by Giacomo Neri and his sons Gianlorenzo and Giovanni. The producer's generational and stylistic versatility is embodied in internationally-renowned Brunellos capable of combining fruity pleasantness, tannic austerity and dense extraction, thanks in part to an approach to maturation that takes into account the typology and vintage. The 2015 version of their Tenuta Nuova put in a superlative performance. It wins you over with its balance, depth, expressive finesse and gustatory tension—its power and generosity bode well for for the next twenty years... The Brunello '15 is right behind, with its bright red fruit. It's firm and sapid, beautifully complex and already quite drinkable. And if the Rosso '18 is one of the most interesting wines of the vintage, the new Giovanni Neri selection, from a 45-year-old vineyard in Sesta, also performed exceptionally well in our finals.

● Brunello di Montalcino Tenuta Nuova '15	3 black glasses	8
● Rosso di Montalcino Giovanni Neri '18	2 black glasses	7
● Brunello di Montalcino '15	2 black glasses	6
● Rosso di Montalcino '18	2 black glasses	5
● Brunello di Montalcino '09	3 white glasses	6
● Brunello di Montalcino '06	3 white glasses	5
● Brunello di Montalcino Cerretalto '07	3 white glasses	8
● Brunello di Montalcino Cerretalto '06	3 white glasses	8
● Brunello di Montalcino Cerretalto '04	3 white glasses	8
● Brunello di Montalcino Cerretalto '01	3 white glasses	8
● Brunello di Montalcino Cerretalto '99	3 white glasses	8
● Brunello di Montalcino Tenuta Nuova '13	3 white glasses	8
● Brunello di Montalcino Tenuta Nuova '06	3 white glasses	8
● Brunello di Montalcino Tenuta Nuova '05	3 white glasses	7
● Brunello di Montalcino Tenuta Nuova '01	3 white glasses	6
● Pietradonice '05	3 white glasses	8

Casisano

LOC. CASISANO
53024 MONTALCINO [SI]
TEL. +39 0577835540
www.casisano.it

ANNUAL PRODUCTION 11,000 bottles
HECTARES UNDER VINE 22.00

This splendid estate overlooks the valley of the Orcia river and the slopes that roll down towards the Abbey of Sant'Antimo. It's here, in the heart of southeast Montalcino, that Tommasi Family Estates decided to establish the nucleus of its new production venture, acquiring the historic Casisano property. In many ways it's a unique area from an environmental and pedoclimatic point of view, qualities that prove perfect for meaty, richly contrasted Sangiovese di Brunello, including their Colombaiolo Riserva, a true hilltop cru matured in 1800 and 2500 liter Slavonian oak. The 2015 version of their Casisano is a great Brunello: it pours an intense ruby colour, anticipating a complex, captivating nose in which ripe morello cherry tones are followed by notes of Mediterranean scrub, undergrowth, spices and a delicate oaky hint. It's firm on the palate, built on wholesome fruit and smooth tannins that fade elegantly on a long finish. We also appreciated the Rosso '18, a wine of character, freshness and a lovely palate.

● Brunello di Montalcino '15	3 black glasses	7
● Rosso di Montalcino '18	2 black glasses	4
● Brunello di Montalcino '12	2 white glasses	7
● Brunello di Montalcino Colombaiolo Ris. '13	2 white glasses	8
● Brunello di Montalcino Colombaiolo Ris. '11	2 white glasses	8
● Rosso di Montalcino '17	2 white glasses	4
● Rosso di Montalcino '16	2 white glasses	4
● Rosso di Montalcino '15	2 white glasses	4

Castelgiocondo

loc. Castelgiocondo
53024 Montalcino [SI]
Tel. +39 057784131
www.frescobaldi.it

PRE-BOOKED VISITS
ANNUAL PRODUCTION 600,000 bottles
HECTARES UNDER VINE 235.00

Overlooked by an ancient tower and small medieval hamlet, Castelgiocondo is a veritable citadel whose viticultural heart is situated in southwest Montalcino. It's a territory historically well-suited to cultivating wine grapes and the Frescobaldi family has made it an increasingly important, strategic part of their Sangiovese da Brunello (and not only). Their wines are distinct for their enfolding and sunny touch. From the first stages of their evolution they are capable of gratifying, gaining in nuance and complexity with time in the bottle. The Riserva Ripe al Convento '14, from Frescobaldi's historic property, is in dazzling form and deservedly takes home Tre Bicchieri. It pours a beautiful, intense and vivid ruby colour, opening on the nose with a rich bouquet in which ripe red and black berries gradually give way to more complex hints of herbs, cocoa and liquorice only to fade on notes of spice and smoke. On the palate it's pervasive, rich, with silky tannins and a long, satisfying finish.

● Brunello di Montalcino Ripe al Convento di Castelgiocondo Ris. '14	🍷🍷🍷 8
● Brunello di Montalcino '15	🍷🍷 6
● Brunello di Montalcino '14	🍷🍷 6
● Brunello di Montalcino '13	🍷🍷 6
● Brunello di Montalcino '12	🍷🍷 6
● Brunello di Montalcino Ripe al Convento di Castelgiocondo Ris. '13	🍷🍷 8
● Rosso di Montalcino Campo ai Sassi '15	🍷🍷 3

★★Castellare di Castellina

loc. Castellare
53011 Castellina in Chianti [SI]
Tel. +39 0577742903
www.castellare.it

CELLAR SALES
PRE-BOOKED VISITS
ACCOMMODATION
ANNUAL PRODUCTION 200,000 bottles
HECTARES UNDER VINE 28.00

The producer's owner is also a shareholder of Gambero Rosso spa. To avoid any conflict of interest, Paolo Panerai has subordinated the possible awarding of Tre Bicchieri (which, in any case, only occurs through a blind tasting) to the attainment of the same rating of excellence (upwards of 90/100) by an independent, international panel. This was the case here.

In a superb vintage for Chianti Classico, their I Sodi di San Niccolò couldn't help but shine. The 2016 offers up a lush fruity background, with spicy hints and touches of pencil lead; in the mouth it's round, deep and juicy, with firm but well-integrated tannins on a broad, still-fruity finish. We also appreciated the Chianti Classico Riserva '17, precise and aromatically vibrant, as well as tonic and rhythmic in its development.

● I Sodi di San Niccolò '16	🍷🍷🍷 8
● Chianti Cl. Ris. '17	🍷🍷 5
● Chianti Cl. '18	🍷🍷 4
● Poggio ai Merli '18	🍷🍷 8
● Chianti Cl. Il Poggiale Ris. '17	🍷 6
● Coniale '16	🍷 8
○ Vin Santo del Chianti Cl. San Niccolò '14	🍷 5
● I Sodi di S. Niccolò '13	🍷🍷🍷 8
● I Sodi di S. Niccolò '12	🍷🍷🍷 8
● I Sodi di S. Niccolò '11	🍷🍷🍷 8
● I Sodi di S. Niccolò '10	🍷🍷🍷 8
● I Sodi di S. Niccolò '09	🍷🍷🍷 8
● I Sodi di S. Niccolò '08	🍷🍷🍷 7
● I Sodi di S. Niccolò '07	🍷🍷🍷 7
● I Sodi di San Niccolò '15	🍷🍷🍷 8
● I Sodi di San Niccolò '14	🍷🍷🍷 8

★★Castello del Terriccio

loc. Terriccio
via Bagnoli, 16
56040 Castellina Marittima [PI]
Tel. +39 050699709
www.terriccio.com

CELLAR SALES
PRE-BOOKED VISITS
ACCOMMODATION
ANNUAL PRODUCTION 200,000 bottles
HECTARES UNDER VINE 65.00

There's important news at a winery made successful and famous by Gian Annibale Rossi di Medelana. It was he who, in 1975, began transforming the producer, focusing attention on the vineyards and the winery. With his death, Vittorio Piozzo di Rosignano Rossi di Medelana, his grandson, has taken over the business. After deciding to leave the world of finance to manage all agricultural activities, he is the current face of the project. The Lupicaia '16 is delicious. It's a blend of Cabernet Sauvignon and Petit Verdot characterized by fresh balsamic scents on the nose, with touches of pepper and red berries of beautiful intensity. On the palate it proves well orchestrated, with enviable balance, a firm finish and a pleasant, fruity encore. The Castello del Terriccio '16, Syrah and Petit Verdot, also impressed: it's rich in fresh spices on the nose, vibrant and balanced on the palate.

Wine	Rating
● Castello del Terriccio '16	🍷🍷 8
● Lupicaia '16	🍷🍷 8
● Tassinaia '17	🍷🍷 5
○ Con Vento '19	🍷 4
● Castello del Terriccio '11	🍷🍷🍷 8
● Castello del Terriccio '07	🍷🍷🍷 8
● Castello del Terriccio '04	🍷🍷🍷 8
● Lupicaia '13	🍷🍷🍷 8
● Lupicaia '11	🍷🍷🍷 8
● Lupicaia '10	🍷🍷🍷 8
● Lupicaia '07	🍷🍷🍷 8
● Lupicaia '06	🍷🍷🍷 8
● Lupicaia '05	🍷🍷🍷 8
● Lupicaia '04	🍷🍷🍷 8
● Castello del Terriccio '15	🍷🍷 8
● Lupicaia '15	🍷🍷 8

Castello del Trebbio

via Santa Brigida, 9
50065 Pontassieve [FI]
Tel. +39 0558304900
www.castellodeltrebbio.it

CELLAR SALES
PRE-BOOKED VISITS
ACCOMMODATION AND RESTAURANT SERVICE
ANNUAL PRODUCTION 320,000 bottles
HECTARES UNDER VINE 60.00
SUSTAINABLE WINERY

In a hilltop territory not far from Florence there's a castle where the Pazzi family hatched a plot to assassinate Lorenzo de' Medici. Today you'll find saffron, cosmetics and especially wine being produced here. The vineyards and olive groves are 'biointegrally' managed, with Sangiovese serving as a cornerstone. It all happens under the direction of Anna Baj Macario and her husband Stefano Casadei, who are also in Tecnovite, a company specialized in planting and managing vineyards and olive groves, in Tenuta Casa Dei in Maremma and in Olianas in Sardinia. The complex Chianti Rufina Lastricato Riserva '16 features tertiary notes of tobacco, leather and earthy hints. Despite this it's a fresh red, with a few hints of mint and aromatic herbs, juniper and berries. The palate is firm, taut, pulpy, with subtle tannins. The enticing Vin Santo '15 is characterized by a classic bouquet of hazelnuts, almonds and citrus notes, coming through long and complex on the palate.

Wine	Rating
● Chianti Rufina Lastricato Ris. '16	🍷🍷 5
● De' Pazzi '17	🍷🍷 4
Vin Santo del Chianti '15	🍷🍷 5
● Chianti Sup. '18	🍷 3
● Chianti Rufina Lastricato Ris. '11	🍷🍷🍷 4*
● Chianti Rufina Lastricato Ris. '15	🍷🍷 5
● Chianti Rufina Lastricato Ris. '14	🍷🍷 5
● Chianti Rufina Lastricato Ris. '12	🍷🍷 5
● Chianti Sup. '15	🍷🍷 3*
○ Congiura '16	🍷🍷 4
● De' Pazzi '15	🍷🍷 4
● De' Pazzi '14	🍷🍷 4
● Pazzesco '16	🍷🍷 5
○ Vin Santo del Chianti '12	🍷🍷 5
○ Vin Santo del Chianti '11	🍷🍷 5

★Castello di Albola

LOC. PIAN D'ALBOLA, 31
53017 RADDA IN CHIANTI [SI]
TEL. +39 0577738019
www.albola.it

CELLAR SALES
PRE-BOOKED VISITS
ANNUAL PRODUCTION 750,000 bottles
HECTARES UNDER VINE 125.00
VITICULTURE METHOD Certified Organic

The Zonin 1821 Group produces great wines at Castello di Albola, wines perfectly in tune with the territory. This is made evident both when tasting older vintages and when encountering the coherence expressed by more recent ones. The stylistic features of this Radda in Chianti winery capture the salient traits of the subzone, expressing balance, freshness and a healthy dose of personality. The prudent use of wood for aging, which is never overwhelming (both when it comes to large barrels and barriques), is not secondary to their success. The Chianti Classico Riserva '17 is, without a doubt, one of the best versions of its kind. Aromas of small red berries, herbs, flint and spices are well defined and fragrant. In the mouth its tannic texture is firm and vivid, well supported by a nice acidic freshness, which ensures a deep, rhythmic palate. The Chianti Classico Gran Selezione Il Solatìo '17 is just a bit tauter on the palate.

● Chianti Cl. Ris. '17	🍷🍷🍷 6
● Chianti Cl. Gran Selezione Il Solatio '17	🍷🍷 8
● Chianti Cl. '18	🍷🍷 5
○ Poggio alle Fate '19	🍷 5
● Acciaiolo '06	🍷🍷🍷 6
● Acciaiolo '04	🍷🍷🍷 6
● Acciaiolo '01	🍷🍷🍷 6
● Chianti Cl. '14	🍷🍷🍷 3*
● Chianti Cl. Gran Sel. '13	🍷🍷🍷 5
● Chianti Cl. Il Solatio Gran Sel. '11	🍷🍷🍷 5
● Chianti Cl. Il Solatio Gran Sel. '10	🍷🍷🍷 5
● Chianti Cl. Le Ellere '08	🍷🍷🍷 3
● Chianti Cl. Ris. '16	🍷🍷🍷 5
● Chianti Cl. Ris. '14	🍷🍷🍷 4*
● Chianti Cl. Ris. '09	🍷🍷🍷 4*
● Chianti Cl. Ris. '08	🍷🍷🍷 4*

★★Castello di Ama

LOC. AMA
53013 GAIOLE IN CHIANTI [SI]
TEL. +39 0577746031
www.castellodiama.com

CELLAR SALES
PRE-BOOKED VISITS
ANNUAL PRODUCTION 300,000 bottles
HECTARES UNDER VINE 90.00

The project that has made the ancient village of Ama a showcase for high contemporary art is one of rare beauty, providing the perfect setting for one of the most prestigious producers of the Chianti Classico appellation. Here wines of comforting continuity and an unmistakable style come to be, paying tribute to their territory of origin with elegance and not infrequently reaching the heights of excellence. In all respects, Castello di Ama is a rare pearl for the district. 2018, one of the best vintages for the appellation, made for an extraordinary Chianti Classico Ama. It exhibits a memorable aromatic and gustatory elegance, truly a great. The Haiku '17, a blend of Sangiovese, Cabernet Franc and Merlot, also impresses with its complex and juicy palate. The Il Chiuso '18, a monovarietal Pinot Nero, also proves well-made: fragrant, sapid and beautifully varietal.

● Chianti Cl. Ama '18	🍷🍷🍷 4*
● Haiku '17	🍷🍷 6
○ Al Poggio '19	🍷🍷 4
● Il Chiuso '18	🍷🍷 5
● L'Apparita '17	🍷🍷 8
⊙ Purple Rose '19	🍷🍷 4
● Chianti Cl. Ama '11	🍷🍷🍷 4*
● Chianti Cl. Bellavista '01	🍷🍷🍷 8
● Chianti Cl. Castello di Ama '05	🍷🍷🍷 5
● Chianti Cl. Castello di Ama '03	🍷🍷🍷 5
● Chianti Cl. Castello di Ama '01	🍷🍷🍷 5
● Chianti Cl. Gran Sel. San Lorenzo '13	🍷🍷🍷 6
● Chianti Cl. La Casuccia '04	🍷🍷🍷 8
● Chianti Cl. La Casuccia '01	🍷🍷🍷 8
● Chianti Cl. San Lorenzo '83	🍷🍷🍷 8
● L'Apparita '01	🍷🍷🍷 8

Castello di Bolgheri

loc. Bolgheri
s.da Lauretta, 7
57020 Castagneto Carducci [LI]
Tel. +39 0565762110
www.castellodibolgheri.eu

CELLAR SALES
PRE-BOOKED VISITS
ACCOMMODATION
ANNUAL PRODUCTION 80,000 bottles
HECTARES UNDER VINE 50.00

The origins of Castello di Bolgheri go way back. The property was in the hands of the Conti della Gherardesca family before passing to the Zileri Dal Verme family together with the surrounding land. In the late 1990s the vineyards were revived, focusing on Bolgheri's principal grape varieties. The vineyards grow on sandy and clay soils, rich in stone, at about 70 meters above sea level. It's a patrimony that guarantees grapes of exceptional quality, which are then rigorously transformed into high-impact wines that exhibit class and identity. Both the Bolgheri wines tasted this year are very good, though our preference is for the Rosso Varvara '18 over the Superiore '17. This is thanks to the year, of course, which, as far as we're concerned, subverts the natural hierarchy of their selection. The latter is more mature and concentrated, refined in its fruity texture, playful but not the least bit simple. In short, it's hard to choose the best.

- Bolgheri Varvàra '18 ▼▼▼ 4*
- Bolgheri Sup. Castello di Bolgheri '17 ▼▼ 6
- Bolgheri Rosso Sup. '16 ▽▽▽ 7
- Bolgheri Sup. Castello di Bolgheri '12 ▽▽▽ 6
- Bolgheri Sup. Castello di Bolgheri '10 ▽▽▽ 6
- Bolgheri Sup. Castello di Bolgheri '09 ▽▽▽ 6
- Bolgheri Sup. Castello di Bolgheri '07 ▽▽▽ 6
- Bolgheri Rosso Sup. '15 ▽▽ 7
- Bolgheri Varvàra '17 ▽▽ 4
- Bolgheri Varvàra '16 ▽▽ 4
- Bolgheri Varvàra '15 ▽▽ 4
- Bolgheri Varvàra '13 ▽▽ 4

★★★Castello di Fonterutoli

loc. Fonterutoli
via Ottone III di Sassonia, 5
53011 Castellina in Chianti [SI]
Tel. +39 057773571
www.mazzei.it

CELLAR SALES
PRE-BOOKED VISITS
ACCOMMODATION AND RESTAURANT SERVICE
ANNUAL PRODUCTION 800,000 bottles
HECTARES UNDER VINE 117.00
SUSTAINABLE WINERY

Castello di Fonterutoli is one of Chianti Classico's historic estates. It's rooted in a multifaceted set of vineyards, which are divided into five zones: Fonterutoli, Siepi, Badiola, Belvedere and Caggio. Their style favours a modern approach, making for wines with complex structures, wines that are plush and well-supported by maturation in small oak barrels. It's a style that we also find at their Maremma, Belguardo estate, but which seems to be gradually shifting to more classic and territorial qualities, especially those wines where Sangiovese dominates. With the 2017 version the Siepi, a blend of Sangiovese and Merlot, once again demonstrates why it's their flagship. Its strong points are its intense and elegant bouquet, which anticipate a soft, broad palate, not lacking in chiaroscuro. The Chianti Classico Gran Selezione '17 features almost overpowering aromas of red berries and spices, with smoky hints on the finish; the palate is pervasive, tight, full of character.

- Chianti Cl. Gran Selezione Castello di Fonterutoli '17 ▼▼ 7
- Marremma Rosso Tenuta Belguardo Tirrenico '16 ▼▼ 4
- Siepi '17 ▼▼ 8
- Chianti Cl. Gran Selezione Badiola '17 ▼▼ 8
- Chianti Cl. Gran Selezione Vicoregio 36 '17 ▼▼ 8
- Chianti Cl. Ris. '17 ▼▼ 5
- Concerto '17 ▼▼ 8
- Poggio Badiola '18 ▼▼ 3
- Chianti Cl. Castello di Fonterutoli '18 ▼ 8
- Mix36 '15 ▽▽▽ 8
- Mix36 '11 ▽▽▽ 8
- Siepi '15 ▽▽▽ 8
- Siepi '13 ▽▽▽ 8
- Siepi '11 ▽▽▽ 8

Castello di Meleto

loc. Meleto
53013 Gaiole in Chianti [SI]
Tel. +39 0577749217
www.castellomeleto.it

CELLAR SALES
PRE-BOOKED VISITS
ACCOMMODATION AND RESTAURANT SERVICE
ANNUAL PRODUCTION 700,000 bottles
HECTARES UNDER VINE 144.00
SUSTAINABLE WINERY

A splendid outpost of Gaiole, Castello di Meleto's origins go as far back as the 13th century. Today it's the symbol of an appealing Chianti Classico winery owned by a pool of investors. In all, the winery covers about a thousand hectares in an engrossing natural landscape. In recent years a major project has been launched, first agronomic and then enological, aimed at increasing the quality and style of their wines. Five farm units with distinct characteristics have been identified: Meleto, San Piero, Casi, Poggiarso and Moci. The aromas of flowers, red berries and spices that distinguish the Chianti Classico '18 are nice and clear—but the wine finds its strong point in a particularly juicy mouth, supple and deliciously drinkable. The Chianti Classico Riserva '17 is also an unmistakable drink, even in the wake of a complicated vintage that sees less freshness in the glass.

Wine	Rating
● Chianti Cl. '18	🍷🍷 3*
● Chianti Cl. Ris. '17	🍷🍷 5
● Camboi '18	🍷 6
● Chianti Cl. Gran Selezione '15	🍷🍷 6
● Chianti Cl. Meleto '16	🍷🍷 3
● Chianti Cl. Meleto '13	🍷🍷 3*
● Chianti Cl. V. Casi Ris. '16	🍷🍷 5
● Chianti Cl. V. Casi Ris. '12	🍷🍷 5
● Chianti Cl. V. Poggiarso Ris. '16	🍷🍷 5

★Castello di Monsanto

via Monsanto, 8
50021 Barberino Val d'Elsa [FI]
Tel. +39 0558059000
www.castellodimonsanto.it

CELLAR SALES
PRE-BOOKED VISITS
ANNUAL PRODUCTION 450,000 bottles
HECTARES UNDER VINE 72.00

Castello di Monsanto's sixty years of history has been marked by pioneering choices, foremost bottling the first cru produced in Chianti Classico (Il Poggio). Then there's the absolute consistency of the Sangiovese grown on the hills of Barberino Val d'Elsa. These are the qualities that characterize Castello di Monsanto, a winery universally recognized as one of the most significant of the entire appellation. Their wines are a clear example of the area's potential: austere just out of the cellar, but highly ageworthy and of sophisticated stylistic elegance. The 2015 version of their Chianti Classico Gran Selezione Il Poggio will likely continue its legacy: aromatically elegant, with fruit meeting spices, flowery sensations and a lightly smoked touch. It has an amazing gustatory energy, rhythmically expressing a rich, pulpy structure. The overall impressions of the fragrant and sapid Chianti Classico Riserva '17 and the Chianti Classico '18 are excellent.

Wine	Rating
● Chianti Cl. Gran Selezione Il Poggio '15	🍷🍷🍷 7
● Chianti Cl. '18	🍷🍷 3
● Chianti Cl. Ris. '17	🍷🍷 3
● Sangioveto '16	🍷 7
● Chianti Cl. '15	🍷🍷🍷 3*
● Chianti Cl. '11	🍷🍷🍷 3*
● Chianti Cl. Cinquantenario Ris. '08	🍷🍷🍷 6
● Chianti Cl. Il Poggio Ris. '13	🍷🍷🍷 7
● Chianti Cl. Il Poggio Ris. '10	🍷🍷🍷 8
● Chianti Cl. Il Poggio Ris. '06	🍷🍷🍷 6
● Chianti Cl. Il Poggio Ris. '88	🍷🍷🍷 5
● Chianti Cl. Ris. '11	🍷🍷🍷 5
● Nemo '01	🍷🍷🍷 6
● Sangioveto '10	🍷🍷🍷 7
● Chianti Cl. '17	🍷🍷 3*
● Chianti Cl. Ris. '16	🍷🍷 3

Castello di Querceto

via Alessandro Francois, 2
50022 Greve in Chianti [FI]
Tel. +39 05585921
www.castellodiquerceto.it

CELLAR SALES
PRE-BOOKED VISITS
ACCOMMODATION
ANNUAL PRODUCTION 600,000 bottles
HECTARES UNDER VINE 60.00

Castello di Querceto has been the François family's home for over a century and represents an important piece in the history of the Chianti Classico appellation. Located in the Greve subzone, in terms of the size of its vineyards and the number of bottles produced, it is undoubtedly one of the most significant wineries in the area. The vineyards unfold on a hillside characterized by a climate that could be defined as continental. As a result freshness serves as a distinctive quality of their main wines, which mature both in small wood barrels and large ones. Particularly fragrant, vibrant aromas characterize the Chianti Classico Riserva '17, which also impresses in the mouth, where it proves a juicy, sapid drink with nice rhythm. The Chianti Classico '18 exhibits a beautiful sylvan-foresty character in its well-defined scents of small red berries and spices, the prelude to a tasty, crunchy and consistently vigorous palate.

Wine	Rating
● Chianti Cl. '18	▼▼ 3*
● Chianti Cl. Ris. '17	▼▼ 4
● Chianti Cl. Gran Selezione La Corte '17	▼▼ 6
● Il Querciolaia '16	▼▼ 6
● Chianti Cl. Gran Selezione Il Picchio '17	▼ 5
● Chianti Cl. '17	▽▽ 3
● Chianti Cl. '13	▽▽ 3
● Chianti Cl. Gran Selezione Il Picchio '16	▽▽ 5
● Chianti Cl. Il Picchio Gran Sel. '12	▽▽ 6
● Chianti Cl. Il Picchio Gran Sel. '11	▽▽ 6
● Chianti Cl. Ris. '16	▽▽ 4
● Chianti Cl. Ris. '13	▽▽ 4
● Chianti Cl. Ris. '12	▽▽ 4
● Il Sole di Alessandro '09	▽▽ 7
● La Corte '10	▽▽ 5

Castello di Radda

loc. Il Becco, 101a
53017 Radda in Chianti [SI]
Tel. +39 0577738992
www.castellodiradda.it

CELLAR SALES
PRE-BOOKED VISITS
ANNUAL PRODUCTION 100,000 bottles
HECTARES UNDER VINE 33.00

The agricultural group headed by the Gussalli Beretta family includes Lo Sparviere in Franciacorta, Orlandi Contucci Ponno in Abruzzo and Castello di Radda in Chianti Classico. The latter has been particularly visible in recent years thanks to some noteworthy wines. A combination of well-suited vineyards of different ages and a minimalist approach in the cellar gives rise to a clearly modern style, making for elegant wines true to their territory of origin. The 2018 is a well made Chianti Classico, of solid and defined expressive consistency, but it's certainly not the first time we've seen that. Aromatically it alternates flowery sensations with small red berries, spices and a light hint of flint, heralding a fragrant, full palate, lively and tasty. The Granbruno '18, a blend of Sangiovese and Merlot, is just a bit more marked by oak, but just as pleasant.

Wine	Rating
● Chianti Cl. '18	▼▼▼ 3*
● Granbruno '18	▼▼ 2*
● Chianti Cl. '15	▽▽▽ 3*
● Chianti Cl. Gran Selezione V. Il Corno '15	▽▽▽ 3*
● Chianti Cl. Gran Selezione V. Il Corno '14	▽▽▽ 6
● Chianti Cl. Ris. '13	▽▽▽ 5
● Chianti Cl. Ris. '12	▽▽▽ 5
● Chianti Cl. Ris. '11	▽▽▽ 6
● Chianti Cl. Ris. '07	▽▽▽ 5
● Chianti Cl. '17	▽▽ 3*
● Chianti Cl. '16	▽▽ 3
● Chianti Cl. Gran Selezione '13	▽▽ 3
● Chianti Cl. Ris. '14	▽▽ 5
● Chianti Cl. Ris. '15	▽ 5
● Guss '14	▽ 6

★Castello di Volpaia

LOC. VOLPAIA
VIA PIER CAPPONI, 2
53017 RADDA IN CHIANTI [SI]
TEL. +39 0577738066
www.volpaia.com

CELLAR SALES
PRE-BOOKED VISITS
ACCOMMODATION AND RESTAURANT SERVICE
ANNUAL PRODUCTION 220,000 bottles
HECTARES UNDER VINE 45.00
VITICULTURE METHOD Certified Organic
SUSTAINABLE WINERY

The Mascheroni Stianti family's estate brings together organic vineyards with expert craftsmanship. Volpaia tends toward elegance, with an impeccably "modern" style, but one that's not lacking in personality and character either. It's a well-established balance that emerges with reassuring continuity in their range of wines, making Castello di Volpaia a benchmark for the Radda in Chianti subzone. Their Chianti Classico Riserva '17 is authoritative, to say the least: aromatically focused and intense, both in its fruitiness and smokiness, in the mouth it proves vivid, firm and flavorful. The Chianti Classico '18 has a graceful structure, but also fragrant aromas and a mouth-watering palate. The Chianti Classico Gran Selezione Coltassala '17 is powerful and juicy, characterized by pleasantly citrus notes.

Wine	Rating
● Chianti Cl. Ris. '17	🍷🍷🍷 6
● Chianti Cl. '18	🍷🍷 4
● Chianti Cl. Gran Selezione Coltassala '17	🍷🍷 8
○ Vin Santo del Chianti Cl. '15	🍷🍷 7
● Balifico '17	🍷 8
● Chianti Cl. Gran Selezione Il Puro Vign. Casanova '16	🍷 8
● Chianti Cl. '16	♡♡♡ 4*
● Chianti Cl. '15	♡♡♡ 4*
● Chianti Cl. '13	♡♡♡ 3*
● Chianti Cl. Il Puro Vign. Casanova Ris. '08	♡♡♡ 8
● Chianti Cl. Ris. '16	♡♡♡ 5
● Chianti Cl. Ris. '13	♡♡♡ 5
● Chianti Cl. Ris. '10	♡♡♡ 5
● Chianti Cl. Ris. '08	♡♡♡ 5

Castello Romitorio

LOC. ROMITORIO, 279
53024 MONTALCINO [SI]
TEL. +39 0577847212
www.castelloromitorio.com

CELLAR SALES
PRE-BOOKED VISITS
ACCOMMODATION
ANNUAL PRODUCTION 150,000 bottles
HECTARES UNDER VINE 30.00

Castello Romitorio's viticultural project is diverse, to say the least: in Montalcino there are the vineyards of Romitorio and Poggio di Sopra, in Maremma there's Ghiaccio, not to mention their parcels in Chianti Senesi. In short, we could say that artist Sandro Chia's choice to acquire the estate in the 1980s has proven much more than a 'whim', even if it's been described as such. Sandro has passed the baton on to his son Filippo, who's supported by Stefano Martini (son of the historic cellarman, Franco). Theirs is a lovely story wrought of modern, gently vigorous Sangiovese. We very much appreciated the Brunello '15, one of the best of the vintage. It's a close-knit, pulpy wine, rich in notes of ripe red and black berries, both on the nose and on the palate, where it exhibits a certain self-assuredness supported by complex notes of cinchona-quinine and medicinal herbs, tobacco and smoky notes that return on an elegant finish. The excellent Filo di Seta '15 is powerful but not ready yet. The Romitòro '18 and other wines tasted also performed well.

Wine	Rating
● Brunello di Montalcino '15	🍷🍷 8
● Brunello di Montalcino Filo di Seta '15	🍷🍷 8
● Romitòro '18	🍷🍷 4
● Rosso di Montalcino '18	🍷 5
● Sant'Antimo Rosso Romito '16	🍷 5
● Brunello di Montalcino '13	♡♡ 8
● Brunello di Montalcino '12	♡♡ 8
● Brunello di Montalcino Filo di Seta '13	♡♡ 8
● Brunello di Montalcino Filo di Seta '12	♡♡ 8
● Brunello di Montalcino Ris. '13	♡♡ 8
● Brunello di Montalcino Ris. '12	♡♡ 8
● Rosso di Montalcino '16	♡♡ 5
● Rosso di Montalcino '15	♡♡ 5

Castello Vicchiomaggio

loc. Le Bolle
via Vicchiomaggio, 4
50022 Greve in Chianti [FI]
Tel. +39 055854079
www.vicchiomaggio.it

CELLAR SALES
PRE-BOOKED VISITS
ACCOMMODATION AND RESTAURANT SERVICE
ANNUAL PRODUCTION 300,000 bottles
HECTARES UNDER VINE 38.00
SUSTAINABLE WINERY

Owned by the Matta family, Castello di Vicchiomaggio has managed to earn a place among Chianti Classico's top producers. The vineyards, which are located on the Florentine side of the appellation in Greve in Chianti, provide the grapes that are then transformed without unnecessarily interfering with the natural process of winemaking. The result is a comforting continuity of quality presented in a range of wines that's reliable and not devoid of character. It's a style that's modern but never over the top. Aging is carried out both in large oak barrels and in barriques. The Amphiarao '18 exhibits a striking originality. It's a blend of Cabernet Sauvignon, Petit Verdot and Sangiovese matured for 12 months in amphora (hence the bizarre name). The nose offers up herbaceous touches, fruity hints and a spicy background; the palate is juicy and fragrant, with a sweet, relaxed finish. The immediately expressive and approachable Chianti Classico Guado Alto '18 is aromatically fragrant, focused on the palate.

- ● Amphiarao '18 — 🍷🍷 6
- ● Chianti Cl. Agostino Petri Ris. '17 — 🍷🍷 5
- ● Chianti Cl. Gran Selezione La Prima '16 — 🍷🍷 7
- ● Chianti Cl. Guado Alto '18 — 🍷🍷 3
- ● FSM '17 — 🍷🍷 8
- ● Sangiovese '16 — 🍷🍷 3
- ● Ripa delle More '17 — 🍷 6
- ● Chianti Cl. Gran Sel. Vigna La Prima '10 — 🍷🍷🍷 7
- ● FSM '07 — 🍷🍷🍷 8
- ● FSM '04 — 🍷🍷🍷 5
- ● Ripa delle More '97 — 🍷🍷🍷 6
- ● Ripa delle More '94 — 🍷🍷🍷 7
- ● Chianti Cl. Agostino Petri Ris. '16 — 🍷🍷 5
- ● Chianti Cl. Guado Alto '17 — 🍷🍷 3*

Castelvecchio

loc. San Pancrazio
via Certaldese, 30
50026 San Casciano in Val di Pesa [FI]
Tel. +39 0558248032
www.castelvecchio.it

CELLAR SALES
PRE-BOOKED VISITS
ACCOMMODATION
ANNUAL PRODUCTION 100,000 bottles
HECTARES UNDER VINE 24.00
VITICULTURE METHOD Certified Organic
SUSTAINABLE WINERY

The noble Cavalcanti family once owned a castle on the hills between San Casciano and Montespertoli. About sixty years ago, Renzo Rocchi acquired ownership of the buildings, built cellars and planted vineyards. Today, it's his grandchildren Filippo and Stefania who manage the entire estate, bringing modern entrepreneurial spirit and passion to their work. Native Sangiovese, Canaiolo Nero, Malvasia del Chianti, Trebbiano, as well as international Merlot, Cabernet Sauvignon and Petit Verdot grapes all grow in their 30 hectares of vineyards. The estate is certified organic and also offers agritourism accommodations. the Chianti Colli Fiorentini Il Castelvecchio '18 pours a ruby red with purple highlights, the prologue to a nose rich in assorted spices and berries; the palate opens well, with juicy texture, liveliness and a racy finish. The Numero Otto '17, an intriguing monovarietal Canaiolo, offers up floral hints, herbs and black berries: in the mouth it has integrated tannins, finishing sapid and clean.

- ● Chianti Colli Fiorentini Il Castelvecchio '18 — 🍷🍷 2*
- ● Chianti Colli Fiorentini V. La Quercia Ris. '17 — 🍷🍷 4
- ● Il Brecciolino '17 — 🍷🍷 5
- ● Numero Otto Canaiolo Nero '17 — 🍷🍷 4
- ● Chianti Santa Caterina '18 — 🍷 2
- ○ San Lorenzo Trebbiano '19 — 🍷 2
- ● Il Brecciolino '15 — 🍷🍷🍷 5
- ● Il Brecciolino '11 — 🍷🍷🍷 5
- ● Chianti Colli Fiorentini V. La Quercia Ris. '16 — 🍷🍷 4
- ● Chianti S. Caterina '15 — 🍷🍷 2*
- ● Il Brecciolino '16 — 🍷🍷 5
- ● Il Brecciolino '13 — 🍷🍷 5
- ● Orme in Rosso '15 — 🍷🍷 4

Castiglion del Bosco

LOC. CASTIGLION DEL BOSCO
53024 MONTALCINO [SI]
TEL. +39 05771913750
www.castigliondelbosco.com

CELLAR SALES
PRE-BOOKED VISITS
ACCOMMODATION AND RESTAURANT SERVICE
ANNUAL PRODUCTION 250,000 bottles
HECTARES UNDER VINE 62.00
VITICULTURE METHOD Certified Organic

It's practically impossible to capture all of Castiglion del Bosco in a few lines. This historic district-estate in northwestern Montalcino was taken over by Massimo Ferragamo in 2003. On the one hand there's their partnership with Rosewood Hotel & Resort, which since 2015 has co-managed its suites and villas, spa, restaurants (Campo del Drago and La Canonica), organic vegetable garden, cooking school and golf club. On the other hand, there's their over sixty hectares of vineyards, which give rise to a range that's constantly growing, especially when it comes to the stylistic definition of their Sangiovese da Brunello. Thanks to a great vintage, their wines exhibit a complete stylistic maturity, faithfully expressing this part of Montalcino as well as the esprit of the maison. Their Brunello '15 is a wine of balance and elegance, playing on classic notes of fruit, with lovely Mediterranean and spicy colors. Finally the Campo del Drago '15 proves to be a Brunello of depth and structure, broad and vertical, with fine-grained tannins.

Wine	Rating	Price
● Brunello di Montalcino Campo del Drago '15	🍷🍷 (black)	8
● Brunello di Montalcino '15	🍷🍷 (black)	6
● Brunello di Montalcino '14	🍷🍷	6
● Brunello di Montalcino '12	🍷🍷	6
● Brunello di Montalcino '11	🍷🍷	6
● Brunello di Montalcino 1100 Ris. '12	🍷🍷	6
● Brunello di Montalcino 1100 Ris. '11	🍷🍷	6
● Brunello di Montalcino Campo del Drago '13	🍷🍷	8
● Brunello di Montalcino Campo del Drago '12	🍷🍷	8
● Brunello di Montalcino Campo del Drago '11	🍷🍷	8
● Brunello di Montalcino Ris. 1100 '10	🍷🍷	6

Cava d'Onice

POD. COLOMBAIO 105
53024 MONTALCINO [SI]
TEL. +39 0577848405
www.cavadonice.it

CELLAR SALES
PRE-BOOKED VISITS
ACCOMMODATION
ANNUAL PRODUCTION 22,000 bottles
HECTARES UNDER VINE 3.60
VITICULTURE METHOD Certified Organic

The Cava d'Onyx brand is relatively recent. Credit goes to Simone Nannetti, who, since he was a boy, has tried to make the most of his father's teachings (for many years he was a cellarman in a Montalcino winery). Nevertheless, Simone began bottling only after putting together a varied and well-rounded set of vineyards. Indeed, his is one of the few wineries in the area that has plots located on the area's four main slopes, an important choice in pursuing a style of Brunello that's contemporary, in the best sense of the word. The Sensis '15 is truly a charming Brunello: precise in its fruitiness, with notes of cherry in the foreground, clear and spicy; on the palate it's youthful but already complex, powerful and dense with elegant tannins and a nice acidity that lends harmony. The Colombaio '15 is also intense and rich, with lovely notes of quinine and tobacco. The Rosso '18 proves fine, harmonious and very classic.

Wine	Rating	Price
● Brunello di Montalcino Sensis '15	🍷🍷 (black)	6
● Brunello di Montalcino Colombaio '15	🍷🍷 (black)	7
● Rosso di Montalcino '18	🍷🍷 (black)	4
● Brunello di Montalcino '14	🍷🍷	7
● Brunello di Montalcino '13	🍷🍷	5
● Brunello di Montalcino Colombaio '13	🍷🍷	7

★Famiglia Cecchi

loc. Casina dei Ponti, 56
53011 Castellina in Chianti [SI]
Tel. +39 057754311
www.famigliacecchi.net

CELLAR SALES
PRE-BOOKED VISITS
RESTAURANT SERVICE
ANNUAL PRODUCTION 8,500,000 bottles
HECTARES UNDER VINE 385.00
SUSTAINABLE WINERY

Cecchi is one of Chianti Classico's essential winemaking brands. Through an emphasis on improving the quality of their wines, especially when it comes to their 'farm selections', the Castellina in Chianti producer has taken a virtuously irreversible leap forward. Credit goes to rigorous stylistic choices, first and foremost the decision to favor a more marked identity. And we shouldn't forget the decision to flank Villa Cerna with a historic Chianti reality such as Villa Rosa, recently acquired in the wake of a growing interest in Gallo Nero. The 2017 version of the Chianti Classico Gran Selezione Villa Rosa '17 leaves no doubt about its excellence. Aromatically it's elegant and sweet, with a lush fruity bouquet accompanied by floral hints, spicy nuances and earthy accents. In the mouth it unfolds pulpy and rhythmic, finishing intense. Good overall definition for the Chianti Classico Riserva di Famiglia '17, a vivid, consistent wine.

Wine	Rating
● Chianti Cl. Gran Selezione Villa Rosa '17	▼▼▼ 6
● Chianti Cl. Riserva di Famiglia '17	▼▼ 5
● Chianti Cl. Villa Cerna Ris. '17	▼ 5
● Chianti Cl. Gran Selezione Villa Rosa '16	▽▽▽ 6
● Chianti Cl. Riserva di Famiglia '15	▽▽▽ 5
● Chianti Cl. Riserva di Famiglia '07	▽▽▽ 5
● Chianti Cl. Villa Cerna Ris. '13	▽▽▽ 5
● Chianti Cl. Villa Cerna Ris. '12	▽▽▽ 5
● Chianti Cl. Villa Cerna Ris. '08	▽▽▽ 5
● Coevo '11	▽▽▽ 8
● Coevo '10	▽▽▽ 7
● Coevo '06	▽▽▽ 7
● Chianti Cl. Riserva di Famiglia '16	▽▽ 5
● Chianti Cl. Villa Cerna Ris. '16	▽▽ 5
● Coevo '16	▽▽ 8

La Cerreta

via Campagna Sud, 143
57020 Sassetta [LI]
Tel. +39 0565794352
www.lacerreta.it

ANNUAL PRODUCTION 20,000 bottles
HECTARES UNDER VINE 8.00
VITICULTURE METHOD Certified Biodynamic

La Cerreta is a true farm where all work is carried out according to the dictates of biodynamic agriculture: horses, pigs, bees and poultry are all raised, without forgetting the production of cheese, honey and fruit. Wine began to become important in 1999, with the first 6 hectares (accompanied by 2 more in 2003). The soil is siliceous-clayey, a makeup that's particularly well suited to grapes such as Vermentino, among the white grapes, Cabernet Sauvignon and Sangiovese for the reds. A monovarietal Vermentino, the Matis '18 offers up aromas of medicinal herbs that combine with notes of apple and white peach, as well as hints of cinnamon; in the mouth it has weight, freshness, and a relaxed, enjoyable finish. The Rio de' Messi '17, Cabernet Sauvignon and a smaller share of Merlot, unveils clear mineral scents, minty notes, hints of lemon verbena, sage and assorted black berries. On the palate it's warm, pervasive, juicy and powerful.

Wine	Rating
○ Matis '18	▼▼ 3
● Rio de' Messi '17	▼▼ 3
● Solatio della Cerreta '16	▼▼ 3
● Spargivento '16	▼▼ 4
● Stanca Vizi '17	▼ 5
○ Matis '15	▽▽ 3
● Rio de' Messi '13	▽▽ 3
● Sangiovese '13	▽▽ 3

Vincenzo Cesani

loc. Pancole, 82d
53037 San Gimignano [SI]
Tel. +39 0577955084
www.cesani.it

CELLAR SALES
PRE-BOOKED VISITS
ACCOMMODATION
ANNUAL PRODUCTION 30,000 bottles
HECTARES UNDER VINE 26.00
VITICULTURE METHOD Certified Organic

In the mid-1950s, many families migrated from Marche to Tuscany, some of whom, including the Cesani family, landed in San Gimignano. Vincenzo started an agricultural activity that today exists in the form of organic viticulture and olive growing. The still family-run business, thanks to the work of Maria Luisa and Letizia, has also dedicated itself to reviving one of the area's traditional products, saffron. Vernaccia remains the cornerstone of their selection, although particular attention is paid to Sangiovese-based reds as well. The Vernaccia Sanice Riserva '17 earned a place in our finals. It has a tantalizing aromatic spectrum in which citrus sensations such as lime and citron stand out amidst vegetal hints of basil and chives, all on a fruity base of apple and damson. The Vernaccia Clamys '18 opens enticing on the palate, delicately salty, appetizing, with a long, pleasant finish: it entices with its hints of saffron and a docile, relaxed body.

Wine	Rating
○ Vernaccia di S. Gimignano Sanice Ris. '17	🍷🍷 3*
○ Vernaccia di S. Gimignano '19	🍷🍷 2*
○ Vernaccia di S. Gimignano Clamys '18	🍷🍷 2*
● Chianti Colli Senesi '19	🍷 2
⊙ Rosato '19	🍷 2
● San Gimignano Rosso Cellori '13	🍷 4
○ Vernaccia di S. Gimignano Sanice Ris. '15	🍷🍷🍷 3*
○ Vernaccia di S. Gimignano Sanice Ris. '14	🍷🍷🍷 3*
● Chianti Colli Senesi '18	🍷🍷 2*
○ Vernaccia di S. Gimignano Clamys '17	🍷🍷 2*
○ Vernaccia di S. Gimignano Clamys '16	🍷🍷 2*
○ Vernaccia di S. Gimignano Sanice Ris. '16	🍷🍷 3*

Giovanni Chiappini

loc. Felciaino
via Bolgherese, 189c
57020 Bolgheri [LI]
Tel. +39 0565765201
www.giovannichiappini.it

CELLAR SALES
PRE-BOOKED VISITS
ANNUAL PRODUCTION 70,000 bottles
HECTARES UNDER VINE 23.00
VITICULTURE METHOD Certified Organic
SUSTAINABLE WINERY

Who knows if the first Chiappini to emigrate to Tuscany from the Marche region imagined what would happen in the years to come? It's difficult to imagine. The fact is that the search for a better future through the cultivation of land has opened up unthinkable scenarios thanks to the vine and wine, so much so that today the winery represents a jewel of the Bolgheri appellation and exhibits increasingly interesting prospects. There has been plenty of progress, such as renovations to their cellar and the decision to focus on an increasingly balanced and precise style. Once again the Lienà Cabernet Franc impressed the most. Evidently the grape is right in the winery's wheelhouse, as they've proven capable of delivering an original and multifaceted red, even with a year like 2017. Rather dark and wrapped in a pleasant toasted texture, fruit is well balanced by herbaceous hints, with a clear minty stroke. Excellent results for the Bolgheri Rosso Felciaino '18 and the Superiore Guado dei Gemoli '17 as well.

Wine	Rating
● Lienà Cabernet Franc '17	🍷🍷 8
● Bolgheri Rosso Felciaino '18	🍷🍷 4
● Bolgheri Rosso Sup. Guado de' Gemoli '17	🍷🍷 8
○ Bolgheri Le Grottine '19	🍷 3
● Bolgheri Rosso Felciaino '17	🍷🍷 4
● Bolgheri Rosso Felciaino '16	🍷🍷 4
● Bolgheri Rosso Felciaino '15	🍷🍷 3
● Bolgheri Rosso Sup. Guado de' Gemoli '16	🍷🍷 8
● Bolgheri Rosso Sup. Guado de' Gemoli '15	🍷🍷 8
● Lienà Cabernet Franc '16	🍷🍷 8
● Lienà Cabernet Franc '15	🍷🍷 8
● Lienà Cabernet Sauvignon '15	🍷🍷 7
● Bolgheri Sup. Guado de' Gemoli '14	🍷 8

Podere La Chiesa

via di Casanova, 66a
56030 Terricciola [PI]
Tel. +39 0587635484
www.poderelachiesa.it

CELLAR SALES
PRE-BOOKED VISITS
ANNUAL PRODUCTION 40,000 bottles
HECTARES UNDER VINE 14.00
VITICULTURE METHOD Certified Organic
SUSTAINABLE WINERY

A couple in life and work, Maurizio Iannantuono and Palma decided to make the most of their passion for wine. They left the IT business and started looking for the right property. The turning point came when they found a beautiful farm on the road to Volterra, where they decided to build the cellar according to modern architectural criteria and functionality, but also aesthetic beauty, so much so that it's become a sort of gallery for exhibitions and events. The Opera in Rosso '15 is a Sangiovese that stands out for its tertiary aromas: a fascinating mix of tobacco, earth, tanned leather and blackberry jam. In the mouth it opens soft, broad, warm in its alcohol, with nice tannins and a balanced finish. The Punto di Vista '19 also delivered. A blend of equal parts Trebbiano and Vermentino, it has a fresh nose, with nuances of apple merging with vegetal hints of basil; on the palate it's subtle, highly drinkable, with a tasty, alluring finish.

- ● Opera in Nero '17 ▼▼ 7
- ○ Punto di Vista '19 ▼▼ 3
- ● Terre di Pisa Rosso Le Redole di Casanova '18 ▼▼ 2*
- ● Terre di Pisa Sangiovese Opera in Rosso '15 ▼▼ 7
- ● Chianti Terre di Casanova '18 ▼ 3
- ● Chianti Terre di Casanova '17 ▽▽ 2*
- ● Chianti Terre di Casanova '12 ▽▽ 2*
- ● Le Redole di Casanova '12 ▽▽ 2*
- ● Le Redole di Casanova '08 ▽▽ 2*
- ● Sabiniano di Casanova '11 ▽▽ 4
- ● Sabiniano di Casanova '08 ▽▽ 4
- ● Sabiniano di Casanova '04 ▽▽ 4
- ○ Taigete '17 ▽▽ 2*
- ● Terre di Pisa Sangiovese Opera in Rosso '14 ▽▽ 7

Le Chiuse

loc. Pullera, 228
53024 Montalcino [SI]
Tel. +39 055597052
www.lechiuse.com

CELLAR SALES
PRE-BOOKED VISITS
ACCOMMODATION
ANNUAL PRODUCTION 30,000 bottles
HECTARES UNDER VINE 8.00
VITICULTURE METHOD Certified Organic

Often remembered as a main site for the Biondi Santi family's legendary reserves, Le Chiuse has for many years been in the hands of Simonetta Valiani, who manages it with her husband, Nicolà Magnelli, and son Lorenzo. Situated in northern Montalcino, it's a practically contiguous strip of Sangiovese wrapped in crus just as renowned, like Montosoli and I Canalicchi, a prestigious territory inextricably bound up with shining interpretations of Sangiovese da Brunello. Here it gets a further boost from biocompatible methods in the vineyard and a minimally-invasive approach in the cellar. The Le Chiuse '15 is exceptionally elegant, classic and sophisticated. A bouquet of red fruit tacks towards subtle hints of tobacco, licorice and spices. On the palate exuberant fruit is elegantly tempered by the harmony of its tannic texture. The Riserva Decennale '10 doesn't betray age, managing to be complex and alluring, clear in its fruit and elegantly evolved in its spicy, tertiary aromas. The Rosso '18 is delicious, dynamic and full.

- ● Brunello di Montalcino '15 ▼▼▼ 7
- ● Brunello di Montalcino Ris. '10 ▼▼ 8
- ● Rosso di Montalcino '18 ▼▼ 4
- ● Brunello di Montalcino '12 ▽▽▽ 7
- ● Brunello di Montalcino '11 ▽▽▽ 7
- ● Brunello di Montalcino '10 ▽▽▽ 7
- ● Brunello di Montalcino '07 ▽▽▽ 7
- ● Brunello di Montalcino Ris. '07 ▽▽▽ 8
- ● Brunello di Montalcino '14 ▽▽ 7
- ● Brunello di Montalcino '13 ▽▽ 7
- ● Rosso di Montalcino '17 ▽▽ 4

Ciacci Piccolomini D'Aragona

FRAZ. CASTELNUOVO DELL'ABATE
LOC. MOLINELLO
53024 MONTALCINO [SI]
TEL. +39 0577835616
www.ciaccipiccolomini.com

CELLAR SALES
PRE-BOOKED VISITS
ACCOMMODATION
ANNUAL PRODUCTION 200,000 bottles
HECTARES UNDER VINE 40.00

Located practically halfway between the Abbey of Sant'Antimo and the hamlet of Castelnuovo dell'Abate, the historic estate of Ciacci Piccolomini is one of the most important in southeast Montalcino. In the mid-1980s it passed to Giuseppe Bianchini, while today it's his children Lucia and Paolo who oversee it, bringing a rigorous focus to the viticultural and expressive attributes of their vineyards. Ferraiole, Egle, Contessa and Colombaio are vinified separately and blended later, with the exception of the cru Vigna di Pianrosso, making for a solid selection of Rossos and Brunellos. The Brunello '15 is pulpy and rich in aromas of ripe, bottled cherries: medicinal herbs, quinine and spices render the bouquet alluring and complex. On the palate it's rich, pulpy, supported by a harmonious acidic-tannic structure. The Pianrosso '15 does a nice job expressing the good vintage, with beautiful tones of tobacco on the nose and smooth tannins that accompany it through a long finish. The Rosso '18 proves elegant and sapid.

Wine	Rating
● Brunello di Montalcino '15	🍷🍷 5
● Brunello di Montalcino Pianrosso '15	🍷🍷 8
● Rosso di Montalcino '18	🍷🍷 4
● Brunello di Montalcino '14	🍷🍷 5
● Brunello di Montalcino '13	🍷🍷 5
● Brunello di Montalcino V. di Pianrosso Ris. '13	🍷🍷 7
● Rosso di Montalcino '17	🍷🍷 4
● Rosso di Montalcino Rossofonte '15	🍷🍷 4

Cinciano

LOC. CINCIANO, 2
53036 POGGIBONSI [SI]
TEL. +39 0577936588
www.cinciano.it

CELLAR SALES
PRE-BOOKED VISITS
ACCOMMODATION AND RESTAURANT SERVICE
ANNUAL PRODUCTION 140,000 bottles
HECTARES UNDER VINE 24.00

Fattoria di Cinciano's vineyards can be found in the part of Chianti Classico that lies nearest to Poggibonsi and Barberino Val d'Elsa. The winery has for some time taken a clear and defined path, not only in terms of quality, but also in terms of consistency and its link with the territory. Quality grapes are cultivated and in the cellar their approach is minimally invasive, with aging carried out in concrete, large oak barrels and small second-use oak barrels, resulting in added personality and style. The Chianti Classico Riserva '17 exhibits vibrant, complex aromas, but it's in the mouth that it changes pace with a juicy palate full of contrast, and a territorial stylistic quality. Some olfactory uncertainty doesn't detract from the overall quality of the Chianti Classico '18, a fresh and tasty wine. The Chianti Classico Gran Selezione '16 is smoky on the nose, robust and tight on the palate.

Wine	Rating
● Chianti Cl. '18	🍷🍷 4
● Chianti Cl. Gran Selezione '16	🍷🍷 6
● Chianti Cl. Ris. '17	🍷🍷 5
● Pietraforte '16	🍷🍷 3
● Chianti Cl. '16	🍷🍷🍷 4*
● Chianti Cl. '15	🍷🍷 3
● Chianti Cl. Gran Sel. '12	🍷🍷 5
● Chianti Cl. Gran Sel. '11	🍷🍷 5
● Chianti Cl. Gran Selezione '15	🍷🍷 6
● Chianti Cl. Gran Selezione '14	🍷🍷 6
● Chianti Cl. Ris. '16	🍷🍷 5
● Chianti Cl. Ris. '15	🍷🍷 5
● Chianti Cl. Ris. '14	🍷🍷 3
● Chianti Cl. Ris. '13	🍷🍷 3*
● Chianti Cl. Ris. '12	🍷🍷 3*
● Chianti Cl. Ris. '11	🍷🍷 3
● Pietraforte '14	🍷🍷 3

Le Cinciole

via Case Sparse, 83
50020 Panzano [FI]
Tel. +39 055852636
www.lecinciole.it

CELLAR SALES
PRE-BOOKED VISITS
ANNUAL PRODUCTION 45,000 bottles
HECTARES UNDER VINE 11.00
VITICULTURE METHOD Certified Organic
SUSTAINABLE WINERY

The winery overseen by Luca and Valeria Orsini deservedly belongs to the tradition of high wine artisanship that has always distinguished the Chianti Classico appellation. Here in the subzone of Panzano the producer cultivates its vineyards organically and ages its wines in large and small oak barrels. The result is a range of wines with a style that's consistent with the territory, one that exhibits comforting quality and well-defined character, combining liveliness and a good propensity for aging. 2016 made for a lovely Petresco. It's a monovarietal Sangiovese that delivers a broad, focused olfactory spectrum amidst fragrant red berries, earthy hints and spices. In the mouth it unfolds full and juicy, coming through well-sustained and satisfying on the palate. Another well-made wine, the sapid Chianti Classico '17, proves redolent of cut grass and red berries. The Cinciorosso '18, a blend of Sangiovese, Merlot and Syrah grapes, is all about drinkability.

Wine	Rating	
● Chianti Cl. '17	🍷🍷	3*
● Petresco '16	🍷🍷	5
● Chianti Cl. A Luigi Ris. '15	🍷🍷	3
● Cinciorosso '18	🍷🍷	3
⊙ Sangiovese Rosato '19	🍷	2
● Camalaione '04	🍸🍸🍸	7
● Chianti Cl. '14	🍸🍸🍸	3*
● Chianti Cl. '12	🍸🍸🍸	3*
● Chianti Cl. Petresco Ris. '01	🍸🍸🍸	5
● Petresco '12	🍸🍸🍸	5
● Chianti Cl. '15	🍸🍸	3*
● Chianti Cl. A Luigi Ris. '14	🍸🍸	3
● Chianti Cl. A Luigi Ris. '12	🍸🍸	3
● Cinciorosso '17	🍸🍸	3
● Cinciorosso '16	🍸🍸	3
● Petresco '15	🍸🍸	5
● Petresco '13	🍸🍸	5

Donatella Cinelli Colombini

loc. Casato,17
53024 Montalcino [SI]
Tel. +39 0577662108
www.cinellicolombini.it

CELLAR SALES
PRE-BOOKED VISITS
ACCOMMODATION AND RESTAURANT SERVICE
ANNUAL PRODUCTION 140,000 bottles
HECTARES UNDER VINE 34.00

Founder of the 'Wine Tourism Movement', creator of Cantine Aperte ('Open Cellars') and a university professor specialized in wine marketing, in 1998 Donatella Cinelli Colombini decided to leave the family business to create her Fattoria del Colle in Trequanda and the Casato Prime Donne in Montalcino, one of the first female-oriented producers. Aged in mid-sized casks and larger 1500-4000 liter barrels, her Brunellos don't conform to any predefined stylistic school, yet they express the appellation's most pervasive and somehow stern qualities. If we had to summarize the Brunello '15 with an adjective it would be 'captivating'. So it is in color, in the elegance and richness of its fruit, in the finesse of its tannic texture and in its long, alluring finish. A masterful performance. The Prime Donne '15 has more depth than texture. It's just a bit marked by alcohol at this stage, but it will improve. The Orcia DOC wines are also very good.

Wine	Rating	
● Brunello di Montalcino '15	🍷🍷🍷	6
● Brunello di Montalcino Prime Donne '15	🍷🍷	7
● Orcia Il Drago e Le Colombe '16	🍷🍷	3
● Orcia Leone Rosso '18	🍷🍷	2*
● Rosso di Montalcino '18	🍷	3
● Brunello di Montalcino '14	🍸🍸	6
● Brunello di Montalcino Prime Donne '13	🍸🍸	7
● Brunello di Montalcino Ris. '13	🍸🍸	8
● Brunello di Montalcino Ris. '12	🍸🍸	8
● Orcia Rosso Cenerentola '16	🍸🍸	5
● Rosso di Montalcino '15	🍸🍸	3

Podere della Civettaja

via di Casina Rossa, 5a
52100 Arezzo
Tel. +39 3397098418
www.civettaja.it

CELLAR SALES
PRE-BOOKED VISITS
ANNUAL PRODUCTION 7,000 bottles
HECTARES UNDER VINE 3.00
VITICULTURE METHOD Certified Organic

After intuiting the potential of Pinot Nero in an area that once hosted the French grape in the late 19th century, Vincenzo Tommasi gave birth to the Casentino revival . It was eventually abandoned due to scarce harvests and replaced with less interesting grapes. But today Tommasi is re-proposing Pinot with excellent results. The climate conditions here are ideal, as are the elevations (500 meters). In the cellar, spontaneous fermentation has resulted in unique wines with a clearly discernible character. Given the complicated vintage, the 2017 version of their Pinot Nero performed well above expectations, further evidence of how this wine and its creator have really managed to square the circle. A multifaceted bouquet sees notes of underbrush and fruits (currants, blueberries and cherries) alternate, enriched by spicy hints and juniper; in the mouth it opens pleasant, light, balanced and elegant in its acidity.

Wine	Rating
● Pinot Nero '17	**YYY** 6
● Pinot Nero '16	YYY 6
● Pinot Nero '14	YYY 6
● Pinot Nero '13	YYY 6
● Pinot Nero '15	YY 6
● Pinot Nero '12	YY 3
● Pinot Nero '11	YY 3

★Tenuta Col d'Orcia

via Giuncheti
53024 Montalcino [SI]
Tel. +39 057780891
www.coldorcia.it

CELLAR SALES
PRE-BOOKED VISITS
ANNUAL PRODUCTION 800,000 bottles
HECTARES UNDER VINE 142.00
VITICULTURE METHOD Certified Organic
SUSTAINABLE WINERY

In Montalcino, where there's been an increasing focus on specific slopes and crus, Col d'Orcia represents a story of awareness and foresight. Immediately after acquiring the estate in the 1970s, in fact, the count Marone Cinzano family began to imagine their first 'single vineyard', the Poggio al Vento Riserva, a wine that best describes the peculiarities of the appellation's south and in particular the sunny, airy area between Sant'Angelo in Colle and the river Orcia. Today, as then, it's the flagship of a range that has many strengths, and not just when it comes to Sangiovese da Brunello. Two of this classic producer's wines reached our finals. The Poggio al Vento '13 is elegant, complex, multifaceted and deep, but with a slightly obscured nose. The Brunello '15 proves enticing, spicy and harmonious and sophisticated—our only qualm is that the palate is too subtle for such a vintage, but the elegance is there. The Nearco '16, Rosso '18 and the rest of the production attest to the maison's great stature.

Wine	Rating
● Brunello di Montalcino '15	**YY** 7
● Brunello di Montalcino Poggio al Vento Ris. '13	**YY** 8
● Rosso di Montalcino '18	**YY** 5
● Sant'Antimo Cabernet Olmaia '15	**YY** 6
○ Sant'Antimo Chardonnay Ghiaie Bianche '18	**YY** 4
● Sant'Antimo Nearco '16	**YY** 5
○ Moscadello di Montalcino V. T. Pascena '15	**Y** 6
● Spezieri '19	**Y** 2
○ Vermentino '19	**Y** 3
● Brunello di Montalcino '14	YY 7
● Brunello di Montalcino Nastagio '13	YY 8
● Brunello di Montalcino Poggio al Vento Ris. '12	YY 8
● Rosso di Montalcino '17	YY 5

Col di Bacche

FRAZ. MONTIANO
S.DA DI CUPI
58051 MAGLIANO IN TOSCANA [GR]
TEL. +39 0564589538
www.coldibacche.com

CELLAR SALES
PRE-BOOKED VISITS
ANNUAL PRODUCTION 80,000 bottles
HECTARES UNDER VINE 13.50

Alberto Carnasciali runs a model winery, one that's been capable of establishing a place in the Maremma winemaking world without unnecessarily shaking things up. It's now more than twenty years old, having gotten its start in 1998 and releasing its first wines in 2004. Today Col di Bacche has managed to earn itself a solid place, to say the least. Indeed, it's grown increasingly self-assured thanks to their impeccable, clearly defined wines. Behind their success there are no shortcuts, just the constant and tireless work of true wine artisans. When tasting the Poggio alle Viole '16, a monovarietal Sangiovese with a strong, austere and Mediterranean profile, the structural depth that emerges is quite notable. It's a wine marked by sensations of ripe red fruit and spices accompanied by smoky, vanilla tones. Fragrant and precise, the Vermentino '19 opens on lime blossom and passion fruit, the prelude to a tasty, dynamic palate rich in contrasts.

Wine	Glasses	Price
● Poggio alle Viole '16	2 black	5
● Morellino di Scansano '19	2 black	3
○ Vermentino '19	2 black	3
● Cupinero '09	3	5
● Morellino di Scansano Rovente '05	3	4
● Morellino di Scansano Rovente Ris. '15	3	5
● Poggio alle Viole '15	3	5
● Cupinero '15	2	5
● Morellino di Scansano '18	2	3
● Morellino di Scansano '17	2	3
● Morellino di Scansano '16	2	3
● Morellino di Scansano '15	2	3*
● Morellino di Scansano Rovente Ris. '16	2	5
● Morellino di Scansano Rovente Ris. '13	2	5
● Poggio alle Viole '14	2	5
○ Vermentino '18	2	3

Fattoria Collazzi

LOC. TAVARNUZZE
VIA COLLERAMOLE, 101
50023 IMPRUNETA [FI]
TEL. +39 0552374902
www.collazzi.it

CELLAR SALES
PRE-BOOKED VISITS
ANNUAL PRODUCTION 80,000 bottles
HECTARES UNDER VINE 32.00

A prestigious villa, whose designs have been attributed to Michelangelo Buonarroti, stands in the central part of the estate owned by the Marchi family, a property that spans over 400 hectares outside Florence. A considerable part of the land is occupied by olive trees, while a carefully tended bee farm gives rise to a small production of whole honey. The wine has gained in notoriety, especially since the nineties when the vineyards were revamped, new, French cultivars were introduced, and the cellars were upgraded. The Collazzi '17 is a blend of mostly Cabernet Sauvignon, with smaller shares of Franc, Merlot and Petit Verdot. It opens on minty notes, then hints of eucalyptus and ripe fruit amidst plum and cherry. The palate is pervaded by a soft, creamy structure, with a proper acidic vein and a long finish. The Ferro '17, 100% Petit Verdot, is captivating, aromatically fresh and racy on the palate.

Wine	Glasses	Price
● Collazzi '17	2 black	6
● Ferro '17	2 black	5
○ Otto Muri '19	2 black	3
● Chianti Cl. I Bastioni '18	1 black	3
● Libertà '18	1 black	3
● Collazzi '16	2	6
● Collazzi '15	2	6
● Collazzi '13	2	6
● Collazzi '11	2	6
● Ferro '16	2	5
● Ferro '15	2	5
● Ferro '12	2	5
● Libertà '17	2	3
● Libertà '16	2	3
○ Otto Muri '18	2	3
○ Otto Muri '17	2	3

Colle di Bordocheo

loc. Segromigno in Monte
via di Piaggiori Basso, 123
55012 Capannori [LU]
Tel. +39 0583929821
www.colledibordocheo.com

CELLAR SALES
PRE-BOOKED VISITS
ACCOMMODATION
ANNUAL PRODUCTION 30,000 bottles
HECTARES UNDER VINE 10.00

Colle di Bordocheo is a lovely, organically-run farm situated in Segromigno in Monte. Here, gorgeous vineyards and olive groves thrive, serving as the foundation for the production of high-quality wine and extra-virgin olive oil. It's an enviable position with breathtaking views of the valley, making it ideal for a farm holiday. Sangiovese, Ciliegiolo and Merlot are grown for their reds, Trebbiano, Vermentino and Chardonnay for their whites. Theirs is a personal production style, capable of giving rise to tasty, intriguing wines. Made with Sangiovese, Canaiolo, Ciliegiolo and Merlot grapes, the Rosso Bordocheo '18 pours a purplish color, the prelude to dark fruity scents, strong yet capable of spicy nuances and earthy hints. In the mouth it's tasty, with nice substance and depth, consistent aromatically. We appreciated the delicious Rosato Sestilia '19, a wine pale in color and iodine in flavor, as well as the Vermentino '19, which is marked by a delicate saltiness and an airy transparency.

Wine	Rating
● Colline Lucchesi Rosso Bordocheo '18	▼▼ 3
○ Colline Lucchesi Vermentino Bordocheo '19	▼▼ 2*
⊙ Sestilia '19	▼▼ 3
○ Bianco dell'Oca '18	▼ 3
● Colline Lucchesi Sangiovese Picchio Rosso '17	▼ 4
○ Bianco dell'Oca '17	▽▽ 3
○ Colline Lucchesi Bianco Bordocheo '18	▽▽ 2*
● Colline Lucchesi Picchio Rosso '13	▽▽ 3
● Colline Lucchesi Picchio Rosso '12	▽▽ 3
● Colline Lucchesi Rosso Bordocheo '17	▽▽ 2*
● Colline Lucchesi Rosso Mille968 '16	▽▽ 5
● Colline Lucchesi Rosso Mille968 '15	▽▽ 5
● Colline Lucchesi Sangiovese Picchio Rosso '16	▽▽ 3*
⊙ Sestilia '18	▽▽ 3

★Colle Massari

loc. Poggi del Sasso
58044 Cinigiano [GR]
Tel. +39 0564990496
www.collemassari.it

CELLAR SALES
PRE-BOOKED VISITS
ACCOMMODATION
ANNUAL PRODUCTION 500,000 bottles
HECTARES UNDER VINE 110.00
VITICULTURE METHOD Certified Biodynamic

Collemassari was founded in 1998 when entrepreneur Claudio Tipa identified, in a little-known area of Maremma, the perfect place to make his life's dream come true. In little more than two decades it's become the headquarters of one of Montecucco's, and Italy's, leading wineries, serving as the centerpiece of a prestigious group that's expanded with acquisitions in Montalcino (Poggio di Sotto, San Giorgio) and Bolgheri (Grattamacco). Their range continues to prove impeccably crafted and marked by notable personality. Probably among the best versions ever produced, the Montecucco Lombrone Riserva '16 features defined, multi-layered aromas in which small red berries alternate with floral hints, flint and spices. In the mouth its tannic structure is dense, tasty and complex, with acidity driving an energetic, deep progression of flavor. The Montecucco Rosso Rigoleto '18 is fragrant in its aromas and flavorful on the palate.

Wine	Rating
● Montecucco Sangiovese Poggio Lombrone Ris. '16	▼▼▼ 6
● Montecucco Rosso Rigoleto '18	▼▼ 3*
● Montecucco Rosso Ris. '17	▼▼ 4
○ Montecucco Vermentino Irisse '19	▼ 4
○ Montecucco Vermentino Melacce '18	▼ 3
● Montecucco Rosso Ris. '16	▽▽▽ 4*
● Montecucco Rosso Ris. '13	▽▽▽ 3*
● Montecucco Sangiovese Lombrone Ris. '11	▽▽▽ 6
● Montecucco Sangiovese Lombrone Ris. '10	▽▽▽ 6
● Montecucco Sangiovese Poggio Lombrone Ris. '14	▽▽▽ 6
● Montecucco Sangiovese Poggio Lombrone Ris. '13	▽▽▽ 6

Colle Santa Mustiola

via delle Torri, 86a
53043 Chiusi [SI]
Tel. +39 057820525
www.poggioaichiari.it

CELLAR SALES
PRE-BOOKED VISITS
ANNUAL PRODUCTION 18,000 bottles
HECTARES UNDER VINE 5.00
SUSTAINABLE WINERY

For some time now, we've grown accustomed to Fabio Cenni's extraordinary wines, which follow in a tradition of great Sangiovese forged in one of Siena and Florence's most prestigious appellations. Colle Santa Mustiola is undoubtedly among those small wineries that represent the backbone of the best of Italian wine. What's more, it's a courageous project. Having developed outside Tuscany's main wine routes, it's marked by unique characteristics, making it an obligatory experience for the most curious and attentive wine lovers. The label has been redesigned but the substance remains the same: Poggio ai Chiari is one of the most original Tuscan Sangioveses. The proof comes from a mature 2012 dominated by tertiaries, with notes of dried herbs and spices—but it's also capable of fresh flashes, with hints of freshly picked berries. The rosé Kernos '19, also made with Sangiovese, is tasty, citrusy and taut, with peppery hints.

Wine	Rating
● Poggio ai Chiari '12	🍷🍷 6
⊙ Kernos Rosato '19	🍷🍷 4
● Poggio ai Chiari '07	YYY 6
● Poggio ai Chiari '06	YYY 6
⊙ Kernos '15	YY 4
⊙ Kernos '15	YY 4
● Poggio ai Chiari '11	YY 6
● Poggio ai Chiari '10	YY 6
● Poggio ai Chiari '09	YY 6
● Poggio ai Chiari '08	YY 6
● Vigna Flavia '13	YY 5
● Vigna Flavia '12	YY 5
● Vigna Flavia '11	YY 5
● Vigna Flavia '10	YY 5

Fattoria Colle Verde

loc. Castello
via di Matraia, 8
55012 Lucca
Tel. +39 0583402310
www.colleverde.it

CELLAR SALES
PRE-BOOKED VISITS
ANNUAL PRODUCTION 30,000 bottles
HECTARES UNDER VINE 7.50
VITICULTURE METHOD Certified Organic

Piero Tartagni and Francesca Pardini chose to live in the countryside for over thirty years only to then transform themselves into wine producers. And so it was that Fattoria Colleverde was born. It's a multifaceted project: a cellar, wine resort and cooking school. The natural scenery offered by the hills of Luca is splendid to say the least. Many things have changed since the beginning of the project. Today agricultural production is certified organic, and biodynamic principles are applied as well. In the cellar, vinification is respectful of the grape, making for clear, well-made and precise wines. Their entire selection put in a good performance, with the Braia delle Ghiandaie leading the way, as usual. The 2017 has more maturity and extraction than the previous version, with toasted hints in the foreground, but it's a wine for laying down, to be tasted after some time. The excellent Nero della Spinosa '17 is fleshy and pleasantly Mediterranean. We also appreciated the Sinòpia '17, an original and fun Cabernet Franc.

Wine	Rating
● Braia delle Ghiandaie '17	🍷🍷 5
● Nero della Spinosa '17	🍷🍷 5
● Sinòpia '17	🍷🍷 8
● Terre di Matraja Rosso '19	🍷 3
● Brania delle Ghiandaie '16	YY 5
● Brania delle Ghiandaie '15	YY 5
● Brania delle Ghiandaie '14	YY 5
● Colline Lucchesi Rosso Brania delle Ghiandaie '13	YY 5
● Colline Lucchesi Rosso Brania delle Ghiandaie '12	YY 5
● Nero della Spinosa '16	YY 5
● Nero della Spinosa '14	YY 5
● Nero della Spinosa '13	YY 5
● Sinòpia '13	YY 8
● Terre di Matraja Rosso '17	YY 3
● Terre di Matraja Rosso '16	YY 3

Collemattoni

FRAZ. SANT'ANGELO IN COLLE
LOC. COLLEMATTONI, 100
53024 MONTALCINO [SI]
TEL. +39 0577844127
www.collemattoni.it

CELLAR SALES
PRE-BOOKED VISITS
ANNUAL PRODUCTION 60,000 bottles
HECTARES UNDER VINE 11.00
VITICULTURE METHOD Certified Organic
SUSTAINABLE WINERY

Marcello Bucci and his family oversee a set of vineyards that's multifaceted, to the say the least. Mainly Sangiovese is cultivated in Sesta, Cava (in Castelnuovo dell'Abate), Orcia (in Sant'Angelo Scalo), Fontelontano and Collemattoni, the property in Sant'Angelo in Colle, in southwest Montalcino, that hosts their original vineyards. These come together favorably in charming, consistent and reliable Brunellos and Rosso. The lovely performance put in by the Brunello '15, which reached our finals, is the proof. It's a modern wine in its stylistic cleanness and focused fruit, but without excesses. The palate is firm and extractive, tannins silky, the finish long and satisfying. The fleshy and satisfying Rosso, with its citrusy nuances and firm body, is also well made.

Wine	Rating
● Brunello di Montalcino '15	▼▼ 6
● Rosso di Montalcino '18	▼▼ 4
● Adone '18	▼ 3
● Brunello di Montalcino '14	▽▽ 6
● Brunello di Montalcino '13	▽▽ 6
● Brunello di Montalcino V. Fontelontano Ris. '13	▽▽ 8
● Rosso di Montalcino '17	▽▽ 4
● Rosso di Montalcino '16	▽▽ 4
● Rosso di Montalcino '15	▽▽ 4
● Rosso di Montalcino '14	▽▽ 4
● Rosso di Montalcino '13	▽▽ 3*

Colognole

LOC. COLOGNOLE
VIA DEL PALAGIO, 15
50065 PONTASSIEVE [FI]
TEL. +39 0558319870
www.colognole.it

CELLAR SALES
PRE-BOOKED VISITS
ACCOMMODATION AND RESTAURANT SERVICE
ANNUAL PRODUCTION 90,000 bottles
HECTARES UNDER VINE 27.00

Cesare and Mario Coda Nunziante, the children of the Countess Gabriella, the last descendent of the Spalletti Trivelli family (who took over the business in 1990), are today leading a multifaceted project consisting of olive groves and farmhouse accommodations, all dedicated to the discovering preserving the centuries-old culture of the territory. Of course the vineyards are notable, situated on the right bank of the Sieve, in Chianti Rufina. Here Sangiovese grapes grow alongside smaller shares of Colorino, Merlot and Chardonnay. For the first time the Chianti Rufina '17 reached our finals. Gentle, fresh and balsamic scents are accompanied by a lively fruitiness (currant, blueberry) and aromatic hints (sage, laurel). In the mouth it opens very well, juicy and supple. It has a balanced mid palate and an appetizing finish. The captivating Sarà Syrah'18 features minty and spicy notes, and a well-defined, relaxed palate.

Wine	Rating
● Chianti Rufina '17	▼▼ 3*
● Chianti Rufina Riserva del Don '16	▼▼ 5
○ Quattro Chiacchiere a Oltrepoggio '18	▼▼ 4
● Sarà Syrah '18	▼▼ 4
● Le Lastre '18	▼ 4
○ Sinopie Chardonnay '18	▼ 2
● Chianti Rufina '15	▽▽ 3
● Chianti Rufina Collezione '16	▽▽ 3
● Chianti Rufina Riserva del Don '15	▽▽ 5
● Chianti Rufina Riserva del Don '12	▽▽ 5
● Chianti Rufina Riserva del Don '11	▽▽ 5
● Chianti Rufina V. Le Rogaie '15	▽▽ 3
○ Quattro Chiacchiere a Oltrepoggio '17	▽▽ 4
○ Quattro Chiacchiere a Oltrepoggio '15	▽▽ 4

Il Colombaio di Santa Chiara

LOC. RACCIANO
VIA SAN DONATO, 1
53037 SAN GIMIGNANO [SI]
TEL. +39 0577942004
www.colombaiosantachiara.it

CELLAR SALES
PRE-BOOKED VISITS
ACCOMMODATION
ANNUAL PRODUCTION 98,000 bottles
HECTARES UNDER VINE 22.00
VITICULTURE METHOD Certified Organic
SUSTAINABLE WINERY

Here in San Gimignano, Mario Logi, who's been working the fields since the early 1950s, developed a farm business initially dedicated to breeding and then to specialized viticulture. Today it's in the hands of his son Alessio, who's involved his brothers Giampiero and Stefano. The idea is that wine is made in the vineyard, while in the cellar it can be improved, but not be transformed. And so it is that soil is treated without the use of pesticides and painstaking care is shown to tending the land, resulting in some of the area's best wines. Once again the producer takes home Tre Bicchieri thanks to the Vernaccia L'Albereta Riserva '17. It's a wine that enchants with its vibrant aromas, initially toasty notes, which open and give way to dried fruit and nuts (almond and hazelnut), then gradually fresher sensations (peach) before closing on floral nuances. The palate is lively, rich in structure but of excellent freshness and acidic backbone, all topped off by a rising finish in crescendo. The Vernaccia Campo della Pieve '18 and Selvabianca '19 are also excellent.

Wine	Rating
○ Vernaccia di San Gimignano L'Albereta Ris. '17	TTT 5
● Chianti Colli Senesi Campale '17	TT 3
○ Vernaccia di San Gimignano Campo della Pieve '18	TT 5
○ Vernaccia di San Gimignano Selvabianca '19	TT 3
⊙ Rosato Cremisi '19	T 2
● San Gimignano Rosso '15	T 5
○ Vernaccia di S. Gimignano Albereta Ris. '13	YYY 3*
○ Vernaccia di S. Gimignano Albereta Ris. '12	YYY 5
○ Vernaccia di S. Gimignano Selvabianca '17	YYY 3*
○ Vernaccia di San Gimignano L'Albereta Ris. '16	YYY 5

Podere Concori

LOC. FIATTONE
VIA PROVINCIALE, 1
55027 GALLICANO [LU]
TEL. +39 0583766039
www.podereconcori.com

CELLAR SALES
PRE-BOOKED VISITS
ANNUAL PRODUCTION 1,000 bottles
HECTARES UNDER VINE 4.00

Podere Concori is Gabriele da Prato's dream-come-true. In the late 1990s Gabriele decided to continue the work of his father, Luigi, while at the same time pursuing a personal direction. After all, there isn't much room for normality in Garfagnana, and even less for shortcuts (or respect for established rules). Thus we find a biodynamic approach, a long-term strategy that replaces myopic thinking. It's a path that bears the hallmarks of Saverio Petrilli, one of the great proponents of the agricultural practice, and now seems to be finding its own footing. The Melograno '18, a Syrah with a small share of traditional grape varieties, is a magnificent red for its grace and expressive purity. A captivating bouquet of small berries and undergrowth is accompanied by a delicate spicy vein: in the mouth, less body opens the way for more flavor, making for a delectable but by no means simple or obvious drink. The excellent Vigna Piezza '17, a Syrah with a fleshy and iodine character, is marked by an elegant spiciness.

Wine	Rating
● Melograno Rosso '18	TT 4
○ Colline Lucchesi Bianco '19	TT 4
● Vigna Piezza '17	TT 5
● Pinot Nero '18	T 5

Il Conventino

FRAZ. GRACCIANO
VIA DELLA CIARLIANA, 25B
53040 MONTEPULCIANO [SI]
TEL. +39 0578715371
www.ilconventino.it

CELLAR SALES
PRE-BOOKED VISITS
ANNUAL PRODUCTION 55,000 bottles
HECTARES UNDER VINE 12.00
VITICULTURE METHOD Certified Organic

Since 2003, Conventino has belonged to the Brini brothers, whose clear, harmonious approach to winemaking is rooted in organic viticulture and calls for absolutely non-invasive production practices. All their wines speak the language of the territory, fully respecting the area's classic grapes (Sangiovese, Colorino, Canaiolo) and more traditional methods, such as maturation in large oak barrels. Their range pursues a delicate, balanced style, constituted of finesse and drinkability, nuances and contrast. The Nobile di Montepulciano Riserva '16 offers up fragrant aromas of undergrowth and violets that gradually fade on notes of tobacco and spices. In the mouth it exhibits measure and character, spirited tannins and nice depth, coming through vivid, tasty and fresh. Sapid and penetrating flavor for the Rosso di Montepulciano '18, a wine redolent of fresh cherries, flowers and raspberries, all anticipating a pleasantly supple and relaxed palate.

Wine	Rating
● Nobile di Montepulciano Ris. '16	🍷🍷 5
● Rosso di Montepulciano '18	🍷🍷 2*
● Nobile di Montepulciano '10	🍷🍷🍷 4*
● Nobile di Montepulciano '16	🍷🍷 4
● Nobile di Montepulciano '15	🍷🍷 4
● Nobile di Montepulciano '13	🍷🍷 4
● Nobile di Montepulciano '12	🍷🍷 4
● Nobile di Montepulciano '11	🍷🍷 4
● Nobile di Montepulciano Ris. '15	🍷🍷 5
● Nobile di Montepulciano Ris. '13	🍷🍷 5
● Nobile di Montepulciano Ris. '12	🍷🍷 5
● Nobile di Montepulciano Ris. '11	🍷🍷 5
● Nobile di Montepulciano Ris. '10	🍷🍷 5
● Rosso di Montepulciano '12	🍷🍷 2*

Corte dei Venti

LOC. PIANCORNELLO, 35
53024 MONTALCINO [SI]
TEL. +39 3473653718
www.lacortedeiventi.it

CELLAR SALES
PRE-BOOKED VISITS
ANNUAL PRODUCTION 20,000 bottles
HECTARES UNDER VINE 5.00

Clara Monaci and Maurizio Machetti's winery is spread over 5 hectares of vineyards in Piancornello, on the southern side of the appellation. It was established in 2011 after Clara inherited the estate from her grandfather. The name attests to how these beautiful vineyards, located between 100-300 meters above sea level, are caressed by sea breezes, which mitigate the heat in summer and drive out humidity in winter, ensuring the ideal conditions for cultivation. This, combined with ferrous-calcareous marl soils, gives rise to elegant, dynamic, fresh, complex Brunellos. Once again an excellent performance for Corte dei Venti's reds. The Brunello '15 is rich in fruity notes, with wild strawberries in the foreground, turning to spicy and smoky sensations. The palate is firm, pervaded by alcohol, its tannins soft and its texture well distributed. The Sant'Antimo Rosso Poggio dei Lecci '17 features juicy fruit and a dense palate; the Rosso '18 is a 'mini' Brunello, delicate and harmonious.

Wine	Rating
● Brunello di Montalcino '15	🍷🍷 8
● Rosso di Montalcino '18	🍷🍷 5
● Sant'Antimo Poggio dei Lecci '17	🍷🍷 3
● Brunello di Montalcino '13	🍷🍷🍷 8
● Brunello di Montalcino '12	🍷🍷🍷 8
● Brunello di Montalcino '14	🍷🍷 8
● Brunello di Montalcino '11	🍷🍷 8
● Brunello di Montalcino Donna Elena Ris. '10	🍷🍷 8
● Brunello di Montalcino Ris. '12	🍷🍷 8
● Rosso di Montalcino '17	🍷🍷 5
● Rosso di Montalcino '16	🍷🍷 5
● Rosso di Montalcino '15	🍷🍷 5
● Sant'Antimo Poggio dei Lecci '16	🍷🍷 3*
● Sant'Antimo Poggio dei Lecci '14	🍷🍷 3

Cortonesi

loc. La Mannella, 322
53024 Montalcino [SI]
Tel. +39 0577848268
www.lamannella.it

PRE-BOOKED VISITS
ANNUAL PRODUCTION 35,000 bottles
HECTARES UNDER VINE 8.00

More and more, Tommaso Cortonesi is leading the production and stylistic choices behind a range overseen together with his father, Marco. From the outset, their wines have been linked to the moods of two quite different parts of Montalcino. In Castelnuovo dell'Abate (in the southeast) there are the plots that give rise to their Brunello I Poggiarelli, while those around the winery (in the north) are used for La Mannella, the historic line for which the producer is still known among a large number of enthusiasts. The Poggiarelli '15 is a gamble: it's intense, rich, concentrated, still marked by wood, but it has excellent texture that we are sure will lead to a brilliant, complex and mature phase in time. The excellent Rosso '18 is immediately expressive and approachable. It's also compact, everything is in its right place, starting with its fresh, crisp red fruit and elegant tannins that make for an extraordinarily intense and enjoyable drink.

Wine	Glasses	Price
● Brunello di Montalcino I Poggiarelli '15	▼▼	5
● Rosso di Montalcino '18	▼▼	3*
● Leonus '18	▼▼	3
● Brunello di Montalcino La Mannella '15	▼	5
● Brunello di Montalcino I Poggiarelli '13	▽▽	5
● Brunello di Montalcino I Poggiarelli '12	▽▽	5
● Brunello di Montalcino La Mannella '14	▽▽	5
● Brunello di Montalcino La Mannella '13	▽▽	5
● Brunello di Montalcino La Mannella '12	▽▽	5
● Rosso di Montalcino '15	▽▽	3*

Fattoria Corzano e Paterno

loc. Corzano
fraz. San Pancrazio
via San Vito di Sopra
50020 San Casciano in Val di Pesa [FI]
Tel. +39 0558248179
www.corzanoepaterno.com

CELLAR SALES
PRE-BOOKED VISITS
ACCOMMODATION
ANNUAL PRODUCTION 85,000 bottles
HECTARES UNDER VINE 19.00
VITICULTURE METHOD Certified Organic

The farm was founded in 1971 by Wendelin Gelpke, who bought the Corzano estate and then added the Paterno property in 1974. From the beginning, their work has centered on wine and oil, without forgetting the production of cheese and their guest accommodations. The winery's history is absolutely charming, focused on the recovery of farmhouses and abandoned land, which have returned to their former glory thanks to the passion of two families. Today it's the founders' descendants who run the business. The main grape cultivated is Sangiovese and the vineyards grow in clayey-calcareous soils. The Chianti Terre di Corzano '18 is a pleasant wine with fruity whiffs of strawberries and cherries; in the mouth it's supple and delicate, closed by fine tannins. The intriguing Sangiovese I Tre Borri '17 features tertiary aromas of tobacco in a mature, fruity profile. The Corzano '17, a blend of Sangiovese, Cabernet and Merlot, is characterized by intense aromas and a relaxed palate.

Wine	Glasses	Price
● Chianti Terre di Corzano '18	▼▼	2*
● Il Corzano '17	▼▼	5
● Sangiovese I Tre Borri '17	▼▼	5
○ Il Corzanello '19	▼	2
○ Il Passito di Corzano '15	▼	6
⊙ Rosato Corzanello '19	▼	2
● Chianti I Tre Borri Ris. '07	▽▽▽	5
● Il Corzano '05	▽▽▽	5
● Chianti I Tre Borri Ris. '14	▽▽	5
● Chianti I Tre Borri Ris. '13	▽▽	5
● I Tre Borri '16	▽▽	5
● Il Corzano '16	▽▽	5
● Il Corzano '15	▽▽	5

Andrea Costanti

loc. Colle al Matrichese
53024 Montalcino [SI]
Tel. +39 0577848195
www.costanti.it

CELLAR SALES
PRE-BOOKED VISITS
ANNUAL PRODUCTION 60,000 bottles
HECTARES UNDER VINE 12.00

Andrea Costanti is the authoritative heir to a historic Sienese family whose name has been bound up with Montalcino and its wines since the 1800s. For almost forty years, Andrea has been overseeing the vineyards of Colle al Matrichese, situated at around 400 meters above sea level on the eastern side of the hill. Divided into the parcels of Casottino and Calbello, the sites are also strongly characterized by their tough, galestrose deposits, which contribute to their aristocratic and long-lived Brunellos, aged in 3000-liter tonneaux and oak. We willingly bet on the positive evolution of this 2015 Brunello. The ingredients of success are all there: great mouthfeel, concentration, exuberance of fruit, tannic richness... We believe, however, it needs time to find the harmony and complexity that are the key stylistic qualities of this Montalcino producer. Wanna bet?

Wine	Rating
● Brunello di Montalcino '15	TT 6
● Brunello di Montalcino '13	YY 6
● Brunello di Montalcino '12	YY 6
● Brunello di Montalcino Ris. '12	YY 8
● Brunello di Montalcino Ris. '10	YY 8
● Rosso di Montalcino '17	YY 4
● Rosso di Montalcino '15	YY 4
● Rosso di Montalcino Vermiglio '14	YY 5

La Cura

loc. Cura Nuova, 12
58024 Massa Marittima [GR]
Tel. +39 0566918094
www.cantinalacura.it

CELLAR SALES
PRE-BOOKED VISITS
ANNUAL PRODUCTION 30,000 bottles
HECTARES UNDER VINE 15.00
SUSTAINABLE WINERY

La Cura, a producer emblematic of the potential of Italy's wine artisans, is situated in a small district between Massa Marittima and Follonica. It's a classic family-run winery, carefully overseen by Enrico Corsi. Their wines have achieved a stylistic identity that's defined by a modern approach and a solid qualitative continuity, factors that, vintage after vintage, confirm and strengthen the winery's place among Maremma's most notable producers. Once again, Enrico Corsi's Merlot demonstrates that it's one of the Maremma's most consistent in qualitative terms. The 2018 version features warm but defined aromas, and it's not without its intriguing nuances, from myrtle to thyme. The palate is broad and fragrant, with a final fruity encore. The slender and more quaffable Colle Bruno '18 offers up aromas of spices and small red fruits, anticipating a supple palate rich in contrasts.

Wine	Rating
● Maremma Toscana Merlot '17	TT 5
● Maremma Toscana Rosso Colle Bruno '18	TT 3
● Maremma Toscana Cabernet Cabernets '18	T 5
● Monteregio di Massa Marittima Rosso Breccerosse '18	T 3
○ Monteregio di Massa Marittima Vermentino Falco Pescatore '19	T 3
● Cabernets '17	YY 5
● Maremma Toscana Rosso Colle Bruno '17	YY 3
● Maremma Toscana Sangiovese Cavaliere d'Italia '18	YY 2*
● Monteregio di Massa Marittima Rosso Breccerosse '17	YY 3

Dal Cero Tenuta Montecchiesi

loc. Montecchio
52044 Cortona [AR]
Tel. +39 0457460110
www.dalcerofamily.it

CELLAR SALES
PRE-BOOKED VISITS
ANNUAL PRODUCTION 300,000 bottles
HECTARES UNDER VINE 65.00

The Dal Cero family's history is a charming one. It all began thanks to Augusto, who, in 1934, founded his first winery in the province of Verona (still owned by the family today). It was Augusto's sons Dario and Giuseppe who decided to move part of production to Tuscany, attracted by the potential of making quality reds, choosing the territory of Cortona. The business grew and consolidated over time. Today, overseeing the estates (now three), are Davide's descendants, Nico and Francesca. Both Syrahs put in good performances. The Klanis '15 has a complex and broad nose in which forest undergrowth meets blueberry and currant as well as spicy notes of pepper. The palate is racy, spirited, with fine tannins and a fresh finish. Red berry sensations, raspberries, hints of vanilla and notes of pepper characterize the Selverello '17, a wine with a subtle, supple, balanced structure. A note of merit for the Versy in Rose '18, a rosé with broad and delicious aromas.

Wine	Rating
● Cortona Syrah Klanis '15	🍷🍷 5
● Sangiovese Montecchiesi '18	🍷🍷 2*
● Selverello '17	🍷🍷 3
⊙ Versy in Rose '18	🍷🍷 5
⊙ Camely '19	🍷 4
⊙ Miraly '19	🍷 3
○ Vermentino Chardonnay Montecchiesi '19	🍷 2
● Cortona Syrah Klanis '13	🍷🍷 5
● Cortona Syrah Selverello '14	🍷🍷 3
● Preziosaterra '15	🍷🍷 3
● Sangiovese '15	🍷🍷 2*
○ Verdonnay '14	🍷🍷 5

De' Ricci

fraz. S.Albino
via Fontecornino, 15
53045 Montepulciano [SI]
Tel. +39 0578798152
www.dericci.it

CELLAR SALES
PRE-BOOKED VISITS
RESTAURANT SERVICE
ANNUAL PRODUCTION 90,000 bottles
HECTARES UNDER VINE 32.00
SUSTAINABLE WINERY

Founded in 2015, the Trabalzini family's winery is one of the most convincing new producers in Nobile di Montepulciano. On the one hand there's the historic cellar of Palazzo Ricci in the Montepulciano city center, on the other there's their vineyards and a modern facility in Fontecornino. Their style privileges finesse and drinkability, nuance and contrast. It's a clearly modern approach that's also in this case twofold: their appellation wines are made with Sangiovese and aged in large oak barrels, the IGTs from international varieties matured in barriques and mid-sized casks. Well-orchestrated aromas for the Nobile di Montepulciano '17, a wine that crosses ripe red berries with hints of violet and spicy nuances. In the mouth its attack is sweet, then it finds energy in a lovely acidic verve, which renders the palate juicy and sapid. Kudos to the Rosso di Montepulciano '18, an aromatically clean wine with a steady and fragrant palate. The enjoyable Vignone '18 is a blend of Merlot and Cabernet Sauvignon.

Wine	Rating
● Nobile di Montepulciano '17	🍷🍷 5
● Il Vignone '17	🍷🍷 5
● Rosso di Montepulciano '18	🍷🍷 3
● Il Severo '16	🍷🍷 3
● Nobile di Montepulciano '16	🍷🍷 5
● Nobile di Montepulciano '15	🍷🍷 5
● Nobile di Montepulciano SorAldo '16	🍷🍷 6
● Nobile di Montepulciano SorAldo '15	🍷🍷 6
● Rosso di Montepulciano '17	🍷🍷 3

Maria Caterina Dei

via di Martiena, 35
53045 Montepulciano [SI]
Tel. +39 0578716878
www.cantinedei.com

CELLAR SALES
PRE-BOOKED VISITS
ACCOMMODATION
ANNUAL PRODUCTION 230,000 bottles
HECTARES UNDER VINE 60.00
SUSTAINABLE WINERY

Maria Caterina Dei has been running the family business herself since 1991. Everything began with the acquisition, in 1964, of the Bossona vineyard, while the Martiena property was taken over in 1973. The first bottles came in 1985 and from then on the Dei brand gradually earned itself an important place in the Nobile di Montepulciano panorama. Their wines are characterized by firm structure, but are always able to unfold with balance and finesse. The Nobile di Montepulciano Madonna della Querce '17 impresses for its fruity and spicy intensity adorned by smoky hints. In the mouth it unfolds broad and pervasive, with dense, tight-knit tannins, giving way to a firm and equally broad finish. The Nobile di Montepulciano '17 is solid and well-crafted, with its lush, fruity nose and juicy, vivid palate. We also appreciated the fragrant and drinkable Rosso di Montepulciano '19.

Wine	Rating
● Nobile di Montepulciano Madonna della Querce '17	TT 8
● Nobile di Montepulciano '17	TT 5
● Nobile di Montepulciano Bossona Ris. '15	TT 7
● Rosso di Montepulciano '19	TT 5
● Nobile di Montepulciano '14	YYY 4*
● Nobile di Montepulciano '13	YYY 4*
● Nobile di Montepulciano Bossona Ris. '13	YYY 6
● Nobile di Montepulciano Bossona Ris. '04	YYY 5
● Nobile di Montepulciano Madonna della Querce '15	YYY 8
● Nobile di Montepulciano '16	YY 5
● Nobile di Montepulciano '15	YY 4
● Nobile di Montepulciano Bossona Ris. '12	YY 6

Fabrizio Dionisio

fraz. Case Sparse Ossaia, 87
loc. Il Castagno
52040 Cortona [AR]
Tel. +39 063223391
www.fabriziodionisio.it

CELLAR SALES
PRE-BOOKED VISITS
ANNUAL PRODUCTION 45,000 bottles
HECTARES UNDER VINE 15.00
SUSTAINABLE WINERY

In the 1970s Sergio Dionisio, Fabrizio's father, chose a farmhouse with seven hectares of vineyards and olive groves on the hills overlooking Cortona. About twenty years later, the purchase of a new plot of land gave the producer its current size, setting off their work in viticulture. Fabrizio, with his wife Alessandra, decided to replant the old vineyards with an addition of Syrah, which does well in area. The first wine came in 2003. Since then they've been tirelessly and scrupulously making clearly Tuscan wines with a strong local identity. The Il Castagno Syrah made its usual appearance in our final tastings, with the 2017 version exhibiting complex aromas, notes of withered rose on a fruity base, then aromatic herbs (marjoram and thyme) and balsamic hints. The palate makes a nice impact, coming through warm, elegant, linear and round, with a rising finish. The Castagnino '19 exhibits a profile more linked to wild berries (and blueberry), with a light, balanced palate.

Wine	Rating
● Cortona Syrah Il Castagno '17	TT 5
● Cortona Syrah Cuculaia '16	TT 7
● Cortona Syrah Il Castagnino '19	TT 3
⊙ Rosa del Castagno '19	T 3
● Cortona Syrah Il Castagno '12	YYY 5
● Cortona Syrah Il Castagno '11	YYY 5
● Cortona Syrah Il Castagno '10	YYY 5
● Cortona Syrah Castagnino '18	YY 3
● Cortona Syrah Castagnino '17	YY 3
● Cortona Syrah Castagnino '16	YY 3
● Cortona Syrah Castagnino '15	YY 3*
● Cortona Syrah Cuculaia '15	YY 7
● Cortona Syrah Cuculaia '13	YY 7
● Cortona Syrah Il Castagno '16	YY 5
● Cortona Syrah Il Castagno '15	YY 5
● Cortona Syrah Il Castagno '14	YY 5
● Cortona Syrah Il Castagno '13	YY 5

Donna Olimpia 1898

FRAZ. BOLGHERI
LOC. MIGLIARINI, 142
57020 CASTAGNETO CARDUCCI [LI]
TEL. +39 0302279601
www.donnaolimpia1898.it

CELLAR SALES
ACCOMMODATION AND RESTAURANT SERVICE
ANNUAL PRODUCTION 250,000 bottles
HECTARES UNDER VINE 45.00
SUSTAINABLE WINERY

It was Guido Folonari's idea to found Donna Olimpia, having decided to develop the family's wine business in Bolgheri as well. Today the group that bears his name is a benchmark for Italian wine, and the coastal estate plays the same role for the appellation. It covers a total of sixty hectares, many of which are vineyards. The varieties cultivated are Cabernet Sauvignon, Cabernet Franc, Merlot, Petit Verdot and Syrah for their reds. Vermentino, Viognier and Petit Manseng form the basis of their whites. The maturation area is the heart of the winery, a space that's accented by a splendid barrique cellar. The wine that impressed us the most was the Bolgheri Rosso '17, in our opinion it's the one that best describes the territory and its grapes. It opens on lovely fruit, expressing sensations of ripe cherry and wild blackberry well enveloped by Mediterranean herbs and balsamic nuances. In the mouth it exhibits nice balance, though without losing sight of fruity sweetness, flavor and freshness.

Wine	Glasses	Price
● Bolgheri Rosso '17	🍷🍷	5
● Bolgheri Rosso Sup. Millepassi '17	🍷🍷	7
● Bolgheri Rosso Campo alla Giostra '17	🍷	5
○ Obizzo '17	🍷	2
● Orizzonte '17	🍷	7
● Bolgheri Rosso Sup. Millepassi '15	🍸🍸🍸	7
● Bolgheri Rosso Sup. Millepassi '13	🍸🍸🍸	6
● Bolgheri Rosso Sup. Millepassi '11	🍸🍸🍸	8
● Bolgheri Rosso '15	🍸🍸	5
● Bolgheri Rosso Campo alla Giostra '16	🍸🍸	5
● Bolgheri Rosso Campo alla Giostra '15	🍸🍸	5
● Bolgheri Rosso Sup. Millepassi '16	🍸🍸	7
○ Obizzo Vermentino '18	🍸🍸	2*
○ Obizzo Vermentino '17	🍸🍸	2*
● Tageto '16	🍸🍸	2*

Duemani

LOC. ORTACAVOLI
56046 RIPARBELLA [PI]
TEL. +39 0583975048
www.duemani.eu

CELLAR SALES
PRE-BOOKED VISITS
ANNUAL PRODUCTION 50,000 bottles
HECTARES UNDER VINE 12.00
VITICULTURE METHOD Certified Biodynamic
SUSTAINABLE WINERY

Luca D'Attoma is a well-known enologist and founder of a consulting firm through which he follows and collaborates with wineries all over Italy. On the hills of Riparbella, overlooking the sea, he's been developing the project conceived with his wife Elena Celli: producing wines according to principles of biodynamic agriculture. For about twenty years they have been cultivating the vines they love the most, from Cabernet Franc to Syrah and Merlot, in a land, by their own definition, extreme, grumpy, wild and magnetic. The result are 'fragrant and tasty' grapes from which 'clean, original, tasty' wines are born.
Tre Bicchieri for the Duemani '17, a monovarietal Cabernet Franc whose broad bouquet spans fresh notes of pepper and balsamic hints by way of black berries, such as blueberry and juniper. Its body is lively, with well-integrated tannins and a firm, persistent finish. The Suisassi '17 also delivers. We appreciated this Syrah for its aromas of tobacco and tanned leather, but also for its balanced, lively palate.

Wine	Glasses	Price
● Duemani '17	🍷🍷🍷	8
● Suisassi '17	🍷🍷	8
● Altrovino '17	🍷🍷	8
● Cifra '18	🍷🍷	5
● G. Punto '18	🍷🍷	8
⊙ Si '19	🍷	6
● Altrovino '15	🍸🍸🍸	6
● Duemani '15	🍸🍸🍸	8
● Duemani '13	🍸🍸🍸	8
● Duemani '12	🍸🍸🍸	8
● Duemani '09	🍸🍸🍸	8
● Suisassi '16	🍸🍸🍸	8
● Suisassi '10	🍸🍸🍸	8
● Altrovino '16	🍸🍸	6
● Duemani '16	🍸🍸	8
● Duemani '14	🍸🍸	8

I Fabbri

loc. Lamole
via Casole, 52
50022 Greve in Chianti [FI]
Tel. +39 339412622
www.ifabbrichianticlassico.it

CELLAR SALES
PRE-BOOKED VISITS
ANNUAL PRODUCTION 35,000 bottles
HECTARES UNDER VINE 11.00
VITICULTURE METHOD Certified Organic

Located on the Florentine side of Greve in Chianti, Lamole is one of the most fascinating and difficult subzones in all of Chianti Classico. The vineyards grow at 650 meters elevation, grapes ripen late and temperature swings are sometimes dizzying. The Grassi sisters' winery represents ones of the purest and most faithful expressions of the peculiarities of this terroir, starting with wines whose grapes are cultivated in the area's characteristic terraces. The style is traditional and charming, marked by acute and ferrous scents, lean structure and generally austere but elegant quality. The expressive essence of the Lamole subzone, in our humble opinion, is captured perfectly in the Chianti Classico Lamole '18. It's a wine that subtly whispers its elegant scents, calling up earth and flowers, with some intriguing whiffs of iron. In the mouth it unfolds subtle but not skeletal, with a truly fresh, rhythmic and enticing palate. The free, easy and fragrant Chianti Classico Olinto '18 exhibits a similar profile.

Wine	Rating
● Chianti Cl. Lamole '18	🍷🍷🍷 4*
● Chianti Cl. Olinto '18	🍷🍷 4
● Chianti Cl. Terra di Lamole '17	🍷🍷 3
● Chianti Cl. Lamole '17	YYY 4*
● Chianti Cl. '16	YY 4
● Chianti Cl. '13	YY 4
● Chianti Cl. Gran Sel. '11	YY 6
● Chianti Cl. Gran Selezione '15	YY 6
● Chianti Cl. Olinto '15	YY 4
● Chianti Cl. Olinto '14	YY 4
● Chianti Cl. Olinto '12	YY 4
● Chianti Cl. Ris. '16	YY 4
● Chianti Cl. Ris. '13	YY 4
● Chianti Cl. Ris. '11	YY 4
● Chianti Cl. Terra di Lamole '16	YY 3
● Chianti Cl. Terra di Lamole '15	YY 3
● Chianti Cl. Terra di Lamole '13	YY 3*

Fabbrica Pienza

loc. Borghetto
53026 Pienza [SI]
Tel. +39 0578810030
www.fabbricapienza.com

CELLAR SALES
PRE-BOOKED VISITS
ANNUAL PRODUCTION 40,000 bottles
HECTARES UNDER VINE 35.00
VITICULTURE METHOD Certified Organic
SUSTAINABLE WINERY

The project was conceived and realized by Philippe Berthera, who bought the estate in 2012, initially as a place for relaxing in an area of great beauty, the Val d'Orcia. Soon, however, a passion for wine took over, so much so that he planted the vineyard, thanks in part to the revival of old vines, and built a beautiful cellar. Today Sangiovese and Syrah are grown for the reds, Vermentino, Marsanne and Viognier for the whites. The name comes from the original building, an old furnace for making terracotta. The Syrah '17 made a good impression: hints of cherry meet dried flowers and black pepper. It opens pleasant in the mouth, with excellent, multifaceted pulp, while the finish proves supple and enticing. The Bianco di Fabbrica '18 is also quite pleasant, calling up almond, with hints of honey, chamomile and rosemary—it's disengaged and fresh on the palate. We also appreciated the excellent Rosso di Fabbrica '18.

Wine	Rating
○ Bianco di Fabbrica '18	🍷🍷 6
● Rosso di Fabbrica '18	🍷🍷 3
● Syrah '17	🍷🍷 5
⊙ Rosato di Fabbrica '19	🍷 2
● Sangiovese di Toscana '17	🍷 5
○ Bianco di Fabbrica '17	YY 6
○ Bianco di Fabbrica '16	YY 6
● Prototipo 470.1 '13	YY 5
● Prototipo 470.2 '14	YY 5
● Prototipo 470.3 Sangiovese '15	YY 8
● Sangiovese '16	YY 5
● Syrah '16	YY 5

Il Falcone

Loc. Falcone, 186
57028 Suvereto [LI]
Tel. +39 0565829331
www.ilfalcone.net

CELLAR SALES
PRE-BOOKED VISITS
ACCOMMODATION
ANNUAL PRODUCTION 40,000 bottles
HECTARES UNDER VINE 10.00

Owned by the Petri family since 1911, Il Falcone is one of Valdicornia's historic farms. The name comes from the hill that hosts the estate, whose presence on land registry maps date back to the early 19th century. Today the property is managed by sisters Paola and Rosa, together with their husbands, Vittorio and Paolo. In 2019 the process of conversion to organic farming began. In addition to wine, oil is also of fundamental importance, thanks to their 4 thousand olive trees. The Vallin dei Ghiri '18 is a very interested Syrah marked by enticing scents of cherry and currant, with pepper and balsamic notes completing the picture. The palate is persuasive, warm, of good weight, making for a juicy, long finish. The Boccalupo '17, a blend of Sangiovese, Giacomino, Cabernet Sauvignon and Merlot, features sanguine notes of pepper and black cherry; the palate is firm and compact, smooth in its tannins, unfolding well on the finish.

Wine	Glasses	Rating
● Suvereto Sangiovese Boccalupo '17	🍷🍷	5
● Vallin dei Ghiri Syrah '18	🍷🍷	5
○ Falcobianco '18	🍷	3
● Falcorosso '18	🍷	3
● Falcorosso '17	🍷🍷	3
● Falcorosso '13	🍷🍷	2*
● Suvereto Boccalupo '14	🍷🍷	6
● Suvereto Sangiovese Boccalupo '16	🍷🍷	5
● Valdicornia Suvereto Boccalupo '12	🍷🍷	4
● Vallin dei Ghiri '15	🍷🍷	7
● Vallin dei Ghiri '13	🍷🍷	5
● Vallin dei Ghiri '12	🍷🍷	5
● Vallin dei Ghiri Syrah '17	🍷🍷	5

Tenuta Fanti

fraz. Castelnuovo dell'Abate
Podere Palazzo, 14
53020 Montalcino [SI]
Tel. +39 0577835795
www.tenutafanti.it

CELLAR SALES
PRE-BOOKED VISITS
ANNUAL PRODUCTION 200,000 bottles
HECTARES UNDER VINE 50.00

Situated in the immediate vicinity of the village of Castelnuovo dell'Abate, an area of reference in southeastern Montalcino, the Fanti family estate is an essential stop for those seeking an interpretation of Brunello that doesn't conform to stereotypes. It's all thanks to Filippo, who, with his daughter Elisa, crafts pleasantly juicy reds from Sangiovese, as one might expect from a warm area that's continually refreshed by the winds and strong temperature swings of nearby Mount Amiata. Filippo and Elisa's 2015 Brunello is a perfect expression of the vintage: it pours a vibrant, ruby red with no extractive forcing. The nose is rich, offering up fresh, ripe red fruit without sagging, elegant nuances of tobacco and smoky notes that herald its complex maturity. The palate is firm, tonic, rich and deep. Well done. The Rosso '18 is a 'mini' Brunello. We appreciated the Sassomagno '18 and found the Brunello Vallocchio '15 a bit less charming.

Wine	Glasses	Rating
● Brunello di Montalcino '15	🍷🍷🍷	6
● Rosso di Montalcino '18	🍷🍷	3*
● Sant'Antimo Rosso Sassomagno '18	🍷🍷	2*
● Brunello di Montalcino Vallocchio '15	🍷	7
● Brunello di Montalcino Vallocchio '13	🍷🍷🍷	7
● Brunello di Montalcino '13	🍷🍷	6
● Brunello di Montalcino '12	🍷🍷	6
● Brunello di Montalcino V. Le Macchiarelle Ris. '13	🍷🍷	6
● Brunello di Montalcino V. Le Macchiarelle Ris. '11	🍷🍷	6
● Rosso di Montalcino '17	🍷🍷	3*
● Rosso di Montalcino '16	🍷🍷	3
● Rosso di Montalcino '15	🍷🍷	3*

Tenuta Le Farnete - Cantagallo

FRAZ. COMEANA
VIA MACIA
59100 CARMIGNANO [PO]
TEL. +39 0571910078
www.tenutacantagallo.it

CELLAR SALES
PRE-BOOKED VISITS
ACCOMMODATION AND RESTAURANT SERVICE
ANNUAL PRODUCTION 65,000 bottles
HECTARES UNDER VINE 40.00
SUSTAINABLE WINERY

The Pierazzuoli family's estate is divided into two sections, one acquired twenty years after the other. The first is Cantagallo, owned since 1970, which extends for 200 hectares on the hills of Vinci. Here Sangiovese and to a lesser extent Merlot, Syrah, Trebbiano, Malvasia and Colorino are cultivated. The center of the estate houses the restaurant, the farm, the winery and a modern oil press. The other, Le Farnete, was purchased in 1990. It occupies 50 hectares in the heart of Carmignano, where Sangiovese, Cabernet Sauvignon and Aleatico grapes are grown. The producer's selection put in a great overall performance, with all the wines presented reaching the threshold of excellence. The best is the Carmignano Riserva '17, with its aromatic spectrum of fruits, especially cherry and blackberry, softened by light, spicy notes of cinnamon and pepper. Good attack in the mouth, wide, balanced structure, creamy and well inserted tannins, and a prolonged, satisfying finish.

Wine	Rating
● Carmignano Ris. '17	▼▼▼ 4*
● Chianti Montalbano Tenuta Cantagallo Il Fondatore Ris. '17	▼▼ 3*
● Barco Reale Le Farnete '19	▼▼ 2*
● Carmignano '18	▼▼ 3
● Chianti Montalbano Tenuta Cantagallo '19	▼▼ 2*
● Chianti Montalbano Tenuta Cantagallo Ris. '17	▼▼ 3
● Gioveto Tenuta Cantagallo '17	▼▼ 4
○ Vin Santo Chianti Montalbano Millarium '14	▼▼ 5
● Carmignano Ris. '16	▽▽▽ 4*
● Carmignano Ris. '15	▽▽▽ 4*
● Carmignano Ris. '14	▽▽▽ 4*
● Chianti Montalbano Tenuta Cantagallo Il Fondatore Ris. '16	▽▽ 2*

Fattoi

LOC. SANTA RESTITUTA
POD. CAPANNA, 101
53024 MONTALCINO [SI]
TEL. +39 0577848613
www.fattoi.it

CELLAR SALES
PRE-BOOKED VISITS
ANNUAL PRODUCTION 60,000 bottles
HECTARES UNDER VINE 11.50

Matured in medium-large Slavonian oak, the Fattoi family's wines are a true homage to the more visceral and gastronomic character of Montalcino's Sangiovese. Their Rosso and Brunello are capable of faithfully reproducing the Mediterranean and sylvan, foresty atmospheres we encounter in Santa Restituta, an area of reference here in the southwestern part of the production zone. Their style, which privileges expressive veracity and naturalness, has been chiseled out over the years by Ofelio together with his sons Lamberto and Leonardo, and his granddaughter Lucia. The Brunello '15, which reached our finals, put in a truly lovely performance. It pours a deep, ruby red, anticipating wholesome, fresh fruit that expresses itself nicely both on the nose, where it's rich and fades on notes of tobacco and wood, and on the palate, where exuberant but fine tannins and a fresh acidic vein lend harmony and pleasantness. The other wines tasted are also enjoyable.

Wine	Rating
● Brunello di Montalcino '15	▼▼ 5
● Rosso della Toscana '18	▼ 4
● Rosso di Montalcino '18	▼ 4
● Brunello di Montalcino '10	▽▽▽ 5
● Brunello di Montalcino Ris. '12	▽▽▽ 7
● Brunello di Montalcino '14	▽▽ 5
● Brunello di Montalcino '13	▽▽ 5
● Brunello di Montalcino '12	▽▽ 5
● Brunello di Montalcino '11	▽▽ 5
● Brunello di Montalcino Ris. '10	▽▽ 7
● Rosso di Montalcino '17	▽▽ 4
● Rosso di Montalcino '16	▽▽ 3
● Rosso di Montalcino '15	▽▽ 3
● Rosso di Montalcino '14	▽▽ 3

Fattoria del Teso

via Poltroniera
55015 Montecarlo [LU]
Tel. +39 0583286288
www.fattoriadelteso.it

CELLAR SALES
PRE-BOOKED VISITS
ANNUAL PRODUCTION 100,000 bottles
HECTARES UNDER VINE 15.00

Fattoria del Teso is one of Montecarlo's historic wineries. Its origins go back to medieval times, while the modern agricultural project took form in the 1970s. The property's lovely main building houses the cellar for aging, while in front we find the rooms for vinification, with fibreglass-lined cement and steel tanks. The vineyards are located at an average elevation of 70 meters, with exposures ranging from northwest to southeast, and host a number of native grapes: Vermentino, Trebbiano Toscano and Verdea among the whites; Sangiovese, Ciliegiolo and Colorino among the reds. A splendid benchmark for the denomination, the Il Montecarlo Rosso '18 bewitches with its elegance and harmony, punctuated by red and black fruits adorned with balsamic streaks. Sapid and racy, it unfolds beautifully in the mouth. The Vinsanto '03 is no less good: bright amber in colour, it's a kaleidoscope of dried fruit, walnutskin, spices, honey and candied orange.

Wine	Rating
● Montecarlo Rosso '18	🍷🍷 3*
○ Montecarlo Vin Santo '03	🍷🍷 6
● Anfidiamante '16	🍷🍷 5
○ Vermentino del Teso '19	🍷🍷 3
○ Montecarlo Bianco '19	🍷 3
● Montecarlo Rosso '16	ΥΥ 3

Fattoria di Piazzano

via di Piazzano, 5
50053 Empoli [FI]
Tel. +39 0571994032
www.fattoriadipiazzano.it

CELLAR SALES
PRE-BOOKED VISITS
ACCOMMODATION
ANNUAL PRODUCTION 150,000 bottles
HECTARES UNDER VINE 33.00
SUSTAINABLE WINERY

Piazzano got its start after the war, thanks to Otello Bettarini, an industrialist from Prato who loves astronomy and identified the property as the perfect place to live out his passion for wine. It was his grandson Riccardo, however, who made the idea concrete, restructuring the land and adopting a modern, efficient organizational approach to production. His work continues today with his children Ilaria and Riccardo, together with Riccardo's wife, Michela. Recent news includes vegan certification. The Ciliegiolo '19 is a very interesting wine, offering up an aromatic bouquet wrought of ripe fruits, cherry and plum, all softened by notes of aromatic herbs. The body is well balanced, juicy, with delicate tannins; it has a fresh acidic vein and excellent depth. The Chianti Riserva '17 also delivers, with its notes of mint and rosemary on the nose, on a fruity plum base: in the mouth it's fresh and pleasantly persistent.

Wine	Rating
● Chianti Ris. '17	🍷🍷 3
● Chianti Sup. Rio Camerata '18	🍷🍷 3
● Ciliegiolo '19	🍷🍷 3
○ Pratile '19	🍷 3
● Ventoso '19	🍷 2
● Blend 1 '15	ΥΥ 4
● Colorino '16	ΥΥ 6
● Messidoro '13	ΥΥ 1*
● Syrah '16	ΥΥ 5
● Syrah '15	ΥΥ 4
● Syrah '11	ΥΥ 4
● Ventoso '13	ΥΥ 1*
○ Vin Santo del Chianti '04	ΥΥ 6

Fattoria Fibbiano

via Fibbiano, 2
56030 Terricciola [PI]
Tel. +39 0587635677
www.fattoria-fibbiano.it

CELLAR SALES
PRE-BOOKED VISITS
ACCOMMODATION AND RESTAURANT SERVICE
ANNUAL PRODUCTION 120,000 bottles
HECTARES UNDER VINE 17.00

The farm and accommodations are located near Terricciola, on the hills between Pisa and Volterra. An area of 75 hectares hosts vineyards and olive groves, as well as woodlands. The origins of the farm date back to the twelfth century, though for more than twenty years it has been owned by Giuseppe Cantoni, who returned to Italy after years of activity abroad in the industrial sector to realize his dream of dedicating himself to agriculture (his sons Matteo and Nicola are now on board). Great attention is paid to forgotten grape varieties like Sanforte, Sangiovese Polveroso and Colombana. The Ciliegiolo '18 unveils an alluring bouquet, with hints of mint and undergrowth in a fruity profile of ripe cherries and spicy notes. In the mouth it opens warm, pervasive, with nicely-distributed tannins and a dry finish. The singular Sanforte '16 is made with the native cultivar of the same name: it features hints of plum and herbs, a robust body and nice length.

Wine	Rating
● Ciliegiolo '18	🍷🍷 4
● L'Aspetto '16	🍷🍷 5
● Sanforte '16	🍷🍷 5
● Terre di Pisa Ceppatella '15	🍷🍷 7
○ Fonte delle Donne '19	🍷 3
⊙ Sofia Rosato '19	🍷 3
● Chianti Sup. Casalini '15	YY 2*
● Ciliegiolo '17	YY 4
● Ciliegiolo '16	YY 4
● Ciliegiolo '15	YY 3
○ Fonte delle Donne '18	YY 3
● L'Aspetto '15	YY 5
● Le Pianette '16	YY 2*
● Le Pianette '15	YY 2*
● Sanforte '15	YY 5
● Sanforte '14	YY 5
● Terre di Pisa Ceppatella '13	YY 6

★Tenute Ambrogio e Giovanni Folonari

loc. Passo dei Pecorai
via di Nozzole, 12
50022 Greve in Chianti [FI]
Tel. +39 055859811
www.tenutefolonari.com

CELLAR SALES
PRE-BOOKED VISITS
ACCOMMODATION
ANNUAL PRODUCTION 1,400,000 bottles
HECTARES UNDER VINE 200.00

The wines of the Nozzole estate in Greve in Chianti, on the Florentine side of Chianti Classico, are characterized by a modern style, marked by the pursuit of ripeness of fruit and weighty structure as well as the discernible presence of oak, all with impeccable technical execution. But Ambrogio and Giovanni Folonari's wines aren't lacking in personality, and not infrequently, the team have delivered absolute excellence. The family have a multifaceted system of wineries: Campo al Mare in Bolgheri, La Fuga in Montalcino and Vigne in Porrona in Maremma. Pure Cabernet Sauvignon, released for the first time in 1987, the Pareto continues its successful journey with the 2017 version as well. It's a monumental wine right from the outset, with pervasive aromas that linger on a luxuriant array of red berries, spices, tobacco and pencil lead. In the mouth it's powerful and mature, with resolved tannins and a broad, sweet finish. The Chianti Classico '18 is a highly enjoyable drink.

Wine	Rating
● Il Pareto '17	🍷🍷🍷 8
● Brunello di Montalcino Tenuta La Fuga '15	🍷🍷 7
● Chianti Cl. '18	🍷🍷 3
● Cabreo Il Borgo '17	🍷 6
● Chianti Cl. Gran Selezione '16	🍷 5
● Chianti Cl. La Forra Ris. '16	🍷 4
○ Le Bruniche '19	🍷 3
● Cabreo Il Borgo '16	YYY 6
● Cabreo Il Borgo '06	YYY 5
● Il Pareto '15	YYY 8
● Il Pareto '09	YYY 7
● Il Pareto '07	YYY 7
● Il Pareto '04	YYY 7
● Il Pareto '01	YYY 7
● Il Pareto '00	YYY 7
● Il Pareto '98	YYY 7

★★Fontodi

fraz. Panzano in Chianti
via San Leolino, 89
50020 Greve in Chianti [FI]
Tel. +39 055852005
www.fontodi.com

CELLAR SALES
PRE-BOOKED VISITS
ACCOMMODATION
ANNUAL PRODUCTION 300,000 bottles
HECTARES UNDER VINE 80.00
VITICULTURE METHOD Certified Organic

Giovanni Manetti's Fontodi, a winery that goes back more than 50 years, is one of Chianti Classico's landmarks. Some of the most significant wines of the appellation have come out, and continue to come out, of the 'Conca d'Oro' vineyards in Panzano, and today, to further expand their work around Gallo Nero, they've added vineyards in the Lamole subzone. Their wines are characterized by a focus on personality and consistency, combined with the ability to express the principle qualities of the production subzones. A famous monvarietal Sangiovese, the 2017 Flaccianello della Pieve exhibits character, featuring aromas ranging from red berries to woodland scrub, from spices to vivid flashes of pencil lead. A ripe, juicy and broad palate follows, finishing intense, once again on fruit. The Chianti Classico '17 is a textbook wine, as enticing aromatically as it is quaffable.

● Chianti Cl. '17	4
● Flaccianello della Pieve '17	8
○ Vin Santo del Chianti Cl. '10	6
● Chianti Cl. Filetta di Lamole '17	5
● Pinot Nero '17	6
● Chianti Cl. Gran Selezione V. del Sorbo '17	6
● Syrah '17	6
● Chianti Cl. '10	4*
● Chianti Cl. Gran Sel. V. del Sorbo '14	6
● Chianti Cl. Gran Selezione V. del Sorbo '16	6
● Flaccianello della Pieve '12	8
● Flaccianello della Pieve '09	8
● Flaccianello della Pieve '08	8
● Flaccianello della Pieve '07	6
● Flaccianello della Pieve '05	6

Fontuccia

via Provinciale, 54
58012 Isola del Giglio [GR]
Tel. +39 0564809576
www.fontuccia.it

ANNUAL PRODUCTION 6,500 bottles
HECTARES UNDER VINE 3.00

Theirs is a time-honored tradition that has been internalized and re-proposed with the necessary 'modern' adjustments (without neglecting the heroic approach that wine-growing on an island imposes and requires). This is the background for this small island winery, owned by the Rossi brothers. The style is openly Mediterranean, to say the least, full of personality and charm, forged with precision, but without resorting to shortcuts of any kind or interfering with the natural process of winemaking. Fontuccia riffs intriguingly on Ansonica. The Caperrosso '19 offers up hints of iodine and flint. On the palate it's rich in minerals, made rhythmic by a well-sustained, delicately salty note. The Cocciuto '19, an Ansonica worked in amphorae, is characterized by aromas of broom and eucalyptus, anticipating a tasty, almost tannic palate. We shouldn't forget the Senti Oh! '19, an assertive Ansonica, and the Saracio Rosso '18, a mix of varieties (some unknown).

○ Capperrosso Senti Oh! '19	4
○ Cocciuto Senti Oh! '19	4
● Saracio '18	6
○ Senti Oh! '19	4
○ Capperrosso Senti Oh! '18	4
○ Capperrosso Senti Oh! '16	4
○ Capperrosso Senti Oh! '15	4
○ N'antro Po' '13	6
○ N'antro Po' Ansonica Passito '18	6
● Saracio '16	6
○ Senti Oh! '18	4
○ Senti Oh! '17	4
○ Senti Oh! '16	4

La Fornace

Pod. Fornace, 154a
53024 Montalcino [SI]
Tel. +39 0577848465
www.agricola-lafornace.it

CELLAR SALES
PRE-BOOKED VISITS
ANNUAL PRODUCTION 15,000 bottles
HECTARES UNDER VINE 4.50

La Fornace's story is a classic in Montalcino: a family-run producer that became the fulfillment of a dream when Fabio Giannetti's grandparents managed to buy the farm where they had worked all their lives as sharecroppers. The first bottling of Rosso and Brunello began in the second half of the 1980s, but it's been of late, especially, that their small range has managed to highlight the attributes of their vineyards, which grow in sandy-clayey soil in the northeast part of the production zone, at elevations of about 400 meters. The Giannetti family's wines once again demonstrates their high levels, earning the producer a place in our main section. The common thread that binds them is power, even if at times it's at the expense of elegance. The Brunello '15 landed in our finals, standing out for its powerful, almost chewy palate and its great length. The Rosso (which comes across like a 'mini' Brunello) is excellent, while the Origini is still a bit stiff and austere.

- Brunello di Montalcino '15 — 6
- Brunello di Montalcino Origini '15 — 6
- Rosso di Montalcino '18 — 4
- Brunello di Montalcino '14 — 6
- Brunello di Montalcino '13 — 6
- Brunello di Montalcino '10 — 6
- Brunello di Montalcino Origini '13 — 6
- Brunello di Montalcino Ris. '11 — 8
- Rosso di Montalcino '17 — 4
- Rosso di Montalcino '16 — 4
- Rosso di Montalcino '14 — 4

Podere Forte

loc. Petrucci, 13
53023 Castiglione d'Orcia [SI]
Tel. +39 05778885100
www.podereforte.it

CELLAR SALES
PRE-BOOKED VISITS
ANNUAL PRODUCTION 12,000 bottles
HECTARES UNDER VINE 15.00
VITICULTURE METHOD Certified Biodynamic
SUSTAINABLE WINERY

Some farms need to be visited more than explained. This is one such case. Just by looking and touching it in person, you can understand the incredible 'universe' conceived and realized by Pasquale Forte, an entrepreneur who chose Val d'Orcia as the ideal place for his agricultural dream. Everything revolves around biodynamic cultivation. Wine is, obviously, the most important and visible product, but they also produce oil, charcuterie, flour and honey, all with the same criteria and all of notable quality. A monovarietal Sangiovese, the Guardiavigna '16 is a marvel. It unveils an original aromatic suite of floral notes, hyacinth, aromatic herbs reminiscent of tarragon, then cherry and green pepper. The palate is consistent, nicely orchestrated and calibrated, long and flavorful. The Amphitheatre '15 is also wonderful. Another Sangiovese, it's perhaps more marked by mature, round sensations, at moments calling up jam and rhubarb.

- Guardiavigna '16 — 8
- Orcia Anfiteatro '15 — 8
- Orcia Petrucci Melo '15 — 8
- Orcia Petruccino '17 — 7
- Orcia Guardiavigna '01 — 8
- Orcia Petruccino '16 — 7
- Guardiavigna '15 — 8
- Guardiavigna '14 — 8
- Guardiavigna '13 — 8
- Guardiavigna '12 — 8
- Guardiavigna '11 — 8
- Guardiavigna '05 — 8
- Orcia Anfiteatro '16 — 8
- Orcia Melo '16 — 8
- Orcia Petrucci '10 — 8
- Orcia Petruccino '15 — 6

Fortulla - Agrilandia

loc. Castiglioncello
s.da Vicinale delle Spianate
57016 Rosignano Marittimo [LI]
Tel. +39 3404524453
www.fortulla.it

CELLAR SALES
PRE-BOOKED VISITS
ACCOMMODATION AND RESTAURANT SERVICE
ANNUAL PRODUCTION 50,000 bottles
HECTARES UNDER VINE 7.00
VITICULTURE METHOD Certified Organic
SUSTAINABLE WINERY

Everything goes back to Fulvio Martini's love for the territory. In 1994 he decided to give life to an uncultivated agricultural area, one characterized by rich biodiversity. In addition to preserving the estate, it was necessary, obviously, to invest in the future. So it was that vineyards and olive groves were planted, in addition to the renovation of a farmhouse to create a hospitality hub. The vines were grafted by hand in soils rich in pebbles, clay and mineral salts; the entire production has been certified organic since 2014. A blend of Cabernet Franc and Sauvignon, the Fortulla '18 features aromas of fresh pepper, with hints of currant and blueberry. On the palate it's pleasant, creamy, enticing, with a long and pleasant finish. The Sorpasso '15 is a similar blend with the addition of Merlot. It impresses with its hints of tomato leaves, then opens on aromas of black berries before unveiling a firm, focused body, coming through fresh on the finish.

Wine	Rating
● Fortulla '18	🍷🍷 4
○ Pelagico '18	🍷🍷 5
● Sorpasso '15	🍷🍷 6
○ Terratico di Bibbona Serpentino '19	🍷🍷 4
⊙ Rosato Epatta '19	🍷 3
○ Pelagico '15	🍷🍷 5
○ Serpentino '16	🍷🍷 4
● Sorpasso '14	🍷🍷 6
● Sorpasso '13	🍷🍷 6
● Sorpasso '12	🍷🍷 6
○ Terratico di Bibbona Serpentino '17	🍷🍷 4

Tenuta La Fortuna

loc. La Fortuna, 83
53024 Montalcino [SI]
Tel. +39 0577848308
www.tenutalafortuna.it

CELLAR SALES
PRE-BOOKED VISITS
ANNUAL PRODUCTION 60,000 bottles
HECTARES UNDER VINE 18.00

The Zannoni family's winery gets its name from a historic estate situated in the northeastern part of Montalcino. Led by the sixth generation (siblings Angelo and Romina), it offers an extremely distinctive range of wines. Some of the grapes used are cultivated on the estate purchased later in the southeastern part of the production zone, near Castelnuovo dell'Abate. In many ways, their vineyards represent a synergistic mix of positions, soils and microclimates, which manifest in La Fortuna's best Rossos and Brunellos, powerful, tasty and vital wines. The favorable 2015 harvest made for two great Brunellos characterized by strength and freshness. The Brunello '15, with its rich aromas of fruit and licorice, has the allure of the champion, thanks in part to the juicy acidity that accompanies it in the mouth, making for a long, satisfying drink. The Giobi strikes an excellent balance between modernity and tradition, highlighting fruit without compromising the complexity of the whole.

Wine	Rating
● Brunello di Montalcino '15	🍷🍷 6
● Brunello di Montalcino Giobi '15	🍷🍷 6
● Rosso di Montalcino '18	🍷 3
● Brunello di Montalcino '14	🍷🍷 6
● Brunello di Montalcino '13	🍷🍷 6
● Brunello di Montalcino '12	🍷🍷 6
● Brunello di Montalcino '10	🍷🍷 6
● Brunello di Montalcino Giobi '13	🍷🍷 6
● Brunello di Montalcino Giobi '12	🍷🍷 6
● Brunello di Montalcino Giobi '10	🍷🍷 6
● Brunello di Montalcino Ris. '13	🍷🍷 7
● Rosso di Montalcino '17	🍷🍷 3
● Rosso di Montalcino '16	🍷🍷 3
● Rosso di Montalcino '11	🍷🍷 3

La Fralluca

loc. Barbiconi, 153
57028 Suvereto [LI]
Tel. +39 0565829076
www.lafralluca.com

CELLAR SALES
PRE-BOOKED VISITS
ANNUAL PRODUCTION 45,000 bottles
HECTARES UNDER VINE 10.00
VITICULTURE METHOD Certified Organic
SUSTAINABLE WINERY

Francesca and Luca worked in the world of fashion and clothing but dreamed of living in Tuscany and making wine. At the top of a hill, in Suvereto, they found an abandoned farmhouse with magnificent views of woods and Mediterranean scrubland. The vineyards were planted and the winery was built. Today, in keeping with principles of sustainability and organic farming, Luca looks after the land, cultivating Sangiovese, Vermentino, Cabernet Franc, Syrah, Viognier, Alicante and Bouschet grapes. Francesca tends to the commercial side of things. The Cabernet Franc '16 reached our finals. On the nose it's characterized by vegetal hints of roasted peppers, which combine with aromatic herbs like bay leaves and rosemary, as well as berries. On the palate it opens pleasant, warm, nicely orchestrated, with an integrated acidic vein and an alluring finish. The Pitis '16 is a delicious monovarietal Syrah that features notes of pepper, tanned leather and red berries on the nose, a lean, lively body in the mouth.

Wine	Rating
● Cabernet Franc '16	🍷🍷 6
○ Bauci Viognier '18	🍷🍷 4
● Fillide '16	🍷🍷 3
● Pitis Syrah '16	🍷🍷 5
○ Filemone Vermentino '19	🍷 3
● Suvereto Sangiovese Ciparisso '16	🍷 5
○ Bauci '15	YY 3
● Cabernet Franc '15	YY 6
○ Elice '16	YY 5
○ Filemone '18	YY 3
● Fillide '15	YY 3
● Fillide '14	YY 3
● Pitis '15	YY 5
● Pitis '14	YY 5

Frascole

loc. Frascole, 27a
50062 Dicomano [FI]
Tel. +39 0558386340
www.frascole.it

CELLAR SALES
PRE-BOOKED VISITS
ACCOMMODATION
ANNUAL PRODUCTION 65,000 bottles
HECTARES UNDER VINE 16.00
VITICULTURE METHOD Certified Organic

Enrico Lippi and his wife, Elisa, are the brains and brawn of this farm, located near the small medieval village of the same name, which grew up around pre-existing buildings dating back to Etruscan and Roman times, surrounded by vineyards and olive groves. The whole family is involved in the production of wine and oil. To a large extent, the vineyards fall within the Chianti Rufina appellation. Here rather high elevations is expressed through their Sangiovese. The desire to experiment has also emerged through grape varieties such as Merlot and Trebbiano, proposed in two versions, and Pinot Nero. The Chianti Rufina Riserva 17 is delicious, with intense mineral hints (flint), fruity sensations (plum) and spicy whiffs (cloves). On the palate it's tasty, firm and balanced in its tannins—it has commendable acidic verve. The Limine '16 is an intriguing monovarietal Merlot characterized by sanguine aromas, fresh notes of resin and stone, all of which bind to its pervasive, harmonious and long palate.

Wine	Rating
● Chianti Rufina Ris. '17	🍷🍷 3*
● Chianti Rufina '18	🍷🍷 2*
● Limine '16	🍷🍷 5
● Pinot Nero '17	🍷🍷 4
● Chianti Rufina '17	YY 2*
● Chianti Rufina '16	YY 2*
● Chianti Rufina '14	YY 2*
● Chianti Rufina '13	YY 2*
● Chianti Rufina Ris. '16	YY 3*
● Chianti Rufina Ris. '15	YY 3*
● Chianti Rufina Ris. '14	YY 3
● Chianti Rufina Ris. '12	YY 3*
○ In Albis sulle bucce '16	YY 5
○ In Albis sulle bucce '15	YY 5
● Pinot Nero '16	YY 4

Tenuta di Frassineto

FRAZ. FRASSINETO
S.DA VICINALE DEL DUCA, 14
52100 AREZZO
TEL. +39 0575367033
www.tenutadifrassineto.com

CELLAR SALES
PRE-BOOKED VISITS
ANNUAL PRODUCTION 60,000 bottles
HECTARES UNDER VINE 30.69

In addition to serving as an exquisite example of 17th-century architecture (even in light of the partial renovations carried out in the 19th century), the monumental villa we find inside Frassineto is of significant historical importance. Its successive owners descended from some very important families, including the Vasaris. The vineyards, which are mostly dedicated to international varieties, represent only a small part of the property, which is used mostly for the cultivation of durum wheat and other grains. The Le Fattorie '17 is a very interesting monovarietal Cabernet Franc characterized by fresh, vegetal aromas, hints of green pepper, minty notes and black berries. In the mouth it's enjoyable, initially round and then increasingly taut, spirited, with a nice, lively persistence. The Rancoli '19 is a highly intriguing monovarietal Vermentino that opts for aromas of tea and honey, then lychee and white peach. It's a forthright, vivid, perfectly adequately drink.

Wine	Rating
○ Frassinoro '19	🍷🍷 2*
● Le Fattorie '17	🍷🍷 4
○ Rancoli '19	🍷🍷 2*
○ Brut M. Cl. '15	🍷 3
● Fontarronco '09	🍷🍷 2*
● Le Fattorie '11	🍷🍷 4
● Maestro della Chiana '11	🍷🍷 4
○ Rancoli '12	🍷🍷 2*
○ Rancoli '07	🍷🍷 2*
○ Vicinale del Duca '07	🍷🍷 4

★Frescobaldi

VIA SANTO SPIRITO, 11
50125 FIRENZE
TEL. +39 05527141
www.frescobaldi.it

CELLAR SALES
PRE-BOOKED VISITS
ANNUAL PRODUCTION 7,500,000 bottles
HECTARES UNDER VINE 923.00

The Frescobaldi family's journey began more than a thousand years ago, that of their wine around 1300. And to speak of more recent times, it should be remembered that in 1855 the family's ancestors introduced vines then unknown in Tuscany, including Cabernet Sauvignon, Merlot, Pinot Nero and Chardonnay. Creativity and research continue today, unfolding across seven estates, on the island of Gorgona, in the vineyards, emerging from wines that speak of the region's diversity while reflecting each single terroir. We were impressed by the consistent quality of all the wines presented for tasting: those from Castello di Nipozzano, those from the Pomino appellation and those from the Castiglioni estate (not to mention the unique wine produced on the island of Gorgona). The Chianti Rufina Nipozzano Riserva '17 took home Tre Bicchieri. On the nose it's fragrant, on the palate it's elegant, balanced and harmonious, long and lingering.

Wine	Rating
● Chianti Rufina Nipozzano Ris. '17	🍷🍷🍷 4*
● Chianti Rufina Nipozzano V. V. Ris. '17	🍷🍷 5
○ Pomino Bianco Benefizio Ris. '18	🍷🍷 5
● Giramonte '16	🍷🍷 8
○ Gorgona '18	🍷🍷 8
● Mormoreto '17	🍷🍷 8
○ Pomino Bianco '19	🍷🍷 3
○ Pomino Brut Leonia '16	🍷🍷 6
● Chianti Rufina Nipozzano V. V. Ris. '16	🍷🍷🍷 5
● Chianti Rufina Nipozzano V. V. Ris. '13	🍷🍷🍷 5
● Chianti Rufina V. V. Ris. '11	🍷🍷🍷 6
● Montesodi '15	🍷🍷🍷 6
● Mormoreto '05	🍷🍷🍷 7
● Mormoreto '01	🍷🍷🍷 7

Fuligni

via Saloni, 33
53024 Montalcino [SI]
Tel. +39 0577848710
www.fuligni.it

CELLAR SALES
PRE-BOOKED VISITS
ANNUAL PRODUCTION 52,000 bottles
HECTARES UNDER VINE 12.00

Divided into various parcels, all vinified separately (San Giovanni, Piano, Ginestreto, Bandita) the Fuligni family's vineyards are mostly concentrated in the Cottimelli enclave, a historic area on the eastern edge of the Montalcino hill. It's a natural passageway towards the north, as testified to by elevations reaching almost 450 meters and its lean, stony soils, but above all by the expansive, compact Brunello produced here after maturation in tonneaux and barrels of various sizes. This year we only tasted one of the producer's wines, but it was a good one. The 2015 version of their Brunello is exemplary for its vigor, freshness, richness of fruit and stylistic cleanness. It has lovely notes of ripe cherry and blackberry, which give way to tobacco and medicinal herbs, nuances of topsoil. In the mouth it's sapid, complex, persistent and deep just as you would expect from an excellent Brunello. Bravo.

Wine	Rating	Price
● Brunello di Montalcino '15	2 black glasses	6
● Brunello di Montalcino '10	3 glasses	6
● Brunello di Montalcino '14	2 glasses	6
● Brunello di Montalcino '13	2 glasses	6
● Brunello di Montalcino '12	2 glasses	6
● Brunello di Montalcino '11	2 glasses	6
● Brunello di Montalcino Ris. '13	2 glasses	8
● Brunello di Montalcino Ris. '12	2 glasses	8
● Rosso di Montalcino Ginestreto '15	2 glasses	4
● Rosso di Montalcino Ginestreto '13	2 glasses	4

La Gerla - Aisna

loc. Canalicchio
pod. Colombaio, 5
53024 Montalcino [SI]
Tel. +39 0577848599
www.lagerla.it

CELLAR SALES
PRE-BOOKED VISITS
ANNUAL PRODUCTION 80,000 bottles
HECTARES UNDER VINE 11.50

Literally 'divine', the Etruscan term Aisna is found prominently displayed on the labels of Alessandro Rossi's wines. It's a relatively recent production project, founded in 2012 after the death of his father, Sergio (well known to wine lovers in Montalcino for having supported his cousin Giulio Consonno in Altesino and Caparzo, before setting up his own winery in La Gerla). Matured in tonneaux and medium-sized barrels, Alessandro's small range of Rossos and Brunellos are made with grapes cultivated in Castelnuovo dell'Abate, Canalicchio and Altesi. It must run in the family. A well-deserved debut for the producer, who immediately hits the mark with three excellent wines. They are all quite similar in that the 2015 harvest conferred a rich, complex style, with the Camponovo, produced in Altesi (north of the town), standing out for its slightly more pronounced acidity and captivating aromas of cherry jam. The Rosso '18 is also excellent. Its aromas and structure call up the idea of a 'mini' Brunello.

Wine	Rating	Price
● Brunello di Montalcino Aisna '15	2 black glasses	6
● Brunello di Montalcino Camponovo '15	2 black glasses	6
● Brunello di Montalcino La Gerla '15	2 black glasses	6
● Poggio gli Angeli La Gerla '18	2 black glasses	3
● Rosso di Montalcino Aisna '18	2 black glasses	3
● Rosso di Montalcino La Gerla '18	2 black glasses	3
● Birba La Gerla '16	1 black glass	4
● Brunello di Montalcino Gli Angeli Ris. '08	2 glasses	7
● Brunello di Montalcino La Gerla '13	2 glasses	6
● Brunello di Montalcino La Gerla '12	2 glasses	6
● Brunello di Montalcino La Gerla '10	2 glasses	5
● Brunello di Montalcino La Gerla '09	2 glasses	5
● Rosso di Montalcino Aisna '16	2 glasses	3
● Rosso di Montalcino La Gerla '15	2 glasses	3
● Rosso di Montalcino La Gerla '14	2 glasses	3
● Rosso di Montalcino La Gerla '13	2 glasses	3

★Tenuta di Ghizzano

FRAZ. GHIZZANO
VIA DELLA CHIESA, 4
56037 PECCIOLI [PI]
TEL. +39 0587630096
www.tenutadighizzano.com

CELLAR SALES
PRE-BOOKED VISITS
ACCOMMODATION
ANNUAL PRODUCTION 80,000 bottles
HECTARES UNDER VINE 20.00
VITICULTURE METHOD Certified Organic

Tenuta di Ghizzano is a natural paradise of over 300 hectares, but only a small part of which are planted with vines. It's a fact that perfectly captures a winery that's intimately linked to its territory and to the principles of sustainability. The property is in the hands of the Venerosi Pesciolini family, who are believed to have arrived in Ghizzano towards the end of the 14th century and are well represented today by Ginevra. It is she who oversees the estate, which has long been managed according to organic and biodynamic protocols. The results speak for themselves, as does their wines' ongoing stylistic evolution. The Nambrot returns and does so to great fanfare. The 2017 harvest was handled with class, giving rise to a wine as powerful as it is balanced and elegant: a Mediterranean nose features jubilant berries and scrubland, a full-bodied yet gentle palate exhibits nice substance and depth. The finish also impresses for its persistence and precision. The Ghizzano '18 isn't far off, proving more smooth and supple, immediately intelligible but truly flavorful.

Wine	Rating
● Nambrot '17	▼▼▼ 6
● Il Ghizzano Rosso '18	▼▼ 3
● Nambrot '09	▽▽▽ 6
● Nambrot '08	▽▽▽ 6
● Nambrot '06	▽▽▽ 6
● Nambrot '05	▽▽▽ 6
● Nambrot '04	▽▽▽ 6
● Nambrot '03	▽▽▽ 6
● Nambrot '01	▽▽▽ 8
● Nambrot '00	▽▽▽ 7
● Terre di Pisa Nambrot '15	▽▽▽ 6
● Terre di Pisa Nambrot '13	▽▽▽ 6
● Terre di Pisa Nambrot '12	▽▽▽ 6
● Veneroso '10	▽▽▽ 5
● Veneroso '07	▽▽▽ 5
● Veneroso '04	▽▽▽ 5
● Veneroso '01	▽▽▽ 5

Giodo

LOC. PODERINO
53024 MONTALCINO [SI]
TEL. +39 3892763222
www.giodo.it

CELLAR SALES
ANNUAL PRODUCTION 20,000 bottles
HECTARES UNDER VINE 5.50
VITICULTURE METHOD Certified Organic
SUSTAINABLE WINERY

Supported by his daughter Bianca, in just a few years Carlo Ferrini has managed to make his personal creation a star of Montalcino. In 2002 he identified Giodo as the ideal place to cultivate three-dimensional Sangiovese: dense, communicative, vigorous and ageworthy. After all, it's one of the best areas in the district. Situated to the south, in Sant'Angelo in Colle and Sant'Antimo, the vineyards reach elevations ranging from 300 to 400 meters above sea level, conditions further highlighted through a tailored production approach, both with Brunello and their Rosso La Quinta. The producer beautifully interpreted the 2015 vintage. It's a contemporary wine, fully expressing the terroir and the year. It pours a lovely, intense ruby colour, while the nose opens rich and luxuriant on notes of ripe red and black berries, then woody sensations and tobacco. The palate is rich, pulpy, supported by a harmonious, acidic structure and soft tannins that accompany it through a long, fresh finish.

Wine	Rating
● Brunello di Montalcino Giodo '15	▼▼▼ 8
● La Quinta '18	▼▼ 8
● Brunello di Montalcino Giodo '13	▽▽▽ 8
● Brunello di Montalcino Giodo '12	▽▽▽ 8
● Brunello di Montalcino Giodo '11	▽▽▽ 8
● Brunello di Montalcino Giodo '14	▽▽ 8
● Giodo '17	▽▽ 6
● Giodo '16	▽▽ 6
● Giodo '15	▽▽ 6
● Giodo '13	▽▽ 6

I Giusti & Zanza

via dei Puntoni, 9
56043 Fauglia [PI]
Tel. +39 058544354
www.igiustiezanza.it

CELLAR SALES
PRE-BOOKED VISITS
ANNUAL PRODUCTION 100,000 bottles
HECTARES UNDER VINE 17.00
VITICULTURE METHOD Certified Organic

Founded in 1996, the Giusti family's winery is situated in Fauglia, on the Pisan Hills, not far from the Tyrrhenian coast. For centuries the area has been known for its agricultural prowess. The vineyards grow in sandy clay (with the presence of gravel), conditions that give rise to wines with a modern edge, capable of expressing the area's potential through approachably pleasant reds and wines of greater extractive complexity. It's worth pointing out that particular attention is paid to sustainable agricultural practices and respect for the ecosystem. The Sangiovese VignaVecchia '17 is a red marked by racy, ripe fruit, well blended with toastiness through maturation in oak. The Cabernet Dulcamara '17 offers up black berries and herbaceous notes, exhibiting nice depth and vibrance in the mouth. Mostly Sangiovese (with a share of Merlot), the Belcore '18 is as dark aromatically as it is elegant and creamy on the palate.

Wine	Rating
● Belcore '18	🍷🍷 3
● Dulcamara '17	🍷🍷 5
● VignaVecchia '17	🍷🍷 8
● Belcore '15	YY 3
● Belcore '13	YY 3
● Dulcamara '16	YY 8
● Dulcamara '15	YY 5
● Dulcamara '13	YY 5
● Dulcamara '12	YY 5
● Nemorino Rosso '18	YY 5
● Nemorino Rosso '16	YY 2*
● Nemorino Rosso '15	YY 2*
● Perbruno '17	YY 6
● Perbruno '16	YY 4
● Perbruno '15	YY 4
● Perbruno '13	YY 4
● Perbruno '12	YY 4

Marchesi Gondi Tenuta Bossi

loc. Bossi
via dello Stracchino, 32
50065 Pontassieve [FI]
Tel. +39 0558317830
www.tenutabossi.com

CELLAR SALES
PRE-BOOKED VISITS
ACCOMMODATION
ANNUAL PRODUCTION 50,000 bottles
HECTARES UNDER VINE 19.00

The Bossi Estate, which has belonged to the Gondi family for centuries, spans 315 hectares in the Chianti Rufina production area on the hills northeast of Florence. Among the grapes grown, in addition to Sangiovese, is a native clone of Colorino, which has been cultivated here for over 100 years, as well as Merlot, Cabernet Sauvignon, Trebbiano Toscano, Chardonnay and Sauvignon Blanc. The grapes, grown with respect for the environment and harvested by hand, are vinified in the ancient vaulted cellars located underground in the villa and partially under the estate vineyards. The delicious Vin Santo Cardinal De Retz '07 features elegant, fruity notes, quince, hazelnuts and surprising wild berry sensations. In the mouth it's silky, elegant, soft, with a long persistence of flavor. The Chianti Rufina Vigna Poggio Diamante Riserva '16 has a vegetal bouquet, with sanguine notes and fruit calling up plum and cherry. On the palate a firm body and fine tannic support give way to a long, clean finish.

Wine	Rating
○ Vin Santo del Chianti Rufina Cardinal de Retz Ris. '07	🍷🍷 5
● Chianti Rufina Villa Bossi V. Poggio Diamante Ris. '16	🍷🍷 4
● Mazzaferrata '15	🍷🍷 4
● Ser Amerigo '15	🍷🍷 4
● Chianti Rufina San Giuliano '18	🍷 3
○ Colli dell'Etruria Centrale Bianco Sassobianco '19	🍷 2
⊙ Violana Rosato '19	🍷 2
● Chianti Rufina San Giuliano '17	YY 3
● Chianti Rufina San Giuliano '16	YY 2*
● Chianti Rufina Villa Bossi Ris. '16	YY 4
● Mazzaferrata '13	YY 4
○ Vin Santo del Chianti Rufina Cardinal de Rez '06	YY 5

★Grattamacco

loc. Lungagnano
57022 Castagneto Carducci [LI]
Tel. +39 0565765069
www.collemassari.it

CELLAR SALES
PRE-BOOKED VISITS
ANNUAL PRODUCTION 120,000 bottles
HECTARES UNDER VINE 16.00
VITICULTURE METHOD Certified Organic

Grattamacco dates back to 1977, making it one of the pioneers of the area and a benchmark brand for Italian wine. Its hilltop vineyards can be found in Castagneto Carducci and Bolgheri, at elevations spanning 100-150 meters above sea level. Since 2002, the estate has been part of the Colle Massari Group, who have helped preserve and develop its heritage and history, thus increasing the winery's value. Their wines are exceptional, faithful to the past but always evolving, capable of representing their territory at the highest level. A pair of 2017 Bolgheri Rossos dueled it out right up to the end. Choosing wasn't easy, as we're talking about two champions. The Superiore Alberello '17 is harmonious, creamy and incredibly elegant, while the Superiore Grattamacco proves vibrant and evenly developing, impressive in its fruity, Mediterranean and balsamic profile. The latter won by a whisker, but we suggest both.

● Bolgheri Rosso Sup. Grattamacco '17	▼▼▼	8
● Bolgheri Rosso Sup. L'Alberello '17	▼▼	8
○ Bolgheri Vermentino '18	▼▼	5
● Bolgheri Rosso Sup. Grattamacco '16	▽▽▽	8
● Bolgheri Rosso Sup. Grattamacco '05	▽▽▽	7
● Bolgheri Sup. Grattamacco '15	▽▽▽	8
● Bolgheri Sup. Grattamacco '14	▽▽▽	8
● Bolgheri Sup. Grattamacco '13	▽▽▽	8
● Bolgheri Sup. Grattamacco '12	▽▽▽	8
● Bolgheri Sup. Grattamacco '10	▽▽▽	7
● Bolgheri Sup. Grattamacco '09	▽▽▽	7
● Bolgheri Sup. Grattamacco '07	▽▽▽	7
● Bolgheri Sup. Grattamacco '06	▽▽▽	7
● Bolgheri Sup. L'Alberello '11	▽▽▽	6
● Bolgheri Rosso Sup. L'Alberello '16	▽▽	8
● Bolgheri Sup. L'Alberello '15	▽▽	8
○ Bolgheri Vermentino '17	▽▽	5

Fattoria di Grignano

via di Grignano, 22
50065 Pontassieve [FI]
Tel. +39 0558398490
www.fattoriadigrignano.com

CELLAR SALES
PRE-BOOKED VISITS
ANNUAL PRODUCTION 200,000 bottles
HECTARES UNDER VINE 53.00
VITICULTURE METHOD Certified Organic
SUSTAINABLE WINERY

Fattoria di Grignano is one of the oldest farms in Rufina, with archaeological finds testifying to human settlements as far back as the Bronze Age, in the 13th century BCE. The first family to own it were the count Guidi family. Later the Medicis arrived and then, for more than 5 centuries, the Gondis. 1971 saw its acquisition by its current owners, the Inghirami family, who in 1999 expanded the property by annexing Pievecchia. Their various expressions of Chianti Rufina were well received during our tastings. The 2017 features classic fruity notes of cherries and raspberries, as well as a touch of minerality that returns on a firm, balanced body. The Poggio Gualtieri Riserva '16 is also notable, with a more complex bouquet, hints of tobacco and tanned leather, well-orchestrated structure and a sapid finish. The captivating Vin Santo '12 offers up notes of dried fruit and nuts, coming through soft and pervasive on the palate.

● Chianti Rufina '17	▼▼	2*
● Chianti Rufina Cardinal Enrico Ris. '15	▼▼	3
● Chianti Rufina Poggio Gualtieri Ris. '16	▼▼	4
● Chianti Rufina Ritratto del Cardinale '17	▼▼	2*
○ Vin Santo del Chianti '12	▼▼	4
● Pietramaggio Rosso '17	▼	3
○ Ricamo '19	▼	2
● Chianti Rufina '15	▽▽	2*
● Chianti Rufina '13	▽▽	2*
● Chianti Rufina '12	▽▽	2*
● Chianti Rufina Poggio Gualtieri Ris. '15	▽▽	4
● Chianti Rufina Poggio Gualtieri Ris. '13	▽▽	4
● Chianti Rufina Poggio Gualtieri Ris. '11	▽▽	4
○ Vin Santo del Chianti Rufina '09	▽▽	4

Guado al Melo

loc. Murrotto, 130a
57022 Castagneto Carducci [LI]
Tel. +39 0565763238
www.guadoalmelo.it

CELLAR SALES
PRE-BOOKED VISITS
ANNUAL PRODUCTION 120,000 bottles
HECTARES UNDER VINE 15.00
SUSTAINABLE WINERY

Guado al Melo is owned by the Scienza family, a leading name in the world of Italian wine. The activity, overseen by Michele, boasts vineyards in some of Bolgheri's most notable areas, on foothills surrounded by Mediterranean scrub and olive trees. Many varieties are grown, from the area's classic grapes to the Mediterranean basin's oldest. Great attention is paid to the grapes themselves, and to white wines in particular, an uncommon direction for the area. The cellar is a true wonder. Of the wines tasted this year, the Bolgheri Rosso Rute '18 impresses for its vibrance and style. It's a wine with splendid Mediterranean scents, with myrtle and curry plant propping up mature, pleasant fruit that unfolds with great consistency on the palate. As smooth as it is deep and sapid at the finish, it wins you over for its long persistence. We also appreciated the broad and complex Bolgheri Bianco Criseo '18.

Wine	Rating	Price
● Bolgheri Rosso Rute '18	🍷🍷🍷	4*
○ Bolgheri Bianco Criseo '18	🍷🍷	5
● Jassarte '17	🍷	5
○ Bolgheri Bianco Criseo '17	🍸🍸🍸	5
● Bolgheri Rosso Sup. Atis '12	🍸🍸🍸	6
○ Bolgheri Bianco Criseo '16	🍸🍸	5
● Bolgheri Rosso Antillo '15	🍸🍸	3
● Bolgheri Rosso Rute '15	🍸🍸	4
● Bolgheri Rosso Rute '13	🍸🍸	5
● Bolgheri Rosso Sup. Atis '13	🍸🍸	6
● Jassarte '15	🍸🍸	5

Guado al Tasso

loc. Bolgheri
s.da Bolgherese km 3,9
57020 Castagneto Carducci [LI]
Tel. +39 0565749735
www.guadoaltasso.it

CELLAR SALES
PRE-BOOKED VISITS
RESTAURANT SERVICE
ANNUAL PRODUCTION 1,700,000 bottles
HECTARES UNDER VINE 320.00

Guado al Tasso belongs to the Antinori family, a benchmark for Italian wine—this alone provides a sense of the quality standards here. And then there's its dimensions: we're talking about a 1,000-hectare property that comprises vineyards, woods and Mediterranean scrub. It's clear that wine-growing is a cornerstone, with the area's classic varieties all cultivated: Merlot, Cabernet Sauvignon, Petit Verdot and Sangiovese for the reds, and mainly Vermentino for the whites. Their wines are stylistically recognizable and well crafted. The Bolgheri Superiore Guado al Tasso '17 is certainly one of the best of the 'hot vintage' versions. The style of the wine and the year deliver a red that's certainly mature, rich in fruit and spices, round and soft, but also capable of balance and dynamism. The Bruciato '18 is racier and and more visceral, even if marked by sweet, fruity timbres as well.

Wine	Rating	Price
● Bolgheri Rosso Guado al Tasso '17	🍷🍷	8
● Bolgheri Rosso Il Bruciato '18	🍷🍷	5
⊙ Bolgheri Rosato Scalabrone '19	🍷	3
● Bolgheri Rosso Cont'Ugo '18	🍷	6
● Bolgheri Sup. Guado al Tasso '01	🍸🍸🍸	8
● Bolgheri Sup. Guado al Tasso '90	🍸🍸🍸	8
⊙ Bolgheri Rosato Scalabrone '16	🍸🍸	3
● Bolgheri Rosso Cont'Ugo '16	🍸🍸	6
● Bolgheri Rosso Guado al Tasso '16	🍸🍸	8
● Bolgheri Rosso Il Bruciato '16	🍸🍸	5
● Bolgheri Rosso Il Bruciato '15	🍸🍸	5
● Bolgheri Rosso Il Bruciato '14	🍸🍸	5
● Bolgheri Rosso Sup. Guado al Tasso '15	🍸🍸	8
● Bolgheri Rosso Sup. Guado al Tasso '09	🍸🍸	8
● Bolgheri Rosso Sup. Guado al Tasso '08	🍸🍸	8
● Bolgheri Sup. Guado al Tasso '13	🍸🍸	8

Gualdo del Re

LOC. NOTRI, 77
57028 SUVERETO [LI]
TEL. +39 0565829888
www.gualdodelre.it

CELLAR SALES
PRE-BOOKED VISITS
ACCOMMODATION AND RESTAURANT SERVICE
ANNUAL PRODUCTION 100,000 bottles
HECTARES UNDER VINE 20.00
VITICULTURE METHOD Certified Organic

Teresa and Nico Rossi's story is a story of love and passion. Today their children, Federico and Valentina, are also involved in the project, bringing a spirit in which youthful enthusiasm is balanced by a sense of continuity with their parents' work. In addition to wine production, over time they've added guest accommodations. The black grape varieties cultivated range from Sangiovese to Merlot, Cabernet Sauvignon, Franc and Aleatico; for the whites, Vermentino and Pinot Bianco are used. Their wines are characterized by opulence and a modern style. The Quinto Re '17 is a monovarietal Merlot characterized by tertiary aromas, from tobacco to tanned leather by way of assorted black berries and toasty hints. The palate has good weight, unfolding warm, with soft tannins and a relaxed finish. The pleasant Cabraia '17 is a Cabernet Franc with a small share of Sauvignon. Occasional balsamic whiffs mark the nose, while in the mouth it surprises for its tannic texture and a balanced body. The Suvereto I'Rennero '17 is also very well made.

Wine	Rating
● Quintoré '17	🍷🍷 8
● Cabraia '17	🍷🍷 8
● Suvereto Merlot I'Rennero '17	🍷🍷 8
⊙ Shiny Rosato '19	🍷 3
● Suvereto Sangiovese Il Gualdo '17	🍷 6
○ Valentina '19	🍷 3
● Quinto Re '16	🥂🥂🥂 8
● Cabraia '16	🥂🥂 6
○ Eliseo Rosso '16	🥂🥂 3
○ Eliseo Rosso '15	🥂🥂 3
● Suvereto Merlot I'Rennero '15	🥂🥂 7
● Suvereto Sangiovese Gualdo del Re '15	🥂🥂 5
● Suvereto Sangiovese Il Guardo '16	🥂🥂 5
○ Valentina '18	🥂🥂 3

Conte Guicciardini Castello di Poppiano

LOC. POPPIANO
VIA FEZZANA, 45/49
50025 MONTESPERTOLI [FI]
TEL. +39 05582315
www.conteguicciardini.it

CELLAR SALES
PRE-BOOKED VISITS
ANNUAL PRODUCTION 270,000 bottles
HECTARES UNDER VINE 130.00
SUSTAINABLE WINERY

Ferdinando and Titti Guicciardini, now helped by Bernardo, oversee three estates: Castello di Poppiano, Massi di Mandorlaia and Belvedere Campòli. The first, on the hills of Montespertoli, has long been the historic family's agricultural center (it's now included in the Chianti Colli Fiorentini production zone). The second is in Scansano, the heart of Morellino, while the third is situated in Panzano and Mercatale (Chianti Classico). Over 200 hectares of vineyards give rise to various types of wine. The Syrah '18 arouses lovely sensations: aromas of berries, tanned leather and black pepper; the palate is warm, rich, juicy and powerful. The finish unfolds progressively, with fleshy, well-distributed tannins. The Historia '17 is an enticing monovarietal Merlot characterized by aromas of black berries, notes of chocolate and cherries in alcohol. The palate is broad, warm, lively, focused and pervasive, with nicely balanced tannins. We also appreciated the classically elegant Riserva Belvedere Campoli '17.

Wine	Rating
● Chianti Cl. Ris. Belvedere Campoli '17	🍷🍷 5
● Chianti Colli Fiorentini Ris. '17	🍷🍷 4
● La Historia '17	🍷🍷 5
● Morellino di Scansano Carbonile Massi di Mandorlaia '19	🍷🍷 2*
● Syrah '18	🍷🍷 4
● Chianti Colli Fiorentini Il Cortile '18	🍷 3
● Scorfano Rosso '19	🍷 3
● Toscoforte '18	🍷 4
● Tricorno '17	🍷 6
○ Vermentino Massi di Mandorlaia '19	🍷 3
● Chianti Cl. Gran Selezione Il Tabernacolo Belvedere Campoli '15	🥂🥂 6
● La Historia '16	🥂🥂 5
● Toscoforte Castello di Poppiano '16	🥂🥂 4

Guicciardini Strozzi

LOC. CUSONA, 5
53037 SAN GIMIGNANO [SI]
TEL. +39 0577950028
www.guicciardinistrozzi.it

CELLAR SALES
PRE-BOOKED VISITS
ANNUAL PRODUCTION 500,000 bottles
HECTARES UNDER VINE 100.00

Guicciardini Strozzi's roots go back a thousand years here at the Cusona Estate in San Gimignano. But its modern history began in the early 1900s, when Francesco Guicciardini, Minister of Agriculture and later Mayor of Florence, transformed the estate into a model winery. In 1933 the father of the current owner, Girolamo Strozzi, first bottled Vernaccia in a Bordeaux bottle. In the 1970s, Girolamo, founder and first president of the Vernaccia Consortium, launched its current phase of growth, which saw the producer expand into Maremma and Bolgheri. The Vernaccia di San Gimignano Riserva '17 opens on aromas of apple, plum, hints of almond and slight grapefruit whiffs. The palate is complex, with an enticing acidity and a delicately salty, long finish. The Vernaccia Titolato '19 is also interesting: initial aromas of pineapple and grapefruit give way to fresher, lemony streaks. In the mouth it's supple and spirited, with good flesh.

Wine	Rating
○ Vernaccia di S. Gimignano Titolato Strozzi '19	▼▼ 2*
○ Vernaccia di San Gimignano Ris. '17	▼▼ 3
○ Arabesque '19	▼ 3
● Sodole '15	▼ 5
○ Arabesque '17	▽▽ 2*
● Chianti Colli Senesi Titolato Strozzi '18	▽▽ 2*
○ San Gimignano Vin Santo '09	▽▽ 5
○ Vernaccia di S. Gimignano '16	▽▽ 2*
○ Vernaccia di S. Gimignano Ris. '15	▽▽ 3
○ Vernaccia di San Gimignano Ris. '16	▽▽ 3

★★Isole e Olena

LOC. ISOLE, 1
50021 BARBERINO VAL D'ELSA [FI]
TEL. +39 0558072763
www.isoleolena.it

CELLAR SALES
PRE-BOOKED VISITS
ANNUAL PRODUCTION 250,000 bottles
HECTARES UNDER VINE 56.00

For over forty years Paolo De Marchi has been working here in Chianti Classico. Piedmontese by origin but by now a true Tuscan, Paolo is one of Gallo Nero's most rigorous winemakers. His work is aimed entirely at pursuing the deepest sense of 'territory', a fact that has played no small part in the winery's success. Their product portfolio comprises Isole and Olena, in addition to wines more closely linked to the traditions of the Barberino Val d'Elsa subzone. They also make wines with international grape varieties, and these also exhibit a strong personality that eschews conventional modes and styles. The Cepparello '17 is an intriguing monovarietal Sangiovese. Aromatically complex, it crosses sanguine hints with ripe red berries and whiffs of forest undergrowth, only to finish with flashes of pencil lead and spices. In the mouth it's broad and dense, as juicy as it is deep, with a very pleasant, delicately salty note emerging on the finish. Impeccable craftsmanship for the Chianti Classico '17, a fragrant, tasty wine.

Wine	Rating
● Cepparello '17	▼▼▼ 8
● Chianti Cl. '17	▼▼ 5
○ Vin Santo del Chianti Classico '09	▼▼ 7
● Collezione Privata Cabernet Sauvignon '16	▼▼ 8
● Collezione Privata Syrah '17	▼▼ 8
● Cepparello '16	▽▽▽ 8
● Cepparello '15	▽▽▽ 8
● Cepparello '13	▽▽▽ 8
● Cepparello '12	▽▽▽ 8
● Cepparello '09	▽▽▽ 8
● Cepparello '07	▽▽▽ 8
● Cepparello '06	▽▽▽ 8
● Cepparello '05	▽▽▽ 8
● Cepparello '03	▽▽▽ 7
● Cepparello '01	▽▽▽ 6
● Cepparello '00	▽▽▽ 6

Istine

LOC. ISTINE
53017 RADDA IN CHIANTI [SI]
TEL. +39 0577733684
www.istine.it

CELLAR SALES
PRE-BOOKED VISITS
ANNUAL PRODUCTION 45,000 bottles
HECTARES UNDER VINE 26.00
VITICULTURE METHOD Certified Organic

Istine has recently emerged in the Chianti Classico panorama, with the first bottles arriving in 2009. As of 2012, the producer changed pace considerably, with Sangiovese being vinified separately according to the area of origin. Bolstered by vineyards in the subzones of Radda and Gaiole in Chianti, Angela Fronti oversees a solid, coherent winery, a fact that's confirmed by wines (all aged in large oak barrels) that exhibit a forthright, authentic style, all in the name of suppleness and elegance. The Chianti Classico Vigna Istine '18 is truly delicious, able to express itself fully aromatically, with fragrance and olfactory detail, managing to hold together complexity and gustatory pleasantness on the palate. We also very much appreciated the Chianti Classico Le Vigne Riserva '17, a wine that's as summery as it is lean and responsive on the palate. The other wines tasted, all decidedly Chianti in style, are also well crafted.

Wine	Rating
● Chianti Cl. V. Istine '18	▼▼▼ 5
● Chianti Cl. Le Vigne Ris. '17	▼▼ 5
● Chianti Cl. '18	▼▼ 3
● Chianti Cl. Casanova dell'Aia '18	▼▼ 5
● Chianti Cl. V. Cavarchione '18	▼▼ 5
● Chianti Cl. Le Vigne Ris. '13	▽▽▽ 3*
● Chianti Cl. V. Cavarchione '16	▽▽▽ 5
● Chianti Cl. V. Istine '15	▽▽▽ 3*
● Chianti Cl. '17	▽▽ 3
● Chianti Cl. '16	▽▽ 3
● Chianti Cl. Casanova dell'Aia '17	▽▽ 4
● Chianti Cl. Le Vigne Ris. '16	▽▽ 4
● Chianti Cl. Le Vigne Ris. '15	▽▽ 3*
● Chianti Cl. V. Cavarchione '17	▽▽ 5
● Chianti Cl. V. Cavarchione '15	▽▽ 3*
● Chianti Cl. V. Istine '17	▽▽ 3*
● Chianti Cl. V. Istine '16	▽▽ 3

Fattoria Kappa

LOC. LE BADIE
VIA ROMA, 118
56040 CASTELLINA MARITTIMA [PI]
TEL. +39 3346619711
andreadimaio1974@gmail.com

CELLAR SALES
PRE-BOOKED VISITS
ANNUAL PRODUCTION 20,000 bottles
HECTARES UNDER VINE 6.00

The farm was founded by Austrian Stefan Klassman and German Manfred Klimek, both journalists. The two, in the late 1990s, bought some plots of land in Pisano in the hopes of launching what would become an important winery, building its physiognomy step by step. Enologist Andrea di Maio later joined the team and today he's still in charge of the vineyard and cellar operations, following the dictates of biodynamic production. The property has recently been enlarged with acquisitions in Volterra. The Kappa '16 is a delicious blend of Merlot, Cabernet Franc and Sauvignon and Syrah. It has a very fine, elegant aromatic profile, with nuances of berries accompanied by hints of pepper, cinnamon, cloves and lavender. In the mouth it's rich and delicious. The same blend, with the addition of Petit Verdot, features in the Lambda '17. Here vegetal tones prevail on the nose, while the palate proves firm and well sustained. The Essenza '16 is also excellent.

Wine	Rating
● Kappa '16	▼▼ 5
● Essenza '16	▼▼ 5
● Lambda '17	▼▼ 3
○ Etabeta '19	▼ 4
○ Etabeta '16	▽▽ 4
● Kappa '15	▽▽ 5
● Kappa '13	▽▽ 5
● Kappa '10	▽▽ 3
● Lambda '13	▽▽ 3
● Rosso '11	▽▽ 3*
● Syrah '12	▽▽ 5

Tenuta La Chiusa

LOC. MAGAZZINI, 93
57037 PORTOFERRAIO [LI]
TEL. +39 0565933046
lachiusa@elbalink.it

CELLAR SALES
PRE-BOOKED VISITS
ACCOMMODATION
ANNUAL PRODUCTION 25,000 bottles
HECTARES UNDER VINE 7.50

The name is intriguing—it derives from the wall that surrounds the estate, 'closing' it in. La Chiusa is part of Elba's wine-growing history, and not only, since Napoleon also set foot during his stay on the island, making for a venture whose roots dates back to the 16th century. Indeed, its cellars go that far back, while the villa was built in the 1800s. Today the property is owned by the Bertozzi Corradi family, who acquired it in 2003 out of a love for the property and a desire to start a radical process of renovation and modernization. Their whites are very pleasant, starting with the Vermentino '19. Enticing in its nuances of white fruit, it unfolds on vegetal hints of chives, bay leaves and citrus notes of mandarin; in the mouth it's generous, well supported by strong acidity. We also appreciated the Ansonica '19, a more intense wine aromatically with peach and orange peel sensations, all carried over on a palate of lovely structure, with a delicately salty vein and an appetizing finish.

Wine	Rating
● Elba Aleatico Passito '18	**YY** 6
○ Elba Ansonica '19	**YY** 2*
○ Elba Bianco '19	**YY** 2*
○ Elba Vermentino '19	**YY** 2*
⊙ Elba Rosato '19	**Y** 3
● Elba Rosso '19	**Y** 2
● Elba Aleatico Passito '17	YY 6
● Elba Aleatico Passito '16	YY 6
○ Elba Ansonica '18	YY 3
○ Elba Ansonica '17	YY 2*
● Elba Rosso Ginevra '17	YY 2*

Lamole di Lamole

LOC. LAMOLE
50022 GREVE IN CHIANTI [FI]
TEL. +39 0559331256
www.lamole.com

CELLAR SALES
PRE-BOOKED VISITS
RESTAURANT SERVICE
ANNUAL PRODUCTION 294,000 bottles
HECTARES UNDER VINE 57.00
SUSTAINABLE WINERY

Lamole di Lamole is certainly the most important winery for the Veneto-based Santa Margherita Group, at least when it comes to adherence to the territory. Both the enological and agronomic choices made here have focused on respect for the peculiarities of one of the most intriguing and particular subzones of Chianti Classico. And so it is that we get wines that are not in the least bit trivial, but rather marked by nice personality making for a clearly modern style that in no way deviates from their territorial identity. Flowery aromas and spicy nuances distinguish the Chianti Classico Gran Selezione Vigneto di Campolungo '16, a juicy and complex wine on the palate, with a broad, sweet finish. The Chianti Classico Etichetta Bianca '17 is pleasant: light and clean aromatically, fresh and expansive in the mouth. A bit of oak holds back the complexity of the Chianti Classico Riserva '16, a firm, austere wine.

Wine	Rating
● Chianti Cl. Gran Selezione Vign. di Campolungo '16	**YYY** 5
● Chianti Cl. Lamole di Lamole Et. Bianca '17	**YY** 3
● Chianti Cl. Ris. '16	**Y** 5
● Lam'oro '15	**Y** 8
● Chianti Cl. Gran Sel. Vign. di Campolungo '10	YYY 5
● Chianti Cl. Lamole di Lamole Et. Bianca '16	YYY 3*
● Chianti Cl. Lamole di Lamole Et. Bianca '13	YYY 3*
● Chianti Cl. Lamole di Lamole Et. Blu '15	YYY 3*
● Chianti Cl. Lamole di Lamole Et. Blu '14	YYY 3*
● Chianti Cl. Lamole di Lamole Et. Blu '12	YYY 3*
● Chianti Cl. Vign. di Campolungo Ris. '09	YYY 5

Lanciola

fraz. Pozzolatico
via Imprunetana, 210
50023 Impruneta [FI]
Tel. +39 055208324
www.lanciola.it

CELLAR SALES
PRE-BOOKED VISITS
ANNUAL PRODUCTION 250,000 bottles
HECTARES UNDER VINE 40.00

Two estates, one owner. The first, on the hills of Impruneta, has belonged to the Guarnieri family for a few decades. It was once the domain of the noble Ricci family, who cultivated the land (including viticulture). Its current owners then consolidated the working of modernizing the property. The acquisition of Villa Le Masse, near Greve, came more recently. At the former, traditional grape varieties coexist with international ones, while at the latter an approach that's in keeping with the traditions of Chianti Classico prevails. Only the wines from the Impruneta estate were presented for tasting this year. The Terricci '17, the estate's historic super Tuscan (Cabernet Sauvignon, Merlot and Sangiovese), put in a good performance. It offers up fine and delicate whiffs of aromatic herbs, tarragon and bay leaf, then currant and blueberry; the body is balanced, not impetuous, standing out for a fresh acidic streak that makes for an enticing drink.

Wine	Rating
● Riccionero '18	🍷🍷 3
● Ricciotto Sangiovese '17	🍷🍷 3
● Terricci '17	🍷🍷 5
● Chianti Colli Fiorentini '18	🍷 2
● Chianti Colli Fiorentini Ris. '16	🍷 3
○ Ricciobianco Chardonnay '19	🍷 3
⊙ Ricciorosa '19	🍷 2
● Chianti Cl. Le Masse di Greve '16	🍷🍷 4
● Chianti Cl. Le Masse di Greve '15	🍷🍷 4
● Chianti Cl. Le Masse di Greve Gran Selezione '16	🍷🍷 4
● Chianti Cl. Le Masse di Greve Ris. '16	🍷🍷 4
● Chianti Colli Fiorentini Lanciola '15	🍷🍷 3
● Ricciotto '13	🍷🍷 4
● Terricci '15	🍷🍷 5
● Terricci '11	🍷🍷 5

LaSelva

loc. Poderone, 10a
58051 Magliano in Toscana [GR]
Tel. +39 0564593077
www.laselva.wine

CELLAR SALES
PRE-BOOKED VISITS
ACCOMMODATION
ANNUAL PRODUCTION 200,000 bottles
HECTARES UNDER VINE 32.00
VITICULTURE METHOD Certified Organic

Despite the fact that Karl Egger's winery, a pioneer of organic farming in Maremma, is relatively young (the new cellar was completed in 2000), they've managed to achieve a reassuring qualitative constancy, and sometimes even excellence. This is due to a defined and well-established production philosophy, which immediately bet on local grape varieties, both red and white, favoring wines that express themselves naturally, without unnecessarily interference in the natural process of winemaking. The result is a range marked more by pleasant drinking than power. The Morellino Colli dell'Uccellina Riserva '17 exhibits warm, fruity and spicy scents, and nice aromatic complexity as well, though the wine finds its strong point in the mouth where it's sapid, juicy and well-sustained. The pleasant Ciliegiolo '17 is marked by fragrances of cherry and plum, nicely adorned by peppery accents. The Morellino di Scansano '19, a wine redolent of juniper and small red berries, proves supple and fluent on the palate.

Wine	Rating
● Maremma Toscana Ciliegiolo '17	🍷🍷 4
● Morellino di Scansano '19	🍷🍷 3
● Morellino di Scansano Colli dell'Uccellina Ris. '17	🍷🍷 4
○ Maremma Toscana Vermentino '19	🍷 3
● Maremma Toscana Ciliegiolo '16	🍷🍷 4
● Maremma Toscana Ciliegiolo '15	🍷🍷 4
● Maremma Toscana Privo '16	🍷🍷 2*
● Morellino di Scansano '18	🍷🍷 3
● Morellino di Scansano '17	🍷🍷 3
● Morellino di Scansano Colli dell' Uccellina Ris. '15	🍷🍷 4
● Morellino di Scansano Colli dell'Uccellina Ris. '13	🍷🍷 3
● Pugnitello '13	🍷🍷 5

La Lastra

FRAZ. SANTA LUCIA
VIA R. DE GRADA, 9
53037 SAN GIMIGNANO [SI]
TEL. +39 0577941781
www.lalastra.it

CELLAR SALES
PRE-BOOKED VISITS
ANNUAL PRODUCTION 58,000 bottles
HECTARES UNDER VINE 7.00
SUSTAINABLE WINERY

Entrepreneurship, corporatism, and profit are less important for Nadia Betti and her husband, Renato Spanu, than respect for the environment and people, territoriality, and a positive work ethic. So it is that, together with a small group of relatives and friends, they founded La Lastra in San Gimignano, where they grow Vernaccia, Sangiovese, Cabernet Sauvignon, and Merlot. In 2000 came a farmstay in Marciano, not far from Siena, where organic farming methods are applied for the cultivation of Canaiolo Nero, Merlot and Cabernet Franc. We very much appreciated the Vernaccia '19: it expresses a complex and unusual aromatic bouquet with floral fragrances of aromatic herbs (tarragon and mint) and assorted white fruits. In the mouth it opens light, drawing strength before reviving, then closing juicy and alluring. The Riserva '18 moves on fresh citrus scents (citron peel), exhibiting a rich but supple body on the palate.

Wine	Rating
○ Vernaccia di S. Gimignano '19	🍷🍷 2*
○ Vernaccia di S. Gimignano Ris. '18	🍷🍷 3
● Canaiolo '18	🍷 3
● Chianti Colli Senesi '17	🍷 2
● Rovaio '17	🍷 4
● Chianti Colli Senesi '15	🍷🍷 2*
● Rovaio '16	🍷🍷 4
○ Vernaccia di S. Gimignano '18	🍷🍷 2*
○ Vernaccia di S. Gimignano '17	🍷🍷 2*
○ Vernaccia di S. Gimignano Ris. '16	🍷🍷 3*
○ Vernaccia di S. Gimignano Ris. '15	🍷🍷 3*
○ Vernaccia di S. Gimignano Ris. '14	🍷🍷 3*

Fattoria Lavacchio

LOC. LAVACCHIO
VIA DI MONTEFIESOLE, 55
50065 PONTASSIEVE [FI]
TEL. +39 0558317472
www.fattorialavacchio.com

CELLAR SALES
PRE-BOOKED VISITS
ACCOMMODATION AND RESTAURANT SERVICE
ANNUAL PRODUCTION 120,000 bottles
HECTARES UNDER VINE 25.00
VITICULTURE METHOD Certified Organic
SUSTAINABLE WINERY

Situated atop Montefiesole, at an elevation of 450 metres and only 18 km from Florence, the Lottero family's Fattoria Lavacchio was the first winery in the Chianti Rufina production area to cultivate grapes, olives, wheat, fruit and vegetables in accordance with the principles of organic farming. When it comes to their wines, for example, there's one made without the addition of sulphite (it's replaced by physical, non-chemical means), yeasts and tannins. Their accommodations are also managed with a low impact on the environment. The Chianti Rufina Cedro '18 is an interesting wine, redolent of blackberry and plum jam, while in the mouth it's youthful, grapey, decidedly floral. Broader and more structured, the Riserva Puro '16 has a specific weight and density but isn't lacking in flavor and dynamism, finishing on appetizing, fruity hints. We also mention the Fontegalli '15, a Merlot and Syrah with pronounced spicy notes.

Wine	Rating
● Chianti Puro Ris. '16	🍷🍷 4
● Chianti Rufina Cedro '18	🍷🍷 2*
● Fontegalli '15	🍷🍷 4
○ Oro del Cedro V. T. '19	🍷🍷 4
● Chianti Puro '18	🍷 2
○ Puro Bianco '19	🍷 2
⊙ Puro Rosato Frizzante '19	🍷 2
● Chianti Rufina Cedro '17	🍷🍷 2*
● Chianti Rufina Cedro '16	🍷🍷 2*
● Chianti Rufina Cedro Ris. '16	🍷🍷 3
● Chianti Rufina Cedro Ris. '15	🍷🍷 3
● Chianti Rufina Ludiè '13	🍷🍷 7
● Chianti Rufina Ludiè Bio '11	🍷🍷 7
● Fontegalli '14	🍷🍷 4
○ Vin Santo del Chianti Rufina '14	🍷🍷 4
○ Vin Santo del Chianti Rufina '11	🍷🍷 4

Podere Le Bèrne

loc. Cervognano
via Poggio Golo, 7
53045 Montepulciano [SI]
Tel. +39 0578767328
www.leberne.it

CELLAR SALES
ANNUAL PRODUCTION 25,000 bottles
HECTARES UNDER VINE 6.00

The Natalini family's Podere Le Berne is without doubt one of the most interesting producers in Montepulciano. Here in Cervognano, probably the most renowned subzone of the area, the winery takes a classic approach to vinification, maturation and aging. By the same token, the traditional grape varieties used for their appellation wines. The style centers on aromatic fragrance and taste. It's an assertive, fine, elegant mix that's topped off by remarkable ageworthiness. The Nobile di Montepulciano '17, one of the best tasted this year, intrigues from the outset: fruit crosses notes of fresh flowers, hints of flint, minty nuances and touches of wild herbs. In the mouth it exhibits plenty of structure, but the palate is well-sustained and made supple by virtue of properly-spirited tannins and acidic verve, which lengthen towards a crisp, balanced finished. Fragrant aromas figure in the highly enjoyable Rosso di Montepulciano '19.

● Nobile di Montepulciano '17	🍷🍷 3*
● Rosso di Montepulciano '19	🍷🍷 2*
● Nobile di Montepulciano Ris. '16	🍷 5
● Nobile di Montepulciano '16	🍷🍷🍷 3*
● Nobile di Montepulciano '15	🍷🍷🍷 3*
● Nobile di Montepulciano '14	🍷🍷 3
● Nobile di Montepulciano '13	🍷🍷 3
● Nobile di Montepulciano '12	🍷🍷 3*
● Nobile di Montepulciano Ris. '12	🍷🍷 5
● Nobile di Montepulciano Ris. '11	🍷🍷 5
● Rosso di Montepulciano '16	🍷🍷 2*
● Rosso di Montepulciano '14	🍷🍷 2*
○ Vin Santo di Montepulciano '10	🍷🍷 6
○ Vin Santo di Montepulciano Occhio di Pernice '07	🍷🍷 7
○ Vin Santo di Montepulciano Occhio di Pernice '06	🍷🍷 7

Tenuta Lenzini

fraz. Gragnano
via della Chiesa, 44
55012 Capannori [LU]
Tel. +39 0583974037
www.tenutalenzini.it

CELLAR SALES
PRE-BOOKED VISITS
ACCOMMODATION
ANNUAL PRODUCTION 60,000 bottles
HECTARES UNDER VINE 14.00
VITICULTURE METHOD Certified Organic

Benedetta Tronci and Michele Guarino chose Gragnano, a heavenly corner of the Lucchesi Hills, for their agricultural endeavor. Their production philosophy calls for a minimally-invasive approach, both in the cellar and in the vineyard, where biodynamic practices are followed. The manor house stands at the centre of the vineyard, an amphitheater cultivated with mainly international grapes. Aging is carried out in steel, concrete or old wooden barrels so as to guarantee the precise pursuit for fruity purity, varietal expression and finesse. The Poggio de' Paoli '17, a blend of Merlot, Cabernet Sauvignon and Franc, Syrah, an Alicante Bouschet that matures in steel, large cask and tonneau for two years, is an elegant and pulpy red, articulated in its aromatic nuances and dynamic in the sip. Young and in the making, La Syrah '18, with its vertical silhouette, its peppery and spicy hints.

● La Syrah '18	🍷🍷 5
● Poggio de' Paoli '17	🍷🍷 4
● La Syrah '16	🍷🍷 5
● La Syrah '15	🍷🍷 5
● La Syrah '13	🍷🍷 5
● Poggio de' Paoli '16	🍷🍷 4
● Poggio de' Paoli '13	🍷🍷 4
● Syrah '12	🍷🍷 5
● Syrah '11	🍷🍷 5
○ Vermignon '18	🍷🍷 4
○ Vermignon '17	🍷🍷 3
○ Vermignon '15	🍷🍷 3
○ Vermignon '14	🍷🍷 3

Leuta

via Pietraia, 21
52044 Cortona [AR]
Tel. +39 3385033560
www.leuta.it

CELLAR SALES
PRE-BOOKED VISITS
ANNUAL PRODUCTION 25,000 bottles
HECTARES UNDER VINE 12.60

After leaving the world of finance, Denis Zeni went from just a few hectares owned by his family in Trentino to the purchase of the Leuta estate in Cortona in 2004. At the time, the 21-hectare property was still uncultivated, but gradually the vineyards came. Now four plots host international varieties like Cabernet Franc, Merlot, Malbec and Syrah, while two others see Sangiovese together with a dozen or so native Tuscan grapes, (there's also a row of Georgian grapes to experiment with). Roses of different colors are planted at the head of each row to distinguish one from the other. The Sangiovese Solitario '16 put in a good performance with its variegated olfactory notes, calling up ripe cherries and aromatic herbs of Mediterranean brush. In the mouth it exhibits a firm body, taut, with proper acidity, and a clean, long finish. The Cabernet Franc Cornelius '16 (only in magnum) intrigues with its hints of green pepper, balsamic notes and berries, all on a smooth, broad gustatory texture, with a fresh, enticing finish.

Wine	Rating	Price
● Cornelius '16	▼▼	8
● Cortona Merlot 1.618 '16	▼▼	5
● Cortona Sangiovese Solitario di Leuta '16	▼▼	6
○ Apostata Bianco '19	▼	7
● Apostata Rosso '19	▼	7
● Cortona Cabernet Franc 2,618 '17	▼	6
● Cortona Syrah 0,618 '17	▼	5
● Malbec '17	▼	6
● Cortona Cabernet Franc 2,618 '16	▽▽	6
● Cortona Cabernet Franc 2,618 '15	▽▽	6
● Cortona Merlot 1.618 '15	▽▽	5
● Cortona Sangiovese Solitario di Leuta '14	▽▽	6
○ Cortona Vin Santo '07	▽▽	8
● Nautilus '15	▽▽	8
● Tau '14	▽▽	4

★Tenuta di Lilliano

loc. Lilliano, 8
53011 Castellina in Chianti [SI]
Tel. +39 0577743070
www.lilliano.com

CELLAR SALES
PRE-BOOKED VISITS
ACCOMMODATION
ANNUAL PRODUCTION 150,000 bottles
HECTARES UNDER VINE 36.00
VITICULTURE METHOD Certified Organic

Tenuta di Lilliano's wines represent some of the best expressions in the southern part of the Castellina in Chianti subzone. The Ruspoli family, who've owned the propety since 1920, have lived through a good part of Chianti Classico's history, preserving a traditional style even while adopting a contemporary production approach. The result is wines in which a classic style is amplified, bringing expressive nuances, together with elegance and finesse, increasingly to the fore. The Chianti Classico Riserva '17 is extremely well crafted. Aromatically it's slightly closed, but a few minutes in the glass are enough to release iron sensations, small red berries and a few spicy and smoky hints. In the mouth it has a sweet attack and a creamy, pervasive, deep development. The Chianti Classico Gran Selezione '17 also delivered, with its mature aromas and taut palate.

Wine	Rating	Price
● Chianti Cl. Ris. '17	▼▼▼	5
● Chianti Cl. Gran Selezione '17	▼▼	5
● Chianti Cl. '18	▼	3
● Chianti Cl. '10	▽▽▽	3*
● Chianti Cl. '09	▽▽▽	3
● Chianti Cl. E. Ruspoli Berlingieri Ris. '85	▽▽▽	8
● Chianti Cl. Gran Sel. '14	▽▽▽	6
● Chianti Cl. Gran Sel. '11	▽▽▽	5
● Chianti Cl. Gran Sel. Ris. '10	▽▽▽	6
● Chianti Cl. Gran Selezione '16	▽▽▽	5
● Chianti Cl. Ris. '15	▽▽▽	5
● Chianti Cl. Ris. '13	▽▽▽	5
● Chianti Cl. '17	▽▽	3*
● Chianti Cl. '16	▽▽	3
● Chianti Cl. Gran Selezione '15	▽▽	5
● Chianti Cl. Ris. '16	▽▽	5

Lisini

FRAZ. SANT'ANGELO IN COLLE
POD. CASANOVA
53024 MONTALCINO [SI]
TEL. +39 0577844040
www.lisini.com

CELLAR SALES
PRE-BOOKED VISITS
ANNUAL PRODUCTION 90,000 bottles
HECTARES UNDER VINE 21.00

The Lisini-Clementi family's deep roots in Montalcino are testified to by the splendid vault where their most ageworthy bottles are kept. It's a saga built on excellent vineyards in the southern part of the production zone, in particular on the route that connects Sesta to Sant'Angelo in Colle, where the soils are lean and rich in iron, as in the case of the Ugolaia cru. The result is a Brunello full of contrast and chiaroscuro, pervasive yet austere, perfect for aging in the bottle after a lengthy stay in medium-sized oak barrels. In the absence of its usual stars (the Riserva and Ugolaia, not produced in the less favorable 2013 vintage), Lisini's line-up was limited to 3 wines. The Brunello di Montalcino '15 didn't disappoint, and topped our preferences. Elegant aromas of tobacco are accompanied by dried herbs and spices combined with hints of fruit and a rich, warm palate endowed with pervasive tannins.

Wine	Rating
● Brunello di Montalcino '15	🍷🍷 6
● Rosso di Montalcino '18	🍷 4
● San Biagio '17	🍷 2
● Brunello di Montalcino '14	🍷🍷 6
● Brunello di Montalcino '13	🍷🍷 6
● Brunello di Montalcino '12	🍷🍷 6
● Brunello di Montalcino Ris. '13	🍷🍷 7
● Brunello di Montalcino Ris. '12	🍷🍷 7
● Brunello di Montalcino Ugolaia '13	🍷🍷 8
● Brunello di Montalcino Ugolaia '12	🍷🍷 8
● Brunello di Montalcino Ugolaia '11	🍷🍷 8
● Rosso di Montalcino '17	🍷🍷 4

Lunadoro

FRAZ. VALIANO
VIA TERRA ROSSA
53045 MONTEPULCIANO [SI]
TEL. +39 348 2215188
www.nobilelunadoro.it

CELLAR SALES
PRE-BOOKED VISITS
ACCOMMODATION
ANNUAL PRODUCTION 60,000 bottles
HECTARES UNDER VINE 12.00
VITICULTURE METHOD Certified Organic

Among the Swiss-owned Schenk Italian Wineries group, we find Lunadoro, a producer situated in Valiano, one of Nobile di Montepulciano's most important subzones. While maintaining the dimensions and approach of a boutique winery, Lunadoro embodies a clearly modern style, well-defined, never trivial, expressed through wines that are consistent with their territory of origin and a constancy that is by now consolidated. At times we even find bottles capable of reaching the heights of excellence. We very much appreciated the Nobile di Montepulciano Pagliareto '17, a juicy wine that's full of contrasts but also able to deliver a lovely aromatic texture amidst flowery and fruity notes well adorned by spicy and somewhat balsamic nuances. The Rosso di Montepulciano Prugnanello '18 also performed well, with its floral and citrus aromas, while in the mouth it exhibits fragrance, flavor and a light structure that amplifies its suppleness.

Wine	Rating
● Nobile di Montepulciano Pagliareto '17	🍷🍷 4
● Rosso di Montepulciano Prugnanello '18	🍷🍷 3
● Nobile di Montepulciano Gran Pagliareto '16	🍷 6
● Nobile di Montepulciano Quercione Ris. '16	🍷 5
● Nobile di Montepulciano Pagliareto '15	🍷🍷🍷 3*
● Nobile di Montepulciano Pagliareto '16	🍷🍷 4
● Nobile di Montepulciano Pagliareto '14	🍷🍷 3*
● Nobile di Montepulciano Pagliareto '13	🍷🍷 3
● Nobile di Montepulciano Quercione Ris. '15	🍷🍷 4
● Nobile di Montepulciano Quercione Ris. '14	🍷🍷 4
● Nobile di Montepulciano Quercione Ris. '12	🍷🍷 4

I Luoghi

Loc. Campo al Capriolo, 201
57022 Castagneto Carducci [LI]
Tel. +39 0565777379
www.iluoghi.it

CELLAR SALES
ANNUAL PRODUCTION 15,000 bottles
HECTARES UNDER VINE 3.80
VITICULTURE METHOD Certified Organic

In Bolgheri, I Luoghi stands out for its distinctly artisan approach. The idea, and everything that has served to make it a reality, can be traced back to Stefano Granata and his wife, Paola, sensitive, empathic people and meticulous vigneron. Their main vineyard, which is divided into two distinct plots, is cultivated without herbicides or chemical products. Their wines are in a stage of stylistic evolution but always good, tasty and original, eschewing conventional modes and styles. The Bolgheri Superiore Campo al Fico '17 is just delicious. The producer's flagship took a year that certainly wasn't easy and transformed it into a notable wine. It's a complex, multifaceted red, aromatically wild and rustic, calling up Mediterranean scrub, and racy on the palate, coming through visceral, flavorful and deep. An excellent performance for the Bolgheri Superiore Podere Ritorti '17, a pervasive, meaty wine, as well.

Wine	Glasses	Price
● Bolgheri Rosso Sup. Campo al Fico '17	▼▼	7
● Bolgheri Rosso Sup. Podere Ritorti '17	▼▼	5
● Franco '16	▼	6
● Bolgheri Sup. Campo al Fico '10	▽▽▽	7
● Bolgheri Sup. Campo al Fico '09	▽▽▽	7
● Bolgheri Sup. Campo al Fico '08	▽▽▽	7
● Bolgheri Sup. Podere Ritorti '13	▽▽▽	5
● Bolgheri Rosso Sup. Campo al Fico '16	▽▽	7
● Bolgheri Rosso Sup. Podere Ritorti '16	▽▽	5
● Bolgheri Sup. Campo al Fico '15	▽▽	7
● Bolgheri Sup. Campo al Fico '13	▽▽	7
● Bolgheri Sup. Podere Ritorti '15	▽▽	5
● Bolgheri Sup. Podere Ritorti '14	▽▽	5

★★Le Macchiole

Loc. Bolgheri
via Bolgherese, 189a
57022 Castagneto Carducci [LI]
Tel. +39 0565766092
www.lemacchiole.it

PRE-BOOKED VISITS
ANNUAL PRODUCTION 190,000 bottles
HECTARES UNDER VINE 28.00

Le Macchiole is one of Bolgheri's historic wineries and one of the most prestigious in terms of quality, style and identity. Their wines, which have become a symbol for character and personality, have contributed to the area's reputation as a great terroir for Italian wine. Cinzia Merli is still at the helm, increasingly supported by her children Elia and Mattia, as well as a team of high-level collaborators. In the vineyards their sights are firmly set on sustainability, while their work in the cellar does away with all the frills, making for an elegant, contemporary range year after year. Once again, this year the Paleo stands out. It's a monovarietal Cabernet Franc, one of the area's true pearls. 2017 gave rise to a wine as vibrant and powerful as it is able to preserve its proverbial elegance, aromatic nuances, the crystalline class of its palate and magnificent texture. The Messorio and Scrio, both 2017s, are right on its heels, while the Bolgheri Rosso '18 also performed well.

Wine	Glasses	Price
● Paleo Rosso '17	▼▼▼	8
● Messorio '17	▼▼	8
● Scrio '17	▼▼	8
● Bolgheri Rosso '18	▼▼	4
● Bolgheri Sup. Paleo '14	▽▽▽	8
● Paleo Rosso '16	▽▽▽	8
● Paleo Rosso '15	▽▽▽	8
● Paleo Rosso '13	▽▽▽	8
● Paleo Rosso '12	▽▽▽	8
● Paleo Rosso '11	▽▽▽	8
● Paleo Rosso '10	▽▽▽	8
○ Bolgheri Bianco Paleo '14	▽▽	6
● Bolgheri Rosso '17	▽▽	4
● Messorio '16	▽▽	8
● Messorio '15	▽▽	8
● Scrio '16	▽▽	8
● Scrio '15	▽▽	8

Le Macioche

S.DA PROV.LE 55 DI SANT'ANTIMO KM 4,850
53024 MONTALCINO [SI]
TEL. +39 0577849168
www.lemacioche.it

CELLAR SALES
PRE-BOOKED VISITS
ACCOMMODATION
ANNUAL PRODUCTION 18,000 bottles
HECTARES UNDER VINE 3.00

Founded in 2016 by Dominga, Marta and Enrica, the Cotarella family brand represents the natural evolution of over 40 years of work in the world of their famous fathers, enologists Renzo and Riccardo. Among the group's gems is Le Macioche, a historic Montalcino estate acquired in 2017 from the Mazzocchi family. Nestled in the hills of Sant'Antimo at elevations of around 450 meters, on land rich in marl, the producer is well known to wine lovers for reds made from mildly dry Sangiovese cultivated in four small vineyards planted in the 1980s. Even if the south-east quadrant of Montalcino, where the hamlet of Sant'Antimo lies, is protected from the sea breezes by Monte Amiata (and therefore enjoys a rather warm climate), the Brunello '15 expresses undeniable qualities of freshness. Elegant aromas of cherries and medicinal herbs are enriched by multifaceted sanguine notes. In the mouth it combines great class with silky, elegant tannins and a long, fresh finish.

Wine	Rating
● Brunello di Montalcino '15	▼▼▼ 8
● Brunello di Montalcino '13	▽▽▽ 7
● Brunello di Montalcino Ris. '13	▽▽▽ 8
● Brunello di Montalcino Ris. '11	▽▽▽ 8
● Brunello di Montalcino '11	▽▽ 7
● Brunello di Montalcino '10	▽▽ 7
● Brunello di Montalcino '09	▽▽ 7
● Brunello di Montalcino '08	▽▽ 7
● Brunello di Montalcino '07	▽▽ 7
● Brunello di Montalcino '06	▽▽ 6
● Brunello di Montalcino '04	▽▽ 6
● Brunello di Montalcino Ris. '06	▽▽ 8
● Brunello di Montalcino Ris. '01	▽▽ 6
● Rosso di Montalcino '13	▽▽ 4
● Rosso di Montalcino '11	▽▽ 4
● Rosso di Montalcino '10	▽▽ 4
● Rosso di Montalcino '09	▽▽ 4

La Madonnina

FRAZ. BOLGHERI
VIA BOLGHERESE, 193
57022 CASTAGNETO CARDUCCI [LI]
TEL. +39 0565763357
www.lamadonninabolgheri.it

ANNUAL PRODUCTION 40,000 bottles
HECTARES UNDER VINE 7.00

A highly worthy venture, the history of La Madonnina is unfolding in a magical place. The estate extends across the western side of the Strada Bolgherese, between the metalliferous hills and the sea, an area bordered by forests, with their unique flora and fauna. The vineyards, which were planted in 2002, host the area's now-classic varieties. These grow in a mix of soils, from clay to sandier terrain. The wines are decidedly modern and of excellent craftsmanship. A restored farmhouse stands out like a jewel on the estate. Among the wines tasted, the authoritative La Madonnina '17 emerged in all its glory. It's a red made with Cabernet Franc, Syrah, Merlot, Cabernet Sauvignon and Petit Verdot, vinified in steel before passing into French oak barriques for 16 months. Full-bodied and juicy, it plays on various aromatic nuances, keeping fruity and toasty embroideries in beautiful harmony, coming through balanced and long on the palate. It finishes pervasive and silky, with smooth tannins and soft flavor.

Wine	Rating
● La Madonnina '17	▼▼▼ 8
● Bolgheri Sup. Opera Omnia '17	▼▼ 8
● Viator '17	▼▼ 8
● Bolgheri Sup. Opera Omnia '16	▽▽ 8

Fattoria di Magliano

LOC. STERPETI, 10
58051 MAGLIANO IN TOSCANA [GR]
TEL. +39 0564593040
www.fattoriadimagliano.it

CELLAR SALES
PRE-BOOKED VISITS
ACCOMMODATION AND RESTAURANT SERVICE
ANNUAL PRODUCTION 300,000 bottles
HECTARES UNDER VINE 50.00
VITICULTURE METHOD Certified Organic

After concluding a career in the footwear sector, in 1997 Agostino Lenci launched a winemaking venture in the heart of Maremma, just a stone's throw from Magliano in Toscana. The first bottles hit the market in 2003 and immediately impressed for their modern style, polished craftsmanship and personality. After a period of tweaking, their range seems to have rediscovered its luster, smoothing out some expressive excesses and relying on a more austere, conscientious style that favors balance over power. The Maremma Vermentino Pagliatura '19 brings together vibrant aromas with a lively, well-sustained palate that's nicely adorned by a delicately salty note. Fragrant and vivid on the palate, the Morellino Heba '18 is characterized by notes of small red fruits and spices, while the balanced Ansonica Brissi '19 offers up beautiful scents of apple, thyme and Mediterranean scrub, introducing a flavorful, vigorous palate.

Wine	Rating
○ Maremma Toscana Vermentino Pagliatura '19	▼▼ 3*
○ Maremma Toscana Ansonica Brissi '19	▼▼ 4
● Morellino di Scansano Heba '18	▼▼ 3
● Maremma Toscana Rosso Altizi '16	▽▽ 5
● Maremma Toscana Sinarra '16	▽▽ 3
● Morellino di Scansano Heba '15	▽▽ 3
● Perenzo '12	▽▽ 6
● Poggio Bestiale '11	▽▽ 5
● Poggio Bestiale '10	▽▽ 5

Malenchini

LOC. GRASSINA
VIA LILLIANO E MEOLI, 82
50015 BAGNO A RIPOLI [FI]
TEL. +39 055642602
www.malenchini.it

CELLAR SALES
PRE-BOOKED VISITS
ANNUAL PRODUCTION 120,000 bottles
HECTARES UNDER VINE 17.00

The estate has been owned by the Malenchini family since 1836, but as far back as the 11th century there was a watchtower on the property, later transformed into a villa by Grand Duke Ferdinando II dei Medici. Today the agricultural side of things is run by Diletta, who oversaw recent organic conversion of the estate. In addition to Sangiovese, which is the cornerstone of production, we find Canaiolo. Once used in blends, today it's also bottled as a monovarietal. The Bruzzico '17 is excellent. A blend of Sangiovese and Cabernet Sauvignon, it offers up notes of ink and pencil lead on the nose, then potpourri and black berries. In the mouth it opens warm, rich, finishing long and enticing. The Canaiolo '19 is an amusing wine characterized by vegetal aromas on the nose, with earthy hints and some spicy whiffs of nutmeg at the fore. On the palate it's subtle, quite fresh, with measured tannins and cherry sensations.

Wine	Rating
● Bruzzico '17	▼▼ 4
● Canaiolo '19	▼▼ 3
● Chianti Colli Fiorentini '18	▼▼ 2*
○ Vin Santo del Chianti '15	▼▼ 4
○ Bianco '19	▼ 2
● Chianti '19	▼ 1*
● Chianti Colli Fiorentini Ris. '17	▼ 3
● Chianti Sup. '18	▼ 2
● Bruzzico '16	▽▽ 4
● Bruzzico '15	▽▽ 4
● Bruzzico '14	▽▽ 4
● Chianti '15	▽▽ 1*
● Chianti Colli Fiorentini '14	▽▽ 2*
● Chianti Colli Fiorentini Ris. '16	▽▽ 2*
○ Vin Santo del Chianti '14	▽▽ 4
○ Vin Santo del Chianti '13	▽▽ 4

Malgiacca

LOC. GRAGNANO
VIA DELLA CHIESA, 45A
55010 CAPANNORI [LU]
TEL. +39 3331840208
www.malgiacca.com

CELLAR SALES
PRE-BOOKED VISITS
ANNUAL PRODUCTION 20,000 bottles
HECTARES UNDER VINE 8.00

Malgiacca is a recent venture, founded on the Lucchese Hills thanks to a friendship involving Lisandro Carmazzi, Luigi Fenoglio, Sarah Richards, Brunella Ponzo and Saverio Petrilli, one of the great experts of biodynamic agriculture in Italy. Their work is based around reviving old vineyards, some abandoned, and the planting of new ones. The producer belongs to LDB, a network of farmers linked by Steinerian practices, which eschew the use of pesticides and herbicides. The wines produced are marked by natural, free expression, pointing up a strong and uncompromising artisan character. The Tingolli '18 is a magnetic white: Trebbiano, Vermentino, Malvasia, Colombana and Viognier macerate partly on the skins for two weeks, then the wine matures for nine months in old oak barrels. Airy, with an exquisite floral and fruity aroma, it also exhibits earthy substance. It's a wine that's as summery as it is austere on its flavorful palate, rich in nuances, welcoming for those who know how to listen.

Wine	Rating
○ Tingolli '18	🍷🍷 5
○ Malgiacca Bianco '19	🍷🍷 3
● Malgiacca Rosso '18	🍷🍷 4

Fattoria Mantellassi

LOC. BANDITACCIA, 26
58051 MAGLIANO IN TOSCANA [GR]
TEL. +39 0564592037
www.fattoriamantellassi.it

CELLAR SALES
PRE-BOOKED VISITS
ANNUAL PRODUCTION 1,000,000 bottles
HECTARES UNDER VINE 99.00
SUSTAINABLE WINERY

More than half a century of winemaking for this Magliano in Toscana producer, which, thanks to the pioneering efforts of Ezio Mantellassi, has contributed a great deal to the success of Morellino and Maremma in Italy and throughout the world. Today the family winery is managed by Ezio's sons Aleardo and Giuseppe, who've managed to maintain the Mantellassi style, bringing together quality and expressive identity in a range that's always highly distinct. The Morellino Le Sentinelle Riserve '16 opens on warm, generous aromas, with a predominantly spicy note accompanied by accents of fresh licorice and black cherry jam. On the palate it proves sapid, with slightly earthy tannins. The Ciliegiolo Maestrale '19, with its fresh and fruity aromatic bouquet, is expansive and full, supported by a lovely acidic verve. Aromatic clarity and drinkability are also hallmarks of the Morellino Mentore '19.

Wine	Rating
● Maremma Toscana Ciliegiolo Maestrale '19	🍷🍷 2*
● Morellino di Scansano Sentinelle Ris. '16	🍷🍷 4
○ Maremma Toscana Vermentino Scalandrino '19	🍷 2
● Morellino di Scansano Mentore '19	🍷 2
● Maremma Toscana Ciliegiolo Maestrale '18	🍷🍷 2* (outline)
● Maremma Toscana Ciliegiolo Maestrale '16	🍷🍷 2* (outline)
○ Maremma Toscana Vermentino Lucumone '18	🍷🍷 2* (outline)
○ Maremma Toscana Vermentino Lucumone '17	🍷🍷 2* (outline)
○ Maremma Toscana Vermentino Scalandrino '18	🍷🍷 2* (outline)

Marchesi Pancrazi Villa di Bagnolo

FRAZ. BAGNOLO
VIA MONTALESE, 156
59013 MONTEMURLO [PO]
TEL. +39 0574652748
www.pancrazi.it

CELLAR SALES
PRE-BOOKED VISITS
ANNUAL PRODUCTION 12,000 bottles
HECTARES UNDER VINE 5.00

Vittorio Pancrazi's story is one of the most beautiful of Tuscan wine. In the 1970s he decided to replant the vineyards on his estate, an old farm that belonged to the Strozzi family. Sangiovese was chosen but the nurseryman, by mistake, supplied rooted cuttings of Pinot Nero: only after a few years did they figure out what had happened, but they also discovered the potential of a vine that until then had never been seriously tested in Tuscany. Since then other territories suitable for the Burgundy vine have been identified, thanks to this providential 'mistake'. The Pinot Nero Villa di Bagnolo '18 earned a place in our finals. It's a characteristic wine in its bouquet of berries, combined with notes of aromatic herbs, thyme and oregano, and sanguine whiffs. The palate is balanced, without excesses, fresh, with a complex finish marked by deep hints of spices and licorice. The intriguing Pinot Nero Monte Ferrato '18, features meaty, vegetal tones on the nose, coming through elegant, responsive and lively in the mouth.

Wine	Rating
● Pinot Nero Villa di Bagnolo '18	🍷🍷 5
● Monte Ferrato Pinot Nero '18	🍷🍷 3
● Pinot Nero Villa di Bagnolo '16	🍷🍷 5
⊙ Rosé di Pinot Nero '19	🍷 2
● Pinot Nero '11	🍸🍸 5
● Pinot Nero Villa di Bagnolo '10	🍸🍸 5

Il Marroneto

LOC. MADONNA DELLE GRAZIE, 307
53024 MONTALCINO [SI]
TEL. +39 0577849382
www.ilmarroneto.it

CELLAR SALES
PRE-BOOKED VISITS
ANNUAL PRODUCTION 30,000 bottles
HECTARES UNDER VINE 6.00
SUSTAINABLE WINERY

A style that transcends a strict focus on quality renders the Mori family's wines more central than ever to contemporary winemaking in Montalcino. Soothing yet fiery, fascinatingly retro and at the same time extraordinarily contemporary in their expression, they bring together the qualities of an area that is in many ways unique: Madonna delle Grazie, a northern cru overlooking Montosoli. But above all, for more than 40 years the producer founded by Giuseppe (and now led by his son Alessandro) has been expressing the best of its 'garagiste' philosophy. The Madonna delle Grazie '15 took home top marks. It's a rich, harmonious wine, with clear, forward fruit that evolves into complexity both on the nose, where it expresses elegant oak, earthy tones of tobacco and spices, and on the palate, where it's pulpy, compact, but softened by elegant acidity and smooth tannins that accompany it right through a long, satisfying finish. The Brunello '15 also delivered.

Wine	Rating
● Brunello di Montalcino Madonna delle Grazie '15	🍷🍷🍷 8
● Brunello di Montalcino '15	🍷🍷 7
● Rosso di Montalcino Ignaccio '17	🍷🍷 5
● Brunello di Montalcino '14	🍸🍸🍸 7
● Brunello di Montalcino Madonna delle Grazie '11	🍸🍸🍸 8
● Brunello di Montalcino Madonna delle Grazie '10	🍸🍸🍸 8
● Brunello di Montalcino Madonna delle Grazie '08	🍸🍸🍸 8
● Brunello di Montalcino '13	🍸🍸 7
● Brunello di Montalcino Madonna delle Grazie '13	🍸🍸 8
● Rosso di Montalcino Ignaccio '16	🍸🍸 5
● Rosso di Montalcino Ignaccio '15	🍸🍸 5

Marzocco di Poppiano

FRAZ. POPPIANO
VIA FEZZANA, 36-38
50025 MONTESPERTOLI [FI]
TEL. +39 0555535259
www.marzoccopoppiano.it

CELLAR SALES
ANNUAL PRODUCTION 30,000 bottles
HECTARES UNDER VINE 35.00

It all began in 1975, when Alberto Chini bought the winery from the count Guicciardini family and began producing, as was customary in those years, a wine made according to tradition, to be sold unbottled. Substantial changes arrived in 2014, with the transfer of management to his daughter Roberta with her husband, Maurizio. This marked the beginning of zoning the land and carrying out a census of the vines, a process through which they've identified old clones of Canaiolo and Malvasia Lunga from Chianti, as well as 4 different types of Sangiovese. The Vigna del Leone '16 put in a good performance. It's a blend of mostly Sangiovese with smaller shares of Canaiolo and Cabernet Sauvignon. It has an elegant, classic nose, with hints of plum and cherry topped off by notes of camphor and cinnamon. In the mouth it opens warm, focused, finishing long with silky tannins. The intriguing Chianti Colli Fiorentini '18 is fruity on the nose, fresh and enjoyable on the palate, calling up iris and ripe cherry sensations.

Wine	Rating
● Chianti Colli Fiorentini '18	🍷🍷 3
● Pretale '16	🍷🍷 4
● V. del Leone '16	🍷🍷 5
● Chianti Ris. '17	🍷 4
● Pretale '15	🍷🍷 4
● Vigna del Leone '15	🍷🍷 5

Cosimo Maria Masini

VIA POGGIO A PINO, 16
56028 SAN MINIATO [PI]
TEL. +39 0571465032
www.cosimomariamasini.it

CELLAR SALES
PRE-BOOKED VISITS
ANNUAL PRODUCTION 50,000 bottles
HECTARES UNDER VINE 14.00
VITICULTURE METHOD Certified Biodynamic
SUSTAINABLE WINERY

Not far from the historic center of San Minato, we find the estate overseen by the Masini family since the year 2000. Various crops are grown, with vineyards occupying about 13 hectares. Tuscany's traditional grape varieties are cultivated along with other, little-known varieties, such as Buonamico, San Colombano and Sanforte. Recently these have been joined by international grapes as well. More important than the presence of lesser-known grapes, however, is the conversion to biodynamic, a philosophy that characterizes the winery as a whole. The Sanforte '18, made with the rare local grape of the same name, impresses. On the nose it expresses floral hints of violet, combined with fruity hints of blackberry. In the mouth it's firm, well built, with a vegetal profile, very fresh and broad. The Daphné '19, Trebbiano with a splash of Malvasia, once again delivered with its mature profile amidst orange peel and medicinal herbs. We appreciated the pleasantly delectable the Matilde Rosato '19. The Annick '19 is also excellent.

Wine	Rating
○ Annick '19	🍷🍷 3
○ Daphné '19	🍷🍷 4
● Sanforte Rosso '18	🍷🍷 2*
● Cosimo '16	🍷 5
⊙ Matilde '19	🍷 2
○ Annick '18	🍷🍷 3
○ Annick '16	🍷🍷 2*
○ Daphné '18	🍷🍷 4
○ Daphné '17	🍷🍷 4
○ Daphné '16	🍷🍷 4
● Nicole '18	🍷🍷 3
● Nicole '17	🍷🍷 3
● Sanforte Rosso '16	🍷🍷 2*
● Sincero '18	🍷🍷 3
● Sincero '17	🍷🍷 3

Masseto

FRAZ. BOLGHERI
57022 CASTAGNETO CARDUCCI [LI]
TEL. +39 056571811
www.masseto.com

ANNUAL PRODUCTION 33,000 bottles
HECTARES UNDER VINE 11.00
SUSTAINABLE WINERY

It still has that new building smell and serves as a model of minimalism, purity and architectural elegance. In addition to being beautiful, the new Masseto winery marks the beginning of an individual journey for Ornellaia's thoroughbred champion. For some time now, we've known that it's as appreciated and prestigious as any wine that can be found on international markets, at least when it comes to Italian producers. And its importance is further evidenced by the aesthetic and functional design that accompanies each new version. We shouldn't forget their 'second vin', the Massetino, either. If the latest versions of their Masseto amaze for their extraction, density and power, the 2017 further explores this deliberately pursued expressive and stylistic profile. It's an incredibly intense, structured wine, supported by broad, fruity tannins, amplified by vigorous toasty hints. Time will have to smooth out its decisive character and many components.

Wine	Rating
● Masseto '17	▼▼ 8
● Massetino '17	▽▽ 8
● Masseto '16	▽▽ 8

★Mastrojanni

FRAZ. CASTELNUOVO DELL'ABATE
POD. LORETO E SAN PIO
53024 MONTALCINO [SI]
TEL. +39 0577835681
www.mastrojanni.com

CELLAR SALES
PRE-BOOKED VISITS
ACCOMMODATION
ANNUAL PRODUCTION 110,000 bottles
HECTARES UNDER VINE 33.00

You say Mastrojanni and immediately you think of two special crus that helped to illuminate the peculiarities of Brunello during a period of transition like the one that preceded its definitive international boom. Vigna Loreto and Vigna Schiena d'Asino are the crown jewels of the winery created by Gabriele in the 1970s and taken over in 2008 by the Illy family. The latter have managed to highlight the attributes of these Castelnuovo dell'Abate vineyards, situated in the heart of southeast Montalcino, through apt technical choices. The Illy family's line-up once again performed at an exceptionally high level overall. At the top is a marvellous Schiena d'Asino '15, a prototype of the great Brunello di Sant'Antimo. It offers up alluring aromas of cherry, tobacco and liquorice, made more complex by spicy hints combined with whiffs of dried flowers. It's a great, austere red for laying down.

Wine	Rating
● Brunello di Montalcino V. Schiena d'Asino '15	▼▼▼ 8
● Brunello di Montalcino '15	▼▼ 5
● Brunello di Montalcino V. Loreto '15	▼▼ 7
● Ciliegiolo '18	▼▼ 6
● San Pio '15	▼▼ 5
● Rosso di Montalcino '18	▼ 5
● Brunello di Montalcino '97	▽▽▽ 7
● Brunello di Montalcino Schiena d'Asino '08	▽▽▽ 8
● Brunello di Montalcino V. Loreto '13	▽▽▽ 7
● Brunello di Montalcino V. Loreto '10	▽▽▽ 7
● Brunello di Montalcino V. Loreto '09	▽▽▽ 7
● Brunello di Montalcino V. Schiena d'Asino '12	▽▽▽ 8
● Brunello di Montalcino V. Schiena d'Asino '10	▽▽▽ 8

Fattorie Melini

loc. Gaggiano
53036 Poggibonsi [SI]
Tel. +39 0577998511
www.cantinemelini.it

CELLAR SALES
PRE-BOOKED VISITS
ANNUAL PRODUCTION 3,300,000 bottles
HECTARES UNDER VINE 136.00

A not insignificant part of the history of Chianti Classico involves the Melini di Poggibonsi brand, which, together with Fattoria Machiavelli di San Casciano Val di Pesa, represents Gruppo Italiano Vini in the Gallo Nero appellation. Exceptional sites for wine-growing, such as Selvanella in Radda in Chianti, make up an extraordinary viticultural patrimony, resulting in a rich range of products. In general, their wines exhibit a comforting consistency, praiseworthy precision and nice personality. Dark, mature aromas feature in the Chianti Classico La Selvanella Riserva '15, a wine that's firm and complex on the palate, and not without length. Nice aromatic complexity introduces the Gran Selezione Vigna di Fontalle '17, which finds its strong point in the mouth thanks to its long, well-sustained palate. The I Coltri '19 is a clean, focused blend of Sangiovese, Cabernet Sauvignon and Merlot characterized by a sapid, immediately expressive palate.

● Chianti Cl. Machiavelli Gran Selezione V. di Fontalle '17	🍷🍷 5
● Chianti Cl. Vign. La Selvanella Ris. '15	🍷🍷 4
● I Coltri '19	🍷🍷 2*
● Chianti Cl. Granaio '18	🍷 2
● Chianti Cl. Machiavelli Solatio del Tani '17	🍷 4
● Chianti Cl. La Selvanella Ris. '06	ΥΥΥ 5
● Chianti Cl. La Selvanella Ris. '03	ΥΥΥ 4
● Chianti Cl. La Selvanella Ris. '01	ΥΥΥ 4
● Chianti Cl. La Selvanella Ris. '00	ΥΥΥ 4
● Chianti Cl. La Selvanella Ris. '99	ΥΥΥ 5
● Chianti Cl. La Selvanella Ris. '90	ΥΥΥ 3*
● Chianti Cl. La Selvanella Ris. '86	ΥΥΥ 4*
● Chianti Cl. Granaio '17	ΥΥ 3*
● Chianti Cl. Machiavelli Solatio del Tani '16	ΥΥ 4

Le Miccine

loc. Le Miccine
s.s. Traversa Chiantigiana
53013 Gaiole in Chianti [SI]
Tel. +39 0577749526
www.lemiccine.com

CELLAR SALES
PRE-BOOKED VISITS
ACCOMMODATION
ANNUAL PRODUCTION 25,000 bottles
HECTARES UNDER VINE 7.00
VITICULTURE METHOD Certified Organic

Le Miccine is situated in the subzone of Gaiole in Chianti. Here the vineyards are cultivated organically without interfering with nature at elevations of almost 400 meters. A similar philosophy has been adopted in the cellar, where their approach is as minimally invasive as possible and aging is carried out in mid-sized casks. From a stylistic point of view, their wines clearly aim to express the qualities of the territory, proving aromatically elegant and forthright, with a lean structure, at times quite subtle. The Chianti Classico Riserva '17 turns on a vibrant, graceful floral bouquet adorned by smoky and spicy hints. In the mouth it's silky and tapered, with a pleasantly vivid finish. The Chianti Classico '18 is a very well-crafted wine, with light and fragrant aromas heralding a juicy gustatory development, rich in contrasts. The Carduus '16 is an enjoyable monovarietal Merlot.

● Chianti Cl. Ris. '17	🍷🍷 5
● Carduus '16	🍷🍷 5
● Chianti Cl. '18	🍷🍷 4
● Chianti Cl. Gran Selezione '16	🍷 4
● Chianti Cl. '16	ΥΥΥ 4*
● Chianti Cl. '15	ΥΥΥ 4*
● Chianti Cl. Ris. '10	ΥΥΥ 5
● Carduus '10	ΥΥ 5
● Chianti Cl. '17	ΥΥ 4
● Chianti Cl. '11	ΥΥ 2*
● Chianti Cl. Don Alberto Ris. '07	ΥΥ 4
● Chianti Cl. Ris. '16	ΥΥ 5
● Chianti Cl. Ris. '15	ΥΥ 5
● Chianti Cl. Ris. '13	ΥΥ 5
● Chianti Cl. Ris. '12	ΥΥ 5
● Chianti Cl. Ris. '09	ΥΥ 2*

Monte Solaio

via di Venturina, 15
57021 Campiglia Marittima [LI]
Tel. +39 0565843291
www.montesolaio.com

CELLAR SALES
PRE-BOOKED VISITS
ANNUAL PRODUCTION 40,000 bottles
HECTARES UNDER VINE 8.50

Owned by Anglo-Italian businessman Claudio Guglielmucci, Monte Solaio is situated in Campiglia Marittima, in Val di Cornia. Castello Bonaria, the center of the farm complex, was founded in the late 18th century in an old hunting lodge, and today, after careful renovation work, it provides guest accommodations. The vineyards, planted in soils rich in minerals, are flanked by wheat and olive trees. For the first time, the Tino Rosso, a blend of Cabernet Sauvignon, Merlot and Petit Verdot, landed in our finals. The 2017 has a multifaceted bouquet, which combines a broad fruitiness with sanguine hints, softened by fresh notes of sage and bay leaf. In the mouth it opens juicy, beautifully broad, rich, with an enticing, long finish. We appreciated the Re del Castello '17, Merlot and Cabernet Franc, for its aromas of licorice and coffee, balanced body and long persistence.

Wine	Rating
● Tino Rosso '17	🍷🍷 3*
● Re del Castello '17	🍷🍷 7
⊙ Sarosa '19	🍷🍷 2*
○ Allegro '19	🍷 3
○ Boccasanta '19	🍷 2
● Collevato '18	🍷 5
● Sassinoro '18	🍷 5
● Re del Castello '16	🍷🍷 7
● Re del Castello '15	🍷🍷 7
● Sassinoro '15	🍷🍷 5
● Tino Rosso '16	🍷🍷 3

★Montenidoli

loc. Montenidoli
53037 San Gimignano [SI]
Tel. +39 0577941565
www.montenidoli.com

CELLAR SALES
ACCOMMODATION
ANNUAL PRODUCTION 100,000 bottles
HECTARES UNDER VINE 24.00
VITICULTURE METHOD Certified Organic

Elisabetta Fagiuoli moved to this part of Tuscany in 1966 together with Sergio Muratori. It was a choice made out of love for the land and the desire to facilitate a dialogue between the elderly and young people in difficulty. In light of these aims, their production philosophy centers on native grape varieties (Vernaccia, Sangiovese, Canaiolo, Trebbiano Gentile and Malvasia Bianca), biodynamic cultivation, and respect for the environment. Their lodging also hosts those who come to study education and viticulture. At times, tasting Elisabetta's great reds (like the Sono Montenidoli '15, a deep, earthy, irresistible wine), we're tempted to rank them at the top. But then we taste her Vernaccias, like the Carato '17, a wine of elegance and extraordinary complexity, a true child of the terroir, or the Tradizionale '19, floral, full-bodied and very fine, and the temptation passes. Hers is the work of a true vigneronne, one who lives in symbiosis with the land, with nature and the rhythm of the seasons. Bravo.

Wine	Rating
○ Vernaccia di S. Gimignano Carato '17	🍷🍷🍷 4*
● Sono Montenidoli '15	🍷🍷 5
○ Vernaccia di S. Gimignano Tradizionale '19	🍷🍷 2*
⊙ Canaiuolo Rosato '19	🍷🍷 3
● Chianti Colli Senesi Il Garrulo '18	🍷🍷 2*
● Colorino '18	🍷🍷 3
○ Il Templare '15	🍷🍷 4
● Montenidoli '18	🍷🍷 4
○ Vernaccia di S. Gimignano Fiore '19	🍷🍷 3
○ Vernaccia di S. Gimignano Carato '16	🍷🍷🍷 4*
○ Vernaccia di S. Gimignano Carato '13	🍷🍷🍷 4*
○ Vernaccia di S. Gimignano Carato '12	🍷🍷🍷 4*
○ Vernaccia di S. Gimignano Carato '11	🍷🍷🍷 4*
○ Vernaccia di S. Gimignano Tradizionale '15	🍷🍷🍷 2*

Monteraponi

loc. Monteraponi
53017 Radda in Chianti [SI]
Tel. +39 0577738208
www.monteraponi.it

CELLAR SALES
PRE-BOOKED VISITS
ACCOMMODATION
ANNUAL PRODUCTION 50,000 bottles
HECTARES UNDER VINE 10.00
VITICULTURE METHOD Certified Organic

The winery owned by Michele Braganti only made its entrance into the Chianti Classico wine scene with the new millennium, but it has immediately made a name for itself thanks to markedly traditional wines that express the best qualities of Radda in Chianti's Sangiovese. Their characteristic trait lies in the aromatic alternation between more intense notes and more nuanced hints, sometimes decidedly autumnal, combined with invigorating, tasty, energetic development. The Baron'Ugo '16 interprets an exceptional vintage in its own way, once again demonstrating that it's a great wine. A blend of Sangiovese, Canaiolo and Colorino, it offers up floral scents adorned by intriguing hints of earth and stone. On the palate it has great flavor, unfolding graceful, dynamic and multifaceted. The delicious Chianti Classico '18 exhibits a frank, generous character, with a fragrant, focused aromatic profile and delectable palate.

Wine	Rating
● Baron'Ugo '16	▼▼▼ 5
● Chianti Cl. '18	▼▼ 4
● Chianti Cl. Il Campitello Ris. '17	▼▼ 7
● Baron'Ugo '13	▽▽▽ 5
● Baron'Ugo '12	▽▽▽ 8
● Chianti Cl. Baron'Ugo Ris. '10	▽▽▽ 7
● Chianti Cl. Baron'Ugo Ris. '09	▽▽▽ 7
● Chianti Cl. Baron'Ugo Ris. '07	▽▽▽ 5
● Chianti Cl. Il Campitello Ris. '16	▽▽▽ 7
● Chianti Cl. Il Campitello Ris. '15	▽▽▽ 7
● Baron'Ugo '15	▽▽ 5
● Chianti Cl. '17	▽▽ 4
● Chianti Cl. '16	▽▽ 4
● Chianti Cl. '13	▽▽ 3
● Chianti Cl. Baron'Ugo Ris. '11	▽▽ 7
● Chianti Cl. Il Campitello Ris. '14	▽▽ 5
● Chianti Cl. Il Campitello Ris. '13	▽▽ 5

Monterinaldi

loc. Lucarelli
53017 Radda in Chianti [SI]
Tel. +39 0577733533
www.monterinaldi.it

ANNUAL PRODUCTION 400,000 bottles
HECTARES UNDER VINE 65.00

Castello di Monterinaldi is located in the Radda in Chianti subzone. This alone could be enough to to give a sense of its production approach, at least according to the most fashionable trends. The estate vineyards are located on some of the area's best hills, while in the cellar winemaking follows classic principles with various options adopted for aging, from large oak barrels to small ones, from concrete to terracotta. It's an approach that results in free, authentic and personal Sangiovese. The Chianti Classico Carpe Testudinem '17 offers up approachable, vibrant aromas. In the mouth it's also on point, coming through juicy, sapid and rich in contrast. A side note for a wine as curious as its name, the Purple Turtle of Tuscany '18, a blend of Sangiovese and Merlot characterized by nice aromatic focus, and a firm, taut palate.

Wine	Rating
● Chianti Cl. Carpe Testudinem '17	▼▼ 4
● Purple Turtle '18	▼▼ 3
● Chianti Cl. '16	▽▽ 3
● Chianti Cl. '15	▽▽ 3
● Chianti Cl. Campopazzo '13	▽▽ 3
● Chianti Cl. Ris. '16	▽▽ 4
● Chianti Cl. Ris. '15	▽▽ 4
● Chianti Cl. Ris. '14	▽▽ 4
● Chianti Cl. Ris. '13	▽▽ 4
● Chianti Cl. Vign. Boscone '16	▽▽ 4
● Chianti Cl. Vign. Boscone '15	▽▽ 4

Monterò

loc. Colle Lupo
58051 Magliano in Toscana [GR]
Tel. +39 3396024802
www.monterò.com

CELLAR SALES
PRE-BOOKED VISITS
ANNUAL PRODUCTION 20,000 bottles
HECTARES UNDER VINE 6.50
VITICULTURE METHOD Certified Organic
SUSTAINABLE WINERY

An abbreviation of Monterozzino, Monterò is located near Magliano in Toscana. The estate is run with passion and enthusiasm by Milena Cacurri, who seems to have found the right direction. Her wines are direct but never banal, appreciable for the way they hold together the typical summeriness and pleasantness that characterize Maremma with finesse and balance. For now we're seeing the best results with their whites, but the house Morellino exhibits notable style and personality. The Invisible '17, a blend of Vermentino and Viogner matured in terracotta, opens on vibrant, fleshy and fruity aromas, with hints of petrol to finish. It's a nice prelude to a dense, delicately salty progression of flavor. The Maremma Vermentino '19 continues on a similarly sapid and vivid track, proving supple, racy and balanced, enriched by nuances of lime blossom and fresh almond. The fragrant and drinkable Morellino di Scansano More '18 also performed well.

Wine	Glasses
○ Maremma Toscana Bianco L'Invisibile '17	TT 6
○ Maremma Toscana Vermentino '19	TT 4
● Morellino di Scansano More '18	TT 4
○ Maremma Toscana Vermentino '18	YY 4
● Maremma Toscana Vermentino '17	YY 3
● Morellino di Scansano More '17	YY 4
● Morellino di Scansano More '16	YY 4
⊙ Tetè '18	YY 3

MonteRosola

loc. Pignano
pod. La Rosola
56048 Volterra [PI]
Tel. +39 058835062
www.monterosola.com

ANNUAL PRODUCTION 8,000 bottles
HECTARES UNDER VINE 19.00

In an area not particularly known for viticulture, Bengt Thomaeus and his wife, Ewa, have achieved the perfect combination of technology, respect for nature and quality agronomic practices. Since 2013, when they took over the property, the total area has expanded to 125 hectares, including 19 vineyards, which grow around a new, futuristic winery. Sangiovese, Merlot, Cabernet Franc and Sauvignon, Syrah, Grechetto, Viogner and Manzoni are all cultivated. For the first time the Indomito '17, a Syrah produced only in magnums, landed in our finals. The nose is enticing with initial notes of rose-water followed by bottled cherries, mint and hints of vanilla. The palate is rich but fresh, with excellent structure. All its components blend well, while a hint of pepper adorns a rising finish. The intriguing Canto della Civetta '17 is a flowery Merlot, soft and pulpy.

Wine	Glasses
● Indomito '17	TT 4
● Canto della Civetta '17	TT 5
● Corpo Notte '17	TT 4
● Crescendo '17	TT 3
● Mastio '18	TT 3
○ Cassero '19	T 2
○ Primo Passo '18	T 3
● Canto della Civetta '16	YY 5
● Corpo Notte '16	YY 4
● Crescendo '16	YY 3
● Indomito '16	YY 4
○ Primo Passo '17	YY 3

Tenuta Monteti

s.da della Sgrilla, 6
58011 Capalbio [GR]
Tel. +39 0564896160
www.tenutamonteti.it

CELLAR SALES
PRE-BOOKED VISITS
ANNUAL PRODUCTION 130,000 bottles
HECTARES UNDER VINE 28.00
SUSTAINABLE WINERY

The Baratta family's Tenuta Monteti is located near Capalbio, in the southernmost part of Maremma wine country. The varieties grown are exclusively international and range from Petit Verdot to Cabernet Franc, from Cabernet Sauvignon to Merlot, all the way to Alicante Bouschet. A modern production approach is natural here, with maturation carried out in small oak barrels of various ages, depending on the wine. The style is rich, with Mediterranean nuances amplifying their wines' personality. A blend of Petit Verdot, Cabernet Franc and Cabernet Sauvignon, the Monteti '16 offers up smoky, spicy aromas on a background of lush fruitiness, well accompanied by fragrance and intensity. In the mouth it's firm, close-woven, pervasive and well-sustained. The Caburnio '16, a blend of Cabernet Sauvignon, Alicante Bouschet and Merlot, also delivered. Slightly herbaceous and earthy on the nose, it unfolds soft and flavorful.

● Monteti '16	🍷🍷🍷 6
● Caburnio '16	🍷🍷 4
⊙ TM Rosé '19	🍷 3
● Caburnio '15	🍷🍷🍷 4*
● Caburnio '14	🍷🍷🍷 3*
● Caburnio '13	🍷🍷 3
● Caburnio '12	🍷🍷 3
● Caburnio '11	🍷🍷 3
● Monteti '15	🍷🍷 6
● Monteti '13	🍷🍷 6
● Monteti '12	🍷🍷 5
● Monteti '11	🍷🍷 5
⊙ TM Rosé '14	🍷🍷 3

Monteverro

s.da Aurelia Capalbio, 11
58011 Capalbio [GR]
Tel. +39 0564890721
www.monteverro.com

CELLAR SALES
PRE-BOOKED VISITS
ANNUAL PRODUCTION 150,000 bottles
HECTARES UNDER VINE 40.00
VITICULTURE METHOD Certified Organic
SUSTAINABLE WINERY

Monteverro is situated in southern Tuscany, just a few kilometers from the sea. Sixty hectares host vineyards and olive groves, as well as Mediterranean scrub and cork oaks. The cellar, partly built inside the slope to obtain natural temperature control, houses the results of a natural and environmentally-friendly winemaking approach. Indeed, here sustainable agriculture and cutting-edge technology come together to make wine from Cabernet Sauvignon and Franc, Merlot, Petit Verdot, Syrah, Grenache, Chardonnay and Vermentino grapes. The Monteverro '17, a blend of mostly Cabernet Franc with a smaller share of Cabernet Sauvignon, is a vibrant red, underpinned aromatically by sanguine notes, dried violet flowers, then currants and green peppers. In the mouth it opens enticing, rich and tasty, with nice tannic texture and an enjoyable finish. The Chardonnay '17 is buttery, rich in tropical fruit, fat and fresh. The Tinata '17, a Rhone-esque blend of Syrah and Grenache, isn't bad either.

● Monteverro '17	🍷🍷 8
○ Chardonnay Monteverro '17	🍷🍷 8
● Tinata '17	🍷🍷 8
● Terra di Monteverro '17	🍷 7
○ Chardonnay '16	🍷🍷 8
○ Chardonnay '13	🍷🍷 8
● Monteverro '16	🍷🍷 8
● Monteverro '14	🍷🍷 8
● Monteverro '13	🍷🍷 8
● Terra di Monteverro '16	🍷🍷 7
● Terra di Monteverro '14	🍷🍷 7
● Terra di Monteverro '13	🍷🍷 7
● Terra di Monteverro '12	🍷🍷 7
● Tinata '15	🍷🍷 8
● Tinata '14	🍷🍷 8
● Tinata '13	🍷🍷 8
● Tinata '12	🍷🍷 8

★★Montevertine

loc. Montevertine
53017 Radda in Chianti [SI]
Tel. +39 0577738009
www.montevertine.it

PRE-BOOKED VISITS
ANNUAL PRODUCTION 85,000 bottles
HECTARES UNDER VINE 19.00

Tuscan and Italian wine would not be what they are today without the work of Sergio Manetti and his son Martino. When in the 1970s Sergio decided to try his hand at winemaking, the area was in a state of semi-abandonment and few believed that a rebirth of local wines was possible. Since then, Montevertine has seen some of the most accomplished bottles in the entire territory, and the trend continues. Their wines are capable of an expressiveness that's as rare as it is coherent, with an original style that still adheres fervently to tradition. A child of a difficult vintage, the 2017 version of their Pergole Torte intrigues. As always, the wine will offer up its most intricate details with time, but we can already attest to its quality. It's not the first time that we've talked up their Piano del Ciampolo—the 2018 is superbly pleasant, to say the least. A juicy and vibrant Montervertine '17 completes the trio.

● Le Pergole Torte '17	🍷🍷🍷 8
● Montevertine '17	🍷🍷 6
● Pian del Ciampolo '18	🍷🍷 4
● Le Pergole Torte '16	🍷🍷🍷 8
● Le Pergole Torte '15	🍷🍷🍷 8
● Le Pergole Torte '13	🍷🍷🍷 8
● Le Pergole Torte '12	🍷🍷🍷 8
● Le Pergole Torte '11	🍷🍷🍷 8
● Le Pergole Torte '10	🍷🍷🍷 8
● Le Pergole Torte '09	🍷🍷🍷 8
● Le Pergole Torte '07	🍷🍷🍷 8
● Le Pergole Torte '04	🍷🍷🍷 8
● Le Pergole Torte '03	🍷🍷🍷 7
● Le Pergole Torte '01	🍷🍷🍷 8
● Montevertine '14	🍷🍷🍷 6
● Montevertine '04	🍷🍷🍷 5
● Montevertine '01	🍷🍷🍷 5

Vignaioli del Morellino di Scansano

loc. Saragiolo
58054 Scansano [GR]
Tel. +39 0564507288
www.vignaiolidiscansano.it

CELLAR SALES
PRE-BOOKED VISITS
ANNUAL PRODUCTION 2,500,000 bottles
HECTARES UNDER VINE 600.00
SUSTAINABLE WINERY

Founded in 1972 as a response to the crisis in the mining sector and conducted with passionate commitment by experts and simple farmers alike, the Cantina Vignaioli del Morellino in Maremma is now on its way to becoming a modern cooperative producer, demonstrating an admirable consistency of quality thanks to wines that are impeccably crafted and true to type. Their wide and multifaceted portfolio includes DOC Maremma, thus completing a range that represents this special territory in southern Tuscany. This year the Scansano cooperative submitted a solid selection for tasting. The Morellino Roggiano Riserva '17 features clear, well-delineated aromas in which red berries alternate with floral hints and spicy nuances. In the mouth it's juicy and supple, maintaining depth and length. The Sicomoro Riserva '17 also delivers, coming through sapid with a nice mix of fruit and well-balanced oak.

● Morellino di Scansano Roggiano '18	🍷🍷 2*
● Morellino di Scansano Roggiano Ris. '17	🍷🍷 4
● Morellino di Scansano Sicomoro Ris. '17	🍷🍷 4
○ Bianco di Pitigliano Sup. Rasenno '19	🍷 2
○ Maremma Toscana Ansonica '19	🍷 3
● Maremma Toscana Ciliegiolo Capoccia '19	🍷 2
● Scantianum Sangiovese '19	🍷 2
○ Scantianum Vermentino '19	🍷 2
● Vin del Fattore Governo all'Uso Toscano '19	🍷 3
● Morellino di Scansano Roggiano Ris. '15	🍷🍷 3*
● Morellino di Scansano Sicomoro Ris. '15	🍷🍷 4
● Morellino di Scansano Vignabenefizio '17	🍷🍷 3
● Scantianum Sangiovese '18	🍷🍷 2*

Giacomo Mori

FRAZ. PALAZZONE
P.ZZA SANDRO PERTINI, 8
53040 SAN CASCIANO DEI BAGNI [SI]
TEL. +39 0578227005
www.giacomomori.it

CELLAR SALES
PRE-BOOKED VISITS
ACCOMMODATION
ANNUAL PRODUCTION 45,000 bottles
HECTARES UNDER VINE 12.00
VITICULTURE METHOD Certified Organic

Managed by Giacomo Mori, Palazzone operates in an area historically well suited to Sangiovese, even if outside Tuscany's classic, more prestigious winemaking districts. Since 1995 this small producer, situated not far from San Casciano dei Bagni, has been making wines that exhibit a reassuring constancy, with a defined style and a strong Chianti character that focuses on drinkability and balance without unnecessarily interfering with the natural process of winemaking. A mix of barriques and large wood barrels are used judiciously. The Chianti '18 is an approachably pleasant wine redolent of fresh cherries, freshly cut grass and spices; in the mouth it attacks sweet and vivid, unfolding with broad flavor and crisp tannins. Despite a somewhat complicated year, the Chianti Castelrotto Riserva '17 also convinced, offering up well-balanced aromas and generous flavor, coming through dynamic and juicy on the palate, with a solid, fruity and spicy finish.

Wine	Rating
● Chianti '18	🍷🍷 3
● Chianti Castelrotto Ris. '17	🍷🍷 4
● Chianti '15	🍷🍷 2*
● Chianti '11	🍷🍷 2*
● Chianti '10	🍷🍷 2*
● Chianti Castelrotto Ris. '16	🍷🍷 3
● Chianti Castelrotto Ris. '15	🍷🍷 3
● Chianti Castelrotto Ris. '14	🍷🍷 3
● Chianti Castelrotto Ris. '13	🍷🍷 3
● Chianti Castelrotto Ris. '11	🍷🍷 3
○ Vin Santo del Chianti '08	🍷🍷 6

Tenuta Moriniello

VIA SANTO STEFANO, 40
50050 MONTAIONE [FI]
TEL. +39 3483198880
www.tenutamoriniello.com

CELLAR SALES
PRE-BOOKED VISITS
ACCOMMODATION
ANNUAL PRODUCTION 50,000 bottles
HECTARES UNDER VINE 20.00
VITICULTURE METHOD Certified Organic

Here in the heart of Tuscany, on the rolling hills of Montaione, Beniamino Moriniello identified and bought an estate, setting out to improve the vineyards and cellar. Now he oversees the property with his children Tania and Luigi, bringing great care to his work. Sangiovese, Canaiolo, Ciliegiolo, Colorino, Cabernet Sauvignon, Cabernet Franc, Merlot, Petit Verdot, Syrah, Sauvignon Blanc and Gewurztraminer all give rise to wines that at times call up authentic regional tradition and in others express a more international style. The Gobbo Nero, a monovarietal Syrah, once again lives up to expectations. The 2017 exhibits enticing olfactory notes amidst berries, currants and raspberries, fresh sensations of mint and tarragon, finishing on peppery spices. The palate is inviting, linear, simple but not insubstantial, with a long finish. The Le Fate Furbe '19, made with Sauvignon and Gewürztraminer, is an expressive wine of great intensity.

Wine	Rating
● Chianti Fortebraccio Ris. '17	🍷🍷 3
● Il Gobbo Nero '17	🍷🍷 4
○ Le Fate Furbe '19	🍷🍷 3
● Chianti La Pieve '19	🍷 2
● Chianti Fortebraccio Ris. '16	🍷🍷 3
● Chianti Fortebraccio Ris. '15	🍷🍷 3
● Chianti La Pieve '18	🍷🍷 2*
● Il Gobbo Nero '16	🍷🍷 4
● Il Gobbo Nero '15	🍷🍷 4
● Il Gobbo Nero '13	🍷🍷 4
○ Le Fate Furbe '17	🍷🍷 3
● Rosso del Pievano '13	🍷🍷 4
● Syrah Gobbo Nero '11	🍷🍷 3

Morisfarms

loc. Cura Nuova
Fattoria Poggetti
58024 Massa Marittima [GR]
Tel. +39 0566919135
www.morisfarms.it

CELLAR SALES
PRE-BOOKED VISITS
ACCOMMODATION
ANNUAL PRODUCTION 300,000 bottles
HECTARES UNDER VINE 70.00

Morisfarms has two main vineyard plots, Fattoria Poggetti in Monteregio di Massa Marittima and Poggio la Mozza (in the Morellino di Scansano appellation) and is one of the most important producers of the Maremma winemaking panorama. The Massa Marittima winery has always delivered wines with a comforting consistency in quality, deservedly earning a place among Tuscany's most reliable wineries. An aromatic profile marked by luscious, vibrant, dark fruit, the Morellino di Scansano '19 stands out for its supple, sapid and soft palate. A blend of Sangiovese, Cabernet Sauvignon and Syrah, the Avvoltore '16 delivers concentrated, potent aromas led by spicy oak, which also emerges on a close-woven, almost austere palate. We also appreciated the approachably pleasant and smooth Maremma Rosso Mandriolo '19.

● Avvoltore '16	🍷🍷 6
● Morellino di Scansano '19	🍷🍷 2*
● Maremma Toscana Rosso Mandriolo '19	🍷 2
○ Vermentino '19	🍷 2
● Avvoltore '06	🍷🍷🍷 5
● Avvoltore '04	🍷🍷🍷 5
● Avvoltore '01	🍷🍷🍷 5
● Avvoltore '00	🍷🍷🍷 5
● Avvoltore '99	🍷🍷🍷 5
● Avvoltore '15	🍷🍷 6
● Maremma Toscana Mandriolo '15	🍷🍷 1*
● Maremma Toscana Rosso Mandriolo '18	🍷🍷 2*
● Morellino di Scansano '17	🍷🍷 2*
● Morellino di Scansano '16	🍷🍷 2*
● Morellino di Scansano Ris. '16	🍷🍷 4

Mormoraia

loc. Sant'Andrea, 15
53037 San Gimignano [SI]
Tel. +39 0577940096
www.mormoraia.it

CELLAR SALES
PRE-BOOKED VISITS
ACCOMMODATION
ANNUAL PRODUCTION 230,000 bottles
HECTARES UNDER VINE 40.00

In 1980, the Passoni family became owners of the ancient convent La Mormoraia. After renovation of the houses and vineyards, the inauguration of its farmstay accommodations and first cellar, expansion of its vineyards and olive groves and the introduction of modern equipment for wine production, the estate now covers an area of over 100 hectares, 10 of which are olive groves. In addition to Vernaccia, Sangiovese, Cabernet Sauvignon and Franc, Merlot and Syrah are cultivated. In 2012 the estate converted to organic. The Vernaccia Antalis Riserva '17 is outstanding, thanks to a lively bouquet in which citrus notes of lemon and mandarin combine with vegetal hints of tea, floral whiffs of chamomile, basil sensations and yellow peach. In the mouth it opens flavorful, weighty, fresh in its acidity and persistent. The Vernaccia Suavis '19 features characteristic aromas of almond and apple, and a balanced body.

○ Vernaccia di S. Gimignano Antalis Ris. '17	🍷🍷 3*
● Chianti Colli Senesi Haurio '18	🍷🍷 2*
○ Vernaccia di S. Gimignano Ostrea '18	🍷🍷 3
○ Vernaccia di S. Gimignano Suavis '19	🍷🍷 3
⊙ Gaudium Rosato '19	🍷 2
○ Vernaccia di S. Gimignano E' ReZet Mattia Barzaghi '11	🍷🍷🍷 3*
○ Vernaccia di S. Gimignano Ostrea '17	🍷🍷🍷 3*
● Chianti Colli Senesi Haurio '16	🍷🍷 2*
● Chianti Colli Senesi Haurio '15	🍷🍷 2*
○ Vernaccia di S. Gimignano Antalis Ris. '16	🍷🍷 3
○ Vernaccia di S. Gimignano Ostrea '16	🍷🍷 3
○ Vernaccia di S. Gimignano Ris. '14	🍷🍷 3*
○ Vernaccia di S. Gimignano Suavis '18	🍷🍷 3
○ Vernaccia di S. Gimignano Suavis '17	🍷🍷 2*

Fabio Motta

Vigna al Cavaliere, 61
57022 Castagneto Carducci [LI]
Tel. +39 0565773041
www.mottafabio.it

CELLAR SALES
PRE-BOOKED VISITS
ANNUAL PRODUCTION 23,000 bottles
HECTARES UNDER VINE 6.50

Now an internationally-known winemaker, Fabio Motta is one of Bolgheri's recent revelations. After graduating in agriculture and gaining experience in the winery under Michele Satta, he started his project, one that's now solid in terms of stylistic definition and overall organization. Here at the foot of Castagneto Carducci, in Le Pievi, their red grapes are grown, while in Fornacelle we find the whites, starting with Vermentino. The style approaches the territory with a personal vision and careful hands. By now the Bolgheri Superiore Le Gonnare is a benchmark for the appellation. A difficult 2017 was managed with class, making for a red that's certainly vibrant and mature, but also elegant and rich in detail, capable of a mobile, flavorful, beautiful texture. The Bolgheri Bianco Nova '19 is fragrant and delicately salty, while the Bolgheri Pieve and Lo Scudiere '18 also put in excellent performances.

- ● Bolgheri Rosso Sup. Le Gonnare '17 TTT 8
- ○ Bolgheri Bianco Nova '19 TT 4
- ● Bolgheri Rosso Pievi '18 TT 4
- ● Lo Scudiere '18 TT 5
- ● Bolgheri Rosso Sup. Le Gonnare '16 YYY 8
- ● Bolgheri Rosso Sup. Le Gonnare '15 YYY 8
- ● Bolgheri Sup. Le Gonnare '13 YYY 8
- ○ Bolgheri Bianco Nova '17 YY 4
- ○ Bolgheri Bianco Nova '16 YY 4
- ● Bolgheri Rosso Pievi '16 YY 4
- ● Bolgheri Rosso Pievi '15 YY 4

Tenute Silvio Nardi

loc. Casale del Bosco
53024 Montalcino [SI]
Tel. +39 0577808332
www.tenutenardi.com

CELLAR SALES
PRE-BOOKED VISITS
ANNUAL PRODUCTION 250,000 bottles
HECTARES UNDER VINE 80.00

Emilia Nardi continues tirelessly in the visionary work begun by her father, Silvio, who after WW II decided to invest in Montalcino. It was a forward-thinking choice, to say the least, in light of today's boom, and resulted in of one of the most solid producers in the area. Everything revolves around the thirty or so plots cultivated, especially those associated with Casale del Bosco (in the northwest) and Manachiara (in the east), which lends its name to their Brunello cru. For some time now, the Nardi family have been producing 3 distinct Brunellos in Montalcino. After the first historic wine, in 1995 they unveiled the Manachiara and later, in 2004, the Poggio Doria, wines heralding from two territories that are diametrically opposed in terms of climate and terrain. The Manachiara, from Castelnuovo dell'Abate, speaks the language of fruit and power, coming through more timidly in its youth. The Poggio Doria is a decidedly modern wine.

- ● Brunello di Montalcino '15 TT 6
- ● Brunello di Montalcino Poggio Doria '15 TT 8
- ● Brunello di Montalcino V. Manachiara '15 TT 8
- ● Chianti dei Colli Senesi '18 TT 2*
- ● Brunello di Montalcino Manachiara '99 YYY 7
- ● Brunello di Montalcino Manachiara '97 YYY 7
- ● Brunello di Montalcino '14 YY 6
- ● Brunello di Montalcino '11 YY 6
- ● Brunello di Montalcino Poggio Doria '12 YY 8
- ● Brunello di Montalcino V. Manachiara '12 YY 8
- ● Rosso di Montalcino '17 YY 3
- ● Rosso di Montalcino '16 YY 3
- ● Rosso di Montalcino '15 YY 3

Nittardi

Loc. Nittardi
53011 Castellina in Chianti [SI]
Tel. +39 0577740269
www.nittardi.com

CELLAR SALES
PRE-BOOKED VISITS
ACCOMMODATION
ANNUAL PRODUCTION 120,000 bottles
HECTARES UNDER VINE 38.00
VITICULTURE METHOD Certified Organic

We find the Femfert family's estate in Castellina, on the border between the provinces of Siena and Florence, surrounded by woods. It took its first steps in the early 1980s, thanks to the passion of Peter and his wife, Stefania Canali. The property, which revolves around a medieval watchtower owned by Michelangelo Buonarroti, and its vineyards, have been perfectly restored. Thanks to the Femfert family's passion for contemporary art, Nittardi is also a fascinating exhibition space. Today Leon Femfert is at the helm, bolstered by the recent acquisition of 17 lovely hectares in Maremma. Nittardi's wines have a clear, territorial and modern character. We very much appreciated the Chianti Classico Riserva '17, a wine that offers lush, sweet fruit on the nose, well supported by spicy and oaky touches. It's also elegant on the palate: flavorful, broad and relaxed, closing clear and long on fruit and spices. The Casanuova '18 and the Maremma Nectar Dei '16 are worth taking note of.

Wine	Glasses	Price
● Chianti Cl. Ris. '17	▼▼	6
● Chianti Cl. Casanuova di Nittardi '18	▼▼	4
● Maremma Toscana Ad Astra '18	▼▼	3
● Nectar Dei '16	▼▼	7
● Chianti Cl. Belcanto '18	▼	4
● Chianti Cl. Belcanto '15	▽▽▽	4*
● Chianti Cl. Ris. '13	▽▽▽	6
● Ad Astra '15	▽▽	3
● Chianti Cl. Casanuova di Nittardi '14	▽▽	4
● Chianti Cl. Ris. '15	▽▽	6
● Chianti Cl. V. Doghessa '17	▽▽	6
● Nectar Dei '14	▽▽	7

★Orma

via Bolgherese
57022 Castagneto Carducci [LI]
Tel. +39 0575477857
www.ormawine.it

ANNUAL PRODUCTION 50,000 bottles
HECTARES UNDER VINE 5.50
SUSTAINABLE WINERY

The Arezzo entrepreneur Antonio Moretti Cuseri has several projects in the world of wine. Among these, Podere Orma deserves a special place. It is the Bolgheri branch of a group that includes Tenuta Setteponti and Feudo Maccari, and has proven capable of standing out from the rest. It may be just five hectares of vineyards on clayey soils rich in pebbles, but its reputation far exceeds the few bottles produced. The style is inspired by the area's traditions, but isn't afraid to pursue original expressions of extreme charm and elegance either. A blend of Merlot, Cabernet Sauvignon and Franc matured for at least 12 months in barriques, Orma is one of the territory's great wines. Rich in red and black fruits, from ripe cherries to blueberries, it exhibits a well-integrated toastiness and excellent grain, combining sapidity, solid structure and a highly flavorful finish. The Bolgheri Passi di Orma '18 is simpler but very pleasant.

Wine	Glasses	Price
● Orma '18	▼▼▼	8
● Bolgheri Rosso Passi di Orma '18	▼▼	5
● Orma '17	▽▽▽	8
● Orma '16	▽▽▽	8
● Orma '14	▽▽▽	8
● Orma '13	▽▽▽	8
● Orma '12	▽▽▽	8
● Orma '11	▽▽▽	8
● Orma '10	▽▽▽	7
● Orma '09	▽▽▽	6
● Orma '08	▽▽▽	6
● Orma '07	▽▽▽	5
● Orma '06	▽▽▽	6
● Bolgheri Rosso '15	▽▽	8
● Bolgheri Rosso Passi di Orma '17	▽▽	5
● Bolgheri Rosso Passi di Orma '16	▽▽	5

★★Ornellaia

FRAZ. BOLGHERI
LOC. ORNELLAIA, 191
57022 CASTAGNETO CARDUCCI [LI]
TEL. +39 056571811
www.ornellaia.it

PRE-BOOKED VISITS
ANNUAL PRODUCTION 1,000,000 bottles
HECTARES UNDER VINE 115.00
SUSTAINABLE WINERY

Ornellaia is one of Italy's most prestigious brands, one that's extremely well known and appreciated all over the world. It took shape in the 1980s, earning universal acclaim in just a short time. Naturally, behind its success lie the vineyards themselves, half-hidden at the foot of the Bolgheri hills, an area that's kissed by the cool sea breeze in the summer months and protected from the coldest winds in winter. The soils are of marine, alluvial and volcanic origin, and in many cases vary from parcel to parcel. Today their wines are compelling, able to speak a language that resonates at an international level. The Bolgheri Superiore Ornellaia '17, their flagship wine, serves as a benchmark for the territory and Italian enology throughout the world. A modern red, it combines intensity of fruit, accentuated by the vintage, with a toasty profile that's as fine as it is decisive, able to accompany its fragrances, and the palate, on hints of vanilla. The white version, another 2017, is also very good.

Wine	Rating
● Bolgheri Rosso Sup. Ornellaia '17	▼▼▼ 8
○ Bolgheri Ornellaia Bianco '17	▼▼ 8
○ Bolgheri Bianco Poggio alle Gazze '18	▼▼ 5
● Bolgheri Rosso Le Serre Nuove '18	▼▼ 6
● Bolgheri Rosso Sup. Ornellaia '16	▽▽▽ 8
● Bolgheri Sup. Ornellaia '14	▽▽▽ 8
● Bolgheri Sup. Ornellaia '13	▽▽▽ 8
● Bolgheri Sup. Ornellaia '07	▽▽▽ 8
● Bolgheri Sup. Ornellaia '05	▽▽▽ 8
● Bolgheri Sup. Ornellaia '04	▽▽▽ 8
● Bolgheri Sup. Ornellaia '02	▽▽▽ 8
● Bolgheri Sup. Ornellaia '01	▽▽▽ 8
● Bolgheri Sup. Ornellaia '99	▽▽▽ 8
● Bolgheri Rosso Le Serre Nuove '17	▽▽ 6
● Bolgheri Rosso Le Serre Nuove '16	▽▽ 6
● Bolgheri Sup. Ornellaia '15	▽▽ 8
○ Ornellaia Bianco '16	▽▽ 8

Siro Pacenti

LOC. PELAGRILLI, 1
53024 MONTALCINO [SI]
TEL. +39 0577848662
www.siropacenti.it

CELLAR SALES
PRE-BOOKED VISITS
ANNUAL PRODUCTION 60,000 bottles
HECTARES UNDER VINE 22.00

A historic family of Montalcino wine, the Pacentis, with their various generational branches, have created several notable estates. Among these is undoubtedly the winery founded by Siro in the 1970s and now led by Giancarlo. Here there's an increased focus on highlighting the specific temperaments of the area. In fact, the vineyards of the original block, Pelagrilli (in the north), were later accompanied by those of Piancornello in the south, allowing for a Sangiovese da Brunello that is in many ways complementary in its combination of power and juice. The tastings of the last few years provide a summary of almost three decades of research carried out by Giancarlo in the name of smoothing out his Brunellos' tannins during vinification. The Vecchievigne has great structure and consistent, fruity flesh, nicely balancing tannins. A long aftertaste testifies to maturation in small oak barrels. Although the Pelagrilli plays the finesse card, all their wines are particularly ageworthy.

Wine	Rating
● Brunello di Montalcino V. V. '15	▼▼ 8
● Brunello di Montalcino Pelagrilli '15	▼▼ 7
● Rosso di Montalcino '18	▼▼ 5
● Brunello di Montalcino '97	▽▽▽ 7
● Brunello di Montalcino '96	▽▽▽ 7
● Brunello di Montalcino '95	▽▽▽ 7
● Brunello di Montalcino '88	▽▽▽ 7
● Brunello di Montalcino PS Ris. '07	▽▽▽ 8
● Brunello di Montalcino V. V. '10	▽▽▽ 8
● Brunello di Montalcino Pelagrilli '14	▽▽ 6
● Brunello di Montalcino Pelagrilli '13	▽▽ 6
● Brunello di Montalcino Pelagrilli '12	▽▽ 6
● Brunello di Montalcino Pelagrilli '11	▽▽ 6
● Brunello di Montalcino PS Ris. '10	▽▽ 8
● Brunello di Montalcino V. V. '14	▽▽ 8
● Brunello di Montalcino V. V. '11	▽▽ 8
● Rosso di Montalcino '17	▽▽ 5

Pagani de Marchi

loc. La Nocera
via della Camminata, 2
56040 Casale Marittimo [PI]
Tel. +39 0586653016
www.paganidemarchi.com

CELLAR SALES
PRE-BOOKED VISITS
ANNUAL PRODUCTION 35,000 bottles
HECTARES UNDER VINE 6.50

The Pagani de Marchi family's story is an interesting one. In the mid-1990s they decided to transform the land overlooking their country house into vineyards, and things went quite well. The territory proved to be particularly fertile, after all, even in ancient times it was dedicated to agriculture, as evidenced by the 7th-century BC remains found in the tombs. Gradually the producer has grown, increasing the area under vine and the wines proposed; in 2009 they undertook a path linked to organic farming. The two 2017 Casalvecchios, both made with Cabernet Sauvignon, prove quite pleasant. In the 'traditional' version, its olfactory sensations are linked to berries and hints of licorice, while the body is balanced, sapid and quite long. The amphora version offers up fresh aromas of curry plant, mint and black berries; the palate is subtle, harmonious and clean.

○ Blumea '19	🍷🍷 3
● Casa Nocera '16	🍷🍷 5
● Casalvecchio '17	🍷🍷 5
● Casalvecchio Anfora '17	🍷🍷 7
● Olmata '17	🍷🍷 4
● Montescudaio Montaleo '18	🍷 2
● Montescudaio Principe Guerriero '17	🍷 4
● Casa Nocera '15	🍷🍷 5
● Casa Nocera '13	🍷🍷 5
● Casa Nocera '10	🍷🍷 5
● Casalvecchio '16	🍷🍷 5
● Casalvecchio '13	🍷🍷 5
● Montescudaio Montaleo '12	🍷🍷 2*
● Montescudaio Principe Guerriero '16	🍷🍷 4
● Montescudaio Principe Guerriero '13	🍷🍷 4
○ Vermentino Blumea '16	🍷🍷 3

Pakravan-Papi

loc. Ortacavoli Nuova
via del Commercio
56046 Riparbella [PI]
Tel. +39 0586786076
www.pakravan-papi.it

CELLAR SALES
PRE-BOOKED VISITS
ANNUAL PRODUCTION 40,000 bottles
HECTARES UNDER VINE 15.00

We have Enzo Papi and Amineh Pakravan to thank for this lovely producer. The two met in Florence as volunteers after the 1966 flood, and they never left each other again. The farm property had been abandoned for many years, even if it had a certain agricultural background. After acquiring enough to have a sufficient surface area to start out with, starting in the 2000s, they began planting vines and building the winery. The Campo del Pari is a pleasant Merlot blend (various amounts of Sangiovese and Cabernet Sauvignon). The 2014 version offers up vibrant, fruity aromas of raspberry and currant, then spicy hints. In the mouth it's pleasant, broad and linear, rather soft and clean. The Cancellaia di Riparbella '14 is an interesting blend of equal parts Cabernet Franc and Cabernet Sauvignon. Here balsamic notes prevail, while the palate comes through clear, focused and tasty.

● Campo del Pari '14	🍷🍷 6
● Cancellaia '14	🍷🍷 5
○ Ribellante '18	🍷🍷 3
○ Serra dei Cocci '18	🍷🍷 3
○ Malvasia di Riparbella '19	🍷 3
● Beccacciaia '12	🍷🍷 5
● Campo del Pari '13	🍷🍷 6
● Cancellaia '13	🍷🍷 5
● Sangiovese Gabbriccio '12	🍷🍷 3
○ Serra dei Cocci '14	🍷🍷 3
○ Valdimare Bianco '14	🍷🍷 3

Il Palagione

LOC. PALAGIONE
VIA PER CASTEL SAN GIMIGNANO, 36
53037 SAN GIMIGNANO [SI]
TEL. +39 0577953134
www.ilpalagione.com

CELLAR SALES
PRE-BOOKED VISITS
ACCOMMODATION
ANNUAL PRODUCTION 60,000 bottles
HECTARES UNDER VINE 16.00
VITICULTURE METHOD Certified Organic

The farm from which the estate takes its name dates back to the late 16th century. The Comotti family, originally from Lombardy, bought it in 1995 and immediately started renovating the existing buildings, as well as planting the vineyards. They were ahead of their time with organic cultivation, with certification coming in 2007. The next step was building a modern and technologically current winery; the final piece was the acquisition of more land in 2014 . The wines submitted put in a nice overall performance, above all the Vernaccias. The Lyra '17 sees buttery, pervasive sensations dominate on the nose, all propped up by ripe fruits, such as lychee, before closing on hints of white pepper. The body is soft, creamy, with lovely length. The Lei '17 features vegetal sensations of tea and chamomile, then candied apple and toasted almond. In the mouth it exhibits nice weight and freshness, with an encore of aromatic herbs.

Wine	Rating
● Chianti Colli Senesi Caelum '18	TT 2*
○ Vernaccia di San Gimignano Lei '17	TT 3
○ Vernaccia di San Gimignano Lyra '17	TT 3
○ Vernaccia di San Gimignano Ori Ris. '18	TT 3
● Chianti CS Drago Ris. '17	T 3
⊙ San Gimignano Rosato Sunrosé '19	T 2
● San Gimignano Rosso Ares '15	T 4
● Trevite '19	T 2
○ Vernaccia di S. Gimignano Hydra '19	T 2
○ Vernaccia di S. Gimignano Hydra '18	YY 2*
○ Vernaccia di San Gimignano Lyra '16	YY 3
○ Vernaccia di San Gimignano Ori Ris. '17	YY 3
○ Vernaccia di San Gimignano Ori Ris. '15	YY 3

La Palazzetta

LOC. CASTELNUOVO DELL'ABATE
POD. LA PALAZZETTA, 1P
53024 MONTALCINO [SI]
TEL. +39 0577835531
www.palazzettafanti.com

CELLAR SALES
PRE-BOOKED VISITS
ACCOMMODATION
ANNUAL PRODUCTION 70,000 bottles
HECTARES UNDER VINE 28.00
VITICULTURE METHOD Certified Organic
SUSTAINABLE WINERY

Situated in southeast Montalcino, in the enclave of Castelnuovo dell'Abate, with a magnificent view of the Abbey of Sant'Antimo, La Palazzetta is the Fanti family's headquarters. Founded by Flavio and Carla in the late 80s, it has since consolidated with the full-time involvement of their children Luca and Tea. The core of their range centers on local Sangiovese, with their Brunello and Rosso standing out for an innovative touch usually softened by bottle aging. The Fanti family is back in our main section thanks to a range without weak points, with the Visconti 2015 standing out. Rich in aromas of cherry jam and hints of blood oranges, this Brunello, created by Carla Visconti (Flavio's wife), shines for the delicacy of its tannins. Without upsetting the house style, the Brunello '15 comes across as richer and fleshier. Among the two Rosso di Montalcinos, the Fanti stands out for its complexity.

Wine	Rating
● Brunello di Montalcino Visconti '15	TT 5
● Brunello di Montalcino '15	TT 5
● I Bruciati '18	TT 2*
● Rosso di Montalcino '18	TT 3
● Rosso di Montalcino Visconti '18	TT 3
● Sant'Antimo Rosso '16	T 2
● Brunello di Montalcino '13	YY 5
● Brunello di Montalcino '11	YY 5
● Brunello di Montalcino '10	YY 5
● Brunello di Montalcino Ris. '13	YY 6
● Rosso di Montalcino '17	YY 3
● Rosso di Montalcino '16	YY 3
● Rosso di Montalcino '12	YY 3

Palazzo

Loc. Palazzo, 144
53024 Montalcino [SI]
Tel. +39 0577849226
www.aziendapalazzo.it

CELLAR SALES
PRE-BOOKED VISITS
ANNUAL PRODUCTION 21,000 bottles
HECTARES UNDER VINE 4.00
VITICULTURE METHOD Certified Biodynamic

The vineyards of the Palazzo estate are easily recognizable for the sandy-marl soils that characterize the eastern Montalcino hillside. For over thirty years these conditions have set the pace for the project founded by Cosimo and Antonietta Loia and later consolidated by their children Angelo and Elia. It's all thanks to their Brunello and Rosso, which are appreciated for their density and propensity to age. Matured both in barriques and large casks, they often find a placid and compelling dimension with time in the bottle, even in versions that are initially darker. Even if the Rosso di Montalcino '15 didn't repeat last year's exploit (when it earned Tre Bicchieri), their selection is still of excellent quality. The Brunello '15 and Cosimo '15 both exhibit a decisive, pervasive alcoholic warmth. The latter still needs time for oak and tannins to blend into the mix completely. For its part, the Brunello delivers harmonious aromas of plum and cherry, and more docile tannins.

Wine	Rating
● Brunello di Montalcino '15	🍷🍷 6
● Brunello di Montalcino Cosimo '15	🍷🍷 6
● Rosso di Montalcino '15	YYY 3*
● Brunello di Montalcino '14	YY 6
● Brunello di Montalcino '13	YY 6
● Brunello di Montalcino '10	YY 6
● Brunello di Montalcino Ris. '13	YY 7
● Brunello di Montalcino Ris. '12	YY 7
● Brunello di Montalcino Ris. '10	YY 7
● Rosso di Montalcino '17	YY 3
● Rosso di Montalcino '16	YY 3

Panizzi

Loc. Santa Margherita, 34
53037 San Gimignano [SI]
Tel. +39 0577941576
www.panizzi.it

CELLAR SALES
PRE-BOOKED VISITS
ACCOMMODATION
ANNUAL PRODUCTION 210,000 bottles
HECTARES UNDER VINE 50.00

Panizzi, one of San Gimignano's most representative wineries, was founded by Giovanni Panizzi in the 1980s and is now owned by Simone Niccolai. It was the first in the area to develop Vernaccia and bring out the grape's ageworthiness, pushing many other producers to focus on quality. Today, while the area's whites continue to serve as a solid base, the winery is pursuing new directions, experimenting with different approaches to vinification and grapes that are less common to area, such as Pinot Nero. Simone Niccolai's winery is back with Tre Bicchieri thanks to the Vernaccia Riserva '16. It's a wine with a complex, multifaceted bouquet, with floral nuances of broom and chamomile followed by notes of apricot and peach, fresh hints of mint and citron peel. The palate exhibits good weight, the right density, proper acid backbone and a long finish—it's a wine of great aromatic consistency. The Vernaccia Vigna Santa Margherita '18 also performs on high levels.

Wine	Rating
○ Vernaccia di S. Gimignano Ris. '16	🍷🍷🍷 5
○ Vernaccia di San Gimignano V. Santa Margherita '18	🍷🍷 3*
● Chianti Colli Senesi Vertunno Ris. '15	🍷🍷 2*
● San Gimignano Pinot Nero '18	🍷🍷 2*
⊙ Ceraso Rosato '19	🍷 2
○ Vernaccia di S. Gimignano '19	🍷 3
○ Vernaccia di S. Gimignano Ris. '07	YYY 5
○ Vernaccia di S. Gimignano Ris. '05	YYY 5
○ Vernaccia di S. Gimignano Ris. '98	YYY 4*
○ Vernaccia di S. Gimignano '18	YY 3
○ Vernaccia di S. Gimignano Ris. '15	YY 5
○ Vernaccia di S. Gimignano Ris. '14	YY 5
○ Vernaccia di San Gimignano V. Santa Margherita '17	YY 3
○ Vernaccia di San Gimignano V. Santa Margherita '16	YY 3

Parmoleto

loc. Montenero d'Orcia
pod. Parmoletone, 44
58040 Castel del Piano [GR]
Tel. +39 0564954131
www.parmoleto.it

CELLAR SALES
PRE-BOOKED VISITS
ACCOMMODATION AND RESTAURANT SERVICE
ANNUAL PRODUCTION 22,000 bottles
HECTARES UNDER VINE 6.00

On the hills of Castel del Piano, near Monte Amiata, the Sodi family have been cultivating their small vineyard since 1990, producing wines marked by good overall quality. When the Montecucco appellation was born, the producer followed suit, working to maximize the value of the area's Sangiovese. Their range exhibits an interesting stylistic profile, combining a traditional approach with targeted modernist forays, especially when it comes to the use of oak, which in some cases steals the limelight. The Montecucco Rosso '17 features dark aromas of cherry and morello, all reinforced by spicy hints and soft, earthy sensations. In the mouth it's well-sustained and rich in contrasts, marked by flavorful, punchy tannins, which render the wine dynamic. Fragrant and well crafted, the Montecucco Vermentino Carabatto '19 offers up floral aromas, citrus and Mediterranean scrub, while unfolding pleasantly fresh, sapid and balanced on the palate.

Wine	Rating
● Montecucco Rosso '17	🍷🍷 2*
○ Montecucco Vermentino Carabatto '19	🍷🍷 2*
● Maremma Toscana Syrah '18	🍷 3
● Montecucco Sangiovese Ris. '16	🍷 3
● Sormonno '18	🍷 4
● Montecucco Rosso '16	🍷🍷 2*
● Montecucco Sangiovese '14	🍷🍷 3
● Montecucco Sangiovese '13	🍷🍷 3
● Montecucco Sangiovese '12	🍷🍷 3
● Montecucco Sangiovese Ris. '15	🍷🍷 3*
● Montecucco Sangiovese Ris. '13	🍷🍷 3*
● Montecucco Sangiovese Ris. '12	🍷🍷 3
● Montecucco Sangiovese Ris. '11	🍷🍷 3*
● Montecucco Sangiovese Ris. '10	🍷🍷 3
○ Montecucco Vermentino Carabatto '18	🍷🍷 2*

Tenuta La Parrina

fraz. Albinia
s.da vicinale della Parrina
58015 Orbetello [GR]
Tel. +39 0564862626
www.parrina.it

CELLAR SALES
PRE-BOOKED VISITS
ACCOMMODATION AND RESTAURANT SERVICE
ANNUAL PRODUCTION 100,000 bottles
HECTARES UNDER VINE 60.00
SUSTAINABLE WINERY

Parrina is a multifaceted agricultural business, a winery and an appellation itself, The Spinola family has been leading the producer since the end of the nineteenth century, overseeing a brand that has contributed greatly to the development of Maremma wine country. Their style is clearly modern and, above all, privileges drinkability and aromatic approachability. There is, however, no lack of more ambitious wines in their densely populated portfolio, some of which reach the heights of excellence. The well-crafted Ansonica '19 opens on aromas of flint and iodine, all amplified by a fresh flavor that closes on a beautiful saline note. The Parrina Sangiovese '19 is excellent, bolstered by an aromatic suite in which floral and fruity suggestions merge well with spicy and smoky notes. On the palate it's pleasantly well-sustained and dense. The rest of their range also delivers, especially the whites.

Wine	Rating
○ Costa dell'Argentario Ansonica '19	🍷🍷🍷 3*
● Parrina Sangiovese '19	🍷🍷 3*
○ Parrina Bianco Vialetto '19	🍷 2
○ Poggio della Fata '19	🍷 3
○ Costa dell'Argentario Ansonica '17	🍷🍷🍷 3*
● Parrina Sangiovese '18	🍷🍷🍷 3*
○ Costa dell'Argentario Ansonica '18	🍷🍷 3*
○ Costa dell'Argentario Ansonica '16	🍷🍷 3
○ Costa dell'Argentario Ansonica '15	🍷🍷 3
● Parrina Rosso Muraccio '17	🍷🍷 4
● Parrina Rosso Muraccio '16	🍷🍷 4
● Parrina Rosso Muraccio '14	🍷🍷 3*
● Parrina Sangiovese '16	🍷🍷 2*
● Parrina Sangiovese Ris. '16	🍷🍷 5
○ Parrina Vermentino '16	🍷🍷 3
○ Poggio della Fata '15	🍷🍷 3

Tenuta Perano

s.da di San Donato in Perano
53013 Gaiole in Chianti [SI]
Tel. +39 0577749563
www.frescobaldi.com

ANNUAL PRODUCTION 500,000 bottles
HECTARES UNDER VINE 52.00

The Frescobaldi family chose Gaiole in Chianti to leave their mark on the terroir of Chianti Classico as well. Perano is a beautiful, 250-hectare estate (52 of which are under vine), rented out in 2014 and subsequently purchased. The vineyards form an amphitheater, surrounded by woods, and grow in soil rich in pebbles. This, combined with the elevations (400-600 meters above sea level) means that the Sangiovese here ripens rather late, making for elegant, expansive wines. The Gran Selezione Rialzi '16, made with grapes from a vineyard in the upper part of the estate (hence its name, 'rialzo' means 'on high'), did well in our finals. In the mouth it opens with a soft, broad profile, a nice pulpiness of fruit, smooth tannins, beautiful notes of pomegranate and vanilla, and oaky tones. Tannins are elegant, but on the whole it's still quite astringent on the finish, needing a bit more time to evolve. In the meantime, we recommend the excellent Chianti Classico '17, a rich and pulpy wine, spicy and immediately enjoyable.

● Chianti Cl. Gran Selezione Rialzi '16	🍷🍷	6
● Chianti Cl. '17	🍷🍷	3
● Chianti Cl. Gran Selezione Rialzi '15	🍷🍷🍷	6
● Chianti Cl. '16	🍷🍷	3
● Chianti Cl. Ris. '16	🍷🍷	5

Perazzeta

fraz. Montenero d'Orcia
via della Piazza
58033 Castel del Piano [GR]
Tel. +39 3803545477
www.perazzeta.it

CELLAR SALES
PRE-BOOKED VISITS
ANNUAL PRODUCTION 100,000 bottles
HECTARES UNDER VINE 19.00

Purchased in 2016 by the Narducci family, this Montenero d'Orcia producer makes wines capable of standing shoulder-to-shoulder with the area's best. The winery got its start in 1998 and immediately bet on the then-young Montecucco appellation, putting together a range that has Sangiovese as its cornerstone, though we shouldn't forget Cabernet Sauvignon, Merlot, Syrah and Vermentino. Their style gives concrete form to a measured mix of tradition and modernity, with the use of oak divided between barriques and large barrels. The Montecucco Rosso '16 features fragrant aromas, with lush fruitiness alternating with spicy hints and more balsamic nuances. In the mouth it's juicy, sapid and vivid. We find a nice interpretation of Maremma's white grape 'par excellence' in the Montecucco Vermentino '19, a wine redolent of aromatic herbs and lime blossoms with light citrus touches. Flavorful in the mouth, it's both rhythmic and well sustained.

● Montecucco Rosso 11 23 Ris. '16	🍷🍷	4
○ Montecucco Vermentino '19	🍷🍷	2*
● Maremma Terre dei Bocci '11	🍷🍷	3
● Montecucco Rosso Alfeno '17	🍷🍷	2*
● Montecucco Rosso Alfeno '15	🍷🍷	2*
● Montecucco Rosso Alfeno '14	🍷🍷	2*
● Montecucco Rosso Alfeno '12	🍷🍷	2*
● Montecucco Sangiovese Licurgo Ris. '13	🍷🍷	5
● Montecucco Sangiovese Licurgo Ris. '12	🍷🍷	4
● Montecucco Sangiovese Licurgo Ris. '11	🍷🍷	4
● Montecucco Sangiovese Terre dei Bocci '15	🍷🍷	3
● Montecucco Sangiovese Terre dei Bocci '14	🍷🍷	3

Petra

loc. San Lorenzo Alto, 131
57028 Suvereto [LI]
Tel. +39 0565845308
www.petrawine.it

CELLAR SALES
PRE-BOOKED VISITS
ANNUAL PRODUCTION 350,000 bottles
HECTARES UNDER VINE 94.00
SUSTAINABLE WINERY

Vittorio Moretti's passion for wine took him from Franciacorta to Val di Cornia. After his success with sparkling wines, his entrepreneurial curiosity drove him towards Tuscany. Not far from Suvereto and the sea we find his futuristic, representative and well-equipped winery (conceived and designed by Mario Botta) and its surrounding vineyards. Everything is now overseen with the same intense passion by Francesca, who's committed to creating wines that tell the story of the territory through a combination of native and international grape varieties. The Petra '17 earned a place in our finals. This blend of Cabernet Sauvignon and Merlot features captivating aromas, with minty whiffs that peep out on a fruity blackcurrant and raspberry background, topped off by spicy nuances of juniper. In the mouth it's soft, elegant, with a nice finish. We also appreciated the Quercegobbe '17 with its notes of myrtle and rosemary on a vital, rich palate.

● Petra '17	TT	7
● Alto '17	TT	5
● Potenti '17	TT	5
● Quercegobbe '17	TT	5
● Hebo '18	T	3
● Petra Rosso '16	YYY	8
● Petra Rosso '15	YYY	8
● Petra Rosso '14	YYY	8
● Petra Rosso '13	YYY	8
● Petra Rosso '12	YYY	8
● Alto '16	YY	6
● Colle al Fico '16	YY	6
● Potenti '16	YY	6
● Quercegobbe '16	YY	6
● Suvereto Hebo '17	YY	3

★Fattoria Petrolo

fraz. Mercatale Valdarno
via Petrolo, 30
52021 Bucine [AR]
Tel. +39 0559911322
www.petrolo.it

CELLAR SALES
PRE-BOOKED VISITS
ACCOMMODATION
ANNUAL PRODUCTION 85,000 bottles
HECTARES UNDER VINE 31.00
VITICULTURE METHOD Certified Organic

The farm has been managed by the Bazzocchi-Sanjust family since 1947, when the grandfather of the current owner, Luca Sanjust, bought the 272-hectare estate in an area that has always been marked by quality wine production. In addition to producing wines and extra-virgin olive oil, they now offer elegant accommodations in a very well-maintained natural setting. The turning point for wine production came in the mid-1980s with the revival of the vineyards and the modernization of the cellar. Today their desire to experiment is emerging through the vinification and aging of certain wines in amphora. The Galatrona '17 is a monovarietal Merlot redolent of minerals, ink, pencil lead and ripe black berries. The palate shows nice weight, coming through juicy, elegant and broad. The Boggina A '18 is also excellent. A Sangiovese (matured in terracotta amphorae), it features a fresh bouquet of aromatic herbs, then fruity hints of cherry. In the mouth it's warm, silky in its tannic texture, with lingering olfactory sensations.

● Valdarno di Sopra Merlot Galatrona '17	TTT	8
● Valdarno di Sopra Sangiovese Bòggina A '18	TT	6
○ Bòggina B '18	TT	6
● Valdarno di Sopra Sangiovese Bòggina C '18	TT	6
● Valdarno di Sopra Pietraviva Torrione '18	T	4
● Galatrona '12	YYY	8
● Galatrona '11	YYY	8
● Torrione '11	YYY	5
● Valdarno di Sopra Galatrona '14	YYY	8
● Valdarno di Sopra Galatrona '13	YYY	8
○ Bòggina B '17	YY	6
● Valdarno di Sopra Sangiovese Bòggina A '17	YY	6
● Valdarno di Sopra Sangiovese Bòggina C '17	YY	6

★Piaggia

LOC. POGGETTO
VIA CEGOLI, 47
59016 POGGIO A CAIANO [PO]
TEL. +39 0558705401
www.piaggia.com

CELLAR SALES
PRE-BOOKED VISITS
ANNUAL PRODUCTION 75,000 bottles
HECTARES UNDER VINE 15.00

The estate's vineyards are situated in the municipalities of Poggio a Caiano and Carmignano, and fall within the Carmignano DOCG appellation. The original site was purchased in the mid 1970s by Mauro Vannucci, and just a few years later he decided to look after its vineyards. Today, after other acquisitions, the property has grown to 25 hectares, 15 of which are planted with vines. Sangiovese, Merlot, Cabernet Sauvignon and Cabernet Franc are all grown. Silvia, Mauro's daughter, now runs the estate. By now the winery is a fixture in the Tre Bicchieri club, and it's almost always the Carmignano Riserva that does the honors. The 2017 bewitches the nose with an assorted bouquet of cherry and blackberry, amplified by a delicate balsamic vein and balanced by alluring sanguine hints. Pleasant on the palate, balanced in its elements, it lingers enduringly, with an aftertaste on pleasant spicy notes.

Wine	Rating
● Carmignano Ris. '17	🍷🍷🍷 6
● Poggio de' Colli '17	🍷🍷 8
● Carmignano Il Sasso '18	🍷🍷 4
● Carmignano Ris. '16	🍷🍷🍷 6
● Carmignano Ris. '15	🍷🍷🍷 6
● Carmignano Ris. '14	🍷🍷🍷 6
● Carmignano Ris. '13	🍷🍷🍷 6
● Carmignano Ris. '12	🍷🍷🍷 6
● Carmignano Ris. '11	🍷🍷🍷 6
● Carmignano Ris. '08	🍷🍷🍷 5
● Carmignano Ris. '07	🍷🍷🍷 5
● Carmignano Ris. '99	🍷🍷🍷 5
● Carmignano Ris. '98	🍷🍷🍷 5
● Carmignano Sasso '07	🍷🍷🍷 4
● Il Sasso '01	🍷🍷🍷 4
● Poggio de' Colli '11	🍷🍷🍷 7
● Poggio de' Colli '10	🍷🍷🍷 6

Piancornello

LOC. PIANCORNELLO
53024 MONTALCINO [SI]
TEL. +39 0577844105
www.piancornello.it

CELLAR SALES
PRE-BOOKED VISITS
ANNUAL PRODUCTION 50,000 bottles
HECTARES UNDER VINE 10.00

Without a doubt Piancornello is one of the most charming parts of Montalcino, in particular the wide strip of vineyards that unfolds in the south. A volcanic hill overlooking the Orcia and Asso rivers at around 250 meters elevation, with Mount Amiata protecting the horizon, it's characterized by steep, rocky slopes as well as a sunny climate and constant breezes. It's the perfect setting for the Monaci-Pieri family, owners of the estate since the 1950s, to make the persuasive, tasty Brunello that we've grown so accustomed to. If there were any doubt, Claudio Monaci once again demonstrates his skill for Sangiovese in Montalcino. Taking advantage of the fresh 2018 vintage, Piancornello amazes with an elegant, classic Rosso that puts fruit on center stage, finding its strong point in a subtle, sophisticated tannic weave. Still a bit rough, the powerful and warm Brunello '15 proves rich in aromas of camphor and licorice.

Wine	Rating
● Rosso di Montalcino '18	🍷🍷 4
● Brunello di Montalcino '15	🍷🍷 7
● Brunello di Montalcino '13	🍷🍷🍷 6
● Brunello di Montalcino '10	🍷🍷🍷 6
● Brunello di Montalcino '06	🍷🍷🍷 6
● Brunello di Montalcino '99	🍷🍷🍷 6
● Brunello di Montalcino '12	🍷🍷 6
● Brunello di Montalcino '11	🍷🍷 6
● Brunello di Montalcino '09	🍷🍷 6
● Brunello di Montalcino '08	🍷🍷 6
● Brunello di Montalcino '07	🍷🍷 6
● Brunello di Montalcino '04	🍷🍷 6
● Brunello di Montalcino Ris. '06	🍷🍷 6
● Brunello di Montalcino Ris. '04	🍷🍷 6
● Rosso di Montalcino '15	🍷🍷 3
● Rosso di Montalcino '11	🍷🍷 3
● Rosso di Montalcino '08	🍷🍷 3*

Pianirossi

loc. Porrona
pod. Santa Genoveffa, 1
58044 Cinigiano [GR]
Tel. +39 0564990573
www.pianirossi.it

CELLAR SALES
PRE-BOOKED VISITS
ACCOMMODATION AND RESTAURANT SERVICE
ANNUAL PRODUCTION 50,000 bottles
HECTARES UNDER VINE 14.00
SUSTAINABLE WINERY

Stefano Sincini's winemaking project seems to have found the right direction. The modernist approach that characterized the winery's early days has been shifted and their wines now embrace a more dynamic, convincing style. Located on the hills of Porrona, near Cinigiano, the producer is also looking more closely at Montecucco DOC so as to accompany the IGT wines that have distinguished their range so far. It's a choice to focus on territory and one that will soon be bearing fruit. The work done with Sangiovese is paying off, as evidenced by two successful Montecuccos made with Tuscany's prince grape. The Rosso Sidus '17 features vibrant aromas, which cross fruity hints, notes of spices and a light smokiness. In the mouth it develops balanced and well-sustained, with a vivid, sapid finish. The Sangiovese La Fonte '17 is also well made, exhibiting a greater share of oak and a riper fruitiness.

Wine	Rating
● Montecucco Rosso Sidus '17	3*
● Montecucco Sangiovese La Fonte '17	5
● Pianirossi '17	6
● Solus '16	4*
● Montecucco Rosso Sidus '16	2*
● Montecucco Rosso Sidus '15	2*
● Montecucco Sangiovese La Fonte '16	5
● Montecucco Sangiovese La Fonte '15	5
● Montecucco Sidus '14	2*
● Montecucco Sidus '13	2*
● Pianirossi '16	6
● Pianirossi '12	6
● Pianirossi '11	6
● Solus '14	3
● Solus '12	3
● Solus '11	4

Tenute Piccini

loc. Piazzole, 25
53011 Castellina in Chianti [SI]
Tel. +39 057754011
www.tenutepiccini.it

ANNUAL PRODUCTION 15,000,000 bottles
HECTARES UNDER VINE 470.00

Since the late-19th century a family and brand have been bringing passion to the world of wine. The original seven hectares in the heart of Chianti are now part of a group of five estates, three of which are in Tuscany, one in Basilicata and one in Sicily. Almost thirty different types of wine are produced, with Tuscan reds representing great quantity and fine quality, especially their Sangioveses, which tend to tradition but occasionally exhibit a modern streak (both in terms of taste and aesthetics). Their whites range from the classic Vernaccia to Vermentino. We very much appreciated the Chianti Classico GS 6.38 '16. Intriguing nose of peppers, cherries and assorted spices, from cinnamon to cloves rise up out of the glass. The palate exhibits commendable balance, great aromatic consistency and a lively finish with nice length. The Vino in Musica '16, a blend of equal parts Sangiovese and Cabernet Sauvignon, proves pleasant with fresh vegetal notes and wild berries.

Wine	Rating
● Chianti Cl. Gran Selezione Valiano 6.38 '16	5
● Vino in Musica '16	4
● Chianti Cl. Valiano '17	3
● M.T. Il Pacchia '18	2*
⊙ M.T. Rosato Tenuta Moraia '19	2*
○ M.T. Vermentino Tenuta Moraia '19	2*
● Chianti Cl. Valiano Poggio Teo '17	4
● Chianti Cl. Gran Selezione Valiano 6.38 '15	5
● Chianti Cl. Montegiachi Ris. Geografico '15	4
● Chianti Cl. Valiano '15	3*
● Chianti Cl. Valiano Poggio Teo '16	4
● Chianti Cl. Valiano Poggio Teo '15	4
● Il Pacchia '16	2*
● Sasso al Poggio '16	3

Pietroso

Loc. Pietroso, 257
53024 Montalcino [SI]
Tel. +39 0577848573
www.pietroso.it

CELLAR SALES
PRE-BOOKED VISITS
ANNUAL PRODUCTION 30,000 bottles
HECTARES UNDER VINE 5.00

That wine resembles its makers is an often abused cliché, but it's certainly true when it comes to Gianni Pignattai. Assisted by his wife, Cecilia, as well as their children Andrea and Gloria, he seems to transfer in an entirely natural way his inspired determination into a battery of Rossos and Brunellos that's constantly growing for its consistency and distinctiveness. Four properties are situated throughout Montalcino: Colombaiolo to the south, Fornello and Montosoli to the north, and near the cellar we find their original vineyards (on the western edge of Collina Centrale). Like all Montalcino's vigneron, this year Gianni Pignattai found himself having to present two vintages that were, for different reasons, difficult: the warm 2015 and the cool, rainy 2018. In fact, the Brunello '15 offers an opulent nose with aromas of jam and tannins that are still a bit dry and edgy on the palate. For its part, the Rosso '18 is austere and slightly immature. Both wines will benefit from a longer stay in the bottle.

Wine	Rating
● Brunello di Montalcino '15	▼▼ 6
● Rosso di Montalcino '18	▼ 4
● Brunello di Montalcino '14	▽▽▽ 6
● Brunello di Montalcino '09	▽▽▽ 6
● Brunello di Montalcino '13	▽▽ 6
● Brunello di Montalcino '12	▽▽ 6
● Brunello di Montalcino '11	▽▽ 6
● Brunello di Montalcino '10	▽▽ 6
● Brunello di Montalcino '04	▽▽ 5
● Brunello di Montalcino Ris. '10	▽▽ 6
● Rosso di Montalcino '17	▽▽ 4
● Rosso di Montalcino '16	▽▽ 4
● Rosso di Montalcino '15	▽▽ 4
● Rosso di Montalcino '14	▽▽ 4
● Rosso di Montalcino '11	▽▽ 3*
● Villa Montosoli '15	▽▽ 7
● Villa Montosoli '13	▽ 7

Pieve Santo Stefano

Loc. Sardini
55100 Lucca
Tel. +39 0583394115
www.pievedisantostefano.com

CELLAR SALES
PRE-BOOKED VISITS
ACCOMMODATION
ANNUAL PRODUCTION 45,000 bottles
HECTARES UNDER VINE 10.60
SUSTAINABLE WINERY

Francesca Bogazzi and Antoine Hiriz's winemaking project continues to offer comfortingly reliable quality. The producer's now well-defined style features elegant, balanced and pleasantly drinkable wines. The main varieties used are Sangiovese and Ciliegiolo, with honed support from Cabernet Franc, Merlot and Syrah. A production approach that's never unnecessarily complex is complemented by aging in large and small oak barrels, which situates their wines in a contemporary style but one that's decidedly removed from the excesses of modern winemaking. The Villa Sardini '18 is herbaceous on the nose with a soft, fragrant red fruitiness, peppery hints, and slightly balsamic nuances. In the mouth it unfolds fresh and juicy—a sapid, vibrant drink. The Ludovico Sardini '16 is marked by darker tones and oak, with a close-woven, firm structure. The Lippo '17, a blend of Merlot and Cabernet Franc, proves to have a warmer, sweeter impact.

Wine	Rating
● Colline Lucchesi Ludovico Sardini '16	▼▼ 4
● Colline Lucchesi Villa Sardini '18	▼▼ 2*
● Lippo '17	▼▼ 4
● Colline Lucchesi Ludovico Sardini '15	▽▽ 4
● Colline Lucchesi Ludovico Sardini '13	▽▽ 4
● Colline Lucchesi Ludovico Sardini '12	▽▽ 4
● Colline Lucchesi Villa Sardini '17	▽▽ 2*
● Colline Lucchesi Villa Sardini '16	▽▽ 2*
● Colline Lucchesi Villa Sardini '15	▽▽ 2*
● Colline Lucchesi Villa Sardini '13	▽▽ 2*
● Lippo '16	▽▽ 4
● Lippo '15	▽▽ 4
● Lippo '14	▽▽ 4
● Ludovico Sardini '12	▽▽ 3

Pinino

Loc. Pinino, 327
53024 Montalcino [SI]
Tel. +39 0577849381
www.pinino.com

CELLAR SALES
PRE-BOOKED VISITS
ANNUAL PRODUCTION 90,000 bottles
HECTARES UNDER VINE 16.00

A splendid hillock overlooking Montosoli in the heart of northern Montalcino: this was the site chosen by the 'double couple' formed by Austrians Andrea and Hannes Gamon, and Spaniards Max and Silvia Hernandez. With the help of Enrico Furi and Maurizio Bianchini, in 2003 they bought the estate created by the notary Tito Costanti at the end of the 19th century, then added the Canchi vineyards in the northeast. Together they give rise to bright, wild Sangiovese reds aged in barriques and barrels of different sizes. In the absence of the Brunello Riserva (not produced in the 2014 vintage), the winery presented three different Brunellos. This year our preference goes to the Cupio '15, the most modern and youthful of the winery's crus. It has very clear, fruity scents with spicy traces, and an elegant, expansive palate. More austere sensations characterize the Vigna Pinino. The complex, potent Rosso '18 is a true 'mini' Brunello.

Wine	Rating
● Brunello di Montalcino Cupio '15	▼▼ 5
● Brunello di Montalcino V. Pinino '15	▼▼ 6
● Rosso di Montalcino '18	▼▼ 3
● Brunello di Montalcino '15	▼ 6
● Brunello di Montalcino '14	▽▽ 6
● Brunello di Montalcino '13	▽▽ 6
● Brunello di Montalcino '11	▽▽ 7
● Brunello di Montalcino '10	▽▽ 6
● Brunello di Montalcino '09	▽▽ 6
● Brunello di Montalcino Cupio '14	▽▽ 5
● Brunello di Montalcino Cupio '13	▽▽ 5
● Brunello di Montalcino Pinino '07	▽▽ 6
● Brunello di Montalcino Pinone Ris. '12	▽▽ 7
● Brunello di Montalcino Pinone Ris. '10	▽▽ 8
● Brunello di Montalcino Pinone Ris. '07	▽▽ 7
● Rosso di Montalcino '16	▽▽ 3*
● Rosso di Montalcino '11	▽▽ 3

Podere dell'Anselmo

Loc. Anselmo
via Anselmo Panfi, 12
50025 Montespertoli [FI]
Tel. +39 0571671951
www.poderedellanselmo.it

CELLAR SALES
PRE-BOOKED VISITS
ACCOMMODATION AND RESTAURANT SERVICE
ANNUAL PRODUCTION 40,000 bottles
HECTARES UNDER VINE 13.00
VITICULTURE METHOD Certified Organic
SUSTAINABLE WINERY

The Forconi family have been involved in agriculture since the early 19th century, with specialization in wine arriving more recently. Fabrizio, its current owner, has overseen replanting of the vineyards, opting for a higher density of vines per hectare and equipping the cellar with modern equipment. Organic conversion had already taken place in 2012, pointing up a longstanding commitment to preserving the local environment. In addition to wine, they produce extra-virgin olive oil. Their farm stay accommodations are particularly well developed. The Pax '16 is a highly pleasant blend of Sangiovese, Colorino, Cabernet Franc and Cabernet Sauvignon. Hints of blackberry and currant adorned by spicy hints rise up on a minty, balsamic backdrop. On the palate it's creamy, with smooth tannins and a fresh finish. The Terre di Bracciatica '17, a blend of mostly Sangiovese with a splash of Cabernet Sauvignon, features a classic bouquet of cherry and underbrush.

Wine	Rating
● Era Ora '16	▼▼ 4
● Francò '17	▼▼ 6
● Pax '16	▼▼ 6
● Terre di Bracciatica '17	▼▼ 2*
○ Vin Santo del Chianti Dedicato alla Gioia Ris. '11	▼▼ 5
○ Anselmino '19	▼ 2
● Chianti Montespertoli '18	▼ 2
● Chianti Montespertoli Ingannamatti Ris. '16	▼ 3
● Chianti Montespertoli Ingannamatti Ris. '15	▽▽ 3
● Era Ora '15	▽▽ 4
● Pax '12	▽▽ 6
● Terre di Bracciatica '16	▽▽ 2*
● Terre di Bracciatica '14	▽▽ 2*
○ Vin Santo del Chianti Ris. '09	▽▽ 5

Tenuta Podernovo

via Podernuovo, 13
56030 Terricciola [PI]
Tel. +39 0587655173
www.tenutapodernovo.it

CELLAR SALES
PRE-BOOKED VISITS
ACCOMMODATION
ANNUAL PRODUCTION 140,000 bottles
HECTARES UNDER VINE 25.00
VITICULTURE METHOD Certified Organic

Tenuta Podernovo belongs to the Lunelli family, owners of the Ferrari wineries in Trento and Castelbuono in Umbria. It is a truly beautiful estate, nestled on a hillock planted with vines in the municipality of Terricciola, in the Pisan Hills. The vines grow in sandy soils, rich in fossil deposits, while the winemaking process unfolds in a cellar built with particular attention to the landscape. Their wines are in an exceptional period of qualitative and stylistic growth, both their entry-level wines and their premium offerings. Once again the Teuto delivers, even in the case of a year as complicated as 2017. It's a Sangiovese-based red that includes a share of Merlot and a drop of Cabernet, matured in large barrels and mid-sized casks. It features vibrant, fruity aromas of mulberry, with hints of roasted coffee and refreshing herbaceous and balsamic sensations. On the palate it's tight, with hints of raspberry gelée.

Wine	Rating
● Teuto '17	🍷🍷 5
● Aliotto '17	🍷🍷 3
● Auritea '17	🍷🍷 8
● Auritea '16	ꝎꝎꝎ 8
● Aliotto '16	ꝎꝎ 3
● Aliotto '15	ꝎꝎ 3
● Auritea '15	ꝎꝎ 8
● Teuto '16	ꝎꝎ 5
● Teuto '15	ꝎꝎ 5

Podernuovo a Palazzone

loc. Le Vigne, 203
53040 San Casciano dei Bagni [SI]
Tel. +39 057856056
www.podernuovoapalazzone.com

ANNUAL PRODUCTION 130,000 bottles
HECTARES UNDER VINE 20.00
SUSTAINABLE WINERY

Giovanni Bulgari is the owner of Podernuovo in Palazzone, having founded the winery with his father Paolo. In love with country life, they decided to invest in a territory straddling Lazio, Umbria and Tuscany, one that wasn't so well known, but certainly extraordinary. The first steps were taken in 2004, with the removal of the existing, though abandoned, vineyards, and the planting of new rows. Sangiovese was the main grape chosen, but there are also international varieties such as Cabernet and Petit Verdot, in addition to Italy's Montepulciano. The first bottles were released in 2012. The Argirio '16 is a highly pleasant monovarietal Cabernet Franc with a captivating nose. It offers up earthy sensations, aromatic herbs (bay leaves) and spices, with a balsamic hint of juniper. The body is plastic, balanced, with fine, well-calibrated tannins and a refreshing finish—an excellent drink. The appealing Sotirio '15, 100% Sangiovese, is mineral and fruity, with a lively, subtle and long body.

Wine	Rating
● Argirio '16	🍷🍷 6
● Sotirio '15	🍷🍷 7
● Therra '15	🍷🍷 5
○ Bianco Nico Leo '18	🍷 2
● Argirio '13	ꝎꝎ 6
● Therra '13	ꝎꝎ 5

Poggerino

LOC. POGGERINO, 6
53017 RADDA IN CHIANTI [SI]
TEL. +39 0577738958
www.poggerino.com

CELLAR SALES
PRE-BOOKED VISITS
ACCOMMODATION
ANNUAL PRODUCTION 60,000 bottles
HECTARES UNDER VINE 12.20
VITICULTURE METHOD Certified Organic

A winery run by siblings Piero and Benedetta Lanza, Poggerino represents the best of the Radda in Chianti subzone, at least if you are looking for Chianti Classico that's capable of combining texture, density and elegance. In short, here they produce judiciously modern Sangiovese reds capable of blending the typical features of the area with a certain fullness and roundness, without excesses, and striking a notable, overall balance. Their vineyards are cultivated organically, while in the cellar aging is carried out in barriques and mid-sized casks. The Chianti Classico Bugialla Riserva '17 successfully interprets the difficult vintage: on the nose it's vibrant, marked by lush fruitiness and toasty notes, while in the mouth it develops broad, with oak in the foreground, making for a compact, vivid palate. Dark aromas characterize the Chianti Classico '18, which finds its strong point on the palate where it proves a docile, fragrant drink.

Wine	Rating	Price
● Chianti Cl. Bugialla Ris. '17	🍷🍷	6
● Chianti Cl. '18	🍷🍷	4
● Chianti Cl. Bugialla Ris. '13	YYY	5
● Chianti Cl. Bugialla Ris. '12	YYY	5
● Chianti Cl. Bugialla Ris. '09	YYY	5
● Chianti Cl. Bugialla Ris. '08	YYY	5
● Chianti Cl. Ris. '90	YYY	4*
● Chianti Cl. '16	YY	4
● Chianti Cl. '15	YY	4
● Chianti Cl. '13	YY	4
● Chianti Cl. '12	YY	3*
● Chianti Cl. Bugialla Ris. '16	YY	6
● Chianti Cl. Bugialla Ris. '15	YY	6
● Chianti Cl. Bugialla Ris. '14	YY	6
● Chianti Cl. Bugialla Ris. '10	YY	5

Poggio al Tesoro

FRAZ. DONORATICO
VIA DEL FOSSO, 33
57022 CASTAGNETO CARDUCCI [LI]
TEL. +39 0565773051
www.poggioaltesoro.it

CELLAR SALES
PRE-BOOKED VISITS
ANNUAL PRODUCTION 500,000 bottles
HECTARES UNDER VINE 67.50

The Allegrini brand is among Italian wine's absolute leaders, starting with the parent company in Valpolicella. From the great red wines of Verona, like Amarone, to the best of Bolgheri, there wasn't far to go. We can say, in fact, that today the family's Tuscan winery is among the most reputable in the area. The soils on which their grapes grow are quite mixed, from areas rich in pebbles and clay to more sandy types. By now their wines are impeccable and rich in personality, starting with truly charming aromatic profiles. The Bolgheri Rosso Il Seggio '17 performed quite well: fresh both in terms of aroma and taste, it manages to maintain its Mediterranean profile while flesh turns creamy and rich in juice, accompanied by cosseting tannins. It's made with Merlot, Cabernet Sauvignon and Franc, and Petit Verdot grapes from their four main vineyards. The Superiore Sondraia '17 sees notes of printer's ink and black berry fruit stand out on a rather extractive profile.

Wine	Rating	Price
● Bolgheri Rosso Il Seggio '17	🍷🍷	4
● Bolgheri Rosso Sup. Sondraia '17	🍷🍷	7
○ Bolgheri Vermentino Solosole '19	🍷🍷	4
● Mediterra '18	🍷🍷	3
⊙ Bolgheri Rosato Cassiopea '19	🍷	3
● Bolgheri Rosso Sup. Dedicato a Walter '16	🍷	7
● Bolgheri Rosso Sup. Sondraia '16	YYY	7
● Bolgheri Rosso Sup. Sondraia '15	YYY	7
● Bolgheri Sup. Sondraia '14	YYY	5
● Bolgheri Sup. Sondraia '13	YYY	5
● Bolgheri Rosso Sup. Dedicato a Walter '15	YY	7
○ Bolgheri Vermentino Solosole '18	YY	4

★Poggio Antico

Loc. Poggio Antico
53024 Montalcino [SI]
Tel. +39 0577848044
www.poggioantico.com

CELLAR SALES
PRE-BOOKED VISITS
RESTAURANT SERVICE
ANNUAL PRODUCTION 120,000 bottles
HECTARES UNDER VINE 32.00

In many ways the enclave that has for decades given rise to Poggio Antico's original Brunellos is unique. On the one hand, there's the influence of the nearby Tyrrhenian Sea and its sunny position in western Montalcino, on the other there's its breezy mesoclimate and elevations that reach almost 500 meters. It's a special mix of Mediterranean grace and hillside finesse that led the Belgian holding company AtlasInvest to acquire the estate from Paola Godler and Alberto Montefiori, entrusting Federico Trost and Pier Giuseppe D'Alessandro with technical oversight of their new direction. The performance put in by Poggio Antico's wines can reassure everyone: the change of ownership hasn't had any repercussions. We appreciated the Brunello '15 for its complexity on the nose, where aromas of red berries stand out together with tobacco, all enriched by hints of coffee cream. All their wines are characterized by the terroir's fresh acidity, and a rich, fruity pulp that counteracts tannic presence, but the Altero is still evolving towards an optimal olfactory harmony.

- ● Brunello di Montalcino '15 — TT 8
- ● Brunello di Montalcino Altero '15 — TT 8
- ● Rosso di Montalcino '18 — TT 5
- ● Brunello di Montalcino '05 — YYY 7
- ● Brunello di Montalcino '88 — YYY 7
- ● Brunello di Montalcino '85 — YYY 7
- ● Brunello di Montalcino Altero '09 — YYY 7
- ● Brunello di Montalcino Altero '07 — YYY 8
- ● Brunello di Montalcino Altero '06 — YYY 8
- ● Brunello di Montalcino Altero '04 — YYY 8
- ● Brunello di Montalcino Altero '99 — YYY 8
- ● Brunello di Montalcino Ris. '01 — YYY 7
- ● Brunello di Montalcino Ris. '85 — YYY 7
- ● Brunello di Montalcino '13 — YY 8
- ● Brunello di Montalcino Altero '13 — YY 8
- ● Rosso di Montalcino '17 — YY 5
- ● Rosso di Montalcino '16 — YY 5

Poggio Argentiera

fraz. Alberese
s.da Banditella Due
58100 Grosseto
Tel. +39 3484952767
www.poggioargentiera.com

CELLAR SALES
PRE-BOOKED VISITS
ACCOMMODATION
ANNUAL PRODUCTION 200,000 bottles
HECTARES UNDER VINE 22.00
VITICULTURE METHOD Certified Organic

The winery got its start in 1997 with the purchase of the Adua farm, a property dating back to the land reclamation of the early 1900s. The choice was to invest in Morellino di Scansano, though the property expanded in 2001 thanks to another plot called Keeling, in addition to further acquisitions that brought Poggio Argentiera to its current size. Part of the vineyards are located close to the sea, on loamy and sandy soils, while the rest can be found in the hills, on decidedly stony terrain. The Capatosta '17, made with Sangiovese and Alicante, landed in our finals. A variegated bouquet sees sensations of Mediterranean scrub together with tobacco, coffee and ripe cherries. On the palate it's polished, austere with an intriguing balsamic finish. The Poggio Raso '17 also delivered. It's a Cabernet Franc with aromas of oregano, plum, pepper and minty hints; the palate is compact, with hints of licorice and ripe berries emerging. We shouldn't forge their well-made 2019 Morellinos either.

- ● Capatosta '17 — TT 2*
- ● Morellino di Scansano '19 — TT 3
- ● Morellino di Scansano Bellamarsilia '19 — TT 4
- ● Poggio Raso '17 — TT 5
- ● Maremmante '19 — T 4
- ○ Vermentino '19 — T 3
- ● Finisterre '07 — YYY 6
- ● Maremmante '16 — YY 4
- ● Maremmante '15 — YY 2*
- ● Morellino di Scansano Bellamarsilia '16 — YY 4
- ● Morellino di Scansano Bellamarsilia '13 — YY 3*
- ● Morellino di Scansano Capatosta '15 — YY 6
- ● Morellino di Scansano Capatosta '13 — YY 5
- ● Podere Adua '16 — YY 5

Fattoria Poggio Capponi

via Montelupo, 184
50025 Montespertoli [FI]
Tel. +39 0571671914
www.poggiocapponi.it

CELLAR SALES
PRE-BOOKED VISITS
ACCOMMODATION
ANNUAL PRODUCTION 200,000 bottles
HECTARES UNDER VINE 32.00

It turns out that Poggio Capponi is both beautiful and cinematic. Because of its architecture and the natural landscape, the estate has been chosen as the setting for successful films. The Rousseau Colzi family has owned it for almost a century, producing wine, oil and wheat here on the hills near Florence. Many varieties are cultivated, from Tuscany's most common red varieties (such as Sangiovese, Colorino, Canaiolo), to international grapes (Merlot, Syrah, Alicante Bouchet), to white cultivars like Trebbiano, Chardonnay, San Colombano, Malvasia and Vermentino. The Chianti '18 is surprising in a positive way. It features a multifaceted aromatic suite in which cherry prevails, nicely adorned by sensations of aromatic herbs, such as thyme and mint. In the mouth it opens supple, generous but without excesses, with nice supporting acidity and a clean, progressively unfolding finish. We very much appreciated the Sovente '19 as well. It's a monovarietal Chardonnay characterized by notes of tropical fruits, white pepper and plenty of juice.

Wine	Rating
○ Bianco di Binto '19	▼▼ 2*
● Chianti '18	▼▼ 2*
● Chianti Montespertoli Petriccio Ris. '17	▼▼ 3
○ Sovente Chardonnay '19	▼▼ 2*
○ Vin Santo del Chianti '12	▼▼ 6
● Chianti Ris. '17	▼ 3
● Michelangelo '19	▼ 2
⊙ Rosé '19	▼ 2
○ Bianco di Binto '18	▽▽ 2*
● Chianti Ris. '16	▽▽ 3
○ Sovente Chardonnay '18	▽▽ 2*
○ Sovente Chardonnay '16	▽▽ 2*
● Tinorso '16	▽▽ 3
● Tinorso '15	▽▽ 3
○ Vin Santo del Chianti '16	▽▽ 6

★Poggio di Sotto

fraz. Castelnuovo dell'Abate
loc. Poggio di Sotto
53024 Montalcino [SI]
Tel. +39 0577835502
www.collemassari.it

CELLAR SALES
PRE-BOOKED VISITS
ANNUAL PRODUCTION 30,000 bottles
HECTARES UNDER VINE 16.00
VITICULTURE METHOD Certified Organic

Situated at elevations of around 450 meters on tough soils rich in clay and marl, Poggio di Sotto is one of the most important outposts of Castelnuovo dell'Abate, the human and production capital of Montalcino's southeast. The passage from founder Piero Palmucci to the Tipa family has given a further boost to the stylistic awareness with which their magnificent 'Sangiovese Grosso' trio is made. Their Rosso, Brunello and Brunello Riserva are all unmistakable for their fruity clarity, extractive grace and three-dimensional depth of flavor. Thanks to two splendid Sangiovese di Montalcinos, the winery once again demonstrates why it's one of the appellation's leaders. A well-deserved Tre Bicchieri for the Brunello '15, which opens on fruity notes of cherry, continuing with hints of tobacco and liquorice and closing on enticing, sanguine sensations. In the mouth it impresses, culminating in a finale of great personality. True to its fame, the Rosso '17 proves powerful and sophisticated, as always.

Wine	Rating
● Brunello di Montalcino '15	▼▼▼ 8
● Rosso di Montalcino Ciampoleto Tenuta San Giorgio '18	▼▼ 3*
● Brunello di Montalcino Ugolforte Tenuta San Giorgio '15	▼▼ 7
● Rosso di Montalcino '17	▼▼ 8
● Brunello di Montalcino '14	▽▽▽ 8
● Brunello di Montalcino '12	▽▽▽ 8
● Brunello di Montalcino '11	▽▽▽ 8
● Brunello di Montalcino '10	▽▽▽ 8
● Brunello di Montalcino '07	▽▽▽ 8
● Brunello di Montalcino '04	▽▽▽ 8
● Brunello di Montalcino '99	▽▽▽ 8
● Brunello di Montalcino Ris. '12	▽▽▽ 8
● Brunello di Montalcino Ris. '07	▽▽▽ 8
● Brunello di Montalcino Ris. '99	▽▽▽ 8
● Brunello di Montalcino Ris. '95	▽▽▽ 8

Poggio La Noce

loc. Ontignano
via Paiatici, 29
50014 Fiesole [FI]
Tel. +39 0556549113
www.poggiolanoce.com

CELLAR SALES
PRE-BOOKED VISITS
ANNUAL PRODUCTION 10,000 bottles
HECTARES UNDER VINE 2.50
VITICULTURE METHOD Certified Organic

Many Florentines don't know it, but Poggio La Noce is located in the municipality of Fiesole, surrounded by greenery just a few kilometers from the city. The property is the dream-come-true of Claire Beliard and Enzo Schiano, a couple in life and work, who in 1999 bought the land to plant the vineyards. They have clear ideas about agriculture, and since as far back as 2006 production has been certified organic. Their grapes grow in soils mainly composed of marl and alberese, rich in pebbles and limestone. Made with Sangiovese and Colorino, the Gigetto '17 features a multifaceted bouquet of camphor, red and black wild berries. In the mouth it opens silky, flowing fresh, calibrated, with a captivating aftertaste of cherry. The Gigiò '17, mostly Sangiovese, offers up suggestions of rosemary, hazelnut and ripe cherries; on the palate it shows lovely verve, dynamism and cleanness. The Paonazzo '16 and the Vin Santo Occhio di Pernice '13 are also excellent.

Wine	Rating
● Gigetto '17	🍷🍷 4
● Gigiò '16	🍷🍷 6
● Paonazzo '16	🍷🍷 7
● Vin Santo del Chianti Occhio di Pernice '13	🍷🍷 5
⊙ Pinko Pallino '19	🍷 3
○ Spumante Metodo Ancestrale Frizzante Rosato Pet Golò '19	🍷 4
● Gigetto '16	🍸🍸 4
● Gigetto '15	🍸🍸 4
● Gigino '16	🍸🍸 5
● Gigino '15	🍸🍸 5
● Gigiò '15	🍸🍸 6
● Vin Santo del Chianti Occhio di Pernice Ejià '11	🍸🍸 5

Poggio Landi

loc. Podere Belvedere
fraz. Torrenieri
s.da prov.le 71
53024 Montalcino [SI]
Tel. +39 0577042736

ANNUAL PRODUCTION 90,000 bottles
HECTARES UNDER VINE 74.00

Poggio Landi is a renowned Montalcino winery that for some years now has been part of Alejandro Bulgheroni Family Vineyards Italia. The viticultural and territorial context in which they operate is multifaceted, to say the least, and expressed through their increasingly persuasive range. In the hills they've chosen to diversify the elevations, positions and microclimates of their vineyards. This allows them to vary the harvest times and expressive characteristics of the Sangiovese used for their Brunello, which matures in 3000 and 5400 liter French oak barrels. Poggio Landi, like Podere Brizio (also in Montalcino), is growing in quality. This year's tastings made a positive impression. The Brunello '15, made through spontaneous fermentation without selected yeasts, punches above its weight, with delicious aromas of cherry and plum, but also medicinal herbs and a juicy and deep palate, where the tannic texture is progressive and refined.

Wine	Rating
● Brunello di Montalcino '15	🍷🍷 7
● Brunello di Montalcino Podere Brizio '15	🍷🍷 6
● Rosso di Montalcino Podere Brizio '18	🍷🍷 4
● Rosso di Montalcino '18	🍷 4
● Brunello di Montalcino '13	🍸🍸 7
● Brunello di Montalcino '12	🍸🍸 7
● Brunello di Montalcino Ris. '13	🍸🍸 7
● Brunello di Montalcino Ris. '12	🍸🍸 7
● Rosso di Montalcino '17	🍸🍸 4
● Rosso di Montalcino '16	🍸🍸 4

Podere Poggio Scalette

LOC. RUFFOLI
VIA BARBIANO, 7
50022 GREVE IN CHIANTI [FI]
TEL. +39 0558546108
www.poggioscalette.it

CELLAR SALES
PRE-BOOKED VISITS
ANNUAL PRODUCTION 60,000 bottles
HECTARES UNDER VINE 13.50

Owned by the Fiore family since 1991, Poggio Scalette is situated on the Ruffoli hill in the subzone of Greve in Chianti, a place historically well suited to wine-growing. The producer embarked on a path of sustainable agriculture, one with a very low environmental impact. Their wines are part of the district's enological history, especially the 'Supertuscan' label. It's a style that is still very much alive and aptly characterizes their approach, although today new directions seem to be emerging. The Capogatto, a blend of Merlot, Cabernet Sauvignon, Cabernet Franc and Petit Verdot, is a clear homage to the Bordeaux model. The 2017 sees richly spicy and fruity aromas introduce a well-balanced gustatory progression, dynamic and full of contrast. The historic monovarietal Sangiovese, Il Carbonaione '17, is also impeccably executed, with just a few notes of oak in excess. The Piantonaia '17, 100% Merlot, proves pervasive and tasty.

- ● Capogatto '17 ▼▼ 7
- ● Il Carbonaione '17 ▼▼ 7
- ● Piantonaia '17 ▼▼ 8
- ● Chianti Cl. '18 ▼ 3
- ● Il Carbonaione '08 ▽▽▽ 6
- ● Il Carbonaione '05 ▽▽▽ 6
- ● Il Carbonaione '03 ▽▽▽ 7
- ● Il Carbonaione '00 ▽▽▽ 7
- ● Il Carbonaione '98 ▽▽▽ 6
- ● Il Carbonaione '96 ▽▽▽ 6
- ● Capogatto '16 ▽▽ 7
- ● Capogatto '15 ▽▽ 7
- ● Capogatto '14 ▽▽ 7
- ● Chianti Cl. '17 ▽▽ 3
- ● Chianti Cl. '15 ▽▽ 3
- ● Il Carbonaione '14 ▽▽ 7
- ● Il Carbonaione '11 ▽▽ 6

Poggio Sorbello

FRAZ. CENTOIA
LOC. CASE SPARSE, 168
52044 CORTONA [AR]
TEL. +39 3395447059
www.poggiosorbello.it

CELLAR SALES
ANNUAL PRODUCTION 10,000 bottles
HECTARES UNDER VINE 9.00
SUSTAINABLE WINERY

The winery belongs to the family of Felice Baldetti, who settled this strip of land straddling the provinces of Arezzo, Siena and Perugia in the early 20th century. In the mid-1990s, the groundwork for a modern winery was laid. The planting of new vines drew on both native varieties and international cultivars, while the next turning point came in 2014, with the construction of their current cellar. Their wines are the result of a careful selection of the grapes harvested, with the rest being sold. The interesting Syrah Gortinaia '17 surprises the nose with vegetal notes of tomato leaves, then cherry and spicy hints of nutmeg. The palate is linear, fresh, simple—an excellent drink. We appreciated the Merlot Donetto '17 for its spicy aromas of cinnamon and cloves, all on a bed of red berries. Soft in the mouth, it's juicy and warm, highly drinkable.

- ● Boschi ai Filari '17 ▼▼ 3
- ● Cortona Merlot Donetto '17 ▼▼ 4
- ● Cortona Syrah Gortinaia '17 ▼▼ 4
- ● Cortona Cabernet Sauvignon Fossa Granaia '17 ▼ 4
- ● Boschi ai Filari '16 ▽▽ 3
- ● Boschi ai Filari '15 ▽▽ 3
- ● Cortona Cabernet Sauvignon Fossa Granaia '16 ▽▽ 4
- ● Cortona Cabernet Sauvignon Fossa Granaia '15 ▽▽ 4
- ● Cortona Syrah Gortinaia '16 ▽▽ 4
- ● Cortona Syrah Gortinaia '15 ▽▽ 4

Tenuta Il Poggione

Fraz. Sant'Angelo in Colle
Loc. Monteano
53024 Montalcino [SI]
Tel. +39 0577844029
www.tenutailpoggione.it

CELLAR SALES
PRE-BOOKED VISITS
ACCOMMODATION
ANNUAL PRODUCTION 600,000 bottles
HECTARES UNDER VINE 127.00

Owned by the Franceschi family for five generations, the properties of Il Poggione are concentrated in the southern part of Montalcino, particularly in Sant'Angelo in Colle, a well-suited area. More than a hundred hectares of vineyards are cultivated mainly with Sangiovese (with small amounts of Merlot, Vermentino and Chardonnay), making it one of the area's historic agricultural juggernauts. Overseen with skillful mastery by Fabrizio Bindocci, their commendable range of wines is led by generous, captivating Brunellos. These mature in 3000 and 5000 liter French oak barrels. Poggione's 2015 is a generous, exuberant Brunello, rich in notes of red fruit and spices, then veering to oak. It's intense and pulpy on the palate, characterized by vivacious tannins that are still struggling to find the right harmony. It's just a matter of time. The Rosso '18 is very pleasant in its red berry sensations and chocolaty hints, but the whole range is quite valid, from their classic bubbly to the Vin Santo Riserva.

Wine	Rating
● Brunello di Montalcino '15	▼▼ 7
⊙ Marchesa Clementina Rosé Pas Dosé M. Cl.	▼▼ 5
○ Moscadello Frizzante '19	▼▼ 4
● Rosso di Montalcino '18	▼▼ 4
○ Sant'Antimo Vin Santo Ris. '07	▼▼ 7
● Il Poggione '18	▼ 2
⊙ Lo Sbrancato '19	▼ 3
● Brunello di Montalcino '14	▽▽ 7
● Brunello di Montalcino '13	▽▽ 7
● Brunello di Montalcino '12	▽▽ 7
● Rosso di Montalcino '17	▽▽ 4
● Rosso di Montalcino '16	▽▽ 4
● Rosso di Montalcino '14	▽▽ 4

★★Poliziano

Fraz. Montepulciano Stazione
via Fontago, 1
53045 Montepulciano [SI]
Tel. +39 0578738171
www.carlettipoliziano.com

CELLAR SALES
PRE-BOOKED VISITS
ANNUAL PRODUCTION 650,000 bottles
HECTARES UNDER VINE 145.00

Founded in 1961 from an original plot of 22 hectares, Poliziano has grown a lot over the years. But it's not just its increase in size that highlights the importance of the estate within Nobile di Montepulciano: since the 1980s Federico Carletti has been building a real top player among Italian producers. It is one of few wineries that represents the rise of Tuscan wine and with it completely new and highly competitive paradigms. The Nobile Le Caggiole once again proves to be a benchmark for Montepulciano. The 2017 version also performs on a very high level, with a fruity and spicy aromatic profile of great finesse and intensity, heralding a juicy palate, at times almost velvety and highly pleasant. The Nobile Asinone '17 is no less good, but it's their entire range that shines for its reliability and expressive consistency.

Wine	Rating
● Nobile di Montepulciano Le Caggiole '17	▼▼▼ 4*
● Nobile di Montepulciano Asinone '17	▼▼ 7
● Nobile di Montepulciano '17	▼▼ 5
● Rosso di Montepulciano '19	▼▼ 3
● Cortona Merlot In Violas '16	▼ 5
● Le Stanze '17	▼ 7
● Maremma Toscana Cabernet Mandrone di Lohsa '17	▼ 5
● Nobile di Montepulciano '09	▽▽▽ 4*
● Nobile di Montepulciano Asinone '14	▽▽▽ 7
● Nobile di Montepulciano Asinone '12	▽▽▽ 7
● Nobile di Montepulciano Le Caggiole '16	▽▽▽ 4*
● Nobile di Montepulciano Le Caggiole '15	▽▽▽ 4*

Pomona

LOC. POMONA, 39
S.DA CHIANTIGIANA
53011 CASTELLINA IN CHIANTI [SI]
TEL. +39 0577740473
www.fattoriapomona.it

CELLAR SALES
PRE-BOOKED VISITS
ACCOMMODATION
ANNUAL PRODUCTION 16,000 bottles
HECTARES UNDER VINE 4.70
VITICULTURE METHOD Certified Organic

Chianti's defining feature is the fact that vineyards share the landscape with olive trees and oaks, a fact that the most demanding wine lovers hope to encounter in the glass. Villa Pomona pretty much sums all of this up. The winery overseen by Monica Raspi, which applies organic protocols in the countryside and a minimally-invasive approach in the cellar, is in fact one of the best examples of enological craftsmanship in Castellina in Chianti, consistently proving to be among the most notable of the appellation in terms of coherence and quality. Although the child of a complicated vintage (to say the least), the Chianti Classico '17 certainly doesn't exhibit a predictable profile. Aromatically it's clear and well delineated, with vibrant, well-sustained fruit, even on the palate, where it proves forthright, balanced and not without contrast. We also appreciated the pleasant, well-made Cabernet Sauvignon '18, with its generous and generally broad palate, and a spicy aromatic suite adorned by herbaceous hints.

Wine	Rating
● Chianti Cl. '17	🍷🍷 3*
● Cabernet Sauvignon '18	🍷🍷 3
● Piero Rosso '18	🍷 2
● Chianti Cl. '13	YYY 3*
● Chianti Cl. '12	YYY 3*
● Chianti Cl. Ris. '16	YYY 4*
● Chianti Cl. Ris. '14	YYY 4*
● Chianti Cl. '16	YY 3*
● Chianti Cl. '15	YY 3
● Chianti Cl. '14	YY 3
● Chianti Cl. '11	YY 3
● Chianti Cl. Ris. '15	YY 4
● Chianti Cl. Ris. '13	YY 4
● Chianti Cl. Ris. '12	YY 4
● Chianti Cl. Ris. '11	YY 4
● Chianti Cl. Ris. '10	YY 4
● Piero Rosso '16	YY 3

Tenuta Le Potazzine

LOC. LE PRATA, 262
53024 MONTALCINO [SI]
TEL. +39 0577846168
www.lepotazzine.it

CELLAR SALES
PRE-BOOKED VISITS
RESTAURANT SERVICE
ANNUAL PRODUCTION 50,000 bottles
HECTARES UNDER VINE 4.70

If Le Potazzine's Sangiovese were a painting, it would have lively pastel colors, starting with the name itself. Indeed, Sofia and Viola Gorelli's grandmother used the term 'potazzina', a local bird, as a term of endearment for the pair when they were young. Today they are at the helm, together with their mother, Gigliola Giannetti. But above all, theirs is an expressive identity made up of floral clarity, citrus finesse and harmony, all of which we find regularly in their Rosso and Brunello, made with grapes cultivated in Le Prata (where the cellar is located, at about 500 meters above sea level) and Sant'Angelo in Colle. Leading the line-up presented this year is a magnificent Rosso di Montalcino '18. It enchants for the peculiarity of its aromas and strong olfactory personality, and for the carefree seriousness of its palate. The nose features fascinating balsamic and minty whiffs, while the palate exhibits a nice, sapid sensation. The Brunello sees a vibrant, harmonic nose rich in hints of fruit followed by a long palate on a background of alcohol.

Wine	Rating
● Rosso di Montalcino '18	🍷🍷 4
● Brunello di Montalcino '15	🍷🍷 7
● Brunello di Montalcino '10	YYY 7
● Brunello di Montalcino '08	YYY 7
● Brunello di Montalcino Ris. '11	YYY 8
● Brunello di Montalcino Ris. '06	YYY 8
● Brunello di Montalcino '14	YY 7
● Brunello di Montalcino '13	YY 7
● Brunello di Montalcino '12	YY 7
● Brunello di Montalcino '11	YY 7
● Brunello di Montalcino '09	YY 7
● Rosso di Montalcino '16	YY 4
● Rosso di Montalcino '15	YY 4
● Rosso di Montalcino '14	YY 4
● Rosso di Montalcino '13	YY 4
● Rosso di Montalcino '12	YY 4

Tenuta Prima Pietra

loc. I Prati
56046 Riparbella [PI]
Tel. +39 05771913750
www.tenutaprimapietra.com

ANNUAL PRODUCTION 40,000 bottles
HECTARES UNDER VINE 11.00

After Castiglion del Bosco, Massimo Ferragamo acquired another estate on the Pisan Hills. It's Prima Pietra, which boasts 11 hectares dedicated to international varieties in a beautiful position. Here, at 450 meters above sea level, the vineyards face east, looking out towards the nearby Tyrrhenian Sea. The characteristics of the clay-rich soils, the play of air currents, and considerable temperature fluctuations lend structure, depth and finesse to Prima Pietra's wines. Their beautiful, new cellar was recently completed. Even with a complicated vintage like 2017, their vineyards have reached a period of peak maturity and are giving rise to excellent grapes, as evidenced by our tastings. This red, made primarily with Merlot and Cabernet Sauvignon (with splashes of Cabernet Franc and Petit Verdot), pours a beautiful, dark and deep ruby red. The nose is tightly woven with black fruits, such as plum, blackberry and blackcurrant, then notes of chocolate, mint and cigar box. The palate is compact and pulpy, its fruit creamy and crunchy, making for a sapid, soft wine.

● Prima Pietra '17	🍷🍷 8
● Prima Pietra '16	🍷🍷 8
● Prima Pietra '15	🍷🍷 8

★Fattoria Le Pupille

fraz. Istia d'Ombrone
loc. Piagge del Maiano, 92a
58100 Grosseto
Tel. +39 0564409517
www.fattorialepupille.it

CELLAR SALES
PRE-BOOKED VISITS
ACCOMMODATION
ANNUAL PRODUCTION 450,000 bottles
HECTARES UNDER VINE 80.00

Fattoria Le Pupille has done plenty for the territory, so much so that it's become virtually synonymous with Morellino, especially abroad. This is, in a nutshell, the value of Elisabetta Geppetti's winery, which has managed to offer an extremely solid range of wines consistently since 1985. Generous oak is a defining characteristic, along with the pursuit of ripe fruit and a strong pressure accompanied by easier drinking, even when it comes to their weightier wines. These last are consistently among the best in Maremma. Warm and satisfying on the palate, the Saffredi '17 exhibits a lush fruitiness on the nose, accompanied by spices and smoky hints. The highly drinkable Morellino di Scansano '19 is as fragrant and sapid in the mouth as it is open and vivid aromatically. The Morellino di Scansano Riserva '17 features floral aromas that cross with toasty hints and Mediterranean scrub. The new Syrah, a 2015, is outstanding, exhibiting plenty of character and lovely spicy hints.

● Morellino di Scansano '19	🍷🍷 3*
● Saffredi '17	🍷🍷 8
● Syrah '15	🍷🍷 8
● Morellino di Scansano Ris. '17	🍷🍷 4
● Pelofino '19	🍷 2
● Poggio Valente Sangiovese '17	🍷 6
● Morellino di Scansano Poggio Valente '04	🍷🍷🍷 5
● Morellino di Scansano Poggio Valente '99	🍷🍷🍷 5
● Morellino di Scansano Ris. '15	🍷🍷🍷 4*
● Saffredi '14	🍷🍷🍷 8
● Saffredi '13	🍷🍷🍷 8
● Saffredi '05	🍷🍷🍷 8
● Saffredi '04	🍷🍷🍷 8
● Saffredi '03	🍷🍷🍷 8
● Saffredi '02	🍷🍷🍷 7

La Querce

via Imprunetana per Tavarnuzze, 41
50023 Impruneta [FI]
Tel. +39 0552011380
www.laquerce.com

CELLAR SALES
PRE-BOOKED VISITS
ACCOMMODATION
ANNUAL PRODUCTION 35,000 bottles
HECTARES UNDER VINE 7.60

The Marchi family's La Querce is comprised of 42 hectares of vineyards that enjoy favorable expositions, especially at midday. On the property, which is situated on a hill overlooking Impruneta, in Chianti Colli Fiorentini, the use of chemicals is kept to a minimum. 8 hectares are cultivated with Sangiovese, Canaiolo, Colorino and Merlot, at times matured in terracotta. There are 2 cellars, one for vinification and maturing, the other for aging, under the villa. There are guest accommodations as well The La Querce '16 is a delicious blend of Sangiovese with a splash of Colorino. It has an enticing aromatic bouquet in which notes of curry plant and myrtle prevail on a well-calibrated fruity background. On the palate it proves firm, with a nicely crafted tannic weave, a supple body and a weighty finish. The aromatically captivating Canaiolo Belrosso '19 is a juicy, highly drinkable wine.

Wine	Rating
● La Querce '16	▼▼ 5
● Belrosso '19	▼▼ 2*
● Dama Rosa Canaiolo Passito '18	▼▼ 5
● M Merlot '15	▼▼ 6
● Chianti Colli Fiorentini La Torretta Ris. '17	▼ 3
● Chianti Colli Fiorentini La Torretta Ris. '15	▽▽▽ 3*
● La Querce '11	▽▽▽ 5
● Chianti Colli Fiorentini La Torretta Ris. '16	▽▽ 3
● Chianti Sorrettole '16	▽▽ 2*
● Chianti Sorrettole '15	▽▽ 2*
● La Querce '15	▽▽ 5
● La Querce '12	▽▽ 5
● La Querce '10	▽▽ 5

★Querciabella

via di Barbiano, 17
50022 Greve in Chianti [FI]
Tel. +39 05585927777
www.querciabella.com

CELLAR SALES
PRE-BOOKED VISITS
ANNUAL PRODUCTION 300,000 bottles
HECTARES UNDER VINE 112.00
VITICULTURE METHOD Certified Organic

Querciabella is part of Chianti Classico's epic history, at least since the start of the so-called Tuscan wine 'Renaissance'. Founded in 1974 by Giuseppe 'Pepito' Castiglioni, and now run by his son Sebastiano, it has been cultivating its vineyards organically since 1988 and biodynamically since 2000. In 1997 they acquired 30 hectares of vineyards in Maremma, near the Alberese Park. The original plots are located on the Ruffoli hill, which rises up to 600 meters elevation in Greve in Chianti area and overlooks the beautiful Lamole. Historically associated with elegance, the Camartina is a blend of Sangiovese and Cabernet Sauvignon. With the 2016 version, we find the wine in excellent form: aromatically it's broad and sweet, with a nuanced and unobtrusive contribution of oak. In the mouth it unfolds with softness, proving persistent and nicely rhythmic. The pleasantly tasty Mongrana '17 is a blend of Sangiovese, Cabernet Sauvignon and Merlot produced in Maremma.

Wine	Rating
● Camartina '16	▼▼ 8
● Mongrana '17	▼▼ 3
○ Batàr '18	▼ 8
● Chianti Cl. '18	▼ 5
● Chianti Cl. Ris. '17	▼ 6
○ Batàr '98	▽▽▽ 8
● Camartina '07	▽▽▽ 8
● Camartina '06	▽▽▽ 7
● Camartina '05	▽▽▽ 7
● Camartina '04	▽▽▽ 7
● Camartina '03	▽▽▽ 8
● Camartina '01	▽▽▽ 8
● Camartina '00	▽▽▽ 8
● Camartina '99	▽▽▽ 8
● Camartina '97	▽▽▽ 8
● Camartina '95	▽▽▽ 8

Le Ragnaie

LOC. LE RAGNAIE
53024 MONTALCINO [SI]
TEL. +39 0577848639
www.leragnaie.com

CELLAR SALES
PRE-BOOKED VISITS
ACCOMMODATION
ANNUAL PRODUCTION 80,000 bottles
HECTARES UNDER VINE 15.50
VITICULTURE METHOD Certified Organic

Few wineries in Montalcino have focused on the study, mapping and value of individual vineyard areas with the same determination shown in recent years by Riccardo and Jennifer Campinoti. A project that goes well beyond the crus proposed in their range so far, and not only Brunello, it involves Fornace (from Loreto di Castelnuovo dell'Abate, in the southeast), Petroso (Scarnacuoia, west of Colle Centrale), Passo del Lume Spento and Ragnaie VV (from the sites closest to the winery). We should also add, as of 2015, Casanovina Montosoli (from the hill of the same name in the north). Even if the performance put in by Le Ragnaie's wines wasn't as smooth as usual, there were two that stood out, in particular, during our tastings, the Brunello '15 and the Fornace '15. The former plays on elegance and finesse, as well as the harmony of its various components, making for a classy Brunello. The Fornace speaks a different language: it has much more complex aromas, calling up dried flowers, and drier tannins.

Wine	Rating	
● Brunello di Montalcino '15	▼▼	7
● Brunello di Montalcino Casanovina Montosoli '15	▼▼	8
● Brunello di Montalcino Fornace '15	▼▼	8
● Troncone '17	▼▼	4
○ Bianco '18	▼	4
○ Civitella '18	▼	4
● Rosso di Montalcino '17	▼	5
● Brunello di Montalcino Fornace '08	▽▽▽	8
● Brunello di Montalcino V. V. '13	▽▽▽	8
● Brunello di Montalcino V. V. '11	▽▽▽	8
● Brunello di Montalcino V. V. '10	▽▽▽	8
● Brunello di Montalcino V. V. '07	▽▽▽	5
● Rosso di Montalcino '16	▽▽▽	5
● Brunello di Montalcino Fornace '13	▽▽	8
● Passo del Lume Spento '15	▽▽	4
● Troncone '16	▽▽	4

Podere La Regola

LOC. ALTAGRANDA
S.DA REG.LE 68 KM 6,400
56046 RIPARBELLA [PI]
TEL. +39 0586698145
www.laregola.com

CELLAR SALES
PRE-BOOKED VISITS
ANNUAL PRODUCTION 100,000 bottles
HECTARES UNDER VINE 25.00
VITICULTURE METHOD Certified Organic

The Nuti family bought the first plot of land in 1900, in an area where they've been making wine for at least two thousand years. Today brothers Luca and Flavio are renovating the property and its management for the purposes of better organization and efficiency while also respecting the environment. Their philosophy is captured in the new winery, a minimalist building that's well-integrated with the landscape. Here Sangiovese, Merlot, Cabernet Franc and Sauvignon, Syrah, Vermentino, Manseng, Chardonnay, Sauvignon Blanc and Viognier grapes are all vinified. The La Regola '17 is an excellent monovarietal Cabernet Franc characterized by sensations of fresh earth and undergrowth, roasted pepper and small wild berries. It has warmth but also dynamism on the palate, coming through smooth on the tannic side, well blended in all its components, combining substance and character. The Vallino '17, mainly Cabernet Sauvignon and Sangiovese, stands out for its fresh fruity notes and superb drinkability.

Wine	Rating	
● La Regola '17	▼▼▼	8
● Vallino '17	▼▼	5
○ Lauro '16	▼	5
○ Spumante Brut M. Cl. '15	▼	5
○ Steccaia '19	▼	3
● La Regola '16	▽▽▽	8
● La Regola '15	▽▽▽	7
● La Regola '14	▽▽	7
● Ligustro '17	▽▽	4
○ Steccaia '17	▽▽	4
● Strido '15	▽▽	8
● Strido '12	▽▽	8
● Vallino '16	▽▽	5
● Vallino '15	▽▽	5

★★Barone Ricasoli

LOC. MADONNA A BROLIO
53013 GAIOLE IN CHIANTI [SI]
TEL. +39 05777301
www.ricasoli.com

CELLAR SALES
PRE-BOOKED VISITS
ACCOMMODATION
ANNUAL PRODUCTION 2,500,000 bottles
HECTARES UNDER VINE 235.00

Here stands a castle whose origins go back almost a thousand years. The Ricasoli family, documented wine merchants as far back as the late 15th century, have lived in it since time immemorial. And then there's the story of Bettino, the "iron baron" inventor of the famous "Chianti formula". These are just a few of the highlights of the history of this authentic Italian 'château'. In more recent times they've distinguished themselves for a forward-thinking zoning project that further evidences the dynamism faithfully expressed by wines conceived with a modern but intimately 'Chianti' approach. The Chianti Classico Gran Selezione Colledilà '17 is elegant, and behaves like a great wine. Aromatically it's focused, playing on a cross between red berries, spices, earthy hints and accents of pyrite. In the mouth it's rich in contrasts, lively and deep. The Gran Selezione CeniPrimo '17 is no less good, with a rougher but equally charming character, as is the Chianti Classico Brolio Riserva '17.

Wine	Rating
● Chianti Cl. Gran Selezione Colledilà '17	TTT 8
● Chianti Cl. Brolio Ris. '17	TT 6
● Chianti Cl. Gran Selezione CeniPrimo '17	TT 8
● Chianti Cl. Brolio '18	TT 5
● Chianti Cl. Gran Selezione Roncicone '17	TT 8
● Chianti Cl. Rocca Guicciarda Ris. '17	TT 5
● Chianti Cl. Brolio Bettino '17	T 5
● Casalferro '08	YYY 8
● Chianti Cl. Brolio Bettino '15	YYY 5
● Chianti Cl. Castello di Brolio '07	YYY 8
● Chianti Cl. Castello di Brolio '06	YYY 8
● Chianti Cl. Colledilà '10	YYY 7
● Chianti Cl. Gran Selezione Colledilà '13	YYY 8
● Chianti Cl. Gran Selezione Colledilà '11	YYY 8
● Chianti Cl. Rocca Guicciarda Ris. '12	YYY 5

Ridolfi

LOC. MERCATALI
53024 MONTALCINO [SI]
TEL. +39 0577 1698333
www.ridolfimontalcino.it

ANNUAL PRODUCTION 110,000 bottles
HECTARES UNDER VINE 19.00
SUSTAINABLE WINERY

Purchased in 2011 by Venetian industrialist Giuseppe Valter Peretti, this winery (once owned by the noble Ridolfi family) is expertly managed by Gianni Maccari. Situated in Mercatali, it rises up to around 300 meters elevation on the northeast side of the hill that hosts the village of Brunello. Four wines, stylistically differentiated, are dedicated to the territory's principal typology: 2500 and 3500-liter barrels for the 'standard-label' version and the Mercatale, Slavonian and French oak for their Lincontro, barriques for the Donna Rebecca. And so it is that the winery now begins to show its enormous potential, taking home Tre Bicchieri, with a subtle, sophisticated and complex Brunello '15 doing the honors. Aromas of fruit and tobacco give way to a vibrant, dynamic palate, a faithful expression of the terroir. The Fiero '17, a blend of Merlot and Sangiovese aged for about 18 months, shines with its sensations of pepper and plum, and its rich palate. For us Ridolfi is 2021's Up-and-Coming Winery.

Wine	Rating
● Brunello di Montalcino '15	TTT 5
● Fiero '17	TT 5
● Rosso di Montalcino '18	T 4
● Brunello di Montalcino '14	YY 5
● Brunello di Montalcino Donna Rebecca '14	YY 5
● Rosso di Montalcino '17	YY 4

★Riecine

loc. Riecine
53013 Gaiole in Chianti [SI]
Tel. +39 0577749098
www.riecine.it

CELLAR SALES
PRE-BOOKED VISITS
ANNUAL PRODUCTION 60,000 bottles
HECTARES UNDER VINE 11.00
VITICULTURE METHOD Certified Organic

The winery's profile is that of a classic Chianti Classico producer, a solid expression of the craftsmanship that characterizes the appellation. In addition to representing a sociological paradigm, Riecine has also managed to establish itself as one of the best enological expressions of the Gaiole in Chianti subzone, where quality and a sense of a territory are decidedly at home. The producer's style, especially in recent times, has become so clear and distinctive as to serve as a model. A great vintage for a great version of La Gioia, a monovarietal Sangiovese. The 2016 features fragrant fruit that crosses subtly smoky hints, spices and whiffs of flint. In the mouth it's simply perfect: balanced, juicy and endless. The Chianti Classico '18 also delivers, proving fresh and sapid. The highly drinkable Sangiovese Riecine '16 is redolent of flowers on slightly earthy hints.

● La Gioia '16	🍷🍷🍷 8
● Chianti Cl. '18	🍷🍷 3*
● Riecine '16	🍷🍷 8
⊙ Palmina Rosè '19	🍷🍷 3
● Chianti Cl. '17	🍷🍷🍷 3*
● Chianti Cl. Ris. '15	🍷🍷🍷 5
● Chianti Cl. Ris. '99	🍷🍷🍷 7
● Chianti Cl. Ris. '88	🍷🍷🍷 6
● Chianti Cl. Ris. '86	🍷🍷🍷 6
● La Gioia '04	🍷🍷🍷 6
● La Gioia '01	🍷🍷🍷 6
● La Gioia '98	🍷🍷🍷 6
● La Gioia '95	🍷🍷🍷 6
● Chianti Cl. '16	🍷🍷 3
● Chianti Cl. Ris. '16	🍷🍷 5
● La Gioia '15	🍷🍷 6
● Riecine '15	🍷🍷 3*

Podere Le Ripi

loc. Le Ripi
53021 Montalcino [SI]
Tel. +39 0577835641
www.podereleripi.com

CELLAR SALES
PRE-BOOKED VISITS
ANNUAL PRODUCTION 80,000 bottles
HECTARES UNDER VINE 26.00
VITICULTURE METHOD Certified Biodynamic
SUSTAINABLE WINERY

It's rather difficult to present in an orderly manner all of Podere Le Ripi's wines. Despite offering a range that is little more than 'garagiste', there are about 10 different Brunellos, Rossos and Toscana IGTs. It's much better, therefore, to once again underline the visionary power behind everything—the vision brought about by Francesco Illy when he arrived in Castelnuovo dell'Abate, the heart of southeast Montalcino. Their precise production philosophy also comprises biodynamic management, plot-based selection and their evocative 'golden cellar'. Podere Le Ripi's range is large and varied, and features plenty of personality, but this year we were able to taste only three wines. Among these the Rosso Sogni e Follia '16 stood out, combining great olfactory finesse with tightly-woven yet soft tannins. A superb Rosso di Montalcino, it emulates its older brother and matures for 30 months in barrels. The Brunello '15 is also excellent.

● Rosso di Montalcino Sogni e Follia '16	🍷🍷 5
● Brunello di Montalcino '15	🍷🍷 7
● Amore e Follia '18	🍷 5
● Brunello di Montalcino Lupi e Sirene Ris. '13	🍷🍷🍷 8
● Brunello di Montalcino Lupi e Sirene '12	🍷🍷 6
● Brunello di Montalcino Lupi e Sirene Ris. '10	🍷🍷 6
● Cielo d'Ulisse '14	🍷🍷 6
● Rosso di Montalcino '11	🍷🍷 5
● Rosso di Montalcino Sogni e Follia '15	🍷🍷 5

★Rocca delle Macìe

LOC. LE MACÌE, 45
53011 CASTELLINA IN CHIANTI [SI]
TEL. +39 05777321
www.roccadellemacie.com

CELLAR SALES
PRE-BOOKED VISITS
ACCOMMODATION AND RESTAURANT SERVICE
ANNUAL PRODUCTION 2,700,000 bottles
HECTARES UNDER VINE 206.00
SUSTAINABLE WINERY

It is not just the quality and style of Rocca delle Macìe's wines, which have taken a considerable leap forward, that convinces. An overall shift has involved multiple facets of their production approach, from the grape varieties used, with Sangiovese playing a leading role and international varieties occupying a discernible place in the winery's portfolio, to their vineyard, which has undergone radical renovation, and the increasing use of large oak barrels instead of barriques. Finesse and lightness distinguish the Sant'Alfonso '18, a Chianti Classico with multifaceted aromas and sweet attack in the mouth, followed by a flavorful development. The Chianti Classico Gran Selezione Sergio Zingarelli '16 is a bit more influenced by oak, but still delivers multifaceted, polished aromas across a juicy, gustatory progression. The Chianti Classico Zingarelli Family '18 is enjoyable and fresh, the Riserva '17 firm and convincing.

● Chianti Cl. Tenuta S. Alfonso '18	🍷🍷🍷 6
● Chianti Cl. Gran Selezione Sergio Zingarelli '16	🍷🍷 8
● Chianti Cl. Famiglia Zingarelli '18	🍷🍷 5
● Chianti Cl. Famiglia Zingarelli Ris. '17	🍷🍷 6
● Chianti Cl. Ser Gioveto Ris. '16	🍷 8
● Roccato '16	🍷 8
● Chianti Cl. '16	ΨΨΨ 3*
● Chianti Cl. Famiglia Zingarelli Ris. '16	ΨΨΨ 5
● Chianti Cl. Famiglia Zingarelli Ris. '09	ΨΨΨ 3*
● Chianti Cl. Fizzano Ris. '10	ΨΨΨ 5
● Chianti Cl. Gran Sel. Riserva di Fizzano '14	ΨΨΨ 6
● Chianti Cl. Gran Sel. Riserva di Fizzano '13	ΨΨΨ 6
● Chianti Cl. Gran Sel. Sergio Zingarelli '11	ΨΨΨ 8

Rocca di Castagnoli

LOC. CASTAGNOLI
53013 GAIOLE IN CHIANTI [SI]
TEL. +39 0577731004
www.roccadicastagnoli.com

CELLAR SALES
PRE-BOOKED VISITS
ACCOMMODATION AND RESTAURANT SERVICE
ANNUAL PRODUCTION 500,000 bottles
HECTARES UNDER VINE 87.00
SUSTAINABLE WINERY

A well-defined and coherent stylistic approach favors the balance and finesse that we've come to expect of Chianti Classico. This is probably the fundamental characteristic of Rocca di Castagnoli's wines, which have proven capable of capturing and highlighting the different nuances of the territory where they are produced. Here in the heart of the Gaiole in Chianti subzone, grapes ripen a bit later while the soils alternate between marl and alberese. Their Capraia wines, on the other hand, come from Castellina in Chianti. The Chianti Classico Gran Selezione Capraia Effe 55 '16 behaves like an important wine, revealing a close-knit, multifaceted structure, combined with airy, complex aromas. Gustatory freshness and aromatic clarity characterize the Chianti Classico Capraia '18. The Chianti Classico Capraia Riserva '17 is also impeccable for the way it channels a pervasive olfactory spectrum into a sapid, focused wine.

● Chianti Cl. Gran Selezione Capraia Effe 55 '16	🍷🍷🍷 6
● Chianti Cl. Capraia '18	🍷🍷 4
● Chianti Cl. Capraia Ris. '17	🍷🍷 5
● Chianti Cl. Gran Selezione Stielle '16	🍷🍷 6
● Chianti Cl. Poggio a' Frati Ris. '17	🍷🍷 5
● Chianti Cl. Rocca di Castagnoli '18	🍷🍷 4
● Buriano '16	🍷 6
● Chianti Cl. Capraia Ris. '07	ΨΨΨ 4
● Chianti Cl. Poggio a' Frati Ris. '08	ΨΨΨ 4
● Chianti Cl. Poggio a' Frati Ris. '06	ΨΨΨ 4*
● Chianti Cl. Poggio ai Frati Ris. '04	ΨΨΨ 4
● Chianti Cl. Rocca di Castagnoli '17	ΨΨΨ 3*
● Chianti Cl. Tenuta di Capraia Ris. '06	ΨΨΨ 4*
● Chianti Cl. Tenuta di Capraia Ris. '05	ΨΨΨ 4
● Stielle '00	ΨΨΨ 7
● Chianti Cl. Capraia '17	ΨΨ 4

★Rocca di Frassinello

loc. Giuncarico
58023 Gavorrano [GR]
Tel. +39 056688400
www.roccadifrassinello.it

CELLAR SALES
PRE-BOOKED VISITS
ACCOMMODATION
ANNUAL PRODUCTION 400,000 bottles
HECTARES UNDER VINE 90.00
SUSTAINABLE WINERY

The producer's owner is also a shareholder of Gambero Rosso spa. To avoid any conflict of interest, Paolo Panerai has subordinated the possible awarding of Tre Bicchieri (which, in any case, only occurs through a blind tasting) to the attainment of the same rating of excellence (upwards of 90/100) by an independent, international panel. This was the case here.

The Maremma Baffo Nero '17, a monovarietal Merlot, stands out (not for the first time) among this Gavorrano producer's selection. Dark aromas span ripe fruit and hints of pencil lead, spicy nuances, tobacco, chocolate and vanilla. In the mouth, the wine has enters broad and sweet, making you feel its powerful structure, with crisp, tightly-wound tannins, and a broad, deep finish. The Poggio alla Guardia '18 is more approachable in its Mediterranean aromas and dense, juicy palate. The rest of their selection also proves sound.

● Maremma Toscana Baffonero '17	🍷🍷🍷	8
● Maremma Toscana Poggio alla Guardia '18	🍷🍷	3
● Maremma Toscana Rocca di Frassinello '18	🍷🍷	8
● Maremma Toscana Le Sughere di Frassinello '18	🍷	5
● Maremma Toscana Ornello '18	🍷	4
○ Maremma Toscana Vermentino '19	🍷	3
● Baffonero '12	🍷🍷🍷	8
● Maremma Toscana Baffonero '16	🍷🍷🍷	8
● Maremma Toscana Baffonero '14	🍷🍷🍷	8
● Maremma Toscana Baffonero '13	🍷🍷🍷	8
● Maremma Toscana Rocca di Frassinello '17	🍷🍷🍷	8
● Maremma Toscana Rocca di Frassinello '15	🍷🍷🍷	6

Rocca di Montemassi

loc. Pian del Bichi
fraz. Montemassi
s.da prov.le Sant'Anna
58036 Roccastrada [GR]
Tel. +39 0564579700
www.roccadimontemassi.it

CELLAR SALES
PRE-BOOKED VISITS
ACCOMMODATION
ANNUAL PRODUCTION 480,000 bottles
HECTARES UNDER VINE 180.00
SUSTAINABLE WINERY

Maremma's Rocca di Montemassi, which is part of the Zonin 1821 Group, is situated in an area that crosses Mediterranean scrub and metalliferous hills, as well as experiencing the effects of the nearby sea. It enjoys unique light, a warm climate with good day-night temperature swings and siliceous-clayey soils rich in minerals. The varieties cultivated were chosen with these characteristics in mind, from classic regional varieties such as Vermentino and Sangiovese to international cultivar, all of which have proven capable of adapting to this part of southern Tuscany. The Maremma Rosso Sassabruna '18 features a well-defined aromatic profile in which fragrant notes of red fruit alternate with smoky, spicy nuances. On the palate it opens sweet and full, only to unfold with flavor and balance, and finish in crescendo. The Sangiovese Le Focaie '19 is crisp, sapid and fragrant, a wine of immediate pleasantness, decidedly delectable and supple. The white wines in their selection also prove sound, as the Vermentino Calasole '19 demonstrates.

● Maremma Toscana Rosso Sassabruna '18	🍷🍷	5
● Maremma Toscana Rosso '17	🍷🍷	8
● Maremma Toscana Sangiovese Le Focaie '19	🍷🍷	4
○ Maremma Toscana Vermentino Calasole '19	🍷🍷	4
● Maremma Toscana Rocca di Montemassi '13	🍷🍷🍷	5
● Rocca di Montemassi '10	🍷🍷🍷	5
● Rocca di Montemassi '09	🍷🍷🍷	5
● Maremma Rocca di Montemassi '12	🍷🍷	5
● Maremma Toscana Rosso '16	🍷🍷	7
● Maremma Toscana Rosso Sassabruna '17	🍷🍷	4
● Maremma Toscana Rosso Sassabruna '16	🍷🍷	5
● Maremma Toscana Sassabruna '14	🍷🍷	3*

Roccapesta

LOC. MACERETO, 9
58054 SCANSANO [GR]
TEL. +39 0564599252
www.roccapesta.com

CELLAR SALES
PRE-BOOKED VISITS
ANNUAL PRODUCTION 100,000 bottles
HECTARES UNDER VINE 26.50

Roccapesta is one of the most interesting producers in Maremma, and especially in the Morellino di Scansano appellation. Alberto Tanzini, owner of the winery, has immediately grasped the potential of these hills, focusing on tradition without useless experiments, starting with aging in large oak barrels. His Sangiovese is austere, robust, rich in character and exhibs an original stroke. His is a serious and respectful path that shows how the grumpy Tuscan grape can be multifaceted and complex even at these latitudes. This Scansano producer gave us a great version of the Morellino Calestaia Riserva, a wine that perfectly interprets the more coherent side of Maremma Sangiovese. The 2016 offers up fragrant scents of violets, cherries, earthy hints and flint, sensations that, in the mouth, link up with spirited tannins and lively acidity. The palate flows with rhythm, fragrance and flavor. The more approachable Morellino'18 is a delectable, tantalizing wine, irresistibly drinkable.

- ● Morellino di Scansano Calestaia Ris. '16 ▼▼▼ 6
- ● Morellino di Scansano '18 ▼▼ 5
- ● Maremma Toscana Masca '18 ▼ 2
- ● Morellino di Scansanp Ribeo '19 ▼ 2
- ● Morellino di Scansano Calestaia Ris. '11 ▽▽▽ 5
- ● Morellino di Scansano Calestaia Ris. '10 ▽▽▽ 5
- ● Morellino di Scansano Calestaia Ris. '09 ▽▽▽ 5
- ● Morellino di Scansano Ribeo '15 ▽▽▽ 3*
- ● Morellino di Scansano Ris. '16 ▽▽▽ 5
- ● Morellino di Scansano Ris. '13 ▽▽▽ 4*
- ● Morellino di Scansano '13 ▽▽ 3*
- ● Morellino di Scansano Ribeo '14 ▽▽ 3*
- ● Morellino di Scansano Ris. '15 ▽▽ 5

★★Ruffino

P.LE RUFFINO, 1
50065 PONTASSIEVE [FI]
TEL. +39 05583605
www.ruffino.it

CELLAR SALES
PRE-BOOKED VISITS
ANNUAL PRODUCTION 18,000,000 bottles
HECTARES UNDER VINE 550.00

Owned by the American giant Constellation Brands, Ruffino concentrates its most important vineyards in Tuscany, overseeing Greppone Mazzi in Montalcino, Santedame, Gretolaio, Montemasso and Poggio Casciano in Chianti Classico, and La Solatia in Monteriggioni, in Siena. Production volumes are large, obviously, but quality is consistent and widespread throughout the winery's entire portfolio, with some bottles positioned firmly at the absolute top. Many exhibit impeccable craftsmanship, without sacrificing character and personality. The Chianti Classico Ducale Riserva '17 is a wine of impeccable craftsmanship: it unveils a focused aromatic suite, complex and clean, a coherent prelude to a palate that tends towards creaminess and juiciness. The Chianti Classico Tenuta Sante Dame '18 is a sapid, immediately pleasant drink, decidedly in accordance with its type. The concentrated and austere Chianti Classico Gran Selezione Riserva Ducale Oro '16 is also notable.

- ● Chianti Cl. Ducale Ris. '17 ▼▼▼ 4*
- ● Chianti Cl. Gran Selezione Riserva Ducale Oro '16 ▼▼ 6
- ● Chianti Cl. Tenuta Santedame '18 ▼▼ 4
- ● Alauda '16 ▼ 8
- ● Brunello di Montalcino Greppone Mazzi '05 ▽▽▽ 6
- ● Chianti Cl. Gran Selezione Riserva Ducale Oro '15 ▽▽▽ 6
- ● Chianti Cl. Gran Selezione Riserva Ducale Oro '14 ▽▽▽ 6
- ● Chianti Cl. Riserva Ducale Oro '04 ▽▽▽ 5
- ● Chianti Cl. Riserva Ducale Oro '01 ▽▽▽ 5
- ● Chianti Cl. Riserva Ducale Oro '00 ▽▽▽ 5
- ● Modus '04 ▽▽▽ 5
- ● Romitorio di Santedame '00 ▽▽▽ 7
- ● Romitorio di Santedame '99 ▽▽▽ 7

Salcheto

via di Villa Bianca, 15
53045 Montepulciano [SI]
Tel. +39 0578799031
www.salcheto.it

CELLAR SALES
PRE-BOOKED VISITS
ACCOMMODATION AND RESTAURANT SERVICE
ANNUAL PRODUCTION 350,000 bottles
HECTARES UNDER VINE 58.00
VITICULTURE METHOD Certified Organic
SUSTAINABLE WINERY

Salcheto, led by Michele Manelli, has focused heavily on uncompromising choices, especially in terms of respect for the environment and sustainability. It was a difficult road, but one that seems to have proven the Sant'Albino (southern Nobile di Montepulciano) producer right. Year after year, their wines express increasingly consolidated quality alongside a focused stylistic approach, privileging character and personality without ever betraying territorial identity. Vibrant, with lovely gustatory energy, the Nobile di Montepulciano '17 also features vivid and well-delineated aromas ranging from fruit to herbs, spices and balsamic hints. The Rosso di Montepulciano '19, which exhibits plenty of fragrance, is absolutely enjoyable. Both the Chianti Biskero '19 and the Obvius '19, a monovarietal Sangiovese, prove approachably pleasant, making for an experience that's 'all in on fruit'.

Wine	Rating
● Nobile di Montepulciano '17	🍷🍷🍷 4*
● Nobile di Montepulciano Ris. '16	🍷🍷 5
● Rosso di Montepulciano '19	🍷🍷 3
● Chianti Biskero '19	🍷 2
● Obvius Rosso '19	🍷 3
● Nobile di Montepulciano '16	🍷🍷🍷 4*
● Nobile di Montepulciano '14	🍷🍷🍷 4*
● Nobile di Montepulciano '10	🍷🍷🍷 4*
● Nobile di Montepulciano '97	🍷🍷🍷 3*
● Nobile di Montepulciano Salco '11	🍷🍷🍷 6
● Nobile di Montepulciano Salco '10	🍷🍷🍷 5
● Nobile di Montepulciano Salco Evoluzione '06	🍷🍷🍷 6
● Nobile di Montepulciano Salco Evoluzione '01	🍷🍷🍷 6
● Nobile di Montepulciano Ris. '15	🍷🍷 5

Podere Salicutti

pod. Salicutti, 174
53024 Montalcino [SI]
Tel. +39 0577847003
www.poderesalicutti.it

CELLAR SALES
PRE-BOOKED VISITS
ACCOMMODATION
ANNUAL PRODUCTION 15,000 bottles
HECTARES UNDER VINE 4.00
VITICULTURE METHOD Certified Organic

Sorgente, Teatro, Piaggione: these are the three vineyard plots that make up the Salicutti Estate and that have each given rise to a Brunello cru since 2015. This is the natural evolution of a journey that began in 1990 with Francesco Leanza, who was involved in production even after selling the estate to the Eichbauer family. The resulting wines represent various expressions of a terroir as special as that which unfolds between Castelnuovo dell'Abate and the Abbey of Sant'Antimo, in the most rustic part of southeastern Montalcino. Their buoyant wines mature in 1000 and 2000-liter oak barrels. Tasting and comparing three crus from the same area reveals significant differences. With the 2015 Piaggione and Teatro selections, notes of tobacco and medicinal herbs combine with ripe red fruit, while the Sorgente is a whirlwind of fresh cherries and spices. The latter stands out on the palate by virtue of its lively acidity; the Teatro, for its part, plays on delicate balances, while the Piaggione opts for the power of alcohol.

Wine	Rating
● Brunello di Montalcino Sorgente '15	🍷🍷 8
● Brunello di Montalcino Teatro '15	🍷🍷 8
● Brunello di Montalcino Piaggione '15	🍷🍷 8
● Rosso di Montalcino '17	🍷 6
● Brunello di Montalcino '97	🍷🍷🍷 7
● Brunello di Montalcino '13	🍷🍷 7
● Brunello di Montalcino Piaggione Ris. '13	🍷🍷 8
● Rosso di Montalcino '16	🍷🍷 4
● Rosso di Montalcino '15	🍷🍷 4
● Rosso di Montalcino Sorgente '11	🍷🍷 5

★Salvioni

P.ZZA CAVOUR, 19
53024 MONTALCINO [SI]
TEL. +39 0577848499
www.aziendasalvioni.com

PRE-BOOKED VISITS
RESTAURANT SERVICE
ANNUAL PRODUCTION 15,000 bottles
HECTARES UNDER VINE 4.00

The Salvioni family's wines derive from an unmistakable geological and territorial jigsaw puzzle, the three parcels of La Cerbaiola. It's a historic estate situated on the southeastern edge of Montalcino, at 400 meters elevation on calcareous, marl and stony soils. But the powerful and visceral character of their Brunellos, produced through spontaneous fermentation and maturation in 2000-liter Slavonian oak barrels, cannot be fully appreciated without considering the personality of its creators, Giulio and Mirella, who are assisted on a permanent basis by their children Davide and Alessia. For decades, year after year, Salvioni's Sangioveses have been thrilling lovers of ageworthy reds. The 2015 vintage is already soft and dense in its tannins, so much so that it offers a sensation of pleasant density on the palate, much like caressing velvet with your fingers. Still youthful and recalcitrant, the Rosso '18 will smooth out its rough edges in a few months.

Wine	Rating
● Brunello di Montalcino '15	🍷🍷 8
● Rosso di Montalcino '18	🍷🍷 8
● Brunello di Montalcino '12	YYY 8
● Brunello di Montalcino '09	YYY 8
● Brunello di Montalcino '06	YYY 8
● Brunello di Montalcino '04	YYY 8
● Brunello di Montalcino '00	YYY 8
● Brunello di Montalcino '99	YYY 8
● Brunello di Montalcino '97	YYY 8
● Brunello di Montalcino '90	YYY 8
● Brunello di Montalcino '89	YYY 8
● Brunello di Montalcino '88	YYY 8
● Brunello di Montalcino '87	YYY 8
● Brunello di Montalcino '85	YYY 8
● Rosso di Montalcino '17	YYY 8
● Brunello di Montalcino '13	YY 8
● Brunello di Montalcino '11	YY 8

San Benedetto

LOC. SAN BENEDETTO, 4A
53037 SAN GIMIGNANO [SI]
TEL. +39 3386958705
www.agrisanbenedetto.com

CELLAR SALES
PRE-BOOKED VISITS
ACCOMMODATION
ANNUAL PRODUCTION 40,000 bottles
HECTARES UNDER VINE 25.00

There's a long history behind the producer owned by the Giannelli family, one that began in 1826 in the district of San Gimignano. They cultivated vines, olive trees and arable land, as well as looking after livestock—in short, a history common to many farms of the time. After more than a century, with the end of sharecropping, the land was purchased by brothers Dario and Giuseppe and in 1975 the first part of the cellar was built. But it was only in 1998 that the producer got its present name and began focusing on wine, a specialization that is, by now, well-defined. The Vernaccia '17 is quite pleasant. A lovely gold color is the prelude to hints of candied orange, peach, lemon and gentle spices. In the mouth it opens soft, then comes through vital and fresh, with pronounced flavor and a delicious finish. The Vermentino '19 is interesting, with vegetal notes and herbs accompanied by tea and tropical hints of mango. On the palate it has a racy body, vivid freshness and nice length.

Wine	Rating
● Chianti Ris. '16	🍷🍷 4
○ Vermentino '19	🍷🍷 2*
○ Vernaccia di San Gimignano Ris. '17	🍷🍷 3
⊙ Rosato '19	🍷 2
○ Vernaccia di San Gimignano '19	🍷 2
○ Vermentino '18	YY 2*
○ Vermentino '17	YY 2*
○ Vernaccia di San Gimignano '17	YY 2*
○ Vernaccia di San Gimignano Ris. '16	YY 3
○ Vernaccia di San Gimignano Ris. '15	YY 4
○ Vernaccia di San Gimignano Ris. '13	YY 2*

Podere San Cristoforo

Fraz. Bagno
via Forni
58023 Gavorrano [GR]
Tel. +39 3358212413
www.poderesancristoforo.it

CELLAR SALES
PRE-BOOKED VISITS
ACCOMMODATION
ANNUAL PRODUCTION 60,000 bottles
HECTARES UNDER VINE 17.00
VITICULTURE METHOD Certified Organic
SUSTAINABLE WINERY

Podere San Cristoforo is characterized by biodynamic vineyard management and a minimally-invasive production approach that involves aging mostly in small oak barrels, resulting in Sangiovese with a strong personality. Owned by Lorenzo Zonin, this Gavorrano winery makes some of the most summery, frank wines in Maremma, demonstrating that the difficult Tuscan grape, if well interpreted, can express qualities of finesse and complexity even in areas that tend to be warm. Stylistically, the Sangiovese Carandelle '16 hits the mark. An elegant, highly supple, sapid and rhythmic wine, multifaceted aromas marked by chiaroscuro reemerge on the palate. The Amaranto '18 is also measured and quite elegant, with slightly compressed primaries, but a tasty and enticing palate. The Vermentino Luminoso '19 is interesting, endowed with nice gustatory energy and aromatic intensity.

Wine	Rating
● Maremma Toscana Sangiovese Carandelle '18	▼▼ 5
● Maremma Toscana Sangiovese Amaranto '18	▼▼ 4
● Ameri Governo all'Uso Toscano '18	▼ 8
○ Maremma Toscana Vermentino Luminoso '19	▼ 4
● Podere San Cristoforo Petit Verdot '18	▼ 8
● Ameri Governo all'Uso Toscano '15	▽▽▽ 6
● Maremma Toscana Podere San Cristoforo '13	▽▽▽ 3*
● Maremma Toscana Sangiovese Carandelle '15	▽▽▽ 3*
● Maremma Toscana Sangiovese Amaranto '16	▽▽ 3*
● San Cristoforo '17	▽▽ 6
● San Cristoforo '16	▽▽ 6
● San Cristoforo '12	▽▽ 5

Fattoria San Donato

Loc. San Donato, 6
53037 San Gimignano [SI]
Tel. +39 0577941616
www.sandonato.it

CELLAR SALES
PRE-BOOKED VISITS
ACCOMMODATION AND RESTAURANT SERVICE
ANNUAL PRODUCTION 70,000 bottles
HECTARES UNDER VINE 20.00
VITICULTURE METHOD Certified Organic

Umberto Lenzi founded this producer in 1932, in a small medieval village of great charm and value. Today it's run by his grandson Umberto Fenzi, who, after gaining experience under his mother, is sharing the stage with his wife, Federica, and daughters Angelica Benedetta and Fiamma. It's a close-knit team that also oversees guest accommodations, the cultivation of spelt and chickpeas, and the production of oil. Their main activity, however, remains, of course, looking after their vineyards and selling wine. The Vernaccia Benedetta Riserva '17 made a pleasant impression: buttery tones rise up to the nose along with hints of lychee, white peach and apple. Its soft body has a fresh acidic vein and a juicy finish. The Vernaccia Angelica '18 is also pleasant, appetizing, with citrus tones and notes of mint prevailing on the nose, and a rich palate of nice weight. The Chianti Colli Senesi Fede Riserva '17 is fruity, enticing to the nose, fresh and enjoyable—a fine drink.

Wine	Rating
● Chianti Colli Senesi Fede Ris. '16	▼▼ 3
○ Vernaccia di S. Gimignano Angelica '18	▼▼ 3
○ Vernaccia di S. Gimignano Benedetta Ris. '17	▼▼ 3
● Chianti Colli Senesi Fiamma '16	▼ 3
⊙ Rosato '19	▼ 3
● San Gimignano Arrigo Merlot '16	▼ 4
● San Gimignano Syrah Arrigo '16	▼ 4
○ Vermentino '19	▼ 3
○ Vernaccia di S. Gimignano '19	▼ 2
● Chianti Colli Senesi '12	▽▽ 2*
○ San Gimignano Vin Santo '11	▽▽ 5
○ Vernaccia di S. Gimignano Angelica '12	▽▽ 3
○ Vernaccia di S. Gimignano Benedetta Ris. '13	▽▽ 3*

★San Felice

loc. San Felice
53019 Castelnuovo Berardenga [SI]
Tel. +39 057739911
www.agricolasanfelice.it

CELLAR SALES
PRE-BOOKED VISITS
ACCOMMODATION AND RESTAURANT SERVICE
ANNUAL PRODUCTION 900,000 bottles
HECTARES UNDER VINE 140.00

San Felice has had a presence in the Chianti Classico appellation for over fifty years and its wines are heavily influenced by the microclimate of the Castelnuovo Berardenga subzone. Distinguished by generous structure, they exhibit pronounced drinkability and aren't lacking in character or personality either. The property, which is owned by the Allianz insurance group, also comprises the Campogiovanni estate in Montalcino and the Perolla estate in Maremma, thus forming a productive mosaic that includes some of the most important areas of Tuscan wine country. San Felice's 2018 is certainly one of the best Chianti Classicos of the vintage. A forthright, fragrant nose of red berries sees hints of smoke and flint. It unfolds in the mouth with rhythm, liveliness and flavor. We tasted a lovely version of the Vigorello '16 as well. The 'father' of all Supertuscans, it's a blend of Cabernet Sauvignon, Merlot and Petit Verdot with mature aromas adorning a complex, well-sustained palate. The Brunello Campogiovanni '15 is also excellent.

Wine	Rating	Price
● Chianti Cl. '18	🍷🍷🍷	3*
● Vigorello '16	🍷🍷	6
● Brunello di Montalcino Campogiovanni '15	🍷🍷	7
● Chianti Cl. Il Grigio Ris. '17	🍷🍷	3
● Chianti Cl. Gran Selezione Poggio Rosso '16	🍷	5
● Pugnitello '16	🍷	6
● Rosso di Montalcino Campogiovanni '18	🍷	3
● Chianti Cl. '13	🍷🍷🍷 (previous)	3*
● Chianti Cl. Gran Sel. Il Grigio da San Felice '11	🍷🍷🍷 (previous)	5
● Chianti Cl. Gran Selezione Poggio Rosso '15	🍷🍷🍷 (previous)	5
● Chianti Cl. Il Grigio Ris. '15	🍷🍷🍷 (previous)	3*
● Vigorello '13	🍷🍷🍷 (previous)	6

San Ferdinando

loc. Ciggiano
via Gargaiolo, 33
52041 Civitella in Val di Chiana [AR]
Tel. +39 3287216738
www.sanferdinando.eu

CELLAR SALES
PRE-BOOKED VISITS
ACCOMMODATION
ANNUAL PRODUCTION 50,000 bottles
HECTARES UNDER VINE 10.00

Situated in Val di Chiana, San Ferdinando is one of the most authentic, original and centered producers operating in Arezzo, thanks to the Grifoni family and their collaborators, all of whom have proven capable of producing a wine that is as contemporary as it is bound up with the area's traditions. Hence the decision to cultivate only native grapes, which are often transformed into monovarietals through minimally-invasive methods that respect nature. Each bottle expresses the variety, the territory and the stylistic approach of those who made it. We very much appreciated the Vermentino '19, with its continental, austere profile. On the nose it features fresh aromas of citrus fruits (citron) and medicinal plants, with exquisite, pebbly minerals. The palate is clearly linear but rich, aromatically consistent and of lovely persistence. The Pugnitello '16 also delivers, coming through spicy and satisfying. As usual, we also appreciated the Ciliegiolo '19—the rosé version as well.

Wine	Rating	Price
● Pugnitello '16	🍷🍷	4
○ Vermentino '19	🍷🍷	3*
● Chianti Podere Gamba '18	🍷🍷	3
● Ciliegiolo '19	🍷🍷	3
⊙ Ciliegiolo Rosato '19	🍷🍷	2*
○ Vermentino '16	🍷🍷🍷 (previous)	3*
● Ciliegiolo '15	🍷🍷 (previous)	2*
● Ciliegiolo '12	🍷🍷 (previous)	2*
● Ciliegiolo '10	🍷🍷 (previous)	2*
● Pugnitello '13	🍷🍷 (previous)	3
● Sangiovese '10	🍷🍷 (previous)	3
○ Vermentino '18	🍷🍷 (previous)	3*
○ Vermentino '17	🍷🍷 (previous)	3*

★★★Tenuta San Guido

FRAZ. BOLGHERI
LOC. LE CAPANNE, 27
57022 CASTAGNETO CARDUCCI [LI]
TEL. +39 0565762003
www.sassicaia.com

PRE-BOOKED VISITS
RESTAURANT SERVICE
ANNUAL PRODUCTION 780,000 bottles
HECTARES UNDER VINE 90.00

If today there is such a thing as 'Bolgheri wine', numerous wineries that offer it and all the related industries, much of the credit goes to the Incisa della Rocchetta family. They are the ones who literally invented this territory, at least in terms of wine production, infusing it with strength through Tenuta San Guido and the Sassicaia myth. Their wines continues to shine, indeed shine as brightly as ever (as demonstrated by recent vintages) proving increasingly impressive, defined, recognizable and coherent in their grandeur. Proof of the validity of this direction, if still needed, comes in the form of a stratospheric 2017, and not only because it was such a complicated year (to say the least). It's a crystal-clear wine, highly transparent and nuanced aromatically, of rare elegance in the mouth, with a graceful texture and an alluring, tasty, very deep finish. Just on its heels, the Guidalberto '18 proves fragrant and juicy, while the Le Difese '18 also put in an excellent performance.

● Bolgheri Sup. Sassicaia '17	🍷🍷🍷	8
● Guidalberto '18	🍷🍷	6
● Le Difese '18	🍷🍷	4
● Bolgheri Sassicaia '15	🍷🍷🍷	8
● Bolgheri Sassicaia '14	🍷🍷🍷	8
● Bolgheri Sassicaia '13	🍷🍷🍷	8
● Bolgheri Sassicaia '12	🍷🍷🍷	8
● Bolgheri Sassicaia '11	🍷🍷🍷	8
● Bolgheri Sassicaia '10	🍷🍷🍷	8
● Bolgheri Sassicaia '06	🍷🍷🍷	8
● Bolgheri Sassicaia '05	🍷🍷🍷	8
● Bolgheri Sassicaia '04	🍷🍷🍷	8
● Bolgheri Sassicaia '03	🍷🍷🍷	8
● Bolgheri Sassicaia '02	🍷🍷🍷	8
● Bolgheri Sup. Sassicaia '16	🍷🍷🍷	8
● Guidalberto '04	🍷🍷🍷	6
● Guidalberto '17	🍷🍷	6

Tenuta San Jacopo

LOC. CASTIGLIONCELLI, 151
52022 CAVRIGLIA [AR]
TEL. +39 055966003
www.tenutasanjacopo.it

CELLAR SALES
PRE-BOOKED VISITS
ACCOMMODATION
ANNUAL PRODUCTION 25,000 bottles
HECTARES UNDER VINE 40.00
VITICULTURE METHOD Certified Organic

In a strip of Tuscany straddling Valdarno and Chianti that was once the scene of bitter battles between Florence and Siena, we find a winery whose history dates back to the early 18th century, a past testified to by a beautiful historic villa, farmhouses and cellar. After purchasing the property in 2002, the Cattaneo brothers began reviving the vineyards, adopting organic farming practices almost immediately. And so it is that we get to enjoy sincere wines made with Sangiovese, Montepulciano, Pinot Nero, Trebbiano and Chardonnay grapes. A monovarietal Montepulciano, the Caprilius '16 features an intriguing, spicy nose, adorned by hints of aromatic herbs and black fruits (blueberries). In the mouth it shows elegance, finesse and depth, as well as a juicy, decisive finish. The version of their Trebbiano Erboli '18 matured in oak is also lovely, offering up notes of chamomile well supported by hints of citrus lemon, as well as apple and damson; in the mouth it's balanced, sapid, with a delicately salty finish that gradually unfolds.

● Caprilius '16	🍷🍷	4
○ Erboli Trebbiano '18	🍷🍷	3
○ Quarto di Luna '19	🍷🍷	2*
● Vigna del Mulinaccio '17	🍷🍷	5
● Chianti Classico Poggio ai Grilli Ris. '17	🍷	3
● Chianti Cl. Poggio ai Grilli '05	🍷🍷	2*
○ Erboli Trebbiano '17	🍷🍷	3
● Orma Del Diavolo '16	🍷🍷	4
● Orma del Diavolo '11	🍷🍷	3
● Orma del Diavolo '05	🍷🍷	3*
○ Quarto di Luna '18	🍷🍷	2*
○ Quarto di Luna '14	🍷🍷	2*
○ Quarto di Luna '12	🍷🍷	2*
● Vigna del Mulinaccio '16	🍷🍷	5

San Polo

Loc. Podernovi, 161
53024 Montalcino [SI]
Tel. +39 0577835101
www.poggiosanpolo.com

CELLAR SALES
PRE-BOOKED VISITS
ANNUAL PRODUCTION 150,000 bottles
HECTARES UNDER VINE 17.00

Located in the heart of Podernovi, a benchmark for eastern Montalcino, Podere San Polo is one of the emblematic properties managed by Valpolicella's Allegrini family. A natural terrace overlooking the enclave of Sant'Antimo and Mount Amiata at around 450 meters elevation, its clayey-calcareous soils prove to be nothing short of excellent for producing solid, pleasant Sangiovese reds. Vinified in concrete, they mature both in small wood barrels and in Slavonian and Allier oak. Marilisa Allegrini's 2015 Brunellos shine, in particular the two premium selections: Vignavecchia and Podernovi. The style is decidedly modern with new and toasted oak used liberally to accompany mature and exuberant fruit. The Vignavecchia boasts greater complexity and balance, thanks to its lively and juicy acidity. The Podernovi is just a bit more austere, contrasting with the peacefulness of the less powerful Brunello di Montalcino '15.

- ● Brunello di Montalcino Vignavecchia '15 TTT 8
- ● Brunello di Montalcino '15 TT 7
- ● Brunello di Montalcino Podernovi '15 TT 8
- ● Rosso di Montalcino '18 TT 3
- ● Brunello di Montalcino '14 YY 7
- ● Brunello di Montalcino '13 YY 7
- ● Brunello di Montalcino '12 YY 6
- ● Brunello di Montalcino '11 YY 6
- ● Brunello di Montalcino '10 YY 6
- ● Brunello di Montalcino Ris. '12 YY 8
- ● Brunello di Montalcino Ris. '10 YY 7
- ● Brunello di Montalcino Vignavecchia Ris. '13 YY 8
- ● Rosso di Montalcino '17 YY 3
- ● Rosso di Montalcino '15 YY 3*

Tenuta San Vito

via San Vito, 59
50056 Montelupo Fiorentino [FI]
Tel. +39 057151411
www.san-vito.com

CELLAR SALES
PRE-BOOKED VISITS
ACCOMMODATION AND RESTAURANT SERVICE
ANNUAL PRODUCTION 150,000 bottles
HECTARES UNDER VINE 29.00
VITICULTURE METHOD Certified Organic
SUSTAINABLE WINERY

Tenuta San Vito was one of the first producers in the area to embrace principles of organic cultivation. It was 1985 when it happened, thanks to Laura Drighi, daughter of owner Roberto, who in 1960 had built the estate, developing the cultivation of vines and olive trees. In the late 1980s they began focusing on their agritourism activities through renovation of the farmhouses. Today it's Neri Gazulli, Roberto's grandson, who's carrying on their work, giving a nice boost to wine production. The newcomer Poggio Alto '18 was well received during our tastings. A blend of Sangiovese, Canaiolo and Colorino, it's characterized by a fruity nose, with nuances of black pepper, mace and pencil lead. The palate is warm, focused, compact and fresh, with a slightly tousled but pleasant finish. The amber Vin Santo '13 bewitches with its notes of dried figs, dates and hints of almonds—it's a velvety, creamy, dense wine that lingers in the mouth.

- ● Chianti Colli Fiorentini Darno '18 TT 3
- ● Poggio Alto '18 TT 4
- ○ Vin Santo del Chianti Malmantico '13 TT 6
- ⊙ 7794 Brut Rosé '19 T 4
- ○ Amantiglio '19 T 3
- ● Chianti Colli Fiorentini Darno '17 YY 3
- ● Chianti Colli Fiorentini Darno '16 YY 2*
- ● Chianti dei Colli Fiorentini Darno '12 YY 2*
- ● Chianti San Vito '15 YY 2*
- ● Colle dei Mandorli '16 YY 6
- ● Colle dei Mandorli '15 YY 6
- ● Colle dei Mandorli '11 YY 6
- ● Poggio Alto '13 YY 4
- ○ Vin Santo del Chianti Malmatico '07 YY 5

Sant'Agnese

LOC. CAMPO ALLE FAVE, 1
57025 PIOMBINO [LI]
TEL. +39 0565277069
www.santagnesefarm.it

CELLAR SALES
PRE-BOOKED VISITS
ANNUAL PRODUCTION 20,000 bottles
HECTARES UNDER VINE 6.00
SUSTAINABLE WINERY

Paolo Gigli's life in wine production has been a great adventure. He's the driving force behind the business founded by his father, a man determined to retire to the countryside after a life spent in other activities. Paolo was immediately passionate about the project, so much so that he left his job in politics to devote himself full-time to wine-growing. Today he's a true jack-of-all-trades, personally overseeing the work in the vineyard while also looking after things in the cellar, signing off on a reliable and consistently territorial range of wines. The I Fiori Blu '15 put in a good performance. It's a monovarietal Cabernet Sauvignon redolent of pencil lead, tanned leather, ash, tomato leaf and plum. In the mouth it comes through firm and substantive, rigid on the attack but relaxed on the finish. The curious Spirto '15, made with Merlot grapes, offers up aromas of oregano, basil, bay leaf and cumin, all grafted on a fruity background of raspberries. In the mouth it has a creamy, warm, pervasive attack, continuing with a fresh acidic streak.

Wine	Rating
● I Fiori Blu '15	TT 6
○ L'Etrange '18	TT 4
● Spirto '15	TT 5
⊙ A Rose is a Rose '19	T 2
○ Kalendamaia '19	T 3
● I Fiori Blu '13	YY 6
○ Kalendamaia '18	YY 2*
○ Kalendamaia '16	YY 2*
● Rubido '16	YY 2*
● Rubido '15	YY 2*
● Spirto '10	YY 5

★Podere Sapaio

VIA DEL FOSSO, 31
57022 CASTAGNETO CARDUCCI [LI]
TEL. +39 0438430440
www.sapaio.it

CELLAR SALES
PRE-BOOKED VISITS
ANNUAL PRODUCTION 110,000 bottles
HECTARES UNDER VINE 26.00
VITICULTURE METHOD Certified Organic

Massimo Piccin, descending from a family of entrepreneurs from Veneto, personifies the Sapaio project. Passionate and sensitive, in a relatively short time he was able to build a winery capable of distinguishing itself in Bolgheri. The estate comprises a total of forty hectares on sandy-calcareous soils, the basis for a modern but increasingly graceful enological style. Increasingly measured extraction and aging in wood (compared to the beginning) makes for wines of crystalline class. Because of the vintage, the Bolgheri Rosso Volpolo '18 earns the pleasure of surpassing its older brother, the Sapaio '17. The latter certainly represents an authoritative interpretation of a controversial year, but the finesse, immediate elegance and juicy drinkability of the former made us believers. It's a racy wine, with sweet and sapid flesh that unfolds clear and compact before a decisive finish.

Wine	Rating
● Bolgheri Rosso Volpolo '18	TTT 5
● Sapaio '17	TT 6
● Bolgheri Rosso Sup. '13	YYY 7
● Bolgheri Rosso Sup. '12	YYY 7
● Bolgheri Rosso Sup. '11	YYY 7
● Bolgheri Rosso Sup. Sapaio '16	YYY 7
● Bolgheri Sup. Sapaio '10	YYY 6
● Bolgheri Sup. Sapaio '09	YYY 6
● Bolgheri Sup. Sapaio '08	YYY 6
● Bolgheri Sup. Sapaio '07	YYY 6
● Bolgheri Sup. Sapaio '06	YYY 6
● Sapaio '15	YYY 6
● Bolgheri Rosso Volpolo '17	YY 5
● Bolgheri Volpolo '16	YY 5
● Bolgheri Volpolo '15	YY 5
● Bolgheri Volpolo '12	YY 4

Fattoria Sardi

FRAZ. MONTE SAN QUIRICO
VIA DELLA MAULINA, 747
55100 LUCCA
TEL. +39 0583341230
www.fattoriasardi.com

CELLAR SALES
PRE-BOOKED VISITS
ACCOMMODATION
ANNUAL PRODUCTION 130,000 bottles
HECTARES UNDER VINE 19.00
VITICULTURE METHOD Certified Organic

Fattoria Sardi is situated in an enchanting landscape, perched on the narrow hills between the Apuan Alps, the Apennines and the Tyrrhenian Sea. The vineyards are located between the Freddana and Serchio rivers, on loamy and sandy soils in the lower parts, clayey with the presence of pebbles and gravel along the more steep slopes. Speaking of natural resources, it should be noted that the young owners have worked to develop a sustainable project that's clean, respectful of the terroir. Their wines are fragrant, tasty, always highly elegant. Great attention is paid to their rosés, a typology for which the area seems very well suited. These last earned reviews that were positive, to say the least, a sign that their great work is bearing fruit. We particularly appreciated the Le Cicale '19, a wine whose splendid aromatic profile is characterized by notes of medlar, mandarin peel and confectioner's sugar. To be really great, a vibrant and pulpy palate needs only a bit of dryness and backbone. A good performance for the fun and enjoyable Pet-Nat '19 as well.

Wine	Rating
⊙ Le Cicale '19	🍷🍷 5
⊙ Rosé '19	🍷🍷 3
● Colline Lucchesi Rosso Vallebuia '19	🍷 4
● Colline Lucchesi Sebastiano '17	🍷 5
○ Colline Lucchesi Vermentino '19	🍷 3
○ Pet Nat Bianco Metodo Ancestrale '19	🍷 3
● Colline Lucchesi Mille968 '16	YY 5
● Colline Lucchesi Sebastiano '15	YY 5
○ Colline Lucchesi Vermentino '18	YY 3
⊙ Le Cicale '18	YY 5
⊙ Le Cicale '17	YY 5
⊙ Le Cicale '16	YY 4
○ Pet-Nat Frizzante '17	YY 3
○ Pet-Nat Frizzante '16	YY 3
⊙ Rosé '18	YY 3

Sassotondo

FRAZ. SOVANA
LOC. PIAN DI CONATI, 52
58010 SORANO [GR]
TEL. +39 0564614218
www.sassotondo.it

CELLAR SALES
PRE-BOOKED VISITS
ANNUAL PRODUCTION 50,000 bottles
HECTARES UNDER VINE 12.00
VITICULTURE METHOD Certified Organic

Edoardo Ventimiglia, a former documentary filmmaker from Rome, and his agronomist wife, Carla Benini began producing wines in this corner of Maremma around the mid-1990s, founding a pioneering project in Sassotondo. The current direction is rooted foremost in the rigorous application of organic viticulture and the zoning of the farm plots, while in the cellar spontaneous fermentation and long macerations are preferred, with maturation carried out both in terracotta and oak (barriques and large barrels, which are increasingly used). The Bianco di Pitigliano Superiore Vigna Isolina '19 brings together olfactory suggestions of aromatic herbs and wild flowers, hints of honey, spices and quince, only to unveil a pleasantly juicy, dynamic palate that's rich in contrast. The Ciliegiolo '19 is fragrant and drinkable, while the Ciliegiolo Monte Calvo '18 features a delectable palate enriched by a peppery and balsamic complexity.

Wine	Rating
○ Bianco di Pitigliano Superiore V. Isolina '19	🍷🍷 4
● Maremma Toscana Ciliegiolo '19	🍷🍷 3
● Maremma Toscana Ciliegiolo Monte Calvo '18	🍷🍷 6
● Maremma Toscana Ciliegiolo Poggio Pinzo '18	🍷 6
● Maremma Toscana Ciliegiolo San Lorenzo '17	🍷 6
○ Numero Sei '18	🍷 7
● Maremma Toscana Ciliegiolo '17	YY 3
● Maremma Toscana Ciliegiolo Poggio Pinzo '17	YY 6
● Maremma Toscana Ciliegiolo San Lorenzo '16	YY 6
● Maremma Toscana Ciliegiolo San Lorenzo '15	YY 6

Michele Satta

loc. Vigna al Cavaliere, 61b
57022 Castagneto Carducci [LI]
Tel. +39 0565773041
www.michelesatta.com

CELLAR SALES
PRE-BOOKED VISITS
ANNUAL PRODUCTION 150,000 bottles
HECTARES UNDER VINE 20.00

Michele Satta's winery is one of Bolgheri's historic producers, and the man who gives it its name is certainly one of the area's pioneers. Founded in 1983, it has consistently taken original paths, starting with a passion for Sangiovese. Today Michele's son Giacomo is taking on a more and more central role, so much so that their production style appears to be in decisive evolution, with wines that are increasingly personal and tasty, the result of practices that are attentive to nature and respectful of the grapes. In the cellar experiments with amphora seem to have convinced the owners and so we're seeing an increase in its use. The Marianova '17 is an original Bolgheri Superiore in every way. It doesn't use 'Bordeaux' grapes, being the result of a blend of Syrah and Sangiovese. It's also vinified in oak before going into barriques and then 750-liter amphorae. Mature and impressive, with toasted notes still in the foreground, it's marked by a juicy, sapid mouthfeel, a bit held back by dense, pronounced tannins.

Wine	Rating	Price
● Bolgheri Rosso Sup. Marianova '17	🍷🍷	8
● Bolgheri Rosso Sup. Piastraia '17	🍷🍷	6
● Cavaliere '17	🍷	6
○ Bolgheri Bianco Giovin Re '17	🍷🍷	6
● Bolgheri Rosso '15	🍷🍷	4
● Bolgheri Rosso '13	🍷🍷	3
● Bolgheri Rosso Sup. I Castagni '12	🍷🍷	8
● Bolgheri Rosso Sup. Marianova '16	🍷🍷	8
● Bolgheri Rosso Sup. Marianova '15	🍷🍷	8
● Bolgheri Rosso Sup. Piastraia '15	🍷🍷	6
● Bolgheri Sup. Piastraia '14	🍷🍷	6
● Cavaliere '15	🍷🍷	6
● Syrah '12	🍷🍷	5

Fattoria Selvapiana

loc. Selvapiana, 43
50068 Rufina [FI]
Tel. +39 0558369848
www.selvapiana.it

CELLAR SALES
PRE-BOOKED VISITS
ANNUAL PRODUCTION 220,000 bottles
HECTARES UNDER VINE 60.00

Now that it's entirely certified organic, Fattoria Selvapiana has completed a journey that began in 1990. The property, which comprises vineyards, olive groves and woodlands, spans three municipalities: Rufina, Pelago and Pontassieve. Most of the vineyards, those of the oldest part of the estate, are situated around the villa, with their new cellar, inaugurated in 2005, nearby. Here Sangiovese reigns supreme, with small islands of Syrah, Merlot and Cabernet Sauvignon appearing on a historic estate, one of Chianti Rufina's most representative. The Chianti Rufina '18 put in a good performance. Clear, focused notes of cherry are accompanied by minerals hints and fresh nuances of aromatic herbs (sage and tarragon); in the mouth it opens pleasant, linear, sapid, while the finish sees polished, tasty tannins. Vegetal notes prevail in the Pomino Rosso '17: green pepper opens the dance, then comes cherry and ripe plum. The palate is supple and racy, with nice flesh.

Wine	Rating	Price
● Chianti Rufina '18	🍷🍷	3
● Fornace '16	🍷🍷	5
● Pomino Rosso Villa Petrognano '17	🍷🍷	2*
○ Pomino Bianco Villa Petrognano '19	🍷	2
● Chianti Rufina '17	🍷🍷	3
● Chianti Rufina '16	🍷🍷	2*
● Chianti Rufina '15	🍷🍷	2*
● Chianti Rufina Bucerchiale Ris. '13	🍷🍷	5
● Chianti Rufina Bucerchiale Ris. '12	🍷🍷	5
● Chianti Rufina Vign. Bucerchiale Ris. '16	🍷🍷	5
● Chianti Rufina Vign. Bucerchiale Ris. '15	🍷🍷	5
● Chianti Rufina Vign. Erci '16	🍷🍷	3
● Fornace '15	🍷🍷	5

Sensi - Fattoria Calappiano

fraz. Cerbaia, 107
51035 Lamporecchio [PT]
Tel. +39 057382910
www.sensivini.com

CELLAR SALES
PRE-BOOKED VISITS
ANNUAL PRODUCTION 2,000,000 bottles
HECTARES UNDER VINE 100.00
VITICULTURE METHOD Certified Organic
SUSTAINABLE WINERY

One of the Medici family's historical-architectural treasures is now owned by the Sensi family. For more than 120 years in the world of wine, first as merchants, then as producers, they have overseen this Montalbano winery situated in the provinces of Florence, Prato and Pistoia. The grapes cultivated on the 60-hectares of organically managed vineyards are Chianti's classic varieties: Sangiovese, Canaiolo, Colorino, Malvasia Bianca and Trebbiano, in addition to Chardonnay. More recently, varieties such as Pugnitello, Ciliegiolo and Petit Manseng have also been rediscovered. The Lungarno '17, a blend of Cabernet Sauvignon, Merlot and Colorino, features an aromatic profile wrought of berries (currant and blueberry), with balsamic and minty hints supporting spicy notes of vanilla, cloves and cinnamon. The palate is soft, pervasive, tannins and alcohol nicely in step, an elegant acidic backbone and succulent finish. The Collegonzi '17 also performs at high levels.

Wine	Glasses	Price
● Collegonzi Sangiovese Fattoria Calappiano '17	2 (black)	6
● Lungarno '17	2 (black)	7
● Chianti Dalcampo Ris. '17	2 (black)	3
● Chianti Sup. Vegante '18	2 (black)	3
● Rosso di Montalcino Villa al Cortile '18	2 (black)	3
○ Vernaccia di San Gimignano Collegiata '19	2 (black)	2*
● Bolgheri Sabbiato '17	1 (black)	5
● Chianti Vinciano '19	1 (black)	5
● Chianti Vinciano Ris. '17	1 (black)	6
● Governato '18	1 (black)	7
● Morellino di Scansano Pretorio '19	1 (black)	3
● Ninfato '19	1 (black)	3
● Collegonzi Sangiovese Fattoria Calappiano '16	2 (white)	6

Serraiola

fraz. Frassine
loc. Serraiola
58025 Monterotondo Marittimo [GR]
Tel. +39 0566910026
www.serraiola.it

CELLAR SALES
PRE-BOOKED VISITS
ANNUAL PRODUCTION 40,000 bottles
HECTARES UNDER VINE 12.00

Fiorella Lenzi is a 'donna del vino' who experienced Maremma's enological development first hand, producing wines of good character and notable quality. From a stylistic point of view, her range exhibits a firm, well-balanced profile, with generous, Mediterranean reds and whites of pleasant drinkability. As is not uncommon for the area, sometimes we notice an excessive presence of oak, but their direction appears increasingly defined and conscientious. The Sassonero '19 features a fragrant nose of red fruit adorned with spicy hints. In the mouth it's smooth and tasty—quite delicious. 100% Sangiovese, the Lentisco '18 offers up vibrant aromas of morello cherry supported by smoky hints, with a wide and juicy progression of flavor. The Campo Montecristo '18 is a monovarietal Merlot with sweet and full aromas. In the mouth it unfolds with a pleasant softness and nice dynamism.

Wine	Glasses	Price
● Maremma Toscana Rosso Sassonero '19	2 (black)	2*
● Campo Montecristo '18	2 (black)	5
● Lentisco '18	2 (black)	3
○ Maremma Toscana Bianco Violina '19	1 (black)	3
● Shiraz '18	1 (black)	4
○ Vermentino '19	1 (black)	3
● Campo Montecristo '16	2 (white)	5
● Campo Montecristo '15	2 (white)	5
● Campo Montecristo '14	2 (white)	5
● Lentisco '17	2 (white)	3
● Lentisco '16	2 (white)	3
● Lentisco '15	2 (white)	3
● Lentisco '14	2 (white)	3
● Shiraz '16	2 (white)	4
○ Vermentino '18	2 (white)	3

Sesti - Castello di Argiano

Fraz. Sant'Angelo in Colle
loc. Castello di Argiano
53024 Montalcino [SI]
Tel. +39 0577843921
www.sestiwine.com

CELLAR SALES
PRE-BOOKED VISITS
ANNUAL PRODUCTION 61,000 bottles
HECTARES UNDER VINE 9.00

We repeat ourselves, but when it comes to the Castello di Argiano one can only start from the enchanted, almost dreamlike beauty that welcomes those who enter the southwestern end of Montalcino to explore the place chosen by the Sesti family as their production center. It's an area immersed in Mediterranean scrub, influenced by sea breezes and sandy soils rich in tufa, a singular environment that's reflected in their multiform, Sangiovese-based range of wines. The result is a gracefully wild Brunello that makes enological considerations seem superfluous. Even though they're missing that crowning stroke, the winery submitted a worthy line-up. Obviously, Brunello takes center stage. The 2015 version brought out the warm aspects of Argiano through Mediterranean aromas, calling up tobacco and medicinal herbs, enriched by fruity and spicy notes of oak. In the mouth fine tannins are balanced by the warmth of alcohol. The cosseting Rosso di Montalcino and the unexpected Rosato are also of note.

Wine	Rating
● Brunello di Montalcino '15	▼▼ 6
● Grangiovese '18	▼▼ 2*
⊙ Rosato '19	▼▼ 2*
● Rosso di Montalcino '18	▼▼ 4
○ Sauvignon '19	▼ 3
● Brunello di Montalcino '06	▽▽▽ 6
● Brunello di Montalcino Phenomena Ris. '07	▽▽▽ 8
● Brunello di Montalcino Phenomena Ris. '01	▽▽▽ 8
● Brunello di Montalcino Ris. '04	▽▽▽ 8
● Rosso di Montalcino '16	▽▽▽ 4*
● Brunello di Montalcino Phenomena Ris. '13	▽▽ 8
● Brunello di Montalcino Phenomena Ris. '10	▽▽ 8
● Rosso di Montalcino '17	▽▽ 4

★Tenuta Sette Ponti

via Sette Ponti, 71
52029 Castiglion Fibocchi [AR]
Tel. +39 0575477857
www.tenutasetteponti.it

CELLAR SALES
PRE-BOOKED VISITS
ACCOMMODATION
ANNUAL PRODUCTION 250,000 bottles
HECTARES UNDER VINE 60.00
VITICULTURE METHOD Certified Organic
SUSTAINABLE WINERY

The estate, which is located in a charming corner of Tuscany, in Florence and Arezzo, takes its name from the number of bridges over the Arno River that meet on the street where it's located. It has been owned by the Moretti Cuseri family since the 1950s, when architect Alberto bought it from Margherita and Maria Cristina di Savoia. It was Antonio, Alberto's son and a fashion entrepreneur, who consolidated the property's wine production. The vineyards are managed organically and include not only Sangiovese, but also many international varieties, such as Cabernet Sauvignon and Merlot. The Oreno '18, a blend of Merlot, Cabernet Sauvignon and Petit Verdot, is truly delicious. Tomato leaf on the nose, then green pepper and mineral notes, but also horseradish and marjoram. The palate, with its balsamic whiffs, exhibits nice weight and calibrated tannins with a smoky aftertaste. We also appreciated the Crognolo '18, a Sangiovese with a splash of Merlot. It's a fresh wine and an enticing drink.

Wine	Rating
● Oreno '18	▼▼▼ 8
● Chianti V. di Pallino Ris. '18	▼▼ 3
● Crognolo '18	▼▼ 5
● Oreno '17	▽▽▽ 8
● Oreno '16	▽▽▽ 8
● Oreno '15	▽▽▽ 8
● Oreno '12	▽▽▽ 7
● Oreno '11	▽▽▽ 7
● Oreno '10	▽▽▽ 7
● Oreno '09	▽▽▽ 7
● Oreno '05	▽▽▽ 7
● Oreno '00	▽▽▽ 5
● Valdarno di Sopra V. dell'Impero '13	▽▽▽ 8
● Crognolo '15	▽▽ 5
● Oreno '13	▽▽ 8
● Valdarno di Sopra Sangiovese Vigna dell'Impero '16	▽▽ 8

Solaria - Cencioni Patrizia

pod. Capanna, 102
53024 Montalcino [SI]
Tel. +39 0577849426
www.solariacencioni.com

CELLAR SALES
PRE-BOOKED VISITS
ANNUAL PRODUCTION 35,500 bottles
HECTARES UNDER VINE 9.00

Launched in 1989 from a part of the estate founded by Giuseppe Cencioni in the 1950s, Solaria has, over time, become one of the most appreciated producers in the area, thanks primarily to the relentless work carried out by Patrizia. Assisted full-time by the new generation, she oversees the vineyards that grow on a sort of natural plateau on the southeast side of Montalcino, at around 300 meters above sea level on clayey-tufa soils. These soil and climate conditions help frame the energy of Brunello wines matured in 2500 and 4000-liter Slavonian oak. Patrizia Cencioni has taken all the right turns, culminating this year in two fantastic 2015 Brunellos, in particular the 30 Anni (produced to celebrate the producer's birthday). Made with grapes from their oldest vineyards, then aged for three years in large Slavonian oak barrels, it's a gem of complexity, redolent of cherry, licorice and camphor, with a palate that lingers on beautifully wedded tannins and pulp.

● Brunello di Montalcino '15	🍷🍷 6
● Brunello di Montalcino 30 anni '15	🍷🍷 8
● Rosso di Montalcino '18	🍷🍷 3
● Solarianne '17	🍷🍷 5
⊙ Rosato '19	🍷 3
● Brunello di Montalcino '14	🍷🍷 6
● Brunello di Montalcino '13	🍷🍷 6
● Brunello di Montalcino '12	🍷🍷 6
● Brunello di Montalcino '10	🍷🍷 5
● Brunello di Montalcino 123 Ris. '13	🍷🍷 8
● Brunello di Montalcino 123 Ris. '10	🍷🍷 8
● Rosso di Montalcino '17	🍷🍷 3*
● Rosso di Montalcino '16	🍷🍷 3
● Rosso di Montalcino '15	🍷🍷 3
● Rosso di Montalcino '12	🍷🍷 4

Fattoria Sorbaiano

loc. Sorbaiano
56040 Montecatini Val di Cecina [PI]
Tel. +39 0588028054
www.fattoriasorbaiano.it

CELLAR SALES
PRE-BOOKED VISITS
ACCOMMODATION
ANNUAL PRODUCTION 60,000 bottles
HECTARES UNDER VINE 27.00
VITICULTURE METHOD Certified Organic

Sorbaiano is one of the most important producers operating in an appellation that was, at one time, one of Pisano's primary DOC zones, but today is need a true revival: Montescudaio. Mainly vines are grown on the farm, but there are also olive trees and arable land. Of late they've been focusing heavily on hospitality as well. It's a strategic position, near the crags of Volterra and close enough to the sea so that the climate proves particularly well-suited to viticulture and good living. The Pian del Conte '17 is a classic Sangiovese blend with a share of Cabernet Sauvignon. On the nose it offers up aromas of freshly-dug earth and undergrowth, plum and balsamic whiffs. The palate is firm, dynamic on the acidic side, with well-coordinated tannins and a finish that unfolds progressively. 100% Merlot, the Febo '17 proves enjoyable on the nose with hints of blueberries and peppers along with fresh notes of lemon verbena; on the palate it's pervasive and creamy, broad and powerful.

● Febo '17	🍷🍷 6
● Montescudaio Rosso delle Miniere '17	🍷🍷 5
○ Montescudaio Vin Santo '12	🍷🍷 6
● Pian del Conte '17	🍷🍷 4
○ Montescudaio Bianco '19	🍷 2
● Montescudaio Rosso '18	🍷 2
○ Montescudaio Bianco '14	🍷🍷 2*
● Montescudaio Rosso '13	🍷🍷 2*
● Montescudaio Rosso delle Miniere '12	🍷🍷 5
○ Montescudaio Vin Santo '08	🍷🍷 5

Talenti

FRAZ. SANT'ANGELO IN COLLE
LOC. PIAN DI CONTE
53024 MONTALCINO [SI]
TEL. +39 0577844064
www.talentimontalcino.it

CELLAR SALES
PRE-BOOKED VISITS
ANNUAL PRODUCTION 100,000 bottles
HECTARES UNDER VINE 21.00

The Talenti family's vineyards are concentrated in the enclave of Sant'Angelo in Colle, at the center of southwest Montalcino. They constitute the Pian di Conte estate, purchased by Pierluigi in the early 1980s and now run by his grandson Riccardo. It's a natural terrace over the Orcia river characterized by elevations spanning 200-400 meters, as well as a composite of clay, limestone and sea sand. It's a pedoclimatic puzzle that we find in their solid and bright Rosso and Brunello, wines that derive from mixed maturation in tonneaux and medium-sized oak barrels. This selection, created with the 2015 harvest, is dedicated to the founder Pierluigi Talenti. It comes from a vineyard of almost two hectares, located in Sant'Angelo in Colle at about 400 meters above sea level. Matured for 24 months in mid-sized, French oak casks, the Piero is a Brunello of great extractive richness, holding nothing back: the palate is bold and tannic, though not lacking in freshness and harmony, enlivened by aromas of black berries and cocoa.

● Brunello di Montalcino Piero '15	🍷🍷 8
● Brunello di Montalcino '15	🍷🍷 8
● Rosso di Montalcino '18	🍷🍷 4
● Rispollo '17	🍷 2
● Trefolo '13	🍷 2
● Brunello di Montalcino '04	🍷🍷🍷 8
● Brunello di Montalcino '88	🍷🍷🍷 8
● Brunello di Montalcino Pian di Conte Ris. '13	🍷🍷🍷 7
● Brunello di Montalcino Ris. '99	🍷🍷🍷 6
● Brunello di Montalcino Trentennale '11	🍷🍷🍷 8
● Brunello di Montalcino V. del Paretaio Ris. '01	🍷🍷🍷 6
● Brunello di Montalcino '14	🍷🍷 6
● Brunello di Montalcino '13	🍷🍷 6
● Rosso di Montalcino '17	🍷🍷 3*

★Tenimenti Luigi d'Alessandro

VIA MANZANO, 15
52042 CORTONA [AR]
TEL. +39 0575618667
www.tenimentidalessandro.it

CELLAR SALES
PRE-BOOKED VISITS
ACCOMMODATION AND RESTAURANT SERVICE
ANNUAL PRODUCTION 130,000 bottles
HECTARES UNDER VINE 37.00
VITICULTURE METHOD Certified Organic

The journey began in 1967, with the purchase of the estate by the D'Alessandro family, but the turning point came in 2013, when the Calabresi family, who had been a partner since 2007, took over the entire property. Since then, Filippo Calabresi has been in charge, obtaining organic certification in 2016 and applying the knowledge accumulated during his stays in France, California and Oregon. The grapes in which he's chosen to invest are Syrah and Viognier, but it is, above all, their production style that has undergone a major transformation. The Bosco '16 is a delicious, monovarietal Syrah characterized by intriguing notes of candied orange, medicinal herbs and lively fruit (currant and cherry). On the palate it exhibits energy, with focused tannins, a fresh acidic vein, and a finish of lovely, sapid vitality. We also appreciated the Rosso '18, where citrus sensations return combined with hints of tarragon and marjoram on a cherry base. In the mouth it's assertive, standing out for its excellent tension and drinkability.

● Cortona Syrah Il Bosco '16	🍷🍷 6
● Migliara '16	🍷🍷 8
● Rosso '18	🍷🍷 3
○ Fontarca '18	🍷 5
● Cortona Il Bosco '09	🍷🍷🍷 6
● Cortona Il Bosco '06	🍷🍷🍷 6
● Cortona Il Bosco '04	🍷🍷🍷 5
● Cortona Il Bosco '03	🍷🍷🍷 5
● Cortona Il Bosco '01	🍷🍷🍷 6
● Cortona Syrah Il Bosco '12	🍷🍷🍷 6
● Cortona Syrah Migliara '08	🍷🍷🍷 8
● Cortona Syrah Migliara '07	🍷🍷🍷 8
● Podere Il Bosco '97	🍷🍷🍷 5
● Podere Il Bosco '95	🍷🍷🍷 5
● Cortona Syrah Il Bosco '15	🍷🍷 6
● Migliara '15	🍷🍷 8
● Syrah '17	🍷🍷 3

Tenuta di Canneto

FRAZ. CANNETO
VIA ROMA, 7
56040 MONTEVERDI MARITTIMO [PI]
TEL. +39 0565784927
www.tenutacanneto.it

CELLAR SALES
PRE-BOOKED VISITS
ANNUAL PRODUCTION 35,000 bottles
HECTARES UNDER VINE 30.00

The estate is very large, about a thousand hectares, but only 30 of those are under vine, all carefully chosen so as to identify the best plots. All this in a village of a few inhabitants, in an area where it's easy to detect the marine influence on the climate. The cellar was built in 2009 so that it could operate with the utmost care and have the necessary space for vinification by plot. Olive trees and the breeding of Chianina meat round out production. The Pian di Contessa '17, a monovarietal Merlot, was very well received. The nose expresses a vegetal bouquet wrought of myrtle, sage, bay leaves, and spicy notes of pepper and juniper, all on a background of black fruit. In the mouth it stands out for its balanced body, refreshing acid backbone and a creamy, docile structure. The Santabarbara '18 is an excellent Bordeaux blend (with added Syrah) that features cherry aromas and a focused palate. The Pietriccio '18 is also well made.

Wine	Rating
● Merlot Pian di Contessa '17	🍷🍷 5
● Pietriccio '18	🍷🍷 3
● Santabarbara '18	🍷🍷 3
○ Lillatro Garbato '19	🍷 3
● Merlot Podere Capannelle '12	ΥΥ 5
● Syrah Podere Vizzate '12	ΥΥ 3*

Tenuta di Castelfalfi

LOC. CASTELFALFI
50050 MONTAIONE [FI]
TEL. +39 0571890190
www.castelfalfi.it

CELLAR SALES
PRE-BOOKED VISITS
ACCOMMODATION AND RESTAURANT SERVICE
ANNUAL PRODUCTION 50,000 bottles
HECTARES UNDER VINE 25.00
VITICULTURE METHOD Certified Organic

The estate is part of a tourist center that includes restaurants, hotels, villas and golf courses. It's located in an area equidistant from Florence, Siena and Pisa, with special care taken when it comes to quality agricultural production. Their work follows the dictates of organic cultivation, with wines and oils representing the peaks of excellence, not to mention arable land that's used in part for the production of craft beers and pasta flours. With the 2016 harvest, Poggio alla Fame reaches peaks not achieved before. A monovarietal Sangiovese, it offers up a captivating olfactory suite of rain-soaked earth, violets and plums, combined with a juicy, pulpy body, fine tannins and appetizing sapidity. The Poggio Nero '16, a blend of Cabernet Sauvignon, Merlot and Alicante, features an aromatic bouquet in which blackberries and cherries meet nuances of chocolate and coffee. Pleasant on the palate, it has a delicate texture and tasty finish.

Wine	Rating
● Poggio alla Fame '16	🍷🍷 4
● Chianti Cercaia Ris. '16	🍷🍷 3
● Chianti Cerchiaia '19	🍷🍷 2*
● Poggionero '16	🍷🍷 4
● Poggio alla Fame '15	ΥΥ 4
● Poggio alla Fame '13	ΥΥ 5
○ Poggio I Soli '18	ΥΥ 2*
● Poggionero '15	ΥΥ 4
● Poggionero '14	ΥΥ 3
● Poggionero '11	ΥΥ 3
○ Rancoli Vermentino '15	ΥΥ 2*
● San Piero '16	ΥΥ 2*

Tenuta di Sesta

fraz. Castelnuovo dell'Abate
loc. Sesta
53024 Montalcino [SI]
Tel. +39 0577835612
www.tenutadisesta.it

CELLAR SALES
PRE-BOOKED VISITS
ANNUAL PRODUCTION 150,000 bottles
HECTARES UNDER VINE 30.00

Founded in the 1960s by Giuseppe Ciacci, Tenuta di Sesta gets its name from one of southern Montalcino's most well-known areas. One of few veteran producers operating in the district, today it's led by Andrea and Francesca together with their father, Giovanni. The family have managed to go further in bringing out the unique attributes of their vineyards, situated at around 350 meters above sea level on calcareous soils, rich in clay and iron. It's here that the grapes for their Brunello are cultivated. An unexpectedly pure wine aged in medium-sized oak barrels, it's also long-lived. Even in the absence of their Riserva, the Ciacci family still demonstrate why they're a leader in the appellation, hitting a bullseye with their Brunello '15. It's a wine that manages to combine two qualities that are usually opposed: richness and freshness. The latter is found in its fruity aromas, while the former emerges on notes of tobacco and liquorice. On the palate, its acidic-tannic backbone contrasts perfectly with its sweet, fruity pulp.

● Brunello di Montalcino '15	🍷🍷🍷 8
● Rosso di Montalcino '18	🍷🍷 5
● Poggio d'Arna '17	🍷🍷 4
● Brunello di Montalcino Duelecci Est Ris. '13	🍷🍷🍷 8
● Brunello di Montalcino Duelecci Ovest Ris. '12	🍷🍷🍷 7
● Brunello di Montalcino Ris. '10	🍷🍷🍷 7
● Brunello di Montalcino '14	🍷🍷 8
● Brunello di Montalcino '13	🍷🍷 8
● Brunello di Montalcino '10	🍷🍷 5
● Brunello di Montalcino '09	🍷🍷 5
● Brunello di Montalcino Ris. '11	🍷🍷 7
● Brunello di Montalcino Ris. '09	🍷🍷 7
● Rosso di Montalcino '17	🍷🍷 5
● Rosso di Montalcino '15	🍷🍷 3*
● Rosso di Montalcino '13	🍷🍷 3

Tenuta di Trinoro

via Val d'Orcia, 15
53047 Sarteano [SI]
Tel. +39 0578267110
www.vinifranchetti.com

PRE-BOOKED VISITS
ANNUAL PRODUCTION 90,000 bottles
HECTARES UNDER VINE 23.00

A few years ago Andrea Franchetti fell in love with this corner of Val d'Orcia near the border with Lazio. It's a land without wine traditions, but Andrea sensed it had potential. After experiences at important producers, he felt ready to realize his dream, planting the first Bordeaux varieties and building a winery. The first vintage came in 1997. The characterful, intense style of his range has carved out an important place among international wines. Andrea, who collaborates today with his cousin Carlo, makes wines characterized by an unmistakable style. They're concentrated, rich wines (uncompromisingly so), yet marked by a balance and elegance that are, at times, remarkable. This is the case with the Campo di Camagi '18, an extraordinary Cabernet Franc made with grapes from a single vineyard. Lush, powerful, deep and balanced, it expresses all the unique attributes of the domaine. Their other wines all perform at outstanding levels.

● Campo di Camagi Cabernet Franc '18	🍷🍷🍷 8
○ Bianco di Trinoro '18	🍷🍷 7
● Tenuta di Trinoro '17	🍷🍷 8
● Campo di Magnacosta Cabernet Franc '18	🍷🍷 8
● Campo di Tenaglia Cabernet Franc '18	🍷🍷 8
● Le Cupole '18	🍷🍷 5
● Sancaba Pinot Nero '18	🍷🍷 7
● Tenuta di Trinoro '08	🍷🍷🍷 8
● Tenuta di Trinoro '04	🍷🍷🍷 8
● Tenuta di Trinoro '03	🍷🍷🍷 8
● Palazzi '16	🍷🍷 8
● Tenuta di Trinoro '16	🍷🍷 8
● Tenuta di Trinoro '15	🍷🍷 8
● Tenuta di Trinoro '14	🍷🍷 8

★Tenute del Cerro

FRAZ. ACQUAVIVA
VIA GRAZIANELLA, 5
53045 MONTEPULCIANO [SI]
TEL. +39 0578767722
www.fattoriadelcerro.it

CELLAR SALES
PRE-BOOKED VISITS
ACCOMMODATION AND RESTAURANT SERVICE
ANNUAL PRODUCTION 1,300,000 bottles
HECTARES UNDER VINE 181.00

The Unipol insurance group's Tuscan wineries operate under the 'umbrella' of Tenute del Cerro: La Poderina in Montalcino, Monterufoli in Monteverdi Marittimo nel Pisano and the Fattoria del Cerro in Montepulciano (as well as Còlpetrone, in Umbria). The Montepulciano winery undoubtedly represents the symbol of this complex enoic mosaic, having produced some important wines for over forty years, and having contributed the growth and success of the Nobile appellation in years that were crucial from a public relations point of view, to say the least. A wine characterized by unabashedly fruity aromas, sweet and concentrated, adorned by hints of oak, the Nobile di Montepulciano '17 unveils a close-woven and well-sustained palate right up through a broad finish still on sweet fruit. Darker and spicy olfactory timbres feature in the Nobile di Montepulciano Riserva '16, a wine that's full, complex and pervasive on the palate.

- Nobile di Montepulciano '17 — TTT 4*
- Nobile di Montepulciano Ris. '16 — TT 5
- Nobile di Montepulciano Antica Chiusina '16 — T 6
- Rosso di Montepulciano '19 — T 3
- Nobile di Montepulciano '16 — YYY 4*
- Nobile di Montepulciano '15 — YYY 4*
- Nobile di Montepulciano '14 — YYY 3*
- Nobile di Montepulciano '11 — YYY 3*
- Nobile di Montepulciano '10 — YYY 3*
- Nobile di Montepulciano Ris. '12 — YYY 4*
- Nobile di Montepulciano Ris. '11 — YYY 4*
- Nobile di Montepulciano Ris. '06 — YYY 4
- Nobile di Montepulciano Vign. Antica Chiusina '00 — YYY 6
- Nobile di Montepulciano Vign. Antica Chiusina '99 — YYY 6

Terenzi

LOC. MONTEDONICO
58054 SCANSANO [GR]
TEL. +39 0564599601
www.terenzi.eu

CELLAR SALES
PRE-BOOKED VISITS
ACCOMMODATION
ANNUAL PRODUCTION 350,000 bottles
HECTARES UNDER VINE 60.00

The Terenzi family of Milan arrived in Maremma in the early 2000s, founding a solid and convincing producer that, to some extent, has shaken up the Morellino di Scansano appellation. The winery adopted a business strategy that has become a model, one characterized by choices that are always on the mark, both in the cellar and in the vineyard, in pursuit of a style that eschews excesses. It's a style that's bound up with the territory while skillfully combining tradition and modern approaches. Once again the Morellino Madrechiesa Riserva emerges as one of the best in its class, thanks to a monumental 2016. Aromas range from violet to cherry, undergrowth and spices, while on the palate its rhythm is marked by a lovely acidic verve, all exalted across a flavorful finish. The Morellino Purosangue Riserva '17 is darker aromatically and more sustained by oak.

- Morellino di Scansano Madrechiesa Ris. '16 — TTT 5
- Morellino di Scansano '19 — TT 3
- Morellino di Scansano Purosangue Ris. '17 — TT 4
- Francesca Romana '16 — YYY 5
- Morellino di Scansano Madrechiesa Ris. '15 — YYY 5
- Morellino di Scansano Madrechiesa Ris. '14 — YYY 5
- Morellino di Scansano Madrechiesa Ris. '13 — YYY 5
- Morellino di Scansano Madrechiesa Ris. '12 — YYY 5
- Morellino di Scansano Madrechiesa Ris. '11 — YYY 5

Terradonnà

LOC. NOTRI, 78
57028 SUVERETO [LI]
TEL. +39 0565838702
www.terradonna.it

CELLAR SALES
PRE-BOOKED VISITS
ANNUAL PRODUCTION 26,000 bottles
HECTARES UNDER VINE 7.00

This small and well-organized winery in the hills of Suvereto has more than half a century of history behind it. The Rossi family's Terradonnà passed from mother to daughter Annalisa in 2000 (the name means land donated from woman to woman). The first wine saw the light of day in 2002, since then their selection has grown and diversified, with each bottle expressing the qualities of a territory situated just a few kilometers from the coast. Sangiovese, Cabernet Sauvignon, Merlot and Syrah grapes are cultivated for their reds and rosés, while Vermentino, Trebbiano, Clarette and Ansonica form the basis of their whites. The Okenio '17 put in a good performance. It's a monovarietal Cabernet characterized by notes of roasted coffee and spicy hints of cloves, all on a complex background of ripe fruits, blackberry and plum. In the mouth it opens well: warm and creamy, with an enticing acidic background and a long finish. The Bixbi '18, made with Syrah and Sangiovese, is grapey, youthful on the nose and fun on the palate by virtue of a pronounced vitality.

Wine	Rating
● Bixbi '18	TT 3
● Giaietto '18	TT 2*
● Prasio '17	TT 3
● Spato '17	TT 3
● Val di Cornia Cabernet Sauvignon Okenio '17	TT 5
○ Faden '19	T 2
○ Kalsi '19	T 2
⊙ Sysa '19	T 3
● Bixbi '15	YY 3
● Giaietto '16	YY 2*
○ Kalsi '18	YY 2*
● Prasio '16	YY 3
● Prasio '15	YY 3*
● Spato '16	YY 3
● Spato '15	YY 3

Fattoria Terre del Marchesato

FRAZ. BOLGHERI
LOC. SANT'UBERTO, 164
57022 CASTAGNETO CARDUCCI [LI]
TEL. +39 0565749752
www.terredelmarchesato.com

CELLAR SALES
PRE-BOOKED VISITS
ACCOMMODATION
ANNUAL PRODUCTION 120,000 bottles
HECTARES UNDER VINE 16.00

Terre del Marchesato belongs to the Fuselli family, who personally oversee the property. Lying from east to west, and rather dense, the vineyards unfold around the farm in an area marked by extremely unique characteristics: Ferruggini, in the middle of Bolgheri, where we find some of the appellation's most prestigious wineries. The producer's style is closely linked to the peculiar character of the soils here, which are rich in medium-textured clay, infused with sand and silt. This year we particularly appreciated an early drinker, the Inedito 2019. Decidedly fresh and juicy, this red perfectly balances fruit, delicate aromatic herbs and spicy sensations, which adorn both the nose and palate. The Bolgheri Superiore Marchesale '17 is also excellent, but the whole battery shines, from the Maurizio Fuselli Petit Verdot '17 to the Tarabuso of the same year.

Wine	Rating
● Bolgheri Marchesale Sup. '17	TT 6
● Inedito '17	TT 2*
● Maurizio Fuselli Petit Verdot '17	TT 8
● Tarabuso '17	TT 5
● Aldone '17	T 8
● Bolgheri Rosso Emilio I '18	T 3
● Aldone '14	YY 7
● Aldone '13	YY 7
● Bolgheri Rosso Emilio I '13	YY 3
● Marchesale '14	YY 6
● Marchesale '13	YY 6
● Marchesale '12	YY 7
○ Nobilis '13	YY 5

Terre dell'Etruria Il Poderone

Loc. Poderone Cà de Frati
58051 Magliano in Toscana [GR]
Tel. +39 0564593011
www.terretruria.it

CELLAR SALES
PRE-BOOKED VISITS
ANNUAL PRODUCTION 150,000 bottles
HECTARES UNDER VINE 97.00

Terre dell'Etruria - Il Poderone was established in 2014, in Magliano in Toscana. But despite the cooperative's young age, it's taken a decidedly clear direction. Without pursuing lofty goals, they've made pure, polished wines, immediately pleasant and drinkable, the center of production. Theirs are simple wines, but not banal, perfectly in keeping with what Maremma has always produced, both in terms of the recent past and historically. Fragrant red fruit and slight hints of Mediterranean scrub enliven the Morellino di Scansano Giogo '19, a wine whose palate is tasty and relaxed. Full and juicy, the Ciliegiolo Briglia '19 is characterized by aromas of berries well adorned with peppery and balsamic nuances. The Vermentino Marmato '19 is also impeccable, with lime blossoms and citrus fruits alternating on the nose, all anticipating a fragrant, vivid palate.

Wine	Rating
● Maremma Toscana Ciliegiolo Briglia '19	🍷🍷 2*
○ Maremma Toscana Vermentino Marmato '19	🍷🍷 2*
● Morellino di Scansano Giogo '19	🍷🍷 2*
○ Brumoso Vermentino Ancestrale Frizzante '19	🍷 2
○ Antico Borgo Ansonica '18	♢♢ 2*
● Briglia Ciliegiolo '14	♢♢ 2*
● Maremma Toscana Ciliegiolo Briglia '18	♢♢ 2*
● Morellino di Scansano Giogo '18	♢♢ 2*

La Togata

Fraz. Sant'Angelo in Colle
Loc. Tavernelle
53024 Montalcino [SI]
Tel. +39 0668803000
www.brunellolatogata.com

CELLAR SALES
PRE-BOOKED VISITS
ANNUAL PRODUCTION 120,000 bottles
HECTARES UNDER VINE 19.00
VITICULTURE METHOD Certified Organic
SUSTAINABLE WINERY

The agricultural and stylistic project carved out in recent years by Jeanneth Angel and her family is inextricably bound up with the particular attributes of the plots cultivated in Sant'Angelo in Colle, a bona fide center of production in southwest Montalcino. Lavacchio, Montosoli and Pietrafocaia—these are sites that dialog favorably in La Togata's varied range of Brunellos. In recent years they've stood out for their character and distinctiveness. Aged in both small wood barrels and 1500/2000-liter Slavonian oak, they share the same mobile, plush qualities. It's nice to get lost in the bizzare names of Togata's large line-up of Rossos and Brunello di Montalcinos. This year two 2015s topped our preferences, the Seconda Stella a Destra and the Togata dei Togati. The latter is aromatically elegant and complex, with red fruit meeting tobacco sensations. On the palate it stands out for its great harmony . The former is suitable for those who love powerful and pleasantly austere reds that are good for laying down.

Wine	Rating
● Brunello di Montalcino La Togata dei Togati '15	🍷🍷 8
● Brunello di Montalcino Seconda Stella a Destra '15	🍷🍷 8
● Barengo '15	🍷🍷 4
● Brunello di Montalcino Carillon '15	🍷🍷 7
● Brunello di Montalcino Jacopus '15	🍷🍷 6
● Brunello di Montalcino La Togata '15	🍷🍷 7
● Rosso di Montalcino Carillon '18	🍷🍷 4
● Rosso di Montalcino Jacopus '18	🍷🍷 3
● Azzurreta '15	🍷 5
● Brunello di Montalcino Notte di Note '15	🍷 6
● Rosso di Montalcino La Togata '18	🍷 4
● Brunello di Montalcino Carillon '14	♢♢ 6
● Brunello di Montalcino Jacopus '14	♢♢ 6
● Rosso di Montalcino Carillon '17	♢♢ 4
● Rosso di Montalcino La Togata '17	♢♢ 4

Tolaini

LOC. VALLENUOVA
S.DA PROV.LE 9 DI PIEVASCIATA, 28
53019 CASTELNUOVO BERARDENGA [SI]
TEL. +39 0577356972
www.tolaini.it

CELLAR SALES
PRE-BOOKED VISITS
ANNUAL PRODUCTION 250,000 bottles
HECTARES UNDER VINE 50.00
SUSTAINABLE WINERY

The Chianti wine cellar that bears the surname of its founder, Pierluigi Tolaini, who unfortunately passed away recently, has been producing wines in Chianti Classico for almost twenty years. In that time they've succeeded in achieving good visibility in a highly competitive area. Situated in the Castelnuovo Berardenga subzone, today the producer offers a range of wines in which appellation offerings are occupying more and more space with respect to Bordeaux blends and monovarietals. The style is modern, but interpreted with measure, eschewing excesses. A fragrant palate and focused aromas distinguish the Chianti Classico Vallenuova '18, an extraordinarily fine wine with a vital, rich, enjoyable palate. The interesting Chianti Classico Gran Selezione Vigneto Montebello Sette '16 finds its strong point in its truly crystalline aromas. Even in the mouth it shows the stuff of a great wine, especially for its juice, but a bit too much oak is slowing it down at this stage.

● Chianti Cl. Vallenuova '18	🍷🍷🍷 3*
● Chianti Cl. Gran Selezione V. Montebello Sette '16	🍷🍷 5
● Valdisanti '16	🍷🍷 5
● Al Passo '17	🍷 4
● Al Passo '14	🥂🥂🥂 4*
● Picconero '10	🥂🥂🥂 8
● Picconero '09	🥂🥂🥂 8
● Valdisanti '08	🥂🥂🥂 8
● Al Passo '16	🥂🥂 4
● Al Passo '15	🥂🥂 4
● Chianti Cl. Gran Selezione V. Montebello Sette '15	🥂🥂 5
● Chianti Cl. Gran Selezione V. Montebello Sette '14	🥂🥂 5
● Picconero '15	🥂🥂 8
● Valdisanti '15	🥂🥂 5

Fattoria La Torre

S.DA PROV.LE DI MONTECARLO, 7
55015 MONTECARLO [LU]
TEL. +39 058322981
www.fattorialatorre.it

CELLAR SALES
PRE-BOOKED VISITS
ACCOMMODATION AND RESTAURANT SERVICE
ANNUAL PRODUCTION 43,500 bottles
HECTARES UNDER VINE 6.50

The Celli family have a long tradition of winemaking, with documents testifying to the fact all the way back to 1887. In more recent times, the original premises have been renovated, leading to a well-equipped cellar in line with modern enological principles. In the vineyard they've adopted a modern approach as well, with higher planting density in order to obtain grapes of greater concentration and richness. In addition to wine, they have well-developed guest accommodations. The Stringaio '18 is a very pleasant blend of Syrah and Cabernet Sauvignon. Aromas of fruits, raspberries and cherries, merge with spicy notes of pepper and hints of aromatic herbs on the nose. It's soft on the palate, creamy, with very fine tannins, measured acidity and an enjoyable finish. The Vermentino '19 features fresh citrus notes of lemon and grapefruit, accompanied by hints of white peach and calamint; its pervasive body is lively and enticing.

● Esse Syrah '17	🍷🍷 5
⊙ Montecarlo Ison Brut Rosé	🍷🍷 3
○ Montecarlo Vermentino '19	🍷🍷 2*
● Stringaio '18	🍷🍷 3
○ Montecarlo Bianco '19	🍷 2
○ Altair '15	🥂🥂 3
● Esse '10	🥂🥂 7
● Esse '07	🥂🥂 7
● Esse '01	🥂🥂 7
● Esse Syrah '13	🥂🥂 5
○ Montecarlo Bianco '11	🥂🥂 2*
● Stringaio '14	🥂🥂 3
● Stringaio '07	🥂🥂 3

Torre a Cona

LOC. SAN DONATO IN COLLINA
VIA TORRE A CONA, 49
50067 RIGNANO SULL'ARNO [FI]
TEL. +39 055699000
www.torreacona.com

CELLAR SALES
PRE-BOOKED VISITS
ACCOMMODATION
ANNUAL PRODUCTION 80,000 bottles
HECTARES UNDER VINE 18.00

One of the most beautiful 18th-century villas in central Italy was purchased in 1935 by the Rossi di Montelera family. The restoration and maintenance work, which began after the Second World War, culminated in a complex tourist and wine-growing project. Their enological style focuses on varietal character and territorial expression through limited production volumes and grapes cultivated exclusively in the estate vineyards, a fact that's particularly important considering that it's an area characterized by a unique microclimate with exceptional temperature swings, with cool nights and sunny days. The Chianti Colli Fiorentini Badia a Corte Riserva '17 is delicious. A splendid aromatic suite of elderberry herbs, ferrous hints and assorted fruits rise up out of the glass. In the mouth it opens pleasant—tannins are perceptible but well integrated, with balanced acidity and a long finish. The Terre di Cino '16, a monovarietal Sangiovese, features hints of blueberry, eucalyptus and resin.

Wine	Rating
● Chianti Colli Fiorentini Badia a Corte Ris. '17	🍷🍷 5
● Terre di Cino '16	🍷🍷 5
● Casamaggio Colorino '18	🍷🍷 5
● Il Merlot '17	🍷🍷 5
● Chianti Colli Fiorentini '18	🍷 3
● Chianti Colli Fiorentini Badia a Corte Ris. '16	🍷🍷🍷 4*
● Chianti Colli Fiorentini Badia a Corte Ris. '15	🍷🍷🍷 4*
● Chianti Colli Fiorentini Badia a Corte Ris. '13	🍷🍷🍷 4*
● Vin Santo del Chianti Occhio di Pernice Fonti e Lecceta '11	🍷🍷🍷 6
● Chianti Colli Fiorentini Badia a Corte Ris. '12	🍷🍷 4
● Il Merlot '16	🍷🍷 4

Oliviero Toscani

VIA PERETA, 10
56040 CASALE MARITTIMO [PI]
TEL. +39 0586652050
www.otwine.com

PRE-BOOKED VISITS
ANNUAL PRODUCTION 80,000 bottles
HECTARES UNDER VINE 15.00

Photographer Oliviero Toscani bought the estate in the late 1960s and decided to move there in 1980, launching its agricultural operations. Today his son Rocco runs the business, which is quite multifaceted (pigs, horses and carrier pigeons are all bred), but their vineyards play a key role. Here in the metalliferous hills of Casale Marittimo, rich in iron and minerals, we find a beautiful amphitheatre-shaped vineyard, situated at elevations spanning 220 and 320 meters. It seems to us that their range is going through a strong period of growth, demonstrating increased conscientiousness. I Toscani '18 is a wine marked by freshness and a joyful expressiveness of fruit. It's a blend of Syrah and Teroldego, which make for aromas of blackberry, blueberry and pepper, a juicy palate and a commendable tannic grain at the finish. The OT '16 is more complex and herbaceous, while the Lumeo '18 features a dynamic, supple vegetal stroke. The Vieni via con Me '17 isn't too shabby either.

Wine	Rating
● I Toscani '18	🍷🍷 3*
● Lumeo '18	🍷🍷 5
● OT '16	🍷🍷 6
● Vieni Via con Me '17	🍷🍷 6
● OT '13	🍷🍷 6
● OT '11	🍷🍷 6
● Quadrato Rosso '15	🍷🍷 5

Travignoli

via Travignoli, 78
50060 Pelago [FI]
Tel. +39 0558361098
www.travignoli.com

CELLAR SALES
PRE-BOOKED VISITS
ANNUAL PRODUCTION 250,000 bottles
HECTARES UNDER VINE 70.00

Est. 500 B.C. That's the date of an Etruscan stele, found on the estate, in which a banquet with wine vases is depicted. A lot has changed in these 2500 years and the Busi family, owners of this 90-hectare farm at the confluence of the Arno and Sieve rivers since the 1800s, now bring a modern management approach to their vineyards and olive groves. Here in Chianti Rufina 70 hectares host primarily Sangiovese, but there's also Cabernet Sauvignon, Merlot and Chardonnay. The Chianti Rufina Tegolaia Riserva '17 features a nose of nice freshness ranging from ripe fruit (plum and cherry) to a few hints of pepper; notes of aromatic herbs complete the picture. The palate exhibits good weight, with measured tannins and a slightly compressed finish. The Gavignano '19, Chardonnay with a splash of Sauvignon, offers up apple sensations together with apricot and hints of thyme. In the mouth it's spirited, racy, with a fresh acidic backbone.

Wine	Rating
● Chianti Rufina Tegolaia Ris. '17	TT 3
○ Gavignano '19	TT 2*
⊙ Rosato '19	T 2
● Chianti Rufina '17	YY 2*
● Chianti Rufina '16	YY 2*
● Chianti Rufina Governo '17	YY 3
● Chianti Rufina Governo '16	YY 2*
● Chianti Rufina Tegolaia Ris. '16	YY 3*
● Chianti Rufina Tegolaia Ris. '15	YY 3*
● Chianti Rufina Tegolaia Ris. '13	YY 3*
● Chianti Rufina Tegolaia Ris. '12	YY 3
● Chianti Rufina Tegolaia Ris. '11	YY 3
○ Gavignano '17	YY 2*
○ Gavignano	YY 2*
○ Vin Santo Chianti Rufina '10	YY 4
○ Vin Santo Chianti Rufina '09	YY 4

Tenuta Trerose

fraz. Valiano
via della Stella, 3
53040 Montepulciano [SI]
Tel. +39 0577804101
www.tenutatrerose.it

CELLAR SALES
PRE-BOOKED VISITS
ANNUAL PRODUCTION 650,000 bottles
HECTARES UNDER VINE 102.00

With increasing consistency the Bertani Domains Group's Tenuta Trerose has been offering a range of wines characterized by a solid and defined style. Their selection expresses the incessant work being done in developing Montepulciano's Sangiovese, as well as its propensity for excellence, and doing so with personality and constancy. Valiano is one of Nobile di Montepulciano's most important subzones, and the winery seems to have found the right key for best interpreting this area. The Nobile di Montepulciano Santa Caterina delivers a notable interpretation of the 2017 vintage. Multifaceted aromas of fruits, flowers and mineral hints blend well with slight nuances of pepper and cocoa. Even in the mouth it proves balanced, unfolding succulently while acidic verve delivers freshness and dynamism. The Simposio '16 also reached our finals.

Wine	Rating
● Nobile di Montepulciano Santa Caterina '17	TT 5
● Nobile di Montepulciano Simposio Ris. '16	TT 6
● Rosso di Montepulciano Salterio '19	TT 3
● Nobile di Montepulciano Simposio '97	YYY 5
● Nobile di Montepulciano Simposio Ris. '15	YYY 6
● Nobile di Montepulciano S. Caterina '14	YY 4
● Nobile di Montepulciano Santa Caterina '16	YY 4
● Nobile di Montepulciano Santa Caterina '15	YY 4
● Nobile di Montepulciano Santa Caterina '12	YY 4

★Tua Rita

LOC. NOTRI, 81
57028 SUVERETO [LI]
TEL. +39 0565829237
www.tuarita.it

CELLAR SALES
PRE-BOOKED VISITS
ANNUAL PRODUCTION 250,000 bottles
HECTARES UNDER VINE 41.00

In the 1980s, Rita Tua and Virgilio Bisti bought a country house in Val di Cornia with some land around it so as to make wine. Since then the area under vine has increased and a well-functioning farm has been established. Their daughter Simena and her husband, Stefano Frascolla, have completed the conversion to organic farming of the property, where they grow Sangiovese, Cabernet Sauvignon, Syrah, Merlot, Vermentino, Traminer, Riesling and Chardonnay. A few years ago they also began renting Poggio Argentiera in Maremma. The Giusto di Notri '17, made with Cabernet, earned a place in our finals. Highly extracted and compressed aromatically, it progressively unveils its vegetal part amidst nuances of pepper, hints of preserves and minty talc. In the mouth it shows nice attack, coming through pulpy and extractive but not heavy, with decisive grip and a fine, mineral finish. A blend of Sangiovese, Cabernet Sauvignon, Merlot and Syrah, the Rosso dei Notri '19 is also rich and enticing.

- ● Giusto di Notri '17 **YY** 8
- ● Perlato del Bosco '18 **YY** 5
- ● Rosso dei Notri '19 **YY** 4
- ○ Perlato del Bosco Vermentino '19 **Y** 3
- ● Giusto di Notri '16 YY 8
- ● Giusto di Notri '15 YY 8
- ● Giusto di Notri '14 YY 8
- ● Giusto di Notri '13 YY 8
- ● Perlato del Bosco '17 YY 5
- ● Perlato del Bosco Rosso '16 YY 5
- ● Perlato del Bosco Rosso '15 YY 5
- ○ Perlato del Bosco Vermentino '18 YY 3
- ○ Perlato del Bosco Vermentino '16 YY 3
- ● Rosso dei Notri '16 YY 4

Uccelliera

FRAZ. CASTELNUOVO DELL'ABATE
POD. UCCELLIERA, 45
53020 MONTALCINO [SI]
TEL. +39 0577835729
www.uccelliera-montalcino.it

CELLAR SALES
PRE-BOOKED VISITS
ANNUAL PRODUCTION 60,000 bottles
HECTARES UNDER VINE 6.00

Generous, summery and at yet endowed with a sapid backbone: Uccelliera's Sangiovese adheres perfectly to the profile we'd expect from Castelnuovo dell'Abate, a district situated at the southeastern edge of Montalcino. The warm and breezy mesoclimate, elevations below 250 meters and clayey-sandy soils are all aptly interpreted by Andrea Cortonesi, a winemaker who's always avoided set techniques, preferring a tailored approach in which vinification and maturation are carried out in relation to the characteristics of the season. It is not for nothing that Andrea is as proud of his Rosso di Montalcino as he is of his Brunellos. Indeed, the former often outperforms the latter in our tastings. Here these are actually two different wines. The Rosso matures for less than six months in oak, and tries to preserve fruit as much as possible, while the Brunello, which ages at least two years in oak, pursues complexity. The Rosso '18 gratifies the nose and palate with its full, cherry aromas and pulpy body.

- ● Rosso di Montalcino '18 **YY** 4
- ● Brunello di Montalcino '15 **YY** 6
- ● Brunello di Montalcino Voliero '15 **YY** 6
- ● Rosso di Montalcino Voliero '18 **Y** 4
- ● Brunello di Montalcino '10 YYY 6
- ● Brunello di Montalcino '08 YYY 7
- ● Brunello di Montalcino Ris. '97 YYY 8
- ● Rosso di Montalcino '16 YYY 4*
- ● Rosso di Montalcino '15 YYY 4*
- ● Rosso di Montalcino '14 YYY 4*
- ● Brunello di Montalcino '14 YY 6
- ● Brunello di Montalcino '13 YY 6
- ● Brunello di Montalcino '12 YY 6
- ● Brunello di Montalcino Ris. '12 YY 8
- ● Brunello di Montalcino Voliero '12 YY 6
- ● Rosso di Montalcino '17 YY 4
- ● Rosso di Montalcino Voliero '15 YY 4

Val delle Corti

FRAZ. LA CROCE
LOC. VAL DELLE CORTI, 141
53017 RADDA IN CHIANTI [SI]
TEL. +39 0577738215
www.valdellecorti.it

CELLAR SALES
PRE-BOOKED VISITS
ACCOMMODATION
ANNUAL PRODUCTION 30,000 bottles
HECTARES UNDER VINE 6.00
VITICULTURE METHOD Certified Organic

The winery owned by Roberto Bianchi is not only one of the most intriguing in Chianti Classico, it's also one of the most convincing in the Radda in Chianti subzone. Their wines have an unmistakable style: clear, essential and unhesitating. It's difficult to find an interpretation of Sangiovese that's so coherent and has been so capable of positioning this area of Gallo Nero so firmly among Italy's most important winemaking territories. Theirs are reds of great pleasantness but, at the same time, complex and never trivial, even when at their most approachable. Just one wine was presented this year by Val delle Corti, but it was a good one. The Chianti Classico '17 is one of the most successful of the vintage, demonstrating once again the Radda sub-zone's prowess for viticulture. Its aromatic suite is crystal clear, alternating citrus notes with darker hints of fruit and earth. In the mouth it shows substance and rhythm, depth and flavor.

Wine	Glasses	Price
● Chianti Cl. '17	🍷🍷🍷	4*
● Chianti Cl. '13	ΨΨΨ	4*
● Chianti Cl. '12	ΨΨΨ	4*
● Chianti Cl. '11	ΨΨΨ	3*
● Chianti Cl. '10	ΨΨΨ	3*
● Chianti Cl. '09	ΨΨΨ	2*
● Chianti Cl. Ris. '16	ΨΨΨ	5
● Chianti Cl. Ris. '14	ΨΨΨ	5
● Chianti Cl. '16	ΨΨ	4
● Chianti Cl. '15	ΨΨ	4
● Chianti Cl. '14	ΨΨ	4
● Chianti Cl. '05	ΨΨ	2*
● Chianti Cl. Ris. '15	ΨΨ	5
● Chianti Cl. Ris. '13	ΨΨ	5
● Chianti Cl. Ris. '11	ΨΨ	5
● Chianti Cl. Ris. '09	ΨΨ	5
● Chianti Cl. Ris. '07	ΨΨ	4

Val di Suga

LOC. VAL DI CAVA
53024 MONTALCINO [SI]
TEL. +39 0577804101
www.valdisuga.it

CELLAR SALES
PRE-BOOKED VISITS
ANNUAL PRODUCTION 270,000 bottles
HECTARES UNDER VINE 55.00

Vigna del Lago in the northeast, Vigna Spuntali in the southwest, Poggio al Granchio in the southeast—these three sets of vineyards form the backbone of the Bertani Domains group's mapping of Montalcino in Val di Suga. The effort, which is aimed at highlighting differences in soil, climate and expression, comes together in three Brunello crus (which accompany the regular, 'standard-label' version). Each calls for a different approach as far as maturation is concerned (barriques, cone vats, oval barrels and 5000/6000-liter Slavonian oak). In the expert hands of Andrea Lonardi, Val di Suga's wines tell tales that are as diverse as they are charming. Among this year's superlative selection it was difficult to choose the best. The Poggio al Granchio offers up aromas of ripe fruit and nice flesh, but needs time to open up completely. The Vigna del Lago shines for its aromatic and gustatory harmony. The Vigna Spuntali wins out, with its aromas of tobacco and red fruit, its class and finesse, with a long, sapid finish. Tre Bicchieri.

Wine	Glasses	Price
● Brunello di Montalcino V. Spuntali '15	🍷🍷🍷	8
● Brunello di Montalcino Poggio al Granchio '15	🍷🍷	7
● Brunello di Montalcino V. del Lago '15	🍷🍷	8
● Brunello di Montalcino '15	🍷🍷	6
● Rosso di Montalcino '18	🍷🍷	4
● Brunello di Montalcino V. del Lago '95	ΨΨΨ	8
● Brunello di Montalcino V. del Lago '93	ΨΨΨ	8
● Brunello di Montalcino V. del Lago '90	ΨΨΨ	8
● Brunello di Montalcino V. Spuntali '95	ΨΨΨ	8
● Brunello di Montalcino V. Spuntali '93	ΨΨΨ	8
● Brunello di Montalcino Val di Suga '07	ΨΨΨ	5
● Brunello di Montalcino '14	ΨΨ	6
● Brunello di Montalcino Poggio al Granchio '13	ΨΨ	7
● Brunello di Montalcino V. del Lago '13	ΨΨ	8
● Brunello di Montalcino V. Spuntali '13	ΨΨ	8

Tenuta Valdipiatta

via della Ciarliana, 25a
53045 Montepulciano [SI]
Tel. +39 0578757930
www.valdipiatta.it

CELLAR SALES
PRE-BOOKED VISITS
ACCOMMODATION
ANNUAL PRODUCTION 100,000 bottles
HECTARES UNDER VINE 23.00
VITICULTURE METHOD Certified Organic
SUSTAINABLE WINERY

Miriam Caporali's Tenuta Valdipiatta is one of Nobile di Montepulciano's most notable wineries, a producer that's managed to confer its wines with a distinct identity characterized by finesse and elegance rather than concentration and roundness. Their wines are sometimes prone to hardness and austerity, but time always smooths things out. Their vineyards are managed organically while unnatural interference with the natural process of winemaking and shortcuts are eschewed in the cellar. Aging is carried out in a favorable mix of large and small oak barrels. The Nobile di Montepulciano '17 features flowery aromas, wild herbs and chocolaty hints. On the palate it unfolds on fine tannins, but still vivid and close-knit, not without character, finishing long and juicy. More concentrated but flavorful, we also appreciated the Nobile Vigna d'Alfiero '17, though it's just a bit held back by oak. The pleasantly varietal Pinot Nero '18 isn't particularly complex but tasty nevertheless.

● Nobile di Montepulciano '17	TT	5
● Nobile di Montepulciano V. d'Alfiero '17	TT	6
● Pinot Nero '18	TT	5
● Rosso di Montepulciano '18	T	3
● Nobile di Montepulciano Ris. '90	YYY	5
● Nobile di Montepulciano V. d'Alfiero '99	YYY	5
● Chianti Colli Senesi Tosca '15	YY	2*
● Nobile di Montepulciano '14	YY	4
● Nobile di Montepulciano Ris. '15	YY	6
● Nobile di Montepulciano Ris. '13	YY	6
● Nobile di Montepulciano V. d'Alfiero '16	YY	6
● Pinot Nero '15	YY	4
● Rosso di Montepulciano '17	YY	3
● Rosso di Montepulciano '16	YY	3

★Tenuta di Valgiano

via di Valgiano, 7
55015 Lucca
Tel. +39 0583402271
www.valgiano.it

CELLAR SALES
PRE-BOOKED VISITS
ANNUAL PRODUCTION 60,000 bottles
HECTARES UNDER VINE 15.00
VITICULTURE METHOD Certified Biodynamic

Valgiano is, first and foremost, a place of unparalleled beauty. Undoubtedly this is one of the keys to understanding the history of the private and professional partnership between Moreno Petrini and Laura di Collobiano, as the lines between life and work here are blurred, both for the owners as for their collaborators. Among these last, we should mention Saverio Petrilli, a true 'pope' of biodynamic agriculture in Italy, a figure who's been decisive in driving the success of Valgiano's great wines over time. A great vintage and a great version of the Tenuta di Valgiano. This 2016 sparkler offers up pure fruit that blends in with sensations of undergrowth and elegant spices. On the palate it's magnetic, three-dimensional, silky and very tasty in a tannic weave that lengthens the back palate. Truly one of the best ever versions of this gem. The Palistorti Bianco '19 plays on less texture, thus leaving room for rich flavor.

● Colline Lucchesi Tenuta di Valgiano '16	TTT	8
○ Palistorti Bianco '19	TT	5
● Colline Lucchesi Tenuta di Valgiano '15	YYY	8
● Colline Lucchesi Tenuta di Valgiano '13	YYY	8
● Colline Lucchesi Tenuta di Valgiano '12	YYY	6
● Colline Lucchesi Tenuta di Valgiano '11	YYY	6
● Colline Lucchesi Tenuta di Valgiano '10	YYY	6
● Colline Lucchesi Tenuta di Valgiano '09	YYY	6
● Colline Lucchesi Tenuta di Valgiano '08	YYY	6
● Colline Lucchesi Tenuta di Valgiano '07	YYY	6
● Colline Lucchesi Tenuta di Valgiano '06	YYY	6
● Colline Lucchesi Tenuta di Valgiano '05	YYY	6
● Colline Lucchesi Tenuta di Valgiano '04	YYY	6
● Colline Lucchesi Tenuta di Valgiano '03	YYY	6
● Colline Lucchesi Tenuta di Valgiano '01	YYY	8
● Colline Lucchesi Palistorti Rosso '15	YY	5

Valle di Lazzaro

LOC. VALLE DI LAZZARO, 103
57037 PORTOFERRAIO [LI]
TEL. +39 0565916387
www.valledilazzaro.com

CELLAR SALES
PRE-BOOKED VISITS
ANNUAL PRODUCTION 12,000 bottles
HECTARES UNDER VINE 4.00

For many years passionate winemaker Stefano Farkas operated in Panzano, in Chianti Classico's Conca d'Oro. Then came an encounter with the island of Elba and a desire to change direction while continuing his passion. Hence the choice to create a small farm and a vineyard, in Portoferraio, in the Valle di Lazzaro, to be managed without excessive complications. In keeping with Elban tradition, he started with Aleatico, and then made room for several white grape varieties. The alluring Ansonica '19 offers up aromas of apple, apricot, peach and hints of aromatic herbs. On the palate it makes a nice impact, coming through pulpy, warm, elegant and lively, making for a tasty, rising finish. The Vermentino '19 is also quite pleasant: mineral hints are followed by vegetal whiffs, all of which continue on a fresh, dynamic palate. Kudos to the Sangiovese '18 as well, with its hints of cherry and Mediterranean scrub, and a racy body, fresh and sapid on the finish.

Wine	Rating
○ Elba Ansonica Lazarus '19	🍷🍷 3
● Elba Sangiovese Lazarus '18	🍷🍷 3
○ Elba Vermentino Lazarus '19	🍷🍷 3
○ Chardonnay Lazarus '18	🍷🍷 4
○ Elba Ansonica '17	🍷🍷 3
○ Elba Ansonica '16	🍷🍷 3
○ Elba Ansonica Lazarus '18	🍷🍷 3
● Elba Sangiovese Lazarus '16	🍷🍷 3*
○ Elba Vermentino '17	🍷🍷 3
○ Elba Vermentino '16	🍷🍷 3
○ Elba Vermentino Lazarus '18	🍷🍷 3

Vallepicciola

S.DA PROV.LE 9 DI PIEVASCIATA, 21
53019 CASTELNUOVO BERARDENGA [SI]
TEL. +39 05771698718
www.vallepicciola.com

CELLAR SALES
PRE-BOOKED VISITS
ANNUAL PRODUCTION 250,000 bottles
HECTARES UNDER VINE 95.00

Vallepicciola is an ambitious venture created by Bruno Bolfo, an entrepreneur in love with the beauty of the Tuscan hills. In a few years Bolfo has managed to create a lovely, solid estate that extends for 265 hectares (100 of which are vineyards) in Castelnuovo Berardenga. He also equipped the property with an evocative, modern cellar. Here you won't only find Sangiovese, but also large quantities of international varieties so as to exploit every peculiarity of the different terroirs. Major projects take time, and this year Vallepicciola made a nice impression in a moment of technical change and stylistic redefinition. The Gran Selezione Lapina '16, a complex, elegant, deep red, topped our preferences and earned itself a place in our finals. The Chianti Classico '18 is a rich, spicy, fleshy Chianti Classico. The Pievasciata '18, a blend of Sangiovese and international grapes, features spicy, oaky hints.

Wine	Rating
● Chianti Cl. Gran Selezione Lapina '16	🍷🍷 6
● Chianti Cl. '18	🍷🍷 4
● Pievasciata '18	🍷🍷 3
● Quercegrosse Merlot '17	🍷🍷 6
● Boscobruno Pinot Nero '17	🍷 6
● Chianti Cl. Ris. '17	🍷 5
● Chianti Cl. '17	🍷🍷🍷 4*
● Boscobruno Pinot Nero '16	🍷🍷 6
● Boscobruno Pinot Nero '15	🍷🍷 6
● Chianti Cl. '16	🍷🍷 4
● Chianti Cl. '15	🍷🍷 4
● Chianti Cl. Gran Selezione '15	🍷🍷 3*
● Chianti Cl. Ris. '16	🍷🍷 5
● Pievasciata '16	🍷🍷 3
● Quercegrosse Merlot '15	🍷🍷 6

Varramista

Loc. Varramista
via Ricavo
56020 Montopoli in Val d'Arno [PI]
Tel. +39 057144711
www.varramista.it

CELLAR SALES
PRE-BOOKED VISITS
ACCOMMODATION
ANNUAL PRODUCTION 35,000 bottles
HECTARES UNDER VINE 13.00

Varramista's eventful history goes back more than 500 years and reaches up to the present day with the Piaggio and Agnelli families, who made it their country residence. In the 1990s, Giovanni Alberto Agnelli, president of Piaggio, chose the property as his country home, overseeing conversion of the vineyards and focusing on Syrah as its cornerstone. After Giovannino's untimely death, wine continues to be the symbol of the estate's quality and style. Sangiovese and Grenache grapes also grow on their four plots. This year we particularly appreciated the Sterpato '17, a Sangiovese with added shares Merlot and Cabernet. It's a fragrant red, with nice structure, deep and sapid. Tannins are present but never bend on bitter notes, rather lengthening the palate and delivering an appealing finish. The Montecarlo Varramista '15 proves multifaceted, despite some foregrounded tertiaries.

Wine	Rating
● Sterpato '17	🍷🍷 3*
● Varramista '15	🍷🍷 7
● Varramista '00	YYY 6
● Chianti Monsonaccio '15	YY 3
● Chianti Monsonaccio '12	YY 2*
● Frasca '15	YY 5
● Frasca '13	YY 4
● Frasca Rosso '11	YY 3
● Sterpato '16	YY 3
● Sterpato '12	YY 2*
● Sterpato '11	YY 2*
● Syrah '11	YY 6
● Varramista '13	YY 7

Vecchia Cantina di Montepulciano

via Provinciale, 7
53045 Montepulciano [SI]
Tel. +39 0578716092
www.vecchiacantinadimontepulciano.com

CELLAR SALES
PRE-BOOKED VISITS
ANNUAL PRODUCTION 7,000,000 bottles
HECTARES UNDER VINE 1000.00
VITICULTURE METHOD Certified Organic

Vecchia Cantina di Montepulciano is one of the oldest cooperatives in Tuscan wine-country, having been founded in 1937. Today it has 400 members who work an extremely mixed set of vineyards spanning two regions (Tuscany and Umbria) and three provinces (Siena, Arezzo and Perugia). But Nobile di Montepulciano is by far their main wine, and Vecchia Cantina is its largest producer in terms of bottles produced annually. This year a number of wines from their selection stood out during our tastings. The Nobile Cantina del Redi '17 features red berries on the nose, accompanied by spices, heralding a juicy, relaxed palate. The Nobile Poggio Stella '17 is a modern wine, impeccably crafted. The highly drinkable and fragrant Rosso di Montepulciano Cantina del Redi '19 pairs well with the Vecchia Cantina del Redi '19. This last is a bit simpler, perhaps, but enjoyable nevertheless.

Wine	Rating
● Nobile di Montepulciano Cantina del Redi '17	🍷🍷 5
● Nobile di Montepulciano Poggio Stella '17	🍷🍷 5
● Rosso di Montepulciano Cantina del Redi '19	🍷🍷 3
● Nobile di Montepulciano '17	🍷 4
● Nobile di Montepulciano Poggio Stella Ris. '15	🍷 5
● Rosso di Montepulciano '19	🍷 2
● Nobile di Montepulciano '14	YY 3
● Nobile di Montepulciano Briareo Ris. Cantina dei Redi '15	YY 5
● Nobile di Montepulciano Cantina del Redi '13	YY 4
● Orbaio Cantina dei Redi '16	YY 5
● Orbaio Redi '15	YY 5

I Veroni

VIA TIFARITI, 5
50065 PONTASSIEVE [FI]
TEL. +39 0558368886
www.iveroni.it

CELLAR SALES
PRE-BOOKED VISITS
ACCOMMODATION
ANNUAL PRODUCTION 110,000 bottles
HECTARES UNDER VINE 20.00
VITICULTURE METHOD Certified Organic

The farm, situated in Chianti Rufina on the hills of Pontassieve, was replanted with select Sangiovese clones and then with international and white grape varieties (there are also 50 hectares of olive groves). Their vin santo barrel storage area is preserved in the historic, 18th-century villa. But antiquity is everywhere here, starting with the name. Indeed, 'Verone' in old Tuscan dialect means 'terrace', and the farm was full of terraces. Their accommodation facilities occupy the spaces of a beautiful, well-restored farmhouse. The Chianti Rufina Quona Riserva '17, with its floral notes of geranium, medicinal herbs and ripe cherries, earned a place in our finals, coming through juicy, suppy and racy on the palate, with a beautiful gustatory persistence. We also appreciated the 'standard-label' 2018 and the surprising Alba di Paola '19. The latter, a blend of Sangiovese, Trebbiano, Malvasia and Canaiolo Bianco vinified off the skins, features a captivating bouquet and lively body.

Wine	Rating
● Chianti Rufina Vign. Quona Ris. '17	🍷🍷 5
○ Alba di Paola '19	🍷🍷 3
● Chianti Rufina I Domi '18	🍷🍷 3
● Rosso Toscana '18	🍷🍷 2*
○ Vin Santo del Chianti Rufina '10	🍷🍷 5
● Chianti Rufina Vign. Quona Ris. '15	🍷🍷🍷 5
● Chianti Rufina I Domi '17	🍷🍷 3
● Chianti Rufina I Domi '16	🍷🍷 3
● Chianti Rufina Quona Ris. '14	🍷🍷 5
● Chianti Rufina Ris. '13	🍷🍷 5
● Chianti Rufina Ris. '12	🍷🍷 4
● Chianti Rufina Vign. Quona Ris. '16	🍷🍷 5
● Vin Santo del Chianti Rufina Occhio di Pernice '09	🍷🍷 6
○ Vin Santo del Chianti Rufina Occhio di Pernice '08	🍷🍷 6

Vignamaggio

VIA PETRIOLO, 5
50022 GREVE IN CHIANTI [FI]
TEL. +39 055854661
www.vignamaggio.com

CELLAR SALES
PRE-BOOKED VISITS
ACCOMMODATION AND RESTAURANT SERVICE
ANNUAL PRODUCTION 250,000 bottles
HECTARES UNDER VINE 67.00
VITICULTURE METHOD Certified Organic
SUSTAINABLE WINERY

Vignamaggio, one of the most important wineries in Greve in Chianti, has played a significant role in the Chianti Classico appellation for over thirty years. The winery's style favors the pursuit of structure and richness of fruit, accompanied by a proper share of oak (both large and small barrels are used). This choice is, however, carried out with grace and measure, so much so that elegance is never lacking in their selection. Indeed, their wines are also capable of achieving the heights of excellence. The lean, dynamic Chianti Classico Terre di Prenzano '17 offers up clear, mature aromas accompanied by a particularly flavorful and appetizing palate. The Chianti Classico Gherardino Riserva '16 features aromas of red berries, earthy hints and flowers, while the palate comes through juicy and spirited by virtue of some pleasant hardness. We also appreciated the Chianti Classico Gran Selezione Monna Lisa '16, austere and complex, with just a little oak still to be integrated.

Wine	Rating
● Chianti Cl. Terre di Prenzano '17	🍷🍷 3*
● Cabernet Franc '16	🍷🍷 8
● Chianti Cl. Gherardino Ris. '16	🍷🍷 5
● Chianti Cl. Gran Selezione Monna Lisa '16	🍷🍷 6
● Chianti Cl. Monna Lisa Ris. '99	🍷🍷🍷 5
● Chianti Cl. Monna Lisa Ris. '95	🍷🍷🍷 5
● Cabernet Franc '15	🍷🍷 8
● Cabernet Franc '13	🍷🍷 8
● Chianti Cl. Gherardino Ris. '15	🍷🍷 5
● Chianti Cl. Gran Selezione Monna Lisa '15	🍷🍷 6
● Chianti Cl. Gran Selezione Monna Lisa Ris. '13	🍷🍷 6
● Chianti Cl. Terre di Prenzano '16	🍷🍷 3*
● Chianti Cl. Terre di Prenzano '15	🍷🍷 3*
● Chianti Cl. Terre di Prenzano '14	🍷🍷 3

Amantis

FRAZ. MONTENERO D'ORCIA
LOC. COLOMBAIO BIRBE
58040 CASTEL DEL PIANO [GR]
TEL. +39 3461402687
www.agricolaamantis.com

ANNUAL PRODUCTION 55,000 bottles
HECTARES UNDER VINE 6.00
SUSTAINABLE WINERY

- ● Montecucco Sangiovese '16 — 4

Antico Colle

VIA PROVINCIALE, 9
53040 MONTEPULCIANO [SI]
TEL. +39 0578707828
www.anticocolle.it

CELLAR SALES
PRE-BOOKED VISITS
ANNUAL PRODUCTION 150,000 bottles
HECTARES UNDER VINE 30.00

- ● Nobile di Montepulciano '17 — 3
- ● Nobile di Montepulciano Il Saggio Ris. '15 — 5

Poderi Arcangelo

LOC. CAPEZZANO
VIA SAN BENEDETTO, 26
53037 SAN GIMIGNANO [SI]
TEL. +39 0577944404
www.poderiarcangelo.it

CELLAR SALES
PRE-BOOKED VISITS
ANNUAL PRODUCTION 50,000 bottles
HECTARES UNDER VINE 23.00
VITICULTURE METHOD Certified Organic

- ● Chianti Colli Senesi '18 — 2*
- ○ Vernaccia di San Gimignano Primo Angelo '19 — 2*
- ● Chianti Il Cantastorie '17 — 2

Armilla

VIA TAVERNELLE, 6
53024 MONTALCINO [SI]
TEL. +39 0577816012
www.armillawine.com

ANNUAL PRODUCTION 12,000 bottles
HECTARES UNDER VINE 3.00

- ● Brunello di Montalcino '15 — 6
- ● Rosso di Montalcino '18 — 4

Fattoria di Bagnolo

LOC. BAGNOLO
VIA IMPRUNETANA PER TAVARNUZZE, 48
50023 IMPRUNETA [FI]
TEL. +39 0552313403
www.bartolinibaldelli.it

CELLAR SALES
PRE-BOOKED VISITS
ANNUAL PRODUCTION 25,000 bottles
HECTARES UNDER VINE 10.00

- ● Chianti Colli Fiorentini '18 — 2*
- ● Chianti Colli Fiorentini Ris. '17 — 4
- ⊙ Rosato Maralò '19 — 2

I Balzini

LOC. PASTINE, 19
50021 BARBERINO VAL D'ELSA [FI]
TEL. +39 0558075503
www.ibalzini.it

CELLAR SALES
PRE-BOOKED VISITS
ANNUAL PRODUCTION 70,000 bottles
HECTARES UNDER VINE 12.00
SUSTAINABLE WINERY

- ● I Balzini Black Label '17 — 6
- ● I Balzini White Label '17 — 5
- ● I Balzini Green Label '18 — 3
- ⊙ I Balzini Pink Label '18 — 2

La Banditaccia

FRAZ. MONTICELLO AMIATA
LOC. BANDITACCIA
58044 CINIGIANO [GR]
TEL. +39 3474167275
www.banditaccia.com

CELLAR SALES
PRE-BOOKED VISITS
ACCOMMODATION AND RESTAURANT SERVICE
ANNUAL PRODUCTION 28,000 bottles
HECTARES UNDER VINE 5.18
VITICULTURE METHOD Certified Organic

- ○ Malandrino Vermentino '19 ᴛᴛ 2*
- ● Montecucco Sangiovese V. Allegra '18 ᴛᴛ 5
- ● Polesse Merlot '18 ᴛ 4

Giacomo Baraldo

P.ZZA MATTEOTTI, 4
53040 SAN CASCIANO DEI BAGNI [SI]
TEL. +39

- ● Il Bossolo '17 ᴛᴛ 5
- ○ Il Pergola '18 ᴛᴛ 5
- ○ L'Affacciatoio '18 ᴛᴛ

Batzella

LOC. BADIA, 227
57024 CASTAGNETO CARDUCCI [LI]
TEL. +39 3393975888
www.batzella.com

CELLAR SALES
PRE-BOOKED VISITS
ACCOMMODATION
ANNUAL PRODUCTION 55,000 bottles
HECTARES UNDER VINE 8.00

- ○ Bolgheri Bianco Mezzodì '19 ᴛᴛ 3
- ● Bolgheri Rosso Peàn '17 ᴛᴛ 4
- ● Bolgheri Superiore Tam '16 ᴛ 5

Belpoggio - Bellussi

FRAZ. CASTELNUOVO DELL'ABATE
LOC. BELLARIA
53024 MONTALCINO [SI]
TEL. +39 0423983411
www.belpoggio.it

PRE-BOOKED VISITS
ANNUAL PRODUCTION 36,000 bottles
HECTARES UNDER VINE 5.00
SUSTAINABLE WINERY

- ● Brunello di Montalcino '15 ᴛᴛ 6
- ● Di Paolo Rosso '19 ᴛᴛ 4

Le Bertille

VIA DELLE COLOMBELLE, 7
53045 MONTEPULCIANO [SI]
TEL. +39 0578758330
www.lebertille.com

CELLAR SALES
PRE-BOOKED VISITS
ACCOMMODATION
ANNUAL PRODUCTION 65,000 bottles
HECTARES UNDER VINE 14.00
SUSTAINABLE WINERY

- ● Nobile di Montepulciano Ris. '16 ᴛᴛ 5
- ● Nobile di Montepulciano '17 ᴛ 4
- ● Rosso di Montepulciano '17 ᴛ 2

Villa Bibbiani

LOC. BIBBIANI
50050 CAPRAIA E LIMITE [FI]
TEL. +39 3383195652
www.villabibbiani.it

CELLAR SALES
PRE-BOOKED VISITS
ANNUAL PRODUCTION 50,000 bottles
HECTARES UNDER VINE 20.00

- ● Chianti Montalbano '18 ᴛᴛ 3
- ● Montereggi '18 ᴛᴛ 6
- ● Pulignano Sangiovese '18 ᴛᴛ 6
- ● Treggiaia '18 ᴛᴛ 5

Bindi Sergardi

loc. Poggiolo
Fattoria I Colli, 2
53035 Monteriggioni [SI]
Tel. +39 0577309107
www.bindisergardi.it

CELLAR SALES
PRE-BOOKED VISITS
ACCOMMODATION AND RESTAURANT SERVICE
ANNUAL PRODUCTION 100,000 bottles
HECTARES UNDER VINE 103.00

- ● Chianti Cl. Gran Selezione Mocenni 89 '16 🍷🍷6
- ● Chianti Cl. La Ghirlanda '17 🍷🍷3
- ● Chianti Cl. Ser Gardo '16 🍷🍷4
- ● Chianti Cl. Calidonia Ris. '16 🍷4

Il Borghetto

loc. Montefiridolfi
via Collina Sant'Angelo, 21
50026 San Casciano in Val di Pesa [FI]
Tel. +39 0558244442
www.borghetto.org

CELLAR SALES
PRE-BOOKED VISITS
ACCOMMODATION
ANNUAL PRODUCTION 14,000 bottles
HECTARES UNDER VINE 5.00

- ● Bilaccio '16 🍷🍷5
- ● Monte de Sassi '16 🍷🍷3
- ● Montigiano '18 🍷🍷4
- ● Clante '16 🍷6

Borratella

loc. Borratella
53013 Gaiole in Chianti [SI]
Tel. +39 3394107545
www.borratella.com

ANNUAL PRODUCTION 30,000 bottles
HECTARES UNDER VINE 5.50

- ● Chianti Cl. '17 🍷🍷3
- ● Chianti Cl. Ris. '17 🍷🍷5
- ● Yaro '17 🍷5

Brancatelli

loc. Casa Rossa, 2
57025 Piombino [LI]
Tel. +39 056520655
www.brancatelli.eu

CELLAR SALES
PRE-BOOKED VISITS
ACCOMMODATION AND RESTAURANT SERVICE
ANNUAL PRODUCTION 75,000 bottles
HECTARES UNDER VINE 15.00
VITICULTURE METHOD Certified Organic

- ⊙ Loren '19 🍷🍷2*
- ● Mila Sangiovese '16 🍷🍷5
- ○ Ansonica Splendente '19 🍷🍷3
- ● Mila Sangiovese '18 🍷5

Ca' Marcanda

loc. Santa Teresa, 272
57022 Castagneto Carducci [LI]
Tel. +39 0565763809
info@camarcanda.com

CELLAR SALES
PRE-BOOKED VISITS
ANNUAL PRODUCTION 450,000 bottles
HECTARES UNDER VINE 120.00

- ● Bolgheri Rosso Camarcanda '17 🍷🍷8
- ● Bolgheri Rosso Magari '18 🍷🍷6

Calafata

p.zzale Arrigoni, 2
55100 Lucca
Tel. +39 0583 430939
info@calafata.it

ANNUAL PRODUCTION 13,000 bottles
HECTARES UNDER VINE 10.00

- ● Chianti Iarsera Sup. '17 🍷🍷4
- ○ Gronda '18 🍷🍷4
- ● Majulina '18 🍷🍷4

Il Calamaio

VIA DELLE GAVINIE, 1707
55100 LUCCA
TEL. +39 3408503670
www.ilcalamaiovini.it

ANNUAL PRODUCTION 7,000 bottles
HECTARES UNDER VINE 2.00

- ● Antenato V. V. '18 ŸŸ3
- ● Poiana '17 ŸŸ3
- ● Soffio '19 Ÿ3

Tenuta Le Calcinaie

LOC. SANTA LUCIA, 36
53037 SAN GIMIGNANO [SI]
TEL. +39 0577943007
www.tenutalecalcinaie.it

CELLAR SALES
PRE-BOOKED VISITS
ANNUAL PRODUCTION 60,000 bottles
HECTARES UNDER VINE 9.50
VITICULTURE METHOD Certified Organic

- ● Chianti Colli Senesi Santa Maria Ris. '15 ŸŸ4
- ○ Vernaccia di S. Gimignano V. ai Sassi Ris. '17 ŸŸ3
- ○ Vernaccia di S. Gimignano '19 Ÿ2

Le Calle

FRAZ. POGGI DEL SASSO
LOC. LA CAVA
58044 CINIGIANO [GR]
TEL. +39 3489307565
www.lecalle.it

CELLAR SALES
PRE-BOOKED VISITS
ACCOMMODATION
ANNUAL PRODUCTION 26,000 bottles
HECTARES UNDER VINE 7.00
VITICULTURE METHOD Certified Organic

- ● Montecucco Rosso Campo Rombolo '18 ŸŸ3
- ● Montecucco Sangiovese Poggio d'Oro Ris. '16 ŸŸ5
- ● Montecucco Sangiovese Poggio d'Oro '17 Ÿ3

Campo al Pero

FRAZ. DONORATICO
VIA DEL CASONE UGOLINO, 12
57022 CASTAGNETO CARDUCCI [LI]
TEL. +39 0565774329
www.campoalpero.it

- ● Bolgheri Rosso '18 ŸŸ4
- ● Bolgheri Rosso Dorianae '17 ŸŸ4
- ● Bolgheri Rosso Zephyro '18 ŸŸ4

Campo del Monte Eredi Benito Mantellini

VIA TRAIANA, 53A
52028 TERRANUOVA BRACCIOLINI [AR]
TEL. +39 0554684135
www.campodelmonte.it

CELLAR SALES
PRE-BOOKED VISITS
ACCOMMODATION
HECTARES UNDER VINE 7.50

- ● Valdarno di Sopra Cabernet Sauvignon Rodos '16 ŸŸ4
- ○ Valdarno di Sopra Pratomagno Isei '15 ŸŸ5

Cantina Canaio

LOC. FARNETA
52044 CORTONA [AR]
TEL. +39 0575604866
cantinacanaio@libero.it

ANNUAL PRODUCTION 6,000 bottles
HECTARES UNDER VINE 1.50

- ● Cortona Syrah Il Calice '17 ŸŸ4
- ● Cortona Syrah Terra Solla '17 ŸŸ5

Cantalici

FRAZ. CASTAGNOLI
VIA DELLA CROCE, 17/19
53013 GAIOLE IN CHIANTI [SI]
TEL. +39 0577731038
www.cantalici.it

CELLAR SALES
PRE-BOOKED VISITS
ANNUAL PRODUCTION 46,000 bottles
HECTARES UNDER VINE 30.00

- ● Chianti Cl. '16 — 🍷🍷 3
- ● Chianti Cl. Messer Ridolfo Ris. '16 — 🍷🍷 4
- ● Chianti Cl. Baruffo '17 — 🍷 3

Capanne Ricci

FRAZ. SANT'ANGELO IN COLLE
LOC. CASELLO
53024 MONTALCINO [SI]
TEL. +39 0564902063
www.tenimentiricci.it

ANNUAL PRODUCTION 40,000 bottles
HECTARES UNDER VINE 12.00

- ● Rosso di Montalcino '18 — 🍷🍷 3*
- ● Brunello di Montalcino '15 — 🍷🍷 6
- ● Ricciolo '19 — 🍷 2

Caparsa

LOC. CASE SPARSE CAPARSA, 47
53017 RADDA IN CHIANTI [SI]
TEL. +39 0577738174
www.caparsa.it

CELLAR SALES
PRE-BOOKED VISITS
ACCOMMODATION
ANNUAL PRODUCTION 40,000 bottles
HECTARES UNDER VINE 12.08
VITICULTURE METHOD Certified Organic
SUSTAINABLE WINERY

- ● Chianti Cl. Caparsa '17 — 🍷🍷 5
- ● Chianti Cl. Caparsino Ris. '17 — 🍷🍷 6

Fattoria Casa di Terra

FRAZ. BOLGHERI
LOC. LE FERRUGGINI, 162A
57022 CASTAGNETO CARDUCCI [LI]
TEL. +39 0565749810
www.fattoriacasaditerra.com

CELLAR SALES
PRE-BOOKED VISITS
ACCOMMODATION
ANNUAL PRODUCTION 180,000 bottles
HECTARES UNDER VINE 44.50

- ● Bolgheri Rosso Sup. Maronea '17 — 🍷🍷 6
- ● Lenaia '18 — 🍷🍷 2*
- ● Bolgheri Rosso Moreccio '18 — 🍷 3

Casa Emma

LOC. SAN DONATO IN POGGIO
S.DA PROV.LE DI CASTELLINA IN CHIANTI, 3
50021 BARBERINO VAL D'ELSA [FI]
TEL. +39 0558072239
www.casaemma.com

CELLAR SALES
PRE-BOOKED VISITS
RESTAURANT SERVICE
ANNUAL PRODUCTION 90,000 bottles
HECTARES UNDER VINE 31.00
VITICULTURE METHOD Certified Organic
SUSTAINABLE WINERY

- ● Chianti Cl. Ris. '16 — 🍷🍷 5
- ● Chianti Cl. '18 — 🍷 3
- ● Chianti Cl. Gran Selezione '16 — 🍷 5

Tenuta Casadei

LOC. SAN ROCCO
57028 SUVERETO [LI]
TEL. +39 05651933605
www.tenutacasadei.it

CELLAR SALES
PRE-BOOKED VISITS
ANNUAL PRODUCTION 130,000 bottles
HECTARES UNDER VINE 24.00
VITICULTURE METHOD Certified Biodynamic
SUSTAINABLE WINERY

- ● Filare 18 '18 — 🍷🍷 6
- ○ Incanto '19 — 🍷🍷 3
- ● Filare 41 '19 — 🍷 6
- ● Sogno Mediterraneo '18 — 🍷 4

Casale Pozzuolo

loc. Borgo Santa Rita
58044 Cinigiano [GR]
Tel. +39 0564902019
www.casalepozzuolo.it

CELLAR SALES
PRE-BOOKED VISITS
ACCOMMODATION
ANNUAL PRODUCTION 15,000 bottles
HECTARES UNDER VINE 4.50

- ● Montecucco Sangiovese Rosso della Porticcia '18 — ΨΨ 3*

Podere Casanova

s.da prov.le 326 Est, 196
53045 Montepulciano [SI]
Tel. +39 0429841418
www.poderecasanovavini.com

CELLAR SALES
PRE-BOOKED VISITS
ACCOMMODATION
ANNUAL PRODUCTION 140,000 bottles
HECTARES UNDER VINE 18.00

- ● Nobile di Montepulciano '17 — ΨΨ 4
- ● Nobile di Montepulciano Settecento '16 — ΨΨ 5
- ● Nobile di Montepulciano Ris. '15 — Ψ 5
- ● Rosso di Montepulciano '18 — Ψ 2

Podere Casina

fraz. Istia d'Ombrone
Piagge del Maiano
58040 Grosseto
Tel. +39 0564408210
www.poderecasina.com

PRE-BOOKED VISITS
ACCOMMODATION
ANNUAL PRODUCTION 55,000 bottles
HECTARES UNDER VINE 11.00

- ● Aione '17 — ΨΨ 5
- ● Morellino di Scansano '19 — ΨΨ 3
- ○ Argenteo Vermentino '19 — Ψ 3

Castagnoli

loc. Castagnoli
53011 Castellina in Chianti [SI]
Tel. +39 0577740446
castagnoli@valdelsa.net

CELLAR SALES
PRE-BOOKED VISITS
ANNUAL PRODUCTION 30,000 bottles
HECTARES UNDER VINE 9.00

- ● Chianti Cl. Terrazze Ris. '17 — ΨΨ 5
- ● Chianti Cl. '18 — ΨΨ 4
- ● Salita '16 — Ψ 6

Tenuta Casteani

loc. Casteani
pod. Fabbri
58023 Gavorrano [GR]
Tel. +39 0566871050
www.casteani.it

CELLAR SALES
PRE-BOOKED VISITS
ACCOMMODATION AND RESTAURANT SERVICE
ANNUAL PRODUCTION 80,000 bottles
HECTARES UNDER VINE 14.00
SUSTAINABLE WINERY

- ● Maremma Toscana Rosso Turione '18 — ΨΨ 3
- ○ Maremma Toscana Vermentino Serin '19 — ΨΨ 2*

Castello della Mugazzena

loc. Fola
via Tresana Paese, 103
54012 Tresana [MS]
Tel. +39 3357906553
www.castellodellamugazzena.it

ANNUAL PRODUCTION 4,000 bottles
HECTARES UNDER VINE 3.00

- ○ Pantagruel '18 — ΨΨ 4
- ● Gargantua '18 — ΨΨ 5

Castello della Paneretta

LOC. MONSANTO
S.DA DELLA PANERETTA, 35
50021 BARBERINO VAL D'ELSA [FI]
TEL. +39 0558059003
www.paneretta.it

CELLAR SALES
PRE-BOOKED VISITS
ACCOMMODATION
ANNUAL PRODUCTION 10,000 bottles
HECTARES UNDER VINE 22.50

- Chianti Cl. '17 3
- Chianti Cl. Ris. '16 4

Castello di Starda

LOC. STARDA, 1
53013 GAIOLE IN CHIANTI [SI]
TEL. +39 0577744017
info@castellodistarda.it

- Chianti Cl. Malaspina Ris. '16 6
- Chianti Cl. Malaspina '18 3

Castello di Vicarello

LOC. VICARELLO, 1
58044 CINIGIANO [GR]
TEL. +39 0564990718
www.castellodivicarellovini.com

CELLAR SALES
PRE-BOOKED VISITS
ACCOMMODATION AND RESTAURANT SERVICE
ANNUAL PRODUCTION 15,000 bottles
HECTARES UNDER VINE 6.50
VITICULTURE METHOD Certified Organic

- Castello di Vicarello '16 8
- Terre di Vico '16 7
- Merah '18 5

Castello La Leccia

LOC. LA LECCIA
53011 CASTELLINA IN CHIANTI [SI]
TEL. +39 0577743148
www.castellolaleccia.com

CELLAR SALES
PRE-BOOKED VISITS
ANNUAL PRODUCTION 30,000 bottles
HECTARES UNDER VINE 13.50

- Chianti Cl. '17 3*
- Vivaio del Cavaliere '18 3

Castello Tricerchi

LOC. ALTESI
53024 MONTALCINO [SI]
TEL. +39 3472501884
www.castellotricerchi.com

CELLAR SALES
PRE-BOOKED VISITS
ANNUAL PRODUCTION 40,000 bottles
HECTARES UNDER VINE 13.00

- Brunello di Montalcino A.D. 1441 '15 8
- Brunello di Montalcino '15 6
- Rosso di Montalcino '18 4

Castelsina

LOC. OSTERIA, 54A
53048 SINALUNGA [SI]
TEL. +39 0577663595
www.castelsina.it

CELLAR SALES
PRE-BOOKED VISITS
ANNUAL PRODUCTION 2,000,000 bottles
HECTARES UNDER VINE 400.00

- Chianti '19 2*
- Chianti Ris. '18 2*
- Cugnale '18 3
- Sangiovese '19 2

I Cavallini

loc. Cavallini
58014 Manciano [GR]
Tel. +39 0564609008
www.icavallini.it

ACCOMMODATION
ANNUAL PRODUCTION 25,000 bottles
HECTARES UNDER VINE 9.50

● Maremma Toscana Alicante '18	🍷🍷 4
● Maremma Toscana Ciliegiolo '18	🍷🍷 3
● Morellino di Scansano '19	🍷🍷 3
○ Maremma Toscana Vermentino Diaccio '19	🍷 3

Centolani

loc. Friggiali
s.da Maremmana
53024 Montalcino [SI]
Tel. +39 0577849454
www.tenutafriggialiepietranera.it

CELLAR SALES
PRE-BOOKED VISITS
ACCOMMODATION
ANNUAL PRODUCTION 260,000 bottles
HECTARES UNDER VINE 70.00

● Le Cacce '16	🍷🍷 4
● Rosso di Montalcino '18	🍷🍷 4
● Terre di Focaia '16	🍷 4

Ceralti

via dei Ceralti, 77
57022 Castagneto Carducci [LI]
Tel. +39 0565763989
www.ceralti.com

CELLAR SALES
PRE-BOOKED VISITS
ACCOMMODATION
ANNUAL PRODUCTION 50,000 bottles
HECTARES UNDER VINE 9.00
VITICULTURE METHOD Certified Organic

● Bolgheri Sup. Alfeo '17	🍷🍷 5
● Bolgheri Sup. Sonoro '17	🍷🍷 7

Chiesina di Lacona

fraz. Lacona
via Santa Maria, 209e
57031 Capoliveri [LI]
Tel. +39 0565964216

○ Elba Ansonica '19	🍷🍷 3
○ Elba Vermentino '19	🍷🍷 3
○ Elba Bianco '19	🍷 3

Fattoria Cigliano di Sopra

via Cigliano, 30
50026 San Casciano dei Bagni [SI]
Tel. +39 055828861
www.ciglianodisopra.it

● Chianti Cl. '18	🍷🍷 4

Cincinelli

p.zza della Vittoria, 11
52010 Capolona [AR]
Tel. +39 3356913678
www.aziendaagricolacincinelli.it

PRE-BOOKED VISITS
ACCOMMODATION
ANNUAL PRODUCTION 20,000 bottles
SUSTAINABLE WINERY

● Chianti '18	🍷🍷 3
● Mandorli '17	🍷🍷 5
● Cinci '16	🍷 3
● Il Legato '16	🍷 6

Il Colle

loc. Il Colle 102b
53024 Montalcino [SI]
Tel. +39 0577848295
ilcolledicarli@katamail.com

CELLAR SALES
PRE-BOOKED VISITS
ANNUAL PRODUCTION 18,000 bottles
HECTARES UNDER VINE 7.00

- Brunello di Montalcino '15 — 🍷🍷 6
- Rosso di Montalcino '18 — 🍷 5

Colle delle 100 bottiglie

loc. La Maolina
fraz. San Concordio di Moriano
via Bevilacqua, 100
55100 Lucca
Tel. +39 3924636248
www.colledelle100bottiglie.com

- Pigne Bordò '18 — 🍷🍷 3
- Segale '17 — 🍷🍷 4

Collelceto

loc. Camigliano
pod. La Pisana
53024 Montalcino [SI]
Tel. +39 0577816606
www.collelceto.it

CELLAR SALES
PRE-BOOKED VISITS
ANNUAL PRODUCTION 22,000 bottles
HECTARES UNDER VINE 6.00

- Brunello di Montalcino '15 — 🍷🍷 6
- Lo Spepo '18 — 🍷 2
- Rosso di Montalcino '18 — 🍷 4

La Collina dei Lecci

loc. Vallafrico
53024 Montalcino [SI]
Tel. +39 0577849287
collina@pacinimauro.com

SUSTAINABLE WINERY

- Brunello di Montalcino '15 — 🍷🍷 5
- Rosso di Montalcino '18 — 🍷 2

Le Colline di Sopra

via delle Colline, 17
56040 Montescudaio [PI]
Tel. +39 0586650377
www.collinedisopra.com

CELLAR SALES
PRE-BOOKED VISITS
ANNUAL PRODUCTION 20,000 bottles
HECTARES UNDER VINE 16.00
VITICULTURE METHOD Certified Organic
SUSTAINABLE WINERY

- Chianti Me Ris. '17 — 🍷🍷 4
- Sopra Cabernet Franc '16 — 🍷🍷 6
- Sopra Petit Verdot '16 — 🍷🍷 6

Tenuta di Collosorbo

fraz. Castelnuovo dell'Abate
loc. Villa a Sesta, 25
53024 Montalcino [SI]
Tel. +39 0577835534
www.collosorbo.com

CELLAR SALES
PRE-BOOKED VISITS
ANNUAL PRODUCTION 100,000 bottles
HECTARES UNDER VINE 27.00

- Brunello di Montalcino '15 — 🍷🍷 6
- Rosso di Montalcino '18 — 🍷🍷 4
- Sant'Antimo '18 — 🍷 3

Contucci

via del Teatro, 1
53045 Montepulciano [SI]
Tel. +39 0578757006
www.contucci.it

CELLAR SALES
PRE-BOOKED VISITS
ACCOMMODATION
ANNUAL PRODUCTION 100,000 bottles
HECTARES UNDER VINE 21.00

- ● Rosso di Montepulciano '19 — 🍷🍷 2*
- ● Nobile di Montepulciano Palazzo Contucci '16 — 🍷 6

Corte Pavone

loc. Corte Pavone
53024 Montalcino [SI]
Tel. +39 0577848110
www.loacker.net

CELLAR SALES
PRE-BOOKED VISITS
ANNUAL PRODUCTION 80,000 bottles
HECTARES UNDER VINE 17.00
VITICULTURE METHOD Certified Organic

- ● Brunello di Montalcino Fiore del Vento '15 — 🍷🍷 8
- ● Brunello di montalcino Fiore di Meliloto '15 — 🍷🍷 8
- ● Brunello di Montalcino '15 — 🍷 8
- ● Brunello di Montalcino Campo Marzio '15 — 🍷 8

Dario Di Vaira

loc. Bolgheri
via Bolgherese, 275a
57022 Castagneto Carducci [LI]
Tel. +39 0565763511
www.agriturismoeucaliptus.com

CELLAR SALES
PRE-BOOKED VISITS
ACCOMMODATION AND RESTAURANT SERVICE
ANNUAL PRODUCTION 30,000 bottles
HECTARES UNDER VINE 8.00
SUSTAINABLE WINERY

- ○ Bolgheri Bianco Rapè '19 — 🍷🍷 3
- ● Bolgheri Rosso Clarice '18 — 🍷🍷 3
- ○ Bolgheri Vermentino Le Pinete '19 — 🍷 3

Diadema

via Imprunetana per Tavarnuzze, 21
50023 Impruneta [FI]
Tel. +39 0552313963
www.diadema-wine.com

CELLAR SALES
PRE-BOOKED VISITS
ACCOMMODATION
ANNUAL PRODUCTION 80,000 bottles
HECTARES UNDER VINE 40.00

- ● Diadema Rosso '18 — 🍷🍷 8
- ● Inprunetis '18 — 🍷🍷 7
- ○ D'Amare Bianco '19 — 🍷 4
- ● D'Amare Rosso '18 — 🍷 5

Donna Olga

loc. Friggiali
s.da Maremmana
53024 Montalcino [SI]
Tel. +39 0577849454
www.tenutedonnaolga.it

CELLAR SALES
PRE-BOOKED VISITS
ACCOMMODATION
ANNUAL PRODUCTION 25,000 bottles
HECTARES UNDER VINE 11.00

- ● Rosso di Montalcino '18 — 🍷🍷 3

Donne Fittipaldi

loc. Bolgheri
via Bolgherese, 198
57022 Castagneto Carducci [LI]
Tel. +39 0565762175
www.donnefittipaldi.it

ANNUAL PRODUCTION 60,000 bottles
HECTARES UNDER VINE 9.50

- ● Bolgheri Rosso '18 — 🍷🍷 5
- ● Bolgheri Rosso Sup. '17 — 🍷🍷 6
- ○ Lady F Orpicchio Bianco '18 — 🍷 5

L'Erta di Radda

Case Sparse Il Corno, 25
53017 Radda in Chianti [SI]
Tel. +39 3284040500
www.ertadiradda.it

ANNUAL PRODUCTION 22,000 bottles
HECTARES UNDER VINE 5.00
VITICULTURE METHOD Certified Organic

- ● Chianti Cl. '18 🍷🍷 3*
- ● Chianti Cl. Ris. '17 🍷 5

Le Falene

loc. Il Fontino
58023 Gavorrano [GR]
Tel. +39 3336533306
valdelbosco@gmail.com

ANNUAL PRODUCTION 4,000 bottles
HECTARES UNDER VINE 2.00

- ● Cabernet Franc '17 🍷🍷 5
- ○ Le Falene Bianco '18 🍷🍷 3
- ● Le Falene Rosso '17 🍷 5

Falzari

via del Fondaccio 19
50059 Vinci [FI]
Tel. +39 3296354731
www.vini-falzari.it

- ● Chianti Selengaia '16 🍷🍷 3
- ○ Tinnari '17 🍷🍷 3
- ● Pilandra '16 🍷 4

Fattoria di Fiano - Ugo Bing

loc. Fiano
via Firenze, 11
50052 Certaldo [FI]
Tel. +39 0571669048
www.ugobing.it

CELLAR SALES
PRE-BOOKED VISITS
ANNUAL PRODUCTION 150,000 bottles
HECTARES UNDER VINE 22.00

- ● Chianti Colli Fiorentini '18 🍷🍷 2*
- ● Chianti Colli Fiorentini Ris. '17 🍷🍷 3
- ● Fianesco '16 🍷🍷 5
- ● Chianti Ris. '16 🍷 2

Fietri

loc. Fietri
53010 Gaiole in Chianti [SI]
Tel. +39 0577734048
www.fietri.com

CELLAR SALES
ACCOMMODATION
ANNUAL PRODUCTION 15,000 bottles
HECTARES UNDER VINE 8.00
VITICULTURE METHOD Certified Organic

- ● Chianti Cl. '17 🍷🍷 3
- ● Dedicato a Benedetta '18 🍷🍷 4
- ● Più di 1 Luna '16 🍷🍷 5
- ○ Hic et Nunc '19 🍷 3

La Fiorita

fraz. Castelnuovo dell'Abate
Podere Bellavista
53024 Montalcino [SI]
Tel. +39 0577835657
www.lafiorita.com

CELLAR SALES
PRE-BOOKED VISITS
ANNUAL PRODUCTION 35,000 bottles
HECTARES UNDER VINE 7.00

- ● Rosso di Montalcino '18 🍷🍷 5
- ● Brunello di Montalcino Fiore di No '15 🍷 7
- ⊙ Ninfalia '19 🍷 5

Le Fonti - Panzano

FRAZ. PANZANO IN CHIANTI
LOC. LE FONTI
50022 GREVE IN CHIANTI [FI]
TEL. +39 055852194
www.fattorialefonti.it

CELLAR SALES
PRE-BOOKED VISITS
ANNUAL PRODUCTION 45,000 bottles
HECTARES UNDER VINE 8.81
VITICULTURE METHOD Certified Organic

- ● Chianti Cl. Ris. '16 — 🍷🍷4
- ● Chianti Cl. '17 — 🍷🍷3
- ● Chianti Cl. Gran Selezione '17 — 🍷5
- ● Fontissimo '16 — 🍷5

Le Fornacelle

LOC. SAN BENEDETTO 46
53037 SAN GIMIGNANO [SI]
TEL. +39 0577944958
www.fornacelle.com

- ● Chianti Colli Senesi '19 — 🍷🍷2*
- ○ Vernaccia di San Gimignano Fiore Ris. '18 — 🍷🍷4
- ○ Vernaccia di San Gimignano '19 — 🍷2

Podere Fortuna

VIA SAN GIUSTO A FORTUNA, 7
50038 SCARPERIA E SAN PIERO [FI]
TEL. +39 3714139429
www.podereFortuna.com

CELLAR SALES
PRE-BOOKED VISITS
ACCOMMODATION
ANNUAL PRODUCTION 25,000 bottles
HECTARES UNDER VINE 6.00
SUSTAINABLE WINERY

- ● Fortuni '16 — 🍷🍷5
- ○ Greto alla Macchia '18 — 🍷🍷5
- ⊙ Rosé '18 — 🍷3

Fossacolle

LOC. TAVERNELLE, 7
53024 MONTALCINO [SI]
TEL. +39 0577816013
www.fossacolle.it

CELLAR SALES
PRE-BOOKED VISITS
ANNUAL PRODUCTION 20,000 bottles
HECTARES UNDER VINE 2.50

- ● Brunello di Montalcino '15 — 🍷🍷6
- ● Riesci '16 — 🍷🍷3
- ● Rosso di Montalcino '18 — 🍷4

Fattoria di Fugnano

VIA FUGNANO, 52
53037 SAN GIMIGNANO [SI]
TEL. +39 0577940012
www.fattoriadifugnano.com

CELLAR SALES
PRE-BOOKED VISITS
ACCOMMODATION AND RESTAURANT SERVICE
ANNUAL PRODUCTION 100,000 bottles
HECTARES UNDER VINE 26.00

- ○ Vernaccia di San Gimignano Da Fugnano '19 — 🍷🍷2*
- ○ Vernaccia di San Gimignano Donna Gina '18 — 🍷🍷3

Gagliole

LOC. GAGLIOLE, 42
53011 CASTELLINA IN CHIANTI [SI]
TEL. +39 0577740369
www.gagliole.com

CELLAR SALES
PRE-BOOKED VISITS
ANNUAL PRODUCTION 35,000 bottles
HECTARES UNDER VINE 9.90

- ● Chianti Cl. Rubiolo '18 — 🍷🍷3*
- ● Gagliole Rosso '16 — 🍷🍷6

Godiolo

via dell'Acquapuzzola, 13
53045 Montepulciano [SI]
Tel. +39 0578757251
www.godiolo.it

CELLAR SALES
PRE-BOOKED VISITS
ACCOMMODATION AND RESTAURANT SERVICE
ANNUAL PRODUCTION 25,000 bottles
HECTARES UNDER VINE 6.00

- ● Nobile di Montepulciano '16 — 3*

Tenuta di Gracciano della Seta

fraz. Gracciano
via Umbria, 59
53045 Montepulciano [SI]
Tel. +39 0578708340
www.graccianodellaseta.com

CELLAR SALES
PRE-BOOKED VISITS
ANNUAL PRODUCTION 90,000 bottles
HECTARES UNDER VINE 19.00
VITICULTURE METHOD Certified Organic
SUSTAINABLE WINERY

- ● Nobile di Montepulciano '17 — 4
- ● Rosso di Montepulciano '18 — 3
- ● Nobile di Montepulciano Ris. '16 — 5

Il Grappolo

loc. Sant'Angelo in Colle
via Traversa dei Monti
53020 Montalcino [SI]
Tel. +39 0574813730
www.ilgrappolofortius.it

ANNUAL PRODUCTION 100,000 bottles
HECTARES UNDER VINE 7.00

- ● Brunello di Montalcino '15 — 5
- ● Rosso di Montalcino '18 — 3

Guidi 1929

via Liguria
53036 Poggibonsi [SI]
Tel. +39 0577936356
www.guidi1929.com

CELLAR SALES
PRE-BOOKED VISITS
ANNUAL PRODUCTION 100,000 bottles
HECTARES UNDER VINE 14.00
SUSTAINABLE WINERY

- ○ Vernaccia di San Gimignano '19 — 2*
- ○ Vernaccia di San Gimignano Aurea Ris. '17 — 2*
- ● Chianti '19 — 2
- ⊙ Rosato '19 — 2

Icario

via delle Pietrose, 2
53045 Montepulciano [SI]
Tel. +39 0578758845
www.icario.it

CELLAR SALES
PRE-BOOKED VISITS
ANNUAL PRODUCTION 110,000 bottles
HECTARES UNDER VINE 20.00

- ● Nobile di Montepulciano Vitaroccia Ris. '15 — 5
- ● Nobile di Montepulciano '16 — 4
- ● Rosso di Montepulciano '18 — 2

La Lupinella

fraz. Sovigliana
via Pietramarina 53
50053 Vinci [FI]
Tel. +39 05717091
info@lalupinella.com

- ● La Lupinella Rossa '18 — 3
- ● La Lupinella Sangiovese '18 — 5
- ○ La Lupinella Bianca '19 — 5
- ⊙ La Lupinella Rosa '19 — 3

Maurizio Lambardi

LOC. CANALICCHIO DI SOTTO, 8
53024 MONTALCINO [SI]
TEL. +39 0577848476
www.lambardimontalcino.it

CELLAR SALES
PRE-BOOKED VISITS
ANNUAL PRODUCTION 17,000 bottles
HECTARES UNDER VINE 6.50

- ● Rosso di Montalcino '17 — 🍷🍷4
- ● Brunello di Montalcino '15 — 🍷🍷8

La Lecciaia

LOC. VALLAFRICO
53024 MONTALCINO [SI]
TEL. +39 0583928366
www.lecciaia.it

PRE-BOOKED VISITS
ANNUAL PRODUCTION 200,000 bottles
HECTARES UNDER VINE 16.00

- ● Pugnitello '18 — 🍷🍷3
- ● Rosso di Montalcino '18 — 🍷🍷3
- ● Brunello di Montalcino '15 — 🍷6
- ● Brunello di Montalcino V. Manapetra '15 — 🍷6

Tenuta Luce

LOC. CASTELGIOCONDO
53024 MONTALCINO [SI]
TEL. +39 0577 84131
www.lucedellavite.com

CELLAR SALES
PRE-BOOKED VISITS
ACCOMMODATION AND RESTAURANT SERVICE
ANNUAL PRODUCTION 470,000 bottles
HECTARES UNDER VINE 88.00
VITICULTURE METHOD Certified Organic
SUSTAINABLE WINERY

- ● Brunello di Montalcino Luce '15 — 🍷🍷8
- ● Luce '17 — 🍷🍷8
- ● Lucente '17 — 🍷🍷6

Podere Il Macchione

FRAZ. GRACCIANO
VIA PROVINCIALE, 18
53045 MONTEPULCIANO [SI]
TEL. +39 0578 758595
www.podereilmacchione.it

CELLAR SALES
PRE-BOOKED VISITS
ANNUAL PRODUCTION 20,000 bottles
HECTARES UNDER VINE 6.00

- ● Nobile di Montepulciano '16 — 🍷🍷5
- ● Rosso di Montepulciano '18 — 🍷4

Maciarine

S.DA PROV.LE DI POGGIOFERRO
58038 SEGGIANO [GR]
TEL. +39 3487155650
www.maciarine.it

CELLAR SALES
PRE-BOOKED VISITS
ANNUAL PRODUCTION 15,000 bottles
HECTARES UNDER VINE 3.90
SUSTAINABLE WINERY

- ● Montecucco Rosso '18 — 🍷🍷3*
- ● Maremma Toscana Rosso Tordaio '18 — 🍷🍷2*
- ● Montecucco Sangiovese Ris. '15 — 🍷🍷4

Macinatico

LOC. SAN BENEDETTO 56-58
53037 SAN GIMIGNANO [SI]
TEL. +39 3388850426
www.macinatico1.it

- ● Baluan '18 — 🍷🍷4
- ● Chianti Massi Ris. '16 — 🍷🍷4
- ● Sangiovese '18 — 🍷🍷1*
- ○ Vernaccia di San Gimignano '18 — 🍷2

La Magia

loc. La Magia
53024 Montalcino [SI]
Tel. +39 0577835667
www.fattorialamagia.it

ANNUAL PRODUCTION 80,000 bottles
HECTARES UNDER VINE 15.00

- Brunello di Montalcino '15 ƔƔ 6
- Rosso di Montalcino '18 ƔƔ 3

Podere Marcampo

loc. San Cipriano
56048 Volterra [PI]
Tel. +39 058885393
www.poderemarcampo.com

CELLAR SALES
PRE-BOOKED VISITS
ACCOMMODATION AND RESTAURANT SERVICE
ANNUAL PRODUCTION 18,000 bottles
HECTARES UNDER VINE 5.00
VITICULTURE METHOD Certified Organic
SUSTAINABLE WINERY

- Giusto alle Balze '17 ƔƔ 5
- Marcampo '17 ƔƔ 3
- Severus '17 ƔƔ 4

Martoccia

loc. Martoccia
53024 Montalcino [SI]
Tel. +39 0577 848540
www.poderemartoccia.it

ANNUAL PRODUCTION 85,000 bottles
HECTARES UNDER VINE 15.00

- Brunello di Montalcino '15 ƔƔ 6
- Luca '14 ƔƔ 6
- Rosso di Montalcino '18 Ɣ 3

Máté

loc. Santa Restituta
53024 Montalcino [SI]
Tel. +39 0577847215
www.matewine.com

CELLAR SALES
PRE-BOOKED VISITS
ACCOMMODATION
ANNUAL PRODUCTION 25,000 bottles
HECTARES UNDER VINE 6.50
VITICULTURE METHOD Certified Organic

- Banditone Syrah '16 ƔƔ 7
- Brunello di Montalcino '15 ƔƔ 6

Giorgio Meletti Cavallari

via Casone Ugolino, 12
57022 Castagneto Carducci [LI]
Tel. +39 0565775620
www.giorgiomeletticavallari.it

CELLAR SALES
PRE-BOOKED VISITS
ACCOMMODATION
ANNUAL PRODUCTION 40,000 bottles
HECTARES UNDER VINE 10.00

- ○ Bolgheri Bianco Borgeri '19 ƔƔ 3
- Bolgheri Rosso Borgeri '18 ƔƔ 3
- Bolgheri Rosso Sup. Impronte '17 Ɣ 5

Metinella

fraz. Sant'Albino
via Fontelellera, 21a
53045 Montepulciano [SI]
Tel. +39 0305780877
www.metinella.it

CELLAR SALES
PRE-BOOKED VISITS
RESTAURANT SERVICE
ANNUAL PRODUCTION 80,000 bottles
HECTARES UNDER VINE 25.00

- Nobile di Montepulciano Burberosso '17 ƔƔ 5

Micheletti

MARCACCIO, 58
57022 CASTAGNETO CARDUCCI [LI]
TEL. +39 3803295193
www.michelettiwine.com

PRE-BOOKED VISITS
ANNUAL PRODUCTION 30,000 bottles
HECTARES UNDER VINE 5.00

- Bolgheri Sup. Guardione '17 — 🍷🍷 5
- Bolgheri Rosso Dalleo '18 — 🍷🍷 4
- Bolgheri Sup. Poggiomatto '17 — 🍷🍷 5

Mocali

LOC. MOCALI
53024 MONTALCINO [SI]
TEL. +39 0577849485
www.mocali.eu

CELLAR SALES
PRE-BOOKED VISITS
ANNUAL PRODUCTION 120,000 bottles
HECTARES UNDER VINE 9.00
VITICULTURE METHOD Certified Organic
SUSTAINABLE WINERY

- Brunello di Montalcino '15 — 🍷🍷 6
- Brunello di Montalcino V. delle Raunate '15 — 🍷🍷 6
- Maremma Toscana Ciliegiolo Alpan Suberli '19 — 🍷🍷 3

Podere Monastero

LOC. MONASTERO
53011 CASTELLINA IN CHIANTI [SI]
TEL. +39 0577740436
www.poderemonastero.com

CELLAR SALES
PRE-BOOKED VISITS
ACCOMMODATION
ANNUAL PRODUCTION 7,000 bottles
HECTARES UNDER VINE 3.00

- La Pineta '18 — 🍷🍷 6
- Campanaio '18 — 🍷🍷 6

La Montanina

LOC. MONTI IN CHIANTI, 25
53020 GAIOLE IN CHIANTI [SI]
TEL. +39 0577280074
www.aziendaagricolalamontanina.it

- Agosto di Monti '16 — 🍷🍷 3
- Nebbiano '18 — 🍷🍷 3
- Chianti Cl. '18 — 🍷 3

Montenero

FRAZ. MONTENERO D'ORCIA
LOC. PODERE MARINELLI, 74
58033 CASTEL DEL PIANO [GR]
TEL. +39 3493701998
www.montenerowinery.com

CELLAR SALES
PRE-BOOKED VISITS
ANNUAL PRODUCTION 45,000 bottles
HECTARES UNDER VINE 7.00

- Montecucco Sangiovese '16 — 🍷🍷 3
- Montecucco Rosso '17 — 🍷 3
- Pampano Ciliegiolo '16 — 🍷 6

Muralia

LOC. IL POGGIARELLO
FRAZ. STICCIANO
VIA DEL SUGHERETO
58036 ROCCASTRADA [GR]
TEL. +39 0564577223
www.muralia.it

CELLAR SALES
PRE-BOOKED VISITS
ACCOMMODATION AND RESTAURANT SERVICE
ANNUAL PRODUCTION 65,000 bottles
HECTARES UNDER VINE 14.00
VITICULTURE METHOD Certified Organic
SUSTAINABLE WINERY

- Manolibera '18 — 🍷🍷 2*
- Maremma Toscana Sangiovese Altana '18 — 🍷🍷 3

Nardi

LOC. CIGNAN ROSSO
53011 CASTELLINA IN CHIANTI [SI]
TEL. +39 3315622266
www.nardiviticoltori.it

- Chianti Cl. '18 — 🍷🍷 4
- Baccheri '18 — 🍷🍷 2*
- Chianti Cl. Ris. '17 — 🍷🍷 5

Le Novelire

LOC. CAMPO ALLA CAPANNA, 216
57022 CASTAGNETO CARDUCCI [LI]
TEL. +39 3479828633
www.lenovelire.it

HECTARES UNDER VINE 4.00
SUSTAINABLE WINERY

- Bolgheri Sup. Re Diale '17 — 🍷🍷 7
- Bolgheri Sup. Re Vignon '17 — 🍷🍷 7
- Re Stigio '18 — 🍷🍷 4

Oliviera

S.DA PROV.LE 102 DI VAGLIAGLI, 36
53019 CASTELNUOVO BERARDENGA [SI]
TEL. +39 3498950188
www.oliviera.it

ANNUAL PRODUCTION 30,000 bottles
HECTARES UNDER VINE 9.00

- Chianti Cl. Campo di Mansueto '18 — 🍷🍷 3
- Chianti Cl. Settantanove Ris. '17 — 🍷🍷 3
- Chianti Cl. '18 — 🍷 3

Fattoria Ormanni

LOC. ORMANNI, 1
53036 POGGIBONSI [SI]
TEL. +39 0577937212
www.ormanni.it

CELLAR SALES
PRE-BOOKED VISITS
ACCOMMODATION
ANNUAL PRODUCTION 120,000 bottles
HECTARES UNDER VINE 68.00

- Canaiolo '19 — 🍷🍷 3
- Chianti Cl. Borro del Diavolo Ris. '16 — 🍷🍷 5
- Chianti Cl. '17 — 🍷 3

Orsumella

LOC. MONTEFIRIDOLFI
VIA COLLINA 52
50026 SAN CASCIANO IN VAL DI PESA [FI]
TEL. +39 3395852557
www.orsumella.it

- Chianti Cl. Corte Rinieri Ris. '16 — 🍷🍷 4
- Chianti Cl. '17 — 🍷🍷 3

Otto Ettari

LOC. MONTENERO D'ORCIA
VIA GIACOMO BRODOLINI
58033 CASTEL DEL PIANO [GR]
TEL. +39 3939368584
ottoettari@gmail.com

CELLAR SALES
PRE-BOOKED VISITS
ANNUAL PRODUCTION 40,000 bottles
HECTARES UNDER VINE 6.00

- Montecucco Sangiovese '16 — 🍷🍷 3*
- Montecucco Sangiovese Ris. '16 — 🍷 5

Tenute Palagetto

via Monteoliveto, 46
53037 San Gimignano [SI]
Tel. +39 0577943090
www.palagetto.it

CELLAR SALES
PRE-BOOKED VISITS
ACCOMMODATION
ANNUAL PRODUCTION 250,000 bottles
HECTARES UNDER VINE 44.00

- ● San Gimignano Sangiovese '16 🍷🍷 5
- ○ Vernaccia di S. Gimignano Ris. '16 🍷🍷 3
- ○ Vernaccia di S. Gimignano V. Santa Chiara '19 🍷 2

Le Palaie

via del Molino, 200-208
56036 Peccioli [PI]
Tel. +39 3473608923
www.lepalaie.it

CELLAR SALES
PRE-BOOKED VISITS
ACCOMMODATION
ANNUAL PRODUCTION 40,000 bottles
HECTARES UNDER VINE 15.00

- ● Gatta Ci Cova '18 🍷🍷 2*
- ● Sotterfugio '16 🍷🍷 7

Il Palazzone

loc. Le Due Porte, 245
53024 Montalcino [SI]
Tel. +39 0577846142
www.ilpalazzone.com

CELLAR SALES
PRE-BOOKED VISITS
ANNUAL PRODUCTION 12,000 bottles
HECTARES UNDER VINE 3.96

- ● Brunello di Montalcino '15 🍷🍷 6

Paradiso di Cacuci

loc. Paradiso, 323
53020 Montalcino [SI]
Tel. +39 3519892059
www.paradisodicacuci.com

- ● Brunello di Montalcino '15 🍷🍷 7
- ● Pavla '17 🍷🍷 5
- ● Rosso di Montalcino '18 🍷 5

Piandaccoli

via Paganelle, 7
50041 Calenzano [FI]
Tel. +39 0550750005
www.piandaccoli.it

CELLAR SALES
PRE-BOOKED VISITS
ANNUAL PRODUCTION 100,000 bottles
HECTARES UNDER VINE 20.00
SUSTAINABLE WINERY

- ● Foglia Tonda del Rinascimento '17 🍷🍷 6
- ● Pugnitello del Rinascimento '17 🍷🍷 6
- ● Chianti Cosmus '17 🍷 2

Le Pianore

fraz. Monticello Amiata
loc. Podere Maladina, 1
58044 Cinigiano [GR]
Tel. +39 3355371513
www.lepianore.it

CELLAR SALES
PRE-BOOKED VISITS
ACCOMMODATION AND RESTAURANT SERVICE
ANNUAL PRODUCTION 7,000 bottles
HECTARES UNDER VINE 1.30
VITICULTURE METHOD Certified Organic
SUSTAINABLE WINERY

- ● Montecucco Rosso Tiniatus '18 🍷🍷 3*
- ● Periodico '18 🍷🍷 4

Piemaggio

LOC. FIORAIE
53011 CASTELLINA IN CHIANTI [SI]
TEL. +39 0577740658

CELLAR SALES
ANNUAL PRODUCTION 40,000 bottles
HECTARES UNDER VINE 11.50
SUSTAINABLE WINERY

- ● Chianti Cl. Le Fioraie '16 — 🍷🍷 4

Agostina Pieri

FRAZ. SANT'ANGELO SCALO
LOC. PIANCORNELLO
53024 MONTALCINO [SI]
TEL. +39 0577844163
www.pieriagostina.it

ANNUAL PRODUCTION 45,000 bottles
HECTARES UNDER VINE 10.78

- ● Brunello di Montalcino '15 — 🍷🍷 6
- ● Rosso di Montalcino '18 — 🍷🍷 3

Piombaia Rossi Cantini

LOC. PIOMBAIA 230
53024 MONTALCINO [SI]
TEL. +39 0577847197
www.piombaia.com

CELLAR SALES
PRE-BOOKED VISITS
ACCOMMODATION AND RESTAURANT SERVICE
ANNUAL PRODUCTION 25,000 bottles
HECTARES UNDER VINE 12.50

- ● Brunello di Montalcino '15 — 🍷🍷 6
- ● Rosso di Montalcino '18 — 🍷 3

Podere Conca

FRAZ. BOLGHERI
VIA BOLGHERESE, 196
57022 CASTAGNETO CARDUCCI [LI]
TEL. +39 3896077754
www.podereconcabolgheri.it

CELLAR SALES
PRE-BOOKED VISITS
ANNUAL PRODUCTION 15,000 bottles
HECTARES UNDER VINE 5.00

- ● Bolgheri Rosso Agapanto '18 — 🍷🍷 4
- ○ Elleboro '19 — 🍷🍷 3

Podere Montale

S.DA POGGIOFERRO
58038 SEGGIANO [GR]
TEL. +39 3471182842
www,poderemontale.it

CELLAR SALES
PRE-BOOKED VISITS
ACCOMMODATION
ANNUAL PRODUCTION 100,000 bottles
HECTARES UNDER VINE 17.50
SUSTAINABLE WINERY

- ● Montecucco Sangiovese La Casetta Ris. '16 — 🍷🍷 8
- ● Montecucco Sangiovese '16 — 🍷 6

Podere Sette

LOC. FERRUGGINI, 162
57022 CASTAGNETO CARDUCCI [LI]
TEL. +39 0565749810
www.poderesette.com

SUSTAINABLE WINERY

- ● Bolgheri Rosso L'Invidio '18 — 🍷🍷 4
- ● Bolgheri Sup. Il Superbo '17 — 🍷🍷 6

Poderi del Paradiso

LOC. STRADA, 21A
53037 SAN GIMIGNANO [SI]
TEL. +39 0577941500
www.poderidelparadiso.it

CELLAR SALES
PRE-BOOKED VISITS
ACCOMMODATION
ANNUAL PRODUCTION 130,000 bottles
HECTARES UNDER VINE 27.00

- ● San Gimignano Rosso Bottaccio '17 — 🍷🍷 3
- ○ Vernaccia di S. Gimignano Biscondola '18 — 🍷🍷 3
- ○ Vernaccia di S. Gimignano '19 — 🍷 2

La Poderina

FRAZ. CASTELNUOVO DELL'ABATE
LOC. PODERINA
53020 MONTALCINO [SI]
TEL. +39 0577835737
www.lapoderina.it

CELLAR SALES
PRE-BOOKED VISITS
ACCOMMODATION
ANNUAL PRODUCTION 120,000 bottles
HECTARES UNDER VINE 37.00

- ● Brunello di Montalcino '15 — 🍷🍷 7
- ● Rosso di Montalcino '18 — 🍷 4

Poggio Grande

LOC. POGGIO GRANDE, 11
53023 CASTIGLIONE D'ORCIA [SI]
TEL. +39 3388677637
www.aziendapoggiogrande.it

CELLAR SALES
PRE-BOOKED VISITS
ANNUAL PRODUCTION 22,000 bottles
HECTARES UNDER VINE 6.50

- ● Orcia Sangiovese Sesterzo Ris. '16 — 🍷🍷 5
- ● Orcia Scorbutico '17 — 🍷🍷 3

Tenuta Poggio Rosso

FRAZ. POPULONIA
LOC. POGGIO ROSSO, 1
57025 PIOMBINO [LI]
TEL. +39 056529553
www.tenutapoggiorosso.it

CELLAR SALES
PRE-BOOKED VISITS
ACCOMMODATION
ANNUAL PRODUCTION 35,000 bottles
HECTARES UNDER VINE 6.00

- ● Fufluna '19 — 🍷🍷 3
- ● Velthune '17 — 🍷🍷 6
- ○ Feronia '19 — 🍷 4
- ○ Phylika '19 — 🍷 3

Villa Poggio Salvi

LOC. POGGIO SALVI
53024 MONTALCINO [SI]
TEL. +39 0577847121
www.villapoggiosalvi.it

PRE-BOOKED VISITS
ANNUAL PRODUCTION 250,000 bottles
HECTARES UNDER VINE 43.00

- ● Brunello di Montalcino '15 — 🍷🍷 6
- ○ Moscadello di Montalcino V. T. Aurico '06 — 🍷🍷 4
- ● Tosco '19 — 🍷🍷 2*
- ● Brunello di Montalcino Pomona '15 — 🍷 6

Poggio Stenti

LOC. MONTENERO D'ORCIA
POD. STENTI, 26A
58033 CASTEL DEL PIANO [GR]
TEL. +39 0564954171
www.poggiostenti.com

CELLAR SALES
PRE-BOOKED VISITS
RESTAURANT SERVICE
ANNUAL PRODUCTION 20,000 bottles
HECTARES UNDER VINE 6.00

- ● Montecucco Sangiovese Pian di Staffa Ris. '16 — 🍷🍷 3*
- ○ Montecucco Vermentino '19 — 🍷 2

Fattoria di Poggiopiano

FRAZ. GIRONE
VIA DEI BASSI, 13
50061 FIESOLE [FI]
TEL. +39 0556593020
www.poggiopiano.it

CELLAR SALES
PRE-BOOKED VISITS
ACCOMMODATION
ANNUAL PRODUCTION 30,000 bottles
HECTARES UNDER VINE 4.50
VITICULTURE METHOD Certified Organic
SUSTAINABLE WINERY

○ Erta al Mandorlo '19	🍷🍷 3
● Poggio Galardi in Anfora '16	🍷🍷 4
○ VinOrange '17	🍷🍷 6

Fabrizio Pratesi

LOC. SEANO
VIA RIZZELLI, 10
59011 CARMIGNANO [PO]
TEL. +39 0558704108
www.pratesivini.it

CELLAR SALES
PRE-BOOKED VISITS
RESTAURANT SERVICE
ANNUAL PRODUCTION 70,000 bottles
HECTARES UNDER VINE 14.00

● Carmignano Il Circo Rosso Ris. '17	🍷🍷 6
● Carmignano Carmione '18	🍷 4

Fattoria di Rignana

VIA DI RIGNANA, 15
50022 GREVE IN CHIANTI [FI]
TEL. +39 055852065
www.rignana.it

CELLAR SALES
PRE-BOOKED VISITS
ACCOMMODATION AND RESTAURANT SERVICE
ANNUAL PRODUCTION 40,000 bottles
HECTARES UNDER VINE 13.50
VITICULTURE METHOD Certified Organic

● Chianti Cl. '17	🍷🍷 3
● Chianti Cl. Ris. '16	🍷🍷 4
● Il Riccio Rosso '16	🍷 5

Tenute delle Ripalte

LOC. RIPALTE
57031 CAPOLIVERI [LI]
TEL. +39 056594211
www.tenutadelleripalte.it

CELLAR SALES
PRE-BOOKED VISITS
ACCOMMODATION AND RESTAURANT SERVICE
ANNUAL PRODUCTION 60,000 bottles
HECTARES UNDER VINE 15.00
SUSTAINABLE WINERY

● Elba Aleatico Passito Alea Ludendo '16	🍷🍷 6
○ Le Riparlte Vermentino '19	🍷🍷 3
○ Bianco Mediterraneo Le Ripalte '17	🍷 3
⊙ Rosato delle Ripalte '19	🍷 3

Tenuta Roccaccia

VIA POGGIO CAVALLUCCIO
58017 PITIGLIANO [GR]
TEL. +39 0564617020
www.tenutaroccaccia.it

CELLAR SALES
PRE-BOOKED VISITS
ACCOMMODATION
ANNUAL PRODUCTION 130,000 bottles
HECTARES UNDER VINE 30.00
VITICULTURE METHOD Certified Organic

○ Bianco di Pitigliano Sup. Oroluna '19	🍷🍷 2*
○ Solechiaro Vermentino '19	🍷🍷 3
○ Maremma Toscana Trebbiano Prezioso '19	🍷 3

Fattoria San Felo

LOC. PAGLIATELLI DI SOTTO
58051 MAGLIANO IN TOSCANA [GR]
TEL. +39 05641950121
www.fattoriasanfelo.it

ANNUAL PRODUCTION 100,000 bottles
HECTARES UNDER VINE 30.00

● Morellino di Scansano Lampo '18	🍷🍷 3
● Maremma Toscana Rosso Balla la Vecchia '18	🍷 2

San Filippo

loc. San Filippo, 134
53024 Montalcino [SI]
Tel. +39 0577847176
www.sanfilippomontalcino.com

ANNUAL PRODUCTION 50,000 bottles
HECTARES UNDER VINE 10.50

● Brunello di Montalcino Le Lucére '15	🍷🍷 6
● Rosso di Montalcino '18	🍷🍷 3
● Brunello di Montalcino '15	🍷 6

San Luciano Vini

loc. San Luciano, 90
52048 Monte San Savino [AR]
Tel. +39 0575848518
www.sanlucianovini.it

CELLAR SALES
PRE-BOOKED VISITS
ACCOMMODATION
ANNUAL PRODUCTION 350,000 bottles
HECTARES UNDER VINE 63.00
SUSTAINABLE WINERY

● Colle Carpito '17	🍷🍷 3
○ Luna di Monte '18	🍷🍷 2*
○ Resico '18	🍷🍷 3
● Boschi Salviati '16	🍷 5

Fabbrica di San Martino

via Pieve Santo Stefano, 2511
55100 Lucca
Tel. +39 3476247497
www.fabbricadisanmartino.it

CELLAR SALES
PRE-BOOKED VISITS
ACCOMMODATION
ANNUAL PRODUCTION 13,000 bottles
HECTARES UNDER VINE 2.00
VITICULTURE METHOD Certified OrganicCertified Biodynamic

● Arcipressi '17	🍷🍷 3
● Montecarlo Rosso Ris. '16	🍷🍷 4

Podere Sanlorenzo

pod. Sanlorenzo, 280
53024 Montalcino [SI]
Tel. +39 3396070930
www.poderesanlorenzo.net

CELLAR SALES
PRE-BOOKED VISITS
ANNUAL PRODUCTION 18,000 bottles
HECTARES UNDER VINE 4.50

● Brunello di Montalcino Bramante '15	🍷🍷 6
● Rosso di Montalcino '18	🍷 3

Tenuta Sanoner

loc. Sant'Anna
fraz. Bagno Vignoni
53027 San Quirico d'Orcia [SI]
Tel. +39 05771698707
www.tenuta-sanoner.it

● Orcia Sangiovese Aetos '18	🍷🍷 5
● Orcia Sangiovese Aetos Ris. '17	🍷🍷 7

Fattoria Santavenere Triacca

s.da per Pienza, 39
53045 Montepulciano [SI]
Tel. +39 0578757774
www.triacca.com

CELLAR SALES
PRE-BOOKED VISITS
ANNUAL PRODUCTION 160,000 bottles
HECTARES UNDER VINE 37.00

● Nobile di Montepulciano '16	🍷🍷 4
● Nobile di Montepulciano Poderuccio '16	🍷🍷 5

SassodiSole

FRAZ. TORRENIERI
LOC. SASSO DI SOLE, 85
53024 MONTALCINO [SI]
TEL. +39 0577834303
www.sassodisole.it

CELLAR SALES
PRE-BOOKED VISITS
ANNUAL PRODUCTION 45,000 bottles
HECTARES UNDER VINE 10.00
SUSTAINABLE WINERY

- ● Brunello di Montalcino '15 — 🍷🍷 8
- ● Brunello di Montalcino Bruno '15 — 🍷🍷 8
- ● Orcia Sangiovese '18 — 🍷🍷 4
- ⊙ Rosato Brut — 🍷 7

Paolina Savignola

LOC. PETRIOLO
VIA PETRIOLO, 58
50022 GREVE IN CHIANTI [FI]
TEL. +39 0558546036
www.savignolapaolina.it

CELLAR SALES
PRE-BOOKED VISITS
ACCOMMODATION
ANNUAL PRODUCTION 35,000 bottles
HECTARES UNDER VINE 6.00

- ● Chianti Cl. Gran Selezione 360° '17 — 🍷🍷 3*
- ● Chianti Cl. Ora '18 — 🍷🍷 4
- ● Chianti Cl. Ris. '17 — 🍷 4

Scopetone

LOC. LA MELINA, 285
53024 MONTALCINO [SI]
TEL. +39 0577848713

- ● Brunello di Montalcino '15 — 🍷🍷 7
- ● Rosso di Montalcino '17 — 🍷🍷 4

Signano

LOC. SANTA MARGHERITA, 36
53037 SAN GIMIGNANO [SI]
TEL. +39 0577941085
www.casolaredibucciano.com

CELLAR SALES
PRE-BOOKED VISITS
ANNUAL PRODUCTION 80,000 bottles
HECTARES UNDER VINE 25.00

- ○ Vernaccia di S. Gimignano La Ginestra Ris. '17 — 🍷🍷 3
- ○ Vernaccia di S. Gimignano Poggiarelli '19 — 🍷🍷 2*
- ○ Vernaccia di S. Gimignano '19 — 🍷 2

Le Sode di Sant'Angelo

LOC. MONTEBAMBOLI
58024 MASSA MARITTIMA [GR]
TEL. +39 0758358574
www.sodesantangelo.com

- ● Maremma Toscana Sangiovese Sassi Dautore '18 — 🍷🍷 3
- ○ Maremma Toscana Vermentino Le Gessaie '19 — 🍷🍷 3

Fattoria Le Spighe

LOC. ALBINIA
FRAZ. SAN DONATO
S.DA PROV.LE 81 OSA
58015 ORBETELLO [GR]
TEL. +39 0564886325
www.agriturismolespighe.it

CELLAR SALES
ACCOMMODATION AND RESTAURANT SERVICE
ANNUAL PRODUCTION 20,000 bottles
HECTARES UNDER VINE 4.00

- ○ Maremma Toscana Ansonica Giragira '19 — 🍷🍷 3
- ● Maremma Toscana Rosso Eccolo '17 — 🍷🍷 4
- ○ Maremma Toscana Bianco Eraora '19 — 🍷 3
- ○ Maremma Toscana Bianco Ullallà '19 — 🍷 3

Borgo La Stella

LOC. VAGLIAGLI
B.GO LA STELLA, 60
53017 RADDA IN CHIANTI [SI]
TEL. +39 0577740699
www.borgolastella.com

ANNUAL PRODUCTION 21,000 bottles
HECTARES UNDER VINE 4.50

- Chianti Cl. Gran Selezione '17 — 🍷🍷 4
- Chianti Cl. '17 — 🍷🍷 3
- Chirone '17 — 🍷 4

Stomennano

LOC. BORGO STOMENNANO
53035 MONTERIGGIONI [SI]
TEL. +39 0577304033
www.stomennano.it

CELLAR SALES
PRE-BOOKED VISITS
ACCOMMODATION
ANNUAL PRODUCTION 50,000 bottles
HECTARES UNDER VINE 25.00
SUSTAINABLE WINERY

- Chianti Cl. '18 — 🍷🍷 5

Fattoria della Talosa

VIA TALOSA, 8
53045 MONTEPULCIANO [SI]
TEL. +39 0578758277
www.talosa.it

CELLAR SALES
PRE-BOOKED VISITS
ANNUAL PRODUCTION 100,000 bottles
HECTARES UNDER VINE 33.00

- Nobile di Montepulciano '17 — 🍷🍷 4
- Nobile di Montepulciano Filai Lunghi '17 — 🍷🍷 6
- Rosso di Montepulciano '19 — 🍷 2

Agricola Tamburini

VIA CATIGNANO, 106
50050 GAMBASSI TERME [FI]
TEL. +39 0571680235
www.agricolatamburini.it

CELLAR SALES
PRE-BOOKED VISITS
ANNUAL PRODUCTION 90,000 bottles
HECTARES UNDER VINE 30.00
VITICULTURE METHOD Certified Organic

- Brunello di Montalcino Somnio '15 — 🍷🍷 6
- Il Moraccio '16 — 🍷🍷 4
- Chianti The Boss '17 — 🍷 2
- Il Massiccio '15 — 🍷 2

Terra Quercus Francesco D'Alessandro

LOC. IL MANDOLETO
VIA DEL MANDOLETO, 12
53047 SARTEANO [SI]
TEL. +39 0578265286
www.terraquercus.it

PRE-BOOKED VISITS
ACCOMMODATION
ANNUAL PRODUCTION 5,000 bottles
HECTARES UNDER VINE 3.50
VITICULTURE METHOD Certified Organic
SUSTAINABLE WINERY

- Quarta Luna '16 — 🍷🍷 6
- Scherzo '18 — 🍷🍷 4

Teruzzi

LOC. CASALE, 19
53037 SAN GIMIGNANO [SI]
TEL. +39 0577940143
www.teruzzieputhod.it

CELLAR SALES
PRE-BOOKED VISITS
ANNUAL PRODUCTION 1,000,000 bottles
HECTARES UNDER VINE 94.00

- ○ Vernaccia di S. Gimignano Sant'Elena Ris. '17 — 🍷🍷 3
- ○ Vernaccia di San Gimignano Isola Bianca '19 — 🍷 2

La Torre

loc. La Torre
fraz. Sant'Angelo in Colle
53020 Montalcino [SI]
Tel. +39 3406765126
www.brunellodimontalcinolatorre.it

- Brunello di Montalcino '15 — 🍷🍷 6
- Rosso di Montalcino '17 — 🍷🍷 4

Le Torri

via San Lorenzo a Vigliano, 31
50021 Barberino Val d'Elsa [FI]
Tel. +39 0558076161
www.letorri.net

CELLAR SALES
PRE-BOOKED VISITS
ACCOMMODATION AND RESTAURANT SERVICE
ANNUAL PRODUCTION 170,000 bottles
HECTARES UNDER VINE 28.00
SUSTAINABLE WINERY

- Magliano '17 — 🍷🍷 5
- San Lorenzo '17 — 🍷🍷 5
- Chianti Colli Fiorentini '18 — 🍷 2
- Chianti Colli Fiorentini Ris. '16 — 🍷 3

Trevisan

via C. S. Pietraia, 182
52044 Cortona [AR]
Tel. +39 3343361004
www.ereditrevisan.it

PRE-BOOKED VISITS
ANNUAL PRODUCTION 10,000 bottles
HECTARES UNDER VINE 2.50
SUSTAINABLE WINERY

- Cortona Syrah Candito '17 — 🍷🍷 5
- Cortona Syrah SoloSyrah '18 — 🍷🍷 3
- ⊙ SoloSyrah Rosa '19 — 🍷 3

Fattoria Uccelliera

via Roncione, 9
56042 Crespina Lorenzana [PI]
Tel. +39 050662747
www.uccelliera.com

CELLAR SALES
PRE-BOOKED VISITS
ACCOMMODATION
ANNUAL PRODUCTION 100,000 bottles
HECTARES UNDER VINE 16.00

- 7 Dieci Syrah '16 — 🍷🍷 4
- ○ Lupinaio '19 — 🍷🍷 3
- Tyche '19 — 🍷🍷 2*
- Castellaccio '16 — 🍷 5

Usiglian Del Vescovo

via Usigliano, 26
56036 Palaia [PI]
Tel. +39 0587468000
www.usigliandelvescovo.it

CELLAR SALES
PRE-BOOKED VISITS
RESTAURANT SERVICE
ANNUAL PRODUCTION 130,000 bottles
HECTARES UNDER VINE 23.00
VITICULTURE METHOD Certified Organic
SUSTAINABLE WINERY

- Il Grullaio '18 — 🍷🍷 3*
- Il Barbiglione '16 — 🍷🍷 6
- MilleEottantatre '16 — 🍷🍷 8

Giovanni Valentini

loc. Valpiana
pod. Fiordaliso, 69
58024 Massa Marittima [GR]
Tel. +39 0566918058
www.agricolavalentini.it

CELLAR SALES
PRE-BOOKED VISITS
ACCOMMODATION
ANNUAL PRODUCTION 55,000 bottles
HECTARES UNDER VINE 7.00
SUSTAINABLE WINERY

- Maremma Toscana Rosso Vivoli '17 — 🍷🍷 4
- ○ Vermentino '19 — 🍷🍷 2*

Valvirginio

via Nuova del Virginio, 34
50025 Montespertoli [FI]
Tel. +39 0571659127
www.collifiorentini.it

CELLAR SALES
PRE-BOOKED VISITS
ANNUAL PRODUCTION 1,000,000 bottles
HECTARES UNDER VINE 1500.00
VITICULTURE METHOD Certified Organic
SUSTAINABLE WINERY

- ● Chianti Valvirginio Ris. '15 — 🍷🍷 2*
- ○ Vin Santo del Chianti Santa Pazienza '10 — 🍷🍷 4
- ● Chianti Valvirginio '19 — 🍷 2

Vecchie Terre di Montefili

via San Cresci, 45
50022 Panzano [FI]
Tel. +39 055853739
www.vecchieterredimontefili.com

CELLAR SALES
PRE-BOOKED VISITS
ANNUAL PRODUCTION 40,000 bottles
HECTARES UNDER VINE 13.50

- ● Anfiteatro '16 — 🍷🍷 7
- ● Bruno di Rocca '16 — 🍷🍷 6
- ● Chianti Cl. Gran Selezione '16 — 🍷🍷 6
- ● Chianti Cl. '17 — 🍷 3

I Vicini

fraz. Pietraia di Cortona
loc. Case Sparse 38 A
52044 Cortona [AR]
Tel. +39 0575678507
www.ivicinicortona.it

CELLAR SALES
PRE-BOOKED VISITS
ACCOMMODATION
ANNUAL PRODUCTION 66,000 bottles
HECTARES UNDER VINE 10.00

- ● Cortona Merlot Laudario '17 — 🍷🍷 3
- ● Cortona Syrah Laudario '16 — 🍷🍷 4

Villa al Cortile

loc. Poderuccio
53024 Montalcino [SI]
Tel. +39 057754011
www.tenutepiccini.it

ANNUAL PRODUCTION 45,000 bottles
HECTARES UNDER VINE 12.00

- ● Brunello di Montalcino '15 — 🍷🍷 6

Villa La Ripa

loc. Antria, 38
52100 Arezzo
Tel. +39 057523330
www.villalaripa.it

CELLAR SALES
PRE-BOOKED VISITS
ANNUAL PRODUCTION 10,000 bottles
HECTARES UNDER VINE 5.00
SUSTAINABLE WINERY

- ● Peconio '17 — 🍷🍷 3
- ● Psyco '17 — 🍷🍷 5
- ○ Namastè '19 — 🍷 2

Villa Le Corti

loc. Le Corti
via San Piero di Sotto, 1
50026 San Casciano in Val di Pesa [FI]
Tel. +39 055829301
www.principecorsini.com

CELLAR SALES
PRE-BOOKED VISITS
ACCOMMODATION
ANNUAL PRODUCTION 150,000 bottles
HECTARES UNDER VINE 50.00
VITICULTURE METHOD Certified Organic

- ● Chianti Cl. Gran Selezione Zac '16 — 🍷🍷 7
- ○ Vin Santo del Chianti Cl. Sant'Andrea '05 — 🍷🍷 6

Villa Le Prata

loc. Le Prata, 261
53024 Montalcino [SI]
Tel. +39 0577848325
www.villaleprata.com

CELLAR SALES
PRE-BOOKED VISITS
ANNUAL PRODUCTION 15,000 bottles
HECTARES UNDER VINE 4.00

- ● Brunello di Montalcino '15 — 🍷🍷 6

Fattoria Villa Saletta

loc. Montanelli
via E. Fermi, 14
56036 Palaia [PI]
Tel. +39 0587628121
www.villasaletta.com

ANNUAL PRODUCTION 50,000 bottles
HECTARES UNDER VINE 21.00

- ● 980 AD '16 — 🍷🍷 8
- ● Saletta Giulia '16 — 🍷🍷 8
- ● Saletta Riccardi '16 — 🍷🍷 8
- ● Chiave di Saletta '16 — 🍷 6

Villa Sant'Anna

fraz. Abbadia di Montepulciano
via della Resistenza, 143
53045 Montepulciano [SI]
Tel. +39 0578708017
www.villasantanna.it

CELLAR SALES
PRE-BOOKED VISITS
ANNUAL PRODUCTION 80,000 bottles
HECTARES UNDER VINE 18.00

- ● Nobile di Montepulciano '16 — 🍷🍷 4
- ● Nobile di Montepulciano Poldo '16 — 🍷🍷 5

Villanoviana

loc. Sant'Uberto
fraz. Bolgheri
via Santa Maddalena, 172b
57022 Castagneto Carducci [LI]
Tel. +39 05861881227
www.villanoviana.it

CELLAR SALES
PRE-BOOKED VISITS
ACCOMMODATION
ANNUAL PRODUCTION 30,000 bottles
HECTARES UNDER VINE 4.00
VITICULTURE METHOD Certified Organic

- ● Cabernet Franc '17 — 🍷🍷 6
- ● Bolgheri Rosso Imeneo '18 — 🍷🍷 6
- ● Bolgheri Rosso Sup. Sant' Uberto '17 — 🍷🍷 7

I Vini di Maremma

loc. Marina di Grosseto
loc. Prile
58046 Grosseto
Tel. +39 056434426
www.ivinidimaremma.it

CELLAR SALES
PRE-BOOKED VISITS
ANNUAL PRODUCTION 350,000 bottles
HECTARES UNDER VINE 530.00
VITICULTURE METHOD Certified Organic

- ○ Maremma Toscana Bianco Brut Marbriò — 🍷🍷 3
- ● Maremma Toscana Ciliegiolo Alberese '18 — 🍷🍷 3
- ○ Maremma Toscana Ansonica '19 — 🍷 2
- ○ Maremma Toscana Vermentino '19 — 🍷 2

Fattoria Viticcio

via San Cresci, 12a
50022 Greve in Chianti [FI]
Tel. +39 055854210
www.viticcio.com

CELLAR SALES
PRE-BOOKED VISITS
ACCOMMODATION
ANNUAL PRODUCTION 250,000 bottles
HECTARES UNDER VINE 60.00
VITICULTURE METHOD Certified Organic

- ● Chianti Cl. '17 — 🍷🍷 3
- ● Chianti Cl. Gran Sel. Prunaio '16 — 🍷🍷 6
- ● Chianti Cl. Ris. '16 — 🍷🍷 4
- ● Monile '16 — 🍷 6

MARCHE

Lockdown and the subsequent effects of the virulent 2020 pandemic set off alarm bells on many of Marche's farms. The backbone of the regional production system is made up of small and medium-sized businesses, capitalised but not indebted (or at least with sustainable debt) and with extensive access to family labor, as well as cooperatives that are generally managed in a prudent manner. This structure allowed it to withstand the blow but nevertheless put a new emphasis on some issues that need to be addressed. First and foremost, the need to increase its added value. It's unthinkable that even in its best areas, such as Matelica, Castelli di Jesi, Conero and Piceno, Marche's grapes aren't as remunerative as they could be. It's for this reason that the region must work on communicating the quality level achieved, as attested to in part by our Tre Bicchieri. It would also be a good idea to implement new forms of sales (rather than focusing exclusively on small, local markets). E-commerce, wine clubs and large-scale distribution networks can no longer be ignored. Looking at the names that hold the region's flag high, a brilliant debut for Riccardo Baldi's La Staffa and the Darini family's Cantina Cològnola-Tenuta Musone both stand out. Roberto Venturi and Marco Casolanetti's Oasi degli Angeli are back in the limelight after a few years of absence. Kudos to last year's debutants in the 'Tre Bicchieri Club', namely Vignamato and Pantaleone, who took home that always-difficult second gold. While we can't say that it comes as a surprise, we saw standout performances from Montecappone - Mirizzi, Valter 'Roccia' Mattoni, Emanuele Dianetti, Tenuta Santori, Bisci, Collestefano and Marotti Campi. And finally, we close by mentioning the region's pillars, true champions of constancy over time, wineries like Umani Ronchi, Belisario, Fazi Battaglia-Tenute San Sisto, Poderi Mattioli, Velenosi, Le Caniette, Tenuta Spinelli and Leo Felici, who was also last year's Grower of the Year.

Maria Letizia Allevi

via Pescolla
63081 Castorano [AP]
Tel. +39 3494063412
www.vinimida.it

CELLAR SALES
PRE-BOOKED VISITS
ANNUAL PRODUCTION 16,000 bottles
HECTARES UNDER VINE 5.00
VITICULTURE METHOD Certified Organic

Piceno is replete with small family producers, such as the one led by Maria Letizia Allevi together with her husband, Roberto Corradetti. It's a winery that makes use of vineyards with different exposures. The area's classic grapes are cultivated and then processed in a small but well-sized (and even better equipped) cellar. The resulting wines exhibit a strong territorial identity, aromatically focused—linear whites aged in steel and full-bodied reds matured in barriques. These last release an inexhaustible fruity energy over time. Made with a clone of Alicante, the Arsi '17 is a whirlwind of spices and iodine notes accompanied by floral and herb nuances; it has a graceful body in the mouth, even if with slightly prickly tannins. The Offida Pecorino '19 is also excellent: meadow herbs and green olives reverberate in a tasty and well-sustained palate. The Mida Rosato is back in good form, and with the 2019 vintage it finds the expressiveness of its best versions. The Mida Passerina '19, rather acidulous and saline, is a new selection.

Wine	Rating
● Arsi '17	▼▼ 8
○ Offida Pecorino Mida '19	▼▼ 3*
⊙ Mida Rosato '19	▼▼ 3
○ Mida Passerina '19	▼ 3
○ Mida Pecorino Pas Dosé M. Cl. '18	▼ 4
● Offida Rosso Mida '17	▼ 4
○ Offida Pecorino Mida '16	▽▽▽ 3*
● Arsi '16	▽▽ 8
○ Offida Pecorino Mida '18	▽▽ 3
○ Offida Pecorino Mida '17	▽▽ 3*
○ Offida Pecorino Mida '15	▽▽ 3
● Offida Rosso Mida '16	▽▽ 4
● Offida Rosso Mida '15	▽▽ 4
● Offida Rosso Mida '14	▽▽ 3
● Offida Rosso Mida '13	▽▽ 3
● Offida Rosso Mida '11	▽▽ 4

Aurora

loc. Santa Maria in Carro
c.da Ciafone, 98
63073 Offida [AP]
Tel. +39 0736810007
www.viniaurora.it

CELLAR SALES
PRE-BOOKED VISITS
ACCOMMODATION
ANNUAL PRODUCTION 52,000 bottles
HECTARES UNDER VINE 10.50
VITICULTURE METHOD Certified Organic

What seemed a utopian dream of a return to the land and an economy based on the principles of subsistence in the late 1970s, today appears to us as an extraordinarily modern vision. Aurora's five partners have always pursued simplicity, taking inspiration from traditional practices, while taking pains not to pollute or make profit the ultimate goal. The wines produced are the natural result of this approach, organic management with strong biodynamic inflections, an emphasis on territorial identity and great character, all at exemplary prices. No Barricadiero this year, but reds were well represented by the Rosso Piceno Superiore '18, a wine marked by pleasantly coarse tannins and authentic varietal expression. The same characteristics, with more wild accents, feature in the Piceno '19. Length and aromatic complexity characterize the Fiobbo '18, a wine streaked with pleasant evolved traits. The Fiorina '18 is a crisp and relaxed Bucciato made with Malvasia.

Wine	Rating
○ Falerio '19	▼▼ 2*
○ Fiorina '18	▼▼ 3
○ Offida Pecorino Fiobbo '18	▼▼ 3
● Rosso Piceno '19	▼▼ 2*
● Rosso Piceno Sup. '18	▼▼ 3
⊙ Rosato '19	▼ 2
● Barricadiero '10	▽▽▽ 4*
● Barricadiero '09	▽▽▽ 4
● Barricadiero '06	▽▽▽ 4
● Barricadiero '04	▽▽▽ 3
● Barricadiero '03	▽▽▽ 3*
● Barricadiero '02	▽▽▽ 3
● Barricadiero '01	▽▽▽ 3*
● Offida Rosso Barricadiero '11	▽▽▽ 4*
● Barricadiero '16	▽▽ 4
○ Offida Pecorino Fiobbo '17	▽▽ 3
● Rosso Piceno Sup. '17	▽▽ 3

★Belisario

via Aristide Merloni, 12
62024 Matelica [MC]
Tel. +39 0737787247
www.belisario.it

CELLAR SALES
PRE-BOOKED VISITS
ANNUAL PRODUCTION 1,200,000 bottles
HECTARES UNDER VINE 300.00

Behind the name Belisario is a cooperative winery that brings together many growers from upper Vallesina. In the battle for market share, it wields a number of wines whose main assets are quality, territorial identity, large-scale distribution and accessible prices. Among their diverse range, various interpretations of Verdicchio stand out. Thanks to the grape's well-known versatility, it gives rise to a selection of fresh and tasty standard-label wines, as well as complex reserves, not to mention sparklers and passitos. The Verdicchio Cambrugiano Riserva '17 is a chiaroscuro of aniseed, light smoky scents, sweet almonds and mineral sensations; in the mouth it's taut and elegant, nuanced yet deep. The flavorful energy of the weighty Verdicchio Meridia '17 and the sapid raciness of the Verdicchio Del Cerro '19, a wine that's crystal clear in its aromas, are no less good, but all their Matelicas shine.

Wine	Rating
○ Verdicchio di Matelica Cambrugiano Ris. '17	TTT 3*
○ Verdicchio di Matelica Del Cerro '19	TT 2*
○ Verdicchio di Matelica Meridia '17	TT 3*
○ Verdicchio di Matelica Anfora '19	TT 2*
○ Verdicchio di Matelica Valbona '19	TT 2*
○ Verdicchio di Matelica Vign. B. '19	TT 3
● Colli Maceratesi Rosso San Leopardo Ris. '16	T 3
○ Esino Bianco '19	T 2
○ Verdicchio di Matelica Animologico '19	T 4
○ Verdicchio di Matelica Cambrugiano Ris. '16	YYY 3*
○ Verdicchio di Matelica Cambrugiano Ris. '14	YYY 3*
○ Verdicchio di Matelica Vign. B. '15	YYY 3*

Bisci

via Fogliano, 120
62024 Matelica [MC]
Tel. +39 0737787490
www.bisci.it

CELLAR SALES
PRE-BOOKED VISITS
ANNUAL PRODUCTION 90,000 bottles
HECTARES UNDER VINE 20.00
VITICULTURE METHOD Certified Organic

A lot of teamwork has gone into this winery's rebirth: the innovative vision of Mauro and Tito Bisci, who took over the from its two founders (i.e. father Giuseppe and uncle Pierino), Aroldo Bellelli's deep agronomic and enological knowledge, a young and motivated team. The Fogliano cru and the vineyards at the foot of Monte San Vicino guarantee consistently high-quality grapes, which are then vinified and matured in steel or concrete vats. Sangiovese and a little bit of Merlot add diversity to a mostly white range. The absence of the Fogliano wasn't a problem in light of the splendid performance put in by the Verdicchio Senex Riserva '15. It enchants with its multifaceted nose, elegant layers of aniseed, aromatic herbs, river stones and hawthorn flowers; in the mouth it's harmonious in its gait and three-dimensional on the finish. The Matelica '19 is fresh, subtle on the palate, but of vivid, delicately salty acidic tension.

Wine	Rating
○ Verdicchio di Matelica Senex Ris. '15	TTT 6
○ Verdicchio di Matelica '19	TT 3*
● Villa Castiglioni '16	TT 3
○ Verdicchio di Matelica '18	YYY 3*
○ Verdicchio di Matelica Vign. Fogliano '15	YYY 4*
○ Verdicchio di Matelica Vign. Fogliano '13	YYY 3*
○ Verdicchio di Matelica Vign. Fogliano '10	YYY 3*
○ Verdicchio di Matelica Vign. Fogliano '08	YYY 3*
○ Verdicchio di Matelica '17	YY 3*
○ Verdicchio di Matelica Senex Ris. '10	YY 4
○ Verdicchio di Matelica Vign. Fogliano '17	YY 4

Boccadigabbia

loc. Fontespina
c.da Castelletta, 56
62012 Civitanova Marche [MC]
Tel. +39 073370728
www.boccadigabbia.com

CELLAR SALES
PRE-BOOKED VISITS
ANNUAL PRODUCTION 100,000 bottles
HECTARES UNDER VINE 25.00
SUSTAINABLE WINERY

International grapes are cultivated just a few kilometers from the Adriatic, near the winery. Cabernet Sauvignon, Merlot, Pinot Nero and Chardonnay provide a sense of the history behind Boccadigabbia, an estate whose roots go back to the 19th-century Napoleonic period. At La Floriana, just outside Macerata, traditional grape varieties such as Maceratino, Verdicchio, Sangiovese and Montepulciano are grown. Elvio Alessandri creates clear, classically-styled wines, with the use of steel for their standard-label wines and small French oak for their more ambitious, long-lived versions. A monovarietal Montepulciano, the Tenuta La Floriana Rosso '15 is modern, polished in its tannins, with a full spectrum of black cherries and aromatic herbs accompanied by smoky strokes. Among the two Ribonas the Le Grane '19 stands out with its minerality wrought of sulphurous hints and a decisive sapidity on the palate. The 'basic' version sees fresh accents of mint and an emphasis on drinkability. The Roseò '19 is a captivating rosé made with Pinot Nero.

Wine	Rating
● Tenuta La Floriana Rosso '15	🍷🍷 6
○ Colli Maceratesi Ribona '19	🍷🍷 3
○ Colli Maceratesi Ribona Le Grane '19	🍷🍷 3
● Pix '15	🍷🍷 6
⊙ Roseò '19	🍷🍷 2*
○ Garbì '19	🍷 2
○ Montalperti '18	🍷 4
● Akronte '98	♀♀♀ 7
● Akronte '97	♀♀♀ 7
● Akronte '95	♀♀♀ 7
● Akronte '94	♀♀♀ 7
● Akronte '93	♀♀♀ 7
● Akronte Cabernet '92	♀♀♀ 7
● Akronte '15	♀♀ 8
○ Colli Maceratesi Ribona Le Grane '18	♀♀ 3*
⊙ Roseò '18	♀♀ 2*
● Rosso Piceno '16	♀♀ 3

Borgo Paglianetto

loc. Pagliano, 393
62024 Matelica [MC]
Tel. +39 073785465
www.borgopaglianetto.it

CELLAR SALES
PRE-BOOKED VISITS
ANNUAL PRODUCTION 100,000 bottles
HECTARES UNDER VINE 29.00
VITICULTURE METHOD Certified Organic
SUSTAINABLE WINERY

With a series of increasingly convincing wines and a varied range, Borgo Paglianetto is one of the most representative wineries in Matelico. Their whites offer, in a crescendo of structure linked to the ripening of the grapes, an effective combination of the acid and mineral qualities that characterize sharper Verdicchio wines and the solidity of more powerful, complex versions. Behind them is a serious project focusing on local cultivars and an approach to vinification that emphasizes stylistic precision. Medium-size oak is reserved only for Matesis. The Matelica Jera Riserva '16 has a seductive fruity streak, which turns into a rather soft, tasty and tenacious palate. The Petrara '19 plays on fresher tones and rhythmic acidic flashes, with a delicate saltiness that's characteristic of Matelica. The Vertis '18 features a slightly sugary entrance in the mouth, which is contrasted by a delicate sapid backbone; The Terravignata '19 offers up white fragrances of flowers and minerals across a fine, supple palate.

Wine	Rating
○ Verdicchio di Matelica Jera Ris. '16	🍷🍷 4
○ Verdicchio di Matelica Petrara '19	🍷🍷 3*
○ Verdicchio di Matelica Terravignata '19	🍷🍷 2*
○ Verdicchio di Matelica Vertis '18	🍷🍷 3
○ Verdicchio di Matelica Jera Ris. '15	♀♀♀ 4*
○ Verdicchio di Matelica Petrara '16	♀♀♀ 2*
○ Verdicchio di Matelica Vertis '16	♀♀♀ 3*
○ Verdicchio di Matelica Ergon '18	♀♀ 3
○ Verdicchio di Matelica Ergon '16	♀♀ 3*
○ Verdicchio di Matelica Ergon '15	♀♀ 3
○ Verdicchio di Matelica M. Cl. Brut	♀♀ 5
○ Verdicchio di Matelica Petrara '18	♀♀ 3*
○ Verdicchio di Matelica Petrara '17	♀♀ 2*
○ Verdicchio di Matelica Terravignata '18	♀♀ 2*
○ Verdicchio di Matelica Terravignata '17	♀♀ 2*
○ Verdicchio di Matelica Vertis '17	♀♀ 3*
○ Verdicchio di Matelica Vertis '15	♀♀ 3

Brunori

V.LE DELLA VITTORIA, 103
60035 JESI [AN]
TEL. +39 0731207213
www.brunori.it

CELLAR SALES
PRE-BOOKED VISITS
ANNUAL PRODUCTION 50,000 bottles
HECTARES UNDER VINE 7.00

The Brunori family hold a special place in the hearts of all Verdicchio lovers, in particular for the tenacity with which they've faced their long journey. Founded in 1956, the winery has come a long ways, and all without being distracted by the various fashions of the day. Giorgio and his son Carlo have always personally managed the San Nicolò cru (in San Paolo di Jesi), which gives rise to two Verdicchios. These are made according to a classic approach, fermented off the skins before maturing in concrete. The Classico San Nicolò Riserva '18 expresses subtle aromas, intimately varietal in their echoes of aniseed, almond and lime blossom; the palate maintains its freshness, has an invigorating acidic backbone, unfolding long and supple. More time in the bottle will probably lend that share of complexity that seems to be missing today. The Classico Superiore San Nicolo '19 is more direct and immediately expressive in its fruity and iodine mix. The Classico Le Gemme '19 is easy, sapid and drinkable, but well made as always.

Wine	Rating
○ Castelli di Jesi Verdicchio Cl. San Nicolò Ris. '18	🍷🍷 3*
○ Verdicchio dei Castelli di Jesi Cl. Le Gemme '19	🍷🍷 2*
○ Verdicchio dei Castelli di Jesi Cl. Sup. San Nicolò '19	🍷🍷 2*
○ Castelli di Jesi Verdicchio Cl. San Nicolò Ris. '16	🍷🍷 3
○ Verdicchio dei Castelli di Jesi Cl. Le Gemme '18	🍷🍷 2*
○ Verdicchio dei Castelli di Jesi Cl. Le Gemme '17	🍷🍷 2*
○ Verdicchio dei Castelli di Jesi Cl. Sup. San Nicolò '18	🍷🍷 2*
○ Verdicchio dei Castelli di Jesi Cl. Sup. San Nicolò '17	🍷🍷 2*

★Bucci

FRAZ. PONGELLI
VIA CONA, 30
60010 OSTRA VETERE [AN]
TEL. +39 071964179
www.villabucci.com

CELLAR SALES
PRE-BOOKED VISITS
ANNUAL PRODUCTION 120,000 bottles
HECTARES UNDER VINE 31.00
VITICULTURE METHOD Certified Organic

Giorgio Grai passed away in late 2019. A decades-long partnership with Ampelio Bucci, the tempestuous and creative amalgam of their ideas, their indissoluble friendship, all created the Villa Bucci Riserva, the winery's flagship Verdicchio and an unmistakable icon of an austere, elegant style. Life goes on at Pongelli anyway: Ampelio and his well-established team will do everything to keep the work going and carry on his teachings, making wines that live up to his legacy. In this round of tastings, their flagship was missing, since presentation of the Villa Bucci Riserva '18 has been postponed until the next edition. Among the newly released wines we find the Verdicchio Classico Bucci '19 with its usual aromas of meadow herbs, subtle almond and floral accents, all of which translate into a palate of calibrated structural depth. The Rosso Piceno Pongelli '18 is redolent of flowers and morello cherries, offering a palate that has some youthful contours but is full of character.

Wine	Rating
● Rosso Piceno Tenuta Pongelli '18	🍷🍷 3
○ Verdicchio dei Castelli di Jesi Cl. Sup. '19	🍷🍷 3
○ Castelli di Jesi Verdicchio Cl. Villa Bucci Ris. '17	🍷🍷🍷 6
○ Castelli di Jesi Verdicchio Cl. Villa Bucci Ris. '14	🍷🍷🍷 6
○ Castelli di Jesi Verdicchio Cl. Villa Bucci Ris. '13	🍷🍷🍷 6
○ Castelli di Jesi Verdicchio Cl. Villa Bucci Ris. '12	🍷🍷🍷 6
○ Castelli di Jesi Verdicchio Cl. Villa Bucci Ris. '10	🍷🍷🍷 6
○ Verdicchio dei Castelli di Jesi Cl. Sup. '16	🍷🍷🍷 3*
○ Verdicchio dei Castelli di Jesi Cl. Villa Bucci Ris. '09	🍷🍷🍷 6

Le Canà

via Molino Vecchio, 4
63063 Carassai [AP]
Tel. +39 0734930054
www.lecana.it

ANNUAL PRODUCTION 40,000 bottles
HECTARES UNDER VINE 25.00
VITICULTURE METHOD Certified Organic

Gabriele Polini is the owner of a large winery, active for more than a century, that historically dealt in significant volumes of bulk wine. But Giuseppe's children Paola, Luca and Alessandra wanted to diversify the family business, choosing a smaller size and the way of the bottle. To this end, they chose more than 20 hectares, some overlooking the Aso valley and others closer to Val Menocchia, in a territory very well suited to wine-growing. The style, which is still in the process of being consolidated, privileges olfactory clarity and generous structure, though without sacrificing dynamism of flavor. The Pecorino Tornavento '19 is an engaging drink wrought of vibrant citrus notes and a flavorful palate—complexity is somewhat lacking but it's none the worse for it. The same goes for the Rosso Piceno Superiore Davore '15, a wine that's well integrated and pulpy on the palate. The Doravera '19 is a vibrant rosé made with Merlot and Montepulciano grapes.

Wine	Rating
⊙ Doravera '19	▼▼ 2*
○ Offida Pecorino Tornavento '19	▼▼ 3
● Rosso Piceno Sup. Davore '15	▼▼ 3
○ Offida Pecorino Retemura '18	▼ 4
○ Quies '19	▼ 2
● Rosso Piceno Infernaccio '19	▼ 2
⊙ Doravera '18	▽▽ 2*
○ Offida Pecorino Tornavento '18	▽▽ 3
● Rosso Piceno Sup. Davore '16	▽▽ 3

Le Caniette

c.da Canali, 23
63065 Ripatransone [AP]
Tel. +39 07359200
www.lecaniette.it

CELLAR SALES
PRE-BOOKED VISITS
ANNUAL PRODUCTION 60,000 bottles
HECTARES UNDER VINE 16.00
VITICULTURE METHOD Certified Organic

Despite the great success of their wines and an overall level of quality that's consistently at the top, brothers Luigino and Giovanni Vagnoni have no intention of growing at any cost. Only native grapes are cultivated (organically for many years now), and they've got plenty of room to work in a beautiful cellar surrounded by vineyards. Their wines have a personal style to them; they're appealingly modern in the way they perfectly blend symmetry and superb drinkability. Yet another outstanding performance for the Piceno Superiore Morellone: the 2016 features a complex nose that touches on all the classic registers, with a peculiar wild accent that's soon incorporated into its bouquet. The palate is magnificent, expansive and harmonious. The Nero di Vite '12 is highly elegant, complex, with a dense but completely resolved tannic texture. The Cinabro '16 (100% Alicante) seems a little more evolved than other versions, but remains a wine of undisputed charm. An obligatory mention for the Rosso Bello '18, which has never been so tasty and supple.

Wine	Rating
● Piceno Sup. Morellone '16	▼▼▼ 4*
● Cinabro '16	▼▼ 8
● Piceno Nero di Vite '12	▼▼ 6
● Piceno Rosso Bello '18	▼▼ 2*
○ Offida Pecorino Iosonogaia Nonsonolucrezia '18	▼▼ 5
○ Offida Pecorino Veronica '19	▼▼ 3
○ Lucrezia '19	▼ 2
⊙ Sinopia Rosato Extra Brut	▼ 3
● Piceno Morellone '10	▽▽▽ 4*
● Piceno Morellone '08	▽▽▽ 4*
● Piceno Sup. Morellone '15	▽▽▽ 4*
● Piceno Sup. Morellone '13	▽▽▽ 4*
● Piceno Sup. Morellone '12	▽▽▽ 4*

Carminucci

via San Leonardo, 39
63013 Grottammare [AP]
Tel. +39 0735735869
www.carminucci.com

CELLAR SALES
ANNUAL PRODUCTION 350,000 bottles
HECTARES UNDER VINE 46.00
VITICULTURE METHOD Certified Organic

Bolstered by extensive experience in the sector, Piero and Giovanni Carminucci, father and son, are at the helm of a family business founded almost a century ago. Serious, well-trained professionals, they're flanked by a first-rate staff who oversee their many hectares of vineyards in Offida and Grottammare. The large cellar, which can be found on a hill at the entrance of the Valtesino valley, is perfectly equipped to handle high volumes, with steel tanks reserved for whites and small oak barrels dedicated to their premium reds. When it comes to Offida Pecorino, the Belato '19 is at the top of the typology. Fresh aromas of citrus fruits and meadow herbs rise up to the nose, all well blended on a full, decisive palate that manages to lengthen through the finish. The Casta '19 (from Passerina grapes) moves on a similar track: it's less structured, but highly smooth on the palate. The award for best red goes to the Naumakos '17. The result of extended maturation, it offers up broad sensations of wild cherry and toasty hints; in the mouth it's full-bodied, rounded and pulpy.

○ Offida Pecorino Belato '19	🍷🍷 2*
○ Casta '19	🍷🍷 2*
○ Chardonnay Naumakos '18	🍷🍷 2*
● Rosso Piceno Sup. Naumakos '17	🍷🍷 2*
○ Falerio Grotte sul Mare '19	🍷 1*
⊙ Grotte sul Mare Rosato '19	🍷 2
○ Offida Pecorino Il Veglio '19	🍷 3
● Paccaosso '16	🍷 7
● Rosso Piceno Grotte sul Mare '19	🍷 2
○ Falerio Grotte sul Mare '18	🍷🍷 1*
● Novanta '14	🍷🍷 7
○ Offida Pecorino Belato '18	🍷🍷 2*
○ Offida Pecorino Belato '17	🍷🍷 2*
● Rosso Piceno Grotte sul Mare '17	🍷🍷 2*
● Rosso Piceno Sup. Naumakos '16	🍷🍷 2*
● Rosso Piceno Sup. Naumakos '15	🍷🍷 2*

CasalFarneto

via Farneto, 12
60030 Serra de' Conti [AN]
Tel. +39 0731889001
www.casalfarneto.it

CELLAR SALES
PRE-BOOKED VISITS
ANNUAL PRODUCTION 80,000 bottles
HECTARES UNDER VINE 43.00

Casalfarneto has made the production of high-quality Verdicchio a central goal. The different versions offered touch all the expressive timbres of the Jesina cultivar convincingly and with a clear stylistic vision. Paolo Togni and Danilo Solustri, the winery's owner and director (respectively), have extensive experience in the field and have succeeded in instilling in their range an enviable consistence in quality. In their work, they are helped by vineyards planted in what many consider true crus of the Esino river's left bank and by a modern, perfectly equipped winery. When it comes to Verdicchio, the Grancasale Superiore '18 topped our preferences: appealing aromas of yellow-fleshed fruit, gooseberries and bergamot peel are followed by a well-orchestrated palate supported by solid backbone. The Crisio Riserva '17 exhibits aromatic breadth but also some vegetal traits accentuated by a delicately bitterish finish. The Cimaio '17 is a persuasive late-harvest wine reminiscent of candied fruit.

○ Verdicchio dei Castelli di Jesi Cl. Sup. Grancasale '18	🍷🍷 3*
○ Castelli di Jesi Verdicchio Cl. Crisio Ris. '17	🍷🍷 4
○ Cimaio '17	🍷🍷 5
● Rosso Piceno Cimaré '18	🍷🍷 2*
○ Verdicchio dei Castelli di Jesi Cl. Sup. Fontevecchia '19	🍷🍷 2*
○ Castelli di Jesi Verdicchio Cl. Crisio Ris. '13	🍷🍷🍷 3*
○ Castelli di Jesi Verdicchio Cl. Crisio Ris. '12	🍷🍷🍷 3*
○ Verdicchio dei Castelli di Jesi Cl. Sup. Grancasale '16	🍷🍷🍷 3*
○ Verdicchio dei Castelli di Jesi Cl. Sup. Grancasale '13	🍷🍷🍷 3*

Castignano Cantine dal 1960

c.da San Venanzo, 31
63072 Castignano [AP]
Tel. +39 0736822216
www.cantinedicastignano.com

CELLAR SALES
PRE-BOOKED VISITS
ANNUAL PRODUCTION 600,000 bottles
HECTARES UNDER VINE 500.00
VITICULTURE METHOD Certified Organic

They're celebrating in San Venanzo di Castignano as the local wine producing cooperative is turning 60. For a person, such an achievement might be a chance to pull in the oars and think about rest, but here it's the opposite. A young team, led by President Omar Traini, is preparing new projects to protect and develop their vineyards. The range relies on the great classics of Piceno tradition, from Passerina to Pecorino and Montepulciano, but there are international cultivars as well. The Rebo '17 put in a lovely and unexpected performance. Produced to celebrate the winery's sixtieth anniversary, it features vivid fruitiness and controlled flavor, tapered and well-adorned by its tannic texture. Red sensations of flowers and fruits also characterize the Offida Gran Maestro '15, a wine that's rounded and persistent on the palate. The two Pecorinos exhibit reliable quality, with the Montemisio '19 proving flavorful and focused in its aromas of white peach, while the Destriero '19 is more citrusy and racy on the palate.

Wine	Rating	
● Offida Rosso Gran Maestro '15	▼▼	3*
● Rebo Sessantesimo Anniversario '17	▼▼	5
○ Falerio Pecorino Destriero '19	▼▼	2*
○ Notturno	▼▼	2
○ Offida Pecorino Montemisio '19	▼▼	2*
● Rosso Piceno Sup. Destriero '18	▼▼	2*
○ Passerina '19	▼	2
● Rosso Piceno '19	▼	1*
● Templaria '18	▼	2
○ Offida Passerina Bio '18	▽▽	3
○ Offida Pecorino Montemisio '18	▽▽	2*
● Offida Rosso Gran Maestro '14	▽▽	3*
● Rosso Piceno Bio '18	▽▽	3
● Rosso Piceno Sup. Bio '17	▽▽	3
● Rosso Piceno Sup. Destriero '17	▽▽	2*
○ Terre di Offida Passerina Brut '18	▽▽	2*

Castrum Morisci

via Molino, 16
63826 Moresco [FM]
Tel. +39 3400820708
www.castrummorisci.it

CELLAR SALES
PRE-BOOKED VISITS
ANNUAL PRODUCTION 30,000 bottles
HECTARES UNDER VINE 7.00
VITICULTURE METHOD Certified Organic

Situated halfway up the hill on the left bank of the Aso river, David Pettinari's winery relies on the cultivation of local grapes, even if during the planting phase some rows of less traditional or rare grapes were added, such as Garofanata (used for a Charmat sparkler). Their wine names mention local districts and indicate that they've aged for six months in terracotta amphorae. The labels with numbers indicate that maturation was carried out in steel. Their range features several original wines. The best examples are their 2019 Pecorinos. The Gallicano is a bit rustic and marked by sensations of grain, but it has a full and flavorful palate; the 003 offers up notes of aromatic herbs on a fragrant palate. The Padreterno '19 (Vermentino and aromatic grapes) make you think of candied citrus fruits—this fresh sensation lends vigor to its easy palate. The Testamozza and 237, both 2019s based on Sangiovese, feature intense spicy and floral hints. A vigorous fruity character marks the Collefrenato '18, a wine made with Montepulciano and Bordeaux grapes.

Wine	Rating	
● 237 '19	▼▼	3
⊙ 326 '19	▼▼	3
● Collefrenato '18	▼▼	5
○ Falerio Pecorino 003 '19	▼▼	3
○ Falerio Pecorino Gallicano '19	▼▼	4
○ Padreterno '19	▼▼	4
● Testamozza '19	▼▼	4
○ 102 Passerina '19	▼	3
○ Garofanata Extra Dry '19	▼	3
○ Falerio Pecorino 003 '18	▽▽	3
○ Falerio Pecorino 003 '17	▽▽	3
○ Falerio Pecorino 003 '16	▽▽	3
○ Falerio Pecorino Gallicano '18	▽▽	5
○ Falerio Pecorino Gallicano '17	▽▽	5
○ Padreterno '17	▽▽	5
● Rosso Piceno Sangiovese Testamozza '16	▽▽	5

Giacomo Centanni

c.da Aso, 159
63062 Montefiore dell'Aso [AP]
Tel. +39 0734938530
www.vinicentanni.it

CELLAR SALES
PRE-BOOKED VISITS
RESTAURANT SERVICE
ANNUAL PRODUCTION 100,000 bottles
HECTARES UNDER VINE 40.00
VITICULTURE METHOD Certified Organic

The valley of the Aso river is characterized by a remarkable propensity for fruit-growing, made possible by its fertile soil, sunshine, and breezy climate (thanks to the presence of the Adriatic Sea). The Centanni family, owners of land in the hills, have gone all in on viticulture. Giacomo's entry into the business after his studies in enology has led to wines of a rather rich style, with marked scents and remarkable energy. All this without ever failing to adhere to the principles of organic farming. The Primodelia '17 is a substantive red, based on Montepulciano, characterized by broad and persistent fruity aromas: the palate goes all in on the pleasantness of its texture and plushiness. We also appreciated the two Pecorinos. The Offida '19 is approachable and flavorful, while the Affinato in Legno '18 is more complex amidst citrus hints and a lean, juicy palate. The Purocentanni line represents their wines made without added sulfites. Here the Rosso '19 stands out with its precise hints of cherries on a pulpy, alcohol-rich palate.

○ Offida Pecorino '19	🍷🍷	3
○ Offida Pecorino Affinato in Legno '18	🍷🍷	4
● Primodelia '17	🍷🍷	6
● Purocentanni Rosso '19	🍷🍷	3
○ Falerio '19	🍷	2
○ Falerio Pecorino Purocentanni '19	🍷	3
○ Passerina Brut	🍷	3
● Monte Floris '15	🍸🍸	3
○ Offida Passerina '16	🍸🍸	2*
○ Offida Pecorino '18	🍸🍸	3
○ Offida Pecorino '17	🍸🍸	3
○ Offida Pecorino '16	🍸🍸	3
○ Offida Pecorino '15	🍸🍸	2*
○ Offida Pecorino Affinato in Legno '17	🍸🍸	4
○ Offida Pecorino Affinato in Legno '16	🍸🍸	4
○ Offida Pecorino Affinato in Legno '15	🍸🍸	4
● Rosso Piceno Rosso di Forca '16	🍸🍸	2*

Cignano

loc. Isola di Fano
via Ada Negri, 50
61034 Fossombrone [PU]
Tel. +39 0721727124
www.cignano.com

CELLAR SALES
PRE-BOOKED VISITS
ANNUAL PRODUCTION 22,000 bottles
HECTARES UNDER VINE 15.00
VITICULTURE METHOD Certified Organic

Cignano is the name of the yellow sandstone hill where Fabio Bucchini's vineyards grow. Above, the view opens onto unspoilt countryside, with little human presence—here woodlands alternate with arable land. The cellar is situated at the bottom of the valley, next to the family home. For vinification and aging they rely on the enological talent of Marco Gozzi, who offers a range of original wines, though without sacrificing their bond with tradition and territory. This is helped by time—indeed, there was no hurry to put their wines on the market, except for the Irrequieto '19, a pleasant Brut Charmat. Among the still whites, the Bianchello San Leone '18 topped our preferences. It's persuasive but rhythmic on the palate, calling up sensations of flowers and aniseed, enriched at the end by a hint of licorice. The Bianco Assoluto '18 is another soft, round Bianchello, commendably complex in its hints of broom and bee's wave.

○ Bianchello del Metauro Bianco Assoluto '18	🍷🍷	2*
○ Bianchello del Metauro Sup. San Leone '18	🍷🍷	3
○ Irrequieto Brut '19	🍷🍷	3
○ Bianchello del Metauro Sup. Superbo Ancestrale '16	🍷	6
○ Bianchello del Metauro Sup. San Leone '17	🍸🍸	2*
○ Bianchello del Metauro Sup. Superbo Ancestrale '17	🍸🍸	6

Tenuta Cocci Grifoni

loc. San Savino
c.da Messieri, 12
63038 Ripatransone [AP]
Tel. +39 073590143
www.tenutacoccigrifoni.it

CELLAR SALES
PRE-BOOKED VISITS
ACCOMMODATION
ANNUAL PRODUCTION 400,000 bottles
HECTARES UNDER VINE 50.00
SUSTAINABLE WINERY

Guido Cocci Grifoni, a charismatic figure, deserves credit for his defense of native grapes, and the work of rediscovering Pecorino (which he himself revived at the foot of Monte Vettore, in an old vineyard, and replicated from there through massal selection). The recently renovated cellar is now a small jewel of winemaking and hospitality. Leading the project are Guido's daughters: Marilena is in charge of administration, while Paola serves both as enologist and coordinator of the technical-viticultural side of things. The absence of their most important reds left room for the wine dedicated to the founder, made with grapes from their best plot, to shine. The 2015 features a subtle nose of aniseed and balsamic hints. These follow through on a compact, complex palate marked by a long sapid streak. The Colle Vecchio '18 offers up notes of wild herbs and green olive on a floral background, all of which reemerge on a commendably vibrant palate. We also appreciated the fresh and enjoyable Tarà '19, a wine characterized by a citrusy acidity.

○ Offida Pecorino Guido Cocci Grifoni '15	▼▼ 6
○ Falerio Pecorino Tarà '19	▼▼ 2*
○ Offida Pecorino Colle Vecchio '18	▼▼ 3
○ Passerina Brut Tarà '19	▼ 3
● Rosso Piceno Sup. San Basso '17	▼ 2
● Rosso Piceno Tarà '19	▼ 2
○ San Basso Passerina '19	▼ 2
○ Offida Pecorino Guido Cocci Grifoni '14	▽▽▽ 6
○ Offida Pecorino Guido Cocci Grifoni '13	▽▽▽ 4*
○ Offida Pecorino Colle Vecchio '17	▽▽ 3
○ Offida Pecorino Colle Vecchio '16	▽▽ 3
● Offida Rosso Il Grifone '13	▽▽ 5
● Rosso Piceno Sup. San Basso '15	▽▽ 2*
○ Terre di Offida Passerina Passito San Basso '13	▽▽ 2*

Col di Corte

via San Pietro, 19a
60036 Montecarotto [AN]
Tel. +39 073189435
www.coldicorte.it

CELLAR SALES
PRE-BOOKED VISITS
ANNUAL PRODUCTION 40,000 bottles
HECTARES UNDER VINE 11.50
VITICULTURE METHOD Certified Organic
SUSTAINABLE WINERY

Montecarotto is the perfect capital for Verdicchio on the Esino river's left bank, and Col di Corte is certainly among the producers that lend prestige to the territory. Founded in 2011, from the outset the winery has adhered convincingly to the dictates of organic agriculture, gradually enriching them through biodynamically inspired practices as well. In the cellar Giacomo Rossi and Claudio Caldaroni have transmitted a freedom of expression that infuses their wines with a distinct and authentic character. The bottles presented in this edition were all made through spontaneous fermentation in steel. The two versions of their Verdicchio Classico Superiore stand out: Anno Uno '19 has a jovial character, with sensations of aniseed followed by a flavorful, deliciously supple palate. The Tobia '18 delivers marked aromas of almond on a rather rich, soft, persistent palate. The always-amusing Lancestrale, a sparkling rosé made with Montepulciano grapes, calls up pomegranate on the nose, while in the mouth it proves relaxed and delicately salty.

⊙ Lancestrale	▼▼ 4
○ Verdicchio dei Castelli di Jesi Cl. Anno Uno '19	▼▼ 2*
○ Verdicchio dei Castelli di Jesi Cl. Sup. Vign. di Tobia '18	▼▼ 4
● Esino Rosso '17	▼ 3
○ Sant'Ansovino '18	▼ 5
○ Castelli di Jesi Verdicchio Cl. Sant'Ansovino Ris. '16	▽▽ 5
⊙ Lancestrale	▽▽ 4
○ Verdicchio dei Castelli di Jesi Cl. Anno Uno '18	▽▽ 2*
○ Verdicchio dei Castelli di Jesi Cl. Anno Uno '17	▽▽ 2*
○ Verdicchio dei Castelli di Jesi Cl. Sup. Vign. di Tobia '17	▽▽ 4

Collestefano

LOC. COLLE STEFANO, 3
62022 CASTELRAIMONDO [MC]
TEL. +39 0737640439
www.collestefano.com

CELLAR SALES
PRE-BOOKED VISITS
ACCOMMODATION
ANNUAL PRODUCTION 120,000 bottles
HECTARES UNDER VINE 17.50
VITICULTURE METHOD Certified Organic

Fabio Marchionni gives life to wines of sparkling precision, fully consistent with the stylistic idea of more saline and linear Matelica. Twenty years of experience go into his production approach, which features the use of steel vats. And if we taste two or more different vintages of Verdicchio Collestefano, we regularly find a perfect reading of the season. In short, his are true 'vineyard wines', always organic and the result of attentive viticulture. The cool nights that preceded the harvest compensated for the heat of 2019. And so it is that the Collestefano exhibits its distinct mountain profile, recognizable in its sensations of flowers, stones and grapefruit, all consistently present on a palate that's fuller than usual, capable of providing an extraordinary intensity of flavor without losing anything in terms of smoothness. It's a memorable version, destined to bring together different sensibilities.

Wine	Rating
○ Verdicchio di Matelica Collestefano '19	🍷🍷🍷 2*
○ Verdicchio di Matelica Collestefano '18	🍷🍷🍷 2*
○ Verdicchio di Matelica Collestefano '15	🍷🍷🍷 2*
○ Verdicchio di Matelica Collestefano '14	🍷🍷🍷 2*
○ Verdicchio di Matelica Collestefano '13	🍷🍷🍷 2*
○ Verdicchio di Matelica Collestefano '12	🍷🍷🍷 2*
○ Verdicchio di Matelica Collestefano '10	🍷🍷🍷 2*
○ Verdicchio di Matelica Collestefano '07	🍷🍷🍷 2*
○ Verdicchio di Matelica Collestefano '06	🍷🍷🍷 2*
○ Verdicchio di Matelica Collestefano '17	🍷🍷 2*
○ Verdicchio di Matelica Collestefano '16	🍷🍷 2*
○ Verdicchio di Matelica Collestefano '11	🍷🍷 2*
○ Verdicchio di Matelica Extra Brut M. Cl. '13	🍷🍷 3*

Collevite

VIA VALLE CECCHINA, 9
63077 MONSAMPOLO DEL TRONTO [AP]
TEL. +39 0735767050
www.collevite.com

CELLAR SALES
PRE-BOOKED VISITS
ANNUAL PRODUCTION 300,000 bottles
HECTARES UNDER VINE 160.00
VITICULTURE METHOD Certified Organic

Founded in 2006 by a group of growers already active in local cooperatives, Collevite makes use of a large body of vineyards in some of Piceno's best suited areas. Winemaking, carried out with the technical support of Fabrizio Ciufoli, takes place in their Monsampolo cellar, making for a range of pleasant wines, modern in their territorial identity, characterized by good structure on the palate and favorable prices. In 2016 the Ripawine project was created, a sort of 'luxury brand' that features their most ambitious bottles. The Trufo '17, a Rosso Piceno Superiore from their Ripawine line, put in a nice performance. Sensations of black plum, wild cherries and aromatic herbs precede a juicy, pervasive yet tasty palate. We also recommend the Offida Rosso Klausura '17 of the same line, a spicy wine that's quite healthy in its fruit. Among the Collevite, the Pecorino Villa Piatti '19 stand out together with the original Falerio Pecorino Nature '19 and the tasty Offida Rosso Villa Piatti '17.

Wine	Rating
● Rosso Piceno Sup. Trufo Ripawine '17	🍷🍷 5
○ Falerio Pecorino Nature '19	🍷🍷 3
○ Offida Pecorino Villa Piatti '19	🍷🍷 2*
● Offida Rosso Klausura Ripawine '16	🍷🍷 5
● Offida Rosso Villa Piatti '17	🍷🍷 3
● Rosso Piceno Sup. Il Caimano '16	🍷🍷 2*
○ Offida Passerina Villa Piatti '19	🍷 2
○ Offida Pecorino Geko Ripawine '19	🍷 5
○ Falerio Pecorino Nature '18	🍷🍷 3
○ Offida Pecorino Villa Piatti '18	🍷🍷 2*
● Offida Rosso Villa Piatti '16	🍷🍷 3

Cantina dei Colli Ripani

C.DA TOSCIANO, 28
63065 RIPATRANSONE [AP]
TEL. +39 07359505
www.colliripani.it

CELLAR SALES
PRE-BOOKED VISITS
ANNUAL PRODUCTION 1,300,000 bottles
HECTARES UNDER VINE 650.00
VITICULTURE METHOD Certified Organic

Colli Ripani is an important benchmark for many micro-vineyards scattered throughout the Picene hills, providing a valid outlet for the efforts of the growers operating here. Enologist Marco Pignotti transforms the grapes of the cooperative's many members into wines with nice varietal adherence, skillfully meeting the needs of a wide audience of enthusiasts without falling into banality. If steel hosts their whites and rosés, their reds mature in wood barrels of varying sizes. The Castellano '17, a Rosso Piceno Superiore, put in a nice performance, calling up red berries adorned by wild and vegetal nuances; in the mouth it comes through sapid and authentic, made complex by the first tertiary notes. The Offida Rosso Leo Ripano '15 is more modern in its extraction and fruit, all clearly discernible on its generous, dry palate. The complex and fascinating Anima Mundi '11 is a Passerina that revives the ancient tradition of Vin Santo style passitos.

- ● Offida Rosso Leo Ripano '15 — 🍷🍷 3
- ● Rosso Piceno Sup. Castellano '17 — 🍷🍷 2*
- ○ Terre di Offida Passerina Passito Anima Mundi '11 — 🍷🍷 5
- ⊙ Il Vicolo '19 — 🍷 2
- ○ Offida Pecorino Mercantino '19 — 🍷 2
- ● Diavolo e Vento '13 — 🍷🍷 5
- ○ Falerio Pecorino Cap. 9 '17 — 🍷🍷 2*
- ○ Offida Pecorino Condivio '16 — 🍷🍷 5
- ○ Offida Pecorino Mercantino '18 — 🍷🍷 2*
- ● Offida Rosso Leo Ripano '13 — 🍷🍷 3*
- ● Rosso Piceno Sup. Castellano '13 — 🍷🍷 2*

Cològnola - Tenuta Musone

LOC. COLOGNOLA, 22A BIS
62011 CINGOLI [MC]
TEL. +39 0733616438
www.tenutamusone.it

CELLAR SALES
PRE-BOOKED VISITS
ANNUAL PRODUCTION 180,000 bottles
HECTARES UNDER VINE 33.00
VITICULTURE METHOD Certified Organic

In last year's edition, we were able to report on the growth of Walter and Serena Darini's winery. This upward trajectory has been made possible thanks to certain fruitful choices, like cultivating only Verdicchio and Montepulciano and drawing on them for a variety of wines (forged in their well-equipped cellar). We only complained about the lack of a star performer, one that could reward the work done by enologist Gabriele Villani and his staff, who've proven adept at a classic style of vinification (and second fermentation in the bottle, for their two Metodo Classicos). And their most consistent, iconic wine, the Verdicchio Classico Superiore Ghiffa, takes home top marks. The 2018 version expresses varietal characteristics with great finesse, drawing strength from the contrast between a softer mid palate and a long, sapid finish, which closes on hints of balsam, aniseed and liquorice. An excellent performance for the Cingulum '18 as well, a persuasive Verdicchio Passito redolent of peach jam. We also appreciated the clear and focused Montepulciano Buraco '15.

- ○ Verdicchio dei Castelli di Jesi Cl. Sup. Ghiffa '18 — 🍷🍷🍷 3*
- ○ Verdicchio dei Castelli di Jesi Passito Cingulum '18 — 🍷🍷 5
- ● Buraco '15 — 🍷🍷 4
- ○ Verdicchio dei Castelli di Jesi Brut Musa M. Cl. '18 — 🍷🍷 3
- ○ Verdicchio dei Castelli di Jesi Extra Brut Darini M. Cl. '14 — 🍷🍷 5
- ○ Verdicchio dei Castelli di Jesi Cl. Sup. Incauto '19 — 🍷 3
- ○ Verdicchio dei Castelli di Jesi Cl. Sup. Via Condotto '19 — 🍷 2
- ⊙ Via Rosa '19 — 🍷 2
- ○ Verdicchio dei Castelli di Jesi Cl. Sup. Ghiffa '17 — 🍷🍷 3
- ○ Verdicchio dei Castelli di Jesi Cl. Sup. Via Condotto '18 — 🍷🍷 2*

Colonnara

A Mandriole, 2
0034 Cupramontana [AN]
el. +39 0731780273
ww.colonnara.it

ELLAR SALES
RE-BOOKED VISITS
NNUAL PRODUCTION 1,200,000 bottles
ECTARES UNDER VINE 160.00

or more than 60 years Colonnara has een a rock for Cupramontana's grape rowers. For many small, family operations, s presence has held at bay the temptation) uproot their vineyards. The producer has lso given a significant boost to Le Marche's sparkling wines, both when it omes to Metodo Classico and Charmat. At he center of it all is the native cultivar par xcellence, Verdicchio. Here it's offered in nany versions, taking advantage of the arying pedoclimates and considerable levations. The Metodo Classico Ubaldo Rosi Riserva '14 is one of the region's best parkling wines: the finesse of aniseed, lmond and balsam fragrances are ollowed by a creamy palate, soft but with a leep, sapid flavor. The Luigi Ghislieri Brut, a rue 'best-buy' among bubbly, exhibits reat consistency and even greater rinkability. The Verdicchio Cl. Tufico Riserva '16 is full-bodied, finishing on hints f camphor.

○ Verdicchio dei Castelli di Jesi Brut M. Cl. Ubaldo Rosi Ris. '14	TT 5
○ Castelli di Jesi Verdicchio Cl. Tùfico Ris. '16	TT 3
● Tornamagno '15	TT 3
○ Verdicchio dei Castelli di Jesi Brut M. Cl. Luigi Ghislieri	TT 4
○ Figurin Brut Rosé	T 3
○ Verdicchio dei Castelli di Jesi Brut Cuvée Tradition	T 3
○ Verdicchio dei Castelli di Jesi Cl. Lyricus '19	T 2
○ Verdicchio dei Castelli di Jesi Cl. Sup. Cuprese '18	T 2
○ Verdicchio dei Castelli di Jesi Brut M. Cl. Ubaldo Rosi Ris. '13	YY 5

Colpaola

loc. Colpaola
fraz. Braccano

62024 Matelica [MC]
Tel. +39 0737768300
www.cantinacolpaola.it

CELLAR SALES
ANNUAL PRODUCTION 50,000 bottles
HECTARES UNDER VINE 10.00
VITICULTURE METHOD Certified Organic

The elevation listed on the label of Francesco Porcarelli and Stefania Peppoloni's wines is more than a minor detail. At 650 meters, Tenuta Colpaola's vineyards are the highest in the district of Matelica. Situated in a panoramic position of unquestionable charm, they're surrounded by woodlands adorned with broom. Aroldo Bellelli has been entrusted with the task of obtaining a white wine with the Verdicchio cultivated around the manor house, while Laura Migliorelli oversees aspects related to sales and marketing. The 2019 vintage gave rise to a Matelica with clear, mineral scents accompanied by pure hints of citrus and wild flowers, all brought out through maturation in steel. In the mouth it shows pronounced acidity and a delicately salty pluck, all well supported by adequate structure: the effect is a fresh, tasty palate that's not without sapid flashes, finishing long and fading on clear hints of grapefruit.

○ Verdicchio di Matelica '19	TTT 3*
○ Verdicchio di Matelica '18	YYY 3*
○ Verdicchio di Matelica '17	YY 2*
○ Verdicchio di Matelica '15	YY 2*
○ Verdicchio di Matelica '14	YY 2*

Il Conte Villa Prandone

c.da Colle Navicchio, 28
63033 Monteprandone [AP]
Tel. +39 073562593
www.ilcontevini.it

CELLAR SALES
PRE-BOOKED VISITS
ANNUAL PRODUCTION 250,000 bottles
HECTARES UNDER VINE 50.00

The name refers to the winery's founder, Amilcare De Angelis, also as 'lu kont'. In the 1980s he and his son Marino took over the land they'd been working as sharecroppers and went out on their own. Marino's four sons transformed the operation into a modern organization, increasing the hectares under vine on Navicchio Hill, a sunny, south-facing slope. Theirs is a modern range that privileges a certain intensity, especially the reds, while of late their whites have gained notably in terms of aromatic freshness. It is, therefore, no coincidence that the citrusy Pecorino Navicchio '19, with its fragrant and alluring palate, topped our preferences. But the Pecorino Aurato '19 didn't skimp on flavor and suppleness either, even though it has a simpler olfactory spectrum. The Passerina Caveceppo '19 (not to be confused with the IGT of the same name) is equally captivating. Among the reds, we appreciated the LuKont '17, a Montepulciano with a robust and generous palate.

○ Offida Pecorino Navicchio '19	🍷🍷 3*
○ Falerio Pecorino Aurato '19	🍷🍷 2*
● LuKont '17	🍷🍷 6
○ Offida Passerina Cavaceppo '19	🍷🍷 3
○ Cavaceppo '19	🍷 2
● Donello '19	🍷 3
● IX Prandone '16	🍷 8
⊙ Rosato '19	🍷 2
● Rosso Piceno Conte Rosso '19	🍷 2
⊙ Venere&Azzurra Brut Rosé	🍷 3
○ Vizius '19	🍷 2
● Zipolo '17	🍷 5
● LuKont '15	🍸🍸 6
○ Offida Pecorino Navicchio '18	🍸🍸 3
● Piceno Sup. Marinus '17	🍸🍸 3
● Piceno Sup. Marinus '16	🍸🍸 3
● Zipolo '16	🍸🍸 5

Tenuta De Angelis

via San Francesco, 10
63030 Castel di Lama [AP]
Tel. +39 073687429
www.tenutadeangelis.it

CELLAR SALES
PRE-BOOKED VISITS
ANNUAL PRODUCTION 500,000 bottles
HECTARES UNDER VINE 50.00
VITICULTURE METHOD Certified Organic

The decades spent working large quantities of Piceno grapes have given the Fausti-De Angelis family formidable experience with Montepulciano and Sangiovese, the grapes they use to make their reds. Nowadays, the entire estate, including the single, contiguous tract that forms the backdrop to the picturesque church of Santa Maria della Rocca di Offida, is managed according to organic principles. In the cellar, winemaking is traditional, but the range is contemporary in style. The Rosso Anghelos '17 exhibits nice aromatic complexity amidst red berries smoky streaks and a spicy wake; the palate has calibrated density, tightened on the finish by close-knit tannins. The Rosso Piceno Superiore Oro '17 expresses the warmth of the vintage through vibrant notes of blackcurrant syrup and a rounded palate, nicely structured and embellished by sweet tannins. The Rosso Piceno Sup. '18 is sapid and spicy. This year also saw the debut of their Oro Bianco '18, a dynamic and persistent Pecorino, matured in barriques, that has some excessive toastiness.

● Offida Rosso Anghelos '17	🍷🍷 4
● Rosso Piceno '19	🍷🍷 2*
● Rosso Piceno Sup. '18	🍷🍷 2*
● Rosso Piceno Sup. Oro '17	🍷🍷 3
○ Offida Passerina '19	🍷 2
○ Offida Pecorino Oro Bianco '18	🍷 4
○ Offida Pecorino Quiete '19	🍷 3
● Anghelos '01	🍸🍸🍸 4
● Anghelos '99	🍸🍸🍸 4*
● Rosso Piceno Sup. Oro '15	🍸🍸🍸 3*
○ Offida Pecorino '18	🍸🍸 2*
○ Offida Pecorino Quiete '18	🍸🍸 3
● Offida Rosso Anghelos '16	🍸🍸 4
● Offida Rosso Anghelos '15	🍸🍸 4
● Rosso Piceno Sup. '17	🍸🍸 2*
● Rosso Piceno Sup. '16	🍸🍸 2*
● Rosso Piceno Sup. Oro '16	🍸🍸 3*

Degli Azzoni

via Don Minzoni, 26
62010 Montefano [MC]
Tel. +39 0733850219
www.degliazzoni.it

CELLAR SALES
PRE-BOOKED VISITS
ANNUAL PRODUCTION 100,000 bottles
HECTARES UNDER VINE 130.00
SUSTAINABLE WINERY

If in the past wine was only a part of a broader agricultural project, of late the Degli Azzoni family have not spared energy nor resources in making it a central part of their Marche estate. A well-trained technical staff, led by agronomist Gianfranco Canullo and enologist Salvatore Lovo, is working to implement the dictates of organic farming, selecting the best plots among their large set of vineyards to obtain wines that are increasingly distinct by virtue of their territorial identity. The Montepulciano Passatempo '16 remains their flagship: distinct notes of black cherry and spices follow through on a full palate, with a compact but rounded tannic texture. The San Donato '17, a classic blend of Montepulciano and Sangiovese, also performs well with its vivid palate and pleasantly rustic sensations. For a relaxed drink we went to the approachable Rosso Evasione '19, a gently fruity wine, while the Phagalus '17 proves to be a mature Merlot with nice depth.

● Passatempo '16	🍷🍷 4
● Colli Maceratesi Rosso Evasione '19	🍷🍷 2*
● Phagalus '17	🍷🍷 3
● Rosso Piceno San Donato '17	🍷🍷 2*
○ Beldiletto Brut	🍷 2
○ Carrodoro '19	🍷 2
○ Colli Maceratesi Ribona '19	🍷 2
○ Colli Maceratesi Passito Sultano '16	🍷🍷 4
○ Colli Maceratesi Ribona '18	🍷🍷 2*
○ Colli Maceratesi Ribona '17	🍷🍷 2*
● Colli Maceratesi Rosso Evasione '17	🍷🍷 2*
○ Grechetto '18	🍷🍷 2*
○ Grechetto '17	🍷🍷 2*
● Merlot '16	🍷🍷 2*
● Passatempo '15	🍷🍷 4
● Rosso Piceno '15	🍷🍷 2*

Fattoria Dezi

c.da Fontemaggio, 14
63839 Servigliano [FM]
Tel. +39 0734710090
www.fattoriadezi.com

CELLAR SALES
PRE-BOOKED VISITS
ANNUAL PRODUCTION 45,000 bottles
HECTARES UNDER VINE 15.00

Founded in 1975, Fattoria Dezi has never betrayed its roots as a family-run artisan producer. Brothers Davide and Stefano represent the driving force behind production: the first is responsible for the 15 hectares of land planted with the area's classic grapes, the second oversees work in the cellar. Their style favors lengthy maturation, structural density and a certain freedom of expression: stern reds worked in barriques and full-bodied, highly pleasant whites aged in concrete. It no longer comes as a surprise just how good the Pecorino Servigliano P is. The 2018 features an olfactory suite of yellow plums and a long, juicy, pervasive finish. The Solagne '19 (Verdicchio) offers up nuances of barley sugar and yellow fruits, all on an invigorating palate. Among the reds the Regina del Bosco '17 winds handily. It's a Montepulciano with characteristic hints of morello cherry and plum, all streaked with smoky notes across a full-bodied, austere palate. Time will do it good.

○ Falerio Pecorino Servigliano P. '18	🍷🍷 3*
● Dezio '18	🍷🍷 3
● Regina del Bosco '17	🍷🍷 6
○ Solagne '19	🍷🍷 3
● Solo '17	🍷 6
● Regina del Bosco '06	🍷🍷🍷 6
● Regina del Bosco '05	🍷🍷🍷 6
● Regina del Bosco '03	🍷🍷🍷 6
● Solo Sangiovese '05	🍷🍷🍷 6
● Solo Sangiovese '01	🍷🍷🍷 5
● Solo Sangiovese '00	🍷🍷🍷 6
● Dezio '17	🍷🍷 3
○ Falerio Pecorino Servigliano P. '17	🍷🍷 3*
● Regina del Bosco '16	🍷🍷 6
● Regina del Bosco '15	🍷🍷 6
○ Solagne '17	🍷🍷 3

Di Sante

via Antinori, 28
61032 Fano [PU]
Tel. +39 0721866212
www.disantevini.it

CELLAR SALES
PRE-BOOKED VISITS
ANNUAL PRODUCTION 80,000 bottles
HECTARES UNDER VINE 30.00
VITICULTURE METHOD Certified Organic

In 1980 Roberto Di Sante transformed the family hobby, making wine, into a profession. His son Tommaso oversaw a period of growth, planting new hectares on the hills of Carignano and building a modern cellar. Mainly Pesaro's traditional grapes are cultivated, but international varieties are present as well. The dry and breezy microclimate, influenced by the Adriatic Sea, allows for the use of organic methods without taking forced measures: in the winery classic vinification is carried out in steel, with barrels of different sizes used only for the Sangiovese Timoteo Riserva. The 2017 version mixes fruity sensations, at times wild, making for a tasty, authentically rustic wine. Its youthful variant, the Sangiovese Gazza '19, is approachable and enjoyable in its pronounced floral vein. The two 2019 Bianchellos exhibit greater elegance: with the Giglio you can feel the greater ripeness of the grapes, all in favor of aromatic and gustatory intensity; the Gazza is supple, tart and easygoing.

○ Bianchello del Metauro Gazza '19	TT 2*
○ Bianchello del Metauro Sup. Giglio '19	TT 2*
● Colli Pesaresi Sangiovese Gazza '19	TT 2*
● Colli Pesaresi Sangiovese Timoteo Ris. '17	TT 2*
⊙ Agape Dry Rosé	T 2
○ Gemma '19	T 2
⊙ Illa '19	T 2

Emanuele Dianetti

c.da Vallerosa, 25
63063 Carassai [AP]
Tel. +39 3383928439
www.dianettivini.it

CELLAR SALES
PRE-BOOKED VISITS
ANNUAL PRODUCTION 23,000 bottles
HECTARES UNDER VINE 5.00

Emanuele Dianetti is a young banker who gave up his suit and tie as soon as he could in favor of his overalls—a sort of backward journey towards his family's agricultural origins, to which he's closely attached. In little more than a decade he has gradually increased the hectares under vine with the help of his mother, Giuliana. Val Menocchia's cool mesoclimate has allowed him to infuse his wines with a crystalline aromatic quality and a dynamic acidic backbone. This time it's the Pecorino Vignagiulia '19 that stands out: sophisticated in its aromas, in the mouth it offers a gritty energy that merges wonderfully vibrant tension and fruity pulp. This year marked the debut of the Pecorino Luciano '18. Matured in mid-sized casks, it offers up a complex mixture of gunpowder, yellow fruit and ginger, all of which follow through on an energetic, multifaceted palate. The Michelangelo '16, made with Alicante, is even more elegant and supple, though we shouldn't forget the solid Offida Rosso Vignagiulia '17 with its fruity, toasty profile.

○ Offida Pecorino Vignagiulia '19	TTT 3*
● Michelangelo '16	TT 8
○ Offida Pecorino Luciano '18	TT 7
● Offida Rosso Vignagiulia '17	TT 6
● Piceno '18	T 3
● Offida Rosso Vignagiulia '16	YYY 5
● Offida Rosso Vignagiulia '14	YYY 5
● Offida Rosso Vignagiulia '13	YYY 5
● Michelangelo '15	YY 8
● Michelangelo '14	YY 8
○ Offida Pecorino Vignagiulia '18	YY 3*
○ Offida Pecorino Vignagiulia '16	YY 3*
○ Offida Pecorino Vignagiulia '15	YY 3*
○ Offida Pecorino Vignagiulia '14	YY 3*
● Offida Rosso Vignagiulia '15	YY 5
● Offida Rosso Vignagiulia '12	YY 4

Andrea Felici

c.da Sant'Isidoro, 28
62021 Apiro [MC]
Tel. +39 0733611431
www.andreafelici.it

CELLAR SALES
PRE-BOOKED VISITS
ANNUAL PRODUCTION 74,000 bottles
HECTARES UNDER VINE 12.00
VITICULTURE METHOD Certified Organic

Leopardo Felici has embodied the "Grower of the Year" prize awarded in last year's version of our guide. Indeed, he took it as reason to do even better, to take on even more responsibility. As always, he's advised by his father, Andrea, and assisted by the technical skill of Aroldo Bellelli, slowly and carefully overseeing the development of the new Verdicchio plots near his historic San Francesco vineyard. In the cellar everything is proceeding as usual, with old concrete tanks used for his Cantico Riserva and steel tanks used for the Superiore. A great interpretation of the vintage, the Il Cantico della Figura Riserva doesn't bear the marks of the torrid 2017 summer, exhibiting instead a typically fresh profile that mixes anise, almond, mint and citrus peels. The first mineral tones streak its succulent palate, dynamic yet extraordinarily supple. The Verdicchio Classico Superiore Andrea Felici '19 sees simpler aromas but similar gustatory energy.

○ Castelli di Jesi Verdicchio Cl. V. Il Cantico della Figura Ris. '17	🍷🍷🍷 6
○ Verdicchio dei Castelli di Jesi Cl. Sup. Andrea Felici '19	🍷🍷 3*
○ Castelli di Jesi Verdicchio Cl. Il Cantico della Figura Ris. '12	🍷🍷🍷 4*
○ Castelli di Jesi Verdicchio Cl. Il Cantico della Figura Ris. '11	🍷🍷🍷 4*
○ Castelli di Jesi Verdicchio Cl. Il Cantico della Figura Ris. '10	🍷🍷🍷 4*
○ Castelli di Jesi Verdicchio Cl. V. Il Cantico della Figura Ris. '16	🍷🍷🍷 6
○ Castelli di Jesi Verdicchio Cl. V. Il Cantico della Figura Ris. '15	🍷🍷🍷 6
○ Castelli di Jesi Verdicchio Cl. V. Il Cantico della Figura Ris. '13	🍷🍷🍷 6

Filodivino

via Serra, 46
60030 San Marcello [AN]
Tel. +39 0731026139
www.filodivino.it

CELLAR SALES
PRE-BOOKED VISITS
ACCOMMODATION AND RESTAURANT SERVICE
ANNUAL PRODUCTION 60,000 bottles
HECTARES UNDER VINE 19.50
VITICULTURE METHOD Certified Organic

Alberto Gandolfi mainly oversees the resort, while Gian Mario Bongini is responsible for wine production: these are the two souls that animate Filodivino, a project that spared no expense in terms of beauty, efficiency, functionality. The cellar, a small, extraordinarily well-equipped architectural jewel, is surrounded by vineyards of Verdicchio and Lacrima Nera. These provide the grapes for a reliable range overseen by enologist Matteo Chiucconi. The Verdicchio Classico Dino Riserva '17 opens on sensations of almond, highlighting nice energy on the palate, where sensations of dried fruit are consistently maintained throughout a long finish. The Classico Superiore Matto '19 has citrus tones and a palate characterized by an effective, sapid suppleness. The interesting Coccio '18 is the first release of a Bucciato made with amphora-aged Verdicchio: it calls up notes of ripe apricots on a weighty, harmonious palate. We also appreciated the Lacrima di Morro d'Alba Diana '18.

○ Castelli di Jesi Verdicchio Cl. Dino Ris. '17	🍷🍷 4
○ Coccio '18	🍷🍷 5
● Lacrima di Morro d'Alba Diana '18	🍷🍷 3
○ Verdicchio dei Castelli di Jesi Cl. Sup. Matto '19	🍷🍷 3
○ Verdicchio dei Castelli di Jesi Cl. Sup. Serra 46 '19	🍷 2
○ Castelli di Jesi Verdicchio Cl. Dino Ris. '15	🍷🍷 4
⊙ Filodivino Rosato '18	🍷🍷 2*
○ Verdicchio dei Castelli di Jesi Cl. Sup. Filotto '17	🍷🍷 3
○ Verdicchio dei Castelli di Jesi Cl. Sup. Matto '18	🍷🍷 3
○ Verdicchio dei Castelli di Jesi Cl. Sup. Matto '17	🍷🍷 3

Fiorano

c.da Fiorano, 19
63067 Cossignano [AP]
Tel. +39 073598247
www.agrifiorano.it

CELLAR SALES
PRE-BOOKED VISITS
ACCOMMODATION
ANNUAL PRODUCTION 45,000 bottles
HECTARES UNDER VINE 8.50
VITICULTURE METHOD Certified Organic
SUSTAINABLE WINERY

Paolo Beretta and Paola Massi, creators of Fiorano, definitely believe in associations. Paolo is a leading figure at Fivi and one of the founders of Terroir Marche, a sort of regional consortium for producers who share the same philosophy and way of working. Activism goes hand in hand with their commitment to the winery: manicured vineyards in a landscape of great beauty and integrity are behind a dynamic and territorial range of wines, all prepared without sacrificing aromatic intensity. The Donna Orgilla '19 shines once again. It's a vivid, polished Pecorino with long strokes of citrus fruits and meadow herbs. The Giulia Erminia '18, the version matured in tonneau, alternates oaku notes with grapefruit sensations on a palate invigorated by sapidity. The Rosso Piceno Superiore Terre di Giobbe '17 proves deliciously fruity, while the Gallo Otto '17 (a blend of Montepulciano and Syrah worked in amphorae) exhibits an original aromatic profile that reemerges on a taut, austere palate.

Wine	Rating
○ Offida Pecorino Donna Orgilla '19	🍷🍷 3*
● Gallo Otto '17	🍷🍷 7
○ Giulia Erminia '18	🍷🍷 5
● I Paoli '19	🍷🍷 2*
⊙ Kami '19	🍷🍷 2*
● Rosso Piceno Sup. Terre di Giobbe '17	🍷🍷 3
● Ser Balduzio '15	🍷 5
○ Offida Pecorino Donna Orgilla '14	🍷🍷🍷 3*
○ Giulia Erminia '17	🍷🍷 5
○ Giulia Erminia '14	🍷🍷 2*
○ Offida Pecorino Donna Orgilla '17	🍷🍷 3
○ Offida Pecorino Donna Orgilla '16	🍷🍷 3*
○ Offida Pecorino Giulia Erminia '16	🍷🍷 5
● Sangiovese '18	🍷🍷 2*
● Ser Balduzio '13	🍷🍷 5

Fiorini

fraz. Barchi
via Giardino Campioli, 5
61038 Terre Roveresche
Tel. +39 072197151
www.fioriniwines.it

CELLAR SALES
PRE-BOOKED VISITS
ACCOMMODATION
ANNUAL PRODUCTION 200,000 bottles
HECTARES UNDER VINE 45.00
VITICULTURE METHOD Certified Organic

The collaboration between Carla Fiorini, owner and enologist, and consultant Emiliano Falsini hasn't distorted the winery's reputation as a guardian of local tradition. If anything, it has enriched it with new ideas, providing that extra something in terms of originality, complexity and constancy. For some years now, all the grapes used have been organic. Local varieties dominate, while their work in the cellar sees a more casual but apt use of small barrels, as well as techniques aimed at greater gustatory vigor. The Tenuta Campioli '19 is a characterful Bianchello, fluid and flavorful, with a knack for improving over time. Matured in mid-sized casks, the Bianchello Superiore Andy '18 features a delectable gustatory richness. The Sangiovese Luigi Fiorini Riserva '16 put in a nice performance, proving properly complex and multifaceted; the Bartis '17 (Sangiovese with small amounts of Montepulciano and Cabernet) is marked by dark fruit sensations—on the palate it's weighty, but a bit austere in its tannins. The Monsavium '12 has charm to sell.

Wine	Rating
○ Bianchello del Metauro Sup. Andy '18	🍷🍷 3
○ Bianchello del Metauro Sup. Tenuta Campioli '19	🍷🍷 2*
● Colli Pesaresi Rosso Bartis '17	🍷🍷 3
● Colli Pesaresi Sangiovese Luigi Fiorini Ris. '16	🍷🍷 4
○ Monsavium Passito '12	🍷🍷 5
● Roy '18	🍷🍷 4
○ Bianchello del Metauro Sup. Andy '16	🍷🍷 3
○ Bianchello del Metauro Sup. Tenuta Campioli '18	🍷🍷 2*
○ Bianchello del Metauro Sup. Tenuta Campioli '17	🍷🍷 2*
● Colli Pesaresi Rosso Bartis '16	🍷🍷 3
○ Monsavium Passito '11	🍷🍷 5

Cantine Fontezoppa

c.da San Domenico, 38
62012 Civitanova Marche [MC]
Tel. +39 0733790504
www.cantinefontezoppa.com

CELLAR SALES
PRE-BOOKED VISITS
ACCOMMODATION AND RESTAURANT SERVICE
ANNUAL PRODUCTION 290,000 bottles
HECTARES UNDER VINE 38.00

Mosè Ambrosi's overflowing energy has revitalized Fontezoppa, bringing a more lively touch to their catalog of wines. The producer has two faces: the 'mountain' one draws on Serrapetrona's Vernaccia Nera and Pinot Nero, while the 'Mediterranean' side is linked to their vineyards in Civitanova Marche, a few kilometers from the Adriatic Sea, where we also find their modern and well-equipped winery. Their wines are styled according to an idea of immediate pleasantness, but they're also capable of depth, especially when it comes to Metodo Classico bubbly. The Ribona Metodo Classico Dosaggio Zero '16 features proper olfactory complexity and a dry, smooth palate that's embellished by a delicately salty finish. The Rosato Extra Brut '16 (Pinot Nero and Vernaccia) has pronounced backbone, subtle flavor and vibrant sapidity. The Ribona '19 was less convincing than usual. With its hints of blueberries and white chocolate, the Cascià '10 (Vernaccia) proves to be one of Le Marche's most original and balanced passitos.

Wine	Rating
● I Terreni di San Severino Passito Cascià '10	🍷🍷 6
○ Colli Maceratesi Ribona Dosaggio Zero M. Cl. '16	🍷🍷 4
⊙ Extra Brut Rosé M. Cl. '16	🍷🍷 5
● Carapetto '16	🍷 5
○ Colli Maceratesi Ribona '19	🍷 3
○ Falerio Pecorino Joco '19	🍷 2
● Serrapetrona Morò '17	🍷 5
● Serrapetrona Pepato '17	🍷 3
○ Colli Maceratesi Ribona '18	🍷🍷 3*
○ Colli Maceratesi Ribona '16	🍷🍷 3*
○ Colli Maceratesi Ribona Dosaggio Zero M. Cl. '15	🍷🍷 4
○ Colli Maceratesi Ribona Dosaggio Zero M. Cl. '14	🍷🍷 4
● I Terreni di San Severino Passito Cascià '09	🍷🍷 6

★★Gioacchino Garofoli

via Carlo Marx, 123
60022 Castelfidardo [AN]
Tel. +39 0717820162
www.garofolivini.it

CELLAR SALES
PRE-BOOKED VISITS
ANNUAL PRODUCTION 1,400,000 bottles
HECTARES UNDER VINE 50.00

Garofoli is one of the few wineries in Le Marche with a century-old history. The turning point in terms of quality came about thanks to brothers Carlo and Gianfranco, who since the end of the 1980s have drawn on their experience and new technology in the cellar to develop a range grounded in Verdicchio and Montepulciano del Conero. Today a number of wines are made, making for a complete and varied selection, with a style that we can now call 'classic'. A special mention goes to their Metodo Classico, a typology they've been exploring since the mid-1970s, putting them well ahead of their time. The Podium '18 remains the best of their diverse portfolio of Verdicchios: finesse and olfactory complexity reverberate on a composite, cadenced and soft palate. The Selezione GG Riserva '10 has charm to sell, proving mouthfilling and fruity, unscathed by the many years spent aging. The delicious Macrina '19 and the spicy Piancarda '17 are valid and conveniently prized. The Brut Metodo Classico Riserva '16 features balsamic echoes and creamy bead.

Wine	Rating
○ Castelli di Jesi Verdicchio Cl. Selezione Gioacchino Garofoli Ris. '10	🍷🍷 7
○ Verdicchio dei Castelli di Jesi Cl. Sup. Podium '18	🍷🍷 4
○ Castelli di Jesi Verdicchio Cl. Serra Fiorese Ris. '16	🍷🍷 4
● Rosso Conero Piancarda '17	🍷🍷 3
○ Verdicchio dei Castelli di Jesi Brut M. Cl. Ris. '16	🍷🍷 4
○ Verdicchio dei Castelli di Jesi Cl. Sup. Macrina '19	🍷🍷 2*
○ Verdicchio dei Castelli di Jesi Pas Dosé M. Cl. Ris. '11	🍷🍷 4
○ Verdicchio dei Castelli di Jesi Passito Brumato '09	🍷🍷 4
⊙ Kòmaros '19	🍷 2
○ Verdicchio dei Castelli di Jesi Cl. Sup. Podium '16	🍷🍷🍷 4*

Guerrieri

via San Filippo, 24
61030 Piagge [PU]
Tel. +39 0721890152
www.aziendaguerrieri.it

CELLAR SALES
PRE-BOOKED VISITS
ANNUAL PRODUCTION 250,000 bottles
HECTARES UNDER VINE 50.00

The Conti Guerrieri estate is one of the oldest in Le Marche. A significant area is cultivated on the Metauro river's right bank, making for a large estate that also includes arable land and extra-virgin olive oil. After a few less-than-brilliant vintages, Luca and his son Alberto have decided to give new life to their wine business by looking to a more modern style, one wrought of immediate pleasantness and smooth intensity of fruit. Significant maturation and the use of various sizes of wood barrels lends complexity and originality. Among the wines submitted, only the Bianchello Superiore Celso '19 is fermented in steel. It has fleshy sensations of yellow fruits and a delicious concentration of flavor. The Guerriero del Mare '18 (Bianchello) is a successful late-harvest wine: creamy, rich, with a sapid stroke at the end to balance sensations of honey and peach puree. We also appreciated the light, delicately salty Sangiovese Galileo Riserva '17.

- ● Colli Pesaresi Sangiovese Galileo Ris. '17 🍷🍷 3*
- ○ Bianchello del Metauro Sup. Celso '19 🍷🍷 3
- ○ Guerriero Bianco '18 🍷🍷 3
- ○ Guerriero del Mare '18 🍷🍷 5
- ● Guerriero della Terra '17 🍷🍷 5
- ● Guerriero Nero '18 🍷🍷 3
- ○ Bianchello del Metauro Celso '13 🍷🍷 2*
- ○ Bianchello del Metauro Sup. Celso '18 🍷🍷 2*
- ● Colli Pesaresi Sangiovese '16 🍷🍷 2*
- ● Colli Pesaresi Sangiovese Galileo Ris. '16 🍷🍷 3
- ● Colli Pesaresi Sangiovese Galileo Ris. '14 🍷🍷 3
- ● Colli Pesaresi Sangiovese Galileo Ris. '13 🍷🍷 3
- ● Colli Pesaresi Sangiovese Galileo Ris. '11 🍷🍷 3
- ● Guerriero Nero '15 🍷🍷 3

Conte Leopardi Dittajuti

via Marina II, 4
60026 Numana [AN]
Tel. +39 0717390116
www.conteleopardi.com

CELLAR SALES
PRE-BOOKED VISITS
ANNUAL PRODUCTION 350,000 bottles
HECTARES UNDER VINE 49.00

Piervittorio Leopardi's estate has been undergoing organic conversion since 2018. This choice was not an easy one given its size, but it's been facilitated by the favorable microclimate that characterizes the hamlet of Coppo di Numana: warm, dry and at the same time tempered by the breeze that blows in constantly from the nearby Adriatic Sea. Here Montepulciano doesn't struggle to ripen, and represents the backbone of the winery's range. The large cellar allows for the creation of several versions, differentiated according to harvesting time and subsequent maturation in small barrels. The Conero Pigmento Riserva '17 topped our preferences. The vintage made for very ripe but well-proportioned fruit, with a close-knit and rounded tannic mesh. The youthful verve of the Rosso Conero Fructus '19 also impressed: focused hints of ripe cherries give way to a compact, generously intense palate. The Antichi Poderi del Conte '18 maintains nice freshness expressed on a fruity palate .

- ● Conero Pigmento Ris. '17 🍷🍷 5
- ● Rosso Conero Antichi Poderi del Conte '18 🍷🍷 2*
- ● Rosso Conero Fructus '19 🍷🍷 3
- ○ Bianco del Coppo '19 🍷 3
- ○ Falerio Risacca '19 🍷 2
- ● Lacrima di Morro d'Alba '19 🍷 3
- ⊙ Rose del Coppo '19 🍷 3
- ● Rosso Conero Casirano '18 🍷 4
- ● Rosso Conero Talismano '19 🍷 3
- ● Rosso Conero Villa Marina '18 🍷 3
- ○ Verdicchio dei Castelli di Jesi Cl. Castelverde '19 🍷 3
- ● Conero Pigmento Ris. '16 🍷🍷 5
- ● Rosso Conero Antichi Poderi del Conte '17 🍷🍷 2*

Roberto Lucarelli

loc. Ripalta
via Piana, 20
61030 Cartoceto [PU]
Tel. +39 0721893019
www.robertolucarelli.com

CELLAR SALES
PRE-BOOKED VISITS
ANNUAL PRODUCTION 250,000 bottles
HECTARES UNDER VINE 50.00

Over time, Roberto Lucarelli has found the right balance between safeguarding the Metauro valley's traditional grape varieties and developing international ones. Their agronomic work aims to harvest grapes when quite ripe, without sacrificing acidity. In the cellar, it's about bringing out the fruity character of the different cultivars through proper temperature control. Their wines prove dynamic, with clear aromatic expression and a solid tendency towards complexity of flavor. Pinot Nero is grown in the vineyards planted on the promontory of Monte San Bartolo. Their Sangioveses put in a nice performance. The Insieme Riserva '16 features spicy sensations and a dark mineral vein, the prelude to a vibrant palate, amply invigorated by sapidity. The Goccione '17 blends hints of black cherry and rain-soaked earth on a background of more sauvage sensations, all on an energetic palate. The elegant Pinot Nero Terre di Fuocaia '18 exhibits an expansive palate; the Bianchello La Ripe '19 comes through supple and tasty in the mouth.

○ Bianchello del Metauro La Ripe '19	🍷🍷 2*
● Colli Pesaresi Focara Pinot Nero Terre di Fuocaia '18	🍷🍷 4
● Colli Pesaresi Sangiovese Goccione '17	🍷🍷 3
● Colli Pesaresi Sangiovese Insieme Ris. '16	🍷🍷 5
● Colli Pesaresi Focara Pinot Nero Terre di Fuocaia Ris. '16	🍷 6
● Colli Pesaresi Sangiovese La Ripe '18	🍷 2
○ Bianchello del Metauro La Ripe '18	🍷🍷 2*
○ Bianchello del Metauro Sup. Rocho '18	🍷🍷 2*
○ Bianchello del Metauro Sup. Rocho '17	🍷🍷 2*

Mario Lucchetti

via Santa Maria del Fiore, 17
60030 Morro d'Alba [AN]
Tel. +39 073163314
www.mariolucchetti.it

CELLAR SALES
PRE-BOOKED VISITS
ANNUAL PRODUCTION 180,000 bottles
HECTARES UNDER VINE 30.00
VITICULTURE METHOD Certified Organic

Undoubtedly Mario Lucchetti was one of the first to believe in of Lacrima Nera. The location of his Santa Maria del Fiore vineyards, in a cru known for its potential, allowed him to deepen his understanding of the grape over many years. Today the vineyards are cultivated organically and are marked by the usual dichotomy between Verdicchio and Lacrima. Today the winery is overseen by his son Paolo, an advocate of a style that brings out varietal characteristics through the preservation of acidity. This is accomplished through fermentation in steel and concrete in their renovated, modern cellar. Both their Verdicchios delivered: the Classico Superiore Vigna Vittoria '19 goes in on a delicate saltiness and deep acidity, while the Classico Birbacciò '19 proves more fruity, soft and savory, though without sacrificing suppleness. The Lacrima Sup. Guardengo '18 features olfactory finesse and a serious, straight, energetic palate—a bit austere but characterful. We also appreciated the Lacrima Fiore '19: redolent of flowers, it exhibits a pronounced, linear backbone.

● Lacrima di Morro d'Alba Sup. Guardengo '18	🍷🍷 3
○ Verdicchio dei Castelli di Jesi Cl. Birbacciò '19	🍷🍷 2*
○ Verdicchio dei Castelli di Jesi Cl. Sup. V. Vittoria '19	🍷🍷 3
● Lacrima di Morro d'Alba Fiore '19	🍷 2
● Lacrima di Morro d'Alba Fiore '18	🍷🍷 2*
● Lacrima di Morro d'Alba Sup. Guardengo '17	🍷🍷 3
● Lacrima di Morro d'Alba Sup. Guardengo '16	🍷🍷 3
● Lacrima di Morro d'Alba Sup. Guardengo '15	🍷🍷 3
● Lacrima di Morro d'Alba Sup. Guardengo '11	🍷🍷 3
○ Verdicchio dei Castelli di Jesi Cl. Sup. V. Vittoria '18	🍷🍷 2*

Mancini

FRAZ. MOIE
VIA PIANELLO, 5
60030 MAIOLATI SPONTINI [AN]
TEL. +39 0731702975
www.manciniwines.it

CELLAR SALES
PRE-BOOKED VISITS
ANNUAL PRODUCTION 130,000 bottles
HECTARES UNDER VINE 20.00

Like many producers in the Esino valley, Benito Mancini's winery, active since 1960, is based on a multifaceted family organization, with his three sons employed today in various capacities. Massimo Mancini is the production manager and the figure who interacts with their historical consultant, Sergio Paolucci, one of Italy's most important Verdicchio experts. Jesi dominates in the vineyards behind the cellar, but there are also small amounts of Montepulciano and Sangiovese used for their Rosso Piceno and Charmat Brut Rosé. The Verdicchio Classico Superiore Villa Talliano '19 stands out by virtue of its great sapid intensity and broad aromatic spectrum: the amalgam discerned on the palate, with its peculiar, soft touch and acidic backbone, make it one of the best of the vintage. We also appreciated the Verdicchio Riserva '17: accentuated notes of almonds and lemon give way to an invigorating, tapered palate marked by long, coherent persistence. The Santa Lucia '19 is a fragrant, standard-label Verdicchio, simple and refreshing.

○ Castelli di Jesi Verdicchio Cl. Ris. '17	🍷🍷	5
○ Verdicchio dei Castelli di Jesi Cl. Sup. Talliano '19	🍷🍷	3*
○ Brut	🍷	2
⊙ Brut Rosé	🍷	2
● Rosso Piceno Panicale '17	🍷	3
○ Verdicchio dei Castelli di Jesi Cl. Santa Lucia '19	🍷	2
○ Castelli di Jesi Verdicchio Cl. Ris. '16	🍸🍸	5
○ Castelli di Jesi Verdicchio Cl. Ris. '14	🍸🍸	5
○ Verdicchio Castelli di Jesi Cl. S. Lucia '17	🍸🍸	2*
○ Verdicchio Castelli di Jesi Cl. Sup. Villa Talliano '17	🍸🍸	3
○ Verdicchio dei Castelli di Jesi Cl. Santa Lucia '18	🍸🍸	2*

Clara Marcelli

VIA FONTE VECCHIA, 8
63081 CASTORANO [AP]
TEL. +39 073687289
www.claramarcelli.it

PRE-BOOKED VISITS
ANNUAL PRODUCTION 40,000 bottles
HECTARES UNDER VINE 10.00
VITICULTURE METHOD Certified Organic

When it comes to vinifying their organically grown grapes, Emanuele and Daniele Colletta have been following Marco Casolanetti's advice for several years. The result is a full-bodied interpretation of the Piceno terroir that can, at times, exhibit a bit of closure at the beginning, a characteristic that's easily overcome by allowing the wine to breathe. After all, patience and slowness are elements inherent in their way of working: from ripening the grapes to aging in barriques, depending on the wine, making for a range that will get your attention. The Ruggine '14 (Alicante) doesn't hide the cool vintage's vegetal side, but adorns it with sensations of Asian spices and Mediterranean scrub; the palate has fiber and gustatory mobility, making for a wine of great personality. The K'un '17 (Montepulciano) scatters brushstrokes of morello cherry, fresh meat and burnt wood, only to reveal an extractive palate, a bit austere in its tight tannic weave. The Piceno Superiore '17 is a bit lighter and more characterful.

● Ruggine '14	🍷🍷	8
● K'un '17	🍷🍷	3
○ Offida Pecorino Irata '18	🍷🍷	3
● Rosso Piceno Sup. '17	🍷🍷	3
● K'un '16	🍸🍸	3
● K'un '13	🍸🍸	3
● K'un '12	🍸🍸	3
● K'un '11	🍸🍸	3
○ Offida Pecorino Irata '17	🍸🍸	3
● Rosso Piceno Sup. '16	🍸🍸	3
● Ruggine '13	🍸🍸	8
● Ruggine '11	🍸🍸	8

Marotti Campi

via Sant'Amico, 14
60030 Morro d'Alba [AN]
Tel. +39 0731618027
www.marotticampi.it

CELLAR SALES
PRE-BOOKED VISITS
ACCOMMODATION
ANNUAL PRODUCTION 260,000 bottles
HECTARES UNDER VINE 70.00

Lorenzo Marotti Campi's winery is in top form. Undisputed skill in vineyard management has made for a diverse range and a modern style in which drinkability and fruit go hand in hand. Indeed, the approach has been so successful that top wines like their Salmariano and Orgiolo have become both trend setters and role models. None of this has been by chance. It's due to the long and painstaking work carried out by the producer together with Roberto Potentini, their technical consultant from the outset. The Verdicchio Salmariano Riserva has never been a featherweight, yet it skillfully circumvents the trap of the hot 2017 vintage: on the nose it exhibits great varietal adherence, with a foreground of almonds well adorned by white fruits, aniseed and balsams; on the palate it comes through vivid and harmonious. We also appreciated the other Verdicchios: both the Classico Albiano '19 and the Classico Superiore Luzano '19 are imbued with playful fragrance and delectable drinkability. The Lacrima Superiore Orgiolo '18 is excellent, despite some vegetal notes.

Wine	Rating
○ Castelli di Jesi Verdicchio Cl. Salmariano Ris. '17	3*
● Lacrima di Morro d'Alba Rubico '19	2*
● Lacrima di Morro d'Alba Sup. Orgiolo '18	3
○ Verdicchio dei Castelli di Jesi Cl. Albiano '19	1*
○ Verdicchio dei Castelli di Jesi Cl. Sup. Luzano '19	2*
○ Verdicchio dei Castelli di Jesi Cl. Sup. Volo d'Autunno '19	5
● Xyris	2
⊙ Brut Rosé	3
⊙ Regina d'Inverno '19	5
⊙ Rosato '19	2
● Lacrima di Morro d'Alba Sup. Orgiolo '17	3*

Poderi Mattioli

via Farneto, 17a
60030 Serra de' Conti [AN]
Tel. +39 0731878676
www.poderimattioli.it

CELLAR SALES
PRE-BOOKED VISITS
ANNUAL PRODUCTION 40,000 bottles
HECTARES UNDER VINE 6.50
VITICULTURE METHOD Certified Organic

At a certain point, the young Mattioli brothers began considering the idea of no longer selling grapes despite a long family history in the sector. The bunches being cultivated in their decidedly strong vineyards, like the one planted in 1971, were just too good. Thanks to Giordano's agronomic skill and Giacomo's enological expertise, they had no difficulty in crafting Castelli di Jesi of great stature and creating a high quality production style. The only deviation from the theory of 'everything Verdicchio' is the presence of a little Chardonnay, which is used in in their Metodo Classico blends. You won't find the Verdicchio Lauro Riserva reviewed below, as it wasn't produced in 2017, but the Ylice '18 will make you feel better about it. A seductive version is all anise and almond adorned with balsamic nuances and the first mineral echoes. The palate comes through harmonious and relaxed, the prelude to a tenacious finish. We also appreciated the delicately salty, crisp and linear Dosaggio Zero '15, which is characterized by aromas of citrus fruits and bread crust.

Wine	Rating
○ Verdicchio dei Castelli di Jesi Cl. Sup. Ylice '18	3*
○ M. Cl. Dosaggio Zero '15	5
○ Castelli di Jesi Verdicchio Cl. Lauro Ris. '16	4*
○ Castelli di Jesi Verdicchio Cl. Lauro Ris. '15	4*
○ Castelli di Jesi Verdicchio Cl. Lauro Ris. '13	3*
○ Verdicchio dei Castelli di Jesi Cl. Sup. Ylice '16	3*
○ Verdicchio dei Castelli di Jesi Cl. Sup. Ylice '12	2*
○ Verdicchio dei Castelli di Jesi Cl. Sup. Ylice '14	3

Valter Mattoni

via Pescolla, 1
63030 Castorano [AP]
Tel. +39 073687329
www.valtermattoni.it

CELLAR SALES
PRE-BOOKED VISITS
ANNUAL PRODUCTION 8,500 bottles
HECTARES UNDER VINE 8.50

Valter 'Roccia' Mattoni's wine venture came about by chance: an old family vineyard that he didn't want to uproot, a burning passion for wine (as a consumer), the friendship and advice of Marco Casolanetti (of Oasi degli Angeli)... The first bottles were makeshift, but they quickly become cult classics. All the enthusiasm convinced Valter to prepare a small structure where he could work on his own, without having to rely on others. Production increased, while the support of his many customers has never waned—thus the 'legend' grows with every harvest. Yet another monumental version of the Montepulciano Arshura: the 2017 pours an indomitable blood-red color. It's a wine that's not silk, but wool, warming and protecting deeply with its close-woven, impenetrable texture. The Rossobordò '16 (Alicante) is a marvel: fruity, firm, deep. The Trebbien '18 (Trebbiano) is that forthright, tasty white that you'd want on your table everyday.

Wine	Glasses	
● Arshura '17	▼▼▼	5
● Rossobordò '16	▼▼	8
○ Trebbien '18	▼▼	4
● Cosecose '19	▼	3
● Arshura '16	▽▽▽	5
● Arshura '11	▽▽▽	3*
● Arshura '14	▽▽	5
● Arshura '13	▽▽	5
● Arshura '12	▽▽	5
● Cosecose '16	▽▽	3
● Rossobordò '15	▽▽	8
● Rossobordò '14	▽▽	8
● Rossobordò '13	▽▽	8
● Rossobordò '12	▽▽	8
○ Trebbien '17	▽▽	4
○ Trebbien '16	▽▽	4
○ Trebbien '15	▽▽	4

★La Monacesca

c.da Monacesca
62024 Matelica [MC]
Tel. +39 0733672641
www.monacesca.it

CELLAR SALES
PRE-BOOKED VISITS
ANNUAL PRODUCTION 160,000 bottles
HECTARES UNDER VINE 33.00

For many years Aldo Cifola's winery has served as a flagship for the territory. With commendable constancy, they've produced some of Matelica's most identifiable wines, born of a style that has always privileged expressive pleasantness, with clear and varietal aromas brought out by significant maturation and aging in steel tanks only. Theirs are interpretations capable of facing the test of time, even growing in complexity with prolonged stays in the bottle. The Matelica '19 exhibits a welcome resoluteness in the glass: nuances of white and yellow fruits, linked by the irreplaceable presence of sweet almond, sensations that emerge with clarity on the palate, where the wine proves pulpy yet endowed with the right suppleness. The Mirum Riserva '18, on the other hand, seemed more linear than usual in its scents of candied lemon, apple and beeswax, then slightly contracted by its generous structure—presumably it will improve in the coming months.

Wine	Glasses	
○ Verdicchio di Matelica '19	▼▼	3*
○ Verdicchio di Matelica Mirum Ris. '18	▼▼	5
○ Verdicchio di Matelica Mirum Ris. '16	▽▽▽	5
○ Verdicchio di Matelica Mirum Ris. '15	▽▽▽	5
○ Verdicchio di Matelica Mirum Ris. '14	▽▽▽	5
○ Verdicchio di Matelica Mirum Ris. '12	▽▽▽	5
○ Verdicchio di Matelica Mirum Ris. '11	▽▽▽	5
○ Verdicchio di Matelica Mirum Ris. '10	▽▽▽	4*
○ Verdicchio di Matelica Mirum Ris. '09	▽▽▽	4
○ Verdicchio di Matelica Mirum Ris. '08	▽▽▽	4
○ Verdicchio di Matelica Mirum Ris. '07	▽▽▽	4*
○ Verdicchio di Matelica Mirum Ris. '06	▽▽▽	4
○ Verdicchio di Matelica Mirum Ris. '04	▽▽▽	4
○ Verdicchio di Matelica Mirum Ris. '02	▽▽▽	3

Montecappone - Mirizzi

via Colle Olivo, 2
60035 Jesi [AN]
Tel. +39 0731205761
www.montecappone.com

CELLAR SALES
PRE-BOOKED VISITS
ANNUAL PRODUCTION 150,000 bottles
HECTARES UNDER VINE 42.50

On some labels you will find the words Mirizzi: it's the surname of Gianluca, the man who oversees the wine venture launched by his family in 1968. In 2015 Gianluca decided to buy a plot of land in Monteroberto, to create his own line as well, all produced in the same well-equipped cellar in Jesi. Here we cover both wineries. The Montecappone range, which is wider, privileges immediate expressiveness and aromatic freshness, in part through slightly early harvests and fermentation at low temperatures. Mirizzi is more structured, playing on a freer, more personal style. The Verdicchio Ergo Sum Riserva '16 Mirizzi debuts with a bang: aged at length on the fine lees in concrete, it opens on subtly whispered, complex notes of aniseed, aromatic herbs and candied orange peel, amplified then by a rhythmic palate of rising intensity. Montecappone unveiled a fruity and tasty Verdicchio Classico Superiore Federico II 1194 '18, with the very fruity and plush Tabano '19 performing just as well.

○ Castelli di Jesi Verdicchio Cl. Ergo Sum Ris. Mirizzi '16	3 glasses 8
○ Verdicchio dei Castelli di Jesi Cl. Sup. Federico II A. D. 1194 '18	2 glasses 5
○ Tabano '19	2 glasses 5
○ Verdicchio dei Castelli di Jesi Cl. Sup. Ergo Mirizzi '18	2 glasses 5
○ Verdicchio dei Castelli di Jesi M. Cl. Extra Brut Mirizzi '17	2 glasses 5
○ La Breccia '19	1 glass 4
● Rosso Piceno '19	1 glass 2
○ Verdicchio dei Castelli di Jesi Cl. '19	1 glass 2
○ Verdicchio dei Castelli di Jesi Cl. Sup. Muntobe '19	1 glass 3
○ Castelli di Jesi Verdicchio Cl. Utopia Ris. '16	3 white glasses 5

Alessandro Moroder

via Montacuto, 121
60029 Ancona
Tel. +39 071898232
www.moroder.wine

CELLAR SALES
PRE-BOOKED VISITS
RESTAURANT SERVICE
ANNUAL PRODUCTION 150,000 bottles
HECTARES UNDER VINE 38.00
VITICULTURE METHOD Certified Organic
SUSTAINABLE WINERY

Conero's history is bound up with the work done by this winery, which operates on its slopes. Alessandro Moroder knows well that just being in an advantageous position isn't enough to stay competitive and in line with modern trends. That's why, together with his sons Marco and Mattia (by now an integral part of the business), he decided at the right time to invest in his vineyards, converting everything to organic. A collaboration with enologist Marco Gozzi makes for wines that express a close bond with the territory, one that's also explored through spontaneous fermentation. The Conero Riserva '16 (not to be confused with the Dorico, which wasn't presented this year) makes for an authentic Montepulciano in its alluring olfactory suite of plum, cherries, meat and burnt wood; in the mouth it has energy and depth, all entrusted to a close-knit weave of supple tannins. The Rosso Conero '17 opens on ripe red fruits, sensations that follow through on a warm, somewhat rustic, appetizing palate. We also appreciated the original and ageworthy Rosa '19.

● Conero Ris. '16	2 glasses 5
⊙ Rosa di Moroder '19	2 glasses 2*
● Rosso Conero '17	2 glasses 2*
● Conero Dorico Ris. '15	3 white glasses 5
● Conero Dorico Ris. '05	3 white glasses 5
● Rosso Conero Dorico '93	3 white glasses 5
● Rosso Conero Dorico '90	3 white glasses 5
● Rosso Conero Dorico '88	3 white glasses 5
● Conero Dorico Ris. '16	2 white glasses 5
● Conero Dorico Ris. '13	2 white glasses 5
● Conero Ris. '15	2 white glasses 5
● Conero Ris. '13	2 white glasses 5
● Rosso Conero '16	2 white glasses 2*
● Rosso Conero Aiòn '18	2 white glasses 2*
● Rosso Conero Aiòn '17	2 white glasses 2*
● Rosso Conero Zero '17	1 white glass 2

Fattoria Nannì

C.DA ARSICCI
62021 APIRO [MC]
TEL. +39 3406225930
www.fattorianannì.it

CELLAR SALES
PRE-BOOKED VISITS
ANNUAL PRODUCTION 30,000 bottles
HECTARES UNDER VINE 8.50
VITICULTURE METHOD Certified Organic

The cellar was built on the site of the former owner's house (Nannì, who has since passed away). It overlooks a multicolored landscape formed by Monte San Vicino, a panorama adorned with snow in winter and many shades of green in summer. The altimeter registers elevations of 450 meters, but the Apennine breezes play an important role for the vegetation and harvests here. It's up to Roberto Cantori to decide how to manage the old and new vineyards, in which only one variety is cultivated, the undisputed protagonist, Verdicchio. A slightly early harvest preserved the delicately salty vigor of the Classico Superiore Origini '19, protecting what is one of its unique traits. At the same time it detracts from its weight somewhat: the result is a lean, vital wine characterized by hints of citrus fruits and stones, interspersed with herbaceous wisps. The Arsicci '19, is a lively and supple second-label wine marked by a focused, floral aromatic profile and gustatory nuances of fresh almond on a subtle, vibrant palate.

- ○ Verdicchio dei Castelli di Jesi Cl. Sup. Origini '19 — 3*
- ○ Verdicchio dei Castelli di Jesi Cl. Sup. Arsicci '19 — 2*
- ○ Verdicchio dei Castelli di Jesi Cl. Sup. Origini '18 — 3*
- ○ Verdicchio dei Castelli di Jesi Cl. Sup. Arsicci '18 — 2*
- ○ Verdicchio dei Castelli di Jesi Cl. Sup. Origini '17 — 3
- ○ Verdicchio dei Castelli di Jesi Cl. Sup. Origini '16 — 3

★Oasi degli Angeli

C.DA SANT'EGIDIO, 50
63012 CUPRA MARITTIMA [AP]
TEL. +39 0735778569
www.kurni.it

CELLAR SALES
PRE-BOOKED VISITS
ANNUAL PRODUCTION 5,000 bottles
HECTARES UNDER VINE 16.00

In order to understand the importance of Marco Casolanetti for Le Marche's wine, one must imagine the region without him and his winery, Oasi degli Angeli. Probably we wouldn't have known the weightier and more contemporary side of Montepulciano. The same holds for 'bordò', the Alicante clone (synonym of Grenache) present in the territory for decades but that had fallen into disuse. Finally, without Marco, there wouldn't have been that virtuous movement named 'Piceni Invisibili', which has paved the way for the small producers who are, today, at the forefront. 2017 proved to be a great year for the Kupra (Alicante). It opens on the nose with a floral vein intertwined with complex sensations of spices, herbs and toasty wisps; the palate comes through compact and silky. The Kurni '18 (Montepulciano) exhibits its usual fruit-forward profile, entering sweet on the palate only to unleash a dense sapidity.

- ● Kupra '17 — 8
- ● Kurni '18 — 8
- ● Kupra '13 — 8
- ● Kupra '12 — 8
- ● Kupra '10 — 8
- ● Kurni '10 — 8
- ● Kurni '09 — 8
- ● Kurni '08 — 8
- ● Kurni '07 — 8
- ● Kurni '04 — 8
- ● Kurni '03 — 8
- ● Kurni '02 — 8
- ● Kurni '01 — 8
- ● Kurni '00 — 8
- ● Kurni '98 — 8
- ● Kurni '97 — 8

Officina del Sole

C.DA MONTEMILONE, 1
63833 MONTEGIORGIO [FM]
TEL. +39 0734277334
www.officinadelsole.it

CELLAR SALES
PRE-BOOKED VISITS
ACCOMMODATION AND RESTAURANT SERVICE
ANNUAL PRODUCTION 75,000 bottles
HECTARES UNDER VINE 14.00

Officina del Sole is an enchanting resort surrounded by fruit trees, vineyards and olive groves. Among the various facilities scattered throughout the panoramic hill, there's also a large underground wine cellar. Assisted by Roberto Potentini (their external consultant), Davide Di Chiara oversees the vineyards, cultivating a mix of native and international grapes, giving rise to a series of wines that are drinkable, aromatically focused and contemporary in style. All the wines presented in this edition are fermented in steel. Both their Pecorinos, which are considerably different despite the similar name, put in good performances. The Franco '19 goes all in on vigor and citrus sapidity, while the Franco Franco '18 is, as usual, characterized by considerable structural strength. The Trecentosessanta Brut is a long Charmat produced in-house without excessive softness and with a nice, delicately salty stroke to close. The Rosso Frutto '19 (Syrah and Lacrima) features spicy and herbaceous hints on a subtle, tannic palate.

Wine	Rating
○ Falerio Pecorino Franco '19	🍷🍷 3
○ Falerio Pecorino Franco Franco '18	🍷🍷 5
○ Trecentosessanta Brut '18	🍷🍷 3
○ Leiè '19	🍷 2
● Rosso Frutto '19	🍷 2
○ Falerio Pecorino Franco '18	♡♡ 3*
○ Falerio Pecorino Franco '17	♡♡ 3
○ Falerio Pecorino Franco Franco '17	♡♡ 5
○ Falerio Pecorino Franco Franco '15	♡♡ 5
○ Offida Pecorino Franco Franco '16	♡♡ 5
● Tignium '16	♡♡ 6
● Tignium '15	♡♡ 6

Pantaleone

VIA COLONNATA ALTA, 118
63100 ASCOLI PICENO
TEL. +39 3478757476
www.pantaleonewine.com

PRE-BOOKED VISITS
ANNUAL PRODUCTION 60,000 bottles
HECTARES UNDER VINE 19.00
VITICULTURE METHOD Certified Organic

Once there, amidst broom and thickets, you wouldn't think you're just a few minutes from the Ascoli Piceno city center—on the contrary, the feeling is that of being immersed in a pleasant hillside town. Nazzareno Pantaloni planted a few rows of vines here without great ambitions, but together with his daughters Francesca and Federica, and his son-in-law Giuseppe Infriccioli, he's made Pantaleone into a model winery. Only traditional grapes are cultivated in the estate vineyards, which give rise to wines of brilliant aromatic expression, all prepared in a small and well-equipped cellar. The Pecorino Onirocep '19 unabashedly unveils its mountain identity in its profile of herbaceous notes, medicinal herbs and citrus. In the mouth it exhibits a vibrant vigor, tidiness and character. The La Ribalta '16 (from Alicante, known as 'bordò' in Piceno), features sensations of Mediterranean scrub and orange peel on a silky palate. The Atto I '18 isn't to be overlooked—this Sangiovese is characterized by nice acidic freshness, healthy fruit and saline nuances.

Wine	Rating
○ Falerio Pecorino Onirocep '19	🍷🍷🍷 3*
● La Ribalta '16	🍷🍷 8
● Atto I '18	🍷🍷 3
⊙ Pivuàn '19	🍷🍷 2*
○ Chicca '19	🍷 2
○ Falerio Pecorino Onirocep '18	♡♡♡ 3*
● Boccascena '15	♡♡ 3
● Boccascena '12	♡♡ 3
○ Chicca '18	♡♡ 2*
○ Chicca '16	♡♡ 2*
○ Falerio Pecorino Onirocep '16	♡♡ 3*
○ Falerio Pecorino Onirocep '15	♡♡ 2*
○ Falerio Pecorino Onirocep '14	♡♡ 2*
● La Ribalta '13	♡♡ 8
● Ribalta '12	♡♡ 8

Pievalta

via Monteschiavo, 18
60030 Maiolati Spontini [AN]
Tel. +39 0731705199
www.pievalta.it

CELLAR SALES
PRE-BOOKED VISITS
ANNUAL PRODUCTION 70,000 bottles
HECTARES UNDER VINE 34.00
VITICULTURE METHOD Certified Biodynamic
SUSTAINABLE WINERY

The most important piece of news for the winery owned by Barone Pizzini and managed by Alessandro Fenino is the purchase of a vineyard in Le Busche, in Montecarotto, considered one of the best crus on the Esino river's left bank. It will flank recent new plantings on Monte Follonica in San Paolo di Jesi, giving life to a diversified set of Verdicchio vineyards. As for the rest, the shift to biodynamic winemaking continues: spontaneous fermentation, a minimally-invasive approach, and painstaking attention at every production stage. An excellent performance for the Verdicchio Classico Superiore Tre Ripe '19, a blend of grapes grown in three areas (Maiolati, Montecarotto, San Paolo). It's an easygoing wine, marked by citrus juiciness and a palate inclined to pleasant drinkability. The San Paolo '17 features characteristic almond hints and some vegetal wisps on a well-orchestrated palate. Nice sapidity as well. The Perlugo Dosaggio Zero is characterized by distinct acidity, a bit raw.

Wine	Rating
○ Verdicchio dei Castelli di Jesi Cl. Sup. Tre Ripe '19	🍷🍷 2*
○ Castelli di Jesi Verdicchio Cl. San Paolo Ris. '17	🍷🍷 3
○ Perlugo Dosaggio Zero M. Cl.	🍷 3
○ Verdicchio dei Castelli di Jesi Passito Curina '18	🍷 4
○ Castelli di Jesi Verdicchio Cl. San Paolo Ris. '16	🍷🍷🍷 3*
○ Castelli di Jesi Verdicchio Cl. San Paolo Ris. '15	🍷🍷🍷 3*
○ Castelli di Jesi Verdicchio Cl. San Paolo Ris. '13	🍷🍷🍷 3*
○ Castelli di Jesi Verdicchio Cl. San Paolo Ris. '10	🍷🍷🍷 3*
○ Verdicchio dei Castelli di Jesi Cl. Sup. Pievalta '09	🍷🍷🍷 2*

Il Pollenza

c.da Casone, 4
62029 Tolentino [MC]
Tel. +39 0733961989
www.ilpollenza.it

CELLAR SALES
PRE-BOOKED VISITS
ANNUAL PRODUCTION 300,000 bottles
HECTARES UNDER VINE 80.00
SUSTAINABLE WINERY

The wonderful estate created by Aldo Brachetti Peretti, a wealthy oil businessman, has never lacked in attention and care when it comes to its considerable vineyards. The same is true of winemaking and aging in the cellar. A technical staff led by Giovanni Campodonico and Carlo Ferrini (as external consultant) draws on a variety of cultivars. If in the past their interest centered on international varieties, today they've begun focusing on Le Marche's traditional grapes. The Cosmino '17 topped our preferences. It's a Bordeaux-style Cabernet Franc in its tannic density, adorned with hints of blueberries, green peppers and spicy wood. The Pollenza '17 (a blend, mostly Cabernet Sauvignon) expresses the power and warmth of the vintage on a full, toasty palate, with a pervasive alcoholic presence and calibrated polyphenolic texture. But the whole battery shines.

Wine	Rating
● Cosmino '17	🍷🍷 5
⊙ ABP Pas Dosé M. Cl Rosé '13	🍷🍷 5
○ Colli Maceratesi Ribona Angera '19	🍷🍷 3
⊙ Didì '19	🍷🍷 3
● Il Pollenza '17	🍷🍷 8
● Porpora '17	🍷🍷 3
● Il Pollenza '15	🍷🍷🍷 8
● Il Pollenza '12	🍷🍷🍷 8
● Il Pollenza '11	🍷🍷🍷 7
● Il Pollenza '10	🍷🍷🍷 7
● Il Pollenza '09	🍷🍷🍷 7
● Il Pollenza '07	🍷🍷🍷 7
● Cosmino '16	🍷🍷 5
● Cosmino '15	🍷🍷 5
● Il Pollenza '16	🍷🍷 8
● Porpora '16	🍷🍷 3
● Porpora '15	🍷🍷 3

Tenute Priori e Galdelli

via Fondiglie, 15a
60030 Rosora [AN]
Tel. +39 0731813266
www.prioriegaldelli.it

CELLAR SALES
PRE-BOOKED VISITS
ANNUAL PRODUCTION 15,000 bottles
HECTARES UNDER VINE 20.00

The road from Rosora to Tassanare offers charming views, such as the silhouette of San Vicino and the wooded spurs of the Gola della Rossa. It climbs and descends gently along many vineyards, including those of Andrea Priori. Today Andrea leads a producer founded in 1974 by his grandfather Giuseppe and by Elia Galdelli. Over time, the small artisan scale of things hasn't changed, but the support of expert enologist Sergio Paolucci has allowed the winery to forge a complete range, one that exhibits with increasing constancy the varietal qualities and expressive temperament of the wines. The Castrum Rosorij '18 put in a great performance, but that shouldn't be a surprise for Verdicchio's most ardent fans, those who appreciate its racy flavor, satisfying juiciness and delicate aniseed finish. The Verdicchio Metodo Classico Brut '14 is a concentrate of citrus and delicately salty acidity; the Passito Akmé '15 blends aromas of peach jam and camphor on a velvety palate. Made with Montepulciano, the fruit forward Cometa '15 comes through vigorous in the mouth.

Wine	Rating
○ Verdicchio dei Castelli di Jesi Cl. Sup. Castrum Rosorij '18	🍷🍷 2*
● Cometa '15	🍷🍷 5
○ Verdicchio dei Castelli di Jesi Brut M. Cl. '14	🍷🍷 4
○ Verdicchio dei Castelli di Jesi Passito Akmé '15	🍷🍷 3

Provima

via Raffaello, 1c
62024 Matelica [MC]
Tel. +39 073784013
www.cantineprovima.it

CELLAR SALES
PRE-BOOKED VISITS
ANNUAL PRODUCTION 200,000 bottles
HECTARES UNDER VINE 120.00

Provima can boast a couple of significant records. Founded in 1932, it is the oldest winery in Matelica; at the same time it's remembered as the first cooperative led by a woman, Giovanna Censi Mancia, elected in 1978. Today Sabrina Orlandi leads its 180 members, while Denis Cingolani serves as manager, acting as a link between elements of production. Together they are helping to bring about clear improvements in terms of personality and varietal adherence. The four Matelicas presented all share a soft pleasantness. The Egos '19 has a clear, elegant olfactory profile accompanied by a soft and substantive palate. The Materga Riserva '18 features hints of almond and flowers; in the mouth it's pervasive, pure. Among the reds we preferred the Vocabolo Rosso '18, a blend of Merlot, Petit Verdot and Sangiovese with a spicy and herbaceous aromatic profile and a pulpy palate marked by acute tannins.

Wine	Rating
○ Verdicchio di Matelica '19	🍷🍷 2*
○ Verdicchio di Matelica Egos '19	🍷🍷 2*
○ Verdicchio di Matelica Materga Ris. '18	🍷🍷 3
○ Verdicchio di Matelica Terramonte '19	🍷🍷 3
● Vocabolo Rosso '18	🍷🍷 3
○ Anno Domini 1579	🍷 2
● Egos Rosso '17	🍷 2

Sabbionare

via Sabbionare, 10
60036 Montecarotto [AN]
Tel. +39 0731889004
www.sabbionare.it

CELLAR SALES
PRE-BOOKED VISITS
ANNUAL PRODUCTION 70,000 bottles
HECTARES UNDER VINE 24.00

The layers of sand that dominate Donatella Paoloni's main vineyard mark the subsoil of the entire district that descends from Montecarotto to Serra De' Conti, lending a warm and dry quality to the grapes. Rows of Verdicchio thrive here, having little difficulty in spawning healthy and ripe bunches under the watch of Pierluigi Donna, a reputed agronomist. Sergio Paolucci transforms the grapes into wines that are exemplary in their varietal expression, powerful and tasty, with clear, focused aromas enhanced by vinification in steel. For their Montepulciano and their Passito, on the other hand, barriques are used. The Sabbionare '19 is a polished, long Verdicchio that unfolds progressively. As usual it's released when very young, and we're sure that it will improve after a further stay in the bottle. The Verdicchio Filetto '19, made with grapes from a different vineyard, is deliberately simpler and more streamlined. We were impressed with the integrity of fruit exhibited by the Cromia '17, a Montepulciano with a share of Merlot.

Wine	Rating
○ Verdicchio dei Castelli di Jesi Cl. Sup. Sabbionare '19	🍷🍷 3*
● Cromìa '17	🍷🍷 3
○ Verdicchio dei Castelli di Jesi Cl. Il Filetto '19	🍷 1*
○ Verdicchio dei Castelli di Jesi Passito Poesia '18	🍷 4
○ Verdicchio dei Castelli di Jesi Cl. Sup. Sabbionare '15	🍷🍷🍷 2*
○ Verdicchio dei Castelli di Jesi Cl. Il Filetto '18	🍷🍷 1*
○ Verdicchio dei Castelli di Jesi Cl. Sup. Sabbionare '18	🍷🍷 3
○ Verdicchio dei Castelli di Jesi Cl. Sup. Sabbionare '17	🍷🍷 3
○ Verdicchio dei Castelli di Jesi Cl. Sup. Sabbionare '16	🍷🍷 3*

Saladini Pilastri

via Saladini, 5
63078 Spinetoli [AP]
Tel. +39 0736899534
www.saladinipilastri.it

CELLAR SALES
PRE-BOOKED VISITS
ANNUAL PRODUCTION 800,000 bottles
HECTARES UNDER VINE 150.00
VITICULTURE METHOD Certified Organic

The origins of the Count Saladino Saladini Pilastri family date back to the year 1000, but their vast estate has been dedicated to wine production for 35 years. A carpet of vines unfold seamlessly in Spinetoli and Monteprandone, hosting primarily white varieties such as Trebbiano, Pecorino and Passerina, even if the winery has hitched its name to blends of Sangiovese and Montepulciano. Their various Rosso Picenos mature in small barrels housed in their large, recently renovated cellar. The Superiore Vigna Monteprandone '18 opens on floral sensations, which becomes hints of morello cherries and black pepper; in the mouth it's still austere in its tannic grip but its texture, mature and robust, will find the right expansion over time. The Piediprato '18 is also without soft spots, relying instead on a sapid development. We also appreciated the taut and citrusy Pecorino '19.

Wine	Rating
○ Offida Pecorino '19	🍷🍷 3
● Rosso Piceno Piediprato '18	🍷🍷 3
● Rosso Piceno Sup. V. Monteprandone '18	🍷🍷 5
○ Falerio Pecorino Palazzi '19	🍷 3
● Rosso Piceno '19	🍷 2
● Rosso Piceno Sup. Montetinello '18	🍷 4
● Rosso Piceno Sup. V. Monteprandone '00	🍷🍷🍷 3
● Pregio del Conte '16	🍷🍷 4
● Rosso Piceno Sup. Montetinello '17	🍷🍷 4
● Rosso Piceno Sup. Montetinello '16	🍷🍷 4
● Rosso Piceno Sup. V. Monteprandone '17	🍷🍷 5
● Rosso Piceno Sup. V. Monteprandone '16	🍷🍷 5
● Rosso Piceno Sup. V. Monteprandone '15	🍷🍷 5

Poderi San Lazzaro

FRAZ. B.GO MIRIAM
C.DA SAN LAZZARO, 88
63073 OFFIDA [AP]
TEL. +39 0736889189
www.poderisanlazzaro.it

CELLAR SALES
PRE-BOOKED VISITS
ANNUAL PRODUCTION 50,000 bottles
HECTARES UNDER VINE 9.00
VITICULTURE METHOD Certified Organic

Paolo Capriotti is a 'one man band', overseeing everything himself. Only traditional varieties are cultivated, for some time now organically, on his nine hectares of vineyards in Ciafone. The recently-constructed cellar is well equipped, with ample space for small wood barrels, a rather popular tool, but one that does not overly mark his wines' aromatic profiles. Indeed, his range seeks to bring out the full ripeness of fruit with little enological intervention. Temperament and territoriality are, in fact, the key elements inherent in every bottle. The Bordò '16 (Alicante) delivers fascinating sensations of Asian spices and Mediterranean scrub on a palate of polished tannins: a pity for the 'garagiste' number of bottles produced. The Offida Rosso Grifola '15 reveals hints of plum, cherries and cocoa; in the mouth it's powerful, with a dry finish. The well-made Pecorino Pistillo '19 sees notes of candied lemon and aniseed at the service of a palate endowed with a superb progression of flavor.

Wine	Rating
● Bordò '16	▼▼ 7
○ Offida Pecorino Pistillo '19	▼▼ 3
● Offida Rosso Grifola '15	▼▼ 5
● Piceno Sup. Podere 72 '17	▼ 4
● Offida Rosso Grifola '11	▽▽▽ 4*
● Bordò '15	▽▽ 7
● Bordò '13	▽▽ 7
● Bordò '12	▽▽ 7
○ Offida Pecorino Pistillo '16	▽▽ 2*
● Offida Rosso Grifola '12	▽▽ 4
● Piceno Sup. Podere 72 '13	▽▽ 2*
● Piceno Sup. Podere 72 '12	▽▽ 2*
● Rosso Piceno Sup. Podere 72 '16	▽▽ 3
● Rosso Piceno Sup. Podere 72 '14	▽▽ 3

Fattoria San Lorenzo

VIA SAN LORENZO, 6
60036 MONTECAROTTO [AN]
TEL. +39 073189656
www.fattoriasanlorenzo.com

CELLAR SALES
PRE-BOOKED VISITS
ANNUAL PRODUCTION 80,000 bottles
HECTARES UNDER VINE 24.00
VITICULTURE METHOD Certified Organic

Natalino Crognaletti is an amiable and passionate vine grower. All his vitality reverberates in wines marked by highly personal organoleptic profiles, obtained through a biodynamically-inspired agricultural approach. Made with Verdicchio, and occasionally other native grapes, such as Trebbiano, his whites are aged in concrete. Measured maturation and glycerine-scented profiles are hallmarks, all enlivened by pure, light and airy traces integrated perfectly in the aromatic spectrum. The reds rely on the harmonizing effects of time for complexity and fullness. Produced only in magnums, the Campo delle Oche Integrale '15 exhibits exciting energy and fruitiness, despite the significant alcohol. The slightly salty and mineral features of the Il Solleone '13 (Montepulciano) also echo in the weighty Il San Lorenzo '06 (Syrah), a wine endowed with charming hints of black pepper. But the whole range is characterized by an authentically rural and artisan profile, brought out by the alluring Di Gino '19.

Wine	Rating
○ Campo delle Oche Integrale '15	▼▼ 8
● Il San Lorenzo '06	▼▼ 8
● Il Solleone '13	▼▼ 5
● Artù '16	▼▼ 3
○ Bianco Di Gino '19	▼▼ 2*
○ Campo delle Oche '16	▼▼ 3
○ Le Oche '18	▼▼ 3
● La Gattara '15	▼ 4
● Artù '15	▽▽ 3
○ Il San Lorenzo '04	▽▽ 6
● Paradiso '12	▽▽ 4
○ Verdicchio dei Castelli di Jesi Cl. Le Oche '16	▽▽ 3
○ Verdicchio dei Castelli di Jesi Cl. Sup. Campo delle Oche '14	▽▽ 4
● Il Solleone '11	▽ 5

★Tenute San Sisto Fazi Battaglia

via Roma, 117
60031 Castelplanio [AN]
Tel. +39 073181591
www.fazibattaglia.it

CELLAR SALES
PRE-BOOKED VISITS
ANNUAL PRODUCTION 1,000,000 bottles
HECTARES UNDER VINE 130.00

In acquiring Fazi Battaglia from its previous owners, Bertani Domains didn't just limit itself to maximizing the advantages that come with the brand's notoriety and historical value. On the contrary, through long term projects it provided for the modernization of parts of its large cellar and restructuring of its vineyards. The work revolves around Verdicchio, which culminates in the Tenute San Sisto project, their flagship wine whose grapes are cultivated in the beautiful vineyard of the same name. The absence of the new San Sisto left room for the Verdicchio Massaccio '18 to shine. It expresses all its accomplished richness of taste and takes home top marks. Made with slightly overripe grapes, and aged in concrete, it delivers a variegated nose: yellow summer fruits, thyme, candied orange peel, a spicy nuance interwoven with toasted almonds. The palate has an alluring energy and a vivid contrast between softness and lively flavor.

○ Verdicchio dei Castelli di Jesi Cl. Sup. Massaccio '18	🍷🍷🍷 4*
○ Verdicchio dei Castelli di Jesi Cl. Sup. Fazi Battaglia '19	🍷🍷 2*
○ Verdicchio dei Castelli di Jesi Cl. Titulus Fazi Battaglia '19	🍷 2
○ Castelli di Jesi Verdicchio Cl. San Sisto Ris. '17	🍷🍷🍷 5
○ Castelli di Jesi Verdicchio Cl. San Sisto Ris. '16	🍷🍷🍷 5
○ Castelli di Jesi Verdicchio Cl. San Sisto Ris. '15	🍷🍷🍷 5
○ Castelli di Jesi Verdicchio Cl. San Sisto Ris. '14	🍷🍷🍷 4*
○ Verdicchio dei Castelli di Jesi Cl. Titulus Fazi Battaglia '18	🍷🍷 2*

Cantina Sant'Isidoro

fraz. Colbuccaro di Corridonia
c.da Colle Sant'Isidoro, 5
62014 Corridonia [MC]
Tel. +39 0733201283
www.cantinasantisidoro.it

CELLAR SALES
PRE-BOOKED VISITS
ANNUAL PRODUCTION 25,000 bottles
HECTARES UNDER VINE 14.50

The old stately villa, restored by the Foresi family, is bordered by woods: a hill overlooking the Chienti valley and the Fiastra river, where the recently built wine cellar is also located. The nearby vineyards are home to a large number of grapes, both local (Maceratino, Sangiovese, Pecorino and Montepulciano) and international. Verdicchio, on the other hand, is cultivated on a hectare rented in Matelica. Technical support is entrusted to Roberto Potentini. Their selection of whites, the only wines presented this year, is more and more reliable. Original profiles emerge, as is the case with the Isidoro '19 (Pecorino): green nuances blend with mineral sensations on a palate rich in contrast. Among their Ribonas, we appreciated the complexity of the Paucis '18, soft on the palate but resolute in its fruitiness. We also found the Metodo Classico Zero Dosage '16 quite pleasant with its creamy palate, in which orange peel and sage nuances stand out.

○ Colli Maceratesi Ribona Dosaggio Zero M. Cl. '16	🍷🍷 4
○ Colli Maceratesi Ribona Paucis '18	🍷🍷 3
○ Isidoro '19	🍷🍷 2*
○ Verdicchio di Matelica Piedicolle '19	🍷🍷 2*
○ Colli Maceratesi Ribona Pausula '19	🍷 2
○ Pinotto '18	🍷 3
○ Colli Maceratesi Ribona Paucis '17	🍷🍷 3
○ Colli Maceratesi Ribona Pausula '18	🍷🍷 2*
○ Verdicchio di Matelica Piedicolle '18	🍷🍷 2*

Santa Barbara

B.GO MAZZINI 35
60010 BARBARA [AN]
TEL. +39 0719674249
www.santabarbara.it

CELLAR SALES
PRE-BOOKED VISITS
ANNUAL PRODUCTION 900,000 bottles
HECTARES UNDER VINE 40.00

Over the years Stefano Antonucci has built up an immense range of wines, covering most of the region's appellations and all its typologies. The style is openly modern, with approachable pleasantness characterizing their simplest wines while texture, complexity and outstanding longevity mark their premium versions. Stefano has been apt at transmitting his vision, entrusting production of his undoubtedly successful wines to a team of professionals led by the Rotatori brothers and enologist Pierluigi Lorenzetti. The Tardivo ma non Tardo Riserva '18 is a Verdicchio that blends pleasantness of taste, aromatic freshness and a nice, spherical, long finish. The Verdicchio Stefano Antonucci '18 offers up notes of anise and white peach on a fragrant, soft, not too complex palate. The Pathos '18 has made progress: complex, evenly developing, more sapid than fruity. We also appreciated the pleasantly compact Rosso Piceno Maschio da Monte '18.

Wine	Rating
○ Castelli di Jesi Verdicchio Cl. Tardivo ma non Tardo Ris. '18	▼▼ 6
● Pathos '18	▼▼ 6
○ Verdicchio dei Castelli di Jesi Passito Lina '18	▼▼ 5
● Mossi '18	▼▼ 5
● Mossone '18	▼▼ 8
○ Offida Pecorino '19	▼▼ 3
● Rosso Piceno Il Maschio da Monte '18	▼▼ 5
○ Verdicchio dei Castelli di Jesi Arnaldo '15	▼▼ 5
○ Verdicchio dei Castelli di Jesi Cl. Le Vaglie '19	▼▼ 3
○ Verdicchio dei Castelli di Jesi Cl. Sup. Stefano Antonucci '18	▼▼ 4
○ Animale Celeste '19	▼ 3
⊙ Sensuade '19	▼ 3
○ Verdicchio dei Castelli di Jesi Ste' '19	▼ 2

Tenuta Santori

C.DA MONTEBOVE, 14
63065 RIPATRANSONE [AP]
TEL. +39 3469559465
www.tenutasantori.it

CELLAR SALES
PRE-BOOKED VISITS
ANNUAL PRODUCTION 50,000 bottles
HECTARES UNDER VINE 17.00
VITICULTURE METHOD Certified Organic

Marco Santori is young but has already demonstrated a sense of measure. A thousand projects are swirling through his head, but he knows that it would take a lot of energy to carry them all out at the same time. At the moment priority has been given to renovating the house at the top of the hill, which will act as a new management/reception center and offers a panoramic view of the beautiful, surrounding hills. After all, he had already equipped himself with a large, modern underground cellar to work the grapes from his private vineyards, planted mostly with Piceno's classics. The Offida Pecorino '19 is once again marked by airy strokes of flowers, stones and citrus fruits all on an exquisite canvas, interwoven with a firm acid backbone and perfect alcohol. It's a compendium of style and elegance. Their portfolio is well represented by the Rosso Piceno Superiore '17, a wine that builds on the fruity generosity of Montepulciano, and by the Offida Passerina '19, all sparkling citrus and sea salt.

Wine	Rating
○ Offida Pecorino '19	▼▼▼ 3*
○ Offida Passerina '19	▼▼ 2*
● Rosso Piceno Sup. '17	▼▼ 3
● Offida Rosso '17	▼ 4
○ Offida Pecorino '18	▽▽▽ 3*
○ Offida Pecorino '17	▽▽▽ 3*
○ Offida Pecorino '16	▽▽▽ 3*
○ Offida Passerina '18	▽▽ 2*
○ Offida Passerina '17	▽▽ 2*
○ Offida Passerina '16	▽▽ 2*
● Rosso Piceno Sup. '16	▽▽ 3*
● Rosso Piceno Sup. '15	▽▽ 3

Sartarelli

via Coste del Molino, 24
60030 Poggio San Marcello [AN]
Tel. +39 073189732
www.sartarelli.com

CELLAR SALES
PRE-BOOKED VISITS
ANNUAL PRODUCTION 300,000 bottles
HECTARES UNDER VINE 55.00
SUSTAINABLE WINERY

Even though organic farming methods aren't applied in its many vineyards (all Verdicchio and situated in the best production areas), Sartarelli has implemented a processing protocol that guarantees the absence of pesticide residues in its wines. Recent restructuring has led to this Coste del Molino winery becoming one of the best in Le Marche, thanks in part to a classic approach to vinification that sees the exclusive use of steel barrels. The resulting range is differentiated according to the time of harvesting. The Balciana is their only single-cru Verdicchio. Made with overripe grapes, the 2018 offers up fascinating notes of orange peel, toasted almond and aromatic herbs, the prelude to a creamy palate, rich in contrast between its pervasive mid palate and a final, lush sapidity. The Tralivio '18, ripe in fruit and soft, has made progress, while the Sartarelli Classico '19 exhibits appreciable energy and polished aromatic definition.

Wine	Rating
○ Verdicchio dei Castelli di Jesi Cl. Sup. Balciana '18	🍷🍷 5
○ Verdicchio dei Castelli di Jesi Cl. Sartarelli '19	🍷🍷 2*
○ Verdicchio dei Castelli di Jesi Cl. Sup. Tralivio '18	🍷🍷 3
○ Sartarelli Brut	🍷 3
○ Verdicchio dei Castelli di Jesi Cl. Sup. Balciana '09	🍸🍸🍸 5
○ Verdicchio dei Castelli di Jesi Cl. Sup. Balciana '04	🍸🍸🍸 5
○ Verdicchio dei Castelli di Jesi Cl. Sup. Contrada Balciana '98	🍸🍸🍸 5
○ Verdicchio dei Castelli di Jesi Cl. Sup. Contrada Balciana '97	🍸🍸🍸 5

Alberto Serenelli

loc. Pietralacroce
via Bartolini, 2
60129 Ancona
Tel. +39 07135505
www.albertoserenelli.com

CELLAR SALES
PRE-BOOKED VISITS
ANNUAL PRODUCTION 27,500 bottles
HECTARES UNDER VINE 7.00

In Le Marche it's difficult to find a producer who doesn't know Alberto Serenelli. An extrovert character, strong-headed, he operates out of a small garage-style cellar in Pietralacroce, just outside Ancona, according to his own vision of wine. His peculiar, rich and polished style, chiseled out over time thanks in part to the advice of Sergio Paolucci, is made possible through the vinification of ripe grapes cultivated on the farms of Varano and Candia, ideal for Montepulciano. The Giorgio Alberto '17 opens on toasty notes, which can be traced back to the small oak barrels used for aging, but just a few turns in the glass are enough to bring out Montepulciano's fleshy fruit and the peppery spiciness of Syrah—the palate is dense in flavor, though not disproportionately so. The Rosso Conero Marro '16 features a robust tannic architecture, but isn't lacking in dynamism. Matured in amphora, the Alberto Serenelli '17 is a soft, long Verdicchio redolent of yellow fruit.

Wine	Rating
● Giorgio Alberto '17	🍷🍷 8
● Rosso Conero Marro '16	🍷🍷 4
○ Verdicchio dei Castelli di Jesi Cl. Alberto Serenelli '17	🍷🍷 8
○ Biancospino '19	🍷 4
● Rosso Conero Varano '17	🍷 8
○ Biancospino '18	🍸🍸 4
● Giorgio Alberto '16	🍸🍸 7
● Rosso Conero Marro '15	🍸🍸 4
● Rosso Conero Marro '13	🍸🍸 4
○ Verdicchio dei Castelli di Jesi Cl. Sora Elvira '18	🍸🍸 4
○ Verdicchio dei Castelli di Jesi Cl. Sora Elvira '16	🍸🍸 4
○ Verdicchio dei Castelli di Jesi Cl. Sora Elvira '13	🍸🍸 3

Fattoria Serra San Martino

via San Martino, 1
60030 Serra de' Conti [AN]
Tel. +39 0731878025
www.serrasanmartino.eu

CELLAR SALES
PRE-BOOKED VISITS
ANNUAL PRODUCTION 16,000 bottles
HECTARES UNDER VINE 3.00
VITICULTURE METHOD Certified Organic

In 1999 Thomas and Kirsten Weydemann gave in to the charm of the Marche countryside, and moved from Germany after magnificently renovating an old farmhouse. At the same time they built a Lilliputian cellar and planted three hectares with red grape varieties. Today the whole farm is biodynamically managed. The wines, which mature in concrete or small wood barrels, show character and complexity, making for a brilliant and original interpretation of the grapes. The Paonazzo '15 is a Syrah aged in concrete for 21 months. Clear notes of tapenade and black pepper rise up to the nose, all expressed on a graceful, firm palate, whose depth is brought out by silky tannins. The Costa dei Zoppi '15 is a Merlot aged 22 months in small barrels. Its fruit is vivid and intact—it's not too complex, but compelling on the palate. The Roccuccio '16, a blend (mostly Montepulciano), offers up sensations of black fruit on a generous palate.

Wine	Rating
● Il Paonazzo '15	🍷🍷 5
● Costa dei Zoppi '15	🍷🍷 4
● Roccuccio '16	🍷🍷 3
● Il Paonazzo '13	ΩΩ 5
● Il Paonazzo '12	ΩΩ 5
● Lysipp '12	ΩΩ 5
● Lysipp '11	ΩΩ 5
● Lysipp '10	ΩΩ 5
● Roccuccio '13	ΩΩ 3
● Roccuccio '12	ΩΩ 3

Sparapani - Frati Bianchi

via Barchio, 12
60034 Cupramontana [AN]
Tel. +39 0731781216
www.fratibianchi.it

CELLAR SALES
PRE-BOOKED VISITS
RESTAURANT SERVICE
ANNUAL PRODUCTION 60,000 bottles
HECTARES UNDER VINE 18.00

Construction of the beautiful, red-walled cellar, clearly visible along the road that leads from the base of the Cupramontana valley to Apiro, has resolved the problems caused by the narrow spaces of the old facility, located in the same building that houses the family restaurant. However, nothing of the artisan approach has been lost, and the three Sparapani siblings continue to oversee the winery founded by their father, Settimio. The vineyards, located at various elevations on the side of the hill that hosts the Hermitage of the White Friars (which inspired the name), give rise to deep wines, expressions of a sapid, flavorful Verdicchio, as tradition would have it. It's a profile that perfectly matches the Il Classico Superiore Priore '18. A certain gustatory mobility drives its development, facilitating the smoothness of its palate, which closes on notes of peach and subtle traces of almond. The Salerna '19 does its job as a 'basic' Verdicchio, making for easy drinking.

Wine	Rating
○ Verdicchio dei Castelli di Jesi Cl. Sup. Il Priore '18	🍷🍷 3*
○ Verdicchio dei Castelli di Jesi Cl. Salerna '19	🍷 2
○ Verdicchio dei Castelli di Jesi Cl. Sup. Il Priore '16	ΩΩΩ 3*
○ Verdicchio dei Castelli di Jesi Cl. Sup. Il Priore '14	ΩΩΩ 2*
○ Verdicchio dei Castelli di Jesi Cl. Sup. Il Priore '13	ΩΩΩ 2*
○ Verdicchio dei Castelli di Jesi Cl. Sup. Il Priore '12	ΩΩΩ 2*
○ Verdicchio dei Castelli di Jesi Cl. Sup. Il Priore '06	ΩΩΩ 2*
○ Castelli di Jesi Verdicchio Cl. Donna Cloe Ris. '16	ΩΩ 5

Tenuta Spinelli

via Lago, 2
63032 Castignano [AP]
Tel. +39 0736821489
www.tenutaspinelli.it

CELLAR SALES
PRE-BOOKED VISITS
ACCOMMODATION
ANNUAL PRODUCTION 62,000 bottles
HECTARES UNDER VINE 14.00

Simone Spinelli never stops. Driven by a lively enthusiasm, he started an ambitious project to renovate the premises. Collectively, they will form a small village that will include a wine cellar and reception for guests/tourists. When it comes to his vineyards, in addition to the rows of Pecorino that have been in production for years near the Sanctuary of Montemisio, his higher plots on Castel di Croce, which enjoy a mountain climate, are entering full swing. Clear citrus scents, linear profiles and notable sapidity (that's never disruptive), are the elements that characterize his wines. The Pecorino Artemisia '19 doesn't miss a chance to put in another memorable performance. The main features are the same: aromas of yellow fruits and citrus, a hint of wild herbs, great acid backbone on the palate. The favorable vintage added aromatic clarity and a textbook palatal brilliance. The interesting Pinot Nero '17, a personal interpretation of the grape, offers up a delicate flutter of red fruits on a gentle, juicy palate.

○ Offida Pecorino Artemisia '19	🍷🍷🍷 3*
● Simone Spinelli Pinot Nero '17	🍷🍷 7
○ Eden '19	🍷 2
○ Offida Pecorino Artemisia '18	ΨΨΨ 3*
○ Offida Pecorino Artemisia '17	ΨΨΨ 2*
○ Offida Pecorino Artemisia '16	ΨΨΨ 2*
○ Offida Pecorino Artemisia '15	ΨΨΨ 2*
○ Offida Pecorino Artemisia '14	ΨΨΨ 2*
○ Offida Pecorino Artemisia '13	ΨΨΨ 2*
○ Offida Pecorino Artemisia '12	ΨΨΨ 2*
○ Eden '18	ΨΨ 2*
○ Eden '17	ΨΨ 2*
○ Eden '15	ΨΨ 2*
○ Eden '13	ΨΨ 2*
○ Offida Pecorino Artemisia '11	ΨΨ 2*
● Simone Spinelli Pinot Nero '16	ΨΨ 7

La Staffa

via Castellaretta, 19
60039 Staffolo [AN]
Tel. +39 0731779810
www.vinilastaffa.it

CELLAR SALES
PRE-BOOKED VISITS
ANNUAL PRODUCTION 45,000 bottles
HECTARES UNDER VINE 10.00
VITICULTURE METHOD Certified Organic

Passionate, tireless, ambitious. These are the qualities that best describe Riccardo Baldi, a thirty-something now firmly established as one of Verdicchio's most inspired interpreters. Through experience, his already solid preparation seems to have found a clear direction: spontaneous fermentations now have that extra olfactory finesse and vivid sapid backbone, without the defects of the past. Great care is shown for the individual plot blends, which are managed in steel and concrete. The territory of Staffolo is expressed without mediation, as is demonstrated by dazzling wines. Starting with the iconic Rincrocca Riserva '17: despite the warm vintage, it exhibits an elegant varietal intimacy and assertive palate, with a very long finish marked by an alluring, delicate salinity. The Verdicchio Selva di Sotto Riserva '17 is even more complex and multifaceted, but needs more time to fully integrate all its components. The Classico Superiore La Staffa '19 is also notable.

○ Castelli di Jesi Verdicchio Cl. Rincrocca Ris. '17	🍷🍷🍷 4*
○ Castelli di Jesi Verdicchio Cl. Selva di Sotto Ris. '17	🍷🍷 8
○ Verdicchio dei Castelli di Jesi Cl. Sup. La Staffa '19	🍷🍷 3*
○ Mai Sentito	🍷 2
○ Castelli di Jesi Verdicchio Cl. Rincrocca Ris. '16	ΨΨ 4
○ Castelli di Jesi Verdicchio Cl. Selva di Sotto Ris. '15	ΨΨ 8
○ Verdicchio dei Castelli di Jesi Cl. Sup. La Staffa '18	ΨΨ 3
○ Verdicchio dei Castelli di Jesi Cl. Sup. La Staffa '17	ΨΨ 3
○ Verdicchio dei Castelli di Jesi Cl. Sup. La Staffa '16	ΨΨ 2*

Tenuta di Tavignano

LOC. TAVIGNANO
62011 CINGOLI [MC]
TEL. +39 0733617303
www.tenutaditavignano.it

CELLAR SALES
PRE-BOOKED VISITS
ANNUAL PRODUCTION 100,000 bottles
HECTARES UNDER VINE 31.00
SUSTAINABLE WINERY

Stefano Aymerich and his granddaughter Ondine de la Feld spare no effort in bringing prestige to Castelli di Jesi. Their crystalline wines exhibit a modern varietal expression and remarkable ageworthiness, even if they're grounded in a profile of absolute pleasantness. To achieve this they make the most of the amphitheatre of vineyards planted at the end of the last century up on a high ridge, a divide between the Musone and Esino rivers. Set in the splendid estate, their cellar is spacious and fully equipped. The barrique cellar in the manor house is dedicated only to red wines. The Verdicchio Classico Superiore Misco '19 features the usual olfactory finesse, open and pleasant hints of flowers, white fruits and a delicate note of aniseed in the background; the palate moves harmoniously, all in favor of a high-profile drinkability. The Verdicchio Villa Torre '19 is more vivid in flavor and gustatory dynamism, but less cohesive and elegant. The focused Metodo Classico Zero Dosage '15 had a nice debut.

Wine	Rating
○ Verdicchio dei Castelli di Jesi Cl. Sup. Misco '19	🍷🍷 4
○ Verdicchio dei Castelli di Jesi Cl. Sup. Villa Torre '19	🍷🍷 3
⊙ Rosato '19	🍷 3
● Rosso Piceno Cervidoni '18	🍷 3
○ Verdicchio dei Castelli di Jesi Dosaggio Zero M. Cl. '15	🍷 6
○ Verdicchio dei Castelli di Jesi Cl. Sup. Misco '17	🍷🍷🍷 3*
○ Verdicchio dei Castelli di Jesi Cl. Sup. Misco '16	🍷🍷🍷 3*
○ Verdicchio dei Castelli di Jesi Cl. Sup. Misco '15	🍷🍷🍷 3*
○ Verdicchio dei Castelli di Jesi Cl. Sup. Misco '14	🍷🍷🍷 3*

Tenuta dell'Ugolino

LOC. CASTELPLANIO
VIA COPPARONI, 32
60031 CASTELPLANIO [AN]
TEL. +39 0731812569
www.tenutaugolino.it

CELLAR SALES
PRE-BOOKED VISITS
ANNUAL PRODUCTION 70,000 bottles
HECTARES UNDER VINE 12.00
SUSTAINABLE WINERY

Andrea Petrini and Matteo Foroni have enlarged their vineyards in recent years, but have never succumbed to the temptation to expand the ampelographic range and abandon their total dedication to Verdicchio. The only exception is a single hectare of Sangiovese and Montepulciano, but the backbone of production, overseen with the technical support of Aroldo Bellelli, is still represented by two still whites matured in steel. They're flanked by a pleasant Charmat sparkler and a few bottles of a passito (offered only in favorable vintages). The Verdicchio Classico Le Piaole '19 exhibits a simple though effective stylistic profile wrought of varietal aromas of almond crossed by floral and herbaceous whiffs; in the mouth it maintains a measured tension. Finer and denser, the Verdicchio Classico Superiore Balluccio '18 proves complex in its aromatic spectrum of anise, medlar and citrus fruits, coming through full yet delicious and persistent on the palate.

Wine	Rating
○ Verdicchio dei Castelli di Jesi Cl. Sup. Vign. del Balluccio '18	🍷🍷 4
○ Maltempo Brut	🍷🍷 4
○ Verdicchio dei Castelli di Jesi Cl. Le Piaole '19	🍷🍷 3
○ Verdicchio dei Castelli di Jesi Cl. Sup. Vign. del Balluccio '17	🍷🍷🍷 4*
○ Verdicchio dei Castelli di Jesi Cl. Le Piaole '18	🍷🍷 3
○ Verdicchio dei Castelli di Jesi Cl. Le Piaole '17	🍷🍷 2*
○ Verdicchio dei Castelli di Jesi Cl. Sup. Vign. del Balluccio '16	🍷🍷 3*
○ Verdicchio dei Castelli di Jesi Cl. Sup. Vign. del Balluccio '15	🍷🍷 3*
○ Verdicchio dei Castelli di Jesi Cl. Sup. Vign. del Balluccio '12	🍷🍷 3*

Terra Fageto

via Valdaso, 52
63827 Pedaso [FM]
Tel. +39 0734931784
www.terrafageto.it

CELLAR SALES
PRE-BOOKED VISITS
ANNUAL PRODUCTION 100,000 bottles
HECTARES UNDER VINE 35.00
VITICULTURE METHOD Certified Organic

Terra Fageto's 35 hectares of vineyards are scattered throughout the municipalities of Campofilone, Pedaso and Altidona. The north-facing slopes are dedicated to white grape varieties, which allows them to preserve their aromatic freshness, while the warmer, sunnier vineyards, some of which overlook the Adriatic, are reserved for red grapes, which have no difficulty in ripening, even a late cultivar such as Montepulciano. The new and well-equipped winery is situated along the Valdaso, in a central position with respect to the production sites. The Fenèsia '19 represents the more immediately expressive and tasty citrus side of Pecorino, with its crystalline aromas and superb drinkability. The Pecorino Salsedine '18 (20% aged in barriques) has greater complexity, a soft touch and strong fruity sensations. The Eva '19 is a slightly herbaceous Falerio, but with a racy profile. The Colle del Buffo '18, wrongly indicated in the last edition (it was the 2017), offers up aromas of black berries on a palate of well-calibrated intensity.

○ Falerio Eva '19	🍷🍷 2*
○ Offida Pecorino Fenèsia '19	🍷🍷 3
○ Offida Pecorino Salsedine '18	🍷🍷 4
● Rosso Piceno Colle del Buffo '18	🍷🍷 3
○ Letizia Passerina '19	🍷 2
● Rosso Piceno Rusus '17	🍷 3
○ Offida Pecorino Fenèsia '18	🍷🍷 3
○ Offida Pecorino Fenèsia '17	🍷🍷 3
○ Offida Pecorino Fenèsia '16	🍷🍷 3
● Rosso Piceno Rusus '16	🍷🍷 3
● Rosso Piceno Rusus '15	🍷🍷 3
● Rosso Piceno Rusus '14	🍷🍷 3

Fattoria Le Terrazze

via Musone, 4
60026 Numana [AN]
Tel. +39 0717390352
www.fattorialeterrazze.it

CELLAR SALES
PRE-BOOKED VISITS
ANNUAL PRODUCTION 90,000 bottles
HECTARES UNDER VINE 16.00

Thanks to a beautiful estate and a history that spans the whole of the last century, Antonio Terni's winery is one of the best known brands in Conero. Their premium wines draw on Montepulciano, but for many years now they've also shown a willingness to draw on international varieties such as Chardonnay, Syrah and Merlot. Federico Curtaz serves as their outside consultant, for both the agronomic and enological side. The Conero Sassi Neri Riserva '18 has fruity intensity to sell. Punctuated by toasty hints, the palate avoids heaviness or tannic over-extraction, making for a commendable drink. The Chaos '16 (Montepulciano, Merlot and Syrah) exhibits more mature fruit and an invigorating, slightly salty palate. A few overtones of greenness don't slow down the character of the Rosso Conero '17. Pink Fluid '19 features a balanced consistency of flavor, while the Donna Giulia Brut '18 impresses with its delicious drinkability.

● Chaos '16	🍷🍷 5
● Conero Sassi Neri Ris. '16	🍷🍷 5
⊙ Donna Giulia Brut Rosé M. Cl. '18	🍷🍷 4
⊙ Pink Fluid '19	🍷🍷 2*
● Rosso Conero Le Terrazze '17	🍷🍷 2*
● Rosso Conero Praeludium '19	🍷🍷 2*
○ Le Cave Chardonnay '19	🍷 2
● Chaos '04	🍷🍷🍷 5
● Chaos '01	🍷🍷🍷 6
● Chaos '97	🍷🍷🍷 6
● Conero Sassi Neri Ris. '04	🍷🍷🍷 5
● Rosso Conero Sassi Neri '02	🍷🍷🍷 5
● Rosso Conero Sassi Neri '99	🍷🍷🍷 5
● Rosso Conero Sassi Neri '98	🍷🍷🍷 5
● Rosso Conero Visions of J '01	🍷🍷🍷 7
● Rosso Conero Visions of J '97	🍷🍷🍷 7

Terre Cortesi Moncaro

VIA PIANOLE, 7A
63036 MONTECAROTTO [AN]
TEL. +39 073189245
www.moncaro.com

CELLAR SALES
PRE-BOOKED VISITS
RESTAURANT SERVICE
ANNUAL PRODUCTION 7,500,000 bottles
HECTARES UNDER VINE 1200.00
SUSTAINABLE WINERY

The fact that the region's best appellations are represented among their roster of wines doesn't come as a surprise: Moncaro is based in Montecarotto, but it brings together three cooperative wineries situated in the region's most important areas (Castelli di Jesi, Conero and Piceno) and merged them into a single producer. Doriano Marchetti, president for many years, together with his well-established team, make a range of fragrant and pleasant wines, rounded, intelligible and certainly appreciated on international markets. The Verdicchio Classico Vigna Novali Riserva '16 topped our preferences: elegant in its aromas of almond and citrus peel, it has a creamy, relaxed palate and a long finish. Excellent performance for their 2019 Verdicchio Classicos as well: the Le Vele proves highly drinkable, the Sup. Fondiglie is fragrant and balanced, while the Superiore Verde Ca' Ruptae combines olfactory breadth and tension. From their southern vineyards come the Pecorino and Passerina Ofithe '19, both of which adeptly combine suppleness and flavor.

Wine	Rating
○ Castelli di Jesi Verdicchio Cl. V. Novali Ris. '16	🍷🍷 4
○ Offida Passerina Ofithe '19	🍷🍷 2*
○ Offida Pecorino Ofithe '19	🍷🍷 3
○ Verdicchio dei Castelli di Jesi Cl. Le Vele '19	🍷🍷 3
○ Verdicchio dei Castelli di Jesi Cl. Sup. Fondiglie '19	🍷🍷 3
○ Verdicchio dei Castelli di Jesi Cl. Sup. Verde Ca' Ruptae '19	🍷🍷 3
● Conero Vign. del Parco Ris. '12	🍷 4
● Piceno Sup. Terrazzano '16	🍷 3
○ Verdicchio dei Castelli di Jesi Passito Tordiruta '16	🍷 5
○ Castelli di Jesi Verdicchio Cl. V. Novali Ris. '10	🍷🍷🍷 3*
● Rosso Piceno Sup. Roccaviva '12	🍷🍷🍷 2*

★★Umani Ronchi

VIA ADRIATICA, 12
60027 OSIMO [AN]
TEL. +39 0717108019
www.umanironchi.com

CELLAR SALES
PRE-BOOKED VISITS
ANNUAL PRODUCTION 2,900,000 bottles
HECTARES UNDER VINE 240.00
VITICULTURE METHOD Certified Organic
SUSTAINABLE WINERY

The figure that most stands out most when looking at Michele Bernetti's winery is the size of its vineyards. It's a significant asset for a project of this magnitude and whose presence reaches into all world markets. The vision goes back to the producer's founder, Massimo, who always championed a personal approach to agronomy. Various vineyards scattered throughout Castelli di Jesi, Conero and Abruzzo are managed through increasingly careful and respectful agricultural practices, giving rise to a solid, modern, multifaceted range. The Conero Campo San Giorgio Riserva '16 is spectacular: black berries, sanguine hints, delicate saltiness and spiciness, it's a deep, progressively unfolding mix of undeniable charm. The Verdicchio Classico Superiore Vecchie Vigne '18, although fine and harmonious, needs a bit more time. The Verdicchio Classico Superiore Casal di Serra '19, another highly expressive wine, features firm gustatory texture. The Maximo '18 is a seductive passito made with botrytised Sauvignon.

Wine	Rating
● Conero Campo San Giorgio Ris. '16	🍷🍷🍷 7
○ Maximo '18	🍷🍷 5
○ Verdicchio dei Castelli di Jesi Cl. Sup. Casal di Serra '19	🍷🍷 3*
○ Verdicchio dei Castelli di Jesi Cl. Sup. V. V. '18	🍷🍷 5
○ Castelli di Jesi Verdicchio Cl. Plenio Ris. '17	🍷🍷 4
● Conero Cumaro Ris. '16	🍷🍷 5
○ La Hoz Brut Nature M.Cl. '15	🍷🍷 5
⊙ La Hoz Nature M. Cl. Rosé	🍷🍷 5
○ LH2 Extra Brut M. Cl.	🍷🍷 4
● Pelago '16	🍷🍷 5
● Rosso Conero San Lorenzo '18	🍷🍷 3
● Rosso Conero Serrano '19	🍷🍷 2*
○ Verdicchio dei Castelli di Jesi Cl. Villa Bianchi '19	🍷🍷 2*

La Valle del Sole

via San Lazzaro, 46
63035 Offida [AP]
Tel. +39 0736889658
www.lavalledelsoleoffida.com

PRE-BOOKED VISITS
ACCOMMODATION AND RESTAURANT SERVICE
ANNUAL PRODUCTION 40,000 bottles
HECTARES UNDER VINE 11.00
VITICULTURE METHOD Certified Organic

If we had to draw up a list of the Piceno wineries that are full-fledged artisans, we certainly couldn't leave out the work done by the Di Nicolòs, a family committed full-time to making wine and providing hospitality in their farmstay accommodations. Alessia and Silvano look after the vineyards planted on the sunny ridge that descends slowly from Offida towards the Tronto valley, where exclusively native varieties are organically cultivated. The cellar houses steel and concrete tanks, while (large volume) wood barrels are reserved entirely for their reds. Both the 2019 whites are harvested slightly early and macerated briefly on the skins. As a result they develop very fresh, fluid and dynamic aromas. The citrusy and invigorating Pecorino is more assertive than the Offida Passerina, which is marked by vegetal overtones. The well-made Rosato '19 offers up notes of cherries and aromatic herbs. The Rosso Piceno Superiore '17 is a little overripe aromatically, but well-structured.

Wine	Rating
○ Offida Pecorino '19	🍷🍷 3
⊙ Rosato '19	🍷🍷 3
● Rosso Piceno Sup. '17	🍷🍷 3
○ Offida Passerina '19	🍷 2
○ Offida Pecorino '18	🍷🍷 3*
○ Offida Pecorino '17	🍷🍷 3
○ Offida Pecorino '16	🍷🍷 3
○ Offida Pecorino '15	🍷🍷 2*
○ Offida Pecorino '11	🍷🍷 2*
● Offida Rosso '15	🍷🍷 4
● Offida Rosso '14	🍷🍷 4
● Rosso Piceno Sup. '16	🍷🍷 3*
● Rosso Piceno Sup. '15	🍷🍷 3

Vigneti Vallorani

c.da La Rocca, 28
63079 Colli del Tronto [AP]
Tel. +39 3477305485
www.vignetivallorani.com

CELLAR SALES
PRE-BOOKED VISITS
ANNUAL PRODUCTION 25,000 bottles
HECTARES UNDER VINE 6.00
VITICULTURE METHOD Certified Organic
SUSTAINABLE WINERY

The Vallorani family have been working the same land for over a century. Rocco and Stefano first got their degrees and then returned to their old vineyards to serve as guardians of tradition. They manage the rows of vines according to rigorous organic principles, while during vinification nothing is off limits: amphorae, maceration, used barriques, lengthy aging on the lees. But for them, no enological instrument or technique should overwhelm the identity of the territory and the variety, but integrate harmoniously. The result is a range that certainly gets one's attention. Floral and oaky on the nose, the Piceno Superiore Polisia '16 then swings to more complex aromas, the prelude to a dry, spirited, bold palate. The Koné 16 is even better, with aromatic herbs giving way to sensations of Asian spices and plum; the palate is both alluring and austere at the same time. The Fric '18 (slightly macerated Trebbiano and Malvasia) unveils appetizing sensations on a supple palate, with clear hazelnut hints emerging.

Wine	Rating
○ LeFric '18	🍷🍷 3
● Piceno Sup. Konè '16	🍷🍷 4
● Piceno Sup. Polisia '16	🍷🍷 3
○ Offida Passerina Zaccarì '15	🍷 5
○ Falerio Avora '18	🍷🍷 3
○ Falerio Avora '16	🍷🍷 3
○ LeFric '16	🍷🍷 3
○ Offida Passerina Zaccarì '14	🍷🍷 5
● Rosso Piceno Sup. Polisia '14	🍷🍷 3

★Velenosi

LOC. MONTICELLI
VIA DEI BIANCOSPINI, 11
63100 ASCOLI PICENO
TEL. +39 0736341218
www.velenosivini.com

CELLAR SALES
PRE-BOOKED VISITS
ANNUAL PRODUCTION 2,500,000 bottles
HECTARES UNDER VINE 192.00

With the new Controguerra estate now operating at full capacity, Velenosi can offer a vast range of wines, with the best appellations in the north and south of Tronto, straddling Marche and Abruzzo, represented. Smooth, contemporary wines are appreciated both in the territory and halfway around the world, in restaurants and shops. This expansion, and the clear vision that underlies it, has been made possible by Angela Velenosi's ten years at the helm. Today she's joined by her daughter Marianna, always ready to forge new distribution channels while consolidating existing ones. It's difficult to dislodge the Rosso Piceno Superiore Roggio del Filare from its throne: the 2017 offers up clear fruity accents adorned with spicy nuances and well-blended toasty notes; the palate comes through relaxed, juicy, fully-resolved in its tannic texture. The Pecorino Rêve '18 and Villa Angela '19 both deserve mentioning, with the former proving more multi-layered and the latter exhibiting great pleasantness.

Wine	Glasses	Price
● Rosso Piceno Sup. Roggio del Filare '17	🍷🍷🍷	6
○ Offida Pecorino Rêve '18	🍷🍷	5
⊙ Cerasuolo d'Abruzzo Prope '19	🍷🍷	2*
○ Falerio V. Solaria '19	🍷🍷	3
● Lacrima di Morro d'Alba Sup. Querciantica '19	🍷🍷	3
● Montepulciano d'Abruzzo Colline Teramane Verso Sera '17	🍷🍷	7
● Montepulciano d'Abruzzo Prope '18	🍷🍷	3
○ Offida Pecorino Villa Angela '19	🍷🍷	3
● Offida Rosso Ludi '17	🍷🍷	6
⊙ Rosé '19	🍷🍷	2*
● Rosso Piceno Sup. Brecciarolo '18	🍷🍷	3
⊙ The Rose Brut M. Cl. '14	🍷🍷	5
○ Velenosi Gran Cuvée Brut M. Cl. '14	🍷🍷	5
○ Verdicchio dei Castelli di Jesi Cl. Querciantica '19	🍷🍷	3

Roberto Venturi

VIA CASE NUOVE, 1A
60010 CASTELLEONE DI SUASA [AN]
TEL. +39 3381855566
www.viniventuri.it

CELLAR SALES
PRE-BOOKED VISITS
ANNUAL PRODUCTION 60,000 bottles
HECTARES UNDER VINE 8.00

In 1998 Filiberto Venturi was making wine in a cramped building in Castelleone di Suasa, a town north of the classic Verdicchio area. But the grapes from Jesi did well there, and only a few years later his son Roberto decided to take the plunge, building a new cellar and adding some rented plots in Montecarotto, near the Le Busche cru. Verdicchio is still cultivated in the original vineyards, along with Moscato, Aleatico and Montepulciano, and the winery has become a consolidated producer of modern, relaxed wines. The Verdicchio Classico Superiore Qudì '18 (not to be confused with the Riserva of the same name) takes home our highest marks. On the nose it unveils sophisticated nuances of anise and almond, all of which reemerge on a progressively unfolding, rhythmic and deep palate. The Qudì Riserva '17 features balsamic and yellow citrus notes, while in the mouth it proves tasty. We also appreciated the pleasant hints of lemon peel and musk that characterize the quaffable Desiderio '19 (Moscato).

Wine	Glasses	Price
○ Verdicchio dei Castelli di Jesi Cl. Sup. Qudì '18	🍷🍷🍷	3*
○ Castelli di Jesi Verdicchio Qudì Ris. '17	🍷🍷	5
○ Desiderio '19	🍷🍷	3
● Squarciafico '17	🍷🍷	4
● Balsamino '19	🍷	2
○ Verdicchio dei Castelli di Jesi Cl. Sup. Qudì '15	🍷🍷🍷 (white)	3*
○ Verdicchio dei Castelli di Jesi Cl. Sup. Qudì '13	🍷🍷🍷 (white)	2*
○ Castelli di Jesi Verdicchio Qudì Ris. '16	🍷🍷 (white)	5
● Squarciafico '16	🍷🍷 (white)	3
○ Verdicchio dei Castelli di Jesi Cl. Sup. Qudì '17	🍷🍷 (white)	3*
○ Verdicchio dei Castelli di Jesi Cl. Sup. Qudì '16	🍷🍷 (white)	3*

Vicari

via Pozzo Buono, 3
60030 Morro d'Alba [AN]
Tel. +39 073163164
www.vicarivini.it

CELLAR SALES
PRE-BOOKED VISITS
ANNUAL PRODUCTION 120,000 bottles
HECTARES UNDER VINE 28.00

The entire winery is grounded in the untiring passion of Vico Vicari and the solid experience of his father, Nazzareno. Valentina, Vico's sister, is in charge of sales, representing their image around the world. The vineyards, including the recently planted plots, see only Verdicchio and Lacrima Nera, rows of vines that wind along the Pozzo Buono district, where their renovated cellar and drying loft are located. The wines are all aged in steel and easily recognizable for their structural density, a quality that's evident even in the simplest versions. The Insolito '18 is a Verdicchio characterized by sweet scents of almond and white fruits, all of which reemerge in the mouth with the usual gustatory energy; the Capofila '19 plays on a simpler, more immediately expressive profile, though without skimping on flavor. The Oltretempo Riserva '16 features nuances of dried fruit on a rich and pervasive palate. The Lacrima Dasempre '19 unveils clear, floral aromas and black cherry on a round, broad palate.

○ Castelli di Jesi Verdicchio Cl. Oltretempo del Pozzo Buono Ris. '16	🍷🍷 5
● Lacrima di Morro d'Alba Dasempre del Pozzo Buono '19	🍷🍷 2*
○ Verdicchio dei Castelli di Jesi Cl. Capofila del Pozzo Buono '19	🍷🍷 2*
○ Verdicchio dei Castelli di Jesi Cl. Sup. L'Insolito del Pozzo Buono '18	🍷🍷 3
● Lacrima di Morro d'Alba Passito Amaranto del Pozzo Buono '18	🍷 5
⊙ Sfumature del Pozzo Buono Brut M. Cl. '16	🍷 5
○ Verdicchio dei Castelli di Jesi Cl. Sup. Insolito del Pozzo Buono '15	🍷🍷🍷 3*

Vignamato

via Battinebbia, 4
60038 San Paolo di Jesi [AN]
Tel. +39 0731779197
www.vignamato.com

CELLAR SALES
PRE-BOOKED VISITS
ANNUAL PRODUCTION 100,000 bottles
HECTARES UNDER VINE 27.00

Maurizio Ceci inherited the business from his father and had the strength to usher it into modern times through the belief that order in the vineyard and cellar is essential. His son Andrea has made the most of that legacy, and at the beautiful family estate everything runs smoothly. Great attention is shown in the vineyards, where mostly Verdicchio is cultivated together with other local varieties, and throughout all stages of production and aging, all carried out with the technical support of Pierluigi Lorenzetti. Repeating last year's performance wasn't an easy feat for the Verdicchio Ambrosia Riserva, especially in light of the hot 2017 vintage, yet the wine left no doubt. Complex and multifaceted, it skillfully manages its weighty texture without betraying structure. We also appreciated the Verdicchio Classico Superiore Versiano '19, a wine that proves true to type in its aromas of aniseed and well sized on the palate—it was a bit youthful at the time of tasting, but there are clear margins for growth. The delicious Versus '19 is the best Incrocio Bruni 54 in Le Marche.

○ Castelli di Jesi Verdicchio Cl. Ambrosia Ris. '17	🍷🍷🍷 4*
○ Verdicchio dei Castelli di Jesi Cl. Sup. Versiano '19	🍷🍷 3
○ Versus '19	🍷🍷 2*
● Campalliano '18	🍷 3
○ Castelli di Jesi Verdicchio Cl. Ambrosia Ris. '16	🍷🍷🍷 3*
○ Castelli di Jesi Verdicchio Cl. Ambrosia Ris. '15	🍷🍷 3*
○ Verdicchio dei Castelli di Jesi Cl. Sup. Versiano '18	🍷🍷 3
○ Verdicchio dei Castelli di Jesi Cl. Sup. Versiano '17	🍷🍷 3*
○ Verdicchio dei Castelli di Jesi Cl. Valle delle Lame '17	🍷🍷 2*

Accadia

FRAZ. CASTELLARO
C.DA AMMORTO, 19
60048 SERRA SAN QUIRICO [AN]
TEL. +39 073185172
www.accadiavini.it

CELLAR SALES
PRE-BOOKED VISITS
ANNUAL PRODUCTION 40,000 bottles
HECTARES UNDER VINE 9.00

- ● Riverbero '14 🍷🍷 5
- ○ Verdicchio dei Castelli di Jesi Cl. Sup. Conscio '18 🍷🍷 4
- ○ Evelyn '18 🍷 4

Stefano Bolognini

C.DA LAURETO, 1A
60030 MORRO D'ALBA [AN]
TEL. +39 3386412143
www.cantinabolognini.it

ANNUAL PRODUCTION 20,000 bottles
HECTARES UNDER VINE 10.00

- ● Lacrima di Morro d'Alba Sup. Sidoro '18 🍷🍷 3
- ○ Verdicchio dei Castelli di Jesi Cl. Olà '18 🍷🍷 2*
- ● Lacrima di Morro d'Alba Osvà '19 🍷 2

Broccanera

FRAZ. MONTALE DI ARCEVIA, 190C
60011 ARCEVIA [AN]
TEL. +39 0731075144
www.broccanera.it

CELLAR SALES
PRE-BOOKED VISITS
ANNUAL PRODUCTION 25,000 bottles
HECTARES UNDER VINE 3.50
VITICULTURE METHOD Certified Organic

- ○ Verdicchio dei Castelli di Jesi Dosaggio Zero M. Cl. '14 🍷🍷 5
- ○ Verdicchio dei Castelli di Jesi Suprino '18 🍷🍷 3

La Calcinara

FRAZ. CANDIA
VIA CALCINARA, 102A
60131 ANCONA
TEL. +39 3285552643
www.lacalcinara.it

CELLAR SALES
PRE-BOOKED VISITS
ANNUAL PRODUCTION 42,000 bottles
HECTARES UNDER VINE 13.00
SUSTAINABLE WINERY

- ⊙ Mun '19 🍷🍷 3
- ● Rosso Conero Il Cacciatore di Sogni '18 🍷🍷 3

Campo di Maggio

FRAZ. PAGLIARE DEL TRONTO
VIA FORMALE, 24
63078 SPINETOLI [AP]
TEL. +39 3493110296
www.cantinacampodimaggio.it

CELLAR SALES
PRE-BOOKED VISITS
ANNUAL PRODUCTION 15,000 bottles
HECTARES UNDER VINE 7.00
VITICULTURE METHOD Certified Organic

- ○ Offida Pecorino Cardofonte '19 🍷🍷 3
- ● Rosso Piceno Masciù '19 🍷 2
- ● Rosso Piceno Sup. Sorgemoro '16 🍷 3

Cantina di Esanatoglia

LOC. CIMA, 25
62024 ESANATOGLIA [MC]
TEL. +39 3348239376
www.cantinadiesanatoglia.it

ANNUAL PRODUCTION 10,000 bottles
HECTARES UNDER VINE 2.20

- ○ Planck '19 🍷🍷 3
- ○ Verdicchio di Matelica Passo Pajano '19 🍷🍷 3
- ● Case Quagna '18 🍷 3

Casa Lucciola

voc. Casalucciola, 42
62024 Matelica [MC]
Tel. +39 3381783572
www.casalucciola.it

ANNUAL PRODUCTION 6,500 bottles
HECTARES UNDER VINE 4.00

○ Verdicchio di Matelica '19 🍷🍷 3*

Cavalieri

via Raffaello, 1
62024 Matelica [MC]
Tel. +39 073784859
www.cantinacavalieri.it

PRE-BOOKED VISITS
ANNUAL PRODUCTION 15,000 bottles
HECTARES UNDER VINE 8.24

● Pinot Nero '18 🍷🍷 4
○ Verdicchio di Matelica Fornacione '18 🍷 3

Enrico Ceci

via Santa Maria D'Arco, 7
60038 San Paolo di Jesi [AN]
Tel. +39 0731779033
www.cecienrico.it

CELLAR SALES
PRE-BOOKED VISITS
ANNUAL PRODUCTION 10,000 bottles
HECTARES UNDER VINE 9.00
SUSTAINABLE WINERY

● Rosso Piceno Santa Maria d'Arco '16 🍷🍷 2*
○ Verdicchio dei Castelli di Jesi Cl. Sup. Santa Maria d'Arco '18 🍷🍷 3

Cherri d'Acquaviva

via Roma, 40
63075 Acquaviva Picena [AP]
Tel. +39 0735764416
www.vinicherri.it

CELLAR SALES
PRE-BOOKED VISITS
ANNUAL PRODUCTION 160,000 bottles
HECTARES UNDER VINE 33.00

○ Offida Pecorino Altissimo '19 🍷🍷 3
○ Passerina '19 🍷🍷 2*
⊙ Ancella '19 🍷 2
● Offida Rosso Tumbulus '15 🍷 4

La Collina delle Fate

loc. San Venanzio, 88
61034 Fossombrone [PU]
Tel. +39 0721726334
www.collinadellefate.com

○ Adagio '14 🍷🍷 5
○ Alcaico '13 🍷🍷 5
○ Alfresco '18 🍷🍷 4

Crespaia

loc. Prelato, 8
61032 Fano [PU]
Tel. +39 0721862383
www.crespaia.it

CELLAR SALES
PRE-BOOKED VISITS
ANNUAL PRODUCTION 40,000 bottles
HECTARES UNDER VINE 10.00
VITICULTURE METHOD Certified Organic

○ Bianchello del Metauro Sup. Chiaraluce '18 🍷🍷 3
● Colli Pesaresi Sangiovese Nerognolo '17 🍷🍷 3
○ Bianchello del Metauro '19 🍷 2

Fioretti Brera

via della Stazione, 48
60022 Castelfidardo [AN]
Tel. +39 335373896
www.fiorettibrera.it

ANNUAL PRODUCTION 10,000 bottles
HECTARES UNDER VINE 3.50
VITICULTURE METHOD Certified Organic

- ● Conero Rigo 23 Ris. '17 — 🍷🍷 5
- ○ Arghilos '18 — 🍷🍷 3
- ● Rosso Conero Faustì '18 — 🍷 3

Esther Hauser

c.da Coroncino, 1a
60039 Staffolo [AN]
Tel. +39 0731770203
www.estherhauser.it

CELLAR SALES
PRE-BOOKED VISITS
ANNUAL PRODUCTION 6,000 bottles
HECTARES UNDER VINE 1.00

- ● Il Cupo '17 — 🍷🍷 5
- ● Il Ceppo '17 — 🍷 4

Podere L' Infinito

c.da San Martino, 1
60039 Staffolo [AN]
Tel. +39 3391068724
www.poderelinfinito.it

ANNUAL PRODUCTION 15,000 bottles
HECTARES UNDER VINE 5.00
VITICULTURE METHOD Certified Organic

- ○ Verdicchio dei Castelli di Jesi Cl. Sup. Cor de Leone '19 — 🍷🍷 4
- ○ Verdicchio dei Castelli di Jesi Cl. Sup. Eclissi di Luglio '19 — 🍷🍷 2*

Lanari

fraz. Varano
via Pozzo, 142
60029 Ancona
Tel. +39 0712861343
www.lanarivini.it

CELLAR SALES
PRE-BOOKED VISITS
ANNUAL PRODUCTION 50,000 bottles
HECTARES UNDER VINE 13.00

- ● Conero Aretè Ris. '17 — 🍷🍷 6
- ● Conero Fibbio Ris. '17 — 🍷🍷 5
- ● Rosso Conero '18 — 🍷🍷 3

Filippo Maraviglia

loc. Pianné, 593
62024 Matelica [MC]
Tel. +39 0737786340
www.vinimaraviglia.com

CELLAR SALES
PRE-BOOKED VISITS
ACCOMMODATION
ANNUAL PRODUCTION 30,000 bottles
HECTARES UNDER VINE 27.00

- ○ Verdicchio di Matelica Alarico '19 — 🍷🍷 2*
- ○ Verdicchio di Matelica Grappoli d'Oro Ris. '17 — 🍷🍷 3
- ○ Verdicchio di Matelica Archè '18 — 🍷 4

La Marca di San Michele

via Torre, 13
60034 Cupramontana [AN]
Tel. +39 0731781183
www.lamarcadisanmichele.com

CELLAR SALES
PRE-BOOKED VISITS
ACCOMMODATION
ANNUAL PRODUCTION 35,000 bottles
HECTARES UNDER VINE 6.00
VITICULTURE METHOD Certified Organic
SUSTAINABLE WINERY

- ○ Verdicchio dei Castelli di Jesi Cl. Sup. Capovolto '19 — 🍷🍷 3

Maurizio Marchetti

FRAZ. PINOCCHIO
VIA DI PONTELUNGO, 166
60131 ANCONA
TEL. +39 071897386
www.marchettiwines.it

CELLAR SALES
PRE-BOOKED VISITS
ANNUAL PRODUCTION 65,000 bottles
HECTARES UNDER VINE 22.00

● Rosso Conero Due Amici '18	🍷🍷 4
○ Verdicchio dei Castelli di Jesi Cl. Sup. Tenuta del Cavaliere '19	🍷🍷 3

Enzo Mecella

VIA DANTE, 112
60044 FABRIANO [AN]
TEL. +39 073221680
www.enzomecella.com

CELLAR SALES
PRE-BOOKED VISITS
ANNUAL PRODUCTION 90,000 bottles
HECTARES UNDER VINE 12.00

○ Verdicchio di Matelica Godenzia '18	🍷🍷 5
○ Verdicchio di Matelica Sainale '18	🍷🍷 4

Monte Torto - San Floriano

LOC. CASENUOVE
VIA DI JESI, 343
60027 OSIMO [AN]
TEL. +39 0731205764
www.montetorto.it

CELLAR SALES
ANNUAL PRODUCTION 13,000 bottles
HECTARES UNDER VINE 6.30

● Casone '16	🍷🍷 3
● Floriano '18	🍷🍷 2*
● Bartolo '19	🍷 2
○ Monticello '19	🍷 2

Claudio Morelli

V.LE ROMAGNA, 47B
61032 FANO [PU]
TEL. +39 0721823352
www.claudiomorelli.it

CELLAR SALES
PRE-BOOKED VISITS
ANNUAL PRODUCTION 110,000 bottles
HECTARES UNDER VINE 40.00

○ Bianchello del Metauro La V. delle Terrazze '19	🍷🍷 2*
○ Bianchello del Metauro Sup. Borgo Torre '19	🍷🍷 3

Tenuta Piano di Rustano

VIA GIOVANNI XXII, 1
62022 CASTELRAIMONDO [MC]
TEL. +39 3393217530
www.pianidirustano.it

ANNUAL PRODUCTION 20,000 bottles
HECTARES UNDER VINE 9.00

○ Verdicchio di Matelica Torre del Parco '19	🍷🍷 3*
○ Verdicchio di Matelica Brut M. Cl. Cavalier Vincenzo '17	🍷 5

Tenute Pieralisi Monte Schiavo

FRAZ. MONTESCHIAVO
VIA VIVAIO
60030 MAIOLATI SPONTINI [AN]
TEL. +39 0731700385
www.monteschiavo.it

CELLAR SALES
PRE-BOOKED VISITS
ANNUAL PRODUCTION 950,000 bottles
HECTARES UNDER VINE 103.00
SUSTAINABLE WINERY

○ Verdicchio dei Castelli di Jesi Cl. Nativo '18	🍷🍷 2*
○ Verdicchio dei Castelli di Jesi Cl. Coste del Molino '19	🍷 2

Tenute Recchi Franceschini

c.da Valle Bianca
63068 Montalto delle Marche [AP]
Tel. +39 3662786985
www.riservalamarna.it

CELLAR SALES
PRE-BOOKED VISITS
ACCOMMODATION
ANNUAL PRODUCTION 9,000 bottles
HECTARES UNDER VINE 8.00

- ○ Offida Pecorino Petraiae '18 🍷🍷 3*
- ○ Offida Passerina Notturno '18 🍷🍷 3
- ● Rosso Piceno Donna Eugenia '15 🍷 3

Tenute Rio Maggio

c.da Vallone, 41
63014 Montegranaro [FM]
Tel. +39 0734889587
www.riomaggiovini.it

CELLAR SALES
PRE-BOOKED VISITS
ANNUAL PRODUCTION 90,000 bottles
HECTARES UNDER VINE 10.00

- ○ Falerio Pecorino Colle Monteverde '19 🍷🍷 3
- ● Rosso Piceno Rio '18 🍷🍷 2*
- ● Rosso Piceno Granarijs '16 🍷 4
- ○ Telusiano '19 🍷 3

San Filippo

loc. Borgo Miriam
c.da Ciafone, 17a
63035 Offida [AP]
Tel. +39 0736889828
www.vinisanfilippo.it

CELLAR SALES
PRE-BOOKED VISITS
ANNUAL PRODUCTION 100,000 bottles
HECTARES UNDER VINE 55.00
VITICULTURE METHOD Certified Organic

- ○ Offida Pecorino '19 🍷🍷 3
- ● Offida Rosso Lupo del Ciafone '16 🍷🍷 4
- ○ Offida Passerina '19 🍷 2

Santa Cassella

c.da Santa Cassella, 7
62018 Potenza Picena [MC]
Tel. +39 0733671507
www.santacassella.it

CELLAR SALES
PRE-BOOKED VISITS
ANNUAL PRODUCTION 70,000 bottles
HECTARES UNDER VINE 32.00

- ○ Colli Maceratesi Ribona '19 🍷🍷 2*
- ● Conte Leopoldo '16 🍷🍷 3
- ● Rosso Piceno '17 🍷🍷 2*
- ○ Donna Angela '19 🍷 3

Selvagrossa

fraz. Borgo S. Maria
s.da Selvagrossa, 37
61020 Pesaro
Tel. +39 0721202923
www.selvagrossa.it

CELLAR SALES
PRE-BOOKED VISITS
ANNUAL PRODUCTION 32,000 bottles
HECTARES UNDER VINE 4.00

- ● Trimpilin '16 🍷🍷 4
- ○ Cuchén '19 🍷 2
- ● Muschén '18 🍷 2

Le Stroppigliose

loc. Stroppigliosi, 9
62022 Castelraimondo [MC]
Tel. +39 3898208660
www.pietramaula.it

CELLAR SALES
ACCOMMODATION AND RESTAURANT SERVICE
ANNUAL PRODUCTION 6,000 bottles
HECTARES UNDER VINE 3.00
VITICULTURE METHOD Certified Organic
SUSTAINABLE WINERY

- ○ Verdicchio di Matelica Arpìa '19 🍷🍷 2*
- ○ Verdicchio di Matelica Cavallo '18 🍷🍷 4

Terracruda

via Serre, 28
61040 Fratte Rosa [PU]
Tel. +39 0721777412
www.terracruda.it

CELLAR SALES
PRE-BOOKED VISITS
ACCOMMODATION
ANNUAL PRODUCTION 130,000 bottles
HECTARES UNDER VINE 22.00

○ Bianchello del Metauro Boccalino '19	🍷🍷 2*
● Pergola Rosso Vettina '18	🍷🍷 2*
○ Bianchello del Metauro Sup. Campodarchi '18	🍷 3

Terre di Serrapetrona

via Colli, 7/8
62020 Serrapetrona [MC]
Tel. +39 0733908329
www.terrediserrapetrona.it

CELLAR SALES
PRE-BOOKED VISITS
ACCOMMODATION AND RESTAURANT SERVICE
ANNUAL PRODUCTION 90,000 bottles
HECTARES UNDER VINE 17.00

● Serrapetrona Robbione '13	🍷🍷 5
● Vernaccia di Serrapetrona Dolce Vernaccianera	🍷🍷 3
● Sommo Passito '12	🍷 3

Le Vigne di Franca

c.da Santa Petronilla, 69
63900 Fermo
Tel. +39 3356512938
www.levignedifranca.it

CELLAR SALES
ANNUAL PRODUCTION 30,000 bottles
HECTARES UNDER VINE 4.50

● Rubrum '17	🍷🍷 3
● Crismon '17	🍷 4
○ Lumes '19	🍷 3

Vignedileo - Tre Castelli

via San Francesco, 2a
60039 Staffolo [AN]
Tel. +39 0731779283
www.vignedileo.it

CELLAR SALES
PRE-BOOKED VISITS
ANNUAL PRODUCTION 250,000 bottles
HECTARES UNDER VINE 36.00

● Lalocco '15	🍷🍷 3
○ Verdicchio di Castelli di Jesi Cl. Sup. Frocco '18	🍷🍷 3
○ Verdicchio di Castelli di Jesi Cl. '19	🍷 2

Cantina Volverino

c.da Santa Croce, 11a
62010 Mogliano [MC]
Tel. +39 0733557130
www.cantinavolverino.it

CELLAR SALES
PRE-BOOKED VISITS
ACCOMMODATION
ANNUAL PRODUCTION 5,000 bottles
HECTARES UNDER VINE 2.50

● La Cavalletta Gialla '17	🍷🍷 2*
● Rosso Piceno La Rana Chiazzata '18	🍷🍷 3
● La Civetta Rossa '16	🍷 4

Zaccagnini

via Salmagina, 9/10
60039 Staffolo [AN]
Tel. +39 0731779892
www.zaccagnini.it

CELLAR SALES
PRE-BOOKED VISITS
ACCOMMODATION AND RESTAURANT SERVICE
ANNUAL PRODUCTION 250,000 bottles
HECTARES UNDER VINE 35.00

○ Verdicchio dei Castelli di Jesi Cl. Sup. Z '19	🍷🍷 3*
○ Verdicchio dei Castelli di Jesi Cl. Sup. Salmàgina '19	🍷🍷 3

UMBRIA

Umbria may be small, but beauty and excellence are certainly not lacking. The portrait of Umbria that emerges this year, in spite of its size, is that of a great land where you can cultivate very different varieties that, depending on the terroir, can express just as many different styles. Despite the fact that Montefalco is growing year by year, both in size and importance (thanks in part to the impeccable work carried out by the consortium), the district is anything but Sagrantino centered. First of all, in these parts Montefalco Rosso is growing before our eyes. Don't be fooled into thinking it's the younger brother of Sagrantino—this is a different wine, characterful, made primarily with Sangiovese. From North to South we're seeing strong results: the great historical appellations, such as Orvieto and Torgiano, are being relaunched, with some surprising varieties getting attention (especially Trebbiano Spoletino in the Spoleto area and Ciliegiolo in Narni). Grechetto has been elevated with producers focusing, rightfully, on its aging potential. All this can be summed up very well by the Tre Bicchieri awarded this year, in our 2021 version of the guide, 14 in all (the same number as last year, but with some new additions). Briziarelli surprised the commission with a great Trebbiano '19; the Tudernum cooperative presented a splendid Grechetto '18; Castelbuono sees it's first Tre Bicchieri with their Riserva di Montefalco Rosso; and Romanelli grabbed a gold with their Medeo (it's the first time for this Sagrantino). The multi-award winning producer Antonelli was also recognized with a new wine, the Molino dell'Attone (a true cru). Obviously we shouldn't overlook the region's classics, starting with Cervaro della Sala. Antinori's prestigious white wine, with the 2018 vintage, conquers its 30th Tre Bicchieri: a truly exceptional record for the region. It's echoed by the Vigna Monticchio di Lungarotti, with its 16th recognition. Among the younger producers that have already made a good impression, we'd like to mention Leonardo Bussoletti in Narni, Roccafiore in Todi, Bellafonte in Montefalco, and Barberani in Orvieto. Last, but not least, an obligatory mention for Caprai. It's an exemplary producer in terms of quality and sustainability, fundamental for the rebirth of Sagrantino. Even in the absence of its 25 Anni (their most prestigious red) Caprai rose to the top of Collepiano.

Adanti

via Belvedere, 2
06031 Bevagna [PG]
Tel. +39 0742360295
www.cantineadanti.com

CELLAR SALES
PRE-BOOKED VISITS
ANNUAL PRODUCTION 160,000 bottles
HECTARES UNDER VINE 30.00
SUSTAINABLE WINERY

The manor house, which is surrounded by vineyards, serves as the symbol of a winery that represents tradition and classicism, rigour in production, but also a degree of freedom when it comes to expressing the natural qualities of the territory. The cellar can be found in the villa. Here oak barrels are used judiciously and yeasts are only indigenous varieties. The result can be seen in a selection of austere wines, that offer up their best after a few years, though without losing the traces of youth and the essence of Montefalco. The Domenico, made with carefully selected Montefalco Sagrantino, landed a place in our finals. 10 years after harvest, the wine shows no signs of pulling back aromatically, on the contrary. The nose unfolds amidst black fruit and spicy hints, dried flowers and undergrowth. The palate is long and gratifying, tannins certainly present, but never bitter or harsh. The Sagrantino '14 is more Mediterranean, playing on freshness. Finally, the Passito '11 proves pleasant and balanced.

Wine	Rating
● Montefalco Sagrantino Il Domenico '10	🍷🍷 6
● Montefalco Rosso Ris. '15	🍷🍷 4
● Montefalco Sagrantino '14	🍷🍷 5
● Montefalco Sagrantino Passito '11	🍷🍷 6
⊙ Amanter '19	🍷 2
○ Montefalco Bianco Arquata '19	🍷 2
○ Montefalco Grechetto '19	🍷 2
● Montefalco Rosso '16	🍷 2
● Montefalco Sagrantino Arquata '08	🍷🍷🍷 6
● Montefalco Sagrantino Arquata '06	🍷🍷🍷 5
● Montefalco Sagrantino Arquata '05	🍷🍷🍷 5
● Montefalco Rosso Arquata '15	🍷🍷 3*
● Montefalco Rosso Ris. '14	🍷🍷 4
● Montefalco Sagrantino '13	🍷🍷 5
● Montefalco Sagrantino Arquata '13	🍷🍷 6

Antonelli - San Marco

loc. San Marco, 60
06036 Montefalco [PG]
Tel. +39 0742379158
www.antonellisanmarco.it

CELLAR SALES
PRE-BOOKED VISITS
ACCOMMODATION
ANNUAL PRODUCTION 320,000 bottles
HECTARES UNDER VINE 52.00
VITICULTURE METHOD Certified Organic
SUSTAINABLE WINERY

San Marco is one of Montefalco's best areas for wine-growing. It's here that the Antonelli family work, managing to bring out all the area's potential through the expert cultivation of Sagrantino and Sangiovese, but also Trebbiano Spoletino and Grechetto. Research and experimentation are part of their approach, but it's respect for nature and tradition that prevail in wines that combine artisan workmanship with clear varietal expression. The Molino dell'Attone '15, their new Sagrantino, impresses with its cleanness and complexity. Right out of the gate, the palate exhibits the qualities of a champion: it's supple and dynamic, the finish is distinguished by depth as well. Another excellent wine is the Trebium '19, a decidedly sapid Trebbiano Spoletino. The Montefalco Rosso '17 is juicy and pleasant, the Sagrantino Passito '14 sweet and delicately salty.

Wine	Rating
● Montefalco Sagrantino Molino dell'Attone '15	🍷🍷🍷 6
● Montefalco Rosso '17	🍷🍷 3*
● Baiocco Sangiovese '19	🍷🍷 2*
● Contrario '17	🍷🍷 3
● Montefalco Sagrantino Passito '14	🍷🍷 5
○ Spoleto Trebbiano Spoletino Anteprima Tonda '18	🍷🍷 4
○ Trebbiano Spoletino Trebium '19	🍷🍷 3
● Montefalco Rosso Ris. '16	🍷 4
● Montefalco Sagrantino '15	🍷 5
● Montefalco Sagrantino Chiusa di Pannone '15	🍷 6
● Montefalco Rosso Ris. '15	🍷🍷🍷 4*
○ Spoleto Trebbiano Spoletino Anteprima Tonda '16	🍷🍷🍷 4*
● Montefalco Rosso '16	🍷🍷 3*

Argillae

voc. Pomarro, 45
05010 Allerona [TR]
Tel. +39 0763624604
www.argillae.eu

CELLAR SALES
PRE-BOOKED VISITS
ANNUAL PRODUCTION 70,000 bottles
HECTARES UNDER VINE 38.00
SUSTAINABLE WINERY

Argillae is an estate of some 220 hectares (38 of which are under vine) that winds through the hills north of Orvieto, in Allerona and Ficulle, on clay and limestone soils. Here the appellation's classic grapes are cultivated in terrain enriched by fossils and shells from the Pliocene era. The winery follows principles of sustainability, as embodied by the use of renewable energy and strictly organic material in the vineyard. Their wines reflect the territory of origin—they're clean and precise, and not devoid of character. The Primo d'Anfora, a unique white fermented with the skins and matured in amphora, earned a place in our finals. A 2018, it features a complex nose of ripe white fruit and dried flowers, the prelude to a sapid and slightly tannic palate. We also appreciated the Grechetto '19, a wine that goes all in on chamomile and wild herbs. The Orvieto Superiore '19 isn't too far behind.

Wine	Rating
○ Primo d'Anfora '18	🍷🍷 6
○ Grechetto '19	🍷🍷 3
○ Orvieto Sup. '19	🍷 2
○ Grechetto '16	YY 2*
○ Grechetto '14	YY 2*
○ Grechetto '12	YY 2*
○ Orvieto '18	YY 2*
○ Orvieto '16	YY 2*
○ Orvieto '15	YY 2*
○ Orvieto '13	YY 2*
○ Orvieto '12	YY 2*
○ Orvieto '11	YY 2*
○ Orvieto Cl. Panata '14	YY 2*
○ Orvieto Cl. Sup. Panata '18	YY 4
○ Orvieto Cl. Sup. Panata '17	YY 4
● Sinuoso '15	YY 2*

Barberani

loc. Vocabolo Mignattaro, 26
fraz. Cerreto
05023 Baschi [TR]
Tel. +39 0763341820
www.barberani.it

CELLAR SALES
PRE-BOOKED VISITS
ACCOMMODATION
ANNUAL PRODUCTION 300,000 bottles
HECTARES UNDER VINE 55.00
VITICULTURE METHOD Certified Organic
SUSTAINABLE WINERY

More than a winery, Barberani is a large family business led by Bernardo and Niccolò, close brothers who deal with the commercial side of things and production respectively. For as far back as anyone can remember, vineyard management has followed the dictates of organic farming and great dedication is shown towards highlighting the Orvieto's unique attributes in the bottle. The family has always believed in the area and the wines are there to prove it: finesse and elegance are on display, while drinkability is a common thread throughout a selection that in some cases also prove highly ageworthy. The Luigi e Giovanna once again demonstrates that it's a superb white, both locally and nationally. It's an Orvieto Classico Superiore '17 that surprises for its olfactory complexity: fresh and dried fruit, pastry-shop sensations, saffron and sweet spices anticipate a fresh, fragrant, deep and extremely clean palate. Tre Bicchieri. The Orvieto Castagnolo '19 is simple, but characterful. The Foresco '18 is expertly crafted.

Wine	Rating
○ Orvieto Cl. Sup. Luigi e Giovanna '17	🍷🍷🍷 5
● Foresco '18	🍷🍷 3
○ Orvieto Cl. Sup. Castagnolo '19	🍷🍷 3
● Aleatico Passito '11	🍷 6
● Lago di Corbara Rosso Villa Monticelli '04	YYY 4
○ Orvieto Cl. Sup. Luigi e Giovanna '16	YYY 5
○ Orvieto Cl. Sup. Luigi e Giovanna '13	YYY 5
○ Orvieto Cl. Sup. Luigi e Giovanna Villa Monticelli '11	YYY 5
○ Orvieto Cl. Sup. Muffa Nobile Calcaia '10	YYY 5
○ Orvieto Muffa Nobile Calcaia '15	YYY 6
○ Grechetto '18	YY 3
○ Moscato Passito '15	YY 6
○ Orvieto Cl. Sup. Castagnolo '18	YY 3
○ Orvieto Cl. Sup. Luigi e Giovanna '15	YY 5

Tenuta Bellafonte

loc. Torre del Colle
via Colle Nottolo, 2
06031 Bevagna [PG]
Tel. +39 0742710019
www.tenutabellafonte.it

CELLAR SALES
PRE-BOOKED VISITS
ACCOMMODATION
ANNUAL PRODUCTION 35,000 bottles
HECTARES UNDER VINE 11.00
SUSTAINABLE WINERY

Bellafonte is just over 10 years old, but the winery has already carved out a place in Montefalco's history. Its creator is Peter Heilbron, who entered the world of wine with very clear ideas, immediately standing out for the few bottles produced (two whites and two reds), all of which are focused on the area's varieties. Sustainable viticulture in the vineyard, precision that's never invasive in the cellar: large barrels, indigenous yeasts and measured extraction makes for wines of character that are always distinguished by elegance and drinkability, enjoyable in youth but ageworthy as well. This year the Montefalco Sagrantino is missing from their selection, as it's still aging. But it was replaced by a great Montefalco Rosso: the Pomontino '18. Youthful and graceful, it exhibits great suppleness and dynamism, perfect tannins and a juicy palate. Delicious aromas calls up red berries. Indubitably a Tre Bicchieri. Among the whites we appreciated the Arneto '18, a highly charming Trebbiano Spoletino.

Wine	Glasses	Price
● Montefalco Rosso Pomontino '18	🍷🍷🍷	6
○ Trebbiano Spoletino Arnèto '18	🍷🍷	4
○ Montefalco Bianco Sperella '19	🍷	2
● Montefalco Rosso Pomontino '17	🍷🍷🍷	6
● Montefalco Sagrantino '09	🍷🍷🍷	6
● Montefalco Sagrantino Collenottolo '14	🍷🍷🍷	6
● Montefalco Sagrantino Collenottolo '13	🍷🍷🍷	6
● Montefalco Sagrantino Collenottolo '11	🍷🍷🍷	6
● Montefalco Sagrantino Collenottolo '10	🍷🍷🍷	6
○ Arnèto '17	🍷🍷	4
○ Arnèto '16	🍷🍷	4
○ Arnèto '14	🍷🍷	5
● Montefalco Sagrantino Collenottolo '15	🍷🍷	6
● Montefalco Sagrantino Collenottolo '12	🍷🍷	6

Bocale

loc. Madonna della Stella
via Fratta Alzatura
06036 Montefalco [PG]
Tel. +39 0742399233
www.bocale.wine

CELLAR SALES
PRE-BOOKED VISITS
ANNUAL PRODUCTION 25,000 bottles
HECTARES UNDER VINE 4.20

Bocale is the the Valentini family's nickname, a piece of dialect that refers to the common mug used for wine and oil. It represents an agricultural tradition that's small in numbers (fewer than five hectares under vine), but great in terms of quality consistency and territorial identity. Three red wines are produced (two Sagrantinos and one Montefalco Rosso), as well as a Trebbiano Spoletino. This last, a traditional white grape in these parts, is increasingly a focus of production. And we start with a white. The Spoletino '19 features a bouquet of medlar, wild flowers and orange blossom, the palate is sapid, slightly marked by sensations of grape skin, with a fresh finish. The delicious Montefalco Sagrantino Ennio '16 offers up hints of tobacco and plum, with dense but never bitter or contracted tannins. We conclude with the Montefalco Rosso '18, a supple and juicy wine—simple but never banal.

Wine	Glasses	Price
● Montefalco Rosso '18	🍷🍷	3
● Montefalco Sagrantino Ennio '16	🍷🍷	6
○ Spoleto Trebbiano Spoletino '19	🍷🍷	3
● Montefalco Rosso '17	🍷🍷	3
● Montefalco Rosso '16	🍷🍷	3*
● Montefalco Rosso '15	🍷🍷	3
● Montefalco Rosso '14	🍷🍷	3
● Montefalco Sagrantino '16	🍷🍷	5
● Montefalco Sagrantino '15	🍷🍷	5
● Montefalco Sagrantino '14	🍷🍷	5
● Montefalco Sagrantino '13	🍷🍷	5
● Montefalco Sagrantino Ennio '15	🍷🍷	7
○ Trebbiano Spoletino '15	🍷🍷	3

Briziarelli

via Colle Allodole, 10
06031 Bevagna [PG]
Tel. +39 0742360036
www.cantinebriziarelli.it

CELLAR SALES
PRE-BOOKED VISITS
ACCOMMODATION AND RESTAURANT SERVICE
ANNUAL PRODUCTION 235,000 bottles
HECTARES UNDER VINE 30.00

The link between Briziarelli and agriculture dates back at least to 1906, the year in which Pio founded the business, betting on Montefalco. Their wine project, launched in the 2000s, is more recent. 30 hectares of vineyards are cultivated, while their new cellar, built in 2012, is at the vanguard in terms of architecture and winemaking. Their range fully respects the varietal and territorial character of the wines, combining technical precision with a contemporary vision, serving as a perfect mirror of the cellar itself. The Mattone Bianco '19, made with Trebbiano Spoletino, is clear, focused and expressive on the nose, offering up aromas of fresh almond and white flowers, yellow fruit and aromatic herbs, while the palate flows well all the way through, holding together beautiful freshness and flavor. Tre Bicchieri. The red Dunarobba '18, a pleasant blend of equal parts Merlot and Sangiovese, combines suppleness, intensity and character. The other wines tasted are all well made.

Wine	Rating
○ Mattone Bianco Trebbiano '19	🍷🍷🍷 3*
● Montefalco Rosso Dunarobba '18	🍷🍷 3*
● Montefalco Rosso '17	🍷 3
● UnoNoveZeroSei '15	🍷 5
● Montefalco Rosso Mattone Ris. '16	🍷🍷🍷 5
● Montefalco Rosso '15	🍷🍷 3
● Montefalco Rosso Mattone '12	🍷🍷 4
● Montefalco Rosso Mattone Ris. '15	🍷🍷 5
● Montefalco Sagrantino '15	🍷🍷 5
● Montefalco Sagrantino '14	🍷🍷 5

Leonardo Bussoletti

loc. Miriano
s.da delle Pretare, 62
05035 Narni [TR]
Tel. +39 0744715687
www.leonardobussoletti.it

PRE-BOOKED VISITS
ANNUAL PRODUCTION 40,000 bottles
HECTARES UNDER VINE 9.00
VITICULTURE METHOD Certified Organic

Leonardo Bussoletti is a skilled vigneron but also an enlightened producer who has managed to lend prestige to the entire Narni territory through wines made with the area's classic cultivars: Ciliegiolo and Grechetto. Just a few exchanges with Leonardo is enough to get an appreciation for his burning passion for viticulture and winemaking, all faithfully reflected in his fine and elegant wines, which are endowed with character, flavor and length. Delectable when young, they grow more complex and austere with age. They are bottles to experience over time, thanks in part to their accessible prices, to say the least. The selection presented this year performed quite well, as usual, starting with the red 05035 '19, a youthful and graceful Ciliegiolo di Narni that stands out for its succulent, pleasant, satisfying and long palate. The real champion this year, however, is the Brecciaro '18. Made with carefully selected Ciliegiolo grapes, it offers up vibrant notes of black fruit and spices. The palate masterfully balances acidity, flavor and tannins. Tre Bicchieri.

Wine	Rating
● Brecciaro Ciliegiolo '18	🍷🍷🍷 3*
● 05035 Ciliegiolo '19	🍷🍷 3*
○ Colle Ozio Grechetto '19	🍷🍷 3
○ 05035 Bianco '19	🍷 2
● 05035 Rosso '16	🍷🍷🍷 2*
● Brecciaro Ciliegiolo '14	🍷🍷🍷 3*
○ Colle Ozio Grechetto '12	🍷🍷🍷 3*
● Ramici Ciliegiolo '16	🍷🍷🍷 5
● 05035 Ciliegiolo '18	🍷🍷 3*
● 05035 Ciliegiolo '17	🍷🍷 2*
● Brecciaro Ciliegiolo '17	🍷🍷 3
○ Colle Murello '18	🍷🍷 3
○ Colle Ozio Grechetto '16	🍷🍷 3*

★★Arnaldo Caprai

loc. Torre, 1
06036 Montefalco [PG]
Tel. +39 0742378802
www.arnaldocaprai.it

CELLAR SALES
PRE-BOOKED VISITS
ACCOMMODATION
ANNUAL PRODUCTION 1,000,000 bottles
HECTARES UNDER VINE 136.00
SUSTAINABLE WINERY

In our thirty years of publishing this guide, we thought we'd said everything about Caprai, but the producer, a leader in Montefalco, continues to evolve and take on new challenges. It's currently overseen by Marco, heir to Arnaldo (who founded the winery in the 1970s), though for some time now Caprai has also benefited from the technical expertise of a high-caliber enologist like Michel Rolland. Their extensive range, which draws on just under 150 hectares of vineyards, manages to balance precision with a contemporary approach, though without undermining the varietal principles that are a true expression of the territory, especially when it comes to 'king' Sagrantino. Waiting for the new version of their Sagrantino 25 Anni, we 'settled' for the Collepiano '16. It's a second-tier wine on paper only, considering its complexity and structure: tobacco, tanned leather, roots and black fruit herald a close-knit palate where tannins take center stage, enriching an energetic drink. We also appreciated their other reds, starting with the Montefalco Rosso Vigna Flaminia Maremmana '18.

Wine	Rating
● Montefalco Sagrantino Collepiano '16	🍷🍷🍷 7
● Montefalco Rosso V. Flaminia Maremmana '18	🍷🍷 4
○ Chardonnay '19	🍷🍷 5
○ Colli Martani Grechetto Grecante '19	🍷🍷 4
○ Cuvée Secrète '18	🍷🍷 7
● Montefalco Rosso '18	🍷🍷 4
● Montefalco Sagrantino Valdimaggio '16	🍷🍷 7
○ Sauvignon '19	🍷 5
● Montefalco Sagrantino 25 Anni '15	🍷🍷🍷 8
● Montefalco Sagrantino 25 Anni '14	🍷🍷🍷 8
● Montefalco Rosso V. Flaminia Maremmana '17	🍷🍷 4
● Montefalco Sagrantino Collepiano '14	🍷🍷 7
● Montefalco Sagrantino Valdimaggio '15	🍷🍷 7

La Carraia

loc. Tordimonte, 56
05018 Orvieto [TR]
Tel. +39 0763304013
www.lacarraia.it

CELLAR SALES
PRE-BOOKED VISITS
ANNUAL PRODUCTION 700,000 bottles
HECTARES UNDER VINE 119.00

La Carraia, a lovely and historic Orvieto producer, has been offering a reliable range of wines for many years, wines that represent a sincere expression of their territory of origin. Envisioned and built by the Gialletti family, the winery avails itself of a valuable partnership with the Cotarellas, with enologist Riccardo overseeing production. Many wines are produced, both with native grapes (including their delicious Orvietos) and international varieties (which give rise to various IGTs). This year it's their reds that stand out. The Querciascura '13 is a monovarietal Sangiovese, close-woven and full-bodied but still rhythmic on the palate: notes of black fruit and leather ensure complexity on the nose, while the palate features pervasive tannins and discernible acidity. The Tizzonero '17 is another Sangiovese, but includes other local grapes as well. More youthful and leaner, it still has the character of a great red. Finally the Solcato '17 proves to be an interesting Bordeaux blend (plus Sangiovese).

Wine	Rating
● Querciascura '13	🍷🍷 4
● Solcato '17	🍷🍷 3
● Tizzonero '17	🍷🍷 3
○ Conte Marzio '17	🍷 4
○ Orvieto Cl. Sup. Poggio Calvelli '19	🍷 2
● Fobiano '03	🍷🍷🍷 4
● Fobiano '99	🍷🍷🍷 4*
● Fobiano '98	🍷🍷🍷 4*
○ Le Basque '18	🍷🍷 3
○ Le Basque '17	🍷🍷 3*
○ Le Basque '16	🍷🍷 3
● Merlot '18	🍷🍷 2*
○ Orvieto Cl. Sup. Poggio Calvelli '18	🍷🍷 2*
○ Orvieto Cl. Sup. Poggio Calvelli '17	🍷🍷 2*
○ Orvieto Cl. Sup. Poggio Calvelli '16	🍷🍷 2*
● Solcato '16	🍷🍷 3
● Solcato '15	🍷🍷 3

★★★Castello della Sala

Loc. Sala
05016 Ficulle [TR]
Tel. +39 076386127
www.antinori.it

CELLAR SALES
ANNUAL PRODUCTION 800,000 bottles
HECTARES UNDER VINE 170.00

The value of Orvieto's wine has always been known to the Marquis Antinori family. In fact, when they wanted to invest in a territory for white wines, they focused on Ficulle, creating the Castello della Sala and, in just a few years, making Cervaro known as a great national white wine, a true pearl. The winery's recent history proves that it's been able to maintain an enviable consistency of quality, expanding the range and focusing more and more on Orvieto, with wines capable of interpreting the spirit of the times in a fluid way. Elegant, fine and graceful: thanks to a fresh vintage, the 2018 Cervaro della Sala once again demonstrates that it's a true prize. Broad in its nuances of apricot, wild herbs and flowers, its pervasive palate is crossed by beautiful acidic freshness. Long and very clean at the finish. Tre Bicchieri. The Bramito della Sala '19, another Chardonnay, is also well made. Among the reds this year the fresh and graceful Pinot Nero '17 stands out.

Wine	Rating
○ Cervaro della Sala '18	🍷🍷🍷 7
○ Bramito della Sala '19	🍷🍷 4
○ Muffato della Sala '16	🍷🍷 6
● Pinot Nero della Sala '17	🍷🍷 7
○ Conte della Vipera '19	🍷 5
○ Orvieto Cl. Sup. San Giovanni della Sala '19	🍷 3
○ Cervaro della Sala '17	🍷🍷🍷 7
○ Cervaro della Sala '16	🍷🍷🍷 6
○ Cervaro della Sala '15	🍷🍷🍷 6
○ Cervaro della Sala '07	🍷🍷🍷 6
○ Cervaro della Sala '06	🍷🍷🍷 6
○ Cervaro della Sala '05	🍷🍷🍷 6
○ Cervaro della Sala '04	🍷🍷🍷 6

Cantina Cenci

fraz. San Biagio della Valle
voc. Anticello, 50
06072 Marsciano [PG]
Tel. +39 3805198980
www.cantinacenci.it

CELLAR SALES
PRE-BOOKED VISITS
ANNUAL PRODUCTION 30,000 bottles
HECTARES UNDER VINE 6.00
VITICULTURE METHOD Certified Organic
SUSTAINABLE WINERY

Led today by explosive winemaker Giovanni, Cenci is situated a few kilometers south of Perugia, in an area that has always been well suited to agriculture. 6 of the property's 40 hectares are planted with vineyards, on clayey and sandy soils rich in limestone, in an area that as far back as the late-7th century was settled by Olivetan monks. Production is divided between central Italy's traditional varieties (Sangiovese, Grechetto and Trebbiano) and international grapes. Their wines exhibit technical precision and an artisan spirit. A white and a red were the most interesting wines tasted this year. The Anticello Grechetto '19 is redolent of apricot, wild flowers, aromatic herbs and spices; the palate is sapid, slightly marked by sensations of grape skin, coming through firm and rich, but acidic freshness balances it all. The Piantata '18 is a graceful and highly drinkable monovarietal Sangiovese: small berries rise up to the nose, while the palate comes through rhythmic and juicy. Their other wines are all well made.

Wine	Rating
○ Anticello '19	🍷🍷 3
● Piantata Sangiovese '18	🍷🍷 5
○ Àlago Stellato '19	🍷 3
● Sanbiagio '18	🍷 3
○ Alago Stellato '15	🍷🍷 2*
○ Anticello '16	🍷🍷 2*
○ Anticello '15	🍷🍷 2*
○ Anticello '14	🍷🍷 2*
○ Anticello Laghetto '18	🍷🍷 3
● Ascheria '16	🍷🍷 3
○ Giole '15	🍷🍷 2*
● Piantata '17	🍷🍷 4
● Piantata '16	🍷🍷 4
● Piantata '15	🍷🍷 4
● Piantata '14	🍷🍷 4
● Piantata R '16	🍷🍷 6
● Sanbiagio '17	🍷🍷 3

Le Cimate

FRAZ. CASALE
LOC. CECAPECORE, 41
06036 MONTEFALCO [PG]
TEL. +39 0742290136
www.lecimate.it

CELLAR SALES
PRE-BOOKED VISITS
ACCOMMODATION AND RESTAURANT SERVICE
ANNUAL PRODUCTION 900,000 bottles
HECTARES UNDER VINE 27.70
SUSTAINABLE WINERY

The Bartoloni family's Le Cimate gets its name from the hilltops that characterize Montefalco. The winery was founded in 2011 by Paolo, heir to a family that has been involved in agriculture since 1800. Almost 28 hectares of land are cultivated both with the area's classic grape varieties and with certain international varieties used mainly in wines with a typical geographical indication. The clayey soils see a notable presence of limestone, resulting in modern wines that are technically impeccable. In recent years, they're also increasingly racy and varietal. The two Trebbiano Spoletino whites impressed. The 2019 is undoubtedly the more complex and balanced: despite its young age there's no lack of flowery sensations and mountain herbs. In the mouth it's sapid and fragrant, while its olfactory suite reemerges clearly. We also appreciated the Riserva del Cav. Bartoloni 2018, a selection that's released two years after the harvest.

Wine	Rating
○ Trebbiano Spoletino '19	🍷🍷 3*
○ Spoleto Trebbiano Spoletino Sup. Riserva del Cavalier Bartoloni '18	🍷🍷 4
● Montefalco Sagrantino '15	🍷 5
● Montefalco Rosso '15	🍷🍷 3
● Montefalco Sagrantino '14	🍷🍷 5
● Montefalco Sagrantino '13	🍷🍷 5
● Montefalco Sagrantino '12	🍷🍷 5
○ Trebbiano Spoletino '18	🍷🍷 3
○ Trebbiano Spoletino '17	🍷🍷 3
○ Trebbiano Spoletino '15	🍷🍷 3

Colle Ciocco

VIA B. GOZZOLI 1/5
06036 MONTEFALCO [PG]
TEL. +39 0742379859
www.colleciocco.it

CELLAR SALES
PRE-BOOKED VISITS
ANNUAL PRODUCTION 45,000 bottles
HECTARES UNDER VINE 15.00

The hill on which it's situated gives its name to this small but interesting Montefalco winery. Its origins date back to the 1930s, when Settimio Spacchetti founded the farm dedicated to wine, oil and crop production. Now it's his heirs Lamberto and Eliseo who carry on the work on the 20-hectare property (15 of these are planted with vines). Sagrantino is a key player. It's flanked by Sangiovese, a protagonist in the production of their Montefalco Rosso. They've also made space for whites, with Trebbiano Spoletino, Montefalco Bianco, Chardonnay and Viognier cultivated as well. And the Tempestivo '19, a selection of Trebbiano Spoletino, shined during our tastings: a complex nose plays on dried herbs and candied orange peel, while the palate proves sapid and rhythmic. But the real champion this year is the Montefalco Sagrantino '15: though not lacking in structure, its body perfectly balances tannins, acidic freshness and sapidity. Supple and deep, it rewards the palate.

Wine	Rating
● Montefalco Sagrantino '15	🍷🍷 5
● Montefalco Rosso '16	🍷🍷 3
○ Spoleto Trebbiano Spoletino Tempestivo '19	🍷🍷 3
○ Montefalco Grechetto Clarignano '18	🍷 3
○ Montefalco Bianco '18	🍷🍷 3
● Montefalco Rosso '15	🍷🍷 3
● Montefalco Sagrantino '14	🍷🍷 5
● Montefalco Sagrantino '12	🍷🍷 5
● Montefalco Sagrantino '11	🍷🍷 5
○ Spoleto Trebbiano Spoletino Tempestivo '18	🍷🍷 3
○ Spoleto Trebbiano Spoletino Tempestivo '17	🍷🍷 3

Fattoria Colleallodole

via Colleallodole 3
06031 Bevagna [PG]
Tel. +39 0742361897
www.fattoriacolleallodole.com

CELLAR SALES
PRE-BOOKED VISITS
ANNUAL PRODUCTION 70,000 bottles
HECTARES UNDER VINE 25.00

Colleallodole is the district and cru in Bevagna after which the farm is named, even if the signature that stands out on the label is the Antano family's. It was Milziade who strongly believed in Montefalco, and his heirs continue the work here, looking after an authentically crafted line of wines, remaining faithful to tradition both in the vineyard (only local grapes are cultivated on the hilly land rich in clay here) and in the cellar, where indigenous yeasts are used, while maceration and maturation are carried out in a way that's ideal for the red grapes. The battery of wines presented this year performed at a high level, with the Colle Allodole '17 leading the way. Made with select Sagrantino, it's characterized by tremendous olfactory complexity, with perky notes of red fruit accompanied by sweet spices. The palate is supple, despite edgy tannins, thanks to its pace-setting freshness. The Montefalco Sagrantino '17 and the Rosso '18 are also excellent. We found the Passito '17 charming.

Wine	Rating	Price
● Montefalco Sagrantino Colleallodole '17	🍷🍷	8
● Montefalco Rosso '18	🍷🍷	3
● Montefalco Sagrantino '17	🍷🍷	6
● Montefalco Sagrantino Passito '17	🍷🍷	7
● Montefalco Rosso Ris. '17	🍷	5
● Montefalco Rosso '17	🍷🍷 (white)	3
● Montefalco Rosso '16	🍷🍷 (white)	3
● Montefalco Sagrantino '16	🍷🍷 (white)	6
● Montefalco Sagrantino Passito '16	🍷🍷 (white)	7
● Montefalco Sagrantino Passito '15	🍷🍷 (white)	7

Decugnano dei Barbi

loc. Fossatello, 50
05018 Orvieto [TR]
Tel. +39 0763308255
www.decugnano.it

CELLAR SALES
PRE-BOOKED VISITS
ANNUAL PRODUCTION 130,000 bottles
HECTARES UNDER VINE 32.00

The Barbi family's winery is a benchmark for Orvieto and beyond, for its beauty, history and modern approach. The beautiful hills overlooking Lake Corbara are home to the area's traditional grapes, which thrive in a soil rich in fossil material and shells. The cellar cave where their Metodo Classico is stored is charming (to say the least), while the facilities dedicated to their line of whites and reds are more modern. Theirs are wines of great drinkability and finesse, fully embodying the terroir of origin amidst minerality and sapidity. The general level of their range is excellent. Their Metodo Classicos dominated, while tasting of their most important Orvieto was postponed until next year (it will age a few months longer). Among the reds, the Decugnano '17 stands out for its close-knit weave, with soft, smooth tannins. The Orvieto Villa Barbi '19 is also top-notch. The elegant Dosaggio Zero once again demonstrates the producer's growing mastery of sparkling wines.

Wine	Rating	Price
○ Orvieto Cl. Villa Barbi '19	🍷🍷🍷	3*
● Il Decugnano Rosso '17	🍷🍷	3*
○ Brut M. Cl. '15	🍷🍷	5
○ Dosaggio Zero M. Cl.	🍷🍷	5
○ Maris '16	🍷🍷	4
⊙ Tramonto d'Estate '19	🍷	4
○ Orvieto Cl. Sup. Il Bianco '17	🍷🍷🍷 (white)	4*
○ Orvieto Cl. Sup. Il Bianco '16	🍷🍷🍷 (white)	4*
○ Orvieto Cl. Sup. Il Bianco '15	🍷🍷🍷 (white)	4*
○ Orvieto Cl. Sup. Il Bianco '12	🍷🍷🍷 (white)	3*
○ Orvieto Cl. Sup. Il Bianco '18	🍷🍷 (white)	4
○ Orvieto Cl. Villa Barbi '18	🍷🍷 (white)	3

Di Filippo

voc. Conversino, 153
06033 Cannara [PG]
Tel. +39 0742731242
www.vinidifilippo.com

CELLAR SALES
PRE-BOOKED VISITS
ANNUAL PRODUCTION 227,000 bottles
HECTARES UNDER VINE 35.00
VITICULTURE METHOD Certified Organic
SUSTAINABLE WINERY

Roberto Di Filippo is the brains and brawn of the beautiful winery that bears his name. A project based on sustainability and biodiversity translates into sincere, genuine wines, technically impeccable (Roberto is a highly skilled enologist) and able to respect the territories of provenance. The vineyards lie in two different areas. On the one hand there's Montefalco, where Sagrantino reigns, on the other there's Colli Martani, where Sangiovese and Grechetto prevail. Here we also review the wines submitted by Di Filippo's Plani Arche winery, where the producer has adopted the same philosophy. Their reds put in an excellent performance, starting with Sagrantino. We very much appreciated the Etnico, but even more so the classic 2015 version. Slightly smoky, earthy and black fruit notes rise up to the nose—in the mouth close-woven tannins are evident but without contracting the palate. It's a wine worthy of our finals. The Passito, another 2015, also delivered. Two years after harvest, the Farandola stands out, as does the delicious Trebbiano Spoletino '18.

Wine	Rating
● Montefalco Sagrantino Passito '15	🍷🍷 6
● Montefalco Rosso Sallustio '16	🍷🍷 3
● Montefalco Sagrantino '15	🍷🍷 6
● Montefalco Sagrantino Etnico '15	🍷🍷 5
○ Trebbiano Spoletino Farandola '18	🍷🍷 2*
⊙ Villa Conversino Rosato '19	🍷🍷 2*
● Villa Conversino Rosso '19	🍷🍷 2*
● Colli Martani Sangiovese Properzio Ris. '17	🍷 4
○ Grechetto '19	🍷 2
● Montefalco Rosso '18	🍷 3
● Sangiovese '19	🍷 2
○ Villa Conversino Bianco '19	🍷 2
● Colli Martani Vernaccia di Cannara '17	🍸🍸 5
○ Grechetto '18	🍸🍸 2*
● Montefalco Rosso '17	🍸🍸 3*

Cantina Dionigi

voc. Madonna della Pia, 92
06031 Bevagna [PG]
Tel. +39 0742360395
www.cantinadionigi.it

CELLAR SALES
PRE-BOOKED VISITS
ACCOMMODATION
ANNUAL PRODUCTION 40,000 bottles
HECTARES UNDER VINE 6.00

Situated in Bevagna, this historic farm in Sagrantino has been dedicated to wine production since 1896. A terrace overlooks the surrounding valleys, amidst vineyards and woods. Here traditional practices continue, both in the vineyard and in the cellar. The simple approach makes for sincere and genuine interpretations, expressions of nature and the culture of the area. Many wines are proposed, some in accordance with local appellations, others made with international grapes. Moraiolo extra-virgin olive oil completes their range of products. Without a doubt the whites proved to be the most impressive of the lot this year, starting with the Goccio '19, a sapid Trebbiano Spoletino and an appealing drink. The Vigna del Brillo '19, a varietal Grechetto from Montefalco, is also delicious. But we shouldn't forget the Chiarina '19, a pervasive and fruity Chardonnay. The rest of their selection also did well.

Wine	Rating
○ Chiarina Chardonnay '19	🍷🍷 3
○ Colli Martani Grechetto V. del Brillo '19	🍷🍷 3
○ Goccio '19	🍷🍷 3
⊙ Rosagrà Rosato '19	🍷🍷 4
● Montefalco Rosso '17	🍷 3
● Montefalco Sagrantino '13	🍷 5
● Montefalco Sagrantino Passito '16	🍷 5
○ Sestum Moscato Secco '17	🍷 3
○ Colli Martani Grechetto V. del Brillo '16	🍸🍸 3
● Merlot Passito Civico 92 '11	🍸🍸 3
● Montefalco Rosso '12	🍸🍸 3
● Montefalco Rosso Ris. '11	🍸🍸 3
● Montefalco Sagrantino Passito '12	🍸🍸 5
○ Passo Greco '11	🍸🍸 3
○ Scialo '11	🍸🍸 3

Duca della Corgna

via Roma, 236
06061 Castiglione del Lago [PG]
Tel. +39 0759652493
www.ducadellacorgna.it

CELLAR SALES
PRE-BOOKED VISITS
ANNUAL PRODUCTION 280,000 bottles
HECTARES UNDER VINE 55.00

Located in Castiglion del Lago (home of the winery and sales point), Duca della Corgna is a benchmark cooperative for the winemakers of Lake Trasimeno. Over the years it's managed to develop a focus on quality, thanks to a respectable managerial staff supported by experienced technicians. The strength of production lies with a grape from the Grenache family but known in the area by the name 'Gamay'. Many versions are produced, from the most delicious vintages to selections with a few years under their belts. Once again the selection submitted didn't disappoint. A number of very good wines were tasted, including the Baccio del Rosso '19. Delicious notes of blackberries and wild strawberries give way to a fresh, supple palate adorned by delicate tannins. The Riserva di Gamay '17 also delivers. The juicy Etichetta Nera del Divina Villa offers up sensations of roses and currants. Finally, among the whites, the new Poggio alla Macchia '18, made with Grechetto, stands out.

● C. del Trasimeno Baccio del Rosso '19	🍷🍷 2*
○ C. del Trasimeno Grechetto Nuricante '19	🍷🍷 3
○ C. del Trasimeno Grechetto Poggio alla Macchia '18	🍷🍷 6
○ Colli del Trasimeno Grechetto Ascanio '19	🍷🍷 2*
● Trasimeno Gamay Divina Villa Ris. '17	🍷🍷 3
○ C. del Trasimeno Baccio del Bianco '19	🍷 2
● C. del Trasimeno Rosso Corniolo Ris. '17	🍷 5
● Trasimeno Gamay Divina Villa '19	🍷 3
○ Ascanio '18	🍷🍷 2*
● C. del Trasimeno Baccio del Rosso '18	🍷🍷 2*
● C. del Trasimeno Rosso Corniolo Ris. '16	🍷🍷 4
● Trasimeno Gamay Divina Villa Ris. '16	🍷🍷 3

Goretti

fraz. Pila
s.da del Pino, 4
06132 Perugia
Tel. +39 075607316
www.vinigoretti.com

PRE-BOOKED VISITS
ANNUAL PRODUCTION 300,000 bottles
HECTARES UNDER VINE 50.00

A family-run business now on its fourth generation, Goretti has its roots in the early-20th century. It's now located just outside Perugia, producing wines that are technically well crafted, faithfully reflecting the varieties used (both native and international), Production is spread over two areas. Part of the property is cultivated around the historic winery, in the Pila estate, while other rows are located in the Montefalco appellations (their Le Mura Saracene line). Given the spaces dedicated to reception and hospitality, tastings, guided tours and cooking classes are organized in their cellar. The Montefalco Rosso Le Mura Saracene '18 is excellent. Fresh and vibrant, it offers up aromas of small fruits and spicy hints. Among the whites the Grechetto dei Colli Perugini '19 stands out: acidity and flavor accompany notes of yellow fruit and wild flowers. Another high level wine is the Arringatore '16, a blend of Sangiovese, Merlot and Ciliegiolo. The rest of their selection also proves well made.

○ Colli Perugini Grechetto '19	🍷🍷 2*
● Colli Perugini Rosso L'Arringatore '16	🍷🍷 5
● Montefalco Rosso Le Mure Saracene '18	🍷🍷 3
● Fontanella Rosso '18	🍷 2
● Montefalco Sagrantino '16	🍷 5
● Colli Perugini Rosso L'Arringatore '16	🍷🍷 5
● Colli Perugini Rosso L'Arringatore '14	🍷🍷 5
● Colli Perugini Rosso L'Arringatore '09	🍷🍷 3
○ Il Moggio '14	🍷🍷 3
● Montefalco Sagrantino '15	🍷🍷 3*
● Montefalco Sagrantino Le Mure Saracene '14	🍷🍷 3*
● Montefalco Sagrantino Le Mure Saracene '11	🍷🍷 3*

Tenute Lunelli - Castelbuono

VOC. CASTELLACCIO, 9
06031 BEVAGNA [PG]
TEL. +39 0742361670
www.tenutelunelli.it

CELLAR SALES
PRE-BOOKED VISITS
ANNUAL PRODUCTION 134,500 bottles
HECTARES UNDER VINE 32.00
VITICULTURE METHOD Certified Organic
SUSTAINABLE WINERY

The Umbrian Lunelli family's winery is about to turn twenty. These historic producers from Trentino (and owners of the great Ferrari sparkling wine brand) have bet on Montefalco with over 30 organically farmed hectares in Bevagna. Their range is dominated by local grapes such as Sagrantino and Sangiovese, with smaller shares of international cultivars used for their Rosso. The Carapace, a splendid architectural design by Arnaldo Pomodoro, surrounds the cellar. It may be a hub of technology, but it's always aimed at respect for the qualities of the grapes and territory. Three reds were presented this year, all outstanding. The Lampante '17 is a Montefalco Rosso Riserva of great complexity: it's impossible not to notice the scents of blackberry, currant and black pepper, all in perfect harmony with a fruity, supple, creamy and dynamic palate. We very much appreciated the youthful Ziggurat '18 and the Sagrantino Carapace '16 as well.

- ● Montefalco Rosso Lampante Ris. '17 — 🍷🍷🍷 5
- ● Montefalco Rosso Ziggurat '18 — 🍷🍷 3*
- ● Montefalco Sagrantino Carapace '16 — 🍷🍷 6
- ● Montefalco Rosso Ziggurat '17 — 🍷🍷🍷 4*
- ● Montefalco Rosso Ziggurat '16 — 🍷🍷🍷 4*
- ● Montefalco Rosso Lampante Ris. '16 — 🍷🍷 5
- ● Montefalco Rosso Lampante Ris. '13 — 🍷🍷 5
- ● Montefalco Sagrantino Carapace '15 — 🍷🍷 6

★Lungarotti

V.LE G. LUNGAROTTI, 2
06089 TORGIANO [PG]
TEL. +39 075988661
www.lungarotti.it

CELLAR SALES
PRE-BOOKED VISITS
ACCOMMODATION AND RESTAURANT SERVICE
ANNUAL PRODUCTION 2,500,000 bottles
HECTARES UNDER VINE 250.00

If the prestige of Umbrian wine is universally recognized, much of the credit must go to the Lungarotti family who have always managed to craft outstanding wines while interpreting the challenges of the sector. Indeed, they are among the few who've been able to adapt without betraying their deep roots. Production is bound up with both the centuries-old estate of Torgiano (where the parent winery is located) and the vineyards of Montefalco, an area where the winery has been focusing of late. Both 2017s stand out. The Sagrantino is rich and gratifying, both on the nose and on the palate, while the Montefalco Rosso proves a fresh and graceful drink. The prize, however, is always the historic Vigna Monticchio. For sure the favorable 2016 vintage contributed to making it so elegant and sophisticated, with a nose that touches on small fruits and spices, while the palate comes through fresh and supple, very long, with perfectly integrated tannins and acidity.

- ● Torgiano Rosso Rubesco V. Monticchio Ris. '16 — 🍷🍷🍷 6
- ● Montefalco Sagrantino '17 — 🍷🍷 5
- ○ M. Cl. Extra Brut 60 Mesi '14 — 🍷🍷 8
- ● Montefalco Rosso '17 — 🍷🍷 3
- ● San Giorgio '17 — 🍷🍷 5
- ○ Torgiano Bianco Torre di Giano '19 — 🍷🍷 2*
- ● Torgiano Rosso Rubesco '18 — 🍷🍷 3
- ● Torgiano Rosso Rubesco V. Monticchio Ris. '15 — 🍷🍷🍷 6
- ● Torgiano Rosso Rubesco V. Monticchio Ris. '13 — 🍷🍷🍷 6
- ● San Giorgio '16 — 🍷🍷 6

Madeleine

RAZ. SCHIFANOIA
.DA MONTINI, 38
)5035 NARNI [TR]
TEL. +39 0744040427
www.cantinalamadeleine.it

CELLAR SALES
PRE-BOOKED VISITS
ANNUAL PRODUCTION 35,000 bottles
HECTARES UNDER VINE 6.40

As they say, 'Make way for youth'. And so it s that siblings Giulia and Francesco find hemselves leading the winery acquired by heir parents Linda and Massimo D'Alema. The brand has remained the same, but a ot has changed in the name of modernization. Mostly non-native grape varieties are cultivated and an international style prevails. They haven't neglected the small patch of land that hosts their seven hectares of vineyards, but rather brought out its best qualities through Pinot Nero, Cabernet Franc and notable Metodo Classico sparklers. And a sparkling wine reached our finals. It's the Il Nerosé 60 (referring to the number of months spent on the lees), a wine that delivers great complexity and length, first in its mix of wild strawberry sensations and hints of pastry, then on a palate where bead and freshness are balanced. Another interesting wine is the Pinot Nero '18, a wine that's graceful in its Mediterranean scents. The Sfide '18 is delicious and pervasive.

◐ Nerosè60 M. Cl.	TT 7
● Pinot Nero '18	TT 6
◐ Nerosé Brut	TT 5
● Sfide '18	TT 3
● NarnOt '15	YY 6
● Pinot Nero '17	YY 6
● Pinot Nero '16	YY 6
● Pinot Nero '15	YY 6
● Pinot Nero '14	YY 6
● Sfide '17	YY 3

Madrevite

LOC. VAIANO
VIA CIMBANO, 36
06061 CASTIGLIONE DEL LAGO [PG]
TEL. +39 0759527220
www.madrevite.com

CELLAR SALES
PRE-BOOKED VISITS
ACCOMMODATION AND RESTAURANT SERVICE
ANNUAL PRODUCTION 25,000 bottles
HECTARES UNDER VINE 11.00
SUSTAINABLE WINERY

Slightly more than 10 hectares of land, an artisan approach and territory: these are the foundations of Madrevite. It's a vision that comes together in a diverse range of white, rosé and red wines (plus a delicious Metodo Ancestrale sparkler) made from both traditional and non-native grape varieties. The main focus is on Gamay, a vine that shares only the name with the Beaujolais grape, belonging instead to the Grenache family. There's also room for Syrah, Sangiovese, Grechetto and Trebbiano Spoletino, making for a selection of distinctive wines closely linked to the microclimate of the lake. Once again the C'osa '18, indubitably one of the best Trasimeno Gamays on the market, lands a place in our finals. Both the nose and palate play on Mediterranean notes, with everything supported by a beautiful acidity. The palate unfolds towards a highly sapid finish—masterfully long. We also appreciated the youthful 2019 version of this unique lake wine.

● Trasimeno Gamay C'osa '18	TT 5
● Trasimeno Gamay '19	TT 5
○ Futura Metodo Ancestrale '19	T 3
○ Il Reminore '19	T 3
● Trasimeno Rosso Glanio '17	T 2
○ Trasimeno Grechetto Èlvé '19	T 5
○ Il Reminore '18	YY 3
● Trasimeno Gamay C'osa '17	YY 5
○ Trasimeno Grechetto Èlvé '18	YY 5

Moretti Omero

Loc. San Sabino, 20
06030 Giano dell'Umbria [PG]
Tel. +39 074290426
www.morettiomero.it

CELLAR SALES
PRE-BOOKED VISITS
ACCOMMODATION AND RESTAURANT SERVICE
ANNUAL PRODUCTION 75,000 bottles
HECTARES UNDER VINE 13.00
VITICULTURE METHOD Certified Organic

Omero Moretti is a skilled and passionate vinedresser who, with the help of his family, cultivates about 13 hectares of vineyards according to organic farming principles. The producer has already passed the quarter-century mark and, in recent years, it's proven capable of forging wines with an artisan style, true expressions of the terroir from which they come. Sometimes there are small inaccuracies, but for their production philosophy it's preferable to follow the course of nature (starting with the vintage) than compromise the unique identity of the wine. A wide range is offered, all falling within the Montefalco appellation. The delicious Sagrantino '16 is among the best versions tasted in recent years: the nose is a whirlwind of blueberry and currant, the palate is fresh, with acidity lending support and driving it towards a long finish. Among the whites we particularly appreciated the Montefalco Bianco '19, with its notes of medlar and its distinct sapidity. The slightly aromatic but dry 'Grechetto e Malvasia' '19, a wine marked by perfect tension, isn't too shabby either.

● Montefalco Sagrantino '16	▼▼ 5
○ Grechetto e Malvasia '19	▼▼ 3
○ Montefalco Bianco '19	▼▼ 3
● Montefalco Rosso '17	▼ 3
○ Sui Lieviti Frizzante	▼ 3
● Argo Passito '12	▽▽ 5
○ Montefalco Bianco '17	▽▽ 3
○ Montefalco Bianco '15	▽▽ 3
● Montefalco Rosso '15	▽▽ 3*
● Montefalco Sagrantino '14	▽▽ 5
● Montefalco Sagrantino '13	▽▽ 5
● Montefalco Sagrantino '12	▽▽ 5
● Montefalco Sagrantino Vignalunga '14	▽▽ 7
● Montefalco Sagrantino Vignalunga '12	▽▽ 7
○ Nessuno '17	▽▽ 3

Enrico Neri

Loc. Bardano, 28
05018 Orvieto [TR]
Tel. +39 3933313844
www.neri-vini.it

CELLAR SALES
PRE-BOOKED VISITS
ACCOMMODATION
ANNUAL PRODUCTION 65,000 bottles
HECTARES UNDER VINE 50.00
SUSTAINABLE WINERY

The Neri family founded their farm in the 1950s with the purchase of about 50 hectares of vineyards and olive groves. Now the winery is run by Enrico, who oversees a range that first saw the light of day in 2000 after many long seasons of grape harvesting. Everything revolves around Orvieto and its traditional grapes while trying to bring out the peculiar expressive characteristics linked to its marine soils, which are rich in shells, fossils and mineral salts. It's a unique geology that's respected by a technically well executed, authentic and racy selection of wines. Once again their selection delivers, both the whites and reds. The Americo '18 is a monovarietal Merlot that grows in Orvieto's clay soil. It's compact and full-bodied, but not lacking in juiciness and suppleness. The Vardano '18 is a sapid Grechetto characterized by sensations of grape skin and ripe apple aromas. Finally the Ca' Viti is a territorial Orvieto '19 that stands out for its distinct sapidity and iodine hints.

● Americo '18	▼▼ 3
○ Orvieto Cl. Sup. Ca' Viti '19	▼▼ 3
○ Vardano Grechetto '18	▼▼ 4
○ Barrage Extra Brut '16	▼ 5
● Rosso dei Neri '19	▼ 3
● Americo '16	▽▽ 3
○ Bardano '18	▽▽ 3
○ Orvieto Cl. Sup. Ca' Viti '18	▽▽ 3*
○ Orvieto Cl. Sup. Ca' Viti '17	▽▽ 2*

La Palazzola

LOC. VASCIGLIANO
05039 STRONCONE [TR]
TEL. +39 0744609091
www.lapalazzola.it

CELLAR SALES
ANNUAL PRODUCTION 150,000 bottles
HECTARES UNDER VINE 28.00

Stefano Grilli is a charismatic vigneron who has transformed the family farm into a winery where experimentation is constantly being carried out. Second fermentation in the bottle is the part on which he's bet the most and, over the years, the producer has become a touchstone for the typology. Several sparklers are produced, in addition to their original late-harvest wines and stills made with international varieties. Theirs are fascinating, characterful interpretations, not without some pleasant imperfections. Indeed that's precisely what sets them apart from the pack. The Vin Santo Occhio di Pernice '13 is truly a great wine for the typology. Splendid oxidative notes light up the nose in a blaze of licorice, dried and candied fruit, hints of undergrowth and dried leaves. It's sweet, but never cloying, endlessly deep. We also appreciated the two sparkling wines: the Metodo Ancestrale '15 (from Pinot Nero) and the Gran Cuvée '16 (from Pinot Nero and Chardonnay).

Wine	Glasses	Price
○ Vin Santo Occhio di Pernice Amelia '13	▼▼	5
○ M. Cl. Gran Cuvée Brut '16	▼▼	5
⊙ Rosé Brut Metodo Ancestrale '15	▼▼	4
● Rubino '16	▼	5
● Merlot '97	▽▽▽	4*
○ Amelia Vin Santo Caratelli al Pozzo '13	▽▽	5
○ Amelia Vin Santo Caratelli al Pozzo '11	▽▽	5
● Amelia Vin Santo Occhio di Pernice '12	▽▽	5
○ Gran Cuvée Brut '13	▽▽	4
○ Riesling Brut '15	▽▽	4
○ Riesling Brut Metodo Ancestrale '12	▽▽	3*
○ Riesling Brut Metodo Ancestrale '11	▽▽	3
⊙ Rosé Brut '10	▽▽	4
● Syrah '14	▽▽	4
○ Verdello '14	▽▽	3*

Palazzone

LOC. ROCCA RIPESENA, 68
05019 ORVIETO [TR]
TEL. +39 0763344921
www.palazzone.com

CELLAR SALES
PRE-BOOKED VISITS
ACCOMMODATION AND RESTAURANT SERVICE
ANNUAL PRODUCTION 130,000 bottles
HECTARES UNDER VINE 24.00
SUSTAINABLE WINERY

Led by Giovanni Dubini, Palazzone is one of the Orvieto wineries that most believed in the area. A focus on the territory centers on highlighting the attributes of the its traditional grapes, which are explored through a stylistically precise style that's also faithful to the great white wine terroir. Freshness and sapidity accompany a remarkable capacity for aging, making for thrills even years after vintage. It's all carried out with that special mix of humility and sensitivity that only the great vigneron possess. The 2019 whites stand out among the lot. The Campo del Guardiano was absent, but we appreciated both the Terre Vineate and the Grechetto. The real surprise, however, was the Musco '17. Made with Procanico, Verdello and Malvasia grown in a single vineyard, it matures first in chestnut, then in glass demijohns. Candied citrus and spices, mountain flowers and helichrysum rise up to the nose; on the palate it's sapid, slightly marked by sensations of grape skin, and very long.

Wine	Glasses	Price
○ Musco '17	▼▼	6
○ Grechetto '19	▼▼	3
○ Orvieto Cl. Sup. Terre Vineate '19	▼▼	3
○ Orvieto Cl. Sup. Muffa Nobile '17	▼	5
● Piviere '18	▼	3
○ Viognier '19	▼	3
○ Musco '16	▽▽	6
○ Orvieto Cl. Sup. Campo del Guardiano '17	▽▽	4
○ Orvieto Cl. Sup. V. T. '17	▽▽	4
● Piviere '16	▽▽	3
○ Viognier '18	▽▽	3

F.lli Pardi

via G. Pascoli, 7/9
06036 Montefalco [PG]
Tel. +39 0742379023
www.cantinapardi.it

CELLAR SALES
PRE-BOOKED VISITS
ANNUAL PRODUCTION 56,000 bottles
HECTARES UNDER VINE 11.00

This Pardi family's history in the textile industry goes way back, and they've invested with the same determination in the wine sector. The winery, which is situated in Montefalco, carries on exemplary work with Sagrantino, delving deeper and deeper into the potential of veritable estate crus. With meticulous care they've managed to express the nuances of the various soil types and positions. Their Montefalco Rosso and whites have also consistently proven excellent. Pardi's entire selection put in a superlative performance, with two wines landing in our finals, the Sagrantino and the Sacrantino, both 2016s. They impress for their finesse, elegance and depth. The Spoletino '18 is a concentrate of marine and iodine scents, the prelude to a sapid and pervasive palate. We also appreciated the simpler, but impeccable, Colle di Giove '19 and Montefalco Rosso '18.

● Montefalco Sagrantino '16	🍷🍷 6
● Montefalco Sagrantino Sacrantino '16	🍷🍷 6
○ Colle di Giove '19	🍷🍷 2*
● Montefalco Rosso '18	🍷🍷 3
○ Spoleto Trebbiano Spoletino '18	🍷🍷 4
● Montefalco Sagrantino Sacrantino '14	YYY 6
○ Montefalco Grechetto '18	YY 2*
● Montefalco Rosso Ris. '16	YY 4
● Montefalco Sagrantino '15	YY 5
○ Spoleto Trebbiano Spoletino '17	YY 4

Cantina Peppucci

loc. Sant'Antimo
fraz. Petroro, 4
06059 Todi [PG]
Tel. +39 0758947439
www.cantinapeppucci.com

CELLAR SALES
PRE-BOOKED VISITS
ACCOMMODATION
ANNUAL PRODUCTION 70,000 bottles
HECTARES UNDER VINE 12.50

We find Peppucci in the hills of Todi, surrounded by vineyards in a landscape of unquestionable charm. The manor house also hosts their production facility, which the family has utilized with such determination that in recent years they've become an absolute benchmark for regional wine-growing. Young Filippo manages the daily work, focusing mainly on Grechetto, an absolute cornerstone in these parts. Among their reds, however, a number of different varieties are treated, from international Cabernet Sauvignon to an interesting 'outsider' Sagrantino. The I Rovi '18, a Grechetto di Todi, once again demonstrates that it's their great white wine. Notes of white flowers, citrus peel and aromatic herbs rise up out of the glass; the palate is fresh and lean, with sapidity driving it towards a precise, clean finish. We also appreciated the Grechetto Montorsolo '19, which proves pleasant in its jovial simplicity, as well as a convincing and personal interpretation of Sagrantino, the l'Altro Io '15.

○ Todi Grechetto I Rovi '18	🍷🍷 5
● Altro Io '15	🍷🍷 5
○ Todi Grechetto Montorsolo '19	🍷🍷 2*
● Todi Rosso Petroro 4 '19	🍷 2
○ Todi Grechetto I Rovi '16	YYY 5
● Giovanni '13	YY 4
● Giovanni '12	YY 4
○ Todi Grechetto Sup. I Rovi '17	YY 5
● Todi Rosso Petroro 4 '18	YY 2*
● Todi Rosso Petroro 4 '17	YY 2*

Perticaia

Loc. Casale
06036 Montefalco [PG]
Tel. +39 0742379014
www.perticaia.it

CELLAR SALES
PRE-BOOKED VISITS
ANNUAL PRODUCTION 250,000 bottles
HECTARES UNDER VINE 50.00
SUSTAINABLE WINERY

There are now many wineries operating in Montefalco, but some of them must be considered essential benchmarks. Among these we'd have to count Perticaia, founded by Guido Guardigli twenty years ago and now managed by a group of local entrepreneurs. The winery is located in the lovely town of Casale, an area highly suited to the area's principal reds, with Sagrantino and Sangiovese serving as cornerstones. Soil and microclimate are also favorable to Trebbiano Spoletino and it's this traditional grape that's provided the most surprises of late. In this edition, however, we saw a very different side. Some wines presented were already tasted last year. But we still appreciated the Montefalco Rosso Riserva, a wine of superb body, made harmonious by sapidity and tannins that are never contracted or bitter. The nose is a whirlwind of black fruit, spices and minty hints. We also appreciated the Del Posto, a dynamic, highly flavorful Spoletino.

● Montefalco Rosso Ris. '16	🍷🍷 4
○ Spoleto Trebbiano Spoletino Del Posto '18	🍷🍷 4
○ Spoleto Trebbiano Spoletino '19	🍷 3
● Montefalco Rosso '15	🍷🍷 3
● Montefalco Rosso '14	🍷🍷 3
● Montefalco Sagrantino '15	🍷🍷 5
● Montefalco Sagrantino '14	🍷🍷 5
● Montefalco Sagrantino '13	🍷🍷 5
● Montefalco Sagrantino '12	🍷🍷 5
⊙ Rosato Cos'é '16	🍷🍷 2*
○ Spoleto Trebbiano Spoletino '18	🍷🍷 2*
○ Spoleto Trebbiano Spoletino '15	🍷🍷 2*
○ Spoleto Trebbiano Spoletino Del Posto '17	🍷🍷 2*
● Umbria Rosso '16	🍷🍷 2*

Pomario

Loc. Pomario
06066 Piegaro [PG]
Tel. +39 0758358579
www.pomario.it

CELLAR SALES
PRE-BOOKED VISITS
RESTAURANT SERVICE
ANNUAL PRODUCTION 15,000 bottles
HECTARES UNDER VINE 8.00
VITICULTURE METHOD Certified Organic
SUSTAINABLE WINERY

Harvest after harvest, Pomario is carving out an important place in the region. Founded 15 years ago by the Spalletti Trivelli family, the small producer operates in an impressive landscape, with the main vineyards located at about 500 meters above sea level, amidst Mediterranean scrub and rock. Here on the border with Tuscany, in the town of Piegaro, the microclimate, combined with the soil, leaves its marks on the wines. In the cellar everything is carried out in the name of environmental sustainability, respecting each wine's varietal and territorial characteristics. Once again at the top of the rankings we find the Sariano '17, a superbly fresh red made with Sangiovese. Blood-scented sensations of iron, bark and noble resins stand out on the nose, anticipating a pervasive and austere palate. Made with Sangiovese and a share of Merlot, the Rubicola '19 proves youthful and juicy. The Arale '19, finally, is a particular white made with macerated Trebbiano and Malvasia grapes.

● Sariano '17	🍷🍷 4
○ Arale '19	🍷🍷 4
● Rubicola '19	🍷🍷 2*
○ Batticoda '19	🍷 2
○ Arale '17	🍷🍷 4
○ Arale '15	🍷🍷 4
○ Arale '14	🍷🍷 4
○ Batticoda '18	🍷🍷 2*
○ Muffato delle Streghe '16	🍷🍷 6
○ Muffato delle Streghe '15	🍷🍷 6
● Rubicola '18	🍷🍷 2*
● Rubicola '17	🍷🍷 2*
● Sariano '16	🍷🍷 3*
● Sariano '15	🍷🍷 3
● Sariano '13	🍷🍷 3
● Sariano '12	🍷🍷 3
● Sariano '11	🍷🍷 3

Roccafiore

FRAZ. CHIOANO
VOC. COLLINA, 110A
06059 TODI [PG]
TEL. +39 0758942746
www.roccafiorewines.com

CELLAR SALES
PRE-BOOKED VISITS
ACCOMMODATION AND RESTAURANT SERVICE
ANNUAL PRODUCTION 120,000 bottles
HECTARES UNDER VINE 15.00
SUSTAINABLE WINERY

Here they don't just produce wine. There's also a resort with restaurant and a spa as well as beautiful wood flats. At Roccafiore everything is studied down to the last detail. But above all, we find deep respect for the environment and an emphasis on sustainability that are perfectly expressed in their wines. Stylistically impeccable, clear, focused and elegant, they transmit the character and peculiarities of Todi's vineyards, especially when it comes to Grechetto, which is offered in different versions. It's a wine that can be appreciated both when young and after a few years in the bottle. Once again the Grechetto FiorFiore proves to be a great wine. The 2018 manages to combine complexity and elegance, depth and sophistication: sensations of aromatic herbs and citrus herald a fresh and flavorful palate. A well deserved Tre Bicchieri. The Collina d'Oro '19 also delivers. Made with Moscato Giallo grapes, it's a sweet wine of great balance. The other wines tasted also exhibit fine craftsmanship.

○ Fiorfiore Grechetto '18	🍷🍷🍷 4*
○ Collina d'Oro '19	🍷🍷 5
● Il Roccafiore '17	🍷🍷 3
● Prova d'Autore '17	🍷🍷 5
○ Fiordaliso Grechetto '19	🍷 2
● Melograno Sangiovese '18	🍷 2
○ Fiorfiore '16	ΥΥΥ 4*
● Il Roccafiore '16	ΥΥΥ 3*
○ Todi Grechetto Sup. Fiorfiore '14	ΥΥΥ 3*
○ Bianco Fiordaliso '18	ΥΥ 2*
○ Collina d'Oro '18	ΥΥ 5
○ Collina d'Oro '17	ΥΥ 5
○ Fiorfiore '17	ΥΥ 4
● Il Roccafiore '15	ΥΥ 3*
● Prova d'Autore '16	ΥΥ 5
● Prova d'Autore '15	ΥΥ 5
● Rosso Melograno '16	ΥΥ 2*

Romanelli

LOC. COLLE SAN CLEMENTE, 129A
06036 MONTEFALCO [PG]
TEL. +39 0742371245
www.romanelli.se

CELLAR SALES
PRE-BOOKED VISITS
ANNUAL PRODUCTION 48,000 bottles
HECTARES UNDER VINE 7.50
VITICULTURE METHOD Certified Organic

The Romanelli family's farm is a solid agricultural producer founded in the late seventies. Of late, it has distinguished itself for a range wines that's interesting, to say the least, proving capable of faithfully transmitting the territory of Montefalco, especially when it comes to their reds. If the remarkable structure of their wines is always mitigated by freshness and flavor, much of the credit has to go to their vineyards. Located in Colle San Clemente, on clay, silt soil at elevations of around 350 meters, they are complemented in the cellar by an approach that favors long maceration, which facilitates balanced extraction. The selection presented this year is truly surprising, with two wines making it to our finals. The Medeo '16 is a Sagrantino of great elegance and finesse: the nose is a whirlwind of fruit and spices, the palate is pervasive and silky, with tannins discernible but well integrated. Le Tese '18 is a sapid, characterful Trebbiano Spoletino. The other reds tasted are also very good.

● Montefalco Sagrantino Medeo '16	🍷🍷🍷 8
○ Spoleto Trebbiano Spoletino Le Tese '18	🍷🍷 5
● Montefalco Rosso '17	🍷🍷 3
● Montefalco Rosso Molinetta Ris. '16	🍷🍷 5
● Montefalco Sagrantino '16	🍷🍷 6
○ Colli Martani Grechetto '19	🍷 3
● Montefalco Sagrantino '11	ΥΥΥ 5
● Montefalco Sagrantino '10	ΥΥΥ 5
○ Colli Martani Grechetto '18	ΥΥ 2*
○ Le Tese Trebbiano Spoletino '17	ΥΥ 4
○ Le Tese Trebbiano Spoletino '16	ΥΥ 4
● Montefalco Rosso '16	ΥΥ 3
● Montefalco Rosso Molinetta Ris. '15	ΥΥ 5
● Montefalco Sagrantino '15	ΥΥ 5
● Montefalco Sagrantino '14	ΥΥ 5
● Montefalco Sagrantino Medeo '15	ΥΥ 8

Scacciadiavoli

LOC. CANTINONE, 31
06036 MONTEFALCO [PG]
TEL. +39 0742371210
www.scacciadiavoli.it

CELLAR SALES
PRE-BOOKED VISITS
ANNUAL PRODUCTION 250,000 bottles
HECTARES UNDER VINE 40.00
SUSTAINABLE WINERY

If we want to talk about Scacciadiavoli's origins, we'd have to go back two centuries, to when Prince Ugo Boncompagni Ludovisi brought an impressive winemaking complex to life. Since the 1950s the winery has been in the hands of the Panbuffetti family and it's now managed by three siblings. The turning point came in the 2000s, with the modernization of production and a desire to focus on territorial identity. The vineyards, which grow in clayey soils at 400 meters above sea level, can be found on different hillsides in the municipalities of Montefalco, Gualdo Cattaneo and Giano dell'Umbria. This year's selection put in an excellent performance, especially the reds. The Sagrantino '16 is a true prize. Aromas of black pepper, plum and resins give way to a close-woven, austere palate, with tannins discernible but not contracted, lending rhythm and depth. The Passito '16, which perfectly harmonizes sweetness and savoriness, also delivers. We also appreciated the Montefalco Rosso '17.

Wine	Rating	
● Montefalco Sagrantino '16	▼▼	5
● Montefalco Rosso '17	▼▼	3
● Montefalco Sagrantino Passito '16	▼▼	5
○ Montefalco Bianco '18	▼	3
○ Montefalco Grechetto '19	▼	2
● Montefalco Sagrantino '10	▽▽▽	5
○ Montefalco Bianco '17	▽▽	3
○ Montefalco Bianco '14	▽▽	3
○ Montefalco Bianco '13	▽▽	3
● Montefalco Rosso '15	▽▽	3
● Montefalco Rosso '12	▽▽	3
● Montefalco Sagrantino '15	▽▽	5
● Montefalco Sagrantino '13	▽▽	5
● Montefalco Sagrantino '12	▽▽	5
● Montefalco Sagrantino '11	▽▽	5
● Montefalco Sagrantino '09	▽▽	5
● Montefalco Sagrantino Passito '12	▽▽	5

Sportoletti

VIA LOMBARDIA, 1
06038 SPELLO [PG]
TEL. +39 0742651461
www.sportoletti.com

CELLAR SALES
PRE-BOOKED VISITS
ANNUAL PRODUCTION 210,000 bottles
HECTARES UNDER VINE 25.00
SUSTAINABLE WINERY

Sportoletti was founded in the late 1970s and immediately chose to pursue quality. To do this it's dedicated resources to continuously modernizing and updating the property and its management, both when it comes to the vineyard and the cellar. Native and international grapes, all grown on the beautiful hills of Spello, form the groundwork. The result is a range of modern and technically well-made wines, impeccably clean and able to respect the varieties used. Five wines were presented: two whites, two reds and a passito. The Assisi Rosso '19 is a simple but not trivial wine, juicy on the palate and characterized by clean, precise olfactory sensations. It's worth more than the price tag. The Grechetto '19 is excellent, citrusy, with notes of aromatic herbs. The Villa Fidelia Bianco '18 isn't afraid to age—two years after harvest it's still intact and dynamic. The Villa Fidelia Rosso '18 also performed well.

Wine	Rating	
○ Assisi Grechetto '19	▼▼	2*
● Assisi Rosso '19	▼▼	2*
○ Villa Fidelia Bianco '18	▼▼	3
○ Villa Fidelia Passito '18	▼	4
● Villa Fidelia Rosso '18	▼	4
● Villa Fidelia Rosso '98	▽▽▽	4*
○ Assisi Grechetto '18	▽▽	1*
● Assisi Rosso '15	▽▽	2*
● Assisi Rosso '14	▽▽	2*
○ Villa Fidelia Bianco '17	▽▽	3
○ Villa Fidelia Bianco '16	▽▽	3
○ Villa Fidelia Bianco '15	▽▽	3
○ Villa Fidelia Bianco '14	▽▽	3
● Villa Fidelia Rosso '17	▽▽	4
● Villa Fidelia Rosso '16	▽▽	4
● Villa Fidelia Rosso '15	▽▽	4
● Villa Fidelia Rosso '14	▽▽	4

★Giampaolo Tabarrini

FRAZ. TURRITA
06036 MONTEFALCO [PG]
TEL. +39 0742379351
www.tabarrini.com

CELLAR SALES
PRE-BOOKED VISITS
ANNUAL PRODUCTION 70,000 bottles
HECTARES UNDER VINE 16.00
SUSTAINABLE WINERY

Around here Giampaolo Tabarrini needs no introduction. He's an explosive presence in the vineyard, even more so in the cellar, especially now that his new, large underground structure allows for perfect execution, capturing in the bottle the attributes of his grapes. Giampaolo is convinced of wine's territorial value, which is why he proposes some three different Sagrantinos, all referring back to their respective vineyard of origin. These exhibit power and drinkability, have character in spades and have even conquered international markets. Reds dominate, but his white Trebbiano Spoletino mustn't be missed. And this year it's precisely this wine that stood out as the best tasted. The Adarmando '18 is truly paradigmatic for the typology. The nose is unique, going all in on iodine notes and smoky hints, which anticipate aromas of herbs and flowers. The palate is highly sapid, lean, unfolding linearly, while the finish comes through clean, almost spicy, and very long. Among the reds we appreciated both the Campo alla Cerqua and the Colle alle Macchie '16.

○ Adarmando Trebbiano Spoletino '18	🍷🍷🍷 4*
● Montefalco Sagrantino Campo alla Cerqua '16	🍷🍷 7
● Montefalco Sagrantino Colle alle Macchie '16	🍷🍷 7
⊙ Bocca di Rosa '19	🍷🍷 2*
● Montefalco Rosso Boccatone '17	🍷🍷 4
● Montefalco Sagrantino Colle Grimaldesco '16	🍷🍷 5
● Montefalco Sagrantino Passito '11	🍷 7
○ Adarmando '16	🍷🍷🍷 4*
○ Adarmando '15	🍷🍷🍷 4*
○ Adarmando Trebbiano Spoletino '17	🍷🍷🍷 4*
● Montefalco Sagrantino Campo alla Cerqua '12	🍷🍷🍷 6
● Montefalco Sagrantino Campo alla Cerqua '11	🍷🍷🍷 6

Terre de la Custodia

LOC. PALOMBARA
06035 GUALDO CATTANEO [PG]
TEL. +39 0742929586
www.terredelacustodia.it

CELLAR SALES
PRE-BOOKED VISITS
ANNUAL PRODUCTION 1,000,000 bottles
HECTARES UNDER VINE 160.00
SUSTAINABLE WINERY

The Farchioni family lead an important agri-food group in which flour and beer are flanked by the their main product, oil, and their Terre de la Custodia wine brand. Focused mainly on traditional grape varieties, it features a modern, precise enological style that's managed to conquer certain foreign markets in an impressive way. Their vineyards are divided between Montefalco (where Sagrantino, Sangiovese and Grechetto are cultivated) and Colli Martani, which gives rise to their Metodo Classico sparkler. The Montefalco Sagrantino '16 earned a place in our finals. Bolstered by an excellent vintage, the great Umbrian red unleashes aromas of spices, noble resins and black fruit; the palate comes through dense, while tannins are present, but never bitter. We also appreciated the Grechetto '19, fresh and sapid, with notes of mint and white fruit. Finally, the Montefalco Rosso Riserva '17 proves warm and pervasive, creamy, with notes of cherry, plum, black pepper and undergrowth. The Rosato '19 is pleasant and on point.

● Montefalco Sagrantino '16	🍷🍷 6
○ Montefalco Grechetto '19	🍷🍷 3
● Montefalco Rosso Ris. '17	🍷🍷 5
⊙ Rosato '19	🍷 2
● Montefalco Sagrantino '15	🍷🍷🍷 6
○ Colli Martani Grechetto '14	🍷🍷 2*
○ Colli Martani Grechetto Plentis '14	🍷🍷 3
○ Colli Martani Spumante Gladius Sublimis	🍷🍷 4
○ Montefalco Bianco Plentis '17	🍷🍷 3
● Montefalco Rosso '12	🍷🍷 4
● Montefalco Rosso Ris. '13	🍷🍷 5
● Montefalco Rosso Rubium Ris. '16	🍷🍷 5
● Montefalco Rosso Rubium Ris. '15	🍷🍷 5
● Montefalco Rosso Rubium Ris. '14	🍷🍷 5
● Montefalco Sagrantino '11	🍷🍷 6
○ Sublimis Gladius Brut M. Cl. '10	🍷🍷 4

Terre Margaritelli

fraz. Chiusaccia
loc. Miralduolo
06089 Torgiano [PG]
Tel. +39 0757824668
www.terremargaritelli.com

CELLAR SALES
PRE-BOOKED VISITS
ACCOMMODATION
ANNUAL PRODUCTION 120,000 bottles
HECTARES UNDER VINE 52.00
VITICULTURE METHOD Certified Organic

The Margaritelli family deals in the world of wood as well as the production of quality wine within the district of Torgiano. In recent years, especially, the level of their wines has grown notably, exhibiting a more territorial character and pleasantness. The appellation's classic grapes (Sangiovese and Grechetto) are flanked by traditional varieties from central Italy and international cultivars. Moreover, their main activity (wood) has allowed them to experiment with the best oak for the maturation of their premium wines. This year they submitted a top-notch selection for tasting. The Pictoricius '17 is a highly sophisticated Torigano Riserva. Compact and full-bodied on the palate, it still has some youthful roughness. Tannins need to blend with its rich matière, but freshness and flavor are certainly well represented. The Malot '17, made with Cabernet Sauvignon and Merlot grapes, is also very good. Among the whites, the Greco di Renabianca '19 stands out.

● Malot '17	▼▼ 4
● Torgiano Rosso Pictoricius Ris. '17	▼▼ 8
○ Greco di Renabianca '19	▼▼ 4
● Lab '19	▼▼ 3
○ Pietramala '19	▼ 2
● Roccascossa '18	▼ 2
● Simon de Brion '19	▼ 3
⊙ Thadea Brut Rosé	▼ 3
○ Torgiano Bianco Costellato '19	▼ 3
● Torgiano Rosso Freccia degli Scacchi Ris. '17	▼ 5
● Torgiano Rosso Miràntico '18	▼ 3
● Torgiano Rosso Pinturicchio Ris. '16	▽▽▽ 5
● Torgiano Rosso Freccia degli Scacchi Ris. '16	▽▽ 5
● Torgiano Rosso Mirantico '17	▽▽ 2*

Todini

fraz. Rosceto
voc. Collina 29/1
06059 Todi [PG]
Tel. +39 075887122
www.wearetodini.com

CELLAR SALES
PRE-BOOKED VISITS
ACCOMMODATION AND RESTAURANT SERVICE
ANNUAL PRODUCTION 250,000 bottles
HECTARES UNDER VINE 70.00

Founded in the sixties at the behest of entrepreneur Franco Todini, this Todi business has developed various activities, from wine to hospitality (with a boutique hotel, spa and restaurant), not to mention farm produce and a natural zoo where many species live freely. In recent years, their aim has been to revive winemaking, which draws on the district's classic grape varieties (foremost Grechetto and Sangiovese) and is starting to bear fruit in a convincing way. The Bianco del Cavaliere '19, 100% Grechetto, earned a place in our finals. Redolent of medlar and yellow flowers, a nice touch of citrus and mountain herbs also emerge, while acidity and flavor dominate the palate. The Consolare '16, a red made with Sangiovese, Merlot and Cabernet Sauvignon, proves close-knit and austere. We also appreciated the Laudato '18, a rich and pervasive white.

○ Bianco del Cavaliere '19	▼▼ 3*
● Consolare '16	▼▼ 6
○ Laudato '18	▼▼ 5
● Rubro '18	▼ 4
○ Bianco del Cavaliere '18	▽▽ 3
○ Grechetto di Todi Bianco del Cavaliere Sup. '16	▽▽ 3
○ Laudato '17	▽▽ 3*
○ Marte Bianco '15	▽▽ 2*
● Marte Rosso '15	▽▽ 3
● Nero della Cervara '13	▽▽ 5
● Rubro '16	▽▽ 3
● Sangiovese di Todi '15	▽▽ 1*
○ Todi Grechetto '15	▽▽ 2*
○ Todi Grechetto Sup. Bianco del Cavaliere '14	▽▽ 3
● Todi Sangiovese '14	▽▽ 4

Tudernum

Loc. Pian di Porto, 146
06059 Todi [PG]
Tel. +39 0758989403
www.tudernum.it

CELLAR SALES
PRE-BOOKED VISITS
ACCOMMODATION AND RESTAURANT SERVICE
ANNUAL PRODUCTION 1,000,000 bottles
HECTARES UNDER VINE 180.00

As with other regions, in Umbria there's no shortage of commendable cooperative wineries. Through painstaking work in collaboration with local growers, Tudernum shapes quality wines capable of capturing varietal peculiarities and territorial identity. Without a doubt the credit goes to the entire management team, who do an outstanding job following production, marketing and sales. In this regard, it's worth pointing out the accessible prices (to say the least) that characterize a range focused mainly on the Montefalco and Todi denominations. The Colle Nobile '18 is a great Grechetto di Todi. The variety is fully expressed, starting with the nose, a whirlwind of medicinal herbs, citrus peel and yellow flowers; the palate has flavor to sell, but everything is well integrated. Tre Bicchieri. The rest of their selection also performed on high levels, starting with the Fidenzio, a Montefalco Sagrantino that hearkens back to the favorable 2016 vintage. We found all the 2019s very pleasant.

○ Todi Grechetto Sup. Colle Nobile '18	🍷🍷🍷 2*
● Montefalco Sagrantino Fidenzio '16	🍷🍷 5
○ Todi Bianco '18	🍷🍷 2*
○ Todi Grechetto '19	🍷🍷 2*
● Todi Rosso '19	🍷🍷 2*
● Todi Sangiovese '17	🍷 2
● Montefalco Sagrantino Fidenzio '12	🍷🍷🍷 4*
○ Colli Martani Grechetto di Todi Sup. Colle Nobile '17	🍷🍷 2*
● Montefalco Rosso Fidenzo '16	🍷🍷 4
● Montefalco Sagrantino Fidenzio '15	🍷🍷 4
● Montefalco Sagrantino Fidenzio '14	🍷🍷 4
○ Todi Grechetto Sup. Colle Nobile '16	🍷🍷 2*
● Todi Rosso '18	🍷🍷 2*
● Todi Rosso Sup. Rojano '16	🍷🍷 3
○ Todi Bianco '18	🍷 2

Tenuta Le Velette

Fraz. Canale di Orvieto
Loc. Le Velette, 23
05019 Orvieto [TR]
Tel. +39 076329090
www.levelette.it

CELLAR SALES
PRE-BOOKED VISITS
ANNUAL PRODUCTION 270,000 bottles
HECTARES UNDER VINE 109.00
SUSTAINABLE WINERY

Le Velette avails itself of 100 hectares of vineyards in Orvieto, in an area characterized by volcanic soil. It's a producer that, over the years, has managed to offer wines that are technically impeccable, owing to the terroir of provenance, but also intelligible to international consumers. The property is owned by the Bottai family, who have created an extremely well-functioning cellar adorned with historic 'aging caves'. Charming and worth a visit, they also serve as the perfect place to better appreciate Le Velette's reliable portfolio of wines. Among the reds, the Calanco '15 stands out. Made with Sangiovese and Cabernet, it features herbaceous aromas and a compact, fresh palate. The Rosso di Spicca '18, a blend of mostly Sangiovese (with a share of Canaiolo), is also excellent. Among the whites we particularly appreciated the Sauvignon Traluce '19, the Orvieto Lunato '19 and the Sole Uve '17, a Grechetto of great character.

● Calanco '15	🍷🍷 4
○ Orvieto Cl. Sup. Lunato '19	🍷🍷 2*
● Rosso Orvietano Rosso di Spicca '18	🍷🍷 2*
○ Sole Uve '17	🍷🍷 3
○ Traluce '19	🍷🍷 3
● Accordo Sangiovese '15	🍷 3
○ Orvieto Cl. Berganorio '19	🍷 2
● Calanco '03	🍷🍷🍷 4
● Calanco '95	🍷🍷🍷 4*
● Gaudio '03	🍷🍷🍷 4
● Calanco '13	🍷🍷 4
● Gaudio '14	🍷🍷 4
○ Orvieto Cl. Berganorio '18	🍷🍷 2*
○ Orvieto Cl. Berganorio '17	🍷🍷 2*
○ Orvieto Cl. Sup. Lunato '18	🍷🍷 2*
○ Orvieto Cl. Sup. Lunato '17	🍷🍷 2*
○ Sole Uve '16	🍷🍷 3

Villa Mongalli

via della Cima, 52
06031 Bevagna [PG]
Tel. +39 0742360703
www.villamongalli.com

CELLAR SALES
ACCOMMODATION
ANNUAL PRODUCTION 70,000 bottles
HECTARES UNDER VINE 15.00

Before tasting their wines, we suggest a visit to the cellar. It's immersed in an enchanting landscape, where nature is interspersed with undulating vineyards. The producer focuses on Montefalco through an approach that privileges indigenous yeasts, measured extraction and attentive maceration. The result guarantees elegance and drinkability, even with Sagrantino, which is proposed in two interesting versions. The whites feature Trebbiano Spoletino, a variety that's increasingly central to their selection. This year Villa Mongalli submitted an outstanding selection. The harmonious and balanced Sagrantino Della Cima '16 is redolent of tobacco, noble resins, spices and undergrowth, while the palate features close-knit, though not astringent, tannins; acidity lends freshness, making for a long, clean drink. Both the Trebbiano Spoletinos submitted are delicious, with the Minganna '18 proving more assertive in its notes of candied citrus and curry plant. We found the Montefalco Rosso Le Grazie '18 to be very pleasant.

● Montefalco Sagrantino della Cima '16	TT 8
○ Calicanto Trebbiano Spoletino '19	TT 5
○ Minganna Trebbiano Spoletino '18	TT 6
● Montefalco Rosso Le Grazie '18	TT 5
● Colcimino '17	T 7
● Montefalco Sagrantino Pozzo del Curato '16	T 7
● Montefalco Sagrantino Colcimino '08	YYY 3*
● Montefalco Sagrantino Della Cima '10	YYY 8
● Montefalco Sagrantino Della Cima '06	YYY 6
● Montefalco Sagrantino Pozzo del Curato '09	YYY 6
○ Calicanto '18	YY 5
● Montefalco Rosso Le Grazie '17	YY 5
● Montefalco Sagrantino Pozzo del Curato '15	YY 8
● Montefalco Sagrantino Della Cima '15	Y 8

Zanchi

s.da prov.le Amelia-Orte Km 4,610
05022 Amelia [TR]
Tel. +39 0744970011
www.cantinezanchi.it

CELLAR SALES
PRE-BOOKED VISITS
ANNUAL PRODUCTION 70,000 bottles
HECTARES UNDER VINE 35.00
VITICULTURE METHOD Certified Organic
SUSTAINABLE WINERY

Fifty years have passed since its foundation and Zanchi continues to make wines of great charm, obtained with a craftsman's approach while eschewing conventional modes and styles. Here in Amelia, in the south of Umbria, for three generations they've been producing wines using native grapes, and some international ones as well, according to a sustainable and environmentally friendly approach (both in the vineyard and the cellar). Their range is wide, divided equally between whites and reds, while some bottles hit the market several years after vintage, thus demonstrating the aging potential of certain local grapes. Two wines stood out during our tastings. The Carmìno '19 is youthful and juicy Ciliegiolo di Amelia with great character. Then there's the Majolo '15, a Malvasia white. The courageous decision to release it five years after harvest paid off as the wine features an original expressiveness. Varietal notes interweave with flowery and fruity sensations, while a fresh palate comes through slightly tannic with a sapid finish.

● Amelia Ciliegiolo Carmìno '19	TT 2*
○ Majolo '15	TT 5
● Amelia Rosso Sciurio Ris. '12	T 4
○ Arvore Grechetto '19	T 2
● Lu Aleatico '17	T 3
○ Vignavecchia Trebbiano '15	T 5
● Amelia Ciliegiolo Carmìno '18	YY 2*
● Amelia Ciliegiolo Carmìno '17	YY 2*
● Amelia Ciliegiolo Carmìno '16	YY 2*
○ Amelia Grechetto Arvore '17	YY 2*
○ Amelia Grechetto Arvore '16	YY 2*
● Amelia Rosso Armané '13	YY 2*
● Amelia Rosso Sciurio Ris. '09	YY 4
○ Arvore Grechetto '18	YY 2*
● Lu Aleatico '16	YY 3
○ Majolo '10	YY 5
○ Vignavecchia '12	YY 5

Cantina Altarocca

loc. Rocca Ripesena, 62
05018 Orvieto [TR]
Tel. +39 0763344210
www.cantinaaltarocca.com

CELLAR SALES
PRE-BOOKED VISITS
ACCOMMODATION AND RESTAURANT SERVICE
ANNUAL PRODUCTION 50,000 bottles
HECTARES UNDER VINE 11.00
VITICULTURE METHOD Certified Organic
SUSTAINABLE WINERY

- ● Lavico '17 🍷🍷 4
- ○ Orvieto Cl. Sup. Albaco '19 🍷🍷 3
- ○ Orvieto Cl. Arcosesto '19 🍷 2
- ● Rosso d'Altarocca Merlot '17 🍷 6

Bartoloni

loc. Case Sparse
fraz. Moriano
06030 Giano dell'Umbria [PG]
Tel. +39 074290286
info@cantinabartoloni.it

CELLAR SALES
PRE-BOOKED VISITS
ACCOMMODATION
ANNUAL PRODUCTION 40,000 bottles
HECTARES UNDER VINE 8.00

- ● Montefalco Rosso '17 🍷🍷 3
- ● Il Nobile Sangiovese '18 🍷 3

Benedetti & Grigi

loc. La Polzella
06036 Montefalco [PG]
Tel. +39 0742379136
www.benedettiegrigi.it

CELLAR SALES
ANNUAL PRODUCTION 400,000 bottles
HECTARES UNDER VINE 68.00

- ○ Spoleto Trebbiano Spoletino '19 🍷🍷 3*
- ○ La Gaita del Falco Bianco '19 🍷🍷 2*
- ● Montefalco Sagrantino La Gaita del Falco '15 🍷🍷 4

Bigi

loc. Ponte Giulio
05018 Orvieto [TR]
Tel. +39 0763315888
www.cantinebigi.it

PRE-BOOKED VISITS
ANNUAL PRODUCTION 3,500,000 bottles
HECTARES UNDER VINE 194.00

- ○ Orvieto Cl. '19 🍷🍷 1*
- ○ Orvieto Cl. Torricella '19 🍷🍷 2*
- ○ Vipra Bianca '19 🍷 2
- ● Vipra Rossa '19 🍷 2

Carini

loc. Canneto
fraz. Colle Umberto
s.da del Tegolaro, 3
06133 Perugia
Tel. +39 0756059495
www.agrariacarini.it

CELLAR SALES
PRE-BOOKED VISITS
ANNUAL PRODUCTION 40,000 bottles
HECTARES UNDER VINE 16.00
VITICULTURE METHOD Certified Organic

- ○ C. del Trasimeno Rile '19 🍷🍷 2*
- ● Tegolaro '16 🍷🍷 5
- ⊙ Le Cupe '19 🍷 3
- ○ Poggio Canneto '19 🍷 3

Castelgrosso

fraz. Torregrosso
via Lex Spoletina, 1
06044 Castel Ritaldi [PG]
Tel. +39 3397821406
www.agricolacastelgrosso.com

CELLAR SALES
PRE-BOOKED VISITS
ACCOMMODATION
ANNUAL PRODUCTION 30,000 bottles
HECTARES UNDER VINE 10.00

- ● Montefalco Rosso '16 🍷🍷 2*
- ○ Spoleto Trebbiano Spoletino Sup. '18 🍷🍷 2*

Castello di Corbara

loc. Corbara, 7
05018 Orvieto [TR]
Tel. +39 0763304035
www.castellodicorbara.it

CELLAR SALES
PRE-BOOKED VISITS
ANNUAL PRODUCTION 200,000 bottles
HECTARES UNDER VINE 100.00

- ● Lago di Corbara Cabernet Sauvignon '18 🍷🍷 3
- ○ Orvieto Cl. Sup. '19 🍷🍷 2*
- ○ Orzalume Grechetto Sauvignon '19 🍷🍷 3
- ● Sangiovese Merlot '19 🍷🍷 2*

Castello di Magione

v.le Cavalieri di Malta, 31
06063 Magione [PG]
Tel. +39 0755057319
www.sagrivit.it

CELLAR SALES
PRE-BOOKED VISITS
ANNUAL PRODUCTION 200,000 bottles
HECTARES UNDER VINE 42.00

- ● Colli del Trasimeno Morcinaia '17 🍷🍷 5
- ● Sangiovese '19 🍷🍷 2*
- ○ Grechetto '19 🍷 2

Castello di Montegiove

fraz. Montegiove
via Beata Angelina, 1
05010 Montegabbione [TR]
Tel. +39 0763837473
www.castellomontegiove.com

CELLAR SALES
PRE-BOOKED VISITS
ACCOMMODATION
ANNUAL PRODUCTION 45,000 bottles
HECTARES UNDER VINE 11.28
SUSTAINABLE WINERY

- ● Rosso Orvietano Elicius '13 🍷🍷 4
- ● Rosso Orvietano Mi.Mo.So '12 🍷🍷 3
- ● Rosso Orvietano Gatto Gatto '18 🍷 2
- ● Rosso Orvietano Mi.Mo.So '13 🍷 3

Chiorri

loc. Sant'Enea
via Todi, 100
06132 Perugia
Tel. +39 075607141
www.chiorri.it

CELLAR SALES
PRE-BOOKED VISITS
ACCOMMODATION AND RESTAURANT SERVICE
ANNUAL PRODUCTION 100,000 bottles
HECTARES UNDER VINE 25.00
SUSTAINABLE WINERY

- ● Saliato '17 🍷🍷 3
- ● Sangiovese '18 🍷🍷 2*
- ○ Titus '19 🍷 2

Cocco

loc. Poggetto, 6c
06036 Montefalco [PG]
Tel. +39 3471916207
www.coccomontefalco.it

ANNUAL PRODUCTION 10,000 bottles
HECTARES UNDER VINE 3.50

- ● Montefalco Sagrantino '15 🍷🍷 4
- ● Montefalco Rosso '16 🍷🍷 3

Colle Uncinano

loc. Uncinano
06049 Spoleto [PG]
Tel. +39 3803454401
www.colleuncinano.com

- ○ Brut '18 🍷🍷 3
- ● Sangiovese '16 🍷🍷 2*
- ○ Spoleto Trebbiano Spoletino Sup. '17 🍷 3

★Còlpetrone

fraz. Marcellano
via Ponte la Mandria, 8/1
06035 Gualdo Cattaneo [PG]
Tel. +39 074299827
www.colpetrone.it

CELLAR SALES
PRE-BOOKED VISITS
ANNUAL PRODUCTION 200,000 bottles
HECTARES UNDER VINE 63.00

○ Grechetto '19	🍷🍷 2*
● Montefalco Rosso '16	🍷 3

Custodi

loc. Canale
v.le Venere
05018 Orvieto [TR]
Tel. +39 076329053
www.cantinacustodi.com

CELLAR SALES
PRE-BOOKED VISITS
ANNUAL PRODUCTION 65,000 bottles
HECTARES UNDER VINE 40.00

○ Orvieto Cl. Belloro '19	🍷🍷 2*
○ Orvieto Cl. Sup. V. del Prete '19	🍷🍷 3
● Piancoleto '19	🍷 2

Fongoli

loc. San Marco di Montefalco
06036 Montefalco [PG]
Tel. +39 0742378930
www.fongoli.com

CELLAR SALES
PRE-BOOKED VISITS
ACCOMMODATION
ANNUAL PRODUCTION 100,000 bottles
HECTARES UNDER VINE 27.00
VITICULTURE METHOD Certified Organic

○ Biancofongoli '19	🍷🍷 4
○ Laetitia Bullarum Trebbiano Spoletino '19	🍷🍷 5
○ Maceratum '19	🍷 6
● Rossofongoli '19	🍷 4

I Girasoli di Sant'Andrea

fraz. Niccone
loc. Molino Vitelli
06019 Umbertide [PG]
Tel. +39 0759410798
www.igirasolidisantandrea.it

CELLAR SALES
PRE-BOOKED VISITS
RESTAURANT SERVICE
ANNUAL PRODUCTION 100,000 bottles
HECTARES UNDER VINE 40.00
VITICULTURE METHOD Certified Organic

● Filare 78 '16	🍷🍷 4
● Prugnano '15	🍷🍷 2*
● Syrah '19	🍷 3

Cantina Lapone

s.da del Lapone, 8
05018 Orvieto [TR]
Tel. +39 347 5472898
cantinalapone.com

ANNUAL PRODUCTION 30,000 bottles
HECTARES UNDER VINE 20.00
SUSTAINABLE WINERY

● Merlot '19	🍷🍷 3
○ Orvieto Cl. L'Escluso '19	🍷🍷 3
● Lo Stregone '18	🍷 4
● Merlot '18	🍷 3

Mevante

via Madonna della neve 1
06031 Bevagna [PG]
Tel. +39 3498057501
info@agricolamevante.com

CELLAR SALES
PRE-BOOKED VISITS
ANNUAL PRODUCTION 60,000 bottles
HECTARES UNDER VINE 15.00

● Montefalco Sagrantino '16	🍷🍷 5
○ Trebbiano Spoletino Birbanteo '19	🍷🍷 3
○ Trebbiano Spoletino Birbanteo Sur Lie '18	🍷🍷 4
● Montefalco Rosso '18	🍷 3

Montioni

via le della Vittoria, 34
06036 Montefalco [PG]
Tel. +39 0742379214
www.gabrielemontioni.it

CELLAR SALES
PRE-BOOKED VISITS
ACCOMMODATION
ANNUAL PRODUCTION 30,000 bottles
HECTARES UNDER VINE 5.00

○ Grechetto '19	🍷🍷 2*
● Montefalco Rosso '18	🍷🍷 3
● Montefalco Sagrantino '16	🍷🍷 4
● Montefalco Sagrantino Ma.Gia '16	🍷🍷 7

Domenico Pennacchi Terre di Capitani

fraz. Marcellano
via Sant'Angelo, 10
06035 Gualdo Cattaneo [PG]
Tel. +39 0742920069
pennacchidomenico@tiscalinet.it

CELLAR SALES
PRE-BOOKED VISITS
ANNUAL PRODUCTION 12,000 bottles
HECTARES UNDER VINE 6.00

● Colli di Fontivecchie Rosso '16	🍷🍷 3
● Montefalco Rosso '18	🍷🍷 3
● Montefalco Sagrantino '11	🍷🍷 5
● Montefalco Rosso Ris. '17	🍷 4

Pucciarella

loc. Villa di Magione
via Case Sparse, 39
06063 Magione [PG]
Tel. +39 0758409147
www.pucciarella.it

CELLAR SALES
PRE-BOOKED VISITS
ACCOMMODATION
ANNUAL PRODUCTION 250,000 bottles
HECTARES UNDER VINE 60.00
SUSTAINABLE WINERY

● C. del Trasimeno Rosso Sant'Anna Ris. '16	🍷🍷 3
○ C. del Trasimeno Vin Santo '16	🍷🍷 4
○ Arsiccio '19	🍷 3

Sandonna

loc. Selve
s.da della Stella Polare
05024 Giove [TR]
Tel. +39 07441926176
www.cantinasandonna.com

CELLAR SALES
PRE-BOOKED VISITS
ANNUAL PRODUCTION 28,000 bottles
HECTARES UNDER VINE 6.20

● Ciliegiolo di Narni '19	🍷🍷 2*
⊙ Gocciola '19	🍷 2
○ Grechetto '19	🍷 2
● Selve di Giove '17	🍷 4

Sasso dei Lupi

via Carlo Faina, 18
06055 Marsciano [PG]
Tel. +39 0758749523
www.sassodeilupi.it

CELLAR SALES
PRE-BOOKED VISITS
ANNUAL PRODUCTION 400,000 bottles
HECTARES UNDER VINE 150.00

● Colli Perugini Rosso Secondoatto '18	🍷🍷 2*
○ Sestavia '19	🍷🍷 2*
⊙ Epoi '19	🍷 3
● L'Intruso '18	🍷 2

La Spina

fraz. Spina
via Emilio Alessandrini, 1
06072 Marsciano [PG]
Tel. +39 0758738120
www.cantinalaspina.it

CELLAR SALES
PRE-BOOKED VISITS
ANNUAL PRODUCTION 17,000 bottles
HECTARES UNDER VINE 2.20
SUSTAINABLE WINERY

● A Fortiori '17	🍷🍷 5
○ Filare Maiore '18	🍷🍷 3
● RossoSpina '17	🍷🍷 3
○ Eburneo '19	🍷 2

Tenuta ColFalco

loc. Belvedere
fraz. Montepennino
via Valle Cupa
06036 Montefalco [PG]
Tel. +39 0742379679
www.tenutacolfalco.it

CELLAR SALES
PRE-BOOKED VISITS
ACCOMMODATION
ANNUAL PRODUCTION 35,000 bottles
HECTARES UNDER VINE 5.50
SUSTAINABLE WINERY

- ● Montefalco Sagrantino '16 — 🍷🍷 5
- ● Montefalco Sagrantino Passito '14 — 🍷🍷 5
- ● Merlot '18 — 🍷 3
- ○ Montefalco Grechetto '19 — 🍷 2

Tenute Baldo

via degli Olmi, 9
06083 Bastia Umbra [PG]
Tel. +39 0758001501
www.broccatelligalli.it

CELLAR SALES
PRE-BOOKED VISITS
ACCOMMODATION AND RESTAURANT SERVICE
ANNUAL PRODUCTION 2,000,000 bottles
HECTARES UNDER VINE 75.00

- ● Montefalco Sagrantino '15 — 🍷🍷 6
- ● Montefalco Sagrantino La Preda del Falco '15 — 🍷🍷 7
- ○ Spoleto Trebbiano Spoletino Bosso '19 — 🍷🍷 3

Terre de' Trinci

via Fiamenga, 57
06034 Foligno [PG]
Tel. +39 0742320165
www.terredetrinci.com

CELLAR SALES
PRE-BOOKED VISITS
ANNUAL PRODUCTION 500,000 bottles
HECTARES UNDER VINE 300.00

- ● Cajo '16 — 🍷🍷 3
- ● Montefalco Rosso '17 — 🍷🍷 3
- ● Montefalco Sagrantino Ugolino '15 — 🍷🍷 5
- ○ Trincia Trebbiano Spoletino '19 — 🍷 2

Terre di San Felice

via Antiluzzo, 26
06044 Castel Ritaldi [PG]
Tel. +39 3386798326
www.terredisanfelice.it

- ● Assiolo Rosso '17 — 🍷🍷 2*
- ● Montefalco Rosso Ris. '17 — 🍷🍷 3
- ● Montefalco Rosso '17 — 🍷 3
- ● Montefalco Sagrantino '16 — 🍷 4

Valdangius

loc. S. Marco
via Case Sparse, 84
06036 Montefalco [PG]
Tel. +39 3334953595
www.cantinavaldangius.it

ANNUAL PRODUCTION 15,000 bottles
HECTARES UNDER VINE 5.50
SUSTAINABLE WINERY

- ○ Filium Trebbiano Spoletino '18 — 🍷🍷 5
- ○ Spoleto Trebbiano Spoletino Campo de Pico '19 — 🍷🍷 3

La Veneranda

loc. Montepennino snc
06036 Montefalco [PG]
Tel. +39 0742951630
www.laveneranda.com

PRE-BOOKED VISITS
ANNUAL PRODUCTION 100,000 bottles
HECTARES UNDER VINE 16.00
SUSTAINABLE WINERY

- ○ Montefalco Grechetto '19 — 🍷🍷 3
- ● Riccardo I '18 — 🍷🍷 2*
- ● Montefalco Sagrantino '16 — 🍷 4

LAZIO

Lazio continues to go in its own direction, driven more by individual producers and brands than by territorial identities and DOC appellations. Of the 30 DOCs and DOCGs, only 2 or 3 seem to have a purpose and a quality that can be considered concrete, and are, more or less, safe havens for ordinary consumers (perhaps none for true wine enthusiasts). Lazio doesn't claim to have 'strong' appellations like in Tuscany or Piedmont, but it should be pointed out that in about 20 years nearby Campania has managed to move from areas linked mainly to individual producers to territories and appellations that have come together extremely well. In Lazio, on the other hand, the direction seems to be much the same as many years ago, with individual wineries creating a quality image that can end up overwhelming any reference to the territory. It's striking, for example, that only a third of the wines that obtained at least Due Bicchieri have a designation of origin. We don't want to unconditionally defend the system of appellations which, especially in recent years, has had its share of contradictions, but we believe it's right to point out that even apart from DOCs and DOCGs, there are very few areas in the region where a 'virtuous' cycle of emulation has been tried, linking producers so as to build the idea of a quality territory. It's a shame, especially in these difficult times. In terms of the Tre Bicchieri awarded, there's a new addition, Sodale Famiglia Cotarella's Merlot. And after a few years, the Anthium is once again back in the limelight, drawing on Bellone, an indigenous grape that's giving rise to increasingly interesting wines, from the hills of Cori to the sands of Anzio and Nettuno, as is the Fiorano Rosso, a splendid blend of Bordeaux grapes made on the outskirts of Rome. After a year of absence, San Giovenale's extraordinary Habemus, a 'Rodaniano' blend, is back. Sergio Mottura's Poggio della Costa, which continues to be the standard bearer of Grechetto in Lazio, put in a lovely performance, as did Castel de Paolis's Frascati Superiore and Poggio Le Volpi's Roma Rosso Edizione Limitata (these last were the only DOC wines on the list).

Marco Carpineti

S.DA PROV.LE VELLETRI-ANZIO, 3
04010 CORI [LT]
TEL. +39 069679860
www.marcocarpineti.com

CELLAR SALES
PRE-BOOKED VISITS
ANNUAL PRODUCTION 300,000 bottles
HECTARES UNDER VINE 55.00
VITICULTURE METHOD Certified Organic

Marco Carpineti, with the help of his children Paolo and Isabella, doesn't know how to rest on his laurels and continues to pull out new innovations. In the vineyard, he introduced Abbuoto (the legendary grape of the ancient Roman Caecubum wine) to his Bassiano vineyards at 550 meters elevation, whose first vintage should be in 2021; in the cellar, he has gradually eliminated selected yeasts in favor of spontaneous fermentation for all wines and uses amphorae for Nero Buono as well as Bellone. The Nzù Bellone '17 confirms that Marco is going in the right direction with his use of amphorae for this grape variety. Its nose highlights notes of white plum, citron and quince, leading into a rich palate with nice staying power and an intense, spicy finish. Their Kius Extra Brut Rosé '16 also proved excellent. This Metodo Classico made with Nero Buono features notes of wild berries and assertive, elegant and creamy bubbles, proving long and pleasant.

⊙ Kius Extra Brut Rosé '16	TT 5
○ Nzù Bellone '17	TT 5
● Capolemole Rosso '17	TT 3
○ Kius Brut '17	TT 4
○ Moro '18	TT 4
○ Capolemole Bianco '19	T 2
● Nzù Nero Buono '17	T 5
● Tufaliccio '19	T 2
○ Capolemole Bianco '18	YY 2*
● Capolemole Rosso '16	YY 3
○ Kius Brut '16	YY 4
⊙ Kius Extra Brut Rosé '15	YY 5
○ Moro '17	YY 3*
○ Moro '16	YY 3*
○ Nzù Bellone '16	YY 5
○ Nzù Bellone '15	YY 5

Casale del Giglio

LOC. LE FERRIERE
S.DA CISTERNA-NETTUNO KM 13
04100 LATINA
TEL. +39 0692902530
www.casaledelgiglio.it

CELLAR SALES
PRE-BOOKED VISITS
ANNUAL PRODUCTION 1,707,000 bottles
HECTARES UNDER VINE 164.00
SUSTAINABLE WINERY

From Ponza to Satrico, Anzio, Olevano and Amatrice, Antonio Santarelli and Paolo Tiefenthaler's attention has always been focused on enhancing the enclave of territories where respect for nature, quality grape varieties and man's work come together in perfect synergy. This idea embraces safeguarding the past (like the excavations of a second-century Roman villa on the Ferriere property), while paying attention to what is new (the first vintage in 2020 for Pecorino di Amatrice and the planting of new Sauvignon clones). The Anthium Bellone is back on top. The 2019 version offers up notes of peach, melon and candied citron, making for a consistent, sapid, lingering palate, with nice texture. The other two impressive wines were Radix Bellone '16, which macerates and rests in amphorae, with overtones of grapefruit, yellow flowers and beeswax, full-bodied and sapid with notable depth, and the fresh, taut Faro della Guardia Biancolella '19, with tones of Mediterranean scrub and yellow fruit.

○ Anthium '19	TTT 3*
○ Faro della Guardia Biancolella '19	TT 5
○ Radix Bellone '16	TT 7
⊙ Albiola '19	TT 2*
○ Antinoo '18	TT 4
○ Aphrodisium '19	TT 5
● Madreselva '17	TT 4
● Mater Matuta '17	TT 7
○ Petit Manseng '19	TT 3
● Matidia '18	T 3
● Merlot '18	T 2
○ Viognier '19	T 3
○ Antium Bellone '15	YYY 4*
○ Antium Bellone '14	YYY 4*
○ Biancolella Faro della Guardia '13	YYY 5
○ Faro della Guardia Biancolella '18	YYY 5
○ Faro della Guardia Biancolella '16	YYY 5

Casale della Ioria

loc. La Gloria
s.da prov.le 118 Anagni-Paliano
03012 Anagni [FR]
Tel. +39 077556031
www.casaledellaioria.com

CELLAR SALES
PRE-BOOKED VISITS
ANNUAL PRODUCTION 75,000 bottles
HECTARES UNDER VINE 38.00
VITICULTURE METHOD Certified Organic
SUSTAINABLE WINERY

We have already mentioned Paolo Perinelli's merits in developing Cesanese, both as a variety and a DOCG, but there's no harm underlining that his first simple, but fundamental, insight was that quality originates in the vineyard. An excellent position in terms of exposure and elevation (400 meters), Guyot-trained vineyards with the right density (about 5000 plants per hectare), almost 40-year-old vineyards alongside newer ones, the use of techniques with a low impact on the environment: this combination is respected by the cellar practices, leading to some of the best results in the area. Sometimes the winery's star wine doesn't compare to its "supporting actors". This year we were won over by the Cesanese del Piglio Superiore Tenuta della Ioria '18, with its tones of bramble, black fruit, spice and Mediterranean scrub, leading into a close-focused palate, with well-managed tannins and pleasant finish. The Riserva Torre del Piano '18 proves well made, with nice freshness and staying power, though the tannins are a bit rugged.

Wine	Rating
● Cesanese del Piglio Sup. Tenuta della Ioria '18	🍷🍷 3*
● Cesanese del Piglio Sup. Torre del Piano Ris. '18	🍷🍷 4
● Cesanese del Piglio Campo Novo '19	🍷 2
○ Colle Bianco '19	🍷 2
● Olivella '14	🍷 2
○ Passerina Extra Dry	🍷 2
● Cesanese del Piglio Sup. Tenuta della Ioria '17	🍷🍷 3
● Cesanese del Piglio Sup. Tenuta della Ioria '16	🍷🍷 3
● Cesanese del Piglio Sup. Torre del Piano Ris. '17	🍷🍷 4
● Cesanese del Piglio Sup. Torre del Piano Ris. '16	🍷🍷 4
● Cesanese del Piglio Sup. Torre del Piano Ris. '15	🍷🍷 4

Casale Marchese

via di Vermicino, 68
00044 Frascati [RM]
Tel. +39 069408932
www.casalemarchese.it

CELLAR SALES
PRE-BOOKED VISITS
ANNUAL PRODUCTION 150,000 bottles
HECTARES UNDER VINE 40.00

For two centuries, the Carletti family have owned Casale Marchese, an estate covering about 60 hectares, growing mainly olives and grapes in the heart of the Frascati appellation. They cultivate traditional local grapes, including the black varieties Malvasia Puntinata, Malvasia di Candia, Trebbiano Toscano, Greco, Bombino and Bellone, alongside Bordeaux ones (Merlot, Cabernet Sauvignon and Cabernet Franc), and Chardonnay for whites. Their wines are modern with close-focused aromas making up their personal style. The Frascati Superiore '19 is a classic: with excellent typical aromas of sage, citrus and Mediterranean scrub, a medium-bodied palate and a supple finish, with typical almondy tones. Their Clemens '19 proves richer and fuller. This equal blend of Chardonnay and Malvasia Puntinata exhibits notes of tropical fruit, especially mango and papaya. The Rosso Eminenza '19 was also well made, with pleasant tones of red fruit.

Wine	Rating
○ Frascati Sup. '19	🍷🍷 2*
○ Clemens '19	🍷🍷 3
● Rosso Eminenza '19	🍷🍷 3
○ Frascati Sup. Quarto Marchese '19	🍷 3
● Marchese de' Cavalieri '18	🍷 4
○ Clemens '14	🍷🍷 3
○ Frascati Sup. '18	🍷🍷 2*
○ Frascati Sup. '15	🍷🍷 2*
○ Frascati Sup. '14	🍷🍷 2*
○ Frascati Sup. Quarto Marchese '17	🍷🍷 3

Castel de Paolis

via Val de Paolis
00046 Grottaferrata [RM]
Tel. +39 069412560
www.casteldepaolis.com

CELLAR SALES
PRE-BOOKED VISITS
RESTAURANT SERVICE
ANNUAL PRODUCTION 90,000 bottles
HECTARES UNDER VINE 11.00

This winery lies at the gates of Rome on the ruins of the Medieval castle it is named after. The castle, in turn, was built on Roman remains, which include a tank where red wines age today. In 1985, Giulio Santarelli involved Professor Attilio Scienza in a project to rediscover the territory, which combined promoting native varieties with experiments on international varieties. His range of wines features lovely technical precision within a traditional framework. Once again, we found the Frascati Superiore (the territory's flagship wine) typical and well made. Meadow herbs, almonds and citrus on the nose follow onto a consistent, round palate, with a sapidity that makes it supple and long. Their Campo Vecchio '19 proves less spacious, but still pleasant, with notes of ripe fruit and hints of citron and almonds. The Campo Vecchio Rosso '16, on the other hand, plays on vegetal overtones of Mediterranean scrub.

Wine	Rating
○ Frascati Sup. '19	▼▼▼ 3*
○ Campo Vecchio '19	▼▼ 3
● Campo Vecchio Rosso '16	▼▼ 3
○ Frascati Sup. '18	▽▽▽ 3*
○ Donna Adriana '17	▽▽ 4
○ Donna Adriana '16	▽▽ 4
○ Donna Adriana '15	▽▽ 4
○ Frascati Campo Vecchio '18	▽▽ 3
○ Frascati Campo Vecchio '16	▽▽ 2*
○ Frascati Sup. '17	▽▽ 3*
○ Frascati Sup. '16	▽▽ 3
○ Frascati Sup. '15	▽▽ 3
● I Quattro Mori '15	▽▽ 6
● I Quattro Mori '14	▽▽ 5
○ Muffa Nobile '16	▽▽ 5
○ Muffa Nobile '15	▽▽ 5
● Rosathea '16	▽▽ 5

Cincinnato

via Cori - Cisterna, km 2
04010 Cori [LT]
Tel. +39 069679380
www.cincinnato.it

CELLAR SALES
PRE-BOOKED VISITS
ACCOMMODATION AND RESTAURANT SERVICE
ANNUAL PRODUCTION 900,000 bottles
HECTARES UNDER VINE 268.00
SUSTAINABLE WINERY

A team established over the years (Nazareno Milita, Carlo Morettini, Fabio and Mattia Bigolin and Giovanna Trisorio) has made this cooperative into a leading example and they mean to keep improving. It's worth mentioning the new Nero Buono and Bellone vineyards, organic certification in 2018, the new temperature-controlled storeroom and FOSS technology to analyze grapes, must and wine in real time, which safeguards quality as well as the professionalism of the grape growers' work. This year the most gratifying wines were those made with Bellone grapes, especially the Metodo Classico ones. The Brut di Bellone '16 comes through rich and full-bodied, with aromas of citrus and confectioner's cream. The bubbles reveal remarkable elegance, making for an inviting palate. The creamy, supple Korì Bellone Pas Dosé '16 exhibits slightly less character than the Brut. The Castore '19 proves well made, as is the rest of their range.

Wine	Rating
○ Brut di Bellone M. Cl. '16	▼▼ 2*
○ Castore '19	▼▼ 2*
○ Cori Bianco Illirio '19	▼▼ 2*
○ Korì Bellone Pas Dosé '16	▼▼ 4
● Arcatura '18	▼ 2
● Ercole Nero Buono '17	▼ 3
○ Pantaleo '19	▼ 2
● Pollùce '18	▼ 2
● Arcatura '17	▽▽ 2*
○ Castore '17	▽▽ 2*
○ Cori Bianco Illirio '18	▽▽ 2*
○ Cori Bianco Illirio '17	▽▽ 2*
○ Enyo Bellone '17	▽▽ 3
● Kora Nero Buono '15	▽▽ 4
○ Pantaleo '18	▽▽ 2*

Damiano Ciolli

via del Corso
00035 Olevano Romano [RM]
Tel. +39 069563334
www.damianociolli.it

CELLAR SALES
PRE-BOOKED VISITS
ANNUAL PRODUCTION 25,000 bottles
HECTARES UNDER VINE 5.00
SUSTAINABLE WINERY

Damiano Ciolli grew up in Olevano Romano, dividing his time between the house and cellar, in the company of his grandfather Guido and father Costantino. He has transformed the bulk-wine-producing, family-run winery into a leading producer in the territory. In 2001, Damiano began to bottle wine from his grandfather's old vineyard, a single hectare planted with Cesanese. Today, he and his partner and winemaker Letizia Rocchi produce two versions of Cesanese: one is fresh and approachable while the other displays more structure and combines the best characteristics of the soil, microclimate and variety. The Cesanese di Olevano Romano Silene '18 shows great density: the nose reveals captivating hints of undergrowth and red fruit, which follow through onto the elegant, pleasant palate, accompanied by licorice notes. The palate is fresh and determined with good length. The flavorsome, deep Cirsium '16 features a palate with marked notes of black fruit and spice.

Wine	Rating
● Cesanese di Olevano Romano Silene '18	🍷🍷 3*
● Cesanese di Olevano Romano Cirsium Ris. '16	🍷🍷 5
● Cesanese di Olevano Romano Silene '17	🍷🍷🍷 3*
● Cesanese di Olevano Romano Cirsium Ris. '15	🍷🍷 5
● Cesanese di Olevano Romano Cirsium Ris. '14	🍷🍷 5
● Cesanese di Olevano Romano Cirsium Ris. '13	🍷🍷 5
● Cesanese di Olevano Romano Sup. Silene '16	🍷🍷 3*
● Cesanese di Olevano Romano Sup. Silene '15	🍷🍷 3

Antonello Coletti Conti

via Vittorio Emanuele, 116
03012 Anagni [FR]
Tel. +39 0775728610
www.coletticonti.it

CELLAR SALES
PRE-BOOKED VISITS
ANNUAL PRODUCTION 20,000 bottles
HECTARES UNDER VINE 20.00

Jokingly (but not too much!), Antonello Coletti Conti loves to say that he even sleeps in his vineyard at certain times of the year. This helped him notice a biotype of Cesanese d'Affile, with very small berries, among his vine rows. He replanted it in a new small vineyard of 1.2 hectares and is hoping it will open up new prospects in this historic vineyard in Lazio. While awaiting imminent separate vinification, the vineyard produces grapes used in the blend of their two Cesanese wines. As has often happened in recent years, Hernicus was the more impressive of Coletti Conti's two Cesanese del Piglio Superiore 2018 wines. Elegant aromas of wild black berries and overtones of spice and undergrowth pave the way to a smooth, close-focused palate, with a pleasant, juicy finish. The Romanico is a wine designed to express its best in a few years; it's denser and more close-knit, but a bit less determined than the Hernicus.

Wine	Rating
● Cesanese del Piglio Sup. Hernicus '18	🍷🍷 3*
● Cesanese del Piglio Sup. Romanico '18	🍷🍷 5
● Cesanese del Piglio Romanico '11	🍷🍷🍷 5
● Cesanese del Piglio Romanico '07	🍷🍷🍷 5
● Cesanese del Piglio Sup. Hernicus '14	🍷🍷🍷 3*
● Cesanese del Piglio Sup. Hernicus '12	🍷🍷🍷 3*
● Cesanese del Piglio Sup. Hernicus '17	🍷🍷 3*
● Cesanese del Piglio Sup. Hernicus '16	🍷🍷 3
● Cesanese del Piglio Sup. Hernicus '15	🍷🍷 3*
● Cesanese del Piglio Sup. Romanico '17	🍷🍷 5
● Cesanese del Piglio Sup. Romanico '16	🍷🍷 5
● Cesanese del Piglio Sup. Romanico '14	🍷🍷 5
● Cesanese del Piglio Sup. Romanico '13	🍷🍷 5
● Cosmato '17	🍷🍷 5
● Cosmato '16	🍷🍷 5
○ Passerina del Frusinate Hernicus '17	🍷🍷 3

★★Falesco Famiglia Cotarella

S.S. Cassia Nord km 94,155
01027 Montefiascone [VT]
Tel. +39 07449556
www.falesco.it

CELLAR SALES
PRE-BOOKED VISITS
ACCOMMODATION
ANNUAL PRODUCTION 3,650,000 bottles
HECTARES UNDER VINE 330.00

The family's first winery was set up in the 1960s in Upper Viterbo by Antonio and Domenico Cotarella. Since then, its pathway has been mapped out by the family's trademark features combined with a desire to focus on the territory. Falesco was officially founded in 1979 by Renzo and Riccardo, with the aim of livening up local production. Today the generational transfer sees their respective daughters, Dominga, Marta and Enrica, play a key role. They have carried on the winery's production philosophy, which consists in technically impeccable wines with character. This year our favorite was the Sodale '18, a monovarietal Merlot that impressed with the great balance between red fruit and sweet spices. Its plush, lively and well-orchestrated palate is very lingering. Their full, sapid Ferentano, which centers on white fruit, also deserves a mention. The Tellus Syrah is a cert, with fresh, pleasant notes of small black fruit. The same method for their approachable Rosé di Syrah, from the same line.

Wine	Rating
● Sodale '18	🍷🍷🍷 5
○ Ferentano '18	🍷🍷 5
● Marciliano '17	🍷🍷 7
⊙ Soré '19	🍷🍷 4
● Appunto Rosso '19	🍷🍷 2*
○ Est! Est!! Est!!! di Montefiascone Poggio dei Gelsi '19	🍷🍷 2*
● I Cento Umbri '19	🍷🍷 2*
● Messidoro '19	🍷🍷 2*
○ Soente Viognier '19	🍷🍷 4
● Tellus Syrah '19	🍷🍷 3
⊙ Tellus Syrah Rosé '19	🍷🍷 3
● Trentanni '18	🍷🍷 4
● Vitiano Rosso '19	🍷🍷 2*
○ Est! Est!! Est!!! di Montefiascone Brut Best	🍷 2
○ Tellus Chardonnay '19	🍷 3

Fontana Candida

via Fontana Candida, 11
00040 Monte Porzio Catone [RM]
Tel. +39 069401881
www.fontanacandida.it

CELLAR SALES
PRE-BOOKED VISITS
RESTAURANT SERVICE
ANNUAL PRODUCTION 2,000,000 bottles
HECTARES UNDER VINE 221.00

Fontana Candida, owned by Gruppo Italiano Vini, has played a key role in Castelli Romani winemaking for over sixty years. In addition to several hectares cultivated by historic grape growers, there are 25 hectares of owned vineyards in the Frascati appellation (including their 13-hectare Santa Teresa vineyard, whose grapes are used to make their historic wine), located at 200 to 400 meters elevation on volcanic soils, rich in minerals and microelements. They mainly grow Malvasia Puntinata, Malvasia di Candia, Trebbiano Toscano and Greco, to produce technically well-made wines. The Frascati Superiore Luna Mater Riserva '19 is back on top. It offers up impressive aromas of white flowers, peach and citrus, coming through fresh with nice drive. The Frascati Superiore Vigneto Santa Teresa is also in good form, featuring notes of sage, passion fruit and citron. Their Merlot Kron '17 is also well made, with hints of cherry and sweet spices leading to a consistent, plush palate with notes of tobacco and hay.

Wine	Rating
○ Frascati Sup. Luna Mater Ris. '19	🍷🍷 4
○ Frascati Secco Terre dei Grifi '19	🍷🍷 2*
○ Frascati Sup. Secco Vign. Santa Teresa '19	🍷🍷 2*
● Kron '17	🍷🍷 4
○ Frascati Secco '19	🍷 2
○ Frascati Sup. Luna Mater Ris. '18	🍷🍷 4
○ Frascati Sup. Luna Mater Ris. '17	🍷🍷 3*
○ Frascati Sup. Secco Vign. Santa Teresa '18	🍷🍷 3
○ Frascati Sup. Secco Vign. Santa Teresa '17	🍷🍷 3
○ Frascati Sup. Vign. Santa Teresa '16	🍷🍷 2*
● Kron '16	🍷🍷 4
○ Roma Malvasia Puntinata '17	🍷🍷 2*

Formiconi

loc. Farinella
00021 Affile [RM]
Tel. +39 3470934541
www.cantinaformiconi.com

CELLAR SALES
PRE-BOOKED VISITS
ANNUAL PRODUCTION 13,000 bottles
HECTARES UNDER VINE 4.00
SUSTAINABLE WINERY

Set up less than 20 years ago, the winery of brothers Livio, Walter and Vito Formiconi can count on a family estate dating back to the end of the 19th century, with four hectares of vineyards situated at over 600 meters elevation, on clayey, calcareous soils. Cesanese d'Affile is the absolute protagonist, alongside small amounts of Malvasia. They produce only three wines, aiming to combine typicity, territoriality and precise winemaking. Once again, the "basic" Cisanium '19 convinced us the most of the two Cesanese di Affile wines; it offers up aromas of black fruit and bramble, while the palate exhibits rich tannins typical of the variety, alongside hints of fresh wild berries, making for a determined finish and pleasant palate. The Riserva Capozzano '18, on the other hand, still shows signs of barrique aging, which confers spicy notes on the nose and a palate still a bit closed, rugged and difficult to read.

Wine	Rating
● Cesanese di Affile Cisinianum '19	🍷🍷 3*
● Cesanese di Affile Capozzano Ris. '18	🍷🍷 4
○ Enea Malvasia '19	🍷 3
● Cesanese di Affile Capozzano Ris. '17	🍷🍷 4
● Cesanese di Affile Capozzano Ris. '16	🍷🍷 4
● Cesanese di Affile Cisinianum '18	🍷🍷 3
● Cesanese di Affile Cisinianum '17	🍷🍷 3*
● Cesanese di Affile Cisinianum '15	🍷🍷 3*

Antiche Cantine Migliaccio

via Pizzicato
04027 Ponza [LT]
Tel. +39 3392822252
www.antichecantinemigliaccio.it

CELLAR SALES
PRE-BOOKED VISITS
ANNUAL PRODUCTION 10,000 bottles
HECTARES UNDER VINE 3.00

When Carlo di Borbone colonized the island of Ponza in 1743, he entrusted Punta Fieno to Pietro Migliaccio. The Neapolitan brought the typical grape varieties from Ischia: Biancolella, Forastera, Guarnaccia, Aglianico and Piedirosso, the same ones that Emanuele Vittorio and his wife Luciana gave a new lease of life to in 2000. They were very old varieties that had remained ungrafted and free to proliferate far from any kind of contamination. The result has been a fruitful marriage between nature and modern techniques, made possible by the support of winemaker Vincenzo Mercurio. The white wines are up to their usual very high standard. The Fieno Bianco '19 charmed us with its citrus and iodine aromas, sapid notes and palate redolent of Mediterranean scrub, with overtones of almond and white flowers. The lively, approachable Biancolella '19 showed great freshness and sapidity, with a pleasantly aromatic finish. We also appreciated the plucky Fieno Rosato '19, with its notes of flowers and small red fruit.

Wine	Rating
○ Biancolella di Ponza '19	🍷🍷 5
○ Fieno di Ponza Bianco '19	🍷🍷 4
⊙ Fieno di Ponza Rosato '19	🍷🍷 4
○ Fieno di Ponza Bianco '17	🍷🍷🍷 4*
○ Biancolella di Ponza '18	🍷🍷 5
○ Biancolella di Ponza '17	🍷🍷 5
○ Biancolella di Ponza '16	🍷🍷 5
○ Biancolella di Ponza '15	🍷🍷 5
○ Biancolella di Ponza '14	🍷🍷 5
○ Fieno di Ponza Bianco '18	🍷🍷 4
○ Fieno di Ponza Bianco '16	🍷🍷 4
○ Fieno di Ponza Bianco '15	🍷🍷 4
⊙ Fieno di Ponza Rosato '18	🍷🍷 4
⊙ Fieno di Ponza Rosato '17	🍷🍷 4
⊙ Fieno di Ponza Rosato '16	🍷🍷 4
● Fieno di Ponza Rosso '18	🍷🍷 4
● Fieno di Ponza Rosso '13	🍷🍷 4

★Sergio Mottura

LOC. POGGIO DELLA COSTA, 1
01020 CIVITELLA D'AGLIANO [VT]
TEL. +39 0761914533
www.motturasergio.it

CELLAR SALES
PRE-BOOKED VISITS
ACCOMMODATION AND RESTAURANT SERVICE
ANNUAL PRODUCTION 97,000 bottles
HECTARES UNDER VINE 37.00
VITICULTURE METHOD Certified Organic

Sergio Mottura, who has always been set on experimentation and research to reappraise native grapes, is a pioneer of organic farming. He moved from his native Piedmont to Civitella d'Agliano, which has become an iconic area for Grechetto over the years. He has identified and selected three different clones of this renowned variety from Alta Tuscia. But he also grows several other varieties, ranging from local Procanico and Verdello grapes to international ones, like Chardonnay and Pinot Nero, to produce high-quality wines. In the absence of the Latour a Civitella (not produced in 2018), we liked the splendid Poggio della Costa '19: a citrusy, slightly spicy nose, a full-bodied, fruity, sapid palate with a long, taut finish. Despite its apparent simplicity, Orvieto Secco '19 proved a top-level wine: yellow fruit, citrus and a gutsy mineral note supporting the palate. Other wines that delivered were their Orvieto Tragugnano, with notes of bergamot orange, and the long, complex Sergio Mottura Brut '11.

○ Poggio della Costa '19	🍷🍷🍷 4*
○ Orvieto Secco '19	🍷🍷 3*
○ Orvieto Tragugnano '19	🍷🍷 4
○ Sergio Mottura Brut M. Cl. '11	🍷🍷 6
⊙ Civitella Rosato '19	🍷 3
● Civitella Rosso '19	🍷 3
○ Grechetto Latour a Civitella '11	🍷🍷🍷 4*
○ Grechetto Poggio della Costa '14	🍷🍷🍷 3*
○ Grechetto Poggio della Costa '10	🍷🍷🍷 3*
○ Grechetto Poggio della Costa '09	🍷🍷🍷 3*
○ Grechetto Poggio della Costa '08	🍷🍷🍷 3*
○ Poggio della Costa '18	🍷🍷🍷 4*
○ Poggio della Costa '17	🍷🍷🍷 4*
○ Poggio della Costa '16	🍷🍷🍷 3*
○ Poggio della Costa '15	🍷🍷🍷 3*
○ Poggio della Costa '12	🍷🍷🍷 3*
○ Poggio della Costa '11	🍷🍷🍷 3*

Omina Romana

VIA FONTANA PARATA, 75
00049 VELLETRI [RM]
TEL. +39 0696430193
www.ominaromana.com

CELLAR SALES
PRE-BOOKED VISITS
ANNUAL PRODUCTION 130,000 bottles
HECTARES UNDER VINE 80.00
SUSTAINABLE WINERY

The symbol of this winery owned by a German, Anton Börner, is a phoenix, the fire bird reborn from its ashes to a new life. It represents his aim to regenerate quality wines in this region. The estate is situated in Velletri, on volcanic hills to the south of Rome. This area has been studied by the University of Geisenheim and the Faculty of Agriculture and Enology in Florence to help Börner achieve the excellent quality he is looking for. He has given his wines a purely international style, with the help of winemakers Simone Sarnà and Claudio Gori. Ars Magna Cabernet Franc '17, with its lovely impact, was particularly convincing this year. It comes through fresh, crisp and very pleasant, with a palate playing entirely on notes of small black fruit and ripe peppers. The rest of their selection also delivered: the well-made reds include Ceres Anesidora I, a rich, pleasant, vegetal and spicy blend of Cabernet Sauvignon and Franc. The Viognier proved the most pleasant of their whites, featuring sweet wood sensations and herbs.

● Ars Magna Cabernet Franc '17	🍷🍷 8
○ Ars Magna Viognier '19	🍷🍷 8
● Ceres Anesidora I '17	🍷🍷 8
● Cesanese '17	🍷 6
○ Hermes Diactoros II '19	🍷 4
● Ars Magna Merlot '15	🍷🍷 8
○ Bellone Brut '14	🍷🍷 4
● Cabernet Franc Linea Ars Magna '13	🍷🍷 8
● Cabernet Sauvignon '11	🍷🍷 7
● Ceres Anesidora I '15	🍷🍷 8
● Diana Nemorensis I '12	🍷🍷 6
● Hermes Diactoros '13	🍷🍷 4
● Janus Geminus I '15	🍷🍷 8
● Merlot '13	🍷🍷 7
● Merlot '12	🍷🍷 7

Tenuta La Pazzaglia

loc. Pazzaglia
s.da di Bagnoregio, 4
01024 Castiglione in Teverina [VT]
Tel. +39 3486610038
www.tenutalapazzaglia.it

CELLAR SALES
PRE-BOOKED VISITS
ACCOMMODATION
ANNUAL PRODUCTION 56,000 bottles
HECTARES UNDER VINE 12.00

The members of the Verdecchia family have in common an unusual tenacity and determination. In 1990, they purchased an abandoned farmhouse on the border between Lazio, Umbria and Tuscany, fully recognizing its potential. It was a new life choice carried forward by the three siblings Laura, Maria Teresa and Pierfrancesco, with the help of winemaker Daniele di Mambro. In order to increase quality and quantity, they have decided to concentrate their efforts on Grechetto and aim to bring out all of its potential. As shown by the Poggio Triale '18, which has given us a lovely expression of the territory and Grechetto variety: the nose offers up floral and citrusy tones, while the palate comes through juicy, sapid and pleasantly long, with refreshing notes of passion fruit and grapefruit. The 2018 version of the 109 Grechetto rests in amphorae, making for a sapid, juicy wine, with notes of citrus and white flowers. The reds submitted proved very sound.

○ Poggio Triale '18	🍷🍷 3*
○ 109 Grechetto Anfora '18	🍷🍷 3
● Aurelius '18	🍷 2
● Palagio '18	🍷 2
○ 109 Grechetto '18	🍷🍷 3*
○ 109 Grechetto '17	🍷🍷 3*
○ 109 Grechetto '16	🍷🍷 3*
○ Il Corno '16	🍷🍷 2*
○ Miadimia '18	🍷🍷 3
○ Poggio Triale '17	🍷🍷 3
○ Poggio Triale '16	🍷🍷 3
○ Poggio Triale '15	🍷🍷 3

Pietra Pinta

via Le Pastine km 20,200
04010 Cori [LT]
Tel. +39 069678001
www.pietrapinta.com

CELLAR SALES
PRE-BOOKED VISITS
ACCOMMODATION AND RESTAURANT SERVICE
ANNUAL PRODUCTION 300,000 bottles
HECTARES UNDER VINE 33.00
VITICULTURE METHOD Certified Organic
SUSTAINABLE WINERY

As the farm's motto goes, 'an eye on the future and a territory in the heart'. Past, present and future all merge in this lovely winery created over the years by the Ferretti family, a legacy that streches back to the 1800s. Great winemaking territories rich in history (from Cori to Ninfa), continual research on native and international grape varieties, comfortable farmhouse accommodation with cozy rooms and lots of space outdoors for catering. The cellar and olive press use the most modern technology in order to respect and bring out the best of their grapes. This estate's wines are always sound. This year we particularly liked the Nero Buono '18, with its spicy aromas of black fruit and palate rich in pulp and body, well supported by acidity, making it long and fresh. The approachable, pleasant Bellone '19 and the Viognier '19, with its tones of yellow peach and melon, good body and volume, also proved well made.

○ Bellone '19	🍷🍷 2*
● Nero Buono '18	🍷🍷 2*
○ Viognier '19	🍷🍷 2*
○ Chardonnay '19	🍷 2
● Colle Amato Nero Buono '16	🍷 3
○ Costa Vecchia Bianco '19	🍷 2
● Costa Vecchia Rosso '18	🍷 2
○ Malvasia Puntinata '19	🍷 2
○ Sauvignon '19	🍷 2
● Shiraz '18	🍷 2
● Colle Amato Nero Buono '15	🍷🍷 3
● Costa Vecchia Rosso '17	🍷🍷 2*
○ Viognier '18	🍷🍷 2*

★Poggio Le Volpi

via Colle Pisano, 27
00078 Monte Porzio Catone [RM]
Tel. +39 069426980
www.poggiolevolpi.com

CELLAR SALES
PRE-BOOKED VISITS
RESTAURANT SERVICE
ANNUAL PRODUCTION 300,000 bottles
HECTARES UNDER VINE 145.00

Manlio Mergè laid the first stone of the winery in 1920, when he began to produce and sell bulk wine. The step from local to national winery was taken by his son Armando, but the real leap in quality came with Felice, who made Poggio Le Volpi one of the leading wineries in Lazio in 1996. It is located in Monte Porzio Catone, a few kilometers from Rome, where the winery's 35 hectares of vineyards find the old volcanic soils give excellent results and make for wines maked by nice territorial expression. The Roma Rosso Edizione Limitata was convincing again this year. The well-made 2017 version features notes of small black fruits and sweet spices, finishing with a rich, caressing, sapid palate. The Baccarossa, a monovarietal Nero Buono, impressed once again, with its captivating nose and a palate exhibiting tones of Mediterranean scrub, cloves and quina. Of their whites, Malvasia Puntinata '19 proved typical and pleasant, revealing notes of melon, sage and white fruit.

Wine	Rating
● Roma Rosso Ed. Limitata '17	TTT 5
● Baccarossa '18	TT 6
○ Roma Malvasia Puntinata '19	TT 5
○ Donnaluce '19	T 5
⊙ Roma Rosato '19	T 5
● Baccarossa '15	YYY 5
● Baccarossa '13	YYY 4*
● Baccarossa '11	YYY 4*
○ Frascati Sup. Epos '13	YYY 2*
○ Frascati Sup. Epos '11	YYY 2*
○ Frascati Sup. Epos '10	YYY 2*
○ Frascati Sup. Epos '09	YYY 2*
○ Frascati Sup. Epos Ris. '15	YYY 3*
● Roma Rosso Ed. Limitata '16	YYY 5
● Roma Rosso Ed. Limitata '15	YYY 5
● Baccarossa '17	YY 6
● Baccarossa '16	YY 5

Tenuta Ronci di Nepi

via Ronci, 2072
01036 Nepi [VT]
Tel. +39 0761555125
www.roncidinepi.it

CELLAR SALES
PRE-BOOKED VISITS
ANNUAL PRODUCTION 100,000 bottles
HECTARES UNDER VINE 30.00

Arturo Improta's Tenuta Ronci di Nepi stretches over thirty hectares in the hills of the Ronci valley, in southernmost Tuscia Viterbese, in the Valle del Treja nature reserve and the municipality of Nepi. It was founded in 2004, although winemaking dates began back to the 1980s. The vineyards lie on volcanic soil with marked components of tuff. Though production focused on international grapes in the early years , for some time now they have turned to typical local varieties like Grechetto, Montepulciano and Sangiovese. The excellent Grechetto '19 offers up aromas of citrus and white fruit, with spicy overtones and a fresh, close-focused, sapid and very pleasant palate. The Manti '19, a Chardonnay with nice body and weight, and the rich, complex Rosso di Né '16, a Sangiovese with 30% of Cabernet Sauvignon and Merlot, featuring marked overtones of undergrowth and black fruit, also turned out quite well.

Wine	Rating
○ Grechetto '19	TT 3*
○ Manti '19	TT 4
● Rosso di Nè '16	TT 3
○ Argento '19	T 1*
○ O' di Nè '19	T 3
● Ronci '16	T 5
● Veste Porpora '17	T 3
○ Chardonnay Manti '15	YY 4
○ Grechetto '18	YY 3
○ O' di Nè '17	YY 3

San Giovenale

Loc. La Macchia
01010 Blera [VT]
Tel. +39 066877877
www.sangiovenale.it

CELLAR SALES
PRE-BOOKED VISITS
ACCOMMODATION AND RESTAURANT SERVICE
ANNUAL PRODUCTION 9,000 bottles
HECTARES UNDER VINE 10.00
VITICULTURE METHOD Certified Organic
SUSTAINABLE WINERY

Low yields per hectare lead to limited, but high-quality production. These have been Emanuele Pangrazi's guidelines since he set up the winery about fifteen years ago. His aim has always been to create a wine that, regardless of the variety used, is able to bring out the character of this part of Tuscia, which benefits from the influence of the nearby Tyrrhenian Sea. The vineyard is planted with international varieties, Syrah, Grenache, Carignano and Cabernet Franc, which make for wines with unique characteristics. Their Habemus '18 is truly splendid. This Grenache-heavy Rhone blend shows a surprising ability to express depth, freshness, complexity and approachability all at the same time. Spices and black fruit alternate with Mediterranean scrub and wild berries, exhibiting a sapid finish and extraordinary palate. We are confidently waiting for the still developing Habemus Cabernet '17, made with Cabernet Franc grapes and featuring overtones of herbs.

Wine	Rating
● Habemus '18	TTT 8
● Habemus Cabernet '17	TT 8
● Habemus '16	YYY 7
● Habemus '15	YYY 7
● Habemus '14	YYY 7
● Habemus '17	YY 7
● Habemus '13	YY 7
● Habemus '12	YY 7
● Habemus '11	YY 7
● Habemus '10	YY 4
● Habemus Cabernet '16	YY 8
● Habemus Cabernet '15	YY 8
● Habemus Cabernet '14	YY 8
● Habemus Cabernet '13	YY 8

Tenuta di Fiorano

via di Fioranello, 19
00134 Roma
Tel. +39 0679340093
www.tenutadifiorano.it

CELLAR SALES
PRE-BOOKED VISITS
ACCOMMODATION AND RESTAURANT SERVICE
ANNUAL PRODUCTION 40,000 bottles
HECTARES UNDER VINE 12.00
VITICULTURE METHOD Certified Organic

The Tenuta di Fiorano stretches across the ancient Appian Way, in a bucolic estate steeped in history and run by Alessandrojacopo Boncompagni Ludovisi today. It was his uncle Alberico who first got the bug for winemaking in the 1940s. He decided to plant Cabernet Sauvignon and Merlot for red wines, Malvasia di Candia and Sémillon, now replaced by Grechetto and Viognier, for whites. The experience came to an end in 1998, but Alessandrojacopo picked up the reins again in later years in order to create complex and fascinating wines that stand the test of time. All the wines submitted were top level. This year the rich, elegant Fiorano Rosso '15 deserves the vote of excellence, with its aromas of small black fruit, ripe cherry and slight spicy nuances. The palate comes through fresh and complex, with very elegant tannins and great length. The very elegant Fiorano Bianco '18 offers up floral, citrus and acacia honey overtones, with a fresh, plush and long palate. Lastly, their two Fioranello wines proved fresh and pleasant-drinking.

Wine	Rating
● Fiorano Rosso '15	TTT 8
○ Fiorano Bianco '18	TT 6
○ Fioranello Bianco '19	TT 3
● Fioranello Rosso '18	TT 4
○ Fiorano Bianco '17	YYY 6
○ Fiorano Bianco '16	YYY 6
○ Fiorano Bianco '13	YYY 5
○ Fiorano Bianco '12	YYY 4*
○ Fiorano Bianco '10	YYY 5
● Fiorano Rosso '12	YYY 7
● Fiorano Rosso '11	YYY 7
○ Fioranello Bianco '18	YY 3
○ Fioranello Bianco '17	YY 3
● Fioranello Rosso '17	YY 4
● Fioranello Rosso '16	YY 4
● Fiorano Rosso '14	YY 8
● Fiorano Rosso '13	YY 8

Giovanni Terenzi

FRAZ. LA FORMA
VIA FORESE, 13
03010 SERRONE [FR]
TEL. +39 0775594286
www.viniterenzi.com

CELLAR SALES
PRE-BOOKED VISITS
ANNUAL PRODUCTION 120,000 bottles
HECTARES UNDER VINE 12.00

Giovanni Terenzi and his wife Santa have run this family winery for over half a century and are helped today by their children. The vineyards contain almost 60-year-old vines and are located on volcanic, calcareous soils. Apart from a few rows of Sangiovese, they are almost exclusively planted with the two varieties that distinguish this territory: Cesanese (mostly the di Affile biotype) and Passerina. The wines submitted are traditional, with good structure and complexity. This year, the Cesanese del Piglio Superiore Colle Forma '18 proved one of the best in the appellation and made it to our finals. It offers up full, immediately expressive aromas of red fruit and undergrowth. The consistent, remarkably dense palate exhibits the tannins typical of the variety in the foreground, but is well-orchestrated with a long, convincing finish. Their well-made Riserva Vajoscuro '18 comes through pleasant, with nice fruit, but isn't as complex as the Colle Forma.

Wine	Rating
● Cesanese del Piglio Sup. Colle Forma '18	🍷🍷 4
● Cesanese del Piglio Sup. Vajoscuro Ris. '18	🍷🍷 5
⊙ Rosato '19	🍷 2
○ Villa Santa Passerina del Frusinate '19	🍷 2
○ Zerli Passerina del Frusinate '18	🍷 4
● Cesanese del Piglio Sup. Colle Forma '15	YY 3
● Cesanese del Piglio Sup. Vajoscuro Ris. '17	YY 5
● Cesanese del Piglio Sup. Vajoscuro Ris. '16	YY 5
● Cesanese del Piglio Vajoscuro Ris. '15	YY 4
● Cesanese del Piglio Velobra '15	YY 3*
○ Zerli Passerina del Frusinate '17	YY 5

Valle Vermiglia

VIA A. GRAMSCI, 7
00197 ROMA
TEL. +39 3487221073
www.vallevermiglia.it

CELLAR SALES
ANNUAL PRODUCTION 30,000 bottles
HECTARES UNDER VINE 8.00
SUSTAINABLE WINERY

On the slopes of Monte Tuscolo, we find the Eremo Tuscolano dei Camaldolesi di Monte Corona, a cloistered complex that gives its name to the only wine produced by the Valle Vermiglia winery. The vineyards, immersed in the woods surrounding the complex, produce grapes that Mario Masini transforms into Frascati Superiore. In just a few years, it has become an emblem of this appellation, which owes a lot to his family: in 1996 his uncle Pietro Campili fought for DOC recognition for Frascati, while in 2011 Mario battled to obtain the DOCG. The 2019 version of the Frascati Superiore Eremo Tuscolano offers up aromas of white fruit and kumquat, followed by hints of sage and rosemary. The sapid palate exhibits nice texture and freshness, with consistent notes of citrus and Mediterranean scrub—it's a long, pleasant wine.

Wine	Rating
○ Frascati Sup. Eremo Tuscolano '19	🍷🍷 3*
○ Frascati Sup. Eremo Tuscolano '17	YYY 3*
○ Frascati Sup. Eremo Tuscolano '16	YYY 3*
○ Frascati Sup. Eremo Tuscolano '13	YYY 3*
○ Frascati Sup. Eremo Tuscolano '18	YY 3*
○ Frascati Sup. Eremo Tuscolano '15	YY 3*
○ Frascati Sup. Eremo Tuscolano '14	YY 3*
○ Frascati Sup. Eremo Tuscolano '12	YY 3*

L'Avventura Produttori di Felicità

loc. Civitella, 3
03010 Piglio [FR]
Tel. +39 0775503051
www.agriavventura.it

CELLAR SALES
PRE-BOOKED VISITS
ACCOMMODATION AND RESTAURANT SERVICE
ANNUAL PRODUCTION 40,000 bottles
HECTARES UNDER VINE 22.00
VITICULTURE METHOD Certified Organic
SUSTAINABLE WINERY

- ● Cesanese del Piglio Sup. Amor '18 — 🍷🍷 5
- ● Cesanese del Piglio Sup. Picchiatello '18 — 🍷🍷 4
- ● Cesanese del Piglio Campanino '18 — 🍷 3
- ⊙ Rosato del Frusinate '19 — 🍷 3

CantinAmena

fraz. Campoleone
via Cisternense, 17
00075 Lanuvio [RM]
Tel. +39 0645557063
www.cantinamena.it

- ● Arcana '18 — 🍷🍷 3
- ○ Divitia '19 — 🍷 3
- ● Patientia '18 — 🍷 5
- ● Roma Rosso '18 — 🍷 3

Capizucchi

via Ardeatina
00134 Roma
Tel. +39
www.capizucchi.it

HECTARES UNDER VINE 25.00

- ● Mater Divini Amoris Merlot '18 — 🍷🍷 3
- ○ Roma Bianco 753 A.C. '19 — 🍷🍷 2*
- ● Roma Rosso 753 A.C. '19 — 🍷🍷 2*
- ● Roma Rosso Mater Divini Amoris '17 — 🍷 3

Capodarco

via del Grottino
00046 Grottaferrata [RM]
Tel. +39 0694549191
www.agricolturacapodarco.it

- ○ Frascati Sup. Philein '19 — 🍷🍷 2*
- ● Don Franco Rosso del Fondatore '19 — 🍷 2
- ○ San Nilo — 🍷 2

Casa Divina Provvidenza

via dei Frati, 140
00048 Nettuno [RM]
Tel. +39 069851366
www.casadivinaprovvidenza.it

CELLAR SALES
PRE-BOOKED VISITS
RESTAURANT SERVICE
ANNUAL PRODUCTION 100,000 bottles
HECTARES UNDER VINE 35.00
SUSTAINABLE WINERY

- ○ Nettuno Cacchione '19 — 🍷🍷 3
- ● Cesanese '18 — 🍷 4
- ○ Nettuno Cacchione Neroniano '19 — 🍷 2
- ● Roma Rosso '19 — 🍷 3

Tenuta Colfiorito

s.da prov.le 40a
00024 Castel Madama [RM]
Tel. +39 0774449396
www.colfio.it

CELLAR SALES
PRE-BOOKED VISITS
ACCOMMODATION
ANNUAL PRODUCTION 20,000 bottles
HECTARES UNDER VINE 4.50
VITICULTURE METHOD Certified Organic

- ○ Sorgente '19 — 🍷🍷 2*
- ○ Il Trovatore '19 — 🍷 3
- ○ Loggia '19 — 🍷 3
- ● Masnadiero '17 — 🍷 4

Corte dei Papi

loc. Colletonno
03012 Anagni [FR]
Tel. +39 0775769271
www.cortedeipapi.it

CELLAR SALES
PRE-BOOKED VISITS
ANNUAL PRODUCTION 60,000 bottles
HECTARES UNDER VINE 25.30

- ● Cesanese del Piglio Colle Ticchio '19 — 🍷🍷 3
- ● Cesanese del Piglio Ottavo Cielo '18 — 🍷 5
- ○ Passerina '19 — 🍷 3

Paolo e Noemia D'Amico

loc. Palombaro
fraz. Vaiano

01024 Castiglione in Teverina [VT]
Tel. +39 0761948034
www.paoloenoemiadamico.net

CELLAR SALES
PRE-BOOKED VISITS
RESTAURANT SERVICE
ANNUAL PRODUCTION 180,000 bottles
HECTARES UNDER VINE 31.00
SUSTAINABLE WINERY

- ● Seiano '19 — 🍷🍷 2*
- ● Villa Tirrena '15 — 🍷🍷 3
- ● Notturno dei Calanchi '15 — 🍷 5
- ○ Orvieto Noe dei Calanchi '19 — 🍷 2

Doganieri Miyazaki

fraz. Vaiano, 3
01024 Castiglione in Teverina [VT]
Tel. +39 3332807985
www.doganierimiyazaki.com

CELLAR SALES
PRE-BOOKED VISITS
ANNUAL PRODUCTION 7,000 bottles
HECTARES UNDER VINE 1.20

- ○ Airi '18 — 🍷🍷 3
- ○ Âme V. T. '18 — 🍷 5
- ⊙ U '18 — 🍷 3

Federici

via Santa Apollaria Vecchia, 30
00039 Zagarolo [RM]
Tel. +39 0695461022
www.vinifederici.com

CELLAR SALES
PRE-BOOKED VISITS
ANNUAL PRODUCTION 350,000 bottles
HECTARES UNDER VINE 3.00

- ○ Le Coste '19 — 🍷🍷 2*
- ○ Roma Malvasia Puntinata '19 — 🍷🍷 3
- ○ Bellone '19 — 🍷 2
- ● Roma Rosso '19 — 🍷 3

Gaffino

via Ardeatina , km 24.650
00040 Ardea [RM]
Tel. +39 0687606038
info@cantinagaffino.it

- ○ Fojetta '19 — 🍷🍷 3
- ● Opimiam '17 — 🍷🍷 3
- ● Cardinale '19 — 🍷 3
- ● Roma Rosso '17 — 🍷 3

Donato Giangirolami

fraz. Le Ferriere
via del Cavaliere, 1414
04100 Latina
Tel. +39 3358394890
www.donatogiangirolami.it

CELLAR SALES
PRE-BOOKED VISITS
ANNUAL PRODUCTION 80,000 bottles
HECTARES UNDER VINE 38.00
VITICULTURE METHOD Certified Organic

- ○ Cardito '19 — 🍷🍷 2*
- ○ Nynphe Ancestrale M. Cl. '16 — 🍷🍷 2*
- ○ Propizio '19 — 🍷🍷 2*
- ○ Regius '19 — 🍷 2

La Giannettòla

via Campoleone, 104
00049 Velletri [RM]
Tel. +39 0637500300
www.lagiannettola.com

- ○ Roma Malvasia Puntinata Il Laschetto '19 — 2 glasses, 3
- ● Il Frangente '19 — 1 glass, 3
- ● L'Ardente '18 — 1 glass, 3
- ○ La Brezza '19 — 1 glass, 2

Marcella Giuliani

loc. Vico Moricino
via Anticolana
03012 Anagni [FR]
Tel. +39 3913481031
www.marcellagiuliani.com

CELLAR SALES
PRE-BOOKED VISITS
ANNUAL PRODUCTION 35,000 bottles
HECTARES UNDER VINE 10.70
VITICULTURE METHOD Certified Organic

- ● Cesanese del Piglio Sup. Dives '17 — 2 glasses, 4
- ● Cesanese del Piglio '19 — 1 glass, 3
- ○ Passerina del Frusinate Dante '19 — 1 glass, 2

Cantina Imperatori

via Pietra Porzia, 14
00044 Frascati [RM]
Tel. +39 3394586822
www.cantinaimperatori.it

CELLAR SALES
ANNUAL PRODUCTION 40,000 bottles
HECTARES UNDER VINE 5.00

- ○ Viognier '19 — 2 glasses, 4
- ● Cesanese '17 — 1 glass, 5
- ○ Segreto Verde Anfora Trebbiano Verde '19 — 1 glass, 5
- ○ Segreto Verde Trebbiano Verde '19 — 1 glass, 4

Antica Cantina Leonardi

via del Pino, 12
01027 Montefiascone [VT]
Tel. +39 0761826028
www.cantinaleonardi.it

CELLAR SALES
PRE-BOOKED VISITS
RESTAURANT SERVICE
ANNUAL PRODUCTION 150,000 bottles
HECTARES UNDER VINE 30.00

- ● Don Carlo '17 — 2 glasses, 3
- ● Nero di Lava '18 — 2 glasses, 3
- ○ Est! Est!! Est!!! di Montefiascone Poggio del Cardinale '19 — 1 glass, 2

Mazziotti

loc. Melona Bonvino
via Cassia, km 110
01023 Bolsena [VT]
Tel. +39 0761799049
www.mazziottiwines.com

CELLAR SALES
PRE-BOOKED VISITS
ANNUAL PRODUCTION 150,000 bottles
HECTARES UNDER VINE 31.00

- ● Volgente '17 — 2 glasses, 3
- ○ Est Est Est di Montefiascone Cl. '19 — 1 glass, 1*
- ● Merlot '19 — 1 glass, 2
- ○ Terre di Melona V.T. '19 — 1 glass, 3

Monti Cecubi

c.da Porcignano, 3
04020 Itri [LT]
Tel. +39 3285550198
www.monticecubi.it

CELLAR SALES
PRE-BOOKED VISITS
ACCOMMODATION
ANNUAL PRODUCTION 20,000 bottles
HECTARES UNDER VINE 20.00
VITICULTURE METHOD Certified Organic
SUSTAINABLE WINERY

- ● Caecubum '17 — 2 glasses, 4
- ● Filari San Raffaele Abbuoto '18 — 1 glass, 3
- ● Terrae d'Itrj '18 — 1 glass, 2
- ○ Thymos '19 — 1 glass, 2

Nuova Cantina di Genazzano Martino V

s.s. 155, km 55,500
00030 Genazzano [RM]
Tel. +39 069579121
www.martinoquinto.it

CELLAR SALES
PRE-BOOKED VISITS
ANNUAL PRODUCTION 150,000 bottles
HECTARES UNDER VINE 50.00

○ Ottonese '18	🍷🍷 3
○ Bellone '18	🍷 2
● Cesanese '18	🍷 2
○ Passerina '18	🍷 2

Antonella Pacchiarotti

via Roma, 14
01024 Grotte di Castro [VT]
Tel. +39 0763796852
www.vinipacchiarotti.it

CELLAR SALES
PRE-BOOKED VISITS
ANNUAL PRODUCTION 10,000 bottles
HECTARES UNDER VINE 3.50
SUSTAINABLE WINERY

● Cavarosso '18	🍷🍷 3
⊙ Ramatico '18	🍷 3

I Pampini

loc. Acciarella
s.da Foglino, 1126
04100 Latina
Tel. +39 0773643144
www.ipampini.it

CELLAR SALES
PRE-BOOKED VISITS
ANNUAL PRODUCTION 22,000 bottles
HECTARES UNDER VINE 7.00
VITICULTURE METHOD Certified Organic

○ Bellone Non Filtrato '19	🍷🍷 3
○ Bellone '19	🍷 2
○ Legionarius '19	🍷 2

Pileum

via Casalotto
03010 Piglio [FR]
Tel. +39 3663129910
www.pileum.it

CELLAR SALES
PRE-BOOKED VISITS
ACCOMMODATION
ANNUAL PRODUCTION 56,000 bottles
HECTARES UNDER VINE 15.00
VITICULTURE METHOD Certified Organic

● Cesanese del Piglio Sup. Bolla di Urbano Ris. '18	🍷🍷 5
● Cesanese del Piglio Sup. Pilarocca Ris. '16	🍷 4
○ Passerina La Fattoria '18	🍷 2

Le Rose

via Ponte Tre Armi, 25
00045 Genzano di Roma [RM]
Tel. +39 0693709671
www.aziendaagricolalerose.com

CELLAR SALES
PRE-BOOKED VISITS
ANNUAL PRODUCTION 70,000 bottles
HECTARES UNDER VINE 10.00
VITICULTURE METHOD Certified Organic
SUSTAINABLE WINERY

○ Artemisia '19	🍷🍷 4
○ La Faiola Bianco '19	🍷 5
○ Petit Manseng '19	🍷 3
○ Tre Armi '19	🍷 3

Cantine San Marco

loc. Vermicino
via di Mola Cavona, 26/28
00044 Frascati [RM]
Tel. +39 069409403
www.sanmarcofrascati.it

CELLAR SALES
PRE-BOOKED VISITS
ANNUAL PRODUCTION 1,500,000 bottles
HECTARES UNDER VINE 32.00

○ Frascati Crio 8 '19	🍷🍷 2*
● Roma Rosso Romae '16	🍷🍷 3
○ Roma Bianco Romae '19	🍷 3
● Solomerlot '19	🍷 2

Sant'Andrea

LOC. BORGO VODICE
VIA RENIBBIO, 1720
04019 TERRACINA [LT]
TEL. +39 0773755028
www.cantinasantandrea.it

CELLAR SALES
PRE-BOOKED VISITS
ANNUAL PRODUCTION 1,000,000 bottles
HECTARES UNDER VINE 100.00

- ● Sogno '14 🍷🍷4
- ○ Circeo Bianco Dune '18 🍷2
- ○ Moscato di Terracina Secco Oppidum '19 🍷2

Sant'Eufemia

VIA ROMA, 97
04012 CISTERNA DI LATINA [LT]
TEL. +39 069682367
www.aziendaagricolasanteufemia.com

- ⊙ Nuvola '19 🍷🍷4
- ○ Ventinove '19 🍷🍷3
- ○ Chiò '19 🍷3
- ○ Ultimo Colle '19 🍷3

Tenuta Sant'Isidoro

LOC. TARQUINIA
LOC. PORTACCIA
01016 TARQUINIA [VT]
TEL. +39 0766869716
www.santisidoro.net

CELLAR SALES
PRE-BOOKED VISITS
ANNUAL PRODUCTION 65,000 bottles
HECTARES UNDER VINE 57.00

- ● Tarquinia Rosso Larth '19 🍷🍷1*
- ○ Soraluisa '19 🍷3
- ● Soremidio '18 🍷4
- ● Terzolo '19 🍷2

Tenuta Santa Lucia

VIA SANTA LUCIA
02047 POGGIO MIRTETO [RI]
TEL. +39 076524616
www.tenutasantalucia.com

CELLAR SALES
PRE-BOOKED VISITS
RESTAURANT SERVICE
ANNUAL PRODUCTION 180,000 bottles
HECTARES UNDER VINE 35.00
SUSTAINABLE WINERY

- ● Morrone Syrah '17 🍷🍷5
- ○ Falanghina '19 🍷2
- ○ Pecorino '19 🍷2
- ⊙ Rosamiooo '19 🍷2

Stefanoni

VIA STEFANONI, 48
01027 MONTEFIASCONE [VT]
TEL. +39 0761825651
www.cantinastefanoni.it

CELLAR SALES
PRE-BOOKED VISITS
ANNUAL PRODUCTION 100,000 bottles
HECTARES UNDER VINE 10.00

- ○ Brut M. Cl. '17 🍷🍷4
- ● Fanum '17 🍷🍷3
- ● Colle de Poggeri Aleatico '19 🍷3
- ○ Moscato Colle de Poggeri '19 🍷2

Tenuta Tre Cancelli

FRAZ. DUE CASETTE
VIA DELLA PISCINA, 3
00052 CERVETERI [RM]
TEL. +39 0639732012
www.tenutatrecancelli.com

CELLAR SALES
PRE-BOOKED VISITS
ANNUAL PRODUCTION 60,000 bottles
HECTARES UNDER VINE 18.00

- ● Cerveteri Rosso Pacha '18 🍷🍷2*
- ● Siborio Sangiovese '16 🍷🍷5
- ○ Cerveteri Procanico Mastarna '19 🍷2
- ● Roma Rosso 753 '18 🍷2

Trebotti

s.da della Poggetta, 9
01024 Castiglione in Teverina [VT]
Tel. +39 07611986704
www.trebotti.it

CELLAR SALES
PRE-BOOKED VISITS
ACCOMMODATION
ANNUAL PRODUCTION 45,000 bottles
HECTARES UNDER VINE 10.00
VITICULTURE METHOD Certified Organic
SUSTAINABLE WINERY

- ● Gocce '17 🍷🍷 4
- ⊙ 3S Aleatico Sostenibile Senza Solfiti '19 🍷 3
- ● 3S Sangiovese Sostenibile Senza Solfiti '17 🍷 3

Casale Vallechiesa

via Pietra Porzia, 19/23
00044 Frascati [RM]
Tel. +39 069417270
www.casalevallechiesa.it

CELLAR SALES
PRE-BOOKED VISITS
ANNUAL PRODUCTION 300,000 bottles
HECTARES UNDER VINE 13.00

- ○ Frascati Sup. Heredio Ris. '18 🍷🍷 7
- ○ Solomia '19 🍷🍷 3
- ○ Frascati Sup. Heredio '19 🍷 3
- ● Soraya '19 🍷 4

Villa Caviciana

loc. Tojena Caviciana
01025 Grotte di Castro [VT]
Tel. +39 0763798212
www.villacaviciana.com

CELLAR SALES
PRE-BOOKED VISITS
ANNUAL PRODUCTION 60,000 bottles
HECTARES UNDER VINE 20.00
VITICULTURE METHOD Certified Biodynamic

- ⊙ Tadzio '19 🍷🍷 2*
- ○ Filippo '19 🍷 2
- ● Letizia '16 🍷 3
- ○ Lorenzo Brut '19 🍷 3

Villa Gianna

loc. Borgo San Donato
s.da Maremmana
04010 Sabaudia [LT]
Tel. +39 0773250034
www.villagianna.it

PRE-BOOKED VISITS
ACCOMMODATION
ANNUAL PRODUCTION 900,000 bottles
HECTARES UNDER VINE 75.00
SUSTAINABLE WINERY

- ○ Vigne del Borgo Bellone '19 🍷🍷 2*
- ● Vigne del Borgo Shiraz '19 🍷🍷 2*
- ○ Moscato di Terracina Amabile '19 🍷 2
- ● Rudestro '18 🍷 2

Villa Simone

via Frascati Colonna, 29
00078 Monte Porzio Catone [RM]
Tel. +39 069449717
www.villasimone.it

CELLAR SALES
PRE-BOOKED VISITS
ANNUAL PRODUCTION 200,000 bottles
HECTARES UNDER VINE 21.00
SUSTAINABLE WINERY

- ○ Frascati Sup. Villa dei Preti '19 🍷🍷 3
- ● Syrah '18 🍷🍷 3
- ○ Frascati '19 🍷 2
- ○ Frascati Sup. Vign. Filonardi Ris. '18 🍷 4

Vinea Domini

loc. Frattocchie
via del Divino Amore, 115
00040 Marino [RM]
Tel. +39 0693022211
www.gottodoro.it

CELLAR SALES
PRE-BOOKED VISITS

- ○ Frascati Sup. '19 🍷🍷 3
- ● Roma Rosso '17 🍷🍷 2*
- ● Cesanese del Piglio '18 🍷 3

ABRUZZO

The Adriatic lying open ahead of you, with your back to the peaks of Majella. This is the image that we have every time we taste a wine from Abruzzo. The region's geography is special, with vineyards that unfold amidst natural wonders: there are plots that hear the sound of the sea, others enjoy the silence of the mountains. Within just a few square kilometers we find sea, glaciers, hills, natural parks. It's here that we find 29,530 hectares of vineyards, with Montepulciano d'Abruzzo taking center stage. It's a great red, capable of expressing all the complexity of such a varied and heterogeneous territory. 14 Tre Bicchieri were awarded in this edition of the guide, 5 are Montepulcianos, ranging from the fresh and fragrant wines of the mountains, shaped by the cold winds and rock, to richer and more powerful wines spawned by sun and clay, to more delicately salty sensations as we get nearer to the coast. Valentini delivers with an interpretation of great character, the 2015—it's flanked by Castorani, Illuminati, Tollo and Valle Reale. Some 3 Cerasuolo d'Abruzzos were recognized. Among these Cataldi Madonna stands out with their Piè delle Vigne '18, which is also our Rosé of the Year for its sumptuous performance. It's a wine that combines extraordinary complexity, expressive lightness and rare drinkability. A real treat for the palate. They're accompanied by 2 other solid producers, Terraviva and Pepe, who are back in the limelight after some time. Together they make for a trio of rosés 'd'auteur'. Pecorino, a white that has benefited from commercial success in recent years by focusing on more complex and mineral fragrances, is clearly growing in quality. It's the Riesling of the Adriatic, giving rise to wines that are increasingly honed and focused, capable of evolving over time with surprising grace. 4 Tre Bicchieri went to Pecorinos: the Codice Vino, Villa Medoro, Masciarelli and Feudo Antico. Finally, Trebbiano d'Abruzzo earned 2 golds for the appellation, and they happen to be particularly ageworthy versions: Agriverde's Trebbiano Solàrea and Testa di Torre dei Beati's excellent Bianchi Grilli.

Agriverde

LOC. CALDARI
VIA STORTINI, 32A
66026 ORTONA [CH]
TEL. +39 0859032101
www.agriverde.it

CELLAR SALES
PRE-BOOKED VISITS
RESTAURANT SERVICE
ANNUAL PRODUCTION 900,000 bottles
HECTARES UNDER VINE 65.00
VITICULTURE METHOD Certified Organic
SUSTAINABLE WINERY

Deep historical roots and a gaze fixed on the future: these are Agriverde's defining characteristics. Founded by the Di Carlo family in the first half of the nineteenth century, the turning point came under Giannicola, who in the mid-1980s felt that the future of his winery was with organic management. Among the first Italian producers to adopt agro-compatible protocols, both in terms of cultivation and their relais / spa, today the Di Carlo family avail themselves of vineyards in the municipalities of Caldari, Ortona, Rogatti, Frisa and Crecchio, on the Teatine Hills. The 2018 version of their Trebbiano Solàrea put in a great performance, exhibiting a profile of yellow fruit with elegant mineral strokes. In the mouth it finds flavor on a racy and supple palate of great energy. The Montepulciano Caldaria '17 is just as good: ripe black berries are framed by a light toastiness, the palate is sapid and juicy, with dense, fine-grained tannins.

Wine	Rating
○ Trebbiano d'Abruzzo Solàrea '18	🍷🍷🍷 4*
● Montepulciano d'Abruzzo Caldaria '17	🍷🍷 3*
⊙ Cerasuolo d'Abruzzo Natum Biovegan '19	🍷🍷 2*
● Montepulciano d'Abruzzo Natum Biologico Vegano '19	🍷🍷 3
○ Eikos Pecorino '19	🍷 3
● Montepulciano d'Abruzzo Eikos '17	🍷 3
○ Passerina Riseis '19	🍷 3
● Montepulciano d'Abruzzo Plateo '04	🍷🍷🍷 6
● Montepulciano d'Abruzzo Plateo '01	🍷🍷🍷 6
● Montepulciano d'Abruzzo Plateo '00	🍷🍷🍷 6
● Montepulciano d'Abruzzo Plateo '98	🍷🍷🍷 5
● Montepulciano d'Abruzzo Plateo Ris. '15	🍷🍷🍷 6
● Montepulciano d'Abruzzo Solàrea '03	🍷🍷🍷 4
● Montepulciano d'Abruzzo Riseis '17	🍷🍷 3*
● Montepulciano d'Abruzzo Riseis '13	🍷🍷 3*

F.lli Barba

LOC. SCERNE
S.DA ROTABILE PER CASOLI
64025 PINETO [TE]
TEL. +39 0859461020
www.fratellibarba.it

CELLAR SALES
PRE-BOOKED VISITS
ACCOMMODATION
ANNUAL PRODUCTION 400,000 bottles
HECTARES UNDER VINE 62.00
SUSTAINABLE WINERY

The operational base of the Barba brothers' winery is situated in Scerne di Pineto: it's here that Giovanni, Domenico and Vincenzo continue the work started by Cavalier Luigi in the 1950s, when the latter decided to leave sharecropping in favor of direct management. Today their more than 60 hectares of vineyards unfold on the warm Teramane Hills, in Casal Thaulero, Colle Morino and Vignafranca. The wines, made with Montepulciano, Trebbiano and Pecorino grapes, represent a modern interpretation of regional classics. We found this year's battery of wines less impressive less than last year's, but two interesting Montepulcianos stand out: I Vasari Old Vines '17 combines floral sensations with characteristic aromas of black berries and whiffs of sweet spices, while the palate comes through full-bodied and voluminous; the Yang '18 brings out certain vegetal sensations on a toasty, relaxed background. The Montepulciano Collemorino '19 plays more on drinkability and suppleness.

Wine	Rating
● Montepulciano d'Abruzzo Collemorino '19	🍷🍷 2*
● Montepulciano d'Abruzzo Colline Teramane Yang '17	🍷🍷 3
● Montepulciano d'Abruzzo I Vasari Old Vines '17	🍷🍷 5
● Montepulciano d'Abruzzo I Vasari '10	🍷🍷🍷 5
● Montepulciano d'Abruzzo I Vasari '09	🍷🍷🍷 5
● Montepulciano d'Abruzzo I Vasari '08	🍷🍷🍷 5
● Montepulciano d'Abruzzo Vignafranca '07	🍷🍷🍷 3*
● Montepulciano d'Abruzzo Vignafranca '06	🍷🍷🍷 3*
○ Trebbiano d'Abruzzo '06	🍷🍷🍷 4*
⊙ Montepulciano d'Abruzzo Cerasuolo Vignafranca '14	🍷🍷 2*
● Montepulciano d'Abruzzo Colle Morino '14	🍷🍷 2*

Barone Cornacchia

c.da Torri, 19
64010 Torano Nuovo [TE]
Tel. +39 0861887412
www.baronecornacchia.it

CELLAR SALES
PRE-BOOKED VISITS
ACCOMMODATION
ANNUAL PRODUCTION 250,000 bottles
HECTARES UNDER VINE 50.00
VITICULTURE METHOD Certified Organic

Filippo and Caterina Cornacchia, together with their father Piero, are the latest heirs of a long tradition dating back to the 16th century, when the family received from the Viceroy of Naples their baronial title and the responsibility of controlling the fiefdoms around the Fortress of Civitella, the heart of the Teramo Hills. Today the main plots are located in what was once a hunting reserve, in the Torri di Torano Nuovo district, where the winery and the most of its 50 hectares of organically managed vineyards are located. Here we find Abruzzo's classic grapes: Trebbiano, Pecorino, Passerina and Montepulciano. This year they're only missing that crowning stroke, but the overall performance was among the best in the region. Indeed, their range proves solid in all respects, starting with their Montepulcianos: the Casanova '18 features nice fruity pulp and energy; the Vigna Le Coste Riserva '17 exhibits a compact aromatic profile and discreet elegance, despite the warm vintage; the Colline Teramane Vizzaro Riserva '16 has nice volume and texture.

○ Controguerra Pecorino Casanova '19	🍷🍷 3
● Montepulciano d'Abruzzo Casanova '18	🍷🍷 3
● Montepulciano d'Abruzzo V. Le Coste '17	🍷🍷 5
● Montepulciano d'Abruzzo Colline Teramane Vizzaro '16	🍷🍷 5
○ Trebbiano d'Abruzzo Sup. Casanova '19	🍷🍷 3
⊙ Cerasuolo d'Abruzzo Sup. Casanova '19	🍷 3
○ Controguerra Passerina Casanova '19	🍷 3
● Controguerra Rosso Colle Cupo '18	🍷 5
○ Controguerra Pecorino Casanova '17	🍷🍷 3
● Controguerra Rosso Colle Cupo '17	🍷🍷 5
● Controguerra Rosso Colle Lupo '16	🍷🍷 5
● Montepulciano d'Abruzzo V. Le Coste '16	🍷🍷 5
● Montepulciano d'Abruzzo V. Le Coste '15	🍷🍷 5
● Montepulciano d'Abruzzo Colline Teramane Vizzaro '15	🍷🍷 5

★Castorani

via Castorani, 5
65020 Alanno [PE]
Tel. +39 0852012513
www.castorani.it

CELLAR SALES
PRE-BOOKED VISITS
ACCOMMODATION AND RESTAURANT SERVICE
ANNUAL PRODUCTION 600,000 bottles
HECTARES UNDER VINE 80.00
VITICULTURE METHOD Certified Organic
SUSTAINABLE WINERY

Alanno is a small town on the Pescaresi Hills, an area that rises up from the Adriatic Sea towards the Majella. In 1793 the surgeon Raffaele Castorani built the farm that today constitutes the heart of the property a few kilometres outside the town. The estate, whose owners include the famous former Formula 1 driver Jarno Trulli, is currently a leader in regional wine-growing thanks to a modern vision that has led to its many wines, especially those made with native grapes, becoming known all over the world. Pencil lead, plum, blueberries and sweet spices form the aromatic spectrum of the Montepulciano Amorino '16, a wine that unfolds in the mouth with excellent elongation supported by fine tannic texture and perfectly calibrated oak. The Trebbiano Cadetto '19 performs just as well. Redolent of flowery meadows and yellow citrus fruits, it develops elegant and vibrant on the palate. But all their wines, as a whole, work well together.

● Montepulciano d'Abruzzo Amorino '16	🍷🍷🍷 3*
○ Trebbiano d'Abruzzo Cadetto '19	🍷🍷 2*
○ Abruzzo Pecorino Sup. Amorino '19	🍷🍷 3
● Montepulciano d'Abruzzo Lupaia '17	🍷🍷 2*
○ Trebbiano d'Abruzzo Podere Castorani Ris. '18	🍷🍷 3
○ Lupaia Trebbiano Spontaneo '19	🍷 2
● Montepulciano d'Abruzzo Cadetto '18	🍷 2
● Montepulciano d'Abruzzo Amorino '13	🍷🍷🍷 3*
● Montepulciano d'Abruzzo Amorino '12	🍷🍷🍷 3*
● Montepulciano d'Abruzzo Casauria Podere Castorani Ris. '15	🍷🍷🍷 5
● Montepulciano d'Abruzzo Podere Castorani Ris. '14	🍷🍷🍷 5
● Montepulciano d'Abruzzo Amorino '15	🍷🍷 3
● Montepulciano d'Abruzzo Cadetto '17	🍷🍷 2*
● Montepulciano d'Abruzzo Lupaia '16	🍷🍷 2*

★★Cataldi Madonna

loc. Madonna del Piano
67025 Ofena [AQ]
Tel. +39 0862954252
www.cataldimadonna.com

CELLAR SALES
PRE-BOOKED VISITS
ANNUAL PRODUCTION 230,000 bottles
HECTARES UNDER VINE 30.00
VITICULTURE METHOD Certified Organic
SUSTAINABLE WINERY

Ofena is commonly nicknamed 'il forno d'Abruzzo' (the Abruzzo oven) because of the high temperature peaks reached in summer. Here continental climates are characterized by dizzying temperature fluctuations, which benefit the vineyards of Cataldi Madonna, where only native grape varieties are grown: Montepulciano, Trebbiano and Pecorino. The changeover from one generation to the next went smoothly, and now it's up to the enthusiasm of young Giulia to take the centuries-old family business into the future, with her father Luigi, "the professor", continuing to supervise the work being carried out. The Piè delle Vigne '18 is an extraordinary Cerasuolo. It already delivers plenty of satisfaction today, and it's destined to improve exponentially in the bottle. Fresh balsamic sensations are accompanied by a characteristic note of pencil lead, all of which adorns hints of small black berries: fragrant, juicy and intense, it has character and drinkability to sell. It's our Rosé of the Year. The Montepulciano Malandrino '18 is also delicious.

Wine	Rating
⊙ Cerasuolo d'Abruzzo Piè delle Vigne '18	TTT 5
● Montepulciano d'Abruzzo Malandrino '18	TT 3*
⊙ Cerasuolo d'Abruzzo Malandrino '19	TT 3
○ Giulia Pecorino '19	TT 3
○ Trebbiano d'Abruzzo Malandrino '19	TT 2*
⊙ Cataldino '18	T 3
● Montepulciano d'Abruzzo Luì '17	T
⊙ Cerasuolo d'Abruzzo Piè delle Vigne '16	YYY 5
⊙ Cerasuolo d'Abruzzo Piè delle Vigne '15	YYY 5
● Montepulciano d'Abruzzo Malandrino '13	YYY 3*
● Montepulciano d'Abruzzo Malandrino '12	YYY 3*
○ Pecorino '11	YYY 5
○ Pecorino Frontone '13	YYY 5
○ Supergiulia Pecorino '17	YYY 5

Cerulli Spinozzi

s.s. 150 del Vomano km 17,600
64020 Canzano [TE]
Tel. +39 086157193
www.cerullispinozzi.it

CELLAR SALES
PRE-BOOKED VISITS
ACCOMMODATION
ANNUAL PRODUCTION 200,000 bottles
HECTARES UNDER VINE 53.00

The union between 2 of the most important families of Abruzzo, the Spinozzi (a feudal family), and the Cerulli Irelli (merchants), dates back to the early 20th century. In 2003 brothers Vincenzo and Francesco Cerulli Irelli decided to create their own winery, availing themselves of 2 vineyards, one a 35-hectare tract in Canzano, the other 18 hectares on the hills of Mosciano, both territories of the Vomano valley, in the Colline Teramane. Today management is entrusted to Enrico, Vincenzo's son. Together with his staff, he creates territorial and contemporary wines. This year the Pecorino Cortalto '18 took home the award for the best wine of the house, offering up delicate salty sensations combined with nuances of lime. On the palate it's got a nice, fruity attack, and sapid development with a rising finish. The Colline Teramane Torre Migliori '15 was also received well: blackberry and plum are accompanied by an almost balsamic herbaceous note, just detectable, while in the mouth it proves dense in fine-grained tannins, exhibiting volume and intensity.

Wine	Rating
⊙ Cersauolo d'Abruzzo Sup. Cortalto '19	TT 2*
○ Cortalto Pecorino '18	TT 2*
● Montepulciano d'Abruzzo Colline Teramane Cortalto '17	TT 3
● Montepulciano d'Abruzzo Colline Teramane Torre Migliori '15	TT 3
○ Trebbiano d'Abruzzo Gruè '19	TT 1*
⊙ Cerasuolo d'Abruzzo Gruè '19	T 1*
● Montepulciano d'Abruzzo Colline Teramane Gruè '18	T 2
○ Trebbiano d'Abruzzo Torre Migliori '18	T 3
● Montepulciano d'Abruzzo '18	YY 2*
● Montepulciano d'Abruzzo '13	YY 2*
● Montepulciano d'Abruzzo Almorano '18	YY 1*
● Montepulciano d'Abruzzo Colline Teramane Cortalto '15	YY 2*
○ Trebbiano d'Abruzzo '18	YY 2*

Chiusa Grande

C.DA CASALI
65010 NOCCIANO [PE]
TEL. +39 085847460
www.chiusagrande.com

CELLAR SALES
PRE-BOOKED VISITS
RESTAURANT SERVICE
ANNUAL PRODUCTION 600,000 bottles
HECTARES UNDER VINE 70.00
VITICULTURE METHOD Certified Organic
SUSTAINABLE WINERY

We are happy to have the lovely winery created by Franco D'Eusanio in 1994 in the main section of our guide. The vineyards are situated in various districts in the provinces of Pescara and Chieti (Nocciano, Cugnoli, Civitaquana, Loreto Aprutino and Casacanditella), at elevations ranging from 200 to 350 meters above sea level, on different types of soils. The variety of pedoclimatic conditions and grapes, both native and non, is expressed in a wide and multifaceted range. We found the Montepulciano In Petra '17 to be the most convincing wine during this round of tastings. It's made following the ancient custom of vinifying the must in stone vats of various shapes and sizes, with grapes fermented after destemming and crushing. The result is a red with a spicy bouquet, redolent of wild cherry and pine needles, unraveling on a progressive, dynamic palate by virtue of its freshness and fine, subtle tannins.

Wine	Rating
● Montepulciano d'Abruzzo In Petra '17	🍷🍷 5
● Montepulciano d'Abruzzo Roccosecco '15	🍷🍷 3
○ Trebbiano d'Abruzzo Perla Bianca '15	🍷🍷 5
⊙ Cerasuolo d'Abruzzo Tatà '19	🍷 3

Cirelli

LOC. TRECIMINIERE
VIA COLLE SAN GIOVANNI, 1
64032 ATRI [TE]
TEL. +39 0858700106
www.agricolacirelli.com

CELLAR SALES
PRE-BOOKED VISITS
ACCOMMODATION AND RESTAURANT SERVICE
ANNUAL PRODUCTION 26,000 bottles
HECTARES UNDER VINE 5.00
VITICULTURE METHOD Certified Organic

For just over 15 years, here in Atri, in the heart of the Teramo Hills, Francesco Cirelli has been building an all-round agricultural business that focuses on respect for the territory and the environment. All crops are grown organically, while the vineyards are dedicated to native varieties, namely Montepulciano, Trebbiano and Pecorino. Spontaneous fermentation, use of amphorae and an artisan approach are all expressed through his wines, which are increasingly popular among wine lovers. The Anfora line was missing in this round of tastings, but it was replaced by a new foray: the Amphora 15+16+17, Bianco and Rosa. A blend of three different vintages makes for two extremely charming wines. But the best results came from the Pecorino La Collina Biologica '19: sensations of tea leaves, mown grass, touches of ginger and citron peel mix in a bouquet that anticipates great character and freshness in the mouth.

Wine	Rating
○ La Collina Biologica Pecorino '19	🍷🍷 3*
○ Amphora Bianco	🍷🍷 7
⊙ Amphora Rosa	🍷🍷 7
⊙ Cerasuolo d'Abruzzo La Collina Biologica '19	🍷🍷 2*
● Montepulciano d'Abruzzo La Collina Biologica '19	🍷🍷 2*
○ Trebbiano d'Abruzzo La Collina Biologica '19	🍷🍷 2*
⊙ Cerasuolo d'Abruzzo La Collina Biologica '18	🍷🍷 2*
○ La Collina Biologica Pecorino '17	🍷🍷 3
● Montepulciano d'Abruzzo La Collina Biologica '18	🍷🍷 2*
● Montepulciano d'Abruzzo La Collina Biologica '16	🍷🍷 2*
○ Trebbiano d'Abruzzo Amphora '17	🍷🍷 5

Codice Vino

LOC. CALDARI
66026 ORTONA [CH]
TEL. +39 0859031342
www.codicevino.it

ANNUAL PRODUCTION 90,200 bottles
SUSTAINABLE WINERY

Costola di Codice Citra, Codice Vino is a new initiative undertaken at the behest of Valentino Di Campli, president of the powerful Ortona cooperative. Developed in accordance with the scientific guidance of Attilio Scienza and the enological advice of Riccardo Cotarella, the project aims to identify the best vineyards among those cultivated by its many members, with a careful eye to zoning and precision viticulture. The range is divided into two lines: the 'Monovarietali' (for graceful and dynamic wines), and 'Codice Oro' (for their premium selections). And it's Tre Bicchieri right out of the gate for the Tegèo '18, a Pecorino Superiore characterized by a clearly Mediterranean profile. Golden in color, broad and fragrant aromatically, it calls up yellow fruits, tropical and white flowers on the nose, coming through with a dense and pervasive flavor on the palate, while still fresh and crisp. We also appreciated the Torre Passo '17, a skillfully textured and spicy Montepulciano marked by hints of plum jam and toasty notes.

○ Abruzzo Pecorino Sup. Tegèo '18	▼▼▼ 4*
● Montepulciano d'Abruzzo Teatro Torrepasso '17	▼▼ 6
○ Abruzzo Passerina Sup. Coda d'Oro '18	▼▼ 4
⊙ Cerasuolo d'Abruzzo Solante '19	▼▼ 5
⊙ Cerasuolo d'Abruzzo '18	▽▽ 3
● Montepulciano d'Abruzzo '17	▽▽ 3*

Contesa

S.DA DELLE VIGNE, 28
65010 COLLECORVINO [PE]
TEL. +39 0858205078
www.contesa.it

CELLAR SALES
PRE-BOOKED VISITS
RESTAURANT SERVICE
ANNUAL PRODUCTION 260,000 bottles
HECTARES UNDER VINE 45.00
SUSTAINABLE WINERY

Rocco Pasetti's winery, created in Collecorvino, in the Terra dei Vestini subzone of the Pescaresi Hills, is celebrating its 20th anniversary. The cellar, surrounded by its own vineyards (mostly native grapes), hosts steel tanks, oak barrels, barriques and large barrels, all of which allows for a variegated approach to aging. Three lines of wines are offered: Contesa, Collecorvino and Vini d'Autore. The arrival of a new generation of family has brought a breath of fresh air to the producer, though without distorting their focus on territorial identity—indeed, if anything, it has brought further emphasis. This time around we especially appreciated the whites: the 2019 version of the Trebbiano d'Abruzzo Fermentazione Spontanea is delicious, offering up notes of hay, Mediterranean herbs and citrus peel. On the palate it's racy, infused with an acidic-sapid freshness that lends vitality and energy. The Pecorino '19 tends to aromas of basil, thyme and white flowers, opening the way to a powerful palate streaked with citrus nuances.

○ Abruzzo Pecorino '19	▼▼ 3
○ Abruzzo Pecorino Sup. Aspetta Primavera '19	▼▼ 4
○ Trebbiano d'Abruzzo Fermentazione Spontanea '19	▼▼ 3
⊙ Cerasuolo d'Abruzzo '19	▼ 2
● Montepulciano d'Abruzzo Ris. '16	▼ 4
● Montepulciano d'Abruzzo Ris. '08	▽▽▽ 3*
○ Abruzzo Pecorino Sup. Aspetta Primavera '18	▽▽ 5
● Montepulciano d'Abruzzo '17	▽▽ 2*
● Montepulciano d'Abruzzo '16	▽▽ 2*
● Montepulciano d'Abruzzo Ris. '15	▽▽ 4
● Montepulciano d'Abruzzo Ris. '13	▽▽ 4
● Montepulciano d'Abruzzo Terre dei Vestini Chiedi alla Polvere Ris. '13	▽▽ 4

D'Alesio

via Gaglierano, 73
65013 Città Sant'Angelo [PE]
Tel. +39 08596713
www.sciarr.com

CELLAR SALES
PRE-BOOKED VISITS
RESTAURANT SERVICE
ANNUAL PRODUCTION 70,000 bottles
HECTARES UNDER VINE 16.00
VITICULTURE METHOD Certified Organic
SUSTAINABLE WINERY

Situated in the hinterland of Città Sant'Angelo, on the Pescaresi Hills, from the outset the winery (Est. 2007) chose to focus immediately on organic certification for its entire production. It was a choice made by Mario and Giovanni, heirs to their grandfather's agricultural legacy and now managers of the family business. Indeed, the 'Tenuta del Professore' line, which form part of their range together with 'D'Alesio' and 'Sciarr', is dedicated to him: a dozen wines with a strong territorial character, born out of the region's native grapes. In the absence of the Trebbiano Tenuta del Professore, their range is led by the Montepulciano Riserva (of the same line). It opens with beautiful oaky and toasty notes joined by crisp black berries; on the palate it's vibrant, dense in its austere, tannic texture. The Pecorino Superiore '17 also delivered—already elegant on the nose, it offers up pleasant hints of flint and wet stones, while notes of white flowers anticipate a dynamic, flavorful palate.

Wine	Rating
○ Abruzzo Pecorino Sup. '17	🍷🍷 2*
● Montepulciano d'Abruzzo Tenuta del Professore Ris. '15	🍷🍷 6
○ Abruzzo Montonico	🍷 3
○ Abruzzo Pecorino Sup. '15	🍷🍷 2*
● Montepulciano d'Abruzzo '17	🍷🍷 4
● Montepulciano d'Abruzzo '15	🍷🍷 4
○ Trebbiano d'Abruzzo Tenuta del Professore '13	🍷🍷 5

Tenuta I Fauri

via Foro, 8
66010 Ari [CH]
Tel. +39 0871332627
www.tenutaifauri.it

CELLAR SALES
PRE-BOOKED VISITS
ACCOMMODATION
ANNUAL PRODUCTION 150,000 bottles
HECTARES UNDER VINE 35.00
SUSTAINABLE WINERY

Chieti, Francavilla al Mare, Miglianico, Villamagna, Bucchianico and Ari: these are the municipalities that host the vineyards (currently being converted to organic) overseen by Valentina and Luigi Di Camillo. The pair are now firmly at the helm of the producer created by their father, Domenico, in the late seventies. While Valentina oversees the commercial side of things (lately she has also been working on two accommodation facilities to welcome wine lovers and tourists), Luigi transforms the grapes into wines that make expressiveness and territoriality their defining characteristics. The Trebbiano Baldovino '19, one of the best in the region, missed Tre Bicchieri by a hair's breadth. Mineral sensations are accompanied by citrus nuances and herbaceous notes reminiscent of mowed lawn; on the palate it's got an almost balsamic attack, showing rhythm and great mobility. The Cerasuolo Baldovino '19 is delectable: cherry and raspberry pulp teases the nose, while the mouth comes through juicy and fresh.

Wine	Rating
⊙ Cerasuolo d'Abruzzo Baldovino '19	🍷🍷 2*
○ Trebbiano d'Abruzzo Baldovino '19	🍷🍷 2*
○ Abruzzo Pecorino '19	🍷🍷 3
● Montepulciano d'Abruzzo Baldovino '18	🍷🍷 2*
● Montepulciano d'Abruzzo Ottobre Rosso '18	🍷🍷 2*
○ Passerina '19	🍷 2
○ Pecorino Brut	🍷 3
○ Abruzzo Pecorino '18	🍷🍷🍷 3*
○ Abruzzo Pecorino '14	🍷🍷🍷 2*
○ Abruzzo Pecorino '13	🍷🍷🍷 2*
● Montepulciano d'Abruzzo Baldovino '17	🍷🍷 2*
● Montepulciano d'Abruzzo Baldovino '15	🍷🍷 2*
● Montepulciano d'Abruzzo Rosso dei Fauri '15	🍷🍷 5
○ Trebbiano d'Abruzzo Baldovino '18	🍷🍷 2*

Feudo Antico

via Crocevecchia, 101
66010 Tollo [CH]
Tel. +39 0871969128
www.feudoantico.it

CELLAR SALES
ANNUAL PRODUCTION 80,000 bottles
HECTARES UNDER VINE 20.00
VITICULTURE METHOD Certified Organic

Founded as a DOC appellation in 2008 and 'promoted' to DOCG in 2019, Tullum is the smallest Italian appellation in terms of size. But it has a very important standard bearer: Feudo Antico, a winery that has focused and continues to focus on the territory's potential like few others. Unlike many other Abruzzo cooperatives, here we are dealing with a small producer: about fifty members oversee 20 hectares of vineyards, bringing painstaking attention and respect for nature and the environment to their work while following principles of organic farming. The Tullum Pecorino Bio is back to form with Tre Bicchieri. The 2019 version offers up a bouquet of yellow flowers, herbs and white-fleshed fruits, all of which follow-through on a tense palate, sapid and long, all in on citrus nuances. The Casadonna Pecorino '19 is a whirlwind of salt and lemon, unleashing electrically on the palate. The Montepulciano d'Abruzzo Bio '19 is true to type in its notes of dark fruits and embers.

Wine	Rating
○ Tullum Pecorino Biologico '19	🍷🍷🍷 3*
○ Casadonna Pecorino '19	🍷🍷 7
● Montepulciano d'Abruzzo Organic '19	🍷🍷 3
○ Tullum Passerina '19	🍷🍷 4
○ Tullum Pecorino '19	🍷🍷 3
● Tullum Rosso '16	🍷🍷 3
● Tullum Rosso Ris. '16	🍷 5
○ Casadonna Pecorino '15	ΥΥΥ 7
● Montepulciano d'Abruzzo Organic '18	ΥΥΥ 3*
○ Tullum Pecorino Biologico '17	ΥΥΥ 3*
○ Casadonna Pecorino '18	ΥΥ 7
○ Casadonna Pecorino '17	ΥΥ 7
○ Casadonna Pecorino '14	ΥΥ 7
○ Tullum Pecorino '14	ΥΥ 3*
○ Tullum Pecorino Biologico '16	ΥΥ 3*
● Tullum Rosso Ris. '14	ΥΥ 5

Il Feuduccio di Santa Maria D'Orni

loc. Feuduccio
66036 Orsogna [CH]
Tel. +39 0871891646
www.ilfeuduccio.it

CELLAR SALES
PRE-BOOKED VISITS
ANNUAL PRODUCTION 150,000 bottles
HECTARES UNDER VINE 50.00

In 1995 Gaetano Lamaletto, a successful entrepreneur in Venezuela who'd returned to Abruzzo, started work on the creation of a model winery. The name comes from the feud of Santa Maria d'Orni where the vineyards are located, in the Orsogna area on the Teatine Hills. Today at the helm are Gaetano's son, Camillo, and his grandson Gaetano Junior. Together with Rocco Cipollone they oversee the property, including a five-story underground cellar that houses a varied range of wines organized into different stylistic lines. An excellent performance for all Feuduccio's wines, including a great version of the Montepulciano Ursonia. The 2016 vintage gave rise to a red in which toasty and spicy notes of oak blend perfectly with ripe plum and blackberry; in the mouth it's concentrated without being heavy, thanks to calibrated tannic extraction and a bursting sapidity, which guides the palate towards a beautiful finish on blood orange. The Pecorino Ursonia '19 is multifaceted and linear.

Wine	Rating
● Montepulciano d'Abruzzo Ursonia '16	🍷🍷 5
⊙ Cerasuolo d'Abruzzo Feuduccio '19	🍷🍷 3
● Montepulciano d'Abruzzo Il Feuduccio '17	🍷🍷 3
○ Pecorino '19	🍷🍷 2*
○ Trebbiano d'Abruzzo Feuduccio '19	🍷🍷 3
○ Trebbiano d'Abruzzo Ursonia '18	🍷🍷 5
○ Ursonia Pecorino '18	🍷🍷 6
● Montepulciano d'Abruzzo Ursonia '13	ΥΥΥ 4*
○ Fonte Venna Pecorino '17	ΥΥ 2*
⊙ Fonte Venna Rosato '17	ΥΥ 2*
● Montepulciano d'Abruzzo '17	ΥΥ 3
● Montepulciano d'Abruzzo Ursonia '15	ΥΥ 5
○ Pecorino '18	ΥΥ 2*
○ Pecorino '16	ΥΥ 2*
○ Trebbiano d'Abruzzo '18	ΥΥ 3
○ Ursonia Pecorino '17	ΥΥ 6

Fontefico

VIA DIFENZA, 38
66054 VASTO [CH]
TEL. +39 3284113619
www.fontefico.it

CELLAR SALES
PRE-BOOKED VISITS
RESTAURANT SERVICE
ANNUAL PRODUCTION 45,000 bottles
HECTARES UNDER VINE 15.00
VITICULTURE METHOD Certified Organic
SUSTAINABLE WINERY

Managed by brothers Emanuele and Nicola Alteri, Fontefico avails itself of about 15 hectares of vineyards cultivated with organic methods. Located on the promontory of Punta Penna, they benefit from the fresh winds and mesoclimate of the nearby Adriatic Sea. Each wine is the result and expression of the grapes grown on their four properties: Vigna Bianca (Pecorino and Trebbiano), Le Coste (dedicated to Aglianico), Vigna del Pozzo and Il Pàstino (both home to Montepulciano). The pair of rosés were the best wines received. The Cerasuolo Fossimatto '19 features an intriguing aromatic profile, with roses and pine needles at the fore, while in the mouth it's juicy and pleasantly salty. Balsamic whiffs and notes of wild strawberries characterize the non-vintage Febbre d'Abruzzo: fleshy, spicy, round, fragrant and beautiful fullness. The Canaglia '19 exhibits the classic profile of a sunny, energetic, powerful Pecorino.

Wine	Rating	Price
○ Abruzzo Pecorino Sup. La Canaglia '19	▼▼	3
⊙ Cerasuolo d'Abruzzo Sup. Fossimatto '19	▼▼	3
⊙ Febbre d'Abruzzo	▼▼	5
● Montepulciano d'Abruzzo Cocca di Casa '17	▼	3
● Montepulciano d'Abruzzo Titinge Ris. '15	▼	5
○ Trebbiano d'Abruzzo Sup. Portarispetto '18	▼	2
○ Abruzzo Pecorino Sup. La Canaglia '17	▽▽	3
○ Abruzzo Pecorino Sup. La Canaglia '16	▽▽	2*
○ Abruzzo Pecorino Sup. La Foia '16	▽▽	5
● Montepulciano d'Abruzzo Cocca di Casa '16	▽▽	3
● Montepulciano d'Abruzzo Cocca di Casa '14	▽▽	3
○ Trebbiano d'Abruzzo Sup. Portarispetto '15	▽▽	2*

★Dino Illuminati

C.DA SAN BIAGIO, 18
64010 CONTROGUERRA [TE]
TEL. +39 0861808008
www.illuminativini.it

CELLAR SALES
PRE-BOOKED VISITS
ANNUAL PRODUCTION 1,150,000 bottles
HECTARES UNDER VINE 130.00

True patriarchs of Abruzzo's viticulture, the Illuminati family cultivate a vineyard that falls within the Montepulciano d'Abruzzo Colline Teramane and Controguerra appellations. The brand was founded at the end of the 19th century with Nicola, but the turning point came in the 1970s thanks to Cavalier Dino's decision to start bottling. At the helm today are his sons Lorenzo and Stefano, who have further strengthened a range that's differentiated according to the origin of the grapes and processing methods, with powerful Montepulciano reds standing out among their offerings. The Colline Teramane Zanna Riserva returns and the 2015 once again grabs Tre Bicchieri. Introduced by a dark aromatic profile of pencil lead, cocoa beans and coffee berries, in the mouth it develops dense, with very close-knit tannins. The Riparosso '19, a more supple Montepulciano, is delicious as usual: ripe cherry and black cherry anticipate a pulpy, fragrant palate.

Wine	Rating	Price
● Montepulciano d'Abruzzo Colline Teramane Zanna Ris. '15	▼▼▼	5
● Montepulciano d'Abruzzo Riparosso '19	▼▼	2*
⊙ Cerasuolo d'Abruzzo Lumeggio di Rosa '19	▼▼	2*
○ Controguerra Passerina '19	▼▼	2*
○ Controguerra Bianco Costalupo '19	▼	2
○ Controguerra Bianco Lumeggio di Bianco '19	▼	2
○ Controguerra Pecorino '19	▼	2
● Montepulciano d'Abruzzo Lumeggio di Rosso '19	▼	2
● Montepulciano d'Abruzzo Colline Teramane Zanna Ris. '13	▽▽▽	5
● Montepulciano d'Abruzzo Colline Teramane Zanna Ris. '11	▽▽▽	5
● Montepulciano d'Abruzzo Ilico '17	▽▽▽	2*

Inalto

VIA DEL GIARDINO, 7
67025 OFENA [AQ]
TEL. +39 0862956618
www.inaltovini.it

ANNUAL PRODUCTION 32,000 bottles
HECTARES UNDER VINE 12.50

The name alone (literally 'on high') gives you an idea of what the project created by Adolfo De Cecco some years ago is all about: only hillside vineyards to bring out the elegance of Abruzzo's native grapes. The starting point was 8 hectares of vineyards in Ofena, the intention being to expand the estate. After the purchase of another 4 hectares in the Subequana Valley, new plots are being sought out in L'Aquila, again between 400-800 meters above sea level, with the aim of creating real crus. For now their whites have earned the most accolades, though we appreciated the airy, graceful and harmonious Rosso '16. The excellent Pecorino '18 is just starting to unveil its complexity and nuance, pointing to a favorable evolution: hints of petrol and flint give way to a flavorful, elegant palate marked by a superb, mineral profile. The Bianco '18 is full and intense; a good performance from their juicy and pulpy Cerasuolo '18 as well.

Wine	Rating
○ Abruzzo Bianco '18	🍷🍷 5
○ Pecorino '18	🍷🍷 5
⊙ Cerasuolo d'Abruzzo '18	🍷🍷 5
● Inalto Rosso '16	🍷🍷 5
⊙ Cerasuolo d'Abruzzo Sup. '19	🍷 5
● Montepulciano d'Abruzzo '18	🍷 5

Tommaso Masciantonio

C.DA CAPRAFICO, 35
66043 CASOLI [CH]
TEL. +39 0871897457
www.trappetodicaprafico.com

PRE-BOOKED VISITS
ACCOMMODATION
ANNUAL PRODUCTION 8,000 bottles
HECTARES UNDER VINE 10.00
VITICULTURE METHOD Certified Organic

The impressions from the last edition's tastings were fully confirmed this year. Tommaso Masciantonio, heir to a long tradition of olive growers, is also a serious winemaker. And so it is that Trappeto di Caprafico has become an all around quality brand, including a selection of Pecorino and Montepulciano from splendid vineyards situated at the foot of Majella, on the Teatine hills of Casoli and Guardiagrele. It's an area with centuries-old agricultural roots, expressed through a small range, but one that's increasingly interesting for its territorial identity and stylistic consistency. Made with grapes from old, pergola vineyards, the Pecorino Superiore Mantica '17 is redolent of lemon pulp and mountain herbs, all infused with light, elegant floral traces that bind to its taut, sapid, fresh palate. We also appreciated the Pecorino Jernare, with its balsamic and citrus profile, and soft, delicately salty flavor.

Wine	Rating
○ Abruzzo Pecorino Sup. Mantica V. Di Caprafico '17	🍷🍷 4
○ Abruzzo Pecorino Jernare V. di Caprafico '19	🍷🍷 3
○ Abruzzo Pecorino Sup. Mantica V. Di Caprafico '15	🍷🍷 4
● Montepulciano d'Abruzzo Sciatò V. Di Caprafico '15	🍷🍷 3

★★★Masciarelli

via Gamberale, 2
66010 San Martino sulla Marrucina [CH]
Tel. +39 087185241
www.masciarelli.it

CELLAR SALES
PRE-BOOKED VISITS
ACCOMMODATION
ANNUAL PRODUCTION 2,500,000 bottles
HECTARES UNDER VINE 300.00

When it comes to Abruzzo's wine, few producers have had international success like the one created in 1981 by Gianni Masciarelli and now run by his wife, Marina, together with their daughter Miriam. It's a project that involves the region's four provinces, with an incredible variety of territories, soil and climates covered, with vineyards ranging from the Adriatic to the slopes of Gran Sasso, making for powerful and modern wines. These are organized across five different production lines that see their outstanding daily drinkers flanked by ambitious and austere selections. It's not surprising that a wine from their Castello di Semivicoli line earns yet another accolade. This time it's the Pecorino '19: sensations of iodine, citrus peel and hay mark its aromatic bouquet, which follows through to a tasty, clear and focused palate. The Montepulciano Villa Gemma Ris. '15 is faithful to classic, modern interpretations of the grape: oaky notes adorn ripe black fruit on a full-bodied palate.

- ○ Abruzzo Pecorino Castello di Semivicoli '19 — 🍷🍷🍷 3*
- ● Montepulciano d'Abruzzo Villa Gemma Ris. '15 — 🍷🍷 8
- ○ Chardonnay Marina Cvetic '18 — 🍷🍷 5
- ● Marina Cvetic Merlot '17 — 🍷🍷 5
- ○ Abruzzo Malvasia Iskra Marina Cvetic '18 — 🍷 4
- ● Marina Cvetic Cabernet Sauvignon '15 — 🍷 6
- ● Marina Cvetic Syrah '17 — 🍷 5
- ● Montepulciano d'Abruzzo Marina Cvetic '05 — 🥂🥂🥂 4
- ● Montepulciano d'Abruzzo Villa Gemma '06 — 🥂🥂🥂 7
- ○ Trebbiano d'Abruzzo Castello di Semivicoli '18 — 🥂🥂🥂 5
- ○ Trebbiano d'Abruzzo Castello di Semivicoli '15 — 🥂🥂🥂 5

Camillo Montori

loc. Piane Tronto, 80
64010 Controguerra [TE]
Tel. +39 0861809900
www.montorivini.it

CELLAR SALES
PRE-BOOKED VISITS
ACCOMMODATION AND RESTAURANT SERVICE
ANNUAL PRODUCTION 600,000 bottles
HECTARES UNDER VINE 50.00

If Controguerra has become one of the wine capitals of Abruzzo, part of the credit goes to Camillo Montori, a producer that epitomizes a tradition of wine producers active as early as the 1800's. The turning point came in the 1960s and 1970s, when the brand left the regional borders and reached shelves all over the world thanks to wise vineyard management and measured technical innovation, a recipe that results in decidedly classic wines. This is especially true of those made with the territory's classic grapes: Montepulciano, Trebbiano and Pecorino. We found this year's battery less brilliant than in the past. The best wine is, undoubtedly, the Trebbiano Fonte Cupa '19: aromas of straw and yellow citrus fruits mix with mineral hints, while the palate unfolds in a relaxed way. We also appreciated the Passerina Fonte Cupa '19: iodine and aromatic herbs anticipate a fresh, flavorful, vital palate.

- ○ Fonte Cupa Passerina '19 — 🍷🍷 2*
- ● Montepulciano d'Abruzzo Colline Teramane Fonte Cupa Ris. '13 — 🍷🍷 5
- ○ Trebbiano d'Abruzzo Fonte Cupa '19 — 🍷🍷 2*
- ⊙ Cerasuolo d'Abruzzo Fonte Cupa '19 — 🍷 2
- ● Montepulciano d'Abruzzo Colline Teramane '15 — 🍷 2
- ○ Pecorino '19 — 🍷 3
- ⊙ Cerasuolo d'Abruzzo Fonte Cupa '16 — 🥂🥂🥂 2*
- ⊙ Cerasuolo d'Abruzzo Fonte Cupa '18 — 🥂🥂 2*
- ⊙ Cerasuolo d'Abruzzo Fonte Cupa '17 — 🥂🥂 2*
- ○ Fonte Cupa Pecorino '17 — 🥂🥂 3
- ● Montepulciano d'Abruzzo Fonte Cupa '15 — 🥂🥂 2*
- ○ Trebbiano d'Abruzzo Fonte Cupa '18 — 🥂🥂 2*

Fattoria Nicodemi

c.da Veniglio, 8
64024 Notaresco [TE]
Tel. +39 085895493
www.nicodemi.com

CELLAR SALES
PRE-BOOKED VISITS
ANNUAL PRODUCTION 200,000 bottles
HECTARES UNDER VINE 30.00
VITICULTURE METHOD Certified Organic

The large single vineyard that extends over the hills of Contrada Veniglio, in Notaresco, enjoys the best that Teramano has to offer in terms of soil and climate: rich clayey-calcareous terrain, elevations of around 300 meters, the Adriatic coast just ten kilometers away, Gran Sasso's breezes tickling the vines during the summer evenings. Elena and Alessandro are adept at transmitting all this in their wines, using the area's native grape varieties of course. As a whole, their selection put in a convincing performance (to say the least), with two Montepulciano Colline Teramane earning a place in our finals: the Neromoro Ris. '16 and Le Murate '18. The first impressed for its intriguing floral and spicy sensations, which accompany more characteristic hints of black fruit and pencil lead; the palate is graceful and elegant with polished tannins. We appreciated the second, foremost, for its notable aromatic and gustatory cleanness.

Wine	Rating
● Montepulciano d'Abruzzo Colline Teramane Neromoro Ris. '16	🍷🍷 5
● Montepulciano d'Abuzzo Colline Teramane Le Murate '18	🍷🍷 3*
⊙ Cerasuolo d'Abruzzo Le Murate '19	🍷🍷 2*
● Montepulciano d'Abruzzo Colline Teramane Notàri '18	🍷🍷 4
○ Trebbiano d'Abruzzo Le Murate '19	🍷🍷 2*
○ Trebbiano d'Abruzzo Sup. Notàri '18	🍷🍷 3
○ Trebbiano d'Abruzzo Cocciopesto '18	🍷 3
● Montepulciano d'Abruzzo Colline Teramane Neromoro Ris. '09	🍷🍷🍷 5
● Montepulciano d'Abruzzo Colline Teramane Neromoro Ris. '03	🍷🍷🍷 5
● Montepulciano d'Abruzzo Colline Teramane Notàri '17	🍷🍷🍷 4*
○ Trebbiano d'Abruzzo Sup. Notàri '15	🍷🍷🍷 3*

Orlandi Contucci Ponno

loc. Piana degli Ulivi, 1
64026 Roseto degli Abruzzi [TE]
Tel. +39 0858944049
www.orlandicontucciponno.com

CELLAR SALES
PRE-BOOKED VISITS
ANNUAL PRODUCTION 185,000 bottles
HECTARES UNDER VINE 31.00

Orlandi Ponno was among those that helped take Abruzzo's wine in a new direction in the 1990s. Bolstered by its past, in 2007 the winery became part of the Gussalli Beretta group, which after investing in Franciacorta and Chianti Classico (and then Langa and Alto Adige) decided to acquire the property and relaunch it. Here in Roseto, just a stone's throw from the Adriatic, the vineyards benefit from predominantly calcareous soil. Territorial varieties such as Montepulciano and Trebbiano are cultivated together with international grapes. We tasted two very well made selections from their Montepulciano Colline Teramane. It takes a while to open in the glass, but then the Regia Specula '17 releases the grape's classic notes, combining aromas of ripe plum with elegant hints of pencil lead; wide and voluminous on the palate, it's supported by abundant tannins. The Riserva '15 is more austere in its notes of medicinal herbs, which follow through on a palate that's close-knit but fresh at the finish.

Wine	Rating
● Montepulciano d'Abruzzo Colline Teramane La Regia Specula '17	🍷🍷 3*
● Montepulciano d'Abruzzo Colline Teramane Ris. '15	🍷🍷 5
○ Abruzzo Pecorino Sup. '19	🍷🍷 2*
○ Trebbiano d'Abruzzo Sup. Colle della Corte '19	🍷🍷 2*
⊙ Cerasuolo d'Abruzzo Sup. Vermiglio '19	🍷 3
● Montepulciano d'Abruzzo Colline Teramane La Regia Specula '16	🍷🍷 3*
● Montepulciano d'Abruzzo Colline Teramane La Regia Specula '15	🍷🍷 3
● Montepulciano d'Abruzzo Colline Teramane Ris. '13	🍷🍷 5
○ Trebbiano d'Abruzzo Sup. Colle della Corte '18	🍷🍷 2*
○ Trebbiano d'Abruzzo Sup. Colle della Corte '16	🍷🍷 2*

Pasetti

LOC. C.DA PRETARO
VIA SAN PAOLO, 21
66023 FRANCAVILLA AL MARE [CH]
TEL. +39 08561875
www.pasettivini.it

CELLAR SALES
PRE-BOOKED VISITS
ACCOMMODATION
ANNUAL PRODUCTION 600,000 bottles
HECTARES UNDER VINE 75.00

The Pasetti family are a historic name in the world of Abruzzo's wine, and Francavilla al Mare is the center of their enological operations. The grapes used are cultivated in hillside vineyards, in particular in Pescosansonesco and Capestrano, which are situated within the Gran Sasso and Monti della Laga National Park (whose logo can also be found on the back labels). Today, the fourth generation of family are leading the producer, bringing a breath of fresh air without distorting a contemporary style, one that strikes the right balance between innovation and territorial identity. The Montepulciano d'Abruzzo '17 interprets the grape in a way that's effective in its simplicity: bay leaf, juniper, ripe black berries and balsamic nuances open the way to a tasty palate, one that plays on drinkability and freshness, with tannins setting the pace, lending pleasant contrast. We also appreciated the graceful and sapid Pecorino Collecivetta '17, a wine that's herbaceous in its sensations of hay and meadow.

Wine	Rating	Price
○ Abruzzo Pecorino Sup. Collecivetta '18	TT	3
● Montepulciano d'Abruzzo '17	TT	2*
○ Testarossa Bianco '18	TT	4
○ Abruzzo Pecorino Collecivetta '17	YY	3
○ Abruzzo Pecorino Collecivetta '15	YY	3
○ Abruzzo Pecorino Collecivetta '14	YY	3
● Montepulciano d'Abruzzo '16	YY	2*
● Montepulciano d'Abruzzo '12	YY	2*
● Montepulciano d'Abruzzo Testarossa '11	YY	4
○ Trebbiano d'Abruzzo Madonnella '17	YY	3
○ Trebbiano d'Abruzzo Madonnella '15	YY	5

Emidio Pepe

VIA CHIESI, 10
64010 TORANO NUOVO [TE]
TEL. +39 0861856493
www.emidiopepe.com

CELLAR SALES
PRE-BOOKED VISITS
ACCOMMODATION AND RESTAURANT SERVICE
ANNUAL PRODUCTION 80,000 bottles
HECTARES UNDER VINE 15.00
VITICULTURE METHOD Certified Biodynamic
SUSTAINABLE WINERY

1964 was the year in which Emidio Pepe, drawing on his father's and grandfather's teachings, began bottling his own wines. Torano Nuovo, a district on the Teramo Hills, immediately became a pilgrimage destination for those wanting to meet that producer, a man who's at times a bit shy, but is able to tame Montepulciano and transform it into great, ageworthy reds. Even today, Emidio supervises all the work in the winery, carried out with determination and success by his daughters Daniela and Sofia and his granddaughter Chiara. The Cerasuolo d'Abruzzo '19, one of the most fascinating in the region, put in a performance to remember. After opening on smoky and spicy notes, it comes through with dazzling vitality and freshness on the palate, proving rhythmic and vibrant, with creamy, intense, rich red fruit, finishing supple, rich in verve and flavor. An excellent performance for the Pecorino as well, a wine that's vivid in its hints of freshly cut grass and ginger. The Trebbiano d'Abruzzo is more mature in its broad, juicy profile.

Wine	Rating	Price
⊙ Cerasuolo d'Abruzzo '19	TTT	5
○ Pecorino '18	TT	6
○ Trebbiano d'Abruzzo '18	TT	5
● Montepulciano d'Abruzzo '18	T	6
● Montepulciano d'Abruzzo '17	YY	6
● Montepulciano d'Abruzzo '15	YY	6
● Montepulciano d'Abruzzo '13	YY	6
● Montepulciano d'Abruzzo '12	YY	6
○ Pecorino '17	YY	6
⊙ Rosato '18	YY	5
○ Trebbiano d'Abruzzo '17	YY	5
○ Trebbiano d'Abruzzo '14	YY	5
○ Trebbiano d'Abruzzo '13	YY	5

Tenuta Terraviva

via del Lago, 19
64018 Tortoreto [TE]
Tel. +39 0861786056
www.tenutaterraviva.it

CELLAR SALES
PRE-BOOKED VISITS
ANNUAL PRODUCTION 80,000 bottles
HECTARES UNDER VINE 22.00
VITICULTURE METHOD Certified Organic

The winery was founded in the 1970s by Gabriele Marano, who decided to combine his work as a building contractor with that of a winemaker. The turning point came in 2006, when the producer passed into the hands of Gabriele's daughter Pina and her husband Pietro Topi. They slowly transformed the estate by turning towards organic farming and deliberately adopting artisan winemaking techniques carried out with indigenous yeasts and spontaneous fermentation. Today Montepulciano, Trebbiano, Cerasuolo and Pecorino give rise to wines marked by character, energy and sincerity. Terraviva is back with Tre Bicchieri thanks to a superlative 2019 version of the Cerasuolo Giusi. Freshly ground black pepper, ripe strawberry and pencil lead accompany an intriguing rustic touch: its multi-faceted aromatic profile anticipates a relaxed, juicy, rhythmic and energetic palate. The Pecorino 'Ekwo '19 also impresses with its aromas of lemon pulp and wet stones: in the mouth it exhibits a great sapid intensity and penetrating development.

⊙ Cerasuolo d'Abruzzo Giusi '19	🍷🍷🍷 2*
○ Abruzzo Pecorino 'Ekwo '19	🍷🍷 3*
○ Abruzzo Passerina 12.1 '19	🍷🍷 3
○ Abruzzo Pecorino '19	🍷🍷 2*
● Montepulciano d'Abruzzo MPH '17	🍷🍷 5
○ Trebbiano d'Abruzzo '19	🍷🍷 2*
○ Trebbiano d'Abruzzo Sup. Mario's 46 '18	🍷🍷 3
● Montepulciano d'Abruzzo Luì '13	🍷🍷🍷 3*
○ Trebbiano d'Abruzzo Sup. Mario's 44 '16	🍷🍷🍷 3*
○ Abruzzo Pecorino 'Ekwo '17	🍷🍷 3
⊙ Cerasuolo d'Abruzzo Giusi '18	🍷🍷 2*
⊙ Cerasuolo d'Abruzzo Giusi '16	🍷🍷 2*
● Montepulciano d'Abruzzo Luì '15	🍷🍷 3
○ Trebbiano d'Abruzzo Mario's 45 '17	🍷🍷 3

Tiberio

c.da La Vota
65020 Cugnoli [PE]
Tel. +39 0858576744
www.tiberio.it

CELLAR SALES
PRE-BOOKED VISITS
ANNUAL PRODUCTION 90,000 bottles
HECTARES UNDER VINE 30.00

It was 1999 when Riccardo Tiberio discovered an old abandoned vineyard in Trebbiano. He was so enamored that he bought it, thus laying the foundations for his winery. The revival of the old vines, the careful selection of clones and the planting of new plots were the first steps towards creating a producer that today is among Abruzzo's most solid, one managed by siblings Cristiana and Antonio in Cugnoli, an area straddling Gran Sasso and Majella. Here calcareous soils, strong day-night temperature swings and mild, constant air circulation prove ideal for the slow and gradual ripening of the grapes. We very much appreciated the Montepulciano d'Abruzzo '18: burnt embers, pepper, crisp black fruit and pencil lead adorn a vital, energetic palate, juicy, precise in its tannic texture. The Cerasuolo '19 also delivered, with small, ripe red berries and mineral nuances opening the way to a pulpy palate, highly fragrant and pleasant. We mustn't underestimate the Pecorino '19 and Trebbiano '19 either.

⊙ Cerasuolo d'Abruzzo '19	🍷🍷 3*
● Montepulciano d'Abruzzo '18	🍷🍷 3*
○ Pecorino '19	🍷🍷 3
○ Trebbiano d'Abruzzo '19	🍷🍷 3
● Montepulciano d'Abruzzo '13	🍷🍷🍷 2*
○ Pecorino '16	🍷🍷🍷 3*
○ Pecorino '15	🍷🍷🍷 3*
○ Pecorino '13	🍷🍷🍷 3*
○ Pecorino '12	🍷🍷🍷 3*
○ Pecorino '11	🍷🍷🍷 3*
○ Pecorino '10	🍷🍷🍷 3
⊙ Cerasuolo d'Abruzzo '18	🍷🍷 3
⊙ Cerasuolo d'Abruzzo '17	🍷🍷 3
○ Pecorino '18	🍷🍷 3*
○ Pecorino '17	🍷🍷 3*
○ Trebbiano d'Abruzzo '18	🍷🍷 3*
○ Trebbiano d'Abruzzo '17	🍷🍷 3

Cantina Tollo

via Garibaldi, 68
66010 Tollo [CH]
Tel. +39 087196251
www.cantinatollo.it

CELLAR SALES
ANNUAL PRODUCTION 13,000,000 bottles
HECTARES UNDER VINE 3200.00

One of Italy's most important wine cooperatives, Tollo was founded in 1960 by a small group driven by the desire to elevate the quality of Abruzzo's wine to the highest standards. Today 13 million bottles are produced by virtue of over 3,200 hectares of vineyards. And the original 19 members have grown to just under a thousand. Production has been entrusted to Riccardo Brighigna for some time now—it's his job to transform this viticultural patrimony into a wide and varied range of wines divided into different lines. And with this year, 6 vintages of the Montepulciano Mo have earned Tre Bicchieri. The '16 version offers up delicate floral scents, a touch of vanilla berry and ripe black cherry, but also something more austere, reminiscent of black olives and burnt wood. In the mouth it's solid in its tannic texture, with a pleasant finish in which fruity sensations return for an encore. The tasty, supple and relaxed Trebbiano Tre '19 also landed in our finals.

Wine	Rating
● Montepulciano d'Abruzzo Mo Ris. '16	🍷🍷🍷 3*
○ Trebbiano d'Abruzzo Tre '19	🍷🍷 3*
○ Abruzzo Pecorino '19	🍷🍷 5
⊙ Cerasuolo d'Abruzzo Hedòs '19	🍷🍷 3
● Montepulciano d'Abruzzo Colle Secco Rubì '16	🍷🍷 2*
○ Peco Pecorino '19	🍷🍷 3
● Montepulciano d'Abruzzo Bio '19	🍷 2
● Montepulciano d'Abruzzo Cagiòlo Ris. '09	🍷🍷🍷 4*
● Montepulciano d'Abruzzo Mo Ris. '15	🍷🍷🍷 3*
● Montepulciano d'Abruzzo Mo Ris. '13	🍷🍷🍷 3*
● Montepulciano d'Abruzzo Mo Ris. '12	🍷🍷🍷 2*
● Montepulciano d'Abruzzo Mo Ris. '11	🍷🍷🍷 2*
● Montepulciano d'Abruzzo Mo' Ris. '14	🍷🍷🍷 3*
○ Trebbiano d'Abruzzo C'Incanta '11	🍷🍷🍷 4*
○ Trebbiano d'Abruzzo C'Incanta '10	🍷🍷🍷 4*

★Torre dei Beati

c.da Poggioragone, 56
65014 Loreto Aprutino [PE]
Tel. +39 0854916069
www.torredeibeati.it

CELLAR SALES
PRE-BOOKED VISITS
ANNUAL PRODUCTION 100,000 bottles
HECTARES UNDER VINE 20.00
VITICULTURE METHOD Certified Organic
SUSTAINABLE WINERY

Loreto Aprutino in Poggioragone: it's here that you'll find the winery overseen by Adriana Galasso and her husband, Fausto Albanesi, a pair who've been working together since 1999. Their vineyards, which host Montepulciano, Trebbiano and Pecorino and have been organically cultivated from the outset, give rise to great Abruzzo wine. The sea is just over twenty kilometres away, the soil is clayey-calcareous, and the Gran Sasso keeps the air cool. These qualities result in healthy grapes that are transformed into energetic, sunny, assertive wines. We're not shy about saying that the Bianchi Grilli per la Testa '18 is the most exhilarating Trebbiano d'Abruzzo tasted this year. Rich and multifaceted on the nose amidst citron peel, balsamic herbs and yellow flowers, the palate is energetic and racy yet intense—pervasive and alluring. Aromas of flint, medlar and hay feature in the Pecorino '18 (from the same line), a wine marked by a powerful, sapid palate.

Wine	Rating
○ Trebbiano d'Abruzzo Bianchi Grilli per la Testa '18	🍷🍷🍷 4*
○ Abruzzo Pecorino Bianchi Grilli per la Testa '18	🍷🍷 4
○ Abruzzo Pecorino Giocheremo con i Fiori '19	🍷🍷 3
⊙ Cerasuolo d'Abruzzo Rosa-ae '19	🍷🍷 2*
● Montepulciano d'Abruzzo '18	🍷🍷 3
● Montepulciano d'Abruzzo Cocciapazza '17	🍷 5
○ Abruzzo Pecorino Giocheremo con I Fiori '17	🍷🍷🍷 3*
⊙ Cerasuolo d'Abruzzo Rosa-ae '18	🍷🍷🍷 2*
● Montepulciano d'Abruzzo Cocciapazza '10	🍷🍷🍷 4*
○ Trebbiano d'Abruzzo Bianchi Grilli per la Testa '14	🍷🍷🍷 4*

La Valentina

via Torretta, 52
65010 Spoltore [PE]
Tel. +39 0854478158
www.lavalentina.it

CELLAR SALES
PRE-BOOKED VISITS
ANNUAL PRODUCTION 350,000 bottles
HECTARES UNDER VINE 40.00
VITICULTURE METHOD Certified Organic
SUSTAINABLE WINERY

Since they started working at their winery, brothers Sabatino, Roberto and Andrea Di Properzio have overseen all stages of production with dedication and meticulousness, earning La Valentina a strong reputation. Their vineyards, which have been cultivated organically since the beginning, can be found in different territories characterized by sun, sea and mountain breezes. Spoltore and Cavaticchi are near the Adriatic coast, while Scafa, San Valentino and Alanno are further inland and closer to the Apennines. It's Luca D'Attoma's job to transform these grapes into modern yet territorial wines. While we usually prefer their reds, this year the Trebbiano d'Abruzzo Spelt '18 stood out with a superlative performance. Mountain meadow, citrus fruits and iodine accents rise up out of the glass, it unfolds tasty and elegant on the palate by virtue of its commendable mineral backbone. We also appreciated the close-knit and full-bodied Montepulciano Spelt Riserva '17: a dark olfactory profile touches on black berries and pencil lead.

Wine	Glasses	Score
● Montepulciano d'Abruzzo Spelt Ris. '17	🍷🍷	4
○ Trebbiano d'Abruzzo Spelt '18	🍷🍷	4
⊙ Cerasuolo d'Abruzzo Spelt '19	🍷🍷	3
● Montepulciano d'Abruzzo Binomio Ris. '16	🍷🍷	5
● Montepulciano d'Abruzzo Terre dei Vestini Bellovedere Ris. '16	🍷🍷	6
○ Pecorino '19	🍷🍷	2*
⊙ Cerasuolo d'Abruzzo '19	🍷	2
○ Trebbiano d'Abruzzo '19	🍷	2
● Montepulciano d'Abruzzo Spelt '08	ΥΥΥ	3*
● Montepulciano d'Abruzzo Spelt '07	ΥΥΥ	3
● Montepulciano d'Abruzzo Spelt '05	ΥΥΥ	3
● Montepulciano d'Abruzzo Spelt Ris. '15	ΥΥΥ	4*
● Montepulciano d'Abruzzo Spelt Ris. '11	ΥΥΥ	4*
● Montepulciano d'Abruzzo Spelt Ris. '10	ΥΥΥ	3*

★★★Valentini

via del Baio, 2
65014 Loreto Aprutino [PE]
Tel. +39 0858291138

ANNUAL PRODUCTION 50,000 bottles
HECTARES UNDER VINE 70.00

In the letters received from Francesco Paolo Valentini in recent years, all rigorously hand-written, it is increasingly evident that climate change is a central concern and an important consideration when it comes to the practices adopted in the vineyard and cellar. His Abruzzo pergola of vineyards seems to be the best way to protect the grapes from ever hotter seasons, while the best grapes, destined for totemic bottles with yellow labels, are fewer and fewer. This was one of those rare occasions where we had the pleasure of tasting all three of their wines (the last time was ten years ago, for the 2011 edition of the guide). The Montepulciano '15 is in great form—it's a red that uniquely combines the grape's fleshiness, complexity and power with a consummate elegance, resulting in a deep, sapid palate. The Cerasuolo '19 and Trebbiano '16 are also rousing.

Wine	Glasses	Score
● Montepulciano d'Abruzzo '15	🍷🍷🍷	8
⊙ Cerasuolo d'Abruzzo '19	🍷🍷	7
○ Trebbiano d'Abruzzo '16	🍷🍷	8
● Montepulciano d'Abruzzo '13	ΥΥΥ	8
● Montepulciano d'Abruzzo '12	ΥΥΥ	8
● Montepulciano d'Abruzzo '06	ΥΥΥ	8
⊙ Montepulciano d'Abruzzo Cerasuolo '09	ΥΥΥ	6
⊙ Montepulciano d'Abruzzo Cerasuolo '08	ΥΥΥ	6
○ Trebbiano d'Abruzzo '15	ΥΥΥ	8
○ Trebbiano d'Abruzzo '13	ΥΥΥ	8
○ Trebbiano d'Abruzzo '12	ΥΥΥ	6
○ Trebbiano d'Abruzzo '11	ΥΥΥ	6
○ Trebbiano d'Abruzzo '10	ΥΥΥ	6
○ Trebbiano d'Abruzzo '09	ΥΥΥ	6
○ Trebbiano d'Abruzzo '08	ΥΥΥ	6
○ Trebbiano d'Abruzzo '07	ΥΥΥ	6

★Valle Reale

LOC. SAN CALISTO
65026 POPOLI [PE]
TEL. +39 0859871039
www.vallereale.it

CELLAR SALES
PRE-BOOKED VISITS
ANNUAL PRODUCTION 197,000 bottles
HECTARES UNDER VINE 46.00
VITICULTURE METHOD Certified Biodynamic
SUSTAINABLE WINERY

The winery established by Leonardo Pizzolo dates back to the late 1990s. From Verona he moved to a magical part of Abruzzo, an uncontaminated area with the protected natural parks of Gran Sasso, Majella and Sirente-Velino all nearby. Biodynamic principles are applied in the vineyards while an artisanal approach has been adopted in the cellar, making for characterful, territorial wines, from their basic offerings to their 'cru' (Sant'Eusanio, San Calisto, Vigna del Convento, Vigneto di Popoli), which benefit from the added complexity. Their line-up put in a performance for the ages, with the Montepulciano Vigneto Sant'Eusanio '18 serving as that crowning stroke. A certain, genuine rusticity gives way to black fruit, balsamic and peppery whiffs, which make for a taut, mineral palate marked by close-knit tannins. Long and bright on the palate, the Trebbiano Vigneto di Popoli '18 plays on aromas of hay and chamomile.

- ● Montepulciano d'Abruzzo Vign. Sant'Eusanio '18 — TTT 6
- ○ Trebbiano d'Abruzzo Vign. di Popoli '18 — TT 7
- ⊙ Cerasuolo d'Abruzzo Vign. Sant'Eusanio Giorno '19 — TT 6
- ● Montepulciano d'Abruzzo '19 — TT 5
- ● Montepulciano d'Abruzzo Vign. di Popoli '15 — TT 7
- ● Montepulciano d'Abruzzo Vign. di Sant'Eusanio '16 — YYY 4*
- ● Montepulciano d'Abruzzo Vign. Sant'Eusanio '17 — YYY 4*
- ○ Trebbiano d'Abruzzo V. del Convento di Capestrano '15 — YYY 6
- ○ Trebbiano d'Abruzzo V. del Convento di Capestrano '14 — YYY 5

Valori

VIA TORQUATO AL SALINELLO, 8
64027 SANT'OMERO [TE]
TEL. +39 087185241
www.vinivalori.it

PRE-BOOKED VISITS
ANNUAL PRODUCTION 150,000 bottles
HECTARES UNDER VINE 26.00
VITICULTURE METHOD Certified Organic
SUSTAINABLE WINERY

Luigi Valori's wines continue to represent a clear interpretation of the Teramane Hills, an area mainly dedicated to the production of Montepulciano d'Abruzzo. Founded in 1996, the producer avails itself of about 15 hectares, which extend in the districts of Sant'Omero and Controguerra, on the border with Le Marche. Their vineyards, which have been cultivated according to organic principles for several years now, give rise to 5 wines, with native grapes prevailing (with the exception of a reserve based on Merlot). Cocoa beans, toasty notes, ripe blackberry and plum constitute the olfactory spectrum of the Montepulciano Colline Teramane Chiamami Quando Piove '15, a dense, close-woven wine in the mouth, pervasive yet fresh across a long finish on sensations of blood oranges. Highly fragrant, the Montepulciano Call Chiamami Quando Piove '17 manages to be supple, vibrant and juicy despite the hot year. It's also worth mentioning the excellent performances put in by the Pecorino '19 and Cerasuolo '19.

- ○ Abruzzo Pecorino Chiamami Quando Piove '19 — TT 3
- ● Montepulciano d'Abruzzo Chiamami Quando Piove '17 — TT 2*
- ● Montepulciano d'Abruzzo Colline Teramane Chiamami Quando Piove '15 — TT 2*
- ○ Abruzzo Pecorino Octava Dies '18 — T 1*
- ⊙ Cerasuolo d'Abruzzo Chiamami Quando Piove '19 — T 2
- ● Montepulciano d'Abruzzo V. Sant' Angelo '03 — YYY 4
- ○ Abruzzo Pecorino Chiamami Quando Piove '18 — YY 3
- ⊙ Cerasuolo d'Abruzzo Chiamami Quando Piove '18 — YY 2*
- ● Montepulciano d'Abruzzo Colline Teramane V. Sant'Angelo '15 — YY 4

★Villa Medoro

c.da Medoro
64030 Atri [TE]
Tel. +39 0858708139
www.villamedoro.it

CELLAR SALES
PRE-BOOKED VISITS
ACCOMMODATION
ANNUAL PRODUCTION 300,000 bottles
HECTARES UNDER VINE 100.00

Federica Morricone, who represents the third generation of family, draws on three estates, Medoro, Fontanelle and Fonte Corvo, for her grapes. Here on the hills of Atri, in Teramano, the Adriatic exercises a strong influence on property's 100 hectares of Montepulciano, Trebbiano, Pecorino, Passerina and Montonico. All stages of production are painstakingly followed from the vineyards to the cutting-edge cellar where modern wines are forged, making for a convincing synthesis between tradition and modern approaches. The Pecorino 8½ '19 just fell short of Tre Bicchieri. Redolent of herbs, peach tobacco and jasmine on the nose, in the mouth it retains beautiful fragrance across an elegant, taut, flavorful, alluring palate. The Pecorino '19 offers up aromas of hay and citrus fruits, coming through fruity on the palate with notable cleanness of flavor. A combination of ripe black berries and spices characterize the Montepulciano '19, a compact wine, intact, that clearly expresses the power of the grape.

Wine	Rating
○ 8½ Pecorino '19	▼▼▼ 3*
⊙ Cerasuolo d'Abruzzo '19	▼▼ 2*
● Montepulciano d'Abruzzo '19	▼▼ 2*
○ Pecorino '19	▼▼ 2*
○ Passerina '19	▼ 2
○ Trebbiano d'Abruzzo '19	▼ 2
● Montepulciano d'Abruzzo '18	▽▽▽ 2*
● Montepulciano d'Abruzzo '14	▽▽▽ 2*
● Montepulciano d'Abruzzo Colline Teramane Adrano '12	▽▽▽ 4*
● Montepulciano d'Abruzzo Colline Teramane Adrano '10	▽▽▽ 4*
● Montepulciano d'Abruzzo Colline Teramane Adrano '09	▽▽▽ 4*
● Montepulciano d'Abruzzo Rosso del Duca '12	▽▽▽ 3*
○ Pecorino '17	▽▽▽ 2*

Ciccio Zaccagnini

c.da Pozzo
65020 Bolognano [PE]
Tel. +39 0858880195
www.cantinazaccagnini.it

CELLAR SALES
PRE-BOOKED VISITS
ANNUAL PRODUCTION 5,000,000 bottles
HECTARES UNDER VINE 300.00

Constantly being at the forefront in the competitive world of Abruzzo wine is not easy. Yet Zaccagnini, led by Marcello (son of the founder Ciccio) together with his cousin Concezio Marulli, is one of the wineries that seems to succeed best. Part of their success lies with a substantial property situated between Majella and the Adriatic Sea, on the Pescaresi Hills, but it's mostly thanks to intelligent management of their selection. Alongside their basic wines, which are as approachable as they are effective, it's possible to find more ambitious selections, without forgetting their forays into sparkling and non-sulphite wines. Aromatic herbs, lime and grapefruit characterize the aromatic profile of the new Chronicon Pecorino, a 2019 that releases all the grape's spirited energy across a palate that's firm in its structure and flavor. The other Chronicon, the Montepulciano '18, is just as well made: classic aromas of black fruit and pencil lead are accompanied by an original and appealing floral hint; on the palate it comes through spicy, fresh and relaxed.

Wine	Rating
○ Abruzzo Pecorino Chronicon '19	▼▼ 3*
● Montepulciano d'Abruzzo Chronicon '18	▼▼ 3
● Montepulciano d'Abruzzo Il Vino del Tralcetto '18	▼▼ 2*
⊙ Cerasuolo d'Abruzzo Il Vino del Tralcetto '19	▼ 3
● Clematis Passito Rosso '14	▼ 7
● Montepulciano d'Abruzzo Terre di Casauria S. Clemente Ris. '16	▼ 5
⊙ Cerasuolo d'Abruzzo Myosotis '16	▽▽▽ 3*
● Montepulciano d'Abruzzo Chronicon '13	▽▽▽ 3*
● Montepulciano d'Abruzzo S. Clemente Ris. '12	▽▽▽ 5
● Montepulciano d'Abruzzo S. Clemente Ris. '11	▽▽▽ 5
○ Abruzzo Bianco San Clemente '17	▽▽ 4
⊙ Cerasuolo d'Abruzzo Myosotis '18	▽▽ 3
● Montepulciano d'Abruzzo Chronicon '16	▽▽ 3

Ausonia

c.da Nocella
64032 Atri [TE]
Tel. +39 0859071026
www.ausoniawines.com

ANNUAL PRODUCTION 35,000 bottles
HECTARES UNDER VINE 11.50

- ⊙ Cerasuolo d'Abruzzo Apollo '19 — 🍷🍷 3
- ● Montepulciano d'Abruzzo Colline Teramane Nostradamus Ris. '15 — 🍷🍷 5
- ○ Trebbiano d'Abruzzo Apollo '18 — 🍷🍷 3

Tenute Barone di Valforte

c.da Piomba, 11
64028 Silvi Marina [TE]
Tel. +39 0859353432
www.baronedivalforte.it

CELLAR SALES
PRE-BOOKED VISITS
ANNUAL PRODUCTION 280,000 bottles
HECTARES UNDER VINE 50.00

- ⊙ Cerasuolo d'Abruzzo Valforte Rosé '19 — 🍷🍷 2*
- ○ Trebbiano d'Abruzzo Villa Chiara '19 — 🍷🍷 2*
- ○ Abruzzo Pecorino '19 — 🍷 2
- ● Montepulciano d'Abruzzo Ris. '15 — 🍷 4

Bove

via Roma, 216
67051 Avezzano [AQ]
Tel. +39 086333133
info@cantinebove.it

CELLAR SALES
PRE-BOOKED VISITS
ANNUAL PRODUCTION 1,200,000 bottles
HECTARES UNDER VINE 60.00

- ⊙ Cerasuolo d'Abruzzo Fiori Chiari '19 — 🍷🍷 1*
- ● Montepulciano d'Abruzzo Feudi d'Albe '18 — 🍷🍷 1*
- ● Montepulciano d'Abruzzo Indio '15 — 🍷🍷 3
- ● Montepulciano d'Abruzzo Poggio d'Albe '16 — 🍷 2

Casal Thaulero

c.da Cucullo, 32
66026 Ortona [CH]
Tel. +39 0859032533
www.casalthaulero.it

CELLAR SALES
PRE-BOOKED VISITS
ANNUAL PRODUCTION 2,000,000 bottles
HECTARES UNDER VINE 500.00
SUSTAINABLE WINERY

- ● Montepulciano d'Abruzzo Duca Thaulero Ris. '15 — 🍷🍷 4
- ● Montepulciano d'Abruzzo Orsetto Oro '17 — 🍷🍷 3
- ○ Abruzzo Pecorino Sup. Duca Thaulero '19 — 🍷 4

Casalbordino

c.da Termine, 38
66021 Casalbordino [CH]
Tel. +39 0873918107
www.vinicasalbordino.com

CELLAR SALES
PRE-BOOKED VISITS
ANNUAL PRODUCTION 6,000,000 bottles
HECTARES UNDER VINE 1400.00

- ● Montepulciano d'Abruzzo Collezione Bordino '18 — 🍷🍷 2*
- ● Montepulciano d'Abruzzo Terre Sabelli '17 — 🍷🍷 1*
- ○ Villa Adami Pecorino '19 — 🍷 2

Centorame

fraz. Casoli di Atri
via delle Fornaci
64030 Atri [TE]
Tel. +39 0858709115
www.centorame.it

CELLAR SALES
PRE-BOOKED VISITS
ANNUAL PRODUCTION 100,000 bottles
HECTARES UNDER VINE 12.00
SUSTAINABLE WINERY

- ○ Trebbiano d'Abruzzo S. Michele '19 — 🍷🍷 3
- ● Montepulciano d'Abruzzo Castellum Vetus '18 — 🍷 4

Ciavolich

C.DA SALMACINA, 11
65014 LORETO APRUTINO [PE]
TEL. +39 0858289002
www.ciavolich.com

CELLAR SALES
PRE-BOOKED VISITS
ACCOMMODATION AND RESTAURANT SERVICE
ANNUAL PRODUCTION 200,000 bottles
HECTARES UNDER VINE 30.00

- ⊙ Cerasuolo d'Abruzzo Fosso Cancelli '19 🍷🍷 5
- ○ Trebbiano d'Abruzzo Fosso Cancelli '18 🍷🍷 5
- ○ Aries Pecorino '19 🍷 3

Codice Citra

C.DA CUCULLO
66026 ORTONA [CH]
TEL. +39 0859031342
www.citra.it

CELLAR SALES
PRE-BOOKED VISITS
ANNUAL PRODUCTION 24,000,000 bottles
HECTARES UNDER VINE 6000.00

- ○ Abruzzo Pecorino Sup. Ferzo '19 🍷🍷 3*
- ● Montepulciano d'Abruzzo Caroso Ris. '17 🍷🍷 4
- ● Montepulciano d'Abruzzo Teate Ferzo Ris. '16 🍷🍷 3

Antonio Costantini Fattoria Colline Verdi

S.DA MIGLIORI, 20
65013 CITTÀ SANT'ANGELO [PE]
TEL. +39 0859699169
www.costantinivini.it

CELLAR SALES
PRE-BOOKED VISITS
ANNUAL PRODUCTION 450,000 bottles
HECTARES UNDER VINE 50.00

- ● Montepulciano d'Abruzzo '17 🍷🍷 2*
- ○ Trebbiano d'Abruzzo Febe '19 🍷🍷 1*
- ⊙ Cerasuolo d'Abruzzo Febe '19 🍷 1*

Adele De Antoniis

LOC. GARRUFO
VIA METELLA NUOVA, 56
64027 SANT'OMERO [TE]
TEL. +39 0861887087
www.deantoniisadele.it

PRE-BOOKED VISITS
ACCOMMODATION
ANNUAL PRODUCTION 10,000 bottles
HECTARES UNDER VINE 6.00
SUSTAINABLE WINERY

- ● Montepulciano d'Abruzzo Colline Teramane Himerio '16 🍷🍷 4
- ○ Trebbiano d'Abruzzo Sup. Le Coste '19 🍷🍷 3
- ⊙ Cerasuolo d'Abruzzo Sassello '19 🍷 3

F.lli De Luca

C.DA CASTEL DI SETTE, 33
66030 MOZZAGROGNA [CH]
TEL. +39 0872578677
www.cantinedeluca.it

CELLAR SALES
PRE-BOOKED VISITS
ACCOMMODATION AND RESTAURANT SERVICE
ANNUAL PRODUCTION 250,000 bottles
HECTARES UNDER VINE 27.00
SUSTAINABLE WINERY

- ○ Armannia Pecorino '19 🍷🍷 2*
- ● Montepulciano d'Abruzzo Dirè '16 🍷🍷 2*
- ○ Trebbiano d'Abruzzo Sipario '19 🍷 2

Lepore

C.DA CIVITA, 29
64010 COLONNELLA [TE]
TEL. +39 086170860
www.vinilepore.it

CELLAR SALES
PRE-BOOKED VISITS
ANNUAL PRODUCTION 330,000 bottles
HECTARES UNDER VINE 43.00

- ⊙ Cerasuolo d'Abruzzo Lunadea '19 🍷🍷 2*
- ● Montepulciano d'Abruzzo Colline Teramane Re '15 🍷🍷 3
- ○ Trebbiano d'Abruzzo Lunadea '19 🍷 2

Francesco Massetti

C.DA GIARDINO
64010 COLONNELLA [TE]
TEL. +39 3297266209
www.vinimassetti.it

CELLAR SALES
PRE-BOOKED VISITS
ANNUAL PRODUCTION 9,500 bottles
HECTARES UNDER VINE 5.50
VITICULTURE METHOD Certified Organic

⊙ C'è '19 — 🍷🍷 5
○ Mezzo Pieno '19 — 🍷🍷 5
● Montepulciano d'Abruzzo Quarantacinque '18 — 🍷🍷 6

Tommaso Olivastri

VIA QUERCIA DEL CORVO, 37
66038 SAN VITO CHIETINO [CH]
TEL. +39 087261543
www.viniolivastri.com

CELLAR SALES
PRE-BOOKED VISITS
ANNUAL PRODUCTION 30,000 bottles
HECTARES UNDER VINE 15.00

⊙ Cerasuolo d'Abruzzo Marcantonio '19 — 🍷🍷 3
● Montepulciano d'Abruzzo La Carrata '15 — 🍷 5

La Quercia

C.DA COLLE CROCE
64020 MORRO D'ORO [TE]
TEL. +39 0858959110
www.vinilaquercia.it

CELLAR SALES
PRE-BOOKED VISITS
ANNUAL PRODUCTION 200,000 bottles
HECTARES UNDER VINE 46.50
SUSTAINABLE WINERY

⊙ Cerasuolo d'Abruzzo Peladi '19 — 🍷🍷 1*
● Montepulciano d'Abruzzo '16 — 🍷🍷 2*
● Montepulciano d'Abruzzo Primamadre '14 — 🍷🍷 2*
○ Santapupa Pecorino '19 — 🍷 2

Vigneti Radica

VIA PIANA MOZZONE, 4
66010 TOLLO [CH]
TEL. +39 0871962227
www.vignetiradica.it

CELLAR SALES
PRE-BOOKED VISITS
ACCOMMODATION
ANNUAL PRODUCTION 120,000 bottles
HECTARES UNDER VINE 26.00
SUSTAINABLE WINERY

○ Pecorino '19 — 🍷🍷 3
⊙ Rosato '19 — 🍷🍷 3
● Tullum Rosso '16 — 🍷🍷 3
○ Trebbiano d'Abruzzo '19 — 🍷 4

San Giacomo

C.DA NOVELLA, 51
66020 ROCCA SAN GIOVANNI [CH]
TEL. +39 0872620504
www.cantinasangiacomo.it

CELLAR SALES
PRE-BOOKED VISITS
ACCOMMODATION
ANNUAL PRODUCTION 60,000 bottles
HECTARES UNDER VINE 300.00
VITICULTURE METHOD Certified Organic

● Montepulciano d'Abruzzo Casino Murri 14° Ris. '16 — 🍷🍷 3
○ Trebbiano d'Abruzzo Casino Murri 14° '19 — 🍷🍷 2*
○ Casino Murri Pecorino '19 — 🍷 2

San Lorenzo Vini

C.DA PLAVIGNANO, 2
64035 CASTILENTI [TE]
TEL. +39 0861999325
www.sanlorenzovini.com

CELLAR SALES
PRE-BOOKED VISITS
ACCOMMODATION AND RESTAURANT SERVICE
ANNUAL PRODUCTION 800,000 bottles
HECTARES UNDER VINE 150.00
SUSTAINABLE WINERY

○ Casabianca Pecorino Passerina Fermentazione Spontanea '19 — 🍷🍷 3
● Montepulciano d'Abruzzo Colline Teramane Escol Ris. '15 — 🍷🍷 5

Strappelli

via Torri, 16
64010 Torano Nuovo [TE]
Tel. +39 0861887402
www.cantinastrappelli.it

CELLAR SALES
PRE-BOOKED VISITS
ANNUAL PRODUCTION 65,000 bottles
HECTARES UNDER VINE 10.00
VITICULTURE METHOD Certified Organic

○ Controguerra Pecorino Soprano '19	🍷🍷 3
○ Trebbiano d'Abruzzo '19	🍷🍷 3
⊙ Cerasuolo d'Abruzzo '19	🍷 3

Nic Tartaglia

via Oratorio, 28
65020 Alanno [PE]
Tel. +39 3339484475
www.nictartaglia.com

CELLAR SALES
ANNUAL PRODUCTION 25,000 bottles
HECTARES UNDER VINE 12.00

● Montepulciano d'Abruzzo '17	🍷🍷 3
○ Trebbiano d'Abruzzo '19	🍷🍷 3
● Montepulciano d'Abruzzo Selva delle Mura '15	🍷 4

Tenuta del Priore Col del Mondo

via Masseria Flaiani, 1
65010 Collecorvino [PE]
Tel. +39 0858207162
www.tenutadelpriore.it

CELLAR SALES
PRE-BOOKED VISITS
ANNUAL PRODUCTION 280,000 bottles
HECTARES UNDER VINE 39.00

● Montepulciano d'Abruzzo Kerrias Col del Mondo '17	🍷🍷 5
● Montepulciano d'Abruzzo Terre dei Vestini Col del Mondo '17	🍷🍷 3

Terra d'Aligi - Spinelli

loc. Piazzano
via Piana La Fara, 90
66041 Atessa [CH]
Tel. +39 0872897916
www.terradaligi.it

CELLAR SALES
PRE-BOOKED VISITS
ANNUAL PRODUCTION 550,000 bottles
HECTARES UNDER VINE 50.00

⊙ Cerasuolo d'Abruzzo '19	🍷🍷 3
● Montepulciano d'Abruzzo '18	🍷🍷 2*
● Montepulciano d'Abruzzo Tatone '17	🍷🍷 3
○ Zite Pecorino '19	🍷 2

Terzini

via Roma, 52
65028 Tocco da Casauria [PE]
Tel. +39 0859158147
www.cantinaterzini.it

CELLAR SALES
PRE-BOOKED VISITS
ANNUAL PRODUCTION 200,000 bottles
HECTARES UNDER VINE 22.00

● Montepulciano d'Abruzzo Dumì '18	🍷🍷 3
○ Trebbiano d'Abruzzo '19	🍷 4

Vigna Madre

loc. Caldari
via Stortini 32/a
66026 Ortona [CH]
Tel. +39 3405506930
www.vignamadre.it

CELLAR SALES
PRE-BOOKED VISITS
ANNUAL PRODUCTION 200,000 bottles
HECTARES UNDER VINE 65.00
VITICULTURE METHOD Certified Organic
SUSTAINABLE WINERY

○ Becco Reale Pecorino '19	🍷🍷 3
⊙ Cerasuolo d'Abruzzo Capo Le Vigne '19	🍷🍷 3
● Montepulciano d'Abruzzo Capo Le Vigne '17	🍷🍷 4

MOLISE

Molise is often described as a border territory, a passageway between zones and regions. We think that's a bit superficial. Certainly it shares some similarities with neighboring areas. There's no doubt this is true in terms of orography and climate, for example, as well as cultural and gastronomic traditions. But it's equally true that Molise's communities manage to maintain their own, strong identity. And its ampelography mirrors that. If on the one hand the region 'borrows' its Montepulciano, Aglianico, Malvasia, Falanghina, and Greco grapes from Campania, Abruzzo, and Puglia, the wines made from these grapes have little to do with their neighboring counterparts. They reveal subtly their Mediterranean or mountain profiles, austere or light qualities, which can be traced back to the different production areas that unfold here between the Meta and Matese mountains and the Adriatic Coast. All this under the banner of Tintilia, the region's true native grape, which every year gives rise to increasingly focused and interesting wines. More and more, we're seeing a focus on territorial expression, all marked by the preservation of the cultivar's characteristics. To this end, hats off to Claudio Cipressi, Antonio Grieco (Tenimenti Grieco) and Michele Travaglini (Tenute Martarosa) for having presented delicious wines that just by a hair's breadth missed Tre Bicchieri. It's an award that once again goes exclusively to the region's most historic producer, Di Majo Norante, whose Don Luigi put in another super performance. It's a red of great tannic structure and Mediterranean warmth. So all is well in Molise? Not quite. Last year we pointed out that too few producers participate in our selections. Unfortunately, we have to make the same complaint again this year. We'd like to be able to increase the space dedicated to the region's best wineries, but to do so we need to have a larger base to work with. In the coming years we hope to work towards this goal. We hope Molise's producers do as well.

Claudio Cipressi

C.DA MONTAGNA, 11B
86030 SAN FELICE DEL MOLISE [CB]
TEL. +39 3351244859
www.claudiocipressi.it

CELLAR SALES
PRE-BOOKED VISITS
ACCOMMODATION
ANNUAL PRODUCTION 45,000 bottles
HECTARES UNDER VINE 15.00
VITICULTURE METHOD Certified Organic
SUSTAINABLE WINERY

Claudio Cipressi cultivates his vineyards on the harshest inland hills in the province of Campobasso, in San Felice del Molise. The winery's vineyards obtained organic certification in 2014 and are located at almost 600 meters elevation. Of the 15 hectares planted with vines, 12 are dedicated to Tintilia, the native variety used to make several wines. The rest of the vineyards are divided between Montepulciano, Falanghina and Trebbiano. Various winemaking methods are used in the cellar, but all of them aim for concreteness and territoriality. An excellent version of Macchiarossa reached our finals: the 2016 vintage made for a wine with very clean balsamic, minty aromas and a touch of aniseed, merging with ripe strawberry and Ferrovia cherry. The palate reveals nice continuity and round, well-defined tannins. Their Collequinto comes through juicy and delectable. This rosé made with Tintilia grapes plays on great aromatic fragrance and a pleasant palate. Their Falanghina Voira is also well-made.

● Molise Tintilia Macchiarossa '16	🍷🍷 5
⊙ Molise Tintilia Rosato Collequinto '19	🍷🍷 5
○ Voira Falanghina '19	🍷🍷 4
● Molise Rosso Decimo '18	🍷 4
○ Molise Trebbiano Le Scoste '18	🍷 4
○ Settevigne Falanghina '19	🍷 4
● Molise Tintilia 66 '13	♀♀ 7
● Molise Tintilia 66 '12	♀♀ 7
● Molise Tintilia Macchiarossa '14	♀♀ 5
● Molise Tintilia Macchiarossa '12	♀♀ 4
● Molise Tintilia Macchiarossa '11	♀♀ 4
● Molise Tintilia Settevigne '15	♀♀ 4
● Molise Tintilia Settevigne '14	♀♀ 4
● Molise Tintilia Settevigne '13	♀♀ 4

★Di Majo Norante

FRAZ. NUOVA CLITERNIA
VIA V. RAMITELLO, 4
86042 CAMPOMARINO [CB]
TEL. +39 087557208
www.dimajonorante.com

CELLAR SALES
PRE-BOOKED VISITS
ANNUAL PRODUCTION 800,000 bottles
HECTARES UNDER VINE 140.00
VITICULTURE METHOD Certified Organic

The Di Majo Norante family's property is a place where history and territory come together to produce wine. It stands on the ancient estate of the Marquises of Santa Cristina, in Campomarino, an area that spans southern Abruzzo, Daunia and Samnium. Alessio currently manages the 120 hectares of the winery's vineyards: he is his father's worthy successor, who has brought a breath of modernity to production, based mainly on the use of native varieties. The Molise Rosso Don Luigi Riserva, a monovarietal Montepulciano, offers up clear notes of ripe morello cherry, juniper berries and licorice. It shows nice cohesion between alcoholic power and close-knit tannins, on an intense and remarkably lingering palate. The Tintilia '18 exhibits overtones of medicinal herbs and blackberry jam, while the palate proves meaty and full of character. The Contado '16 is an Aglianico with great structure, volume and power.

● Molise Rosso Don Luigi Ris. '16	🍷🍷🍷 6
● Biferno Rosso Ramitello '16	🍷🍷 3
● Molise Aglianico Contado Ris. '16	🍷🍷 3
● Molise Tintilia '18	🍷🍷 3
○ Molise Greco '19	🍷 2
○ Molise Moscato Bianco Passito Apianae '16	🍷 5
● Sangiovese '19	🍷 2
● Molise Aglianico Biorganic '11	♀♀♀ 2*
● Molise Aglianico Contado Ris. '14	♀♀♀ 3*
● Molise Aglianico Contado Ris. '10	♀♀♀ 3*
● Molise Aglianico Contado Ris. '09	♀♀♀ 3*
● Molise Rosso Don Luigi Ris. '15	♀♀♀ 5
● Molise Rosso Don Luigi Ris. '12	♀♀♀ 5
● Molise Rosso Don Luigi Ris. '11	♀♀♀ 5
● Molise Tintilia '16	♀♀♀ 3*
● Molise Tintilia '13	♀♀♀ 3*

Tenimenti Grieco

c.da Difensola
86045 Portocannone [CB]
Tel. +39 0875590032
www.tenimentigrieco.it

CELLAR SALES
PRE-BOOKED VISITS
ANNUAL PRODUCTION 700,000 bottles
HECTARES UNDER VINE 85.00

Vintage after vintage, it is becoming one of the leading wineries in the region. Tenimenti Grieco is the result of significant renewal in the vineyards of the former Flocco farm that Antonio Grieco took over in 2013. The vineyards are planted with varieties ranging from native grapes such as Falanghina, Montepulciano and Tintilia, to international ones like Sauvignon, Pinot Bianco, Chardonnay, Cabernet, Merlot and Syrah. Over 80 hectares of vineyards are scattered over the slopes of Portocannone, overlooking the Adriatic. They produce a selection of refreshing, easy-drinking wines. The whole selection submitted this year performed really well at our tasting tables. Their Tintilia 200 Metri was outstanding: it opens with aromas of juniper berries, black pepper, Mediterranean scrub and black cherries, which give way to a juicy, fragrant, relaxed, supple and graceful palate. Rosemary and bay are followed by sweet spices and black fruit in their Molise Rosso I Costali, a monovarietal Montepulciano with nice pulp.

Wine	Rating
● MoliseTintilia 200 Metri '19	ŦŦ 3*
● Biferno Rosso Bosco delle Guardie '17	ŦŦ 3
● Molise Rosso I Costali '18	ŦŦ 3
● Molise Aglianico Passo alle Tremiti '17	Ŧ 3
○ Molise Falanghina Passo alle Tremiti '19	Ŧ 3
● Lenda Aglianico '15	ΨΨ 5
⊙ Molise Rosato Passo alle Tremiti '15	ΨΨ 3
● Molise Rosso I Costali '17	ΨΨ 3
● Molise Rosso Monterosso I Costali '16	ΨΨ 3*
● Molise Rosso Passo alle Tremiti '15	ΨΨ 3*
● Molise Tintilia '14	ΨΨ 2*
● Molise Tintilia 200 Metri '18	ΨΨ 2*
● Molise Tintilia 200 Metri '17	ΨΨ 2*
● Molise Tintilia 200 Metri '16	ΨΨ 2*
● Molise Tintilia 200 Metri '15	ΨΨ 2*
● Triassi '15	ΨΨ 5

Tenute Martarosa

fraz. Nuova Cliternia
via Madonna Grande, 11
86042 Campomarino [CB]
Tel. +39 087557156
www.tenutemartarosa.com

CELLAR SALES
ANNUAL PRODUCTION 50,000 bottles
HECTARES UNDER VINE 20.00

Tenute Martarosa is a young winery, founded by Michele Travaglini in Campomarino, in 2016. But the history of this estate dates back to 1938, the year the first bush-trained vineyards were planted in Martarosa with the aim of selling grapes; two generations later, Michele fulfilled his dream to produce his own wines from about twenty hectares of owned vineyards. He grows Tintilia, Montepulciano, Moscato and Fiano grapes to produce six wines. The Tintilia has reached our finals for the second year running, just grazing the most important goal: nuances of strawberry, cherry, white pepper and red roses pave the way for a palate with subtle, silky tannins. It features a vaguely iron-like development and a fragrant, enthralling finish. The Antico Podere '17 is a monovarietal Montepulciano exhibiting graceful floral, fruity and spicy aromas, followed by very close-knit, nicely-textured tannins.

Wine	Rating
● Molise Tintilia '18	ŦŦ 3*
○ Molise Fiano '19	ŦŦ 3
○ Molise Moscato '19	ŦŦ 3
● Molise Rosso Antico Podere '17	ŦŦ 3
○ Due Versure Bianco '19	Ŧ 2
● Due Versure Rosso '18	Ŧ 2
⊙ Molise Tintilia Rosato '19	Ŧ 3
● Molise Tintilia '16	ΨΨ 3*

Borgo di Colloredo

FRAZ. NUOVA CLITERNIA
VIA COLLOREDO, 15
86042 CAMPOMARINO [CB]
TEL. +39 087557453
www.borgodicolloredo.com

CELLAR SALES
PRE-BOOKED VISITS
ACCOMMODATION AND RESTAURANT SERVICE
ANNUAL PRODUCTION 230,000 bottles
HECTARES UNDER VINE 80.00
SUSTAINABLE WINERY

- ● Aglianico '16 🍷🍷 3
- ○ Biferno Bianco Gironia '19 🍷🍷 3
- ○ Molise Falanghina Campo in Mare '19 🍷 3

Catabbo

C.DA PETRIERA
86046 SAN MARTINO IN PENSILIS [CB]
TEL. +39 0875604945
www.catabbo.it

CELLAR SALES
ANNUAL PRODUCTION 150,000 bottles
HECTARES UNDER VINE 54.00
VITICULTURE METHOD Certified Organic

- ● Molise Rosso I Diecettari '17 🍷🍷 3
- ● Petriera Montepulciano '19 🍷🍷 2*
- ○ Molise Falanghina Colle del Limone '19 🍷 3
- ● Molise Tintilia Ris. '15 🍷 5

Cantine Salvatore

C.DA VIGNE
86049 URURI [CB]
TEL. +39 0874830656
www.cantinesalvatore.it

CELLAR SALES
PRE-BOOKED VISITS
ANNUAL PRODUCTION 80,000 bottles
HECTARES UNDER VINE 20.00
SUSTAINABLE WINERY

- ● Molise Rosso Biberius '17 🍷🍷 2*
- ● Molise Tintilia Rutilia '17 🍷🍷 3
- ● Ti.A.Mo. '16 🍷🍷 3
- ○ Molise Falanghina Nysias '19 🍷 3

Cantina San Zenone

C.DA PIANA DEI PASTINI
86036 MONTENERO DI BISACCIA [CB]
TEL. +39 3477998397
www.cantinasanzenone.it

CELLAR SALES
PRE-BOOKED VISITS
ANNUAL PRODUCTION 150,000 bottles
HECTARES UNDER VINE 300.00
VITICULTURE METHOD Certified Organic

- ● Il Viandante Rosso '17 🍷🍷 2*
- ● Molilse Tintilia '17 🍷🍷 5
- ● Nonno Matteo '17 🍷🍷 4

Terresacre

C.DA MONTEBELLO
86036 MONTENERO DI BISACCIA [CB]
TEL. +39 0875960191
www.terresacre.net

CELLAR SALES
PRE-BOOKED VISITS
ACCOMMODATION AND RESTAURANT SERVICE
ANNUAL PRODUCTION 100,000 bottles
HECTARES UNDER VINE 35.00

- ● Molise Rosso Neravite '17 🍷🍷 2*
- ● Molise Rosso Rispetto '16 🍷🍷 5

Campi Valerio

LOC. SELVOTTA
86075 MONTERODUNI [IS]
TEL. +39 0865493043
www.campi-valerio.it

CELLAR SALES
PRE-BOOKED VISITS
ANNUAL PRODUCTION 100,000 bottles
HECTARES UNDER VINE 5.00

- ● Molise Rosso Calidio '17 🍷🍷 2*
- ● Molise Rosso Sannazzaro '17 🍷🍷 3
- ● Tintilia del Molise Opalia '16 🍷🍷 4

CAMPANIA

In Campania there are rare flavors to be discovered. By virtue of its mind-boggling biodiversity, these flavors are everywhere, in Campania's wines as well as its dishes. Here is the food ever delicious. And you can taste it in the glass. The area under vine? 24,200 hectares, and in our guide we cover 106 wineries, with a number of new entries, from small, artisanal wineries to large producers whose output reaches millions of bottles per year. In a panorama that's varied (to say the least) the constants in the bottle are Campania's marine sensations and Mediterranean profile. We think of its islands, the vines that grow on the slopes of Vesuvius, the vineyards overlooking the sea in Cilento, or those wonderful patches of vineyards in the form of terraces on the Amalfi Coast. But there are also the hills of Benevento and Irpinia, with its terrain rich in marine sediment, crossed by layers of tuff and limestone. And in Caserta the influence of the volcano returns to lend a darker, sapid rhythm to the wines. This year Campania snatches 23 Tre Bicchieri. We welcome 2 wineries to the club: Tenuta Scuotto (thanks to their 2019 Fiano d'Avellino), and Fiorentino (thanks to an excellent 2015 Taurasi). The district of Irpinia took the lead with 12 Tre Bicchieri. It's followed by Sannio with 4 awards, 3 in the Salerno area, 2 in Caserta, and 2 for the Phlegraean Fields (in this case in the province of Naples). Fiano di Avellino once again reigns supreme, but Greco di Tufo and Falanghina, both in Sannio and in the Phlegraean Fields, are keeping the momentum going thanks to a good 2019 vintage. We're also seeing good signs from Taurasi. For years it hadn't been able to reach 4 golds, but this time was different thanks to interpretations that aren't focusing strictly on power. Finally, we'd like to mention a few red Due Bicchieri, excellent wines that reached our finals. We start with Passo delle Tortore's Greco di Tufo Le Arcaie, the best version in our guide. Then there's Nanni Copè's recent addition, the lovely white Polveri della Scarrupata. We shouldn't forget the unique, mature and smoky Terra di Lavoro by Galardi or the delicately salty, sulphurous and powerful texture of Angelo Muto's Greco di Tufo Miniere. Casebianche's La Matta Dosaggio Zero is a carefree Fiano that undergoes second fermentation, and dances in the bottle. Contrade di Taurasi's Grecomusc' is redolent of mountain herbs. Finally, we wanted to point out a Fiano produced in one of the most evocative places on the planet, Punta Tresino, in Cilento. Here San Giovanni produces a Fiano that's so close to the sea you can hear the waves breaking when you drink it.

Agnanum

VIA VICINALE ABBANDONATA AGLI ASTRONI, 3
80125 NAPOLI
TEL. +39 3385315272
www.agnanum.it

CELLAR SALES
PRE-BOOKED VISITS
ANNUAL PRODUCTION 25,000 bottles
HECTARES UNDER VINE 7.50

Agnanum nurtures vines planted on volcanic hills in the Cratere degli Astroni nature reserve. In the 1960s, Gennaro Moccia decided to devote a large part of his work to an area that was barely known for winemaking at the time: Campi Flegrei. Then the baton passed to his son Raffaele, a hard-headed vigneron and key figure at this expert winery with terraced vineyards located on the steep hills of the Astroni Natural Park. Work in the vineyards is done exclusively by hand and water is provided by digging out small hollows near the ungrafted vines. The Campi Flegrei Falanghina '19 stood out in our tastings. It exhibits an exquisite sapid intensity and citrusy enthusiasm, zippy aromas and a lively palate, with a close-focused smoky influence. The Falanghina Sabbia Vulcanica 'a Ren 'e Lav' 18 features particularly intense aromas redolent of tomato leaf and catmint, while the finish offers up a slightly spicy overtone.

Wine	Rating
○ Campi Flegrei Falanghina '19	🍷🍷 3*
● Campi Flegrei Pér 'e Palumm '18	🍷🍷 4
○ Falanghina Sabbia Vulcanica 'a Ren' e 'Lav' '18	🍷🍷 3
○ Campi Flegrei Falanghina V. delle Volpi '17	🍷 3
○ Campi Flegrei Falanghina '18	YYY 3*
● Campi Flegrei Piedirosso '16	YYY 4*
● Campi Flegrei Piedirosso '15	YYY 4*
○ Campi Flegrei Falanghina '17	YY 3*
○ Campi Flegrei Falanghina V. delle Volpi '16	YY 3
● Campi Flegrei Pér 'e Palumm '18	YY 4
● Campi Flegrei Pér 'e Palumm '17	YY 4

Alois

LOC. AUDELINO
VIA RAGAZZANO
81040 PONTELATONE [CE]
TEL. +39 0823876710
www.vinialois.it

CELLAR SALES
PRE-BOOKED VISITS
ANNUAL PRODUCTION 300,000 bottles
HECTARES UNDER VINE 30.00
SUSTAINABLE WINERY

The Alois family have always specialized in packaging precious fabrics, but over the years their name has become associated with production of Casavecchia and Pallagrello, historic wines in Caserta winemaking. Brothers Michele and Massimo run the winery today, helped by winemaker Carmine Valentino. Together they have given vinegrowing in Monti Caiatini a new lease of life by promoting this part of Campania all over the world. Worth mentioning is their new wine, Vigna Morrone, a Pallagrello Bianco bearing the name of the vineyard the grapes are grown in. This year, Alois' new addition takes home Tre Bicchieri. The Pellagrello Bianco Morrone '18 offers up a generous, complex profile with toasty, spicy overtones on a citrusy background. In the mouth it features nice pulp and a classy, sapid finish. Their Caiati '19 plays more on fruit, exhibiting aromas of peach and lime and a very pleasant, juicy, supple palate. The Trebulanum and two wines made with Falanghina also impressed.

Wine	Rating
○ Morrone Pallagrello Bianco '18	🍷🍷🍷 6
○ Caiatì '19	🍷🍷 3*
● Campole '18	🍷🍷 3
● Casavecchia di Pontelatone Trebulanum Ris. '15	🍷🍷 5
○ Fiano di Avellino Donna Paolina '19	🍷🍷 4
● Ponte Pellegrino Aglianico '19	🍷🍷 5
○ Ponte Pellegrino Falanghina '19	🍷🍷 3
○ Caulino '19	🍷 3
● Cunto Pallagrello Nero '17	🍷 4
● Settimo '18	🍷 3
○ Caiatì Pallagrello Bianco '17	YYY 4*
○ Caulino '18	YY 3
● Cunto Pallagrello Nero '16	YY 4
● Ponte Pellegrino Aglianico '18	YY 5
○ Ponte Pellegrino Falanghina '18	YY 3

Cantine Astroni

via Sartania, 48
80126 Napoli
Tel. +39 0815884182
www.cantineastroni.com

CELLAR SALES
PRE-BOOKED VISITS
RESTAURANT SERVICE
ANNUAL PRODUCTION 330,000 bottles
HECTARES UNDER VINE 25.00
VITICULTURE METHOD Certified Organic
SUSTAINABLE WINERY

Cantine Astroni promotes the Campi Flegrei territory by virtue of a centuries-old tradition and terraced vineyards perched on the external slopes of the Astroni crater. A total of 25 hectares are tended to under the direct supervision of Gerardo Vernazzaro, his wife Emanuela Russo and his cousin Vincenzo. This is an extraordinary landscape, caressed by the sea and made up of layers of lapillus and ash, which make for very authentic wines. Their range is always more complex and complete and this year they have a new entry to add to their historic plots of land: the Campi Flegrei Tenuta Jossa, a limited-edition white wine made with Falanghina and Fiano grapes fermented in amphorae. The Piedirosso Colle Rotondella '19 takes home Tre Bicchieri. It's a delicious wine in its fragrances of pomegranate and its enticing, peppery whiffs. On the palate it's sapid, delicately smoky, with a fresh, long and citrusy finish. A new addition, the Tenuta Jossa, features a deep gustatory phase on sensations of sulfur, coming through rich, savory and highly characterful.

Wine	Rating
● Campi Flegrei Piedirosso Colle Rotondella '19	🍷🍷🍷 3*
○ Campi Flegrei Bianco Tenuta Jossa '18	🍷🍷 5
○ Campi Flegrei Falanghina Colle Imperatrice '19	🍷🍷 3
○ Lacryma Christi del Vesuvio Bianco Cratere Bianco '19	🍷🍷 3
● Lacryma Christi del Vesuvio Rosso Cratere Rosso '19	🍷🍷 3
○ Campi Flegrei Falanghina V. Astroni '15	🍷🍷🍷 3*
○ Campi Flegrei Falanghina Colle Imperatrice '18	🍷🍷 2*
○ Campi Flegrei Falanghina V. Astroni '17	🍷🍷 3
● Campi Flegrei Piedirosso Tenuta Camaldoli Ris. '16	🍷🍷 3*
○ Strione '15	🍷🍷 4

Bambinuto

via Cerro
83030 Santa Paolina [AV]
Tel. +39 0825964634
www.cantinabambinuto.com

PRE-BOOKED VISITS
ANNUAL PRODUCTION 25,000 bottles
HECTARES UNDER VINE 6.00

Tastings done throughout the year confirm how suitable the wines produced by Marilena Aufiero are for long aging. Her Greco di Tufo wines still prove full of energy, with a very unusual taste, after ten years. It all began in 2006 when Marilena convinced her parents to vinify their own grapes grown on two particularly good plots of winemaking land located in the municipality of Santa Paolina, Paoloni and Picoli respectively, at over 500 meters of elevation, on soils rich in clay and layers of limestone. Aglianico, on the other hand, is grown in Toppole near Montemiletto. The two whites proposed in this edition performed at high levels. The Greco di Tufo Picoli '18 expresses the best of the typology in terms of sapid energy, structure and fullness of flavour. It has a savory profile, spirited, with a finish rich in energy and citrusy hints. Slightly leaner and balsamic, the excellent Greco di Tufo '18 proves fresh in its aromas of lime and aniseed, with a nicely linear, refreshing palate.

Wine	Rating
○ Greco di Tufo Picoli '18	🍷🍷 4
● Aglianico 212.4 Toppole '18	🍷🍷 3
○ Greco di Tufo '18	🍷🍷 2*
○ Greco di Tufo '15	🍷🍷 2*
○ Greco di Tufo '14	🍷🍷 2*
○ Greco di Tufo '13	🍷🍷 2*
○ Greco di Tufo '12	🍷🍷 3
○ Greco di Tufo Picoli '17	🍷🍷 4
○ Greco di Tufo Picoli '16	🍷🍷 4
○ Greco di Tufo Picoli '15	🍷🍷 4
○ Greco di Tufo Picoli '13	🍷🍷 4
○ Greco di Tufo Picoli '11	🍷🍷 4
○ Greco di Tufo Picoli '10	🍷🍷 4
○ Irpinia Falanghina Insania '15	🍷🍷 2*
● Taurasi '07	🍷🍷 5

Bosco de' Medici

via Antonio Segni, 43
80045 Pompei [NA]
Tel. +39 3382828234
www.boscodemedici.com

CELLAR SALES
PRE-BOOKED VISITS
ACCOMMODATION AND RESTAURANT SERVICE
ANNUAL PRODUCTION 25,000 bottles
HECTARES UNDER VINE 8.00

This well-organized, dynamic winery in the southern part of Vesuvius also includes a lovely resort. Here at the heart of archeological excavations in Pompeii, the history of Ancient Roman wine merges with the Florentine dynasty of the Medici. In 1567, during the days of the Kingdom of Naples, Luigi de' Medici entrusted to his favorite nephew Giuseppe the task of improving the quality of the family wines. Today, that tradition has been taken up again and developed by Giuseppe Palomba and Antonio Monaco. Since 2014, they have been making wine under a brand that has come along way among enthusiasts. The Pompeii Bianco, made with Caprettone, once again demonstrates that it's one of the best whites in the region. The 2019 features a rich, mature profile that plays nicely on delicately toasted almond and ginger, as well as juicy, fragrant yellow fruit. It has structure and a sapid energy, making for a fresh, well-sustained finish. Aromas of wild cherry, tobacco and roots characterize the Pompeii Rosso '19, made with Piedirosso grapes.

Wine	Rating
○ Pompeii Bianco '19	🍷🍷 4
● Pompeii Rosso '19	🍷🍷 3
○ Lacryma Christi del Vesuvio Bianco Lavaflava '19	🍷 3
○ Pompeii Bianco '18	🍷🍷🍷 3*
○ Dressel 19.2 '17	🍷🍷 3
○ Lacryma Christi del Vesuvio Bianco Lavaflava '18	🍷🍷 3
● Lacryma Christi del Vesuvio Rosso Lavarubra '15	🍷🍷 3
○ Pompeii Bianco '15	🍷🍷 3*
● Pompeii Rosso '18	🍷🍷 3

I Cacciagalli

s.da prov.le 91 - Borgonuovo- Cipriani
81057 Teano [CE]
Tel. +39 0823875216
www.icacciagalli.it

CELLAR SALES
PRE-BOOKED VISITS
ACCOMMODATION
ANNUAL PRODUCTION 20,000 bottles
HECTARES UNDER VINE 9.00
VITICULTURE METHOD Certified Organic

There is always a good reason to stop off in Teano, in upper Caserta, to visit Diana Iannaccone and her husband Mario Bosco. Here the olive trees, chestnuts and vineyards are cultivated under biodynamic management. The stars of the show are the local native varieties Falanghina, Fiano, Aglianico and Pallagrello Nero.
Fermentation takes place with native yeasts and the white wines undergo long maceration in concrete and amphorae with stainless steel closures. Their wide range of wines exhibits an original style and territoriality. Don't miss the Bistrot 26, open in the center of Teano. The Zagreo '18 took home Tre Bicchieri. In opens a bit fuzzy on notes of yeast, wheat and orange peel before unfolding on the palate with a rare energy, on sapid sensations of vibrant freshness, with a graceful, flavorful texture. The result is a wine of rare drinkability and complexity. The Pellerosa, a focused and expressive Aglianico rosé, is also delicious, spanning fruity and spicy sensations with grace and vividness.

Wine	Rating
○ Zagreo '18	🍷🍷🍷 4*
⊙ Pellerosa '18	🍷🍷 4
● Phos '18	🍷🍷 4
● Sphaeranera '18	🍷 4
○ Zagreo '15	🍷🍷🍷 4*
○ Aorivola '18	🍷🍷 3
○ Aorivola '16	🍷🍷 3
● Lucno '13	🍷🍷 4
⊙ Pellerosa '17	🍷🍷 4
● Phos '17	🍷🍷 4
● Phos '15	🍷🍷 4
● Sphaeranera '17	🍷🍷 4
● Sphaeranera '15	🍷🍷 4
○ Zagreo '17	🍷🍷 4
○ Zagreo '14	🍷🍷 4
○ Zagreo '13	🍷🍷 4

Antonio Caggiano

C.DA SALA
83030 TAURASI [AV]
TEL. +39 082774723
www.cantinecaggiano.it

CELLAR SALES
PRE-BOOKED VISITS
RESTAURANT SERVICE
ANNUAL PRODUCTION 165,000 bottles
HECTARES UNDER VINE 30.00

Meeting Antonio Caggiano is a unique experience, thanks to his fascinating personal history, his love for the land and for Taurasi. He is passionate about photography and travel and, in 1990, he decided to build a cellar made entirely of local stone; then he began to tend the old vineyards under the supervision of Professor Luigi Moio. Today, his son Giuseppe, Pino to his friends, plays a fundamental role in the winery, juggling production of Fiano di Avellino, Greco di Tufo and Taurasi. It's worth mentioning their historic wine Vigna Macchia dei Goti, one of the most profound and long-lived crus in the Taurasi appellation. The 2016 version takes home Tre Bicchieri by virtue of its deep, multi-layered gustative texture in which earthy aromas are accompanied by roots and tanned leather; the palate is powerful, voluminous but well supported by a lively acidity, making for a rich and dynamic red. As usual, the Salae Domini, a more direct and approachable Aglianico, also delivers.

Wine	Rating
● Taurasi V. Macchia dei Goti '16	🍷🍷🍷 6
○ Fiano di Avellino Béchar '19	🍷🍷 3
○ Greco di Tufo Devon '19	🍷🍷 3
● Irpinia Campi Taurasini Salae Domini '17	🍷🍷 5
○ Mel	🍷🍷 6
○ Falanghina '19	🍷 3
○ Fiano di Avellino Béchar '13	🍸🍸🍸 3*
● Taurasi V. Macchia dei Goti '14	🍸🍸🍸 6
● Taurasi V. Macchia dei Goti '08	🍸🍸🍸 5
● Taurasi V. Macchia dei Goti '04	🍸🍸🍸 5
● Taurasi V. Macchia dei Goti '99	🍸🍸🍸 5
● Taurasi V. Macchia dei Goti Ris. '15	🍸🍸🍸 6
○ Fiano di Avellino Béchar '17	🍸🍸 3
● Irpinia Aglianico Taurì '18	🍸🍸 3
● Irpinia Aglianico Taurì '17	🍸🍸 2*
○ Mel	🍸🍸 5

Cantine dell'Angelo

VIA SANTA LUCIA, 32
83010 TUFO [AV]
TEL. +39 3384512965
www.cantinedellangelo.com

CELLAR SALES
PRE-BOOKED VISITS
ANNUAL PRODUCTION 18,000 bottles
HECTARES UNDER VINE 5.00

The Greco specialists. The history of the Muto family is linked to the production of Greco di Tufo. The owner, Angelo, is the third generation to devote his work to the vineyard, with the invaluable support of Maria Nuzzolo. Five hectares of vineyards are dedicated to the DOCG, located in part on ancient sulfur mines, and give rise to original, multifaceted Greco. Torrefavale and Miniere, their only wines, manage to capture the soul of the place in the glass: vigorous and exuberant, driven by sapidity and freshness, steering toward rocky whiffs intensified by strong sulfur notes in the Miniere. And it's the Miniere that does the honors in our finals. It's one of the region's most complex drinks. As usual, aromatically it's a bit restless and tousled, but the palate is simply amazing for its intensity, expansiveness, savoriness and endless finish. The Torrefavale sees a similar gustatory profile, but it's even more mature, with a horizontal development in which aromas of peach, citron and honey emerge on a nice, smoky background.

Wine	Rating
○ Greco di Tufo Miniere '18	🍷🍷 4
○ Greco di Tufo Torrefavale '18	🍷🍷 5
○ Greco di Tufo '09	🍸🍸🍸 3*
○ Greco di Tufo Miniere '16	🍸🍸🍸 4*
○ Greco di Tufo '14	🍸🍸 3
○ Greco di Tufo '13	🍸🍸 3
○ Greco di Tufo '11	🍸🍸 3
○ Greco di Tufo '10	🍸🍸 3
○ Greco di Tufo Miniere '17	🍸🍸 4
○ Greco di Tufo Torrefavale '17	🍸🍸 5
○ Greco di Tufo Torrefavale '16	🍸🍸 5
○ Greco di Tufo Torrefavale '15	🍸🍸 3
○ Greco di Tufo Torrefavale '14	🍸🍸 3
○ Greco di Tufo Torrefavale '13	🍸🍸 3*

Casa Setaro

via Bosco del Monaco, 34
80040 Trecase [NA]
Tel. +39 0818628956
www.casasetaro.it

CELLAR SALES
PRE-BOOKED VISITS
RESTAURANT SERVICE
ANNUAL PRODUCTION 75,000 bottles
HECTARES UNDER VINE 12.00
VITICULTURE METHOD Certified Organic
SUSTAINABLE WINERY

Casa Setaro is where Massimo and his wife, Maria Rosaria, both live and work. It's a real house-cum-cellar that bears witness to the strong link between family and the Neapolitan wine culture. Here in the town of Trecase, on the slopes of Vesuvius, native varieties such as Caprettone and Piedirosso are made into two different versions of wine. The vineyards are located at 350 meters of elevation, on volcanic soils, inside the Vesuvius national park: Massimo scrupulously follows the vines, which are located in two areas of the park: Tirrone della Guardia and Bosco del Monaco. We start with the Rosato Munazei '19, a wine that entices right from its pale color, opening in the glass on hints of pomegranate and pepper, light but at the same time expressive—a convincing drink. We also appreciated the 2019 Rosso Munazei, with its aromas of pencil lead and licorice; in the mouth it has juice and a sapid pluck. The Caprettone Metodo Classico Pietrafumante '17 is original in its aromatic weave and improving in terms of bead.

Wine	Rating
⊙ Lacryma Christi del Vesuvio Rosato Munazei '19	TT 3
● Lacryma Christi del Vesuvio Rosso Munazei '19	TT 3
○ Pietrafumante Brut M. Cl. '17	TT 5
● Lacryma Christi del Vesuvio Rosso Don Vincenzo '15	T 4
○ Campanelle '17	YY 2*
○ Caprettone Brut M. Cl. '14	YY 4
○ Caprettone Brut M. Cl. '13	YY 4
○ Falanghina Campanelle '16	YY 2*
● Lacryma Christi del Vesuvio Rosso Don Vincenzo '14	YY 4
● Lacryma Christi del Vesuvio Rosso Don Vincenzo Ris. '14	YY 4
○ Pietrafumante Brut '16	YY 5
● Vesuvio Piedirosso Fuocoallegro '17	YY 3

Casebianche

c.da Case Bianche, 8
84076 Torchiara [SA]
Tel. +39 0974843244
www.casebianche.eu

CELLAR SALES
PRE-BOOKED VISITS
ANNUAL PRODUCTION 35,000 bottles
HECTARES UNDER VINE 5.50
VITICULTURE METHOD Certified Organic
SUSTAINABLE WINERY

Pleasantly-unpolished, fragrant and drinkable. Betty Iurio and Pasquale have revolutionized style in Campania, playing on wines with unusual drinkability that faithfully express the territory at the same time. Architects by profession, they began to tend the family vineyards in Torchiara, in Cilento, in 2000, putting to good use the soils rich in gravel and clay between Monte Stella, the Acquasanta river and the sea. Here, the vine rows of Aglianico, Barbera, Piedirosso, Fiano, Trebbiano and Malvasia are all cultivated under organic management. Endowed with energy and precise stylistic definition, their bottle-fermented wines are their pride and joy. Just take the La Matta '19, a Fiano redolent of citron, ginger and hay; the palate is juicy, sapid, smoky, unfolding lively and with great character. The Fric is more a life philosophy than a wine: whiffs of pomegranate and blood orange reveal the cheerful, light-hearted side of Aglianico.

Wine	Rating
○ La Matta Dosaggio Zero '19	TT 4
○ Cilento Fiano Cumalè '19	TT 3
⊙ Il Fric '19	TT 4
○ Iscadoro '18	T 4
⊙ Il Fric '16	YYY 3*
● Pashka' '17	YYY 4*
○ Cilento Fiano Cumalè '12	YY 2*
● Cilento Rosso Dellemore '17	YY 3
● Cilento Rosso Dellemore '16	YY 3
● Cilento Rosso Dellemore '15	YY 3
⊙ Il Fric '18	YY 4
⊙ Il Fric '17	YY 4
⊙ Il Fric '15	YY 3
○ La Matta Dosaggio Zero '16	YY 3
○ La Matta Dosaggio Zero '15	YY 3*
● Pashkà '18	YY 4
● Pashkà '16	YY 3

Tenuta Cavalier Pepe

via Santa Vara
83050 Sant'Angelo all'Esca [AV]
Tel. +39 082773766
www.tenutapepe.it

CELLAR SALES
PRE-BOOKED VISITS
ACCOMMODATION AND RESTAURANT SERVICE
ANNUAL PRODUCTION 450,000 bottles
HECTARES UNDER VINE 60.00
SUSTAINABLE WINERY

Following his entrepreneurial success in Belgium, Angelo Pepe decided to reinvest in his land of origin, Irpinia. In just a few years, he remapped the future of his family by setting up a cellar equipped with a lovely area for receiving visitors, run by his daughter Milena, who has a diploma in enology and lots of experience in Rhone and Burgundy. Today the Pepe family's wines are distributed in both Italy and abroad and include the most successful appellations in the territory of Irpinia, thanks to 60 hectares of vines. The vineyards extend between the territory of Sant'Angelo all'Esca, Montefusco, Torrioni and Luogosano. The Fiano di Avellino Refiano '19 landed in our finals by virtue of its elegant aromatic profile, playing on sensations of yellow fruit, roasted almond, and a steady structure that traces our a complex, characterful parabola of flavor. Fresh whiffs of mandarin and sage characterize the Greco di Tufo '19, a wine that's tonic and lively on the palate, with a clearly sapid finish.

Wine	Rating
○ Fiano di Avellino Refiano '19	▼▼ 3*
○ Greco di Tufo Nestor '19	▼▼ 3
● Irpinia Aglianico Terra del Varo '16	▼▼ 2*
○ Irpinia Coda di Volpe Bianco di Bellona '19	▼ 3
○ Irpinia Falanghina Santa Vara '18	▼ 4
○ Fiano di Avellino Brancato '17	▽▽ 5
○ Fiano di Avellino Brancato '16	▽▽ 3
○ Fiano di Avellino Refiano '16	▽▽ 3
○ Fiano di Avellino Refiano '15	▽▽ 3
○ Greco di Tufo Grancare '15	▽▽ 5
○ Greco di Tufo Grancare Sel. '16	▽▽ 7
○ Greco di Tufo Nestor '18	▽▽ 5
○ Greco di Tufo Nestor '17	▽▽ 5
○ Greco di Tufo Nestor '16	▽▽ 3
● Taurasi Opera Mia '13	▽▽ 8
● Taurasi Opera Mia '12	▽▽ 5

★Colli di Lapio

via Arianiello, 47
83030 Lapio [AV]
Tel. +39 0825982184
www.collidilapio.it

CELLAR SALES
PRE-BOOKED VISITS
ANNUAL PRODUCTION 60,000 bottles
HECTARES UNDER VINE 12.00

The Lady of Fiano lives in Arianello, in the municipality of Lapio, the cradle of one of Italy's great white wines: Fiano di Avellino, which obtained DOCG recognition in 2003. Together with her children Carmela and Federico, she has given a new lease of life to a wine that benefits from grapes grown at 600 meters of elevation. This confers pure, fresh aromas redolent of mountain herbs and sparkling acidity that gives us a long, sharpish dynamism. The Fiano and Greco are exclusively made in steel, while Aglianico ages in oak barrels. All the wines are made from grapes grown in their own vineyards. Tre Bicchieri for the Fiano di Avellino '19, a wine that has plenty of tricks up its sleeve. Aromatically it calls up the freshness of aniseed and freshly roasted hazelnut, its fruit is both ripe and fragrant, the palate creamy, enlivened by a focused acidic tension that lengthens its flavor towards a long, balsamic finish. The Irpinia Campi Taurasini Donna Chiara continues to improve: the 2018 is pleasant, dynamic and juicy.

Wine	Rating
○ Fiano di Avellino '19	▼▼▼ 4*
● Irpinia Campi Taurasini Donna Chiara '18	▼▼ 3
○ Greco di Tufo Alèxandros '19	▼ 3
● Taurasi Andrea '15	▼ 5
○ Fiano di Avellino '18	▽▽▽ 4*
○ Fiano di Avellino '16	▽▽▽ 4*
○ Fiano di Avellino '15	▽▽▽ 4*
○ Fiano di Avellino '14	▽▽▽ 4*
○ Fiano di Avellino '13	▽▽▽ 4*
○ Fiano di Avellino '10	▽▽▽ 4
○ Fiano di Avellino '09	▽▽▽ 4
○ Fiano di Avellino '08	▽▽▽ 4*
○ Fiano di Avellino '07	▽▽▽ 4
○ Fiano di Avellino '05	▽▽▽ 4
○ Fiano di Avellino '04	▽▽▽ 4
○ Fiano di Avellino '17	▽▽ 4

Contrade di Taurasi

via Municipio, 41
83030 Taurasi [AV]
Tel. +39 082774483
www.cantinelonardo.it

CELLAR SALES
PRE-BOOKED VISITS
ANNUAL PRODUCTION 15,000 bottles
HECTARES UNDER VINE 5.00
VITICULTURE METHOD Certified Organic

The Di Lonardo family comes from a long farming tradition, but it was only in 1998 that Alessandro decided to move their winemaking business up a gear, by creating their own brand. Together with his daughter Antonella and her husband Flavio Castaldo, he manages just a few hectares of vineyards in the hills of Taurasi, Bonito and Mirabella Eclano, where the star of the show is Aglianico, of course. They produce territorial wines, made with fermentation done using native yeasts. For the first time the Taurasi t31 lands a place in our finals. The 2012 is a mature, highly complex Taurasi with hints of undergrowth and resin, rich in fruit, with dense and well-extracted tannins. The finish comes through balsamic and long. The Grecomusc '18 once again proves highly alluring. It's very fine white in its aromas of mountain herbs, fresh its sensations of anise and mint, with a measured, ethereal palate—a truly classy drink.

Wine	Rating
○ Grecomusc' '18	▼▼ 4
● Taurasi t31 '12	▼▼ 8
○ Grecomusc' '15	▽▽▽ 5
○ Grecomusc' '12	▽▽▽ 4*
○ Grecomusc' '10	▽▽▽ 4*
● Taurasi '10	▽▽▽ 6
● Taurasi '04	▽▽▽ 6
● Taurasi Coste '11	▽▽▽ 8
● Taurasi Coste '08	▽▽▽ 7
● Taurasi Vigne d'Alto '12	▽▽▽ 8
○ Grecomusc' '17	▽▽ 5
○ Grecomusc' '16	▽▽ 5
○ Grecomusc' '14	▽▽ 5
● Irpinia Aglianico '16	▽▽ 4
● Taurasi '15	▽▽ 6
● Taurasi '12	▽▽ 6
● Taurasi Coste '12	▽▽ 8

★Marisa Cuomo

via G. B. Lama, 16/18
84010 Furore [SA]
Tel. +39 089830348
www.marisacuomo.com

CELLAR SALES
PRE-BOOKED VISITS
RESTAURANT SERVICE
ANNUAL PRODUCTION 109,000 bottles
HECTARES UNDER VINE 18.00

The vineyards belonging to Marisa Cuomo and her husband Andrea Ferraioli stretch across an area of rare beauty, above the hairpin bends of the Amalfi coast. They grow native varieties: Piedirosso and Sciascinoso for red wines and Ripoli, Fenile and Ginestra to produce the flagship white, Fiorduva, the only wine aged in barriques for about three months. Their children Dora and Raffaele work alongside their parents: the 18 hectares are all tended without using weedkillers. The Fiorduva put in an excellent performance. The 2019 version of this white calls up broad hints of Mediterranean scrub, with summery, soft and clear aromas, and juicy fruit on a spicy background that's just evident. The finish is long and elegantly expressed. The Ravello Bianco '19 is delicious in its interweaving of citrus and herbaceous sensations, fragrant and complex. The Furore Bianco '19 entices with its suite of yellow flowers—a highly pleasant drink.

Wine	Rating
○ Costa d'Amalfi Furore Bianco Fiorduva '19	▼▼▼ 7
○ Costa d'Amalfi Ravello Bianco '19	▼▼ 3*
○ Costa d'Amalfi Furore Bianco '19	▼▼ 4
● Costa d'Amalfi Ravello Rosso Ris. '17	▼▼ 5
○ Costa d'Amalfi Furore Bianco '15	▽▽▽ 4*
○ Costa d'Amalfi Furore Bianco '10	▽▽▽ 4
○ Costa d'Amalfi Furore Bianco Fiorduva '18	▽▽▽ 7
○ Costa d'Amalfi Furore Bianco Fiorduva '17	▽▽▽ 7
○ Costa d'Amalfi Furore Bianco Fiorduva '16	▽▽▽ 7
○ Costa d'Amalfi Furore Bianco Fiorduva '14	▽▽▽ 7
○ Costa d'Amalfi Furore Bianco Fiorduva '10	▽▽▽ 6

Cantine di Marzo

via Gaetano Di Marzo, 2
83010 Tufo [AV]
Tel. +39 0825998022
www.cantinedimarzo.it

CELLAR SALES
PRE-BOOKED VISITS
ANNUAL PRODUCTION 120,000 bottles
HECTARES UNDER VINE 20.00

Back in 1647, Scipione Di Marzo abandoned Nola, ravaged by plague, and moved to Tufo to start producing wine. When you visit the 17th-century cellars, you get an idea of the extraordinary legacy taken up by the Di Somma family. Ferrante heads the winery today, adding luster to 20 hectares of private vineyards dedicated mainly to Greco. These stretch across the districts of Santa Lucia, San Paolo di Tufo and Santa Paolina. Their range includes approachable fruity wines, ones made with grapes grown on small plots, fermented in steel, and a Metodo Classico made with Greco. The Greco di Tufo '19 made it into our finals. It's a pleasantly rustic wine in its almond sensations and whiffs of sage, characteristic in its pronounced sapidity, with juicy, vigorous fruit. In the mouth it shows plenty of determination. We also appreciated the Vigna Ortale '18, with its pronounced marine hints—it's an appetizing wine with a bright future. More vibrant vegetal notes characterize the Vigna Serrone '18, while the Vigna Laure '18 proves softer and creamier.

Wine	Rating
○ Greco di Tufo '19	▼▼ 2*
○ Greco di Tufo V. Ortale '18	▼▼ 3*
○ Greco di Tufo V. Laure '18	▼▼ 3
○ Greco di Tufo V. Serrone '18	▼▼ 4
○ 1930 Extra Brut M. Cl.	▼ 4
● Taurasi '16	▼ 4
○ Greco di Tufo '16	▽▽▽ 2*
○ Fiano di Avellino Donatus '13	▽▽ 3*
○ Greco di Tufo '18	▽▽ 2*
○ Greco di Tufo '15	▽▽ 2*
○ Greco di Tufo Colle Serrone '16	▽▽ 3*
○ Greco di Tufo Somnium Scipionis '13	▽▽ 5
○ Greco di Tufo Somnium Scipionis '12	▽▽ 5
○ Greco di Tufo V. Laure '17	▽▽ 3
○ Greco di Tufo V. Laure '16	▽▽ 3*
○ Greco di Tufo V. Ortale '17	▽▽ 3
○ Greco di Tufo V. Ortale '16	▽▽ 3*

Di Meo

c.da Coccovoni, 1
83050 Salza Irpina [AV]
Tel. +39 0825981419
www.dimeo.it

CELLAR SALES
PRE-BOOKED VISITS
RESTAURANT SERVICE
ANNUAL PRODUCTION 380,000 bottles
HECTARES UNDER VINE 30.00
SUSTAINABLE WINERY

The Di Meo family's winery was already operating in the 1980s. It was one of the first in Irpinia to produce bottled wine and to focus on the longevity of their whites. Roberto, the family winemaker, as well as president of Assoenologi Campania, has even put them on the market 15 years after the vintage, in order to demonstrate the indomitable character of these lands. Today their very sound, wide selection includes whites and reds with consistent quality standards. The Fiano vineyards stretch across clayey-calcareous soils at about 550 meters of elevation, while the Greco ones come under the municipalities of Santa Paolina and Tufo; lastly, Aglianico resides in the highest areas of Montemarano at 650 meters.. We very much appreciated the Greco di Tufo G '19, rich and savory as expected, with delicate sensations of yellow flowers, expansive and long on the palate. The juicy and focused Fiano di Avellino is delicious in its spicy overtones of ginger and white pepper, with hints of wheat. We also appreciated the extracted and complex Taurasi Vigna Olmo Riserva '13.

Wine	Rating
○ Greco di Tufo G '19	▼▼▼ 3*
○ Fiano di Avellino F '19	▼▼ 3*
● Taurasi V. Olmo Ris. '13	▼▼ 6
● Aglianico '17	▼ 3
○ Fiano di Avellino Alessandra '12	▽▽▽ 3*
● Taurasi Ris. '06	▽▽▽ 5
● Aglianico A '16	▽▽ 3
○ Coda di Volpe C '17	▽▽ 2*
○ Coda di Volpe C '16	▽▽ 2*
○ Fiano di Avellino F '18	▽▽ 3
○ Fiano di Avellino F '15	▽▽ 3*
○ Greco di Tufo G '18	▽▽ 3
○ Greco di Tufo G '17	▽▽ 3
○ Greco di Tufo G '07	▽▽ 3
○ Greco di Tufo Vittoria '07	▽▽ 4
● Taurasi Sel. Hamilton Ris. '09	▽▽ 7
● Taurasi V. Olmo Ris. '10	▽▽ 5

Donnachiara

LOC. PIETRACUPA
VIA STAZIONE
83030 MONTEFALCIONE [AV]
TEL. +39 0825977135
www.donnachiara.com

CELLAR SALES
PRE-BOOKED VISITS
ACCOMMODATION
ANNUAL PRODUCTION 200,000 bottles
HECTARES UNDER VINE 27.00
VITICULTURE METHOD Certified Organic
SUSTAINABLE WINERY

Ilaria Petitto has demonstrated her ability in running this winery in Irpinia. It is named after Chiara Mazzoleni, a noblewoman from Campania who married surgeon Antonio Petitto, with the lovely Torre Le Nocelle estate in Irpinia making up part of her dowry. With the help of winemaker Riccardo Cotarella, Ilaria produces a neat range of wines that embrace the main appellations in Irpinia. She exploits the potential of Aglianico, Greco and Fiano and promotes them on the main world markets with professionalism and determination. The Taurasi '16 offers up ripe aromas of cherries and blackberries on a lovely background of spices. In the mouth it has creamy tannins, a rather pronounced smoky profile and steady length thanks to its vivid acidity, only to finish on fruit and an encore of spices. Among the whites, this year, the Fiano di Avellino '19 stands out for its delicately herbaceous hints and its sapid, pulpy palate.

Wine	Rating
● Taurasi '16	🍷🍷🍷 6
○ Fiano di Avellino '19	🍷🍷 3
● Aglianico '19	🍷 2
○ Fiano di Avellino Empatia '19	🍷 4
○ Greco di Tufo '19	🍷 3
○ Resilienza Falanghina '18	🍷 3
● Aglianico '16	🍷🍷🍷 3*
○ Fiano di Avellino Empatia '18	🍷🍷🍷 4*
○ Greco di Tufo '16	🍷🍷🍷 3*
● Aglianico '18	🍷🍷 3
○ Falanghina '15	🍷🍷 2*
○ Falanghina Resilienza '17	🍷🍷 2*
○ Greco di Tufo '15	🍷🍷 3
● Irpinia Aglianico '17	🍷🍷 3
○ Irpinia Coda di Volpe '15	🍷🍷 3
● Taurasi Ris. '12	🍷🍷 7

I Favati

P.ZZA BARONE DI DONATO
83020 CESINALI [AV]
TEL. +39 0825666898
www.cantineifavati.it

CELLAR SALES
PRE-BOOKED VISITS
ANNUAL PRODUCTION 100,000 bottles
HECTARES UNDER VINE 21.00

Rosanna Petrozziello runs the winery, together with Piersabino and Giancarlo Favati. This proud woman with an Irpinian soul tends her vineyards on the southern side of the Sabato river, where the calcareous-clay soils make for full-bodied, expressive wines. Their fame has been established over the years with Pietramara, the Fiano cru in Atripalda, where the cool climate meets soil rich in minerals and sulphur; the Greco Terrantica is made with grapes from Montefusco, while the Cretarossa, an Aglianico, is from San Mango sul Calore. They get invaluable help from Vincenzo Mercurio, a who's able to interpret the mood of Irpinia. Tre Bicchieri for the Fiano di Avellino Pietramara '19, a white made complete by the way it perfectly balances structure and acidity; in the mouth it has the usual sapid pluck and juicy yellow fruit, expanding with class and finesse. We also appreciated the Greco di Tufo Terrantica '19, a wine that charms with its hints of chamomile and peach; on the palate it features tension together with sensations of sea salt.

Wine	Rating
○ Fiano di Avellino Pietramara '19	🍷🍷🍷 5
○ Greco di Tufo Terrantica '19	🍷🍷 4
● Irpinia Campi Taurasini Cretarossa '17	🍷🍷 3
○ Cabrì Fiano Extra Brut	🍷 3
● Taurasi TerzoTratto '15	🍷 5
○ Fiano di Avellino Pietramara '18	🍷🍷🍷 5
○ Fiano di Avellino Pietramara '17	🍷🍷🍷 5
○ Fiano di Avellino Pietramara '16	🍷🍷🍷 5
○ Fiano di Avellino Pietramara '15	🍷🍷🍷 5
○ Fiano di Avellino Pietramara '13	🍷🍷🍷 3*
○ Fiano di Avellino Pietramara '12	🍷🍷🍷 3*
○ Fiano di Avellino Pietramara '14	🍷🍷 3*
○ Greco di Tufo Terrantica '17	🍷🍷 3*
○ Greco di Tufo Terrantica '16	🍷🍷 3*
● Taurasi TerzoTratto Et. Bianca Ris. '10	🍷🍷 7

Benito Ferrara

FRAZ. SAN PAOLO, 14A
83010 TUFO [AV]
TEL. +39 0825998194
www.benitoferrara.it

CELLAR SALES
PRE-BOOKED VISITS
ANNUAL PRODUCTION 55,000 bottles
HECTARES UNDER VINE 13.00

Their vineyards stretch across the district of San Paolo, in the municipality of Tufo, an area famous for the production of some of the most intense and complex Greco wines. Benito Ferrara quickly understood the potential of this territory and the importance of making monovarietal Greco and Aglianico wines, the latter grown in Montemiletto. Gabriella Ferrara and her husband Sergio Ambrosino run the winery today, with a total of 13 hectares. The jewel in the crown is their Greco cru Vigna Cicogna, situated at 500 meters of elevation, on soils rich in clay and stones with large amounts of sulfur, ideal for long bottle aging. The 2019 version is commendable. Aromatically it calls up medicinal herbs, with an almondy streak and quite evident white fruits. The palate is elegant, creamy, rich in flavor, with nice final length. The Greco di Tufo Terra d'Uva '19 is of good quality, more immediately expressive in its citrus hints, vibrant and fresh on a balsamic finish.

Wine	Rating
○ Greco di Tufo V. Cicogna '19	🍷🍷 4
○ Fiano d'Avellino Sequenzha '19	🍷🍷 4
○ Greco di Tufo Terra d'Uva '19	🍷🍷 4
● Irpinia Aglianico V. Quattro Confini '17	🍷🍷 3
● Taurasi V. Quattro Confini '15	🍷 6
○ Greco di Tufo V. Cicogna '15	🍷🍷🍷 4*
○ Greco di Tufo V. Cicogna '14	🍷🍷🍷 4*
○ Greco di Tufo V. Cicogna '13	🍷🍷🍷 5
○ Greco di Tufo V. Cicogna '12	🍷🍷🍷 4*
○ Greco di Tufo V. Cicogna '10	🍷🍷🍷 4
○ Greco di Tufo V. Cicogna '09	🍷🍷🍷 4
○ Fiano d'Avellino Sequenzha '17	🍷🍷 4
○ Greco di Tufo Terra d'Uva '18	🍷🍷 4
○ Greco di Tufo Terra d'Uva '17	🍷🍷 4
○ Greco di Tufo V. Cicogna '18	🍷🍷 4
○ Greco di Tufo V. Cicogna '17	🍷🍷 4

★★Feudi di San Gregorio

LOC. CERZA GROSSA
83050 SORBO SERPICO [AV]
TEL. +39 0825986683
www.feudi.it

CELLAR SALES
PRE-BOOKED VISITS
RESTAURANT SERVICE
ANNUAL PRODUCTION 3,500,000 bottles
HECTARES UNDER VINE 300.00
VITICULTURE METHOD Certified Organic

Feudi di San Gregorio began production in 1986, in Sorbo Serpico. In just a few years they met with their first success and became a benchmark on a regional and national level. Antonio Capaldo is at the helm, supported by Pierpaolo Sirch in managing the wide range of vineyards. Production embraces the main regional appellations, while the Dubl brand, their line of sparkling wines, has reached maturity. Over the years, Feudi has crossed borders, with the purchase of the Basilisco brand in Basilicata and Campo alle Comete in Tuscany. We very much appreciated the Taurasi, with its elegant tannic texture: it's a creamy wine, vibrant in its whiffs of small red berries. Its spicy background is well calibrated, the finish long with nice aromatic freshness. The Serpico '15, a beautifully crafted and long Aglianico, features nice character and a tasty, spicy profile. The Rosato Visione is getting better, the Dubl Esse Dosaggio Zero again delivers.

Wine	Rating
● Taurasi Piano di Montevergine Ris. '15	🍷🍷 6
○ Dubl Esse M. Cl. Dosaggio Zero	🍷🍷 6
○ Fiano di Avellino Pietracalda '19	🍷🍷 4
○ Greco di Tufo Cutizzi '19	🍷🍷 4
● Irpinia Aglianico Serpico '15	🍷🍷 8
⊙ Irpinia Rosato Visione '19	🍷🍷 3
● Taurasi '16	🍷🍷 5
⊙ Dubl Esse Rosé M. Cl. Dosaggio Zero	🍷 6
○ Fiano di Avellino Pietracalda '09	🍷🍷🍷 3
○ Greco di Tufo Cutizzi '12	🍷🍷🍷 3*
○ Greco di Tufo Cutizzi '10	🍷🍷🍷 3
○ Greco di Tufo Cutizzi '07	🍷🍷🍷 3*
● Taurasi '13	🍷🍷🍷 5
● Taurasi Piano di Montevergine Ris. '14	🍷🍷🍷 6
● Taurasi Piano di Montevergine Ris. '13	🍷🍷🍷 6
● Taurasi Piano di Montevergine Ris. '07	🍷🍷🍷 6

Fiorentino

c.da Barbassano
83052 Paternopoli [AV]
Tel. +39 082771463
www.fiorentinovini.it

CELLAR SALES
PRE-BOOKED VISITS
ANNUAL PRODUCTION 15,000 bottles
HECTARES UNDER VINE 5.00
SUSTAINABLE WINERY

Gianni Fiorentino has built a model cellar, made entirely out of wood, in full compliance with bioarchitecture techniques. He has followed in his family's footsteps: it was his grandfather Luigi who purchased land in Paternopoli, with the fruits of his labor on his return from the United States. Today, these lands are managed by Gianni. The star of the show is Aglianico, which is not just a decision based on family tradition, but to meet the needs of the grape variety itself: the volcanic soils here give rise to the most authentic Taurasi wine, which manages to express its true character. The Taurasi '15 took full advantage of a good year, offering up elegant toasty notes amidst coffee, pepper and earthy sensations; on the palate it's rich and mature, well supported by acidity and freshness, making for a long, complex gustatory weave. The rest of the range is also on point, in particular the Flavia rosé, a delicious wine in its overtones of red berries and blood orange.

Wine	Rating	Price
● Taurasi '15	🍷🍷🍷	5
● Irpinia Aglianico Celsì '15	🍷	3
○ Irpinia Coda di Volpe Zirpoli '19	🍷	2
⊙ Irpinia Rosato Flavia '19	🍷	3
● Irpinia Aglianico Celsì '14	🥂🥂	3
● Irpinia Aglianico Celsì '12	🥂🥂	3
● Taurasi '14	🥂🥂	5
● Taurasi '13	🥂🥂	5
● Taurasi '12	🥂🥂	5

Fontanavecchia

via Fontanavecchia, 7
82030 Torrecuso [BN]
Tel. +39 0824876275
www.fontanavecchia.info

CELLAR SALES
PRE-BOOKED VISITS
ACCOMMODATION AND RESTAURANT SERVICE
ANNUAL PRODUCTION 175,000 bottles
HECTARES UNDER VINE 20.00

Libero Rillo has given a new lease of life to the winery his father Orazio set up on the slopes of Monte Taburno in 1990. The twenty hectares of vineyards are mainly planted with Falanghina (with wines made several vintages ago), as well as Aglianico, Piedirosso, Fiano and Greco. The whites exhibit great management of harvest times and are fermented in steel, while the reds show spot-on extraction, correct dosage of wood and good supporting acidity. Tre Bicchieri for the Falanghina del Sannio Taburno '19, a wine redolent of green tea leaves and lime. It shows generous, juicy fruit amidst a profile of great freshness and drinkability, the finish coming through long on whiffs of aniseed and mint. The Falanghina Libero '14 once again demonstrates the variety's aging potential, alternating whiffs of ripe apple with an intriguing, spicy background. On the palate it stands out for its nice supporting acidity and complex, deep finish.

Wine	Rating	Price
○ Falanghina del Sannio Taburno '19	🍷🍷🍷	3*
○ Falanghina del Sannio Libero '14	🍷🍷	5
○ Sannio Fiano '19	🍷🍷	3
● Aglianico del Taburno '18	🍷	3
○ Sannio Greco '19	🍷	3
○ Falanghina del Sannio Taburno '18	🥂🥂🥂	3*
○ Falanghina del Sannio Taburno '16	🥂🥂🥂	3*
○ Falanghina del Sannio Taburno '15	🥂🥂🥂	2*
○ Falanghina del Sannio Taburno '14	🥂🥂🥂	2*
○ Falanghina del Sannio Taburno '13	🥂🥂🥂	2*
○ Falanghina del Sannio Taburno '12	🥂🥂🥂	2*
○ Sannio Taburno Falanghina Libero '07	🥂🥂🥂	5
● Aglianico del Taburno V. Cataratte Ris. '10	🥂🥂	5
○ Falanghina del Sannio Facetus V. T. '12	🥂🥂	3*
○ Falanghina del Sannio Taburno '17	🥂🥂	3*

Fonzone

Loc. Scorzagalline
83052 Paternopoli [AV]
Tel. +39 08271730100
www.fonzone.it

CELLAR SALES
PRE-BOOKED VISITS
ANNUAL PRODUCTION 57,000 bottles
HECTARES UNDER VINE 22.00
SUSTAINABLE WINERY

Lorenzo Fonzone Caccese's winery always proves well-organized. A surgeon by profession, he founded the winery in 2005 in Paternopoli, in the heart of the Taurasi appellation. The technologically avant-garde, underground cellar is perfectly integrated into the surrounding territory, while weedkillers are not used in the vineyard: grassing over is done every year, grass is sown to safeguard the biodiversity of soil and plants. Production embraces all the main appellations in Irpinia, from Taurasi, rich in fruit and concentration, to dynamic whites with vibrant freshness. The Fonzone family are back with Tre Bicchieri thanks to the Greco di Tufo '19, a highly fragrant wine in its almond sensations and hints of Mediterranean scrub; on the palate it exhibits a firm structure, both savory and citrusy, unfolding steadily towards a long finish. The Taurasi Scorzagalline Riserva '13 is characterized by ripe fruit, vibrant whiffs of cocoa and root, coming through powerful but also creamy and well balanced on the palate. The other wines tasted are also well made.

Wine	Rating	Price
○ Greco di Tufo '19	TTT	3*
● Taurasi Scorzagalline Ris. '13	TT	5
○ Fiano di Avellino '19	TT	3
○ Irpinia Fiano Sequoia '18	TT	5
○ Fiano di Avellino '16	YYY	3*
○ Greco di Tufo '13	YYY	3*
○ Fiano di Avellino '18	YY	3*
○ Fiano di Avellino '17	YY	3
○ Greco di Tufo '18	YY	3
○ Greco di Tufo '17	YY	3*
● Irpina Aglianico '14	YY	3
● Irpinia Campi Taurasini '15	YY	3
○ Irpinia Fiano Sequoia '17	YY	5

La Fortezza

Loc. Tora II, 20
82030 Torrecuso [BN]
Tel. +39 0824886155
www.lafortezzasrl.it

CELLAR SALES
PRE-BOOKED VISITS
ANNUAL PRODUCTION 900,000 bottles
HECTARES UNDER VINE 65.00

Enzo Rillo's winery was set up in 2006, when the entrepreneur decided to purchase about thirty hectares of vineyards on the eastern side of the Taburno Camposauro regional park, in the district of Torrecuso. He started by cultivating Fiano and Falanghina, but his passion (and success) drove him to expand the vineyard, which totals about 65 hectares today, with a range of varieties including Greco and Aglianico. Their sound selection includes both the traditional Classic line, and the more free-and-easy and approachable Noi Beviamo Con La Testa line. We appreciated the 2016 Aglianico del Taburno for its firm structure, well played on ripe, fragrant, dark fruit. Spiciness is well balanced, its tannins soft, the finish comes through clear, well sustained and nicely expressed. The 2019 Greco also has character, with aromas of yellow flowers on the nose and a palate of body and flavor, as expected for the typology. We also appreciated the pleasant and fragrant Piedirosso and Falanghina.

Wine	Rating	Price
● Aglianico del Taburno Enzo Rillo '16	TT	3
○ Sannio Greco '19	TT	3
● Sannio Piedirosso '19	TT	3
● Aglianico del Taburno Enzo Rillo Ris. '12	T	6
○ Falanghina Brut Maleventum	T	3
○ Falanghina del Sannio Taburno '19	T	3
○ Sannio Fiano '19	T	3
● Aglianico del Taburno '14	YY	3
● Aglianico del Taburno '12	YY	3
● Aglianico del Taburno Ris. '11	YY	4
● Aglianico del Taburno Ris. '07	YY	4
○ Sannio Fiano '17	YY	2*
○ Sannio Fiano '15	YY	2*
○ Sannio Greco '17	YY	2*
○ Sannio Greco '16	YY	2*
○ Sannio Greco '15	YY	2*

Masseria Frattasi

FRAZ. VARONI
VIA FRATTASI, 1
82016 MONTESARCHIO [BN]
TEL. +39 0824834392
www.masseriafrattasi.it

CELLAR SALES
PRE-BOOKED VISITS
ANNUAL PRODUCTION 120,000 bottles
HECTARES UNDER VINE 30.00

We can certainly count the Cecere Clemente family among those who have made vinegrowing history in Campania: they have been making wine in the Montesarchio countryside, on the southern part of the calcareous massif of Taburno, since 1576, while the complex currently housing the cellar is an old building dating back to 1779. What's more, Don Antonio was the man who rediscovered and developed Falanghina di Bonea, a variety that continues to be a main element in their most iconic wines. The 2019 Falanghina del Sannio Taburno Donnalaura performed well during our tastings. It's a fragrant wine in its aromas of citrus and rocky, mineral hints. The palate exhibits a supple, linear texture, well governed by a sapid presence. The Kapnios, an Aglianico with structure, proves mature and spicy on the finish. Sensations of black olives and marine whiffs feature in the 2018 Capri Rosso.

Wine	Rating
● Capri Rosso '18	🍷🍷 8
○ Falanghina del Sannio Taburno V. T. Donnalaura '19	🍷🍷 5
● Kapnios Aglianico '17	🍷🍷 8
○ Chy Chardonnay 890 '19	🍷 5
○ Coda di Volpe '19	🍷 5
● Aglianico del Taburno Iovi Tonant '16	🍷🍷 6
● Aglianico del Taburno Iovi Tonant '15	🍷🍷 6
○ Falanghina del Sannio Bonea '18	🍷🍷 2*
○ Falanghina del Sannio Taburno Bonea '16	🍷🍷 3
○ Falanghina del Sannio Taburno Donnalaura '18	🍷🍷 5
○ Taburno Falanghina '12	🍷🍷 2*
○ Taburno Falanghina di Bonea '12	🍷🍷 3
○ Taburno Falanghina di Bonea '11	🍷🍷 2*
● Taburno Iovi Tonant '09	🍷🍷 6

★Galardi

FRAZ. SAN CARLO
S.DA PROV.LE SESSA-MIGNANO
81037 SESSA AURUNCA [CE]
TEL. +39 08231440003
www.terradilavoro.it

CELLAR SALES
PRE-BOOKED VISITS
ANNUAL PRODUCTION 30,000 bottles
HECTARES UNDER VINE 10.00
VITICULTURE METHOD Certified Organic

The district of San Carlo di Sessa Aurunca: these are the geographical coordinates you need to reach the Fontana Galardi estate, which produces one of the most iconic reds in the region: the Terre di Lavoro, a blend of Aglianico and Piedirosso grapes grown on volcanic, alluvial soils in the area, with a marked presence of limestone. The creators of this wine are Luisa Murena, Arturo Celentato and Francesco and Dora Catello, who added another wine just three vintages ago, this time a monovarietal Piedirosso: the Terre di Rosso. The 2018 version of the Terra di Lavoro exhibits a broad and mature character. Aromatically it calls up freshly ground coffee, pepper, and ripe Ferrovia cherries. The palate is rich, developing broad, with a vibrant, smoky stroke. The finish is still evolving, with spices dominating. The Terra di Rosso '18, a particularly juicy Pieridorosso, is more immediately expressive, with sweet, creamy tannins.

Wine	Rating
● Terra di Lavoro '18	🍷🍷 7
● Terra di Rosso '18	🍷🍷 5
● Terra di Lavoro '13	🍷🍷🍷 7
● Terra di Lavoro '11	🍷🍷🍷 7
● Terra di Lavoro '10	🍷🍷🍷 7
● Terra di Lavoro '09	🍷🍷🍷 7
● Terra di Lavoro '08	🍷🍷🍷 7
● Terra di Lavoro '07	🍷🍷🍷 7
● Terra di Lavoro '06	🍷🍷🍷 7
● Terra di Lavoro '05	🍷🍷🍷 7
● Terra di Lavoro '04	🍷🍷🍷 7
● Terra di Lavoro '03	🍷🍷🍷 6
● Terra di Lavoro '02	🍷🍷🍷 6
● Terra di Lavoro '99	🍷🍷🍷 6
● Terra di Rosso '17	🍷🍷🍷 5

La Guardiense

c.da Santa Lucia, 104/106
82034 Guardia Sanframondi [BN]
Tel. +39 0824864034
www.laguardiense.it

CELLAR SALES
PRE-BOOKED VISITS
RESTAURANT SERVICE
ANNUAL PRODUCTION 5,000,000 bottles
HECTARES UNDER VINE 1500.00

When dealing with a winery of this size, you need to start with the figures. Today, La Guardiense totals 1500 hectares of vineyards, 600 of which are planted with Falanghina (the true flagship variety) and about a thousand members. These are impressive figures if we compare them to the 1960s, when the founding grape growers numbered just 33. Work in the cellar is done under the supervision of Riccardo Cotarella, who also dictates the production guidelines of the vinegrowers. Tre Bicchieri for the Falanghina Janare Senete '19, a wine that unleashes aromas of citrus, peach and mint. In the mouth it's juicy, full, pleasantly drinkable. Jasmine whiffs and a supple, dynamic palate feature in the Fiano Janare '19. The wines from their Aicon line also perform at high levels: the Falanghina is vibrant, fleshy, the Aglianico rich in balsamic sensations and supported by graceful tannins.

Wine	Glasses	Price
○ Falanghina del Sannio Janare Senete '19	🍷🍷🍷	3*
○ Falanghina del Sannio Aicon '19	🍷🍷	2*
● Sannio Aglianico Aicon '18	🍷🍷	2*
● Sannio Aglianico Janare Lucchero '17	🍷🍷	3
○ Sannio Fiano Janare '19	🍷🍷	2*
○ Falanghina del Sannio Brut Aicon '18	🍷	3
⊙ Sannio Aglianico Rosato Ambra Rosa '19	🍷	3
● Sannio Guardia Sanframondi Aglianico Cantari Janare Ris. '15	🍷	4
○ Falanghina del Sannio Janare '15	YYY	2*
○ Falanghina del Sannio Janare Senete '18	YYY	3*
○ Falanghina del Sannio Janare Senete '17	YYY	3*

Salvatore Molettieri

c.da Musanni, 19b
83040 Montemarano [AV]
Tel. +39 082763722
www.salvatoremolettieri.com

CELLAR SALES
PRE-BOOKED VISITS
ANNUAL PRODUCTION 65,000 bottles
HECTARES UNDER VINE 13.00

The Molettieri family comes from a long winemaking tradition: four generations of vinegrowers right down to Salvatore, who decided to vinify grapes from his own vineyards in 1983, which had previously been sold to third parties. The winery is located between Montemarano and Castelfranci, in the heart of Irpinia, at about 600 meters of elevation. Here, Fiano, Greco and especially Aglianico grapes produce powerful, rich, indomitable wines in the early years, which guarantee satisfaction if awaited with patience. The 2013 Taurasi Vigna Cinque Querce Taurasi takes home Tre Bicchieri. It's a deep wine in its characteristic earthy and spicy hints. It has strength and sapid pluck to sell, all on a nicely distributed gustatory texture, topped off by a finish of great character and length. The 2012 Taurasi Vigna Cinque Querce Riserva is also delicious, even more vibrant in its smoky whiffs and dense tannic structure. The Greco di Tufo is definitely making progress—the 2018 exhibits flavor and detail.

Wine	Glasses	Price
● Taurasi V. Cinque Querce '13	🍷🍷🍷	6
○ Greco di Tufo '18	🍷🍷	3
● Taurasi V. Cinque Querce Ris. '12	🍷🍷	7
○ Fiano d'Avellino Apianum '18	🍷	3
● Irpinia Rosso Ischia Piana '17	🍷	3
● Taurasi Renonno '14	🍷	5
● Taurasi Renonno '08	YYY	5
● Taurasi V. Cinque Querce '05	YYY	6
● Taurasi V. Cinque Querce '04	YYY	6
● Taurasi V. Cinque Querce '01	YYY	5
● Taurasi V. Cinque Querce Ris. '05	YYY	7
● Taurasi V. Cinque Querce Ris. '04	YYY	7
● Taurasi V. Cinque Querce Ris. '01	YYY	7
● Aglianico Cinque Querce '10	YY	4
● Taurasi V. Cinque Querce '09	YY	6
● Taurasi V. Cinque Querce Ris. '11	YY	7
● Taurasi V. Cinque Querce Ris. '08	YY	7

★★Montevetrano

FRAZ. CAMPIGLIANO
VIA MONTEVETRANO, 3
84099 SAN CIPRIANO PICENTINO [SA]
TEL. +39 089882285
www.montevetrano.it

CELLAR SALES
PRE-BOOKED VISITS
ACCOMMODATION
ANNUAL PRODUCTION 70,000 bottles
HECTARES UNDER VINE 5.00

Few vinegrowers have succeeded as well as Silvia Imparato in combining perspective and an international setting with a firm territorial base. Since 1991, she has been blending Aglianico, Cabernet Sauvignon and Merlot at San Cipriano Picentino to make Montrevetrano, one of the most iconic wines in southern winemaking. She works with Riccardo Cotarella, who has followed the winery since it first began. During recent vintages, Silvia has decided to expand her range; today there are three wines, with the addition of Core Rosso (Aglianico) and Core Bianco (Fiano and Greco). For the first time the Core Bianco takes home Tre Bicchieri. 2019 made for a wine with fresh and fragrant fruit, multifaceted in its citrus and smoky overtones, with a taut, tasty palate. The finish is precise and balanced. The Montevetrano '18 features a balsamic profile and a steady palate, with well-calibrated oak and a finish that's rich in juice and fine spices.

Wine	Rating
○ Core Bianco '19	🍷🍷🍷 4*
● Montevetrano '18	🍷🍷 8
● Core Rosso '17	🍷🍷 4
● Montevetrano '17	🍷🍷🍷 8
● Montevetrano '14	🍷🍷🍷 7
● Montevetrano '12	🍷🍷🍷 7
● Montevetrano '11	🍷🍷🍷 7
● Montevetrano '10	🍷🍷🍷 7
● Montevetrano '09	🍷🍷🍷 7
● Montevetrano '08	🍷🍷🍷 7
● Montevetrano '07	🍷🍷🍷 7
● Montevetrano '06	🍷🍷🍷 7
● Montevetrano '05	🍷🍷🍷 7
● Montevetrano '04	🍷🍷🍷 7
● Montevetrano '03	🍷🍷🍷 7
● Montevetrano '02	🍷🍷🍷 7
● Montevetrano '01	🍷🍷🍷 7

Mustilli

VIA CAUDINA, 10
82019 SANT'AGATA DE' GOTI [BN]
TEL. +39 0823718142
www.mustilli.com

CELLAR SALES
PRE-BOOKED VISITS
ACCOMMODATION AND RESTAURANT SERVICE
ANNUAL PRODUCTION 100,000 bottles
HECTARES UNDER VINE 15.00

The history of the winery's production is indissolubly linked to the production of Falanghina in Sant'Agata dei Goti. Credit is due to the engineer, Leonardo Mustilli, who realized its potential and was the first to bottle this wine in far-off 1979. The debut bottle is now kept in the underground cellars of the historic Rainone palace, dug out of the rock and interconnected by an impressive network of underground tufaceous tunnels. The cellar is currently run by his daughters, Paola and Anna Chiara, with the winemaking consultancy of Fortunato Sebastiano, who gives his signature interpretation to Falanghina and Piedirosso in this part of Campania. The Falanghina Vigna Segreta '18 earns Tre Bicchieri, impressing with its perfectly rhythmic, sapid palate, and a citrus profile adorned by hints of yellow flowers. Everything is in balance amidst freshness, structure and acidity; the finish comes through long and well sustained. The Piedirosso Artus '18 also made an appearance in our finals—it's just slightly more mature than in past editions.

Wine	Rating
○ Falanghina del Sannio Sant'Agata dei Goti V. Segreta '18	🍷🍷🍷 4*
● Sannio Sant'Agata dei Goti Piedirosso Artus '18	🍷🍷 4
○ Sannio Greco '19	🍷🍷 3
○ Falanghina del Sannio '19	🍷 3
○ Falanghina Frizzante Regina Isabella '19	🍷 3
● Sannio Aglianico '18	🍷 3
● Sannio Piedirosso '19	🍷 3
● Sannio Sant'Agata dei Goti Aglianico Cesco di Nece '17	🍷 4
● Sannio Sant'Agata dei Goti Piedirosso Artus '17	🍷🍷🍷 5
● Sannio Sant'Agata dei Goti Piedirosso Artus '16	🍷🍷🍷 5
● Sannio Sant'Agata dei Goti Piedirosso Artus '15	🍷🍷🍷 4*

Nanni Cope'

via Tufo, 3
81041 Vitulazio [CE]
Tel. +39 3487478459
www.nannicope.it

CELLAR SALES
ANNUAL PRODUCTION 10,000 bottles
HECTARES UNDER VINE 3.50
VITICULTURE METHOD Certified Organic
SUSTAINABLE WINERY

Giovanni Ascione has done what a lot of us would have loved to do. He set aside his pen and career as a journalist to try his hand in the vineyard and to put his intuition and skill as a taster to practice. The results are extraordinary, his Sabbie di Sopra il Bosco has become a model of excellence on a national level in just a few years and is successfully exported all over the world despite its limited production. His fairy-tale story has become a significant event in Campania winemaking, but last year he sold the vineyards and is now ready for another challenge. His latest creation, the Polveri della Scarrupata '18, is poignant. A blend of Fiano, Falanghina and Asprinio, it's one of the best whites in Italy. It opens delicate on hints of basil, aniseed and citron. The palate comes through weighty, the attack precise and creamy, only to unfold a deep, sapid weave of unique energy and expressive detail. The finish is musky, just a bit spicy, of singular length and complexity.

Wine	Rating
○ Polveri della Scarrupata '18	🍷🍷 6
● Sabbie di Sopra il Bosco '17	🍷🍷🍷 6
● Sabbie di Sopra il Bosco '16	🍷🍷🍷 6
● Sabbie di Sopra il Bosco '15	🍷🍷🍷 5
● Sabbie di Sopra il Bosco '14	🍷🍷🍷 5
● Sabbie di Sopra il Bosco '12	🍷🍷🍷 5
● Sabbie di Sopra il Bosco '11	🍷🍷🍷 5
● Sabbie di Sopra il Bosco '10	🍷🍷🍷 5
● Sabbie di Sopra il Bosco '09	🍷🍷🍷 5
○ Polveri della Scarrupata '16	🍷🍷 6
● Sabbie di Sopra il Bosco '13	🍷🍷 5
● Sabbie di Sopra il Bosco '08	🍷🍷 5
● Sabbie di Sopra il Bosco r12 '12	🍷🍷 6

Cantine Olivella

via Zazzera, 28
80048 Sant'Anastasia [NA]
Tel. +39 0815311388
www.cantineolivella.com

CELLAR SALES
ANNUAL PRODUCTION 86,400 bottles
HECTARES UNDER VINE 12.00
SUSTAINABLE WINERY

Andrea Cozzolino, Ciro Giordano and Domenico Ceriello have strongly focused on the Vesuvius territory and particularly on the potential of a barely known white grape variety: Catalanesca. The cellar is located in Sant'Anastasia, at the foot of Monte Somma, inside the Vesuvius national park. It is named after an ancient source of the Olivella river that provided Charles III of Spain's royal palace in Portici with water. In addition to Catalanesca, they also make wines with Piedirosso and Caprettone grapes, using old farming techniques such as offshoot reproduction, locally called "pass annanz". The Katà '19 stands out for its marked aromatic character, more vibrant than usual, with hints of lime accompanied by exotic fruit and Mediterranean herbs; in the mouth it proves sapid and juicy. The well-made Lacryma Christi Biano '19 comes through intense, fuller rather than linear. The Vesuvio Rosso '17 features multifaceted, smoky tones, with hints of ash, pencil lead and tomato leaf, while on the palate it shows character and generous texture.

Wine	Rating
○ Katà Catalanesca '19	🍷🍷 3
○ Lacryma Christi del Vesuvio Bianco Lacrimabianco '19	🍷🍷 3
● Vesuvio Rosso '17	🍷🍷 5
○ Vesuvio Bianco Emblema '19	🍷 3
● Vesuvio Piedirosso Vipt '17	🍷 3
⊙ Vesuvio Rosato Ereo '19	🍷 4
○ Catalanesca Kata '16	🍷🍷 3
○ Katà Catalanesca '17	🍷🍷 3
○ Lacryma Christi del Vesuvio Bianco Emblema '16	🍷🍷 3

Ciro Picariello

via Marroni, 18a
83010 Summonte [AV]
Tel. +39 3478885625
www.ciropicariello.it

PRE-BOOKED VISITS
ANNUAL PRODUCTION 55,000 bottles
HECTARES UNDER VINE 15.00
SUSTAINABLE WINERY

When you say "Ciro Picariello" you immediately think of Fiano di Avellino, a spontaneous association of ideas as rarely happens in the wine world. And yet, the history of this winery is quite recent: it began in 2004 with the Montefredane and Summonte vineyards, about fifteen hectares between 500 and 650 meters of elevation. But this indissoluble link between man and grape variety does not just come from the harvests done over time, but rather from the organization that the vinegrower gives to his work: sustainable practices that respect the vineyard environment and an artisan's sensibility in the cellar. The only bottle presented in this edition of the guide earned a place in our finals. We're talking about the Fiano di Avellino '19, a wine redolent of wild herbs, fresh almond and aniseed. In the mouth it offers up fragrant white fruit of nice intensity, coming through both pulpy and beautifully sapid. The finish is linear and well sustained, with a fresh and minty final whiff.

Wine	Rating
○ Fiano di Avellino '19	🍷🍷 4
○ Fiano di Avellino '14	🍷🍷🍷 4*
○ Fiano di Avellino '10	🍷🍷🍷 3*
○ Fiano di Avellino '08	🍷🍷🍷 3*
○ Brut Contadino	🍷🍷 4
○ Fiano di Avellino '18	🍷🍷 4
○ Fiano di Avellino '17	🍷🍷 4
○ Fiano di Avellino '15	🍷🍷 4
○ Fiano di Avellino Ciro 906 '13	🍷🍷 4
○ Fiano di Avellino Ciro 906 '12	🍷🍷 4

La Pietra di Tommasone

s.da prov.le Fango, 98
80076 Lacco Ameno [NA]
Tel. +39 0813330330
www.tommasonevini.it

CELLAR SALES
PRE-BOOKED VISITS
ANNUAL PRODUCTION 100,000 bottles
HECTARES UNDER VINE 16.50

Antonio Monti and his daughter Lucia (winemaker at the winery in Lacco Ameno, on the northern slope of Ischia) are guardians of the island's viticulture, which boasts centuries of tradition, a unique range of native varieties and mesmerizingly enchanting landscapes. Their vineyards comprise a mosaic of several scattered little plots of land, the result of constant work to safeguard the territory: in fact, over the years much abandoned land has been recovered and today the vineyard surface area amounts to about 17 hectares, divided into 14 small estates. The Per'e Palummo Tenuta Monte Zunta '18, from a vineyard situated at 450 meters above sea level, earned a place in our finals. It charms with its floral fragrances, scents of violets and cherries. In the mouth it's mature, steady, bolstered by graceful oak with a finish slightly spicy in peppery hints. Interwoven earthy and marine sensations feature in the Pithecusa Rosso, a blend of Aglianico and Piedirosso. Fresher aromas of citrus and the sea for the Biancolella Tenuta dei Preti '19.

Wine	Rating
● Ischia Per'e Palummo Tenuta Monte Zunta '18	🍷🍷 5
○ Ischia Biancolella '19	🍷🍷 3
○ Ischia Biancolella Tenuta dei Preti '19	🍷🍷 4
● Pithecusa Rosso '17	🍷🍷 4
● Pignanera '16	🍷 5
⊙ Rosamonti '19	🍷 3
○ Ischia Biancolella '17	🍷🍷🍷 2*
○ Epomeo Bianco Pithecusa '18	🍷🍷 3
● Epomeo Rosso '14	🍷🍷 3
○ Ischia Biancolella '18	🍷🍷 2*
○ Ischia Biancolella Tenuta dei Preti '18	🍷🍷 4
○ Ischia Biancolella Tenuta dei Preti '17	🍷🍷 4
● Ischia Per' e Palummo '17	🍷🍷 3
● Ischia Per'e Palummo Tenuta Monte Zunta '17	🍷🍷 5
⊙ Rosamonti '18	🍷🍷 2*

★Pietracupa

c.da Vadiaperti, 17
83030 Montefredane [AV]
Tel. +39 0825607418
pietracupa@email.it

CELLAR SALES
PRE-BOOKED VISITS
ANNUAL PRODUCTION 50,000 bottles
HECTARES UNDER VINE 7.50

Sabino Loffredo possesses all the traits of an artist. He's not hot on organization, he's instinctive, creative, passionate and undoubtedly talented. In the past decade he has proved to be one of the most virtuous and consistent producers of white wines in Italy, thanks to wines that travel with extraordinary ease and accomplish truly unique changes in pace. His Greco and Fiano wines are sharpish and well-honed, with coherent high acidity and mountains aromas. In the absence of the 2019 Fiano and Greco, to be released next year, we make mention of the Taurasi '15, which arrived in our finals by virtue of its ripe, fleshy red fruit. Sensations of cherry and blood orange chase each other on a palate supported by creamy tannins—it's a harmonious wine, full of detail. The Cupo also made it into our finals. Delicate in its hints of chamomile and almond, it shows vibrant freshness on the palate, closing on a long trail of citrus and aniseed. The highly drinkable Falanghina '19 is fresh, breezy in its sensations of grapefruit and freshly mown grass.

Wine	Rating
○ Cupo '18	🍷🍷 5
● Taurasi '15	🍷🍷 5
○ Falanghina '19	🍷🍷 3
○ Cupo '10	🍷🍷🍷 5
○ Cupo '08	🍷🍷🍷 5
○ Fiano di Avellino '13	🍷🍷🍷 3*
○ Fiano di Avellino '12	🍷🍷🍷 3*
○ Greco '18	🍷🍷🍷 4*
○ Greco di Tufo '17	🍷🍷🍷 3*
○ Greco di Tufo '15	🍷🍷🍷 3*
○ Greco di Tufo '14	🍷🍷🍷 3*
○ Greco di Tufo '10	🍷🍷🍷 3*
○ Greco di Tufo '09	🍷🍷🍷 3*
○ Greco di Tufo '08	🍷🍷🍷 3*
○ Greco di Tufo '07	🍷🍷🍷 3*
● Taurasi '10	🍷🍷🍷 5

Fattoria La Rivolta

c.da Contrada Rivolta
82030 Torrecuso [BN]
Tel. +39 0824872921
www.fattorialarivolta.com

CELLAR SALES
PRE-BOOKED VISITS
ACCOMMODATION
ANNUAL PRODUCTION 180,000 bottles
HECTARES UNDER VINE 29.00
VITICULTURE METHOD Certified Organic

We find the Cotroneo family at the helm of one of the most beautiful estates in Benevento. They have been producing a wide, varied and consistent selection of wines since 1997. Their 29 hectares of certified organic vineyards comprise the main appellations of Samnite vinegrowing. The winery features a well-defined style: the fragrant, intense whites are fermented in steel, while the reds exhibit a richer profile and manage to combine spices and concentration. This year we tasted a solid and convincing selection. The Aglianico del Taburno '18 is truly commendable, combining a spicy profile of coffee and tobacco with ripe, juicy fruit; the palate is full, dynamic, with a lovely sapid energy. Redolent of orange blossom and citron, the Sannio Greco '19 comes through sapid and fragrant in the mouth; the Coda di Volpe '19 also delivers. Among the reserves, this year we point out the Terra di Rivolta '17, with its ripe fruit and a dense, rich, powerful palate.

Wine	Rating
● Aglianico del Taburno '18	🍷🍷 3*
● Aglianico del Taburno Terra di Rivolta Ris. '17	🍷🍷 6
○ Sannio Coda di Volpe '19	🍷🍷 3
○ Sannio Greco '19	🍷🍷 3
○ Falanghina del Sannio Taburno '19	🍷 3
○ Sannio Fiano '19	🍷 3
● Simbiosi Rosso '17	🍷 5
● Aglianico del Taburno '10	🍷🍷🍷 3*
● Aglianico del Taburno Terra di Rivolta Ris. '08	🍷🍷🍷 5
○ Falanghina del Sannio Taburno '16	🍷🍷🍷 2*
● Aglianico del Taburno Terra di Rivolta Ris. '12	🍷🍷 5
● Aglianico del Taburno Terra di Rivolta Ris. '11	🍷🍷 5

Rocca del Principe

VIA ARIANIELLO, 9
83030 LAPIO [AV]
TEL. +39 08251728013
www.roccadelprincipe.it

CELLAR SALES
PRE-BOOKED VISITS
ANNUAL PRODUCTION 40,000 bottles
HECTARES UNDER VINE 7.00

The winery was founded in 2004 by the husband and wife team Ercole Zarella and Aurelia Fabrizio. It is located in Lapio, a small town in the hills of Irpinia known as one of the Fiano d'Avellino crus. The climate of this territory is influenced by the nearby Monti Picentini that accentuate the day-night temperature swings; in addition, the soils are of volcanic origin, rich in pumice, with perfect soil and climate conditions for Fiano to ripen in. This variety is the winery's masterpiece and is made into several versions; one of these, the Tognano, is made with grapes grown in a very select plot of land, a cru within a cru. The Fiano di Avellino Tognano '17 handily took home Tre Bicchieri, enchanting with its aromatic purity on minty notes, fresh hazelnut, almond, and a whiff of spices. The palate fits like a glove for its texture and long, unabashedly elegant persistence. We also appreciated the Fiano di Avellino '18 in its marine sensations and wild herb hints, coming through pleasantly linear on the palate, with vivid acidic verve and a final touch of ginger.

○ Fiano di Avellino Tognano '17	🍷🍷🍷 5
○ Fiano di Avellino '18	🍷🍷 4
● Taurasi Aurelia '16	🍷🍷 5
○ Fiano di Avellino '14	🥂🥂🥂 3*
○ Fiano di Avellino '13	🥂🥂🥂 3*
○ Fiano di Avellino '12	🥂🥂🥂 3*
○ Fiano di Avellino '10	🥂🥂🥂 3*
○ Fiano di Avellino '08	🥂🥂🥂 2*
○ Fiano di Avellino '07	🥂🥂🥂 2*
○ Fiano di Avellino Tognano '16	🥂🥂🥂 5
○ Fiano di Avellino Tognano '15	🥂🥂🥂 5
○ Fiano di Avellino '17	🥂🥂 4
○ Fiano di Avellino '16	🥂🥂 4
○ Fiano di Avellino '15	🥂🥂 3*
○ Fiano di Avellino Tognano '14	🥂🥂 3*

Ettore Sammarco

VIA CIVITA, 9
84010 RAVELLO [SA]
TEL. +39 089872774
www.ettoresammarco.it

CELLAR SALES
PRE-BOOKED VISITS
ANNUAL PRODUCTION 66,000 bottles
HECTARES UNDER VINE 13.00

As heroic viticulture is at the center of a lot of discussions about wine today, we think it very fitting to talk about Ettore Sammarco, who was already cultivating his grueling terraced vineyards in Ravello back in the 1960s. Today, his son Bartolo works alongside him and together they tend the 13 hectares of vineyards, divided into several small plots that reach 500 meters of elevation in the Monte Brusara vineyard. The Campania Apennines of Monte Lattari and the sea breezes create wines with a Mediterranean style, made exclusively with native grapes. The Ravello Bianco Selva delle Monache '19 earned a place in our finals, with its sweet scents of yellow fruit and Mediterranean scrub; in the mouth it's creamy, long and expansive, with hints of citron. The Ravello Rosso Riserva '16 is a red of remarkable aromatic persistence, characteristic in its whiffs of small red and black berries, nicely concentrated. The Rosato Selva delle Monache, one of the best of its kind in the region, once again delivers.

○ Costa d'Amalfi Ravello Bianco Selva delle Monache '19	🍷🍷 3*
⊙ Costa d'Amalfi Ravello Rosato Selva delle Monache '19	🍷🍷 3
● Costa d'Amalfi Ravello Rosso Selva delle Monache Ris. '16	🍷🍷 3
○ Costa d'Amalfi Bianco Terre Saracene '19	🍷 3
⊙ Costa d'Amalfi Rosato Terre Saracene '19	🍷 3
○ Costa d'Amalfi Ravello Bianco Selva delle Monache '17	🥂🥂🥂 3*
○ Costa d'Amalfi Ravello Bianco V. Grotta Piana '15	🥂🥂🥂 4*
○ Costa d'Amalfi Ravello Bianco Selva delle Monache '18	🥂🥂 3*

Tenuta San Francesco

FRAZ. CORSANO
VIA SOFILCIANO, 18
84010 TRAMONTI [SA]
TEL. +39 089876748
www.vinitenutasanfrancesco.com

CELLAR SALES
PRE-BOOKED VISITS
ACCOMMODATION
ANNUAL PRODUCTION 40,000 bottles
HECTARES UNDER VINE 10.00

The winery of the Bove, D'Avino and Giordano families originated in one of the most fascinating areas of the Amalfi coast, which is both harsh and arduous at the same time. In fact, several micro-plots of vineyards (almost fifty) lie on terraces marked by ferociously steep slopes, with elevations ranging from 300 to 700 meters. Grown with the hundred-year-old ungrafted pergola system training, we find typical local varieties such as Aglianico, Tintore and Piedirosso for reds and Pepella, Falanghina and Ginestra for whites. The Costa d'Amalfi Bianco Per Eva '18 landed a place in our finals. Elegant in its Mediterranean timbre, it offers up hints of musk, sea breeze and thyme. The palate is multifaceted, deep, with an elegant stride, coming through flavorful on the finish, delicately smoky. The charming E' Iss, a Tintore redolent of roots and licorice, is richer and more extracted than usual, while the 2016 Rosso 4 Spine proves more immediately expressive in its fruity profile.

○ Costa d'Amalfi Bianco Per Eva '18	🍷🍷 4
○ Costa d'Amalfi Tramonti Bianco '19	🍷🍷 2*
● Costa d'Amalfi Tramonti Rosso Quattrospine Ris. '16	🍷🍷 5
● È Iss Tintore Prephilloxera '17	🍷🍷 5
● Costa d'Amalfi Tramonti Rosso '17	🍷 3
● È Iss Tintore Prephilloxera '16	🍷🍷🍷 5
○ Costa d'Amalfi Bianco Per Eva '17	🍷🍷 4
○ Costa d'Amalfi Tramonti Bianco '17	🍷🍷 2*
○ Costa d'Amalfi Tramonti Bianco Per Eva '16	🍷🍷 4
● Costa d'Amalfi Tramonti Rosso '16	🍷🍷 3
● Costa d'Amalfi Tramonti Rosso Quattrospine Ris. '15	🍷🍷 5
● È Iss Tintore Prephilloxera '14	🍷🍷 5

San Giovanni

C.DA TRESINO
84048 CASTELLABATE [SA]
TEL. +39 0974965136
www.agricolasangiovanni.it

CELLAR SALES
PRE-BOOKED VISITS
ACCOMMODATION
ANNUAL PRODUCTION 20,000 bottles
HECTARES UNDER VINE 4.00

Mario Corrado and Ida Budetta's winery is located in a place of dazzling beauty: the house-cum-cellar is the result of low environmental-impact renovations of a farmhouse immersed in the Cilento natural park, in Punta Tresino, in the municipality of Castellabate. Just four hectares of vineyards are divided into two plots of land: one is completely surrounded by classic woods of Mediterranean scrub, while the other one, right in front of the cellar, overlooks the sea, reaping the benefits of sea breezes. We only find native grapes among their vine rows: Fiano, Greco, Aglianico and Piedirosso. The four wines presented this year all achieved high scores, starting with two excellent Fiano whites. The Tresinus is redolent of hay, calling up excellent buffalo mozzarella and wheat in its smoky stroke; in the mouth it's sapid, rich, unfolding expansively on the palate. The Paestum '19 is also delicious. A sunny and bright Fiano, it's exquisitely Mediterranean in its aromas and flavor. The reds are also of good quality, both the Maroccia, a juicy and spicy wine, and the Ficonera, a supple and lean Piedirosso.

○ Paestum Bianco '19	🍷🍷 3*
○ Tresinus Fiano '19	🍷🍷 4
● Maroccia '15	🍷🍷 5
● Ficonera '17	🍷 5
○ Paestum Bianco '15	🍷🍷🍷 2*
○ Tresinus Fiano '12	🍷🍷🍷 3*
○ Aureus '15	🍷🍷 5
● Castellabate '16	🍷🍷 3
● Ficonera '14	🍷🍷 5
○ Paestum Bianco '17	🍷🍷 3
○ Paestum Bianco '16	🍷🍷 3*
○ Paestum Bianco '14	🍷🍷 2*
○ Tresinus Fiano '18	🍷🍷 4
○ Tresinus Fiano '17	🍷🍷 4
○ Tresinus Fiano '16	🍷🍷 4
○ Tresinus Fiano '15	🍷🍷 3

San Salvatore 1988

via Dioniso
84050 Giungano [SA]
Tel. +39 08281990900
www.sansalvatore1988.it

CELLAR SALES
ACCOMMODATION AND RESTAURANT SERVICE
ANNUAL PRODUCTION 160,000 bottles
HECTARES UNDER VINE 23.00
VITICULTURE METHOD Certified Biodynamic

San Salvatore is a wide-ranging project. There's winemaking, of course, but the whole agronomic and gastronomic chain is covered. It was Giuseppe Pagano who left the hotel business and decided to channel his energy, experience and passion into San Salvatore. So yes, there's wine but not only: they also breed buffalos, produce mozzarella, olives and grains. There are food services as well. It's all part of a microcosm in which respect for the environment serves as a guiding light. The Pian di Stio '19 grabbed Tre Bicchieri by virtue of its clear marine sensations, calling up hay and lemon peel. In the mouth it shows a linear profile, with an assertive acidity and a finish on whiffs of Mediterranean herbs. The Trentenare, also a Fiano, features juicy fruit and a pleasant, expansive palate. Among their Aglianico reds, the Omaggio a Gillo Dorfles '16 stands out for its intensity and aromatic breadth, while the Ceraso '19 proves fresh and immediately expressive.

Wine	Rating
○ Pian di Stio '19	🍷🍷🍷 4*
○ Trentenare '19	🍷🍷 3*
● Ceraso '19	🍷🍷 3
○ Falanghina '19	🍷🍷 3
● Omaggio a Gillo Dorfles '16	🍷🍷 6
● Jungano '18	🍷 3
⊙ Vetere Rosato '19	🍷 3
○ Pian di Stio '18	🍷🍷🍷 4*
○ Pian di Stio '17	🍷🍷🍷 4*
○ Pian di Stio '14	🍷🍷🍷 4*
○ Pian di Stio '13	🍷🍷🍷 4*
○ Pian di Stio '12	🍷🍷🍷 3*
○ Trentenare '16	🍷🍷🍷 3*
○ Trentenare '15	🍷🍷🍷 3*
○ Calpazio '18	🍷🍷 3
● Jungano '17	🍷🍷 3
○ Trentenare '18	🍷🍷 3*

Sanpaolo di Claudio Quarta

fraz. c.da San Paolo
via Aufieri, 25
83010 Torrioni [AV]
Tel. +39 0832704398
www.claudioquarta.it

CELLAR SALES
PRE-BOOKED VISITS
ANNUAL PRODUCTION 250,000 bottles
HECTARES UNDER VINE 20.00
SUSTAINABLE WINERY

After a lifetime experimenting with biotechnology all over the world, Claudio Quarta decided to return to Italy in 2005 to start a new life as a vinegrower. He bought three estates, two in Puglia and one in Irpinia, in Contrada San Paolo di Torrioni. With his daughter Alessandra (young, enthusiastic and an inexhaustible source of new ideas), he produces typical, local wines with his own grapes as well of those cultivated by other trusted growers: the Fiano from Lapio and Candida, the Aglianico from Castelfranci and Taurasi, and lastly the Greco from Tufo, the winery's iconic wine. Once again Tre Bicchieri for the Quarta family. The Greco di Tufo '19, named after the winery's founder, is fascinating. The 2019 offers up a profile of mountain herbs, a whiff of white pepper and ginger. In the mouth it's creamy, with juicy white fruit and a soft, multifaceted and long finish. Redolent of sage and bay leaves, we also appreciated the Greco di Tufo '19, which comes through fragrant and taut on the palate where it unveils a progression of vibrant freshness.

Wine	Rating
○ Greco di Tufo Claudio Quarta Special Edition '19	🍷🍷🍷 4*
○ Greco di Tufo '19	🍷🍷 3*
○ Fiano di Avellino '19	🍷🍷 3
○ Toto Bianco '19	🍷🍷 3
○ Falanghina '19	🍷 2
○ Foxtail Coda di Volpe Passito '18	🍷 5
● Toto Rosso '18	🍷 3
○ Greco di Tufo Claudio Quarta '13	🍷🍷🍷 6
○ Greco di Tufo Claudio Quarta '12	🍷🍷🍷 6
○ Falanghina '18	🍷🍷 2*
○ Greco di Tufo '17	🍷🍷 3
○ Greco di Tufo Claudio Quarta '18	🍷🍷 4
○ Greco di Tufo Claudio Quarta '17	🍷🍷 6
○ Totò Bianco '18	🍷🍷 5
● Totò Rosso '17	🍷🍷 5

Sclavia

LOC. MARIANELLO
VIA CASE SPARSE
81040 LIBERI [CE]
TEL. +39 3357406773
www.sclavia.com

CELLAR SALES
PRE-BOOKED VISITS
ANNUAL PRODUCTION 50,000 bottles
HECTARES UNDER VINE 13.00
VITICULTURE METHOD Certified Organic
SUSTAINABLE WINERY

White and black Pallagrello and Casavecchia: these are the ingredients for Andrea Granito and Lello Ferrara's wines. In 2003, they set up the winery in the Liberi countryside, on the Monti Trebulani, on a piece of land in Upper Caserta, where the soils benefit from ancient volcanic influences. The attention they pay to the environment and safeguarding the territory has helped them obtain organic certification for their whole vineyard, comprising 13 hectares at about 500 meters of elevation. This year they submitted a smaller line-up than usual. The 2019 Granite is a Casavecchia that exhibits a very pleasant, juicy, fruity texture with a classic, peppery profile in the background and a steady, enjoyable expansion on the palate. The Montecardillo is a fleshy, full-bodied Pallagrello Nero characterized by a slightly more pronounced smokiness and a dense tannic texture.

● Granito '19	TT 3
● Pallagrello Nero Montecardillo '19	TT 3
○ Calù Pallagrello Bianco '18	YY 3
○ Calù Pallagrello Bianco '17	YY 3*
○ Calù Pallagrello Bianco '16	YY 3*
○ Calù Pallagrello Bianco '15	YY 3*
● Casavecchia di Pontelatone Liberi '15	YY 5
○ Don Ferdinando '15	YY 5
● Granito '12	YY 3
● Granito Casavecchia '15	YY 3
● Liberi '14	YY 5
● Liberi '12	YY 5
○ Pallarè '15	YY 5

Tenuta Scuotto

C.DA CAMPOMARINO, 2/3
83030 LAPIO [AV]
TEL. +39 08251851965
www.tenutascuotto.it

CELLAR SALES
PRE-BOOKED VISITS
ANNUAL PRODUCTION 40,000 bottles
HECTARES UNDER VINE 3.00

After his success as an entrepreneur in the graphic design field, Eduardo Scuotto decided to follow his ever-burning passion for winegrowing. So in 2009 he purchased a cellar and vineyards in Lapio, on Monte Tuoro, in the heart of the Fiano di Avellino appellation, and began to produce typical local wines. Vintage after vintage, the results have become more precise and finely-tuned and the winery is leading the way in this competitive area of Campania. The range includes Greco, Aglianico and Falanghina wines, in addition to the above-mentioned Fiano. It's the Scuotto family's turn to take home Tre Bicchieri, thanks to the 2019 Fiano di Avellino, a wine redolent of wild herbs, vivid in its marine hints. On the palate it exhibits full, fragrant fruit, with a delicately smoky background to enrich its profile. We also appreciated the Greco di Tufo, a richer and fatter wine characterized by overtones of olives and citron, well supported by a lively supporting acidity and a light tannic touch that's typical of the grape.

○ Fiano di Avellino '19	TTT 3*
○ Greco di Tufo '19	TT 3
⊙ Rosato Malgrè '19	T 3
○ Falanghina '16	YY 3
○ Fiano di Avellino '18	YY 3*
○ Fiano di Avellino '16	YY 2*
○ Greco di Tufo '18	YY 3
○ Greco di Tufo '17	YY 3*
○ Greco di Tufo '16	YY 3*
○ Oi Nì '17	YY 5
● Taurasi '12	YY 5

La Sibilla

FRAZ. BAIA
VIA OTTAVIANO AUGUSTO, 19
80070 BACOLI [NA]
TEL. +39 0818688778
www.sibillavini.com

CELLAR SALES
PRE-BOOKED VISITS
ANNUAL PRODUCTION 70,000 bottles
HECTARES UNDER VINE 9.50

Campi Flegrei is an area that has fascinated man since ancient times and even today it continues to intrigue and attract attention, also from a winegrowing point of view. Vincenzo di Meos' winery originated here, with soils of volcanic origin, a primitive mix of ash and lapillus, breezes from the nearby Tyrrhenian sea and ungrafted vineyards. Vincenzo's recipe for creating wine includes territory, a personal style based on limited cellar operations and enhancing the character of native grape varieties. The Falangina Cruna DeLago caps off a very positive and convincing performance, taking home Tre Bicchieri. The 2018 sees sensations of intense hay combine with peat, a whiff of spices and ripe, multifaceted fruit. In the mouth it's fat, rich, but made dynamic by a very intense and deep savory texture. The basic Falanghina once again demonstrates that it's a more supple, linear wine. The Vigna Madre is growing in definition, while the two Piedirossos complete a solid, complete range.

Wine	Rating	Price
○ Campi Flegrei Falanghina Cruna deLago '18	🍷🍷🍷	5
○ Campi Flegrei Falanghina '19	🍷🍷	4
● Campi Flegrei Piedirosso '19	🍷🍷	3
● Campi Flegrei Piedirosso V. Madre '18	🍷🍷	4
○ Campi Flegrei Falanghina '13	🍷🍷🍷 (outline)	2*
○ Campi Flegrei Falanghina Cruna deLago '15	🍷🍷🍷 (outline)	4*
○ Campi Flegrei Falanghina Cruna deLago '17	🍷🍷 (outline)	5
○ Campi Flegrei Falanghina Cruna deLago '16	🍷🍷 (outline)	5
● Campi Flegrei Piedirosso '18	🍷🍷 (outline)	4

Luigi Tecce

C.DA TRINITÀ, 6
83052 PATERNOPOLI [AV]
TEL. +39 3492957565
ltecce@libero.it

PRE-BOOKED VISITS
ANNUAL PRODUCTION 10,000 bottles
HECTARES UNDER VINE 5.50

Harmony: this is the first word that leaps to mind when we think of Luigi Tecce and his Aglianico. Luigi tends his vineyard here in the high hills between Paternopoli and Castelfranci, the elect area for this red variety from Irpinia. The grapes grown on these five hectares are subjected to different kinds of ripening, maceration and aging depending on the season: the materials, wood sizes and timings change. What doesn't change is the character of his wines: capricious and unsettled at the start, but guaranteeing satisfaction for those who are patient. The Taurasi Puro Sangue Riserva '15, a mature and complex red, earned a place in our finals. Rich in leather and liquorice sensations, lively in it sapidity, it proves complex and multifaceted in its fleshy fruit. Even more compact but charming, the Taurasi Poliphemo Riserva '15 impresses with its linear, austere and deep tannins. The excellent Rosato La Cyclope surprises with its mature and expressive profile amidst aromas of blood orange and spices, and its characterful finish.

Wine	Rating	Price
⊙ Irpinia Rosato La Cyclope '18	🍷🍷	3*
● Taurasi Puro Sangue Ris. '15	🍷🍷	6
● Taurasi Poliphemo V. V. Ris. '15	🍷🍷	8
● Taurasi Poliphemo '08	🍷🍷🍷 (outline)	6
● Taurasi Poliphemo '07	🍷🍷🍷 (outline)	6
● Taurasi Puro Sangue Ris. '14	🍷🍷🍷 (outline)	6
● Irpinia Campi Taurasini Satyricon '15	🍷🍷 (outline)	4
● Irpinia Campi Taurasini Satyricon '14	🍷🍷 (outline)	4
● Irpinia Campi Taurasini Satyricon '13	🍷🍷 (outline)	4
● Irpinia Campi Taurasini Satyricon '12	🍷🍷 (outline)	5
● Taurasi Poliphemo '13	🍷🍷 (outline)	6
● Taurasi Poliphemo '12	🍷🍷 (outline)	6
● Taurasi Poliphemo '11	🍷🍷 (outline)	6
● Taurasi Poliphemo V. V. Ris. '14	🍷🍷 (outline)	6

Tenuta del Meriggio

c.da Serra, 79/81a
83038 Montemiletto [AV]
Tel. +39 0825962282
www.tenutadelmeriggio.it

CELLAR SALES
PRE-BOOKED VISITS
ANNUAL PRODUCTION 65,000 bottles
HECTARES UNDER VINE 23.00
SUSTAINABLE WINERY

Bruno Pizza's over 20 hectares of vineyards, located in the best areas of Irpinia, are undeniably enviable: Fiano comes from Lapio, Aglianico from Montemiletto, Paternopoli and Castelfranci, while Greco can only come from Tufo and Santa Paolina. The winery was only set up just over ten years ago, but has already made its way in this competitive area of Irpinia thanks to clean, fragrant and distinctive wines that are both varietal and territorial. Elegant in its aromas of chamomile and broom, the Fiano di Avellino Colle delle Ginestre '18 also proves multifaceted in its sapid texture, steadily unfolding towards a broad finish. Vibrant aromas of rosemary and green tea characterize the Fiano di Avellino '19; on the palate it offers up generous fruit and an acidity that enlivens its fragrance and freshness.

○ Fiano di Avellino Colle delle Ginestre '18	🍷🍷 4
○ Fiano di Avellino '19	🍷🍷 3
● Irpinia Campi Taurasini '17	🍷🍷 2*
○ Falanghina '19	🍷 3
○ Greco di Tufo Colle dei Lauri '19	🍷 4
● Irpinia Aglianico '16	🍷 3
○ Fiano di Avellino '17	🍷🍷🍷 3*
○ Fiano di Avellino '18	🍷🍷 3*
○ Greco di Tufo '18	🍷🍷 3
○ Greco di Tufo '17	🍷🍷 3
● Taurasi '14	🍷🍷 5

Terre Stregate

loc. Santa Lucia
82034 Guardia Sanframondi [BN]
Tel. +39 0824817857
www.terrestregate.it

CELLAR SALES
PRE-BOOKED VISITS
ANNUAL PRODUCTION 130,000 bottles
HECTARES UNDER VINE 22.00

Armando Iacobucci gave new a lease of life to the old family tradition by adding winemaking to the oil press activity in 2004. He renovated the cellar belonging to his grandfather and created Terre Stregate. Today his children run the farm: Carlo looks after work in the vineyards, while Filomena deals with sales. The vineyards are located in Guardia Sanframondi and the vine rows are planted with local native grapes: Fiano, Greco and Aglianico for powerful, firmly-structured red wines and, of course, Falanghina, the true ambassador of this territory. Tre Bicchieri for the Falanghina del Sannio '19. Aromatically it calls up freshly cut grass and citrus, while the palate comes through juicy, full, multifaceted and nicely expansive. The Sannio Aglianico Manent '17 also convinces with its sensations of wild berries and pepper; a firm palate gives way to a flavorful, tasty, delicately spicy finish.

○ Falanghina del Sannio Svelato '19	🍷🍷🍷 3*
● Sannio Aglianico Manent '17	🍷🍷 2*
○ Cara Cara Falanghina '17	🍷 6
⊙ Rosato Attimo '19	🍷 2
○ Sannio Fiano Genius Loci '19	🍷 3
○ Sannio Greco Aurora '19	🍷 2
○ Falanghina del Sannio Svelato '18	🍷🍷🍷 3*
○ Falanghina del Sannio Svelato '17	🍷🍷🍷 2*
○ Falanghina del Sannio Svelato '16	🍷🍷🍷 2*
○ Falanghina del Sannio Svelato '15	🍷🍷🍷 2*
○ Falanghina del Sannio Svelato '14	🍷🍷🍷 2*
○ Falanghina del Sannio Svelato '13	🍷🍷🍷 2*
○ Caracara Falanghina '16	🍷🍷 6
● Costa del Duca Aglianico '15	🍷🍷 7
○ Falanghina Trama '18	🍷🍷 2*

Terredora Di Paolo

via Serra
83030 Montefusco [AV]
Tel. +39 0825968215
www.terredora.com

CELLAR SALES
PRE-BOOKED VISITS
ACCOMMODATION
ANNUAL PRODUCTION 700,000 bottles
HECTARES UNDER VINE 200.00

Walter Mastroberardino's business venture began in 1994 and is carried forward today by his hard-headed children, Daniela and Paolo. Together they manage the largest vineyards in southern Italy, 200 hectares in the best subzones of Irpinia: Lapio, Montemiletto, Montefalcione, Santa Paolina, Montefusco, Pietradefusi. These territories are some of the best winemaking areas in the region, where Aglianico, Fiano, Greco, Falanghina and Coda di Volpe are grown. Their wine range is divided into three lines: Le Grandi Riserve, Le Selezioni and I Classici, which include technically exemplary, clean and focused wines. Their Taurasi selections stand out, in particular the Taurasi Pago dei Fusi, vintage 2012, a wine that features smoky notes, elegant hints of coffee and pepper. The palate is close-knit and juicy, fading on sapid sensations. The Taurasi CampoRe '09 is evolved aromatically but still lively and energetic, while intense balsamic hints feature in the Taurasi Fatica Contadina '14. Clear sensations of small berries characterize the Corte di Giso, a wine that's austere and pulpy in the mouth.

Wine	Glasses	Price
● Irpinia Aglianico Corte di Giso '17	TT	3
● Taurasi CampoRe Ris. '09	TT	7
● Taurasi Fatica Contadina '14	TT	5
● Taurasi Pago dei Fusi '12	TT	5
○ Fiano di Avellino Campore '16	T	5
○ Greco di Tufo Loggia della Serra '19	T	3
● Corte di Giso Aglianico '15	YY	2*
○ Fiano di Avellino '17	YY	5
○ Greco di Tufo Loggia della Serra '17	YY	3
● Taurasi Fatica Contadina '12	YY	5
● Taurasi Pago dei Fusi '11	YY	5
● Taurasi Pago dei Fusi '10	YY	5

Traerte

c.da Vadiaperti
83030 Montefredane [AV]
Tel. +39 0825607270
info@traerte.it

CELLAR SALES
PRE-BOOKED VISITS
ANNUAL PRODUCTION 81,000 bottles
HECTARES UNDER VINE 6.00

Raffaele Troisi, a true vigneron, inherited the estate from his father Antonio, one of the first vinegrowers in Montefredane to start vinifying his own grapes. In this part of Irpinia, Fiano rules the roost, but years ago, Troisi decided to return another variety to its former glory, which had only been used for blending until then: Coda di Volpe. Their selection, Torama, is constantly among the best interpretations in the region; character, sapidity, marked acidity, these characteristics are found in all the winery's range. A decidedly convincing line-up demonstrated the excellent work being done. The Greco di Tufo Tornante '19 is still lagging behind aromatically, but the palate exhibits a singular sapid energy, steady acidity and a long final expansion. The Fiano di Avellino Aiperti '19 offers up aromas of orange blossom and Chinese magnolia, unfolding confidently, made rhythmic by fragrant fruit, closing on balsamic hints. The Irpinia Coda di Volpe Torama '19 is the best of its kind, evocative in its whiffs of hazelnut.

Wine	Glasses	Price
○ Fiano di Avellino Aipierti '19	TT	5
○ Greco di Tufo Tornante '19	TT	5
○ Fiano di Avellino '19	TT	3
○ Greco di Tufo '19	TT	3
○ Irpinia Coda di Volpe '19	TT	2*
○ Irpinia Coda di Volpe Torama '19	TT	5
○ Greco di Tufo Tornante '18	YYY	5
○ Fiano di Avellino Aipierti '17	YY	5
○ Fiano di Avellino Aipierti '16	YY	5
○ Greco di Tufo '17	YY	3
○ Greco di Tufo Tornante '17	YY	5
○ Irpinia Coda di Volpe '17	YY	2*
○ Irpinia Coda di Volpe Torama '18	YY	5
○ Irpinia Coda di Volpe Torama '17	YY	5
○ Irpinia Coda di Volpe Torama '16	YY	5

★Villa Matilde Avallone

S.DA ST.LE DOMITIANA, 18
81030 CELLOLE [CE]
TEL. +39 0823932088
www.villamatilde.it

CELLAR SALES
PRE-BOOKED VISITS
ACCOMMODATION AND RESTAURANT SERVICE
ANNUAL PRODUCTION 700,000 bottles
HECTARES UNDER VINE 130.00
SUSTAINABLE WINERY

The history of Villa Matilde goes hand in hand with wine made in the Massico hills, the heart of ancient Falerno wine. It all began in the 1960s, when the lawyer Francesco Paolo Avallone, founder of the winery, set up complex archeological work (in collaboration with the Faculty of Agriculture of the University of Naples) to identify the grapes used by the Romans to produce wine. Today, Salvatore and Maria Ida head the winery. As well as carrying forward their father Francesco's winemaking concept, they have expanded production to embrace the main appellations, including territories in Irpinia and Benevento. The two Falerno del Massico reserves earned the highest marks. The Vigna Caracci '17 is a charming white capable of combining intensity, power and structure across a ripe, sapid, fruity weave with a delicately toasty finish rich in flavor. Vibrant in its smoky notes, the Falerno Vigna Camarato delivers fleshy, ripe fruit.

○ Falerno del Massico Bianco V. Caracci '17	🍷🍷 5
○ Falanghina Sinuessa '19	🍷🍷 2*
○ Falerno del Massico Bianco '19	🍷🍷 3
● Falerno del Massico Rosso V. Camarato Ris. '15	🍷🍷 8
○ Mata Extra Brut M. Cl.	🍷🍷 5
● Roccaleoni Aglianico '17	🍷🍷 3
● Stregamora Piedirosso '19	🍷🍷 3
● Cecubo '15	🍷 5
○ Fiano di Avellino Montelapio '19	🍷 3
○ Greco di Tufo Daltavilla '19	🍷 3
⊙ Mata Brut M. Cl. Rosé	🍷 5
● Taurasi Fusonero '16	🍷 6
● Taurasi Pietrafusa '16	🍷 5
⊙ Terre Cerase '19	🍷 3
● Falerno del Massico Camarato '05	🍷🍷🍷 (white) 6

Villa Raiano

LOC. CERRETO
VIA BOSCO SATRANO, 1
83020 SAN MICHELE DI SERINO [AV]
TEL. +39 0825595663
www.villaraiano.com

CELLAR SALES
PRE-BOOKED VISITS
RESTAURANT SERVICE
ANNUAL PRODUCTION 270,000 bottles
HECTARES UNDER VINE 27.00
VITICULTURE METHOD Certified Organic

Founded in 1996, the winery underwent renewal in 2009, starting with the building of a cellar that is perfectly integrated into the surrounding landscape, among vineyards and woods, on a hill dominating the valley of the Sabato river. This important winery in Irpinia is run by the brothers Sabino and Simone Basso and their brother-in-law Paolo Sibillo, who tend the vineyards with certified organic methods. The almost 30 owned hectares are divided among native grapes grown to produce the classic appellations of the territory, making for reliable and very impressive wines. Once again, the producer submitted a line-up to remember. Tre Bicchieri go to the Fiano di Avellino Alimata '18, a classic wine in its fresh aromas of cut grass and almond, with a citrusy, smoky, decidedly graceful quality—it has balance and a distinct aromatic fragrance. The Fiano di Avellino Bosco Satrano '18 is also excellent, bright and crystalline in its fruity profile, finishing on balsamic sensations. Green tea and fresh hazelnut feature in the Fiano di Avellino Ventidue of the same vintage.

○ Fiano di Avellino Alimata '18	🍷🍷🍷 5
○ Fiano di Avellino Bosco Satrano '18	🍷🍷 5
○ Fiano di Avellino Ventidue '18	🍷🍷 5
○ Greco di Tufo '19	🍷🍷 4
○ Greco di Tufo Ponte dei Santi '18	🍷🍷 5
● Taurasi '15	🍷🍷 5
● Irpinia Campi Taurasini Costa Baiano '16	🍷 4
○ Fiano di Avellino 22 '13	🍷🍷🍷 (white) 4*
○ Fiano di Avellino Alimata '15	🍷🍷🍷 (white) 4*
○ Fiano di Avellino Alimata '10	🍷🍷🍷 (white) 4
○ Fiano di Avellino Bosco Satrano '17	🍷🍷🍷 (white) 4*
○ Fiano di Avellino Ventidue '16	🍷🍷🍷 (white) 4*
○ Fiano di Avellino Alimata '17	🍷🍷 (white) 4
○ Fiano di Avellino Ventidue '17	🍷🍷 (white) 4

Abbazia di Crapolla

LOC. AVIGLIANO
VIA SAN FILIPPO, 2
80069 VICO EQUENSE [NA]
TEL. +39 3383517280
www.abbaziadicrapolla.it

ANNUAL PRODUCTION 12,000 bottles
HECTARES UNDER VINE 2.00
SUSTAINABLE WINERY

● Sabato	🍷🍷 5
○ Sireo Bianco '18	🍷🍷 5
○ Poizzo '18	🍷 5

Aia delle Monache

S.DA PROV.LE 327 KM 1,700
81010 CASTEL CAMPAGNANO [CE]
TEL. +39 3339843706
www.aiadellemonache.it

CELLAR SALES
ANNUAL PRODUCTION 15,000 bottles
HECTARES UNDER VINE 3.00
SUSTAINABLE WINERY

○ Radegonda '17	🍷🍷 5
○ Intruso Brillo col Naso All'insù Asprinio '19	🍷 3

Antico Castello

C.DA POPPANO, 11BIS
83050 SAN MANGO SUL CALORE [AV]
TEL. +39 3408062830
www.anticocastello.com

CELLAR SALES
PRE-BOOKED VISITS
ACCOMMODATION AND RESTAURANT SERVICE
ANNUAL PRODUCTION 50,000 bottles
HECTARES UNDER VINE 10.00
SUSTAINABLE WINERY

○ Irpinia Fiano Orfeo '19	🍷🍷 3
● Taurasi '15	🍷🍷 5
○ Irpinia Falanghina Demetra '19	🍷 2
○ Irpinia Greco Ermes '19	🍷 3

Cantine Barone

VIA GIARDINO, 2
84070 RUTINO [SA]
TEL. +39 0974830463
www.cantinebarone.it

CELLAR SALES
PRE-BOOKED VISITS
ACCOMMODATION
ANNUAL PRODUCTION 100,000 bottles
HECTARES UNDER VINE 12.00
VITICULTURE METHOD Certified Organic

○ Cilento Fiano Una Mattina '19	🍷🍷 2*
⊙ Primula Rosa '19	🍷 2

Boccella

VIA SANT'EUSTACHIO
83040 CASTELFRANCI [AV]
TEL. +39 082772574
www.boccellavini.it

CELLAR SALES
PRE-BOOKED VISITS
ANNUAL PRODUCTION 10,000 bottles
HECTARES UNDER VINE 5.00
VITICULTURE METHOD Certified Organic

○ Casefatte Fiano '18	🍷🍷 2*
● Irpinia Campi Taurasini Rasott '17	🍷🍷 3
● Taurasi Sant'Eustachio '15	🍷 5

Borgodangelo

LOC. C.DA BOSCO SELVA
S.DA 52 KM 10,00
83050 SANT'ANGELO ALL'ESCA [AV]
TEL. +39 082773027
www.borgodangelo.it

CELLAR SALES
PRE-BOOKED VISITS
RESTAURANT SERVICE
ANNUAL PRODUCTION 30,000 bottles
HECTARES UNDER VINE 9.00
SUSTAINABLE WINERY

⊙ Irpinia Rosato '19	🍷🍷 2*
● Taurasi Ris. '13	🍷🍷 4
○ Fiano di Avellino '19	🍷 2
● Taurasi '14	🍷 4

Cantina dei Monaci

fraz. Santa Lucia, 80
83030 Santa Paolina [AV]
Tel. +39 0825964350
www.cantinadeimonaci.it

CELLAR SALES
PRE-BOOKED VISITS
ANNUAL PRODUCTION 60,000 bottles
HECTARES UNDER VINE 7.50

○ Greco di Tufo Decimo Sesto '18	🍷🍷 4
● Irpinia Aglianico Santa Lucia '17	🍷🍷 4
○ Greco di Tufo '19	🍷 3
● Taurasi Monaco Rosso '15	🍷 5

Cantina del Barone

via Nocelleto, 21
83020 Cesinali [AV]
Tel. +39 0825666751
www.cantinadelbarone.it

CELLAR SALES
PRE-BOOKED VISITS
ANNUAL PRODUCTION 30,000 bottles
HECTARES UNDER VINE 2.50

○ Particella 928 '18	🍷🍷 3

Cantine del Mare

via Cappella IV, trav. 6
80070 Monte di Procida [NA]
Tel. +39 0815233040
www.cantinedelmare.it

CELLAR SALES
PRE-BOOKED VISITS
ANNUAL PRODUCTION 35,000 bottles
HECTARES UNDER VINE 11.00

○ Campi Flegrei Falanghina '18	🍷🍷 2*
● Campi Flegrei Piedirosso Terrazze Romane '18	🍷🍷 3
○ Campi Flegrei Falanghina Torrefumo '18	🍷 3

Casa di Baal

fraz. Macchia
via Tiziano, 14
84096 Montecorvino Rovella [SA]
Tel. +39 089981143
www.casadibaal.it

CELLAR SALES
PRE-BOOKED VISITS
ANNUAL PRODUCTION 28,000 bottles
HECTARES UNDER VINE 5.00
VITICULTURE METHOD Certified Organic
SUSTAINABLE WINERY

○ Fiano di Baal '18	🍷🍷 4
⊙ Il Tocco di Baal '19	🍷🍷 3
○ Bianco di Baal '19	🍷 3

Case d'Alto

via Piave,1
83035 Grottaminarda [AV]
Tel. +39 3397000779
info@casedalto.it

CELLAR SALES
ANNUAL PRODUCTION 10,000 bottles
HECTARES UNDER VINE 6.50
VITICULTURE METHOD Certified Organic

○ Fiano di Avellino Eclissi '18	🍷 3
○ Fiano Rifermentato in Bottiglia '15	🍷 3

Tenute Casoli

via Roma, 28
83040 Candida [AV]
Tel. +39 082522433
www.tenutecasoli.it

CELLAR SALES
PRE-BOOKED VISITS
ACCOMMODATION AND RESTAURANT SERVICE
ANNUAL PRODUCTION 20,000 bottles
HECTARES UNDER VINE 13.00

○ Greco di Tufo Le Crete '19	🍷🍷 3
○ Fiano di Avellino Kryos '19	🍷 3
● Irpinia Aglianico Kataros '18	🍷 3
● Taurasi Armonia '14	🍷 6

Castelle

S.DA NAZIONALE SANNITICA, 48
82037 CASTELVENERE [BN]
TEL. +39 0824940232
www.castelle.it

ANNUAL PRODUCTION 60,000 bottles
HECTARES UNDER VINE 7.00

○ Falanghina del Sannio '19	🍷🍷 4
● Camaiola '19	🍷 2
● Sannio Barbera '16	🍷 2

Elena Catalano

C.DA MONTE PINO
82100 BENEVENTO
TEL. +39 082444318
www.elenacatalano.it

ANNUAL PRODUCTION 25,000 bottles
HECTARES UNDER VINE 10.00
SUSTAINABLE WINERY

○ Falanghina del Sannio Taburno '19	🍷🍷 3
● Sannio Aglianico '18	🍷🍷 3
● Aglianico del Taburno Monte Pino '16	🍷 4
○ Sannio Taburno Coda di volpe '19	🍷 3

Cautiero

C.DA ARBUSTI
82030 FRASSO TELESINO [BN]
TEL. +39 3387640641
www.cautiero.it

CELLAR SALES
ACCOMMODATION
ANNUAL PRODUCTION 18,000 bottles
HECTARES UNDER VINE 4.00
VITICULTURE METHOD Certified Organic

○ Falanghina del Sannio Fois '19	🍷🍷 2*
○ Erba Bianca '18	🍷 2
● Fois Rosso Sannio '17	🍷 3
⊙ Vita Nuova '19	🍷 2

Cenatiempo Vini d'Ischia

VIA BALDASSARRE COSSA, 84
80077 ISCHIA [NA]
TEL. +39 081981107
www.vinicenatiempo.it

CELLAR SALES
PRE-BOOKED VISITS
ANNUAL PRODUCTION 70,000 bottles
HECTARES UNDER VINE 4.00

○ Ischia Biancolella '19	🍷🍷 3*
○ Ischia Biancolella Kalimera '18	🍷🍷 4
○ Ischia Forastera '19	🍷 4
● Ischia Per' 'e Palummo '19	🍷 3

Rossella Cicalese

VIA PAPALEONE, 575
84025 EBOLI [SA]
TEL. +39 3663645380
info@aziendaagricolacicalese.it

CELLAR SALES
ACCOMMODATION AND RESTAURANT SERVICE
ANNUAL PRODUCTION 20,000 bottles
HECTARES UNDER VINE 6.00
SUSTAINABLE WINERY

● Aglianico Evoli '18	🍷🍷 3
○ Cilento Fiano Fluminè '19	🍷🍷 3

Colli di Castelfranci

C.DA BRAUDIANO
83040 CASTELFRANCI [AV]
TEL. +39 082772392
www.collidicastelfranci.com

CELLAR SALES
PRE-BOOKED VISITS
ACCOMMODATION AND RESTAURANT SERVICE
ANNUAL PRODUCTION 150,000 bottles
HECTARES UNDER VINE 25.00

● Irpinia Campi Taurasini Vadantico '15	🍷🍷 4
○ Irpinia Fiano Paladino '15	🍷🍷 6
○ Fiano di Avellino Pendino '19	🍷 4
● Taurasi Alta Valle '13	🍷 7

Contrada Salandra

FRAZ. COSTE DI CUMA
VIA TRE PICCIONI, 40
80078 POZZUOLI [NA]
TEL. +39 0815265258
contradasalandra@gmail.com

CELLAR SALES
PRE-BOOKED VISITS
ANNUAL PRODUCTION 20,000 bottles
HECTARES UNDER VINE 4.50

○ Campi Flegrei Falanghina '18	🍷🍷 3*
● Campi Flegrei Piedirosso '17	🍷🍷 3

Cuomo - I Vini del Cavaliere

VIA FEUDO LA PILA, 16
84047 CAPACCIO PAESTUM [SA]
TEL. +39 0828725376
www.vinicuomo.com

CELLAR SALES
PRE-BOOKED VISITS
RESTAURANT SERVICE
ANNUAL PRODUCTION 25,000 bottles
HECTARES UNDER VINE 4.00

● Cilento Aglianico Granatum '18	🍷🍷 3
○ Leukòs Fiano '19	🍷🍷 3
● Poseidon Primitivo '19	🍷🍷 3
⊙ Rosato Paistom '19	🍷🍷 3

Viticoltori De Conciliis

LOC. QUERCE, 1
84060 PRIGNANO CILENTO [SA]
TEL. +39 0974831090
www.viticoltorideconciliis.it

CELLAR SALES
PRE-BOOKED VISITS
ANNUAL PRODUCTION 200,000 bottles
HECTARES UNDER VINE 21.00
VITICULTURE METHOD Certified Organic
SUSTAINABLE WINERY

● Bacioilcielo Rosso '18	🍷🍷 2*
○ Cilento Fiano Donnaluna '19	🍷🍷 3
● Donnaluna Aglianico '17	🍷🍷 3
○ Fiano Perella '16	🍷 3

Dryas

VIA TOPPOLE, 10
83030 MONTEFREDANE [AV]
TEL. +39 3472392634
www.cantinadryas.it

ANNUAL PRODUCTION 7,400 bottles
HECTARES UNDER VINE 2.00

○ Brut M. Cl. '15	🍷🍷 5
○ Brut M. Cl.	🍷🍷 5
○ Griseo '19	🍷🍷 3

Farro

LOC. FUSARO
VIA VIRGILIO, 16/24
80070 BACOLI [NA]
TEL. +39 0818545555
www.cantinefarro.it

CELLAR SALES
PRE-BOOKED VISITS
ANNUAL PRODUCTION 207,000 bottles
HECTARES UNDER VINE 20.00

○ Campi Flegrei Falanghina '19	🍷🍷 2*
● Campi Flegrei Piedirosso '18	🍷🍷 2*
⊙ Campi Flegrei Piedirosso Depiè Rosé '19	🍷 2

Cantine Federiciane Monteleone

FRAZ. SAN ROCCO
VIA ANTICA CONSOLARE CAMPANA, 34
80016 MARANO DI NAPOLI [NA]
TEL. +39 0815765294
www.federiciane.it

CELLAR SALES
PRE-BOOKED VISITS
ANNUAL PRODUCTION 200,000 bottles
HECTARES UNDER VINE 15.00

● Penisola Sorrentina Gragnano '19	🍷🍷 2*
● Penisola Sorrentina Lettere '19	🍷 2
● Roccia Madre '17	🍷 4

Francesca Fiasco

loc. Campanaro Km 32, 100
84055 Felitto [SA]
Tel. +39 3381563628
info@francescafiasco.com

CELLAR SALES
PRE-BOOKED VISITS
ANNUAL PRODUCTION 20,000 bottles
HECTARES UNDER VINE 7.00

● Difesa Rosso '16	🍷🍷 5
● Ersa Rosso '17	🍷🍷 4
● Mèrcuri Rosso '16	🍷🍷 8
● Lapazio '19	🍷 5

Filadoro

c.da Cerreto, 19
83030 Lapio [AV]
Tel. +39 0825982536
www.filadoro.it

CELLAR SALES
PRE-BOOKED VISITS
ANNUAL PRODUCTION 40,000 bottles
HECTARES UNDER VINE 6.00

○ Fiano di Avellino '19	🍷🍷 3*
○ Santàri Fiano '18	🍷 5
● Taurasi '13	🍷 5

Raffaele Guastaferro

via A. Gramsci
83030 Taurasi [AV]
Tel. +39 3341551543
info@guastaferro.it

CELLAR SALES
ANNUAL PRODUCTION 10,000 bottles
HECTARES UNDER VINE 7.00

● Taurasi Primum Ris. '15	🍷🍷 7
○ Fulgeo Grecomusc' '19	🍷 4

Historia Antiqua

via Variante Est s.s 7Bis, 75
83030 Manocalzati [AV]
Tel. +39 0825675240
www.historiaantiqua.it

CELLAR SALES
PRE-BOOKED VISITS
ANNUAL PRODUCTION 90,000 bottles
HECTARES UNDER VINE 40.00

○ Greco di Tufo '19	🍷🍷 4
○ Irpinia Falanghina '19	🍷🍷 3
○ Fiano di Avellino '19	🍷 4
● Taurasi '15	🍷 6

Cantine Iorio

via Scauzone, 2
82030 Torrecuso [BN]
Tel. +39 3483772727
www.cantineiorio.it

CELLAR SALES
ANNUAL PRODUCTION 300,000 bottles
HECTARES UNDER VINE 0.00

● Sannio Aglianico '18	🍷🍷 2*
○ Falanghina del Sannio Spumante Extra Dry	🍷 2
● Sannio Barbera '19	🍷 2

Lunarossavini

via V. Fortunato, P.I.P. Lotto 10
84095 Giffoni Valle Piana [SA]
Tel. +39 3286232323
www.viniepassione.it

CELLAR SALES
PRE-BOOKED VISITS
ANNUAL PRODUCTION 50,000 bottles
HECTARES UNDER VINE 4.50

● Borgomastro Aglianico '16	🍷🍷 2*
○ Quartara '17	🍷🍷 5

Salvatore Martusciello

via Spinelli, 4
80010 Quarto [NA]
Tel. +39 0818766123
www.salvatoremartusciello.it

ANNUAL PRODUCTION 70,000 bottles
HECTARES UNDER VINE 2.00

- ○ Asprinio d'Aversa Trentapioli Brut '19 ŸŸ 3
- ● Campi Flegrei Piedirosso Settevulcani '19 Ÿ 3
- ● Penisola Sorrentina Gragnano Ottouve '19 Ÿ 3
- ● Penisola Sorrentina Lettere Ottouve '19 Ÿ 3

Cantina Mito

c.da Mito
83051 Nusco [AV]
Tel. +39 3488069745
www.cantinamito.it

ANNUAL PRODUCTION 40,000 bottles
HECTARES UNDER VINE 9.00

- ● Dunsogno Aglianico '16 ŸŸ 5
- ● Taurasi Amato '16 ŸŸ 7

Fattoria Monserrato 1973

c.da La Francesca
82100 Benevento
Tel. +39 0864565041
www.monserrato1973.it

CELLAR SALES
ANNUAL PRODUCTION 20,000 bottles
HECTARES UNDER VINE 12.00

- ● Rintocco Aglianico '19 ŸŸ 3
- ● Sannio Barbera '19 ŸŸ 4

Montesole

fraz. Serra
83030 Montefusco [AV]
Tel. +39 0825963972
www.montesole.it

PRE-BOOKED VISITS
ACCOMMODATION AND RESTAURANT SERVICE
ANNUAL PRODUCTION 700,000 bottles
HECTARES UNDER VINE 65.00
SUSTAINABLE WINERY

- ○ Greco di Tufo '19 ŸŸ 3
- ● Irpinia Aglianico '15 ŸŸ 2*
- ● Sairus Aglianico '15 ŸŸ 4
- ○ Irpinia Falanghina '19 Ÿ 2

Raffaele Palma

loc. San Vito
via Arsenale, 8
84010 Maiori [SA]
Tel. +39 3357601858
www.raffaelepalma.it

CELLAR SALES
PRE-BOOKED VISITS
ACCOMMODATION
ANNUAL PRODUCTION 20,000 bottles
HECTARES UNDER VINE 6.00
VITICULTURE METHOD Certified Organic

- ○ Costa d'Amalfi Bianco Puntacroce '18 ŸŸ 5
- ● Costa d'Amalfi Rosso Montecorvo '16 Ÿ 5

Gennaro Papa

p.zza Limata, 2
81030 Falciano del Massico [CE]
Tel. +39 0823931267
www.gennaropapa.it

CELLAR SALES
PRE-BOOKED VISITS
ANNUAL PRODUCTION 26,500 bottles
HECTARES UNDER VINE 6.00
SUSTAINABLE WINERY

- ● Falerno del Massico Primitivo Campantuono '17 ŸŸ 6
- ● Falerno del Massico Primitivo Conclave '18 Ÿ 4

Passo delle Tortore

C.DA VERTECCHIA
83030 PIETRADEFUSI [AV]
TEL. +39 3355946330
www.passodelletortore.it

CELLAR SALES
PRE-BOOKED VISITS
HECTARES UNDER VINE 5.50

- ○ Greco di Tufo Le Arcaie '19 — 4
- ○ Fiano di Avellino Bacio delle Tortore '19 — 4
- ○ Irpinia Falanghina Piano del Cardo '19 — 4

Perillo

C.DA VALLE, 19
83040 CASTELFRANCI [AV]
TEL. +39 082772252
cantinaperillo@libero.it

CELLAR SALES
PRE-BOOKED VISITS
ANNUAL PRODUCTION 20,000 bottles
HECTARES UNDER VINE 5.00

- ● Taurasi '10 — 6

Porto di Mola

S.S. 430, KM 16,200
81050 ROCCA D'EVANDRO [CE]
TEL. +39 0823925801
www.portodimola.it

CELLAR SALES
PRE-BOOKED VISITS
ANNUAL PRODUCTION 300,000 bottles
HECTARES UNDER VINE 50.00

- ○ Galluccio Bianco Petratonda '19 — 3
- ● Peppì '17 — 3
- ○ Collelepre '19 — 3
- ● Galluccio Rosso Camporoccio '17 — 3

Andrea Reale

FRAZ. GETE
VIA CARDAMONE, 75
84010 TRAMONTI [SA]
TEL. +39 089856144
www.aziendaagricolarealeandrea.it

CELLAR SALES
PRE-BOOKED VISITS
ACCOMMODATION AND RESTAURANT SERVICE
ANNUAL PRODUCTION 18,000 bottles
HECTARES UNDER VINE 2.50
VITICULTURE METHOD Certified Organic

- ○ Costa d'Amalfi Tramonti Bianco Aliseo '19 — 4
- ● Costa d'Amalfi Tramonti Rosso Borgo di Gete '16 — 7

Regina Viarum

VIA VELLARIA
81030 FALCIANO DEL MASSICO [CE]
TEL. +39 0823931299
www.reginaviarum.com

CELLAR SALES
PRE-BOOKED VISITS
ANNUAL PRODUCTION 19,000 bottles
HECTARES UNDER VINE 5.00
VITICULTURE METHOD Certified Organic
SUSTAINABLE WINERY

- ● Falerno del Massico Primitivo Zer05 '16 — 3*

Tenuta Sarno 1860

C.DA SERRONI, 4B
83100 AVELLINO
TEL. +39 082526161
www.tenutasarno1860.it

ANNUAL PRODUCTION 15,000 bottles
HECTARES UNDER VINE 6.00

- ○ Fiano di Avellino '18 — 4

Lorenzo Nifo Sarrapochiello

via Piana, 62
82030 Ponte [BN]
Tel. +39 0824876450
www.nifo.eu

CELLAR SALES
PRE-BOOKED VISITS
ANNUAL PRODUCTION 90,000 bottles
HECTARES UNDER VINE 18.00
VITICULTURE METHOD Certified Organic

○ Sannio Taburno Greco '19	🍷🍷 2*
○ Falanghina del Sannio Taburno '19	🍷 2

Cantina di Solopaca

via Bebiana, 44
82036 Solopaca [BN]
Tel. +39 0824977921
www.cantinasolopaca.it

CELLAR SALES
PRE-BOOKED VISITS
ANNUAL PRODUCTION 700,000 bottles
HECTARES UNDER VINE 1300.00

○ Falanghina del Sannio Identitas '19	🍷🍷 3*
○ Falanghina del Sannio '19	🍷 2
○ Falanghina del Sannio Brut	🍷 2

Sorrentino Vini

via Rio, 26
80042 Boscotrecase [NA]
Tel. +39 0818584963
www.sorrentinovini.com

CELLAR SALES
PRE-BOOKED VISITS
ACCOMMODATION AND RESTAURANT SERVICE
ANNUAL PRODUCTION 240,000 bottles
HECTARES UNDER VINE 35.00
VITICULTURE METHOD Certified Organic

○ Lacryma Christi del Vesuvio Bianco V. Lapillo '18	🍷🍷 3
○ Vesuvio Caprettone Benita '31 '19	🍷🍷 3
● Don Paolo '16	🍷 5

Telaro

loc. Calabritto
via Cinque Pietre, 2
81044 Galluccio [CE]
Tel. +39 0823925841
www.vinitelaro.it

CELLAR SALES
PRE-BOOKED VISITS
ANNUAL PRODUCTION 550,000 bottles
HECTARES UNDER VINE 70.00
VITICULTURE METHOD Certified Organic

● Bariletta '19	🍷🍷 3
● Calivierno '17	🍷🍷 5
○ Galluccio Bianco Ripa Bianca '19	🍷🍷 3
● Galluccio Rosso Ara Mundi Ris. '16	🍷 5

Tempere

via San Sebastiano
84037 Sant'Arsenio [SA]
Tel. +39 0975396202
www.vino-tempere.it

CELLAR SALES
PRE-BOOKED VISITS
ACCOMMODATION AND RESTAURANT SERVICE
ANNUAL PRODUCTION 8,000 bottles
HECTARES UNDER VINE 3.00

● Aglianico Tempere '15	🍷🍷 6
● Aglianico Tempere '16	🍷 6
○ Monteroro Fiano '19	🍷 4

Terre del Principe

p.zza Municipio, 4
81010 Castel Campagnano [CE]
Tel. +39 0823867126
www.terredelprincipe.com

CELLAR SALES
PRE-BOOKED VISITS
ANNUAL PRODUCTION 20,000 bottles
HECTARES UNDER VINE 7.00
VITICULTURE METHOD Certified Organic
SUSTAINABLE WINERY

● Ambruco '16	🍷🍷 5
○ Fontanavigna '19	🍷🍷 3
○ Le Serole '18	🍷 5

Terre di Tora

via Roma, 8
81044 Tora e Piccilli [CE]
Tel. +39 3396615759
www.terreditora.com

ANNUAL PRODUCTION 15,000 bottles
HECTARES UNDER VINE 3.00

- ● Adalaris '17 — 🍷🍷 6
- ● Rebalto '17 — 🍷🍷 7

Torelle

loc. Torelle
via Nazionale Appia, 1
81037 Sessa Aurunca [CE]
Tel. +39 392185208
www.vinitorelle.com

ANNUAL PRODUCTION 12,000 bottles
HECTARES UNDER VINE 4.00

- ○ Falanghina '19 — 🍷🍷 2*
- ● Falerno del Massico Rosso '15 — 🍷🍷 3

Torricino

loc. Torricino, 5
via Nazionale
83010 Tufo [AV]
Tel. +39 0825998119
www.torricino.it

CELLAR SALES
PRE-BOOKED VISITS
ANNUAL PRODUCTION 40,000 bottles
HECTARES UNDER VINE 8.00
SUSTAINABLE WINERY

- ○ Fiano di Avellino '19 — 🍷🍷 4
- ○ Greco di Tufo '19 — 🍷🍷 4
- ● Taurasi Cevotiempo '16 — 🍷🍷 6
- ○ Fiano di Avellino Serrapiano '19 — 🍷 5

Vestini Campagnano Poderi Foglia

via Costa dell'Aia, 9
81044 Conca della Campania [CE]
Tel. +39 0823679087
www.vestinicampagnano.it

CELLAR SALES
PRE-BOOKED VISITS
ANNUAL PRODUCTION 80,000 bottles
HECTARES UNDER VINE 7.00
VITICULTURE METHOD Certified Organic

- ● Kajanero '19 — 🍷🍷 2*
- ○ Pallagrello Bianco '19 — 🍷 3
- ○ Pallagrello Bianco Le Òrtole '19 — 🍷 4
- ● Pallagrello Nero '18 — 🍷 5

Villa Diamante

via Toppole, 16
83030 Montefredane [AV]
Tel. +39 3476791469
villadiamante1996@gmail.com

CELLAR SALES
PRE-BOOKED VISITS
ANNUAL PRODUCTION 10,000 bottles
HECTARES UNDER VINE 4.50

- ○ Fiano di Avellino V. della Congregazione '18 — 🍷🍷 5

Villa Dora

s.da prov.le Zabatta, 252
80040 Terzigno [NA]
Tel. +39 0815295016
www.cantinevilladora.it

CELLAR SALES
PRE-BOOKED VISITS
RESTAURANT SERVICE
ANNUAL PRODUCTION 60,000 bottles
HECTARES UNDER VINE 15.00
VITICULTURE METHOD Certified Organic

- ○ Lacryma Christi del Vesuvio Bianco V. del Vulcano '18 — 🍷🍷 5

BASILICATA

Basilicata is one of Italy's emerging wine territories, even if it's a region where wine (and high-quality wine at that) has been produced for at least 2 millennia. Aglianico, southern Italy's great red grape variety was probably born right here in the hills at the foot of Mount Vulture, where in Roman times the Aelia family had extensive land holdings and marketed their wines (Allianicum) throughout the empire. Despite this, the region's location, and the resourcefulness of its neighbors (who did a better job mastering trade routes), has meant that these lands have remained somewhat secluded, are still to be discovered, even if an event like the Matera European Capital of Culture in 2019 brought millions of visitors to appreciate its artistic treasures, landscapes and its cultural patrimonies, including its wine. This year we tasted many excellent wines from Basilicata, and we awarded 6 of them, all Aglianico del Vulture. Matera is growing fast and you don't have to be a fortune-teller to predict that pretty soon we'll be seeing other great wines being produced alongside the great red cultivated at the foot of the volcano. Names like Elena Fucci, Re Manfredi, Grifalco and Cantine del Notaio are already known to wine lovers. And this year we welcome 2 producers to the exclusive 'Tre Bicchieri' club: Terra dei Re, with their excellent Aglianico del Vulture Nocte '16, and Donato D'Angelo, an emblematic figure for the appellation, with his Aglianico del Vulture '17.

Basilisco

via delle Cantine
85022 Barile [PZ]
Tel. +39 0972771033
www.basiliscovini.it

CELLAR SALES
PRE-BOOKED VISITS
ANNUAL PRODUCTION 55,000 bottles
HECTARES UNDER VINE 25.00
VITICULTURE METHOD Certified Organic
SUSTAINABLE WINERY

Viviana Malafarina is at the helm of this solid winery in Basilicata, owned by the Feudi di San Gregorio group since 2011. The cellar is in an old palazzo in the heart of Barile. Their 25 hectares of vineyards, cultivated under organic management, are located in the Macarico and Gelosia crus, between 450 and 600 meters of elevation, on soils of the now extinct Monte Vulture volcano. Pierpoalo Sirch is in charge of vineyard management, which means cutting-edge vinegrowing, manual grape harvesting and precise, separate vinification for each plot of land. The 2017 vintage of Teodosio, Basilisco's historic wine, is in great form. This concentrated, rich red features intense aromas of cherry and ripe morello, spruced up by vegetal overtones and spicy nuances. The pleasant palate impressed for its structure, elegance and soft tannins. Also performing well were their Superiore Cruà '16, with a close-focused, Mediterranean profile, and Fontanelle '16, with a more rustic character, still a bit spirited.

Wine	Rating
● Aglianico del Vulture Teodosio '17	TT 3*
● Aglianico del Vulture Sup. Cruà '16	TT 5
● Aglianico del Vulture Sup. Fontanelle '16	TT 5
○ Sophia '19	T 3
● Aglianico del Vulture Basilisco '09	YYY 5
● Aglianico del Vulture Basilisco '08	YYY 5
● Aglianico del Vulture Basilisco '07	YYY 5
● Aglianico del Vulture Basilisco '06	YYY 5
● Aglianico del Vulture Basilisco '04	YYY 5
● Aglianico del Vulture Basilisco '01	YYY 5
● Aglianico del Vulture Sup. Cruà '13	YYY 5
● Aglianico del Vulture Sup. Cruà '15	YY 5
● Aglianico del Vulture Sup. Fontanelle '13	YY 5
● Aglianico del Vulture Teodosio '16	YY 3*

Battifarano

c.da Cerrolongo, 1
75020 Nova Siri [MT]
Tel. +39 0835536174
www.battifarano.com

CELLAR SALES
PRE-BOOKED VISITS
ACCOMMODATION
ANNUAL PRODUCTION 70,000 bottles
HECTARES UNDER VINE 33.00
SUSTAINABLE WINERY

The Battifarano family has owned this splendid farm in Nova Siri for over five centuries. Today, Vincenzo and his son Francesco Paolo run the estate. They are both agronomists and look after every aspect of the farm, which also offers rural accommodation. The vineyards stretch along the Ionian coast of Basilicata, almost reaching the border with Calabria, covering a total of 33 hectares with good exposure, lying on soils rich in clay and sand. Putting aside frivolous comments on the name (from the local river that flows through the estate), the 2017 Toccaculo (you can look it up) is a complex blend of Cabernet, Primitivo and Merlot. It reached our finals thanks to its lovely concentration, rich aromas of red fruit, balance and elegant tannins. The same positive verdict goes to their intense, spicy Akratos '18. However, their whole range is worth tasting.

Wine	Rating
● Matera Primitivo Akratos '18	TT 2*
● Toccaculo '17	TT 2*
○ Matera Greco Le Paglie '19	T 2
⊙ Matera Rosato Akratos '19	T 2
● Matera Moro Curaffanni Ris. '16	YY 3*
● Matera Moro Torre Bollita '17	YY 3*
● Matera Moro Torre Bollita '07	YY 2
● Matera Primitivo Akratos '17	YY 2*
● Matera Primitivo Akratos '15	YY 2*
● Matera Primitivo Akratos '14	YY 2*
● Matera Primitivo Akratos '11	YY 2*
● Toccaculo '16	YY 2*
○ Matera Greco Le Paglie '18	Y 2

Cantine del Notaio

via Roma, 159
85028 Rionero in Vulture [PZ]
Tel. +39 0972723689
www.cantinedelnotaio.it

CELLAR SALES
PRE-BOOKED VISITS
ANNUAL PRODUCTION 470,000 bottles
HECTARES UNDER VINE 40.00

At the end of the 1990s, Gerardo Giuratrabocchetti and his wife Marcella decided to take up the family's winemaking activity again, cultivating a patrimony of about 40 hectares of vineyards in Rionero, Barile, Ripacandida, Maschito and Ginestra. The very original names of the wines are inspired by his father's job as a notary. The picturesque modern cellar is located in Ripacandida, but the barriques rest in the 17th-century caves, dug out of tuff beneath the soil in Rionero by Franciscan monks, where humidity and temperature are constant throughout the year. Several wines stood out at our tastings this year, including the 2018 version of Repertorio, which reveals the more seductive, supple side of Aglianico. It proves rich in tones of red fruit, with a full, lean body, smooth tannins and is spurred toward a long, balanced finish by fresh acidity that enriches the palate. An excellent 2015 version of their other great wine, La Firma, comes through deep, complex and full of somber, super-ripe overtones.

- ● Aglianico del Vulture Il Repertorio '18 — 🍷🍷🍷 6
- ● Aglianico del Vulture Sup. La Firma '15 — 🍷🍷 8
- ● Aglianico del Vulture Macarico '18 — 🍷🍷 3
- ○ Il Preliminare '19 — 🍷🍷 5
- ○ L'Autentica '18 — 🍷🍷 7
- ● La Scrittura '19 — 🍷🍷 5
- ○ Xjnestra Macarico '19 — 🍷🍷 2*
- ⊙ Il Rogito '19 — 🍷 5
- ● L'Atto '19 — 🍷 5
- ● Aglianico del Vulture Il Repertorio '17 — 🍷🍷🍷 4*
- ● Aglianico del Vulture Il Repertorio '16 — 🍷🍷🍷 4*
- ● Aglianico del Vulture Il Repertorio '15 — 🍷🍷🍷 4*
- ● Aglianico del Vulture Il Repertorio '14 — 🍷🍷🍷 4*
- ● Aglianico del Vulture Il Repertorio '13 — 🍷🍷🍷 4*
- ● Aglianico del Vulture Il Repertorio '12 — 🍷🍷🍷 4*
- ● Aglianico del Vulture La Firma '10 — 🍷🍷🍷 6

Masseria Cardillo

loc. Cardillo
s.s. 407 Basentana, km 97,5
75012 Bernalda [MT]
Tel. +39 0835748992
www.masseriacardillo.it

CELLAR SALES
ACCOMMODATION AND RESTAURANT SERVICE
ANNUAL PRODUCTION 50,000 bottles
HECTARES UNDER VINE 20.00

Metaponto has always been great land for farming and producing quality wines. Here we find the estate of brothers Rocco and Giovanni Graziadei, heirs to a family tradition dating back to the 17th century. In addition to a range of excellent products (including oil, cereals and livestock), the Graziadei brothers also cultivate 20 hectares of vineyards lying on calcareous soils, where the climate benefits from the vicinity to the Ionian Sea, which enriches their wines with a pleasant Mediterranean sapidity. The Rubra '17 is one of the best versions ever of this wine. It exhibits a lovely dark ruby color and an intense nose of ripe cherry, morello, spices and Mediterranean herbs. It comes through round, full-bodied and warm on the palate. Their Primitivo Vigna Giadi '19 proves spicy, balanced and fresh. The rest of their wines impressed as well.

- ● Aglianico del Vulture Rubra '17 — 🍷🍷 3*
- ○ Ovo Di Elena '19 — 🍷🍷 2*
- ● Vigna Giadì '19 — 🍷🍷 2*
- ⊙ Bacche Rosa '19 — 🍷 2
- ● Aglianico del Vulture Rubra '15 — 🍷🍷 3*
- ● Aglianico del Vulture Rubra '06 — 🍷🍷 3
- ● Baruch Primitivo '15 — 🍷🍷 5
- ● Matera Moro Malandrina '15 — 🍷🍷 3
- ● Matera Moro Malandrina '06 — 🍷🍷 3
- ● Tittà '15 — 🍷🍷 2*
- ● Tittà '10 — 🍷🍷 2*
- ● Vigna Giadì '08 — 🍷🍷 2

Donato D'Angelo di Filomena Ruppi

via Padre Pio, 10
85028 Rionero in Vulture [PZ]
Tel. +39 0972724602
www.donatodangelo.it

CELLAR SALES
PRE-BOOKED VISITS
ANNUAL PRODUCTION 150,000 bottles
HECTARES UNDER VINE 20.00

The winery got its start in 2001 with the purchase of about twenty hectares in Barile, Ripacandida and Maschito, mostly planted with Aglianico. Today it's run by Filomena Ruppi and her husband Donato D'Angelo, a key figure in the recent history of Aglianico del Vulture, thanks to decades of experience at his family's winery. Production is limited (around 150 thousand bottles a year), focusing on the territory's main grape, and follows a classic style, leading to structured, generous, long-lived wines. The style of Donato D'Angelo's reds goes beyond fads and trends. This is demonstrated by their splendid 2017 version of Donato D'Angelo, featuring rare cleanliness and elegance. It's not a dark, extractive wine, playing on fine, elegant, clean fruit. It exhibits very smooth tannins and a very lingering aromatic length. In other words ... Burgundy.

Wine	Glasses	Score
• Aglianico del Vulture Donato D'Angelo '17	▼▼▼	4*
• Aglianico del Vulture Calice '18	▼▼	3
• Balconara '17	▼	4
• Balconara '09	▽▽▽	4*
• Aglianico del Vulture '16	▽▽	4
• Aglianico del Vulture Donato D'Angelo '14	▽▽	3*
• Aglianico del Vulture Donato D'Angelo '13	▽▽	3*
• Aglianico del Vulture Donato D'Angelo '12	▽▽	3*
• Aglianico del Vulture Donato D'Angelo '11	▽▽	4
• Balconara '15	▽▽	4

★Elena Fucci

c.da Solagna del Titolo
85022 Barile [PZ]
Tel. +39 3204879945
www.elenafuccivini.com

CELLAR SALES
PRE-BOOKED VISITS
ANNUAL PRODUCTION 28,000 bottles
HECTARES UNDER VINE 7.00
VITICULTURE METHOD Certified Organic
SUSTAINABLE WINERY

Winemaker Elena Fucci is a key figure on Basilicata's modern winemaking scene. After graduating, she gave a new lease of life to the business that her grandfather Generoso started in the 1960s as an artisan activity, in the Valle del Titolo di Barile. Also working at the winery are Elena's husband, Andrea Manzano, who deals with sales, and her father, Salvatore. The cellar draws on cutting-edge technology and was designed according to sustainable architecture. Their seven hectares of fairly old vineyards are located in the upper part of the Solagna del Titolo district, at the foot of Monte Vulture. With the 2018 vintage, Elena Fucci bags the highest score. The Titolo '18 is in dazzling form: it features a lovely, non-wavering, ruby-red color and a nose that opens with aromas ranging from small fruits and cherries to ripe plums, made livelier and more complex by elegant nuances of Mediterranean scrub, coffee and delicately balsamic overtones. The palate proves rich, solidly built and continuous, without being heavy. Great length and fruit.

Wine	Glasses	Score
• Aglianico del Vulture Titolo '18	▼▼▼	8
• Aglianico del Vulture Titolo '17	▽▽▽	8
• Aglianico del Vulture Titolo '16	▽▽▽	6
• Aglianico del Vulture Titolo '15	▽▽▽	6
• Aglianico del Vulture Titolo '14	▽▽▽	6
• Aglianico del Vulture Titolo '13	▽▽▽	6
• Aglianico del Vulture Titolo '12	▽▽▽	5
• Aglianico del Vulture Titolo '11	▽▽▽	5
• Aglianico del Vulture Titolo '10	▽▽▽	5
• Aglianico del Vulture Titolo '09	▽▽▽	5
• Aglianico del Vulture Titolo '08	▽▽▽	6
• Aglianico del Vulture Titolo '07	▽▽▽	6
• Aglianico del Vulture Titolo '06	▽▽▽	5
• Aglianico del Vulture Titolo '05	▽▽▽	5

Grifalco

LOC. PIAN DI CAMERA
85029 VENOSA [PZ]
TEL. +39 097231002
www.grifalcovini.com

CELLAR SALES
PRE-BOOKED VISITS
ANNUAL PRODUCTION 70,000 bottles
HECTARES UNDER VINE 15.00
VITICULTURE METHOD Certified Organic
SUSTAINABLE WINERY

This beautiful winery founded by Fabrizio Piccin has now passed into the hands of his sons, Lorenzo and Andrea: the former, a winemaker, follows production, while the latter deals with sales, aided by their ever-present mother, Cecilia. This passion has been passed down from parents to children, who are committed to cultivating the fascinating, complex Aglianico grape. The organic vineyards stretch across Ginestra, Maschito, Rapolla and Venosa, each one presenting different soil and climate features, which are enhanced by separate vinification, making for wines full of charm and personality. The Gricos didn't disappoint this year, either: the 2018 gives us another great version of Aglianico. The complex nose conveys red fruit interweaved with notes of pencil lead, ink and delicately smoky nuances. The generous, succulent palate closes on notes of fruit. We appreciated their other wines as well.

- ● Aglianico del Vulture Gricos '18 ▼▼▼ 3*
- ● Aglianico del Vulture Sup. DaGinestra '16 ▼▼ 6
- ● Aglianico del Vulture Sup. DaMaschito '16 ▼▼ 6
- ● Aglianico del Vulture '18 ▼ 5
- ● Aglianico del Vulture Gricos '17 ▽▽▽ 3*
- ● Aglianico del Vulture Gricos '14 ▽▽▽ 3*
- ● Aglianico del Vulture Gricos '16 ▽▽ 3*
- ● Aglianico del Vulture Gricos '15 ▽▽ 3*
- ● Aglianico del Vulture Gricos '13 ▽▽ 3*
- ● Aglianico del Vulture Gricos '11 ▽▽ 2*
- ● Aglianico del Vulture Grifalco '17 ▽▽ 4
- ● Aglianico del Vulture Grifalco '12 ▽▽ 3*
- ● Aglianico del Vulture Grifalco '09 ▽▽ 3

Michele Laluce

VIA ROMA, 21
85020 GINESTRA [PZ]
TEL. +39 0972646145
www.vinilaluce.com

CELLAR SALES
PRE-BOOKED VISITS
ANNUAL PRODUCTION 40,000 bottles
HECTARES UNDER VINE 7.00
SUSTAINABLE WINERY

Michele Laluce is the epitome of the passionate vinegrower. Since 2001, he has skilfully managed the old family vineyards: about 6 hectares at 400 meters elevation on the slopes of Monte Vulture. He produces an interesting range of wines—made with Aglianico, of course. The recent arrival of his daughter Maddalena, a winemaker, has not tainted the authenticity of these products, but adds an elegant and expressive clarity to their precise and exquisitely artisanal range, year after year. The Aglianico S'Adatt is probably the wine that best represents the winery today. This solidly-built red full of character is fermented and aged in steel, which maintains clean fruit and confers extraordinary freshness and a pleasant palate. Supple tannins and good grip support the fruity overtones and nice length. The Superiore Le Drude '14, aged in large wood, proves elegant and well-orchestrated.

- ● Aglianico del Vulture Le Drude '14 ▼▼ 5
- ● Aglianico del Vulture S'Adatt '14 ▼▼ 2*
- ○ Morbino Bianco '18 ▼▼ 3
- ● Aglianico del Vulture Le Drude '13 ▽▽ 5
- ● Aglianico del Vulture Le Drude '12 ▽▽ 5
- ● Aglianico del Vulture Le Drude '08 ▽▽ 5
- ● Aglianico del Vulture Le Drude '07 ▽▽ 6
- ● Aglianico del Vulture Le Drude '06 ▽▽ 4
- ● Aglianico del Vulture Zimberno '12 ▽▽ 3
- ● Aglianico del Vulture Zimberno '08 ▽▽ 3
- ● Aglianico del Vulture Zimberno '06 ▽▽ 4

Martino

via La Vista, 2a
85028 Rionero in Vulture [PZ]
Tel. +39 0972721422
www.martinovini.com

CELLAR SALES
PRE-BOOKED VISITS
ANNUAL PRODUCTION 250,000 bottles
HECTARES UNDER VINE 30.00

It has been a long, complicated route in the world of wine for the Martino family. This journey began at the end of the 19th century and was further consolidated by Don Martino, who started making and bottling wine under his own brand in the 1940s. The turning point in quality came with the current owner, Armando, helped by his daughter Carolin. The current premises employ modern technology for production and an underground cellar in tuff stone for aging, while the vineyards also extend into Matera. Aglianico is made into red, white and rosé wines, though they also grow white varieties, such as Greco, Malvasia, Moscato and Chardonnay. This historic winery's Aglianico del Vulture Superiore Riserva '14 made it into our finals this year. The classy red bears witness to Martino's growing efforts towards achieving excellence. It's a velvety, fresh, elegant, sapid and well-orchestrated red. The Oraziano '15 and their other wines also impressed.

● Aglianico del Vulture Sup. Ris. '14	🍷🍷 7
● Aglianico del Vulture Bel Poggio '15	🍷🍷 2*
● Aglianico del Vulture Oraziano '15	🍷🍷 5
● Aglianico del Vulture Pretoriano '15	🍷 5
○ Sincerità '19	🍷 2
● Aglianico del Vulture '14	🍷🍷 3*
● Aglianico del Vulture Bel Poggio '10	🍷🍷 2*
● Aglianico del Vulture Oraziano '13	🍷🍷 5
● Aglianico del Vulture Oraziano '12	🍷🍷 5
● Aglianico del Vulture Oraziano '10	🍷🍷 5
● Aglianico del Vulture Pretoriano '09	🍷🍷 5
● Aglianico del Vulture Sup. Ris. '13	🍷🍷 7

★Paternoster

c.da Valle del Titolo
85022 Barile [PZ]
Tel. +39 0972770224
www.paternostervini.it

CELLAR SALES
PRE-BOOKED VISITS
ANNUAL PRODUCTION 150,000 bottles
HECTARES UNDER VINE 20.00
VITICULTURE METHOD Certified Organic

This historic winery, founded in 1925 by Anselmo Paternoster, is now owned by the Tommasi group. They wanted to send out a strong sign of continuity by confirming professionals such as Vito Paternoster and Fabio Mecca, to add new drive and coherence to the project. The vineyards extend over several winemaking districts in Barile and Macarico, making for a style that renders the richness and intensity of Aglianico a veritable trademark, known and esteemed all over the world. The two flagship wines, Don Anselmo and Rotondo, confirm the great ageworthiness of the area's reds. Without their Don Anselmo, which will age for a further year in the cellar, it was down to the 2017 vintage Aglianico from the Rotondo cru to uphold the good name of the historic winery in Barile. This solidly-built, concentrated, fruit-rich red really impressed in our finals. Their Syntesi '18 expresses the territory rather well: a generous red, full of character, with rich tannins and good balance.

● Aglianico del Vulture Rotondo '17	🍷🍷 5
● Aglianico del Vulture Synthesi '18	🍷🍷 3
● Aglianico del Vulture Giuv '17	🍷 2
○ Vulcanico '19	🍷 3
● Aglianico del Vulture Don Anselmo '16	🍷🍷🍷 6
● Aglianico del Vulture Don Anselmo '15	🍷🍷🍷 6
● Aglianico del Vulture Don Anselmo '13	🍷🍷🍷 6
● Aglianico del Vulture Don Anselmo '09	🍷🍷🍷 6
● Aglianico del Vulture Don Anselmo Ris. '05	🍷🍷🍷 6
● Aglianico del Vulture Rotondo '11	🍷🍷🍷 5
● Aglianico del Vulture Rotondo '01	🍷🍷🍷 5
● Aglianico del Vulture Rotondo '00	🍷🍷🍷 5
● Aglianico del Vulture Rotondo '15	🍷🍷 5
● Aglianico del Vulture Rotondo '13	🍷🍷 5
● Aglianico del Vulture Rotondo '12	🍷🍷 5
● Aglianico del Vulture Synthesi '17	🍷🍷 3*

★Re Manfredi Cantina Terre degli Svevi

loc. Pian di Camera
85029 Venosa [PZ]
Tel. +39 097231263
www.cantineremanfredi.it

CELLAR SALES
PRE-BOOKED VISITS
RESTAURANT SERVICE
ANNUAL PRODUCTION 235,000 bottles
HECTARES UNDER VINE 110.00

This winery owned by Gruppo Italiano Vini was set up in 1998; today it is run by Paolo Montrone, with the help of winemaker Pietro Bertè. It is named after King Manfred, son of Frederick II, who once ruled these lands. The vineyards (110 hectares in total) cross Venosa, Maschito and Barile, at 400-550 meters elevation. Aglianico is certainly the winery's undisputed star, with small amounts of Müller Thurgau and Traminer Aromatico completing the range. The wine that obtained the umpteenth acknowledgment for this prestigious winery is made with a selection of the best grapes grown in the Serpara vineyard in Maschito, the great Vulture cru. It exhibits a bright, deep, ruby-red color, a complex, charming nose dominated by berries and Mediterranean essences, an assertive, plush, balanced palate and a very lingering finish. Great job.

● Aglianico del Vulture Sup. Serpara '16	🍷🍷🍷 5
● Aglianico del Vulture Taglio del Tralcio '18	🍷🍷 3*
● Aglianico del Vulture Re Manfredi '17	🍷🍷 5
● Aglianico del Vulture Re Manfredi '16	ΥΥΥ 5
● Aglianico del Vulture Re Manfredi '15	ΥΥΥ 5
● Aglianico del Vulture Re Manfredi '13	ΥΥΥ 6
● Aglianico del Vulture Re Manfredi '11	ΥΥΥ 4*
● Aglianico del Vulture Re Manfredi '10	ΥΥΥ 4*
● Aglianico del Vulture Re Manfredi '05	ΥΥΥ 4
● Aglianico del Vulture Re Manfredi '99	ΥΥΥ 4*
● Aglianico del Vulture Serpara '10	ΥΥΥ 5
● Aglianico del Vulture Sup. Serpara '12	ΥΥΥ 5
● Aglianico del Vulture Vign. Serpara '03	ΥΥΥ 4*
● Aglianico del Vulture Sup. Serpara '15	ΥΥ 5

Taverna

c.da Tratturo Regio
75020 Nova Siri [MT]
Tel. +39 0835877310
www.cantinetaverna.wine

CELLAR SALES
PRE-BOOKED VISITS
ACCOMMODATION AND RESTAURANT SERVICE
ANNUAL PRODUCTION 50,000 bottles
HECTARES UNDER VINE 20.00

Pasquale Lunati is at the helm of this family farm that covers an area of 250 hectares. Twenty hectares are dedicated to vineyards, located in a fabulous position between the Pollino massif and the Ionian Sea. They also produce other crops and raise livestock. Since the end of the 1980s, an ambitious development program has brought more famous international varieties alongside native varieties, such as Greco and Primitivo. The building of a modern cellar and the arrival of consultant winemaker, Emiliano Falsini, has produced tangible results in recent vintages. The excellent 2018 version of Matera Primitivo I Sassi features a lovely dark color, body and the right concentration, but it's crisp, dry and sapid with a lovely palate. We also liked their Greco San Basile '19, which proved crisp, spirited and sapid, but full of fruity notes at the same time. Their white, sulfite-free Sens02 '19 was also interesting.

○ Matera Greco San Basile '19	🍷🍷 3
● Matera Primitivo I Sassi '18	🍷🍷 3
● Il Lagarino '18	🍷 4
⊙ Primitivo Rosato Maddalena '19	🍷 2
○ SenS02 Bianco '19	🍷 2
● Aglianico del Vulture Loukania '11	ΥΥ 4
● Il Lucano '16	ΥΥ 4
● Matera I Sassi '15	ΥΥ 3
● Matera Moro I Sassi '14	ΥΥ 3
● Matera Moro I Sassi '11	ΥΥ 3*
● Matera Primitivo I Sassi '17	ΥΥ 3
● Matera Primitivo I Sassi '16	ΥΥ 3*
● Primitivo '12	ΥΥ 3*
⊙ Primitivo Rosato Maddalena '17	ΥΥ 2*
● Senso2 Rosso '18	ΥΥ 3

Terra dei Re

via Monticchio km 2,700
85028 Rionero in Vulture [PZ]
Tel. +39 0972725116
www.terradeire.com

CELLAR SALES
PRE-BOOKED VISITS
ACCOMMODATION AND RESTAURANT SERVICE
ANNUAL PRODUCTION 70,000 bottles
HECTARES UNDER VINE 11.00
SUSTAINABLE WINERY

This lovely winery set up in 2000 is a joint venture between the Leone and Rabasco families; today it's moving at full speed. The modern cellar is located in the municipality of Rionero in Vulture, where the wine matures in volcanic underground caves, while the hectares planted with organic vineyards extend between Rionero, Barile, Melfi and Rapolla. Recent projects include a Pinot Nero vineyard at 800 meters of elevation, which makes for extremely pleasant expressions. Their style is marked by rich, intense and powerful wines: the star of the show is Aglianico del Vulture. Reorganization in recent years and changes in the winery's technical management have produced good results. The Aglianico Nocte '16 is elegant, deep, complex and solidly built and wins the winery's first Tre Bicchieri. While the new vintages of their other selections age in the cellar, we can recommend the fruity, fresh red, Lerà '19, and its white counterpart.

Wine	Rating
● Aglianico del Vulture Nocte '16	TTT 4*
● Lerà '19	TT 2*
○ Lerà Malvasia '19	T 2
● Aglianico del Vulture Divinus '04	YY 4
● Aglianico del Vulture Divinus '03	YY 4
● Aglianico del Vulture Divinus '01	YY 4
● Aglianico del Vulture Nocte '15	YY 4
● Aglianico del Vulture Nocte '10	YY 4
● Aglianico del Vulture Sup. Divinus '13	YY 4
● Aglianico del Vulture Sup. Divinus '12	YY 4
⊙ Lerà Rosato '18	YY 2*
● Vulcano 800 '15	YY 4
● Vulcano 800 Pinot Nero '17	YY 5

Cantina di Venosa

loc. Vignali
via Appia
85029 Venosa [PZ]
Tel. +39 097236702
www.cantinadivenosa.it

CELLAR SALES
PRE-BOOKED VISITS
ANNUAL PRODUCTION 1,000,000 bottles
HECTARES UNDER VINE 800.00
SUSTAINABLE WINERY

There are 400 grape grower members behind this historic cooperative founded in 1957, totaling 800 hectares of vineyards located in Venosa, Ripacandida, Maschito and Ginestra (the municipality with the most hectares under vine in the region); Aglianico prevails here, with Moscato and Malvasia completing the range of whites. Their flagship selections, which draw on their best plots, are Aglianico del Vulture Terre di Orazio, Carato Venusio and Verbo—rich, intense wines with sapid energy. Aglianico del Vulture Verbo '18 made it to our finals thanks to its intact fruit, rich texture, velvety tannins and lovely length. Alongside it is a very successful 2018 version of Baliaggio, a succulent, soft red with lovely nuances of herbs and Mediterranean scrub, and a Malvasia Verbo '19, with intense aromatic overtones.

Wine	Rating
● Aglianico del Vulture Verbo '18	TT 3*
● Aglianico del Vulture Baliaggio '18	TT 2*
● Aglianico del Vulture Terre di Orazio '18	TT 4
○ Verbo Malvasia '19	TT 3
⊙ Terre di Orazio Rosé '19	T 3
⊙ Verbo Rosé '19	T 3
● Aglianico del Vulture Carato Venusio '12	YY 6
● Aglianico del Vulture Gesualdo da Venosa '13	YY 5
● Aglianico del Vulture Gesualdo da Venosa '11	YY 5
● Aglianico del Vulture Sup. Carato Venusio '12	YY 6
● Aglianico del Vulture Terre di Orazio '17	YY 4
● Aglianico del Vulture Verbo '17	YY 3*

Alovini

s.da prov.le 123 bis km 7,350
85013 Genzano di Lucania [PZ]
Tel. +39 0971776372
www.alovini.it

CELLAR SALES
PRE-BOOKED VISITS
ANNUAL PRODUCTION 170,000 bottles
HECTARES UNDER VINE 18.00

- ● Aglianico del Vulture Alvolo '17 ΨΨ 4
- ● Aglianico del Vulture Armand '17 ΨΨ 3
- ● Cabànico '17 ΨΨ 3

Cantina Di Barile

s.da st.le 93
85022 Barile [PZ]
Tel. +39 0972770386
www.coviv.it

CELLAR SALES
PRE-BOOKED VISITS
ANNUAL PRODUCTION 130,000 bottles
HECTARES UNDER VINE 100.00

- ● Aglianico del Vulture Vetusto '16 ΨΨ 7
- ● Aglianico del Vulture '16 Ψ 3

Cantine Strapellum

c.da Scavone Lotti. 14/15
85028 Rionero in Vulture [PZ]
Tel. +39 0972083446
www.cantinestrapellum.com

CELLAR SALES
PRE-BOOKED VISITS
ANNUAL PRODUCTION 80,000 bottles
HECTARES UNDER VINE 21.00

- ● Aglianico del Vulture Fosso del Tiglio '16 ΨΨ 2*
- ○ Fiano Kline '19 Ψ 2
- ○ Il Nibbio Bianco '17 Ψ 3

Eleano

fraz. Pian dell'Altare
s.da prov.le 8
85028 Ripacandida [PZ]
Tel. +39 0972722273
www.eleano.it

CELLAR SALES
PRE-BOOKED VISITS
ACCOMMODATION
ANNUAL PRODUCTION 53,000 bottles
HECTARES UNDER VINE 7.50

- ● Aglianico del Vulture Eleano '17 ΨΨ 5

Eubea

s.da prov.le 8
85020 Ripacandida [PZ]
Tel. +39 3284312789
www.agricolaeubea.com

CELLAR SALES
PRE-BOOKED VISITS
ANNUAL PRODUCTION 40,000 bottles
HECTARES UNDER VINE 20.00
VITICULTURE METHOD Certified Organic

- ● Aglianico del Vulture Covo dei Briganti '18 ΨΨ 6
- ● Aglianico del Vulture Ròinos '18 Ψ 8

Masseria Lanzolla

loc. Masseria Lanzolla
75023 Montalbano Jonico [MT]
Tel. +39 0835691197
www.masserialanzolla.it

CELLAR SALES
PRE-BOOKED VISITS
ACCOMMODATION
ANNUAL PRODUCTION 100,000 bottles
HECTARES UNDER VINE 25.00
SUSTAINABLE WINERY

- ● Matera Moro Mons Albius '16 ΨΨ 2*
- ● Matera Primitivo Primebacche '16 ΨΨ 2*
- ● Monade '16 Ψ 2

Cantine Madonna delle Grazie

LOC. VIGNALI
VIA APPIA
85029 VENOSA [PZ]
TEL. +39 097235704
www.cantinemadonnadellegrazie.it

CELLAR SALES
PRE-BOOKED VISITS
ANNUAL PRODUCTION 18,000 bottles
HECTARES UNDER VINE 8.00
VITICULTURE METHOD Certified Organic

- ● Aglianico del Vulture Bauccio '15 ΨΨ 4
- ● Aglianico del Vulture Liscone '15 ΨΨ 3

Musto Carmelitano

VIA PIETRO NENNI, 23
85020 MASCHITO [PZ]
TEL. +39 097233312
www.mustocarmelitano.it

CELLAR SALES
PRE-BOOKED VISITS
ACCOMMODATION AND RESTAURANT SERVICE
ANNUAL PRODUCTION 25,000 bottles
HECTARES UNDER VINE 6.00
VITICULTURE METHOD Certified Organic

- ● Aglianico del Vulture Serra del Prete '17 ΨΨ 4
- ● Aglianico del Vulture '17 ΨΨ 6
- ● Aglianico del Vulture Pian del Moro '16 Ψ 4

Tenuta Parco dei Monaci

C.DA PARCO DEI MONACI
75100 MATERA
TEL. +39 0835259546
www.tenutaparcodeimonaci.it

PRE-BOOKED VISITS
ACCOMMODATION
ANNUAL PRODUCTION 20,000 bottles
HECTARES UNDER VINE 5.00
SUSTAINABLE WINERY

- ● Matera Moro Spaccasassi '17 ΨΨ 5
- ● Matera Primitivo Monacello '18 ΨΨ 4
- ⊙ Matera Rosato Rosapersempre '19 Ψ 3

Quarta Generazione

C.DA MACARICO
85022 BARILE [PZ]
TEL. +39 3342039805
www.quartagenerazione.com

ANNUAL PRODUCTION 20,000 bottles
HECTARES UNDER VINE 3.00
VITICULTURE METHOD Certified Organic

- ● Aglianico del Vulture '18 ΨΨ 4

Regio Cantina

LOC. PIANO REGIO
85029 VENOSA [PZ]
TEL. +39 057754011
www.tenutepiccini.it

CELLAR SALES
PRE-BOOKED VISITS
ANNUAL PRODUCTION 90,000 bottles
HECTARES UNDER VINE 15.00
VITICULTURE METHOD Certified Organic

- ● Aglianico del Vulture Donpà '17 ΨΨ 4
- ● Aglianico del Vulture Genesi '18 ΨΨ 2*

Vitis in Vulture

C.SO GIUSTINO FORTUNATO, 159
85024 LAVELLO [PZ]
TEL. +39 097283983
www.vitisinvulture.com

ANNUAL PRODUCTION 50,000 bottles
HECTARES UNDER VINE 100.00

- ● Aglianico del Vulture Forentum '17 ΨΨ 3
- ● Aglianico del Vulture Sup. Forentum '16 ΨΨ 3
- ○ Labellum Chardonnay '19 ΨΨ 2*

PUGLIA

For years now we've been talking about Puglia's constant and continuous growth—this year we can once again attest to the fact. Indeed, the number of producers reviewed in our main section is now 44 (compared to 36 last year), thanks to a quality that can be found throughout the region.

It's true that in places this growth is more evident than in others, as can be seen in Gioia del Colle and Manduria. In short, despite the difficult times we're facing, it's a positive trajectory, and we believe that comes down to a couple of things. The first is that attention has grown for the way of cultivating and working Primitivo. The grape is increasingly a benchmark for its quality characteristics, its ability to best express the territories of origin and its expressive versatility, a versatility that allows producers to make wines of great quality both when the grapes used come from bush-trained vines and when they come from young vines. The result is wines that are clearly different but can be excellent for their respective typologies. The second is the growth of the importance and quality of Puglia's denominated wines, which lend prominence not only to the cultivar, but also to the territory (whereas until recently most producers focused on their individual brands). When it comes to the Tre Bicchieri awarded, there is an absolute newbie: Terre dei Vaaz, a young winery in Gioia del Colle in its second year of production that won us over with its Onirico '18, a monovarietal Primitivo (not denominated). We close with a criticism, completed ignored, that we've been leveling for some years now: in Puglia there is now an 'invasion of the heavy weights', or rather, ultra-heavy bottles (those weighing over a kilo), in the erroneous belief that such bottles are 'prestigious'. The result is that bottles weighing almost 2 kilograms travel around the world in defiance of any idea of sustainability, especially the resulting carbon footprint. It's simply unacceptable, in particular for producers who proudly bear the 'organic certification' logo.

Amastuola

via Appia Km 632,200
74016 Massafra [TA]
Tel. +39 0998805668
www.amastuola.it

CELLAR SALES
PRE-BOOKED VISITS
ACCOMMODATION AND RESTAURANT SERVICE
ANNUAL PRODUCTION 360,000 bottles
HECTARES UNDER VINE 109.00
VITICULTURE METHOD Certified Organic
SUSTAINABLE WINERY

Situated in the heart of the Terra delle Gravine Regional Natural Park, the Montanaro family's winery is housed within a large, 15th-century masseria with a closed courtyard, and is surrounded by more than 100 hectares of organic vineyards. The large property hosts the territory's classic grapes, such as Primitivo or Malvasia, as well as international ones, like Merlot and Chardonnay. All the wines proposed are technically well made, with particular attention paid to the pleasantness and richness of fruit. The Primitivo Lamarossa '17, a wine marked by notes of flowers and red fruit, proves clear, focused and assertive, marked by a lovely typicity. Their Capocanale '17, a sapid Merlot, has nice structure and freshness, playing more on vegetal hints and black fruit, while the Calaprice '19, a delectable blend of Sauvignon, Chardonnay and Fiano, surprised us for its pleasantness and aromatic brilliance. Finally, the Aglianico Ondarosa '19, a sapid, spicy rosé, also proves well made.

○ Calaprice '19	🍷🍷 2*
● Capocanale '17	🍷🍷 3
● Lamarossa '17	🍷🍷 3
⊙ Ondarosa '19	🍷🍷 2*
● L'Onda del Tempo '17	🍷 3
● Primitivo '18	🍷 3
○ Salento Bianco '19	🍷 2
● Aglianico '13	🍷🍷 3
● Centosassi '15	🍷🍷 5
● Lamarossa '15	🍷🍷 2*
● Lamarossa '14	🍷🍷 2*
● Onda del Tempo '16	🍷🍷 3
● Vignatorta '13	🍷🍷 2*

Giuseppe Attanasio

via per Oria, 13
74024 Manduria [TA]
Tel. +39 0999737121
www.primitivo-attanasio.com

ANNUAL PRODUCTION 15,000 bottles
HECTARES UNDER VINE 7.00

The Attanasio family's small winery has been bottling its own products for twenty years now, and should be considered one of Primitivo di Manduria's top producers. A few hectares of vineyards planted with Apulian bush-trained vines lie on a substratum of calcareous tufa rock, making for a range based entirely around Primitivo - the only grape cultivated in the estate vineyards. The result is a handful of traditional wines in which typicity and territorial identity come together with traction and complexity. The Primitivo di Manduria Dolce Naturale is once again at the top of its class. The 2015 is generous on the nose, with notes of aromatic herbs, gingerbread, cinnamon, bottled cherries and chocolate, while a long and pleasant palate exhibits vigor and nice structure. The Primitivo di Manduria Riserva Ventesima Vendemmia '14 is also charming, with hints of cinnamon and Mediterranean scrub on the nose and a palate marked by considerable depth, finishing fruity, long and juicy.

● Primitivo di Manduria Dolce Naturale '15	🍷🍷 5
● Primitivo di Manduria Ventesima Vendemmia Ris. '14	🍷🍷 6
● Primitivo di Manduria '14	🍷🍷 5
⊙ Primitivo Rosato '19	🍷🍷 3
● Primitivo di Manduria '15	🍷🍷 5
● Primitivo di Manduria '13	🍷🍷 5
● Primitivo di Manduria Dolce Naturale '18	🍷🍷 5
● Primitivo di Manduria Dolce Naturale '13	🍷🍷 5
● Primitivo di Manduria Dolce Naturale '12	🍷🍷 5
● Primitivo di Manduria Ris. '13	🍷🍷 6
⊙ Primitivo Rosato '18	🍷🍷 3
⊙ Primitivo Rosato '16	🍷🍷 3

Cantele

S.DA PROV.LE SALICE SALENTINO-SAN DONACI KM 35,600
73010 GUAGNANO [LE]
TEL. +39 0832705010
www.cantele.it

CELLAR SALES
PRE-BOOKED VISITS
ANNUAL PRODUCTION 1,500,000 bottles
HECTARES UNDER VINE 48.00

For over forty years the Cantele family's winery, run by cousins Luisa, Gianni, Paolo and Umberto, has been one of Puglia's best known producers. Today it offers a wide range of modern wines, technically well crafted, while not lacking in typicity or pleasantness. The vineyards are located in Guagnano, Montemesola and San Pietro Vernotico on a predominantly red soil. In addition to Chardonnay, which gives rise to some of Cantele's historic wines, the area's traditional grape varieties are cultivated. The Salice Salentino Rosso Riserva is back at the top of their range. The 2017 features strong hints of blackberries and blueberries on the nose, while the palate exhibits pluck and tension, with a long, crisp finish rich in fruit. The Negroamaro Rosato '19 is pleasant and fresh in its floral notes and hints of red berries, while the Teresa Manara Chardonnay Five September '18 is interesting and complex. Both the classic Amativo '17 and the gutsy Rohesia Malvasia Bianca '19 also prove well made.

Wine	Rating
● Salice Salentino Rosso Ris. '17	🍷🍷 2*
● Amativo '17	🍷🍷 4
⊙ Negroamaro Rosato '19	🍷🍷 2*
○ Rohesia Malvasia Bianca '19	🍷🍷 2*
○ Teresa Manara Chardonnay Cinque Settembre '18	🍷🍷 4
● Fanòi Negroamaro '15	🍷 6
● Fanòi Primitivo '15	🍷 6
⊙ Rohesia Negroamaro Rosato '19	🍷 3
● Rohesia Susumaniello '18	🍷 2
○ Teresa Manara Chardonnay '19	🍷 3
● Teresa Manara Negroamaro '17	🍷 3
○ Verdeca '19	🍷 2
● Amativo '07	🍷🍷🍷 4*
● Amativo '03	🍷🍷🍷 3*
● Salice Salentino Rosso Ris. '09	🍷🍷🍷 2*

★Carvinea

LOC. PEZZA D'ARENA
VIA PER SERRANOVA
72012 CAROVIGNO [BR]
TEL. +39 3483738581
www.carvinea.com

CELLAR SALES
PRE-BOOKED VISITS
ACCOMMODATION AND RESTAURANT SERVICE
ANNUAL PRODUCTION 70,000 bottles
HECTARES UNDER VINE 10.00
VITICULTURE METHOD Certified Organic

In fewer than twenty years, Beppe di Maria has managed to build a winery whose success can't be in doubt. The small range of wines offered by Carvinea exhibits great aromatic clarity and technical precision, proving pleasant and rich in fruit. Their vineyards, which surround the cellar in the countryside of Carovigno, enjoy the salty and iodine-rich air that blows in off the two seas, the Ionian and the Adriatic, on either side of Salento. The territory's traditional grapes are grown: Negroamaro, Ottavianello and Primitivo. The Otto '18, a monovarietal Octavianello, affirms its remarkable charm, playing on floral and berry notes, with a palate that's both fresh and nicely textured. Black fruits and undergrowth characterize the well-crafted Negroamaro '18, while the Primitivo of the same vintage is pleasant, playing on fruit. The Merularosa '19 is once again gratifyingly fresh in its tones of pomegranate and currant.

Wine	Rating
● Otto '18	🍷🍷🍷 5
⊙ Merularosa '19	🍷🍷 3
● Negroamaro '18	🍷🍷 3
● Primitivo '18	🍷🍷 3
○ Lucerna '19	🍷 3
⊙ Ottorosa '19	🍷 3
● Frauma '08	🍷🍷🍷 4
● Merula '11	🍷🍷🍷 3*
● Negroamaro '17	🍷🍷🍷 5
● Negroamaro '14	🍷🍷🍷 5
● Negroamaro '13	🍷🍷🍷 5
● Negroamaro '11	🍷🍷🍷 3*
● Otto '16	🍷🍷🍷 4*
● Primitivo '15	🍷🍷🍷 5
● Sierma '09	🍷🍷🍷 5

Castello Monaci

VIA CASE SPARSE
73015 SALICE SALENTINO [LE]
TEL. +39 0831665700
www.castellomonaci.it

CELLAR SALES
PRE-BOOKED VISITS
RESTAURANT SERVICE
ANNUAL PRODUCTION 1,900,000 bottles
HECTARES UNDER VINE 210.00

The Memmo family has been overseeing Castello Monaci, the winery at the gates of Salice Salentino (now part of Gruppo Italiano Vini), for four generations now. More than 200 hectares of vineyards are divided into three estates located on different soils: sandy (close to the sea, where white grapes are grown), iron-rich red soil (where Primitivo is cultivated), and clay-tuff (where various native red grapes are grown). A wide range of well-made and modern wines is offered. This year the Petraluce Verdeca '19 is particularly good, with green citrus tones on the nose, and a taut, plucky, pleasant palate. The Salice Salentino Liante '19 also put in a good performance, with its hints of spices and Mediterranean scrub, and a sapid and fruity palate. The classic Kreos, a Negroamaro rosé, is smooth and pleasantly gratifying, while the Primitivo Pilùna '19 proves fresh and fruity. As usual the rest of their selection also did well.

Wine	Rating
⊙ Kreos '19	🍷🍷 2*
○ Petraluce '19	🍷🍷 2*
● Pilùna '19	🍷🍷 2*
● Salice Salentino Rosso Liante '19	🍷🍷 2*
○ Acante '19	🍷 2
● Coribante '18	🍷 2
○ Heos '19	🍷 2
● Maru '19	🍷 2
○ Moscatello Selvatico Passito '19	🍷 3
● Artas '07	🍸🍸🍸 5
● Artas '06	🍸🍸🍸 4
● Artas '05	🍸🍸🍸 4*
● Artas '04	🍸🍸🍸 3*
⊙ Kreos '18	🍸🍸 2*
● Maru '18	🍸🍸 2*
● Pilùna '18	🍸🍸 2*
○ Simera '18	🍸🍸 2*

Giancarlo Ceci

C.DA SANT'AGOSTINO
76123 ANDRIA [BT]
TEL. +39 0883565220
www.giancarloceci.com

PRE-BOOKED VISITS
ANNUAL PRODUCTION 350,000 bottles
HECTARES UNDER VINE 60.00
VITICULTURE METHOD Certified Biodynamic
SUSTAINABLE WINERY

The estate of Giancarlo Ceci comprises more than 200 hectares situated at 250 meters above sea level, in Andria and Castel del Monte (this last hosts a large contiguous vineyard that benefits from the presence of the nearby sea). For eight generations the Ceci family have been producing wine here. Today in the vineyard, cultivated organically since 1988 and biodynamic since 2011, we find the area's classic grapes, foremost Nero di Troia. Their wines are modern, with freshness and aromatic precision serving as their distinct stylistic features. The Castel del Monte Rosso Parco Grande '19 opens with notes of cherries and black fruits accompanied by spicy hints, while the palate exhibits pluck, immediately gratifying sensations and nice length. The rosé Castel del Monte Bombino Nero Parchitello '19 is pleasant and floral, while the the Castel del Monte Chardonnay Pozzo Sorgente '19 offers up citrus tones on the nose and an expansive palate. The rest of their selection also did well.

Wine	Rating
● Castel del Monte Rosso Parco Grande '19	🍷🍷 2*
⊙ Castel del Monte Bombino Nero Parchitello '19	🍷🍷 2*
○ Castel del Monte Chardonnay Pozzo Sorgente '19	🍷🍷 3
● Almagia Zero Solfiti Aggiunti '19	🍷 2
○ Castel del Monte Bombino Bianco Panascio '19	🍷 2
○ Clara Fiano '18	🍷 4
○ Castel del Monte Bombino Bianco Panascio '17	🍸🍸 2*
⊙ Castel del Monte Bombino Nero Rosato Parchitello '17	🍸🍸 2*
● Castel del Monte Rosso Parco Grande '18	🍸🍸 2*
○ Moscato di Trani Dolce Rosalia '18	🍸🍸 4

★Tenute Chiaromonte

B.GO ANNUNZIATA
70021 ACQUAVIVA DELLE FONTI [BA]
TEL. +39 080768156
www.tenutechiaromonte.com

CELLAR SALES
PRE-BOOKED VISITS
ANNUAL PRODUCTION 150,000 bottles
HECTARES UNDER VINE 45.00

Tenute Chiaromonte is among those producers leading the rebirth of the Gioia del Colle appellation and its Primitivo. The estate's vineyards are located at elevations of over 300 meters in Gioia del Colle, mainly on calcareous soils rich in minerals. The attention paid to the old bush-trained vines has led Nicola Chiaromonte and Paolo Montanaro to manage about 10 hectares of Primitivo that go back more than 60 years. The wines produced are among the most alluring and complex on the market. Yet another excellent performance from the 2017 version of their Contrada Barbatto. Hints of berries and white mulberry are followed by a fresh, taut palate rich in fruit, finishing on great sapidity and length. Equally successful but different in style, the Riserva '15 proves richer,fuller, expansive yet assertive. The fresh and approachable Elè '18 proves well made, as does the Donna Carlotta '17, a rich but balanced sweet wine. It's also worth mentioning the debut of their Chiaromonte Ancestrale Rosé '17, a truly promising Pinot Nero Metodo Classico.

Wine	Rating
● Gioia del Colle Primitivo Muro Sant'Angelo Contrada Barbatto '17	🍷🍷🍷 5
● Gioia del Colle Primitivo Ris. '15	🍷🍷 8
⊙ Chiaromonte Ancestrale M. Cl. Rosé '17	🍷🍷 6
● Donna Carlotta '17	🍷🍷 4
● Elè '18	🍷🍷 3
○ Kimìa Fiano '19	🍷🍷 3
⊙ Kimìa Pinot Nero Rosato '19	🍷🍷 3
● Le Maschere Primitivo '18	🍷🍷 2*
⊙ Kimìa Primitivo Rosato '19	🍷 3
● Gioia del Colle Primitivo Muro Sant'Angelo Contrada Barbatto '16	YYY 5
● Gioia del Colle Primitivo Muro Sant'Angelo Contrada Barbatto '15	YYY 5
● Gioia del Colle Primitivo Muro Sant'Angelo Contrada Barbatto '14	YYY 5

Coppi

S.DA PROV.LE TURI - GIOIA DEL COLLE
70010 TURI [BA]
TEL. +39 0808915049
www.vinicoppi.it

CELLAR SALES
PRE-BOOKED VISITS
RESTAURANT SERVICE
ANNUAL PRODUCTION 900,000 bottles
HECTARES UNDER VINE 100.00
VITICULTURE METHOD Certified Organic

Lisia, Miriam and Doni Coppi run the family business established in 1976 by their father, Antonio, who took over a winery founded in 1882. The vineyards are all located in Turi and Gioia del Colle and about half are bush-trained vines. All the wines produced, which exhibit a modern style, good territorial identity and aromatic precision, are made using native grapes: Primitivo, Aleatico, Malvasia Nera and Negroamaro for the reds; Falanghina, Malvasia Bianca and Verdeca for the whites. Back at the top of their range with a 2017, the Gioia del Colle Primitivo Senatore is a sapid, plucky wine with nice body and volume, offering up spicy sensations and black fruits. Their other Primitivos also delivered, even if they're of varying styles. If the Don Antonio '18 is rich and marked by ripe fruit, the Siniscalco '18 is nicely fresh, long and quite supple. Finally, the Negroamaro Rosato Coré '19, with its floral and wild strawberry sensations, proves highly pleasant and drinkable.

Wine	Rating
● Gioia del Colle Primitivo Senatore '17	🍷🍷🍷 5
⊙ Coré '19	🍷🍷 2*
● Don Antonio Primitivo '18	🍷🍷 3
● Siniscalco Primitivo '18	🍷🍷 2*
● Vinaccero Aleatico '16	🍷🍷 3
● Cantonovo Primitivo '19	🍷 3
○ Guiscardo Falanghina '19	🍷 3
● Pellirosso Negroamaro '19	🍷 2
● Sannace Malvasia Nera '18	🍷 2
○ Serralto Malvasia Bianca '19	🍷 2
● Don Antonio Primitivo '17	YYY 3*
● Gioia del Colle Primitivo Senatore '15	YYY 5
● Gioia del Colle Primitivo Senatore '11	YYY 5
● Gioia del Colle Primitivo Senatore '10	YYY 3*

Crifo - Cantina di Ruvo di Puglia

via Madonna delle Grazie, 8a
70037 Ruvo di Puglia [BA]
Tel. +39 0803601611
www.cantinacrifo.it

CELLAR SALES
PRE-BOOKED VISITS
ANNUAL PRODUCTION 2,000,000 bottles
HECTARES UNDER VINE 1500.00

Founded in 1960 by 27 members, this cooperative winery now has about 1100 members and cultivates some 1500 hectares of land. The vineyards are located in the Murgia of Bari, in a hilly area (in the Castel del Monte appellation, in particular), and exclusively native grapes are grown. In addition to Nero di Troia, cornerstones include Bombino Bianco, Bombino Nero and the almost-extinct Moscatello Selvatico. The wines produced are modern, with a particular attention to richness of fruit and drinkability. The Castel del Monte Nero di Troia Augustale Riserva '15 is splendid with its aromas of black berries, floral nuances and a fruity, deep palate, with a long, juicy finish. The Castel del Monte Rosato Terre del Crifo '19 is also well made with its notes of wild strawberries, and a sapid, smooth palate, as is the fresh and approachable Bellagriffi Moscatello Selvatico '19, with its varietal notes of sage and hints of tropical fruit.

Wine	Rating
● Castel del Monte Nero di Troia Augustale Ris. '15	TT 5
○ Bellagriffi '19	TT 3
⊙ Castel del Monte Rosato Terre del Crifo '19	TT 3
● Castel del Monte Bombino Nero Augustale '19	T 3
● Squarcione '19	T 4
● Terre del Crifo Nero di Troia '19	T 3
⊙ Castel del Monte Rosato '18	YY 1*
● Nero di Troia '18	YY 3

★Cantine Due Palme

via San Marco, 130
72020 Cellino San Marco [BR]
Tel. +39 0831617865
www.cantineduepalme.it

CELLAR SALES
PRE-BOOKED VISITS
ACCOMMODATION AND RESTAURANT SERVICE
ANNUAL PRODUCTION 17,000,000 bottles
HECTARES UNDER VINE 2500.00

Founded by Angelo Maci in 1989, this large cooperative's growers (more than 1,000) cultivate 2500 hectares of vineyards. A part of these are managed directly by the co-op's vast team of experts, who operate in various facilities (in addition to the one in Cellino San Marco). Their range encompasses all the region's most important appellations, and is successfully exported throughout the world. Due Palme recently acquired Castello di Cellino San Marco. The property will be open to whomever and represent the producer to the public. When it comes to their wines, the Salice Salentino Selvarossa always has a place of honour. This year we resist the temptation to reward it to make room for a wine of great depth: the 1943 del Presidente, a blend of Primitivo and Aglianico from a historic, bush-trained vineyard that goes back more than 50 years. It has concentration, elegance, fruit, smooth tannins and a very long aromatic persistence. But from the new Seraia line to their more classic wines, the entire range is commendable.

Wine	Rating
● 1943 del Presidente '18	TTT 8
● Salice Salentino Rosso Selvarossa Ris. '17	TT 6
● Selvamara Negroamaro '17	TT 4
● Ettamiano Primitivo '18	TT 3
● Salice Salentino Rosso Selvarossa Terra Ris. '12	TT 5
● Seraia Negroamaro e Cabernet Sauvignon '19	TT 3
● Seraia Negroamaro e Malvasia Nera '19	TT 3
● Seraia Negroamaro e Merlot '19	TT 3
● Seraia Negroamaro e Primitivo '19	TT 3
● Seraia Negroamaro e Syrah '19	TT 3
● Serre Susumaniello '19	TT 4
● Salice Salentino Rosso Selvarossa Ris. '16	YYY 4*

Tenute Eméra di Claudio Quarta

FRAZ. MARINA DI LIZZANO
C.DA PORVICA, SDA. PROV.LE 124
74020 LIZZANO [TA]
TEL. +39 0832704398
www.claudioquarta.it

CELLAR SALES
PRE-BOOKED VISITS
RESTAURANT SERVICE
ANNUAL PRODUCTION 400,000 bottles
HECTARES UNDER VINE 55.00
SUSTAINABLE WINERY

15 years have passed since Claudio Quarta decided to exchange his research role and career as a biotechnology entrepreneur for harvesting grapes and making wine. Today, together with his daughter Alessandra, he manages two wineries in Puglia (in addition to the Sanpaolo winery in Irpinia). Tenute Eméra is made up of 50 hectares near Lizzano, while Cantina Moros is just over a hectare in Guagnano. Their traditionally-styled range of wines pursues, above all, pleasantness and richness of fruit. This year we find the Salice Salentino Rosso Riserva Moros '17 at the fore, a wine from that hectare of old bush-trained vines in Guagnano. The nose features hints of fresh black fruits followed by light, spicy notes. The palate is consistent, assertive and sapid, with a long, pleasant finish. The Anima di Chardonnay Révolution '18 is also intriguing, combining buttery, balsamic tones with a gutsy palate and a fresh, citrus finish.

Wine	Rating
● Salice Salentino Rosso Moros Ris. '17	🍷🍷 4
○ Anima di Chardonnay R Revolution '18	🍷🍷 3
● Sud del Sud '18	🍷🍷 3
○ Amure '19	🍷 3
○ Bianco di Negroamaro '19	🍷 3
⊙ La Vigne en Rose '19	🍷 3
● Lizzano Negroamaro Sup. Anima di Negroamaro '17	🍸🍸 2*
● Lizzano Negroamaro Sup. Anima di Negroamaro '16	🍸🍸 2*
● Primitivo di Manduria Anima di Primitivo '16	🍸🍸 3*
⊙ Rose '18	🍸🍸 3
● Salice Salentino Rosso Moros Ris. '16	🍸🍸 4
● Sud del Sud '17	🍸🍸 3
● Sud del Sud '16	🍸🍸 3

Felline

S.DA COMUNALE SANTO STASI I, 4B
74024 MANDURIA [TA]
TEL. +39 0999711660
www.agricolafelline.it

CELLAR SALES
PRE-BOOKED VISITS
ANNUAL PRODUCTION 1,000,000 bottles
HECTARES UNDER VINE 120.00
VITICULTURE METHOD Certified Organic
SUSTAINABLE WINERY

For over a quarter of a century, Gregory Perrucci has been among those leading a revival in the winemaking traditions of Salento, especially through the recovery and development of old Apulian bush-trained vines. The vineyards are situated in various parts of the Primitivo di Manduria appellation and on different types of soil, from sandy ones, near the sea, to rocky terrain, from red to black soil. The wines are modern, elegant, rich in fruit and exhibit great aromatic clarity. With the 2018 version, the Primitivo di Manduria Sinfarosa Zinfandel once again proves that it's a flagship for the appellation, and one of the region's best. Hints of Mediterranean scrub and black fruits give way to a palate that's complex yet pleasant, making for a wine that manages to combine fullness and ease of drinking. Fresh and approachable, with light vegetal notes, the Nero di Troia Trullari '19 performed well, as did the always-juicy, fruity and highly drinkable Alberello '19.

Wine	Rating
● Primitivo di Manduria Sinfarosa Zinfandel '18	🍷🍷🍷 4*
● Alberello '19	🍷🍷 2*
● Alcione '19	🍷🍷 2*
⊙ Cicala Rosé '19	🍷🍷 2*
● Malvasia Nera '19	🍷🍷 2*
● Sangiovese Primitivo '19	🍷🍷 2*
● Segnavento '19	🍷🍷 2*
● Trullari Nero di Troia '19	🍷🍷 2*
● I Monili '19	🍷 2
● Primitivo di Manduria Terra Rossa '19	🍷 3
○ Verdeca '19	🍷 2
● Primitivo di Manduria Sinfarosa Zinfandel '15	🍸🍸🍸 3*
● Primitivo di Manduria Zinfandel Sinfarosa Terra Nera '17	🍸🍸🍸 4*

Gianfranco Fino

via Piave, 12
74028 Sava [TA]
Tel. +39 0997773970
www.gianfrancofino.it

PRE-BOOKED VISITS
ANNUAL PRODUCTION 20,000 bottles
HECTARES UNDER VINE 21.00
SUSTAINABLE WINERY

Founded about 15 years ago around an old, one-hectare vineyard, Gianfranco Fino and Simona Natale's winery now oversees 21 hectares, some of which are rented, all planted with bush-trained vines that, in many cases, go back more than 50 years. Primitivo dominates along with a small amount of Negroamaro. When it comes to the vineyard, their approach is strongly anchored to tradition, while their enological style and production approach is progressive, especially when it comes to the Es. As usual Simona and Gianfranco only submitted the Es for tasting. This monovarietal Primitivo comes from 60-year-old vineyards that grow in red soil, with a yield of about 20 quintals per hectare and nine-month maturation in small, half new barrels. The 2018 features classic hints of black fruits and Mediterranean scrub, while the palate, dense but also balanced, proves surprisingly fresh, with a sapid, long and very pleasant finish.

● Es '18	🍷🍷	7
● Primitivo di Manduria Es '12	YYY	7
● Primitivo di Manduria Es '11	YYY	7
● Primitivo di Manduria Es '10	YYY	6
● Primitivo di Manduria Es '09	YYY	6
● Primitivo di Manduria Es '08	YYY	6
● Primitivo di Manduria Es '07	YYY	6
● Primitivo di Manduria Es '06	YYY	5
● Es '17	YY	7
● Es '16	YY	7
● Es '15	YY	7
● Primitivo di Manduria Dolce Naturale Es + Sole '12	YY	7
● Primitivo di Manduria Es '14	YY	7
● Primitivo di Manduria Es '13	YY	7

Vito Donato Giuliani

via Gioia Canale, 18
70010 Turi [BA]
Tel. +39 0808915335
www.vitivinicolagiuliani.com

ANNUAL PRODUCTION 100,000 bottles
HECTARES UNDER VINE 40.00

Founded more than eighty years ago, the Giuliani family's winery has played a lead role in the Gioia del Colle appellation's great success, thanks to a modern production approach that's attentive to technical precision and territorial identity. Their vineyards are situated in Turi and Gioia del Colle, in the heart of Murgia Barese, where the mineral-rich karst terrain consists of a thin layer of red soil spread over a rocky base. Always one of the appellation's best, the 2017 Gioia del Colle Primitivo Baronaggio Riserva offers up notes of black berry fruits and curious nuances of curry, while a juicy, sapid palate comes through with nice pulp and freshness. The Gioia del Colle Primitivo Lavarossa '17 also delivered, playing more on tones of berries and cinchona. In the mouth it's plucky, with a pleasant, slightly bitterish finish.

● Gioia del Colle Primitivo Baronaggio Ris. '17	🍷🍷	5
● Gioia del Colle Primitivo Lavarossa '17	🍷🍷	3
● Trelamie '19	🍷	3
● Gioia del Colle Primitivo Baronaggio Ris. '15	YYY	5
○ Chiancaia '18	YY	3
○ Chiancaia '17	YY	3
● Gioia del Colle Aleatico Cantone di Cristo '15	YY	4
● Gioia del Colle Baronaggio Ris. '13	YY	5
● Gioia del Colle Primitivo Baronaggio Ris. '16	YY	5
● Gioia del Colle Primitivo Lavarossa '14	YY	3
● Gioia del Colle Primitivo Lavarossa '13	YY	3
● Gioia del Colle Primitivo Lavarossa '12	YY	3*

Cantine Paolo Leo

via Turturano, 21
72025 San Donaci [BR]
Tel. +39 0831635073
www.paololeo.it

CELLAR SALES
PRE-BOOKED VISITS
ACCOMMODATION
ANNUAL PRODUCTION 3,000,000 bottles
HECTARES UNDER VINE 45.00
VITICULTURE METHOD Certified Organic

The Leo family's winery offers a wide range, over forty wines made with grapes from their own vineyards and from estates managed for several years in collaboration with trusted growers. Their private plots are all located in the municipality of San Donaci, on tufaceous and calcareous soils, and are mostly bush-trained vines. The wines proposed are modern, technically impeccable, often rich in fruit, and are marked by a particular attention to varietal expression. The Orfeo Negroamaro is back at the top with a 2018 redolent of black berry fruits, porcini mushrooms and Mediterranean scrub. On the palate it exhibits nice texture, firmness and sapidity, with a long finish in which black berry sensations reemerge. The 350 Alture Verdeca '18 proves well made, with tones of blood orange, nice pulp and acidity, as does the Primitivo di Manduria Passo del Cardinale '19, a spicy wine rich in fruit.

Wine	Rating
● Orfeo Negroamaro '18	🍷🍷🍷 5
○ 350 Alture Minutolo '18	🍷🍷 3
○ 350 Alture Verdeca '18	🍷🍷 3
● Primitivo di Manduria Passo del Cardinale '19	🍷🍷 3
○ Alture Bianco d'Alessano '18	🍷 3
○ Numen '19	🍷 4
● Orfeo Negroamaro '16	🍷🍷🍷 5
● Orfeo Negroamaro '15	🍷🍷🍷 4*
● Primitivo di Manduria Passo del Cardinale '14	🍷🍷🍷 3*
● Taccorosso Negroamaro '15	🍷🍷🍷 6
● Orfeo Negroamaro '17	🍷🍷 5
● Primitivo di Manduria Passo del Cardinale '18	🍷🍷 3
● Primitivo di Manduria Passo del Cardinale '17	🍷🍷 3

★Leone de Castris

via Senatore de Castris, 26
73015 Salice Salentino [LE]
Tel. +39 0832731112
www.leonedecastris.com

PRE-BOOKED VISITS
ACCOMMODATION AND RESTAURANT SERVICE
ANNUAL PRODUCTION 2,500,000 bottles
HECTARES UNDER VINE 300.00
SUSTAINABLE WINERY

Leone de Castris is a symbol of Salento winemaking, having a number of estates throughout the municipalities of Salice Salentino, Campi and Guagnano. Half of these are planted with bush-trained vines, with both native and international varieties cultivated. The result is a wide range, with over forty different wines produced, all technically well made and marked by a modern approach. Approachable selections rich in fruit alternative with wines that are more complex and ageworthy. The splendid Five Roses 76th Anniversary '19 is elegant on the nose, with floral hints and notes of small berries, while the palate is long, fine and fresh—highly drinkable and pleasant. The Five Roses '19 is a bit softer than its older brother but still delivers convincingly. The Lemos Susumaniello '19, with its spicy tones and hints of black fruits, exhibits freshness and good pulp, while the Salice Salentino Rosso Riserva Donna Lisa '17 plays more on tones of ripe fruit, proving rich and structured.

Wine	Rating
⊙ Five Roses 76° Anniversario '19	🍷🍷 3*
● Salice Salentino Rosso Donna Lisa Ris. '17	🍷🍷 5
⊙ Five Roses '19	🍷🍷 2*
● Il Lemos Susumaniello '19	🍷🍷 2*
⊙ Salice Salentino Brut Rosé M.Cl. Five Roses '17	🍷🍷 4
⊙ Salice Salentino Brut Rosé M.Cl. Five Roses Anniversario '15	🍷🍷 4
● Elo Veni '19	🍷 2
● Primitivo di Manduria Villa Santera '19	🍷 2
⊙ Villa Santera '17	🍷 3
⊙ Five Roses 74° Anniversario '17	🍷🍷🍷 3*
● Salice Salentino Rosso Donna Lisa Ris. '16	🍷🍷🍷 5
● Salice Salentino Rosso Per Lui Ris. '15	🍷🍷🍷 6

Masseria Li Veli

s.da prov.le Cellino-Campi, km 1
72020 Cellino San Marco [BR]
Tel. +39 0831618259
www.liveli.it

CELLAR SALES
PRE-BOOKED VISITS
ANNUAL PRODUCTION 500,000 bottles
HECTARES UNDER VINE 36.00
SUSTAINABLE WINERY

The vineyards of Masseria Li Veli, owned by the Falvo family, are divided into two estates. One is next to the cellar, outside Cellino San Marco, where the soil is sandy and red and mainly red grape varieties are grown on Apulian bush-trained vines. The other is the Valle d'Itria, where white grapes are grown. The wines produced, often monovarietals, are modern, with particular attention to the varietal expression of the various cultivars used. With the 2019 version, the Askos Verdeca once again confirms its reputation as one of Puglia's best whites. Fresh scents of citrus fruits, Mediterranean scrub and lavender are followed by a rich, assertive palate, sapid and long. The Askos Malvasia Nera '18 is highly pleasant, slightly aromatic, rich in fruit and easy to drink, while the Salice Salentino Riserva Pezzo Morgana '17 plays more on spicy notes on the nose, with a palate of solid structure and nice verve.

Wine	Rating
○ Askos Verdeca '19	🍷🍷🍷 4*
● Salice Salentino Rosso Pezzo Morgana Ris. '17	🍷🍷 4
● Askos Malvasia Nera '18	🍷🍷 4
● Askos Primitivo '18	🍷🍷 4
● Askos Susumaniello '19	🍷🍷 4
⊙ Askos Susumaniello Rosato '19	🍷 4
○ Askos Verdeca '18	🍷🍷🍷 4*
○ Askos Verdeca '17	🍷🍷🍷 3*
● Masseria Li Veli '10	🍷🍷🍷 5
● Aleatico Passito '10	🍷🍷 8
● Askos Susumaniello '18	🍷🍷 4
⊙ Askos Susumaniello Rosato '18	🍷🍷 3
⊙ Askos Susumaniello Rosato '17	🍷🍷 2*
● Masseria Li Veli '17	🍷🍷 7
● Salice Salentino Rosso Pezzo Morgana Ris. '16	🍷🍷 4

Cantina Sociale di Lizzano

c.so Europa, 34/39
74020 Lizzano [TA]
Tel. +39 0999552013
www.cantinelizzano.it

CELLAR SALES
PRE-BOOKED VISITS
ANNUAL PRODUCTION 1,000,000 bottles
HECTARES UNDER VINE 500.00

Founded in 1959, today the cooperative comprises 400 growers, who cultivate about 500 hectares of vineyards, mostly located on the area's characteristic red soil. Here we find the region's classic grapes (Primitivo, Negroamaro, Malvasia Nera, Moscato), with a notable presence of bush-trained vines. Their style is modern, attentive to richness of fruit and pleasantness. This year they presented a superb line-up. The Lizzano Negroamaro Manorossa '18 features hints of black berries, spices and pencil lead on the nose, while on the palate it comes through rich in fruit, nicely balancing tannins and acidity, with a long, juicy finish. The Primitivo di Manduria Manonera '17 is just as good, with its red fruit sensations and nuances of curry, standing out on the palate for its energy, length and sapidity.

Wine	Rating
● Lizzano Negroamaro Manorossa '18	🍷🍷 6
● Primitivo di Manduria Manonera '17	🍷🍷 6
● Primitivo di Manduria Dolce Naturale Mandoro '17	🍷🍷 6
● Primitivo di Manduria Macchia '17	🍷 2

Masca del Tacco

VIA TRIPOLI, 5/7
72020 ERCHIE [BR]
TEL. +39 0831759786
www.mascadeltacco.com

ANNUAL PRODUCTION 300,000 bottles
HECTARES UNDER VINE 140.00

At Masca del Tacco, Felice Mergè (owner of Poggio Le Volpi in the Castelli Romani) avails himself of a large estate in the triangle formed by the municipalities of Erchie, Veglie and Torricella. The territory's traditional grapes, such as Primitivo, Negroamaro or Susumaniello, are accompanied by certain international varieties, such as Cabernet Sauvignon, Pinot Nero and Chardonnay. The modern and technically well-made wines offered pursue fruit and fullness. The 2017 version of the Primitivo di Manduria Piano Chiuso 26 27 63 Riserva affirms its role as the winery's flagship, with its scents of black fruits accompanied by spicy notes and an aromatically coherent, dense palate marked by an unexpected tannic vein, all closing with nice persistence and length. We found the Ro'si Pinot Nero Rosato '19 pleasant, with its floral, sweet citrus tones, and a fresh, drinkable palate.

Wine	Rating
● Primitivo di Manduria Piano Chiuso 26 27 63 Ris. '17	🍷🍷🍷 5
⊙ Ro'Si '19	🍷🍷 5
○ L'Uetta '19	🍷 4
● Primitivo di Manduria Piano Chiuso 26 27 63 Ris. '16	YYY 5
○ L'Uetta '18	YY 4
● Primitivo di Manduria Li Filitti Ris. '15	YY 4
● Primitivo di Manduria Li Filitti Ris. '11	YY 4
● Primitivo di Manduria Lu Rappaio '17	YY 4
● Primitivo di Manduria Lu Rappaio '15	YY 4
● Primitivo di Manduria Piano Chiuso 26 27 63 Ris. '15	YY 4
⊙ Ro'si '17	YY 3

Morella

VIA PER UGGIANO, 147
74024 MANDURIA [TA]
TEL. +39 0999791482
www.morellavini.com

CELLAR SALES
PRE-BOOKED VISITS
ANNUAL PRODUCTION 30,000 bottles
HECTARES UNDER VINE 20.00
VITICULTURE METHOD Certified Biodynamic

Lisa Gilbee and Gaetano Morella's winery was founded 20 years ago with the aim of developing and promoting Manduria's extraordinary patrimony of old vineyards. Thus Lisa and Gaetano purchased 5 hectares of red soil about 2 kilometers from the sea, where the bush-trained vines of Primitivo go back anywhere from 35 to 80 years. Today the hectares covered have quadrupled, but the attention to quality and care in the vineyard and the cellar have remained unchanged, as evidenced by the decision to follow biodynamic principles. The producer's two flagship wines always perform at a high level. The Primitivo La Signora '17 features hints of black fruits, spices and roots, while the palate proves juicy, full and sapid. The Primitivo Old Vines '17, on the other hand, offers up notes of Mediterranean scrub and blackcurrant followed by a palate of nice persistence and depth, coming through long and assertive. The pleasant and fruity Negroamaro Primitivo '18 proves well made, as does the Mezzarosa '19, a fresh, approachable wine.

Wine	Rating
● La Signora Primitivo '17	🍷🍷 6
● Old Vines Primitivo '17	🍷🍷 6
⊙ Mezzarosa Rosato '19	🍷🍷 3
● Negroamaro Primitivo '18	🍷🍷 4
● Malbek Primitivo '17	🍷 4
○ Mezzogiorno '19	🍷 3
● La Signora Primitivo '10	YYY 6
● La Signora Primitivo '07	YYY 5
● Old Vines Primitivo '09	YYY 5
● Old Vines Primitivo '08	YYY 5
● Old Vines Primitivo '07	YYY 5
● La Signora Primitivo '15	YY 6
● La Signora Primitivo '13	YY 6
● Old Vines Primitivo '16	YY 6
● Old Vines Primitivo '15	YY 6
● Old Vines Primitivo '14	YY 6
● Old Vines Primitivo '13	YY 6

Mottura Vini del Salento

p.zza Melica, 4
73058 Tuglie [LE]
Tel. +39 0833596601
www.motturavini.it

PRE-BOOKED VISITS
ANNUAL PRODUCTION 2,500,000 bottles
HECTARES UNDER VINE 120.00

Founded in 1927 by Pasquale Mottura, today this family-run producer is managed by Barbara, the fourth generation. Their main facility is in Tuglie, on a late-19th century property, while the vineyards are situated on a large tract bordered by the Cellino San Marco, Campi Salentina, Salice Salentino and Squinzano. Here, on mainly red soil with layers of limestone and clay, they cultivate espalier and old bush-trained vines (which go back some 60 years). The region's typical grapes are grown while the wines proposed, divided into different lines, are traditionally styled. Barbara Mottura's winery enters our main section thanks to an excellent overall performance, starting with the Primitivo di Manduria Le Pitre '18. It's a wine redolent of Mediterranean scrub with notes of black berries, nice body and structure. From the I Classici line, the Rosato '19, a Negroamaro with a splash of Malvasia Nera, stands out, coming through sapid, long and taut, as does the Negroamaro '19, with its whiffs of undergrowth and herbs, and its plucky, dynamic palate.

● I Classici Negroamaro '19	🍷🍷 2*
⊙ I Classici Rosato '19	🍷🍷 2*
● Primitivo di Manduria Le Pitre '18	🍷🍷 3
● Primitivo di Manduria Stilio '18	🍷🍷 3
○ I Classici Fiano '19	🍷 2
● I Classici Primitivo '19	🍷 3
● I Classici Negroamaro '16	🍷🍷 2*
● Negroamaro Le Pitre '13	🍷🍷 5
● Negroamaro Le Pitre '11	🍷🍷 5
● Negroamaro Villa Mottura '15	🍷🍷 3
● Primitivo '18	🍷🍷 3
● Primitivo di Manduria Le Pitre '15	🍷🍷 6
● Primitivo Le Pitre '14	🍷🍷 6
● Primitivo Le Pitre '13	🍷🍷 6
● Salice Salentino Rosso Le Pitre '17	🍷🍷 4

Palamà

via A. Diaz, 6
73020 Cutrofiano [LE]
Tel. +39 0836542865
www.vinicolapalama.com

CELLAR SALES
PRE-BOOKED VISITS
ANNUAL PRODUCTION 200,000 bottles
HECTARES UNDER VINE 15.00
VITICULTURE METHOD Certified Organic
SUSTAINABLE WINERY

For over eighty years now, the Palamà family have been working their own vineyards in Salento, in Cutrofiano and Matino, for the most part Apulian bush-trained vines and only native grapes (Negroamaro, Primitivo, Malvasia Nera, Malvasia Bianca and Verdeca). In recent years their range has grown to include about twenty wines, which are made with the aim of highlighting the quality and characteristics of both the grapes and the territories of origin. By now the Metiusco Rosato is a sure bet. For years one of the best rosés in Puglia, the 2019 confirms its place at the top of regional production. Hints of roses, red currants and cherries give way to a palate with nice volume, and a long, superbly fresh, pleasant finish. The Patrunale '16, a traditionally-styled monovarietal Primitivo, proved a pleasant surprise by virtue of its nice texture and notes of dried figs and cinnamon. The other wines submitted also proved well made.

⊙ Metiusco Rosato '19	🍷🍷 3*
● Patrunale '16	🍷🍷 5
● Metiusco Rosso '19	🍷🍷 3
⊙ Ninì Rosato '19	🍷🍷 2*
● Salice Salentino Rosso Albarossa '18	🍷🍷 2*
● Albarossa '18	🍷 2
○ Metiusco Aleatico '19	🍷 4
○ Metiusco Bianco '19	🍷 3
● Ninì Rosso '19	🍷 2
○ Ninì Verdeca '19	🍷 2
● 75 Vendemmie '11	🍷🍷🍷 4*
● 75 Vendemmie '17	🍷🍷 5
○ Bianco Evoluto '17	🍷🍷 5
● Mavro '17	🍷🍷 4
● Mavro '15	🍷🍷 3*
⊙ Metiusco Rosato '18	🍷🍷 3*
⊙ Metiusco Rosato '17	🍷🍷 3*

Pietraventosa

loc. Parco Largo
s.da vic.le Latta Latta
70023 Gioia del Colle [BA]
Tel. +39 3355730274
www.pietraventosa.it

ANNUAL PRODUCTION 30,000 bottles
HECTARES UNDER VINE 5.40
VITICULTURE METHOD Certified Organic
SUSTAINABLE WINERY

Founded in 2005, Marianna Annio and Raffaele Leo's small winery has managed to establish itself in recent years as one of Gioia del Colle's most interesting producers. The estate is divided into two properties a short distance from each other and both at about 380 meters above sea level: four and a half hectares of espalier vines and one hectare of old, bush-trained vines. The principal grape cultivated is Primitivo, obviously, which is accompanied by small amounts of Aglianico and Malvasia di Candia. Their wines are modern, but of a fascinating expressiveness. The Gioia del Colle Primitivo Riserva '15 offers up notes of ripe black berry fruit and figs, while the palate comes through fresh, with nice vigor and a long, pleasant finish. The rest of their range also proves well made, from the EstRosa '19, a floral and nicely textured Primitivo rosé, to the juicy and plucky Gioia del Colle Primitivo Allegoria '17, to the Ossimoro '17, a long and fresh blend of Primitivo and Aglianico.

Wine	Rating
● Gioia del Colle Primitivo Ris. '15	🍷🍷 5
⊙ EstRosa '19	🍷🍷 3
● Gioia del Colle Primitivo Allegoria '17	🍷🍷 3
● Ossimoro '17	🍷🍷 4
○ Apriti Cielo! '19	🍷 4
● Gioia del Colle Primitivo Ris. '06	ΥΥΥ 4
○ Apriti Cielo! '18	ΥΥ 5
⊙ EstRosa '17	ΥΥ 3*
⊙ EstRosa '16	ΥΥ 3
● Gioia del Colle Primitivo Allegoria '16	ΥΥ 4
● Gioia del Colle Primitivo Ris. '13	ΥΥ 6
● Gioia del Colle Primitivo Ris. '12	ΥΥ 5
● Ossimoro '13	ΥΥ 3
● Volere Volare '17	ΥΥ 3
● Volere Volare '15	ΥΥ 2*

Plantamura

via V. Bodini, 9a
70023 Gioia del Colle [BA]
Tel. +39 3474711027
www.viniplantamura.it

CELLAR SALES
PRE-BOOKED VISITS
ANNUAL PRODUCTION 50,000 bottles
HECTARES UNDER VINE 10.00
VITICULTURE METHOD Certified Organic
SUSTAINABLE WINERY

The winery founded by Mariangela Plantamura and her husband, Vincenzo, organically managed since its foundation in 2002, is completely dedicated to the production of Gioia del Colle Primitivo. Only 3 wines are produced, all from old, bush-trained espalier vineyards in the Gioia countryside, situated at about 350 meters elevation on calcareous-clay terrain covered by a thin layer of red soil. The truly splendid Gioia del Colle Primitivo Riserva '17 is redolent of berries accompanied by nuances of Mediterranean scrub. A juicy, fruity and dynamic palate exhibits lovely tension and length. The spicy, clear and focused Gioia del Colle Primitivo Contrada San Pietro '18 proves well made with its highly fresh finish, as does the Gioia del Colle Primitivo Parco Largo '18, a wine that features notes of black olives and chocolate, and a fresh, fruity, pleasant palate.

Wine	Rating
● Gioia del Colle Primitivo Ris. '17	🍷🍷🍷 4*
● Gioia del Colle Primitivo Contrada San Pietro '18	🍷🍷 3
● Gioia del Colle Primitivo Parco Largo '18	🍷🍷 3
● Gioia del Colle Primitivo Et. Nera Contrada San Pietro '13	ΥΥΥ 3*
● Gioia del Colle Primitivo Et. Nera Contrada San Pietro '12	ΥΥΥ 3*
● Gioia del Colle Primitivo Et. Rossa '11	ΥΥΥ 4*
● Gioia del Colle Primitivo Contrada San Pietro '17	ΥΥ 3
● Gioia del Colle Primitivo Et. Rossa Parco Largo '13	ΥΥ 3*
● Gioia del Colle Primitivo Parco Largo '17	ΥΥ 3*
● Gioia del Colle Primitivo Ris. '15	ΥΥ 4
● Gioia del Colle Primitivo Ris. '13	ΥΥ 3*

Podere 29

loc. Borgo Tressanti
s.da prov.le 544
76016 Cerignola [FG]
Tel. +39 3471917291
www.podere29.it

CELLAR SALES
PRE-BOOKED VISITS
ACCOMMODATION
ANNUAL PRODUCTION 130,000 bottles
HECTARES UNDER VINE 17.00
VITICULTURE METHOD Certified Organic

La Podere 29 was founded in 2003 by Giuseppe Marrano, who took over a property that had previously been managed by the 'Opera Nazionale Combattenti' (a veterans association). Although the land was well suited to viticulture, it had never been cultivated with vines. Today vineyards grow about 10 kilometres from the Margherita di Savoia salt-pans and see the presence mainly of native grapes, foremost Nero di Troia. The wines proposed are modern, with particular attention to richness of fruit and aromatic clarity. The Nero di Troia Gelso d'oro '18 delivered in our finals, offering up spicy notes and black berries; the palate's consistent, with nice persistence and support, and a juicy, convincing finish. Other excellent selections include the Avia Pervia '18, a Primitivo that goes all in on fruit, coming through supple, pleasant and fresh on the palate, and the supple, approachable Unio '19, a blend of Nero di Troia and Primitivo marked by red fruit aromas.

Wine	Rating
● Gelso d'Oro '18	▼▼ 5
● Avia Pervia '18	▼▼ 2*
● Gelso Nero '19	▼▼ 2*
⊙ Unio '19	▼▼ 3
○ Gelso Bianco '19	▼ 3
⊙ Gelso Rosa '19	▼ 2
○ Salina '19	▼ 2
● Avia Pervia '17	▽▽ 2*
● Gelso d'Oro '16	▽▽ 5
● Gelso d'Oro '15	▽▽ 5
● Gelso d'Oro '14	▽▽ 5
● Gelso D'Oro '11	▽▽ 4
● Gelso Nero '18	▽▽ 2*
● Gelso Nero '16	▽▽ 2*
● Gelso Nero '12	▽▽ 2*
⊙ Gelso Rosa '17	▽▽ 2*

★Polvanera

s.da Vicinale Lamie Marchesana, 601
70023 Gioia del Colle [BA]
Tel. +39 080758900
www.cantinepolvanera.it

CELLAR SALES
RESTAURANT SERVICE
ANNUAL PRODUCTION 650,000 bottles
HECTARES UNDER VINE 120.00
VITICULTURE METHOD Certified Organic

The Cassano family's Polvanera comprises a large expanse of vineyards in Gioia del Colle and Acquaviva delle Fonti. Situated at elevations spanning 300 - 450 meters above sea level, the soil here is mainly karst, with a thin layer of land resting directly on living rock. Only native grape varieties are cultivated, the most important being Primitivo, obviously, making for a range of great personality that's also able to express the best of the territory. Yet more proof of the winery's great quality comes in the form of the Gioia del Colle Primitivo 17 Vigneto Montevella. The 2017, with its scents of berries and Mediterranean scrub, is characterized by a consistent, fresh, sapid, long and truly splendid palate. The fruit-forward Gioia del Colle Primitivo 16 Vigneto San Benedetto '17 is also excellent, with its aromas of delicate spices and its nice persistence.

Wine	Rating
● Gioia del Colle Primitivo 17 Vign. Montevella '17	▼▼▼ 6
● Gioia del Colle Primitivo 16 Vign. San Benedetto '17	▼▼ 5
○ Bianco d'Alessano '19	▼▼ 3
● Gioia del Colle Primitivo 14 Vign. Marchesana '17	▼▼ 3
○ Minutolo '19	▼ 3
⊙ Rosato '19	▼ 2
● Gioia del Colle Primitivo 16 Vign. San Benedetto '15	▽▽▽ 5
● Gioia del Colle Primitivo 17 '13	▽▽▽ 5
● Gioia del Colle Primitivo 17 Vign. Montevella '16	▽▽▽ 6
● Gioia del Colle Primitivo 17 Vign. Montevella '14	▽▽▽ 6

Produttori di Manduria

via Fabio Massimo, 19
74024 Manduria [TA]
Tel. +39 0999735332
www.produttoridimanduria.it

CELLAR SALES
PRE-BOOKED VISITS
ANNUAL PRODUCTION 1,400,000 bottles
HECTARES UNDER VINE 900.00
SUSTAINABLE WINERY

Produttori di Manduria has almost reached its 90 birthday and it continues to be a production leader in Manduria and beyond. Almost 400 growers cover about 900 hectares of vineyards, almost half of which are bush-trained. Obviously Primitivo is the principal grape cultivated, occupying more than half the area under vine. It's followed by Negroamaro and other grapes, such as Fiano and Malvasia. The wines proposed are technically well crafted, making for a production that brings together integrity and tradition. Once again the Primitivo di Manduria Lirica confirms it's a top-level wine, with a 2018 redolent of black fruits, cinnamon and rosemary. The palate has body and volume, but it's also smooth, fresh and long. The charming Primitivo di Manduria Dolce Naturale Il Madrigale '17 plays on notes of dried figs, coffee cream and plum jam, while exhibiting a remarkable balance between sweet tones and acidic freshness.

Wine	Rating
● Primitivo di Manduria Lirica '18	▼▼▼ 2*
● Primitivo di Manduria Dolce Naturale Madrigale '17	▼▼ 3*
● Primitivo di Manduria Elegia Ris. '17	▼▼ 4
● Abatemasi '17	▼▼ 4
○ Alice '19	▼▼ 2*
● Primitivo di Manduria Memoria '19	▼▼ 2*
○ Zin '19	▼▼ 2*
● Primitivo di Manduria Lirica '17	▽▽▽ 2*
⊙ Aka '18	▽▽ 2*
⊙ Amoroso '15	▽▽ 2*
● Primitivo di Manduria Dolce Naturale Madrigale '16	▽▽ 4
● Primitivo di Manduria Elegia Ris. '15	▽▽ 5
● Primitivo di Manduria Lirica '16	▽▽ 2*

Rivera

s.da prov.le 231 km 60,500
76123 Andria [BT]
Tel. +39 0883569510
www.rivera.it

CELLAR SALES
PRE-BOOKED VISITS
ANNUAL PRODUCTION 1,100,000 bottles
HECTARES UNDER VINE 75.00

The De Corato family's Rivera, one of Castel del Monte's most important producers, is 70 years old. The estate's vineyards are located on two different soil types: the Coppa, Rivera and Torre di Bocca estates lie on calcareous-tufaceous soils at elevations ranging from 200 to 230 meters above sea level, while Lama di Corvo is characterized by the calcareous- rocky soils of the Alta Murgia at 350 meters elevation. The various wines offered are of great solidity and character, with their most important reds proving particularly well suited to aging. The 2015 version of one of their historic wines, the Castel del Monte Aglianico Cappellaccio Riserva, opens on hints of fresh red fruits, all followed by a gutsy, fresh palate with detectable but fine-grained tannins. Other classic selections also proved well made , from the Castel del Monte Rosso Il Falcone Riserva '15, a floral, expansive wine marked by spicy hints and black berry fruits, to the Moscato di Trani Dolce Naturale Piani di Tufara '18, which does a nice job balancing notes of orange jam with acidity.

Wine	Rating
● Castel del Monte Aglianico Cappellaccio Ris. '15	▼▼ 3*
● Castel del Monte Nero di Troia Puer Apuliae Ris. '15	▼▼ 5
● Castel del Monte Rosso Il Falcone Ris. '15	▼▼ 4
○ Moscato di Trani Dolce Naturale Piani di Tufara '18	▼▼ 2*
○ Castel del Monte Bombino Bianco Marese '19	▼ 2
⊙ Castel del Monte Bombino Nero Pungirosa '19	▼ 2
○ Castel del Monte Chardonnay Lama dei Corvi '19	▼ 3
○ Castel del Monte Chardonnay Preludio n°1 '19	▼ 2
● Castel del Monte Nero di Troia Violante '18	▼ 2

★Tenute Rubino

via E. Fermi, 50
72100 Brindisi
Tel. +39 0831571955
www.tenuterubino.com

CELLAR SALES
PRE-BOOKED VISITS
ANNUAL PRODUCTION 1,200,000 bottles
HECTARES UNDER VINE 290.00

The Rubino family's winery is now a true bedrock for Brindisi winemaking thanks to their constant commitment to both quality and tradition. In addition to their four local estates in the Adriatic ridge and the hinterland of Brindisi province, they've recently added a vineyard in Lizzano, in the Primitivo di Manduria appellation. The grapes grown are mostly native, with particular attention paid to Susumaniello and Primitivo. The Brindisi Rosso Susumaniello Oltremé '18 opens with scents of ripe black fruits accompanied by vegetal nuances, while the palate features nice body and a fruit-forward finish. The well-made Punta Aquila Primitivo '18 proves varietal, with nice volume and fullness, while the Brindisi Negroamaro Rosato Saturnino '19 is fresh and pleasant in its notes of red fruits and sweet citrus fruits—approachably pleasant and highly drinkable.

Wine	Rating
● Brindisi Rosso Susumaniello Oltremé '18	▼▼▼ 4*
⊙ Brindisi Negroamaro Rosato Saturnino '19	▼▼ 3
● Punta Aquila Primitivo '18	▼▼ 3
○ Giancòla '19	▼ 3
○ Salende '19	▼ 3
⊙ Torre Testa Susumaniello Rosato '19	▼ 3
● Oltremé '17	▽▽▽ 4*
● Oltremé '16	▽▽▽ 4*
● Oltremé Susumaniello '15	▽▽▽ 4*
● Torre Testa '13	▽▽▽ 6
● Torre Testa '12	▽▽▽ 6
● Torre Testa '11	▽▽▽ 6
● Torre Testa '02	▽▽▽ 5
● Torre Testa '01	▽▽▽ 5
● Visellio '10	▽▽▽ 4*

Cantina San Donaci

via Mesagne, 62
72025 San Donaci [BR]
Tel. +39 0831681085
www.cantinasandonaci.eu

CELLAR SALES
PRE-BOOKED VISITS
ANNUAL PRODUCTION 800,000 bottles
HECTARES UNDER VINE 543.00

Founded in 1933 by a group of 12 farmers, today this cooperative winery has over 300 members. Their plots are located mainly in the historical part of Salice Salentino, on calcareous-clayey soils, almost entirely Apulian bush-trained vines. The grapes grown are mostly the area's classics, such as Negroamaro, Primitivo and Malvasia Nera. Their range is of a modern style, though it also aims to express the terroir and typicity of the cultivars used. The wines submitted put in an excellent overall performance. The Salice Salentino Salentino Anticaia Riserva '17 sees aromas of Mediterranean scrub followed by a vibrant, tannic palate. The Contrada del Falco '17, a blend of Negroamaro, Primitivo and Malvasia Nera, is fresh in its spicy notes; the Negroamaro Fulgeo '17 features whiffs of aromatic herbs, exhibiting nice energy and tension on the palate, while the Salice Salentino Rosato Anticaia '19 offers up hints of red berries, anticipating a palate of nice structure, with a finish on sensations of orange peel.

Wine	Rating
● Contrada del Falco '17	▼▼ 3
● Fulgeo '17	▼▼ 5
⊙ Salice Salentino Rosato Anticaia '19	▼▼ 2*
● Salice Salentino Rosso Anticaia Ris. '17	▼▼ 3
● Anticaia Negroamaro '19	▼ 2
● Anticaia Primitivo '19	▼ 2
○ Pietra Cava Malvasia '18	▼ 2
● Primitivo di Manduria Primius '18	▼ 3
● Anticaia Negroamaro '14	▽▽ 2*
● Fulgeo '16	▽▽ 5
○ Pietra Cava Malvasia '17	▽▽ 2*
● Posta Vecchia '14	▽▽ 2*
● Salice Salentino Rosso Anticaia '16	▽▽ 3

Cantine San Marzano

via Monsignor Bello, 9
74020 San Marzano di San Giuseppe [TA]
Tel. +39 0999574181
www.sanmarzanowines.com

CELLAR SALES
ANNUAL PRODUCTION 10,000,000 bottles
HECTARES UNDER VINE 1500.00
VITICULTURE METHOD Certified Organic
SUSTAINABLE WINERY

San Marzano's grapes are cultivated by about 1200 growers. The 1500 hectares of terrain covered are located mainly on calcareous soils (with a strong presence of iron oxides) in the municipalities of San Marzano, Sava and Francavilla Fontana. A traditional style of viticulture is adopted, thanks in part to a large quantity of old, bush-trained vines still present in the area, while in the cellar, a resolutely modern approach is taken. The result is a wide range of wines that pursue a balance between richness of alcohol, pleasantness and freshness of fruit. The Primitivo di Manduria Sessantanni '17 offers up classic notes of bottled cherries and black fruit jam followed by a palate of considerable complexity, full, round and beautifully long. The Primitivo di Manduria Anniversario 62° Riserva '17 is also excellent, with hints of damson, plum, licorice and Mediterranean scrub, and a palate that's long and pleasant but also has great mouthfeel. The rest of their selection also proves well made.

Wine	Rating
● Primitivo di Manduria Sessantanni '17	🍷🍷🍷 5
● Primitivo di Manduria Anniversario 62° Ris. '17	🍷🍷 6
○ Talò Verdeca '19	🍷🍷 3
○ Timo Vermentino '19	🍷🍷 2*
⊙ Tramari Rosé di Primitivo '19	🍷🍷 3
○ Edda '19	🍷 4
● F Negroamaro '17	🍷 5
● Primitivo di Manduria Talò '19	🍷 3
● Talò Malvasia Nera '19	🍷 3
● Talò Negroamaro '19	🍷 3
● Primitivo di Manduria Sessantanni '16	🍷🍷🍷 5
● Primitivo di Manduria Sessantanni '15	🍷🍷🍷 5
● Primitivo di Manduria Talò '13	🍷🍷🍷 3*

Conte Spagnoletti Zeuli

fraz. San Domenico
s.da prov.le 231 km 60,000
70031 Andria [BT]
Tel. +39 0883569511
www.contespagnolettizeuli.it

CELLAR SALES
PRE-BOOKED VISITS
ANNUAL PRODUCTION 600,000 bottles
HECTARES UNDER VINE 150.00

The Spagnoletti Zeuli family's historic winery has long been a leader in Castel del Monte. The property is divided into two estates, San Domenico and Zagaria, for a total of 400 hectares, 120 of which are under vine. The area's classic grapes are cultivated, with Nero di Troia followed by Bombino (both white and red), Montepulciano, Aglianico and Fiano. Their decidedly modern wines pursue freshness of fruit and pleasantness. The Castel del Monte line presented this year is truly noteworthy. The Terranera Riserva '16 stands out with its hints of black fruits accompanied by light aromatic herbs—it's a fresh, pleasant wine rich in fruit. The Pezzalaruca '17 delivers sensations of red berry fruits and Mediterranean shrub. The Nero di Troia 23 Settembre Riserva '15 is spicy and juicy, while the Nero di Troia Il Rinzacco Riserva '17 comes through flowery, with notable balance and length.

Wine	Rating
● Castel del Monte Rosso Terranera Ris. '16	🍷🍷 3*
● Castel del Monte Aglianico Ghiandara V. San Domenico '16	🍷🍷 2*
● Castel del Monte Nero di Troia 23 settembre Ris. '15	🍷🍷 6
● Castel del Monte Nero di Troia Il Rinzacco Ris. '17	🍷🍷 3
● Castel del Monte Rosso '19	🍷🍷 2*
● Castel del Monte Rosso Pezzalaruca '17	🍷🍷 2*
● Castel del Monte Bombino Nero Concadoro '19	🍷 2
⊙ Castel del Monte Bombino Nero Rosato Colombaio '19	🍷 2
● Castel del Monte Nero di Troia Vignagrande '17	🍷 2
○ Nevaia Fiano Tenuta Zagaria '18	🍷 2

Cosimo Taurino

s.da prov.le 365 km 1,400
73010 Guagnano [LE]
Tel. +39 0832706490
www.taurinovini.it

CELLAR SALES
PRE-BOOKED VISITS
ANNUAL PRODUCTION 900,000 bottles
HECTARES UNDER VINE 90.00

The winery founded half a century ago by Cosimo Taurino is a bedrock of Apulian winemaking. Credit for its success in Italy and the world goes to Patriglione, who literally redesigned the idea of Negroamaro wines. Today the estate comprises 90 hectares of vineyards in Guagnano, Salice Salentino and San Donaci, 80% of which are bush-trained vines, mainly Negroamaro and Malvasia Negroamaro. Their range is designed to be long-lived and to express the highest potential of the territory. Among the various Negroamaros proposed this year, the Notarpanaro '15 stood out. Rich in character, it's characterized by notes of dried aromatic herbs, peat and spices. On the palate it finishes long and juicy. The Patriglione '15 once again delivers, proving spicy with notes of dried figs on the nose, expansive and pleasant on the palate. We appreciated the well-made Kompà '17, a fruity and persistent wine, as well as the interesting Primitivo 7° Ceppo '19, with its notes of fresh red fruits and Mediterranean scrubland.

Wine	Rating
● Notarpanaro '15	🍷🍷 3*
● 7° Ceppo '19	🍷🍷 3
● Kompà '17	🍷🍷 2*
● Patriglione '15	🍷🍷 7
● A64 Cosimo Taurino '14	🍷 4
● Salice Salentino Rosso Ris. '15	🍷 3
● Patriglione '94	🍷🍷🍷 7
● Patriglione '88	🍷🍷🍷 7
● Patriglione '85	🍷🍷🍷 5
● A64 Cosimo Taurino '13	🍷🍷 4
● Kompà '16	🍷🍷 2*
● Notarpanaro '12	🍷🍷 3*
● Patriglione '14	🍷🍷 7
● Patriglione '13	🍷🍷 7
● Salice Salentino Rosso Ris. '14	🍷🍷 3
⊙ Scaloti '17	🍷🍷 2*

Terre dei Vaaz

via Agostino De Pretis, 9
70100 Sammichele di Bari [BA]
Tel. +39 3488013644
www.terredeivaaz.it

ANNUAL PRODUCTION 33,000 bottles
HECTARES UNDER VINE 8.00

A few years ago five friends decided to set up a winery together in the heart of Murgia, in one of the best areas for cultivating Primitivo, Sanmichele di Bari. They named it after the old family that had founded the town, Vaaz. From the very beginning, their aim has been to produce a few thousand bottles of high quality wine. The first results came last year, with the release of the first vintage, and it earned the winery a place in Italian Wines. With the second vintage Terre dei Vaaz have landed a place in our main section. Both the wines submitted this year delivered. The Oneiric '18 opens with scents of aromatic herbs followed by balsamic nuances of plum and white pepper. The palate comes through close-knit, but also long and pleasantly drinkable. The Ipnotico '18 plays more on tones of ripe black berries, making for a palate of great stuffing and depth, with a full, almost chewy finish.

Wine	Rating
● Onirico '18	🍷🍷🍷 6
● Ipnotico '18	🍷🍷 8
● Ipnotico '17	🍷🍷 7
● Onirico '17	🍷🍷 6

Terrecarsiche 1939

via Maestri del Lavoro 6/8
70013 Castellana Grotte [BA]
Tel. +39 0804962309
www.terrecarsiche.it

PRE-BOOKED VISITS
ANNUAL PRODUCTION 600,000 bottles
HECTARES UNDER VINE 30.00

The Insalata family have been working in the wine sector for four generations, but it was only 10 years ago that they founded their own winery. Terrecarsiche 1939 has its production base, and vineyards, in the Gioia del Colle and Valle d'Itria appellations, but they also offer wines from other territories, thanks to collaborations with trusted growers who get year-round support from the producer. Their wines are unabashedly modern, with particular attention paid to expressing richness of fruit. Once again the Gioia del Colle Primitivo Fanova proves to be among the best wines in the appellation, earning a place in our finals. The 2018 sees fragrances of red fruits and sweet spices followed by a pleasant palate, beautifully long and persistent, playing on notes of ripe fruit. The Gioia Rosa '19, a floral, plucky wine that unfolds with great pleasantness and pace, proves well made, as does the Passaturi Minutolo '19, with its pleasant aromas of sage and rosemary.

- ● Gioia del Colle Primitivo Fanova '18 ▼▼ 3*
- ⊙ Gioia Rosa '19 ▼▼ 3
- ○ Passaturi Minutolo '19 ▼▼ 2*
- ● Telamone '16 ▼ 3
- ○ Verdeca '19 ▼ 2
- ● Gioia del Colle Primitivo Fanova '17 ▽▽ 3
- ● Gioia del Colle Primitivo Fanova '16 ▽▽ 3*
- ● Gioia del Colle Primitivo Fanova Ris. '16 ▽▽ 3*
- ● Gioia del Colle Primitivo Fanova Ris. '15 ▽▽ 3
- ● Nero di Troia '15 ▽▽ 3
- ○ Passaturi '18 ▽▽ 2*
- ○ Verdeca '18 ▽▽ 2*

★Tormaresca

loc. Tofano
c.da Torre d'Isola
76013 Minervino Murge [BT]
Tel. +39 0883692631
www.tormaresca.it

CELLAR SALES
PRE-BOOKED VISITS
ACCOMMODATION
ANNUAL PRODUCTION 3,200,000 bottles
HECTARES UNDER VINE 380.00
VITICULTURE METHOD Certified Organic
SUSTAINABLE WINERY

Founded in 1998 by the Antinori family, Tormaresca has since become a leader among Puglia's wine producers. The estate is divided into two large properties. Bocca di Lupo, which lies within the Castel del Monte appellation, hosts primarily Nero di Troia and Aglianico, while Masseria Maime, in Upper Salento, mostly sees Negroamaro and Primitivo. Their wines bring together technical precision with pleasantness and character. It was something of a subdued year for Tormaresca. The highly pleasant Fichimori '19 is a Negroamaro with a small share of Syrah, a red to drink chilled. Approachably gratifying and highly pleasing, it goes all in on notes of wild berries. The Castel del Monte Aglianico Bocca di Lupo '16 is well made, though needs some more time in the bottle. Hints of black fruits and licorice are followed by a palate of considerable fullness, but with tannins still in the foreground. The rest of their selection also proved sound.

- ● Castel del Monte Aglianico Bocca di Lupo '16 ▼▼ 6
- ● Fichimori '19 ▼▼ 2*
- ⊙ Calafuria '19 ▼ 3
- ○ Chardonnay '19 ▼ 2
- ● Masseria Maime '16 ▼ 4
- ○ Moscato di Trani Kaloro '18 ▼ 3
- ○ Roycello '18 ▼ 3
- ● Castel del Monte Rosso Trentangeli '11 ▽▽▽ 3*
- ● Masseria Maime '12 ▽▽▽ 5
- ● Masseria Maime '08 ▽▽▽ 5
- ● Masseria Maime '07 ▽▽▽ 4
- ● Masseria Maime '06 ▽▽▽ 4
- ● Masseria Maime '05 ▽▽▽ 4*
- ● Torcicoda '11 ▽▽▽ 4*
- ● Torcicoda '10 ▽▽▽ 3*
- ● Torcicoda '09 ▽▽▽ 3

★Torrevento

S.DA PROV.LE 234 KM 10.600
70033 CORATO [BA]
TEL. +39 0808980923
www.torrevento.it

CELLAR SALES
PRE-BOOKED VISITS
ACCOMMODATION AND RESTAURANT SERVICE
ANNUAL PRODUCTION 2,500,000 bottles
HECTARES UNDER VINE 450.00
SUSTAINABLE WINERY

In recent years, Francesco Liantonio's winery has become a stylistic benchmark for the Castel del Monte appellation, thanks to a series of wines in which complexity, freshness and elegance combine with tradition and territorial identity. Most of the estate's vineyards are situated in the Alta Murgia National Park, on rocky limestone, karst soil, while their rented plots are located in the Itria Valley and Salento. In the absence of their most famous wines, such as the Vigna Pedale and Ottagono reserves, two regular, standard-label wines stood out. The Torre del Falco Nero di Troia offers up aromas of black berries and notes of Mediterranean scrub. On the palate it exhibits nice fruit and and an approachable pleasantness, with tannins whose present is felt but still supple. The Castel del Monte Rosso Bolonero, aromatically balsamic with hints of pomegranate and black berries, comes through smooth with nice acidity on the palate. As usual, the rest of their selection also performed well.

Wine	Rating	Price
● Castel del Monte Rosso Bolonero '19	▼▼▼	2*
● Torre del Falco Nero di Troia '19	▼▼	2*
○ Castel del Monte Bianco Pezzapiana '19	▼▼	2*
⊙ Castel del Monte Rosato Primaronda '19	▼▼	2*
● Primitivo di Manduria Ghenos '18	▼▼	3
● Salice Salentino Faneros '18	▼▼	2*
● Salice Salentino Rosso Sine Nomine Ris. '17	▼▼	3
● Matervitae Negroamaro '19	▼	2
● Passione Reale '19	▼	2
● Since 1913 Primitivo '18	▼	5
● Castel del Monte Rosso V. Pedale Ris. '16	▽▽▽	3*
● Castel del Monte Rosso V. Pedale Ris. '15	▽▽▽	3*

Cantine Tre Pini

VIA VECCHIA PER ALTAMURA, S.DA PROV.LE 79 KM 16
70020 CASSANO DELLE MURGE [BA]
TEL. +39 080764911
www.cantinetrepini.com

CELLAR SALES
PRE-BOOKED VISITS
ACCOMMODATION AND RESTAURANT SERVICE
ANNUAL PRODUCTION 70,000 bottles
HECTARES UNDER VINE 10.00
VITICULTURE METHOD Certified Organic
SUSTAINABLE WINERY

Founded in 2012, in the last few years the Plantamura family's Cantine Tre Pini has grown into one of the best wineries in Gioia del Colle. The estate's vineyards are situated at elevations spanning 400 - 450 meters, in the municipalities of Cassano delle Murge and Acquaviva delle Fonti. Primitivo dominates, obviously, though it's flanked by a few other varieties, such as Fiano, Malvasia Bianca and Bombino Nero. The wines produced play mainly on tension, freshness of fruit and pleasantness. As usual, this small producer's wines are of excellent quality. The Gioia del Colle Primitivo Piscina delle Monache '18 is characterized by aromas of blueberries and black plums, sensations followed by a fresh palate of beautiful tension and length with a silky tannic texture—it's complex and pleasant at the same time. The Gioia del Colle Primitivo Riserva '17 offers up notes of black fruits and Mediterranean scrub, coming through juicy with a long finish rich in fruit.

Wine	Rating	Price
● Gioia del Colle Primitivo Piscina delle Monache '18	▼▼	3*
● Gioia del Colle Primitivo Ris. '17	▼▼	5
● Crae '19	▼▼	2*
○ Donna Johanna '19	▼▼	2*
○ Fajano Brut M. Cl. '14	▼	4
⊙ Ventifile Rosé '19	▼	2
● Gioia del Colle Primitivo Ris. '14	▽▽▽	5
● Gioia del Colle Primitivo Ris. '13	▽▽▽	4*
● Gioia del Colle Primitivo Piscina delle Monache '17	▽▽	3
● Gioia del Colle Primitivo Piscina delle Monache '16	▽▽	3*
● Gioia del Colle Primitivo Piscina delle Monache '13	▽▽	3
● Gioia del Colle Primitivo Ris. '16	▽▽	5
● Gioia del Colle Primitivo Ris. '15	▽▽	5

Masseria Trullo di Pezza

c.da Trullo di Pezza
74020 Torricella [TA]
Tel. +39 0999872011
www.trullodipezza.com

CELLAR SALES
PRE-BOOKED VISITS
ACCOMMODATION AND RESTAURANT SERVICE
ANNUAL PRODUCTION 100,000 bottles
HECTARES UNDER VINE 40.00
VITICULTURE METHOD Certified Organic

Sisters Simona and Marika Lacaita founded their winery in 2012, renovating an estate, inherited from their parents, of over 100 hectares. Today 35 hectares of vineyards stretch across calcareous red soil in Torricella, Maruggio, Lizzano and Manduria. Primitivo is the cornerstone, though it's flanked by other grapes historically bound up with the area, such as Negroamaro, Fiano, Aglianico, and a few hectares of international vines such as Syrah and Cabernet Sauvignon. The wines proposed are of a modern style, with particular attention to aromatic clarity. The Scarfoglio '17 delivered in our finals. It's a monovarietal Aglianico with spicy aromas and ripe black berry sensations. The palate exhibits nice fruit, coming through firm, assertive, with a long, sapid finish. Other well made wines include the Primitivo di Manduria Licurti '17, with its scents of plum and rain-soaked earth, nice texture and freshness, and the pleasantly approachable Primitivo Mezzapezza '18, a fruity, supple drink.

Wine	Rating
● Scarfoglio '17	▼▼ 3*
● Mezzapezza '18	▼▼ 2*
● Primitivo di Manduria Licurti '17	▼▼ 3
● Artati '19	▼ 2
○ Dieci Grana '19	▼ 2
● Primitivo di Manduria Pezzale Ris. '15	▼ 5
⊙ Speziale '19	▼ 2

Agricole Vallone

via XXV Luglio, 7
73100 Lecce
Tel. +39 0832308041
www.agricolevallone.it

PRE-BOOKED VISITS
ANNUAL PRODUCTION 490,000 bottles
HECTARES UNDER VINE 170.00
VITICULTURE METHOD Certified Organic
SUSTAINABLE WINERY

Founded in 1934, today the Vallone family's winery is run by Francesco Vallone. The estate is divided into three properties: Iore, in the countryside of San Pancrazio Salentino (in the Salice Salentino appellation), Flaminio (in the Brindisi appellation, where their modern cellar is located), and their vineyards in the historic Castello di Serranova, in the Torre Guaceto Nature Reserve, where we also find their drying loft. The wines produced are an authentic expression of the grape varieties and their territory of provenance. In the absence of their Graticciaia, the producer's most famous and prestigious wine, this year the role of flagship goes to two selections. The Salice Salentino Negroamaro Vereto Riserva '17 is marked by hints of dried aromatic herbs and a juicy palate, finishing fresh and pleasant. The Tenuta Serranova Susumaniello Rosé '19, with its notes of red berries, is a long and pleasant wine with nice stuffing, but it's also smooth and approachable.

Wine	Rating
● Salice Salentino Rosso Vereto Ris. '17	▼▼ 2*
⊙ Tenuta Serranova Susumaniello Rosé '19	▼▼ 3
⊙ Brindisi Rosato V. Flaminio '19	▼ 2
● Susumaniello '18	▼ 2
○ Tenuta Serranova Fiano '19	▼ 3
● Graticciaia '03	▽▽▽ 6
● Graticciaia '01	▽▽▽ 6
⊙ Brindisi Rosato V. Flaminio '13	▽▽ 2*
● Brindisi Rosso V. Flaminio Ris. '12	▽▽ 3
● Castelserranova '14	▽▽ 4
● Castelserranova '13	▽▽ 4
● Graticciaia '15	▽▽ 7
● Graticciaia '13	▽▽ 7
● Graticciaia '12	▽▽ 7
● Susumaniello '17	▽▽ 2*
● Vigna Castello '11	▽▽ 5

Varvaglione 1921

C.DA SANTA LUCIA
74020 LEPORANO [TA]
TEL. +39 0995315370
www.varvaglione.com

CELLAR SALES
PRE-BOOKED VISITS
ACCOMMODATION
ANNUAL PRODUCTION 4,000,000 bottles
HECTARES UNDER VINE 400.00
SUSTAINABLE WINERY

Established 100 years ago, the Varvaglione family's winery, now run by the fourth generation, is one of the most important producers in Tarantino. The winery works with both its own grapes, mainly native cultivars, and those delivered by associated growers, in producing over 30 different wines, which are divided into various lines. Their approach seeks to express both the varietal characteristics of the grapes used and the territory of origin. This year two wines stood out among the Varvaglione family's selection, both from the 'Cosimo Varvaglione Old Vines Private Collection'. The Negroamaro '17 features sensations of ripe red fruits and sweet spices followed by a rich palate that plays more on tones of black fruits, with nice persistence and length, The Primitivo di Manduria '17 is marked by aromas of black plum jam on the nose, with a juicy, sapid palate and a finish in which notes of Mediterranean scrub emerge.

- ● Collezione Privata Cosimo Varvaglione Old Vines Negroamaro '17 — TTT 6
- ● Primitivo di Manduria Collezione Privata Cosimo Varvaglione Old Vines '17 — TT 6
- ⊙ Idea Rosa di Primitivo '19 — TT 3
- ○ 12 e Mezzo Malvasia Bianca '19 — T 2
- ● 12 e Mezzo Primitivo '19 — T 2
- ⊙ Idea '18 — YYY 3*
- ● Negroamaro di Terra d'Otranto Varvaglione Collezione Privata Old Vines '16 — YY 6
- ● Primitivo di Manduria Papale Linea Oro '17 — YY 5
- ● Primitivo di Manduria Papale Linea Oro '15 — YY 5
- ● Primitivo di Manduria Papale Oro '15 — YY 5

Vespa Vignaioli per Passione

FRAZ. C.DA RENI
VIA MANDURIA - AVETRANA KM 3,8
74024 MANDURIA [TA]
TEL. +39 063722120
www.vespavignaioli.it

CELLAR SALES
ANNUAL PRODUCTION 165,000 bottles
HECTARES UNDER VINE 30.00
SUSTAINABLE WINERY

Situated in the Masseria Li Reni, Bruno Vespa and his sons Alessandro and Federico avail themselves of their own private vineyards, which grow in clayey-sandy soils, mainly in the Primitivo di Manduria appellation. Primitivo dominates, obviously, but there's no shortage of other grape varieties, such as Aleatico, Fiano and Negroamaro, which gives rise to a small range of technically impeccable wines. These combine fullness of fruit, good texture and pleasant drinkability. With the 2018 version, the Primitivo di Manduria Raccontami confirms its status as a benchmark. Fragrances of black fruits and spices are followed by a well-balanced palate, which features nice mouthfeel and volume, as well as freshness and pleasantness. The well-made Il Bruno dei Vespa '19 is a monovarietal Primitivo of great precision and aromatic clarity, rich in fruity notes, pleasant and approachable on the palate. As usual, the rest of selection submitted proves impeccable.

- ● Primitivo di Manduria Raccontami '18 — TTT 5
- ● Il Bruno dei Vespa '19 — TT 2*
- ⊙ Flarò '19 — T 2
- ○ Il Bianco dei Vespa '19 — T 2
- ● Il Fedale '17 — T 3
- ● Primitivo di Manduria Il Rosso dei Vespa '19 — T 3
- ● Primitivo di Manduria Raccontami '17 — YYY 5
- ● Primitivo di Manduria Raccontami '16 — YYY 5
- ● Primitivo di Manduria Raccontami '15 — YYY 5
- ● Primitivo di Manduria Raccontami '14 — YYY 5
- ● Primitivo di Manduria Raccontami '13 — YYY 5
- ● Il Bruno dei Vespa '18 — YY 2*
- ● Il Bruno dei Vespa '17 — YY 2*
- ● Primitivo di Manduria Il Rosso dei Vespa '16 — YY 3
- ● Primitivo di Manduria Raccontami '12 — YY 5

Tenuta Viglione

S.DA PROV.LE 140 KM 4,500
70029 SANTERAMO IN COLLE [BA]
TEL. +39 0802123661
www.tenutaviglione.com

CELLAR SALES
PRE-BOOKED VISITS
ACCOMMODATION AND RESTAURANT SERVICE
ANNUAL PRODUCTION 400,000 bottles
HECTARES UNDER VINE 60.00
VITICULTURE METHOD Certified Organic

The Zullo family farm is situated on the border between the provinces of Bari and Taranto, along the ancient Via Appia. The estate's vineyards are located on Murgia's classic calcareous-clay and mineral-rich soils, in Gioia del Colle and Santeramo in Colle. Their grapes range from more traditional varieties, foremost Primitivo (naturally), to international cultivars, making for a range marked by nice territorial identity, with particular attention paid to fullness of fruit and acidic freshness. This year we especially liked the Gioia del Colle Primitivo Sellato '18, broad in its aromas of dried figs, ripe black berries and spices. Fresh and pleasant, it's also got nice mouthfeel and tension. The always-charming Gioia del Colle Primitivo Marpione Riserva '17 plays more on black cherry tones, proving rich in pulp and juicy, but a little less bright than other versions. Some wines from the Maioliche line prove well made, such as the fruity Nero di Troia and the spunky Negroamaro.

Wine	Rating
● Gioia del Colle Primitivo Sellato '18	🍷🍷🍷 3*
● Gioia del Colle Primitivo Marpione Ris. '17	🍷🍷 5
● Maioliche Negroamaro '19	🍷🍷 2*
● Maioliche Nero di Troia '19	🍷🍷 2*
● Susumaniello '19	🍷🍷 3
⊙ Maioliche Rosato Primitivo '19	🍷 2
○ Maioliche Verdeca Brut '19	🍷 2
● Gioia del Colle Primitivo Marpione Ris. '15	🍷🍷🍷 3*
● Gioia del Colle Primitivo Marpione Ris. '13	🍷🍷🍷 3*
● Gioia del Colle Primitivo Marpione Ris. '11	🍷🍷🍷 3*
● Gioia del Colle Primitivo Marpione Ris. '10	🍷🍷🍷 3*

★Conti Zecca

VIA CESAREA
73045 LEVERANO [LE]
TEL. +39 0832925613
www.contizecca.it

CELLAR SALES
PRE-BOOKED VISITS
ANNUAL PRODUCTION 2,800,000 bottles
HECTARES UNDER VINE 320.00
SUSTAINABLE WINERY

The Conti Zecca family have been cultivating the lands of Leverano for over 400 years. Today there are four estates, three in Leverano (Donna Marzia, Santo Stefano and Saraceno) and one in Salice Salentino (Cantalupi), where both the area's native cultivars and various international grapes are grown. The many wines produced are modern, but exhibit a strong link to the territory, always in pursuit of clarity, aromatic precision and the overall integrity of fruit. Once again the Nero confirms its role as their flagship wine. The 2017 version of this historic blend of Negroamaro (70%) and Cabernet Sauvignon features spicy notes and black berries on the nose, sensations followed by a palate with notable tannic structure and a long finish. The Malvasia Calavento '19 is fresh and pleasant in its notes of citrus and Mediterranean scrub, while the Cantalupi Negroamaro '19 is marked by approachably pleasant sensations and varietal nuances. The Leverano Negroamaro Rosso Riserva Liranu '17 proves supple and rich in fruit.

Wine	Rating
○ Calavento '19	🍷🍷 3
● Cantalupi Negroamaro '19	🍷🍷 2*
● Leverano Negroamaro Liranu Ris. '17	🍷🍷 3
● Nero '17	🍷🍷 6
○ Luna '19	🍷 4
○ Mendola '19	🍷 3
● Rifugio Primitivo '18	🍷 3
● Salice Salentino Rosso Cantalupi Ris. '17	🍷 3
● Terra '17	🍷 4
⊙ Venus '19	🍷 3
● Nero '09	🍷🍷🍷 5
● Nero '08	🍷🍷🍷 5
● Nero '07	🍷🍷🍷 5
● Nero '06	🍷🍷🍷 5
● Nero '03	🍷🍷🍷 5
● Nero '02	🍷🍷🍷 5

A Mano

via San Giovanni, 41
70015 Noci [BA]
Tel. +39 0803434872
www.amanowine.com

CELLAR SALES
PRE-BOOKED VISITS
ANNUAL PRODUCTION 235,000 bottles
SUSTAINABLE WINERY

- ○ Fiano Greco '19 — 2*
- ● Primitivo '17 — 2*
- ● Imprint of Mark Shannon Primitivo '17 — 2

Cantina Albea

via Due Macelli, 8
70011 Alberobello [BA]
Tel. +39 0804323548
www.albeavini.com

CELLAR SALES
PRE-BOOKED VISITS
ANNUAL PRODUCTION 380,000 bottles
HECTARES UNDER VINE 40.00

- ● Lui '18 — 5
- ⊙ Petrarosa Special Cuvée '19 — 3
- ○ Locorotondo Sup. Il Selva '19 — 2
- ● Sol '17 — 4

Donato Angiuli

fraz. Montrone
via Principe Umberto, 27
70010 Adelfia [BA]
Tel. +39 0804597130
www.angiulidonato.com

CELLAR SALES
PRE-BOOKED VISITS
ANNUAL PRODUCTION 200,000 bottles
HECTARES UNDER VINE 6.00

- ● Maccone Primitivo '18 — 4
- ○ Maccone Moscato Secco '19 — 1*
- ⊙ Maccone Primitivo Rosato '19 — 6
- ● Nero di Troia '18 — 4

Antica Enotria

loc. Risicata
s.da prov.le 65, km 7
71042 Cerignola [FG]
Tel. +39 0885418462
www.anticaenotria.it

CELLAR SALES
PRE-BOOKED VISITS
ANNUAL PRODUCTION 100,000 bottles
HECTARES UNDER VINE 14.00
VITICULTURE METHOD Certified Organic

- ● Nero di Troia '17 — 3
- ○ Fiano '19 — 3
- ● Il Sale della Terra Nero di Troia '16 — 5
- ● Puragioia Nero di Troia '18 — 3

Antica Masseria Jorche

c.da Palermo
74020 Torricella [TA]
Tel. +39 0999573232
www.jorche.it

CELLAR SALES
PRE-BOOKED VISITS
ACCOMMODATION AND RESTAURANT SERVICE
ANNUAL PRODUCTION 100,000 bottles
HECTARES UNDER VINE 31.00
SUSTAINABLE WINERY

- ● Primitivo di Manduria '17 — 4
- ● Primitivo di Manduria Ris. '16 — 5
- ● Primitivo di Manduria Dolce Naturale Lo Apu '19 — 5

Barsento

s.da vicinale San Giacomo
70015 Noci [BA]
Tel. +39 0804979657
www.cantinebarsento.com

CELLAR SALES
PRE-BOOKED VISITS
RESTAURANT SERVICE
ANNUAL PRODUCTION 100,000 bottles
HECTARES UNDER VINE 30.00
SUSTAINABLE WINERY

- ● Gioia del Colle Primitivo Casaboli Ris. '16 — 5
- ● Ladislao '16 — 4
- ● Il Paturno '18 — 3

Cantine Bonsegna

via A. Volta, 17
73048 Nardò [LE]
Tel. +39 0833561483
www.vinibonsegna.it

CELLAR SALES
PRE-BOOKED VISITS
ANNUAL PRODUCTION 100,000 bottles
HECTARES UNDER VINE 20.00

- ● Terra d'Otranto Negroamaro Baia di Uluzzo '18 — 🍷🍷 2*
- ⊙ Nardò Rosato Narthos '19 — 🍷 2
- ● Nardò Rosso Danze della Contessa '18 — 🍷 2

I Buongiorno

c.so Vittorio Emanuele,73
72012 Carovigno [BR]
Tel. +39 0831996286
www.ibuongiorno.com

CELLAR SALES
RESTAURANT SERVICE
ANNUAL PRODUCTION 37,000 bottles
HECTARES UNDER VINE 10.00
SUSTAINABLE WINERY

- ● Nicolaus '17 — 🍷🍷 4
- ○ Fiano '19 — 🍷🍷 3
- ● Nerisco '17 — 🍷🍷 4

Vigneti Calitro

c.da Papacaniello, 18/19
74028 Sava [TA]
Tel. +39 0999721127
www.vigneticalitro.it

- ● Negroamaro '17 — 🍷🍷 6
- ● Primitivo di Manduria Ausilio '17 — 🍷🍷 5
- ● Ausilio Negroamaro '18 — 🍷 5
- ● Primitivo di Manduria Ris. '16 — 🍷 6

Borgo Turrito

loc. Incoronata
71122 Foggia
Tel. +39 0881810141
www.borgoturrito.it

ANNUAL PRODUCTION 60,000 bottles
HECTARES UNDER VINE 12.00

- ● Lingue di Terra '15 — 🍷🍷 7
- ⊙ CalaRosa '19 — 🍷 2
- ○ Terra Cretosa Falanghina '19 — 🍷 2
- ● Terra Cretosa Nero di Troia '18 — 🍷 2

Caiaffa

s.da vicinale Le Torri
71042 Cerignola [FG]
Tel. +39 3293449555
www.caiaffavini.it

CELLAR SALES
PRE-BOOKED VISITS
ANNUAL PRODUCTION 100,000 bottles
HECTARES UNDER VINE 35.00
VITICULTURE METHOD Certified Organic

- ● Lampyris '15 — 🍷🍷 5
- ● Primitivo '19 — 🍷🍷 3
- ⊙ Acheta '19 — 🍷 3
- ⊙ Troia Rosato '19 — 🍷 2

Cannito

c.da Parco Bizzarro
70025 Grumo Appula [BA]
Tel. +39 080623529
www.agricolacannito.it

CELLAR SALES
PRE-BOOKED VISITS
ANNUAL PRODUCTION 60,000 bottles
HECTARES UNDER VINE 14.00
VITICULTURE METHOD Certified Organic
SUSTAINABLE WINERY

- ● Gioia del Colle Primitivo Drùmon '16 — 🍷🍷 5
- ○ Drùmon Fiano '19 — 🍷 5
- ● Gioia del Colle Primitivo Drùmon Ris. '15 — 🍷 7
- ● Gioia del Colle Primitivo Drùmon S '16 — 🍷 6

Cantolio Manduria

VIA PER LECCE KM 2,5
74024 MANDURIA [TA]
TEL. +39 0999796045
www.cantolio.it

CELLAR SALES
PRE-BOOKED VISITS
RESTAURANT SERVICE
ANNUAL PRODUCTION 500,000 bottles
HECTARES UNDER VINE 800.00
VITICULTURE METHOD Certified Organic

- ● Primitivo di Manduria Primitivo Di Terra '18 — 🍷🍷 3
- ● Primitivo di Manduria Tema Ris. '16 — 🍷🍷 4
- ○ Cleonymus '19 — 🍷 2

Casa Primis

VIA ORTANOVA, KM 0,500
71048 STORNARELLA [FG]
TEL. +39 0885433333
www.casaprimis.com

CELLAR SALES
PRE-BOOKED VISITS
ANNUAL PRODUCTION 120,000 bottles
HECTARES UNDER VINE 23.00
VITICULTURE METHOD Certified Organic
SUSTAINABLE WINERY

- ● Crusta '16 — 🍷🍷 3
- ● Nero di Troia '18 — 🍷🍷 2*
- ○ Bombino Bianco '19 — 🍷 2
- ● Ciliegiolo '19 — 🍷 2

Centovignali

P.ZZA ALDO MORO, 10
70010 SAMMICHELE DI BARI [BA]
TEL. +39 0805768215
www.centovignali.it

CELLAR SALES
PRE-BOOKED VISITS
ANNUAL PRODUCTION 35,000 bottles
HECTARES UNDER VINE 25.00
VITICULTURE METHOD Certified Organic

- ● Gioia del Colle Primitivo Indellicato '18 — 🍷🍷 5
- ● Gioia del Colle Primitivo Pentimone Ris. '18 — 🍷🍷 6
- ○ Albiore Fiano '19 — 🍷 3

Tenuta Cerfeda

C.DA PORVICA, 29000
74123 TARANTO
TEL. +39 3428798195
www.tenutacerfeda.it

VITICULTURE METHOD Certified Organic

- ● Primitivo di Manduria Don Filippo Ris. '12 — 🍷🍷 5
- ● Primitivo di Manduria Mandurino '13 — 🍷🍷 5
- ● Primitivo di Manduria Masseria Vecchia '15 — 🍷 4

Masseria Cuturi

S.DA PROV.LE 137
74024 MANDURIA [TA]
TEL. +39 0999711660
www.masseriacuturi.it

CELLAR SALES
PRE-BOOKED VISITS
ACCOMMODATION
ANNUAL PRODUCTION 60,000 bottles
HECTARES UNDER VINE 30.00
VITICULTURE METHOD Certified Organic

- ⊙ Rosa dei Cuturi '19 — 🍷🍷 3
- ● Chidro '17 — 🍷 4
- ○ Segreto di Bianca '19 — 🍷 3
- ● Tumà Primitivo '19 — 🍷 3

D'Alfonso Del Sordo

C.DA SANT'ANTONINO
71016 SAN SEVERO [FG]
TEL. +39 0882221444
www.dalfonsodelsordo.it

CELLAR SALES
PRE-BOOKED VISITS
RESTAURANT SERVICE
ANNUAL PRODUCTION 250,000 bottles
HECTARES UNDER VINE 35.00
SUSTAINABLE WINERY

- ○ Catapanus '19 — 🍷🍷 3
- ● Guado San Leo '17 — 🍷🍷 5
- ○ Cortecampana '19 — 🍷 3
- ○ Dammisole '19 — 🍷 3

De Falco

via Milano, 25
73051 Novoli [LE]
Tel. +39 0832711597
www.cantinedefalco.it

CELLAR SALES
PRE-BOOKED VISITS
ANNUAL PRODUCTION 300,000 bottles
HECTARES UNDER VINE 20.00

- ⊙ Rosato '19 — 🍷🍷 1*
- ● Squinzano Negroamaro Serre di Sant'Elia '18 — 🍷🍷 2*
- ● Salice Salentino Negroamaro Salore '17 — 🍷 2

Ferri

via Bari, 347
70010 Valenzano [BA]
Tel. +39 0804671753
www.cantineferri.it

CELLAR SALES
PRE-BOOKED VISITS
ANNUAL PRODUCTION 40,000 bottles
HECTARES UNDER VINE 5.00

- ● Mora di Cuti '16 — 🍷🍷 2*
- ● Purpureus '16 — 🍷🍷 3
- ⊙ Rosa di Cuti '19 — 🍷 2
- ○ Sol di Cuti '19 — 🍷 2

Tenute Girolamo

via Noci, 314
74015 Martina Franca [TA]
Tel. +39 0804402141
www.tenutegirolamo.it

CELLAR SALES
PRE-BOOKED VISITS
ANNUAL PRODUCTION 300,000 bottles
HECTARES UNDER VINE 45.00

- ● Conte Giangirolamo '17 — 🍷🍷 6
- ● Monte dei Cocci Primitivo V. T. '18 — 🍷 3
- ● Pizzo Rosso '17 — 🍷 5

Hiso Telaray Libera Terra Puglia

vico dei Cantelmo, 1
72023 Mesagne [BR]
Tel. +39 0831775981
www.hisotelaray.it

CELLAR SALES
ANNUAL PRODUCTION 120,000 bottles
HECTARES UNDER VINE 28.00
VITICULTURE METHOD Certified Organic
SUSTAINABLE WINERY

- ● Antò Primitivo '19 — 🍷🍷 5
- ⊙ Emmedielle '19 — 🍷 3
- ● Renata Fonte '19 — 🍷 5

Franco Ladogana

loc. Orta Nova
fraz. Loc. Passo D'Orta
s.s. 16 km 699+500
71045 Orta Nova [FG]
Tel. +39 0885784335
www.ladoganavini.it

CELLAR SALES
PRE-BOOKED VISITS
ANNUAL PRODUCTION 600,000 bottles
HECTARES UNDER VINE 40.00
VITICULTURE METHOD Certified Organic
SUSTAINABLE WINERY

- ⊙ Versura Rosato '19 — 🍷🍷 2*
- ● Ghort Nero di Troia '19 — 🍷 3
- ● Orta Nova Rosso Tarù '16 — 🍷 3

Cantine Massimo Leone

fraz. Posta San Nicola d'Arpi
via Sprecacenere
71122 Foggia
Tel. +39 0881723674
www.cantinemassimoleone.it

ANNUAL PRODUCTION 70,000 bottles
HECTARES UNDER VINE 10.50

- ● Nero di Troia '18 — 🍷🍷 2*
- ○ Falanghina '19 — 🍷 2
- ⊙ Forme Rosato '19 — 🍷 2
- ● Primitivo '18 — 🍷 3

Alberto Longo

s.da prov.le 5 Lucera-Pietramontecorvino km 4
71036 Lucera [FG]
Tel. +39 0881539057
www.albertolongo.it

CELLAR SALES
PRE-BOOKED VISITS
ANNUAL PRODUCTION 200,000 bottles
HECTARES UNDER VINE 35.00

- ● Cacc'e Mmitte di Lucera '17 — 🍷🍷 3
- ⊙ Donnadele '19 — 🍷 3
- ● Le Cruste '17 — 🍷 4
- ○ Le Fossette '19 — 🍷 3

Menhir Salento

via Salvatore Negro
73020 Bagnolo del Salento [LE]
Tel. +39 0836818199
www.menhirsalento.it

CELLAR SALES
PRE-BOOKED VISITS
RESTAURANT SERVICE
ANNUAL PRODUCTION 1,000,000 bottles
HECTARES UNDER VINE 50.00
SUSTAINABLE WINERY

- ● Pietra Susumaniello '19 — 🍷🍷 3
- ● Calamuri Primitivo '17 — 🍷 3
- ● Filo '17 — 🍷 3
- ⊙ N°Zero Rosato '19 — 🍷 2

Cantine Miali

via Madonnina, 11
74015 Martina Franca [TA]
Tel. +39 0804303222
www.cantinemiali.com

CELLAR SALES
PRE-BOOKED VISITS
ANNUAL PRODUCTION 160,000 bottles
HECTARES UNDER VINE 16.00

- ● Campirossi '15 — 🍷🍷 2*
- ⊙ Ametys Rosato '19 — 🍷 3
- ○ Chardonnay Single Vineyard '19 — 🍷 2
- ○ Martina Franca Dolcimèlo '19 — 🍷 2

Cantine Paradiso

via Manfredonia, 39
71042 Cerignola [FG]
Tel. +39 0885428720
www.cantineparadiso.it

ANNUAL PRODUCTION 200,000 bottles
HECTARES UNDER VINE 30.00

- ● Darione Podere Belmantello Primitivo '19 — 🍷🍷 2*
- ● Posta Piana Primitivo '18 — 🍷🍷 2*
- ● 1954 Primitivo '18 — 🍷 4
- ● Sant'Andrea Primitivo '19 — 🍷 2

Tenuta Patruno Perniola

c.da Marzagaglia
70023 Gioia del Colle [BA]
Tel. +39 3383940830
www.tenutapatrunoperniola.it

CELLAR SALES
PRE-BOOKED VISITS
ACCOMMODATION AND RESTAURANT SERVICE
ANNUAL PRODUCTION 12,000 bottles
HECTARES UNDER VINE 3.00
VITICULTURE METHOD Certified Organic

- ● Lenos '18 — 🍷🍷 3
- ⊙ Ghirigori '19 — 🍷 3
- ○ Striale '19 — 🍷 2

Petra Nevara

via Madonna dell'Arco, 180
74015 Martina Franca [TA]
Tel. +39 3358379386
www.petranevara.com

PRE-BOOKED VISITS
HECTARES UNDER VINE 4.00

- ● Pavone Rosso Primitivo '18 — 🍷🍷 4
- ● Nevaja Negroamaro '18 — 🍷 5
- ⊙ Rosanevara '19 — 🍷 3

Placido Volpone

c.da Monterozzi
71040 Ordona [FG]
Tel. +39 3395847668
www.placidovolpone.it

CELLAR SALES
PRE-BOOKED VISITS
HECTARES UNDER VINE 12.00
VITICULTURE METHOD Certified Organic
SUSTAINABLE WINERY

⊙ Faragola '19	🍷🍷 3
⊙ Rosàntica '19	🍷🍷 3
● Beniamino '16	🍷 5
● Rosone '17	🍷 4

Risveglio Agricolo

c.da Torre Mozza
72100 Brindisi
Tel. +39 0831519948
www.cantinerisveglio.it

CELLAR SALES
PRE-BOOKED VISITS
ANNUAL PRODUCTION 100,000 bottles
HECTARES UNDER VINE 44.00

● 72100 '18	🍷🍷 3
● Eneo '18	🍷🍷 3
● Pecora Nera Nero di Troia '18	🍷 4
● Susu' '18	🍷 3

Rosa del Golfo

via Garibaldi, 18
73011 Alezio [LE]
Tel. +39 0833281045
www.rosadelgolfo.com

CELLAR SALES
PRE-BOOKED VISITS
ANNUAL PRODUCTION 300,000 bottles
HECTARES UNDER VINE 40.00

⊙ Negroamaro Rosato '19	🍷🍷 2*
● Quarantale Mino Calò '17	🍷🍷 5
○ Bolina '19	🍷 2
● Portulano '17	🍷 2

Cantina Sociale Sampietrana

via Mare, 38
72027 San Pietro Vernotico [BR]
Tel. +39 0831671120
www.cantinasampietrana.com

CELLAR SALES
PRE-BOOKED VISITS
ACCOMMODATION
ANNUAL PRODUCTION 1,500,000 bottles
HECTARES UNDER VINE 140.00

● Brindisi Rosso Since 1952 Ris. '17	🍷🍷 3
● Settebraccia '17	🍷🍷 3
⊙ Primitivo Rosato '19	🍷 2
● Salice Salentino Le Monache Ris. '15	🍷 4

Cantine Santa Barbara

via Maternità e Infanzia, 23
72027 San Pietro Vernotico [BR]
Tel. +39 0831652749
www.cantinesantabarbara.it

CELLAR SALES
PRE-BOOKED VISITS
ANNUAL PRODUCTION 2,000,000 bottles
HECTARES UNDER VINE 150.00
VITICULTURE METHOD Certified Organic
SUSTAINABLE WINERY

● Capirussu Primitivo '19	🍷🍷 3
● Sumanero '18	🍷🍷 3
● Salice Salentino Capirrussu '18	🍷 3
● Ursa Major '16	🍷 4

Schola Sarmenti

via Generale Cantore, 37
73048 Nardò [LE]
Tel. +39 0833567247
www.scholasarmenti.it

CELLAR SALES
PRE-BOOKED VISITS
ANNUAL PRODUCTION 240,000 bottles
HECTARES UNDER VINE 41.00
VITICULTURE METHOD Certified Organic

● Cubardi '17	🍷🍷 4
● Nardò Rosso Neriò Ris. '17	🍷🍷 3
○ Cillenza '17	🍷 4
○ Fiano '19	🍷 3

Tagaro

c.da S. Angelo, zona industriale sud
70015 Fasano [BR]
Tel. +39 0804316323
www.tagaro.it

ANNUAL PRODUCTION 600,000 bottles
HECTARES UNDER VINE 40.00
VITICULTURE METHOD Certified Organic

- ● Salice Salentino Sei Caselle '19 🍷🍷 3
- ● U'Cucci Susumaniello '18 🍷🍷 4
- ● Passo del Sud '19 🍷 3
- ● Primitivo di Manduria Muso Rosso '19 🍷 4

Teanum

via Croce Santa, 48
71016 San Severo [FG]
Tel. +39 0882336332
www.teanum.it

CELLAR SALES
PRE-BOOKED VISITS
RESTAURANT SERVICE
ANNUAL PRODUCTION 1,500,000 bottles
HECTARES UNDER VINE 200.00

- ⊙ Favùgnë Rosato '19 🍷🍷 2*
- ● Òtre Primitivo '18 🍷 3
- ● San Severo Rosso Gran Tiati Gold Vintage Ris. '15 🍷 5

Torrequarto

c.da Quarto, 5
71042 Cerignola [FG]
Tel. +39 0885418453
www.torrequarto.com

CELLAR SALES
PRE-BOOKED VISITS
ACCOMMODATION AND RESTAURANT SERVICE
ANNUAL PRODUCTION 400,000 bottles
HECTARES UNDER VINE 50.00

- ● Passione Rosso '17 🍷🍷 3
- ● Tarabuso '18 🍷🍷 3
- ● Tavoliere delle Puglie Nero di Troia Bottaccia '18 🍷 3

La Vecchia Torre

via Marche, 1
73045 Leverano [LE]
Tel. +39 0832925053
www.cantinavecchiatorre.it

CELLAR SALES
PRE-BOOKED VISITS
ANNUAL PRODUCTION 3,500,000 bottles
HECTARES UNDER VINE 1500.00
SUSTAINABLE WINERY

- ● Roccia Rosso '17 🍷🍷 2*
- ● Syrah Primitivo '18 🍷🍷 2*
- ● Barocco Reale '16 🍷 3
- ● Primitivo '17 🍷 2

Vetrere

fraz. Vetrère
s.da prov.le 80 Monteiasi - Montemesola km 16
74123 Taranto
Tel. +39 3402977870
www.vetrere.it

CELLAR SALES
PRE-BOOKED VISITS
ACCOMMODATION
ANNUAL PRODUCTION 150,000 bottles
HECTARES UNDER VINE 37.00

- ● Lago della Pergola '18 🍷🍷 4
- ⊙ Taranta '19 🍷🍷 3
- ○ Cré '19 🍷 4
- ● Livruni '19 🍷 3

Vigneti Reale

via Reale, 55
73100 Lecce
Tel. +39 0832248433
www.vignetireale.it

PRE-BOOKED VISITS
ACCOMMODATION AND RESTAURANT SERVICE
ANNUAL PRODUCTION 180,000 bottles
HECTARES UNDER VINE 85.00
SUSTAINABLE WINERY

- ● Norie Negroamaro '18 🍷🍷 2*
- ● Rudiae Primitivo '19 🍷🍷 3
- ○ Blasi Chardonnay '19 🍷 2
- ⊙ Malvasia Rosato '19 🍷 2

CALABRIA

From a pedoclimatic point of view, Calabria is certainly one of Italy's best regions for growing grapes, thanks to its particular, long and narrow shape, which starts in the north with a series of windy plateaus between the 2 seas, protected from the cold north winds by the Pollino massif, and then narrows drastically down to the south, where the steep hills overlook the sea on both the Ionian and Tyrrhenian coasts, protected high up by the Apennine ridge. In historical terms, towers over much 'nobler' Italian territories. We'll simply point out the fact that Calabrian wine's historical roots go back well before the 8th century B.C. when the first Greek colonizers arrived on the Ionian shore, bringing with them the first bush-trained vines, the use of wine jars and more sophisticated techniques, all attested to by the hundreds of ancient 'palmenti' (a kind of early, stone cellar for winemaking) found throughout the territory. After years of abandonment and a drastic reduction in production, for some years now we've been seeing a gradual return to viticulture. It's mainly young people (women in particular) who are shaking up the sleepy world of Calabrian wine. From our tastings it's clear that 2020, despite everything that went on, will be remembered as the year in which Calabrian viticulture began anew. Never have so many wines earned Tre Bicchieri, and never before were so many so close. It's a true acceleration that's seeing new motivated producers springing up, all well prepared and enthusiastic about the life they've chosen: producing wine in their land, respecting it by practicing organic and biodynamic agriculture, enriching it by cultivating native grapes. Right now Calabria is a true open-air wine laboratory in which history, tradition, the desire for redemption and the firm will of those who are trying to win over critics and the market with their own means and resources are all coming together. To this end, Antonella Lombardo is an exemplary case. Winner of our Grower of the Year Award, she enchanted us with her PiGreco '19. For our part, we invite all those who think that in Italy there won't be any more terroirs to discover after Etna to keep an eye on this region. They may soon change their minds.

Cantine Benvenuto

C.DA ZIOPÀ
89815 FRANCAVILLA ANGITOLA [VV]
TEL. +39 331729 2517
info@cantinebenvenuto.it

CELLAR SALES
PRE-BOOKED VISITS
ANNUAL PRODUCTION 40,000 bottles
HECTARES UNDER VINE 6.00
VITICULTURE METHOD Certified Organic

Sometimes the means, determination and skill are not enough to make great wines: Giovanni Benvenuto knew this all too well when he decided to turn his passion for wine into a career. Nevertheless, he was brave enough to give it a go, and he succeeded, judging by his debut into our Guide. He planned to produce quality wines in a still unknown area of Calabria, growing native grapes using organic methods and natural winemaking. The result is a selection of exciting wines which are impressively close-focused and consistent with respect to the grape variety used. An example is Benvenuto Orange '19, a masterpiece of macerated Zibibbo, out-of-the-box even for the category of "orange" wines. It proves very scented and clean on the nose, with notes of candied citrus fruit, peach, figs and medicinal herbs. The palate develops around a whirling spiral of sapid acidity that enriches its fruit and monumental length.

Wine	Rating
○ Benvenuto Orange Zibibbo '19	🍷🍷 3*
○ Benvenuto Zibibbo '19	🍷🍷 3
○ Mare '19	🍷🍷 3
● Terra '19	🍷🍷 3
⊙ Celeste Rosato '19	🍷 3

Roberto Ceraudo

LOC. MARINA DI STRONGOLI
C.DA DATTILO
88815 CROTONE
TEL. +39 0962865613
www.dattilo.it

CELLAR SALES
PRE-BOOKED VISITS
ACCOMMODATION AND RESTAURANT SERVICE
ANNUAL PRODUCTION 70,000 bottles
HECTARES UNDER VINE 20.00
VITICULTURE METHOD Certified Organic

When Robert Ceraudo began working on his farm, where he cultivates olives and citrus fruit as well as vineyards, he followed the criteria of organic farming at a time when there didn't even exist a certifying body in Italy. Now, over forty years later, that little gem has become the Dattilo estate where his children work alongside him: Susy deals with sales, Antonio is an agronomist, and young Caterina, who studied enology, is an excellent cook, so much so that Dattilo, the restaurant of the same name, is considered one of the best in southern Italy. Tre Bicchieri for Pecorello Grisara '19. Its complex, polished nose features nuances of iodine, mint, citrus, exotic fruit and camomile. The sapid, taut palate exhibits fresh acidity that supports nice, juicy fruit, making for a very lingering finish. Their red Petraro '16 also put in an excellent performance. It offers up cleanly expressed fruit on both the nose and in the mouth, where it's well-supported by sapid acidity.

Wine	Rating
○ Grisara Pecorello '19	🍷🍷🍷 5
● Petraro '16	🍷🍷 5
○ Petelia '19	🍷🍷 4
○ Imyr '19	🍷 5
● Nanà '18	🍷 4
○ Grisara '17	🍸🍸🍸 4*
○ Grisara '16	🍸🍸🍸 4*
○ Grisara '15	🍸🍸🍸 4*
○ Grisara '14	🍸🍸🍸 3*
○ Grisara '13	🍸🍸🍸 3*
○ Grisara '12	🍸🍸🍸 3*
○ Grisara Pecorello '18	🍸🍸🍸 4*
● Dattilo '16	🍸🍸 4
● Dattilo '15	🍸🍸 4
● Dattilo '14	🍸🍸 4
● Petraro '15	🍸🍸 5

Ippolito 1845

via Tirone, 118
88811 Cirò Marina [KR]
Tel. +39 096231106
www.ippolito1845.it

CELLAR SALES
PRE-BOOKED VISITS
ANNUAL PRODUCTION 1,000,000 bottles
HECTARES UNDER VINE 100.00

This large historic winery in Cirò underwent a generational change that affected both their management and philosophy. Vincenzo and Gianluca, with their cousin Paolo, have turned things around in just a few years: they started by remodernizing wood and technology in the cellar; then they worked on pruning and yields in the vineyard to obtain perfectly ripe grapes to produce pleasant wines on the palate that can be easily traced back to their terroir, made with traditional varieties; and lastly they have made the packaging much more appealing today. Mare Chiaro '19 gave a nice performance; it's the first Cirò Bianco to reach our finals. A clean, delicate nose is redolent of citrus, white-fleshed fruit and herbs. The palate comes through sapid, lingering, fresh and gratifying. Their Gaglioppo 160 Anni also delivered, featuring clean balsamic overtones and notes of small red and black fruit on the nose, with a sapid, juicy palate.

Wine	Rating
○ Cirò Bianco Mare Chiaro '19	**YY** 2*
● 160 Anni Gaglioppo '17	**YY** 5
● Cirò Rosso Cl. Sup. Colli del Mancuso Ris. '17	**YY** 3
● Cirò Rosso Cl. Sup. Liber Pater '18	**YY** 2*
● Cirò Rosso Cl. Sup. Ripe del Falco Ris. '12	**YY** 5
● I Mori '18	**YY** 2*
○ Pecorello '19	**YY** 2*
⊙ Pescanera Rosé '19	**YY** 2*
● Calabrise '19	**Y** 2
⊙ Cirò Rosato Mabilia '19	**Y** 2
○ Pecorello '17	YYY 2*
● 160 Anni '13	YY 5
● Cirò Rosso Cl. Sup. Colli del Mancuso Ris. '16	YY 3*
○ Pecorello '16	YY 2*

Cantine Lento

via del Progresso, 1
88040 Amato [CZ]
Tel. +39 096828028
www.cantinelento.it

CELLAR SALES
PRE-BOOKED VISITS
ANNUAL PRODUCTION 500,000 bottles
HECTARES UNDER VINE 70.00

In an area like Lametino, where there are very few wine producers, the winery run by Salvatore Lento, aided by his daughters Danila and Manuela, really stands out. It is a sound and consolidated estate with three different production areas and a cellar built a few years ago, which has enough space for twice their 70 hectares of owned vineyards, and is equipped with the very latest technology. A whole series of logistic problems caused by the pandemic upset all activities this year, including those linked to vinegrowing. Danila, who deals firsthand with the cellar, didn't manage to bottle her best wines. Except for the white Emburga '19, made with Chardonnay and Malvasia, exhibiting aromas of herbs, peach and plum, with a lively, plucky palate. The wines from the Dragone line (their entry level wines) also stood out for their quality and pleasant palate.

Wine	Rating
○ Contessa Emburga '19	**YY** 3
○ Dragone Bianco '19	**YY** 3
⊙ Dragone Rosato '19	**YY** 3
○ Lamezia Greco '19	**YY** 3
○ Contessa Emburga '17	YY 3
● Dragone Rosso '17	YY 3
● Federico II '15	YY 4
● Federico II '14	YY 4
○ Lamezia Greco '18	YY 3
● Lamezia Rosso Salvatore Lento Ris. '15	YY 4
● Lamezia Rosso Salvatore Lento Ris. '14	YY 4
● Lamezia Rosso Salvatore Lento Ris. '13	YY 4
● Magliocco '15	YY 5
● Magliocco '13	YY 5

★Librandi

loc. San Gennaro
s.s. Jonica, 106
88811 Cirò Marina [KR]
Tel. +39 096231518
www.librandi.it

CELLAR SALES
PRE-BOOKED VISITS
ANNUAL PRODUCTION 2,200,000 bottles
HECTARES UNDER VINE 232.00

The second generation of the Librandi family has inherited a thriving winery from their parents, Antonio and Nicodemo: it's a leader in the region, as well as a spearhead of southern Italian winemaking. And we are very pleased to find that the quality of their wines has continued to improve again this year. This is not only true for the top of their range, which is always sound, but also their so-called entry-level wines, which are produced in large quantities and make up the calling card of this self-respecting winery, as well as its economic backbone. The picture that emerged this year was of a selection that's very on point. Tre Bicchieri for Cirò Rosso Duca Sanfelice '18, an archetype of the appellation. The close-focused, tight-knit nose offers up aromas of small red fruit, spices and Mediterranean scrub, while the elegant palate, rich in close-knit, stylish tannins, closes with lovely dark cherries.

Wine	Rating
● Cirò Rosso Cl. Sup. Duca San Felice Ris. '18	🍷🍷🍷 3*
● Gravello '18	🍷🍷 5
○ Cirò Bianco Segno '19	🍷🍷 2*
⊙ Cirò Rosato Segno '19	🍷🍷 2*
○ Critone '19	🍷🍷 2*
○ Efeso '19	🍷🍷 4
○ Le Passule '19	🍷🍷 5
● Megonio '18	🍷🍷 4
⊙ Terre Lontane '19	🍷🍷 2*
● Cirò Rosso Cl. Sup. Duca San Felice Ris. '17	🍷🍷🍷 3* (previous years)
● Gravello '16	🍷🍷🍷 5 (previous years)
● Gravello '14	🍷🍷🍷 5 (previous years)
● Magno Megonio '13	🍷🍷🍷 4* (previous years)
● Magno Megonio '12	🍷🍷🍷 4* (previous years)

Antonella Lombardo

c.da Chiusi snc
89032 Bianco [RC]
Tel. +39 09641901835
www.antonellalombardo.com

ANNUAL PRODUCTION 5,220 bottles
HECTARES UNDER VINE 5.00

An explosive debut for Antonella Lombardo, an enthusiastic vinegrower in Bianco, on the Ionian coast of Calabria. Vines have been cultivated here since the 8th century B.C., when the first Greek colonists brought their grape varieties with them, together with bush-trained vines, the most common training system used in this area today. Antonella personally follows the work in both the vineyards and cellar. Her winery totals five hectares of vineyards under organic management, using cover crops to enrich the mainly clayey-marl and calcareous soils. She is our Grower of the Year. Tre Bicchieri for the dry Greco di Bianco, Pi Greco '19, a wine with an exuberant bouquet ranging from aromas of peach, pineapple, apricot and mint to mineral overtones and sweeter floral references of white roses. The pure, fresh, dynamic palate exhibits nice length with a deep, citrusy finish.

Wine	Rating
○ Pi Greco '19	🍷🍷🍷 5
⊙ Charà '19	🍷🍷 5

Russo & Longo

LOC. SERPITO
88816 STRONGOLI [KR]
TEL. +39 09621905782
www.russoelongo.it

CELLAR SALES
PRE-BOOKED VISITS
ANNUAL PRODUCTION 100,000 bottles
HECTARES UNDER VINE 16.00

This small winery is one of the oldest in Crotone. It was founded at the end of the eighteenth century and run by Felice Russo until the middle of the following century. There has always been a strong bond with the Strongoli territory, which is recognized as one of the best vinegrowing areas in the whole of Calabria. The 20 hectares of owned vineyards are located on steep terraces in a particularly sunny hillside area exposed to the beneficial influence of the sea; the highest plots of land are usually reserved for the production of their top wines. Our tastings confirmed a definite change of gear for this dynamic winery's selection: they are clearly cleaner, more reliable and consistent than last year. The grape blend of their Rosso Jachello '17 (Gaglioppo, Greco Nero and Sangiovese) hit the bullseye. Despite the muscle and lots of fruit, it proves balanced and polished on the nose and, above all, in the mouth.

Wine	Rating	Price
● Jachello '17	🍷🍷	5
⊙ Colli di Ginestra '19	🍷🍷	2*
● Pietra di Tesauro '18	🍷🍷	3
○ Terre di Trezzi '19	🍷🍷	2*
⊙ Alma Risa '19	🍷	3
● Decennio '17	🍷	3
○ Malvasia e Sauvignon '19	🍷	3
○ Passo del Gelso '19	🍷	2
● Decennio '16	🍷🍷 (outline)	3
● Jachello '15	🍷🍷 (outline)	5
○ Ois '18	🍷🍷 (outline)	3*
○ Passo del Gelso '18	🍷🍷 (outline)	2*
○ Terre di Trezzi '18	🍷🍷 (outline)	2*

Santa Venere

LOC. TENUTA VOLTA GRANDE
S.DA PROV.LE 04, KM 10.00
88813 CIRÒ [KR]
TEL. +39 096238519
www.santavenere.com

CELLAR SALES
PRE-BOOKED VISITS
ANNUAL PRODUCTION 150,000 bottles
HECTARES UNDER VINE 25.00
VITICULTURE METHOD Certified Organic

Cirò boasts some of the oldest wineries in southern Italy. This is the thousand-year-old legacy of a territory that was the first in the Italian peninsula subjected to Greek colonization, which brought not only civilization to the area, but also vineyards and advanced winemaking techniques. The winery was founded in the seventeenth century and has come down to modern times firmly in the hands of the Scala family. Today it's run by Giuseppe, who recently completely transformed the whole winery from organic to biodynamic management. Our judgment was totally positive about this winery's selection: well-made, close-focused and, above all, varietal and territorial. Unfortunately, they are just missing a champion to make the difference: in fact, the Cirò Riserva Federico Scala '17 didn't get past our finals. It features an intriguing nose of red fruit, balsam and spices, with a refined, juicy palate supported by acidity and tannins.

Wine	Rating	Price
● Cirò Rosso Cl. Sup. Federico Scala Ris. '18	🍷🍷	5
○ Cirò Bianco '19	🍷🍷	2*
⊙ Cirò Rosato '19	🍷🍷	2*
● Cirò Rosso Cl. Sup. '19	🍷🍷	2*
⊙ SP1 Brut M. Cl. Rosé '18	🍷🍷	5
● Speziale '19	🍷🍷	3
⊙ Scassabarile '19	🍷	3
○ Vescovado '19	🍷	3
● Vurgadà '18	🍷	4
● Cirò Cl. Sup. Federico Scala Ris. '16	🍷🍷 (outline)	5
● Cirò Cl. Sup. Federico Scala Ris. '12	🍷🍷 (outline)	5
● Cirò Rosso Cl. Sup. '18	🍷🍷 (outline)	2*
● Cirò Rosso Federico Scala Ris. '14	🍷🍷 (outline)	5
● Speziale '18	🍷🍷 (outline)	3
● Vurgadà '16	🍷🍷 (outline)	4

Spiriti Ebbri

VIA ROMA, 96
87050 SPEZZANO PICCOLO [CS]
TEL. +39 0984408992
www.spiritiebbri.it

CELLAR SALES
PRE-BOOKED VISITS
ANNUAL PRODUCTION 20,000 bottles
HECTARES UNDER VINE 2.50

When Pierpaolo Greco, Damiano Mele and Michele Scrivano heard about an old vineyard up for rent from an old farmer ten years ago, they decided to go and take a look with the idea of producing their own wine. Imagine their surprise when they discovered that it was no ordinary vineyard, but a reliquary of ancient native Calabrian varieties, all planted together like in the olden days. This is how their first wine, Appianum, was created; today they make seven wines all from native varieties, Magliocco, Gaglioppo and Greco, cultivated naturally, without using chemical substances. This year their flagship wine placed best. Full, extractive, close-woven and graceful, the Appianum '18 opens on the nose with intense fruity aromas of mulberry and blueberry. The palate proves silky, but exhibits just the right touch of sapidity and freshness, while the finish comes through overwhelmingly fruity.

- ● Appianum Rosso '18 — 5
- ● Cotidie Rosato '19 — 3
- ● Cotidie Rosso '18 — 3
- ○ Neostòs Bianco '19 — 4
- ● Neostòs Rosso '18 — 4
- ⊙ Appianum Rosato '19 — 5
- ○ Cotidie Bianco '19 — 3
- ⊙ Neostòs Rosato '19 — 4
- ○ Neostòs Bianco '17 — 4*
- ○ Neostòs Bianco '16 — 4*
- ● Appianum Rosso '17 — 5
- ● Appianum Rosso La Vigna di Alberto '15 — 5
- ● Neostòs Rosso '17 — 4
- ● Neostòs Rosso '16 — 4
- ● Neostòs Rosso '15 — 4

Statti

C.DA LENTI
88046 LAMEZIA TERME [CZ]
TEL. +39 0968456138
www.statti.com

CELLAR SALES
PRE-BOOKED VISITS
RESTAURANT SERVICE
ANNUAL PRODUCTION 500,000 bottles
HECTARES UNDER VINE 100.00

The Baroni Statti family's beautiful farm stretches over 500 hectares of land in Lamezia Terme and produces wine, oil and much more: large areas of land are set aside for grazing the cattle bred here. This is done with the utmost respect for the environment and using green energy they produce themselves thanks to a biogas plant. The quality of their wines is constantly on the up, especially their reds, which we found well-made, clean and finally ready to compete for the highest step of the podium this year. For a few years now, the Statti brothers have been working on developing native grapes in the territory; and it's no coincidence that their Batasarro '17 made it into our finals. This elegant monovarietal Gaglioppo features aromas of cherries, violets and red spices, with a creamy, relaxed palate that plays well on fruit and tannins.

- ● Lamezia Batasarro Ris. '17 — 4
- ● Cauro '17 — 4
- ⊙ Greco Nero '19 — 3
- ○ Lamezia Bianco '19 — 2*
- ⊙ Lamezia Rosato '19 — 2*
- ● Gaglioppo '19 — 3
- ○ Greco '19 — 3
- ● Lamezia Rosso '19 — 2
- ● Batasarro '13 — 4
- ● Batasarro '12 — 4
- ● Gaglioppo '18 — 3
- ● Gaglioppo '17 — 3
- ● Gaglioppo '15 — 2*
- ● Gaglioppo '14 — 2*
- ○ Greco '18 — 3
- ● Lamezia Batasarro Ris. '15 — 4
- ● Lamezia Rosso '18 — 2*

Tenuta del Travale

via Travale, 13
87050 Rovito [CS]
Tel. +39 3937150240
www.tenutadeltravale.it

CELLAR SALES
PRE-BOOKED VISITS
ANNUAL PRODUCTION 14,000 bottles
HECTARES UNDER VINE 2.00
SUSTAINABLE WINERY

The Tenuta del Travale started off as a retreat for Raffaella Ciardullo, who purchased it in 1993 to spend vacations with her family. On the estate there was also a very old vineyard of Nerello Mascalese and Cappuccio, with several of the vines ungrafted. In 2007, realizing that the old vineyard was burning out, Raffaella decided to replant it using those century-old clones, in order to preserve its memory. The first wine from the new vineyard, called Eleuteria (from the Greek for 'freedom'), was sold for the first time in 2014, when the new vineyard was already at full steam and guaranteed quality production. Esmen Tetra '18, a blend of Nerello Mascalese and Cappuccio with close-focused aromas of red and black berries, medicinal herbs and candied violets, wins our Tre Bicchieri at its debut. The polished, close-knit tannins and acidity, guarantee the very elegant palate many years of longevity.

Wine	Rating	Price
● Esmen Tetra '18	3 black glasses	4*
● Eleuteria '17	2 black glasses	6
● Eleuteria '16	2 white glasses	6
● Eleuteria '15	2 white glasses	6
● Eleuteria '14	2 white glasses	6

★Luigi Viola

via Roma, 18
87010 Saracena [CS]
Tel. +39 098134722
www.cantineviola.it

CELLAR SALES
PRE-BOOKED VISITS
ANNUAL PRODUCTION 15,000 bottles
HECTARES UNDER VINE 3.00
VITICULTURE METHOD Certified Organic

One day, Luigi Viola, an elementary school teacher, got it into his head to save an ancient wine produced in his town that was gradually disappearing: Moscato di Saracena. So he bought some vineyards, fitted out a cellar and got the elderly people in his town to explain the archaic production methods of that barely-known wine. A few years ago, Luigi's Moscato won the Tre Bicchieri and much-deserved fame; now there are a dozen producers of this type of wine in Saracena and Luigi is a happy man for having given this local wine its dignity back. The Moscato Passito '19 is probably one of the best versions ever to be produced by this winery. This masterpiece of balance and complexity features a harmonious bouquet of exotic fruit, yellow spices, lavender flowers and chamomile in a very wide range of aromas. The sweet, velvety palate comes through very stylish, while plucky acid combined with ripe fruit is marked by a delicately salty overtone.

Wine	Rating	Price
○ Moscato Passito '19	3 black glasses	6
○ Bianco Margherita '18	2 black glasses	3
● Rosso Viola '16	2 black glasses	3
○ Moscato Passito '18	3 white glasses	6
○ Moscato Passito '17	3 white glasses	6
○ Moscato Passito '14	3 white glasses	6
○ Moscato Passito '13	3 white glasses	6
○ Moscato Passito '12	3 white glasses	6
○ Moscato Passito '11	3 white glasses	6
○ Moscato Passito '10	3 white glasses	6
○ Moscato Passito '09	3 white glasses	6
○ Moscato Passito '08	3 white glasses	6
○ Moscato Passito '07	3 white glasses	6
○ Moscato Passito '16	2 white glasses	6
○ Moscato Passito '15	2 white glasses	6
● Rosso Viola '15	2 white glasses	3

'A Vita

s.s. 106 km 279,800
88811 Cirò Marina [KR]
Tel. +39 3290732473
www.avitavini.it

CELLAR SALES
PRE-BOOKED VISITS
ANNUAL PRODUCTION 15,000 bottles
HECTARES UNDER VINE 8.00

● Cirò Rosso Cl. Sup. Ris. '16	🍷🍷 6
⊙ 'A Vita Rosato '19	🍷 3

Antiche Vigne

via Regina Elena, 110
87054 Rogliano [CS]
Tel. +39 3208194246
www.antichevigne.com

ANNUAL PRODUCTION 72,000 bottles
HECTARES UNDER VINE 15.00

● Savuto Rosso Sup. '14	🍷🍷 3
○ Savuto Bianco Terra di Ginestre '19	🍷 2
⊙ Savuto Rosato Gida '19	🍷 2
● Savuto Rosso Cl. '18	🍷 2

Baccellieri

via Concordia, 4
89032 Bianco [RC]
Tel. +39 3355244570
www.baccellieri.it

ANNUAL PRODUCTION 25,000 bottles
HECTARES UNDER VINE 15.00
VITICULTURE METHOD Certified Organic
SUSTAINABLE WINERY

○ Mantonico Passito '13	🍷🍷 5
● Piroci '17	🍷🍷 3

Brigante

via Sant'Elia, 31
88813 Cirò [KR]
Tel. +39 3334135843
www.vinocirobrigante.it

CELLAR SALES
PRE-BOOKED VISITS
ACCOMMODATION
ANNUAL PRODUCTION 50,000 bottles
HECTARES UNDER VINE 10.00
SUSTAINABLE WINERY

○ Cirò Bianco Phemina '19	🍷🍷 3
● Cirò Rosso Cl. Sup. 0727 Ris. '17	🍷🍷 6
⊙ Zero Rosato '19	🍷🍷 6
⊙ Cirò Rosato Manyarì '19	🍷 3

Caparra & Siciliani

s.s. 106
88811 Cirò Marina [KR]
Tel. +39 0962373319
www.caparraesiciliani.com

CELLAR SALES
PRE-BOOKED VISITS
ANNUAL PRODUCTION 800,000 bottles
HECTARES UNDER VINE 180.00
VITICULTURE METHOD Certified Organic

⊙ Cirò Rosato Le Formelle '19	🍷🍷 2*
● Cirò Rosso Cl. Sup. Volvito Ris. '17	🍷🍷 2*
● Cirò Rosso Cl. Solagi '18	🍷 2
○ Curiale '19	🍷 2

Casa Comerci

fraz. Badia di Nicotera
c.da Comerci, 6
89844 Nicotera [VV]
Tel. +39 09631976077
www.casacomerci.it

CELLAR SALES
PRE-BOOKED VISITS
ANNUAL PRODUCTION 45,000 bottles
HECTARES UNDER VINE 15.00
VITICULTURE METHOD Certified Organic

○ Jancu Greco Bianco '19	🍷🍷 3
○ Rèfulu '19	🍷🍷 3
● 'A Batia '17	🍷 4
● Libìci '18	🍷 4

Tenuta Celimarro

C.DA CELIMARRO
87012 CASTROVILLARI [CS]
TEL. +39 09811926111
www.celimarro.it

CELLAR SALES
PRE-BOOKED VISITS
ANNUAL PRODUCTION 15,000 bottles
HECTARES UNDER VINE 20.00
VITICULTURE METHOD Certified Organic

- ○ Terre di Cosenza Pollino Bianco Greco Bianco '19 — 🍷🍷 3
- ⊙ Terre di Cosenza Pollino Rosato Oltre Tempo '19 — 🍷 3

Cantine De Mare

VIA SAFFO
88811 CIRÒ MARINA [KR]
TEL. +39 3393768853
www.cantinedemare.it

CELLAR SALES
PRE-BOOKED VISITS
ANNUAL PRODUCTION 100,000 bottles
HECTARES UNDER VINE 33.00

- ○ Cirò Bianco Sant'Angelo '19 — 🍷🍷 3
- ● Cirò Rosso Cl. Sup. Altura '18 — 🍷🍷 3
- ○ Pecorello Matto '19 — 🍷🍷 3
- ⊙ Cirò Rosato Prima Luce '19 — 🍷 3

Cantine Elisium

FRAZ. BORGO PARTENOPE
C.DA SERRE, 8
87100 COSENZA
TEL. +39 3281143418
www.cantineelisium.it

CELLAR SALES
PRE-BOOKED VISITS
ACCOMMODATION AND RESTAURANT SERVICE
ANNUAL PRODUCTION 10,000 bottles
HECTARES UNDER VINE 4.50

- ○ Petrara '19 — 🍷🍷 3
- ● Terre di Cosenza Donnici Capumasca '18 — 🍷🍷 6
- ⊙ Ispico '19 — 🍷 3

Colacino Wines

VIA COLLE MANCO
87054 ROGLIANO [CS]
TEL. +39 09841900252
www.colacino.it

CELLAR SALES
PRE-BOOKED VISITS
ANNUAL PRODUCTION 120,000 bottles
HECTARES UNDER VINE 21.00

- ○ Quarto '19 — 🍷🍷 2*
- ○ Savuto Bianco '19 — 🍷🍷 2*
- ● Savuto Sup. Britto '17 — 🍷🍷 4
- ● Savuto Cl. Colle Barabba '19 — 🍷 3

Diana

C.DA MILEO SNC
SARACENA [CS]
TEL. +39 3473892928
www.aziendaagricoladiana.it

- ○ Mileo '19 — 🍷🍷 3*
- ○ Moscato Passito '16 — 🍷🍷 6

Enotria

LOC. SAN GENNARO
S.DA ST.LE JONICA, 106
88811 CIRÒ MARINA [KR]
TEL. +39 0962371181
www.cantinaenotria.wine

CELLAR SALES
PRE-BOOKED VISITS
ANNUAL PRODUCTION 300,000 bottles
HECTARES UNDER VINE 45.00

- ● Cirò Rosso Cl. '18 — 🍷🍷 2*
- ○ 91 '19 — 🍷🍷 3
- ⊙ Punta dei 20 '19 — 🍷🍷 3
- ○ Cirò Bianco '19 — 🍷 2

Ferrocinto

FRAZ. VIGNE
C.DA FERROCINTO
87012 CASTROVILLARI [CS]
TEL. +39 0981415122
www.ferrocinto.it

CELLAR SALES
PRE-BOOKED VISITS
ANNUAL PRODUCTION 700,000 bottles
HECTARES UNDER VINE 45.00
VITICULTURE METHOD Certified Organic

○ Terre di Cosenza Pollino Bianco '19 ŸŸ 3
● Terre di Cosenza Pollino Magliocco '18 Ÿ 4
● Terre di Cosenza Pollino Rosato '19 Ÿ 4

Tenuta Iuzzolini

LOC. FRASSÀ
88811 CIRÒ MARINA [KR]
TEL. +39 0962373893
www.tenutaiuzzolini.it

CELLAR SALES
PRE-BOOKED VISITS
ANNUAL PRODUCTION 1,000,000 bottles
HECTARES UNDER VINE 100.00

● Belfresco '19 ŸŸ 3
● Muranera '18 ŸŸ 4
○ Prima Fila '18 ŸŸ 3
● Principe Spinelli '19 Ÿ 3

Barone Macrì

C.DA MODI
89040 GERACE [RC]
TEL. +39 0964356497
www.baronemacri.it

CELLAR SALES
PRE-BOOKED VISITS
ACCOMMODATION AND RESTAURANT SERVICE
ANNUAL PRODUCTION 30,000 bottles
HECTARES UNDER VINE 11.00
VITICULTURE METHOD Certified Organic

● Terre di Gerace Rosso '19 ŸŸ 2*
○ Terre di Gerace Bianco '19 Ÿ 2
⊙ Terre di Gerace Rosato '19 Ÿ 2

Malena

LOC. PETRARO
S.S. JONICA 106
88811 CIRÒ MARINA [KR]
TEL. +39 096231758
www.malena.it

CELLAR SALES
PRE-BOOKED VISITS
ANNUAL PRODUCTION 220,000 bottles
HECTARES UNDER VINE 16.00

○ Demetra Bianco '19 ŸŸ 2*
● Demetra Rosso '19 ŸŸ 2*
○ Cirò Bianco '19 Ÿ 2
● Cirò Rosso Cl. Sup. Pian della Corte Ris. '17 Ÿ 3

Poderi Marini

LOC. SANT'AGATA
87069 SAN DEMETRIO CORONE [CS]
TEL. +39 3683525028
www.poderimarini.it

CELLAR SALES
PRE-BOOKED VISITS
ANNUAL PRODUCTION 50,000 bottles
HECTARES UNDER VINE 7.00
VITICULTURE METHOD Certified Organic

⊙ Koronè Rosato '19 ŸŸ 2*
● Koronè Rosso '18 ŸŸ 2*
○ Koronè Bianco '19 Ÿ 2

Marrelli Wines

LOC. SANT'ANDREA
VIA DELL'ERICA, 28
88841 ISOLA DI CAPO RIZZUTO [KR]
TEL. +39 0962930276
www.marrelliwines.it

CELLAR SALES
PRE-BOOKED VISITS
ACCOMMODATION AND RESTAURANT SERVICE
ANNUAL PRODUCTION 50,000 bottles
HECTARES UNDER VINE 15.00

⊙ Don Lorenzo '19 ŸŸ 3
○ Donna Dora '19 ŸŸ 3
● Lakinio '18 ŸŸ 4
○ Liberty '19 Ÿ 2

Masseria Falvo 1727

loc. Garga
s.da prov.le Piana
87010 Saracena [CS]
Tel. +39 098138127
www.masseriafalvo.com

CELLAR SALES
ANNUAL PRODUCTION 80,000 bottles
HECTARES UNDER VINE 26.00
VITICULTURE METHOD Certified Organic

- ○ Terre di Cosenza Bianco Ejà '13 ΨΨ 5
- ○ Terre di Cosenza Bianco Pircoca '18 ΨΨ 3
- ○ Terre di Cosenza Bianco Spart '18 ΨΨ 3
- ⊙ Terre di Cosenza Pollino Rosato Cjviz '19 Ψ 3

Tenute Pacelli

c.da Rose
87010 Malvito [CS]
Tel. +39 09841634348
www.tenutepacelli.it

CELLAR SALES
PRE-BOOKED VISITS
ACCOMMODATION
ANNUAL PRODUCTION 18,000 bottles
HECTARES UNDER VINE 9.00
VITICULTURE METHOD Certified Organic
SUSTAINABLE WINERY

- ○ Barone Bianco '18 ΨΨ 2*
- ⊙ Malvarosa '18 ΨΨ 2*

La Pizzuta del Principe

c.da Pizzuta
88816 Strongoli [KR]
Tel. +39 096288252
www.lapizzutadelprincipe.it

CELLAR SALES
PRE-BOOKED VISITS
ACCOMMODATION AND RESTAURANT SERVICE
ANNUAL PRODUCTION 80,000 bottles
HECTARES UNDER VINE 13.00
VITICULTURE METHOD Certified Organic

- ● Scavello Cabernet Sauvignon '18 ΨΨ 2*
- ● Zingamaro '16 ΨΨ 3
- ○ Scavello Chardonnay '19 Ψ 2

Rocca Brettia

fraz. Donnici Inferiore
c.da Verzano snc
87100 Cosenza
Tel. +39 09841524393
www.roccabrettia.com

CELLAR SALES
PRE-BOOKED VISITS
ANNUAL PRODUCTION 13,000 bottles
HECTARES UNDER VINE 4.00

- ● Terre di Cosenza Aglianico '17 ΨΨ 3*
- ○ Svevo Bianco '19 ΨΨ 3
- ● Barbera '17 Ψ 3
- ● Terre di Cosenza Merlot '17 Ψ 3

Fattoria San Francesco

loc. Quattromani
88813 Cirò [KR]
Tel. +39 096232228
www.fattoriasanfrancesco.it

CELLAR SALES
PRE-BOOKED VISITS
ANNUAL PRODUCTION 224,000 bottles
HECTARES UNDER VINE 40.00

- ⊙ Cirò Rosato '19 ΨΨ 2*
- ● Cirò Rosso Cl. '18 ΨΨ 2*
- ⊙ Donna Rosa '19 Ψ 3
- ● Ronco Dei Quattroventi Gaglioppo '17 Ψ 3

Senatore Vini

loc. San Lorenzo
88811 Cirò Marina [KR]
Tel. +39 096232350
www.senatorevini.com

CELLAR SALES
PRE-BOOKED VISITS
ANNUAL PRODUCTION 250,000 bottles
HECTARES UNDER VINE 32.00
VITICULTURE METHOD Certified Organic
SUSTAINABLE WINERY

- ⊙ Cirò Rosato Puntalice '19 ΨΨ 3
- ● Unico Senator '12 ΨΨ 7
- ○ Cirò Bianco Alaei '19 Ψ 2
- ○ Silò '19 Ψ 3

Serracavallo

c.da Serracavallo
87043 Bisignano [CS]
Tel. +39 098421144
www.viniserracavallo.com

CELLAR SALES
PRE-BOOKED VISITS
RESTAURANT SERVICE
ANNUAL PRODUCTION 100,000 bottles
HECTARES UNDER VINE 30.00
VITICULTURE METHOD Certified Organic

○ Petramola '19	🍷🍷 3*
● Terre di Cosenza Colline del Crati Quattro Lustri '19	🍷🍷 3
⊙ Terre di Cosenza Rosato Don Filì '19	🍷🍷 3

Spadafora Wines 1915

zona ind. Piano Lago, 18
87050 Mangone [CS]
Tel. +39 0984969080
www.spadafora1915.it

CELLAR SALES
PRE-BOOKED VISITS
ACCOMMODATION
ANNUAL PRODUCTION 600,000 bottles
HECTARES UNDER VINE 15.00

⊙ Rosaspina '19	🍷🍷 3
○ Terre di Cosenza Donnici Dolcemare '19	🍷🍷 2*
● Terre di Cosenza Magliocco 1915 Anno Domini '17	🍷🍷 4

Terre del Gufo - Muzzillo

c.da Albo San Martino, 22a
87100 Cosenza
Tel. +39 0984780364
www.terredelgufo.it

CELLAR SALES
PRE-BOOKED VISITS
ANNUAL PRODUCTION 25,500 bottles
HECTARES UNDER VINE 3.00

● Terre di Cosenza Portapiana '18	🍷🍷 4
● Timpamara '18	🍷🍷 5

Terre di Balbia

c.da Montino
87042 Altomonte [CS]
Tel. +39 098435359
www.terredibalbia.it

CELLAR SALES
PRE-BOOKED VISITS
ANNUAL PRODUCTION 12,000 bottles
HECTARES UNDER VINE 8.00
VITICULTURE METHOD Certified Organic
SUSTAINABLE WINERY

⊙ Ligrezza '19	🍷🍷 3
● Blandus '18	🍷 4

Val di Neto

loc. Margherita
via delle Magnolie, 71
88900 Crotone
Tel. +39 0962930185
www.cantinavaldineto.com

CELLAR SALES
PRE-BOOKED VISITS
ACCOMMODATION AND RESTAURANT SERVICE
ANNUAL PRODUCTION 50,000 bottles
HECTARES UNDER VINE 20.00

⊙ Amistà '19	🍷🍷 2*
○ Kalypso '19	🍷🍷 2*
● Arkè '18	🍷 3

Zito

loc. Punta Alice
via Scalaretto
88811 Cirò Marina [KR]
Tel. +39 096231853
www.zito.it

CELLAR SALES
PRE-BOOKED VISITS
ANNUAL PRODUCTION 800,000 bottles
HECTARES UNDER VINE 80.00

⊙ Cirò Rosato Casale Difesa '19	🍷🍷 3
● Cirò Rosso Cl. Sup. Lilio Ris. '13	🍷🍷 3
○ Cirò Bianco '19	🍷 1
⊙ Cirò Rosato Imerio '19	🍷 2

SICILY

Everything seemed to be going well in early 2020, with reasonably exciting prospects. Instead, all of a sudden, everything changed: commercial networks were blocked, foreign markets unexpectedly closed. Producers were facing difficulties impossible to imagine even just a short time before. All the island's wine players tried to react, creatively. There were (and there are) problems, but Sicily's wine industry has responded with energy and conviction, despite difficulties that often led to (understandable) delays in bottling. But from our vantage point, the situation is still exciting, for the region's constantly growing overall quality, its liveliness, the technical-cultural evolution of the sector, and the increasingly evident (and winning) combination of terroir and native grapes. We also perceived something else, something important and remarkable that's opening up new horizons. Many producers have undergone (or are undergoing) a generational changeover. New figures are at the helm, dynamic and motivated young people, almost all of whom have expertise and an international vision. They're bringing new life and energy, bolstered by their studies,extensive experiences outside the region and new sensibilities. Another important factor that's creating value for this exciting panorama is Sicily's native grapes. Finally, Catarratto, Grillo, Insolia, Zibibbo, Carricante are treated as great native cultivars capable of giving rise to great wines (in reality and in the minds of the public). Some 26 wines took home Tre Bicchieri this year, testifying to the strength of this wonderful land, a continent in-and-of-itself that, surprisingly, is home to another: Etna. Because of space limitations we can only highlight the new additions: Poggio di Bortolone's Cerasuolo di Vittoria Il Para Para '17, a successful marriage of terroir and native grapes. Tre Bicchieri, for the first time, for Generazione Alessandro's surprising Etna Bianco Trainara '18 as well. Finally, we mention Monteleone (Giulia Monteleone and Benedetto Alessandro) and their Etna Rosso Qubba '18, which also took home a gold. This very positive regional portrait is enriched by a special recognition for Firriato, winners of our Sustainability Award.

Abbazia Santa Anastasia

Loc. Castelbuono
c.da Santa Anastasia
90013 Castelbuono [PA]
Tel. +39 0921671959
www.abbaziasantanastasia.com

CELLAR SALES
PRE-BOOKED VISITS
ACCOMMODATION AND RESTAURANT SERVICE
ANNUAL PRODUCTION 400,000 bottles
HECTARES UNDER VINE 67.50
VITICULTURE METHOD Certified Organic
SUSTAINABLE WINERY

The vineyard has thrived in this magnificent territory since the 12th century, bound up with the cultural and agricultural activities of the beautiful abbey founded by Ruggero d'Altavilla (today a charming country relais). Theatine and Benedictine monks eventually took over management, boosting viticulture and wine (essential in liturgy as the 'blood of Christ'). In 1982 a part of the immense estate—300 hectares, 70 vineyards—was bought by engineer Franco Lena, who was seduced by its beauty. He proceeded to modernized everything in light of the best organic and biodynamic agricultural practices. The Litra '17, a monovarietal Cabernet Sauvignon marked by superb and decisive personality, just fell short of Tre Bicchieri. It pours a dark purplish color, heralding vibrant nuances of berries, bay leaf, walnut skin and conifers; in the mouth it's dynamic and incredibly persistent, embellished by soft tannins. The highly drinkable Santa Anastasia Zibibbo '19, a wine redolent of peach, lavender and citrus fruits, also put in a notable performance.

Wine	Rating
● Sicilia Cabernet Sauvignon Litra '17	▼▼ 6
○ Sicilia Baccante '17	▼▼ 4
● Sicilia Montenero '17	▼▼ 4
● Sicilia Passomaggio '17	▼▼ 4
○ Sicilia Zibibbo '19	▼▼ 4
● Sens(i)nverso Nero d'Avola '17	▼ 6
● Sens(i)nverso Syrah '17	▼ 6
○ Sicilia Sauvignon Sinestesia '19	▼ 4
● Litra '04	▽▽▽ 6
● Litra '01	▽▽▽ 7
● Litra '00	▽▽▽ 7
● Litra '99	▽▽▽ 7
● Litra '97	▽▽▽ 7
● Litra '96	▽▽▽ 6
● Montenero '04	▽▽▽ 4

Alessandro di Camporeale

c.da Mandranova
90043 Camporeale [PA]
Tel. +39 092437038
www.alessandrodicamporeale.it

CELLAR SALES
PRE-BOOKED VISITS
ANNUAL PRODUCTION 240,000 bottles
HECTARES UNDER VINE 40.00
VITICULTURE METHOD Certified Organic

Much appreciated by critics and consumers, this beautiful winery, founded in the early twentieth century, has recently seen significant changes. Brothers Alessandro, Natale, Nino and Rosolino are focusing on the quality and elegance of their wines in pursuit of territorial and varietal expression. The arrival of their young children, bolstered by their studies (including international, law, enology and marketing) has given a further boost to the family management style, all in preparation for the next generational changing of the guard. The extraordinary Catarratto Vigna di Mandranova '18 took home a gold. It's a territorial wine marked by crystalline beauty right from the outset, offering up aromas of citrus fruits, wisteria, medicinal herbs and slate, charming with its perfect balance of fruit and acidity—truly elegant and gratifying. The pulpy, assertive and elegant Grillo Vigna di Mandranova '19 also made it into our finals by virtue of exquisite nuances of peach, iris and grapefruit.

Wine	Rating
○ Sicilia Catarrato V. di Mandranova '18	▼▼▼ 4*
○ Sicilia Grillo V. di Mandranova '19	▼▼ 3*
○ Extra Brut M. Cl. '16	▼▼ 6
○ Sicilia Catarratto Benedè '19	▼▼ 2*
● Sicilia MNRL V. di Mandranova '17	▼▼ 6
● Sicilia Nero d'Avola Donnatà '19	▼▼ 2*
○ Sicilia Sauvignon V. di Mandranova '19	▼▼ 3
● Sicilia Syrah Kaid '18	▼▼ 4
● Sicilia Syrah Kaid V. T. '19	▼▼ 5
○ Sicilia Catarratto V. di Mandranova '16	▽▽▽ 4*
○ Sicilia Grillo V. di Mandranova '18	▽▽▽ 3*
● Sicilia Syrah Kaid '16	▽▽▽ 4*
● Sicilia Syrah Kaid '17	▽▽ 4
● Sicilia Syrah Kaid '15	▽▽ 4

Alta Mora

fraz. Pietramarina
c.da Verzella
95012 Castiglione di Sicilia [CT]
Tel. +39 0918908713
www.altamora.it

PRE-BOOKED VISITS
ANNUAL PRODUCTION 100,000 bottles
HECTARES UNDER VINE 44.00
SUSTAINABLE WINERY

Founded in April 2013, Alberto and Diego Cusumano's adventure on Mt. Etna is now a long-term dream come true. The two brothers' vision was measured and clear: identify certain districts and produce the best suited wines. The entire range is fruit of the volcano, but at the same time it's diverse, with different wines exhibiting distinct personalities. So it is that Alta Mora successfully brings together, at elevations ranging from 500 to 1000 meters, the districts of Guardiola, Feudo di Mezzo, Pietramarina, Solicchiata, Santo Spirito and Verzella, the last of which also hosts a cellar that integrates nicely with the landscape. The Alta Mora Bianco '19 is a singular wine: timid and graceful with its delicate, clear straw-yellow colour streaked with greenish highlights, on the nose it comes through majestic and complex, with elegant nuances of plums and white peach accompanied by medicinal herbs, flowers and citrus fruits. A fine mineral substrate emerges, rendering it highly drinkable and endlessly long. Once again, Tre Bicchieri.

Wine	Rating
○ Etna Bianco Alta Mora '19	TTT 4*
● Etna Rosso Alta Mora Feudo di Mezzo '16	TT 7
● Etna Rosso Alta Mora Guardiola '16	TT 7
⊙ Etna Rosato Alta Mora '19	TT 4
○ Etna Bianco Alta Mora '18	YYY 4*
○ Etna Bianco Alta Mora '17	YYY 4*
○ Etna Bianco Alta Mora '16	YYY 4*
○ Etna Bianco Alta Mora '14	YYY 3*
⊙ Etna Rosato Alta Mora '18	YY 3
⊙ Etna Rosato Alta Mora '17	YY 3
● Etna Rosso Alta Mora '17	YY 4
● Etna Rosso Alta Mora '16	YY 4
● Etna Rosso Alta Mora Feudo di Mezzo '15	YY 4
● Etna Rosso Alta Mora Guardiola '15	YY 4

Assuli

c.da Carcitella
91026 Mazara del Vallo [TP]
Tel. +39 0923547267
www.assuli.it

CELLAR SALES
ANNUAL PRODUCTION 100,000 bottles
HECTARES UNDER VINE 120.00
VITICULTURE METHOD Certified Organic
SUSTAINABLE WINERY

The Caruso family maintains an ancient bond with Western Sicily and its territory. The farm founded by Giacomo Caruso has quickly become an important producer thanks to his son Roberto, who runs the splendid winery with the help of the third generation, his grandson Roberto and children Nicoletta and Michele. About 130 hectares of vineyards span Mazara del Vallo, Castelvetrano, Salemi and Calatafimi-Segesta. 18 hectares near Bosco di Scorace, on hills reaching 600 meters elevation, host native cultivars of excellent quality that will soon enter production. For the second year in a row, the Perricone Furioso delivers. The 2017 is deep and well defined, with elegant earthy and herbaceous nuances, fleshy and persistent on the palate. The Nero d'Avola Besi '17 also made it into our finals. It's complex, with beautifully integrated oak and lovely, round fruit. Intense marine and candied citron notes characterize the Grillo Passito '17; the Insolia Carinda '19 proves pleasantly fresh and mineral.

Wine	Rating
● Sicilia Perricone Furioso '17	TTT 5
● Sicilia Nero d'Avola Besi '17	TT 5
○ Passito di Grillo '17	TT 5
○ Sicilia Grillo Astolfo '18	TT 4
○ Sicilia Grillo Fiordiligi '19	TT 3
○ Sicilia Insolia Carinda '19	TT 3
○ Sicilia Lucido Donna Angelica '18	TT 3
● Sicilia Nero d'Avola Lorlando Ris. '17	TT 5
● Sicilia Nero d'Avola Lorlando '19	TT 3
○ Sicilia Zibibbo Dardinello '19	TT 3
○ Astolfo '15	YYY 4*
● Lorlando '15	YYY 2*
● Lorlando '14	YYY 2*
● Sicilia Nero d'Avola Lorlando '17	YYY 3*
● Sicilia Perricone Furioso '16	YYY 5

Baglio del Cristo di Campobello

loc. c.da Favarotta
s.da st.le 123, km 19,200
92023 Campobello di Licata [AG]
Tel. +39 0922 877709
www.cristodicampobello.it

PRE-BOOKED VISITS
ANNUAL PRODUCTION 300,000 bottles
HECTARES UNDER VINE 35.00

This year Baglio del Cristo is celebrating its twentieth harvest. It's an important milestone for the Bonetta family, passionate winemakers who in 2000 decided to put their long experience in the wine sector to good use. 30 hectares of vineyards unfold along the sunny, shimmering white limestone hills. It's an area that boasts a unique soil and climate, thanks in part to the nearby sea and the fact that its abundant sunshine is greatly amplified by the reflection of the calcareous crystals that make up the soil. The Adénzia Bianco '19, a blend of Inzolia and Chardonnay, made it into our finals. A broad and elegant bouquet of flowers and yellow fruit characterize the nose—its mineral and balsamic aspects are also on display, mint in particular. On the palate it comes through sapid, fresh and well balanced amidst body and acidity, finishing long and lovely. The C'D'C Bianco '19 is a very pleasant drink, with delicious citrus scents that make an encore in its fresh finish.

Wine	Rating
○ Sicila Bianco Adènzia '19	🍷🍷 3*
○ C'D'C' Cristo di Campobello Bianco '19	🍷🍷 2*
● C'D'C' Cristo di Campobello Rosso '19	🍷🍷 2*
○ Sicilia Grillo Lalùci '19	🍷🍷 3
● Sicilia Syrah Lusirà '18	🍷🍷 5
● Lu Patri '09	🥂🥂🥂 5
○ C'D'C' Cristo di Campobello Bianco '18	🥂🥂 2*
● C'D'C' Cristo di Campobello Rosso '18	🥂🥂 2*
○ Sicilia Bianco Adènzia '18	🥂🥂 3
○ Sicilia Bianco Adènzia '16	🥂🥂 3*
○ Sicilia Grillo Lalùci '17	🥂🥂 3*
● Sicilia Rosso Adènzia '17	🥂🥂 3
● Sicilia Syrah Lusirà '17	🥂🥂 5

Baglio di Pianetto

loc. Pianetto
via Francia
90030 Santa Cristina Gela [PA]
Tel. +39 0918570002
www.bagliodipianetto.it

CELLAR SALES
PRE-BOOKED VISITS
ACCOMMODATION AND RESTAURANT SERVICE
ANNUAL PRODUCTION 550,000 bottles
HECTARES UNDER VINE 104.00
SUSTAINABLE WINERY

It was 1997 when Count Paolo Marzotto, a well-known wine entrepreneur from Veneto who recently passed away, decided to invest in a large winery in Sicily to accompany those his group already owned in Italy. The ambitious project involved two different production areas, one in Santa Cristina Gela, just outside Palermo, and the other in Contrada Baroni, in Val di Noto, more than 100 organically farmed hectares in all. For some years now, the Palermo estate has also hosted an elegant wine resort nestled among the vineyards and endowed with a fine local restaurant. The Syraco '17, an elegant monovarietal Syrah, features close-woven, clear scents of spices, red fruits and aromatic herbs. The palate is full and dense, with alluring, smooth tannins, stretching sapid, juicy and long right up to the end. We also appreciated the territorial Nero d'Avola Cembali '16, with its intense nuances of cherries and black pepper, and its ripe, harmonious, pleasant palate.

Wine	Rating
● Syraco '17	🍷🍷 3*
⊙ Baiasyra '19	🍷🍷 3
○ Monreale Bianco Murriali '19	🍷🍷 3
○ Sicilia Bianco Timeo '19	🍷🍷 3
● Sicilia Nero d'Avola Cembali '16	🍷🍷 5
● Sicilia Rosso Viafrancia Ris. '15	🍷🍷 5
○ Sicilia Bianco Ficiligno '19	🍷 3
○ Sicilia Bianco Viafrancia Ris. '18	🍷 4
● Ramione '04	🥂🥂🥂 3*
● Shymer '14	🥂🥂🥂 2*
● Shymer '13	🥂🥂🥂 2*
● Sicilia Rosso Ramione '13	🥂🥂🥂 3*
○ Sicilia Bianco Viafrancia Ris. '16	🥂🥂 4
● Sicilia Rosso Viafrancia Ris. '14	🥂🥂 6

Barone di Villagrande

via del Bosco, 25
95025 Milo [CT]
Tel. +39 3337993868
www.villagrande.it

CELLAR SALES
PRE-BOOKED VISITS
ACCOMMODATION AND RESTAURANT SERVICE
ANNUAL PRODUCTION 90,000 bottles
HECTARES UNDER VINE 28.00
VITICULTURE METHOD Certified Organic
SUSTAINABLE WINERY

They've been going for 300 years and show no signs of slowing down. Indeed, the Nicolosi family have been cultivating vines for ten generations (and the eleventh is ready) with the same passion and enthusiasm. In 1727 Carmelo Nicolosi planted his first rooted cuttings in Milo, on the eastern side of Mount Etna. Now it's Marco Nicolosi's turn to oversee the property, and he's been making major changes of late, modernizing the cellar, opening a beautiful wine resort and redesigning the labels so as to coincide with a significant increase in the quality level of their entire range. Our tastings confirmed not only the craftsmanship of their wines, but also the fact that they're among the most faithful in expressing Etna's terroir-grape combination. An example is the Etna Bianco Superiore Villagrande '17, which offers up notes of Mediterranean herbs, smoked salt and white-fleshed fruit. In the mouth it's also elegant and harmonious, with invigorating fruit that's nicely infused in a full, mature palate.

Wine	Glasses	
○ Etna Bianco Sup. Contrada Villagrande '17	▼▼	8
⊙ Etna Rosato '19	▼▼	5
● Etna Rosso Contrada Villagrande '17	▼▼	8
○ Salina Bianco '19	▼▼	8
○ Etna Bianco Sup. '17	▽▽	3
○ Etna Bianco Sup. Contrada Villagrande '15	▽▽	6
● Etna Rosso '18	▽▽	3
● Etna Rosso '16	▽▽	3
● Etna Rosso '15	▽▽	3
● Etna Rosso Contrada Villagrande '14	▽▽	6
● Etna Rosso Contrada Villagrande '13	▽▽	6
○ Malvasia delle Lipari Passito '14	▽▽	5
○ Malvasia delle Lipari Passito '13	▽▽	5

Tenuta Bastonaca

c.da Bastonaca
97019 Vittoria [RG]
Tel. +39 0932686480
www.tenutabastonaca.it

CELLAR SALES
PRE-BOOKED VISITS
ACCOMMODATION
ANNUAL PRODUCTION 48,000 bottles
HECTARES UNDER VINE 17.00
VITICULTURE METHOD Certified Organic

Silvana Raniolo and her husband, Giovanni Calcaterra, represent a small operation, perfectly suited to the definition of 'boutique winery', synonymous with high quality and artisanal craftsmanship. Of the two estates, the largest (15 hectares of non-irrigated bush-trained vineyards) is situated in one of Cerasuolo di Vittoria's best areas. The second, just 2 hectares, is located on Mount Etna, in Castiglione di Sicilia, in the Piano dei Daini district. Here, on average, the vines go back over 70 years. A strong ecological sensitivity is of great importance. The Sud '18 just missed Tre Bicchieri. It's a commendable blend of Nero d'Avola, Tannat and Grenache, a wine with a strong and multifaceted character that stands out for its extreme stylistic precision and pronounced elegance. Aromatically it's characterized by nuances of blackcurrant, cherry jam, juniper berries and capers, while in the mouth it proves juicy and vibrant, with round, cosseting tannins. The rest of their selection also did well.

Wine	Glasses	
● Sud '18	▼▼	5
● Cerasuolo di Vittoria '18	▼▼	3
○ Etna Bianco '18	▼▼	5
● Etna Rosso '17	▼▼	5
○ Sicilia Grillo '19	▼▼	3
● Sicilia Nero d'Avola '19	▼▼	3
● Vittoria Frappato '19	▼	3
● Cerasuolo di Vittoria '17	▽▽	3
● Cerasuolo di Vittoria '16	▽▽	3
○ Etna Bianco '17	▽▽	5
● Etna Rosso '16	▽▽	5
● Etna Rosso '15	▽▽	4
● Frappato '18	▽▽	3
● Frappato '17	▽▽	3
● Sicilia Nero d'Avola '18	▽▽	3
● Sud '17	▽▽	5
● Sud '16	▽▽	5

★Benanti

via Giuseppe Garibaldi, 361
95029 Viagrande [CT]
Tel. +39 0957893399
www.benanti.it

CELLAR SALES
PRE-BOOKED VISITS
RESTAURANT SERVICE
ANNUAL PRODUCTION 170,000 bottles
HECTARES UNDER VINE 28.00
SUSTAINABLE WINERY

In the late 1980s Giuseppe Benanti commissioned a study on Etna's native grapes by a team that included professors Rocco Di Stefano (from the Institute of Enology in Asti), Jean Siegrist (from INRA in Beaune), enologists Gian Domenico Negro and Alessandro Monchiero, and Sicilian agronomist Salvo Foti. The results of the first small batch fermentations were so encouraging that the first vintage was bottled in 1990 and debuted at Vinitaly 1994. Thus the custom of marketing wines only after lengthy aging in the cellar was inaugurated—it's still used today. After a couple of years of ups and downs, the Benanti seem to have achieved the right balance between vineyard and cellar, an admirable stylistic feature, as well as impeccable definition in all their wines. The Monte Serra '18 is a good example with its pure, light and airy aromas of violet, black berries, iron and medicinal herbs. It's made elegant by virtue of its almost impalpable, but still discernible, fruit.

● Etna Rosso Contrada Monte Serra '18	TT 6
○ Etna Bianco Sup. Pietra Marina '16	TT 8
● Etna Rosso Contrada Cavaliere '18	TT 6
● Etna Rosso Contrada Dafara Galluzzo '18	TT 6
● Nerello Cappuccio '18	TT 5
○ Etna Bianco Sup. Pietramarina '09	YYY 5
○ Etna Bianco Sup. Pietramarina '04	YYY 6
○ Etna Bianco Sup. Pietramarina '02	YYY 5
○ Etna Bianco Sup. Pietramarina '01	YYY 5
○ Etna Bianco Sup. Pietramarina '00	YYY 5
○ Etna Bianco Sup. Pietramarina '99	YYY 4
○ Etna Bianco Sup. Pietramarina '97	YYY 4*
● Etna Rosso Contrada Monte Serra '17	YYY 6
● Etna Rosso Serra della Contessa '06	YYY 7
● Etna Rosso Serra della Contessa '04	YYY 7
● Etna Rosso Serra della Contessa '03	YYY 7

Tenute Bosco

s.da prov.le 64 Solicchiata
95012 Castiglione di Sicilia [CT]
Tel. +39 0957658856
www.tenutebosco.com

CELLAR SALES
PRE-BOOKED VISITS
ANNUAL PRODUCTION 50,000 bottles
HECTARES UNDER VINE 10.00
VITICULTURE METHOD Certified Organic

Sofia Ponzini started off quietly, preferring not to sell her first vintages before facing the market and critics. She wanted to be sure she had reached the goals of high quality and the right balance between terroir and grape that she had set herself when she purchased the century-old Vico vineyard. Time proved her right. Sunny, determined and driven by an unquenchable passion, Sofia continues to offer us notable wines, harvest after harvest. They express her character and style: vital and energetic, but at the same time harmonious and sophisticated in their elegance. Their wines confirm that, when fully respected, the generous terroir of Etna can bring out the varietal peculiarities of its vines. Tre Bicchieri for the Vigna Vico '17, an archetype of Etna's reds with its clear, focused mineral and fruity aromas: elegant and austere on the palate, it opens nicely around a dynamic tannic weave that will support it for a long time to come.

● Etna Rosso V. Vico Prephylloxera '17	TTT 8
○ Etna Bianco Piano dei Daini '19	TT 5
⊙ Etna Rosato Piano dei Daini '19	TT 5
● Etna Rosso Piano dei Daini '18	TT 5
● Etna Rosso V. Vico Prephylloxera '16	YYY 8
● Etna Rosso V. Vico Prephylloxera '15	YYY 8
○ Etna Bianco Piano dei Daini '18	YY 5
○ Etna Bianco Piano dei Daini '17	YY 5
○ Etna Bianco Piano dei Daini '16	YY 5
⊙ Etna Rosato Piano dei Daini '18	YY 5
⊙ Etna Rosato Piano dei Daini '17	YY 5
⊙ Etna Rosato Piano dei Daini '16	YY 5
● Etna Rosso Piano dei Daini '17	YY 5
● Etna Rosso Piano dei Daini '16	YY 5
● Etna Rosso Piano dei Daini '15	YY 5
● Etna Rosso Vigna Vico '14	YY 8

Paolo Calì

fraz. c.da Salmé
via del Frappato, 100
97019 Vittoria [RG]
Tel. +39 0932510082
www.vinicali.it

CELLAR SALES
PRE-BOOKED VISITS
ANNUAL PRODUCTION 90,000 bottles
HECTARES UNDER VINE 15.00

Given the passion for agriculture that Paolo Calì inherited from his father, as a boy the countryside served as a refuge from his studies. As an adult, he flanks his work as a pharmacist with that of the vigneron. The estate is beautiful, currently being converted to organic, and though not near the sea, it's marked by a strong presence of sand dunes, which give rise to subtle, intriguing wines. Paolo believes in 'following nature', thus the yeasts are indigenous, and there are neither filtrations nor stabilizations. The Forfice '16 just fell short of Tre Bicchieri. It's Cerasuolo di Vittoria of great depth and elegance, offering up vibrant notes of black mulberries, peach, capers and topsoil on the nose. In the mouth it exhibits great freshness and energy, perfectly balancing acidity and fruit. The Frappato Mandragola '18 is also excellent. But what stood out most is just how well made all their wines are while admirably expressing the terroir.

Wine	Glasses	Price
● Cerasuolo di Vittoria Cl. Forfice '16	🍷🍷	6
○ Blues Grillo '19	🍷🍷	3
● Cerasuolo di Vittoria Cl. Manene '18	🍷🍷	4
⊙ Osa! Frappato Rosato '19	🍷🍷	4
● Vittoria Frappato Mandragola '18	🍷🍷	3
● Vittoria Nero d'Avola Violino '17	🍷🍷	3
● Vittoria Frappato Pruvenza '17	🍷	6
● Cerasuolo di Vittoria Cl. Forfice '15	ΥΥ	4
● Cerasuolo di Vittoria Cl. Forfice '13	ΥΥ	6
● Jazz '16	ΥΥ	3
● Vittoria Frappato Mandragola '17	ΥΥ	3
● Vittoria Frappato Mandragola '16	ΥΥ	3
● Vittoria Frappato Mandragola '15	ΥΥ	3
● Vittoria Frappato Pruvenza '15	ΥΥ	6
● Vittoria Nero d'Avola Violino '16	ΥΥ	3
● Vittoria Nero d'Avola Violino '12	ΥΥ	3

Caravaglio

via Nazionale, 33
98050 Malfa [ME]
Tel. +39 3398115953
www.caravaglio.it

CELLAR SALES
PRE-BOOKED VISITS
ANNUAL PRODUCTION 50,000 bottles
HECTARES UNDER VINE 12.00
VITICULTURE METHOD Certified Organic
SUSTAINABLE WINERY

It takes a lot of passion to run a winery on a small island, and a lot of patience as well. Since Nino Caravaglio's vineyards are scattered on 40 different plots in Salina's three municipalities, the bureaucracy is multiplied by three. But Nino has always put incredible willpower into his work. Thus his winery has become a solid benchmark not only for the Aeolian Islands but for the whole Sicily, thanks to wines that fully reflect the terroir and to personal, successful interpretations of Malvasia delle Lipari, a wine whose history goes back millennia. Tre Bicchieri for the Malvasia Passito '19, a wine endowed with a seductive Mediterranean bouquet and a very elegant palate, which manages to be soft and velvety, but also fresh and invigorating by virtue of a sapid acidity that accompanies it throughout a long finish. We appreciated all the wines tasted: the excellent Malvasia Secca Infatata '19 easily reached our finals.

Wine	Glasses	Price
○ Malvasia delle Lipari Passito '19	🍷🍷🍷	5
○ Infatata '19	🍷🍷	3*
● Chianu Cruci '19	🍷🍷	3
● Nero du Munti '19	🍷🍷	4
● Palmento di Salina '19	🍷🍷	4
○ Malvasia delle Lipari Passito '18	ΥΥΥ	5
○ Malvasia delle Lipari Passito '17	ΥΥΥ	5
○ Malvasia delle Lipari Passito '16	ΥΥΥ	5
● Chianu Cruci '15	ΥΥ	3
○ Infatata '18	ΥΥ	3
○ Infatata '17	ΥΥ	3
○ Malvasia '18	ΥΥ	5
○ Malvasia '17	ΥΥ	5
○ Occhio di Terra Chianu Cruci '17	ΥΥ	3
● Palmento di Salina '18	ΥΥ	4
● Palmento di Salina '17	ΥΥ	4
○ Rossi di Salina '18	ΥΥ	3

Case Alte

loc. Macellarotto
via Pisciotta, 27
90043 Camporeale [PA]
Tel. +39 3297130750
www.casealte.it

ACCOMMODATION
ANNUAL PRODUCTION 17,000 bottles
HECTARES UNDER VINE 8.00
VITICULTURE METHOD Certified Organic

For 3 generations the Vaccaro family have been cultivating vines in the territory of Camporeale. It all began in the 1950s with Giuseppe, who oversaw a small production of Catarratto and Nerello Mascalese. In the years that followed it grew under his son Calogero, this until 2010, when the cellar was built by his grandson Giuseppe. Agricultural management is organic and native yeasts are used in the cellar, all under the careful technical guidance of Benedetto Alessandro. The vineyards are situated on the hills around Macellarotto, at 500 meters above sea level, the ideal mesoclimate for grapes with superb potential. A classic Catarratto, the 12 Filari '19 performed well in our finals. The nose is broad and complex, delivering floral notes of citrus fruits and subtle mineral nuances; its texture is consistent, with tension, sapidity and length. We also appreciated the very pleasant Grillo 4 Filari '19: peach, grapefruit, green almond accompany a fresh and crisp pulp. The Nero d'Avola 16 Filari '18 is clear and focused in its varietal notes, and fragrant in its delicious fruit.

Wine	Rating
○ Sicilia Catarratto 12 Filari '19	▼▼ 3*
○ Sicilia Grillo 4 Filari '19	▼▼ 3
● Sicilia Nero d'Avola 16 Filari '18	▼▼ 4
○ Sicilia 12 Filari '16	▽▽ 3
● Sicilia 16 Filari '15	▽▽ 3
○ Sicilia 4 Filari '16	▽▽ 3
○ Sicilia Catarratto 12 Filari '18	▽▽ 3
○ Sicilia Catarratto 12 Filari '17	▽▽ 3
○ Sicilia Grillo 4 Filari '18	▽▽ 3
○ Sicilia Grillo 4 Filari '17	▽▽ 3
● Sicilia Nero d'Avola 16 Filari '17	▽▽ 4
● Sicilia Nero d'Avola 16 Filari '16	▽▽ 4

Le Casematte

loc. Faro Superiore
c.da Corso
98163 Messina
Tel. +39 0906409427
www.lecasematte.it

CELLAR SALES
ANNUAL PRODUCTION 40,000 bottles
HECTARES UNDER VINE 11.00
VITICULTURE METHOD Certified Organic
SUSTAINABLE WINERY

On the hills overlooking the Strait of Messina, a few hectares of steep and impervious land are characterized by panoramic terraces. Here 'casematte' (military forts) mark the profile of a tract of vineyards that serve as an example of 'heroic' viticulture. They're owned by accountant Gianfranco Sabbatino and Andrea Barzagli, a well-known former footballer. Their common passion for quality derives from a desire to boost the prestigious DOC Faro, all in pursuit of finesse and style. It's a much appreciated wine for its clarity and elegance. Yet another gold for the Faro '18 (Nerello Mascalese, Cappuccio, Nero d'Avola and Nocera). It pours a seductive ruby-red colour tending towards garnet, heralding rich and complex aromas of black spices, mulberries, chocolate, medicinal herbs and topsoil. On the palate it comes through juicy and elegant, long and cosseting. We appreciated the delicate and subtle Rosematte '19 rosé, while both the Peloro Bianco '19 and the Peloro Rosso '18 also put in notable performances.

Wine	Rating
● Faro '18	▼▼▼ 5
● Nanuci '18	▼▼ 3
⊙ Rosematte Nerello Mascalese '19	▼▼ 3
○ Sicilia Peloro Bianco '19	▼▼ 3
● Sicilia Peloro Rosso '18	▼▼ 3
● Faro '17	▽▽▽ 5
● Faro '16	▽▽▽ 5
● Faro '15	▽▽▽ 5
● Faro '14	▽▽▽ 5
● Faro '13	▽▽▽ 5
● Figliodiennenne '12	▽▽ 2*
● Nanuci '17	▽▽ 3
● Peloro Rosso '17	▽▽ 3
● Peloro Rosso '16	▽▽ 3
● Peloro Rosso '15	▽▽ 2*
● Peloro Rosso '14	▽▽ 2*

Centopassi

via Porta Palermo, 132
90048 San Giuseppe Jato [PA]
Tel. +39 0918577655
www.centopassisicilia.it

CELLAR SALES
PRE-BOOKED VISITS
ACCOMMODATION AND RESTAURANT SERVICE
ANNUAL PRODUCTION 450,000 bottles
HECTARES UNDER VINE 65.00
VITICULTURE METHOD Certified Organic
SUSTAINABLE WINERY

Twenty years ago Consorzio Libera Terra brought to life a beautiful project, transforming a property built with violence and crime into a source of wealth and occupation for the entire community. The winery and the vineyards are, in fact, all confiscated from the mafia. The plots are mainly located in various areas in Alto Belice Corleonese, in the municipalities of Monreale, Camporeale and San Giuseppe Jato, which also hosts the cellar. Centopassi's pride is its selection of crus, ten wines that highlight the attributes of the territory's pedoclimatic diversity. The Grillo Rocce di Pietra Longa '19 features a fine nose of peach and Mediterranean scrub—in the mouth its fruit is taut and fragrant. The floral and citrusy Catarratto Terre Rosse di Giabbascio '19 proves fresh and lively on the palate.. We also appreciated the blend of Grillo and Catarratto, the Giato '19, with its notes of pear and pleasant herbaceous hints. The Cimento di Perricone '18 is characterized by very mature fragrances and elegant, jammy hints.

○ Sicilia Bianco Sup. Giato '19 — TT 2*
○ Sicilia Catarratto Terre Rosse di Giabbascio '19 — TT 3
○ Sicilia Grillo Rocce di Pietra Longa '19 — TT 3
● Argille di Tagghia Via di Sutta '19 — T 3
● Cimento di Perricone '18 — T 3
● Sicilia Merlot Sulla Via Francigena '17 — T 3
● Sicilia Nerello Mascalese Pietre a Purtedda da Ginestra '17 — T 5
● Sicilia Rosso Giato '19 — T 2
○ Tendoni di Trebbiano '18 — T 3
○ Sicilia Catarratto Terre Rosse di Giabbascio '18 — YYY 3*
● Cimento di Perricone '17 — YY 3
○ Sicilia Catarratto Terre Rosse di Giabbascio '17 — YY 3*
● Sicilia Giato Nero d'Avola Perricone '18 — YY 2*

★Cottanera

loc. Iannazzo
s.da prov.le 89
95030 Castiglione di Sicilia [CT]
Tel. +39 0942963601
www.cottanera.it

CELLAR SALES
PRE-BOOKED VISITS
ANNUAL PRODUCTION 350,000 bottles
HECTARES UNDER VINE 65.00

Cottanera Iannazzo is one of Etna's most important producers in terms of quality and surface area. It was founded thanks to the foresight and vision of the late Guglielmo Cambria and his brother Enzo. The grandchildren of the latter, Mariangela, Emanuele and Francesco, are continuing the family adventure, bringing new enthusiasm and the same dedication to their work. In addition to their prized selections made with native cultivars, it's worth mentioning the successful use of international grapes as well (including Cabernet Sauvignon, Merlot and Syrah, which have been present on Etna since the 19th century). Once again all the wines presented exhibit great clarity and focus, elegance and polish, while managing to express the magical Etnean terroir and its cultivars. The Etna Rosso Zottorinoto Ris. '16 earns Tre Bicchieri by virtue of its exceptionally elegant aromas and a mature, smooth, fruity texture that's also extraordinarily invigorating.

● Etna Rosso Zottorinoto Ris. '16 — TTT 8
● Etna Rosso Feudo di Mezzo '17 — TT 6
○ Etna Bianco '19 — TT 3
○ Etna Bianco Barbazzale '19 — TT 5
○ Etna Bianco Calderara '18 — TT 5
⊙ Etna Rosato '19 — TT 2*
● Etna Rosso Barbazzale '19 — TT 3
● Etna Rosso Diciassettesalme '18 — TT 3
● Sicilia L'Ardenza '17 — TT 4
● Sicilia Sole di Sesta '17 — TT 4
● Etna Rosso '11 — YYY 5
● Etna Rosso Feudo di Mezzo '16 — YYY 6
● Etna Rosso Zottorinoto Ris. '14 — YYY 8
● Etna Rosso Zottorinoto Ris. '13 — YYY 8
● Etna Rosso Zottorinoto Ris. '12 — YYY 8
● Etna Rosso Zottorinoto Ris. '11 — YYY 8

★★Cusumano

LOC. C.DA SAN CARLO
S.DA ST.LE 113 KM 307
90047 PARTINICO [PA]
TEL. +39 0918908713
www.cusumano.it

CELLAR SALES
PRE-BOOKED VISITS
ANNUAL PRODUCTION 2,500,000 bottles
HECTARES UNDER VINE 520.00
SUSTAINABLE WINERY

Twenty years ago Alberto and Diego made their debut in the world of wine. Bolstered by a solid family tradition, in a short time they've managed to make Cusumano a benchmark for quality winemaking in Sicily. Five estates constitute a priceless patrimony of diversity. Each vineyard corresponds to a project aimed at developing the relationship between terroir and cultivar, while giving rise to wines unique in elegance and character, from San Carlo to Partinico, Butera, Monreale and the high hills of Bosco di Ficuzza, which provide the grapes for their Salealto, a new blend based on Grillo, Inzolia and Zibibbo. And the Salealto '18 takes home Tre Bicchieri: intriguing on the nose with beautiful aromatic notes, nuances of tropical fruits and an elegant minerality, on the palate it comes through with soft fruit, sapid and long. The Chardonnay Jalé '18, fine and soft, with a harmoniously integrated oak, accompanied it in our finals. The Nero d'Avola Sagana '17 proves defined and intense on the nose, invigorating and vibrant on the palate.

Wine	Rating
○ Salealto Tenuta Ficuzza '18	🍷🍷🍷 6
○ Sicilia Chardonnay Jalé '18	🍷🍷 5
○ Sicilia Bianco Angimbè Tenuta Ficuzza '19	🍷🍷 3
○ Sicilia Grillo Shamaris Tenuta Monte Pietroso '19	🍷🍷 3
● Sicilia Nero d'Avola '19	🍷🍷 2*
● Sicilia Nero d'Avola Disueri Tenuta San Giacomo '19	🍷🍷 3
● Sicilia Nero d'Avola Sàgana Tenuta San Giacomo '17	🍷🍷 5
● Sicilia Syrah '19	🍷🍷 2*
○ Insolia '19	🍷 2
○ Sicilia Lucido '19	🍷 2
○ Sicilia Grillo Shamaris '18	YYY 3*
● Sicilia Nero d'Avola Sàgana '16	YYY 4*
● Sicilia Noà '13	YYY 4*

★★Donnafugata

VIA S. LIPARI, 18
91025 MARSALA [TP]
TEL. +39 0923724200
www.donnafugata.it

CELLAR SALES
PRE-BOOKED VISITS
ANNUAL PRODUCTION 2,700,000 bottles
HECTARES UNDER VINE 410.00
SUSTAINABLE WINERY

Created by the late Giacomo Rallo, a shrewd and visionary entrepreneur, and his wife, Gabriella Anca, a cultured, modern and innovative woman, Donnafugata is a brand of the highest quality, of international renown. Its founding values are ecology, territoriality, elegant wines, respect for tradition and, at the same time, an ability to see 'beyond'—values that, today, bond Gabriella even more to her children, Josè and Antonio. Production sites and plots can be found throughout Sicily, from Contessa Entellina to Marsala and Pantelleria, from Cerasuolo di Vittoria to Etna. We are used to great performances from this iconic producer, yet every year we still marvel. The Ben Ryè '17 is incredible, the nectar of a moving, sumptuous, sensual sweetness. On the nose it calls up pears and candied apricots, orange peel, dried figs and lavender, while in the mouth the opulence of its fruit harmonizes perfectly with a formidable, contrasting freshness.

Wine	Rating
○ Passito di Pantelleria Ben Ryé '17	🍷🍷🍷 8
● Etna Rosso Fragore Contrada Montelaguardia '17	🍷🍷 8
● Cerasuolo di Vittoria Floramundi '18	🍷🍷 4
● Etna Rosso Contrada Marchesa '17	🍷🍷 8
● Etna Rosso Sul Vulcano '17	🍷🍷 5
● Sicilia Mille e una Notte '16	🍷🍷 8
○ Sicilia Zibibbo Lighea '19	🍷🍷 3
● Tancredi '17	🍷🍷 5
● Vittoria Frappato Bell'Assai '18	🍷🍷 4
○ Passito di Pantelleria Ben Ryé '16	YYY 7
○ Passito di Pantelleria Ben Ryé '15	YYY 7
○ Passito di Pantelleria Ben Ryé '14	YYY 7
○ Passito di Pantelleria Ben Ryé '12	YYY 7
○ Passito di Pantelleria Ben Ryé '11	YYY 7

Duca di Salaparuta

via Nazionale, s.s. 113
90014 Casteldaccia [PA]
Tel. +39 091945201
www.duca.it

CELLAR SALES
PRE-BOOKED VISITS
ANNUAL PRODUCTION 9,000,000 bottles
HECTARES UNDER VINE 165.00
SUSTAINABLE WINERY

Acquired in 2001 by the ILLVA group of Saronno, the three famous historic brands, Corvo, Duca di Salaparuta and Florio, represent Sicilian success stories in which aristocratic elegance, entrepreneurial skill, beauty and an innovative worldview have merged over time. The new ownership has been committed to developing the personalities and characteristics of the wines and terroirs underlying the three different producers, combining modernity with authentic tradition. Their wine tourism initiatives have also been of considerable importance and success. The Sciaranèra Vajasindi '18 is a fine Pinot Nero characterized by elegant hints of cherry, wild strawberries and peach; pleasant and lively in the mouth, it has gentle, alluring tannins. An excellent performance for the Marsala Superiore Dolce Oltre Cento '17 as well, with its elegant bouquet of dried fruit and nuts, walnut, figs and medicinal herbs—sweet and tempting, it bewitches with its pleasantly oxidative complexity.

Wine	Rating
● Calanìca Frappato '19	🍷🍷 2*
○ Marsala Sup. Dolce Oltre Cento '17	🍷🍷 4
○ Marsala Sup. Semisecco Ambra Donna Franca Ris.	🍷🍷 6
○ Marsala Vergine Baglio Florio '02	🍷🍷 5
● Sciaranera Pinot Nero Vajasindi '18	🍷🍷 3
○ Calanìca Grillo '19	🍷 2
○ Kados '19	🍷 3
○ Morsi di Luce	🍷 5
● Nawàri Pinot Nero '17	🍷 6
○ Sentiero del Vento Suor Marchesa '19	🍷 3
● Duca Enrico '03	🍷🍷🍷 6
● Duca Enrico '01	🍷🍷🍷 6
● Duca Enrico '92	🍷🍷🍷 6
● Duca Enrico '90	🍷🍷🍷 6

★Feudi del Pisciotto

c.da Pisciotto
93015 Niscemi [CL]
Tel. +39 09331930280
www.castellare.it

CELLAR SALES
PRE-BOOKED VISITS
ACCOMMODATION
ANNUAL PRODUCTION 200,000 bottles
HECTARES UNDER VINE 45.00

The owner of this producer is also a shareholder of Gambero Rosso spa. To avoid any conflict of interest, Paolo Panerai has subordinated the possible awarding of Tre Bicchieri (which, in any case, only occurs through a blind tasting), to the attainment of the same rating of excellence (upwards of 90/100) by an independent, international panel. This was the case here. Feudi is a lovely, dynamic winery. In addition to its modern cellar, the property is endowed with an elegant wine resort characterized by a magnificent, 18th-century 'palmento' with 8 vats. The entire range of wines tasted performed notably well. Tre Bicchieri for the elegant Cerasuolo Giambattista Valli '18, with its clear aromas of red berries, humus and aromatic herbs, and its invigorating, juicy and fleshy palate, all well supported by an elegant tannic weave. The Chardonnay Alberta Ferretti '18, with its broad and complex olfactory profile performed well, coming through taut and plucky on the palate.

Wine	Rating
● Cerasuolo di Vittoria Giambattista Valli '18	🍷🍷🍷 4*
○ Alberta Ferretti Chardonnay '18	🍷🍷 4
● Baglio del Sole Nero d'Avola '18	🍷🍷 2*
● Carolina Marengo Kisa Frappato '18	🍷🍷 4
○ Gianfranco Ferré Passito '18	🍷🍷 5
○ Gurra di Mare Tirsat '18	🍷🍷 4
● L'Eterno '18	🍷🍷 7
● Missoni Cabernet Sauvignon '18	🍷🍷 4
○ Sicilia Grillo Carolina Marengo Kisa '18	🍷🍷 4
● Sicilia Nero d'Avola Versace '18	🍷🍷 4
● Valentino Merlot '18	🍷🍷 4
○ Baglio del Sole Inzolia '19	🍷 2
○ Baglio del Sole Inzolia Catarratto '19	🍷 2
● Baglio del Sole Merlot Syrah '18	🍷 2

Feudo Arancio

c.da Portella Misilbesi
92017 Sambuca di Sicilia [AG]
Tel. +39 0925579000
www.feudoarancio.it

CELLAR SALES
PRE-BOOKED VISITS
ACCOMMODATION
ANNUAL PRODUCTION 6,000,000 bottles
HECTARES UNDER VINE 700.00
SUSTAINABLE WINERY

Long an important local producer, since 1904 Mezzacorona has written memorable chapters in Trentino's enological and economic history. In contemporary times, thanks to the far-sightedness of its administrators, Mezzacorona has grown into an international giant. In Sicily they have two properties, one on Lake Arancio, in Sambuca di Sicilia, and the other in Acate, in Ragusa, both outstanding terroirs. Their goals have always been clear: to produce quality wines that closely reflect the two territories and so with the lowest possible environmental impact. Not all their wines were ready at the time of the tasting. We appreciated very much, however, those that arrived, starting with the soft and cosseting Cantadoro Riserva '17 (Nero d'Avola and Cabernet Sauvignon), an aromatically dark and deep wine marked by vibrant hints of cherry, black pepper, mulberries and medicinal herbs. We found the Nero d'Avola '19 just as good. True to type, it offers up sensations of blackcurrant, capers and plum.

Wine	Rating
● Sicilia Rosso Cantodoro Ris. '17	🍷🍷 4
○ Sicilia Bianco Dalila Ris. '18	🍷🍷 4
○ Sicilia Grillo '19	🍷🍷 3
○ Sicilia Inzolia '19	🍷🍷 3
● Sicilia Nero d'Avola '19	🍷🍷 3
○ Barone d'Albius '15	🍷🍷 5
● Cantodoro Ris. '16	🍷🍷 3
○ Sicilia Dalila Ris. '17	🍷🍷 4
○ Sicilia Dalila Riserva '16	🍷🍷 4
○ Sicilia Grillo '18	🍷🍷 3
○ Sicilia Grillo '17	🍷🍷 3
○ Sicilia Grillo Tinchitè '18	🍷🍷 3
● Sicilia Hedonis Ris. '16	🍷🍷 4
● Sicilia Hedonis Ris. '15	🍷🍷 4
○ Sicilia Inzolia '18	🍷🍷 3
○ Sicilia Inzolia '17	🍷🍷 3

★Feudo Maccari

s.da prov.le Noto-Pachino km 13,5
96017 Noto [SR]
Tel. +39 0931596894
www.feudomaccari.it

CELLAR SALES
PRE-BOOKED VISITS
ANNUAL PRODUCTION 280,000 bottles
HECTARES UNDER VINE 60.00
VITICULTURE METHOD Certified Organic
SUSTAINABLE WINERY

Antonio Moretti's Sicilian estate (his son Amedeo is now chipping in) is one the most beautiful in the Val di Noto valley. The old farmhouses have been perfectly restored with the area's classic rural colors—red and ochre—and around the vineyards, all rigorously bush-trained, the traditional dry stone walls have been restored. In addition to Nero d'Avola, which the Moretti family have been focusing on since the first harvest, they're achieving good results with the area's Grillo, a grape they've invested heavily in. All the wines presented confirmed the high level of quality achieved by this prestigious winery in recent years, but that's not all—we are pleased to underline the excellent value offered by their range. Yet another Tre Bicchieri for the Saia '18, an elegant, varietal and territorial Nero d'Avola. The balsamic and long Nero d'Avola Neré '18, with its iodine nuances, also earned a place in our finals.

Wine	Rating
● Sicilia Nero d'Avola Saia '18	🍷🍷🍷 4*
● Sicilia Nero d'Avola Nerè '18	🍷🍷 3*
○ Family and Friends Bianco '19	🍷🍷 5
● Family and Friends Rosso '18	🍷🍷 5
○ Sicilia Grillo Olli '19	🍷🍷 3
● Sicilia Syrah Maharis '17	🍷🍷 5
● Saia '14	🍷🍷🍷 4*
● Saia '13	🍷🍷🍷 4*
● Saia '12	🍷🍷🍷 4*
● Saia '11	🍷🍷🍷 4*
● Saia '10	🍷🍷🍷 4*
● Saia '08	🍷🍷🍷 4*
● Saia '07	🍷🍷🍷 4*
● Saia '06	🍷🍷🍷 4
● Sicilia Nero d'Avola Saia '17	🍷🍷🍷 4*
● Sicilia Nero d'Avola Saia '16	🍷🍷🍷 4*
● Sicilia Saia '15	🍷🍷🍷 4*

Feudo Montoni

c.da Montoni Vecchi
92022 Cammarata [AG]
Tel. +39 091513106
www.feudomontoni.it

CELLAR SALES
PRE-BOOKED VISITS
ANNUAL PRODUCTION 215,000 bottles
HECTARES UNDER VINE 30.00
VITICULTURE METHOD Certified Organic
SUSTAINABLE WINERY

As far back as 1469, the year in which the 'baglio' (an enclosed Sicilian farmstead) was built by the Aragonese Abatellis family, the estate was renowned for its viticultural prowess. In the late 19th century the Sireci family, its current owners, began the patient work of developing the estate's vineyards through massal selection. Fabio, who represents the third generation, started producing on his own, bringing the same passion as his predecessors. The vineyards are organically cultivated, while care and artisan techniques characterize their approach in the cellar. The Perricone Vigna del Core '18 earned a place in our finals with its intense, ripe mulberry fruitiness, fine green notes of capers and a juicy fruit texture that features a pleasant balsamic encore. The Nero d'Avola Vrucara '16 proves elegant and focused in its varietal notes, smooth and round, coming through clear and long on the finish. The Grillo Vigna della Timpa '19 offers up deliciously fresh and sapid peach and almond.

Wine	Glasses	Price
● Sicilia Perricone V. del Core '18	🍷🍷	4
○ Sicilia Grillo V. della Timpa '19	🍷🍷	3
⊙ Sicilia Nerello Mascalese Rose di Adele '19	🍷🍷	4
● Sicilia Nero d'Avola V. Lagnusa '18	🍷🍷	4
● Sicilia Nero d'Avola Vrucara '16	🍷🍷	5
○ Sicilia Inzolia dei Fornelli '19	🍷	3
○ Sicilia Catarratto V. del Masso '18	YY	4
○ Sicilia Catarratto V. del Masso '17	YY	4
○ Sicilia Grillo V. della Timpa '18	YY	3
○ Sicilia Grillo V. della Timpa '17	YY	3
○ Sicilia Inzolia dei Fornelli '17	YY	3
● Sicilia Nero d'Avola V. Lagnusa '16	YY	4
● Sicilia Nero d'Avola V. Lagnusa '15	YY	4
● Sicilia Nero d'Avola Vrucara '15	YY	5
● Sicilia Nero d'Avola Vrucara '14	YY	5
● Sicilia Perricone V. del Core '15	YY	4

★★Firriato

via Trapani, 4
91027 Paceco [TP]
Tel. +39 0923882755
www.firriato.it

CELLAR SALES
PRE-BOOKED VISITS
ANNUAL PRODUCTION 6,000,000 bottles
HECTARES UNDER VINE 470.00
VITICULTURE METHOD Certified Organic
SUSTAINABLE WINERY

The first Italian winery to have 'zero impact' in terms of greenhouse gas emissions, Firriato represents Sicily's three main terroirs: the sea (with the island of Favignana), the hills (with vineyards in the Trapani countryside) and the mountains (with Cavanera Etnea). In this last they've identified a cru at 650 meters above sea level on the northeast side of the volcano, with ungrafted vines dating back to the second half of the 19th century (certified by the University of Palermo and genetic profiling by the CNR). The precious grapes give rise to the Signum Aetnae reserve, yet another feather in the cap for the Di Gaetano family. While waiting for the precious Etna cru, the Ribeca '15 enchants with its complexity and elegance. It's an intense and deep Perricone, silky and infinitely long in the mouth. The Favinia La Muciara '18 is excellent: fresh, rich and summery in its notes of Mediterranean scrub. For the outstanding work carried out in the vineyard, this year Firriato receives our Award for Sustainable Viticulture.

Wine	Glasses	Price
● Sicilia Perricone Ribeca '15	🍷🍷🍷	5
○ Favinia La Muciara '18	🍷🍷	5
○ Etna Bianco Cavanera Ripa di Scorciavacca '18	🍷🍷	5
○ Etna Bianco Le Sabbie dell'Etna '19	🍷🍷	4
● Etna Rosso Le Sabbie dell'Etna '18	🍷🍷	4
○ Quater Vitis Bianco '19	🍷🍷	4
○ Sicilia Bianco BayAmore Bianco di Bianchi '19	🍷🍷	3
○ Sicilia Bianco Santagostino Baglio Sorià '19	🍷🍷	4
● Sicilia Camelot '15	🍷🍷	5
● Sicilia Rosso Santagostino Baglio Sorìa '15	🍷🍷	4

Fondo Antico

FRAZ. RILIEVO
S.DA FIORAME, 54A
91100 TRAPANI
TEL. +39 0923864339
www.fondoantico.it

CELLAR SALES
PRE-BOOKED VISITS
ANNUAL PRODUCTION 400,000 bottles
HECTARES UNDER VINE 80.00

The origins of the ancient 'baglio' (an enclosed Sicilian farmstead) and more than 100 hectares of terrain, mostly under vine, go back to the early 19th century, when the estate was used as the summer residence for the Polizzotti-Scuderi family, pharmacists for generations who were also passionate agricultural entrepreneurs. At the time the main crop was wheat—it was only in the early 20th century that conversion to viticulture begin. In 1995 Giuseppe Polizzotti completely revolutionized the property by building a new and modern cellar to produce and market wines under his brand name. The adept Lorenza Scianna submitted a superb selection, demonstrating that she's found her way not only with Grillo, long a cornerstone, but also when it comes to their reds. The Per Te Perricone '18 made it into our finals, offering up sensations of mulberries and violets on the nose. In the mouth it's well governed by a sapid and plucky acidity that brings out its lovely, compact and juicy fruit.

● Per Te Perricone '18	🍷🍷 3*
○ Bello Mio Zibibbo '19	🍷🍷 3
○ Sicilia Chardonnay Lumiére '19	🍷🍷 3
○ Sicilia Grillo Parlante '19	🍷🍷 3
● Sicilia Syrah Le Clay '18	🍷🍷 3
⊙ Sicilia Aprile '19	🍷 2
● Sicilia Nero d'Avola Nenè '19	🍷 2
○ Baccadoro '16	🍸🍸 3*
○ Bello Mio '17	🍸🍸 3
○ Bello Mio Zibibbo '18	🍸🍸 3
○ Il Coro di Fondo Antico '16	🍸🍸 3
⊙ Memorie '16	🍸🍸 4
● Per Te Perricone '17	🍸🍸 3
○ Sicilia Grillo Parlante '18	🍸🍸 3
○ Sicilia Grillo Parlante '17	🍸🍸 3*
● Sicilia Nero d'Avola '16	🍸🍸 2*
● Sicilia Nero d'Avola Nenè '17	🍸🍸 2*

Generazione Alessandro

C.DA BORRIGLIONE
95015 LINGUAGLOSSA [CT]
TEL. +39 092437038
www.generazionealessandro.it

CELLAR SALES
PRE-BOOKED VISITS
ANNUAL PRODUCTION 18,500 bottles
HECTARES UNDER VINE 10.00

A new promising property of 10 hectares, 8 already under vine, the sum of 4 estates and districts on northeast Etna, at elevations averaging close to 700 meters: Pontale Palino, Piano Filici, Sciaramanica and Borriglione. The vineyards go back anywhere from 10 to 70 years, while the grapes (only native cultivars) are vinified in an ancient, though now restored, 'palmento' in Borriglione. We find 3 talented young cousins, Benedetto, Anna and Benedetto Alessandro at the helm of this remarkable producer. Once active in the family business, today they're fully autonomous and independent. The Etna Bianco '18 Trainara (80% Carricante and 20% Catarratto) handily earns Tre Bicchieri. Vibrant and elegant on the nose, it offers up sophisticated mineral nuances accompanied by citrus fruits, white peach and medicinal herbs. It's a wine of superior character and quality, infinitely refreshing and complex. The fine and deep Etna Rosso Croceferro '18 is right on its heels.

○ Etna Bianco Trainara '18	🍷🍷🍷 4*
● Etna Rosso Croceferro '18	🍷🍷 4

Tenuta Gorghi Tondi

c.da San Nicola
91026 Mazara del Vallo [TP]
Tel. +39 0923719741
www.gorghitondi.it

CELLAR SALES
PRE-BOOKED VISITS
ANNUAL PRODUCTION 800,000 bottles
HECTARES UNDER VINE 130.00
VITICULTURE METHOD Certified Organic
SUSTAINABLE WINERY

In April 2020 Michele Sala, father of Annamaria and Clara and a leading figure in the Sicilian wine business, passed away. In 2000 he and his wife, Doretta, founded this winery, entrusting its management to their daughters. The vineyards and cellar are situated in an area of astonishing beauty, between the sea of Mazara, the Preola Lake Reserve and Gorghi Tondi. Their 130 hectares of vineyards are organically cultivated, with great attention paid to sustainability during production, as evidenced by the Contrade line, produced and bottled without added sulphur dioxide. The Nero d'Avola Sorante '17 landed a place in our finals with its focused, varietal aromas of capers and mulberries; in the mouth it's round, juicy and long. The Frappato Dumè '19 once again delivered, proving fresh and fragrant on the palate. We also appreciated the very well-made Nero d'Avola Rosé Metodo Charmat Palmares, the Catarratto Midor '19 with its nice, crisp peach fruit, and the pleasant, fine aromas of the Zibibbo Rajah '19.

● Sicilia Nero d'Avola Sorante '17	▼▼ 3*
⊙ Palmarés Rosé Extra Dry	▼▼ 3
○ Sicilia Catarratto Midor '19	▼▼ 2*
● Sicilia Frappato Dumè '19	▼▼ 3
○ Sicilia Zibibbo Rajah '19	▼▼ 4
○ Grillo d'Oro Passito '16	▼ 7
○ Sicilia Grillo Kheirè '19	▼ 4
○ Grillo d'Oro Passito '15	▽▽ 7
● Sicilia Frappato Dumè '18	▽▽ 3
● Sicilia Frappato Dumè '17	▽▽ 3
○ Sicilia Grillo Kheirè '18	▽▽ 4
● Sicilia Syrah Segreante '16	▽▽ 4
● Sicilia Syrah Segreante '15	▽▽ 4
○ Sicilia Zibibbo Rajah '18	▽▽ 4
○ Sicilia Zibibbo Rajah '17	▽▽ 4
○ Sicilia Zibibbo Rajah '16	▽▽ 4

Graci

loc. Passopisciaro
c.da Feudo di Mezzo
95012 Castiglione di Sicilia [CT]
Tel. +39 3487016773
www.graci.eu

CELLAR SALES
PRE-BOOKED VISITS
ANNUAL PRODUCTION 65,000 bottles
HECTARES UNDER VINE 18.00
VITICULTURE METHOD Certified Organic

Alberto Graci's organically cultivated vineyards span five prestigious districts around Passopisciaro, on the northeast side of Etna, a terroir known for its absolute quality. The cellar is located in an ancient baglio (enclosed Sicilian farmstead), on the border between Arcurìa and Feudo di Mezzo. Moving up towards the top of the volcano we find Muganazzi and Santo Spirito, where in 2019 a hectare of Carricante was planted. Finally, at 1000 meters, lies Barbabecchi, which hosts 100-year-old ungrafted vines. In early 2020 the first Idda wines were released, the result of a collaboration between Alberto and Angelo Gaja. The Bianco Arcuria '18 handily took home Tre Bicchieri: complex, clear and focused on the nose, oak harmonizes beautifully with fruity citrus and plum. In the mouth it's self-assured, with close-knit pulp accompanied by a mineral encore of noble finesse. The Arcuria Rosso '18 also made it into our finals. A subtle, elegant bouquet of peach and small red fruits rise up to the nose—in the mouth it's creamy and long, with a clear finish.

○ Etna Bianco Arcuria '18	▼▼▼ 6
● Etna Rosso Arcurìa '18	▼▼ 6
○ Etna Bianco '19	▼▼ 3
⊙ Etna Rosato '19	▼▼ 3
● Etna Rosso '18	▼▼ 3
● Etna Rosso Feudo di Mezzo '18	▼▼ 6
○ Etna Bianco '10	▽▽▽ 4*
○ Etna Bianco Arcuria '11	▽▽▽ 5
○ Etna Bianco Quota 600 '10	▽▽▽ 5
● Etna Rosso '16	▽▽▽ 3*
● Etna Rosso Arcurìa '17	▽▽▽ 6
● Etna Rosso Arcurìa '13	▽▽▽ 6
● Etna Rosso Arcurìa '12	▽▽▽ 6
○ Etna Bianco '18	▽▽ 3
○ Etna Bianco Arcuria '17	▽▽ 6
● Etna Rosso '17	▽▽ 3
● Etna Rosso Feudo di Mezzo '17	▽▽ 6

Lisciandrello

via Case Nuove, 31
90048 San Giuseppe Jato [PA]
Tel. +39 3395917618
www.aziendalisciandrello.com

ANNUAL PRODUCTION 30,000 bottles
HECTARES UNDER VINE 6.00

Giuseppe Lisciandrello, one of the best-known and most well-stocked wine merchants in Sicily (and beyond), spent more than a quarter century selling wines produced by others, from all over the world. In 2015 he took over a beautiful 6-hectare estate (and cellar) in Monreale, in the district of Cerasa, at 550 meters elevation, where day-night temperature swings are notable and snow is a common occurrence in winter. His companions in the venture are Luciano Tocco, a real 'man of action', and Benedetto Alessandro, one of the most brilliant Sicilian enologists of the nouvelle vague. This year some of their wines are missing, but the ones presented are absolutely commendable. The highly drinkable Jàto '18 is excellent. Made with Catarratto cultivated on high, on the nose it offers up vibrant aromas of yellow flowers, citrus zest, ripe peach and wafts of flint. On the palate it proves deep and elegant, sapid and racy. We also appreciated the bewitching Nerello Mascalese '17, which features elegant hints of cherry and fine, silky tannins.

Wine	Rating
○ Monreale Jàto '18	🍷🍷 4
○ Etna Bianco Carricante '18	🍷🍷 4
● Nerello Mascalese '17	🍷🍷 3
○ Carricante '16	🍷🍷 4
○ Cataratto '16	🍷🍷 4
○ Chardonnay '16	🍷🍷 4
○ Chardonnay '15	🍷🍷 3
● Nerello Mascalese '16	🍷🍷 3*
● Nerello Mascalese '15	🍷🍷 3
○ Sicilia Carricante '17	🍷🍷 4
○ Sicilia Chardonnay '17	🍷🍷 4

Monteleone

c.da Cuba
95012 Castiglione di Sicilia [CT]
Tel. +39 334 5772422
www.monteleonetna.com

ANNUAL PRODUCTION 6,000 bottles
HECTARES UNDER VINE 3.00

While very young, Giulia Monteleone has already had two lives. The first she lived as a talented, active, competent, trustworthy wine journalist. In the second she met Benedetto Alessandro, one of the most brilliant young winemakers in the region, an enologist bolstered by significant periods of study outside Sicily, extensive experiences abroad, a knowledge of languages, and an international mindset. Etna has come into play in both their personal and work lives: 6 hectares (so far only 3 under vine) in Cuba, Pontale Palino and Sant'Alfio, at elevations ranging from 500 to 900 meters. The Etna Rosso Qubba '18 handily took home Tre Bicchieri. A wine with a strong personality, on the nose sophisticated, subtle peach aromas alternate with elegant slate. On the palate it comes through juicy and lively, with sweet, alluring tannins. The sapid and crisp Etna Bianco '19, which offers up fragrances of white plum and grapefruit, proves excellent, as does the gratifying and characterful Etna Rosso Rumex '18, with its ripe fruity sensations of black cherry, violet and blueberries.

Wine	Rating
● Etna Rosso Qubba '18	🍷🍷🍷 7
● Etna Bianco '19	🍷🍷 5
● Etna Rosso '18	🍷🍷 6
● Etna Rosso Rumex '18	🍷🍷 7
● Etna Bianco Anthemis '18	🍷🍷 6
● Etna Rosso '17	🍷🍷 6
● Etna Rosso Cuba '17	🍷🍷 6

Cantine Nicosia

via Luigi Capuana, 65
95039 Trecastagni [CT]
Tel. +39 0957806767
www.cantinenicosia.it

CELLAR SALES
PRE-BOOKED VISITS
RESTAURANT SERVICE
ANNUAL PRODUCTION 1,800,000 bottles
HECTARES UNDER VINE 240.00
VITICULTURE METHOD Certified Organic
SUSTAINABLE WINERY

The Nicosia family have been cultivating vineyards on Etna with continued success since 1898. In addition to operating in this benchmark territory, in recent times they've made major investments in the province of Ragusa, acquiring a vast estate in one of the best areas of Cerasuolo di Vittoria. The producer aims to maximize the value of local grapes and various terroirs through sustainable production practices, highlighted by an organic-vegan approach of national renown. This year the wines from their new, Etnean Monte San Nicolò (situated at 600 meters above sea level) are remarkable. A prestigious and key player in the territory, which the Nicosia family have known in depth for over a century, this historic producer continues to grow when it comes to the quality of their wines. Ethereal, bewitching, vibrant, the Lenza di Munti Rosso 720 slm '17 won us over by virtue of its sophisticated aromas of red berries and slate. The elegant white version of the same wine is practically on the same level .

Wine	Rating
● Etna Rosso Lenza di Munti 720 slm '17	🍷🍷🍷 3*
○ Etna Bianco Lenza di Munti 720 slm '19	🍷🍷 3*
○ Etna Bianco Contrada Monte Gorna '16	🍷🍷 6
○ Etna Bianco Contrada Monte San Nicolò '19	🍷🍷 4
○ Etna Bianco Fondo Filara Contrada Monte Gorna '19	🍷🍷 4
○ Etna Brut Sosta Tre Santi Collezione di Famiglia M. Cl. '16	🍷🍷 5
⊙ Etna Rosato Vulkà '19	🍷🍷 3
● Etna Rosso Contrada Monte Gorna Ris. '14	🍷🍷 6
● Etna Rosso Contrada Monte San Nicolò '18	🍷🍷 4
● Etna Rosso Fondo Filara Contrada Monte Gorna '18	🍷🍷 4
● Sicilia Frappato Fondo Filara '19	🍷🍷 3
● Etna Rosso Vign. Monte Gorna Ris. '13	🍷🍷🍷 6

Arianna Occhipinti

fraz. Pedalino
s.da prov.le 68 Vittoria-Pedalino km 3,3
97019 Vittoria [RG]
Tel. +39 09321865519
www.agricolaocchipinti.it

CELLAR SALES
PRE-BOOKED VISITS
ANNUAL PRODUCTION 130,000 bottles
HECTARES UNDER VINE 22.00
VITICULTURE METHOD Certified Organic
SUSTAINABLE WINERY

In just over three decades Arianna Occhipinti has become an icon of Sicilian wine, loved for her talent, stubbornness and passion. But above all, she's loved for her good, indeed outstanding, wines. They are marked by their strong personality, authenticity, originality, and a refusal to conform. In short they are 'Arianna's wines'. The latest pieces of news are, respectively, the acquisition of a new estate in Chiaramonte Gulfi and the "Contrade Project", already in place, which aims to clearly distinguish the wines of three different terroirs: Pettineo, Fossa di Lupo and Bombolieri. Their high-quality range of wines proves unique in style. We very much appreciated the juicy and fleshy Frappato '18, a vibrant, meaty and fragrant wine redolent of ripe cherries and sweet Asian spices. It just fell missed out on Tre Bicchieri. The dark and deep Grotte Alte '15 is a pleasantly austere, elegant and classy drink, highly generous and persistent.

Wine	Rating
● Il Frappato '18	🍷🍷 5
● BB Vino di Contrada '17	🍷🍷 7
● Cerasuolo di Vittoria Cl. Grotte Alte '15	🍷🍷 7
● FL Vino di Contrada '17	🍷🍷 7
● PT Vino di Contrada '17	🍷🍷 7
● Siccagno '17	🍷🍷 6
● Il Frappato '12	🍷🍷🍷 5
● Il Frappato '11	🍷🍷🍷 5
● SP 68 Rosso '15	🍷🍷🍷 3*
● Cerasuolo di Vittoria Cl. Grotte Alte '14	🍷🍷 7
● Cerasuolo di Vittoria Cl. Grotte Alte '13	🍷🍷 7
● Cerasuolo di Vittoria Cl. Grotte Alte '10	🍷🍷 7
● Il Frappato '17	🍷🍷 5
● Il Frappato '16	🍷🍷 5

Tenute Orestiadi

v.le Santa Ninfa
91024 Gibellina [TP]
Tel. +39 092469124
www.tenuteorestiadi.it

CELLAR SALES
PRE-BOOKED VISITS
ACCOMMODATION
ANNUAL PRODUCTION 1,200,000 bottles
HECTARES UNDER VINE 120.00
VITICULTURE METHOD Certified Organic
SUSTAINABLE WINERY

This important cooperative producer was founded in the wake of the terrible earthquake that struck the Belìce Valley in 1968. The reaction was to focus on quality, with commitment, passion and absolute dedication as a foundation. The hard work that followed was favorably wed to beauty and art, embodied by the Orestiadi Foundation, one of the Mediterranean's most significant cultural entities. Their success was achieved through delicious, characterful wines, expressions of the various terroirs. Their recent arrival on Mount Etna was another piece of good news. The Bianco di Ludovico Riserva '17 (Catarratto with a drop of Chardonnay) is in great form. Generous, soft and gratifying, it offers up fragrances of lemon, citron, white flowers and herbs. We also appreciated the characterful Etna Rosso '16, made with grapes from the eastern estate of La Gelsomina. The nose features lovely, ripe, fruity sensations of black cherries accompanied by liquorice and spices. True to type and territorial, the palate is marked by cosseting, silky tannins.

Wine	Rating
○ Etna Bianco La Gelsomina '19	🍷🍷 3
● Etna Rosso La Gelsomina '16	🍷🍷 3
⊙ La Gelsomina Brut M. Cl. Rosé	🍷🍷 5
○ Pacènzia Zibibbo V. T.	🍷🍷 4
● Paxmentis Syrah Passito '18	🍷🍷 4
● Sicilia Frappato '18	🍷🍷 3
○ Sicilia Il Bianco di Ludovico Ris. '17	🍷🍷 4
○ La Gelsomina Brut Blanc de Noirs M. Cl.	🍷 5
● Sicilia Nero d'Avola '18	🍷 3
● Sicilia Perricone '18	🍷 3
● Sicilia Frappato '17	ΥΥ 3
● Sicilia Frappato '16	ΥΥ 3
● Sicilia Nero d'Avola '16	ΥΥ 3
● Sicilia Perricone '17	ΥΥ 3
● Sicilia Perricone '16	ΥΥ 3
○ Sicilia Zibibbo '18	ΥΥ 3

★Palari

loc. Santo Stefano Briga
c.da Barna
98137 Messina
Tel. +39 090630194
www.palari.it

ANNUAL PRODUCTION 50,000 bottles
HECTARES UNDER VINE 7.00

Happy 30th! It was 1990 when Salvatore Geraci semi-clandestinely bottled his first Palari. They were clarets, and the corks had to be bought in a hardware store because he'd forgotten to order them. The iconic Burgundy bottle with the golden sun (for which the wine is known throughout the world) would only arrive in 1994, when the first vintage was sold commercially. For Salvatore, however, time doesn't seem to have passed. He's still the same jovial Peter Pan of Italian wine, cultured, ironic, elegant, always around for all the Kensington Gardens of the world. This year Salvatore, in full harmony with his brother Giampiero (who's always been in charge of the technical side of the business, both in the vineyard and in the cellar) has decided to let the Faro Palari age in the bottle for another year. That didn't overshadow the Rosso del Soprano '17, however, which offers up charming marine sensations, cardamom and cherry scents on the nose, coming through invigorating, deep and sapid on the palate.

Wine	Rating
● Rosso del Soprano '17	🍷🍷 4
● Faro Palari '14	ΥΥΥ 6
● Faro Palari '12	ΥΥΥ 6
● Faro Palari '11	ΥΥΥ 6
● Faro Palari '09	ΥΥΥ 6
● Faro Palari '08	ΥΥΥ 6
● Faro Palari '07	ΥΥΥ 6
● Faro Palari '06	ΥΥΥ 6
● Faro Palari '05	ΥΥΥ 6*
● Faro Palari '04	ΥΥΥ 7
● Faro Palari '03	ΥΥΥ 6
● Faro Palari '02	ΥΥΥ 6
● Faro Palari '01	ΥΥΥ 6
● Rosso del Soprano '15	ΥΥΥ 4*
● Rosso del Soprano '11	ΥΥΥ 4*
● Rosso del Soprano '10	ΥΥΥ 4*
● Rosso del Soprano '07	ΥΥΥ 4

Palmento Costanzo

loc. Passopisciaro
c.da Santo Spirito
95012 Castiglione di Sicilia [CT]
Tel. +39 0942983239
www.palmentocostanzo.com

CELLAR SALES
PRE-BOOKED VISITS
RESTAURANT SERVICE
ANNUAL PRODUCTION 90,000 bottles
HECTARES UNDER VINE 20.00
VITICULTURE METHOD Certified Organic
SUSTAINABLE WINERY

You can't help but notice the brown volcanic sands, the result of crumbling ancient lava, that characterize the Costanzo family's beautiful estate, a property where environmental concerns are at the fore. Here on the north side of Etna, in contrada Santo Spirito, a hamlet of Passopisciaro, in Castiglione di Sicilia, the various terraced vineyards grow at elevations ranging from 650 to 800 meters. As a whole the estate is striking, with a modern winery coexisting alongside a perfectly functional, 19th-century palmento that's been carefully restored according to principles of bio-architecture. Careful work of extraordinary precision has allowed the producer to define some excellent crus. A well-deserved Tre Bicchieri for the magnificent Contrada S. Spirito particella 468. Redolent of blackcurrant, juniper berries, mountain herbs and flint, it's a wine of great elegance, with lovely, invigorating fruit, and spectacular tannins. The other wines tasted also delivered.

Wine	Glasses	Price
● Etna Rosso Contrada Santo Spirito Part. 468 '16	▼▼▼	6
● Etna Rosso Contrada Santo Spirito Part. 464 '16	▼▼	6
● Etna Rosso Nero di Sei '16	▼▼	5
○ Etna Bianco di Sei '19	▼▼	5
○ Etna Bianco Mofete '19	▼▼	3
⊙ Etna Rosato Mofete '19	▼▼	3
● Etna Rosso Contrada Santo Spirito '17	▼▼	6
● Etna Rosso Contrada Santo Spirito Part. 466 '16	▼▼	6
● Etna Rosso Mofete '17	▼▼	3
○ Etna Bianco di Sei '17	▽▽▽	5
⊙ Etna Rosato Mofete '18	▽▽▽	3*
● Etna Rosso Mofete '14	▽▽	3*
● Etna Rosso Prefillossera '16	▽▽	8

Passopisciaro

loc. Passopisciaro
c.da Guardiola
95030 Castiglione di Sicilia [CT]
Tel. +39 0578267110
www.vinifranchetti.com

CELLAR SALES
ANNUAL PRODUCTION 75,000 bottles
HECTARES UNDER VINE 26.00

in 2000 Andrea Franchetti took up the challenge of interpreting an extraordinary terroir dominated by unpredictable, ancestral forces: that of Etna. It was the beginning of a process of revival that still has wide margins for growth. An emphasis on the pedoclimatic diversity of the Contrade, the result of extensive research, showed great intuition. The vineyards are located on the northern slope, reaching 550 meters elevation in Chiappemacine and 1000 meters in Rampante. In addition to Nerello Mascalese, they cultivate Petit Verdot, Cesanese d'Affile and Chardonnay, the source of their new Contrada PC. The 2018 vintage gave rise to a thrilling Passorosso, which took home Tre Bicchieri thanks to the finesse and complexity of its bouquet, marked by a focused minerality; in the mouth it exhibits wonderful texture and incomparable elegance of fruit. Clear, focused notes of pomegranate and peach characterize the Contrada G '18, a wine that's pleasantly invigorating on the palate. We also appreciated the silky Contrada R '18 with its charming flowery sensations.

Wine	Glasses	Price
● Etna Rosso Passorosso '18	▼▼▼	5
● Contrada C '18	▼▼	8
● Contrada G '18	▼▼	8
● Contrada P '18	▼▼	8
○ Contrada PC '18	▼▼	8
● Contrada R '18	▼▼	8
● Contrada S '18	▼▼	8
● Franchetti '17	▼▼	8
○ Passobianco '18	▼▼	5
● Contrada C '17	▽▽▽	6
● Contrada G '11	▽▽▽	8
● Contrada P '10	▽▽▽	7
● Contrada P '09	▽▽▽	7
● Contrada Sciaranuova '15	▽▽▽	6
● Passopisciaro '04	▽▽▽	5
● Contrada Guardiola '16	▽▽	6
● Contrada S '17	▽▽	6

Carlo Pellegrino

via del Fante, 39
91025 Marsala [TP]
Tel. +39 0923719911
www.carlopellegrino.it

CELLAR SALES
PRE-BOOKED VISITS
ANNUAL PRODUCTION 5,500,000 bottles
HECTARES UNDER VINE 150.00
SUSTAINABLE WINERY

It was 1880 when Paolo Pellegrino, a notary public passionate about viticulture, started his winery. Seven generations of family followed, leaving their mark on Sicily's economic and enological history. The entrepreneurial vision has always been the same: maximize the value of the terroir (today there are four estates), highlight the innate attributes of each wine and cultivar, prepare for the future through a forward-thinking vision while connecting it to the present and bringing out the best tradition. Their historic selection of Marsala is commendable, as usual. Among the (few) wines submitted, we very much appreciated the Il Salinaro '19, a highly elegant and mineral Grillo redolent of orange blossom and wisteria—on the palate it comes through remarkably fresh and drinkable. The Gibelé '19 once again demonstrates that it's a highly pleasant wine, aromatic, fine and vibrant, marked by Mediterranean herbs and citron. The sweet, seductive and harmonious Passito Nes '18 also delivered.

Wine	Rating
○ Gibelè '19	🍷🍷 3
○ Passito di Pantelleria Nes '18	🍷🍷 6
○ Sicilia Grillo Il Salinaro '19	🍷🍷 3
○ Marsala Sup. Ambra Semisecco Ris. '85	🥂🥂🥂 4*
○ Marsala Vergine Ris. '81	🥂🥂🥂 6
○ Passito di Pantelleria Nes '09	🥂🥂🥂 5
● Tripudium Rosso Duca di Castelmonte '09	🥂🥂🥂 4*
● Duca di Castelmonte Tripudium Rosso '16	🥂🥂 5
● Gazzerotta '16	🥂🥂 4
○ Gibelè '18	🥂🥂 4
○ Passito di Pantelleria Nes '17	🥂🥂 7
○ Passito di Pantelleria Nes '16	🥂🥂 5
○ Passito di Pantelleria Nes '15	🥂🥂 7
● Rinazzo '16	🥂🥂 4

★Pietradolce

fraz. Solicchiata
c.da Rampante
95012 Castiglione di Sicilia [CT]
Tel. +39 3484037792
www.pietradolce.it

ANNUAL PRODUCTION 50,000 bottles
HECTARES UNDER VINE 20.00

With the latest acquisitions in Feudo di Mezzo, this charming estate, one of Sicily's most famous, has grown to comprise more than 30 hectares of vineyards. The new underground cellar is so well integrated into the landscape that in the direction of the hill, it's truly difficult to know where one begins and the other ends. Inside, together with the most modern technology, we find many works of art, such as those by Alfio Bonanno, a world-famous exponent of 'Land Art' or the beautiful sculpture 'Pietre d'Acqua' by Veronese artist Giorgio Vigna. Once again, the selection submitted proves to be of the highest quality: Tre Bicchieri for the Vigna Barbagalli '17, a wine of metaphysical beauty, with a broad and alluring bouquet of sweet spices, fruits and dark citrus notes veined with elegant mineral nuances. The palate thrills for its elegant and persistent texture. We also appreciated the Archineri Rosso '18, also very complex on the nose, full, vital and marked by rare length on the palate.

Wine	Rating
● Etna Rosso Barbagalli '17	🍷🍷🍷 8
● Etna Rosso Archineri '18	🍷🍷 6
● Etna Rosso Contrada Rampante '18	🍷🍷 6
○ Etna Bianco Archineri '19	🍷🍷 6
○ Etna Bianco Pietradolce '19	🍷🍷 4
⊙ Etna Rosato Archineri '19	🍷🍷 6
● Etna Rosso Contrada Santo Spirito '18	🍷🍷 6
● Etna Rosso Pietradolce '19	🍷🍷 4
○ Sant'Andrea Carricante '17	🍷🍷 8
● Etna Rosso Archineri '10	🥂🥂🥂 5
● Etna Rosso Contrada Rampante '16	🥂🥂🥂 6
● Etna Rosso V. Barbagalli '16	🥂🥂🥂 8
● Etna Rosso V. Barbagalli '14	🥂🥂🥂 8
● Etna Rosso V. Barbagalli '13	🥂🥂🥂 8
● Etna Rosso V. Barbagalli '12	🥂🥂🥂 8
● Etna Rosso V. Barbagalli '11	🥂🥂🥂 8
● Etna Rosso V. Barbagalli '10	🥂🥂🥂 8

★★★Planeta

C.DA DISPENSA
92013 MENFI [AG]
TEL. +39 091327965
www.planeta.it

PRE-BOOKED VISITS
ACCOMMODATION AND RESTAURANT SERVICE
ANNUAL PRODUCTION 2,500,000 bottles
HECTARES UNDER VINE 395.00
SUSTAINABLE WINERY

Year after year Francesca, Alessio and Santi Planeta's vision is strengthening and growing. They continue to deliver quality while promoting authentic Sicilian values through interesting initiatives. Six cellars and five terroirs fully represent the island's diversity. From the original site of Ulmo and Dispensa in Menfi, to Baronia in Capo Milazzo, Dorilli in Vittoria, Buonivini in Noto and Feudo di Mezzo on Mount Etna, theirs has been an exciting journey that elegantly narrates the relationship between cultivar, nature and territory. The Syrah Maroccoli '16 landed a place in our finals: complex and deep on the nose, it's focused in its fruity notes of currant and blueberry, with elegant spicy and balsamic nuances; in the mouth its fruit is round, long and clear. The Chardonnay '18 also delivered, proving rich in texture, which harmonizes nicely with its measured oak. Fine mineral and plum jam notes feature in the pulpy Santa Cecilia '17.

○ Sicilia Menfi Chardonnay '18	TT 5
● Sicilia Menfi Syrah Maroccoli '16	TT 3*
● Cerasuolo di Vittoria Cl. Dorilli '17	TT 4
○ Etna Bianco '19	TT 3
● Etna Rosso '19	TT 3
● Noto Nero d'Avola Santa Cecilia '17	TT 5
○ Sicilia Carricante Brut M. Cl '17	TT 4
○ Sicilia Carricante Eruzione 1614 '18	TT 4
○ Sicilia Menfi Alastro '19	TT 3
○ Sicilia Menfi Grillo Terebinto '19	TT 3
● Sicilia Nocera '18	TT 3
○ Sicilia Noto Allemanda '19	TT 3
● Cerasuolo di Vittoria Cl. Dorilli '14	YYY 3*
● Cerasuolo di Vittoria Cl. Dorilli '13	YYY 3*
○ Etna Bianco '16	YYY 3*
● Menfi Syrah Maroccoli '14	YYY 4*

Poggio di Bortolone

FRAZ. ROCCAZZO
VIA BORTOLONE, 19
97010 CHIARAMONTE GULFI [RG]
TEL. +39 0932921161
www.poggiodibortolone.it

CELLAR SALES
PRE-BOOKED VISITS
RESTAURANT SERVICE
ANNUAL PRODUCTION 80,000 bottles
HECTARES UNDER VINE 15.00
SUSTAINABLE WINERY

Pierluigi ('Pigi') Cosenza safeguards and cultivates the family's land in Chiaramonte Gulfi. Here on the plateaus and alluvial soils of the Para Para and Mazzarronello rivers, 15 of the estate's 50 hectares are under vine. Situated in the heart of the Cerasuolo di Vittoria Classico DOCG, the property hosts mainly Nero d'Avola and Frappato, but there are also international grapes such as Syrah, Cabernet Sauvignon and Petit Verdot. There are still a few patches of Grosso Nero, an endangered cultivar that once contributed to their Cerasuolo blend. The Cerasuolo Para Para '17 is magnificent. It took home Tre Bicchieri with its character, elegant bouquet of cherry preserves, sweet spices and citron; its fruit is pleasant, lively and round, the finish impeccable. A blend of Syrah and Cabernet, the Addamanera '19 features lovely green, fruity and marine notes, while the Rosachiara '19, a Frappato and Nero d'Avola rosé, proves very fresh and clear.

● Cerasuolo di Vittoria Il Para Para '17	TTT 5
● Addamanera '19	TT 3
⊙ Sicilia Rosato Rosachiara '19	TT 3
● Cerasuolo di Vittoria V. Para Para '05	YYY 4
● Cerasuolo di Vittoria V. Para Para '02	YYY 4*
● Addamanera '17	YY 3*
● Cerasuolo di Vittoria Cl. Contessa Costanza '16	YY 3
● Cerasuolo di Vittoria Cl. Poggio di Bortolone '17	YY 3
● Cerasuolo di Vittoria Cl. Poggio di Bortolone '16	YY 3
● Cerasuolo di Vittoria Il Para Para '16	YY 4
● Sicilia Rosso Pigi '17	YY 5
● Sicilia Rosso Pigi '14	YY 5
● Vittoria Frappato '18	YY 3
● Vittoria Frappato '16	YY 3

Principi di Butera

c.da Deliella
93011 Butera [CL]
Tel. +39 0934347726
www.principidibutera.it

CELLAR SALES
PRE-BOOKED VISITS
ANNUAL PRODUCTION 800,000 bottles
HECTARES UNDER VINE 180.00
SUSTAINABLE WINERY

The appellation dates back to 1543, when the Branciforte family received the title of Princes of Butera from Philip II, King of Spain. A period of decay during the 20th century was followed by a revival at the behest of the Zonin family, who restored the estate's 320 hectares as well as the ancient baglio (an enclosed Sicilian farmstead). About 170 hectares of vineyards unfold across calcareous hills. Here a sunny microclimate is mitigated by winds from the nearby Gulf of Gela to the south and Mount Dessueri to the northeast, ideal conditions for conferring elegance and personality to their wines. We appreciated the intensity and definition of the Grillo Diamanti '19. A lovely nose of citrus fruits, plums and medlars emanates from the glass; in the mouth its fruit is fragrant and taut. Clear and fine in its floral hints, the Chardonnay '19 also delivered with its pleasant flavor. The very well-crafted Metodo Classico Pas Dosé '17 is made with Nero d'Avola fermented off-the-skins: elegant varietal notes of plum and capers give way to a fresh and lively palate.

Wine	Rating
○ Nero d'Avola Pas Dosé M. Cl. '17	🍷🍷 6
○ Sicilia Chardonnay '19	🍷🍷 3
○ Sicilia Grillo Diamanti '19	🍷🍷 3
○ Nero d'Avola Pas Dosé M. Cl. 36 Mesi '16	🍷 6
○ Sicilia Inzolia Carizza '19	🍷 3
● Sicilia Nero d'Avola Amira '18	🍷 4
● Sicilia Syrah Butirah '18	🍷 4
● Cabernet Sauvignon '00	🍷🍷🍷 5
● Deliella '12	🍷🍷🍷 6
● Deliella '05	🍷🍷🍷 6
● Deliella '02	🍷🍷🍷 7
● Deliella '00	🍷🍷🍷 6
● Sicilia Deliella '13	🍷🍷🍷 6
● Sicilia Nero d'Avola Deliella '16	🍷🍷🍷 6
● Sicilia Syrah '15	🍷🍷🍷 3*

Rallo

via Vincenzo Florio, 2
91025 Marsala [TP]
Tel. +39 0923721633
www.cantinerallo.it

CELLAR SALES
PRE-BOOKED VISITS
ANNUAL PRODUCTION 420,000 bottles
HECTARES UNDER VINE 110.00
VITICULTURE METHOD Certified Organic

Rooted in the best of Sicily's enological history, this commendable winery, founded in 1860 by Diego Rallo, immediately established itself on international markets. Acquired by the Vesco family in 1997, it's benefited from its new owners' enthusiasm and expertise. Given their commitment to high quality organic farming, they've provided a clear example of how to produce elegant, pleasing, fine wines. Guided authoritatively by Andrea Vesco, who brings a solid ecological sensitivity, they avail themselves of plots in Alcamo, Pantelleria and Marsala, with this last hosting their charming, historic cellars. We tasted a formidable version of the Al Quasar dry Zibibbo. The 2019 barged its way to Tre Bicchieri by virtue of its overt personality. Delicious, vibrant and complex aromas span lavender and orange zest, medicinal herbs and iris. In the mouth it's rich and playful, vibrant, sumptuously multifaceted and elegant, alluring in its length, seductive. The other wines tasted are also excellent.

Wine	Rating
○ Sicilia Zibibbo Al Qasar '19	🍷🍷🍷 3*
○ Alcamo Beleda '19	🍷🍷 4
○ Marsala Sup. Semisecco Mille	🍷🍷 6
○ Marsala Vergine Soleras Venti Anni Ris.	🍷🍷 5
○ Orange AV 01 Catarratto '19	🍷🍷 4
○ Sicilia Grillo Bianco Maggiore '19	🍷🍷 3
○ Sicilia Insolia Evrò '19	🍷🍷 3
○ Alcamo Beleda '17	🍷🍷🍷 4*
○ Alcamo Beleda '15	🍷🍷🍷 4*
○ Alcamo Beleda '13	🍷🍷🍷 2*
○ Bianco Maggiore '12	🍷🍷🍷 3*
○ Sicilia Bianco Maggiore '18	🍷🍷🍷 3*
○ Sicilia Bianco Maggiore '16	🍷🍷🍷 3*
○ Sicilia Bianco Maggiore '14	🍷🍷🍷 3*
○ Al Qasar Zibibbo '16	🍷🍷 3*
○ Al Qasar Zibibbo '15	🍷🍷 3*

Tenute Rapitalà

c.da Rapitalà
90043 Camporeale [PA]
Tel. +39 092437233
www.rapitala.it

CELLAR SALES
PRE-BOOKED VISITS
ANNUAL PRODUCTION 2,200,000 bottles
HECTARES UNDER VINE 163.00

The hills that slope down from Camporeale towards the Gulf of Castellammare represent the terroir of reference for the winery founded in 1968 by Hugues Bernard de La Gatinais and Gigi Guarrasi (now headed by their son Laurent under Gruppo Italiano Vini). These lands have deep roots in viticulture, while the varieties cultivated range from native grapes like Catarratto, Grillo and Nero d'Avola to international cultivars like Chardonnay, Viognier, Syrah, Cabernet Sauvignon and Pinot Nero. Recently a vineyard of Nerello Mascalese was acquired in Randazzo, on the northeast of Etna. The Grand Cru '18 is an outstanding Chardonnay: it won over our tasters with its alluring bouquet of vanilla, white flowers and tropical fruits—oak serves as a backdrop without being invasive. In the mouth it's soft, fresh and balsamic. The late-harvest Catarratto and Sauvignon Cielo d'Alcamo '19 performed at its highest levels yet: elegant, buttery and harmonious in the sweetness of its lively fruit.

○ Conte Hugues Bernard De La Gatinais Grand Cru '18	TT 5
○ Alcamo Bianco I Templi '19	TT 2*
○ Alcamo Cl. V. Casalj '19	TT 3
○ Alcamo V. T. Cielo Dalcamo '19	TT 4
○ Piano Maltese Bianco '19	TT 2*
○ Sicilia Grillo I Templi '19	TT 2*
○ Bouquet '19	T 2
○ Sicilia Grillo Viviri '19	T 2
● Sicilia Syrah Sire Nero '19	T 2
○ Conte Hugues Bernard de la Gatinais Grand Cru '10	YYY 4*
● Hugonis '01	YYY 6
● Solinero '03	YYY 5
● Solinero '00	YYY 5
● Hugonis '16	YY 5
● Sicilia Nero d'Avola Alto Nero '17	YY 3

Riofavara

fraz. Rio Favara
s.da prov.le 49 Ispica-Pachino
97014 Ispica [RG]
Tel. +39 0932705130
www.riofavara.it

CELLAR SALES
PRE-BOOKED VISITS
ACCOMMODATION
ANNUAL PRODUCTION 45,000 bottles
HECTARES UNDER VINE 20.00
VITICULTURE METHOD Certified Organic
SUSTAINABLE WINERY

Founded in 1920, the Padova family's business is situated in Val di Noto, in Ispica and Pachino, home to two traditional DOC wines, Eloro Nero d'Avola and Moscato di Noto. The white calcareous soils of the area and a unique mesoclimate regulated by the wind, makes for grapes characterized by a unique sunniness and personality. Wine production, which dates back to 1994, calls for organic cultivation and non-invasive methods in the cellar. New vineyards have recently entered production, 11 hectares in Pachino planted with Nero d'Avola, Moscato and some 'ancient' cultivars. While waiting for the new version of their Sciavé, the Eloro Nero d'Avola Spaccaforno '16 made it into our finals by virtue of its charmingly territorial aromas, with notes of mulberry jam, bay leaf, capers and anchovies all discernible; in the mouth it's round and fresh, clean and long. The Moscato secco Mizzica '19 featured a nice aromatic encore, while the charming new blend of ancient cultivars, the Nsajàr '19, proves fresh and spirited in its fruit.

● Eloro Spaccaforno '16	TT 3*
○ Moscato di Noto Mizzica '19	TT 3
○ Nsajàr Recunu '19	TT 6
⊙ Sicilia Rosato '19	TT 3
○ Sicilia Extra Brut M. Cl. '18	T 7
● Eloro Nero d'Avola Sciavè '16	YY 5
● Eloro Nero d'Avola Sciavè '13	YY 5
● Eloro Nero d'Avola Spaccaforno '15	YY 4
○ Marzaiolo '18	YY 3
○ Marzaiolo '17	YY 3
○ Marzaiolo '16	YY 3
○ Moscato di Noto Mizzica '18	YY 3
○ Moscato di Noto Mizzica '17	YY 3
○ Moscato di Noto Mizzica '16	YY 3
○ Moscato di Noto Notissimo '16	YY 3

★Girolamo Russo

loc. Passopisciaro
via Regina Margherita, 78
95012 Castiglione di Sicilia [CT]
Tel. +39 3283840247
www.girolamorusso.it

CELLAR SALES
PRE-BOOKED VISITS
ANNUAL PRODUCTION 65,000 bottles
HECTARES UNDER VINE 15.00
VITICULTURE METHOD Certified Organic

Giuseppe Russo personally oversees the family vineyards located in the Etnean equivalent of the Côte d'Or. Here the ancient lava flows ('sciare') on the northeastern slopes of the volcano overlook the Alcantara river valley. Their 15 hectares are distributed across three districts in Randazzo and Passopisciaro: San Lorenzo, Feudo and Feudo di Mezzo, at elevations ranging from 650 to 780 meters above sea level. Giuseppe integrates organic cultivation with Etna's traditional vine growing techniques. The grapes are vinified separately so as to bring out the differences and personality of each cru. The whites put in a fine performance, demonstrating their quality. The Nerina '19 landed a place in our finals—it's fragrant and focused in its notes of aromatic herbs, with clear, harmonious fruit. The new San Lorenzo '19, with its elegant, smoky mineral nuances and pleasant creaminess in the mouth, was also well received. However it was the maturity, elegant complexity and smoothness of the Rosso San Lorenzo '18 that most stood out, earning the wine Tre Bicchieri.

● Etna Rosso San Lorenzo '18	▼▼▼	6
○ Etna Bianco Nerina '19	▼▼	5
○ Etna Bianco San Lorenzo '19	▼▼	5
⊙ Etna Rosato '19	▼▼	4
● Etna Rosso 'A Rina '18	▼▼	4
● Etna Rosso Feudo di Mezzo '18	▼▼	6
● Etna Rosso Calderara Sottana '18	▼	4
● Etna Rosso Feudo '18	▼	6
● Etna Rosso 'A Rina '15	▽▽▽	4*
● Etna Rosso 'A Rina '12	▽▽▽	3*
● Etna Rosso Feudo '11	▽▽▽	5
● Etna Rosso Feudo '10	▽▽▽	5
● Etna Rosso Feudo '07	▽▽▽	5
● Etna Rosso Feudo di Mezzo '16	▽▽▽	6
● Etna Rosso San Lorenzo '14	▽▽▽	6
● Etna Rosso San Lorenzo '13	▽▽▽	5
● Etna Rosso San Lorenzo '09	▽▽▽	5

Cantine Settesoli

s.s. 115
92013 Menfi [AG]
Tel. +39 092577111
www.cantinesettesoli.it

CELLAR SALES
PRE-BOOKED VISITS
ANNUAL PRODUCTION 20,000,000 bottles
HECTARES UNDER VINE 6000.00

The fact that December 21, 1958 was a beautiful day was seen as a good omen. Indeed, on that day 68 farmers gave life to a new cooperative by planting a vineyard where there had once been citrus fruits, cotton and wheat. Luck was on their side—the winery strengthened and grew into the economic and social benchmark it is today. Now Settesoli has over 2,000 members and manages 6,000 hectares. Its brands are widespread throughout the world and are synonymous with high quality. Its success is the result of collective effort and the forward-thinking vision of its directors, first Diego Planeta and now Giuseppe Bursi. The consistent quality of their range rewards the work started many years ago, and a far-sighted vision that has never sought shortcuts. An exemplary Nero d'Avola, the Cartagho '18, earned top marks (a performance we're used to by now). Elegant and fine, characterized by intense nuances of bay leaf, tobacco, plum and mulberry jam, it's streaked with fascinating iodine timbres. An excellent debut for the two Etnas as well.

● Sicilia Mandrarossa Cartagho '18	▼▼▼	3*
● Etna Rosso Mandrarossa Sentiero delle Gerle '16	▼▼	4
○ Etna Bianco Mandrarossa Sentiero delle Gerle '18	▼▼	4
○ Santannella Mandrarossa '19	▼▼	3
○ Sicilia Bertolino Soprano '18	▼▼	3
○ Sicilia Mandrarossa Urra di Mare '19	▼▼	3
● Sicilia Nero d'Avola Terre del Sommacco '17	▼▼	3
● Mandrarossa Cavadiserpe '16	▽▽▽	3*
● Sicilia Mandrarossa Cartagho '17	▽▽▽	3*
● Sicilia Mandrarossa Cartagho '16	▽▽▽	3*
● Sicilia Mandrarossa Cartagho '14	▽▽▽	3*
● Timperosse Mandrarossa '14	▽▽▽	3*

★★Tasca d'Almerita

C.DA REGALEALI
90129 SCLAFANI BAGNI [PA]
TEL. +39 0916459711
www.tascadalmerita.it

CELLAR SALES
PRE-BOOKED VISITS
ACCOMMODATION AND RESTAURANT SERVICE
ANNUAL PRODUCTION 2,124,000 bottles
HECTARES UNDER VINE 370.19
SUSTAINABLE WINERY

Lucio Tasca d'Almerita has often been called 'the last Gattopardo', but in truth he's never been a champion of the decadent immobility of the Sicilian nobility depicted by his cousin Tomasi di Lampedusa in his masterpiece. 'If we want everything to remain as it is, everything must change', the most quoted aphorism in Sicilian literature doesn't hold true for Count Lucio, who's never stood still. Indeed, he has worked since he was a lad to innovate and expand the winery, investing so much that through a combination of terroir, grape and ecology he's succeeded in creating wines of great quality. An outstanding range provides a litmus test for a producer that helped shaped the history of Italian enology. The Chardonnay Vigna San Francesco '18, the Tasca family's historic wine (in the mid-20th century they were among the first to plant the cultivar in Sicily) stood out, earning Tre Bicchieri. The 2018 proves highly elegant in its olfactory expression, invigorating, sophisticated and subtle on the palate.

○ Sicilia Chardonnay V. San Francesco Tenuta Regaleali '18	🍷🍷🍷 6
● Etna Rosso Tascante Contrada Sciaranuova V. V. '17	🍷🍷 8
● Contea di Sclafani Rosso del Conte Tenuta Regaleali '16	🍷🍷 7
● Etna Rosso Tascante Contrada Pianodario '17	🍷🍷 6
● Etna Rosso Tascante Contrada Sciaranuova '17	🍷🍷 6
● Etna Rosso Tascante Ghiaia Nera '18	🍷🍷 4
○ Sicilia Bianco Nozze d'Oro Tenuta Regaleali '18	🍷🍷 4
● Sicilia Cabernet Sauvignon V. San Francesco Tenuta Regaleali '17	🍷🍷 6
● Sicilia Rosso Cygnus Tenuta Regaleali '17	🍷🍷 4
○ Vigna di Paola Tenuta Capofaro '19	🍷🍷 6

Tenuta di Fessina

FRAZ. ROVITTELLO
VIA NAZIONALE 120, 22
95012 CASTIGLIONE DI SICILIA [CT]
TEL. +39 3357220021
www.tenutadifessina.com

CELLAR SALES
PRE-BOOKED VISITS
ACCOMMODATION AND RESTAURANT SERVICE
ANNUAL PRODUCTION 70,000 bottles
HECTARES UNDER VINE 13.00
SUSTAINABLE WINERY

Tragically, a bicycle accident took Roberto Silva, successful entrepreneur and husband of Silvia Maestrelli, away from us. Roberto didn't like to make appearances, but he was as attached to Fessina as Silvia was, so much so that he always offered encouragement and support. From the beginning of Silvia's adventure on Etna, Roberto was there, sharing in all the choices, even the most difficult ones. Together they'd recently decided to expand and modernize the winery, acquiring new vineyards while opening a wine resort. Management is entrusted to two young and talented technicians, Benedetto Alessandro and Jacopo Maniaci. The red Moscamento 1911, vintage 2017, took home top marks. Made with grapes from an ancient vineyard on the north side of Mount Etna (planted in 1911), it's a highly complex and deep wine, as only old vineyards can deliver: clear and focused amidst ferrous and fruity sensations, it exhibits a rock solid palate that nicely balances fragrance of fruit with a vibrant, sapid acidity. As usual, the whites are very good as well.

● Etna Rosso Erse Contrada Moscamento 1911 '17	🍷🍷🍷 5
○ Etna Bianco A' Puddara '18	🍷🍷 6
○ Etna Bianco Erse '19	🍷🍷 5
○ Etna Bianco Il Musmeci Contrada Caselle '17	🍷🍷 8
○ Etna Rosso Erse '18	🍷🍷 4
● Sicilia Nerello Cappuccio Laeneo '18	🍷🍷 4
○ Etna Rosato Erse '19	🍷 4
○ Etna Bianco A' Puddara '17	🍷🍷🍷 5
○ Etna Bianco A' Puddara '16	🍷🍷🍷 5
○ Etna Bianco A' Puddara '13	🍷🍷🍷 5
○ Etna Bianco A' Puddara '12	🍷🍷🍷 5
○ Etna Bianco A' Puddara '11	🍷🍷🍷 5
○ Etna Bianco A' Puddara '10	🍷🍷🍷 5
○ Etna Bianco A' Puddara '09	🍷🍷🍷 5
● Etna Rosso Musmeci '07	🍷🍷🍷 6

Terra Costantino

VIA GARIBALDI, 417
95029 VIAGRANDE [CT]
TEL. +39 095434288
www.terracostantino.it

CELLAR SALES
PRE-BOOKED VISITS
ACCOMMODATION
ANNUAL PRODUCTION 55,000 bottles
HECTARES UNDER VINE 10.00
VITICULTURE METHOD Certified Organic
SUSTAINABLE WINERY

Dino and Fabio Costantino's beautiful winery is situated on the southeast side of Etna. Founded in 1699, all the vineyards are located around the coeval palmento wine cellar in contrada Blandano, Viagrande. The area is just a stone's throw from the Ionian Sea, whose cool breezes play an important role in the microclimate on this side of the volcano, amplifying temperature swings during summer nights. The Costantino family, who were among the first to pursue organic farming on Etna, have always cultivated with great attention to the environment and biodiversity. The Etna Bianco De Aetna '18 made it into our finals. It's a wine that fully reflects the combination of volcanic terroir and varieties used, right from its bouquet, which calls up aniseed and white peach sensations on a lovely, mineral-saline background. In the mouth a sapid and fresh acidity manages to support its commendable fruit. The fresh, fruity and mineral rosé De Aetna '19 is a highly enjoyable drink.

Wine	Rating
○ Etna Bianco De Aetna '18	TT 5
⊙ Etna Rosato De Aetna '19	TT 4
● Etna Rosso De Aetna '18	TT 4
⊙ Rasola '19	TT 3
○ Etna Bianco Contrada Blandano '16	YY 5
○ Etna Bianco Contrada Blandano '15	YY 5
○ Etna Bianco Contrada Blandano '14	YY 5
○ Etna Bianco De Aetna '17	YY 3
● Etna Rosso Contrada Blandano '16	YY 5
● Etna Rosso Contrada Blandano '15	YY 5
● Etna Rosso Contrada Blandano '14	YY 5
● Etna Rosso De Aetna '17	YY 3*
● Etna Rosso De Aetna '16	YY 3*
● Etna Rosso De Aetna '15	YY 3
● Etna Rosso De Aetna '14	YY 3
● Etna Rosso De Aetna '13	YY 3

Terrazze dell'Etna

C.DA BOCCA D'ORZO
95036 RANDAZZO [CT]
TEL. +39 0916236343
www.terrazzedelletna.it

CELLAR SALES
PRE-BOOKED VISITS
ANNUAL PRODUCTION 120,000 bottles
HECTARES UNDER VINE 38.00

Amidst chestnut and oak woods, the immense slopes descend along the back of Mount Etna. It's a landscape shaped by the formidable energy and tenacious patience of farmers who have literally carved terraced vineyards out of lava. Bowled over by the beauty of Bocca d'Orzo, Nino Bevilacqua decided to found the family producer here. The vineyards, which are located between 600 and 950 meters elevation, mainly host Nerello Mascalese (some vines of which go back as far as 60 years), together with Cappuccio, Chardonnay, Pinot Nero and Petit Verdot. The Cuvée 50 Mesi repeats last year's performance, worthy of our finals, with the 2015 vintage: a complex nose offers up elegant notes of peanut butter and broom; in the mouth it's creamy, exhibiting delicate and persistent bead. Pleasant mineral hints and red berry notes feature in the Rosé Brut '17, with a nice encore on the palate where it's fresh and sapid. More mature and complex aromas characterize the classy Rosé Brut 50 Mesi '15. We also appreciated the pleasant Cuvée Brut '17.

Wine	Rating
○ Cuvée Brut 50 Mesi '15	TT 5
○ Cuvée Brut '17	TT 5
⊙ Cuvée Brut 50 Mesi Rosé '15	TT 5
⊙ Rosé Brut '17	TT 5
⊙ Etna Rosato '18	T 3
● Etna Rosso Cirneco '09	YYY 6
● Etna Rosso Cirneco '08	YYY 5
○ Cuvée Brut '16	YY 5
○ Cuvée Brut '15	YY 5
○ Cuvée Brut '14	YY 5
○ Cuvée Brut 50 Mesi '14	YY 5
○ Cuvée Brut 50 Mesi '12	YY 5
⊙ Rosé Brut '16	YY 5
⊙ Rosé Brut '15	YY 5
⊙ Rosé Brut '14	YY 5
⊙ Rosé Brut 50 Mesi '14	YY 5
⊙ Rosé Brut 50 Mesi '12	YY 5

Girolamo Tola & C.

via Giacomo Matteotti, 2
90047 Partinico [PA]
Tel. +39 0918781591
www.vinitola.it

ANNUAL PRODUCTION 180,000 bottles
HECTARES UNDER VINE 55.00

The new cellar, centrally located with respect to the plots cultivated in Bosco Falconeria, Giambascio and Grassuri Dairoldi, in the provinces of Palermo and Trapani, has afforded more breathing space to this successful family producer, which is highly appreciated on international markets. Modern equipment, comfortable tasting rooms and larger spaces now provide the ideal conditions for bringing out the best of their artisan approach to winemaking, which is overseen with passion by Mimmo Tola and his son Francesco, who's fresh off his studies in economics and management. The level of their whites and reds is constantly growing. Vibrant and territorial, the Nero d'Avola '19 offers up fragrant, fruity aromas of black cherries and spices. The surprising Grysos '18 is a Pinot Nero of great pleasantness and drinkability. The Nero d'Avola Black Label '18, with its decisive yet soft tannins, put in a notable performance, while the peachy rosé Costarosa '19, a sapid and mineral mix of red grapes, proves just as good.

Wine	Glasses	Price
⊙ Costarosa '19	TT	3
○ GranDuca Chardonnay '18	TT	3
● Grysos Pinot Nero '18	TT	6
● Nero d'Avola Syrah '17	TT	3
○ Sicilia Grillo '19	TT	2*
○ Sicilia Grillo Catarratto Chimaera Bianco '19	TT	2*
● Sicilia Nero d'Avola '19	TT	3
● Sicilia Nero d'Avola Black Label '18	TT	3
○ White Label Chardonnay Insolia '19	TT	3
○ Catarratto '18	YY	2*
○ Catarratto Insolia '18	YY	2*
○ Chardonnay Insolia '17	YY	2*
● Nero d'Avola Black Label '17	YY	3
● Nero D'Avola Syrah '16	YY	3
○ Sicilia Grillo '18	YY	2*
● Sicilia Nero d'Avola '18	YY	3

Tornatore

fraz. Verzella
via Pietramarina, 8a
95012 Castiglione di Sicilia [CT]
Tel. +39 3662641380
www.tornatorewine.com

CELLAR SALES
PRE-BOOKED VISITS
ANNUAL PRODUCTION 120,000 bottles
HECTARES UNDER VINE 45.00

Francesco Tornatore's winery is one of the most beautiful on Etna, marked by an enormous potential for growth, both in terms of quality (already very high) and production volumes. Francesco began his journey by starting from his roots, a five-hectare farm of vineyards that his father cultivated in Trimarchisa. Like a good entrepreneur, however, he did so with the future in mind. So it was that, in addition to Nerello Mascalese, he planted 25 hectares of Carricante. It was a brilliant intuition for a cultivar that's not particularly common on the north side of the volcano. Here it's thriving. If it's true that the reliability of a winery is measured by the quality of its basic wines, we can certainly say that this is one of the most reliable on Etna. Tre Bicchieri for the Etna Bianco Pietrarizzo '19, complex and fine on the nose, with a dense, elegant and remarkably long palate. The Etna Rosso '18 also made it into our finals. It's a wine of territorial expression with clear and invigorating fruit, making for a highly pleasant drink.

Wine	Glasses	Price
○ Etna Bianco Pietrarizzo '19	TTT	5
● Etna Rosso '18	TT	4
○ Etna Bianco '19	TT	4
⊙ Etna Rosato '19	T	4
● Etna Rosso '17	YYY	4*
● Etna Rosso '15	YYY	4*
● Etna Rosso Trimarchisa '16	YYY	6
○ Etna Bianco '18	YY	4
○ Etna Bianco '17	YY	4
○ Etna Bianco '16	YY	4
○ Etna Bianco Pietrarizzo '18	YY	5
○ Etna Bianco Pietrarizzo '17	YY	5
● Etna Rosso '16	YY	4
● Etna Rosso Ris. '14	YY	4
● Etna Rosso Trimarchisa '17	YY	6

Valle dell'Acate

C.DA BIDINI
97011 ACATE [RG]
TEL. +39 0932874166
www.valledellacate.it

CELLAR SALES
PRE-BOOKED VISITS
ACCOMMODATION
ANNUAL PRODUCTION 350,000 bottles
HECTARES UNDER VINE 80.00
VITICULTURE METHOD Certified Organic
SUSTAINABLE WINERY

Since 2019 the winery has been managed exclusively by Gaetana, who represents the sixth generation of Jacono family to cultivate the lands of Feudo Bidini. The terroir of reference is situated in the heart of the Cerasuolo di Vittoria Classico DOCG zone, the hills marked by the course of the Dirillo river. Here seven different types of soil have been identified, from yellow clay-sand to white-limestone, where their 'Bidis' Chardonnay grows, to black-pebbles, which host Frappato, and the red-orange terrain of the Iri da Iri cru. Fascinating iodine mineral notes and Mediterranean herbs characterize the Grillo Zagra '19, a wine that performed admirably with its highly pleasant palate, fresh, sapid and long. The new Bellifolli Bianco '19, a blend of Inzolia, Moscato and Fiano, features nice gustatory tension. The Nero d'Avola Bellifolli '19 is captivating in its varietal aromas; as always the Il Frappato '19 proves fragrant in its fruit.

Wine	Glasses
● Cerasuolo di Vittoria Cl. '18	4
○ Sicilia Bianco Bellifolli '19	3
○ Sicilia Grillo Zagra '19	3
○ Sicilia Insolia Bellifolli '19	3
● Sicilia Nero d'Avola Bellifolli '19	3
● Sicilia Rosso Bellifolli '19	3
● Vittoria Frappato Il Frappato '19	3
● Cerasuolo di Vittoria Cl. '17	4
● Cerasuolo di Vittoria Cl. '15	4
● Cerasuolo di Vittoria Cl. '14	4
○ Sicilia Insolia Bellifolli '18	3
● Sicilia Nero d'Avola Il Moro '15	4
● Sicilia Nero d'Avola Tanè '15	6
● Sicilia Nero d'Avola Bellifolli '18	3
● Sicilia Syrah Bellifolli '17	3
● Vittoria Frappato Il Frappato '18	3
● Vittoria Frappato Il Frappato '17	3

Zisola

C.DA ZISOLA
96017 NOTO [SR]
TEL. +39 057773571
www.mazzei.it

CELLAR SALES
PRE-BOOKED VISITS
ANNUAL PRODUCTION 120,000 bottles
HECTARES UNDER VINE 30.00
SUSTAINABLE WINERY

It was Filippo Mazzei's love for Sicily (Noto in particular) that inspired the family, already owners of the famous Castello di Fonterutoli in Chianti and the Tenuta di Belguardo in Maremma, to found their estate here. When Filippo first saw Zisola, it had almost been entirely abandoned. Only a beautiful citrus grove, partly dedicated to the cultivation of pink grapefruit, had managed to endure. He proceeded to restore the picturesque, 18th-century baglio (an enclosed Sicilian farmstead), create a new cellar and, most importantly, plant 30 hectares of vines, mainly Nero d'Avola. The Azisa '19, a blend of Catarratto and Grillo, deservedly earned a place in our finals. An explosive bouquet of citrus fruits, iodine hints, aromatic herbs and almonds give way to a fresh, delicately salty palate of rare pleasantness. The reds are also delicious, the elegant Nero d'Avola, with its fruity, graceful palate, in particular. The Doppiozeta '17 is simpler but no less pleasant, while the Zisola '18 offers up pleasant notes of mulberry.

Wine	Glasses
○ Sicilia Azisa '19	3*
● Noto Doppiozeta '17	6
● Noto Nero d'Avola Zisola '18	4
● Sicilia Achilles '17	6
● Achilles '16	6
● Achilles '15	4
● Effe Emme '15	6
● Effe Emme '13	6
● Noto Doppiozeta '15	6
● Noto Doppiozeta '14	6
● Noto Effe Emme '14	6
● Noto Nero d'Avola Zisola '17	4
● Noto Zisola '14	4
● Noto Zisola Doppiozeta '13	6
○ Sicilia Azisa '18	3
○ Sicilia Azisa '17	3
○ Sicilia Azisa '15	3

Al-Cantàra

loc. cda. Feudo S. Anastasia
s.da prov.le 89
95036 Randazzo [CT]
Tel. +39 095339430
www.al-cantara.it

CELLAR SALES
PRE-BOOKED VISITS
ACCOMMODATION
ANNUAL PRODUCTION 100,000 bottles
HECTARES UNDER VINE 14.00
SUSTAINABLE WINERY

- ○ 'A Nutturna '19 🍷🍷 4
- ○ Etna Bianco Luci Luci '18 🍷🍷 5
- ○ Etna Bianco Occhi di Ciumi '19 🍷🍷 3
- ● Muddichi di Suli '17 🍷🍷 4

Ampelon

c.da Calderara
95036 Randazzo [CT]
Tel. +39 3459196437
www.viniampelon.it

CELLAR SALES
ANNUAL PRODUCTION 50,000 bottles
HECTARES UNDER VINE 7.00
SUSTAINABLE WINERY

- ○ Etna Bianco Ampelon '19 🍷🍷 3
- ● Etna Rosso Le Caldere '16 🍷🍷 5
- ● Etna Rosso Passo alle Sciare '17 🍷🍷 4

Avide - Vigneti & Cantine

c.da Mastrella, 346
97013 Comiso [RG]
Tel. +39 0932967456
www.avide.it

CELLAR SALES
PRE-BOOKED VISITS
ANNUAL PRODUCTION 250,000 bottles
HECTARES UNDER VINE 68.00

- ● Cerasuolo di Vittoria Barocco '13 🍷🍷 5
- ● 1607 Frappato '19 🍷 3
- ● Cerasuolo di Vittoria Cl. Etichetta Nera '17 🍷 3
- ● Sigillo Rosso '15 🍷 5

Barone Sergio

loc. Noto
via Cavour, 29
96018 Pachino [SR]
Tel. +39 0902927878
www.baronesergio.it

CELLAR SALES
PRE-BOOKED VISITS
ANNUAL PRODUCTION 100,000 bottles
HECTARES UNDER VINE 30.00

- ● Eloro Nero d'Avola Barone Sergio '18 🍷🍷 3
- ○ Sicilia Grillo Alègre '19 🍷🍷 2*
- ○ Sicilia Moscato Moscà '19 🍷🍷 3
- ○ Alluccà Moscato '19 🍷 3

Battiato

via Carlo Cattaneo, 25
95010 Santa Venerina [CT]
Tel. +39 3491090748
www.battiatovini.it

- ● Etna Rosso ElloNero '17 🍷🍷 4

Tenuta Benedetta

c.da Petto Dragone
95015 Linguaglossa [CT]
Tel. +39 3342720047
www.tenutabenedetta.it

CELLAR SALES
ANNUAL PRODUCTION 10,000 bottles
HECTARES UNDER VINE 2.50

- ● Unico di Benedetta '16 🍷🍷 7
- ○ Etna Bianco di Mariagrazia '17 🍷 6
- ● Etna Rosso di Laura '16 🍷 6
- ● Unico di Benedetta '15 🍷 7

Birgi

C.DA BIRGI NIVALORO
91025 MARSALA [TP]
TEL. +39 0923966736
www.cantinebirgi.it

CELLAR SALES
PRE-BOOKED VISITS
ACCOMMODATION AND RESTAURANT SERVICE
ANNUAL PRODUCTION 1,000,000 bottles
HECTARES UNDER VINE 2500.00
VITICULTURE METHOD Certified Organic

○ Sicilia Merlot Kinisia Ris. '17	🍷🍷 4
● Sicilia Nero d'Avola Trisole '19	🍷🍷 2*
● Sicilia Nero d'Avola V. T. Unico '18	🍷🍷 4
○ Sicilia Zibibbo Trisole '19	🍷 2

Biscaris

VIA MARESCIALLO GIUDICE, 52
97011 ACATE [RG]
TEL. +39 0932990762
www.biscaris.it

CELLAR SALES
ANNUAL PRODUCTION 50,000 bottles
HECTARES UNDER VINE 10.00
VITICULTURE METHOD Certified Biodynamic

● Cerasuolo di Vittoria '19	🍷🍷 3
● Frappato '19	🍷🍷 2*

Calcagno

FRAZ. PASSOPISCIARO
VIA REGINA MARGHERITA,153
95012 CASTIGLIONE DI SICILIA [CT]
TEL. +39 3387772780
www.vinicalcagno.it

CELLAR SALES
PRE-BOOKED VISITS
ANNUAL PRODUCTION 13,000 bottles
HECTARES UNDER VINE 3.00

○ Etna Bianco Ginestra '19	🍷🍷 5
⊙ Etna Rosato Romice delle Sciare '19	🍷🍷 5
⊙ Etna Rosato Romice delle Sciare '18	🍸 5

Cambria

LOC. C.DA SAN FILIPPO
VIA VILLA ARANGIA
98054 FURNARI [ME]
TEL. +39 0941840214
www.cambriavini.com

CELLAR SALES
PRE-BOOKED VISITS
ACCOMMODATION
ANNUAL PRODUCTION 100,000 bottles
HECTARES UNDER VINE 25.00

● Kio Nocera Passito '17	🍷🍷 5
○ Sicilia Chardonnay '17	🍷 4
● Sicilia Syrah '17	🍷 5

CVA Canicattì

C.DA AQUILATA
92024 CANICATTÌ [AG]
TEL. +39 0922829371
www.cvacanicatti.it

CELLAR SALES
PRE-BOOKED VISITS
ANNUAL PRODUCTION 900,000 bottles
HECTARES UNDER VINE 1000.00

● Diodoros '16	🍷🍷 4
○ Sicilia Grillo Fileno '19	🍷🍷 2*
● Sicilia Nero d'Avola Aynat '16	🍷🍷 5
○ Sicilia Grillo Aquilae Bio '19	🍷 2

Palmento Carranco

FRAZ. VERZELLA
C.DA CARRANCO
95012 CASTIGLIONE DI SICILIA [CT]
TEL. +39 00390173626100
www.palmentocarranco.com

ANNUAL PRODUCTION 35,000 bottles
HECTARES UNDER VINE 7.00
SUSTAINABLE WINERY

○ Etna Bianco Villa dei Baroni '19	🍷🍷 5
● Etna Rosso Villa dei Baroni '17	🍷 5

Caruso & Minini

VIA SALEMI, 3
91025 MARSALA [TP]
TEL. +39 0923982356
www.carusoeminini.it

CELLAR SALES
PRE-BOOKED VISITS
ANNUAL PRODUCTION 1,200,000 bottles
HECTARES UNDER VINE 120.00
VITICULTURE METHOD Certified Organic
SUSTAINABLE WINERY

- ● Nino '11 — 🍷🍷 6
- ○ Sicilia Catarratto Naturalmente Bio '19 — 🍷🍷 3
- ○ Sicilia Grillo Naturalmente Bio '19 — 🍷🍷 3
- ● Naturalmente Bio Perricone '19 — 🍷 3

Casa Grazia

FRAZ. C.DA BRUCAZZI
ZONA IND.LE 2° STRADA
93012 GELA [CL]
TEL. +39 0933919465
www.casagrazia.com

CELLAR SALES
ANNUAL PRODUCTION 60,000 bottles
HECTARES UNDER VINE 50.00
VITICULTURE METHOD Certified Organic

- ● Cerasuolo di Vittoria Victorya 1607 '18 — 🍷🍷 5
- ○ Sicilia Grillo Zahara '19 — 🍷🍷 5
- ○ Sicilia Moscato Adoré '19 — 🍷🍷 5
- ● Sicilia Frappato Laetitya '19 — 🍷 5

Tenuta di Castellaro

FRAZ. QUATTROPANI
VIA CAOLINO
98055 LIPARI [ME]
TEL. +39 035233337
www.tenutadicastellaro.it

CELLAR SALES
PRE-BOOKED VISITS
ANNUAL PRODUCTION 25,000 bottles
VITICULTURE METHOD Certified Organic

- ● Nero Ossidiana '17 — 🍷🍷 5
- ○ Bianco Pomice '19 — 🍷🍷 5
- ● Corinto '18 — 🍷🍷 5
- ⊙ Rosa Caolino '19 — 🍷 3

Cantine Colosi

LOC. PACE DEL MELA
FRAZ. GIAMMORO
98042 MESSINA
TEL. +39 0909385549
www.cantinecolosi.it

PRE-BOOKED VISITS
ANNUAL PRODUCTION 100,000 bottles
HECTARES UNDER VINE 10.00

- ○ Malvasia delle Lipari Dolce Naturale Nurah '16 — 🍷🍷 5
- ○ Malvasia delle Lipari Na'jm '16 — 🍷🍷 5
- ○ Passito '16 — 🍷🍷 5

Contrada Santo Spirito di Passopisciaro

FRAZ. PASSOPISCIARO
C.DA SANTO SPIRITO
95012 CASTIGLIONE DI SICILIA [CT]
TEL. +39 0575477857
www.contradasantospiritodipassopisciaro.it

ANNUAL PRODUCTION 7,000 bottles
HECTARES UNDER VINE 4.00

- ● Etna Rosso Animardente '16 — 🍷🍷 6

Agricola Cortese

C.DA SABUCI, SDA. PRO.VLE 3, KM 11
97019 VITTORIA [RG]
TEL. +39 09321846555
www.agricolacortese.com

CELLAR SALES
PRE-BOOKED VISITS
ANNUAL PRODUCTION 70,000 bottles
HECTARES UNDER VINE 12.00
VITICULTURE METHOD Certified Organic
SUSTAINABLE WINERY

- ○ Nostru Carricante '19 — 🍷🍷 3
- ○ Nostru Catarratto Lucido '19 — 🍷🍷 3
- ● Nostru Nerello Mascalese '19 — 🍷 3
- ○ Vanedda '18 — 🍷 4

Coste Ghirlanda

LOC. PIANA DI GHIRLANDA
91017 PANTELLERIA [TP]
TEL. +39 3333913695
www.costeghirlanda.it

CELLAR SALES
PRE-BOOKED VISITS
RESTAURANT SERVICE
ANNUAL PRODUCTION 25,000 bottles
HECTARES UNDER VINE 11.00

○ Silenzio '18 — 🍷🍷 6
● Sicilia Alicante Ghirlanda '17 — 🍷🍷 6

Curto

LOC. C.DA SULLA
S.DA ST.LE 115 ISPICA - ROSOLINI KM 358
97014 ISPICA [RG]
TEL. +39 0932950161
www.curto.it

CELLAR SALES
PRE-BOOKED VISITS
ANNUAL PRODUCTION 70,000 bottles
HECTARES UNDER VINE 30.00

● Eloro Nero d'Avola '19 — 🍷🍷 3
○ Poiano '19 — 🍷🍷 2*
● Ikano '17 — 🍷 3

Gianfranco Daino

VIA CROCE DEL VICARIO, 115
95041 CALTAGIRONE [CT]
TEL. +39 093358226
www.vinidaino.it

CELLAR SALES
PRE-BOOKED VISITS
ANNUAL PRODUCTION 18,000 bottles
HECTARES UNDER VINE 2.44

● Suber '17 — 🍷🍷 7

Gaspare Di Prima

LOC. LAGO ARANCIO
VIA G. GUASTO, 27
92017 SAMBUCA DI SICILIA [AG]
TEL. +39 0925941201
www.cantinadiprima.com

CELLAR SALES
PRE-BOOKED VISITS
ANNUAL PRODUCTION 50,000 bottles
HECTARES UNDER VINE 38.00
VITICULTURE METHOD Certified Organic

● Sicilia Pepita Rosso '18 — 🍷🍷 2*
● Syrah '18 — 🍷🍷 2*
● Sicilia Grillo Il Grillo del Lago '19 — 🍷 2
● Sicilia Nero d'Avola Gibilmoro '17 — 🍷 3

Feudo Disisa

LOC. GRISÌ
FRAZ. C.DA DISISA
S.DA PROV.LE 30, KM 6
90040 MONREALE [PA]
TEL. +39 0916127109
www.feudodisisa.it

CELLAR SALES
PRE-BOOKED VISITS
ANNUAL PRODUCTION 150,000 bottles
HECTARES UNDER VINE 150.00
VITICULTURE METHOD Certified Organic

○ Monreale Lu Bancu '19 — 🍷🍷 3
○ Sicilia Chardonnay '18 — 🍷🍷 4
⊙ Sicilia Grecu di Livanti '19 — 🍷🍷 3
○ Sicilia Chara '19 — 🍷 3

Edomé

LOC. PASSOPISCIARO
C.DA FEUDO DI MEZZO
95012 CASTIGLIONE DI SICILIA [CT]
TEL. +39 3911709974
www.cantinedome.com

CELLAR SALES
ANNUAL PRODUCTION 17,000 bottles
HECTARES UNDER VINE 3.00

○ Etna Bianco Aitna V. Nica '19 — 🍷🍷 5
● Etna Rosso Aitna Feudo di Mezzo '16 — 🍷🍷 5

Cantine Ermes

c.da Salinella, s.s. 188, km 45,5
91029 Santa Ninfa [TP]
Tel. +39 092469124
www.cantineermes.it

ANNUAL PRODUCTION 12,000,000 bottles
HECTARES UNDER VINE 10554.00
VITICULTURE METHOD Certified Organic
SUSTAINABLE WINERY

- ● Vento di Mare Bio Nero d'Avola Cabernet Sauvignon '19 — 🍷🍷 2*
- ○ Vento di Mare Grillo '19 — 🍷🍷 2*
- ● Vento di Mare Nerello Mascalese '19 — 🍷🍷 3

Fazio Wines

fraz. Fulgatore
via Capitano Rizzo, 39
91010 Erice [TP]
Tel. +39 0923811700
www.faziowines.it

CELLAR SALES
PRE-BOOKED VISITS
ANNUAL PRODUCTION 820,000 bottles
HECTARES UNDER VINE 100.00
SUSTAINABLE WINERY

- ○ Trenta Salmi Catarratto '18 — 🍷🍷 3
- ○ Erice Grillo Aegades '19 — 🍷 3
- ● Erice Nero d'Avola Torre dei Venti '19 — 🍷 4
- ● Sicilia Nero d'Avola Gàbal '18 — 🍷 4

Fischetti

fraz. Rovittello
via Via Nazionale, 2
95012 Castiglione di Sicilia [CT]
Tel. +39 3341272527
www.fischettiwine.it

CELLAR SALES
PRE-BOOKED VISITS
ACCOMMODATION
ANNUAL PRODUCTION 5,000 bottles
HECTARES UNDER VINE 3.00

- ○ Etna Bianco Muscamento '19 — 🍷🍷 6
- ⊙ Etna Rosato Muscamento '19 — 🍷🍷 6
- ● Etna Rosso Muscamento '15 — 🍷 5

Tenuta Gatti

c.da Cuprani
98064 Librizzi [ME]
Tel. +39 0941368173
www.tenutagatti.com

CELLAR SALES
PRE-BOOKED VISITS
ANNUAL PRODUCTION 40,000 bottles
HECTARES UNDER VINE 15.00
VITICULTURE METHOD Certified Organic

- ○ Mamertino Bianco Catalina '18 — 🍷🍷 3

Giasira

c.da Ritillini
96019 Rosolini [SR]
Tel. +39 0931501700
www.lagiasira.it

CELLAR SALES
PRE-BOOKED VISITS
ANNUAL PRODUCTION 30,000 bottles
HECTARES UNDER VINE 7.00
VITICULTURE METHOD Certified Organic

- ○ Aurantium '16 — 🍷🍷 4
- ○ Giasira Bianco '19 — 🍷🍷 3
- ○ Keration '19 — 🍷🍷 3
- ● Morhum Nerello Mascalese '17 — 🍷 3

Hauner

loc. Santa Maria
via G.Grillo, 61
98123 Messina
Tel. +39 0906413029
www.hauner.it

CELLAR SALES
PRE-BOOKED VISITS
ANNUAL PRODUCTION 80,000 bottles
HECTARES UNDER VINE 18.00

- ○ Malvasia delle Lipari Passito Carlo Hauner Ris. '17 — 🍷🍷 8
- ● Carlo Hauner '18 — 🍷 4
- ○ Iancura '19 — 🍷 2

Hibiscus

c.da Tramontana
90010 Ustica [PA]
Tel. +39 0918449543
www.agriturismohibiscus.com

CELLAR SALES
PRE-BOOKED VISITS
ACCOMMODATION
ANNUAL PRODUCTION 10,000 bottles
HECTARES UNDER VINE 3.00

- ○ Grotta dell'Oro '19 — 🍷🍷 4
- ○ Onde di Sole '19 — 🍷🍷 4
- ○ Zhabib Passito '19 — 🍷🍷 4
- ⊙ L'Isola Rosato '19 — 🍷 2

Incarrozza

loc. c.da Carrozza
s.da prov.le 12/II km 1
95045 Misterbianco [CT]
Tel. +39 3488749305
www.incarrozzavini.com

ANNUAL PRODUCTION 20,000 bottles
HECTARES UNDER VINE 8.00

- ⊙ Alicante Rosato '18 — 🍷🍷 4
- ● San Nicola Syrah '12 — 🍷🍷 4
- ● Fra' Anselmo Perricone '15 — 🍷 5
- ○ Uve d'Agosto Bianco '17 — 🍷 3

Tenute Lombardo

c.da Cusatino
93100 Caltanissetta
Tel. +39 09341935148
www.tenutelombardo.it

PRE-BOOKED VISITS
ANNUAL PRODUCTION 120,000 bottles
HECTARES UNDER VINE 30.00

- ○ Sicilia Catarratto Bianco d'Altura '19 — 🍷🍷 2*
- ● Sicilia Nero d'Avola Nero d'Altura '17 — 🍷🍷 2*
- ● Unànime Rosso '18 — 🍷🍷 3
- ● Sicilia Eimi '16 — 🍷 3

Maggiovini

via Filippo Bonetti, 35
97019 Vittoria [RG]
Tel. +39 0932984771
www.maggiovini.com

CELLAR SALES
PRE-BOOKED VISITS
ACCOMMODATION
ANNUAL PRODUCTION 400,000 bottles
HECTARES UNDER VINE 50.00
VITICULTURE METHOD Certified Organic
SUSTAINABLE WINERY

- ● Amongae '16 — 🍷🍷 4
- ○ Sicilia Grillo V. di Pettineo '18 — 🍷🍷 3
- ● Vittoria Frappato V. di Pettineo '19 — 🍷🍷 3
- ● Cerasuolo di Vittoria Cl. V. di Pettineo '17 — 🍷 2

Marino Vini

via Alfieri, 51
90043 Camporeale [PA]
Tel. +39 3886537642
www.marinovini.it

CELLAR SALES
PRE-BOOKED VISITS
RESTAURANT SERVICE
ANNUAL PRODUCTION 50,000 bottles
HECTARES UNDER VINE 15.00
VITICULTURE METHOD Certified Organic
SUSTAINABLE WINERY

- ○ Benì Cataratto Chardonnay '19 — 🍷🍷 3
- ○ Sicilia Grillo Flavì '19 — 🍷🍷 3
- ● Sicilia Rosso Krìmisos '19 — 🍷🍷 3
- ○ Sicilia Bianco Krenè '19 — 🍷 3

Masseria del Feudo

c.da Grottarossa
93100 Caltanissetta
Tel. +39 0934830885
www.masseriadelfeudo.it

CELLAR SALES
PRE-BOOKED VISITS
ACCOMMODATION
ANNUAL PRODUCTION 100,000 bottles
HECTARES UNDER VINE 12.00
VITICULTURE METHOD Certified Organic

- ○ Sicilia Grillo '19 — 🍷🍷 2*
- ⊙ Sicilia Rosé Cotì '19 — 🍷🍷 3
- ○ Sicilia Inzolia '19 — 🍷 2
- ● Sicilia Nero d'Avola '18 — 🍷 2

Cantina Modica di San Giovanni

c.da Bufalefi
96017 Noto [SR]
Tel. +39 09311805181
www.vinidinoto.it

CELLAR SALES
PRE-BOOKED VISITS
RESTAURANT SERVICE
ANNUAL PRODUCTION 80,000 bottles
HECTARES UNDER VINE 40.00
SUSTAINABLE WINERY

● Eloro Nero d'Avola Arà '13	🍷🍷 3
○ Lupara '19	🍷🍷 2*
○ Moscato di Noto Dolcenoto '19	🍷🍷 3
● Eloro Nero d'Avola Filinona '14	🍷 2

Morgante

c.da Racalmare
92020 Grotte [AG]
Tel. +39 0922945579
www.morgantevini.it

CELLAR SALES
ANNUAL PRODUCTION 310,000 bottles
HECTARES UNDER VINE 52.00

● Sicilia Nero d'Avola Don Antonio '17	🍷🍷 6
○ Bianco di Morgante '19	🍷 3
● Sicilia Nero d'Avola '18	🍷 3
⊙ Sicilia Rosè di Morgante '19	🍷 2

Tenuta Morreale Agnello

c.da Fauma
92100 Agrigento
Tel. +39 347 6028029
www.tenutamorrealeagnello.it

ANNUAL PRODUCTION 50,000 bottles
HECTARES UNDER VINE 60.00
VITICULTURE METHOD Certified Organic
SUSTAINABLE WINERY

○ Sicilia Grillo Sephora '19	🍷🍷 2*
● Terre di Fauma Nero d'Avola '18	🍷🍷 2*
● Sephora Merlot '17	🍷 3
○ Vigna di Sopra Zibibbo '19	🍷 2

Cantine Mothia

via Giovanni Falcone, 22
91025 Marsala [TP]
Tel. +39 0923737295
www.cantinemothia.it

CELLAR SALES
PRE-BOOKED VISITS
ANNUAL PRODUCTION 100,000 bottles
HECTARES UNDER VINE 25.00

○ Sicilia Grillo Mosaikon '19	🍷🍷 2*
○ Vela Latina '19	🍷🍷 2*

Musita

c.da Passo Clacara
91018 Salemi [TP]
Tel. +39 092468576
www.musita.it

○ Sicilia Catarratto Regieterre '19	🍷🍷 3
○ Sicilia Zibibbo Passito Passopasso '18	🍷🍷 5
○ Sicilia Bianco Passocalcara '17	🍷 5
● Sicilia Rosso Passocalcara Ris. '14	🍷 4

Antica Tenuta del Nanfro

c.da Nanfro San Nicola Le Canne
95041 Caltagirone [CT]
Tel. +39 093360744
www.nanfro.com

CELLAR SALES
PRE-BOOKED VISITS
ANNUAL PRODUCTION 65,000 bottles
HECTARES UNDER VINE 39.00
VITICULTURE METHOD Certified Organic

● Cerasuolo di Vittoria Sammauro '18	🍷🍷 3
● Vittoria Frappato '19	🍷🍷 3
● Vittoria Nero d'Avola Strade '16	🍷🍷 3
○ Strade Insolia '19	🍷 3

Mimmo Paone

FRAZ. SCALA
C.SO SICILIA, 61
98040 TORREGROTTA [ME]
TEL. +39 0909981101
www.paonevini.it

CELLAR SALES
PRE-BOOKED VISITS
ANNUAL PRODUCTION 250,000 bottles
HECTARES UNDER VINE 70.00

- ○ Malvasia delle Lipari Passito '16 — 🍷🍷 6
- ○ Sicilia Grillo Di Volà '19 — 🍷🍷 2*
- ● Funnari Nero d'Avola '16 — 🍷 2
- ○ Mamertino Bianco '19 — 🍷 3

Pietracava

VIA LUIGI STURZO, 16
93011 BUTERA [CL]
TEL. +39 3392410117
www.pietracavawines.it

ANNUAL PRODUCTION 30,000 bottles
HECTARES UNDER VINE 15.00

- ● Kalpis '17 — 🍷🍷 4
- ○ Sicilia Grillo Pioggia di Luce '19 — 🍷🍷 3
- ● Sicilia Nero D'Avola Septimo '17 — 🍷🍷 3
- ○ Sicilia Chardonnay Idria '18 — 🍷 3

Pupillo

C.DA LA TARGIA
96100 SIRACUSA
TEL. +39 0931494029
www.pupillowines.com

CELLAR SALES
PRE-BOOKED VISITS
ANNUAL PRODUCTION 35,000 bottles
HECTARES UNDER VINE 20.00

- ○ Moscato di Siracusa Solacium '19 — 🍷🍷 4
- ○ Siracusa Bianco Podere 27 '19 — 🍷🍷 3
- ○ Siracusa Cyane '19 — 🍷🍷 3
- ○ Siracusa Bianco Damarete '19 — 🍷 3

Quignones

LOC. C.DA SANT'OLIVA
S.S. 123 KM 31.900
92027 LICATA [AG]
TEL. +39 0922773744
www.quignones.it

CELLAR SALES
PRE-BOOKED VISITS
ANNUAL PRODUCTION 30,000 bottles
HECTARES UNDER VINE 28.00

- ○ Largasia Insolia Chardonnay '19 — 🍷🍷 3
- ⊙ Sicilia Nero d'Avola Rosato Fimmina '19 — 🍷🍷 2*

Ramaddini Vignaioli a Marzamemi

FRAZ. MARZAMEMI
C.DA LETTIERA
96018 PACHINO [SR]
TEL. +39 09311847100
www.feudoramaddini.com

CELLAR SALES
PRE-BOOKED VISITS
RESTAURANT SERVICE
ANNUAL PRODUCTION 100,000 bottles
HECTARES UNDER VINE 20.00
VITICULTURE METHOD Certified Organic

- ○ Ramà Catarratto '19 — 🍷🍷 2*
- ○ Sicilia Grillo Nassa '19 — 🍷🍷 3
- ● Noto Rosso Ramà '18 — 🍷 2
- ● Sicilia Syrah Note Nere '18 — 🍷 3

Tenuta Sallier de La Tour

FRAZ. CAMPOREALE
C.DA PERNICE
90046 MONREALE [PA]
TEL. +39 0916459711
www.tascadalmerita.it

PRE-BOOKED VISITS
ANNUAL PRODUCTION 260,000 bottles
HECTARES UNDER VINE 40.00
SUSTAINABLE WINERY

- ● Monreale Syrah La Monaca '18 — 🍷🍷 4
- ● Sicilia Nero d'Avola '18 — 🍷🍷 2*
- ⊙ Sicilia Rosato Madamarosè '19 — 🍷🍷 3
- ○ Sicilia Grillo '19 — 🍷 2

Santa Tresa

C.DA SANTA TERESA
97019 VITTORIA [RG]
TEL. +39 09321846555
www.santatresa.com

CELLAR SALES
PRE-BOOKED VISITS
ANNUAL PRODUCTION 250,000 bottles
HECTARES UNDER VINE 39.00
VITICULTURE METHOD Certified Organic

- ● Cerasuolo di Vittoria '18 — 🍷🍷 3
- ● Rina Russa Frappato '19 — 🍷🍷 3
- ⊙ Rosa di Santa Tresa '19 — 🍷🍷 3
- ○ Sicilia Bianco Rina Ianca '19 — 🍷 3

Il Serralh

C.DA LA SERRAGLIA
91017 PANTELLERIA [TP]
TEL. +39 3335058930
ilserralh@tiscali.it

- ○ Passito di Pantelleria Alma Noctis '09 — 🍷🍷 6
- ○ Pantelleria Yle '19 — 🍷🍷 4

Solidea

C.DA KADDIUGGIA
91017 PANTELLERIA [TP]
TEL. +39 0923913016
www.solideavini.it

CELLAR SALES
PRE-BOOKED VISITS
ANNUAL PRODUCTION 12,000 bottles
HECTARES UNDER VINE 5.00

- ○ Ilios '19 — 🍷🍷 3
- ○ Passito di Pantelleria '19 — 🍷🍷 5

Salvatore Tamburello

VIA BORSELLINO, 22
91020 POGGIOREALE [TP]
TEL. +39 3398605865
www.salvatoretamburello.it

PRE-BOOKED VISITS
ANNUAL PRODUCTION 15,000 bottles
HECTARES UNDER VINE 12.00
VITICULTURE METHOD Certified Organic

- ○ Sicilia Catarratto 797 N '19 — 🍷🍷 3
- ○ Sicilia Grillo 204 N '19 — 🍷🍷 3
- ● Sicilia Nero d'Avola 306 N '17 — 🍷 3
- ● Sicilia Nero d'Avola 306 '17 — 🍷 3

Tenute di Nuna

LOC. FORNAZZO
95010 SANT'ALFIO [CT]
TEL. +39 3493001213
www.terredinuna.com

- ○ Etna Bianco Nuna '16 — 🍷🍷 5
- ○ Etna Bianco Nuna '17 — 🍷🍷 5
- ○ Etna Bianco Nuna '15 — 🍷🍷 5

Terresikane

C.DA TURCHIOTTO
93011 BUTERA [CL]
TEL. +39 3273872386
www.terresikane.com

CELLAR SALES
PRE-BOOKED VISITS
ACCOMMODATION
ANNUAL PRODUCTION 90,000 bottles
HECTARES UNDER VINE 21.00

- ● Sicilia Nero d'Avola Frasciano '18 — 🍷🍷 4
- ● Sicilia Nero d'Avola Merlot Il Sikano '18 — 🍷 3

Torre Mora

s.da di collegamento tra SS120 e SR Mareneve
95012 Castiglione di Sicilia [CT]
Tel. +39 057754011
www.tenutepiccini.it

PRE-BOOKED VISITS
ANNUAL PRODUCTION 76,000 bottles
HECTARES UNDER VINE 13.00
VITICULTURE METHOD Certified Organic

- ○ Etna Bianco Scalunera '19 — 🍷🍷 4
- ⊙ Etna Rosato Scalunera '19 — 🍷🍷 5
- ● Etna Rosso Chiuse Vidalba '16 — 🍷🍷 6
- ● Etna rosso Cauru '19 — 🍷 3

Feudo Vagliasindi

loc. C.da Feudo Sant'Anastasia
s.da prov.le 89
95036 Randazzo [CT]
Tel. +39 0957991823
www.feudovagliasindi.it

- ● Nerello Cappuccio '17 — 🍷🍷 4
- ⊙ Etna Rosato '18 — 🍷 3
- ● Etna Rosso '16 — 🍷 4
- ● Etna Rosso '15 — 🍷 4

Tenuta Valle delle Ferle

c.da Valle delle Ferle
95041 Caltagirone [CT]
Tel. +39 3288359712
www.valledelleferle.it

CELLAR SALES
PRE-BOOKED VISITS
RESTAURANT SERVICE
ANNUAL PRODUCTION 12,000 bottles
HECTARES UNDER VINE 10.00

- ● Cerasuolo di Vittoria Tenuta Valle delle Ferle '17 — 🍷🍷 5
- ● Vittoria Frappato '17 — 🍷🍷 5
- ● Vittoria Nero D'Avola '17 — 🍷🍷 5

Villa Moreri

via Ugo Foscolo, 7
90144 Palermo
Tel. +39 3332128127
caffarellistudio@gmail.com

SUSTAINABLE WINERY

- ○ Mamertino Guzman '19 — 🍷🍷 3*

Vinisola

c.da Kazzen, 11
91017 Pantelleria [TP]
Tel. +39 3356042155
www.vinisola.it

CELLAR SALES
PRE-BOOKED VISITS
ANNUAL PRODUCTION 35,000 bottles
HECTARES UNDER VINE 6.50

- ○ A Mano Libera '19 — 🍷🍷 5
- ○ Passito di Pantelleria Arbaria '15 — 🍷🍷 5
- ⊙ Vòta e Firrìa '18 — 🍷🍷 4
- ○ Pantelleria Bianco Zefiro '18 — 🍷 3

Vivera

c.da Martinella
95015 Linguaglossa [CT]
Tel. +39 095643837
www.vivera.it

CELLAR SALES
PRE-BOOKED VISITS
ANNUAL PRODUCTION 120,000 bottles
HECTARES UNDER VINE 30.00
VITICULTURE METHOD Certified Organic

- ○ A'Mami '17 — 🍷🍷 4
- ○ Altrove '19 — 🍷🍷 3
- ○ Etna Bianco Salisire Contrada Martinella '16 — 🍷🍷 4

SARDINIA

As we know, numbers leave no room for ambiguity. That's why it's important to start with them, to unpack the balance sheet for Sardinia in this new edition of Italian Wines. Of the 400 wines evaluated, 200 earned Due Bicchieri, 48 entered our final tastings and 15 took home our highest award. It's a record, one that, in light of the number of wines tasted, makes the region one of Italy's best for quality (at least in our opinion). It's an even more remarkable fact if you think that just over 10 years ago only a handful of Sardinian wines ever won Tre Bicchieri. Was it a great year then? No doubt there are many bright spots, though there are shadows as well. If one the one hand there's no doubt about the quality of Sardinia's wine, its adherence to the territory (by way of its cultivars) and, last but not least, the aging potential of certain wines, there's still much to be done in terms of marketing, communication and commercialization. Wine (we will never tire of saying) is a global game. Whether it's made by a small artisan producer, a large cooperative, or a historic private brand, wine is an ambassador for the territory. But the game can only be won through teamwork, collective efforts in name of the island, to be able to face international markets without fear or hesitation. And in this respect, there's still work to be done. Indeed, it's no coincidence that some appellations, especially those that span the entire region, are obsolete and do nothing to highlight the attributes of individual territories. But without the work of the protection consortia, which only really exist on paper, nothing will change. That said, let's enjoy this year's great result and focus on the Tre Bicchieri awarded, which summarize the quality of the whole island. From north to south, we find Cannonaus of great elegance and finesse, playing on aromatic complexity and great drinkability. Then there are its sapid and mineral Vermentinos, fruit of different terroirs, its pervasive, Mediterranean Carignanos and certain Bovales that are as structured as they are balanced. And finally there's Sardinia's great, immortal wine, Vernaccia di Oristano. This year 2 reached the peaks of excellence, Silvio Carta's Riserva '68 and the Antico Gregori '76. The latter, a masterpiece, is our Sweet Wine of the Year.

★★Argiolas

via Roma, 28/30
09040 Serdiana [CA]
Tel. +39 070740606
www.argiolas.it

CELLAR SALES
PRE-BOOKED VISITS
ANNUAL PRODUCTION 2,200,000 bottles
HECTARES UNDER VINE 230.00

Without a doubt one of Sardinia's great wineries, Argiolas is capable of producing more than two million bottles, but doing it while offering quality across their entire range, from their daily-drinking wines to their most prestigious selections. Behind it all is the Argiolas family, who are as united as ever, with the third generation now at the helm. Their wines are all made with grapes cultivated in the south, mostly Serdiana, in the sub-region of Parteolla, though there are some properties in Sulcis as well. Thanks in part to a great 2016 vintage, we tasted an excellent version of their Turriga: this year their most important wine offers up notes of Mediterranean scrub, red berries, spices and touches of undergrowth. The palate is lean, despite its structure, coming through clean and elegant at the finish. Tre Bicchieri. We also appreciated the Korem, another top red (made mainly with Bovale). Here tannins are more imposing but this doesn't detract from drinkability.

Wine	Rating
● Turriga '16	🍷🍷🍷 8
● Korem Bovale '17	🍷🍷 5
● Carignano del Sulcis Is Solinas Ris. '17	🍷🍷 4
○ Nasco di Cagliari Iselis '19	🍷🍷 3
○ Vermentino di Sardegna Merì '19	🍷🍷 3
● Carignano del Sulcis Cardanera '19	🍷 4
○ Vermentino di Sardegna Is Argiolas '19	🍷 3
● Cannonau di Sardegna Senes Ris. '13	🍷🍷🍷 5
● Cannonau di Sardegna Senes Ris. '12	🍷🍷🍷 5
● Turriga '15	🍷🍷🍷 8
● Turriga '11	🍷🍷🍷 8
● Turriga '10	🍷🍷🍷 8
● Cannonau di Sardegna Senes Ris. '16	🍷🍷 5
● Cannonau di Sardegna Senes Ris. '14	🍷🍷 5
○ Vermentino di Sardegna Cerdeña '16	🍷🍷 7

Audarya

loc. Sa Perdera
s.s. 466 km 10,100
09040 Serdiana [CA]
Tel. +39 070 740437
www.audarya.it

CELLAR SALES
PRE-BOOKED VISITS
ANNUAL PRODUCTION 280,000 bottles
HECTARES UNDER VINE 40.00

A young winery and young owners. In just a few years Audarya has managed to carve out a prominent place in Sardinia. Credit goes to siblings Salvatore and Nicoletta Pala, who have managed to carry forth a family tradition and transform it into an innovative producer. The cellar and adjacent vineyards are located a few kilometers from Serdiana. Traditional grapes are cultivated, focusing on the most widespread varieties, as well as Bovale, Nuragus and Nasco, three cultivars that are leading to excellent results. A white and a red wine earned a place in our finals, with the Nuracada getting the upper hand and taking home Tre Bicchieri. We appreciated the great elegance of the Bovale '18, it's a wine redolent of red fruit and spices, with an elegant, deep palate—highly drinkable but also characterful and plucky. The Camminera '19 is a great Vermentino produced in the south of the island. Fragrances of wild flowers and white fruit give way to a fresh, pervasive palate.

Wine	Rating
● Nuracada Bovale '18	🍷🍷🍷 5
○ Vermentino di Sardegna Camminera '19	🍷🍷 3*
● Cannonau di Sardegna '19	🍷🍷 3
⊙ Cannonau di Sardegna Rosato '19	🍷🍷 2*
○ Nuragus di Cagliari '19	🍷🍷 2*
● Monica di Sardegna '19	🍷 2
○ Vermentino di Sardegna '19	🍷 2
● Nuracada Bovale '17	🍷🍷🍷 5
○ Bisai '18	🍷🍷 5
● Cannonau di Sardegna '18	🍷🍷 3
● Cannonau di Sardegna '17	🍷🍷 3
○ Malvasia di Cagliari Estissa '18	🍷🍷 4
● Nuracada Bovale '16	🍷🍷 5
○ Vermentino di Sardegna Camminera '18	🍷🍷 3*

Cantina di Calasetta

via Roma, 134
09011 Calasetta [SU]
Tel. +39 078188413
www.cantinadicalasetta.it

CELLAR SALES
PRE-BOOKED VISITS
ANNUAL PRODUCTION 100,000 bottles
HECTARES UNDER VINE 300.00

Calasetta is a small cooperative winery that bases its production on the island of Sant'Antioco and its vineyards. Here in the heart of Sulcis, Carignano is still grown on its own root, in sandy soils, with some vineyards going back over a hundred years. Several reds are produced—these are differentiated according to the age of the vines and the type of aging. Their very well-made wines are faithful to the territory of origin and sold at very competitive prices. Vermentino and Moscato complete the range. None of their Carignanos disappointed. The most convincing are, for different reasons, the Piede Franco and Aìna. The first, made with grapes from only pre-phylloxera vines and fermented entirely in steel, expresses all the purity the grape has to offer when cultivated in sandy soils: creamy tannins, aromas of scrub and ripe fruit, distinct sapidity. The second is a 2017 Riserva. It's more close-knit and full-bodied, with alcohol lending warmth and pervasiveness—its rich structure endures right up through the finish. Among the whites we appreciated the Cala di Seta '19.

● Carignano del Sulcis Àina Ris. '17	🍷🍷 4
● Carignano del Sulcis Piede Franco '18	🍷🍷 3
● Carignano del Sulcis Tupei '18	🍷🍷 2*
○ Vermentino di Sardegna Cala di Seta '19	🍷🍷 2*
● Carignano del Sulcis Maccòri '19	🍷 2
● Carignano del Sulcis Rosato Rassetto '19	🍷 2
● Carignano del Sulcis Àina Ris. '16	🍷🍷 4
● Carignano del Sulcis Maccòri '18	🍷🍷 2*
● Carignano del Sulcis Piede Franco '17	🍷🍷 3*
● Carignano del Sulcis Piede Franco '15	🍷🍷 2*
● Carignano del Sulcis Tupei '16	🍷🍷 2*
○ Moscato di Cagliari In Fundu '17	🍷🍷 3
○ Vermentino di Sardegna Cala di Seta '18	🍷🍷 2*

★Capichera

s.s. Arzachena-Sant'Antonio, km 4
07021 Arzachena [SS]
Tel. +39 078980612
www.capichera.it

CELLAR SALES
PRE-BOOKED VISITS
ANNUAL PRODUCTION 250,000 bottles
HECTARES UNDER VINE 50.00
SUSTAINABLE WINERY

This prestigious brand is well known in Sardinia, Italy and the world, but over the years the number of bottles produced hasn't grown significantly. The Ragnedda family have always preferred to focus on their wonderful vineyards, trying to raise quality year after year while identifying individual crus for Vermentino whites that transmit the territory's soul, as well as the wine's aging potential. Their range is rounded out by some notable reds made with Carignano grapes and Syrah, a variety that has found an ideal habitat here. We really are spoilt for choice when it comes to Capichera's range. Three wines perform at absolute top levels with the late-harvest version getting the best of it. Three years after vintage, the great Vermentino white won over our tasting panel by virtue of its multifaceted, complex nose, which plays on anise and almond, white flowers and candied citrus peel. Supple and deep in the mouth, it exhibits fresh acidity and a charming sapid touch.

○ Capichera V. T. '17	🍷🍷🍷 8
○ Capichera '18	🍷🍷 6
● Mantenghja '15	🍷🍷 8
● Assajé '17	🍷🍷 6
⊙ També Rosato '19	🍷🍷 4
○ Vermentino di Gallura Vign'Angena '19	🍷🍷 5
○ Capichera '14	🍷🍷🍷 6
○ Capichera '13	🍷🍷🍷 6
○ Capichera '12	🍷🍷🍷 6
○ Capichera '11	🍷🍷🍷 6
○ Capichera '10	🍷🍷🍷 5
○ Capichera V. T. '16	🍷🍷🍷 8
○ Vermentino di Gallura Vigna'Ngena '17	🍷🍷🍷 5
○ Vermentino di Gallura Vigna'Ngena '10	🍷🍷🍷 5

Silvio Carta

via Roma, 2
09070 Baratili San Pietro [OR]
Tel. +39 +39 0783410314
www.silviocarta.it

CELLAR SALES
PRE-BOOKED VISITS
ANNUAL PRODUCTION 83,500 bottles
HECTARES UNDER VINE 8.00
VITICULTURE METHOD Certified Organic
SUSTAINABLE WINERY

Silvio Carta has deep roots. It was founded in 1929 in Baratili San Pietro, a small village in Oristano. The aim was to promote Vernaccia di Oristano, a unique and highly valued wine obtained through long aging in barrels. Since 1973 Elio Carta (Silvio's son) has overseen the winery which, in the meantime, has also specialized in quality spirits and liqueurs. Every year we taste several of this historic producer's old Vernaccia Reserves, and there are always a few surprises. The Riserva 1968 had to be full of surprises. Just thinking of a wine that's over fifty years old gives you the shivers. But, as we have said many times, Vernaccia is a great wine that's capable of astonishing especially over the long (very long) term. Its explosion of aromas can be perceived as soon as you open the bottle, before it even gets in the glass: dried fruit, Asian spices, medicinal herbs and a clear salty note flood the nose. The palate, which is also marked by a charming salinity, is endless.

Wine	Rating	Price
○ Vernaccia di Oristano Ris. '68	🍷🍷🍷	8
○ Vermentino di Gallura Sup. Serenata '19	🍷🍷	3
○ Vernaccia di Oristano Ris. '06	🍷🍷	8
● Cagnulari Po Tui '18	🍷	3
● Monica di Sardegna Po Tui '18	🍷	3
○ Vernaccia di Oristano Ris. '03	🍷🍷 (outline)	6
○ Vernaccia di Oristano Ris. '01	🍷🍷 (outline)	6

Giovanni Maria Cherchi

loc. Sa Pala e Sa Chessa
07049 Usini [SS]
Tel. +39 079380273
www.vinicolacherchi.it

CELLAR SALES
PRE-BOOKED VISITS
ANNUAL PRODUCTION 170,000 bottles
HECTARES UNDER VINE 30.00

Usini's development passed (and continues to pass) through Cherchi, a producer that, over the years, has managed to surprise with their Vermentino (produced in different versions), but also with Cagnulari, a wine obtained from the grape of the same name present only in this area. Their wines communicate well with the terroir of origin, whose unique features are represented by higher elevations, calcareous soils and sea breezes. There's also a Cannonau, a passito and a Metodo Classico made with Vermentino grapes. Once again the selection presented didn't disappoint, especially the 2018 reds. Among them the Luzzana (a blend of Cagnulari and Cannonau) stands out with its complex nose of black fruit, and a close-knit, compact palate. Tannins are round and soft, joined by excellent freshness and, owing to a delicately salty touch, it finishes clean and long. The Cannonau di Sardegna also delivers. The Billia line is always a sure bet (and at the right price). Among the whites we appreciated the excellent Tuvaoes 30 Vendemmie.

Wine	Rating	Price
● Luzzana '18	🍷🍷	4
● Cagnulari Billia '19	🍷🍷	3
● Cannonau di Sardegna '18	🍷🍷	3
○ Vermentino di Sardegna Billia '19	🍷🍷	2*
○ Vermentino di Sardegna Tuvaoes '19	🍷🍷	3
○ Vermentino di Sardegna Tuvaoes 30 Vendemmie	🍷🍷	3
○ Vermentino di Sardegna Filighe Brut M. Cl. '15	🍷	3
○ Vermentino di Sardegna Tuvaoes '16	🍷🍷🍷 (outline)	3*
○ Vermentino di Sardegna Tuvaoes '88	🍷🍷🍷 (outline)	4*
● Cagnulari '18	🍷🍷 (outline)	3
● Cannonau di Sardegna '16	🍷🍷 (outline)	3*
● Luzzana '17	🍷🍷 (outline)	4

Chessa

via San Giorgio
07049 Usini [SS]
Tel. +39 3283747069
www.cantinechessa.it

CELLAR SALES
PRE-BOOKED VISITS
ANNUAL PRODUCTION 43,000 bottles
HECTARES UNDER VINE 15.00

Giovanna Chessa is a skilled and passionate producer who has bet everything on the territory of Usini, and she's got plenty to show for it. Her range focuses on Vermentino and Cagnulari, the two varieties that here manage to best express the territory. The calcareous and clayey soils, the hilltop vineyards long caressed by breezes, and a production approach aimed at preserving the natural qualities of the grapes, make for wines of great finesse and drinkability, fresh and elegant, able to evolve well over time. The range is completed by a Moscato Passito and a notable IGT made with Cagnulari and Cannonau. This last, the Lugherra, wasn't submitted because it's still aging. In the meantime, however, we tasted one of the best versions of Cagnulari ever presented: fascinating notes of wild berries and sweet spices rise up, with blood-scented, iron sensations making an appearance as well. The palate comes through lean and highly elegant, though without betraying the grape's strength. The Mattariga is always a sure bet.

Wine	Rating
● Cagnulari '19	▼▼ 3*
○ Vermentino di Sardegna Mattariga '19	▼▼ 3
● Cagnulari '18	▽▽ 3*
● Cagnulari '16	▽▽ 3
● Cagnulari '15	▽▽ 3
● Cagnulari '14	▽▽ 3
● Cagnulari '13	▽▽ 3
○ Kentàles	▽▽ 5
● Lugherra '16	▽▽ 5
○ Vermentino di Sardegna Mattariga '18	▽▽ 3
○ Vermentino di Sardegna Mattariga '16	▽▽ 3
○ Vermentino di Sardegna Mattariga '15	▽▽ 3
○ Vermentino di Sardegna Mattariga '14	▽▽ 3

Attilio Contini

via Genova, 48/50
09072 Cabras [OR]
Tel. +39 0783290806
www.vinicontini.it

CELLAR SALES
PRE-BOOKED VISITS
ANNUAL PRODUCTION 1,000,000 bottles
HECTARES UNDER VINE 110.00
VITICULTURE METHOD Certified Organic
SUSTAINABLE WINERY

Founded in the late 1800s by Attilio Contini, and still managed by the family, this is certainly one of the most important wineries on the island. The reins are now in the hands of the fourth generation, Alessandro and Mauro. The winery contributed to developing Oristano's wine, starting with vinification of the enological jewel that is Vernaccia di Oristano, which they've never abandoned. Indeed, entering the historic cellar means being able to taste old Vernaccia reserves that go back to the 1950s. But production certainly doesn't stop at the great oxidative wine, theirs is a vast range that comprises all the island's main varieties. It's true that, when it comes to certain wines everything else goes on the back burner. For the first time the Antico Gregori is being released with the vintage displayed. The 1976 is an incredible wine, of masterful complexity, endless on the palate. After several decades it still has so much to say. For us it's one of the best versions of Vernaccia di Oristano tasted in this guide's 30 years. Tre Bicchieri. It's our Meditation Wine of the Year.

Wine	Rating
○ Vernaccia di Oristano Antico Gregori '76	▼▼▼ 8
● Cannonau di Sardegna Cl. 'Inu Ris. '16	▼▼ 4
● Cannonau di Sardegna Sartiglia '18	▼▼ 3
○ Karmis '19	▼ 3
● Maluentu '18	▼ 3
○ Vermentino di Sardegna Pariglia '19	▼ 2
● Barrile '13	▽▽▽ 7
● Barrile '11	▽▽▽ 6
○ Pontis '00	▽▽▽ 4
○ Vernaccia di Oristano Antico Gregori	▽▽▽ 7
○ Vernaccia di Oristano Ris. '88	▽▽▽ 4*
○ Vernaccia di Oristano Ris. '71	▽▽▽ 5
● Cannonau di Sardegna 'Inu Ris. '13	▽▽ 4
● Cannonau di Sardegna Sartiglia '17	▽▽ 3
● I Giganti Rosso '16	▽▽ 5

Antonella Corda

s.s. 466 Km 6,8
09040 Serdiana [CA]
Tel. +39 0707966300
www.antonellacorda.it

CELLAR SALES
PRE-BOOKED VISITS
ANNUAL PRODUCTION 50,000 bottles
HECTARES UNDER VINE 15.00

2016 was the first vintage for Antonella Corda, and the winemaker immediately left her mark with her first Tre Bicchieri and our Up-and-Coming Winery award. Four years later she's consolidated her range of Cannonau, Vermentino and Nuragus and focused increasingly on wines of great drinkability and elegance. All this starts with painstaking work in the vineyard and identifying the most suitable plots (all of which are now being converted to organic). These three wines are now joined by a very special white IGT, made with Vermentino grapes, vinified in amphora with maceration on the skins. We'll start with the latter. The 2018 Ziru is truly superb. Unique in its aromas of candied citrus, dried fruit and nuts, wildflowers and iodine, in the mouth it's marked by sensations of grape peel, but never bitter or astringent—freshness and sapidity support the palate, leading it to a beautiful finish. Another great wine is the Cannonau di Sardegna '18: fresh, elegant, subtle and lean, it's an exemplary Cannonau.

Wine	Rating
● Cannonau di Sardegna '18	TT 5
○ Ziru '18	TT 6
○ Nuragus di Cagliari '19	TT 4
○ Vermentino di Sardegna '19	TT 4
● Cannonau di Sardegna '17	YYY 3*
● Cannonau di Sardegna '16	YYY 3*
○ Nuragus di Cagliari '18	YY 3
○ Nuragus di Cagliari '17	YY 2*
○ Vermentino di Sardegna '18	YY 3
○ Vermentino di Sardegna '17	YY 3

Cantine di Dolianova

loc. Sant'Esu
s.s. 387 km 17,150
09041 Dolianova [SU]
Tel. +39 070744101
www.cantinedidolianova.it

CELLAR SALES
PRE-BOOKED VISITS
ANNUAL PRODUCTION 4,000,000 bottles
HECTARES UNDER VINE 1200.00

Dolianova is the largest cooperative winery on the island and can boast sizable production volumes, made possible thanks to dozens of growers who cultivate the grapes from Parteolla, just a stone's throw from Cagliari. In the last few years the winery has managed to renew itself, with changes concerning the image, quality and range of wines offered. The results were not long in coming, both when it comes to their simpler wines and (indeed especially) concerning their selections rooted in the great native grapes of the south. Some two wines made it into our final round of tastings. One is this year's great new release, the Ju '17. A blend of native grapes, it's a full wine of great complexity, modern in style and marked by hints of menthol, chocolate, spices and black fruit. On the palate it's impressive, only slightly contracted at the back. Another standout is the Terresicci '15, a unique, Mediterranean wine made with Sardinian Barbera. We also appreciated the Prendas and Anzenas, Vermentino and Cannonau, respectively.

Wine	Rating
● Ju '17	TT 6
● Terresicci '15	TT 5
● Cannonau di Sardegna Anzenas '18	TT 2*
⊙ Cannonau di Sardegna Rosato Rosada '19	TT 2*
○ Càralis Chardonnay Brut M. Cl.	TT 3
○ Montesicci '18	TT 3
○ Vermentino di Sardegna Prendas '19	TT 2*
○ Càralis Malvasia Demi Sec	T 2
● Monica di Sardegna Arenada '17	T 2
○ Nuragus di Cagliari Perlas '19	T 2
● Terresicci '14	YYY 5
● Cannonau di Sardegna Blasio Ris. '13	YY 3
○ Nuragus di Cagliari Perlas '18	YY 2*
○ Vermentino di Sardegna Prendas '18	YY 2*

Cantina Dorgali

via Piemonte, 11
08022 Dorgali [NU]
Tel. +39 078496143
www.cantinadorgali.com

CELLAR SALES
PRE-BOOKED VISITS
ANNUAL PRODUCTION 1,500,000 bottles
HECTARES UNDER VINE 600.00
SUSTAINABLE WINERY

The local cooperative Dorgali takes its name from the small village on the eastern side of the island. It's a beautiful area for wine grape cultivation, situated not far from the Tyrrhenian coast, where the hills and headlands host vineyards and centuries-old olive trees. Cannonau is, without a doubt, the primary variety grown here in the appellation's classic heart, and the vines are still bush-trained. Dorgali's wide range comprises whites, some delicious Rosé Cannonau bubbly and sweet, late-harvest selections as well. Truly competitive prices. It was the D53, a highly drinkable and characteristic Sardinian Cannonau, that most surprised during our tastings, with the 2016 earning a place in our finals. On the nose it features notes of myrtle, undergrowth, red fruit and spices, while the palate comes through fresh and sapid, paving the way for a deep, clean palate. The Icoré is a younger Cannonau, but no less charming. Blackberry and currant dominate the nose, heralding a gentle, smooth palate. As usual we appreciated the Hortos '14, a blend of Cannonau and Syrah.

Wine	Rating	
● Cannonau di Sardegna Cl. D 53 '16	**YY**	5
● Cannonau di Sardegna Icorè '18	**YY**	2*
● Hortos '14	**YY**	6
● Bardia '19	**Y**	3
⊙ Cannonau di Sardegna Rosato Filieri '19	**Y**	2
○ Vermentino di Sardegna Cala Luna '19	**Y**	2
○ Vermentino di Sardegna Filine '19	**Y**	2
● Cannonau di Sardegna Cl. D 53 '15	YY	5
● Cannonau di Sardegna Tunila '17	YY	2*
● Cannonau di Sardegna V. di Isalle '16	YY	2*
● Cannonau di Sardegna Vigna di Isalle '17	YY	2*
● Hortos '13	YY	6
⊙ Cannonau di Sardegna Rosato Filieri '18	Y	2

Fradiles

loc. Creccheri
via S. Pertini, 2
08030 Atzara [NU]
Tel. +39 3331761683
paolo.savoldo@gmail.com

CELLAR SALES
PRE-BOOKED VISITS
ANNUAL PRODUCTION 20,000 bottles
HECTARES UNDER VINE 12.00
SUSTAINABLE WINERY

Fradiles is a small artisan producer led by Paolo Savoldo, a young and passionate winemaker. Here in the heart of Mandrolisai, an appellation based on three grape varieties (Cannonau, Bovale and Monica), we find old bush-trained vines and elevations surpassing 700 meters above sea level. The wines proposed, which are very traditional, reflect the variety and area of origin, and never disappoint in terms of finesse and pleasantness. Different versions of Mandrolisai are offered, according to age. There's also a monovarietal Bovale. Two wines in the finals make for a major success story for this small Atzara producer. The new Angraris '16, a Mandrolisai Superiore of the highest quality, perfectly balances softness and acidity. The nose is close-woven and multifaceted, anticipating a pulpy palate, where tannins set the rhythm, lending the right hardness. The Antiogu, another 2016, is graceful and juicy, with perfect extraction. We also appreciated the Istentu and the Fradiles, a young, dynamic wine.

Wine	Rating	
● Mandrolisai Sup. Angraris '16	**YY**	8
● Mandrolisai Sup. Antiogu '16	**YY**	4
● Mandrolisai Fradiles '18	**YY**	3
● Mandrolisai Sup. Istentu '16	**YY**	5
○ Funtanafrisca '19	**Y**	4
● Mandrolisai Sup. Antiogu '11	YYY	5
● Bagadìu '17	YY	3
● Bagadìu '16	YY	3
● Bagadiu '13	YY	4
● Bagadìu Bovale '15	YY	3
● Mandrolisai Azzàra '16	YY	2*
● Mandrolisai Fradiles '17	YY	3*
● Mandrolisai Fradiles '16	YY	3
● Mandrolisai Fradiles '15	YY	3*
● Mandrolisai Sup. Antiogu '15	YY	4
● Mandrolisai Sup. Antiogu '14	YY	4

★Giuseppe Gabbas

via Trieste, 59
08100 Nuoro
Tel. +39 078433745
www.gabbas.it

CELLAR SALES
PRE-BOOKED VISITS
ANNUAL PRODUCTION 70,000 bottles
HECTARES UNDER VINE 15.00

The years pass but Giuseppe Gabbas, driven by his innate passion, continues to work the estate's vineyards, all located around the cellar not far from Nuoro. Here, Cannonau vine the undisputed king and Giuseppe, harvest after harvest, has been able to offer versions faithful to the variety and territory, but that also manage to exhibit finesse and elegance, simplicity and character. The credit goes to painstaking work in the vineyard, the prelude to a simple, minimally-invasive approach in the cellar. Three wines were submitted this year, all of excellent quality. Once again the Dule proves to be a model for the typology. The 2017 version of the Cannonau di Sardegna Classico offers up aromas of blackberry, blackcurrant and black pepper, with flowery notes making an appearance as well. On the palate it's lean, pervasive, warm but never burning. It surprises for its aromatic polish and focused finish. Yet again, Tre Bicchieri. The Lillové, a young, juicy and dynamic version of Cannonau, is always a sure bet. We also appreciated the fresh and iodine Manzanile '19.

- ● Cannonau di Sardegna Cl. Dule '17 — 🍷🍷🍷 4*
- ● Cannonau di Sardegna Lillové '19 — 🍷🍷 3
- ○ Vermentino di Sardegna Manzanile '19 — 🍷 3
- ● Cannonau di Sardegna Cl. Dule '16 — YYY 4*
- ● Cannonau di Sardegna Cl. Dule '15 — YYY 4*
- ● Cannonau di Sardegna Cl. Dule '13 — YYY 4*
- ● Cannonau di Sardegna Cl. Dule '12 — YYY 4*
- ● Cannonau di Sardegna Cl. Dule '11 — YYY 4*
- ● Cannonau di Sardegna Dule Ris. '10 — YYY 4*
- ● Cannonau di Sardegna Dule Ris. '09 — YYY 3*
- ● Cannonau di Sardegna Dule Ris. '08 — YYY 3*
- ● Cannonau di Sardegna Dule Ris. '07 — YYY 3*
- ● Cannonau di Sardegna Dule Ris. '06 — YYY 3*
- ● Cannonau di Sardegna Dule Ris. '05 — YYY 3*
- ● Cannonau di Sardegna Lillové '18 — YY 3
- ● Cannonau di Sardegna Lillové '17 — YY 2*
- ● Cannonau di Sardegna Lillové '16 — YY 2*

Cantina Gallura

via Val di Cossu, 9
07029 Tempio Pausania
Tel. +39 079631241
www.cantinagallura.com

CELLAR SALES
PRE-BOOKED VISITS
ANNUAL PRODUCTION 1,300,000 bottles
HECTARES UNDER VINE 350.00

Gallura is one of the three great cooperative producers operating in the area. Over the years it's managed to develop and promote the viticulture of northeast Sardinia through its main grape variety, Vermentino. A wide range of wines are produced, starting with whites, which are differentiated according to aging and vineyard position. Their Vermentino di Gallura, which is offered at competitive prices, is always a guarantee of excellent quality. We also make note of some good sparkling wines, including the traditionally-styled Moscato di Tempio. The Canayli, the producer's historic wine, now comes in two versions: the simpler is delicious, expressing aromas of almond and white flowers, medlar and citrus. Then there's the late-harvest version, also a 2019, which plays more on richness and roundness, though without losing the freshness and minerality of a proper Gallura. We also appreciated the aforementioned Moscato di Tempio Spumante, a real champion among sweet sparklers.

- ○ Moscato di Tempio Pausania Spumante Dolce — 🍷🍷 2*
- ○ Vermentino di Gallura Canayli V. T. '19 — 🍷🍷 4
- ○ Vermentino di Gallura Sup. Canayli '19 — 🍷🍷 2*
- ● Karana '19 — 🍷 2
- ⊙ Campos '18 — YY 2*
- ● Cannonau di Sardegna Templum '16 — YY 2*
- ● Karana '17 — YY 2*
- ○ Vermentino di Gallura Canayli V. T. '17 — YY 4
- ○ Vermentino di Gallura Piras '18 — YY 2*
- ○ Vermentino di Gallura Piras '17 — YY 2*
- ○ Vermentino di Gallura Piras '16 — YY 2*
- ○ Vermentino di Gallura Sup. Canayli '18 — YY 2*

Cantina Giba

via Principe di Piemonte, 16
09010 Giba [SU]
Tel. +39 0781689718
www.cantinagiba.it

CELLAR SALES
ANNUAL PRODUCTION 100,000 bottles
HECTARES UNDER VINE 15.00

Situated in the deep south of the island, Giba (the name comes from the small village where the winery was born) is as small as it is charming. Here the approach centers on highly territorial wines, sometimes a pinch imprecise, but marked by plenty of character. It all starts with Carignano del Sulcis grapes grown on old bushed-trained vines that produce very limited yields. There's also Vermentino (from Sulcis as well), and a very special Metodo Classico rosè that's also made with Carignano. Once again the authentic and alluring 6Mura (Carignano del Sulcis Riserva) won us over and earned Tre Bicchieri. Made with grapes from old vineyards, it has masterly tannic extraction. Oak isn't discernible at all, leaving room for red fruit and charming hints of scrub. In the mouth, despite its warmth, sapidity/acidity is nicely balanced, and the finish comes through long. We also appreciated the Vermentino di Sardegna, made with grapes grown entirely in Sulcis.

- ● Carignano del Sulcis 6 Mura Ris. '17 — 5
- ● Carignano del Sulcis Giba '19 — 2*
- ○ Vermentino di Sardegna 6 Mura '19 — 4
- ⊙ Carignano del Sulcis Rosato '19 — 2
- ● Carignano del Sulcis 6Mura '12 — 5
- ● Carignano del Sulcis 6Mura '11 — 5
- ● Carignano del Sulcis 6Mura '10 — 5
- ● Carignano del Sulcis 6Mura '09 — 5
- ● Carignano del Sulcis 6Mura Ris. '16 — 5
- ● Carignano del Sulcis 6Mura Ris. '15 — 5
- ● Carignano del Sulcis Giba '17 — 2*
- ● Carignano del Sulcis Giba '16 — 2*
- ○ Vermentino di Sardegna 6Mura '18 — 4
- ○ Vermentino di Sardegna Giba '18 — 3
- ○ Vermentino di Sardegna Giba '17 — 2*

Luca Gungui

c.so Vittorio Emanuele, 21
08024 Mamoiada [NU]
Tel. +39 3473320735
cantinagungui@tiscali.it

ANNUAL PRODUCTION 3,437 bottles
HECTARES UNDER VINE 2.30

A great number of wineries have sprung up in Mamoiada in recent years, testifying to a unique, valuable territory. Cannonau reigns supreme, and the area is a concentration of old, bush-trained vines cultivated at elevations of over 700 meters. A few years ago Luca Gungui also decided to invest in his land here and in viticulture. For now he's producing two wines, a red and a rosé. Territorial expression isn't lacking, nor is drinkability and elegance, and that's why, despite the small quantities produced, we're listing his winery here in our main section. This year we tasted two wines, both 2019s. The Cannonau di Sardegna Berteru proves to be a superb representative of the typology, fresh and perky in its tones of dried rose and red fruit, it has a juicy palate and nice length. It's subtler and leaner than previous years, but still very charming. En Rose, as its name suggests, is the rosé version (also Cannonau). Vital and supple, it's redolent of wild strawberry and lily of the valley.

- ● Cannonau di Sardegna Berteru '19 — 6
- ⊙ Cannonau di Sardegna Berteru En Rose '19 — 8
- ● Cannonau di Sardegna Berteru '18 — 6
- ● Cannonau di Sardegna Berteru '17 — 6
- ● Cannonau di Sardegna Berteru '16 — 6
- ⊙ Cannonau di Sardegna Berteru En Rose '18 — 8
- ● Cannonau di Sardegna Berteru Ris. '15 — 8

Antichi Poderi Jerzu

via Umberto I, 1
08044 Jerzu [OG]
Tel. +39 078270028
www.jerzuantichipoderi.it

CELLAR SALES
PRE-BOOKED VISITS
ANNUAL PRODUCTION 1,500,000 bottles
HECTARES UNDER VINE 750.00

Antichi Poderi di Jerzu is a historic and indubitably important cooperative winery. It operates smack in the middle of Ogliastra, a district capable of delivering great wines, true testaments to the prowess of the eastern coast. Cannonau is the undisputed king, and the they can boast one of the great regional appellation's three subzones. Several years ago the winery invested heavily in quality, with a precise program aimed at maximizing the value of their grapes (implemented through zoning). The range also includes whites made with Vermentino. Two Cannonau Reserves led our tastings, both 2017s. The Chuèrra is a modern red. You can still discern a note of oak, but fruit and varietal sensations are well represented. Close-knit and full-bodied, it has a nice, clean finish. The Josto Miglior also delivered, despite being slightly contracted due to weighty tannins. Their younger wines all prove well made.

Wine	Rating
● Cannonau di Sardegna Chuèrra Ris. '17	🍷🍷 5
⊙ Cannonau di Sardegna Isara '19	🍷🍷 2*
● Cannonau di Sardegna Josto Miglior Ris. '17	🍷🍷 5
● Cannonau di Sardegna Bantu '19	🍷 2
● Cannonau di Sardegna Jerzu Marghìa '18	🍷 4
● Monica di Sardegna Camalda '19	🍷 2
○ Vermentino di Sardegna Lucean le Stelle '19	🍷 3
○ Vermentino di Sardegna Telavè '19	🍷 2
● Cannonau di Sardegna Josto Miglior Ris. '09	🍷🍷🍷 4*
● Cannonau di Sardegna Josto Miglior Ris. '05	🍷🍷🍷 4
● Radames '01	🍷🍷🍷 5
● Cannonau di Sardegna Chuèrra Ris. '16	🍷🍷 5

Tenuta La Sabbiosa

loc. Cussorgia
Case Sparse
09011 Calasetta [SU]
Tel. +39 3921493397
www.tenutalasabbiosa.com

RESTAURANT SERVICE
ANNUAL PRODUCTION 20,000 bottles
HECTARES UNDER VINE 7.00
VITICULTURE METHOD Certified Organic
SUSTAINABLE WINERY

This lovely, charming winery got its start a few years ago thanks to the efforts of Tessa Gelisio and Massimo Pusceddu. Situated on the island of Sant'Antioco, as the name suggests, they draw on valuable plots of old, bush-trained vines cultivated on sandy soil ('sabbiosa' means 'sandy' in Italian).. Only Carignano is grown, while its production is based on organic farming principles and a focus on environmental sustainability. Since the first vintage two wines have been made, both Carignano del Sulcis, though this year they've added a Superiore, made with their best grapes. The latter is the wine that surprised the most during our tastings. The 2 is a Superiore of great depth and complexity. At this stage it's still slightly marked by oak, but underneath its texture is incredible. On the nose notes of red fruit emerge along with myrtle, cistus and balsamic nuances. In the mouth it's creamy and pervasive, deep and clear. A great debut. We also appreciated the drinkable Bio for its pleasantness.

Wine	Rating
● Carignano del Sulcis Sup. 2 '17	🍷🍷 8
● Carignano del Sulcis Il Bio '18	🍷🍷 5
● Carignano del Sulcis Il Bio '17	🍷🍷 5
● Carignano del Sulcis Il Bio '16	🍷🍷 5
● Carignano del Sulcis Il Doc '17	🍷🍷 5
● Carignano del Sulcis Il Doc '16	🍷🍷 5

Andrea Ledda

via Musio, 13
07043 Bonnanaro [SS]
Tel. +39 079845060
www.vitivinicolaledda.com

CELLAR SALES
PRE-BOOKED VISITS
ANNUAL PRODUCTION 25,000 bottles
HECTARES UNDER VINE 24.00

Andrea Ledda's winery is divided into three estates. The winery got its start in Bonnanaro, Andrea's birthplace, then came the planting of the volcanic soils of Tenuta Pelao, where elevations surpass 700 meters. The property is completed by the Matteu Estate in Arzachena, one of Gallura's most beautiful vineyards. Elegance, finesse and drinkability are on display, complemented by the character of each territory. This is evident especially when it comes to Vermentino, which is cultivated on all three estates. They decided to age their wines for a while longer, so tasting of the entire range has been postponed until next year. Currently the vintages reviewed last year are on the market, so we've listed them below in white glasses. Once again we tasted the Soliànu '18 and a year later it's in excellent form. Floral and fruity scents are still vibrant, its flavor is invigorating and supple—no signs of pulling back. Truly a great confirmation of its quality.

Wine	Rating
○ Vermentino di Gallura Sup. Soliànu - Tenuta Matteu '18	𝕐𝕐𝕐 5
○ Vermentino di Sardegna Azzesu - Tenuta del Vulcano Pelao '17	𝕐𝕐𝕐 7
● Cannonau di Sardegna Cerasa - Tenuta Monte Santu '16	𝕐𝕐 6
● Cannonau di Sardegna Cerasa - Tenuta Monte Santu '15	𝕐𝕐 6
○ Vermentino di Gallura Soliànu - Tenuta Matteu '16	𝕐𝕐 5
○ Vermentino di Gallura Sup. Soliànu - Tenuta Matteu '17	𝕐𝕐 5
○ Vermentino di Sardegna Azzesu - Tenuta del Vulcano Pelao '18	𝕐𝕐 7
○ Vermentino di Sardegna Giaru - Tenuta Monte Santu '18	𝕐𝕐 3
○ Vermentino di Sardegna Giaru - Tenuta Monte Santu '17	𝕐𝕐 3

Masone Mannu

loc. Su Canale
s.s. 199 km 48
07020 Monti [SS]
Tel. +39 078947140
www.tenutamasonemannu.it

CELLAR SALES
PRE-BOOKED VISITS
ANNUAL PRODUCTION 70,000 bottles
HECTARES UNDER VINE 30.00
SUSTAINABLE WINERY

After several changes of ownership, the winery was acquired a few years ago by an entrepreneur from Romagna, already owner of the Tenuta Mara. Certainly we can say that it's in excellent hands and, given the value of the wines it has always produced, as well as its vineyards, it will continue to do well. The new owners are directing Masone Mannu towards sustainability through great efforts in the vineyard and a minimally-invasive production approach. Freshness, energy and exceptional territorial identity are their wines' defining traits. Two wines, a white and a red, made it into our finals. The first is the Vermentino di Gallura Superiore Costarenas '19, fragrant in its aromas of medlar and white flowers, invigorating and very fresh on the palate. Even more amazing is the Entu '16, a dense and complex red characterized by notes of blackberry, plum and cherry, and a palate nicely supported by acidity, all accompanied by a charming salinity. In the end the latter had the upper hand and took home Tre Bicchieri. Among the rest we appreciated the Zurria '18, a fresh and lively red.

Wine	Rating
● Entu '16	🍷🍷🍷 5
○ Vermentino di Gallura Sup. Costarenas '19	🍷🍷 4
⊙ Zeluiu Rosato '19	🍷🍷 3
● Zurria '18	🍷🍷 3
○ Vermentino di Gallura Petrizza '19	🍷 3
○ Vermentino di Gallura Sup. Costarenas '18	𝕐𝕐𝕐 4*
○ Vermentino di Gallura Sup. Costarenas '16	𝕐𝕐𝕐 3*
● Cannonau di Sardegna Zòjosu '15	𝕐𝕐 3*
● Entu '15	𝕐𝕐 5
○ Vermentino di Gallura Petrizza '18	𝕐𝕐 3
○ Vermentino di Gallura Petrizza '17	𝕐𝕐 3
○ Vermentino di Gallura Sup. Costarenas '17	𝕐𝕐 4

Cantina Mesa

loc. Su Baroni
09010 Sant'Anna Arresi [CA]
Tel. +39 0781965057
www.cantinamesa.com

CELLAR SALES
PRE-BOOKED VISITS
ANNUAL PRODUCTION 700,000 bottles
HECTARES UNDER VINE 78.00

Founded by Gavino Sanna, Mesa is currently owned by the Santa Margherita group. Their philosophy hasn't changed and the winery continues to offer an impressive range focused on the territory, the heart of Sulcis, and on drinkable, clean wines. When it comes to reds, Carignano comes in different versions according to the vineyard age, though there's also Cannonau and Syrah, which have found an ideal habitat here. Among the whites, Vermentino is central, and has proven capable of thrilling even several years after the harvest. And a Vermentino made for a lovely surprise this year.. The Opale '19 is a triumph of aromas amidst white flowers, citrus fruits, almond and herbs. The palate is sapid, invigorating, nor does the finish disappoint for its cleanness and depth. The Buio Buio '17, a complex and characteristic Carignano del Sulcis, fared even better in its sensations of scrubland and red fruit. Creamy and pervasive in the mouth, a proper backbone helps the palate unfold. The regular, standard-label vintage versions, Buio and Giunco, are pleasant, though simpler.

● Carignano del Sulcis Buio Buio Ris. '17	🍷🍷 5
○ Vermentino di Sardegna Opale '19	🍷🍷 5
● Brace Cagnulari '17	🍷🍷 4
● Brama Syrah '18	🍷🍷 4
○ Vermentino di Sardegna Giunco '19	🍷🍷 3
● Carignano del Sulcis Buio '19	🍷 3
● Buio Buio '10	🍷🍷🍷 4*
● Carignano del Sulcis Buio Buio Ris. '13	🍷🍷🍷 5
● Carignano del Sulcis Buio Buio Ris. '12	🍷🍷🍷 5
● Brace Cagnulari '15	🍷🍷 4
● Brama Syrah '15	🍷🍷 4
● Carignano del Sulcis Buio '15	🍷🍷 3
● Carignano del Sulcis Buio Buio Ris. '16	🍷🍷 5
● Carignano del Sulcis Buio Buio Ris. '15	🍷🍷 5
● Carignano del Sulcis Sup. Gavino '16	🍷🍷 5
○ Vermentino di Sardegna Giunco '18	🍷🍷 3
○ Vermentino di Sardegna Opale '17	🍷🍷 4

Cantina di Mogoro Il Nuraghe

s.s. 131 km 62
09095 Mogoro [OR]
Tel. +39 0783990285
www.cantinadimogoro.it

CELLAR SALES
PRE-BOOKED VISITS
ANNUAL PRODUCTION 850,000 bottles
HECTARES UNDER VINE 480.00

Nuraghe, a cooperative winery operating in the Campidano plain, avails itself of vineyards and growers in the municipality of Mogoro and all the surrounding areas, up to lower Oristano. Here the indigenous white grape variety Semidano has always been a cornerstone (it even has a small DOC, Mogoro, dedicated to it). The winery produces several versions, including the Puisteris, which is released several years after harvest. The other grape on which it focuses is Bovale, especially that from the nearby Terralba DOC zone. And it's a Bovale that most surprised our tasting panel: the Cavaliere Sardo is a Terralba Riserva '16 of great depth. Complexity is guaranteed by musky tones of myrtle, undergrowth and black pepper, while the palate exhibits character and backbone, nicely balancing tannins and body as it unfolds. While waiting for the new Puisteris, we mention another Semidano di Mogoro, the young, fresh and citrusy Anastasia '19, a truly pleasant wine. Finally the Tiernu, another Bovale, is a great daily drinker.

○ Semidano di Mogoro Anastasia '19	🍷🍷 2*
● Terralba Bovale Cavaliere Sardo '16	🍷🍷 2*
● Terralba Bovale Tiernu '18	🍷🍷 2*
○ Nuragus di Cagliari Mugarò '19	🍷 2
○ Vermentino di Sardegna Don Giovanni '19	🍷 2
● Cannonau di Sardegna Vignaruja '15	🍷🍷 2*
○ Semidano di Mogoro Anastasia '18	🍷🍷 2*
○ Semidano di Mogoro Sup. Puistèris '17	🍷🍷 4
○ Vermentino di Sardegna Don Giovanni '18	🍷🍷 2*

Mura

LOC. AZZANIDÒ, 1
07020 LOIRI PORTO SAN PAOLO [SS]
TEL. +39 3402602507
vini.mura@tiscali.it

CELLAR SALES
PRE-BOOKED VISITS
RESTAURANT SERVICE
ANNUAL PRODUCTION 50,000 bottles
HECTARES UNDER VINE 12.00

This small but delightful Gallura producer is well managed by two members of the Mura family. Marianna, enologist, oversees the vineyard and production, while Salvatore is dedicated to the commercial side. Their wines are a distillation of Gallura—you can feel the freshness of the mesoclimate, mitigated by sea breezes, as well as the minerality of its granitic soil. Vermentino is the undisputed king, but reds are also well represented. Their wines, in addition to balance and precision, exhibit great aging potential. As release of their reds has been postponed until next year (in the name of further aging), we dedicated ourselves to their whites, the Mura brothers' true specialty. Dedicated to the wine's 10-year anniversary, the charming Sienda Il Decennio is made with select Vermentino grapes and produced only during the best vintages. Two years after harvest its aromas are still intact and clean, its varietal qualities are still visible and the first tertiary notes are just beginning to emerge. The Sienda and Cheremi 2019 are also very good.

Wine	Rating
○ Sienda il Decennio '18	🍷🍷 6
○ Vermentino di Gallura Cheremi '19	🍷🍷 3
○ Vermentino di Gallura Sup. Sienda '19	🍷🍷 5
○ Vermentino di Gallura Sup. Sienda '13	🍷🍷🍷 3*
● Cannonau di Sardegna Cortes '16	🍷🍷 3
○ Vermentino di Gallura Cheremi '18	🍷🍷 3
○ Vermentino di Gallura Cheremi '16	🍷🍷 3
○ Vermentino di Gallura Cheremi '12	🍷🍷 3
○ Vermentino di Gallura Sienda '15	🍷🍷 4
○ Vermentino di Gallura Sup. Sienda '18	🍷🍷 3*
○ Vermentino di Gallura Sup. Sienda '16	🍷🍷 3
○ Vermentino di Gallura Sup. Sienda '14	🍷🍷 3*

Olianas

LOC. PORRUDDU
08030 GERGEI [CA]
TEL. +39 0558300411
www.olianas.it

CELLAR SALES
PRE-BOOKED VISITS
ANNUAL PRODUCTION 170,000 bottles
HECTARES UNDER VINE 24.00
VITICULTURE METHOD Certified Organic
SUSTAINABLE WINERY

Olianas was created by Stefano Casadei (enologist and winemaker in Tuscany) and his business partner, Erminio Olianas. For some time they've chosen to invest in Sardinia, in Gergei, an area once populated by vineyards and Mediterranean scrub. Thanks to the duo, the plots have been revived through a highly sustainable, internal protocol called 'Biointegrale'. No chemicals are used and animals help work the vineyards, starting with geese for weeding. In the cellar a minimally-invasive approach is adopted and there are interesting forays into the use of amphorae. Once again an excellent performance for Gergei's classic wines. Their premium selections are undoubtedly the best: the Riserva '17, a Cannonau di Sardegna, offers up notes of tobacco and undergrowth—the palate is close-woven but never contracted. The Perdixi, an Igt (mainly Bovale), is also vibrant and complex: notes of tanned leather and iron nuances alternate with black fruit and spices, while the palate proves supple. The young Cannonau di Sardegna '19 is delicious, as usual.

Wine	Rating
● Cannonau di Sardegna '19	🍷🍷 3
● Cannonau di Sardegna Ris. '17	🍷🍷 4
● Perdixi '18	🍷🍷 4
○ Vermentino di Sardegna '19	🍷 3
● Cannonau di Sardegna '16	🍷🍷 3
● Cannonau di Sardegna '15	🍷🍷 3
● Cannonau di Sardegna Ris. '16	🍷🍷 4
● Cannonau di Sardegna Ris. '15	🍷🍷 4
⊙ Olianas '18	🍷🍷 3
● Perdixi '16	🍷🍷 4

Cantina Oliena

via Nuoro, 112
08025 Oliena [NU]
Tel. +39 0784287509
www.cantinasocialeoliena.it

ANNUAL PRODUCTION 300,000 bottles
HECTARES UNDER VINE 180.00

Situated in Oliena, the small village in Nuoro after which it's named, this is one of Sardinia's smallest cooperative wineries. Production is based solely on Cannonau di Sardegna, a DOC that can be used here in the Nepente subzone of Oliena. In recent years the commitment of their entire staff (technical and commercial) has been impressive, and the results are evident. Their wines are a pure expression of the area, with drinkability and finesse on display, and some versions showing excellent results even over the long term. For us the most convincing of an excellent lot was the Irilai, a 2015 Nepente Classico. Varietal in its aromas of red fruit and dried rose, it manages to express strength and vigor on the palate without renouncing suppleness and dynamism. The younger Nepente di Oliena (this year proposed in the 2018 vintage) is always a sure bet, as is the Corrasi, a powerful and complex 2014 reserve. Finally, we recommend the Logheri, a highly expressive white made with native grapes that exhibits a calibrated sweetness.

Wine	Rating
● Cannonau di Sardegna Dionisi '17	TT 2*
● Cannonau di Sardegna Nepente di Oliena '18	TT 2*
● Cannonau di Sardegna Nepente di Oliena Corrasi Ris. '14	TT 4
● Cannonau di Sardegna Nepente di Oliena Irilai '15	TT 3
● Lanaitto '18	TT 2*
○ Logheri	TT 6
⊙ OroRosa Brut Rosé	T 5
● Cannonau di Sardegna Nepente di Oliena '16	YY 2*
● Cannonau di Sardegna Nepente di Oliena '15	YY 2*
● Cannonau di Sardegna Nepente di Oliena Corrasi Ris. '13	YY 4
● Cannonau di Sardegna Nepente di Oliena Irilai '14	YY 3

Pala

via Verdi, 7
09040 Serdiana [CA]
Tel. +39 070740284
www.pala.it

CELLAR SALES
PRE-BOOKED VISITS
ANNUAL PRODUCTION 490,000 bottles
HECTARES UNDER VINE 98.00

Pala is an impressive producer that has contributed to making the territory of Serdiana famous and prestigious. It's led by Mario Pala and his family, with the valuable help of Fabio Angius, Mario's commercial director and right-hand man. Their wines do a fine job transmitting the territory and share a charming, characteristic and subtle sapidity. In addition to Serdiana, the winery makes use of plots in Terralbese. Here they cultivate Bovale, still ungrafted, on sandy soils. Their entire range delivers, from the simpler wines of the Silenzi line on up. Once again we tasted an impeccable selection, as evidenced by several finalists, including the 'usual' Stellato. The 2019 version of this Vermentino di Sardegna impresses for its textbook olfactory complexity and a long, progressive palate in which sapidity contrasts well with the grape's classic aromas. The Nature '19, with its cloudiness and sediments, is charming. Among their excellent reds, we appreciated the Essentija '17.

Wine	Rating
○ Vermentino di Sardegna Stellato '19	TTT 4*
○ Stellato Nature '19	TT 6
● Cannonau di Sardegna I Fiori '19	TT 3
○ Entemari '17	TT 5
● Essentija '17	TT 3
● S'Arai '17	TT 5
○ Vermentino di Sardegna I Fiori '19	TT 3
⊙ Chiaro di Stelle '19	T 3
● Monica di Sardegna I Fiori '19	T 3
○ Nuragus di Cagliari I Fiori '19	T 2
● Cannonau di Sardegna Ris. '12	YYY 3*
● Cannonau di Sardegna Ris. '11	YYY 3*
○ Vermentino di Sardegna Stellato '18	YYY 4*
○ Vermentino di Sardegna Stellato '17	YYY 4*
○ Vermentino di Sardegna Stellato '16	YYY 4*

Cantina Pedres

VIA MINCIO, 42 Z.I. SETT.7
07026 OLBIA
TEL. +39 0789595075
www.cantinapedres.it

CELLAR SALES
PRE-BOOKED VISITS
ANNUAL PRODUCTION 500,000 bottles
HECTARES UNDER VINE 80.00
SUSTAINABLE WINERY

Pedres is managed with passion and determination by Antonella Mancini (heir to an important Sardinian wine family) and her husband, an enologist. Together they manage 80 hectares of vineyards, which give rise to about 500,000 bottles. Primarily Vermentino di Gallura is produced in different versions, the result of a pure, minimalist style that aims to bring out all the essence of Gallura's granitic soil and mesoclimate. In short, fresh and highly drinkable wines, but always deep and pleasant. In addition to whites, they produce interesting reds and various Metodo Italiano sparklers. The Vermentino di Gallura Thilibas stood out during our tastings. This white Superiore '19 is distinguished by its fine, elegant nose, which goes all in on floral and citrus notes. The palate is graceful and persistent, deep and rhythmic, with measured acidity that lends frankness and vigor. We also appreciated the two Cannonau reds: the Sulitài is delicious, even if very young, while the Cerasio proves more mature and complex.

Wine	Rating
○ Vermentino di Gallura Sup. Thilibas '19	🍷🍷 4
● Cannonau di Sardegna Cerasio '18	🍷🍷 4
● Cannonau di Sardegna Sulitài '19	🍷🍷 3
○ Vermentino di Gallura Pedres Brut '18	🍷🍷 3
○ Vermentino di Gallura Sangusta '19	🍷🍷 3
● Cannonau di Sardegna Desigio '19	🍷 3
○ Moscato di Sardegna Assolo '19	🍷 3
○ Vermentino di Gallura Brino '19	🍷 3
○ Vermentino di Sardegna Desigio '19	🍷 2
○ Vermentino di Gallura Sup. Thilibas '10	🍷🍷🍷 (white) 3*
○ Vermentino di Gallura Sup. Thilibas '09	🍷🍷🍷 (white) 3*
○ Vermentino di Gallura Brino '18	🍷🍷 (white) 3
○ Vermentino di Gallura Sangusta '18	🍷🍷 (white) 3
○ Vermentino di Gallura Sup. Thilibas '17	🍷🍷 (white) 4

Tenute Perdarubia

LOC. PRANU MANNU
S.DA PROV.LE 56, KM 7,1
08040 TALANA [NU]
TEL. +39 3296333122
www.tenuteperdarubia.com

CELLAR SALES
PRE-BOOKED VISITS
ANNUAL PRODUCTION 20,000 bottles
HECTARES UNDER VINE 20.00
VITICULTURE METHOD Certified Organic

Founded in the late 1940s at the behest of decorated citizen Mario Mereu Perdarubia, this winery has always focused on Cannonau, cultivated on its own root, ungrafted, in accordance with tradition. After a period of inactivity, the third generation of family have resumed production and sales, continuing to focus on their historic vineyards, which express Ogliastra's characteristic aromas and flavors. 20 hectares give rise to 3 wines marked by authenticity and tradition. Undoubtedly this was a year to remember. The wines presented (especially the reds) stood out during our tastings, and not just by a little. The Naniha is a Cannonau of great freshness, redolent of small berries and spices. A floral touch makes an appearance, anticipating a graceful, elegant palate, fresh and deep. Just what we want from a young Cannonau di Sardegna. Tre Bicchieri. The Perdarubia is also at the top of its game—another year of aging has made for a more full-bodied and pervasive wine.

Wine	Rating
● Cannonau di Sardegna Naniha '18	🍷🍷🍷 4*
● Cannonau di Sardegna Cl. Perdarubia '17	🍷🍷 5
○ Vermentino di Sardegna Lanùra '19	🍷 3
● Cannonau di Sardegna Nanhia '16	🍷🍷 (white) 4

F.lli Puddu

loc. Orbuddai
08025 Oliena [NU]
Tel. +39 0784288457
info@aziendapuddu.it

ANNUAL PRODUCTION 70,000 bottles
HECTARES UNDER VINE 30.00
VITICULTURE METHOD Certified Organic

The Puddu brothers' solid farm business produces high quality cured meats and quality wine. Organic farming focuses mainly on Cannonau, which in this area draws on the Nepente di Oliena sub-zone. Their wines are authentic and very traditional. They also age very well and strike up a lovely harmony between cleanness, stylistic precision and the peculiarities resulting from soil and microclimate. Their range sees Nepente offered in various versions (amidst select wines and reserves), white wines from Vermentino and bubbly produced with native grapes. Three wines were submitted, all Nepente di Oliena from different vintages. The Pro Vois is the producer's prized-pony, a reserve made with a careful selection of Cannonau grapes. The 2015 made for a wine of great complexity and depth, exemplary in its ticipity and frankness. Autumn tones dominate the nose, amidst dry leaves, spices, ripe fruit and undergrowth, while the palate flows impeccably, urged on by freshness and silky tannins. Tre Bicchieri.

- ● Cannonau di Sardegna Nepente di Oliena Pro Vois Ris. '15 — 🍷🍷🍷 5
- ● Cannonau di Sardegna Nepente di Oliena Carros '16 — 🍷🍷 3
- ● Cannonau di Sardegna Nepente di Oliena Tiscali '18 — 🍷🍷 3
- ● Cannonau di Sardegna Nepente di Oliena Pro Vois Ris. '14 — 🍷🍷🍷 5
- ● Cannonau di Sardegna Nepente di Oliena Tiscali '17 — 🍷🍷 3
- ● Cannonau di Sardegna Nepente di Oliena Tiscali '16 — 🍷🍷 3*
- ⊙ Cannonau di Sardegna Rosato Nepente di Oliena Biriai '18 — 🍷🍷 3

Quartomoro di Sardegna

via Dino Poli, 31
09092 Arborea [OR]
Tel. +39 3467643522
www.quartomoro.it

CELLAR SALES
PRE-BOOKED VISITS
ANNUAL PRODUCTION 50,000 bottles
HECTARES UNDER VINE 11.00

Quartomoro is overseen by Piero Cella and his wife. It's the result of Piero's experience as an enological consultant, and a connoisseur of the island's territories and grapes. His aim is to develop old vineyards and lesser-known varieties, as well as experiment with ancestral winemaking techniques on the best known cultivars. The result is fascinating, to say the least, with wines of extreme character, convincing and pure. There's a wide range, though volumes are limited, including reds, whites and some sparkling wines that undergo a second fermentation in the bottle. The BVL, from the Memorie di Vite line, is delicious. Made with Bovale, this red impressed by virtue of a textbook taste-olfactory complexity. Myrtle and plum aromas, cherry and black pepper herald a close-knit, compact and deep palate. Among the whites we appreciated the ARV, made with Arvesionadu: white fruit, lemon peel and wildflowers give way to a sapid palate slightly marked by sensations of grape peel. The rest of their selection also proves charming and well made.

- ● BVL Memorie di Vite '18 — 🍷🍷 4
- ○ ARV Memorie di Vite '19 — 🍷🍷 4
- ○ Q Brut M. Cl. — 🍷🍷 4
- ○ Orriu Vernaccia sulle Bucce '19 — 🍷 3
- ● BVL Memorie di Vite '17 — 🍷🍷 4
- ● BVL Memorie di Vite '16 — 🍷🍷 4
- ● Cannonau di Sardegna CNS Memorie di Vite '16 — 🍷🍷 4
- ● Cannonau di Sardegna Memorie di Vite CNS '15 — 🍷🍷 4
- ○ Orriu Vernaccia sulle Bucce '18 — 🍷🍷 3
- ○ SMD Memorie di Vite '18 — 🍷🍷 3
- ○ Vermentino di Sardegna VRM Memorie di Vite '16 — 🍷🍷 4
- ○ Vermentino di Sardegna VRM Memorie di Vite '14 — 🍷🍷 4

Santa Maria La Palma

FRAZ. SANTA MARIA LA PALMA
07041 ALGHERO [SS]
TEL. +39 079999008
www.santamarialapalma.it

CELLAR SALES
PRE-BOOKED VISITS
ANNUAL PRODUCTION 4,000,000 bottles
HECTARES UNDER VINE 650.00

Santa Maria La Palma is a large cooperative in northwest Sardinia. In recent years the producer has undergone a general overhaul that has benefited both the image of the wines and, above all, their quality. Cannonau, Cagnulari and Vermentino are the three main varieties. They are offered in various versions, from their simpler lines to select wines and reserves. There's also room for bubbly, which they've always believed in. Finally, it's worth mentioning certain historic selections, everyday wines sold at honest prices, but of undisputed quality. Despite the wide range of wines produced, only 4 wines were submitted for tasting this year. All of them were recently introduced on the market and are the result of rigorous grape selection. Without a doubt the most interesting is the Ràfia '18, a Vermentino di Sardegna with great sapidity and intense aromas. The Cannonau di Sardegna Redìt Riserva '17 is also intriguing, as is the Recònta, another 2017 (but made with Cagnulari grapes). Another interesting new product is the Akenta Cuvée 71 '19.

- ○ Vermentino di Sardegna Ràfia '18 — 🍷🍷 5
- ● Alghero Cagnulari Recònta Ris. '17 — 🍷🍷 4
- ● Cannonau di Sardegna Redit Ris. '17 — 🍷🍷 3
- ○ Vermentino di Sardegna Akènta Cuvée 71 '19 — 🍷🍷 3
- ● Cannonau di Sardegna R Ris. '15 — 🍷🍷🍷 3*
- ● Alghero Cagnulari '16 — 🍷🍷 3
- ● Alghero Cagnulari '14 — 🍷🍷 3
- ● Alghero Cagnulari Recònta Ris. '16 — 🍷🍷 4
- ● Alghero Rosso Cabirol '14 — 🍷🍷 2*
- ● Cannonau di Sardegna '17 — 🍷🍷 3
- ● Cannonau di Sardegna Redit Ris. '16 — 🍷🍷 3*
- ● Cannonau di Sardegna Valmell '17 — 🍷🍷 2*
- ● Cannonau di Sardegna Valmell '16 — 🍷🍷 2*
- ○ Vermentino di Sardegna Ràfia '17 — 🍷🍷 5

★★Cantina Santadi

VIA GIACOMO TACHIS, 14
09010 SANTADI [SU]
TEL. +39 0781950127
www.cantinadisantadi.it

CELLAR SALES
PRE-BOOKED VISITS
ANNUAL PRODUCTION 1,740,000 bottles
HECTARES UNDER VINE 603.00

The territory of Sulcis began developing many years ago thanks to Santadi. By virtue of its quality, made possible through a strong relationship with its growers, the cooperative has served as an example for the other 'social wineries' that now constitute a major asset for the island. Here everything centers on Carignano, bush-trained in sandy soil (at times ungrafted). Thus theirs is a range dedicated almost exclusively to reds, with the local grape offered in various versions. The Terre Brune remains a real class act in its category and this year it once again earned Tre Bicchieri. The 2016 vintage was also favorable in Sulcis, making for a wine marked by great balance, playing on aromatic complexity and harmony of taste. Its younger brother, the Rocca Rubia, always does its thing well, and once again proves superb, especially considering its price. An excellent performance from the Cannonau di Sardegna Noras.

- ● Carignano del Sulcis Sup. Terre Brune '16 — 🍷🍷🍷 7
- ● Cannonau di Sardegna Noras Cl. '17 — 🍷🍷 4
- ● Carignano del Sulcis Grotta Rossa '18 — 🍷🍷 2*
- ● Carignano del Sulcis Rocca Rubia Ris. '17 — 🍷🍷 4
- ● Festa Noria — 🍷🍷 6
- ○ Nuragus di Cagliari Pedraia '19 — 🍷🍷 2*
- ○ Solais Brut M. Cl. — 🍷🍷 5
- ○ Vermentino di Sardegna Cala Silente '19 — 🍷🍷 3
- ○ Villa di Chiesa '18 — 🍷 5
- ● Carignano del Sulcis Sup. Terre Brune '15 — 🍷🍷🍷 7
- ○ Vermentino di Sardegna Cala Silente '18 — 🍷🍷 3

Sardus Pater

via Rinascita, 46
09017 Sant'Antioco [SU]
Tel. +39 0781800274
www.cantinesarduspater.com

CELLAR SALES
PRE-BOOKED VISITS
ANNUAL PRODUCTION 400,000 bottles
HECTARES UNDER VINE 250.00

Sardus Pater is a cooperative in Sant'Antioco, an island in the southwest of the region connected to Sardinia through an artificial isthmus. Smack in the middle of the Carignano del Sulcis DOC zone, here the sandy terrain hosts plenty of old vineyards (some of which are ungrafted). In addition to Carignano (produced in different versions, from regular, standard-labels vinified entirely in steel to reserves and dessert wines) their range also includes Vermentino (there's a good sparkler) as well as sweets from Moscato and Nasco. This year's new release concerns the company's 70th anniversary and, not for nothing, it's called 'Sardus Pater Settantenario'. The result of a careful selection of Carignano grapes harvested in 2016, it's rich, ripe, elegant, with notes of pencil lead and dark fruit. The palate is supple, crossed by a subtle sapid vein. We very much appreciated the other three Carignanos proposed as well: a fresher and more immediately expressive version (the Nur '18), the reserve (Is Arenas '18) and the superiore (Arruga '17).

Wine	Rating
● Sardus Pater Settantenario '16	🍷🍷 5
● Carignano del Sulcis Is Arenas Ris. '18	🍷🍷 5
● Carignano del Sulcis Nur '18	🍷🍷 3
● Carignano del Sulcis Sup. Arruga '17	🍷🍷 6
● Carignano del Sulcis Is Solus '19	🍷 3
○ Elat '19	🍷 3
○ Vermentino di Sardegna Brut AD 49 M. Cl. '16	🍷 5
○ Vermentino di Sardegna Lugore '19	🍷 4
○ Vermentino di Sardegna Terre Fenicie '19	🍷 3
● Carignano del Sulcis Is Arenas Ris. '09	🍷🍷🍷 4*
● Carignano del Sulcis Is Arenas Ris. '08	🍷🍷🍷 4*
● Carignano del Sulcis Is Arenas Ris. '07	🍷🍷🍷 3*
● Carignano del Sulcis Is Arenas Ris. '06	🍷🍷🍷 3*
● Carignano del Sulcis Sup. Arruga '09	🍷🍷🍷 6
● Carignano del Sulcis Sup. Arruga '07	🍷🍷🍷 5

Giuseppe Sedilesu

via Vittorio Emanuele II, 64
08024 Mamoiada [NU]
Tel. +39 078456791
www.giuseppesedilesu.com

CELLAR SALES
PRE-BOOKED VISITS
ANNUAL PRODUCTION 100,000 bottles
HECTARES UNDER VINE 20.00

This great wine family have brought so much (and continues to bring) lustre to Mamoiada. Founded by Giuseppe Sedilesu (to whom a wine is dedicated), it's now on the third generation. Everything revolves around sustainability, which takes into account environmental and social protections through viticulture. Their wines are a mirror of the territory: the result of old, bush-trained vines that benefit from elevations of over 700 meters. In the cellar their simple approach aims to let through—or better yet, to highlight—what nature has to offer. The Mamuthone is one of the winery's symbols, and for us the 2017 is one of the best versions ever. It's redolent of scrub, medicinal herbs, black fruit and spices. The palate is velvety, but fresh, pervasive, yet sapid, advancing in a crescendo of chiaroscuro, charming and endless. It's a true champion that represents the best of Mamoiada. Tre Bicchieri. But it's not the only one to amaze: the Ballu Tundu '15 proves a textbook reserve.

Wine	Rating
● Cannonau di Sardegna Mamuthone '17	🍷🍷🍷 4*
● Cannonau di Sardegna Ballu Tundu Ris. '15	🍷🍷 5
● Cannonau di Sardegna Carnevale Ris. '17	🍷🍷 5
● Cannonau di Sardegna Sartiu '19	🍷🍷 3
○ Granazza '19	🍷🍷 3
⊙ Cannonau di Sardegna Erèssia '19	🍷 3
● Cannonau di Sardegna Mamuthone '15	🍷🍷🍷 3*
● Cannonau di Sardegna Mamuthone '12	🍷🍷🍷 3*
● Cannonau di Sardegna Mamuthone '11	🍷🍷🍷 3*
● Cannonau di Sardegna Mamuthone '08	🍷🍷🍷 3*
○ Perda Pintà '09	🍷🍷🍷 4
○ Perda Pintà '07	🍷🍷🍷 5
● Cannonau di Sardegna Ballu Tundu Ris. '14	🍷🍷 6

★★Tenute Sella & Mosca

Loc. I Piani
07041 Alghero [SS]
Tel. +39 079997700
www.sellaemosca.com

CELLAR SALES
PRE-BOOKED VISITS
ANNUAL PRODUCTION 5,000,000 bottles
HECTARES UNDER VINE 560.00

A few years after the arrival of Terra Moretti, we're seeing the results of a true revolution at this historic Alghero winery. The contiguous, 500-hectare vineyard is being converted to organic, the range has expanded (and features some new, interesting labels, which the Alghero-based designer Antonio Marras had a hand in) and quality has been strengthened. Two grapes dominate: Torbato, which is available in several versions, and Cabernet Sauvignon, which gives rise to the producer's great red, the Marquis di Villamarina. Without a doubt, the extra year of aging paid off for the Catore '18. This selection of Torbato grapes landed a place in our finals and surprised our tasting panel: aromatically it ranges from notes of wild flowers to nuances of aromatic herbs, while the palate comes through close-knit and sapid. A very well-deserved Tre Bicchieri. Their other prized wine is just as good. The Marquis of Villamarina once again demonstrates that it's a great island Cabernet Sauvignon.The rest of their selection is all very well made.

Wine	Glasses	Price
○ Alghero Torbato Catore '18	TTT	5
● Alghero Marchese di Villamarina '16	TT	6
○ Alghero Torbato Brut	TT	3
● Cannonau di Sardegna Mustazzo '17	TT	5
● Carignano del Sulcis Terre Rare Ris. '16	TT	3
○ Vermentino di Gallura Sup. Monteoro '19	TT	3
○ Vermentino di Sardegna Ambat '18	TT	5
○ Vermentino di Sardegna Cala Reale '19	T	3
○ Alghero Torbato Catore '17	YYY	5
○ Alghero Torbato Terre Bianche Cuvée 161 '18	YYY	3*
○ Alghero Torbato Terre Bianche Cuvée 161 '16	YYY	3*
○ Alghero Torbato Terre Bianche Cuvée 161 '15	YYY	4*

Siddùra

Loc. Siddùra
07020 Luogosanto [SS]
Tel. +39 0796513027
www.siddura.com

CELLAR SALES
PRE-BOOKED VISITS
ACCOMMODATION AND RESTAURANT SERVICE
ANNUAL PRODUCTION 200,000 bottles
HECTARES UNDER VINE 37.00
SUSTAINABLE WINERY

Founded by Massimo Ruggero and Nathan Gottesdiener (administrator and president, respectively), from the beginning Siddùra has set itself the goal of producing great wines that mirror this beautiful section of Gallura. Indeed, the estate has taken its name from the area itself, not far from the village of Luogasanto. The cellar is situated in the heart of their main vineyards, and represents a hub of technology. Everything revolves around the vineyard and is aimed at highlighting the attributes of the area's grapes, starting with Vermentino. And a Vermentino proves to be the best wine of the lot. Released a year after harvest, the Maìa exhibits vitality and depth. The nose fully expresses Gallura, with hints of iodine, herbaceous traces and white fruit, while the palate comes through fresh and sapid. Just a pinch of complexity prevents it from going all the way. The reds are also delicious, from the fresh and creamy Cannonau Fòla to the Bàcco and Tiros.

Wine	Glasses	Price
○ Vermentino di Gallura Sup. Maìa '18	TT	4
● Bàcco Cagnulari '17	TT	5
● Cannonau di Sardegna Fòla Ris. '17	TT	5
● Tiros '16	TT	6
⊙ Cannonau di Sardegna Rosato Nudo '19	T	4
○ Vermentino di Gallura Sup. Maìa '15	YYY	4*
○ Vermentino di Gallura Sup. Maìa '14	YYY	4*
● Cannonau di Sardegna Fòla '15	YY	5
⊙ Cannonau di Sardegna Rosato Nudo '17	YY	2*
○ Vermentino di Gallura Spèra '18	YY	3
○ Vermentino di Gallura Spèra '17	YY	3
○ Vermentino di Gallura Sup. Maìa '17	YY	4
○ Vermentino di Gallura Sup. Maìa '16	YY	4

Su Entu

S.DA PROV.LE KM 1,800
09025 SANLURI
TEL. +39 070 93571206
www.cantinesuentu.com

CELLAR SALES
PRE-BOOKED VISITS
ANNUAL PRODUCTION 240,000 bottles
HECTARES UNDER VINE 32.00

Founded at the behest of Salvatore Pilloni, a classic entrepreneur, Su Entu has contributed to giving new life to the viticulture of Marmilla, a southern sub-region. The cellar, situated on a hill overlooking the vineyards, is a charming, modern facility. The exterior takes environmental sustainability into account, while the interior provides ample space for reception and events. Over the years, their wines have achieved excellent quality, with local varieties serving as cornerstones (Cannonau, Vermentino, Bovale and Moscato). There are also forays using international grapes. Several outstanding wines were presented, all of them modern in style. The first-rate Su' Nico '18 is a monovarietal Bovale with spicy, chocolaty aromas and a close-knit, soft palate. Even if slightly marked by oak, fruit is well represented, a sign of its good youth. From the same vintage, the Su' Anima proves to be a fresh and graceful Cannonau di Sardegna. The Su' Diterra, their other noteworthy red, is a blend that goes all in on Mediterranean fragrances.

Wine	Rating
● Su' Nico '18	▼▼▼ 5
● Cannonau di Sardegna Su'Anima '18	▼▼ 3
○ Su'Aro '19	▼▼ 3
● Su'Diterra '18	▼▼ 3
○ Su'Luci Passito '18	▼ 5
● Su'Oltre '17	▼ 5
○ Vermentino di Sardegna Su'Imari '19	▼ 3
● Bovale '16	▽▽▽ 5
● Cannonau di Sardegna '16	▽▽ 3
● Su'Oltre '16	▽▽ 3*
○ Vermentino di Sardegna '16	▽▽ 3
○ Vermentino di Sardegna Su'Orma '17	▽▽ 3*

Surrau

S.DA PROV.LE ARZACHENA - PORTO CERVO
07021 ARZACHENA [SS]
TEL. +39 078982933
www.vignesurrau.it

CELLAR SALES
PRE-BOOKED VISITS
ANNUAL PRODUCTION 300,000 bottles
HECTARES UNDER VINE 50.00
SUSTAINABLE WINERY

Surrau is indubitably one of the producers that has most convinced of late. Credit goes to Tino Demuro and his staff, true children of Gallura, who've managed to bottle impressive wines while also developing a concrete commercial strategy that's slowly gaining the producer recognition worldwide. Hospitality is also priority, thanks to a lovely cellar, open year round, which hosts exhibitions, conferences and meetings of all kinds. Their range comprises whites made with Vermentino, some very interesting reds, and some admirable Metodo Classico sparklers. The Cannonau di Sardegna Sincaru '18 is a red of great finesse and elegance adorned by sensations of scrubland and some smoky hints. The palate is lean and juicy, deep and clean. The Vermentino di Gallura Superiore Sciala '19 features vibrant notes of orange blossom and lime, curry plant and rosemary. In the mouth freshness is well represented, combined with good flavor, driving the palate towards a very long finish. Tre Bicchieri. The Branu '19 is also worthy of note.

Wine	Rating
○ Vermentino di Gallura Sup. Sciala '19	▼▼▼ 5
● Cannonau di Sardegna Sincaru '18	▼▼ 5
● Cannonau di Sardegna Sincaru Ris. '17	▼▼ 5
● Surrau '18	▼▼ 4
○ Vermentino di Gallura Branu '19	▼▼ 3
● Cannonau di Sardegna Sincaru Ris. '14	▽▽▽ 5
● Surrau '09	▽▽▽ 4*
○ Vermentino di Gallura Sup. Sciala '18	▽▽▽ 5
○ Vermentino di Gallura Sup. Sciala '17	▽▽▽ 5
○ Vermentino di Gallura Sup. Sciala '15	▽▽▽ 5
○ Vermentino di Gallura Sup. Sciala '14	▽▽▽ 5
○ Vermentino di Gallura Sup. Sciala '13	▽▽▽ 5
○ Vermentino di Gallura Sup. Sciala '12	▽▽▽ 5
● Cannonau di Sardegna Sincaru Ris. '16	▽▽ 5
● Cannonau di Sardegna Sincaru Ris. '15	▽▽ 5
○ Vermentino di Gallura Branu '18	▽▽ 3

Tenuta l'Ariosa

LOC. PREDDA NIEDDA SUD
S.DA 15
07100 SASSARI
TEL. +39 079261905
www.lariosa.it

ANNUAL PRODUCTION 40,000 bottles
HECTARES UNDER VINE 9.00

The Rau family are behind Tenuta l'Ariosa, an agricultural business founded in the mid-1920s. The producer is specialized in quality liqueurs and spirits, but in the last few years they've been focusing on wine through a major initiative, one that's grown in quality year after year. The wines are made with native grape varieties, with a keen focus on Sardinia's northwest regions. Excellent drinkability and aromatic finesse are hallmarks of the entire range, which is made up of both whites and reds, as well as a sweet wine made with Moscato. The high level of the range presented makes Ariosa one of the most important wineries reviewed in the guide. At the top of the list is the elegant and dynamic Assolo '19, a fresh and juicy Cannonau. This is how a young red must be, and it's no coincidence that it made it into our finals. Another wine that impressed is the Pèdrastella, made with native grapes. It's close-knit, but fresh and sapid, exhibiting character and authenticity. Among the whites we appreciated the Galatea '19, a Vermentino with clear iodine hints.

● Cannonau di Sardegna Assolo '19	🍷🍷 3*
● Cannonau di Sardegna Llunes Ris. '17	🍷🍷 3
● Pedrastella '18	🍷🍷 4
● Sass'Antico Cagnulari '17	🍷🍷 4
○ Vermentino di Sardegna Arenu '19	🍷🍷 3
○ Vermentino di Sardegna Galatea '19	🍷🍷 3
● Cannonau di Sardegna Assolo '18	🍷🍷 3
● Cannonau di Sardegna Assolo '15	🍷🍷 3
○ Vermentino di Sardegna Arenu '17	🍷🍷 3
○ Vermentino di Sardegna Galatea '18	🍷🍷 3

Cantina Sociale della Vernaccia

LOC. RIMEDIO
VIA ORISTANO, 6A
09170 ORISTANO
TEL. +39 078333383
www.vinovernaccia.com

CELLAR SALES
PRE-BOOKED VISITS
ANNUAL PRODUCTION 260,000 bottles
HECTARES UNDER VINE 120.00

This small cooperative owes everything to the area's flagship wine, Vernaccia di Oristano. In recent years quality has grown across their entire range, from whites made with Vermentino to Cannonau, Nieddera and Monica reds. But of course Vernaccia continues to play a prominent role. It's produced in a traditional version (oxidative, aged in barrels and released several years after harvesting), as well as a fresh, standard-label version. For some years now they've also produced a special, bottle-fermented sparkling wine. There's no new Riserva di Vernaccia to review, but we still encountered several excellent wines during our tastings. Above all the Corash, a tasty 2016 Cannonau di Sardegna reserve, stood out. Myrtle, plum and sweet spices anticipate an austere and bold palate in which freshness lends balance, and makes the difference. We also appreciated two whites, both 2019s, one a Vermentino (Is Arutas), the other a Vernaccia (Terresinis). The Montiprama also put in a notable performance.

● Cannonau di Sardegna Corash Ris. '16	🍷🍷 3
● Montiprama Nieddera '17	🍷🍷 3
⊙ Seu '19	🍷🍷 2*
○ Terresinis Vernaccia '19	🍷🍷 2*
○ Vermentino di Sardegna Is Arutas '19	🍷🍷 2*
○ Aristanis M. Cl. Brut	🍷 3
● Cannonau di Sardegna Maiomone '18	🍷 2
● Monica di Sardegna Don Efisio '18	🍷 2
⊙ Seu Rosé Brut	🍷 2
○ Vermentino di Sardegna Spumante Is Arutas Brut	🍷 2
● Cannonau di Sardegna Corash Ris. '15	🍷🍷 3
● Cannonau di Sardegna Maimone '17	🍷🍷 2*
● Cannonau di Sardegna Maiomone '15	🍷🍷 2*
⊙ Seu '18	🍷🍷 2*

1Sorso - Leonardo Bagella

loc. Trunconi
07037 Sorso [SS]
Tel. +39 3471274211
www.1sorso.it

CELLAR SALES
PRE-BOOKED VISITS
ANNUAL PRODUCTION 20,000 bottles
HECTARES UNDER VINE 12.00
SUSTAINABLE WINERY

- ● Mario Millenovecento28 Cagnulari '18 🍷🍷 6
- ○ Millenovecento64 Moscato '19 🍷🍷 4
- ○ Vermentino di Sardegna Olieddu '19 🍷🍷 5
- ● Cannonau di Sardegna '19 🍷 4

Cantina Berritta

loc. Vallata di Oddoene
via Kennedy, 108
08022 Dorgali [NU]
Tel. +39 078495372
www.cantinaberritta.it

CELLAR SALES
PRE-BOOKED VISITS
ANNUAL PRODUCTION 30,000 bottles
HECTARES UNDER VINE 11.00
VITICULTURE METHOD Certified Organic
SUSTAINABLE WINERY

- ● Cannonau di Sardegna Cl. Monte Tundu '17 🍷🍷 4
- ● Cannonau di Sardegna Baillanu '16 🍷🍷 5
- ● Cannonau di Sardegna Thurcalesu '18 🍷🍷 4

Cantina Canneddu

via Manno, 69
08024 Mamoiada [NU]
Tel. +39 3496852916
www.cantinacanneddu.it

CELLAR SALES
PRE-BOOKED VISITS
ACCOMMODATION
ANNUAL PRODUCTION 8,000 bottles
HECTARES UNDER VINE 2.50
VITICULTURE METHOD Certified Organic

- ● Cannonau di Sardegna Zibbo '18 🍷🍷 5
- ○ Delissia '19 🍷 5

Cantine Carboni

via Umberto, 163
08036 Ortueri [NU]
Tel. +39 078466213
www.vinicarboni.it

PRE-BOOKED VISITS
ANNUAL PRODUCTION 25,000 bottles
HECTARES UNDER VINE 13.00
SUSTAINABLE WINERY

- ● Mandrolisai Sup. Balente '16 🍷🍷 6
- ● Balente '18 🍷 4
- ○ Helios '19 🍷 4

Cantina Castiadas

loc. Olia Speciosa
09040 Castiadas [CA]
Tel. +39 0709949004
www.cantinacastiadas.com

CELLAR SALES
PRE-BOOKED VISITS
ANNUAL PRODUCTION 120,000 bottles
HECTARES UNDER VINE 150.00

- ● Cannonau di Sardegna Capo Ferrato Rei '17 🍷🍷 3
- ● Parolto '16 🍷🍷 4
- ○ Vermentino di Sardegna Notteri '19 🍷 3

Ferruccio Deiana

loc. Su Leunaxi
via Gialeto, 7
09040 Settimo San Pietro [CA]
Tel. +39 070749117
www.ferrucciodeiana.it

CELLAR SALES
PRE-BOOKED VISITS
ANNUAL PRODUCTION 430,000 bottles
HECTARES UNDER VINE 120.00

- ● Cannonau di Sardegna Sileno Ris. '16 🍷🍷 4
- ● Monica di Sardegna Karel '18 🍷🍷 2*
- ● Ajana '16 🍷 6
- ○ Vermentino di Sardegna Arvali '19 🍷 3

Eminas

via Vittorio Emanuele II, 71
08024 Mamoiada [NU]
Tel. +39 3476800377
www.eminas.it

PRE-BOOKED VISITS
ANNUAL PRODUCTION 6,000 bottles
HECTARES UNDER VINE 9.00

- ● Cannonau di Sardegna '17 🍷🍷 4
- ⊙ Cannonau di Sardegna Rosato Izza '19 🍷 4

Francesco Fiori

via Ossi, 10
07049 Usini [SS]
Tel. +39 3381949246
www.vinifiori.it

CELLAR SALES
HECTARES UNDER VINE 6.00

- ○ Vermentino di Sardegna Serra Aspridda '19 🍷🍷 3
- ● Cagnulari Serra Juales '18 🍷🍷 3

Tenute Fois Accademia Olearia

loc. Ungias Galantè Lotto E1, zona D2
07041 Alghero [SS]
Tel. +39 079980394
www.accademiaolearia.com

CELLAR SALES
ANNUAL PRODUCTION 10,000 bottles
HECTARES UNDER VINE 11.00

- ○ Vermentino di Sardegna Chlamys '19 🍷🍷 3

I Garagisti di Sorgono

via Logudoro, 1
08038 Sorgono [NU]
Tel. +39 3470868122
www.garagistidisorgono.com

PRE-BOOKED VISITS
ANNUAL PRODUCTION 24,000 bottles
HECTARES UNDER VINE 9.00

- ● Manca '17 🍷🍷 6
- ● Parisi '17 🍷🍷 5
- ● Uras '17 🍷🍷 6
- ● Murru '17 🍷 5

Cantina Giogantinu

via Milano, 30
07022 Berchidda [SS]
Tel. +39 079704163
www.giogantinu.it

CELLAR SALES
PRE-BOOKED VISITS
ANNUAL PRODUCTION 1,500,000 bottles
HECTARES UNDER VINE 320.00

- ● Nastarrè '19 🍷🍷 2*
- ○ Vermentino di Gallura Giogantinu '19 🍷 2
- ○ Vermentino di Gallura Lunghente '18 🍷 3

Jankara

via Arzacehna, 19
07030 Sant'Antonio di Gallura [SS]
Tel. +39 3287577060
www.vinijankara.com

CELLAR SALES
PRE-BOOKED VISITS
ANNUAL PRODUCTION 31,000 bottles
HECTARES UNDER VINE 9.00

- ● 755mt '18 🍷🍷 7
- ● Cannonau di Sardegna '18 🍷🍷 5
- ● Colli del Limbara Lu Nieddu '18 🍷 5
- ○ Vermentino di Gallura Sup. '19 🍷 4

Antonella Ledà d'Ittiri

fraz. Fertilia
loc. Arenosu, 23
07041 Alghero [SS]
Tel. +39 079999263
www.ledadittiri.it

CELLAR SALES
PRE-BOOKED VISITS
ACCOMMODATION
ANNUAL PRODUCTION 18,000 bottles
HECTARES UNDER VINE 5.50
SUSTAINABLE WINERY

- ● Alghero Cagnulari Cigala '19 🍷🍷 3
- ● Ginjol '19 🍷🍷 3
- ● Margallò '19 🍷🍷 3

Li Duni

loc. Li Parisi
07030 Badesi [SS]
Tel. +39 0799144480
www.cantinaliduni.it

CELLAR SALES
PRE-BOOKED VISITS
ANNUAL PRODUCTION 40,000 bottles
HECTARES UNDER VINE 20.00
SUSTAINABLE WINERY

- ○ Vermentino di Gallura Sup. Amabile Nozzinnà '18 🍷🍷 5
- ○ Vermentino di Gallura Sup. Renabianca '19 🍷🍷 3

Cantina del Mandrolisai

c.so IV Novembre, 20
08038 Sorgono [NU]
Tel. +39 078460113
www.cantinadelmandrolisai.com

CELLAR SALES
PRE-BOOKED VISITS
ANNUAL PRODUCTION 200,000 bottles
HECTARES UNDER VINE 80.00

- ● Mandrolisai Sup. Kent'Annos '15 🍷🍷 4

Meana Terre del Mandrolisai

via Roma, 129
08030 Meana Sardo [NU]
Tel. +39 3498797817
www.cantinameana.it

ANNUAL PRODUCTION 35,000 bottles
HECTARES UNDER VINE 12.00

- ⊙ Mandrolisai Rosato Parèda '19 🍷🍷

Abele Melis

via Santa Suina, 3
09098 Terralba [OR]
Tel. +39 0783851090
melis.vini@tiscali.it

CELLAR SALES
PRE-BOOKED VISITS
ANNUAL PRODUCTION 100,000 bottles
HECTARES UNDER VINE 35.00

- ● Bovale '18 🍷🍷 2*
- ● Terralba Bovale Dominariu '17 🍷🍷 3
- ○ Vermentino di Sardegna Iocalia '19 🍷 2

Mora&Memo

via Giuseppe Verdi, 9
09040 Serdiana [CA]
Tel. +39 3311972266
www.moraememo.it

CELLAR SALES
PRE-BOOKED VISITS
ANNUAL PRODUCTION 35,000 bottles
HECTARES UNDER VINE 37.00
VITICULTURE METHOD Certified Organic

- ● Cannonau di Sardegna Nau '19 🍷🍷 4
- ○ Vermentino di Sardegna Tino '19 🍷🍷 4
- ○ Vermentino di Sardegna Tino Sur Lie '19 🍷 3

Nuraghe Crabioni

LOC. LU CRABIONI
07037 SORSO [SS]
TEL. +39 3468292457
www.nuraghecrabioni.com

CELLAR SALES
PRE-BOOKED VISITS
ANNUAL PRODUCTION 60,000 bottles
HECTARES UNDER VINE 35.00
SUSTAINABLE WINERY

- ● Cannonau di Sardegna Crabioni '18 🍷🍷 3*
- ○ Sussinku Bianco '18 🍷🍷 3
- ● Sussinku Cagnulari '18 🍷🍷 5
- ○ Vermentino di Sardegna '19 🍷🍷 3

Orgosa

LOC. LUCURIÒ
08027 ORGOSOLO [NU]
TEL. +39 3397784958
mgorgosolo@tiscali.it

CELLAR SALES
PRE-BOOKED VISITS
ANNUAL PRODUCTION 9,000 bottles
HECTARES UNDER VINE 3.00

- ● Cannonau di Sardegna '19 🍷🍷 4

Poderi Parpinello

LOC. JANNA DE MARE
S.S. 291
07100 SASSARI
TEL. +39 3465915194
www.poderiparpinello.it

ANNUAL PRODUCTION 250,000 bottles
HECTARES UNDER VINE 32.00

- ○ Alghero Torbato Cento Gemme '19 🍷🍷 3
- ● Cagnulari '18 🍷🍷 4
- ● Cannonau di Sardegna San Costantino '18 🍷🍷 3

Pedra Majore

VIA ROMA, 106
07020 MONTI [SS]
TEL. +39 078943185
www.pedramajore.it

CELLAR SALES
PRE-BOOKED VISITS
ANNUAL PRODUCTION 155,000 bottles
HECTARES UNDER VINE 50.00

- ○ Vermentino di Gallura Le Conche '19 🍷🍷 2*
- ○ Vermentino di Gallura Sup. Hysony '19 🍷🍷 4
- ○ Vermentino di Gallura I Graniti '19 🍷 3

Giuliana Puligheddu

P.ZZA COLLEGIO, 5
08025 OLIENA [NU]
TEL. +39 0784287734
www.agricolapuligheddu.it

CELLAR SALES
PRE-BOOKED VISITS
ANNUAL PRODUCTION 5,000 bottles
HECTARES UNDER VINE 3.00
VITICULTURE METHOD Certified Organic

- ● Cannonau di Sardegna Cl. Cupanera '17 🍷🍷 5

Viticoltori Romangia

VIA MARINA, 5
07037 SORSO [SS]
TEL. +39 079351666
www.cantinaromangia.it

CELLAR SALES
PRE-BOOKED VISITS
ANNUAL PRODUCTION 65,000 bottles
HECTARES UNDER VINE 60.00

- ● Oro Dry '19 🍷🍷 4
- ● Pietra '18 🍷🍷 3
- ○ Vermentino di Sardegna Sabbia '19 🍷🍷 3

Sa Raja

via Sa Raja
07020 Telti [SS]
Tel. +39 3458080429
www.saraja.it

PRE-BOOKED VISITS
ANNUAL PRODUCTION 86,000 bottles
HECTARES UNDER VINE 49.00

● Cannonau di Sardegna '19	🍷🍷 3
○ Vermentino di Sardegna '19	🍷🍷 3
● Carignano del Sulcis '19	🍷 4

Consorzio San Michele

loc. San Michele
07022 Berchidda [SS]
Tel. +39 078957817
www.consorziosanmichele.com

CELLAR SALES
PRE-BOOKED VISITS
ANNUAL PRODUCTION 50,000 bottles
HECTARES UNDER VINE 10.00

○ Vermentino di Gallura Invidia Gallurese '18	🍷🍷 3
○ Vermentino di Gallura Sinfonia Gallurese '18	🍷🍷 3

Tenute Smeralda

via Kennedy, 21
09040 Donori [CA]
Tel. +39 3387446524
www.tenutesmeralda.it

ANNUAL PRODUCTION 45,000 bottles
HECTARES UNDER VINE 7.00

● Sapienti '17	🍷🍷 4
● Rubinus '18	🍷 5
○ Vermentino di Sardegna Smeralda '19	🍷 3

Agricola Soi

via Cucchesi, 1
08030 Nuragus [CA]
Tel. +39 3488140084
www.agricolasoi.it

CELLAR SALES
PRE-BOOKED VISITS
ANNUAL PRODUCTION 16,000 bottles
HECTARES UNDER VINE 4.00

● Cannonau di Sardegna '16	🍷🍷 4
● Lun '17	🍷🍷 3
○ Nuragus di Cagliari Nurà '19	🍷 4

Tenute Soletta

loc. Signor'Anna
07040 Codrongianos [SS]
Tel. +39 079435067
www.tenutesoletta.it

CELLAR SALES
PRE-BOOKED VISITS
ACCOMMODATION AND RESTAURANT SERVICE
ANNUAL PRODUCTION 100,000 bottles
HECTARES UNDER VINE 15.00
VITICULTURE METHOD Certified Organic
SUSTAINABLE WINERY

○ Hermes '18	🍷🍷 5
○ Vermentino di Sardegna Chimera '19	🍷🍷 4
○ Vermentino di Sardegna Sardo '19	🍷 3

Cantina Tani

loc. Conca Sa Raighina, 2
07020 Monti [SS]
Tel. +39 3386432055
www.cantinatani.it

CELLAR SALES
PRE-BOOKED VISITS
ACCOMMODATION AND RESTAURANT SERVICE
ANNUAL PRODUCTION 65,000 bottles
HECTARES UNDER VINE 18.00

● Serranu '16	🍷🍷 8
○ Vermentino di Gallura Meoru '19	🍷🍷 3

Tenute Gregu

LOC. GIUNCHEDDU
07023 CALANGIANUS [SS]
TEL. +39 3480364383
www.tenutegregu.com

ANNUAL PRODUCTION 50,000 bottles
HECTARES UNDER VINE 30.00

- ○ Vermentino di Gallura Rias '19 — ΨΨ 3
- ○ Vermentino di Gallura Sup. Selenu '19 — ΨΨ 3
- ⊙ Cannonau di Sardegna Rosato Sirè '19 — Ψ 3

Cantina Tondini

LOC. SAN LEONARDO
07023 CALANGIANUS [SS]
TEL. +39 079661359
www.cantinatondini.it

CELLAR SALES
PRE-BOOKED VISITS
ANNUAL PRODUCTION 80,000 bottles
HECTARES UNDER VINE 25.00

- ○ Vermentino di Gallura Sup. Karagnanj '19 — ΨΨ 4
- ○ Vermentino di Gallura Sup. Katala '19 — ΨΨ 3
- ● Amjonis '19 — Ψ 4

Cantina Trexenta

V.LE PIEMONTE, 40
09040 SENORBÌ [CA]
TEL. +39 0709808863
www.cantinatrexenta.it

CELLAR SALES
ANNUAL PRODUCTION 1,000,000 bottles
HECTARES UNDER VINE 250.00

- ● Cannonau di Sardegna Goimajor '19 — ΨΨ 2*
- ○ Vermentino di Sardegna Contissa '19 — ΨΨ 2*
- ○ Sant'Efis '17 — Ψ 4
- ○ Vermentino di Sardegna Monteluna '19 — Ψ 2

Cantina del Vermentino Monti

VIA SAN PAOLO, 2
07020 MONTI [SS]
TEL. +39 078944012
www.vermentinomonti.it

CELLAR SALES
PRE-BOOKED VISITS
ANNUAL PRODUCTION 2,000,000 bottles
HECTARES UNDER VINE 500.00

- ○ Vermentino di Gallura Funtanaliras '19 — ΨΨ 3
- ○ Vermentino di Gallura Sup. Aghiloia Oro '19 — ΨΨ 2*
- ○ Vermentino di Gallura Frizzante Balari '19 — Ψ 2

Vigna du Bertin

C.SO AGOSTINO TAGLIAFICO, 49
09014 CARLOFORTE [SU]
TEL. +39 3391381464
www.vignadubertincarloforte.com

CELLAR SALES
PRE-BOOKED VISITS
ANNUAL PRODUCTION 10,000 bottles
HECTARES UNDER VINE 2.00
SUSTAINABLE WINERY

- ● Carignano del Sulcis Mandediu Ris. '16 — ΨΨ 6
- ⊙ Rosé du Bertin '19 — ΨΨ 5
- ● Carignano del Sulcis Bertin '19 — Ψ 5
- ○ Vermentino di Sardegna Ribotta '19 — Ψ 5

Vigne Rada

FRAZ. MONTE PEDROSU
REG. GUARDIA GRANDE, 12
07041 ALGHERO [SS]
TEL. +39 3274259136
www.vignerada.com

ANNUAL PRODUCTION 28,000 bottles
HECTARES UNDER VINE 7.00

- ● Alghero Cagnulari Arsenale '17 — ΨΨ 6
- ● Cannonau di Sardegna Riviera '17 — Ψ 5

INDEX
wineries in alphabetical order